Endsheet Pictures

Left-hand page

The temple area of Jerusalem as it likely appeared in the first century C.E.

Right-hand page

Jesus answering Jews who endeavored to trap him with a question about paying taxes

Inset: A denarius—the kind to which Jesus referred in his reply. It bears the likeness of Tiberius

INSIGHT
ON THE SCRIPTURES

**Volume 2: Jehovah - Zuzim
and Index**

Insight on the Scriptures English (it-2-E)
Made in the United States of America

JEHOVAH (Je·ho'vah) [the causative form, the imperfect state, of the Heb. verb *ha·wah'* (become); meaning "He Causes to Become"]. The personal name of God. (Isa 42:8; 54:5) Though Scripturally designated by such descriptive titles as "God," "Sovereign Lord," "Creator," "Father," "the Almighty," and "the Most High," his personality and attributes—who and what he is—are fully summed up and expressed only in this personal name.—Ps 83:18.

Correct Pronunciation of the Divine Name. "Jehovah" is the best known English pronunciation of the divine name, although "Yahweh" is favored by most Hebrew scholars. The oldest Hebrew manuscripts present the name in the form of four consonants, commonly called the Tetragrammaton (from Greek *te·tra-,* meaning "four," and *gram'ma,* "letter"). These four letters (written from right to left) are יהוה and may be transliterated into English as *YHWH* (or, *JHVH*).

The Hebrew consonants of the name are therefore known. The question is, Which vowels are to be combined with those consonants? Vowel points did not come into use in Hebrew until the second half of the first millennium C.E. (See HEBREW, II [Hebrew Alphabet and Script].) Furthermore, because of a religious superstition that had begun centuries earlier, the vowel pointing found in Hebrew manuscripts does not provide the key for determining which vowels should appear in the divine name.

Superstition hides the name. At some point a superstitious idea arose among the Jews that it was wrong even to pronounce the divine name (represented by the Tetragrammaton). Just what basis was originally assigned for discontinuing the use of the name is not definitely known. Some hold that the name was viewed as being too sacred for imperfect lips to speak. Yet the Hebrew Scriptures themselves give no evidence that any of God's true servants ever felt any hesitancy about pronouncing his name. Non-Biblical Hebrew documents, such as the so-called Lachish Letters, show the name was used in regular correspondence in Palestine during the latter part of the seventh century B.C.E.

Another view is that the intent was to keep non-Jewish peoples from knowing the name and possibly misusing it. However, Jehovah himself said that he would 'have his name declared in all the earth' (Ex 9:16; compare 1Ch 16:23, 24; Ps 113:3; Mal 1:11, 14), to be known even by his adversaries. (Isa 64:2) The name was in fact known and used by pagan nations both in pre-Common Era times and in the early centuries of the Common Era. (*The Jewish Encyclopedia,* 1976, Vol. XII, p. 119) Another claim is that the purpose was to protect the name from use in magical rites. If so, this was poor reasoning, as it is obvious that the more mysterious the name became through disuse the more it would suit the purposes of practicers of magic.

When did the superstition take hold? Just as the reason or reasons originally advanced for discontinuing the use of the divine name are uncertain, so, too, there is much uncertainty as to when this superstitious view really took hold. Some claim that it began following the Babylonian exile (607-537 B.C.E.). This theory, however, is based on a supposed reduction in the use of the name by the later writers of the Hebrew Scriptures, a view that does not hold up under examination. Malachi, for example, was evidently one of the last books of the Hebrew Scriptures written (in the latter half of the fifth century B.C.E.), and it gives great prominence to the divine name.

Many reference works have suggested that the name ceased to be used by about 300 B.C.E. Evidence for this date supposedly was found in the absence of the Tetragrammaton (or a transliteration of it) in the Greek *Septuagint* translation of the Hebrew Scriptures, begun about 280 B.C.E. It is true that the most complete manuscript copies of the *Septuagint* now known do consistently follow the practice of substituting the Greek words *Ky'ri·os* (Lord) or *The·os'* (God) for the Tetragrammaton. But these major manuscripts date back only as far as the fourth and fifth centuries C.E. More ancient copies, though in fragmentary form, have been discovered that prove that the *earliest* copies of the *Septuagint* did contain the divine name.

One of these is the fragmentary remains of a papyrus roll of a portion

Silver piece using the divine name; found at Jerusalem and evidently dating to the seventh or sixth century B.C.E.

of Deuteronomy, listed as P. Fouad Inventory No. 266. (PICTURE, Vol. 1, p. 326) It regularly presents the Tetragrammaton, written in square Hebrew characters, in each case of its appearance in the Hebrew text being translated. This papyrus is dated by scholars as being from the first century B.C.E., and thus it was written four or five centuries earlier than the manuscripts mentioned previously.—See *NW* appendix, pp. 1562-1564.

When did the Jews in general actually stop pronouncing the personal name of God?

So, at least in written form, there is no sound evidence of any disappearance or disuse of the divine name in the B.C.E. period. In the first century C.E., there first appears some evidence of a superstitious attitude toward the name. Josephus, a Jewish historian from a priestly family, when recounting God's revelation to Moses at the site of the burning bush, says: "Then God revealed to him His name, which ere then had not come to men's ears, and of which I am forbidden to speak." (*Jewish Antiquities,* II, 276 [xii, 4]) Josephus' statement, however, besides being inaccurate as to knowledge of the divine name prior to Moses, is vague and does not clearly reveal just what the general attitude current in the first century was as to pronouncing or using the divine name.

The Jewish Mishnah, a collection of rabbinic teachings and traditions, is somewhat more explicit. Its compilation is credited to a rabbi known as Judah the Prince, who lived in the second and third centuries C.E. Some of the Mishnaic material clearly relates to circumstances prior to the destruction of Jerusalem and its temple in 70 C.E. Of the Mishnah, however, one scholar says: "It is a matter of extreme difficulty to decide what historical value we should attach to any tradition recorded in the Mishnah. The lapse of time which may have served to obscure or distort memories of times so different; the political upheavals, changes, and confusions brought about by two rebellions and two Roman conquests; the standards esteemed by the Pharisean party (whose opinions the Mishnah records) which were not those of the Sadducean party . . .—these are factors which need to be given due weight in estimating the character of the Mishnah's statements. Moreover there is much in the contents of the Mishnah that moves in an atmosphere of academic discussion pursued for its own sake, with (so it would appear) little pretence at recording historical usage." (*The Mishnah,* translated by

H. Danby, London, 1954, pp. xiv, xv) Some of the Mishnaic traditions concerning the pronouncing of the divine name are as follows:

In connection with the annual Day of Atonement, Danby's translation of the Mishnah states: "And when the priests and the people which stood in the Temple Court heard the Expressed Name come forth from the mouth of the High Priest, they used to kneel and bow themselves and fall down on their faces and say, 'Blessed be the name of the glory of his kingdom for ever and ever!'" (*Yoma* 6:2) Of the daily priestly blessings, *Sotah* 7:6 says: "In the Temple they pronounced the Name as it was written, but in the provinces by a substituted word." *Sanhedrin* 7:5 states that a blasphemer was not guilty 'unless he pronounced the Name,' and that in a trial involving a charge of blasphemy a substitute name was used until all the evidence had been heard; then the chief witness was asked privately to 'say expressly what he had heard,' presumably employing the divine name. *Sanhedrin* 10:1, in listing those "that have no share in the world to come," states: "Abba Saul says: Also he that pronounces the Name with its proper letters." Yet, despite these negative views, one also finds in the first section of the Mishnah the positive injunction that "a man should salute his fellow with [the use of] the Name [of God]," the example of Boaz (Ru 2:4) then being cited.—*Berakhot* 9:5.

Taken for what they are worth, these traditional views may reveal a superstitious tendency to avoid using the divine name sometime before Jerusalem's temple was destroyed in 70 C.E. Even then, it is primarily the priests who are explicitly said to have used a substitute name in place of the divine name, and that only in the provinces. Additionally the historical value of the Mishnaic traditions is questionable, as we have seen.

There is, therefore, no genuine basis for assigning any time earlier than the first and second centuries C.E. for the development of the superstitious view calling for discontinuance of the use of the divine name. The time did come, however, when in reading the Hebrew Scriptures in the original language, the Jewish reader substituted either 'Adho·nai' (Sovereign Lord) or 'Elo·him' (God) rather than pronounce the divine name represented by the Tetragrammaton. This is seen from the fact that when vowel pointing came into use in the second half of the first millennium C.E., the Jewish copyists inserted the vowel points for either 'Adho·nai' or 'Elo·him' into the Tetragrammaton, evidently to warn the reader to say those words in place of pronouncing the divine name. If using the Greek *Septuagint* translation of the He-

Excerpts from the Psalms, Dead Sea Scroll.
The Tetragrammaton appears repeatedly
in distinctive ancient Hebrew characters

brew Scriptures in *later* copies, the reader, of course, found the Tetragrammaton completely replaced by *Ky·ri·os* and *The·os'.*—See LORD.

Translations into other languages, such as the Latin *Vulgate,* followed the example of these later copies of the Greek *Septuagint.* The Catholic *Douay Version* (of 1609-1610) in English, based on the Latin *Vulgate,* therefore does not contain the divine name, while the *King James Version* (1611) uses LORD or GOD (in capital and small capitals) to represent the Tetragrammaton in the Hebrew Scriptures, except in four cases.

What is the proper pronunciation of God's name?

In the second half of the first millennium C.E., Jewish scholars introduced a system of points to represent the missing vowels in the consonantal Hebrew text. When it came to God's name, instead of inserting the proper vowel signs for it, they put other vowel signs to remind the reader that he should say *'Adho·nai'* (meaning "Sovereign Lord") or *'Elo·him'* (meaning "God").

The Codex Leningrad B 19ᴬ, of the 11th century C.E., vowel points the Tetragrammaton to read *Yehwah', Yehwih',* and *Yeho·wah'.* Ginsburg's edition of the Masoretic text vowel points the divine

name to read *Yeho·wah'.* (Ge 3:14, ftn) Hebrew scholars generally favor "Yahweh" as the most likely pronunciation. They point out that the abbreviated form of the name is Yah (Jah in the Latinized form), as at Psalm 89:8 and in the expression *Ha·lelu-Yah'* (meaning "Praise Jah, you people!"). (Ps 104:35; 150:1, 6) Also, the forms *Yehoh', Yoh, Yah,* and *Ya'hu,* found in the Hebrew spelling of the names Jehoshaphat, Joshaphat, Shephatiah, and others, can all be derived from Yahweh. Greek transliterations of the name by early Christian writers point in a somewhat similar direction with spellings such as *I·a·be'* and *I·a·ou·e',* which, as pronounced in Greek, resemble Yahweh. Still, there is by no means unanimity among scholars on the subject, some favoring yet other pronunciations, such as "Yahuwa," "Yahuah," or "Yehuah."

Since certainty of pronunciation is not now attainable, there seems to be no reason for abandoning in English the well-known form "Jehovah" in favor of some other suggested pronunciation. If such a change were made, then, to be consistent, changes should be made in the spelling and pronunciation of a host of other names found in the Scriptures: Jeremiah would be changed to *Yir·meyah',* Isaiah would become *Yesha'·ya'hu,* and Jesus would be either *Yehoh·shu'a'* (as in Hebrew) or *I·e·sous'* (as in Greek). The purpose of words is to transmit thoughts; in English the name Jehovah identifies the true God, transmitting this thought more satisfactorily today than any of the suggested substitutes.

Importance of the Name. Many modern scholars and Bible translators advocate following the tradition of eliminating the distinctive name of God. They not only claim that its uncertain pronunciation justifies such a course but also hold that the supremacy and uniqueness of the true God make unnecessary his having a particular name. Such a view receives no support from the inspired Scriptures, either those of pre-Christian times or those of the Christian Greek Scriptures.

The Tetragrammaton occurs 6,828 times in the Hebrew text printed in *Biblia Hebraica* and *Biblia Hebraica Stuttgartensia*. In the Hebrew Scriptures the *New World Translation* contains the divine name 6,973 times, because the translators took into account, among other things, the fact that in some places the scribes had replaced the divine name with *'Adho·nai'* or *'Elo·him'*. (See *NW* appendix, pp. 1561, 1562.) The very frequency of the appearance of the name attests to its importance to the Bible's Author, whose name it is. Its use throughout the Scriptures far outnumbers that of any of the titles, such as "Sovereign Lord" or "God," applied to him.

Noteworthy, also, is the importance given to names themselves in the Hebrew Scriptures and among Semitic peoples. Professor G. T. Manley points out: "A study of the word 'name' in the O[ld] T[estament] reveals how much it means in Hebrew. The name is no mere label, but is significant of the real personality of him to whom it belongs. . . . When a person puts his 'name' upon a thing or another person the latter comes under his influence and protection."—*New Bible Dictionary,* edited by J. D. Douglas, 1985, p. 430; compare *Everyman's Talmud,* by A. Cohen, 1949, p. 24; Ge 27:36; 1Sa 25:25; Ps 20:1; Pr 22:1; see NAME.

"God" and "Father" not distinctive. The title "God" is neither personal nor distinctive (one can even make a god of his belly; Php 3:19). In the Hebrew Scriptures the same word (*'Elo·him'*) is applied to Jehovah, the true God, and also to false gods, such as the Philistine god Dagon (Jg 16:23, 24; 1Sa 5:7) and the Assyrian god Nisroch. (2Ki 19:37) For a Hebrew to tell a Philistine or an Assyrian that he worshiped "God ['*Elo·him'*]" would obviously not have sufficed to identify the Person to whom his worship went.

In its articles on Jehovah, *The Imperial Bible-Dictionary* nicely illustrates the difference between *'Elo·him'* (God) and Jehovah. Of the name Jehovah, it says: "It is everywhere a *proper* name, denoting the personal God and him only; whereas Elohim partakes more of the character of a *common* noun, denoting usually, indeed, but not necessarily nor uniformly, the Supreme. . . . The Hebrew may say *the* Elohim, the true God, in opposition to all false gods; but he never says *the* Jehovah, for Jehovah is the name of the true God only. He says again and again *my* God . . . ; but never *my* Jehovah, for when he says *my God,* he means Jehovah. He speaks of the God of Israel, but never of the Jehovah of Israel, for there is no other Jehovah. He speaks of the living God, but never of the living Jehovah, for he cannot conceive of Jehovah as other than living."—Edited by P. Fairbairn, London, 1874, Vol. I, p. 856.

The same is true of the Greek term for God, *The·os'*. It was applied alike to the true God and to such pagan gods as Zeus and Hermes (Roman Jupiter and Mercury). (Compare Ac 14:11-15.) Presenting the true situation are Paul's words at 1 Corinthians 8:4-6: "For even though there are those who are called 'gods,' whether in heaven or on earth, just as there are many 'gods' and many 'lords,' there is actually to us one God the Father, out of whom all things are, and we for him." The belief in numerous gods, which makes essential that the true God be distinguished from such, has continued even into this 20th century.

Paul's reference to "God the Father" does not mean that the true God's name is "Father," for the designation "father" applies as well to every human male parent and describes men in other relationships. (Ro 4:11, 16; 1Co 4:15) The Messiah is given the title "Eternal Father." (Isa 9:6) Jesus called Satan the "father" of certain murderous opposers. (Joh 8:44) The term was also applied to gods of the nations, the Greek god Zeus being represented as the great father god in Homeric poetry. That "God the Father" has a name, one that is distinct from his Son's name, is shown in numerous texts. (Mt 28:19; Re 3:12; 14:1) Paul knew the personal name of God, Jehovah, as found in the creation account in Genesis, from which Paul quoted in his writings. That name, Jehovah, distinguishes "God the Father" (compare Isa 64:8), thereby blocking any attempt at merging or blending his identity and person with that of any other to whom the title "god" or "father" may be applied.

Not a tribal god. Jehovah is called "the God of Israel" and 'the God of their forefathers.' (1Ch 17:24; Ex 3:16) Yet this intimate association with the Hebrews and with the Israelite nation gives no reason for limiting the name to that of a tribal god, as some have done. The Christian apostle Paul wrote: "Is he the God of the Jews only? Is he not also of people of the nations? Yes, of people of the nations also." (Ro 3:29) Jehovah is not only "the God of the whole earth" (Isa 54:5) but also the God of the universe, "the Maker of heaven and earth." (Ps 124:8) Jehovah's covenant with Abraham, nearly 2,000 years earlier than Paul's day, had promised blessings for people of all nations, showing God's interest in all mankind.—Ge 12:1-3; compare Ac 10:34, 35; 11:18.

Jehovah God eventually rejected the unfaithful nation of fleshly Israel. But his name was to continue among the new nation of spiritual Israel, the Christian congregation, even when that new nation began to embrace non-Jewish persons in its membership. Presiding at a Christian assembly in Jerusalem, the disciple James therefore spoke of God as having "turned his attention to the [non-Jewish] nations to take out of them *a people for his name.*" As proof that this had been foretold, James then quoted a prophecy in the book of Amos in which Jehovah's name appears twice.—Ac 15:2, 12-14; Am 9:11, 12.

In the Christian Greek Scriptures. In view of this evidence it seems most unusual to find that the extant manuscript copies of the original text of the Christian Greek Scriptures do not contain the divine name in its full form. The name therefore is also absent from most translations of the so-called New Testament. Yet the name does appear in these sources in its abbreviated form at Revelation 19:1, 3, 4, 6, in the expression "Alleluia" or "Hallelujah" (*KJ, Dy, JB, AS, RS*). The call there recorded as spoken by spirit sons of God to "Praise Jah, you people!" (*NW*) makes clear that the divine name was not obsolete; it was as vital and pertinent as it had been in the pre-Christian period. Why, then, the absence of its full form from the Christian Greek Scriptures?

Why is the divine name in its full form not in any available ancient manuscript of the Christian Greek Scriptures?

The argument long presented was that the inspired writers of the Christian Greek Scriptures made their quotations from the Hebrew Scriptures on the basis of the *Septuagint,* and that, since this version substituted *Ky′ri·os* or *The·os′* for the Tetragrammaton, these writers did not use the name Jehovah. As has been shown, this argument is no longer valid. Commenting on the fact that the oldest fragments of the Greek *Septuagint do* contain the divine name in its Hebrew form, Dr. P. Kahle says: "We now know that the Greek

Bible text [the *Septuagint*] as far as it was written by Jews for Jews did not translate the Divine name by *kyrios,* but the Tetragrammaton written with Hebrew or Greek letters was retained in such MSS [manuscripts]. It was the Christians who replaced the Tetragrammaton by *kyrios,* when the divine name written in Hebrew letters was not understood any more." (*The Cairo Geniza,* Oxford, 1959, p. 222) When did this change in the Greek translations of the Hebrew Scriptures take place?

It evidently took place in the centuries following the death of Jesus and his apostles. In Aquila's Greek version, dating from the second century C.E., the Tetragrammaton still appeared in Hebrew characters. Around 245 C.E., the noted scholar Origen produced his *Hexapla,* a six-column reproduction of the inspired Hebrew Scriptures: (1) in their original Hebrew and Aramaic, accompanied by (2) a transliteration into Greek, and by the Greek versions of (3) Aquila, (4) Symmachus, (5) the *Septuagint,* and (6) Theodotion. On the evidence of the fragmentary copies now known, Professor W. G. Waddell says: "In Origen's *Hexapla* . . . the Greek versions of Aquila, Symmachus, and LXX [*Septuagint*] all represented *JHWH* by ΠΙΠΙ; in the second column of the *Hexapla* the Tetragrammaton was written in Hebrew characters." (*The Journal of Theological Studies,* Oxford, Vol. XLV, 1944, pp. 158, 159) Others believe the original text of Origen's *Hexapla* used Hebrew characters for the Tetragrammaton in *all* its columns. Origen himself stated that "in the most accurate manuscripts THE NAME occurs in Hebrew characters, yet not in today's Hebrew [characters], but in the most ancient ones."

As late as the fourth century C.E., Jerome, the translator of the Latin *Vulgate,* says in his prologue to the books of Samuel and Kings: "And we find the name of God, the Tetragrammaton [i.e., יהוה], in certain Greek volumes even to this day expressed in ancient letters." In a letter written at Rome, 384 C.E., Jerome states: "The ninth [name of God] is the Tetragrammaton, which they considered [*a·nek·pho′ne·ton*], that is, unspeakable, and it is written with these letters, Iod, He, Vau, He. Certain ignorant ones, because of the similarity of the characters, when they would find it in Greek books, were accustomed to read ΠΙΠΙ [Greek letters corresponding to the Roman letters PIPI]."—*Papyrus Grecs Bibliques,* by F. Dunand, Cairo, 1966, p. 47, ftn. 4.

The so-called Christians, then, who "replaced the Tetragrammaton by *kyrios*" in the *Septuagint* copies, were not the early disciples of Jesus. They were persons of later centuries, when the foretold apostasy was well developed and had corrupted the purity of Christian teachings.—2Th 2:3; 1Ti 4:1.

Used by Jesus and his disciples. Thus, in the days of Jesus and his disciples the divine name very definitely appeared in copies of the Scriptures, both in Hebrew manuscripts and in Greek manuscripts. Did Jesus and his disciples use the divine name in speech and in writing? In view of Jesus' condemnation of Pharisaic traditions (Mt 15:1-9), it would be highly unreasonable to conclude that Jesus and his disciples let Pharisaic ideas (such as are recorded in the Mishnah) govern them in this matter. Jesus' own name means "Jehovah Is Salvation." He stated: "I have come in the name of my Father" (Joh 5:43); he taught his followers to pray: "Our Father in the heavens, let your name be sanctified" (Mt 6:9); his works, he said, were done "in the name of my Father" (Joh 10:25); and, in prayer on the night of his death, he said he had made his Father's name manifest to his disciples and asked, "Holy Father, watch over them on account of your own name" (Joh 17:6, 11, 12, 26). In view of all of this, when Jesus quoted the Hebrew Scriptures or read from them he certainly used the divine name, Jehovah. (Compare Mt 4:4, 7, 10 with De 8:3; 6:16; 6:13; also Mt 22:37 with De 6:5; and Mt 22:44 with Ps 110:1; as well as Lu 4:16-21 with Isa 61:1, 2.) Logically, Jesus' disciples, including the inspired writers of the Christian Greek Scriptures, would follow his example in this.

Why, then, is the name absent from the extant manuscripts of the Christian Greek Scriptures or so-called New Testament? Evidently because by the time those extant copies were made (from the third century C.E. onward) the original text of the writings of the apostles and disciples had been altered. Thus later copyists undoubtedly replaced the divine name in Tetragrammaton form with *Ky'ri·os* and *The·os'*. (PICTURE, Vol. 1, p. 324) This is precisely what the facts show was done in later copies of the *Septuagint* translation of the Hebrew Scriptures.

Restoration of the divine name in translation. Recognizing that this must have been the case, some translators have included the name Jehovah in their renderings of the Christian Greek Scriptures. *The Emphatic Diaglott,* a 19th-century translation by Benjamin Wilson, contains the name Jehovah a number of times, particularly where the Christian writers quoted from the Hebrew Scriptures. But as far back as the 14th cen-

tury the Tetragrammaton had already begun to be used in translations of the Christian Scriptures into Hebrew, beginning with the translation of Matthew into Hebrew that was incorporated in the work *'E'ven bo'chan* by Shem-Tob ben Isaac Ibn Shaprut. Wherever Matthew quoted from the Hebrew Scriptures, this translation used the Tetragrammaton in each case of its occurrence. Many other Hebrew translations have since followed the same practice.

As to the properness of this course, note the following acknowledgment by R. B. Girdlestone, late principal of Wycliffe Hall, Oxford. The statement was made before manuscript evidence came to light showing that the Greek *Septuagint* originally contained the name Jehovah. He said: "If that [*Septuagint*] version had retained the word [Jehovah], or had even used one Greek word for *Jehovah* and another for *Adonai,* such usage would doubtless have been retained in the discourses and arguments of the N. T. Thus our Lord, in quoting the 110th Psalm, instead of saying, 'The Lord said unto my Lord,' might have said, '*Jehovah* said unto *Adoni.*'"

Proceeding on this same basis (which evidence now shows to have been actual fact) he adds: "Supposing a Christian scholar were engaged in translating the Greek Testament into Hebrew, he would have to consider, each time the word Κύριος occurred, whether there was anything in the context to indicate its true Hebrew representative; and this is the difficulty which would arise in translating the N. T. into all languages if the title *Jehovah* had been allowed to stand in the [*Septuagint* translation of the] O. T. The Hebrew Scriptures would be a guide in many passages: thus, wherever the expression 'the angel of the Lord' occurs, we know that the word Lord represents *Jehovah;* a similar conclusion as to the expression 'the word of the Lord' would be arrived at, if the precedent set by the O. T. were followed; so also in the case of the title 'the Lord of Hosts.' Wherever, on the contrary, the expression 'My Lord' or 'Our Lord' occurs, we should know that the word *Jehovah* would be inadmissible, and *Adonai* or *Adoni* would have to be used." (*Synonyms of the Old Testament,* 1897, p. 43) It is on such a basis that translations of the Greek Scriptures (mentioned earlier) containing the name Jehovah have proceeded.

Outstanding, however, in this regard is the *New World Translation,* used throughout this work, in which the divine name in the form "Jehovah" appears 237 times in the Christian Greek Scriptures. As has been shown, there is sound basis for this.

Early Use of the Name and Its Meaning. Exodus 3:13-16 and 6:3 are often misapplied to mean that Jehovah's name was first revealed to Moses sometime prior to the Exodus from Egypt. True, Moses raised the question: "Suppose I am now come to the sons of Israel and I do say to them, 'The God of your forefathers has sent me to you,' and they do say to me, 'What is his name?' What shall I say to them?" But this does not mean that he or the Israelites did not know Jehovah's name. The very name of Moses' mother Jochebed means, possibly, "Jehovah Is Glory." (Ex 6:20) Moses' question likely was related to the circum-stances in which the sons of Israel found themselves. They had been in hard slavery for many decades with no sign of any relief. Doubt, discour-agement, and weakness of faith in God's power and purpose to deliver them had very likely infil-trated their ranks. (Note also Eze 20:7, 8.) For Moses simply to say he came in the name of "God" (*'Elo·him'*) or the "Sovereign Lord" (*'Adho·nai'*) therefore might not have meant much to the suf-fering Israelites. They knew the Egyptians had their own gods and lords and doubtless heard taunts from the Egyptians that their gods were superior to the God of the Israelites.

A few of the many translations of the Christian Greek Scriptures that have included the divine name

עַל־כֵּן לֹא תֶהְיוּ פְתָאִים 17
כִּי־אֵם מְבִינִים מַה הִיא
יְהֹוָה:

Novum Testamentum Domini Nostri Iesu Christi, *translated by Elias Hutter (Hebrew section); published in Nuremburg; 1599; Ephesians 5:17*

The New Testament of Our Lord and Saviour Jesus Christ, *translated by John Eliot (Massachuset language); published in Cambridge, Mass.; 1661; Matthew 21:9*

29. The Jesus answered him, verily first it exists, hear, O Israel, Jehovah our God, one Jehovah he exists,

30. and thou shalt love Jehovah thy God, with all thy heart, and with all thy soul, and with all thy mind, and with all thy strength,

A Literal Translation of the New Testament . . . From the Text of the Vatican Manuscript, *by Herman Heinfetter; published in London; 1863; Mark 12:29, 30*

An die Römer XV 52

33 Loblieder singen;" und an einem andern Or-te: "Freuet euch ihr Nationen mit dem Volke 10 Jehovahs! Lobet den Herrn alle Heyden, prei-11 set ihn alle Völker!" Und in einer Stelle Jesaias: "Aus Isai wird ein Zweig aufsbros-12 sen, und ein Beherrscher der Nationen her-13 kommen, dem sie sich anvertrauen werden."*

Der Gott, auf den wir hoffen, erfülle euch mit Freude und Gleichgesinntheit, aufdaß euere Hofnung durch die Kraft des heiligen Geistes immer stärker und vollkommner werde.

Sämtliche Schriften des Neuen Testaments, *translated by Johann Jakob Stolz (German); published in Zurich; 1781-1782; Romans 15:11*

Then, too, we must keep in mind that names then had real meaning and were not just "labels" to identify an individual as today. Moses knew that Abram's name (meaning "Father Is High (Exalted)") was changed to Abraham (meaning "Father of a Crowd (Multitude)"), the change being made because of God's purpose concerning Abraham. So, too, the name of Sarai was changed to Sarah and that of Jacob to Israel; in each case the change revealed something fundamental and prophetic about God's purpose concerning them. Moses may well have wondered if Jehovah would now reveal himself under some new name to throw light on his purpose toward Israel. Moses' going to the Israelites in the "name" of the One who sent him meant being the representative of that One, and the greatness of the authority with which Moses would speak would be determined by or be commensurate with that name and what it represented. (Compare Ex 23:20, 21; 1Sa 17:45.) So, Moses' question was a meaningful one.

God's reply in Hebrew was: 'Eh·yeh' 'Asher' 'Eh·yeh'. Some translations render this as "I AM THAT I AM." However, it is to be noted that the Hebrew verb ha·yah', from which the word 'Eh·yeh' is drawn, does not mean simply "be." Rather, it means "become," or "prove to be." The reference here is not to God's self-existence but to what he has in mind to become toward others. Therefore, the *New World Translation* properly renders the above Hebrew expression as "I SHALL PROVE TO BE WHAT I SHALL PROVE TO BE." Jehovah thereafter added: "This is what you are to say to the sons of Israel, 'I SHALL PROVE TO BE has sent me to you.'" —Ex 3:14, ftn.

That this meant no change in God's name, but only an additional insight into God's personality, is seen from his further words: "This is what you are to say to the sons of Israel, 'Jehovah the God of your forefathers, the God of Abraham, the God of Isaac and the God of Jacob, has sent me to you.' This is my name to time indefinite, and this is the memorial of me to generation after generation." (Ex 3:15; compare Ps 135:13; Ho 12:5.) The name Jehovah comes from the Hebrew verb ha·wah', "become," and actually means "He Causes to Become." This reveals Jehovah as the One who, with progressive action, causes himself to become the Fulfiller of promises. Thus he always brings his purposes to realization. Only the true God could rightly and authentically bear such a name.

This aids one in understanding the sense of Jehovah's later statement to Moses: "I am Jehovah. And I used to appear to Abraham, Isaac and Jacob as God Almighty, but as respects my name Jehovah I did not make myself known to them." (Ex 6:2, 3) Since the name Jehovah was used many times by those patriarchal ancestors of Moses, it is evident that God meant that he manifested himself to them in the capacity of Jehovah only in a limited way. To illustrate this, those who had known the man Abram could hardly be said to have really *known* him as *Abraham* (meaning "Father of a Crowd (Multitude)") while he had but one son, Ishmael. When Isaac and other sons were born and began producing offspring, the name Abraham took on greater meaning or import. So, too, the name Jehovah would now take on expanded meaning for the Israelites.

To "know," therefore, does not necessarily mean merely to be acquainted with or cognizant of something or someone. The foolish Nabal knew David's name but still asked, "Who is David?" in the sense of asking, "What does he amount to?" (1Sa 25:9-11; compare 2Sa 8:13.) So, too, Pharaoh had said to Moses: "Who is Jehovah, so that I should obey his voice to send Israel away? I do not know Jehovah at all and, what is more, I am not going to send Israel away." (Ex 5:1, 2) By that, Pharaoh evidently meant that he did not know Jehovah as the true God or as having any authority over Egypt's king and his affairs, nor as having any might to enforce His will as announced by Moses and Aaron. But now Pharaoh and all Egypt, along with the Israelites, would come to know the real meaning of that name, the person it represented. As Jehovah showed Moses, this would result from God's carrying out His purpose toward Israel, liberating them, giving them the Promised Land, and thereby fulfilling His covenant with their forefathers. In this way, as God said, "You will certainly know that I am Jehovah your God." —Ex 6:4-8; see ALMIGHTY.

Professor of Hebrew D. H. Weir therefore rightly says that those who claim Exodus 6:2, 3 marks the first time the name Jehovah was revealed, "have not studied [these verses] in the light of other scriptures; otherwise they would have perceived that by *name* must be meant here not the two syllables which make up the word Jehovah, but the idea which it expresses. When we read in Isaiah, ch. lii. 6, *'Therefore my people shall know my name;'* or in Jeremiah, ch. xvi. 21, *'They shall know that my name is Jehovah;'* or in the Psalms, Ps. ix. [10, 16], *'They that know thy name shall put their trust in thee;'* we see at once that to know Jehovah's name is something very different from knowing the four letters of which it is composed. It is to know by experience that Jehovah really is what his name declares him to be. (Compare also Is. xix. 20, 21; Eze. xx. 5, 9; xxxix. 6, 7; Ps. lxxxiii.

[18]; lxxxix. [16]; 2 Ch. vi. 33.)"—*The Imperial Bible-Dictionary*, Vol. I, pp. 856, 857.

Known by the first human pair. The name Jehovah was not first revealed to Moses, for it was certainly known by the first man. The name initially appears in the divine Record at Genesis 2:4 after the account of God's creative works, and there it identifies the Creator of the heavens and earth as "Jehovah God." It is reasonable to believe that Jehovah God informed Adam of this account of creation. The Genesis record does not mention his doing so, but then neither does it explicitly say Jehovah revealed Eve's origin to the awakened Adam. Yet Adam's words upon receiving Eve show he had been informed of the way God had produced her from Adam's own body. (Ge 2:21-23) Much communication undoubtedly took place between Jehovah and his earthly son that is not included in the brief account of Genesis.

Eve is the first human specifically reported to have used the divine name. (Ge 4:1) She obviously learned that name from her husband and head, Adam, from whom she had also learned God's command concerning the tree of the knowledge of good and bad (although, again, the record does not directly relate Adam's passing this information on to her).—Ge 2:16, 17; 3:2, 3.

As is shown in the article ENOSH, the start that was made of "calling on the name of Jehovah" in the day of Adam's grandson Enosh was evidently not done in faith and in a divinely approved manner. For between Abel and Noah only Jared's son Enoch (not Enosh) is reported to have 'walked with the true God' in faith. (Ge 4:26; 5:18, 22-24; Heb 11:4-7) Through Noah and his family, knowledge of the divine name survived into the post-Flood period, beyond the time of the dispersion of peoples at the Tower of Babel, and was transmitted to the patriarch Abraham and his descendants.—Ge 9:26; 12:7, 8.

The Person Identified by the Name. Jehovah is the Creator of all things, the great First Cause; hence he is uncreated, without beginning. (Re 4:11) "In number his years are beyond searching." (Job 36:26) It is impossible to place an age upon him, for there is no starting point from which to measure. Though ageless, he is properly called "the Ancient of Days" since his existence stretches endlessly into the past. (Da 7:9, 13) He is also without future end (Re 10:6), being incorruptible, undying. He is therefore called "the King of eternity" (1Ti 1:17), to whom a thousand years are but as a night watch of a few hours.—Ps 90:2, 4; Jer 10:10; Hab 1:12; Re 15:3.

Despite his timelessness, Jehovah is preeminently a historical God, identifying himself with specific times, places, persons, and events. In his dealings with mankind he has acted according to an exact timetable. (Ge 15:13, 16; 17:21; Ex 12:6-12; Ga 4:4) Because his eternal existence is undeniable and the most fundamental fact in the universe, he has sworn by it in oaths, saying, "As I am alive," thereby guaranteeing the absolute certainty of his promises and prophecies. (Jer 22:24; Zep 2:9; Nu 14:21, 28; Isa 49:18) Men, too, took oaths, swearing by the fact of Jehovah's existence. (Jg 8:19; Ru 3:13) Only senseless ones say: "There is no Jehovah."—Ps 14:1; 10:4.

Descriptions of his presence. Since he is a Spirit beyond the power of humans to see (Joh 4:24), any description of his appearance in human terms can only approximate his incomparable glory. (Isa 40:25, 26) While not actually seeing their Creator (Joh 1:18), certain of his servants were given inspired visions of his heavenly courts. Their description of his presence portrays not only great dignity and awesome majesty but also serenity, order, beauty, and pleasantness.—Ex 24:9-11; Isa 6:1; Eze 1:26-28; Da 7:9; Re 4:1-3; see also Ps 96:4-6.

As can be noted, these descriptions employ metaphors and similes, likening Jehovah's appearance to things known to humans—jewels, fire, rainbow. He is even described as though he had certain human features. While some scholars make a considerable issue out of what they call the anthropomorphological expressions found in the Bible—as references to God's "eyes," "ears," "face" (1Pe 3:12), "arm" (Eze 20:33), "right hand" (Ex 15:6), and so forth—it is obvious that such expressions are necessary for the description to be humanly comprehensible. For Jehovah God to set down for us a description of himself in spirit terms would be like supplying advanced algebraic equations to persons having only the most elementary knowledge of mathematics, or trying to explain colors to a person born blind.—Job 37:23, 24.

The so-called anthropomorphisms, therefore, are never to be taken literally, any more than other metaphoric references to God as a "sun," "shield," or "Rock." (Ps 84:11; De 32:4, 31) Jehovah's sight (Ge 16:13), unlike that of humans, does not depend on light rays, and deeds done in utter darkness can be seen by him. (Ps 139:1, 7-12; Heb 4:13) His vision can encompass all the earth (Pr 15:3), and he needs no special equipment to see the growing embryo within the human womb. (Ps 139:15, 16) Nor does his hearing depend on sound waves in an atmosphere, for he can "hear" expressions though uttered voicelessly in the heart. (Ps

19:14) Man cannot successfully measure even the vast physical universe; yet the physical heavens do not embrace or enclose the place of God's residence, and much less does some earthly house or temple. (1Ki 8:27; Ps 148:13) Through Moses, Jehovah specifically warned the nation of Israel not to make an image of Him in the form of a male or of any kind of created thing. (De 4:15-18) So, whereas Luke's account records Jesus' reference to expelling demons "by means of God's finger," Matthew's account shows that Jesus thereby referred to "God's spirit," or active force.—Lu 11:20; Mt 12:28; compare Jer 27:5 and Ge 1:2.

Personal qualities revealed in creation. Certain facets of Jehovah's personality are revealed by his creative works even prior to his creation of man. (Ro 1:20) The very act of creation reveals his love. This is because Jehovah is self-contained, lacking nothing. Hence, although he created hundreds of millions of spirit sons, not one could add anything to his knowledge or contribute some desirable quality of emotion or personality that He did not already possess in superior degree.—Da 7:9, 10; Heb 12:22; Isa 40:13, 14; Ro 11:33, 34.

This, of course, does not mean that Jehovah does not find pleasure in his creatures. Since man was made "in God's image" (Ge 1:27), it follows that the joy a human father finds in his child, particularly one who shows filial love and acts with wisdom, reflects the joy that Jehovah finds in his intelligent creatures who love and wisely serve Him. (Pr 27:11; Mt 3:17; 12:18) This pleasure comes, not from any material or physical gain, but from seeing his creatures willingly hold to his righteous standards and show unselfishness and generosity. (1Ch 29:14-17; Ps 50:7-15; 147:10, 11; Heb 13:16) Contrariwise, those who take a wrong course and show contempt for Jehovah's love, who bring reproach on his name and cruel suffering to others, cause Jehovah to 'feel hurt at his heart.' —Ge 6:5-8; Ps 78:36-41; Heb 10:38.

Jehovah also finds pleasure in the exercise of his powers, whether in creation or otherwise, his works always having a real purpose and a good motive. (Ps 135:3-6; Isa 46:10, 11; 55:10, 11) As the Generous Giver of "every good gift and every perfect present," he takes delight in rewarding his faithful sons and daughters with blessings. (Jas 1:5, 17; Ps 35:27; 84:11, 12; 149:4) Yet, though he is a God of warmth and feeling, his happiness is clearly not dependent upon his creatures, nor does he sacrifice righteous principles for sentimentality.

Jehovah also showed love in granting his first-created spirit Son the privilege of sharing with him in all further works of creation, both spirit and material, generously causing this fact to be made known with resultant honor to his Son. (Ge 1:26; Col 1:15-17) He thus did not weakly fear the possibility of competition but, rather, displayed complete confidence in his own rightful Sovereignty (Ex 15:11) as well as in his Son's loyalty and devotion. He allows his spirit sons relative freedom in the discharge of their duties, on occasion even permitting them to offer their views on how they might carry out particular assignments. —1Ki 22:19-22.

As the apostle Paul pointed out, Jehovah's invisible qualities are also revealed in his material creation. (Ro 1:19, 20) His vast power is staggering to the imagination, huge galaxies of billions of stars being but 'the work of his fingers' (Ps 8:1, 3, 4; 19:1), and the richness of his wisdom displayed is such that, even after thousands of years of research and study, the understanding that men have of the physical creation is but "a whisper" compared with mighty thunder. (Job 26:14; Ps 92:5; Ec 3:11) Jehovah's creative activity toward the planet Earth was marked by logical orderliness, following a definite program (Ge 1:2-31), making the earth—as astronauts in our 20th century have called it—a jewel in space.

As revealed to man in Eden. As what kind of person did Jehovah reveal himself to his first human children? Certainly Adam in his perfection would have had to concur with the later words of the psalmist: "I shall laud you because in a fear-inspiring way I am wonderfully made. Your works are wonderful, as my soul is very well aware." (Ps 139:14) From his own body—outstandingly versatile among earthly creatures—on outward to the things he found around him, the man had every reason to feel awesome respect for his Creator. Each new bird, animal, and fish; each different plant, flower, and tree; and every field, forest, hill, valley, and stream that the man saw would impress upon him the depth and breadth of his Father's wisdom and the colorfulness of Jehovah's personality as reflected in the grand variety of his creative works. (Ge 2:7-9; compare Ps 104:8-24.) All of man's senses—sight, hearing, taste, smell, and touch—would communicate to his receptive mind the evidence of a most generous and thoughtful Creator.

Nor were Adam's intellectual needs, his need for conversation and companionship, forgotten, as his Father provided him with an intelligent feminine counterpart. (Ge 2:18-23) They both could well have sung to Jehovah, as did the psalmist: "Rejoicing to satisfaction is with your face; there is pleasantness at your right hand forever." (Ps 16:8, 11) Having been the object of so much love, Adam and Eve should certainly have known that "God is love," the source and supreme example of love. —1Jo 4:16, 19.

Most important, Jehovah God supplied man's spiritual needs. Adam's Father revealed himself to his human son, communicating with him, giving him divine assignments of service, the obedient performance of which would constitute a major part of man's worship.—Ge 1:27-30; 2:15-17; compare Am 4:13.

A God of moral standards. Man early came to know Jehovah not merely as a wise and bountiful Provider but also as a God of morals, one holding to definite standards as to what is right and what is wrong in conduct and practice. If, as indicated, Adam knew the account of creation, then he also knew Jehovah had divine standards, for the account says of his creative works that Jehovah saw that "it was very good," hence meeting his perfect standard.—Ge 1:3, 4, 12, 25, 31; compare De 32:3, 4.

Without standards there could be no means for determining or judging good and bad or for measuring and recognizing degrees of accuracy and excellence. In this regard, the following observations from the *Encyclopædia Britannica* (1959, Vol. 21, pp. 306, 307) are enlightening:

"Man's accomplishments [in establishing standards] . . . pale into insignificance when compared with standards in nature. The constellations, the orbits of the planets, the changeless normal properties of conductivity, ductility, elasticity, hardness, permeability, refractivity, strength, or viscosity in the materials of nature, . . . or the structure of cells, are a few examples of the astounding standardization in nature."

Showing the importance of such standardization in the material creation, the same work says: "Only through the standardization found in nature is it possible to recognize and classify . . . the many kinds of plants, fishes, birds or animals. Within these kinds, individuals resemble each other in minutest detail of structure, function and habits peculiar to each. [Compare Ge 1:11, 12, 21, 24, 25.] If it were not for such standardization in the human body, physicians would not know whether an individual possessed certain organs, where to look for them . . . In fact, without nature's standards there could be no organized society, no education and no physicians; each depends upon underlying, comparable similarities."

Adam saw much stability in Jehovah's creative works, the regular cycle of day and night, the steady downward course of the water in Eden's river in response to the force of gravity, and countless other things that gave proof that Earth's Creator is not a God of confusion but of order. (Ge 1:16-18; 2:10; Ec 1:5-7; Jer 31:35, 36; 1Co 14:33) Man surely found this helpful in carrying out his assigned work and activities (Ge 1:28; 2:15), being able to plan and work with confidence, free from anxious uncertainty.

In view of all of this, it should not have seemed strange to intelligent man that Jehovah should set standards governing man's conduct and his relations with his Creator. Jehovah's own splendid workmanship set the example for Adam in his cultivating and caring for Eden. (Ge 2:15; 1:31) Adam also learned God's standard for marriage, that of monogamy, and of family relationship. (Ge 2:24) Especially stressed as essential for life itself was the standard of *obedience* to God's instructions. Since Adam was humanly perfect, perfect obedience was the standard Jehovah set for him. Jehovah gave his earthly son the opportunity to demonstrate love and devotion by obedience to His command to abstain from eating of one of the many fruit trees in Eden. (Ge 2:16, 17) It was a simple thing. But Adam's circumstances then were simple, free from the complexities and confusion that have since developed. Jehovah's wisdom in this simple test was emphasized by the words of Jesus Christ some 4,000 years later: "The person faithful in what is least is faithful also in much, and the person unrighteous in what is least is unrighteous also in much."—Lu 16:10.

This orderliness and the standards set would not detract from man's enjoyment of life but would contribute to it. As the encyclopedia article on standards, mentioned earlier, observes regarding the material creation: "Yet with this overwhelming evidence of standards none charges nature with monotony. Although a narrow band of spectral wave lengths forms the foundation, the available variations and combinations of colour to delight the eye of the observer are virtually without limit. Similarly, all of the artistry of music comes to the ear through another small group of frequencies." (Vol. 21, p. 307) Likewise, God's requirements for the human pair allowed them all the freedom that a righteous heart could desire. There was no need to hem them in with a multitude of laws and regulations. The loving example set for them by their Creator and their respect and love for him would protect them from exceeding the proper bounds of their freedom.—Compare 1Ti 1:9, 10; Ro 6:15-18; 13:8-10; 2Co 3:17.

Jehovah God, therefore, by his very Person, his ways, and his words, was and is the Supreme Standard for all the universe, the definition and the sum of all goodness. For that reason his Son when on earth could say to a man: "Why do you call me good? Nobody is good, except one, God." —Mr 10:17, 18; also Mt 19:17; 5:48.

Name to Be Sanctified and Vindicated. All things relating to God's person are holy; his personal name, Jehovah, is holy and hence is to be sanctified. (Le 22:32) To sanctify means "to make holy, set apart or hold as sacred," and therefore not to use as something common, or ordinary. (Isa 6:1-3; Lu 1:49; Re 4:8; see SANCTIFICATION.) Because of the Person it represents, Jehovah's name is "great and fear-inspiring" (Ps 99:3, 5), "majestic," and "unreachably high" (Ps 8:1; 148:13), worthy of being regarded with awe (Isa 29:23).

Profanation of the name. The evidence is that the divine name was so regarded until events in the garden of Eden brought about its profanation. Satan's rebellion brought God's name and reputation into question. To Eve, he claimed to speak for God in telling her what "God knows," while at the same time he cast doubt on God's command, expressed to Adam, concerning the tree of the knowledge of good and bad. (Ge 3:1-5) Being divinely commissioned and being the earthly head through whom God communicated instructions to the human family, Adam was Jehovah's representative on earth. (Ge 1:26, 28; 2:15-17; 1Co 11:3) Those serving in such capacity are said to 'minister in Jehovah's name' and 'speak in his name.' (De 18:5, 18, 19; Jas 5:10) Thus, while his wife Eve had already profaned Jehovah's name by her disobedience, Adam's doing so was an especially reprehensible act of disrespect for the name he represented.—Compare 1Sa 15: 22, 23.

The supreme issue a moral one. It is evident that the spirit son who became Satan knew Jehovah as a God of moral standards, not as a capricious, erratic person. Had he known Jehovah as a God given to uncontrolled, violent outbursts, he could only have expected immediate, on-the-spot extermination for the course he took. The issue Satan raised in Eden, therefore, was not simply a test of Jehovah's mightiness or power to destroy. Rather, it was a moral issue: that of God's moral right to exercise universal sovereignty and require implicit obedience and devotion of all of his creatures in all places. Satan's approach to Eve reveals this. (Ge 3:1-6) Likewise, the book of Job relates how Jehovah brings out into the open before all his assembled angelic sons the extent of the posi-

tion taken by his Adversary. Satan made the claim that the loyalty of Job (and, by implication, of any of God's intelligent creatures) toward Jehovah was not wholehearted, not based on true devotion and genuine love.—Job 1:6-22; 2:1-8.

Thus, the question of integrity on the part of God's intelligent creatures was a secondary, or subsidiary, issue arising out of the primary issue of God's right to universal sovereignty. These questions would require time in order for the veracity or falsity of the charges to be demonstrated, for the heart attitude of God's creatures to be proved, and thus for the issue to be settled beyond any doubt. (Compare Job 23:10; 31:5, 6; Ec 8:11-13; Heb 5:7-9; see INTEGRITY; WICKEDNESS.) Jehovah thus did not immediately execute the rebellious human pair nor the spirit son who raised the issue, and so the two foretold 'seeds,' representing opposite sides of the issue, would come into existence.—Ge 3:15.

That this issue still remained alive when Jesus Christ was on earth is seen from his confrontation with Satan in the wilderness after Jesus' 40-day fast. The serpentlike tactics employed by Jehovah's Adversary in his temptation efforts toward God's Son followed the pattern seen in Eden some 4,000 years earlier, and Satan's offer of rulership over earthly kingdoms made clear that the issue of universal sovereignty had not changed. (Mt 4:1-10) The book of Revelation reveals the continuance of the issue down until the time when Jehovah God declares the case closed (compare Ps 74:10, 22, 23) and executes righteous judgment upon all opposers, by his righteous Kingdom rule bringing complete vindication and sanctification to his holy name.—Re 11:17, 18; 12:17; 14:6, 7; 15:3, 4; 19:1-3, 11-21; 20:1-10, 14.

Why is the sanctification of God's name of primary importance?

The entire Bible account revolves around this issue and its settlement, and makes manifest Jehovah God's primary purpose: the sanctification of his own name. Such sanctification would require a cleansing of God's name of all reproach and false charges, that is, a vindicating of it. But, much more than that, it would require the honoring of that name as sacred by all intelligent creatures in heaven and earth. This, in turn, would mean their recognizing and respecting Jehovah's sovereign position, doing so willingly, wanting to serve him, delighting to do his divine will, because of love for him. David's prayer to Jehovah at Psalm 40:5-10 well expresses such attitude and true sanctification of Jehovah's name. (Note the apostle's application of portions of this psalm to Christ Jesus at Heb 10:5-10.)

Upon the sanctification of Jehovah's name, therefore, depend the good order, peace, and well-being of all the universe and its inhabitants. God's Son showed this, at the same time pointing out Jehovah's means for accomplishing his purpose, when he taught his disciples to pray to God: "Let your name be sanctified. Let your kingdom come. Let your will take place, as in heaven, also upon earth." (Mt 6:9, 10) This primary purpose of Jehovah provides the key for understanding the reason behind God's actions and his dealings with his creatures as set forth in the entire Bible.

Thus, we find that the nation of Israel, whose history forms a large part of the Bible record, was selected to be a 'name people' for Jehovah. (De 28:9, 10; 2Ch 7:14; Isa 43:1, 3, 6, 7) Jehovah's Law covenant with them laid prime importance on their giving exclusive devotion to Jehovah as God and not taking up his name in a worthless way, "for Jehovah will not leave the one unpunished who takes up his name in a worthless way." (Ex 20:1-7; compare Le 19:12; 24:10-23.) By his display of his power to save and power to destroy when liberating Israel from Egypt, Jehovah's name was "declared in all the earth," its fame preceding Israel in their march to the Promised Land. (Ex 9:15, 16; 15:1-3, 11-17; 2Sa 7:23; Jer 32:20, 21) As the prophet Isaiah expressed it: "Thus you led your people in order to make a beautiful name for your own self." (Isa 63:11-14) When Israel showed a rebellious attitude in the wilderness, Jehovah dealt mercifully with them and did not abandon them. However, he revealed his primary reason in saying: "I went acting for the sake of my own name that it might not be profaned before the eyes of the nations."—Eze 20:8-10.

Throughout the history of that nation, Jehovah kept the importance of his sacred name before them. The capital city, Jerusalem, with its Mount Zion was the place Jehovah chose "to place his name there, to have it reside." (De 12:5, 11; 14:24, 25; Isa 18:7; Jer 3:17) The temple built in that city was the 'house for Jehovah's name.' (1Ch 29:13-16; 1Ki 8:15-21, 41-43) What was done at that temple or in that city, for good or for bad, inevitably affected Jehovah's name and would be given attention by him. (1Ki 8:29; 9:3; 2Ki 21:4-7) The profaning of Jehovah's name there would bring certain destruction upon the city and lead to the casting away of the temple itself. (1Ki 9:6-8;

Jer 25:29; 7:8-15; compare Jesus' actions and words at Mt 21:12, 13; 23:38.) Because of these facts, the plaintive petitions of Jeremiah and Daniel on behalf of their people and city urged that Jehovah grant mercy and help 'for his own name's sake.'—Jer 14:9; Da 9:15-19.

In foretelling his restoration of his name people to Judah and their cleansing, Jehovah again made clear to them his main concern, saying: "And I shall have compassion on my holy name." "'Not for your sakes am I doing it, O house of Israel, but for my holy name, which you have profaned among the nations where you have come in.' 'And I shall certainly sanctify my great name, which was being profaned . . . ; and the nations will have to know that I am Jehovah,' is the utterance of the Sovereign Lord Jehovah, 'when I am sanctified among you before their eyes.'"—Eze 36:20-27, 32.

These and other scriptures show that Jehovah does not exaggerate mankind's importance. All men being sinners, they are justly worthy of death, and it is only by God's undeserved kindness and mercy that any will gain life. (Ro 5:12, 21; 1Jo 4:9, 10) Jehovah owes nothing to mankind, and life everlasting for those who attain it will be a gift, not wages earned. (Ro 5:15; 6:23; Tit 3:4, 5) True, he has demonstrated unparalleled love toward mankind. (Joh 3:16; Ro 5:7, 8) But it is contrary to Scriptural fact and a putting of matters in wrong perspective to view human salvation as if it were the all-important issue or the criterion by which God's justice, righteousness, and holiness can be measured. The psalmist expressed the true perspective of matters when he humbly and wonderingly exclaimed: "O Jehovah our Lord, how majestic your name is in all the earth, you whose dignity is recounted above the heavens! . . . When I see your heavens, the works of your fingers, the moon and the stars that you have prepared, what is mortal man that you keep him in mind, and the son of earthling man that you take care of him?" (Ps 8:1, 3, 4; 144:3; compare Isa 45:9; 64:8.) The sanctification of Jehovah God's name rightly means more than the life of all mankind. Thus, as God's Son showed, man should love his human neighbor as he loves himself, but he must love God with his whole heart, mind, soul, and strength. (Mr 12:29-31) This means loving Jehovah God more than relatives, friends, or life itself. —De 13:6-10; Re 12:11; compare the attitude of the three Hebrews at Da 3:16-18; see JEALOUS, JEALOUSY.

This Scriptural view of matters should not repel persons but, rather, should cause them to appreciate the true God all the more. Since Jehovah could, in full justice, put an end to all sinful mankind, this exalts all the more the greatness of his mercy and undeserved kindness in saving some of mankind for life. (Joh 3:36) He takes no pleasure in the death of the wicked (Eze 18:23, 32; 33:11), yet neither will he allow the wicked to escape the execution of his judgment. (Am 9:2-4; Ro 2:2-9) He is patient and long-suffering, with salvation in view for obedient ones (2Pe 3:8-10), yet he will not tolerate forever a situation that brings reproach upon his lofty name. (Ps 74:10, 22, 23; Isa 65:6, 7; 2Pe 2:3) He shows compassion and is understanding regarding human frailties, forgiving repentant ones "in a large way" (Ps 103:10-14; 130:3, 4; Isa 55:6, 7), yet he does not excuse persons from the responsibilities they rightly bear for their own actions and the effects these have on themselves and their families. They reap what they have sown. (De 30:19, 20; Ga 6:5, 7, 8) Thus, Jehovah shows a beautiful and perfect balance of justice and mercy. Those having the proper perspective of matters as revealed in his Word (Isa 55:8, 9; Eze 18:25, 29-31) will not commit the grave error of trifling with his undeserved kindness or 'missing its purpose.'—2Co 6:1; Heb 10:26-31; 12:29.

Unchanging in Qualities and Standards. As Jehovah told the people of Israel: "I am Jehovah; I have not changed." (Mal 3:6) This was some 3,500 years after God's creation of mankind and some 1,500 years from the time of God's making the Abrahamic covenant. While some claim that the God revealed in the Hebrew Scriptures differs from the God revealed by Jesus Christ and by the writers of the Christian Greek Scriptures, examination shows this claim to be without any foundation. Of God, the disciple James rightly said: "With him there is not a variation of the turning of the shadow." (Jas 1:17) There was no 'mellowing' of Jehovah God's personality during the centuries, for no mellowing was needed. His severity as revealed in the Christian Greek Scriptures is no less nor his love any greater than it was at the beginning of his dealings with mankind in Eden.

The seeming differences in personality are in reality merely different aspects of the same unchanging personality. These result from the differing circumstances and persons dealt with, calling for different attitudes or relationships. (Compare Isa 59:1-4.) It was not Jehovah, but Adam and Eve, who changed; they put themselves in a position where Jehovah's unchangeable righteous standards allowed no further dealings with them as members of his beloved universal family. Being perfect, they were fully responsible for their deliberate wrongdoing (Ro 5:14) and hence beyond the limits of divine mercy, although

Jehovah showed them undeserved kindness in starting them out with clothing and allowing them to live for centuries outside the sanctuary of Eden and bring forth offspring before they finally died from the effects of their own sinful course. (Ge 3:8-24) After their eviction from Eden all divine communication with Adam and his wife apparently ceased.

Why he can deal with imperfect humans. Jehovah's just standards allowed for his dealing differently with Adam and Eve's offspring than with their parents. Why? For the reason that Adam's offspring *inherited* sin, hence involuntarily started life as imperfect creatures with a built-in inclination toward wrongdoing. (Ps 51:5; Ro 5:12) Thus, there was basis for mercy toward them. Jehovah's first prophecy (Ge 3:15), spoken at the time of pronouncing judgment in Eden, showed that the rebellion of his first human children (as well as that of one of his spirit sons) had not embittered Jehovah nor dried up the flow of his love. That prophecy pointed in symbolic terms toward a righting of the situation produced by the rebellion and a restoration of conditions to their original perfection, the full significance being revealed millenniums later.—Compare the symbolisms of the "serpent," the "woman," and the "seed" at Re 12:9, 17; Ga 3:16, 29; 4:26, 27.

Adam's descendants have been permitted to continue on earth for thousands of years, though imperfect and in a dying condition, never able to free themselves from sin's deadly grip. The Christian apostle Paul explained Jehovah's reason for allowing this, saying: "For the creation was subjected to futility, not by its own will but through him that subjected it [that is, Jehovah God], on the basis of hope that the creation itself also will be set free from enslavement to corruption and have the glorious freedom of the children of God. For we know that all creation keeps on groaning together and being in pain together until now." (Ro 8:20-22) As shown in the article FOREKNOWLEDGE, FOREORDINATION, there is nothing to indicate that Jehovah chose to use his powers of discernment to foresee the original pair's deflection. However, once it took place, Jehovah foreordained the means for correcting the wrong situation. (Eph 1:9-11) This sacred secret, originally locked up in the symbolic prophecy in Eden, was finally fully revealed in Jehovah's only-begotten Son, sent to earth that he might "bear witness to the truth" and "by God's undeserved kindness might taste death for every man."—Joh 18:37; Heb 2:9; see RANSOM.

God's dealing with and blessing certain descendants of the sinner Adam, therefore, marked no change in Jehovah's standards of perfect righteousness. He was not thereby approving their sinful state. Because his purposes are absolutely certain of fulfillment, Jehovah "calls the things that are not as though they were" (as in naming Abram "Abraham," meaning "Father of a Crowd (Multitude)" while he was yet childless). (Ro 4:17) Knowing that in his due time (Ga 4:4) he would provide a ransom, the legal means for forgiving sin and removing imperfection (Isa 53:11, 12; Mt 20:28; 1Pe 2:24), Jehovah consistently could deal with and have in his service imperfect men, inheritors of sin. This was because he had the just basis for 'counting,' or reckoning, them as righteous persons because of their faith in Jehovah's promises and, eventually, in the fulfillment of those promises in Christ Jesus as the perfect sacrifice for sins. (Jas 2:23; Ro 4:20-25) Thus, Jehovah's provision of the ransom arrangement and its benefits gives striking testimony not only of Jehovah's love and mercy but also of his fidelity to his exalted standards of justice, for by the ransom arrangement he exhibits "his own righteousness in this present season, that he might be righteous even when declaring righteous the man [though imperfect] that has faith in Jesus."—Ro 3:21-26; compare Isa 42:21; see DECLARE RIGHTEOUS.

Why the 'God of peace' fights. Jehovah's statement in Eden that he would put enmity between the seed of his Adversary and the seed of "the woman" did not change Him from being the 'God of peace.' (Ge 3:15; Ro 16:20; 1Co 14:33) The situation then was the same as in the days of the earthly life of his Son, Jesus Christ, who, after referring to his union with his heavenly Father, said: "Do not think I came to put peace upon the earth; I came to put, not peace, but a sword." (Mt 10:32-40) Jesus' ministry brought divisions, even within families (Lu 12:51-53), but it was because of his adherence to, and proclamation of, God's righteous standards and truth. Division resulted because many individuals hardened their hearts against these truths while others accepted them. (Joh 8:40, 44-47; 15:22-25; 17:14) This was unavoidable if the divine principles were to be upheld; but the blame lay with the rejecters of what was right.

So, too, enmity was foretold to come because Jehovah's perfect standards would allow for no condoning of the rebellious course of Satan's "seed." God's disapproval of such ones and his blessing of those holding to a righteous course would have a divisive effect (Joh 15:18-21; Jas 4:4), even as in the case of Cain and Abel.—Ge 4:2-8; Heb 11:4; 1Jo 3:12; Jude 10, 11; see CAIN.

The rebellious course chosen by men and wicked angels constituted a challenge to Jehovah's rightful sovereignty and to the good order of all the universe. Standing up to this challenge has required Jehovah to become "a manly person of war" (Ex 15:3-7), defending his own good name and righteous standards, fighting on behalf of those who love and serve him, and executing judgment upon those meriting destruction. (1Sa 17:45; 2Ch 14:11; Isa 30:27-31; 42:13) He does not hesitate to use his almighty power, devastatingly at times, as at the Flood, in the destruction of Sodom and Gomorrah, and in the delivery of Israel from Egypt. (De 7:9, 10) And he has no fear of making known any of the details of his righteous warfare; he makes no apologies, having nothing for which to be ashamed. (Job 34:10-15; 36:22-24; 37:23, 24; 40:1-8; Ro 3:4) His respect for his own name and the righteousness it represents, as well as his love for those who love him, compels him to act.—Isa 48:11; 57:21; 59:15-19; Re 16:5-7.

The Christian Greek Scriptures portray the same picture. The apostle Paul encouraged fellow Christians, saying: "The God who gives peace will crush Satan under your feet shortly." (Ro 16:20; compare Ge 3:15.) He also showed the rightness of God's repaying tribulation to those causing tribulation for his servants, bringing everlasting destruction upon such opposers. (2Th 1:6-9) This was in harmony with the teachings of God's Son, who left no room for doubt as to his Father's uncompromising determination forcibly to end all wickedness and those practicing it. (Mt 13:30, 38-42; 21:42-44; 23:33; Lu 17:26-30; 19:27) The book of Revelation is replete with descriptions of divinely authorized warring action. All of this, however, in Jehovah's wisdom ultimately leads to the establishment of an enduring, universal peace, solidly founded on justice and righteousness.—Isa 9:6, 7; 2Pe 3:13.

Dealings with fleshly and spiritual Israel. Similarly, much of the difference in content between the Hebrew Scriptures and the Christian Greek Scriptures is because the former deal mainly with Jehovah's dealings with fleshly Israel, whereas the latter, to a large extent, lead up to and portray his dealings with spiritual Israel, the Christian congregation. Thus, on the one hand, we have a nation whose millions of members are such solely by virtue of fleshly descent, a conglomerate of the good and the bad. On the other hand, we have a spiritual nation formed of persons drawn to God through Jesus Christ, persons who show love for truth and right and who personally and voluntarily dedicate themselves to the doing of Jehovah's will. Logically, God's dealings and relations with the two groups would differ and the first group would reasonably call forth more expressions of Jehovah's anger and severity than would the second group.

Yet it would be a grave error to miss the upbuilding and comforting insight into Jehovah God's personality that his dealings with fleshly Israel provide. These give sterling examples proving that Jehovah is the kind of Person he described himself to Moses as being: "Jehovah, Jehovah, a God merciful and gracious, slow to anger and abundant in loving-kindness and truth, preserving loving-kindness for thousands, pardoning error and transgression and sin, but by no means will he give exemption from punishment, bringing punishment for the error of fathers upon sons and upon grandsons, upon the third generation and upon the fourth generation."—Ex 34:4-7; compare Ex 20:5.

Though balanced by justice, it is in reality Jehovah's love, patience, and long-suffering that are the outstanding facets of his personality as revealed in the history of Israel, a highly favored people who, in their majority, proved remarkably "stiff-necked" and "hardhearted" toward their Creator. (Ex 34:8, 9; Ne 9:16, 17; Jer 7:21-26; Eze 3:7) The strong denunciations and condemnation repeatedly leveled against Israel by Jehovah through his prophets only serve to emphasize the greatness of his mercy and the amazing extent of his long-suffering. At the end of over 1,500 years of bearing with them, and even after his own Son was slain at the instigation of religious leaders of the nation, Jehovah continued to favor them for a period of three and a half more years, mercifully causing the preaching of the good news to be restricted to them, granting them yet further opportunity to gain the privilege of reigning with his Son—an opportunity that repentant thousands accepted.—Ac 2:1-5, 14-41; 10:24-28, 34-48; see SEVENTY WEEKS.

Jesus Christ evidently referred to Jehovah's previously quoted statement as to 'bringing punishment to later descendants of offenders' when he said to the hypocritical scribes and Pharisees: "You say, 'If we were in the days of our forefathers, we would not be sharers with them in the blood of the prophets.' Therefore you are bearing witness against yourselves that you are sons of those who murdered the prophets. Well, then, *fill up the measure of your forefathers.*" (Mt 23:29-32) Despite their pretensions, by their course of action such ones demonstrated their approval of the wrong deeds of their forefathers and proved that they themselves continued to be among 'those hating Jehovah.' (Ex 20:5; Mt 23:33-36; Joh 15:23, 24) Thus, they, unlike the Jews who repented and heeded the words of God's Son, suffered the cumulative effect of God's judgment when, years later, Jerusalem was besieged and destroyed and most of its population died. They could have escaped but chose not to avail themselves of Jehovah's mercy.—Lu 21:20-24; compare Da 9:10, 13-15.

His personality reflected in his Son. In every respect Jesus Christ was a faithful reflection of the beautiful personality of his Father, Jehovah God, in whose name he came. (Joh 1:18; Mt 21:9; Joh 12:12, 13; compare Ps 118:26.) Jesus said: "The Son cannot do a single thing of his own initiative, but only what he beholds the Father doing. For whatever things that One does, these things the Son also does in like manner." (Joh 5:19) It follows, therefore, that the kindness and compassion, the mildness and warmth, as well as the strong love for righteousness and hatred of wickedness that Jesus displayed (Heb 1:8, 9), are all qualities that the Son had observed in his Father, Jehovah God. —Compare Mt 9:35, 36 with Ps 23:1-6 and Isa 40:10, 11; Mt 11:27-30 with Isa 40:28-31 and Isa 57:15, 16; Lu 15:11-24 with Ps 103:8-14; Lu 19:41-44 with Eze 18:31, 32; Eze 33:11.

Every lover of righteousness who reads the inspired Scriptures and who truly comes to "know" with understanding the full meaning of Jehovah's name (Ps 9:9, 10; 91:14; Jer 16:21) has every reason, therefore, to love and bless that name (Ps 72:18-20; 119:132; Heb 6:10), praise and exalt it (Ps 7:17; Isa 25:1; Heb 13:15), fear and sanctify it (Ne 1:11; Mal 2:4-6; 3:16-18; Mt 6:9), trust in it (Ps 33:21; Pr 18:10), saying with the psalmist: "I will sing to Jehovah throughout my life; I will make melody to my God as long as I am. Let my musing about him be pleasurable. I, for my part, shall rejoice in Jehovah. The sinners will be finished off from the earth; and as for the wicked, they will be no longer. Bless Jehovah, O my soul. Praise Jah, you people!"—Ps 104:33-35.

JEHOVAH HIMSELF IS THERE.
This expression translates *Yehwah' Sham'mah,* applied to the city seen by the prophet Ezekiel in his vision recorded in chapters 40 through 48. (Eze 48:35) The visionary city is depicted as foursquare (4,500 long cubits to a side [2,331 m; 7,650 ft]) and as having 12 gates, each bearing the name of one of the tribes of Israel. (Eze 48:15, 16, 31-34) The visionary city of Ezekiel's prophecy is to belong to "all the house of Israel." (Eze 45:6) The name Jehovah-Shammah, or "Jehovah Himself Is There," would signify a representational presence of God like that expressed in other texts, such as Psalm 46:5; 132:13, 14; Isaiah 24:23; Joel 3:21; and Zechariah 2:10, 11, where Jehovah, whom 'the

heaven of the heavens cannot contain,' is spoken of as though residing in an earthly city or place. —1Ki 8:27; see also CHIEFTAIN.

JEHOVAH IS OUR RIGHTEOUSNESS.

The expression translated from the two words *Yehwah' Tsidh·qe'nu,* found at Jeremiah 23:6 and 33:16.

Jeremiah 23:5, 6 is a Messianic prophecy describing the future king sprouting from David's line to "execute justice and righteousness in the land." Since he rules as God's representative (even as David, and others, sat "upon Jehovah's throne" as God's anointed king; 1Ch 29:23), the prophecy says, "This is his name with which he will be called, Jehovah Is Our Righteousness." There is no basis for claiming, as some have, that this means that Jesus, the Messiah, and Jehovah are the same, forming one God. This can be seen from the fact that the similar Messianic prophecy at Jeremiah 33:14-16 applies the identical expression to Jerusalem, saying: "And this is what she will be called, Jehovah Is Our Righteousness." In both cases the expression shows that God's name, Jehovah, placed both upon his promised king and upon his chosen capital, is a guarantee of their righteousness. Moreover, the justice and righteousness emanating from or expressed by these sources are the product of full devotion to Jehovah and his divine will, bringing Jehovah's blessing and direction.

JEHOVAH-JIREH

(Je·ho'vah-ji'reh) [Jehovah Will See To [It]; Jehovah Will Provide]. A place on one of the mountains in the land of Moriah where Abraham found a ram caught in a thicket and subsequently offered it instead of Isaac. Abraham viewed this ram as Jehovah's provision and therefore named the place Jehovah-jireh. Ancient tradition links this location with the site of Solomon's temple.—Ge 22:2, 13, 14; see MORIAH.

JEHOVAH-NISSI

(Je·ho'vah-nis'si). The name of the memorial altar erected by Moses after Israel's successful battle against the Amalekites at Rephidim.—Ex 17:8, 13-16.

The name means "Jehovah Is My Signal Pole," deriving *nis·si'* from *nes* (signal pole). The Greek *Septuagint* translators understood *nis·si'* to be derived from *nus* (flee for refuge) and rendered it "Jehovah Is My Refuge," while in the Latin *Vulgate* it was thought to be derived from *na·sas'* (hoist; lift up) and was rendered "Jehovah Is My Exaltation."—Ex 17:15, ftn.

JEHOVAH OF ARMIES.

This expression, found 283 times, with variations, in the Scriptures, translates the Hebrew *Yeho·wah' tseva-*

'ohth'. The prophetic books, particularly Isaiah, Jeremiah, and Zechariah, contain by far the majority of its occurrences. Paul and James, quoting from or alluding to the prophecies, used the expression (transliterated into Greek) in their writings.—Ro 9:29; Jas 5:4; compare Isa 1:9.

The Hebrew word *tsa·va''* (singular; plural, *tseva·'ohth'*) basically means a literal army of soldiers, or combat forces, as at Genesis 21:22; Deuteronomy 20:9, and many other texts. However, the term is also used in a figurative sense as in "the heavens and the earth and all their army," or "the sun and the moon and the stars, all the army of the heavens." (Ge 2:1; De 4:19) The plural form (*tseva·'ohth'*) is employed a number of times as applying to the Israelite forces, as at Exodus 6:26; 7:4; Numbers 33:1; Psalms 44:9; 60:10. Some scholars believe that the "armies" in the expression "Jehovah of armies" include not only the angelic forces but also the Israelite army and the inanimate heavenly bodies. However, it appears that the "armies" signified are primarily, if not exclusively, the angelic forces.

When Joshua saw an angelic visitor near Jericho and asked him if he was for Israel or for the enemy side, the reply was, "No, but I—as prince of the army of Jehovah I have now come." (Jos 5:13-15) The prophet Micaiah told Kings Ahab and Jehoshaphat, "I certainly see Jehovah sitting upon his throne and all the army of the heavens standing by him, to his right and to his left," clearly referring to Jehovah's spirit sons. (1Ki 22:19-21) The use of the plural form in "Jehovah of armies" is appropriate, inasmuch as the angelic forces are described not only in divisions of cherubs, seraphs, and angels (Isa 6:2, 3; Ge 3:24; Re 5:11) but also as forming organized groups, so that Jesus Christ could speak of having "more than twelve legions of angels" available at his call. (Mt 26:53) In Hezekiah's plea to Jehovah for help he called him "Jehovah of armies, the God of Israel, sitting upon the cherubs," evidently alluding to the ark of the covenant and the cherub figures on its cover, symbolizing Jehovah's heavenly throne. (Isa 37: 16; compare 1Sa 4:4; 2Sa 6:2.) Elisha's fearful servant was reassured by a miraculous vision in which he saw the mountains around the besieged city of Elisha's residence "full of horses and war chariots of fire," part of Jehovah's angelic hosts. —2Ki 6:15-17.

The expression "Jehovah of armies" thus conveys the sense of power, the power held by the Sovereign Ruler of the universe, who has at his command vast forces of spirit creatures. (Ps 103: 20, 21; 148:1, 2; Isa 1:24; Jer 32:17, 18) It thus commands deep respect and awe, while at the same time being a source of comfort and encouragement to Jehovah's servants. David, alone and unaided by any earthly military force, challenged the formidable Philistine Goliath in "the name of Jehovah of armies, the God of the battle lines of Israel." (1Sa 17:45) Not only in times of literal battle but also in all other trialsome situations or occasions of importance God's people as a whole and as individuals could take courage and hope from recognizing the majesty of Jehovah's sovereign position, reflected in his control over the mighty forces serving from his heavenly courts. (1Sa 1:9-11; 2Sa 6:18; 7:25-29) The use of the expression "Jehovah of armies" by the prophets supplied yet one more reason for those hearing the prophecies to be certain of their fulfillment.

JEHOVAH'S DAY.   See DAY OF JEHOVAH.

JEHOVAH-SHALOM   (Je·ho′vah-sha′lom) [Jehovah Is Peace]. The name given to the altar that Gideon built at Ophrah W of the Jordan. After having seen Jehovah's angel, Gideon feared that he would die. But he was assured: "Peace be yours. Do not fear. You will not die." Out of gratitude, Gideon built the altar, evidently not for sacrifice, but as a memorial to Jehovah.—Jg 6:22-24.

JEHOZABAD   (Je·hoz′a·bad) [probably, Jehovah Has Endowed].

1. The second of Obed-edom's eight sons included among the sanctuary gatekeepers.—1Ch 26:1, 4, 5, 13, 15.

2. A Benjamite officer over 180,000 in King Jehoshaphat's army.—2Ch 17:17, 18.

3. An accomplice in the slaying of King Jehoash of Judah. Jehozabad and Jozacar, servants of Jehoash, put the king to death because he had murdered Jehoiada's son Zechariah. They themselves were killed by Jehoash's son and successor, Amaziah. Jehozabad was the son of a Moabitess named Shimrith (likely the same as Shomer).—2Ki 12:20, 21; 2Ch 24:20-22, 25-27; 25:1, 3.

JEHOZADAK   (Je·hoz′a·dak) [probably, Jehovah Pronounces Righteous], **JOZADAK** (Jo′za·dak) [shortened form of Jehozadak]. The shorter form is used in Nehemiah, the longer form elsewhere.

Father of High Priest Jeshua (or Joshua). (Ezr 3:2; Hag 1:12; Zec 6:11) Jehozadak was taken into exile after Nebuchadnezzar killed his father, the chief priest Seraiah, and thus through him the high-priestly line was preserved.—1Ch 6:14, 15; 2Ki 25:18-21; Ne 12:26.

JEHU   (Je′hu) [possibly, Jehovah Is He].

1. A Benjamite of the city of Anathoth who came as a volunteer to serve with David. David was then at Ziklag as a refugee from King Saul. Jehu was among the mighty men "armed with the bow, using the right hand and using the left hand with stones or with arrows in the bow."—1Ch 12:1-3.

2. A prophet, the son of Hanani. He foretold the destruction of the house of Baasha, king of Israel. (1Ki 16:1-4, 7, 12) More than 33 years later, a prophet by the same name (and hence, perhaps the same person) reproved King Jehoshaphat of Judah for his friendship with and assistance to wicked King Ahab of Israel. (2Ch 19:1-3) At 2 Chronicles 20:34 Jehoshaphat's history is said to be written "among the words of Jehu the son of Hanani, which were inserted in the Book of the Kings of Israel."

3. The son of Jehoshaphat (not King Jehoshaphat of Judah) and grandson of Nimshi. (2Ki 9:14) Jehu ruled as king of Israel from about 904 to 877 B.C.E. During the reign of King Ahab of Israel, Elijah the prophet had fled to Mount Horeb to escape death at the hands of Ahab's wife Jezebel. God commanded Elijah to go back and to anoint three men: Elisha as Elijah's successor, Hazael as king of Syria, and Jehu as king of Israel. (1Ki 19:15, 16) Elijah anointed Elisha (or, appointed him; see ANOINTED, ANOINTING). However, the anointing of Jehu remained for Elijah's successor Elisha actually to perform.

Was this leaving of Jehu's anointing to Elisha due to procrastination on Elijah's part? No. A while after giving Elijah the command, Jehovah told him that the calamity on Ahab's house (to be executed by Jehu) would not come in Ahab's day, but in the days of Ahab's son. (1Ki 21:27-29) So it is evident that the delay was by Jehovah's guidance and not because of laxity on Elijah's part. But Jehovah timed the anointing exactly right, when the opportunity was ripe for Jehu to put the anointing immediately into effect by action. And, in harmony with Jehu's decisive and dynamic personality, he did not lose a moment, but acted immediately.

The due time came. It was a time of war. Ahab was dead and his son Jehoram was ruling. Israel's army was gathered at Ramoth-gilead, keeping guard against the forces of Hazael, the king of Syria. Jehu was there as one of the military commanders. (2Ki 8:28; 9:14) He and his adjutant Bidkar, as soldiers in the army of Ahab, had been present when Elijah had denounced Ahab, prophesying that Jehovah would 'repay Ahab in the tract of land belonging to Naboth.' This tract had been taken by Ahab after his wife Jezebel had brought about Naboth's murder.—1Ki 21:11-19; 2Ki 9:24-26.

As Israel's military force kept guard at Ramoth-gilead, King Jehoram of Israel was at Jezreel recovering from wounds he had received at the hands of the Syrians at Ramah. The king of Judah, Ahaziah, was also there. He was a nephew of Jehoram of Israel, for his mother was Athaliah the sister of Jehoram of Israel and the daughter of Ahab and Jezebel. King Ahaziah had come to Jezreel on a visit to his sick uncle, Jehoram.—2Ki 8:25, 26, 28, 29.

Jehu's Anointing. Elisha called one of the sons of the prophets, his attendant, telling him to take a flask of oil, go to the Israelite camp at Ramoth-gilead, there anoint Jehu, and flee. Elisha's attendant obeyed, calling Jehu away from the other officers into a house, where he anointed him and stated Jehu's commission to destroy the entire house of Ahab. Then the attendant fled, as Elisha had directed.—2Ki 9:1-10.

On coming out of the house, Jehu tried to pass off the matter lightly, as though the prophet had said nothing of importance. But the men saw from his appearance and manner that something of significance had occurred. On being pressed, Jehu revealed that he had been anointed as king of Israel; on hearing this pronouncement, the army immediately proclaimed him king.—2Ki 9:11-14.

Destruction of the House of Ahab. Giving orders to keep the matter secret from Jezreel, Jehu rode furiously toward that city. (2Ki 9:15, 16) Messengers sent out from Jezreel by Jehoram to inquire "Is there peace?" were sent to the rear of Jehu's men. As "the heaving mass" of Jehu's horsemen and chariots came closer, the chariot driving of Jehu "with madness" identified him to the watchman on the tower. Jehoram the king of Israel and son of Ahab became suspicious and rode out in his war chariot, reaching Jehu at Naboth's tract of land. Jehu shot him with an arrow and, recalling the prophecy of Elijah, commanded his adjutant Bidkar to throw his body into the field of Naboth. Then Jehu continued on into the city of Jezreel. Apparently Ahab's grandson Ahaziah, who had come out of the city with Jehoram, tried to make his way back to his own capital, Jerusalem, but got only as far as Samaria and hid there. He was captured later and taken to Jehu near the town of Ibleam, not far from Jezreel. Jehu ordered his men to kill him in his war chariot. They wounded him mortally, on the way up to Gur, near Ibleam, but he escaped and fled to Megiddo, where he died. Then he was taken to Jerusalem and buried there.—2Ki 9:17-28; 2Ch 22:6-9.

On Jehu's arrival in Jezreel, Ahab's widow Jezebel called out: "Did it go all right with Zimri the killer of his lord?" (See 1Ki 16:8-20.) But Jehu, unmoved by this veiled threat, called upon the court officials to throw her down. They complied. Her blood spattered on the wall, and Jehu trampled her under his horses. Possibly giving a further insight into Jehu's character is the terse statement in the account, "After that he came on in and ate and drank," then commanded her burial. In the meantime Jezebel had been eaten by the dogs, which circumstance brought back to Jehu's mind Elijah's prophetic expression concerning her death.—2Ki 9:30-37; 1Ki 21:23.

Jehu wasted no time in pursuing the completion of his mission. He challenged the men of Samaria to set one of Ahab's 70 sons on the throne and fight. But in fear they expressed loyalty to Jehu. Jehu boldly tested their loyalty by saying: "If you belong to me, . . . take the heads of the men that are sons of your lord and come to me tomorrow at this time at Jezreel." The next day messengers appeared, carrying in baskets the 70 heads, which Jehu commanded to be put in two heaps at the gate of Jezreel until morning. After this Jehu killed all of Ahab's distinguished men, his acquaintances, and his priests. Then he slaughtered 42 other men, the brothers of Ahab's grandson King Ahaziah of Judah. Thus he destroyed also the sons of Jehoram of Judah, the husband of wicked Jezebel's daughter Athaliah.—2Ki 10:1-14.

Great steps had been taken toward ridding Israel of Baal worship, but Jehu had much yet to do, and he went about it with characteristic promptness and zeal. On his ride to Samaria he encountered Jehonadab, a Rechabite. It may be recalled that the descendants of this man were later commended by Jehovah through the prophet Jeremiah for their faithfulness. (Jer 35:1-16) Jehonadab expressed himself as being on Jehu's side in his fight against Baalism and went along, assisting Jehu. All left over of those related to or connected with Ahab in Samaria were destroyed.—2Ki 10:15-17.

Baal Worshipers Annihilated. Next, by the ruse of calling a great gathering for the worship of Baal, Jehu got all of Israel's Baal worshipers to assemble at the house of Baal. After ascertaining that there were no worshipers of Jehovah present, Jehu commanded his men to put to death everyone in the house. They thereafter destroyed the sacred pillars of Baal and pulled down the house, setting it aside for privies, for which the site was used down to the day of Jeremiah, writer of the account in the book of Kings. The record reads:

"Thus Jehu annihilated Baal out of Israel." (2Ki 10:18-28) However, later on Baal worship again gave trouble in both Israel and Judah.—2Ki 17:16; 2Ch 28:2; Jer 32:29.

Likely to keep the ten-tribe kingdom of Israel distinct from the kingdom of Judah with its temple of Jehovah at Jerusalem, King Jehu let the calf worship remain in Israel with its centers at Dan and Bethel. "And Jehu himself did not take care to walk in the law of Jehovah the God of Israel with all his heart. He did not turn aside from the sins of Jeroboam with which he caused Israel to sin." —2Ki 10:29, 31.

Nevertheless, for Jehu's zealous and thorough work in eradicating Baalism and in executing Jehovah's judgments on the house of Ahab, Jehovah rewarded Jehu with the promise that four generations of his sons would sit upon the throne of Israel. This was fulfilled in Jehu's descendants Jehoahaz, Jehoash, Jeroboam II, and Zechariah, whose rule ended in his assassination in about 791 B.C.E. The dynasty of Jehu therefore reigned over Israel for about 114 years.—2Ki 10:30; 13:1, 10; 14:23; 15:8-12.

Why was the house of Jehu held accountable by God for bloodshed, when Jehovah had commissioned Jehu as his executioner?

However, after Jehu's day, by the prophet Hosea, Jehovah said: "For yet a little while and I must hold an accounting for the acts of bloodshed of Jezreel against the house of Jehu, and I must cause the royal rule of the house of Israel to cease." (Ho 1:4) This bloodguilt on Jehu's house could not be for his carrying out the commission to destroy the house of Ahab, for God commended him for this. Neither could it be because he destroyed Ahaziah of Judah and his brothers. By their family connections, namely, the marriage of Jehoram of Judah, the son of King Jehoshaphat, to Athaliah, the daughter of Ahab and Jezebel, the royal line of Judah was contaminated with an infiltration of the wicked house of Omri.

Rather, the key to the matter seems to lie in the statement that Jehu let calf worship continue in Israel and did not walk in the law of Jehovah with all his heart. Probably Jehu came to believe that independence from Judah could be maintained only through religious separation. Like other kings of Israel, he sought to secure his position by perpetuating calf worship. This was really an expression of lack of faith in Jehovah, who had made it

possible for Jehu to become king. So, it may be that, apart from the proper execution of Jehovah's judgment against the house of Ahab, the wrong motivations that prompted Jehu to let calf worship remain also caused him to spill blood.

The real power of the kingdom of Israel was broken when Jehu's house fell, the kingdom lasting only about 50 years longer. Only Menahem, who struck down Zechariah's murderer Shallum, had a son who succeeded him on the throne. This son, Pekahiah, was assassinated, as was his murderer and successor Pekah. Hoshea, Israel's last king, went into captivity to the king of Assyria. —2Ki 15:10, 13-30; 17:4.

The primary sin of Israel all along was its practice of calf worship. This led to the drawing of the nation away from Jehovah, with consequent deterioration. So the guilt for the "bloodshed of Jezreel" was one of the things, along with murdering, stealing, adultery, and other crimes, that really found its root in the false worship in which the rulers permitted the people to indulge. Finally God had to "cause the royal rule of the house of Israel to cease."—Ho 1:4; 4:2.

Syria and Assyria Harass Israel. Because of not turning fully to Jehovah and walking in his ways, Jehu had to face trouble from Hazael, the king of Syria, all the days of his rule. Hazael took territory piece by piece from Israel's domain on the other side of the Jordan. (2Ki 10:32, 33; Am 1:3, 4) At the same time the Assyrian threat to Israel's existence mounted.

Assyrian Inscriptions Name Jehu. In inscriptions of Shalmaneser III, king of Assyria, he claims to have received tribute from Jehu. The inscription reads: "The tribute of Jehu (Ia-ú-a), son of Omri (Hu-um-ri); I received from him silver, gold, a golden saplu-bowl, a golden vase with pointed bottom, golden tumblers, golden buckets, tin, a staff for a king, (and) wooden puruhtu [the meaning of the latter word being unknown]." (Ancient Near Eastern Texts, edited by J. B. Pritchard, 1974, p. 281) (Actually, Jehu was not the son of Omri. But from Omri's time the expression was sometimes used to designate the kings of Israel, doubtless because of Omri's prowess and his building of Samaria, which continued as Israel's capital until the fall of that ten-tribe kingdom to Assyria.)

Along with this same inscription on what is known as the Black Obelisk is a pictorial representation, perhaps of an emissary of Jehu, bowing before Shalmaneser and offering tribute. Some commentators remark that this is the first pictorial portrayal of Israelites, as far as is known. However, we cannot be absolutely sure of the truthfulness of Shalmaneser's claim. Also, the appearance of the figure in the picture cannot be relied on to be an accurate likeness of an Israelite, for these nations may have depicted their enemies as undesirable in appearance, much as drawings or pictures today portray people of an enemy nation as weak, grotesque, or hateful.

4. The son of Obed of the family of Jerahmeel, a descendant of Hezron, son of Perez, who was born to Judah by Tamar. This Jehu's line came through Jarha, an Egyptian slave. Sheshan, a descendant of Jerahmeel, had no sons, so he gave to Jarha his daughter as wife. The son born to them was Attai, an ancestor of Jehu.—1Ch 2:3-5, 25, 34-38.

5. A Simeonite, the son of Joshibiah. In the days of King Hezekiah of Judah he was among the chieftains of the Simeonite families who struck down the Hamites and the Meunim living in the vicinity of Gedor and who dwelt thereafter in the place of these people with their flocks.—1Ch 4:24, 35, 38-41.

JEHUBBAH (Je·hub′bah). A leading member of the tribe of Asher.—1Ch 7:34, 40.

JEHUCAL (Je·hu′cal) [Jehovah Is Able; Jehovah Prevails], **JUCAL** (Ju′cal) [shortened form of Jehucal, meaning "Jehovah Is Able; Jehovah Prevails"]. A prince sent by King Zedekiah to ask Jeremiah to pray for Judah. (Jer 37:3) This son of Shelemiah and three other influential princes had Jeremiah put into the miry cistern because his preaching was, as they put it, "weakening the hands of the men of war," as well as the hands of the people in general.—Jer 38:1-6.

JEHUD (Je′hud). A site in the territory of Dan (Jos 19:40, 45) usually identified with el-Yehudiyeh (Yehud), some 13 km (8 mi) E of Tel Aviv-Yafo. The Greek *Septuagint* (Vatican MS. No. 1209), though, uses "Azor" instead of "Jehud." (Jos 19:45) Therefore some scholars link Jehud with a tell near Yazur (Azor), about 6 km (3.5 mi) ESE of Tel Aviv-Yafo. It is believed that this is the place called Azuru in Sennacherib's annals.

JEHUDI (Je·hu′di) [A Jew; Of (Belonging to) Judah]. An officer of King Jehoiakim sent by the princes of Judah to bring to them Baruch with Jeremiah's scroll. When Jehudi later read the same roll to Jehoiakim, the king cut it up and burned it, piece by piece, until the whole scroll was destroyed.—Jer 36:14, 21-23, 27, 32.

Jehudi was a great-grandson of Cushi. (Jer 36:14) His name and that of his ancestor are thought by some to denote that he was not a Jew by birth, but a proselyte, his great-grandfather's name suggesting that the family was from Cush, or Ethiopia. However, those of the generations in between both have typical Jewish names (Nethaniah his father and Shelemiah his grandfather), and even the name Cushi itself is elsewhere found as a proper name of a natural-born Jew. (Zep 1:1) So Jehudi was most likely simply a proper name given at birth and not a name first acquired as a proselyte.

JEIEL (Je·i′el).

1. A descendant of Jacob's son Reuben.—1Ch 5:1, 7.

2. A Benjamite who, together with his family (wife Maacah and ten sons), was a settler of Gibeon; an ancestor of King Saul. (1Ch 8:29; 9:35-39) Apparently the same as Abiel.—1Sa 9:1; see ABIEL No. 1.

3. One of David's mighty men; son of Hotham the Aroerite.—1Ch 11:26, 44.

4. A Levite, both a gatekeeper and a musician, who participated in the musical celebration when the Ark was first brought to Jerusalem and thereafter played in front of the tent that contained it. —1Ch 15:17, 18, 21, 28; 16:1, 4, 5 (the second occurrence of the name in vs 5).

5. Another Levite musician who performed the same services as No. 4. (1Ch 16:5, the first occurrence of the name in that verse) He is called Jaaziel at 1 Chronicles 15:18 and Aziel in 15:20.

6. A Levitical descendant of Asaph and ancestor of the Levite who encouraged King Jehoshaphat and the inhabitants of Judah and Jerusalem not to fear their enemies, for Jehovah would be with his people.—2Ch 20:14-17.

7. The secretary who registered and numbered King Uzziah's army.—2Ch 26:11.

8. One of the chief Levites who made a very large contribution of animals for King Josiah's great Passover celebration.—2Ch 35:1, 9.

9. A descendant of Adonikam who made the trip with Ezra from Babylon to Jerusalem in 468 B.C.E.—Ezr 8:1, 13.

10. One of the sons of Nebo who sent away their foreign wives and sons in Ezra's day.—Ezr 10:43, 44.

JEKABZEEL (Je·kab′ze·el) [God Has Collected]. An alternate form of the name Kabzeel. (Ne 11:25) This was a city in the southern part of Judah and is tentatively identified with Khirbet

Hora, about 10 km (6 mi) ENE of Beer-sheba.—See KABZEEL.

JEKAMEAM
(Jek·a·me′am) [May the People Rise Up]. The fourth son of Hebron, a Kohathite Levite, and founder of a Levitical paternal house that survived at least until David's reign.—1Ch 23:12, 19; 24:23, 30b, 31.

JEKAMIAH
(Jek·a·mi′ah) [Jah Has Raised Up].
1. A descendant of Judah and son of Shallum. —1Ch 2:3, 41.
2. One of the sons born to King Jehoiachin (Jeconiah) during his Babylonian exile.—1Ch 3:17, 18.

JEKUTHIEL
(Je·ku′thi·el). A descendant of Judah and "father of Zanoah." (1Ch 4:1, 18) Zanoah is the name of a city rather than a person in its other occurrence (Jos 15:56, 57), so Jekuthiel as its "father" was likely the father of those who settled there, or was himself its founder or chief settler.

JEMIMAH
(Je·mi′mah). The first of Job's three daughters born after his great test. Jemimah and her sisters, the most beautiful women in all the land, received an inheritance in among their seven brothers.—Job 42:13-15.

JEMUEL
(Jem·u′el) [possibly, Day of God]. The first-named son of Simeon and one of the "seventy" numbered among Jacob's household "who came into Egypt." (Ge 46:10, 27; Ex 6:15) In other accounts he is called Nemuel.—Nu 26:12; 1Ch 4:24.

JEPHTHAH
(Jeph′thah) [May [God] Open; [God] Has Opened]. A judge of Israel, of the tribe of Manasseh. (Nu 26:29; Jg 11:1) He administered justice over the territory of Gilead for six years perhaps during the priesthood of Eli and the early life of Samuel. (Jg 12:7) Jephthah's reference to "three hundred years" of Israelite control E of the Jordan would seem to place the start of his six-year judgeship around 1173 B.C.E.—Jg 11:26.

Jephthah a Legitimate Son. The mother of Jephthah was "a prostitute woman," not meaning, however, that Jephthah was born of prostitution or was illegitimate. His mother *had been* a prostitute prior to her marriage as a secondary wife to Gilead, just as Rahab had once been a prostitute but later married Salmon. (Jg 11:1; Jos 2:1; Mt 1:5) That Jephthah was not illegitimate is proved by the fact that his half brothers by Gilead's primary wife drove him out so that he would not share in the inheritance. (Jg 11:2) Additionally, Jephthah later became the accepted leader of the men of Gilead (of whom Jephthah's half brothers

seemed to be foremost). (Jg 11:11) Moreover, he offered a sacrifice to God at the tabernacle. (Jg 11:30, 31) None of these things would have been possible for an illegitimate son, for the Law specifically stated: "No illegitimate son may come into the congregation of Jehovah. Even to the tenth generation none of his may come into the congregation of Jehovah."—De 23:2.

Jephthah was evidently the firstborn of Gilead. Consequently he would normally have inherited two portions in the property of his father Gilead (who apparently was dead at the time Jephthah's half brothers drove him out) and would also have been the head of the family. Only by illegally driving him away could Jephthah's half brothers deprive him of his rightful inheritance, for even though the firstborn son of a father was the son of a secondary wife, or even a less-favored wife, he was, nevertheless, to receive the firstborn's rights. —De 21:15-17.

"Idle Men" Gather to Jephthah. When Jephthah was driven away by his half brothers he took up dwelling in the land of Tob, a region E of Gilead, apparently outside the borders of Israel. Here Jephthah would be on the frontier, exposed to Israel's foreign enemies, particularly Ammon. "Idle men," that is, men evidently made idle or put out of employment by Ammonite harassment, and revolting against servitude to Ammon, came to Jephthah and put themselves under his command. (Jg 11:3) The people living in the territory E of the Jordan River (the tribes of Reuben, Gad, and half of Manasseh) were mainly cattle raisers, and the forays of the Ammonite raiders (who even crossed the Jordan at times) had apparently taken away the possessions and the means of livelihood from many of the inhabitants of Gilead. —Jg 10:6-10.

Ammonites Threaten War. For 18 years oppression by the Ammonites continued. This was permitted by God because the Israelites had unfaithfully turned to serving the gods of the nations round about. But now the sons of Israel were brought to their senses, repenting of their folly and calling on Jehovah for help. They began to do away with their idols and to serve Jehovah. At this point Ammon gathered together in Gilead for large-scale warfare. (Jg 10:7-17; 11:4) This fact indicates that it was actually the great invisible enemy of God, Satan the Devil, who incited the pagan nations against Israel and that the real issue was worship of the true God.—Compare Re 12:9; Ps 96:5; 1Co 10:20.

Israel gathered its forces at Mizpah. The half brothers of Jephthah were evidently prominent among the older men of Gilead. (Jg 10:17; 11:7) They saw the need for proper leadership and direction. (Jg 10:18) They realized that they must be under the headship of a God-appointed man if they were to defeat Ammon. (Jg 11:5, 6, 10) Undoubtedly Jephthah and his men had been performing exploits in Tob, suggesting that he was God's designated choice. (Jg 11:1) The men of Gilead decided to go to Jephthah, whom they had despised, to ask him to be their head.

Jephthah Becomes Head of Gilead. Jephthah agreed to lead them in the fight against Ammon on one condition: if Jehovah gave him victory, he would continue as head after returning from the fight. His insistence on this was not a selfish demand. He had shown himself concerned with the fight in behalf of God's name and his people. Now, if he defeated Ammon, it would prove that God was with him. Jephthah wanted to make sure that God's rule would not be forsaken again once the crisis had passed. Also, if he was indeed Gilead's firstborn son, he was only establishing his legal right as head of the house of Gilead. The covenant was then concluded before Jehovah in Mizpah. Here again Jephthah showed that he looked to Jehovah as Israel's God and King and their real Deliverer.—Jg 11:8-11.

Jephthah, a man of action, lost no time in exercising vigorous leadership. He sent a message to the king of Ammon, pointing out that Ammon was the aggressor in invading Israel's land. The king replied that it was land Israel had taken from Ammon. (Jg 11:12, 13) Here Jephthah showed himself to be, not a mere rough, uncultured warrior, but a student of history and particularly of God's dealings with his people. He refuted the Ammonite argument, showing that (1) Israel did not molest Ammon, Moab, or Edom (Jg 11:14-18; De 2:9, 19, 37; 2Ch 20:10, 11); (2) Ammon had not possessed the disputed land at the time of the Israelite conquest, because it was in the hands of the Canaanite Amorites and God had given their king, Sihon, and his land into Israel's hand; (3) Ammon had not disputed Israel's occupation for the past 300 years; therefore, on what valid basis could they do so now?—Jg 11:19-27.

Jephthah got at the heart of the matter when he showed that the issue revolved around the matter of worship. He declared that Jehovah God had given Israel the land and that for this reason they would not give an inch of it to worshipers of a false god. He called Chemosh the god of Ammon. Some have thought this to be an error. But, although Ammon had the god Milcom, and though Chemosh was a god of Moab, those related nations worshiped many gods. Solomon even wrongly

brought the worship of Chemosh into Israel because of his foreign wives. (Jg 11:24; 1Ki 11:1, 7, 8, 33; 2Ki 23:13) Furthermore, "Chemosh" may mean "Subduer, Conqueror," according to some scholars. (See *Gesenius's Hebrew and Chaldee Lexicon,* translated by S. Tregelles, 1901, p. 401.) Jephthah may have called attention to this god as being given credit by the Ammonites for 'subduing' or 'conquering' others and giving them land.

Jephthah's Vow. Jephthah now saw that a fight with Ammon was God's will. With God's spirit energizing him, he led his army to the fight. Similar to Jacob's action some 600 years previously, Jephthah made a vow, demonstrating his wholehearted desire for Jehovah's direction and attributing any success he would have to Jehovah. (Jg 11:30, 31; Ge 28:20-22) Jehovah heard his vow with favor, and the Ammonites were subdued. —Jg 11:32, 33.

Did Jephthah have in mind human sacrifice when he vowed to present as a burnt offering the first one coming out of his house?

Some critics and scholars have condemned Jephthah for his vow, having the view that Jephthah followed the practice of other nations, offering up his daughter by fire as a human burnt offering. But this is not the case. It would be an insult to Jehovah, a disgusting thing in violation of his law, to make a literal human sacrifice. He strictly commanded Israel: "You must not learn to do according to the detestable things of those nations. There should not be found in you anyone who makes his son or his daughter pass through the fire . . . For everybody doing these things is something detestable to Jehovah, and on account of these detestable things Jehovah your God is driving them away from before you." (De 18:9-12) Jehovah would curse, not bless, such a person. The very ones Jephthah was fighting, the Ammonites, practiced human sacrifice to their god Molech. —Compare 2Ki 17:17; 21:6; 23:10; Jer 7:31, 32; 19:5, 6.

When Jephthah said: "It must also occur that the one coming out, who comes out of the doors of my house to meet me . . . must also become Jehovah's," he had reference to a person and not an animal, since animals suitable for sacrifice were not likely kept in Israelite homes, to have free run there. Besides, the offering of an animal would not show extraordinary devotion to God. Jephthah knew that it might well be his daughter who would come out to meet him. It must be borne in mind that Jehovah's spirit was on Jephthah at the time; this would prevent any rash vow on Jephthah's part. How, then, would the person coming out to meet Jephthah to congratulate him on his victory "become Jehovah's" and be offered up "as a burnt offering"?—Jg 11:31.

Persons could be devoted to Jehovah's exclusive service in connection with the sanctuary. It was a right that parents could exercise. Samuel was one such person, promised to tabernacle service by a vow of his mother Hannah before his birth. This vow was approved by her husband Elkanah. As soon as Samuel was weaned, Hannah offered him at the sanctuary. Along with him, Hannah brought an animal sacrifice. (1Sa 1:11, 22-28; 2:11) Samson was another child specially devoted to God's service as a Nazirite.—Jg 13:2-5, 11-14; compare the father's authority over a daughter as outlined in Nu 30:3-5, 16.

When Jephthah brought his daughter to the sanctuary, which was in Shiloh at that time, he undoubtedly accompanied his presentation of her with an animal burnt offering. According to the Law, a burnt offering was slaughtered, skinned, and cut up; the intestines and shanks were washed; and its body, head and all, was burned on the altar. (Le 1:3-9) The wholeness of such offering represented full, unqualified, wholehearted dedication to Jehovah, and when it accompanied another offering (as, for example, when the burnt offering followed the sin offering on the Day of Atonement), it constituted an appeal to Jehovah to accept that other offering.—Le 16:3, 5, 6, 11, 15, 24.

It was a real sacrifice on the part of both Jephthah and his daughter, for he had no other child. (Jg 11:34) Therefore no descendant of his would carry on his name and his inheritance in Israel. Jephthah's daughter was his only hope for this. She wept, not over her death, but over her "virginity," for it was the desire of every Israelite man and woman to have children and to keep the family name and inheritance alive. (Jg 11:37, 38) Barrenness was a calamity. But Jephthah's daughter "never had relations with a man." Had these words applied only to the time prior to the carrying out of the vow, they would have been superfluous, for she is specifically said to have been a virgin. That the statement has reference to the fulfilling of the vow is shown in that it follows the expression, "He carried out his vow that he had made toward her." Actually, the record is pointing out that also *after* the vow was carried out she

maintained her virginity.—Jg 11:39; compare renderings in *KJ; Dy; Yg; NW*.

Moreover, Jephthah's ·daughter was visited "from year to year" by her companions to 'give her commendation.' (Jg 11:40) The Hebrew word *ta-nah'*, used here, also occurs at Judges 5:11, and in that text is variously rendered "recount" (*NW*), "rehearse" (*KJ*), "recounted" (*AT*), "repeat" (*RS*). The word is defined in *A Hebrew and Chaldee Lexicon* (edited by B. Davies, 1957, p. 693) as "to repeat, to rehearse." At Judges 11:40 the *King James Version* renders the term "lament," but the margin reads "talk with." As Jephthah's daughter served at the sanctuary, doubtless like other Nethinim ("Given Ones" devoted to sanctuary service), there was much she could do. These persons served in gathering wood, drawing water, doing repair work, and undoubtedly performing many other tasks as assistants to the priests and Levites there.—Jos 9:21, 23, 27; Ezr 7:24; 8:20; Ne 3:26.

Ephraimites Resist Jephthah. The Ephraimites, who considered themselves the dominant tribe of northern Israel (including Gilead), proudly refused to acknowledge Jephthah and sought to justify themselves. So they worked up a false charge as an excuse for taking offense against him. A like attitude had been shown by them years before, in Judge Gideon's time. (Jg 8:1) They claimed that Jephthah failed to call them to the fight against Ammon, and they threatened to burn Jephthah's house over him.—Jg 12:1.

Jephthah replied that he had called them but they had refused to respond. He argued: *"Jehovah gave them [Ammon] into my hand. So why have you come up against me this day to fight against me?"* (Jg 12:2, 3) The Ephraimites contended about Jephthah's forces: "Men escaped from Ephraim is what you are, O Gilead, inside of Ephraim, inside of Manasseh." (Jg 12:4) By this they may have been slurring Jephthah by reference to his formerly being driven out and having associated with him "idle men," unemployed, as 'fugitives.'—Jg 11:3.

In the fight that ensued, Ephraim was beaten and routed. Jephthah's men stopped them at the fords of the Jordan. When the fleeing Ephraimites tried to conceal their identity, their pronunciation gave them away. When tested by being asked to say the word "Shibboleth," they were unable to pronounce the harsh "sh" but could only form a soft "Sibboleth." For taking rebellious action against one whom Jehovah had appointed for their salvation, 42,000 Ephraimites lost their lives. —Jg 12:5, 6.

Approved by God. At 1 Samuel 12:11 Jephthah is named as being sent by Jehovah as a deliverer, and at Hebrews 11:32 he is listed among the faithful "cloud of witnesses."—Heb 12:1.

JEPHUNNEH (Je·phun′neh).

1. Father of the Judean spy Caleb and, likely, the father of Kenaz. (Nu 13:2, 3, 6; 1Ch 4:15; Jg 1:13) Jephunneh was a Kenizzite associated with the tribe of Judah.—Jos 14:6, 14.

2. A prominent member of the tribe of Asher. —1Ch 7:38, 40.

JERAH (Je′rah) [Lunar Month]. A "son" of Joktan whose descendants may have settled somewhere in S Arabia.—Ge 10:26-29; 1Ch 1:20; see JOKTAN.

JERAHMEEL (Je·rah′me·el) [May God Show Mercy; God Has Shown Mercy].

1. The firstborn of Judah's grandson Hezron. The royal and Messianic lineage passed through Jerahmeel's brother Ram (apparently the same as Arni). An extensive genealogy is included for Jerahmeel's descendants, some of whom inhabited the southern part of Judah.—1Ch 2:4, 5, 9-15, 25-42; 1Sa 27:10; Lu 3:33.

2. Son or descendant of a Merarite Levite named Kish.—1Ch 24:26, 29; 23:21.

3. One of the three men sent by King Jehoiakim in his fifth year to seize Jeremiah and Baruch. They returned empty-handed, however, for Jehovah kept his faithful servants concealed.—Jer 36:9, 26.

Since Jehoiakim's successor and presumed firstborn Jehoiachin was only about 12 years old during his father's fifth year of rule, other sons of Jehoiakim were likely still younger, too young to be sent on such a mission as Jerahmeel's. (2Ki 23:36; 24:6, 8) Therefore, Jerahmeel's being called "the son of the king" might mean, not that he was an offspring of the king, but that he was a member of the royal household or an official of royal descent.

Of interest is the discovery of a seal impression, said to be from the seventh century B.C.E., that reads: "Belonging to Jerahmeel the king's son." —*Israel Exploration Journal,* Jerusalem, 1978, Vol. 28, p. 53.

JERAHMEELITES (Je·rah′me·el·ites) [Of (Belonging to) Jerahmeel]. The descendants of Judah through Jerahmeel son of Hezron. (1Ch 2:4, 9, 25-27, 33, 42) The Jerahmeelites lived in the southern part of Judah, apparently in the same general region as the Amalekites, Geshurites, and Girzites whom David raided while residing among the Philistines as a fugitive from King Saul. When returning from such raids, David would ambiguously report that these raids had been made "upon the south of Judah and upon the south of the Jerahmeelites and upon the south of the Kenites." Philistine King Achish, therefore, assumed that David had raided Israelites, thus making himself a stench to his countrymen and enhancing his value to Achish. (1Sa 27:7-12) In reality, David later shared spoils of war with the older men "in the cities of the Jerahmeelites."—1Sa 30:26, 29.

JERBOA [Heb., ′akh·bar′]. The Hebrew word ′akh·bar′, variously rendered "mouse," "rat," "jerboa," and "jumping rodent," is understood by many scholars as possibly embracing all varieties of rats, mice, and related animals such as the jerboa. However, a Hebrew and Aramaic lexicon by Koehler and Baumgartner gives the meaning of the Hebrew term as "jerboa."

The jerboa is a jumping rodent that somewhat resembles a miniature kangaroo and is still encountered in the arid parts of the Middle East. The desert jerboa (*Jaculus jaculus*) has a body length of from 10 to 15 cm (4-6 in.) and weighs 50 to 70 g (1.8-2.5 oz). Their ears and eyes are large. The

The jerboa resembles a miniature kangaroo

front limbs are short, but the two hind limbs measure about two thirds of the total head and body length. The tail is the longest part of the animal and terminates in a small brush. This nocturnal animal prefers desert lands, spending the hot day in its underground burrow but venturing forth during the cooler night to procure food.

Although the Arabs inhabiting the Syrian desert use the jerboa for food, it was legally unclean to the Israelites. (Le 11:29) But it seems that apostate Israelites ignored this prohibition of the Law.—Isa 66:17, ftn.

Jerboas are destructive to grain and other crops. During the time the sacred Ark was in the territory of the Philistines, the divinely sent plague of jerboas brought the land to ruin.—1Sa 6:4, 5, 11, 18.

JERED (Je′red). A descendant of Judah and "father" of those who settled Gedor.—1Ch 4:1, 18; see ATROTH-BETH-JOAB.

JEREMAI (Jer′e·mai) [shortened form of Jeremoth or of Jeremiah]. A postexilic Israelite, one of the seven sons or descendants of Hashum who had taken foreign wives but sent them away. —Ezr 10:25, 33, 44.

JEREMIAH (Jer·e·mi′ah) [possibly, Jehovah Exalts; or, Jehovah Loosens [likely from the womb]].

1. A Benjamite who joined David when he was at Ziklag. He was among David's mighty men. —1Ch 12:1-4.

2. One of the sons of Gad who gathered to David "at the place difficult to approach in the wilderness" when David was a refugee from Saul. He was the fifth among these "valiant, mighty men . . . whose faces were the faces of lions, and they were like the gazelles upon the mountains for speed." Of these Gadite heads of David's army, it is said: "The least one was equal to a hundred, and the greatest to a thousand." They "crossed the Jordan in the first month when it was overflowing all its banks, and they then chased away all those of the low plains, to the east and to the west." —1Ch 12:8-15.

3. The tenth one of the Gadite heads in David's army, as described in No. 2.—1Ch 12:13, 14.

4. One of the heads of paternal houses in the section of the tribe of Manasseh E of the Jordan in the days of the kings. The Reubenites, the Gadites, and the half tribe of Manasseh E of the Jordan (among them being this Jeremiah's descendants) "began to act unfaithfully toward the God of their forefathers and went having immoral intercourse with the gods of the peoples of the land, whom God had annihilated from before them. Consequently the God of Israel stirred up the spirit of Pul the king of Assyria even the spirit of Tilgath-pilneser the king of Assyria, so that [in the days of Pekah, king of Israel] he took into exile those of the Reubenites and of the Gadites and of the half tribe of Manasseh and brought them to Halah and Habor and Hara and the river Gozan."—1Ch 5:23-26; 2Ki 15:29.

5. A man of the town of Libnah, a priestly city. He was the father of King Josiah's wife Hamutal, who was the mother of Kings Jehoahaz and Zedekiah (Mattaniah).—2Ki 23:30, 31; 24:18; Jer 52:1; Jos 21:13; 1Ch 6:57.

6. A prophet, the son of Hilkiah, a priest of Anathoth, a city of the priests located in Benjamin's territory less than 5 km (3 mi) NNE of the Temple Mount in Jerusalem. (Jer 1:1; Jos 21:13, 17, 18) Jeremiah's father, Hilkiah, was not the high priest of that name, who was of the line of Eleazar. Jeremiah's father was very likely of the line of Ithamar and possibly descended from Abiathar, the priest whom King Solomon dismissed from priestly service.—1Ki 2:26, 27.

Commissioned as Prophet. Jeremiah was called to be a prophet when a young man, in 647 B.C.E., in the 13th year of the reign of King Josiah of Judah (659-629 B.C.E.). Jehovah told him: "Before I was forming you in the belly I knew you, and before you proceeded to come forth from the womb I sanctified you. Prophet to the nations I made you." (Jer 1:2-5) He was therefore one of the few men for whose birth Jehovah assumed responsibility—intervening by a miracle or by a guiding providence—that they might be his special servants. Among these men are Isaac, Samson, Samuel, John the Baptizer, and Jesus.—See FOREKNOWLEDGE, FOREORDINATION.

When Jehovah spoke to him, Jeremiah showed diffidence. He replied to God: "Alas, O Sovereign Lord Jehovah! Here I actually do not know how to speak, for I am but a boy." (Jer 1:6) From this remark of his, and comparing his boldness and firmness during his prophetic ministry, it can be seen that such unusual strength was not a thing inherent in Jeremiah, but actually came from full reliance on Jehovah. Truly Jehovah was with him "like a terrible mighty one," and it was Jehovah who made Jeremiah "a fortified city and an iron pillar and copper walls against all the land." (Jer 20:11; 1:18, 19) Jeremiah's reputation for courage and boldness was such that some during Jesus' earthly ministry took him to be Jeremiah returned to life.—Mt 16:13, 14.

Writings. Jeremiah was a researcher and a historian as well as a prophet. He wrote the book bearing his name and is also generally credited with writing the books of First and Second Kings, covering the history of both kingdoms (Judah and Israel) from the point where the books of Samuel left off (that is, in the latter part of David's reign over all Israel) down to the end of both kingdoms. His chronology of the period of the kings, using the method of comparison or collation of the reigns of Israel's and Judah's kings, helps us to establish the dates of certain events with accuracy. After the fall of Jerusalem, Jeremiah wrote the book of Lamentations.

Strong Denunciatory Message. Jeremiah was no chronic complainer. Rather, he showed himself to be loving, considerate, and sympathetic. He exercised fine control and marvelous endurance and was moved to great sadness by the conduct of his people and the judgments they suffered.—Jer 8:21.

Actually, it was Jehovah who made the complaint against Judah, and justifiably so, and Jeremiah was under obligation to declare it unremittingly, which he did. Also, it must be borne in mind that Israel was God's nation, bound to him by covenant and under his law, which they were grossly violating. As basis and solid ground for Jeremiah's denunciations, Jehovah repeatedly pointed to the Law, calling attention to the responsibility of the princes and the people and recounting wherein they had broken the Law. Time and again Jehovah called attention to the things he, through his prophet Moses, had warned them would come upon them if they refused to listen to his words and broke his covenant.—Le 26; De 28.

Courage, Endurance, Love. Jeremiah's courage and endurance were matched by his love for his people. He had scathing denunciations and fearful judgments to proclaim, especially to the priests, prophets, and rulers and to those who took "the popular course" and had developed "an enduring unfaithfulness." (Jer 8:5, 6) Yet he appreciated that his commission was also "to build and to plant." (Jer 1:10) He wept over the calamity that was to come to Jerusalem. (Jer 8:21, 22; 9:1) The book of Lamentations is an evidence of his love and concern for Jehovah's name and people. In spite of cowardly, vacillating King Zedekiah's treacherousness toward him, Jeremiah pleaded with him to obey the voice of Jehovah and continue living. (Jer 38:4, 5, 19-23) Furthermore, Jeremiah had no self-righteous attitude but included

himself when acknowledging the wickedness of the nation. (Jer 14:20, 21) After his release by Nebuzaradan, he hesitated to leave those being taken into Babylonian exile, perhaps feeling that he should share their lot or desiring to serve their spiritual interests further.—Jer 40:5.

At times in his long career Jeremiah became discouraged and required Jehovah's assurance, but even in adversity he did not forsake calling on Jehovah for help.—Jer 20.

Associations. Through all of his more than 40 years of prophetic service, Jeremiah was not abandoned. Jehovah was with him to deliver him from his enemies. (Jer 1:19) Jeremiah took delight in Jehovah's word. (Jer 15:16) He avoided association with those who had no consideration for God. (Jer 15:17) He found good associates among whom he could do 'building up' work (Jer 1:10), namely, the Rechabites, Ebed-melech, and Baruch. Through these friends he was assisted and delivered from death, and more than once Jehovah's power was manifested in protecting him.—Jer 26:7-24; 35:1-19; 36:19-26; 38:7-13; 39:11-14; 40:1-5.

Dramatic Illustrations. Jeremiah performed several small dramas as symbols to Jerusalem of her condition and the calamity to come to her. There was his visit to the house of the potter (Jer 18:1-11), and the incident of the ruined belt. (Jer 13:1-11) Jeremiah was commanded not to marry; this served as a warning of the "deaths from maladies" of the children who would be born during those last days of Jerusalem. (Jer 16:1-4) He broke a flask before the older men of Jerusalem as a symbol of the impending smashing of the city. (Jer 19:1, 2, 10, 11) He repurchased a field from his paternal uncle's son Hanamel as a figure of the restoration to come after the 70 years' exile, when fields would again be bought in Judah. (Jer 32:8-15, 44) Down in Tahpanhes, Egypt, he hid large stones in the terrace of bricks at the house of Pharaoh, prophesying that Nebuchadnezzar would set his throne over that very spot.—Jer 43:8-10.

A True Prophet. Jeremiah was acknowledged as God's true prophet by Daniel, who, by a study of Jeremiah's words concerning the 70 years' exile, was able to strengthen and encourage the Jews regarding the nearness of their release. (Da 9:1, 2; Jer 29:10) Ezra called attention to the fulfillment of his words. (Ezr 1:1; see also 2Ch 36:20, 21.) The apostle Matthew pointed to a fulfillment of one of Jeremiah's prophecies in the days of Jesus' young childhood. (Mt 2:17, 18; Jer 31:15) The apostle Paul spoke of the prophets, among whom was Jeremiah, from whose writings he quoted, at Hebrews 8:8-12. (Jer 31:31-34) Of these men, the same writer said, "the world was not worthy of them," and "they had witness borne to them through their faith."—Heb 11:32, 38, 39.

7. Son of Habazziniah and father of Jaazaniah; evidently a family head and one of the Rechabites whom the prophet Jeremiah tested, at Jehovah's command, by bringing them into one of the dining rooms of the temple and offering them wine to drink. They refused, in obedience to the command that had been laid upon them more than two centuries previously by their forefather Jonadab (Jehonadab) the son of Rechab. For this, Jehovah promised: "There will not be cut off from Jonadab the son of Rechab a man to stand before me always."—Jer 35:1-10, 19.

8. A priest (or one representing the priestly house of that name) who returned from Babylonian exile in 537 B.C.E. with Governor Zerubbabel and High Priest Jeshua.—Ne 12:1.

9. A priest (or one representing a household by that name) among those attesting by seal the "trustworthy arrangement" entered into before Jehovah by Nehemiah and the princes, priests, and Levites, to walk in God's law. If the name stands for a house rather than an individual, this may be the same as No. 8.—Ne 9:38; 10:1, 2, 29.

10. A priest (or a priestly house) appointed to one of the thanksgiving choirs walking in procession on the wall of Jerusalem from the Gate of the Ash-heaps to the right, toward the Water Gate, eventually meeting the other choir at the temple. (Ne 12:31-37) In the days of Joiakim, Hananiah was head of the paternal house of Jeremiah. (Ne 12:12) If the name Jeremiah here stands for a house and not for an individual, this may be the same as No. 8.

JEREMIAH, BOOK OF. Prophecies and a historical record written by Jeremiah at the direction of Jehovah. Jeremiah was commissioned as prophet in the 13th year of King Josiah (647 B.C.E.) to warn the southern kingdom, Judah, of her impending destruction. This was less than a century after the prophet Isaiah's activity and the fall of Israel, the northern kingdom, to the Assyrians.

Arrangement. The book is not arranged chronologically, but, rather, according to subject matter. Dating is presented where necessary, but the majority of the prophecies are applicable to the nation of Judah throughout the general period of the reigns of Josiah, Jehoahaz, Jehoiakim, Jehoiachin, and Zedekiah. God repeatedly told Jeremiah that the nation was incorrigibly wicked, be-

yond reform. Yet those with right hearts were given full opportunity to reform and find deliverance. As to being prophetic for our day, the arrangement does not affect the understanding and application of Jeremiah's writings.

When Written. For the most part, the book of Jeremiah was not written at the time he declared the prophecies. Rather, Jeremiah evidently did not put any of his proclamations into writing until he was commanded by Jehovah, in the fourth year of King Jehoiakim (625 B.C.E.), to dictate all the words given him by Jehovah to date. This included not only words spoken about Judah in Josiah's time but also proclamations of judgment on all the nations. (Jer 36:1, 2) The resulting scroll was burned by Jehoiakim when Jehudi read it to him. But Jeremiah was ordered to write it over, which he did through his secretary Baruch, with many additional words.—36:21-23, 28, 32.

The remainder of the book was evidently added later, including the introduction, which mentions the 11th year of Zedekiah (Jer 1:3), other prophecies that Jeremiah wrote down at the time he was to deliver them (30:2; 51:60), and the letter to the exiles in Babylon (29:1). Additionally, the proclamations uttered during the reign of Zedekiah and the accounts of the events after Jerusalem's fall, down to about 580 B.C.E., were added later. It may be that, although the scroll written by Baruch was the basis for a large part of the book, Jeremiah afterward edited and arranged it when adding later sections.

Authenticity. The authenticity of Jeremiah is generally accepted. Only a few critics have challenged it on the basis of the differences in the Hebrew Masoretic text and the Greek *Septuagint* as found in the Alexandrine Manuscript. There are more variations between the Hebrew and the Greek texts of the book of Jeremiah than in any other book of the Hebrew Scriptures. The Greek *Septuagint* is said to be shorter than the Hebrew text by about 2,700 words, or one eighth of the book. The majority of scholars agree that the Greek translation of this book is defective, but that does not lessen the reliability of the Hebrew text. It has been suggested that the translator may have had a Hebrew manuscript of a different "family," a special recension, but critical study reveals that this apparently was not the case.

The fulfillment of the prophecies recorded by Jeremiah, together with their content, strongly testifies to the book's authenticity. Among the numerous prophecies of Jeremiah are those listed on the chart on page 34.

Principles and Qualities of God. Besides the fulfillments that we have listed, the book sets forth principles that should guide us. It stresses that formalism is of no value in God's eyes but that he desires worship and obedience from the heart. The inhabitants of Judah are told not to trust in the temple and its surrounding buildings and are admonished: "Get yourselves circumcised to Jehovah, and take away the foreskins of your hearts." —Jer 4:4; 7:3-7; 9:25, 26.

The book furnishes many illustrations revealing God's qualities and his dealings with his people. Jehovah's great loving-kindness and mercy are exemplified in his delivering a remnant of his people and finally restoring them to Jerusalem, as prophesied by Jeremiah. God's appreciation and consideration for those showing kindness to his servants and his being the Rewarder of those who seek him and show obedience are highlighted in his care for the Rechabites, for Ebed-melech, and for Baruch.—Jer 35:18, 19; 39:16-18; 45:1-5.

Jehovah is brilliantly portrayed as the Creator of all things, the King to time indefinite, the only true God. He is the only one to be feared, the Corrector and Director of those calling on his name, and the one under whose denunciation no nation can hold up. He is the Great Potter, in whose hand individuals and nations are as clay pottery, for him to work with or destroy as he pleases.—Jer 10; 18:1-10; Ro 9:19-24.

The book of Jeremiah reveals that God expects the people bearing his name to be a glory and a praise to him and that he considers them close to him. (Jer 13:11) Those who prophesy falsely in his name, saying "peace" to those with whom God is not at peace, have to account to God for their words, and they will stumble and fall. (6:13-15; 8:10-12; 23:16-20) Those standing before the people as priests and prophets have great responsibility before God, for, as he told those in Judah: "I did not send the prophets, yet they themselves ran. I did not speak to them, yet they themselves

---

HIGHLIGHTS OF JEREMIAH

A record of Jehovah's judgment proclamations through Jeremiah, as well as an account of the prophet's own experiences and of Babylon's destruction of Jerusalem

Writing was begun about 18 years before Jerusalem fell, and was completed some 27 years after that event

Youthful Jeremiah is commissioned as a prophet

He will have "to tear down" as well as "build" and "plant"

Jehovah will strengthen him for the commission (1:1-19)

Jeremiah fulfills his commission "to tear down"

He exposes the wickedness in Judah and proclaims the certainty of Jerusalem's destruction; the presence of the temple will not save the unfaithful nation; God's people will be exiles for 70 years in Babylon (2:1-3: 13; 3:19–16:13; 17:1–19:15; 24:1–25:38; 29:1-32; 34:1-22)

Judgments are announced against Zedekiah and Jehoiakim, as well as against false prophets, unfaithful shepherds, and faithless priests (21:1–23:2; 23:9-40; 27: 1–28:17)

Jehovah foretells humiliating defeats of many nations, including the Babylonians (46:1–51:64)

Jeremiah carries out his assignment "to build" and "to plant"

He points to the restoration of an Israelite remnant and the raising up of "a righteous sprout" (3:14-18; 16:14-21; 23:3-8; 30:1–31:26; 33:1-26)

He also announces that Jehovah will conclude a new covenant with his people (31:27-40)

At Jehovah's direction, Jeremiah buys a field in order to illustrate the certainty that Israel will return from exile (32:1-44)

He assures the Rechabites that they will survive, because they obeyed their forefather Jehonadab; their obedience shows up Israel's disobedience to Jehovah (35:1-19)

He reproves Baruch and strengthens him with the assurance of surviving the coming calamity (45:1-5)

Jeremiah suffers because of his bold prophesying

He is struck and placed in the stocks overnight (20:1-18)

A plot is hatched to kill him for proclaiming the destruction of Jerusalem, but the princes deliver him (26:1-24)

The king burns Jeremiah's scroll; Jeremiah is falsely accused of deserting to the Babylonians and is arrested and confined (36:1–37:21)

Finally, he is put into a miry cistern to die; Ebed-melech rescues him and is promised protection during the coming destruction of Jerusalem (38:1-28; 39:15-18)

Events from the fall of Jerusalem until the flight into Egypt

Jerusalem falls; King Zedekiah is captured, his sons are slain, and he is blinded and taken to Babylon (52:1-11)

The temple and great houses of Jerusalem are burned, and most of the people are led off into exile (39:1-14; 52:12-34)

Gedaliah is appointed governor over the few Israelites remaining, but he is assassinated (40:1–41:9)

Fearful, the people flee to Egypt; Jeremiah warns that Egypt itself will fall and that calamity will overtake them in that land (41:10–44:30)

PROPHECIES RECORDED BY JEREMIAH

Ones That He Saw Fulfilled

The captivity of Zedekiah and destruction of Jerusalem by Nebuchadnezzar, king of Babylon (Jer 20:3-6; 21:3-10; 39:6-9)

The dethronement and death in captivity of King Shallum (Jehoahaz) (Jer 22:11, 12; 2Ki 23:30-34; 2Ch 36:1-4)

The taking captive of King Coniah (Jehoiachin) to Babylon (Jer 22:24-27; 2Ki 24:15, 16)

The death, within one year, of the false prophet Hananiah (Jer 28:16, 17)

Some of the Rechabites and Ebed-melech the Ethiopian surviving Jerusalem's destruction (Jer 35:19; 39:15-18)

Others Concerning Which History Records Fulfillment

Egypt invaded, conquered by Nebuchadrezzar (Nebuchadnezzar) (Jer 43:8-13; 46:13-26)

The return of the Jews and rebuilding of the temple and the city after 70 years' desolation (Jer 24:1-7; 25:11, 12; 29:10; 30:11, 18, 19; compare 2Ch 36:20, 21; Ezr 1:1; Da 9:2.)

Ammon laid waste (Jer 49:2)

Edom cut off as a nation (Jer 49:17, 18) (With the death of the Herods, Edom became extinct as a nation.)

Babylon to become a permanent desolation (Jer 25:12-14; 50:35, 38-40)

Those Having Significant Spiritual Fulfillment, as Indicated in the Christian Greek Scriptures

A new covenant made with the house of Israel and the house of Judah (Jer 31:31-34; Heb 8:8-13)

David's house not to lack a man on the throne of the kingdom forever (Jer 33:17-21; Lu 1:32, 33)

Fall of Babylon the Great an enlargement and symbolic application of Jeremiah's words against ancient Babylon, as the following comparisons show: Jer 50:2—Re 14:8; Jer 50:8; 51:6, 45—Re 18:4; Jer 50:15, 29—Re 18:6, 7; Jer 50:23—Re 18:8, 15-17; Jer 50:38—Re 16:12; Jer 50:39, 40; 51:37—Re 18:2; Jer 51:8—Re 18:8-10, 15, 19; Jer 51:9, 49, 56—Re 18:5; Jer 51:12—Re 17:16, 17; Jer 51:13—Re 17:1, 15; Jer 51:48—Re 18:20; Jer 51:55—Re 18:22, 23; Jer 51:63, 64—Re 18:21

prophesied. But if they had stood in my intimate group, then they would have made my people hear my own words, and they would have caused them to turn back from their bad way and from the badness of their dealings."—23:21, 22.

As in other books of the Bible, God's holy nation is considered to be in relationship to him as a wife, and unfaithfulness to him is "prostitution." (Jer 3:1-3, 6-10; compare Jas 4:4.) Jehovah's own loyalty to his covenants, however, is unbreakable. —Jer 31:37; 33:20-22, 25, 26.

Many are the fine principles and illustrations in the book, upon which the other Bible writers have drawn for reference. And many other pictorial and prophetic patterns are found that have application and vital meaning to the modern-day Christian and his ministry.

JEREMOTH (Jer'e·moth) [from a root meaning "be high (exalted)"].

1. A descendant of Benjamin through his son Becher.—1Ch 7:6, 8.

2. A Benjamite head of a family that lived in Jerusalem; one of Beriah's "sons."—1Ch 8:14-16, 28.

3. Son of Mushi and grandson of Merari in the tribe of Levi. The paternal house founded by this person, whose name is also spelled "Jerimoth," was included in David's rearrangement of the Levitical service organization.—1Ch 23:21, 23; 24:30, 31.

4. A son of Heman in the Levitical branch of Kohathites. During David's reign, Jeremoth (Jerimoth) was selected by lot to head the 15th of the 24 divisions of sanctuary musicians.—1Ch 6:33; 25:1, 4, 8, 9, 22.

5, 6, 7. Three Israelites, of the sons of Elam, Zattu, and Bani respectively, who sent away their foreign wives and sons in Ezra's day.—Ezr 10:25-27, 29, 44.

JERIAH (Je·ri'ah) [May Jehovah See; Jehovah Has Seen]. Son or descendant of Kohath's son Hebron. (1Ch 23:12, 19) Jeriah or his paternal house is mentioned in connection with David's organization of the Levites (1Ch 24:23, 30, 31) and, when appointed over territory E of the Jordan, is called the head of the Hebronites. In this instance his name is spelled "Jerijah."—1Ch 26:31, 32.

JERIBAI (Jer'i·bai) [May He Contend; He Has Conducted [Our] Legal Case]. One of David's mighty men; son of Elnaam.—1Ch 11:26, 46.

JERICHO (Jer'i·cho) [possibly, Moon City]. The first Canaanite city W of the Jordan to be conquered by the Israelites. (Nu 22:1; Jos 6:1, 24, 25) It is identified with Tell es-Sultan (Tel Yeriho) about 22 km (14 mi) ENE of Jerusalem. Nearby Tulul Abu el-'Alayiq is considered to be the site of first-century Jericho. Lying about 250 m (820 ft) below sea level in the Jordan Valley, Jericho has a subtropical climate. Today oranges, bananas, and figs are cultivated in the area and, as anciently, palms still thrive there.

Firstfruits of Israel's Conquest. At the end of their 40 years of wandering in the wilderness, the Israelites came to the Plains of Moab. There, opposite Jericho, Moses ascended Mount Nebo and viewed the Promised Land, including Jericho, "the city of the palm trees," and its plain.—Nu 36:13; De 32:49; 34:1-3.

After Moses' death Joshua sent two spies to Jericho. Concealed by Rahab, they avoided detection and afterward escaped from the city by means of a rope through the window of her house situated atop Jericho's wall. For three days the two men hid themselves in the nearby mountainous region, after which they forded the Jordan and returned to the Israelite camp.—Jos 2:1-23.

Great must have been the fear of Jericho's king and its inhabitants as they heard about or witnessed the miraculous damming up of the flooding Jordan, enabling the Israelites to cross on dry ground. Afterward, although the Israelite males underwent circumcision and had to recover from its effects before being in a good position to defend themselves, no one dared to attack them at Gilgal. Unmolested, the Israelites also observed the Passover on the desert plain of Jericho.—Jos 5:1-10.

Later, near Jericho, an angelic prince appeared to Joshua and outlined the procedure for taking the city, which was then tightly shut up on account of the Israelites. Obediently, once a day for six days the Israelite military force went forth, followed by seven priests continually blowing the horns, behind whom were the priests carrying the Ark, and finally the rear guard—all marching around Jericho. But on the seventh day they marched around the city seven times. At the blowing of the horns on the final march around Jericho, the people shouted a great war cry, and the city's walls began to fall flat.—Jos 5:13–6:20.

The Israelites then rushed into Jericho, devoting its inhabitants and all domestic animals to destruction. But on account of the kindness shown by Rahab in hiding the spies, she and her relatives, safe in her house atop the portion of the wall that had not fallen, were preserved alive. The entire city was burned, only the gold and silver being turned over to Jehovah's sanctuary. (Jos 6:20-25) However, one Israelite, Achan, stole a gold bar, some silver, and a fine garment and then hid the items under his tent. Thereby he brought death upon himself and his entire family.—Jos 7:20-26.

Later Historical References. The destroyed city of Jericho subsequently became part of Benjamite territory bordering on Ephraim and Manasseh. (Jos 16: 1, 7; 18:12, 21) Not long thereafter some kind of settlement apparently sprang up at the site. It was captured by Moab's King Eglon and remained under his control for 18 years. (Jg 3:12-30) In the time of King David a settlement continued to exist at Jericho. (2Sa 10:5; 1Ch 19:5) But not until Ahab's reign did Hiel the Bethelite actually rebuild Jericho. The prophetic curse pronounced by Joshua over 500 years earlier was then fulfilled, Hiel losing Abiram his firstborn as he laid the foundation and Segub his youngest son when he put up the doors.—Jos 6:26; 1Ki 16:34.

During this same general period some of "the sons of the prophets" resided at Jericho. (2Ki 2:4, 5) After Jehovah took the prophet Elijah away in a

Excavation of walls of ancient Jericho

windstorm, Elisha remained at Jericho for a time and healed the city's water supply. (2Ki 2:11-15, 19-22) The water of 'Ain es-Sultan (traditionally, the fountain that Elisha healed) has been described as sweet and pleasant and irrigates the gardens of modern Jericho.

In the time of wicked Judean King Ahaz, Jehovah permitted the Israelite armies under King Pekah to inflict a humiliating defeat upon unfaithful Judah, killing 120,000 and taking 200,000 captives. But Jehovah's prophet Oded met the returning victors and warned them not to enslave the captives. Accordingly, the captives, after being clothed and fed, were taken to Jericho and released.—2Ch 28:6-15.

After the fall of Jerusalem in 607 B.C.E., King Zedekiah fled in the direction of Jericho but was overtaken and captured by the Babylonians in the desert plains of Jericho. (2Ki 25:5; Jer 39:5; 52:8) Following the release from Babylonian exile, 345 "sons of Jericho" were among those returning with Zerubbabel in 537 B.C.E. and apparently settled at Jericho. (Ezr 2:1, 2, 34; Ne 7:36) Later, some of the men of Jericho assisted in rebuilding the wall of Jerusalem.—Ne 3:2.

Toward the close of the year 32 and the beginning of 33 C.E., Jericho figured in Jesus' ministry. Near this city Jesus Christ healed the sight of blind Bartimaeus and his companion. (Mr 10:46; Mt 20:29; Lu 18:35; see BARTIMAEUS.) At Jericho, Jesus also met Zacchaeus and thereafter was a guest at his home. (Lu 19:1-7) Earlier in Judea, when giving his illustration of the neighborly Samaritan, Jesus alluded to the road from Jerusalem to Jericho. (Lu 10:30) This road, according to ancient historical testimony, was frequented by robbers.

Have archaeologists found evidence of the destruction of Jericho in the days of Joshua?

Professor John Garstang, leader of an English expedition at Tell es-Sultan between 1929 and 1936, found that what he considered to be one of the cities built on the site had been subjected to intense fires and its walls had fallen. This city he identified with the Jericho of Joshua's time and assigned its destruction to about 1400 B.C.E. Although some scholars today still endorse Garstang's conclusions, others interpret the evidence differently. Writes archaeologist G. Ernest Wright: "The two walls which surrounded the summit of the old city, which Garstang . . . believed were destroyed by earthquake and fire in Joshua's time,

were discovered to date from the 3rd millennium and to represent only two of some fourteen different walls or wall-components built successively during that age." (Biblical Archaeology, 1963, pp. 79, 80) Many feel that little, if anything, remains of the Jericho that existed in Joshua's time, earlier excavations at the site having removed what might have survived from the time of its destruction. As Professor Jack Finegan notes: "There is now, therefore, virtually no evidence at the site by which to try to determine at what date Joshua might have taken Jericho."—Light From the Ancient Past, 1959, p. 159.

For this reason numerous scholars date the fall of Jericho on circumstantial evidence, and suggested dates span a period of about 200 years. In view of such uncertainty, Professor Merrill F. Unger fittingly observes: "Scholars also must be extremely wary of attaching undue authority to archeologists' estimates of dates and interpretation of data. That the fixing of dates and the conclusions drawn from archeological findings often depend on subjective factors is amply demonstrated by the wide divergences between competent authorities on these matters."—Archaeology and the Old Testament, 1964, p. 164.

Therefore, the fact that the interpretations of archaeologists do not agree with Biblical chronology in pointing to 1473 B.C.E. as the date for Jericho's destruction is no reason for concern. The difference in the viewpoint of Garstang and other archaeologists about Jericho illustrates the need for caution in accepting archaeological testimony regardless of whether it seems to confirm or to contradict the Bible record and its chronology.

JERIEL (Je'ri·el) [May God See; God Has Seen]. Son of Tola, and head of a paternal house in the tribe of Issachar.—1Ch 7:1, 2.

JERIJAH. See JERIAH.

JERIMOTH (Jer'i·moth) [from a root meaning "be high (exalted)"].

1. A son or descendant of Benjamin's firstborn Bela, and a valiant, mighty man.—1Ch 7:6, 7.

2. A Benjamite warrior who supported David while he was at Ziklag outlawed by King Saul. —1Ch 12:1, 2, 5.

3. A Merarite Levite.—1Ch 24:26, 30; see JEREMOTH No. 3.

4. A Kohathite Levite.—1Ch 6:33; 25:4; see JEREMOTH No. 4.

5. The prince over the tribe of Naphtali during David's rule; son or descendant of Azriel.—1Ch 27:19, 22.

6. A son of David whose daughter married King Rehoboam. (2Ch 11:18) As Jerimoth is not included in the listings of David's sons by his named wives, he might have been a son by a concubine or by an unnamed wife. (2Sa 5:13) Jerimoth was apparently married to his cousin Abihail, the daughter of David's oldest brother Eliab.—2Ch 11:18; 1Sa 17:13.

7. One of the Levite commissioners caring for the generous contribution, tithe, and holy things brought in during Hezekiah's reign.—2Ch 31: 12, 13.

JERIOTH   (Jer′i·oth) [from a root verb meaning "quiver"]. It is likely that Jerioth was a concubine or handmaid of Caleb who bore some of his sons credited to "Azubah his wife." First Chronicles 2:18 reads: "Caleb . . . became father to sons by Azubah his wife and by Jerioth; and these were her sons."

JEROBOAM   (Jer′o·bo′am). Two kings of Israel whose reigns were separated by some 130 years.

1. First king of the ten-tribe kingdom of Israel; the son of Nebat, one of Solomon's officers in the village of Zeredah; of the tribe of Ephraim. Apparently at an early age Jeroboam was left fatherless, to be raised by his widowed mother Zeruah.—1Ki 11:26.

When Solomon observed that Jeroboam was not only a valiant, mighty man but also a hard worker, he put him in charge of the compulsory labor force of the house of Joseph. (1Ki 11:28) Subsequently, Jeroboam was approached by God's prophet Ahijah with startling news. After tearing his own new garment into 12 pieces, the prophet told Jeroboam to take ten of them in symbol of how Jehovah would rip Solomon's kingdom in two and make Jeroboam king over ten of the tribes. This, however, was to be merely a governmental division and not also a departure from true worship as centered at the temple in Jerusalem, the capital of the southern kingdom. So Jehovah assured Jeroboam that he would bless and prosper his reign and build him a lasting house of successors provided he kept God's laws and commandments.—1Ki 11:29-38.

Possibly it was upon learning of these events that Solomon sought to kill Jeroboam. However, Jeroboam fled to Egypt, and there under the sheltering protection of Pharaoh Shishak he remained until the death of Solomon.—1Ki 11:40.

The news of Solomon's death in about 998 B.C.E. brought Jeroboam quickly back to his homeland, where he joined his people in demanding that Solomon's son Rehoboam lighten their burdens if he wanted their support of his new kingship. Rehoboam, however, disregarded the good advice of the older counselors in preference to that of younger men his own age who told him to increase the workload of the people. The ten tribes responded to this harshness by making Jeroboam their king. In reality, this "turn of affairs took place at the instance of Jehovah, in order that he might indeed carry out his word that Jehovah had spoken by means of Ahijah."—1Ki 12:1-20; 2Ch 10:1-19.

The newly installed king Jeroboam immediately set about building up Shechem as his royal capital, and E of Shechem, on the other side of the Jordan, he fortified the settlement of Penuel (Peniel), the place where Jacob had wrestled with an angel. (1Ki 12:25; Ge 32:30, 31) Seeing his subjects streaming up to the temple in Jerusalem to worship, Jeroboam envisioned that in time they might switch their allegiance to Rehoboam and then they would kill him. So he decided to put a stop to this by establishing a religion centered around two golden calves, which he set up, one at Bethel in the south, the other at Dan in the north. He also set up his own non-Aaronic priesthood, composed of those among the people in general who were willing to procure the office by offering one bull and seven rams. These then served "for the high places and for the goat-shaped demons and for the calves that he had made." Jeroboam also invented special 'holy days' and personally led the people in sacrificing to his newly created gods.—1Ki 12:26-33; 2Ki 23:15; 2Ch 11:13-17; 13:9.

On one such occasion when Jeroboam was about to offer up sacrificial smoke on his altar at Bethel, Jehovah's spirit caused a certain man of God to reprove the king for his detestable idolatry, and when the king ordered this servant of God seized, the altar split open, spilling its ashes, and the king's hand dried up. Not until the man of God softened Jehovah's anger was the hand restored, but even after that Jeroboam continued in his blasphemous defiance of Jehovah. (1Ki 13:1-6, 33, 34) His introducing calf worship constituted "the sins of Jeroboam," sins of which other Israelite kings became guilty by perpetuating this apostate worship.—1Ki 14:16; 15:30, 34; 16:2, 19, 26, 31; 22:52; 2Ki 3:3; 10:29, 31; 13:2, 6, 11; 14:24; 15:9, 18, 24, 28; 17:21-23.

In the 18th year of Jeroboam's reign Rehoboam died, but the warring that had gone on between the two nations continued during the three-year reign of Rehoboam's son Abijam (Abijah), who succeeded him. (1Ki 15:1, 2, 6; 2Ch 12:15) On one occasion Abijah assembled 400,000 to battle against Jeroboam's forces twice the size. Despite Jeroboam's superior force and his clever ambush strategy, he was badly beaten. He lost 500,000 men and many of his Ephraimite towns and was greatly humiliated. Judah's victory was because Abijah and his men trusted in Jehovah and cried to him for help.—2Ch 13:3-20.

To add to Jeroboam's calamity, his son Abijah fell deathly sick, whereupon the king had his wife disguise herself, and then he sent her with a gift to the old prophet Ahijah, now blind, to inquire whether the child would recover. The answer was 'No.' Additionally the prediction was made that every male heir of Jeroboam would be cut off, and with the exception of this son, in whom Jehovah found something good, none of Jeroboam's offspring would have a decent burial, but, instead, their carcasses would be eaten either by the dogs or by fowl.—1Ki 14:1-18.

Shortly thereafter, in about 977 B.C.E., "Jehovah dealt [Jeroboam] a blow, so that he died," bringing to an end his 22-year reign. (2Ch 13:20; 1Ki 14:20) His son Nadab succeeded him to the throne for two years before being killed by Baasha, who also cut off every breathing thing of Jeroboam's house. In this way his dynasty was abruptly terminated "according to Jehovah's word," and "on account of the sins of Jeroboam."—1Ki 15:25-30.

2. King of Israel; son and successor of Jehoash, and great-grandson of Jehu. As the 14th ruler of the northern kingdom Jeroboam II reigned for 41 years, starting in about 844 B.C.E. (2Ki 14:16, 23) Like so many of his predecessors he did what was bad in Jehovah's eyes by perpetuating the calf worship of Jeroboam I.—2Ki 14:24.

Notice is taken of a special genealogical registration, evidently made during the reign of Jeroboam II. (1Ch 5:17) However, the outstanding achievement of his reign was the restoration of land that had earlier been lost by the kingdom. In fulfillment of Jonah's prophecy, Jeroboam "restored the boundary of Israel from the entering in of Hamath clear to the sea of the Arabah [Dead Sea]." He is also credited with restoring "Damascus and Hamath to Judah in Israel." (2Ki 14:25-28) This may mean that Jeroboam made the kingdoms of Damascus and Hamath tributary, as they had once been to Judah during the reigns of David and Solomon.—Compare 2Sa 8:5-10; 1Ki 4:21; 2Ch 8:4.

In the wake of these successes doubtless came a wave of material prosperity for the northern kingdom. But at the same time the nation continued in its spiritual decline. The prophets Hosea and Amos had some harsh criticism to offer rebellious

Jeroboam and his supporters for their outright apostasy, as well as their immoral conduct —fraud, thievery, fornication, murder, oppression, idolatry, and other God-dishonoring practices. (Ho 1:2, 4; 4:1, 2, 12-17; 5:1-7; 6:10; Am 2:6-8; 3:9, 12-15; 4:1). Particularly pointed was Jehovah's warning to Jeroboam by the mouth of his prophet Amos: "I will rise up against the house of Jeroboam with a sword."—Am 7:9.

After Jeroboam's death, his son Zechariah ascended the throne. (2Ki 14:29) However, there was a gap of 11 years between Jeroboam's death and the six-month rule credited to Zechariah, the last of Jehu's dynasty. Possibly because Zechariah was very young or for some other reason, his kingship was not fully established or confirmed as his until about 792 B.C.E.

JEROHAM (Je·ro'ham) [May He Be Shown Mercy].

1. Father of Elkanah and grandfather of Samuel; descendants of the Levite Kohath.—1Sa 1:1, 19, 20; 1Ch 6:22, 27, 34, 38.

2. A Benjamite of Gedor whose two "sons" were named among David's "helpers in the warfare" while he was at Ziklag under Saul's restrictions. —1Ch 12:1, 2, 7.

3. Father of Azarel the prince of the tribe of Dan under King David.—1Ch 27:1, 22.

4. Father of Azariah, one of the army chiefs who helped Jehoiada install Jehoash as king. —2Ch 23:1, 11.

5. A descendant of Benjamin whose six named "sons" became heads of families living in Jerusalem. (1Ch 8:1, 26-28) Possibly the same as No. 3.

6. Benjamite forefather of Ibneiah, who lived in Jerusalem after the exile. (1Ch 9:7, 8) Possibly the same as No. 2.

7. Father or forefather of Adaiah, a priest who lived in Jerusalem after the Babylonian exile. —1Ch 9:3, 10, 12; Ne 11:4, 12.

JERUBBAAL (Jer·ub·ba'al) [Let Baal Make a Legal Defense (Contend)].

The name given to Gideon son of Joash the Abi-ezrite after he had torn down his father's altar to Baal and the wooden sacred pole by it; then, on an altar built to Jehovah, Gideon sacrificed a bull belonging to his father, using the pieces of the sacred pole as fuel. —Jg 6:11, 25-27.

Early next morning the men of Ophrah, on discovering what had been done, were highly incensed. Accordingly they inquired and, finding that Gideon had done this thing, demanded that he be put to death. Gideon's father Joash took the side of Gideon, saying: "Will you be the ones to make a legal defense for Baal to see whether you yourselves may save him? Whoever makes a legal defense for him ought to be put to death even this morning. If he is God, let him make a legal defense for himself, because someone has pulled down his altar." The Bible account continues: "And he began to call him Jerubbaal on that day, saying: 'Let Baal make a legal defense in his own behalf, because someone has pulled down his altar.'"—Jg 6:28-32.

Gideon is called Jerubbesheth at 2 Samuel 11:21. —See GIDEON.

JERUBBESHETH (Je·rub'be·sheth) [Let the Shameful Thing Make a Legal Defense (Contend)]. The name of Judge Gideon found at 2 Samuel 11:21. Evidently this is a form of Jerubbaal, the name given to Gideon by his father Joash when Gideon pulled down the altar of Baal. (Jg 6:30-32) Some scholars believe that the writer of Second Samuel replaced ba''al with the Hebrew word for "shame" (bo'sheth) in order not to use the name of the false god Baal as part of a proper name.—See GIDEON.

JERUEL (Je·ru'el) [possibly, Laid (Erected) by God]. A wilderness apparently situated somewhere between the cities of Tekoa and En-gedi. Its exact location and extent are today unknown. —2Ch 20:2, 16, 20.

JERUSALEM (Je·ru'sa·lem) [Possession (Foundation) of Twofold Peace]. The capital city of the ancient nation of Israel from the year 1070 B.C.E. onward. Following the division of the nation into two kingdoms (997 B.C.E.), Jerusalem continued as the capital of the southern kingdom of Judah. Throughout the Scriptures there are more than 800 references to Jerusalem.

Name. The earliest recorded name of the city is "Salem." (Ge 14:18) Whereas some try to associate the meaning of the name Jerusalem with that of a West Semitic god named Shalem, the apostle Paul shows that "Peace" is the true meaning of the latter half of the name. (Heb 7:2) The Hebrew spelling of this latter half suggests a dual form, hence "Twofold Peace." In Akkadian (Assyro-Babylonian) texts the city was called Urusalim (or Ur-sa-li-im-mu). On this basis some scholars give the meaning of the name as "City of Peace." But the Hebrew form, which logically ought to govern, apparently means "Possession (Foundation) of Twofold Peace."

Many other expressions and titles were used in the Scriptures to refer to the city. The psalmist on one occasion uses the earlier name, "Salem." (Ps 76:2) Other appellations were: "city of Jehovah" (Isa 60:14), "town of the grand King" (Ps 48:2; compare Mt 5:35), "City of Righteousness" and "Faithful Town" (Isa 1:26), "Zion" (Isa 33:20), and "holy city" (Ne 11:1; Isa 48:2; 52:1; Mt 4:5). The name "el Quds," meaning "Holy City," is still the popular name for it in Arabic. The name shown on present-day maps of Israel is Yerushalayim.

Location. Comparatively remote from principal international trade routes, Jerusalem lay on the edge of an arid wilderness (the Wilderness of Judah), its water supplies being limited. Nevertheless, two internal trade routes did intersect near the city. One ran in a N-S direction along the top of the plateau forming the "backbone" of ancient Palestine, and this route linked together such cities as Dothan, Shechem, Bethel, Bethlehem, Hebron, and Beer-sheba. The second route ran in an E-W direction from Rabbah (modern 'Amman), cut through torrent valleys to the Jordan River basin, ascended the steep Judean slopes, and then wound down the western slopes to the Mediterranean Coast and the seaport town of Joppa. Additionally, Jerusalem was centrally located for the whole area of the Promised Land, hence appropriate for a state administration center.

Lying about 55 km (34 mi) inland from the Mediterranean Sea and some 25 km (16 mi) due W of the northern end of the Dead Sea, Jerusalem rests among the hills of the central mountain range. (Compare Ps 125:2.) Its altitude of about 750 m (2,500 ft) above sea level made it one of the highest capital cities in the world at that time. Its "loftiness" is mentioned in the Scriptures, and travelers had to 'go up' from the coastal plains to reach the city. (Ps 48:2; 122:3, 4) The climate is pleasant, with cool nights, an average annual temperature of 17° C. (63° F.), and an average annual rainfall of about 63 cm (25 in.), the rain falling mainly between November and April.

Despite its height, Jerusalem does not stand up above the surrounding terrain. The traveler gets a full view of the city only when quite close. To the E, the Mount of Olives rises about 800 m (2,620 ft). North of it, Mount Scopus reaches about 820 m (2,690 ft), and the encircling hills on the S and W rise as high as 835 m (2,740 ft). These elevations give a view of the situation in relation to the Temple Mount (c. 740 m [2,430 ft]).

In times of war, this situation would seem to constitute a serious disadvantage. Any drawback, however, was compensated for by the city's being surrounded on three sides by steep-walled valleys: the torrent valley of Kidron on the east and the Valley of Hinnom on the south and west. A central valley, apparently referred to by Josephus as the Tyropoeon Valley (or "the Valley of the Cheesemakers"), bisected the city area into eastern and western hills or spurs. (*The Jewish War*, V, 136 [iv, 1]) This central valley has filled in considerably throughout the centuries, but a visitor still must make a rather sharp descent to a central hollow and then climb up the other side when crossing the city. There is evidence that, in addition to the N-S central valley, two smaller E-W valleys, or depressions, further divided the hills, one cutting across the eastern hill and the other across the western.

The steep valley walls seem to have been incorporated into the city's defensive wall system in all periods. The only side of the city lacking in natural defense was that on the N, and here the walls were made especially strong. When attacking the city in 70 C.E., General Titus, according to Josephus, was faced with three successive walls on that side.

Water Supply. Jerusalem's inhabitants suffered from serious food shortages in siege, but evidently had no great water problem. For, in spite of its nearness to the arid Judean Wilderness, the city had access to a constant supply of fresh water and had adequate storage facilities within the city walls.

Two springs, En-rogel and Gihon, were located near the city. The first lay a little S of the junction of the Kidron and Hinnom valleys. While a valuable source of water, its position made it inaccessible during times of attack or siege. The Gihon spring lay on the W side of the Kidron Valley, alongside what came to be called the City of David. Though outside the city walls, it was close enough that a tunnel could be excavated and a shaft sunk, enabling the city's inhabitants to draw water without going outside the protective walls. This was done early in the city's history, according to the archaeological evidence. In 1961 and 1962, excavations revealed a substantial early wall, situated *below* the upper end, or entrance, of the tunnel, hence enclosing it. It is thought to be the wall of the old Jebusite city.

Over the years, additional tunnels and canals were formed to channel Gihon's waters. One channel ran from the mouth of the cave of the Gihon spring down the valley and around the end of the SE hill to a pool located at the junction of the Hinnom Valley with the central or Tyropoeon Valley. According to what has been found, it was in the form of a trench, covered with flat stones, and tunneled through the hillside at points. Openings at intervals allowed for water to be drawn off for irrigation of the valley terraces below. The canal's gradient of about 4 or 5 millimeters per meter (less than 0.2 in. per yd) produced a slow gentle flow, reminding one of "the waters of the Shiloah that are going gently." (Isa 8:6) It is suggested that this canal, unprotected and vulnerable, was constructed during Solomon's reign, when peace and security were predominant.

Jerusalem's homes and buildings were evidently equipped with underground cisterns, supplementing the supply of water from springs. Rainwater collected from the roofs was stored therein, kept clean and cool. The temple area seems to have had particularly large cisterns, archaeologists claiming to have plotted 37 cisterns there with a total capacity of about 38,000 kl (10,000,-000 gal), one cistern alone estimated as capable of holding 7,600 kl (2,000,000 gal).

Over the centuries a number of aqueducts, or conduits, were built, in order to provide water for Jerusalem. Tradition ascribes to Solomon the construction of a conduit from the "Pools of Solomon" (three reservoirs SW of Bethlehem) to the temple enclosure at Jerusalem. At Ecclesiastes 2:6, Solomon says: "I made pools of water for myself, to irrigate with them the forest." Such a large undertaking as the building of the pools could well have included the building of a conduit for the larger supply of water that would be needed at Jerusalem after the temple services were instituted. However, there is no evidence, other than tradition, to support the Solomonic origin of a conduit from the Pools of Solomon to Jerusalem. A number of aqueducts can still be traced. One conduit constructed to carry water from springs in the Wadi 'Arrub 20 km (12 mi) SSW of Jerusalem to the Pools of Solomon is possibly the one alluded to by Josephus, who says that it was constructed by Pontius Pilate with temple treasury funds. (*Jewish Antiquities*, XVIII, 60 [iii, 2]; *The Jewish War*, II, 175 [ix, 4]) Of the two aqueducts leading from the Pools of Solomon to Jerusalem, the lower one is the older, possibly dating from the time of Herod or of the Hasmonaeans. This aqueduct passed under the village of Bethlehem and ran on to the Temple Mount over "Wilson's Arch."

Archaeological Research. Though much research and excavation have been carried out, few concrete facts have been determined as to the city of Bible times. Various factors have restricted investigation or limited its value. Jerusalem has had almost continuous occupation in the Common Era, thus severely reducing the area available for excavation. Then, too, the city was destroyed a number of times, with new cities built on top of the ruins and often made, in part, from material of those ruins. The piling up of debris and rubble, in some places about 30 m (100 ft) deep, has obscured the early contours of the site and made the interpretation of the excavated evidence a precarious task. Some wall sections, pools, water tunnels, and ancient tombs have been unearthed, but very little written material. Principal archaeological discoveries have come from the SE hill, which now lies outside the city walls.

The main sources of information regarding the ancient city, therefore, remain the Bible and the description of the first-century city given by Jewish historian Josephus.

Early History. The first historical mention of the city comes in the decade between 1943 and 1933 B.C.E., when Abraham's encounter with Melchizedek took place. Melchizedek was "king of Salem" and "priest of the Most High God." (Ge 14:17-20) However, the origins of the city and of the population that composed it are as wrapped in obscurity as is the origin of its king-priest Melchizedek.—Compare Heb 7:1-3.

Apparently another event in Abraham's life involved the vicinity of Jerusalem. Abraham was commanded to offer up his son Isaac on "one of the mountains" in "the land of Moriah." The temple built by Solomon was erected on "Mount Moriah" on a site that previously had been a threshing floor. (Ge 22:2; 2Ch 3:1) Thus, the Bible apparently links the place of Abraham's attempted sacrifice with the mountainous region around Jerusalem. (See MORIAH.) Whether Melchizedek was still living then is not revealed; but Salem likely remained friendly territory for Abraham.

The Amarna Tablets, written by Canaanite rulers to their Egyptian overlord, include seven letters from the king or governor of Jerusalem (Urusalim). These letters were written prior to the Israelite conquest of Canaan. Thus, Jerusalem, in the approximately 465-year period between Abraham's meeting with Melchizedek and the Israelite conquest, had become the possession of pagan Hamitic Canaanites and was under the domination of the Hamitic Egyptian Empire.

The account of Joshua's sweeping conquest of Canaan lists Adoni-zedek, king of Jerusalem, among the confederate kings attacking Gibeon. His name (meaning "(My) Lord Is Righteousness") closely parallels that of Jerusalem's earlier King Melchizedek ("King of Righteousness"), but Adoni-zedek was no worshiper of the Most High God, Jehovah.—Jos 10:1-5, 23, 26; 12:7, 8, 10.

In the allotting of tribal territories, Jerusalem was on the boundary between Judah and Benjamin, the specific border running along the Valley of Hinnom. This would place at least what comprised the later "City of David," situated on the ridge between the Kidron and Tyropoeon valleys, within the territory of Benjamin. Apparently the Canaanite city had additional settlements, or "suburbs," however, and part of the settled area may have overlapped into Judah's territory to the W and S of the Valley of Hinnom. Judah is credited with the initial capture of Jerusalem at Judges 1:8, but after the invading forces moved on, the Jebusite inhabitants apparently remained (or returned) in sufficient force to form a later pocket of resistance that neither Judah nor Benjamin could break. Thus, of both Judah and Benjamin it is said that the 'Jebusites continued dwelling with them in Jerusalem.' (Jos 15:63; Jg 1:21) This situation continued for some four centuries, and the city was at times referred to as "Jebus," "a city of foreigners."—Jg 19:10-12; 1Ch 11:4, 5.

During the United Kingdom. King Saul's headquarters were at Gibeah in the territory of Benjamin. King David's capital city was first at Hebron in Judah, about 30 km (19 mi) SSW of Jerusalem. After ruling there a total of seven and a half years (2Sa 5:5), he determined to transfer the capital to Jerusalem. This was by divine direction (2Ch 6:4-6), Jehovah having spoken centuries earlier of the 'site where He would choose to place his name.'—De 12:5; 26:2; compare 2Ch 7:12.

It seems that the Jebusites at that time had their city on the southern end of the eastern spur. They were confident of the impregnability of their fortress city, with its natural defenses of steep valley walls on three sides and, probably, special fortifications on the north. It was known as "the place difficult to approach" (1Ch 11:7), and the Jebusites taunted David that even 'the blind and the lame of the city' could hold off his attacks. But David conquered the city, his attack being spearheaded by Joab, who evidently gained entry into the city by means of "the water tunnel." (2Sa 5:6-9; 1Ch 11:4-8) Scholars are not entirely certain of the meaning of the Hebrew term here rendered "water tunnel," but generally accept this or similar terms ("water shaft," *RS, AT;* "gutter," *JP*) as the most likely meaning. The brief account does not state just how the city's defenses were breached. Since the discovery of the tunnel and shaft leading to the Gihon spring, the popular view is that Joab led men up this vertical shaft, through the sloping tunnel and into the city in a surprise attack. (PICTURE, Vol. 2, p. 951) By whatever means, the city was taken and David moved his capital there (1070 B.C.E.). The Jebusite stronghold now came to be known as "the City of David," also called "Zion."—2Sa 5:7.

David began a building program within the area, apparently also improving the city's defenses. (2Sa 5:9-11; 1Ch 11:8) "The Mound" (Heb., *ham·Mil·loh'*) referred to here (2Sa 5:9) and in later accounts (1Ki 9:15, 24; 11:27) was some geographic or structural feature of the city, well known then but unidentifiable today. When David later transferred the sacred "ark of Jehovah" from the house of Obed-edom to Jerusalem, the city became the religious, as well as administrative, center of the nation.—2Sa 6:11, 12, 17; see BURIAL, BURIAL PLACES; DAVID, CITY OF; MOUND.

There is no record of Jerusalem's being attacked by enemy forces during David's reign, as he carried the battle to his foes. (Compare 2Sa 5:17-25; 8:1-14; 11:1.) On one occasion, however, David saw fit to abandon the city before the advance of rebel forces led by his own son, Absalom. The king's retreat may have been to avoid having blood shed in civil war at this place where Jehovah's name rested. (2Sa 15:13-17) Whatever the motive for the retreat, it led to the fulfillment of the inspired prophecy spoken by Nathan. (2Sa 12:11; 16:15-23) David did not allow the ark of the covenant to be evacuated with him but ordered the faithful priests to return it to the city, God's chosen location. (2Sa 15:23-29) The description of the initial part of David's flight as recorded at 2 Samuel chapter 15 outlines well the geographic features of the area on the E of the city.

Toward the close of his rule, David began preparing construction materials for the temple. (1Ch 22:1, 2; compare 1Ki 6:7.) The hewn stones prepared may have been quarried in that area, for the bedrock of Jerusalem itself is easily cut and chiseled to size and shape, yet, upon exposure to the weather, hardens into durable and attractive building stones. There is evidence of an ancient quarry near the present Damascus Gate, vast quantities of rock having been cut out there in the course of time.

A further view of the layout of the terrain around Jerusalem, this time to the E and S, is given in the account of the anointing of Solomon by order of aged King David. Another son, Adonijah, was at the spring of En-rogel, plotting to seize the kingship, when Solomon was anointed at the spring of Gihon. The distance between the two points was short enough (c. 700 m; 2,300 ft) that Adonijah and his coconspirators heard the noise of the horn and celebrations at Gihon.—1Ki 1:5-9, 32-41.

Solomon's reign saw considerable building (and perhaps rebuilding) done within the city and expansion of its limits. (1Ki 3:1; 9:15-19, 24; 11:27; compare Ec 2:3-6, 9.) The temple, his outstanding construction work, with its associated courtyards was built on Mount Moriah on the eastern ridge but N of "the City of David," evidently in the area of the present-day Dome of the Rock. (2Ch 3:1; 1Ki 6:37, 38; 7:12) Other major buildings nearby were Solomon's own house or palace, the cedarwood House of the Forest of Lebanon, the Porch of Pillars, and the judicial Porch of the Throne. (1Ki 7:1-8) This building complex was apparently situated S of the temple on the gradual slope running down toward "the City of David."—MAP, Vol. 1, p. 752; PICTURE, Vol. 1, p. 748.

Divided Kingdom (997-607 B.C.E.). Jeroboam's rebellion split the nation into two kingdoms, and Jerusalem was left as the capital of two tribes, Benjamin and Judah, under Solomon's son Rehoboam. Levites and priests also moved to the city where Jehovah's name rested, thereby strengthening Rehoboam's kingship. (2Ch 11:1-17) Jerusalem was now no longer at the geographic center of the kingdom, being only a few miles from the border of the hostile northern ten-tribe kingdom. Within five years of Solomon's death, the city experienced the first of a number of invasions. King Shishak of Egypt attacked the kingdom of Judah, doubtless viewing it as vulnerable in its reduced state. Because of national unfaithfulness, he succeeded in entering Jerusalem, carrying off temple treasures and other valuables. Only because of repentance was a measure of divine protection granted, preventing actual ruin to the city.—1Ki 14:25, 26; 2Ch 12:2-12.

During faithful King Asa's reign, King Baasha of the northern kingdom made an unsuccessful attempt to build up strength on Judah's northern frontier in order to seal it off and prevent communication with Jerusalem (and possibly expressions of loyalty to the Judean kingdom by any of his subjects). (1Ki 15:17-22) The continuance of pure worship under the rule of Asa's son Jehoshaphat brought divine protection and great benefits to the city, including improved provisions for the handling of legal cases.—2Ch 19:8-11; 20:1, 22, 23, 27-30.

Throughout the remainder of Jerusalem's history as the capital of the Judean kingdom, this pattern continued. True worship brought Jehovah's blessing and protection; apostasy led to grave problems and vulnerability to attack. The reign of Jehoshaphat's unfaithful son Jehoram (913-c. 907 B.C.E.) saw the city invaded and looted a second time by an Arab-Philistine combine, this despite the strong defense walls. (2Ch 21:12-17) In the next century the deflection from a righteous course by King Jehoash resulted in Syrian forces 'beginning to invade Judah and Jerusalem,' the context implying that they were successful in entering the city. (2Ch 24:20-25) During Amaziah's apostasy the northern kingdom of Israel invaded Judah, and broke down about 180 m (590 ft) of the vital northern wall between the Corner Gate (in the NW corner) and the Ephraim Gate (to the E of the Corner Gate). (2Ch 25:22-24) It is possible that, at some point prior to this, the city had expanded across the central valley onto the western ridge.

King Uzziah (829-778 B.C.E.) made notable additions to the city's defenses, fortifying the (NW) Corner Gate and the Valley Gate (at the SW corner) with towers, as well as a tower at "the Buttress" ("the Angle," *RS, JB;* "the Turning," *JP*), apparently some part of the eastern wall not far from the royal buildings, either those of David or of Solomon. (2Ch 26:9; Ne 3:24, 25) Uzziah also equipped the towers and corners with "engines of war," perhaps mechanical catapults for shooting arrows and large stones. (2Ch 26:14, 15) His son Jotham continued the building program.—2Ch 27:3, 4.

Faithful King Hezekiah, ruling after his father, the apostate Ahaz, did cleansing and repair work in the temple area and arranged a great Passover celebration that drew worshipers to Jerusalem from all over the land, the northern kingdom included. (2Ch 29:1-5, 18, 19; 30:1, .10-26) This stimulus for true worship, however, was soon followed by attack from pagan quarters, mockers of the true God whose name rested on Jerusalem. In 732 B.C.E., eight years after Assyria's conquest of the northern kingdom of Israel, Assyrian King Sennacherib made a scythelike sweep through Palestine, diverting some troops to threaten Jerusalem. (2Ch 32:1, 9) Hezekiah had readied the city for a siege. He stopped up the water sources outside the city to hide them and make things difficult for the enemy, strengthened the walls, and fortified them. (2Ch 32:2-5, 27-30) It would seem that "the conduit" for bringing water into the city from the spring of Gihon was already constructed at this time, possibly being a peacetime project. (2Ki 20:20; 2Ch 32:30) If, as believed, it was the conduit that includes the tunnel cut through the side of the Kidron Valley with its termination at the Pool of Siloam in the Tyropoeon Valley, then it was no minor project to be completed in a few days. (See ARCHAEOLOGY [Palestine and Syria]; GIHON No. 2.) At any rate, the city's strength lay not in its defensive systems and supplies but in the protective power of Jehovah God, who said: "And I shall certainly defend this city to save it for my own sake and for the sake of David my servant." (2Ki 19:32-34) The miraculous destruction of 185,000 Assyrian troops sent Sennacherib scurrying back to Assyria. (2Ki 19:35, 36) When the campaign account was recorded in the Assyrian annals, it boasted of Sennacherib's shutting Hezekiah up inside Jerusalem like a 'bird in a cage,' but it made no claim of capturing the city.—See SENNACHERIB.

The reign of Manasseh (716-662 B.C.E.) brought further wall construction along the Kidron Valley. It also saw the nation drift farther from true worship. (2Ch 33:1-9, 14) His grandson Josiah temporarily reversed this decline, and during his rule the Valley of Hinnom, used by idolatrous persons for vile ceremonies, was "made unfit for worship," likely desecrated by being made into a city garbage dump. (2Ki 23:10; 2Ch 33:6) "The Gate of the Ash-heaps" apparently opened out onto this valley. (Ne 3:13, 14; see GEHENNA; HINNOM, VALLEY OF.) During Josiah's time "the second quarter" ("the new town," *JB*) of the city receives initial mention. (2Ki 22:14; 2Ch 34:22) This "second quarter" is generally understood to be the section of the city lying W or NW of the temple area.—Zep 1:10.

After Josiah's death, the situation deteriorated rapidly for Jerusalem, as four unfaithful kings followed each other in succession. In King Jehoiakim's eighth year Judah came into vassalage to Babylon. Jehoiakim's revolt three years later provoked a successful Babylonian siege of Jerusalem, after which the city's treasures were looted and the then king, Jehoiachin, and other citizens were deported. (2Ki 24:1-16; 2Ch 36:5-10) Babylon's appointee, King Zedekiah, tried to throw off the Babylonian yoke, and in his ninth year (609 B.C.E.) Jerusalem again came under siege. (2Ki 24:17-20; 25:1; 2Ch 36:11-14) An Egyptian military force sent to relieve Jerusalem succeeded in drawing off the besiegers only temporarily. (Jer 37:5-10) True to Jehovah's prophecy through Jeremiah, the Babylonians returned and renewed the siege. (Jer 34:1, 21, 22; 52:5-11) Jeremiah spent the latter part of the siege imprisoned in "the Courtyard of the Guard" (Jer 32:2; 38:28), connected with "the King's House." (Ne 3:25) Finally, 18 months from the start of the siege with its accompanying starvation, disease, and death, the walls of Jerusalem were breached, in Zedekiah's 11th year, and the city was taken.—2Ki 25:2-4; Jer 39:1-3.

Desolation and Restoration. The city walls were breached on Tammuz 9, 607 B.C.E. A month later, on Ab 10, Nebuchadnezzar's agent, Nebuzaradan, entered the conquered city and began demolition work, burning the temple and other buildings and proceeding to pull down the city walls. Jerusalem's king and most of her people were exiled to Babylon and her treasures were carried away as plunder.—2Ki 25:7-17; 2Ch 36:17-20; Jer 52:12-20; PICTURE, Vol. 2, p. 326.

The statement by archaeologist Conder that "the history of the ruined city remains a blank until Cyrus" is true not only of Jerusalem but also of the entire realm of the kingdom of Judah. Unlike the Assyrians, the Babylonian king moved no replacement peoples into the conquered region. A period of 70 years of desolation set in, even as prophesied.—Jer 25:11; 2Ch 36:21.

In "the first year" (evidently as ruler over Babylon) of Cyrus the Persian (538 B.C.E.) the royal decree went forth freeing the exiled Jews to "go up to Jerusalem, which is in Judah, and rebuild the house of Jehovah the God of Israel." (Ezr 1:1-4) The people who made the long trip to Jerusalem, carrying temple treasures with them, included 42,360 males, besides slaves and professional singers. They arrived in time to celebrate the Festival of Booths in Tishri (September-October) 537 B.C.E. (Ezr 2:64, 65; 3:1-4) Temple rebuilding got under way under Governor Zerubbabel's direction and, after serious interference and the infiltration of some apathy among the returned Jews, was finally completed by March of 515 B.C.E. More exiles returned with priest-scribe Ezra in 468 B.C.E., bringing additional things "to beautify the house of Jehovah, which is in Jerusalem" (Ezr 7:27), this by authorization of King Artaxerxes (Longimanus). The treasures brought by them were evidently worth more than $43,000,-000.—Ezr 8:25-27.

About a century and a half after Nebuchadnezzar's conquest, the walls and gates of the city were still broken down. Nehemiah obtained permission from Artaxerxes to go to Jerusalem and remedy this situation. (Ne 2:1-8) The account that follows of Nehemiah's nighttime survey and of his apportioning the construction work to different family groups is a major source of information about the layout of the city at that time, especially of its gates. (Ne 2:11-15; 3:1-32; see GATE, GATEWAY.) This rebuilding was in fulfillment of Daniel's prophecy and established the year that marked the start of the 70 prophetic "weeks" involving the coming of the Messiah. (Da 9:24-27) Despite harassment, in the short space of 52 days, in the year 455 B.C.E., they ringed Jerusalem with a wall and gates.—Ne 4:1-23; 6:15; 7:1; see SEVENTY WEEKS ("The Going Forth of the Word").

Jerusalem was now "wide and great, [but] there were few people inside it." (Ne 7:4) Following the public reading of Scriptures and celebrations in "the public square that was before the Water Gate" on the E side of the city (Ne 3:26; 8:1-18), arrangements were made to build up the city's population by bringing in one Israelite out of every ten to dwell there. This was done by casting lots, but additionally there were evidently volunteers. (Ne 11:1, 2) A spiritual cleansing work was done to put the city's population on a sound foundation as regards true worship. (Ne 12:47–13:3) Nehemiah's governorship lasted 12 years or more and embraced a trip to the Persian king's court. Upon his return to Jerusalem, he found need for further cleansing. (Ne 13:4-31) With the vigorous rooting out of apostasy he effected, the record of the Hebrew Scriptures closes, sometime after the year 443 B.C.E.

Hellenic and Maccabean Control. The changeover from Medo-Persian to Greek control came in 332 B.C.E. when Alexander the Great marched through Judah. The Greek historians make no mention of Alexander's entry into Jerusalem. Yet the city did come under Greek dominion, and it is reasonable to assume that it was not completely bypassed by Alexander. Josephus, in the first century C.E., records the Jewish tradition that, upon approaching Jerusalem, Alexander was met by the Jewish high priest and was shown the divinely inspired prophecies recorded by Daniel foretelling the lightning conquests by Greece. (*Jewish Antiquities*, XI, 326-338 [viii, 4, 5]; Da 8:5-7, 20, 21) Whatever the case, Jerusalem seems to have survived the change in control free of any damage.

Following Alexander's death, Jerusalem and Judea came under the control of the Ptolemies, who ruled out of Egypt. In 198 B.C.E. Antiochus the Great, ruling in Syria, after taking the fortified city of Sidon, captured Jerusalem, and Judah became a dominion of the Seleucid Empire. (Compare Da 11:16.) Jerusalem lay under Seleucid rule for 30 years. Then, in the year 168 B.C.E., Syrian King Antiochus IV (Epiphanes), in his attempt to Hellenize completely the Jews, dedicated Jerusalem's temple to Zeus (Jupiter) and profaned the altar by an unclean sacrifice. (1 Maccabees 1:57, 62; 2 Maccabees 6:1, 2, 5; PICTURES, Vol. 2, p. 335) This led to the Maccabean (or Hasmonaean) revolt. After a three-year struggle, Judas Maccabaeus gained control of the city and temple and rededicated Jehovah's altar to true worship on the anniversary of its profanation, Chislev 25, 165 B.C.E.

—1 Maccabees 4:52-54; 2 Maccabees 10:5; compare Joh 10:22.

The war against the Seleucid rulers had not ended. The Jews appealed to Rome for help and thus a new power came on the Jerusalem scene in about 160 B.C.E. (1 Maccabees 8:17, 18) Now Jerusalem began to come under the influence of the expanding Roman Empire. About 142 B.C.E., Simon Maccabaeus was able to make Jerusalem the capital of a region ostensibly free from subservience to or taxation by Gentile nations. Aristobulus I, Jerusalem's high priest, even assumed the title of king in 104 B.C.E. He was not, however, of the Davidic line.

Jerusalem was no 'city of peace' during this period. Internal quarrels, fired by selfish ambitions and worsened by rival religious factions—Sadducees, Pharisees, Zealots, and others—gravely weakened the city. A violent quarrel between Aristobulus II and his brother Hyrcanus resulted in Rome's being called on to arbitrate the dispute. Under General Pompey, Roman forces besieged Jerusalem in 63 B.C.E. for three months in order to enter the city and settle the dispute. Twelve thousand Jews reportedly died, many at the hands of fellow Israelites.

It is in Josephus' account of Pompey's conquest that the archway across the Tyropoeon Valley is first mentioned. It served as a link between the eastern and western halves of the city and gave those on the western half direct access to the temple area.

The Idumean Antipater (II) was now installed as Roman governor for Judea, a Maccabean being left as high priest and local ethnarch in Jerusalem. Later, Antipater's son Herod (the Great) was appointed by Rome as "king" over Judea. He did not get control of Jerusalem until 37 or 36 B.C.E., from which date his rule effectively began.

Under Herod the Great. Herod's rule was marked by an ambitious building program, and the city enjoyed considerable prosperity. A theater, gymnasium, and hippodrome (PICTURE, Vol. 2, p. 535), as well as other public buildings, were added. Herod also built a well-fortified royal palace (PICTURE, Vol. 2, p. 538), evidently on the W side of the city S of the present-day Jaffa Gate, where archaeologists believe they have found the foundation of one of the towers. Another fortress, the Tower of Antonia, lay near the temple and was connected with it by a passageway. (PICTURE, Vol. 2, p. 535; *Jewish Antiquities*, XV, 424 [xi, 7]) The Roman garrison could thus gain quick access to the temple area, as likely occurred when soldiers rescued Paul from a mob there.—Ac 21: 31, 32.

Herod's greatest work, however, was the reconstruction of the temple and its building complex. Beginning in his 18th year (*Jewish Antiquities*, XV, 380 [xi, 1]), the holy house itself was completed in a year and a half, but the work on the adjoining buildings and courtyards went on long after his death. (Joh 2:20) The total area encompassed was about double that of the previous temple area. Part of the wall of the temple courtyard apparently still stands, known today as the Western Wall, or the Wailing Wall. Archaeologists date the lower courses of huge 0.9-m-high (3 ft) blocks as from Herod's construction.

From 2 B.C.E. to 70 C.E. The Christian Greek Scriptures now carry forward the description of events involving Jerusalem. Jesus' birth took place, not at Jerusalem, but at nearby Bethlehem, "David's city." (Lu 2:10, 11) Nevertheless, the astrologers' later report about the birth of the "king of the Jews" caused Herod and "all Jerusalem along with him" to become agitated. (Mt 2:1-3) Shortly after issuing his infamous decree ordering the killing of Bethlehem's babes, Herod died, evidently in the year 1 B.C.E. (See HEROD No. 1.) His son Archelaus inherited rulership over Jerusalem and Judea as well as other areas. Rome later removed Archelaus for misdemeanors; thereafter governors who were directly appointed by Rome ruled, as did Pontius Pilate during Jesus' ministry. —Lu 3:1.

Jesus was taken to Jerusalem 40 days after birth and presented at the temple as Mary's firstborn. Aged Simeon and Anna rejoiced at seeing the promised Messiah, and Anna spoke of him "to all those waiting for Jerusalem's deliverance." (Lu 2:21-38; compare Le 12:2-4.) How many other times he was taken to Jerusalem during his childhood years is not stated, only one visit, made when he was 12, being specifically recorded. He then engaged in a discussion with teachers in the temple area, thus being occupied in the 'house of his Father,' in the chosen city of his Father.—Lu 2:41-49.

After his baptism and during his three-and-a-half-year ministry Jesus periodically visited Jerusalem; he certainly was there for the three annual festivals, attendance at which was obligatory for all Jewish males. (Ex 23:14-17) Much of his time, however, was spent outside the capital, as he preached and taught in Galilee and other regions of the land.

Aside from the temple area, where Jesus frequently taught, few other specific points in the city are mentioned in connection with his ministry. The Pool of Bethzatha with its five colonnades

(Joh 5:2) is thought to be the one that was unearthed just N of the temple area. (See BETHZATHA.) The Pool of Siloam is located on a slope of the southern part of the eastern ridge, receiving its water from the spring of Gihon through the conduit and tunnel attributed to Hezekiah. (Joh 9:11; PICTURE, Vol. 2, p. 949) It is with regard to Jesus' final visit to Jerusalem that a more detailed picture is given.—MAP, Vol. 2, p. 742; PICTURES, Vol. 2, p. 743.

Six days prior to the Passover festival of 33 C.E., Jesus came to Bethany, on the eastern side of the Mount of Olives. The next day, Nisan 9, as Jehovah's anointed King, he approached the capital city, mounted on the colt of an ass, in fulfillment of the prophecy of Zechariah 9:9. (Mt 21:1-9) Coming down the Mount of Olives, he paused to view the city and wept over it, graphically foretelling the coming siege and desolation it would undergo. (Lu 19:37-44) Upon his entering the city, likely through a gate in the eastern wall, the whole city was "set in commotion," for news would spread quickly throughout the relatively small area.—Mt 21:10.

During the remaining time, in which he spent the days in Jerusalem and the nights in Bethany (Lu 21:37, 38), Jesus cleansed the temple area of commercialists (Mt 21:12, 13), as he had done some three years earlier. (Joh 2:13-16) On Nisan 11 he was with four of his disciples on the Mount of Olives, from which the city and its temple could be viewed, when he gave his great prophecy regarding Jerusalem's coming destruction and "the conclusion of the system of things," as well as of his presence. (Mt 24; Mr 13; Lu 21) On Nisan 13 Peter and John arranged for the Passover meal in an upper room in Jerusalem where, that evening (the start of Nisan 14), Jesus celebrated the meal with his apostles. After his discussion with them, they left the city, crossed "the winter torrent of Kidron," and climbed the slopes of the Mount of Olives to the garden called Gethsemane. (Mt 26:36; Lu 22:39; Joh 18:1, 2) Gethsemane means "Oil Press," and olive trees of great age are yet to be found on the slope. But the exact location of the garden is today a matter of conjecture. —See GETHSEMANE.

Arrested that night, Jesus was led back into Jerusalem to priests Annas and Caiaphas and to the Sanhedrin hall for trial. (Mt 26:57–27:1; Joh 18:13-27) From there, at dawn, he was taken to Pilate at "the governor's palace" (Mt 27:2; Mr 15: 1, 16) and then to Herod Antipas, who was also in Jerusalem at that time. (Lu 23:6, 7) Finally, he was returned to Pilate for final judgment at "The Stone Pavement," called "Gab'ba·tha" in Hebrew. —Lu 23:11; Joh 19:13; see STONE PAVEMENT.

Golgotha, meaning "Skull [Place]," was the site of Jesus' impalement. (Mt 27:33-35; Lu 23:33) Though it obviously lay outside the city walls, probably toward the N, the site cannot now be identified with certainty. (See GOLGOTHA.) The same is true of the site of Jesus' burial.—PICTURES, Vol. 2, p. 948.

"The potter's field to bury strangers," purchased with the bribe money Judas threw back to the priests (Mt 27:5-7), is traditionally identified with a site on the S side of the Hinnom Valley near its junction with the Kidron. Many tombs are found in this area.—See AKELDAMA.

During the apostolic period. Following his resurrection, Jesus gave orders to his disciples not to leave Jerusalem at that time. (Lu 24:49; Ac 1:4) This was to be the starting point for preaching repentance for forgiveness of sins on the basis of Christ's name. (Lu 24:46-48) Ten days after his ascension to heaven, the disciples, gathered together in an upper room, received the anointing by holy spirit. (Ac 1:13, 14; 2:1-4) Jerusalem was crowded with Jews and proselytes from all parts of the Roman Empire, in attendance at the Festival of Pentecost. The witnessing done by the spirit-filled Christians resulted in thousands becoming baptized disciples. With thousands bearing witness to their faith, it is no wonder the angry religious leaders cried: "Look! you have filled Jerusalem with your teaching." (Ac 5:28) Miracles performed added power to the testimony, as, for example, the healing of the lame beggar at "the temple door that was called Beautiful," likely the E gate of the Court of Women.—Ac 3:2, 6, 7.

Even after the witnessing began to spread out from Jerusalem to "Samaria and to the most distant part of the earth" (Ac 1:8), Jerusalem continued to be the location of the governing body of the Christian congregation. Persecution early caused 'all except the apostles to be scattered throughout the regions of Judea and Samaria.' (Ac 8:1; compare Ga 1:17-19; 2:1-9.) From Jerusalem, certain apostles and disciples were sent out to aid new groups of believers, as at Samaria. (Ac 8:14; 11:19-22, 27) Saul of Tarsus (Paul) soon found it advisable to cut short his first visit to Jerusalem as a Christian because of attempts to murder him. (Ac 9:26-30) But there were also periods of calm. (Ac 9:31) Here Peter reported to the Christian assembly about God's acceptance of Gentile believers and here, too, the issue of circumcision and related matters were settled.—Ac 11:1-4, 18; 15:1, 2, 22-29; Ga 2:1, 2.

Jesus had called Jerusalem "the killer of the prophets and stoner of those sent forth to her." (Mt 23:37; compare vss 34-36.) Though many of her citizens showed faith in God's Son, the city as a whole continued to follow the pattern of the past. For this, 'her house was abandoned to her.' (Mt 23:38) In 66 C.E. a Jewish revolt brought Roman forces under Cestius Gallus to the city, surrounding it and making a thrust right up to the temple walls. Suddenly Cestius Gallus withdrew for no apparent reason. This allowed Christians to put into action Jesus' instructions: "Then let those in Judea begin fleeing to the mountains, and let those in the midst of [Jerusalem] withdraw, and let those in the country places not enter into her." (Lu 21:20-22) Eusebius, in his *Ecclesiastical History* (III, v, 3), states that the Christians fled from Jerusalem and the whole land of Judea to a city of Perea that was called Pella.

Jerusalem's relief as a result of the Roman withdrawal was short-lived, as it had been when the Babylonians temporarily withdrew to deal with the Egyptians near the end of King Zedekiah's reign. Under General Titus the Roman forces returned in 70 C.E. in increased numbers and laid siege to the city, now crowded with Passover celebrants. Siege banks were thrown up by the Romans, and a continuous wall or fence was erected around the entire city to prevent escape by day or night. This, too, fulfilled Jesus' prophecy. (Lu 19:43) Within the city rival factions quarreled and fought, much of the food supply was destroyed, and those caught attempting to leave the city were slain as traitors. Josephus, the source of this information, relates that in time the famine became so grave that the people were reduced to eating wisps of hay and leather, even their own children. (Compare La 2:11, 12, 19, 20; De 28:56, 57.) Titus' offers of peace were consistently rejected by the stubborn city leaders.

Eventually the walls were systematically breached by the Romans, and their troops invaded the city. (PICTURE, Vol. 2, p. 752) Despite orders to the contrary, the temple was burned and gutted. According to Josephus, this took place on the anniversary of Nebuchadnezzar's destruction of the first temple centuries earlier. His account also states that the repository of the archives, housing the genealogical records of tribal and family descent and inheritance rights, was put to the fire. (*The Jewish War*, VI, 250, 251 [iv, 5]; II, 426-428 [xvii, 6]; VI, 354 [vi, 3]) Thus, the legal means for establishing the lineage of members of the Messianic tribe of Judah and the priestly tribe of Levi came to an end.

In just 4 months and 25 days, from April 3 to August 30, 70 C.E., the conquest had been effected. Thus, the tribulation, though intense, was remarkably short. The unreasoning attitude and actions of the Jews within the city doubtless contributed to this shortness. Though Josephus puts the number of dead at 1,100,000, there were survivors. (Compare Mt

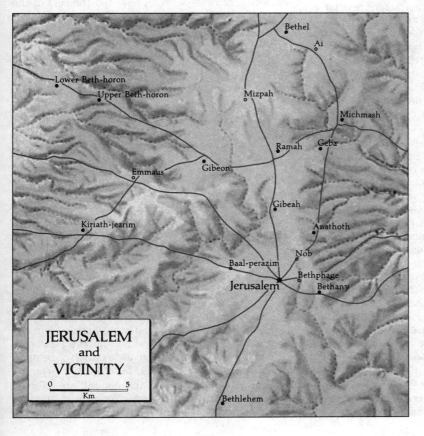

JERUSALEM
and
VICINITY

0 —————— 5
Km

Bethel
Ai
Lower Beth-horon
Upper Beth-horon
Mizpah
Michmash
Ramah   Geba
Emmaus   Gibeon
Gibeah
Kiriath-jearim
Anathoth
Nob
Baal-perazim
Bethphage
Jerusalem   Bethany
Bethlehem

*Bronze prutah minted
during the Jewish war against Rome,
proclaiming "Freedom of Zion"*

24:22.) Ninety-seven thousand captives were taken, many of whom were sent as slaves to Egypt or were killed by sword or beasts in the theaters of the Roman provinces. This, too, fulfilled divine prophecy.—De 28:68.

The entire city was demolished, with only the towers of Herod's palace and a portion of the western wall left standing as evidence to later generations of the defensive strength that had availed nothing. Josephus remarks that, apart from these remnants, "the rest of the wall encompassing the city was so completely levelled to the ground as to leave future visitors to the spot no ground for believing that it had ever been inhabited." (*The Jewish War,* VII, 3, 4 [i, 1]) A relief on the Arch of Titus in Rome depicts Roman soldiers carrying off sacred vessels of the ruined temple.—Compare Mt 24:2; PICTURE, Vol. 2, p. 752.

Later Periods. Jerusalem remained virtually desolate until about 130 C.E., when Emperor Hadrian ordered the building of a new city, named Aelia Capitolina. This provoked a Jewish revolt by Bar Kokhba (132-135 C.E.), which succeeded for a time but was then crushed. Jews were not allowed in the Roman-built city for nearly two centuries. In the fourth century, Constantine the Great's mother Helena visited Jerusalem and began the identification of the many so-called holy sites and shrines. Later the Muslims captured the city. Today there are two Islamic structures on the Temple Mount. Late in the seventh century Caliph 'Abd al-Malik ibn Marwan built the Dome of the Rock on or near the temple site. Although also called a mosque, it is in reality a shrine. South of the Dome of the Rock is the present-day el-Aqsa mosque constructed near the beginning of the seventh century on the site of an earlier building.

For further information concerning geographic locations related to Jerusalem, see such articles as:

EN-ROGEL; KIDRON, TORRENT VALLEY OF; MAKTESH; OLIVES, MOUNT OF; OPHEL; TEMPLE; and ZION.

The City's Significance. Jerusalem was far more than the capital of an earthly nation. It was the only city in all the earth upon which Jehovah God placed his name. (1Ki 11:36) After the ark of the covenant, associated with God's presence, was transferred there, and even more so when the temple sanctuary, or house of God, was constructed there, Jerusalem became Jehovah's figurative 'residence,' his "resting-place." (Ps 78:68, 69; 132: 13, 14; 135:21; compare 2Sa 7:1-7, 12, 13.) Because the kings of the Davidic line were God's anointed, sitting upon "Jehovah's throne" (1Ch 29:23; Ps 122:3-5), Jerusalem itself was also called "the throne of Jehovah"; and those tribes or nations turning to it in recognition of God's sovereignty were, in effect, being congregated to the name of Jehovah. (Jer 3:17; Ps 122:1-4; Isa 27: 13) Those hostile to or fighting against Jerusalem were, in actuality, opposing the expression of God's sovereignty. This was certain to occur, in view of the prophetic statement at Genesis 3:15.

Jerusalem therefore represented the seat of the divinely constituted government or typical kingdom of God. From it went forth God's law, his word, and his blessing. (Mic 4:2; Ps 128:5) Those working for Jerusalem's peace and its good were

*Bronze sestertius commemorating Roman
conquest of Judea; front, Emperor Vespasian;
reverse, "IVDAEA CAPTA" (Judea captured)*

therefore working for the success of God's righteous purpose, the prospering of his will. (Ps 122:6-9) Though situated among Judah's mountains and doubtless of impressive appearance, Jerusalem's true loftiness and beauty came from the way in which Jehovah God had honored and glorified it, that it might serve as "a crown of beauty" for him.—Ps 48:1-3, 11-14; 50:2; Isa 62:1-7.

Since Jehovah's praise and his will are effected primarily by his intelligent creatures, it was not the buildings forming the city that determined his continued use of the city but the people in it, rulers and ruled, priests and people. (Ps 102:18-22; Isa 26:1, 2) While these were faithful, honoring Jehovah's name by their words and life course, he blessed and defended Jerusalem. (Ps 125:1, 2; Isa 31:4, 5) Jehovah's disfavor soon came upon the people and their kings because of the apostate course the majority followed. For this reason Jehovah declared his purpose to reject the city that had borne his name. (2Ki 21:12-15; 23: 27) He would remove "support and stay" from the city, resulting in its becoming filled with tyranny, with juvenile delinquency, with disrespect for men in honorable positions; Jerusalem would suffer abasement and severe humiliation. (Isa 3:1-8, 16-26) Even though Jehovah God restored the city 70 years after permitting its destruction by Babylon, making it again beautiful as the joyful center of true worship in the earth (Isa 52:1-9; 65:17-19), the people and their leaders reverted to their apostate course once more.

Jehovah preserved the city until the sending of his Son to earth. It had to be there for the Messianic prophecies to be fulfilled. (Isa 28:16; 52:7; Zec 9:9) Israel's apostate course was climaxed in the impalement of the Messiah, Jesus Christ. (Compare Mt 21:33-41.) Taking place as it did at Jerusalem, instigated by the nation's leaders with popular support, this made certain God's complete and irreversible rejection of the city as representing him and bearing his name. (Compare Mt 16: 21; Lu 13:33-35.) Neither Jesus nor his apostles foretold any restoration by God of earthly Jerusalem and its temple to come after the city's divinely decreed destruction, which occurred in 70 C.E.

Yet the name Jerusalem continued to be used as symbolic of something greater than the earthly city. The apostle Paul, by divine inspiration, revealed that there is a "Jerusalem above," which he speaks of as the "mother" of anointed Christians. (Ga 4:25, 26) This places the "Jerusalem above" in the position of a wife to Jehovah God the great Father and Life-Giver. When earthly Jerusalem was used as the chief city of God's chosen nation, it, too, was spoken of as a woman, married to God, being tied to him by holy bonds in a covenant relationship. (Isa 51:17, 21, 22; 54:1, 5; 60:1, 14) It thus stood for, or was representative of, the entire congregation of God's human servants. "Jerusalem above" must therefore represent the entire congregation of Jehovah's loyal spirit servants.

New Jerusalem. In the inspired Revelation, the apostle John records information concerning the "new Jerusalem." (Re 3:12) In vision John sees this "holy city" as "coming down out of heaven

from God and prepared as a bride adorned for her husband." This is in relation to the vision he sees of "a new heaven and a new earth." This "bride" was said to be "the Lamb's wife." (Re 21:1-3, 9-27) Other apostolic writings apply the same figure to the Christian congregation of anointed ones. (2Co 11:2; Eph 5:21-32) In Revelation chapter 14 "the Lamb" Christ Jesus is depicted as standing on Mount Zion, a name also associated with Jerusalem (compare 1Pe 2:6), and with him are 144,000 having his name and the name of his Father written on their foreheads.—Re 14:1-5; see NEW JERUSALEM.

Unfaithful Jerusalem. Since much that is said concerning Jerusalem in the Scriptures is in condemnation of her, it is clear that only when faithful did Jerusalem symbolize Jehovah's heavenly organization and, at times, the true Christian congregation, "the Israel of God." (Ga 6:16) When unfaithful, it was pictured as a prostitute and an adulterous woman; it became like the pagan Amorites and Hittites that once controlled the city. (Eze 16:3, 15, 30-42) As such, it could only represent apostates, those following a 'prostitute' course of infidelity to the God whose name they claim to bear.—Jas 4:4.

It can thus be seen that "Jerusalem" is used in a multiple sense, and the context must in each case be considered to gain correct understanding.—See APPOINTED TIMES OF THE NATIONS.

JERUSHA(H) (Je·ru′sha[h]) [He Has Taken Possession]. Mother of King Jotham; wife of Uzziah; daughter of Zadok.—2Ki 15:32, 33; 2Ch 27:1, 2.

JESHAIAH (Je·sha′iah) [Jehovah Is Salvation].

1. A Levitical descendant of Moses through Eliezer, and an ancestor of the Shelomoth whom David appointed as one of his treasurers.—1Ch 23:15; 26:24-26.

2. A Levite musician of "the sons of Jeduthun," selected by lot to head the 8th of the 24 Davidic musical groups.—1Ch 25:1, 3, 15.

3. A Benjamite whose distant descendant lived in Jerusalem during Nehemiah's governorship. —Ne 11:4, 7.

4. Head of the paternal house of Elam in whose group were 70 males accompanying Ezra on the return to Jerusalem.—Ezr 8:1, 7.

5. A Merarite Levite who also returned with Ezra from Babylon.—Ezr 8:1, 19.

6. A descendant of King David; grandson of Governor Zerubbabel.—1Ch 3:1, 19, 21.

JESHANAH (Jesh′a·nah) [Old [Town]]. A place mentioned along with Mizpah as indicating the location of the stone that Samuel set up and called "Ebenezer." (1Sa 7:12) Jeshanah was one of the cities captured by Judean King Abijah (980-978 B.C.E.) from Jeroboam the king of Israel. (2Ch 13:19) It is considered to be identical with the Isana referred to by Josephus as the site of Herod the Great's victory over General Pappus. (*Jewish Antiquities,* XIV, 458 [xv, 12]) The name Isana seems to be preserved in Burj el-Isaneh, about 8 km (5 mi) NNE of Bethel. This place has therefore been suggested as a possible identification for ancient Jeshanah.

JESHARELAH (Jesh·a·re′lah). A 'son of Asaph' listed among the musicians and singers in David's time. (1Ch 25:1, 9, 14) He is probably the same as Asharelah.—1Ch 25:2.

JESHEBEAB (Je·sheb′e·ab) [May the Father Continue to Dwell; or, possibly, Jehovah Has Brought the Father Back]. The priest whose paternal house was selected by lot for the 14th course when David had the priestly services divided up. —1Ch 24:6, 13.

JESHER (Je′sher) [Uprightness]. A son of Caleb the son of Hezron; of the tribe of Judah.—1Ch 2:3-5, 18.

JESHIMON (Je·shi′mon) [Desert].

1. A bare wilderness area seemingly at the NE end of the Dead Sea, in which area Beth-jeshimoth was perhaps located. Apparently Pisgah and Peor overlooked Jeshimon.—Nu 21:20; 23:28; Jos 12:1-3.

2. A region near Ziph, situated N of the Wilderness of Maon. It would appear that Jeshimon included part of the Wilderness of Judah and lay a few miles SE of Hebron. In this area of naked, chalky hills, David and his men hid from King Saul.—1Sa 23:19, 24; 26:1, 3; see JUDAH, WILDERNESS OF.

JESHISHAI (Je·shish′ai) [from a root meaning "aged"]. A descendant of Gad.—1Ch 5:11, 14.

JESHOHAIAH (Jesh·o·hai′ah). A Simeonite chieftain, one of those who expanded their territory at the expense of the Hamites during the days of King Hezekiah.—1Ch 4:24, 34-41.

JESHUA (Jesh′u·a) [possibly a shortened form of Jehoshua, meaning "Jehovah Is Salvation"].

1. An Aaronic priest in David's time. The 9th of the 24 divisions of the Aaronic priesthood as arranged by David was assigned to the house of Jeshua. Probably the same house is listed among those returning with Zerubbabel from Babylonian exile in 537 B.C.E.—1Ch 24:1, 11, 31; Ezr 2:1, 36; Ne 7:39.

2. One of the Levites assigned to be in charge of distributing the tithes and contributions in the priests' cities; also to priests who were serving in the sanctuary during the service period of their divisions; these priests brought along with them their sons from three years old and upward when they came to serve at the sanctuary, and the children ate with the family in one of the sanctuary's dining rooms.—2Ch 31:15, 16.

3. An Israelite of the family of Pahath-moab, some of whose descendants returned from Babylonian exile with Zerubbabel.—Ezr 2:1, 2, 6; Ne 7:11.

4. A high priest (called Joshua in Haggai and Zechariah), son of Jehozadak and grandson of Seraiah. (Ezr 3:8; Ne 12:26; 1Ch 6:14) He was of the house of Eleazar.—See Ezr 7:1-5 for the genealogy from Eleazar to Seraiah.

When Nebuchadnezzar destroyed Jerusalem he put to death Seraiah, who was high priest then, and took Jehozadak captive to Babylon. (2Ki 25:18-21; 1Ch 6:14, 15; Ne 7:7) Jeshua returned from Babylon in 537 B.C.E. with Zerubbabel and served as high priest to the restored Jewish remnant. (Ezr 2:2; 5:2; Hag 1:1) Thus the highpriestly line was preserved by Jehovah, so that Israel had the services of high priests from the restoration until the coming of the Messiah. Jeshua took the lead, along with Zerubbabel, in setting up the altar, then in rebuilding the temple, encouraged by the prophets Haggai and Zechariah. (Ezr 3:2; 5:1, 2) He stood by Zerubbabel in opposing the adversaries of the temple reconstruction. —Ezr 4:1-3.

Some of the older ones among the returned Israelites had seen the glory of Solomon's temple and tended to view the rebuilt temple as nothing in comparison. Haggai the prophet was sent to speak to Zerubbabel and Joshua (Jeshua), telling them that the glory of the later house would become greater than that of the former one. Jehovah would do this by bringing in "the desirable things of all the nations."—Hag 2:1-4, 7, 9.

The prophet Zechariah was given a vision in which he beheld Joshua (Jeshua) the high priest standing before the angel of Jehovah, and Satan at his right hand to resist him. "Joshua" was given a change from befouled garments to robes of state and a clean turban. Then "Joshua" was told of God's servant Sprout.—Zec 3:1-8.

At another time Jehovah told Zechariah to put a

crown on Joshua's (Jeshua's) head and to say to him: "Here is the man whose name is Sprout. . . . And he himself will build the temple of Jehovah, . . . and he must become a priest upon his throne." This prophecy certainly applied to someone future for, under the Law, priesthood and kingship were strictly separate, and High Priest Joshua never ruled as king over Israel.—Zec 6:11-13.

5. The head of a Levitical house, some of whom returned from Babylonian exile with Zerubbabel in 537 B.C.E. (Ezr 2:40; Ne 7:43) If not another person by the same name, a representative of Jeshua's house signed the "trustworthy arrangement" entered into by the priests, princes, and people to walk in God's law. He was the son of Azaniah (Ne 9:38; 10:1, 9) and probably the same as the Jeshua mentioned at Nehemiah 12:8, 24.

"Jozabad the son of Jeshua," one of the Levites to whom Ezra turned over the silver, gold, and vessels for the house of God, was probably a member of this Jeshua's house.—Ezr 8:33.

Ezer son of Jeshua, a prince of Mizpah, who worked under Nehemiah in repairing Jerusalem's wall, may have been of the same family.—Ne 3:19.

6. One of the Levite supervisors of the temple rebuilding.—Ezr 3:9.

7. One of the Levites reading and explaining the Law to the people and taking the lead in worship, under Ezra's direction. Perhaps of the same house as No. 5.—Ne 8:7; 9:4, 5.

8. A town in the southern part of Judah where some of the repatriated Jewish remnant dwelt. Its site is identified by some scholars as Tell es-Sa'weh (Tel Yeshu'a), about 15 km (9 mi) ENE of Beer-sheba. (Ne 11:25, 26) It may be the Shema of Joshua 15:26, and possibly the Sheba of Joshua 19:2.

JESHURUN (Jesh'u·run) [Upright One]. An

honorary title for Israel. In the Greek *Septuagint* "Jeshurun" becomes a term of affection, it being rendered "beloved." The designation "Jeshurun" should have reminded Israel of its calling as Jehovah's covenant people and therefore of its obligation to remain upright. (De 33:5, 26; Isa 44:2) At Deuteronomy 32:15 the name Jeshurun is used ironically. Instead of living up to its name Jeshurun, Israel became intractable, forsook its Maker, and despised its Savior.

JESIMIEL (Je·sim'i·el) [May God Set (Ap-

point); God Has Set (Appointed)]. One of the Simeonite chieftains who, in King Hezekiah's day, extended their territory to the E of the Valley of Gedor.—1Ch 4:24, 34-41.

JESSE (Jes'se) [shortened form of Isshiah,

meaning "Jehovah Makes Forget"; or, possibly, a shortened form of Abishai]. Father of King David of the tribe of Judah; grandson of Ruth and Boaz and a link in the genealogical line from Abraham to Jesus. (Ru 4:17, 22; Mt 1:5, 6; Lu 3:31, 32) Jesse fathered eight sons, one of whom apparently died before producing any sons of his own, which may account for the omission of his name from the genealogies of Chronicles. (1Sa 16:10, 11; 17:12; 1Ch 2:12-15) The two sisters of David, Abigail and Zeruiah, are nowhere called Jesse's daughters, but one is called "the daughter of Nahash." (1Ch 2:16, 17; 2Sa 17:25) It may be that Nahash was the former husband of Jesse's wife, making her girls half sisters to Jesse's sons, unless Nahash is another name for Jesse, or even the name of his wife, as some have suggested.

Jesse was a sheep owner living at Bethlehem. After King Saul turned away from true worship, Jehovah sent Samuel to Jesse's home to anoint one of his sons as king. Jesse brought in the seven older boys, but when Jehovah chose none of these Jesse was obliged to call his youngest son David from pasturing the sheep; this son was Jehovah's choice.—1Sa 16:1-13.

When Saul summoned David to play the soothing harp for him, aged Jesse sent along a generous gift and later granted permission for David to remain some time in attendance at Saul's court. (1Sa 16:17-23; 17:12) Later, when it appears that David was back again tending the sheep, Jesse sent him with some provisions for the three oldest boys, who were in Saul's army. (1Sa 17:13, 15, 17, 18, 20) During the time David was outlawed by Saul, Jesse and his wife were given asylum in Moab.—1Sa 22:3, 4.

Often David is called "the son of Jesse," disparagingly, by persons such as Saul, Doeg, Nabal, and Sheba (1Sa 20:27, 30, 31; 22:7-9, 13; 25:10; 2Sa 20:1; 1Ki 12:16; 2Ch 10:16), but more respectfully in other instances, for example, by David himself, Ezra, and Jehovah God.—1Sa 16:18; 17:58; 2Sa 23:1; 1Ch 10:14; 12:18; 29:26; Ps 72:20; Lu 3:32; Ac 13:22.

The prophetic promise that "the root of Jesse" would 'stand up as a signal for the peoples' and would judge in righteousness finds fulfillment in Christ Jesus, the one who, because he is immortal, keeps the genealogical line of Jesse alive.—Isa 11:1-5, 10; Ro 15:8, 12.

JESUS (Je'sus) [Lat. form of the Gr. *I·e·sous'*,

which corresponds to the Heb. *Ye·shu'a'* or *Yehoh·shu'a'* and means "Jehovah Is Salvation"]. Jewish historian Josephus of the first century C.E. mentions some 12 persons, other than those in the Bible record, bearing that name. It also appears in the Apocryphal writings of the last centuries of the B.C.E. period. It therefore appears that it was not an uncommon name during that period.

1. The name *I·e·sous'* appears in the Greek text of Acts 7:45 and Hebrews 4:8 and applies to Joshua, the leader of Israel following Moses' death. —See JOSHUA No. 1.

2. An ancestor of Jesus Christ, evidently in his mother's line. (Lu 3:29) Some ancient manuscripts here read "Jose(s)."—See GENEALOGY OF JESUS CHRIST.

3. Jesus Christ.—See JESUS CHRIST.

4. A Christian, evidently Jewish, and fellow worker of Paul. He was also called Justus.—Col 4:11.

JESUS CHRIST.

The name and title of the Son of God from the time of his anointing while on earth.

The name Jesus (Gr., *I·e·sous'*) corresponds to the Hebrew name Jeshua (or, in fuller form, Jehoshua), meaning "Jehovah Is Salvation." The name itself was not unusual, many men being so named in that period. For this reason persons often added further identification, saying, "Jesus the Nazarene." (Mr 10:47; Ac 2:22) Christ is from the Greek *Khri·stos'*, the equivalent of the Hebrew *Ma·shi'ach* (Messiah), and means "Anointed One." Whereas the expression "anointed one" was properly applied to others before Jesus, such as Moses, Aaron, and David (Heb 11:24-26; Le 4:3; 8:12; 2Sa 22:51), the position, office, or service to which these were anointed only prefigured the superior position, office, and service of Jesus Christ. Jesus is therefore preeminently and uniquely "the Christ, the Son of the living God."—Mt 16:16; see CHRIST; MESSIAH.

Prehuman Existence. The person who became known as Jesus Christ did not begin life here on earth. He himself spoke of his prehuman heavenly life. (Joh 3:13; 6:38, 62; 8:23, 42, 58) John 1:1, 2 gives the heavenly name of the one who became Jesus, saying: "In the beginning the Word [Gr., *Lo'gos*] was, and the Word was with God, and the Word was a god ["was divine," *AT; Mo;* or "of divine being," *Böhmer; Stage* (both German)]. This one was in the beginning with God." Since Jehovah is eternal and had no beginning (Ps 90:2; Re 15:3), the Word's being with God from "the beginning" must here refer to the beginning of Jehovah's creative works. This is confirmed by other texts identifying Jesus as "the firstborn of all creation," "the beginning of the creation by God."

(Col 1:15; Re 1:1; 3:14) Thus the Scriptures identify the Word (Jesus in his prehuman existence) as God's first creation, his firstborn Son.

That Jehovah was truly the Father or Life-Giver to this firstborn Son and, hence, that this Son was actually a creature of God is evident from Jesus' own statements. He pointed to God as the Source of his life, saying, "I live because of the Father." According to the context, this meant that his life resulted from or was caused by his Father, even as the gaining of life by dying men would result from their faith in Jesus' ransom sacrifice.—Joh 6:56, 57.

If the estimates of modern-day scientists as to the age of the physical universe are anywhere near correct, Jesus' existence as a spirit creature began thousands of millions of years prior to the creation of the first human. (Compare Mic 5:2.) This firstborn spirit Son was used by his Father in the creation of all other things. (Joh 1:3; Col 1:16, 17) This would include the millions of other spirit sons of Jehovah God's heavenly family (Da 7:9, 10; Re 5:11), as well as the physical universe and the creatures originally produced within it. Logically, it was to this firstborn Son that Jehovah said: "Let us make man in our image, according to our likeness." (Ge 1:26) All these other created things were not only created "through him" but also "for him," as God's Firstborn and the "heir of all things."—Col 1:16; Heb 1:2.

Not a co-Creator. The Son's share in the creative works, however, did not make him a co-Creator with his Father. The power for creation came from God through his holy spirit, or active force. (Ge 1:2; Ps 33:6) And since Jehovah is the Source of all life, all animate creation, visible and invisible, owes its life to him. (Ps 36:9) Rather than a co-Creator, then, the Son was the agent or instrumentality through whom Jehovah, the Creator, worked. Jesus himself credited God with the creation, as do all the Scriptures.—Mt 19:4-6; see CREATION.

Wisdom personified. What is recorded concerning the Word in the Scriptures fits remarkably the description given at Proverbs 8:22-31. There wisdom is personified, represented as though able to speak and act. (Pr 8:1) Many professed Christian writers of the early centuries of the Common Era understood this section to refer symbolically to God's Son in his prehuman state. In view of the texts already considered, there can be no denying that that Son was "produced" by Jehovah "as the beginning of his way, the earliest of his achievements of long ago," nor that the Son was "beside [Jehovah] as a master worker" during earth's creation, as described in these verses of Proverbs. It is true that in Hebrew, which assigns gender to its nouns (as do many other languages), the word for "wisdom" is always in the feminine gender. This would continue to be the case even though wisdom is personified and so would not rule out wisdom's being used figuratively to represent God's firstborn Son. The Greek word for "love" in the expression "God is love" (1Jo 4:8) is also in the feminine gender but that does not make God feminine. Solomon, the principal writer of Proverbs (Pr 1:1), applied the title *qo·he′leth* (congregator) to himself (Ec 1:1) and this word is also in the feminine gender.

Wisdom is manifest only by being expressed in some way. God's own wisdom was expressed in creation (Pr 3:19, 20) but *through* his Son. (Compare 1Co 8:6.) So, too, God's wise purpose involving mankind is made manifest through, and summed up in, his Son, Jesus Christ. Thus, the apostle could say that Christ represents "the power of God and the wisdom of God" and that Christ Jesus "has become to us wisdom from God, also righteousness and sanctification and release by ransom."—1Co 1:24, 30; compare 1Co 2:7, 8; Pr 8:1, 10, 18-21.

How he is the "only-begotten Son." Jesus' being called the "only-begotten Son" (Joh 1:14; 3:16, 18; 1Jo 4:9) does not mean that the other spirit creatures produced were not God's sons, for they are called sons as well. (Ge 6:2, 4; Job 1:6; 2:1; 38:4-7) However, by virtue of his being the sole *direct* creation of his Father, the firstborn Son was unique, different from all others of God's sons, all of whom were created or begotten by Jehovah *through* that firstborn Son. So "the Word" was Jehovah's "only-begotten Son" in a particular sense, even as Isaac was Abraham's "only-begotten son" in a particular sense (his father already having another son but not by his wife Sarah).—Heb 11:17; Ge 16:15.

Why called "the Word." The name (or, perhaps, title) "the Word" (Joh 1:1) apparently identifies the function that God's firstborn Son performed after other intelligent creatures were formed. A similar expression is found at Exodus 4:16, where Jehovah says to Moses concerning his brother Aaron: "And he must speak for you to the people; and it must occur that he will serve as a mouth to you, and you will serve as God to him." As spokesman for God's chief representative on earth, Aaron served as "a mouth" for Moses. Likewise with the Word, or Logos, who became Jesus Christ. Jehovah evidently used his Son to convey information and instructions to others of his fam-

ily of spirit sons, even as he used that Son to deliver his message to humans on earth. Showing that he was God's Word, or Spokesman, Jesus said to his Jewish listeners: "What I teach is not mine, but belongs to him that sent me. If anyone desires to do His will, he will know concerning the teaching whether it is from God or I speak of my own originality."—Joh 7:16, 17; compare Joh 12:50; 18:37.

Doubtless on many occasions during his prehuman existence as the Word, Jesus acted as Jehovah's Spokesman to persons on earth. While certain texts refer to Jehovah as though directly speaking to humans, other texts make clear that he did so through an angelic representative. (Compare Ex 3:2-4 with Ac 7:30, 35; also Ge 16:7-11, 13; 22:1, 11, 12, 15-18.) Reasonably, in the majority of such cases God spoke through the Word. He likely did so in Eden, for on two of the three occasions where mention is made of God's speaking there, the record specifically shows someone was with Him, undoubtedly his Son. (Ge 1:26-30; 2:16, 17; 3:8-19, 22) The angel who guided Israel through the wilderness and whose voice the Israelites were strictly to obey because 'Jehovah's name was within him,' may therefore have been God's Son, the Word.—Ex 23:20-23; compare Jos 5:13-15.

This does not mean that the Word is the only angelic representative through whom Jehovah has spoken. The inspired statements at Acts 7:53, Galatians 3:19, and Hebrews 2:2, 3 make clear that the Law covenant was transmitted to Moses by angelic sons of God other than his Firstborn.

Jesus continues to bear the name "The Word of God" since his return to heavenly glory.—Re 19: 13, 16.

Why do some Bible translations refer to Jesus as "God," while others say he was "a god"?

Some translations render John 1:1 as saying: "In the beginning was the Word, and the Word was with God, and the Word was God." Literally the Greek text reads: "In beginning was the word, and the word was toward the god, and god was the word." The translator must supply capitals as needed in the language into which he translates the text. It is clearly proper to capitalize "God" in translating the phrase "the god," since this must identify the Almighty God with whom the Word was. But the capitalizing of the word "god" in the second case does not have the same justification.

The *New World Translation* renders this text: "In the beginning the Word was, and the Word was with God, and the Word was a god." True, there is no indefinite article (corresponding to "a" or "an") in the original Greek text. But this does not mean one should not be used in translation, for Koine, or common Greek, *had no indefinite article*. Hence, throughout the Christian Greek Scriptures, translators are obliged to use the indefinite article or not according to their understanding of the meaning of the text. All English translations of those Scriptures do contain the indefinite article hundreds of times; yet most do not use it at John 1:1. Nevertheless, its use in the rendering of this text has sound basis.

First, it should be noted that the text itself shows that the Word was *"with* God," hence could not *be* God, that is, be the Almighty God. (Note also vs 2, which would be unnecessary if vs 1 actually showed the Word to be God.) Additionally, the word for "god" (Gr., *the·os'*) in its second occurrence in the verse is significantly without the definite article "the" (Gr., *ho*). Regarding this fact, Ernst Haenchen, in a commentary on the Gospel of John (chapters 1-6), stated: "[*the·os'*] and [*ho the·os'*] ('god, divine' and 'the God') were not the same thing in this period. . . . In fact, for the . . . Evangelist, only the Father was 'God' ([*ho the·os'*]; cf. 17:3); 'the Son' was subordinate to him (cf. 14:28). But that is only hinted at in this passage because here the emphasis is on the proximity of the one to the other . . . . It was quite possible in Jewish and Christian monotheism to speak of divine beings that existed alongside and under God but were not identical with him. Phil 2:6-10 proves that. In that passage Paul depicts just such a divine being, who later became man in Jesus Christ . . . Thus, in both Philippians and John 1:1 it is not a matter of a dialectical relationship between two-in-one, but of a personal union of two entities."—*John 1,* translated by R. W. Funk, 1984, pp. 109, 110.

After giving as a translation of John 1:1c "and divine (of the category divinity) was the Word," Haenchen goes on to state: "In this instance, the verb 'was' ([*en*]) simply expresses predication. And the predicate noun must accordingly be more carefully observed: [*the·os'*] is not the same thing as [*ho the·os'*] ('divine' is not the same thing as 'God')." (pp. 110, 111) Elaborating on this point, Philip B. Harner brought out that the grammatical construction in John 1:1 involves an anarthrous predicate, that is, a predicate noun without the definite article "the," preceding the verb, which construction is primarily qualitative in meaning and indicates that "the *logos* has the nature of *theos.*" He further stated: "In John 1:1 I think that the qualitative force of the predicate is so prominent that the noun [*the·os'*] cannot be regarded as definite." (*Journal of Biblical Literature,* 1973, pp. 85, 87) Other translators, also recognizing that the Greek term has qualitative force and describes the nature of the Word, therefore render the phrase: "the Word was divine."—*AT; Sd;* compare *Mo;* see *NW* appendix, p. 1579.

The Hebrew Scriptures are consistently clear in showing that there is but one Almighty God, the Creator of all things and the Most High, whose name is Jehovah. (Ge 17:1; Isa 45:18; Ps 83:18) For that reason Moses could say to the nation of Israel: "Jehovah our God is one Jehovah. And you must love Jehovah your God with all your heart and all your soul and all your vital force." (De 6:4, 5) The Christian Greek Scriptures do not contradict this teaching that had been accepted and believed by God's servants for thousands of years, but instead they support it. (Mr 12:29; Ro 3:29, 30; 1Co 8:6; Eph 4:4-6; 1Ti 2:5) Jesus Christ himself said, "The Father is greater than I am" and referred to the Father as his God, "the only true God." (Joh 14:28; 17:3; 20:17; Mr 15:34; Re 1:1; 3:12) On numerous occasions Jesus expressed his inferiority and subordination to his Father. (Mt 4:9, 10; 20:23; Lu 22:41, 42; Joh 5:19; 8:42; 13:16) Even after Jesus' ascension into heaven his apostles continued to present the same picture.—1Co 11:3; 15:20, 24-28; 1Pe 1:3; 1Jo 2:1; 4:9, 10.

These facts give solid support to a translation such as "the Word was a god" at John 1:1. The Word's preeminent position among God's creatures as the Firstborn, the one through whom God created all things, and as God's Spokesman, gives real basis for his being called "a god" or mighty one. The Messianic prophecy at Isaiah 9:6 foretold that he would be called "Mighty God," though not the Almighty God, and that he would be the "Eternal Father" of all those privileged to live as his subjects. The zeal of his own Father, "Jehovah of armies," would accomplish this. (Isa 9:7) Certainly if God's Adversary, Satan the Devil, is called a "god" (2Co 4:4) because of his dominance over men and demons (1Jo 5:19; Lu 11:14-18), then with far greater reason and propriety is God's firstborn Son called "a god," "the only-begotten god" as the most reliable manuscripts of John 1:18 call him.

When charged by opposers with 'making himself a god,' Jesus' reply was: "Is it not written in your Law, 'I said: "You are gods"'? If he called 'gods' those against whom the word of God came, and yet the Scripture cannot be nullified, do you say to me whom the Father sanctified and dispatched into the world, 'You blaspheme,' because I said, I am God's Son?" (Joh 10:31-37) Jesus there quoted from Psalm 82, in which human judges, whom God condemned for not executing justice, were called "gods." (Ps 82:1, 2, 6, 7) Thus, Jesus showed the unreasonableness of charging him with blasphemy for stating that he was, not God, but God's Son.

This charge of blasphemy arose as a result of Jesus' having said: "I and the Father are one." (Joh 10:30) That this did not mean that Jesus claimed to be the Father or to be God is evident from his reply, already partly considered. The oneness to which Jesus referred must be understood in harmony with the context of his statement. He was speaking of his works and his care of the "sheep" who would follow him. His works, as well as his words, demonstrated that there was unity, not disunity and disharmony, between him and his Father, a point his reply went on to emphasize. (Joh 10:25, 26, 37, 38; compare Joh 4:34; 5:30; 6:38-40; 8:16-18.) As regards his "sheep," he and his Father were likewise at unity in their protecting such sheeplike ones and leading them to everlasting life. (Joh 10:27-29; compare Eze 34:23, 24.) Jesus' prayer on behalf of the unity of all his disciples, including future ones, shows that the oneness, or union, between Jesus and his Father was not as to identity of person but as to purpose and action. In this way Jesus' disciples could "all be one," just as he and his Father are one.—Joh 17:20-23.

In harmony with this, Jesus, responding to a question by Thomas, said: "If you men had known me, you would have known my Father also; from this moment on you know him and have seen him," and, in answer to a question from Philip, Jesus added: "He that has seen me has seen the Father also." (Joh 14:5-9) Again, Jesus' following explanation shows that this was so because he faithfully represented his Father, spoke the Father's words, and did the Father's works. (Joh 14:10, 11; compare Joh 12:28, 44-49.) It was on this same occasion, the night of his death, that Jesus said to these very disciples: "The Father is greater than I am."—Joh 14:28.

The disciples 'seeing' the Father in Jesus can also be understood in the light of other Scriptural examples. Jacob, for instance, said to Esau: "I have seen your face as though seeing God's face in that you received me with pleasure." He said this because Esau's reaction had been in harmony with Jacob's prayer to God. (Ge 33:9-11; 32:9-12) After God's interrogation of Job out of a windstorm had

clarified that man's understanding, Job said: "In hearsay I have heard about you, but now my own eye does see you." (Job 38:1; 42:5; see also Jg 13:21, 22.) The 'eyes of his heart' had been enlightened. (Compare Eph 1:18.) That Jesus' statement about seeing the Father was meant to be understood figuratively and not literally is evident from his own statement at John 6:45 as well as from the fact that John, long after Jesus' death, wrote: "No man has seen God at any time; the only-begotten god who is in the bosom position with the Father is the one that has explained him."—Joh 1:18; 1Jo 4:12.

What did Thomas mean when he said to Jesus, "My Lord and my God"?

On the occasion of Jesus' appearance to Thomas and the other apostles, which had removed Thomas' doubts of Jesus' resurrection, the now-convinced Thomas exclaimed to Jesus: "My Lord and my God! [literally, "The Lord of me and the God (ho The·os´) of me!"]." (Joh 20:24-29) Some scholars have viewed this expression as an exclamation of astonishment spoken to Jesus but actually directed to God, his Father. However, others claim the original Greek requires that the words be viewed as being directed to Jesus. Even if this is so, the expression "My Lord and my God" would still have to harmonize with the rest of the inspired Scriptures. Since the record shows that Jesus had previously sent his disciples the message, "I am ascending to my Father and your Father and to my God and your God," there is no reason for believing that Thomas thought Jesus was the Almighty God. (Joh 20:17) John himself, after recounting Thomas' encounter with the resurrected Jesus, says of this and similar accounts: "But these have been written down that you may believe that Jesus is the Christ the Son of God, and that, because of believing, you may have life by means of his name."—Joh 20:30, 31.

So, Thomas may have addressed Jesus as "my God" in the sense of Jesus' being "a god" though not the Almighty God, not "the only true God," to whom Thomas had often heard Jesus pray. (Joh 17:1-3) Or he may have addressed Jesus as "my God" in a way similar to expressions made by his forefathers, recorded in the Hebrew Scriptures, with which Thomas was familiar. On various occasions when individuals were visited or addressed by an angelic messenger of Jehovah, the individuals, or at times the Bible writer setting out the account, responded to or spoke of that angelic messenger as though he were Jehovah God.

(Compare Ge 16:7-11, 13; 18:1-5, 22-33; 32:24-30; Jg 6:11-15; 13:20-22.) This was because the angelic messenger was acting for Jehovah as his representative, speaking in his name, perhaps using the first person singular pronoun, and even saying, "I am the true God." (Ge 31:11-13; Jg 2:1-5) Thomas may therefore have spoken to Jesus as "my God" in this sense, acknowledging or confessing Jesus as the representative and spokesman of the true God. Whatever the case, it is certain that Thomas' words do not contradict the clear statement he himself had heard Jesus make, namely, "The Father is greater than I am."—Joh 14:28.

His Birth on Earth. Prior to Jesus' birth on earth, angels had appeared on this planet in human form, apparently materializing suitable bodies for the occasion, then dematerializing them after completing such assignments. (Ge 19:1-3; Jg 6:20-22; 13:15-20) They thus remained spirit creatures, merely employing a physical body temporarily. This, however, was not the case with the coming of God's Son to earth to become the man Jesus. John 1:14 says that "the Word became flesh and resided among us." For that reason he could call himself "the Son of man." (Joh 1:51; 3:14, 15) Some draw attention to the expression "resided [literally, "tented"] among us" and claim this shows Jesus was, not a true human, but an incarnation. However, the apostle Peter uses a similar expression about himself, and Peter was obviously not an incarnation.—2Pe 1:13, 14.

The inspired Record says: "But the birth of Jesus Christ was in this way. During the time his mother Mary was promised in marriage to Joseph, she was found to be pregnant by holy spirit before they were united." (Mt 1:18) Prior to this, Jehovah's angelic messenger had informed the virgin girl Mary that she would 'conceive in her womb' as the result of God's holy spirit coming upon her and His power overshadowing her. (Lu 1:30, 31, 34, 35) Since actual conception took place, it appears that Jehovah God caused an ovum, or egg cell, in Mary's womb to become fertile, accomplishing this by the transferal of the life of his firstborn Son from the spirit realm to earth. (Ga 4:4) Only in this way could the child eventually born have retained identity as the same *person* who had resided in heaven as the Word, and only in this way could he have been an actual son of Mary and hence a genuine *descendant* of her forefathers Abraham, Isaac, Jacob, Judah, and King David and legitimate *heir* of the divine promises made to them. (Ge 22:15-18; 26:24; 28:10-14; 49:10; 2Sa 7:8, 11-16; Lu 3:23-34; see GENEALOGY OF JESUS CHRIST.) It is likely, therefore, that the child born resembled its Jewish mother in certain physical characteristics.

Mary was a descendant of the sinner Adam, hence herself imperfect and sinful. The question therefore is raised as to how Jesus, Mary's "firstborn" (Lu 2:7), could be perfect and free from sin in his physical organism. While modern geneticists have learned much about laws of heredity and about dominant and recessive characteristics, they have had no experience in learning the results of uniting perfection with imperfection, as was the case with Jesus' conception. From the results revealed in the Bible, it would appear that the perfect male life-force (causing the conception) canceled out any imperfection existent in Mary's ovum, thereby producing a genetic pattern (and embryonic development) that was perfect from its start. Whatever the case, the operation of God's holy spirit at the time guaranteed the success of God's purpose. As the angel Gabriel explained to Mary, "power of the Most High" overshadowed her so that what was born was holy, God's Son. God's holy spirit formed, as it were, a protective wall so that no imperfection or hurtful force could damage, or blemish, the developing embryo, from conception on.—Lu 1:35.

Since it was God's holy spirit that made the birth possible, Jesus owed his human life to his heavenly Father, not to any man, such as his adoptive father Joseph. (Mt 2:13-15; Lu 3:23) As Hebrews 10:5 states, Jehovah God 'prepared a body for him,' and Jesus, from conception onward, was truly "undefiled, separated from the sinners."—Heb 7:26; compare Joh 8:46; 1Pe 2:21, 22.

The Messianic prophecy at Isaiah 52:14, which speaks of "the disfigurement as respects his appearance," therefore must apply to Jesus the Messiah only in a figurative way. (Compare vs 7 of the same chapter.) Though he was perfect in physical form, the message of truth and righteousness that Jesus Christ boldly proclaimed made him repulsive in the eyes of hypocritical opposers, who claimed to see in him an agent of Beelzebub, a man possessed of a demon, a blasphemous fraud. (Mt 12:24; 27:39-43; Joh 8:48; 15:17-25) In a similar way the message proclaimed by Jesus' disciples later caused them to be "a sweet odor" of life to receptive persons, but an odor of death to those rejecting their message.—2Co 2:14-16.

Time of Birth, Length of Ministry. Jesus evidently was born in the month of Ethanim (September-October) of the year 2 B.C.E., was baptized about the same time of the year in 29 C.E., and died about 3:00 p.m. on Friday, the 14th day of the spring month of Nisan (March-

April), 33 C.E. The basis for these dates is as follows:

Jesus was born approximately six months after the birth of his relative John (the Baptizer), during the rule of Roman Emperor Caesar Augustus (31 B.C.E.–14 C.E.) and the Syrian governorship of Quirinius (see REGISTRATION for the probable dates of Quirinius' administration), and toward the close of the reign of Herod the Great over Judea.—Mt 2:1, 13, 20-22; Lu 1:24-31, 36; 2:1, 2, 7.

His birth in relation to Herod's death. While the date of Herod's death is a debated one, there is considerable evidence pointing to 1 B.C.E. (See HEROD No. 1 [Date of His Death]; CHRONOLOGY [Lunar eclipses].) A number of events intervened between the time of Jesus' birth and Herod's death. These included Jesus' circumcision on the eighth day (Lu 2:21); his being brought to the temple in Jerusalem 40 days after birth (Lu 2:22, 23; Le 12:1-4, 8); the journey of the astrologers "from eastern parts" to Bethlehem (where Jesus was no longer in a manger but in a house—Mt 2:1-11; compare Lu 2:7, 15, 16); Joseph and Mary's flight to Egypt with the young child (Mt 2:13-15); followed by Herod's realization that the astrologers had not followed his instructions, and the subsequent slaughter of all boys in Bethlehem and its districts under the age of two years (indicating that Jesus was not then a newborn infant). (Mt 2:16-18) Jesus' birth taking place in the fall of 2 B.C.E. would allow for the time required by these events intervening between his birth and the death of Herod, likely in 1 B.C.E. There is, however, added reason for placing Jesus' birth in 2 B.C.E.

Relationship to John's ministry. Further basis for the dates given at the start of this section is found at Luke 3:1-3, which shows that John the Baptizer began his preaching and baptizing in "the fifteenth year of the reign of Tiberius Caesar." That 15th year ran from the latter half of 28 C.E. to August or September of 29 C.E. (See TIBERIUS.) At some point in John's ministry, Jesus went to him and was baptized. When Jesus thereafter commenced his own ministry he was "about thirty years old." (Lu 3:21-23) At the age of 30, the age at which David became king, Jesus would no longer be subject to human parents.—2Sa 5:4, 5; compare Lu 2:51.

According to Numbers 4:1-3, 22, 23, 29, 30, those going into sanctuary service under the Law covenant were "from thirty years old upward." It is reasonable that John the Baptizer, who was a Levite and son of a priest, began his ministry at the same age, not at the temple, of course, but in the special assignment Jehovah had outlined for him. (Lu 1:1-17, 67, 76-79) The specific mention (twice) of the age difference between John and Jesus and the correlation between the appearances and messages of Jehovah's angel in announcing the births of the two sons (Lu 1) give ample basis for believing that their ministries followed a similar timetable, that is, the start of John's ministry (as the forerunner of Jesus) being followed about six months later by the commencement of Jesus' ministry.

On this basis, John's birth occurred 30 years before he began his ministry in Tiberius' 15th year, hence somewhere between the latter half of 3 B.C.E. and August or September of 2 B.C.E., with Jesus' birth following about six months later.

Evidence for three-and-a-half-year ministry. Through the remaining chronological evidence an even more definite conclusion can be reached. This evidence deals with the length of Jesus' ministry and time of death. The prophecy at Daniel 9:24-27 (discussed fully in the article SEVENTY WEEKS) points to the appearance of the Messiah at the start of the 70th "week" of years (Da 9:25) and his sacrificial death in the middle or "at the half" of the final week, thereby ending the validity of the sacrifices and gift offerings under the Law covenant. (Da 9:26, 27; compare Heb 9:9-14; 10:1-10.) This would mean a ministry of three and a half years' duration (half of a "week" of seven years) for Jesus Christ.

For Jesus' ministry to have lasted three and a half years, ending with his death at Passover time, would require that that period include four Passovers in all. Evidence for these four Passovers is found at John 2:13; 5:1; 6:4; and 13:1. John 5:1 does not specifically mention the Passover, referring only to "a ["the," according to certain ancient manuscripts] festival of the Jews." There is, however, good reason to believe this refers to the Passover rather than to any other of the annual festivals.

Earlier, at John 4:35, Jesus is mentioned as saying that there were "yet four months before the harvest." The harvest season, particularly the barley harvest, got under way about Passover time (Nisan 14). Hence Jesus' statement was made four months before that or about the month of Chislev (November-December). The postexilic Festival of Dedication came during Chislev but it was not one of the great festivals requiring attendance at Jerusalem. (Ex 23:14-17; Le 23:4-44) Celebration was held throughout the land in the many synagogues, according to Jewish tradition. (See FESTIVAL OF DEDICATION.) Later, at John 10:22, Jesus is specifically mentioned as attending one such Festival of Dedication in Jerusalem; however, it appears that he had already been in that area since the earlier Festival of Booths, hence had not gone there especially for that purpose. Different from this, John 5:1 clearly implies that it was the particular "festival of the Jews" that caused Jesus to go from Galilee (Joh 4:54) to Jerusalem.

The only other festival between Chislev and Passover time was that of Purim, held in Adar (February-March), about one month before Passover. But the postexilic Feast of Purim was likewise celebrated throughout the land in homes and synagogues. (See PURIM.) So, the Passover seems to be the most likely "festival of the Jews" referred to at John 5:1, Jesus' attendance at Jerusalem then being in conformity to God's law to Israel. It is true that John thereafter records only a few events before the next mention of the Passover (Joh 6:4), but a consideration of the chart of the Main Events of Jesus' Earthly Life will show that John's coverage of Jesus' early ministry was very abbreviated, many events already discussed by the other three evangelists being passed over. In fact, the great amount of activity of Jesus as recorded by these other evangelists (Matthew, Mark, and Luke) lends weight to the conclusion that an annual Passover did indeed intervene between those recorded at John 2:13 and 6:4.

Time of his death. The death of Jesus Christ took place in the spring, on the Passover Day, Nisan (or Abib) 14, according to the Jewish calendar. (Mt 26:2; Joh 13:1-3; Ex 12:1-6; 13:4) That year the Passover occurred on the sixth day of the week (counted by the Jews as from sundown on Thursday to sundown on Friday). This is evident from John 19:31, which shows that the following day was "a great" sabbath. The day after Passover was always a sabbath, no matter on what day of the week it came. (Le 23:5-7) But when this special Sabbath coincided with the regular Sabbath (the seventh day of the week), it became "a great one." So Jesus' death took place on Friday, Nisan 14, by about 3:00 p.m.—Lu 23:44-46.

Summary of evidence. Summing up, then, since Jesus' death took place in the spring month of Nisan, his ministry, which began three and a half years earlier according to Daniel 9:24-27, must have begun in the *fall*, about the month of Ethanim (September-October). John's ministry (initiated in Tiberius' 15th year), then, must have begun in the *spring* of the year 29 C.E. John's birth therefore would be placed in the spring of the year 2 B.C.E., Jesus' birth would come about six months later in the fall of 2 B.C.E., his ministry would start about 30 years later in the fall of 29 C.E., and his death would come in the year 33 C.E. (on Nisan 14 in the spring, as stated).

No basis for winter date of birth. The popular date of December 25 as the day of Jesus' birth therefore has no basis in Scripture. As many reference works show, it stems from a pagan holiday. Regarding the origin for the celebration of the day December 25, the Jesuit scholar Urbanus Holzmeister wrote:

"Today it is commonly admitted that the occasion for the celebration of the day December 25 was the festival that the pagans were celebrating on this day. Petavius [French Jesuit scholar, 1583-1652] already has rightly observed that on December 25 was celebrated 'the birthday of the unconquered sun.'

"Witnesses for this festival are: (a) The *Calendar* of Furius Dionysius Filocalus, composed in the year 354 [C.E.], in which it is noted: 'December 25, the B(irthday) of the unconquered (Sun).' (b) The calendar of astrologer Antiochus (composed about 200 [C.E.]): 'Month of December . . . 25 . . . The birthday of the Sun; daylight increases.' (c) Caesar Julian [Julian the Apostate, emperor 361-363 C.E.] recommended the games that were celebrated at the end of the year in honor of the sun, which was called 'the unconquered sun.'"—*Chronologia vitae Christi* (Chronology of the Life of Christ), Pontificium Institutum Biblicum, Rome, 1933, p. 46.

Perhaps the most obvious evidence of the incorrectness of the December 25 date is the Scriptural fact that shepherds were in the fields tending their flocks on the night of Jesus' birth. (Lu 2:8, 12) Already by the autumn month of Bul (October-November) the rainy season was starting (De 11:14), and flocks were brought into protected shelters at night. The next month, Chislev (the ninth month of the Jewish calendar, November-December), was a month of cold and rain (Jer 36:22; Ezr 10:9, 13), and Tebeth (December-January) saw the lowest temperatures of the year, with occasional snows in the highlands area. The presence of shepherds in the fields at night therefore harmonizes with the evidence pointing to the early autumn month of Ethanim as the time of Jesus' birth.—See BUL; CHISLEV.

Also weighing against a December date is that it would be most unlikely for the Roman emperor to choose such a wintry, rainy month as the time for his Jewish subjects (often rebellious) to travel "each one to his own city" to be registered.—Lu 2:1-3; compare Mt 24:20; see TEBETH.

Early Life. The record of Jesus' early life is very brief. Born in Bethlehem of Judea, King David's native city, he was taken to Nazareth in

Galilee after the family returned from Egypt—all of this in fulfillment of divine prophecy. (Mt 2:4-6, 14, 15, 19-23; Mic 5:2; Ho 11:1; Isa 11:1; Jer 23:5) Jesus' adoptive father, Joseph, was a carpenter (Mt 13:55) and evidently of little means. (Compare Lu 2:22-24 with Le 12:8.) Thus Jesus, who on his first day of human life had slept in a stable, evidently spent his childhood in quite humble circumstances. Nazareth was not historically prominent, though near to two principal trade routes. It may have been looked down upon by many Jews.—Compare Joh 1:46; see PICTURES, Vol. 2, p. 539; NAZARETH.

Of the first years of Jesus' life nothing is known except that "the young child continued growing and getting strong, being filled with wisdom, and God's favor continued upon him." (Lu 2:40) In course of time the family grew as four sons and some daughters were born to Joseph and Mary. (Mt 13:54-56) So, Mary's "firstborn" son (Lu 2:7) did not grow up as an only child. This doubtless explains why his parents could begin a return journey from Jerusalem without realizing for a while that Jesus, their oldest child, was missing from the group. This occasion, with Jesus' visit (as a 12-year-old) to the temple, where he engaged in a discussion with the Jewish teachers that left them amazed, is the only incident of his early life recounted in some detail. (PICTURE, Vol. 2, p. 538) Jesus' reply to his worried parents when they located him there shows that Jesus knew the miraculous nature of his birth and realized his Messianic future. (Lu 2:41-52) Reasonably, his mother and his adoptive father had passed on to him the information obtained through the angelic visitations as well as through the prophecies of Simeon and Anna, spoken when the first trip was made to Jerusalem 40 days after Jesus' birth.—Mt 1:20-25; 2:13, 14, 19-21; Lu 1:26-38; 2:8-38.

There is nothing to indicate that Jesus had or exercised any miraculous powers during his childhood years, as the fanciful stories recorded in certain apocryphal works, such as the so-called Gospel of Thomas, pretend. The changing of water to wine at Cana, performed during his ministry, was "the beginning of his signs." (Joh 2:1-11) Likewise, while among the family in Nazareth, Jesus evidently did not make a showy display of his wisdom and superiority as a perfect human, as is perhaps indicated by the fact that his half brothers did not exercise faith in him during his ministry as a human, as well as by the disbelief most of the population of Nazareth showed toward him.—Joh 7:1-5; Mr 6:1, 4-6.

Yet Jesus was evidently well known by the people of Nazareth (Mt 13:54-56; Lu 4:22); his splendid qualities and personality must certainly have been noted, at least by those appreciative of righteousness and goodness. (Compare Mt 3:13, 14.) He regularly attended the synagogue services each Sabbath. He was educated, as is shown by his ability to find and read sections from the Sacred Writings, but he did not attend the rabbinic schools of "higher learning."—Lu 4:16; Joh 7:14-16.

The brevity of the record concerning these early years is because Jesus had not yet been anointed by Jehovah as "the Christ" (Mt 16:16) and had not commenced carrying out the divine assignment awaiting him. His childhood and the growing-up process, like his birth, were necessary, though incidental, means to an end. As Jesus later stated to Roman Governor Pilate: "For this I have been born, and for this I have come into the world, that I should bear witness to the truth."—Joh 18:37.

His Baptism.   The outpouring of holy spirit at the time of Jesus' baptism marked the time of his becoming in actual fact the Messiah, or Christ, God's Anointed One (the use of this title by angels when announcing his birth evidently being in a prophetic sense; Lu 2:9-11, note also vss 25, 26). For six months John had been 'preparing the way' for "the saving means of God." (Lu 3:1-6) Jesus, now "about thirty years old," was baptized over John's initial objections, voiced because John till then had been baptizing only repentant sinners. (Mt 3:1, 6, 13-17; Lu 3:21-23) Jesus, however, was sinless; hence his baptism testified instead to his presenting himself to do his Father's will. (Compare Heb 10:5-9.) After Jesus had 'come up from the water,' and while he was praying, "he saw the heavens being parted," God's spirit descended upon Jesus in bodily shape like a dove, and Jehovah's voice was heard from heaven, saying: "You are my Son, the beloved; I have approved you." —Mt 3:16, 17; Mr 1:9-11; Lu 3:21, 22.

God's spirit poured out upon Jesus doubtless illuminated his mind on many points. His own expressions thereafter, and particularly the intimate prayer to his Father on Passover night, 33 C.E., show that Jesus recalled his prehuman existence and the things he had heard from his Father and the things he had seen his Father do, as well as the glory that he himself had enjoyed in the heavens. (Joh 6:46; 7:28, 29; 8:26, 28, 38; 14:2; 17:5) It may well have been that the memory of these things was restored to him at the time of his baptism and anointing.

Jesus' anointing with holy spirit appointed and commissioned him to carry out his ministry of preaching and teaching (Lu 4:16-21) and also to serve as God's Prophet. (Ac 3:22-26) But, over and above this, it appointed and commissioned him as Jehovah's promised King, the heir to David's throne (Lu 1:32, 33, 69; Heb 1:8, 9) and to an everlasting Kingdom. For that reason he could later tell Pharisees: "The kingdom of God is in your midst." (Lu 17:20, 21) Similarly, Jesus was anointed to act as God's High Priest, not as a descendant of Aaron, but after the likeness of King-Priest Melchizedek.—Heb 5:1, 4-10; 7:11-17.

Jesus had been God's Son from the time of his birth, even as the perfect Adam had been the "son of God." (Lu 3:38; 1:35) The angels had identified Jesus as God's Son from his birth onward. So, when, after Jesus' baptism, his Father's voice was heard saying, "You are my Son, the beloved; I have approved you" (Mr 1:11), it seems reasonable that this declaration accompanying the anointing flow of God's spirit was more than just an acknowledgment of Jesus' identity. The evidence is that Jesus was then begotten or brought forth by God as his *spiritual* Son, "born again," as it were, with the right to receive life once more as a spirit Son of God in the heavens.—Compare Joh 3:3-6; 6:51; 10:17, 18; see BAPTISM; ONLY-BEGOTTEN.

His Vital Place in God's Purpose. Jehovah God saw fit to make his firstborn Son the central, or key, figure in the outworking of all His purposes (Joh 1:14-18; Col 1:18-20; 2:8, 9), the focal point on which the light of all prophecies would concentrate and from which their light would radiate (1Pe 1:10-12; Re 19:10; Joh 1:3-9), the solution to all the problems that Satan's rebellion had raised (Heb 2:5-9, 14, 15; 1Jo 3:8), and the foundation upon which God would build all future arrangements for the eternal good of His universal family in heaven and earth. (Eph 1:8-10; 2:20; 1Pe 2:4-8) Because of the vital role he thus plays in God's purpose, Jesus could say, rightly and without exaggeration: "I am the way and the truth and the life. No one comes to the Father except through me."—Joh 14:6.

The "sacred secret." God's purpose as revealed in Jesus Christ remained a "sacred secret [or, mystery] . . . kept in silence for long-lasting times." (Ro 16:25-27) For over 4,000 years, since the rebellion in Eden, men of faith had awaited the fulfillment of God's promise of a "seed" to bruise the head of the serpentlike Adversary and thereby to bring relief to mankind. (Ge 3:15) For nearly 2,000 years they had hoped in Jehovah's covenant with Abraham for a "seed" who would "take possession of the gate of his enemies" and by means of whom all nations of the earth would bless themselves.—Ge 22:15-18.

Finally, when "the full limit of the time arrived," God sent forth his Son" and through him revealed the meaning of the "sacred secret," gave the definitive answer to the issue raised by God's Adversary (see JEHOVAH [The supreme issue a moral one]), and provided the means for redeeming obedient mankind from sin and death through the ransom sacrifice of his Son. (Ga 4:4; 1Ti 3:16; Joh 14:30; 16:33; Mt 20:28) Thereby Jehovah God cleared away any uncertainty or ambiguity regarding his purposes in the minds of his servants. For that reason the apostle says that "no matter how many the promises of God are, they have become Yes by means of [Jesus Christ]."—2Co 1:19-22.

The "sacred secret" did not simply involve an identification of God's Son as such. Rather it involved the role he was assigned in the framework of God's foreordained purpose, and the revelation and execution of that purpose through Jesus Christ. This purpose, so long a secret, was "for an administration at the full limit of the appointed times, namely, to gather all things together again in the Christ, the things in the heavens and the things on the earth."—Eph 1:9, 10.

The "sacred secret" bound up in Christ Jesus has as one of its aspects his heading a new heavenly government; its membership is to be formed of persons (Jews and non-Jews) taken from among earth's population, and its domain is to embrace both heaven and earth. Thus, in the vision at Daniel 7:13, 14, one "like a son of man" (a title later applied frequently to Christ—Mt 12:40; 24:30; Lu 17:26; compare Re 14:14) appears in Jehovah's heavenly courts and is given "rulership and dignity and kingdom, that the peoples, national groups and languages should all serve even him." The same vision, however, shows that "the holy ones of the Supreme One" are also to share with this "son of man" in his Kingdom, rulership, and grandeur. (Da 7:27) While Jesus was on earth, he selected from among his disciples the first prospective members of his Kingdom government and, after they had 'stuck with him in his trials,' covenanted with them for a Kingdom, praying to his Father for their sanctification (or being made "holy ones") and requesting that "where I am, they also may be with me, in order to behold my glory that you have given me." (Lu 22:28, 29; Joh 17:5, 17, 24) Because of being thus united with Christ, the Christian congregation also plays a part in the "sacred secret," as is later expressed by the inspired apostle.—Eph 3:1-11; 5:32; Col 1:26, 27; see SACRED SECRET.

"Chief Agent of life." As an expression of his Father's undeserved kindness, Christ Jesus laid down his perfect human life in sacrifice. This made possible the union of Christ's chosen followers with him in his heavenly reign and also made possible the arrangement for earthly subjects of his Kingdom rule. (Mt 6:10; Joh 3:16; Eph 1:7; Heb 2:5; see RANSOM.) He thereby became "the Chief Agent ["Prince," *KJ; JB*] of life" for all mankind. (Ac 3:15) The Greek term here used means, basically, "chief leader," a related word being applied to Moses (Ac 7:27, 35) as "ruler" in Israel.

Hence, as the "chief leader" or "pioneer of Life" (*Mo*), Jesus Christ introduced a new and essential element for gaining eternal life in the sense of being an intermediary or go-between, but he is such in an administrative sense as well. He is God's High Priest who can effect full cleansing from sin and liberation from sin's death-dealing effects (Heb 3:1, 2; 4:14; 7:23-25; 8:1-3); he is the appointed Judge into whose hands all judgment is committed, so that he judiciously administers his ransom benefits to individuals among mankind according to their worthiness to live under his kingship (Joh 5:22-27; Ac 10:42, 43); through him the resurrection of the dead also comes. (Joh 5:28, 29; 6:39, 40) Because Jehovah God so ordained to use his Son, "there is no salvation in anyone else, for there is not another name under heaven that has been given among men by which we must get saved."—Ac 4:12; compare 1Jo 5:11-13.

Since this aspect of Jesus' authority is also embraced in his "name," his disciples, as representatives of the Chief Agent of life, by that name could heal persons of their infirmities resulting from inherited sin and they could even raise the dead. —Ac 3:6, 15, 16; 4:7-11; 9:36-41; 20:7-12.

The full significance of his "name." It can be seen that, while Jesus' death on a torture stake plays a vital part in human salvation, acceptance of this is by no means all that is involved in 'putting faith in the name of Jesus.' (Ac 10:43) Following his resurrection, Jesus informed his disciples, "All authority has been given me in heaven and on the earth," thereby showing that he heads a government of universal domain. (Mt 28:18) The apostle Paul made clear that Jesus' Father has "left nothing that is not subject to him [Jesus]," with the evident exception of "the one who subjected all things to him," that is, Jehovah, the Sovereign God. (1Co 15:27; Heb 1:1-14; 2:8) Jesus Christ's "name," therefore, is more excellent than that of God's angels, in that his name embraces or stands for the vast executive authority that Jehovah has

placed in him. (Heb 1:3, 4) Only those who willingly recognize that "name" and bow to it, subjecting themselves to the authority it represents, will gain life eternal. (Ac 4:12; Eph 1:19-23; Php 2:9-11) They must, sincerely and without hypocrisy, line up with the standards Jesus exemplified and, in faith, obey the commands he gave.—Mt 7:21-23; Ro 1:5; 1Jo 3:23.

What is the "name" of Jesus on account of which Christians are hated by all nations?

Illustrating this other aspect of Jesus' "name" is his prophetic warning that his followers would be "objects of hatred by all the nations on account of my name." (Mt 24:9; also Mt 10:22; Joh 15:20, 21; Ac 9:15, 16) Clearly, this would be, not because his name represented that of a Ransomer or Redeemer, but because it represented God's appointed Ruler, the King of kings, to whom all nations should bow in submission or else experience destruction.—Re 19:11-16; compare Ps 2:7-12.

So, too, it is certain that when demons gave in to Jesus' command to get out of persons they possessed, they did so, not on the basis of Jesus' being a sacrificial Lamb of God, but on account of the authority for which his name stood as the anointed representative of the Kingdom, the one with authority to call for, not merely one legion, but a dozen legions of angels, capable of expelling any demons who might stubbornly resist the order to leave. (Mr 5:1-13; 9:25-29; Mt 12:28, 29; 26:53; compare Da 10:5, 6, 12, 13.) Jesus' faithful apostles were authorized to use his name to expel demons, both before and after his death. (Lu 9:1; 10:17; Ac 16:16-18) But when the sons of Jewish priest Sceva tried to use Jesus' name in this way, the wicked spirit challenged their right to appeal to the authority the name represented and caused the possessed man to attack and maul them.—Ac 19:13-17.

When Jesus' followers referred to his "name" they frequently employed the expression "the Lord Jesus" or "our Lord Jesus Christ." (Ac 8:16; 15:26; 19:5, 13, 17; 1Co 1:2, 10; Eph 5:20; Col 3:17) They recognized him as their Lord not only because he was their divinely appointed Repurchaser and Owner by virtue of his ransom sacrifice (1Co 6:20; 7:22, 23; 1Pe 1:18, 19; Jude 4) but also because of his kingly position and authority. It was in the full regal as well as priestly authority represented by Jesus' name that his followers preached (Ac 5:29-32, 40-42), baptized disciples

(Mt 28:18-20; Ac 2:38; compare 1Co 1:13-15), disfellowshipped immoral persons (1Co 5:4, 5), and exhorted and instructed the Christian congregations they shepherded (1Co 1:10; 2Th 3:6). It follows, then, that those approved for life by Jesus could never put faith in, or render allegiance to, some other "name" as representing God's authority to rule but must show unbreakable loyalty to the "name" of this divinely commissioned King, the Lord Jesus Christ.—Mt 12:18, 21; Re 2:13; 3:8; see APPROACH TO GOD.

'Bearing Witness to the Truth.' To Pilate's question, "Well, then, are you a king?", Jesus replied: "You yourself are saying that I am a king. For this I have been born, and for this I have come into the world, that I should bear witness to the truth. Everyone that is on the side of the truth listens to my voice." (Joh 18:37; see LEGAL CASE [Jesus' Trial].) As the Scriptures show, the truth to which he bore witness was not just truth in general. It was the all-important truth of what God's purposes were and are, truth based on the fundamental fact of God's sovereign will and His ability to fulfill that will. By his ministry Jesus revealed that truth, contained in "the sacred secret," as being God's Kingdom with Jesus Christ, the "son of David," serving as King-Priest on the throne. This was also the essence of the message proclaimed by angels prior to and at the time of his birth in Bethlehem of Judea, the city of David. —Lu 1:32, 33; 2:10-14; 3:31.

The accomplishment of his ministry in bearing witness to the truth required more of Jesus than merely talking, preaching, and teaching. Besides shedding his heavenly glory to be born as a human, he had to fulfill all the things prophesied about him, including the shadows, or patterns, contained in the Law covenant. (Col 2:16, 17; Heb 10:1) To uphold the truth of his Father's prophetic word and promises, Jesus had to live in such a way as to make that truth become reality, fulfilling it by what he said and did, how he lived, and how he died. Thus, he had to *be* the truth, in effect, the embodiment of the truth, as he himself said he was.—Joh 14:6.

For this reason the apostle John could write that Jesus was "full of undeserved kindness and truth" and that, though "the Law was given through Moses, the undeserved kindness and the truth came to be through Jesus Christ." (Joh 1:14, 17) By means of his human birth, his presenting himself to God by baptism in water, his three and a half years of public service in behalf of God's Kingdom, his death in faithfulness to God, his resurrection to heaven—by all these historical events—God's

truth arrived, or "came to be," that is, came to realization. (Compare Joh 1:18; Col 2:17.) The whole career of Jesus Christ was therefore a 'bearing witness to the truth,' to the things to which God had sworn. Jesus was thus no *shadow* Messiah or Christ. He was the *real* one promised. He was no *shadow* King-Priest. He was, in substance and fact, the true one that had been prefigured. —Ro 15:8-12; compare Ps 18:49; 117:1; De 32:43; Isa 11:10.

This truth was the truth that would 'set men free' if they showed themselves to be "on the side of the truth" by accepting Jesus' role in God's purpose. (Joh 8:32-36; 18:37) To ignore God's purpose concerning his Son, to build hopes on any other foundation, to form conclusions regarding one's life course on any other basis would be to believe a lie, to be deceived, to follow the leading of the father of lies, God's Adversary. (Mt 7:24-27; Joh 8:42-47) It would mean 'to die in one's sins.' (Joh 8:23, 24) For this reason Jesus did not hold back from declaring his place in God's purpose.

True, he instructed his disciples, even with sternness, not to broadcast his Messiahship to the public (Mt 16:20; Mr 8:29, 30) and rarely referred to himself directly as the Christ except when in privacy with them. (Mr 9:33, 38, 41; Lu 9:20, 21; Joh 17:3) But he boldly and regularly drew attention to the evidence in the prophecies and in his works that proved he was the Christ. (Mt 22:41-46; Joh 5:31-39, 45-47; 7:25-31) On the occasion of talking to a Samaritan woman at a well, Jesus, "tired out from the journey," identified himself to her, perhaps to excite curiosity among the townsfolk and draw them out from the town to him, which was the result. (Joh 4:6, 25-30) The mere claim of Messiahship would mean nothing if not accompanied by the evidence, and in the end, faith was required on the part of those seeing and hearing if they were to accept the conclusion to which that evidence unerringly pointed.—Lu 22:66-71; Joh 4:39-42; 10:24-27; 12:34-36.

Tested and Perfected. Jehovah God demonstrated supreme confidence in his Son in charging him with the mission of going to earth and serving as the promised Messiah. God's purpose that there be a "seed" (Ge 3:15), the Messiah, who would serve as the sacrificial Lamb of God, was foreknown to Him "before the founding of the world" (1Pe 1:19, 20), an expression considered under the heading FOREKNOWLEDGE, FOREORDINATION (Foreordination of the Messiah). The Bible record, however, does not state at what point Jehovah designated or informed the specific individual chosen to fill this role, whether at the time of the rebellion in Eden or at some later time. The requirements,

MAIN EVENTS OF JESUS' EARTHLY LIFE
The Four Gospels Set in Chronological Order

Time	Place	Event	Matthew	Mark	Luke	John
		Leading Up to Jesus' Ministry				
3 B.C.E.	Jerusalem, temple	Birth of John the Baptizer foretold to Zechariah			1:5-25	
c. 2 B.C.E.	Nazareth; Judea	Birth of Jesus foretold to Mary, who visits Elizabeth			1:26-56	
2 B.C.E.	Judean hill country	Birth of John the Baptizer; later, his desert life			1:57-80	
2 B.C.E., c. Oct. 1	Bethlehem	Birth of Jesus (the Word, through whom all other things had come into existence) as descendant of Abraham and of David	1:1-25		2:1-7	1:1-5, 9-14
	Near Bethlehem	Angel announces good news; shepherds visit babe			2:8-20	
	Bethlehem; Jerusalem	Jesus circumcised (8th day), presented in temple (40th day)			2:21-38	
1 B.C.E. or 1 C.E.	Jerusalem; Bethlehem; Nazareth	Astrologers; flight to Egypt; babes killed; Jesus' return	2:1-23		2:39, 40	
12 C.E.	Jerusalem	Twelve-year-old Jesus at the Passover; goes home			2:41-52	
29, spring	Wilderness, Jordan	Ministry of John the Baptizer	3:1-12	1:1-8	3:1-18	1:6-8, 15-28
		The Beginning of Jesus' Ministry				
29, fall	Jordan River	Baptism and anointing of Jesus, born as a human in David's line but declared to be the Son of God	3:13-17	1:9-11	3:21-38	1:32-34
	Judean Wilderness	Fasting and temptation of Jesus	4:1-11	1:12, 13	4:1-13	
	Bethany beyond Jordan	John the Baptizer's testimony concerning Jesus				1:15, 29-34
	Upper Jordan Valley	First disciples of Jesus				1:35-51
	Cana of Galilee; Capernaum	Jesus' first miracle; he visits Capernaum				2:1-12
30, Passover	Jerusalem	Passover celebration; drives traders from temple				2:13-25
	Jerusalem	Jesus' discussion with Nicodemus				3:1-21
	Judea; Aenon	Jesus' disciples baptize; John to decrease				3:22-36
	Tiberias	John imprisoned; Jesus leaves for Galilee	4:12; 14:3-5	1:14; 6:17-20	3:19, 20; 4:14	4:1-3
	Sychar, in Samaria	En route to Galilee, Jesus teaches the Samaritans				4:4-43
		Jesus' Great Ministry in Galilee				
	Galilee	First announces, "The kingdom of the heavens has drawn near"	4:17	1:14, 15	4:14, 15	4:44, 45
	Nazareth; Cana; Capernaum	Heals boy; reads commission; rejected; moves to Capernaum	4:13-16		4:16-31	4:46-54
	Sea of Galilee, near Capernaum	Call of Simon and Andrew, James and John	4:18-22	1:16-20	5:1-11	
	Capernaum	Heals demoniac, also Peter's mother-in-law and many others	8:14-17	1:21-34	4:31-41	
	Galilee	First tour of Galilee, with the four now called	4:23-25	1:35-39	4:42, 43	
	Galilee	Leper healed; multitudes flock to Jesus	8:1-4	1:40-45	5:12-16	
	Capernaum	Heals paralytic	9:1-8	2:1-12	5:17-26	
	Capernaum	Call of Matthew; feast with tax collectors	9:9-17	2:13-22	5:27-39	
	Judea	Preaches in Judean synagogues			4:44	

Time	Place	Event	Matthew	Mark	Luke	John
31, Passover	Jerusalem	Attends feast; heals man; rebukes Pharisees				5:1-47
	Returning from Jerusalem(?)	Disciples pluck ears of grain on the Sabbath	12:1-8	2:23-28	6:1-5	
	Galilee; Sea of Galilee	Heals hand on Sabbath; retires to seashore; heals	12:9-21	3:1-12	6:6-11	
	Mountain near Capernaum	The 12 are chosen as apostles		3:13-19	6:12-16	
	Near Capernaum	The Sermon on the Mount	5:1–7:29		6:17-49	
	Capernaum	Heals army officer's servant	8:5-13		7:1-10	
	Nain	Raises widow's son			7:11-17	
	Galilee	John in prison sends disciples to Jesus	11:2-19		7:18-35	
	Galilee	Cities reproached; revelation to babes; yoke kindly	11:20-30			
	Galilee	Feet anointed by sinful woman; illustration of debtors			7:36-50	
	Galilee	Second preaching tour of Galilee, with the 12			8:1-3	
	Galilee	Demoniac healed; league with Beelzebub charged	12:22-37	3:19-30		
	Galilee	Scribes and Pharisees seek a sign	12:38-45			
	Galilee	Christ's disciples his close relatives	12:46-50	3:31-35	8:19-21	
	Sea of Galilee	Illustrations of sower, weeds, others; explanations	13:1-53	4:1-34	8:4-18	
	Sea of Galilee	Windstorm stilled in the crossing of the lake	8:18, 23-27	4:35-41	8:22-25	
	Gadara, SE of Sea of Galilee	Two demoniacs healed; swine possessed by demons	8:28-34	5:1-20	8:26-39	
	Probably Capernaum	Jairus' daughter raised; woman healed	9:18-26	5:21-43	8:40-56	
	Capernaum(?)	Heals two blind men and a mute demoniac	9:27-34			
	Nazareth	Revisits city where reared, and is again rejected	13:54-58	6:1-6		
	Galilee	Third tour of Galilee, expanded as apostles sent	9:35–11:1	6:6-13	9:1-6	
	Tiberias	John the Baptizer beheaded; Herod's guilty fears	14:1-12	6:14-29	9:7-9	
32, near Passover (Joh 6:4)	Capernaum(?); NE side Sea of Galilee	Apostles return from preaching tour; 5,000 fed	14:13-21	6:30-44	9:10-17	6:1-13
	NE side Sea of Galilee; Gennesaret	Attempt to crown Jesus; he walks on sea; cures	14:22-36	6:45-56		6:14-21
	Capernaum	Identifies "bread of life"; many disciples fall away				6:22-71
32, after Passover	Probably Capernaum	Traditions that make void God's Word	15:1-20	7:1-23		7:1
	Phoenicia; Decapolis	Near Tyre, Sidon; then to Decapolis; 4,000 fed	15:21-38	7:24–8:9		
	Magadan	Sadducees and Pharisees again seek a sign	15:39–16:4	8:10-12		
	NE side Sea of Galilee; Bethsaida	Warns against leaven of Pharisees; heals blind	16:5-12	8:13-26		
	Caesarea Philippi	Jesus the Messiah; foretells death, resurrection	16:13-28	8:27–9:1	9:18-27	
	Probably Mt. Hermon	Transfiguration before Peter, James, and John	17:1-13	9:2-13	9:28-36	
	Caesarea Philippi	Heals demoniac that disciples could not heal	17:14-20	9:14-29	9:37-43	
	Galilee	Again foretells his death and resurrection	17:22, 23	9:30-32	9:43-45	
	Capernaum	Tax money miraculously provided	17:24-27			
	Capernaum	Greatest in Kingdom; settling faults; mercy	18:1-35	9:33-50	9:46-50	
	Galilee; Samaria	Leaves Galilee for Festival of Booths; everything set aside for ministerial service	8:19-22		9:51-62	7:2-10

Time	Place	Event	Matthew	Mark	Luke	John
		Jesus' Later Ministry in Judea				
32, Festival of Booths	Jerusalem	Jesus' public teaching at Festival of Booths				7:11-52
	Jerusalem	Teaching after Festival; cures blind				8:12–9:41
	Probably Judea	The 70 sent to preach; their return, report			10:1-24	
	Judea; Bethany	Tells of neighborly Samaritan; at home of Martha, Mary			10:25-42	
	Probably Judea	Again teaches model prayer; persistence in asking			11:1-13	
	Probably Judea	Refutes false charge; shows generation condemnable			11:14-36	
	Probably Judea	At Pharisee's table, Jesus denounces hypocrites			11:37-54	
	Probably Judea	Discourse on God's care; faithful steward			12:1-59	
	Probably Judea	Heals crippled woman on Sabbath; three illustrations			13:1-21	
32, Festival of Dedication	Jerusalem	Jesus at Festival of Dedication; Fine Shepherd				10:1-39
		Jesus' Later Ministry East of the Jordan				
	Beyond Jordan	Many put faith in Jesus				10:40-42
	Perea (beyond Jordan)	Teaches in cities, villages, moving toward Jerusalem			13:22	
	Perea	Kingdom entrance; Herod's threat; house desolate			13:23-35	
	Probably Perea	Humility; illustration of grand evening meal			14:1-24	
	Probably Perea	Counting the cost of discipleship			14:25-35	
	Probably Perea	Illustrations: lost sheep, lost coin, prodigal son			15:1-32	
	Probably Perea	Illustrations: unrighteous steward, rich man and Lazarus			16:1-31	
	Probably Perea	Forgiveness and faith; good-for-nothing slaves			17:1-10	
	Bethany	Lazarus raised from the dead by Jesus				11:1-46
	Jerusalem; Ephraim	Caiaphas' counsel against Jesus; Jesus withdraws				11:47-54
	Samaria; Galilee	Heals and teaches en route through Samaria, Galilee			17:11-37	
	Samaria or Galilee	Illustrations: importunate widow, Pharisee and tax collector			18:1-14	
	Perea	Swings down through Perea; teaches on divorce	19:1-12	10:1-12		
	Perea	Receives and blesses children	19:13-15	10:13-16	18:15-17	
	Perea	Rich young man; illustration of laborers in vineyard	19:16–20:16	10:17-31	18:18-30	
	Probably Perea	Third time Jesus foretells his death, resurrection	20:17-19	10:32-34	18:31-34	
	Probably Perea	Request for James' and John's seating in Kingdom	20:20-28	10:35-45		
	Jericho	Passing through Jericho, he heals two blind men; visits Zacchaeus; illustration of the ten minas	20:29-34	10:46-52	18:35–19:28	
		Jesus' Final Ministry at Jerusalem				
Nisan 8, 33	Bethany	Arrives at Bethany six days before Passover				11:55–12:1
Nisan 9	Bethany	Feast at Simon the leper's house; Mary anoints Jesus; Jews come to see Jesus and Lazarus	26:6-13	14:3-9		12:2-11

Time	Place	Event	Matthew	Mark	Luke	John
Nisan 9 (cont'd)	Bethany-Jerusalem	Christ's triumphal entry into Jerusalem	21:1-11, 14-17	11:1-11	19:29-44	12:12-19
Nisan 10	Bethany-Jerusalem	Barren fig tree cursed; second temple cleansing	21:18, 19, 12, 13	11:12-17	19:45, 46	
	Jerusalem	Chief priests and scribes scheme to destroy Jesus		11:18, 19	19:47, 48	
	Jerusalem	Discussion with Greeks; unbelief of Jews				12:20-50
Nisan 11	Bethany-Jerusalem	Barren fig tree found withered	21:19-22	11:20-25		
	Jerusalem, temple	Christ's authority questioned; illustration of two sons	21:23-32	11:27-33	20:1-8	
	Jerusalem, temple	Illustrations of wicked cultivators, marriage feast	21:33–22:14	12:1-12	20:9-19	
	Jerusalem, temple	Catch questions on tax, resurrection, commandment	22:15-40	12:13-34	20:20-40	
	Jerusalem, temple	Jesus' silencing question on Messiah's descent	22:41-46	12:35-37	20:41-44	
	Jerusalem, temple	Scathing denunciation of scribes and Pharisees	23:1-39	12:38-40	20:45-47	
	Jerusalem, temple	The widow's mite		12:41-44	21:1-4	
	Mount of Olives	Prediction of Jerusalem's fall; Jesus' presence; end of system	24:1-51	13:1-37	21:5-38	
	Mount of Olives	Illustrations of ten virgins, talents, sheep and goats	25:1-46			
Nisan 12	Jerusalem	Religious leaders plot Jesus' death	26:1-5	14:1, 2	22:1, 2	
	Jerusalem	Judas bargains with priests for Jesus' betrayal	26:14-16	14:10, 11	22:3-6	
Nisan 13 (Thursday afternoon)	Near and in Jerusalem	Arrangements for the Passover	26:17-19	14:12-16	22:7-13	
Nisan 14	Jerusalem	Passover feast eaten with the 12	26:20, 21	14:17, 18	22:14-18	
	Jerusalem	Jesus washes the feet of his apostles				13:1-20
	Jerusalem	Judas identified as traitor and is dismissed	26:21-25	14:18-21	22:21-23	13:21-30
	Jerusalem	Memorial supper instituted with the 11	26:26-29	14:22-25	22:19, 20, 24-30	[1Co 11: 23-25]
	Jerusalem	Denial by Peter and dispersion of apostles foretold	26:31-35	14:27-31	22:31-38	13:31-38
	Jerusalem	Helper; mutual love; tribulation; Jesus' prayer				14:1–17:26
	Gethsemane	Agony in the garden; Jesus' betrayal and arrest	26:30, 36-56	14:26, 32-52	22:39-53	18:1-12
	Jerusalem	Trial by Annas, Caiaphas, Sanhedrin; Peter denies	26:57–27:1	14:53–15:1	22:54-71	18:13-27
	Jerusalem	Judas the betrayer hangs himself	27:3-10		[Ac 1:18, 19]	
	Jerusalem	Before Pilate, then Herod, and then back to Pilate	27:2, 11-14	15:1-5	23:1-12	18:28-38
	Jerusalem	Delivered to death, after Pilate seeks his release	27:15-30	15:6-19	23:13-25	18:39–19:16
(c. 3:00 p.m., Friday)	Golgotha, Jerusalem	Jesus' death on a torture stake, and accompanying events	27:31-56	15:20-41	23:26-49	19:16-30
	Jerusalem	Jesus' body removed from the torture stake and buried	27:57-61	15:42-47	23:50-56	19:31-42
Nisan 15	Jerusalem	Priests and Pharisees get guard for tomb	27:62-66			
Nisan 16	Jerusalem and vicinity	Jesus' resurrection and events of that day	28:1-15	16:1-8	24:1-49	20:1-25
	Jerusalem; Galilee	Subsequent appearances of Jesus Christ	28:16-20	[1Co 15:5-7]	[Ac 1:3-8]	20:26–21:25
Iyyar 25	Mount of Olives, near Bethany	Jesus' ascension, 40th day after his resurrection	[Ac 1:9-12]		24:50-53	

particularly that of the ransom sacrifice, ruled out the use of any imperfect human, but not of a perfect spirit son. Out of all his millions of spirit sons, Jehovah selected one to take on the assignment: his Firstborn, the Word.—Compare Heb 1:5, 6.

God's Son willingly accepted the assignment. This is evident from Philippians 2:5-8; he "emptied himself" of his heavenly glory and spirit nature and "took a slave's form" in submitting to the transferal of his life to the earthly, material, human plane. The assignment before him represented a tremendous responsibility; so very much was involved. By remaining faithful he would prove false Satan's claim, recorded in the case of Job, that under privation, suffering, and test, God's servants would deny Him. (Job 1:6-12; 2:2-6) As the firstborn Son, Jesus, of all God's creatures, could give the most conclusive answer to that charge and the finest evidence in favor of his Father's side in the larger issue of the rightfulness of Jehovah's universal sovereignty. Thereby he would prove to be "the Amen . . . , the faithful and true witness." (Re 3:14) If he failed, he would reproach his Father's name as none other could.

In selecting his only-begotten Son, Jehovah, of course, was not 'laying his hands hastily upon him,' with the risk of being 'a sharer in possible sins,' for Jesus was no novice likely to get "puffed up with pride and fall into the judgment passed upon the Devil." (Compare 1Ti 5:22; 3:6.) Jehovah 'fully knew' his Son from his intimate association with him during countless ages past (Mt 11:27; compare Ge 22:12; Ne 9:7, 8) and could therefore assign him to fulfill the unerring prophecies of His Word. (Isa 46:10, 11) Thus God was not arbitrarily or automatically guaranteeing "certain success" for his Son simply by placing him in the role of the prophesied Messiah (Isa 55:11), in the manner that the theory of predestinarianism claims.

While the Son had never undergone a test like that now before him, he had demonstrated his faithfulness and devotion in other ways. He had already had great responsibility as God's Spokesman, the Word. Yet he never misused his position and authority, as did God's earthly spokesman Moses on one occasion. (Nu 20:9-13; De 32:48-51; Jude 9) Being the One through whom all things were made, the Son was a god, "the only-begotten god" (Joh 1:18), hence held a position of glory and preeminence in relation to all others of God's spirit sons. Yet he did not become haughty. (Contrast Eze 28:14-17.) So, it could not be said that the Son had not already proved his loyalty, humility, and devotion in many respects.

To illustrate, consider the test placed upon God's first human son, Adam. That test did not involve enduring persecution or suffering, but only maintaining obedient respect for God's will in regard to the tree of the knowledge of good and bad. (Ge 2:16, 17; see TREES.) Satan's rebellion and temptation were not part of the test as originally given by God but came as an added feature, from a source foreign to God. Nor did the test, when given, call for any human temptation, as resulted to Adam from Eve's deflection. (Ge 3:6, 12) This being so, Adam's test could have been effected without any outside temptation or influence toward wrongdoing, the whole matter resting with Adam's heart —his love for God and his freedom from selfishness. (Pr 4:23) Proving faithful, Adam would have been privileged to take fruit of "the tree of life and eat and live to time indefinite" as a tested, approved human son of God (Ge 3:22), all of this without having been subjected to vile influence and temptation, persecution, or suffering.

It may also be noted that the spirit son who became Satan by defecting from God's service did not do so because anyone had persecuted him or tempted him to do wrong. Certainly not God, for 'He does not try anyone with evil things.' Yet that spirit son failed to maintain loyalty, allowed himself to be "drawn out and enticed by his own desire," and sinned, becoming a rebel. (Jas 1:13-15) He failed the test of love.

The issue raised by God's Adversary, however, required that the Son, as the promised Messiah and future King of God's Kingdom, now undergo a test of integrity under new circumstances. This test and the sufferings it entailed were also necessary for his being "made perfect" for his position as God's High Priest over mankind. (Heb 5:9, 10) To meet the requirements for full installation as the Chief Agent of salvation, God's Son was "obliged to become like his 'brothers' [those who became his anointed followers] in all respects, that he might become a merciful and faithful high priest." He must endure hardships and sufferings, so that he might be "able to come to the aid of those who are being put to the test," able to sympathize with their weaknesses as one who had "been tested in all respects like ourselves, but without sin." Though perfect and sinless, he would still be "able to deal moderately with the ignorant and erring ones." Only through such a High Priest could imperfect humans "approach with freeness of speech to the throne of undeserved kindness, [to] obtain mercy and find undeserved kindness for help at the right time."—Heb 2:10-18; 4:15–5:2; compare Lu 9:22.

Still a free moral agent. Jesus himself said that all the prophecies concerning the Messiah were certain of realization, "must be fulfilled." (Lu 24:44-47; Mt 16:21; compare Mt 5:17.) Yet this certainly did not relieve God's Son of the weight of responsibility, nor did it eliminate his freedom of choice—either to be faithful or unfaithful. The matter was not one-sided, resting solely with the Almighty God, Jehovah. His Son must do his part to make the prophecies come true. God assured the certainty of the prophecies by his wise choice of the one to fill the assignment, "the Son of his love." (Col 1:13) That his Son still retained and exercised his own free will while a human on earth is clear. Jesus spoke of his own will, showed that he was voluntarily submitting himself to his Father's will (Mt 16:21-23; Joh 4:34; 5:30; 6:38), and consciously worked toward the fulfillment of his assignment as laid out in his Father's Word. (Mt 3:15; 5:17, 18; 13:10-17, 34, 35; 26:52-54; Mr 1:14, 15; Lu 4:21) The fulfillment of other prophetic features, of course, was not under Jesus' control, some taking place after his death. (Mt 12:40; 26: 55, 56; Joh 18:31, 32; 19:23, 24, 36, 37) The record of the night preceding his death strikingly reveals the intense personal effort it took on his part to subject his own will to the superior will of the One wiser than himself, his Father. (Mt 26:36-44; Lu 22:42-44) It also reveals that, though perfect, he keenly recognized his human dependence upon his Father, Jehovah God, for strength in time of need.—Joh 12:23, 27, 28; Heb 5:7.

Jesus therefore had much to meditate on, and to fortify himself for, during the 40 days he spent fasting (as Moses had) in the wilderness following his baptism and anointing. (Ex 34:28; Lu 4:1, 2) He there had a direct encounter with the serpentlike Adversary of his Father. Using tactics similar to those in Eden, Satan the Devil tried to induce Jesus to display selfishness, to exalt himself, and to deny his Father's sovereign position. Unlike Adam, Jesus ("the last Adam") kept integrity and, by consistently citing his Father's declared will, caused Satan to withdraw, "until another convenient time."—Lu 4:1-13; 1Co 15:45.

His Works and Personal Qualities. Because both "the undeserved kindness and the truth" were to come to be through Jesus Christ, he had to get out among the people, let them hear him, see his works and qualities. Thus they might recognize him as the Messiah and put faith in his sacrifice when he died for them as "the Lamb of God." (Joh 1:17, 29) He personally visited Palestine's many regions, covering hundreds of miles on foot. He talked to people on lakeshores and hillsides as well as in cities and villages, synagogues and temple, marketplaces, streets and houses (Mt 5:1, 2; 26:55; Mr 6:53-56; Lu 4:16; 5:1-3; 13:22, 26; 19:5, 6), addressing large crowds and individuals, men and women, old and young, rich and poor.—Mr 3:7, 8; 4:1; Joh 3:1-3; Mt 14:21; 19:21, 22; 11:4, 5.

The accompanying chart presents a suggested manner in which the four accounts of Jesus' earthly life can be coordinated chronologically. It also gives an understanding of the various "campaigns" or tours he carried out during his ministry of three and a half years.

Jesus set an example for his disciples by being hardworking, rising early, serving on into the night. (Lu 21:37, 38; Mr 11:20; 1:32-34; Joh 3:2; 5:17) More than once he spent the night in prayer, as he did the night before giving the Sermon on the Mount. (Mt 14:23-25; Lu 6:12–7:10) Another time, after serving during the night, he rose while it was still dark and headed for a lonely place to pray. (Mr 1:32, 35) His privacy often interrupted by the crowds, he, nevertheless, "received them kindly and began to speak to them about the kingdom of God." (Lu 9:10, 11; Mr 6:31-34; 7:24-30) He experienced tiredness, thirst, and hunger, at times forgoing food for the sake of the work to be done.—Mt 21:18; Joh 4:6, 7, 31-34; compare Mt 4:2-4; 8:24, 25.

Balanced view of material things. He was not, however, an ascetic, practicing self-denial to an extreme degree without regard for the circumstances at hand. (Lu 7:33, 34) He accepted many invitations to meals and even banquets, visiting the homes of persons of some wealth. (Lu 5:29; 7:36; 14:1; 19:1-6) He contributed to the enjoyment at a wedding by changing water into fine wine. (Joh 2:1-10) And he appreciated good things done for him. When Judas expressed indignation at Lazarus' sister Mary's use of a pound of perfumed oil (worth over $220, or about a year's wages of a laborer) to anoint Jesus' feet and professed concern for the poor who could have benefited from the sale of the oil, Jesus said: "Let her alone, that she may keep this observance in view of the day of my burial. For you have the poor always with you, but me you will not have always." (Joh 12:2-8; Mr 14:6-9) The inner garment he wore when arrested, "woven from the top throughout its length," was evidently a quality garment. (Joh 19:23, 24) Nevertheless, Jesus always gave spiritual things first place and was never overly concerned about material things, even as he counseled others.—Mt 6:24-34; 8:20; Lu 10:38-42; compare Php 4:10-12.

Courageous Liberator. Great courage, manliness, and strength are evident throughout his ministry. (Mt 3:11; Lu 4:28-30; 9:51; Joh 2:13-17;

10:31-39; 18:3-11) Like Joshua, King David, and others, Jesus was a fighter for God's cause and on behalf of lovers of righteousness. As the promised "seed," he had to face the enmity of the 'seed of the serpent,' doing battle with them. (Ge 3:15; 22:17) He waged offensive warfare against the demons and their influence on men's minds and hearts. (Mr 5:1-13; Lu 4:32-36; 11:19-26; compare 2Co 4:3, 4; Eph 6:10-12.) Hypocritical religious leaders showed they were actually in opposition to God's sovereignty and will. (Mt 23:13, 27, 28; Lu 11:53, 54; Joh 19:12-16) Jesus thoroughly defeated them in a series of verbal encounters. He wielded "the sword of the spirit," God's Word, with strength, perfect control, and strategy—cutting through subtle arguments and traplike questions that his opposers advanced, putting them 'in a corner' or on the 'horns of a dilemma.' (Mt 21:23-27; 22:15-46) He fearlessly exposed them for what they were: teachers of human traditions and formalisms, blind leaders, a generation of vipers, and children of God's Adversary, who is the prince of the demons and a murderous liar. —Mt 15:12-14; 21:33-41, 45, 46; 23:33-35; Mr 7:1-13; Joh 8:40-45.

In all of this, Jesus was never foolhardy, sought no trouble, and avoided unnecessary danger. (Mt 12:14, 15; Mr 3:6, 7; Joh 7:1, 10; 11:53, 54; compare Mt 10:16, 17, 28-31.) His courage was based on faith. (Mr 4:37-40) He did not lose control of himself but remained calm when vilified and mistreated, "committing himself to the one who judges righteously."—1Pe 2:23.

By his courageous fight for the truth and by bringing light to the people concerning God's purpose, Jesus, as one greater than Moses, fulfilled the prophetic role of Liberator. He proclaimed freedom to the captives. (Isa 42:1, 6, 7; Jer 30:8-10; Isa 61:1) Though many held back for selfish reasons and out of fear of the element in power (Joh 7:11-13; 9:22; 12:42, 43), others gained courage to break free of their chains of ignorance and slavish subservience to false leaders and false hopes. (Joh 9:24-39; compare Ga 5:1.) As faithful Judean kings had waged campaigns to eliminate false worship from the realm (2Ch 15:8; 17:1, 4-6; 2Ki 18:1, 3-6), so, too, the ministry of Jesus, God's Messianic King, had a devastating effect on false religion in his day. —Joh 11:47, 48.

For further information regarding the earthly ministry of Jesus Christ, see MAPS, Vol. 2, pp. 540, 541.

Depth of feeling and warmth. But Jesus was also a man of great feeling, a requirement for serving as God's High Priest. His perfection did not make him hypercritical or arrogant and overbearing (as were the Pharisees) toward the imperfect, sin-laden persons among whom he lived and worked. (Mt 9:10-13; 21:31, 32; Lu 7:36-48; 15:1-32; 18:9-14) Even children could feel at ease with him, and when using a child as an example, he did not merely stand the child before his disciples but also "put his arms around it." (Mr 9:36; 10:13-16) He proved himself a real friend and affectionate companion to his followers, 'loving them to the end.' (Joh 13:1; 15:11-15) He did not use his authority to be demanding and to add to the people's burdens but, rather, said: "Come to me, all you who are toiling . . . I will refresh you." His disciples found him "mild-tempered and lowly in heart," his yoke kindly and his load light.—Mt 11:28-30.

Priestly duties included care for the physical and spiritual health of the people. (Le 13-15) Pity and compassion moved Jesus to help the people suffering from illness, blindness, and other afflictions. (Mt 9:36; 14:14; 20:34; Lu 7:11-15; compare Isa 61:1.) The death of his friend Lazarus and the resulting grief to Lazarus' sisters caused Jesus to 'groan and give way to tears.' (Joh 11:32-36) Thus, in an anticipatory way, Jesus the Messiah 'carried the sicknesses and bore the pains' of others, doing so at the cost of power from himself. (Isa 53:4; Lu 8:43-48) He did so not only in fulfillment of prophecy but because 'he *wanted* to.' (Mt 8:2-4, 16, 17) More important, he brought them spiritual health and forgiveness of sins, being authorized to do so because, as the Christ, he was foreordained to provide the ransom sacrifice, in fact was already undergoing the baptism into death that would terminate on the torture stake.—Isa 53:4-8, 11, 12; compare Mt 9:2-8; 20:28; Mr 10:38, 39; Lu 12:50.

"Wonderful Counselor." The priest was responsible for the education of the people in God's law and will. (Mal 2:7) Also, as the royal Messiah, the foretold "twig out of the stump of Jesse [David's father]," Jesus had to manifest 'the spirit of Jehovah in wisdom, counsel, mightiness, knowledge, along with the fear of Jehovah.' Thereby God-fearing persons would find "enjoyment by him." (Isa 11:1-3) The unparalleled wisdom found in the teachings of Jesus, who was "more than Solomon" (Mt 12:42), is one of the most powerful evidences that he was indeed the Son of God and that the Gospel accounts could not be the mere product of imperfect men's minds or imagination.

Jesus proved himself to be the promised "Wonderful Counselor" (Isa 9:6) by his knowledge of God's Word and will, by his understanding of human nature, by his ability to get to the heart of questions and issues, and by showing the solution to problems of daily living. The well-known Sermon on the Mount is a prime example of this. (Mt 5-7) In it his counsel showed the way to true happiness, how to settle quarrels, how to avoid immorality, how to deal with those showing enmity, the way to practice righteousness free from hypocrisy, the right attitude toward the material things of life, confidence in God's generosity, the golden rule for right relationships with others, the means for detecting religious frauds, and how to build for a secure future. The crowds were "astounded at his way of teaching; for he was teaching them as a person having authority, and not as their scribes." (Mt 7:28, 29) After his resurrection he continued to be the key figure in Jehovah's channel of communication to mankind.—Re 1:1.

Master Teacher. His manner of teaching was remarkably effective. (Joh 7:45, 46) He presented matters of great weight and depth with simplicity, brevity, and clarity. He illustrated his points with things well known to his listeners (Mt 13:34, 35)—to fishermen (Mt 13:47, 48), shepherds (Joh 10:1-17), farmers (Mt 13:3-9), builders (Mt 7:24-27; Lu 14:28-30), merchants (Mt 13:45, 46), slaves or masters (Lu 16:1-9), housewives (Mt 13:33; Lu 15:8), or anyone else (Mt 6:26-30). Simple things, like bread, water, salt, wineskins, old garments, were used as symbols of things of great importance, even as they were so used in the Hebrew Scriptures. (Joh 6:31-35, 51; 4:13, 14; Mt 5:13; Lu 5:36-39) His logic, often expressed through analogies, cleared away misguided objections and put matters in their proper perspective. (Mt 16:1-3; Lu 11:11-22; 14:1-6) He aimed his message primarily at men's hearts, using penetrating questions to cause them to think, arrive at their own conclusions, examine their motives, and make decisions. (Mt 16:5-16; 17:24-27; 26:52-54; Mr 3:1-5; Lu 10:25-37; Joh 18:11) He did not strive to win over the masses but endeavored to awaken the hearts of those sincerely hungering for truth and righteousness.—Mt 5:3, 6; 13:10-15.

Though considerate of the limited understanding of his audience and even of his disciples (Mr 4:33) and though using discernment in how much information to give them (Joh 16:4, 12), he never 'watered down' God's message in an effort to gain popularity or curry favor. His speech was straightforward, even blunt at times. (Mt 5:37; Lu 11: 37-52; Joh 7:19; 8:46, 47) The theme of his message was: "*Repent, . . .* for the kingdom of the heavens has drawn near." (Mt 4:17) As did Jehovah's prophets of earlier times, he plainly told the people of "their revolt, and the house of Jacob [of] their sins" (Isa 58:1; Mt 21:28-32; Joh 8:24), pointing them to the 'narrow gate and the cramped road' that would lead them back to God's favor and life.—Mt 7:13, 14.

"Leader and Commander." Jesus demonstrated his qualifications as "a leader and commander" as well as "a witness to the national groups." (Isa 55:3, 4; Mt 23:10; Joh 14:10, 14; compare 1Ti 6:13, 14.) When the time came for it, several months after beginning his ministry, he went to certain people already known to him and gave them the invitation: "Be my follower." Men abandoned fishing businesses and tax office employment to respond without hesitation. (Mt 4:18-22; Lu 5:27, 28; compare Ps 110:3.) Women contributed time, effort, and material possessions to supply the needs of Jesus and his followers.—Mr 15:40, 41; Lu 8:1-3.

This small group formed the nucleus of what would become a new "nation," spiritual Israel. (1Pe 2:7-10) Jesus spent an entire night praying for his Father's guidance before selecting 12 apostles, who, if faithful, would become pillars in that new nation, like the 12 sons of Jacob in fleshly Israel. (Lu 6:12-16; Eph 2:20; Re 21:14) As Moses had 70 men associated with him as representatives of the nation, Jesus later assigned 70 more disciples to the ministry. (Nu 11:16, 17; Lu 10:1) Thereafter Jesus concentrated special attention on these disciples in his teaching and instruction, even the Sermon on the Mount being delivered principally for them, as its contents reveal.—Mt 5:1, 2, 13-16; 13:10, 11; Mr 4:34; 7:17.

He fully accepted the responsibilities of his headship, took the lead in every respect (Mt 23:10; Mr 10:32), assigned his disciples responsibilities and tasks in addition to their preaching work (Lu 9:52; 19:29-35; Joh 4:1-8; 12:4-6; 13:29; Mr 3:9; 14:12-16), encouraged and reproved (Joh 16:27; Lu 10:17-24; Mt 16:22, 23). He was a commander, and the chief of his commands was that they 'love one another even as he had loved them.' (Joh 15:10-14) He was able to control crowds numbering into the thousands. (Mr 6:39-46) The steady, helpful training he gave his disciples, men for the most part of humble position and education, was extremely effective. (Mt 10:1–11:1; Mr 6:7-13; Lu 8:1) Later, men of high station and learning were to wonder at the apostles' forceful, confident speech; and as "fishers of men," they enjoyed amazing results—persons by the thousands responded to their preaching. (Mt 4:19; Ac 2:37, 41; 4:4, 13; 6:7) Their grasp of Bible principles, carefully implanted in their hearts by Jesus, enabled them to be real shepherds of the flock in later years. (1Pe 5:1-4) Thus, Jesus, in the short span of three and a half years, laid the sound foundation for a unified international congregation with thousands of members drawn from many races.

Able Provider and Righteous Judge. That his rule would bring prosperity surpassing that of Solomon's was evident from his ability to direct the fishing operations of his disciples with overwhelming success. (Lu 5:4-9; compare Joh 21: 4-11.) The feeding of thousands of persons by this man born in Bethlehem (meaning "House of Bread"), as well as his converting water into fine wine, was a small foretaste of the future banquet that God's Messianic Kingdom would provide "for all the peoples." (Isa 25:6; compare Lu 14:15.) His rule not only would end poverty and hunger but would even result in the 'swallowing up of death.' —Isa 25:7, 8.

There was every reason, as well, to trust in the justice and righteous judgment his government would bring, in harmony with the Messianic prophecies. (Isa 11:3-5; 32:1, 2; 42:1) He showed the utmost respect for law, particularly that of his God and Father, but also for that of "the superior authorities" allowed to operate on earth in the form of secular governments. (Ro 13:1; Mt 5:17-19; 22:17-21; Joh 18:36) He rejected the effort to inject him into the current political scene by 'making him king' through popular acclaim. (Joh 6:15; compare Lu 19:11, 12; Ac 1:6-9.) He did not overstep the bounds of his authority. (Lu 12:13, 14) No one could 'convict him of sin'; this was not merely because he had been born perfect but because he exercised constant care to observe God's Word. (Joh 8:46, 55) Righteousness and faithfulness girded him like a belt. (Isa 11:5) His love of righteousness was coupled with a hatred of wickedness, hypocrisy, and fraud, as well as indignation toward those who were greedy and callous toward the sufferings of others. (Mt 7:21-27; 23:1-8, 25-28; Mr 3:1-5; 12:38-40; compare vss 41-44.) Meek and lowly ones could take heart, because his rule would wipe out injustice and oppression.—Isa 11:4; Mt 5:5.

He showed keen discernment of principles, of the real meaning and purpose of God's laws, emphasizing "the weightier matters" thereof, "justice and mercy and faithfulness." (Mt 12:1-8; 23:23, 24) He was impartial, displaying no favoritism, even though he felt particular affection for one of his disciples. (Mt 18:1-4; Mr 10:35-44; Joh 13:23; compare 1Pe 1:17.) Though one of his last acts while dying on the torture stake was to show concern for his human mother, his fleshly family

ties never took priority over his spiritual relationships. (Mt 12:46-50; Lu 11:27, 28; Joh 19:26, 27) As foretold, his handling of problems was never superficial, based on "any mere appearance to his eyes, nor [was his reproof] simply according to the thing heard by his ears." (Isa 11:3; compare Joh 7:24.) He was able to see into men's hearts, discern their thinking, reasoning, and motives. (Mt 9:4; Mr 2:6-8; Joh 2:23-25) And he kept his ear tuned to God's Word and sought, not his own will, but that of his Father; this assured that, as God's appointed Judge, his decisions would always be right and righteous.—Isa 11:4; Joh 5:30.

Outstanding Prophet. Jesus fulfilled the requirements of a prophet like, but greater than, Moses. (De 18:15, 18, 19; Mt 21:11; Lu 24:19; Ac 3:19-23; compare Joh 7:40.) He foretold his own sufferings and manner of death, the scattering of his disciples, the siege of Jerusalem, and the utter destruction of that city and its temple. (Mt 20:17-19; 24:1–25:46; 26:31-34; Lu 19:41-44; 21:20-24; Joh 13:18-27, 38) In connection with these latter events, he included prophecies to be fulfilled at the time of his presence, when his Kingdom would be in active operation. And, like the earlier prophets, he performed signs and miracles as evidence from God that he was divinely sent. His credentials surpassed those of Moses— he calmed the stormy sea of Galilee; walked on its waters (Mt 8:23-27; 14:23-34); healed the blind, the deaf, and the lame, as well as those with sicknesses as grave as leprosy; and even raised the dead.—Lu 7:18-23; 8:41-56; Joh 11:1-46.

Superb example of love. The quality that predominates through all these aspects of Jesus' personality is love—Jesus' love for his Father above all and also for his fellow creatures. (Mt 22:37-39) Love was therefore to be the distinguishing mark identifying his disciples. (Joh 13: 34, 35; compare 1Jo 3:14.) His love was not sentimentality. Though he expressed strong feeling, Jesus was always guided by principle (Heb 1:9); his Father's will was his supreme concern. (Compare Mt 16:21-23.) He proved his love for God by keeping God's commandments (Joh 14:30, 31; compare 1Jo 5:3) and by seeking to glorify his Father at all times. (Joh 17:1-4) On his final night with his disciples, he spoke of love and loving nearly thirty times, three times repeating the command that they "love one another." (Joh 13: 34; 15:12, 17) He told them: "No one has love greater than this, that someone should surrender his soul in behalf of his friends. You are my friends if you do what I am commanding you."—Joh 15:13, 14; compare Joh 10:11-15.

In proof of his love for God and for imperfect mankind, he then let himself be "brought just like a sheep to the slaughtering," submitting to trials, being slapped, hit with fists, spit on, scourged with a whip, and finally, nailed to a stake between criminals. (Isa 53:7; Mt 26:67, 68; 27:26-38; Mr 14:65; 15:15-20; Joh 19:1) By his sacrificial death he exemplified and expressed God's love toward men (Ro 5:8-10; Eph 2:4, 5) and enabled men to have absolute belief in his own unbreakable love for his faithful disciples.—Ro 8:35-39; 1Jo 3:16-18.

Since the portrait of God's Son obtainable through the written record, admittedly brief (Joh 21:25), is grand, the reality must have been far grander. His heartwarming example of humility and kindness, coupled with strength for righteousness and justice, gives assurance that his Kingdom government will be all that men of faith through the centuries have longed for, in fact, that it will surpass their highest expectations. (Ro 8:18-22) In all respects he exemplified the perfect standard for his disciples, one far different from that of worldly rulers. (Mt 20:25-28; 1Co 11:1; 1Pe 2:21) He, their Lord, washed their feet. Thus, he set the pattern of thoughtfulness, consideration, and humility that would characterize his congregation of anointed followers, not only on earth but also in heaven. (Joh 13:3-15) Though heaven-high on their thrones and sharing 'all authority in heaven and earth' with Jesus during Christ's Thousand Year Reign, they must humbly care for and lovingly serve the needs of his subjects on earth.—Mt 28:18; Ro 8:17; 1Pe 2:9; Re 1:5, 6; 20:6; 21:2-4.

Declared Righteous and Worthy. By his entire life course of integrity to God, including his sacrifice, Jesus Christ accomplished the "one act of justification" that proved him qualified to serve as God's anointed King-Priest in heaven. (Ro 5:17, 18) By his resurrection from the dead to life as a heavenly Son of God, he was "declared righteous in spirit." (1Ti 3:16) Heavenly creatures proclaimed him "worthy to receive the power and riches and wisdom and strength and honor and glory and blessing," as one who was both lionlike in behalf of justice and judgment and also lamblike in giving himself as a sacrifice for the saving of others. (Re 5:5-13)He had accomplished his primary purpose of sanctifying his Father's name. (Mt 6:9; 22:36-38) This he did, not just by using that name, but by revealing the Person it represents, displaying his Father's splendid qualities —his love, wisdom, justice, and power—enabling persons to know or experience what God's name stands for. (Mt 11:27; Joh 1:14, 18; 17:6-12) And above all, he did it by upholding Jehovah's universal sovereignty, showing that his own Kingdom government would be based solidly on that Supreme Source of authority. Therefore it could be said of him: "God is your throne forever."—Heb 1:8.

The Lord Jesus Christ is thus "the Chief Agent and Perfecter of our faith." By his fulfillment of prophecy and his revelation of God's future purposes, as well as by what he said and did and was, he provided the solid foundation on which true faith must rest.—Heb 12:2; 11:1.

JETHER (Je'ther) [from a root meaning "more than enough; overflow"].

1. Moses' father-in-law Jethro is called Jether in the Masoretic text at Exodus 4:18.—See JETHRO.

2. A descendant of Judah through Perez. Jether died without sons.—1Ch 2:4, 5, 25, 26, 28, 32.

3. The first-named son of Ezrah; descendant of Judah.—1Ch 4:17.

4. A descendant of Asher. (1Ch 7:30, 38) He is likely the same as Ithran in verse 37; the names are quite similar in Hebrew.

5. The firstborn son of Gideon. Jether apparently accompanied his father in the pursuit and capture of the Midianite kings Zebah and Zalmunna, but when ordered to slay them, the young Jether feared to draw his sword. (Jg 8:20) After Gideon died, Jether was killed by his half brother Abimelech.—Jg 9:5, 18.

6. Father of David's onetime army chief Amasa. (1Ki 2:5, 32) Second Samuel 17:25 in the Masoretic text calls him Ithra and says that he was an Israelite, but 1 Chronicles 2:17 calls him an Ishmaelite, possibly because he lived for a time among the Ishmaelites.

JETHETH (Je'theth). A sheik of Edom, descendant of Esau.—Ge 36:40-43; 1Ch 1:51; see TIMNA No. 3.

JETHRO (Jeth'ro) [from a root meaning "more than enough; overflow"]. Moses' father-in-law, a Kenite. (Ex 3:1; Jg 1:16) Jethro is also called Reuel. (Nu 10:29) Jethro may have been a title, whereas Reuel was a personal name. However, it was not uncommon for an Arabian chief to have two or even more names, as is attested to by many inscriptions. Jethro is spelled "Jether" in the Masoretic text at Exodus 4:18.

Jethro was "the priest of Midian." Being head of a large family of at least seven daughters and one named son (Ex 2:15, 16; Nu 10:29), and having the responsibility not only to provide for his family materially but also to lead them in worship, he is appropriately called "the priest [or chieftain] of Midian." This of itself does not necessarily indicate worship of Jehovah God; but Jethro's ancestors may have had true worship inculcated in them, and some of this perhaps continued in the family. His conduct suggests at least a deep respect for the God of Moses and Israel.—Ex 18:10-12.

Jethro's association with his future son-in-law began shortly after Moses fled from Egypt in 1553 B.C.E. Moses assisted Jethro's daughters in watering their father's flocks, and this they reported to their father, who, in turn, extended hospitality to Moses. Moses then took up living in Jethro's household and eventually married his daughter Zipporah. After some 40 years of caring for Jethro's flocks in the vicinity of Mount Horeb (Sinai), Moses was summoned by Jehovah back to Egypt, and he returned with his father-in-law's good wishes.—Ex 2:15-22; 3:1; 4:18; Ac 7:29, 30.

Later Jethro received report of Jehovah's great victory over the Egyptians, and at once he came to Moses at Horeb, bringing along Zipporah and Moses' two sons; it was indeed a very warm reunion. Jethro responded to Moses' review of Jehovah's mighty saving acts by blessing God and confessing: "Now I do know that Jehovah is greater than all the other gods." He then offered up sacrifices to the true God. (Ex 18:1-12) The next day, Jethro observed Moses listening to the problems of the Israelites "from the morning till the evening." Perceiving how exhausting this was for both Moses and the people, Jethro suggested a system of delegating authority. 'Train other capable and worthy men as chiefs over tens, fifties, hundreds, and thousands to decide cases, so that you will hear only what they cannot handle.' Moses agreed, and later Jethro returned to his own land. —Ex 18:13-27.

Jethro's son Hobab was requested by Moses to be a scout. Apparently with some persuasion, he responded, and some of his people entered the Promised Land with Israel. (Nu 10:29-33) Judges 4:11 calls Hobab the father-in-law of Moses rather than his brother-in-law, and this has caused difficulty in understanding. However, the Hebrew expression normally rendered "father-in-law" can in a broader sense denote any male relative by marriage and so could also be understood as "brother-in-law." To say that Hobab instead of Jethro was Moses' father-in-law would disagree with other texts. If Hobab were another name for Jethro, as some suggest, it would also mean that two men, father and son, bore the name Hobab. On the other hand, Hobab, as a leading member of the next generation of Kenites, might be used in this text as a representative of his father.—See HOBAB.

JETUR (Je'tur). A son of Ishmael (Ge 25:13-15; 1Ch 1:31) and forefather of a people against whom the Israelites warred. (1Ch 5:18, 19) It is possible that Jetur's descendants were the Ituraeans.—Lu 3:1; see ITURAEA.

JEUEL (Je·u'el).

1. A Levite who helped in cleansing the temple during Hezekiah's reign; a descendant of Elizaphan.—2Ch 29:13, 15, 16.

2. A postexilic resident of Jerusalem; head of the Judean paternal house of Zerah.—1Ch 9:3-6, 9; Ge 46:12.

JEUSH (Je'ush) [possibly, May He Lend Aid].

1. A son of Esau by his Hivite wife Oholibamah. Jeush was born in Canaan, but later the family moved to Edom.—Ge 36:2, 5-8, 14, 18; 1Ch 1:35.

2. A descendant of Benjamin; a warrior and founder of a tribal family.—1Ch 7:6, 10.

3. A Gershonite Levite; son of Shimei. As both Jeush and his brother Beriah had very few sons, their descendants in David's time merged to form one paternal house.—1Ch 23:7, 10, 11.

4. The first-named son of King Rehoboam, presumably by his wife Mahalath. Because Rehoboam loved a different wife more, Jeush was passed up in the royal succession.—2Ch 11:18-23.

5. A Benjamite; one of King Saul's descendants. —1Ch 8:33, 39.

JEUZ (Je'uz) [He Has Counseled (Advised)]. A family head in the tribe of Benjamin; son of Shaharaim by his wife Hodesh.—1Ch 8:1, 8-10.

JEW(ESS) [Of (Belonging to) Judah]. A person belonging to the tribe of Judah. The name is not used in the Bible account prior to the fall of the ten-tribe kingdom of Israel. The southern kingdom was called Judah, and the people were called sons of Judah or the tribe of the sons of Judah. The first one to use the name Jews was the writer of the books of Kings, doubtless Jeremiah, whose prophetic service began in 647 B.C.E. (See 2Ki 16:6; 25:25.) After the exile the name was applied to any Israelites returning (Ezr 4:12; 6:7; Ne 1:2; 5:17) and, finally, to all Hebrews throughout the world, to distinguish them from the Gentile nations. (Es 3:6; 9:20) Gentile men who accepted the Jewish faith and became circumcised proselytes also declared themselves Jews. (Es 8:17) However, in the Hebrew Scriptures the expression "alien resident" may refer to one who had adopted the religion of the Jews (Jer 22:3), and even in the Christian Greek Scriptures such are distinguished at times by the term "proselytes." (Ac 2:10; 6:5; 13:43) The term "Jewess" is used at Acts 24:24.

When Jesus was a young child, the astrologers came, inquiring: "Where is the one born king of the Jews?" (Mt 2:1, 2) On Jesus' torture stake Pilate put the title "Jesus the Nazarene the King of the Jews."—Joh 19:19.

Figurative Use. The apostle Paul, in arguing that the Jews were mistaken in their pride of fleshly descent and in relying on the works of the Law to find favor with God, said: "For he is not a Jew who is one on the outside, nor is circumcision that which is on the outside upon the flesh. But he is a Jew who is one on the inside, and his circumcision is that of the heart by spirit, and not by a written code. The praise of that one comes, not from men, but from God." (Ro 2:28, 29) Here Paul, by a play on the meaning of the name Judah, shows that the real basis for praise from God is being a servant of God from the heart, by spirit. This argument parallels his reasoning in Romans chapter 4, that the true seed of Abraham are those with the faith of Abraham. He further points out that in the Christian congregation nationality is of no consequence, for "there is neither Jew nor Greek [Gentile]." (Ga 3:28) The resurrected Jesus Christ spoke to the congregation at Smyrna, comforting them with regard to the persecution they were receiving, to a great extent at the hands of the Jews, saying: "I know . . . the blasphemy by those who say they themselves are Jews, and yet they are not but are a synagogue of Satan."—Re 2:9.

JEWELRY. See JEWELS AND PRECIOUS STONES; ORNAMENTS.

JEWELS AND PRECIOUS STONES.

A jewel may be a precious stone, a gem (a cut and polished precious or semiprecious stone), or a decorative ornament made of precious metal (principally gold or silver) set with such stones. Jewels have been worn by both men and women from early Biblical days for purposes of adornment. Today the diamond, emerald, ruby, and sapphire are strictly considered to be precious stones, whereas other rare and beautiful stones are viewed as semiprecious. However, the Hebrew term rendered "precious stone" has a broader application, as is shown at Ezekiel 28:12, 13. These precious stones are distinguished from other minerals chiefly because they are rare, beautiful, and durable.

The first Biblical reference to any precious stone is at Genesis 2:11, 12, where Havilah is identified as a land containing good gold, "bdellium gum and the onyx stone."

Wealth was partially measured by one's possession of precious stones; such kings as Solomon and Hezekiah apparently had them in great quantity. (1Ki 10:11; 2Ch 9:10; 32:27) Precious stones were given as gifts (1Ki 10:2, 10; 2Ch 9:1, 9), might constitute part of war booty (2Sa 12:29, 30; 1Ch 20:2), and, as among the ancient Tyrians, were used as articles of trade (Eze 27:16, 22). In an inspired dirge concerning "the king of Tyre," Ezekiel stated: "Every precious stone was your covering, ruby, topaz and jasper; chrysolite, onyx and jade; sapphire, turquoise and emerald; and of gold was the workmanship of your settings and your sockets in you." (Eze 28:12, 13) Symbolic Babylon the Great is represented as being richly adorned with precious stones.—Re 17:3-5; 18:11-17.

While the ancients rounded and polished precious stones, generally they do not seem to have angled, or faceted, them, as do craftsmen of modern times. The emery stone (corundum) or emery powder was employed by the Hebrews and Egyptians to polish precious stones. Often these were sculptured and engraved. The Hebrews apparently knew how to engrave precious stones long before their bondage in Egypt, where engraving was also an art. Judah's seal ring had evidently been engraved. (Ge 38:18) For further discussions of ancient jewelry and ornaments, see ANKLET; BEADS; BRACELET; BROOCH; EARRING; NECKLACE; NOSE RING; ORNAMENTS; RING.

Uses Associated With Worship. The Israelites, in the wilderness, were privileged to contribute various valuable things for the tabernacle and the high priest's ephod and breastpiece, no doubt contributing articles that the Egyptians had given to them when urging them to depart. (Ex 12:35, 36) These included "onyx stones and setting stones for the ephod and for the breastpiece." (Ex 25:1-7; 35:5, 9, 27) The high priest's ephod had two onyx stones on the shoulder pieces, with the names of 6 of the 12 tribes of Israel inscribed on each stone. "The breastpiece of judgment" was embellished with four rows of precious stones, the account stating: "A row of ruby, topaz and emerald was the first row. And the second row was turquoise, sapphire and jasper. And the third row was lesh'em stone, agate and amethyst. And the fourth row was chrysolite and onyx and jade. They were set with settings of gold in their fillings." The name of one of Israel's 12 tribes was inscribed on each of these stones.—Ex 39:6-14; 28:9-21; see BREASTPIECE.

Though Jehovah would not permit David to build the temple in Jerusalem (1Ch 22:6-10), the aged king joyfully prepared valuable materials for its construction, including "onyx stones, and stones to be set with hard mortar, and mosaic pebbles, and every precious stone, and alabaster stones in great quantity." He made substantial contributions of materials, and the people in general also contributed. (1Ch 29:2-9) When Solomon built the temple, he "overlaid the house with precious stone for beauty," or studded it with precious stones.—2Ch 3:6.

Figurative Use. The apostle Paul, after identifying Jesus Christ as the foundation on which Christians should build, mentioned building materials of various kinds in connection with the Christian ministry. He indicated that the choice materials would include figurative "precious stones" capable of withstanding the force of "fire."—1Co 3:10-15.

Precious stones are sometimes used Scripturally to symbolize qualities of heavenly or spiritual things or persons. The heavens were opened for Ezekiel, and in two visions he beheld four winged living creatures accompanied by four wheels, the appearance of each wheel being likened to "the glow of chrysolite," that is, having a hue of yellow or possibly green. (Eze 1:1-6, 15, 16; 10:9) Later, Daniel saw an angel, "a certain man clothed in linen," whose "body was like chrysolite."—Da 10:1, 4-6.

Ezekiel also, when beholding a vision of Jehovah's glory, saw "something in appearance like sapphire stone [a deep blue], the likeness of a throne." (Eze 1:25-28; 10:1) The glory of Jehovah God himself is likened to the dazzling beauty of gemstones, for when the apostle John beheld God's heavenly throne, he said: "The one seated is, in appearance, like a jasper stone and a precious red-colored stone, and round about the throne there is a rainbow like an emerald in appearance." —Re 4:1-3, 9-11.

"The holy city, New Jerusalem," that is, "the Lamb's wife," is represented as having a radiance "like a most precious stone, as a jasper stone shining crystal-clear." The 12 foundations of its wall "were adorned with every sort of precious stone," a different stone for each foundation: jasper, sapphire, chalcedony, emerald, sardonyx, sardius, chrysolite, beryl, topaz, chrysoprase, hyacinth, and amethyst. The city's 12 gates were 12 pearls.—Re 21:2, 9-21; see CORAL and separate articles on individual types of precious stones.

JEZANIAH (Jez·a·ni′ah) [probably a shortened form of Jaazaniah, meaning "Jehovah Has Given Ear"]. A chief of the Judean military force among those submitting to Gedaliah's brief administration in 607 B.C.E. (Jer 40:8, 9; 42:1) Jezaniah is also called Azariah (Jer 43:2) and Jaazaniah.—2Ki 25:23.

JEZEBEL (Jez′e·bel) [from Phoenician, possibly meaning "Where Is the Lofty One [that is, the prince]?"].

1. Wife of Ahab, a king of Israel in the latter half of the tenth century B.C.E. She was a domineering queen who proved to be a strong advocate of Baalism at the expense of Jehovah's worship. In this she was like her father Ethbaal, the king of Sidon, evidently the one identified by the ancient historian Menander (according to Josephus' *Against Apion,* I, 116, 123 [18]) as a priest of Astarte (Ashtoreth) who gained the throne by murdering his own king.—1Ki 16:30, 31.

Quite likely Ahab's marriage to this pagan princess Jezebel was for political reasons, without regard for the disastrous religious consequences. And after his having made such an alliance, it was only the next logical step in pleasing his devout Baal-worshiping wife to build a temple and altar for Baal, erect a phallic "sacred pole," and then join her in this idolatrous worship. In all of this, Ahab did more to offend Jehovah than all the kings of Israel prior to him.—1Ki 16:32, 33.

Jezebel, not satisfied that Baal worship was officially approved by the throne, endeavored to exterminate the worship of Jehovah from the land. To that end she ordered all the prophets of Jehovah killed, but God warned Elijah to escape across the Jordan, and Obadiah, the palace steward, hid a hundred others in caves. (1Ki 17:1-3; 18:4, 13) Some time later Elijah again fled for his life when Jezebel, by personal messenger, vowed to kill him.—1Ki 19:1-4, 14.

There came to be 450 prophets of Baal and 400 prophets of the sacred pole, all of whom Jezebel cared for and fed from her own royal table at the State's expense. (1Ki 18:19) But in spite of her fanatic efforts to obliterate the worship of Jehovah, Jehovah revealed that, in the end, 'all the knees that had not bent down to Baal, and every mouth that had not kissed him' amounted to 7,000 persons.—1Ki 19:18.

In Jezebel's treatment of Naboth, we are given another view of this woman's wicked character, a character that was extremely selfish, unscrupulous, arrogant, cruel. When Ahab began to sulk and pout because Naboth refused to sell him his hereditary vineyard, this unscrupulous woman shamelessly overstepped her husband's headship and arrogantly declared: "I myself shall give you the vineyard of Naboth." (1Ki 21:1-7) With that she wrote letters, signed and sealed in the name of Ahab, ordering the older men and nobles of Naboth's hometown to arrange for good-for-nothing fellows falsely to accuse Naboth of cursing God and the king and then to take Naboth out and stone him to death. In this way Naboth was put to death by a perversion of justice. Ahab then seized the vineyard and prepared to turn it into a vegetable garden.—1Ki 21:8-16.

For such wanton disregard for righteousness, Jehovah decreed that Ahab and his line of descent would be removed in a clean sweep of destruction. "Without exception no one has proved to be like Ahab, who sold himself to do what was bad in the eyes of Jehovah, whom Jezebel his wife egged on." Hence, Jehovah's judgment against Jezebel: "The very dogs will eat up Jezebel."—1Ki 21:17-26.

In the course of time Ahab died and was succeeded first by Jezebel's son Ahaziah, who ruled for two years, and then by another of her sons, Jehoram, who ruled for the next 12 years before Ahab's dynasty finally ended. (1Ki 22:40, 51-53; 2Ki 1:17; 3:1) During the reigns of these sons, Jezebel, now in the role of queen mother, continued to influence the land with her fornications and sorceries. (2Ki 9:22) Her influence was even felt in Judah to the S, where her wicked daughter Athaliah, who had married Judah's king, perpetuated the Jezebel spirit in that southern kingdom for another six years after her mother's death.—2Ki 8:16-18, 25-27; 2Ch 22:2, 3; 24:7.

When the news reached Jezebel that Jehu had killed her reigning son Jehoram and was on his way to Jezreel, she artfully painted her eyes, adorned her hair, and framed herself in an upper window overlooking the palace square. There she greeted the conqueror upon his triumphal entry, saying: "Did it go all right with Zimri the killer of his lord?" This sarcastic greeting was probably a veiled threat, for Zimri, after killing his king and usurping the throne, committed suicide seven days later when his life was threatened.—2Ki 9:30, 31; 1Ki 16:10, 15, 18.

Jehu's response to this hostile reception was: "Who is with me? Who?" When two or three court officials looked out, he commanded, "Let her drop!" In the violence of the fall, her blood splattered the wall and the horses, and she was trodden underfoot, presumably by the horses. Shortly thereafter when men came to bury this "daughter of a king," why, they found the scavenger dogs had already practically disposed of her, just as "the word of Jehovah that he spoke by means of his servant Elijah" had foretold, leaving only the skull, the feet, and the palms of her hands as evidence that all that Jehovah says comes true.—2Ki 9:32-37.

2. That "woman" in the congregation of Thyatira who called herself a prophetess. This "woman" no doubt was given the name Jezebel because her wicked conduct resembled that of Ahab's wife. Not only did this "woman" teach false religion and mislead many to commit fornication and idolatry but she also callously refused to repent. For this reason "the Son of God" declared she would be thrown into a sickbed and her children would be killed, to show that each one receives according to one's deeds.—Re 2:18-23.

JEZER (Je′zer) [He Has Formed]. The third-listed son of Naphtali; founder of the family of Jezerites.—Ge 46:24; Nu 26:48, 49; 1Ch 7:13.

JEZERITES (Je′zer·ites) [Of (Belonging to) Jezer]. A family of Naphtali that sprang from Jezer.—Nu 26:48, 49.

JEZIEL (Je′zi·el). A Benjamite son of Azmaveth who sided with David when he was outlawed by Saul.—1Ch 12:1-3.

JEZREEL (Jez′re·el) [God Will Sow Seed], **JEZREELITE** (Jez′re·el·ite).

1. A descendant of Judah; possibly the forefather of the inhabitants of Jezreel (No. 3) or its principal settler.—1Ch 4:1, 3.

2. Son of the prophet Hosea by his wife Gomer (Ho 1:3, 4); for the prophetic significance of "Jezreel," see No. 4.

3. An unidentified city in the mountainous region of Judah, perhaps founded by No. 1. (Jos 15:20, 48, 56) This Jezreel doubtless was the home of David's wife Ahinoam.—1Sa 25:43; 27:3.

4. A city on the border of Issachar's territory. (Jos 19:17, 18) Today Jezreel is identified with Zer′in (Tel Yizre′el), located about 11 km (7 mi) NNE of Jenin (En-gannim). Just to the SE lies a crescent-shaped ridge of limestone hills traditionally identified with Mount Gilboa.

During the latter half of the tenth century B.C.E., Jezreel served as the royal residence for Israel's King Ahab and his successor Jehoram, although Samaria was the actual capital of the northern kingdom. (1Ki 18:45, 46; 21:1; 2Ki 8:29) In the vineyard of Naboth near the palace at Jezreel, the prophet Elijah uttered Jehovah's judgment against the house of Ahab. (1Ki 21:17-29) The prophecy was fulfilled. Jehu slew Ahab's son King Jehoram and then had his corpse thrown into the tract of Naboth's field. Ahab's wife Jezebel became food for the scavenger dogs of Jezreel when she was dropped from a window at Jehu's command. The heads of Ahab's 70 sons, executed by their caretakers in Samaria, were piled up in two heaps at the gate of Jezreel. None of Ahab's distinguished men, acquaintances, and priests at Jezreel escaped.—2Ki 9:22-37; 10:5-11.

Hosea's Prophecy. The words of Jehovah to Hosea (1:4) regarding "the acts of bloodshed of Jezreel" are not to be understood as referring to Jehu's destroying Ahab's ungodly house. Jehu was used as Jehovah's instrument in executing divine judgment. However, it may well be that the wrong motivations that were behind Jehu's continuing to let calf worship remain also caused him to make himself guilty of bloodshed.—2Ki 10:30, 31.

The prophetic name Jezreel, by which Jehovah instructed Hosea to call his son by Gomer, pointed to a future accounting against the house of Jehu. God would "sow seed" in that he would cause a scattering of it. The accounting against Jehu's house came when Jehu's great-great-grandson Zechariah, after ruling for six months, was murdered and the assassin Shallum seized the throne. (2Ki 15:8-10) Thus ended the dynasty of Jehu. About 50 years later, in 740 B.C.E., when the northern kingdom fell to Assyria and its inhabitants were exiled, the royal rule of the house of Israel ceased completely. At that time "the bow of Israel," that is, its military strength, was definitely broken. The prophecy had indicated that this would take place in the Low Plain of Jezreel, perhaps because the Assyrians gained a decisive victory there.—Ho 1:4, 5.

However, through his prophet Hosea, Jehovah also pointed to a favorable meaning of Jezreel. By regathering the remnant of Israel and Judah and then bringing his people back to their land, Jehovah would sow seed, causing them to increase in numbers there.—Ho 1:11; 2:21-23; compare Zec 10:8-10.

5. The geographic area embraced by the Low Plain of Jezreel. This designation is often restricted to the low plain extending in a southeasterly direction from the city of Jezreel in Issachar to Beth-shean on the western edge of the Jordan Valley. But the designation "Valley of Jezreel" is also used today to include the low plain W of Jezreel, the Plain of Esdraelon (the Greek form of the Hebrew Jezreel). Therefore, in the broad sense the "Valley of Jezreel" includes the whole plain from the Carmel Range to the Jordan River.

Situated at the edge of a rocky descent, the city of Jezreel (Zer'in) overlooks the entire eastern part of the Low Plain of Jezreel, extending southeastward for nearly 19 km (12 mi) and measuring about 3 km (2 mi) in width. In the time of Joshua this area was controlled by Canaanites having a strong, well-equipped chariotry. (Jos 17:16) It was also in the Low Plain of Jezreel that Gideon and his 300 men witnessed Jehovah's saving hand as the enemy forces of the Midianites, Amalekites, and Easterners turned against one another in confusion. (Jg 6:33; 7:12-22) Later, the Israelite army under King Saul, when facing the enemy Philistines, encamped by the spring in Jezreel (perhaps 'Ain Jalud on the NW spur of Mount Gilboa or 'Ain el-Meiyiteh below the town of Zer'in). Thereafter, from Jezreel report was received about the deaths of Saul and his son Jonathan. (1Sa 29:1, 11; 2Sa 4:4) Jezreel and its vicinity then came to be part of the territory ruled by Saul's son Ish-bosheth. (2Sa 2:8, 9) And while Solomon reigned, the assignment of the deputy Baana included the fertile Plain of Jezreel.—1Ki 4:7, 12.

JIDLAPH (Jid'laph). The seventh listed of the eight sons borne to Nahor by his wife Milcah. Jidlaph was therefore a nephew of Abraham and an uncle to Isaac's wife Rebekah.—Ge 22:20-23; 24:67.

JOAB (Jo'ab) [Jehovah Is Father].

1. Son of Seraiah, a descendant of Kenaz of the tribe of Judah. Joab was "the father of Geharashim" (meaning "Valley of Craftsmen"), "for," says the Bible account, "craftsmen are what they became." Evidently Joab was "father" or founder of the community of craftsmen living in the valley.—1Ch 4:1, 13, 14; see GE-HARASHIM.

2. The second of three sons of David's sister or half sister Zeruiah (possibly the daughter of David's mother by an earlier marriage to Nahash; 2Sa 17:25). Joab was therefore the nephew of David. His brothers were Abishai and Asahel. (2Sa 8:16; 1Ch 2:13-16) In identifying these three men, the mother's name is recorded rather than the father's, because she was David's sister; thus the relationship of David to the three men is made clear.

Characteristics. Joab was an able general, a man of organizational ability, resourceful, and decisive. On the other hand, he was an ambitious opportunist, vengeful, cunning, and at times unscrupulous.

Joab was at the head of David's men at the time Ish-bosheth the son of Saul ruled over all Israel with the exception of the tribe of Judah, which clung to David. (2Sa 2:10) The servants of Ish-bosheth and those of David were drawn up against one another at the Pool of Gibeon, Ish-bosheth's forces being under command of Saul's uncle Abner, who had been responsible for putting Ish-bosheth on the throne. As the men sat facing one another, Abner suggested a combat between 12 men from each side. When they grabbed hold of one another by the head, each ran his opponent through with the sword, all falling down dead together. (2Sa 2:12-16) Since the issue was not settled by the combat, a full-scale battle resulted. A count afterward revealed that Ish-bosheth's forces lost 360 men, and David's, only 20.—2Sa 2:30, 31.

During the fight, as Abner fled, Joab's fleet-footed brother Asahel pursued Abner. Despite re-monstrances and warnings from Abner, Asahel persisted until finally Abner thrust backward with the butt end of his spear, piercing him through. (2Sa 2:18-23) Reaching the hill of Ammah, Abner and his men gathered on its top, from which Abner made appeal to stop the fighting in order to avoid bitterness and endless slaughter. Joab here demonstrated practical wisdom by heeding the appeal and returning to David at Hebron.—2Sa 2:24-28, 32.

Slays Abner in vengeance.   Joab's desire for vengeance, nevertheless, smoldered in him, and he waited for opportunity to satisfy it. In the meantime he engaged in a drawn-out war with Saul's house, which constantly declined, while Da-vid grew stronger. Eventually Abner, offended at Ish-bosheth over a personal matter, made a cove-nant with David, promising to bring all Israel over to David's side. (2Sa 3:6-21) Joab strongly dis-agreed with the transaction, charging Abner with being a spy. But pretending friendship for Abner, Joab caught Abner off guard and slew him in revenge for his brother Asahel. He may also have felt that he was at the same time eliminating a possible rival for the post of commander of David's army.—2Sa 3:22-27.

When David heard of the murder, he disclaimed guilt for his own house before all Israel and said: "May it whirl back upon the head of Joab and upon the entire house of his father, and let there not be cut off from Joab's house a man with a running discharge or a leper [one diseased] or a man taking hold of the twirling spindle [perhaps, one crippled] or one falling by the sword or one in need of bread!" David did not act at this time against Joab and Abishai, who connived with Joab in the mur-der, because, as he said: "I today am weak al-though anointed as king, and these men, the sons of Zeruiah, are too severe for me. May Jehovah repay the doer of what is bad according to his own badness."—2Sa 3:28-30, 35-39.

Commander of the Armies of Israel.   After David had been anointed as king of all Israel, he went up against Jerusalem (Jebus). The Jebusites taunted David, thinking that their position was unassailable. But David saw that the city was vulnerable through its water tunnel. Hence, he offered the position as "head and prince" to any-

one who would climb up the tunnel and be first to strike the Jebusites. Joab went up, the city fell to David, and Joab was rewarded with the high position of commander of the armies of Israel. (2Sa 5:6-8; 8:16; 20:23; 1Ch 11:4-8) As com-mander, Joab had a body of ten personal atten-dants bearing his weapons, among whom was the mighty man Naharai the Berothite.—2Sa 18:15; 1Ch 11:39.

After David's conquest of Edom, Joab remained there for six months in an effort to destroy every male among them. (2Sa 8:13, 14; 1Ki 11:14-17) Later, Joab manifested military leadership in the fight with the Ammonites and Syrians, putting his brother Abishai in charge of one division, to defeat a pincer movement of the enemy forces. (2Sa 10:8-14; 1Ch 19:6-16) He doubtless played a large part in the other battles fought by David against the Philistines, the Moabites, and others.

Supports David's kingship.   At the siege of Rabbah of Ammon, Joab appeared to evince loyal-ty to David as Jehovah's anointed king. He took "the city of waters," possibly meaning that part of the city containing its water supply or the fort protecting its water supply. With this vital part of the city taken, the capital city could not hold out much longer, and surrender would be inevitable. Instead of pressing the siege of the city to a successful climax by himself, Joab (whether actu-ally out of respect for the king, for Israel's good, or for his own advancement) seemed to show the proper regard for his earthly sovereign. He said that he preferred to have Jehovah's anointed king complete the capture of the enemy's royal city and earn the fame for this exploit, even though he, Joab, had done the vital preliminary work.—2Sa 12:26-31; 1Ch 20:1-3.

Cooperates in bringing Uriah's death.   It was during the siege of Rabbah that David sent a letter by Uriah telling Joab to place Uriah in the heaviest part of the battle so that he would be killed. Joab went along with the arrangement in full coopera-tion, but in his report to the king on the outcome of the battle, he adroitly used the fact to block David from reprimanding him because he had lost valiant men in the battle by sending them too close to the city wall. In his report Joab said: "Some of the servants of the king died; and your servant Uriah the Hittite also died." As Joab had calculated, David's answer contained no tone of displeasure but one of encouragement to Joab. —2Sa 11:14-25; see DAVID.

Helps, then opposes, Absalom.   It was Joab who, after Absalom had been in banishment for three years for slaying his half brother Amnon, sent a woman from Tekoa to David, putting words in her mouth to appeal for Absalom's return. The appeal was successful, and Joab brought Absalom back to Jerusalem, though David would not see Absalom. Two years later Absalom repeatedly requested Joab to come and approach the king in his behalf, but Joab declined. Finally Absalom resorted to the device of setting Joab's barley field afire, which brought a quick and angry response from Joab. Absalom was then able to give the reason for his act, and he induced Joab to see the king to bring about restoration of Absalom to David's favor.—2Sa 13:38; 14:1-33.

Though Joab supported Absalom's cause in achieving his return, when Absalom rebelled, Joab supported David. David placed Joab in charge of a third part of his men, with strict orders to deal gently with Absalom. But during the fight Joab disobeyed David's order and killed Absalom. (2Sa 18:1-17) Here, as in some other cases, he put his own judgment ahead of theocratic orders through God's anointed king. But he had the courage to speak in a bold, direct manner to David afterward, when David's mourning for Absalom endangered the unity of the kingdom.—2Sa 19:1-8.

Removed, Then Reinstated, as Army Chief. Evidently because of Joab's disobedience in the killing of Absalom, David replaced Joab as chief of the army, appointing Amasa. (2Sa 19:13) Amasa, however, did not prove to be the general that Joab had been. When commanded by David to call the men of Judah together to fight the rebel Sheba the son of Bichri, Amasa called Judah, but he came later than the time appointed by David. Because the matter was urgent, David commissioned Abishai to go after Sheba, saying, "That he may not actually find for himself fortified cities and escape before our eyes." In the ensuing fight, Joab appears to have taken the lead as he had done when army chief. At the siege of Abel of Beth-maacah that followed, the citizens of the town threw Sheba's head over the wall at Joab's bidding, and Joab spared the city, withdrawing and returning to Jerusalem.—2Sa 20:1-7, 14-22.

Murders Amasa. During the pursuit of Sheba, Joab committed a grave crime. As Amasa (who was his cousin; 2Sa 17:25; 1Ch 2:16, 17) came to meet him near Gibeon, Joab let his sword fall out of its sheath. Picking it up, he held it conveniently in his left hand as he took hold of Amasa's beard with his right hand, as if to kiss him. Because Amasa was off guard, Joab was able to kill him with one thrust of his sword. It is true that Joab may have had some distrust of Amasa because he

had headed Absalom's rebellious army; but be that as it may, Joab, the opportunist, seized on a time of emergency and strife to advance his personal career by murdering his rival. David may have deferred action against Joab because of Amasa's recent connections with Absalom and the fact that Joab had only recently fought the rebel forces of Absalom under Amasa's leadership. According to Joab's ambitious wishes, he was again made head of the army.—2Sa 20:8-13, 23.

Why did David fail to execute Joab when he murdered Abner, and why did he reappoint Joab as general over the army after he had also murdered Amasa, who had been made general to replace Joab? The Bible does not say. If it was weakness in enforcing God's law, it may have been because of the strength and influence of Joab and his family in the army. Or there may have been other circumstances that the Bible does not relate. At any rate, it must be remembered that David, though not executing Joab for some reason, whether good or bad, did not forgive him, but he charged Solomon his son and successor to see that Joab paid for his badness.

Takes incomplete census. At another time David was incited by Satan to take an illegal census of the people. Joab remonstrated with David, to no avail. But he did not complete the work, leaving out the tribes of Levi and Benjamin "because the king's word had been detestable to Joab."—1Ch 21:1-6; 2Sa 24:1-9; see REGISTRATION.

Joins Adonijah's attempt to take throne. Despite his previous service under David, when David became old and sick, Joab forsook David and joined the conspiracy of David's son Adonijah. (1Ki 1:18, 19) Perhaps he did this because he felt that, with Adonijah as king, he would be the power behind the throne, or it may be that he felt more sure of his position with Adonijah than with Solomon. When he heard that Solomon had been made king by David, he forsook Adonijah. (1Ki 1:49) Later, when Adonijah was killed, Joab ran to the tent of Jehovah and took hold of the horns of the altar. (1Ki 2:28) This furnished no sanctuary for him, for he was a deliberate murderer; therefore Solomon sent Benaiah to execute him there. Thus Solomon carried out David's deathbed counsel to him not to let the gray hairs of Joab go down in peace to Sheol, because of the bloodguilt on Joab for his murder of Abner and Amasa, "two men more righteous and better than he was." Joab was buried in his own house in the wilderness. Thereafter Benaiah was made head of the army.—1Ki 2:5, 6, 29-35; 11:21.

The 60th psalm, a psalm of David, is devoted, in its latter verses (8-12), to Joab's victory over the Edomites.—See the superscription of this psalm.

3. The head of a family of "sons of Pahath-moab," some of whom returned in 537 B.C.E. from Babylonian exile, with Zerubbabel.—Ezr 2:1, 2, 6; Ne 7:6, 7, 11.

4. At Ezra 8:1, 9, "sons of Joab" are listed among those returning with Ezra in 468 B.C.E. At that time Obadiah the son of Jehiel was family head. In this text they are not connected with the house of Pahath-moab, but it is possible that they are of the same family or were related to No. 3.

JOAH (Jo'ah) [Jehovah Is Brother (Companion)].

1. One of the Levitical gatekeepers assigned in David's day to guard duty over the storehouses; the third son of Obed-edom.—1Ch 26:1, 4, 12-15.

2. A Levite descended from Gershom (Gershon); son of Zimmah. (1Ch 6:19b-21) He is possibly the same Joah who, with his son, helped dispose of the unclean objects that Hezekiah had removed from the temple at the beginning of his reign.—2Ch 29:1, 3, 12, 16.

3. One of the committee of three sent by King Hezekiah to hear what the Assyrian messenger Rabshakeh would say but who were not to answer his charges and brags. Joah and his two companions did, however, ask Rabshakeh to speak to them in the Syrian tongue, which they themselves understood, rather than in the Jews' language in the hearing of others on the city wall. With their clothes ripped apart, they reported his threats to Hezekiah. (2Ki 18:18, 26, 36, 37; Isa 36:3, 11, 21, 22) The construction of the text, "Joah the son of Asaph the recorder," allows for either Joah or Asaph to be "the recorder," but it is more likely that Joah himself held this office, just as the two with him are also described by their office.

4. The recorder by whom King Josiah sent money to the workers to repair the temple; son of Joahaz.—2Ch 34:8-11.

JOAHAZ (Jo'a·haz) [shortened form of Jehoahaz, meaning "May Jehovah Take Hold; Jehovah Has Taken Hold"].

1. Variant spelling of the name of Jehoahaz, king of Israel, as found in certain translations (*AS, JP, Ro, RS*) of 2 Kings 14:1. There the Masoretic text reads *Yoh·'a·chaz'*, but on the authority of Hebrew manuscripts that read *Yehoh·'a·chaz'*, other translations (*AT, JB, Mo, NW*) render the name Jehoahaz.—See JEHOAHAZ No. 2.

2. Father of King Josiah's recorder Joah.—2Ch 34:1, 8.

3. Variant spelling, at 2 Chronicles 36:2, of the name of Jehoahaz, the son and successor of Josiah, king of Judah. Here certain translations (*AS, AT, JP, Ro*) follow the Masoretic text and read Joahaz, whereas others (*KJ, JB, Mo, NW*) read Jehoahaz. —See JEHOAHAZ No. 3.

JOANAN (Jo·an'an) [shortened form of Jehohanan, meaning "Jehovah Has Shown Favor; Jehovah Has Been Gracious"]. An ancestor of Jesus' mother Mary; listed apparently as grandson of Zerubbabel.—Lu 3:23, 27.

JOANNA (Jo·an'na) [shortened feminine form of Jehohanan, meaning "Jehovah Has Shown Favor; Jehovah Has Been Gracious"]. One of several women whom Jesus Christ cured of infirmities and who then became his followers, ministering to him and his apostles from their own possessions. (Lu 8:1-3) Joanna was apparently with the women present at Jesus' impalement. Having prepared spices and oil to take to his tomb, these women were among the first to find that he had been resurrected. The 11 apostles, however, found their report difficult to believe. (Lu 23:49, 55, 56; 24:1-11) Joanna's husband Chuza was steward of Herod Antipas.—Lu 8:3.

JOASH (Jo'ash). This name is spelled two ways in Hebrew, though only as "Joash" in English. The first and more common, *Yoh·'ash'*, is a shortened form of Jehoash. Numbers 1 and 5 listed below are the other spelling, *Yoh·'ash'*.

1. A Benjamite in the family line of Becher. —1Ch 7:6, 8.

2. A descendant of Judah through his third-named son Shelah.—1Ch 2:3; 4:21, 22.

3. The father of Judge Gideon; an Abi-ezrite of the tribe of Manasseh. (Jg 6:11, 15; 7:14; 8:13, 32) Joash was evidently a man of considerable means and influence in the community, possessing an altar dedicated to Baal, also a "sacred pole," and having a household of servants. When his son Gideon secretly tore down this altar and sacred pole, and in their place built an altar to Jehovah upon which he sacrificed a seven-year-old bull, the citizens of the place demanded that Joash hand over his son to be put to death. Joash's answer was: "If [Baal] is God, let him make a legal defense for himself." And with that Joash began calling his son Jerubbaal.—Jg 6:25-32; 8:29.

4. One of the mighty men of the tribe of Benjamin that joined David's forces at Ziklag when the latter was outlawed by Saul; son or descendant of Shemaah.—1Ch 12:1-3.

5. A chief appointed by King David to oversee the oil supplies.—1Ch 27:28, 31.

6. One of those into whose custody the faithful prophet Micaiah was committed for imprisonment by Ahab. He is designated "the king's son." (1Ki 22:26, 27; 2Ch 18:25, 26) This expression may refer to an offspring of King Ahab or it could denote an official of royal descent or someone else closely connected with the royal household.

7. Shortened form of Jehoash, king of Judah and son of Ahaziah. (2Ki 11:2, 3, 21) Joash as an alternate spelling for Jehoash occurs many times in the Masoretic Hebrew text, as is pointed out in footnotes of the *New World Translation*.—2Ki 12: 19; 1Ch 3:11; 2Ch 24:1, 2; see JEHOASH No. 1.

8. Shortened form of Jehoash, king of Israel, son of Jehoahaz and grandson of Jehu. (2Ki 14:1, 8, 9) This alternate spelling (Joash) often occurs in the Masoretic text.—2Ki 13:9, 12, 13; 2Ch 25:17, 18, 21; Ho 1:1; Am 1:1; see JEHOASH No. 2.

JOB [Object of Hostility]. A man living in the land of Uz, in what is now Arabia. (Job 1:1) God said concerning Job: "There is no one like him in the earth, a man blameless and upright, fearing God and turning aside from bad." (Job 1:8) This would indicate that Job lived in Uz at about the time that his distant cousins, the 12 tribes of Israel, were in slavery down in the land of Egypt. By then Joseph the son of Jacob (Israel) had died (1657 B.C.E.) after he had endured much unjust suffering but had kept his blamelessness toward Jehovah God. Moses had not yet risen up as Jehovah's prophet to lead the 12 tribes of Israel out of Egyptian slavery. Between Joseph's death and the time when Moses by his conduct showed himself to be blameless and upright, there was no human with integrity like Job's. It was likely during this period that the conversations involving Job took place between Jehovah and Satan.—Job 1:6-12; 2:1-7.

Moses is generally credited with writing the account of Job's experiences. He could have known about Job when he spent 40 years in Midian and may have heard of Job's final outcome and death when Israel was near Uz toward the end of its wilderness journey. If Moses completed the book of Job about the time of Israel's entry into the Promised Land in 1473 B.C.E. (probably not long after Job's death), this would place the time of Job's trial about 1613 B.C.E., for Job lived 140 years after his trial was over.—Job 42:16, 17.

Job was a relative of Abraham, both being descendants of Shem. Though not an Israelite, Job was a worshiper of Jehovah. He was "the greatest of all the Orientals," possessing great wealth. His family consisted of his wife, seven sons, and three daughters. (Job 1:1-3) He conscientiously performed duties as a priest for his family, offering sacrifices to God in their behalf.—Job 1:4, 5.

Job was a figure of importance in the gate of the city, even aged men and princes giving him respect. (Job 29:5-11) He sat as an impartial judge, executing justice as a champion of the widow, and was like a father to the fatherless boy, the afflicted, and those who had no help. (Job 29:12-17) He kept himself clean from immorality, greedy materialism, and idolatry, and he was generous to the poor and needy.—Job 31:9-28.

Job's Integrity. Job's integrity to Jehovah was challenged by Satan. Then Jehovah, with confidence in that integrity and knowing His own ability to recover and reward Job, permitted Satan to test Job's integrity to the limit, but he did not allow Satan to kill Job. Although Satan, through various means, took away first Job's livestock and servants and then his children (Job 1:13-19), Job never charged God with folly or wrongdoing. Neither did he turn away from God, even when pressure was brought upon him by his own wife and by others. (Job 1:20-22; 2:9, 10) He spoke the truth about God. (Job 42:8) He accepted reproof for being too anxious to declare himself righteous and neglecting to vindicate God (Job 32:2), and he acknowledged his sins to God.—Job 42:1-6.

Jehovah loved Job. At the end of Job's faithful course under test, God constituted him a priest for his three companions who had contended with him, and God restored Job to his former status. He again had a fine family (evidently by the same wife) and double the wealth he had previously possessed. All his relatives and former associates returned to pay respect to him and to bring him gifts. (Job 42:7-15) He lived to see his sons and his grandsons to four generations.—Job 42:16.

Through the prophet Ezekiel, God pointed to Job as an example of righteousness. (Eze 14:14, 20) His patient endurance of suffering is set before Christians as a pattern, and his happy outcome is pointed to as magnifying Jehovah's affection and mercy. (Jas 5:11) The account of his trialsome experience gives great comfort and strength to Christians, and many Bible principles are highlighted and illuminated by the book bearing his name.

JOB, BOOK OF. Written by Moses, according to both Jewish and early Christian scholars. Its poetry, language, and style indicate that it was originally written in Hebrew. The many similarities to the Pentateuch in the prose portion of the book tend to point to Moses as the writer. During his 40-year stay in Midian, Moses could have had access to the facts about Job's trial, and he likely learned of the outcome of Job's life when Israel came near Uz on the way to the Promised Land, in 1473 B.C.E.

Arrangement. The book of Job is unique in that it consists largely of a debate between a true servant of Jehovah God and three others who claimed to serve God but who erred in doctrine in their attempts to correct Job. Job, they mistakenly thought, was being punished by God for some grievous hidden sin. Thus, arguing on this basis, they actually became Job's persecutors. (Job 19:1-5, 22) The debate consists of a series of three rounds of speeches, in which all four speakers participate, except that Zophar does not speak in the last round having been silenced by Job's argument. Thereafter all are corrected by Jehovah's spokesman Elihu and finally by God himself.

It is clear, therefore, that one has to bear in mind when reading or quoting from the book that the arguments presented by Eliphaz, Bildad, and Zophar are erroneous. At times these three companions of Job state true facts, but in a setting and with an application that is wrong. Satan used this tactic against Jesus Christ when he "took him along into the holy city, and he stationed him upon the battlement of the temple and said to him: 'If you are a son of God, hurl yourself down; for it is written, "He will give his angels a charge concerning you, and they will carry you on their hands, that you may at no time strike your foot against a stone."' Jesus said to him: 'Again it is written, "You must not put Jehovah your God to the test."'"—Mt 4:5-7.

The companions of Job said that God punishes the wicked. This is true. (2Pe 2:9) But they concluded that all suffering a person undergoes is a result of sins on his part—that God is thereby

---

HIGHLIGHTS OF JOB

The account of Job's experiences when Satan challenged his integrity before Jehovah

Likely recorded by Moses during Israel's wandering in the wilderness, although the trial of Job must have occurred some years before Moses' birth

---

Job's prosperity and well-being end when Jehovah grants Satan permission to test Job (1:1–2:10)

Satan claims that Job's uprightness is motivated simply by self-interest

Job loses cattle, flocks, and his ten children all in one day, but he keeps integrity

He is then afflicted with a loathsome, painful disease but refuses to curse God; thus, Job remains faithful

Eliphaz, Bildad, and Zophar, three companions of Job, come together by appointment to "sympathize" with him (2:11–3:26)

They sit around him in silence for seven days

Job breaks the silence, cursing the day of his birth

He wonders why God allows him to go on living

The three so-called comforters debate at length with Job (4:1–31:40)

They contend that he is suffering because of his sins, arguing that Job must be in the wrong since God is treating him as an enemy

They try to persuade Job of this by resorting to false reasoning and slander and by appealing to tradition and visions they claim to have seen

The three companions urge Job to confess his wrongdoing and change his ways; then, they say, he will regain his former prosperity

Job insists that he is upright; he does not understand why Jehovah allows him to suffer, but he silences the false counsel of his three companions

In his final words, Job contrasts his former days as a respected elder with his present period of affliction and humiliation; he points out how careful he has been to avoid sin

Elihu, a young bystander, corrects Job and his companions (32:1–37:24)

He shows that Job was in the wrong when he justified himself rather than God, and he upbraids Job's three companions for failing to answer Job correctly

Elihu upholds Jehovah's justice, impartiality, glory, and almightiness

Jehovah himself now speaks out of a windstorm (38:1–42:6)

Jehovah asks where Job was when the earth was created, and whether he understands the wonderful ways of wild things, thus demonstrating man's littleness in comparison with God's greatness

He then asks whether Job should find fault with Him

Job admits that he spoke without a proper understanding; he repents "in dust and ashes"

Job's trial ends, and his integrity is rewarded (42:7-17)

Jehovah expresses displeasure to Eliphaz, Bildad, and Zophar because they spoke untruthfully; he directs them to make sacrifices and to ask Job to pray on their behalf

Job is healed when he prays for his companions

He comes to be blessed with twice as much in flocks and herds as formerly, as well as with ten more children, seven sons and three daughters

administering punishment to him. Suffering, they said, is an evidence that an individual has specially sinned. They spoke untruthfully concerning God. (Job 42:7) They slandered Him. As they presented God, he was lacking in mercy. Their claim was that God has no delight in the integrity-keeping man and that he has no trust in His servants, even in angels. This denies the many Scriptural statements revealing Jehovah's love for his intelligent servants. An example of God's confidence and trust in his faithful worshipers is seen in his conversations with Satan, in which he called attention to Job and expressed the greatest confidence in Job's loyalty when giving the Devil permission to test Job. Note, however, that he protected Job's life. (Job 2:6) The Christian writer James says of God's dealings with Job: "Jehovah is very tender in affection and merciful."—Jas 5:11.

Importance. The book of Job is essential, in conjunction with Genesis 3:1-6 and other scriptures, in revealing the great issue of the righteousness of God in his exercise of sovereignty as well as the manner in which the integrity of God's earthly servants is involved in the issue. This issue Job did not understand, but he, nevertheless, did not allow his three companions to make him doubt that he had been a man of integrity. (Job 27:5) He did not understand why his calamity came upon him, since he was no practicer of sin. He was off balance on the matter of self-justification, no doubt being pushed farther in that direction by the constant charges of his three companions. He

was also mistaken in insisting on receiving an answer from God as to why he was suffering, when he should have realized that no one can rightly say to Jehovah: "Why did you make me this way?" (Ro 9:20) Nevertheless, Jehovah mercifully answered Job, both through his servant Elihu and by speaking to Job from the windstorm. The book therefore strongly drives home the

Book of Job	Point of comparison	Other Bible references
3:17-19	The dead know not anything but are as those asleep	Ec 9:5, 10; Joh 11:11-14; 1Co 15:20
10:4	God does not judge from man's viewpoint	1Sa 16:7
10:8, 9, 11, 12	God's great care in forming man	Ps 139:13-16
12:23	God lets the nations grow powerful and even unite against him so that he can justly destroy them at one stroke	Re 17:13, 14, 17
14:1-5	Man is born in sin and in bondage to death	Ps 51:5; Ro 5:12
14:13-15	Resurrection of the dead	1Co 15:21-23
17:9	The righteous one is not stumbled, no matter what others do	Ps 119:165
19:25	Jehovah's purpose to redeem (repurchase, release) faithful mankind	Ro 3:24; 1Co 1:30
21:23-26	All men subject to the same eventuality; all are the same in death	Ec 9:2, 3
24:3-12	Affliction by wicked; Christians so treated	2Co 6:4-10; 11:24-27
24:13-17	Wicked love darkness rather than light; light terrifies them	Joh 3:19
26:6	All things are exposed before the eyes of Jehovah	Heb 4:13
27:8-10	Apostate one will not genuinely call on God nor be heard by him	Heb 6:4-6
27:12	Those seeing "visions" of own heart, not from God, utter vain things	Jer 23:16
27:16, 17	The righteous will inherit the wealth amassed by the wicked	De 6:10, 11; Pr 13:22
Chap 28	Man cannot find the true wisdom from 'book of divine creation,' only from God and fear of him	Ec 12:13; 1Co 2:11-16
30:1, 2, 8, 12	Worthless, senseless idlers are used to persecute God's servants	Ac 17:5
32:22	Bestowing unscriptural titles is wrong	Mt 23:8-12
34:14, 15	Life of all flesh is in Jehovah's hand	Ps 104:29, 30; Isa 64:8; Ac 17:25, 28
34:19	Jehovah is not partial	Ac 10:34
34:24, 25	Jehovah takes down, sets up rulers as he wills	Da 2:21; 4:25
36:24; 40:8	Declaring of God's righteousness the important thing	Ro 3:23-26
42:2	With God all things are possible	Mt 19:26
42:3	God is unsearchable in wisdom	Isa 55:9; Ro 11:33

Other noteworthy comparisons are: Job 7:17 and Ps 8:4; Job 9:24 and 1Jo 5:19; Job 10:8 and Ps 119:73; Job 26:8 and Pr 30:4; Job 28:12, 13, 15-19 and Pr 3:13-15; Job 39:30 and Mt 24:28.

wrongness of attempting to justify oneself before God.—Job 40:8.

Authenticity and Value. Ezekiel refers to Job, and James makes mention of him. (Eze 14:14, 20; Jas 5:11) Arguing powerfully for the book's canonicity is the fact that the Jews accepted it as of equal authority with the other inspired books of the Hebrew Scriptures, even though Job was not an Israelite.

Perhaps the strongest evidence of the book's genuineness exists in its harmony with the rest of the Bible. It also reveals much about the beliefs and customs of patriarchal society. More than that, it greatly helps the Bible student to get a better understanding of Jehovah's purposes through a comparison with other Bible statements. There are a remarkable number of points that are parallel in thought with other Bible passages, and some of these are listed on the accompanying chart.

JOBAB (Jo'bab).

1. A descendant of Shem through Joktan. (Ge 10:21, 25, 29; 1Ch 1:23) The exact region settled by the offspring of Jobab is not known today.

2. "Son of Zerah from Bozrah"; an Edomite monarch who reigned sometime before Saul ruled as Israel's first king. Jobab succeeded "Bela the son of Beor" to the throne.—Ge 36:31-34; 1Ch 1:43-45.

3. King of Madon, a city in northern Palestine. Jobab and other monarchs joined Jabin the king of Hazor in an offensive against the Israelites but suffered defeat at the waters of Merom.—Jos 11:1-8; 12:19.

4. Son of the Benjamite Shaharaim by his wife Hodesh.—1Ch 8:1, 8, 9.

5. A descendant of the Benjamite Shaharaim through Elpaal.—1Ch 8:1, 8, 11, 18.

JOCHEBED (Joch'e·bed) [possibly, Jehovah Is Glory].

A daughter of Levi who married Amram of the same tribe and became the mother of Miriam, Aaron, and Moses. (Ex 6:20; Nu 26:59) Jochebed was a woman of faith; she trusted in her God Jehovah. In defiance of Pharaoh's decree she refused to kill her baby, later named Moses, and after three months, when he could no longer be concealed in the house, she placed him in an ark of papyrus and put it among the reeds along the bank of the Nile. Pharaoh's daughter found the baby and claimed him for herself, but, as it worked out, Moses' own mother was asked to nurse him. As the child grew, Jochebed, together with her husband, was very diligent to teach her children the principles of pure worship, as is reflected in their later lives.—Ex 2:1-10.

According to the Masoretic text, Jochebed was the sister of Amram's father Kohath; that is to say, Amram married his aunt, which was not unlawful at the time. (Ex 6:18, 20) However, some scholars believe that Jochebed was Amram's cousin rather than his aunt, for the Greek *Septuagint* so reads, conveying the same idea as the Syriac *Peshitta* and Jewish traditions. For example, Exodus 6:20 reads in part: "Jochabed the daughter of his father's brother." (*LXX*, Bagster) "Amram took his uncle's daughter Jokhaber." (*La*) "When Amram married he took his cousin Jokabad." (*Fn*) "Amram married a kinswoman of his called Jochabed." (*Kx*) A footnote of Rotherham on the expression "his father's sister" says: "Prob[ably] merely a female member of his father's family." Thomas Scott in his *Explanatory Notes* (1832) says: "According to the Septuagint and the Jewish traditions, Jochebed was *cousin*, not *aunt* to Amram." "The best critics suppose that Jochebed was the *cousin-german* of Amram, and not his *aunt.*" (Clarke's *Commentary*) When Numbers 26:59 says Jochebed was "Levi's daughter," it could mean "granddaughter," as in so many other places in the Scriptures where "son" is used to denote a "grandson." In his translation, F. Fenton comments that the expression 'born to Levi' in this same verse, "in the Hebrew idiom of language, does not mean to Levi personally, but simply a descendant of the Tribe. The length of time makes it impossible for her to have been Levi's personal child."

If, on the other hand, the Masoretic text is correct at Exodus 6:20, Jochebed was Amram's aunt and not his cousin. Granting the possibility that Jochebed's father was Levi, her mother must have been someone younger than Kohath's mother. In this case Jochebed, though only a half sister to Kohath, would have been an aunt to Amram.

JODA (Jo'da).

Ancestor of Jesus' mother Mary; listed third in descent from Zerubbabel.—Lu 3:26, 27.

JOED (Jo'ed) [Jehovah Is a Witness].

A Benjamite whose descendant Sallu was a postexilic resident of Jerusalem.—Ne 11:4, 7.

JOEL (Jo'el) [Jehovah Is God].

1. A descendant of Issachar and family head in his tribe.—1Ch 7:1-4.

2. A descendant of Levi's son Kohath; "son of Azariah" and forefather of No. 5.—1Ch 6:36-38.

3. A Reubenite whose descendant Beerah was taken into exile by Assyrian King Tiglath-pileser (Tiglath-pileser III).—1Ch 5:3-10.

4. A headman of the Gadites living in Bashan. —1Ch 5:11, 12.

5. The firstborn son of the prophet Samuel; a descendant of No. 2 and father of Heman the Levitical singer. (1Ch 6:28, 33, 36; 15:17) Joel and his younger brother Abijah had been appointed by their father to be judges, but their dishonesty in office gave the people an excuse to ask for a human king.—1Sa 8:1-5.

At 1 Chronicles 6:28 the Masoretic text (and certain translations) says "Vashni" was Samuel's firstborn. Scholars, however, generally agree that "Joel" was in the original Hebrew, a reading retained by the Syriac *Peshitta* and the Lagardian edition of the Greek *Septuagint.* (Compare 1Sa 8:2.) Similarity between "Joel" and the ending of a preceding word in the text ("Samuel") possibly caused a scribe inadvertently to drop the name "Joel" altogether. Seemingly, he then mistook the Hebrew word *wehash·she·ni'* (meaning "and the second [son]") for the proper name "Vashni" and inserted the letter *waw* (and) before the name Abijah.

6. One of David's mighty men; brother of Nathan.—1Ch 11:26, 38.

7. A Gershonite Levite of the house of Ladan; son of Jehiel(i). (1Ch 23:7, 8) Joel the chief and 130 of his brothers sanctified themselves and helped bring the ark of the covenant to Jerusalem. (1Ch 15:4, 7, 11-14) Joel and his brother Zetham were later appointed as overseers of the sanctuary treasures.—1Ch 26:21, 22.

8. A prince, during David's reign, of that part of Manasseh W of the Jordan; son of Pedaiah.—1Ch 27:20-22.

9. A prophet of Jehovah and writer of the Bible book bearing his name. He was the son of Pethuel. —Joe 1:1; see JOEL, BOOK OF.

10. A Kohathite Levite; son of Azariah. In the first year of Hezekiah, Joel helped take the unclean objects removed from the temple by the priests to the Kidron Valley for disposal.—2Ch 29:1, 3, 12, 15, 16.

11. One of several Simeonite chieftains who, in Hezekiah's day, took by force the land of certain Hamites and the Meunim to expand their pasturage.—1Ch 4:24, 35, 38-41.

12. One of the sons of Nebo who dismissed their foreign wives and sons in Ezra's day.—Ezr 10:43, 44.

13. An overseer of those Benjamites living in Jerusalem during Nehemiah's governorship; son of Zichri.—Ne 11:4, 7-9.

JOEL, BOOK OF.

An inspired book of the Hebrew Scriptures written by "Joel the son of Pethuel." (Joe 1:1) Virtually nothing is known about this prophet's life. From his references to Judah, Jerusalem, and Jehovah's house there, it may be inferred that he prophesied in Judah and perhaps resided in Jerusalem. (1:9, 14; 2:17, 32; 3:1, 2, 16-20) The fact that he mentioned "the low plain of Jehoshaphat" (3:2, 12) implies that he wrote his book after Jehovah's great victory on behalf of King Jehoshaphat. But the exact period involved is in question.

Time of Writing. Scholars variously assign the book of Joel dates from before 800 B.C.E. to about 400 B.C.E. Regarding their arguments in favor of a late or an early composition for the book, *The International Standard Bible Encyclopaedia* (edited by James Orr, 1960, Vol. III, p. 1690) observes: "Many of the arguments adduced are of a negative kind, i.e. consideration of what the prophet does *not* mention or refer to [including the Chaldeans, the Assyrians, a Judean king, and the ten-tribe kingdom], and the argument from silence is notoriously precarious." Similarly, whether Joel quoted other prophets or was quoted by them cannot be established with certainty. A date after the Babylonian exile would be indicated if Joel (2:32) quoted Obadiah (17). On the other hand, not only Obadiah but even the much earlier prophet Amos (compare Joe 3:16 with Am 1:2) may have quoted from Joel. This would mean that Joel wrote his book no later than the time of Uzziah (Am 1:1), perhaps about 820 B.C.E. Though not conclusive, the place occupied by the book of Joel in the Hebrew canon between Hosea and Amos seems to favor the earlier period.

Authenticity. The Jews did not question the canonicity of the book of Joel but placed it second among the "minor" prophets. It also harmonizes completely with the rest of the Scriptures, as is evident from the numerous parallels between Joel and other Bible books. (Compare Joe 2:2 with Zep 1:14, 15; Joe 2:4, 5, 10 with Re 9:2, 7-9; Joe 2:11 with Mal 4:5; Joe 2:12 with Jer 4:1; Joe 2:13 with Ex 34:6, Nu 14:18, Ps 86:15, and 106:45; Joe 2:31 with Isa 13:9, 10, Mt 24:29, 30, and Re 6:12-17.) The fulfillment of Joel's prophecies furnishes another argument for its authenticity. As foretold, Tyre, Philistia, and Edom experienced Jehovah's judgments. (Joe 3:4, 19; for details, see EDOM, EDOMITES; PHILISTIA, PHILISTINES; TYRE.) On the day of Pentecost in the year 33 C.E., the apostle Peter showed that the outpouring of God's spirit upon the disciples of Jesus Christ was a fulfillment of Joel's prophecy. (Joe 2:28-32; Ac 2:17-21) Later,

---

HIGHLIGHTS OF JOEL

A vivid prophecy emphasizing Jehovah's vengeance and his mercy

Written possibly about 820 B.C.E., nine years after Uzziah became king and about a century after Jehovah's great victory over Moab, Ammon, and the inhabitants of Seir in the days of Jehoshaphat

Locust invasion to strip the land; the day of Jehovah is near (1:1–2:11)

The coming plague will be talked about for generations

The vegetation of the land will be stripped so that grain and drink offerings will cease at Jehovah's house

Priests are told to mourn and cry to Jehovah for help

Jehovah's day is marked by a destructive invasion of "his military force"

Israel invited to return to Jehovah; His spirit to be poured out (2:12-32)

The inhabitants of Zion are invited to "come back" to

Jehovah; he will restore their prosperity and protect them from "the northerner"

Jehovah will pour out his spirit on his people, and he will give portents in the heavens and on earth before his "great and fear-inspiring day"

Those calling on Jehovah's name will escape during his great day

The nations will be judged in "the low plain of Jehoshaphat" (3:1-21)

The nations will be judged for mistreating God's people

They are challenged to prepare themselves for war against Jehovah and to come down to the low plain of Jehoshaphat; there they will be crushed like grapes in a winepress

At that time Jehovah will be a refuge for his people

Egypt and Edom will become a wilderness, whereas Judah will be inhabited and produce abundantly; Jehovah will reside in Zion

---

the apostle Paul applied the prophetic words found at Joel 2:32 to both Jews and non-Jews who call upon Jehovah in faith.—Ro 10:12, 13.

JOELAH (Jo·eʹlah). One of the warriors who came to David at Ziklag; son of Jeroham of Gedor. —1Ch 12:1, 7.

JOEZER (Jo·eʹzer) [Jehovah Is Help]. One of the warriors who joined David at Ziklag when he was still under restrictions due to Saul; a Korahite. —1Ch 12:1, 2, 6.

JOGBEHAH (Jogʹbe·hah). One of the fortified cities with stone flock pens that were built or rebuilt by the Gadites before their crossing the Jordan to assist in the conquest of Canaan. (Nu 32:34-36) At a later period Judge Gideon's forces passed Jogbehah prior to their surprise attack on the Midianite camp at Karkor. (Jg 8:10, 11) Jogbehah is identified with el-Jubeihat, situated about 1,050 m (3,440 ft) above sea level and some 10 km (6 mi) NW of modern ʽAmman (Rabbah).

JOGLI (Jogʹli) [May Jehovah Uncover (Reveal)]. A Danite whose son Bukki was chieftain of the tribe of Dan for dividing up the land of Canaan. —Nu 34:18, 22, 29.

JOHA (Joʹha) [shortened form of Jehohanan, meaning "Jehovah Has Shown Favor; Jehovah Has Been Gracious"].

1. One of David's mighty men; a Tizite.—1Ch 11:26, 45.

2. Head of a Benjamite family in Jerusalem; son or descendant of Beriah.—1Ch 8:1, 16, 28.

JOHANAN (Jo·haʹnan) [shortened form of Jehohanan, meaning "Jehovah Has Shown Favor; Jehovah Has Been Gracious"]. The English name John stems from this Hebrew name.

1. An ambidextrous, mighty Benjamite, one of the skilled warriors who joined David at Ziklag. —1Ch 12:1-4.

2. A Gadite officer, one of 11 exceptional fighters who came to David's side in the wilderness. —1Ch 12:8, 12-15.

3. A high priest. It was likely his son Azariah who was high priest when King Uzziah acted presumptuously.—1Ch 6:9, 10; 2Ch 26:19, 20.

4. Firstborn son of King Josiah. (1Ch 3:15) Since he is nowhere mentioned in connection with succession to the throne of Judah, as are his three younger brothers, he must have died before his father's death.—2Ki 23:30, 34; 24:17; Jer 22:11; see JOSIAH No. 1.

5. One of the chiefs of the military forces remaining in Judah after the general deportation to Babylon in the summer of 607 B.C.E. This son of Kareah readily supported the appointment of Gedaliah and, on learning of Ishmael's plot to assassinate the governor, asked Gedaliah for permission to kill Ishmael secretly but was denied it. (Jer 40:7, 8, 13-16) Gedaliah was assassinated, Johanan led the forces to avenge him, and persons whom Ishmael had taken captive were recovered; but the assassin himself escaped to Ammon. (Jer 41:11-16) Fearing reprisals from the Babylonians, Johanan and the others asked the prophet Jeremi-

ah what they should do, but, rather than follow Jehovah's advice to remain in the land, they fled to Egypt, taking Jeremiah with them.—Jer 42:1–43:7; 2Ki 25:23-26.

6. Son of Hakkatan and head of the 110 males of the paternal house of Azgad who returned with him to Jerusalem, accompanying Ezra in 468 B.C.E.—Ezr 8:1, 12.

7. Grandson of Eliashib, the high priest contemporary with Nehemiah. His being called Jonathan in Nehemiah 12:11 is probably due to a scribal error, as the names "Johanan" and "Jonathan" are very similar in Hebrew. Johanan is mentioned in Nehemiah 12:22, 23 and in a letter found among the Elephantine Papyri, where he is addressed as high priest.—*Jewish Antiquities,* by F. Josephus, XI, 297 (vii, 1).

8. Son of Elioenai; Johanan appears in a list of the house of David that includes Zerubbabel and his descendants.—1Ch 3:1, 10, 19, 24.

JOHN [English equivalent of Jehohanan, meaning "Jehovah Has Shown Favor; Jehovah Has Been Gracious"].

1. John the Baptizer, son of Zechariah and Elizabeth; the forerunner of Jesus. Both of John's parents were of the priestly house of Aaron. Zechariah was a priest of the division of Abijah.—Lu 1:5, 6.

Miraculous Birth. In the year 3 B.C.E., during the assigned time of service of the division of Abijah, it became Zechariah's turn to enjoy the rare privilege of offering incense in the sanctuary. As he stood before the altar of incense, the angel Gabriel appeared with the announcement that he would have a son, who was to be called John. This son would be a lifetime Nazirite, as Samson had been. He was to be great before Jehovah, to go before Him "to get ready for Jehovah a prepared people." John's birth would be by a miracle of God, since Zechariah and Elizabeth were both of advanced age.—Lu 1:7-17.

When Elizabeth was six months pregnant, she was visited by her relative Mary, then pregnant by holy spirit. As soon as she heard her relative's greeting, Elizabeth's unborn child leapt in her womb, and filled with holy spirit, she acknowledged that the child to be born to Mary would be her "Lord."—Lu 1:26, 36, 39-45.

At the birth of Elizabeth's child, the neighbors and relatives wanted to call it by its father's name, but Elizabeth said: "No, indeed! but he shall be called John." Then its father was asked what he wanted the child to be called. As the angel had said, Zechariah had been unable to speak from the time of Gabriel's announcement to him, so he wrote on a tablet: "John is its name." Then Zechariah's mouth was opened so that he began to speak. At this all recognized that the hand of Jehovah was with the child.—Lu 1:18-20, 57-66.

Beginning of His Ministry. John spent the early years of his life in the hill country of Judea, where his parents lived. He "went on growing and getting strong in spirit, and he continued in the deserts until the day of showing himself openly to Israel." (Lu 1:39, 80) According to Luke, John began his ministry in the 15th year of the reign of Tiberius Caesar. John would have been then about 30 years old. Though there is no record that John engaged in priestly service at the temple, this was the age for priests to enter into full duty. (Nu 4: 2, 3) Augustus died on August 17, 14 C.E., and Tiberius was named emperor by the Roman Senate on September 15; thus his 15th year would run from the latter part of 28 C.E. to August or September of 29 C.E. Since Jesus (also at the age of about 30) presented himself for baptism in the autumn, John, six months older, must have begun his ministry in the spring of 29 C.E.—Lu 3:1-3, 23.

John began his preaching in the Wilderness of Judea, saying: "Repent, for the kingdom of the heavens has drawn near." (Mt 3:1, 2) He wore clothing of camel hair and a leather girdle around his loins, similar to the dress of the prophet Elijah. John's food consisted of insect locusts and wild honey. (2Ki 1:8; Mt 3:4; Mr 1:6) He was a teacher and was, accordingly, called "Rabbi" by his disciples.—Joh 3:26.

Purpose of His Work. John preached baptism for forgiveness of sins for those repenting, confining his baptism to Jews and proselytes to the Jews' religion. (Mr 1:1-5; Ac 13:24) John's being sent was a manifestation of God's loving-kindness toward the Jews. They were in covenant relationship with Jehovah but were guilty of sins committed against the Law covenant. John brought to their attention that they had broken the covenant, and he urged honesthearted ones to repentance. Their water baptism symbolized this repentance. Then they were in line to recognize the Messiah. (Ac 19:4) All sorts of persons came to John to be baptized, including harlots and tax collectors. (Mt 21:32) There also came to the baptism Pharisees and Sadducees, against whom John directed a scathing message of denunciation and to whom he spoke of the judgment that was near at hand. He did not spare them, calling them "offspring of vipers" and pointing out that their reliance on fleshly descent from Abraham was of no value. —Mt 3:7-12.

John taught those coming to him that they should share things and not commit extortion, that they should be satisfied with their provisions and harass no one. (Lu 3:10-14) He also taught his baptized followers how to pray to God. (Lu 11:1) At this time "the people were in expectation and all were reasoning in their hearts about John: 'May he perhaps be the Christ?'" John denied that he was and declared that the One to follow him would be far greater. (Lu 3:15-17) When priests and Levites came to him in Bethany across the Jordan, they asked if he was Elijah or if he was "The Prophet," and he confessed that he was not. —Joh 1:19-28.

John performed no miracles, as had Elijah (Joh 10:40-42), yet he came with the spirit and power of Elijah. He performed a powerful work in 'turning the hearts of fathers to children and the disobedient ones to the practical wisdom of righteous ones.' He fulfilled the purpose for which he had been sent, "to get ready for Jehovah a prepared people." Indeed, 'many of the sons of Israel he turned back to Jehovah their God.' (Lu 1:16, 17) He went before Jehovah's representative, Jesus Christ.

John Introduces "the Lamb of God." In the autumn of 29 C.E., Jesus came to John to be baptized. John at first objected, knowing his own sinfulness and the righteousness of Jesus. But Jesus insisted. God had promised John a sign so that he could identify the Son of God. (Mt 3:13; Mr 1:9; Lu 3:21; Joh 1:33) When Jesus was baptized, the sign was fulfilled: John saw God's spirit coming down upon Jesus and heard God's own voice declaring Jesus to be His Son. Evidently no others were present at Jesus' baptism.—Mt 3:16, 17; Mr 1:9-11; Joh 1:32-34; 5:31, 37.

For about 40 days after his baptism, Jesus was in the wilderness. On His return, John pointed Jesus out to his disciples as "the Lamb of God that takes away the sin of the world." (Joh 1:29) The following day Andrew and another disciple, probably John the son of Zebedee, were introduced to the Son of God. (Joh 1:35-40) Thus John the Baptizer, as a faithful "doorkeeper" to the Israelite sheepfold, began to turn his disciples over to "the fine shepherd."—Joh 10:1-3, 11.

While Jesus' disciples did baptizing in Judean country, John was also baptizing in Aenon near Salim. (Joh 3:22-24) When a report came to John that Jesus was making many disciples, John did not become jealous but replied: "This joy of mine has been made full. That one must go on increasing, but I must go on decreasing."—Joh 3:26-30.

Closing Days of His Ministry. This statement of John's proved to be true. After a year or more of active ministry, John was forcibly taken out of the field. He was thrown into prison by Herod Antipas because John had reproved Antipas for his adulterous marriage to Herodias, whom he had taken away from his brother Philip. Antipas, nominally a Jewish proselyte accountable to the Law, was afraid of John, knowing him to be a righteous man.—Mr 6:17-20; Lu 3:19, 20.

When John was in prison he heard of Jesus' performing powerful works, including resurrecting a widow's son at Nain. Desiring verification from Jesus himself, he sent two of his disciples to ask Jesus: "Are you the Coming One, or are we to expect a different one?" Jesus did not answer directly; but before John's disciples he healed many persons, even casting out demons. Then he told the disciples to report that the blind, deaf, and lame were being healed and that the good news was being preached. Thus, not by mere words, but by the testimony of Jesus' works, John was comforted and reassured that Jesus was truly the Messiah (Christ). (Mt 11:2-6; Lu 7:18-23) After John's messengers had left, Jesus revealed to the crowds that John was more than a prophet, that he was, in fact, the one of whom Jehovah's prophet Malachi had written. He also applied the prophecy of Isaiah 40:3 to John, as John's father Zechariah had previously done.—Mal 3:1; Mt 11:7-10; Lu 1:67, 76; 7:24-27.

Jesus Christ also explained to his disciples that John's coming was a fulfillment of the prophecy at Malachi 4:5, 6, that God would send Elijah the prophet before the coming of the great and fear-inspiring day of Jehovah. Nevertheless, great as John was ("Among those born of women there has not been raised up a greater than John the Baptist"), he would not be one of "the bride" class who will share with Christ in his heavenly Kingdom rule (Re 21:9-11; 22:3-5), for, Jesus said, "a person that is a lesser one in the kingdom of the heavens is greater than he is." (Mt 11:11-15; 17:10-13; Lu 7:28-30) Indirectly Jesus also defended John against the charge that John had a demon.—Mt 11:16-19; Lu 7:31-35.

Some time after this occasion, Herodias carried out her grudge against John. During Herod's birthday celebration the daughter of Herodias delighted Herod with her dancing, upon which Herod swore to her that he would give her whatever she asked. Influenced by her mother, she asked for the head of John. Herod, out of regard for his oath and for those present, granted her request. John was beheaded in prison and his head was delivered on a platter to the girl, who brought it to her mother. John's disciples later came and removed John's body and buried him, reporting the matter to Jesus.—Mt 14:1-12; Mr 6:21-29.

After John's death Herod heard of Jesus' ministry of preaching, healing, and casting out demons. He was frightened, fearing that Jesus was actually John who had been raised from the dead. Thereafter he greatly desired to see Jesus, not to hear his preaching, but because he was not sure of this conclusion.—Mt 14:1, 2; Mr 6:14-16; Lu 9:7-9.

John's Baptism Ends. John's baptism continued until Pentecost day, 33 C.E., when the holy spirit was poured out. From that time on, baptism "in the name of the Father and of the Son and of the holy spirit" was preached. (Mt 28:19; Ac 2:21, 38) Those who thereafter were baptized in John's baptism had to be rebaptized in the name of the Lord Jesus in order to become receivers of holy spirit.—Ac 19:1-7.

2. Father of the apostle Simon Peter. At John 1:42 and 21:15-17 he is called John, according to the Sinaitic Manuscript and the "Old Latin" versions. Some manuscripts and versions call him Jona. Jesus calls him Jonah at Matthew 16:17.

3. The apostle John, son of Zebedee and Salome (compare Mt 27:55, 56; Mr 15:40) and brother of the apostle James—likely James' younger brother, as James is usually named first where both are mentioned. (Mt 10:2; Mr 3:14, 16, 17; Lu 6:14; 8:51; 9:28; Ac 1:13) Zebedee married Salome of the house of David, possibly the natural sister of Mary the mother of Jesus.

Background. John's family seems to have been fairly well situated. His father Zebedee employed hired men in his fishing business, in which he was partner with Simon. (Mr 1:19, 20; Lu 5:9, 10) Zebedee's wife Salome was among the women who accompanied and ministered to Jesus when he was in Galilee (compare Mt 27:55, 56; Mr 15:40, 41), and she took part in bringing spices to prepare Jesus' body for burial. (Mr 16:1) John evidently had a house of his own.—Joh 19:26, 27.

Zebedee and Salome were faithful Hebrews, and the evidence indicates that they raised John in the teaching of the Scriptures. He is generally understood to be the disciple of John the Baptizer that was with Andrew when John announced to them: "See, the Lamb of God!" His ready acceptance of Jesus as the Christ reveals that he had a knowledge of the Hebrew Scriptures. (Joh 1:35, 36, 40-42) While it is never stated that Zebedee became a disciple of either John the Baptizer or of Christ, it appears that he offered no resistance to

his two sons' becoming full-time preachers with Jesus.

When John and Peter were brought before the Jewish rulers, they were viewed as "unlettered and ordinary." This did not mean, however, that they had no education or were unable to read and write, but meant that they had not received their training at the rabbinic schools. It is stated, rather, that "they began to recognize about them that they used to be with Jesus."—Ac 4:13.

Becomes Christ's Disciple. After being introduced to Jesus as the Christ in the fall of 29 C.E., John undoubtedly followed Jesus into Galilee and was an eyewitness to His first miracle at Cana. (Joh 2:1-11) He may have accompanied Jesus from Galilee to Jerusalem, and again on his return through Samaria to Galilee, for the vividness of his account seems to stamp it as that of an eyewitness to the events described. However, the record does not so state. (Joh 2-5) Nevertheless, John did not leave his fishing business for some time after becoming acquainted with Jesus. In the following year, as Jesus walked alongside the Sea of Galilee, James and John were in the boat with their father Zebedee repairing their nets. He called them to the full-time work of being "fishers of men," and the account by Luke informs us: "So they brought the boats back to land, and abandoned everything and followed him." (Mt 4:18-22; Lu 5:10, 11; Mr 1:19, 20) Later they were selected to be apostles of the Lord Jesus Christ.—Mt 10:2-4.

John was one of the three most intimately associated with Jesus. Peter, James, and John were taken to the mountain of transfiguration. (Mt 17:1, 2; Mr 9:2; Lu 9:28, 29) They only of the apostles were allowed to enter the house of Jairus with Jesus. (Mr 5:37; Lu 8:51) They were privileged to be the ones taken by Jesus farther than the others into the garden of Gethsemane on the night of his betrayal, although at that time even they did not realize the full significance of the occasion, falling asleep three times and being awakened by Jesus. (Mt 26:37, 40-45; Mr 14:33, 37-41) John occupied the position next to Jesus at his last Passover and the institution of the Lord's Evening Meal. (Joh 13:23) He was the disciple who, at Jesus' death, received the signal honor of being entrusted with the care of Jesus' mother.—Joh 21:7, 20; 19:26, 27.

Identifying John in His Gospel. In John's Gospel he never refers to himself by his name John. He is spoken of either as one of the sons of Zebedee or as the disciple whom Jesus used to love. When he speaks of John the Baptizer, unlike the other Gospel writers he calls the Baptizer only "John." This would be more natural for one of the same name to do, since no one would misunderstand about whom he was speaking. Others would have to use a surname or title or other descriptive terms to distinguish whom they meant, as John himself does when speaking of one of the Marys. —Joh 11:1, 2; 19:25; 20:1.

Viewing John's writing in this light, it becomes evident that he himself was the unnamed companion of Andrew to whom John the Baptizer introduced Jesus Christ. (Joh 1:35-40) After Jesus' resurrection John passed Peter by as they ran to the tomb to investigate the report that Jesus had risen. (Joh 20:2-8) He was privileged to see the resurrected Jesus that same evening (Joh 20:19; Lu 24:36) and again the following week. (Joh 20:26) He was one of the seven who went back to fishing and to whom Jesus appeared. (Joh 21:1-14) John was also present at the mountain in Galilee after Jesus rose from the dead, and he personally heard the command: "Make disciples of people of all the nations."—Mt 28:16-20.

John's Later History. After Jesus' ascension John was in Jerusalem at the assembling of about 120 disciples when Matthias was chosen by lot and reckoned along with the 11 other apostles. (Ac 1:12-26) He was present at the outpouring of the spirit on the day of Pentecost and saw 3,000 added to the congregation on that day. (Ac 2:1-13, 41) He, along with Peter, stated before the Jewish rulers the principle followed by the congregation of God's people: "Whether it is righteous in the sight of God to listen to you rather than to God, judge for yourselves. But as for us, we cannot stop speaking about the things we have seen and heard." (Ac 4:19, 20) Again, he joined the other apostles in telling the Sanhedrin: "We must obey God as ruler rather than men."—Ac 5:27-32.

After Stephen's death at the hands of enraged Jews, great persecution arose against the congregation in Jerusalem, and the disciples were scattered. But John, with the other apostles, remained in Jerusalem. When the preaching of Philip the evangelizer moved many in Samaria to accept the word of God, the governing body dispatched Peter and John to assist these new disciples to receive the holy spirit. (Ac 8:1-5, 14-17) Paul later said that John was one of those in Jerusalem "who seemed to be pillars" of the congregation. John, as a member of the governing body, gave Paul and Barnabas "the right hand of sharing together" as they were sent on their mission to preach to the nations (Gentiles). (Ga 2:9) In about 49 C.E., John was present at the conference of the governing body on the issue of circumcision for Gentile converts.—Ac 15:5, 6, 28, 29.

While Jesus Christ was still on earth he had indicated that John would survive the other apostles. (Joh 21:20-22) And John did serve Jehovah faithfully for some 70 years. Toward the end of his life he was exiled on the isle of Patmos, where he came to be "for speaking about God and bearing witness to Jesus." (Re 1:9) This proves that he was energetically active in preaching the good news, even at a very old age (in about 96 C.E.).

While on Patmos, John was favored with the marvelous vision of Revelation, which he faithfully wrote down. (Re 1:1, 2) It is generally believed that he was exiled by Emperor Domitian and was released by Domitian's successor, Emperor Nerva (96-98 C.E.). According to tradition, he went to Ephesus, where he wrote his Gospel and his three letters entitled the First, Second, and Third of John, about 98 C.E. Traditionally, it is believed that he died at Ephesus in about 100 C.E. during the reign of Emperor Trajan.

Personality. Scholars have generally concluded that John was a nonactive person, sentimental, and introspective. As one commentator puts it: "John, with his contemplative, stately, ideal mind, went angel-like through life." (Lange's *Commentary on the Holy Scriptures,* translated and edited by P. Schaff, 1976, Vol. 9, p. 6) They base their evaluation of John's personality on the fact that John speaks so much about love, and because he does not appear so prominently in the Acts of Apostles as do Peter and Paul. Also, they note that he seems to have let Peter take the lead in speaking when they were together.

It is true that when Peter and John were together, Peter was always foremost as the spokesman. But the accounts do not say that John was *silent.* Rather, when before the rulers and older men both Peter and John spoke without fear. (Ac 4:13, 19) Likewise, John spoke boldly, as did the other apostles before the Sanhedrin, although Peter is specifically mentioned by name. (Ac 5:29) And as to being the active, energetic type, did he not anxiously outrun Peter in reaching Jesus' tomb? —Joh 20:2-8.

Early in their ministry as apostles, Jesus gave the surname Boanerges (meaning "Sons of Thunder") to John and his brother James. (Mr 3:17) This title certainly does not denote any soft sentimentality or lack of vigor but, rather, dynamism of personality. When a Samaritan village refused to receive Jesus, these "Sons of Thunder" were ready to call down fire from heaven to annihilate its inhabitants. Previously, John had tried to prevent a man from expelling demons in Jesus' name. Jesus gave reproof and correction in each case. —Lu 9:49-56.

The two brothers on those occasions showed misunderstanding and, to a great extent, lacked the balance and the loving, merciful spirit that they later developed. Nevertheless, on these two occasions the brothers manifested a spirit of loyalty and a decisive, vigorous personality that, channeled in the right direction, made them strong, energetic, faithful witnesses. James died a martyr's death at the hands of Herod Agrippa I (Ac 12:1, 2), and John endured as a pillar "in the tribulation and kingdom and endurance in company with Jesus" as the last living apostle.—Re 1:9.

When James and John apparently got their mother to request that they sit next to Christ in his Kingdom, they demonstrated an ambitious spirit that made the other apostles indignant. But it afforded Jesus a fine opportunity to explain that the one great among them would be the one who served the others. Then he pointed out that even He came to minister and to give his life a ransom for many. (Mt 20:20-28; Mr 10:35-45) However selfish their desire was, the incident reveals their faith in the reality of the Kingdom.

Certainly if John's personality had been as it is painted by religious commentators—weak, impractical, lacking in energy, introverted—Jesus Christ would not likely have used him to write the stirring, powerful book of Revelation, in which Christ repeatedly encourages Christians to be conquerors of the world, tells of the good news to be preached worldwide, and issues forth the thunderous judgments of God.

It is true that John speaks about love more than the other Gospel writers. This does not give evidence of any soft sentimentality. Conversely, love is a strong quality. The entire Law and the Prophets were based on love. (Mt 22:36-40) "Love never fails." (1Co 13:8) Love "is a perfect bond of union." (Col 3:14) Love, of the kind that John advocates, sticks to principle and is capable of strong reproof, correction, and discipline, as well as kindness and mercy.

Wherever he appears in the three synoptic Gospel accounts, as well as in all of his own writings, John always manifests the same strong love and loyalty toward Jesus Christ and his Father Jehovah. Loyalty and hatred of that which is bad are manifest in his noting of bad motives or traits in the actions of others. He alone tells us that it was Judas who grumbled at Mary's use of expensive ointment to anoint Jesus' feet and that the reason for Judas' complaint was that he carried the mon-

ey box and was a thief. (Joh 12:4-6) He points out that Nicodemus came to Jesus 'under cover of night.' (Joh 3:2) He notes the serious flaw in Joseph of Arimathea, that he was "a disciple of Jesus but a secret one out of his fear of the Jews." (Joh 19:38) John could not countenance the fact that anyone could profess to be a disciple of his Master and yet be ashamed of it.

John had developed the fruits of the spirit to a far greater degree when he wrote his Gospel and letters than when he was a young man newly associated with Jesus. He was certainly not displaying the trait that was manifest when he had asked for a special seat in the Kingdom. And in his writings we can find expression of his maturity and good counsel to help us to imitate his faithful, loyal, energetic course.

4. John Mark. One of Jesus' disciples and the writer of the Good News According to Mark. He is often called Mark the Evangelist. Mark was his surname. The home of his mother Mary in Jerusalem was a gathering place for the disciples. (Ac 12:12) He accompanied Paul and Barnabas on Paul's first missionary tour (Ac 12:25; 13:5), but he left them at Perga in Pamphylia and returned to Jerusalem. (Ac 13:13) On this account Paul later refused to take Mark along on his next tour, so Barnabas went in another direction, taking Mark with him. (Ac 15:36-41) Mark, however, evidently proved later that he was a reliable and diligent worker, for Paul wrote to Timothy from Rome, where he was imprisoned: "Take Mark and bring him with you, for he is useful to me for ministering."—2Ti 4:11; see MARK, I.

5. A Jewish ruler (possibly a relative of the chief priest Annas) who shared with Annas and Caiaphas in having the apostles Peter and John arrested and brought before them. Though they had proof of Peter's miracle in healing a lame man, they commanded Peter and John to stop their preaching and further threatened them. But having no ground on which to take action against the apostles and being afraid of the people, they released them.—Ac 3:1-8; 4:5-22.

JOHN, GOOD NEWS ACCORDING TO.

An account of Jesus Christ's earthly life and ministry, the last of the four to be written.

Writership. Though the book does not name its writer, it has been almost universally acknowledged that it was written by the hand of the apostle John. From the beginning, his writership was not challenged, except by a small group in the second century who objected on the ground that they considered the book's teachings unorthodox, but not because of any evidence concerning writership. Only since the advent of modern "critical" scholarship has John's writership been challenged anew.

The internal evidence that the apostle John, the son of Zebedee, was indeed the writer consists of such an abundance of proofs from various viewpoints that it overwhelms any arguments to the contrary. Only a very limited number of points are mentioned here, but the alert reader, with these in mind, will find a great many more. A few are:

(1) The writer of the book was evidently a Jew,

as is indicated by his familiarity with Jewish opinions.—Joh 1:21; 6:14; 7:40; 12:34.

(2) He was a native dweller in the land of Palestine, as is indicated by his thorough acquaintance with the country. The details mentioned concerning places named indicate personal knowledge of them. He referred to "Bethany across the Jordan" (Joh 1:28) and 'Bethany near Jerusalem.' (11:18) He wrote that there was a garden at the place where Christ was impaled and a new memorial tomb in it (19:41), that Jesus "spoke in the

HIGHLIGHTS OF JOHN

The apostle John's account of the life of Jesus, highlighting the theme that Jesus is the Christ the Son of God, by means of whom eternal life is possible

Written about 98 C.E., more than 30 years after the last of the other three Gospels and 65 years after the death of Jesus

The Word becomes flesh and is identified as the Lamb of God, God's Son, and the Christ (1:1-51)

The Word, who was in the beginning with God, resides among men but is rejected by his people; those who accept him are given authority to become God's children

John the Baptizer testifies that Jesus is God's Son and the Lamb of God that takes away the sin of the world

Andrew and then others become convinced that Jesus is the Christ

Jesus' miracles and preaching demonstrate that he is the Christ, through whom eternal life is attainable (2:1-6:71)

Jesus turns water into wine in Cana

He tells Nicodemus that God sent His only-begotten Son so that faithful ones may have everlasting life

He speaks to a Samaritan woman about the spiritual water that imparts everlasting life, and he identifies himself as the Christ

Jesus performs healing miracles; the Jews object when a healing takes place on the Sabbath, and they want to kill him

Proclaiming that those who believe him have everlasting life, Jesus foretells the resurrection of all in the memorial tombs

He miraculously feeds about 5,000 men; when the crowd wants to make him king, he withdraws; when the people keep following him, he identifies himself as the bread that came down from heaven and tells them they will have to eat his flesh and drink his blood if they want everlasting life

Hostility to the Son of God intensifies (7:1-12:50)

Jesus boldly preaches in temple area although the chief priests and the Pharisees are seeking to seize him

Jesus announces that he is the light of the world and that the truth can make his listeners free, but they try to stone him

On the Sabbath, Jesus heals a man who was born blind; the Pharisees are furious

Jesus identifies himself as the fine shepherd, explaining that his sheep listen to his voice; the Jews again try to stone him

The resurrection of Lazarus fills the Jewish religious leaders with fear; they determine that both Jesus and Lazarus must die

Jesus rides into Jerusalem and is hailed as King by the crowd but not by the Pharisees

At the final Passover, Jesus gives parting counsel to his followers (13:1-17:26)

He washes their feet to teach humility and gives "a new commandment," that they should love one another as he loved them

He identifies himself as the way, the truth, and the life; he promises to send the holy spirit to his disciples after his departure

To bear fruit, his followers must remain at one with him, the true vine; but they will be persecuted

Jesus prays for his followers and reports to his Father that he has finished the work assigned to him, making His name manifest

Jesus is arrested, rejected by Jewish nation, and impaled (18:1-19:42)

In Gethsemane, Jesus is arrested; he is led before Annas, Caiaphas, and then Pilate

He tells Pilate that His kingdom is no part of this world

When Pilate's efforts to release him are frustrated, Jesus is impaled and dies

Joseph of Arimathea and Nicodemus care for his burial

Evidence of resurrection of Jesus concludes John's proof that this one really is the Christ (20:1-21:25)

Jesus is seen by Mary Magdalene, then by the rest of the disciples, including Thomas

In Galilee, he performs one final miracle, providing a miraculous catch of fish, and then he gives the commission: "Feed my little sheep"

treasury as he was teaching in the temple" (8:20), and that "it was wintertime, and Jesus was walking in the temple in the colonnade of Solomon" (10:22, 23).

(3) The writer's own testimony and the factual evidence show that he was an eyewitness. He names individuals who said or did certain things (Joh 1:40; 6:5, 7; 12:21; 14:5, 8, 22; 18:10); he is detailed about the times of events (4:6, 52; 6:16; 13:30; 18:28; 19:14; 20:1; 21:4); he factually designates numbers in his descriptions, doing so unostentatiously.—1:35; 2:6; 4:18; 5:5; 6:9, 19; 19:23; 21:8, 11.

(4) The writer was an apostle. No one but an apostle could have been eyewitness to so many events associated with Jesus' ministry; also his intimate knowledge of Jesus' mind, feelings, and reasons for certain actions reveals that he was one of the party of 12 who accompanied Jesus throughout his ministry. For example, he tells us that Jesus asked Philip a question to test him, "for he himself knew what he was about to do." (Joh 6:5, 6) Jesus knew "in himself that his disciples were murmuring." (6:61) He knew "all the things coming upon him." (18:4) He "groaned in the spirit and became troubled." (11:33; compare 13:21; 2:24; 4:1, 2; 6:15; 7:1.) The writer was also familiar with the apostles' thoughts and impressions, some of which were wrong and were corrected later.—2:21, 22; 11:13; 12:16; 13:28; 20:9; 21:4.

(5) Additionally, the writer is spoken of as "the disciple whom Jesus used to love." (Joh 21:20, 24) He was evidently one of the three most intimate apostles that Jesus kept nearest to him on several occasions, such as the transfiguration (Mr 9:2) and the time of his anguish in the garden of Gethsemane. (Mt 26:36, 37) Of these three apostles, James is eliminated as the writer because of his being put to death about 44 C.E. by Herod Agrippa I. There is no evidence whatsoever for such an early date for the writing of this Gospel. Peter is ruled out by having his name mentioned alongside "the disciple whom Jesus used to love."—Joh 21:20, 21.

Authenticity. The Gospel of John was accepted as canonical by the early Christian congregation. It appears in nearly all the ancient catalogs, being there accepted without query as authentic. The epistles of Ignatius of Antioch (c. 110 C.E.) contain clear traces of his use of John's Gospel, as do also the writings of Justin Martyr a generation later. It is found in all the most important codices of the Christian Greek Scriptures— the Sinaitic, Vatican, Alexandrine, Ephraemi, Bezae, Washington I, and Koridethi codices—as well as in all the early versions. A fragment of this Gospel containing part of John chapter 18 is contained in the John Rylands Papyrus 457 (P^{52}), of the first half of the second century. Also parts of chapters 10 and 11 are found in the Chester Beatty Papyrus No. 1 (P^{45}), and a large part of the whole book is found in the Bodmer Papyrus No. 2 (P^{66}) of the early third century.

When and Where Written. It is generally thought that John had been released from exile on the island of Patmos and was in or near Ephesus, about 100 km (60 mi) from Patmos, at the time he wrote his Gospel, about 98 C.E. Roman Emperor Nerva (96-98 C.E.) recalled many who had been exiled at the close of the reign of his predecessor Domitian. John may have been among these. In the Revelation that John received on Patmos, Ephesus was one of the congregations to which he was commanded to write.

John had reached a very old age, being probably about 90 or 100 when he wrote his Gospel. He was undoubtedly familiar with the other three accounts of Jesus' earthly life and ministry, also the Acts of Apostles and the letters written by Paul, Peter, James, and Jude. He had had opportunity to see Christian doctrine fully revealed and had seen the effects of its preaching to all nations. He also had seen the beginning of "the man of lawlessness." (2Th 2:3) He had witnessed many of Jesus' prophecies already fulfilled, notably the destruction of Jerusalem and the end of that Jewish system of things.

Purpose of John's Gospel. John, inspired by holy spirit, was selective in the events he chose to chronicle, because, as he says: "To be sure, Jesus performed many other signs also before the disciples, which are not written down in this scroll," and, "There are, in fact, many other things also which Jesus did, which, if ever they were written in full detail, I suppose, the world itself could not contain the scrolls written."—Joh 20:30; 21:25.

With these things in mind, John states his purpose for writing the account he was led by inspiration to write, in which he repeated little that had been written before: "But these have been written down that you may believe that Jesus is the Christ the Son of God, and that, because of believing, you may have life by means of his name."—Joh 20:31.

John emphasized the fact that what he wrote was real and true and that it had actually taken place. (Joh 1:14; 21:24) His Gospel is a valuable addition to the Bible canon as the actual eyewitness evidence from the last living apostle of Jesus Christ.

Widely Published. The Good News According to John has been the most widely published of any part of the Bible. Thousands of copies of the

Gospel of John have been separately printed and distributed, apart from its being included in copies of the complete Bible.

Value. In harmony with the Revelation, in which Jesus Christ states that he is "the beginning of the creation by God" (Re 3:14), John points out that this One was with God "in the beginning" and that "all things came into existence through him." (Joh 1:1-3) Throughout the Gospel he stresses the intimacy of this only-begotten Son of God with his Father, and he quotes many of Jesus' statements revealing that intimacy. Throughout the book we are kept aware of the Father-Son relationship, the subjection of the Son, and the worship of Jehovah as God by his Son. (Joh 20:17) This closeness qualified the Son to reveal the Father as no one else could and as God's servants of ages past never realized. And John highlights the affectionate love of the Father for the Son and for those who become God's sons by exercising faith in the Son.

Jesus Christ is presented as God's channel of blessing to mankind and the only way of approach to God. He is revealed as the One through whom undeserved kindness and truth come (Joh 1:17), also as "the Lamb of God" (1:29), "the only-begotten Son of God" (3:18), "the bridegroom" (3:29), "the true bread from heaven" (6:32), "the bread of God" (6:33), "the bread of life" (6:35), "living bread" (6:51), "the light of the world" (8:12), "the Son of man" (9:35), "the door" of the sheepfold (10:9), "the fine shepherd" (10:11), "the resurrection and the life" (11:25), "the way and the truth and the life" (14:6), and "the true vine" (15:1).

Jesus Christ's position as King is stressed (Joh 1:49; 12:13; 18:33), also his authority as Judge (5:27) and the power of resurrection granted him by his Father. (5:28, 29; 11:25) John reveals Christ's role in sending the holy spirit as a "helper," to act in the capacities of remembrancer or reminder, witness bearer for Him, and teacher. (14:26; 15:26; 16:14, 15) But John does not allow the reader to lose sight of the fact that it is actually God's spirit, emanating from God and sent by His authority. Jesus made it clear that the holy spirit could not come in such capacity unless he went to the Father, who is greater than he is. (16:7; 14:28) Then his disciples would do even greater works, for the reason that Christ would again be with his Father and would answer requests asked in his own name, all for the purpose of bringing glory to the Father.—14:12-14.

John reveals Jesus Christ also as the sacrificial ransom for mankind. (Joh 3:16; 15:13) His title "Son of man" reminds us of his being most closely related to man by becoming flesh, being man's kinsman, and by reason of this, as foreshadowed in the Law, the repurchaser and avenger of blood. (Le 25:25; Nu 35:19) Christ told his disciples that the ruler of this world had no hold on him but that he had conquered the world and, as a result, the world was judged and its ruler was to be cast out. (Joh 12:31; 14:30) Jesus' followers are encouraged to conquer the world by keeping loyalty and integrity to God as Jesus did. (Joh 16:33) This harmonizes with the Revelation that John had received, in which Christ repeats the need to conquer and promises rich heavenly rewards alongside him to those in union with him.—Re 2:7, 11, 17, 26; 3:5, 12, 21.

The Spurious Passage at John 7:53–8:11. These 12 verses have obviously been added to the original text of John's Gospel. They are not found in the Sinaitic Manuscript or the Vatican Manuscript No. 1209, though they do appear in the sixth-century Codex Bezae and later Greek manuscripts. They are omitted, however, by most of the early versions. It is evident that they are not part of John's Gospel. One group of Greek manuscripts places this passage at the end of John's Gospel; another group puts it after Luke 21:38, supporting the conclusion that it is a spurious and uninspired text.

JOHN, THE LETTERS OF. These letters were among the last portions of the inspired Scriptures to be put in writing. Although the name of the apostle John nowhere appears within these letters, scholars have generally been in agreement with the traditional view that the writer of The Good News According to John and the three letters entitled the First, Second, and Third of John are by the same hand. There are many similarities between them and the fourth Gospel.

The authenticity of these letters is well established. The internal evidence testifies to their harmoniousness with the rest of the Scriptures. Also, many early writers give testimony to their genuineness. Polycarp seems to quote from 1 John 4:3; Papias is said by Eusebius to have testified to the first letter, as did Tertullian and Cyprian; and it is contained in the Syriac *Peshitta*. Clement of Alexandria seemingly indicates knowledge of the other two letters; Irenaeus apparently quotes from 2 John 10, 11; Dionysius of Alexandria, according to Eusebius, alludes to them. These latter-mentioned writers also testify to the authenticity of First John.

Very likely John wrote the letters from Ephesus about 98 C.E., near the time when he wrote his Gospel account. The frequent expression "little [or,

HIGHLIGHTS OF FIRST JOHN

A vigorous treatise designed to safeguard Christians against apostate influences

Written by the apostle John about 98 C.E., after Revelation and not long before John's death

Beware of falsehoods being spread about Jesus

Jesus' having come in the flesh is confirmed by his having been heard, seen, and touched (1:1-4)

Anyone denying that Jesus is the Christ is a liar, an antichrist; anointed believers know the truth and do not need to listen to a different teaching (2:18-29)

Any inspired expression denying that Jesus Christ came in the flesh is not from God; many false prophets have gone forth (4:1-6)

Anyone denying that Jesus is God's Son is rejecting the Father's own testimony about his Son (5:5-12)

Christians do not lead sinful lives

If we avoid the darkness and walk in the light, Jesus' blood cleanses us from sin (1:5-7)

If we *do* commit a sin, we should confess our wrong, and we will be cleansed on the basis of Jesus' sacrifice (1:8–2:2)

Christians do not *practice* sin; practicers of sin originate with the Devil; children of God seek righteousness and shun sin (3:1-12; 5:18, 19)

Christians are encouraged to pray for their brother if he falls into sin—as long as it is not a sin "so as to incur death" (5:16, 17)

Love for God and for fellow Christians will safeguard us

He who loves his brother is walking in the light and will not stumble (2:9-11)

To have the love of the Father, a Christian must do His will and avoid loving the world and its attractions (2:15-17)

Genuine love for the brothers shows that one has passed over from death to life; if we do not show love for our brothers by helping them when they are in need, there is no love of God in us (3:13-24)

Christians should love one another because God is love; we love Him because he loved us first; if a Christian claims to love God but hates his brother, he is a liar (4:7–5:2)

---

young] children" seems to indicate that they were written in his old age.

First John. This letter is written more in the style of a treatise, since it has neither a greeting nor a conclusion. In the second chapter John addresses fathers, young children, and young men, denoting that it was not a personal letter to an individual. It was very likely intended for a congregation or congregations and, in fact, applies to the entire association of those in union with Christ.—1Jo 2:13, 14.

John was the last living apostle. It had been more than 30 years since the last of the other letters of the Christian Greek Scriptures had been written. Soon the apostles would all be off the scene. Years before this time, Paul had written to Timothy that he would not be with him much longer. (2Ti 4:6) He urged Timothy to keep holding the pattern of healthful words and to commit to faithful men the things he had heard from Paul, so that these men could, in turn, teach others. —2Ti 1:13; 2:2.

The apostle Peter had warned of false teachers who would arise from within the congregation, bringing in destructive sects. (2Pe 2:1-3) Additionally, Paul had told the overseers of the congregation in Ephesus (where John's letters were later written) that "oppressive wolves" would enter in, not treating the flock with tenderness. (Ac 20:29, 30) He foretold the great apostasy with its "man of lawlessness." (2Th 2:3-12) In 98 C.E. it was, therefore, as John said: "Young children, it is the last hour, and, just as you have heard that antichrist is coming, even now there have come to be many antichrists; from which fact we gain the knowledge that it is the last hour." (1Jo 2:18) Consequently, the letter was most timely and of vital importance for the strengthening of the faithful Christians as a bulwark against the apostasy.

Purpose. However, John did not write merely to refute false teachings. Rather, his main purpose was to strengthen the faith of the early Christians in the truths they had received; often he contrasted these truths with the false teachings. Possibly, First John was sent as a circular letter to all the congregations in the area. This view is supported by the writer's frequent use of the Greek plural form for "you."

His argument is orderly and forceful, as the following consideration of the letter will show. The letter has strong emotional appeal, and it is clear that John wrote out of his great love for the truth and his abhorrence of error—his love for light and hatred of darkness.

Three primary themes. John dealt extensively with three themes in particular in his first letter: the antichrist, sin, and love.

Regarding the antichrist, he spoke very plainly. He said: "These things I write you about those who are trying to mislead you." (1Jo 2:26) These men were denying that Jesus Christ was the Son of God that had come in the flesh. He explained that they were once with the congregation but had gone out in order that it might be shown that they were not of "our sort." (2:19) They were not the loyal, loving sort that "have faith to the preserving alive of the soul" but were the sort "that shrink back to destruction."—Heb 10:39.

As to sin, some of the high points made are: (1) We all sin, and those who say they do not sin do not have the truth and are making God out to be a liar (1Jo 1:8-10); (2) we are all to strive against sin (2:1); (3) God has provided a propitiatory sacrifice for sins by Jesus Christ, whom we have as a helper with the Father (2:1; 4:10); (4) those who are true Christians do not make a practice of sin—they do not carry on sin, although they may commit an act of sin at times (2:1; 3:4-10; 5:18); (5) there are two kinds of sin, the kind that can be forgiven and the willful, deliberate kind that is not forgivable (5:16, 17).

On the subject of love, John writes more freely. He declares: (1) God is love (1Jo 4:8, 16); (2) God showed his love by having his Son die as a propitiatory sacrifice for our sins; also, by providing through Christ that his anointed ones become children of God (3:1; 4:10); (3) the love of God and Christ puts us under obligation to show love to our brothers (3:16; 4:11); (4) the love of God means to observe his commandments (5:2, 3); (5) perfect love throws fear outside, removing restraint from freeness of speech to God (4:17, 18); (6) love of brothers is not just a matter of words but of deeds, giving them things that we have if they are in need (3:17, 18); (7) anyone who hates his brother is a manslayer (3:15); and (8) Christians are not to love the world and the things in it (2:15).

Second John. The second letter of John opens with the words: "The older man to the chosen lady and to her children." (2Jo 1) Thus, in a tactful way, John indicates that he is the writer. He was indeed an "older man," being, by this time, about 90 or 100 years of age. He was also older in the sense of Christian growth and was a 'pillar' of the congregation.—Ga 2:9.

It is thought by some that this letter to "the chosen lady" is addressed to one of the Christian congregations and that the children are spiritual children, the children of the "sister" (2Jo 13) being members of another congregation. On the other hand, some hold the idea that it actually was addressed to an individual, perhaps named Kyria (Greek for "lady").

Many of the points made by John in his second letter are abbreviations of thoughts from his first

---

HIGHLIGHTS OF SECOND JOHN

A letter addressed to "the chosen lady"—perhaps an individual or possibly a congregation

Written by the apostle John about 98 C.E.

Go on walking in the truth (vss 1-6)

John and all others who know the truth love "the chosen lady" and her children who are walking in the truth

He encourages her to continue to cultivate love

Love means "walking according to his commandments"

Be on guard against deceivers (vss 7-13)

Deceivers deny that Jesus Christ came in the flesh

Believers must avoid anyone not remaining in the teaching of Christ; they must not receive such a person into their homes or even say a greeting to him; otherwise they may become sharers in his wicked works

---

letter. He speaks of the truth that remains in those who really know it and of the undeserved kindness and peace from God. He rejoices that some continue to 'walk in the truth.' They show love for one another and keep God's commandments. However, deceivers have gone forth into the world, the antichrist denying that God's Son came in the flesh. (Compare 2Jo 7 and 1Jo 4:3.) In 2 John 10, 11 he adds to the instruction in his first letter, showing the action that members of the congregation should take toward those who push ahead of the teaching of the Christ and who come with a teaching of their own or of men. John commands that such should not be greeted or received into the Christian's home.

Third John. The third letter was from "the older man" to Gaius, with greetings to others in the congregation. It was written in customary letter style. It is so like the first and second letters in style and material that it was clearly written by the same person, namely, the apostle John. Just who Gaius was is not certain. While there are several persons by this name mentioned in the Scriptures, this may have been yet another Gaius, since the letter was written 30 years or more after Acts, Romans, and First Corinthians, where the name Gaius also appears.—Ac 19:29; 20:4; Ro 16:23; 1Co 1:14.

John urges Christian hospitality and says that one Diotrephes, who liked to have the first place in the congregation, did not receive the messages from John or other responsible ones with respect, nor did Diotrephes demonstrate any respect for other traveling representatives of the early Christian congregation. He even wanted to throw out of the congregation those who did receive such brothers hospitably. Therefore John mentioned that if he came personally, as he hoped to do, he would set this matter straight. (3Jo 9, 10) He commends to Gaius a faithful brother named Demetrius, who may have been the bearer of the letter, urging Gaius to receive hospitably those who went forth to build up the Christian congregations.

Throughout the three letters we find emphasized Christian unity, love for God shown by keeping his commandments, avoiding the darkness and walking in the light, showing love for the brothers, and continuing to walk in the truth. Even in his old age, this "older man" John was thus a great source of encouragement and strength to the congregations in Asia Minor and to all Christians reading his letters.

HIGHLIGHTS OF THIRD JOHN

An inspired letter to Gaius that can benefit all Christians

Written by the apostle John around 98 C.E., about the same time as his other two letters

---

We are obligated to be hospitable to fellow Christians (vss 1-8)

John experienced great joy when traveling brothers reported about Gaius' walking in the truth and about his love, evidently expressed in his receiving them hospitably

We are "fellow workers in the truth" if we show hospitality to brothers who go forth in behalf of God's name

Be an imitator, not of bad, but of what is good (vss 9-14)

Diotrephes, liking to have the first place, refuses to accept anything from John with respect

He will not receive traveling brothers and tries to expel anyone who wants to show hospitality to them

Avoid copying what is bad; imitate what is good

JOIADA   (Joi'a·da) [shortened form of Jehoiada, meaning "May Jehovah Know"].

1. Son of Paseah who helped repair the Gate of the Old City when Nehemiah had Jerusalem's wall rebuilt.—Ne 3:6.

2. Great-grandson of Jeshua and father of Johanan (Jonathan) in the postexilic high-priestly line. (Ne 12:10, 11, 22) One of Joiada's sons defiled himself and his priesthood by marrying a daughter of Sanballat the Horonite, for which Nehemiah chased him away.—Ne 13:28, 29.

JOIAKIM   (Joi'a·kim) [shortened form of Jehoiakim, possibly meaning "Jehovah Raises Up"]. Son and evidently the successor of postexilic High Priest Jeshua. (Ne 12:10, 12, 26) He evidently held office at the time Ezra returned. (*Jewish Antiquities,* XI, 121 [v, 1]) However, by the time of Nehemiah's arrival later (455 B.C.E.), Joiakim's son Eliashib had become high priest.—Ne 3:1.

JOIARIB   (Joi'a·rib) [shortened form of Jehoiarib, meaning "May Jehovah Contend; Jehovah Has Conducted [Our] Legal Case"].

1. Head of a paternal house of priests; also called Jehoiarib. (1Ch 24:6, 7) Representatives of his house (or another priest with the same name) were contemporaries of Zerubbabel, Nehemiah, and Joiakim.—Ne 12:1, 6; 11:4, 10; 12:12, 19, 26.

2. An "instructor" in Ezra's time.—Ezr 8:16.

3. A Judahite ancestor of Maaseiah.—Ne 11:5.

JOKDEAM   (Jok'de·am) [meaning, possibly, People's Burning]. A city in the mountainous region of Judah. (Jos 15:20, 48, 56) The site is perhaps to be identified with Khirbet Raq'a (Horvat Raq'a), about 7 km (4.5 mi) S of Hebron.

JOKIM   (Jo'kim) [shortened form of Jehoiakim, possibly meaning "Jehovah Raises Up"]. A descendant of Judah through his third son Shelah.—1Ch 2:3; 4:21, 22.

JOKMEAM   (Jok'me·am) [Let the People Raise (or, Rise) Up].

1. An Ephraimite city given to the Kohathites. (1Ch 6:66, 68) At Joshua 21:22, Jokmeam is evidently called "Kibzaim," perhaps another or earlier name for the same site. Its location is today unknown.

2. A region bordering on the territory under the jurisdiction of Ahilud's son Baana, one of Solomon's 12 deputies. (1Ki 4:12) It may be the same as Jokneam.

JOKNEAM   (Jok'ne·am). A city in Carmel conquered by Joshua. (Jos 12:7, 22) Originally assigned to the tribe of Zebulun (Jos 19:10, 11), Jokneam subsequently was given to the Merarite Levites. (Jos 21:34) Today it is usually identified with Tell Qeimun (Tel Yoqne'am), on a mound at the foot of Mount Carmel about 11 km (7 mi) NW of Megiddo and overlooking the Valley of Jezreel. At 1 Kings 4:12 "Jokmeam" may possibly be a spelling error for "Jokneam."

JOKSHAN   (Jok'shan) [from a root meaning "lay a snare"]. A descendant of Abraham by Keturah; the progenitor of Sheba and Dedan.—Ge 25:1-3; 1Ch 1:32.

JOKTAN (Jok'tan). A descendant of Eber, brother of Peleg, and father of 13 sons. (Ge 10:25-29; 1Ch 1:19-23) The names of some of Joktan's descendants appear to have survived at various places in S and SW Arabia. It has been suggested that Joktan was the progenitor of the original peoples of Arabia, as distinguished from the tribes descended from the sons of Abraham by Hagar and Keturah. The geographic limits of the territory inhabited by Joktan's descendants are Biblically described as running "from Mesha as far as Sephar" (Ge 10:30), but the exact area covered is uncertain.

JOKTHEEL (Jok'the·el).

1. A city of Judah in the Shephelah (Jos 15:20, 33, 38), the exact location of which city is today unknown.

2. The Edomite city of Sela, which was conquered by Judean King Amaziah and renamed Joktheel.—2Ki 14:1, 7; see SELA No. 2.

JONADAB. See JEHONADAB, JONADAB.

JONAH (Jo'nah) [Dove].

1. "Son of Amittai"; a prophet of Jehovah from Gath-hepher (2Ki 14:25), a border city in the territory of Zebulun. (Jos 19:10, 13) In fulfillment of Jehovah's word spoken through Jonah, Israel's King Jeroboam II succeeded in restoring "the boundary of Israel from the entering in of Hamath clear to the sea of the Arabah [the Salt Sea]." (2Ki 14:23-25; compare De 3:17.) So it appears that Jonah served as a prophet to the ten-tribe kingdom sometime during the reign of Jeroboam II. He is evidently the same person Jehovah commissioned to proclaim judgment against Nineveh (Jon 1:1, 2) and, therefore, also the writer of the book bearing his name.

Instead of following through on his assignment to preach to the Ninevites, Jonah decided to run away from it. At the seaport of Joppa, he secured passage on a ship bound for Tarshish (generally associated with Spain) over 3,500 km (2,200 mi) W of Nineveh.—Jon 1:1-3; 4:2.

After boarding the decked vessel, Jonah fell fast asleep in its "innermost parts." Meanwhile, the mariners, faced with a divinely sent tempestuous wind that threatened to wreck the ship, cried to their gods for aid and cast articles overboard to lighten the vessel. The ship captain awakened Jonah, urging him also to call on his "god." Finally the mariners cast lots to determine on whose account the storm had arisen. Evidently Jehovah then caused the lot to single out Jonah. Upon being questioned, Jonah confessed to having been unfaithful to his commission. Not wanting others to perish on his account, he requested that he be thrown into the sea. When all efforts to get back to land failed, the mariners did to Jonah according to his word, and the sea stopped its raging.—Jon 1:4-15.

As Jonah sank beneath the waters, seaweed wound around his head. Finally his drowning sensation ceased, and he found himself inside a large fish. Jonah prayed to Jehovah, glorifying him as Savior and promising to pay what he had vowed. On the third day the prophet was vomited out onto dry land.—Jon 1:17–2:10.

Is it reasonable to believe that the Ninevites would repent in sackcloth at the warning of Jonah?

Commissioned a second time to go to Nineveh, he undertook the long journey there. "Finally Jonah started to enter into the city the walking distance of one day, and he kept proclaiming and saying: 'Only forty days more, and Nineveh will be overthrown.'" (Jon 3:1-4) Whether Jonah knew Assyrian or was miraculously endowed with ability to speak that language is not revealed in the Bible. He may even have spoken Hebrew, his proclamation later being interpreted by one(s) knowing the language. If spoken in Hebrew, Jonah's words could have aroused great curiosity, with many wondering just what this stranger was saying.

Some critics think it incredible that the Ninevites, including the king, responded to Jonah's preaching. (Jon 3:5-9) In this regard the remarks of commentator C. F. Keil are of interest: "The powerful impression made upon the Ninevites by Jonah's preaching, so that the whole city repented in sackcloth and ashes, is quite intelligible, if we simply bear in mind the great susceptibility of Oriental races to emotion, the awe of one Supreme Being which is peculiar to all the heathen religions of Asia, and the great esteem in which soothsaying and oracles were held in Assyria from the very earliest times . . . ; and if we also take into calculation the circumstance that the appearance of a foreigner, who, without any conceivable personal interest, and with the most fearless boldness, disclosed to the great royal city its godless ways, and announced its destruction within a very short period with the confidence so characteristic of the God-sent prophets, could not fail to make a powerful impression upon the minds of the people, which would be all the stronger if the report of the miraculous working of the prophets of Israel had penetrated to Nineveh."—*Commentary on the Old Testament*, 1973, Vol. X, Jonah 3:9, pp. 407, 408.

After 40 days had passed and still nothing had happened to Nineveh, Jonah was highly displeased that Jehovah had not brought calamity upon the city. He even prayed for God to take away his life. But Jehovah answered Jonah with the question: "Have you rightly become hot with anger?" (Jon 3:10–4:4) The prophet subsequently left the city and, later, erected a booth for himself. There, to the E of Nineveh, Jonah watched to see what would befall the city.—Jon 4:5.

When a bottle-gourd plant miraculously grew to provide shade for Jonah, the prophet was very pleased. But his rejoicing was short-lived. The next day, early in the morning, a worm injured the plant, causing it to dry up. Deprived of its shade, Jonah was subjected to a parching east wind and the hot sun beating down upon his head. Again, he asked to die.—Jon 4:6-8.

By means of this bottle-gourd plant Jonah was taught a lesson in mercy. He felt sorry for the bottle-gourd plant, probably wondering why it had to die. Yet Jonah had neither planted nor cared for it. On the other hand, being the Creator and Sustainer of life, Jehovah had much more reason to feel sorry for Nineveh. The value of its inhabitants and that of the cattle was far greater than that of one bottle-gourd plant. Therefore, Jehovah asked Jonah: "For my part, ought I not to feel sorry for Nineveh the great city, in which there exist more than one hundred and twenty thousand men who do not at all know the difference between their right hand and their left, besides many domestic animals?" (Jon 4:9-11) That Jonah must have got the point is indicated by the candid portrayal of his own experiences.

It may be that sometime later Jonah met at least one of the persons who had been aboard the ship from Joppa, possibly at the temple in Jerusalem, and learned from him about the vows made by the mariners after the storm abated.—Jon 1:16; compare Jon 2:4, 9; see JONAH, BOOK OF; NINEVEH.

2. Father of the apostles Peter and Andrew (Mt 16:17; Joh 1:40-42); also called John at John 1:42; 21:15-17 in certain manuscripts.

JONAH, BOOK OF.

The only book in the Hebrew Scriptures dealing exclusively with the commission of a prophet of Jehovah to proclaim in and for a non-Israelite city a message of doom, and which proclamation resulted in that city's repentance. The experiences related in this book were unique to its writer, Jonah the son of Amittai. Evidently being the same person as the Jonah of 2 Kings 14:25, he must have prophesied during the reign of Israel's King Jeroboam II (c. 844-804 B.C.E.). It is therefore reasonable to place the events recorded in the book of Jonah in the ninth century B.C.E.—See JONAH No. 1.

Authenticity. Because of the supernatural character of many events mentioned in the book of Jonah, it has often been attacked by Bible critics. The raising of the tempestuous wind and its quick cessation, the fish swallowing Jonah and three days later vomiting the prophet out unharmed, and the sudden growth and death of a gourd plant have all been labeled unhistorical because such things do not happen today. This contention might have a basis if the book of Jonah claimed that they were ordinary occurrences back then. But it does not do so. It relates events in the life of one who was specially commissioned by God. Therefore, those maintaining that these things simply could not have happened must deny either the existence of God or his ability to affect natural forces and plant, animal, and human life in a special way for his purpose.—See Mt 19:26.

What sort of sea creature could possibly have swallowed Jonah?

A favorite contention in the past was that no sea creature could swallow a man. But this argument is not valid. The sperm whale, having a mammoth square-shaped head that constitutes about one third of its length, is fully capable of swallowing a man whole. (Walker's *Mammals of the World,* revised by R. Nowak and J. Paradiso, 1983, Vol. II, p. 901) Interestingly, there is evidence that the seaport of Joppa anciently was a headquarters for whalers. On the other hand, it is possible that the great white shark was the fish that swallowed Jonah. One of these that was caught in 1939 contained two whole 2-m-long (6 ft) sharks in its stomach—each about the size of a man. And the great white sharks have roamed all the seas, including the Mediterranean. (*Australian Zoological Handbook,* The Fishes of Australia, by G. P. Whitley, Sydney, 1940, Part 1—The Sharks, p. 125; *The Natural History of Sharks,* by R. H. Backus and T. H. Lineaweaver III, 1970, pp. 111, 113) It should be noted, however, that the Bible simply states: "Jehovah appointed a great fish to swallow Jonah," the kind of fish not being specified. (Jon 1:17) So it cannot be determined just what "fish" might have been involved. In fact, man's knowledge of the creatures inhabiting the seas and oceans is rather incomplete. Noted the magazine *Scientific American* (September 1969, p. 162): "As it has in the past, further exploration of the abyssal realm will undoubtedly reveal undescribed creatures including members of groups thought long extinct."

Some feel that the authenticity of the book of Jonah is in question because there is no confirmation of this prophet's activity in Assyrian records.

Actually, though, the absence of such information should not be surprising. It was customary for nations of antiquity to extol their successes, not their failures and humiliations, and also to eradicate anything unfavorable to them. Moreover, since not all ancient records have been preserved or found, no one can say with certainty that an account of what happened in Jonah's time never existed.

The lack of certain details (such as the name of the Assyrian king and the exact spot where Jonah was spewed onto dry land) has been cited as yet another proof that the book of Jonah is not true history. This objection, however, ignores the fact that all historical narratives are condensed accounts, the historian recording only such information as he deemed important or necessary for his purpose. As commentator C. F. Keil fittingly observes: "There is not a single one of the ancient historians in whose works such completeness as this can be found: and still less do the biblical historians aim at communicating such things as have no close connection with the main object of their narrative, or with the religious significance of the facts themselves."—*Commentary on the Old Testament,* 1973, Vol. X, Introduction to Jonah, p. 381.

Since archaeological evidence has been interpreted as indicating that the walls surrounding ancient Nineveh were only about 13 km (8 mi) in circumference, it is claimed that the book of Jonah

---

HIGHLIGHTS OF JONAH

The experiences of Jonah when he was assigned to prophesy to a pagan people, the inhabitants of Nineveh

It was written about 844 B.C.E., some 100 years before Assyria took Israel into exile

Jonah's flight (1:1–2:10)

Jonah is commissioned to warn the Ninevites of Jehovah's anger but takes passage on a ship bound for Tarshish

A tremendous storm arises and rouses fear of shipwreck

Fearful mariners cry to their gods, try to lighten the ship, and then cast lots to determine on whose account they face calamity

The lot singles out Jonah; he tells the mariners to cast him overboard since the tempest is on his account

The sailors, unwilling to do this, try to get the vessel back to land; when this fails, they hurl Jonah into the sea; the storm promptly abates

In the water, Jonah is swallowed by a big fish

From inside the fish's belly, he prays to Jehovah and promises to pay what he has vowed

Finally, Jonah is vomited out onto dry land

Jonah goes to Nineveh (3:1–4:11)

Jehovah again instructs Jonah to go to Nineveh to proclaim His warning

Jonah goes to Nineveh and announces that the city will be overthrown in 40 days

The Ninevites repent; as directed by the king, they cover their animals and themselves with sackcloth and cry out to God for mercy; Jehovah 'feels regret' over the foretold calamity

Jonah becomes furiously angry that Nineveh is to be spared; he erects a booth outside the city, sits in its shade, and awaits developments

Jehovah causes a bottle-gourd plant to spring up and provide Jonah with welcome shade; the next day a worm strikes the plant and it dries up; using Jonah's reaction to this, Jehovah explains to Jonah why He showed mercy to the more than 120,000 inhabitants of Nineveh

exaggerates the size of the city when describing it as being a walking distance of three days. (Jon 3:3) This, however, is not a valid reason for questioning the Scriptural reference. Both in Biblical and modern usage the name of a city can include its suburbs. In fact, Genesis 10:11, 12 shows that Nineveh, Rehoboth-Ir, Calah, and Resen constituted "the great city."

The fact that Jonah did not write in the first person has been used to discredit the book. But this argument does not take into account that it was common for Bible writers to refer to themselves in the third person. (Ex 24:1-18; Isa 7:3; 20:2; 37:2, 5, 6, 21; Jer 20:1, 2; 26:7, 8, 12; 37:2-6, 12-21; Da 1:6-13; Am 7:12-14; Hag 1:1, 3, 12, 13; 2:1, 10-14, 20; Joh 21:20) Even ancient secular historians, including Xenophon and Thucydides, did this. Yet it is noteworthy that the genuineness of their accounts has never been called into question on this basis.

By its opening statement, "the word of Jehovah began to occur," the book of Jonah lays claim to being from God. (Jon 1:1) The Jews have from earliest times accepted this and other prophetic books similarly introduced (Jer 1:1, 2; Ho 1:1; Mic 1:1; Zep 1:1; Hag 1:1; Zec 1:1; Mal 1:1) as genuine. This in itself provides a good case for its authenticity. As has been noted: "It is in fact inconceivable . . . that the Jewish authorities would have received such a book into the canon of Scripture without the most conclusive evidence of its genuineness and authenticity."—*The Imperial Bible-Dictionary,* edited by P. Fairbairn, London, 1874, Vol. I, p. 945.

Further, this book is in complete harmony with the rest of the Scriptures. It attributes salvation to Jehovah (Jon 2:9; compare Ps 3:8; Isa 12:2; Re 7:10), and the narrative illustrates Jehovah's mercy, long-suffering, patience, and undeserved kindness in dealing with sinful humans.—Jon 3:10; 4:2, 11; compare De 4:29-31; Jer 18:6-10; Ro 9:21-23; Eph 2:4-7; 2Pe 3:9.

Another evidence testifying to the authenticity of this Bible book is its candor. Jonah's improper attitude toward his commission and concerning God's action in sparing the Ninevites is not covered over.

The most conclusive evidence, though, is provided by the Son of God himself. Said he: "No sign will be given [this generation] except the sign of Jonah the prophet. For just as Jonah was in the belly of the huge fish three days and three nights, so the Son of man will be in the heart of the earth three days and three nights. Men of Nineveh will rise up in the judgment with this generation and will condemn it; because they repented at what Jonah preached, but, look! something more than Jonah is here." (Mt 12:39-41; 16:4) The resurrection of Christ Jesus was to be just as real as Jonah's deliverance from the belly of the fish. And the generation that heard Jonah's preaching must have been just as literal as the generation that heard what Christ Jesus said. Mythical men of Nineveh could never rise up in the judgment and condemn an unresponsive generation of Jews.

JONAM (Jo'nam). An ancestor of Jesus' mother Mary. Jonam was a descendant of David through Nathan and perhaps lived around the time of King Asa.—Lu 3:23, 30, 31.

JONATHAN (Jon'a·than) [Jehovah Has Given]. An English rendering of two Hebrew names, *Yohna·than'* and the longer form *Yehoh·na·than'.*—See JEHONATHAN.

1. A Levite who served as priest in connection with false worship at the house of Micah in Ephraim and later with the Danites. The account in Judges chapters 17 and 18 repeatedly refers to a young Levite who, at Judges 18:30, is called "Jonathan the son of Gershom, Moses' son." That he was earlier described as "of the family of Judah" may refer simply to the fact that he resided in Bethlehem in the territory of Judah.—Jg 17:7.

Wandering Jonathan eventually came to the home of Micah in the mountains of Ephraim. Micah had set up a carved image in his home. Jonathan agreed to serve as priest for the household even though he was not of the family of Aaron and an image was being used in worship. Later five Danites seeking a place for a section of the tribe to settle met Jonathan. They asked him to inquire of God whether they would be successful, and he gave them a favorable response in the name of Jehovah.

When the main body of 600 Danite men, as well as their families and livestock, passed by Micah's house on their way north, they took the objects of worship including the carved image. They also induced selfish Jonathan to throw in his lot with them, to become their priest and not just priest for a family. (Jg 17:7–18:21) Jonathan "and his sons became priests to the tribe of the Danites until the day of the land's being taken into exile." (Jg 18:30) Some commentators have applied this to a conquest of the district, such as by Tiglath-pileser III, or all of the northern tribes in 740 B.C.E. (2Ki 15:29; 17:6) However, since Samuel evidently wrote Judges, an earlier application must be intended. Judges 18:31 mentions that the Danites kept the carved image "set up for themselves all the days that the house of the true God continued in Shiloh." This suggests a time period for the application of the preceding verse, and it strengthens the view that Jonathan's family served as priests until the Ark was captured by the Philistines. It has been contended that verse 30 should read, 'until the day of the ark's being taken into exile.' (1Sa 4:11, 22) But this conclusion about the duration of the priesthood of Jonathan's family may be correct even without altering the reading, for verse 30 may be taking the view that the land, in a sense, was carried into exile when the Ark was captured.

2. Eldest and favorite son of Benjamite King Saul, evidently by Ahinoam the daughter of Ahimaaz. (1Sa 14:49, 50) Jonathan is chiefly noted for his unselfish friendship for and support of David as Jehovah's king-designate.

Jonathan is first mentioned in the early years of Saul's reign as a valiant commander of a thousand warriors. (1Sa 13:2) He thus would probably be at least 20 then and hence at least approaching 60 when he died in about 1078 B.C.E. (Nu 1:3) David was 30 at the time of Jonathan's death. (1Sa 31:2; 2Sa 5:4) Hence, during their friendship Jonathan was evidently some 30 years David's senior. Jonathan's being a grown young man when Saul became king might help to explain his temperament and outlook. During his formative years he well may have been influenced by his father who, up to the time of being chosen as king, displayed modesty, obedience, and a respect for Jehovah and his arrangements.—1Sa 9:7, 21, 26; 10:21, 22.

In the opening notice of Jonathan, he courageously and successfully led a thousand poorly armed men against the Philistine garrison at Geba. In response the enemy collected at Michmash. Secretly Jonathan and his armor-bearer left Saul and his men and approached the enemy outpost. By this act alone Jonathan displayed his valor, his ability to inspire confidence in others, and yet his recognition of Jehovah's leading, for his actions depended on a sign from God. The two bold fighters struck down about 20 Philistines, which led to a full-scale battle and victory for Israel. (1Sa 13: 3–14:23) As the fighting was proceeding, Saul rashly swore a curse on anyone eating before the battle ended. Jonathan was unaware of this and he ate some wild honey. Later, when confronted by Saul, Jonathan did not shrink back from dying for having partaken of the honey. Yet he was redeemed by the people, who recognized that God was with him that day.—1Sa 14:24-45.

These exploits clearly prove that Jonathan was a courageous, capable, and manly warrior. He and Saul well deserved being described as "swifter than the eagles" and "mightier than the lions." (2Sa 1:23) He was skilled as an archer. (2Sa 1:22; 1Sa 20:20) His manly qualities may have especially endeared him to Saul. It is apparent that they were very close. (1Sa 20:2) This did not, though, overshadow Jonathan's zeal for God and loyalty to his friend David.

David had been introduced into the king's court to play music for Saul, since Jehovah's spirit had departed from the king and had been replaced by a bad spirit—something Jonathan may have noted. Though young, David was "a valiant, mighty man and a man of war," and Saul "got to loving him very much, and he came to be his armor-bearer."—1Sa 16:14-23.

Jonathan's special friendship with David dates from soon after he killed Goliath. That fearless act in defense of Jehovah's people must have particularly moved Jonathan. Hearing David's account of it, "Jonathan's very soul became bound up with the soul of David, and Jonathan began to love him as his own soul." (1Sa 18:1) The two courageous warriors and devoted servants of God "proceeded to conclude a covenant" of friendship. Jonathan could see that David had God's spirit. (1Sa 18:3) He did not jealously view him as a rival, as did Saul. Instead, his respect for God's way of handling matters was a fine example for his younger friend. He did not act on Saul's desire to kill David but, rather, warned David and tried to intercede. When David was forced to flee, Jonathan met him and made a covenant to the effect that David would protect him and his household.—1Sa 19: 1–20:17.

Jonathan again spoke to Saul about David, but it nearly cost him his life, for in a fit of rage Saul hurled a spear at his own son. According to arrangement, Jonathan and David met in a field where ostensibly the king's son had gone to practice archery. (1Sa 20:24-40) The two friends renewed their bond of affection and "began kissing each other and weeping for each other," as other men are noted to have done and even as is done in some lands today. (1Sa 20:41; Ge 29:13; 45:15; Ac 20:37) Later Jonathan was able to contact David for the last time at Horesh and he strengthened "his hand in regard to God"; they renewed their covenant.—1Sa 23:16-18.

There is no Biblical indication that Jonathan shared with his father in his expeditions against David. But in the battle against God's enemies, the Philistines, Jonathan fought to the death, dying on the same day as two of his brothers and his father. The Philistines hung the corpses on the walls at Beth-shan. However, valiant men of Jabesh-gilead removed them and buried them at Jabesh. Later David moved the bones of Saul and Jonathan to Zela. (1Sa 31:1-13; 2Sa 21:12-14; 1Ch 10:1-12) David deeply lamented the death of his close friend Jonathan, even chanting over Saul and Jonathan the dirge entitled "The Bow." (2Sa 1:17-27) King David showed special kindness to Jonathan's lame son Mephibosheth, who was five years old at his father's death. He eventually had a permanent place at the king's table. (2Sa 4:4; 9:10-13) Jonathan's line continued for generations.—1Ch 8:33-40.

3. A son of High Priest Abiathar and one who served as a courier when David fled Jerusalem during Absalom's revolt but who apparently later sided with rebellious Adonijah. Jonathan's father Abiathar traveled with David when the future king was outlawed by Saul, and later he was made high priest. At the time of Absalom's usurpation, David sent Abiathar and Zadok back to the capital so they could supply information. Abiathar's priestly son Jonathan is here first brought into the Biblical account. He and Ahimaaz the son of Zadok were to carry vital messages from their fathers and from Hushai to David. (2Sa 15:27-29, 36) The two couriers could not enter the city without being recognized, so they waited at a spring or well named En-rogel near the city. When Absalom seemed to accept Hushai's counsel, word was sent to the two waiting messengers, Jonathan and Ahimaaz. They sped to convey word to the king. Spotted and pursued, they were almost apprehended. With the help of a woman, they hid in a well until the danger was past and then went to David and advised him to cross over the Jordan. —2Sa 17:15-22.

In David's closing days his son Adonijah conspired to become king instead of Solomon, and Abiathar linked up with him. Perhaps being influenced by his father's lead, Jonathan evidently defected to the side of Adonijah. It was Jonathan who brought to the banqueting usurper the disquieting news that David had foiled the plot by making Solomon the king. The Bible does not say anything further about Jonathan. He may have shared his father's banishment, but whatever occurred, the office of high priest did not continue in his family.—1Ki 1:41-43; 2:26, 27.

4. Nephew of King David who struck down a giant who taunted Israel at Gath. (2Sa 21:20, 21; 1Ch 20:6, 7) This Jonathan is listed as the son of King David's brother Shimea, or Shimei. Since

there is a Jehonadab mentioned at 2 Samuel 13:3 as the son of David's brother Shimeah, some commentators feel that the same individual is intended.—See JEHONADAB No. 1.

5. One of David's mighty men of the military forces. He was the son of Shagee the Hararite. —2Sa 23:8, 32; 1Ch 11:26, 34.

6. A son of Uzziah, in charge of King David's treasures "in the field, in the cities and in the villages and in the towers," as distinct from the king's treasures in Jerusalem. (1Ch 27:25) Jonathan is mentioned after royal treasurer Azmaveth and before those responsible to care for specific assignments such as the vineyards or the olive groves.—1Ch 27:25-28.

7. A man of understanding, a secretary and a counselor for King David. (1Ch 27:32) In the Masoretic text Jonathan's relationship to David is indicated by the Hebrew word *dohdh,* which generally means "uncle." But in view of two references in the Scriptures to a nephew of David named Jonathan, it is likely that the word is here used in the wider sense of "relative," here being "brother's son" or "nephew." (*Ro; AS,* ftn; *NW*) He would thus be the same as No. 4.

8. One of the military chiefs in the field when Nebuchadnezzar conquered Jerusalem in 607 B.C.E.; a son of Kareah and brother of Johanan. After Gedaliah had been put in charge of the people left in the land, Jonathan and the other military leaders from the field went to him and were reassured of safety. (Jer 40:7-10) Evidently Jonathan was also among those who delivered to Gedaliah the warning that he chose to ignore about the danger of assassination.—Jer 40:13-16.

9. One of the two sons of Jada and a descendant of Judah through Hezron and Jerahmeel. His brother Jether died without sons, but Jonathan had two, Peleth and Zaza.—1Ch 2:3, 25, 26, 28, 32, 33.

10. An Israelite of the family of Adin whose son Ebed returned to Jerusalem from Babylon with Ezra in 468 B.C.E.—Ezr 8:1, 6.

11. Son of Asahel who perhaps opposed Ezra's proposal that the returned Jews put away their foreign wives. It has been suggested, however, that this opposition was not to Ezra's suggestion but to the procedure adopted for carrying it out. —Ezr 10:15, ftn.

12. Son of Joiada and grandson of High Priest Eliashib. (Ne 12:10, 11) It is thought that actually verse 11 should read "Johanan" instead of "Jonathan" since Nehemiah 12:22, 23 refers to Johanan as "son of Eliashib" and "son" can signify "grandson."—See JOHANAN No. 7.

13. Priest who was head of the paternal house of Malluchi in the days of High Priest Joiakim. —Ne 12:12, 14.

14. Son of Shemaiah of the family of Asaph and father of Zechariah, a priestly trumpeter in the procession that marched upon the rebuilt wall of Jerusalem.—Ne 12:31, 35, 36.

JOPPA (Jop′pa) [Beautiful (Pretty) [City]]. An ancient seaport about 55 km (34 mi) WNW of Jerusalem. Modern Yafo (Arabic, Jaffa; merged with Tel Aviv in 1950 and now called Tel Aviv-Yafo) occupies the ancient site. The city is situated on a rocky hill rising to a height of about 35 m (115 ft). Its harbor, the only natural one between Mount Carmel and the border of Egypt, is formed by a low ledge of rocks about 100 m (330 ft) from the coast. The harbor may be entered either through a narrow gap in the rocky ledge or at the open but shallow north end. Rocks bar access from the south.

Joppa was on the border of Dan's original territory, although not necessarily a part of it. (Jos 19:40, 41, 46) However, Judges 5:17 associates Dan with ships, and this may imply that the Danites actually controlled the seaport of Joppa.

In view of King Solomon's extensive commercial intercourse with other nations (1Ki 10:22, 28, 29), likely the harbor facilities at Joppa were improved. It was to Joppa that the Tyrians floated rafts of timber from the forests of Lebanon, to be used in temple construction. (2Ch 2:16) Later, the prophet Jonah, seeking to flee from his assignment, boarded a ship at Joppa to go to Tarshish. (Jon 1:3) After the Babylonian exile, Joppa again served as the harbor for receiving cedar timbers from Lebanon for use in temple rebuilding.—Ezr 3:7.

In the first century C.E., a Christian congregation existed at Joppa. Dorcas (Tabitha), a woman 'abounding in good deeds and gifts of mercy,' was associated with that congregation. Upon her death Peter came from nearby Lydda on request, and he subsequently resurrected Dorcas. As news of this mir-

acle spread throughout Joppa, many became believers. (Ac 9:36-42) For quite a few days, Peter stayed at Joppa, being entertained by a certain Simon, a tanner, who had his house by the sea. (Ac 9:43; 10:6) It was on the roof of Simon's house that Peter, while in a trance, received divine revelation concerning the propriety of preaching to non-Jews, just in time to receive the messengers from the Gentile Cornelius. Consequently, Peter did not hesitate to go to Caesarea with these messengers. Also, six Jewish brothers, apparently from Joppa, accompanied him.—Ac 10:9-45; 11:5-14.

JORAH. See HARIPH.

JORAI (Jo′rai). A descendant of Gad who is mentioned in a genealogical listing along with other "heads of the house of their forefathers." —1Ch 5:11, 13, 15.

JORAM (Jo′ram) [shortened form of Jehoram, meaning "Jehovah Is High (Exalted)"].

1. Son of King Toi of Hamath. Joram was sent with costly gifts made of gold, silver, and copper, along with his father's congratulations, to King David when the latter defeated Hadadezer the king of Zobah. David, in turn, accepted and sanc-

Modern-day port of Yafo; in this city
Peter was given a vision that prepared him
to preach to Gentiles

tified the gifts to Jehovah. (2Sa 8:5, 9-11) In a parallel account Joram's name is spelled Hadoram. —1Ch 18:9-11.

2. A descendant of Levite Eliezer, Moses' son; he apparently lived when David was king.—1Ch 26:24, 25; Ex 18:2-4.

3. King of Israel for 12 years; son of Ahab. Usually he is identified by the longer form of his name, Jehoram. (2Ki 3:1) Only in three chapters do we find the short form in the Masoretic text. —2Ki 8:16, ftn, 17-29; 9:14, ftn, 15-29; 2Ch 22:5, ftn, 6, 7; see JEHORAM No. 2.

4. King of Judah for eight years; son of Jehoshaphat. The Masoretic text has his name at times in the short form. (2Ki 8:21, 23, 24; 11:2; 1Ch 3:11, ftn) The shortened form is also found in the Westcott and Hort Greek Text, but a few translations give assistance in understanding by rendering the full name.—Mt 1:8, *NW, Sawyer, TC, We;* see JEHORAM No. 3.

JORDAN

(Jor′dan). The main river of the Promised Land, forming a natural border between most of E and W Palestine. (Jos 22:25) Anciently the Jordan proper began its course upon its exit from the Hula Basin, a swamp area and lake now drained. The area N of the Hula Basin is characterized by numerous watercourses, the sources of the Jordan. The three principal streams that form the Jordan, from E to W, are the Nahr Banyas (Nahal Hermon), the Nahr el-Leddan (Nahal Dan), and the Nahr Hasbani (Nahal Senir). The Yarmuk and the Jabbok are the Jordan's main tributaries from the E. Today most of the Jordan is a very muddy stream.

Upon emerging from the Hula Basin, the Jordan flows somewhat peacefully for about 3 km (2 mi) but then rushes through basalt gorges on its way to the Sea of Galilee. From the southern end of the Sea of Galilee, the Jordan snakes its way to the Dead Sea for some 320 km (200 mi), although the airline distance is only about 105 km (65 mi). —PICTURE, Vol. 1, p. 334.

Within a distance of some 16 km (10 mi) between the Hula Basin and the Sea of Galilee, the Jordan falls some 270 m (890 ft). As it continues its course from the Sea of Galilee to the Dead Sea, the Jordan forms 27 cascading rapids and drops about 180 m (590 ft) more.

Below the Sea of Galilee, the Jordan flows through a valley measuring some 6 to 13 km (3.5 to 8 mi) across. But at Jericho this valley has a width of about 22 km (14 mi). It is through the valley's lower level (the *Zor*), with a width of about 0.5 to 3 km (0.3 to 2 mi), that the Jordan turns and twists through dense thickets of thorns and thistles, vines and bushes, oleanders, tamarisks, willows, and poplars. Anciently, lions roamed in "the proud thickets along the Jordan." (Jer 49:19; 50:44; Zec 11:3) Wolves and jackals can still be found there. The summers are extremely hot and humid in this jungle, with temperatures climbing well above 38° C. (100° F.). And in the spring, as the snow melts on Mount Hermon, the Jordan floods the *Zor.*

The upper level of the valley (the *Ghor*) lies as much as 46 m (150 ft) above the Jordan's jungle and is separated from it by bare and eroded grayish marl hills. The portion of the *Ghor* extending some 40 km (25 mi) S of the Sea of Galilee contains cultivated land and pastures. Aside from this, most of the *Ghor* is uncultivated. However, in the time of Abraham and Lot, before the destruction of Sodom and Gomorrah, apparently much more of it was productive, especially in the vicinity of the Dead Sea.—Ge 13:10, 11.

The Jordan's shallow waters and its numerous rapids and whirlpools render it unnavigable. Reportedly, there are at least 60 places where it is possible to wade across the river when not at flood stage. In ancient times control of the river's fords was militarily advantageous, as they were the main means for crossing the Jordan.—Jg 3:28; 12:5, 6.

Usually the portion of the Jordan below the Sea of Galilee averages from 1 to 3 m (3 to 10 ft) in depth and is approximately 27 to 30 m (90 to 100 ft) wide. But in the spring the Jordan overflows its banks and is then much wider and deeper. (Jos 3:15) At flood stage it would not have been safe for the Israelite nation of men, women, and children to cross the Jordan, especially not near Jericho. The current there is so swift that in more recent times bathers have actually been swept away. However, Jehovah miraculously dammed up the Jordan, making it possible for the Israelites to cross on dry land. (Jos 3:14-17) Centuries later a like miracle occurred once for Elijah while in the company of Elisha, and once for Elisha alone.—2Ki 2:7, 8, 13, 14.

The Jordan also figured in the miraculous healing of Naaman. Helped to the right viewpoint by his servants, Naaman, who regarded the rivers of Damascus as better than all the waters of Israel, obediently bathed seven times in the Jordan. After the seventh time he was completely healed of his leprous condition.—2Ki 5:10-14.

In the first century C.E., John the Baptizer immersed many repentant Jews in the waters of the

Jordan. He also had the privilege of baptizing Jesus, the perfect Son of God, there.—Mt 3:1, 5, 6, 13-17; see DISTRICT OF THE JORDAN.

JORIM (Jo'rim). A descendant of King David through Nathan, and an ancestor of Jesus' mother Mary. (Lu 3:23, 29-31) Jorim may have lived while Uzziah was king of Judah.

JORKEAM (Jor'ke·am). Apparently a Judean site 'fathered,' or founded, by Raham.—1Ch 2:44.

JOSECH (Jo'sech). A forefather of Jesus' mother Mary. Josech was a distant descendant of David through Nathan, and the fourth generation after Zerubbabel, placing him at about the end of the Hebrew Scripture era.—Lu 3:23, 26, 27, 31.

JOSEPH (Jo'seph) [shortened form of Josiphiah meaning "May Jah Add (Increase); Jah Has Added (Increased)"].

1. The first of Jacob's two sons by his beloved wife Rachel. (Ge 35:24) At his birth, Rachel, because of having been barren, exclaimed: "God has taken away my reproach!" She then called his name Joseph, saying: "Jehovah is adding another son to me," that is, another son besides Dan and Naphtali, whom Rachel had accepted as her own although they were borne by her maidservant Bilhah. (Ge 30:3-8, 22-24) At this time Jacob was evidently 91 years old.—Compare Ge 41:46, 47, 53, 54; 45:11; 47:9.

Some six years later Jacob left Paddan-aram with his entire family to return to the land of Canaan. (Ge 31:17, 18, 41) Upon learning that his brother Esau was coming to meet him with 400 men, Jacob divided off his children, wives, and concubines, placing Rachel and Joseph in the rear, the safest position. (Ge 33:1-3) Joseph and his mother therefore were the last to bow before Esau.—Ge 33:4-7.

Thereafter Joseph resided with the family at Succoth, Shechem (Ge 33:17-19), and Bethel respectively. (Ge 35:1, 5, 6) Later, on the way from Bethel to Ephrath (Bethlehem), Joseph's mother Rachel died while giving birth to Benjamin.—Ge 35:16-19.

Hated by His Half Brothers. At the age of 17, Joseph, in association with the sons of Jacob by Bilhah and Zilpah, tended sheep. While doing so, he, although their junior, did not share in their wrongdoing but dutifully brought a bad report about them to his father.—Ge 37:2.

Jacob came to love Joseph more than all his other sons, he being a son of his old age. Joseph's adherence to right may also have contributed to his becoming the special object of his father's affection. Jacob had a long striped garment, perhaps such as was worn by persons of rank, made for his son. As a result, Joseph came to be hated by his half brothers. Later, when he related a dream that pointed to his gaining the preeminence over them, his brothers were incited to further hatred. A second dream even indicated that not only his brothers but also his father and mother (apparently not Rachel, as she was already dead, but perhaps the household or Jacob's principal living wife) would bow down to him. For relating this dream, Joseph was rebuked by his father, and the jealousy of his brothers intensified. The fact that Joseph spoke about his dreams does not mean that he entertained feelings of superiority. He was merely making known what God had revealed to him. Jacob may have recognized the prophetic nature of the dreams, for he "observed the saying."—Ge 37:3-11.

On another occasion, Jacob, then at Hebron, requested that Joseph check on the welfare of the flock and his brothers while they were in the vicinity of Shechem. In view of their animosity, this would not have been a pleasant assignment for Joseph. Yet unhesitatingly he said: "Here I am!" From the Low Plain of Hebron he then set out for Shechem. Informed by a man there that his brothers had left for Dothan, Joseph continued on his way. When they caught sight of him at a distance, his brothers began scheming against him, saying: "Look! Here comes that dreamer. And now come and let us kill him and pitch him into one of the waterpits . . . Then let us see what will become of his dreams." (Ge 37:12-20) The firstborn, Reuben, however, desired to thwart the murderous plot and urged that they not kill Joseph but throw him into a dry waterpit. When Joseph arrived they stripped him of his long striped garment and followed through on Reuben's recommendation. Subsequently, as a caravan of Ishmaelites came to view, Judah, in Reuben's absence, persuaded the others that, rather than kill Joseph, it would be better to sell him to the passing merchants.—Ge 37:21-27.

Sold Into Slavery. Despite Joseph's plea for compassion, they sold him for 20 silver pieces. (Ge 37:28; 42:21) Later, they deceived Jacob into believing that Joseph had been killed by a wild beast. So grieved was aged Jacob over the loss of his son that he refused to be comforted.—Ge 37:31-35.

Eventually the merchants brought Joseph into Egypt and sold him to Potiphar, the chief of Pharaoh's bodyguard. (Ge 37:28, 36; 39:1) This purchase by the Egyptian Potiphar was not unusual, ancient papyrus documents indicating that Syrian slaves (Joseph was half Syrian [Ge 29:10; 31:20]) were valued highly in that land.

As Joseph had been diligent in furthering his father's interests, so also as a slave he proved himself to be industrious and trustworthy. With Jehovah's blessing, everything that Joseph did turned out successfully. Potiphar therefore finally entrusted to him all the household affairs. Joseph thus appears to have been a superintendent, a post mentioned by Egyptian records in association with the large homes of influential Egyptians. —Ge 39:2-6.

Resists Temptation. Meanwhile Joseph had come to be a very handsome young man. Consequently Potiphar's wife became infatuated with him. Repeatedly she asked him to have relations with her. But Joseph, trained in the way of righteousness, refused, saying: "How could I commit this great badness and actually sin against God?" This, however, did not end the danger for Joseph. Archaeological evidence indicates that the arrangement of Egyptian houses appears to have been such that a person had to pass through the main part of the house to reach the storerooms. If Potiphar's house was laid out similarly, it would have been impossible for Joseph to avoid all contact with Potiphar's wife.—Ge 39:6-10.

Finally Potiphar's wife took advantage of what she considered to be an opportune time. While there were no other men in the house and while Joseph was caring for the household business, she grabbed hold of his garment, saying: "Lie down with me!" But Joseph left his garment in her hand and fled. At that she began to scream and made it appear that Joseph had made immoral advances toward her. On her relating this to her husband, the enraged Potiphar had Joseph thrown into the prison house, the one where the king's prisoners were kept under arrest.—Ge 39:11-20.

In Prison. It appears that initially Joseph was treated severely in prison. "With fetters they afflicted his feet, into irons his soul came." (Ps 105: 17, 18) Later, however, the chief officer of the prison house, because of Joseph's exemplary conduct under adverse circumstances and the blessing of Jehovah, placed him in a position of trust over the other prisoners. In this capacity the prisoner Joseph again showed himself to be an able administrator by seeing to it that all the work was done.—Ge 39:21-23.

Thereafter, when two of Pharaoh's officers, the chief of the cupbearers and the chief of the bakers, were put into the same prison, Joseph was assigned to wait upon them. In the course of time, both of these men had dreams, which Joseph, after ascribing interpretation to God, explained to them. The cupbearer's dream pointed to his being restored to his position in three days. Joseph therefore requested that the cupbearer remember him and mention him to Pharaoh so that he might be released from prison. He explained that he had been kidnapped from "the land of the Hebrews" and had done nothing deserving of imprisonment. Probably so as not to cast a bad reflection on his family, Joseph chose not to identify the kidnappers. Subsequently he interpreted the baker's dream to mean that he would be put to death in three days. Both dreams were fulfilled three days later on the occasion of Pharaoh's birthday. This doubtless strengthened Joseph as to the certain fulfillment of his own dreams and aided him to continue enduring. By that time some 11 years had already passed since his being sold by his brothers.—Ge 40:1-22; compare Ge 37:2; 41: 1, 46.

Before Pharaoh. Again restored to his position, the cupbearer forgot all about Joseph. (Ge 40:23) However, at the end of two full years, Pharaoh had two dreams that none of Egypt's magic-practicing priests and wise men could interpret. It was then that the cupbearer brought Joseph to Pharaoh's attention. At once Pharaoh sent for Joseph. In keeping with Egyptian custom, Joseph, before going before Pharaoh, shaved and changed his garments. Also in this case he did not take any credit to himself but ascribed interpretation to God. He then explained that both of Pharaoh's dreams pointed to seven years of plenty to be followed by seven years of famine. Additionally, he recommended measures for alleviating the future conditions of famine.—Ge 41:1-36.

In agreement with the Bible's report that Pharaoh had a chief cupbearer, grape harvesting and winemaking are depicted in a tomb in Thebes

Made Second Ruler of Egypt. Pharaoh recognized in 30-year-old Joseph the man wise enough to administer affairs during the time of plenty and the time of famine. Joseph was therefore constituted second ruler in Egypt, Pharaoh giving Joseph his own signet ring, fine linen garments, and a necklace of gold. (Ge 41:37-44, 46; compare Ps 105:17, 20-22.) This manner of investiture is attested by Egyptian inscriptions and murals. It is also of interest that from ancient Egyptian records it is known that several Canaanites were given high positions in Egypt and that Joseph's change in name to Zaphenath-paneah is not without parallel. Joseph was also given Asenath the daughter of Potiphera (from Egyptian, meaning "He Whom Ra Has Given") the priest of On as a wife.—Ge 41:45.

Thereafter Joseph toured the land of Egypt and prepared to administer affairs of state, later storing great quantities of foodstuffs during the years of plenty. Before the famine arrived, his wife Asenath bore him two sons, Manasseh and Ephraim. —Ge 41:46-52.

Half Brothers Come to Buy Food. Then the famine came. Since it extended far beyond Egypt's borders, people from surrounding lands came to buy food from Joseph. Eventually even his ten half brothers arrived and bowed low to him, thus partially fulfilling Joseph's two previous dreams. (Ge 41:53–42:7) However, they did not recognize him, dressed as he was in royal attire and speaking to them through an interpreter. (Ge 42:8, 23) Feigning not to know them, Joseph accused them of being spies, upon which charge they asserted that they were ten brothers, that they had left behind at home their father and their younger brother, and that another brother was no more. But Joseph insisted that they were spies and put them in custody. On the third day he said to them: "Do this and keep alive. I fear the true God. If you are upright, let one of your brothers be kept bound in your house of custody [apparently the one in which all ten had been in custody], but the rest of you go, take cereals for the famine in your houses. Then you will bring your youngest brother to me, that your words may be found trustworthy; and you will not die."—Ge 42:9-20.

In view of these developments, Joseph's half brothers began to sense divine retribution on them for having sold him into slavery years earlier. In front of their brother, whom they still did not recognize, they discussed their guilt. On overhearing their words reflecting repentance, Joseph was so emotionally overcome that he had to leave their presence and weep. On returning, he had Simeon bound until such time as they would come back with their youngest brother.—Ge 42:21-24.

Half Brothers Come With Benjamin. When Joseph's nine half brothers told Jacob what had happened in Egypt and when it was discovered that the money of all of them was back in their sacks, all became very much afraid, and their father gave expression to grief. Only the severity of the famine, coupled with Judah's assurance for the safe return of Benjamin, moved Jacob to allow his youngest son to accompany the others back to Egypt.—Ge 42:29–43:14.

Upon arriving there, they were reunited with Simeon, and much to their surprise, all were invited to have dinner with the food administrator. When Joseph came they presented him with a gift, prostrated themselves to him, and after answering his inquiries concerning their father,

Grain harvesting and storing as depicted in an Egyptian tomb. Genesis refers to abundant grain harvest in Egypt

again bowed down to him. On seeing his full brother Benjamin, Joseph was so aroused emotionally that he left their presence and gave way to tears. After that he was able to control his feelings and had the noon meal served. The 11 brothers were seated at their own table according to age, and Benjamin was given portions five times greater than the others. Likely Joseph did this to test his brothers as to any hidden jealousies. But they gave no evidence of such.—Ge 43:15-34.

As on the previous visit, Joseph had each one's money put back in his bag (Ge 42:25), and additionally he had his silver cup placed in Benjamin's bag. After they had got under way, he had them overtaken and charged with stealing his silver cup. Perhaps to impress upon them its great value to him and the serious nature of their supposed crime, the man over Joseph's house was to say to them: "Is not this the thing that my master drinks from and by means of which he expertly reads omens?" (Ge 44:1-5) Of course, since all of this was part of a ruse, there is no basis for believing that Joseph actually used the silver cup to read omens. Apparently Joseph wanted to represent himself as an administrator of a land to which true worship was foreign.

Great must have been the consternation of his brothers when the cup was found in Benjamin's bag. With garments ripped apart, they returned to Joseph's house and bowed before him. Joseph told them that all except Benjamin were free to go. But this they did not want to do, showing that the envious spirit that had moved them about 22 years earlier to sell their brother was gone. Judah eloquently pleaded their case, offering to take Benjamin's place lest their father die from grief because of Benjamin's failure to return.—Ge 44:6-34.

Joseph Reveals His Identity. Joseph was so affected by Judah's plea that he could no longer contain himself. After requesting all strangers to leave, he identified himself to his brothers. Although greatly mistreated by them formerly, he harbored no animosity. Said he: "Now do not feel hurt and do not be angry with yourselves because you sold me here; because for the preservation of life God has sent me ahead of you. For this is the second year of the famine in the midst of the earth, and there are yet five years in which there will be no plowing time or harvest. Consequently God sent me ahead of you in order to place a remnant for you men in the earth and to keep you alive by a great escape. So now it was not you who sent me here, but it was the true God." (Ge 45:1-8)

Joseph's forgiveness was genuine, for he wept over and kissed all his brothers.—Ge 45:14, 15.

Thereafter Joseph, according to Pharaoh's orders, provided wagons for his brothers so that they might bring Jacob and his entire household to Egypt. Additionally he gave them presents and provisions for the journey. And, in parting, he encouraged them not to get "exasperated at one another on the way."—Ge 45:16-24.

Joseph's Father Comes to Egypt. Jacob at first could not believe that his son Joseph was still alive. But, when finally convinced, 130-year-old Jacob exclaimed: "Ah, let me go and see him before I die!" Later, at Beer-sheba while on the way to Egypt with his entire household, Jacob, in vision, received divine approval for the move and was also told: "Joseph will lay his hand upon your eyes." So Joseph was to be the one to close Jacob's eyes after his death. Since the firstborn customarily did this, Jehovah thereby revealed that Joseph was to receive the right as firstborn.—Ge 45: 25–46:4.

Having been advised of his father's coming by Judah, who had been sent in advance, Joseph got his chariot ready and went to meet Jacob at Goshen. Then, with five of his brothers, Joseph came to Pharaoh. As directed by Joseph, his brothers identified themselves as herders of sheep and requested to reside as aliens in the land of Goshen. Pharaoh granted their request, and Joseph, after introducing his father to Pharaoh, settled Jacob and his household in the very best of the land. (Ge 46:28–47:11) Thus, wisely and lovingly Joseph made the best of an Egyptian prejudice against shepherds. It resulted in safeguarding Jacob's family from being contaminated by Egyptian influence and eliminated the danger of their being completely absorbed by the Egyptians through marriage. From then on Jacob and his entire household were dependent on Joseph. (Ge 47: 12) In effect, all bowed down to Joseph as Pharaoh's prime minister, fulfilling Joseph's prophetic dreams in a remarkable way.

Effect of Famine on Egyptians. As the famine continued, the Egyptians gradually exhausted all their money and their livestock in exchange for food. Finally they even sold their land and themselves as slaves to Pharaoh. Then Joseph settled them in cities, doubtless to facilitate the distribution of grain. Apparently, though, this resettlement in cities was a temporary measure. Since the Egyptians had to return to their fields to sow seed, logically they would again dwell in their former houses. Once they were again enjoying a harvest from the land, the Egyptians, according to

Joseph's decree, were required to give a fifth of their produce to Pharaoh for using the land. The priests, however, were exempted.—Ge 47:13-26.

Jacob Blesses Joseph's Sons. About 12 years after the famine ended, Joseph brought his two sons, Manasseh and Ephraim, before Jacob. It was then that Jacob indicated that the right of firstborn was to be Joseph's, Ephraim and Manasseh being viewed as equals of Jacob's direct sons. So from Joseph were to spring two distinct tribes, with two separate tribal inheritances. Though it displeased Joseph, Jacob, in blessing Ephraim and Manasseh, kept his right hand placed on the younger, Ephraim. By giving the preference to Ephraim, he prophetically indicated that the younger would become the greater.—Ge 47:28, 29; 48:1-22; see also De 21:17; Jos 14:4; 1Ch 5:1.

Jacob Blesses Joseph and Other Sons. Later, Jacob, on his deathbed, called all his sons to him and blessed them individually. He likened Joseph to "the offshoot of a fruit-bearing tree." That "fruit-bearing tree" was the patriarch Jacob himself, and Joseph became one of the prominent branches. (Ge 49:22) Though harassed by archers and an object of animosity, Joseph's bow "was dwelling in a permanent place, and the strength of his hands was supple." (Ge 49:23, 24) This could have been said of Joseph personally. His half brothers harbored animosity and figuratively shot at him to destroy him. Yet Joseph repaid them with mercy and loving-kindness, these qualities being like arrows that killed their animosity. The enemy archers did not succeed in killing Joseph nor in weakening his devotion to righteousness and brotherly affection.

Prophetically, though, Jacob's words could apply to the tribes that were to spring from Joseph's two sons, Ephraim and Manasseh, and their future battles. (Compare De 33:13, 17; Jg 1:23-25, 35.) It is of interest that the tribe of Ephraim produced Joshua (Hoshea; Jehoshua), Moses' successor and the leader of the fight against the Canaanites. (Nu 13:8, 16; Jos 1:1-6) Another descendant of Joseph, Gideon of the tribe of Manasseh, with the help of Jehovah, defeated the Midianites. (Jg 6:13-15; 8:22) And Jephthah, evidently also of the tribe of Manasseh, subdued the Ammonites.—Jg 11:1, 32, 33; compare Jg 12:4; Nu 26:29.

Other aspects of Jacob's prophetic blessing also find a parallel in Joseph's experiences. When Joseph, instead of taking vengeance, made provision for the entire household of Jacob, or Israel, he was as a shepherd and a stone of support to Israel. Since Jehovah had guided matters so that he could serve in this capacity, Joseph had come from the hands of the "powerful one of Jacob." Being from God, Joseph had Jehovah's help. He was with the Almighty in that he was on Jehovah's side and therefore was a recipient of his blessing.—Ge 49: 24, 25.

The blessing of Jehovah also was to be experienced by the tribes to descend from Joseph through Ephraim and Manasseh. Said Jacob: "He [the Almighty] will bless you with the blessings of the heavens above, with the blessings of the watery deep lying down below, with the blessings of the breasts and womb." (Ge 49:25) This assured Joseph's descendants of needed water supplies from heaven and from underground, as well as a large population.—Compare De 33:13-16; Jos 17:14-18.

The blessings that Jacob pronounced upon his beloved son Joseph were to be like an ornament to the two tribes to spring from Joseph. These blessings were to be an ornament superior to the blessings of forests and springs that adorn the eternal mountains and the indefinitely lasting hills. They were to be a permanent blessing, continuing upon the head of Joseph and of those descended from him just as long as mountains and hills continued.—Ge 49:26; De 33:16.

Joseph was "singled out from his brothers" because God chose him to perform a special role. (Ge 49:26) He had distinguished himself by displaying excellence of spirit and ability to oversee and organize. It was therefore appropriate that special blessings descend upon the crown of his head.

After Jacob finished blessing his sons, he died. Joseph then fell upon his father's face and kissed him. In compliance with Jacob's wish to be buried in the cave of Machpelah, Joseph had the Egyptian physicians embalm his father's body in preparation for the trip to Canaan.—Ge 49:29–50:13.

Attitude Toward His Brothers. Subsequent to their return from burying Jacob, Joseph's half brothers, still plagued by guilty consciences, feared that Joseph might take revenge, and they pleaded for forgiveness. At that, Joseph burst into tears, comforting and reassuring them that there was no reason for fear: "Do not be afraid, for am I in the place of God? As for you, you had evil in mind against me. God had it in mind for good for the purpose of acting as at this day to preserve many people alive. So now do not be afraid. I myself shall keep supplying you and your little children with food."—Ge 50:14-21.

Death. Joseph survived his father by about 54 years, reaching the age of 110 years. It was his privilege to see even some of his great-grandsons. Before his death, Joseph, in faith, requested that his bones be taken to Canaan by the Israelites at the time of their Exodus. At death, Joseph's body was embalmed and placed in a coffin.—Ge 50:22-26; Jos 24:32; Heb 11:22.

The Name Joseph Given Prominence. In view of Joseph's prominent position among the sons of Jacob, it was most appropriate that his name was sometimes used to designate all the tribes of Israel (Ps 80:1) or those that came to be included in the northern kingdom. (Ps 78:67; Am 5:6, 15; 6:6) His name also figures in Bible prophecy. In Ezekiel's prophetic vision, the inheritance of Joseph is a double portion (Eze 47:13), one of the gates of the city "Jehovah Himself Is There" bears the name Joseph (Eze 48:32, 35), and with reference to the reunifying of Jehovah's people, Joseph is spoken of as chief of the one part of the nation and Judah as chief of the other part. (Eze 37:15-26) Obadiah's prophecy indicated that "the house of Joseph" would share in the destruction of "the house of Esau" (Ob 18), and that of Zechariah pointed to Jehovah's saving "the house of Joseph." (Zec 10:6) Rather than Ephraim, Joseph appears as one of the tribes of spiritual Israel.—Re 7:8.

The fact that Joseph is listed at Revelation 7:8 suggests that Jacob's deathbed prophecy would have an application to spiritual Israel. It is noteworthy, therefore, that the Powerful One of Jacob, Jehovah God, provided Christ Jesus as the Fine Shepherd who laid down his life for "the sheep." (Joh 10:11-16) Christ Jesus is also the foundation cornerstone upon which God's temple composed of spiritual Israelites rests. (Eph 2:20-22; 1Pe 2:4-6) And this Shepherd and Stone is with the Almighty God.—Joh 1:1-3; Ac 7:56; Heb 10:12; compare Ge 49:24, 25.

Parallels Between Joseph and Christ. Numerous parallels may be noted between the life of Joseph and that of Christ Jesus. As Joseph had been singled out as the special object of his father's affection, so also had Jesus. (Compare Mt 3:17; Heb 1:1-6.) Joseph's half brothers were hostile toward him. Similarly, Jesus was rejected by his own, the Jews (Joh 1:11), and his fleshly half brothers at first did not exercise faith in him. (Joh 7:5) Joseph's ready obedience in complying with his father's will in checking on his half brothers parallels Jesus' willingly coming to earth. (Php 2:5-8) The bitter experiences that this mission resulted in for Joseph were comparable to what befell Jesus, particularly when abused and finally put to death on a torture stake. (Mt 27:27-46) As Joseph's half brothers sold Joseph to the Midianite-Ishmaelite caravan, so the Jews delivered up Jesus to the Roman authority for execution. (Joh 18:35) Both Joseph and Jesus were refined and prepared for their lifesaving roles through suffering. (Ps 105:17-19; Heb 5:7-10) The elevation of Joseph to the position of food administrator in Egypt and the saving of life resulting therefrom finds a parallel in Jesus' exaltation and his becoming a Savior of both Jews and non-Jews. (Joh 3:16, 17; Ac 5:31) The scheme of Joseph's brothers to harm him proved to be God's means of saving them from starvation. Likewise, the death of Jesus provided the basis for salvation.—Joh 6:51; 1Co 1:18.

2. Father of Igal, the spy of the tribe of Issachar sent out by Moses from the Wilderness of Paran. —Nu 13:2, 3, 7.

3. A Levite "of the sons of Asaph" designated by lot during David's reign to be in the first of 24 service groups of musicians.—1Ch 25:1, 2, 9.

4. "Son of Jonam"; ancestor of Christ Jesus in the lineage of his earthly mother Mary. (Lu 3:30) Joseph was a descendant of David and lived before the destruction of Jerusalem by the Babylonians.

5. One among those dismissing their foreign wives and sons at Ezra's exhortation.—Ezr 10: 10-12, 42, 44.

6. A priest of the paternal house of Shebaniah during the time of High Priest Joiakim, Governor Nehemiah, and Ezra the priest.—Ne 12:12, 14, 26.

7. "Son of Mattathias" and ancestor of Jesus Christ on the maternal side. (Lu 3:24, 25) Joseph lived years after the Babylonian exile.

8. Son of a certain Jacob; adoptive father of Christ Jesus, husband of Mary, and later, the natural father of at least four sons, James, Joseph, Simon, and Judas, besides daughters. (Mt 1:16; 13:55, 56; Lu 4:22; Joh 1:45; 6:42) Joseph was also called the son of Heli (Lu 3:23), this evidently being the name of his father-in-law. Ever obedient to divine direction, righteous Joseph adhered closely to the Mosaic Law and submitted to the decrees of Caesar.

A carpenter by trade and a resident of Nazareth, Joseph had rather limited financial resources. (Mt 13:55; Lu 2:4; compare Lu 2:24 with Le 12:8.) He was engaged to the virgin girl Mary (Lu 1:26, 27), but before they were united in marriage she became pregnant by holy spirit. Not wanting to make her a public spectacle, Joseph intended to divorce her secretly. (See DIVORCE.) However, upon receiving an explanation from Jehovah's angel in a dream, Joseph took Mary to his home as his legal wife. Nevertheless, he refrained from having relations with her until after the birth of her miraculously begotten son.—Mt 1:18-21, 24, 25.

In obedience to the decree of Caesar Augustus for persons to get registered in their own cities, Joseph, as a descendant of King David, traveled with Mary to Bethlehem of Judea. There Mary gave birth to Jesus and laid him in a manger, because other accommodations were not available. That night shepherds, having been informed by an angel concerning the birth, came to see the newborn infant. About 40 days later, as required by the Mosaic Law, Joseph and Mary presented Jesus at the temple in Jerusalem along with an offering. Both Joseph and Mary wondered as they heard aged Simeon's prophetic words about the great things Jesus would do.—Lu 2:1-33; compare Le 12:2-4, 6-8.

It appears that sometime after this, while residing in a house at Bethlehem, Mary and her young son were visited by some Oriental astrologers. (Although Luke 2:39 might seem to indicate that Joseph and Mary returned to Nazareth right after presenting Jesus at the temple, it must be remembered that this scripture is part of a highly condensed account.) Divine intervention prevented their visit from bringing death to Jesus. Warned in a dream that Herod was seeking to find the child to destroy it, Joseph heeded divine instructions to flee with his family to Egypt.—Mt 2:1-15.

After the decease of Herod, Jehovah's angel again appeared in a dream to Joseph, saying: "Get up, take the young child and its mother and be on your way into the land of Israel." However, hearing that Herod's son Archelaus was ruling in his father's stead, he feared to return to Judea, and "being given divine warning in a dream, he withdrew into the territory of Galilee, and came and dwelt in a city named Nazareth."—Mt 2:19-23.

Each year Joseph took his whole family with him to attend the Passover celebration at Jerusalem. On one occasion they were returning to Nazareth when, after covering a day's distance from Jerusalem, Joseph and Mary found that the 12-year-old Jesus was missing. Diligently they searched for him and finally found him at the temple in Jerusalem, listening to and questioning the teachers there.—Lu 2:41-50.

The Scriptural record is silent on the extent of the training Joseph gave to Jesus. Doubtless, though, he contributed to Jesus' progressing in wisdom. (Lu 2:51, 52) Joseph also taught him carpentry, for Jesus was known both as "the carpenter's son" (Mt 13:55) and as "the carpenter."—Mr 6:3.

Joseph's death is not specifically mentioned in the Scriptures. But it seems that he did not survive Jesus. Had he lived beyond Passover time of 33 C.E., it is unlikely that the impaled Jesus would have entrusted Mary to the care of the apostle John.—Joh 19:26, 27.

9. A half brother of Jesus Christ. (Mt 13:55; Mr 6:3) Like his other brothers, Joseph at first did not exercise faith in Jesus. (Joh 7:5) Later, however, Jesus' half brothers, doubtless including Joseph, became believers. They are mentioned as being with the apostles and others after Jesus' ascension to heaven, so they were likely among the group of about 120 disciples assembled in an upper room at Jerusalem when Matthias was chosen by lot as a replacement for unfaithful Judas Iscariot. It appears that later this same group of about 120 received God's spirit on the day of Pentecost in 33 C.E.—Ac 1:9–2:4.

10. A wealthy man from the Judean city of Arimathea and a reputable member of the Jewish Sanhedrin. Although a good and righteous man who was waiting for God's Kingdom, Joseph, because of his fear of unbelieving Jews, did not openly identify himself as a disciple of Jesus Christ. However, he did not vote in support of the Sanhedrin's unjust action against Christ Jesus. Later, he courageously asked Pilate for Jesus' body and, along with Nicodemus, prepared it for burial and then placed it in a new rock-cut tomb. This tomb was situated in a garden near the place of impalement and belonged to Joseph of Arimathea.—Mt 27:57-60; Mr 15:43-46; Lu 23:50-53; Joh 19:38-42.

11. One put up along with Matthias as a candidate for the office of oversight vacated by the unfaithful Judas Iscariot. Joseph, also called Barsabbas (perhaps a family name or merely an additional name) and surnamed Justus, was a witness of the work, miracles, and resurrection of Jesus Christ. However, Matthias, not Joseph, was chosen by lot to replace Judas Iscariot before Pentecost of 33 C.E. and came to be "reckoned along with the eleven apostles."—Ac 1:15–2:1.

12. A Levite surnamed Barnabas and a native of Cyprus. (Ac 4:36, 37) He was a close associate of the apostle Paul.—See BARNABAS.

JOSES (Jo'ses) [from Heb., a shortened form of Josiphiah, meaning "May Jah Add (Increase); Jah Has Added (Increased)"]. Brother of James the Less and son of Mary. (Mt 27:56; Mr 15:40, 47; see JAMES No. 3.) Instead of "Joses," some ancient manuscripts read "Joseph."

JOSHAH (Jo'shah). One of the Simeonite chieftains who, in the days of King Hezekiah, conquered a portion of territory from the Hamites and Meunim in order to have more pasture ground.—1Ch 4:24, 34, 38-41.

JOSHAPHAT
(Josh'a·phat) [shortened form of Jehoshaphat, meaning "Jehovah Is Judge"].

1. One of David's loyal warriors; a Mithnite.—1Ch 11:26, 43.

2. A priest and one of the seven trumpeters who accompanied the ark of the covenant to Jerusalem.—1Ch 15:24, 25.

JOSHAVIAH
(Josh·a·vi'ah) [possibly from Joshibiah, meaning "Jah Causes to Dwell"]. A leading warrior in David's army; son of Elnaam.—1Ch 11:26, 46.

JOSHBEKASHAH
(Josh·be·kash'ah) [possibly from roots meaning "in whom affliction remains"]. Head of the 17th group of musicians at Jehovah's house; a son of Heman.—1Ch 25:1, 4, 9, 24.

JOSHEB-BASSHEBETH
(Jo'sheb-bas·she'-beth). The head one of David's three most outstanding mighty men. (2Sa 23:8) At 1 Chronicles 11:11 he is called Jashobeam, which is probably the more correct form. There are other scribal difficulties with the text in 2 Samuel 23:8, making it necessary for the obscure Hebrew in the Masoretic text (which appears to read, "He was Adino the Eznite") to be corrected to read "He was brandishing his spear." (*NW*) Other modern translations read similarly. (*AT; RS; Mo; Ro*, ftn; *JB*) Thus Samuel is made to agree with the book of Chronicles and with the construction pattern in this section of material. It is "the three" that are being discussed, but to introduce another name, Adino, makes four. Additionally, each of the three mighty men has one of his deeds credited to him, so if the overpowering of the 800 were attributed to someone else, there would be no deed credited here to Josheb-basshebeth (Jashobeam).—See JASHOBEAM No. 2.

There is a possibility that the deed ascribed to Josheb-basshebeth at 2 Samuel 23:8 is not the same as that mentioned at 1 Chronicles 11:11. This may explain why the Samuel account speaks of 800 slain, whereas the Chronicles account refers to 300 slain.

JOSHIBIAH
(Josh·i·bi'ah) [meaning "Jah Causes to Dwell"]. A Simeonite whose descendant joined a territory-expansion campaign.—1Ch 4:24, 35, 38-41.

JOSHUA
(Josh'u·a) [shortened form of Jehoshua, meaning "Jehovah Is Salvation"].

1. Son of Nun; an Ephraimite who ministered to Moses and was later appointed as his successor. (Ex 33:11; De 34:9; Jos 1:1, 2) The Scriptures portray Joshua as a bold and fearless leader, one who was confident in the certainty of Jehovah's promises, obedient to divine direction, and determined to serve Jehovah in faithfulness. His original name was Hoshea, but Moses called him Joshua or Jehoshua. (Nu 13:8, 16) The Bible record, however, does not reveal just when Hoshea came to be known as Joshua.

Leads Fight Against the Amalekites. In the year 1513 B.C.E., when the Israelites encamped at Rephidim shortly after their miraculous deliverance from Egypt's military might at the Red Sea, the Amalekites launched an unprovoked attack on them. Joshua was then appointed by Moses as commander in the fight against the Amalekites. Under his able leadership, the Israelites, with divine assistance, vanquished the foe. Subsequently Jehovah decreed ultimate annihilation for the Amalekites, instructing Moses to make a written record about this and to propound it to Joshua.—Ex 17:8-16.

Serves as Moses' Attendant. Later, at Mount Sinai, Joshua, as Moses' attendant, likely was one of the 70 older men who were privileged to see a magnificent vision of Jehovah's glory. Thereafter Joshua accompanied Moses partway up Mount Sinai but apparently did not enter the cloud, since Moses alone was commanded to do so. (Ex 24:9-18) Both he and Moses remained on Mount Sinai for 40 days and 40 nights. At the end of this period, while descending Mount Sinai with Moses, Joshua mistook the sound of Israel's singing in connection with their idolatrous calf worship as "a noise of battle." Doubtless he shared Moses' indignation when he caught sight of the golden calf and perhaps even assisted in its destruction.—Ex 32:15-20.

By engaging in calf worship, the Israelites broke the solemn covenant they had made with Jehovah God. This may have prompted Moses to move his tent ("the tent of meeting") from the area where the people encamped, as Jehovah had not yet forgiven them for their sin and was therefore no longer in the midst of Israel. Perhaps to prevent Israelites from entering the tent of meeting in their unclean state, Joshua remained there whenever Moses returned to the Israelite camp.—Ex 33:7-11; 34:9.

At a later time, when Moses, on account of the murmurings of the people, felt that his load was too great, Jehovah directed that he select 70 older men to assist him. These older men were then to go to the tent of meeting. But two of them, Eldad and Medad, doubtless for a valid reason, remained in the camp. When God's spirit became operative upon the 68 assembled at the tent of meeting, Eldad and Medad likewise began acting as prophets in the camp. News of this was quickly brought to Moses. Then Joshua, feeling jealous for his lord, urged that Moses restrain them. Since Eldad and Medad had apparently received the spirit apart from Moses' mediation, Joshua may have felt that this detracted from the authority of his lord. But Moses corrected Joshua, saying: "I wish that all of Jehovah's people were prophets, because Jehovah would put his spirit upon them."—Nu 11:10-29; compare Mr 9:38, 39.

Spies Out the Promised Land. It was sometime after this that the Israelites encamped in the Wilderness of Paran. From there Moses sent out 12 men to spy out the Promised Land, one of these men being Joshua (Hoshea, or Jehoshua). Forty days later only Joshua and Caleb brought back a good report. The other ten spies disheartened the people, claiming that Israel could never hope to defeat the powerful inhabitants of Canaan. Consequently rebellious murmuring broke out in the camp. Joshua and Caleb then ripped their garments apart and, as they tried to allay the people's fears, cautioned them against rebellion. But their courageous words reflecting full confidence in Jehovah's ability to fulfill his word were to no avail. In fact, "all the assembly talked of pelting them with stones."—Nu 13:2, 3, 8, 16, 25–14:10.

For their rebellion Jehovah sentenced the Israelites to wander in the wilderness for 40 years until all the registered males (not including the Levites, who were not registered among the other Israelites for military duty; Nu 1:2, 3, 47) from 20 years old upward died off. Of the registered males, Joshua and Caleb alone were to enter the Promised Land, whereas the ten unfaithful spies were to die by a scourge from Jehovah.—Nu 14:27-38; compare Nu 26:65; 32:11, 12.

Appointed as Moses' Successor. Toward the close of Israel's wandering in the wilderness, Moses and Aaron, for failing to sanctify Jehovah respecting the miraculous provision of water at Kadesh, also lost the privilege of entering the Promised Land. (Nu 20:1-13) Therefore, Jehovah instructed Moses to commission Joshua as his successor. In the immediate presence of the new high priest, Aaron's son Eleazar, and before the assembly of Israel, Moses placed his hands upon Joshua. Although appointed as Moses' successor, Joshua was not to be like him in knowing Jehovah "face to face." Not all of Moses' dignity was transferred to Joshua but only that which was needed for him to have the respect of the nation. Rather than the more direct communication Moses had been able to enjoy with Jehovah, "face to face" as it were, Joshua was to consult the high priest, to whom had been entrusted the Urim and Thummim by which the divine will could be ascertained.—Nu 27:18-23; De 1:37, 38; 31:3; 34:9, 10.

As divinely directed, Moses gave certain instructions and encouragement to Joshua so that he might faithfully discharge his commission. (De 3:21, 22, 28; 31:7, 8) Finally, as the time of his death was nearing, Moses was to station himself with Joshua at the tent of meeting. Jehovah then commissioned Joshua, confirming the earlier appointment made by the imposition of Moses' hands. (De 31:14, 15, 23) Subsequently Joshua participated in some way in writing and teaching the Israelites the song that was given to Moses by inspiration.—De 31:19; 32:44.

Activities as Moses' Successor. After Moses' death Joshua prepared to enter the Promised Land. He dispatched officers so that these might instruct the Israelites about getting ready to cross the Jordan three days from then; he reminded the Gadites, Reubenites, and the half tribe of Manasseh of their obligation to assist in the conquest of the land; and he sent out two men to spy out Jericho and the surrounding area.—Jos 1:1–2:1.

Following the return of the two spies, the Israelites left Shittim and encamped near the Jordan. On the next day Jehovah miraculously dammed up the Jordan, permitting the nation to cross on dry ground. To memorialize this event, Joshua set up 12 stones in the middle of the riverbed and 12 stones at Gilgal, Israel's first encampment W of the Jordan. He also made flint knives for circumcising all the Israelite males born in the wilderness. Thus some four days later they were in a fit condition to observe the Passover.—Jos 2:23–5:11.

Thereafter, while near Jericho, Joshua met an angelic prince from whom he received instruction about the procedure to be followed in taking that city. Joshua handled matters accordingly and, after devoting Jericho to destruction, pronounced a prophetic curse on its future rebuilder, which was fulfilled over 500 years later. (Jos 5:13–6:26; 1Ki 16:34) Next he moved against Ai. At first, the Israelite force of some 3,000 men suffered defeat, Jehovah having withheld his aid because of Achan's disobediently taking spoil from Jericho for personal use. Subsequent to Israel's stoning of Achan and his household for this sin, Joshua employed an ambush against Ai and reduced the city to a desolate mound.—Jos 7:1–8:29.

It was then that the entire congregation of Israel, including women, children, and alien residents, went to the vicinity of Mount Ebal. There at Mount

Ebal, Joshua built an altar according to the specifications outlined in the Law. As half of the congregation stood in front of Mount Gerizim and the other half in front of Mount Ebal, Joshua read to them the "law, the blessing and the malediction." "There proved to be not a word of all that Moses had commanded that Joshua did not read aloud." —Jos 8:30-35.

After returning to their Gilgal camp, Joshua and the chieftains of Israel had a visit from Gibeonite messengers. Recognizing that Jehovah was fighting for the Israelites, the Gibeonites, through trickery, succeeded in concluding a covenant of peace with Joshua. When the actual facts came to light, however, Joshua constituted them slaves. News of what the Gibeonites had done also reached Adoni-zedek the king of Jerusalem. For this reason he and four other Canaanite kings launched a punitive expedition against them. In response to an appeal from the Gibeonites for aid, Joshua staged an all-night march from Gilgal. Jehovah then fought for Israel in defense of the Gibeonites, indicating that he did not disapprove of the covenant that had earlier been made with them. More of the enemy forces perished as a result of a miraculous hailstorm than died in the actual warfare. Jehovah even listened to Joshua's voice in lengthening the daylight hours for the battle.—Jos 9:3–10:14.

Joshua followed up this God-given victory by capturing Makkedah, Libnah, Lachish, Eglon, Hebron, and Debir, thus breaking the power of the Canaanites in the southern part of the land. Next, the northern Canaanite kings, under the leadership of Jabin the king of Hazor, assembled their forces at the waters of Merom to fight against Israel. Though faced with horses and chariots, Joshua was divinely encouraged not to give way to fear. Again Jehovah granted victory to the Israelites. As instructed, Joshua hamstrung the horses and burned the chariots of the enemy. Hazor itself was consigned to the fire. (Jos 10: 16–11:23) Thus, within a period of about six years (compare Nu 10:11; 13:2, 6; 14:34-38; Jos 14:6-10), Joshua defeated 31 kings and subjugated large sections of the Promised Land.—Jos 12:7-24; MAP, Vol. 1, p. 737.

Now came the time for distributing the land to the individual tribes. This was done initially from Gilgal, under the supervision of Joshua, High Priest Eleazar, and ten other divinely appointed representatives. (Jos 13:7; 14:1, 2, 6; Nu 34:17-29) After the tabernacle was located at Shiloh, the apportioning of the land by lot continued from there. (Jos 18:1, 8-10) Joshua himself received the city of Timnath-serah in the mountainous region of Ephraim.—Jos 19:49, 50.

Final Admonition to Israelites, and Death. Toward the end of his life, Joshua assembled Israel's older men, its heads, judges, and officers, admonishing them to serve Jehovah in faithfulness and warning them of the consequences of disobedience. (Jos 23:1-16) He also called together the entire congregation of Israel, reviewed Jehovah's past dealings with their forefathers and the nation, and then appealed to them to serve Jehovah. Said Joshua: "Now if it is bad in your eyes to serve Jehovah, choose for yourselves today whom you will serve, whether the gods that your forefathers who were on the other side of the River served or the gods of the Amorites in whose land you are dwelling. But as for me and my household, we shall serve Jehovah." (Jos 24:1-15) Thereafter the Israelites renewed their covenant to obey Jehovah.—Jos 24:16-28.

At the age of 110 years, Joshua died and was buried at Timnath-serah. The good effect of his unswerving loyalty to Jehovah is evident from the fact that "Israel continued to serve Jehovah all the days of Joshua and all the days of the older men who extended their days after Joshua."—Jos 24:29-31; Jg 2:7-9.

2. Owner of a field at Beth-shemesh where the sacred Ark first came to rest and was exposed to view after being returned by the Philistines.—1Sa 6:14, 18.

3. Chief of Jerusalem in the time of King Josiah. It appears that high places used for false worship were located near Joshua's residence, but Josiah had these pulled down.—2Ki 23:8.

4. Son of Jehozadak; the first high priest to serve the repatriated Israelites following their return from Babylonian exile. (Hag 1:1, 12, 14; 2:2-4; Zec 3:1-9; 6:11) In the Bible books of Ezra and Nehemiah, he is called Jeshua.—See JESHUA No. 4.

JOSHUA, BOOK OF. This Bible book provides a vital link in the history of the Israelites by showing how God's promises to the patriarchs Abraham, Isaac, and Jacob were fulfilled. Probably covering a period of more than 20 years (1473-c. 1450 B.C.E.), it tells of the conquest of Canaan, followed by the distribution of the land to the Israelites; and it concludes with Joshua's discourses encouraging faithfulness to Jehovah.

The fact that the book contains ancient names for cities (Jos 14:15; 15:15) and detailed instructions and then relates how these were carried out indicates that it is a contemporary record. (For examples see Jos 1:11-18; 2:14-22; 3:2–4:24; 6:22, 23.) In fact, the writer identifies himself as living at the same time as Rahab of Jericho and therefore as an eyewitness.—6:25.

Authenticity. In the estimation of some, however, the book of Joshua is not true history. This view is primarily based on the assumption that, since the miracles mentioned in the book are foreign to recent human experience, they could not have happened. It therefore calls into question God's ability to perform miracles, if not also his existence, as well as the writer's integrity. For the writer to have embellished his account with fiction while presenting himself as an eyewitness would have made him guilty of deliberate deceit. Surely it is illogical to conclude that a book that honors God as the Fulfiller of his word (Jos 21:43-45), encourages faithfulness to him (23:6-16; 24:14,

---

HIGHLIGHTS OF JOSHUA

The record of how Jehovah gave the land of Canaan to Israel, in fulfillment of his oath to their forefathers

Events of the first 20 years or so following the death of Moses at the end of Israel's wandering in the wilderness

Joshua prepares Israel to enter Canaan, sends out spies (1:1–2:24)

Jehovah commissions Joshua to lead the Israelites into the land

Joshua commands that Israel be instructed to get ready to cross the Jordan

He sends spies out to investigate the land and the city of Jericho

When these are in Jericho they are hidden by Rahab, who is promised that she and all in her house who obey the instructions given will be spared in the coming destruction of Jericho

Israel crosses the Jordan River dry-shod (3:1–5:12)

The people sanctify themselves in preparation for crossing the Jordan

Priests carrying the Ark step into the river first; the river is miraculously dammed up some distance upstream, and the Israelites cross dry-shod

To memorialize the crossing, 12 stones are taken from the river and set up at Gilgal; another 12 stones are set up where the priests stood in the riverbed

Israelite males born in the wilderness are circumcised; a Passover is celebrated; the provision of manna ceases, and Israel begins to eat the produce of the land

The conquest of Jericho is followed by defeat at Ai (5:13–8:35)

The angelic prince of Jehovah's army appears to Joshua; Jehovah tells Joshua how to fight against Jericho

For six days in succession the Israelites march once daily around the city; on the seventh day they march around it seven times; upon the final round they give a loud shout, Jericho's walls fall, and the city is devoted to destruction

Achan takes for himself some of what has been devoted to destruction

Because of this sin, Jehovah withdraws his aid and Israel suffers defeat at Ai; Achan's sin is uncovered, and he and his household are stoned

The second attack against Ai succeeds with Jehovah's blessing

Joshua builds an altar at Mount Ebal and reads the Law to the people

The Gibeonites sue for peace, while others are destroyed (9:1–12:24)

The inhabitants of Gibeon, hearing of Israel's successes, shrewdly trick Joshua into making a covenant with them

Five kings unite to attack the Gibeonites, but Israel comes to Gibeon's aid; Jehovah hurls great hailstones and miraculously lengthens the daylight hours, causing utter defeat for the attackers

The Israelites under Joshua capture cities in the SW and the S

They are victorious over a coalition of kings in the N

Land is apportioned among tribes of Israel (13:1–22:34)

Reuben, Gad, and half tribe of Manasseh have territory E of the Jordan

Caleb receives Hebron; the tribes of Judah, Ephraim, and other half of Manasseh are assigned a land inheritance by lot

The tabernacle is set up at Shiloh, and lots are drawn there to determine land inheritances for the remaining tribes

The Levites receive 48 cities, 13 of which are priestly cities; 6 cities of refuge are set aside

Men of Reuben, Gad, and half tribe of Manasseh build an altar at the Jordan; its purpose is misunderstood until they explain that it is to serve as a memorial of faithfulness to Jehovah

Joshua urges Israel to serve Jehovah faithfully (23:1–24:33)

Advanced in years, Joshua calls an assembly of Israel's leaders and exhorts them to remain faithful to Jehovah

At an assembly in Shechem, he reviews God's dealings and encourages Israel to fear Jehovah and serve him alone; they express their determination to do so and reaffirm their covenant obligations

Joshua dies

15, 19, 20, 23), and openly acknowledges Israel's failures was produced by a false witness.—7:1-5; 18:3.

No one can deny that the Israelite nation came into existence and occupied the land described in the book of Joshua. Likewise, there is no valid basis for challenging the truthfulness of that book's account concerning the way in which the Israelites gained possession of Canaan. Neither the psalmists (Ps 44:1-3; 78:54, 55; 105:42-45; 135:10-12; 136:17-22), nor Nehemiah (Ne 9: 22-25), nor the first Christian martyr Stephen (Ac 7:45), nor the disciple James (Jas 2:25), nor the learned apostle Paul (Ac 13:19; Heb 4:8; 11:30, 31) doubted its authenticity. And 1 Kings 16:34 records the fulfillment of Joshua's prophetic curse uttered about 500 years earlier at the time of Jericho's destruction.—Jos 6:26.

Writer. Some scholars, although acknowledging that the book was written in or near the time of Joshua, reject the traditional Jewish view that Joshua himself wrote it. Their main objection is that some of the events recorded in the book of Joshua also appear in the book of Judges, which commences with the words, "And after the death of Joshua." (Jg 1:1) Nevertheless, this opening statement is not necessarily a time indicator for all the events found in the Judges account. The book is not arranged in strict chronological order, for it mentions an event that definitely is placed before Joshua's death. (Jg 2:6-9) Therefore, some things, such as the capture of Hebron by Caleb (Jos 15:13, 14; Jg 1:9, 10), Debir by Othniel (Jos 15:15-19; Jg 1:11-15), and Leshem, or Laish (Dan), by the Danites (Jos 19:47, 48; Jg 18:27-29), could likewise have taken place before Joshua's death. Even the action of the Danites in setting up an idolatrous image at Laish could reasonably fit Joshua's time. (Jg 18:30, 31) In his concluding exhortation, Joshua told the Israelites: "Remove the gods that your forefathers served on the other side of the River and in Egypt, and serve Jehovah." (Jos 24:14) Had idolatry not existed, this statement would have had little meaning.

Logically, then, with the exception of the concluding portion that reports his death, the book may be attributed to Joshua. As Moses had recorded the happenings of his lifetime, so it would have been fitting for Joshua to do likewise. The book itself reports: "Then Joshua wrote these words in the book of God's law."—Jos 24:26.

Not Contradictory. Some have felt that the book is contradictory in making it appear that the land was completely subdued by Joshua while at the same time reporting that much of it remained to be taken. (Compare Jos 11:16, 17, 23; 13:1.) But such seeming discrepancies are easily resolved when one bears in mind that there were two distinct aspects in the conquest. First, national warfare under Joshua's leadership broke the power of the Canaanites. Next, individual and tribal action was required to take full possession of the land. (17:14-18; 18:3) Probably while Israel was warring elsewhere, the Canaanites reestablished themselves in cities such as Debir and Hebron so that these had to be retaken by individual or tribal effort.—Compare Jos 11:21-23 with Jos 14:6, 12; 15:13-17.

JOSIAH   (Jo·si′ah) [if related to an Arabic root, May Jehovah Heal; Jehovah Has Healed].

1. Son of Judean King Amon by Jedidah the daughter of Adaiah. (2Ki 22:1) Josiah had at least two wives, Hamutal and Zebidah. (2Ki 23:31, 34, 36) Of his four sons mentioned in the Bible, only the firstborn, Johanan, did not rule as king over Judah.—1Ch 3:14, 15.

After the assassination of his father and the execution of the conspirators, eight-year-old Josiah became king of Judah. (2Ki 21:23, 24, 26; 2Ch 33:25) Some six years later Zebidah gave birth to Josiah's second son, Jehoiakim. (2Ki 22:1; 23:36) In the eighth year of his reign, Josiah sought to learn and to do Jehovah's will. (2Ch 34:3) It was also about this time that Jehoahaz (Shallum), Josiah's son by Hamutal, was born.—2Ki 22:1; 23:31; Jer 22:11.

During his 12th year as king, Josiah began a campaign against idolatry that apparently extended into the 18th year of his reign. Altars used for false worship were torn down and desecrated by burning human bones upon them. Also, sacred poles, graven images, and molten statues were destroyed. Josiah even extended his efforts as far as the northern part of what had once been territory of the ten-tribe kingdom but had been desolated because of the Assyrian conquest and subsequent exile. (2Ch 34:3-8) Evidently Zephaniah's and Jeremiah's denunciations of idolatry had a good effect.—Jer 1:1, 2; 3:6-10; Zep 1:1-6.

After King Josiah completed cleansing the land of Judah and while he was having Jehovah's temple repaired, High Priest Hilkiah found "the book of Jehovah's law by the hand of Moses," doubtless the original copy. Entrusted by Hilkiah with this sensational find, Shaphan the secretary reported on the progress of the temple repair work and thereafter read the book to Josiah. On hearing God's word, this faithful king ripped his garments apart and then commissioned a five-man delegation to inquire of Jehovah on his behalf and on behalf of the people. The delegation went to the prophetess Huldah, then dwelling in Jerusalem, and brought back a report to this effect: 'Calamity will come as a consequence of disobedience to Jehovah's Law. But because you, King Josiah, humbled yourself, you will be gathered to your graveyard in peace and will not see the calamity.' —2Ki 22:3-20; 2Ch 34:8-28; see HULDAH.

Subsequently Josiah assembled all the people of Judah and Jerusalem, including the older men, the priests, and the prophets, and read God's Law to them. After this, they concluded a covenant of faithfulness before Jehovah. Then followed a second and evidently a more intensive campaign against idolatry. The foreign-god priests of Judah and Jerusalem were put out of business, and Levite priests who had become involved in improper worship at high places were deprived of the privilege of serving at Jehovah's altar. The high places built centuries earlier during Solomon's reign were made completely unfit for worship. In fulfillment of a prophecy uttered about 300 years previously by an unnamed man of God, Josiah pulled down the altar built by Israel's King Jeroboam at Bethel. The high places were removed not only at Bethel but also in the other cities of Samaria, and the idolatrous priests were sacrificed on the altars where they had officiated.—1Ki 13:1, 2; 2Ki 23:4-20; 2Ch 34:33.

In the 18th year of his reign, Josiah arranged for the celebration of the Passover, on Nisan 14. It transcended any Passover that had been observed since the days of the prophet Samuel. Josiah himself contributed 30,000 Passover victims and 3,000 head of cattle.—2Ki 23:21-23; 2Ch 35:1-19.

About four years later Josiah became father to Mattaniah (Zedekiah) by his wife Hamutal.—2Ki 22:1; 23:31, 34, 36; 24:8, 17, 18.

Toward the close of Josiah's 31-year reign (659-629 B.C.E.), Pharaoh Necho led his army northward to the aid of the Assyrians. For a reason not revealed in the Bible, King Josiah disregarded "the words of Necho from the mouth of God" and tried to turn the Egyptian forces back at Megiddo, but he was mortally wounded in the attempt. He was brought back to Jerusalem in a war chariot and died either en route or upon arrival there. Josiah's death brought much grief to his subjects. "All Judah and Jerusalem were mourning over Josiah. And Jeremiah began to chant over Josiah; and all the male singers and female singers keep talking about Josiah in their dirges down till today."—2Ch 35:20-25; 2Ki 23: 29, 30; see ASSYRIA (The fall of the empire).

Although three of Josiah's sons and one grand-

son ruled as kings over Judah, none of them imitated his fine example of turning to Jehovah with all his heart, soul, and vital force. (2Ki 23:24, 25, 31, 32, 36, 37; 24:8, 9, 18, 19) This also indicates that although Josiah's efforts had removed the outward appendages of idolatry, the people generally had not returned to Jehovah with a complete heart. Consequently, future calamity was certain.—Compare 2Ki 23:26, 27; Jer 35:1, 13-17; 44:15-18.

2. "Son of Zephaniah" residing at Jerusalem after the exile, probably the same as Hen.—Zec 6: 10, 14.

JOSIPHIAH (Jo·si·phi'ah) [May Jah Add (Increase); Jah Has Added (Increased)]. A member of the paternal house of Bani whose son Shelomith, as head of the paternal house, went to Jerusalem with Ezra in 468 B.C.E.—Ezr 8:1, 10.

JOTBAH (Jot'bah) [from a root meaning "go well; prove satisfactory; do good"]. The home of Haruz, maternal grandfather of Judean King Amon. (2Ki 21:19) Jotbah is often identified with modern Khirbet Jefat (Horvat Yodefat), about 15 km (9 mi) N of Nazareth.

JOTBATHAH (Jot'ba·thah) [from a root that means "go well; prove satisfactory; do good"]. A well-watered wilderness encampment of the Israelites. (Nu 33:33, 34; De 10:7) Its exact location cannot be determined. However, 'Ain Tabah ('En Yotvata), located in a swampy depression about 40 km (25 mi) N of Ezion-geber, has been suggested as a possible identification.

JOTHAM (Jo'tham) [Jehovah Is Perfect; or, May Jehovah Complete].

1. A descendant of Judah designated as a 'son' of Jahdai.—1Ch 2:47.

2. Youngest son of Judge Gideon (Jerubbaal) residing at Ophrah. (Jg 8:35; 9:5) After Gideon's death, Abimelech, his son by a slave girl, murdered all of Gideon's other sons, his half brothers, that is, all but Jotham, who had concealed himself. Thereafter, when the landowners of Shechem made Abimelech their king, Jotham stationed himself atop Mount Gerizim and, by means of an illustration involving trees, pronounced a prophetic malediction upon the landowners of Shechem and upon Abimelech. Subsequently Jotham fled and took up residence at Beer.—Jg 9:6-21, 57.

3. Son of Judean King Uzziah (Azariah) by Jerusha(h) the daughter of Zadok. (2Ki 15:32, 33; 1Ch 3:12; 2Ch 27:1; Mt 1:9) After Uzziah was struck with leprosy when he became angry at the

priests because of being reproved by them for unlawfully invading the temple and attempting to offer up incense, Jotham began caring for the kingly duties in his father's stead. But apparently not until Uzziah's death did 25-year-old Jotham begin his 16-year rule (777-762 B.C.E.).—2Ki 15:5, 7, 32; 2Ch 26:18-21, 23; 27:8.

Isaiah, Hosea, and Micah served as prophets in the time of Jotham. (Isa 1:1; Ho 1:1; Mic 1:1) Although his subjects engaged in improper worship at high places, Jotham personally did what was right in Jehovah's eyes.—2Ki 15:35; 2Ch 27:2, 6.

Much construction work was done during Jotham's reign. He erected the upper gate of the temple, did considerable building on the wall of Ophel, also built cities in the mountainous region of Judah as well as fortified places and towers in the woodlands.—2Ch 27:3-7.

But Jotham did not enjoy a peaceful reign. He warred with the Ammonites and finally triumphed over them. As a result, for three years they paid a yearly tribute of 100 silver talents ($660,600) and 10,000 cor measures (2,200 kl; 62,500 bu) both of wheat and of barley. (2Ch 27:5) During Jotham's reign the land of Judah also began to experience military pressures from Syrian King Rezin and Israelite King Pekah.—2Ki 15:37.

At his death Jotham was buried in the City of David, and his son Ahaz, who had been about four years old when Jotham became king, ascended the throne of Judah.—2Ch 27:7–28:1.

Since Jotham ruled only 16 years, the reference at 2 Kings 15:30 to the "twentieth year of Jotham" evidently is to be understood to mean the 20th year after his becoming king, that is, the fourth year of Ahaz. The writer of the Kings account may

Signet ring bearing the name Jotham

have chosen not to introduce Jotham's successor Ahaz at this point because of yet having to supply details about Jotham's reign.

JOURNEY. The word "journey" is often used in the Bible to designate a general distance covered. (Ge 31:23; Ex 3:18; Nu 10:33; 33:8) The distance covered in a day depended on the means of transport used and the conditions and terrain encountered by the traveler. An average day's journey on land was perhaps 32 km (20 mi) or more. But a "sabbath day's journey" was far less. (Mt 24:20) Acts 1:12 indicates that a "sabbath day's journey" separated Jerusalem from the Mount of Olives. Probably because of reckoning from two different starting points, Josephus gives this distance once as five furlongs (925 m; 3,034 ft) and another time as six furlongs (1,110 m; 3,640 ft). Rabbinic sources, on the basis of Joshua 3:4, indicate a "sabbath day's journey" to be 2,000 cubits (890 m; 2,920 ft).

JOY. The emotion excited by the acquisition or expectation of good; state of happiness; exultation. The Hebrew and Greek words used in the Bible for joy, exultation, rejoicing, and being glad express various shades of meaning, different stages or degrees of joy. The verbs involved express the inner feeling and the outward manifestation of joy and variously mean "be joyful; exult; shout for joy; leap for joy."

Jehovah God and Jesus Christ. Jehovah is called "the happy God." (1Ti 1:11) He creates and works with joy for himself and his creatures. What he brings about makes him joyful. (Ps 104:31) He wants his creatures likewise to enjoy his works and to enjoy their own work. (Ec 5:19) Since he is the Source of all good things (Jas 1:17), all intelligent creatures, both mankind and angels, can find their chief enjoyment in coming to know him. (Jer 9:23, 24) King David said: "Let my musing about him be pleasurable. I, for my part, shall rejoice in Jehovah." (Ps 104:34) He also sang: "The righteous one will rejoice in Jehovah and will indeed take refuge in him; and all the upright in heart will boast." (Ps 64:10) The apostle Paul urged Christians to take joy at all times in their knowledge of Jehovah and his dealing with them, writing to them: "Always rejoice in the Lord ['Jehovah,' in several versions]. Once more I will say, Rejoice!" —Php 4:4.

Jesus Christ, who was the intimate one of Jehovah, knows him best (Mt 11:27), and he is able to explain Him to his followers. (Joh 1:18) Jesus is therefore joyful, being called "the happy and only Potentate." (1Ti 6:14, 15) Out of love for his Father, he is eager to do always the things that please Him. (Joh 8:29) Therefore, when there was set before him the task of coming to earth, suffering, and dying in order that he might vindicate Jehovah's name, "for the joy that was set before him he endured a torture stake, despising shame." (Heb 12:2) He also had great love for and joy in mankind. The Scriptures, personifying him in his prehuman existence as wisdom, represent him as saying: "Then I came to be beside [Jehovah] as a master worker, and I came to be the one he was specially fond of day by day, I being glad before him all the time, being glad at the productive land of his earth, and the things I was fond of were with the sons of men."—Pr 8:30, 31.

Jesus desired his followers to have the same joy, telling them: "These things I have spoken to you, that my joy may be in you and your joy may be made full." The angels had joy at the creation of the earth. (Joh 15:11; 17:13; Job 38:4-7) They also view the course of God's people, taking joy in their faithful course and especially exulting when an individual turns from his sinful ways to the pure worship and service of God.—Lu 15:7, 10.

What makes God joyful. Jehovah's heart can be made glad by his servants because of their faithfulness and loyalty to him. Satan the Devil has constantly challenged the rightfulness of God's sovereignty and the integrity of all those serving God. (Job 1:9-11; 2:4, 5; Re 12:10) To them apply the words: "Be wise, my son, and make my heart rejoice, that I may make a reply to him that is taunting me." (Pr 27:11) Jehovah's people in the earth can cause God to rejoice by faithfulness and loyalty to him.—Isa 65:19; Zep 3:17.

A Fruit of the Spirit. Since Jehovah is the Source of joy and he desires joyfulness for his people, joy is a fruit of his holy spirit. Joy is named immediately after love in the list at Galatians 5:22, 23. The apostle wrote to the Christians at Thessalonica: "You became imitators of us and of the Lord, seeing that you accepted the word under much tribulation with *joy of holy spirit.*" (1Th 1:6) Accordingly, Paul counseled the Christians at Rome that the Kingdom of God "means righteousness and peace and joy with holy spirit."—Ro 14:17.

True joy is a quality of the heart and can affect the whole body for good. "A joyful heart has a good effect on the countenance," and "a heart that is joyful does good as a curer [or, "does good to the body"]," says the wise writer of Proverbs.—Pr 15:13; 17:22, ftn.

Joy in God's Service. What Jehovah asks of his servants is not burdensome. (1Jo 5:3) He wants them to enjoy his service. His people Israel were to enjoy the seasonal festivals that he arranged for them, and they were to rejoice in other aspects of their life and worship of God. (Le 23:40; De 12:7, 12, 18) They were to speak out about God joyfully. (Ps 20:5; 51:14; 59:16) If they did not serve with joy of heart, there was something wrong with their hearts and their appreciation of his loving-kindness and goodness. Therefore he warned what would take place if they became disobedient and took no joy in serving him: "All these maledictions will certainly come upon you . . . because you did not listen to the voice of Jehovah your God by keeping his commandments and his statutes . . . And they must continue on you and your offspring . . . due to the fact that you did not serve Jehovah your God with rejoicing and joy of heart for the abundance of everything."—De 28:45-47.

The Christian, no less, should enjoy his service to God. Otherwise, something is lacking in heart appreciation. (Ps 100:2) "The joy of Jehovah is your stronghold," said one of God's faithful servants. (Ne 8:10) The good news the Christian proclaims was announced by God's angel as "good news of a great joy that all the people will have." (Lu 2:10) Jehovah's name upon his witnesses and the truth as found in the Bible should themselves be a joy to them. The prophet Jeremiah said: "Your word becomes to me the exultation and the rejoicing of my heart; for your name has been called upon me, O Jehovah God of armies."—Jer 15:16.

Moreover, Jehovah's just, right judicial decisions put into effect in the Christian congregation and in the lives of Christians are cause for joy, especially in a time when the world has thrown justice and righteousness to the ground. (Ps 48:11) Then, too, the marvelous hope ahead surely gives strong ground for joyfulness. ("Rejoice in the hope"; Ro 12:12; Pr 10:28.) Their salvation is a basis for joy. (Ps 13:5) Additionally, there is the joy that the servant of God has in those whom he aids in coming to the knowledge and service of Jehovah. (Php 4:1; 1Th 2:19) Meeting together and working together with God's people is one of the greatest joys.—Ps 106:4, 5; 122:1.

Persecution a cause for joy. For the Christian who guards his heart, even persecution, though not in itself enjoyable, should be viewed with joy, for endurance of it with integrity is a victory. God will help the faithful one. (Col 1:11) Additionally, it is proof that one is approved by God. Jesus said that when reproach and persecution come, the Christian should "leap for joy."—Mt 5:11, 12; Jas 1:2-4; 1Pe 4:13, 14.

Other Joys Provided by God. Jehovah has provided many other things that mankind may enjoy day by day. Some of these are marriage (De 24:5; Pr 5:18), being father or mother of a righteous and wise child (Pr 23:24, 25), food (Ec 10:19; Ac 14:17), wine (Ps 104:14, 15; Ec 10:19), and the multitudinous things of His creation (Jas 1:17; 1Ti 6:17).

False or Nonlasting Joys. Jesus speaks of some who would hear the truth and receive it with joy but without getting the real sense of it. Such do not cultivate the implanted word in their hearts and, as a consequence, soon lose their joy by being stumbled when tribulation or persecution arises on account of the word. (Mt 13:20, 21) Joy based on materialism is a false joy that is in error and will be short-lived. Also, a person rejoicing over the calamity of another, even of one who hates him, must account to Jehovah for his sin. (Job 31:25-30; Pr 17:5; 24:17, 18) A young man is foolish to think that enjoyment of life requires that he give in to following "the desires incidental to youth." (2Ti 2:22; Ec 11:9, 10) Similarly, love of merriment will bring one into a bad situation. (Pr 21:17; Ec 7:4) Even the Christian who exults in comparing himself with others is in error. Rather, he should prove what his own work is and have cause for exultation in himself alone.—Ga 6:4.

Everlasting Joy. Jehovah promised to restore his people Israel after their exile in Babylon. He did bring them back to Jerusalem in 537 B.C.E., and they greatly rejoiced when the temple foundation was laid. (Isa 35:10; 51:11; 65:17-19; Ezr 3:10-13) But Isaiah's prophecy (65:17) has a greater fulfillment in the establishment of "a new heaven and a new earth," in which arrangement all mankind will have joy forever under the "New Jerusalem."—Re 21:1-3.

Under present conditions, wickedness, sickness, and death prevent full and undiminished joy. But in harmony with the Bible rule, "A wise king is scattering wicked people," Jesus Christ as King will bring an end to all enemies of God and of righteousness. (Pr 20:26; 1Co 15:25, 26) Thus all obstacles to complete joy will be removed, for even "death will be no more, neither will mourning nor outcry nor pain be anymore." (Re 21:4) Sorrow for those who have died will be completely gone, removed by the resurrection of the dead. This knowledge comforts Christians even today, who, on this account, do not "sorrow just as the rest also do who have no hope."—1Th 4:13, 14; Joh 5:28, 29.

JOZABAD (Jo′za·bad) [shortened form of Jehozabad, probably meaning "Jehovah Has Endowed"].

1. A warrior who joined David at Ziklag; a Gederathite.—1Ch 12:1-4.

2, 3. Two persons with this name were among the headmen of Manasseh who deserted to David when he was at Ziklag and became chiefs in his army.—1Ch 12:20, 21.

4. A commissioner appointed by King Hezekiah to assist in caring for the tithes, contributions, and holy things brought in by the people; no doubt a Levite.—2Ch 31:12, 13.

5. A Levite chief who contributed many sheep and cattle for King Josiah's great Passover celebration.—2Ch 35:1, 9, 18.

6. One of the postexilic Levites into whose hand Ezra and his party weighed out all the precious items that had been brought with them from Babylon to Jerusalem in 468 B.C.E. (Ezr 8:33, 34) See Nos. 8, 9, and 10.

7. A son or descendant of Pashhur, and one of the priests who dismissed their foreign wives and sons.—Ezr 10:22, 44.

8. One of the Levites whom Ezra successfully encouraged to send away their foreign wives. (Ezr 10:10, 11, 23, 44) Possibly the same as Nos. 6, 9, and 10.

9. One of the Levites associated with Ezra and Nehemiah who read and explained the Law to the people. (Ne 8:7-9) Possibly the same as Nos. 6, 8, and 10.

10. A Levite "over the outside business" of the rebuilt temple. (Ne 11:15, 16) Possibly the same as Nos. 6, 8, and 9.

JOZACAR (Jo′za·car) [Jehovah Has Remembered]. A servant of King Jehoash of Judah. He and his companion Jehozabad killed their ruler in reprisal for the death of Zechariah and perhaps other sons of High Priest Jehoiada. However, Jehoash's son and successor Amaziah, in turn, avenged his father's death by striking down Jozacar and his accomplice. Jozacar was the son of Shimeath, an Ammonitess. He is also called Zabad.—2Ki 12:20, 21; 2Ch 24:20-22, 25-27; 25:1, 3.

JOZADAK. See JEHOZADAK, JOZADAK.

JUBAL (Ju′bal) [possibly, Ram]. Son of Lamech and Adah; descendant of Cain. As "founder of all those who handle the harp and the pipe," Jubal may have invented both stringed and wind instruments, or perhaps he 'founded' a profession, which gave considerable impetus to the progress of music.—Ge 4:17-21.

JUBILEE. The year following each cycle of seven 7-year periods, counting from Israel's entry into the Promised Land. The Hebrew word yoh·vel′

(or, *yo·vel'*) means "ram's horn," and this refers to the sounding of a ram's horn during that 50th year to proclaim liberty throughout the land. —Le 25:9, 10, ftn; see HORN.

Starting with the time of entering the Promised Land, the nation of Israel was to count six years during which time the land was sown, cultivated, and harvested; but the seventh year was to be a sabbath year, during which the land must lie fallow. In the seventh year no sowing or pruning could be done. Even the growth from kernels of grain spilled during the harvest of the previous year could not be reaped, and grapes were not to be gathered from the unpruned vines. Grain and fruit that grew of itself would be available to the owner, his slaves, hired laborers, alien residents, and the poor. Domestic animals and wild beasts also were allowed to eat of it. (Le 25:2-7; Ex 23:10, 11) Seven of these seven-year periods (7 × 7 = 49) were to be counted, and the following year, the 50th, was to be a Jubilee year.

The Jubilee shared features of the sabbatical year. The land again had complete rest. The same regulations applied to the produce of the land. (Le 25:8-12) This meant that the produce of the 48th year of each 50-year cycle would be the primary source of food for that year and for a little over two years following, until the harvest of the 51st, or the year after the Jubilee. Jehovah's special blessing on the sixth year resulted in a crop yield sufficient to furnish food through the Sabbath year. (Le 25:20-22) Similarly, God provided a bountiful and sufficient harvest in the 48th year to supply the nation through the Sabbath year, the Jubilee that followed, and the next year until harvesttime, if the Jews kept his Law.

The Jubilee was in a sense an entire year of festival, a year of liberty. The keeping of it would demonstrate Israel's faith in their God Jehovah and would be a time of thanksgiving and happiness in his provisions.

It was on the tenth day of the seventh month (in the month of Tishri), on the Day of Atonement, that the horn (*shoh·phar'*, or *sho·phar'*, a curved, animal horn) was sounded, proclaiming liberty throughout the land. This meant freedom for the Hebrew slaves, many of whom had sold themselves because of debt. Such release normally would not come until the seventh year of servitude (Ex 21:2), but the Jubilee provided liberty even for those who had not yet served for six years. All hereditary land possessions that had been sold (usually because of financial reverses) were returned, and each man returned to his family and his ancestral possession. No family was to sink into the depths of perpetual poverty. Every family was to have its honor and respect. Even a person who squandered his substance could not forever lose his inheritance for his posterity. After all, the land was really Jehovah's, and the Israelites themselves were alien residents and settlers from Jehovah's standpoint. (Le 25:23, 24) If the nation kept God's laws, then, as he said, "No one should come to be poor among you."—Le 25:8-10, 13; De 15:4, 5.

By reason of the Jubilee law, none of the land could be sold in perpetuity. God provided that if a man sold any land of his hereditary possession, the sale price was to be gauged according to the number of years left until the Jubilee. The same rate was in effect when hereditary land was repurchased by its owner. In effect, a sale of land, therefore, was actually only the sale of the use of the land and its produce for the number of years left until Jubilee year. (Le 25:15, 16, 23-28) This applied to houses in unwalled settlements, which were counted as the open country; but houses in walled cities were not included in property returned at Jubilee. Exceptions to this were the houses of the Levites, whose only possessions were the houses and the pasture grounds around the Levite cities. These had their houses returned at Jubilee; the pasture ground of Levite cities could not be sold.—Le 25:29-34.

The wonderful provision of the Jubilee year can better be appreciated when one considers not only the beneficial results to the individual Israelites but especially the effect on the nation as a whole. When the Jubilee arrangement was properly observed, the nation was restored in the Jubilee year to the full and proper theocratic state that God purposed and established at the beginning. Government was on a sound basis. The national economy would always be stable, and the nation would have no crushing debt. (De 15:6) The Jubilee brought about a stable standard of land values and also prevented a great internal debt and its resultant false prosperity that brings inflation, deflation, and business depression.

The Jubilee law, when obeyed, preserved the nation from gravitating to the sad state that we observe today in many lands, where there are virtually only two classes, the extremely rich and the extremely poor. The benefits to the individual strengthened the nation, for none would be underprivileged and crushed into unproductiveness by a bad economic situation, but all could contribute their talents and abilities to the national welfare. With Jehovah providing blessings of the yield of the ground and with the education that was provided, Israel, while obedient, would enjoy the perfect government and prosperity that only the true theocracy could provide.—Isa 33:22.

The Law was read to the people on Sabbath years, particularly during the Festival of Booths, or Ingathering. (De 31:10-12) They should thereby have been drawn closer to Jehovah and should have maintained their freedom. Jehovah warned the Israelites that they would suffer tragedy if they were disobedient and repeatedly ignored his laws (which included those pertaining to the Sabbath and Jubilee years).—Le 26:27-45.

Starting the count of years with the entry of the Israelites into the Promised Land, their first Jubilee year began in Tishri of 1424 B.C.E. (Le 25:2-4, 8-10) Between the time of entering the Promised Land in 1473 B.C.E. and the fall of Jerusalem in 607 B.C.E., the Israelites were obligated to celebrate 17 Jubilees. But it is a sad commentary on their history that they did not appreciate Jehovah as their King. They eventually violated his commands, including the Sabbath laws, and suffered the loss of the blessings he arranged for them. Their failure brought reproach on God before the nations of the world and hindered them from realizing the excellence of his theocratic government.—2Ch 36:20, 21.

Symbolic Meaning.   There are allusions to the Jubilee arrangement in the Christian Greek Scriptures. Jesus Christ said he came to "preach a release to the captives." (Lu 4:16-18) He later said with regard to liberation from bondage to sin: "If the Son sets you free, you will be actually free." (Joh 8:36) Because spirit-anointed Christians were declared righteous for life and were begotten as sons of God beginning with Pentecost of 33 C.E., the apostle Paul could thereafter write: "The law of that spirit which gives life in union with Christ Jesus has set you free from the law of sin and of death." (Ro 8:2) During Christ's Thousand Year Reign, others, too, as indicated at Romans 8:19-21, "will be set free from enslavement to corruption" and, after proving their loyalty to Jehovah under test, will "have the glorious freedom of the children of God." They will be liberated from inborn sin and from the death to which it leads. The custody of the earth itself will be returned to true worshipers, to be cared for in harmony with Jehovah's original purpose for mankind.—Re 21:4; Ge 1:28; Isa 65:21-25.

JUCAL   (Ju'cal) [a shortened form of Jehucal, meaning "Jehovah Is Able; Jehovah Prevails"]. "Son of Shelemiah"; one of the princes of Judah

who asked that the prophet Jeremiah be executed for weakening the hands of the warriors.—Jer 38:1-4.

JUDAH   (Ju'dah) [Lauded; [Object of] Laudation].

1. Jacob's fourth son by his wife Leah. (Ge 29:35; 1Ch 2:1) After spending about nine years of his life at Haran in Paddan-aram, Judah was taken with all of Jacob's household to Canaan. (Compare Ge 29:4, 5, 32-35; 30:9-12, 16-28; 31: 17, 18, 41.) Subsequently he resided with his father at Succoth and then at Shechem. After his sister Dinah was violated by Hamor's son, and Simeon and Levi had avenged her by killing all the males of Shechem, Judah evidently shared in plundering the city.—Ge 33:17, 18; 34:1, 2, 25-29.

Relationship to Joseph.   In the course of time, because Jacob favored him, Joseph came to be hated by Judah and his other half brothers. Their hatred intensified after Joseph related two dreams that pointed to his becoming their superior. Therefore, when Jacob sent Joseph to check on his half brothers as they cared for the flocks, they, upon seeing him from a distance, plotted to kill him. But at the suggestion of Reuben, who had in mind saving Joseph's life, they pitched him into a dry waterpit.—Ge 37:2-24.

Thereafter, as a caravan of Ishmaelites came into view, Judah, apparently in Reuben's absence, convinced the others that, instead of murdering Joseph, it would be better to sell him to the passing merchants. (Ge 37:25-27) Despite Joseph's plea for compassion, they sold him for 20 silver pieces (if shekels, $44). (Ge 37:28; 42:21) Although the indications are that Judah's main concern was to save Joseph's life and that the sale itself afterward proved to be a blessing for all concerned, Judah, like the others, was guilty of a grave sin that long burdened his conscience. (Ge 42:21, 22; 44:16; 45:4, 5; 50:15-21) (Under the Mosaic Law later given to the Israelites, this offense carried the death penalty; Ex 21:16.) Afterward Judah also joined the others in deceiving Jacob into thinking that Joseph had been killed by a wild beast. (Ge 37:31-33) Judah was then about 20 years old.

Judah's Family.   It seems that after this incident Judah left his brothers. He took up tenting near Hirah the Adullamite, and apparently a friendly relationship developed between them. During this time Judah married the daughter of the Canaanite Shua. By her he had three sons, Er, Onan, and Shelah. The youngest, Shelah, was born at Achzib.—Ge 38:1-5.

Later, Judah selected Tamar as a wife for his

firstborn Er. But on account of his badness, Er was executed by Jehovah. Judah then instructed his second son, Onan, to perform brother-in-law marriage. But Onan, although having relations with Tamar, "wasted his semen on the earth so as not to give offspring to his brother." For this Jehovah also slew him. Judah then recommended that Tamar return to her father's house and wait until Shelah matured. Yet, even after Shelah had grown up, Judah, seemingly reasoning that his youngest son might die, did not give him in marriage to Tamar.—Ge 38:6-11, 14.

Therefore, subsequent to Judah's becoming a widower, Tamar, on learning that her father-in-law was going to Timnah, disguised herself as a prostitute and then seated herself at the entrance of Enaim on the road Judah would be traversing. Not recognizing his daughter-in-law and assuming her to be a prostitute, Judah had relations with her. When it later came to light that Tamar was pregnant, Judah demanded that she be burned as a harlot. But upon the presentation of the evidence that he himself had made her pregnant, Judah exclaimed: "She is more righteous than I am, for the reason that I did not give her to Shelah my son." Thus unwittingly Judah had taken the place of Shelah in fathering legal offspring. Some six months later Tamar gave birth to the twins Perez and Zerah. Judah had no further relations with her.—Ge 38:12-30.

To Egypt for Food. Sometime later reports reached famine-stricken Canaan that food was available in Egypt. Consequently, at Jacob's direction, ten of his sons, including Judah, went there for food. At this time their half brother Joseph was serving as Egypt's food administrator. Whereas Joseph immediately knew them, they did not recognize him. Joseph accused them of being spies and warned them not to return without Benjamin, whom they mentioned in denying that they were spies. Joseph also had one of his half brothers, Simeon, bound and held as a hostage.—Ge 42:1-25.

Understandably, Jacob, presuming that he had lost both Joseph and Simeon, was unwilling to let Benjamin accompany his other sons to Egypt. Reuben's emotional statement that Jacob could put his own two sons to death if he did not return Benjamin carried insufficient weight, perhaps because he had proved himself to be unreliable by violating his father's concubine. (Ge 35:22) Finally Judah succeeded in getting his father's consent by promising to be surety for Benjamin.—Ge 42:36-38; 43:8-14.

Homeward bound, after having bought cereals in Egypt, Jacob's sons were overtaken by Joseph's steward and accused of theft (actually a ruse by Joseph). When the supposedly stolen item was found in Benjamin's bag, the men returned and entered Joseph's house. It was Judah who then answered the charge and eloquently and earnestly pleaded in behalf of Benjamin and for the sake of his father, requesting that he be constituted a slave in Benjamin's stead. So moved was Joseph by Judah's sincere plea that he could no longer control his emotions. Thereafter, alone with his brothers, Joseph identified himself. After pardoning them for having sold him into slavery, Joseph instructed his half brothers to get Jacob and then return to Egypt, as the famine was to continue for five more years.—Ge 44:1-45:13.

Later, as Jacob and his entire household neared Egypt, Jacob "sent Judah in advance of him to Joseph to impart information ahead of him to Goshen."—Ge 46:28.

Superior Among His Brothers. By his concern for his aged father and his noble effort to preserve Benjamin's freedom at the cost of his own, Judah proved himself to be superior among his brothers. (1Ch 5:2) No longer was he the Judah who in his youth had shared in plundering the Shechemites and who had been party to wronging his half brother Joseph and then deceiving his own father. His fine qualities of leadership entitled Judah, as one of the heads of the 12 tribes of Israel, to receive a superior prophetic blessing from his dying father. (Ge 49:8-12) Its fulfillment is considered below.

2. The tribe that sprang from Judah. About 216 years after Judah came to Egypt with Jacob's household, the tribe's able-bodied men from 20 years old upward had increased to 74,600, a number greater than that of any other of the 12 tribes. (Nu 1:26, 27) At the end of the 40 years of wandering in the wilderness, Judah's registered males had increased by 1,900.—Nu 26:22.

It was under the direction of Judean Bezalel and his Danite assistant Oholiab that the tabernacle and its furnishings and utensils were constructed. (Ex 35:30-35) After its erection, Judah, along with the tribes of Issachar and Zebulun, encamped on the E side of the sanctuary.—Nu 2:3-8.

Early Evidence of His Leadership. Jacob's prophetic blessing had assigned a leading role to Judah (Ge 49:8; compare 1Ch 5:2), and its fulfillment is confirmed even by the early history of the tribe. Under the leadership of its chieftain Nahshon, Judah led the march through the wilderness. (Nu 2:3-9; 10:12-14) Also, this tribe produced Caleb, one of the two faithful spies who were privileged to reenter the Promised Land.

Though advanced in years, Caleb had an active share in conquering the land allotted to Judah. The tribe itself was divinely designated to take the lead in the fight against the Canaanites, and it did so in association with the Simeonites. (Nu 13:6, 30; 14:6-10, 38; Jos 14:6-14; 15:13-20; Jg 1:1-20; compare De 33:7.) Later, Judah, again on the basis of divine authorization, led the punitive military action against Benjamin.—Jg 20:18.

Judah's Inheritance. The territory allotted to the tribe of Judah was bounded by Benjamite territory on the N (Jos 18:11), the Salt Sea (Dead Sea) on the E (Jos 15:5), and the Great Sea (Mediterranean) on the W (Jos 15:12). The S boundary appears to have extended in a southwesterly direction from the southernmost point of the Dead Sea to the ascent of Akrabbim; proceeding from there, it continued over to Zin, ran northward near Kadesh-barnea, and finally crossed over to the Mediterranean by way of Hezron, Addar, Karka, Azmon, and the torrent valley of Egypt. (Jos 15:1-4) The portion of this territory centering primarily around Beer-sheba was assigned to the Simeonites. (Jos 19:1-9) The Kenites, a non-Israelite family related to Moses by marriage, also began residing in Judean territory.—Jg 1:16.

Several distinct natural regions were within the assigned boundaries of ancient Judah. The Negeb, much of which is a plateau between 450 and 600 m (1,500 and 2,000 ft) above sea level, lies to the S. Along the Mediterranean stretches the Plain of Philistia, with its sand dunes that sometimes penetrate the shore for as much as 6 km (3.5 mi). In early times this rolling plain was a region of vineyards, olive groves, and grainfields. (Jg 15:5) Just E of it rises a hilly area, cleft by numerous valleys, that attains an altitude of about 450 m (1,500 ft) above sea level in the S. This is the Shephelah (meaning "Lowland"), a region anciently covered with sycamore trees. (1Ki 10:27) It is a lowland when compared with the mountainous region of Judah, which lies farther to the E and has elevations varying from about 600 to more than 1,000 m (2,000 to 3,300 ft) above sea level. The barren hills occupying the eastern slope of the Judean mountains constitute the Wilderness of Judah.

Under the leadership of Joshua, the power of the Canaanites had apparently been broken in the territory given to Judah. However, since evidently no garrisons were established, the original inhabitants appear to have returned to such cities as Hebron and Debir, probably while the Israelites were warring elsewhere. Therefore, these places had to be recaptured. (Compare Jos 12:7, 10, 13; Jg 1:10-15.) But the inhabitants of the low plain, with their well-equipped chariotry, were not dispossessed. This doubtless included the Philistines of Gath and Ashdod.—Jos 13:2, 3; Jg 1:18, 19.

From the Judges to Saul. During the turbulent period of the Judges, Judah, like the other tribes, repeatedly fell victim to idolatry. Therefore, Jehovah allowed surrounding nations, particularly the Ammonites and the Philistines, to make inroads on the territory of Judah. (Jg 10:6-9) In Samson's day, not only had the Judeans lost all control over the Philistine cities of Gaza, Ekron, and Ashkelon but the Philistines had actually become their overlords. (Jg 15:9-12) Apparently not until Samuel's time was Judean territory recovered from the Philistines.—1Sa 7:10-14.

After Saul of the tribe of Benjamin was anointed by Samuel as Israel's first king, the Judeans fought loyally under his leadership. (1Sa 11:5-11; 15:3, 4) Most frequent were the battles against the Philistines (1Sa 14:52), who again seem to have got the upper hand over the Israelites. (1Sa 13:19-22) But gradually their power was reduced. With Jehovah's help, Saul and his son Jonathan gained victories over them in the area extending from Michmash to Aijalon. (1Sa 13:23–14:23, 31) When the Philistines later invaded Judah, they again suffered defeat after the young Judean shepherd David killed their champion Goliath. (1Sa 17:4, 48-53) Subsequently King Saul placed David, who had earlier been anointed as Israel's future king, over the Israelite warriors. In this capacity David loyally supported Saul and gained further victories over the Philistines. (1Sa 18:5-7) At this time the tribe of Judah was like "a lion cub," not yet having attained regal power in the person of David.—Ge 49:9.

When Saul came to view David as a threat to his kingship and outlawed him, David still remained loyal to Saul as Jehovah's anointed. Never did he side with the enemies of Israel nor did he personally harm Saul or allow others to do so. (1Sa 20:30, 31; 24:4-22; 26:8-11; 27:8-11; 30:26-31) Instead, David fought against Israel's enemies. On one occasion David saved the Judean city of Keilah from the Philistines.—1Sa 23:2-5.

Fulfillment of Jacob's Blessing in David. Finally God's due time came for the transfer of royal power from the tribe of Benjamin to the tribe of Judah. At Hebron, after Saul's death, the men of Judah anointed David as king. But the other tribes stuck with the house of Saul and made his son Ish-bosheth king over them. Repeated clashes occurred between these two kingdoms until the strongest supporter of Ish-bosheth, Abner, defected to David. Not long thereafter Ish-bosheth was murdered.—2Sa 2:1-4, 8, 9; 3:1–4:12.

When David subsequently gained the kingship over all Israel, the 'sons of Jacob,' that is, all the tribes of Israel, lauded Judah and prostrated themselves to his representative as ruler. Therefore, David was also able to move against Jerusalem though it was basically in Benjamite territory and, after capturing the stronghold of Zion, to make it his capital. For the most part David conducted himself in a commendable way. So through him, the tribe of Judah was lauded for such qualities as justice and righteousness, and also for its services to the nation, including the maintenance of national security, as Jacob had foretold in his deathbed blessing. The hand of Judah was truly on the back of his enemies as David subdued the Philistines (who had twice sought to overthrow him as king in Zion), as well as the Moabites, Syrians, Edomites, Amalekites, and Ammonites. Thus, under David, Israel's boundaries were at last extended to their God-ordained limits.—Ge 49:8-12; 2Sa 5:1-10, 17-25; 8:1-15; 12:29-31.

By reason of the everlasting covenant for a Kingdom made with David, the tribe of Judah possessed the scepter and the commander's staff for 470 years. (Ge 49:10; 2Sa 7:16) But only during the reigns of David and Solomon was there a united kingdom, with all the tribes of Israel prostrating themselves before Judah. On account of Solomon's apostatizing toward the close of his reign, Jehovah ripped ten tribes away from the next Judean king, Rehoboam, and gave these to Jeroboam. (1Ki 11:31-35; 12:15-20) Only the Levites and the tribes of Benjamin and Judah remained loyal to the house of David.—1Ki 12:21; 2Ch 13:9, 10.

3. Judah as a kingdom, including the tribe of Benjamin. (2Ch 25:5) After Solomon's death the other ten tribes formed an independent kingdom under the Ephraimite Jeroboam.

Not long thereafter, in the fifth year of Rehoboam, Egypt's King Shishak invaded the kingdom of Judah as far as Jerusalem and captured fortified cities en route.—1Ki 14:25, 26; 2Ch 12:2-9.

For a period of some 40 years during the reigns of Judean Kings Rehoboam, Abijam (Abijah), and Asa, repeated conflicts occurred between the kingdoms of Judah and Israel. (1Ki 14:30; 15:7, 16) But Asa's successor Jehoshaphat formed a marriage alliance with wicked King Ahab of Israel. While this meant peace between the two kingdoms, the marriage of Jehoshaphat's son Jehoram to Ahab's daughter Athaliah proved to be disas-

trous for Judah. Under Athaliah's influence, Jehoram became guilty of rank apostasy. During his reign the Philistines and the Arabs invaded Judah and took captive and killed all of his sons except Jehoahaz (Ahaziah), the youngest. When Ahaziah became king, he likewise followed the directives of wicked Athaliah. After Ahaziah's violent death, Athaliah killed all the royal offspring. But, undoubtedly by divine providence, the infant Jehoash, rightful heir to the throne of David, was hidden and therefore survived. Meanwhile the usurper Athaliah ruled as queen until her execution at the command of High Priest Jehoiada. —2Ch 18:1; 21:1, 5, 6, 16, 17; 22:1-3, 9-12; 23:13-15.

Though his reign started out well, Jehoash departed from true worship after the death of High Priest Jehoiada. (2Ch 24:2, 17, 18) Jehoash's son, Amaziah, likewise failed to continue in a righteous course. During his reign, after years of peaceful coexistence, the ten-tribe kingdom and the kingdom of Judah again met in battle, with the latter suffering a humiliating defeat. (2Ch 25:1, 2, 14-24) With the exception of his invading the sanctuary, the next Judean king, Uzziah (Azariah), did what was right in Jehovah's eyes. His successor Jotham proved to be a faithful king. But Jotham's son Ahaz became notorious for practicing large-scale idolatry.—2Ch 26:3, 4, 16-20; 27:1, 2; 28:1-4.

During Ahaz' reign Judah suffered from invasions by the Edomites and the Philistines, as well as by the northern kingdom and Syria. The Syro-Israelite combine even threatened to unseat Ahaz and constitute a man not of the Davidic line as king of Judah. Although assured by the prophet Isaiah that this would not happen, faithless Ahaz bribed Assyrian King Tiglath-pileser III to come to his aid. This unwise move brought the heavy yoke of Assyria upon Judah.—2Ch 28:5-21; Isa 7:1-12.

Hezekiah, Ahaz' son, restored true worship and rebelled against the king of Assyria. (2Ki 18:1-7) Consequently Sennacherib invaded Judah and captured many fortified cities. But Jerusalem was never taken, for in one night the angel of Jehovah slew 185,000 in the camp of the Assyrians. Humiliated, Sennacherib returned to Nineveh. (2Ki 18:13; 19:32-36) Some eight years earlier, in 740 B.C.E., the ten-tribe kingdom had come to its end with the fall of its capital Samaria to the Assyrians.—2Ki 17:4-6.

Judah's next king, Hezekiah's son Manasseh, revived idolatry. However, upon being taken as a captive to Babylon by the king of Assyria, he repented and, after his return to Jerusalem, undertook religious reforms. (2Ch 33:10-16) But his son Amon reverted to idolatry.—2Ch 33:21-24.

The last sweeping campaign against idolatry came during the reign of Amon's son Josiah. However, it was then too late for genuine repentance to be effected among the people in general. Therefore, Jehovah decreed the complete desolation of Judah and Jerusalem. Finally, Josiah himself was killed in an attempt to turn the Egyptian forces back at Megiddo as they were on their way to assist the king of Assyria at Carchemish.—2Ki 22:1–23:30; 2Ch 35:20.

The last four Judean kings, Jehoahaz, Jehoiakim, Jehoiachin, and Zedekiah proved to be bad rulers. Pharaoh Nechoh deposed Jehoahaz, laid a heavy fine on the land of Judah, and made Jehoahaz' brother Jehoiakim king. (2Ki 23:31-35) Later, apparently after eight years of his reign, Jehoiakim was made a vassal to Nebuchadnezzar the king of Babylon, who had earlier defeated the Egyptians at Carchemish. For three years Jehoiakim served the king of Babylon but then rebelled. (2Ki 24:1; Jer 46:2) Thereafter Nebuchadnezzar, evidently intending to take the rebellious king as a prisoner to Babylon, came against Jerusalem. (2Ch 36:6) However, Jehoiakim never was taken to Babylon, for he died in a manner not disclosed in the Bible. Subsequently Jehoiachin became king. After ruling for only three months and ten days, he voluntarily surrendered to Nebuchadnezzar and, along with other members of the royal family and thousands of his subjects, went into Babylonian exile. Then Nebuchadnezzar placed Jehoiachin's uncle, Zedekiah, on the throne of Judah. —2Ki 24:6, 8-17; 2Ch 36:9, 10.

In his ninth year as vassal king, Zedekiah rebelled and looked to Egypt's military might for support against Babylon. (2Ki 24:18–25:1; 2Ch 36:11-13; Eze 17:15-21) Nebuchadnezzar, therefore, marched his armies toward Judah. For 18 months Jerusalem was subjected to siege until its walls were finally breached. Although Zedekiah fled, he was captured, his sons were slaughtered before him, and he was then blinded. The next month most of the survivors were taken into exile. Over the few remaining lowly people of Judah, Gedaliah was appointed as governor. But following his assassination, the people fled to Egypt. Thus in the seventh month of 607 B.C.E. the land of Judah was completely desolated.—2Ki 25:1-26; for details see articles on the individual kings.

Rulership Not Lost. This calamitous end for the kingdom of Judah, however, did not mean that the scepter and commander's staff had departed from the tribe for all time. According to Jacob's

deathbed prophecy, the tribe of Judah was to produce the permanent royal heir, Shiloh (meaning "He Whose It Is; He To Whom It Belongs"). (Ge 49:10) Appropriately, therefore, before the overthrow of the kingdom of Judah, Jehovah, through Ezekiel, directed these words to Zedekiah: "Remove the turban, and lift off the crown. This will not be the same. Put on high even what is low, and bring low even the high one. A ruin, a ruin, a ruin I shall make it. As for this also, it will certainly become no one's until he comes who has the legal right, and I must give it to him." (Eze 21:26, 27) The one having the legal right, as indicated by the angel Gabriel's announcement to the virgin Jewess Mary some 600 years later, is none other than Jesus, the Son of God. (Lu 1:31-33) It is, therefore, fitting that Jesus Christ bears the title "the Lion that is of the tribe of Judah."—Re 5:5.

Compared With the Northern Kingdom. The kingdom of Judah enjoyed far greater stability and also lasted about 133 years longer than did the northern kingdom. Several factors contributed to this. (1) On account of God's covenant with David, the royal line remained unbroken, whereas in the northern kingdom fewer than half of the kings had their own sons succeed them. (2) The continuance of the Aaronic priesthood at the temple in Jerusalem had Jehovah's blessing and made it easier for the unfaithful nation to return to their God. (2Ch 13:8-20) On the other hand, in the northern kingdom the institution and continuance of calf worship was deemed necessary for the preservation of independence from Judah, and apparently for this reason no efforts were ever made to eradicate it. (1Ki 12:27-33) (3) Four of the 19 Judean kings, Asa, Jehoshaphat, Hezekiah, and Josiah, were outstanding in their devotion to true worship and instituted major religious reforms.

However, the history of both kingdoms illustrates the folly of disregarding Jehovah's commands and trusting in military alliances for security. Also, Jehovah's long-suffering with his disobedient people is highlighted. Time and again he sent his prophets to encourage repentance among the people, but often their warnings were not heeded. (Jer 25:4-7) Among the prophets serving in Judah were Shemaiah, Iddo, Azariah, Oded, Hanani, Jehu, Eliezer, Jahaziel, Micah, Hosea, Isaiah, Zephaniah, Habakkuk, and Jeremiah. —See Israel Nos. 2 and 3.

After the Exile. In 537 B.C.E., when Cyrus' decree permitting the Israelites to return to the land of Judah and there rebuild the temple went into effect, apparently representatives from the various tribes came back to their homeland. (Ezr

1:1-4; Isa 11:11, 12) In fulfillment of Ezekiel 21:27, never did a king of the Davidic line administer the affairs of the repatriated people. It is also noteworthy that no mention is made of tribal jealousies, indicating that Ephraim and Judah had indeed become one.—Isa 11:13.

4. Apparently the same as the Levite Hodaviah, or Hodevah, who returned to Jerusalem with Zerubbabel.—Ezr 2:40; 3:9; Ne 7:43.

5. A Levite listed among those returning with Zerubbabel.—Ne 12:1, 8.

6. A Levite among those dismissing their foreign wives and sons.—Ezr 10:23, 44.

7. A Benjamite resident of Jerusalem serving there in a supervisory capacity after the exile. —Ne 11:7, 9.

8. One in the inaugural march arranged by Nehemiah after the completion of Jerusalem's wall.—Ne 12:31, 34.

9. A priestly musician in the inaugural march. —Ne 12:31, 35, 36.

JUDAH, WILDERNESS OF. The generally uninhabited, barren eastern slope of the Judean mountains. (Jg 1:16) This wilderness region, extending about 16 to 24 km (10 to 15 mi) in width, begins not far E of the Mount of Olives and stretches some 80 km (50 mi) along the W coast of the Dead Sea. It mainly consists of smooth and rounded barren hills of soft chalk, cleft by torrent valleys and ravines. (PICTURE, Vol. 1, p. 335) Toward the Dead Sea the rounded hills give way to rocky gorges, and the sea itself is faced by a wall of jagged cliffs. Dropping some 1,200 m (3,900 ft) in 24 km (15 mi), this wilderness is shielded from the rain-bearing W winds and therefore receives only limited rainfall. At the same time it is at the mercy of the dry winds that sweep in from the E. But when it does rain, water rushes through the otherwise dry torrent valleys, and for a few weeks in the rainy season the wilderness produces meager vegetation.

David, who sought refuge from Saul in the Wilderness of Judah, described it as "a land dry and exhausted, where there is no water." (Ps 63: Sup, 1) No stream has its source in the heart of this arid region, and no surface water runs there. In sharp contrast, the stream issuing forth from Ezekiel's visionary temple flowed through this wilderness and supported trees in abundance along its banks.—Eze 47:1-10.

It was undoubtedly into the desolate Wilderness of Judah that the 'goat for Azazel' was sent on the annual Atonement Day after being led there from the temple at Jerusalem. (Le 16:21, 22) In the first century C.E., John the Baptizer began his ministry in a section of this region N of the Dead Sea. (Mt 3:1-6) Apparently somewhere in this same wilderness Christ Jesus was tempted by the Devil. —Mt 4:1.

JUDAISM (Ju'da·ism). The Jewish religious system. (Ga 1:13, 14) In the first century C.E., Judaism in its various forms was not based exclusively on the Hebrew Scriptures. One of the most prominent divisions of Judaism, that of the Sadducees, rejected the Scriptural teaching of the resurrection and denied the existence of angels. (Mt 12:18-27; Ac 23:8) Although the Pharisees, who formed yet another important branch of Judaism, sharply disagreed with the Sadducees on this (Ac 23:6-9), they were guilty of making God's Word invalid because of their many unscriptural traditions. (Mt 15:1-11) Not the Law, which was actually a tutor leading to Christ (Ga 3:24), but these unscriptural traditions made it difficult for many to accept Christ. The Law itself was good and holy (Ro 7:12), but the traditions of men served to enslave the Jews. (Col 2:8) It was an ardent zeal for 'the traditions of his fathers' that caused Saul (Paul) to be a vicious persecutor of Christians. —Ga 1:13, 14, 23; see PHARISEES; SADDUCEES.

JUDAS (Ju'das) [from Heb., a form of the name Judah].

1. An ancestor of Jesus in the line from Nathan through Mary. The son of Joseph and father of Symeon, Judas was the seventh generation from David's son Nathan and so lived prior to the Babylonian exile.—Lu 3:30, 31.

2. Judas the Galilean, referred to by Gamaliel in his address to the Sanhedrin. (Ac 5:37) At the time of the registration identified with Quirinius governor of Syria in 6 C.E., Judas led a Jewish uprising. Josephus mentions him a number of times and states that he "incited his countrymen to revolt, upbraiding them as cowards for consenting to pay tribute to the Romans and tolerating mortal masters, after having God for their lord. This man was a sophist who founded a sect of his own, having nothing in common with the others." (*The Jewish War*, II, 118 [viii, 1]) In one place Josephus called Judas a Gaulanite, which some would relate to an area E of the Sea of Galilee. Yet in other places the same historian says Judas was a Galilean, as did Gamaliel. (*Jewish Antiquities*, XVIII, 3 [i, 1]; XVIII, 23 [i, 6]) These rebels stressed liberty, but they did not succeed in getting it. Judas "perished, and all those who were obeying him were scattered abroad." (Ac 5:37)

Some of his descendants were also involved in uprisings.—*The Jewish War*, II, 433-440 (xvii, 8); VII, 253 (viii, 1).

3. One of the 12 apostles, also called Thaddaeus and "Judas the son of James." In the listings of the apostles in Matthew 10:3 and Mark 3:18, James the son of Alphaeus and Thaddaeus are linked together. In the listings at Luke 6:16 and Acts 1:13 Thaddaeus is not included; instead we find "Judas the son of James," leading to the conclusion that Thaddaeus is another name for the apostle Judas. The possibility of confusing two apostles named Judas might be a reason why the name Thaddaeus is sometimes used. Some translators render Luke 6:16 and Acts 1:13, "Judas the *brother* of James," since the Greek does not give the exact relationship. But the Syriac *Peshitta* does supply the word "son." Consequently, numerous modern translations read "Judas the *son* of James." (*RS, AT, NW, La*) The only Biblical reference to Judas alone is at John 14:22. This verse refers to him as "Judas, not Iscariot," thus providing a means of distinguishing which Judas spoke.

In the *King James Version* at Matthew 10:3 "Lebbaeus, whose surname was" is inserted before "Thaddaeus." This is based on the Received Text, but the Westcott and Hort text omits this, for it is not in manuscripts such as the Sinaitic.

4. Judas Iscariot, the son of Simon and the infamous apostle who betrayed Jesus. The Bible provides little direct information about the family and background of Judas. Both he and his father were called Iscariot. (Lu 6:16; Joh 6:71) This term has commonly been understood to indicate that they were from the Judean town of Kerioth-hezron. If this is so, then Judas was the only Judean among the 12 apostles, the rest being Galileans.

Judas is introduced into the Gospel accounts in the listing of the apostles sometime after Passover 31 C.E. and about a year and a half after Jesus began his ministry. (Mr 3:19; Lu 6:16) It is logical to conclude that Judas had been a disciple for a time before Jesus made him an apostle. Many writers paint an entirely black picture of Judas, but evidently for a while he had been a disciple who found favor with God and with Jesus; his very selection as an apostle indicates that. Furthermore, he was entrusted with caring for the common finances of Jesus and the 12. That reflects favorably on his dependability at the time and his ability or education, especially since Matthew had had experience with money and figures but did not receive this assignment. (Joh 12:6; Mt 10:3) Nonetheless, Judas did become completely, inex-cusably corrupt. No doubt it is for this reason that he is placed last in the list of the apostles and is described as the Judas "who later betrayed him" and "who *turned* traitor."—Mt 10:4; Lu 6:16.

Became Corrupt. Near Passover 32 C.E., Judas, with the other apostles, was sent out preaching. (Mt 10:1, 4, 5) Shortly after Judas' return, and less than a year after he had been made an apostle, he was publicly denounced by Christ, though not by name. Some disciples left Jesus, being shocked over his teachings, but Peter said that the 12 would stick with Christ. In response Jesus acknowledged that he had chosen the 12 but said: "One of you *is* a slanderer [Gr., *di·a'bo·los*, meaning "devil" or "slanderer"]." The account explains that the one who already was a slanderer was Judas, who "was going to betray him, although one of the twelve."—Joh 6:66-71.

In connection with this incident John says: "From the beginning Jesus knew . . . who was the one that would betray him." (Joh 6:64) From Hebrew Scripture prophecies Christ knew that he would be betrayed by a close associate. (Ps 41:9; 109:8; Joh 13:18, 19) God also, by use of his foreknowledge, had seen that such a one would turn traitor, but it is inconsistent with God's qualities and past dealings to think that Judas had to fail, as if he were predestined. (See FOREKNOWLEDGE, FOREORDINATION.) Rather, as already mentioned, at the beginning of his apostleship Judas was faithful to God and to Jesus. Thus Christ must have meant that "from the beginning" of when Judas started to go bad, started to give in to imperfection and sinful inclinations, Jesus recognized it. (Joh 2:24, 25; Re 1:1; 2:23) Judas must have known he was the "slanderer" Jesus mentioned, but he continued to travel with Jesus and the faithful apostles and apparently he made no changes.

The Bible does not discuss in detail the motives for his corrupt course, but an incident that occurred on Nisan 9, 33 C.E., five days before Jesus' death, sheds light on the matter. At Bethany in the house of Simon the leper, Mary, Lazarus' sister, anointed Jesus with perfumed oil worth 300 denarii, about a year's wages for a laborer. (Mt 20:2) Judas strongly objected that the oil could have been sold and the money "given to the poor people." Evidently other apostles merely assented to what seemed to be a valid point, but Jesus rebuked them. Judas' real reason for objecting was that he cared for the money box and he "was a thief . . . and used to carry off the monies" put in the box. So Judas was a greedy, practicing thief. —Joh 12:2-7; Mt 26:6-12; Mr 14:3-8.

Betrayal Price. Judas was undoubtedly stung by Jesus' rebuke about the use of money. At this time "Satan entered into Judas," likely in the sense that the traitorous apostle gave himself in to the will of the Devil, allowing himself to be a tool to carry out Satan's design to stop Christ. A few days later, on Nisan 12, Judas went to the chief priests and temple captains to see how much they would pay him to betray Jesus, again showing his avarice. (Mt 26:14-16; Mr 14:10, 11; Lu 22:3-6; Joh 13:2) The chief priests had that day met together with "the older men of the people," the influential men of the Sanhedrin. (Mt 26:3) The temple captains may have been brought in because of their influence and to lend legal flavor to any planned arrest of Jesus.

Why did the Jewish religious leaders offer just 30 pieces of silver for the betrayal of Jesus?

Thirty pieces of silver ($66, if shekels) was the price offered. (Mt 26:14, 15) The sum fixed by the religious leaders appears designed to show their contempt of Jesus, viewing him as of little value. According to Exodus 21:32, the price of a slave was 30 shekels. Carrying this forward, for his work as a shepherd of the people, Zechariah was paid "thirty pieces of silver." Jehovah scorned this as a very meager amount, regarding the wages given to Zechariah as an estimation of how the faithless people viewed God himself. (Zec 11:12, 13) Consequently, in offering just 30 pieces of silver for Jesus, the religious leaders made him out to be of little value. At the same time, though, they were fulfilling Zechariah 11:12, treating Jehovah as of low value by doing this to the representative he had sent to shepherd Israel. Corrupt Judas "consented [to the price], and he began to seek a good opportunity to betray [Jesus] to them without a crowd around."—Lu 22:6.

Last Night With Jesus. In spite of having turned against Christ, Judas continued to associate with him. He gathered with Jesus and the apostles on Nisan 14, 33 C.E., for the celebration of the Passover. While the Passover meal was in process Jesus ministered to the apostles, humbly washing their feet. Hypocritical Judas allowed Jesus to do that to him. But Jesus said, "Not all of you are clean." (Joh 13:2-5, 11) He also stated that one of the apostles there at the table would betray him. Perhaps so as not to appear guilty, Judas asked if he was the one. As a further identification, Jesus gave Judas a morsel and told him to do

quickly what he was doing.—Mt 26:21-25; Mr 14:18-21; Lu 22:21-23; Joh 13:21-30.

Immediately Judas left the group. A comparison of Matthew 26:20-29 with John 13:21-30 indicates that he departed before Jesus instituted the celebration of the Lord's Evening Meal. Luke's presentation of this incident evidently is not in strict chronological order, for Judas had definitely left by the time Christ commended the group for having stuck with him; that would not fit Judas, nor would he have been taken into the "covenant . . . for a kingdom."—Lu 22:19-30.

Judas later found Jesus together with the faithful apostles in the garden of Gethsemane, a place the betrayer knew well, for they had met there before. He led a great crowd, including Roman soldiers and a military commander. The mob had clubs and swords as well as torches and lamps, which they would need if clouds covered the full moon or if Jesus was in the shadows. The Romans probably would not recognize Jesus, so, according to a prearranged sign, Judas greeted Christ and in an act of hypocrisy "kissed him very tenderly," thus identifying him. (Mt 26:47-49; Joh 18:2-12) Later Judas felt the enormity of his guilt. In the morning he attempted to return the 30 pieces of silver, but the chief priests refused to take them back. Finally, Judas threw the money into the temple.—Mt 27:1-5.

Death. According to Matthew 27:5, Judas hanged himself. But Acts 1:18 says, "pitching head foremost he noisily burst in his midst and all his intestines were poured out." Matthew seems to deal with the *mode* of the attempted suicide, while Acts describes the *result*. Combining the two accounts, it appears that Judas tried to hang himself over some cliff, but the rope or tree limb broke so that he plunged down and burst open on the rocks below. The topography around Jerusalem makes such an event conceivable.

Also related to his death is the question of who bought the burial field with the 30 pieces of silver. According to Matthew 27:6, 7, the chief priests decided they could not put the money in the sacred treasury so *they* used it to buy the field. The account in Acts 1:18, 19, speaking about Judas, says: "This very man, therefore, purchased a field with the wages for unrighteousness." The answer seems to be that the priests purchased the field, but since Judas provided the money, it could be credited to him. Dr. A. Edersheim pointed out: "It was not lawful to take into the Temple-treasury, for the purchase of sacred things, money that had been unlawfully gained. In such cases the Jewish Law provided that the money was to be restored to the donor, and, if he insisted on giving it, that he should be induced to spend it for something for the public weal [well-being]. . . . By a fiction of law the money was still considered to be Judas', and to have been applied by him in the purchase of the well-known 'potter's field.'" (*The Life and Times of Jesus the Messiah,* 1906, Vol. II, p. 575) This purchase worked to fulfill the prophecy at Zechariah 11:13.

The course that Judas chose was a deliberate one, involving malice, greed, pride, hypocrisy, and scheming. He afterward felt remorse under the burden of guilt, as a willful murderer might at the result of his crime. Yet Judas had of his own volition made a bargain with those who Jesus said made proselytes that were subjects of Gehenna twice as much as themselves, who were also liable to "the judgment of Gehenna." (Mt 23:15, 33) On the final night of his earthly life, Jesus himself said, actually about Judas: "It would have been finer for that man if he had not been born." Later Christ called him "the son of destruction."—Mr 14:21; Joh 17:12; Heb 10:26-29.

Replacement. Between Jesus' ascension and the day of Pentecost 33 C.E., Peter, applying the prophecy in Psalm 109:8, explained to a group of about 120 assembled disciples that it seemed appropriate to select a replacement for Judas. Two candidates were proposed and lots were cast, resulting in Matthias being chosen "to take the place of this ministry and apostleship, from which Judas deviated to go to his own place."—Ac 1:15, 16, 20-26.

5. One of Jesus' four half brothers. (Mt 13:55; Mr 6:3) Evidently he was with his three brothers and his mother Mary early in Jesus' ministry when, at Cana, Jesus performed a miracle, and he later traveled with Jesus and his disciples to Capernaum for a short stay. (Joh 2:1-12) Well over a year later he apparently accompanied Mary and his brothers when they sought out Jesus. (Mt 12:46) Nonetheless, in 32 C.E., Jesus' brothers, including Judas, were "not exercising faith in him." (Joh 7:5) Shortly before dying, Jesus turned his believing mother over to the care of the apostle John, strongly suggesting that neither Judas nor his brothers had yet become disciples. (Joh 19:26, 27) Perhaps it was the resurrection of Christ that helped convince Judas, though, because he was among the apostles and others who, between the time of Jesus' ascension and the day of Pentecost 33 C.E., met together and persisted in prayer. (Ac 1:13-15) Logically, then, Judas would have been among the believers who first received holy spirit. Evidently Judas is the same as the Jude who,

about 65 C.E., wrote the Bible book by that name. —See JUDE.

6. A man of Damascus who had a home on the street Straight. While blind immediately after his conversion, Saul (Paul) resided in Judas' home, and it was there that Ananias was sent to lay his hands on Saul. (Ac 9:11, 17) The account does not say whether Judas was a disciple at the time, but this seems unlikely since Ananias and others who were disciples hesitated to approach Saul in view of his reputation as a persecutor, yet Judas accepted Saul into his home.—Ac 9:13, 14, 26.

7. Judas, also called Barsabbas, was one of the two disciples sent by the governing body in Jerusalem to accompany Paul and Barnabas when they delivered the letter about circumcision (c. 49 C.E.). Both Judas and his companion Silas were considered "leading men among the brothers." (Ac 15: 22) The letter was addressed to "those brothers in Antioch and Syria and Cilicia." Judas and Silas were mentioned only as being in Antioch, and there is no record that they went farther. They were to confirm by word of mouth the message in the letter. Judas was a 'prophet,' and as a visiting speaker he gave many discourses to the brothers in Antioch, encouraging and strengthening them. —Ac 15:22, 23, 27, 30-32.

Acts 15:33 indicates that Judas and Silas returned to Jerusalem after they had "passed some time" with the Christians in Antioch. Certain manuscripts (such as Codex Ephraemi, Codex Bezae) contain verse 34, reading, with variations: "But it seemed good to Silas to remain there further; however Judas alone departed for Jerusalem." This verse is omitted in older reliable manuscripts (Sinaitic, Alexandrine, Vatican MS. No. 1209). Probably it was a marginal note intended to explain verse 40, and in time it crept into the main text.

Some commentators have suggested that Judas called Barsabbas was the brother of "Joseph called Barsabbas," a disciple proposed to take the place of Judas Iscariot. (Ac 1:23) But there is no evidence supporting this, other than mere similarity in name. Judas is not mentioned again in the Bible after he returned to Jerusalem.

JUDE [from Heb., a form of the name Judah]. "A slave of Jesus Christ, but a brother of James." This is the way the writer of the inspired letter bearing his name introduces himself. Apparently he was not the same person as "Judas the son of James," one of the 11 faithful apostles of Jesus Christ. (Lu 6:16) He speaks of himself as "a slave," not an apostle, of Jesus Christ; also he refers to the apostles in the third person as "they."—Jude 1, 17, 18.

Though the Christian Greek Scriptures speak of other persons called Jude or Judas, this Bible writer distinguished himself from the others by mentioning the name of his brother. (See JUDAS No. 5.) From this it may be inferred that his brother James was well known among Christians. Only one person by that name appears to have been outstandingly prominent. The apostle Paul referred to this James as one of the "pillars" of the Jerusalem congregation and as "the brother of the Lord." (Ga 1:19; 2:9; see also Ac 12:17; 15:13-21.) Therefore, Jude, or Judas, was evidently a half brother of Christ Jesus. (Mt 13:55; Mr 6:3) Yet humbly he did not seek to capitalize on his fleshly relationship to the Son of God but calls himself "a slave of Jesus Christ."

Almost nothing is known about Jude's life. Early in the ministry of Christ Jesus, Jude may have been among those saying: "He has gone out of his mind." (Mr 3:21) In any event, Jude and his other brothers did not then exercise faith in Christ Jesus.—Joh 7:5.

However, after his resurrection, Jesus appeared to his half brother James. (1Co 15:7) Doubtless this had much to do with convincing not only James but also Jude and his other brothers that Jesus was indeed the Messiah. Therefore, even before Pentecost of 33 C.E. they were persisting in prayer with the 11 faithful apostles and others in an upper room at Jerusalem. It appears that they were also among the some 120 persons assembled on the occasion that Matthias was chosen by lot to replace the unfaithful Judas Iscariot. (Ac 1:14-26) If this is the case, it would indicate that they received the holy spirit on the day of Pentecost.—Ac 2:1-4.

JUDE, THE LETTER OF.

An inspired letter of the Christian Greek Scriptures written by Jude, a brother of James and therefore evidently also a half brother of Jesus Christ. (See JUDE.) Addressed to "the called ones who are loved in relationship with God the Father and preserved for Jesus Christ," this general letter was evidently to be circulated to all Christians.—Jude 1.

At the time Jude wrote his letter a threatening situation had developed. Immoral, animalistic men had slipped in among Christians and were 'turning the undeserved kindness of God into an excuse for loose conduct.' For this reason Jude did not, as he had originally intended, write about the salvation that Christians called to God's heavenly Kingdom hold in common. Instead, directed by God's spirit, he provided exhortation to help fellow believers to cope successfully with corruptive influences inside the congregation. Jude admonished them to "put up a hard fight for the faith" by resisting immoral persons, by maintaining pure worship and fine conduct, and by "praying with holy spirit." (Jude 3, 4, 19-23) Drawing upon such examples as the angels that sinned, the inhabitants of Sodom and Gomorrah, Cain, Balaam, and Korah, Jude forcefully proved that Jehovah's judgment will be executed upon ungodly persons just as certainly as it was upon the unfaithful angels and wicked men of former times. He also exposed the baseness of those who were trying to defile Christians.—Jude 5-16, 19.

Unique Information. Though short, Jude's letter contains some information not found elsewhere in the Bible. It alone mentions the archangel Michael's dispute with the Devil over Moses' body and the prophecy uttered centuries earlier by Enoch. (Jude 9, 14, 15) Whether Jude received this information through direct revelation or by reliable transmission (either oral or written) is not known. If the latter was the case, this may explain the presence of a similar reference to Enoch's prophesying in the apocryphal book of Enoch (thought to have been written probably sometime during the second and first centuries B.C.E.). A common source could have furnished the basis for the statement in the inspired letter as well as in the apocryphal book.

Place and Time of Writing. Likely Jude wrote his letter from Palestine, as there is no record of his ever having left this land. It is possible to arrive at an approximate date for the letter on the basis of internal evidence. The fact that Jude mentions neither Cestius Gallus' coming against Jerusalem (66 C.E.) nor the fall of that city to the Romans under Titus (70 C.E.) suggests that he wrote before the year 66 C.E. Had even a part of Jesus' prophecy regarding Jerusalem's destruction been fulfilled (Lu 19:43, 44), Jude doubtless would have included this execution of divine judgment as another warning example. Since Jude seemingly quoted from Peter's second letter about ridiculers appearing "in the last time" (compare 2Pe 3:3 with Jude 18), it may be inferred that he wrote his letter later, in about 65 C.E.

Authenticity. The Bible book of Jude was accepted as canonical by early Scripture catalogers. Among these from the second through the fourth centuries C.E. were Clement of Alexandria, Tertullian, Origen, Eusebius, Cyril of Jerusalem, Athanasius, Epiphanius, Gregory of Nazianzus, Philastrius, Jerome, and Augustine. The letter is also included in the Muratorian Fragment (c. 170 C.E.).

JUDEA

(Ju·de'a) [from Heb., Of (Belonging to) Judah]. The exact boundaries of this region of Palestine are uncertain. Seemingly Judea em-

HIGHLIGHTS OF JUDE

Concise, powerful warning against wicked ones who would infiltrate the congregation

Probably written about 65 C.E., more than 30 years after the death and resurrection of Christ

A situation calling for Christian endurance (vss 1-4)

Ungodly men have slipped into congregation and are using God's undeserved kindness as an excuse for loose conduct

Christians must put up a hard fight for the faith

Attitudes, conduct, and people to guard against (vss 5-16)

Not to be forgotten is the fact that Israelites saved from Egypt who later lacked faith were destroyed

Angels that forsook their proper position were punished

Grossly immoral Sodom and Gomorrah suffered the judgment of everlasting fire

Despite these examples, some endeavor to bring similar practices into the congregation

Michael was not abusive, even when speaking with the Devil; but these men 'speak abusively of glorious ones'

They are following the bad examples of Cain, Balaam, and Korah

They pose a threat comparable to rocks hidden below water; like waterless clouds and dead, uprooted trees, they produce nothing beneficial

Enoch prophesied God's judgment against such ungodly sinners

These men are murmurers, complainers, self-centered, as well as deceptive flatterers

How Christians can resist this bad influence (vss 17-25)

Remember, the apostles foretold the presence of such men in "the last time"

Christians should stand out as different from them, building themselves up on the foundation of faith, praying with holy spirit, keeping themselves in God's love, waiting for Jesus' mercy to be expressed

They should also help others, showing mercy to doubters, saving them by snatching them out of the fire

---

braced an area of approximately 80 km (50 mi) from east to west and about 50 km (30 mi) from north to south. Samaria lay to the north and Idumea to the south. The Dead Sea and the Jordan Valley formed the eastern boundary. However, when Idumean territory was included in Judea, the southern boundary appears to have extended from below Gaza in the west to Masada in the east.

At Matthew 19:1 the reference to Jesus' leaving Galilee and coming to "the frontiers of Judea across the Jordan" may mean that Jesus departed from Galilee, crossed the Jordan, and entered Judea by way of Perea.

Herod the Great was the "king of Judea" at the time John the Baptizer and Jesus were born. (Lu 1:5) Earlier, Herod had been constituted king of Judea by the Roman senate. His dominions were later increased and at the time of his death included Judea, Galilee, Samaria, Idumea, Perea, and other regions. Herod the Great's son Archelaus inherited the rulership over Judea, Samaria, and Idumea. (Compare Mt 2:22, 23.) But subsequent to his banishment Judea came under the administration of Roman governors having their official residence at Caesarea. With the exception of the brief reign of Herod Agrippa I as king over Palestine (Ac 12:1), governors administered the affairs of Judea until the Jewish revolt in 66 C.E.

Toward the close of the first century B.C.E., in fulfillment of prophecy, the promised Messiah, Jesus, was born at Bethlehem in Judea. (Mt 2:3-6; Lu 2:10, 11) After the visit of some Oriental astrologers, Jesus' adoptive father Joseph, having been alerted by an angel in a dream concerning Herod the Great's intent to destroy the child, fled with his family to Egypt. Following Herod's death Joseph did not return to Judea but settled at Nazareth in Galilee. This was because Herod's son Archelaus then ruled over Judea and also on account of the divine warning given to Joseph in a dream.—Mt 2:7-23.

In the spring of 29 C.E., when John the Baptizer began his work in preparation for Messiah's coming, Judea was under the jurisdiction of Roman Governor Pontius Pilate. Many, including Judeans, heard John's preaching in the Wilderness of Judea and were baptized in symbol of repentance. (Mt 3:1-6; Lu 3:1-16) At the time Jesus commenced his ministry less than eight months later, inhabitants of Judea were given further opportunity to return to Jehovah with a complete heart. For a time Jesus' disciples even immersed more persons than John the Baptizer. (Joh 3:22; 4:1-3) After Jesus departed for Galilee great crowds from Jerusalem and Judea followed him and thus benefited from his ministry there. (Mt 4:25; Mr 3:7; Lu 6:17) Like the Galileans, many of these Judeans doubtless had their initial interest aroused by what they saw Jesus doing in Jerusalem at the festival (Passover, 30 C.E.). (Joh 4:45) News of Jesus' miracles in Galilee, such as the resurrection of the only son of a widow at Nain, also spread throughout Judea. —Lu 7:11-17.

However, intense opposition came against Jesus from the religious leaders of Judea. These appear to have wielded greater influence over the Judeans than over the Galileans. Already from Passover time of 31 C.E. onward Jesus was no longer safe in Judea. (Joh 5:1, 16-18; 7:1) Nevertheless, he attended the festivals at Jerusalem and used the opportunity to preach. (Joh 7:10-13, 25, 26, 32; 10:22-39) It was probably in Judea, after the Festival of Booths in 32 C.E., that Jesus sent out the 70. (Lu 10:1-24) Later, despite previous attempts to stone him, Jesus, on learning that his friend Lazarus had died, decided to go to Judea. Jesus' subsequent resurrection of Lazarus at Bethany was used by the religious leaders as a further reason to seek his death. Some of them said: "If we let him alone this way, they will all put faith in him, and the Romans will come and take away both our place and our nation."—Joh 11:5-8, 45-53.

While the synoptic Gospels deal mainly with Jesus' ministry in Galilee (likely because of better response there), Jesus did not neglect Judea. Otherwise his enemies could not have stated before Pilate: "He stirs up the people by teaching throughout all Judea, even starting out from Galilee to here."—Lu 23:5.

After the death and resurrection of Christ Jesus, Jerusalem and Judea continued to receive a thorough witness. (Ac 1:8) On the day of Pentecost, 33 C.E., Judeans were doubtless among the 3,000 that responded to Peter's preaching and were baptized. Afterward the Christian congregation at Jerusalem continued to enjoy increases. (Ac 2) But this was not without opposition. (Ac 4:5-7, 15-17; 5:17, 18, 40; 6:8-12) After the stoning of the Christian Stephen, such bitter persecution came that "all except the apostles were scattered throughout the regions of Judea and Samaria." (Ac 8:1) But, instead of being a hindrance, this scattering resulted in spreading the Christian message, and apparently new congregations were formed in Judea and elsewhere. (Ac 8:4; Ga 1:22) Following the conversion of the persecutor Saul of Tarsus, "the congregation throughout the whole of Judea and Galilee and Samaria entered into a period of peace, being built up; and as it walked in the fear of Jehovah and in the comfort of the holy spirit it kept on multiplying." (Ac 9:31) The former persecutor, the apostle Paul himself, preached in Jerusalem and Judea. (Ac 26:20) Through the activities of Paul and others, new congregations of Christians were established, and the apostles and older men of the Jerusalem congregation served

as a governing body for all of these.—Ac 15:1-33; Ro 15:30-32.

Apparently many of the Jewish Christians living in Judea were poor. It therefore must have been very encouraging for them to benefit from the voluntary relief measures organized in their behalf by their Christian brothers in other parts of the earth. (Ac 11:28-30; Ro 15:25-27; 1Co 16:1-3; 2Co 9:5, 7) As they continued their faithful service the Jewish Christians in Judea suffered much persecution from unbelieving fellow countrymen. (1Th 2:14) Finally, in 66 C.E., when the Roman armies under Cestius Gallus withdrew from Jerusalem, these Christians, in obedience to Jesus' prophetic words, fled from Jerusalem and Judea to the mountains, thereby escaping the terrible destruction visited upon Jerusalem in 70 C.E.—Mt 24:15, 16; Mr 13:14; Lu 21:20, 21.

JUDGE.   Men raised up by Jehovah to deliver his people prior to the period of Israel's human kings were known as judges. (Jg 2:16) Moses, as mediator of the Law covenant and God-appointed leader, judged Israel for 40 years. But the period of Judges, as usually viewed, began with Othniel, sometime after the death of Joshua, and extended until Samuel the prophet. Samuel is not usually counted among the Judges. So the period of the Judges extended about 300 years.—Jg 2:16; Ac 13:20.

The judges were selected and appointed by Jehovah from various tribes of Israel. Between Joshua and Samuel, 12 judges (not including Deborah) are named, as follows:

Judge	Tribe	Judge	Tribe
Othniel	Judah	Jair	Manasseh
Ehud	Benjamin	Jephthah	Manasseh
Shamgar	(?)	Ibzan	Zebulun (?)
Barak	Naphtali (?)	Elon	Zebulun
Gideon	Manasseh	Abdon	Ephraim
Tola	Issachar	Samson	Dan

The exact area over which each of the judges exercised jurisdiction and the dates of their judgeships cannot in every case be determined. Some may have judged contemporaneously in different sections of Israel, and there were periods of oppression intervening.—See MAP, Vol. 1, p. 743; COURT, JUDICIAL; JUDGMENT DAY; also judges of Israel under individual names.

JUDGES, BOOK OF.   A Bible book that basically covers a period of some 330 years between Israel's conquest of Canaan and the beginning of the monarchy. Earlier, the Israelites had been forewarned that their failure to drive out the in-

HIGHLIGHTS OF JUDGES

A vigorous account of the deliverances that Jehovah repeatedly performed for Israel through the Judges when Israel abandoned idolatrous practices and earnestly sought his help

Likely written by Samuel, the book covers about 330 years between the conquest of Canaan and the beginning of the monarchy

Background for conditions prevailing during time of the Judges (1:1–3:6)

After Joshua's death, the tribes of Israel fail to drive the remaining inhabitants of Canaan out of the land

Instead, they intermarry with these pagans and are ensnared by their false religion

Jehovah abandons them to their foes; but from time to time he raises up Judges to deliver them

Deliverances from oppression when Israel abandoned false worship and called out to Jehovah for help (3:7–16:31)

Through Othniel, Israel is delivered from an eight-year subjugation to the Mesopotamian king Cushan-rishathaim

The 18-year domination by Moabite King Eglon ends when he is killed by Ehud, who then assembles an Israelite army and subdues the Moabites

Shamgar single-handedly strikes down 600 Philistines, thus saving Israel

Barak, encouraged by the prophetess Deborah, defeats Jabin, thus ending his 20-year oppression of Israel; Jabin's army chief, Sisera, is killed by Jael, the wife of Heber the Kenite; Deborah and Barak commemorate this victory in song

Gideon is commissioned to deliver Israel from seven-year harassment by Midianites; Jehovah grants victory after he reduces Gideon's army to just 300 men; Gideon subsequently refuses kingship

Tola judges Israel for 23 years, and Jair judges for 22 years

Israel suffers at the hands of the Ammonites; Jehovah provides deliverance through Jephthah, who subsequently carries out his vow to surrender his only child, a daughter, to Jehovah's service

Ibzan, Elon, and Abdon judge Israel a combined total of about 25 years

Jehovah gives Samson enormous strength and uses him to release Israel from a 40-year domination by the Philistines; his betrothal to a Philistine woman from Timnah gives him occasions to act against them; his betrayal by Delilah eventually leads to a situation in which he kills more Philistines at his death than he had killed in his lifetime

Further undesirable situations that developed during the time of the Judges (17:1–21:25)

In Ephraim, Micah sets up an image in his home and employs a young Levite as a priest

Certain Danites come to Micah's house and later steal his idolatrous objects; they also take the Levite to serve as their priest

Men of the Benjamite city of Gibeah are guilty of a mass sex crime against the concubine of a Levite; failure to hand over the guilty ones for punishment prompts the other tribes to undertake a punitive war against Benjamin; the tribe is almost annihilated

---

habitants of the land, as divinely commanded, would lead to their adopting the debased religious practices of the Canaanites. Finally this would result in Jehovah's disfavor and his abandoning them to their enemies. (Ex 23:32, 33; 34:11-17; Nu 33:55; De 7:2-5) The historical record found in the book of Judges shows how the warning became a reality. However, rather than deal extensively with Israel's unfaithfulness and the resultant foreign oppression, the book primarily relates the exploits of the judges and the marvelous deliverances Jehovah performed by means of them. Thus Jehovah's saving ability and his long-suffering, mercy, undeserved kindness, and justice are highlighted. The judges themselves stand out as sterling examples of faith.—Heb 11:32-34, 39, 40.

Arrangement. Judges is linked with the preceding Bible book by its opening words, "And after the death of Joshua." However, some of the happenings narrated therein evidently occurred before Joshua died. For example, Judges 2:6 reads:

"When Joshua sent the people away, then the sons of Israel went their way, each to his inheritance, to take possession of the land." So it appears that Judges 1:1–3:6 serves as an introduction, the writer having drawn on events taking place before and after Joshua's death in order to provide the historical background for the account that follows. The section running from chapter 3, verse 7, to the end of chapter 16 is, basically, in chronological order and relates the activities of 12 judges (not including Deborah) and concluding with Samson. The last part of the book could be termed an appendix and fits a period much earlier than Samson's judgeship. The capture of Laish by the Danites could reasonably have taken place before Joshua's death. (Compare Jos 19:47; Jg 18:27-29.) The mass sex crime of the men of Gibeah and subsequent events resulting in the near extermination of the tribe of Benjamin probably occurred not many years after Joshua's death. (Jg 19:1–21:25; Jos 24:31) This would allow sufficient time for the Benjamites to have increased from about 600 men (Jg 20:47) to nearly 60,000 warriors by the time of David's reign. —1Ch 7:6-12.

Writer and Time of Composition. Internal evidence provides a basis for determining when the book of Judges was written. It was compiled while a king ruled over Israel. Otherwise, the writer, when referring to the past, would not have said: "In those days there was no king in Israel." (Jg 17:6; 18:1; 19:1; 21:25) Yet it was at a time when the Jebusites still inhabited Jerusalem. (Jg 1:21) Since, in 1070 B.C.E., David captured "the stronghold of Zion" (a part of Jerusalem) from the Jebusites and transferred his capital there (2Sa 5:6-9), the book of Judges must have been committed to writing before that date, probably during Saul's reign. At that time Samuel was the main advocate of true worship and, as Jehovah's prophet, would have been the logical one to have recorded this book.

Authenticity. That the book of Judges rightly occupies a place in the Bible canon there can be no question. It is frank and honest, and it does not hide Israel's gross sins. Throughout, the book gives glory and honor, not to the human judges, but to Jehovah God as Israel's real Deliverer. It shows that God's spirit empowered the judges (Jg 3:9, 10; 6:34; 11:29; 13:24, 25; 14:6, 19; 15:14, 18; 16:20, 28-30) and they, in turn, recognized Jehovah as Judge (11:27) and King (8:23). Other inspired Bible books refer to events recorded therein.—1Sa 12:9-11; 2Sa 11:21; Ps 83:9-12; Isa 9:4; 10:26; Heb 11:32-34.

JUDGMENT DAY.

A specific "day," or period, when particular groups, nations, or mankind in general are called to account by God. It may be a time when those already judged to be deserving of death are executed, or the judgment may afford opportunity for some to be delivered, even to everlasting life. Jesus Christ and his apostles pointed to a future "Judgment Day" involving not only the living but also those who had died in the past.—Mt 10:15; 11:21-24; 12:41, 42; 2Ti 4:1, 2.

Past Times of Judgment. At various times in the past Jehovah called peoples and nations to account for their actions and executed his judgments by bringing destruction. Such executional judgments were not arbitrary demonstrations of brute force or overwhelming power. In some instances the Hebrew word translated "judgment" (mish·pat') is also rendered "justice" and "what is right." (Ezr 7:10; Ge 18:25) The Bible emphasizes that Jehovah "is a lover of righteousness and jus-

tice," so his executional judgments involve both of those qualities.—Ps 33:5.

Sometimes the executional judgments came as a result of the wicked conduct of people in their daily lives. Sodom and Gomorrah are an example of this. Jehovah inspected the cities and determined that the sin of the inhabitants was very heavy; he decided to bring the cities to ruin. (Ge 18:20, 21; 19:14) Later Jude wrote that those cities underwent "the judicial punishment [Gr., di'ken; "judgment," Da; "justice," Yg; "retributive justice," ED] of everlasting fire." (Jude 7) So those cities experienced a "day" of judgment.

Jehovah conducted a legal case against ancient Babylon, the longtime enemy of God and his people. Because of being unnecessarily cruel to the Jews, not intending to release them after the 70-year exile, and crediting Marduk with the victory over God's people, Babylon was in line for an executional judgment. (Jer 51:36; Isa 14:3-6, 17; Da 5:1-4) That came to Babylon in 539 B.C.E. when it was overthrown by the Medes and Persians. Because the judgment to be executed was Jehovah's, such a period could be referred to as "the day of Jehovah."—Isa 13:1, 6, 9.

Similarly, Jeremiah prophesied that God would "put himself in judgment" with Edom, among others. (Jer 25:17-31) Hence the nation that had shown hatred for Jehovah and his people experienced destructive judgment in "the day of Jehovah."—Ob 1, 15, 16.

When Judah and Jerusalem became unfaithful and merited God's disapproval, he promised to "execute in the midst of [her] judicial decisions." (Eze 5:8) In 607 B.C.E. "the day of Jehovah's fury" came with an execution of his destructive judgment. (Eze 7:19) However, another "day," or time, of judgment on Jerusalem was foretold. Joel prophesied an outpouring of spirit before "the great and fear-inspiring day of Jehovah." (Joe 2:28-31) Under inspiration Peter, on the day of Pentecost 33 C.E., explained that they were then experiencing a fulfillment of that prophecy. (Ac 2:16-20) The destructive "day of Jehovah" came in 70 C.E. when the Roman armies executed divine judgment upon the Jews. As Jesus foretold, those were "days for meting out justice."—Lu 21:22; see DESTRUCTION.

Future Times of Executional Judgment. Aside from Hebrew Scripture prophecies, the Bible definitely mentions a number of future judgment days that are executional. Revelation points to the time when "Babylon the Great" will be completely burned with fire. This judicial punishment is due to her fornication with the nations and her being drunk with the blood of the witnesses of Jesus. (Re 17:1-6; 18:8, 20; 19:1, 2) Mentioning another executional judgment, Peter drew upon what occurred in Noah's day and foretold a "day of judgment and of destruction of the ungodly men." (2Pe 3:7) Revelation speaks of such a destruction as being executed by "The Word of God," who will strike the nations with a long sword. (Re 19:11-16; compare Jude 14, 15.) Also, in the first century the Devil already had judgment passed on him, and the demons he leads knew that they would be put into the abyss, as will Satan. (1Ti 3:6; Lu 8:31; Re 20:1-3) Thus it follows that the judgment awaiting them is simply the execution of a judgment that has already been decided upon.—Jude 6; 2Pe 2:4; 1Co 6:3.

May or May Not Be Condemnatory. Most of the occurrences of "judgment" (Gr., *kri'sis* and *kri'ma*) in the Christian Greek Scriptures clearly carry the force of condemnatory, or adverse, judgment. In John 5:24, 29 "judgment" is set in contrast with "life" and "everlasting life," plainly implying a condemnatory judgment that means utter loss of life—death. (2Pe 2:9; 3:7; Joh 3:18, 19) However, not all adverse judgment leads inevitably to destruction. Illustrating this are Paul's remarks at 1 Corinthians 11:27-32 about celebrating the Lord's Evening Meal. If a person did not discern properly what he was doing, he could eat or drink "judgment against himself." Then Paul adds: "When we are judged, we are disciplined by Jehovah, that we may not become condemned with the world." Thus one might receive adverse judgment but because of repenting not be destroyed forever.

Furthermore, the possibility of a judgment that is not condemnatory is apparent from 2 Corinthians 5:10. About those manifest before the judgment seat it says: "Each one [will] get his award . . . according to the things he has practiced, whether it is good or vile." The judging mentioned in Revelation 20:13 evidently results in a favorable outcome for many. Of the dead judged, those receiving an adverse judgment are hurled into "the lake of fire." The rest, though, come through the judgment, being "found written in the book of life."—Re 20:15.

Judgment Day of Personal Accountability. Pre-Christian Hebrews were acquainted with the idea that God would hold them personally accountable for their conduct. (Ec 11:9; 12:14) The Christian Greek Scriptures explain that there will be a specific future period, or "day," when mankind, both the living and those who died in the past, will individually be judged.—2Ti 4:1, 2.

Identity of the judges. In the Hebrew Scriptures Jehovah is identified as "the Judge of all the earth." (Ge 18:25) Similarly, in the Christian Greek Scriptures he is called "the Judge of all." (Heb 12:23) He has, though, deputized his Son to do judging for him. (Joh 5:22) The Bible speaks of Jesus as "appointed," "decreed," and "destined" to do judging. (Ac 10:42; 17:31; 2Ti 4:1) That Jesus is thus authorized by God resolves any seeming contradiction between the text that says that individuals will "stand before the judgment seat of God" and the verse that says they will "be made manifest before the judgment seat of the Christ." —Ro 14:10; 2Co 5:10.

Jesus also told his apostles that when he would sit down on his throne in the "re-creation," they would "sit upon twelve thrones" to do judging. (Mt 19:28; Lu 22:28-30) Paul indicated that Christians who had been "called to be holy ones" will judge the world. (1Co 1:2; 6:2) Also, the apostle John saw in vision the time when some received "power of judging." (Re 20:4) In view of the above texts, this evidently includes the apostles and the other holy ones. Such a conclusion is borne out by the remainder of the verse, which speaks of those who rule with Christ for the Millennium. These then will be royal judges with Jesus.

The fine quality of the judging that will take place on Judgment Day is assured, for Jehovah's "judgments are true and righteous." (Re 19:1, 2) The kind of judging that he authorizes is also righteous and true. (Joh 5:30; 8:16; Re 1:1; 2:23) There will be no perverting of justice or hiding of the facts.

Resurrection is involved. When using the expression "Judgment Day," Jesus brought into the picture a resurrection of the dead. He mentioned that a city might reject the apostles and their message, and said: "It will be more endurable for the land of Sodom and Gomorrah on Judgment Day than for that city." (Mt 10:15) This projected the matter into the future and naturally suggested that the people of Sodom and Gomorrah would then be alive by means of resurrection. (Compare Mt 11:21-24; Lu 10:13-15.) Even clearer are Jesus' statements that the "men of Nineveh will rise up in the judgment" and "the queen of the south will be raised up in the judgment." (Mt 12:41, 42; Lu 11:31, 32) The Biblical statements about Jesus' judging "the living and the dead" can be viewed in the light of the fact that resurrection is involved in Judgment Day.—Ac 10:42; 2Ti 4:1.

A final indication that many being examined on Judgment Day will be resurrected ones is the information in Revelation 20:12, 13. Individuals are seen "standing before the throne." The dead are mentioned and so is the fact that death and Hades gave up those dead in them. Such ones are judged.

Time for Judgment Day. In John 12:48 Christ linked the judging of persons with "the last day." Revelation 11:17, 18 locates a judging of the dead as occurring after God takes his great power and begins ruling in a special way as king. Additional light on the matter comes from the sequence of events recorded in Revelation chapters 19 and 20. There one reads of a war in which the "King of kings" kills "the kings of the earth and their armies." (Earlier in Revelation [16:14] this is called "the war of the great day of God the Almighty.") Next Satan is bound for a thousand years. During that thousand years royal judges serve with Christ. In the same context, resurrection and the judging of the dead are mentioned. This, then, is an indication of the time when Judgment Day comes. And it is not impossible from a Scriptural standpoint for a thousand-year period to be viewed as a "day," for such an equation is stated in the Bible.—2Pe 3:8; Ps 90:4.

Basis for judgment. In describing what will take place on earth during the time of judgment, Revelation 20:12 says that the resurrected dead will then be "judged out of those things written in the scrolls according to their deeds." Those resurrected will not be judged on the basis of the works done in their former life, because the rule at Romans 6:7 says: "He who has died has been acquitted from his sin."

However, Jesus said that unwillingness to take note of his powerful works and repent or unresponsiveness to God's message would make it hard for some to endure Judgment Day.—Mt 10:14, 15; 11:21-24.

JUDGMENTS. See JUDICIAL DECISIONS.

JUDGMENT SEAT. Usually a raised outdoor platform, approached by steps, from which seated officials could address the crowds and announce their decisions. (Mt 27:19; Joh 19:13; Ac 12:21; 25:6, 10, 17) What is thought by some to have been the judgment seat (called the Bema) at Corinth, where Paul appeared before Gallio, was built of white and blue marble. (Ac 18:1, 12, 16, 17) Alongside it were two waiting rooms with mosaic floors and marble benches.

Jehovah God has committed all judging to his Son (Joh 5:22, 27), and therefore all must appear before 'the judgment seat of Christ.' (2Co 5:10) This is also rightly called "the judgment seat of God" in that Jehovah is the Originator of the arrangement and judges by means of his Son. —Ro 14:10.

JUDICIAL DECISIONS. Judgment rendered by one(s) in authority. (2Sa 8:15; 1Ki 3:16-28; 10:9; 2Ki 25:6; 2Ch 19:8-10) Jehovah God, as Judge, Statute-Giver, and King (Isa 33:22), gave to the nation of Israel an extensive code of laws. His decisions on matters of law furnished guidelines for deciding matters involving individuals and the nation's internal and external affairs. —See COURT, JUDICIAL; LAW; LEGAL CASE.

Many of these judicial decisions were given to the nation of Israel at Mount Sinai. (Ne 9:13) But at times certain situations called for a special judicial decision. For example, when Manassite Zelophehad was survived by daughters only, a question arose regarding whether they should receive an inheritance. Jehovah then rendered a decision that covered the case and afterward served as a statute for handling like situations. (Nu 27:1-11; 36:1-12; see also Le 24:10-16.) Similarly, a judicial decision made by David about the distribution of spoils of war set a legal precedent.—1Sa 30:23-25.

By designating certain common but extremely harmful acts as capital offenses, the divinely given judicial decisions stood out as unique among the laws of contemporary nations. Surrounding peoples engaged in bestiality, sodomy, incest, and other degraded practices that were injurious to mental, physical, and spiritual well-being. (Le 18:6-30; 20:10-23) Therefore, Jehovah's judicial decisions, if obeyed, would have elevated the nation of Israel. With Jehovah's blessing, Israel's strict adherence to his commands would have resulted in observable benefits, causing other nations to say: "This great nation is undoubtedly a wise and understanding people." (De 4:4-6) Since these were really a blessing to Israel (Le 25:18, 19; De 4:1; 7:12-15; 30:16), it is not surprising that the psalmist prayed that he might be taught Jehovah's judicial decisions. (Ps 119:108) He so much appreciated them that he praised Jehovah for his judicial decisions seven times a day (Ps 119:164), even getting up at midnight to thank God for them.—Ps 119:62.

However, although good, righteous, and holy, the judicial decisions of the Law merely served as a tutor leading to Christ. That Law covenant was replaced by the new covenant. (Ro 7:12; Ga 3:24; Heb 8:7-13) So it is to be expected that obedience to the commands, or judicial decisions, associated with the new covenant would result in far grander blessings than those natural Israel experienced under the Law.—Joh 13:34, 35; 1Co 6:9-11; 1Pe 1:14, 15, 22, 23; 2:9, 10; 1Jo 5:3.

JUDITH (Ju′dith) [feminine form of Judah]. A wife of Esau; daughter of Beeri the Hittite and a constant source of bitterness to Isaac and Rebekah. (Ge 26:34, 35) She is perhaps the same as Oholibamah at Genesis 36:2.

JULIA (Ju′li·a). A member of the congregation at Rome to whom Paul sent greetings. (Ro 16:15) Julia may have been the wife or sister of Philologus.

JULIUS (Ju′li·us). A Roman army officer or centurion of the band of Augustus in whose custody Paul traveled to Rome. (Ac 27:1; see ARMY OFFICER; AUGUSTUS, BAND OF.) From the beginning of the voyage, Julius apparently appreciated that Paul was not an ordinary prisoner and showed him kindness, for example, letting him go ashore to visit friends at Sidon. However, when Paul later suggested that for the time being their continuing on would be perilous, Julius listened to the contrary opinion of the pilot and the shipowner. Later Julius' soldiers prevented the escape of the sailors, in keeping with Paul's words: "Unless these men remain in the boat, you cannot be saved." When shipwreck occurred, Julius, by not letting the soldiers kill the prisoners, saved Paul's life.—Ac 27:1-44.

JUNIAS (Ju′ni·as). A recipient of special greetings in Paul's letter to the Romans (16:7). Andronicus and Junias were his "relatives." While the Greek word used here can mean "fellow-countryman," the primary meaning is "blood relative of the same generation." The two were Paul's "fellow captives," possibly having been in prison with him somewhere. Paul calls them both "men of note among the apostles," perhaps recalling their fine reputation with the apostles. They were 'in union with Christ longer than Paul himself was,' indicating early discipleship.

JUNIPER.

1. [Heb., *berohsh′*]. The Hebrew term for this tree has been given various meanings, such as "fir," "cypress"; however, some lexicographers recommend the juniper tree on good basis. (See *Lexicon in Veteris Testamenti Libros*, by L. Koehler and W. Baumgartner, Leiden, 1958, p. 148; *The Interpreter's Dictionary of the Bible*, edited by G. A. Buttrick, 1962, Vol. 2, p. 293.) Since the tree was imported from Lebanon by King Solomon (1Ki 5:8-10; 9:11; 2Ch 2:8), it may be identified with the *Juniperus excelsa*, a tall, robust evergreen growing up to 20 m (66 ft) in height, with spreading branches, small scalelike leaves, and dark, small, globular fruit. It is highly fragrant. The timber from this juniper tree is greatly valued for its durability.

The *Juniperus excelsa* is a native of Lebanon and is regularly associated with that land, being included with other trees as the "glory of Lebanon." (2Ki 19:23; Isa 14:8; 37:24; 60:13) The psalmist spoke of the juniper trees as the "house," or nesting place, of storks. (Ps 104:17) Juniper wood was used extensively in the temple built by Solomon. (2Ch 3:5) The leaves of the main doors were made of juniper wood (1Ki 6:34), and the floor was overlaid with it. (1Ki 6:15) It is elsewhere spoken of as being used for rafters (Ca 1:17), planking for ships (Eze 27:5), spear shafts (Na 2:3), and musical instruments (2Sa 6:5). As a luxuriant tree, it is used in the restoration prophecies to describe the beauty and fruitful fertility to be brought to the land of God's people.—Isa 41:19; 55:13; 60:13.

2. [Heb., *′aroh·′er′* or *′ar·′ar′*]. The Arabic word *′ar′ar* aids in identifying this tree as probably the *Juniperus phoenicia*, a shrublike tree to be found in the Sinai region and also in the area of the Desert of Edom. The root word in the Hebrew from which the tree's name is drawn has the idea of "nakedness" or being "stripped" (compare Ps 102:17), and this dwarf juniper is correspondingly described as of rather gloomy appearance, growing in rocky parts of the desert and on crags. It is fittingly used in the book of Jeremiah when comparing the man whose heart turns away from Jehovah with "a solitary tree [*′ar·′ar′*] in the desert plain," and also in warning the Moabites to take flight and become "like a juniper tree [*ka·′aroh·′er′*] in the wilderness."—Jer 17:5, 6; 48:1, 6 (see, however, ftn).

JURISDICTIONAL DISTRICT. An administrative division of a realm under the control of a central government. (Es 1:16; 2:3, 18) The Bible mentions jurisdictional districts in connection with Israel, Babylon, and Medo-Persia. (1Ki 20:14-19; Es 1:1-3; Da 3:1, 3, 30) The Hebrew and Aramaic word for "jurisdictional district" (*medhi·nah′*) comes from the root verb *din*, meaning "judge."

Daniel the prophet was made ruler over all the jurisdictional district of Babylon, perhaps the principal one that included the city of Babylon. (Da 2:48) His three Hebrew companions, Shadrach, Meshach, and Abednego, were also appointed to serve in administrative capacities in this district. (Da 2:49; 3:12) Elam appears to have been another Babylonian jurisdictional district. (Da 8:2) Possibly because of having lived in the jurisdictional district of Babylon, the repatriated Jewish exiles are called "sons of the jurisdictional district." (Ezr 2:1; Ne 7:6) Or, this designation may allude to their being inhabitants of the Medo-Persian jurisdictional district of Judah.—Ne 1:3.

At least during the reign of Ahasuerus (Xerxes I) the Medo-Persian Empire consisted of 127 jurisdictional districts, from India to Ethiopia. Jews were scattered throughout this vast realm. (Es 1:1; 3:8; 4:3; 8:17; 9:2, 30) The land of Judah, with its own governor and lesser administrative heads, was itself one of the 127 jurisdictional districts. (Ne 1:3; 11:3) Seemingly, however, Judah was part of a still larger political division administered by a higher governmental official. Apparently this official directed any serious complaints concerning the districts under his jurisdiction to the king and then waited for royal authorization to act. Also, lesser officials could request that the activities of a particular jurisdictional district be investigated. (Ezr 4:8-23; 5:3-17) When authorized by the king, jurisdictional districts could receive money from the royal treasury, and the royal decrees were sent by means of couriers to the various parts of the empire. (Ezr 6:6-12; Es 1:22; 3:12-15; 8:10-14) Therefore, all the inhabitants of the jurisdictional districts were familiar with the laws and decrees of the central government.—Compare Es 4:11.

The system of jurisdictional districts existing in nations of antiquity often made the lot of the subject peoples more difficult. This fact is acknowledged by the wise writer of Ecclesiastes (5:8).—See PROVINCE.

JUSHAB-HESED (Ju'shab-he'sed). One of Zerubbabel's sons.—1Ch 3:19, 20.

JUSTICE. The maintenance or administration of what is right in a fair and impartial way and according to a standard. The Hebrew word *mishpat'*, often translated "justice" or "judgment" (*NW, RS*), may also convey the idea of a particular plan (Ex 26:30), custom (Ge 40:13), rule (2Ch 4:20), or regular procedure (Le 5:10) for doing things.

The two Hebrew words most frequently translated "justice" in the *King James Version* (*tse'dheq* and *tsedha·qah'*) are usually rendered "righteousness" in the *New World Translation*. (Ge 18:19; Job 8:3) Whereas justice has legal associations, basically there is no distinction between justice and righteousness.—Compare Am 5:24.

One Greek word translated "in harmony with justice" (*NW*) designates something that is "just" (*KJ, RS*) or deserved. (Ro 3:8; Heb 2:2) "Judgment" and "vengeance" are the primary meanings

of two other Greek words sometimes rendered "justice."—Mt 12:20, *NW, RS;* Lu 18:7, *NW.*

The supreme Judge and Statute-Giver (Isa 33:22), Jehovah God, "is a lover of righteousness and justice." (Ps 33:5) "Justice and abundance of righteousness he will not belittle." (Job 37:23) This guarantees that he will never abandon his loyal ones. (Ps 37:28) Jehovah shows no partiality in dealing with his creatures, but he accepts and bestows his blessing upon all those fearing him and practicing righteousness. (Ac 10:34, 35) Individuals and nations are punished or rewarded according to their acts. (Ro 2:3-11; Eph 6:7-9; Col 3:22–4:1) Jehovah's justice is also balanced with mercy, thus providing opportunity for men and nations to turn from their wicked ways and thereby escape the execution of his adverse judgments. —Jer 18:7-10; Eze 33:14-16; see DECLARE RIGHTEOUS.

Jehovah's wisdom is far superior to that of imperfect humans, and man, not God, must learn the path of justice. (Isa 40:14) Thus man is in no position to judge God's acts as just or unjust, but must learn to conform his thinking to the standard of justice that Jehovah has revealed in his Word. Said God to the Israelites: "As for my ways, are they not adjusted right, O house of Israel? Are not the ways of you people the ones that are not adjusted right?" (Eze 18:29) Also, Jehovah's creatorship rules out all basis for questioning the rightness of his activities.—Ro 9:20, 21; see also Job 40:8–41:34.

Therefore, Jehovah has always rightly required that those desiring to gain his approval acquaint themselves with his standard of justice and follow it. (Isa 1:17, 18; 10:1, 2; Jer 7:5-7; 21:12; 22:3, 4; Eze 45:9, 10; Am 5:15; Mic 3:9-12; 6:8; Zec 7:9-12) Like God, they must be impartial, as a failure in this regard is unjust and violates the law of love. (Jas 2:1-9) However, the exercise of justice according to God's standard is not a burden; man's happiness actually depends on it. (Ps 106:3; compare Isa 56:1, 2.) This truth was acknowledged by the famous English jurist Blackstone: "[God] has so intimately connected, so inseparably interwoven the laws of eternal justice with the happiness of each individual, that the latter cannot be attained but by observing the former; and, if the former be punctually obeyed, it cannot but induce the latter."—*Chadman's Cyclopedia of Law,* 1912, Vol. I, p. 88.

The proper exercise of justice by governmental authority likewise contributes to the happiness and well-being of its subjects. (Compare Pr 29:4.) Since justice will always be exercised by Christ

Jesus as King of God's Kingdom and by all those serving in administrative capacities under him, his loyal subjects will find pleasure in submitting themselves to his righteous rule.—Isa 9:6, 7; 32:1, 16-18; 42:1-4; Mt 12:18-21; Joh 5:30; compare Pr 29:2.

Concerning the administration of justice and the principles involved, see COURT, JUDICIAL; LAW; LEGAL CASE.

JUSTICES.
Persons responsible for deciding legal cases. At Job 31:11, 28 the phrase "for attention by the justices" is used in an adjective sense to describe errors calling for judgment. Thus in these verses *An American Translation* reads "a heinous sin" (vs 11) and "a heinous crime" (vs 28), instead of "an error for [attention by] the justices." The "error" under consideration in verse 11 is adultery (vss 9, 10), a crime that in Job's time may have been judged by the older men at the city gate. (Compare Job 29:7.) However, the "error" of verse 28 involves materialism and secret idolatry (vss 24-27), wrongs of mind and heart that cannot be established at the mouth of witnesses. Therefore, no human justices could determine guilt. Job, though, apparently recognized that God could judge such wrongs and that they were serious enough to warrant his judgment.

JUSTIFICATION.
See DECLARE RIGHTEOUS.

JUSTUS
(Jus'tus) [from Lat., meaning "Just; Upright; Righteous"].

1. The surname of Joseph Barsabbas. Justus and Matthias were the two candidates suggested as possible replacements for Judas Iscariot as an apostle. The lot fell to Matthias. Even though Justus was not chosen, his being considered for the office shows he was a mature disciple of Jesus Christ.—Ac 1:23-26.

2. A Corinthian believer whose home adjoined the synagogue. Because of Jewish opposition, Paul "transferred" to the house of Titius Justus, that is, he continued his preaching there; his residence remained with Aquila and Priscilla.—Ac 18:1-7.

3. A Jewish fellow worker of the apostle Paul. Justus, also called Jesus, was one of those who strengthened Paul during his first imprisonment in Rome and who sent along his greetings to the Colossians.—Col 4:10, 11.

JUTTAH
(Jut'tah) [probably, Extended (or, Stretched-Out) Place]. A site in the mountainous region of Judah given to "the sons of Aaron" as a priestly city. (Jos 15:20, 48, 55; 21:13, 16) Juttah is identified with modern Yatta, situated on a ridge about 10 km (6 mi) S of Hebron.

K

KABZEEL
(Kab'ze·el) [God Has Collected]. A city in the southern part of Judah. (Jos 15:21) It is tentatively identified with Khirbet Hora (Horvat Hur), about 10 km (6 mi) ENE of Beer-sheba. The Hebrew text of 2 Samuel 23:20 and 1 Chronicles 11:22 has been variously understood to mean that Kabzeel was (1) the home of the distinguished warrior Benaiah, (2) the home of one of his progenitors or the place where such a one performed notable deeds, or (3) the scene for Benaiah's many deeds. (Compare *AS; KJ; JB; Le; NW; RS.*) An alternate form, "Jekabzeel," appears at Nehemiah 11:25 in a listing of postexilic settlements in Judah.

KADESH
(Ka'desh) [Holy Place], **KADESH-BARNEA** (Ka'desh-bar'ne·a) [Holy Place of Barnea]. An Israelite wilderness encampment situated at the extremity of Edomite territory near "the way to Shur," perhaps the modern Darb el-Shur extending from Hebron to Egypt. (Ge 16:7, 14; Nu

20:14-16 [Heb. *'ir* (city) at Nu 20:16 may simply mean encampment; compare Nu 13:19.]) Apparently 11 days' travel distance by way of Mount Seir separated Kadesh-barnea from Horeb.—De 1:2.

Kadesh is spoken of as being located in both the Wilderness of Paran and the Wilderness of Zin. Possibly Zin and Paran were adjoining wildernesses that met at Kadesh, and therefore, the site could be referred to as lying in either one. Or, the Wilderness of Zin may have been part of the larger Wilderness of Paran. (Nu 13:26; 20:1) In Abraham's time the place was known both as En-mishpat and as Kadesh. (Ge 14:7; 20:1) It is perhaps the same site as Kedesh.—Jos 15:21, 23.

'Ain Qedeis, about 80 km (50 mi) SSW of Beer-sheba, has been suggested as a possible identification for Kadesh. In the midst of a desolate wilderness (compare De 1:19), the pure and sweet water of the spring at Qedeis supports an oasis of grass, shrubs, and trees. There are also two other springs in the vicinity, 'Ain el-Qudeirat and 'Ain el-Qeseimeh. Today the largest of the three springs is 'Ain el-Qudeirat, and for this reason some favor identifying it with Kadesh-barnea. However, 'Ain Qedeis is the most easterly spring. Consequently, the identification of 'Ain Qedeis with Kadesh-barnea seems to be more in line with the description of the E-W course of Canaan's southern boundary: Kadesh-barnea ('Ain Qedeis?), Hazzar-addar ('Ain el-Qudeirat?), and Azmon ('Ain el-Qeseimeh?).—Nu 34:3-5.

If the Israelites did encamp in this area, because of the vast multitude they doubtless used all three springs. For example, the encampment just before crossing the Jordan spread out "from Beth-jeshimoth to Abel-shittim." (Nu 33:49) That was a distance of about 8 km (5 mi), according to the suggested sites for those places. The distance from Kadesh-barnea ('Ain Qedeis) to Azmon ('Ain el-Qeseimeh) is about 14 km (8.5 mi); and to Hazzar-addar ('Ain el-Qudeirat) is 9 km (5.5 mi). So, for them to have used all three springs is not an unreasonable possibility. It is also possible that the whole area was called Kadesh-barnea with the name preserved in the SE spring.—See ADDAR No. 2; AZMON.

In the second year after their Exodus from Egypt, the Israelites pulled away from Hazeroth and encamped at Kadesh-barnea. (Compare Nu 10:11, 12, 33, 34; 12:16; 13:26.) Moses then sent 12 men to spy out the Promised Land. Ten of these spies brought back a bad report, resulting in rebellious murmurings among the Israelites. Jehovah, therefore, sentenced the nation to wander in the wilderness. Israel's subsequent attempt to take Canaan without divine approval and direction brought humiliating defeat. (Nu 13:1-16, 25-29; 14:1-9, 26-34, 44, 45; 32:7-13; De 1:41-45) For some time thereafter the Israelites stayed at Kadesh-barnea. (De 1:46) But it was not Jehovah's purpose for them to remain there. Earlier he had said to them: "While the Amalekites and the Canaanites are dwelling in the low plain, you people make a turn tomorrow [a Heb. idiom meaning "later on," as at Ex 13:14] and pull away to march to the wilderness by way of the Red Sea."—Nu 14:25.

Accordingly, the Israelites left Kadesh-barnea and walked about in the wilderness for 38 years. (De 2:1, 14) It seems that during these years they spent time at some 18 different places, this being the number of camp stages listed after the Israelites left Hazeroth. (Compare Nu 12:16–13:3, 25, 26; 33:16-36.) Although Israel encamped at Ka-

desh after departing from Hazeroth, Numbers 33:18 does not mention Kadesh after Hazeroth. This may have been an intentional omission or perhaps, as some have suggested in the past, Kadesh may be the same as Rithmah.

Finally the Israelites appear to have returned to Kadesh in the first month of the 40th year after the Exodus. (Nu 20:1; 33:36-39) Moses' sister Miriam died there. Later, Moses and Aaron lost the privilege of entering the Promised Land for failing to sanctify Jehovah in connection with the miraculous provision of water for the Israelites encamped at Kadesh. From there Moses subsequently asked Edom's permission to pass through its territory. (Nu 20:1-17) This request was denied, and seemingly the Israelites remained a while longer at Kadesh (Nu 20:18; Jg 11:16, 17) before moving on toward the Promised Land by way of Mount Hor. (Nu 20:22; 33:37) When they reached the Plains of Moab, E of the Jordan, Jehovah designated Kadesh-barnea as a part of the southern border of the Promised Land. (Nu 33:50; 34:4) Later, the Israelites under Joshua conquered the area extending from Kadesh-barnea to Gaza (Jos 10:41), and Kadesh-barnea came to be on the southern boundary of Judah.—Jos 15:1-4.

Psalm 29:8 speaks of Jehovah's voice as causing the Wilderness of Kadesh 'to writhe.' The allusion may be to a violent storm that rushes from the mountains of the N to the region of Kadesh in the S and there blows about the sands in such a way as to give the appearance of a writhing wilderness.

KADMIEL (Kad'mi·el) [God Confronts; God Goes in Front]. A Levite returning to Jerusalem (with Zerubbabel) accompanied by members of his family. (Ezr 2:1, 2, 40; Ne 7:6, 7, 43; 12:1, 8, 24) Kadmiel and his sons helped supervise the temple reconstruction.—Ezr 3:9.

The time period between the return from Babylonian exile (537 B.C.E.) and the confession of the nation's sins against Jehovah in Nehemiah's day (455 B.C.E.), which was followed by the attesting by seal of the "trustworthy arrangement" (Ne 9:4, 5, 38; 10:1, 9, 10), does not allow for the same Kadmiel to be identified with all these affairs. No doubt a representative of Kadmiel's house participated in these latter two events.

KADMONITES (Kad'mon·ites) [from a root meaning "east"]. A people listed among other nations whose lands Jehovah promised to Abram's seed. (Ge 15:18-21) They were evidently a pastoral or nomadic tribe, like the Kenites and Kenizzites with whom they are mentioned. (Ge 15:19)

The exact location of their territory is uncertain, although it is suggested that they inhabited the Syrian desert between Palestine-Syria and the Euphrates River.

The Hebrew name of this people (*qadh·moh·ni'*) has the same form as the adjective *qadh·moh·ni'* (eastern, Eze 47:18); thus some suggest that it may merely mean "Easterners." (Jg 8:10) However, the fact that this Hebrew term is used as a name at Genesis 15:19 shows that it can refer to a specific tribe.

KAIN (Ka'in) [from a root meaning "produce; acquire; buy"].

1. A name employed in a proverbial utterance of Balaam to refer to the tribe of the Kenites. (Nu 24:22) It is rendered "the Kenites" at Judges 4:11. —See KENITE.

2. A city in the mountainous region of Judah. (Jos 15:1, 48, 57) It is identified with en-Nebi Yaqin, about 6 km (3.5 mi) SE of Hebron.

KAIWAN (Kai'wan). Apparently a star-god, as indicated by the fact that the name Kaiwan is put in a parallelism with "the star of your god." (Am 5:26) Evidently the Akkadian star *kaimanu* or *kaiwanu* is meant, since this occurs in Akkadian inscriptions as the name of Saturn (a star-god). In the Masoretic text the name was intentionally vowel pointed to correspond with the Hebrew word *shiq·quts'* (disgusting thing). In the Greek *Septuagint,* "Kaiwan" is rendered *Rhai·phan',* presumably the Egyptian designation for Saturn; and in Stephen's quotation, at Acts 7:43, *Rhom·pha'* appears in the Westcott and Hort Greek text.—See ASTROLOGERS; REPHAN.

KALLAI (Kal'lai). A priest in the days of the high priest Joiakim. He was the head of the paternal house of Sallai.—Ne 12:12, 20, 26.

KAMON (Ka'mon). The burial place of Judge Jair. (Jg 10:5) Josephus speaks of Kamon as "a city of Gilead." (*Jewish Antiquities,* V, 254 [vii, 6]) This seems to fit the Scriptural reference to Jair's being a "Gileadite." (Jg 10:3) Two locations E of the Jordan are commonly presented for ancient Kamon. One is Qamm, about 18 km (11 mi) SE of the Sea of Galilee. But its ruins give no evidence of habitation before Roman times. The other suggestion is the site of the less impressive ruins of undetermined antiquity at Qumeim, about 3 km (2 mi) farther S.

KANAH (Ka'nah) [Reed; Cane].

1. A torrent valley that served as a boundary between Ephraim and Manasseh. (Jos 16:8; 17:9)

Today it is usually linked with the Wadi Qanah (Nahal Qana). This small stream rises in the hill country a few kilometers SW of Nablus and, as the Wadi Ishkar, flows in a southwesterly direction and then joins the Wadi Yarkon (Nahal Yarqon), which empties into the Mediterranean Sea N of Tel Aviv-Yafo. However, some scholars believe that in Joshua's day the lower course of the Wadi Qanah perhaps flowed directly into the Mediterranean at a point about 10 km (6 mi) farther N.

2. A boundary city of Asher. (Jos 19:24, 28) It is generally identified with modern Qana, about 12 km (7.5 mi) ESE of Tyre.

KAPH [כ; final, ך]. The 11th letter of the Hebrew alphabet. In sound *kaph* corresponds to *kh* when not having the point (daghesh lene) in it; but with this point in it (כּ), it becomes hard like the English "k." In the Hebrew, it is the initial letter in each of the eight verses of Psalm 119:81-88. The letters *kaph* [כ] and *behth* [ב] are similar in appearance.

KAREAH (Ka·re'ah) [Bald; Baldness]. A man of Judah whose sons Johanan and Jonathan were chiefs of military forces in Judah. This was at the time Gedaliah was commissioned by the king of Babylon to govern the Judeans who had not been taken into Babylonian exile following the destruction of Jerusalem in 607 B.C.E.—2Ki 25:21-23; Jer 40:7, 8.

KARKA (Kar'ka) [Floor]. A site on Judah's S boundary between Addar (No. 2) and Azmon. (Jos 15:1-3) The exact location is today uncertain. Some scholars tentatively identify it with a well-built pool discovered at the confluence of Wadi el-'Ain and Wadi Umm Hashim, about 4 km (2.5 mi) ESE of Azmon ('Ain el-Qeseimeh).—See KADESH, KADESH-BARNEA.

KARKOR (Kar'kor). The campsite E of the Jordan from which the remaining forces of Midianite Kings Zebah and Zalmunna were routed by Judge Gideon's surprise military maneuver. (Jg 8:10, 11) Karkor's exact location is today unknown.

KARTAH (Kar'tah) [from a root meaning "town"]. A city given to the Merarite Levites out of the inheritance of Zebulun. (Jos 21:34) Some consider it to be the same as Kattath.—Jos 19:15.

KARTAN (Kar'tan) [form of Kiriathaim, meaning "Double Town"]. A city of Naphtali given to the Gershonite Levites. (Jos 21:27, 32) It is apparently called Kiriathaim at 1 Chronicles 6:76. Kartan is usually identified with Khirbet el-Qureiyeh, about 21 km (13 mi) WNW of the Hula Basin.

KATTATH (Kat'tath). A city of Zebulun (Jos 19:10, 15), often considered to be the same as Kitron.—Jg 1:30.

KEDAR (Ke'dar) [from a root meaning "be dark"].

1. One of the 12 sons of Ishmael.—Ge 25: 13-15; 1Ch 1:29-31.

2. An Arab tribe descended from Ishmael's son Kedar and classed with "the sons of the East." Their land is also called Kedar. (Jer 2:10; 49:28, 29) A nomadic and pastoral people, having herds of sheep, goats, and camels (Isa 60:7; Jer 49:28, 29), the Kedarites evidently inhabited the Syro-Arabian desert E of Palestine in the NW part of the Arabian Peninsula. The reference to "the settlements that Kedar inhabits" (Isa 42:11), while possibly referring to temporary encampments, may instead indicate that a portion of them were somewhat settled. Perhaps because of their importance among the Arab tribes, the name of Kedar in later times came to apply to desert tribes in general. In the Targums and in rabbinic literature, Arabia itself is sometimes called Kedar.

The Shulammite girl of The Song of Solomon likened her swarthy appearance to "the tents of Kedar" (Ca 1:5, 6; compare Ps 120:5), these likely being made of black goat's hair, as are the tents of many modern-day Bedouin. Ezekiel's prophecy mentions "the chieftains of Kedar" along with the Arabs as merchants of male lambs, rams, and he-goats for the commercial city of Tyre.—Eze 27:21.

During the time of Assyria's dominance in the Middle East, the prophet Isaiah foretold the sudden decline of Kedar's glory, her mighty bowmen being reduced to a mere remnant. (Isa 21:16, 17) The Kedarites are evidently the *Qidri* or *Qadri* referred to in Assyrian records of warring campaigns. Assyrian King Ashurbanipal includes them with the *Aribi* (Arabs) and Nebaioth (compare Isa 60:7) in one campaign account and boasts of the asses, camels, and sheep taken from them as booty.

At a later time, Nebuchadnezzar, king of Babylon, struck down Kedar. (Jer 49:28, 29) The monarch's conquest of N Arabia is mentioned by Babylonian historian Berossus, quoted by Josephus. —*Against Apion*, I, 129, 133 (19).

A silver bowl (considered to be of the fifth century B.C.E.) found at Tell el-Maskhutah in Egypt bears the Aramaic inscription: "Qanu son of Geshem, king of Kedar." The Geshem meant in this case may possibly be "Geshem the Arabian" who opposed the work of rebuilding Jerusalem's wall in Nehemiah's day.—Ne 2:19; 6:1, 2, 6.

Assyrian records indicate that at the shrine of King Hazail of Kedar there were images of the following false deities: Atarsamain (the Assyrians identified her with Ishtar Dilbat), Dai, Nahai, Ruldaiu, Atarquruma, and Abirillu. A star of gold decorated with precious stones served as a symbol of the goddess Atarsamain. According to the Babylonian Talmud (*Ta'anit* 5b), the people of Kedar also worshiped water.

KEDEMAH (Ked'e·mah) [Eastward; Toward the East]. A son of Ishmael, named last in order at Genesis 25:15 and 1 Chronicles 1:31. In fulfillment of Jehovah's promise to Abraham (Ge 17:20), Kedemah was one of the 12 chieftains produced by Ishmael.

KEDEMOTH (Ked'e·moth) [from a root meaning "east"]. The name applied to a city E of the Jordan and apparently also to the wilderness surrounding it. From the Wilderness of Kedemoth, Moses sent messengers to Amorite King Sihon, requesting permission to pass through his land. (De 2:26, 27) Originally given to the Reubenites, Kedemoth was later assigned to the Merarite Levites. (Jos 13:15, 18; 21:34, 36, 37; 1Ch 6:77-79) Scholars generally favor as a possible identification one of the tells near where the torrent valley of Arnon begins, such as Qasr ez-Za'faran, situated about 16 km (10 mi) NE of what is thought to be the site of ancient Dibon.

KEDESH (Ke'desh) [Holy Place].

1. A city in southern Judah (Jos 15:21, 23), possibly the same as Kadesh-barnea.—See KA-DESH, KADESH-BARNEA.

2. A city of Naphtali given to the Gershonites and set aside as a city of refuge. (Jos 20:7; 21:32, 33; 1Ch 6:71, 76) Because of its location it was also called "Kedesh-naphtali" (Jg 4:6) and "Kedesh in Galilee." (Jos 20:7) Apparently the residence of Judge Barak, Kedesh served as the rallying point for his 10,000 men from Naphtali and Zebulun prior to their victory over the Canaanite army under Sisera. (Jg 4:6, 10) Centuries later the city was conquered by Assyrian King Tiglath-pileser III during the rule of Israel's King Pekah (c. 778-759 B.C.E.).—2Ki 15:29.

Kedesh has been identified with Tell Qades (Tel Qedesh), a mound overlooking a small, fertile plain about 20 km (12 mi) SW of Dan.

3. A site in Issachar assigned to "the sons of Gershom" (1Ch 6:71, 72), seemingly the same as the "Kishion" mentioned in the parallel list at Joshua 21:28. Tell Abu Qedeis (Tel Qedesh), about 4 km (2.5 mi) SE of Megiddo, has been suggested as a possible identification. This would seem to fit

Joshua 12:21, 22, where Kedesh appears to be placed in the vicinity of Megiddo and Jokneam. Since Barak defeated Sisera in the Megiddo area (Jg 5:19), it may have been near this Kedesh (and not No. 2) that Jael killed Canaanite army chief Sisera in her tent.—Jg 4:11, 17, 21.

KEHELATHAH (Ke·he·la′thah) [from a root meaning "congregation"]. One of the places where the Israelites encamped while wandering in the wilderness. (Nu 33:22, 23) Its exact location is today unknown.

KEILAH (Kei′lah). A fortified Judean city in the Shephelah. (Jos 15:20, 33, 44; 1Sa 23:7) Keilah was perhaps founded or, at one time, governed by some Calebite(s). (1Ch 4:15, 19) It is commonly identified with Khirbet Qila (Qeila), situated on a hill about 14 km (8.5 mi) NW of Hebron. As in the region of ancient Keilah, today grain is cultivated in the vicinity of Khirbet Qila.—Compare 1Sa 23:1.

David, while outlawed by King Saul, saved Keilah from falling to the Philistines. Yet afterward he and his men had to escape from the city to avoid being surrendered to Saul's army by the landowners of Keilah.—1Sa 23:5, 8-13.

The city was reoccupied after the Babylonian exile. At the time that Jerusalem's walls were being repaired under Nehemiah's direction, there were two half districts of Keilah, each with its own "prince."—Ne 3:17, 18.

KELAIAH (Ke·lai′ah). Another name for the Levite Kelita, a contemporary of Ezra the priest. —Ezr 10:23; see KELITA No. 1.

KELITA (Ke·li′ta) [possibly from a root meaning "too short" [that is, dwarfed]].

1. One of the Levites of Ezra's day who recognized their guilt in taking foreign wives and therefore sent them away. He is also called Kelaiah. (Ezr 10:23, 44) Possibly the same as Nos. 2 and 3.

2. A Levite who assisted Ezra in "explaining the law to the people" in 455 B.C.E.—Ne 8:7, 8; see No. 1.

3. A Levite whose descendant, if not he himself, attested by seal the "trustworthy arrangement" of Nehemiah's time. (Ne 9:38; 10:1, 9, 10) If Kelita himself, rather than a descendant, was present when this agreement was made, he may have been the same as No. 1 or No. 2.

KEMUEL (Kem·u′el).

1. A son of Abraham's brother Nahor and his wife Milcah; hence, Abraham's nephew. He had a son named Aram.—Ge 22:20, 21.

2. Son of Shiphtan and a chieftain of the tribe of Ephraim. He was one of the 12 men appointed by Jehovah through Moses to divide the land of Canaan among the Israelites, representing the tribe of Ephraim in this undertaking.—Nu 34:16-29.

3. A Levite who was the father of Hashabiah, leader over the tribe of Levi in David's day.—1Ch 27:16, 17.

KENAN (Ke′nan) [from a root meaning "produce; acquire; buy"]. The son of Enosh, grandson of Seth, and great-grandson of Adam. He was the father of Mahalalel and lived 910 years. (Ge 5:3-14; 1Ch 1:1, 2) Kenan is evidently referred to as "Cainan, son of Enosh," in Luke's listing of Jesus' genealogy.—Lu 3:37, 38.

KENATH (Ke′nath). A site E of the Jordan captured by Nobah, probably a Manassite, who thereafter called it by his own name. (Nu 32:42) But the designation "Nobah" perhaps did not stick, for later "Kenath" is reported to have been taken by Geshur and Syria. (1Ch 2:23) Kenath is identified with the ruins at Kanaouat (or Canatha), about 90 km (60 mi) SSE of Damascus and 7 km (4.5 mi) NW of modern Soueida. Kanaouat was one of the original ten cities of the Decapolis.

KENAZ (Ke′naz).

1. One of the sons of Esau's son Eliphaz and a sheik in the land of Edom.—Ge 36:11, 15, 42, 43; 1Ch 1:36, 53.

2. The father of Othniel and Seraiah and brother to Caleb son of Jephunneh.—Jos 15:17; Jg 1:13; 3:9, 11; 1Ch 4:13.

3. A descendant of Caleb the son of Jephunneh through Elah.—1Ch 4:15.

KENITE (Ken′ite). A member of a people residing in Canaan or its vicinity in the days of Abram (Abraham). The Scriptures, however, provide no definite genealogical link for determining their origin.—Ge 15:18-21.

While some scholars, on the basis of a similar Aramaic word, consider "Kenite" to mean "smith," this is uncertain. The Bible itself does not speak of the Kenites as smiths, but it does appear to indicate that at least some of them were shepherds. (Compare Ex 2:15, 16; 3:1; Jg 1:16.) Another suggestion links the term "Kenite" with a Hebrew word meaning "nest," and this would fit the description of the Kenites' dwelling place, or 'nest,' as being "set on the crag."—Nu 24:21.

At the time Moses fled from Egypt to the land of Midian, he married into a Kenite family living there. When the setting of an account involves their residence in Midian, members of this family are called Midianites; in other cases they are referred to as Kenites. This suggests that Moses' father-in-law Jethro, "the priest of Midian," and his brother-in-law Hobab may have been Midianites from a geographic standpoint. (Ex 2:15, 16; 3:1; 18:1; Nu 10:29, 30; Jg 1:16) On the other hand, if Moses' relatives were racial descendants of Midian, then they may have been called Kenites because of belonging to a Kenite branch, or family, of the Midianites, thus making them racially distinct from the Kenites existing in Abraham's time before the birth of Midian.

When the Israelites were about to leave the region of Mount Sinai, Moses requested that Hobab accompany them to serve as "eyes," or as a scout, for the nation because of his knowledge of the area. Although declining at first, Hobab apparently did go along, for the Kenites are later mentioned as taking up residence in the Wilderness of Judah to the S of Arad.—Nu 10:29-32; Jg 1:16.

At a later period Heber the Kenite separated himself from the other Kenites and pitched his tent at Kedesh. (Jg 4:11; see KEDESH No. 3.) When the Canaanite forces were overthrown, Sisera "fled on foot to the tent of Jael the wife of Heber the Kenite, for there was peace between Jabin the king of Hazor and the household of Heber the Kenite." However, there Sisera's life ended at Jael's hand.—Jg 4:17-21; 5:24-27.

In the days of King Saul some Kenites were residing among the Amalekites. Therefore Saul, when about to make war against the Amalekites, urged the Kenites to separate themselves to escape calamity. This kindness was extended because the Kenites had themselves "exercised loving-kindness with all the sons of Israel at the time of their coming up out of Egypt." (1Sa 15:5, 6; compare Ex 18:8, 9; Nu 10:29-33.) Later, David told Achish that he had made a raid "upon the south of the Kenites." (1Sa 27:10) But this was part of a subterfuge. Actually, the Kenites were on friendly terms with the Israelites. Thus, when David plundered Ziklag he sent some of the spoil "to those in the cities of the Kenites," probably in the mountainous region of southern Judah.—1Sa 30:29.

Families of scribes residing at Jabez were Kenites "that came from Hammath the father of the house of Rechab." (1Ch 2:55) They are mentioned in connection with descendants of Judah.—1Ch 2:3.

The fact that the Kenites lived in association with different peoples at various times and places may imply that this nomadic or seminomadic people was not entirely absorbed by any other tribe or people.

The Bible does not specifically report what happened to the Kenites, also called Kain. Balaam's proverbial utterance concerning them posed the question: "How long will it be till Assyria will carry you away captive?" (Nu 24:21, 22) So it may be that some Kenites lived in the northern kingdom of Israel and surrounding areas and were taken captive along with them by the Assyrians.—2Ki 15:29; 17:6.

KENIZZITE (Ken′iz·zite) [Of (Belonging to) Kenaz].

1. Member of a non-Israelite people in or near Canaan whose territory was promised by Jehovah to Abram's seed. (Ge 15:18, 19) The Kenizzites evidently moved into the Negeb from the SE, possibly spreading over part of Edom as well as what became southern Judah, doing so prior to the Israelite conquest of the Promised Land.

The Kenizzites have been linked by some scholars with the Kenaz who was a sheik of Edom descended from Esau through Eliphaz (Ge 36: 15, 16), and thus are viewed as a prominent Edomite family. There is, however, uncertainty as to the actual identity of the patronymic ancestor of the Kenizzites since the Bible itself does not provide details in this regard. The fact that, in Abram's time, Jehovah listed the Kenizzites among those occupying territory that was to become the possession of Abram's seed (Ge 15:18, 19) does not favor the view that the Kenizzites were descendants of Esau, who had not then been born.

2. Faithful Caleb is called "the son of Jephunneh the Kenizzite." (Nu 32:12; Jos 14:6, 14) Jephunneh could have descended from some member of the non-Israelite Kenizzites (Ge 15:18, 19) who associated with the descendants of Jacob (Israel), marrying an Israelite wife. However, more likely the name Kenizzite in his case derives from some ancestral Judean family head named Kenaz, even as Caleb's brother was so named.—Jos 15:17; Jg 1:13; 1Ch 4:13.

KEREN-HAPPUCH (Ker′en-hap′puch) [possibly, Horn of the Black (Eye) Paint [that is, a receptacle for makeup]]. The third and youngest of the daughters born to Job after his great test and suffering had ended and Jehovah had blessed him. (Job 42:12-14) The name may be suggestive of beautiful eyes, or it may be indicative of her great beauty generally, as "no women were found as pretty as Job's daughters in all the land." (Job 42:15) The bluish-white metallic substance antimony produces a brilliant black color that was used by Oriental women of Biblical days to dye their eyelashes and perhaps their eyebrows, or it was used to color the edges of their eyelids, thus making the eyes appear large and lustrous.—See 2Ki 9:30; Jer 4:30.

KERIOTH (Ke·ri·oth) [Towns]. A place mentioned in two prophecies against Moab. (Jer 48:24; Am 2:2) The meaning of its name may indicate that the city was comprised of several smaller towns. Kerioth's exact location is uncertain. Some scholars tentatively suggest Saliya, a site about 16 km (10 mi) ESE of Dibon and N of the Arnon. Others believe that Kerioth is perhaps the same as Ar, S of Arnon. This view seems to find some support in the fact that Ar and Kerioth, although figuring as principal cities (compare Am 2:1-3; De 2:9, 18), do not appear together in lists of Moabite towns.—Compare Isa 15 and 16; Jer 48.

The Moabite Stone, although giving no hint as to the location of Kerioth, does indicate that the god Chemosh had a sanctuary there.

KERIOTH-HEZRON (Ke·ri·oth-hez'ron)[Towns of Hezron]. Another name for Hazor (No. 3), a town of Judah that has tentatively been identified with Khirbet el-Qaryatein (Tel Qeriyyot), about 20 km (12 mi) S of Hebron.—Jos 15:25.

KEROS (Ke'ros) [possibly, Stooped Over]. The founder of a family of Nethinim, some of whose descendants were among those returning to Jerusalem and Judah with Zerubbabel after the Babylonian exile.—Ezr 2:1, 2, 43, 44; Ne 7:6, 7, 46, 47.

KESIL CONSTELLATION (Ke'sil) [Heb., kesil', "stupid"]. Though this word is used many times in its basic sense of "stupid" (compare Ps 49:10; 92:6; Pr 1:22), yet the context in four places (Job 9:9; 38:31; Am 5:8; and Isa 13:10 [here in the plural]) indicates its use to designate a stellar body or group.

The term is generally considered to apply to Orion, also called the hunter, a very prominent constellation containing the giant stars Betelgeuse and Rigel. The Latin *Vulgate* translated *kesil'* as "Orion" in Job 9:9 and Amos 5:8. Most translations imitate the Latin *Vulgate* in viewing *kesil'* as referring to Orion. The ancient Targum and Syriac versions read "giant," and this corresponds to the Arabic name for the Orion constellation, *gabbar*, or "strong one" (Hebrew equivalent, *gib·bohr'*).

The term is used at Amos 5:8 in connection with the reproof of Israel for failing to search for the true God Jehovah, the Maker of the heavenly constellations. At Isaiah 13:9, 10, where the plural *kesi·leh·hem'* (their constellations of Kesil) is used, the description is of "the day of Jehovah," in which proud and haughty tyrants will be abased and the celestial bodies will cease to give their light.

KETURAH (Ke·tu'rah) [from a root meaning "make sacrificial smoke"]. A wife of Abraham and the mother of six of his sons, Zimran, Jokshan, Medan, Midian, Ishbak, and Shuah, ancestors of various N Arabian peoples dwelling to the S and E of Palestine.—Ge 25:1-4.

Keturah is specifically referred to as "Abraham's concubine" at 1 Chronicles 1:32, and quite apparently she and Hagar are meant at Genesis 25:6, where reference is made to the sons of Abraham's "concubines." Keturah was therefore a secondary wife who never attained the same position as Sarah the mother of Isaac, through whom the promised Seed came. (Ge 17:19-21; 21:2, 3, 12; Heb 11:17, 18) While "Abraham gave everything he had to Isaac," the patriarch gave gifts to the sons of his concubines and then "sent them away from Isaac his son, while he was still alive, eastward, to the land of the East."—Ge 25:5, 6.

It has been contended that Abraham took Keturah as a concubine prior to Sarah's death, some thinking it improbable that he would have six sons by one woman after he was about 140 years old and that he would then survive to see them attain an age at which he might send them away. However, Abraham lived for more than 35 years after Sarah's death, dying at the age of 175 years. (Ge 25:7, 8) So he could well have taken Keturah as a wife, had six sons by her, and seen them grow up before he died. Also, it seems proper to consider Abraham's general regard for Sarah's feelings, which makes it unlikely that he would risk the possibility of further discord in the household (comparable to that involving Hagar and Ishmael) by taking another concubine during Sarah's lifetime. The order of events as set forth in the book of Genesis is quite conclusive in indicating that it was after Sarah's death that Abraham took Keturah as his wife.—Compare Ge 23:1, 2; 24:67; 25:1.

It was only because their reproductive powers were miraculously revived that Abraham and Sarah were able to have a son, Isaac, in their old age. (Heb 11:11, 12) Evidently, such restored powers enabled Abraham to become father to six more sons by Keturah when he was even more advanced in age.

KEY

KEY. An instrument used to lock or unlock doors and gates. "Key" is used both literally and figuratively in the Bible.

The key of Biblical times was often a flat piece of wood having pins that corresponded to holes in a bolt that was inside the door of a home. Such a key served to push the bar or bolt inside the door, instead of being turned in the lock as is the modern key. The key was often carried in the girdle or was fastened to some other object and carried over the shoulder.—Isa 22:22.

Egyptian keys of bronze or iron have been found, consisting of a straight shank approximately 13 cm (5 in.) long, with three or more projecting teeth at the end. The Romans also used metal keys, including some of the type made to turn in locks. Keys of bronze have been discovered in Palestine.

Moabite King Eglon used a lock and key for the door of his roof chamber. (Jg 3:15-17, 20-25) Certain postexilic Levites were entrusted with temple guard service, being placed "in charge of the key, even to open up from morning to morning."—1Ch 9:26, 27.

Figurative Use. In the figurative vein the Bible uses the term "key" to symbolize authority, government, and power. Eliakim, elevated to a position of trust and honor, had "the key of the house of David" put upon his shoulder. (Isa 22:20-22) In the Middle East, in more recent times, a large key upon a man's shoulder identified him as a person of consequence or importance. Anciently, a king's adviser, entrusted with the power of the keys, might have general supervision of the royal chambers and might also decide on any candidates for the king's service. In the angelic message to the congregation in Philadelphia the exalted Jesus Christ is said to have "the key of David," and he is the one "who opens so that no one will shut, and shuts so that no one opens." (Re 3:7, 8) As the Heir of the covenant made with David for the Kingdom, Jesus Christ has committed to him the government of the household of faith and the headship of spiritual Israel. (Lu 1:32, 33) By his authority, symbolized by "the key of David," he can open or shut figurative doors, or opportunities and privileges.—Compare 1Co 16:9; 2Co 2:12, 13.

How did Peter use "the keys of the kingdom" that were entrusted to him?

Jesus said to Peter: "I will give you the keys of the kingdom of the heavens, and whatever you may bind on earth will be the thing bound in the heavens, and whatever you may loose on earth will be the thing loosed in the heavens." (Mt 16:19) The identification of these keys logically must be based on other Scriptural information. Jesus made another reference to the subject of keys when he said to the religious leaders, versed in the Law, "You took away the key of knowledge; you yourselves did not go in, and those going in you hindered!" (Lu 11:52) A comparison of this text with Matthew 23:13 indicates that the 'going in' referred to is with regard to entrance into "the kingdom of the heavens." Thus, the use of the word "key" in Jesus' statement to Peter indicated that Peter would have the privilege of initiating a program of instruction that would open up special opportunities with respect to the Kingdom of the heavens.

Different from the hypocritical religious leaders of that time, Peter clearly did use divinely provided knowledge to help persons to 'enter into the kingdom,' notably on three occasions. One was on the day of Pentecost 33 C.E., when Peter, under inspiration, revealed to a gathered multitude that Jehovah God had resurrected Jesus and exalted him to His own right hand in the heavens and that Jesus, in that royal position, had poured out holy spirit on his assembled disciples. As a result of this knowledge and acting upon Peter's exhortation, "Repent, and let each one of you be baptized in the name of Jesus Christ for forgiveness of your sins, and you will receive the free gift of the holy spirit," about 3,000 Jews (and Jewish converts) took the step that led to their becoming prospective members of "the kingdom of the heavens." Other Jews subsequently followed their example. —Ac 2:1-41.

On another occasion Peter and John were sent to the Samaritans, who had not received the holy spirit even though they had been baptized. However, the two apostles "prayed for them" and "went laying their hands upon them," and they received holy spirit.—Ac 8:14-17.

The third occasion of Peter's being used in a special way to introduce persons into privileges as Kingdom heirs was when he was sent to the home of the Gentile Cornelius, an Italian centurion. By divine revelation Peter recognized and declared God's impartiality as regards Jews and Gentiles and that people of the nations, if God fearing and doers of righteousness, were now as acceptable to God as their Jewish counterparts. While Peter was presenting this knowledge to his Gentile hearers, the heavenly gift of the holy spirit came upon them and they miraculously spoke in tongues.

They were subsequently baptized and became the first prospective members of "the kingdom of the heavens" from among the Gentiles. The unlocked door of opportunity for Gentile believers to become members of the Christian congregation thereafter remained open.—Ac 10:1-48; 15:7-9.

Matthew 16:19 may be rendered with grammatical correctness: "Whatever you may bind on earth will be the thing bound [or, the thing already bound] in the heavens, and whatever you may loose on earth will be the thing loosed [or, the thing already loosed] in the heavens." The translation by Charles B. Williams here reads: "Whatever you forbid on earth must be what is already forbidden in heaven, and whatever you permit on earth must be what is already permitted in heaven." Greek scholar Robert Young's literal translation reads: "Whatever thou mayest bind upon the earth shall be having been bound in the heavens, and whatever thou mayest loose upon the earth shall be having been loosed in the heavens." Since other texts make clear that the resurrected Jesus remained the one true Head over the Christian congregation, it is obvious that his promise to Peter did not mean Peter's dictating to heaven what should or should not be loosed but, rather, Peter's being used as heaven's instrument in the unlocking, or loosing, of certain determined things.—1Co 11:3; Eph 4:15, 16; 5:23; Col 2:8-10.

"Key of the abyss." At Revelation 9:1-11 the vision is presented of "a star" out of heaven to whom "the key of the pit of the abyss" is given and who opens that pit and releases a swarm of locusts, their king being "the angel of the abyss." Since the abyss, as shown at Romans 10:6, 7, evidently includes Hades (though it is not limited to Hades), it appears that "the key of the pit of the abyss" includes "the keys of death and of Hades" possessed by the resurrected Jesus Christ, as stated at Revelation 1:18. These "keys" are undoubtedly symbolic of Jesus' authority to free persons from a restraint that is beyond the power of anyone but God or his authorized representative. The "keys" therefore include authority to resurrect persons literally, freeing them from the confines of the grave, as well as to release persons from a figurative death state. (Joh 5:24-29; compare Re 11:3-12; see DEATH [Change in spiritual state or condition].) The last-recorded use of "the key of the abyss" is at Revelation 20:1-7, where the vision describes an angel with that key casting Satan into the abyss, shutting and sealing it over him for a thousand years. At the close of that period Satan is released from his "prison," evidently by the use of the "key" of authority.—See ABYSS.

KEZIAH (Ke·zi'ah) [possibly, Cassia]. The second of the three daughters of Job born after his severe trial and subsequent restoration and blessing by Jehovah. (Job 42:14) The Hebrew word for "cassia" was used as a feminine name, likely because of the fragrance of cassia, and may have been given to this girl as an indication of her beauty.—Job 42:15.

KIBROTH-HATTAAVAH (Kib'roth-hat·ta'a·vah) [Burial Places of the Craving]. The site of an Israelite wilderness encampment, where the mixed crowd expressed selfish longing for the food of Egypt. (Nu 11:4; 33:16, 17; De 9:22) It is generally identified with Rueis el-Eberij, about halfway between Jebel Musa, the traditional site of Mount Sinai, and Hazeroth. There Jehovah miraculously provided a month's supply of quail for the entire camp. (Nu 11:19, 20, 31) But the people were so greedy that "the one collecting least gathered ten homers" (2,200 L; 62 bu). The record says that while "the meat was yet between their teeth, before it could be chewed, . . . Jehovah began striking at the people with a very great slaughter." Instead of denoting literal chewing of a mouthful, this may mean before the entire provision of meat could be "exhausted" or "consumed" (*AT, RS*), because the Hebrew word translated "chewed" basically means "cut off." (Compare Joe 1:5.) After this the dead were buried, and the place therefore came to be called Kibroth-hattaavah.—Nu 11:32-35.

KIBZAIM (Kib'za·im) [A Double Collecting Together (Gathering)]. An Ephraimite city given to the Kohathite Levites. (Jos 21:20-22) At 1 Chronicles 6:68 it is apparently called Jokmeam.

KID. See GOAT.

KIDNAPPING. Seizing, carrying away, and detaining a person against his will through unlawful force, fraud, or intimidation. Kidnapping was a crime carrying the penalty of capital punishment under the Mosaic Law. If a person were to steal or kidnap a man and sell him, or if the kidnapped individual was found with him, the kidnapper was to be put to death. (Ex 21:16; De 24:7) Prior to the giving of this law to Israel, Jacob's son Joseph, sold into slavery, was a victim of kidnapping. (Ge 37:27, 28; 40:15) God later turned this act into a blessing for Joseph in Egypt, and Joseph forgave his brothers for their wicked deed.—Ge 45:4, 5.

In writing to Timothy, the apostle Paul made the observation that "law is promulgated, not for a righteous man," but for lawless persons, including kidnappers.—1Ti 1:8-11.

KIDNEYS

KIDNEYS. Twin organs located in the lower back. Their function is to filter impurities from the blood. Regarding the Hebrew word *kela·yohth'* (kidneys), J. N. Oswalt wrote: "When used figuratively, the term refers to the innermost aspects of personality." (*Theological Wordbook of the Old Testament,* edited by R. Laird Harris, 1980, Vol. 1, p. 440; compare Ps 7:9, ftn.) The same is true of the Greek word *ne·phroi'* (kidneys).—Re 2:23, ftn.

As with all the organs of the body, the kidneys were directly designed by Jehovah God the Creator. (Ps 139:13) In sacrificial animals, the fat around the kidneys was considered especially choice and was specifically mentioned as something that was to be made to smoke on the altar along with the kidneys in communion sacrifices (Le 3:10, 11; 9:19, 20), sin offerings (Le 4:8, 9; 8: 14, 16; 9:10), and guilt offerings (Le 7:1, 4). In the installation of the priesthood, the kidneys of the ram of installation were first waved and then burned on the altar. (Ex 29:22, 24, 25; Le 8:25, 27, 28) In this significance of choiceness, Moses spoke of Jehovah as feeding his people Israel with "the kidney fat of wheat."—De 32:14.

Because of their position deep in the body, the kidneys are among the most inaccessible organs. With good reason, therefore, the Bible uses the term to represent the deepest thoughts and emotions of one's personality. A wound in the kidneys would be a very deep wound, either literally or figuratively considered. (Job 16:13; Ps 73:21; La 3:13) At times kidneys are mentioned in close connection with the heart, which is used figuratively for the total inner person.—Jer 11:20; 17: 10; 20:12; see HEART.

Our Creator knows the makeup of man in the most thorough and intimate way. Therefore, Jehovah is said to test out "heart and kidneys," even as his Son also searches "the kidneys and hearts." (Ps 7:9; Re 2:23) Just as one refines silver, Jehovah can "refine" the kidneys and heart of a person so he may become right before God, being made more sensitive to Jehovah's ways.—Ps 26:2; 66:10.

At Psalm 16:7 David wrote: "I shall bless Jehovah, who has given me advice. Really, during the nights my kidneys have corrected me." God's advice reached the innermost recesses of David's being as a worshiper of the true God. Because it had settled so deeply within, the "advice" was identified with the "kidneys," and thus it could be said that the kidneys corrected David.

God's Word, although it might be on the lips of the wicked ones, does not reach down to the innermost aspects of their personality. Thus, regarding the wicked ones, Jeremiah 12:2 says: "They keep going ahead; they have also produced fruit. You are near in their mouth, but far away from their kidneys." This parallels the scripture at Isaiah 29:13, quoted by Jesus at Matthew 15:7, 8, which says the same thing about the heart of the wicked, thus showing that at times "heart" and "kidneys" are used in a corresponding way.

KIDRON, TORRENT VALLEY OF (Kid'ron) [possibly from a root meaning "be dark"]. A deep valley that separates Jerusalem from the Mount of Olives and runs first southeastward and then southward along the city. Waterless even in winter, except in case of an especially heavy rain, the Kidron Valley (Nahal Qidron) starts some distance to the N of Jerusalem's walls. At first a broad and shallow valley, it continues to narrow and deepen. By the time it is opposite the former temple area, it is approximately 30 m (100 ft) deep and 120 m (390 ft) wide. Farther to the S the Kidron Valley was joined by the Tyropoeon Valley and the Valley of Hinnom respectively. From then on it continued southeastward across the arid Wilderness of Judah to the Dead Sea. The modern name applied to the valley's lower course is Wadi en-Nar (meaning "Fire Wadi"), indicating that it is hot and dry most of the time.

Opposite Jerusalem, rock-cut tombs occupy the steep and rocky slopes of the valley's E side. On its W side, about midway between the former temple area and the junction of the Tyropoeon and Kidron valleys, is the spring of Gihon. (See GIHON No. 2.) Not far from this spring the Kidron Valley widens and forms an open space. It has been suggested that this open area may correspond to the ancient "king's garden."—2Ki 25:4.

King David, when fleeing from rebellious Absalom, crossed the Kidron Valley on foot. (2Sa 15:14, 23, 30) For cursing David on that occasion, Shimei was later restricted by Solomon to Jerusalem and was not permitted to cross the Kidron Valley under pain of death. (1Ki 2:8, 9, 36, 37) It was this same valley that Jesus traversed on his way to the garden of Gethsemane. (Joh 18:1) During the reigns of Judean Kings Asa, Hezekiah, and Josiah, the Kidron Valley was used as a place of disposal for appendages of idolatry. (1Ki 15:13; 2Ki 23:4, 6, 12; 2Ch 15:16; 29:16; 30:14) It also served as a place of burial. (2Ki 23:6) This made the Kidron Valley an unclean area, and it is therefore significant that Jeremiah's prophecy pointed to a time when, by contrast, "all the terraces as far as the torrent valley of Kidron" would be "something holy to Jehovah."—Jer 31:40.

KILN. A heating chamber designed for processing various materials. Kilns of ancient times were used for baking bricks, firing pottery, and processing lime. Unlike the modern meaning of the English term "kiln," the Hebrew word *kiv·shan'* does not embrace structures classified as ovens. —See OVEN.

In view of the progress made in pre-Flood times in the forging of copper and iron tools (Ge 4:22), kilns were likely developed at an early point in man's history. Though not directly mentioned, there is evidence for their use in Nimrod's day. When about to build the city of Babel and its tower in the land of Shinar, the post-Flood people said: "Come on! Let us make bricks and bake them with a burning process." (Ge 11:3) Ancient Babylonian ruins reveal the use of kiln-fired bricks from ancient times. Such durable bricks were used in the more important structures for veneered walls and for paved areas. Some houses excavated at Ur (Abraham's onetime residence) have the lower level built with burnt bricks, while the second story was evidently of sun-dried bricks. Sun-dried bricks, while not as durable as kiln-fired bricks, were inexpensive, easy to manufacture, and satisfactory in dry climates. —See BRICK.

Egyptian pottery kilns were shaped like a tapered chimney, with a perforated baffle between the fire pit below and the firing chamber above. The pottery was placed in this chamber before the fuel was ignited. The correct firing of the kiln was a trade secret among Egyptian potters, and skill was required to bring out the desired qualities in the finished products. The draft created by the air rushing from the fireplace up the flue drew the fire through the baffle perforations and allowed it to circulate around the pottery before passing out at the top of the stack.

In preparation for His sixth blow against Egypt and its proud Pharaoh, Jehovah commanded Moses and Aaron: "Take for yourselves both hands full of soot from a kiln, and Moses must toss it toward the heavens in Pharaoh's sight." Complying with these instructions, "they took the soot of a kiln and stood before Pharaoh, and Moses tossed it toward the heavens, and it became boils with blisters, breaking out on man and beast." —Ex 9:8-10.

Palestinian kilns, or furnaces, discovered at Megiddo, measuring about 2.5 by 3 m (8 by 10 ft), are U-shaped. In this type, the fireplace is located in the bend of the enclosure. Evidently, the draft entering below the fireplace door forced the flames through the two firing chambers and out the two flues located at the rear of the kiln.

Limekilns. Limekilns were used in ancient Palestine because of the abundance of limestone. More recently in that land such kilns have been built on hillsides, the hill forming part of the rear wall. The kilns have been constructed of rough stones without mortar, the spaces between the stones being filled with clay but with a large open flue at the top. After the interior was properly packed with crushed limestone, a hot fire made from brush would be started in the fireplace at the base of the kiln. The strong draft entering through a tunnel in the bottom of the kiln would carry the flames up through the limestone, heating it until it was converted into lime. This process would normally continue for several days. —See LIME.

The first direct Biblical reference to a kiln is at Genesis 19:28. There the black voluminous smoke of a kiln is used to describe the scene Abraham saw when he looked down upon the burning cities of Sodom and Gomorrah and all the District and observed that "thick smoke ascended from the land like the thick smoke of a kiln!"

When the Israelites gathered at the base of Mount Sinai to 'meet the true God,' the awe-inspiring spectacle before their eyes included Mount Sinai's smoking all over, "due to the fact that Jehovah came down upon it in fire; and its smoke kept ascending like the smoke of a kiln, and the whole mountain was trembling very much." —Ex 19:18.

The rendering of 2 Samuel 12:31 in the *King James Version* makes it appear that David caused Ammonite captives to "pass through the brick-kiln," but the sense of the Hebrew text, by a correction of one letter, appears to be that he "made them serve at brickmaking." —*NW; AT; RS*.

KIMAH CONSTELLATION. This term is used at Job 9:9; 38:31; and Amos 5:8 to refer to a celestial constellation. It is usually considered to refer to the Pleiades, a star group formed of seven large stars and other smaller ones, enveloped in nebulous matter and situated about 300 light-years from the sun. At Job 38:31 Jehovah asks Job if he can "tie fast the bonds of the Kimah constellation," and some relate this to the compactness of the Pleiades cluster, the star cluster most likely to be noted by the naked eye. While the identification of the particular constellation intended is indefinite, the sense of the question asked evidently is whether a mere man can bind together in a cluster a group of stars so that they comprise a permanent constellation. Thus, by this question, Jehovah brought home to Job man's inferiority when compared with the Universal Sovereign.

KIN, KINSMAN.

KIN, KINSMAN. Relative, either by common ancestry or by marriage. Kinsman has special reference to a male relative. There are several words in the original Bible languages having the following meanings and usages.

Go·'el' (from Heb. *ga·'al'*, meaning "redeem" or "buy back") has reference to the nearest male relative with the right of a repurchaser or an avenger of blood. Willful murderers were to be put to death by "the avenger of blood." (Nu 35:16-19) Boaz' relationship to Naomi and Ruth was that of "a repurchaser." (Ru 2:20; 3:9, 12, 13; 4:1, 3, 6, 8, 14) Jehovah himself, the Great Father or Life-Giver, is both an Avenger and a Repurchaser for his servants.—Ps 78:35; Isa 41:14; 43:14; 44:6, 24; 48:17; 54:5; 63:16; Jer 50:34.

She·'er' (Heb., meaning "organism") has reference to a fleshly relative or blood relative. God's laws forbade having sexual relations with a close "blood relation," such as one's aunt. (Le 18:6-13; 20:19) If a fellow Israelite fell into debt to an alien, then a brother, an uncle, a cousin, or any other "blood relative" could buy him back. (Le 25:47-49) Or if one died having no sons, daughters, brothers, or uncles, then the next closest "blood relation" received the inheritance.—Nu 27:10, 11.

Qa·rohv' (Heb., meaning "near") includes not only one closely related but also an intimate acquaintance. If a brother became so poor that he had to sell his possessions, then one "closely related" had to buy them back for him. (Le 25:25) Job grieved that his "intimate acquaintances" had left him, and David lamented that his "close acquaintances" also stood aloof.—Job 19:14; Ps 38:11.

Terms related to *ya·dha'* (Heb., meaning "know," "be acquainted") could mean a kinsman or just an acquaintance. Naomi had "a kinsman of her husband" named Boaz. Jehu executed all of Ahab's house including his "acquaintances."—Ru 2:1; 2Ki 10:11.

In the Christian Greek Scriptures *syg·ge·nes'* refers to a relative by blood, but it is never used in speaking of the relation between parents and children. Following this rule, note that Jesus said to his followers: "You will be delivered up even by parents and brothers and relatives [*syg·ge·non'*] and friends." (Lu 21:16) When the 12-year-old Jesus was missing, his parents began looking for him among "the relatives." (Lu 2:44) When you spread a feast, Jesus counseled, do not invite your "relatives" who could pay you back but, rather, the poor people. (Lu 14:12-14) When Peter brought the good news of salvation to Cornelius, his "relatives" were also present. (Ac 10:24) Paul, in his letter to the Romans, referred to the Israelites collectively as well as a number of individuals as his "relatives."—Ro 9:3; 16:7, 11, 21.

KINAH (Ki'nah). A city of southern Judah. (Jos 15:21, 22) Some identify it with Khirbet Taiyib (Horvat Tov), about 30 km (19 mi) ENE of Beer-sheba. The name seems to be preserved in Wadi el-Qeini nearby.

KIND. The creation record found in the first chapter of Genesis reveals that Jehovah God created earth's living things "according to their kinds." (Ge 1:11, ftn) Toward the end of the sixth creative day the earth was supplied with a great variety of basic created "kinds," which included very complex forms of life. These were endowed with the capacity for reproducing offspring "according to their kind(s)" in a fixed, orderly manner.—Ge 1:12, 21, 22, 24, 25; 1Co 14:33.

The Biblical "kinds" seem to constitute divisions of life-forms wherein each division allows for cross-fertility within its limits. If so, then the boundary between "kinds" is to be drawn at the point where fertilization ceases to occur.

In recent years, the term "species" has been applied in such a manner as to cause confusion when it is compared with the word "kind." The basic meaning of "species" is "a sort; kind; variety." In biologic terminology, however, it applies to any group of interfertile animals or plants mutually possessing one or more distinctive characteristics. Thus, there could be many such species or varieties within a single division of the Genesis "kinds."

Although the Bible creation record and the physical laws implanted in created things by Jehovah God allow for great diversity within the created "kinds," there is no support for theories maintaining that new "kinds" have been formed since the creation period. The unchangeable rule that "kinds" cannot cross is a biologic principle that has never been successfully challenged. Even with the aid of modern laboratory techniques and manipulation, no new "kinds" have been formed. Besides, the crossing of created "kinds" would interfere with God's purpose for a separation between family groups and would destroy the individuality of the various kinds of living creatures and things. Hence, because of the distinct discontinuity apparent between the created "kinds," each basic group stands as an isolated unit apart from other "kinds."

From the earliest human record until now, the evidence is that dogs are still dogs, cats continue to be cats, and elephants have been and will always be elephants. Sterility continues to be the delimiting factor as to what constitutes a "kind."

This phenomenon makes possible, through the test of sterility, the determining of the boundaries of all the "kinds" in existence today. Through this natural test of fertilization it is possible to uncover the primary relationships within animal life and plant life. For example, sterility presents an impassable gulf between man and the animals. Breeding experiments have demonstrated that appearance is no criterion. Man and the chimpanzee may look somewhat similar, have comparable types of muscles and bones; yet the complete inability of man to hybridize with the ape family proves that they are two separate creations and not of the same created "kind."

Although hybridization was once hoped to be the best means of bringing about a new "kind," in every investigated case of hybridization the mates were always easily identified as being of the same "kind," such as in the crossing of the horse and the donkey, both of which are members of the horse family. Except in rare instances, the mule thus produced is sterile and unable to continue the variation in a natural way. Even Charles Darwin was forced by the facts to admit: "The distinctness of specific forms and their not being blended together by innumerable transitional links, is a very obvious difficulty." (*Origin of Species*, 1902, Part 2, p. 54) This still remains true.

Whereas specific created *"kinds"* may number only in the hundreds, there are many more varieties of animals and plants on the earth. Modern research has indicated that hundreds of thousands of different plants are members of the same family. Similarly, in the animal kingdom, there may be many varieties of cats, all belonging to one cat family or feline "kind." The same is true of men, of cattle, and of dogs, allowing for great diversity within each "kind." But the fact remains that no matter how many varieties occur in each family, none of these "kinds" can commingle genetically.

Geological research provides clear evidence that the fossils held to be among the earliest specimens of a certain creature are very similar to their descendants alive today. Cockroaches found among the supposed earliest fossil insects are virtually identical to modern ones. Fossil "bridges" between "kinds" are totally lacking. Horses, oak trees, eagles, elephants, walnuts, ferns, and so forth, all continue within the same "kinds" without evolving into other "kinds." The testimony of the fossils is in full accord with the Bible's history of creation, which shows that Jehovah created the living things of the earth in great numbers and "according to their kinds" during the final creative days.—Ge 1:20-25.

From the foregoing, it becomes apparent that Noah could get all the necessary animals into the ark for preservation through the Flood. The Bible does not say that he had to preserve alive every *variety* of the animals. Rather, it states: "Of the flying creatures according to their kinds and of the domestic animals according to their kinds, of all moving animals of the ground according to their kinds, two of each will go in there to you to preserve them alive." (Ge 6:20; 7:14, 15) Jehovah God knew it was necessary to save only representative members of the different "kinds," since they would reproduce in variety after the Flood.—See ARK No. 1.

Following the recession of the floodwaters, these comparatively few basic "kinds" emerged from the ark and spread out over the surface of the earth, eventually producing many variations of their "kinds." Although many new varieties have come into existence since the Flood, the surviving "kinds" have remained fixed and unchanged, in harmony with the unchangeable word of Jehovah God.—Isa 55:8-11.

KINDNESS. The quality or state of taking an active interest in the welfare of others; friendly and helpful acts or favors. The principal word for "kindness" in the Christian Greek Scriptures is *khre·sto'tes*. Jehovah God takes the lead and is the best example of one showing kindness in so many ways toward others, even toward the unthankful and wicked, encouraging them to repentance. (Lu 6:35; Ro 2:4; 11:22; Tit 3:4, 5) Christians, in turn, under the kindly yoke of Christ (Mt 11:30), are urged to clothe themselves with kindness (Col 3:12; Eph 4:32) and to develop the fruitage of God's spirit, which includes kindness. (Ga 5:22) In this way they recommend themselves as God's ministers. (2Co 6:4-6) "Love is . . . kind."—1Co 13:4.

"Kindness" (or, reasonableness; literally, yieldingness; Gr., *e·pi·ei·ki'a*) is an outstanding characteristic of Christ Jesus. (2Co 10:1, ftn) Paul was treated with unusual "human kindness" (literally, affection for mankind; Gr., *phi·lan·thro·pi'a*) by the inhabitants of Malta.—Ac 28:2, ftn.

Loving-Kindness of God. As in the Christian Greek Scriptures so also in the Hebrew Scriptures, frequent mention is made of kindness. The Hebrew word *che'sedh*, when used in reference to kindness, occurs 245 times. The related verb *cha·sadh'* means "act in loyalty (or, loving-kindness)" and carries with it more than just the thought of tender regard or kindness stemming from love, though it includes such traits. (Ps 18:25, ftn) *Che'sedh* is kindness that lovingly attaches itself to an object until its purpose in connection with that object is realized. According to the *Theological Dictionary of the Old Testament, che'sedh* "is active, social, and enduring. . . . [*Che'sedh*] always designates not just a human attitude, but also the act that emerges from this attitude. It is an act that preserves or promotes life. It is intervention on behalf of someone suffering misfortune or distress. It is demonstration of friendship or piety. It pursues what is good and not what is evil." (Edited by G. J. Botterweck and H. Ringgren, 1986, Vol. 5, p. 51) Hence, *che'sedh* is more comprehensively rendered "loving-kindness," or, because of the fidelity, solidarity, and proved loyalty associated with it, an alternate translation would be "loyal love." In the plural number it may be rendered "loving-kindnesses," "acts of loyal love," "full loving-kindness," or "full loyal love."—Ps 25:6, ftn; Isa 55:3, ftn.

Loving-kindness is a precious quality of Jehovah God in which he delights, and it is manifest in all his dealings with his servants. (Ps 36:7; 62:12; Mic 7:18) Were this not the case, they would have perished long ago. (La 3:22) Thus, Moses could plead in behalf of rebellious Israel, both on the basis of Jehovah's great name and because He is a God of loving-kindness.—Nu 14:13-19.

The Scriptures show that Jehovah's loving-kindness, or loyal love, is displayed in a variety of ways and under different circumstances—in acts of deliverance and preservation (Ps 6:4; 119:88, 159), as a safeguard and protection (Ps 40:11; 61:7; 143:12), and as a factor bringing relief from troubles (Ru 1:8; 2:20; Ps 31:16, 21). Because of it one may be recovered from sin (Ps 25:7), sustained, and upheld. (Ps 94:18; 117:2) By it God's chosen ones are assisted. (Ps 44:26) God's loving-kindness was magnified in the cases of Lot (Ge 19:18-22), Abraham (Mic 7:20), and Joseph (Ge 39:21). It was also acknowledged in the choice of a wife for Isaac.—Ge 24:12-14, 27.

With the development of the nation of Israel and thereafter, Jehovah's loving-kindness in connection with his covenant continued to be magnified. (Ex 15:13; De 7:12) This was true in David's case (2Sa 7:15; 1Ki 3:6; Ps 18:50), as it was also with Ezra and those with him (Ezr 7:28; 9:9), and likewise with "thousands" of others (Ex 34:7; Jer 32:18). In support of the kingdom covenant with David, Jehovah continued to express his loving-kindness even after Jesus died, for He resurrected this "loyal one" in fulfillment of the prophecy: "I will give you the loving-kindnesses to David that are faithful."—Ps 16:10; Ac 13:34; Isa 55:3.

It is this loving-kindness on the part of Jehovah that draws individuals to him. (Jer 31:3) They trust in it (Ps 13:5; 52:8), hope in it (Ps 33:18, 22), pray for it (Ps 51:1; 85:7; 90:14; 109:26; 119:41), and are comforted by it (Ps 119:76). They also give thanks to Jehovah for his loving-kindness (Ps 107:8, 15, 21, 31), they bless and praise him for it (Ps 66:20; 115:1; 138:2), and they talk to others about it (Ps 92:2). Like David, they should never try to hide it (Ps 40:10), for it is good (Ps 69:16; 109:21) and it is a great source of rejoicing. (Ps 31:7) Certainly this divine loving-kindness is like a pleasant pathway in which to walk.—Ps 25:10.

In other Bible texts the overflowing abundance of God's loving-kindness (Ps 5:7; 69:13; Jon 4:2), its greatness (Nu 14:19), and its permanence (1Ki 8:23) are emphasized. It is as high as the heavens (Ps 36:5; 57:10; 103:11; 108:4), fills the earth (Ps 33:5; 119:64), and is extended to a thousand generations (De 7:9) and "to time indefinite" (1Ch 16:34, 41; Ps 89:2; Isa 54:8, 10; Jer 33:11). In Psalm 136 all 26 verses repeat the phrase, 'Jehovah's loving-kindness is to time indefinite.'

Often this wonderful characteristic of Jehovah, his loving-kindness, is associated with other magnificent qualities—God's mercy, graciousness, truth, forgiveness, righteousness, peace, judgment, and justice.—Ex 34:6; Ne 9:17; Ps 85:10; 89:14; Jer 9:24.

Loving-Kindness of Man. From the above it is apparent that those wishing to have God's approval must "love kindness" and "carry on with one another loving-kindness and mercies." (Mic 6:8; Zec 7:9) As the proverb says, "The desirable thing in earthling man is his loving-kindness," and it brings him rich rewards. (Pr 19:22; 11:17) God remembered and was pleased with the loving-kindness shown during Israel's youth. (Jer 2:2) But when it became "like the morning clouds and like the dew that early goes away," Jehovah was not pleased, for "in loving-kindness I have taken delight, and not in sacrifice," he says. (Ho 6:4, 6) Lacking loving-kindness, Israel was reproved, the reproof itself actually being a loving-kindness on God's part. (Ho 4:1; Ps 141:5) Israel was also advised to return to God by demonstrating loving-kindness and justice. (Ho 12:6) Such traits should be manifest at all times if one is to find favor in the sight of God and man.—Job 6:14; Pr 3:3, 4.

Instances in the Bible are numerous where individuals showed loving-kindness toward others. Sarah, for example, showed such loyal love toward her husband when they were in enemy territory, protecting him by saying he was her brother. (Ge 20:13) Jacob asked Joseph to exercise the same toward him by promising not to bury him in Egypt. (Ge 47:29; 50:12, 13) Rahab requested that the Israelites show her loving-kindness by preserving her household alive, even as she had similarly treated the Israelite spies. (Jos 2:12, 13) Boaz commended Ruth for exercising it (Ru 3:10), and Jonathan asked David to show it toward him and his household.—1Sa 20:14, 15; 2Sa 9:3-7.

The motives and circumstances that prompt persons to show kindness or loving-kindness vary a great deal. Incidental acts of kindness may reflect customary hospitality or a tendency toward warmheartedness, yet may not necessarily indicate godliness. (Compare Ac 27:1, 3; 28:1, 2.) In the case of a certain man belonging to the city of Bethel, the kindness offered him really was in payment for favors expected of him in return. (Jg 1:22-25) At other times acts of loving-kindness were requested of recipients of past favors, perhaps because of the dire circumstances of the petitioner. (Ge 40:12-15) But sometimes persons failed to pay such debts of loving-kindness. (Ge 40:23; Jg 8:35) As the proverb shows, a multitude of men will proclaim their loving-kindness, but few are faithful to carry it out. (Pr 20:6) Saul and David both remembered the loving-kindness that others had shown (1Sa 15:6, 7; 2Sa 2:5, 6), and it seems that the kings of Israel gained some sort of reputation for loving-kindness (1Ki 20: 31), perhaps in comparison with the pagan rulers. However, on one occasion David's display of loving-kindness was rebuffed through a misinterpretation of the motives behind it.—2Sa 10:2-4.

Law, Paul says, was not made for righteous persons but for bad people, who, among other things, are lacking in loving-kindness. (1Ti 1:9) The Greek word *a·no'si·os*, here rendered "lacking loving-kindness," also has the sense of "disloyal." —2Ti 3:2.

Undeserved Kindness. The Greek word *kha'-ris* occurs more than 150 times in the Greek Scriptures and is rendered in a variety of ways, depending on the context. In all instances the central idea of *kha'ris* is preserved—that which is agreeable (1Pe 2:19, 20) and winsome. (Lu 4:22) By extension, in some instances it refers to a kind gift (1Co 16:3; 2Co 8:19) or the kind manner of the giving. (2Co 8:4, 6) At other times it has reference to the credit, gratitude, or thankfulness that an especially kind act calls forth.—Lu 6:32-34; Ro 6:17; 1Co 10:30; 15:57; 2Co 2:14; 8:16; 9:15; 1Ti 1:12; 2Ti 1:3.

On the other hand, in the great majority of occurrences, *kha'ris* is rendered "grace" by most English Bible translators. The word "grace," how-

ever, with some 14 different meanings does not convey to most readers the ideas contained in the Greek word. To illustrate: In John 1:14, where the *King James Version* says "the Word was made flesh . . . full of grace and truth," what is meant? Does it mean "gracefulness," or "favor," or what?

Scholar R. C. Trench, in *Synonyms of the New Testament,* says *kha'ris* implies "a favour freely done, without claim or expectation of return—the word being thus predisposed to receive its new emphasis [as given it in the Christian writings] . . . , to set forth the entire and absolute freeness of the loving-kindness of God to men. Thus Aristotle, defining [*kha'ris*], lays the whole stress on this very point, that it is conferred freely, with no expectation of return, and finding its only motive in the bounty and free-heartedness of the giver." (London, 1961, p. 158) Joseph H. Thayer in his lexicon says: "The word [*kha'ris*] contains the idea of *kindness which bestows upon one what he has not deserved* . . . the N. T. writers use [*kha'ris*] pre-eminently of that kindness by which God bestows favors even upon the ill-deserving, and grants to sinners the pardon of their offences, and bids them accept of eternal salvation through Christ." (*A Greek-English Lexicon of the New Testament,* 1889, p. 666) *Kha'ris* is closely related to another Greek word, *kha'ri·sma,* concerning which William Barclay's *New Testament Wordbook* (1956, p. 29) says: "The whole basic idea of the word [*kha'ri·sma*] is that of a free and undeserved gift, of something given to a man unearned and unmerited."—Compare 2Co 1:11, *Int.*

When *kha'ris* is used in the above sense, in reference to kindness bestowed on one who does not deserve it, as is true with the kindnesses extended by Jehovah, "undeserved kindness" is a very good English equivalent for the Greek expression.—Ac 15:40; 18:27; 1Pe 4:10; 5:10, 12.

A worker is entitled to what he has worked for, his pay; he expects his wages as a right, as a debt owed him, and payment of it is no gift or special undeserved kindness. (Ro 4:4) But for sinners condemned to death (and we are all born as such) to be released from that condemnation and to be declared righteous, this is indeed kindness that is totally undeserved. (Ro 3:23, 24; 5:17) If it is argued that those born under the Law covenant arrangement were under a greater condemnation to death, because such covenant showed them up as sinners, then it should be remembered that greater undeserved kindness was extended to the Jews in that salvation was first offered to them. —Ro 5:20, 21; 1:16.

This special manifestation of undeserved kindness on God's part toward mankind in general was the release by ransom from condemnation through the blood of Jehovah's beloved Son, Christ Jesus. (Eph 1:7; 2:4-7) By means of this undeserved kindness God brings salvation to all sorts of men (Tit 2:11), something that the prophets had spoken about. (1Pe 1:10) Paul's reasoning and argument, therefore, is sound: "Now if it is by undeserved kindness, it is no longer due to works; otherwise, the undeserved kindness no longer proves to be undeserved kindness."—Ro 11:6.

Paul, more than any other writer, mentioned God's undeserved kindness—more than 90 times in his 14 letters. He mentions the undeserved kindness of God or of Jesus in the opening salutation of all his letters with the exception of Hebrews, and in the closing remarks of each letter, without exception, he again speaks of it. Other Bible writers make similar reference in the opening and closing of their writings.—1Pe 1:2; 2Pe 1:2; 3:18; 2Jo 3; Re 1:4; 22:21.

Paul had every reason for emphasizing Jehovah's undeserved kindness, for he had formerly been "a blasphemer and a persecutor and an insolent man." "Nevertheless," he explains, "I was shown mercy, because I was ignorant and acted with a lack of faith. But the undeserved kindness of our Lord abounded exceedingly along with faith and love that is in connection with Christ Jesus." (1Ti 1:13, 14; 1Co 15:10) Paul did not spurn such undeserved kindness, as some have foolishly done (Jude 4), but he gladly accepted it with thanksgiving and urged others also who accept it 'not to miss its purpose.'—Ac 20:24; Ga 2:21; 2Co 6:1.

KING. A sovereign who has authority to rule over others. Jehovah is the supreme King, possessing unlimited power and authority. The kings of Judah were subordinate kings who represented His sovereignty on earth. Like them, Jesus Christ is a subordinate King, but with far greater power than those earthly kings, because Jehovah has put him in the position of ruling the universe. (Php 2:9-11) Jesus Christ has therefore been made "King of kings and Lord of lords."—Re 19:16; see JESUS CHRIST; KINGDOM.

Early Kings. Among earthly rulers a king is a male sovereign invested with supreme authority over a city, a tribe, a nation, or an empire, and he usually rules for life. Nimrod, a descendant of Ham, was the first human king of Bible record. He ruled over a kingdom that included several cities in Mesopotamia. He was a rebel against Jehovah's sovereignty.—Ge 10:6, 8-10.

Canaan and the countries surrounding it had kings in the days of Abraham, long before the Israelites did. (Ge 14:1-9) Kings are also found from the earliest times among the Philistines, Edomites, Moabites, Midianites, Ammonites, Syrians, Hittites, Egyptians, Assyrians, Babylonians, Persians, Greeks, and Romans. Many of these kings ruled over limited domains such as a city-state. Adoni-bezek, for example, boasted that he had conquered 70 of such kings.—Jg 1:7.

The first human king noted in the Bible as being righteous was Melchizedek, king-priest of Salem. (Ge 14:18) Aside from Jesus Christ, who is King and High Priest combined, Melchizedek is the only God-approved ruler to have held both offices. The apostle Paul points out that God used Melchizedek as a typical representation of Christ. (Heb 7:1-3; 8:1, 6) No other faithful servant of God, not even Noah, attempted to be a king, and God appointed none of them until Saul was anointed at His direction.

Israelite Kings. Initially Jehovah ruled Israel as an invisible King through various agencies, first through Moses and later through human Judges from Othniel to Samson. (Jg 8:23; 1Sa 12:12) Eventually the Israelites clamored for a king in order to be like the nations around them. (1Sa 8:5-8, 19) Under the legal provision embodied in the Law covenant for a divinely appointed human king, Jehovah appointed Saul of the tribe of Benjamin through the prophet Samuel. (De 17:14-20; 1Sa 9:15, 16; 10:21, 24) Because of disobedience and presumptuousness, Saul lost Jehovah's favor and the opportunity to provide a dynasty of kings. (1Sa 13:1-14; 15:22-28) Turning then to the tribe of Judah, Jehovah selected David the son of Jesse to be the next king of Israel. (1Sa 16:13; 17:12) For faithfully supporting Jehovah's worship and laws, David was privileged to establish a dynasty of kings. (2Sa 7:15, 16) The Israelites reached a peak of prosperity under the reign of Solomon, a son of David.—1Ki 4:25; 2Ch 1:15.

During the reign of Solomon's son Rehoboam, the nation was split into two kingdoms. The first king of the northern, ten-tribe kingdom, generally spoken of as Israel, was Jeroboam the son of Nebat of the tribe of Ephraim. (1Ki 11:26; 12:20) Disobediently he turned the worship of his people to golden calves. For this sin he came under Jehovah's disfavor. (1Ki 14:10, 16) A total of 20 kings ruled in the northern kingdom from 997 to 740 B.C.E., beginning with Jeroboam and ending with Hoshea the son of Elah. In the southern kingdom, Judah, 19 kings reigned from 997 to 607 B.C.E., beginning with Rehoboam and ending with Zedekiah. (Athaliah, a usurper of the throne and not a king, is not counted.)—See BURIAL, BURIAL PLACES; CHRONOLOGY.

Divinely appointed representatives. Jehovah appointed the kings of his people, and they were to act as his royal agents, sitting, not on their own thrones, but on "the throne of the kingship of Jehovah," that is, as representatives of his theocratic rule. (1Ch 28:5; 29:23) Contrary to the practice of some Oriental peoples in those days, the nation of Israel did not deify their kings. All the kings of Judah were regarded as being the anointed ones of Jehovah, although the record does not specifically state that each individual king was literally anointed with oil when he ascended the throne. Literal anointing oil is recorded as being used when a new dynasty was established, when the throne was disputed in David's old age as well as in the days of Jehoash, and when an older son was passed over for a younger son at the time Jehoahaz was enthroned. (1Sa 10:1; 16:13; 1Ki 1:39; 2Ki 11:12; 23:30, 31, 34, 36) It seems likely, nevertheless, that such anointing was the regular practice.

The king of Judah was chief administrator of national affairs, as a shepherd of the people. (Ps 78:70-72) He generally took the lead in battle. (1Sa 8:20; 2Sa 21:17; 1Ki 22:29-33) He also acted as the higher court in the judiciary, except that the high priest would consult Jehovah for decisions on some matters of state and on certain matters in which the decision was very difficult or evidence at the mouth of witnesses was insufficient.—1Ki 3:16-28.

Kingly restraints. The restraints placed upon the king in the exercise of his authority were his own fear of God, the law of God, which he was bound to obey, and the persuasive influence of the prophets and the priests as well as the advisory counsel of the older men. He was required to write for himself a copy of the Law and to read in it all the days of his life. (De 17:18, 19) He was, as Jehovah's special servant and representative, responsible to Jehovah. There were, sad to relate, many Judean kings who broke through these restraints and ruled despotically and wickedly. —1Sa 22:12, 13, 17-19; 1Ki 12:12-16; 2Ch 33:9.

Religious leader. Although the king was prevented by law from being a priest, he was supposed to be the chief nonpriestly supporter of Jehovah's worship. At times the king blessed the nation in Jehovah's name and represented the people in prayer. (2Sa 6:18; 1Ki 8:14, 22, 54, 55) Besides being responsible for safeguarding the religious life of the people from idolatrous intrusions, he had the authority to dismiss an unfaithful high priest, as King Solomon did when High Priest Abiathar supported Adonijah's seditious attempt to take the throne.—1Ki 1:7; 2:27.

Wives and property. The marriage and family customs of the Judean kings included the practice of having a plurality of wives and concubines, although the Law stipulated that the king was not to multiply wives to himself. (De 17:17) The concubines were considered to be crown property and were passed on to the successor to the throne along with the rights and property of the king. To marry or take possession of one of the deceased king's concubines was tantamount to publishing a claim to the throne. Hence, Absalom's having relations with the concubines of his father, King David, and Adonijah's requesting as wife Abishag, David's nurse and companion in his old age, were equivalent to claims on the throne. (2Sa 16:21, 22; 1Ki 2:15-17, 22) These were treasonable acts.

Aside from the king's personal estate, spoils of war, and gifts (1Ch 18:10), other sources of revenue were developed. These included special taxation of the produce of the land for the royal table, tribute from subjugated kingdoms, toll on traveling merchants passing through the land, and commercial ventures, such as the trading fleets of Solomon.—1Ki 4:7, 27, 28; 9:26-28; 10:14, 15.

Instability of Northern Kingdom. In the northern kingdom of Israel the principle of hereditary succession was observed except when it was interfered with by assassination or revolt. The practice of false religion kept the northern kingdom in a constant state of unrest that contributed to frequent assassinations of its kings and usurpation of the throne. Only two dynasties lasted more than two generations, those of Omri and Jehu. Not being under the Davidic kingdom covenant, none of the kings of the northern kingdom sat on "the throne of the kingship of Jehovah" as the anointed of Jehovah.—1Ch 28:5.

Gentile Kings and Subordinate Kings. Babylonian kings were officially consecrated as monarchs over all the Babylonian Empire by grasping the hand of the golden image of Marduk. This was done by Cyrus the Great in order to gain control over the Babylonian Empire without having to conquer the entire empire by military action.

Other kings came to their thrones through appointment by a higher king, such as the one who conquered the territory. It was a frequent practice for kings to rule conquered domains through tributary native kings of lesser rank. By this process Herod the Great became a tributary king of Rome over Judea (Mt 2:1), and Aretas the king of the Nabataeans was confirmed by Rome in his tributary kingdom.—2Co 11:32.

Non-Israelite kings were less accessible to their subjects than those who ruled God's people. The

Israelite kings evidently mingled quite freely with their people. The Gentile kings were often very remote. To enter the inner court of the Persian king without express permission automatically made that one liable to death unless the king gave his specific approval by extending his scepter, as was done with Esther. (Es 4:11, 16) The Roman emperor, however, was available for audience on the appeal of a Roman citizen from a decision made by a lower judge, but only after a process of going through many lower officials.—Ac 25: 11, 12.

KINGDOM. Basically, a royal government; also the territory and peoples under the rule of a king or, less frequently, under a female monarch or queen. Often the kingship was hereditary. The sovereign ruler might bear other titles such as Pharaoh or Caesar.

Kingdoms of ancient times, as today, had various symbols of royalty. There was generally a capital city or place of the king's residence, a royal court, a standing army (though perhaps quite reduced in size in times of peace). The word "kingdom," as used in the Bible, does not of itself reveal anything definite as to the governmental structure, the territorial extent, or the authority of the monarch. Kingdoms ranged in size and influence from the mighty world powers such as Egypt, Assyria, Babylon, Medo-Persia, Greece, and Rome, on down to small city-kingdoms such as those in Canaan at the time of the Israelite conquest. (Jos 12:7-24) The governmental structure also might vary considerably from kingdom to kingdom.

The first kingdom of human history, that of Nimrod, seems to have been initially a city-kingdom, later extending its realm to include other cities, its base remaining at Babel. (Ge 10:9-11) Salem, over which King-Priest Melchizedek ruled in the first kingdom with divine approval, was also apparently a city-kingdom. (Ge 14:18-20; compare Heb 7:1-17.) Larger kingdoms embraced an entire region, such as the kingdoms of Edom, Moab, and Ammon. The great empires, ruling vast areas and having other kingdoms tributary to them, generally seem to have arisen or grown out of small city-states or tribal groups that eventually combined under a dominant leader. Such coalitions were sometimes of a temporary nature, often formed for war against a common foe. (Ge 14:1-5; Jos 9:1, 2; 10:5) Vassal kingdoms frequently enjoyed a considerable degree of autonomy, or self-rule, though subject to the will and demands of the suzerain power.—2Ki 17:3, 4; 2Ch 36:4, 10.

Broad Usage. In Scriptural use the term "kingdom" may refer to specific aspects of a royal government. It can refer to the realm or geographic area over which sovereignty is exercised. The royal realm thus included not merely the capital city but the entire domain, embracing any subordinate or tributary kingdoms.—1Ki 4:21; Es 3:6, 8.

"Kingdom" may refer in a general way to any or all human governments, whether actually headed by a king or not.—Ezr 1:2; Mt 4:8.

It may signify kingship, the royal office or position of the king (Lu 17:21), with its accompanying dignity, power, and authority. (1Ch 11:10; 14:2; Lu 19:12, 15; Re 11:15; 17:12, 13, 17) Children of the king may be referred to as "the offspring of the kingdom."—2Ki 11:1.

The Israelite Kingdom. The Law covenant given through Moses to the nation of Israel made provision for a kingdom rule. (De 17:14, 15) The individual heading the kingdom was empowered and given royal dignity, not for personal exaltation, but to serve for the honor of God and the good of his Israelite brothers. (De 17:19, 20; compare 1Sa 15:17.) Nevertheless, when the Israelites in course of time requested a human king, the prophet Samuel warned of the demands such a ruler would make upon the people. (1Sa 8) The kings of Israel seem to have been more approachable and more accessible to their subjects than were the monarchs of most ancient Oriental kingdoms.—2Sa 19:8; 1Ki 20:39; 1Ch 15:25-29.

Though the kingdom of Israel began with a king from the line of Benjamin, Judah thereafter became the royal tribe, in keeping with Jacob's deathbed prophecy. (1Sa 10:20-25; Ge 49:10) A royal dynasty was established in David's line. (2Sa 2:4; 5:3, 4; 7:12, 13) When the kingdom was 'ripped away' from Solomon's son Rehoboam, ten tribes formed a northern kingdom, while Jehovah God retained one tribe, Benjamin, to remain with Judah, "in order that David my servant may continue having a lamp always before me in Jerusalem, the city that I have chosen for myself to put my name there." (1Ki 11:31, 35, 36; 12:18-24) Though the Judean kingdom fell to the Babylonians in 607 B.C.E., the legal right to rule eventually passed on to the rightful heir, the "son of David," Jesus Christ. (Mt 1:1-16; Lu 1:31, 32; compare Eze 21:26, 27.) His Kingdom was to be endless.—Isa 9:6, 7; Lu 1:33.

A royal organization developed in Israel to administer the interests of the kingdom. It consisted of an inner circle of advisers and ministers of state (1Ki 4:1-6; 1Ch 27:32-34), as well as various governmental departments with their respective overseers to administer crown lands, supervise the economy, and supply the needs of the royal court.—1Ki 4:7; 1Ch 27:25-31.

While the kings of Israel in the Davidic line could issue specific orders, the actual legislative power rested with God. (De 4:1, 2; Isa 33:22) In all things the king was responsible to the true Sovereign and Lord, Jehovah. Wrongdoing and waywardness on the part of the king would bring divine sanctions. (1Sa 13:13, 14; 15:20-24) Jehovah at times communicated with the king himself (1Ki 3:5; 11:11); at other times he gave him instructions and counsel or reproof through appointed prophets. (2Sa 7:4, 5; 12:1-14) The king could also draw upon the wise counsel of the body of older men. (1Ki 12:6, 7) The enforcement of instructions or reproof, however, rested, not with the prophets or older men, but with Jehovah.

When the king and the people faithfully adhered to the Law covenant given them by God, the nation of Israel enjoyed a degree of individual freedom, material prosperity, and national harmony unparalleled by other kingdoms. (1Ki 4:20, 25) During the years of Solomon's obedience to Jehovah, the Israelite kingdom was widely renowned and respected, having many tributary kingdoms and benefiting from the resources of many lands. —1Ki 4:21, 30, 34.

Jehovah God's kingship, while visibly expressed for a time through the Israelite kingdom, is one of universal sovereignty. (1Ch 29:11, 12) Whether acknowledged by the peoples and kingdoms of mankind or not, his kingship is absolute and unalterable, and all the earth is part of his rightful domain. (Ps 103:19; 145:11-13; Isa 14:26, 27) By virtue of His creatorship, Jehovah exercises his sovereign will in heaven and on earth, according to his own purposes, answerable to no one (Jer 18:3-10; Da 4:25, 34, 35), yet always acting in harmony with his own righteous standards.—Mal 3:6; Heb 6:17, 18; Jas 1:17.

KINGDOM OF GOD.

The expression and exercise of God's universal sovereignty toward his creatures, or the means or instrumentality used by him for this purpose. (Ps 103:19) The phrase is used particularly for the expression of God's sovereignty through a royal government headed by his Son, Christ Jesus.

The word rendered "kingdom" in the Christian Greek Scriptures is *ba·si·lei′a,* meaning "a kingdom, realm, the region or country governed by a king; kingly power, authority, dominion, reign; royal dignity, the title and honour of king." (*The Analyt-*

ical Greek Lexicon, 1908, p. 67) The phrase "the kingdom of God" is used frequently by Mark and Luke, and in Matthew's account the parallel phrase "the kingdom of the heavens" appears some 30 times.—Compare Mr 10:23 and Lu 18:24 with Mt 19:23, 24; see HEAVEN (Spiritual Heavens); KINGDOM.

The government of God is, in structure and function, a pure theocracy (from Gr. *the·os′,* god, and *kra′tos,* a rule), a rule by God. The term "theocracy" is attributed to Jewish historian Josephus of the first century C.E., who evidently coined it in his writing *Against Apion* (II, 164, 165 [16]). Of the government established over Israel in Sinai, Josephus wrote: "Some peoples have entrusted the supreme political power to monarchies, others to oligarchies, yet others to the masses. Our lawgiver, however, was attracted by none of these forms of polity, but gave to his constitution the form of what—if a forced expression be permitted—may be termed a 'theocracy [Gr., *the·o·kra·ti′an*],' placing all sovereignty and authority in the hands of God." To be a pure theocracy, of course, the government could not be ordained by any human legislator, such as the man Moses, but must be ordained and established by God. The Scriptural record shows this was the case.

Origin of the Term. The term "king" (Heb., *me′lekh*) evidently came into use in human language after the global Flood. The first earthly kingdom was that of Nimrod "a mighty hunter in opposition to Jehovah." (Ge 10:8-12) Thereafter, during the period down to Abraham's time, city-states and nations developed and human kings multiplied. With the exception of the kingdom of Melchizedek, king-priest of Salem (who served as a prophetic type of the Messiah [Ge 14:17-20; Heb 7:1-17]), none of these earthly kingdoms represented God's rule or were established by him. Men also made kings of the false gods they worshiped, attributing to them the ability to grant power of rulership to humans. Jehovah's application of the title "King [*Me′lekh*]" to himself, as found in the post-Flood writings of the Hebrew Scriptures, therefore meant God's making use of the title men had developed and employed. God's use of the term showed that he, and not presumptuous human rulers or man-made gods, should be looked to and obeyed as "King."—Jer 10:10-12.

Jehovah had, of course, been Sovereign Ruler long before human kingdoms developed, in fact before humans existed. As the true God and as their Creator, he was respected and obeyed by angelic sons numbering into the millions. (Job 38:4-7; 2Ch 18:18; Ps 103:20-22; Da 7:10) By whatever title, then, he was, from the beginning of creation, recognized as the One whose will was rightfully supreme.

God's Rulership in Early Human History. The first human creatures, Adam and Eve, likewise knew Jehovah as God, the Creator of heaven and earth. They recognized his authority and his right to issue commands, to call upon people to perform certain duties or to refrain from certain acts, to assign land for residence and cultivation, as well as to delegate authority over others of his creatures. (Ge 1:26-30; 2:15-17) Though Adam had the ability to coin words (Ge 2:19, 20), there is no evidence that he developed the title "king [me′-lekh]" to apply it to his God and Creator, although he recognized Jehovah's supreme authority.

As revealed in the initial chapters of Genesis, God's exercise of his sovereignty toward man in Eden was benevolent and not unduly restrictive. The relationship between God and man called for obedience such as the obedience a son renders to his father. (Compare Lu 3:38.) Man had no lengthy code of laws to fulfill (compare 1Ti 1:8-11); God's requirements were simple and purposeful. Nor is there anything to indicate that Adam was made to feel inhibited by constant, critical supervision of his every action; rather, God's communication with perfect man seems to have been periodic, according to need.—Ge chaps 1-3.

A new expression of God's rulership purposed. The first human pair's open violation of God's command, instigated by one of God's spirit sons, was actually rebellion against divine authority. (Ge 3:17-19; see TREES [Figurative Use].) The position taken by God's spirit Adversary (Heb., sa-tan′) constituted a challenge calling for a test, the issue being the rightfulness of Jehovah's universal sovereignty. (See JEHOVAH [The supreme issue a moral one].) The earth, where the issue was raised, is fittingly the place where it will be settled.—Re 12:7-12.

At the time of pronouncing judgment upon the first rebels, Jehovah God spoke a prophecy, couched in symbolic phrase, setting forth his purpose to use an agency, a "seed," to effect the ultimate crushing of the rebel forces. (Ge 3:15) Thus, Jehovah's rulership, the expression of his sovereignty, would take on a new aspect or expression in answer to the insurrection that had developed. The progressive revelation of "the sacred secrets of the kingdom" (Mt 13:11) showed that this new aspect would involve the formation of a subsidiary government, a ruling body headed by a deputy ruler. The realization of the promise of the "seed" is in the kingdom of Christ Jesus in

union with his chosen associates. (Re 17:14; see JESUS CHRIST [His Vital Place in God's Purpose].) From the time of the Edenic promise forward, the progressive development of God's purpose to produce this Kingdom "seed" becomes a basic theme of the Bible and a key to understanding Jehovah's actions toward his servants and toward mankind in general.

God's delegating vast authority and power to creatures (Mt 28:18; Re 2:26, 27; 3:21) in this way is noteworthy inasmuch as the question of the integrity of all God's creatures, that is, their wholehearted devotion to him and their loyalty to his headship, formed a vital part of the issue raised by God's Adversary. (See INTEGRITY [Involved in the supreme issue].) That God could confidently entrust any of his creatures with such remarkable authority and power would in itself be a splendid testimony to the moral strength of his rule, contributing to the vindication of Jehovah's name and position and exposing the falsity of his adversary's allegations.

Need for divine government manifested. The conditions that developed from the time of the start of human rebellion until the time of the Flood clearly illustrated mankind's need for divine headship. Human society soon had to contend with disunity, bodily assault, and murder. (Ge 4:2-9, 23, 24) To what extent the sinner Adam, during his 930 years of life, exercised patriarchal authority over his multiplying descendants is not revealed. But by the seventh generation shocking ungodliness evidently existed (Jude 14, 15), and by the time of Noah (born about 120 years after Adam's death) conditions had deteriorated to the point that "the earth became filled with violence." (Ge 6:1-13) Contributing to this condition was the unauthorized interjection of spirit creatures into human society, contrary to God's will and purpose.—Ge 6:1-4; Jude 6; 2Pe 2:4, 5; see NEPHILIM.

Though earth had become a focus of rebellion, Jehovah did not relinquish his dominion over it. The global Flood was evidence that God's power and ability to enforce his will on earth, as in any part of the universe, continued. During the pre-Flood period he likewise demonstrated his willingness to guide and govern the actions of those individuals who sought him, such as Abel, Enoch, and Noah. Noah's case in particular illustrates God's exercise of rulership toward a willing earthly subject, giving him commands and direction, protecting and blessing him and his family, as well as evidencing God's control over the other earthly creation—animals and birds. (Ge 6:9–7:16) Jehovah likewise made clear that he would not allow alienated human society to corrupt the earth endlessly; that he had not restricted himself as to executing his righteous judgment against wrong-doers when and as he saw fit. Additionally he demonstrated his sovereign ability to control earth's various elements, including its atmosphere.—Ge 6:3, 5-7; 7:17–8:22.

The early post-Flood society and its problems. Following the Flood, a patriarchal arrangement apparently was the basic structure of human society, providing a measure of stability and order. Mankind was to "fill the earth," which called not merely for procreating but for the steady extension of the area of human habitation throughout the globe. (Ge 9:1, 7) These factors, of themselves, would reasonably have had a limiting effect on any social problems, keeping them generally within the family circle and making unlikely the friction that frequently develops where density of population or crowded conditions exist. The unauthorized project at Babel, however, called for an opposite course, for a concentrating of people, avoiding being "scattered over all the surface of the earth." (Ge 11:1-4; see LANGUAGE.) Then, too, Nimrod departed from the patriarchal rule and set up the first "kingdom" (Heb., *mam·la·khah'*). A Cushite of the family line of Ham, he invaded Shemite territory, the land of Asshur (Assyria), and built cities there as part of his realm.—Ge 10:8-12.

God's confusion of human language broke up the concentration of people on the Plains of Shinar, but the pattern of rulership begun by Nimrod was generally followed in the lands to which the various families of mankind migrated. In the days of Abraham (2018-1843 B.C.E.), kingdoms were active from Asian Mesopotamia on down to Egypt, where the king was titled "Pharaoh" rather than *Me'lekh*. But these kingships did not bring security. Kings were soon forming military alliances, waging far-ranging campaigns of aggression, plunder, and kidnapping. (Ge 14:1-12) In some cities strangers were subject to attack by homosexuals.—Ge 19:4-9.

Thus, whereas men doubtless banded together in concentrated communities in search of security (compare Ge 4:14-17), they soon found it necessary to wall their cities and eventually fortify them against armed attack. The earliest secular records known, many of them from the Mesopotamian region where Nimrod's kingdom had originally operated, are heavy with accounts of human conflict, greed, intrigue, and bloodshed. The most ancient non-Biblical law records found, such as those of Lipit-Ishtar, Eshnunna, and Hammurabi,

show that human living had become very complex, with social friction producing problems of theft, fraud, commercial difficulties, disputes about property and payment of rent, questions regarding loans and interest, marital infidelity, medical fees and failures, assault and battery cases, and many other matters. Though Hammurabi called himself "the efficient king" and "the perfect king," his rule and legislation, like that of the other ancient political kingdoms, was incapable of solving the problems of sinful mankind. (*Ancient Near Eastern Texts,* edited by J. B. Pritchard, 1974, pp. 159-180; compare Pr 28:5.) In all these kingdoms religion was prominent, but not the worship of the true God. Though the priesthood collaborated closely with the ruling class and enjoyed royal favor, this brought no moral improvement to the people. The cuneiform inscriptions of the ancient religious writings are devoid of spiritual uplift or moral guidance; they betray the gods worshiped as quarrelsome, violent, lustful, not governed by righteous standards or purpose. Men needed Jehovah God's kingdom if they were to enjoy life in peace and happiness.

Toward Abraham and His Descendants. True, those individuals who looked to Jehovah God as their Head were not without their personal problems and frictions. Yet they were helped to solve these or to endure them in a way conforming to God's righteous standards and without becoming degraded. They were afforded divine protection and strength. (Ge 13:5-11; 14:18-24; 19:15-24; 21:9-13, 22-33) Thus, after pointing out that Jehovah's "judicial decisions are in all the earth," the psalmist says of Abraham, Isaac, and Jacob: "They happened to be few in number, yes, very few, and alien residents in [Canaan]. And they kept walking about from nation to nation, from one kingdom to another people. [Jehovah] did not allow any human to defraud them, but on their account he reproved kings, saying: 'Do not you men touch my anointed ones, and to my prophets do nothing bad.'" (Ps 105:7-15; compare Ge 12:10-20; 20:1-18; 31:22-24, 36-55.) This, too, was proof that God's sovereignty over earth was still in effect, enforceable by him in harmony with the development of his purpose.

The faithful patriarchs did not attach themselves to any of the city-states or kingdoms of Canaan or other lands. Rather than seek security in some city under the political rule of a human king, they lived in tents as aliens, "strangers and temporary residents in the land," in faith "awaiting the city having real foundations, the builder and maker of which city is God." They accepted God as their Ruler, waited for his future heavenly arrangement, or agency, for governing the earth, solidly founded on his sovereign authority and will, though the realization of this hope was then "afar off." (Heb 11:8-10, 13-16) Thus, Jesus, already anointed by God to be king, could later say: "Abraham . . . rejoiced greatly in the prospect of seeing my day, and he saw it and rejoiced."—Joh 8:56.

Jehovah brought the development of his promise regarding the Kingdom "seed" (Ge 3:15) a step farther by the establishing of a covenant with Abraham. (Ge 12:1-3; 22:15-18) In connection therewith, he foretold that 'kings would come' from Abraham (Abram) and his wife. (Ge 17:1-6, 15, 16) Though the descendants of Abraham's grandson Esau formed sheikdoms and kingdoms, it was to Abraham's other grandson, Jacob, that God's prophetic promise of kingly descendants was repeated.—Ge 35:11, 12; 36:9, 15-43.

Formation of the Israelite nation. Centuries later, at the due time (Ge 15:13-16), Jehovah God acted on behalf of Jacob's descendants, now numbering into the millions (see EXODUS [The Number Involved in the Exodus]), protecting them during a campaign of genocide by the Egyptian government (Ex 1:15-22) and finally freeing them from harsh slavery to Egypt's regime. (Ex 2:23-25) God's command to Pharaoh, delivered through his agents Moses and Aaron, was spurned by the Egyptian ruler as proceeding from a source with no authority over Egyptian affairs. Pharaoh's repeated refusal to recognize Jehovah's sovereignty brought demonstrations of divine power in the form of plagues. (Ex 7 to 12) God thereby proved that his dominion over earth's elements and creatures was superior to that of any king in all the earth. (Ex 9:13-16) He climaxed this display of sovereign power by destroying Pharaoh's forces in a way that none of the boastful warrior kings of the nations could ever have duplicated. (Ex 14:26-31) With real basis, Moses and the Israelites sang: "Jehovah will rule as king to time indefinite, even forever."—Ex 15:1-19.

Thereafter Jehovah gave added proof of his dominion over earth, its vital water resources, and its bird life, and he showed his ability to guard and sustain his nation even in arid and hostile surroundings. (Ex 15:22–17:15) Having done all of this, he addressed the liberated people, telling them that, by obedience to his authority and covenant, they could become his special property out of all other peoples, "because the whole earth belongs to me." They could become "a kingdom of priests and a holy nation." (Ex 19:3-6) When they went on record as willing subjects of his sover-

eignty, Jehovah acted as Kingly Legislator by giving them royal decrees in a large body of laws, accompanying this by dynamic and awe-inspiring evidence of his power and glory. (Ex 19:7–24:18) A tabernacle or tent of meeting, and particularly its ark, was to indicate the presence of the invisible heavenly Head of State. (Ex 25:8, 21, 22; 33:7-11; compare Re 21:3.) Although Moses and other appointed men judged the majority of cases, guided by God's law, Jehovah intervened personally at times to express judgments and apply sanctions against lawbreakers. (Ex 18:13-16, 24-26; 32:25-35) The ordained priesthood acted to maintain good relations between the nation and its heavenly Ruler, helping the people in their efforts to conform to the high standards of the Law covenant. (See PRIEST.) Thus the government over Israel was a genuine theocracy.—De 33:2, 5.

As God and Creator, holding the right of "eminent domain" over all the earth, as well as being "the Judge of all the earth" (Ge 18:25), Jehovah had assigned the land of Canaan to Abraham's seed. (Ge 12:5-7; 15:17-21) As Chief Executive, he now ordered the Israelites to carry out the forcible expropriation of the territory held by the condemned Canaanites, as well as his death sentence against them.—De 9:1-5; see CANAAN, CANAANITE No. 2 (Conquest of Canaan by Israel).

The period of the Judges. For three and a half centuries after Israel's conquest of Canaan's many kingdoms, Jehovah God was the nation's only king. During varying periods, Judges, chosen by God, led the nation or portions thereof in battle and in peace. Judge Gideon's defeat of Midian brought a popular request that he become the nation's ruler, but he refused, acknowledging Jehovah as the true ruler. (Jg 8:22, 23) His ambitious son Abimelech briefly established kingship over a small segment of the nation, but this ended in personal disaster.—Jg 9:1, 6, 22, 53-56.

Of this general period of the Judges, the comment is made: "In those days there was no king in Israel. As for everybody, what was right in his own eyes he was accustomed to do." (Jg 17:6; 21:25) This does not imply that there was no judicial restraint. Every city had judges, older men, to handle legal questions and problems and to mete out justice. (De 16:18-20; see COURT, JUDICIAL.) The Levitical priesthood functioned as a superior guiding force, educating the people in God's law, the high priest having the Urim and Thummim by which to consult God on difficult matters. (See HIGH PRIEST; PRIEST; URIM AND THUMMIM.) So, the individual who availed himself of these provisions, who gained knowledge of God's law and applied it, had a sound guide for his conscience. His doing "what was right in his own eyes" *in such case* would not result in bad. Jehovah allowed the people to show a willing or unwilling attitude and course. There was no human monarch over the nation supervising the work of the city judges or commanding the citizens to engage in particular projects or marshaling them for defense of the nation. (Compare Jg 5:1-18.) The bad conditions that developed, therefore, were chargeable to the unwillingness of the majority to heed the word and law of their heavenly King and to avail themselves of his provisions. —Jg 2:11-23.

A Human King Requested. Nearly 400 years from the time of the Exodus and over 800 years from the making of God's covenant with Abraham, the Israelites requested a human king to lead them, even as the other nations had human monarchs. Their request constituted a rejection of Jehovah's own kingship over them. (1Sa 8:4-8) True, the people properly expected a kingdom to be established by God in harmony with his promise to Abraham and to Jacob, already cited. They had further basis for such hope in Jacob's deathbed prophecy concerning Judah (Ge 49:8-10), in Jehovah's words to Israel after the Exodus (Ex 19:3-6), in the terms of the Law covenant (De 17:14, 15), and even in part of the message God caused the prophet Balaam to speak (Nu 24:2-7, 17). Samuel's faithful mother Hannah expressed this hope in prayer. (1Sa 2:7-10) Nevertheless, Jehovah had not fully revealed his "sacred secret" regarding the Kingdom and had not indicated when his due time for its establishment would arrive nor what the structure and composition of that government would be—whether it would be earthly or heavenly. It was therefore presumptuous on the part of the people now to demand a human king.

The menace of Philistine and Ammonite aggression evidently contributed to the Israelites' desire for a visible royal commander-in-chief. They thus displayed a lack of faith in God's ability to protect, guide, and provide for them, as a nation or as individuals. (1Sa 8:4-8) The people's motive was wrong; yet Jehovah God granted their request not for their sake primarily but to accomplish his own good purpose in the progressive revelation of the "sacred secret" of his future Kingdom by the "seed." Human kingship would bring its problems and expense for Israel, however, and Jehovah laid the facts before the people.—1Sa 8:9-22.

The kings thereafter appointed by Jehovah were to serve as God's earthly agents, not diminishing in the least Jehovah's own sovereignty over the nation. The throne was actually Jehovah's, and they sat thereon as deputy kings. (1Ch 29:23) Jehovah commanded the anointing of the first king, Saul (1Sa 9:15-17), at the same time exposing the lack of faith the nation had displayed. —1Sa 10:17-25.

For the kingship to bring benefits, both king and nation must now respect God's authority. If they unrealistically looked to other sources for direction and protection, they and their king would be swept away. (De 28:36; 1Sa 12:13-15, 20-25) The king was to avoid reliance on military strength, the multiplying of wives for himself, and being dominated by the lust for wealth. His kingship was to operate entirely within the framework of the Law covenant. He was under divine orders to write his own copy of that Law and read it daily, that he might keep a proper fear of the Sovereign Authority, stay humble, and hold to a righteous course. (De 17:16-20) To the extent that he did this, loving God wholeheartedly and loving his neighbor as himself, his rule would bring blessings, with no real cause for complaint due to oppression or hardship. But, as with the people, so now with their kings, Jehovah allowed the rulers to demonstrate what their hearts contained, their willingness or unwillingness to recognize God's own authority and will.

David's Exemplary Rule. Disrespect by the Benjamite Saul for the superior authority and arrangements of "the Excellency of Israel" brought divine disfavor and cost his family line the throne. (1Sa 13:10-14; 15:17-29; 1Ch 10:13, 14) With the rule of Saul's successor, David of Judah, Jacob's deathbed prophecy saw further fulfillment. (Ge 49:8-10) Though David committed errors through human weakness, his rule was exemplary because of his heartfelt devotion to Jehovah God and his humble submission to divine authority. (Ps 51:1-4; 1Sa 24:10-14; compare 1Ki 11:4; 15:11, 14.) At the time of receiving contributions for the temple construction, David prayed to God before the congregated people, saying: "Yours, O Jehovah, are the greatness and the mightiness and the beauty and the excellency and the dignity; for everything in the heavens and in the earth is yours. Yours is the kingdom, O Jehovah, the One also lifting yourself up as head over all. The riches and the glory are on account of you, and you are dominating everything; and in your hand there are power and mightiness, and in your hand is ability to make great and to give strength to all. And now, O our God, we are thanking you and praising your beauteous name." (1Ch 29:10-13)

His final counsel to his son Solomon also illustrates David's fine viewpoint of the relationship between the earthly kingship and its divine Source.—1Ki 2:1-4.

On the occasion of bringing the ark of the covenant, associated with Jehovah's presence, to the capital, Jerusalem, David sang: "Let the heavens rejoice, and let the earth be joyful, and let them say among the nations, 'Jehovah himself has become king!'" (1Ch 16:1, 7, 23-31) This illustrates the fact that, though Jehovah's rulership dates from the beginning of creation, he can make specific expressions of his rulership or establish certain agencies to represent him that allow for his being spoken of as 'becoming king' at a particular time or occasion.

The covenant for a kingdom. Jehovah made a covenant with David for a kingdom to be established everlastingly in his family line, saying: "I shall certainly raise up your seed after you, . . . and I shall indeed firmly establish his kingdom. . . . And your house and your kingdom will certainly be steadfast to time indefinite before you; your very throne will become one firmly established to time indefinite." (2Sa 7:12-16; 1Ch 17:11-14) This covenant in force toward the Davidic dynasty provided further evidence of the outworking of God's Edenic promise for his Kingdom by the foretold "seed" (Ge 3:15) and supplied additional means for identifying that "seed" when he should come. (Compare Isa 9:6, 7; 1Pe 1:11.) The kings appointed by God were anointed for their office, hence the term "messiah," meaning "anointed one," applied to them. (1Sa 16:1; Ps 132:13, 17) Clearly, then, the earthly kingdom Jehovah established over Israel served as a type or small-scale representation of the coming Kingdom by the Messiah, Jesus Christ, "son of David."—Mt 1:1.

Decline and Fall of the Israelite Kingdoms. Because of failure to adhere to Jehovah's righteous ways, conditions at the end of just three reigns and the start of the fourth produced strong discontent that led to revolt and a split in the nation (997 B.C.E.). A northern kingdom and a southern one resulted. Jehovah's covenant with David nevertheless continued in force toward the kings of the southern kingdom of Judah. Over the centuries, faithful kings were rare in Judah, and were completely lacking in the northern kingdom of Israel. The northern kingdom's history was one of idolatry, intrigue, and assassinations, kings often following one another in rapid succession. The people suffered injustice and oppression. About 250 years from its start, Jehovah allowed the

king of Assyria to crush the northern kingdom (740 B.C.E.) because of its course of rebellion against God.—Ho 4:1, 2; Am 2:6-8.

Though the kingdom of Judah enjoyed greater stability because of the Davidic dynasty, the southern kingdom eventually surpassed the northern kingdom in its moral corruption, despite the efforts of God-fearing kings, such as Hezekiah and Josiah, to roll back the decline toward idolatry and rejection of Jehovah's word and authority. (Isa 1:1-4; Eze 23:1-4, 11) Social injustice, tyranny, greed, dishonesty, bribes, sexual perversion, criminal attacks, and bloodshed, as well as religious hypocrisy that converted God's temple into a "cave of robbers"—all of these were decried by Jehovah's prophets in their warning messages delivered to rulers and people. (Isa 1:15-17, 21-23; 3:14, 15; Jer 5:1, 2, 7, 8, 26-28, 31; 6:6, 7; 7:8-11) Neither the support of apostate priests nor any political alliance made with other nations could avoid the coming crash of that unfaithful kingdom. (Jer 6:13-15; 37:7-10) The capital city, Jerusalem, was destroyed and Judah was laid waste by the Babylonians in 607 B.C.E.—2Ki 25:1-26.

Jehovah's kingly position remains unmarred. The destruction of the kingdoms of Israel and Judah in no way reflected on the quality of Jehovah God's own rulership; in no way did it indicate weakness on his part. Throughout the history of the Israelite nation, Jehovah made clear that his interest was in *willing* service and obedience. (De 10:12-21; 30:6, 15-20; Isa 1:18-20; Eze 18:25-32) He instructed, reproved, disciplined, warned, and punished. But he did not use his power to force either the king or the people to follow a righteous course. The bad conditions that developed, the suffering experienced, the disaster that befell them, were all of their own making, because they stubbornly hardened their hearts and insisted on following an independent course, one that was stupidly damaging to their own best interests. —La 1:8, 9; Ne 9:26-31, 34-37; Isa 1:2-7; Jer 8:5-9; Ho 7:10, 11.

Jehovah exhibited his Sovereign power by holding in abeyance the aggressive, rapacious powers of Assyria and Babylon until his own due time, even maneuvering them so that they acted in fulfillment of his prophecies. (Eze 21:18-23; Isa 10:5-7) When Jehovah finally removed his defenses from around the nation, it was an expression of his righteous judgment as Sovereign Ruler. (Jer 35:17) The desolation of Israel and Judah came as no shocking surprise to God's obedient servants who were forewarned by his prophecies. The abasing of haughty rulers exalted Jehovah's own "splendid superiority." (Isa 2:1, 10-17) More than all of this, however, he had demonstrated his ability to protect and preserve individuals who looked to him as their King, even when they were surrounded by conditions of famine, disease, and wholesale slaughter, as well as when they were persecuted by those hating righteousness.—Jer 34:17-21; 20:10, 11; 35:18, 19; 36:26; 37:18-21; 38:7-13; 39:11–40:5.

Israel's last king was warned of the coming removal of his crown, representing anointed kingship as Jehovah's royal representative. That anointed Davidic kingship would no longer be exercised "until he comes who has the legal right, and I [Jehovah] must give it to him." (Eze 21:25-27) Thus, the typical kingdom, now in ruins, ceased to function, and attention was again directed forward, toward the coming "seed," the Messiah.

Political nations, such as Assyria and Babylon, devastated the apostate kingdoms of Israel and Judah. Though God speaks of himself as 'raising up' or 'bringing' them against those condemned kingdoms (De 28:49; Jer 5:15; 25:8, 9; Eze 7:24; Am 6:14), this was evidently in a sense similar to God's 'hardening' the heart of Pharaoh. (See FORE-KNOWLEDGE, FOREORDINATION [Concerning individuals].) That is, God 'brought' these attacking forces by permitting them to carry out the desire already in their heart (Isa 10:7; La 2:16; Mic 4:11), removing his protective 'hand' from over the objects of their ambitious greed. (De 31:17, 18; compare Ezr 8:31 with Ezr 5:12; Ne 9:28-31; Jer 34:2.) The apostate Israelites, stubbornly refusing to subject themselves to Jehovah's law and will, thus were given 'liberty to the sword, pestilence, and famine.' (Jer 34:17) But the attacking pagan nations did not thereby become approved of God, nor did they have 'clean hands' before him in their ruthless destruction of the northern and southern kingdoms, the capital city of Jerusalem, and its sacred temple. Hence, Jehovah, the Judge of all the earth, could rightly denounce them for 'pillaging his inheritance' and could doom them to suffer the same desolation they had wreaked on his covenant people.—Isa 10:12-14; 13:1, 17-22; 14:4-6, 12-14, 26, 27; 47:5-11; Jer 50:11, 14, 17-19, 23-29.

Visions of Kingdom of God in Daniel's Day.

The prophecy of Daniel in its entirety emphatically stresses the theme of the Universal Sovereignty of God, further clarifying Jehovah's purpose. Living in exile in the capital of the world power that overthrew Judah, Daniel was used by God to reveal the significance of a vision had by the Babylonian monarch, a vision that foretold the march of world powers and their eventual demolition by the everlasting Kingdom of Jehovah's own establishment. Doubtless to the amazement of his royal court, Nebuchadnezzar, the very conqueror of Jerusalem, was now moved to prostrate himself in homage to Daniel the exile and to acknowledge Daniel's God as "a Lord of kings." (Da 2:36-47) Again, by Nebuchadnezzar's dream vision of the 'chopped-down tree,' Jehovah forcefully made known that "the Most High is Ruler in the kingdom of mankind and that to the one whom he wants to, he gives it and he sets up over it even the lowliest one of mankind." (Da 4; see the discussion of this vision under APPOINTED TIMES OF THE NATIONS.) Through the fulfillment of the dream as it related to him, imperial ruler Nebuchadnezzar once more was brought to recognize Daniel's God as "the King of the heavens," the One who "is doing according to his own will among the army of the heavens and the inhabitants of the earth. And there exists no one that can check his hand or that can say to him, 'What have you been doing?'"—Da 4:34-37.

Toward the close of Babylon's international dominance, Daniel saw prophetic visions of successive empires, beastlike in their characteristics; he saw also Jehovah's majestic heavenly Court in session, passing judgment on the world powers, decreeing them unworthy of rulership; and he beheld "someone like a son of man . . . [being] given rulership and dignity and kingdom, that the peoples, national groups and languages should all serve even him" in his "indefinitely lasting rulership that will not pass away." He witnessed as well the war waged against "the holy ones" by the final world power, calling for its annihilation, and the giving of "the kingdom and the rulership and the grandeur of the kingdoms under all the heavens . . . to the people who are the holy ones of the Supreme One," Jehovah God. (Da 7, 8) Thus, it became evident that the promised "seed" would involve a governmental body with not only a kingly head, the "son of man," but also associate rulers, "the holy ones of the Supreme One."

Toward Babylon and Medo-Persia.

God's inexorable decree against mighty Babylon was carried out suddenly and unexpectedly; her days were numbered and brought to a finish. (Da 5:17-30) During the Medo-Persian rule that followed, Jehovah made further revelation concerning the Messianic Kingdom, pointing to the time of Messiah's appearance, foretelling his being "cut off," as well as a second destruction of the city of Jerusalem and its holy place. (Da 9:1, 24-27; see SEVENTY WEEKS.) And, as he had done during the

Babylonian rule, Jehovah God again demonstrated his ability to protect those recognizing his sovereignty in the face of official anger and the threat of death, exhibiting his power over both earthly elements and wild beasts. (Da 3:13-29; 6:12-27) He caused Babylon's gates to swing wide open on schedule, allowing his covenant people to have the freedom to return to their own land and rebuild Jehovah's house there. (2Ch 36:20-23) Because of his act of liberating his people, the announcement could be made to Zion, "Your God has become king!" (Isa 52:7-11) Thereafter, conspiracies against his people were thwarted and misrepresentation by subordinate officials and adverse governmental decrees were overcome, as Jehovah moved various Persian kings to cooperate with the carrying out of his own sovereign will.—Ezr 4-7; Ne 2, 4, 6; Es 3-9.

Thus, for thousands of years the changeless, irresistible purpose of Jehovah God moved forward. Regardless of the turn of events on earth, he proved to be ever in command of the situation, always ahead of opposing man and devil. Nothing was allowed to interfere with the perfect outworking of his purpose, his will. The nation of Israel and its history, while serving to form prophetic types and forecasts of the future dealings of God with men, also illustrated that without wholehearted recognition and submission to divine headship there can be no lasting harmony, peace, and happiness. The Israelites enjoyed the benefits of having in common such things as ancestry, language, and country. They also faced common foes. But only as long as they loyally and faithfully worshiped and served Jehovah God did they have unity, strength, justice, and genuine enjoyment of life. When the bonds of relationship with Jehovah God weakened, the nation deteriorated rapidly.

The Kingdom of God 'Draws Near.' Since the Messiah was to be a descendant of Abraham, Isaac, and Jacob, a member of the tribe of Judah, and a "son of David," he had to have a human birth; he had to be, as Daniel's prophecy declared, "a son of man." When the "full limit of the time arrived," Jehovah God sent forth his Son, who was born of a woman and who fulfilled all the legal requirements for the inheritance of "the throne of David his father." (Ga 4:4; Lu 1:26-33; see GENEALOGY OF JESUS CHRIST.) Six months before his birth, John, who became the Baptizer and who was to be Jesus' forerunner, had been born. (Lu 1:13-17, 36) The expressions of the parents of these sons showed they were living in eager anticipation of divine acts of rulership. (Lu 1:41-55, 68-79) At Jesus' birth, the words of the angelic

deputation sent to announce the meaning of the event also pointed to glorious acts by God. (Lu 2:9-14) So, too, the words of Simeon and Anna at the temple expressed hope in saving acts and liberation. (Lu 2:25-38) Both the Biblical record and secular evidence reveal that a general feeling of expectation prevailed among the Jews that the coming of the Messiah was drawing near. With many, however, interest was primarily in gaining freedom from the heavy yoke of Roman domination.—See MESSIAH.

John's commission was to 'turn back the hearts' of persons to Jehovah, to his covenants, to "the privilege of fearlessly rendering sacred service to him with loyalty and righteousness," thereby getting ready for Jehovah "a prepared people." (Lu 1:16, 17, 72-75) He told the people in no uncertain terms that they were facing a time of judgment by God, that 'the kingdom of the heavens had drawn near,' making urgent their turning away repentantly from their course of disobedience to God's will and law. This again emphasized Jehovah's standard of having only *willing* subjects, persons who both recognize and appreciate the rightness of his ways and laws.—Mt 3:1, 2, 7-12.

The Messiah came when Jesus presented himself to John for baptism and was then anointed by God's holy spirit. (Mt 3:13-17) He thereby became the King-Designate, the One recognized by Jehovah's Court as having the legal right to the Davidic throne, a right that had not been exercised during the preceding six centuries. (See JESUS CHRIST [His Baptism].) But Jehovah additionally brought this approved Son into a covenant for a heavenly Kingdom, in which Jesus would be both King and Priest, as Melchizedek of ancient Salem had been. (Ps 110:1-4; Lu 22:29; Heb 5:4-6; 7:1-3; 8:1; see COVENANT.) As the promised 'seed of Abraham,' this heavenly King-Priest would be God's Chief Agent for blessing persons of all nations.—Ge 22:15-18; Ga 3:14; Ac 3:15.

Early in his Son's earthly life, Jehovah had manifested his kingly power on Jesus' behalf. God diverted the Oriental astrologers who were going to inform tyrannical King Herod of the young child's whereabouts, and he caused Jesus' parents to slip away into Egypt before Herod's agents carried out the massacre of infants in Bethlehem. (Mt 2:1-16) Since the original prophecy in Eden had foretold enmity between the promised "seed" and the 'seed of the serpent,' this attempt on Jesus' life could only mean that God's Adversary, Satan the Devil, was trying, however futilely, to frustrate Jehovah's purpose.—Ge 3:15.

After some 40 days in the Judean Wilderness,

the baptized Jesus was confronted by this principal opponent of Jehovah's sovereignty. By some means, the spirit Adversary conveyed to Jesus certain subtle suggestions designed to draw him into acts violating Jehovah's expressed will and word. Satan even offered to give to the anointed Jesus dominion over all earthly kingdoms *without a struggle and without any need for suffering on Jesus' part*—in exchange for one act of worship toward himself. When Jesus refused, acknowledging Jehovah as the one true Sovereign from whom authority rightly proceeds and to whom worship goes, God's Adversary began drawing up other plans of war strategy against Jehovah's Representative, resorting to the use of human agents in various ways, as he had done long before in the case of Job.—Job 1:8-18; Mt 4:1-11; Lu 4:1-13; compare Re 13:1, 2.

In what way was God's Kingdom 'in the midst' of those to whom Jesus preached?

Trusting in Jehovah's power to protect him and grant him success, Jesus entered his public ministry, announcing to Jehovah's covenant people that "the appointed time has been fulfilled," resulting in the approach of the Kingdom of God. (Mr 1: 14, 15) In determining in what sense the Kingdom was "near," his words to certain Pharisees may be noted, namely, that "the kingdom of God is in your midst." (Lu 17:21) Commenting on this text, *The Interpreter's Dictionary of the Bible* observes: "Although frequently cited as an example of Jesus' 'mysticism' or 'inwardness,' this interpretation rests chiefly upon the old translation, 'within you,' [KJ, Dy] understood in the unfortunate modern sense of 'you' as singular; the 'you' ([hy·mon']) is plural (Jesus is addressing the Pharisees—vs. 20) . . . The theory that the kingdom of God is an inner state of mind, or of personal salvation, runs counter to the context of this verse, and also to the whole NT presentation of the idea." (Edited by G. A. Buttrick, 1962, Vol. 2, p. 883) Since "kingdom [ba·si·lei'a]" can refer to the "royal dignity," it is evident that Jesus meant that he, God's royal representative, the one anointed by God for the kingship, was in their midst. Not only was he present in this capacity but he also had authority to perform works manifesting God's kingly power and to prepare candidates for positions within his coming Kingdom rule. Hence the 'nearness' of the Kingdom; it was a time of tremendous opportunity.

Government with power and authority. Jesus' disciples understood the Kingdom to be an actual government of God, though they did not comprehend the reach of its domain. Nathanael said to Jesus: "Rabbi, you are the Son of God, you are King of Israel." (Joh 1:49) They knew the things foretold about "the holy ones" in the prophecy of Daniel. (Da 7:18, 27) Jesus directly promised his apostolic followers that they would occupy "thrones." (Mt 19:28) James and John sought certain privileged positions in the Messianic government, and Jesus acknowledged that there would be such privileged positions, but he stated that the assigning of these rested with his Father, the Sovereign Ruler. (Mt 20:20-23; Mr 10:35-40) So, whereas his disciples mistakenly limited Messiah's kingly rule to earth and specifically to fleshly Israel, even doing so on the day of the resurrected Jesus' ascension (Ac 1:6), they correctly understood that it referred to a governmental arrangement.—Compare Mt 21:5; Mr 11:7-10.

Jehovah's kingly power toward his earthly creation was visibly demonstrated in many ways by his royal Representative. By God's spirit, or active force, his Son exercised control over wind and sea, vegetation, fish, and even over the organic elements in food, causing the food to be multiplied. These powerful works caused his disciples to develop deep respect for the authority that he had. (Mt 14:23-33; Mr 4:36-41; 11:12-14, 20-23; Lu 5:4-11; Joh 6:5-15) Even more profoundly impressive was his exercise of God's power over human bodies, healing afflictions ranging from blindness to leprosy, and restoring the dead to life. (Mt 9:35; 20:30-34; Lu 5:12, 13; 7:11-17; Joh 11:39-47) Healed lepers he sent to report to the divinely authorized, but generally unbelieving, priesthood, as "a witness to them." (Lu 5:14; 17:14) Finally, he showed God's power over superhuman spirits. The demons recognized the authority invested in Jesus and, rather than risk a decisive test of the power backing him up, they acceded to his orders to release persons possessed by them. (Mt 8:28-32; 9:32, 33; compare Jas 2:19.) Since this powerful expulsion of demons was by God's spirit, this meant that the Kingdom of God had really "overtaken" his listeners.—Mt 12:25-29; compare Lu 9:42, 43.

All of this was solid proof that Jesus had kingly authority and that this authority came from no earthly, human, political source. (Compare Joh 18:36; Isa 9:6, 7.) Messengers from the imprisoned John the Baptizer, as witnesses of these powerful works, were instructed by Jesus to go back to John and tell him what they had seen and heard as confirmation that Jesus was indeed "the

Coming One." (Mt 11:2-6; Lu 7:18-23; compare Joh 5:36.) Jesus' disciples were seeing and hearing the evidence of Kingdom authority that the prophets had longed to witness. (Mt 13:16, 17) Moreover, Jesus was able to delegate authority to his disciples so that they could exercise similar powers as his appointed deputies, thereby giving force and weight to their proclamation, "The kingdom of the heavens has drawn near."—Mt 10:1, 7, 8; Lu 4:36; 10:8-12, 17.

Entrance Into the Kingdom. Jesus emphasized the special period of opportunity that had thus arrived. Of his forerunner John the Baptizer, Jesus said: "Among those born of women there has not been raised up a greater than John the Baptist; but a person that is a lesser one in the kingdom of the heavens is greater than he is. But from the days of John the Baptist until now the kingdom of the heavens is the goal toward which men press [bi·a′ze·tai], and those pressing forward [bi·a·stai′] are seizing it. [Compare AT; also the Zürcher Bibel (German).] For all, the Prophets and the Law, prophesied until John." (Mt 11:10-13) Thus, the days of John's ministry, which were soon to end with his execution, marked the close of one period, the start of another. Of the Greek verb bi·a′zo·mai used in this text, Vine's Expository Dictionary of Old and New Testament Words says, "The verb suggests forceful endeavour." (1981, Vol. 3, p. 208) Regarding Matthew 11:12, German scholar Heinrich Meyer states: "In this way is described that eager, irresistible striving and struggling after the approaching Messianic kingdom . . . So eager and energetic (no longer calm and expectant) is the interest in regard to the kingdom. The [bi·a·stai′] are, accordingly, believers [not enemy attackers] struggling hard for its possession."—Meyer's Critical and Exegetical Handbook to the Gospel of Matthew, 1884, p. 225.

Membership in the Kingdom of God, therefore, would not be easy to gain, not like approaching an open city with little or nothing to make entrance difficult. Rather, the Sovereign, Jehovah God, had placed barriers to shut out any not worthy. (Compare Joh 6:44; 1Co 6:9-11; Ga 5:19-21; Eph 5:5.) Those who would enter must traverse a narrow road, find the narrow gate, keep on asking, keep on seeking, keep on knocking, and the way would be opened. They would find the way to be "narrow" in that it restricts those who follow it from doing things that would result in injury to themselves or others. (Mt 7:7, 8, 13, 14; compare 2Pe 1:10, 11.) They might figuratively have to lose an eye or a hand to gain entrance. (Mr 9:43-47) The Kingdom would be no plutocracy in which one could buy the King's favor; it would be a difficult thing for a rich man (Gr., plou′si·os) to enter. (Lu 18:24, 25) It would be no worldly aristocracy; prominent position among men would not count. (Mt 23:1, 2, 6-12, 33; Lu 16:14-16) Those apparently "first," having an impressive religious background and record, would be "last," and the 'last would be first' to receive the favored privileges connected with that Kingdom. (Mt 19:30–20:16) The prominent but hypocritical Pharisees, confident of their advantageous position, would see reformed harlots and tax collectors enter the Kingdom before them. (Mt 21:31, 32; 23:13) Though calling Jesus "Lord, Lord," all hypocritical persons disrespecting the word and will of God as revealed through Jesus would be turned away with the words: "I never knew you! Get away from me, you workers of lawlessness."—Mt 7:15-23.

Those gaining entrance would be those putting material interests secondary and seeking first the Kingdom and God's righteousness. (Mt 6:31-34) Like God's anointed King, Christ Jesus, they would love righteousness and hate wickedness. (Heb 1:8, 9) Spiritually minded, merciful, purehearted, peaceable persons, though the objects of reproach and persecution by men, would become prospective members of the Kingdom. (Mt 5:3-10; Lu 6:23) The "yoke" Jesus invited such ones to take upon themselves meant submission to his kingly authority. It was a kindly yoke, however, with a light load for those who were "mild-tempered and lowly in heart" as was the King. (Mt 11:28-30; compare 1Ki 12:12-14; Jer 27:1-7.) This should have had a heartwarming effect on his listeners, assuring them that his rule would have none of the undesirable qualities of many earlier rulers, both Israelite and non-Israelite. It gave them reason to believe that his rule would bring no burdensome taxation, forced servitude, or forms of exploitation. (Compare 1Sa 8:10-18; De 17:15-17, 20; Eph 5:5.) As Jesus' later words showed, not only would the Head of the coming Kingdom government prove his unselfishness to the point of giving his life for his people but all those associated with him in that government would also be persons who sought to serve rather than be served.—Mt 20:25-28; see JESUS CHRIST (His Works and Personal Qualities).

Willing submission vital. Jesus himself had the deepest respect for the Sovereign will and authority of his Father. (Joh 5:30; 6:38; Mt 26:39) As long as the Law covenant was in effect, his Jewish followers were to practice and advocate obedience to it; any taking an opposite course would be rejected as regards his Kingdom. This respect and obedience, however, must be from the heart, not a mere formal or one-sided observing of the Law with emphasis on specific acts required, but the observing of basic principles inherent therein involving justice, mercy, and faithfulness. (Mt 5:17-20; 23:23, 24) To the scribe who acknowledged Jehovah's unique position and who recognized that "loving him with one's whole heart and with one's whole understanding and with one's whole strength and this loving one's neighbor as oneself is worth far more than all the whole burnt offerings and sacrifices," Jesus said, "You are not far from the kingdom of God." (Mr 12:28-34) Thus, in all respects Jesus made clear that Jehovah God seeks only willing subjects, those who prefer his righteous ways and desire fervently to live under his Sovereign authority.

Covenant relationship.　On his last night with his disciples, Jesus spoke to them of a "new covenant" to become operative toward his followers as a result of his ransom sacrifice (Lu 22:19, 20; compare 12:32); he himself would serve as the Mediator of that covenant between Jehovah the Sovereign and Jesus' followers. (1Ti 2:5; Heb 12: 24) Additionally, Jesus made a personal covenant with his followers "for a kingdom," that they might join him in his royal privileges.—Lu 22: 28-30; see COVENANT.

Conquest of the world.　Although Jesus' subsequent arrest, trials, and execution made his kingly position appear weak, in reality it marked a powerful fulfillment of God's prophecies and was allowed by God for that reason. (Joh 19:10, 11; Lu 24:19-27, 44) By his loyalty and integrity until death, Jesus proved that "the ruler of the world," God's Adversary, Satan, had "no hold" on him and that Jesus had indeed "conquered the world." (Joh 14:29-31; 16:33) Additionally, even while his Son was impaled on the stake, Jehovah gave evidence of his superior power: The light of the sun was blacked out for a time; there was also a strong earthquake and the ripping in two of the large curtain in the temple. (Mt 27:51-54; Lu 23:44, 45) On the third day thereafter, he gave far greater evidence of his Sovereignty when he resurrected his Son to spirit life, despite the puny efforts of men to prevent the resurrection by posting guards before Jesus' sealed tomb.—Mt 28:1-7.

"The Kingdom of the Son of His Love."　Ten days after Jesus' ascension to heaven, on Pentecost of 33 C.E., his disciples had evidence that he had been "exalted to the right hand of God" when Jesus poured out holy spirit upon them. (Ac 1:8, 9; 2:1-4, 29-33) The "new covenant" thus became operative toward them, and they became the nucleus of a new "holy nation," spiritual Israel.—Heb 12:22-24; 1Pe 2:9, 10; Ga 6:16.

Christ was now sitting at his Father's right hand and was the Head over this congregation. (Eph 5:23; Heb 1:3; Php 2:9-11) The Scriptures show that from Pentecost 33 C.E. onward, a spiritual kingdom was set up over his disciples. When writing to first-century Christians at Colossae, the apostle Paul referred to Jesus Christ as already having a kingdom: "[God] delivered us from the authority of the darkness and transferred us into the kingdom of the Son of his love."—Col 1:13; compare Ac 17:6, 7.

Christ's kingdom from Pentecost of 33 C.E. onward has been a spiritual one ruling over spiritual Israel, Christians who have been begotten by God's spirit to become the spiritual children of God. (Joh 3:3, 5, 6) When such spirit-begotten Christians receive their heavenly reward, they will no longer be earthly subjects of the spiritual kingdom of Christ, but they will be kings with Christ in heaven.—Re 5:9, 10.

"Kingdom of Our Lord and of His Christ." The apostle John, writing toward the close of the first century C.E., foresaw through a divine revelation the future time when Jehovah God, by means of his Son, would make a new expression of divine rulership. At that time, as in the time of David's bringing the Ark up to Jerusalem, it would be said that Jehovah 'has taken his great power and begun ruling as king.' This would be the time for loud voices in heaven to proclaim: "The kingdom of the world did become the kingdom of our Lord and of his Christ, and he will rule as king forever and ever."—Re 11:15, 17; 1Ch 16:1, 31.

It is "our Lord," the Sovereign Lord Jehovah, who asserts his authority over "the kingdom of the world," setting up a new expression of his sovereignty toward our earth. He gives to his Son, Jesus Christ, a subsidiary share in that Kingdom, so that it is termed "the kingdom of our Lord and of his Christ." This Kingdom is of greater proportions and bigger dimensions than "the kingdom of the Son of his love," spoken of at Colossians 1:13. "The kingdom of the Son of his love" began at Pentecost 33 C.E. and has been over Christ's anointed disciples; "the kingdom of our Lord and of his Christ" is brought forth at the end of "the appointed times of the nations" and is over all mankind on earth.—Lu 21:24.

Upon receiving a share in "the kingdom of the world," Jesus Christ takes necessary measures to clean out opposition to God's sovereignty. The initial action takes place in the heavenly realm; Satan and his demons are defeated and cast down to the earthly realm. This results in the proclamation: "Now have come to pass the salvation and the power and the kingdom of our God and the authority of his Christ." (Re 12:1-10) During the short period of time remaining to him, this principal Adversary, Satan, continues to fulfill the prophecy at Genesis 3:15 by warring against "the remaining ones" of the "seed" of the woman, "the holy ones" due to govern with Christ. (Re 12:13-17; compare Re 13:4-7; Da 7:21-27.) Jehovah's "righteous decrees" are made manifest, nevertheless, and his expressions of judgment come as plagues upon those opposing him, resulting in the destruction of mystic Babylon the Great, the prime persecutor on earth of God's servants. —Re 15:4; 16:1–19:6.

Thereafter "the kingdom of our Lord and of his Christ" sends its heavenly armies against the rulers of all earthly kingdoms and their armies in an Armageddon fight, bringing them to an end. (Re 16:14-16; 19:11-21) This is the answer to the petition to God: "Let your kingdom come. Let your will take place, as in heaven, also upon earth." (Mt 6:10) Satan is then abyssed and a thousand-year period begins in which Christ Jesus and his associates rule as kings and priests over earth's inhabitants.—Re 20:1, 6.

Christ "hands over the kingdom." The apostle Paul also describes the rule of Christ during his presence. After Christ resurrects his followers from death, he proceeds to bring "to nothing all government and all authority and power" (logically referring to all government, authority, and power in opposition to God's sovereign will). Then, at the end of his Millennial Reign, he "hands over the kingdom to his God and Father," subjecting himself to the "One who subjected all things to him, that God may be all things to everyone." —1Co 15:21-28.

Since Christ "hands over the kingdom to his God and Father," in what sense is his Kingdom "everlasting," as repeatedly stated in the Scriptures? (2Pe 1:11; Isa 9:7; Da 7:14; Lu 1:33; Re 11:15) His Kingdom "will never be brought to ruin"; its accomplishments will endure forever; he will eternally be honored for his role as Messianic King. —Da 2:44.

During the Thousand Year Reign, Christ's rule toward earth involves priestly action toward obedient mankind. (Re 5:9, 10; 20:6; 21:1-3) By this means the dominion of sin and death as kings over obedient mankind, subjected to their "law," ends; undeserved kindness and righteousness are the ruling factors. (Ro 5:14, 17, 21) Since sin and death are to be completely removed from earth's inhabitants, this also brings to an end the need for Jesus' serving as "a helper with the Father" in the sense of providing propitiation for the sins of imperfect humans. (1Jo 2:1, 2) That brings mankind back to the original status enjoyed when the perfect man Adam was in Eden. Adam while perfect needed no one to stand between him and God to make propitiation. So, too, at the termination of Jesus' Thousand Year Rule, earth's inhabitants will be both in position and under responsibility to answer for their course of action before Jehovah God as the Supreme Judge, without recourse to anyone as legal intermediary, or helper. Jehovah, the Sovereign Power, thus becomes "all things to everyone." This means that God's purpose to "gather all things together again in the Christ, the things in the heavens and the things on the earth," will have been fully realized.—1Co 15:28; Eph 1:9, 10.

Jesus' Millennial Rule will have fully accomplished its purpose. Earth, once a focus of rebellion, will have been restored to a full, clean, and undisputed position in the realm, or domain, of the Universal Sovereign. No subsidiary kingdom will remain between Jehovah and obedient mankind.

Following this, however, a final test is made of the integrity and devotion of all such earthly subjects. Satan is loosed from his restraint in the abyss. Those yielding to his seduction do so on the same issue raised in Eden: the rightfulness of God's sovereignty. This is seen by their attacking "the camp of the holy ones and the beloved city." Since that issue has been judicially settled and declared closed by the Court of heaven, no prolonged rebellion is permitted in this case. Those failing to stand loyally on God's side will not be able to appeal to Christ Jesus as a 'propitiatory helper,' but Jehovah God will be "all things" to them, with no appeal or mediation possible. All rebels, spirit and human, receive the divine sentence of destruction in "the second death."—Re 20:7-15.

KINGS, BOOKS OF.

Books of the Holy Scriptures relating the history of Israel from the last days of King David until the release of King Jehoiachin from prison in Babylon.

Originally the two books of Kings comprised one roll called Kings (Heb., *Mela·khim'*), and in the Hebrew Bible today they are still counted as one book, the fourth in the section known as the Former Prophets. In the Greek *Septuagint* the Books of the Kings were called Third and Fourth Kingdoms, the Books of Samuel having been designated First and Second Kingdoms. In the Latin *Vulgate* these books were together known as the four books of Kings because Jerome preferred the name *Regum* (Kings), in harmony with the Hebrew title, to the literal translation of the *Septuagint* title *Regnorum* (Kingdoms). Division into two books in the *Septuagint* became expedient because the Greek translation with vowels required almost twice as much space as did Hebrew, in which no vowels were used until the second half of the first millennium of the Common Era.

The division between Second Samuel and First Kings has not always been at the same place in the Greek versions. Lucian, for one, in his recension of the *Septuagint,* made the division so that First Kings commenced with what is 1 Kings 2:12 in our present-day Bibles.

Writing of the Books.   Although the name of the writer of the books of Kings is not given in the two accounts, Scriptural indications and Jewish

---

HIGHLIGHTS OF FIRST KINGS

A concise summary of the history of both the kingdom of Judah and the kingdom of Israel from the last days of David until the death of Jehoshaphat

Originally the first book of Kings was part of one scroll with Second Kings

---

Solomon is known for outstanding wisdom at the start of his rule, but he ends up in apostasy

Nathan, by decisive action, blocks Adonijah's attempt to be king in Israel; Solomon is enthroned (1:5–2:12)

Asked by Jehovah what he desires, Solomon requests wisdom; he is additionally granted riches and glory (3:5-15)

Divinely given wisdom is evident in Solomon's handling of the case of two prostitutes, each claiming to be the mother of the same baby boy (3:16-28)

King Solomon and Israel under his rule prosper; the king's unparalleled wisdom is world famous (4:1-34; 10:14-29)

Solomon builds Jehovah's temple and later a palace complex; then all the older men of Israel gather for the inauguration (5:1–8:66)

Jehovah sanctifies the temple, assures Solomon of permanence of the royal line, but warns against unfaithfulness (9:1-9)

The queen of Sheba comes to see Solomon's wisdom and prosperity for herself (10:1-13)

In old age, Solomon is influenced by his many foreign wives and goes after foreign gods (11:1-8)

The nation is split in two; calf worship is instituted to prevent those in the northern kingdom from going up to Jerusalem

Because of Solomon's apostasy, Jehovah foretells division of the nation (11:11-13)

After Solomon's death, his son Rehoboam threatens to impose a heavier yoke on the people; ten tribes revolt and make Jeroboam king (12:1-20)

Jeroboam establishes worship of golden calves in the northern kingdom to prevent his subjects from going to Jerusalem for worship and possibly wanting to reunite the kingdom (12:26-33)

The southern kingdom, Judah, has both good kings and bad ones

Rehoboam and Abijam after him allow detestable false worship (14:21-24; 15:1-3)

Abijam's son Asa and his son Jehoshaphat actively promote true worship (15:9-15; 22:41-43)

The northern kingdom, Israel, is marred by power struggles, assassinations, and idolatry

Jeroboam's son Nadab becomes king; Baasha assassinates him and seizes the throne (15:25-30)

Baasha's son Elah succeeds to the throne and is assassinated by Zimri; Zimri commits suicide when facing defeat by Omri (16:6-20)

Omri's victory leads to civil war; Omri finally triumphs, becomes king, and later builds Samaria; his sins are even worse than those of earlier kings (16:21-28)

Ahab becomes king and marries the daughter of Ethbaal, king of the Sidonians; he introduces Baal worship into Israel (16:29-33)

Wars between Judah and Israel end with an alliance

Wars take place between Jeroboam and both Rehoboam and Abijam; Baasha fights against Asa (15:6, 7, 16-22)

Jehoshaphat makes an alliance with Ahab (22:1-4, 44)

Jehoshaphat and Ahab battle together against Ramothgilead; Ahab is killed (22:29-40)

Prophetic activity in Israel and Judah

Ahijah foretells ripping of ten tribes away from David's house; later he proclaims Jehovah's judgment against Jeroboam (11:29-39; 14:7-16)

Shemaiah conveys Jehovah's word that Rehoboam and his subjects should not fight against the rebellious ten tribes (12:22-24)

A man of God announces Jehovah's judgment against the altar for calf worship at Bethel (13:1-3)

Jehu the son of Hanani pronounces Jehovah's judgment against Baasha (16:1-4)

Elijah foretells a prolonged drought in Israel; during the drought, he miraculously extends the food supply of a widow and resurrects her son (17:1-24)

Elijah proposes a test on Mount Carmel to determine who is the true God; when Jehovah is proved true, the Baal prophets are killed; Elijah flees for his life from Ahab's wife Jezebel, but Jehovah sends Elijah to anoint Hazael, Jehu, and Elisha (18:17–19:21)

Micaiah foretells Ahab's defeat in battle (22:13-28)

tradition point to Jeremiah. Many Hebrew words and expressions found in these two books appear elsewhere in the Bible only in Jeremiah's prophecy. The books of Kings and the book of Jeremiah complement each other; events, as a rule, are briefly covered in one if they are fully described in the other. Absence of any mention of Jeremiah in the books of Kings, although he was a very prominent prophet, could be expected if Jeremiah was the writer, because his activities were detailed in the book bearing his name. The books of Kings tell of conditions in Jerusalem after the exile had begun, indicating that the writer had not been taken to Babylon, even as Jeremiah was not.—Jer 40:5, 6.

Some scholars see in the books of Kings what they consider to be evidence of the work of more than one writer or compiler. However, except for variation because of the sources used, it must be observed that the language, style, vocabulary, and grammar are uniform throughout.

First Kings covers a period of about 129 years, commencing with the final days of King David, about 1040 B.C.E., and running through to the death of Judean King Jehoshaphat in about 911 B.C.E. (1Ki 22:50) Second Kings begins with Ahaziah's reign (c. 920 B.C.E.) and carries through to the end of the 37th year of Jehoiachin's exile, 580 B.C.E., a period of about 340 years. (2Ki 1:1, 2; 25:27-30) Hence the combined accounts of the

HIGHLIGHTS OF SECOND KINGS

Continuation of the history of Judah and of Israel begun in First Kings; it reaches to the destruction of Samaria and then of Jerusalem, due to unfaithfulness

The writing of it was likely completed in Egypt about 27 years after Jerusalem's destruction by Babylon

After Elijah, Elisha serves as Jehovah's prophet

Elijah predicts Ahaziah's death; he also calls down fire upon two disrespectful military chiefs and their companies of 50 sent to get the prophet (1:2-17)

Elijah is taken away in a windstorm; Elisha receives his official garment (2:1-13)

Elisha divides the Jordan and heals water in Jericho; his inspired advice saves the allied armies of Israel, Judah, and Edom from perishing for lack of water and results in defeat of Moabites; he increases a widow's oil supply, resurrects a Shunammite woman's son, renders poisonous stew harmless, multiplies a gift of bread and grain, heals Naaman of leprosy, announces that Naaman's leprosy would come upon greedy Gehazi and his offspring, and causes a borrowed axhead to float (2:14–6:7)

Elisha warns the king of Israel in advance of surprise attacks by the Syrians; a Syrian force comes to seize him but is stricken with temporary mental blindness; the Syrians besiege Samaria, and Elijah is blamed for the resulting famine; he foretells the end of the famine (6:8–7:2)

The commission given to Elijah is completed when Elisha tells Hazael that he will become king of Syria and sends a messenger to anoint Jehu as king over Israel (8:7-13; 9:1-13)

Jehu acts against Ahab's house, eradicating Baal worship from Israel (9:14–10:28)

Elisha, on his deathbed, is visited by Jehu's grandson King Jehoash; he foretells three victories over Syria (13:14-19)

Israel's disrespect for Jehovah leads to exile in Assyria

The calf worship started by Jeroboam continues during the reigns of Jehu and his offspring—Jehoahaz, Jehoash, Jeroboam II, and Zechariah (10:29, 31; 13:6, 10, 11; 14:23, 24; 15:8, 9)

During Israel's final days, King Zechariah is assassinated by Shallum, Shallum by Menahem, Menahem's son Pekahiah by Pekah, and Pekah by Hoshea (15:8-30)

During Pekah's reign, Tiglath-pileser III, king of Assyria, exiles many Israelites; in the ninth year of Hoshea, Samaria is destroyed and Israel is taken into exile because of disrespecting Jehovah; Israel's territory is populated by other peoples (15:29; 17:1-41)

Religious reforms in Judah bring no lasting change; Babylon destroys Jerusalem and takes God's people into exile

Jehoram of Judah marries Athaliah, daughter of Ahab and Jezebel; Jehoram apostatizes, as does his son Ahaziah after him (8:16-27)

When Ahaziah dies, Athaliah tries to kill off the seed of David so that she herself can rule; Jehoash, son of Ahaziah, is rescued by his aunt and eventually made king; Athaliah is killed (11:1-16)

As long as High Priest Jehoiada lives and advises him, Jehoash restores true worship, but 'sacrificing on the high places' persists during his reign and that of his successors—Amaziah, Azariah (Uzziah), and Jotham (12:1-16; 14:1-4; 15:1-4, 32-35)

Jotham's son Ahaz practices idolatry; Ahaz' son Hezekiah makes good reforms, but these are undone by the subsequent bad reigns of Manasseh and Amon (16:1-4; 18:1-6; 21:1-22)

Amon's son Josiah undertakes firm measures to rid the land of idolatry; he is killed in a battle with Pharaoh Nechoh (22:1–23:30)

Judah's last four kings are unfaithful: Josiah's son Jehoahaz dies in captivity in Egypt; Jehoahaz' brother Jehoiakim reigns after him; Jehoiakim's son and successor Jehoiachin is carried into Babylonian exile; Jehoiakim's brother Zedekiah reigns until Jerusalem is conquered by the Babylonians and most survivors of the conquest are taken into exile (23:31–25:21)

books of Kings cover about four and a half centuries of Hebrew history. As the events recorded therein include those up to 580 B.C.E., these books could not have been completed before this date, and because there is no mention of the termination of the Babylonian exile, they, as one roll, were undoubtedly finished before that time.

The place of writing for both books appears to have been, for the most part, Judah, because most of the source material would be available there. However, Second Kings was logically completed in Egypt, where Jeremiah was taken after the assassination of Gedaliah at Mizpah.—Jer 41:1-3; 43:5-8.

The books of Kings have always had a place in the Jewish canon and are accepted as canonical. There is good reason for this, because these books carry forward the development of the foremost Bible theme, the vindication of Jehovah's sovereignty and the ultimate fulfillment of his purpose for the earth, by means of his Kingdom under Christ, the promised Seed. Moreover, three leading prophets, Elijah, Elisha, and Isaiah, are given prominence, and their prophecies are shown to have had unerring fulfillments. Events recorded in the books of Kings are referred to and elucidated elsewhere in the Scriptures. Jesus refers to what is written in these books three times—regarding Solomon (Mt 6:29), the queen of the south (Mt 12:42; compare 1Ki 10:1-9), and the widow of Zarephath and Naaman (Lu 4:25-27; compare 1Ki 17:8-10; 2Ki 5:8-14). Paul mentions the account concerning Elijah and the 7,000 men who did not bend the knee to Baal. (Ro 11:2-4; compare 1Ki 19:14, 18.) James speaks of Elijah's prayers for drought and rain. (Jas 5:17, 18; compare 1Ki 17:1; 18:45.) These references to the actions of individuals described in the books of Kings vouch for the canonicity of these writings.

The books of Kings were largely compiled from written sources, and the writer shows clearly that he referred to these outside sources for some of his information. He refers to "the book of the affairs of Solomon" (1Ki 11:41), "the book of the affairs of the days of the kings of Judah" (1Ki 15:7, 23), and "the book of the affairs of the days of the kings of Israel" (1Ki 14:19; 16:14).

One of the oldest extant Hebrew manuscripts containing the books of Kings in full is dated 1008 C.E. The Vatican No. 1209 and the Alexandrine Manuscript contain the books of Kings (in Greek), but the Sinaitic Manuscript does not. Fragments of the books of Kings evidently dating from the B.C.E. period have been found in the Qumran caves.

The framework of these books shows that the writer or compiler gave pertinent facts about each king for the purpose of chronology and to reveal God's estimate, favorable or unfavorable, of each king. The relationship of their reigns to the worship of Jehovah stands out as the most important factor. After considering the reign of Solomon, there is, with some exceptions, a general set pattern for describing each reign, as two parallel lines of history are interwoven. For the kings of Judah there is usually given first an introductory synchronism with the contemporaneous king of Israel, then the age of the king, the length of his reign, the place of rule, and the name and home of his mother, the latter being an item of interest and importance because at least some of the kings of Judah were polygamous. In concluding the account for each king, the source of the information, the burial of the king, and the name of his successor are given. Some of the same details are provided for each king of Israel, but the king's age at the time of his accession and the name and home of his mother are not given. Information supplied in First and Second Kings has been very useful in the study of Bible chronology.—See CHRONOLOGY.

The books of Kings are more than just annals or a recital of events as in a chronicle. They report the facts of history with an explanation of their significance. Eliminated from the account, it seems, is anything that does not have direct bearing on the developing purpose of God and that does not illustrate the principles by which Jehovah deals with his people. The faults of Solomon and the other kings of Judah and Israel are not disguised but are related with the utmost candor.

Archaeological Evidence. The discovery of numerous artifacts has furnished certain confirmation that the books of Kings are historically and geographically accurate. Archaeology, as well as living proof today, confirms the existence of the cedar forests of Lebanon, from which Solomon obtained timbers for his building projects in Jerusalem. (1Ki 5:6; 7:2) Evidence of industrial activity has been found in the basin of the Jordan N of the Jabbok, where Succoth and Zarethan once stood.—1Ki 7:45, 46.

Shishak's invasion of Judah in Rehoboam's time (1Ki 14:25, 26) is confirmed by the Pharaoh's own record on the walls of the temple of Karnak in Egypt. A black limestone obelisk of Assyrian King Shalmaneser III found at Nimrud in 1846 depicts perhaps an emissary of Jehu bowing before Shalmaneser, an incident that, though not mentioned in the books of Kings, adds testimony to the historicity of Israel's King Jehu. The extensive building works of Ahab, including "the house of ivory that he built" (1Ki 22:39), are well attested by the ruins found at Samaria.

The Moabite Stone relates some of the events involved in King Mesha's revolt against Israel, giving the Moabite monarch's version of what took place. (2Ki 3:4, 5) This alphabetic inscription also contains the Tetragrammaton.

The name Pekah is found in an annalistic text credited to Tiglath-pileser III. (2Ki 15:27) The campaign of Tiglath-pileser III against Israel is mentioned in his royal annals and in an Assyrian building inscription. (2Ki 15:29) The name Hoshea has also been deciphered from inscriptions of Tiglath-pileser's campaign.—2Ki 15:30; *Ancient Near Eastern Texts,* edited by J. Pritchard, 1974, pp. 282-284.

While some of Assyrian King Sennacherib's engagements are mentioned in his annals, the angelic destruction of his army of 185,000 when it threatened Jerusalem is not mentioned (2Ki 19:35), and we would not expect to find in his boastful records an account of this overwhelming setback. Notable archaeological confirmation of the last statement in the books of Kings has been found in cuneiform tablets excavated at Babylon. These indicate that *Ja'ukinu* (Jehoiachin) was imprisoned in Babylon and mention that he was provided with rations from the royal treasury. —2Ki 25:30; *Ancient Near Eastern Texts,* p. 308.

Fulfillments of Prophecy. The books of Kings contain various prophecies and point to striking fulfillments. For example, 1 Kings 2:27 shows the fulfillment of Jehovah's word against the house of Eli. (1Sa 2:31-36; 3:11-14) Prophecies regarding Ahab and his house were fulfilled. (Compare 1Ki 21:19-21 with 1Ki 22:38 and 2Ki 10:17.) What was foretold concerning Jezebel and her remains came true. (Compare 1Ki 21:23 with 2Ki 9:30-36.) And the facts of history confirm the veracity of the prophesied destruction of Jerusalem.—2Ki 21:13.

Among the many points highlighted in the books of Kings is the importance of adherence to Jehovah's requirements and the dire consequences of ignoring his just laws. The two books of Kings forcefully verify the predicted consequences of both obedience and disobedience to Jehovah God.

KING'S ROAD. The road from which the Israelites promised not to depart if allowed to pass through Edomite territory and the Amorite realm of King Sihon. (Nu 20:17; 21:21, 22; De 2:26, 27) This road must have extended from the Gulf of 'Aqaba at least as far as the Jabbok, the apparent

N boundary of Sihon's territory, and many believe that it ran as far N as Damascus and generally corresponded to the paved Roman highway built by Emperor Trajan in the second century C.E. With the exceptions of needed adjustments for modern traffic, the present-day road called Tariq es-Sultan(i) closely follows the ancient Roman highway, portions of which still exist.

Apparently the northern portion of this road from Heshbon to Ashtaroth was called "the way of Bashan."—Nu 21:33; De 3:1.

KINSMAN. See KIN, KINSMAN.

KIR. The place from which the Aramaeans came to Syria, although not necessarily their original home. (Am 9:7) Through his prophet Amos (1:5), Jehovah indicated that the Aramaeans would return to Kir, but as exiles. This prophecy was fulfilled when Tiglath-pileser III, after being bribed by Judean King Ahaz to do so, captured Damascus, the Aramaean capital, and led its inhabitants into exile at Kir.—2Ki 16:7-9.

Isaiah 22:5, 6 depicts Kir as readying itself against "the valley of the vision" (thought to represent Jerusalem). This prophecy is generally understood to have been fulfilled at the time of Assyrian King Sennacherib's campaign against Judah. Because Kir is associated with Elam in this text, some have suggested that it must have been located in the same general area as Elam, E of the Tigris River. (Compare Isa 21:2, where Elam's known geographic neighbor Media is similarly coupled with Elam.) The Greek *Septuagint* does not use "Kir" in any of the previously cited texts but employs several different words for the Hebrew *qir.* The actual location thus remains uncertain.

KIR-HARESETH (Kir-har′e·seth). Apparently another name for Kir of Moab, a city usually identified with modern Karak.—2Ki 3:25; Isa 16:7; see KIR OF MOAB.

KIR-HERES (Kir-he′res). Evidently an alternate name for Kir-Hareseth or Kir of Moab, a city commonly linked with modern Karak.—Jer 48:31, 36; see KIR OF MOAB.

KIRIATH (Kir′i·ath) [Town]. A city of Benjamin usually thought to be the same as Kiriath-jearim. Some scholars believe that the name Kiriath-jearim appeared in the original Hebrew text at Joshua 18:28, as it does in the Alexandrine Manuscript (*LXX*).—See KIRIATH-JEARIM.

KIRIATHAIM (Kir·i·a·tha′im) [Double Town].

1. A city E of the Jordan, built or rebuilt by the Reubenites. (Nu 32:37; Jos 13:15, 19) At a later

period the city came under Moabite control. It is mentioned in the prophecies of Jeremiah (48:1) and Ezekiel (25:9) as a city of Moab that would experience calamity. Earlier, Moabite King Mesha of the tenth century B.C.E. boasted about building Qaryaten (apparently Kiriathaim).

Scholars usually situate it in the area near Quraiyat, about 10 km (6 mi) WNW of Dibon. The remains found there, however, do not date prior to the first century B.C.E., so the exact location is uncertain.

2. A site in Naphtali given to the Levitical Gershonites (1Ch 6:71, 76) and called Kartan in Joshua 21:32.—See KARTAN.

KIRIATH-ARBA (Kir′i·ath-ar′ba) [Town of Arba]. The ancient name for the city of Hebron. The name was even used after the Babylonian exile. (Ne 11:25) This city, as its name suggests, appears to have been founded by Arba, "the great man among the Anakim."—Jos 14:15; see HEBRON No. 3.

KIRIATH-BAAL (Kir′i·ath-ba′al) [Town of Baal]. An alternate name for the Judean city of Kiriath-jearim. This place is usually identified with Deir el-'Azar (Tel Qiryat Ye'arim), about 9 km (5.5 mi) S of Upper Beth-horon.—Jos 15:60; 18:14; see KIRIATH-JEARIM.

KIRIATH-HUZOTH (Kir′i·ath-hu′zoth) [Town of Streets]. A site probably located in Moab somewhere between the Arnon River and Bamoth-baal. (Nu 22:36, 39, 41) Its exact location is today unknown.

KIRIATH-JEARIM (Kir′i·ath-je′a·rim) [Town of Forests]. A Hivite city associated with the Gibeonites (Jos 9:17), also known as Baalah (Jos 15:9), Baale-judah (2Sa 6:2), and Kiriath-baal (Jos 15:60). Kiriath-jearim later came to belong to Judah and bordered on Benjamite territory. (Jos 15:1, 9; 18:11, 14; Jg 18:12) Apparently descendants of Judah through Caleb settled there.—1Ch 2:3, 50, 52, 53.

In the 12th century B.C.E., sometime after being returned by the Philistines, the Ark was taken to Kiriath-jearim at the request of the men of nearby Beth-shemesh. It apparently remained there until it was moved by King David to Jerusalem some 70 years later.—1Sa 6:20–7:2; 1Ch 13:5, 6; 16:1; 2Ch 1:4.

Jeremiah's contemporary, the prophet Urijah, was the son of Shemaiah of Kiriath-jearim. (Jer 26:20) Descendants of those who had lived in the city were also represented among those returning from Babylonian exile.—Ezr 2:1, 2, 25; Ne 7:6, 7, 29.

Deir el-'Azar (Tel Qiryat Ye'arim) is the place commonly suggested as corresponding to the Biblical description of Kiriath-jearim as a city of the mountainous region (Jos 15:48, 60) on the border between Judah and Benjamin in the vicinity of the other Gibeonite cities. This site is strategically situated atop a hill about 14 km (8.5 mi) ENE of Beth-shemesh and about 13 km (8 mi) WNW of Jerusalem. This location approximately fits Eusebius' placing Kiriath-jearim once as 9 Roman miles (13 km; 8 mi) and another time as 10 Roman miles (15 km; 9 mi) from Jerusalem. Also, the fact that Deir el-'Azar lies in what at one time seems to have been a well-wooded region accords nicely with the name Kiriath-jearim, "Town of Forests."

KIRIATH-SANNAH (Kir′i·ath-san′nah) [Town of Sannah]. An alternate name for Debir, a Judean city assigned to the Aaronic priests, about 13 km (8 mi) SW of Hebron. (Jos 15:49; 21:13, 15) Some consider Kiriath-sannah to be a copyist's error in the spelling of Kiriath-sepher.—See DEBIR No. 2.

KIRIATH-SEPHER (Kir′i·ath-se′pher) [Town of the Book]. The ancient name of Debir, a priestly city in the territory of Judah, about 13 km (8 mi) SW of Hebron.—Jos 15:15, 16; 21:13, 15; Jg 1:11, 12; see DEBIR No. 2.

KIR OF MOAB. An important city of Moab, probably a onetime capital. The Aramaic Targum consistently refers to Kir (of Moab), Kir-hareseth, and Kir-heres as Karak, indicating that these are but alternative names for the same place. "Kir of Moab" is therefore usually identified with modern Karak. (Isa 15:1) This city is situated on a small plateau over 900 m (3,000 ft) above sea level and about 35 km (22 mi) S of Dibon. Steep valleys separate most of Karak from the loftier neighboring mountains.

Toward the close of the tenth century B.C.E. the allied forces of Israel, Judah, and Edom attacked Kir-hareseth. If the site is correctly identified with Karak, it was doubtless from the nearby mountains that slingers bombarded the city with stones. Although Kir-hareseth evidently was not taken, the battle went hard against the king of Moab. For some unstated reason he, along with 700 warriors, sought to break through the battle lines in order to reach the king of Edom but was unsuccessful. As a last resort, it appears that the king of Moab publicly sacrificed his own firstborn son, probably to appease the god Chemosh. (2Ki 3:5, 9, 25-27) The Hebrew text (2Ki 3:27) may also be understood to refer to the firstborn son of the king of Edom, and some suggest that this is alluded to at Amos 2:1. But this is less likely.

Isaiah's prophecy indicated that the Moabites would mourn for Kir-hareseth's raisin cakes, perhaps a principal product of the city's trade. (Isa 16:6, 7) Isaiah also spoke of his being boisterous like a harp over Moab and Kir-hareseth. As the strings of a harp vibrate with sound, so Isaiah's inward parts were moved by the message of woe for Kir-hareseth.—Isa 16:11; see also Jer 48: 31, 36.

KISH.

1. A Merarite Levite who was the son of Mahli and brother of Eleazar. As Eleazar died without sons, having had only daughters, the sons of Kish took these heiresses as wives. One of "the sons of Kish" was Jerahmeel.—1Ch 23:21, 22; 24:29.

2. A Benjamite; the son of Jeiel and his wife Maacah. (1Ch 8:29, 30) His brother Ner was the grandfather of Saul, Israel's first king. (1Ch 9:35-39) Apparently Kish's father Jeiel was also called Abiel.—See ABIEL No. 1.

3. A Benjamite who was the father of King Saul. (1Sa 14:51; Ac 13:21) He was a wealthy member of the family of the Matrites. (1Sa 9:1; 10:21) This Kish was the son of Ner and grandson of Jeiel (Abiel), thus being the nephew of the Kish mentioned above and the brother of Abner. (1Ch 8:29-33; 9:35-39) However, 1 Samuel 9:1 calls him the son of Abiel, apparently using the term "son" to represent him, not as the immediate son of Abiel (Jeiel), but rather as his grandson.

The home of Kish was evidently at Gibeah, in Benjamin (1Sa 10:26), although his burial place was in Zela. (2Sa 21:14) The only event mentioned in the Bible regarding Kish concerns his sending his son Saul and an attendant out to search for some lost she-asses.—1Sa 9:3, 4.

4. A Levite of King Hezekiah's time; son of Abdi of the sons of Merari. Kish was one of the Levites who helped to cleanse the temple in the first year of Hezekiah's reign.—2Ch 29:1-5, 12-17.

5. A Benjamite ancestor of Esther's cousin Mordecai.—Es 2:5-7.

KISHI (Kish'i) [shortened form of Kushaiah]. Apparently the same person as the Merarite Levite Kushaiah, father of the musician Ethan.—1Ch 6:19, 44; 15:17.

KISHION (Kish'i·on). A boundary city of Issachar assigned to the Gershonites. (Jos 19:17, 18, 21:27, 28) "Kedesh," found at 1 Chronicles 6:72, appears to be an alternate name for Kishion.—See KEDESH No. 3.

KISHON, TORRENT VALLEY OF (Ki'shon). A stream identified as the Nahr el-Muqatta' (Nahal Qishon). The Kishon winds its way in a northwesterly direction from the hills near Taanach through the Plain of Jezreel, or Esdraelon ('Emeq Yizre'el), and, after flowing through a narrow gorge between Mount Carmel and a spur of the Galilean hills, enters the Plain of Acco (Acre) before finally emptying into the Mediterranean. The airline distance from the Kishon's sources to its mouth at the Bay of Acco is about 37 km (23 mi). Approximately 6 m (20 ft) wide in the spring, the portion of the Kishon flowing through the Plain of Jezreel increases in width by some 3 m (10 ft) in the western section of the plain. The Kishon's greatest width of about 20 m (66 ft) is reached in the Plain of Acco. With the exception of about the last 10 km (6 mi) of its course, the Kishon is usually dry during the summer. But in the rainy season it becomes a rushing torrent, flooding its banks and sweeping everything in its path. The plain through which the Kishon flows then becomes a marshy region.

In the time of Barak and Deborah the torrent valley of Kishon figured in the deliverance of the Israelites from Canaanite oppression. Barak and his troops took a position on Mount Tabor, this action drawing army chief Sisera, with his well-equipped forces and 900 chariots, to the Kishon. (Jg 4:6, 7, 12, 13) The Israelites appeared to be at a military disadvantage. Yet, when directed to do so, Barak and his 10,000 men descended from Mount Tabor to engage the enemy in battle. Jehovah God then intervened. "From heaven did the stars fight, from their orbits they fought against Sisera."—Jg 4:14, 15; 5:20.

According to the traditional Jewish view expressed in the writings of Josephus, "there came up a great tempest with torrents of rain and hail; and the wind drove the rain in the faces of the Canaanites, obscuring their vision, so that their bows and their slings were of no service to them." (*Jewish Antiquities*, V, 205 [v, 4]) Such a downpour would have turned the ground to mud, immobilizing chariots and causing horses to sink into the mire and the enemy to flee in terror before Barak's men. By whatever means, with Jehovah's help, "all the camp of Sisera fell by the edge of the sword. Not as much as one remained." (Jg 4:15, 16; see also Ps 83:9, 10.) Apparently the treacherous torrent of Kishon swept the corpses of the enemy away. (Jg 5:21) Sisera himself escaped on foot, to suffer inglorious death by the hand of a woman, Jael the wife of Heber the Kenite.—Jg 4:17-21.

Later, during the reign of Israel's King Ahab, the prophet Elijah slaughtered 450 prophets of Baal at the torrent valley of Kishon.—1Ki 18: 22, 40.

"The waters of Megiddo" (Jg 5:19) and "the torrent valley that is in front of Jokneam" (Jos 19:11) are considered to be the Kishon.

KISS. In Biblical times the act of kissing or touching one's lips to those of another (Pr 24:26), to another person's cheek, or, in an exceptional case, even to his feet (Lu 7:37, 38, 44, 45) served as a token of affection or respect. Kissing was common not only between male and female relatives (Ge 29:11; 31:28) but also between male relatives. (Ge 27:26, 27; 45:15; Ex 18:7; 2Sa 14:33) It was likewise a gesture of affection between close friends.—1Sa 20:41, 42; 2Sa 19:39.

Kissing might accompany a blessing. (Ge 31:55) Aged Israel, or Jacob, kissed and embraced Joseph's sons, Ephraim and Manasseh, before blessing their father and them. (Ge 48:8-20) When the patriarch later finished giving commands to his 12 sons he expired, and "Joseph fell upon the face of his father and burst into tears over him and kissed him." (Ge 49:33–50:1) Samuel kissed Saul when anointing him as Israel's first king.—1Sa 10:1.

A fond greeting included kissing, perhaps accompanied by weeping and embracing. (Ge 33:4) The father of the returning prodigal of Jesus Christ's illustration fell upon his son's neck and "tenderly kissed him." (Lu 15:20) Kissing also went with a loving farewell. (Ge 31:55; Ru 1:9, 14) When the apostle Paul was about to depart from Miletus, the older men of the Ephesian congregation were so moved that they wept and "fell upon Paul's neck and tenderly kissed him."—Ac 20: 17, 37.

The Bible makes brief reference to kisses associated with love between the sexes. (Ca 1:2; 8:1) In giving advice to guard against the devices of a wicked woman, the book of Proverbs warns of the seductive kiss of a prostitute.—Pr 7:13.

Kisses could be hypocritical. Absalom, shrewdly seeking power, kissed men who drew near to bow down to him. (2Sa 15:5, 6) Treacherous Joab's kiss meant death to unsuspecting Amasa. (2Sa 20:9, 10) Also, it was with a deceitful kiss that Judas Iscariot betrayed Jesus Christ.—Mt 26:48, 49; Mr 14:44, 45.

False Worship. Kissing as an act of adoration toward false gods was forbidden by Jehovah, who mentions 7,000 men who did not bend the knee to Baal and kiss him. (1Ki 19:18) Ephraim was reproved for making idols and saying: "Let the sacrificers who are men kiss mere calves." (Ho 13:1-3) The Greeks and Romans had the practice of throwing a kiss with the hand to their idols, if these were inaccessible, and in this way they also greeted the rising sun. Job 31:27 may allude to a similar idolatrous practice.

The "Holy Kiss." Among early Christians there was the "holy kiss" (Ro 16:16; 1Co 16:20; 2Co 13:12; 1Th 5:26) or "kiss of love" (1Pe 5:14), possibly bestowed on individuals of the same sex. This early Christian form of greeting may correspond to the ancient Hebrew practice of greeting one with a kiss. Though the Scriptures provide no details, the "holy kiss" or "kiss of love" evidently reflected the wholesome love and unity prevailing in the Christian congregation.—Joh 13:34, 35.

Figurative Use. Kissing, as representing a demonstration of respect and devotion, is mentioned in the inspired advice to "serve Jehovah with fear" and "kiss the son, that He may not become incensed and you may not perish from the way." (Ps 2:11, 12) Persons responding favorably and submitting to the one God appoints as King and his Kingdom will realize great blessings when it can be said: "Righteousness and peace—they have kissed each other," because the connection of the two will be as evident to all as is the close association of affectionate friends.—Ps 85:10.

KITE [Heb., 'ai·yah', "black kite"; da·'ah', "red kite"; and perhaps dai·yah', "glede," likely a variety of kite]. The kite is a bird of prey and scavenger combined. Both the black kite and the red kite, the common varieties found in Palestine, are included among the unclean birds according to the Law. (Le 11:13, 14; De 14:12, 13) The Deuteronomy list contains ra·'ah' in place of da·'ah', as in Leviticus, but this is considered to be probably due to a scribal substitution of the Hebrew equivalent of "r" (ר) for "d" (ד), the letters being very similar in appearance.

The Hebrew name 'ai·yah' is believed to be in imitation of the piercing cry of the black kite (classified by ornithologists as Milvus migrans).

The original meaning of the Hebrew name da·'ah' is uncertain, but it is suggested that it indicates a "swooping or darting flight," as in the expression "he came darting [from Heb., da·'ah'] upon the wings of a spirit" (Ps 18:10), and in references to the 'pouncing' of the eagle. (De 28: 49; Jer 48:40; 49:22) The name thus points to a bird of prey, and Koehler and Baumgartner (Lexicon in Veteris Testamenti Libros, Leiden, 1958, p. 198) suggest the red kite (Milvus milvus).

Job uses the black kite as an example of superior sharp-sightedness, while showing that man's ingenuity and his search for wealth lead him into underground paths that even the farseeing birds of prey cannot see.—Job 28:7.

Most black kites pass through Palestine to spend the winter in Africa. An increasing number winter in Israel. They build their nests in the forks of tall trees and store food in the nest before laying eggs. The red kite, a rare winter visitor, is a reddish-brown bird, barred with black, with a grayish-white head.

KITRON (Kit'ron) [from a root meaning "make sacrificial smoke"]. A city from which the Zebulunites failed to expel the Canaanite inhabitants. (Jg 1:30) Although various sites have been suggested, none is certain. This ancient city in Zebulun may be the same as Kattath.—Jos 19:15.

KITTIM (Kit'tim). Kittim is listed as one of the four "sons" of Javan, although the name appears only in the plural form in all Scriptural references. (Ge 10:4; 1Ch 1:7) The name thereafter is used to represent a people and region.

Josephus (*Jewish Antiquities,* I, 128 [vi, 1]) referred to Kittim as "Chethimos" and associated it with Cyprus and with "the name *Chethim* given by the Hebrews to all islands and to most maritime countries." The ancient Phoenicians referred to the people of Cyprus as *Kitti.* Modern authorities generally agree with such identification of Kittim with Cyprus.

The city of Kition (Citium) on the SE coast of Cyprus is best known as a Phoenician colony, and so some scholars have viewed the listing of Kittim among the descendants of Japheth as out of place. (Ge 10:2, 4; 1Ch 1:5, 7) However, the evidence shows that the Phoenicians were relative latecomers to Cyprus and their colony at Kition is considered to date from only about the ninth century B.C.E. Thus, after *The New Encyclopædia Britannica* (1987, Vol. 3, p. 332) identifies Kition as the "principal Phoenician city in Cyprus," it adds: "The earliest remains at Citium are those of an Aegean colony of the Mycenaean Age (*c.* 1400-1100 BC)."—See also Vol. 16, p. 948.

That Kittim may embrace other areas in addition to the island of Cyprus is indicated by Josephus' statement, quoted earlier, about the Hebrew usage of the term as embracing other Mediterranean islands and countries bordering the sea, Cyprus being but the nearest (to Palestine) of the Kittim lands. This seems to be borne out by the references to the "islands" or "coastlands" of Kittim at Ezekiel 27:6 and Jeremiah 2:10. Some commen-

Black kite; a bird not suitable for food, according to the Mosaic Law

tators consider that Kittim is also used in this larger sense at Numbers 24:24, where the prophet Balaam, who lived contemporaneously with Moses, foretold that "ships from the coast of Kittim" would afflict Assyria and Eber but that the attacker would eventually perish. This view would allow for the attack perhaps to originate from the seacoast region of Macedonia, from which country Alexander the Great advanced, conquering the land of "Asshur" (Assyria-Babylonia) along with the Medo-Persian Empire; others suggest that the attackers were Romans from the Mediterranean coastlands of Italy. The Latin *Vulgate* uses "Italy" in place of "Kittim" at Numbers 24:24, and the Targum of Onkelos reads "Romans"; but the Apocryphal book of 1 Maccabees (1:1, *JB*) uses Kittim to represent the land of Macedonia.

In Isaiah's pronouncement against Tyre, Kittim (likely Cyprus) is the point at which the eastbound ships of Tarshish receive the news of Tyre's downfall, and "the virgin daughter of Sidon" is told by Jehovah to "cross over to Kittim itself," in a vain effort to find refuge. (Isa 23:1, 11, 12) This is in harmony with the historical evidence for Phoenician colonies in Cyprus at the time of Isaiah's prophesying (c. 778–a. 732 B.C.E.). An inscription of Sennacherib relates the flight of King Luli of

Sidon to the island of *Iadnana* (Cyprus) as the result of the Assyrian attack. (*Ancient Near Eastern Texts,* edited by J. Pritchard, 1974, pp. 287, 288) Similarly, many from Tyre evidently sought haven in Cyprus during Nebuchadnezzar's 13-year siege of Tyre, in fulfillment of Isaiah's proclamation.

Final mention of Kittim (by that name) comes in Daniel's prophecy of the rivalry between the "king of the north" and "king of the south," where an attack by the "king of the north" is thwarted by "the ships of Kittim."—Da 11:30; see CYPRUS.

KNEADING TROUGH.

A shallow and generally portable bowl-shaped vessel. It was usually made of wood but sometimes was earthenware or was made of bronze. In it flour and water were mixed and worked into dough. In preparing leavened bread, the mass was usually leavened by working in a piece of sourdough saved from a previous baking. The mass of dough was left to rise in the kneading trough before baking. (Ge 18:6; 1Sa 28:24) The usual method was to knead the dough with one's hands, though the Egyptians also used their feet at times, when kneading dough in a large trough.—Ho 7:4.

The size of the kneading bowl, or trough, varied considerably. However, one earthenware type often used was a bowl approximately 25 cm (10 in.) in diameter and about 8 cm (3 in.) deep.

Bread was an important part of the Hebrew diet and was baked regularly. Hence, the kneading trough was an essential item among the Israelites and other peoples of antiquity. The frogs that covered Egypt during the second blow brought upon it by Jehovah in Moses' day entered the homes and were even found in the kneading troughs. (Ex 8:3) The Israelites, later leaving Egypt hurriedly, "carried their flour dough before it was leavened, with their kneading troughs wrapped up in their mantles upon their shoulder." (Ex 12:33, 34) Since the kneading trough was an important vessel in the home, having to do with the preparing of the 'daily bread,' Jehovah's blessing upon it evidently signified an assured sufficiency of food in the home, while his curse upon it represented hunger.—De 28:1, 2, 5, 15, 17.

KNEE, KNEEL.

This joint in the leg is important for support of the body. Hence, wobbling or enfeebled knees portray weakness; and knocking knees, fear.—Job 4:4; Ps 109:24; Isa 35:3; Da 5:6; Heb 12:12.

All except 300 of Gideon's 10,000 men bent down upon their knees to drink, apparently putting their faces down to the water. In this position they could not be alert, prepared in case of a surprise attack. They were more concerned with slaking their thirst than with the issue at hand. On the other hand, the 300 remained on their feet, picking up the water and lapping it out of their hands, alert, watchful, ready. The 9,700 negligent ones were therefore dismissed.—Jg 7:3, 5-8.

Figuratively, a child said to be 'born upon the knees' of a person other than the mother, and thus enjoying that one's favor and care, was acknowledged as that person's child, or descendant, just as Bilhah's child was counted as Rachel's.—Ge 30:3-6; compare Ge 50:23.

Jehovah promised restoration for his people and likened them to children of Zion, or Jerusalem, who would be 'fondled upon the knees,' that is, well cared for, brought back into a favored state. —Isa 66:12, 13.

Kneeling. The Hebrew word for "kneel" (*ba·rakh′*) possibly has the same root as the one for "blessing," which may indicate that at least at times blessings were conferred upon persons while they knelt.

While imploring favor. A person might kneel as an act of respect or to implore favor, as when a "chief of fifty" representing King Ahaziah knelt before Elijah to plead for his life and that of the men accompanying him. (2Ki 1:13, 14) It was on bended knee that a leper entreated Jesus to make him clean.—Mr 1:40-42; also 10:17-22.

During prayer. True worshipers often knelt when praying to God, this posture being a suitable indication of their humility. (Ezr 9:5; Ac 9:36, 40; 21:3-6) Solomon assumed a kneeling position before the congregation of Israel during his prayer at the temple's dedication. (2Ch 6:13) Despite a royal decree that for 30 days petition should be made only to King Darius, Daniel knelt in prayer to Jehovah three times a day, doing so while the windows of his roof chamber were open toward Jerusalem. (Da 6:6-11) Jesus Christ himself furnished an example of kneeling in prayer to Jehovah. In the garden of Gethsemane on the night of his betrayal, Jesus "bent his knees and began to pray."—Lu 22:41.

Practicers of false religion knelt before idols of their gods. But in Elijah's day there were still 7,000 faithful persons in Israel, 'all the knees that had not bent down to Baal.'—1Ki 19:18; Ro 11:4.

Obeisance or acknowledgment of high station. Kneeling may denote obeisance or recognition of a superior's high position. Soldiers knelt before Jesus and did obeisance to him, doing so, however, in mockery.—Mt 27:27-31; Mr 15:16-20.

Jehovah has granted the faithful resurrected

Jesus Christ a superior position and a name that is above every other name, "so that in the name of Jesus every knee should bend of those in heaven and those on earth and those under the ground." All who gain life must bend their knees in worship to Jehovah in the name of Jesus Christ and acknowledge him as Lord to God's glory. This includes "those under the ground," evidently showing that those resurrected from the grave also come under this requirement.—Php 2:9-11; Joh 5:28, 29; Eph 1:9, 10.

Primarily, recognition of Jehovah's supremacy and sovereignty is required of those desiring divine favor. Jehovah has declared: "By my own self I have sworn . . . that to me every knee will bend down." (Isa 45:23; Ro 14:10-12) Appropriately, therefore, the psalmist fervently urged fellow Israelites: "O come in, let us worship and bow down; let us kneel before Jehovah our Maker."—Ps 95:6; see ATTITUDES AND GESTURES.

KNIFE.

A single- or double-edged cutting implement. Knives used in Biblical lands in times past were made of stone (particularly of flint), copper, bronze, or iron.

The Hebrew term *ma·'akhe'leth,* which literally refers to an instrument for eating, is also applied to large knives such as those employed in cutting up the carcasses of sacrificial animals. A "slaughtering knife" (Heb., *ma·'akhe'leth*) was the instrument faithful Abraham took in hand when about to sacrifice Isaac (Ge 22:6, 10), and the same type was used by a certain Levite to cut the body of his dead concubine into 12 pieces. (Jg 19:29) Also, Proverbs 30:14 speaks of "a generation whose teeth are swords and whose jawbones are slaughtering knives," thus employing the same Hebrew term as a figure of rapaciousness.

"Flint knives" were made by Joshua for use in circumcising the sons of Israel at Gibeath-haaraloth. (Jos 5:2-4) The Hebrew term designating these knives is *che'rev,* generally rendered "sword." (See Jos 5:2, ftn.) The common "Canaanite" flint knife was about 15 cm (6 in.) in length and had a raised center ridge and a double edge.

Scribes and secretaries of ancient times used a type of knife to sharpen their reed pens and to make erasures. Jeremiah 36:23 tells of the use of a "secretary's knife" to tear apart a roll of a book prepared by Jeremiah at Jehovah's direction.

Many ancient knives of copper have a straight blade from 15 to 25 cm (6 to 10 in.) in length; some with curved tips have also been discovered. Handles were often one piece with the blade. Other handles were made of wood and were fastened to the blade.

Proverbs 23:1, 2 makes figurative reference to a knife, recommending the 'putting of a knife to one's throat' when eating with a king, evidently emphasizing the need to restrain one's appetite in such a circumstance.

KNOB.

An ornamental part of the golden lampstand used in the tabernacle; designated by the Hebrew word *kaph·tohr',* or *kaph·tor',* evidently referring to a round protrusion. (Ex 25:31-36; 37:17-22) These "knobs" alternated with the ornamental blossoms on the main stem and on each of the six branches of the lampstand. Some of the knobs seem to have formed a boss, or projecting support, for these branches. They are discernible on the lampstand as depicted in the relief on the Arch of Titus (in Rome), where Roman soldiers are shown carrying spoils from the temple in Jerusalem, destroyed in 70 C.E.

KNOWLEDGE.

Essentially, knowledge means familiarity with facts acquired by personal experience, observation, or study. The Bible strongly urges the seeking for and treasuring of right knowledge, recommending it rather than gold. (Pr 8:10; 20:15) Jesus stressed the importance of truly knowing him and his Father, and knowledge is repeatedly emphasized in the books of the Christian Greek Scriptures.—Joh 17:3; Php 1:9; 2Pe 3:18.

Source of Knowledge. Jehovah is actually the basic Source of knowledge. Life, of course, is from him and life is essential for one's having any knowledge. (Ps 36:9; Ac 17:25, 28) Furthermore, God created all things, so human knowledge is based on a study of God's handiwork. (Re 4:11; Ps 19:1, 2) God also inspired his written Word, from which man can learn the divine will and purposes. (2Ti 3:16, 17) Thus the focal point of all true knowledge is Jehovah, and a person seeking it ought to have a fear of God that makes him careful not to incur Jehovah's displeasure. Such fear is the beginning of knowledge. (Pr 1:7) Such godly fear puts one in position to gain accurate knowledge, whereas those who do not consider God readily draw wrong conclusions from the things that they observe.

The Bible repeatedly links Jehovah and knowledge, calling him "a God of knowledge" and describing him as "perfect in knowledge."—1Sa 2:3; Job 36:4; 37:14, 16.

The role that Jehovah has assigned to his Son in the outworking of His purposes is of such importance that it can be said of Jesus: "Carefully concealed in him are all the treasures of wisdom and of knowledge." (Col 2:3) Unless a person exercises faith in Jesus Christ as God's Son, he cannot grasp the real meaning of the Scriptures and see how God's purposes are working out in harmony with what He has foretold.

One is helped to appreciate more fully the meaning and importance of knowledge by examining the Hebrew and Greek words often translated "knowledge" as well as by noting the relationship between knowledge and wisdom, understanding, thinking ability, and discernment.

Meaning of Term. In the Hebrew Scriptures a number of words (nouns) that can be translated "knowledge" are related to the basic verb *ya·dha'*, signifying "know (by being told)," "know (by observing)," "know (by personal acquaintance or experience)," or "be experienced, skillful." The exact shade of meaning, and often the way each word should be translated, must be determined by the context. For instance, God said that he 'knew' Abraham and so was sure that that man of faith would command his offspring correctly. Jehovah was not saying simply that he was aware that Abraham existed but, rather, that He had become well acquainted with Abraham, for he had observed Abraham's obedience and interest in true worship over many years.—Ge 18:19, *NW, La;* Ge 22:12; compare JEHOVAH (Early Use of the Name and Its Meaning).

As with the verb *ya·dha'* (know), the principal Hebrew word rendered "knowledge" (*da'ath*) carries the basic idea of knowing facts or having information, but at times it includes more than that. For example, Hosea 4:1, 6 says that at a certain time there was no "knowledge of God" in Israel. That does not mean that the people were not aware that Jehovah was God and that he had delivered and led the Israelites in the past. (Ho 8:2) But by their course of murdering, stealing, and committing adultery, they showed that they rejected real knowledge because they were not acting in harmony with it.—Ho 4:2.

Ya·dha' sometimes denotes sexual intercourse, as at Genesis 4:17, where some translations render it literally "knew" (*KJ; RS; Ro*), whereas others suitably say that Cain "had intercourse" with his wife. (*AT; Mo; NW*) The Greek verb *gi·no'sko* is used similarly at Matthew 1:25 and Luke 1:34.

After Adam and Eve ate the forbidden fruit (Ge 2:17; 3:5, 6), Jehovah said to his associate in creative work (Joh 1:1-3): "Here the man has become like one of us in *knowing* good and bad." (Ge 3:22) This apparently did not mean merely having knowledge of what was good and what was bad for them, for the first man and woman had such knowledge by reason of God's com-

mands to them. Furthermore, God's words at Genesis 3:22 could not pertain to their now knowing what was bad by experience, for Jehovah said that they had become like him and he has not learned what is bad by doing it. (Ps 92:14, 15) Evidently, Adam and Eve got to know what was good and what was bad in the special sense of now judging for themselves what was good and what was bad. They were idolatrously placing their judgment above God's, disobediently becoming a law to themselves, as it were, instead of obeying Jehovah, who has both the right and the wisdom necessary to determine good and bad. So their independent knowledge, or standard, of good and bad was not like that of Jehovah. Rather, it was one that led them to misery.—Jer 10:23.

In the Christian Greek Scriptures there are two words commonly translated "knowledge," *gno'sis* and *e·pi'gno·sis.* Both are related to the verb *gi·no'sko,* which means "know; understand; perceive." The way this verb is used in the Bible, though, shows that it can indicate a favorable relationship between the person and one he "knows." (1Co 8:3; 2Ti 2:19) Knowledge (*gno'sis*) is put in a very favorable light in the Christian Greek Scriptures. However, not all that men may call "knowledge" is to be sought, because philosophies and views exist that are "falsely called 'knowledge.'" (1Ti 6:20). The recommended knowledge is about God and his purposes. (2Pe 1:5) This involves more than merely having facts, which many atheists have; a personal devotion to God and Christ is implied. (Joh 17:3; 6:68, 69) Whereas having knowledge (information alone) might result in a feeling of superiority, our knowing "the love of the Christ which surpasses knowledge," that is, knowing this love by experience because we are personally imitating his loving ways, will balance and give wholesome direction to our use of any information we may have gained.—Eph 3:19.

E·pi'gno·sis, a strengthened form of *gno'sis* (*e·pi',* meaning "additional"), can often be seen from the context to mean "exact, accurate, or full knowledge." Thus Paul wrote about some who were learning (taking in knowledge) "yet never able to come to an accurate knowledge ["a real knowledge," *TC;* "a personal knowledge," *Ro;* "clear, full knowledge," *Da* ftn] of truth." (2Ti 3:6, 7) He also prayed that ones in the Colossian congregation, who obviously had some knowledge of God's will, for they had become Christians, "be filled with the accurate knowledge of his will in all wisdom and spiritual comprehension." (Col 1:9) Such accurate knowledge should be sought by all Christians (Eph 1:15-17; Php 1:9; 1Ti 2:3, 4), it being important in putting on "the new personality" and in gaining peace.—Col 3:10; 2Pe 1:2.

Related Attributes. Frequently in the Bible, knowledge is linked with other attributes such as wisdom, understanding, discernment, and thinking ability. (Pr 2:1-6, 10, 11) Grasping the basic differences between these greatly illuminates many texts. It is to be acknowledged, though, that the original words involved cannot be said to match invariably certain English words. The setting and the use of a word affect the sense. Nonetheless, certain interesting differences emerge when one notes the Bible's references to knowledge, wisdom, understanding, discernment, and thinking ability.

Wisdom. Wisdom is the ability to put knowledge to work, or to use it, the intelligent application of learning. A person might have considerable knowledge but not know how to use it because of lacking wisdom. Jesus linked wisdom with accomplishment in saying: "Wisdom is proved righteous by its works." (Mt 11:19) Solomon asked for and received from God not just knowledge but also wisdom. (2Ch 1:10; 1Ki 4:29-34) In the case of two women who claimed the same child, Solomon had knowledge of a mother's devotion to her child; he displayed wisdom by using his knowledge to settle the dispute. (1Ki 3:16-28) "Wisdom is the prime thing," for without it knowledge is of little value. (Pr 4:7; 15:2) Jehovah abounds in and provides both knowledge and wisdom.—Ro 11:33; Jas 1:5.

Understanding. Understanding is the ability to see how the parts or aspects of something relate to one another, to see the entire matter and not just isolated facts. The Hebrew root verb *bin* has the basic meaning "separate" or "distinguish," and it is often rendered "understand" or "discern." It is similar with the Greek *sy·ni'e·mi.* Thus at Acts 28:26 (quoting Isa 6:9, 10) it could be said that the Jews heard but did not understand, or did not put together. They did not grasp how the points or thoughts fitted together to mean something to them. Proverbs 9:10, in saying that "knowledge of the Most Holy One is what understanding is," shows that true understanding of anything involves appreciation of its relation to God and his purposes. Because a person with understanding is able to connect new information to things he already knows, it can be said that "to the understanding one knowledge is an easy thing." (Pr 14:6) Knowledge and understanding are allied, and both are to be sought.—Pr 2:5; 18:15.

Discernment. A Hebrew word frequently rendered "discernment" (*tevu·nah'*) is related to the word *bi·nah',* translated "understanding." Both appear at Proverbs 2:3, which the translation by The Jewish Publication Society renders: "If thou call for understanding, and lift up thy voice for discernment . . . " As with understanding, discernment involves seeing or recognizing things, but it emphasizes distinguishing the parts, weighing or evaluating one in the light of the others. A person who unites knowledge and discernment controls what he says and is cool of spirit. (Pr 17:27) The one opposing Jehovah displays lack of discernment. (Pr 21:30) Through his Son, God gives discernment (full understanding or insight).—2Ti 2:1, 7, *NW, NE.*

Thinking ability. Knowledge is also related to what is sometimes translated "thinking ability" (Heb., *mezim·mah'*). The Hebrew word can be used in a bad sense (evil ideas, schemes, devices) or a favorable one (shrewdness, sagacity). (Ps 10:2; Pr 1:4) Thus the mind and thoughts can be directed to an admirable, upright end, or just the opposite. By paying close attention to the way Jehovah does things and by inclining one's ears to all the various aspects of His will and purposes, a person safeguards his own thinking ability, directing it into right channels. (Pr 5:1, 2) Properly exercised thinking ability, harmonious with godly wisdom and knowledge, will guard a person against being ensnared by immoral enticements. —Pr 2:10-12.

Caution in Gaining Knowledge. Solomon apparently put knowledge in a negative light when saying: "For in the abundance of wisdom there is an abundance of vexation, so that he that increases knowledge increases pain." (Ec 1:18) This would appear contrary to the general view of knowledge one finds in the Bible. However, Solomon here stresses again the vanity of human endeavors in all matters other than the carrying out of God's commands. (Ec 1:13, 14) Thus, a man may gain knowledge and wisdom in many fields, or he may explore deeply some specialized field, and such knowledge and wisdom may be proper in themselves, though not directly related to God's declared purpose. Yet, with such increased knowledge and wisdom the man may well become more keenly aware of how limited his opportunities are to use his knowledge and wisdom because of his short life span and because of the problems and bad conditions that confront and oppose him in imperfect human society. This is vexing, producing a painful sense of frustration. (Compare Ro 8:20-22; Ec 12:13, 14; see ECCLESIASTES.) Thus, too, the knowledge obtained by 'devotion to many books,' unless tied in with and put to use in the carrying out of God's commands, is "wearisome to the flesh."—Ec 12:12.

KOA (Koʹa). A people or region mentioned with Pekod and Shoa at Ezekiel 23:23 and foretold by Jehovah to supply part of the enemy forces that would assault unfaithful Jerusalem and Judah. Koa was probably located E of Babylonia and has been generally linked with the *Qutu,* a people who resided E of the Tigris on the steppes between the upper ʹAdhaim and Diyala rivers. The *Qutu* are frequently coupled with the *Sutu* (perhaps the Shoa of Eze 23:23) in Assyrian inscriptions, such records showing them as fighting against Assyria.

KOHATH (Koʹhath). The second named of the three sons of Levi (Ge 46:11; Ex 6:16; 1Ch 6:1) and father of Amram, Izhar, Hebron, and Uzziel. (Ex 6:18; Nu 3:19; 1Ch 6:2) He was the progenitor of the Kohathites, one of the three main divisions of the Levites. (Nu 3:17, 27) He was likely born in the land of Canaan and is listed among the 66 souls who "came to Jacob into Egypt." (Ge 46:8, 11, 26; see, however, BENJAMIN No. 1.) Kohath's descendants included Moses, Aaron, Miriam (Ex 6:18, 20; Nu 26:58, 59), and rebellious Korah. (Nu 16:1-3) Kohath lived 133 years.—Ex 6:18.

KOHATHITE (Koʹhath·ite) [Of (Belonging to) Kohath]. A descendant of the family head Kohath, who was one of the three sons of Levi. (Ge 46:11; Nu 26:57) The "Kohathites" or "sons of Kohath" were divided into four families, these being descendants of the four sons of Kohath: the Amramites, the Izharites, the Hebronites, and the Uzzielites. (Nu 3:19, 27) Their chieftain at the time of Israel's encampment at Mount Sinai (1513 B.C.E.) was Elizaphan the son of Uzziel.—Nu 3:30.

Moses and Aaron were Kohathites of the Amramite family (Ex 6:18, 20); rebellious Korah was a Kohathite of the family of the Izharites (Nu 16:1), as was the faithful prophet Samuel.—1Sa 1:1, 19, 20; 1Ch 6:33-38.

The census taken in the Wilderness of Sinai revealed that there were 8,600 males a month old and upward belonging to the families of the Kohathites. (Nu 3:27, 28) According to some manuscripts of the Greek *Septuagint,* the figure is 8,300. When the smaller number is added to the 7,500 and the 6,200 of Numbers 3:22, 34, the sum total is 22,000—the very figure found in Numbers 3:39. Their males between 30 and 50 years of age "who entered into the service group for the service in the tent of meeting" numbered 2,750.—Nu 4:34-37.

During the wilderness trek, the Kohathites were assigned to camp on the S side of the tabernacle (Nu 3:29), between it and the encampment of the tribes of Reuben, Simeon, and Gad. (Nu 2:10, 12, 14) The Kohathites had the privilege and responsibility of transporting the ark of the covenant, the table of showbread, the lampstand, the altars, and the utensils of the holy place, as well as the screen of the Most Holy (Nu 3:30, 31), after these items were packed and covered by Aaron and his sons, who were also Kohathites. The Kohathites other than Aaron and his sons were not allowed to see the utensils even for a moment or to touch the holy place, for doing so would mean death. (Nu 4:4-15, 20) Though Israel provided the Levites with cattle and wagons for transporting the tabernacle equipment, the Kohathites were not given any. Doubtless because of the sacredness of their burdens, they carried their loads on the shoulder. (Nu 7:2-9) They were the last of the Levites to pull away from an encampment.—Nu 10:17-21.

After the conquest of Canaan, when the Levites were assigned certain cities, the Kohathites received 23; the "sons" of Aaron (that is, the Kohathites) were assigned 13 cities out of the territories of Judah, Simeon, and Benjamin, and the rest of the Kohathites were assigned 10 other cities from the territories of Ephraim, Dan, and the half tribe of Manasseh.—Jos 21:1-5, 9-26; 1Ch 6:54-61, 66-70.

Heman, a Kohathite of the family of Izhar, was given a position by David in connection with the singing at Jehovah's sanctuary. (1Ch 6:31-38) One hundred and twenty Kohathites under Uriel their chief were among those whom David appointed to bring the ark of Jehovah from the house of Obed-edom to Jerusalem, on which occasion Heman figured prominently in the music and singing. (1Ch 15:4, 5, 11-17, 19, 25) According to First Chronicles, when David divided the Levites into courses, or divisions, some Kohathites were singers (25:1, 4-6) and gatekeepers (26:1-9); others were in charge of the stores and things made holy (26:23-28); and some acted as officers, judges, and administrators. (26:29-32) Certain Kohathites looked after baking and the preparation of layer bread for the Sabbath.—1Ch 9:31, 32.

The Kohathites praised Jehovah upon learning that he would give Judah under Jehoshaphat victory over the combined forces of Ammon, Moab, and Seir. (2Ch 20:14-19) Kohathite Levites participated in cleansing the house of Jehovah in King Hezekiah's day. (2Ch 29:12-17) Also, Kohathites Zechariah and Meshullam were among those acting as overseers when King Josiah repaired the temple.—2Ch 34:8-13.

KOLAIAH (Ko·laiʹah).

1. Father of the false prophet Ahab who was among the Jews in Babylonian exile before

Jerusalem's destruction in 607 B.C.E.—Jer 29:21; see AHAB No. 2.

2. A Benjamite and apparent ancestor of a certain Sallu residing in Jerusalem in Nehemiah's day after the Babylonian exile.—Ne 11:4, 7.

KORAH (Ko'rah) [possibly, Bald; Baldness].

1. One of Esau's three sons by his Hivite wife Oholibamah; born in Canaan prior to Esau's withdrawal to the mountainous region of Seir. (Ge 36:2, 5-8, 14; 1Ch 1:35) Korah was a sheik of the land of Edom.—Ge 36:18.

A "sheik Korah" is listed at Genesis 36:16 as a son of Eliphaz and grandson of Esau. However, the name does not appear among the descendants of Eliphaz at Genesis 36:11, 12 or 1 Chronicles 1:36. The Samaritan *Pentateuch* omits the name at Genesis 36:16, and some scholars suggest its appearance in the Masoretic text may be the result of a copyist's error.

2. One of the sons of Hebron of the tribe of Judah.—1Ch 2:43.

3. A Kohathite Levite of the family of Izhar. (Ex 6:16, 18, 21; 1Ch 6:1, 2, 22 [Amminadab was perhaps an alternative name for Izhar.]) During Israel's wilderness trek Korah rebelled against the authority of Moses and Aaron, doing so in league with the Reubenites Dathan, Abiram, and On, as well as 250 "chieftains of the assembly" or "men of fame." (Nu 16:1, 2) They contended that "the whole assembly are all of them holy and Jehovah is in their midst," asking, "Why, then, should you lift yourselves up above the congregation of Jehovah?" (Nu 16:3-11) Moses later sent to call Dathan and Abiram, but they refused to be present, thinking Moses had no right to summon them. (Nu 16:12-15) Korah, his assembly, and High Priest Aaron were told to present themselves before Jehovah, all supplied with fire holders and burning incense.—Nu 16:16, 17.

The following day Korah and the 250 men with him, all carrying fire holders with burning incense, stood at the entrance of the tent of meeting with Moses and Aaron. Jehovah's glory appeared to all the assembly and God spoke to Moses and Aaron, telling them to separate themselves from the midst of the assembly, "that I may exterminate them in an instant." However, Moses and Aaron interceded for the people, and God then directed Moses to have the assembly get away from the tabernacles of Korah, Dathan, and Abiram. This was done. (Nu 16:18-27) Shortly thereafter, "the earth proceeded to open its mouth and to swallow up them and their households and all humankind that belonged to Korah and all the goods." They and all that belonged to them went down alive into Sheol, and the earth covered them over.—Nu 16:28-34.

Those who were before the tent of meeting with the incense-filled fire holders did not escape, for "a fire came out from Jehovah and proceeded to consume the two hundred and fifty men offering the incense." (Nu 16:35) Korah himself was with them at that time and thus perished in that fire from God.—Nu 26:10.

The fire holders of those who conspired with Korah were made into metal plates with which to overlay the altar. This was done "because they presented them before Jehovah, so that they became holy; and they should serve as a sign to the sons of Israel." (Nu 16:36-40) Despite this powerful evidence of divine judgment, the very next day the whole assembly of Israel murmured against Moses and Aaron, complaining, "You men, you have put Jehovah's people to death." This gave rise to indignation on God's part, and despite the pleas of Moses and Aaron, 14,700 died as a result of a scourge from Jehovah, halted only after Aaron made atonement for the people. (Nu 16:41-50) Thereafter, Aaron's priestly position was confirmed by the budding of his rod.—Nu 17.

That the sons of Korah did not follow their father in rebellion seems apparent from the Bible record, for it states: "However, the sons of Korah did not die." (Nu 26:9-11) Korah's descendants later became prominent in Levitical service.—See KORAHITE.

The writer of the book of Jude linked Cain, Balaam, and Korah together when warning Christians to guard against animalistic men who "have perished in the rebellious talk of Korah!" Korah evidently sought glory for himself. He challenged Jehovah's appointments, becoming a rebel, and thus justly suffered death as a consequence of his improper course of action.—Jude 10, 11.

KORAHITE (Ko'rah·ite) [Of (Belonging to) Korah]. A descendant of Korah, who rebelled in Moses' day. The Korahites were a paternal house of the Kohathite Levites and descended from Korah through his three sons Assir, Elkanah, and Abiasaph. (Ex 6:18, 21, 24; Nu 16:1-3) "The sons of Korah did not die" with their father (Nu 26:10, 11), evidently because they did not follow him in rebellion.

In the census of Israel taken on the Plains of Moab, "the family of the Korahites" was registered with the Levite families. (Nu 26:57, 58) When David was still under restrictions imposed by King Saul, certain Korahites were among the mighty men who joined him at Ziklag. (1Ch 12:1, 6) The Levitical singer Heman and the prophet Samuel were Korahites (1Ch 6:33-38), and King David organized members of Heman's family as singers. (1Ch 15:16, 17; 16:37, 41, 42; 25:1, 4-6) Korahites were among the gatekeepers for the house of Jehovah (1Ch 26:1-9, 19), and in Jehoshaphat's day "Levites of the sons of the Kohathites and of the sons of the Korahites rose up to praise Jehovah the God of Israel with an extraordinarily loud voice," because of promised deliverance from the combined forces of Moab, Ammon, and Seir.—2Ch 20:14-19.

The superscriptions of Psalms 42, 44-49, 84, 85, 87, and 88 specifically mention the sons of Korah. Though their forefather had been rebellious, Jehovah did not hold the sons of Korah accountable for his error, and because of their faithfulness they were blessed and honored with temple service.

KORE   (Ko're) [possibly, Bald; Baldness].

1. A Kohathite Levite "of the sons of Asaph" and a descendant of Korah. (Ex 6:16, 18, 21; 1Ch 9:19; 26:1) Shallum, one of "the doorkeepers of the tent," is described as "the son of Kore the son of Ebiasaph the son of Korah," at 1 Chronicles 9:19. This text does not mention all the generations between Shallum and Ebiasaph, but the names given belong in this one genealogy. First Chronicles 26:1 calls the gatekeeper Meshelemiah "the son of Kore."

2. A Levite, "the son of Imnah" and "the gatekeeper to the east" of the temple in King Hezekiah's day. He was "in charge of the voluntary offerings of the true God, to give Jehovah's contribution and the most holy things," and had other men under his control.—2Ch 31:14-16.

KOZ   [Thorn]. A descendant of Judah. Koz "became father to Anub and Zobebah and the families of Aharhel the son of Harum."—1Ch 4:1, 8.

KUSHAIAH   (Kush·a'iah). A Levite of the family of Merari and the father or ancestor of Ethan, one of the group of Levite singers and musicians of David's day. (1Ch 15:16, 17) Kushaiah is evidently called Kishi at 1 Chronicles 6:44.

KYRIOS.   See LORD.

L

LAADAH   (La'a·dah). A descendant of Judah and the second named of Shelah's two sons. He is referred to as "the father of Mareshah."—1Ch 4:21.

LABAN   (La'ban) [White].

1. The grandson of Abraham's brother Nahor. He was the son of Bethuel and the brother of Rebekah (Ge 24:15, 29; 28:5), and he was the father of Leah and Rachel. (Ge 29:16) Laban resided at the city of Haran in Paddan-aram, an area of Mesopotamia.—Ge 24:10; 27:43; 28:6; 29:4, 5.

Laban is called "the son of Bethuel the Syrian [literally, "the Aramaean"]." He is also referred to as "Laban the Syrian." (Ge 28:5; 25:20; 31:20, 24) This designation is fitting in view of the fact that he was a resident of Paddan-aram, which means "Plain (Flatland) of Aram (Syria)." Laban was a Semite dwelling in a region occupied by persons speaking Aramaic, a Semitic language.

To the vicinity just mentioned, aged Abraham sent his servant to find a wife for Isaac. (Ge 24:1-4, 10) When Laban heard Rebekah's account of her encounter with Abraham's servant and saw the gifts she had been given, he went running to the servant, addressed him as one blessed by Jehovah, and extended hospitality to him. (Ge 24:28-32) Laban subsequently took a leading part in the negotiations concerning the marriage of Rebekah, the approval for the marriage coming from both him and his father, Bethuel.—Ge 24:50-61.

Years later, to escape Esau's vengeance and to obtain a wife, Jacob traveled to the home of his uncle Laban at Haran. (Ge 27:41–28:5) By this time Laban had two daughters, Leah and Rachel (Ge 29:16), and possibly also sons. (Ge 31:1) Laban made an agreement with Jacob that for seven years of service he would receive Laban's younger daughter Rachel as wife. However, Laban tricked Jacob on his wedding night by substituting the older daughter Leah for Rachel, brushing Jacob's protests aside by appealing to local custom and then offering Rachel to Jacob as a second wife, if Jacob would serve him for an additional seven years.—Ge 29:13-28.

When Jacob finally wished to depart, Laban urged him to remain and continue serving him for wages. (Ge 30:25-28) The agreement was that Jacob could keep for himself all the speckled and color-patched sheep, the dark-brown sheep among the young rams, and any color-patched and speckled she-goats. (Ge 30:31-34) But Jacob's later words to Leah and Rachel and also to Laban (Ge 31:4-9, 41) indicate that during succeeding years Laban frequently altered this original agreement when it turned out that Jacob's flocks were increasing greatly. Laban's attitude toward Jacob was not the same as formerly, and at Jehovah's direction Jacob decided to return to his homeland with his family and flocks.—Ge 31:1-5, 13, 17, 18.

On the third day after Jacob's secret departure, Laban learned of it and pursued Jacob, catching up with him in the mountainous region of Gilead. However, a warning from God prevented Laban from harming Jacob. (Ge 31:19-24) When they met, Laban and Jacob quarreled. Jacob pointed to his 20 years of faithful service and hard work and showed how Laban had dealt with him unfairly, changing his wages ten times.—Ge 31:36-42.

Laban was very concerned about retrieving the teraphim, or household idols, which Rachel, unknown to Jacob, had stolen. These he was unable to find, for Rachel kept them concealed. Laban may have become influenced in his religious ideas by the moon-worshiping people among whom he dwelt, and this may be indicated by his use of omens and his possession of teraphim. However, it should be noted that it was likely more than merely religious reasons that made Laban so anxious to locate and retrieve the teraphim. Tablets unearthed at Nuzi near Kirkuk, Iraq, reveal that, according to the laws of patriarchal times in that particular area, possession of such household idols by a woman's husband could give him the right to appear in court and claim the estate of his deceased father-in-law. Hence, Laban may have thought that Jacob himself stole the teraphim in order to dispossess Laban's own sons later. This may explain why, on failing to locate the household gods, Laban was anxious to conclude an agreement with Jacob that would ensure that Jacob would not go back with the household gods after Laban's death to deprive his sons of their inheritance.—Ge 31:30-35, 41-52.

Laban made a covenant of family peace with Jacob, and to memorialize it, a stone pillar and a heap of stones were set up. Using Hebrew, Jacob called the heap Galeed, meaning "Witness Heap." Laban called it Jegar-sahadutha, using an Aramaic, or Syrian, expression having the same meaning. It was also called "The Watchtower." (Ge 31:43-53) After bidding his grandchildren and daughters farewell, Laban returned home, and the Bible record makes no further mention of him. —Ge 31:54, 55.

2. A place mentioned at Deuteronomy 1:1 in relation to "the desert plains in front of Suph." The exact location of Laban is unknown.

LABDANUM (lab'da·num). A soft, black or dark-brown gum that exudes from the leaves and branches of several varieties of *Cistus*, or rockrose. The gum has a bitter taste but a fragrant odor. It is used in perfumes and, at one time, was also extensively employed in medicine. With reference to this substance the ancient Greek historian Herodotus (III, 112) wrote: "It is gathered from the beards of he-goats, where it is found sticking like gum, having come from the bushes on which they browse. It is used in many sorts of unguents [ointments], and is what the Arabs burn chiefly as incense."—Translation by G. Rawlinson.

The Hebrew word *nekho'th'* designates this item carried by a caravan of Ishmaelites to whom Joseph was sold and one of the fine products that Jacob told his sons to take as a gift to one who was ruler in Egypt. (Ge 37:25; 43:11) *Nekho'th'* has been variously rendered "spices" (*KJ*), "gum" (*AT, RS*), "tragacanth" (*Da*), "resin" (*Mo*), and, as defined by Koehler and Baumgartner, "labdanum" (*NW*).—*Lexicon in Veteris Testamenti Libros*, Leiden, 1958, p. 615.

LABOR.   See FORCED LABOR; HIRED LABORER.

LABOR PAINS.   The tribulation associated with giving birth. God expressed to the first woman, Eve, after she had sinned, what the result would be as to childbearing. If she had remained obedient, God's blessing would have continued upon her and childbearing would have been an unmixed joy, for, "the blessing of Jehovah—that is what makes rich, and he adds no pain with it." (Pr 10:22) But now, as a general rule, the imperfect functioning of the body would bring pain. Accordingly, God said (as often the things that he *permits* are said to be *done* by him): "I shall greatly increase the pain of your pregnancy; in birth pangs you will bring forth children."—Ge 3:16.

The Hebrew expression in this passage of Scripture is, literally, "your pain and your pregnancy" and is rendered by some translations "thy sorrow and thy conception." (*KJ; Yg*) But the grammatical form used is called hendiadys, in which two words are connected by "and" though one thing is meant. Modern translations render the expression accordingly. (*AT; Mo; RS*) So it is not stated that conception would necessarily increase, but that the pain would.

It is true that the pain of pregnancy and childbearing may be relieved by medical treatment and may even be prevented to some extent by care and preparatory methods. But, generally, childbirth remains a physically distressing experience.—Ge 35:16-20; Isa 26:17.

Symbolic Use. Despite labor pains associated with childbearing, there is happiness attendant upon the birth of a child. When Jesus Christ spoke intimately with his apostles on the evening before his death, he used this circumstance as an illustration. He explained to them that he was going to leave them and then went on to say: "Most truly I say to you, You will weep and wail, but the world will rejoice; you will be grieved, but your grief will be turned into joy. A woman, when she is giving birth, has grief, because her hour has arrived; but when she has brought forth the young child, she remembers the tribulation no more because of the joy that a man has been born into the world. You also, therefore, are now, indeed, having grief; but I shall see you again and your hearts will rejoice, and your joy no one will take from you."—Joh 16:20-22.

This painful time did come upon them for parts of three days, when they doubtless wept and 'afflicted their souls' by fasting. (Lu 5:35; compare Ps 35:13.) But early on the morning of the third day, Nisan 16, and for 40 days after that, the resurrected Jesus appeared to certain of the disciples. Imagine their joy! On the day of Pentecost, the 50th day from Jesus' resurrection, God's holy spirit was poured out upon them, and they became joyful witnesses of his resurrection, first in Jerusalem and later in distant parts of the earth. (Ac 1:3, 8) And no one could take their joy away. —Joh 16:22.

The psalmist described a gathering of kings as they viewed the splendor and magnificence of God's holy city Zion, with its towers and ramparts of strength. He says: "They themselves saw; and so they were amazed. They got disturbed, they were sent running in panic. Trembling itself took hold of them there, birth pangs like those of a woman giving birth." (Ps 48:1-6) The psalm apparently describes an actual occurrence in which enemy kings were panic stricken in a projected attack on Jerusalem.

Jeremiah, in prophesying defeat to come upon mighty Babylon, told of a people from the north, the report about whom would cause the king of Babylon to have severe pains, like a woman giving birth. This was fulfilled when Cyrus came against Babylon and particularly when the mysterious handwriting appeared on the wall at Babylonian King Belshazzar's feast. This the prophet Daniel interpreted to Belshazzar as portending the imme-

diate fall of Babylon to the Medes and Persians. —Jer 50:41-43; Da 5:5, 6, 28.

Concerning the coming of "Jehovah's day," the apostle Paul explained that it would be when the cry of "Peace and security!" is being proclaimed. Then "sudden destruction is to be instantly upon them just as the pang of distress upon a pregnant woman; and they will by no means escape." (1Th 5:2, 3) Labor pains come suddenly, the exact day and hour not being foreknown. The pains first are about 15 to 20 minutes apart, becoming closer together as labor advances. In most cases the time of labor is relatively short, especially in its second stage, but once labor pains begin, the woman knows that a birth is approaching and that the ordeal must be undergone. There is no "escape."

In the apostle John's vision in Revelation he saw a heavenly woman crying out "in her pains and in her agony to give birth." The child born was "a son, a male, who is to shepherd all the nations with an iron rod." In spite of the dragon's efforts to devour it, "her child was caught away to God and to his throne." (Re 12:1, 2, 4-6) The son's being caught away by God would denote God's acceptance of the child as his own, even as it was customary in ancient times to present a newborn child before its father for acceptance. (See BIRTH.) It would follow that the "woman" is God's "wife," the "Jerusalem above," the "mother" of Christ and his spiritual brothers.—Ga 4:26; Heb 2:11, 12, 17.

God's heavenly "woman" would, of course, be perfect, and the birth would be without literal pain. The labor pains would, therefore, symbolically indicate that the "woman" would realize that the birth was at hand; she would be in expectation of it shortly.—Re 12:2.

Who would this "son, a male," be? He was to "shepherd all the nations with an iron rod." This was foretold of God's Messianic King, at Psalm 2:6-9. But John saw this vision long after Christ's birth on earth and his death and resurrection. The vision would therefore appear to refer to the birth of the Messianic Kingdom in the hands of God's Son Jesus Christ, who, on being raised from the dead, "sat down at the right hand of God, from then on awaiting until his enemies should be placed as a stool for his feet."—Heb 10:12, 13; Ps 110:1; Re 12:10.

This was an expected event, and as the time drew near, the expectation of it in heaven and on earth would become great, for fulfilled prophecy would be a sure indication of its nearness. So it would be, as the apostle pointed out to Christians, with the coming of "Jehovah's day": "Now as for the times and the seasons, brothers, you need nothing to be written to you." "You, brothers, you are not in darkness, so that that day should overtake you as it would thieves."—1Th 5:1, 4.

LACHISH (La'chish). A Judean city in the Shephelah. (Jos 15:21, 33, 39) Lachish is identified with Tell ed-Duweir (Tel Lakhish), a mound surrounded by valleys and lying some 24 km (15 mi) W of Hebron. Anciently this site occupied a strategic position on the principal road linking Jerusalem with Egypt. At one time the city covered an area of about 8 ha (20 acres) and perhaps had a population numbering between 6,000 and 7,500 persons.

At the time of Israel's conquest of Canaan, Japhia the king of Lachish joined four other kings in a military offensive against Gibeon, a city that had made peace with Joshua. (Jos 10:1-5) In response to Gibeon's appeal for aid, the Israelite army staged an all-night march from Gilgal. With Jehovah's help, they defeated the Canaanite alliance, trapped the kings themselves in a cave, and thereafter executed them. (Jos 10:6-27; 12:11) Later, the city of Lachish was taken in less than two days of fighting and its inhabitants were slain. Also, Horam the king of Gezer, who came to the aid of Lachish, suffered defeat.—Jos 10:31-35.

Some archaeologists link Israel's campaign against Lachish with a thick layer of ash uncovered at Tell ed-Duweir, in which, among other things, a scarab of Ramses was found. But the Bible does not state that the city was burned, as it does in the case of Jericho (Jos 6:24, 25), Ai (Jos 8:28), and Hazor (Jos 11:11). Rather, Joshua 11:13 seems to indicate that the Israelites rarely burned "cities standing on their own mounds." So there is no Scriptural basis for placing the destruction causing the ash layer in the time of Joshua and then dating the Israelite conquest of Canaan accordingly. It is also noteworthy that the Ramses to whom the scarab should be assigned cannot be definitely ascertained. At least one archaeologist attributed the scarab to Ramses III and advanced the thought that Lachish was destroyed by the Philistines in the 12th century B.C.E.

During Rehoboam's reign (997-981 B.C.E.) Lachish was strengthened militarily. (2Ch 11:5-12) Later, in about 830 B.C.E., King Amaziah fled to Lachish to escape conspirators but was pursued and put to death there.—2Ki 14:19; 2Ch 25:27.

Besieged by Sennacherib. Lachish was besieged by Assyrian King Sennacherib in 732 B.C.E. From there he sent Rabshakeh, Tartan, and Rabsaris with a heavy military force to Jerusalem in an effort to move King Hezekiah to surrender.

Through his chief spokesman Rabshakeh, Sennacherib defied Jehovah and later sent messengers to Jerusalem with letters of continued taunt and threat designed to bring about Hezekiah's surrender. This defiance of Jehovah God finally led to the annihilation by God's angel of 185,000 Assyrian warriors in one night.—2Ki 18:14, 17-35; 19:8-13, 32-35; Isa 36:1-20; 37:8-13, 33-36.

A portrayal of the siege of Lachish, from Sennacherib's palace at Nineveh, indicates that the city was encompassed by a double wall having towers at regular intervals and that palms, grapes, and figs flourished in the surrounding hilly area. The scene showing Sennacherib receiving the spoils of Lachish is accompanied by the following inscription: "Sennacherib, king of the world, king of Assyria, sat upon a *nimedu* -throne and passed in review the booty (taken) from Lachish (*La-ki-su*)."—*Ancient Near Eastern Texts*, edited by J. B. Pritchard, 1974, p. 288.

Captured by Babylonians. When the Babylonians under Nebuchadnezzar overran Judah (609-607 B.C.E.), Lachish and Azekah were the last two fortified cities to fall before Jerusalem was taken. (Jer 34:6, 7) What are known as the Lachish Letters (written on pottery fragments, 18 of which were found at Tell ed-Duweir in 1935 and 3 more in 1938) appear to relate to this period. One of these letters, evidently directed by a military outpost to the commander at Lachish, reads in part: "We are watching for the signals of Lachish, according to all the indications which my lord hath given, for we cannot see Azekah." This message suggests that Azekah had already been taken so that no signals were received from there. It is also of interest that nearly all the legible Lachish Letters contain words such as "May יהוה [Yahweh or Jehovah] cause my lord to hear this very day tidings of good!" (Lachish Ostracon IV) This shows that the divine name was then in common use. —*Ancient Near Eastern Texts*, p. 322.

After Judah and Jerusalem lay desolate for 70 years, Lachish was reoccupied by the returning Jewish exiles.—Ne 11:25, 30.

Prophetic Mention. At Micah 1:13, Lachish is addressed prophetically: "Attach the chariot to the team of horses, O inhabitress of Lachish. The beginning of sin was what she was to the daughter of Zion, for in you the revolts of Israel have been found." These words constitute part of a picture of defeat and appear to suggest that Lachish prepare for flight. The "sin" of Lachish is not discussed elsewhere in Scripture. Perhaps a form of idolatry introduced in Jerusalem originated at

Lachish. Or, the sin possibly involved Judah's reliance on horses and chariots, which may have been received at Lachish from Egypt.

LADAN (La'dan).

1. An Ephraimite ancestor of Joshua.—1Ch 7:22, 26, 27.

2. A Gershonite Levite from whom several paternal houses originated. (1Ch 23:7-9; 26:21) He evidently was also called Libni.—Ex 6:17.

LADDER. The only Biblical reference to a ladder is at Genesis 28:12, where the Hebrew term *sul·lam'* applies to a ladder Jacob beheld in a dream. The patriarch saw a ladder (or perhaps what looked like a rising flight of stones) stationed upon the earth, with its top reaching up to the heavens. God's angels were ascending and descending on the ladder, and a representation of Jehovah God was above it. (Ge 28:13) This ladder with the angels upon it indicates the existence of communication between earth and heaven and that angels minister in an important way between God and those having his approval.

When Jesus said to his disciples, "Most truly I say to you men, You will see heaven opened up and the angels of God ascending and descending to the Son of man," he may have had in mind Jacob's vision.—Joh 1:51.

Scaling ladders were part of siege equipment used during warfare and are frequently depicted on Egyptian and Assyrian monuments. A relief from Nineveh shows the Assyrians employing siege ladders when assaulting Lachish.

Ladders served other purposes in ancient times, as in the building trades. For instance, they are shown on the Ur-Nammu stele depicting the construction of a ziggurat. Also, in an Assyrian relief from Tell Halaf, considered to be of the ninth century B.C.E., a man is shown climbing a date-palm tree by means of a ladder.

LADY. See QUEEN.

LAEL (La'el) [Belonging to God]. A Levite and the father of Eliasaph, the chieftain of the paternal house for the Gershonites during Israel's trek in the wilderness.—Nu 3:24.

LAHAD (La'had). A descendant of Judah and the second named of Jahath's two sons.—1Ch 4:1, 2.

LAHMAM (Lah'mam). A Judean city in the Shephelah. (Jos 15:20, 33, 40) It is usually identified with Khirbet el-Lahm (Horvat Lehem), about 5 km (3 mi) E of Lachish.

LAHMI (Lah'mi) [My Bread]. The brother of Goliath the Gittite. The account at 1 Chronicles 20:5 reads, in part, "Elhanan the son of Jair got to strike down Lahmi the brother of Goliath the Gittite," during a war with the Philistines. However, in a parallel text at 2 Samuel 21:19 the reading is: "Elhanan the son of Jaare-oregim the Bethlehemite got to strike down Goliath the Gittite." In the latter text it appears that *'eth-lach·mi'* (in English, "Lahmi," the Hebrew term *'eth* merely denoting that Lahmi is the object of a verb) was misread by a copyist to be *behth hal·lach·mi'* ("Bethlehemite"). Therefore the original probably read, "got to strike down Lahmi," just as the parallel text at 1 Chronicles 20:5 reads. This would make the two texts harmonize on this point. Lahmi, then, was evidently the brother of the Goliath that David killed. On the other hand, it is possible that there were two Goliaths.—See GOLIATH.

LAISH (La'ish) [Lion].

1. A man from Gallim, the father of Palti (Paltiel), to whom Saul gave as a wife his daughter Michal, previously the wife of David.—1Sa 25:44; 2Sa 3:15.

2. A northern Canaanite city destroyed by the Danites, who thereafter rebuilt it and gave it the name of Dan (Jg 18:27-29); also called Leshem. —Jos 19:47; see DAN No. 3.

LAISHAH (La'i·shah) [Lion]. A town in the territory of Benjamin identified by F.-M. Abel (*Géographie de la Palestine*, Paris, 1938, Vol. II, p. 368) with 'Isawiya, about 2.5 km (1.5 mi) NNE of the Temple Mount in Jerusalem. Isaiah's prophetic foreview of the rampaging Assyrian, as he advances village by village, calls on Laishah to "pay attention" to the coming attack.—Isa 10:30.

LAKE OF FIRE. This expression occurs only in the book of Revelation and is clearly symbolic. The Bible gives its own explanation and definition of the symbol by stating: "This means *the second death,* the lake of fire."—Re 20:14; 21:8.

The symbolic quality of the lake of fire is further evident from the context of references to it in the book of Revelation. Death is said to be hurled into this lake of fire. (Re 20:14, 20) Death obviously cannot be literally burned. Moreover, the Devil, an invisible spirit creature, is thrown into the lake. Being spirit, he cannot be hurt by literal fire.—Re 20:10; compare Ex 3:2 and Jg 13:20.

Since the lake of fire represents "the *second death*" and since Revelation 20:14 says that both "death and Hades" are to be cast into it, it is evident that the lake cannot represent the death man has inherited from Adam (Ro 5:12), nor does it refer to Hades (Sheol). It must, therefore, be symbolic of another kind of death, one that is without reversal, for the record nowhere speaks of the "lake" as giving up those in it, as do Adamic death and Hades (Sheol). (Re 20:13) Thus, those not found written in "the book of life," unrepentant opposers of God's sovereignty, are hurled into the lake of fire, meaning eternal destruction, or the second death.—Re 20:15.

While the foregoing texts make evident the symbolic quality of the lake of fire, it has been used by some persons to support belief in a literal place of fire and torment. Revelation 20:10 has been appealed to, because it speaks of the Devil, the wild beast, and the false prophet as being "tormented day and night forever and ever" in the lake of fire. However, this cannot refer to actual conscious torment. Those thrown into the lake of fire undergo "the second death." (Re 20:14) In death there is no consciousness and, hence, no feeling of pain or suffering.—Ec 9:5.

In the Scriptures fiery torment is associated with destruction and death. For example, in the Greek *Septuagint* translation of the Hebrew Scriptures the word for torment (*ba·sa·nos*) is several times used with reference to punishment by death. (Eze 3:20; 32:24, 30) Similarly, concerning Babylon the Great, the book of Revelation says, "the kings of the earth . . . will weep and beat themselves in grief over her, when they look at the smoke from the burning of her, while they stand at a distance because of their fear of her torment [Gr., *ba·sa·ni·smou'*]." (Re 18:9, 10) As to the meaning of the torment, an angel later explains: "Thus with a swift pitch will Babylon the great city be hurled down, and she will never be found again." (Re 18:21) So, fiery torment here is parallel with destruction, and in the case of Babylon the Great, it is everlasting destruction. —Compare Re 17:16; 18:8, 15-17, 19.

Therefore, those who are 'tormented forever' (from Gr., *ba·sa·ni'zo*) in the lake of fire undergo "second death" from which there is no resurrection. The related Greek word *ba·sa·ni·stes'* is translated 'jailer' in Matthew 18:34. (*RS, NW, ED;* compare vs 30.) Thus those hurled into the lake of fire will be held under restraint, or "jailed," in death throughout eternity.—See GEHENNA; TORMENT.

LAKKUM (Lak'kum). A boundary site of Naphtali. (Jos 19:32, 33) It is possibly Khirbet Kushsha (Horvat Kush), by the Jordan River just S of the Sea of Galilee.

LAMB.   See SHEEP.

LAME, LAMENESS.   A physical handicap that prevents a person from walking normally. Lameness may date from birth because of congenital deformities (Ac 3:2; 14:8), but most cases are caused by accidents or diseases.

Aaronic Priesthood.   A lame person who was a descendant of Aaron could not serve in the priesthood, although he was allowed to eat from the things provided for the priesthood for their sustenance. (Le 21:16-23) Jehovah set a high standard of physical fitness for his priesthood, for these represented him at his sanctuary. (Le 21:17-23) So, too, Christ, the great High Priest, was "loyal, guileless, undefiled, separated from the sinners."—Heb 7:26.

Sacrifices.   It was also forbidden, under the Law, to offer as a sacrifice any animal with a defect of lameness, because these foreshadowed the perfect sacrifice of Christ. (De 15:21; Le 22:19, 20) This law was violated by the apostate Israelites, for which God reproved them, saying: "When you present a lame animal [for sacrificing, you say]: 'It is nothing bad.' Bring it near, please, to your governor. Will he find pleasure in you, or will he receive you kindly? . . . Can I take pleasure in it at your hand?" (Mal 1:8, 13) The apostle evidently applies this requirement in a spiritual way to Christians, entreating them: "Present your bodies a sacrifice living, holy, acceptable to God, a sacred service with your power of reason."—Ro 12:1.

Jacob's Lameness.   When Jacob was about 97 years old, he had the experience of grappling all night with a materialized angel of God. He prevailed in detaining the angel until the angel gave him a blessing. During the contest, the angel touched the socket of Jacob's thigh joint, throwing it out of place. The result was that Jacob walked with a limp. (Ge 32:24-32; Ho 12:2-4) Jacob thereafter had a reminder that, although he had "contended with God [God's angel] and with men so that [he] at last prevailed," as the angel said, he did not in reality defeat a powerful angel of God. It was only by God's purpose and permission that Jacob was allowed to contend with the angel, so as to provide proof of Jacob's great appreciation of the need of God's blessing.

Consideration.   The Scriptures inculcate consideration for the lame. Job remarked that, even in his prosperous state, "feet to the lame one I was." (Job 29:15) Jesus and his disciples had compassion for the sick and lame, performing many cures of such persons.—Mt 11:4, 5; 15:30, 31; 21:14; Ac 3:1-10; 8:5-7; 14:8-10.

Illustrative and Figurative Uses.   The Jebusites illustrated their boastful confidence in the security of their citadel when they taunted David:

"'You will not come in here, but the blind and the lame ones will certainly turn you away,' they thinking: 'David will not come in here.'" They may have actually placed such persons on the wall as defenders, as is stated by Josephus (*Jewish Antiquities*, VII, 61 [iii, 1]), and this may be the reason why David said: "Anyone striking the Jebusites, let him, by means of the water tunnel, make contact with both the lame and the blind, hateful to the soul of David!" These lame and blind ones were the symbol of the Jebusites' insult to David and, more seriously, their taunt against the armies of Jehovah. David hated the Jebusites, along with their lame and blind, for such arrogance. He may actually have been calling the Jebusite leaders themselves 'the lame and blind,' in derision. —2Sa 5:6-8.

As to the statement in verse 8, "That is why they say: 'The blind one and the lame one will not come into the house,'" several explanations have been offered. In the text this statement is not attributed to David and may mean that others developed this proverbial saying with regard to those who, like the Jebusites, boasted or were overconfident of their secure position. Or, the saying might have meant, 'No one who holds intercourse with disagreeable people like the Jebusites will enter.' Others would render the text, "because the blind and the lame continued to say, He shall not come into this house," or, "Because they had said, even the blind and the lame, He shall not come into the house."—Barrett's *Synopsis of Criticisms*, London, 1847, Vol. II, Part II, p. 518; *KJ* margin.

On a later occasion, Elijah asked the Israelites: "How long will you be limping upon two different opinions? If Jehovah is the true God, go following him; but if Baal is, go following him." At that time the Israelites were claiming to worship Jehovah but at the same time were worshiping Baal. Their course was unsteady and halting, like that of a lame man. During the contest that ensued, when the prophets of Baal were vainly trying from morning till noon to get their god to answer them, "they kept limping around the altar that they had made." This may be a mocking description of the ritualistic dance or hobble of the fanatical Baal worshipers, or it may be that they limped because of their tiredness from the long, futile ritual.—1Ki 18:21-29.

Limping, lameness, and stumbling are used in figures of speech to denote halting irregularity or unsteadiness in one's course of life, purpose, or speech. Bildad, supposedly warning Job of dangers ahead for him, said of a person taking a wicked course: "Disaster stands ready to make him limp." (Job 18:12) In a similar figure David and Jeremiah spoke of their enemies as waiting for them to make an unsteady step, watching for them to limp, so that, as Jeremiah's foes said, "we may prevail against him and take our revenge upon him." (Jer 20:10; Ps 38:16, 17) The enemies of Jesus Christ wanted to see him stumble, or limp, in his speech so as to entrap him.—Mt 22:15.

Proverbial usage. "As one that is mutilating his feet [which would make him lame], as one that is drinking mere violence, is he that is thrusting matters into the hand of someone stupid," said wise King Solomon. Truly, the man employing a stupid person to handle any project for him is doing crippling violence to his own interests. He is certain to see his proposed work collapse, with damage to himself.—Pr 26:6.

The Proverbs continue with a like illustration: "Have the legs of the lame one drawn up water? Then there is a proverb in the mouth of stupid people." (Pr 26:7) In ancient times, especially in cities built upon mounds, it was often necessary to climb down a ladder or a long stairway to bring water up from a well. A stupid person trying to speak or apply a proverb is as clumsy and ineffective as a lame man trying to carry water up a stairway.

God's ancient nation. In speaking of the restoration of his people, Jehovah promised to strengthen them to leave Babylon and to undertake the hazardous journey back to desolated Jerusalem. Any spiritual lameness, hesitancy, or indecision would be removed. Through the prophet Isaiah, God encouraged them: "At that time the lame one will climb up just as a stag does." (Isa 35:6) God's nation had limped and suffered a fall into captivity, but "in that day," said Jehovah, "I will gather her that was limping; . . . and I shall certainly make her that was limping a remnant, and her that was removed far off a mighty nation."—Mic 4:6, 7; Zep 3:19.

Further comforting his people, Jehovah promised, as their King, to protect them from aggressors. He described the helplessness of Zion's enemies as a ship with its tacklings loosed, its mast wobbling, and its sail gone. Then he said: "At that time even spoil [of the enemy] in abundance will have to be divided up; the lame ones themselves will actually take a big plunder." There would be so much spoil that even those not usually able to have part in taking plunder would at that time be able to share.—Isa 33:23.

Consideration for spiritually lame ones. The Christian writer of the letter to the Hebrews pointed out that among them were many spiritually immature ones, who should be making better progress. (Heb 5:12-14) Then, after speaking of discipline, he said: "Keep making straight paths for your feet, that what is lame may not be put out of joint, but rather that it may be healed." (Heb 12:13) Even stronger ones should carefully watch how they walk in their Christian course, so that the weaker, spiritually "lame" ones would not stumble or injure themselves. If those stronger in faith used their spiritual freedom to do certain things that were lawful, those weaker in faith might be stumbled by their actions.—Ro 15:1.

The apostle Paul sets forth as an example of this principle the matter of eating and drinking. (Ro 14:13-18, 21) In this passage he counsels, in part: "Make this your decision, not to put before a brother a stumbling block or a cause for tripping." He says: "It is well not to eat flesh or to drink wine or do anything over which your brother stumbles."—Compare 1Co 8:7-13.

On the other hand, the apostle shows, a Christian should strengthen his own spiritual 'legs' so that he will not limp or be stumbled by what occurs or by what someone else does. He should make himself strong so as to keep steady in the Christian course. Paul says: "Let the one eating not look down on the one not eating, and let the one not eating not judge the one eating, for God has welcomed that one." (Ro 14:3) This principle was expressed by the psalmist: "Abundant peace belongs to those loving your law, and for them there is no stumbling block." (Ps 119:165) Those loving God's law will not be caused to limp with spiritual lameness over any matter.

Complete Healing. Lameness has caused many tears. Just as Jesus Christ healed many lame and maimed persons when he was on earth, even restoring dried-up body parts (Mr 3:1, 5; compare Lu 22:50, 51), by means of "a new heaven" God's Son will again perform similar cures. This he will accomplish completely as High Priest and King appointed by God, wiping out every tear from the eyes of humankind.—Mt 8:16, 17; Re 21:1, 4.

LAMECH   (La′mech).

1. The son of Methushael and a descendant of Cain. (Ge 4:17, 18) His lifetime and Adam's overlapped. Lamech had two wives, Adah and Zillah, at the same time and is the first polygamist of Bible record. (Ge 4:19) By Adah he had sons named Jabal, "the founder of those who dwell in tents and have livestock," and Jubal, "the founder of all those who handle the harp and the pipe." (Ge 4:20, 21) By Zillah, Lamech became the father of Tubal-cain, "the forger of every sort of tool of copper and iron," and a daughter named Naamah. —Ge 4:22.

The poem that Lamech composed for his wives (Ge 4:23, 24) reflects the violent spirit of that day. Lamech's poem ran: "Hear my voice, you wives of Lamech; give ear to my saying: A man I have killed for wounding me, yes, a young man for giving me a blow. If seven times Cain is to be avenged, then Lamech seventy times and seven." Evidently Lamech was presenting a case of self-defense, pleading that his act was not one of deliberate murder, like that of Cain. Lamech claimed that, in defending himself, he had killed the man who struck and wounded him. Therefore, his poem stood as a plea for immunity against anyone desiring to get revenge against him for killing his attacker.

It appears that none of Cain's descendants, which would include Lamech's offspring, survived the Flood.

2. A descendant of Seth; son of Methuselah and father of Noah. (Ge 5:25, 28, 29; 1Ch 1:1-4) The lifetimes of this Lamech and Adam likewise overlapped. Lamech had faith in God, and after calling his son's name Noah (probably meaning "Rest; Consolation"), he uttered the words: "This one will bring us comfort from our work and from the pain of our hands resulting from the ground which Jehovah has cursed." (Ge 5:29) These words found fulfillment when the curse on the ground was lifted during Noah's lifetime. (Ge 8:21) Lamech had other sons and daughters. He lived 777 years, dying about five years before the Flood. (Ge 5:30, 31) His name is listed in the genealogy of Jesus Christ at Luke 3:36.

LAMEDH   [ל] (la′medh).

The 12th letter in the Hebrew alphabet. *La′medh* corresponds generally to the English "l." In the Hebrew, the psalmist uses this letter at the beginning of each of the eight verses at Psalm 119:89-96.

LAMENTATIONS, BOOK OF.

In Biblical days lamentations, or dirges, were composed and chanted for deceased friends (2Sa 1:17-27), devastated nations (Am 5:1, 2), and ruined cities (Eze 27:2, 32-36). The book of Lamentations furnishes an inspired example of such mournful composition. It consists of five lyrical poems (in five chapters) lamenting the destruction of Jerusalem at Babylonian hands in 607 B.C.E.

The book acknowledges that Jehovah justly brought punishment upon Jerusalem and Judah because of the error of his people. (La 1:5, 18) It also highlights God's loving-kindness and mercy and shows that Jehovah is good to the one hoping in him.—La 3:22, 25.

Name. In the Hebrew this book is named by the opening word *'Eh·khah'!*, which means "How!" The *Septuagint* translators called the book *Thre'-noi*, meaning "Dirges; Laments." In the Babylonian Talmud (*Bava Batra* 14*b*) it is identified by the term *Qi·nohth'*, meaning "Dirges; Elegies," and it is called *Lamentationes* (Latin) by Jerome. The English name Lamentations comes from this latter title.

Place in the Bible Canon. In the Hebrew canon the book of Lamentations is usually counted in among the five *Meghil·lohth'* (Rolls), consisting of The Song of Solomon, Ruth, Lamentations, Ecclesiastes, and Esther. However, in ancient copies of the Hebrew Scriptures the book of Lamentations is said to have followed the book of Jeremiah, as it does in English Bibles of today.

Writer. In the Greek *Septuagint* this book is introduced with the words: "And it occurred that, after Israel had been taken captive and Jerusalem had been desolated, Jeremiah sat down weeping and lamented with this lamentation over Jerusalem and said." The Targums also identify Jeremiah as the writer, introducing it as follows: "Jeremiah the prophet and great priest said." The introduction in the Clementine recension of the Latin *Vulgate* is: "And it occurred that, after Israel had been led away into captivity and Jerusalem was deserted, Jeremiah the prophet sat weeping and wailed with this lamentation over Jerusalem;

and sighing with a bitter spirit, and moaning woefully, he said."

Style. The five chapters of the book of Lamentations consist of five poems, the first four of which are acrostics. The Hebrew alphabet has 22 distinct letters (consonants) and in each of the first four chapters of Lamentations successive verses begin with different ones of the 22 letters of the Hebrew alphabet. Chapters 1, 2, and 4 each have 22 verses arranged alphabetically according to the Hebrew alphabet, verse 1 beginning with the first Hebrew letter *'a'leph*, verse 2 commencing with the second letter, *behth*, and so forth, to the end of the alphabet. Chapter 3 has 66 verses, and in it three successive verses begin with the same Hebrew letter before passing on to the next letter.

In chapters 2, 3, and 4 there is a reversal of the letters *'a'yin* and *pe'* (there they are not in the same order as in Lamentations 1 and Ps 119). But this does not mean that the inspired writer of Lamentations made a mistake. It has been observed in a consideration of this matter: "Still less does the irregularity in question permit of being attributed to an oversight on the part of the composer . . . , for the irregularity is repeated in three poems. It is rather connected with another circumstance. For we find in other alphabetic poems also, especially the older ones, many deviations from the rule, which undeniably prove that the composers bound themselves rigorously by the order of the alphabet only so long as it fitted in to

---

HIGHLIGHTS OF LAMENTATIONS

Five poems lamenting the tragedy that befell Jerusalem and its inhabitants in 607 B.C.E. at the hands of the Babylonians

Written by Jeremiah immediately after the destruction of Jerusalem

Jerusalem is personified as a widow bereaved of her children, with no one to give comfort (1:1-22)

She acknowledges that her sin against Jehovah is the reason for her distress

She prays for the Almighty to punish those who rejoice over her suffering

Jehovah has acted in anger against Jerusalem (2:1-22)

He has thrown Jerusalem down "from heaven to earth"

He has spurned his sanctuary and shown no respect for king and priest

As a result, passersby are amazed at what has happened to the city that was "the perfection of prettiness"

The "able-bodied man," representing the nation, speaks of his affliction, yet expresses hope (3:1-66)

He describes his present desperate situation

Nevertheless, he is confident that Jehovah will hear his people's prayers and show mercy

Terrible effects of the siege of Jerusalem (4:1-22)

Death by the sword was better than death from the famine; women even ate their own children

Fleeing survivors were relentlessly pursued in mountainous and wilderness regions

Jehovah is petitioned to note the people's suffering and to restore them to favor (5:1-22)

His people's hereditary possession has been given to strangers

They have been shamed and debased

They pray for Jehovah to bring them back to himself even though he rejected them with indignation

the course of thought without any artificiality." (*Commentary on the Old Testament,* by C. F. Keil and F. Delitzsch, 1973, Vol. VIII, The Lamentations of Jeremiah, p. 338) Among examples then cited are Psalm 34, where the *waw* verse is lacking, and Psalm 145, which omits the *nun* verse. The fact that strict adherence to the alphabetic arrangement of Hebrew letters is not present in these inspired writings should cause no concern. While the use of acrostics undoubtedly served as a memory aid, the message was of primary importance, and thought content took precedence over any literary device.

Lamentations chapter 5 is not an acrostic poem, though it does contain 22 verses, the same number as the distinct letters of the Hebrew alphabet.

Time of Composition. The vividness of Lamentations shows that the book was written shortly after Jerusalem's fall in 607 B.C.E., while the events of the Babylonian siege and burning of Jerusalem were still fresh in the mind of Jeremiah. There is general agreement that the book of Lamentations was penned soon after Jerusalem's fall, and it is reasonable to conclude that the writing of it was completed in 607 B.C.E.

Fulfillment of Prophecy. Fulfilled in Jerusalem's experience as vividly portrayed in the book of Lamentations were the words of Deuteronomy 28:63-65. The fulfillment of various other divine prophecies and warnings is also shown in this book. For example, compare Lamentations 1:2 with Jeremiah 30:14; Lamentations 2:17 with Leviticus 26:17; Lamentations 2:20 with Deuteronomy 28:53.

Contents. In the first chapter, beginning with verse 12, Jeremiah personifies Jerusalem, God's covenant "woman" Zion, as speaking. (Isa 62:1-6) She is now desolate, as though widowed and bereft of her children, a captive woman put into forced labor as a slave. In chapter 2, Jeremiah himself speaks. In chapter 3, Jeremiah pours out his feelings, transferring them to the figure of the nation as an "able-bodied man." In chapter 4, Jeremiah continues his lament. In the fifth chapter, the inhabitants of Jerusalem are pictured as speaking. The expressions of acknowledgment of sin, the hope and confidence in Jehovah, and the desire to turn to the right way, as portrayed throughout, were not the actual feelings of the majority of the people. However, there was a remnant like Jeremiah. So the view expressed in the book of Lamentations is a true evaluation of Jerusalem's situation as God saw it.

The book of Lamentations is therefore a true and valuable record, inspired by God.

LAMP. A vessel used to produce artificial light. It has a wick for burning flammable liquids such as oil, the wick drawing up the fluid by capillary attraction to feed the flame. Wicks were made of flax (Isa 42:3; 43:17), peeled rush, or hemp. Olive oil was the fluid generally burned in ancient lamps (Ex 27:20), though oil from the terebinth tree was also used.

The five discreet virgins of Jesus' illustration each had a lamp and a receptacle containing oil. (Mt 25:1-4) Those who came to arrest Jesus were also carrying lamps and torches.—Joh 18:3.

*Ancient lamp decorated
with a stylized menorah*

Ordinarily, household lamps were made of earthenware, although bronze lamps have also been discovered in Palestine. The common Canaanite lamp was shaped like a saucer, having a rounded bottom and vertical rim. (PICTURES, Vol. 2, p. 952) Its rim was slightly pinched on one side, where the wick rested. Sometimes the rim was pinched at the four corners, providing four places for wicks. In time, lamps were made in somewhat different shapes, some being closed except for two holes, one on top (near the center) for filling the vessel with oil and the other being a spout for holding the wick. Certain lamps had a loop handle at the end opposite the spout, sometimes in a horizontal, but more often in a vertical position. The Greco-Roman type frequently bore mythological human or animal forms, but the Jews made lamps bearing such designs as vine leaves or scrolls.

Early saucer lamps were generally a shade of brown. Varieties made in the first century C.E. were of various colors, including light brown, red orange, and gray. Also, there were those of Roman times that were covered with red glaze.

The lamps generally used in homes and other buildings might be placed in a niche in the wall, or on a shelf on a wall or pillar, or they might be suspended from the ceiling by means of a cord. Sometimes they were placed on clay, wooden, or metal stands. Such lampstands permitted the light to radiate throughout the room.—2Ki 4:10; Mt 5:15; Mr 4:21.

There is no evidence that the candle as we know it today was used in Bible times. Whereas the flammable wax or fat of a modern candle is kept in the solid state until melted by the proximity of the flame, lamp oil, a liquid, was used in Biblical days. Hence, frequent rendering by the *King James Version* of the Hebrew *ner* and the Greek word *ly'khnos* as "candle" is inappropriate, as at Job 29:3 and Luke 11:33, where modern translations (such as *AT, NW, RS*) fittingly use "lamp."

Sanctuary Use. In Israel's tabernacle, the lampstand was made of gold and differed in design from common household lampstands. Made according to Jehovah God's instructions (Ex 25:31), it was ornamented with alternating knobs and blossoms and had three branches on each side of a central shaft, thus providing for seven holders in which small lamps were placed. Only fine beaten olive oil was used in these lamps. (Ex 37:17-24; 27:20) Later, Solomon had ten golden lampstands and a number of silver lampstands made for temple use.—1Ki 7:48, 49; 1Ch 28:15; 2Ch 4:19, 20; 13:11.

Jehovah a Lamp and Source of Light. Jehovah is the paramount Source of light and guidance. David, after being delivered out of the hand of his enemies and of Saul, said: "You are my lamp, O Jehovah, and it is Jehovah that makes my darkness shine." (2Sa 22:29) In the Psalms a slightly different expression is used: "You yourself will light my lamp, O Jehovah," there picturing Jehovah as the one kindling the lamp that David carried to light his way.—Ps 18:28.

Jesus Christ. In the heavenly New Jerusalem, as seen by the apostle John in vision, "night will not exist." The city's light is not that of the sun and moon, for Jehovah God's glory directly lights up the city, just as the cloud of light that the Hebrews called the Shechinah illuminated the Most Holy of the ancient tabernacle and temple. (Le 16:2; compare Nu 9:15, 16.) And the Lamb,

Jesus Christ, is its "lamp." This "city" will shed its spiritual light down upon the nations, the inhabiters of the "new earth," for their guidance.—Re 21:22-25.

Kings of the Line of David. Jehovah God established King David on the throne of Israel, and David proved to be a wise guide and leader of the nation, under God's direction. He was therefore called "the lamp of Israel." (2Sa 21:17) In his kingdom covenant with David, Jehovah promised: "Your very throne will become one firmly established to time indefinite." (2Sa 7:11-16) Accordingly, the dynasty, or family line, of rulers from David through his son Solomon was as a "lamp" to Israel.—1Ki 11:36; 15:4; 2Ki 8:19; 2Ch 21:7.

When King Zedekiah was dethroned and taken captive to Babylon to die there, it appeared that "the lamp" was extinguished. But Jehovah had not abandoned his covenant. He merely held rulership on the throne in abeyance "until he comes who has the legal right." (Eze 21:27) Jesus Christ, the Messiah, the "son of David," was heir to that throne forever. Thus "the lamp" of David will never go out. Jesus is therefore an everlasting lamp as the one who possesses the Kingdom forever.—Mt 1:1; Lu 1:32.

God's Word. Because "man must live, not on bread alone, but on every utterance coming forth through Jehovah's mouth" (Mt 4:4), His commandments are like a lamp, lighting the way of God's servants in the darkness of this world. The psalmist declared: "Your word is a lamp to my foot, and a light to my roadway." (Ps 119:105) King Solomon said: "For the commandment is a lamp, and a light the law is, and the reproofs of discipline are the way of life."—Pr 6:23.

The apostle Peter had seen many prophecies concerning Jesus Christ fulfilled, and he had been personally present at Jesus' transfiguration on the mountain. In view of all of this, Peter could say: "Consequently we have the prophetic word made more sure; and you are doing well in paying attention to it as to a lamp shining in a dark place, until day dawns and a daystar rises, in your hearts." (2Pe 1:19) The Christian was encouraged, therefore, to allow the light of God's prophetic Word to illuminate his heart. Then it would furnish guidance in the safe way "until day dawns and a daystar rises."

God's Servants. In the year 29 C.E., John the son of Zechariah, a priest, came, announcing: "Repent, for the kingdom of the heavens has drawn near." (Mt 3:1, 2; Lu 1:5, 13) Israel had turned away from obedience to the Law, and John was sent preaching repentance and pointing to the

Lamb of God. He succeeded in turning many of the sons of Israel back to Jehovah their God. (Lu 1:16) Consequently, Jesus said of John: "That man was a burning and shining lamp, and you for a short time were willing to rejoice greatly in his light. But I have the witness greater than that of John, for the very works that my Father assigned me to accomplish, the works themselves that I am doing, bear witness about me that the Father dispatched me."—Joh 5:35, 36.

Jesus also said to his disciples: "You are the light of the world. A city cannot be hid when situated upon a mountain. People light a lamp and set it, not under the measuring basket, but upon the lampstand, and it shines upon all those in the house. Likewise let your light shine before men, that they may see your fine works and give glory to your Father who is in the heavens." (Mt 5:14-16) The servant of God should appreciate the reason for which he is given the light, and he should realize that it would be utterly foolish and disastrous for him to refuse to let it shine from him as from a lamp.

Other Figurative Uses. What a person depends upon to light his way is symbolized by a lamp. With such a figure the proverb contrasts the righteous and the wicked, saying: "The very light of the righteous ones will rejoice; but the lamp of the wicked ones—it will be extinguished." (Pr 13:9) The light of the righteous continually becomes more brilliant, but however brilliantly the lamp of the wicked appears to shine and however prosperous his way may seem as a consequence, God will see to it that he ends up in darkness, where his foot will certainly stumble. Such an outcome is ahead for the person calling down evil on his father and mother.—Pr 20:20.

One's 'lamp being extinguished' also means that there is no future for him. Another proverb says: "There will prove to be no future for anyone bad; the very lamp of wicked people will be extinguished."—Pr 24:20.

Bildad, when implying that Job was hiding some secret wickedness, said of the wicked: "A light itself will certainly grow dark in his tent, and in it his own lamp will be extinguished." Farther on in his argument Bildad adds: "He will have no posterity and no progeny among his people." In the light of the fact that Solomon was said to be a lamp that God gave to David his father, the putting out of one's lamp may carry the thought that such a person would have no progeny to take over his inheritance.—Job 18:6, 19; 1Ki 11:36.

One's eye is, figuratively, a "lamp." Jesus said: "The lamp of the body is the eye. If, then, your eye is simple [sincere; all one way; in focus; generous], your whole body will be bright; but if your eye is wicked, your whole body will be dark." (Mt 6:22, 23, ftn) The eye is like a lamp, because with it the body can walk about without stumbling and without bumping into anything. Jesus, of course, had in mind 'the eyes of the heart' (Eph 1:18), as his words in the context show.

Proverbs 31:18, in saying of the good wife: "Her lamp does not go out at night," uses a figurative expression meaning that she works industriously at night and even rises before dawn for further work.—Compare Pr 31:15.

According to Proverbs 20:27, "the breath of earthling man is the lamp of Jehovah, carefully searching all the innermost parts of the belly." By what a person "breathes out," or gives vent to, whether good or bad expressions, he reveals, or sheds light on, his personality or inmost self. —Compare Ac 9:1.

LAMPSTAND. A stand or support for an oil-burning lamp or lamps. Though mentioning lampstands in homes and other buildings (2Ki 4:10; Da 5:5; Lu 8:16; 11:33), the Bible's emphasis is primarily on the lampstands associated with true worship.

In the Tabernacle. Jehovah directed Moses in vision to make for use in the tabernacle a lampstand (Heb., *menoh·rah'*; Gr., *ly·khni'a*) 'of pure gold, of hammered work.' Together with its lamps and utensils it was to weigh one talent. (Ex 25:31, 39, 40; 37:17, 24; Nu 8:4; Heb 9:2) This would equal about 34 kg (92 lb t), with a value, in modern terms, of $385,350.

Design. This luminary for "the Holy Place," the anterior compartment of the tabernacle (Heb 9:2), was composed of a central stem, with six branches. These branches curved upward from opposite sides of the main shaft. The central shaft, or stem, was decorated with four sculptured cups shaped like almond flowers, with knobs and flower blossoms alternating. The kind of flower represented in the flower blossoms is not certain; the Hebrew word used can mean any flower. The branches each had three cups, with knobs and flowers alternating. The description may indicate that the knobs on the central stem came at the point where the branches joined the stem. Lamps burning fine beaten olive oil were placed at the top of the main stem and on the end of each branch. Accessories consisted of snuffers, fire holders, and oil vessels.—Ex 25:31-38; 37:18-23; Le 24:2; Nu 4:9.

The actual construction of the lampstand was done under the oversight of Bezalel of the tribe of

Judah and Oholiab of the tribe of Dan. (Ex 31:1-11; 35:30-35) These men were doubtless good craftsmen, possibly learning the trade while slaves in Egypt. But Jehovah now put his spirit upon them so that the work could be perfectly done, exactly according to the pattern revealed and spoken to Moses.—Ex 25:9, 40; 39:43; 40:16.

Use. Moses "placed the lampstand in the tent of meeting in front of the table, on the side of the tabernacle to the south." Evidently it was parallel with the south side of the tent (left-hand side as one entered), opposite the table of showbread. The light shone "on the area in front of the lampstand," thus illuminating the Holy Place, which contained also the golden altar of incense.—Ex 40:22-26; Nu 8:2, 3.

At the time Moses completed setting up the tabernacle, on Nisan 1, 1512 B.C.E., he followed Jehovah's instructions to light the lamps. (Ex 40:1, 2, 4, 25) Later on, Aaron did so (Nu 8:3), and thereafter he (and future high priests) set the lampstand in order "from evening to morning before Jehovah constantly." (Le 24:3, 4) When Aaron dressed the lamps "morning by morning" and when he lit them "between the two evenings," he also offered incense on the golden altar.—Ex 30:1, 7, 8.

The lampstand, with the other tabernacle utensils, was transported during the wilderness journey by the Kohathite family of the tribe of Levi. First, however, the priests had to cover the articles, because, as Jehovah warned, nonpriestly persons "must not come in to see the holy things for the least moment of time, and so they have to die." The lampstand with its accessories was covered with a blue cloth and then put into a covering of sealskin and put onto a bar for carrying.—Nu 4:4, 9, 10, 15, 19, 20.

In the account relating King David's bringing the ark of the covenant to Mount Zion, there is no mention of the lampstand. Evidently it remained in the tabernacle in the various locations where the tabernacle came to be situated.

In the Temples. David gave to Solomon the architectural plans for the temple, which plans he had received by inspiration. These included directions for lampstands of gold and lampstands of silver. (1Ch 28:11, 12, 15, 19) There were ten golden lampstands, and they were placed "five to the right and five to the left," or five on the south side and five on the north side as one faced east, in the Holy of the temple. (1Ki 7:48, 49; 2Ch 4:20) All ten of these were "of the same plan." (2Ch 4:7) They were perhaps much larger than the one that had been in the tabernacle, commensurate with the increased dimensions of the temple and its other furnishings, such as "the molten sea." (2Ch 3:3, 4; 1Ki 7:23-26) The silver lampstands were undoubtedly used in courtyards or rooms other than the Holy and the Most Holy, for the furnishings of these two rooms were of gold. As in the tabernacle, the lamps of the golden lampstands were lighted up "evening by evening," constantly. —2Ch 13:11.

When the temple was destroyed by the Babylonians in 607 B.C.E., the lampstands were among

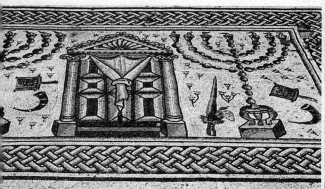

Jewish portrayals of the temple lampstand (on a column pillar at the right; on a synagogue floor above) have a base design very different from what is shown on the Arch of Titus

the gold and silver items taken from the house of Jehovah.—Jer 52:19.

Temple rebuilt by Zerubbabel. The Scriptures provide no information about lampstands in the temple rebuilt by Zerubbabel. However, Josephus says that Antiochus (Epiphanes) "stripped the temple, carrying off . . . the golden lampstands." (*Jewish Antiquities,* XII, 250 [v, 4]) The Apocryphal book of Maccabees mentions a "lampstand" being removed, necessitating the making of a new one.—1 Maccabees 1:21-23; 4:49, 50, *JB.*

Temple rebuilt by Herod. The magnificence of the temple rebuilt by Herod would give basis for assuming that this temple must also have contained lampstands equal in beauty and costliness to those in Solomon's temple. We have no mention of them in the Scriptures, however. Evidence of such a lampstand is found in its mention by Josephus and its representation on a bas-relief in an interior vault of the triumphal Arch of Titus in Rome. On this arch are depicted certain items taken from Jerusalem when it was destroyed by the Romans in 70 C.E. Josephus claimed to have been an eyewitness of this triumphal procession of Emperor Vespasian and his son Titus. Josephus speaks of the procession carrying "a lampstand, likewise made of gold, but constructed on a different pattern from those which we use in ordinary life. Affixed to a pedestal was a central shaft, from which there extended slender branches, arranged trident-fashion, a wrought lamp being attached to the extremity of each branch; of these there were seven."—*The Jewish War,* VII, 148, 149 (v, 5).

No one can say for certain today whether the lampstand depicted on the Arch of Titus looks exactly the same as the original from the temple in Jerusalem. Differences in opinion concern mainly the form of the base, made up of two parallel polygonal cases, the smaller one above the larger. One viewpoint is that the Roman representation on the arch is accurate but that Herod himself had changed its design from the traditional Jewish form of a triangular, or tripod, base in a "westernizing" campaign to please the Romans. Other scholars disagree that the representation is exact. Decorative panels on the base display eagles and sea monsters, which they cite as an apparent violation of the second commandment.

Some conclude that the original temple lampstand stood on three legs, basing this in part on the numerous representations of the lampstand from different parts of Europe and the Middle East dating from the third to the sixth centuries that show a tripod base, a few with animal feet. The oldest representation of the lampstand appears on

coins of Antigonus II, who reigned 40-37 B.C.E. Though not well preserved, one specimen seems to indicate that the base consisted of a plate with feet. In 1969, a representation of the temple lampstand was found incised in plaster in a house excavated in the old city of Jerusalem. The schematic drawing indicates seven branches and a triangular base, all ornamented with knobs separated by two parallel lines. In the Tomb of Jason, discovered in Jerusalem in 1956 and dated to the beginning of the first century B.C.E., archaeologists found designs of a seven-branched lampstand scratched into plaster. The lower sections seem to be stuck into a box or stand.

Thus, on the basis of these archaeological findings, some object to the appearance of the base of the lampstand on the Arch of Titus and suggest among other possibilities that the carvings are a Roman artist's conception influenced by Jewish designs familiar to him from other sources.

Figurative Use. The prophet Zechariah saw in vision an unusual golden lampstand. As with the lampstand prepared for the tabernacle, it had seven lamps, but these lamps had seven pipes, which scholars understand in a distributive sense to mean a pipe to each lamp. Also, on top of the lampstand there was a bowl. Apparently a continuous supply of oil was provided for the lamps through the pipes leading to them. The oil evidently came from the two olive trees the prophet saw alongside the lampstand.—Zec 4:2, 3, 12.

Jehovah God, through the glorified Jesus Christ, gave to the apostle John a vision in which he saw "seven golden lampstands, and in the midst of the lampstands someone like a son of man." This one, whose description reveals him to be Jesus Christ, explained to John that the lampstands meant seven congregations. (Re 1:1, 12, 13, 20) These visionary lampstands were probably like the one that lighted the tabernacle so that the priests could perform their duties there. The use of such to represent congregations is in harmony with Jesus' words to those who are dedicated servants of God: "You are the light of the world." (Mt 5:14) As the One "who walks in the midst of the seven golden lampstands," he oversees all their activity as light-bearers.—Re 2:1.

In counseling the congregation at Ephesus, Christ warned that he would remove the lampstand from its place, unless they repented. This would doubtless mean that they would no longer be used to shed the light of truth in that area, but that their light would go out.—Re 2:1-5; compare Mt 6:22, 23.

The final mention of lampstands in the Bible bears certain similarities to Zechariah's vision. "Two witnesses" who were to prophesy in sackcloth were said to be symbolized by "the two olive trees and the two lampstands."—Re 11:3, 4.

LANCE. See ARMS, ARMOR.

LANDOWNER. From very early times, property rights of landowners or landholders (Heb., *be'a·lim'*, literally, *owners*) have been recognized. Abraham bargained with Ephron the Hittite for a burial place for his wife Sarah, finally buying a field for a stated sum, the transaction being legalized before the townspeople. (Ge 23:1-20) During a famine in Egypt, Joseph bought land for Pharaoh from Egyptian landowners, in exchange for food. (Ge 47:20-26) God's faithful servant Job, living in the land of Uz, possessed inheritable property, doubtless including land, that he gave to his sons and daughters. (Job 1:4; 42:15) However, Jehovah is the Supreme Landowner, and his dealings demonstrate that humans are accountable to him for the way they use his property.—Ps 24:1; 50:10-12.

In Israel. When Jehovah brought Israel into Canaan he exercised his right as Lord and Owner of the whole earth to dispossess the Canaanites, who were, in effect, squatters on the land. (Jos 3:11; 1Co 10:26) The period of God's tolerating their holding the land had run out. Although more than 450 years previously God had promised the land to Abraham's seed, he had told Abraham: "The error of the Amorites [a term sometimes used for all the Canaanite tribes] has not yet come to completion." (Ge 15:7, 8, 12-16) Therefore, as the Christian martyr Stephen told the Jews, God "did not give [Abraham] any inheritable possession in it, no, not a footbreadth; but he promised to give it to him as a possession, and after him to his seed, while as yet he had no child."—Ac 7:5.

Israel was not to fight wars of aggression, continuing to expand its territory by taking the property of surrounding nations. Jehovah warned Israel that they must respect the property rights of certain nations to whom he had assigned land. These nations were Edom, Moab, and Ammon, related to the Israelites through Esau (Edom) and Lot (Moab and Ammon).—De 2:4, 5, 9, 19.

Promised Land held in trust. Even the people Israel, to whom God had given the land for them to enjoy as landowners, were told by Jehovah that they were not actually *owners* of it but only held it in trust. He said concerning the sale of a family land estate: "So the land should not be sold in perpetuity, because the land is mine. For you are alien residents and settlers from my standpoint." (Le 25:23) God had ousted the Canaanites from the land for their disgusting practices. He warned he would also take away all title from Israel and drive them out of the land if they followed such practices, and when they later did, they were sent into exile. (Le 18:24-30; 25:18, 19; 26:27-33; Jer 52:27) After 70 years of desolation of their land, from 607 to 537 B.C.E., God mercifully reestablished them, but this time under Gentile domination. Eventually, in 70 C.E., the Romans completely destroyed Jerusalem and scattered its people.

Within the nation, tribes were assigned sections of the land or cities inside the boundaries of other tribes. Priests and Levites had cities with pasture grounds. (Jos 15-21) In turn, within the tribes families were allotted inheritances. These divisions became smaller as families subdivided their own allotments because of increase in numbers. This resulted in thorough cultivation and use of the land. Inheritances were not allowed to circulate from one tribe to another. To prevent this, women who inherited land (because there were no living brothers) had to marry within the tribe to hold their inheritance.—Nu 36:1-12.

If a man died without having a son, his brother (or, if no brothers, his nearest of kin) could marry his widow to bring forth offspring from her. The man marrying the widow could also repurchase the dead man's inheritance, if it had been sold. (Ru 4:9, 10, 13-17) The woman's firstborn would take the name, not of his actual father, but of the widow's first husband, thus possessing the land inheritance and keeping the man's name alive over his inheritance in Israel.—De 25:5, 6.

The Jubilee year. God had said to Israel: "No one should come to be poor among you." (De 15:4, 5) The Jubilee year, as long as observed, prevented the nation from sinking into a situation where only two classes existed, the very rich and the very poor. On every 50th year (counted from the time of Israel's entering Canaan), every man returned to his inheritance, and any land he had sold was to be restored to him. Because of this law, the price of land decreased every year as the Jubilee approached. Actually, the buyer, in a sense, only leased the land, the price depending on the number of crops until the Jubilee year. (Le 25:13-16, 28) Even a buyer of another's inheritance could not necessarily hold it until the Jubilee. If the original owner acquired enough money, he could repurchase the land. Also, any repurchaser (close relative) could repurchase it for the original owner.—Le 25:24-27.

A man could not be forced to sell his property.

Neither did the principle of eminent domain apply in Israel. This was illustrated in the refusal of Naboth to sell a field of his inheritance to King Ahab.—1Ki 21:1-4, 17-19; compare Eze 46:18.

The Levites. As a protection to the Levites, their fields could not be sold; this was because Levites had no individual land inheritance—they had been given only houses in the Levite cities and the pasture grounds surrounding them. If a Levite sold his *house* in a Levite city, the right of repurchase continued for him, and in the Jubilee, at the latest, it was returned to him.—Le 25:32-34.

As the productive land yielded fruitage, the Great Proprietor of all the land was not to be left out of the picture. By means of the tithing arrangement, a tenth of the produce was to be used to support the Levites in their important functions related to Jehovah's worship, thus spiritually benefiting all Israel.—Nu 18:21-24; De 14:22-29.

The sanctuary. The sanctuary of Jehovah could also become a landholder by reason of fields "sanctified" to Jehovah; that is, the produce of these fields went to the sanctuary for a period of time designated by the owner or possessor. (Le 27:16-19) If a field that was "sanctified" by the owner was not repurchased, but was sold to another man, that field would become the permanent possession of the sanctuary at the time of the Jubilee. (Le 27:20, 21) Also, fields "devoted" to the sanctuary by their owners remained the permanent possession of the sanctuary.—Le 27:28.

In the Christian Congregation. The Bible makes it clear that individual property rights were recognized in the Christian congregation. When the congregation was established, on Pentecost day, 33 C.E., many Jews and proselytes of the Jewish religion from other lands had gathered at Jerusalem to observe the festival. A large number of these were present to hear Peter's discourse and began to be believers in Christ. (Ac 2:1, 5, 9-11, 41, 42, 47) They remained to learn more. So the Christians voluntarily sold possessions and distributed the proceeds to help these visiting ones and others who were needy. They had "all things in common." (Ac 2:44-46) This was not socialism or communism, but a *voluntary sharing* for the purpose of aiding persons interested in the good news and in furthering the spread of it.

Later, for similar reasons, and partly because of persecution of the Christians by Jerusalem's rulers, this practice continued, under the spirit and undeserved kindness of God. Fields were sold and the proceeds brought to the apostles, who administered the assistance program. (Ac 4:31-37) But each Christian's property was his own and his rights were inviolable; he was under no compulsion to put property into a common pool. It was counted as a privilege to do so, not a duty. It was right motive that dominated and moved these generous Christians.

In the case of Ananias and Sapphira, however, a hypocritical show was made in order to get plaudits and honor of men. They conspired together to sell a field and to give only part of the proceeds to the apostles, with the claim that they were generously giving up all the possession. Peter, by direction of holy spirit, discerned what they were doing. He did *not* say, 'Why did you not *give* us *all* the money you received for the field?' as if they were under obligation to do so. Rather, he said: "Ananias, why has Satan emboldened you to play false to the holy spirit and to hold back secretly some of the price of the field? As long as it remained with you did it not remain yours, and after it was sold did it not continue in your control? Why was it that you purposed such a deed as this in your heart? You have played false, not to men, but to God."—Ac 5:1-4.

About three hours later, when Sapphira came in, not knowing what had happened, she made the same claim, and Peter replied: "Why was it agreed upon between you two to make a test of the spirit of Jehovah?" (Ac 5:7-9) Their sin was in lying to Jehovah, making a mockery of him and his congregation, as if God's spirit were not upon it. (Ga 6:7) It was not that they were compelled to part with their property in some sort of communal arrangement.

Jehovah's Ownership Must Be Recognized. Since Jehovah is the Owner of all the land, the landowner on earth must respect his possession and use it properly. Otherwise it will become a ruin and he will eventually suffer complete loss of it. (Pr 24:30-34) Even nations must recognize this fact. (Isa 24:1-6; Jer 23:10) Eventually those who ignore this principle will themselves be ruined. —Re 11:18.

Recognition of God's real ownership will also prevent one from trying to gain possession of land in a greedy or wrongful way. (Pr 20:21; 23:10, 11) When Israel departed from God's law, there were men against whom God expressed condemnation, saying: "Woe to the ones joining house to house, and those who annex field to field until there is no more room and you men have been made to dwell all by yourselves in the midst of the land!"—Isa 5:8; Mic 2:1-4.

On the other hand, Jesus said: "Happy are the mild-tempered ones, since they will inherit the earth." (Mt 5:5; Ps 37:9, 22, 29) He taught his followers to pray to God: "Let your kingdom come. Let your will take place, as in heaven, also upon earth." (Mt 6:10) Under the Kingdom sovereignty of the Great Landowner himself, those holding land in trust for him in faithfulness are to experience the full joy of ownership in complete security. God stated his viewpoint of proper conditions as regards land ownership when he gave restoration prophecies through the mouths of Isaiah and Micah. These indicate what situation he will bring about when his 'will takes place on earth.' He said of his people: "They will certainly build houses and have occupancy; and they will certainly plant vineyards and eat their fruitage. They will not build and someone else have occupancy; they will not plant and someone else do the eating." "And they will actually sit, each one under his vine and under his fig tree, and there will be no one making them tremble."—Isa 65:21, 22; Mic 4:4; see PEOPLE OF THE LAND (EARTH).

LANGUAGE.

Any means, vocal or other, by which feelings or thoughts are expressed or communicated. Generally, however, language means a body of words and the methods of combining these as understood by a community of people. The Hebrew and Greek words for "tongue" signify "language." (Jer 5:15, ftn; Ac 2:11, *Int*) The Hebrew term for "lip" is used in a similar way.—Ge 11:1, ftn.

Language, of course, is most intimately associated with the mind, which employs the speech organs—throat, tongue, lips, and teeth—as its instruments. (See TONGUE.) Thus, the *Encyclopædia Britannica* (1959 edition) states: "Thinking and words go together. For thinking, to be clear, has to rely upon names [or nouns] and their various associations with one another. . . . While some minor reservations are justifiable there is an overwhelming mass of evidence . . . that fortifies the contention stated above—no words, no thinking." (Vol. 5, p. 740) Words are man's principal means of receiving, storing, manipulating, and transmitting information.

Origin of Speech. The first human, Adam, was created with a vocabulary, as well as with the ability to coin new words and thus expand his vocabulary. Without a God-given vocabulary the newly created man would have been no more able to comprehend verbal instructions from his Creator than were the unreasoning animals. (Ge 1:27-30; 2:16-20; compare 2Pe 2:12; Jude 10.) So, while only intelligent man of all earth's creatures has the ability of true speech, language did not originate with man but with man's All-Wise Creator, Jehovah God.—Compare Ex 4:11, 12.

On the origin of language, the well-known lexicographer Ludwig Koehler wrote: "There has been, especially in former times, much speculation as to how human speech 'came into being'. Writers strove to explore 'animal language'. For animals also are able to express audibly by sounds and groups of sounds their feelings and sensations, such as contentment, fear, emotion, threat, anger, sexual desire and satisfaction in its fulfilment, and perhaps many other things. However manifold these [animal] expressions may be, . . . they lack concept and thought, the essential domain of human language." After showing how men can explore the physiological aspect of human speech, he adds: "But what actually happens in speech, how the spark of perception kindles the spirit of the child, or of mankind generally, to become the spoken word, eludes our grasp. Human speech is a secret; it is a divine gift, a miracle."—*Journal of Semitic Studies,* Manchester, 1956, p. 11.

Language had been employed for untold ages prior to man's appearance on the universal scene. Jehovah God communicated with his heavenly firstborn Son and evidently used him in communicating with his other spirit sons. Hence that firstborn Son was called "the Word." (Joh 1:1; Col 1:15, 16; Re 3:14) The apostle Paul made inspired reference to "tongues of men and of angels." (1Co 13:1) Jehovah God speaks to his angelic creatures in their 'tongue' and they 'carry out his word.' (Ps 103:20) Since He and his spirit sons are not reliant upon an atmosphere (which makes possible the sound waves and vibrations necessary for human speech), angelic language is obviously beyond human conception or attainment. As God's messengers, angels therefore employed human language to talk with men, and angelic messages are recorded in Hebrew (Ge 22:15-18), Aramaic (Da 7:23-27), and Greek (Re 11:15), the cited texts being written in those languages respectively.

What accounts for the diversity of languages?

According to language academies, about 3,000 tongues are spoken today throughout the earth. Some are spoken by hundreds of millions of persons, others by fewer than a thousand. Though the ideas expressed and communicated may be basically the same, there are many ways to express them. The Bible history alone explains the origin of this strange diversity in human communication.

Up until some point after the global Flood, all mankind "continued to be of one language [literally, "lip"] and of one set of words." (Ge 11:1) The Bible indicates that the language later called Hebrew was that original "one language." (See HEBREW, II.) As will be shown, this does not mean that all other languages stemmed from and are related to Hebrew but that Hebrew *preceded* all other languages.

The Genesis account describes the uniting of some part of the post-Flood human family in a project that opposed God's will as stated to Noah and his sons. (Ge 9:1) Instead of spreading out and 'filling the earth,' they determined to centralize human society, concentrating their residence on a site in what became known as the Plains of Shinar in Mesopotamia. Evidently this was also to become a religious center, with a religious tower.—Ge 11:2-4.

Almighty God gave their presumptuous project a setback by breaking up their unity of action, accomplishing this by confusing their common language. This made impossible any coordinated work on their project and led to their scattering to all parts of the globe. The confusion of their language would also hinder or slow down future progress in a wrong direction, a God-defying direction, since it would limit mankind's ability to combine its intellectual and physical powers in ambitious schemes and also make it difficult to draw upon the accumulated knowledge of the different language groups formed—knowledge, not from God, but gained through human experience and research. (Compare Ec 7:29; De 32:5.) So, while it introduced a major divisive factor into human society, the confusion of human speech actually benefited human society in retarding the attainment of dangerous and hurtful goals. (Ge 11:5-9; compare Isa 8:9, 10.) One has only to consider certain developments in our own times, resulting from accumulated secular knowledge and man's misuse thereof, to realize what God foresaw long ago would develop if the effort at Babel were allowed to go unhindered.

Philology, the comparative study of languages, generally classifies languages into distinct "families." The "parent" language of each major family usually has not been identified; much less is there any evidence pointing to any one "parent" language as the source of all the thousands of tongues now spoken. The Bible record does not say that all languages descended, or branched off, from Hebrew. In what is commonly called the Table of Nations (Ge 10), the descendants of Noah's sons (Shem, Ham, and Japheth) are listed

and in each case are grouped 'according to their families, according to their tongues, in their lands, by their nations.' (Ge 10:5, 20, 31, 32) It appears, therefore, that, when miraculously confusing human language, Jehovah God produced, not dialects of Hebrew, but a number of completely new languages, each capable of expressing the full range of human feeling and thought.

Thus, after God confused their language, not only did the builders at Babel lack "one set of words" (Ge 11:1), one common vocabulary, but they also lacked a common grammar, a common way of expressing the relationship between words. Professor S. R. Driver stated: "Languages, however, differ not only in grammar and roots, but also . . . in the manner in which ideas are built up into a sentence. Different races do not *think* in the same way; and consequently the forms taken by the sentence in different languages are not the same." (*A Dictionary of the Bible*, edited by J. Hastings, 1905, Vol. IV, p. 791) Thus, different languages require quite different thought patterns, making it difficult for a new learner to 'think in the language.' (Compare 1Co 14:10, 11.) This is also why a *literal* translation of something said or written in an unfamiliar language may seem illogical, often causing persons to say, "But it doesn't make sense!" So, it appears that, when Jehovah God confused the speech of those at Babel, he first blotted out all memory of their previous common language and then introduced into their minds not only new vocabularies but also changed thought patterns, producing new grammars.—Compare Isa 33:19; Eze 3:4-6.

We find, for example, that certain languages are *monosyllabic* (made up of words of only one syllable), such as Chinese. By contrast, the vocabularies of a number of other languages are formed largely by *agglutination*, that is, by joining words placed side by side, as in the German word *Hausfriedensbruch*, which means literally "house peace breakage," or, in a form more understandable to the English-speaking mind, "trespass." In some languages syntax, the order of the words in the sentence, is very important; in others it matters little. So, too, some languages have many conjugations (verb forms); others, such as Chinese, have none. Countless differences could be cited, each requiring an adjustment in mental patterns, often with great effort.

Apparently the original languages resulting from divine action at Babel in course of time produced related dialects, and the dialects frequently developed into separate languages, their relationship to their "sister" dialects or to the "parent" language sometimes becoming almost indistinguishable. Even Shem's descendants, who apparently did not figure among the crowd at Babel, came to speak not only Hebrew but also Aramaean, Akkadian, and Arabic. Historically, various factors have contributed to the change in languages: separation due to distance or geographic barriers, wars and conquests, a breakdown in communications, and immigration by those of another language. Because of such factors ancient major languages have fragmented, certain tongues have partially merged with others, and some languages have disappeared completely and have been replaced by those of the invading conquerors.

Language research provides evidence in harmony with the preceding information. *The New Encyclopædia Britannica* says: "The earliest records of written language, the only linguistic fossils man can hope to have, go back no more than about 4,000 or 5,000 years." (1985, Vol. 22, p. 567) An article in *Science Illustrated* of July 1948 (p. 63) states: "Older forms of the languages known today were far more difficult than their modern descendants . . . man appears not to have begun with a simple speech, and gradually made it more complex, but rather to have gotten hold of a tremendously knotty speech somewhere in the unrecorded past, and gradually simplified it to the modern forms." Linguist Dr. Mason also points out that "the idea that 'savages' speak in a series of grunts, and are unable to express many 'civilized' concepts, is very wrong," and that "many of the languages of non-literate peoples are far more complex than modern European ones." (*Science News Letter*, September 3, 1955, p. 148) The evidence is thus against any evolutionary origin of speech or of ancient languages.

Concerning the focal point from which the spreading of ancient languages began, Sir Henry Rawlinson, Oriental language scholar, observed: "If we were to be thus guided by the mere intersection of linguistic paths, and independently of all reference to the scriptural record, we should still be led to fix on the plains of Shinar, as the focus from which the various lines had radiated." —*The Journal of the Royal Asiatic Society of Great Britian and Ireland*, London, 1855, Vol. 15, p. 232.

Among the major "families" listed by modern philologists are: Indo-European, Sino-Tibetan, Afro-Asian, Japanese and Korean, Dravidian, Malayo-Polynesian, and Black African. There are many tongues that till now defy classification. Within each of the major families there are many subdivisions, or smaller families. Thus, the Indo-European family includes Germanic, Romance (Italic), Balto-Slavic, Indo-Iranian, Greek, Celtic, Albanian, and Armenian. Most of these smaller families, in turn, have several members. Romance languages, for example, embrace French, Spanish, Portuguese, Italian, and Romanian.

From Abraham Onward. Abraham the Hebrew evidently had no difficulty in conversing with the Hamitic people of Canaan. (Ge 14:21-24; 20:1-16; 21:22-34) No use of interpreters is mentioned, but then, neither is such use mentioned when Abraham went to Egypt. (Ge 12:14-19) He probably knew Akkadian (Assyro-Babylonian) because of having lived in Ur of the Chaldeans. (Ge 11:31) Akkadian for a time was an international language. It is possible that the people of Canaan, living in relative proximity to the Semitic peoples of Syria and Arabia, were to a degree bilingual. Then, too, the alphabet gives clear evidence of its being of Semitic origin, and this could also have exercised considerable influence toward the use of Semitic tongues by persons of other language groups, particularly rulers and officials.—See CANAAN, CANAANITE No. 2 (Language); WRITING.

Jacob also apparently communicated easily with his Aramaean relatives (Ge 29:1-14), though their terminology differed on occasion.—Ge 31:46, 47.

Joseph, who likely learned Egyptian while a slave of Potiphar, employed an interpreter when first talking with his Hebrew brothers upon their arrival in Egypt. (Ge 39:1; 42:6, 23) Moses, raised in Pharaoh's courts, doubtless knew several languages, Hebrew, Egyptian, probably Akkadian, and perhaps others.—Ex 2:10; compare verses 15-22.

Aramaic in time replaced Akkadian as the lingua franca, or international language, being used even in correspondence with Egypt. However, by the time of Assyrian King Sennacherib's attack on Judah (732 B.C.E.), Aramaic (ancient Syrian) was not understood by the majority of Jews, though Judean officials understood it. (2Ki 18:26, 27) So, too, the Chaldean language of the Semitic Babylonians, who finally conquered Jerusalem in 607 B.C.E., sounded like those "stammering with their lips" to the Jews. (Isa 28:11; Da 1:4; compare De 28:49.) Although Babylon, Persia, and other world powers carved out huge empires and brought under their control people of many languages, they did not eliminate the divisive barrier of language differences.—Da 3:4, 7; Es 1:22.

Nehemiah showed great concern upon learning that the sons of mixed marriages among the returned Jews did not know "Jewish" (Hebrew). (Ne 13:23-25) His concern was for pure worship, as he recognized the importance of understanding the Sacred Scriptures (till then available only in Hebrew) when these were read and discussed. (Compare Ne 13:26, 27; 8:1-3, 8, 9.) Oneness of language in itself would also be a unifying force among the people. The Hebrew Scriptures doubtless were a major factor in the stability of the Hebrew language. During the thousand-year period of their being written, virtually no change in language is noted.

When Jesus was on earth, Palestine had become, to a considerable extent, a polyglot, or multilingual, region. There is solid evidence that the Jews still retained their use of Hebrew, but Aramaic and Koine were also spoken. Latin, too, appeared on official inscriptions of the Roman rulers of the land (Joh 19:20) and was doubtless heard from Roman soldiers stationed there. As to the language generally spoken by Jesus, see ARAMAIC; also HEBREW, II.

On the day of Pentecost, 33 C.E., the holy spirit was poured out on the Christian disciples in Jerusalem, and they suddenly began speaking in many languages that they had never studied and learned. Jehovah God had demonstrated at Babel his miraculous ability to place different vocabularies and different grammars in the minds of people. At Pentecost he did so again but with a major difference, for the Christians suddenly gifted with the power to speak new languages did not forget their original tongue, Hebrew. God's spirit here was also effecting a very different purpose, not of confusing and scattering but of enlightening and drawing together persons of honest heart into Christian unity. (Ac 2:1-21, 37-42) From then on God's covenant people were a multilingual people, but the barrier created by language difference was overcome because their minds were filled with the common or mutual language of the truth. In unity they spoke in praise of Jehovah and his righteous purposes by Christ Jesus. Thus, the promise at Zephaniah 3:9 saw a fulfillment as Jehovah God gave "peoples the change to a pure language, in order for them all to call upon the name of Jehovah, in order to serve him shoulder to shoulder." (Compare Isa 66:18; Zec 8:23; Re 7:4, 9, 10.) For this to be so, they should "all speak in agreement" and be "fitly united in the same mind and in the same line of thought."—1Co 1:10.

The 'purity' of the language spoken by the Christian congregation was also because of its being free from words expressing malicious bitterness, anger, wrath, screaming, and similar abusive language, as well as being free from deceit, obscenity, and corruptness. (Eph 4:29, 31;

1Pe 3:10) Christians were to put language to its most exalted use, praising their Creator and upbuilding their neighbor with wholesome, truthful speech, especially the good news about God's Kingdom. (Mt 24:14; Tit 2:7, 8; Heb 13:15; compare Ps 51:15; 109:30.) As the time neared for God to execute his judicial decision upon all the nations of the world, Jehovah would enable many more to speak that pure language.

The Bible began to be written in the Hebrew language, and some portions were later recorded in Aramaic. Then, in the first century of the Common Era, the remainder of the Sacred Scriptures were written in Koine, or common Greek (though Matthew wrote his Gospel first in Hebrew). By then a translation had also been made of the Hebrew Scriptures into Greek. Called the *Septuagint*, it was not an inspired translation but, nevertheless, was used by the Christian writers of the Bible in numerous quotations. (See INSPIRATION.) So, too, the Christian Greek Scriptures and eventually the whole Bible came to be translated into other languages, among the earliest being Latin, Syriac, Ethiopic, Arabic, and Persian. As of the present time, the Bible, the whole or in part, is available in upwards of 1,800 languages. This has facilitated the proclamation of the good news and thus has contributed to overcoming the barrier of language divisions for the purpose of uniting people of many lands in pure worship of their Creator.

LAODICEA (La·o·di·ce'a), **LAODICEANS** (La·o·di·ce'ans). A city in the western part of Asia Minor, the ruins of which lie near Denizli, about 150 km (90 mi) E of Ephesus. It was known earlier as Diospolis and Rhoas but was evidently rebuilt in the third century B.C.E. by the Seleucid ruler Antiochus II and named after his wife Laodice. Situated in the fertile valley of the Lycus River, Laodicea lay at the junction of major trade routes and was linked by roads with cities such as Ephesus, Pergamum, and Philadelphia.

Laodicea enjoyed great prosperity as a manufacturing city and as a banking center. Indicative of the city's great wealth is the fact that when it suffered extensive earthquake damage in the reign of Nero, it was able to rebuild without any financial assistance from Rome. (Tacitus' *Annals,* XIV, XXVII) The glossy black wool of Laodicea and the garments made therefrom were widely known. The seat of a famous medical school, this city probably also produced the eye medicine known as Phrygian powder. One of the main deities venerated at Laodicea was Asclepius, a god of medicine.

This city had a major disadvantage. Unlike the nearby city of Hierapolis, with its hot springs famed for their healing properties, and Colossae, with its refreshing cold water, Laodicea had no permanent water supply. From a considerable distance away, water had to be piped to Laodicea and likely was lukewarm on reaching the city. For the initial part of the distance the water was conveyed by means of an aqueduct and then, closer to the city, through cubical stone blocks that were bored through the middle and cemented together.

Laodicea seems to have had a considerable number of Jews. According to a letter from Laodicean magistrates (as quoted by Josephus), the Jews, in compliance with the injunction of Gaius Rabirius, were allowed to observe their Sabbaths and other sacred rites. (*Jewish Antiquities,* XIV, 241-243 [x, 20]) At least some of the Jews there were quite wealthy. This may be deduced from the fact that, when Governor Flaccus ordered the confiscation of the annual contributions that were meant for the temple at Jerusalem, the amount reportedly was found to be more than 20 pounds of gold.

In the first century C.E., a Christian congregation existed at Laodicea and apparently met in the home of Nympha, a Christian sister there. Doubtless the efforts of Epaphras contributed to the establishment of that congregation. (Col 4:12, 13, 15) Also, the effects of Paul's work at Ephesus likely reached as far as Laodicea. (Ac 19:10) Although not ministering there personally, Paul was nevertheless concerned about the Laodicean congregation and even wrote a letter to them. (Col 2:1; 4:16) However, some scholars believe that Paul's letter may have been simply a duplicate of the one he sent to Ephesus. Of course, that is only a theory, an effort to account for the fact that the Bible contains no letter from Paul to the Laodiceans, although Paul wrote to them. The letter to Laodicea may simply have contained information not necessary for us today, or it may have repeated points adequately covered in other canonical letters.

The congregation at Laodicea was one of the seven in Asia Minor to which the glorified Jesus Christ, in a revelation to John, addressed personal messages. (Re 1:11) At that time, toward the close of the first century C.E., the Laodicean congregation had little to commend it. Though materially rich, it was spiritually poor. Instead of the literal gold handled by the Laodicean bankers, instead of the garments of glossy black wool made locally, instead of the eye medicine doubtless produced by the Laodicean medical profession, instead of the boiling hot medicinal waters from the springs of nearby Hierapolis, the Laodicean congregation needed things like these in a spiritual sense. It needed "gold refined by fire" to enrich its personality (compare 1Co 3:10-14; 1Pe 1:6, 7), white outer garments to give it an irreproachable Christian appearance with no unchristian features that were as shameful as bodily nakedness. (Compare Re 16:15; 19:8.) It needed to have spiritual "eyesalve" applied to take away its blindness to Bible truth and Christian responsibilities. (Compare Isa 29:18; 2Pe 1:5-10; 1Jo 2:11.) It could buy these things from Christ Jesus, the one knocking at the door, if it let him in hospitably to entertain him. (Compare Isa 55:1, 2.) It needed to become stimulatingly hot (compare Ps 69:9; 2Co 9:2; Tit 2:14) or refreshingly cold (compare Pr 25:13, 25), but not to stay lukewarm.—Re 3:14-22.

LAPPIDOTH (Lap·pi·doth) [possibly, Torches; Lightning Flashes]. The husband of the Israelite prophetess Deborah.—Jg 4:4.

LASEA (La·se′a). A Cretan city near the harbor called Fair Havens. (Ac 27:8) Lasea is usually identified with ruins situated about 8 km (5 mi) E of modern Kaloi Limniones (Fair Havens).

LASHA (La′sha). A place mentioned in the earliest Canaanite boundary description. (Ge 10:19) Its exact location is uncertain. Either Lasha was "near" Zeboiim (*NW; JP* [1962 ed.]) or the Canaanite boundary extended from the area around Zeboiim "as far as" Lasha. (*AT; RS; JB*) On the basis of Jerome's identification and Jewish tradition, many place Lasha at Callirrhoe, near the eastern shore of the Dead Sea below the Wadi Zarqa Ma′in. Others link Lasha with Laish (Dan).

LASSHARON (Las·shar′on). A royal Canaanite city whose king was defeated by the Israelites under Joshua. (Jos 12:7, 8, 18) Lassharon is often linked with the district called Sarona, situated, according to Eusebius, between Mount Tabor and the Sea of Galilee. Possibly modern Sarona (Sharona), about 10 km (6 mi) SW of Tiberias, marks the ancient site.

LAST DAYS. In Bible prophecy, "last days" or comparable expressions such as "final part of the days" were used to designate a time when events of history culminate. (Eze 38:8, 16; Da 10:14) The content of the prophecy fixes the starting point of the "final part of the days" when the foretold events would begin to occur. Those living at the time of the prophecy's fulfillment could therefore be spoken of as living in the "last days" or the "final part of the days." Depending upon the nature of the prophecy, this may be a period covering just a few years or many and can apply to widely separated time periods.

Jacob's Deathbed Prophecy. When Jacob said to his sons, "Gather yourselves together that I may tell you what will happen to you in the final part of the days" or "in days to come" (*AT*), he meant in that future time when his words would begin undergoing fulfillment. (Ge 49:1) Over two centuries earlier Jehovah had stated to Jacob's grandfather Abram (Abraham) that his offspring would suffer affliction for 400 years. (Ge 15:13) Therefore, in this case, the future time referred to by Jacob as "the final part of the days" could not begin until after the 400 years of affliction ended. (For details on Genesis 49, see the articles on the sons of Jacob under their respective names.) A later application of the prophecy that would involve the spiritual "Israel of God" could also be expected.—Ga 6:16; Ro 9:6.

Balaam's Prophecy. It was before the Israelites entered the Promised Land that the prophet Balaam said to Moab's King Balak: "Do come, let me advise you what this people [Israel] will do to your people afterward in the end of the days. . . . A star will certainly step forth out of Jacob, and a scepter will indeed rise out of Israel. And he will certainly break apart the temples of Moab's head and the cranium of all the sons of tumult of war." (Nu 24:14-17) In the initial fulfillment of this prophecy, the "star" proved to be King David, the subduer of the Moabites. (2Sa 8:2) Evidently, therefore, in that fulfillment of this particular prophecy, "the end of the days" began with David's becoming king. Since David foreshadowed Jesus as Messianic King, the prophecy would also apply to Jesus at the time when he subdues his enemies.—Isa 9:7; Ps 2:8, 9.

The Prophecy of Isaiah and Micah. At Isaiah 2:2 and Micah 4:1 the words "final part of the days" introduce a prophecy about the time when people from all nations would stream to "the mountain of the house of Jehovah." In a typical fulfillment, between 29 C.E. and 70 C.E., during the final part of the days of the Jewish system of things, Jehovah's worship was exalted above the lofty elevation that pagan nations gave to their false gods. The King, Jesus Christ, made "a breakthrough" in elevating true worship, and he was followed, first by a remnant of the nation of Israel, and then by people from all nations. (Isa 2:2; Mic 2:13; Ac 10:34, 35) In an antitypical fulfillment, in the final part of the days of this system of things, Jehovah's worship has been elevated heaven high. The King, Jesus Christ, has led the remnant of spiritual Israel to pure worship, and they have

been followed by a great crowd out of all nations. —Re 7:9.

Last Days of the Jewish System of Things. Less than three and a half years before the non-Jews became part of the Christian congregation, God's spirit was poured out on faithful Jewish disciples of Jesus Christ. At that time Peter explained that this was in fulfillment of Joel's prophecy, saying: "'And in the *last days*,' God says, 'I shall pour out some of my spirit upon every sort of flesh . . . And I will give portents in heaven above and signs on earth below, blood and fire and smoke mist; the sun will be turned into darkness and the moon into blood before the great and illustrious day of Jehovah arrives.'" (Ac 2:16-20) In this case "the last days" preceded "the great and illustrious day of Jehovah," which "day" apparently brought "the last days" to their conclusion. (Compare Zep 1:14-18; Mal 4:5; Mt 11:13, 14; see DAY OF JEHOVAH.) Since Peter addressed natural Jews and Jewish proselytes, his words must have had particular reference to them and evidently indicated that they were living in "the last days" of the then-existing Jewish system of things with its center of worship at Jerusalem. Earlier, Christ Jesus himself had foretold the destruction of Jerusalem and its temple (Lu 19:41-44; 21:5, 6), which occurred in 70 C.E.

It must have been also with reference to the end of the Jewish system of things that Christ Jesus was spoken of as appearing and carrying on his activity "at the end of the times" or "at the end of these days." (1Pe 1:20, 21; Heb 1:1, 2) This is confirmed by the words of Hebrews 9:26: "But now he [Jesus] has manifested himself once for all time at the conclusion of the systems of things to put sin away through the sacrifice of himself."

Last Days Associated With the Apostasy. The words "last days" or comparable expressions are sometimes used in connection with the apostasy that was to be experienced within the Christian congregation. Wrote the apostle Paul to Timothy: "The inspired utterance says definitely that in later periods of time some will fall away from the faith, paying attention to misleading inspired utterances and teachings of demons." (1Ti 4:1; compare Ac 20:29, 30.) In a later letter to Timothy, Paul again discussed this point and spoke of future "last days." Because of the abandonment of right conduct by people then, these were to be "critical times hard to deal with" or, more literally, 'fierce appointed times.' (*Int*) After describing in detail the wayward course and perverted attitudes to prevail among persons living at that time, Paul continued: "From these arise those men who slyly work their way into households and lead as their captives weak women loaded down with sins, led by various desires, always learning and yet never able to come to an accurate knowledge of truth." (2Ti 3:1-7) Next Paul contrasted such corrupt persons with Timothy, who had closely followed the apostle's teaching, and encouraged him to 'continue in the things that he had learned and been persuaded to believe.' (2Ti 3:8-17; see also 2Ti 4:3-5.) Thus from the context it is clear that the apostle was informing Timothy well in advance about future developments among professed Christians and describing what fruitage such apostasy would finally yield.

Similarly, the apostle Peter provided advance knowledge to fellow Christians about pressures from within the congregation: "There will also be false teachers among you. These very ones will quietly bring in destructive sects and will disown even the owner that bought them, bringing speedy destruction upon themselves. Furthermore, many will follow their acts of loose conduct." (2Pe 2:1, 2) This same warning is echoed in Jude's words encouraging Christians "to put up a hard fight for the faith": "As for you, beloved ones, call to mind the sayings that have been previously spoken by the apostles of our Lord Jesus Christ, how they used to say to you: 'In the last time there will be ridiculers, proceeding according to their own desires for ungodly things.'" (Jude 3, 17, 18) Toward the close of the first century C.E., apostate elements were clearly in evidence. In our day the full fruitage of such apostasy is clearly evident; the "last days" to which Paul referred have arrived.

"The Conclusion of the System of Things." However, as Jesus Christ had foretold, the apostasy did not take in the entire body of Christians; the true, loyal ones were to be as "wheat" associated with "weeds." After Christ's presence begins, invisible, in spirit, and during "the conclusion of the system of things" then existing, a clear separation and demarcation was to be made evident. The "weeds," "the sons of the wicked one," were to be 'collected out of the kingdom of the Son of man.' This cleaning out of the true Christian congregation would leave a field of clean wheat; the false, imitation Christians would be outside the true Christian congregation. Whereas the weedlike ones would finally be pitched into "the fiery furnace," the wheatlike ones would "shine as brightly as the sun in the kingdom of their Father." (Mt 13:24-30, 37-43) This definitely pointed to the concluding portion of the system of things under Satan's wicked rule, preceding its destruction.

Furthermore, the illustration suggested that the apostasy would bear its full fruitage of wickedness during "the conclusion of the system of things" under Satan's control. Reasonably, therefore, at that time the conditions described by the writers of the Christian Greek Scriptures as marking "the last days" would be in evidence on a large scale among professed Christians. There would be increasing lawlessness and disobedience to parents. Persons would be "lovers of pleasures rather than lovers of God, having a form of godly devotion but proving false to its power." (2Ti 3:2-5) Also, there would be "ridiculers with their ridicule, proceeding according to their own desires and saying: 'Where is this promised presence of his? Why, from the day our forefathers fell asleep in death, all things are continuing exactly as from creation's beginning.'"—2Pe 3:3, 4.

The prophetic illustration of Jesus also showed that time had to pass before the weedlike ones would become fully manifest, finally to be destroyed. Since the apostles knew this, their use of "last days" and like expressions in connection with the apostasy did not mean that they expected Jesus' presence and the subsequent destruction of the ungodly right away. As Paul pointed out to the Thessalonians: "However, brothers, respecting the presence of our Lord Jesus Christ and our being gathered together to him, we request of you not to be quickly shaken from your reason nor to be excited either through an inspired expression or through a verbal message or through a letter as though from us, to the effect that the day of Jehovah is here. Let no one seduce you in any manner, because it will not come unless the apostasy comes first and the man of lawlessness gets revealed, the son of destruction."—2Th 2:1-3.

"Last Day." The Bible also refers to a "last day," during which the resurrection of the dead is to take place. (Joh 6:39, 40, 44; 11:24; compare Da 12:13.) At John 12:48 this "last day" is associated with a time of judgment. Obviously, therefore, it denotes a time of a far more distant future than the end of the apostolic period.—Compare 1Th 4:15-17; 2Th 2:1-3; Re 20:4-6, 12.

LAST SUPPER.   See LORD'S EVENING MEAL.

LATIN.   A language belonging to the Indo-European family and the parent of the Romance languages, namely, Italian, Spanish, French, Portuguese, and Romanian. The last half of the second century C.E. saw a move on the part of the religious powers of Rome to have Latin replace Greek as the language of the Roman bishopric. Among the results of this was the production of the Latin *Vulgate,* by Jerome of the fourth century C.E., second only to the Greek *Septuagint* as a noted ancient Bible translation.

Latin was the language of Imperial Rome and hence, when Jesus Christ was on earth, it was the official language of Palestine, though not the popular language of the people. It is therefore not surprising to find some Latinisms in the Christian Greek Scriptures. The word "Latin" itself occurs but once in the Bible, at John 19:20, where we are told that the inscription placed above Jesus on the torture stake was written in Hebrew, Greek, and Latin.

Latin in the Christian Greek Scriptures occurs in various forms. They contain over 40 proper Latin names of persons and places, such as Aquila, Luke, Mark, Paul, Caesarea, and Tiberias. In this part of the Bible are found Greek equivalents of some 30 Latin words of military, judicial, monetary, and domestic nature, such as *centurio* (Mr 15:39, army officer), *denarius* (Mt 20:2), and *speculator* (Mr 6:27, body guardsman). Certain Latin expressions or idioms also occur, such as "wishing to satisfy the crowd" (Mr 15:15) and "taking sufficient security." (Ac 17:9) The syntax, or pattern of phrases and sentences, sometimes suggests Latin influence. However, the amount of this is disputed by various scholars.

Latinisms are found mostly in Mark and Matthew, Mark having used them more than any other Bible writer. This lends credence to the belief that he wrote his Gospel in Rome and mainly for Gentiles, particularly the Romans. Paul made little use of Latinisms; none occur in the Greek *Septuagint.*

The appearance of Latinisms in the Scriptures is of more than academic interest to Bible lovers. It is in keeping with what the Bible shows about Palestine's being occupied by Rome when Jesus Christ was on earth. Further, the use of these Latinisms by the best secular Greek writers of the same period argues that the Christian Scriptures were indeed produced during the times about which they tell. This fact, therefore, further testifies to the authenticity of the Christian Greek Scriptures.

LATTICE. A framework consisting of crossed strips of wood, or laths, forming a network and generally used to cover a window. For centuries window lattices have been common in the Middle East. They have served to keep houses cool by blocking out the direct rays of the sun, while allowing for ventilation, and they also have contributed favorably to the general appearance of buildings. Some houses of Biblical times had ground-floor windows facing an inner courtyard and others facing the street. The latter were usually high up on the wall or in the roof chamber and were latticed.

A person in the house could look out through a latticed window and see what was taking place out of doors without being seen from the outside. In the song of Deborah and Barak, the mother of slain Sisera is represented as futilely looking out from a window and watching for her son "from the lattice." (Jg 5:1, 28) It was from a window through a lattice that it was possible for an observer to look down on "a young man in want of heart" as he came in contact with a prostitute. (Pr 7:6-13) Also, in The Song of Solomon (2:9), reference is made to "gazing through the windows, glancing through the lattices."

Some window lattices were evidently hinged so that they could be opened or closed. The windows of Daniel's roof chamber, from which he could be seen praying to Jehovah three times daily, may have had lattices that could be opened or shut. —Da 6:10.

LAUGHTER. The Hebrew words for laughter (*tsechoq'* and the parallel form *sechoq'*) are, according to Gesenius, onomatopoeic, that is, they are imitative of the sound of laughter (as are the written English interjections "ho-ho" and "ha-ha"). Isaac's name, *yits·chaq',* also meaning "Laughter," has this same mimetic quality.

Both Abraham and Sarah laughed at the angelic announcements that they would have a son in their old age. Abraham was not reproved for laughing but Sarah was, and she even tried to deny her laughter. It therefore appears that Abraham's laughter was the result of joy at the amazing prospect of having a son by Sarah in his old age. But Sarah's laughter evidently was because the same amazing prospect struck her as somewhat humorous; the thought of a woman of her age, till now sterile, having a child apparently brought a somewhat incongruous picture to her mind. (Ge 17:17; 18:9-15) In neither case, however, did the laughter represent scorn or deliberate mocking, and both are recorded as demonstrating faith in God's promise. (Ro 4:18-22; Heb 11:1, 8-12) When this son was born, the parents were no doubt delighted, for this had been their hearts' desire for years. Abraham named their son, after which Sarah said: "God has prepared laughter for me: everybody hearing of it will laugh at me." (Ge 21:1-7) Others were undoubtedly amazed and delighted on hearing of the good news of Abraham and Sarah's blessing at the hand of Jehovah.

When Appropriate. Jehovah is "the happy God" and wants his servants to be happy. (1Ti 1:11) However, the Scriptures show that laughter is fitting only at certain times. There is "a time to weep and a time to laugh." (Ec 3:1, 4) The wise man, King Solomon, counsels us: "Go, eat your food with rejoicing and drink your wine with a good heart, because already the true God has found pleasure in your works." However, there is no real cause for rejoicing if one's activity shows disregard for the righteous ways of God.—Ec 9:7.

When Inappropriate. The thing of importance is to live so that one achieves a good name with Jehovah. Therefore, in this system of things, laughter may at times be most inappropriate, even harmful. Solomon, in his experiment "to lay hold on folly until I could see what good there was to the sons of mankind in what they did," said in his heart: "Do come now, let me try you out with rejoicing. Also, see good." But he discovered that this was a vain pursuit. He found that mirth and laughter in themselves are not truly satisfying, for they fail to produce real and lasting happiness. There must be a true foundation for enduring, upbuilding joy. Solomon voiced his feelings: "I said to laughter: 'Insanity!' and to rejoicing: 'What is this doing?'"—Ec 2:1-3.

Solomon illustrates the wisdom of not merely living for the pursuit of enjoyment. He says: "Better is it to go to the house of mourning than to go to the banquet house, because that is the end of all mankind; and the one alive should take it to his heart." This is no recommendation for sadness as superior to rejoicing. It refers to a specific time, to the time when a person has died and the house is in mourning. Go there to console the sad survivors rather than callously forget them and feast and revel. Visiting the mourners would not only comfort the bereaved but also induce the visitor to remember life's brevity, to know that the death that has come to this house will come to all soon enough and that those living should keep it in mind. It is while a person is still living that he can make a good name, not when he is dying. And a good name with God is the only thing of real value to the dying.—Ec 7:2; Ge 50:10; Joh 11:31.

Solomon goes on to say: "Better is vexation than laughter, for by the crossness of the face the heart becomes better." (Ec 7:3) Laughter is good medicine, but there are times when we must soberly view our life and the way we are living it. If we see we are wasting too much time in frivolous feasting and not making a good name by doing good works, we have reason to be vexed with ourselves, to be sorry, and to change; it will make our heart better. It will help us make a good name so that the day of our death or the time of our final inspection by God and Christ will be better for us than the day of our birth.—Ec 7:1.

"The heart of the wise ones is in the house of mourning, but the heart of the stupid ones is in the house of rejoicing," Solomon goes on to say. "Better is it to hear the rebuke of someone wise than to be the man hearing the song of the stupid ones." (Ec 7:4, 5) The wise heart in a house where one has died is attuned to the seriousness that is natural in a house of bereavement, and it influences the wise heart to watch how one's life is lived, but the careless mood in a place of revelry appeals to the foolish heart and causes life to be faced with a shallow, reckless spirit. If a person is straying from right paths, the rebuke of a wise man will put him back in the way of life by correcting him and enabling him to make a good name for himself. But how can hearing a fool's song or empty flattery that conceals faults and hardens us in a wrong course be helpful? It would induce us to keep on making a bad name, not correcting us into ways leading to a good name with Jehovah.

"For as the sound of thorns under the pot, so is the laughter of the stupid one; and this too is vanity." (Ec 7:6) Thorns flame up quickly but are just as quickly burned to ashes. They may not last long enough to finish cooking what is in the pot, in such a case not accomplishing the task for which the fire is lit. Their showy, noisy, blazing crackling thus proves futile and vain. And so are the frivolous gigglings and follies of the fool. Also, the very sound of a fool's laughter grates on the ears, being inappropriate for the time or the occasion, and tends to discourage rather than encourage. It helps no one to advance in the serious task of making a good name that God will remember and thereby to ensure that 'the day of death will be better than the day of birth.'

Laughter Changed to Mourning. In his Sermon on the Mount, Jesus Christ said: "Happy are you who weep now, because you will laugh," and, "Woe, you who are laughing now, because you will mourn and weep." (Lu 6:21, 25) Jesus was evidently pointing out that those who were sad because of bad religious conditions then prevailing in Israel could have their weeping changed to laughter by faith in Him, whereas those enjoying laughter and life with no concern for the future would find their laughter changed to mourning. (Compare Lu 16:19-31.) In writing to Christians, Jesus' half brother James urged worldly-minded

Christians: "Give way to misery and mourn and weep. Let your laughter be turned into mourning, and your joy into dejection. Humble yourselves in the eyes of Jehovah, and he will exalt you." (Jas 4:4, 9, 10) Such exaltation would bring genuine happiness.

To Express Derision. Laughter figures prominently in the Scriptures as an expression of derision. The Hebrew verb *tsa·chaq'* (laugh) also has the meaning "poke fun; make a laughingstock." —Ge 21:9; 39:14.

Even members of the animal creation are depicted as laughing in scorn. The female ostrich is represented as laughing at the pursuing horse and its rider (because of her speed), and the horse as laughing at dread when going into battle (because of his strength and fearlessness). (Job 39:13, 18, 19, 22) Leviathan (the crocodile) is said to laugh at the rattling of a javelin, because of his heavy armor.—Job 41:1, 29.

Servants of God have had to endure much derisive laughter against them. Job said: "One who is a laughingstock to his fellowman I become." (Job 12:4; 30:1) Jeremiah was an object of laughter all day long among his contemporaries. (Jer 20:7) Jesus Christ himself was laughed at scornfully before raising the daughter of Jairus from death. (Mt 9:24; Mr 5:40; Lu 8:41-53) Yet, all who knew the strength and wisdom of God and were obedient to him had good reason to be happy.—Mt 5:11, 12.

Jehovah God is described as laughing in derision at the nations, at their boastful words, which come to nothing, and at the confusion their foolish course against him brings. (Ps 59:8) He knows his own power and purposes, and he laughs at the puny, futile opposition they bring against him and his people. (Ps 2:1-4) A wise person surely wants to avoid having Jehovah laugh at him. (Pr 1:26) While Jehovah has no pleasure in the death of the wicked (Eze 18:23, 32), he is unworried over their plots against his people and laughs because he sees the day of deliverance for the righteous, in which the schemes of the wicked will fail and wickedness will be ended forever.—Ps 37:12, 13, 20.

LAUNDRYMAN.

One who in Bible times washed used clothing and who also processed new cloth by bleaching and shrinking it and removing the oils in preparation for dyeing. In Hebrew the term is evidently from a root meaning "trample," that is, to wash by stamping with the feet to loosen the dirt. (Mal 3:2; see BATHING.) The Greek word for "clothes cleaner" (*gna·pheus'*) is related to *gna'phos* (prickly teasel; carding comb) and refers to one who dresses new cloth or washes and scours soiled garments.

Clothes cleaners of ancient times were likely able to whiten their clothing considerably by cleaning and bleaching. Yet, when describing the incomparable whiteness of Jesus' garments at the transfiguration scene, Mark says: "His outer garments became glistening, far whiter than any clothes cleaner on earth could whiten them."—Mr 9:3.

Alkali. In Hebrew the word for alkali is *ne'ther*, a carbonate of soda, also called natron. It is termed "mineral alkali," to distinguish it from "vegetable alkali." Natron was a native grade of the chemical, commercial grades of which are known as soda ash and sal soda. Its effervescence when mixed with a weak acid is alluded to at Proverbs 25:20. Though in some translations it is called "niter" (nitre), it should not be confused with modern niter (nitre), also called saltpeter, which may be either potassium or sodium nitrate.

By itself or as a soap builder this alkali is a very effective cleaner. This fact adds force to Jehovah's words as to the depth of Israel's sinfulness: "Though you should do the washing with alkali and take to yourself large quantities of lye, your error would certainly be a stain before me."—Jer 2:22.

The ancient world obtained this alkali from several sources of supply—from lakes or from deposits in Syria, India, Egypt, and along the southeastern shores of the Dead Sea. It is reported that, in addition to using it as a detergent, the Egyptians and others substituted it for yeast in breadmaking, employed it as a tenderizer when boiling meat, mixed it with vinegar for a toothache cure, and used it in embalming.

Lye. The Hebrew word *bo·rith'*, translated "lye" (in some translations, "soap"), refers to a vegetable alkali as distinguished from *ne'ther*, the so-called mineral alkali. The distinction was not one of chemical composition but, rather, was based on the difference in the source of supply. At Jeremiah 2:22 both words occur in the same verse. Chemically the lye of Bible times was sodium carbonate or potassium carbonate, depending on whether the vegetation from which the ashes were obtained was grown near the sea on saline soil or grown inland. The chemicals in the ashes were separated by leaching or filtering with water. This lye is different from the modern-day chemical termed "lye," the very caustic potassium hydroxide. The ancient laundryman's lye was used not only for clothes cleaning (Mal 3:2) but also for the reduction of such metals as lead and silver.—Isa 1:25.

Potash. The Hebrew word *bor* is translated "potash" (*NW*), "soap" (*Yg*), "lye" (*AT*), at Job 9:30. There it is spoken of as being used for cleansing the hands. This cleanser is thought to be either potassium carbonate or sodium carbonate. The way it was made gives it the name potash: wood *ashes* were first leached, then the solution was boiled down in *pots.*

LAUNDRYMAN'S FIELD.
Apparently an area close to the city of Jerusalem where laundrymen worked.

Isaiah and his son Shear-jashub were to meet King Ahaz by the "highway of the laundryman's field"; later, Sennacherib's emissaries came to the same vicinity. (2Ki 18:17; Isa 7:3; 36:2) While this "highway of the laundryman's field" was obviously outside the city, it was near enough that the taunts of Sennacherib's messengers could be heard by those on the city walls.—2Ki 18:18, 26, 27; Isa 36:1, 2.

A "conduit" is mentioned in connection with the "highway of the laundryman's field." This could not refer to what is called Hezekiah's tunnel, as that had not yet been constructed in Ahaz' day. The conduit therefore seems to have been one that ran through the torrent valley of Kidron down to the S end of the City of David. The laundryman's field appears to have been located either in this part of the valley or somewhat farther S, near the suggested site of En-rogel.

LAUREL
[Heb., *'o'ren*]. An evergreen, often growing as a shrub but capable of heights up to some 15 m (50 ft). The entire tree (leaves, bark, roots, and fruit) contains an oil long employed in medicine. The leaves are oblong and leathery, with a glossy upper side.

This tree is mentioned as the last of several trees in Isaiah 44:14; it is the only reference to the tree in the Hebrew Scriptures. *Lexicon in Veteris Testamenti Libros* (by L. Koehler and W. Baumgartner, Leiden, 1958, p. 88) identifies the name with the laurel tree (*Laurus nobilis*), also commonly called the sweet bay tree. (See also *The Interpreter's Dictionary of the Bible,* edited by G. A. Buttrick, 1962, Vol. 2, p. 293.) The *Laurus nobilis* is found from the coast on up into the middle mountain regions of Palestine and grows in other Mediterranean countries as well.

Laurel leaves were used by the ancient Greeks to form wreaths, which they placed on the heads of victors in the Pythian Games and also extended to those holding certain offices as a symbol of distinction.

LAW.
"1. The principles and regulations emanating from a government and applicable to a people, whether in the form of legislation or of custom and policies recognized and enforced by judicial decision. 2. Any written or positive rule, or collection of rules, prescribed under the authority of the state or nation." (*The American College Dictionary,* edited by C. L. Barnhart, 1966) "A divine commandment or a revelation of the will of God . . . the whole body of God's commandments or revelations: the will of God . . . : a rule of right living or good conduct esp[ecially] when conceived as having the sanction of God's will, of conscience or the moral nature, or of natural justice."—*Webster's Third New International Dictionary,* 1981.

The word "law," in the Hebrew Scriptures, is translated primarily from the Hebrew word *toh·rah',* related to the verb *ya·rah',* meaning "direct, teach, instruct." In some cases it is translated from the Aramaic term *dath.* (Da 6:5, 8, 15) Other words translated in the *King James Version* as "law" are *mish·pat'* (judicial decision, judgment), and *mits·wah'* (commandment). In the Greek Scriptures the word *no'mos,* from the verb *ne'mo* (deal out, distribute), is translated "law."

Jehovah God is designated as the Source of law, the Supreme Lawgiver (Isa 33:22), the Sovereign, delegating authority (Ps 73:28; Jer 50:25; Lu 2:29; Ac 4:24; Re 6:10), without whose permission or allowance no authority can be exercised. (Ro 13:1; Da 4:35; Ac 17:24-31) His throne is established on righteousness and judgment. (Ps 97:1, 2) The stated will of God becomes law to his creatures.—See LEGAL CASE.

Law to Angels. Angels, higher than man, are subject to the law and commandments of God. (Heb 1:7, 14; Ps 104:4) Jehovah even commanded and restricted his adversary Satan. (Job 1:12; 2:6) Michael the archangel recognized and respected Jehovah's position as Supreme Judge when he said, in dispute with the Devil: "May Jehovah rebuke you." (Jude 9; compare Zec 3:2.) The glorified Jesus Christ has all the angels placed under his authority by Jehovah God. (Heb 1:6; 1Pe 3:22; Mt 13:41; 25:31; Php 2:9-11) Thus, by Jesus' command, an angelic messenger was sent to John. (Re 1:1) Yet, at 1 Corinthians 6:3 the apostle Paul speaks of the spiritual brothers of Christ as designated to judge angels, evidently because they are to share in some way in executing judgment upon wicked spirits.

Law of Divine Creation. One of the definitions of law given in *Webster's Third New International Dictionary* is "the observed regularity of nature." As Creator of all things in heaven and earth (Ac 4:24; Re 4:11), Jehovah has established laws governing all created things. Job 38:10 speaks of a "regulation" on the sea; Job 38:12, of 'commanding the morning'; and Job 38:31-33 calls attention to star constellations and to "the statutes of the heavens." The same chapter points to God as governing the light, snow, hail, clouds, rain, dew, and lightning. Continuing to chapters 39 through 41, God's care for the animal kingdom is shown, and the birth, life cycles, and habits of animals are attributed to regulations laid down by God, not to any evolutionary "adaptation." In fact, in the very creating of life-forms, God incorporated the law that each was to bring forth "according to its kind," making evolution impossible. (Ge 1:11, 12, 21, 24, 25) Man also brought forth sons "in his likeness, in his image." (Ge 5:3) At Psalm 139:13-16 the embryonic growth of a child in the womb is spoken of, its parts being written down "in [Jehovah's] book" before any of them actually existed. Job 26:7 describes Jehovah as "hanging the earth upon nothing." Scientists today attribute the earth's position in space primarily to the interaction of the law of gravity and the law of centrifugal force.

Law to Adam. In the garden of Eden, Adam and Eve were commanded by God concerning their duties (1) to fill the earth, (2) to subdue it, and (3) to have in subjection all other living creatures of earth, sea, and air. (Ge 1:28) They were given laws as to their diet, granting them the seed-bearing vegetation and fruit as food. (Ge 1:29; 2:16) However, Adam was given a command that prohibited eating from the tree of the knowledge of good and bad (Ge 2:17); this command was transmitted to Eve. (Ge 3:2, 3) Adam is referred to as a transgressor and a trespasser because he violated a stated law.—Ro 5:14, 17; 4:15.

Laws to Noah; Patriarchal Law. Noah was given commandments relative to the building of the ark and the saving of his family. (Ge 6:22) After the Flood he was given laws that allowed the adding of flesh to man's diet; declared the sacredness of life and therefore of blood, in which is the life; prohibited the eating of blood; condemned murder; and instituted capital punishment for this crime.—Ge 9:3-6.

The patriarch was a family head and ruler. Jehovah is designated as the great Family Head, or Patriarch, "the Father, to whom every family in heaven and on earth owes its name." (Eph 3:14, 15) Noah, Abraham, Isaac, and Jacob are outstanding examples of patriarchs. These were especially dealt with by Jehovah. Abraham was given the command to circumcise all the males of his household as a sign of God's covenant with him. (Ge 17:11, 12) He observed Jehovah's "commands," "statutes," and "laws." He knew Jehovah's way to do righteousness and judgment and he laid these commands on his household.—Ge 26:4, 5; 18:19.

The laws that governed the patriarchs were also generally understood and partially reflected in the laws of the nations at that time, all of which nations sprang from the three sons of Noah, the patriarch. For example, the Pharaoh of Egypt knew that it was wrong to take another man's wife (Ge 12:14-20), as did the kings of the Philistines in the cases of Sarah and Rebekah.—Ge 20:2-6; 26:7-11.

In the days of Moses, the Israelites were in slavery to Egypt. They had voluntarily gone into Egypt during Jacob's lifetime but were enslaved after Jacob's son, the prime minister Joseph, had died. So, in effect, they were sold into slavery for nothing. Jehovah, in harmony with the patriarchal law of redemption and of the priority of the firstborn son, told Pharaoh, by the mouth of Moses and Aaron: "Israel is my son, my firstborn. And I say to you: Send my son away that he may serve me. But should you refuse to send him away, here I am killing your son, your firstborn." (Ex 4:22, 23) No redemption price was necessary for this release, nor was any given to Egypt. And when the Israelites left their slave masters, the Egyptians, "Jehovah gave the people favor in the eyes of the Egyptians, so that these granted them what was asked; and they stripped the Egyptians." (Ex 3:21; 12:36) They had entered the land with the approval of the Pharaoh, not as captives of war to be enslaved, but as free people. The enslavement had been unjust, so evidently Jehovah was seeing to it that they were now given wages for their labor.

The family was held responsible for violations of law by individual members. The patriarchal head was the responsible representative; he was blamed for wrongs of his family and was required to punish individual wrongdoers in the family. —Ge 31:30-32.

Marriage and birthright. Parents governed the arrangement of marriage for their sons and daughters. (Ge 24:1-4) The paying of a bride-price was common. (Ge 34:11, 12) Among the worshipers of Jehovah, intermarriage with idolaters was disobedience and was against the interests of the family.—Ge 26:34, 35; 27:46; 28:1, 6-9.

The birthright was reserved for the firstborn, belonging to him by inheritance. This included receiving a double portion of the estate. However, it could be transferred by the family head, the father. (Ge 48:22; 1Ch 5:1) The oldest son normally became the patriarchal head when the father died. Sons, after marriage, could establish households separate from the father's headship and could themselves become family heads.

Morals. Fornication was disgraceful and punishable, especially in cases of engaged persons or married persons (adultery). (Ge 38:24-26; 34:7) Brother-in-law marriage was practiced when a man died without a son. His brother then had the responsibility to take the widow as his wife, and the firstborn of their union would inherit the dead man's estate and carry on his name.—De 25:5, 6; Ge 38:6-26.

Property. Generally there seems to have been no holding of individual property, aside from a few personal belongings; all herds, household goods, and equipment were held in common by the family.—Ge 31:14-16.

On the basis of related historical evidence, some scholars believe that, in transferring land, the buyer was shown the land from a vantage point, the exact boundaries being designated. When the buyer said, "I see," he indicated legal acceptance. When Jehovah gave Abraham the promise of receiving the land of Canaan, Abraham was first told to look in all four directions. Abraham did not say, "I see," perhaps because God said that he would give the Promised Land to Abraham's *seed,* later on. (Ge 13:14, 15) Moses, as the legal representative of Israel, was told to "see" the land, which, if the view just discussed is correct, would indicate legal transfer of the land to Israel, for them to take it under Joshua's leadership. (De 3:27, 28; 34:4; consider also Satan's offer to Jesus at Mt 4:8.) Another action appearing to have similar legal flavor was: walking across the land or entering it for the purpose of taking possession. (Ge 13:17; 28:13) In certain ancient documents, the number of trees on a piece of land was listed at each real-estate sale.—Compare Ge 23:17, 18.

Custody. Legal responsibility came when an individual promised to keep or 'guard' a person, animal, or thing. (Ge 30:31) Reuben, as the firstborn of Jacob, was responsible in the case of Joseph's disappearance. (Ge 37:21, 22, 29, 30) The custodian was to give sufficient care to what was in his charge. He had to restore animals stolen, but not those that died of themselves or that were lost through events beyond his control, such as a raid by armed sheep rustlers. If an animal was killed by a wild beast, evidence of the torn animal had to be produced to clear the custodian of responsibility.—Ge 37:12-30, 32, 33; Ex 22:10-13.

Slavery. Slaves might be purchased or might be such through birth to slave parents. (Ge 17:12, 27) Slaves could enjoy a very honored position in the patriarchal household, as was the case with Abraham's servant Eliezer.—Ge 15:2; 24:1-4.

Law of God to Israel—The Law of Moses. Jehovah gave Israel the Law through Moses as mediator, in the Wilderness of Sinai, 1513 B.C.E. At the inauguration of the Law at Mount Horeb there was an awe-inspiring demonstration of Jehovah's power. (Ex 19:16-19; 20:18-21; Heb 12:18-21, 25, 26) The covenant was validated by the blood of bulls and goats. The people presented communion offerings, and they heard the book of the covenant read to them, after which they agreed to be obedient to all that Jehovah had spoken. Many of the earlier patriarchal laws were incorporated in the Law given through Moses.—Ex 24:3-8; Heb 9:15-21; see COVENANT.

The first five books of the Bible (Genesis through Deuteronomy) are often referred to as the Law. Sometimes this term is used with reference to the entire inspired Hebrew Scriptures. Generally, however, the Jews considered the entire Hebrew Scriptures to be composed of three sections, "the law of Moses," "the Prophets," and "Psalms." (Lu 24:44) Commands that came through the prophets were binding upon Israel.

Jehovah was identified in the Law as absolute Sovereign and also as King in a special way. Since Jehovah was both God and King of Israel, disobedience to the Law was both a religious offense and lèse-majesté, an offense against the Head of State, which in this case was against the King Jehovah. David, Solomon, and their successors on the throne of Judah were said to sit on "Jehovah's throne." (1Ch 29:23) Human kings and rulers in Israel were bound by the Law, and when they became despotic they were law violators accountable to God. (1Sa 15:22, 23) Kingship and priesthood were separate, this separation constituting a balance of power and a safeguard against tyranny. It kept the Israelites ever mindful that Jehovah was their God and real King. Each individual's relationship to God and to his fellowman was defined by the Law, and each individual could approach God through the priestly arrangement.

Under the Law, the Israelites could have become "a kingdom of priests and a holy nation." (Ex 19: 5, 6) The Law's demands of exclusive devotion to Jehovah, its absolute prohibition of any form of interfaith, and its regulations concerning religious cleanness and diet constituted a "wall" to keep the nation outstandingly separate from other nations. (Eph 2:14) A Jew could hardly enter a Gentile tent

SOME FEATURES OF THE LAW COVENANT

THEOCRATIC GOVERNMENT

Jehovah God is the Supreme Sovereign (Ex 19:5; 1Sa 12:12; Isa 33:22)

King to sit on "Jehovah's throne," representing Him (1Ch 29:23; De 17:14, 15)

Other officers (chieftains of tribes; chiefs of thousands, of hundreds, of fifties, and of tens) were selected on the basis of their fear of God, as well as their trustworthiness and incorruptibility (Ex 18:21, 25; Nu 1:44)

Respect was due to all who exercised God-given authority: officers, priests, judges, parents (Ex 20:12; 22:28; De 17:8-13)

RELIGIOUS OBLIGATIONS

(These were summed up in the greatest commandment in the Law—to love Jehovah with one's whole heart, mind, soul, and strength; De 6:5; 10:12; Mr 12:30)

Worship was to go only to Jehovah (Ex 20:3; 22:20; De 5:7)

Love should be a powerful motivating factor in one's relationship with God (De 6:5, 6; 10:12; 30:16)

All were to fear God so as not to disobey him (Ex 20:20; De 5:29)

God's name was not to be taken up in a worthless way (Ex 20:7; De 5:11)

They could approach him only in the way he approved (Nu 3:10; Le 10:1-3; 16:1)

All were obligated to keep the Sabbath (Ex 20:8-11; 31:12-17)

Congregating for worship (De 31:10-13)

All males were required to assemble three times a year: Passover and Festival of Unfermented Cakes, Festival of Weeks, and Festival of Booths (De 16:16; Le 23:1-43)

Man who deliberately neglected to keep Passover was "cut off" (Nu 9:13)

Supporting priesthood

Levites received a tithe, or tenth, of all the produce of the land from the other tribes (Nu 18:21-24)

Levites had to give to the priesthood a tithe made up of the very best of what they received (Nu 18:25-29)

Offering of sacrifices (Heb 8:3-5; 10:5-10)

Various offerings outlined in the Law: regular burnt offerings (Le chap 1; Nu chap 28), communion offerings (Le chap 3; 19:5), sin offerings (Le chap 4; Nu 15:22-29), guilt offerings (Le 5:1–6:7), grain offerings (Le chap 2), drink offerings (Nu 15:5, 10), wave offerings (Le 23:10, 11, 15-17)

Practices of false religion forbidden

Idolatry (Ex 20:4-6; De 5:8-10)

Making cuts in one's flesh for the dead or tattooing one's body (Le 19:28)

Planting a tree as a sacred pole (De 16:21)

Bringing things detestable, devoted to destruction, into one's house (De 7:26)

Speaking of revolt against Jehovah (De 13:5)

Advocating false worship (De 13:6-10; 17:2-7)

Going over to false worship (De 13:12-16)

Devoting offspring to false gods (Le 18:21, 29)

Spiritism, sorcery (Ex 22:18; Le 20:27; De 18:9-14)

DUTIES OF PRIESTHOOD

(In fulfilling their duties, the priests were assisted by the Levites; Nu 3:5-10)

Teach the Law of God (De 33:8, 10; Mal 2:7)

Serve as judges, applying divine law (De 17:8, 9; 19:16, 17)

Offer sacrifices on behalf of the people (Le chaps 1-7)

Use Urim and Thummim to inquire of God (Ex 28:30; Nu 27:18-21)

MEMBERSHIP IN THE CONGREGATION OF ISRAEL

Membership in congregation of Israel not limited to those born into the nation

Persons of other nations could become circumcised worshipers

Such alien residents were bound to keep all the terms of the Law covenant (Le 24:22)

Restrictions limiting membership in congregation of Israel

No man castrated by crushing testicles or having male member cut off (De 23:1)

No illegitimate son or his descendants to "tenth generation" (De 23:2)

No Ammonite or Moabite (evidently males) to time indefinite, because they would not extend hospitality but opposed Israel at the time of the Exodus from Egypt (De 23:3-6)

Sons born to Egyptians "as the third generation" could be admitted (De 23:7, 8)

JUDICIAL SYSTEM

(Laws governing legal cases highlighted Jehovah's justice and mercy. Judges were given latitude to show mercy, depending on the circumstances. These laws also kept the nation uncontaminated and protected the welfare of each individual Israelite)

Judges

Priests, kings, and other men appointed as judges (Ex 18:25, 26; De 16:18; 17:8, 9; 1Ki 3:6, 9-12; 2Ch 19:5)

Standing before judges was regarded as standing before Jehovah (De 1:17; 19:16, 17)

Hearing cases

Ordinary cases were submitted to judges (Ex 18:21, 22; De 25:1, 2; 2Ch 19:8-10)

If lower court could not make decision, case would go to higher courts (Ex 18:25, 26; 1Ki 3:16, 28)

Exceptional or hard cases that were taken to priests:

Cases of jealousy or unchastity of wife (Nu 5:12-15)

When witness charged another with revolt (De 19:16, 17)

When a violent deed or one causing bloodshed was committed, or when decision was hard or it was disputed (De 17:8, 9; 21:5)

When man was found slain in field and murderer could not be identified (De 21:1-9)

Witnesses

At least two witnesses required to establish truth (De 17:6; 19:15; compare Joh 8:17; 1Ti 5:19)

Hands of witnesses were to be the first to come upon guilty person in putting him to death. This was deterrent to false, hasty, or careless testimony (De 17:7)

Testifying falsely

Perjury was strictly forbidden (Ex 20:16; 23:1; De 5:20)

If false accusation against another person, false witness would receive punishment schemed for accused (De 19:16-19)

Bribery, partiality in judgment

Bribery prohibited (Ex 23:8; De 27:25)

Perverting justice forbidden (Ex 23:1, 2, 6, 7; Le 19:15, 35; De 16:19)

Holding a person in custody was done only when case was difficult and had to be decided by Jehovah (Le 24:11-16, 23; Nu 15:32-36)

Punishments

Strokes—limited to 40, to avoid disgraceful beating (De 25:1-3; compare 2Co 11:24)

Death by stoning—then body might be put on a stake as one accursed (De 13:10; 21:22, 23)

Retaliation—retribution, a like punishment (Le 24:19, 20)

Damages: If a person's animal damaged the property of another person (Ex 22:5; 21:

35, 36); if a person kindled fire that damaged another's property (Ex 22:6); if a person killed another's domestic animal (Le 24:18, 21; Ex 21:33, 34); if a person unintentionally appropriated to his own use something "holy," such as tithes or sacrifices (Le 5:15, 16); if a person deceived an associate about something in his charge or a deposit in hand or a robbery or something found, swearing falsely concerning these things (Le 6:2-7; Nu 5:6-8)

Cities of refuge

Accidental manslayer could flee to nearest one (Nu 35:12-15; De 19:4, 5; Jos 20:2-4)

Then trial was held in jurisdiction where incident occurred

One found to be an unintentional manslayer had to live in city of refuge until the death of the high priest (Nu 35:22-25; Jos 20:5, 6)

A deliberate murderer was put to death (Nu 35:30, 31)

MARRIAGE, FAMILY RELATIONSHIPS, SEXUAL MORALITY

(The Law safeguarded Israel by preserving the sacred status of marriage and family life)

Marriage, first performed by Jehovah (Ge 2:18, 21-24)

Husband was owner of his wife but was answerable to God for how he dealt with her (De 22:22; Mal 2:13-16)

Polygamy was permitted but was regulated so as to safeguard wife and her offspring (De 21:15-17; Ex 21:10)

Marriage was compulsory after seduction (unless father of girl forbade it) (Ex 22:16, 17; De 22:28, 29)

Levirate marriage was the arrangement in which a man married his brother's widow if his deceased brother died sonless; the man failing to do so was reproached (De 25:5-10)

Marriage alliances with aliens were forbidden (Ex 34:12-16; De 7:1-4), but marriage with captive women was permitted (De 21:10-14)

Women who were heirs of land were to marry only within tribe (Nu 36:6-9)

Divorce

Only husband was allowed to divorce (for something indecent on wife's part); he was required to give wife written certificate of divorce (De 24:1-4)

No divorce allowed if husband had married wife after seducing her (De 22:28, 29)

Man could not remarry woman he divorced after she had married again and her second husband divorced her or died (De 24:1-4)

Adultery carried death penalty for both guilty parties (Ex 20:14; De 22:22)

Incest

An Israelite man could not marry any of the following: His mother, stepmother, or a secondary wife of his father (Le 18:7, 8; 20:11; De 22:30; 27:20); his sister or half sister (Le 18:9, 11; 20:17; De 27:22); his granddaughter (Le 18:10); his aunt (either his mother's sister or his father's sister) (Le 18:12, 13; 20:19); his aunt by marriage (either his father's brother's wife or his mother's brother's wife) (Le 18:14; 20:20); his daughter-in-law (Le 18:15; 20:12); his daughter, stepdaughter, stepdaughter's daughter, stepson's daughter, mother-in-law (Le 18:17; 20:14; De 27:23); brother's wife (Le 18:16; 20:21), except in levirate marriage (De 25:5, 6); his wife's sister during his wife's lifetime (Le 18:18)

An Israelite woman could not marry any of the following: Her son or her stepson (Le 18:7, 8; 20:11; De 22:30; 27:20); her brother or half brother (Le 18:9, 11; 20:17; De 27:22); her grandfather (Le 18:10); her nephew (either her brother's son or her sister's son) (Le 18:12, 13; 20:19); her nephew (either her husband's brother's son or her husband's sister's son) (Le 18:14; 20:20); her father-in-law (Le 18:15; 20:12); her father, stepfather, mother's stepfather, father's stepfather, son-in-law (Le 18:7, 17; 20:14; De 27:23); her husband's brother (Le 18:16; 20:21), except in levirate marriage (De 25:5, 6); her sister's husband during her sister's lifetime (Le 18:18)

Penalty for incest: death (Le 18:29; 20:11, 12, 14, 17, 20, 21)

Intercourse during menstruation

If a man and a woman deliberately cohabited during menstruation, they were cut off in death (Le 18:19; 20:18)

Husband who unwittingly had intercourse with wife during such uncleanness (perhaps at unexpected beginning of menstruation) was unclean seven days (Le 15:19-24)

Parent-child relationships

Parents (especially fathers) were commanded to teach children God's Law (De 6:6-9, 20-25; 11:18-21; Isa 38:19)

Children to honor parents (Ex 20:12; 21:15, 17; Le 19:3; De 5:16; 21:18-21; 27:16)

Wearing dress of opposite sex (to deceive for immoral purposes) was prohibited (De 22:5)

Sodomy carried death penalty for both persons involved (Le 18:22; 20:13)

Bestiality resulted in death for person and beast (Ex 22:19; Le 18:23, 29; 20:15, 16; De 27:21)

Indecent assault (woman in husband's fight grabbed hold of other man's privates) punished by amputation of her hand, instead of penalty of like for like, out of Jehovah's regard for her reproductive powers and her husband's right to have children by her (De 25:11, 12)

BUSINESS PRACTICES

(The Law encouraged both honesty in business dealings and respect for the home and property of others)

Ownership of land

Land was allotted to families (Nu 33:54; 36:2)

Land not sold permanently but reverted to owner at Jubilee; its sale value was based on the number of crops until Jubilee (Le 25:15, 16, 23-28)

If there was a sale, nearest kinsman had right to buy (Jer 32:7-12)

The state did not have right to seize one's land inheritance for public purposes simply by paying compensation (1Ki 21:2-4)

Share of Levites consisted of cities and their pasture grounds

Of the 48 cities allotted, 13 were priestly cities (Nu 35:2-5; Jos 21:3-42)

Field of pasture ground of a Levite city could not be sold; it belonged to city, not to individuals (Le 25:34)

If man sanctified (set aside the use or production of) part of a field to Jehovah (sanctuary use, priesthood), the standard for estimating its value was that the area of ground seeded by a homer of barley would be worth 50 shekels of silver; the value diminished proportionately according to number of years left until next Jubilee (Le 27:16-18)

If sanctifier wanted to buy it back, he had to add 20 percent to the estimated value (Le 27:19)

If he did not buy it back but sold it to another man, at the Jubilee it became the possession of the priest as holy to Jehovah (Le 27:20, 21)

If a man sanctified to Jehovah part of field he had purchased from another, at Jubilee it returned to original holder (Le 27:22-24)

If a man "devoted" anything of his own property ("devoted" things were permanently and solely for sanctuary use or for destruction; Jos 6:17; 7:1, 15; Eze 44:29), it could not be sold or bought back; it remained Jehovah's (Le 27:21, 28, 29)

Redemption of property

All land returned to original possessor at time of Jubilee (with previously noted exceptions) (Le 25:8-10, 15, 16, 24-28)

Levites could redeem their houses in Levite cities at any time (Le 25:32, 33)

Jubilee year: began on Day of Atonement, in 50th year; counting started from year Israelites entered land (Le 25:2, 8-19)

Inheritance

Firstborn son inherited double share of property (De 21:15-17)

When there was no son, inheritance went to daughters. (Nu 27:6-8) If man had neither sons nor daughters, it went to his brothers, to his father's brothers, or to his nearest blood relative (Nu 27:9-11)

Scales, weights, and measures

Jehovah demanded honesty and accuracy (Le 19:35, 36; De 25:13-15)

Cheating was detestable to him (Pr 11:1)

Debts

At end of every seven years, Hebrew brothers were released from debts (De 15:1, 2)

Could press foreigner for payment of debt (De 15:3)

Security for a loan

If a person took a person's outer garment as security for a loan, he must not keep it overnight (The poor often slept in the garment for lack of other bedclothes) (Ex 22:26, 27; De 24:12, 13)

A person could not enter another man's house to get a pledge or something as a security for a loan. He had to remain outside the house and let the person bring it out to him (This maintained the inviolability of the man's domain) (De 24:10, 11)

One could not take a hand mill or its upper grindstone for security (The person then could not grind grain to feed himself and his family) (De 24:6)

MILITARY LAWS

(These laws regulated Israel's God-ordained warfare in the Promised Land. Wars of selfish aggression or conquest beyond God-given limits were strictly forbidden)

Wars

To be only wars of Jehovah (Nu 21:14; 2Ch 20:15)

Soldiers were sanctified before going into battle (1Sa 21:1-6; compare Le 15:16, 18)

Age of soldiers

Twenty years old and upward (Nu 1:2, 3; 26:1-4)

According to *Jewish Antiquities,* III, 288 (xii, 4), by Josephus, they served until 50 years of age

Exemptions from military service:

Levites, as ministers of Jehovah (Nu 1:47-49; 2:33)

Man who had not inaugurated newly built house or had not used newly planted vineyard (De 20:5, 6; compare Ec 2:24; 3:12, 13)

Man who had become engaged and had not yet taken his wife. The newly married man continued exempt for one year (Man had the right to have heir and to see this heir) (De 20:7; 24:5)

Man who was fearful (He would tend to break down morale of fellow soldiers) (De 20:8; Jg 7:3)

Cleanliness was required in camp (since soldiers were sanctified for warfare) (De 23:9-14)

No women were allowed as camp followers for sex relations; relations with women were abstained from during campaign. This ensured religious and physical cleanliness (Le 15:16; 1Sa 21:5; 2Sa 11:6-11)

No raping of women among enemy was allowed, for this would be fornication; and no marriage with such women was permitted until campaign was over. This provided for religious cleanliness and it also was an inducement for enemy surrender, for they would be assured that their women would not be molested (De 21:10-13)

Military procedures against enemy cities

If city that was attacked belonged to one of seven nations of land of Canaan (mentioned at De 7:1), all inhabitants were to be devoted to destruction. (De 20:15-17; Jos 11:11-14; De 2:32-34; 3:1-7) If left in the land, these would be a danger to continued relationship of Israel with Jehovah God. He had let them live in land until their iniquity came to completion (Ge 15:13-21)

For cities not belonging to the seven nations, terms of peace would first be proclaimed. (De 20:10, 15) If city surrendered, inhabitants were put to forced labor. If they did not surrender, all males and all women not virgins were killed. Others were spared as captives. (De 20:11-14; compare Nu 31:7, 17, 18.) Killing all men removed danger of later revolt by city and also marriage of these men to Israelite women. These measures also helped to avoid phallic worship and diseases among Israelites

Trees producing food could not be cut down and used for siegeworks (De 20:19, 20)

Chariots were burned; horses were hamstrung to incapacitate them for battle, and later they were killed (Jos 11:6)

DIETARY AND SANITARY LAWS

(These served to keep the Israelites separate from pagan nations, to promote cleanliness and health, and to remind them of their holiness to God; Le 19:2)

Use of blood

Eating of blood was strictly forbidden. (Ge 9:4; Le 7:26; 17:12; De 12:23-25) Penalty for violation: death (Le 7:27; 17:10)

Life (soul) is in the blood (Le 17:11, 14)

SOME FEATURES OF THE LAW COVENANT (*con't*)

Blood of slaughtered animal had to be poured out on ground like water and covered with dust (Le 17:13; De 12:16)

No animal dying of itself or found dead could be eaten (because it was unclean and had not been properly bled) (De 14:21)

Only legal uses: put upon altar for atonement; used for prescribed cleansing purposes (Le 17:11, 12; De 12:27; Nu 19:1-9)

Use of fat

No fat could be eaten; fat belonged to Jehovah (Le 3:16, 17; 7:23, 24)

Eating fat of offering brought death penalty (Le 7:25)

Slaughtered animals

In wilderness, any domestic animals that were to be slaughtered were to be brought to tabernacle. They would be eaten as communion sacrifices (Le 17:3-6)

Penalty for violation: death (Le 17:4, 8, 9)

Wild clean animals caught in hunting could be killed on the spot; blood had to be poured out (Le 17:13, 14)

After entering Promised Land, clean animals could be slaughtered for food in the place of a person's residence if he was far from the sanctuary, but blood had to be poured on ground (De 12:20-25)

Animals, fish, insects permitted for food:

Every creature that splits hoof, forming a cleft therein, and chews cud (Le 11:2, 3; De 14:6)

Everything in the waters that has fins and scales (Le 11:9-12; De 14:9, 10)

Insects and winged swarming creatures that go upon all fours and have leaper legs: migratory locust, edible locust, cricket, and grasshopper (all according to their kinds) (Le 11:21, 22)

Animals, fish, birds, swarming creatures prohibited for food:

Animals: camel, rock badger, hare, pig (Le 11:4-8; De 14:7, 8)

Fish and other swarming creatures in the water that have no fins or scales (Le 11:10)

Birds and flying creatures: eagle, osprey, black vulture, red kite, black kite, glede, raven, ostrich, owl, gull, falcon, little owl, long-eared owl, swan, pelican, vulture, cormorant, stork, heron, hoopoe, bat, any winged swarming creature that goes on all fours (that is, having locomotion in the manner of animals that walk on four legs). The factors determining which flying creatures were designated ceremonially "unclean" are not expressly stated in the Bible. While most of the "unclean" birds were birds of prey or scavengers, not all of them were (De 14:12-19; Le 11:13-20; see Birds and articles on individual birds)

Swarming creatures on the earth: mole rat, jerboa, lizard, gecko fanfoot, large lizard, newt, sand lizard, chameleon, any creature that goes upon the belly, on all fours (style of locomotion), or on any great number of feet (Le 11:29, 30, 42)

Animal that died of itself or was already dead or torn by wild beast (Le 17:15, 16; De 14:21; Ex 22:31)

Animals presented as vow or voluntary offerings, communion sacrifice could be eaten on day offered and on second but not on third day; penalty for violation, death. Thanksgiving sacrifice to be eaten on *that* day; none to be saved over until morning (second day). Passover must not be left over; what was not eaten was to be burned (Le 7:16-18; 19:5-8; 22:29, 30; Ex 12:10)

Things causing uncleanness:

Emission of semen

Person had to bathe and was unclean until evening (Le 15:16; De 23:10, 11)

Garment touched by semen was washed and was unclean until evening (Le 15:17)

Husband and wife, after having intercourse, had to bathe and were unclean until evening (Le 15:18)

Childbirth

Woman was unclean 7 days after bearing a male, plus 33 days (first 7 days, unclean to all, as in menstruation; 33 days unclean only in relation to touching holy things such as sacrificial meals or coming into the holy place) (Le 12:2-4)

If child was female, woman unclean 14 days, plus 66 (Le 12:5)

Woman's menstruation (Le 12:2)

Woman unclean seven days in regular menstruation; during entire period of abnormal or extended discharge of blood, plus seven days (Le 15:19, 25, 28)

During her uncleanness anything on which she sat or lay down was unclean (Le 15:20)

Person who touched her or her bed or what she sat on had to wash garments and bathe and was unclean until evening (Le 15:21-23)

If her menstrual impurity came to be upon a man, he was unclean seven days, and any bed upon which he would lie was unclean (Le 15:24)

Anytime she had running discharge she was unclean (Le 15:25)

Safeguards against disease

Leprosy and other plagues

Priest determined whether it was leprosy or not (Le 13:2)

Person was quarantined seven days and then examined; if plague had stopped, quarantined seven more days (Le 13:4, 5, 21, 26); if plague did not spread then, he was pronounced clean (Le 13:6); if plague spread, it was leprosy (Le 13:7, 8)

If leprous, person had to have garments torn, let his head become ungroomed, cover over mustache (or upper lip), call out "Unclean, unclean!" Dwelt isolated outside camp until plague cured (Le 13:45, 46; Nu 5:2-4)

Genital discharge (evidently due to diseased condition) (Le 15:2, 3)

Bed or articles that such a person would sit or lie on were unclean (Le 15:4)

Anyone who touched the affected person, his bed, or whatever he was sitting on was unclean, or if affected person spat on another, he was rendered unclean (Le 15:5-11)

If touched by one having running discharge, earthenware vessels were smashed, wooden one was rinsed with water (Le 15:12)

After discharge stopped, person was unclean seven days (Le 15:13)

Cleanness of military camp was safeguarded by requiring that excrement be deposited outside the camp and be covered over (De 23:12, 13)

Regulations concerning bodies of dead persons

Touching corpse, bone, or burial place of human made one unclean seven days (even when on open field). (Nu 19:11, 16) Death for refusing to purify self (Nu 19:12, 13) (See cleansing procedure at Nu 19:17-19)

All who were in or came into tent containing dead person were unclean as was any opened vessel there on which no lid was tied down (Nu 19:14, 15)

Regulations concerning bodies of dead animals

The body of a clean animal that died of itself made the one who carried it, touched it, or ate it unclean; the dead body of any unclean animal made the one who touched it unclean. Cleansing was required (Le 11:8, 11, 24-31, 36, 39, 40; 17:15, 16)

Bodies of unclean animals would make items such as vessels, jar stands, ovens, garments, skins, and sackcloth unclean by contact (Le 11:32-35)

Spoil taken from city

Everything that could be processed with fire had to be so processed (metals), then purified by water for cleansing; other things had to be washed (Nu 31:20, 22, 23)

OTHER OBLIGATIONS INVOLVING FELLOW CREATURES

(The Law specified that "you must love your fellow as yourself"; Le 19:18. Jesus indicated that this was the second greatest commandment in the Law; Mt 22:37-40)

Toward fellow Israelites

Love was to be shown; murder was forbidden (Ex 20:13; Ro 13:9, 10)

Must not take vengeance or hold a grudge against one's fellowman (Le 19:18)

Care for the poor (Ex 23:6; Le 25:35, 39-43)

Care for widows and orphans (Ex 22:22-24; De 24:17-21; 27:19)

Respect for property

Stealing was forbidden; compensation was required (Ex 20:15; 22:1-4, 7)

Wrongful desire for property and possessions belonging to one's fellowman was forbidden (Ex 20:17)

Consideration for the handicapped

Could not ridicule or call down evil upon deaf person; he could not defend himself against statements he could not hear (Le 19:14)

One who put an obstacle in the way of blind person or misled him was cursed (Le 19:14; De 27:18)

Toward alien residents: they were not to be mistreated (Ex 22:21; 23:9; Le 19:33, 34; De 10:17-19; 24:14, 15, 17; 27:19)

Toward slaves

Hebrew slave was released in seventh year of his (or her) servitude or at Jubilee year, whichever came first. During slavery, to be treated as hired laborer, with consideration (Ex 21:2; De 15:12; Le 25:10)

If man came in with wife, she went out or was freed with him (Ex 21:3)

If master gave him a wife (evidently a foreigner) while he was in slavery, only he went free; if this wife had borne him children, she and children remained property of master (Ex 21:4)

On freeing Hebrew slave, master had to give him gift according to his ability to give (De 15:13-15)

Slave could be flogged by master. (Ex 21:20, 21) If maimed, was given freedom. (Ex 21:26, 27) If slave died under his master's beating, master could be punished by death; judges would decide the penalty (Ex 21:20; Le 24:17)

Toward animals

If one came upon a domestic animal in distress, he was obligated to help it, even if it belonged to an enemy of his (Ex 23:4, 5; De 22:4)

Beasts of burden were not to be overworked or mistreated (De 22:10; compare Pr 12:10)

Bull not to be muzzled when threshing, so that it could feed on the grain it was threshing (De 25:4; compare 1Co 9:7-10)

FEATURES OF LAW COVENANT (con't)

A person was not to take both a mother bird and her eggs, thereby wiping out family (De 22:6, 7)

A person was not to slaughter a bull or a sheep and its young on the same day (Le 22:28)

PURPOSES SERVED BY THE LAW

It made transgressions manifest; it showed that the Israelites needed to be forgiven of their transgressions and that a greater sacrifice was required that could really atone for their sins (Ga 3:19)

As a tutor, it safeguarded and disciplined the Israelites, preparing them for the Messiah as their instructor (Ga 3:24)

Various aspects of the Law were shadows that represented greater things to come; these shadows helped righthearted Israelites to identify the Messiah, since they could see how he fulfilled these prophetic patterns (Heb 10:1; Col 2:17)

or house or eat with Gentiles without becoming religiously unclean. In fact, when Jesus was on earth, even entering a Gentile house or building was thought to make a Jew unclean. (Joh 18:28; Ac 10:28) The sanctity of life and the dignity and honor of the family, of marriage, of person, were protected. Additional effects, which could be considered incidental to the religious separation that the Law covenant accomplished, were the health benefits and the protection from diseases common to the nations around the Israelites. The laws of moral cleanness, physical sanitation, and diet undoubtedly had a salutary effect when they were obeyed.

But the real purpose of the Law was, as stated by the apostle Paul, "to make transgressions manifest, until the seed should arrive." It was a "tutor leading to Christ." It pointed to Christ as the objective aimed at ("Christ is the end of the Law"). It revealed that all humans, including the Jews, are under sin and that life cannot be obtained by "works of law." (Ga 3:19-24; Ro 3:20; 10:4) It was "spiritual," from God, and "holy." (Ro 7:12, 14) At Ephesians 2:15 it is called "the Law of commandments consisting in decrees." It was a standard of perfection, marking the one who could keep it as perfect, worthy of life. (Le 18:5; Ga 3:12) Since imperfect humans could not keep the Law, it showed that "all have sinned and fall short of the glory of God." (Ro 3:23) Only Jesus Christ kept it blamelessly.—Joh 8:46; Heb 7:26.

The Law also served as "a shadow of the good things to come," and things connected with it were "typical representations," causing Jesus and the apostles to call upon it often to explain heavenly things and matters concerning Christian doctrine and conduct. Therefore, it provides an essential and necessary field of study for the Christian. —Heb 10:1; 9:23.

Jesus said that the whole Law hung upon the two commandments, to love God and to love one's neighbor. (Mt 22:35-40) It is interesting that in the book of Deuteronomy (where the Law was modified somewhat to govern Israel's new circumstances upon settling in the Promised Land) the Hebrew words for "love," "loved," and so forth, appear more than 20 times.

The Ten Words (Ex 34:28), or the Ten Commandments, were the basic part of the Law but were combined with about 600 other laws, all of which were of equal force and binding power upon the Israelites. (Jas 2:10) The first four of the Ten Commandments defined man's relationship to God; the fifth, to God and to parents; and the last five, to one's fellowman. These last five were named in apparent order of severity of harm done to one's fellowman: murder, adultery, stealing, bearing false witness, and covetousness or selfish desire. The tenth commandment makes the Law unique in comparison with the laws of all other nations in that it prohibits selfish desire, a command in reality enforceable only by God. It actually got at the cause of violation of all the other commandments.—Ex 20:2-17; De 5:6-21; compare Eph 5:5; Col 3:5; Jas 1:14, 15; 1Jo 2:15-17.

The Law contained many principles and guiding statutes. The judges were given latitude to investigate and consider motives and attitude of violators, along with the circumstances surrounding the violation. A deliberate, disrespectful, or unrepentant violator received the full penalty. (Nu 15:30, 31) In other cases a lighter judgment might be determined. For example, whereas a murderer was to be put to death without fail, an accidental manslayer could receive mercy. (Nu 35:15, 16) The owner of a bull that habitually gored people and that killed a man might die; or the judges might impose a ransom. (Ex 21:29-32) The difference between a deliberate thief and a wrongdoer who voluntarily confessed evidently accounts for the difference between the penalty stated at Exodus 22:7 and that of Leviticus 6:1-7.

Law of Conscience. The Bible shows this results from persons having 'the law written in their hearts.' Those not under a direct law from God, such as the Law given through Moses, are shown to be "a law to themselves," for their consciences cause them to be "accused or even excused" in their own thoughts. (Ro 2:14, 15) Many just laws in pagan societies reflect this conscience, originally placed in their forefather Adam and passed down through Noah.—See CONSCIENCE.

At 1 Corinthians 8:7 the apostle Paul says that lack of accurate Christian knowledge could result in a weak conscience. Conscience can be a good guide or a poor one, depending upon the knowledge and training of the individual. (1Ti 1:5; Heb 5:14) One's conscience can be defiled and, therefore, can mislead. (Tit 1:15) Some, by constantly going contrary to conscience, cause it to become like insensitive scar tissue, and consequently no safe guide to follow.—1Ti 4:1, 2.

"Law of the Christ." Paul wrote: "Go on carrying the burdens of one another, and thus fulfill the law of the Christ." (Ga 6:2) While the Law covenant was terminated at Pentecost, 33 C.E. ("since the priesthood is being changed, there comes to be of necessity a change also of the law"; Heb 7:12), Christians come "under law toward Christ." (1Co 9:21) This law is called "the perfect law that belongs to freedom," "the law of a free people," "the law of faith." (Jas 1:25; 2:12; Ro 3:27) Such a new law had been foretold by God through the prophet Jeremiah when he spoke of a new covenant and the writing of his law on the hearts of his people.—Jer 31:31-34; Heb 8:6-13.

Like Moses, the mediator of the Law covenant, Jesus Christ is Mediator of the new covenant. Moses wrote the Law in code form, but Jesus did not personally put a law down in writing. He talked and put his law into the minds and hearts of his disciples. Neither did his disciples set down laws in the form of a code for Christians, classifying the laws into categories and subheadings. Nonetheless, the Christian Greek Scriptures are full of laws, commands, and decrees that the Christian is bound to observe.—Re 14:12; 1Jo 5:2, 3; 4:21; 3:22-24; 2Jo 4-6; Joh 13:34, 35; 14:15; 15:14.

Jesus gave instruction to his disciples to preach the 'good news of the kingdom.' His command is found at Matthew 10:1-42; Luke 9:1-6; 10:1-12. At Matthew 28:18-20 a new command was given to Jesus' disciples to go, not to the Jews only, but to all nations, to make disciples and baptize them with a new baptism, "in the name of the Father and of the Son and of the holy spirit, teaching them to observe all the things I have commanded you." Thus, with divine authorization Jesus taught and issued commands while on earth (Ac 1:1, 2) as well as after his ascension. (Ac 9:5, 6; Re 1:1-3) The entire book of Revelation consists of prophe-cies, commands, admonition, and instruction to the Christian congregation.

The "law of the Christ" covers the whole course and scope of the Christian's life and work. By the help of God's spirit the Christian can follow the commands in order to be judged favorably by that law, for it is "the law of that spirit which gives life in union with Christ Jesus."—Ro 8:2, 4.

"Law of God." The apostle Paul speaks of the Christian's fight as influenced by two factors, "the law of God" and "the law of my mind"—"the law of that spirit which gives life" on one side and "sin's law," or "the law of sin and of death," on the other. Paul describes the conflict, saying that fallen flesh infected with sin is enslaved to "sin's law." "The minding of the flesh means death," but "God, by sending his own Son in the likeness of sinful flesh and concerning sin, condemned sin in the flesh." With the help of God's spirit the Christian can win the fight—by exercising faith in Christ, putting to death the practices of the body, and living according to the spirit's direction—and can gain life.—Ro 7:21–8:13.

Law of Sin and Death. The apostle Paul argues that, because of the sin of mankind's father Adam, "death ruled as king" from Adam to the time of Moses (when the Law was given) and that the Law made transgressions manifest, making men chargeable with sin. (Ro 5:12-14; Ga 3:19) This rule, or law of sin, working in imperfect flesh exercises power over it, making it incline toward violation of God's law. (Ro 7:23; Ge 8:21) Sin causes death. (Ro 6:23; 1Co 15:56) The law of Moses could not overcome the rule of kings sin and death, but freedom and victory come by means of the undeserved kindness of God through Jesus Christ.—Ro 5:20, 21; 6:14; 7:8, 9, 24, 25.

"Law of Faith." The "law of faith" is contrasted with "that of works." Man cannot attain to righteousness by his own works or those of the Law of Moses, as though earning righteousness as pay for works, but righteousness comes by faith in Jesus Christ. (Ro 3:27, 28; 4:4, 5; 9:30-32) James says, however, that such faith will be accompanied by works that result from one's faith and are in harmony with it.—Jas 2:17-26.

Law of Husband. A married woman is under obligation to "the law of her husband." (Ro 7:2; 1Co 7:39) The principle of husbandly headship holds true throughout the entire organization of God and has been in operation among those worshiping God as well as among many other peoples. God occupies the position of a husband to his "woman," "the Jerusalem above." (Ga 4:26, 31; Re 12:1, 4-6, 13-17) The Jewish national organization was in the relationship of a wife to Jehovah as husband.—Isa 54:5, 6; Jer 31:32.

In patriarchal law the husband was the undisputed head of the family, the wife being in submission, though she could make recommendations subject to the husband's approval. (Ge 21:8-14) Sarah called Abraham "lord." (Ge 18:12; 1Pe 3: 5, 6) A head covering was worn by the woman as a sign of her subjection to her husbandly head. —Ge 24:65; 1Co 11:5.

Under the Law given to Israel the wife was in subjection. Her husband could allow or annul vows she made. (Nu 30:6-16) She did not inherit, but went along with the land inheritance, and in the event that the inheritance was repurchased by a kinsman, she was included. (Ru 4:5, 9-11) She could not divorce her husband, but the husband had the right to divorce his wife.—De 24:1-4.

In the Christian arrangement, the woman is required to recognize the man's position and not usurp it. The apostle Paul speaks of the married woman as being under the law of her husband as long as he is alive, but he points out that she is freed by his death, so that she is not an adulteress if she then remarries.—Ro 7:2, 3; 1Co 7:39.

"Kingly Law." The "kingly law" rightly has the prominence and importance among other laws governing human relationships that a king would have among men. (Jas 2:8) The tenor of the Law covenant was love; and "you must love your neighbor as yourself" (the kingly law) was the second of the commandments on which all the Law and the Prophets hung. (Mt 22:37-40) Christians, though not under the Law covenant, are subject to the law of the King Jehovah and his Son, the King Jesus Christ, in connection with the new covenant.

LAWGIVER. A maker of laws; a legislator. The Bible centers attention on Jehovah as the fundamental Lawgiver of the universe.

Jehovah as the Lawgiver. Jehovah is actually the one true Lawgiver in the universe. Attributable to him are the physical laws governing inanimate creation (Job 38:4-38; Ps 104:5-19), and animal life. (Job 39:1-30) Man also, as a creation of Jehovah, is subject to Jehovah's physical laws, and since he is a moral, rational creature, capable of reasoning and of spirituality, he is equally subject to God's moral laws. (Ro 12:1; 1Co 2:14-16) Furthermore, Jehovah's law governs spirit creatures, angels.—Ps 103:20; 2Pe 2:4, 11.

Jehovah's physical laws are unbreakable. (Jer 33:20, 21) Throughout the known visible universe his laws are so stable and reliable that, in areas where scientists have knowledge of these laws, they can calculate the movements of the moon, planets, and other celestial bodies with split-second accuracy. One who goes contrary to the physical laws experiences immediate application of their sanctions. Likewise, the moral laws of God are irrevocable and cannot be circumvented or violated with impunity. They are as sure of enforcement as are His natural laws, though the punishment may not be as immediately enforced. "God is not one to be mocked. For whatever a man is sowing, this he will also reap."—Ga 6:7; 1Ti 5:24.

Before Jehovah gave his law to Israel, how could humans determine God's will for them?

Whereas from Adam's rebellion to the Flood badness increased among the majority of his descendants, some faithful men "kept walking with the true God." (Ge 5:22-24; 6:9; Heb 11:4-7) The only specific commands recorded as given to such men by God are the instructions to Noah in connection with the ark. These Noah obeyed implicitly. (Ge 6:13-22) Nevertheless, there were principles and precedents to guide faithful humans in their "walking with the true God."

They knew of God's bounteous generosity in providing for man in Eden; they saw the evidence of divine unselfishness and loving interest. They knew that the principle of headship was in effect from the start, God's headship over man and the man's headship over woman. They knew of God's assignment of work to man as well as His concern for proper care of the things given to man for his use and enjoyment. They knew that sexual unions were to be between man and woman and that those so uniting were to do so within a marital relationship, that they would 'leave father and mother' to form a lasting union instead of a temporary one (as in fornication). From God's command regarding the use of the trees of the garden of Eden and the tree of the knowledge of good and bad in particular, they could appreciate the principle of ownership rights and due respect for such. They were aware of the bad results coming from the first lie. They knew of God's approval of Abel's course of worship, God's disapproval of Cain's envy and hatred of his brother, and God's punishment of Cain's murder of Abel.—Ge 1:26–4:16.

Thus, even without further specific statements, decrees, or statutes from God, they could draw on these principles and precedents to guide them in different, but related, situations that might develop. Centuries later, Jesus and his apostles viewed pre-Flood matters in this way. (Mt 19:3-9; Joh 8:43-47; 1Ti 2:11-14; 1Jo 3:11, 12) Law means a *rule of action*. By God's words and acts they had the means for knowing something of his way, his standards, and this should be the rule of action, or law, for them to follow. By doing so, they could 'keep on walking with the true God.' Those failing to do so were sinning, 'missing the mark,' even though there was no law code to condemn them.

Following the Flood, God stated to Noah the law, binding on all mankind, that allowed the eating of flesh but prohibited eating of blood, and He stated the principle of capital punishment for murder. (Ge 9:1-6) In the early post-Flood period, men such as Abraham, Isaac, Jacob, and Joseph showed genuine concern for God's way, his rule of action. (Ge 18:17-19; 39:7-9; Ex 3:6) Though God gave certain specific commands to faithful men (Ge 26:5), such as the law of circumcision, there is no record of his giving them a detailed law code to observe. (Compare De 5:1-3.) Nonetheless, they had not only the principles and precepts of the pre-Flood period to guide them but also additional principles and precepts to be drawn from his expressions and dealings with mankind in the post-Flood period.

Thus, although God had not given a detailed law code, as he later did with the Israelites, men were not without some means for determining right and wrong conduct. Idolatry, for example, had not yet been specifically condemned by a stated law. Nonetheless, as the apostle Paul shows, such practice was inexcusable inasmuch as God's "invisible qualities are clearly seen from the world's creation onward, because they are perceived by the things made, even his eternal power and Godship." The venerating and rendering of "sacred service to the creation rather than the One who created" was against all reason. Those following such an empty-headed course would thereafter deviate into other unrighteous practices, such as homosexuality, changing "the natural use of themselves into one contrary to nature." Again, even though no specific law had been given, such practice was obviously contrary to the way of God the Creator, as the very structure of the male and female manifested. Man, having been originally made in God's image, had intelligence sufficient to see these things. Hence, he was responsible before God if he went contrary to God's way; he was sinning, 'missing the mark,' even without a specifically stated law to charge him with guilt.—Ro 1:18-27; compare Ro 5:13.

The Law covenant. Even prior to the Exodus from Egypt, Jehovah had served as the Statute-Giver to his people Israel. (Ex 12:1, 14-20; 13:10) But an outstanding example of his role as Lawgiver to a nation was his institution of the Law covenant. Here, for the first time, was a body of laws in code form governing every facet of life. This covenant making Israel an exclusive people, a nation belonging peculiarly to Him, distinguished Israel from all other nations.—Ex 31:16, 17; De 4:8; Ps 78:5; 147:19, 20.

In a prophetic message forecasting salvation by Jehovah, the prophet Isaiah stated: "Jehovah is our Judge, Jehovah is our Statute-giver ["lawgiver," *AS, Dy, Le, Yg*], Jehovah is our King; he himself will save us." (Isa 33:22) Jehovah therefore constituted the judicial, legislative, and executive power in Israel; the three branches of government were combined in him. Isaiah's prophecy thus gave assurance of complete defense and direction for the nation, for it highlighted the fact that Jehovah was in a full sense the Sovereign Ruler.

In describing Jehovah as Israel's Statute-Giver, or Lawgiver, Isaiah used a form of the Hebrew term *cha·qaq'*, which literally means "hew out" or "inscribe." In discussing this word, the Hebrew lexicon by W. Gesenius explains: "Since the inscribing of decrees and statutes on public tablets and monuments was the part of the lawgiver, this implied also the power of decreeing." (*A Hebrew and English Lexicon of the Old Testament*, translated by E. Robinson, 1836, p. 366) Bible translators have rendered the word "lawgiver," "ruler," and "commander." (Ge 49:10; De 33:21; Jg 5:14; Ps 60:7; 108:8; compare *AT, KJ, NW, RS, Yg.*) Hence, the rendering "Statute-giver" is in accord with one sense of the Hebrew word, and it provides a suitable contrast and completeness at Isaiah 33:22, where the word is included in the same sentence with "Judge" and "King."

God had not given such a detailed law to any other nation or people. Nevertheless, God had originally created man in righteousness and had endowed him with the faculty of conscience. Despite fallen man's inherent imperfection and tendency toward sin, there also remained evidence of his having been made in his Creator's image and likeness as well as evidence of the faculty of conscience. Thus, even among the non-Israelite nations certain rules of action and judicial decrees were developed that reflected to some degree the righteous principles of God.

The apostle Paul describes this in saying: "For instance, all those who sinned without law [that is,

God's law given to his people] will also perish without law; but all those who sinned under law will be judged by law. For the hearers of law are not the ones righteous before God, but the doers of law will be declared righteous. For whenever people of the nations that do not have law do by nature the things of the law, these people, although not having law, are a law to themselves. They are the very ones who demonstrate the matter of the law to be written in their hearts, while their conscience is bearing witness with them and, between their own thoughts, they are being accused or even excused." (Ro 2:12-15) Thus, those nations, though not brought into legal relationship with God, were not sinless but 'missed the mark' of Jehovah's perfect standards. —Compare Ro 3:9.

By giving the Law covenant to Israel, God made clear that all persons, not merely the idolatrous pagans but also the Israelites, were guilty of sin. It served to make the Israelites acutely aware of the many ways in which they failed to measure up to perfect standards. This was "so that every mouth may be stopped and all the world may become liable to God for punishment . . . for by law is the accurate knowledge of sin." (Ro 3:19, 20) Even though an Israelite may have been free from idolatry, may have been abstaining from blood, may not have been guilty of murder, he was still declared guilty of sin by the Law covenant. This was so because the Law covenant now specifically identified a host of actions and even attitudes as sinful. Hence, Paul, viewing himself as if alive in the loins of his forefathers prior to the giving of the Law, says: "Really I would not have come to know sin if it had not been for the Law; and, for example, I would not have known covetousness if the Law had not said: 'You must not covet.' . . . In fact, I was once alive apart from law; but when the commandment arrived, sin came to life again, but I died."—Ro 7:7-9.

Other Lawgivers. When God's Son came to earth, he acknowledged Jehovah as his Lawgiver and God. As a Jew, Jesus himself was born under the Law covenant and was obligated to obey it perfectly. (Ga 4:4, 5) He, in turn, set forth laws for his followers, both when he spoke to them and through holy spirit operating on his followers who wrote the Christian Scriptures. Collectively, these laws are called "the law of the Christ." (Ga 6:2; Joh 15:10-15; 1Co 9:21) This law governs "the Israel of God," his spiritual "nation." (Ga 6:16; 1Pe 2:9) Christ, however, did not originate these laws but got them from the great Lawgiver, Jehovah.—Joh 14:10.

Moses. Although the Bible repeatedly mentions "the law of Moses" (Jos 8:31, 32; 1Ki 2:3; 2Ch 23:18; 30:16), it also acknowledges Jehovah as the actual Lawgiver and Moses as only His instrument and representative in giving the Law to Israel. (2Ch 34:14) Even angels had a share in representing God in this matter, for the Law "was transmitted through angels by the hand of a mediator." Nevertheless, Moses, being Jehovah's appointed mediator of the covenant between God and Israel, is spoken of as if he were the lawgiver.—Ga 3:19; Heb 2:2.

Human rulers as lawgivers. God has not established worldly human governments nor given them their authority, but he has allowed them to exist and has removed them and permitted new ones to come up as it suited his purpose. (De 32:8; Da 4:35; 5:26-31; Ac 17:26; Ro 13:1) Some of these rulers become lawgivers to their nation, state, or community. But their laws and statutes are proper only if made within the framework of and in harmony with the law of the Great Lawgiver, Jehovah God. The famous British jurist Sir William Blackstone said, with reference to God's law governing natural things: "It is binding over all the globe, in all countries, and at all times: no human laws are of any validity, if contrary to this; and such of them as are valid derive all their force, and all their authority, mediately or immediately, from this original." Also, "Upon these two foundations, the law of nature and the law of revelation [found only in the Holy Scriptures], depend all human laws, that is to say, no human laws should be suffered to contradict these."—*Chadman's Cyclopedia of Law*, 1912, Vol. I, pp. 89, 91; compare Mt 22:21; Ac 5:29.

In the Christian congregation. Jesus' half brother James wrote to some Christians who were becoming proud, boastful, and critical of their Christian brothers, saying: "Quit speaking against one another, brothers. He who speaks against a brother or judges his brother speaks against law and judges law. Now if you judge law, you are, not a doer of law, but a judge. One there is that is lawgiver [Gr., no·mo·the'tes] and judge, he who is able to save and to destroy. But you, who are you to be judging your neighbor?" James goes on to speak of those who bragged about what they would do in the future, as though they were independent of circumstances, instead of saying, "If Jehovah wills." (Jas 4:11-16) James had spoken of "the kingly law," "You must love your neighbor as yourself." (Jas 2:8) These Christians, by failing to exhibit love for their neighbor, speaking against him instead, were, in effect, setting themselves up as judges of divine law, as lawgivers or lawmakers.

The apostle Paul had given similar counsel in his letter to the Romans concerning some who were judging others on the basis of such things as what they ate and drank: "Who are you to judge the house servant of another? To his own master he stands or falls. Indeed, he will be made to stand, for Jehovah can make him stand."—Ro 14:4.

In the light of the foregoing, how can Paul's instructions with regard to a serious case of fornication in the congregation at Corinth be viewed? He said: "I for one, although absent in body but present in spirit, have certainly judged already, as if I were present, the man who has worked in such a way as this . . . Do you not judge those inside, while God judges those outside? 'Remove the wicked man from among yourselves.'" He then spoke of judging matters of this life and of those "in the congregation that [they] put in as judges."—1Co 5:1-3, 12, 13; 6:3, 4; compare Joh 7:24.

With authority vested in him as an apostle of Jesus Christ, Paul had responsibility for the cleanness and welfare of the congregations (2Co 1:1; 11:28); so he wrote to those who by appointment of the governing body had authority in the congregation. (Ac 14:23; 16:4, 5; 1Ti 3:1-13; 5:22) They were responsible for keeping the congregation in good standing, as pure in God's sight. These men, in sitting in judgment in the case mentioned, which was an open and flagrant violation of God's law, would not be making themselves judges of the law of God, nor would they be making laws according to their will. They would not be going beyond the boundaries of God-given law. They would be acting according to the law given by the great Statute-Giver, denouncing fornication as unclean. Practicers of such uncleanness could not enter God's Kingdom, according to God's law. (1Co 6:9, 10) They were not fit to remain in association with the congregation of Christ. Yet even then the men responsible for the cleanness of the congregation, by expelling unclean ones, were not executing the penalty that God the Lawgiver himself would execute on those unrepentantly continuing to follow such a course, namely, death.—Ro 1:24-27, 32.

Paul also calls to the attention of Christians that "the holy ones will judge the world" and that "we shall judge angels." Here he is speaking, not of the present time, but of the future, when those who reign in the Kingdom with Christ will serve as heavenly judges, administering the law of God and executing judgment on wicked ones.—1Co 6:1-3; Re 20:6; compare 1Co 4:8.

Moses' blessing of Gad. In Moses' blessing of the tribes of Israel just before his death, "as to Gad he said: 'Blessed is the one widening the borders of Gad. . . . And he [Gad] will pick out the first part for himself, for there the allotment of a statute-giver is reserved.'" (De 33:20, 21) This use of the term "statute-giver" may have the following meaning: Most of the tribes had their inheritance assigned to them by lot, under the direction of Joshua and Eleazar the high priest. But, shortly after the defeat of the Midianites, the tribe of Gad, along with Reuben, had requested land E of the Jordan River. Since these tribes had much livestock, the land was well suited for them. Moses heard their request favorably and granted them this part of the land. (Nu 32:1-5, 20-22, 28) Hence, their portion was an "allotment of a statute-giver," Moses, the lawgiver to Israel.

LAWLESSNESS.   See MAN OF LAWLESSNESS.

LAYING ON OF HANDS.   See HAND.

LAZARUS   (Laz′a·rus) [probably the Gr. form of the Heb. name Eleazar, meaning "God Has Helped"].

1. The brother of Martha and Mary; his resurrection was one of the outstanding miracles performed by Jesus Christ. (Joh 11:1, 2) Jesus had a deep love for this family living at Bethany, "about two miles" from Jerusalem on the road to Jericho. (Joh 11:5, 18, ftn) He had been entertained at their home, perhaps frequently.—Lu 10:38-42.

The two sisters sent word to Jesus, who was at that time across the Jordan River, that their brother Lazarus was very sick. Doubtless they entertained the hope that Jesus would cure him. (Joh 11:3, 21, 32) However, instead of going to Bethany immediately, or curing Lazarus from a distance, as in the case of the manservant of an army officer (Mt 8:5-13), Jesus stayed where he was for two more days. Upon his arrival in the vicinity of Bethany he was met by Martha and then by Mary. Lazarus had expired and had been dead for four days.—Joh 11:6, 17, 20, 30-32.

When speaking to Martha, Jesus took the occasion to stress the resurrection. (Joh 11:23-27) He was soon to give added meaning to his words. Upon arriving at the tomb or cave where Lazarus was interred, Christ ordered that the stone sealing its entrance be taken away. Then in prayer to his heavenly Father, Jesus showed that one reason these events were taking place was "in order that they [the crowd present] might believe that you sent me forth." (Joh 11:38-42) Jesus then called the dead Lazarus out of the tomb, and he emerged, undoubtedly to the astonishment and joy of those present.—Joh 11:43, 44.

This miracle moved many to put faith in Jesus, but it also caused the chief priests and Pharisees to plot his death. The anger of the chief priests was further aroused when a great crowd of Jews came to see not only Jesus but also the resurrected Lazarus. Because of Lazarus, many Jews were putting faith in Jesus, and so the chief priests took counsel to kill Lazarus also. (Joh 11:45-53; 12:1-11) However, there is no Biblical evidence to the effect that these religious foes carried out their evil plans against Lazarus.

John's account of the resurrection of Lazarus has been assailed by some critics of the Bible. They point to the silence of the other Gospel accounts regarding this event. A consideration of the various Gospels will show, however, that even the writers of the synoptic Gospels did not each recount every deed of Jesus. For example, only Luke reported the raising of the son of the widow of Nain. (Lu 7:11-15) John did not customarily repeat what others had recorded. The resurrection of Lazarus is a notable instance of this.

This miracle of Lazarus' resurrection served well as part of Jesus' ministry, both to illustrate the power of the Son of God and to increase faith in him and the resurrection. (Joh 11:4, 41, 42) It evidently occurred near the beginning of the year 33 C.E. The Scriptures do not furnish information as to the circumstances, place, or time of Lazarus' death after his resurrection.—See RESURRECTION (Resurrections before ransom was given).

There is no Biblical statement nor any reason to link the historical Lazarus with the beggar of Jesus' illustration of the rich man and Lazarus.

2. The name given to the beggar in Jesus' illustration commonly known as the parable of the rich man and Lazarus. (Lu 16:19-31) In the *Vulgate* the word "rich" has been rendered by the Latin adjective *dives,* which is often mistakenly used as the proper name of the rich man. However, the Jewish name Lazarus itself was common in ancient times, a fact borne out by ossuary inscriptions.

In the parable, the ulcerous beggar, Lazarus, was put at the gate of the rich man, desiring to be fed with the things that fell from the rich man's sumptuous table. Lazarus subsequently died and was carried off by angels to the bosom position of Abraham (a place comparable to that occupied by a person in ancient times when he reclined in front of another on the same couch during a meal). Abraham had a conversation with the rich man, who had also died, was buried, and was in Hades, existing in torments. "A great chasm" that could not be crossed separated the rich man from Abraham and Lazarus. The rich man's request that Abraham send Lazarus to his five brothers to "give them a thorough witness," in the hope of sparing them the same experience, met with rejection on the grounds that these had "Moses and the Prophets," and, if unwilling to listen to them, "neither will they be persuaded if someone rises from the dead."—See ILLUSTRATIONS.

For Jesus' illustration of the rich man and Lazarus, did he draw on rabbinic beliefs concerning the dead?

Teachers and students of comparative religion have in some cases suggested that in giving this illustration, Jesus Christ drew upon the ancient rabbinic concept and teaching regarding the underworld. Josephus furnishes the following information regarding the then-current view of the Pharisees in this regard: "They believe that souls have power to survive death and that there are rewards and punishments under the earth for those who have led lives of virtue or vice: eternal imprisonment is the lot of evil souls, while the good souls receive an easy passage to a new life." (*Jewish Antiquities,* XVIII, 14 [i, 3]) However, Jesus flatly rejected false teachings, including those of the Pharisees. (Mt 23) Hence, it would have been inconsistent for him to frame his illustration of the rich man and Lazarus according to the outlines of the false rabbinic concept of the underworld. Consequently, it must be concluded that Jesus had in mind the fulfillment of the illustration and framed its details and movement in harmony with the facts of the fulfillment rather than according to any unscriptural teaching.

The context and the wording of the story show clearly that it is a parable and not an actual historical account. Poverty is not being extolled, nor are riches being condemned. Rather, conduct, final rewards, and a reversal in the spiritual status, or condition, of those represented by Lazarus and by the rich man are evidently indicated. The fact that the rich man's brothers rejected Moses and the prophets also shows that the illustration had a deeper meaning and purpose than that of contrasting poverty and the possession of riches.

LAZINESS.   Disinclination or aversion to effort or work; idleness; indolence; slothfulness; sluggishness. The Hebrew verb *'a·tsal'* means "be sluggish." (Jg 18:9) The noun related to this verb is translated "lazy one." (Pr 6:6) The Greek word *o·kne·ros'* means "sluggish, slothful." (Mt 25:26; Ro

12:11, *Int*) Another term, *no·thros'*, means "sluggish, dull."—Heb 5:11; 6:12.

Jehovah and his Son, as the two greatest Workers, hate laziness. Jesus said: "My Father has kept working until now, and I keep working." (Joh 5:17) Throughout God's Word the lazy person is warned and laziness is condemned.

The Lazy Man's Thinking. A description of the lazy man is given in the book of Proverbs. First of all, he throws up barriers in his own mind to justify himself in not starting on a project. "The way of the lazy one is like a brier hedge." (Pr 15:19) He views his task as a road ahead filled with briers, very difficult to traverse. Then he makes ridiculous excuses for his slothfulness, saying: "There is a lion outside! In the midst of the public squares I shall be murdered!" as if a danger that actually does not exist attended the job. (Pr 22:13) Frequently laziness is accompanied by cowardice, a fearful holding back. (Mt 25:26, ftn; 2Ti 1:7) Even though counseled and prompted by others, he turns over on his bed 'like a door on its pivot,' as one who cannot get up. He is too lazy even to feed himself. He "has hidden his hand in the banquet bowl; he has become too weary to bring it back to his mouth." (Pr 26:14, 15; 19:24) But he has deceived himself so that he thinks in his own heart that he is right.

Such an individual indulges in specious and imaginary reasoning. He may think that work will injure his health or that he is too tired. He may feel that 'the world owes him a living.' Or, he puts off a job until "tomorrow." (Pr 20:4) Any little thing he has done may make him feel he has done his part, as much as anyone else. Whereas all diligent men could give a sensible reply to any of such arguments, he is "wiser in his own eyes," feeling that they are the foolish ones for exerting themselves and trying to encourage him to do the same.—Pr 26:13-16.

The lazy person is not one who has "self-sufficiency" or contentment with "sustenance and covering." (1Ti 6:6-8) Rather, he has desires for things, usually for much more than food or clothing. "The lazy one is showing himself desirous, but his soul has nothing." (Pr 13:4) He has no consideration or respect for his fellowman, but he is willing to let someone else do his work, even to let another person provide him with the things he desires.—Pr 20:4.

The Reward of Laziness. While the lazy individual may think he will get busy later, the reward of his laziness suddenly catches up with him and it is too late, for, he is told: "A little more sleep, a little more slumbering, a little more folding of the hands in lying down, and your poverty will certainly come just like some rover, and your want like an armed man."—Pr 6:9-11.

Whether taken literally or figuratively, the description of the lazy man's situation is true: "I passed along by the field of the lazy individual and by the vineyard of the man in need of heart. And, look! all of it produced weeds. Nettles covered its very surface, and its stone wall itself had been torn down." "Through great laziness the beamwork sinks in, and through the letting down of the hands the house leaks."—Pr 24:30, 31; Ec 10:18.

Whoever hires the lazy person, or whoever he represents, is bound to be disappointed and vexed and will suffer loss, for, "as vinegar to the teeth and as smoke to the eyes, so the lazy man is to those sending him forth."—Pr 10:26.

The slothful one's laziness will eventually bring dire results to him, for "the very craving of the lazy will put him to death." His craving is for things he does not deserve or that are wrong. He may come to ruin in trying to get them. At any rate, his craving with laziness turns him away from God the Source of life.—Pr 21:25.

The Christian who is lazy is not cultivating the fruitage of the spirit, which will enliven and activate (Ac 18:25), but is actually bringing himself into trouble. He is catering to the desires of the flesh. He may soon be "walking disorderly," "not working at all but meddling with what does not concern" him.—2Th 3:11.

How Viewed in the Christian Congregation. In the early Christian congregation an arrangement was established to give material help to needy ones, especially to widows. It seems that some of the younger widows expressed themselves as desirous of using their freedom as widows to engage zealously in the Christian ministry. (Compare 1Co 7:34.) Evidently some were given material assistance. But instead of properly using the greater freedom and additional time thus afforded them, they became idle, unoccupied, and began to gad about. They became gossipers and meddlers in other people's affairs, talking of things they ought not. For this reason the apostle Paul instructed the overseer Timothy not to put such persons on the list for aid but to let them marry and use their energies and abilities in rearing children and managing a household.—1Ti 5:9-16.

In the matter of material assistance in the Christian congregation, the Bible rule is: "If anyone does not want to work, neither let him eat." (2Th 3:10) The family head must provide for his household, and the wife must not eat "the bread of laziness."—Pr 31:27; 1Ti 5:8.

Avoid Laziness in Study and in the Ministry. Counsel is given against laziness regarding studying and getting a deeper understanding of God's purposes as well as in engaging in the Christian ministry. The apostle Paul reproved some unprogressive Hebrew Christians, pointing out: "You have become dull [sluggish] in your hearing. For, indeed, although you ought to be teachers in view of the time, you again need someone to teach you from the beginning the elementary things of the sacred pronouncements of God; and you have become such as need milk, not solid food." (Heb 5:11, 12) He also admonishes: "Do not loiter [be slothful] at your business. Be aglow with the spirit."—Ro 12:11.

Jesus foretold that there would be a class of persons claiming to be his servants who would become sluggish and wicked, not working to increase the Master's interests in the earth. The Master, on his return, would take away from them the interests committed to their care and would have them thrown as a "good-for-nothing slave" "into the darkness outside."—Mt 25:18, 24-30.

LEAD. One of the heavier metallic elements, having the specific gravity 11.34. The dull-gray metal was useful as weight on fishlines and nets and for heavy lids, or covers. Moses poetically sang in triumph that the Egyptians "sank like lead [Heb., 'o·phe'reth]" in the Red Sea. (Ex 15:10) The Greek verb translated 'sound' at Acts 27:28 (bo-li'zo) literally means "heave the lead." The Hebrew word translated "plummet" in Amos 7:7, 8 ('anakh') may mean "lead" or "tin." For permanency and legibility, liquid lead was sometimes poured into engravings on stone—a practice dating at least to Job's day. (Job 19:23, 24) "Soldering" (Heb., de'veq) is mentioned at Isaiah 41:7 in connection with the making of idols, but whether the solder was made of lead and tin, as today, is not known.

The most common source of lead was galena, a lead sulfide ore. It was mined in the Arabah between the S end of the Dead Sea and the Gulf of 'Aqaba. Tarshish (Spain) was another source of supply. (Eze 27:12) Lead ore had to be smelted in a furnace like the ores of other metals. (Jer 6:29; Eze 22:18-20; compare Nu 31:22, 23.) The first step in the refining process converted lead sulfide to lead oxide, which was itself sometimes used as a pottery glaze, as is evidenced in the ruins of Egypt and Nineveh.—See REFINE, REFINER.

LEADER, NOBLE, PRINCE. Several Hebrew words may be translated variously as "leader," "noble," and "prince." Those appearing most frequently are as follows:

Na·ghidh', meaning "leader," is applied to Saul and David in connection with their being designated as kings over Israel and to Hezekiah as the king of Judah, with the responsibility of shepherding Jehovah's people. (1Sa 9:16; 25:30; 2Sa 5:2; 2Ki 20:5) The tribe of Judah was selected by Jehovah to be leader of the 12 tribes of Israel, and it was from Judah that the kingly dynasty of David came.—1Ch 28:4; Ge 49:10; Jg 1:2.

Jesus is referred to as "Messiah the Leader" and "a leader and commander to the national groups," at Daniel 9:25 and Isaiah 55:4. He counseled his disciples: "Neither be called 'leaders,' for your Leader [ka·the·ge·tes'] is one, the Christ." (Mt 23: 10) As regards the Christian congregation, Jesus Christ is the only one rightly bearing the title "Leader," because no imperfect human is the leader of true Christians; they follow Christ. While there are those who 'take the lead' in God's service, they are not titled "leader" or addressed as such, and their example is to be followed only as they imitate Christ.—1Co 11:1; Heb 13:7.

Na·dhiv', meaning "noble," "willing one," "generous one," is used at Numbers 21:18, paralleling the term "princes," for the willing ones of Israel who excavated a well in the wilderness. It also describes the volunteer contributors to the tabernacle construction. (Ex 35:5) As used at Job 12:21, positions of prominence and power are indicated. —See also Ps 83:9-11.

The Hebrew word cho·rim', meaning "nobles," is used for certain men of influence in a city of the ten-tribe kingdom of Israel (1Ki 21:8, 11) and for Jews who held authority under the Persian Empire. (Ne 5:7; 13:17) Many of the nobles of Judah and Jerusalem, including Daniel and his companions, were taken as exiles to Babylon by King Nebuchadnezzar in 617 B.C.E., and others were slaughtered by him in 607 B.C.E.—Jer 27:20; 39:6; Da 1:3, 6.

Sar, meaning "prince," "chief," is drawn from a verb meaning "exercise dominion." (Jg 9:22, ftn) While it is often translated "prince," it does not necessarily apply to the son of a king or a person of royal rank in every instance. The tribal heads of Israel were called "princes." (1Ch 27:22) Those holding high office under Pharaoh of Egypt and King Nebuchadnezzar of Babylon were so titled. (Ge 12:15; Jer 38:17, 18, 22; Es 3:12) An army chief might be termed a sar. (Ne 2:9) Jehovah is called "the Prince of the army" and "the Prince of princes," at Daniel 8:11, 25. Michael the archangel is "the great prince who is standing in behalf of the sons of [Daniel's] people." (Da 12:1) Invisible demon princes governing the world powers of

Persia and Greece are mentioned at Daniel 10:13, 20.—Compare Eph 6:12.

Psalm 45, verses 6 and 7 of which are applied to Christ Jesus by the apostle Paul (Heb 1:8, 9), contains the statement: "In place of your forefathers there will come to be your sons, whom you will appoint as princes in all the earth." (Ps 45:16) Of Abraham, Isaac, and Jacob, men in Christ's ancestral line of descent, it is written: "In faith all these died, although they did not get the fulfillment of the promises, but they saw them afar off and welcomed them." (Heb 11:8-10, 13) The rule of Christ involves his having not only subordinate kings and priests in heaven (Re 20:6) but also 'princely' representatives on earth carrying out the king's directions. (Compare Heb 2:5, 8.) Isaiah 32:1, 2 is clearly part of a Messianic prophecy and describes the benefits rendered by such "princes" under the Kingdom rule.—See CHIEFTAIN; HEAD (Ruling Position); RULER.

LEAH (Le′ah) [possibly related to an Akkadian word meaning "cow," or to an Arabic word meaning "wild cow"]. The older daughter of Laban, the grandnephew of Abraham. Laban was the brother of Rebekah, Jacob's mother, so Leah was Jacob's cousin. (Ge 22:20-23; 24:24, 29; 29:16) Leah was not as beautiful as her younger sister Rachel; it especially was noted that her eyes lacked luster, or were dull (weak). (Ge 29:17) In the case of Oriental women, bright or lustrous eyes especially are considered to be an evidence of beauty.—Compare Ca 1:15; 4:9; 7:4.

Leah became Jacob's first wife because, at night, Laban deceived Jacob by giving him Leah as a wife instead of Rachel, whom Jacob loved. Jacob protested his being tricked, but Laban argued that it was not the custom of the place to give the younger daughter in marriage before the firstborn. Leah likely was veiled, in keeping with the ancient Oriental custom of heavily veiling a prospective bride, and this doubtless contributed to the success of the ruse. Jacob had served seven years with Rachel in mind, but for this work he received Leah. Rachel was granted to him after he celebrated a week of seven days with Leah, but Jacob had to work seven more years to pay for Rachel.—Ge 29:18-28.

The account tells us that Leah was "hated." (Ge 29:31, 33) But it also recounts that, after he had finally got Rachel, Jacob "expressed more love for Rachel than for Leah." (Ge 29:30) Undoubtedly Jacob did not hold malicious hatred for Leah but viewed Rachel more lovingly, as his favorite wife. He continued to care for Leah and to have relations with her. Leah's being "hated," therefore,

would merely mean that Jacob loved her less than Rachel.—See HATE.

Leah became the mother of seven of Jacob's children, his six sons Reuben, Simeon, Levi, Judah, Issachar, and Zebulun and a daughter, Dinah. (Ge 29:32-35; 30:16-21) Accordingly, Leah is named at Ruth 4:11 along with Rachel as one of those who "built the house of Israel." Leah had the honor of having borne Levi, who became the founder of Israel's priestly tribe, and Judah, who became the father of the nation's royal tribe.

Leah and her children accompanied Jacob when he left Paddan-aram and returned to Canaan, the land of his birth. (Ge 31:11-18) Before Jacob met Esau en route, he protectively divided off the children to Leah and to Rachel and their maidservants, putting the maidservants and their children foremost, followed by Leah and her children, with Rachel and Joseph to their rear. (Ge 33:1-7) Leah's children accompanied Jacob into Egypt, but the Bible account does not say that she did so. (Ge 46:15) The time, place, and circumstances of her death are not furnished, but she may have died in Canaan. Whatever the case, the patriarch had her body taken to the family burial place, the cave in the field of Machpelah. Jacob's instructions respecting his own remains show that it was his desire to be buried where Abraham and Sarah, Isaac and Rebekah, and Leah had been buried. —Ge 49:29-32.

LEAVEN. A substance added to dough or liquids to cause fermentation, especially a portion of fermenting dough preserved for baking purposes. This type of leavening agent is specified by the Hebrew word se′or′ ("sourdough"; Ex 12:15) and by the Greek word zy′me ("leaven"; Lu 13:21). A leavened thing is designated by the Hebrew word cha·mets′.—Le 2:11.

Wine, the fermented juice of grapes or other fruit, has long been known to mankind. Of course, wine ferments without the addition of leaven.

The early Egyptians made beer, which requires a leavening agent for its production, and they baked both leavened and unleavened bread. The Hebrews were likely familiar with "wheat beer." (Isa 1:22; Ho 4:18, NW; Lexicon in Veteris Testamenti Libros, by L. Koehler and W. Baumgartner, Leiden, 1958, p. 646) Wild yeast that might be obtained from the spores of certain fungus growths may have served as one of the leavening agents for these products. Excavations in Egypt have yielded porous bread containing dead yeast cells. The Egyptians are also said to have used natron (sodium carbonate) in making bread. Sodium carbonate would not bring about the process of fermentation as did sourdough, but it would provide gas bubbles to make the bread rise. In Egypt, as in Israel, the primary practice in bread-making seems to have been to save some dough from a batch, let it ferment, and use the resulting sourdough to leaven a fresh batch.

In God's Law to Israel.   No grain offering that the Israelites presented by fire to Jehovah was to be made of "a leavened thing." (Le 2:11) However, leaven could be used in connection with thanks-giving communion offerings, in which the offerer voluntarily made the presentation in a spirit of thankfulness for Jehovah's many blessings. The meal was to be one of cheerfulness; leavened bread was normally eaten on happy occasions. Along with the meat (that is, the animal) offered, and the unfermented cakes, he would bring ring-shaped cakes of leavened bread, which were not put on the altar but were eaten by the offerer and by the officiating priest.—Le 7:11-15.

At the presentation of the firstfruits of the wheat harvest, on the day of Pentecost, the high priest waved before Jehovah two loaves of leav-ened wheat bread. (Le 23:15-21) It is noteworthy that, on Pentecost day, 33 C.E., the first members of the Christian congregation, namely, the disci-ples of Jesus Christ taken from among the Jews, were anointed with holy spirit. Jesus Christ, as Jehovah's great High Priest, was able to present before God the first of his spirit-begotten brothers. These were taken from sinful mankind. (Ac 2:1-4, 41) About three years and four months later, the first uncircumcised Gentile converts to Christiani-ty, Cornelius and his household, were anointed with holy spirit, thereby being presented before God. These were likewise from sinful humankind. —Ac 10:24, 44-48; Ro 5:12.

The Festival of Unfermented Cakes occupied the seven days following Passover day, namely Abib, or Nisan, 15-21. During those days nothing leav-ened nor any sourdough was even to be found in the Israelites' houses or "seen" with them. (Ex 12:14-20; 13:6, 7; 23:15) This served to remind them of their hasty deliverance from Egypt by Jehovah's hand, when they did not have time to wait for their dough to ferment but, in their hurry, carried it with them along with their kneading troughs.—Ex 12:34.

Symbolic Significance.   "Leaven" is used in the Bible to denote sin or corruption. Jesus Christ told his disciples: "Watch out for the leaven of the Pharisees and Sadducees," and, "Watch out for the leaven of the Pharisees, which is hypocrisy." The disciples at first did not understand that Jesus was

using a symbolism, but they finally discerned that he was warning them to be on guard against false doctrine and hypocritical practices, "the *teaching* of the Pharisees and Sadducees," which teaching had a corrupting effect. (Mt 16:6, 11, 12; Lu 12:1) He also mentioned Herod (evidently including his party followers) in one of his warnings, saying: "Keep your eyes open, look out for the leaven of the Pharisees and the leaven of Herod." (Mr 8:15) Jesus boldly denounced the Pharisees as hyp-ocrites concerned with outward show. (Mt 23:25-28) He pointed out the wrong doctrinal viewpoint of the Sadducees. He exposed the hy-pocrisy and political treachery of the party follow-ers of Herod.—Mt 22:15-21; Mr 3:6.

The apostle Paul employed the same symbolism when he commanded the Christian congregation in Corinth to expel an immoral man from the congregation, stating: "Do you not know that a little leaven ferments the whole lump? Clear away the old leaven, that you may be a new lump, according as you are free from ferment. For, in-deed, Christ our passover has been sacrificed." He then clearly showed what he meant by "leaven": "Consequently let us keep the festival, not with old leaven, neither with leaven of badness and wick-edness, but with unfermented cakes of sincerity and truth." (1Co 5:6-8) Paul here was drawing on the pictorial meaning of the Jewish Festival of Unfermented Cakes, which immediately followed the Passover celebration. Just as a bit of sour-dough soon causes the whole lump, or batch, of bread to be leavened, so the congregation as a body would become unclean in Jehovah's eyes if they did not clear out this corrupting influence of the immoral man. They must act to get the "leav-en" out of their midst, just as the Israelites could have no leaven in their houses during the festival.

Leaven was associated with corruption even in the minds of peoples of antiquity other than the Hebrews. For instance, Plutarch, a Greek biogra-pher, spoke of it as "itself also the product of corruption, and produces corruption in the dough with which it is mixed."—*Moralia*, IV, "The Roman Questions," 109.

Because of the negative aspects associated with leaven, Jesus evidently had in mind corrupting elements when he said: "The kingdom of the heavens is like leaven, which a woman took and hid in three large measures of flour, until the whole mass was fermented." (Mt 13:33; Lu 13:20, 21) The Scriptures do indicate that corruption of truth would be brought about by individuals pro-fessing to be in line for membership in the heav-enly Kingdom.—Ac 20:29, 30; 1Ti 4:1-3.

It was with irony that Jehovah told transgressing Israel in Amos' day: "From what is leavened make a thanksgiving sacrifice to smoke, and proclaim voluntary offerings." (Am 4:5) God was telling them that all their worship at Bethel and at Gilgal was transgression against him, so they might as well go ahead and offer leavened as well as unleavened bread on the altar—hold nothing back. It would all still be in vain because they were committing idolatry.

LEBANAH (Le·ba'nah) [White; Full Moon].

Founder of a family whose sons or descendants were among the Nethinim returning with Zerubbabel from Babylonian exile.—Ezr 2:1, 2, 43, 45; Ne 7:46, 48.

LEBANON (Leb'a·non) [White [Mountain]].

Generally, the westernmost of the two ranges forming the mountain system of Lebanon. Perhaps its name is derived from the light color of its limestone cliffs and summits or from the fact that the range's upper slopes are covered with snow during a major part of the year. (Jer 18:14) Extending from NNE to SSW for about 160 km (100 mi) along the Mediterranean Sea, the Lebanon chain parallels the Anti-Lebanon Range for about 100 km (60 mi). The two ranges are separated by a long, fertile valley, the Beqa' (Coele-Syria), measuring between 10 and 16 km (6 and 10 mi) in width. (Jos 11:17; 12:7) Through this valley the Orontes River courses northward, whereas the Litani (its lower course being called Nahr el-Kasimiye) flows southward and curves around the southern end of the Lebanon range. The Nahr el-Kebir (Eleutherus) flows past the northern end of the Lebanon chain.

With few exceptions, the foothills of the Lebanon Range rise almost directly from the Mediterranean Sea, leaving only a narrow coastal plain. The summits of this range average between 1,800 and 2,100 m (6,000 and 7,000 ft) in elevation, with two peaks towering over 900 m (3,000 ft) higher. Both the eastern and the western slopes of the range are steep.

Its eastern slopes are quite barren and have practically no important streams. But the well-watered western slopes are cleft by streams and gorges. (Compare Ca 4:15.) The terraced lower slopes on the W side support grain, vineyards, and fruit orchards, as well as mulberry, walnut, and olive trees. (Compare Ho 14:5-7.) Pines thrive in the rich soil of the sandstone layer, and at the higher elevations a few small groves of majestic cedars are to be found. These trees anciently covered the range and their wood was used for a variety of purposes. (1Ki 6:9; Ca 3:9; Eze 27:5; see CEDAR.) Ash, cypress, and juniper trees are also native to the Lebanon Range. (1Ki 5:6-8; 2Ki 19:23; Isa 60:13) Among the animals inhabiting this region are jackals, gazelles, hyenas, wolves, and bears. In ancient times both the forests and the wildlife were more abundant; the region was a haunt for lions and leopards. (Ca 4:8; Isa 40:16) Possibly it was the fragrance of its great forests that was known as "the fragrance of Lebanon." —Ca 4:11.

The Lebanon region was not conquered by the Israelites under Joshua's leadership, but it came to be the NW border of the land. (De 1:7; 3:25; 11:24; Jos 1:4; 9:1) The pagan inhabitants of this area, however, served to test Israel's faithfulness to Jehovah. (Jg 3:3, 4) Centuries later, King Solomon exercised jurisdiction over a part of Lebanon and there did building work. (1Ki 9:17-19; 2Ch 8:5, 6) Possibly one of his construction projects included "the tower of Lebanon, which is looking out toward Damascus." (Ca 7:4; some, however, understand this to refer to one of the peaks of Lebanon.) At this time Hiram the king of Tyre controlled another portion of Lebanon, from which he supplied Solomon with cedar and juniper timbers. —1Ki 5:7-14.

Illustrative Use. Many of the Scriptural references to Lebanon are associated with its fruitfulness (Ps 72:16; Isa 35:2) and luxuriant forests, particularly its majestic cedars. (Ps 29:5) Often Lebanon is used in a figurative way. It is depicted as if in a state of abashment, sympathizing with the land of Judah that had been despoiled by the Assyrian forces. (Isa 33:1, 9) The Assyrian army itself, however, was to experience calamity, being felled like trees of Lebanon. (Isa 10:24-26, 33, 34) Disastrous effects resulting from Jehovah's judgment are compared to the withering of the blossom of Lebanon. (Na 1:4) However, the turning of Lebanon's forest into a fruitful orchard is alluded to in a restoration prophecy and illustrates a complete reversal of matters.—Isa 29:17, 18.

Jehovah, through Jeremiah, "said concerning the house of the king of Judah, 'You are as Gilead to me, the head of Lebanon.'" (Jer 22:6) "The house" appears to designate the palace complex. (Jer 22:1, 5) Situated as it was on an eminence, the palace's location was lofty and magnificent, like Lebanon. Also, cedarwood had been used extensively in the construction of the various royal edifices there. (1Ki 7:2-12) King Jehoiakim, who heard the words recorded at Jeremiah 22:6, had himself used cedar paneling for his luxurious palace. (Jer 22:13-15) Therefore, the palace area was like a magnificent forest of cedar buildings and could appropriately be compared to Lebanon and to heavily wooded Gilead. Jehovah warned Judah that if King Jehoiakim, his servants, and the people did not render justice, the 'house would become a mere devastation' (Jer 22:1-5) and those dwelling in figurative Lebanon (Jerusalem), "being nested in the cedars," would experience calamity. —Jer 22:23; see also Eze 17:2, 3.

Similarly, the desire of Assyrian King Sennacherib to "ascend the height of mountainous regions, the remotest parts of Lebanon," and to "cut down its lofty cedars" appears to allude to his intentions concerning Jerusalem. (Isa 37:21-24) The prophetic words regarding the violence done to Lebanon (Hab 2:17) may refer to calamity in store for Jerusalem. Or they are perhaps to be understood literally as denoting the depletion of Lebanon's forests through the ravages of war.—Compare Isa 14:5-8.

Zechariah's prophecy (10:10) pointed to the time when Jehovah would bring his people back to the land of Gilead and Lebanon. In this case Lebanon may refer to the territory W of the Jordan, as Gilead designates the land E of the Jordan.

LEBAOTH (Le·ba′oth) [Lionesses]. A city in the southern part of the territory of Judah (Jos 15:21, 32), apparently also called Beth-lebaoth and assigned as such to the tribe of Simeon.—Jos 19:1, 2, 6; see BETH-LEBAOTH.

LEB-KAMAI (Leb-ka′mai) [Heart of Those Rising Up Against Me]. This appears to be a cryptographic name for Chaldea, or Kas·dim′. It occurs only at Jeremiah 51:1, in a statement regarding what Jehovah would do to Babylon and the inhabitants of Chaldea. The term is employed there in keeping with a system called athbash, in which the last letter of the Hebrew alphabet (taw) represents the first letter thereof ('a′leph), the second-last letter (shin) represents the second (behth), and so forth. Hence, at Jeremiah 51:1 the real name (Kas·dim′) is disguised by forming the Hebrew word Lev qa·mai′ (Leb-kamai). For "Leb-kamai" the Greek Septuagint has "the Chaldeans" and the Targums read "the land of the Chaldeans."

LEBONAH (Le·bo′nah). A place mentioned as a reference point in connection with the location of Shiloh. (Jg 21:19) It is tentatively identified with el-Lubban (Lubban Sharqiya), about 5 km (3 mi) WNW of the suggested site of Shiloh. However, the Bible's placing of Shiloh "toward the south of Lebonah" may indicate that originally the city was farther E than this suggested site.

LECAH (Le′cah). Probably a descendant of Judah through Er. (1Ch 4:21) On the basis of the context, it has been suggested that Lecah was a village, but the location of such a place is unknown.

LEECH [Heb., 'alu·qah′]. A bloodsucking worm with a flat, segmented body that tapers at both ends but is broadest toward the posterior part. Leeches measure from over 1 cm (0.5 in.) to over 10 cm (4 in.) in length. These creatures have a disk, or sucker, at each end of the body, the one at the head end being equipped with biting jaws.

Leeches are found in great numbers in many streams and rivers of the Middle East. The young of one variety (Limnatis nilotica), when swallowed with the drinking water, attach themselves to the nasal cavities, larynx, or epiglottis of their host. They grow rapidly and are not easily removed. Their presence can hinder breathing and this, as well as loss of blood, sometimes proves fatal to the victim.

Sole mention is made of the leech (Heb., 'alu·qah′) at Proverbs 30:15, where the reference is to insatiable greed, it being stated that "the leeches have two daughters that cry: 'Give! Give!'" The Commentary by F. C. Cook suggests that the leech's greed is here viewed as "its daughter," spoken of in the plural to express intensity. Others consider the "two daughters" to be a reference to the two lips of its bloodsucking disk. A leech may consume three times its own weight in blood, a strong anticoagulant in its saliva ensuring a continuous flow from the victim.

LEEK [Heb., cha·tsir′]. One of the items of diet for which the mixed crowd and the Israelites longed while in the wilderness. (Nu 11:4, 5) The Hebrew word cha·tsir′, rendered "leeks" in this text, may possibly come from the same root as the identical Hebrew word translated "green grass." (Isa 40:7, 8) This item of diet is listed along with onions and garlic, specific plant foods very similar to leeks, indicating that a definite vegetable, rather than grass in general, is meant. Also, from ancient times leeks have enjoyed great popularity in Egypt and are still commonly eaten there as well as in Palestine.

The leek (Allium porrum) is much like the onion but is distinguished from the latter by its milder flavor, slender cylindrical shape, and juicy, grass-like leaves measuring about 2.5 cm (1 in.) in width. The flower stem, terminating in a large compact ball of flowers, may attain a height of about 0.6 m (2 ft). The bulbs and leaves of this biennial plant are cooked as a vegetable and used as a seasoning; they are also eaten raw.

LEG. The limb of a man or an animal used to support the body and for walking. In connection with the installation of the priesthood, the right leg of "the ram of the installation" constituted a part of the "wave offering." (Le 8:22, 25-27) In certain sacrifices, the right hind leg, evidently the choice upper part of it, was also given as a sacred portion to the officiating priest. (Le 7:32-34; 10:12, 14, 15) The front leg, the "shoulder" or "shoulder blade" (literally, "arm"), is also mentioned as a portion for the priests, at Numbers 6:19 and Deuteronomy 18:3.

Insects having "leaper legs" (Heb., kera·'a'yim) were the only winged swarming creatures designated by the Law as clean for food. (Le 11:21) Elsewhere, the same Hebrew term refers to the "shanks" of animals.—See SHANK.

Jehovah prophetically told Babylon: "Strip off the flowing skirt. Uncover the leg. Cross over the rivers." (Isa 47:1, 2) Instead of being a pampered queen who is served, she figuratively had to uncover her legs to the hip to wade barefoot as a captive across the rivers through which her conquerors would drag her.

Legs were also used figuratively to represent mightiness or human swiftness and power. At Psalm 147:10 we read: "Not in the mightiness of the horse does [Jehovah] take delight, nor in the legs of the man does he find pleasure." At Proverbs 26:7 lame legs are referred to as a symbol of uselessness or incapacity.

It appears to have been a Roman custom to perform a coup de grace by breaking the legs of criminals condemned to die on the stake in order to shorten their miseries. The soldiers, at the Jews' request, broke the legs of the men impaled on stakes alongside Jesus Christ but, finding Jesus already dead, did not break his legs. Consequently, the prophecy at Psalm 34:20 was fulfilled. —Joh 19:31-36; compare Ex 12:46; Nu 9:12.

LEGAL CASE. A matter to be settled in a judicial court; a legal hearing or trial. The principal Hebrew verb having to do with legal cases is riv, meaning "quarrel; contend; conduct a legal case." (Ge 26:20; De 33:8; Pr 25:8) The noun form is rendered "controversy; dispute; case at law; legal case." (Ex 23:2; De 17:8; Ps 35:23; Isa 34:8) The Hebrew word din (judgment) is sometimes rendered "legal case; legal claim; legal contest." (Job 35:14; Ps 140:12; Pr 22:10) A legal case, among God's servants, had as its primary purpose the satisfying of the divine requirements and, secondarily, the rendering of justice to the person or persons involved, along with compensation where such was due. God considered himself involved in even personal offenses between humans, as is noted in Moses' words to Israelite judges at Deuteronomy 1:16, 17.

A legal case was conducted in the garden of Eden, to bring out the facts of that case and the issues involved, to establish them as a matter of public record, and also to pass sentence on the offenders. Jehovah called Adam and Eve before him for questioning. Though he knew all, he held a hearing, made the charges clear, brought out the facts by questioning, and gave them an opportunity to make expression in their own defense. He obtained a confession from the offenders. Jehovah then made his decision in the matter and, with justice and undeserved kindness, applied the law, exercising mercy toward Adam and Eve's unborn offspring by deferring the execution of the death sentence upon the offenders for a time.—Ge 3:6-19.

Jehovah God the Supreme Judge here set the pattern for all further judicial proceedings among his people. (Ge 3:1-24) Legal cases conducted according to God's judicial regulations were for the finding and discussion of facts for the purpose of rendering justice—where possible, justice tempered with mercy. (De 16:20; Pr 28:13; compare Mt 5:7; Jas 2:13.) The entire procedure was meant to keep the nation of Israel uncontaminated and to provide for the individual welfare of its members as well as that of the alien residents and settlers among them. (Le 19:33, 34; Nu 15:15, 16; De 1:16, 17) The Law given to the nation contained within it the procedure that was to be followed in civil cases and also in cases of misdemeanor or crime (including those against God and the State), misunderstandings, personal quarrels, and troubles on the individual, family, tribal, and national levels.

Procedure. If cases of dispute were personal in nature, the disputants were encouraged to avoid quarrels and to settle matters privately. (Pr 17:14; 25:8, 9) If they could not come to an agreement, they could appeal to the judges. (Mt 5:25) Jesus gave such counsel. (Mt 18:15-17) There was no formal or complicated procedure in conducting legal cases, either during the pre-Mosaic period or under the Law, although some formalism did creep in after the establishment of the Sanhedrin. Nevertheless, cases were conducted in an orderly and purposeful manner. The courts were open to women, to slaves, and to the alien resident, so that justice might be administered to all. (Job 31:13, 14; Nu 27:1-5; Le 24:22) The accused would be present when testimony was presented against him and could make his defense. No equivalent of a public prosecutor appears in either patriarchal or Israelite courts; neither was an attorney for the defense necessary. Proceedings were without court costs to the litigants.

A person with a civil matter or a complainant in a criminal matter would bring his case to the judges. The other party would be called, witnesses were gathered together, and the hearing was conducted usually in a public place, most often at the city gates. (De 21:19; Ru 4:1) The judges would question the litigants and examine the evidence and testimony. They would render a verdict without delay unless evidence was lacking, or if the matter was too difficult, the judges would refer the case to a higher court. Sentences, such as flogging and the death penalty, were carried out immediately. There was no provision in the Law for imprisonment. Custody was employed only in a case in which Jehovah had to be consulted for a decision.—Le 24:12; see COURT, JUDICIAL; CRIME AND PUNISHMENT.

Guilt always brought liability; there were no exceptions. Guilt could not be overlooked. Wherever the Law demanded it, punishment had to be administered or, in some cases, compensation made. Then the guilty one, in order to make peace with God, was required to present an offering at the sanctuary. Sacrifices for atonement were required in any case of guilt. (Le 5:1-19) Even unintentional sin brought guilt, and offerings had to be made for atonement. (Le 4:1-35) In certain wrongdoings, including deception, fraud, and extortion, where a person voluntarily repented and confessed, he had to make compensation and also present a guilt offering.—Le 6:1-7.

Evidence. If a person was a witness to apostate acts, sedition, murder, which defiled the land, or certain other serious crimes, he was under obligation to report it and to testify to what he knew, or he would be subject to divine curse, publicly proclaimed. (Le 5:1; De 13:8; compare Pr 29:24; Es 6:2.) One witness was not enough to establish a matter, however. Two or more were required. (Nu 35:30; De 17:6; 19:15; compare Joh 8:17, 18; 1Ti 5:19; Heb 10:28.) Witnesses were commanded by the Law to speak the truth (Ex 20:16; 23:7), and were, in some cases, put under oath. (Mt 26:63) This would especially be so when the one on whom suspicion fell was the only witness to the matter. (Ex 22:10, 11) Since those in a legal case before the judges or at the sanctuary for judgment of a matter were regarded as standing before Jehovah, witnesses were to recognize that they were accountable to God. (Ex 22:8; De 1:17; 19:17) A witness was not to accept a bribe,

allow anyone wicked to persuade him to speak untruthfully, or scheme violence. (Ex 23:1, 8) He was not to let his testimony be swayed by pressure of a crowd or by the wealth or poverty of those involved in the case. (Ex 23:2, 3) Even the closest family relationship was not to hold one back from testifying against a wicked violator of the law, such as an apostate or rebellious one. —De 13:6-11; 21:18-21; Zec 13:3.

One who proved to be a false witness received the punishment that the person accused would have received if found guilty. (De 19:17-21) Witnesses in all capital convictions were required to throw the first stone in the execution of the convicted one. Thus witnesses were enjoined by law to demonstrate their zeal for true, clean worship and for clearing out what was bad in Israel. This would also act as a deterrent to false testimony. It would take a very callous person to make a false accusation, knowing that he had to be the first to act in putting the accused to death.—De 17:7.

Material and circumstantial evidence. In case livestock had been entrusted to the care of another, the responsible one could bring in the torn body of an animal that had been killed by a wild beast as evidence, and that would thereby relieve him of liability. (Ex 22:10-13) If a married woman was accused by her husband of falsely claiming to be a virgin at the time of marriage, the girl's father could bring the mantle from the marriage bed as evidence of her virginity to present before the judges in order to clear her of the charge. (De 22:13-21) Even under patriarchal law, material evidence was acceptable in some cases. (Ge 38:24-26) Circumstances were given consideration as evidence. If an engaged girl was attacked in the city, failure on her part to scream was deemed evidence of willful submission and guilt.—De 22:23-27.

Secret adultery. A man suspecting his wife of secret adultery, for which he had no confession or eyewitness, could take her before the priest, where she would be judged by Jehovah, who saw and who knew all the facts. It was not a trial by ordeal. There was nothing in the *procedure itself* that would harm the woman or make manifest her innocence or guilt, but it was Jehovah who judged the woman and made known his verdict. If she was innocent, she would be unharmed and was to be made pregnant by her husband. If she was guilty, her reproductive organs would be affected so that she would be incapable of pregnancy. If there had been the required two witnesses, the matter would not have been taken to Jehovah in this manner, but she would have been adjudged guilty by the judges and stoned to death.—Nu 5:11-31.

Documents. Records, or documents, of various kinds were used. A husband was required to give his wife a certificate of divorce when putting her away. (De 24:1; Jer 3:8; compare Isa 50:1.) Genealogical records were available, as we see particularly in First Chronicles. Mention is made of deeds registering the sale of real estate. (Jer 32:9-11) Historical annals were in existence from the beginning of human history. (Ge 5:1; 6:9) Many letters were written, some of which may have been retained and may have figured in legal cases.—2Sa 11:14; 1Ki 21:8-14; 2Ki 10:1; Ne 2:7.

Jesus' Trial. The greatest travesty of justice ever committed was the trial and sentencing of Jesus Christ. Prior to his trial the chief priests and older men of the people took counsel together with a view to putting Jesus to death. So the judges were prejudiced and had their minds made up on the verdict before ever the trial took place. (Mt 26:3, 4) They bribed Judas to betray Jesus to them. (Lu 22:2-6) Because of the wrongness of their actions, they did not arrest him in the temple in the daytime, but they waited until they could act under cover of darkness and then sent a crowd armed with clubs and swords to arrest him in an isolated place outside the city.—Lu 22:52, 53.

Jesus was then taken first to the house of Annas, the ex-high priest, who still wielded great authority, his son-in-law Caiaphas being the high priest at the time. (Joh 18:13) There Jesus was questioned and was slapped in the face. (Joh 18:22) Next he was led bound to Caiaphas the high priest. False witnesses were sought by the chief priests and the whole Sanhedrin. Many such witnesses came forward but could not agree on their testimony, except two who twisted Jesus' words recorded at John 2:19. (Mt 26:59-61; Mr 14:56-59) Finally Jesus was put under oath by the high priest and questioned as to whether he was the Christ the Son of God. When Jesus answered in the affirmative and alluded to the prophecy at Daniel 7:13, the high priest ripped his garments and called upon the court to find Jesus guilty of blasphemy. This verdict was rendered, and he was sentenced to death. After this they spit in his face and hit him with their fists, taunting him, contrary to the Law.—Mt 26:57-68; Lu 22:66-71; compare De 25:1, 2 with Joh 7:51 and Ac 23:3.

After this illegal night trial the Sanhedrin met early in the morning to confirm their judgment and for a consultation. (Mr 15:1) Jesus was now led, again bound, to the governor's palace, to Pilate, since they said: "It is not lawful for us to kill anyone." (Joh 18:31) Here Jesus was charged with forbidding the paying of taxes to Caesar and with saying that he himself was Christ a king. Blasphemy against the God of the Jews would not have been so serious a charge in the eyes of the Romans, but sedition would. Pilate, after making futile attempts to get Jesus to testify against himself, told the Jews that he found no crime in him. Discovering, however, that Jesus was a Galilean, Pilate was happy to send him to Herod, who had jurisdiction over Galilee. Herod questioned Jesus, hoping to see a sign performed by him, but Jesus refused. Herod then discredited Jesus, making fun of him, and sent him back to Pilate.—Lu 23:1-11.

Pilate now tried to release Jesus in harmony with a custom of that time, but the Jews refused, calling for the release of a seditionist and murderer instead. (Joh 18:38-40) Pilate therefore had Jesus scourged, and the soldiers again mistreated him. After this, Pilate brought Jesus outside and tried to get his release, but the Jews insisted: "Impale him! Impale him!" Finally he issued the order to have Jesus impaled.—Mt 27:15-26; Lu 23:13-25; Joh 19:1-16.

What laws of God did the Jewish priests violate by the way they handled the trial of Jesus Christ?

The following are some of the laws of God that were flagrantly violated by the Jews in the trial of Christ: bribery (De 16:19; 27:25); conspiracy and the perversion of judgment and justice (Ex 23:1, 2, 6, 7; Le 19:15, 35); bearing false witness, in which matter the judges connived (Ex 20:16); letting a murderer (Barabbas) go, thereby bringing blood-guilt upon themselves and upon the land (Nu 35:31-34; De 19:11-13); mob action, or 'following a crowd to do evil' (Ex 23:2, 3); in crying out for Jesus to be impaled, they were violating the law that prohibited following the statutes of other nations and that also prescribed no torture but that provided that a criminal be stoned or put to death *before* being hung on a stake (Le 18:3-5; De 21:22); they accepted as king one not of their own nation, but a pagan (Caesar), and rejected the King whom God had chosen (De 17:14, 15); and finally, they were guilty of murder (Ex 20:13).

LEGION. The name by which one of the two demon-possessed men, whom Christ Jesus encountered in the region E of the Sea of Galilee, identified himself. Evidently, though, Legion was not his actual name, as it referred to his being possessed by many demons. Possibly the chief one of these demons caused this man to say that his name was Legion. The fact that in the first century C.E. Roman legions usually consisted of 6,000 men may give some indication of the large number of demons involved. So fierce were the demon-possessed man and his companion that no one dared to pass the area where they had their dwelling among the tombs. Under demon influence the man who said his name was Legion walked about naked, and day and night he cried aloud and slashed himself with stones. All efforts to bind him, even with fetters and chains, were unsuccessful. Christ Jesus, however, freed this man and his companion from the power of the demons. Thereafter the expelled demons took possession of a herd of swine and caused these to rush over a precipice to their death in the Sea of Galilee.—Mt 8:28-34; Mr 5:1-20; Lu 8:26-39; see GADARENES; SWINE.

For details about the Roman legions, see ARMY (Roman).

LEHABIM (Le·ha′bim). A name appearing at Genesis 10:13 and 1 Chronicles 1:11 among the descendants of Ham through Mizraim. Since the Hebrew name is a plural form, many scholars hold that a tribe taking its name from one of Mizraim's sons is meant. (See, however, MIZRAIM.) The Lehabim are generally identified with the Libyans and at least seem to have constituted one of the tribes inhabiting Libya in ancient times. While identification is difficult, they were probably the same as the *Lu·vim′* mentioned elsewhere in the Hebrew text, as at 2 Chronicles 12:3, where the *American Standard Version* reads "Lubim" and other translations read "Libyans."—*Mo; NW; RS.*

LEHI (Le′hi) [Jawbone]. The scene of one or, possibly, two Israelite victories over the Philistines. Its exact location is unknown today. Some identify it with Khirbet es-Siyyaj, which perhaps derives its name from the Greek word *si·a·gon′* (jawbone), less than 3 km (2 mi) E of Beth-shemesh.

At Lehi, Samson struck down a thousand Philistines with the moist jawbone of an ass. Subsequently he called the site Ramath-lehi (meaning "Lofty Place of the Jawbone"), probably to memorialize the victory Jehovah had given him there. (Jg 15:9-19) Originally, though, Lehi may have got its name from the shape of its crags.

Later, according to the rendering of numerous translators, Shammah struck down many Philistines assembled at Lehi. (2Sa 23:11, 12; *AT, JB, NW, RS*) However, the Hebrew term *la·chai·yah′* literally means "into a tent village," and, by a

slight change in vowel pointing, is rendered "to Lehi."

LEMUEL (Lem′u·el) [Belonging to God]. An unidentified king of ancient times whose words are recorded in Proverbs chapter 31. His identity has been the subject of considerable discussion, some commentators suggesting that Lemuel was another name for Solomon. Others identify Lemuel with Hezekiah. The words of King Lemuel constitute "the weighty message that his mother gave to him in correction." (Pr 31:1) However, the time and circumstances of the king's reception of such information from his mother are unknown. This "weighty message" advises against involvement with a bad woman, warns of how intoxicating liquor can pervert judgment, highlights the need to judge righteously, and then describes a good wife.

LENTIL [Heb., *'adha·shah′*]. An annual plant of the legume family that has long been cultivated by man and is still extensively grown in Egypt and Israel, as well as in other lands. (2Sa 17:27, 28; 23:11) This small plant (*Lens esculenta*), measuring from 15 to 46 cm (6 to 18 in.) in height, thrives in light, dry soil. Its compound leaves, generally consisting of six pairs of oblong leaflets, terminate in tendrils. Slender branchlets bear two to four small pealike flowers each. The short pods that develop from the flowers resemble those of the pea, and usually contain two small lens-shaped seeds. The color of the seeds and that of the flowers differs with the variety of lentil plant. The seeds may be reddish brown, gray, or black, and the flowers, white or pale blue. Rich in protein and carbohydrates, the seeds are, as in the past, commonly used for soups. (Ge 25:34) In combination with barley, lentils have been used for making bread. (Compare Eze 4:9.) The plant itself serves well as a fodder for livestock.

LEOPARD [Heb., *na·mer′*; Aramaic, *nemar′*; Gr., *par′da·lis*]. One of the large cats, usually having a light-tan coat with black spots arranged in broken circles. (Jer 13:23) Leopards commonly measure 1.2 m (4 ft) in length, not including the tail. Although even in more recent years several leopards have been killed near Jerusalem, these creatures evidently were found in far greater numbers in ancient Palestine. (Ca 4:8) The cheetah, or hunting leopard, ranked among the fastest of mammals, was also found in Palestine, and the Hebrew designation *na·mer′* may have included this animal as well as the leopard. The cheetah differs from the true leopard in that its claws are only partially retractile and its spots are solid, not ringed.

Under Messiah's rule, the Scriptures foretell, the leopard and the kid will lie down together in peace

In the Scriptures, allusion is made to the swiftness of the leopard (Hab 1:8) and its manner of lying in wait near towns, ready to pounce upon passing domestic animals. (Jer 5:6; Ho 13:7) In sharp contrast with this, the leopard and the kid are depicted as lying down together in peace during Messiah's rule.—Isa 11:6.

At Daniel 7:6, the four-winged, four-headed leopard represents the Grecian World Power, which conquered Medo-Persia with the swiftness of a leopard. Also, the wild beast out of the sea, seen in vision by the apostle John, was basically like a leopard.—Re 13:1, 2; see BEASTS, SYMBOLIC.

The Hebrew word *la'yish*, otherwise translated "lion" (Job 4:11; Pr 30:30), is rendered "leopard" at Isaiah 30:6 (*NW*), the "lion" (*la·vi'*) already having been mentioned in the same text.

LEPROSY. A disease designated in the Bible by the Hebrew term *tsa·ra''ath* and the Greek word *le'pra*. A person afflicted with it is called a leper.

In the Scriptures "leprosy" is not restricted to the disease known by that name today, for it could affect not only humans but also clothing and houses. (Le 14:55) The leprosy of today is otherwise called Hansen's disease, so named because Dr. Gerhard A. Hansen discovered the germ that is generally thought to cause this malady. However, though *tsa·ra''ath* applies to more than the leprosy of today, there is no doubt that human leprosy now called Hansen's disease was in evidence in the Middle East in Biblical times.

Varieties, With Their Effects. Today leprosy, or Hansen's disease, which is only slightly communicable, manifests itself in three basic varieties. One, the nodular type, results in a thickening of one's skin and the forming of lumps, first in the skin on the face and then on other parts of the body. It also produces degenerative effects in mucous membranes of the victim's nose and throat. This is known as black leprosy. Another type is anesthetic leprosy, sometimes called white leprosy. It is not as severe as black leprosy and basically affects the peripheral nerves. It may manifest itself in skin that is painful to the touch, though it can also result in numbness. The third type of leprosy, a mixed kind, combines the symptoms of both forms just described.

As leprosy progresses toward its advanced stage, the swellings that initially develop discharge pus, the hair may fall from one's head and eyebrows, nails may loosen, decay, and fall off. Then the victim's fingers, limbs, nose, or eyes may be slowly eaten away. Finally, in the most serious cases, death ensues. That Biblical "leprosy" certainly included such a serious disease is apparent from Aaron's reference to it as a malady wherein the flesh is "half eaten off."—Nu 12:12.

This description helps one better to appreciate Biblical references to this dread malady and the dire consequences of Uzziah's presumptuous act in improperly endeavoring to offer incense in Jehovah's temple.—2Ki 15:5; 2Ch 26:16-23.

Diagnosis. By means of the Mosaic Law, Jehovah provided Israel with information enabling the priest to diagnose leprosy and to distinguish between it and other less serious skin afflictions. From what is recorded at Leviticus 13:1-46, it can be seen that leprosy might begin with an eruption, a scab, a blotch, a boil, or a scar in one's flesh from fire. Sometimes the symptoms were very clear. The hair in the affected area had turned white, and the malady was seen to be deeper than the skin. For example, a white eruption in the skin might turn the hair white, and raw flesh might appear in the eruption. This meant that one had leprosy and was to be declared unclean. However, in other cases the malady was not deeper than the skin and a period of quarantine was imposed, with subsequent inspection by the priest, who made a final determination in the case.

It was acknowledged that leprosy could reach a stage in which it was not contagious. When it overspread the entire body, all of it having turned white, and living flesh was not in evidence, it was a sign that the diseased action was over and that only the marks of its ravages remained. The priest would then declare the victim clean, the disease posing no further danger to anyone.—Le 13:12-17.

If the leper's malady left him and he was cured, there were arrangements whereby he could ceremonially purify himself, and these included the offering of sacrifice in his behalf by the priest. (Le 14:1-32) But if the priest declared the uncured leper unclean, the leper's garments were to be torn, his head was to become ungroomed, he was to cover the mustache or upper lip, and he was to call out "Unclean, unclean!" He had to dwell in isolation outside the camp (Le 13:43-46), a measure that was taken so that the leper would not contaminate those in the midst of whom Jehovah was tenting. (Nu 5:1-4) It seems that in Biblical times lepers associated with one another or lived in groups, making it possible for them to aid one another.—2Ki 7:3-5; Lu 17:12.

In garments and houses. Leprosy could also affect woolen or linen garments, or an article of skin. The plague might disappear with washing, and there were arrangements for quarantining the article. But where this yellowish-green or reddish plague persisted, malignant leprosy was present and the article was to be burned. (Le 13:47-59) If yellowish-green or reddish depressions appeared in the wall of a house, the priest imposed a quarantine. It might be necessary to tear out affected stones and have the house scraped off inside, the stones and scraped-off mortar being disposed of in an unclean place outside the city. If the plague returned, the house was declared unclean and was pulled down, and the materials were disposed of in an unclean place. But for the house pronounced clean there was an arrangement for purification. (Le 14:33-57) It has been suggested that the leprosy affecting garments or houses was a type of mildew or mold; however, about this there is uncertainty.

As a Sign. One of the signs Jehovah empowered Moses to perform to prove to the Israelites that God had sent him involved leprosy. As instructed, Moses stuck his hand in the upper fold of his garment, and upon his withdrawing it, "his hand was stricken with leprosy like snow!" It was restored "like the rest of his flesh" by his returning it into the upper fold of his garment and withdrawing it once again. (Ex 4:6, 7) Miriam was stricken with "leprosy as white as snow" as a divine act because she spoke against Moses. He begged God to heal her, which was done, but she was quarantined outside the camp for seven days. —Nu 12:1, 2, 9-15.

In Elisha's Time. Naaman the Syrian was "a valiant, mighty man, though a leper [or, struck with skin disease]." (2Ki 5:1, ftn) His pride nearly lost him the opportunity of being cured, but he eventually did as instructed by Elisha, plunging into the Jordan seven times, and "his flesh came back like the flesh of a little boy and he became clean." (2Ki 5:14) He thereupon became a worshiper of Jehovah. However, Elisha's attendant Gehazi greedily acquired a gift from Naaman in the prophet's name, thus misrepresenting his master and, in effect, making the undeserved kindness of God a means of material gain. For his misdeed, Gehazi was stricken with leprosy by God and became "a leper white as snow."—2Ki 5:20-27.

That there were a number of lepers in Israel in Elisha's day is shown by the presence of four Israelite lepers outside Samaria's gates while Elisha was inside the city. (2Ki 7:3) But there was a general lack of faith on the part of the Israelites in this man of the true God, just as the Jews in Jesus' home territory would not accept him. Hence, Christ said: "Also, there were many lepers in Israel in the time of Elisha the prophet, yet not one of them was cleansed, but Naaman the man of Syria."—Lu 4:27.

Healed by Jesus and His Disciples. During his Galilean ministry, Jesus healed a leper described by Luke as "a man full of leprosy." Jesus ordered him to tell nobody and said: "But go off and show yourself to the priest, and make an offering in connection with your cleansing, just as Moses directed, for a witness to them."—Lu 5:12-16; Mt 8:2-4; Mr 1:40-45.

When Christ sent out the 12 apostles, he told them, among other things, "Make lepers clean." (Mt 10:8) Later, while he was going through Samaria and Galilee, Jesus cured ten lepers in a certain village. Only one of them, a Samaritan, "turned back, glorifying God with a loud voice" and fell upon his face at Jesus' feet, thanking him for what had been done in his behalf. (Lu 17:11-19) It may also be noted that Christ was in Bethany at the home of Simon the leper (whom Jesus may have cured) when Mary anointed Jesus with costly perfumed oil a few days before his death.—Mt 26:6-13; Mr 14:3-9; Joh 12:1-8.

LESHEM (Le'shem). Alternate name for the city of Laish, later called Dan.—Jos 19:47; Jg 18:7, 27, 29; see DAN No. 3.

LESHEM STONE (lesh'em). An unidentified precious stone that was placed first in the third row of gems on the high priest's "breastpiece of judgment."—Ex 28:15, 19; 39:12.

Various stones, such as amber, hyacinth, opal, and tourmaline, have been suggested as being identical with "*leshem* stone," but none of these identifications can be substantiated. The *New World Translation* therefore leaves the Hebrew word untranslated as *leshem* stone.

LETTERS. The writing and sending of official, business, and personal letters was a widely used means of communication in ancient times.—2Sa 11:14; 2Ki 5:5-7; 10:1, 2; 2Ch 30:1; Ezr 4:7; Isa 37:14; Jer 29:1; Ac 9:1, 2; 28:21; 2Th 2:2; Heb 13:22.

The Hebrew word *se'pher* refers to anything that is written and has the various meanings "book; letter; writing; certificate; deed; written document." The Greek word *gram'ma* can denote a letter of the alphabet or a written document. (2Co 3:7; Ac 28:21) The Greek term *e·pi·sto·le'* is used only with regard to a written message.—1Co 5:9.

Confidential letters were usually sealed. (1Ki 21:8) Sanballat's disrespectful action in sending an open letter to Nehemiah may have been intended to cause the false charges set forth therein to become public knowledge.—Ne 6:5.

In addition to papyrus, materials employed for letter writing in ancient times included ostraca (small pieces of broken pottery or earthenware) and clay tablets. Thousands of clay tablets have been found in Babylonia and other regions. Washed and cleaned, smooth clay was made into a tablet and, while still wet, it was imprinted by means of a stylus forming wedge-shaped (cuneiform) characters. These tablets were often enclosed in clay envelopes. In the case of contracts, the text was sometimes repeated on the envelope. The envelopes were sealed and then baked in a kiln or dried in the sun to make them hard and durable.—See ARCHAEOLOGY.

Letter writing was often done by professional scribes. As in the Persian court, such scribes were usually on hand to take down official government correspondence. (Es 8:9; Ezr 4:8) Scribes were also to be found in the marketplaces near city gates, where they could be engaged by the populace to write letters and to record business transactions.

Letters were sometimes delivered by messengers (2Ki 19:14), runners (2Ch 30:6), or couriers (Es 3:13; 8:14). Postal service itself seems to have been restricted to official correspondence down to Roman times. So average persons had to rely on traveling acquaintances or merchants to deliver their letters.

Anciently, letters of recommendation were also used. However, the apostle Paul did not need such letters to or from the Christians at Corinth to prove that he was a minister. He had helped them to become Christians and therefore could say: "You yourselves are our letter, inscribed on our hearts and known and being read by all mankind." —2Co 3:1-3.

In the first century C.E., letters from Paul, James, Peter, John, Jude, and the governing body in Jerusalem contributed to the growth and the preservation of the unity and cleanness of the Christian congregation.—Ac 15:22-31; 16:4, 5; 2Co 7:8, 9; 10:8-11.

LETUSHIM (Le·tu'shim) [possibly from a root meaning "sharpen; hammer; forge"]. A name appearing among the descendants of Abraham through Dedan, one of his sons by Keturah. (Ge 25:3) This name has the plural Hebrew ending *im,* as do the names Asshurim and Leummim appearing in the same text. Because of this, many scholars believe that a tribe or people is meant. In view of their relationship to Dedan, this tribe likely located in the Arabian Peninsula, but precise identification is impossible.—See MIZRAIM.

LEUMMIM (Le·um'mim) [Nation Groups; Populations]. A name appearing at Genesis 25:1-3 along with Asshurim and Letushim, all being descendants of Abraham and Keturah through their son Dedan. The use of the plural Hebrew ending *im* in the name Leummim may indicate that it represents a tribe or people. Specific identification of this Dedanite tribe is not possible. It has been suggested, however, that they inhabited some part of Arabia, likely in the vicinity generally assigned to Dedan.—See MIZRAIM.

LEVELING INSTRUMENT. A device used in making surfaces level or at right angles to a plumb line. The "leveling instrument" (Heb., *mish·qe'leth* or *mish·qo'leth*) was employed by carpenters, stonemasons, and other craftsmen of ancient times to achieve horizontal accuracy when building walls and various structures, while the plummet was used to assure vertical accuracy. Egyptian masons seem to have employed a level shaped like the letter "A" with a short plumb line suspended from the apex. Evidently when the hanging line coincided with a center mark on the crossbar, this indicated that the surface on which it was placed was level. The Scriptures furnish no description of leveling instruments, however, and they refer to this device only in figurative ways.

A leveling instrument may be used to construct a building properly or to test its fitness for preservation. Jehovah foretold that he would apply to wayward Jerusalem "the measuring line applied to Samaria and also the leveling instrument applied to the house of Ahab." God had measured and found Samaria and the house of King Ahab to be morally bad or crooked, resulting in their destruction. Likewise, God would judge Jerusalem and its rulers, exposing their wickedness and bringing about the destruction of that city. These events actually occurred in 607 B.C.E. (2Ki 21:10-13; 10:11) Through Isaiah the various wicked braggarts and rulers of the people in Jerusalem were apprised of their coming calamity and of Jehovah's declaration: "I will make justice the measuring line and righteousness the leveling instrument." The standards of true justice and genuine righteousness would reveal who were really God's servants and who were not, resulting in either preservation or destruction.—Isa 28:14-19.

LEVI (Le'vi) [Adherence; Joined].

1. Jacob's third son by his wife Leah, born in Paddan-aram. (Ge 35:23, 26) At his birth Leah said: "Now this time my husband will join himself to me, because I have borne him three sons." The boy was therefore called Levi, the meaning of this name evidently being linked with Leah's hope for a new bond of affection between her and Jacob. (Ge 29:34) Levi became the father of Gershon (Gershom), Kohath, and Merari, founders of the three principal divisions of the Levites.—Ge 46: 11; 1Ch 6:1, 16.

Levi, along with his brother Simeon, took drastic action against the defilers of their sister Dinah. (Ge 34:25, 26, 31) This expression of violent anger was cursed by Jacob, who foretold that Levi's descendants would be scattered in Israel, a prophecy that was fulfilled when the Levites were indeed scattered throughout 48 Levite cities in the territories of Israel's various tribes in the land of Canaan. (Ge 49:7; Jos 21:41) Levi accompanied Jacob into Egypt and died there at 137 years of age.—Ex 1:1, 2; 6:16; see LEVITES.

2. An ancestor of Jesus Christ who is referred to as the "son of Symeon" in the genealogy of Jesus recorded by Luke. He is listed in the line between David and Zerubbabel.—Lu 3:27-31.

3. The "son of Melchi," who is the second person preceding Heli (Mary's father) in Luke's genealogy of Jesus.—Lu 3:23, 24.

4. A tax collector (Mr 2:14; Lu 5:27, 29) who became an apostle of Jesus Christ and was otherwise known as Matthew.—Mt 9:9; 10:2-4; see MATTHEW.

LEVIATHAN [Heb., *liw·ya·than'*]. This Hebrew word occurs six times in the Bible. It is believed to come from a root word meaning "wreath"; hence the name indicates something that is "wreathed," or "gathered into folds." The word is transliterated in most Bible translations.

Since, with the exception of Job 3:8, the references mention water in connection with it, Leviathan appears to signify some form of aquatic creature of great proportions and strength, although not necessarily of one specific kind. Psalm 104:25, 26 describes it as cavorting in the sea where ships travel, and for this reason many suggest that the term here applies to some type of whale. Though whales are rare in the Mediterranean, they are not unknown there, and parts of two whale skeletons can be found in a museum at Beirut in Lebanon. *An American Translation* here says "crocodile" instead of Leviathan. Additionally, the word "sea" (*yam*) by itself is not determinative inasmuch as in Hebrew it can refer to a large inland body of water such as the Sea of Galilee (Sea of Chinnereth) (Nu 34:11; Jos 12:3), or even to the river Nile (Isa 19:5) or the Euphrates.—Jer 51:36.

The description of "Leviathan" at Job 41:1-34 aptly fits the crocodile, and the "sea" of verse 31 may refer to a river such as the Nile or another body of fresh water. It should be noted, however, that some crocodiles, as the Nile crocodiles (*Crocodylus niloticus*), are found along the seacoast and at times go out into the sea some distance from land.

Psalm 74 describes God's record of salvation for his people, and verses 13 and 14 refer symbolically to his deliverance of Israel from Egypt. Here the term "sea monsters [Heb., *than·ni·nim'*, plural of *tan·nin'*]" is used as a parallel expression to "Leviathan," and the crushing of the heads of Leviathan may well refer to the crushing defeat administered to Pharaoh and his army at the time of the Exodus. The Aramaic Targums here give "the strong ones of Pharaoh" in place of "the heads of Leviathan." (Compare Eze 29:3-5, where Pharaoh is likened to a "great sea monster" in the midst of the Nile canals; also Eze 32:2.) Isaiah 27:1 apparently employs Leviathan (*LXX,* "the dragon") as a symbol of an empire, an organization that is international in scope and that is dominated by one who himself is referred to as "serpent" and "dragon." (Re 12:9) The prophecy is one of restoration for Israel, and therefore Jehovah's 'turning attention' to Leviathan must include Babylon. However, verses 12 and 13 consider Assyria and Egypt as well. So, Leviathan here evidently refers to an international organization or empire that is in opposition to Jehovah and his worshipers.

LEVIRATE MARRIAGE. See Brother-in-Law Marriage.

LEVITE CITIES.
The Levites were given no territorial allotment, Jehovah being their inheritance. (Nu 18:20; De 18:1, 2) But God directed that the other tribes of Israel give them a total of 48 cities and surrounding pasture grounds. (Nu 35:1-8) Such cities were ultimately assigned to the Levites (Jos 21:1-8), and 13 of them were priestly cities. (Jos 21:19; see Priests' Cities.) Of the 48 cities, 6 were assigned as cities of refuge for unintentional manslayers.—Jos 20:7-9; see Cities of Refuge.

The scattering of the Levites among the other tribes of Israel was in fulfillment of Jacob's deathbed prophecy.—Ge 49:5-7.

The Levites had the right to repurchase at any time houses they sold within their cities, or these were restored to them during the Jubilee year. But the pasturelands adjacent to their cities were never to be sold.—Le 25:32-34; see Levites.

LEVITES
[Of (Belonging to) Levi]. Descendants of Levi, third son of Jacob by Leah. (Ge 29:32-34) At times the term applies to the whole tribe, but usually it excludes the priestly family of Aaron (Jos 14:3, 4; 21:1-3); thus the expression "priests and Levites" is common. (1Ki 8:4; 1Ch 23:2; Ezr 1:5; Joh 1:19) Priestly duties were confined to the male members of Aaron's family, with the Levites, the rest of the tribe, acting as their assistants. (Nu 3:3, 6-10) This arrangement began with the setting up of the tabernacle, as before this no particular family or tribe was assigned to offer the sacrifices.—Ex 24:5.

Taken as a Ransom for Firstborn. The Levites were chosen by Jehovah in place of all the firstborn of the other tribes. (Ex 13:1, 2, 11-16; Nu 3:41) Counting from a month old upward, there were 22,000 Levite males who could be exchanged for the same number of firstborn males of the other tribes. The census taken in the Wilderness of Sinai revealed that there were 22,273 firstborn

sons in the other tribes. Therefore, God required that a ransom price of five shekels ($11) be given to Aaron and his sons for each of the 273 firstborn in excess of the Levites.—Nu 3:39, 43, 46-51.

Duties. The Levites were made up of three families, from Levi's sons Gershon (Gershom), Kohath, and Merari. (Ge 46:11; 1Ch 6:1) Each of these families was assigned a place near the tabernacle in the wilderness. The Kohathite family of Aaron camped in front of the tabernacle to the east. The other Kohathites camped on the south side, the Gershonites on the west, and the Merarites on the north. (Nu 3:23, 29, 35, 38) Setting up, dismantling, and carrying the tabernacle was the work of the Levites. When it was time to move, Aaron and his sons took down the curtain dividing the Holy from the Most Holy and covered the ark of the testimony, the altars, and other sacred furniture and utensils. The Kohathites then carried these things. The Gershonites transported the tent cloths, coverings, screens, courtyard hangings, and tent cords (evidently the cords of the tabernacle itself), and the Merarites took care of the panel frames, pillars, socket pedestals, tent pins and cords (cords of the courtyard surrounding the tabernacle).—Nu 1:50, 51; 3:25, 26, 30, 31, 36, 37; 4:4-33; 7:5-9.

The work of the Levites was highly organized under David, who appointed supervisors, officers, judges, gatekeepers, and treasurers, as well as a vast number to assist the priests in the temple, the courtyards, and the dining rooms in connection with the offerings, sacrifices, purification work, weighing, measuring, and various guard duties. Levite musicians were organized into 24 groups, similar to the priestly divisions, and served in rotation. Duties were determined by casting lots. In the case of the groups of gatekeepers, the particular gate assignment was chosen in the same way.—1Ch 23, 25, 26; 2Ch 35:3-5, 10.

In Moses' day it was at 30 years of age that a Levite assumed his full duties, such as bearing the tabernacle and its articles when it was being moved. (Nu 4:46-49) Some duties could be performed from the age of 25, but apparently not the laborious service, such as transporting the tabernacle. (Nu 8:24) In King David's time the age was reduced to 20 years. The reason David gave was that the tabernacle (now to be replaced by the temple) would no longer have to be carried about. Assignments of obligatory service terminated at the age of 50 years. (Nu 8:25, 26; 1Ch 23:24-26; see Age.) The Levites needed to be well versed in the Law, often being called upon to read it in public and to teach it to the common people.—1Ch 15:27; 2Ch 5:12; 17:7-9; Ne 8:7-9.

Maintenance. Maintenance of the Levites was mainly by tithes from the other tribes, a tenth of everything produced from the ground and the cattle being given them. The Levites, in turn, passed on a tenth of this to the priests. (Nu 18:25-29; 2Ch 31:4-8; Ne 10:38, 39) Also, though the Levites were exempt from military service, they, along with the priests, shared some of the spoils of battle. (Nu 1:45-49; 31:25-31; see TITHE.) The Levites received no territorial allotment in Canaan, Jehovah being their share. (Nu 18:20) However, other tribes of Israel gave them a total of 48 cities scattered throughout the Promised Land.—Nu 35:1-8.

Provided Supporters of True Worship. The Levites supplied some notable examples of enthusiasm for true worship. This was evident in the golden-calf incident and again when Levites moved out of Jeroboam's territory following the split in the kingdom. (Ex 32:26; 2Ch 11:13, 14) They were also zealous in their support of Kings Jehoshaphat, Hezekiah, and Josiah as well as of Governors Zerubbabel and Nehemiah and the priest-scribe Ezra in their efforts to restore true worship in Israel.—2Ch 17:7-9; 29:12-17; 30:21, 22; 34:12, 13; Ezr 10:15; Ne 9:4, 5, 38.

As a tribe, however, they did not support the Son of God in his work of restoration, although some individual Levites became Christians. (Ac 4:36, 37) Many of the Levite priests became obedient to the faith. (Ac 6:7) With the destruction of Jerusalem and its temple in 70 C.E., the family records of the Levites were lost or destroyed, bringing the Levitical system to an end. But, a "tribe of Levi" constitutes part of spiritual Israel. —Re 7:4, 7.

The name of the tribe is also the basis for the name of the Bible book Leviticus. This book deals extensively with the Levites and their duties.

LEVITICUS.

LEVITICUS. The third book of the Pentateuch, containing laws from God on sacrifices, purity, and other matters connected with Jehovah's worship. The Levitical priesthood, carrying out its instructions, rendered sacred service in "a typical representation and a shadow of the heavenly things."—Heb 8:3-5; 10:1.

Period Covered. Not more than a month is covered by the events given in the book. Most of Leviticus is devoted to listing Jehovah's ordinances rather than recounting various happenings over an extended period of time. The tabernacle's erection on the first day of the first month in the second year of Israel's departure from Egypt is mentioned in the final chapter of Exodus, the book preceding Leviticus. (Ex 40:17) Then, the book of Numbers (immediately following the Leviticus account) in its first verses (1:1-3) begins with God's command to take a census, stated to Moses "on the first day of the second month in the second year of their coming out of the land of Egypt."

When and Where Written. The logical time for the writing of the book would be 1512 B.C.E., at Sinai in the wilderness. Testifying that Leviticus was indeed written in the wilderness are its references that reflect camp life.—Le 4:21; 10:4, 5; 14:8; 17:1-5.

Writer. All the foregoing evidence likewise helps to identify the writer as Moses. He received the information from Jehovah (Le 26:46), and the book's closing words are: "These are the commandments that Jehovah gave Moses as commands to the sons of Israel in Mount Sinai." (27:34) Besides, Leviticus is a part of the Pentateuch, the writer of which is generally acknowledged to be Moses. Not only does the opening "And . . . " of Leviticus indicate its connection with Exodus, and therefore with the rest of the Pentateuch, but the way in which Jesus Christ and the writers of the Christian Scriptures refer to it shows that they knew it to be the writing of Moses and an unquestionable part of the Pentateuch. For example, see Christ's reference to Leviticus 14:1-32 (Mt 8:2-4), Luke's reference to Leviticus 12:2-4, 8 (Lu 2:22-24), and Paul's paraphrasing of Leviticus 18:5 (Ro 10:5).

Dead Sea Leviticus Scrolls. Among the manuscripts found at the Dead Sea, nine contain fragments of the book of Leviticus. Four of them, believed to date from 125 to 75 B.C.E., were written in ancient Hebrew characters that were in use before the Babylonian exile.

Value of the Book. God promised Israel that if they obeyed his voice they would become to him "a kingdom of priests and a holy nation." (Ex 19:6) The book of Leviticus contains a record of God's installing a priesthood for his nation and giving them the statutes that would enable them to maintain holiness in his eyes. Even though Israel was only God's typical "holy nation," whose priests were "rendering sacred service in a typical representation and a shadow of the heavenly things" (Heb 8:4, 5), God's law, if obeyed, would have kept them clean and in line for filling the membership of his spiritual "royal priesthood, a holy nation." (1Pe 2:9) But the disobedience of the majority deprived Israel of filling exclusively the place of membership in the Kingdom of God, as Jesus told the Jews. (Mt 21:43) Nevertheless, the laws set down in the book of Leviticus were of inestimable value to those heeding them.

Through the sanitary and dietary laws, as well as the regulations on sexual morality, they were provided with safeguards against disease and depravity. (Le chaps 11-15, 18) Especially, however, did these laws benefit them spiritually, because they enabled them to get acquainted with Jehovah's holy and righteous ways and they helped them to conform to His ways. (11:44) Furthermore, the regulations set out in this portion of the Bible, as part of the Law, served as a tutor leading believing ones to Jesus Christ, God's great High Priest and the one foreshadowed by the countless sacrifices offered in accord with the Law.—Ga 3:19, 24; Heb 7:26-28; 9:11-14; 10:1-10.

The book of Leviticus continues to be of great value to all today who desire to serve Jehovah acceptably. A study of the fulfillment of its various features in connection with Jesus Christ, the ransom sacrifice, and the Christian congregation is indeed faith strengthening. While it is true that Christians are not under the Law covenant (Heb 7:11, 12, 19; 8:13; 10:1), the regulations set out in the book of Leviticus give them insight into God's viewpoint on matters. The book is, therefore, not a mere recounting of dry, inapplicable details, but a live source of information. By getting a knowledge of how God views various matters, some of which are not specifically covered in the Christian Greek

HIGHLIGHTS OF LEVITICUS

God's laws, especially concerning the service of the priests in Israel, with emphasis, for the benefit of the nation as a whole, on the seriousness of sin and the importance of being holy because Jehovah is holy

Written by Moses in 1512 B.C.E., while Israel was camped at Mount Sinai

Aaronic priesthood is installed and begins to function

Moses carries out the seven-day installation procedure (8:1-36)

On the eighth day, the priesthood begins to function; Jehovah manifests his approval by displaying his glory and consuming the offering on the altar (9:1-24)

Jehovah strikes down Nadab and Abihu for offering illegitimate fire; subsequently the use of alcoholic drinks when one is serving at the sanctuary is forbidden (10:1-11)

Requirements are outlined for those who will serve as priests; regulations are laid down about eating what is holy (21:1–22:16)

Use of sacrifices in maintaining an approved relationship with God

Laws are given regarding animals acceptable as burnt offerings and how they should be prepared for presentation (1:1-17; 6:8-13; 7:8)

Kinds of grain offerings are stipulated as well as how they are to be presented to Jehovah (2:1-16; 6:14-18; 7:9, 10)

Procedure is laid down for handling communion sacrifices; the eating of blood and fat is forbidden (3:1-17; 7:11-36)

Animals are specified for sin offering in the case of a priest, the assembly of Israel, a chieftain, or one of the people; procedure for handling this offering is outlined (4:1-35; 6:24-30)

Laws are given on situations requiring guilt offerings (5:1–6:7; 7:1-7)

Instructions are handed down regarding the offering to be made on the day of the priest's being anointed (6:19-23)

All offerings must be sound; defects making an animal unfit for sacrifice are listed (22:17-33)

Atonement Day procedures are outlined involving the sacrifice of a bull and two goats—one goat for Jehovah and the other for Azazel (16:2-34)

Detailed regulations to safeguard against uncleanness and to maintain holiness

Certain animals are acceptable as clean for food and others are prohibited as unclean; uncleanness results from contact with dead bodies (11:1-47)

A woman should be purified from her uncleanness after giving birth (12:1-8)

Procedures for handling cases of leprosy are detailed (13:1–14:57)

Uncleanness results from sexual discharges, and purification is required (15:1-33)

Holiness must be maintained by respecting sanctity of blood and by shunning incest, sodomy, bestiality, slander, spiritism, and other detestable practices (17:1–20:27)

Sabbaths and seasonal festivals to Jehovah

Sabbath days and years as well as regulations and principles touching the Jubilee are laid down (23:1-3; 25:1-55)

The manner of observing the annual Festival of Unfermented Cakes (following Passover) and the Festival of Weeks (later called Pentecost) is detailed (23:4-21)

The procedure for observing the Day of Atonement and the Festival of Booths is outlined (23:26-44)

Blessings for obedience, maledictions for disobedience

Blessings for obedience will include bountiful harvests, peace, and security (26:3-13)

Maledictions because of disobedience will include disease, defeat by enemies, famine, destruction of cities, desolation of land, and exile (26:14-45)

Scriptures, the Christian can be helped to avoid what displeases God and to do what pleases him.

LIBERTY. See FREEDOM; JUBILEE.

LIBNAH (Lib′nah) [from a root meaning "white"; or, possibly, "storax tree"].

1. An Israelite wilderness encampment. Its location is unknown.—Nu 33:20, 21.

2. A royal Canaanite city taken by Joshua before the conquest of Lachish. (Jos 10:29-32, 39; 12:15) Libnah was one of the cities in the territory of Judah given to "the sons of Aaron." (Jos 15:21, 42; 21:13; 1Ch 6:57) Centuries later King Josiah's father-in-law lived there.—2Ki 23:31; 24:18; Jer 52:1.

At the time of the Edomite revolt in the tenth century B.C.E., Libnah also rebelled against Judean King Jehoram. (2Ki 8:22; 2Ch 21:10) In 732 B.C.E., Assyrian King Sennacherib's army moved from Lachish to Libnah. He had sent a military detachment from Lachish to threaten Jerusalem. While at Libnah, the Assyrians received reports that Tirhakah the king of Ethiopia intended to fight them. Therefore, Sennacherib, to encourage Jerusalem's surrender, sent messengers a second time with intimidating letters to Hezekiah the king of Judah. Subsequently Jehovah's angel slew 185,000 of the Assyrian host, apparently still encamped near Libnah.—2Ki 19:8-35; Isa 37:8-36.

Tell es-Safi has been suggested as a possible identification of ancient Libnah. However, since the weight of evidence points to identifying Tell es-Safi with Gath, contemporary scholars tend to identify Libnah with Tell Bornat (Tel Burena), about 8 km (5 mi) NNE of Lachish.

LIBNI (Lib′ni) [from a root meaning "white"].

1. A grandson of Levi and the son of Gershon (Gershom). (Ex 6:17; 1Ch 6:17) He was the founder of a Levitical family (Nu 3:18, 21; 1Ch 6:19, 20) and was evidently also called Ladan.—1Ch 23:6, 7; 26:21.

2. A Levite who descended from Merari through Mahli.—1Ch 6:29.

LIBNITES [Of (Belonging to) Libni]. A family of Levites who descended from Gershon (Gershom) through his son Libni.—Nu 3:21; 26:58.

LIBYA (Lib′y·a), **LIBYANS** (Lib′y·ans). Ancient Libya occupied an area of northern Africa W of Egypt. Its inhabitants are generally thought to have been designated by the Hebrew term *Lu·vim′*. (2Ch 12:3; "Libyans," *LXX, NW, RS*) If *Lu-*

vim′ is a variant of *Leha·vim′* (Lehabim), this may indicate that at least some of the Libyans descended from Ham through Mizraim. (Ge 10:13) The traditional Jewish view found in the writings of Josephus (*Jewish Antiquities,* I, 130-132 [vi, 2]) makes the Libyans descendants of Ham through Put. (Ge 10:6) Also, the Greek *Septuagint* and the Latin *Vulgate* read "Libyans" in Jeremiah 46:9, Ezekiel 27:10, and 38:5 where the Hebrew text says "Put." It is possible, of course, that descendants of both Put and Mizraim settled in the geographic region of northern Africa that came to be called Libya. This would mean that the designation "Libyans" is more comprehensive than the Hebrew term *Lu·vim′*.

Egypt's King Shishak, regarded as the founder of the "Libyan dynasty," captured numerous cities when he invaded Judah in the fifth year of King Rehoboam (993 B.C.E.). His powerful force of chariots and horsemen included Libyans. Although Jerusalem itself was spared, Shishak stripped the city of its treasures. (1Ki 14:25, 26; 2Ch 12:2-9) About 26 years later (967 B.C.E.), the Libyans were represented among the troops of Zerah the Ethiopian, which penetrated Judah but suffered humiliating defeat. (2Ch 14:9-13; 16:8) In the seventh century B.C.E., the assistance of the Libyans and others was seemingly of no avail in saving the Egyptian city of No-amon from calamity at the hands of the Assyrians. (Na 3:7-10) It was foretold that the Libyans and Ethiopians would be at the "steps" of the "king of the north," implying that these former supporters of Egypt would come under his control.—Da 11:43.

In the year 33 C.E., among the Jews and proselytes at Jerusalem for the Festival of Pentecost were persons from "the parts of Libya, which is toward Cyrene," that is, the western part of Libya. Likely some of these were baptized in response to Peter's discourse and later carried the message of Christianity back to the land of their residence. —Ac 2:10.

LIE. The opposite of truth. Lying generally involves saying something false to a person who is entitled to know the truth and doing so with the intent to deceive or to injure him or another person. A lie need not always be verbal. It can also be expressed in action, that is, a person may be living a lie. The Hebrew verb that conveys the idea of speaking that which is untrue is *ka·zav′*. (Pr 14:5) Another Hebrew verb *sha·qar′* means "deal or act falsely," and the noun form is rendered "lie; deception; falsehood." (Le 19:11; Ps 44:17; Le 19:12; Ps 33:17; Isa 57:4) Hebrew *shaw′*, at times rendered "untruth; falsehood," basically refers to something worthless, vain, valueless. (Ps 12:2; De 5:20; Ps 60:11; 89:47; Zec 10:2) The Hebrew verb ka·chash' (deceive) evidently has the basic meaning "prove disappointing." (Le 19:11; Ho 9:2) The Greek term pseu'dos and related words have to do with lying and falsehood.

The father, or originator, of lying is Satan the Devil. (Joh 8:44) His lie conveyed by means of a serpent to the first woman Eve ultimately brought death to her and to her husband Adam. (Ge 3:1-5, 16-19) That first lie was rooted in selfishness and wrong desire. It was designed to divert the love and obedience of the first human pair to the liar, who had presented himself as an angel of light, a benefactor. (Compare 2Co 11:14.) All other malicious lies uttered since that time have likewise been a reflection of selfishness and wrong desire. People have told lies to escape deserved punishment, to profit at the expense of others, and to gain or maintain certain advantages, material rewards, or the praise of men.

Especially serious have been the religious lies, as they have endangered the future life of persons deceived by them. Said Jesus Christ: "Woe to you, scribes and Pharisees, hypocrites! because you traverse sea and dry land to make one proselyte, and when he becomes one you make him a subject for Gehenna twice as much so as yourselves." (Mt 23:15) The exchange of God's truth for "the lie," the falsehood of idolatry, can cause a person to become a practicer of what is degrading and vile. —Ro 1:24-32.

The case of the religious leaders of Judaism in the time of Jesus' earthly ministry shows what can happen when one abandons the truth. They schemed to have Jesus put to death. Then, when he was resurrected, they bribed the soldiers who had guarded the tomb so they would conceal the truth and spread a lie about the disappearance of Jesus' body.—Mt 12:14; 27:1, 2, 62-65; 28:11-15; Mr 14:1; Lu 20:19.

Jehovah God cannot lie (Nu 23:19; Heb 6:13-18), and he hates "a false tongue." (Pr 6:16-19) His law to the Israelites required compensation for injuries resulting from deception or malicious lying. (Le 6:2-7; 19:11, 12) And a person presenting false testimony was to receive the punishment that he desired to inflict upon another by means of his lies. (De 19:15-21) God's view of malicious lying, as reflected in the Law, has not changed. Those desiring to gain his approval cannot engage in the practice of lying. (Ps 5:6; Pr 20:19; Col 3:9, 10; 1Ti 3:11; Re 21:8, 27; 22:15) They cannot be living a lie, claiming to love God while hating their brother. (1Jo 4:20, 21) For playing false to the holy spirit by lying, Ananias and his wife lost their lives.—Ac 5:1-11.

However, persons who are momentarily overreached in telling a lie do not automatically become guilty of an unforgivable sin. The case of Peter, in denying Jesus three times, illustrates that if a person is truly repentant, God will forgive him. —Mt 26:69-75.

While malicious lying is definitely condemned in the Bible, this does not mean that a person is under obligation to divulge truthful information to people who are not entitled to it. Jesus Christ counseled: "Do not give what is holy to dogs, neither throw your pearls before swine, that they may never trample them under their feet and turn around and rip you open." (Mt 7:6) That is why Jesus on certain occasions refrained from giving full information or direct answers to certain questions when doing so could have brought unnecessary harm. (Mt 15:1-6; 21:23-27; Joh 7:3-10) Evidently the course of Abraham, Isaac, Rahab, and Elisha in misdirecting or in withholding full facts from nonworshipers of Jehovah must be viewed in the same light.—Ge 12:10-19; chap 20; 26:1-10; Jos 2:1-6; Jas 2:25; 2Ki 6:11-23.

Jehovah God allows "an operation of error" to go to persons who prefer falsehood "that they may get to believing the lie" rather than the good news about Jesus Christ. (2Th 2:9-12) This principle is illustrated by what happened centuries earlier in the case of Israelite King Ahab. Lying prophets assured Ahab of success in war against Ramothgilead, while Jehovah's prophet Micaiah foretold disaster. As revealed in vision to Micaiah, Jehovah allowed a spirit creature to become "a deceptive spirit" in the mouth of Ahab's prophets. That is to say, this spirit creature exercised his power upon them so that they spoke, not truth, but what they themselves wanted to say and what Ahab wanted to hear from them. Though forewarned, Ahab preferred to be fooled by their lies and paid for it with his life.—1Ki 22:1-38; 2Ch 18.

LIFE. The principle of life or living; the animate existence, or term of animate existence, of an individual. As to earthly, physical life, things possessing life generally have the capabilities of growth, metabolism, response to external stimuli, and reproduction. The Hebrew word used in the Scriptures is chai·yim', and the Greek word is zo·e'. The Hebrew word ne'phesh and the Greek word psy·khe', both meaning "soul," are also employed to refer to life, not in the abstract sense, but to life as a person or an animal. (Compare the words "soul" and "life," as used at Job 10:1; Ps 66:9; Pr 3:22.) Vegetation has life, the life principle operating in it, but not life as a soul. Life in the fullest sense, as applied to intelligent persons, is perfect existence with the right to it.

Jehovah God the Source. Life has always existed, because Jehovah God is the living God, the Fountain of life, and he has no beginning or end of existence. (Jer 10:10; Da 6:20, 26; Joh 6:57; 2Co 3:3; 6:16; 1Th 1:9; 1Ti 1:17; Ps 36:9; Jer 17:13) The first of his creations was given life, namely, his only-begotten Son, the Word. (Joh 1:1-3; Col 1:15) Through this Son, other living angelic sons of God were created. (Job 38:4-7; Col 1:16, 17) Later, the physical universe was brought into existence (Ge 1:1, 2), and on the third of earth's creative "days" the first forms of physical life: grass, vegetation, and fruit trees. On the fifth day, living earthly souls, sea animals, and winged flying creatures were created, and on the sixth day, land animals and, finally, man.—Ge 1:11-13, 20-23, 24-31; Ac 17:25; see CREATION; DAY.

Consequently, life on earth did not have to wait for some chance combination of chemicals to occur under certain exact conditions. Such a thing has never yet been observed and, in fact, is impossible. Life on earth came to be as the result of a direct command of Jehovah God the Source of life and by the direct action of his Son in carrying out that command. Only life begets life. The Bible account tells us in each instance that the thing created brought forth offspring in its likeness, or, "according to its kind." (Ge 1:12, 21, 25; 5:3) Scientists have found that there is indeed discontinuity between the different 'kinds,' and, except for the question of origin, this has been the chief obstacle to the theory of evolution.—See KIND.

Life-force and breath. In earthly creatures, or "souls," there is both the active life-force, or "spirit" that animates them, and the breath that sustains that life-force. Both spirit (life-force) and breath are provisions from God, and he can destroy life by taking either away. (Ps 104:29; Isa 42:5) At the time of the Flood, animals and humans were drowned; their breath was cut off and the force of life was extinguished. It died out. "Everything in which the breath of the force of life was active [literally, "in which the breath of the active force (spirit) of life [was]"] in its nostrils, namely, all that were on the dry ground, died."—Ge 7:22; compare Robert Young's translation; see SPIRIT.

Organism. All things having life, either spiritual or fleshly, have an organism, or body. Life itself is impersonal, incorporeal, being merely the life principle. In discussing the kind of body with which resurrected persons will come back, the apostle Paul explains that those created for different environments have different bodies. As for those having life on earth, he says: "Not all flesh is the same flesh, but there is one of mankind, and there is another flesh of cattle, and another flesh of birds, and another of fish." He says also that "there are heavenly bodies, and earthly bodies; but the glory of the heavenly bodies is one sort, and that of the earthly bodies is a different sort." —1Co 15:39, 40.

Regarding the difference in the flesh of various earthly bodies, the 1942 edition of the *Encyclopædia Britannica* (Vol. 14, p. 42) says: "Another feature is the chemical individuality everywhere manifest, for each distinct type of organism seems to have some distinctive protein of its own, and some characteristic rate or rhythm of metabolism. Thus under the general quality of persistence amid unceasing metabolism, there is a triad of facts: (1) the building-up that compensates for the breaking-down of proteins, (2) the occurrence of these proteins in a colloidal state and (3) *their specificity from type to type.*"—Italics ours.

Transmission of Life-Force. The life-force in creatures, being started into activity by Jehovah in the first of each kind (for example, in the first human pair), could then be passed on by the procreative process to offspring. In mammals, following conception the mother supplies oxygen and other nourishment until birth, when the infant begins to breathe through its nostrils, to nurse, and later to eat.

When Adam was created, God formed man's body. For that newly created body to live and continue alive, both the spirit (life-force) and breathing were needed. Genesis 2:7 states that God proceeded "to blow into his nostrils the breath [form of *nesha·mah'*] of life, and the man came to be a living soul." "The breath of life" must refer to more than just breath or air moving into the lungs. God evidently provided Adam with both the spirit or spark of life and the breath needed to keep him alive. Now Adam began to have life as a person, to express personality traits, and by his speech and actions he could reveal that he was higher than the animals, that he was a "son of God," made in His likeness and image.—Ge 1:27; Lu 3:38.

The life of man and animals is dependent both on the life-force started off initially in the first of each kind and on breath to sustain that life-force. Biological science testifies to this fact. This is evident in their separation of the process of death into two classifications: *Somatic,* or *systemic death* (sometimes called clinical death), which is the absolute cessation of the functions of the brain, as well as of the circulatory and the respiratory organs (the body as an organized unit is dead), and *death of the tissues* (sometimes termed biological death), the entire disappearance of the vital actions of the ultimate structural constituents of the body. So even though somatic death has taken place, the life-force still lingers in the cells of the body's tissues until eventually every cell dies completely (death of the tissues).

Aging and Death. All forms of vegetable life, as well as animal life, are transitory. A long-standing question among scientists has been, Why does man grow old and die?

Some scientists propose that there is a genetically determined life span for each cell. For support they point to experiments in which cells cultured in an artificial environment were found to stop dividing after about 50 divisions. Other scientists, however, contend that such experiments do not provide insight into why whole organisms age. Various other explanations are offered, including the theory that the brain releases hormones that play a large part in aging and subsequent death. That a person must be cautious about accepting one theory over another is suggested by the comments of Roy L. Walford, M.D., who said: "It's not a cause for alarm or even surprise that Hayflick's paradigm [the theory that aging is built into the cell's genetics] may prove ultimately false, or be replaced by a better but ultimately equally false paradigm. Everything is true for its own time."—*Maximum Life Span*, 1983, p. 75.

In considering the findings and conclusions of scientists, it should be noted that most do not credit life to a Creator. Through their own efforts, they hope to discover the secret of aging and death so as to extend human life indefinitely. They overlook the fact that the Creator himself decreed the death sentence for the first human pair, implementing that sentence in a way that man does not fully understand; similarly, he holds forth the prize of everlasting life to those who exercise faith in his Son.—Ge 2:16, 17; 3:16-19; Joh 3:16.

Adam lost life for himself and offspring. When Adam was created, God placed in the garden of Eden "the tree of life." (Ge 2:9) This tree evidently had no intrinsic life-giving qualities in its fruit, but it represented God's guarantee of life "to time indefinite" to the one whom God would allow to eat of its fruit. Since the tree was put there by God for some purpose, undoubtedly Adam would have been permitted to eat this fruit

after proving faithful to a point that God considered satisfactory and sufficient. When Adam transgressed, he was prevented from having opportunity to eat from the tree, Jehovah saying: "Now in order that he may not put his hand out and actually take fruit also from the tree of life and eat and live to time indefinite,—." Then Jehovah followed his words with action. He would not allow one unworthy of life to live in the garden made for righteous persons and to eat of the tree of life.—Ge 3:22, 23.

Adam, who had enjoyed perfect life contingent on obedience to Jehovah (Ge 2:17; De 32:4), now experienced in himself the workings of sin and its fruitage, death. His life's vigor was strong, nevertheless. Even in his sad situation, cut off from God and true spirituality, he lived 930 years before death overtook him. In the meantime he was able to pass on, not fullness of life, but a measure of life to his posterity, many of whom lived from 700 to 900 years. (Ge 5:3-32) But the process that took place with Adam is described by Jesus' half brother James: "Each one is tried by being drawn out and enticed by his own desire. Then the desire, when it has become fertile, gives birth to sin; in turn, sin, when it has been accomplished, brings forth death."—Jas 1:14, 15.

What Man Needs for Life. Most scientific investigators not only overlook the cause of death in all mankind, but more important, they ignore the prime factor requisite for everlasting life. While it is necessary for the human body to be constantly nourished and refreshed by breathing, drinking, and eating, there is something far more essential for continuance of life. The principle was expressed by Jehovah: "Not by bread alone does man live but by every expression of Jehovah's mouth does man live." (De 8:3) Jesus Christ repeated this statement and also said: "My food is for me to do the will of him that sent me and to finish his work." (Joh 4:34; Mt 4:4) On another occasion he declared: "Just as the living Father sent me forth and I live because of the Father, he also that feeds on me, even that one will live because of me."—Joh 6:57.

When man was created, he was made in God's image, according to his likeness. (Ge 1:26, 27) This, of course, did not mean physical image or appearance, for God is a Spirit, and man is flesh. (Ge 6:3; Joh 4:24) It meant that man, different from the "unreasoning animals" (2Pe 2:12), had reasoning power; he had attributes like those of God, such as love, a sense of justice, wisdom, and power. (Compare Col 3:10.) He had the ability to understand why he existed and his Creator's purpose toward him. Hence he, unlike the animals, was given the capacity for spirituality. He could appreciate and worship his Creator. This capacity created a need in Adam. He needed more than literal food; he had to have spiritual sustenance; his spirituality had to be exercised for his mental and physical welfare.

Consequently, apart from Jehovah God and his spiritual provisions there can be no indefinite continuance of life. As to living forever, Jesus said: "This means everlasting life, their taking in knowledge of you, the only true God, and of the one whom you sent forth, Jesus Christ."—Joh 17:3.

Regeneration. With a view to restoring to mankind perfection of organism and the prospect of eternal life, Jehovah has provided the truth, "the word of life." (Joh 17:17; Php 2:16) Following the truth will lead one to a knowledge of God's provision of Jesus Christ, who gave himself "a ransom in exchange for many." (Mt 20:28) Only through this means can man be restored to full spirituality as well as to physical wholeness.—Ac 4:12; 1Co 1:30; 15:23-26; 2Co 5:21; see RANSOM.

Through Jesus Christ, then, regeneration to life comes. He is called "the last Adam . . . a life-giving spirit." (1Co 15:45) Prophecy designates him as "Eternal Father" (Isa 9:6) and as the one who "poured out his soul to the very death," whose soul is 'set as a guilt offering.' He, as such "Father," is able to regenerate mankind, thus giving life to those who exercise faith in the offering of his soul and are obedient.—Isa 53:10-12.

Hope of men of ancient times. Faithful men of ancient times had the hope of life. The apostle Paul points out this fact. He refers back in time to the offspring of Abraham before the Law was given, and he speaks of himself, a Hebrew, as though he were alive then, in the sense that he was in the loins of his forefathers. He argues: "I was once alive apart from law; but when the commandment arrived, sin came to life again, but I died. And the commandment which was to life, this I found to be to death." (Ro 7:9, 10; compare Heb 7:9, 10.) Men like Abel, Enoch, Noah, and Abraham had hope in God. They believed in the "seed" that would bruise the serpent's head, which would mean deliverance. (Ge 3:15; 22:16-18) They looked forward to God's Kingdom, the "city having real foundations." They believed in a resurrection of the dead to life.—Heb 11:10, 16, 35.

With the giving of the Law, Jehovah stated: "You must keep my statutes and my judicial decisions, which if a man will do, he must also live by means of them." (Le 18:5) Doubtless those Israelites receiving the Law hailed it as offering the hope of life to them. The Law was "holy and righteous" and would mark as completely righteous the one who could live up to its standards fully. (Ro 7:12) But, instead of giving life, the Law showed all Israel, and mankind in general, to be imperfect and sinners. Furthermore, it condemned the Jews to death. (Ga 3:19; 1Ti 1:8-10) Truly, as Paul says, "when the commandment arrived, sin came to life again, but I died." Therefore, life could not come by the Law.

The apostle argues: "If a law had been given that was able to give life, righteousness would actually have been by means of law." (Ga 3:21) Now, the Jews, being condemned by the Law, were not only shown to be sinners as offspring of Adam but were also under an additional disability. For this reason, Christ died on a torture stake, as Paul says: "Christ by purchase released us from the curse of the Law by becoming a curse instead of us, because it is written: 'Accursed is every man hanged upon a stake.'" (Ga 3:13) By removing this obstacle, namely, the curse brought on the Jews by their breaking of the Law, Jesus Christ removed this barrier to life for the Jews, giving them opportunity for life. His ransom could thus benefit them as well as others.

Everlasting life a reward from God. It is evident throughout the Bible that the hope of servants of Jehovah has been to receive everlasting life at God's hands. This hope has encouraged them in maintaining faithfulness. And it is not a selfish hope. The apostle writes: "Moreover, without faith it is impossible to please him well, for he that approaches God must believe that he is and that he becomes the *rewarder* of those earnestly seeking him." (Heb 11:6) He is that kind of God; it is one of the qualities for which he deserves full devotion from his creatures.

Immortality, incorruption, divine life. The Bible speaks of Jehovah as having immortality and incorruption. (1Ti 1:17) He has granted this first to his Son. At the time the apostle Paul wrote to Timothy, Christ was the only one who had been given immortality. (1Ti 6:16) But it is promised to others, those who become Christ's spiritual brothers. (Ro 2:7; 1Co 15:53, 54) Also, these become partakers of "divine nature"; they share with Christ in his glory. (2Pe 1:4) Angels are spirit creatures, but they are not immortal, for those who become wicked demons will be destroyed. —Mt 25:41; Lu 4:33, 34; Re 20:10, 14; see IMMORTALITY; INCORRUPTION.

Earthly life without corruption. What about others of mankind who do not receive heavenly life? The apostle John quotes Jesus as saying: "For

God loved the world so much that he gave his only-begotten Son, in order that everyone exercising faith in him might not be destroyed but have everlasting life." (Joh 3:16) In his parable of the sheep and the goats, those of the nations separated on Jesus' right side as sheep enter "into everlasting life." (Mt 25:46) Paul speaks of "God's sons" and "joint heirs with Christ" and says that "the eager expectation of the creation is waiting for the revealing of the sons of God." Then he says, "the creation itself also will be set free from enslavement to corruption and have the glorious freedom of the children of God." (Ro 8:14-23) Adam when created as a perfect human was a "son [or child] of God." (Lu 3:38) The prophetic vision of Revelation 21:1-4 points to the time of "a new heaven" and "a new earth" and gives the promise that then "death will be no more, neither will there be mourning nor outcry nor pain be anymore." Since this promise is given, not to spirit creatures, but specifically to "mankind," it gives assurance that a new earthly society of humankind living under the "new heaven" will experience restoration of mind and body to fullness of health and everlasting life as earthly "children of God."

In his command to Adam, God implied that if Adam obeyed, he would not die. (Ge 2:17) So with obedient mankind, when man's last enemy, death, is brought to nothing, there will be no sin working in their bodies to bring death. To time indefinite they will not need to die. (1Co 15:26) This bringing of death to nothing takes place at the end of Christ's reign, which the book of Revelation shows is 1,000 years long. Here it is said of those becoming kings and priests with Christ that they "came to life and ruled as kings with the Christ for a thousand years." "The rest of the dead" not coming to life "until the thousand years were ended" must be those alive at the end of the thousand years, but before Satan is released from the abyss and brings the decisive test on mankind. By the end of the thousand years, people on earth will have reached human perfection, being in the condition that Adam and Eve were in before they sinned. Now they will really have life in perfection. Those who thereafter pass the test when Satan is released for a short time from the abyss will be able to enjoy that life forever.—Re 20:4-10.

The Way of Life. Jehovah, the Fountain of life, has revealed the way of life through his Word of truth. The Lord Jesus Christ "shed light upon life and incorruption through the good news." (2Ti 1:10) He told his disciples: "It is the spirit that is life-giving; the flesh is of no use at all. The sayings that I have spoken to you are spirit and are

life." A little later Jesus asked his apostles whether they were going to leave him, as others had. Peter replied: "Lord, whom shall we go away to? You have sayings of everlasting life." (Joh 6:63, 66-68) The apostle John called Jesus "the word of life," and said: "By means of him was life."—1Jo 1:1, 2; Joh 1:4.

From Jesus' words it is evident that human efforts to prolong life indefinitely or theories that certain diets or regimens will bring life to mankind are futile. At best, they can bring improved health only temporarily. The only way of life is obedience to the good news, "the word of life." (Php 2:16) To get life, the individual must keep his mind fixed "on the things above, not on the things upon the earth." (Col 3:1, 2) To his hearers Jesus said: "He that hears my word and believes him that sent me has everlasting life, and he does not come into judgment but has passed over from death to life." (Joh 5:24; 6:40) They are no longer condemned sinners, in the way of death. The apostle Paul wrote: "Therefore those in union with Christ Jesus have no condemnation. For the law of that spirit which gives life in union with Christ Jesus has set you free from the law of sin and of death." (Ro 8:1, 2) John says that a Christian knows he has 'passed from death to life' if he loves his brothers.—1Jo 3:14.

Since "there is not another name under heaven that has been given among men by which we must get saved," the seeker for life must follow Christ. (Ac 4:12) Jesus showed that a person must be conscious of his spiritual need; he must hunger and thirst for righteousness. (Mt 5:3, 6) Not only must he hear the good news but he must exercise faith in Jesus Christ and through him call on the name of Jehovah. (Ro 10:13-15) Following Jesus' example, he will be baptized in water. (Mt 3:13-15; Eph 4:5) He must then keep on seeking the Kingdom and Jehovah's righteousness.—Mt 6:33.

Safeguard the Heart. The person who has become a disciple of Jesus Christ must continue in the way of life. He is warned: "Let him that thinks he is standing beware that he does not fall." (1Co 10:12) He is counseled: "More than all else that is to be guarded, safeguard your heart, for out of it are the sources of life." (Pr 4:23) Jesus showed that it is from the heart that wicked reasonings, adultery, murder, and so forth, emanate. These things would lead to death. (Mt 15:19, 20) Guarding against such heart reasonings by supplying the heart with life-giving spiritual nourishment, the truth from the pure Fountain of life, will keep the heart from going wrong and taking the person out of the way of life.—Ro 8:6; see HEART.

In safeguarding one's life by guarding the heart, the tongue must be controlled. "Death and life are in the power of the tongue, and he that is loving it will eat its fruitage." (Pr 18:21) The reason was explained by Jesus: "The things proceeding out of the mouth come out of the heart, and those things defile a man." (Mt 15:18; Jas 3:5-10) But by proper use of the tongue to praise God and to speak right things, one continues in the way of life.—Ps 34:12-14; 63:3; Pr 15:4.

This Present Life. King Solomon, after trying out everything this life has to offer in the way of riches, houses, gardens, and forms of enjoyment, came to the conclusion: "I hated life, because the work that has been done under the sun was calamitous from my standpoint, for everything was vanity and a striving after wind." (Ec 2:17) Solomon did not hate life itself, for it is a 'good gift and perfect present from above.' (Jas 1:17) Solomon hated the calamitous, vain life that one experiences in living as does the present world of mankind, subject to futility. (Ro 8:20) At the conclusion of his book Solomon gave the exhortation to fear the true God and keep his commandments, which is the way of real life. (Ec 12:13, 14; 1Ti 6:19) The apostle Paul spoke of himself and fellow Christians, saying that, after their strenuous preaching and bearing witness to Christ and the resurrection in the face of persecution, "if in this life only we have hoped in Christ, we are of all men most to be pitied." Why? Because they would have relied on a false hope. "However," Paul continued, "now Christ has been raised up from the dead." "Consequently, my beloved brothers," he concluded, "become steadfast, unmovable, always having plenty to do in the work of the Lord, knowing that your labor is not in vain in connection with the Lord."—1Co 15:19, 20, 58.

Trees of Life. Aside from the tree of life in Eden (Ge 2:9), already discussed herein, the expression "tree[s] of life" occurs several other times in the Scriptures, always in a figurative, or symbolic, sense. Wisdom is called "a tree of life to those taking hold of it," in that it will supply them with that which they need, not only to enjoy their present life but also to receive eternal life, namely, knowledge of God and the insight and good sense to obey his commands.—Pr 3:18; 16:22.

"The fruitage of the righteous one is a tree of life, and he that is winning souls is wise," says another proverb. (Pr 11:30) The righteous person, by speech and example, wins souls, that is, by listening to him, persons get spiritual nourishment, are led to serve God, and receive the life

that God makes possible. Similarly, "the calmness of the tongue is a tree of life, but distortion in it means a breaking down in the spirit." (Pr 15:4) The calm speech of the wise person helps and refreshes the spirit of those hearing him, nourishing good qualities in them, helping them along the way of life, but distortion in the tongue is like bad fruit; it brings trouble and discouragement, damaging those hearing it.

Proverbs 13:12 reads: "Expectation postponed is making the heart sick, but the thing desired is a tree of life when it does come." The fulfillment of a long-awaited desire is strengthening and refreshing, giving renewed vigor.

The glorified Jesus Christ promises the conquering Christian that He will grant him to eat of "the tree of life, which is in the paradise of God." (Re 2:7) Again, in the last verses of the book of Revelation, we read: "And if anyone takes anything away from the words of the scroll of this prophecy, God will take his portion away from the trees of life and out of the holy city, things which are written about in this scroll." (Re 22:19) In the context of these two Scripture texts, Christ Jesus is speaking to those who are conquerors, who will not "be harmed by the second death" (Re 2:11), who will be given "authority over the nations" (Re 2:26), who will be made a "pillar in the temple of my God" (Re 3:12), and who will sit down with Christ in his heavenly throne. (Re 3:21) Therefore the tree or trees could not be literal, for conquerors who eat are those who are partakers of the heavenly calling (Heb 3:1), with places in heaven reserved for them. (Joh 14:2, 3; 2Pe 1:3, 4) The tree(s) would therefore be symbolic of God's provision for sustained life, in this case, the heavenly, immortal life that the faithful ones are given as conquerors with Christ.

There is the mention of "trees of life" in a different context, at Revelation 22:1, 2. Here the nations are shown as partaking of the leaves of the trees for healing purposes. They are alongside the river flowing out from the temple-palace of God, in which is his throne. The picture appears after the scene of the establishing of the new heaven and the new earth and the statement that "the tent of God is with mankind." (Re 21:1-3, 22, 24) Symbolically, then, these would be curative, life-sustaining provisions for humankind, for their eventual everlasting life. The source of such provisions is the royal throne of God and of the Lamb Jesus Christ.

Several references are made to "the scroll of life" or to God's "book." It evidently contains the names of all those who, because of their faith, are in line to receive the grant of everlasting life either in heaven or on earth. It contains the names of Jehovah's servants "from the founding of the world," that is, the world of redeemable mankind. So righteous Abel's is apparently the first name written on "the scroll."—Re 17:8; Mt 23:35; Lu 11: 50, 51.

What is signified by one's name being written in God's "book" or "scroll of life"?

The writing of a person's name in "the book of life" does not predestine that one to eternal life. His name's remaining there depends on his obedience. Thus Moses pleaded with Jehovah for Israel: "Now if you will pardon their sin,—and if not, wipe me out, please, from your book that you have written." Jehovah answered: "Whoever has sinned against me, I shall wipe him out of my book." (Ex 32:32, 33) This indicates that the list of names in "the book" would undergo changes because of disobedience on the part of some, their names being 'wiped' or 'blotted' out from "the book."—Re 3:5.

In the judgment scene at Revelation 20:11-15, during Christ's Millennial Reign "the scroll of life" is shown as opened to receive additional names; scrolls of instruction are also opened. Those who come back in the 'resurrection of the unrighteous' will thus have the opportunity of having their names written on "the scroll of life," provided they obediently perform deeds that are in harmony with the scrolls of instruction. (Ac 24:15) Of course, faithful servants of God who come back in the 'resurrection of the righteous' will already have their names in "the scroll of life." By their loyal obedience to the divine instructions, they will *keep* their names in it.

How does a person get his name *permanently* retained in "the book of life"? For those who are in line to receive heavenly life, it is by 'conquering' this world through faith, proving themselves "faithful even to death." (Re 2:10; 3:5) For those who are in line to receive life on earth, it is by proving loyal to Jehovah through a final, decisive test at the end of Christ's Millennial Reign. (Re 20: 7, 8) Those who maintain integrity through that final test will have their names retained permanently by God in "the book of life," Jehovah thus acknowledging that they are righteous in the complete sense and worthy of the right to everlasting life on earth.—Ro 8:33.

"The Lamb's scroll." "The scroll of life of the Lamb" is a separate scroll, apparently containing only the names of those with whom the Lamb, Jesus Christ, shares his Kingdom rule, including those still on earth who are in line to receive heavenly life. (Re 13:8; compare Re 14:1, 4.) Those enrolled in "the Lamb's scroll" are spoken of as entering the holy city, New Jerusalem, thus becoming part of the heavenly Messianic Kingdom. (Re 21:2, 22-27) Their names are written both in "the Lamb's scroll" and in the other scroll, God's "book of life."—Php 4:3; Re 3:5.

River of Water of Life. In John's vision in the book of Revelation, he saw "a river of water of life, clear as crystal, flowing out from the throne of God and of the Lamb" down the middle of the broad way of the holy city, New Jerusalem. (Re 22:1, 2; 21:2) Water is essential for life. The time setting given in the vision is after the establishment of "a new heaven and a new earth; for the former heaven and the former earth had passed away." (Re 21:1) The context places the flowing of this river after the destruction of the present system of things. The vision speaks of trees alongside the river producing fruit, and of leaves for the curing of the nations. The life-giving waters, then, would be the provisions for life that Jehovah has made through the Lamb, Jesus Christ, for all on earth who will receive life.

After reporting other details of the inspired revelation, John wrote: "The spirit and the bride keep on saying: 'Come!'" and he commanded anyone hearing to say: "Come!" then extending the invitation to anyone thirsting to "take life's water free." Even before the end of the present wicked system of things the spirit and the bride invite persons to *begin* drinking of God's provisions for gaining eternal life through the Lamb of God. Such invited ones also can anticipate drinking from the river of water of life in such a way that they will experience complete healing under the ministrations of the Lamb and his bride after the old system has been destroyed.—Re 22:17.

"Life's Moisture." At Psalm 32:1-5 David shows the happiness that attends forgiveness, though he also reveals the distress experienced before making confession of transgressing to Jehovah and receiving God's pardon. Prior to confessing and while trying to conceal his error, the psalmist is conscience stricken and says: "My life's moisture has been changed as in the dry heat of summer." Attempted repression of a guilty conscience wore him out, and anguish reduced his vigor just as a tree might lose life-giving moisture during a drought or in summer's intense dry heat.

David's words seem to indicate that he experienced ill effects both mentally and physically, or had at least lost most of his joy of life, because of failure to confess his sin. Only confession to Jehovah could bring pardon and relief.—Pr 28:13.

"The Bag of Life." When Abigail appealed to David to turn back from his mission of vengeance upon Nabal, thereby restraining him from entering into bloodguilt, she said: "When man rises up to pursue you and look for your soul, the soul of my lord will certainly prove to be wrapped up in the bag of life with Jehovah your God; but, as for the soul of your enemies, he will sling it forth as from inside the hollow of the sling." (1Sa 25:29-33) Just as a person wraps up something valuable to protect and preserve it, so David's life as an individual was in the hands of the living God, and He would preserve David's life from his enemies, as long as David did not try to bring his salvation by his own hand, but waited on Jehovah. However, the soul of David's enemies God would throw away.

LIFE SPAN. It was God's original purpose that man should live forever. Being perfect, the first man Adam had the opportunity to enjoy a span of life that would never end, subject to obedience to God. (Ge 2:15-17) However, because of disobedience, Adam forfeited that opportunity, and from him all the human race inherited sin and death.—Ro 5:12.

During the Patriarchal Period. During the pre-Flood period, the life span approached a thousand years. (Ge 5:5-29) The people closer to man's original perfection enjoyed greater longevity than those farther removed from it. The longest life on record is that of Methuselah, who lived 969 years. After the Flood, the human life span dropped rapidly.

Some have theorized that the year in the times before the Flood was just a month long. However, there is no Scriptural basis for this view. Had the year been a 30-day month, this would mean that Enosh would have become a father before he was eight years old, and others, such as Kenan, Mahalalel, Jared, and Enoch, would have fathered children before they were six years old. (Ge 5:9, 12, 15, 18, 21) A comparison of Genesis 7:11 with Genesis 8:3, 4 shows that 150 days amounted to five months. The fact that the Bible also mentions the 10th month and, subsequently, one 40-day period and at least two 7-day time periods as passing during this year, indicates the year was 12 months long.—Ge 8:5, 6, 10, 12-14.

Since Moses' Time. About 3,500 years ago Moses wrote concerning the life span: "In themselves the days of our years are seventy years;

LENGTHS OF LIFE OF THE PATRIARCHS		
Name	Genesis	Length of Life
Adam	5:5	930
Seth	5:8	912
Enosh	5:11	905
Kenan	5:14	910
Mahalalel	5:17	895
Jared	5:20	962
Enoch	5:23	365
Methuselah	5:27	969
Lamech	5:31	777
Noah	9:29	950
Shem	11:10, 11	600
Arpachshad	11:12, 13	438
Shelah	11:14, 15	433
Eber	11:16, 17	464
Peleg	11:18, 19	239
Reu	11:20, 21	239
Serug	11:22, 23	230
Nahor	11:24, 25	148
Terah	11:32	205
Abraham	25:7	175
Isaac	35:28	180
Jacob	47:28	147

and if because of special mightiness they are eighty years, yet their insistence is on trouble and hurtful things." (Ps 90:10) The situation in this regard has not changed substantially.

Throughout the centuries, man's efforts to extend his life span have been unsuccessful. However, in many lands *life expectancy* has increased. Hence, James Fries and Lawrence Crapo noted: "The average length of life in the United States has increased from approximately 47 years at the turn of the century to over 73 years today, an increase of more than 25 years. . . . A critical look at these data, however, shows that the increase in life expectancy results from the elimination of premature death rather than by extension of the natural life span."—*Vitality and Aging*, 1981, pp. 74, 75.

Almost 2,000 years ago Jesus Christ stated that nobody "can add a cubit to his life span." (Lu 12:25) However, Jesus also said: "The things impossible with men are possible with God." (Lu 18:27) Through the prophet Isaiah, God had foretold: "Like the days of a tree will the days of my people be." (Isa 65:22) And in Isaiah 25:8 it was foretold that God "will actually swallow up death forever, and the Sovereign Lord Jehovah will certainly wipe the tears from all faces." This promise was repeated in the last book of the Bible: "And [God] will wipe out every tear from their eyes, and death will be no more, neither will mourning nor outcry nor pain be anymore."—Re 21:4.

LIGAMENTS. Strong bands of tissue that connect bones or support organs. Various modern Bible translations render the Greek word *syn·de'smon* (a form of *syn'de·smos*) at Colossians 2:19 as "ligaments" (*ED; NE; NW; RS*), while others translate it either as "sinews" (*Fn; Mo*), "uniting bands" (*Ro*), or merely "bands" (*AS; KJ*). *Syn'de·smos* means "that which binds together, bond of union, fastening" and is used with reference to sinews or ligaments. (*A Greek-English Lexicon*, by H. G. Liddell and R. Scott, revised by H. Jones, Oxford, 1968, p. 1701) This same Greek term is employed in the expressions "bond of unrighteousness" (Ac 8:23), "uniting bond of peace" (Eph 4:3), and "perfect bond of union" (Col 3:14).

In warning against the "mock humility" of one merely professing Christianity, Paul said: "He is not holding fast to the head, to the one from whom all the body, being supplied and harmoniously joined together by means of its joints and ligaments [*syn·de'smon*], goes on growing with the growth that God gives." (Col 2:18, 19) Here the anointed Christian congregation is likened to a body having a head. The interdependence of its members is shown by the comment that it is "harmoniously joined together by means of its joints and ligaments," Paul thus using "ligaments" metaphorically in connection with the spiritual body of Christ, having Jesus as its head. As the head, Jesus supplies the members of the body what they need through the "joints and ligaments," the means and arrangements for supplying spiritual nourishment, as well as communication and coordination. (Compare 1Co 12:12-30; Joh 15:4-10.) In the literal human body every member has a part to play toward its smooth operation and growth, both in receiving nutriment and direction and in passing such on to other members of the body. Circumstances are similar in the case of the congregational body of Christ.

LIGHT. The Hebrew term *'ohr* and the Greek term *phos* refer to that which emanates from a light-giving body such as a lamp (Jer 25:10) or the sun, as well as to the opposite of darkness, literally and figuratively. (Isa 5:20; Joh 11:10, 11) It is generally believed that light consists of energy particles that have wave properties. To this day, however, man still cannot give a complete answer to the question propounded over three millenniums ago by the Creator of light: "Where, now, is the way by which the light distributes itself?" —Job 38:24.

Light from the sun is a combination of colors, with each color having a different wavelength. The color of an object is determined by the partic-

ular portion of the light reflected by its surface. Thus light furnishes the many hues that delight the eye of man. It is also essential for earthly life —plant, animal, and human—to continue.

The Source of Light. Jehovah God is the Former of light and the Creator of darkness. (Isa 45:7) It was on the first creative day that he said: "Let light come to be." (Ge 1:3) Earlier he had created the heavens (including "the great lights" —the sun, moon, and stars; compare Ps 136:7-9) and the earth. (Ge 1:1) So the bringing of light into existence with reference to the earth apparently involved gradually removing whatever had formerly obstructed the sun's rays from reaching this planet. And the "division" between light and darkness must have come about through the rotation of the earth as it moved around the sun. (Ge 1:4, 5) Much later Jehovah plagued the sun-worshiping Egyptians with darkness, a darkness that did not affect the Israelites. (Ex 10:21-23) In leading his people out of Egypt, he provided light by means of a pillar of fire.—Ex 13:21; 14:19, 20; Ps 78:14.

The Scriptures repeatedly associate light with its Creator. Stated the psalmist: "O Jehovah my God, you have proved very great. With dignity and splendor you have clothed yourself, enwrapping yourself with light as with a garment." (Ps 104:1, 2) This declaration harmonizes well with Ezekiel's description of what he saw in vision: "I got to see something like the glow of electrum, like the appearance of fire all around inside thereof, from the appearance of his hips and upward; and from the appearance of his hips and downward I saw something like the appearance of fire, and he had a brightness all around. There was something like the appearance of the bow that occurs in a cloud mass on the day of a pouring rain. That is how the appearance was of the brightness round about. It was the appearance of the likeness of the glory of Jehovah." (Eze 1:27, 28) Centuries earlier, just a partial manifestation of that glory caused Moses' face to emit rays.—Ex 33:22, 23; 34:29, 30.

"God is light and there is no darkness at all in union with him." (1Jo 1:5) He is righteous, upright, and holy (De 32:4; Re 4:8), having nothing in common with the degrading and unclean practices commonly linked with darkness. (Compare Job 24:14-16; 2Co 6:14; 1Th 5:7, 8.) Therefore persons who are walking in the darkness by manifesting hatred for their brother and who are not practicing the truth could never be in union with him.—1Jo 1:6; 2:9-11.

Jehovah is "the Father of the celestial lights." (Jas 1:17) Not only is he the "Giver of the sun for light by day, the statutes of the moon and the stars for light by night" (Jer 31:35) but he is also the Source of all spiritual enlightenment. (2Co 4:6) His law, judicial decisions, and word are a light to those allowing themselves to be guided by them. (Ps 43:3; 119:105; Pr 6:23; Isa 51:4) The psalmist declared: "By light from you we can see light." (Ps 36:9; compare Ps 27:1; 43:3.) Just as the light of the sun continues to get brighter from dawn until "the day is firmly established," so the path of the righteous ones, illuminated by godly wisdom, gets lighter and lighter. (Pr 4:18) To follow the course that Jehovah outlines is to walk in his light. (Isa 2:3-5) On the other hand, when a person looks at things in an impure way or with evil design, he is in great spiritual darkness. As Jesus put it: "If your eye is wicked, your whole body will be dark. If in reality the light that is in you is darkness, how great that darkness is!"—Mt 6:23; compare De 15:9; 28:54-57; Pr 28:22; 2Pe 2:14.

Light and the Son of God. Since his resurrection and ascension to heaven, Christ Jesus, "the King of those who rule as kings and Lord of those who rule as lords," "dwells in unapproachable light." That light is so glorious that it makes it impossible for weak human eyes to behold him. (1Ti 6:15, 16) In fact, one man, Saul (Paul) of Tarsus was blinded by the light from heaven seen by him at the time the glorified Son of God revealed himself to this persecutor of Jesus' followers.—Ac 9:3-8; 22:6-11.

During his earthly ministry Jesus Christ was a light, furnishing spiritual enlightenment concerning God's purposes and will for those who would gain divine favor. (Joh 9:5; compare Isa 42:6, 7; 61:1, 2; Lu 4:18-21.) Initially, only "the lost sheep of the house of Israel" received benefit from that "great light." (Isa 9:1, 2; Mt 4:13-16; 15:24) But spiritual enlightenment was not to be limited just to the natural Jews and proselytes. (Joh 1:4-9; compare Ac 13:46, 47.) When the infant Jesus was presented at the temple, aged Simeon referred to him as "a light for removing the veil from the nations." (Lu 2:32) As Paul explained to the Ephesians, uncircumcised non-Jews had been in the dark respecting God and his purposes: "Formerly you were people of the nations as to flesh; 'uncircumcision' you were called by that which is called 'circumcision' made in the flesh with hands—that you were at that particular time without Christ, alienated from the state of Israel and strangers to the covenants of the promise, and you had no hope and were without God in the world." (Eph 2:11, 12) However, when the good news about the Christ was brought to the non-Jews, those who responded favorably were 'called out of darkness into God's wonderful light.' (1Pe 2:9) But others continued to allow the one who transforms himself into "an angel of light" or enlightenment (2Co 11:14), "the god of this system of things," to blind them so 'that the illumination of the good news about the Christ might not shine through.' (2Co 4:4) They preferred darkness, for they wanted to continue in their selfish course.—Compare Joh 3:19, 20.

Followers of Christ Become Lights. Those who exercised faith in Christ Jesus as "the light of the world" and became his followers themselves came to be "sons of light." (Joh 3:21; 8:12; 12:35, 36, 46) They made known to others the requirements for gaining God's favor and life, doing so "in the light," that is, openly. (Mt 10:27) Similarly, John the Baptizer had served as a light when "preaching baptism in symbol of repentance" and pointing forward to Messiah's coming. (Lu 3:3, 15-17; Joh 5:35) Also, by their fine works, by word and example, followers of Christ let their light shine. (Mt 5:14, 16; compare Ro 2:17-24.) "The fruitage of the light consists of every sort of goodness and righteousness and truth." It therefore exposes the baseness of the shameful works belonging to darkness (fornication, uncleanness of every kind, greediness, and the like) practiced by "the sons of disobedience." As a result these shameful works are seen in their true light and, in the sense of being manifested as things condemned by God, become light themselves. (Eph 5:3-18; compare 1Th 5:4-9.) Equipped with "weapons of the light," the spiritual armor from God, Christians wage warfare "against the governments, against the authorities, against the world rulers of this darkness, against the wicked spirit forces in the heavenly places" and are enabled thereby to stand firm as approved servants of God.—Ro 13:12-14; Eph 6:11-18.

Other Figurative Uses. The Scriptures contain many figurative references to light. Ability to see is meant by the words "the light of my own eyes." (Ps 38:10) For God to "give light" to someone means that he gives them life or allows them to continue living. (Job 3:20, 23; compare Ps 56: 13.) "Children that have seen no light" are those who are born dead. (Job 3:16; compare Ps 49:19.) "It is good for the eyes to see the sun" may be understood to mean 'it is good to be alive.'—Ec 11:7.

Morning light is picturesquely described as 'taking hold of the ends of the earth and shaking the wicked out of it,' because dawn disperses evildoers. Darkness is their "light," for they are accustomed to carrying out their evil deeds under its cover, and this figurative "light" is taken from them by the literal light of dawn.—Job 38:12-15; compare Job 24:15-17.

As the light of the sun is clearly observable, thus Jehovah's adverse judgments are obvious. This is alluded to at Hosea 6:5: "The judgments upon you will be as the light that goes forth."

The 'light of God's face' means divine favor. (Ps 44:3; 89:15) "Lift up the light of your face upon us" is an expression meaning 'show us favor.' (Ps 4:6) Similarly, the favor of a ruler is referred to as "the light of the king's face."—Pr 16:15.

Light may denote brightness or cheerfulness, the opposite of gloom. (Job 30:26) This may explain the words of Job (29:24): "The light of my face they would not cast down." Although others were gloomy and dejected, this did not cause Job to become of like disposition.

A bright prospect, such as salvation or deliverance, is at times referred to under the figure of light. (Es 8:16; Ps 97:11; Isa 30:26; Mic 7:8, 9) Jehovah's causing his glory to shine forth upon Zion pointed forward to her deliverance from a captive state. As a result Zion was to become a source of enlightenment to the nations. (Isa 60:1-3, 19, 20; compare Re 21:24; 22:5.) On the other hand, for the sun, moon, and stars not to give their light would signify calamity.—Isa 13: 10, 11; Jer 4:23; Eze 32:7, 8; Mt 24:29.

LIGHTNING. The brilliant flashes of light resulting from the discharge of atmospheric electricity between clouds or between the clouds and the earth. This phenomenon accompanying a thunderstorm is common in Israel during the rainy periods of spring and fall, especially reaching a peak in the cool months of November or December.

As Creator of the elements necessary for producing lightning, Jehovah is its source. (Job 37:3, 11) He can also control it and apparently has used lightning and means comparable to it to deliver his servants from their enemies as well as to execute his judgments. (2Sa 22:1, 15; Ps 18:14; 77:16-20; Zec 9:14; compare Job 36:32; Ps 97:4; 144:6.) Appropriately, therefore, lightnings are associated with God's throne (Re 4:5; compare Re 11:19) as well as with expressions of divine anger (Re 8:5; 16:18) and are figuratively represented as reporting the accomplishment of their task. (Job 38:35) At Mount Sinai, lightning flashes accompanied awesome physical manifestations of God's presence.—Ex 19:16; 20:18.

Lightning (Heb., ba·raq') is used figuratively to represent the glittering of polished metal. (De 32:41, ftn; Eze 21:10, ftn; Na 3:3; Hab 3:11) At

Nahum 2:4 either the glitter or the great speed of the enemy chariots on Nineveh's streets is meant by the words, "Like the lightnings they keep running." And the radiant faces or appearance of angelic creatures is compared to lightning.—Da 10:5, 6; Mt 28:2, 3; see also Eze 1:14.

Christ Jesus showed that his presence would not be kept secret, even as it is impossible to conceal lightning that "comes out of eastern parts and shines over to western parts." (Mt 24:23-27; Lu 17:20-24) Earlier, when the 70 disciples he had sent out returned with the report that even the demons were subject to them by the use of his name, Jesus alluded to the future ouster of Satan from heaven as a certainty, saying: "I began to behold Satan already fallen like lightning from heaven."—Lu 10:1, 17, 18.

In Luke 11:36 the Greek word for lightning (a·stra·pe') refers to the light or flashing of a lamp.

LIKHI (Lik'hi) [possibly from a root meaning "take"]. A man of the tribe of Manasseh who is named third in the list of Shemida's sons.—1Ch 7:19.

LILY. The Hebrew term shu·shan' and its corresponding Greek equivalent kri'non, both rendered "lily," probably embrace a great variety of flowers, such as the tulips, anemones, hyacinths, irises, and gladioli. According to Koehler and Baumgartner, the Hebrew designation is derived from an Egyptian word meaning "big flower." (Lexicon in Veteris Testamenti Libros, Leiden, 1958, p. 958) The Greek historian Herodotus (II, 92) speaks of the Egyptian lotus as "lily," and many believe that in the Scriptural references to the "lily" or "lily work" in ornamentation, the Egyptian lotus, a water lily, is meant. (1Ki 7:19, 22, 26; 2Ch 4:5) However, in view of the fact that the lotus figured prominently in the false religious symbolism of Egypt, the identification of the lily with the lotus is questionable.

The lilies of the Scriptural record were to be found in the low plain, among thorny weeds, and in pastures where flocks and gazelles grazed. (Ca 2:1, 2, 16; 4:5) They may also have been cultivated in gardens (Ca 6:2, 3), and allusion is made to their sweet fragrance. (Ca 5:13) Possibly with reference to the lily's beauty, Hosea, in foretelling Israel's restoration, spoke of the time when God's people would blossom as a lily.—Ho 14:5.

In de-emphasizing the importance generally attached to material things, Jesus Christ pointed out that not even Solomon in all his glory was as beautifully arrayed as the lilies of the field. It has been suggested that Jesus probably had the anemone in mind. However, he may simply have been referring to lilylike flowers in general, as may be inferred from the fact that "lilies of the field" is used in parallel with "vegetation of the field."—Mt 6:28-30; Lu 12:27, 28.

The significance of the expressions "The Lily," "The Lilies," appearing in the superscriptions of Psalms 45, 60, 69, and 80, is not known.

LIME. A substance, white when pure, that is prepared by burning forms of calcium carbonate such as limestone, shells, or bones. (Am 2:1) Abundant in the mountainous region of Palestine, limestone was converted into lime (calcium oxide) by burning fragments of limestone in conical or cylindrical limekilns. In ancient times lime (Heb., *sidh*) was a principal ingredient in mortar and was used for plastering walls and for whitewashing walls, graves, and so forth. (De 27:4; Eze 13:10; Mt 23:27; Ac 23:3) The Bible also uses the burnings of lime figuratively to represent destruction.—Isa 33:12; see KILN.

LINEN. The thread or cloth made from flax. (Ex 25:4; Jg 15:14) Among the Hebrews, most garments were either woolen or linen. (Le 13:47; Pr 31:13, 22; Ho 2:5, 9) A mixture of the two materials was prohibited by the Law for non-priestly Israelite garments. (De 22:11) Other items made from linen included belts (Jer 13:1) and sails. (Eze 27:7) The Israelites, although evidently manufacturing their own linen, imported some linen from Egypt.—Pr 7:16.

Linen varied in quality, as is indicated by Scriptural references to "fine linen" and "fine fabric." (Eze 16:10; 27:16) The wealthy, kings, and men of high governmental station wore linen of a superior quality. (Ge 41:42; 1Ch 15:27; Es 8:15; Lu 16:19) Jesus' corpse was wrapped in clean, fine linen by Joseph, a rich man of Arimathea.—Mt 27:57-59.

Fine linen yarn spun by Israelite women was used in making the ten tent cloths of the tabernacle, the curtain separating the Holy from the Most Holy, the screen for the entrance of the tabernacle, and the hangings of the courtyard as well as the screen of its gate. (Ex 35:25; 36:8, 35, 37; 38:16, 18) Fine twisted linen was also used in the high priest's girdle, ephod, and breastpiece. (Ex 39:2, 3, 5, 8) Robes of fine linen were likewise made for the other priests. (Ex 39:27-29) In the case of curtains and garments for use in the sanctuary, it seems that linen was the basic cloth used and that dyed wool and gold were embroidered on for decorative effect.—Ex 35:35; 38:23.

Figurative Use. Babylon the Great is depicted as being arrayed in fine linen and purple and scarlet, representing luxury. (Re 18:16) But in the case of the bride of Christ the fine linen of her apparel is clearly said to represent "the righteous acts of the holy ones." Likewise the heavenly armies are shown clothed in white, clean, fine linen, indicative of their carrying on war in righteousness.—Re 19:8, 11, 14; see also Da 10:5; Re 15:6; FLAX.

LINUS (Li'nus). A Christian in Rome named by the apostle Paul as sending greetings to Timothy. (2Ti 4:21) Irenaeus (born about 130 C.E.) and others after him have identified this Linus with an early overseer of Rome who bore the same name, but this identification rests merely on tradition.

LION [Heb., *'ar·yeh'*; *'ari'*; *la·vi''*; *la'yish*; *sha'-chal* (young lion); *kephir'* (maned young lion); *levi·yah'* (lioness); Aramaic, *'ar·yeh'*; Gr., *le'on*]. A large, tawny-colored mammal of the cat family having a long, tufted tail. The distinctive shaggy mane of the male begins to grow when the animal is about three years old. Although now extinct in Palestine, anciently lions were very plentiful there. They were found in the area of the Anti-Lebanon and Hermon ranges (Ca 4:8), the thickets along the Jordan (Jer 49:19; 50:44; Zec 11:3), and in "the land of distress and hard conditions," that is, the wilderness to the S of Judah.—Isa 30:6; compare De 8:15.

There were times when shepherds had to protect the flock from lions. David on one occasion courageously struck down a lion and rescued the sheep it had taken. (1Sa 17:34, 35) This, however, was exceptional. Frequently even "a full number of shepherds" could not frighten away a maned young lion. (Isa 31:4) Sometimes the shepherd recovered merely a portion of the domestic animal from the lion's mouth (Am 3:12), thereby enabling him to present the needed evidence to free him from having to make compensation.—Ex 22:13.

Although David, Samson, and Benaiah single-handedly killed lions (Jg 14:5, 6; 1Sa 17:36; 2Sa 23:20), others did not escape the lion's paw. (2Ki 17:25, 26) Jehovah used lions to execute his judgment on a prophet who had disobeyed him (1Ki 13:24-28) and on a man who refused to cooperate with one of His prophets.—1Ki 20:36.

The Scriptures repeatedly allude to the characteristics and habits of the lion, including its thunderous roar and its growling. (Pr 19:12; 20:2; Am 3:4, 8) The lion does not usually roar when hunting wild animals. However, when trying to prey upon domestic animals in an enclosure, a lion often will roar. The terrifying sound is calculated to cause a stampede to break down the protective fence and to isolate individual animals from the flock. The animal does well in its pacing. (Pr 30:29, 30) Its strength is proverbial. (Jg 14:18; Pr 30:30) A single blow from the lion's powerful paw is enough to break the neck of a small antelope. The lion can kill and carry animals larger than itself, and its short, strong jaws are equipped with teeth of sufficient strength to break large bones. (Ps 58:6; Joe 1:6; Isa 38:13) Little wonder that the lazy man is depicted as excusing his failure to act with the words: "There is a lion outside!" (Pr 22:13; 26:13) However, being carnivorous, lions may perish for lack of prey. (Job 4:11; see also Ps 34:10.) And "a live dog [although despised] is better off than a [once majestic but now] dead lion."—Ec 9:4.

The lion generally spends part of the day sleeping in its lair and does most of its hunting at night. In procuring its food, the animal either resorts to ambush or stalks its prey until close enough to make a short rush. (Job 38:39, 40; Ps 10:9; La 3:10) Then it can move in at a speed of about 65 km/hr (40 mph). In order to gain necessary experience in killing prey, lion cubs begin to accompany their mother on hunts when three months old. They are weaned after six or seven months, reach sexual maturity in their fourth year, and attain full physical size in six years. —Eze 19:2, 3.

Lions have long been hunted by man. Pits and nets were employed to capture them. (Eze 19:3, 4, 9) In ancient Assyria, hunting lions was a favorite sport of the monarch. Either on horseback or in his chariot, the king, armed with bow and arrows, pursued the lions.—PICTURE, Vol. 1, p. 955.

Hungry lions were anciently used to inflict capital punishment. Protected by Jehovah's angel, the prophet Daniel escaped this fate. (Da 6:16, 17, 22, 24; compare Heb 11:33.) In the first century C.E., the apostle Paul was delivered from "the lion's mouth," either literally or figuratively.—2Ti 4:17.

Ornamental and Figurative Use. Engraved lions ornamented the sidewalls of the copper carriages designated for temple use. (1Ki 7:27-36) And the figures of 12 lions lined the steps leading up to Solomon's throne, in addition to the two lions that were standing beside the armrests. (1Ki 10: 19, 20) Also, the temple seen in vision by Ezekiel was adorned with cherubs having two faces, one of a man and the other of a maned young lion. —Eze 41:18, 19.

Most of the Scriptural references to the lion are figurative, or illustrative. The entire nation of Israel (Nu 23:24; 24:9), and individually the tribes of Judah (Ge 49:9) and Gad (De 33:20), were prophetically compared to lions, representative of invincibility and courage in righteous warfare. (Compare 2Sa 17:10; 1Ch 12:8; Pr 28:1.) Jehovah likens himself to a lion in executing judgment on his unfaithful people. (Ho 5:14; 11:10; 13:7-9) And God's foremost judicial officer, Jesus Christ, is "the Lion that is of the tribe of Judah." (Re 5:5) Appropriately, therefore, the lion, as a symbol of courageous justice, is associated with Jehovah's presence and throne.—Eze 1:10; 10:14; Re 4:7.

Because of the lion's fierce, rapacious, and predatory characteristics, the animal was also used to represent wicked ones (Ps 10:9), persons who oppose Jehovah and his people (Ps 22:13; 35:17; 57:4; Jer 12:8), false prophets (Eze 22:25), wicked rulers and princes (Pr 28:15; Zep 3:3), the Babylonian World Power (Da 7:4), and Satan the Devil (1Pe 5:8). And the seven-headed, ten-horned wild beast out of the sea, which derives its authority from Satan, was depicted as having a lion's mouth. (Re 13:2) At Psalm 91:13 the lion and the cobra seem to denote the power of the enemy, the lion being representative of open attack and the cobra of underhanded scheming, or attacks from a concealed place.—Compare Lu 10:19; 2Co 11:3.

At the time the Israelites returned to their homeland in 537 B.C.E., Jehovah evidently protected them from lions and other rapacious beasts along the way. (Isa 35:8-10) In the land itself lions and other predators doubtless had increased during the 70 years of its desolation. (Compare Ex 23:29.) But, evidently because of Jehovah's watch care over his people, the Israelites and their domestic animals apparently did not fall prey to lions as had the foreign peoples whom the king of Assyria settled in the cities of Samaria. (2Ki 17:25, 26) Therefore, from the standpoint of the Israelites, the lion was, in effect, eating straw like a bull, that is, doing no harm to them or their domestic animals. (Isa 65:18, 19, 25) Under Messiah's rulership, however, there comes to be a greater fulfillment of the restoration prophecies. Persons who may at one time have been of a beastly, animalistic, vicious disposition come to be at peace with more docile fellow humans and do not seek to do them harm or injury. Both in a literal and a figurative sense, peace will come to exist between lions and domestic animals.—Isa 11:1-6; see BEASTS, SYMBOLIC.

LIONS' PIT. The place of execution into which the prophet Daniel was thrown but from which he was later removed unharmed, having enjoyed angelic protection. (Da 6:7, 12, 13, 16-24) This pit had an opening that could be covered with a stone. (Da 6:17) It was evidently a sunken or underground place, for Daniel was "lifted up out of the pit."—Da 6:23.

LIP. Being a part of the mouth and having much to do with formation of words, "lip" (Heb., *sa·phah'*; Gr., *khei'los*) is used figuratively for speech or language (Pr 14:3; 1Co 14:21) and is occasionally used in parallelism with "tongue" (Ps 34:13; Pr 12:19) and with "mouth." (Ps 66:14; Pr 18:7) Before the confusion of language at Babel, "all the earth continued to be of one language [literally, "lip"] and of one set of words." (Ge 11:1, 6-9; the same usage is employed at Ps 81:5; Isa 19:18.) God promised through the prophet Zephaniah to give to peoples "the change to a pure language [lip]"; thus they would unitedly speak in praise of Jehovah and his righteous purposes by Christ Jesus.—Zep 3:9; compare Pr 12:19.

The lips are no sure index of what is in the heart, since they can be used by the individual to utter hypocritical speech. (Mt 15:8) However, the lips cannot hide the true condition of the heart from God (Heb 4:13), and they will eventually bring forth what is in the heart.—Pr 26:23-26; Mt 12:34.

Moses wanted to excuse himself from speaking before Pharaoh because he was "uncircumcised in lips," that is, as though his lips had a foreskin over them and hence were too long and thick to utter speech with ease. He may have had some sort of speech impediment. (Ex 6:12, 30) Isaiah, when called by Jehovah, wished to serve but lamented that he was as good as brought to silence because he, a man unclean in lips, had seen Jehovah in vision, and he was unfit to carry God's clean message. Jehovah then caused Isaiah's lips to be cleansed.—Isa 6:5-7; compare Joh 15:3; Isa 52:11; 2Co 6:17.

Hosea's prophecy encouraged Israel to offer to Jehovah "the young bulls" of their lips, representing sacrifices of sincere praise. (Ho 14:2) The apostle Paul alludes to this prophecy when he exhorts fellow believers to offer to God "a sacrifice of praise, that is, the fruit of lips which make public declaration to his name."—Heb 13:15.

Figuratively, "a smooth lip" denotes deceptive speech. (Ps 12:2, 3) Such lips, as well as harsh or lying ones, can be damaging—wounding deeply like a sword or poisoning like a viper. (Ps 59:7; 140:3; Ro 3:13) A person "opening wide his lips" is one who speaks thoughtlessly or unwisely. (Pr 13:3) It can bring him to ruin, for God holds everyone accountable for his words.—De 23:23; Nu 30:6-8; Pr 12:13; compare Job 2:10; Mt 12:36, 37.

LIQUOR, INTOXICATING. See WINE AND STRONG DRINK.

LITTER. A portable couch or bed usually covered with a canopy and curtained in on the sides, designed so that a person of importance, either seated or reclined, can be carried about by men or beasts of burden; a palanquin as used in the Orient. The royal litter of King Solomon was made of Lebanese cedarwood, with silver pillars and supports of gold, and with the seat or cushion upholstered in costly and beautiful wool dyed reddish purple. The interior was richly ornamented, possibly with ebony.—Ca 3:7-10, ftn.

A bier, or portable funeral couch, for transporting the remains of the dead was known as a *so·ros'*.—Lu 7:14.

LIVER. A large glandular organ in vertebrate animals and man that plays a role in digestion and blood chemistry; in man, the largest of the glands. The Hebrew term for the liver (*ka·vedh'*) comes from a root meaning "be heavy." The Hebrew Scriptures use the word "liver" most frequently with reference to the livers of animals prepared by the Israelites for sacrifice. (Ex 29:22; Le 3:4, 10, 15; 4:9) It was "the appendage upon the liver" that was made to smoke on the altar. (Ex 29:13) The *Commentary on the Old Testament*, by C. F. Keil and F. Delitzsch, describes this portion of the liver as "the liver-net, or stomach-net . . . , which commences at the division between the right and left lobes of the liver, and stretches on the one side across the stomach, and on the other to the region of the kidneys. . . . This smaller net is delicate, but not so fat as the larger net; though it still forms part of the fat portions." (1973, Vol. I, The Third Book of Moses, p. 300) In Rashi's comment on Leviticus 3:4, it is defined as "the protecting wall (membrane) over the liver."—*Pentateuch With Targum Onkelos, Haphtaroth and Rashi's Commentary*, translated by M. Rosenbaum and A. Silbermann.

King Solomon's account of the inexperienced youth who succumbs to the enticement of the immoral woman concludes: "All of a sudden he is going after her, . . . until an arrow cleaves open his liver, . . . and he has not known that it involves his very soul." (Pr 7:21-23) This is a very appropriate description, for medical doctors have found that in advanced stages of syphilis (as is true of many other diseases), bacterial organisms overwhelm the liver. The organism (gonococcus) responsible for gonorrhea, another sexually transmitted disease, also in some cases causes severe inflammation of the liver. Severe damage to the liver can, of course, result in death. The liver's vital role to life is acknowledged in that it is used figuratively in depicting profound sorrow.—La 2:11.

King Nebuchadnezzar of Babylon, when looking for guidance as to his military maneuvers, "looked into the liver" as a form of divination.—Eze 21:21; see DIVINATION.

LIZARD

LIZARD [Heb., *tsav*]. Lizards are four-legged reptiles, generally small, with long tails and scaly skin. The lizard's legs are attached far enough out at the sides to enable it to rest its belly on the ground without folding its feet under it. More than 40 kinds are found in Palestine. They are to be found in trees, in warm crevices of rocks, and on walls and ceilings in homes. The lizard is included among the unclean "swarming creatures" at Leviticus 11:29. It is suggested that the Hebrew name for it is derived from a root meaning "cleave to ground." The *Hebrew and English Lexicon of the Old Testament* by Brown, Driver, and Briggs (1980, p. 839) suggests "lizard" as the translation. Evidently the Hebrew term *tsav* at least includes the Agamidae family of lizards, for the equivalent Arabic term *dabb* refers to the Egyptian spiny-tailed lizard (*Uromastix aegyptius*), the largest of the species of Agamidae found in Israel.—See CHAMELEON; GECKO; SAND LIZARD.

Lexicons generally suggest that the Hebrew word *ko'ach* also refers to a kind of lizard. Since the root meaning of the name is "power" or "strength," it may refer to the desert monitor lizard (*Varanus griseus*), a powerful, large lizard. It inhabits dry, sandy desert areas. In Palestine this lizard reaches a length of about 1.2 m (4 ft). It is an eater of carrion and is on the list of "unclean" foods.—Le 11:29, 30.

Another creature listed as unclean for Israelite use as food is referred to by the Hebrew word *cho'met*, at Leviticus 11:30. Some recent translations (*RS; NW*) render this "sand lizard." The sand lizard is possibly a skink.

LOAD

LOAD. See BURDEN.

LOAF

LOAF. The Hebrew word *le'chem* and the Greek word *ar'tos* (both meaning "bread") are also rendered 'loaf.' (1Sa 10:4; Mt 14:17) Bread loaves, generally made from barley or wheat flour (2Ki 4:42; Joh 6:9; compare Ex 34:22 with Le 23:17), were often circular. (Jg 7:13; 1Sa 10:3; Jer 37:21) In fact, the Hebrew word *kik·kar'* (round loaf) literally means "something round." (1Sa 2:36) Of course, loaves were also formed into other shapes. An Egyptian papyrus document mentions over 30 different forms of bread.

Ancient specimens from Bible lands include relatively thin round, oval, triangular, and wedge-shaped cakes or loaves and thick, long loaves. (See BREAD; CAKE.) However, the thick loaves, like those of the Western world, do not appear to have been common in the ancient Middle East. Even today Oriental bread is baked in thin loaves, usually from 1 to 2.5 cm (0.5 to 1 in.) in thickness and about 18 cm (7 in.) in diameter.

Since they were relatively thin and, if unleavened, brittle, loaves of bread were broken rather than cut. So in itself there is nothing special about Jesus' 'breaking' the loaf used at the institution of the Lord's Evening Meal (Mt 26:26), it being the customary way to partake of bread.—Mt 14:19; 15:36; Mr 6:41; 8:6; Lu 9:16; Ac 2:42, 46, *Int.*

LO-AMMI

LO-AMMI (Lo-am'mi) [Not My People]. The name of the second son borne by Hosea's wife Gomer. Jehovah commanded that the child be given this meaningful name to show that He had disowned faithless Israel. (Ho 1:8, 9) It has been suggested that this boy was not Hosea's offspring but a child of Gomer's adultery (Ho 1:2), for when Jezreel was born, it was said that Gomer "bore to *him* [Hosea] a son," whereas regarding Lo-ammi it is merely said that "she proceeded to become pregnant and give birth to a son."—Ho 1:3, 8.

LOAN

LOAN. Anything, especially money, given for temporary use, with expectation of future return or the delivery of an equivalent.

Often very high interest was charged in nations of antiquity, and people unable to repay loans were treated harshly. Interest rates requiring one half of a man's crop for use of a field are known from ancient records, and the requiring that a merchant repay double what he borrowed was not viewed as unlawful. (*Ancient Near Eastern Texts*, edited by J. Pritchard, 1974, pp. 168, 170) At times the treatment of a debtor was very harsh.—*Livy*, II, XXIII, 2-7; compare Mt 18:28-30.

In ancient Israel, however, the situation was quite different. Ordinarily loans of money or foodstuffs were made to poor fellow Israelites who were the victims of financial reverses, and the Law prohibited exacting interest from them. For an Israelite to have accepted interest from a needy fellow Israelite would have meant profiting from that one's adversity. (Ex 22:25; Le 25:35-37; De 15:7, 8; 23:19) Foreigners, though, could be required to pay interest. But even this provision of the Law may have applied to business loans only and not to cases of actual need. Often foreigners were in Israel as transient merchants and could reasonably be expected to pay interest, as they would also be lending to others on interest.—De 23:20.

The Hebrew Scriptures censure the borrower who refuses to repay a loan (Ps 37:21) and at the same time encourage lending to those in need. (De 15:7-11; Ps 37:26; 112:5) Says Proverbs 19:17: "He that is showing favor to the lowly one is lending to Jehovah, and his treatment He will repay to him."

The case of Hannah illustrates that Jehovah repays generously. After 'lending' her only son Samuel to Jehovah for service at the sanctuary in fulfillment of her vow, Hannah was blessed, not with just another son, but with three sons and two daughters.—1Sa 1:11, 20, 26-28; 2:20, 21.

While on earth Christ Jesus reflected the generous spirit of his Father Jehovah and taught others to do likewise. Amplifying the matter of making loans, Jesus said: "If you lend without interest to those from whom you hope to receive, of what credit is it to you? Even sinners lend without interest to sinners that they may get back as much. To the contrary, continue . . . to lend without interest, not hoping for anything back; and your reward will be great, and you will be sons of the Most High, because he is kind toward the unthankful and wicked."—Lu 6:34, 35.

Jesus' Jewish listeners were obligated by the Law to make interest-free loans to needy fellow Israelites. It was not unusual even for sinners to lend without interest to those who would be in position to make repayment. Such lending without interest might even be done with the intent of gaining some favor from the borrower in the future. On the other hand, one desiring to be an imitator of God would do more than a sinner, by lending to needy persons whose economic situation was such that they might never be able to make repayment.

The application of Jesus' words is, of course, limited by circumstances. For example, the obligation to care for the needs of family members takes a prior claim. It would therefore be wrong for anyone to make a loan that would interfere with his obligation to provide life's necessities for his family. (Mr 7:11-13; 1Ti 5:8) Also, the attitude and circumstances of the prospective borrower enter the picture. Is he in need because of his being irresponsible, lazy, and unwilling to accept work although jobs he is able to perform are available? If so, the words of the apostle Paul apply: "If anyone does not want to work, neither let him eat."—2Th 3:10; see DEBT, DEBTOR; INTEREST.

LOATHSOME THING. See DISGUSTING THING, LOATHSOME THING.

LOAVES OF PRESENTATION. See SHOWBREAD.

LOCK.

A device for fastening a door or gate to restrict entrance. (Jg 3:23, 24; Ne 3:3, 6, 13-15) The lock of ancient times usually consisted of a bolt of wood that could slide sideways through a groove in a wooden upright attached to the door. To lock the door, the bolt was pushed into a socket in the doorpost and was secured by wooden or iron pins falling from the upright into holes in the bolt. To unlock the door, a key was inserted to raise the pins, thus enabling the bolt to be brought back to the unlocked position. The socket, or hollow, into which the bolt was inserted is referred to by the Shulammite girl in recounting a dream she had in which her shepherd lover was kept away from her by means of a locked door.—Ca 5:2-5; see KEY.

LOCUST.

Any of a variety of grasshoppers with short antennae or feelers, especially those that migrate in great swarms. Of the several Hebrew words rendered "locust," 'ar·beh' appears most frequently and is understood to refer to the migratory locust, the insect in its fully developed, winged stage. (Le 11:22, ftn) The Hebrew word ye'leq refers to the creeping, wingless locust, that is, one that is at an immature stage of development. (Ps 105:34, ftn; Joe 1:4) The Hebrew term sol·'am' (edible locust) possibly refers to a leaper and not a flier. (Le 11:22, ftn) A locust swarm is denoted by the Hebrew term goh·vai'. (Am 7:1) The Greek word a·kris' is rendered 'insect locust' and 'locust.'—Mt 3:4; Re 9:7.

The locust measures 5 cm (2 in.) or more in length. It is equipped with two pairs of wings, four walking legs, and two much longer leaper legs with broad thighs. The wide, transparent back wings, when not in use, lie folded under the thick membranous front wings. By means of its leaper legs, the insect is able to jump many times the length of its body. (See Job 39:20.) In Scripture the locust is at times used to represent innumerableness.—Jg 6:5; 7:12; Jer 46:23; Na 3:15, 17.

A "Clean" Food. The Law designated locusts as clean for food. (Le 11:21, 22) John the Baptizer, in fact, subsisted on insect locusts and honey. (Mt 3:4) These insects are said to taste something like shrimp or crab and are rich in protein; desert locusts, according to an analysis made at Jerusalem, consist of 75 percent protein. When used for food today, the head, legs, wings, and abdomen are removed. The remaining portion, the thorax, is cooked or eaten raw.

Locust Plagues. In Bible times a locust plague was a severe calamity and, on occasion, an expression of Jehovah's judgment, as was the eighth plague on ancient Egypt. (Ex 10:4-6, 12-19; De 28:38; 1Ki 8:37; 2Ch 6:28; Ps 78:46; 105:34) Locusts, brought by the wind, arrive suddenly, but the sound of their coming, compared in Scripture to that of chariots and of a fire consuming stubble (Joe 1:4; 2:5, 25), can, it is said, be heard at a distance of about 10 km (6 mi). Their flight is largely dependent on the wind, which, when favorable, enables them to cover many kilometers. Locust swarms have even been seen by persons at sea more than 1,600 km (1,000 mi) from land. Unfavorable winds, though, can drive them into the water to their death. (Ex 10:13, 19) The effect of a large swarm in flight (reaching over 1,500 m [5,000 ft] in height) is comparable to a cloud that intercepts the light of the sun.—Joe 2:10.

An invasion of locusts can transform a land from a paradiselike state into a wilderness, for their appetite is voracious. (Joe 2:3) A single migratory locust consumes its own body weight in food in a day; that is proportionately 60 to 100 times as much as a human consumes. They eat not only greenery but also linen, wool, silk, and leather, not even sparing the varnish on the furniture as they penetrate the houses. The daily food consumption of a large swarm has been estimated as equaling that of a million and a half men.

A swarm of locusts progresses like a well-organized, disciplined fighting force, but without king or leader, this testifying to their instinctive wisdom. (Pr 30:24, 27) Even though many perish, the onslaught continues. Fires built to check their advance are extinguished by the bodies of the dead locusts. Water-filled ditches are of no avail in impeding their progress, for these likewise become filled with their dead bodies. (Joe 2:7-9) "There is no known natural enemy that can keep their devastating migrations in check," wrote a zoology professor.—*The New York Times Magazine,* "The Locust War," May 22, 1960, p. 96.

Describing locust plagues in more recent times, *Grzimek's Animal Life Encyclopedia* (1975, Vol. 2, pp. 109, 110) reports: "Several species of spur-throated grasshoppers cause locust plagues even today in Africa and other parts of the world. Their occasional increase to tremendous numbers and widespread migrations caused great damage to food crops in recent times. In 1873-1875 in Europe and 1874-1877 in the U.S.A. the outbreaks were extremely severe. . . . In 1955, a swarm of migratory locusts 250 km long and 20 km wide attacked southern Morocco. Again, in 1961/62, there was a plague there which could not be effectively combated . . . As a result, within five days the locusts

Female locust laying eggs; proportionately, locusts consume 60 to 100 times as much as humans do

had caused damage amounting to more than a billion francs in an area of over 5000 square kilometers. . . . In the five days, the migratory locusts consumed 7000 t of oranges, the equivalent of 60,000 kg per hour. This is more than the yearly consumption of the entire country of France."

Figurative Use. Research indicates that the life span of the locust is between four and six months. Appropriately, therefore, the symbolic locusts of Revelation 9:5 are said to torment men for five months, or what would commonly be their full life span.

When describing Assyria's military men, Nahum 3:16 mentions the locust's stripping off of its skin. The locust sheds its skin five times to reach adult size. At Nahum 3:17 the Assyrian guardsmen and recruiting officers are compared to locusts that camp in stone pens during a cold day but flee when the sun shines forth. The allusion here may be to the fact that cold weather makes the insects numb, causing them to hide in the crevices of walls until such time as they are warmed by the sun's rays, after which they fly away. It is reported that not until their bodies reach about 21° C. (70° F.) can locusts fly.

LOD. A city with dependent towns built either by the Benjamite Elpaal or his "son" Shemed. (1Ch 8:1, 12) After the Jews returned from Babylonian exile Lod was one of their most westerly settlements. (Ezr 2:33; Ne 7:37; 11:35) It is thought to be the same as Lydda, where Peter healed Aeneas. (Ac 9:32-38) Situated in a fertile valley at the southern edge of the Plain of Sharon, el-Ludd (Lod) is about 18 km (11 mi) SE of Joppa. Its location anciently placed the city at the intersection of what is considered to have been the principal route between Egypt and Babylon and the main road from Joppa to Jerusalem. During the Common Era this strategic position exposed the city to ravages by the armies of the Romans, Saracens, Crusaders, and Mongols.

LO-DEBAR (Lo-de′bar). The site where Machir, a contemporary of King David, had his home. (2Sa 9:4, 5; 17:27) Lo-debar is usually thought to be the same as Debir in Gad.—Jos 13:24, 26; see DEBIR No. 4.

LOG. The smallest liquid measure mentioned in the Bible. Talmudic evidence indicates the log to be one twelfth of a hin, or 0.014 bath. On the basis of archaeological findings, the bath is estimated to be 22 L (5.81 gal). If correct, this would give the log measure a capacity of about 0.31 L (0.66 pt). One log measure of oil was part of the prescribed offering by a cleansed leper.—Le 14:2, 10, 12, 15, 21, 24.

LOINS. The abdominal region and the area about the hips. The Bible uses both the Hebrew words *chala·tsa′yim* (loins) and *moth·na′yim* (hips) to refer to this area. (Isa 5:27; 2Ki 4:29) The Greek *o·sphys′* is also applied in the ordinary sense in describing John the Baptizer as clothed about the loins with a leather girdle.—Mt 3:4.

The section of the body designated by the word "loins" contains the reproductive organs; therefore offspring are said to 'come out of the loins.' (Ge 35:11; 1Ki 8:19; Ac 2:30) Paul uses this fact when showing that Jesus' priesthood according to the manner of Melchizedek is superior to Aaron's, in that Levi, Aaron's forefather, was in the loins of Abraham, and in that sense paid tithes to Melchizedek. (Heb 7:5-10; Ge 14:18-20) Paul also argued similarly at Romans 7:9, saying: "I [Paul the Jew, in his forefathers' loins before the Law was given] was once alive apart from law; but when the commandment arrived, sin came to life again, but I died."

To "gird up the loins" meant to gather up the ends of the robes under the sash to facilitate physical activity and came to be used as an expression denoting preparation for vigorous mental or spiritual activity, and at times, it conveyed the idea of strengthening.—Lu 12:35; compare 1Pe 1:13, "Brace up your minds [literally, "Gird up the loins of your mind"] for activity."

At Ephesians 6:14, Christians are told to have their "loins girded about with truth," that is, strengthened by the truth of God's Word as an essential support, just as a tight girding of the physical loins protects them against damage due to extreme stress.

Jehovah foretold the pain and distress of Jerusalem by the figure "every able-bodied man with his hands upon his loins like a female that is giving birth."—Jer 30:6.

The Hebrew word *ke′sel* (loins) appears several times at Leviticus 3:4-15, referring to communion sacrifices. It is also used at Job 15:27 and Psalm 38:7. It is translated "flanks" and "loins" in the *King James Version*.

LOIS (Lo′is). Timothy's grandmother and apparently the mother of his mother Eunice. That she was not Timothy's paternal grandmother is indicated by the Syriac rendering "thy mother's mother." Lois is commended by Paul, who indicates that she was a Christian woman having 'faith without hypocrisy.' (2Ti 1:5) The family's residence apparently was in Lystra. (Ac 16:1, 2) A comparison of 2 Timothy 1:5 with 2 Timothy 3:15 suggests that Lois and Eunice both taught Timothy from the Scriptures.

LONG-SUFFERING. The patient endurance of wrong or provocation, combined with a refusal to give up hope for improvement in the disturbed relationship. Long-suffering therefore has a purpose, looking particularly to the welfare of the one causing the disagreeable situation. It does not mean the condoning of wrong, however. When the purpose for long-suffering is accomplished, or when there is no point in further putting up with the situation, long-suffering ends. It ends either with good to those giving provocation or with action against the wrongdoers. In any case the one exercising long-suffering is not harmed in spirit.

The literal meaning of the Hebrew expression translated "slow to anger" ("long-suffering" in some translations) is "length of nostrils [where anger flares up]." (Ex 34:6; Nu 14:18; see ANGER.) The Greek word *ma·kro·thy·mi′a* (long-suffering) literally means "longness of spirit." (Ro 2:4, *Int*) Both the Hebrew and Greek expressions denote patience, forbearance, slowness to anger. The English word "suffering" in the word "long-suffering" has the sense of "putting up with, permitting, tolerating, holding up, or delaying." "Long-suffering" means more than merely enduring pain or trouble. It does not mean merely "suffering long" but involves deliberate restraint.

The Scriptures reveal God's evaluation of long-suffering and point out the foolishness and bad results of not maintaining "longness of spirit." The long-suffering person may seem weak, but he actually is using discernment. "He that is slow to anger is abundant in discernment, but one that is impatient is exalting foolishness." (Pr 14:29) Long-suffering is better than physical mightiness, and it will accomplish more. "He that is slow to anger is better than a mighty man, and he that is controlling his spirit than the one capturing a city."—Pr 16:32.

The man who is not 'long in spirit,' but who bursts forth without restraint, is open to the invasion of any and all improper thoughts and actions, for: "As a city broken through, without a wall, is the man that has no restraint for his spirit." (Pr 25:28) "All his spirit is what a stupid one lets out, but he that is wise keeps it calm to the last." (Pr 29:11) For these reasons, the wise man counsels not to be 'short in spirit': "Do not hurry yourself in your spirit to become offended, for the taking of offense is what rests in the bosom of the stupid ones."—Ec 7:9.

Jehovah's Long-Suffering. When Jehovah took Moses up into Mount Horeb and showed him some of his glory, he declared before Moses: "Jehovah, Jehovah, a God merciful and gracious, slow to anger and abundant in loving-kindness and truth, preserving loving-kindness for thousands, pardoning error and transgression and sin, but by no means will he give exemption from punishment." (Ex 34:5-7) This truth about Jehovah's slowness to anger was repeated by Moses, David, Nahum, and others.—Nu 14:18; Ne 9:17; Ps 86:15; 103:8; Joe 2:13; Jon 4:2; Na 1:3.

While long-suffering is an attribute of Jehovah, it is always expressed in harmony with his primary attributes of love, justice, wisdom, and power. (1Jo 4:8; De 32:4; Pr 2:6; Ps 62:11; Isa 40:26, 29) Justice is due, first of all, to God's own name. That name must be exalted above all others in the universe; and this is essential for the well-being of all his creatures. The magnifying of his name is one of his chief reasons for long-suffering, as the apostle Paul explains: "If, now, God, although having the will to demonstrate his wrath and to make his power known, tolerated with much long-suffering vessels of wrath made fit for destruction, in order that he might make known the riches of his glory upon vessels of mercy, which he prepared beforehand for glory, namely, us, whom he called not only from among Jews but also from among nations, what of it?" (Ro 9:22-24) God, in exercising long-suffering, is taking out a people for his name. And by means of them he is magnifying himself in all the earth.—Ac 15:14; 1Co 3:9, 16, 17; 2Co 6:16.

God exhibited his long-suffering in the very early part of man's history. Rebellion of the first human couple had brought violation of his law. But instead of executing them immediately, as God could have justly done, in love he displayed long-suffering. This was for their as-yet-unborn descendants, to whom such long-suffering meant everything (his patience means salvation for many [2Pe 3:15]). More important, God also had in view the magnifying of his glory by means of the Seed of promise. (Ge 3:15; Joh 3:16; Ga 3:16) And God not only was long-suffering at that time but he knew that he would have to put up with imperfect mankind for several thousand years of history, delaying punishment against a world at enmity with him. (Jas 4:4) Some have misunderstood and misused God's long-suffering toward them, missing its purpose by viewing it as slowness rather than as loving patience.—Ro 2:4; 2Pe 3:9.

Nowhere is the long-suffering of God more evident than in his dealings with the ancient nation of Israel. (Ro 10:21) Time and again he received them back after they had fallen away, were punished, and repented. They killed his prophets and finally his own Son. They fought the preaching of the good news by Jesus and his apostles. But God's long-suffering was not wasted. There was a remnant that proved faithful. (Isa 6:8-13; Ro 9:27-29; 11:5) He used some of such faithful ones to write his Word under inspiration. (Ro 3:1, 2) The Law he gave showed that all mankind are sinners and need a redeemer, and it pointed to that One who would give his life as a ransom price and who would be exalted to the high position of King. (Ga 3:19, 24) Patterns of that Kingdom and of Christ's priesthood were provided (Col 2:16, 17; Heb 10:1), and examples for us to follow or avoid were set forth. (1Co 10:11; Heb 6:12; Jas 5:10) All these things are essential to mankind for the gaining of everlasting life.—Ro 15:4; 2Ti 3:16, 17.

Jehovah not long-suffering forever. On the other hand, God is long-suffering only as long as it is in harmony with justice, righteousness, and wisdom. The fact that long-suffering is exercised when a bad or provocative situation exists shows that it is meant to give opportunity for those involved in the bad situation to change, to straighten up. When matters come to a point where it is seen that there is no hope of such change, justice and righteousness would be violated if long-suffering should continue. Then God acts in wisdom to remove the bad situation. His patience comes to an end.

An example of this forbearance on God's part and of its coming to an end is found in God's dealing with men before the Flood. A deplorable condition existed, and God said: "My spirit shall not act toward man indefinitely in that he is also flesh. Accordingly his days shall amount to a hundred and twenty years." (Ge 6:3) Later, regarding Israel's misuse of Jehovah's long-suffering, Isaiah said: "But they themselves rebelled and made his holy spirit feel hurt. He now was changed into an enemy of theirs; he himself warred against them."—Isa 63:10; compare Ac 7:51.

For these reasons Christians are entreated not to "accept the undeserved kindness of God and miss its purpose." (2Co 6:1) They are counseled: "Do not be grieving [saddening] God's holy spirit." (Eph 4:30, *Int*) Also, "Do not put out the fire of the spirit." (1Th 5:19) Otherwise they may continue to the point of sin and blasphemy against God's spirit, in effect outraging it, in which case there is no repentance or forgiveness, only destruction. —Mt 12:31, 32; Heb 6:4-6; 10:26-31.

Jesus Christ. Jesus Christ exemplified long-suffering among humans. Of him, the prophet Isaiah wrote: "He was hard pressed, and he was letting himself be afflicted; yet he would not open his mouth. He was being brought just like a sheep to the slaughtering; and like a ewe that before her shearers has become mute, he also would not open his mouth." (Isa 53:7) He put up with the weaknesses of his apostles and the insults and discourtesies heaped upon him by bitter, vicious enemies. Yet he did not retaliate in kind, by word or action. (Ro 15:3) When the apostle Peter acted injudiciously in cutting off the ear of Malchus, Jesus reproved him with the words: "Return your sword to its place, . . . do you think that I cannot appeal to my Father to supply me at this moment more than twelve legions of angels? In that case, how would the Scriptures be fulfilled that it must take place this way?"—Mt 26:51-54; Joh 18:10, 11.

Why is it important for Christians to cultivate long-suffering?

From the foregoing it is evident that long-suffering originates with Jehovah God. It is a fruit of his spirit. (Ga 5:22) Man, made in the image and likeness of God, has a measure of this quality and can develop it by following God's Word and the direction of his holy spirit. (Ge 1:26, 27) Christians are therefore commanded to cultivate and display this quality. (Col 3:12) It is an identifying mark of a minister of God. (2Co 6:4-6) The apostle Paul says: "Be long-suffering toward all." (1Th 5:14) He indicates that it is essential to exercise this quality in order to be pleasing to God. But one's long-suffering is not genuine if it is accompanied by grumbling and complaining. Paul shows that the

commendable thing is to "be long-suffering with joy."—Col 1:9-12.

Aside from the joy that one gets through the practice of long-suffering, the rewards are great. Jehovah is rewarded by having his name glorified. The challenge against the righteousness and rightfulness of God's sovereignty is proved wrong, and he is vindicated. (Ge 3:1-5; Job 1:7-11; 2:3-5) What if he had put Adam, Eve, and Satan to death at the time of the rebellion? Some might have concluded that Satan had a point in his challenge. But by long-suffering, Jehovah gave men the opportunity to prove under test that they prefer his sovereignty over them and that they want to serve him because of his fine qualities, yes, to demonstrate that they prefer Jehovah's sovereignty to complete independence, knowing that it is far better.—Ps 84:10.

Jesus Christ, because of long-suffering in obedience to God, received a most marvelous reward, being exalted to the superior position of kingship and being given "the name that is above every other name," by his Father. (Php 2:5-11) Besides this, he receives a "bride" made up of his spiritual brothers, the New Jerusalem, which is represented as a city, the foundation stones of which have on them the names of the 12 apostles of the Lamb. —2Co 11:2; Re 21:2, 9, 10, 14.

Likewise, the reward is rich for all persons cultivating long-suffering and maintaining it in harmony with God's purpose. (Heb 6:11-15) They have the satisfaction of copying God's quality, of doing God's will, and of having God's approval. Additionally, their long-suffering will bring accomplishment in helping others to know God and to gain everlasting life.—1Ti 4:16.

LOOSE CONDUCT. Acts that reflect a brazen attitude, an attitude betraying disrespect, even contempt for law and authority. The Hebrew word *zim·mah'* is rendered "loose conduct" and "loose morals." (Le 18:17; 19:29) The Greek term *a·sel'-gei·a* (loose conduct) may also be rendered "licentiousness; wantonness; shameless conduct; lewdness of conduct." (Ga 5:19, ftn; 2Pe 2:7, ftn) Neither term is restricted to sexual immorality. The Scriptures classify as loose conduct such things as gang rape (Jg 19:25; 20:6), prostitution (Jer 13:27; Eze 23:44), and bloodshed (Ps 26:9, 10; Eze 22:9; Hos 6:9). "The unprincipled man" is the one who is said to scheme loose conduct, and those to whom such conduct is "like sport" are classed as stupid, or morally worthless.—Isa 32:7; Pr 10:23.

"Out of the Heart." Jesus points out that loose conduct reflects what a person is inside. He says: "From inside, out of the heart of men, injurious reasonings issue forth: fornications, . . . adulteries, . . . loose conduct . . . All these wicked things issue forth from within and defile a man." (Mr 7:20-23) Loose conduct is one of "the works of the flesh," one of the fleshly desires that "carry on a conflict against the soul." "Those who practice such things will not inherit God's kingdom," says God's Word.—Ga 5:19, 21; 1Pe 2:11.

Christians loving the light of truth are told: "As in the daytime let us walk decently, not in revelries and drunken bouts, not in illicit intercourse and loose conduct." (Ro 13:13; Joh 3:19-21) The apostle Peter argues: "For the time that has passed by [before becoming servants of God] is sufficient for you to have worked out the will of the nations when you proceeded in deeds of loose conduct." (1Pe 4:3) The apostle Paul likewise admonishes Christians, describing the course of worldly nations with whom they formerly associated as "in darkness mentally, and alienated from the life that belongs to God . . . Having come to be past all moral sense, they gave themselves over to loose conduct to work uncleanness of every sort with greediness."—Eph 4:17-19.

Nevertheless, some claiming to be servants of God and Christ turn from the way of light and display a brazen, defiant attitude toward divine law and authority. Paul was grieved by those in the Corinthian congregation who had not repented of the "uncleanness and fornication and loose conduct that they [had] practiced," in spite of admonition to the contrary. (2Co 12:21) Peter warned the early Christians that false teachers would come from among their own ranks and that many would follow their acts of loose conduct, bringing reproach upon the way of truth. (2Pe 2: 1, 2) Jesus' words to the congregations in Pergamum and Thyatira, written down by the apostle John about 96 C.E., indicate that Peter's prophecy was to some extent having fulfillment at that time. (Re 2:12, 14, 18, 20) Both Peter and Jude express the judgment coming on practicers of loose conduct.—2Pe 2:17-22; Jude 7.

The argument of some practicers of loose conduct in their attempt to entice and deceive others in the Christian congregation is that God's undeserved kindness is great and that he will overlook their sins, since he recognizes their imperfections and fleshly weakness. But Jesus' half brother Jude spoke of such as being "ungodly men, turning the undeserved kindness of our God into an excuse for loose conduct and proving false to our only Owner and Lord, Jesus Christ." (Jude 4) Such ones' profession of Christianity is meaningless. Their service is unacceptable to God; it is as the wise writer

of Israel said: "The sacrifice of the wicked ones is something detestable. How much more so when one brings it along with loose conduct."—Pr 21:27.

Under the Law, the same viewpoint was expressed against loose conduct. God has not changed on this matter. Loose conduct was legislated against, and the penalty was death. (Le 18:17; 20:14) David appealed to God not to take his life away with "bloodguilty men, in whose hands there is loose conduct."—Ps 26:9, 10.

Through his prophets Jeremiah and Ezekiel, Jehovah warned Israel of his judgments against them for loose conduct practiced both in a physical and a spiritual way.—Jer 13:26, 27; Eze 16:27, 43, 58; 22:9; 23:21-49; 24:13.

LORD. The Greek and Hebrew words rendered "lord" (or such related terms as "sir," "owner," "master") are used with reference to Jehovah God (Eze 3:11), Jesus Christ (Mt 7:21), one of the elders seen by John in vision (Re 7:13, 14), angels (Ge 19:1, 2; Da 12:8), men (1Sa 25:24; Ac 16:16, 19, 30), and false deities (1Co 8:5). Often the designation "lord" denotes one who has ownership or authority and power over persons or things. (Ge 24:9; 42:30; 45:8, 9; 1Ki 16:24; Lu 19:33; Ac 25:26; Eph 6:5) This title was applied by Sarah to her husband (Ge 18:12), by children to their fathers (Ge 31:35; Mt 21:28, 29), and by a younger brother to his older brother (Ge 32:5, 6). It appears as a title of respect addressed to prominent persons, public officials, prophets, and kings. (Ge 23:6; 42:10; Nu 11:28; 2Sa 1:10; 2Ki 8:10-12; Mt 27:63) When used in addressing strangers, "lord," or "sir," served as a title of courtesy.—Joh 12:21; 20:15; Ac 16:30.

Jehovah God. Jehovah God is the "Lord of heaven and earth," being the Universal Sovereign by reason of his Creatorship. (Mt 11:25; Re 4:11) Heavenly creatures speak of him as "Lord," as reported at Revelation 11:15, which says: "Loud voices occurred in heaven, saying: 'The kingdom of the world did become the kingdom of our Lord [Jehovah] and of his Christ.'" Faithful servants of God on earth addressed him as "Sovereign Lord," and this title appears over 300 times in the inspired Scriptures. (Ge 15:2; Re 6:10) He is also appropriately described as "the true Lord." (Isa 1:24) It is at his direction that people are gathered, or harvested, for life. So petitions for more workers to assist in the harvest must be made to him as the "Master [Lord] of the harvest."—Mt 9:37, 38; see NW appendix, pp. 1566-1568.

Jesus Christ. While on earth, Jesus Christ referred to himself as "Lord of the sabbath." (Mt 12:8) Appropriately, he used the Sabbath for doing the work commanded by his heavenly Father. That work included healing the sick. (Compare Mt 8:16, 17.) Jesus knew that the Mosaic Law, with its Sabbath requirement, was "a shadow of the good things to come." (Heb 10:1) In connection with those "good things to come," there is a sabbath of which he is to be the Lord.—See SABBATH DAY ("Lord of the Sabbath").

While Jesus Christ was on earth, persons besides his disciples called him "Lord," or "Sir." (Mt 8:2; Joh 4:11) In these cases the designation was primarily a title of respect or courtesy. However, to his apostles Jesus showed that calling him "Lord" involved more than this. Said he: "You address me, 'Teacher,' and, 'Lord,' and you speak rightly, for I am such." (Joh 13:13) As his disciples, these apostles were his learners, or pupils. Thus he was their Lord, or Master.

Especially after Jesus' death and resurrection did his title Lord take on great significance. By means of his sacrificial death, he purchased his followers, this making them their Owner. (Joh 15:13, 14; 1Co 7:23; 2Pe 2:1; Jude 4; Re 5:9, 10) He was also their King and Bridegroom to whom they were subject as their Lord. (Ac 17:7; Eph 5:22-27; compare Joh 3:28, 29; 2Co 11:2; Re 21:9-14.) When Jehovah rewarded his Son for faithfulness to the point of dying a shameful death on a stake, he "exalted him to a superior position and kindly gave him the name that is above every other name, so that in the name of Jesus every knee should bend of those in heaven and those on earth and those under the ground, and every tongue should openly acknowledge that Jesus Christ is Lord to the glory of God the Father." (Php 2:9-11) Acknowledgment of Jesus Christ as Lord means more than simply calling him "Lord." It requires that an individual recognize Jesus' position and follow a course of obedience. (Compare Joh 14:21.) As Jesus himself said: "Not everyone saying to me, 'Lord, Lord,' will enter into the kingdom of the heavens, but the one doing the will of my Father who is in the heavens will."—Mt 7:21.

Jehovah God also granted immortality to his faithful Son. Therefore, although many men have ruled as kings or lords, only Jesus Christ, the "King of kings and Lord of lords," has immortality.—1Ti 6:14-16; Re 19:16.

Since Jesus has the keys of death and Hades (Re 1:17, 18), he is in position to release mankind from the common grave (Joh 5:28, 29) and from the death inherited from Adam. (Ro 5:12, 18) He is therefore also the 'Lord over the dead,' including King David, one of his earthly ancestors.—Ac 2:34-36; Ro 14:9.

A Title of Respect. The fact that Christians have only the "one Lord" Jesus Christ (Eph 4:5) does not rule out their applying "lord" (or, "sir") to others as a title of respect, courtesy, or authority. The apostle Peter even cited Sarah as a good example for Christian wives because of her obedience to Abraham, "calling him 'lord.'" (1Pe 3:1-6) This was no mere formality on Sarah's part. It was a sincere reflection of her submissiveness, for she spoke of him as such "inside herself." (Ge 18:12) On the other hand, since all Christians are brothers, it would be wrong for them to call one of their number "Leader" or "Lord," viewing that one as a spiritual leader.—Mt 23:8-10; see AXIS LORDS; JEHOVAH; JESUS CHRIST.

The Greek "Kyrios." This Greek word is an adjective, signifying the possessing of power (ky'ros) or authority, and it is also used as a noun. It appears in each book of the Christian Greek Scriptures except Titus and the letters of John. The term corresponds to the Hebrew 'A·dhohn'. As God's created Son and Servant, Jesus Christ properly addresses his Father and God (Joh 20:17) as "Lord" ('Adho·nai' or Ky'ri·os), the One having superior power and authority, his Head. (Mt 11:25; 1Co 11:3) As the one exalted to his Father's right hand, Jesus is "Lord of lords" as respects all except his Father, God the Almighty.—Re 17:14; 19:15, 16; compare 1Co 15:27, 28.

Its use in place of the divine name. During the second or third century of the Common Era, the scribes substituted the words Ky'ri·os (Lord) and The·os' (God) for the divine name, Jehovah, in copies of the Greek Septuagint translation of the Hebrew Scriptures. Other translations, such as the Latin Vulgate, the Douay Version (based on the Vulgate), and the King James Version, as well as numerous modern translations (NE, AT, RS, NIV, TEV, NAB), followed a similar practice. The divine name was replaced by the terms "God" and "Lord," generally in all-capital letters in English to indicate the substitution for the Tetragrammaton, or divine name.

In departing from this practice, the translation committee of the American Standard Version of 1901 stated: "The American Revisers, after a careful consideration, were brought to the unanimous conviction that a Jewish superstition, which regarded the Divine Name as too sacred to be uttered, ought no longer to dominate in the English or any other version of the Old Testament, as it fortunately does not in the numerous versions made by modern missionaries. . . . This personal name [Jehovah], with its wealth of sacred associations, is now restored to the place in the sacred text to which it has an unquestionable claim." —*AS* preface, p. iv.

A number of translations since then (*An, JB* [English and French], *NC, BC* [both in Spanish], and others) have consistently rendered the Tetragrammaton as "Yahweh" or have used a similar form.

Under the heading JEHOVAH (In the Christian Greek Scriptures), evidence is also presented to show that the divine name, Jehovah, was used in the original writings of the Christian Greek Scriptures, from Matthew to Revelation. On this basis, the *New World Translation,* used throughout this work, has restored the divine name in its translation of the Christian Greek Scriptures, doing so a total of 237 times. Other translations had made similar restorations, particularly when translating the Christian Greek Scriptures into Hebrew.

When discussing "Restoring the Divine Name," the New World Bible Translation Committee states: "To know where the divine name was replaced by the Greek words Κύριος and Θεός, we have determined where the inspired Christian writers have quoted verses, passages and expressions from the Hebrew Scriptures and then we have referred back to the Hebrew text to ascertain whether the divine name appears there. In this way we determined the identity to give *Ky'ri·os* and *The·os'* and the personality with which to clothe them." Explaining further, the Committee said: "To avoid overstepping the bounds of a translator into the field of exegesis, we have been most cautious about rendering the divine name in the Christian Greek Scriptures, always carefully considering the Hebrew Scriptures as a background. We have looked for agreement from the Hebrew versions to confirm our rendering." Such agreement from Hebrew versions exists in all the 237 places that the New World Bible Translation Committee has rendered the divine name in the body of its translation.—*NW* appendix, pp. 1564-1566.

The Hebrew "Adhohn" and "Adhonai." The Hebrew word *'a·dhohn'* occurs 334 times in the Hebrew Scriptures. It carries the thought of ownership or headship and is used of God and of men. The plural form *'adho·nim'* sometimes denotes the simple numerical plural and is then translated "lords" or "masters." (Ps 136:3; Isa 26:13) At other places the plural form denotes excellence, or majesty, whether of God or of man (Ps 8:1; Ge 39:2), and in such cases any appositional pronouns or modifying adjectives are in the singular number. (Ps 45:11; 147:5) In some places, two plurals are used side by side to distinguish Jehovah by the plural of excellence from the numerous other lords.—De 10:17; Ps 136:3; compare 1Co 8:5, 6.

The titles *'A·dhohn'* and *'Adho·nim'* are applied to Jehovah 25 times in the Scriptures. In nine places in the Masoretic text, *'A·dhohn'* has the definite article *ha* before it, so limiting application of the title to Jehovah. (Ex 23:17; 34:23; Isa 1:24; 3:1; 10:16, 33; 19:4; Mic 4:13; Mal 3:1) At all six places where *'A·dhohn'* without the definite article refers to Jehovah, it describes him as Lord (Owner) of the earth and so is not ambiguous. (Jos 3:11, 13; Ps 97:5; 114:7; Zec 4:14; 6:5) At the ten places where *'Adho·nim'* is used of Jehovah, the immediate context makes certain his identity.—De 10:17; Ne 8:10; 10:29; Ps 8:1, 9; 135:5; 136:3; 147:5; Isa 51:22; Ho 12:14.

The ending *ai* added to the Hebrew word *'a·dhohn'* is a different form of the plural of excellence. When *'Adho·nai'* appears without an additional suffix in Hebrew, it is used exclusively of Jehovah and indicates that he is the Sovereign Lord. According to *The International Standard Bible Encyclopedia* (1986, Vol. 3, p. 157), "the form highlights the power and sovereignty of Yahweh as 'Lord.'" Its use by men in addressing him suggests submissive acknowledgment of that great fact.—Ge 15:2, 8; De 3:24; Jos 7:7.

Evidently by early in the Common Era the divine name, *YHWH,* had come to be regarded by the Jewish rabbis as too sacred to be pronounced. Instead, they substituted *'Adho·nai'* (sometimes *'Elo·him'*) when reading the Scriptures aloud. The Sopherim, or scribes, went even further by replacing the divine name in the written text with *'Adho·nai'* 134 times (133 in *Biblia Hebraica Stuttgartensia*). From about the fifth to the ninth centuries of our Common Era, the Masoretes copied the text with great care. They noted in the Masora (their notes on the text) where the Sopherim had made such changes. Hence, these 134 changes are known. (For a list see *NW* appendix, p. 1562.) Taking this into account, there remain 306 places where *'Adho·nai'* did originally appear in the text.

The title *'Adho·nai'* is used mostly by the prophets, and much more frequently by Ezekiel than by any other. Nearly every time, he combines it with the divine name to form *'Adho·nai' Yehwih',* "Sovereign Lord Jehovah." Another combination title, appearing 16 times, is *'Adho·nai' Yehwih' tseva·'ohth',* "Sovereign Lord, Jehovah of armies," and all but two of its occurrences (Ps 69:6; Am 9:5) are in Isaiah and Jeremiah. The title is used to reveal Jehovah as the one with the power and determination not only to avenge his oppressed people but also to punish them for their unfaithfulness.

LORD'S DAY.

A definite period of time during which the Lord Jesus Christ brings certain things in connection with God's purpose to a successful conclusion.

In Biblical usage the word "day" may denote a period of time far longer than 24 hours. (Ge 2:4; Joh 8:56; 2Pe 3:8) Contextual evidence indicates that "the Lord's day" of Revelation 1:10 is not a particular 24-hour day. Since it was "by inspiration" that John came to be "in the Lord's day," the reference could not be to some particular day of the week. It would not have been necessary for John to have been inspired to come to a specific day of the week. Therefore, "the Lord's day" must be that future time during which events that John was privileged to see in vision would occur. This included such happenings as the war in heaven and the ouster of Satan, the destruction of Babylon the Great and the kings of the earth and their armies, the binding and abyssing of Satan, the resurrection of the dead, and Christ's Thousand Year Reign.

The context points to Jesus Christ as the Lord whose "day" it is. Immediately after coming to be "in the Lord's day," John heard, not the voice of Almighty God, but that of the resurrected Son of God. (Re 1:10-18) Also, the 'day of the Lord' mentioned at 1 Corinthians 1:8; 5:5; and 2 Corinthians 1:14 is that of Jesus Christ.

LORD'S EVENING MEAL.

A literal meal, commemorative of the death of the Lord Jesus Christ; hence, a memorial of his death. Since it is the only event Scripturally commanded to be memorialized by Christians, it is also properly termed the Memorial. It is sometimes called "the Lord's supper."—1Co 11:20, *KJ.*

The institution of the Lord's Evening Meal is reported on by two apostles who were eyewitnesses and participants, namely, Matthew and John. Mark and Luke, though not present on the occasion, fill in some details. Paul, in giving instructions to the Corinthian congregation, provides enlightenment on some of its features. These sources tell us that, on the evening before his death, Jesus met with his disciples in a large upper room to observe the Passover. (Mr 14:14-16) Matthew reports: "As they continued eating, Jesus took a loaf and, after saying a blessing, he broke it and, giving it to the disciples, he said: 'Take, eat. This means my body.' Also, he took a cup and, having given thanks, he gave it to them, saying: 'Drink out of it, all of you; for this means my "blood of the covenant," which is to be poured out in behalf of many for forgiveness of sins. But I tell you, I will by no means drink henceforth any of this product of the vine until that day when I drink it new with you in the kingdom of my Father.' Finally, after singing praises, they went out to the Mount of Olives."—Mt 26:17-30; Mr 14:17-26; Lu 22:7-39; Joh 13:1-38; 1Co 10:16-22; 11:20-34.

Time of Its Institution. The Passover was always observed on Nisan (Abib) 14, being on or near the day of full moon, inasmuch as the first day of every month (lunar month) in the Jewish calendar was the day of the new moon, as determined by visual observation. Therefore the 14th day of the month would be about the middle of a lunation. The date of Jesus' death is shown in the article JESUS CHRIST (Time of his death) to be Nisan 14, 33 C.E. Concerning the day of his death as reckoned on the Gregorian calendar, astronomical calculations show that there was an eclipse of the moon on Friday, April 3, 33 C.E. (Julian calendar), which would be Friday, April 1, on the Gregorian calendar. (Oppolzer's *Canon of Eclipses,* translated by O. Gingerich, 1962, p. 344) Eclipses of the moon always occur at the time of full moon. This evidence strongly indicates that Nisan 14, 33 C.E., fell on Thursday-Friday, March 31–April 1, 33 C.E., on the Gregorian calendar.

It was on the evening before his death that Jesus observed his last Passover meal and afterward instituted the Lord's Evening Meal. Even before the Memorial meal began, the traitorous Judas was sent out, at which time, according to the record, "it was night." (Joh 13:30) Since the days of the Jewish calendar ran from evening of one day to evening of the next, the Lord's Evening Meal was celebrated also on Nisan 14, on Thursday evening, March 31.—See DAY.

How Often Observed. According to Luke and Paul, when instituting the Memorial of his death Jesus said: "Keep doing this in remembrance of me." (Lu 22:19; 1Co 11:24) From this it is reasonable to understand that Jesus meant that his followers should celebrate the Lord's Evening Meal annually, not more often. The Passover, observed in remembrance of Jehovah's deliverance of Israel from Egyptian bondage in 1513 B.C.E., was commemorated only once a year, on the anniversary date of Nisan 14. The Memorial, also an anniversary, would appropriately be held only on Nisan 14.

Paul quoted Jesus as saying regarding the cup, "Keep doing this, as often as you drink it, in remembrance of me," and added: "For as often as you eat this loaf and drink this cup, you keep proclaiming the death of the Lord, until he arrives." (1Co 11:25, 26) "Often" can refer to something done only once a year, especially when done for many years. (Heb 9:25, 26) Nisan 14 was the day on which Christ gave his literal body as a sacrifice on the torture stake and poured out his lifeblood for forgiveness of sins. Hence, that was the day of "the death of the Lord" and, consequently, the date to commemorate his death thereafter.

The participants in this meal would be "absent from the Lord" and would celebrate the Lord's Evening Meal "often" before their death in faithfulness. Then, following their resurrection to heavenly life, they would be together with Christ and would no longer need a remembrancer of him. Regarding the duration of this observance, "until he arrives," the apostle Paul evidently had reference to Christ's coming again and receiving them into heaven by a resurrection during the time of his presence. This understanding of the matter is clarified by Jesus' words to the 11 apostles later that evening: "If I go my way and prepare a place for you, I am coming again and will receive you home to myself, that where I am you also may be."—Joh 14:3, 4; compare 2Co 5:1-3, 6-9.

Jesus informed the disciples that the wine he had drunk (at this Passover preceding the Memorial) was the last of the product of the vine that he would drink "until that day when I drink it new with you in the kingdom of my Father." (Mt 26:29) Since he would not be drinking literal wine in heaven, he obviously had reference to what wine sometimes symbolized in the Scriptures, namely, joy. Being together in the Kingdom was what they looked forward to with highest anticipation. (Ro 8:23; 2Co 5:2) King David wrote, in song, of Jehovah's provision of "wine that makes the heart of mortal man rejoice," and his son Solomon said: "Wine itself makes life rejoice."—Ps 104:15; Ec 10:19.

The Emblems. Mark relates concerning the bread used by Jesus when instituting the Lord's Evening Meal: "As they continued eating, he took a loaf, said a blessing, broke it and gave it to them, and said: 'Take it, this means my body.'" (Mr 14:22) The loaf of bread was the kind on hand for the Passover meal that Jesus and his disciples had already concluded. This was unleavened bread, as no leaven was permitted in Jewish homes during the Passover and the associated Festival of Unfermented Cakes. (Ex 13:6-10) Leaven is used Scripturally to denote sinfulness. The unleavened quality of the bread is appropriate because it represents Jesus' sinless fleshly body. (Heb 7:26; 9:14; 1Pe 2:22, 24) The unleavened loaf was flat and brittle; so it was broken, as was customary at

meals in those days. (Lu 24:30; Ac 27:35) Earlier, when Jesus miraculously multiplied bread for thousands of persons, he broke it in order to distribute it to them. (Mt 14:19; 15:36) Consequently, the breaking of the Memorial bread apparently had no spiritual significance.

After Jesus had passed the bread, he took a cup and "offered thanks and gave it to them, and they all drank out of it. And he said to them: 'This means my "blood of the covenant," which is to be poured out in behalf of many.'" (Mr 14:23, 24) He used fermented wine, not unfermented grape juice. Biblical references to wine are to literal wine, not to the unfermented juice of the grape. (See WINE AND STRONG DRINK.) Fermented wine, not grape juice, would burst "old wineskins," as Jesus said. Jesus' enemies accused him of being "given to drinking wine," a charge that would mean nothing if the "wine" were mere grape juice. (Mt 9:17; 11:19) Real wine was on hand for the Passover celebration that had been concluded, and it could appropriately be used by Christ in instituting the Memorial of his death. Doubtless the wine was red, for only red wine would be a fitting symbol of blood.—1Pe 1:19.

A Communion Meal. In ancient Israel a man could provide a communion meal. He would bring an animal to the sanctuary, where it was slaughtered. A portion of the animal offered went on the altar for "a restful odor to Jehovah." A portion went to the officiating priest, another portion to the priestly sons of Aaron, and the offerer and his household shared in the meal. (Le 3:1-16; 7:28-36) One who was 'unclean' as defined by the Law was forbidden to eat a communion sacrifice on pain of being "cut off from his people."—Le 7:20, 21.

The Lord's Evening Meal is likewise a communion meal, because there is a sharing together. Jehovah God is involved as the Author of the arrangement, Jesus Christ is the ransom sacrifice, and his spiritual brothers eat the emblems as joint participants. Their eating at "the table of Jehovah" would signify that they are at peace with Jehovah. (1Co 10:21) In fact, communion offerings were sometimes called "peace offerings."—Le 3:1, ftn.

Partakers of the meal, in eating the bread and drinking the wine, acknowledge that they are sharers together in Christ, in complete unity. The apostle Paul says: "The cup of blessing which we bless, is it not a sharing in the blood of the Christ? The loaf which we break, is it not a sharing in the body of the Christ? Because there is one loaf, we, although many, are one body, for we are all partaking of that one loaf."—1Co 10:16, 17.

In thus partaking, these indicate that they are in the new covenant and are receiving the benefits of it, that is, God's forgiveness of sins through Christ's blood. They properly esteem the value of "the blood of the covenant" by which they are sanctified. (Heb 10:29) The Scriptures call them "ministers of a new covenant," serving its ends. (2Co 3:5, 6) And they fittingly partake of the emblematic loaf because they can say: "By the said 'will' we have been sanctified through the offering of the body of Jesus Christ once for all time." (Heb 10:10) They share in Christ's sufferings and in a death like his, a death of integrity. They hope to share in "the likeness of his resurrection," a resurrection to immortal life in a spiritual body.—Ro 6:3-5.

Of each participant in the meal, the apostle Paul writes: "Whoever eats the loaf or drinks the cup of the Lord unworthily will be guilty respecting the body and the blood of the Lord. First let a man approve himself after scrutiny, and thus let him eat of the loaf and drink of the cup. For he that eats and drinks eats and drinks judgment against himself if he does not discern the body." (1Co 11:27-29) Unclean, unscriptural, or hypocritical practices would disqualify one from eating. If he should eat in that condition, he would be eating and drinking judgment against himself. He would be failing to appreciate Christ's sacrifice, its purpose, and its meaning. He would be showing disrespect and contempt for it. (Compare Heb 10:28-31.) Such a person would be in danger of being 'cut off from God's people,' as was the one in Israel who partook of a communion meal in an unclean state.—Le 7:20.

In fact, Paul compares the Lord's Evening Meal to an Israelite communion meal when he speaks first of the partakers sharing together in Christ and then says: "Look at that which is Israel in a fleshly way: Are not those who eat the sacrifices sharers with the altar? . . . You cannot be drinking the cup of Jehovah and the cup of demons; you cannot be partaking of 'the table of Jehovah' and the table of demons."—1Co 10:18-21.

Partakers and Other Attenders at the Meal. Jesus had gathered his 12 apostles, saying to them: "I have greatly desired to eat this passover with you before I suffer." (Lu 22:15) But John's eyewitness account indicates that Jesus dismissed the traitorous Judas before instituting the Memorial meal. During the Passover, Jesus, knowing that Judas was his betrayer, dipped a morsel of the Passover meal and handed it to Judas, instructing him to leave. (Joh 13:21-30) Mark's account also intimates this order of events. (Mr 14:12-25) During the Lord's Evening Meal that followed, Jesus passed the bread and the wine to the 11 remaining apostles, telling them to eat and drink. (Lu 22:19, 20) Afterward he spoke to them as "the ones that have stuck with me in my trials," a further indication that Judas had been dismissed.—Lu 22:28.

There is no evidence that Jesus himself ate the bread thus offered or drank out of the cup during this Memorial meal. The body and blood he gave was in their behalf and for validating the new covenant, through which their sins were removed. (Jer 31:31-34; Heb 8:10-12; 12:24) Jesus had no sins. (Heb 7:26) He mediates the new covenant between Jehovah God and those chosen as Christ's associates. (Heb 9:15; see COVENANT.) Besides the apostles present at that meal, there were to be others making up the spiritual "Israel of God," a "little flock," who would eventually be kings and priests with Christ. (Ga 6:16; Lu 12:32; Re 1:5, 6; 5:9, 10) All of Christ's spiritual brothers on earth, therefore, would be partakers in this meal each time it is celebrated. They are shown to be "certain firstfruits of his creatures" (Jas 1:18), bought from mankind as "firstfruits to God and to the Lamb," and are revealed in John's vision to number 144,000.—Re 14:1-5.

Observers not partaking. The Lord Jesus Christ revealed that, at his presence, there would be persons who would do good to his spiritual brothers, visiting them in time of need and giving them assistance. (Mt 25:31-46) Would these, who might attend the celebration of the Lord's Evening Meal, qualify as partakers of the emblems? The Scriptures say that God will provide, through his holy spirit, evidence and assurance to those qualified to partake of the emblems as "heirs indeed of God, but joint heirs with Christ," that they are God's sons. The apostle Paul writes: "The spirit itself bears witness with our spirit that we are God's children." He goes on to explain that there are others who benefit from God's arrangement for these sons: "For the eager expectation of the creation is waiting for the revealing of the sons of God." (Ro 8:14-21) Since the joint heirs with Christ are to 'rule as kings and priests over the earth,' the Kingdom will benefit those living under it. (Re 5:10; 20:4, 6; 21:3, 4) Those benefiting would naturally be interested in the Kingdom and its development. Such persons therefore would attend and observe the celebration of the Lord's Evening Meal, but not being joint heirs with Christ and spiritual sons of God, they would not partake of the emblems as joint participants in the death of Christ, with hope of resurrection to a heavenly life with him.—Ro 6:3-5.

No Transubstantiation or Consubstantiation.

Jesus still had his fleshly body when offering the bread. This body, whole and entire, was to be offered as a perfect, unblemished sacrifice for sins the next afternoon (of the same day of the Hebrew calendar, Nisan 14). He also retained all his blood for that perfect sacrifice. "He poured out his soul [which is in the blood] to the very death." (Isa 53:12; Le 17:11) Consequently, during the evening meal he did not perform a miracle of transubstantiation, changing the bread into his literal flesh and the wine into his literal blood. For the same reasons, it cannot be truly said that he miraculously caused his flesh and his blood to be present or combined with the bread and wine, as is claimed by those who adhere to the doctrine of consubstantiation.

This is not contradicted by Jesus' words at John 6:51-57. Jesus was not there discussing the Lord's Evening Meal; such an arrangement was not instituted until a year later. The 'eating' and 'drinking' mentioned in this account are done in a figurative sense by exercising faith in Jesus Christ, as is indicated by verses 35 and 40.

Furthermore, eating actual human flesh and blood would be cannibalism. Therefore, Jews who were not exercising faith and who did not properly understand Jesus' statement about eating his flesh and drinking his blood were shocked. This indicated the Jewish view on eating human flesh and blood, as inculcated by the Law.—Joh 6:60.

Additionally, drinking blood was a violation of God's law to Noah, prior to the Law covenant. (Ge 9:4; Le 17:10) The Lord Jesus Christ would never instruct others to violate God's law. (Compare Mt 5:19.) Furthermore, Jesus commanded: "Keep doing this in *remembrance* of me," not in *sacrifice* of me.—1Co 11:23-25.

The bread and the wine are, therefore, emblems, representing Christ's flesh and blood in a symbolic way, just as were his words about eating his flesh and drinking his blood. Jesus had said to those offended by his words: "For a fact, the bread that I shall give is my flesh in behalf of the life of the world." (Joh 6:51) This was given at his death as a sacrifice on the torture stake. His body was buried and was disposed of by his Father before it could see corruption. (Ac 2:31) No one ever ate any of his flesh or blood, literally.

Proper, Orderly Observance.

The Christian congregation at Corinth had got into a bad spiritual state, in some respects, so that, as the apostle Paul said: "Many among you are weak and sickly, and quite a few are sleeping in death." This was to a great extent due to their misunderstanding of the Lord's Evening Meal and its significance. They were failing to respect the sacredness of the occasion. Some brought their supper with them to eat before or during the meeting. Among these were persons who overindulged and became intoxicated, while others in the congregation who had no supper were hungry and felt shamed in the presence of those who had much. With their minds drowsy or on other matters, they were not in condition to partake of the emblems with appreciation. Furthermore, there were divisions in the congregation over the fact that some in their midst favored Peter, others preferred Apollos, and yet others looked to Paul for leadership. (1Co 1:11-13; 11:18) They were failing to appreciate that this occasion was one that should highlight unity. They did not have full realization of the seriousness of the matter, that the emblems represented the body and blood of the Lord and that the meal was in memory of his death. Paul emphasized the grave danger to those who partook without discerning these facts.—1Co 11:20-34.

LO-RUHAMAH

(Lo·ru·ha′mah) [[She Was] Not Shown Mercy]. A girl borne by Gomer, the wife of Hosea. Jehovah told the prophet to give the child this name because He would "no more show mercy again to the house of Israel." God thus indicated his rejection of Israel as a whole. (Ho 1:6-8) Earlier, when Jezreel was born, it was said that Gomer "bore to him [Hosea] a son," but regarding Lo-ruhamah it is only stated that Gomer "proceeded to become pregnant another time and to give birth to a daughter," without direct personal reference to Hosea. Though the account does not specifically say, it has been suggested that this child was the fruit of Gomer's adultery and was not the prophet's own offspring. (Ho 1:2, 3) There is allusion to her symbolic name in Hosea 2:1, 23.

LOT, I.

The casting of lots is an ancient custom for deciding a question at issue. The method used was to cast pebbles or small bits or tablets of wood or of stone into the gathered folds of a garment, "the lap," or into a vase, and then to shake them. The one whose lot fell out or was drawn out was the one chosen. The lot, like the oath, implied a prayer with it. Prayer was either expressed or implied, and Jehovah's intervention was sought and anticipated. Lot (Heb., *goh·ral′*) is used literally and figuratively with the thought of "share" or "portion."—Jos 15:1; Ps 16:5; 125:3; Isa 57:6; Jer 13:25.

Uses. Proverbs 16:33 says: "Into the lap the lot is cast down, but every decision by it is from Jehovah." In Israel the proper use of a lot was to end a controversy: "The lot puts even contentions to rest, and it separates even the mighty from one another." (Pr 18:18) It was not used for sport, play, or gambling. There were no bets, wagers, or stakes—no losses or winnings. It was not done to enrich the temple or the priests, nor was it done for charity. Contrariwise, the Roman soldiers did have selfish gain in mind when, as foretold at Psalm 22:18, they cast lots for Jesus' garments. —Mt 27:35.

The first mention in the Bible of drawing lots is in connection with selecting the goats for Jehovah and for Azazel on Atonement Day. (Le 16:7-10) In Jesus' time this was performed at Herod's temple by the high priest's drawing from a receptacle two lots that were made, it is said, of boxwood or of gold. The lots, respectively marked "For Jehovah" and "For Azazel," were then placed on the heads of the goats.

Lots were drawn to determine the order of service at the temple for the 24 divisions of the priesthood. (1Ch 24:5-18) Here the secretary of the Levites wrote the names of the heads of the paternal houses, and they were evidently picked out in succession. Also, in this manner the Levites were allotted to temple service as singers, gatekeepers, treasurers, and so forth. (1Ch 24:31; chaps 25, 26; Lu 1:8, 9) After the return from exile, lots were used to arrange for the supplying of wood for temple service and to designate who should move into Jerusalem.—Ne 10:34; 11:1.

Although lots are not mentioned directly in connection with the Urim and Thummim placed by Moses in the breastpiece worn by the high priest (Le 8:7-9) and it is not known just what the Urim and Thummim were, nevertheless, they were used to settle a problem in a manner similar to two lots. The Urim and Thummim seem to be connected with the casting of lots at 1 Samuel 14:41, 42. They are sometimes spoken of as sacred lots. When a question important to the nation arose, upon which a decision could not be made, the high priest would stand before Jehovah and receive Jehovah's decision by means of these sacred lots.

Jehovah commanded that the division of the Promised Land among the 12 tribes be performed by casting lots. (Nu 26:55, 56) The book of Joshua gives a detailed discussion of this, the word "lot(s)" occurring more than 20 times in chapters 14 to 21. Lots were drawn before Jehovah at the tent of meeting in Shiloh and under the supervision of Joshua and High Priest Eleazar. (Jos 17:4; 18:6, 8) The Levite cities were also selected by lot. (Jos 21:8) Jehovah obviously caused the lot to fall in harmony with his previous prophecy regarding the general location of the tribes.—Ge 49.

Lots were used to point out offenders. In Jonah's case the mariners cast lots to find out on whose account the storm had come upon them. (Jon 1: 7, 8) By the use of lots, Jonathan was pointed out as the one breaking Saul's foolish oath.—1Sa 14: 41, 42.

Lots were used by the enemies of Israel in dividing war booty and captives. (Joe 3:3; Ob 11) Haman had "Pur, that is, the Lot" cast as a form of divination to determine the auspicious day for the extermination of the Jews throughout the Persian Empire. (Es 3:7) The plural is *pu·rim'*, from which the Festival of Purim, also called the Festival of Lots, gets its name.—Es 9:24-26.

In Time of the Apostles. Lots were used by the disciples of Jesus, along with their prayer, to determine who would fill the place of Judas Iscariot as one of the 12 who had witnessed Jesus' activities and his resurrection; Matthias was chosen. (Ac 1:21-26) The Greek word here is *kle'ros* and is related to the word *kle·ro·no·mi'a*, inheritance. *Kle'ros* is used at Colossians 1:12 and 1 Peter 5:3 in regard to the inheritance, or allotment, that God has given to Christians.

But we do not read of lots being used after Pentecost 33 C.E. for selecting overseers and their assistants or to decide matters of importance. Selection of overseers and their assistants was to be based on the evidence of the fruitage of the holy spirit in their lives (1Ti 3; Tit 1), while other decisions were based on the fulfillment of prophecy, angelic guidance, the principles of God's Word and Jesus' teachings, and the direction of holy spirit. (Ac 5:19-21; 13:2, 3; 14:23; 15:15-19, 28) The apostle Paul states: "All Scripture is inspired of God and beneficial . . . for setting things straight."—2Ti 3:16.

LOT, II. A grandson of Terah and son of Abraham's (Abram's) brother Haran; hence, Abraham's nephew.—Ge 11:27.

Lot's father Haran died in Ur of the Chaldees, and Lot therefore went with Terah, Abram, and Sarai from Ur to the city of Haran, where his grandfather Terah died. (Ge 11:28, 31, 32) Lot then journeyed to Canaan with Abram and Sarai, and he later accompanied them to and from Egypt. (Ge 12:4, 5; 13:1) Because the accumulated possessions of Lot and Abram had become many, when they returned to Canaan the land was unable to sustain them together. Also, quarreling arose between their herdsmen. (Ge 13:5-7) Abram, not wishing to see this continue, suggested that they separate, giving his nephew the choice of land. Lot selected a well-watered area, the whole district of Lower Jordan. He moved his camp to the E and eventually pitched tent near Sodom. (Ge 13:8-12) But Lot did not become like the Sodomites. He proved himself to be a "righteous man" who "by what he saw and heard while dwelling among them from day to day was tormenting his righteous soul by reason of their lawless deeds."—2Pe 2:8.

At the time that four invading confederate kings defeated five local kings, including the king of Sodom, the victors looted the city and took Lot captive. Learning of Lot's plight, Abram mustered 318 slaves, defeated the captors, recovered all the property, and rescued Lot.—Ge 14:1-16.

Visited by Angels. Later, when Lot was visited by two angels at the time of Sodom's impending destruction, he extended hospitality to them. But the men of the city surrounded the house and demanded that the visitors be brought out to them for immoral purposes. Lot sought to protect his guests even to the point of offering his two virgin daughters to the mob. Angered, the mob pressed heavily in on Lot, whereupon his angelic visitors brought him indoors and struck the wicked Sodomites with blindness.—Ge 19:1-11.

Delivered from Sodom. The angels then informed Lot that the outcry against the inhabitants of Sodom had grown loud before Jehovah and that they had been sent to destroy the city. As instructed, Lot warned his prospective sons-in-law, who evidently were intending to take his daughters as wives but had not yet done so. (Compare Ge 19:8, 14.) However, his sons-in-law did not heed his words. (Ge 19:12-14) At dawn the two angels urged prompt departure, hastening it by seizing the hands of Lot, his wife, and his two daughters. In keeping with Lot's request, the angels permitted him to flee to the nearby city of Zoar. After Lot arrived there, Jehovah brought fiery destruction upon Sodom and Gomorrah. However, Lot's wife (who is unnamed in the Scriptures) disobediently "began to look around from behind him," perhaps with longing for the things left behind. For doing so, "she became a pillar of salt."—Ge 19:15-26.

Lot later moved from Zoar and began dwelling in a cave in a mountainous region. The prospective sons-in-law of Lot evidently died in Sodom, so Lot's two daughters were without mates. They caused their father unwittingly to have sexual relations with them while he was under the influence of wine. This they did to preserve offspring from their father. As a result, each daughter had a son, from whom the Moabites and the Ammonites descended.—Ge 19:30-38, ftn; De 2:9, 19.

A Warning. The authenticity of the Scriptural account regarding Lot is attested to by Jesus Christ. He showed that "in the days of the Son of man," or during his presence, circumstances would parallel those of the days of Lot when persons were unconcernedly eating, drinking, buying, selling, planting, and building until fire and sulfur rained down from heaven to destroy them all. Christ showed that at that future time persons should not return to the things behind, and he gave a striking example to show the dire consequences of doing so, by saying: "Remember the wife of Lot."—Lu 17:26-32.

LOTAN (Lo'tan). A son of Seir the Horite and one of the sheiks of Edom. (Ge 36:20, 29) His sons were Hori and Hemam (Homam), and his sister was named Timna.—Ge 36:22; 1Ch 1:38, 39.

LOTS, FESTIVAL OF. See PURIM.

LOTUS TREE [Heb., *tse·'elim'*]. The thorny lotus (*Ziziphus lotus*) is a thickly branched shrub or low tree, often growing to a height of only 1.5 m (5 ft). The leaves are small, oval, and leathery, and at the base of each leaf is a pair of thorns. The only reference to it is at Job 40:21, 22, which speaks of Behemoth (the hippopotamus) as lying in the shade cast by the tree. While this tree is found in dry places in Palestine, *A Dictionary of Life in Bible Times* speaks of it as "flourishing in the hot and humid marshland" of N Africa.—By W. Corswant, Suffolk, 1960, p. 177.

LOUNGE. See BED.

LOVE. A feeling of warm personal attachment or deep affection, as for a friend, for a parent or child, and so forth; warm fondness or liking for another; also, the benevolent affection of God for his creatures or the reverent affection due from them to God; also, the kindly affection properly expressed by God's creatures toward one another; that strong or passionate affection for a person of the opposite sex that constitutes the emotional incentive to conjugal union. One of the synonyms for love is "devotion."

Aside from those meanings, the Scriptures speak also of love guided by principle, as love of righteousness or even love for one's enemies, for whom a person may not have affection. This facet or expression of love is an unselfish devotion to righteousness and a sincere concern for the lasting welfare of others, along with an active expression of this for their good.

The verb *'a·hev'* or *'a·hav'* ("love") and the noun *'a·havah'* ("love") are the words primarily used in

Hebrew to denote love in the foregoing senses, the context determining the sense and degree meant.

The Christian Greek Scriptures mainly employ forms of the words a·ga'pe, phi·li'a, and two words drawn from stor·ge' (e'ros, love between the sexes, not being used). A·ga'pe appears more frequently than the other terms.

Of the noun a·ga'pe and the verb a·ga·pa'o, Vine's Expository Dictionary of Old and New Testament Words says: "Love can be known only from the actions it prompts. God's love is seen in the gift of His Son, I John 4:9, 10. But obviously this is not the love of complacency, or affection, that is, it was not drawn out by any excellency in its objects, Rom. 5:8. It was an exercise of the Divine will in deliberate choice, made without assignable cause save that which lies in the nature of God Himself, cp. Deut. 7:7, 8."—1981, Vol. 3, p. 21.

Regarding the verb phi·le'o, Vine comments: "[It] is to be distinguished from agapao in this, that phileo more nearly represents tender affection. . . . Again, to love (phileo) life, from an undue desire to preserve it, forgetful of the real object of living, meets with the Lord's reproof, John 12:25. On the contrary, to love life (agapao) as used in I Pet. 3:10, is to consult the true interests of living. Here the word phileo would be quite inappropriate." —Vol. 3, pp. 21, 22.

James Strong's Exhaustive Concordance of the Bible, in its Greek dictionary (1890, pp. 75, 76), remarks under phi·le'o: "To be a friend to (fond of [an individual or an object]), i.e. have affection for (denoting personal attachment, as a matter of sentiment or feeling; while [a·ga·pa'o] is wider, embracing espec. the judgment and the deliberate assent of the will as a matter of principle, duty and propriety . . .)."—See AFFECTION.

A·ga'pe, therefore, carries the meaning of love guided, or governed, by principle. It may or may not include affection and fondness. That a·ga'pe may include affection and warmth is evident in many passages. At John 3:35, Jesus said: "The Father loves [a·ga·pai'] the Son." At John 5:20, he said: "The Father has affection for [phi·lei'] the Son." Certainly God's love for Jesus Christ is coupled with much affection. Also Jesus explained: "He that loves [a·ga·pon'] me will be loved [a·ga·pe·the'se·tai] by my Father, and I will love [a·ga·pe'so] him." (Joh 14:21) This love of the Father and of the Son is accompanied by tender affection for such loving persons. Jehovah's worshipers must love him and his Son, as well as one another, in the same way.—Joh 21:15-17.

So, although distinguished by respect for principle, a·ga'pe is not unfeeling; otherwise it would not differ from cold justice. But it is not ruled by feeling or sentiment; it never ignores principle. Christians rightly show a·ga'pe toward others for whom they may feel no affection or fondness, doing so for the welfare of those persons. (Ga 6:10) Yet, though not feeling affection, they do feel compassion and sincere concern for such fellow humans, to the limits and in the way that righteous principles allow and direct.

However, while a·ga'pe refers to love governed by principle, there are good and bad principles. A wrong kind of a·ga'pe could be expressed, guided by bad principles. For example, Jesus said: "If you love [a·ga·pa'te] those loving you, of what credit is it to you? For even the sinners love those loving them. And if you do good to those doing good to you, really of what credit is it to you? Even the sinners do the same. Also, if you lend without interest to those from whom you hope to receive, of what credit is it to you? Even sinners lend without interest to sinners that they may get back as much." (Lu 6:32-34) The principle upon which such ones operate is: 'Do good to me and I will do good to you.'

The apostle Paul said of one who had worked alongside him: "Demas has forsaken me because he loved [a·ga·pe'sas] the present system of things." (2Ti 4:10) Demas apparently loved the world on the principle that love of it will bring material benefits. The apostle John says: "Men have loved [e·ga'pe·san] the darkness rather than the light, for their works were wicked. For he that practices vile things hates the light and does not come to the light, in order that his works may not be reproved." (Joh 3:19, 20) Because it is a truth or principle that darkness helps cover their wicked deeds, they love it.

Jesus commanded: "Love [a·ga·pa'te] your enemies." (Mt 5:44) God himself established the principle, as the apostle Paul states: "God recommends his own love [a·ga'pen] to us in that, while we were yet sinners, Christ died for us. . . . For if, when we were enemies, we became reconciled to God through the death of his Son, much more, now that we have become reconciled, we shall be saved by his life." (Ro 5:8-10) An outstanding instance of such love is God's dealing with Saul of Tarsus, who became the apostle Paul. (Ac 9:1-16; 1Ti 1:15) Loving our enemies, therefore, should be governed by the principle established by God and should be exercised in obedience to his commandments, whether or not such love is accompanied by any warmth or affection.

God. The apostle John writes: "God is love." (1Jo 4:8) He is the very personification of love, which is his dominant quality. The converse is not true, however, that 'love (the abstract quality) is God.' He reveals himself in the Bible as a *Person* and figuratively speaks of his "eyes," "hands," "heart," "soul," and so forth. He also has other attributes, among them justice, power, and wisdom. (De 32:4; Job 36:22; Re 7:12) Moreover, he has the capacity to hate, a quality the very opposite of love. His love of righteousness requires his hatred of wickedness. (De 12:31; Pr 6:16) Love includes the feeling and expression of warm personal affection, which only a *person* can have, or which can be extended toward a *person*. Certainly God's Son Jesus Christ is not an abstract quality; he spoke of being with his Father, working with him, pleasing him, and hearing him, as well as of angels beholding the face of his Father, things impossible with a mere abstract quality.—Mt 10: 32; 18:10; Joh 5:17; 6:46; 8:28, 29, 40; 17:5.

Evidence of his love.   The evidence that Jehovah the Creator and God of the universe is love is abundant. This can be seen in the physical creation itself. With what remarkable care it has been made for the health, pleasure, and welfare of man! Man is made not just to exist but to enjoy eating, to delight in viewing the color and beauty of creation, to enjoy animals as well as the company of his fellowmen, and to find pleasure in the countless other delights of living. (Ps 139:14, 17, 18) But Jehovah has displayed his love even more by making man in his image and likeness (Ge 1:26, 27), with the capacity for love and for spirituality, and by revealing himself to man through his Word and his holy spirit.—1Co 2: 12, 13.

Jehovah's love toward mankind is that of a Father toward his children. (Mt 5:45) He spares nothing that is for their good, no matter what it costs him; his love transcends anything that we can feel or express. (Eph 2:4-7; Isa 55:8; Ro 11:33) His greatest manifestation of love, the most loving thing that a parent can do, he did for mankind. That was the giving of the life of his own faithful, only-begotten Son. (Joh 3:16) As the apostle John writes: "As for us, we love, because he first loved us." (1Jo 4:19) He is, accordingly, the Source of love. John's fellow apostle, Paul, writes: "For hardly will anyone die for a righteous man; indeed, for the good man, perhaps, someone even dares to die. But God recommends his own love to us in that, while we were yet sinners, Christ died for us."—Ro 5:7, 8; 1Jo 4:10.

God's everlasting love.   Jehovah's love for his faithful servants is everlasting; it does not fail or diminish, no matter in what circumstances, high or low, his servants may be, or what things, great or small, may come against them. The apostle Paul exclaimed: "For I am convinced that neither death nor life nor angels nor governments nor things now here nor things to come nor powers nor height nor depth nor any other creation will be able to separate us from God's love that is in Christ Jesus our Lord."—Ro 8:38, 39.

God's sovereignty based on love.   Jehovah glories in the fact that his sovereignty and the support of it by his creatures is based primarily on love. He desires only those who love his sovereignty because of his fine qualities and because it is righteous, who prefer his sovereignty to any other. (1Co 2:9) They choose to serve under his sovereignty rather than try to be independent—this because of their knowledge of him and of his love, justice, and wisdom, which they realize far surpasses their own. (Ps 84:10, 11) The Devil failed in this respect, egotistically seeking independence for himself, as did Adam and Eve. In fact, the Devil challenged God's way of ruling, saying, in effect, that it was unloving, unrighteous (Ge 3:1-5), and that God's creatures served Him not because of love, but through selfishness.—Job 1:8-12; 2:3-5.

Jehovah God allowed the Devil to live and to put his servants, even his only-begotten Son, to the test, to the point of death. God foretold the faithfulness of Jesus Christ. (Isa 53) How could he do this, staking his word on his Son? Because of love. Jehovah knew his Son and knew the love his Son had for Him and for righteousness. (Heb 1:9) He knew his Son most intimately and thoroughly. (Mt 11:27) He had full trust and confidence in the Son's faithfulness. More than that, "love . . . is a perfect bond of union." (Col 3:14) It is the most powerful bond in the universe, perfect love bonding the Son and the Father together unbreakably. For like reasons, God could trust his organization of servants, knowing that love would hold most of them immovably to him under test and that his organization of creatures would never secede in toto.—Ps 110:3.

Jesus Christ.   Because for untold ages Jesus associated most closely with his Father, the Source of love, and knew Him most intimately and thoroughly, he could say: "He that has seen me has seen the Father also." (Joh 14:9; Mt 11:27) Therefore Jesus' love is complete, perfect. (Eph 3:19) He told his disciples: "No one has love greater than this, that someone should surrender his soul in behalf of his friends." (Joh 15:13) He had told them: "I am giving you a new commandment, that you love one another; just as I have loved you, that you also love one another." (Joh 13:34) This commandment was new, in that the Law, under which Jesus and his disciples were at that time, commanded a person: "You must love your fellow [or neighbor] as yourself." (Le 19:18; Mt 22:39) It called for love of others as of oneself but not for a self-sacrificing love that went even to the point of giving one's own life in behalf of another. Jesus' life and death exemplified the love this new commandment called for. In addition to doing good when the occasion arises, the follower of Christ is to take the initiative, under Christ's direction, to help others spiritually and otherwise. He is to work actively for their good. The preaching and teaching of the good news to others, some of whom may be enemies, is one of the greatest expressions of love, for it can result in everlasting life to them. The Christian must 'impart not only the good news of God but also his own soul' in helping and working with those who accept the good news. (1Th 2:8) And he should be ready to surrender his soul (life) in behalf of them.—1Jo 3:16.

How One Acquires Love. Through holy spirit, the first man and woman were created with a measure of this dominant attribute of God, namely love, and with the capacity to extend, enlarge, and enrich that love. Love is a fruit of God's spirit. (Ga 5:22) Godly love is not a quality that one has without knowing why, as may be the case with certain physical or mental abilities, such as physical beauty, talent in music, or similar inherited qualities. Godly love cannot exist in the person apart from knowledge and service of God or apart from meditation and appreciation. Only by cultivating love can one become an imitator of God, the Source of love. (Ps 77:11; Eph 5:1, 2; Ro 12:2) Adam failed to cultivate love of God; he did not progress toward perfection of love. This is shown by his not being in union with God, bound to God by that perfect bond of union. Adam, nevertheless, even though imperfect and sinful, passed on to his offspring, "in his image," the ability and capacity to love. (Ge 5:3) Humankind in general expresses love, but it is often a misguided, deteriorated, twisted love.

Love can be misguided. For these reasons, it is evident that a person can have real, properly directed love only by seeking and following God's spirit and the knowledge that comes from His Word. For example, a parent may have affection for his child. But he may let that love deteriorate or he may be misguided because of sentimentality, giving the child everything and denying him nothing. He may not exercise his parental authority in giving discipline and at times actual chastisement. (Pr 22:15) Such supposed love may actually be family pride, which is selfishness. The

Bible says such a person is exercising, not love, but hate, because he is not taking the course that will save his child's life.—Pr 13:24; 23:13, 14.

This is not the love that comes from God. Godly love causes one to do what is good and beneficial for the other person. "Love builds up." (1Co 8:1) Love is not sentimentality. It is firm, strong, directed by godly wisdom, adhering first of all to that which is chaste, right. (Jas 3:17) God demonstrated this with Israel, whom he punished severely for disobedience, for their own everlasting welfare. (De 8:5; Pr 3:12; Heb 12:6) The apostle Paul says to Christians: "It is for discipline you are enduring. God is dealing with you as with sons. For what son is he that a father does not discipline? . . . Furthermore, we used to have fathers who were of our flesh to discipline us, and we used to give them respect. Shall we not much more subject ourselves to the Father of our spiritual life and live? For they for a few days used to discipline us according to what seemed good to them, but he does so for our profit that we may partake of his holiness. True, no discipline seems for the present to be joyous, but grievous; yet afterward to those who have been trained by it it yields peaceable fruit, namely, righteousness."—Heb 12:7-11.

Knowledge gives love right direction. Love must be directed *first* to God, above all others. Otherwise it will become misdirected and even lead into the worship of a creature or thing. Knowing God's purposes is essential, because a person knows then what is best for his own welfare and that of others and will know how to express love in the proper way. Our love for God is to be with our 'whole heart, mind, soul, and strength.' (Mt 22:36-38; Mr 12:29, 30) It is to be, not merely an outward expression, but a love that reflects the total inner person. Love involves the emotions. (1Pe 1:22) But if the mind is not equipped with knowledge of what true love is and how it acts, love can be expressed in the wrong direction. (Jer 10:23; 17:9; compare Php 1:9.) The mind must know God and his qualities, his purposes, and how he expresses love. (1Jo 4:7) In harmony with this, and since love is the most important quality, dedication to God is to the *person* of Jehovah himself (in whom love is the dominant quality) and is not to a work or a cause. Then, love must be carried out with the soul, every fiber of one's organism; and all one's strength must be put behind that effort.

Love is expansive. The true love that is a fruit of God's spirit is expansive. (2Co 6:11-13) It is not stingy, confined, or circumscribed. It must be shared to be complete. A person must first love

God (De 6:5), his Son (Eph 6:24), and then the whole association of his Christian brothers throughout the world (1Pe 2:17; 1Jo 2:10; 4:20, 21). He must love his wife; and she, her husband. (Pr 5:18, 19; Ec 9:9; Eph 5:25, 28, 33) Love is to be extended to one's children. (Tit 2:4) All mankind, even a person's own enemies, are to be loved, and Christian works are to be exercised toward them. (Mt 5:44; Lu 6:32-36) The Bible, commenting on the fruits of the spirit, of which love is first, says: "Against such things there is no law." (Ga 5:22, 23) This love has no law that can limit it. It may be practiced at any time or place, to any extent, toward those to whom it is due. In fact, the only debt Christians should be owing one another is love. (Ro 13:8) This love for one another is an identifying mark of true Christians.—Joh 13:35.

How Godly Love Acts. Love, such as God is, is so wonderful that it is hard to define. It is easier to tell how it acts. In the following discussion of this fine quality, its application to Christians will be considered. The apostle Paul, in writing on the subject, first emphasizes how essential it is for a Christian believer and then details how it acts unselfishly: "Love is long-suffering and kind. Love is not jealous, it does not brag, does not get puffed up, does not behave indecently, does not look for its own interests, does not become provoked. It does not keep account of the injury. It does not rejoice over unrighteousness, but rejoices with the truth. It bears all things, believes all things, hopes all things, endures all things."—1Co 13:4-7.

"Love is long-suffering and kind." It puts up with unfavorable conditions and wrong actions of others, doing so with a purpose, namely, to work out the eventual salvation of those doing wrong or of others involved in the circumstances, as well as to bring honor and vindication, finally, to God's name. (2Pe 3:15) Love is kind, no matter what the provocation may be. Roughness or harshness on the part of a Christian toward others would not accomplish any good. Nonetheless, love can be firm and act in justice in behalf of righteousness. Those having authority may discipline wrongdoers, but even then, they are to employ kindness. Unkindness would bring benefit neither to the unkind counselor nor to the one doing unrighteousness, but it could separate that one even farther from repentance and right works.—Ro 2:4; Eph 4:32; Tit 3:4, 5.

"Love is not jealous." It is not envious of good things coming to others. It rejoices in seeing a fellowman receive a position of greater responsibility. It does not begrudge even one's enemies receiving good things. It is generous. God makes his rain fall on the righteous and the unrighteous. (Mt 5:45) God's servants who have love are content with their lot (1Ti 6:6-8) and their place, not getting out of place or selfishly seeking the position occupied by another. Satan the Devil selfishly and enviously did get out of place, even desiring worship to be given to him by Jesus Christ.—Lu 4:5-8.

Love "does not brag, does not get puffed up." It does not seek the applause and admiration of creatures. (Ps 75:4-7; Jude 16) The person having love will not push another person down to make himself appear greater. Rather, he will exalt God and will sincerely encourage and build up other persons. (Ro 1:8; Col 1:3-5; 1Th 1:2, 3) He will be happy to see another Christian make advancement. And he will not boast of what he is going to do. (Pr 27:1; Lu 12:19, 20; Jas 4:13-16) He will realize that all he does is due to the strength coming from Jehovah. (Ps 34:2; 44:8) Jehovah told Israel: "Let the one bragging about himself brag about himself because of this very thing, the having of insight and the having of knowledge of me, that I am Jehovah, the One exercising lovingkindness, justice and righteousness in the earth; for in these things I do take delight."—Jer 9:24; 1Co 1:31.

Love "does not behave indecently." It is not ill-mannered. It does not engage in indecent behavior, such as sexual abuses or shocking conduct. It is not rude, vulgar, discourteous, insolent, coarse, or disrespectful to anyone. A person who has love will avoid doing things that, in appearance or actions, disturb his Christian brothers. Paul instructed the congregation at Corinth: "Let all things take place decently and by arrangement." (1Co 14:40) Love will also prompt one to walk honorably in the view of others who are not Christian believers.—Ro 13:13; 1Th 4:12; 1Ti 3:7.

Love "does not look for its own interests." It follows the principle: "Let each one keep seeking, not his own advantage, but that of the other person." (1Co 10:24) Here is where concern for the everlasting welfare of others shows itself. This sincere concern for others is one of the strongest motivating forces in love as well as one of the most effective and beneficial in its results. The possessor of love does not demand that everything be done *his* way. Paul said: "To the weak I became weak, that I might gain the weak. I have become all things to people of all sorts, that I might by all means save some. But I do all things for the sake of the good news, that I may become a sharer of it with others." (1Co 9:22, 23) Neither does love demand its "rights"; it is more concerned with the spiritual welfare of the other person.—Ro 14: 13, 15.

Love "does not become provoked." It does not look for an occasion or an excuse for provocation. It is not moved to outbursts of anger, which is a work of the flesh. (Ga 5:19, 20) One having love is not easily offended by what others say or do. He is not afraid that his personal "dignity" may be injured.

Love "does not keep account of the injury." (Literally, it is not "reckoning the bad thing"; *Int.*) It does not consider itself to be injured and so lay up that injury as something 'on the books of account,' to be settled, or paid off, in due time, in the meantime permitting no relations between the injured and the injurer. That would be a vengeful spirit, condemned in the Bible. (Le 19:18; Ro 12: 19) Love will not impute evil motives to another but will be inclined to make allowances and give others the benefit of the doubt.—Ro 14:1, 5.

Love "does not rejoice over unrighteousness, but rejoices with the truth." Love rejoices with the truth even though it upsets previous beliefs held or statements made. It sticks with God's Word of truth. It always sides with the right, finding no pleasure in wrong, in lies, or in any form of injustice, no matter who the victim is, even if he is an enemy. However, if a thing is wrong or misleading, love does not fear to speak out in the interests of truth and of others. (Ga 2:11-14) Also, it prefers to suffer wrong rather than commit another wrong in an attempt to straighten out the matter. (Ro 12:17, 20) But if another person is properly corrected by one having authority, the loving person will not sentimentally side with the chastised one and find fault with the correction or the authorized one who did the correcting. Such an action would not be an expression of love for the individual. It might gain the favor of the corrected one, but it would harm rather than help him.

Love "bears all things." It is willing to endure, to suffer for righteousness' sake. A literal rendering is, "all things it is covering." (*Int*) A person having love will be slow to expose to others the one who wrongs him. If the offense is not too serious, he will overlook it. Otherwise, when the course recommended by Jesus at Matthew 18:15-17 is applicable, he will follow it. In such cases, if the other person asks forgiveness after the wrong is privately pointed out to him, and repairs the damage, the one having love will show that his forgiveness is real, that it has completely covered the matter, as God has.—Pr 10:12; 17:9; 1Pe 4:7, 8.

Love "believes all things." Love has faith in the things God has said in his Word of truth, even if outward appearances are against it and the unbelieving world scoffs. This love, especially toward God, is a recognition of his truthfulness, based on his record of faithfulness and reliability, just as we know and love a true, faithful friend and do not doubt when he tells us something for which we may not have proof. (Jos 23:14) Love believes all God says, though it may not be able to grasp it thoroughly, and it is willing to wait patiently until the matter is more fully explained or until getting a clear understanding. (1Co 13:9-12; 1Pe 1:10-13) Love also trusts in God's direction of the Christian congregation and his appointed servants and backs up their decisions based on God's Word. (1Ti 5:17; Heb 13:17) However, love is not gullible, for it follows the counsel of God's Word to "test the inspired expressions to see whether they originate with God," and it tests everything by the measuring rule of the Bible. (1Jo 4:1; Ac 17:11, 12) Love produces confidence in one's faithful Christian brothers; a Christian would not suspect them or disbelieve them unless there was absolute proof that they were wrong.—2Co 2:3; Ga 5:10; Phm 21.

Love "hopes all things." It has hope in all the things Jehovah has promised. (Ro 12:12; Heb 3:6) It continues to work, waiting patiently for Jehovah to bring fruitage, to make things grow. (1Co 3:7) A person having love will hope the best for his Christian brothers through any circumstances in which they might be, even though some may be weak in faith. He will realize that if Jehovah is patient with such weak ones, he should certainly adopt the same attitude. (2Pe 3:15) And he continues to assist those he is helping to learn the truth, hoping and waiting for them to be moved by God's spirit to serve him.

Love "endures all things." Love is required for the Christian to keep his integrity toward Jehovah God. Despite whatever the Devil may do to test the soundness of the Christian's devotion and faithfulness to God, love will endure in a way that holds the Christian true to God.—Ro 5:3-5; Mt 10:22.

"Love never fails." It will never come to an end or cease to exist. New knowledge and understanding may correct things we once believed; hope changes as the hoped-for things are realized and new things are hoped for, but love always remains in its fullness and continues to be built up stronger and stronger.—1Co 13:8-13.

"A Time to Love." Love is held back only from those whom Jehovah shows are unworthy of it, or from those set in a course of badness. Love is extended to all persons until they show they are haters of God. Then the time comes for love's expression toward them to end. Both Jehovah God and Jesus Christ love righteousness and hate lawlessness. (Ps 45:7; Heb 1:9) Those who intensely hate the true God are not persons toward whom love is to be expressed. Indeed, it would accomplish no good to continue exercising love toward such ones, for those who hate God will not respond to God's love. (Ps 139:21, 22; Isa 26:10) Therefore God properly hates them and has a time to act against them.—Ps 21:8, 9; Ec 3:1, 8.

Things Not to Be Loved. The apostle John writes: "Do not be loving either the world or the things in the world. If anyone loves the world, the love of the Father is not in him; because everything in the world—the desire of the flesh and the desire of the eyes and the showy display of one's means of life—does not originate with the Father, but originates with the world." (1Jo 2:15, 16) He says, later on, "the whole world is lying in the power of the wicked one." (1Jo 5:19) Accordingly, those who love God hate every wicked way.—Ps 101:3; 119:104, 128; Pr 8:13; 13:5.

While the Bible shows that a husband and wife should love each other and that this love includes the conjugal relationship (Pr 5:18, 19; 1Co 7:3-5), it points out the wrongness of the fleshly, worldly practice of sexual love toward another not one's spouse. (Pr 7:18, 19, 21-23) Another worldly thing is materialism, "love of money" (phi·lar·gy·ri'a, literally, "fondness of silver"; Int), which is a root of all sorts of injurious things.—1Ti 6:10; Heb 13:5.

Jesus Christ warned against seeking glory from men. He scathingly denounced the hypocritical religious leaders of the Jews who liked to pray standing in the synagogues and on the corners of the broad ways to be visible to men and who loved the prominent places at evening meals and the front seats in the synagogues. He pointed out that they had already received in full their reward, that which they loved and desired, namely, honor and glory from men; therefore no reward at all was due them from God. (Mt 6:5; 23:2, 5-7; Lu 11:43) The record reads: "Many even of the rulers actually put faith in [Jesus], but because of the Pharisees they would not confess him, in order not to be expelled from the synagogue; for they loved the glory of men more than even the glory of God."—Joh 12:42, 43; 5:44.

In speaking to his disciples, Jesus said: "He that is fond of [phi·lon'] his soul destroys it, but he that hates his soul in this world will safeguard it for everlasting life." (Joh 12:23-25) A person who prefers to protect his life now rather than to be willing to lay down his life as a follower of Christ will lose out on everlasting life, but one who considers life in this world as secondary, and who loves Jehovah and Christ and their righteousness above everything else, will receive everlasting life.

God hates liars, for they have no love of the truth. He declared to the apostle John in vision: "Outside [the holy city, New Jerusalem] are the dogs and those who practice spiritism and the fornicators and the murderers and the idolaters and everyone liking [phi·lon'] and carrying on a lie."—Re 22:15; 2Th 2:10-12.

One's Love Can Cool Off. Jesus Christ, in telling his disciples of the things ahead, indicated that the love (a·ga'pe) of many who professed belief in God would cool off. (Mt 24:3, 12) The apostle Paul said that, as a feature of the critical times to come, men would become "lovers of money." (2Ti 3:1, 2) It is evident, therefore, that a person can lose sight of right principles and that the proper love he once had can fade away. This emphasizes the importance of constant exercise and development of love by meditation on God's Word and by molding one's life according to His principles.—Eph 4:15, 22-24.

LOVE FEASTS.

The Bible does not describe these love feasts nor does it indicate how often they were held. (Jude 12) They were not commanded by the Lord Jesus Christ or his apostles, and it is apparent that they are not to be considered mandatory or permanent. Some say they were occasions when materially prosperous Christians held banquets to which their poor fellow believers were invited. Together, the fatherless, the widows, the rich, and the less fortunate shared a bountiful table in a spirit of brotherhood.

Tertullian, a writer of the second and third centuries, gives a description of the love feasts, recounting that the participants, before reclining to eat, offered prayer to God. They would eat and drink with moderation, only enough to satisfy hunger and thirst, remembering that even during the night they must worship God. Their conversation was as those who knew that the Lord was listening. Each sang a song, and the feast closed with prayer.—Apology, XXXIX, 16-18.

That these feasts were originally held with good intent is indicated by the word used to describe them—a·ga'pe. A·ga'pe is the Greek word used for the highest form of love, love based on principle. It is the kind of love that the Bible says "God is." (1Jo 4:8) It is listed as a fruit of the spirit at Galatians 5:22 and is described at length in 1 Corinthians 13:4-7.

Not the Lord's Evening Meal. There does not appear to be any basis for connecting such love feasts with the Lord's Evening Meal (Memorial), as some have done, saying that the love feasts took place either before or after the observance of the Memorial. The Lord's Evening Meal is an anniversary taking place yearly on the same day, the 14th day of the lunar month Nisan, whereas the love feasts seem to have taken place often and not necessarily on a regular schedule. After condemning abuses that arose in connection with bringing their suppers to the place where the Lord's Evening Meal was to be celebrated, Paul wrote: "Certainly you do have houses for eating and drinking, do you not? . . . If anyone is hungry, let him eat at home." (1Co 11:22, 34) This was an evening to be observed with seriousness and meditation on its significance and not an occasion for eating and drinking at the meeting place.

Neither are these love feasts the same as the "taking of meals" ("breaking of bread," *KJ*) mentioned at Acts 2:42, 46; 20:7. Bread in those times was usually made in thin cakes. Unleavened bread would be crisp as well. Bread was not cut, but broken, which gave rise to the phrase "breaking bread," with reference oftentimes to the partaking of an ordinary meal.—Ac 2:46, *KJ*, compare *NW*.

Misused by Some. As a literal meal, love feasts became subject to various abuses by those who did not have the proper spiritual outlook. Since they were not commanded by the Lord Jesus Christ or by his apostles but were only a custom, they were later discontinued. Jude's words indicate that some associated on these occasions with bad motives: "These are the rocks hidden below water in your love feasts while they feast with you, shepherds that feed themselves without fear." (Jude 12) Peter indicates the infiltration of evildoers and those teaching false doctrine among true Christians, saying: "They consider luxurious living in the daytime a pleasure. They are spots and blemishes, indulging with unrestrained delight in their deceptive teachings while feasting together with you." (2Pe 2:13) While Christians up to and including the present time have continued to have pleasurable fellowship and have helped one another materially as far as it is within their power, there is no basis for the revival of love feasts as a custom in the Christian congregation.—Jas 1:27; 2:15.

LOVING-KINDNESS. See KINDNESS.

LOYALTY.

In the Hebrew Scriptures, the adjective *cha·sidh'* is used of "someone loyal," or "one of loving-kindness." (Ps 18:25, ftn) The noun *che'-sedh* has reference to kindness but contains more than the thought of tender regard or kindness stemming from love, though it includes such traits. It is kindness that lovingly attaches itself to an object until its purpose in connection with that object is realized. Such is the sort of kindness that God expresses toward his servants and that they express toward him. It therefore comes into the field of loyalty, a righteous, devoted, holy loyalty, and is variously rendered "loving-kindness" and "loyal love."—Ge 20:13; 21:23; see KINDNESS.

In the Greek Scriptures the noun *ho·si·o'tes* and the adjective *ho'si·os* carry the thought of holiness, righteousness, reverence; being devout, pious; the careful observance of all duties toward God. It involves a right relationship with God.

There appear to be no English words that exactly express the full meaning of the Hebrew and Greek words, but "loyalty," including, as it does, the thought of devotion and faithfulness, when used in connection with God and his service, serves to give an approximation. The best way to determine the full meaning of the Bible terms in question is to examine their usage in the Bible.

Jehovah's Loyalty. Jehovah God the Most Holy One, who is devoted to righteousness and who exercises unbreakable loving-kindness toward those who serve him, deals in righteousness and trueness even with his enemies and is eminently dependable. It is said of him: "Great and wonderful are your works, Jehovah God, the Almighty. Righteous and true are your ways, King of eternity. Who will not really fear you, Jehovah, and glorify your name, because you alone are loyal?" (Re 15:3, 4) Because Jehovah's loyalty to righteousness and justice, as well as his love for his people, prompts him to take needed judicial action, an angel was moved to say: "You, the One who is and who was, the loyal One, are righteous, because you have rendered these decisions."—Re 16:5; compare Ps 145:17.

Jehovah is loyal to his covenants. (De 7:9) Because of his covenant with his friend Abraham, he exercised long-suffering and mercy for centuries toward the nation of Israel. (2Ki 13:23) Through his prophet Jeremiah he appealed to Israel: "'Do return, O renegade Israel,' is the utterance of Jehovah. 'I shall not have my face drop angrily upon you people, for I am loyal.'" (Jer 3:12) Those who are loyal to him can rely fully on him. David, in prayer, asked for God's help and said: "With someone loyal you will act in loyalty; with the faultless, mighty one you will deal faultlessly." (2Sa 22:26) In an appeal to the people, David asked them to turn away from what is bad and do what is good, "for," he said, "Jehovah is a lover of justice, and he will not leave his loyal ones. To time indefinite they will certainly be guarded." —Ps 37:27, 28.

Those who are loyal to Jehovah can count on his closeness and his help to the very end of their faithful course, and they can rest in full security, knowing that he will remember them no matter what situation arises. He guards their way. (Pr 2:8) He guards their lives or souls.—Ps 97:10.

Jesus Christ. Jesus Christ when on earth was greatly strengthened in the knowledge that God had caused to be foretold of him that, as God's chief "loyal one," his soul would not be left in Sheol. (Ps 16:10) On the day of Pentecost, 33 C.E., the apostle Peter applied this prophecy to Jesus, saying: "[David] saw beforehand and spoke concerning the resurrection of the Christ, that neither was he forsaken in Hades nor did his flesh see corruption. This Jesus God resurrected, of which fact we are all witnesses." (Ac 2:25-28, 31, 32; compare Ac 13:32-37.) *The Expositor's Greek Testament,* in a comment on Acts 2:27, says that the Hebrew word *cha·sidh'* (used in Ps 16:10) "denotes not only one who is godly and pious, but also one who is the object of Jehovah's loving-kindness." —Edited by W. R. Nicoll, 1967, Vol. II.

Loyalty Required by God. Jehovah requires loyalty of his servants. They must copy him. (Eph 5:1) The apostle Paul tells Christians that they "should put on the new personality which was created according to God's will in true righteousness and loyalty." (Eph 4:24) In recommending prayer in the congregation, he says: "Therefore I desire that in every place the men carry on prayer, lifting up loyal hands, apart from wrath and debates." (1Ti 2:8) Loyalty is an essential quality if a man is to qualify for appointment to serve as an overseer in the congregation of God. —Tit 1:8.

LUCIUS (Lu′cius) [from a Lat. root meaning "light; illumination"].

1. A man of Cyrene who was associated with the Antioch, Syria, congregation when Paul set out from there on his first missionary journey.—Ac 13:1-3.

2. A Christian "relative" of Paul who was with him in Corinth during his third missionary tour when the apostle wrote his letter to the Romans. Lucius joined in sending greetings to Christians in Rome.—Ro 16:21.

LUCK. See GOD OF GOOD LUCK, GOD OF DESTINY.

LUD, LUDIM (Lu′dim).

1. A son of Shem (Ge 10:22; 1Ch 1:17) whose descendants were identified by Josephus (and others) with the Lydians of SW Asia Minor. (*Jewish Antiquities,* I, 143, 144 [vi, 4]) Assyrian inscriptions of the seventh century B.C.E. referred to the Lydians as *Luddu.*

2. A descendant of Ham through Mizraim. (Ge 10:6, 13; 1Ch 1:8, 11) The people descended from this Hamitic Lud are evidently "the Ludim" noted for their proficiency with the bow who, together with Hamitic Put and Cush, were incorporated in Egyptian military forces. (Jer 46:8, 9; compare Eze 30:4, 5.) A similar allusion to the bow-drawing Lud at Isaiah 66:19 would seem to point to the Hamitic Lud, rather than to the Semitic one, as those included among nations far away from Israel. The Ludim who rendered military service for Tyre are more difficult to identify. (Eze 27:3, 10) Their being linked in the text with Put, however, may again point to the Hamitic Ludim.

The texts referred to would logically place the Hamitic Ludim in North Africa, but it is not possible to locate them more definitely. Some scholars situate them in the general vicinity of Libya, but they do so on the basis of an arbitrary alteration of the spelling of the name to Lub instead of Lud.

LUGGAGE. The Hebrew term *keli',* sometimes rendered "luggage" and "baggage," has a broad application. The basic sense of the Hebrew word is "something finished, accomplished, completed." —See ARMS, ARMOR.

An army camp, travelers, those gathering to an assembly away from their homes, and so forth, would have with them the necessary items as luggage, or baggage. (1Sa 10:21, 22; 17:22; 25:9-13) David established the rule in Israel that the men left behind to guard the baggage during military campaigns should share the spoils of victory equally with the fighting men.—1Sa 30:21-25.

Egypt was told to outfit herself for exile by making "baggage for exile," her fall to Babylon being certain, as foretold through the prophet Jeremiah. (Jer 46:13, 19) In broad daylight, as part of a symbolic enactment relating to Jerusalem's coming exile to Babylon, Ezekiel brought "luggage for exile" out of his house.—Eze 12:1-4, 7-11.

LUHITH (Lu′hith) [from a root meaning "tablet; plank"]. A place mentioned in prophecies of doom against Moab. (Isa 15:1, 5; Jer 48:5) Some scholars believe that Luhith was a Moabite city located at the top of an ascent. Identified by

Eusebius and Jerome with a place called Loueitha, Luhith has been linked with either Rujm Madinat er Ras, about 20 km (12 mi) SW of Karak, or nearby Khirbet Fas. Another view is that Luhith was not a city but merely the name of the ascent or slope to be used by the fleeing and weeping Moabite refugees.—Compare Nu 34:4.

LUKE. A physician and faithful companion of the apostle Paul. He was the writer of the Gospel of Luke and of the Acts of Apostles. That Luke was well educated is apparent from his writings. Also, his background as a doctor is noticeable in his use of medical terms.—Lu 4:38; Ac 28:8.

Luke did not speak of himself as an eyewitness of the events in the life of Christ that are recorded in his Gospel account. (Lu 1:2) So, he apparently became a believer sometime after Pentecost of 33 C.E.

In the book of Acts, Luke is referred to in an indirect way by the use of the pronouns "we" and "us." (Ac 16:10-17; 20:5–21:18; 27:1–28:16) He was with Paul at Troas on the apostle's second missionary tour and accompanied him from there to Philippi, where he may have remained until Paul's return on his third missionary journey. Luke accompanied Paul to Judea at the end of that missionary tour (Ac 21:7, 8, 15), and while the apostle was imprisoned for about two years at Caesarea, Luke probably wrote his Gospel account there (c. 56-58 C.E.). He accompanied Paul on his trip to Rome for trial. (Ac 27:1; 28:16) Since the book of Acts covers events from 33 C.E. down through two years of Paul's imprisonment in Rome but does not record the outcome of Paul's appeal to Caesar, Luke likely completed the book of Acts there by about 61 C.E.

Luke joined Paul in sending greetings to Christians at Colossae when Paul wrote to them from Rome (c. 60-61 C.E.), and the apostle identified him as "the beloved physician." (Col 4:14) In writing to Philemon from Rome (c. 60-61 C.E.), Paul included greetings from Luke (Lucas, *KJ*), referring to him as one of his "fellow workers." (Phm 24) That Luke stuck close to Paul and was with him shortly before the apostle's martyrdom is evident from Paul's remark, "Luke alone is with me."—2Ti 4:11.

Some hold that Luke was a Gentile, basing this mainly on Colossians 4:11, 14. Because Paul first mentioned "those circumcised" (Col 4:11) and later referred to Luke (Col 4:14), the implication is drawn that Luke was not of the circumcision and hence was not a Jew. But this is by no means conclusive. Romans 3:1, 2 states that God entrusted his inspired utterances to the Jews. Luke is one of those to whom such inspired utterances were entrusted.

The Scriptures likewise furnish no basis for identifying Luke with the Lucius mentioned at Acts 13:1 or Paul's 'relative' of the same name referred to at Romans 16:21.

LUKE, GOOD NEWS ACCORDING TO. An account primarily relating the events of Jesus' earthly ministry. Its purpose was to present an accurate record in logical order, verifying the certainty of what Theophilus had been taught orally. (Lu 1:3, 4) As suggested by its having a place in the Bible canon, this record was also to benefit many other persons, both Jews and non-Jews. Whereas topical arrangement appears to predominate at times, this Gospel follows a chronological order in general outline.

Writer and Time Written. Although not named therein, the physician Luke (Col 4:14) has generally been credited with the writership of this account. There is written evidence to this effect from as early as the second century C.E., the Gospel being attributed to Luke in the Muratorian Fragment (c. 170 C.E.). Certain aspects of this Gospel may also be viewed as pointing to a well-educated physician as its writer. The vocabulary found therein is more extensive than that of the other three Gospels combined. At times the descriptions of afflictions healed by Jesus are more specific than in the other accounts.—Compare Mt 8:14; Mr 1:30; Lu 4:38; Mt 8:2; Mr 1:40; Lu 5:12.

It was evidently before writing the book of Acts that Luke completed his Gospel. (Ac 1:1, 2) Since he had accompanied Paul to Jerusalem at the end of the apostle's third missionary journey (Ac 21:15-17), he would have been in a good position to trace accurately the things pertaining to Jesus Christ in the very land where the Son of God had carried out his activity. Following Paul's arrest at Jerusalem and during Paul's later imprisonment in Caesarea, Luke would have had many opportunities to interview eyewitnesses and to consult written records. So it is reasonable to conclude that the Gospel may have been written at Caesarea sometime during Paul's confinement there for about two years (c. 56-58 C.E.).—Ac 21:30-33; 23:26-35; 24:27.

Points of Uniqueness. As in the case of the three other Gospels, Luke's account provides abundant evidence that Jesus is indeed the Christ, the Son of God. It reveals Jesus to have been a man of prayer, one who relied fully on his heavenly Father. (Lu 3:21; 6:12-16; 11:1; 23:46) It contains numerous supplementary details, which, when combined with what is found in the three other Gospels, furnish a more complete picture of the events associated with Christ Jesus. Almost all of chapters 1 and 2 are without parallel in the other Gospels. At least six specific miracles and more than twice that number of illustrations are unique to the book. The miracles are: Jesus' causing some of his disciples to have a miraculous catch of fish (5:1-6), his raising a widow's son at Nain (7:11-15), as well as his healing a woman bent double (13:11-13), a man afflicted with drop-sy (14:1-4), ten lepers (17:12-14), and the ear of the high priest's slave (22:50, 51). Among the illustrations are: the two debtors (7:41-47), the neighborly Samaritan (10:30-35), the barren fig tree (13:6-9), the grand evening meal (14:16-24), the lost drachma coin (15:8, 9), the prodigal son (15:11-32), the unrighteous steward (16:1-8), the rich man and Lazarus (16:19-31), and the widow and the unrighteous judge (18:1-8).

HIGHLIGHTS OF LUKE

Luke's account of the life of Jesus, written to confirm the certainty of events surrounding the life of Christ and in a manner that would appeal to people of all nations

The second Gospel written; it was likely recorded between 56 and 58 C.E.

Events preceding Jesus' public ministry (1:1–4:13)

Gabriel announces in advance to Mary that she is to bear the Son of God; at Jesus' birth angels identify him as "Christ the Lord"

At 12 years of age, Jesus questions the teachers at the temple

At his baptism by John, holy spirit comes upon Jesus and a voice from heaven identifies Jesus as God's Son

Satan fails in repeated efforts to tempt Jesus

Jesus' early ministry, largely in Galilee (4:14–9:62)

In a synagogue in Nazareth, Jesus reads his commission from the scroll of Isaiah; hearers attempt to kill him

He teaches in a synagogue in Capernaum, expels a demon, and cures many who are sick

He is challenged on issues such as the forgiveness of sins and healing on the Sabbath

After praying all night, Jesus chooses his 12 apostles

He delivers the Sermon on the Mount

He heals an army officer's slave and resurrects a widow's son

Jesus tells the parables of the two debtors and the sower; he performs more miracles, including the resurrection of Jairus' daughter

The apostles are sent out to preach the Kingdom of God

Peter identifies Jesus as the Christ; soon after, he and two other apostles witness the transfiguration

Jesus' later ministry, largely in Judea and Perea (10:1–19:27)

Jesus sends out the 70 to preach

He tells the parable of the neighborly Samaritan

He teaches his disciples how to pray, then refutes the charge that he expels demons by means of Beelzebub

Jesus warns against materialism and urges disciples to seek God's Kingdom; he speaks of the little flock and the faithful steward

He heals a woman who is bent double and answers objections because this is done on the Sabbath

He shows that those who would be disciples must face up to what it involves

He relates parables, including the ones about the prodigal son and the rich man and Lazarus

Jesus warns his disciples about stumbling others; he illustrates the need for humility

He heals ten lepers, but only one, a Samaritan, returns to thank him

Jesus compares "the days of the Son of man" to the days of Noah and of Lot

He again stresses the need for humility—especially for the rich—then travels to Jericho, where Zacchaeus is converted

Using the parable of the minas, he shows that the Kingdom is not going to come at that time

Jesus' final public ministry, in and around Jerusalem (19:28–24:53)

Jesus rides into Jerusalem and is hailed by the people, but he weeps over the city and foretells its desolation

He ejects the money changers from the temple; then he is confronted with tricky questions about taxes and the resurrection

Foretelling the destruction of the temple and the fall of Jerusalem, Jesus speaks also of the end of the appointed times of the nations

He institutes the Memorial of his death, and afterward he is betrayed; when Peter strikes off the ear of the high priest's slave, Jesus heals the man

Arrested, Jesus is led to the house of the high priest, to the Sanhedrin, and to Pilate; then he is sent to Herod and finally returned to Pilate

Jesus is impaled; on the stake he speaks about Paradise to an evildoer hung with him; as he dies, darkness falls over the earth and the curtain of the sanctuary is rent down the middle

His body is buried, but within three days the resurrected Jesus appears to his followers

Finally, Jesus starts his ascent to heaven before their eyes

Chronological material appearing in this Gospel aids in determining when John the Baptizer and Jesus were born and when they began their respective ministries.—Lu 1:24-27; 2:1-7; 3:1, 2, 23; see REGISTRATION.

Authenticity. Indicative of the authenticity of Luke's Gospel and the harmony between it and other Bible books are the numerous Hebrew Scripture references it contains and the quotations made therein from the Hebrew Scriptures. (Compare Lu 2:22-24; Ex 13:2; Le 12:8; Lu 3:3-6; Isa 40:3-5; Lu 7:27; Mal 3:1; Lu 4:4, 8, 12; De 8:3; 6:13, 16; Lu 4:18, 19; Isa 61:1, 2.) Further testifying to the book's authenticity is the fulfillment of Jesus' prophecy concerning the destruction of Jerusalem and its temple.—Lu 19:41-44; 21:5, 6.

LUMINARY. A source of light; a lamp; a heavenly body from which the earth receives light.

The Genesis account relates that during the fourth creative "day," God caused luminaries to "come to be in the expanse of the heavens." (Ge 1: 14, 19) This does not indicate the coming into existence of light (Heb., *'ohr*) itself, since this is shown to have existed previously. (Ge 1:3) Nor does it state that the sun, moon, and stars were created at this point. The initial verse of the Bible states: "In the beginning God created the heavens and the earth." (Ge 1:1) Thus the heavens with their celestial bodies, including the sun, existed for an undetermined period of time prior to the processes and events stated as occurring during the six creative periods described in the following verses of the first chapter of Genesis.

It should be noted that, whereas Genesis 1:1 states that God "created" (Heb., *ba·ra'*) the heavens and the earth in the beginning, verses 16 and 17 state that, during the fourth creative "day," "God proceeded to *make* [Heb., a form of *'a·sah'*] the two great luminaries, the greater luminary for dominating the day and the lesser luminary for dominating the night, and also the stars. Thus God put them in the expanse of the heavens to shine upon the earth." The Hebrew word *'a·sah'*, often translated "make," can mean simply to establish (2Sa 7:11), appoint (De 15:1), form (Jer 18:4), or prepare (Ge 21:8).

Thus the record here states what the already existing sun, moon, and stars now became in relation to planet Earth. On the first "day" light (Heb., *'ohr*) evidently gradually penetrated the cloud layers still enveloping the earth and would have become visible to an earthly observer, had he been present. (Ge 1:3) On the fourth "day" things changed. The statement that "God put

them in the expanse of the heavens" on that day expresses the fact that God caused the *sources* of light (Heb., *ma·'ohr'*), namely, the sun, moon, and stars, to become discernible in the expanse. Their purpose was to "make a division between the day and the night" and to "serve as signs and for seasons and for days and years." In addition to being signs of God's existence and majesty, by their movements such luminaries enable man to mark accurately the natural seasons, days, and years.—Ge 1:14-18; Ps 74:16; 148:3.

The same Hebrew word (*ma·'ohr'*) is used with reference to the light-bearing equipment in the tabernacle, which employed lighted oil as the means for producing illumination. (Ex 25:6; 27: 20; 35:8, 14, 28; Le 24:2; Nu 4:9) At Proverbs 15:30 it is used figuratively in the expression "brightness of the eyes." Egypt is prophetically warned of a withdrawal of all light by Jehovah's darkening and beclouding all the "luminaries [form of *ma·'ohr'*] of light [*'ohr*] in the heavens." —Eze 32:2, 7, 8.

LUTE. The Hebrew word *sha·lish'* seems to be related to a root signifying "three." (Compare Ex 14:7, ftn.) Hence, the plural form *sha·li·shim'* at 1 Samuel 18:6 has been variously translated as "instruments of three strings" (*Ro*), "three-stringed instruments" (*Yg*), and as favored by some modern lexicons, "lutes" (*NW*). The context of this verse suggests a comparatively light musical instrument, for it was played by Israelite women as they sang and danced in celebration of the victories of King Saul and of David.—1Sa 18:6, 7.

LUZ [Almond Tree].

1. The earlier name of the town of Bethel, evidently given to it by the Canaanite inhabitants. Jacob applied the name Bethel (meaning "House of God") to the site where he received a dream containing a divine revelation; a place where Abraham had previously camped. (Ge 28:16-19; 35:6) Luz is identified with the ruins by the village of Beitin, about 17 km (11 mi) N of Jerusalem. It appears that the name Bethel eventually superseded that of Luz, at the latest by the time of the Israelite conquest of Canaan. (Jg 1:22) Because of the rendering of Joshua 16:2 in the *King James Version* and the *Revised Standard Version* which describes Ephraim's boundary as running "from Beth-el to Luz," some have assumed that these sites were distinct as separate towns. However, other modern translations here read "Beth-el-luz" (*JP*), "Bethel-luz" (*JB*), "Bethel (that is, Luz)" (*AT*), or "Bethel belonging to Luz" (*NW*). After chapter 1 of the book of Judges, the name Luz is no longer used.—See BETHEL No. 1.

The Hebrew word (*luz*) corresponding to the name of the town is also used at Genesis 30:37 with reference to the almond-tree staffs used by Jacob.

2. The name of a city built in "the land of the Hittites" by a man of Bethel (Luz) who cooperated with Israelite fighters of the house of Joseph in bringing about the fall of Bethel. Like Rahab and her family, he and his family were allowed to go unharmed. But, different from Rahab and perhaps indicating that the basis for his services rendered was not a genuine fear and appreciation of Jehovah the God of Israel, the man did not seek to associate himself with Israel, preferring to go to Hittite country and there build his city, which he named Luz, doubtless in memory of his hometown. The Bible does not dignify him by naming him as it does Rahab. (Jg 1:23-26) Some consider it likely that the name of the city at least is reflected in the ruins of el-Louaize, about 20 km (12 mi) ESE of Sidon.

LYCAONIA (Lyc·a·o′ni·a). A region in Asia Minor where the Lycaonian language was spoken. (Ac 14:6-11) The boundaries of Lycaonia fluctuated considerably throughout its history and are uncertain. Basically, in the period during which Lycaonia figured in the Bible record, it lay in the southern part of the Roman province of Galatia and was bounded by Pisidia and Phrygia on the W, Cappadocia on the E, and Cilicia on the S. This area consists of a treeless plain having limited water. Anciently, though, it was reasonably productive and furnished sufficient pasturage for a large number of sheep.

The apostle Paul visited Derbe and Lystra, two cities of Lycaonia, during the course of his first and second missionary journeys. He may also have stopped there on his third missionary tour as he traveled from "place to place through the country of Galatia."—Ac 14:6, 20, 21; 16:1; 18:23.

LYCIA (Ly′ci·a). A mountainous region on the SW coast of Asia Minor. To the NW of Lycia lay Caria; to the N, Phrygia and Pisidia; and to the NE, Pamphylia. The mountains in the territory of ancient Lycia are spurs of the Taurus Range. Particularly in the eastern half of the region, they rise almost directly from the coast. The river valleys, chief of which is that of the Xanthus (modern Koca), are fertile. Vegetation thrives on the hills, and the mountain slopes provide pasture for sheep.

Two Lycian cities, Patara and Myra, are specifically mentioned in connection with the apostle Paul's travels. But there is no record of his doing any preaching there.—Ac 21:1; 27:5.

LYDDA (Lyd′da). Lydda is identified with el-Ludd (modern Lod) in the Plain of Sharon about 18 km (11 mi) SE of Joppa. At Lydda, Peter healed paralyzed Aeneas. This miracle caused many in the vicinity to accept Christianity. (Ac 9:32-35, 38) Lydda is considered to be the same as Lod. —1Ch 8:12, see LOD.

LYDIA (Lyd′i·a). This woman and her household were among the first persons in Europe to accept Christianity as a result of the apostle Paul's activity at Philippi in about 50 C.E. Originally she lived at Thyatira, a city in Asia Minor known for its dyeing industry. Later, at Philippi in Macedonia, Lydia sold purple, either the dye or garments and fabrics colored therewith. It appears that she was the head of her household (this could include slaves and servants), and therefore, she was possibly widowed or single.—Ac 16:14, 15.

"A worshiper of God," Lydia probably was a Jewish proselyte. It may be that there were few Jews and no synagogue at Philippi so that on the Sabbath day she and other devout women assembled by a river outside the city. When the apostle Paul preached to these women, Lydia listened attentively. After being baptized along with her household, she entreated Paul and his companions to stay with her, saying: "If you men have judged me to be faithful to Jehovah, enter into my house." Such genuine offer of hospitality simply could not be refused. The writer of Acts, Paul's traveling companion Luke, adds: "She just made us come." —Ac 16:11-15.

Later, after Paul and Silas were released from prison, they again went to the home of Lydia. There they encouraged the brothers and then left Philippi.—Ac 16:36-40.

Perhaps at least partly because of Lydia's hospitality, Paul wrote to the Philippians: "I thank my God always upon every remembrance of you in every supplication of mine for all of you, as I offer my supplication with joy, because of the contribution you have made to the good news from the first day until this moment."—Php 1:3-5.

LYE. See LAUNDRYMAN.

LYSANIAS (Ly·sa′ni·as) [from a root meaning "loose; loosen"]. The district ruler, or tetrarch, of Abilene when John the Baptizer began his ministry (29 C.E.), during the 15th year of Tiberius Caesar's rule. (Lu 3:1) The Roman tetrarchy of Abilene had its capital at Abila, near Damascus of Syria. An inscription from the time of Tiberius Caesar found there commemorates a temple dedication by a freedman of "Lysanias the tetrarch." (*Corpus Inscriptionum Graecarum*, Vol. 3, No. 4521) Because Josephus refers to a Lysanias executed about 34 B.C.E. by Mark Antony at Cleopatra's instigation, some have charged Luke with inaccuracy. (*Jewish Antiquities*, XV, 92 [iv, 1]) However, Luke did not err, for the Lysanias he mentions is not the same person as the earlier Lysanias (the son of Ptolemy) who, before being executed, ruled, not Abilene, but nearby Chalcis, and who is not called a tetrarch.

LYSIAS. See CLAUDIUS LYSIAS.

LYSTRA (Lys'tra). A city of Lycaonia, a region in the south-central part of Asia Minor. Lystra has been identified with a mound to the N of Hatunsaray, situated in a fertile, well-watered area about 32 km (20 mi) SSW of Konya (Iconium).

It was to Lystra in the Roman province of Galatia that the apostle Paul and Barnabas came after being forced to leave Iconium because of an attempt to have them stoned. The city was then a Roman colony, having earlier been made such by Augustus. The native inhabitants, however, continued to speak the Lycaonian language. After Paul healed a man lame from birth, the crowds concluded that he and Barnabas were incarnated gods, Hermes and Zeus. Barely were they able to restrain the people from sacrificing to them. Later,

however, Jews from Iconium and Pisidian Antioch so stirred up the inhabitants of Lystra against Paul that they stoned him and dragged his body outside the city, imagining him to be dead. Afterward, when surrounded by fellow Christians, Paul got up, entered Lystra, and then, accompanied by Barnabas, left the next day for Derbe.—Ac 14:1, 5-20.

Subsequent to their activity at Derbe, Paul and Barnabas returned to Lystra, Iconium, and Antioch. They strengthened and encouraged the disciples associated with the newly established Christian congregations in those cities and appointed older men.—Ac 14:21-23.

Later, after the circumcision issue was settled by the apostles and older men of the Jerusalem congregation (c. 49 C.E.), Paul again visited Derbe and Lystra. The reference to this at Acts 16:1 could be understood to mean that the young man Timothy resided at either Lystra or nearby Derbe. But the evidence seems to favor Lystra. For while Derbe is not mentioned again in connection with Timothy, Acts 16:2 specifically states that Timothy "was well reported on by the brothers in Lystra and Iconium." (See also 2Ti 3:10, 11.) Timothy had made such good progress that Paul chose him as a traveling companion.—Ac 16:3.

When the apostle Paul visited various places in "the country of Galatia" on his third missionary tour, he may also have stopped at Lystra.—Ac 18:23.

M

MAACAH (Ma'a·cah). The name of several persons and of a kingdom.

[1-9: possibly from a root meaning "squeeze"]

1. A child born to Nahor, Abraham's brother, by his concubine Reumah. The child was evidently a male, as a kingdom and its inhabitants derived their name from this person.—Ge 22:23, 24; 2Sa 10:6, 8.

2. Wife of the Manassite Machir.—1Ch 7:14-16.

3. One of the concubines of Caleb (the son of Hezron) who bore several of his children.—1Ch 2:18, 48, 49.

4. The wife of Jeiel "the father of Gibeon."—1Ch 8:29; 9:35.

5. One of David's wives and the daughter of Talmai the king of Geshur. She was Absalom's mother.—2Sa 3:2, 3; 1Ch 3:1, 2.

6. Father or ancestor of Hanan, a mighty man of David's military forces.—1Ch 11:26, 43.

7. Father or ancestor of Shephatiah, a prince of Israel appointed leader of the Simeonites in David's organization of the king's service.—1Ch 27:1, 16, 22.

8. Father of Achish, king of Gath, to whom Shimei's slaves fled early in Solomon's reign. (1Ki 2:39) This Maacah may be the same person as Maoch of 1 Samuel 27:2.—See MAOCH.

9. Absalom's granddaughter, who was the most beloved wife of Judean King Rehoboam and the mother of King Abijah (Abijam). (2Ch 11:20-22; 1Ki 15:1, 2, 9, 10) She was regarded as "lady" in the kingdom, being queen mother, until her grandson, King Asa, in a restoration of true worship, removed her "because she had made a horrible idol to the sacred pole," or the Asherah. (1Ki 15:9-13; 2Ch 15:16) She is called Micaiah at 2 Chronicles 13:2.

10. A petty kingdom in existence in N Palestine at the time of the Israelite invasion, also called Maacath. The territory of the tribe of Manasseh evidently was to embrace this area, but the record shows that the Israelites did not dispossess the inhabitants of that land, so 'they kept dwelling in the midst of Israel.' (De 3:14; Jos 13:13) Generally associated with the neighboring kingdom of Geshur, Maacah appears to have been located to the N of that kingdom and to have bordered on the region of Bashan. (Jos 12:5) It is usually considered to have occupied the area running from the southern slopes of Mount Hermon down to the Hula Basin and from the Jordan River eastward to the edge of the Syrian Desert, or, basically, the northern part of the present district of Golan.

Maacah was an Aramaean (Syrian) kingdom, its people perhaps descending from Nahor's son of the same name. (Ge 22:24; 1Ch 19:6) When the Ammonites went to war against King David, they hired the services of the king of Maacah, along with others. The small number of troops provided by Maacah, as compared with those of the other allies, may indicate the small size of the Maacathite kingdom. (2Sa 10:6-8) Joab's victory over the Ammonites and their Syrian allies was followed up by a further victory over the Syrians by King David. (2Sa 10:13-19) From later accounts it seems likely that the kingdom of Maacah eventually came under the domination of the kingdom of Damascus.

MAACATH. See MAACAH No. 10.

MAACATHITE (Ma·ac'a·thite) [Of (Belonging to) Maacath [the town]]. Inhabitant of the Aramaean kingdom of Maacah (De 3:14; Jos 12:5; 13:13), one of these being Eshtemoa. (1Ch 4:19) It is suggested that Abel-beth-maacah (meaning "Watercourse of the House of Maacah"), a town in N Palestine, may have been so named because of its proximity to the region occupied by the Maacathites.—1Ki 15:20.

MAADAI (Ma·a·da'i) [shortened form of Maadiah]. An Israelite among "the sons of Bani" who had accepted foreign wives but sent them away in Ezra's day after the Jews returned from Babylonian exile.—Ezr 10:25, 34, 44.

MAADIAH (Ma·a·di'ah) [Jah Decks Himself]. A priest and head of a paternal house accompanying those returning from Babylon with Zerubbabel. (Ne 12:1, 5) Moadiah mentioned at Nehemiah 12:17 may be the same person.

MAAI (Ma'ai). A priest and musician who descended from Asaph and played an instrument of song at the inauguration of Jerusalem's wall in Nehemiah's time.—Ne 12:36.

MAARATH (Ma'a·rath) [Cave; or, Bare Field]. A town assigned to the tribe of Judah. (Jos 15:21, 59) A site near the village of Beit Ummar in the hill country of Judah, 11 km (7 mi) N of Hebron, is considered to be the probable location. Some suggest that Maarath may be a variant name of Maroth.—Mic 1:9, 12.

MAASAI (Ma'a·sai) [possibly a shortened form of Maaseiah]. A priest and descendant of Immer, who returned from Babylonian exile.—1Ch 9:10, 12.

MAASEIAH (Ma·a·sei'ah) [Work of Jehovah].

1. A Levite musician of the second division who played a stringed instrument when the ark of Jehovah was brought from the house of Obed-edom to Jerusalem in David's day.—1Ch 15:17-20, 25.

2. One of "the chiefs of hundreds" who entered a covenant with High Priest Jehoiada in connection with establishing Jehoash as Judah's rightful king in place of the usurper Athaliah.—2Ch 23:1.

3. An officer under the control of Hananiah, a prince of Judah's King Uzziah. He evidently had to do with the registration of Uzziah's military forces.—2Ch 26:11.

4. "The son of the king" (an offspring of Judean King Ahaz or possibly an official of royal descent) who was killed by the Ephraimite Zichri when Pekah of Israel invaded Judah.—2Ch 28:1, 6, 7.

5. The chief of the city of Jerusalem and one of the men King Josiah sent to repair the house of Jehovah.—2Ch 34:8.

6. A priest and the father of a certain Zephaniah, a contemporary of Jeremiah.—Jer 21:1; 29:25; 37:3.

7. Father of Zedekiah; a false prophet of Jeremiah's day.—Jer 29:21.

8. Son of Shallum the doorkeeper and evidently a Levite. A temple dining room was linked with his name.—Jer 35:4.

9. One of the sons of the priests, of the house of Jeshua, among those who had taken foreign wives but who sent them away in Ezra's time.—Ezr 10:18, 19, 44.

10. A priest "of the sons of Harim," among those who had married foreign wives but who sent them away in the time of Ezra.—Ezr 10:21, 44.

11. A priest "of the sons of Pashhur," also among those sending their foreign wives away. —Ezr 10:22, 44.

12. An Israelite "of the sons of Pahath-moab," among those dismissing their foreign wives.—Ezr 10:25, 30, 44.

13. Father or ancestor of a certain Azariah, one of the repairers of Jerusalem's wall under Nehemiah's supervision.—Ne 3:23.

14. A man who stood at Ezra's right hand when he read the Law to the Israelites assembled in Jerusalem.—Ne 8:2, 4.

15. A Levite who assisted the priest Ezra by explaining the Law to the Israelites gathered in Jerusalem.—Ne 8:7.

16. One of "the heads of the people" whose descendant, if not he himself, attested by seal the "trustworthy arrangement" of Nehemiah's time. —Ne 9:38; 10:1, 14, 25.

17. A man of Judah who resided in Jerusalem after the return from Babylonian exile. (Ne 11:4, 5) He may be identical with Asaiah of 1 Chronicles 9:5.—See ASAIAH No. 4.

18. A man of Benjamin who was an ancestor of Sallu, a resident of Jerusalem in Nehemiah's time. —Ne 11:7.

19. A priest who participated in the dedication of Jerusalem's wall in the time of Nehemiah.—Ne 12:41.

20. Another priest participating in the dedication of the wall of Jerusalem in Nehemiah's day. —Ne 12:42.

MAATH (Ma'ath). One of Jesus' ancestors listed in his genealogy as given by Luke.—Lu 3:23, 26.

MAAZ (Ma'az) [shortened form of Ahimaaz]. One of Judah's descendants through Jerahmeel and Ram.—1Ch 2:3, 25, 27.

MAAZIAH (Ma·a·zi'ah) [Jehovah Is a Stronghold].

1. A descendant of Aaron who was made head of the 24th course of priests in David's day.—1Ch 24:1, 18.

2. One of the priests, or a forefather of one, who attested by seal the "trustworthy arrangement" of Nehemiah's time.—Ne 9:38; 10:1, 8.

MACEDONIA, MACEDONIAN (Mac·e·do'-ni·a[n]). A region of SE Europe occupying the central part of what is now known as the Balkan Peninsula. It extended from the Adriatic Sea on the W to the Aegean Sea on the E, and lay N of Achaia. Although having numerous fertile plains, this is chiefly a mountainous area. Anciently, Mac-

edonia served as a vital link between the east and the west. The Roman-built *Via Egnatia* ran from Dyrrachium and Apollonia on the W coast of the peninsula to Neapolis on the E coast, and beyond.

The Macedonians were descendants of Japheth, perhaps through Kittim the son of Javan. (Ge 10:2, 4, 5) Although primarily associated with the island of Cyprus, the name Kittim was anciently also used to refer to other areas. The historian Josephus writes that the Hebrews called the islands and most of the seacoasts (apparently those in the Mediterranean area) *"Chethim."* (*Jewish Antiquities,* I, 128 [vi, 1]) This may account for Macedonia's being called "Cethim" in the Apocryphal book of First Maccabees (1:1 *Dy; Kx*) and provides a possible basis for considering the Macedonians to have been descendants of Kittim.

History. Macedonia attained prominence under the rule of Philip II. He was able to consolidate Macedonia and neighboring regions, and as a result of his victory in the Battle of Chaeronea (338 B.C.E.), Macedonia emerged supreme in relation to the majority of the Greek states. Subsequent to Philip's assassination, his son Alexander (the Great) ascended the throne. Two years later, Alexander commenced his extensive campaign of conquest. By the time of his death at Babylon (323 B.C.E.), Alexander, through his military victories, had built up an empire that extended as far E as India and included Mesopotamia, Syria, Palestine, Egypt, Asia Minor, Thrace, Macedonia, and Greece.—See Da 2:31-33, 39; 7:6; 8:1-7, 20, 21; ALEXANDER No. 1; BEASTS, SYMBOLIC; IMAGE.

When the empire was divided following Alexander's death, Antipater, who had been the regent of Macedonia while Alexander was warring in the east, retained his position. Before his death, Antipater entrusted the regency to Polyperchon instead of to his own son Cassander. Then followed political struggles that finally culminated in Cassander's being recognized as king of Macedonia. His son Alexander succeeded him but not long thereafter was killed by Demetrius Poliorcetes (son of Antigonus Cyclops, one of the generals of Alexander the Great). Again confusion set in. Finally, Antigonus Gonatas, son of Demetrius Poliorcetes, gained possession of the throne. Though driven from his kingdom twice, Antigonus recovered it each time, and Macedonia continued to be ruled by the Antigonids until coming under Roman administration. In the middle of the second century B.C.E., Macedonia became a Roman province. For a time during the first century C.E., it was joined with Achaia, to the S, and Moesia, to the N, to form an imperial province under the legate of Moesia. However, in 44 C.E. Macedonia again became a senatorial province under the jurisdiction of a Roman governor.—See GREECE, GREEKS.

Paul's Ministry. Macedonia was the first area in Europe to be visited by the apostle Paul on his second missionary journey. While at Troas in NW Asia Minor, Paul had a vision. "A certain Macedonian man was standing and entreating him and saying: 'Step over into Macedonia and help us.'" (Ac 16:8, 9) Paul responded to that vision and, with Luke, Timothy, and Silas (if not also other companions), left for Macedonia. After arriving at Neapolis (the port of Philippi in NE Macedonia), Paul went to Philippi and there declared the good news. (Ac 16:11-40) Luke, it appears, remained at Philippi when Paul, Silas, and Timothy journeyed through the Macedonian cities of Amphipolis (about 50 km [30 mi] WSW of Philippi) and Apollonia (about 50 km [30 mi] SW of Amphipolis). Next Paul witnessed in the Macedonian cities of Thessalonica (about 60 km [40 mi] WNW of Apollonia) and Beroea (about 80 km [50 mi] WSW of Thessalonica) respectively. (Ac 17:1-12) On account of threatened mob violence at Beroea, Paul was forced to depart from Macedonia. But he left Silas and Timothy at Beroea so that they might care for the new group of believers there. Silas and Timothy were to join him later. (Ac 17:13-15) Paul, concerned about the welfare of the newly formed congregation at Thessalonica, sent Timothy to encourage the brothers there. (1Th 3:1, 2) Perhaps Timothy joined Paul at Athens, in Achaia, and then was sent back to Thessalonica. But it seems more likely that Paul notified him at Beroea to make the trip to Thessalonica. The good report Timothy brought, upon returning, prompted Paul to write his first letter to the Thessalonians (1Th 3:6; Ac 18:5). His second letter to the Thessalonians followed not long thereafter.

During the course of his third missionary tour, Paul made plans to return to Macedonia. (1Co 16:5-8; 2Co 1:15, 16) Although Paul remained a while longer at Ephesus, he sent Timothy and Erastus to Macedonia in advance. (Ac 19:21, 22) It was after this that the Ephesian silversmith Demetrius stirred up a riot against Paul. The city was thrown into confusion, and as the Ephesians rushed into the theater, they seized and took along "Gaius and Aristarchus, Macedonians, traveling companions of Paul." (Ac 19:23-29) After the uproar subsided, Paul set out for Macedonia. (Ac 20:1) He apparently stopped at Troas. There he was disappointed at not meeting Titus, who had been sent to Corinth, in Achaia, to assist in the collection for the holy ones in Judea. (2Co 2:12, 13) Paul then proceeded to Macedonia, where he was joined by Titus and received word about the way the Corinthians had reacted to the apostle's first letter. (2Co 7:5-7) Subsequently Paul wrote his second letter to the Corinthians and later went south to Greece. He had intended to sail from Greece to Syria, but a plot against him by the Jews caused him to change his plans and to return to Macedonia instead. (Ac 20:2, 3) His traveling companions included three Macedonians, Sopater, Aristarchus, and Secundus.—Ac 20:4.

Although poor themselves, the Macedonian Christians were very generous. They expended themselves beyond their actual ability in making contributions for the needy brothers in Judea. (2Co 8:1-7; compare Ro 15:26, 27; 2Co 9:1-7.) Especially were the Philippians outstanding in supporting Paul's ministry. (2Co 11:8, 9; Php 4:15-17) Even while the apostle was imprisoned at Rome for the first time, the congregation at Philippi sent Epaphroditus to minister to Paul's needs. (Php 2:25-30; 4:18) And the Thessalonians manifested great faith and endurance and, therefore, came to be an example for "all the believers in Macedonia and in Achaia."—1Th 1:1-8; 4:9, 10.

It appears that Paul, after being released from imprisonment at Rome, revisited Macedonia and from there wrote the letter known as First Timothy. (1Ti 1:3) The letter to Titus may also have been written from Macedonia.

MACHBANNAI (Mach'ban·nai). A Gadite mighty man who joined David's band at "the place difficult to approach in the wilderness" and became one of the heads of his army.—1Ch 12:8-14.

MACHBENAH (Mach·be'nah). The name appears in a list of Caleb's descendants through his concubine Maacah, her son Sheva being called "the father of Machbenah and the father of Gibea." (1Ch 2:48, 49) Some commentators, noting that many of the names in this section also occur as names of towns, suggest that Machbenah may be the name of a town founded or 'fathered' by Sheva.

MACHI (Ma'chi) [possibly a shortened form of Machir]. A Gadite and the father of Geuel, one of the 12 Israelites sent to spy out Canaan.—Nu 13:1, 2, 15, 16.

MACHIR (Ma'chir) [from a root meaning "sell"].

1. The first-named son of Manasseh by his Syrian concubine. Machir founded the family of Machirites and is called "the father of Gilead." His wife was Maacah, and he had sons within Joseph's lifetime. (Ge 50:23; Nu 26:29; Jos 17:1; 1Ch 2:21, 23; 7:14-17) "The sons of Machir" captured the

region of Gilead, drove out the Amorites, and were given that district as an inheritance. (Nu 32:39, 40; De 3:15; Jos 13:31) Zelophehad and his daughters were of the Manassite family of Machir. (Nu 27:1; 36:1, 2; Jos 17:3) In the victory song of Deborah and Barak, "Machir" seems to be used poetically for the entire tribe of Manasseh.—Jg 5:1, 14.

2. Son of Ammiel (and resident of Lo-debar) with whom Jonathan's son Mephibosheth resided until David sent for him and made provision for his care. (2Sa 9:4-7, 13) Later, during Absalom's rebellion, Machir was among the persons who supplied King David and his associates with food and other provisions.—2Sa 17:27-29.

MACHIRITES (Ma'chir·ites) [Of (Belonging to) Machir]. A family of the tribe of Manasseh founded by his son Machir.—Nu 26:29; see MA-CHIR No. 1.

MACHNADEBAI (Mach·nad'e·bai). A postexilic Israelite among those who sent away their foreign wives in Ezra's day.—Ezr 10:25, 40, 44.

MACHPELAH (Mach·pe'lah) [from a root meaning "double," possibly indicating that the cave had a double entrance or two recesses or receptacles]. The name used with reference to a field and a cave in the vicinity of Hebron, purchased by Abraham from Ephron the Hittite for 400 silver shekels (c. $880). The cave served as a burial place for Abraham's wife Sarah and for at least five others: Abraham, Isaac, Rebekah, Jacob, and Leah. (Ge 23:14-19; 25:9; 49:30, 31; 50:13) The designation "Machpelah" evidently also applied to the surrounding area.—Ge 23:17.

The burial cave is generally identified with Me'arat HaMakhpela, located in modern Hebron beneath a Moslem mosque within an enclosure called Haram el-Khalil.

At Genesis 23:17 the Hebrew-language term indicating the position of the cave of Machpelah in relation to Mamre has been variously rendered "east of" (RS), "before" (AS), "near" (The Bible in Basic English), "opposite" (JB), and "in front of Mamre" (NW). If the traditional location of Mamre (er-Ramat el-Khalil) is correct, the rendering "east of Mamre" would not be appropriate, since this site lies about 3 km (2 mi) N of modern Hebron. The phrase "Mamre, that is to say, Hebron" (Ge 23:19), may mean that Mamre was in the district of Hebron.

MADAI (Ma'da·i). The third-listed son of Japheth. (Ge 10:2; 1Ch 1:5) He is believed to be the progenitor of the Medes. Because of this under-

standing, elsewhere in the Bible the Hebrew Madai is translated "Medes," or "Media," as at 2 Kings 17:6; 18:11; Esther 1:3; Isaiah 13:17; 21:2; and other texts. The Medes were also called Madaia in Assyro-Babylonian (Akkadian) and Mada in Old Persian. At some point in the past, they established themselves in the Iranian plateau region, settling primarily between the Elburz Mountains (S of the Caspian Sea) and the Zagros Mountains to the E of Assyria. The modern name Iran derives from the word "Aryan," a term used to refer to those of Japhetic descent.

MADMANNAH (Mad·man'nah) [from a root meaning "manure"].

1. This name appears in the list of descendants of Judah through Caleb. Caleb's concubine Maacah is stated to have borne "Shaaph the father of Madmannah." (1Ch 2:49) However, most scholars consider the term "father" to be used here in the sense of "founder" and consider Madmannah in this text to correspond with the town considered below, Shaaph being viewed as the founder or perhaps the rebuilder thereof after its capture. It may be noted that the names of Kiriath-jearim and Bethlehem appear in a similar context in the following verses.—1Ch 2:50, 54.

2. A city in the southern part of the territory of Judah. (Jos 15:21, 31) Although Umm Deimneh may preserve the ancient name, there are no suitable remains at the site. Scholars in recent times favor Khirbet Tatrit, about 15 km (9.5 mi) NE of Beer-sheba. A comparison of Joshua 15:31 with the parallel lists at Joshua 19:5 and 1 Chronicles 4:31 indicates it to be the same as Beth-marcaboth. Beth-marcaboth (meaning "House of the Chariots") may have been a secondary name of Madmannah.—See BETH-MARCABOTH.

MADMEN (Mad'men) [possibly from a root meaning "manure"]. Seemingly a place in Moab foretold to suffer calamity by sword. At Jeremiah 48:2, "You, too, O Madmen, should keep silent," translates the Hebrew phrase gam-madh·men' tid·dom'mi. Many scholars believe that the initial m in madh·men' ("Madmen") was inadvertently repeated from the previous word (gam). Without the initial m, the consonants of Madmen correspond to those of Dimon, and therefore, Madmen is often considered to be the same as Dimon (possibly, Dimna, about 10 km [6 mi] N of Karak). However, perhaps Madmen does not designate an actual location, since the renderings of the Greek Septuagint, Syriac Peshitta, and Latin Vulgate suggest that the ancient Hebrew text read, 'Yes, you [Moab] shall be utterly brought to silence.'

MADMENAH

MADMENAH (Mad·me′nah) [from a root meaning "manure"]. A site in the path of the Assyrian advance toward Jerusalem. (Isa 10:24, 31, 32) Today Madmenah's exact location is unknown. But some tentatively identify it with Shu′fat, about 4 km (2.5 mi) NNW of the Temple Mount in Jerusalem.

MADNESS

MADNESS. Mental derangement, either insanity or a condition of extreme rage or great folly. Various Hebrew and Greek words are employed in the Scriptures to denote such disorders of the mind, whether lasting or temporary. Some of these words seem to be associated with or derived from the weird and sometimes violent or sorrowful cries of persons afflicted with madness.

Madness befell boastful Babylonian King Nebuchadnezzar. In fulfillment of a prophetic dream explained by Daniel, this monarch was stricken with madness at a time of boasting. For seven years he was insane, "and vegetation he began to eat just like bulls." (Da 4:33) His reason gone, Nebuchadnezzar may have imagined that he was a beast, perhaps a bull. Regarding his mental derangement, a French medical dictionary states: "Lycanthropy . . . from [*ly′kos*], *lupus,* wolf; [*an′thro·pos*], *homo,* man. This name was given to the sickness of people who believe themselves to be changed into an animal, and who imitate the voice or cries, the shapes or manners of that animal. These individuals usually imagine themselves transformed into a wolf, a dog or a cat; sometimes also into a bull, as in the case of Nebuchadnezzar." (*Dictionnaire des sciences médicales, par une société de médicins et de chirurgiens,* Paris, 1818, Vol. 29, p. 246) At the end of the seven years, Jehovah restored Nebuchadnezzar's understanding to him.—Da 4:34-37.

Madness and Demon Possession. While not all persons afflicted with madness or insanity are possessed by the demons, logically persons possessed by the demons may be expected to manifest an unbalanced mental state. In the country of the Gerasenes, Jesus encountered a madman who was demon possessed. His haunt was among the tombs, and though he had often been bound with fetters and chains, "the chains were snapped apart by him and the fetters were actually smashed; and nobody had the strength to subdue him." Further, "continually, night and day, he was crying out in the tombs and in the mountains and slashing himself with stones." After Jesus cast out the demons, the man had a "sound mind." (Mr 5:1-17; Lu 8:26-39) However, Christians are kept safe from demon invasion that produces madness if they put on and keep on "the complete suit of armor from God."—Eph 6:10-17.

Feigned Madness. On one occasion, while he was outlawed by King Saul, David sought refuge with Achish the king of Gath. Upon discovering who he was, the Philistines suggested to Achish that David was a security risk, and David became afraid. Consequently, he disguised his sanity by acting insane. He "kept making cross marks on the doors of the gate and let his saliva run down upon his beard." Thinking David was crazy, Achish let him go with his life, as a harmless idiot. David was later inspired to write Psalm 34, in which he thanked Jehovah for blessing this strategy and delivering him.—1Sa 21:10–22:1.

Madness of Opposition to Jehovah. The prophet Balaam foolishly wanted to prophesy against Israel in order to receive money from King Balak of the Moabites, but Jehovah overruled and prevented his efforts. The apostle Peter wrote about Balaam that "a voiceless beast of burden, making utterance with the voice of a man, hindered the prophet's mad course." For Balaam's madness the apostle used the Greek word *pa·ra·phro·ni′a,* which has the thought of "being beside one's mind."—2Pe 2:15, 16; Nu 22:26-31.

Regarding the false prophets of Israel, the prophet Hosea wrote: "The prophet will be foolish, the man of inspired expression will be maddened on account of the abundance of your error, even animosity being abundant." (Ho 9:7) Jehovah brings madness to his opposers and those who reject his wisdom, identifying himself as "the One that makes diviners themselves act crazily," that is, by making their forecasts prove false. (Isa 44: 24, 25) Job said, concerning worldly judges, that Jehovah "makes judges themselves go crazy." —Job 12:17.

Paul compared men who resisted the truth and who tried to corrupt the Christian congregation to Jannes and Jambres, who resisted Moses. He assured: "They will make no further progress, for their madness will be very plain to all, even as the madness of those two men became."—2Ti 3:8, 9.

Madness From Oppression and Confusion. Among the dire consequences the Israelites would suffer for disobedience to Jehovah was being stricken with madness. As a result of the oppressive measures of their conquerors, they would become maddened, responding in an unreasoning way because of frustration. (De 28:28-34) Indeed, King Solomon stated that "mere oppression may make a wise one act crazy."—Ec 7:7.

In prophecy Babylonian King Nebuchadnezzar

was likened to the 'cup of the wine of Jehovah's rage.' This the nations would have to drink, and it would cause them to "shake back and forth and act like crazed men because of the sword that I [Jehovah] am sending among them." (Jer 25:15, 16) Later, in Babylon herself madness would be brought about, her idolaters having horrifying visions, "and because of their frightful visions they [would] keep acting crazy." (Jer 50:35-38) She, too, would have to drink the cup of Jehovah's rage. —Jer 51:6-8.

Extreme Rage. Madness, as used Biblically, can also denote extreme rage. On a sabbath day Jesus cured a man with a withered right hand. The observing scribes and Pharisees thereupon "became filled with madness, and they began to talk over with one another what they might do to Jesus." (Lu 6:6-11) To describe their state of mind, Luke used the Greek word *a·noi·a*, meaning, literally, "mindlessness" (the English word "paranoia" is related to this term). Paul evidently had in mind extreme rage or fury when he admitted that in persecuting Christians he had been "extremely mad against them."—Ac 26:11.

Contrasted With Wisdom. In the book of Ecclesiastes, the congregator reveals that he gave his heart "to knowing wisdom and to knowing madness." (Ec 1:17) His investigation did not restrict itself to considering wisdom but also took into account its opposite as manifested by men. (Ec 7:25) At Ecclesiastes 2:12, Solomon again reveals that he weighed wisdom, madness, and folly. In this way he could determine their contrast in value. He recognized inordinate frivolity as madness, saying, "I said to laughter: 'Insanity!'" for, as compared with wisdom, it was senseless, not producing real happiness.—Ec 2:2.

Commenting on the stupid one's condition of mind, Solomon said: "The start of the words of his mouth is foolishness, and the end afterward of his mouth is calamitous madness." (Ec 10:13) Foolishness may take the form of a trick, which can sometimes be so harmful to its victim that the player of the trick is likened to a madman armed with deadly weapons.—Pr 26:18, 19.

Some have no hope in the resurrection of the dead, thinking that death ends all for everyone. Giving evidence of their unbalanced outlook, they seek only to satisfy their fleshly inclinations and show no concern about doing God's will. Solomon also took note of them, saying: "Because there is one eventuality to all, the heart of the sons of men is also full of bad; and there is madness in their heart during their lifetime, and after it—to the dead ones!"—Ec 9:3.

Illustrative Use. The apostle Paul's authority and apostleship were challenged by some in Corinth whom he sarcastically termed "superfine apostles." (2Co 11:5) In order to bring the Corinthian congregation to their senses, Paul "boasted" about his credentials, his blessings and the things he had experienced in Jehovah's service, proving his claim. This boasting was contrary to the usual speech of a Christian, but Paul had to do it in this case. Hence he spoke of himself as though being 'out of his mind' and said of the so-called superfine apostles: "Are they ministers of Christ? I reply like a madman, I am more outstandingly one."—2Co 11:21-27.

MADON (Ma'don) [from a root verb meaning "judge"]. A royal Canaanite city that leagued itself with Hazor against the Israelites and was subsequently defeated. (Jos 11:1-12; 12:19) Madon is usually identified with Qarn Hattin (Horvat Qarne Hittim), about 8 km (5 mi) WNW of Tiberias. Khirbet Madin, about 1 km (0.6 mi) to the S, seems to preserve the ancient name. However, some question the identification because it is based solely on the similarity of the name of nearby Madin to the Biblical name.

MAGADAN (Mag'a·dan). An area near the Sea of Galilee to which Jesus withdrew after his miraculous feeding of about 4,000 men. (Mt 15:39; manuscripts of more recent date here read "Magdala.") Mark (8:10), according to the best Greek manuscripts, referred to the same territory as "Dalmanutha."—See DALMANUTHA.

No place called Magadan is today known in the region around the Sea of Galilee. However, some scholars believe that Magadan is the same as Magdala. Lending some support to this view is the fact that in Aramaic the letter *l* often replaces the *n* of Hebrew words. Thus Magadan could have been changed to Magdala. Others suggest that "Magdala" perhaps came to appear in more recent copies of the Greek text on account of an attempt to equate Magadan with modern Majdal.

Magdala (possibly Magadan) is considered to be Khirbet Majdal (Migdal), about 6 km (3.5 mi) NNW of Tiberias on the Sea of Galilee. Located near the fork formed by the road running along the Sea of Galilee from Tiberias and the one coming down from the western hills, this site occupies a strategic position. Ruins of a relatively modern tower found there indicate that Majdal once guarded the southern entrance to the Plain of Gennesaret. Both Majdal and Magdala (a form of the Hebrew *migh·dal'*) mean "Tower." This place is often suggested as the home of Mary Magdalene.

MAGBISH (Mag'bish). The name of either a person or a place. Among those returning from Babylonian exile were 156 "sons of Magbish." (Ezr 2:1, 30) Some tentatively identify Magbish with Khirbet el-Mahbiyeh, located about 5 km (3 mi) SW of Adullam.

MAGDALENE, MARY. See MARY No. 3.

MAGDIEL (Mag'di·el) [Choice Things of God]. A descendant of Esau, and one of the sheiks of Edom. (Ge 36:40-43; 1Ch 1:51, 54) Magdiel may have also been the name of a place and a tribe. —See TIMNA No. 3.

MAGGOT [Heb., *rim·mah'*; Gr., *sko'lex*]. The larva, or wormlike stage, of an insect just after leaving the egg. The term "maggot" is applied particularly to the fly larvae found in decaying vegetable or animal matter and in living tissues. The living or putrefying material provides heat for hatching the eggs and nourishment for the maggots.

Maggots have a legless, slender, segmented body that appears to be headless. However, with reference to the head, *The Smithsonian Series* (Vol. 5, p. 343) states: "The tapering end of the body is the head end, but the true head of the maggot is withdrawn entirely into the body. From the aperture where the head has disappeared, which serves the maggot as a mouth, two clawlike hooks project, and these hooks are both jaws and grasping organs to the maggot."

The Scriptures allude to the fact that maggots subsist on dead organic matter. (Job 7:5; 17:14; 21:26; 24:20; Isa 14:11) The miraculous manna, if saved by the Israelites until the morning of the next day, gave off a repulsive odor and developed worms or maggots, except the manna stored up on the sixth day and saved over for the Sabbath. (Ex 16:20, 24) In mentioning the "maggot" in connection with Gehenna, Jesus evidently was alluding to the dump outside the city of Jerusalem where fires consumed the refuse and where worms or maggots subsisted on decaying matter near, but not in, the fire.—Mr 9:48; compare Isa 66:24; see GEHENNA.

The word "maggot" was employed by Bildad to denote someone of little account.—Job 25:6.

MAGIC AND SORCERY. Secret arts and uncanny powers presumably used to accomplish things beyond what is natural—associated with spiritistic, occult powers.

"Black" magic is said to consist of spells, special curses, and "the evil eye" that bring harm to one's enemies. "White" magic, on the other hand, is said by its practicers to produce good results by breaking the spells and canceling the curses. Among some ancient peoples "black" magic was forbidden under penalty of death. The Bible, however, goes a step further and forbids every form of spiritistic magic. (Le 19:26; De 18:9-14) By the use of magic formulas, said to be obtained through supernatural knowledge and wisdom, the practitioner attempts to influence people and alter future events. In this respect magic differs from divination, which attempts only to discover future events rather than influence or change them.—See DIVINATION.

Much of the concept of magic-working sorcery is based on the belief that evil spirits can be induced either to leave or to enter a person, that they can be tricked and deceived, and that they can be captured or trapped in a piece of wood or a clay image. For example, it is claimed that by making magic paths of honey or other agreeable things, the demons can be led around at the will of the magician.

All such notions naturally gave rise to a crafty class of magic-practicing priests, who exercised great power over the lives of the people, extorting large payments from those under their influence on the pretense of possessing supernatural powers over and beyond those of the demons. The people believed that these professional sorcerers could invoke the demons to obey but that the demons had no power over the sorcerers.

These spiritistic practices, so-called sciences, were developed and used by the ancient Chaldeans of Babylonia. Isaiah, in the eighth century B.C.E., tells us that Babylon of his day was rife with sorceries of all sorts. (Isa 47:12-15) More than a century later, in the days of Daniel, the magic-practicing priests were still a part of the Babylonian court. (Da 1:20; 2:2, 10, 27; 4:7; 5:11) This expression "magic-practicing priests" is a literal and explicit translation of the Hebrew.

The Babylonians had a great fear of physically deformed persons called warlocks and witches, in the belief that they were dispensers of "black" magic. The priests, on the other hand, were said to be masters of "white" magic. They believed that the same incantation that made a sick man well if spoken by a priest would kill the man if uttered by a warlock or witch.

It is possible that when people scattered around the earth because of the confusion of languages at Babel, they took with them some concept of such magical arts. (Ge 11:8, 9) Today millions practice the magic of mantra, that is, the mystic formula, hymn, or spellbinding prayer of popular Hinduism. Magic-practicing priests, witch doctors, medicine men, and sorcerers of all sorts are found in many places the world over, as they were among the Egyptians of the 18th century B.C.E., in the days of Joseph. (Ge 41:8, 24) Over two centuries after Joseph was sold into slavery, the magic-practicing priests of Egypt seemingly duplicated to an extent the first two miracles performed by Moses. (Ex 7:11, 22; 8:7) But they were powerless when it came to producing gnats, having to admit that it was "the finger of God!" They were likewise helpless in preventing the plague of boils from afflicting themselves.—Ex 8:18, 19; 9:11.

Condemned by the Bible. The Bible is singularly different from the writings of other ancient people in that its references to uncanny powers and magical arts are all condemnatory. Nowhere does it recommend "white" magic to cancel spells of "black" magic. Rather, it urges faith, prayer, and trust in Jehovah as the protection against unseen "wicked spirit forces" and all their related activities, including magical influences. (Eph 6:11-18) In the Psalms the righteous pray for deliverance from evil; Jesus taught us to pray for deliverance "from the wicked one." (Mt 6:13) The Talmud and the Koran, on the other hand, give way to superstition and fear. The Apocryphal book of Tobit contains absurd passages of magic-working sorcery.—Tobit 6:5, 8, 9, 19; 8:2, 3; 11:8-15; 12:3; see APOCRYPHA (Tobit).

The nation of Israel was, therefore, unlike its contemporaries in this respect, and in order that it might remain so, Jehovah gave his people some very explicit laws concerning those who were intimate with the occult powers. "You must not preserve a sorceress alive." (Ex 22:18) "You must not practice magic." "As for a man or woman in whom there proves to be a mediumistic spirit or spirit of prediction, they should be put to death without fail." (Le 19:26; 20:27) "There should not be found in you . . . a practicer of magic or anyone who looks for omens or a sorcerer, or one who binds others with a spell or anyone who consults a spirit medium."—De 18:10-14.

Jehovah's prophet also declared that God would cut off all those who indulged in sorceries. (Mic 5:12) Certain individuals such as Saul, Jezebel, and Manasseh, who forsook Jehovah and turned to sorceries of one kind or another, are examples of the past not to be copied.—1Sa 28:7; 2Ki 9:22; 2Ch 33:1, 2, 6.

The Christian Greek Scriptures also tell of the prevalence of sorcerers throughout the Roman Empire in the days of Jesus and the apostles. On the island of Cyprus, there was such a one named Bar-Jesus, whom Paul denounced as "full of every sort of fraud and every sort of villainy, . . . son of the Devil." (Ac 13:6-11) There were others, however, such as Simon of Samaria who gave up their magic-working practices and embraced Christianity. (Ac 8:5, 9-13) On one occasion in Ephesus, "quite a number of those who practiced magical arts brought their books together and burned them up before everybody. And they calculated together the prices of them and found them worth fifty thousand pieces of silver [if denarii, $37,200]." (Ac 19:18, 19) Writing to those in Galatia, the apostle Paul included spiritistic occultism among "the works of the flesh," warning them "that those who practice such things will not inherit God's kingdom." (Ga 5:19-21) Outside that glorious Kingdom will be all those who persist in these Babylonish practices. (Re 21:8; 22:15) Together with Babylon the Great, so notorious for misleading the nations by her sorceries, they will all be destroyed.—Re 18:23; see POWER, POWERFUL WORKS (Responsible use of power).

MAGISTRATE. Under the government of Babylon, police magistrates were civil officers in the jurisdictional districts who were learned in the law and exercised limited judicial authority. They were among the officials gathered to bow to Nebuchadnezzar's image of gold.—Da 3:2, 3.

In Roman colonies, the administration of government was in the hands of civil magistrates, generally known in Latin as *duumviri*. There could be 3, 4, usually 5, or even 10 or 12 making up the magisterial board. These had the duties of keeping order, administering finances, trying and judging law violators, and ordering the execution of punishment. Sometimes their names and titles appear on coins issued by a city. Constables, or lictors, were assigned to them to carry out their orders. —See CONSTABLE.

The civil magistrates in the Roman colony of Philippi (Ac 16:12), without a trial, had Paul and Silas put into stocks. The next day, hearing that they were Roman citizens, the magistrates sent constables to release them. But Paul, in order to give public and legal vindication to the good news that he preached, demanded that the magistrates personally release them. The magistrates, fearing trouble with Rome over flogging Roman citizens, entreated Paul and Silas and released them.—Ac 16:19-39.

MAGOG (Ma′gog).

1. A son of Japheth and grandson of Noah. His name appears among the family heads from

whom the initial national groups were dispersed about the earth following the Flood.—Ge 10:1, 2, 5; 1Ch 1:5.

2. A name that occurs in Ezekiel's prophecy concerning the stormlike attack by "Gog of the land of Magog" against Jehovah's regathered people. It appears to be used by the prophet to indicate a land or region in "the remotest parts of the north," out of which Gog's host comes forth, his plundering forces described as "riding on horses, a great congregation, even a numerous military force" employing sword and bow.—Eze 38:2-4, 8, 9, 13-16; 39:1-3, 6.

From the time of the Jewish historian Josephus, it has been suggested that "the land of Magog" related to the Scythian tribes found in NE Europe and Central Asia. (*Jewish Antiquities*, I, 123 [vi, 1]) Classical writers of Greek and Roman times described the Scythians as northern barbarians, rapacious and warlike, equipped with large cavalry forces, well armored, and skilled with the bow. While the name Scythian may originally have been derived from "Ashkenaz," another descendant of Japheth (Ge 10:2, 3), the 1959 edition of the *Encyclopædia Britannica* (Vol. 20, p. 235) states that "throughout classical literature Scythia generally meant all regions to the north and northeast of the Black sea, and a Scythian (*Skuthes*) any barbarian coming from those parts." Other reference works likewise show that the term "Scythian" was used rather flexibly to embrace generally the nomadic tribes N of the Caucasus (the region between the Black and Caspian Seas), similar to the modern use of the term "Tartar." Hence *The New Schaff-Herzog Encyclopedia of Religious Knowledge* comments: "The name 'Scythians' was among the ancients an elastic appellation, and so was the Hebrew '*Magog*.'" —Edited by S. Jackson, 1956, Vol. V, p. 14.

Symbolic Use. The fact that the definite location of "the land of Magog" is left uncertain and indeterminate to us in the Bible (as well as in secular history), along with the prophet's reference to "the final part of the years" (Eze 38:8), and the fact that the described invasion is not known to have taken place literally upon Israel, provide the basis for viewing the prophecy concerning Magog as relating to a future time in the Biblical 'time of the end.' Because of this, many commentators see in it a forecast of the final attack of the world powers upon the Kingdom of God, and they see the land of Magog as representing "the world as hostile to God's people and kingdom."—*Funk and Wagnalls New Standard Bible Dictionary*, 1936, p. 307.

Thus, the land of Magog clearly has a symbolic significance. The fact that the term "Scythian," with which Magog is usually associated, came to be used as a synonym for that which is brutal and degraded would logically seem to point to a fallen state or position of debasement, analogous to the position assigned to Satan and his angels following the war in heaven and from which debased position he wrathfully wages "war with the remaining ones of [the woman's] seed," as described at Revelation 12:7-17.—See GOG No. 2.

3. A term used at Revelation 20:8 in relation to events to occur at the close of the Thousand Year Reign of Christ Jesus and subsequent to the loosing of Satan from the abyss. Instead of referring to a particular land or location, "Gog and Magog" here is used to describe those on earth who yield to the released Adversary's influence and rebel against God's rule as expressed through "the holy ones and the beloved city."—Re 20:3, 7-10.

MAGPIASH (Mag′pi·ash). One of the heads of the people whose descendant, if not he himself, attested by seal the "trustworthy arrangement" of Nehemiah's day.—Ne 9:38; 10:1, 14, 20.

MAHALALEEL. See MAHALALEL No. 1.

MAHALALEL (Ma·hal′a·lel) [possibly, Praise of God].

1. A descendant of Seth through Enosh and Kenan; hence Seth's great-grandson. Mahalalel lived 895 years. (Ge 5:6-17; 1Ch 1:1, 2) In Luke's genealogy of Jesus, he is referred to by the name Mahalaleel.—Lu 3:37, 38.

2. A descendant of Judah through Perez and the ancestor of Athaiah, a resident of Jerusalem after the return from Babylonian exile.—Ne 11:4.

MAHALATH, I (Ma′ha·lath).

1. Ishmael's daughter, the sister of Nebaioth and one of the women Esau took as a wife. (Ge 28:9) She is possibly the same person as the Basemath of Genesis 36:3.

2. A granddaughter of David through his son Jerimoth. She became one of the wives of Rehoboam.—2Ch 11:18.

MAHALATH, II (Ma′ha·lath). Probably a musical term, perhaps one of a technical nature, found in the superscriptions of Psalms 53 and 88. Some believe that this term may be related to a Hebrew root verb meaning "grow weak; fall sick," thereby suggesting a gloomy and melancholy tune. This would harmonize with the somewhat somber content of the two songs, particularly that of Psalm 88.

MAHANAIM

MAHANAIM (Ma·ha·na′im) [Two Camps]. A site E of the Jordan where Jacob, after parting from Laban, encountered a company of angels. Jacob then called the place "Mahanaim." (Ge 32:1, 2) The meaning of the name ("Two Camps") may allude to "the camp of God," as represented by his angels, and to the camp of Jacob. Apparently sometime later a city was built on the site. In the 15th century B.C.E., this city was first assigned to the Gadites and then to the Levite Merarites.—Jos 13:24, 26; 21:34, 38.

While David ruled from Hebron, Mahanaim served as the capital for the rival kingdom of Saul's son and successor Ish-bosheth. This suggests that it was fortified and occupied a strategic position. (2Sa 2:8-11, 29) Evidently in this city Ish-bosheth was assassinated. (2Sa 4:5-7) Later David, fleeing from his rebellious son Absalom, came to Gilead where he was kindly received at Mahanaim. He remained there at the request of his supporters and did not share in the battle that completely defeated Absalom's attempt to seize the throne. (2Sa 17:24–18:16; 19:32; 1Ki 2:8) During the reign of David's son Solomon, Mahanaim was under the jurisdiction of the deputy Ahinadab.—1Ki 4:7, 14.

At The Song of Solomon 6:13 "the dance of two camps" may also be rendered "the dance of Mahanaim" (*AS*) or "the Mahanaim dance." (*AT*) Perhaps the reference is to dancing associated with a certain festival that was held at Mahanaim. —Compare Jg 21:19, 21.

The exact location of Mahanaim is uncertain, but it was E of the Jordan and evidently N of the Jabbok. (2Sa 2:29; Ge 31:21; 32:2, 22) Some suggest Khirbet Mahneh (or, Mihna), about 19 km (12 mi) N of the Jabbok and about the same distance E of the Jordan, but many feel that it is too far N of the Jabbok. Yohanan Aharoni identifies Mahanaim with Tell edh-Dhahab el-Gharbi, on the N bank of the Jabbok, about 12 km (7.5 mi) E of the Jordan.—*The Land of the Bible,* translated and edited by A. Rainey, 1979, pp. 314, 439.

MAHANEH-DAN

MAHANEH-DAN (Ma′ha·neh-dan) [Camp of Dan]. A place once described as lying "between Zorah and Eshtaol" (Jg 13:25) and another time as being located W of Kiriath-jearim. (Jg 18:11, 12) Some believe that these are two different sites, since the suggested locations for Eshtaol and Zorah are a number of miles SW of Kiriath-jearim. In any event, the location(s) of Mahaneh-dan is unknown. Its name means "Camp of Dan" and, therefore, perhaps simply denoted a temporary settlement or a campsite and understandably could have applied to more than one place.

MAHARAI

MAHARAI (Ma′ha·rai) [from a root meaning "hurry; hasten"]. A mighty man of David's military forces and a Netophathite. (2Sa 23:8, 28; 1Ch 11:26, 30) He was a descendant of Zerah and was later put in charge of the division of 24,000 ministering to the king during the tenth month.—1Ch 27:1, 13.

MAHATH

MAHATH (Ma′hath) [possibly from a root meaning "terrify"].

1. A Kohathite Levite and ancestor of Samuel and Heman the singer at the house of Jehovah. —1Ch 6:31-35.

2. One of the Kohathite Levites who aided in cleansing the temple in King Hezekiah's day. (2Ch 29:12, 15, 16) Evidently the same person was made a commissioner under Conaniah and Shimei in charge of "the contribution and the tenth and the holy things" at the temple.—2Ch 31:12, 13.

MAHAVITE

MAHAVITE (Ma′ha·vite). A designation applied to Eliel, one of the mighty men of David's military forces. (1Ch 11:26, 46) The term may have been used to distinguish this person from the Eliel of 1 Chronicles 11:47.

MAHAZIOTH

MAHAZIOTH (Ma·ha′zi·oth). A Kohathite Levite and last mentioned of the 14 sons of Heman. Mahazioth became head of the 23rd service group of temple musicians as organized by David.—1Ch 25:4-6, 8, 9, 30.

MAHER-SHALAL-HASH-BAZ

MAHER-SHALAL-HASH-BAZ (Ma′her-shal′al-hash-baz) [Hurry, O Spoil! He Has Made Haste to the Plunder; or, Hurrying to the Spoil, He Has Made Haste to the Plunder]. The name given to Isaiah's second son at Jehovah's direction.

Jehovah commanded Isaiah to write these prophetic words on a large tablet and have it attested to by reliable witnesses. Thereafter, he instructed the prophet to give this same expression as a name to his newborn son, declaring that before the child could say, "My father!" and "My mother!" the king of Assyria would subjugate Judah's enemies—Damascus and Samaria. (Isa 8:1-4) The prophetic meaning of this name given to Isaiah's second son was fulfilled within the designated time period. During the reign of Israel's King Pekah, the Assyrian monarch Tiglath-pileser III invaded Israel, took many cities, plundered the land, and carried numerous inhabitants into captivity. Thereafter, Pekah was murdered. (2Ki 15:29, 30) The king of Assyria also captured Syria's capital city Damascus, took its people into exile, and put Syrian King Rezin to death. (2Ki 16:9) In this way both of these kings who had conspired against Judah met their end. Later, in

740 B.C.E., the Assyrians overthrew Samaria, removing the apostate Israelites from that city and from the rest of the domain of the northern kingdom of Israel. (2Ki 17:1-6) Thus, this boy born to Isaiah by his wife (whom he terms "the prophetess") proved to be in Israel a truthful and reliable 'sign and miracle' from Jehovah.—Isa 8:3, 18.

MAHLAH (Mah′lah) [from a root meaning "grow weak; fall sick"].

1. One of the daughters of Zelophehad of the tribe of Manasseh. Mahlah and her sisters requested their father's inheritance, since he had no sons but only five daughters. Moses inquired of Jehovah, who ruled that the daughters of Zelophehad should receive it. (Nu 26:28-33; 27:1-11) A subsequent order of Jehovah through Moses required Mahlah and the other daughters of Zelophehad to marry within the tribe of Manasseh, to prevent the inheritance from passing to another tribe. Accordingly, Mahlah and her sisters "became the wives of the sons of their father's brothers." (Nu 36:1-6, 10-12) This judicial decision established a precedent as to inheritance. (Nu 36:7-9) They later presented themselves before Eleazar the priest and Joshua, cited Jehovah's command, and were given "an inheritance in the midst of the brothers of their father."—Jos 17:3, 4.

2. A descendant of Manasseh whose mother was Hammolecheth. It is not stated whether this was a son or a daughter.—1Ch 7:17, 18.

MAHLI (Mah′li) [possibly from a root meaning "grow weak; fall sick"].

1. Levi's grandson, a son of Merari and brother of Mushi. (Ex 6:16, 19; 1Ch 6:19, 29; 24:26) Mahli was the father of Eleazar and Kish and the family head of the Mahlites. (Nu 3:20, 33; 1Ch 23:21; 24:28, 29) His descendant Sherebiah, referred to as "a man of discretion from the sons of Mahli," returned to Jerusalem with Ezra.—Ezr 8:18.

2. A Levite, the son of Mushi, and hence the nephew of Merari's son Mahli.—1Ch 6:47; 23:23; 24:26, 30.

MAHLITES (Mah′lites) [Of (Belonging to) Mahli]. Levites who were descendants of Merari's son Mahli.—Nu 3:17, 20, 33; 26:58.

MAHLON (Mah′lon) [possibly from a root meaning "grow weak; fall sick"]. Son of Elimelech and Naomi. During a famine in the days of the Judges, he moved with his parents from Bethlehem in Judah to Moab. There Mahlon married the Moabitess Ruth, but he died childless. (Ru 1:1-5; 4:10) Ruth returned to Judah with her mother-in-law and, complying with the law of levirate mar-

riage, married Boaz. (Ru 4:9, 10; De 25:5, 6) The resulting family line produced David and led to Jesus Christ.—Ru 4:22; Mt 1:5, 6, 16.

MAHOL (Ma′hol) [from a root meaning "dance; whirl"; or, possibly from a root meaning "play the flute"]. One whose sons' wisdom, though great, was not equal to King Solomon's. (1Ki 4:31) Some view the designation "sons of Mahol" to mean an association of musicians or dancers.—Compare Ps 150:4, where the same Hebrew word is rendered "circle dance."

MAHSEIAH (Mah·sei′ah) [Jah Is a Refuge]. Ancestor of Jeremiah's associate Baruch and of Seraiah the quartermaster.—Jer 32:12; 51:59.

MAIDEN. See VIRGIN.

MAKAZ (Ma′kaz) [possibly from a root meaning "abhor"]. A place under the jurisdiction of one of Solomon's 12 deputies. (1Ki 4:7, 9) Makaz is tentatively identified with Khirbet el-Mukheizin, about 5 km (3 mi) NW of Ekron.

MAKHELOTH (Mak·he′loth) [Congregated Throngs]. One of Israel's wilderness encampments. (Nu 33:25, 26) Location, unidentified.

MAKKEDAH (Mak·ke′dah). A royal Canaanite city in the Shephelah. It was in the cave of Makkedah that the five kings who had allied themselves against the Gibeonites hid and were then temporarily trapped until their execution. Thereafter this cave became their common tomb, and the Israelite army under Joshua captured the city of Makkedah and devoted it to destruction. At the time of the division of the Promised Land, Makkedah was granted to the tribe of Judah.—Jos 10:5-29; 12:7, 8, 16; 15:20, 33, 41.

The exact site of Makkedah is uncertain. It has been tentatively identified with Khirbet el-Kheishum, about 4 km (2.5 mi) NNE of Azekah. Extensive ruins and nearby caves mark the site.

MAKTESH (Mak′tesh) [A Mortar]. Apparently a section of Jerusalem near the Fish Gate and the second quarter. At the time of Judah's calamity, the inhabitants of Maktesh were foretold to howl, since commercial activities would cease there.—Zep 1:1, 2, 10, 11.

The Hebrew word *makh·tesh′* refers to "a mortar" (Pr 27:22) or "a mortar-shaped hollow" (Jg 15:19), and therefore, some translations use "Mortar" instead of "Maktesh" as a proper name. (*AT, JB, RS*) The Targum identifies Maktesh with the Kidron Valley, the deep ravine along Jerusalem's eastern wall. But this valley is not in the vicinity of the more westerly "Fish Gate" and the "second quarter." For this reason Maktesh is generally thought to denote a part of the Central (Tyropoeon) Valley, perhaps its upper portion.

MALACHI (Mal'a·chi). A Hebrew prophet and Bible writer. (Mal 1:1) The Scriptures furnish no information as to his ancestry and personal life. What is known about him is revealed in the book bearing his name. He is therein shown to have been a man of great zeal for the name and worship of Jehovah.

MALACHI, BOOK OF. The final book of the Hebrew Scriptures in modern English Bibles. In the traditional Jewish canon, it is placed last among the writings of the so-called minor prophets but before the Writings (Hagiographa). It constitutes a pronouncement of Jehovah regarding Israel by means of Malachi.—Mal 1:1.

Circumstances in Malachi's Time. At the time Malachi prophesied, a deplorable situation existed among the priests. Contrary to the Law, they were accepting lame, blind, and sick animals for sacrifice on Jehovah's altar. (Mal 1:8; Le 22:19; De 15:21) They failed to give proper direction and instruction to the people, causing many to stumble. (Mal 2:7, 8) When judging matters, they showed partiality. (2:9) All of this had a bad effect on the Israelites in general, causing them to view Jehovah's service as being of little value. (3:14, 15) This is apparent from the fact that the Israelites did not support the temple by paying their tithes. So far had they fallen from their devotion to Jehovah that apparently they were divorcing their wives to marry women worshiping false gods. Also, sorcery, adultery, lying, fraud, and oppression came to exist among the Israelites. (2:11, 14-16; 3:5, 8-10) For this reason Jehovah gave advance warning of his coming to his temple for judgment. (3:1-6) At the same time he encouraged wrongdoers to repent, saying: "Return to me, and I will return to you."—3:7.

Time of Composition. Internal evidence provides a basis for dating the completion of the book of Malachi. It was written after the Babylonian exile, for the Israelites were under the administration of a governor. Worship was carried on at the temple, indicating that it had been rebuilt. (Mal 1:7, 8; 2:3, 13; 3:8-10) This points to a period later than that of Haggai (520 B.C.E.) and Zechariah (520-518 B.C.E.), as these prophets were active in urging the Israelites to complete the temple. (Ezr 5:1, 2; 6:14, 15) Israel's neglect of true worship and its failure to adhere to God's law appear to fit conditions existing when Nehemiah again arrived at Jerusalem sometime after the 32nd year of King Artaxerxes (c. 443 B.C.E.). (Compare Mal 1:6-8; 2:7, 8, 11, 14-16; Ne 13:6-31.) Therefore, like the book of Nehemiah, the book of Malachi may well have been committed to writing after 443 B.C.E.

Harmony With Other Bible Books. This book is in full agreement with the rest of the Scriptures. The apostle Paul quoted from Malachi 1:2, 3 when illustrating that God's choosing depends, "not upon the one wishing nor upon the one running, but upon God, who has mercy." (Ro 9:10-16) Jehovah is identified as the Creator (Mal 2:10; compare Ps 100:3; Isa 43:1; Ac 17:24-26) and as a just, merciful, and unchangeable God who does not leave deliberate wrongdoing unpunished. (Mal 2:2, 3, 17; 3:5-7, 17, 18; 4:1; compare Ex 34:6, 7; Le 26:14-17; Ne 9:17; Jas 1:17.) The importance of God's name is stressed. (Mal 1:5, 11, 14; 4:2; compare De 28:58, 59; Ps 35:27; Mic 5:4.) And encouragement is given to remember the Law of Moses.—Mal 4:4.

The book also directed Israel's attention to the coming of the Messiah and to the day of Jehovah. While it is pointed out that Jehovah would send forth the one called "my messenger," this one would be only the forerunner of the still greater "messenger of the covenant" who would accompany Jehovah. (Mal 3:1) The inspired accounts of Matthew (11:10-14; 17:10-13), Mark (9:11-13), and Luke (1:16, 17, 76) combine to identify Jesus' forerunner John the Baptizer as the "messenger" and the "Elijah" initially meant at Malachi 3:1 and 4:5, 6.

MALCAM (Mal'cam) [Their King].

1. A Benjamite and a son of Shaharaim by his wife Hodesh.—1Ch 8:1, 8, 9.

2. The principal idol god of the Ammonites. (2Sa 12:30; 1Ch 20:1, 2; Jer 49:1, 3) Possibly the same as Milcom, Molech, and Moloch. (1Ki 11:5, 7; Ac 7:43) The name Malcam in the Masoretic text differs from Milcom, "the disgusting thing of the Ammonites," only in the vowel pointing of the Hebrew. (1Ki 11:5) Contrary to the instruction given at Joshua 23:7, the Jews began making sworn oaths by Malcam. (Zep 1:5) It must be determined from context when the Hebrew should be rendered as the name of the god and when as "their king."—Am 1:15; see MOLECH.

MALCHIAH. See MALCHIJAH No. 3.

MALCHIEL (Mal'chi·el) [God Is King; or, My King Is God]. Grandson of Asher and a son of Beriah. (Ge 46:17) He is called "the father of Birzaith" (1Ch 7:31) and was a family head in Israel. —Nu 26:45.

HIGHLIGHTS OF MALACHI

A pronouncement emphasizing accountability to Jehovah God when his requirements are disregarded

Written by the prophet Malachi, evidently some 95 years after the first Jewish exiles returned from Babylon

Jehovah loved Israel, but they despise his name (1:1-14)

Jehovah loved his people just as he loved Jacob, though he hated Esau

Nevertheless, Israel's priests despise God's name, accepting lame and sick animals for sacrifice; they would not give animals like that to a human governor

Priests and people are censured for failure to keep Jehovah's ways (2:1-17)

The priests have departed from God's way, causing many "to stumble in the law," and thus have "ruined the covenant of Levi"

There has been a marrying of foreign wives, and some have dealt treacherously with the wives of their youth by divorcing them

Israelites have wearied God by claiming that he approves of those doing bad

The true Lord will judge and refine his people (3:1-18)

Jehovah will come to the temple with the messenger of the covenant; he will refine and cleanse the Levites, and Judah's gift offering will please Jehovah

Sorcerers, adulterers, those swearing falsely, defrauders, and oppressors will experience a speedy judgment

Bring the whole tenth part into Jehovah's storehouse and thus receive a flood of blessings

A book of remembrance will be written for those fearing Jehovah; His people will discern the distinction between the righteous and the wicked

The coming of the great and fear-inspiring day of Jehovah (4:1-6)

Jehovah's day will bring the complete destruction of the wicked, while 'the sun of righteousness will shine forth' to those fearing God's name

That day will be preceded by a restoration work, to be accomplished by the prophet Elijah

---

MALCHIELITES (Mal'chi·el·ites) [Of (Belonging to) Malchiel]. A family of Asherites that descended from Malchiel.—Nu 26:44, 45.

MALCHIJAH (Mal·chi'jah) [My King Is Jehovah].

1. A Levite who descended from Gershom and who was an ancestor of the Levite musician Asaph.—1Ch 6:39-43.

2. Descendant of Aaron and head of the 5th of the 24 divisions of priests organized by David. —1Ch 24:1, 9.

3. A priest and the father of Pashhur.—1Ch 9:12; Ne 11:12; Jer 21:1; 38:1.

4. "The son of the king" into whose cistern Jeremiah was thrown. (Jer 38:6) In this instance the expression "the son of the king" may denote, not that he was an offspring of the king, but that he was closely connected with the royal household or was an official of royal descent.—See JERAHMEEL No. 3.

5. An Israelite "of the sons of Parosh" among those accepting foreign wives but dismissing them in Ezra's day.—Ezr 10:25, 44.

6. Another Israelite "of the sons of Parosh" among those sending their foreign wives away. Ezr 10:25, 44) The Greek *Septuagint* reads "Hashabiah" instead of "Malchijah" here.

7. A man of Israel "of the sons of Harim" who was among those sending away foreign wives and sons in Ezra's time.—Ezr 10:31, 44.

8. An Israelite, "the son of Harim." Along with Hasshub, he repaired a section of Jerusalem's wall and the Tower of the Bake Ovens after the return from Babylonian exile. (Ne 3:11) He may be the same person as No. 7.

9. Son of Rechab and prince of the district of Beth-haccherem who repaired the Gate of the Ash-heaps during Nehemiah's governorship.—Ne 3:14.

10. Member of the goldsmith guild who repaired part of Jerusalem's wall in Nehemiah's day. —Ne 3:31.

11. A priest who stood at Ezra's left hand when the copyist read the Law before the Israelites in reestablished Jerusalem.—Ne 8:4.

12. One of the priests, or the forefather of one, who attested by seal the "trustworthy arrangement" during Nehemiah's governorship.—Ne 9:38–10:3.

13. A priest who participated in the inauguration ceremonies for Jerusalem's wall as rebuilt under Nehemiah's supervision. (Ne 12:40-42) He may be the same person as No. 11.

MALCHIRAM (Mal·chi'ram) [My King Is High (Exalted)]. One of the sons of King Jeconiah (Jehoiachin) as a prisoner in Babylon.—1Ch 3:17, 18.

MALCHI-SHUA (Mal'chi-shu'a) [My King [Hears My] Cry for Help]. One of King Saul's sons. (1Sa 14:49; 1Ch 8:33; 9:39) He was struck down in battle by the Philistines at Mount Gilboa (1Sa 31:2;

1Ch 10:2), and his corpse (along with those of his brothers Jonathan and Abinadab and that of his father Saul) was fastened by the Philistines on the wall of Beth-shan. However, valiant men of Israel retrieved the bodies, burned them in Jabesh, and buried their bones there.—1Sa 31:8-13.

MALCHUS (Mal′chus) [from a Heb. root meaning "king"]. The high priest's slave who accompanied Judas Iscariot and the crowd to Gethsemane, where Christ was arrested. Peter struck off Malchus' right ear with a sword (Joh 18:10; Mt 26:51; Mr 14:47), but Jesus miraculously healed it. (Lu 22:50, 51) Another slave of the high priest Caiaphas, a relative of Malchus, later recognized Peter, and this led to the apostle's third denial of Christ. —Joh 18:26, 27.

MALEDICTION. Literally, a speaking ill, or evil, against someone, and hence, the opposite of a benediction, or a blessing. The Hebrew word *qelalah′* basically refers to such a malediction and is regularly contrasted with "blessing" in numerous texts. (Ge 27:12, 13; De 11:26-29; Zec 8:13) It is derived from the root verb *qa·lal′*, which literally means "be light"; but, when used in a figurative sense, means "call down evil upon," "treat with contempt." (Ex 18:22; Le 20:9; 2Sa 19:43) This is the word David used when he told Michal he would make himself even more "lightly esteemed" than what she had accused him of doing. (2Sa 6:20-22) Jehovah God used it after the Flood in saying that he would never again "call down evil upon the ground on man's account."—Ge 8:21.

Purpose of Divine Maledictions. One purpose of divine maledictions is to make clear who are and who are not God's approved servants, since the maledictions manifest God's disapproval, even as his blessings manifest his approval. So, in promising Abraham his blessing, Jehovah also stated that "him that calls down evil [a participial form of *qa·lal′*] upon you I shall curse." (Ge 12:3) When the object of the malediction is thus left anonymous, the malediction also serves as a warning guide and a protection for those who wish to gain or retain God's favor. The Mosaic Law specified numerous blessings and maledictions, all of which would result from the application of the Law's statutes and ordinances. (De 28:1, 2, 15) Prior to entry into the Promised Land, Moses emphasized the fact that the nation, as individuals and as a collective group, must choose between the blessing and the malediction and that this they would do by either obedience or disobedience. (De 30:19, 20) Joshua, in essence, repeated this protective exhortation and warning within

the Promised Land. (Compare Jos 8:32-35; 24:14, 15.) Individuals could, therefore, endeavor to avoid coming under the announced maledictions.

The malediction also certifies that there can be no trifling with or despising of God's principles and announced purposes. High Priest Eli became the object of a specific malediction because of weakly allowing his sons to go unrebuked, even though they were "calling down evil upon God." (1Sa 3:13) Jehovah told him the rule that "those honoring me I shall honor, and those despising me will be of little account [from the root form *qalal′*]." (1Sa 2:30) Just recompense for wrongdoing thus accompanies God's malediction. This may be immediate, as in the case of the jeering delinquents upon whom Elisha called down evil in the name of Jehovah (2Ki 2:24), or it may be reserved for a later time, as when God informed King Josiah concerning the calamity due to come on Judah. (2Ki 22:19, 20) Jehovah warned the nation of Israel that violation of his laws would bring inescapable difficulties, saying: "All these maledictions will certainly come upon you and *pursue* you and *overtake* you until you have been annihilated, because you did not listen to the voice of Jehovah your God by keeping his commandments and his statutes that he commanded you." (De 28:45) Although he foretold their desolation and exile in the plainest of terms, they refused to give heed, and thus Jerusalem became "a malediction to all the nations of the earth."—Jer 26:6; 24:9; De 29:27.

Setting Aside of Maledictions. A malediction can be set aside or canceled by Jehovah, but only where his just requirements are properly satisfied. This appears to be the case with the original malediction on the earth that was evidently terminated by the Flood that cleansed the globe of wickedness. (Ge 8:21) Failure to keep the Law covenant brought a malediction on all the nation of Israel, even on those who conscientiously (though imperfectly) tried to keep its terms. The apostle Paul shows that it was for this reason that Christ Jesus died in the manner in which he did —upon a torture stake. (Ga 3:10-13) Thereby Jesus, though he had perfectly observed the Law himself, took upon himself the curse that resulted from the malediction of the Law and that rested on all those under that Law. Deuteronomy 21:23 states: "Because something accursed [literally, a malediction] of God is the one hung up [upon a stake]." Jesus, by being nailed to the stake as a criminal, sentenced (though unjustly) by the Jewish priestly court, in effect became "a curse." Thereafter, when Jesus presented the value of his sacrifice in heaven, the Law was canceled by God.

In accepting the sacrifice, God figuratively nailed the Law to the stake, and the curse accompanying that Law was legally removed. (Col 2:14) Because Jesus' body was viewed as being a malediction, and also to fulfill the Law's requirement so that the Sabbath might not be profaned, the Jews were anxious that Jesus' corpse and those of the malefactors be removed from their stakes before the day ended.—De 21:23; Joh 19:31.

What determines the effectiveness of a malediction?

While individuals may pronounce maledictions, their validity is entirely dependent on God, his principles, and his purposes. It was in vain that Goliath "called down evil upon David by his [false] gods." (1Sa 17:43) Jehovah changed Balaam's proposed malediction into a blessing. (De 23:4, 5; Jos 24:9, 10) Because David recognized that only Jehovah can make a malediction effective, he rejected Abishai's angry request to be allowed to go and 'take off the head' of Shimei, who was abusively calling down evil on David. David said: "Let him alone that he may call down evil, for Jehovah has said so to him! Perhaps Jehovah will see with his eye, and Jehovah will actually restore to me goodness instead of his malediction this day." (2Sa 16:5-12; compare Ps 109:17, 18, 28.) God's Word specifically condemns the calling down of evil on one's parents (Ex 21:17; Le 20:9; Pr 20:20), on God (Ex 22:28; Le 24:11, 14, 15, 23), or on the king (Ec 10:20), and it exposes those who bless with their mouths while "inside themselves they call down evil."—Ps 62:4.

As God's spokesman, Christ Jesus while on earth, in effect, pronounced maledictions on the religious guides and Pharisees for their willful opposition to God's purpose. (Mt 23:13-33) The apostle Peter evidently 'called down evil' upon Ananias and Sapphira for playing false to God, resulting in their immediate death. (Ac 5:1-11) The apostle Paul did somewhat similarly with the false prophet Elymas, the sorcerer, whom he called a "son of the Devil" and an "enemy of everything righteous," and who, thereafter, became temporarily blind. (Ac 13:6-12) These actions had a salutary effect on those witnessing them. Such apostolic powers, however, did not give authority, or license, to others to pronounce maledictions. James warns against Christians' improperly using the tongue for cursing men.—Jas 3:9-12; compare Ps 109:17, 18 with Col 3:8-10.

Whereas history records that in postapostolic times and down through the centuries religious organizations have published many "anathemas" and "interdicts" against individuals, cities, and nations, it also shows that the agent employed to make such malediction effective has invariably been, not the power of God, but the earthly power of a church or of the secular state. In contrast, at Psalm 37:3-9, 22 we are counseled to wait on Jehovah, since "those being blessed by him will themselves possess the earth, but those upon whom evil is called by him will be cut off." Such "cutting-off" is included in the malediction Jesus pronounces on the cursed "goat" class of his prophetic parable at Matthew 25:31-46. In connection with the "new heavens and a new earth," evil is also prophesied to be called down on sinners.—Isa 65:17, 20; see CURSE.

MALLOTHI (Mal·lo′thi) [from a root meaning "make signs; utter"]. A Kohathite Levite and one of the 14 sons of the singer Heman. (1Ch 25:4, 5) The family served as musicians under the direction of their father Heman. When David organized the divisions of the Levites to serve in turns at the house of Jehovah, the 19th lot fell to Mallothi, who assumed the headship of that division of 12 musicians.—1Ch 25:6, 26.

MALLOWS [Heb., ′o·roth′ or ′oh·roth′]. The dwarf mallow is a creeping plant having nearly round, somewhat lobed, saw-edged leaves with long leafstalks. Its flowers are over 1 cm (0.5 in.) across and vary in color from pale blue to white. The flat and circular mucilaginous fruits are commonly called cheeses.

"Mallows" translates the Hebrew word ′o·roth′ (2Ki 4:39; Isa 26:19), considered to be the plural of ′oh·rah′, "light." (Es 8:16; Ps 139:12) According to L. Koehler and W. Baumgartner's *Lexicon in Veteris Testamenti Libros* (Leiden, 1958, p. 90), ′o·roth′ denotes the dwarf mallow (*Malva rotundifolia*). This identification is based on the fact that this plant is very sensitive to light, hence perhaps the Hebrew designation meaning "light-[herbs]." Also, its fruit is edible, thus harmonizing with 2 Kings 4:39.—PICTURE, Vol. 1, p. 543.

MALLUCH (Mal′luch) [from a root meaning "reign as king"; or, "king"].

1. A Merarite Levite and a forefather of the Levitical singer Ethan.—1Ch 6:44-47.

2. One of the priests accompanying Zerubbabel when the Jews returned from Babylonian exile. —Ne 12:1, 2, 7.

3. An Israelite "of the sons of Bani" among those who had accepted foreign wives but who sent them away in the days of Ezra.—Ezr 10:29, 44.

4. An Israelite "of the sons of Harim" among those who had taken foreign wives but who dismissed them in Ezra's time.—Ezr 10:31, 32, 44.

5. One of the priests, or a forefather of one, attesting by seal the "trustworthy arrangement" made in Nehemiah's day.—Ne 9:38–10:4.

6. An Israelite, one of the heads of the people, whose descendant, if not he himself, attested the "trustworthy arrangement" made in the time of Nehemiah.—Ne 9:38; 10:1, 14, 27.

MALLUCHI (Mal'lu·chi). A priestly family whose representative served in the days of High Priest Joiakim, and in the days of Ezra and Governor Nehemiah.—Ne 12:12, 14, 26.

The name Malluchi is in the Masoretic text with the kere, or marginal notation, that it should be read as "Melicu," which latter form is found in the *King James Version*. The Greek *Septuagint* reads "Malluch," which some scholars think was the original form. These scholars suggest (but there is no way of proving it) that the adding of *i* (*yohdh* [·] in Hebrew) at the end of the name came about when the first letter of the following word was unintentionally repeated in manuscript copying.

MALTA (Mal'ta). An island in the Mediterranean lying about 100 km (60 mi) S of Sicily and having an area of about 246 sq km (95 sq mi). It was at Malta that the apostle Paul was shipwrecked, and there he remained for three months. During this time he healed Publius' father and others afflicted with sicknesses.—Ac 28:1, 7-9, 11.

In the past some associated the Greek word rendered "Malta" (*Me·li'te*) with Mljet (or, Italian Meleda) off the coast of Yugoslavia, because anciently this island was called Melita. But tradition and the evidence of Scripture point to Malta as the place where Paul experienced shipwreck. The designation "sea of Adria," where the boat was said to be as it approached Malta, came to include the waters of the Mediterranean E of Sicily and W of Crete, and therefore, it could be said that Malta was bounded by this sea.—Ac 27:27.

Paul's Shipwreck. Sometime after Atonement Day (in September or October) the ship on which Paul was traveling as a prisoner left the Cretan harbor of Fair Havens and was seized by a tempestuous wind (Euroaquilo), apparently from the ENE. It drove the ship away from the coast of Crete to Cauda, and the mariners feared being run aground on the "Syrtis," the quicksands along the shores of northern Africa. (Ac 27:8, 9, 13-17) An ENE wind could not have caused the vessel to drift toward Mljet, about 1,000 km (600 mi) NNW of Cauda. Evidently the boat, after drifting some two

weeks, neared Malta, about 870 km (540 mi) WNW of Cauda.—Ac 27:33; see EUROAQUILO.

What is today called St. Paul's Bay, situated on the NE side of Malta, could have been reached on a WNW course without previously touching any other part of the island of Malta. Perhaps when their trained ears heard breakers dashing against rocky Koura Head, which juts out into the Mediterranean from the eastern side of St. Paul's Bay, the sailors began to suspect that they were approaching land. The depths of "twenty fathoms" and "fifteen fathoms" (a fathom equals 1.8 m; 6 ft) ascertained by them basically correspond to soundings made in the mid-19th century in the St. Paul's Bay area.—Ac 27:27, 28.

Possibly because of being familiar with another of Malta's harbors, the mariners did not recognize the land as Malta even in daylight. The island's largest and best-known harbor is at Valletta, 13 km (8 mi) SE of St. Paul's Bay.—Ac 27:39.

Along the western side of St. Paul's Bay, there are two inlets. Probably at one of these, the sailors hoped to "beach the boat" but were unsuccessful, the reason for the failure (according to the literal Greek text) being their 'having fallen around into a place of two seas.' This may mean that the ship struck "a place where two seas met" (*AS*) or "a shoal washed on each side by the sea." (*NW*) Or, the vessel was caught between crosscurrents and ran aground. (Compare *JB, NE*.) The ship's bow became immovably stuck, perhaps in the mud and clay that lie three fathoms below the surface in parts of St. Paul's Bay, while the stern was broken in pieces by the waves.—Ac 27:39-41.

Paul's experience in Malta. At this time the soldiers determined to kill Paul and the other prisoners. This may have been because of the strict Roman military discipline that held guards accountable for the escape of prisoners under their control. (Compare Ac 12:19; 16:27.) Since the army officer (centurion) restrained the soldiers on account of Paul, all those aboard, numbering 276, survived the shipwreck, either by swimming ashore or getting safely to land upon planks and other floatable items from the wrecked vessel. —Ac 27:37, 42-44.

The non-Greek-speaking inhabitants of Malta showed extraordinary human kindness to the survivors, even building a fire for them so that they might warm themselves. When the apostle Paul placed a bundle of sticks on this fire, a venomous viper came out and fastened itself to his hand. Amazed that Paul did not swell up or die, the people of Malta began to view him as a god.—Ac 28:1-6.

Today there are no vipers indigenous to Malta. Great changes have taken place since the first century C.E. Whereas now Malta is one of the most densely populated islands in the world, with about 1,280 persons per sq km (3,330 per sq mi), extensive wooded areas may have existed there in Paul's time. The population increase would have had a marked effect on the habitats of wildlife. This could easily have caused all vipers to disappear, as was the case in Arran, an island off the SW coast of Scotland. As late as 1853, however, a viper is reported to have been seen near St. Paul's Bay.

MAMMON. See RICHES.

MAMRE (Mam're) [possibly, Well-Fed].

1. An Amorite chieftain who, along with his brothers Aner and Eshcol, supported Abraham in defeating King Chedorlaomer and his allies. The basis for their support was evidently the confederacy into which they had entered with Abraham. —Ge 14:13, 24.

2. A place generally identified with er-Ramat el-Khalil, about 3 km (2 mi) N of Hebron, but thought by some to be farther to the W, in harmony with Genesis 23:17. (See MACHPELAH.) It was the principal place of residence for Abraham and, at least for a time, for Isaac. In the nearby cave of Machpelah, they and their wives as well as Jacob and Leah were eventually buried. (Ge 13:18; 35: 27; 49:29-33; 50:13) The area is well watered with numerous springs. There was a grove of big trees in Mamre in Abraham's time, and here he built an altar to Jehovah. (Ge 13:18) Under one of such trees, he entertained the angels prior to the destruction of Sodom and Gomorrah. (Ge 18:1-8) Here, too, Jehovah's promise was made to him of a son by Sarah. (Ge 18:9-19) From a point near Mamre, it was possible for Abraham to see all the way down to Sodom and there behold the thick smoke billowing up as a result of the fiery destruction of that area.—Ge 19:27-29.

In the area presently identified with Mamre, large trees (usually oaks) have received historical attention from Josephus' time down to the present day. Over the centuries shrines have been set up, usually in connection with an ancient tree presumed to be the one under which Abraham spoke with the angels. Herod the Great built a stone wall around such a traditional site. After his mother-in-law visited the area in the fourth century C.E., Emperor Constantine had a basilica erected there. Thereafter the Muslim conquerors also venerated the area.

MAN. The highest form of earthly life and a product of the Creator, Jehovah God. Jehovah formed the man out of dust from the ground, blew into his nostrils the breath of life, "and the man came to be a living soul." (Ge 2:7; 1Co 15:45) After Adam was created and after he named the animals, Jehovah caused a deep sleep to fall upon him; and while he slept, God took one of Adam's ribs and used it to make the woman. Therefore, when she was presented to the man, Adam could say: "This is at last bone of my bones and flesh of my flesh." He called her Woman, 'ish·shah', "because from man this one was taken." (Ge 2:21-23) Adam later gave her the name Eve (meaning "Living One").—Ge 3:20.

A number of Hebrew and Greek terms refer to man. 'A·dham' means "man; human; earthling man; mankind" (generic); 'ish, "man; an individual; a husband"; 'enohsh', "a mortal man"; ge'ver, "an able-bodied man"; za·khar', "a male"; a few other Hebrew words are also sometimes translated "man." The Greek an'thro·pos means "man; mankind" (generic); a·ner', "a man; a male person; a husband."

Testifying to man's creation by Jehovah God, the apostle Paul told the Athenians: "He made out of one man every nation of men, to dwell upon the entire surface of the earth." (Ac 17:26) Hence, all nations and races have a common origin.

Adam and Eve were created toward the end of the sixth creative "day." (Ge 1:24-31) There are no actual records of ancient man, his writing, agriculture, and other pursuits, extending into the past before 4026 B.C.E., the date of Adam's creation. Since the Scriptures outline man's history from the very creation of the first human pair, there can be no such thing as "prehistoric man." Fossil records in the earth provide no link between man and the animals. Then, too, there is a total absence of reference to any subhumans in man's earliest records, whether these be written documents, cave drawings, sculptures, or the like. The Scriptures make clear the opposite, that man was originally a son of God and that he has degenerated. (1Ki 8:46; Ec 7:20; 1Jo 1:8-10) Archaeologist O. D. Miller observed: "The tradition of the 'golden age,' then, was not a myth. The old doctrine of a subsequent decadence, of a sad degeneracy of the human race, from an original state of happiness and purity, undoubtedly embodied a great, but lamentable truth. Our modern philosophies of history, which begin with the primeval man as a savage, evidently need a new introduction. . . . No; the primeval man was not a savage."—*Har-Moad*, 1892, p. 417.

The Bible reveals that man's original home was "a garden in Eden." (Ge 2:8; see EDEN No. 1.) Its indicated location is relatively near the place of mankind's early post-Flood civilization. The view generally accepted by scholars is expressed by P. J. Wiseman as follows: "All the real evidence we have, that of Genesis, archæology, and the traditions of men, points to the Mesopotamian plain as the oldest home of man. Far Eastern civilization, whether Chinese or Indian, cannot compete with this land in the antiquity of its peoples, for it can easily sustain its claim to be the cradle of civilization."—*New Discoveries in Babylonia About Genesis,* 1949, p. 28.

In what sense is man made "in God's image"?

In disclosing to his "master worker" the divine purpose to create mankind, God said: "Let us make man ['a·dham'] in our image, according to our likeness." (Ge 1:26, 27; Pr 8:30, 31; compare Joh 1:1-3; Col 1:15-17.) Note that the Scriptures do not say that God created man in the image of a wild beast or of a domestic animal or of a fish. Man was made "in God's image"; he was a "son of God." (Lu 3:38) As to the form or shape of God's body, "at no time has anyone beheld God." (1Jo 4:12) No one on earth knows what God's glorious, heavenly, spiritual body looks like, so we cannot liken man's body to God's body. "God is a Spirit."—Joh 4:24.

Nevertheless, man is "in God's image" in that he was created with moral qualities like those of God, namely, love and justice. (Compare Col 3:10.) He also has powers and wisdom above those of animals, so that he can appreciate the things that God enjoys and appreciates, such as beauty and the arts, speaking, reasoning, and similar processes of the mind and heart of which the animals are not capable. Moreover, man is capable of spirituality, of knowing and having communication with God. (1Co 2:11-16; Heb 12:9) For such reasons man was qualified to be God's representative and to have in subjection the forms of creature life in the skies, on the earth, and in the sea.

Being a creation of God, man was originally perfect. (De 32:4) Accordingly, Adam could have bequeathed to his posterity human perfection and opportunity for eternal life on earth. (Isa 45:18) He and Eve were commanded: "Be fruitful and become many and fill the earth and subdue it." As their family increased, they would have cultivated and beautified the earth according to the design of their Creator.—Ge 1:28.

The apostle Paul, in discussing the relative positions of man and woman in God's arrangement, says: "I want you to know that the head of every man is the Christ; in turn the head of a woman is the man; in turn the head of the Christ is God." He then points out that a woman who prays or prophesies in the congregation with her head uncovered shames the one who is her head. To enforce his argument he then states: "For a man ought not to have his head covered, as he is *God's image and glory;* but the woman is man's glory." Man was created first and for some time was alone, being in God's image by himself. The woman was made from the man and was to be subject to the man, a situation unlike that of God, who is subject to no one. Man's headship, nevertheless, comes under the headship of God and Christ.—1Co 11:3-7.

A Free Moral Agent. Being made in God's image, according to His likeness, man was a free moral agent. He had the freedom of choice to do good or bad. By his willing, loving obedience to his Creator, he was in a position to bring honor and glory to God far beyond that which the animal creation could bring. He could intelligently praise God for His wonderful qualities and could support His sovereignty. But Adam's freedom was a relative freedom; it was not absolute. He could continue to live in happiness only if he acknowledged Jehovah's sovereignty. This was indicated by the tree of knowledge of good and bad, from which Adam was forbidden to eat. Eating of it would be an act of disobedience, a rebellion against God's sovereignty.—Ge 2:9, 16, 17.

Since Adam was a "son of God" (Lu 3:38), his relationship to God was that of a son to a father, and he should have obeyed accordingly. Additionally, God created in man an innate desire to render worship. This desire, if perverted, would take man in the wrong direction and would destroy his freedom, bringing him into bondage to what was created instead of to the Creator. This, in turn, would result in man's degradation.

A rebellious spirit son of God caused Adam's wife Eve to sin, and she placed the temptation before Adam, who deliberately entered into rebellion against Jehovah. (Ge 3:1-6; 1Ti 2:13, 14) They became like those whom Paul later described in Romans 1:20-23. By his transgression Adam lost his sonship and perfection and he introduced sin, with imperfection and death, to his offspring, the entire human race. Even at birth, they were in the image of their father Adam, imperfect, with death working in their bodies.—Ge 3:17-19; Ro 5:12; see ADAM No. 1.

"The Man We Are Inside." In speaking of the conflict of the Christian, including that with the fallen, sinful flesh, the Bible uses the expressions "the man I am within," "the man we are inside," and similar phrases. (Ro 7:22; 2Co 4:16; Eph 3:16) These expressions are appropriate because Christians have been "made new in the force actuating [their] mind." (Eph 4:23) The driving force or inclination of their mind is in a spiritual direction. They are making efforts to "strip off the old personality [literally, old man]" and clothe themselves with the "new personality [literally, new (one)]." (Col 3:9, 10; Ro 12:2) In being baptized into Christ, anointed Christians have been "baptized into his death"; the old personality has been impaled, "that [the] sinful body might be made inactive." But until their death in the flesh and their resurrection, the fleshly body is still there to fight the 'spiritual man.' It is a difficult contest, about which Paul says, "In this dwelling house we do indeed groan." But the ransom sacrifice of Jesus Christ covers the sins of the old personality with fleshly desires working in its members, unless these Christians give in and deliberately go the way of the flesh.—Ro 6:3-7; 7:21-25; 8:23; 2Co 5:1-3.

The Spiritual Man. The apostle contrasts the spiritual man with the physical man. He says: "But a physical [literally, soulical] man does not receive the things of the spirit of God, for they are foolishness to him." (1Co 2:14) This "physical man" does not mean merely one living on earth, one with a fleshly body, for, obviously, Christians on earth have fleshly bodies. The physical man here spoken of means one who has no spiritual side to his life. He is "soulical" in that he follows the desires of the human soul to the exclusion of spiritual things.

Paul continues about the "physical man," that he cannot get to know the things of the spirit of God "because they are examined spiritually." Then he says: "However, the spiritual man examines indeed all things, but he himself is not examined by any man." The spiritual man has understanding of the things God reveals; he sees also the wrong position and course of the physical man. But the spiritual man's position, actions, and course of life cannot be understood by the physical man, neither can any man judge the spiritual man, for God only is his Judge. (Ro 14:4, 10, 11; 1Co 4:3-5) The apostle says by way of illustration and argument: "For 'who has come to know the mind of Jehovah, that he may instruct him?'" No one, of course. "But," Paul says of Christians, "we do have the mind of Christ." By getting the mind of Christ,

who reveals Jehovah and his purposes to Christians, they are spiritual men.—1Co 2:14-16.

See OLDER MAN; SON OF MAN.

MANAEN (Man′a·en) [Gr. form of Heb. for Menahem, meaning "One Who Comforts"]. A man who was among the prophets and teachers in the congregation at Antioch. He had been educated with the district ruler Herod (Antipas).—Ac 13:1.

MANAHATH (Man′a·hath) [from a root that means "rest; settle down"].

1. A descendant of Seir through Shobal.—Ge 36:20, 23; 1Ch 1:38, 40.

2. A site to which certain "sons of Ehud" inhabiting Geba were exiled at an unspecified time. (1Ch 8:6) Some tentatively identify it with el-Malha (Manahat), about 6 km (3.5 mi) WSW of the Temple Mount in Jerusalem.

MANAHATHITES (Man·a·ha′thites) [Of (Belonging to) Manahath]. Certain Judeans descended from Caleb and Salma who apparently constituted part of the population of Manahath. (1Ch 2:50, 51, 54; 8:6) The Manahathites may be the same as the Menuhoth mentioned at 1 Chronicles 2:52.

MANASSEH (Ma·nas′seh) [One Making Forgetful; One Who Makes Forget].

1. Joseph's firstborn son and a grandson of Jacob. After Joseph became Egypt's food administrator, Pharaoh gave him Asenath, the daughter of Potiphera the priest of On, as a wife, and she bore Joseph two sons, Manasseh and Ephraim. Joseph named his firstborn Manasseh, because, he said: "God has made me forget all my trouble and all the house of my father."—Ge 41:45, 50-52.

When Jacob blessed Manasseh and Ephraim, he persisted in putting his right hand on Ephraim and his left on Manasseh, thereby placing the younger Ephraim before Manasseh. (Ge 48:13-20) As indicated thereby, Ephraim was to become greater than Manasseh.

Manasseh had sons by a Syrian concubine (1Ch 7:14), and Joseph lived long enough to see the sons of Manasseh's son Machir.—Ge 50:22, 23.

2. The tribe of Israel that descended from Joseph's son Manasseh and consisted of seven tribal families. About a year after the Israelites left Egypt, Manasseh's able-bodied men from 20 years old upward numbered 32,200. (Nu 1:34, 35) This doubtless included Gaddi, one of the ten men bringing back a bad report after spying out the Promised Land. (Nu 13:1, 2, 11, 25-33) By the time a second census was taken nearly four decades later, the tribe's registered males had increased to

52,700, outnumbering Ephraim by 20,200. (Nu 26:28-34, 37) Evidently, therefore, it was with reference to the lesser *future* role of Manasseh that Moses spoke of the "tens of thousands of Ephraim" but the "thousands of Manasseh."—De 33:17.

In the wilderness, the tribe of Manasseh, under the leadership of its chieftain Gamaliel the son of Pedahzur, encamped W of the tabernacle, along with Ephraim and Benjamin. This three-tribe division was third in the order of march.—Nu 1:10, 16; 2:18-24; 7:54; 10:23.

Conquests on Both Sides of Jordan River. When the Israelites defeated Amorite Kings Sihon and Og, Moses granted their conquered land to the Reubenites, the Gadites, and half of the tribe of Manasseh on condition that these tribes participate in the conquest of the territory W of the Jordan. (Nu 32:20-33; 34:14, 15; De 29:7, 8) The northern section of the area E of the Jordan appears to have been taken primarily through Manassite efforts, portions thereof being conquered by Jair, Nobah, and "the sons of Machir." For this reason Moses assigned this region to them.—Nu 32:39-42; De 3:13-15; 1Ch 2:21, 22.

Later, men from "the half tribe of Manasseh" that had received their inheritance did cross the Jordan and shared in the conquest of the land to the west. (Jos 1:12-18; 4:12) They were also among those assembled in front of Mount Gerizim when Joshua "read aloud all the words of the law, the blessing and the malediction." (De 27:12; Jos 8:33, 34) Under the leadership of Joshua, the Israelites broke the power of the Canaanites, defeating 31 kings in the course of about six years. (Jos 12:7-24) Thereafter, although unconquered territory yet remained, Joshua, assisted by High Priest Eleazar and divinely appointed representatives from ten tribes (including the Manassite Hanniel the son of Ephod), divided the land into inheritance portions.—Nu 34:17, 23; Jos 13:1-7.

Land Inheritance. Half of the tribe of Manasseh, of course, already had its inheritance E of the Jordan. It included Bashan and a part of Gilead. (Jos 13:29-31) To the S lay Gad, the border city being Mahanaim. (Jos 13:24-26, 30) This region was chiefly a high plateau, with an average elevation of some 610 m (2,000 ft). Here were located Golan, one of the six cities of refuge, and Beeshterah (Ashtaroth), another Levite city.—Jos 20:8, 9; 21:27; 1Ch 6:71.

The remaining half of the Manassites received as their inheritance territory W of the Jordan. (Jos 17:2, 5) It was bounded by Ephraim on the S, Asher on the NW, Issachar on the NE, and the Mediterranean Sea on the W. From Michmethah the border between Ephraim and Manasseh extended to Tappuah, continued along the torrent valley of Kanah, and terminated at the Mediterranean. (Compare Jos 16:5-8; 17:7-10.) Whereas the Ephraimites had certain enclave cities in Manasseh, the Manassites were assigned enclave cities (Beth-shean, Ibleam, Dor, En-dor, Taanach, and Megiddo, as well as their dependent towns) both in Issachar and Asher. (Jos 16:9; 17:11) The Manassites failed to drive out the Canaanites from these enclave cities but, in time, subjected them to forced labor. (Jos 17:11-13; Jg 1:27, 28; compare 1Ch 7:29.) Two of these enclave cities, Taanach (Aner?) and Ibleam (Bileam or Gath-rimmon?), were assigned to Kohathite Levites.—Jos 21:25, 26; 1Ch 6:70.

History. After the distribution of the land had been completed, Joshua blessed the men of Reuben, Gad, and the eastern "half tribe of Manasseh" and encouraged them to continue serving Jehovah. (Jos 22:1-8) They left Shiloh, crossed the Jordan, and then near that river built an altar. This almost precipitated civil war, as the other tribes regarded this as an act of unfaithfulness and rebellion. However, the issue was settled peaceably when it was explained that the altar had been erected, not for sacrifice, but to serve as a memorial of faithfulness to Jehovah.—Jos 22:9-31.

In a later period Manassite Judge Gideon was the one used by Jehovah to deliver the Israelites from Midianite oppression. (Jg 6:11-16, 33-35; 7:23; 8:22) Jephthah was evidently yet another judge from the tribe of Manasseh. It was during his judgeship that Israel was liberated from Ammonite harassment.—Jg 11:1, 32, 33.

Sometime during the reign of Israel's first king, Saul, the Reubenites, the Gadites, and the eastern "half tribe of Manasseh" gained a decisive victory over the Hagrites and their allies. (1Ch 5:10, 18-22) Also in this general period, Manassites, including men of outstanding valor, were among those who deserted Saul to join David. (1Ch 12:19-21) After the death of Saul and his successor Ish-bosheth, 18,000 Manassites from the region W of the Jordan and other thousands from the area E of the Jordan came to Hebron to make David king over all Israel (1070 B.C.E.).—1Ch 12:31, 37, 38.

Years later, the extensive religious reforms undertaken by Judean King Asa prompted many Manassites to desert the northern kingdom "when they saw that Jehovah his God was with him." (2Ch 15:8, 9) On the occasion of a grand assembly in the 15th year of Asa's reign (963 B.C.E.), they joined with others in making a covenant to search for Jehovah. (2Ch 15:10, 12) Similarly, in the reign of Judean King Hezekiah (745-717 B.C.E.), while many mocked the messengers sent by him to extend the invitation to come to Jerusalem for the Passover celebration, other Manassites were willing to humble themselves and responded favorably. Thereafter these responsive ones shared in destroying appendages of idolatry.—2Ch 30:1, 10, 11, 18; 31:1.

Earlier (c. 760 B.C.E.), Tiglath-pileser (Tilgath-pilneser) III had taken the Manassites living E of the Jordan into exile. (1Ch 5:23-26) About the same time it appears that intertribal conflicts existed between Ephraim and Manasseh. But both tribes were united in their opposition to Judah.—Isa 9:20, 21.

Nearly a century after the ten-tribe kingdom came to its end, Judean King Josiah extended his destruction of altars, incense stands, sacred poles, and images, all used for false worship, to the devastated places of Manasseh and other areas outside Judah (from and after 648 B.C.E.). This Judean king also had repair work done on the temple, the work itself being financed by contributions received from Israelites of various tribes, including Manasseh.—2Ch 34:1-11.

After the return from Babylonian exile (537 B.C.E.), some Manassites resided at Jerusalem.—1Ch 9:1-3.

In Ezekiel's vision, Manasseh's land assignment lay between Naphtali and Ephraim. (Eze 48:4, 5) Manasseh is also represented as one of the tribes of spiritual Israel.—Re 7:6.

3. A name appearing in the Masoretic text at Judges 18:30, because of scribal modification. The account concerns Danite apostasy, and the *New World Translation* says that "Jonathan the son of Gershom, Moses' son, he and his sons became priests to the tribe of the Danites." (See also *AT; Mo; Ro; RS.*) Jewish scribes inserted a suspended letter (*nun* = n) between the first two letters in the original Hebrew name so as to give the reading "Manasseh's" instead of "Moses'," doing so out of regard for Moses. The scribes thus sought to hide the reproach or disgrace that might be brought upon the name of Moses because of Jonathan's action. In addition to the altered Masoretic text, "Manasseh's" appears in the Vatican Manuscript No. 1209 of the Greek *Septuagint* and in the Syriac *Peshitta*. However, "Moses'" is found in the Alexandrine Manuscript of the Greek *Septuagint* and in the Latin *Vulgate* at Judges 18:30.

4. King of Judah who was the son and successor of King Hezekiah. (2Ki 20:21; 2Ch 32:33) Ma-nasseh's mother was Hephzibah. He was 12 years old when he ascended the throne as the 14th king of Judah after David and ruled for 55 years (716-662 B.C.E.) in Jerusalem. (2Ki 21:1) He did what was bad in Jehovah's eyes, rebuilding the high places his father had destroyed, setting up altars to Baal, worshiping "all the army of the heavens," and building false religious altars in two temple courtyards. He made his sons pass through the fire, practiced magic, employed divination, and promoted spiritistic practices. Manasseh also put the graven image of the sacred pole he had made into the house of Jehovah. He seduced Judah and Jerusalem "to do worse than the nations that Jehovah had annihilated from before the sons of Israel." (2Ki 21:2-9; 2Ch 33:2-9) Though Jehovah sent prophets, these were not heeded. Manasseh was also guilty of shedding innocent blood in great quantity (2Ki 21:10-16), which, according to the literature of the Jewish rabbis, included that of Isaiah, who they say was sawed apart at Manasseh's command.—Compare Heb 11:37.

Manasseh was punished for paying no attention to Jehovah's message, the king of Assyria taking him captive to Babylon, one of the Assyrian monarch's royal cities. (2Ch 33:10, 11) 'Manasseh of Judah' is mentioned in Assyrian King Esarhaddon's list of 22 tribute-paying "kings of Hatti, the seashore and the islands." Manasseh's name also appears in a list of kings tributary to Ashurbanipal.—*Ancient Near Eastern Texts*, edited by J. Pritchard, 1974, pp. 291, 294.

While in captivity, Manasseh repented, humbled himself, and prayed to Jehovah. God heard his request for favor and restored him to the kingship in Jerusalem. (2Ch 33:12, 13) Manasseh thereafter "built an outer wall for the City of David," put military chiefs in Judah's fortified cities, and removed the foreign gods and the idol image from Jehovah's house, as well as the altars he had built "in the mountain of the house of Jehovah and in Jerusalem." Manasseh prepared the altar of Jehovah and began to sacrifice upon it, encouraging others also to serve Jehovah. However, the people were still sacrificing on the high places, though to Jehovah. (2Ch 33:14-17) At Manasseh's death, he was succeeded in the kingship by his son Amon.—2Ch 33:20.

5. An Israelite "of the sons of Pahath-moab" who was among those accepting foreign wives and sending them away "along with sons" in Ezra's day.—Ezr 10:30, 44.

6. Another Israelite, "of the sons of Hashum," among those dismissing their foreign wives because of Ezra's zealous stand for pure worship.—Ezr 10:33, 44.

MANASSITES.   See Manasseh No. 2.

MANDRAKE   [Heb., *du·dha·ʹim'*, plural]. A perennial herb of the potato family, with large, ovate, or oblong, dark-green leaves. The leaves of the mandrake (*Mandragora officinarum*) appear to grow directly from the taproot, fan out in a circle, and lie close to the ground. From the center of this circle, the flower stalks grow, each bearing only one white, bluish, or purple flower. The yellowish-red fruit, about the size of a plum, ripens about the time of the Palestinian wheat harvest. (Ge 30:14) It has been described as smelling sweet and fresh like an apple. (See Ca 7:13.) The thick, frequently forked, taproot of the mandrake bears some resemblance to a man's lower limbs. This has given rise to numerous superstitious beliefs and the ascribing of magical powers to the plant.—PICTURE, Vol. 1, p. 544.

In ancient times the fruit of the mandrake was used in medicine as a narcotic and as an antispasmodic. Also, it was, and still is in some parts of the Middle East, regarded as an aphrodisiac and as able to increase human fertility or aid in conception. The Genesis record reports that Rachel agreed to exchange with her sister Leah an opportunity to have the marital due from her husband Jacob for some mandrakes. (Ge 30:14, 15) While the Bible does not reveal her motive, possibly Rachel felt that these would help her conceive, thus ending the reproach of her barrenness. It was, however, not until some years after this incident that she actually became pregnant.—Ge 30:22-24.

MANEH.   See Mina.

MANGER, STALL.   The infant Jesus was laid in a manger and was seen there by shepherds, to whom the angelic announcement of his birth was made. (Lu 2:7, 12, 16) The Greek word for "manger" in this case is *phat'ne,* meaning "feeding place." (Compare Lu 13:15.) *Phat'ne* may also possibly apply to the stall in which animals are kept. The Hebrew term *'e·vus'* is generally understood to mean "manger" and was rendered *phat'ne* in the Greek *Septuagint,* as were three other Hebrew words that have been translated "stalls" (2Ch 32: 28), "enclosures" (Hab 3:17), and "fodder" (Job 6:5).

In Palestine, archaeologists have found large troughs cut out of single pieces of limestone and measuring about 0.9 m (3 ft) in length, 0.5 m (1.5 ft) in width, and 0.6 m (2 ft) in depth. These are thought to have served as mangers. It may also be that, as in more recent times, mangers

were cut in the rock walls of caves that were used for sheltering animals.

MANIFESTATION.   A disclosure, or discernible evidence, a display of authority or power. The Greek term *e·pi·pha·neiʹa,* translated "manifestation," is used in the Scriptures with reference to Jesus Christ's days on earth and especially with regard to various events during his presence in royal power.

God's Son Manifested in Flesh.   It was with respect to "the manifestation of our Savior, Christ Jesus," in the flesh that the apostle Paul wrote the words of 2 Timothy 1:9-11. The sending of God's Son from heaven was to work toward the vindication of Jehovah's name and sovereignty. It was also to result in the 'abolition of death' traceable to Adam and to bring to light the prospect of life and incorruption in heaven for some humans. As a feature of the development of "the sacred secret of this godly devotion," Jesus was "made manifest in flesh." (1Ti 3:16) Paul also called this act of God in sending his Son a 'manifestation' of God's undeserved kindness "which brings salvation to all sorts of men . . . , instructing us to repudiate ungodliness and worldly desires and to live with soundness of mind and righteousness and godly devotion amid this present system of things, while we wait for the happy hope and glorious manifestation of the great God and of the Savior of us, Christ Jesus." (Tit 2:11-13) Christ's manifestation in glory, when accomplished, would also manifest the glory of God, who sent him.

Christ Manifest in Heavenly Glory.   During Christ's presence, he would turn his attention to his spiritual brothers who were sleeping in death. These would be the ones Paul speaks of, along with himself, who "have loved his manifestation" and who would receive the 'crown of righteousness as a reward.' (2Ti 4:8) When the Lord would "descend from heaven with a commanding call, with an archangel's voice and with God's trumpet," the dead in union with Christ would rise first, and Christ would receive them home to himself. He would in this way be powerfully manifested in his glory to them. He would then proceed to make his presence manifest to his brothers yet on earth, and would take them home to himself at the time of their death.—1Th 4:15, 16; Joh 14:3; Re 14:13.

As King and Judge.   When Christ was before Pontius Pilate, he said that his Kingdom was no part of this world, though he did not deny being a king. (Joh 18:36, 37) He did not then manifest himself as a potentate, because the time for taking his Kingdom authority had not arrived. Nevertheless, there would come a time when "the manifestation of our Lord Jesus Christ" would be clearly recognized, when he would exercise authority as "the happy and only Potentate" and "the King of those who rule as kings and Lord of those who rule as lords."—1Ti 6:13-16; Da 2:44; 7:13, 14.

In view of the coming Kingdom and of Christ's manifestation, Paul said to Timothy: "I solemnly charge you before God and Christ Jesus, who is destined to judge the living and the dead, and by his manifestation and his kingdom, preach the word." (2Ti 4:1, 2) The apostle thus pointed to the time when Christ's glorious position in heaven would be made unmistakably manifest, when he would make God's judgments felt in the earth.

In destroying "the man of lawlessness." In writing to Christians in Thessalonica "respecting the presence of our Lord Jesus Christ," Paul urged them not to be shaken from their reason or to be excited by any message "to the effect that the day of Jehovah is here." The symbolic "man of lawlessness," which had been operating for centuries in opposition to God and Christ, would then be brought to nothing "by the manifestation of his presence." This "lawless one" would recognize Christ's presence, not by faith, as would Christians, who loved his manifestation, but by Jesus' power manifested in annihilating those of this composite "man."—2Th 2:1-8; see MAN OF LAWLESSNESS.

Manifestation of the Spirit and the Truth. After the holy spirit was poured out on Christ's disciples, the fact of its invisible operation on these disciples was 'manifested' by visible evidences. Some of these were: the ability to speak in foreign tongues, gifts of healing, and discernment of inspired utterances. (1Co 12:7-10) The apostle Paul also speaks of "making the truth manifest" to others by the good conduct and preaching of Christians.—2Co 4:2.

MANNA (man′na). The main food of the Israelites during their 40-year trek in the wilderness. (Ex 16:35) Manna was first provided by Jehovah in the Wilderness of Sin during the last half of the second month after Israel's coming out of Egypt in 1513 B.C.E. (Ex 16:1-4) It served as food for them until they entered Canaan in 1473 B.C.E. and partook of the produce of the Promised Land.—Jos 5:10-12.

Manna appeared on the ground with the evaporation of a layer of dew that developed in the morning, so that "upon the surface of the wilderness there was a fine flaky thing, fine like hoarfrost upon the earth." When the Israelites first saw it, they said, "What is it?" or, literally, *"man hu'?"* (Ex 16:13-15; Nu 11:9) This is the probable origin of the name, the Israelites themselves beginning to call this food "manna."—Ex 16:31.

Description. Manna was "white like coriander seed" and had the "look" of bdellium gum, a waxlike and transparent substance having a form that resembles a pearl. Its taste was comparable to "that of flat cakes with honey" or "an oiled sweet cake." After being ground in a hand mill or pounded in a mortar, manna was boiled or made into cakes and baked.—Ex 16:23, 31; Nu 11:7, 8.

No natural substance known today fits the Biblical description of manna in every respect, and so there is little basis for identifying it with a known product. This is especially so because miraculous aspects were involved in Jehovah's providing manna for the Israelites. The availability of manna did not depend on the time of year or a particular wilderness location. Although the manna would breed worms and begin to stink on all the other days if kept overnight, the additional omer of manna gathered on the sixth day, to be used as food on the Sabbath, did not spoil. No manna could be found on the Sabbath, this serving to enforce Sabbath observance on the Israelites.—Ex 16:19-30.

The family head either gathered or supervised the gathering of manna for the entire household. Since the manna melted when the sun got hot, he doubtless quickly gathered the approximate supply needed for the household and afterward measured it. Whether little or much was gathered, depending upon the size of the household, the amount collected always proved to be one omer (2.2 L; 2 dry qt) per person. (Ex 16:16-18) The apostle Paul alluded to this when encouraging Christians at Corinth to use their material surplus to offset the material deficiency of their brothers. —2Co 8:13-15.

Purpose. Jehovah let the Israelites go hungry in the wilderness and then furnished manna to teach them "that not by bread alone does man live but by every expression of Jehovah's mouth does man live." Jehovah did this 'in order to humble them and put them to the test so as to do them good in their afterdays.' (De 8:3, 16) When the Israelites tired of manna and began calling it "contemptible bread," Jehovah punished their rebellion by sending poisonous serpents among them, causing the death of many.—Nu 21:5, 6.

The psalmist referred to manna as "the grain of heaven" (Ps 78:24), "bread from heaven" (Ps 105:40), and "the very bread of powerful ones" (Ps 78:25). Angels are described as being "mighty in power" (Ps 103:20) and therefore could be called "powerful ones." This, however, would not mean that angels actually eat manna but that God may have used angelic means in providing it for the Israelites. (Compare Gal 3:19.) Or, since heaven is the dwelling place of the "powerful ones," the expression "bread of powerful ones" may simply point to its heavenly source.

So that future generations might see manna, Aaron was to deposit before Jehovah a jar containing an omer (2.2 L; 2 dry qt) of manna. After the golden ark of the covenant was completed, a "golden jar" of manna was put inside this sacred chest. (Ex 16:32-34; Heb 9:4) About five centuries later, however, when the Ark was transferred from the tent that David had erected for it to the temple that Solomon had built, the golden jar was missing. (2Sa 6:17; 1Ki 8:9; 2Ch 5:10) It had served its purpose.

Symbolic Use. Although the manna was a divine provision (Ne 9:20), it did not sustain the lives of the Israelites forever. Christ Jesus made a point of this, and then he added: "I am the living bread that came down from heaven; if anyone eats of this bread he will live forever; and, for a fact, the bread that I shall give is my flesh in behalf of the life of the world." (Joh 6:30-33, 48-51, 58) Christ's faithful followers avail themselves of this heavenly manna, or "bread of life." They do so in a figurative manner by exercising faith in the redeeming power of Jesus' flesh and blood laid down in sacrifice. Their doing so opens up to them the prospect of living forever, whether in the heavens with Christ or in the earthly Paradise.

Christ also used the jar of manna symbolically when he assured his spirit-anointed followers that those who prove to be conquerors would receive "the hidden manna," an imperishable food supply or that which results from such a supply, in their case, immortality and incorruptibility in heaven. —Re 2:17; 1Co 15:53.

MANOAH (Ma·no'ah). A Danite man of the Shephelah town of Zorah (Jos 15:33) and the father of Judge Samson. Manoah was a devout worshiper of Jehovah.

One day an angel appeared to Manoah's barren wife, announcing that she would give birth to a son who would be a Nazirite of God. Upon being informed of this, Manoah supplicated Jehovah, asking him to send the messenger again in order to instruct them on raising the child. Jehovah answered the prayer and sent the angel a second time. When Manoah offered to set a meal before the messenger, he was told to render up a burnt offering to Jehovah instead, which he did. It was

after this messenger ascended in the flame rising from the altar that Manoah recognized him as being Jehovah's angel. Because of having had this experience, Manoah feared that he and his wife would die. But she allayed his fear, saying: "If Jehovah had been delighted only to put us to death, he would not have accepted a burnt offering and grain offering from our hand, and he would not have shown us all these things, and he would not as now have let us hear anything like this."—Jg 13:2-23.

Years later, Manoah and his wife, 'not knowing that it was from Jehovah,' objected to Samson's desire to marry a Philistine woman of Timnah. (Jg 14:1-4; compare De 7:3, 4.) Subsequently Manoah and his wife accompanied Samson to Timnah, although not going with him as far as the home of the Philistine woman. Therefore they did not witness Samson's killing a young lion with his bare hands. On another occasion Samson, intending to take the Philistine woman to his home, again went with his parents to Timnah. He turned aside to inspect the corpse of the lion that he had slain earlier and found a swarm of bees and honey inside. Upon rejoining his parents, he offered them some of the honey that he had scraped out of the lion's corpse, and they ate it. Thereafter the family apparently continued on their way, and doubtless both parents were present at the banquet arranged by Samson at Timnah.—Jg 14:5-10.

Manoah preceded his son in death, for Samson was buried in the burial place of Manoah between Zorah and Eshtaol.—Jg 16:31.

MAN OF LAWLESSNESS. An expression used by the apostle Paul at 2 Thessalonians 2:2, 3 in warning of the great anti-Christian apostasy that would develop before "the day of Jehovah." The Greek word for "apostasy" here used, a·po·sta·si'a, denotes more than a mere falling away, an indifferent sliding back. It means a defection, a revolt, a planned, deliberate rebellion. In ancient papyrus documents a·po·sta·si'a was used politically of rebels.

A Religious Revolt. This rebellion, however, is not a political one. It is a religious one, a revolt against Jehovah God and Jesus Christ and therefore against the Christian congregation.

Foretold. Other forecasts of this apostasy were made by the apostles Paul and Peter both verbally and in writing, and the Lord Jesus Christ himself warned of its coming. In his illustration of the wheat and the weeds (Mt 13), Jesus said that the Devil would sow "weeds," imitation Christians, "sons of the wicked one," among the "wheat," the "sons of the kingdom." These would exist until the conclusion of the system of things, when they would be identified and 'burned up.'

Paul warned the Christian overseers of Ephesus that after his going away "oppressive wolves" would enter in among true Christians and would not treat the flock with tenderness but would try to draw away "the disciples" after themselves (not just making disciples for themselves but trying to draw away *the* disciples, Christ's disciples). (Ac 20:29, 30) He wrote, at 1 Timothy 4:1-3: "However, the inspired utterance says definitely that in later periods of time some will fall away from the faith, paying attention to misleading inspired utterances and teachings of demons, by the hypocrisy of men who speak lies, marked in their conscience as with a branding iron [feelingless, seared, so that they do not feel any twinges of conscience because of hypocritically speaking lies]; forbidding to marry, commanding to abstain from foods which God created to be partaken of with thanksgiving."

Paul later wrote to Timothy that "there will be a period of time when they will not put up with the healthful teaching, but, in accord with their own desires, they will accumulate teachers for themselves to have their ears tickled; and they will turn their ears away from the truth."—2Ti 4:3, 4.

The apostle Peter drew a parallel between the apostasy from Christianity and that which occurred in the natural house of Israel. He said: "However, there also came to be false prophets among the people, as there will also be false teachers among you. These very ones will quietly bring in destructive sects and will disown even the owner that bought them, bringing speedy destruction upon themselves. Furthermore, many will follow their acts of loose conduct, and on account of these the way of the truth will be spoken of abusively." Peter goes on to point out that these would exploit the congregation but that "the destruction of them is not slumbering."—2Pe 2:1-3.

A composite "man." The "man" of 2 Thessalonians 2:1-12 is, therefore, not an individual, but a composite "man," a collective group, as the foregoing scriptures show, and this "man" was to continue after the apostles' death and exist down until the time of the Lord's presence.

Treason against God. The "lawlessness" that this composite apostate "man" commits is lawlessness against Jehovah God the Universal Sovereign. This "man" is guilty of treason. He is called "the son of destruction," as was Judas Iscariot, the traitor who betrayed the Lord Jesus Christ and who was instrumental in bringing about his death. He, like Judas, is to be annihilated, sent into extinction forever. This "man" is not "Babylon the Great," who also fights against God, for she is a woman, a harlot. However, since he carries on a religious rebellion against God, he is evidently a part of mystic Babylon.—Joh 17:12; Re 17:3, 5.

"The man of lawlessness" sets himself in opposition to God and is therefore a "satan," which means "resister." And, indeed, his "presence is according to the operation of Satan." (2Th 2:9) In the days of the apostle Paul, there was "mystery," or a religious secret, about the identity of this "man of lawlessness." To this day mystery shrouds his identity in the minds of many persons, because his wickedness is practiced under the guise of godly devotion. (2Th 2:7) By his lying teachings contrary to or superseding, as it were, the law of God, "the man of lawlessness" sets himself up over Jehovah God and other 'gods,' mighty ones of the earth, and also against God's holy ones, true spiritual brothers of Jesus Christ. (Compare 2Pe 2:10-13.) Since he is a hypocrite, a false teacher claiming to be Christian, he "sits down in the temple of The God," that is, what such false teachers claim to be that temple.—2Th 2:4.

A restraint. Paul speaks of "the thing that acts as a restraint." (2Th 2:6) It appears that the apostles constituted this restraint. Paul had told the Ephesian overseers that after his going away wolflike men would enter in. (Ac 20:29) He repeatedly wrote admonitions about such apostasy not only here in Second Thessalonians but in many exhortations to Timothy. And he counseled Timothy to commit the things he had heard from Paul to faithful men who would be qualified to teach others. He spoke of the congregation of the living God as being "a pillar and support of the truth." He wanted it built up as strongly as possible before the great apostasy blossomed out.—2Ti 2:2; 1Ti 3:15.

Much later, at the command of Christ, the apostle John was told to write, warning against sects, mentioning especially the sect of Nicolaus and speaking of false prophets like Balaam and of the woman Jezebel who called herself a prophetess. —Re 2:6, 14, 15, 20.

At work in apostles' days. The apostle Paul said that the mystery was "already at work." (2Th 2:7) There were those trying to teach false doctrine, some of these even disturbing the Thessalonian congregation, prompting, in part, the writing of his second letter to them. There were antichrists when John wrote his letters, and doubtless before that. John spoke of "the last hour" of the apostolic period, and said: "Just as you have heard that antichrist is coming, even now there have come to be many antichrists . . . They went out from us, but they were not of our sort; for if they had been of our sort, they would have remained with us. But they went out that it might be shown up that not all are of our sort."—1Jo 2:18, 19; see ANTICHRIST.

Revealed. Following the apostles' death, "the man of lawlessness" came out into the open with his religious hypocrisy and false teachings. (2Th 2:3, 6, 8) According to Paul's words, this "man" would gain great power, operating under Satan's control, performing "every powerful work and lying signs and portents." Persons deceived by the operation of the composite "man of lawlessness" are referred to as "those who are perishing [literally, "destroying themselves"], as a retribution because they did not accept the love of the truth that they might be saved." The apostle shows that they "get to believing the lie" and they will all "be judged because they did not believe the truth but took pleasure in unrighteousness." (2Th 2:9-12; see *Int.*) The judgment is therefore a condemnatory one.—See RESURRECTION (Sin against the holy spirit).

Destroyed. This composite, hypocritical "man of lawlessness" is to be done away with by the Lord Jesus "by the spirit of his mouth" and brought to nothing "by the manifestation of his presence." The annihilation of this wicked opposer of God will be visible, concrete proof that the Lord Jesus Christ is sitting and acting as Judge. He will not judge according to his own standards, hence the destruction "by the spirit of his mouth" evidently means in expression of Jehovah's judgment against this wicked class of persons.—2Th 2:8; compare Re 19:21, as to "the long sword . . . which sword proceeded out of his mouth."

MANSLAYER. See CITIES OF REFUGE; MURDER.

MANTLE. See DRESS.

MANUSCRIPTS OF THE BIBLE.
The Holy Scriptures have a superhuman origin as to content but a human history as to their writing and preservation. Moses began compiling them under divine inspiration in 1513 B.C.E., and the apostle John wrote the final portion thereof more than 1,600 years later. The Bible was not originally one book, but as time passed, a demand arose for copies of its various books. This was so, for instance, after the Babylonian exile, for not all released Jews returned to the land of Judah. Instead, many settled elsewhere, and synagogues sprang up throughout the vast territory of the resultant Jewish Dispersion. Scribes prepared copies of the

Scriptures needed for these synagogues where the Jews gathered to hear the reading of God's Word. (Ac 15:21) In later times, among Christ's followers, conscientious copyists labored to reproduce the inspired writings for the benefit of the multiplying Christian congregations so that there might be an interchange and general circulation of these.—Col 4:16.

Before printing from movable type became common (from the 15th century C.E. onward), the original Bible writings and also copies of them were handwritten. Hence, they are called manuscripts (Latin, *manu scriptus,* "written by hand"). A Bible manuscript is a handwritten copy of the Scriptures, the whole or in part, as distinguished from one that is printed. Bible manuscripts were produced principally in the form of rolls and codices.

Materials. There are leather, papyrus, and vellum manuscripts of the Scriptures. The noted Dead Sea Scroll of Isaiah, for instance, is a leather roll. Papyrus, a type of paper made from the fibers of a water plant, was used for Bible manuscripts in the original languages and for translations thereof until about the fourth century C.E. At that time its use for Bible manuscripts began to be superseded by the use of vellum, a fine grade of parchment generally made from calf, lamb, or goat skins, a further development of the earlier use of animal skins as writing material. Such manuscripts as the renowned Codex Sinaiticus (Sinaitic Manuscript) and the Codex Vaticanus (Vatican Manuscript No. 1209) of the fourth century C.E. are parchment, or vellum, codices.

A palimpsest (Lat., *palimpsestus;* Gr., *pa-lim′pse·stos,* meaning "scraped again") is a manuscript from which earlier writing was removed or scraped off to make room for later writing. A noted Bible palimpsest is the Codex Ephraemi Syri rescriptus of the fifth century C.E. If the earlier writing (the writing scraped off) is the important one on the palimpsest, scholars can often read this erased writing by employing technical means that include the use of chemical reagents and photography. Some manuscripts of the Christian Greek Scriptures are lectionaries, selected Bible readings for use at religious services.

Styles of Writing. Bible manuscripts written in Greek (whether translations of the Hebrew Scriptures, or copies of the Christian Greek Scriptures, or both) can be divided, or classified, as to writing style, which is also an aid in dating them. The older style (employed especially down to the ninth century C.E.) is the uncial manuscript, written in large, separated capital letters. In it there is generally no word separation, and punctuation and accent marks are lacking. The Codex Sinaiticus is such an uncial manuscript. Changes in writing style began to develop in the sixth century, eventually leading (in the ninth century C.E.) to the cursive, or minuscule, manuscript, written in smaller letters, many of which were joined in a running or flowing writing style. The majority of extant manuscripts of the Christian Greek Scriptures have a cursive script. Cursive manuscripts remained in vogue until the inception of printing.

Copyists. As far as is known today, no handwritten original, or autograph, manuscripts of the Bible are in existence. Yet the Bible has been preserved in accurate, reliable form because Biblical copyists in general, accepting the Scriptures as being divinely inspired, sought perfection in their arduous labor of producing manuscript copies of God's Word.

The men who copied the Hebrew Scriptures in the days of Jesus Christ's ministry on earth and for centuries before that time were called scribes (Heb., *soh·pherim'*). Among the early scribes was Ezra, spoken of in the Scriptures as "a skilled copyist." (Ezr 7:6) Later scribes made some deliberate alterations of the Hebrew text. But their scribal successors, the Masoretes, detected these and recorded them in the Masora, or notes appearing in the margins of the Hebrew Masoretic text they produced.

Copyists of the Christian Greek Scriptures also made earnest efforts to reproduce faithfully the text of the Scriptures.

What assurance is there that the Bible has not been changed?

Despite the care exercised by copyists of Bible manuscripts, a number of small scribal errors and alterations crept into the text. On the whole, these are insignificant and have no bearing on the Bible's general integrity. They have been detected and corrected by means of careful scholastic collation or critical comparison of the many extant manuscripts and ancient versions. Critical study of the Hebrew text of the Scriptures commenced toward the end of the 18th century. Benjamin Kennicott published at Oxford (in 1776-1780) the readings of over 600 Masoretic Hebrew manuscripts, and the Italian scholar Giambernardo de Rossi published at Parma comparisons of 731 manuscripts in 1784 to 1798. Master texts of the Hebrew Scriptures were also produced by the German scholar Baer and, more recently, by

C. D. Ginsburg. Hebrew scholar Rudolf Kittel released in 1906 the first edition of his *Biblia Hebraica* (The Hebrew Bible), providing therein a textual study through a footnote service, comparing many Hebrew manuscripts of the Masoretic text. The basic text he used was the Ben Hayim text. But, when the older and superior Ben Asher Masoretic texts became available, Kittel undertook the production of an entirely new third edition, which was completed by his colleagues after his death.

The 7th, 8th, and 9th editions of the *Biblia Hebraica* (1951-1955) furnished the basic text used to render the Hebrew Scriptures into English in the *New World Translation of the Holy Scriptures* originally published in 1950-1960. A new edition of the Hebrew text, namely *Biblia Hebraica Stuttgartensia,* is dated 1977. This edition was used for updating the information presented in the footnotes of the *New World Translation* published in 1984.

The first printed edition of the Christian Greek Scriptures was that appearing in the Complutensian Polyglott (in Greek and Latin), of 1514-1517. Then in 1516 the Dutch scholar Desiderius Erasmus published his first edition of a master Greek text of the Christian Greek Scriptures. It contained many errors, but an improved text thereof was made available through four succeeding editions from 1519 to 1535. Later, Paris printer and editor Robert Estienne, or Stephanus, issued several editions of the Greek "New Testament," based principally on Erasmus' text, but having corrections according to the Complutensian Polyglott (edition of 1522) and 15 late manuscripts. The third edition of Stephanus' Greek text (issued in 1550) became, in effect, the "Received Text" (called *textus receptus* in Latin), which was used for many early English versions, including the *King James Version* of 1611.

Quite noteworthy in more recent times is the master Greek text prepared by J. J. Griesbach, who availed himself of materials gathered by others but who also gave attention to Biblical quotations made by early writers such as Origen. Further, Griesbach studied the readings of various versions, such as the Armenian, Gothic, and Philoxenian. He viewed extant manuscripts as comprising three families, or recensions, the Byzantine, the Western, and the Alexandrian, giving preference to readings in the latter. Editions of his master Greek text were issued between 1774 and 1806, his principal edition of the entire Greek text being published in 1796-1806. Griesbach's text was used for Sharpe's English translation of 1840 and is the Greek text printed in *The Emphatic Diaglott,* by Benjamin Wilson, in 1864.

A Greek master text of the Christian Greek Scriptures that attained wide acceptance is that produced in 1881 by Cambridge University scholars B. F. Westcott and F. J. A. Hort. It was the product of 28 years of independent labor, though they compared notes regularly. Like Griesbach, they divided manuscripts into families and leaned heavily on what they termed the "neutral text," which included the renowned Sinaitic Manuscript and the Vatican Manuscript No. 1209, both of the fourth century C.E. While Westcott and Hort viewed matters as quite conclusive when these manuscripts agreed and especially when they were supported by other ancient uncial manuscripts, they were not bound to that position. They took every conceivable factor into consideration in endeavoring to solve problems presented by conflicting texts; and when two readings were of equal weight, that, too, was indicated in their master text. The Westcott and Hort text was the one used principally in translating the Christian Greek Scriptures into English in the *New World Translation*. However, the New World Bible Translation Committee also consulted other excellent Greek texts, among them Nestle's Greek text (1948).

Commenting on the history of the text of the Christian Greek Scriptures and the results of modern textual research, Professor Kurt Aland wrote: "It can be determined, on the basis of 40 years of experience and with the results which have come to light in examining . . . manuscripts at 1,200 test places: The text of the New Testament has been excellently transmitted, better than any other writing from ancient times; the possibility that manuscripts might yet be found that would change its text decisively is zero."—*Das Neue Testament—zuverlässig überliefert* (The New Testament—Reliably Transmitted), Stuttgart, 1986, pp. 27, 28.

The extant manuscripts of the Christian Scriptures (in Greek and other languages) show textual variations. Variations are to be expected in view of human imperfection and the copying and recopying of manuscripts, especially by many copyists who were not professionals. If certain manuscripts had a common ancestor manuscript, perhaps came from a particular revision of early texts, or were produced in a particular area, they would probably have at least some variations in common, and hence they are said to belong to the same family, or group. On the basis of similarity in such differences, scholars have sought to classify the texts into groups, or families, the number of which has increased with the passing of time, till reference is now made to the Alexandrian, West-

ern, Eastern (Syriac and Caesarean), and the Byzantine texts, represented in various manuscripts or in different readings scattered throughout numerous manuscripts. But despite the variations peculiar to different manuscript families (and the variations within each group), the Scriptures have come down to us in essentially the same form as that of the original inspired writings. The variations of reading are of no consequence as to Bible teachings in general. And scholastic collations have corrected errors of any importance, so that today we enjoy an authentic and reliable text.

Since Westcott and Hort produced their refined Greek text, a number of critical editions of the Christian Greek Scriptures have been produced. Noteworthy among them is *The Greek New Testament* published by the United Bible Societies and now in its third edition. Identical in wording is the 26th edition of the so-called Nestle-Aland text, published in 1979 in Stuttgart, Germany.—See CHRISTIAN GREEK SCRIPTURES.

Manuscripts of Hebrew Scriptures. There are possibly 6,000 manuscripts of all or portions of the Hebrew Scriptures extant today in various libraries. The vast majority contain the Masoretic text and are of the tenth century C.E. or thereafter. The Masoretes (of the second half of the first millennium C.E.) sought to transmit the Hebrew text faithfully and made no changes in the wording of the text itself. However, to preserve the traditional pronunciation of the vowelless consonantal text, they devised systems of vowel pointing and accenting. Additionally, in their Masora, or marginal notes, they drew attention to textual peculiarities and gave corrected readings they considered necessary. It is the Masoretic text that appears in printed Hebrew Bibles of the present day.

Damaged Hebrew Scripture manuscripts used in Jewish synagogues were replaced by verified copies, and the defaced or damaged manuscripts were stored in a genizah (a synagogue storeroom or repository). Finally, when it was full, the manuscripts were removed and ceremoniously buried. Doubtless many ancient manuscripts perished in that way. But the contents of the synagogue genizah in Old Cairo were spared, probably because it was walled up and forgotten for centuries. Following the rebuilding of the synagogue in 1890 C.E., the manuscripts in its genizah were reexamined, and from there fairly complete Hebrew Scripture manuscripts and fragments (some said to be of the sixth century C.E.) found their way into various libraries.

One of the oldest extant fragments containing Biblical passages is the Nash Papyrus, found in

Egypt and preserved at Cambridge, England. Evidently part of an instructional collection, it is of the second or first century B.C.E. and consists of only four fragments of 24 lines of a pre-Masoretic text of the Ten Commandments and some verses of Deuteronomy, chapters 5 and 6.

Since 1947 many Biblical and non-Biblical scrolls have been found in various areas W of the Dead Sea, and these are referred to generally as the Dead Sea Scrolls. Most significant among them are manuscripts discovered in a number of caves in and about the Wadi Qumran (Nahal Qumeran). These are also known as the Qumran texts and evidently once belonged to a Jewish religious community centered at nearby Khirbet Qumran (Horvat Qumeran). The first discovery was made by a Bedouin in a cave about 15 km (9.5 mi) S of Jericho, where he found a number of earthenware jars containing ancient manuscripts. One of these was the now-renowned Dead Sea Scroll of Isaiah (1QIsª), a well-preserved leather roll of the entire book of Isaiah, except for a few gaps. (PICTURE, Vol. 1, p. 322) It contains a pre-Masoretic Hebrew script and has been dated toward the end of the second century B.C.E. Hence, it is about a thousand years older than the oldest extant manuscript of the Masoretic text. However, though showing some differences in spelling and grammatical construction, it does not vary doctrinally from the Masoretic text. Among the documents recovered in the Qumran area are fragments of over 170 scrolls representing parts of all Hebrew Scripture books except Esther, and in the case of some books, more than one copy exists. These manuscript scrolls and fragments are believed to range in date from about 250 B.C.E. to about the middle of the first century C.E., and they exhibit more than one type of Hebrew text, such as a proto-Masoretic text or one underlying the Greek *Septuagint*. Studies of such materials are still in progress.

Among notable vellum Hebrew manuscripts of the Hebrew Scriptures is the Cairo Karaite Codex of the Prophets. It contains the Masora and vocalization, and its colophon indicates that it was completed in about 895 C.E. by the noted Masorete Moses ben Asher of Tiberias. Another significant manuscript (of 916 C.E.) is the Leningrad Codex of the Later Prophets known as the Codex Babylonicus Petropolitanus. The Aleppo Sephardic Codex, once preserved at Aleppo, Syria, and now in Israel, until recently contained the entire Hebrew Scriptures. Its original consonantal text was corrected, punctuated, and furnished with the Masora about 930 C.E. by Aaron ben Asher, son of

Moses ben Asher. The oldest dated manuscript of the complete Hebrew Scriptures in Hebrew is the Leningrad Manuscript No. B 19ᴬ, preserved in the Public Library in Leningrad. It was copied in 1008 C.E. "from the corrected books prepared and annotated by Aaron ben Moses ben Asher the teacher." Another noteworthy Hebrew manuscript is a codex of the Pentateuch preserved in the British Museum (Codex Oriental 4445), consisting of Genesis 39:20 to Deuteronomy 1:33 (except for Nu 7:46-73 and 9:12–10:18, which are lacking or have been supplied by a later hand) and probably dating from the tenth century C.E.

Many manuscripts of the Hebrew Scripture portion of the Bible were written in Greek. Among those of particular note is one in the collection of the Fouad Papyri (Inventory Number 266, belonging to the Société Egyptienne de Papyrologie, Cairo), containing portions of the second half of Deuteronomy according to the *Septuagint*. It is of the first century B.C.E. and shows, in various places, the divine name written in square Hebrew characters within the Greek text. Fragments of Deuteronomy, chapters 23 to 28, are found in Rylands Papyrus iii. 458 of the second century B.C.E., preserved in Manchester, England. Another leading manuscript of the *Septuagint* contains fragments of Jonah, Micah, Habakkuk, Zephaniah, and Zechariah. In this leather scroll, dated to the end of the first century C.E., the divine name is rendered by the Tetragrammaton written in ancient Hebrew characters.—See *NW* appendix, pp. 1562-1564.

Manuscripts of Christian Greek Scriptures. The Christian Scriptures were written in Koine. Though no original autograph manuscripts thereof are known to exist today, according to one calculation, there are some 5,000 extant manuscript copies, whole or in part, of these Scriptures in Greek.

Papyrus manuscripts. Biblical papyri of great importance were among papyrus codices found in Egypt about 1930, their purchase being announced in 1931. Some of these Greek codices (dating from the second to the fourth centuries C.E.) consist of parts of eight Hebrew Scripture books (Genesis, Numbers, Deuteronomy, Isaiah, Jeremiah, Ezekiel, Daniel, and Esther), and three contain portions of 15 books of the Christian Greek Scriptures. Most of these Scriptural papyri were purchased by an American manuscript collector, A. Chester Beatty, and are now preserved in Dublin, Ireland. The rest were acquired by the University of Michigan and by others.

The international designation for Biblical papyri is a capital "P" followed by a small superior number. The Chester Beatty Papyrus No. 1 (P⁴⁵)

consists of parts of 30 leaves from a codex that probably once had about 220 leaves. P⁴⁵ has portions of the four Gospels and the book of Acts. The Chester Beatty Papyrus No. 3 (P⁴⁷) is a fragmentary codex of Revelation containing ten somewhat damaged leaves. These two papyri are believed to be from the third century C.E. Quite noteworthy is the Chester Beatty Papyrus No. 2 (P⁴⁶) believed to be from about 200 C.E. It has 86 somewhat damaged leaves out of a codex that probably had 104 leaves originally, and it still contains nine of Paul's inspired letters: Romans, Hebrews, First Corinthians, Second Corinthians, Ephesians, Galatians, Philippians, Colossians, and First Thessalonians. It is noteworthy that the letter to the Hebrews is included in this early codex. Since Hebrews does not give its writer's name, its composition by Paul has frequently been disputed. But this letter's inclusion in P⁴⁶, evidently consisting of Paul's letters exclusively, indicates that in about 200 C.E., Hebrews was accepted by early Christians as an inspired writing of the apostle Paul. The letter to the Ephesians appears in this codex, thus also refuting arguments that Paul did not write this letter.

At the John Rylands Library, Manchester, England, there is a small papyrus fragment of John's Gospel (some verses of chapter 18) cataloged as Rylands Papyrus 457. It is internationally designated as P⁵². This is the oldest extant manuscript fragment of the Christian Greek Scriptures, having been written in the first half of the second century, possibly about 125 C.E., and thus only a quarter of a century or so after John's death. The fact that a copy of John's Gospel was evidently circulating in Egypt (the place of the fragment's discovery) by that time shows that the good news according to John was really recorded in the first century C.E. and by John himself, not by some unknown writer well along in the second century C.E., after John's death, as some critics once claimed.

The most important addition to the collection of Biblical papyri since the discovery of the Chester Beatty Papyri was the acquisition of the Bodmer Papyri, published between 1956 and 1961. Particularly noteworthy are Papyrus Bodmer 2 (P⁶⁶) and Papyrus Bodmer 14, 15 (P⁷⁵), both written about 200 C.E. Papyrus Bodmer 2 contains a large part of the Gospel of John, while Papyrus Bodmer 14, 15 has much of Luke and John and is textually very close to Vatican Manuscript No. 1209.

Vellum manuscripts. Bible manuscripts written on vellum sometimes include both the Hebrew and Christian Greek Scripture portions of the Bible, though some are only of the Christian Scriptures.

Codex Bezae, designated by the letter "D," is a valuable manuscript of the fifth or sixth century C.E. Though its actual place of origin is unknown, it was acquired in France in 1562. It contains the Gospels, the book of Acts, and only a few other verses, and is an uncial manuscript, written in Greek on the left-hand pages, with a parallel Latin text appearing on the right-hand pages. This codex is preserved at Cambridge University in England, having been presented to that institution by Theodore Beza in 1581.

Codex Claromontanus (D₂) is likewise written in Greek and Latin on opposite pages, Greek on the left and Latin on the right. It contains Paul's canonical letters, including Hebrews, and is considered to be of the sixth century. It was reportedly found in the monastery at Clermont, France, and was acquired by Theodore Beza, but it is now preserved at the Bibliothèque Nationale in Paris.

Among more recently discovered vellum manuscripts of the Christian Greek Scriptures is Codex Washingtonianus I, containing the Gospels in Greek (in the common Western order: Matthew, John, Luke, and Mark). It was obtained in 1906 in Egypt and is preserved at the Freer Gallery of Art, Washington, D.C. The international symbol of this codex is "W," and it is thought to have been written in the fifth century C.E., except that apparently, because of damage, Matthew and part of John were replaced in the seventh century C.E. Codex Washingtonianus II, having the symbol "I," is also in the Freer Collection and contains portions of Paul's canonical letters, including Hebrews. This codex is believed to have been written in the fifth century C.E.

Hebrew and Christian Greek Scriptures. The most important and most complete extant Bible manuscripts in Greek were written on vellum in uncial letters.

Vatican Manuscript No. 1209. The Vatican Manuscript No. 1209 (Codex Vaticanus), designated internationally by the symbol "B," is an uncial codex of the fourth century C.E., possibly produced in Alexandria, and it originally contained the entire Bible in Greek. A corrector of later date retraced the letters, perhaps because the original writing had faded, except that he skipped letters and words he considered incorrect. Originally this codex probably had approximately 820 leaves, of which 759 remain. Most of Genesis is gone, as well as a part of Psalms, Hebrews 9:14 to 13:25, and all of First and Second Timothy, Titus, Philemon, and Revelation. Codex Vaticanus is preserved at the Vatican Library in Rome, Italy, and is known to

Sinaitic Manuscript, of the fourth century C.E., containing much of the Bible in Greek

have been there as early as the 15th century. However, Vatican Library authorities made access to the manuscript extremely difficult for scholars and did not publish a full photographic facsimile of the entire codex until 1889-1890.

Sinaitic Manuscript. The Sinaitic Manuscript (Codex Sinaiticus) is also of the fourth century C.E., but Codex Vaticanus may be a little older. The Sinaitic Manuscript is designated by the symbol ℵ (*'a'leph,* first letter in the Hebrew alphabet), and while it evidently once contained the entire Bible in Greek, part of the Hebrew Scriptures has been lost. However, it has all the Christian Greek Scriptures. Likely this codex originally consisted of 730 leaves, at least, though the whole or parts of just 393 are now verified to be extant. It was discovered (one portion in 1844 and another in 1859) by the Bible scholar Konstantin von Tischendorf at the Monastery of St. Catherine at Mount Sinai. Forty-three leaves of this codex are kept in Leipzig, portions of three leaves are at Leningrad, and 347 leaves are preserved at the British Museum in London. It has been reported that 8 to 14 more leaves were discovered in the same monastery in 1975.

Alexandrine Manuscript. The Alexandrine Manuscript (Codex Alexandrinus), designated by the letter "A," is a Greek uncial manuscript containing most of the Bible, including the book of Revelation. Of possibly 820 original leaves, 773 have been preserved. This codex is generally considered to be of the first half of the fifth century C.E., and it is also preserved in the British Museum.—PICTURE, Vol. 2, p. 336.

Codex Ephraemi Syri rescriptus. The Codex Ephraemi Syri rescriptus (Codex Ephraemi), designated internationally by the letter "C," is also generally considered to have originated in the fifth century C.E. It is written in Greek uncials on vellum and is a rewritten codex, a palimpsest manuscript. The original Greek text was removed, and a number of leaves were then written over with discourses of Ephraem Syrus (the Syrian), rendered in Greek. This was done probably during the 12th century, when there was a scarcity of vellum. However, the underlying text has been deciphered. While "C" evidently once contained all the Scriptures in Greek, just 209 leaves remain, 145 being of the Christian Greek Scriptures. Hence, this codex now contains only portions of Hebrew Scripture books and parts of all books of the Christian Greek Scriptures except Second Thessalonians and Second John. It is preserved at the Bibliothèque Nationale in Paris.

Reliability of the Bible Text. Appreciation of the reliability of the Bible is greatly enhanced when it is realized that, by comparison, there are only very few extant manuscripts of the works of classical secular writers and none of these are original, autograph manuscripts. Though they are only copies made centuries after the death of the authors, present-day scholars accept such late copies as sufficient evidence of the authenticity of the text.

Extant Hebrew manuscripts of the Scriptures were prepared with great care. Respecting the text of the Hebrew Scriptures, scholar W. H. Green observed: "It may be safely said that no other work of antiquity has been so accurately transmitted." (*Archaeology and Bible History*, by J. P. Free, 1964, p. 5) The late Bible text scholar Sir Frederic Kenyon made this reassuring statement in the introduction to his seven volumes entitled *The Chester Beatty Biblical Papyri:* "The first and most important conclusion derived from the examination of them [the Papyri] is the satisfactory one that they confirm the essential soundness of the existing texts. No striking or fundamental variation is shown either in the Old or the New Testament. There are no important omissions or additions of passages, and no variations which affect vital facts or doctrines. The variations of text affect minor matters, such as the order of words or the precise words used. . . . But their essential importance is their confirmation, by evidence of an earlier date than was hitherto available, of the integrity of our existing texts. In this respect they are an acquisition of epoch-making value."—London, 1933, Fasciculus I, p. 15.

Concerning the Christian Greek Scriptures, Sir Frederic Kenyon stated: "The interval then between the dates of original composition and the earliest extant evidence becomes so small as to be in fact negligible, and the last foundation for any doubt that the Scriptures have come down to us substantially as they were written has now been removed. Both the *authenticity* and the *general integrity* of the books of the New Testament may be regarded as finally established."—*The Bible and Archæology*, 1940, pp. 288, 289.

Centuries ago, Jesus Christ, "the faithful and true witness" (Re 3:14), repeatedly and emphatically confirmed the genuineness of the Hebrew Scriptures, as did his apostles. (Lu 24:27, 44; Ro 15:4) Extant ancient versions, or translations, further bespeak the exactness of the preserved Hebrew Scriptures. Manuscripts and versions of the Christian Greek Scriptures bear unassailable testimony to the marvelous preservation and accurate transmission of that portion of God's Word. We are therefore now favored with an authentic, thoroughly reliable Bible text. A thoughtful examination of preserved manuscripts of the Holy Scriptures bears eloquent testimony to their faithful preservation and permanence, giving added meaning to the inspired statement: "The green grass has dried up, the blossom has withered; but as for the word of our God, it will last to time indefinite."—Isa 40:8; 1Pe 1:24, 25.

MAOCH (Ma'och). Father of Achish, king of the Philistine city of Gath, with whom David and his 600 men found refuge from Saul. (1Sa 27:1-3) He may be the same person as the Maacah of 1 Kings 2:39, though such identification is not positive. The name Maacah is quite similar to Maoch, and it is possible that Achish, who was ruling when David was outlawed, was still the Philistine king of Gath at the commencement of Solomon's rule.

MAON (Ma'on).

1. A descendant of Caleb through Shammai. Maon may have been the father of Beth-zur's inhabitants or the principal man or founder of that city.—1Ch 2:42, 45.

2. A city in the mountainous region of Judah. (Jos 15:20, 48, 55) Israel's King Saul pursued David and his men into the wilderness area surrounding Maon. But news of a Philistine raid forced Saul to abandon the chase. (1Sa 23:24-28) Later, David's men were treated inhospitably by Nabal, a rich landowner apparently residing at Maon. (1Sa 25:2-11) This city is identified with Tell Ma'in (Horvat Ma'on [Bi-Yehuda]) atop a high hill about 13 km (8 mi) SSE of Hebron.

MARA (Ma'ra) [Bitter]. The name Mara was suggested by Elimelech's widow for herself to express the bitterness she experienced because of being bereaved of her husband and her sons Mahlon and Chilion. Naomi had left Bethlehem with a husband and two sons (Ru 1:1, 2), but returned from Moab as a saddened, childless widow. At that time her old friends, the women of Bethlehem, asked: "Is this Naomi?" Still grief stricken, she replied: "Do not call me Naomi [meaning "My Pleasantness"]. Call me Mara [meaning "Bitter"], for the Almighty has made it very bitter for me. I was full when I went, and it is empty-handed that Jehovah has made me return."—Ru 1:19-21.

MARAH (Ma'rah) [Bitterness]. One of Israel's early encampments in the Sinai Peninsula. It was named "Marah" because of the unpalatable water found there. (Ex 15:23; Nu 33:8) Although having only recently been delivered from the Egyptians at the Red Sea, the Israelites gave way to faithless murmuring when they were unable to drink the water at Marah. Thereafter, at Jehovah's direction, Moses cast a tree into the water, and the water became sweet. The Bible does not specify the kind of tree, and so there is no basis for identifying it. Of course, Jehovah could have directed Moses to a particular variety having natural properties for sweetening the water. But there is no need to seek a scientific or natural explanation, as the healing of the water was doubtless miraculous.—Ex 15:23-25; compare 2Ki 2:19-22; 4:38-41.

Jehovah used the circumstances at Marah to test the Israelites as to their faith in his ability to care for them. Since bad water can cause disease (2Ki 2:19), the sweetening of the water illustrated Jehovah's ability to preserve the Israelites from the maladies experienced by the Egyptians. The "regulation" Jehovah then taught the Israelites was: Obedience to him as their God would prevent their being afflicted by the maladies he put upon the Egyptians.—Ex 15:25, 26.

Marah is usually identified with 'Ein Hawwara 80 km (50 mi) SSE of modern Suez, just a few miles inland from the Red Sea.

MARBLE. A crystalline limestone (calcium carbonate) of close grain that varies in color, texture, and crystal structure, and that is capable of taking a high polish. Its color ranges from snow white to numerous shades of gray, brown, yellow, red, green, and black. Streaks, or veins, are due to impurities of metal oxides and carbonaceous matter.

Marble apparently was not found in Palestine. Lebanon produced a variety of marbles; but in the Aegean island of Paros and in Arabia, the choicest specimens were found. The Shulammite maiden, in describing her beloved shepherd companion to the ladies-in-waiting at the court of King Solomon, said: "His legs are pillars of marble based on socket pedestals of refined gold." (Ca 5:15) The Persian palace at Shushan in the days of Queen Esther had marble pillars, and its pavement in part was made of black marble. (Es 1:6) Marble is also listed as one of the precious commodities of "the traveling merchants of the earth" who weep over Babylon the Great's fall into destruction.—Re 18:11, 12.

It is uncertain whether Solomon made use of marble in his building program. Josephus says "white marble" was used, but the Hebrew word usually translated "marble" at 1 Chronicles 29:2 probably denotes "alabaster" and is thus rendered in some translations. (*JB, NW; Jewish Antiquities,* VIII, 64 [iii, 2]) This is in agreement with *A Hebrew and English Lexicon of the Old Testament* by Brown, Driver, and Briggs (1980, p. 1010), and *Lexicon in Veteris Testamenti Libros,* by Koehler and Baumgartner (Leiden, 1958, p. 966).

MAREAL (Mar'e·al). A boundary location of Zebulun. (Jos 19:10, 11) Some tentatively identify it with Tell Ghalta (Tel Re'ala), about 6 km (3.5 mi) ENE of Jokneam in the Valley of Jezreel.

MARESHA(H) (Ma·re'sha[h]) [Place at the Head (Summit)].

1. A descendant of Judah who is called the "father" of Hebron. (1Ch 2:3, 42) While it might be concluded that Mareshah was the ancestor of the inhabitants of the city of Hebron, this is unlikely since the Hebron here mentioned had sons and thus was evidently a person.—1Ch 2:43.

2. A descendant of Judah through Shelah. Laadah is identified as "the father of Mareshah." (1Ch 4:21) While it is possible that this Mareshah (or his father Laadah) founded the town of Mareshah, or that he is the same person as the Judahite mentioned above, there is no certainty about these matters.

3. One of a group of nine cities in the Shephelah region of Judah (Jos 15:44), Mareshah occupied a position of strategic importance beside one of the valleys forming a natural route from the coastal plain up into the mountains and to Hebron. It is identified with Tell Sandahannah (Tel Maresha), about 1.5 km (1 mi) S of Beit Jibrin (Bet Guvrin).

King Rehoboam, successor to Solomon, made a fortress city of Mareshah, thereby strengthening Judah's defense against attack from that avenue of approach. (2Ch 11:5, 8) Zerah the Ethiopian swept up from the S with his huge force of a million men and was met at Mareshah by the army of King Asa, and the battle, resulting in a Judean victory by divine assistance, was fought in that area. Asa pursued the defeated Ethiopian force about 35 km (22 mi) to Gerar, SW of Mareshah. (2Ch 14:9-13) Mareshah, also Maresha, was the hometown of the prophet Eliezer, who correctly foretold the failure of King Jehoshaphat's joint maritime enterprise with Ahaziah of Israel. (2Ch 20:35-37) Micah's prophecy, warning apostate Judah and Israel of impending punishment, makes specific reference to Mareshah.—Mic 1:15.

In the postexilic period, Mareshah became known as Marisa and continued to be a site of considerable importance, though it became a Sidonian colony and later an Idumean stronghold. It was finally destroyed by the Parthians in 40 B.C.E.

MARINER. One who navigates or assists in the operation of a ship; a sailor or seaman. (1Ki 9:26, 27; Eze 27:8, 9; Re 18:17-19) The life of ancient mariners was a perilous one. In a storm-tossed sea they were practically helpless. Wrote the psalmist: "Because of the calamity their very soul finds itself melting. They reel and move unsteadily like a drunken man, and even all their wisdom proves confused. And they begin crying out to Jehovah in their distress."—Ps 107:26-28.

Acts 27:15-19 contains a vivid account of the measures taken by mariners during a storm. The skiff, which was towed along and evidently served as a lifeboat when needed, was hoisted aboard. Helps, possibly ropes or chains, were used to undergird the boat, that is, were passed around the hull of the ship and tightened on deck. The gear was lowered. This may mean that the mainsail was reduced. Items were thrown overboard to lighten the vessel, serving to increase the ship's buoyancy.—Compare Jon 1:5; Ac 27:38; see SHIP.

MARK, I. The Roman surname of the son of Mary of Jerusalem. His Hebrew name was John, meaning "Jehovah Has Shown Favor; Jehovah Has Been Gracious." (Ac 12:12, 25) Mark was a cousin of Barnabas, was his traveling companion and that of other early Christian missionaries, and was inspired to write the Gospel bearing his own name. (Col 4:10) Mark is the John Mark mentioned in the book of Acts and the John of Acts 13:5, 13.

He was evidently an early believer in Christ. His mother's home was used as a place of worship by the early Christian congregation, which may mean that both she and Mark became Jesus' followers before Christ's death. (Ac 12:12) Since Mark alone mentions the scantily clad young man who fled on the night of Jesus' betrayal, there is reason to believe that Mark himself was that young man. (Mr 14:51, 52) So it seems likely that Mark was present when the holy spirit was poured out on the some 120 disciples of Christ on Pentecost 33 C.E.—Ac 1:13-15; 2:1-4.

After they had carried out the relief ministration in Jerusalem, Barnabas and Saul (Paul) "returned and took along with them John, the one surnamed Mark." It appears that Mark served as their attendant, perhaps caring for their physical needs while they traveled. (Ac 12:25; 13:5) For some undisclosed reason, when they arrived at Perga in Pamphylia, "John [Mark] withdrew from them and returned to Jerusalem." (Ac 13:13) When Paul later set out on his second missionary journey, though Barnabas was determined to take Mark along, Paul "did not think it proper to be taking this one along with them, seeing that he had departed from them from Pamphylia and had not gone with them to the work." "A sharp burst of anger" ensued, and they separated; Barnabas took Mark with him to Cyprus and Paul took Silas with him through Syria and Cilicia.—Ac 15:36-41.

Some time thereafter, however, whatever breach there was between Paul, Barnabas, and Mark was evidently healed, for Mark was with Paul in Rome and joined him in sending greetings to the Colossian Christians (c. 60-61 C.E.). Paul spoke favorably of him, saying: "Aristarchus my fellow captive sends you his greetings, and so does Mark the cousin of Barnabas, (concerning whom you received commands to welcome him if ever he comes to you)." (Col 4:10) Mark is also among those mentioned by Paul as sending greetings to

Philemon when the apostle wrote to him from Rome (also c. 60-61 C.E.). (Phm 23, 24) Later (c. 65 C.E.), when Paul was again a prisoner in Rome, he specifically asked Timothy to "take Mark and bring him with you, for he is useful to me for ministering."—2Ti 4:11.

John Mark also associated with Peter in Babylon, for he is mentioned as sending greetings in the apostle's first letter (written c. 62-64 C.E.). Peter calls him "Mark my son," perhaps indicating the strong bond of Christian affection that existed between them. (1Pe 5:13; compare 1Jo 2:1, 7.) Thus, Mark, once the cause of difficulty, gained the commendation and trust of prominent servants of God and enjoyed the yet greater privilege of being inspired to write an account of Jesus' ministry. —See JOHN No. 4; MARK, GOOD NEWS ACCORDING TO.

MARK, II. Among non-Israelites, animals and even slaves were branded with a mark as an indication of ownership. In the case of humans, such property marks were placed on a conspicuous part of the body, such as the forehead. Worshipers of false gods at times identified themselves as such by having the mark of their deity on their forehead. However, Jehovah's law to Israel prohibited disfiguring humans with tattoo marks. This served to counteract any idolatrous practices and taught due regard for God's creation.—Le 19:28; see BRAND MARK.

Figurative Use. The Scriptures allude to marks made on humans and refer to these in a figurative sense. In Ezekiel's vision a man with a secretary's inkhorn was commissioned to go through Jerusalem and to 'put a mark [Heb., taw] on those who were sighing and groaning over all the detestable things that were being done in the midst of it.' This action on their part showed that they were righteous persons, servants belonging to Jehovah, and therefore worthy of preservation at the time for the execution of Jehovah's judgment. The figurative mark on their forehead testified to that fact.—Eze 9; compare Eze 9:4, ftn; 2Pe 2:6-8.

On the other hand, in John's vision persons receiving the mark (or, engraving) of the wild beast on their forehead or on their hand were in line for destruction. The mark on the forehead publicly identified them as worshipers of the wild beast and therefore as slaves to it. They were thus shown to be opposers of God, for the wild beast received its authority from the dragon, Satan the Devil. The mark on the hand would logically signify active support of the wild beast, the hand being used to accomplish work.—Re 13:1, 2, 16-18; 14:9, 10; 16:1, 2; 20:4.

See also BOUNDARY MARK.

BABYLON was indeed an impressive city—with towering walls, its Processional Way, the famous Hanging Gardens, and upwards of 50 temples.

Very early in man's history, Babel (later named Babylon) became a prominent center of worship that defied the true God, Jehovah. (Ge 10:9, 10) Jehovah thwarted the purpose of its builders by confusing the people's language and scattering them from there throughout the earth. (Ge 11:4-9) Thus it came about that false worship spread from Babylon to other lands.

Babylon's defiance of Jehovah eventually led to its downfall. In prophecy, Jehovah depicted Babylon as a lion having eagle's wings; he also foretold its fall and its eventual desolation. On October 5, 539 B.C.E., in one night, Babylon was taken by Cyrus the Great, whom Jehovah had foretold by name. Babylon fell in the very manner foretold. Eventually the city became "piles of stones," never to be rebuilt.—Jer 51:37; see Isa 44:27–45:2.

PRINCIPAL CITIES

Babylon: Political and religious capital of the empire; many Jewish exiles were here

Tema: Apparently a second capital, established by King Nabonidus, who left Belshazzar in charge at Babylon

Nineveh: Assyrian capital, which fell to a coalition of Chaldeans and Medes in 632 B.C.E.

Carchemish: Nebuchadnezzar II defeated Egyptian forces here, establishing Babylonian supremacy in Syria

Jerusalem: Became tributary to Babylon in 620 B.C.E. Besieged by Babylonian forces in 618-617 and in 609-607 B.C.E.

Tyre: Capitulated to Babylonian forces after a 13-year siege

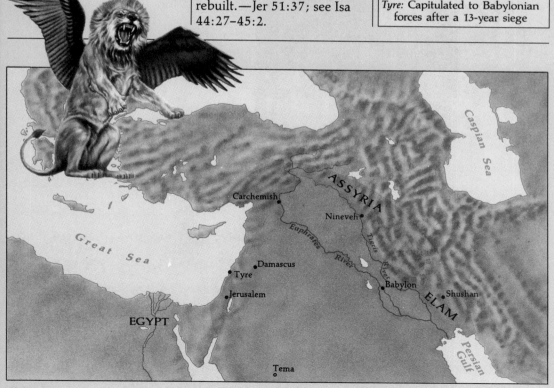

A reconstruction
of the Ishtar Gate

Ziggurat at Ur. The tower
erected at Babel was likely
a religious ziggurat such as this

This inscription sets out the boasting of Nebuchadnezzar II regarding all he did to enlarge and extend Babylon (Compare Da 4:30)

Walls of Babylon. The city appeared to be impregnable. It was protected by a massive system of double walls. A second set of walls surrounded the eastern part of the city; a wall also served as a protection along the eastern bank of the Euphrates, which ran through the city. The temple of Marduk was the central feature of Babylon. Associated with it was the tower of Etemenanki (viewed by some as the Tower of Babel), which reached to a height of 91 m (300 ft)

Decoration from Babylon's Processional Way. Interestingly, Babylon is symbolized in the Bible by a lion (Da 7:4)

Clay model of a sheep's liver, inscribed with omens and magical formulas; used in Babylon for divination (Compare Eze 21:20-22)

Nabonidus, the last supreme monarch of Babylon, with symbols of his gods. Looking to the heavenly bodies, and the gods that were associated with these, did not save Babylon (Isa 47:12-15)

This is claimed to be the oldest remaining example of a horoscope; from Babylonia; believed to date from the fifth century B.C.E.

The ruins of ancient Babylon testify to the reliability of Bible prophecy. Babylon was once "the decoration of kingdoms"; now it is "a desolate waste" (Isa 13:19-22; Jer 50:13)

The fall of Babylon

Nabonidus Chronicle
—a cuneiform tablet that
confirms the sudden fall
of Babylon to Cyrus

ANCIENT Jerusalem enjoyed a unique distinction: It was the only earthly city upon which Jehovah placed his name. (1Ki 11:36) It was also the center for the pure worship of Jehovah. His temple was built there, and for that reason Jerusalem could especially be called God's "resting-place." (Ps 132:13, 14; 135:21) In addition, Jerusalem was the location where the kings of the Davidic line sat on "Jehovah's throne," representing him by administering his laws. —1Ch 29:23.

In contrast, ancient Babylon was the center from which false worship spread to all parts of the earth. It was of special significance, therefore, when Jehovah permitted Babylon to destroy unfaithful Jerusalem. In 620 B.C.E., Jerusalem was made subject to Babylon. (2Ki 24:1) Three years later, in 617 B.C.E., the Babylonians deported many of Jerusalem's inhabitants —its nobility, its mighty men, and its craftsmen—and looted the city's treasures. (2Ch 36:5-10) Finally, the city, along with the temple, was destroyed and thousands of Jews were taken into exile.—2Ch 36:17-20.

Jerusalem's destruction took place in 607 B.C.E., a very significant year from the standpoint of Bible prophecy. Although this date differs from the one used by many Bible commentators, it is used consistently in this publication. Why? Because we give greater weight to the testimony of the Bible than to the conclusions that scholars have drawn from the fragmentary record of history that is available on cuneiform tablets.

Babylonian chronicle that tells of Nebuchadnezzar's capturing Jerusalem, seizing the king, and appointing one of his own choice; 617 B.C.E.

According to some archaeologists, this "Burnt Room" excavated in Jerusalem dates back to the destruction of Jerusalem at the time of Judah's last king

Medo-Persian Empire

THE Medes and the Persians are referred to repeatedly in the Scriptures because they pursued a policy of religious toleration that served to fulfill Bible prophecy.

Jehovah had permitted the Jews to be taken into captivity by Babylon, a nation that did not release captive peoples. Yet, God also had foretold Jewish restoration to their homeland. (Jer 27:22; 30:3) Medo-Persia, referred to in the Bible symbolically as a bear (Da 7:5), served Jehovah's purpose in this regard.

Shortly after Babylon's fall, Persian King Cyrus decreed that the formerly captive Jews could return to their homeland and rebuild Jehovah's temple. (Ezr 1:2-4) Darius I later honored this decree. (Ezr 6:1-11) King Ahasuerus (evidently Xerxes I), when properly informed, signed a decree that thwarted a scheme to exterminate the Jews. (Es 7:3–8:14) In 455 B.C.E., King Artaxerxes Longimanus granted permission for Nehemiah to rebuild Jerusalem's walls, thus beginning the prophetic countdown to the appearance of the Messiah. —Ne 2:3-8; Da 9:25.

PRINCIPAL LOCATIONS

Pasargadae: An early Persian capital

Shushan: Former Elamite capital that became administrative center of the Medo-Persian Empire

Persepolis: A royal city built by Emperors Darius I, Xerxes I, and Artaxerxes Longimanus

Ecbatana: Summer capital of the empire; it had been the capital of Media

Babylon: A royal city of the empire; because of the torrid summer weather, the city seldom served as more than a winter capital

Gaugamela: Site of the defeat of Persia's million-man army by Alexander the Great in 331 B.C.E., thus marking the end of the empire

Relief work showing Medes (with round hats)
and Persians (with fluted hats)

Seal impression of Darius I.
Darius upheld the Jews in their
temple-rebuilding work in Jerusalem

Cyrus Cylinder

Modern Hamadan
(in Iran), the site of
ancient Ecbatana. Here
Cyrus the Great had a
palace. His policy of
religious toleration
greatly benefited
the Jews

Ruins from ancient Persepolis.
Here Darius I, Xerxes I, and Artaxerxes
Longimanus built palaces

Excavations of ancient town area in Shushan

Decorations typical of those that adorned the palace audience hall at Shushan

Mordecai and Esther before King Ahasuerus (evidently Xerxes I)

Exiles Return From Babylon

IN 607 B.C.E. the once-prosperous land of Judah was made "a desolate waste, without an inhabitant," as Jewish captives were led away to exile in Babylon and a remnant fled to Egypt. (Jer 9:11) The God of loving-kindness, though, would not leave his people in exile forever. He foretold that they would "have to serve the king of Babylon seventy years," after which he would deliver a faithful remnant. (Jer 25:11, 12; 29:10-14) And not even the seemingly impregnable world power of Babylon could thwart God's stated purpose. The return of the Jewish exiles demonstrates the unerring accuracy with

Cyrus Cylinder, which states the policy of Cyrus to return captives to their homelands and to aid in restoration of their temples

which Jehovah's prophecies are fulfilled.

Even before the end of the 70 years of exile, Babylon fell, in 539 B.C.E., to the invading armies of Persian King Cyrus. Then, during his first year as ruler of Babylon, Cyrus issued a decree opening the way for the Jewish exiles to return to Jerusalem. (Ezr 1:1-4) A remnant that may have numbered 200,000 (including men, women, and children) made the journey, arriving in Judah in 537 B.C.E. (Ezr 1:5–3:1; 4:1) Thus the 70 years' desolation ended exactly on time!

Not all the exiles returned at that time, however. In 468 B.C.E., another group of returnees accompanied the priest Ezra, who brought to Jerusalem gifts for the temple. (Ezr 7:1–8:32) Then in 455 B.C.E., Nehemiah traveled from Shushan to rebuild Jerusalem's walls. (Ne 2:5, 6, 11) As to the exact route followed by the returnees, the Scriptures are silent. Some reasonable possibilities are shown on the map.

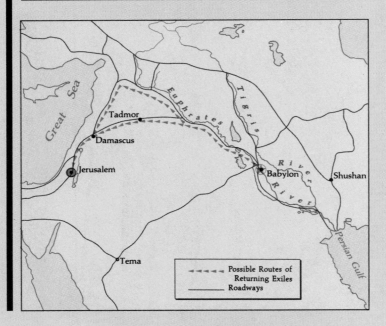

Possible Routes of Returning Exiles
Roadways

Grecian Empire

AMAZING events in Greek history have fulfilled Bible prophecy. Greece seemed an unlikely candidate for world power, as its people were divided into independent tribes and city-states.

But Bible prophecy recorded in the sixth century B.C.E. pointed to a dramatic change. Symbolizing Greece first as a leopard with wings and then as a he-goat with a conspicuous horn, it foretold in an unmistakable way that Greece would trample down the Medo-Persian World Power. It also disclosed that the power of a "conspicuous horn" would be broken and that four others would come up instead of it.—Da 7:6; 8:5-8, 20-22; 11:3, 4.

Alexander the Great proved to be that "conspicuous horn." Beginning in 334 B.C.E., he led a small but well-disciplined Greek army to one victory after another. With lightning speed he conquered Asia Minor, Syria, Palestine, Egypt, and the entire Medo-Persian Empire as far as India. But in just a few years Alexander was dead, and in a relatively short time his empire was split four ways, among four of his generals.

The Grecian Empire was short-lived, but its effects were long-lasting. Before his death, Alexander had introduced Greek culture and the Greek language into all parts of his domain. Common Greek became the lingua franca of many nationalities, and this later contributed to the rapid spread of Christianity throughout the Mediterranean area.

Athens and its acropolis as these now appear. Even after Greece ceased to be a world power, Athens remained an international cultural center

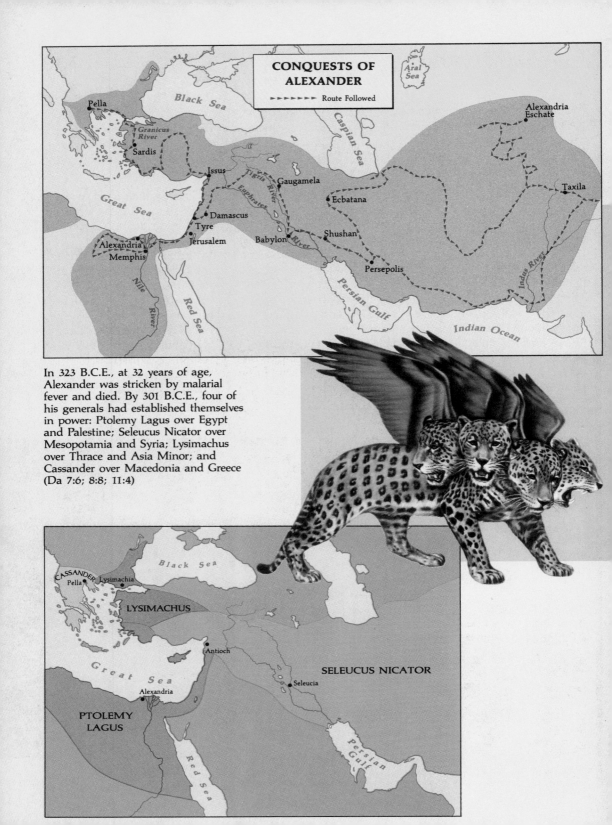

CONQUESTS OF ALEXANDER

▶▶▶▶▶ Route Followed

Aral Sea

Black Sea

Pella

Granicus River

Sardis

Issus

Caspian Sea

Alexandria Eschate

Great Sea

Tigris River

Euphrates

Gaugamela

Ecbatana

Taxila

Damascus

Tyre

Jerusalem

Babylon

River

Shushan

Alexandria

Memphis

Nile River

Red Sea

Persepolis

Persian Gulf

Indus River

Indian Ocean

In 323 B.C.E., at 32 years of age, Alexander was stricken by malarial fever and died. By 301 B.C.E., four of his generals had established themselves in power: Ptolemy Lagus over Egypt and Palestine; Seleucus Nicator over Mesopotamia and Syria; Lysimachus over Thrace and Asia Minor; and Cassander over Macedonia and Greece (Da 7:6; 8:8; 11:4)

CASSANDER

Pella

Lysimachia

Black Sea

LYSIMACHUS

Antioch

Great Sea

Alexandria

Seleucia

SELEUCUS NICATOR

PTOLEMY LAGUS

Red Sea

Persian Gulf

Greek games were associated with Greek religion;
a gymnasium established in Jerusalem thus corrupted Jewish youths

A ceramic platter showing a pig being sacrificed.
In a vicious attempt to defile and to stamp out
the worship of Jehovah, Antiochus IV
(Epiphanes) made such a sacrifice on
an altar built over the large one
in Jehovah's temple in Jerusalem
and then dedicated the temple
to Zeus

Coin bearing
the likeness of
Antiochus IV (Epiphanes)

Ancient Corinth.
Christians in the first-century
congregation here had to
contend with the influence
of Greek philosophy and the
morally corrupting practices
of its religion

The philosopher Plato, of the
fourth century B.C.E., did much
to propagate the Greek notion
of immortality of the soul

The Alexandrine Manuscript, in
Greek, of the fifth century C.E.
Most of the Christian Greek
Scriptures was originally written
in Koine, the common Greek

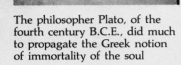

MARK, GOOD NEWS ACCORDING TO.

The divinely inspired record of the ministry of Jesus Christ written by John Mark. This account of "the good news about Jesus Christ" begins with the work of Christ's forerunner, John the Baptizer, and concludes with a report of the circumstances surrounding Jesus' resurrection. Hence, it covers the time from the spring of 29 to the spring of 33 C.E. —Mr 1:1.

This Gospel, the shortest of all four, is a rapid-moving and descriptive record of the ministry of Jesus Christ as the miracle-working Son of God. Frequent is the use of "immediately" or "at once." (Mr 1:10, 12, 18, 21, 29) The account is almost evenly divided between conversation and action.

Source of Information. Ancient tradition indicates that Peter provided the basic information for Mark's Gospel, and this would agree with the fact that Mark was associated with Peter in Babylon. (1Pe 5:13) According to Origen, Mark composed his Gospel "in accordance with Peter's instructions." (*The Ecclesiastical History,* Eusebius, VI, xxv, 3-7) In his work, "Against Marcion" (IV, v), Tertullian says that the Gospel of Mark "may be affirmed to be Peter's, whose interpreter Mark was." (*The Ante-Nicene Fathers,* Vol. III, p. 350) Eusebius gives the statement of "John the presbyter" as quoted by Papias (c. 140 C.E.): "And the Presbyter used to say this, 'Mark became Peter's interpreter and wrote accurately all that he remembered, not, indeed, in order, of the things said or done by the Lord. . . . Mark did nothing wrong in thus writing down single points as he remembered them. For to one thing he gave attention, to leave out nothing of what he had heard and to make no false statements in them.'"—*The Ecclesiastical History,* III, xxxix, 12-16.

John Mark evidently also had other sources of information. Since Jesus' early disciples met in the home of his mother (Ac 12:12), Mark must have been acquainted with persons other than Peter who had known Jesus Christ well, individuals who had seen him doing his work and had heard him preach and teach. Probably being the "certain young man" whom those arresting Christ tried to seize but who "got away naked," Mark himself was apparently not totally without personal contact with Jesus.—Mr 14:51, 52.

Evidently Written With Non-Jews in Mind. While the good news according to Mark would interest and benefit Jewish readers, apparently it was not written specifically for them. It seems to have been composed primarily for non-Jewish readers, especially the Romans. Its conciseness and abrupt character have been viewed as particularly suitable for the intellect of Roman readers. Latin terms are sometimes transliterated into Greek, as when the Greek word *prai·to'ri·on* is used for the Latin term *praetorium.* (Mr 15:16, *Int*) Also, the Greek word *ken·ty·ri'on* is employed for the Latin word *centurio,* an officer in command of a hundred soldiers.—Mr 15:39, *Int.*

The account contains explanations that would not have been necessary for Jewish readers. It indicates that the Jordan was a river and shows that the temple could be seen from the Mount of Olives. (Mr 1:5; 13:3) It mentions that the Pharisees practiced "fasting" and that the Sadducees "say there is no resurrection." (2:18; 12:18) This Gospel also explains that the Passover victim was sacrificed on "the first day of unfermented cakes" and that "Preparation" was "the day before the sabbath."—14:12; 15:42.

Whereas it would not normally have been necessary to explain Semitic terms for Jewish readers in general, Mark's Gospel provides many of such explanations. Interpretations are given for "Boanerges" ("Sons of Thunder"), *"Tal'i·tha cu'mi"* ("Maiden, I say to you, Get up!"), "corban" ("a gift dedicated to God"), and *"E'li, E'li, la'ma sa·bach·tha'ni?"* ("My God, my God, why have you forsaken me?").—Mr 3:17; 5:41; 7:11; 15:34.

Time and Place of Composition. According to ancient tradition, Mark's Gospel was first made public in Rome, this being the testimony of such early writers as Clement, Eusebius, and Jerome. Mark was in Rome during Paul's first imprisonment there. (Col 4:10; Phm 1, 23, 24) Thereafter he was with Peter in Babylon. (1Pe 5:13) Then, during Paul's second imprisonment in Rome, Paul asked that Timothy come soon and bring Mark with him. (2Ti 4:11) Probably Mark did then return to Rome. Since no mention is made of Jerusalem's destruction in fulfillment of Jesus' prophecy, Mark must have compiled his account before that event in 70 C.E. His presence in Rome at least once, and likely twice, during the years 60-65 C.E. suggests that Mark may have completed his Gospel there sometime during those years.

Some Unique Features of Mark's Account. Though largely covering material similar to that of Matthew and Luke, Mark also provides supplementary details. Some of these illuminate how Jesus felt about certain things. He was 'grieved at the insensibility of the hearts' of persons who objected to his healing a man's withered hand on the Sabbath. (Mr 3:5) When Jesus received a poor reception from people in his home territory, "he wondered at their lack of faith." (6:6) And he "felt love" for the rich young man who asked about the requirements for gaining everlasting life.—10:21.

Also unique with Mark's account are certain points regarding the end of Jesus' earthly life. He reports that at Jesus' trial the false witnesses were not in agreement. (Mr 14:59) The passerby impressed into service to carry Jesus' torture stake was Simon of Cyrene, "the father of Alexander and Rufus." (15:21) And Mark relates that Pilate made sure that Jesus was dead before granting permission for Joseph of Arimathea to take the body for burial.—15:43-45.

One of the four illustrations of Jesus found in Mark's Gospel is unique. (Mr 4:26-29) The account mentions at least 19 miracles performed by Jesus Christ. Two of these (the healing of a deaf man who also had a speech impediment and the cure of a certain blind man) are contained only in Mark's Gospel.—Mr 7:31-37; 8:22-26.

References to the Hebrew Scriptures. Although Mark appears to have written primarily for the Romans, this record does contain references to and quotations from the Hebrew Scriptures. The work of John the Baptizer is shown to have been a fulfillment of Isaiah 40:3 and Malachi 3:1. (Mr 1:2-4) Also to be found in the account are instances of Jesus' applying, quoting from, or alluding to the Hebrew Scriptures. These include: Giving God mere lip service (Mr 7:6, 7; Isa 29:13); honoring parents (Mr 7:10; Ex 20:12; 21:17); the creation of man and woman and the institution of marriage (Mr 10:6-9; Ge 1:27; 2:24); various commandments (Mr 10:19; Ex 20:12-16; Le 19:13); Jesus' comments regarding the temple (Mr 11:17; Isa 56:7; Jer 7:11); his statement about being rejected (Mr 12:10, 11; Ps 118:22, 23); Jehovah's words to Moses at the burning thornbush (Mr 12:26; Ex 3:2, 6); the two great commandments on love (Mr 12:29-31; De 6:4, 5; Le 19:18); the prophetic words of Jehovah to David's Lord on the subjugation of foes (Mr 12:36; Ps 110:1); the scattering of Jesus' disciples (Mr 14:27; Zec 13:7); Jesus' statement on being forsaken by God (Mr 15:34; Ps 22:1); his instructions to a healed leper (Mr 1:44; Le 14:10, 11); and his prophetic statement regarding the disgusting thing causing desolation (Mr 13:14; Da 9:27).

The references to the Hebrew Scriptures in Mark's account amply illustrate that Jesus Christ had confidence in them and used those Scriptures in his ministry. The Gospel also provides a basis for becoming better acquainted with the Son of man, who "came, not to be ministered to, but to minister and to give his soul a ransom in exchange for many."—Mr 10:45.

Long and Short Conclusions. Some have thought that Mark 16:8, which ends with the words "and they told nobody anything, for they were in fear," is too abrupt to have been the original ending of this Gospel. However, that need not be concluded in view of Mark's general style. Also, the fourth-century scholars Jerome and Eusebius agree that the authentic record closes with the words "for they were in fear."—Jerome, letter 120, question 3, as published in *Corpus Scriptorum Ecclesiasticorum Latinorum,* Vienna and Leipzig, 1912, Vol. LV, p. 481; Eusebius, "Ad Marinum," I, as published in *Patrologia Græca,* Paris, 1857, Vol. XXII, col. 937.

There are a number of manuscripts and versions that add a long or a short conclusion after these words. The long conclusion (consisting of 12 verses) is found in the Alexandrine Manuscript, the Codex Ephraemi Syri rescriptus, and the Bezae Codices. It also appears in the Latin *Vulgate,* the Curetonian Syriac, and the Syriac *Peshitta.* But it is omitted in the Sinaitic Manuscript, the Vatican Manuscript No. 1209, the Sinaitic Syriac codex, and the Armenian Version. Certain late manuscripts and versions contain the short conclusion. The Codex Regius of the eighth century C.E. has both conclusions, giving the shorter conclusion first. It prefixes a note to each conclusion, saying that these passages are current in some quarters, though it evidently recognized neither of them as authoritative.

In commenting on the long and short conclusions of the Gospel of Mark, Bible translator Edgar J. Goodspeed noted: "The Short Conclusion connects much better with Mark 16:8 than does the Long, but neither can be considered an original part of the Gospel of Mark."—*The Goodspeed Parallel New Testament,* 1944, p. 127.

MARKETPLACE. An open area that served as a center for buying and selling and as a place of public assembly in cities and towns of the ancient Middle East and the Roman world. In Greek and Roman cities, statues and public buildings, including religious edifices, surrounded the open area. It appears that some judicial matters were handled in marketplaces. (Compare Ac 16:19-21.) Also, news, both local and foreign, could be obtained in the marketplace, for it was there that persons congregated and spoke about the latest happenings.—Compare Ac 17:17-21.

In the marketplaces of Palestine, children could be found playing games. (Mt 11:16; Lu 7:32) Unemployed men as well as those who were willing to be hired for a day might be standing around. (Compare Mt 20:3, 4.) The proud scribes and

Pharisees wanted to be noticed by the throngs there and to be greeted in accord with their assumed high station. (Mt 23:2, 6, 7; Mr 12:38; Lu 11:43; 20:46) Upon returning from the market, the tradition-keeping Pharisees and other Jews cleansed themselves by sprinkling before ever eating anything.—Mr 7:3, 4.

While on earth, Christ Jesus healed persons in the marketplaces. (Mr 6:56) And the apostle Paul, at Athens, daily reasoned "in the marketplace with

HIGHLIGHTS OF MARK

Mark's concise, fast-moving account of Jesus' life, presenting Jesus as the miracle-working Son of God

The shortest Gospel, it was the third to be written (c. 60-65 C.E.), evidently with non-Jews in mind

Jesus conducts a vigorous campaign of Kingdom preaching

Jesus is baptized and begins preaching, "The kingdom of God has drawn near" (1:9-11, 14, 15)

He invites Simon, Andrew, James, and John to leave the fishing business and be his followers (1:16-21)

After preaching in the synagogue at Capernaum, he proceeds to preach throughout the whole of Galilee (1:21, 22, 35-39)

Levi, a tax collector, responds to invitation to be Jesus' follower (2:14-17)

Jesus forms a group of 12 apostles to preach (3:13-19)

He uses many illustrations when teaching about the Kingdom of God so that only worthy ones get the full sense of what he says (4:1-34)

Jesus encounters lack of faith while witnessing in his home territory (6:1-6)

He steps up the preaching activity by sending out his apostles (6:7-13)

His activity reaches into Phoenicia and the Decapolis (7:24, 31)

Jesus is transfigured in Kingdom glory (9:1-8)

Outside Jerusalem, he prophesies about 'the coming of the Son of man with great power and glory' (13:1-37)

At the Lord's Evening Meal, Jesus promises that his followers will be with him in the Kingdom (14:12-31)

The miracle-working Son of God

At the synagogue in Capernaum, he frees a man from demon possession; afterward, he heals Simon's mother-in-law and cures many others of various afflictions (1:23-34, 40-42)

By curing a paralytic, Jesus demonstrates his power to forgive sins (2:1-12)

Sufferers crowd in from all parts seeking relief (3:1-12)

After calming a storm on the Sea of Galilee, he expels demons from a man and allows them to enter a herd of swine (4:35–5:17)

He heals a woman suffering from a flow of blood and resurrects Jairus' daughter (5:21-43)

After feeding 5,000 with two fishes and five loaves, Jesus walks on the windswept Sea of Galilee (6:35-52)

He casts a demon from the daughter of a Syrophoenician woman and cures a deaf man having a speech impediment (7:24-37)

He feeds 4,000 with seven loaves; at Bethsaida, he restores sight to a blind man (8:1-9, 22-26)

From a speechless, deaf boy, Jesus expels a demon that had resisted the disciples; he restores sight to a blind beggar at Jericho (9:14-29; 10:46-52)

He curses a fig tree, which subsequently withers (11:12-14, 20)

Opposers of God's Son are unsuccessful

After Satan's efforts at temptation in the wilderness, angels minister to Jesus (1:12, 13)

When scribes of the Pharisees criticize his eating with tax collectors and sinners, Jesus refutes them (2:15-17)

Later the Pharisees object to his disciples plucking heads of grain on the Sabbath and Jesus' healing on the Sabbath; they join the Herodians in wanting to destroy him (2:23–3:6)

Jesus convincingly refutes the accusation that he expels demons by means of Satan (3:20-30)

Jesus' forerunner John the Baptizer is beheaded, but Jesus continues to teach (6:14-29, 34)

Pharisees and scribes protest that his disciples disregard their tradition about hand washing; Jesus exposes their hypocrisy and explains the real source of uncleanness (7:1-23)

Pharisees question Jesus regarding divorce in order to test him, but without success (10:1-12)

Chief priests, scribes, and older men challenge Jesus' authority after he cleanses the temple, but he silences them (11:15-18, 27-33)

He tells the parable of the vineyard to expose the opposition of the religious leaders to God's will and their intent to kill Jesus; these seek to seize him but fear the crowd (12:1-12)

Pharisees and Herodians ask Jesus whether it is right to pay taxes to Caesar; Sadducees pose a difficult question about the resurrection. All fail to trap Jesus (12:13-27)

Judas betrays Jesus; Jesus is arrested and the Sanhedrin judges him worthy of death; nevertheless, he foretells he will 'sit at the right hand of power and come with the clouds of heaven' (14:1, 2, 10, 11, 32-65)

Pilate is pressured into condemning Jesus to death; Jesus dies on the stake and is buried (15:1-47)

Angels announce the resurrection of Jesus (16:1-8)

those who happened to be on hand."—Ac 17:16, 17; see APPIUS, MARKETPLACE OF.

MAROTH (Ma′roth) [from a root meaning "be bitter"]. A town mentioned by the prophet Micah in his prophecy foretelling Jehovah's punishment of Jerusalem and Judah. (Mic 1:12) The location is undetermined; some would identify it with Maarath of Joshua 15:59.

MARRIAGE. The union of a man and a woman as husband and wife according to the standard set out by God. Marriage is a divine institution, authorized and established by Jehovah in Eden. Marriage brings into being the family unit, the family circle. Its basic purpose was the reproducing of the members of the human family, to bring into existence more creatures of the human kind. Jehovah the Creator made male and female and ordained marriage as the proper arrangement for the multiplication of the human race. (Ge 1:27, 28) The first human wedding was performed by Jehovah, as described at Genesis 2:22-24.

Marriage was designed to form a permanent bond of union between man and woman, that they might be mutually helpful to each other. Living together in love and confidence, they could enjoy great happiness. Jehovah created woman as a mate for man by using the man's rib as a base, thereby making woman man's closest fleshly relative on earth, his own flesh. (Ge 2:21) As Jesus pointed out, it was not Adam but God who said, "That is why a man will leave his father and his mother and he must stick to his wife and they must become one flesh." The wording of this text makes it evident that monogamy was the original standard for marriage in the eyes of Jehovah God. —Mt 19:4-6; Ge 2:24.

Marriage was the normal way of life among the Hebrews. There is no word for bachelor in the Hebrew Scriptures. The basic purpose of marriage being to have children, the statement of blessing by Rebekah's family is understandable: "May you become thousands times ten thousand" (Ge 24: 60), also Rachel's appeal to Jacob: "Give me children or otherwise I shall be a dead woman."—Ge 30:1.

Marriage was a matter affecting the family, and not only the family but the entire tribe or patriarchal community, for it could have an effect on the strength of the tribe as well as its economy. It was natural and seemed necessary, therefore, that the selection of a wife and the arrangement of all contractual and financial matters connected with it should be decided upon by the parents or guardians involved, though the consent of the parties was sometimes sought (Ge 24:8) and romantic attachments often accompanied the arrangements. (Ge 29:20; 1Sa 18:20, 27, 28) The initial steps or proposals were generally made by the parents of the young man, but sometimes by the father of the girl, especially if there was a difference of rank.—Jos 15:16, 17; 1Sa 18:20-27.

It seems to have been generally customary for a man to look for a wife within the circle of his own relations or tribe. This principle is indicated by Laban's statement to Jacob: "It is better for me to give [my daughter] to you than for me to give her to another man." (Ge 29:19) Especially was this observed among the worshipers of Jehovah, as exemplified by Abraham when he sent to his relatives in his own country to get a wife for his son Isaac rather than to take one from the daughters of the Canaanites among whom he was dwelling. (Ge 24:3, 4) Marriage to nonworshipers of Jehovah was frowned upon and strongly discouraged. It was a form of disloyalty. (Ge 26:34, 35) Under the Law, marriage alliances with persons of the seven Canaanite nations were prohibited. (De 7:1-4) However, a soldier might marry a captive virgin from another foreign nation after she had undergone a purification period, during which she mourned her dead parents and got rid of all features of her past religious connections.—De 21:10-14.

Bride-Price. Before the marriage contract was concluded, the young man or the father of the young man had to pay to the girl's father the bride-price, or marriage price. (Ge 34:11, 12; Ex 22:16; 1Sa 18:23, 25) This was doubtless regarded as compensation for the loss of the services of the daughter and for the effort and expense required of the parents in caring for and educating her. Sometimes the bride-price was paid in services to the father. (Ge 29:18, 20, 27; 31:15) In the Law there was an established purchase price for an unengaged virgin who was seduced by a man. —Ex 22:16.

Ceremony. As to the wedding itself, the central and characteristic feature was the solemn bringing of the bride from her father's home to her husband's home on the date agreed upon, in which act the significance of marriage as representing admission of the bride into the family of her husband found expression. (Mt 1:24) This constituted the wedding in patriarchal days before the Law. It was altogether a civil affair. There was no religious ceremony or form, and no priest or clergyman officiated or validated the marriage. The bridegroom took the bride to his house or to the tent or house of his parents. The matter was publicly made known, acknowledged, and recorded, and the marriage was binding.—Ge 24:67.

However, as soon as marriage arrangements had been made and the parties were engaged, they were considered bound in marriage. Lot's daughters were still in his house, under his jurisdiction, but the men engaged to them were termed Lot's "sons-in-law who were to take his daughters." (Ge 19:14) Although Samson never married a certain Philistine woman but was only engaged to her, she was spoken of as his wife. (Jg 14:10, 17, 20) The Law stated that if an engaged girl committed fornication, she and the guilty man were to be put to death. If she was violated against her will, the man was to be put to death. However, any case involving an unengaged girl was handled differently.—De 22:22-27.

Marriages were registered. Under the Law marriages, as well as births resulting from the union, were recorded in the official records of the community. For this reason we have an accurate genealogy of Jesus Christ.—Mt 1:1-16; Lu 3:23-38; compare Lu 2:1-5.

Celebration. While the wedding itself had no formal ceremony, there was, nevertheless, a very joyous celebration of weddings in Israel. On the day of the wedding, at her own home the bride usually made elaborate preparations. First she would bathe herself and rub herself with perfumed oil. (Compare Ru 3:3; Eze 23:40.) At times assisted by woman attendants, she put on breastbands and a white robe, often richly embroidered, according to her financial status. (Jer 2:32; Re 19:7, 8; Ps 45:13, 14) She decked herself with ornaments and jewels, if she was able to do so (Isa 49:18; 61:10; Re 21:2), and then covered herself with a light garment, a form of veil, that extended from head to foot. (Isa 3:19, 23) This explains why Laban could so easily practice a deception on Jacob so that Jacob did not know that Laban was giving him Leah instead of Rachel. (Ge 29:23, 25) Rebekah put on a head covering when she approached to meet Isaac. (Ge 24:65) This symbolized the subjection of the bride to the bridegroom—to his authority.—1Co 11:5, 10.

The bridegroom was likewise arrayed in his best attire and often had a handsome headdress and a garland on his head. (Ca 3:11; Isa 61:10) Escorted by his friends, he would leave his house in the evening for the home of the bride's parents. (Mt 9:15) From there the procession, accompanied by musicians and singers and usually by persons bearing lamps, moved toward the home of the bridegroom or to the house of his father.

The people along the route would take great interest in the procession. The voices of the bride and bridegroom would be heard in exultation. Some, particularly maidens bearing lamps, would join the procession. (Jer 7:34; 16:9; Isa 62:5; Mt 25:1) The bridegroom might spend considerable time at his home and, then again, some delay might take place before the procession would leave the home of the bride, so that it would thus be quite late, and some who were waiting along the way might get drowsy and fall asleep, as in Jesus' illustration of the ten virgins. The singing and exultation might be heard quite a distance ahead, those hearing it making the cry: "Here is the bridegroom!" The attendants were ready to greet the bridegroom when he came, and those invited to the marriage supper would enter the house. After the bridegroom and his entourage had gone into the house and closed the door, it was too late for tardy guests to enter. (Mt 25:1-12; 22:1-3; Ge 29:22) It was looked upon as a gross insult to decline the invitation to the marriage feast. (Mt 22:8) The guests might be provided with robes (Mt 22:11), and their respective places at the feast were often designated by the one extending the invitation.—Lu 14:8-10.

Friend of the Bridegroom. "The friend of the bridegroom" had a large share in the arrangements and was looked upon as bringing together the bride and groom. The friend of the bridegroom rejoiced in hearing the voice of the groom conversing with the bride and now could feel happy that his duties had been blessed with a successful conclusion.—Joh 3:29.

Proof of Virginity. After the supper the husband took his bride into the nuptial chamber. (Ps 19:5; Joe 2:16) On the wedding night a cloth or garment was used and then kept or given to the wife's parents so that the marks of the blood of the girl's virginity would constitute legal protection for her in the event she was later charged with lack of virginity or of having been a prostitute prior to her marriage. Otherwise, she could be stoned to death for having presented herself in marriage as a spotless virgin and for bringing great reproach on her father's house. (De 22:13-21) This practice of keeping the cloth has continued among some peoples in the Middle East until recent times.

Privileges and Duties. The husband was head of the house, and the final decision on matters affecting the welfare and economy of the family were left to him. If he felt that the family would be adversely affected, he could even annul a vow of his wife or daughter. This authority evidently also belonged to the man when he was engaged to a woman. (Nu 30:3-8, 10-15) The husband was the lord, master of the household, and was considered the owner (Heb., *ba'al*) of the woman.—De 22:22.

Proverbs 31 describes some of the duties of the wife toward her husband, or owner, which included the household work, the making of and care for clothing, even some of the buying and selling, and general supervision of the household. The woman, while being in subjection and being in a sense the property of the husband, enjoyed a fine status and many privileges. Her husband was to love her, and this was true even if she was a secondary wife or one who had been taken as a captive. She was not to be mistreated and was guaranteed food, clothing, shelter, and the marriage due without diminution. Also, the husband could not constitute the son of the favorite wife as the firstborn at the expense of the son of the "hated" (or less preferred) wife. (Ex 21:7-11; De 21:11, 14-17) Faithful Hebrew men loved their wives, and if the wife was wise and acted in harmony with God's law, often the husband would listen to her or approve of her actions.—Ge 21:8-14; 27:41-46; 28:1-4.

Even the unengaged virgin who was seduced by an unmarried man was protected, for if the father permitted, the seducer had to marry the girl and could never divorce her all his life. (De 22:28, 29) If the wife was formally accused by her husband of not being a virgin at the time of marriage and the charge was proved false, her husband was fined and could never divorce her. (De 22:17-19) The woman who was accused of secret adultery, if innocent, was then to be made pregnant by her husband so that she could bear a child and thereby give public notice of her innocence. The dignity of the wife's person was respected. Intercourse with her during menstruation was forbidden.—Le 18:19; Nu 5:12-28.

Prohibited Marriages. Besides prohibition of marriage alliances with nonworshipers of Jehovah, especially with the seven nations in the land of Canaan (Ex 34:14-16; De 7:1-4), other marriages were prohibited within certain degrees of consanguinity or affinity.—Le 18:6-17.

A high priest was prohibited from marrying a widow, a divorced or violated woman, or a prostitute; he was to marry only a virgin from his people. (Le 21:10, 13, 14) The other priests could not marry a prostitute or violated woman, nor a woman divorced from her husband. (Le 21:1, 7) According to Ezekiel 44:22, they could marry a virgin of the house of Israel or a widow who happened to be the widow of a priest.

If a daughter inherited property, she was not to marry out of her tribe. This prevented the hereditary possession from circulating from tribe to tribe.—Nu 36:8, 9.

Divorce. At the institution of marriage by the Creator, he made no provision for divorce. A man was to stick to his wife, and "they must become one flesh." (Ge 2:24) A man would therefore have one wife who was considered one flesh with him. It was only after man's fall and consequent imperfections and degradation that divorce entered in.

In giving the Law to Israel, God did not at that time choose to enforce the original standard, but he regulated divorce so that it would not bring dissolution of the family arrangement in Israel or work undue hardship. However, at God's due time his original standard was restored. Jesus stated the principle governing the Christian congregation—that "fornication" (Gr., *por·nei'a*) is the only valid ground for divorce. He explained that God did not enforce this standard through Moses out of regard for the hardheartedness of the Israelites. —Mt 19:3-9; Mr 10:1-11.

In the Christian congregation, therefore, aside from death, which automatically breaks the marriage tie, the only other way it may be broken is on the ground of "fornication," which causes the offending one to become one flesh with an illicit partner. It therefore may be used by the innocent party as a ground for dissolving the marriage if that one chooses to do so, and the innocent one may then remarry. (Mt 5:32; Ro 7:2, 3) Aside from making this allowance in case of "fornication" (Gr., *por·nei'a*), the Greek Scriptures counsel Christians not even to separate from their mates, whether believers or unbelievers, and require that if they do, they have no sex relations with anyone else.—1Co 7:10, 11; Mt 19:9.

Under the Law a husband could divorce his wife for something 'indecent' on her part. This, of course, would not include adultery, for it carried a death penalty. It might be such offenses as great disrespect for the husband or for the house of his father, or something bringing reproach upon his household. The husband was required to provide her with a written certificate of divorce, which implies that in the eyes of the community he had to have sufficient grounds on which to divorce her. The certificate being a legal document, there is the implication that it involved consultation with the older men or authorities of his city. The woman could then remarry, the certificate protecting her from any later charge of adultery. No divorce was allowed a man if he had seduced the girl before marriage or if he had falsely charged after marriage that she was deceptive in claiming to be a virgin at the time of their marriage.—De 22:13-19, 28, 29.

After a divorce if a woman married another man and this man later divorced her or died, the original husband could not marry her again. This worked to prevent any scheme to bring about a divorce from the second husband or perhaps even his death so the original couple might remarry. —De 24:1-4.

Jehovah hated an unjust divorce, especially where a faithful worshiper of his was treacherously dealt with in order to arrange for another marriage to a pagan woman who was not a member of his chosen covenant people.—Mal 2:14-16; see DIVORCE.

Polygamy. Since God's original standard for mankind was for the husband and wife to become one flesh, polygamy was not intended, and it is prohibited in the Christian congregation. Overseers and ministerial servants, who are to set the example for the congregation, are to be men having not more than one living wife. (1Ti 3:2, 12; Tit 1:5, 6) This is in harmony with what true marriage is used to picture, namely, the relationship of Jesus Christ and his congregation, the only wife possessed by Jesus.—Eph 5:21-33.

As was the case with divorce, polygamy, while not God's original arrangement, was tolerated until the time of the Christian congregation. Polygamy had a start not long after Adam's deflection. The first Bible mention of it is concerning a descendant of Cain, Lamech, of whom it says: "[He] proceeded to take two wives for himself." (Ge 4:19) Concerning some of the angels, the Bible mentions that before the Flood, "the sons of the true God . . . went taking wives for themselves, namely, all whom they chose."—Ge 6:2.

Concubinage was practiced under patriarchal law and under the Law covenant. A concubine had a legal status; her position was not a matter of fornication or adultery. Under the Law, if a man's firstborn son was the son of his concubine, this son would be the one to receive the firstborn's inheritance.—De 21:15-17.

Concubinage and polygamy no doubt enabled the Israelites to increase at a much faster rate, and therefore, while God did not establish these arrangements but only allowed and regulated them, they served some purpose at the time. (Ex 1:7) Even Jacob, who was tricked into polygamy by his father-in-law, was blessed by having 12 sons and some daughters from his two wives and their handmaidens who became concubines to Jacob. —Ge 29:23-29; 46:7-25.

Christian Marriage. Jesus Christ showed his approval of marriage when he attended the marriage feast in Cana of Galilee. (Joh 2:1, 2) As already stated, monogamy is God's original standard, reestablished by Jesus Christ in the Christian congregation. (Ge 2:24; Mt 19:4-8; Mr 10:2-9) Since man and woman were originally endowed with the ability to express love and affection, the arrangement was to be a happy, blessed, and peaceful one. The apostle Paul uses the illustration of Christ as husband and head of the congregation, his bride. It is a prime example of the tender loving-kindness and care that the husband should have for his wife, loving her as his own body. He also points out that, on the other hand, the wife should have deep respect for her husband. (Eph 5:21-33) The apostle Peter counsels wives to be in subjection to their husbands, appealing to them through chaste conduct, deep respect, and a quiet and mild spirit. He uses Sarah, who called her husband Abraham "lord," as an example to imitate.—1Pe 3:1-6.

Cleanness and loyalty in the marriage bond are emphasized throughout the Christian Greek Scriptures. Paul says: "Let marriage be honorable among all, and the marriage bed be without defilement, for God will judge fornicators and adulterers." (Heb 13:4) He counsels mutual respect between husband and wife and the payment of the marriage due.

'Marry in the Lord' is the apostle's admonition, which is in harmony with the practice of ancient worshipers of God in marrying only those who were likewise true worshipers. (1Co 7:39) However, the apostle gives counsel to those who are not married that they may be able to serve the Lord without distraction if they remain single. He says that, in view of the time, those who get married should live 'as though they had no wives,' in other words, that they should not devote themselves to the marital privileges and responsibilities to the extent of making this their whole life but should seek and serve Kingdom interests, while not excluding their marriage responsibilities. —1Co 7:29-38.

Paul counseled that just because younger widows expressed the intent to devote themselves exclusively to Christian ministerial activities, they were not to be put on the list of those to be cared for by the congregation; it was better for them to remarry. This is because, he says, their sexual impulses may induce them to go contrary to their expression of faith that might lead to their accepting the congregation's financial support as hard workers, while at the same time trying to get a husband as well as becoming unoccupied and meddlers. They would thereby bring themselves under an unfavorable judgment. To marry, bear children, and manage a household, while still maintaining the Christian faith, would effectively occupy them, protecting them against gossiping and talking of things they ought not. This would enable the congregation to help those who were actually widows and who qualified for such aid. —1Ti 5:9-16; 2:15.

Celibacy. The apostle Paul warns that one of the identifying features of the apostasy that was to come would be enforced celibacy, "forbidding to marry." (1Ti 4:1, 3) Some of the apostles were married. (1Co 9:5; Lu 4:38) Paul, in setting forth the qualifications for overseers and ministerial servants in the Christian congregation, says that these men (if married) should have only one wife. —1Ti 3:1, 2, 12; Tit 1:5, 6.

Christians and Civil Marriage Laws. At the present time, in most lands of the earth, marriage is governed by laws of the civil authorities, "Caesar," and the Christian should normally comply with these. (Mt 22:21) The Bible record nowhere sets out the requirement of a religious ceremony or the services of a clergyman. According to the arrangement in Bible times, the requirement would consistently be that a marriage be legalized according to the laws of the land and that marriages and births be registered where such a provision is made by law. Since the "Caesar" governments exercise such control of marriage, the Christian would be obliged to apply to them for the legalizing of a marriage. And even if he should desire to use the adultery of his mate as a Scriptural ground for terminating the marriage, he must obtain a legal divorce if this is possible. A Christian who remarries without due respect for Scriptural and legal requirements, therefore, would be violating God's laws.—Mt 19:9; Ro 13:1.

Marriage and the Resurrection. A group of Jesus' opponents who did not believe in the resurrection asked Jesus a question that was calculated to embarrass him. In answering them, he revealed that "those who have been counted worthy of gaining that system of things and the resurrection from the dead neither marry nor are given in marriage."—Lu 20:34, 35; Mt 22:30.

Symbolic Uses. Throughout the Scriptures, Jehovah speaks of himself as a husband. He considered himself as married to the nation of Israel. (Isa 54:1, 5, 6; 62:4) When Israel rebelled against Jehovah by practicing idolatry or some other form of sin against him, this was spoken of as committing prostitution like an unfaithful wife, providing

cause for his divorcing her.—Isa 1:21; Jer 3:1-20; Ho 2.

In Galatians chapter 4 the apostle Paul likens the nation of Israel to the slave girl Hagar, the concubine of Abraham, and the Jewish people to Hagar's son Ishmael. Just as Ishmael was the son of the secondary wife of Abraham, so the Jews were the children of the secondary "wife" of Jehovah. The tie binding Israel to Jehovah was the Law covenant. Paul likens "Jerusalem above," Jehovah's "woman," to Sarah, Abraham's free wife. Of this free woman "Jerusalem above," Christians are the free spiritual children.—Ga 4:21-31; compare Isa 54:1-6.

As the great Father, Jehovah God, like Abraham, oversees the selection of a bride for his son Jesus Christ—not an earthly woman, but the Christian congregation. (Ge 24:1-4; 2Th 2:13; 1Pe 2:5) The first members of Jesus' congregation were presented to him by "the friend of the bridegroom," John the Baptizer, whom Jehovah had sent ahead of his Son. (Joh 3:28, 29) This congregational bride is "one spirit" with Christ, as his body. (1Co 6:17; Eph 1:22, 23; 5:22, 23) Just as the bride in Israel bathed and adorned herself, Jesus Christ sees that in preparation for marriage his bride is bathed so that she is perfectly clean without a spot or blemish. (Eph 5:25-27) In Psalm 45 and Revelation 21 she is shown as being beautifully adorned for the marriage.

Also in the book of Revelation, Jehovah foretells the time when his Son's marriage would draw near and the bride would be prepared, arrayed in bright, clean, fine linen. He describes those invited to the evening meal of the Lamb's marriage as being happy. (Re 19:7-9; 21:2, 9-21) On the night before his death, Jesus instituted the Lord's Evening Meal, the Memorial of his death, and instructed his disciples to keep observing it. (Lu 22:19) This observance is to be kept "until he arrives." (1Co 11:26) Just as in ancient times the bridegroom arrived at the house of the bride in order to take her from her own parents to the home he had provided for her in the house of his father, so Jesus Christ comes to take his anointed followers from their former earthly home, taking them with him so that where he is they may be also, in his Father's house, in heaven.—Joh 14:1-3.

See BROTHER-IN-LAW MARRIAGE.

MARROW. A soft and fatty vascular tissue that fills the interior cavities of most bones. There are two kinds of marrow, yellow and red. In adults, the long, rounder bones are filled with yellow, or inactive, marrow composed mainly of fat, and the flat bones of the skull, the ribs, the sternum, and the pelvis contain red, or active, marrow. Red marrow plays an important role in the formation of blood. It yields the oxygen-carrying red blood corpuscles, the important clotting agents called platelets, and a large percentage of white corpuscles, which primarily serve as fighters of infection. As a blood-forming organ, the marrow has a direct effect upon an individual's health and vigor. Hence, Job (21:24) appropriately alludes to a well-nourished and healthy person under the figure of one whose bone marrow "is being kept moist."

Animal bone marrow was apparently used for food by the Israelites. (Compare Mic 3:2, 3.) It has a very high nutritional value, being rich in protein, fats, and iron. Jehovah's banquet for all the peoples, therefore, fittingly includes symbolic "well-oiled dishes filled with marrow."—Isa 25:6.

In Hebrews 4:12 "the word of God" is compared to a weapon that is sharper than any two-edged sword and can penetrate the thoughts and motives of an individual, piercing, as it were, clear to the marrow, the innermost part of the bones.

MARSENA
(Mar·se′na). One of seven princes consulted by Ahasuerus on Vashti's refusal to obey.—Es 1:14.

MARS' HILL.
See AREOPAGUS.

MARSHMALLOW
[Heb., chal·la·muth′]. A perennial plant that is closely related to the hollyhock. The woody stems of the marshmallow (Althaea officinalis) measure up to 1.8 m (6 ft) in height. The plant's large, wide leaves are notched and terminate in a sharp point. Both the stems and the leaves are covered with soft downy hair. The pale-pink, five-petal flowers are about 5 cm (2 in.) across. In times of famine, the marshmallow's white carrotlike root has been used for food. The sole Scriptural reference to the marshmallow alludes to its tastelessness.—Job 6:6.

The Hebrew term chal·la·muth′, found only at Job 6:6, has been variously rendered "egg" (AS, KJ), "purslain" (AT), and, as defined in a Hebrew and Aramaic lexicon by L. Koehler and W. Baumgartner, "marsh-mallow" (Lexicon in Veteris Testamenti Libros, Leiden, 1958, p. 304).

MARTHA
(Mar′tha). A Jewess, the sister of Lazarus and Mary of Bethany. (Joh 11:1, 2) Evidently Christ often visited their home when he was in the vicinity of Jerusalem. Bonds of affection existed between him and these three, for it is specifically said: "Now Jesus loved Martha and her sister and Lazarus."—Joh 11:5.

Luke reports that when Jesus entered "a certain village," "a certain woman named Martha received him as guest into the house." (Lu 10:38) On the basis of Matthew 26:6, Mark 14:3, and John 12:1-3, the thought has been advanced that Martha was the wife, or the widow, or even the daughter of Simon the leper. However, the Scriptures do not make any specific statements in support of these views.

On one occasion when Jesus visited the home of Lazarus, Mary, and Martha, Mary "sat down at the feet of the Lord and kept listening to his word," whereas Martha "was distracted with attending to many duties." Martha tried to obtain Mary's assistance, saying: "Lord, does it not matter to you that my sister has left me alone to attend to things? Tell her, therefore, to join in helping me." Obviously Martha was concerned about satisfying Jesus' material needs. But Christ then emphasized the excelling value of spiritual things and gave her kind reproof, saying: "Martha, Martha, you are anxious and disturbed about many things. A few things, though, are needed, or just one. For her part, Mary chose the good portion, and it will not be taken away from her." (Lu 10:38-42) Christ would have been satisfied with one item of food if his doing so would mean that Martha, too, would gain greater advantage from his teaching.

While it may seem that Martha was overly concerned with material things, it should not be concluded that she lacked interest in spiritual matters. After the death of Lazarus, it was Martha who went to meet Jesus as he journeyed to Bethany, while Mary, at first, sat at home (possibly because of grief or because of the many visiting friends). Martha showed faith in Christ when she said that Lazarus would not have died if Jesus had been present. She also acknowledged: "I know he will rise in the resurrection on the last day," showing she believed in the resurrection. During that conversation Jesus explained that he is "the resurrection and the life," pointing out that though one exercising faith in him died, he would come to life. When Christ asked Martha, "Do you believe this?" she clearly showed her faith by replying: "Yes, Lord; I have believed that you are the Christ the Son of God, the One coming into the world." (Joh 11:19-27) This, of course, does not rule out the possibility of her having some doubts as to what Jesus could or would now do in the case of her dead brother. (Compare the apostles' attitude related at Lu 24:5-11.) At Lazarus' tomb, when Christ ordered that the stone be taken away, Martha said: "Lord, by now he must smell, for it is four days." But in response Jesus asked: "Did I not tell you that if you would believe you would see the glory of God?" That she witnessed when her brother was resurrected.—Joh 11:39-44.

After the resurrection of Lazarus, Christ departed. Later, he returned to Bethany and gathered with others, including Martha, Mary, and Lazarus, in the home of Simon the leper. An evening meal had been prepared and again "Martha was ministering." Lazarus was at the table, and it was on that occasion that Mary anointed Jesus with costly perfumed oil. (Joh 12:1-8; Mt 26:6-13; Mr 14:3-9) The Scriptures are silent regarding subsequent events in Martha's life and the time and circumstances of her death.

MARY (Ma′ry) [from the Heb. Miriam, possibly meaning "Rebellious"]. There are six Marys mentioned in the Bible.

1. Mary the mother of Jesus. She was the daughter of Heli, though the genealogy given by Luke lists Mary's husband Joseph as the "son of Heli." Says M'Clintock and Strong's *Cyclopædia* (1881, Vol. III, p. 774): "In constructing their genealogical tables, it is well known that the Jews reckoned wholly by males, rejecting, where the blood of the grandfather passed to the grandson through a daughter, the name of the daughter herself, and counting that daughter's husband for the son of the maternal grandfather (Numb. xxvi, 33; xxvii, 4-7)." It is undoubtedly for this reason the historian Luke says that Joseph was the "son of Heli."—Lu 3:23.

Mary was of the tribe of Judah and a descendant of David. Hence it could be said of her son Jesus that he "sprang from the seed of David *according to the flesh.*" (Ro 1:3) Through his adoptive father Joseph, a descendant of David, Jesus had a *legal* right to David's throne, and through his mother, as the "offspring," "seed," and "root" of David, he held the natural *hereditary* right to "the throne of *David his father.*"—Mt 1:1-16; Lu 1:32; Ac 13:22, 23; 2Ti 2:8; Re 5:5; 22:16.

If tradition is correct, Heli's wife, the mother of Mary, was Anna, whose sister had a daughter named Elizabeth, the mother of John the Baptizer. This tradition would make Elizabeth the cousin of Mary. That Mary was related to Elizabeth, who was "from the daughters of Aaron" of the tribe of Levi, the Scriptures themselves state. (Lu 1:5, 36) Mary's sister, some have thought, was Salome, the wife of Zebedee, whose two sons, James and John, were numbered among Jesus' apostles.—Mt 27:55, 56; Mr 15:40; 16:1; Joh 19:25.

Visited by Angel. About the end of 3 B.C.E., the angel Gabriel was sent by God to the virgin girl Mary in the town of Nazareth. "Good day, highly favored one, Jehovah is with you," was the angel's most unusual greeting. When he told her that she would conceive and give birth to a son called Jesus, Mary, who at the time was only engaged to Joseph, asked, "How is this to be, since I am having no intercourse with a man?" "Holy spirit will come upon you, and power of the Most High will overshadow you. For that reason also what is born will be called holy, God's Son," the angel explained. Thrilled with the prospect, yet with fitting modesty and humility, she replied: "Look! Jehovah's slave girl! May it take place with me according to your declaration."—Lu 1:26-38.

To strengthen her faith further for this momentous experience, Mary was told that her relative Elizabeth, in her old age, was already six months pregnant, because the miraculous power of Jehovah had removed her barrenness. Mary paid her a visit, and when she entered Elizabeth's home the infant in Elizabeth's womb leaped with joy, whereupon she congratulated Mary, saying: "Blessed are you among women, and blessed is the fruit of your womb!" (Lu 1:36, 37, 39-45) Thereupon Mary broke forth in inspired words magnifying Jehovah for his goodness.—Lu 1:46-55.

After a visit of about three months with Elizabeth in the Judean hills, Mary returned to Nazareth. (Lu 1:56) When it came to Joseph's notice (likely through disclosure of the matter to him by Mary) that she was pregnant, he intended to divorce her secretly rather than expose her to public shame. (Engaged persons were viewed as married, and a divorce was required to dissolve the engagement.) But Jehovah's angel appeared, revealing to Joseph that what had been begotten in her was by holy spirit. Joseph thereupon complied with the divine instruction and took Mary as his wife, "but he had no intercourse with her until she gave birth to a son; and he called his name Jesus."—Mt 1:18-25.

Bears Jesus in Bethlehem. As this drama continued to unfold, the decree of Caesar Augustus, compelling everyone to register in the town of his origin, proved providential in its timing, for the prophecy concerning Jesus' birthplace had to be fulfilled. (Mic 5:2) Accordingly, Joseph took Mary, who was "heavy with child," on the strenuous journey of about 150 km (93 mi) from their home in Nazareth in the N to Bethlehem in the S. Because there was no place for them in the lodging room, the birth of the child took place under most humble conditions, with the newborn babe being laid in a manger. This occurred probably about October 1 of the year 2 B.C.E.—Lu 2:1-7; see PICTURES, Vol. 2, p. 537; JESUS CHRIST.

After hearing the angel say: "There was born to

you today a Savior, who is Christ the Lord, in David's city," shepherds hastened to Bethlehem and there found the sign: Mary's babe "bound in cloth bands and lying in a manger." They related to the happy family what the great angelic chorus had sung: "Glory in the heights above to God, and upon earth peace among men of goodwill." So Mary "began to preserve all these sayings, drawing conclusions in her heart."—Lu 2:8-20.

On the eighth day Mary had her son circumcised in obedience to Jehovah's law. On the 40th day she and her husband brought the child to the temple in Jerusalem to make the prescribed offering. The Law required the sacrifice of a young ram and a young pigeon or a turtledove. If the family could not afford the sheep, two turtledoves or two young pigeons were to be offered. That Joseph was a man of poor financial means is indicated by the fact that Mary offered either "a pair of turtledoves or two young pigeons." (Lu 2:21-24; Le 12:1-4, 6, 8) Simeon, a righteous man, upon seeing the child, praised Jehovah for having allowed him to behold the Savior before dying in his old age. Turning to Mary, he said: "Yes, a long sword will be run through the soul of you yourself," not meaning that she would be pierced with a literal sword, but, rather, indicating the pain and suffering she would undergo in connection with her son's foretold death on a torture stake.—Lu 2:25-35.

Returns to Nazareth. Sometime later, an angel warned Joseph of a plot by Herod the Great to kill the young child, and he instructed Joseph to flee with Jesus to Egypt. (Mt 2:1-18) After the death of Herod, the family returned and settled in Nazareth, where, during the ensuing years, Mary bore other children, at least four sons as well as daughters.—Mt 2:19-23; 13:55, 56; Mr 6:3.

Though the Law did not require women to attend, it was Mary's custom to accompany Joseph year by year on the trek of about 150 km (93 mi) to Jerusalem for the annual Passover celebration. (Ex 23:17; 34:23) On one of these trips, in about 12 C.E., the family was returning home when, after going a day's distance from Jerusalem, they discovered that the boy Jesus was missing. His parents immediately returned to Jerusalem to search for him. After three days they found him in the temple listening to and questioning the teachers. Mary exclaimed: "Child, why did you treat us this way? Here your father and I in mental distress have been looking for you." Jesus replied: "Why did you have to go looking for me? Did you not know that I must be in the house of my Father?" Certainly the logical place for God's Son

to be found was the temple, where he could receive Scriptural instruction. Mary "carefully kept all these sayings in her heart."—Lu 2:41-51.

This 12-year-old boy Jesus displayed brilliant learning for his age. "All those listening to him were in constant amazement at his understanding and his answers." (Lu 2:47) Jesus' knowledge and understanding of the Scriptures reflected fine parental training. Mary as well as Joseph must have been very diligent in teaching and training the child, bringing him up in "the discipline and mental-regulating of Jehovah" and cultivating in him appreciation of the custom of attending the synagogue every Sabbath.—Lu 4:16; Eph 6:4.

Respected, Loved by Jesus. After his baptism, Jesus did not show special favoritism toward Mary; he addressed her, not as "mother," but simply as "woman." (Joh 2:4; 19:26) This was in no sense an expression of disrespect, as might be understood from modern-day English usage. In German, for example, the word used in this way denotes madam, Mrs., lady. Mary was Jesus' mother according to the flesh; but since his spirit-begetting at the time of his baptism, he was primarily God's spiritual Son, his "mother" being "the Jerusalem above." (Ga 4:26) Jesus laid emphasis on this fact when Mary and her other children on one occasion interrupted Jesus during a teaching session by asking him to come outside where they were. Jesus let it be known that really his mother and close relatives were those of his spiritual family, that spiritual matters take precedence over fleshly interests.—Mt 12:46-50; Mr 3:31-35; Lu 8:19-21.

When the wine ran out at a wedding in Cana of Galilee and Mary said to Jesus, "They have no wine," he responded: "What have I to do with you, woman? My hour has not yet come." (Joh 2:1-4) Jesus here used an ancient form of question that occurs eight times in the Hebrew Scriptures (Jos 22:24; Jg 11:12; 2Sa 16:10; 19:22; 1Ki 17:18; 2Ki 3:13; 2Ch 35:21; Ho 14:8) and six times in the Greek Scriptures. (Mt 8:29; Mr 1:24; 5:7; Lu 4:34; 8:28; Joh 2:4) Literally translated, the question is: "What to me and to you?" meaning, "What is there in common between me and you?" or, "What do I and you have in common?" or, "What have I to do with you?" In every instance where it is used, the question indicates an objection to the thing suggested, proposed, or suspected. Jesus, therefore, lovingly couched his gentle reproof in this form, indicating to his mother that his direction came not from her but from the Supreme Authority who had sent him. (1Co 11:3) Mary's sensitive and humble nature was quick to catch the point and accept the correction. Stepping back and letting Jesus take the lead, she remarked to the attendants: "Whatever *he* tells you, do."—Joh 2:5.

Mary was standing alongside the torture stake when Jesus was impaled. To her, Jesus was more than a beloved son, he was the Messiah, her Lord and Savior, the Son of God. Mary was apparently a widow by now. Consequently, Jesus, as the firstborn of Joseph's household, discharged his responsibility by asking the apostle John, likely his cousin, to take Mary to his home and look after her as his own mother. (Joh 19:26, 27) Why did Jesus not entrust her to one of his own half brothers? It is not stated that any of them were present. Furthermore, they were not yet believers, and Jesus considered the spiritual relationship more important than the fleshly.—Joh 7:5; Mt 12:46-50.

A Faithful Disciple. The last Biblical notice of Mary shows her to be a woman of faith and devotion still closely associated with other faithful ones after the ascension of Jesus. The 11 apostles, Mary, and others were assembled in an upper chamber, and "with one accord all these were persisting in prayer."—Ac 1:13, 14.

2. Mary the sister of Martha and Lazarus. At Bethany, about 2 Roman miles (2.8 km; 1.7 mi) from the Temple Mount in Jerusalem and on the E slope of the Mount of Olives, Jesus visited the home of these friends for whom he had special affection. (Joh 11:18) During a visit by Jesus in the third year of his ministry, Martha, in her determination to be a good hostess, was overly concerned for Jesus' physical comfort. Mary, on the other hand, showed a different kind of hospitality. She "sat down at the feet of the Lord and kept listening to his word." When Martha complained because her sister was not helping, Jesus commended Mary, saying, "For her part, Mary chose the good portion, and it will not be taken away from her." —Lu 10:38-42.

Sees Lazarus Resurrected. A few months after the aforementioned visit to the home, Lazarus became sick, near to death. So Mary and Martha sent word to Jesus, who was probably somewhere E of the Jordan in Perea. However, by the time Jesus arrived, Lazarus had been dead four days. With the news of Jesus' coming, Martha quickly went to greet him, while Mary "kept sitting at home." Not until Martha returned from the outskirts of the village and whispered to her grief-stricken sister, "The Teacher is present and is calling you," did Mary hasten out to meet him. At his feet she sobbed, "Lord, if you had been here, my brother would not have died." She used exact-

ly the same words as those spoken by her sister when Martha first went to meet Jesus. On seeing Mary's tears and those of the Jews with her, the Master was moved to groan and weep. After Jesus performed the stupendous miracle of raising Lazarus from the dead, "many of the Jews that had come to Mary [to comfort her] . . . put faith in him."—Joh 11:1-45.

Anoints Jesus With Oil. Five days before Jesus' last Passover, he and his disciples were guests again in Bethany, this time at the home of Simon the leper, where Mary and her family also were. Martha was serving the evening meal; Mary again gave her attention to the Son of God. As Jesus was reclining, Mary "took a pound of perfumed oil, genuine nard, very costly" (worth about a year's wages) and poured it on his head and feet. Not generally appreciated at the time, this act done out of love and regard for Jesus in reality signified the preparation for Jesus' death and burial so near at hand. As before, Mary's expression of love was criticized by others, and as before, her love and devotion were defended and greatly appreciated by Jesus. "Wherever this good news is preached in all the world," he declared, "what this woman did shall also be told as a remembrance of her."—Mt 26:6-13; Mr 14:3-9; Joh 12:1-8.

The above incident, Mary's anointing of Jesus, as reported by Matthew, Mark, and John, should not be confused with the anointing mentioned in Luke 7:36-50. The two events have some similarities, yet there are differences. The earlier event, reported by Luke, took place in the northern district of Galilee; the later, in the south at Bethany in Judea. The earlier was in the home of a Pharisee; the later, in that of Simon the leper. The earlier anointing was by an unnamed woman publicly known to be "a sinner," probably a prostitute; the later was by Martha's sister Mary. There was also more than a year's difference in time between the two events.

Some critics complain that John contradicts Matthew and Mark in saying the perfume was poured on Jesus' feet rather than on his head. (Mt 26:7; Mr 14:3; Joh 12:3) Commenting on Matthew 26:7, Albert Barnes says: "There is, however, no contradiction. She probably poured it *both* on his head and his feet. Matthew and Mark having recorded the former, John, who wrote his gospel in part to record events omitted by them, relates that the ointment was also poured on the feet of the Saviour. To pour ointment on the *head* was common. To pour it on the *feet* was an act of distinguished *humility* and attachment to the Saviour, and therefore deserved to be particularly recorded."—*Barnes' Notes on the New Testament,* 1974.

3. Mary Magdalene. Her distinguishing name (meaning "Of (Belonging to) Magdala") likely stems from the town of Magdala (see MAGADAN) on the western shore of the Sea of Galilee about halfway between Capernaum and Tiberias. There is no record of Jesus' ever visiting this town, though he spent a great deal of time in the surrounding area. Nor is it certain that it was Mary's hometown or place of residence. Since Luke refers to her as "Mary *the so-called* Magdalene," some think he implies something special or peculiar. —Lu 8:2.

Jesus expelled seven demons from Mary Magdalene, reason enough for her to put faith in him as the Messiah and for her to back up such faith with outstanding works of devotion and service. She is first mentioned in the account of Jesus' second year of preaching, when he and his apostles were "journeying from city to city and from village to village, preaching and declaring the good news of the kingdom of God." Together with Joanna the wife of Herod's man in charge, Susanna, and other women, Mary Magdalene continued ministering to the needs of Jesus and his apostles out of her own belongings.—Lu 8:1-3.

The most prominent notice of Mary Magdalene is in connection with the death and resurrection of Jesus. When Jesus, as the Lamb of God, was led to the slaughter, she was among the women "who had accompanied Jesus from Galilee to minister to him" and were "viewing from a distance" as Jesus hung on the torture stake. In her company were Jesus' mother Mary, Salome, and also "the other Mary" (No. 4).—Mt 27:55, 56, 61; Mr 15:40; Joh 19:25.

After Jesus' burial, Mary Magdalene and other women went to prepare spices and perfumed oil before the Sabbath began at sundown. Then following the Sabbath, at the break of dawn, on the first day of the week, Mary and the other women brought the perfumed oil to the tomb. (Mt 28:1; Mr 15:47; 16:1, 2; Lu 23:55, 56; 24:1) When Mary saw the tomb was open and apparently empty, she rushed off to tell the startling news to Peter and John, who ran to the tomb. (Joh 20:1-4) By the time Mary got back to the tomb, Peter and John had left, and it was now that she checked inside and was stunned at seeing two angels in white. Then she turned back and saw Jesus standing. Thinking him to be the gardener, she asked where the body was, that she might care for it. When he replied "Mary!" his identity was immediately revealed to her and she impulsively em-

braced him, exclaiming, *"Rab·bo'ni!"* But there was no time now for expressions of earthly affection. Jesus would be with them only a short time. Mary must hasten to inform the other disciples of his resurrection and that Jesus was ascending, as he said, "to my Father and your Father and to my God and your God."—Joh 20:11-18.

4. "The other Mary." She was the wife of Clopas (Alphaeus) (see CLOPAS) and the mother of James the Less and Joses. (Mt 27:56, 61; Joh 19:25) Tradition, though without any Scriptural support, says that Clopas and Joseph, the adoptive father of Jesus, were brothers. If true, that would make this Mary Jesus' aunt, and her sons his cousins.

Mary was not only among the women "who had accompanied Jesus from Galilee to minister to him" but was also one who witnessed his impalement. (Mt 27:55; Mr 15:40, 41) Together with Mary Magdalene, she lingered outside his tomb that bitter afternoon, Nisan 14. (Mt 27:61) On the third day, the two of them and others came to the tomb with spices and perfumed oil for the purpose of rubbing the body of Jesus and, to their alarm, found the tomb open. An angel explained that Christ had risen from the dead, hence he commanded, "Go, tell his disciples." (Mt 28:1-7; Mr 16:1-7; Lu 24:1-10) While they were on their way, the resurrected Jesus appeared to this Mary and the others.—Mt 28:8, 9.

5. Mary the mother of John Mark. She was also the aunt of Barnabas. (Ac 12:12; Col 4:10) Her home was used for a meeting place by the early Christian congregation in Jerusalem. Her son Mark was closely associated with the apostle Peter, who evidently had much to do with Mark's spiritual growth, for Peter speaks of him as "Mark my son." (1Pe 5:13) Peter, upon release from Herod's prison, came directly to her home "where quite a few were gathered together and praying." The house must have been of considerable size, and the presence of a servant girl suggests that Mary was a woman of means. (Ac 12:12-17) Since it was referred to as *her* home, and not her husband's, she probably was a widow.—Ac 12:12.

6. Mary of Rome. She was sent greetings by Paul in his letter to the Romans and was commended for her "many labors" in behalf of the Roman congregation.—Ro 16:6.

MASH. A descendant of Shem through Aram. (Ge 10:22, 23; 1Ch 1:17, *Sy* and six Heb. manuscripts) At 1 Chronicles 1:17 the Masoretic text reads "Meshech" instead of "Mash." But this is probably a scribal error, since Meshach is listed as a "son" of Japheth.—Ge 10:2; 1Ch 1:5.

Some link Mash and his descendants with Mons

Masius, a mountainous region of northern Mesopotamia mentioned by Greek geographer Strabo. (*Geography*, 16, I, 23) Others associate Mash with a part of the Syro-Arabian desert called the "(country of) *Mash*" in Assyrian annals and described as "the desert where parching thirst is at home, where there are not even birds in the sky and wherein neither wild donkeys (nor) gazelles pasture."—*Archaeology and the Old Testament*, by M. F. Unger, 1964, p. 98; *Ancient Near Eastern Texts*, edited by J. B. Pritchard, 1974, p. 299.

MASHAL (Ma'shal). A city of Asher assigned to the Gershonites; apparently an alternate name for Mishal. (Jos 21:27, 30; 1Ch 6:71, 74) Its exact location is unknown.

MASKIL (Mas'kil). This word appears in the superscription of 13 psalms (32, 42, 44, 45, 52, 53, 54, 55, 74, 78, 88, 89, 142) and possibly means "contemplative poem." However, because the meaning of the Hebrew word is not certain, it is left untranslated in many versions. A clue to its sense may be indicated in the fact that a word of similar form is elsewhere translated "acting prudently," 'acting with discretion,' "acting with consideration," "having insight," and so forth.—1Sa 18:14, 15; 2Ch 30:22; Ps 41:1; 53:2.

MASON. A craftsman who builds with brick or stone. (2Ki 12:12; 22:6) The stonemason of ancient times hewed and sawed stones and then used them to construct walls and various kinds of buildings. (2Sa 5:11; 1Ki 7:9-12; 1Ch 22:2; 2Ch 24:12) Other constructions included burial places (Isa 22:16) and water tunnels.—2Ki 20:20.

Among the tools used by masons were the hammer, the ax, the stone saw, the leveling instrument, the measuring line, and the plummet. (1Ki 6:7; 7:9; Isa 28:17; Zec 4:10) As shown on monuments, implements used by Egyptian masons included the mallet and chisel, doubtless also employed by Israelite stonemasons. During construction in Egypt, stones were measured and marked with dark lines, which served as guides for the stonecutters, and each stone's position in the building was designated by a mark or number placed on it.

Ancient masons were able to dress stones so well that it was not necessary to use mortar. To this day it is impossible to insert a knife blade between the massive stones of certain structural remains in Palestine dating from the Herodian period.—See ARCHITECTURE.

MASREKAH (Mas·re'kah). Apparently the home of Samlah, an Edomite king. (Ge 36:31, 36; 1Ch 1:43, 47) The name Masrekah may be pre-

served in the mountain that the Arabs call Jebel el-Mushraq, located about 50 km (30 mi) SW of Ma'an. Eusebius placed Masrekah farther N, nearer the Dead Sea.

MASSA (Mas'sa). A descendant of Abraham through Ishmael. (Ge 25:12-14; 1Ch 1:29, 30) Massa's offspring probably settled somewhere in N Arabia. In the annals of Tiglath-pileser III, Mas'a (Biblical Massa?) is mentioned along with Tema and other locations in N Arabia. (*Ancient Near Eastern Texts*, edited by J. Pritchard, 1974, p. 283) Massa has been linked with the *Ma·sa·noi* located by Greek geographer Ptolemy (second century C.E.) as NE of "Dumah" (the Dumat al-Ghandal area in N Arabia?).

The Hebrew word *mas·sa'* is also found at Proverbs 30:1 (with the definite article *ha*) and at Proverbs 31:1 (without an article). This has given rise to the renderings 'Agur son of Jakeh, of Massa' and 'Lemuel king of Massa.' (Compare *AT, JB, Ro, RS* or their alternate readings.) However, Agur and Lemuel evidently were Israelites, and therefore, *mas·sa'* is appropriately translated "oracle" (*AS*), "declaration" (*Yg*), and "weighty message" (*NW*; compare Pr 30:5, 9; 31:30 with Ps 12:6; Ro 3:1, 2).

MASSAH (Mas'sah) [Testing; Trial]. One of the names for the place near Rephidim where the Israelites received a miraculous supply of water. As instructed by Jehovah, Moses and some of the older men of Israel went to the rock in Horeb. There Moses struck the rock. The water that then began to issue forth flowed as a river there in the wilderness. Moses subsequently named the place Massah (meaning "Testing; Trial") because the Israelites had put Jehovah to the test by their faithless murmuring, and on account of their quarreling, he called it Meribah (meaning "Quarreling"). —Ex 17:1-7; Ps 105:41.

Shortly before his death Moses warned Israel not to put Jehovah to the test as they had done at Massah. (De 6:16; see also De 9:22.) Then, in blessing Israel, he again took note of this event, indicating that it had resulted in testing Levi. (De 33:8) In this case Levi may mean the heads of the tribe, that is, Moses and Aaron.

Later, the psalmist admonished the Israelites not to harden their hearts like the generation that wandered in the wilderness. His reference to Meribah and Massah evidently alludes to Israel's murmuring for water at Rephidim, the incident being representative of their faithless course throughout the entire 40-year period. (Ps 95:8-11) This appears to be the thought conveyed by the quotation of the psalmist's words (from the Greek *Septuagint*) found at Hebrews chapter 3: "Do not harden your hearts as on the occasion of causing bitter anger [Meribah], as in the day of making the test [Massah] in the wilderness, in which your forefathers made a test of me with a trial, and yet they had seen my works for forty years [literally, "and they saw my works forty years"]." (Heb 3:8, 9) Both Psalm 95:8 and Hebrews 3:8 may also include Israel's later murmuring for water at the Meribah in the Kadesh area.—Nu 20:1-13.

MASSIVE TREE.   See BIG TREE, MASSIVE TREE.

MATRED   (Ma'tred) [from a root that means "drive [one] away"]. Mother of Mehetabel, the wife of Edomite King Hadar (Hadad). (Ge 36:31, 39; 1Ch 1:50) At Genesis 36:39 the Syriac *Peshitta* and the Greek *Septuagint* present Matred as the son of Mezahab, but according to the Masoretic text, Matred was Mezahab's daughter.

MATRITES   (Mat'rites) [Of (Belonging to) Matar (Rain [thus born in the rainy season])]. A Benjamite family of which King Saul of Israel was a member. (1Sa 10:21) The *King James Version* uses the name "Matri" (Ma'tri). However, the Hebrew word *mat·ri'* here is accompanied by the definite article. Thus the *New World Translation* appropriately reads "the Matrites," as do other modern translations.—AS; AT; RS.

MATTAN   (Mat'tan) [Gift].
   1. A priest of Baal who was killed before the altars at the house of that false god. This occurred when the people, led by Jehoiada the priest of Jehovah, pulled down the house of Baal and destroyed his altars as well as his images. At that time the usurper Athaliah was put to death, and Jehoash was installed as Judah's king.—2Ki 11:16-21; 2Ch 23:17.
   2. The father of Jeremiah's persecutor Shephatiah.—Jer 38:1, 4-6.

MATTANAH   (Mat'ta·nah) [Gift]. One of Israel's encampments between the Arnon torrent valley and the territory of Sihon the Amorite. (Nu 21:13-21) Khirbet el-Medeiyineh (or, Mudaiyina), about 15 km (9.5 mi) NE of Dibon is tentatively identified with the ancient site.

MATTANIAH   (Mat·ta·ni'ah) [Gift of Jehovah].
   1. A Levite, a son of Heman. He was selected by lot to head the ninth service group of Levitical musicians as arranged by David.—1Ch 25:1, 4, 8, 9, 16.
   2. A Levite of the sons of Asaph and an ancestor of Jahaziel. (2Ch 20:14) He may be the Matta-

niah mentioned in 1 Chronicles 9:15 and Nehemiah 13:13. It may be another Mattaniah or the representative of that house that is mentioned in Nehemiah 12:8; compare Nehemiah 11:17, 22; 12:25.
   3. A Levite descendant of Asaph who assisted in cleansing the house of Jehovah in King Hezekiah's time.—2Ch 29:12-16.
   4. A son of King Josiah and the uncle of King Jehoiachin. He was put on the throne of Judah by Nebuchadnezzar king of Babylon, who changed his name to Zedekiah.—2Ki 24:15-17; see ZEDEKIAH No. 4.
   5. An Israelite among "the sons of Elam" who sent away foreign wives.—Ezr 10:25, 26, 44.
   6. An Israelite among "the sons of Zattu" who sent away foreign wives.—Ezr 10:25, 27, 44.
   7. An Israelite among "the sons of Pahathmoab" who sent away foreign wives.—Ezr 10:25, 30, 44.
   8. An Israelite among "the sons of Bani" who sent away foreign wives.—Ezr 10:25, 34, 37, 44.

MATTATHA   (Mat'ta·tha) [probably a shortened form of the Heb. Mattithiah, meaning "Gift of Jehovah"]. A man of the tribe of Judah who was a son of Nathan and grandson of David. He was an ancestor of Jesus, according to Christ's maternal genealogy recorded by Luke.—Lu 3:23, 31.

MATTATHIAS   (Mat·ta·thi'as) [from the Heb. Mattithiah, meaning "Gift of Jehovah"].
   1. The Greek name applied in the *Septuagint* to the Korahite Levite Mattithiah, Shallum's firstborn.—1Ch 9:31; see MATTITHIAH No. 2.
   2. Greek form used in the *Septuagint* for "Mattithiah," one of "the sons of Jeduthun."—1Ch 25:3; see MATTITHIAH No. 1.
   3. A man of the tribe of Judah who is called the "son of Amos" in the maternal genealogy of Jesus.—Lu 3:23, 25.
   4. Another man of Judah, called the "son of Semein," who lived after the days of Zerubbabel and who is mentioned in Jesus' genealogy recorded by Luke.—Lu 3:23, 26, 27.

MATTATTAH   (Mat'tat·tah) [shortened form of Mattithiah, meaning "Gift of Jehovah"]. An Israelite "of the sons of Hashum" who married foreign wives but dismissed them in the days of Ezra.—Ezr 10:25, 33, 44.

MATTENAI   (Mat·te'nai) [shortened form of Mattaniah, meaning "Gift of Jehovah"].
   1. An Israelite "of the sons of Hashum" who had taken foreign wives but sent them away in Ezra's time.—Ezr 10:25, 33, 44.

2. An Israelite "of the sons of Bani" who sent away their foreign wives in Ezra's day.—Ezr 10: 25, 34, 37, 44.

3. A priest in the days of Joiakim who was the head of the paternal house of Joiarib.—Ne 12: 12, 19.

MATTHAN (Mat'than). An ancestor of Joseph, the adoptive father of Jesus Christ. Matthan may have been Joseph's grandfather.—Mt 1:15, 16.

MATTHAT (Mat'that) [probably a shortened form of the Heb. Mattithiah, meaning "Gift of Jehovah"].

1. A distant ancestor of Jesus Christ through Mary. He is called the "son of Levi" and was one of the persons listed in the period between Zerubbabel and David.—Lu 3:29.

2. A closer ancestor of Jesus through Mary. Her father Heli is referred to as the "son" of this Matthat, who was probably Mary's grandfather. —Lu 3:23, 24.

MATTHEW (Mat'thew) [probably a shortened form of the Heb. Mattithiah, meaning "Gift of Jehovah"]. A Jew, otherwise known as Levi, who became an apostle of Jesus Christ and the writer of the Gospel bearing his name. He was the son of a certain Alphaeus and was a tax collector before becoming one of Jesus' disciples. (Mt 10:3; Mr 2:14; see TAX COLLECTOR.) The Scriptures do not reveal whether Levi also had the name Matthew before becoming a disciple of Jesus, received it at that time, or was given that name by Jesus when he was appointed as an apostle.

It appears that early in his Galilean ministry (30 or early 31 C.E.) Jesus Christ called Matthew from the tax office in or near Capernaum. (Mt 9:1, 9; Mr 2:1, 13, 14) 'Leaving everything behind, Matthew rose up and went following Jesus.' (Lu 5:27, 28) Perhaps to celebrate the receiving of his call to follow Christ, Matthew "spread a big reception feast," attended by Jesus and his disciples as well as many tax collectors and sinners. This disturbed the Pharisees and the scribes, causing them to murmur about Christ's eating and drinking with tax collectors and sinners.—Lu 5:29, 30; Mt 9:10, 11; Mr 2:15, 16.

Later, after the Passover of 31 C.E., Jesus selected the 12 apostles, and Matthew was one of them. (Mr 3:13-19; Lu 6:12-16) Though the Bible makes various references to the apostles as a group, it does not mention Matthew by name again until after Christ's ascension to heaven. Matthew saw the resurrected Jesus Christ (1Co 15:3-6), received parting instructions from him, and saw him ascend to heaven. After this he and the other apos-

tles returned to Jerusalem. The apostles were staying in an upper chamber there, and Matthew is specifically named as being among them, so he must have been one of the some 120 disciples who received the holy spirit on the day of Pentecost 33 C.E.—Ac 1:4-15; 2:1-4.

MATTHEW, GOOD NEWS ACCORDING TO. The inspired account of the life of Jesus Christ written, doubtless in Palestine, by the onetime tax collector Matthew, or Levi. It is the first book in the Christian Greek Scriptures and has since ancient times been viewed as the first Gospel written. Matthew's account commences with the human ancestry of Jesus, followed by his birth, and concludes with Christ's postresurrection commissioning of his followers to go and "make disciples of people of all the nations." (Mt 28:19, 20) Hence, it covers the time between Jesus' birth in 2 B.C.E. and his meeting with his disciples just before his ascension in 33 C.E.

Time of Writing. Subscriptions, appearing at the end of Matthew's Gospel in numerous manuscripts (all being later than the tenth century C.E.), say that the account was written about the eighth year after Christ's ascension (c. 41 C.E.). This would not be at variance with internal evidence. The fact that no reference is made to the fulfillment of Jesus' prophecy respecting Jerusalem's destruction would point to a time of composition prior to 70 C.E. (Mt 5:35; 24:16) And the expression "to this very day" (27:8; 28:15) indicates a lapse of some time between the events considered and the time of writing.

Originally Written in Hebrew. External evidence to the effect that Matthew originally wrote this Gospel in Hebrew reaches as far back as Papias of Hierapolis, of the second century C.E. Eusebius quoted Papias as stating: "Matthew collected the oracles in the Hebrew language." (*The Ecclesiastical History*, III, XXXIX, 16) Early in the third century, Origen made reference to Matthew's account and, in discussing the four Gospels, is quoted by Eusebius as saying that the "first was written . . . according to Matthew, who was once a tax-collector but afterwards an apostle of Jesus Christ, . . . in the Hebrew language." (*The Ecclesiastical History*, VI, XXV, 3-6) The scholar Jerome (of the fourth and fifth centuries C.E.) wrote in his work *De viris inlustribus* (Concerning Illustrious Men), chapter III, that Matthew "composed a Gospel of Christ in Judaea in the Hebrew language and characters for the benefit of those of the circumcision who had believed. . . . Moreover, the Hebrew itself is preserved to this day in the library at Caesarea, which the martyr Pamphilus so diligently collected."—Translation from the Latin text edited by E. C. Richardson and published in the series "Texte und Untersuchungen zur Geschichte der altchristlichen Literatur," Leipzig, 1896, Vol. 14, pp. 8, 9.

It has been suggested that Matthew, after compiling his account in Hebrew, may have personally translated it into Koine, the common Greek.

Information Unique to Matthew's Gospel. An examination of Matthew's account shows that more than 40 percent of the material contained therein is not found in the other three Gospels. Unique is Matthew's genealogy of Jesus (Mt 1:1-16), which takes an approach different from that set out by Luke (Lu 3:23-38). A comparison of the two indicates that Matthew gave the legal genealogy through Jesus' adoptive father Joseph, while Luke apparently gave Jesus' natural genealogy. Other incidents mentioned only in Matthew's account are: Joseph's reaction to Mary's pregnancy, the appearance of an angel to Joseph in a dream (Mt 1:18-25), the visit of the astrologers, the flight to Egypt, the slaughter of the young boys in Bethlehem and its districts (chap 2), and the dream of Pilate's wife regarding Jesus (27:19).

HIGHLIGHTS OF MATTHEW

The apostle Matthew's account of Jesus' life; written primarily with the Jews in mind, this Gospel demonstrates that Jesus is the foretold Messianic King

The first Gospel written, it was likely composed initially in Hebrew about eight years after the death and resurrection of Christ

---

Details of Jesus' life fulfill Messianic prophecies

Jesus is born of a virgin, an offspring of Abraham in David's line, at Bethlehem (1:1-23; 2:1-6)

Baby boys are slaughtered; he is called out of Egypt (2:14-18)

He grows up in Nazareth; John the Baptizer prepares the way for him (2:23–3:3)

He proves to be a light in Galilee (4:13-16)

He performs many miraculous healings (8:16, 17)

He gladly helps the lowly ones (12:10-21)

He teaches, using illustrations; the hearts of many people are unreceptive (13:10-15, 34, 35)

Jesus rides into Jerusalem on the colt of an ass; he is hailed as the Son of David by the crowds but rejected by Jewish "builders" (21:1-11, 15, 42)

Judas betrays him for 30 silver pieces, which money is later used to buy a potter's field (26:14, 15, 48, 49; 27:3-10)

His disciples are scattered (26:31)

Jesus is in the tomb for parts of three days (12:39, 40)

Jesus proclaims the good news of God's Kingdom

After John's arrest, Jesus proclaims: "The kingdom of the heavens has drawn near" (4:12-23)

He visits all the cities and villages of Galilee to preach the good news of the Kingdom (9:35)

He instructs his 12 disciples and sends them out to preach about the Kingdom (10:1–11:1)

He reveals truths about the Kingdom, telling the parables of the sower, the wheat and weeds, the mustard grain, the leaven, treasure hidden in a field, a pearl of high value, a dragnet, workers in a vineyard, two sons, wicked cultivators, and a marriage feast for a king's son (13:3-50; 20:1-16; 21:28-41; 22:1-14)

He answers his disciples' question about the sign of his presence, including in his answer a forecast of global preaching of the Kingdom good news (24:3–25:46)

Jesus exposes the hypocrisy of the religious leaders

He shows that they misrepresent the purpose of the Sabbath and that their traditions invalidate God's Word (12:3-7; 15:1-14)

He exposes their lack of faith, their murderous spirit, their hypocrisy and pride (12:24-42; 16:1-4; 21:43-45; 23:2-36)

He lays bare their utter disregard for justice, mercy, and faithfulness (23:23, 24; 9:11-13)

Jesus gives fine counsel to his followers

In the Sermon on the Mount, Jesus shows why his disciples would be truly happy; he warns against wrath and urges them to make peace with one another and to love even their enemies; he tells of the danger of adulterous thoughts; he counsels against hypocrisy, teaches how to pray, warns against materialism, and advises seeking first God's Kingdom and His righteousness; he cautions his hearers not to be overcritical, tells them to pray constantly, and urges them to realize that the road to life is narrow and that they should produce fine fruits (5:1–7:27)

Jesus encourages humility and warns against stumbling others; he shows how to settle differences (18:1-17, 21-35)

He states the Christian standard for marriage and divorce (19:3-9)

The death and resurrection of God's Son

On Passover night, Jesus institutes the Memorial of his coming death (26:26-30)

Betrayed and arrested, he is judged worthy of death by the Sanhedrin (26:46-66)

He is examined by Pilate, then whipped, mocked, and impaled (27:2, 11-54)

Jesus is buried; he is resurrected and appears to his followers; he commissions them to go and make disciples of people of all nations (27:57–28:20)

At least ten parables, or illustrations, found in Matthew's account are not mentioned in the other Gospels. These include four in chapter 13, those of the weeds in the field, the hidden treasure, the "one pearl of high value," and the dragnet. Others are the illustrations of the unmerciful slave (Mt 18:23-35), the workers in the vineyard (20:1-16), the marriage of the king's son (22:1-14), the ten virgins (25:1-13), and the talents (25:14-30).

At times Matthew provides supplementary details. Although material from the Sermon on the Mount also appears in Luke's account (Lu 6:17-49), Matthew's Gospel is far more extensive in this respect. (Mt 5:1–7:29) Whereas Mark, Luke, and John mention the miraculous feeding of about 5,000 men, Matthew adds "besides women and young children." (Mt 14:21; Mr 6:44; Lu 9:14; Joh 6:10) Matthew mentions two demon-possessed men encountered by Jesus in the country of the Gadarenes, while Mark and Luke refer to only one. (Mt 8:28; Mr 5:2; Lu 8:27) Matthew also tells of two blind men being healed on an occasion, whereas Mark and Luke mention only one. (Mt 20:29, 30; Mr 10:46, 47; Lu 18:35, 38) Of course, all the writers were correct in that at least one person was involved in each incident. But Matthew was often more explicit as to number. This perhaps is to be attributed to his former occupation as a tax collector.

Matthew's Use of the Hebrew Scriptures. It has been estimated that Matthew's Gospel contains about a hundred references to the Hebrew Scriptures. About 40 of these are actual quotations of passages. These include Christ's own quotations from and allusions to the Hebrew Scriptures, among which are the following: a man's enemies to be persons of his own household (Mt 10:35, 36; Mic 7:6); John the Baptizer identified as the "Elijah" to come (Mt 11:13, 14; 17:11-13; Mal 4:5); Jesus' and Jonah's experiences compared (Mt 12:40; Jon 1:17); commandment on honoring parents (Mt 15:4; Ex 20:12; 21:17); rendering lip service to God (Mt 15:8, 9; Isa 29:13); need for two or three witnesses (Mt 18:16; De 19:15); statements on marriage (Mt 19:4-6; Ge 1:27; 2:24); various commandments (Mt 5:21, 27, 38; 19:18, 19; Ex 20:12-16; 21:24; Le 19:18; 24:20; De 19:21); the temple made into "a cave of robbers" (Mt 21:13; Isa 56:7; Jer 7:11); rejection of Jesus, "the stone" that became "the chief cornerstone" (Mt 21:42; Ps 118:22, 23); foes of David's Lord put under his feet (Mt 22:44; Ps 110:1); disgusting thing in the holy place (Mt 24:15; Da 9:27); Jesus' disciples scattered (Mt 26:31; Zec 13:7); Christ apparently forsaken by God (Mt 27:46; Ps 22:1). There are also

Jesus' statements used in resisting Satan's temptations.—Mt 4:4, 7, 10; De 8:3; 6:16, 13.

Interesting, too, is Matthew's inspired application of Hebrew Scripture prophecies to Jesus, proving him to be the promised Messiah. This aspect would have been of particular concern to the Jews, for whom the account seems to have been originally intended. The prophecies include: Jesus' being born of a virgin (Mt 1:23; Isa 7:14); his birth in Bethlehem (Mt 2:6; Mic 5:2); his being called out of Egypt (Mt 2:15; Ho 11:1); the lamentation over the death of slaughtered children (Mt 2:16-18; Jer 31:15); John the Baptizer's preparing the way before Jesus (Mt 3:1-3; Isa 40:3); Jesus' ministry bringing light (Mt 4:13-16; Isa 9:1, 2); his carrying of illnesses (Mt 8:14-17; Isa 53:4); his use of illustrations (Mt 13:34, 35; Ps 78:2); Jesus' entry into Jerusalem on the colt of an ass (Mt 21:4, 5; Zec 9:9); the betrayal of Christ for 30 pieces of silver (Mt 26:14, 15; Zec 11:12).

An Accurate, Beneficial Record. Matthew, being a close associate of Christ during Jesus' later years of life on earth and thus an eyewitness of his ministry, could understandably record a moving and meaningful Gospel. This we possess in the former tax collector's record of the life of Jesus Christ. He was enabled by God's spirit to recall in detail what Jesus said and did on earth. (Joh 14:26) Hence, Matthew accurately portrayed Jesus of Nazareth as the beloved Son of God having divine approval, as the one who came "to minister and to give his soul a ransom in exchange for many," and as the foretold Messianic King who was to arrive in glory. (Mt 20:28; 3:17; 25:31) When on earth, Jesus pointed to his works and could truthfully say: "The poor are having the good news declared to them." (11:5) And today multitudes, both natural Jews and non-Jews, greatly benefit from such Kingdom good news as recorded in Matthew's Gospel.—Mt 4:23, ftn.

MATTHIAS (Mat·thi′as) [probably a shortened form of the Heb. Mattithiah, meaning "Gift of Jehovah"]. The disciple selected by lot to replace Judas Iscariot as an apostle. After Jesus' ascension to heaven, Peter, noting that not only had the psalmist David foretold Judas' deflection (Ps 41:9) but David had also written (Ps 109:8) "his office of oversight let someone else take," proposed to the approximately 120 disciples gathered together that the vacancy of office be filled. Joseph Barsabbas and Matthias were put up for selection; after prayer, lots were cast, and Matthias was chosen. Occurring just a few days prior to the outpouring of holy spirit, this is the last instance reported in the Bible of the lots being resorted to in determining Jehovah's choice in a matter.—Ac 1:15-26.

According to Peter's words (Ac 1:21, 22), Matthias had been a follower of Christ throughout Jesus' three-and-a-half-year ministry, had been closely associated with the apostles, and was quite likely one of the 70 disciples or evangelists whom Jesus sent out to preach. (Lu 10:1) After his selection, he was "reckoned along with the eleven apostles" by the congregation (Ac 1:26), and when the book of Acts immediately thereafter speaks of "the apostles" or "the twelve," Matthias was included. —Ac 2:37, 43; 4:33, 36; 5:12, 29; 6:2, 6; 8:1, 14; 9:27; see PAUL.

MATTITHIAH (Mat·ti·thi'ah) [Gift of Jehovah].

1. A Levite who played a harp when the ark of the covenant was brought to Jerusalem from the house of Obed-edom. (1Ch 15:17-21, 25) Probably this same Mattithiah was one of the Levite musicians whom David put before the Ark "both to call to remembrance and to thank and praise Jehovah the God of Israel" (1Ch 16:4, 5) and was the individual who was later selected by lot from among the sons of Jeduthun to head the 14th division of 12 Levite musicians.—1Ch 25:1, 3, 9, 21.

2. A Kohathite Levite of the family of Korah and the firstborn son of Shallum. This Mattithiah was among the Levites returning from Babylonian exile and "was in the office of trust over the things baked in pans."—1Ch 9:31, 32.

3. A Levite or priest who stood at Ezra's right hand when the copyist read the Law of Moses to the Jews assembled in Jerusalem.—Ne 8:1, 4.

4. An Israelite "of the sons of Nebo" who was among those accepting foreign wives but who sent them away "along with sons" in Ezra's day. —Ezr 10:25, 43, 44.

MATURITY.

The state of being full grown, ripe, complete, as determined by a standard. (See PERFECTION.) The Bible provides the standard for ascertaining what constitutes spiritual maturity (completeness). According to this standard, a mature Christian is one who is not a spiritual babe, often changeable and easily led astray or influenced by others in matters of doctrine. (Eph 4:11-14) Since his perceptive powers are trained, he is able to distinguish both right and wrong. He does not need to be taught elementary things. (Heb 5:11–6:2) He is guided, not by worldly wisdom, but by God's spirit.—1Co 2:6, 10-13, ftn.

Never does the Bible speak about degrees or stages of spiritual maturity or adulthood. However, just as a person continues to grow in knowledge, experience, and discernment after becoming an adult, the mature Christian likewise continues to make progress. Trials that he has can strengthen his faith and endurance. Wrote the disciple James: "Consider it all joy, my brothers, when you meet with various trials, knowing as you do that this tested quality of your faith works out endurance. But let endurance have its work complete, that you may be complete [literally, perfect] and sound in all respects, not lacking in anything." (Jas 1:2-4) Similarly, as adults will vary in physical aspects and in mental abilities and talents, so mature Christians may vary in certain qualities, some being notable in some aspect, such as knowledge, judgment, courage, or generosity; others in another. (Compare 1Co 7:7; 12:4-11, 27-31.) Thus, in considering maturity, it is necessary to take into consideration that special abilities or talents are not the things that determine whether one is a mature Christian or not.

The entire congregational arrangement, with its apostles, prophets, evangelizers, shepherds, and teachers, served to produce mature Christians, spiritual adults. (Eph 4:11-14; compare Col 1:28, 29; 4:12, 13.) Obviously, then, those serving as shepherds and teachers had to be spiritually mature persons, not babes. However, more than spiritual adulthood was required of one appointed as an overseer or a ministerial servant. (1Ti 3:1-9, 12, 13; Tit 1:5-9) For example, one of the requirements for an overseer was that he be "a man presiding over his own household in a fine manner, having children in subjection with all seriousness." (1Ti 3:4) Thus, a man could be mature in certain respects from a spiritual viewpoint, and yet, if his children were rebellious and uncontrollable, he would not qualify for the position of overseer.

MAZZAROTH CONSTELLATION (Maz'zaroth).

The Aramaic Targum equates Mazzaroth with the maz·za·lohth' of 2 Kings 23:5, "constellations of the zodiac," or "twelve signs, or, constellations." (NW; KJ margin) Some believe that the word is derived from a root meaning "engird" and that Mazzaroth refers to the zodiacal circle. However, at Job 38:32 a singular pronoun is used in Hebrew in the expression "in its appointed time," whereas the reference in 2 Kings 23:5 is in the plural. Hence, Mazzaroth appears to refer to a particular constellation rather than to the entire zodiacal circle, but no positive identification is possible at present.

At Job 38:32 Jehovah asks Job: "Can you bring forth the Mazzaroth constellation in its appointed time? And as for the Ash constellation alongside its sons, can you conduct them?" Thus, whatever the identification of these particular constellations may be, God puts the question to Job whether he can control the visible celestial bodies, bringing forth a certain group at its proper season or guiding another constellation in its prescribed heavenly course.

MEAH. See TOWER.

MEAL. Often occasions of happy fellowship and spiritual benefit among the ancient Hebrews and, later, the early Christians. Meals also afforded opportunities for showing love and extending hospitality to others. It appears that the Hebrews and early Christians customarily offered prayers in connection with meals.—1Sa 9:13; Ac 27:35; 1Ti 4:1, 3; see HOSPITALITY; LORD'S EVENING MEAL; LOVE FEASTS.

The Israelites appear to have had two main meals each day, one in the morning and the other in the evening at the close of the workday. (Compare Ru 3:2, 3, 7; 1Ki 17:6.) While many ate their breakfasts at home, others, including fishermen who toiled all night, apparently made it a practice to take some food along when going to work. Fishermen could also prepare some of their catch for breakfast.—Compare Mr 8:14; Joh 21:12, 15.

There is evidence, however, that a meal, perhaps usually a lighter one, was served about noon. (Ac 10:9, 10) Probably at this time persons working in the field stopped to rest and ate some food. —Compare Ru 2:14.

Women customarily served the food. (Joh 12:1-3) But at times they ate their meals in company with men. (1Sa 1:4, 5; Job 1:4) In well-to-do, particularly royal, households servants waited on the tables. King Solomon's table was served by waiters having special attire.—1Ki 10:4, 5; 2Ch 9:3, 4.

Drinks were usually served in individual cups, but food was often placed in a common dish. Those eating might take food with their fingers or use a piece of bread somewhat like a spoon to partake of certain foods.—Mr 14:20; Joh 13:25, 26; see also Pr 26:15.

The postures assumed by persons at meals included reclining and sitting. (Ge 18:4; 27:19; Jg 19:6; Lu 9:14) A relief from the palace of Assyrian King Ashurbanipal depicts him as reclining on a couch and his queen as seated on an elevated chair while feasting. Reclining on couches at meals was apparently also a practice among the Persians. (Es 7:8) Tables and couches were used at least by some Israelites in Ezekiel's time.—Eze 23:41.

During the Time of Jesus' Earthly Ministry. The general Hebrew custom in the first century C.E. was for persons to wash their hands before eating a meal. This was a ritualistic practice among the scribes and Pharisees.—Mr 7:1-8; see WASHING OF HANDS.

At banquets or large feasts in the time of Jesus' earthly ministry, couches were placed around three sides of a table. This left the fourth side free so that those serving the food could gain access to the table. At times four or five persons occupied one couch, but usually the number was three. Those partaking of the meal usually rested on the left elbow, probably on a cushion, with their heads toward the table. Food was normally taken with the right hand. The place of highest importance on a couch was that occupied by the person having no one behind him. To be in the "bosom position" in relation to someone else reclining at a meal meant being in front of him and would also signify having his favor. (Joh 13:23) The individual having a person in the bosom position could easily carry on a confidential conversation with him.

The customary three positions on each couch indicated that a person had the high, middle, or low position on the couch. One having the low position on the third or lowest couch had the lowest position at the meal.—Compare Mt 23:6; Lu 14:7-11.

At least on certain festive occasions a large meal or banquet might be under the supervision of a director (Joh 2:9) and could feature such entertainment as "a music concert and dancing."—Lu 15:25.

Proper View of Meals. It is God's will for man to enjoy food and drink. (Ec 2:24) But excesses are detestable to him. (Pr 23:20, 21; Ec 10:17; Ro 13:13; 1Pe 4:3; see DRUNKENNESS; GLUTTON.) Since partaking of meals in moderation can be most delightful, the condition of one who is joyful at heart is comparable to a continuous feast. (Pr 15:15) Also, a loving atmosphere contributes to the enjoyment of a meal. Says the proverb: "Better is a dish of vegetables where there is love than a manger-fed bull and hatred along with it."—Pr 15:17.

Figurative Use. To eat a meal with someone signified friendship and peace between the persons involved. Therefore one who was privileged to eat regularly at the table of a king was especially favored and enjoyed a very close bond with the monarch. (1Ki 2:7) This relationship Jesus promised his faithful disciples when telling them that they would eat and drink with him in his Kingdom.—Lu 22:28-30; see also Lu 13:29; Re 19:9.

The destruction of those standing in opposition to God provides the occasion for a "great evening meal." This meal is for the birds that will feed on the dead bodies of those slain. (Re 19:15-18) A very different meal is the great banquet for all the peoples mentioned at Isaiah 25:6.

MEARAH (Me·ar'ah) [Cave]. A Sidonian city or district that remained to be conquered after Israel's campaign under Joshua's leadership ended. (Jos 13:2, 4) Two locations have tentatively been suggested. One is the village of Mghairiye, about 10 km (6 mi) NE of Sidon. The other is Mughar Jezzin (Arabic for "Caves of Jezzin"), a district of caves atop the Lebanon Range and E of Sidon.

MEASURE. See WEIGHTS AND MEASURES.

MEASURING LINE. A string, rope, or cord used for measuring. (1Ki 7:15, 23; Am 7:17; Zec 2:1, 2) Some measuring lines were apparently divided into cubits. (2Ch 4:2) The extent of a particular land area was determined by stretching or casting a measuring line upon its surface. (Compare Job 38:4, 5; Ps 78:55; Mic 2:4, 5.) Builders used it, as when laying out a city (Jer 31:38, 39; Zec 1:16), and a wood carver might use it to set the dimensions of an object. (Isa 44:13) On one occasion King David appears to have measured off the vanquished Moabites that were to be put to death from those to be preserved alive.—2Sa 8:2.

Figurative Use. In a figurative sense, "measuring line" denotes a rule, or standard, of action. (Isa 28:10, 13) For example, Jehovah made "justice the measuring line" when dealing with his unfaithful people. (Isa 28:17) His applying the same measuring line to Jerusalem as he had to Samaria pointed to a similar desolation for Jerusalem. (2Ki 21:13; La 2:8) His stretching out "the measuring line of emptiness" on Edom likewise betokened destruction, and the use of this measuring line meant apportioning the land to the animals that would begin to dwell in the desolated areas of Edom.—Isa 34:5-17.

David regarded his relationship with Jehovah as his portion in life. This was a most satisfying inheritance, prompting him to say: "The measuring lines themselves have fallen for me in pleasant places."—Ps 16:5, 6; compare Nu 18:20.

The heavenly bodies testify to God's creative activity, and since their silent testimony fills the earth, the psalmist could say respecting them: "Into all the earth their measuring line has gone out."—Ps 19:1-4; Ro 1:20.

See REED.

MEAT. See FLESH; FOOD; IDOLS, MEATS OFFERED TO.

MEBUNNAI (Me·bun'nai). A mighty man in David's army, a Hushathite. (2Sa 23:27) Apparently he is the same person as the Sibbecai mentioned in 2 Samuel 21:18 and 1 Chronicles 11:29; 20:4; 27:11.

MECHERATHITE (Me·che'rath·ite). A term pertaining to a person or place named Mecherah, to which Hepher, one of David's mighty men, was linked either by descent or former residence. (1Ch 11:26, 36) Some scholars suggest that "Mecherathite" may be a variation of "Maacathite," as at 2 Samuel 23:34.

MECONAH (Me·co'nah) [from a root meaning "firmly establish"]. A town in southern Judah apparently near Ziklag and large enough to have dependent, or "daughter," towns. (Ne 11:25, 28) Precise identification is not possible; most suggested locations are based on textual emendations.

MEDAD (Me'dad). One of the 70 older men of Israel selected to assist Moses during the wilderness trek. While Medad and Eldad had not gone to the tent of meeting with the others, "they were among those written down." Hence, when Jehovah took away some of the spirit that was upon Moses, putting it upon each of the 70 older men, these too received it and began acting as prophets in the camp. (Nu 11:16, 17, 24-26) Though Joshua suggested restraining Medad and Eldad, Moses said: "Are you feeling jealous for me? No, I wish that all of Jehovah's people were prophets, because Jehovah would put his spirit upon them!" —Nu 11:27-29.

MEDAN (Me'dan). One of Abraham's six sons by his concubine Keturah. (Ge 25:1, 2; 1Ch 1:32) The Arabian tribe that descended from Medan has not been identified, and where it settled is unknown. However, "Medan" may be represented in "Badan," a place S of Tema taken by Assyrian King Tiglath-pileser III in the eighth century B.C.E., as the Arabic "m" and "b" are frequently interchanged.

MEDEBA (Med'e·ba). This place is represented by modern Madaba, a town located on a low, gently sloping hill about 20 km (12 mi) E of the northern end of the Dead Sea. The ancient "king's road" linked it with other cities E of the Jordan. (Compare Nu 20:17.) Madaba is situated on a treeless but fertile plain, or plateau. In the plain, "the tableland of Medeba," flocks of sheep and goats find pasturage.—Jos 13:9, 16.

After the Israelites defeated Amorite King Sihon, Medeba came to be in the territory given to the tribe of Reuben. (Jos 13:8, 9, 15, 16) It appears that earlier the Amorites had taken Medeba from the Moabites. (Nu 21:25-30) Several centuries later, in a fight against the Ammonites, the army of King David under Joab's command defeated Aramaean (Syrian) mercenary forces encamped before Medeba.—1Ch 19:6-16.

According to the Moabite Stone (line 8), Israel's King Omri (c. 951-941 B.C.E.) took possession of the "land of Mehedeba (Medeba)." Line 30 of the same monument indicates that Moab's King Mesha rebuilt Medeba and other cities in the area. It may be, however, that the Israelites regained dominion over Medeba when Jeroboam II (c. 844-804 B.C.E.) "restored the boundary of Israel from the entering in of Hamath clear to the sea of the Arabah." (2Ki 14:25) But this would not have been for long, since Isaiah's pronouncement (c. 778–a. 732) against Moab shows that Medeba was by then under the control of the Moabites and it was foretold that the Moabites would 'howl' over the loss of the city.—Isa 15:1, 2.

MEDES, MEDIA.

The Medes were an Aryan race, hence of Japhetic stock and evidently descended from Japheth's son Madai. (Ge 10:2) They were closely related to the Persians in race, language, and religion.

As a people, the Medes do not begin to appear in Biblical history until the eighth century B.C.E., while the first mention of them in available secular records dates from the time of Assyrian King Shalmaneser III, a contemporary of King Jehu (c. 904-877 B.C.E.). Archaeological and other evidence is viewed as indicating their presence on the Iranian Plateau from about the middle of the second millennium B.C.E. onward.

Geography. Though its boundaries undoubtedly fluctuated, the ancient region of Media basically lay W and S of the Caspian Sea, being separated from the coastland of that sea by the Elburz mountain range. In the NW it evidently reached beyond Lake Urmia to the Araxes River valley, while on its W boundary the Zagros Mountains served as a barrier between Media and the land of Assyria and the lowlands of the Tigris; to the E lay a large desert region, and on the S the country of Elam.

The land of the Medes was thus mainly a mountainous plateau averaging from 900 to 1,500 m (3,000 to 5,000 ft) above sea level. A considerable portion of the land is arid steppe, rainfall being generally scanty, though there are several fertile plains that are highly productive. Most of the rivers flow toward the great central desert, where their waters are dissipated into marshes and swamps that dry up in the hot summer and leave salt deposits. Natural barriers made it relatively easy to defend. The western mountain range is the highest, with numerous peaks over 4,270 m (14,000 ft) high, but the tallest single peak, Mount Damavand (5,771 m; 18,934 ft), is found in the Elburz range near the Caspian Sea.

Principal Occupations. Evidently, then as now, most of the people lived in small villages or were nomadic, and stock raising was a principal occupation. Cuneiform texts recounting Assyrian incursions into Media present such a picture and show that the excellent breed of horses raised by the Medes was one of the main prizes sought by the invaders. Herds of sheep, goats, asses, mules, and cows were also pastured on the good grazing grounds of the high valleys. On Assyrian reliefs Medes are sometimes represented as wearing what appear to be sheepskin coats over their tunics and as having high-laced boots, necessary

equipment for pastoral work on the plateaus where the winters brought snow and bitter cold. Archaeological evidence shows that the Medes had capable metalsmiths working in bronze and gold.

History. The Medes left virtually no written records; what is known of them is derived from the Bible record, from Assyrian texts, and also from the classical Greek historians. The Medes appear to have been formed into numerous petty kingdoms under tribal chieftains, and the boastful accounts of Assyrian Emperors Shamshi-Adad V, Tiglath-pileser III, and Sargon II refer to their victories over certain city chieftains of the distant land of the Medes. Following the Assyrian victory over the kingdom of Israel in 740 B.C.E., the Israelites were sent into places of exile in Assyria and "in the cities of the Medes," some of which were then in vassalage to Assyria.—2Ki 17:6; 18:11.

Assyrian efforts to subjugate "the insubmissive Medes" continued under Assyrian King Esar-haddon, son of Sennacherib and evidently a contemporary of King Manasseh of Judah (716-662 B.C.E.). In one of his inscriptions, Esar-haddon speaks of "a district on the border of the salt-desert which lies in the land of the distant Medes, on the edge of Mount Bikni, the lapis-lazuli mountain, . . . powerful chieftains who had not submitted to my yoke,—themselves, together with their people, their riding-horses, cattle, sheep, asses and (Bactrian) camels,—an enormous spoil, I carried off to Assyria. . . . My royal tribute and tax I imposed upon them, yearly."—*Ancient Records of Assyria and Babylonia*, by D. D. Luckenbill, 1927, Vol. II, pp. 215, 216.

According to the Greek historian Herodotus (I, 96), the Medes were formed into a united kingdom under a ruler named Deioces. Some modern historians believe Deioces to be the ruler named Daiaukku in the inscriptions. He was captured and deported to Hamath by Sargon II as a result of one of the Assyrian raids into the region of Media. However, most scholars consider that it was not until the time of Cyaxares (or Kyaxares, a grandson of Deioces according to Herodotus [I, 102, 103]) that the kings of Media began to unite under a particular ruler. Even then they may well have been like the petty kings of Canaan, who at times fought under the direction of a particular king while still maintaining a considerable measure of independence.—Compare Jos 11:1-5.

The Medes had been growing in strength despite Assyrian incursions and now came to constitute Assyria's most dangerous rival. When Nabopolassar of Babylon, the father of Nebuchad-nezzar, rebelled against Assyria, Cyaxares the Mede allied his forces with the Babylonians. Following the Median capture of Asshur in Nabopolassar's 12th year (634 B.C.E.), Cyaxares (called *Ú-ma-kis-tar* in the Babylonian records) met with Nabopolassar by the captured city, and they "made an entente cordiale." (*Assyrian and Babylonian Chronicles*, by A. K. Grayson, 1975, p. 93) Berossus (known through Polyhistor and Abydenus, both quoted by Eusebius) says that Nabopolassar's son, Nebuchadnezzar, married the daughter of the Median king, her name being Amytis (or Amuhea according to Abydenus). (Eusebius, *Chronicorum liber prior*, edited by A. Schoene, Berlin, 1875, col. 29, lines 16-19, col. 37, lines 5-7) Historians disagree, however, as to whether Amytis was the daughter of Cyaxares or of his son Astyages.

With Babylonians defeat Assyria. After further battles against the Assyrians, finally in the 14th year of Nabopolassar (632 B.C.E.) the combined forces of the Medes and the Babylonians conquered Nineveh. (Zep 2:13) Assyrian resistance was transferred to Haran (some 360 km [225 mi]) to the W, but though Assyria received assistance from Egypt, the effort to continue Assyrian rule was ineffectual and the Assyrian Empire was split up between the Medes and the Babylonians. (Na 2:8-13; 3:18, 19) The Medes appear to have taken the northern portion of the territory while the Babylonians took the southern and southwestern portion, including Syria and Palestine. Cyaxares thereafter pushed into Asia Minor as far as the Halys River, where a war with Lydia resulted in a stalemate and the Halys became the far-western boundary of the Median Empire. This empire now extended over the greater part of the Iranian Plateau, northern Mesopotamia, Armenia, and Cappadocia.

Lose dominant position to Persians. At this time the Medes, with their capital at Ecbatana (Ezr 6:2), held the dominant position over the related Persians, who had occupied the area to the S of Media. Greek historians Herodotus (I, 107, 108) and Xenophon (*Cyropaedia*, I, ii, 1) both relate that Cyaxares' successor Astyages (called Ishtumegu in the cuneiform texts) had given his daughter Mandane in marriage to Persian ruler Cambyses, resulting in the birth of Cyrus (II). Cyrus, upon becoming king of Anshan, a Persian province, united the Persian forces in an effort to throw off the Median yoke. The Nabonidus Chronicle indicates that "the army of Ishtumegu [Astyages] revolted" and "in fetters" they delivered him to Cyrus, who thereafter seized the Median capital. (*Ancient Near Eastern Texts*, edited by

J. Pritchard, 1974, p. 305) From this point forward Media merges with Persia to form the Medo-Persian Empire. Thus, the vision received by the prophet Daniel aptly likened the dual power of Medo-Persia to a two-horned ram, the taller of the two horns being "the one that came up afterward," representing the ascendancy of the Persians and their dominance of the empire for the remainder of its existence.—Da 8:3, 20.

The evidence is, however, that Cyrus gave positions of power and authority to the Medes so that they continued to maintain a considerable measure of prominence within his government. Thus, the prophet Daniel interpreted to King Belshazzar the cryptic writing on the wall as predicting the division of the Babylonian Empire and its being given "to the Medes and the Persians," and elsewhere in the book of Daniel the Medes continue to be listed first in the phrase "the law of the Medes and the Persians." (Da 5:28; 6:8, 12, 15) In the following century the book of Esther (Es 1:3, 14, 18, 19) reverses the order, with one exception (Es 10:2) in which the Medes are listed as preceding the Persians historically.

With Persians defeat Babylon. In the eighth century B.C.E., the prophet Isaiah had foretold that Jehovah would arouse against Babylon "the Medes, who account silver itself as nothing and who, as respects gold, take no delight in it. And their bows will dash even young men to pieces." (Isa 13:17-19; 21:2) The term "Medes" here may well include the Persians, even as the classical Greek historians commonly used the term to embrace both Medes and Persians. Their disdaining silver and gold evidently indicates that in Babylon's case conquest was the prime motive with them rather than spoil, so that no bribe or offer of tribute would buy them off from their determined purpose. The Medes, like the Persians, used the bow as a principal weapon. The wooden bows, though sometimes mounted with bronze or copper (compare Ps 18:34), likely 'dashed the young men of Babylon to pieces' by the hail of arrows, individually polished so as to penetrate even deeper. —Jer 51:11.

It may be noted that Jeremiah (51:11, 28) makes reference to "the *kings* of Media" as among those attacking Babylon, the plural perhaps indicating that even under Cyrus, a subordinate Median king or kings may have continued to exist, a situation by no means incompatible with ancient practice. (Compare also Jer 25:25.) Thus, too, we find that when Babylon was captured by the combined forces of Medes, Persians, Elamites, and other neighboring tribes, it was a Mede named Darius who was "made king over the kingdom of the Chaldeans," evidently as an appointee of King Cyrus the Persian.—Da 5:31; 9:1; see DARIUS No. 1.

Conquered by Alexander the Great. In the time of King Ahasuerus (believed to be Xerxes I), reference was still made to "the military force of Persia *and Media,*" the king's privy council was formed of "seven princes of Persia and Media," and the laws were still known as "the laws of Persia and Media." (Es 1:3, 14, 19) In 334 B.C.E. Alexander the Great won his first decisive victories over the Persian forces, and in 330 B.C.E. he occupied Media. Following his death, the southern part of Media came to form part of the Seleucid Empire, while the northern part became an independent kingdom. Though it was dominated variously by the Parthians and by the Seleucid Empire, Greek geographer Strabo indicated that a Median dynasty continued in the first century C.E. (*Geography,* 11, XIII, 1) At Jerusalem, Medes along with Parthians, Elamites, and persons of other nationalities were present at Pentecost in the year 33 C.E. Since they are spoken of as "Jews, reverent men, from every nation," they may have been descendants of those Jews exiled to cities of the Medes following the Assyrian conquest of Israel, or perhaps some were proselytes to the Jewish faith.—Ac 2:1, 5, 9.

By the third century C.E. the Medes had merged with the rest of the nation of the Iranians, thus ceasing to exist as a distinct people.

MEDIATOR. One who interposes between two parties at variance to reconcile them; an intercessor; an intermediary agent, or go-between. In the Scriptures the term is applied to Moses and Jesus, the mediators respectively of the Law covenant and the new covenant.—Ga 3:19; 1Ti 2:5.

Blood Required for Covenant Validation. The inspired writer of the book of Hebrews discusses two principal covenants, the Law covenant and the new covenant. In this discussion he refers to Christ's mediating the new covenant. (Heb 9:15) His words at Hebrews 9:16 have been a subject of controversy among Bible scholars. Accordingly, the text has been rendered in the following ways: "For where a testament is, there must also of necessity be the death of the testator." (*KJ*) "For where a will is involved, the death of the one who made it must be established." (*RS*) "For where a covenant is it is necessary for the death to be brought in of him that hath covenanted." (*Ro*) "For where there is a covenant, the death of the human covenanter needs to be furnished." (*NW*) "For where a covenant is, the death of the covenant-victim to come in is necessary." (*Yg*) "For where a Covenant exists, the Death of that which has ratified it is necessary to be produced." (*ED*) "For where a covenant is, there is a necessity for the death of that which establisheth the covenant."—*The New Testament in an Improved Version.*

The literal rendering as set forth in interlinear translations of the Greek text is as follows: "Where for covenant, death necessity to be borne of the one having made for self covenant." (Heb 9:16, *Int*) "For where there is a covenant, the death there is necessity to be offered of the one making covenant."—*The Interlinear Greek-English New Testament*, translated by Alfred Marshall.

The rendering of *di·a·the′ke* as "covenant" expresses correctly the writer's meaning. The renderings "testament" and "will," found in many versions, are inconsistent with the use of the term in the Greek *Septuagint* as well as in many places in the Christian Greek Scriptures. (Lu 1:72; Ac 3:25; 7:8; Ro 9:4; 11:27; Heb 8:6-10; 12:24) "Will" and "testament" also are out of harmony with what Paul is talking about, as he is speaking of the *Law covenant* and the *new covenant* in the context. Neither the Law covenant nor the new covenant was a "will."

At Hebrews 9:16 the apostle Paul was evidently speaking of covenants between God and man (not man and man) as requiring sacrifices. And it may be noted that, particularly with the Hebrews, approaches to God and covenants with God were regularly based on sacrifices, the victims sacrificed sometimes being cut in pieces on the occasion of entering a covenant. It is quite obvious that the Law covenant and the new covenant required the shedding of blood in order to go into operation or to be effective before God. Otherwise God would not have recognized them as valid, nor dealt with the persons involved on the basis of a covenant relationship. (Heb 9:17) For the validation of the Law covenant, the sacrifice used was that of animals—bulls and goats—these taking the place of Moses, the mediator. (Heb 9:19) For validating the new covenant, the sacrifice was the human life of Jesus Christ.—Lu 22:20; see *NW* appendix, p. 1584.

The Mediator of the Law Covenant. Moses was the mediator of the Law covenant between Jehovah God and the nation of Israel. Jehovah spoke with him "mouth to mouth" (Nu 12:8), although actually Jehovah's angel spoke representatively for God. (Ac 7:38; Ga 3:19; Heb 2:2) Moses was an intermediary spokesman for Jehovah to Israel. (Ex 19:3, 7, 9; 24:9-18) As mediator he was "entrusted with all [Jehovah's] house." (Nu 12:7) In mediating the Law covenant he helped the nation of Israel to keep the covenant and to receive its benefits.

Validation of the Law covenant. The apostle Paul says: "Now there is no mediator where only one person is concerned, but God is only one." (Ga 3:20) In the Law covenant God was one party; the nation of Israel was the other 'party.' Because of their sinful condition, the Israelites were unable to approach God in a covenant. They needed a mediator. Their weakness was demonstrated in their request to Moses: "You speak with us, and let us listen; but let not God speak with us for fear we may die." (Ex 20:19; Heb 12:18-20) Accordingly, Jehovah mercifully constituted Moses mediator of the Law covenant and arranged for animals to be sacrificed to validate the covenant. Moses, of course, was also imperfect and sinful; however, he enjoyed a favorable standing with God, even as Abraham had earlier. (Heb 11:23-28; see DECLARE RIGHTEOUS [How "counted" righteous].) On the occasion of the inauguration of the covenant, Moses officiated, directing the sacrifice of the animals. Then he sprinkled their blood on the scroll or "the book of the covenant." He read the book to the people, setting forth the terms, and the people responded by agreeing to obey. Moses then sprinkled them (doubtless the representative older men) with the blood, saying: "Here is the blood of the covenant that Jehovah has concluded with you as respects all these words."—Ex 24:3-8; Heb 9:18-22.

Inauguration of the priesthood. The designated priests of the house of Aaron could not begin functioning as priests on their own. They had to be installed in office under the direction of God's mediator Moses. When this took place, Nisan 1-7, 1512 B.C.E., Moses anointed the tabernacle and its furniture and utensils and also anointed Aaron with the oil of special composition. After filling the hands of Aaron and his sons with sacrificial materials, Moses waved their filled hands before Jehovah, thereby consecrating them or 'filling their hands with power' for the priesthood. Afterward he spattered them with the anointing oil and blood from the altar. So one function of Moses' mediatorial office was the installing and setting in operation of the priesthood, which was a feature of the Law covenant.—Le 8; Heb 7:11; see INSTALLATION.

Moses also played a significant part in connection with the first services performed by the newly installed priesthood, Nisan 8, 1512 B.C.E., as he directed the procedure and, along with Aaron, blessed the people. (Le 9) Throughout the institution of all things pertaining to the Law covenant, he acted in his official capacity as mediator.

Other mediatorial work. A body of more than 600 laws, including the priestly statutes, was given to Israel through Moses. By the power of God, Moses performed many miracles in behalf of the people. He interceded for them, pleading with Jehovah to spare them for Jehovah's name's sake. (Ex 32:7-14; Nu 14:11-20; 16:20-22; 21:7; De 9:18-20, 25-29; 10:8-11) Moses had the interests of Jehovah's name and also the people's interest at heart even above his concern for his own welfare. —Ex 32:30-33; Nu 11:26-29; 12:9-13.

Parallels in Mediatorships. With respect to those brought into the *new* covenant, we find a situation similar to that of ancient Israel. Christians are also sinners. Since the blood of animals cannot actually remove sins (Heb 10:4), a better sacrifice is necessary. Jesus Christ is that better sacrifice. (Heb 10:5-10) The writer of Hebrews expresses the matter in this way. After mentioning the sacrifices offered under the Law, he says: "How much more will the blood of the Christ . . . cleanse our consciences from dead works that we may render sacred service to the living God? So that is why he is a mediator of a new covenant, in order that, because a death has occurred for their release by ransom from the transgressions under the former covenant, the ones who have been called might receive the promise of the everlasting inheritance. For where there is a covenant, the death of the human covenanter needs to be furnished. For a covenant is valid over dead victims, since it is not in force at any time while the human covenanter is living."—Heb 9:11-17.

Paul goes on to point out that the former covenant was not inaugurated without blood. Moses, in negotiating it, saw that the sacrifices were made and sprinkled the blood on "the book of the covenant." (Heb 9:18-28) Likewise Jesus Christ, God's Mediator for the new covenant, after his sacrifice, appeared before Jehovah God with the value of his blood. Another likeness is that the Law covenant was made with a nation, not with individuals (Ex 24:7, 8), and so, too, the new covenant is made with God's "holy nation," "the Israel of God."—1Pe 2:9; Ga 6:15, 16.

Those for Whom Christ Is Mediator. The apostle Paul declares that there is "one mediator between God and men, a man, Christ Jesus, who gave himself a corresponding ransom for all"—for both Jews and Gentiles. (1Ti 2:5, 6) He mediates the new covenant between God and those taken into the new covenant, the congregation of spiritual Israel. (Heb 8:10-13; 12:24; Eph 5:25-27) Christ became Mediator in order that the ones called "might receive the promise of the everlasting inheritance" (Heb 9:15); he assists, not the angels, but "Abraham's seed." (Heb 2:16) He assists those who are to be brought into the new covenant to become 'adopted' into Jehovah's household of spiritual sons; these eventually will be in heaven as Christ's brothers, becoming a part with him of the seed of Abraham. (Ro 8:15-17, 23-25; Ga 3:29) He has transmitted to them the promised holy spirit, with which spirit they are sealed and are given a token of what is to come, their heavenly inheritance. (2Co 5:5; Eph 1:13, 14) The total number of those who are finally and permanently sealed is revealed in Revelation 7:4-8 as 144,000.

Inauguration of the New Covenant. After Jesus died and was resurrected, he entered into heaven to appear before the person of God to present his offering, the benefits of which go first to those taken into the new covenant. (Heb 9:24) Here he acted both as High Priest and Mediator. In harmony with the pattern followed at the inauguration of the Law covenant, Jesus Christ presented the value of his sacrifice before God in heaven (even as Moses sprinkled the blood on the book of the Law [for God was not personally present there]). Then, on Pentecost day, 33 C.E., Jesus poured out the holy spirit from God on the first ones brought into the new covenant, about 120 persons. Later that day about 3,000, Jews and proselytes, were added to the congregation. (Ac 1:15; 2:1-47; Heb 9:19) And just as Moses read the Law to the people, so Jesus Christ clearly enunciates the terms of the new covenant and its laws to those sharing in it.—Ex 24:3-8; Heb 1:1, 2; Joh 13:34; 15:14; 1Jo 5:1-3.

Holding the offices of Mediator and High Priest, Jesus Christ, being immortal, is always alive and able to plead for those of spiritual Israel approaching God through him, so that he can mediate the new covenant until those persons receiving his mediatorial assistance are saved completely. (Heb 7:24, 25) He is able to conduct matters to the successful completion of the new covenant. Those in the covenant are eventually installed in the heavenly priesthood as underpriests with Christ, their great High Priest.—Re 5:9, 10; 20:6.

Blessings to Mankind in General. While Jesus' mediatorship operates solely toward those in the new covenant, he is also God's High Priest and the Seed of Abraham. In fulfilling his duties in these latter two positions, he will bring blessings to others of mankind, for all the nations are to be blessed by means of Abraham's seed. Those in the new covenant are first blessed by Christ, the primary Seed (Ga 3:16, 29), being brought in as associate members of the seed. Being made kings and priests by reason of the new covenant that he mediated, they will share in administering the blessings of Jesus' sacrifice and of his Kingdom rule to all the nations of the earth. Christ's mediatorship, having accomplished its purpose by bringing "the Israel of God" into this position, thus results in benefits and blessings to all mankind. —Ga 6:16; Ge 22:17, 18.

There are, thus, others not of the 144,000 "sealed" ones who also pray to Jehovah God in the name of Christ, putting faith in the merit of his ransom sacrifice. This sacrifice is not only for those for whom Jesus mediates the new covenant but also for all mankind expressing faith in Christ. (1Jo 2:2) These not in the new covenant also appreciate that "there is not another name under heaven that has been given among men by which we must get saved." (Ac 4:12) They, too, look to Jesus Christ as their great heavenly High Priest, through whom they can approach God and through whose ministration they can get forgiveness of sin. (Heb 4:14-16) Revelation 21:22-24 points out that 'the nations will walk in the light of New Jerusalem,' where Jehovah God is the light and the Lamb Jesus Christ is the lamp.

MEDITATION.

The kind of deep, concentrated thinking in which a person seriously reflects on past experiences, ponders and muses over current matters, or thoughtfully contemplates possible future events.

In order to meditate properly, a person needs to be free from distractions, alone with his thoughts, so to speak. Isaac, for example, went out walking alone in the early evening to meditate, possibly about his coming marriage to Rebekah. (Ge 24:63) It was during the solitude of the night watches that the psalmist meditated on the greatness of his Grand Creator. (Ps 63:6) The meditations of the heart should be focused on beneficial things, on Jehovah's splendor and activities, on things pleasing to him (Ps 19:14; 49:3; 77:12; 143:5; Php 4:8), and not on the devices of the wicked.—Pr 24:1, 2.

By engaging in profitable meditation, one will not be inclined to give foolish answers. He will seriously think out these matters of importance, and as a result, the answers given will be from the heart and will not be something to regret later on. —Pr 15:28.

When Joshua was appointed as the overseer of the nation of Israel, he was instructed to make a copy of Jehovah's law, and he was told (as rendered in many Bible versions) to "meditate" thereon day and night. (Jos 1:8; AS, KJ, JB, RS) The Hebrew word here for "meditate" is ha·ghah'. It basically means "utter inarticulate sounds" and is rendered "moan," 'growl,' 'coo,' and 'mutter.' (Isa 16:7; 31:4; 38:14; 59:3) Ha·ghah' also has the meanings "utter in an undertone" and "meditate." (Ps 35:28; Pr 15:28) The New World Translation appropriately renders the Hebrew term ha·ghah', appearing in Joshua 1:8, "you must in an undertone read." (See also Ps 1:2.) Reading in an undertone would impress more indelibly on the mind the material on which one was meditating. Gesenius's Hebrew and Chaldee Lexicon (translated by S. Tregelles, 1901, p. 215) says of ha·ghah': "Prop[erly] to speak with oneself, murmuring and in a low voice, as is often done by those who are musing."—Compare Ps 35:28; 37:30; 71:24; Isa 8:19; 33:18.

The apostle Paul told Timothy that he should ponder over or be meditating on his conduct, ministry, and teaching. As an overseer, Timothy had to be unusually careful that he taught sound doctrine and that his way of life was exemplary. —1Ti 4:15.

Wrong Meditation. After the apostles Peter and John had been arrested by the captain of the temple and the Jewish rulers had threatened them and charged them not to teach further on the basis of Jesus' name, the apostles returned to the other disciples. These prayed to God, referring to David's prophetic words, saying: "'Why did nations become tumultuous and peoples meditate upon empty things?' . . . Even so, both Herod and Pontius Pilate with men of nations and with peoples of Israel were in actuality gathered together in this city against your holy servant Jesus, whom you anointed, in order to do what things your hand and counsel had foreordained to occur."—Ac 4:1-3, 18, 21, 23-28.

The "empty things" here spoken of are shown by the context to be, not the things that people ordinarily seek in life, but things that are devoid of all good—actually thinking, speaking, and attempting to fight against Jehovah and his servants—utterly futile things.—Ac 4:25.

King David said of those who hated him and sought his death: "Deceptions they keep muttering [form of ha·ghah'] all day long." (Ps 38:12) These meditations were not mere passing thoughts. They were deeply rooted in the heart, their inclination being toward that wicked pursuit. The writer of Proverbs says of such men: "Despoiling is what their heart keeps meditating, and trouble is what their own lips keep speaking."—Pr 24:2.

Jesus said to those hating him: "Why are you

reasoning these things in your *hearts?*" (Mr 2:8) Of all who would 'suppress the truth in an unrighteous way,' the apostle Paul says: "They became empty-headed in their reasonings and their unintelligent heart became darkened." Such meditation proves fatal to those indulging in it.—Ro 1:18, 21.

MEEKNESS. A mildness of temper, without haughtiness or vanity. The mental disposition that enables one to endure injury with patience and without irritation, resentment, or vindictive retaliation. It is a close companion of and seldom found separate from such other virtues as humility, lowliness of mind, and gentleness. (See HUMILITY; MILDNESS.) The Hebrew word translated "meek" ('a·naw') comes from the root 'a·nah', which means "afflict, humble, humiliate."

In the Bible, meekness is emphasized as one's mental attitude first of all toward God, then toward fellow creatures. For example, it is written: "The meek ones will certainly increase their rejoicing in Jehovah himself." (Isa 29:19) Meek persons are teachable—Jehovah "will teach the meek ones his way" (Ps 25:9)—and they are willing to endure discipline from the hand of God, though such is grievous at the time. (Heb 12:4-11) Meekness causes persons to wait upon Jehovah to right the wrongs and injuries unjustly suffered, instead of becoming heated up with anger. (Ps 37:8-11) Such persons are not disappointed, for Jehovah's appointed one, the "twig out of the stump of Jesse," will give reproof in righteousness "in behalf of the meek ones of the earth."—Isa 11:1-4.

Moses. Moses was just such a man, "by far the meekest of all the men who were upon the surface of the ground," one who could take criticism without resentment. (Nu 12:3) The occasion of this comment on his meekness was the time when Miriam and Aaron murmured against Moses. In reality, it was an uncalled-for complaint against Jehovah and one that he quickly took note of and reproved.—Nu 12:1-15.

Some commentators charge that for Moses to record this reference to his own meekness was unjustified self-praise. Other critics claim the statement was added later by someone else, while still others offer this as evidence that Moses did not write the Pentateuch after all. However, Cook's *Commentary* says concerning these words: "When we regard them as uttered by Moses not '*proprio motu* [of his own initiative],' but under the direction of the Holy Spirit which was upon him (cf. xi. 17), they exhibit a certain 'objectivity,' which is a witness at once to their genuineness

and also to their inspiration. There is about these words, as also about the passages in which Moses no less unequivocally records his own faults (cf. xx. 12 sqq.; Ex. iv. 24 sqq.; Deut. i. 37), the simplicity of one who bare witness of himself, but not to himself (cf. St Matt. xi. 28, 29). The words are inserted to explain how it was that Moses took no steps to vindicate himself, and why consequently the Lord so promptly intervened."

Jesus Christ. Jesus demonstrated meekness by enduring all manner of personal injury without a word of complaint, even allowing himself to be led to the slaughter as a lamb without opening his mouth in protest. (Php 2:5-8; Heb 12:2; Ac 8:32-35; Isa 53:7) This Greater-than-Moses also recommended himself to others as a meek or mild-tempered person. (Mt 11:28, 29, *AS, KJ, ED, NW, Ro*) As Isaiah 61:1 foretold, he was anointed with Jehovah's spirit "to tell good news to the meek ones." After reading this prophecy in the synagogue of his hometown of Nazareth, Jesus declared: "Today this scripture that you just heard is fulfilled." (Lu 4:16-21) In thus sending his beloved Son to teach the meek concerning salvation, God was indeed showing them very special favor. —Ps 149:4; Pr 3:34.

Brings Benefits. The invitation expressed by the prophet Zephaniah is still extended to meek persons of the earth: "Seek Jehovah, all you meek ones of the earth, who have practiced His own judicial decision. Seek righteousness, seek meekness [or, humbleness; humility]. Probably you may be concealed in the day of Jehovah's anger." (Zep 2:3, ftn) Above and beyond that are other wonderful promises extended to such ones. For example: "The meek ones themselves will possess the earth, and they will indeed find their exquisite delight in the abundance of peace." (Ps 37:11) In both a spiritual and a literal sense, "the meek ones will eat and be satisfied."—Ps 22:26.

So, in contrast with the wicked who lead the meek astray and seek to destroy them (Am 2:7; 8:4), Jehovah listens to their heartfelt desires by answering their prayers; their hope in Jehovah is not disappointed. (Ps 10:17; 9:18) It is a true proverb, "Better is it to be lowly in spirit with the meek ones than to divide spoil with the self-exalted ones."—Pr 16:19.

MEGIDDO (Me·gid'do). One of the more important cities of the Promised Land, located about 90 km (56 mi) N of Jerusalem and 31 km (19 mi) SE of the modern city of Haifa. It was built on a plot of somewhat over 4 ha (10 acres), atop a mound known today as Tell el-Muteselliim (Tel Megiddo), which rises nearly 21 m (70 ft) above the valley below.—Pictures and Map, Vol. 1, p. 953.

Strategic. Situated in this strategic spot overlooking and dominating the fertile western section of the Jezreel Valley (Plain of Esdraelon, also known as "the valley plain of Megiddo"; 2Ch 35: 22; Zec 12:11), it easily controlled the major trade and military routes that intersected there. Both Biblical history and secular records tell how the armies of many nations fought decisive battles around Megiddo because of its commanding position. Near this site "by the waters of Megiddo," Judge Barak defeated Jabin's mighty forces under Sisera, which included 900 chariots outfitted with iron scythes. (Jg 4:7, 13-16; 5:19) It was at Megiddo that King Ahaziah of Judah died after being mortally wounded near Ibleam on orders of Jehu. (2Ki 9:27) At Megiddo King Josiah of Judah was mortally wounded when he intercepted the Egyptian army under Pharaoh Nechoh that was on its way to help the Assyrians at the river Euphrates. —2Ki 23:29, 30; 2Ch 35:22.

At various times during its long history, as archaeological diggings show, Megiddo was heavily fortified. Ruins have been uncovered showing that it once had walls between 4 and 5 m (13 and 16 ft) thick, which were later increased to more than 7.5 m (25 ft) thick, sections of which were still over 3.3 m (11 ft) high when found.

History. The first mention of Megiddo lists its king among the 31 that Joshua defeated in the initial conquest of the Promised Land. (Jos 12:7, 8, 21, 24) When the land was apportioned, Megiddo, together with its dependent towns, became an enclave city belonging to the tribe of Manasseh, though it was situated in the territory of Issachar. (Jos 17:11; 1Ch 7:29) However, during the period of the Judges, Manasseh was not able to drive the Canaanites out of this stronghold. At best, when Israel became strong, the inhabitants of this city were regimented for forced labor.—Jg 1:27, 28.

Under David's reign, when the boundaries of the kingdom were extended to their full limits, all Canaanite elements within the Promised Land were subjugated, including Megiddo. This allowed Solomon to include Megiddo in the fifth-named district set up to supply the royal household with food one month out of the year.—1Ki 4:7, 8, 12.

Solomon also fortified Megiddo, and it may have become one of his chariot cities where some of his 12,000 steeds were stabled. (1Ki 9:15-19; 10:26) At Megiddo archaeologists have found very extensive remains of what some scholars (but not all) think were stables capable of accommodating upwards of 450 horses. At first these structures were credited to Solomon's time, but many later archaeologists redated them to a later period, perhaps the time of Ahab.

Solomonic gate at Megiddo,
like the ones found at Hazor and Gezer

Zechariah's prophecy (12:11) speaks of a 'great wailing' that occurred "in the valley plain of Megiddo," which may be a reference to the lamentation over King Josiah, who was killed there in battle. (2Ki 23:29, 30) There is a slight difference in the Hebrew spelling of Megiddo here in the book of Zechariah. Instead of the conventional Hebrew spelling *Meghid·doh'*, it is *Meghid·dohn'*, a prolonged form similar to that found at Revelation 16:16.—See HAR–MAGEDON.

MEHETABEL (Me·het'a·bel) [probably, God Does Good].

1. Daughter of the woman Matred and wife of Edomite King Hadar (Hadad).—Ge 36:31, 39; 1Ch 1:50.

2. Ancestor (probably the grandfather) of the Shemaiah hired by Tobiah and Sanballat to try to induce Nehemiah to sin out of fear.—Ne 6:10-14.

MEHIDA (Me·hi'da). Ancestor of a family of Nethinim whose "sons" or descendants returned to Judah from Babylonian exile with Zerubbabel in 537 B.C.E.—Ezr 2:1, 2, 43, 52; Ne 7:54.

MEHIR (Me'hir) [possibly, Price]. A man of the tribe of Judah who was the son of Chelub (Caleb) and "father of Eshton."—1Ch 4:1, 11.

MEHOLATHITE (Me·hol'ath·ite) [Of (Belonging to) Abel-meholah]. The designation for Adriel (a son-in-law of Saul) and his father Barzillai. (1Sa 18:19; 2Sa 21:8) It evidently denotes that they were from the town of Abel-meholah.—See ABEL-MEHOLAH.

MEHUJAEL (Me·hu'ja·el) [Struck by God]. Great-grandson of Cain. Mehujael was the father of Methushael and the grandfather of Lamech (not the Lamech descended from Seth).—Ge 4:17, 18.

MEHUMAN (Me·hu'man). One of the court officials of Persian King Ahasuerus (Xerxes I), who ruled in the days of Mordecai and Esther. Mehuman was named first among the seven court officials ordered by Ahasuerus to bring Queen Vashti into his presence.—Es 1:10, 11.

ME-JARKON (Me-jar'kon) [Waters of the Jarkon]. Some scholars believe that Me-jarkon in the territory of Dan (Jos 19:40, 41, 46) is the Nahr el-'Auja (Nahal Yarqon), which enters the Mediterranean Sea about 6 km (3.5 mi) NNE of Joppa. Its headwaters, among the largest springs in Palestine, surface about 20 km (12 mi) inland near the suggested site of Aphek (No. 3).

Another view is that the original Hebrew text, like the Greek *Septuagint,* may have read 'and on the west [or, on the sea] Jarkon.' Tell Qasileh (Tel Qasila), situated within the limits of Tel Aviv-Yafo (Joppa), has been presented as a possible identification for Jarkon.

MELATIAH (Mel·a·ti'ah) [Jah Has Provided Escape]. A Gibeonite who assisted in repairing part of Jerusalem's wall under Nehemiah's supervision in 455 B.C.E.—Ne 3:7.

MELCHI (Mel'chi) [from Heb., meaning "My King"]. The name of two maternal ancestors of Jesus Christ.

1. The "son" (or descendant) of Addi and father (or ancestor) of Neri.—Lu 3:27, 28.

2. The "son" (or descendant) of Jannai and father (or ancestor) of Levi.—Lu 3:23, 24.

MELCHIZEDEK (Mel·chiz'e·dek) [King of Righteousness]. King of ancient Salem and "priest of the Most High God," Jehovah. (Ge 14:18, 22) He is the first priest mentioned in the Scriptures; he occupied that position sometime prior to 1933 B.C.E. Being the king of Salem, which means "Peace," Melchizedek is identified by the apostle Paul as "King of Peace" and, on the basis of his name, as "King of Righteousness." (Heb 7:1, 2) Ancient Salem is understood to have been the nucleus of the later city of Jerusalem, and its name was incorporated in that of Jerusalem, which is sometimes referred to as "Salem."—Ps 76:2.

After Abram (Abraham) defeated Chedorlaomer and his confederate kings, the patriarch came to the Low Plain of Shaveh or "the king's Low Plain." There Melchizedek "brought out bread and wine" and blessed Abraham, saying: "Blessed be Abram of the Most High God, Producer of heaven and earth; and blessed be the Most High God, who has delivered your oppressors into your hand!" At that Abraham gave the king-priest "a tenth of everything," that is, of "the chief spoils" he had acquired in his successful warfare against the allied kings.—Ge 14:17-20; Heb 7:4.

Christ's Priesthood Typified. In a notable Messianic prophecy the sworn oath of Jehovah to David's "Lord" is: "You are a priest to time indefinite according to the manner of Melchizedek!" (Ps 110:1, 4) This inspired psalm gave the Hebrews reason to regard the promised Messiah as the one in whom the office of priest and king would be combined. The apostle Paul, in the letter to the Hebrews, removed any doubt about the identity of the one foretold, speaking of "Jesus, who has become a high priest according to the manner of Melchizedek forever."—Heb 6:20; 5:10; see COVENANT.

Direct appointment. Jehovah evidently appointed Melchizedek to be a priest. In discussing Jesus' status as the great High Priest, Paul showed that a man does not take the honor "of his own accord, but only when he is called by God, just as Aaron also was." He also explained that "the Christ did not glorify himself by becoming a high priest, but was glorified by him who spoke with reference to him: 'You are my son; I, today, I have become your father,'" and the apostle next applies the prophetic words of Psalm 110:4 to Jesus Christ. —Heb 5:1, 4-6.

'Received tithes from Levi.' Melchizedek's priestly status was not linked with the priesthood of Israel, and as the Scriptures point out, it was higher than the Aaronic priesthood. One factor indicating this is the deference accorded to Melchizedek by Abraham, the forefather of the entire nation of Israel, including the priestly tribe of Levi. Abraham, "Jehovah's friend," who became "the father of all those having faith" (Jas 2:23; Ro 4:11), gave a tenth, or a "tithe," to this priest of the Most High God. Paul shows that the Levites collected tithes from their brothers, who also issued from the loins of Abraham. However, he points out that Melchizedek "who did not trace his genealogy from them took tithes from Abraham," and "through Abraham even Levi who receives tithes has paid tithes, for he was still in the loins of his forefather when Melchizedek met him." Thus, though the Levitical priests received tithes from the people of Israel, they, as represented in their ancestor Abraham, paid tithes to Melchizedek. Furthermore, the superiority of Melchizedek's priesthood is shown in that he blessed Abraham, Paul pointing out that "the less is blessed by the greater." Such factors are among those making Melchizedek a suitable type of the great High Priest Jesus Christ.—Heb 7:4-10.

No predecessors or successors. Paul clearly indicates that perfection was unattainable through the Levitical priesthood, thus necessitating the appearance of a priest "according to the manner of Melchizedek." He points out that Christ sprang from Judah, a nonpriestly tribe, but, citing Jesus' similarity to Melchizedek, shows that he became a priest, "not according to the law of a commandment depending upon the flesh, but according to the power of an indestructible life." Aaron and his sons became priests without an oath, but the priesthood conferred on Christ was ordained by an oath of Jehovah. Also, whereas the Levitical priests kept dying and needed to have successors, the resurrected Jesus Christ "because of continuing alive forever has his priesthood without any successors" and, therefore, is able "to save completely those who are approaching God through him, because he is always alive to plead for them."—Heb 7:11-25.

How was it true that Melchizedek had 'neither beginning of days nor end of life'?

Paul isolated an outstanding fact respecting Melchizedek, in saying of him: "In being fatherless, motherless, without genealogy, having neither a beginning of days nor an end of life, but having been made like the Son of God, he remains a priest perpetually." (Heb 7:3) Like other humans, Melchizedek was born and he died. However, the names of his father and mother are not furnished, his ancestry and posterity are not disclosed, and the Scriptures contain no information about the beginning of his days or the end of his life. Thus, Melchizedek could fittingly foreshadow Jesus Christ, who has an unending priesthood. As Melchizedek had no recorded predecessor or successor in his priesthood, so too Christ was preceded by no high priest similar to himself, and the Bible shows that none will ever succeed him. Furthermore, although Jesus was born in the tribe of Judah and in the kingly line of David, his fleshly ancestry had no bearing on his priesthood, nor was it by virtue of human ancestry that the offices of both priest and king were combined in him. These things were as a result of Jehovah's own oath to him.

A view that appears in the Targums of Jerusalem and of Jonathan and that has gained wide acceptance among the Jews and others is that Melchizedek was Noah's son Shem. Shem was then alive and even outlived Abraham's wife Sarah. Also, Noah specifically blessed Shem. (Ge 9:26, 27) But this identification has not been confirmed. The fact remains that Melchizedek's nationality, genealogy, and offspring are left undisclosed in the Scriptures, and that with good reason, for he could thus typify Jesus Christ, who by Jehovah's sworn oath "has become a high priest according to the manner of Melchizedek forever."—Heb 6:20.

MELEA (Meʹle·a). A maternal ancestor of Jesus Christ who lived not long after King David.—Lu 3:31.

MELECH (Melʹech) [King]. One of the sons of Micah and a descendant of King Saul of Israel, actually, the great-grandson of Saul's son Jonathan.—1Ch 8:33-35; 9:39-41.

MEM [מ; final, ם]. The 13th letter of the Hebrew alphabet. It is one of the five Hebrew letters that have a different form when used as the final letter of a word. In the Hebrew, it appears as the initial letter in each of the eight verses in Psalm 119:97-104; see HEBREW, II.

MEMORIAL. See LORD'S EVENING MEAL.

MEMORIAL TOMB. A burial place in which the remains of a deceased person were placed with the hope that he would be remembered, especially by God.

Concerning the Greek words used to refer to a burial place or tomb, A. T. Robertson in *Word Pictures in the New Testament* (1932, Vol. V, p. 87) states: *"Taphos* (grave) presents the notion of burial (*thapto,* to bury) as in Matt. 23:27, *mnemeion* (from *mnaomai, mimnesko,* to remind) is a memorial (sepulchre as a monument)." Related to *mne·mei'on* is the word *mne'ma,* which appears to have a corresponding meaning, referring also to "a memorial or record of a thing or a dead person, then a sepulchral monument, and hence a tomb." —*Vine's Expository Dictionary of Old and New Testament Words,* 1981, Vol. 2, p. 173.

Such a tomb might be an excavated grave in the ground or, as was often the case among the Hebrews, might be a natural cave or a rock-cut vault. (Compare Ac 7:16 and Ge 23:19, 20.) As has been seen above, whereas the word *ta'phos* (grave) gives emphasis to the idea of *burial,* the words *mne'ma* (tomb) and *mne·mei'on* (memorial tomb) lay stress on the thought of preserving the memory of the deceased person. These latter words, therefore, appear to carry a greater idea of permanence than *ta'phos;* they are related to the Latin word *monumentum.*

It seems evident that Jewish burial tombs were customarily built outside the cities, a major exception being those of the kings. The references to such tombs in the Christian Greek Scriptures would all appear to place them outside the cities, except the reference to David's tomb at Acts 2:29. Being thus withdrawn and also being avoided by the Jews, because of the ceremonial uncleanness connected with them, the areas in which such tombs were located were at times the haunt of crazed or demonized persons.—Mt 8:28; Mr 5:5.

Not Ornate. While serving as a remembrance of the deceased person, the Jewish memorial tombs in general do not appear to have been ornate or ostentatious. Some were so unpretentious and inconspicuous that men might walk upon them without being aware of it. (Lu 11:44) Although it was the custom of the pagan peoples around them to make their tombs as lavish as their circumstances allowed, the early Jewish tombs that have been found are notable for their simplicity. This was because the Jews' worship allowed no veneration of the dead and did not foster any ideas of a conscious existence after death in a spirit world, ideas such as those held by the Egyptians, Canaanites, and Babylonians. Thus, while many critics make the claim that the worship of the nation of Israel was, from early times, syncretistic, that is, resulting from the union of conflicting beliefs and having developed by the addition of tenets and practices from earlier religions, the fundamental resistance to such religious corruption is evidenced once again in the plainness of their tombs. Deviations, however, did occur. Jesus shows that in his day it was the practice of the scribes and Pharisees to decorate the memorial tombs of the prophets and others. (Mt 23:29, 30) Under Greek and Roman influence, the tendency among the wealthy at that time was toward more pretentious tombs.

Aside from the tomb of John the Baptizer (Mr 6:29), the principal tombs considered in the Christian Greek Scriptures are those of Lazarus and of Jesus. Lazarus' tomb was typically Jewish, being a cave with a stone lying against the opening, which opening may have been relatively small, if we conclude that similar tombs found in Palestine are comparable. The context would indicate it was outside the village.—Joh 11:30-34, 38-44.

Jesus' Tomb. The tomb used for Jesus' burial was a new one belonging to Joseph of Arimathea; it was not a cave but had been quarried in a rock-mass situated in a garden not far from the place of Jesus' impalement. The tomb had an entrance requiring a big stone to close it, and this stone apparently was of the circular type sometimes used. (Mt 27:57-60; Mr 16:3, 4; Joh 19:41, 42) It may have had, within it, benchlike shelves cut into the walls or burial niches cut vertically into the wall on which bodies could be placed. —Compare Mr 16:5.

Claims are made for two principal sites as being the original location of Jesus' tomb. One is the traditional site over which the Church of the Holy Sepulchre has been erected. The other site is that known as the Garden Tomb, which is cut out of a huge stone protruding from the side of a hill and is outside even the present city walls. No definite proof exists, however, that either of these places authentically represents the memorial tomb in which Jesus was laid.—See GOLGOTHA.

'Tombs Opened' at Jesus' Death. The text at Matthew 27:52, 53 concerning "the memorial tombs [that] were opened" as the result of an earthquake occurring at the time of Jesus' death has caused considerable discussion, some holding that a resurrection occurred. However, a comparison with the texts concerning the resurrection makes clear that these verses do not describe a resurrection but merely a throwing of bodies out of their tombs, similar to incidents that have taken place in more recent times, as in Ecuador in 1949 and again in Bogotá, Colombia, in 1962, when 200 corpses in the cemetery were thrown out of their tombs by a violent earth tremor.—*El Tiempo,* Bogotá, Colombia, July 31, 1962.

Remembrance by God. In view of the underlying thought of remembrance associated with *mne·mei'on,* the use of this word (rather than *ta'phos*) at John 5:28 with regard to the resurrection of "all those in the memorial tombs" seems particularly appropriate and contrasts sharply with the thought of complete repudiation and effacement from all memory as represented by Gehenna. (Mt 10:28; 23:33; Mr 9:43) The importance attached to burial by the Hebrews (see BURIAL, BURIAL PLACES) is indicative of their concern that they be remembered, primarily by Jehovah God in whom they had faith as "the rewarder of those earnestly seeking him." (Heb 11:1, 2, 6) Inscriptions of the tombs of Israelite origin are very rare and, when found, often consist of only the name. The outstanding kings of Judah left no magnificent monuments with their praises and exploits engraved thereon, as did the kings of other nations. Thus it seems evident that the concern of faithful men of ancient times was that their name be in the "book of remembrance" described at Malachi 3:16.—Compare Ec 7:1; see NAME.

The basic idea of remembrance involved in the original Greek words for "tomb" or "memorial tomb" also gives added meaning to the plea of the thief impaled alongside Jesus to "remember me when you get into your kingdom."—Lu 23:42.

MEMPHIS

MEMPHIS (Mem'phis). One of the capitals of ancient Egypt, identified with the ruins at Mit Rahiney, about 23 km (14 mi) S of Cairo, on the W side of the Nile River. Memphis was for long the most important city in "Lower Egypt" (that is, the Delta region and a small section to the S thereof).

At Hosea 9:6 the city is called *Moph* in the Hebrew text (rendered "Memphis" in most English translations). Elsewhere it is referred to by the Hebrew *Noph.*—Isa 19:13; Jer 2:16; 44:1; 46:14, 19; Eze 30:13, 16.

History. According to legend, recounted by Greek historian Herodotus (II, 99), Memphis was established by a ruler named Menes; no historical evidence has been found, however, for this supposed founder of the "First Dynasty" of Egyptian rulers.

Memphis' geographic situation was ideally suited for a capital city of this land of the Nile. Lying just a little south of the apex of the Delta (that is, the point where the Nile River divides up into its branches), it could exercise control not only over the Delta region to the north but also over the traffic on the Nile. Desert and mountains made difficult any approach to the city from the W, and the Nile itself and the hills beyond served as a protection from the E. Thus, Memphis, on the border between Upper (southern) and Lower (northern) Egypt, anciently held the key to all Egypt, much as modern Cairo does today in a nearby location.

Commercial. The city was a great commercial center throughout its history, declining only after the Greek conquest when Alexandria on the northern coast became the country's most thriving port. According to some historians, Memphis became widely reputed for its glass manufacture, Rome being a principal importer of its wares. Acacia trees were also cultivated in the area to supply wood for making furniture, ships for Egypt's navy, and military weapons.

Political. Politically, also, Memphis held great prominence, particularly during the period Egyptologists call the "Old Kingdom" and on down into the "Middle Kingdom." Most historians believe that the seat of government of the earliest dynasties was at Memphis, though perhaps moving to Thebes (Biblical No-amon, about 480 km [300 mi] farther S) for a time. It seems likely that the capital was still at Memphis when Abraham visited Egypt and had his experience with the ruling Pharaoh.—Ge 12:10-20.

The Biblical evidence seems to indicate that during the Israelites' sojourn in Egypt the Egyptian capital was in Lower (Northern) Egypt within reasonably easy access of the land of Goshen, where the Israelites were dwelling. (Ge 47:1, 2; see GOSHEN No. 1.) Moses' meeting Pharaoh 'by the Nile River' would appear to favor the capital's being at Memphis rather than down in the Delta region (as some suggest), for the Nile split into several branches upon reaching the Delta.—Ex 7:15.

Because of its prominence, Memphis figures in several prophecies involving Egypt. At Jeremiah 2:16, the prophet spoke of Noph (Memphis) and Tahpanes (a city in the Delta region) as "feeding on [Israel] at the crown of the head," that is, stripping Israel and making it as if bald. This meant a humiliation for God's professed people, accompanied by mourning. (Compare 2Ki 2:23; Isa 22:12.) In the case of both the northern kingdom of Israel and the southern kingdom (Judah), Egypt, as here represented by Memphis and Tahpanes, proved to be a futile source of hoped-for aid and support, while at the same time showing itself ready to exploit God's covenant people for selfish advantage.—Ho 7:11; Isa 30:1-3; 2Ki 23:31-35.

Religious. Memphis was a center of religion and of learning in Egypt, but back in the eighth century B.C.E., Isaiah foretold that the vaunted wisdom of the princes (perhaps priestly princes) of Noph (Memphis) would fail and Egypt would be misled. (Isa 19:13) Such counselors evidently fostered a false sense of security in Egypt as regards the aggressive power of Assyria.

Memorials of Ethiopian King Tirhakah's reign over Egypt have been found at Memphis. Though Tirhakah managed to survive his encounter with Assyrian King Sennacherib in Canaan (732 B.C.E.; 2Ki 19:9), Sennacherib's son Esar-haddon later shattered the Egyptian army, forcing them to retreat to Memphis. Esar-haddon's own record of the subsequent conflict reads: "I led siege to Memphis, his [Tirhakah's] royal residence, and conquered it in half a day by means of mines, breaches and assault ladders; I destroyed (it), tore down (its walls) and burnt it down." (*Ancient Near Eastern Texts*, edited by J. Pritchard, 1974, p. 293) Apparently a few years later Egypt's forces retook Memphis, massacring the Assyrian garrison. But Ashurbanipal, son of Esar-haddon, marched into Egypt and drove the rulers out of Memphis and back up the Nile (southward).

When Assyria went into decline in the latter part of the seventh century B.C.E., Memphis came back under full Egyptian control. Following Babylonian King Nebuchadnezzar's desolation of Judah in 607 B.C.E., Jewish refugees fled into Egypt, taking up residence in Memphis and other cities. (Jer 44:1) Through his prophets Jeremiah and Ezekiel, Jehovah condemned them to disaster and foretold that Nebuchadnezzar would strike Egypt a devastating blow, with Memphis (Noph) experiencing the full force of the attack. (Jer 44:11-14; 46:13, 14, 19; Eze 30:10-13) The Babylonian attackers of Memphis would confidently attack the city in broad daylight.—Eze 30:16.

Memphis again came in for a severe defeat at the hands of Persian King Cambyses in 525 B.C.E., thereafter becoming the seat of a Persian satrapy. The city never fully recovered from the effects of this conquest. With the rise of Alexandria under the Ptolemies, Memphis declined steadily and by the seventh century of the Common Era had become vast ruins.

Memphis was among the foremost sacred cities of ancient Egypt, along with nearby On (Heliopolis). (Ge 41:50) Especially important were the shrines dedicated to the god Ptah and to the sacred bull Apis. The god Ptah, according to the "Memphite theology" devised by the priests of Memphis, was the creator (sharing this distinction with other gods such as Thoth, Ra, and Osiris), and his mythological activity apparently was modeled on the actual role of the Pharaoh in human affairs. Classical historians describe the temple of Ptah at Memphis as being periodically enlarged and beautified. Enormous statues adorned it.

The Apis bull, a specially marked live bull, was kept at Memphis and worshiped as the incarnation of the god Osiris, though in certain legends it is also connected with the god Ptah. At its death, public mourning was carried on, and an impressive burial of the bull was made at nearby Saqqara. (When the tomb there was opened in the last century, investigators found the embalmed bodies of over 60 bulls and cows.) The selection of a new Apis bull and its enthronement at Memphis was an equally elaborate ceremony. This worship may have influenced the rebellious Israelites in their idea of worshiping Jehovah through a golden calf. (Ex 32:4, 5) The worship of the foreign goddess Astarte was also prominent at Memphis, and there were temples to Egyptian gods and goddesses such as Hathor, Amon, Imhotep, Isis, Osiris-Sokar, Anubis, and others. This whole array of ancient deities and their idols was due for destruction by divine judgment.—Eze 30:13.

Royal burial sites. Evidence of Memphis' past importance is seen from the vast burial grounds close by the ancient site, these areas containing some 20 pyramids or royal monumental tombs. The prominence of Memphis as a royal burial site doubtless is reflected in Hosea's prophecy against faithless Israel in the eighth century B.C.E., to the effect that "Egypt itself will collect them together; Memphis, for its part, will bury them." (Ho 9:6) Among the pyramids found at Saqqara, near Memphis, is the Step Pyramid built by King Djoser ("Third Dynasty"), considered to be the oldest freestanding stone structure known. Farther to the WNW of Memphis are the far more impressive pyramids of Giza and the Great Sphinx. Today these tombs and similar stone structures are all that remain to indicate Memphis' past religious glory. As foretold, the city has become "a mere object of astonishment."—Jer 46:19.

MEMUCAN (Me·mu'can). The chief spokesman for the seven Medo-Persian princes on the occasion that Vashti refused to obey King Ahasuerus. (Es 1:13-15) Memucan's opinion was that Vashti had wronged not only the king but also the princes and the people of the empire and that she should therefore be removed as queen, so that all wives of the empire might learn to be obedient to their husbands. The king and the other princes agreed with Memucan, and a royal decree to this effect was written among the unchangeable laws of the Medes and Persians.—Es 1:16-22.

These "seven princes of Persia and Media" were "versed in law and legal cases." They were the king's closest advisers, "sitting first in the kingdom." (Es 1:13, 14) That the Persian court had such a council of seven is confirmed by Ezra 7:14.

MENAHEM (Men'a·hem) [One Who Comforts]. Son of Gadi and king of Israel for ten years from about 790 B.C.E. Upon learning that Shallum had assassinated King Zechariah, Menahem went from Tirzah to Samaria and killed the assassin there. He then assumed rulership. Evidently during the early part of his reign Menahem struck down Tiphsah "and all that was in it and its territory out from Tirzah, because it did not open up." The town was apparently reluctant to open its gate to him. (LXX, Vg, Sy) Harsh treatment was meted out to the populace: "All its pregnant women he ripped up."—2Ki 15:10, 13-17.

Menahem did what was bad in Jehovah's eyes. He promoted calf worship, failing to depart from the sins of Jeroboam, the first king of the ten-tribe kingdom. During his reign, King Pul (Tiglath-pileser III) invaded Israel, and Menahem was forced to pay that Assyrian monarch "a thousand talents of silver." ($6,606,000) He acquired this sum by imposing an assessment of 50 silver shekels upon each of "the valiant, mighty men" of Israel. Since a talent of silver equaled about 3,000 shekels, the silver was obtained from about 60,000 persons. Menahem gave the silver to the Assyrian king, "that his hands might prove to be with him to strengthen the kingdom in his own hand." Upon receiving this amount, Pul withdrew from the land.—2Ki 15:19, 20.

Menahem is named in an inscription of Tiglath-pileser III as "Menahem of Samaria" (Me-ni-hi-im-ne alSa-me-ri-na-a-a), being listed there, along with Syrian King Rezon (Ra-hi-a-nu) and King Hiram (Hi-ru-um-mu) of Tyre (different from the Hiram of David's day), as a ruler from whom that Assyrian monarch claims to have received tribute. (Ancient Near Eastern Texts, edited by J. Pritchard, 1974, pp. 282, 283) Menahem died about

781 B.C.E., and his son Pekahiah succeeded him on Israel's throne.—2Ki 15:22.

MENE (Me'ne). The opening word of a cryptic message miraculously inscribed on the plaster wall of King Belshazzar's banquet hall in Babylon on the night of October 5, 539 B.C.E. (Gregorian calendar), just before the city's fall to the Medes and Persians. According to Daniel, who was empowered by Jehovah to read the inscription and give its interpretation, the writing read: "MENE, MENE, TEKEL and PARSIN." (Da 5:25) The inscription evidently consisted only of consonants and required intelligent and proper vocalization, as well as correct interpretation. The words themselves literally mean: "A mina, a mina, a shekel, and half shekels."

In giving the accurate interpretation, Daniel said first: "This is the interpretation of the word: MENE, God has numbered the days of your kingdom and has finished it." (Da 5:26) Even that portion of the message should have made things clear to King Belshazzar. Jehovah had dethroned mighty Nebuchadnezzar, who had been more powerful than Belshazzar. So He should be able to cut down the number of days of Belshazzar's kingship and those of his coregent and father, Nabonidus. Jehovah could bring the dynasty to its end. The word "MENE" appeared twice in the inscription, perhaps because the message applied to both rulers in the kingdom of Babylon at that time, Nabonidus and Belshazzar. However, Daniel, in giving the interpretation, used "MENE" only once, possibly because only Belshazzar was present on this occasion.

The Bible does not reveal why none of Babylon's wise men were able to read the writing. (Da 5:8) It may have been because of the cryptic nature of the message, or the writing itself may have been in a script or language unknown to them.

MENNA (Men'na). A distant maternal ancestor of Jesus Christ, not far removed from David.—Lu 3:31.

MENSTRUATION (men·stru·a'tion). The periodic discharge of the menses (blood, fluid, and some tissue debris) from a woman's uterus. Menstruation of women is generally a monthly experience, occurring about every four weeks. Girls begin menstruating at puberty, and this function normally continues until menopause, each menstrual flow usually lasting from three to five days.

The Scriptures associate menstruation with impurity and uncleanness (Le 12:2; Eze 22:10; 36:17), a form of the Hebrew word relating to it (nid·dah') sometimes being rendered "menstrual impurity." (Le 15:25, 26) A form of another

Hebrew term, *da·weh'*, which can denote illness (La 5:17), is used in the expression "menstruating woman." (Le 15:33; Isa 30:22) Menstruation is also meant by the phrase "the customary thing with women."—Ge 31:35.

"Unclean" Under Law.   According to the Mosaic Law, a woman was considered unclean for seven days during normal menstruation. The bed or any other articles upon which the menstruating woman might lie or sit were also rendered unclean. Anyone touching her or items she had made unclean was required to wash his garments and bathe, and that one remained unclean until the evening. If her menstrual impurity came to be upon a man lying down with her (as when, unwittingly, a husband had sexual relations with his wife at the beginning of menstruation), he was rendered unclean for seven days, and the bed upon which he might lie down was considered unclean.

The woman was also viewed as unclean for the duration of an irregular running discharge of blood or "a flow longer than her menstrual impurity," at which time she made the articles on which she lay or sat as well as persons touching these items unclean. After the abnormal discharge ceased, she was to count seven days, and she then became clean. On the eighth day the woman brought two turtledoves or two young pigeons to the priest, who made atonement for her, presenting one of these creatures to Jehovah as a sin offering and the other as a burnt offering. —Le 15:19-30; see CLEAN, CLEANNESS.

If a man and a woman deliberately cohabited during her menstrual impurity, they were cut off in death. (Le 18:19; 20:18) The prohibiting of sexual union during menstruation probably contributed to health, perhaps preventing, for instance, the occurrence of inflammation in the genital area, simple urethritis. The Israelites also may have been reminded of the sanctity of blood by the Law's regulations involving menstruation or blood flow. These rules were not discriminatory against women, for men were subject to uncleanness by discharges to which they were prone. (Le 15:1-17) Especially did regulations concerning menstruation show Jehovah's consideration for womankind. The Christian husband, though he is not under the Law (Ro 6:14; Eph 2:11-16), also does well to consider his wife's cycles and vicissitudes, dwelling with her "according to knowledge" and assigning her honor "as to a weaker vessel, the feminine one."—1Pe 3:7.

MENUHOTH   (Me·nu'hoth)   [Resting-Places]. According to the Masoretic text, apparently a Judean family descended through Shobal. (1Ch 2:4,

52) But some scholars prefer emending the Hebrew text to read "the Manahathites," as in verse 54. (*JB, Mo*) And a Jewish commentary on Chronicles gives the alternate reading "who supervised half of the resting-places" and notes: "Shobal was in charge of half the caravan stations in the land of Judah."—*Soncino Books of the Bible,* edited by A. Cohen, London, 1952, p. 15

MEONENIM, BIG TREE OF   (Me·on'e·nim) [Those Practicing Magic]. A tree within sight of Shechem, passed by a band of King Abimelech's men before their fight with the landowners of that city. (Jg 9:34-37) "Big tree of Meonenim" translates the Hebrew words *'e·lohn' me'oh·nenim'.* *'E·lohn'* refers to big trees in general, and *me'oh·nenim'* is a participle signifying "those practicing magic." (See De 18:14.) The tree may have been so named because Canaanites or apostate Israelites engaged in magical practices there. Some scholars also link "the big tree of Meonenim" with "the big trees of Moreh" that are similarly described as being in the vicinity of Shechem.—Compare Ge 12:6; 35:4; Jg 9:6.

MEONOTHAI   (Me·o'no·thai). A descendant of Judah who "became father to Ophrah," being either the paternal ancestor of a person named Ophrah or the founder of a place bearing that name.—1Ch 4:1, 14.

MEPHAATH   (Meph'a·ath). A city originally assigned to the Reubenites but subsequently granted to the Merarite Levites. (Jos 13:15, 18; 21:34, 36, 37; 1Ch 6:77-79) In Jeremiah's day, about eight centuries later, Mephaath was under Moabite control. (Jer 48:21, 24) It is possibly identified with Tell Jawa, about 11 km (7 mi) S of 'Amman (Rabbah). Nearby Khirbet Nefa'a (or Qureiyat Nafi') may preserve the ancient name.

MEPHIBOSHETH   (Me·phib'o·sheth).

1. One of King Saul's two sons by Rizpah the daughter of Aiah. (2Sa 21:8) He was among the seven descendants of Saul that David gave to the Gibeonites to atone for Saul's attempt to annihilate them. The Gibeonites exposed Mephibosheth and the six other members of Saul's household "on the mountain before Jehovah," after putting them to death "in the first days of harvest, at the start of the barley harvest." (Compare Nu 25:4.) However, Rizpah acted to keep the fowls and wild beasts away from them, and David later had their bones gathered and buried with those of Saul and Jonathan in the burial place of Kish.—2Sa 21:1-14.

2. Son of Jonathan; grandson of King Saul. When the report about the deaths of Saul and

Jonathan came from Jezreel, Mephibosheth's nurse began to carry the five-year-old boy and flee in panic. At that time he "had a fall and was lamed" in both feet. (2Sa 4:4) For some years thereafter, Mephibosheth lived in the house of Machir the son of Ammiel at Lo-debar. David learned this from Ziba, a former servant in Saul's house. Doubtless remembering his covenant with Jonathan (1Sa 20:12-17, 42), David wished to exercise loving-kindness toward anyone "left over of the house of Saul." Mephibosheth was brought before David, and when the king explained that it was his desire to exercise loving-kindness toward Mephibosheth by returning to him "all the field of Saul" and by having him "eat bread at my table constantly," Mephibosheth responded humbly: "What is your servant, that you have turned your face to the dead dog such as I am?" However, in keeping with David's determination in the matter, Ziba and all those dwelling in his house (including 15 sons and 20 servants) became servants to Mephibosheth, who was given Saul's property. He thereafter resided in Jerusalem and constantly ate at the table of the king.—2Sa 9.

When David fled from Jerusalem because of Absalom's conspiracy, he was met by Ziba, who provided him with supplies. Answering David's inquiries as to the whereabouts of Mephibosheth, Ziba said: "There he is dwelling in Jerusalem; for he said: 'Today the house of Israel will give back to me the royal rule of my father.'" At that, the king told Ziba: "Look! Yours is everything that belongs to Mephibosheth." (2Sa 16:1-4) Mephibosheth came to meet David upon the king's return to Jerusalem, the account saying "he had not attended to his feet nor had he attended to his mustache nor had he washed his garments from the day that the king went away until the day that he came in peace." When David asked why Mephibosheth had not gone with him, Mephibosheth gave the explanation that his servant had tricked him and also said: "So he slandered your servant to my lord the king. But my lord the king is as an angel of the true God" (that is, he would see the matter in its true light). David evidently recognized Mephibosheth's innocence, altering his first decree by saying: "You and Ziba should share in the field." To this Mephibosheth replied: "Let him even take the whole, now that my lord the king has come in peace to his house."—2Sa 19:24-30; compare Pr 18:17; 25:8-10.

When the Gibeonites sought the death of Saul's descendants to atone for that king's evil attempt against them, David felt compassion for Mephibosheth because of the oath of Jehovah between David and Jonathan and spared Mephibosheth. (2Sa 21:7, 8) The Scriptures provide no further information about Mephibosheth, though Saul's family continued in existence to a later generation through Mephibosheth's son Mica (Micah). (2Sa 9:12; 1Ch 9:39-44) Evidently Mephibosheth also had the name Merib-baal, as 1 Chronicles 8:34 and 9:40 would indicate.

MERAB (Me'rab) [from a root meaning "become many (abundant)"]. The older of King Saul's two daughters. (1Sa 14:49) Saul had evidently promised to give one of them in marriage to the man who would defeat Goliath (1Sa 17:25), and it may have been for that reason that he offered Merab to David. After his encounter with Goliath, David proved to be a prudent and successful fighter against the Philistines, so much so that Saul "was scared of him," while the people of Israel and Judah loved him. (1Sa 18:15, 16) In offering Merab to David as a wife, Saul urged him on to continued valor, while thinking to himself, "Do not let my hand come to be upon him, but let the hand of the Philistines come to be upon him," hoping for David's death in battle. David, in humility, hesitated to accept the offer to become the son-in-law of the king. As matters turned out, Saul did not keep his promise, and Merab never became David's wife. The account states that the younger daughter, Michal, "was in love with David," which may imply that Merab was not. At any rate, "it came about that at the time for giving Merab, Saul's daughter, to David, she herself had already been given to Adriel the Meholathite as a wife."—1Sa 18:17-20.

Merab bore five sons to Adriel. However, David later gave these sons and two other members of Saul's household to the Gibeonites, who put all seven to death. This was done to atone for Saul's having tried to annihilate the Gibeonites.—2Sa 21:1-10.

Merab's Sister Rears Her Sons. According to the Masoretic text, 2 Samuel 21:8 speaks of "the five sons of Michal the daughter of Saul whom she bore to Adriel." Yet 2 Samuel 6:23 says that Michal died childless. It appears that some scribes have tried to resolve this difficulty by substituting the name of Merab for Michal at 2 Samuel 21:8. This seems apparent from the fact that the Greek *Septuagint* (Lagardian edition) and two Hebrew manuscripts read "Merab" in this verse. However, a traditional explanation of 2 Samuel 21:8 as it appears in almost all other Hebrew manuscripts is as follows:

Michal's sister Merab was the wife of Adriel and bore him the five sons in question. But Merab died early, and her sister Michal, rejected by David and childless, undertook the rearing, or bringing up, of the five boys. Hence, they were spoken of as Michal's children instead of those of Merab. In harmony with this view of 2 Samuel 21:8, the Bible translation by Isaac Leeser speaks of "the five sons of Michal the daughter of Saul, whom she had brought up for Adriel," and a footnote thereon states: "As Michal was David's wife; but the children were those of Merab, the oldest daughter of Saul, who were probably educated by her sister." The Targums read: "The five sons of Merab (which Michal, Saul's daughter, brought up) which she bare." Other factors, not revealed in the Scriptures, may have a bearing on the way the text was set down.

MERAIAH (Me·rai'ah) [possibly, Rebellious]. A priest and head of the paternal house of Seraiah in the days of Joiakim after the Jews' return from Babylonian exile.—Ne 12:12.

MERAIOTH (Me·ra'ioth) [possibly, Rebellious Ones].

1. A priestly descendant of Aaron through Eleazar; called "the son of Zerahiah."—1Ch 6:3-7, 52; Ezr 7:3, 4.

2. A priest identified as "the son of Ahitub, a leader of the house of the true God" and who appears to be the father of Zadok.—1Ch 9:10, 11; Ne 11:11.

3. Founder of a priestly paternal house, the head of which was Helkai in the days of Joiakim. (Ne 12:12, 15) "Meraioth," which was the name of this house following the Jews' return from Babylonian exile, may be a variation of "Meremoth," the name of one of the priests accompanying Zerubbabel to Jerusalem in 537 B.C.E.—Ne 12:3.

MERARI (Me·rar'i) [from a root meaning "be bitter"]. Son of Levi and brother of Gershon (Gershom) and Kohath. (Ge 46:11; 1Ch 6:1, 16) Since Merari is mentioned in third place among Levi's sons, he may have been the youngest. He was one of the 70 members of Jacob's household "who came into Egypt." (Ge 46:8, 11, 26, 27) Merari had two sons, Mahli and Mushi (Ex 6:19; 1Ch 6:19), and was the founder of the Merarites, one of the three main Levite families.—Nu 26:57.

MERARITES (Me·rar'ites) [Of (Belonging to) Merari]. One of the three major families of Levites, descending from Levi's son Merari through Mahli and Mushi. (Ex 6:16, 19; Nu 3:20; 26:57, 58) The first census of the Israelites in the wilderness listed 6,200 Merarite males from a month old upward, 3,200 of these being from 30 to 50 years

of age and entering the service group "for the service in the tent of meeting." (Nu 3:33, 34; 4:42-45) Their chieftain then was Zuriel, and their encampment was on the N side of the tabernacle. (Nu 3:35) During the wilderness trek the three-tribe division of Judah was first to pull away from an encampment. Then the Gershonites and Merarites "as carriers of the tabernacle pulled away," followed by the three-tribe division of Reuben and then the Kohathite Levites. (Nu 10:14-21) The Merarites were in charge of the panel frames, bars, pillars, and socket pedestals of the tabernacle, as well as "all its utensils and all its service," in addition to the pillars, socket pedestals, tent pins and tent cords of the courtyard. (Nu 3:36, 37) To move these heavy objects, they were supplied with four wagons and eight cattle. In the wilderness they and the Gershonites were "under the hand" of Aaron's son Ithamar.—Nu 7:6-8.

In the division of the Promised Land under Joshua, 12 cities were assigned to the Merarites, four each from the tribal territories of Reuben, Gad, and Zebulun. One of these, Ramoth in Gilead (in the territory of Gad), was a "city of refuge."—Jos 21:7, 34-40; 1Ch 6:63, 77-81.

In David's day 220 Merarites, with Asaiah as their chief, assisted other Levites in bringing the ark of the covenant to Jerusalem from the house of Obed-edom. (1Ch 15:1-6, 25) After the Ark had a resting-place, "David gave positions for the direction of the singing at the house of Jehovah" to certain Merarites. (1Ch 6:31, 44-47) Other Merarites were assigned as gatekeepers.—1Ch 26:1, 10, 19.

Merarites were among the Levites returning from Babylonian exile in 537 B.C.E. (1Ch 9:14) Later (in 468 B.C.E.), Merarites were among the Levites accompanying Ezra from Babylon to Jerusalem.—Ezr 8:1, 18, 19, 31, 32.

During Judean King Hezekiah's reform program, some Merarites were among the Levites who cleansed the temple. (2Ch 29:12, 15) Later, in the seventh century B.C.E., Merarites Jahath and Obadiah were appointed over repairers of the temple by King Josiah.—2Ch 34:12, 13.

MERATHAIM (Mer·a·tha'im) [probably, Double Rebellion]. A designation applying to Babylon or, possibly, to a particular territory in Babylonia. (Jer 50:21, 23, 24) It may allude to the *nar marratu* of Babylonian inscriptions, considered to be the Persian Gulf where the Tigris and Euphrates rivers enter into it. It is evidently a play on the Hebrew verb *ma·rah'* (be rebellious). As a dual form derived from *ma·rah'*, Merathaim may point to the intensity of Babylon's rebellion. From the days of its founder Nimrod, Babylon's course was one of rebellion against Jehovah.—Ge 10:8-10.

MERCHANT.

One who buys and sells or barters with expectation of making a profit; a tradesman or a tradeswoman. The Hebrew term rendered "merchant" literally refers to one who 'travels about' for commercial purposes.—Ge 34: 10, ftn.

Very early in man's history people became skilled in certain fields of endeavor, specializing in their occupation. (Ge 4:20-22) Commerce and trade between them naturally followed, and in the course of events, many individuals, both men and women (Eze 27:3), worked exclusively as merchants and traders handling a great variety of commodities. By the time Abraham reached Canaan early in the second millennium B.C.E., certain mercantile weights and measures were used and recognized. (Ge 23:16) The Mosaic Law commanded that the merchant's measurements be standardized and just.—De 25:13-16; Pr 11:1; 20: 10; Mic 6:11.

Some merchants were shopkeepers; others did business in the cities in marketplaces and bazaars. (Ne 13:20) Some owned fleets of ships that plied the high seas to bring back valuable cargoes of merchandise from distant lands. (Ps 107:23; Pr 31:14) Other traders were travelers who followed the extensive overland trade routes of the ancient world. (1Ki 10:14, 15; 2Ch 9:13, 14) Joseph was sold by his brothers to such traveling merchants headed for Egypt.—Ge 37:25, 28.

All the nations, small and great, had their merchants, and through their activity many were made rich. There were the merchants of Ethiopia (Isa 45:14), of Assyria (Na 1:1; 3:16), of the kingdom of Solomon (1Ki 10:28; 2Ch 1:16), and of Sidon and Tyre (Isa 23:2, 8).

Ezekiel's prophecy describes the city of Tyre as a great commercial center to which the ships and caravans from all parts of the world came and did business. This same prophecy also describes the great variety of merchandise these merchants handled, which enriched this port city, such things as silver, iron, tin, lead, copper articles, horses, mules, ivory, ebony, turquoise, wool, dyed fabrics, corals, rubies, wheat, special foodstuffs, honey, oil, balsam, wine, cassia, cane, garments of woven material, perfumes, precious stones, and gold.—Eze 27:2, 12-25.

The Greek word *em'po·ros* (*po'ros* meaning "journey") refers to a traveling merchant, or one 'on a journey." An example is the traveling merchant in Jesus' illustration who searched for fine pearls of great price. (Mt 13:45) It is the traveling merchants that the symbolic book of Revelation says are made rich by "the great harlot . . . 'Babylon the Great, the mother of the harlots,'" and who weep and mourn over her downfall and destruction. (Re 17:1, 5; 18:3, 11-15) Babylon the Great also has her own traveling merchants, "the top-ranking men of the earth."—Re 18:23.

MERCY.

An expression of kind consideration or pity that brings relief to those who are disadvantaged; tender compassion; also, at times, a lightening of judgment or punishment.

Mercy is a frequent translation of the Hebrew *ra·chamim'* and the Greek *e'le·os* (verb, *e.le·e'o*). An examination of these terms and their usage helps bring out their full flavor and sense. The Hebrew verb *ra·cham'* is defined as meaning "to glow, to feel warm with tender emotion; . . . to be compassionate." (*A Hebrew and Chaldee Lexicon*, edited by B. Davies, 1957, p. 590) According to lexicographer Gesenius: "The primary idea seems to lie in cherishing, soothing, and in a gentle emotion of mind." (*A Hebrew and English Lexicon of the Old Testament*, translated by E. Robinson, 1836, p. 939) The term is closely related to the word for "womb" or can refer to "bowels," which are affected when one feels warm and tender sympathy or pity.—Compare Isa 63:15, 16; Jer 31:20.

In the Scriptures *ra·cham'* is used only once by man toward God, the psalmist saying: "I shall have affection [form of *ra·cham'*] for you, O Jehovah my strength." (Ps 18:1) Between humans, Joseph displayed this quality when "his inward emotions [form of *ra·chamim'*] were excited" toward his brother Benjamin and he gave way to tears. (Ge 43:29, 30; compare 1Ki 3:25, 26.) When people were subjected to the possibility of being dealt with harshly or unfeelingly by captors (1Ki 8:50; Jer 42:10-12) or by officials of superior authority (Ge 43:14; Ne 1:11; Da 1:9), they desired and prayed to become objects of pity or mercy before such ones, hence, to be treated with favor, gentleness, consideration.—Contrast Isa 13:17, 18.

Jehovah's Mercy. The term's most frequent use is with regard to Jehovah's dealings with his covenant people. God showing pity (*ra·cham'*) toward these is compared with a woman showing pity toward the children of her womb and with a father showing mercy toward his sons. (Isa 49:15; Ps 103:13) Since the nation of Israel frequently strayed from righteousness and came into sore straits, they often became especially in need of merciful help. If they showed a right heart attitude and turned to Jehovah, he, though having been angry with them, would express compassion, favor, goodwill. (De 13:17; 30:3; Ps 102:13; Isa 54:7-10; 60:10) His sending his Son to be born in Israel was evidence of a coming "daybreak" of divine compassion and mercy for them.—Lu 1:50-58, 72-78.

The Greek e'le·os conveys some of the sense of the Hebrew ra·chamim'. *Vine's Expository Dictionary of Old and New Testament Words* says: "ELEOS (ἔλεος) 'is the outward manifestation of pity; it assumes need on the part of him who receives it, and resources adequate to meet the need on the part of him who shows it.'" The verb (e·le·e'o) generally conveys the idea of feeling "sympathy with the misery of another, and especially sympathy manifested in act." (1981, Vol. 3, pp. 60, 61) Hence, the blind, the demon-possessed, the leprous, or those whose children were afflicted were among those who evoked e'le·os, the expression of mercy, pity. (Mt 9:27; 15:22; 17:15; Mr 5:18, 19; Lu 17:12, 13) In response to the plea, "Have mercy on us," Jesus performed miracles relieving such ones. He did so, not in a routine, apathetic way, but "moved with pity" (Mt 20:31, 34), the Gospel writer here using a form of the verb *splag·khni'zo·mai*, which is related to *splag'khna*, literally meaning "intestines." (Ac 1:18) This verb expresses the *feeling* of pity, whereas e'le·os refers to the active *manifestation* of such pity, hence an act of mercy.

Not limited to judicial action. In English the word "mercy" quite generally conveys the idea of refraining, exercising restraint, such as in the administering of punishment, this restraint being motivated by compassion or sympathy. Thus, it frequently has a judicial flavor, as when a judge shows clemency in softening the judgment upon a wrongdoer. Since God's exercise of mercy is always in harmony with his other qualities and righteous standards, including his justice and trueness (Ps 40:11; Ho 2:19), and since all men are by inheritance sinful and worthy of receiving sin's payment of death (Ro 5:12; compare Ps 130:3, 4; Da 9:18; Tit 3:5), it is clear that the pardoning of error, or the lightening of judgment or punishment, is frequently involved in God's exercise of mercy. (Ps 51:1, 2; 103:3, 4; Da 9:9; Mic 7:18, 19) However, it can be seen from the preceding information that the Hebrew and Greek terms (ra·chamim'; e'le·os) are not limited to forgiveness or restraint in applying a judicial penalty. Pardon of error of itself is not the mercy generally portrayed by these terms, but, rather, such forgiveness opens the way for that mercy. In expressing mercy, God, of course, never ignores his perfect standards of justice, and for this reason he has

provided the ransom sacrifice through his Son Jesus Christ, making possible the forgiveness of sins with no violation of justice.—Ro 3:25, 26.

Mercy, then, most frequently refers, not to a negative action, a holding back (as of punishment), but to a positive action, to an expression of kind consideration or pity that brings relief to those who are disadvantaged, in need of mercy.

This is well illustrated in Jesus' parable of the Samaritan who saw the traveler lying by the roadside, robbed and beaten. He showed himself "neighbor" to the man because, moved with pity, he "acted mercifully toward him," treating his wounds and caring for him. (Lu 10:29-37) No forgiveness of wrongdoing or judicial proceedings were involved.

Hence, the Scriptures show that the mercifulness of Jehovah God is not a quality that comes into play only when persons are, in effect, "on trial" before him because of having committed some particular wrong. Rather, it is a characteristic quality of God's personality, his normal way of reacting toward those in need, a facet of his love. (2Co 1:3; 1Jo 4:8) He is not like the false gods of the nations—unfeeling, noncompassionate gods. Instead, "Jehovah is gracious and merciful, slow to anger and great in loving-kindness. Jehovah is good to all, and his mercies are over all his works." (Ps 145:8, 9; compare Ps 25:8; 104:14, 15, 20-28; Mt 5:45-48; Ac 14:15-17.) He is "rich in mercy," and the wisdom proceeding from him is "full of mercy." (Eph 2:4; Jas 3:17) His Son, who revealed what his Father is like (Joh 1:18), showed this by his own personality, speech, and acts. When crowds came out to hear him, and even before seeing their reaction to what he would say, Jesus was "moved with pity [form of *splag·khni'zo·mai*]" because they were "skinned and thrown about like sheep without a shepherd."—Mr 6:34; Mt 9:36; compare Mt 14:14; 15:32.

Mankind's need. Obviously, mankind's basic and greatest disability comes from sin, inherited from their forefather Adam. Thus, all are in dire need, in a pitiable state. Jehovah God has acted mercifully toward mankind as a whole by providing the means for them to become free from this great disability and its consequences of sickness and death. (Mt 20:28; Tit 3:4-7; 1Jo 2:2) As a merciful God, he exercises patience because "he does not desire any to be destroyed but desires all to attain to repentance." (2Pe 3:9) Jehovah is desirous of doing good toward all, he prefers this (compare Isa 30:18, 19), he finds 'no delight in the death of the wicked,' and "not out of his own heart has he afflicted or does he grieve the sons of men," as in the destruction of Judah and Jerusalem. (Eze 33:11; La 3:31-33) It is the hardheartedness of persons, their obstinacy and refusal to respond to his graciousness and mercifulness, that obliges him to take a different course toward them, causes his mercies to be "shut off" from flowing toward them.—Ps 77:9; Jer 13:10, 14; Isa 13:9; Ro 2:4-11.

Not to be presumed upon. While Jehovah has great mercy toward those who draw near to him in sincerity, he will by no means exempt from punishment those who are unrepentant and really deserving of punishment. (Ex 34:6, 7) A person cannot presume on God's mercy; he cannot sin with complete impunity or be exempted from the natural results or outworking of his wrong course of action. (Ga 6:7, 8; compare Nu 12:1-3, 9-15; 2Sa 12:9-14.) Jehovah may mercifully show patience and long-suffering, giving persons the opportunity to correct their wrong course; though manifesting disapproval, he may not completely abandon them but may mercifully continue supplying them a measure of aid and direction. (Compare Ne 9:18, 19, 27-31.) But if they do not respond, his patience has its limits and he withdraws his mercy and acts against them for his own name's sake. —Isa 9:17; 63:7-10; Jer 16:5-13, 21; compare Lu 13:6-9.

Not governed by human standards. It is not up to humans to try to establish their own standards or criteria by which God should show mercy. From his heavenly vantage point and in harmony with his own good purpose, with his own long-range view of the future and his ability to read the heart, he 'shows mercy to whom he will show mercy.' (Ex 33:19; Ro 9:15-18; compare 2Ki 13:23; Mt 20:12-15.) At Romans chapter 11 the apostle discusses God's display of unparalleled wisdom and mercy in giving to the Gentiles an opportunity to enter the heavenly Kingdom. The Gentiles were outside the commonwealth of God's nation, Israel, and hence previously not the recipients of the mercies resulting from covenant relationship with God; and they also lived in disobedience to God. (Compare Ro 9:24-26; Ho 2:23.) Paul explains that Israel first had the opportunity but that they were, for the most part, disobedient. This resulted in opening up the way for Gentiles to become part of the promised "kingdom of priests and a holy nation." (Ex 19:5, 6) Paul concludes: "For God has shut them all up together [Jews and Gentiles] in disobedience, that he might show all of them mercy." Through Christ's ransom sacrifice, the Adamic sin working in all mankind could be removed for all those exercising faith (including Gentiles), and through his death on the torture stake the curse of the Law could also be removed

from those under it (the Jews), so that *all* could receive mercy. The apostle exclaims: "O the depth of God's riches and wisdom and knowledge! How unsearchable his judgments are and past tracing out his ways are!"—Ro 11:30-33; Joh 3:16; Col 2:13, 14; Ga 3:13.

Seeking God's Mercy. Those desirous of enjoying the flow of God's mercy must seek him, showing a right heart condition by abandoning their wrong ways and harmful thoughts (Isa 55: 6, 7); they must properly fear him and show appreciation for his righteous precepts (Ps 103:13; 119:77, 156, 157; Lu 1:50); and if they deviate from the righteous course they have been following, they must not try to cover it over but must confess it and manifest genuine contrition and heartfelt sadness (Ps 51:1, 17; Pr 28:13). Another absolute essential is that they themselves be merciful. Jesus said: "Happy are the merciful, since they will be shown mercy."—Mt 5:7.

Gifts of Mercy. The Pharisees showed an unmerciful attitude toward others and were rebuked by Jesus with the words: "Go, then, and learn what this means, 'I want mercy, and not sacrifice.'" (Mt 9:10-13; 12:1-7; compare Ho 6:6.) He placed mercy among the weightier matters of the Law. (Mt 23:23) As noted, while such mercy could embrace judicial clemency, such as the Pharisees might have opportunity to show, perhaps as members of the Sanhedrin, it was not limited to this. More basically it referred to active manifestation of pity or compassion, deeds of mercy.—Compare De 15:7-11.

This mercy might be expressed in material giving. But to count with God, it must be properly motivated, not be mere 'enlightened selfishness.' (Mt 6:1-4) Material things were among the "gifts of mercy [form of *e·le·e·mo·sy'ne*]" in which Dorcas abounded (Ac 9:36, 39), and doubtless also among those of Cornelius, whose gifts together with his prayers brought a favorable hearing with God. (Ac 10:2, 4, 31) Jesus said the failure of the Pharisees was in not giving "as gifts of mercy the things that are inside." (Lu 11:41) Thus true mercy must proceed from the heart.

Jesus and his disciples were notable especially for their merciful giving of spiritual gifts of far greater value than material things. (Compare Joh 6:35; Ac 3:1-8.) Members of the Christian congregation, particularly those acting as 'shepherds' therein (1Pe 5:1, 2), must cultivate the quality of mercy. Both in material and in spiritual ways their mercy should be exercised "with cheerfulness," never begrudgingly. (Ro 12:8) The faith of certain members of the congregation may become weak, causing them to become spiritually ill, even to express doubts. Because these approach the danger of spiritual death, their fellow Christians are exhorted to maintain the flow of mercy to these and help them to avoid a destructive end. While continuing to show mercy to some whose actions have not been proper, they need to be careful not to fall into temptation themselves, being conscious that they must not only love righteousness but also hate what is bad. Hence their mercy does not imply any condoning of wrong.—Jude 22, 23; compare 1Jo 5:16, 17; see GIFTS OF MERCY.

Mercy Exults Triumphantly Over Judgment. The disciple James states: "For the one that does not practice mercy will have his judgment without mercy. Mercy exults triumphantly over judgment." (Jas 2:13) The context shows that he is developing the thoughts expressed earlier as to true worship, including the expression of mercy in caring for those afflicted, and in not showing favoritism and discriminating against the poor in favor of the rich. (Jas 1:27; 2:1-9) His following words also indicate this, as they deal with the needs of brothers "in a naked state and lacking the food sufficient for the day." (Jas 2:14-17) Hence, his words correspond to those of Jesus, that it is the merciful who will be shown mercy. (Mt 5:7; compare Mt 6:12; 18:32-35.) When brought into judgment by God, those who have been merciful —showing pity or compassion, and giving active aid to those in need—will, in turn, be shown mercy by God, and thus their mercy will in effect triumph over any adverse judgment that might otherwise be leveled against them. As the proverb states: "He that is showing favor to the lowly one is lending to Jehovah, and his treatment He will repay to him." (Pr 19:17) The point made by James is corroborated by many other texts. —Compare Job 31:16-23, 32; Ps 37:21, 26; 112:5; Pr 14:21; 17:5; 21:13; 28:27; 2Ti 1:16, 18; Heb 13:16.

The Mercy of God's High Priest. The book of Hebrews explains why Jesus, as the High Priest far greater than any priest of the Aaronic line, had to become a man, suffer, and die: "Consequently he was obliged to become like his 'brothers' in all respects, that he might become a merciful and faithful high priest in things pertaining to God, in order to offer propitiatory sacrifice for the sins of the people." Having suffered under test, "he is able to come to the aid of those who are being put to the test." (Heb 2:17, 18) Because of having the record of Jesus' life, his words and deeds, those addressing themselves to God through Jesus can do so with confidence. "For we have as high priest, not one who cannot sympathize with our weak-

nesses, but one who has been tested in all respects like ourselves, but without sin. Let us, therefore, approach with freeness of speech to the throne of undeserved kindness, that we may obtain mercy and find undeserved kindness for help at the right time."—Heb 4:15, 16.

Jesus' sacrificing his own life was an outstanding act of mercy and love. In his heavenly position as High Priest, he gave evidence of his mercifulness, as in his dealings with Paul (Saul), showing him mercy because of Paul's ignorance. Paul states: "Nevertheless, the reason why I was shown mercy was that by means of me as the foremost case Christ Jesus might demonstrate all his longsuffering for a sample of those who are going to rest their faith on him for everlasting life." (1Ti 1:13-16) Even as Jesus' Father, Jehovah God, showed mercy many times to Israel in saving them from their enemies, freeing them from their oppressors, and bringing them into a peaceful, prosperous state, so, too, Christians may have firm hope in the mercy to be expressed through God's Son. Hence Jude writes: "Keep yourselves in God's love, while you are waiting for the mercy of our Lord Jesus Christ with everlasting life in view." (Jude 21) God's wonderful mercy through Christ encourages true Christians not to give up in their ministry and to carry it out in an unselfish way. —2Co 4:1, 2.

Merciful Treatment of Animals. Proverbs 12:10 says: "The righteous one is caring for the soul of his domestic animal, but the mercies of the wicked ones are cruel." Whereas the righteous person knows the needs of his animals and has a feeling for their welfare, the wicked person's mercies are not stirred up by these needs. According to the selfish, unfeeling principles of the world, the treatment of one's animals is based only on what benefit one might gain from them. What the wicked person would consider adequate care might actually be cruel treatment. (Contrast Ge 33:12-14.) The righteous person's concern for his animals finds precedent in God's own care for them as part of his creation.—Compare Ex 20:10; De 25:4; 22:4, 6, 7; 11:15; Ps 104:14, 27; Jon 4:11.

Mercy and Kindness. Other words closely associated with and frequently used in connection with the terms ra·chamim' and e'le·os are the Hebrew che'sedh (Ps 25:6; 69:16; Jer 16:5; La 3:22) and the Greek kha'ris (1Ti 1:2; Heb 4:16; 2Jo 3), meaning, respectively, "loving-kindness (loyal love)" and "undeserved kindness." Che'sedh differs from ra·chamim' in that it stresses devotion or loyal loving attachment to the object of the kindness, whereas ra·chamim' lays emphasis on the tender sympathy or pity felt. Similarly the principal difference between *kha'ris* and *e'le·os* is that *kha'ris* expresses especially the idea of a free and undeserved gift, thus emphasizing the free-heartedness and generosity of the giver, whereas *e'le·os* stresses the merciful response to the needs of those afflicted or disadvantaged. Thus, *kha'ris* (undeserved kindness) was shown by God to his own Son when he "kindly gave [*e·kha·ri'sa·to*] him the name that is above every other name." (Php 2:9) This kindness was motivated not by pity but by God's loving generosity.—See KINDNESS.

MERED (Me'red) [Rebellion]. A son of Ezrah mentioned in the genealogy of the tribe of Judah. Mered had an Egyptian wife, Bithiah the daughter of Pharaoh, by whom Mered had sons. (1Ch 4:1, 17, 18) The "Jewish" wife mentioned in verse 18 may have been another wife of Mered.

MEREMOTH (Mer'e·moth).

1. One of the head priests accompanying Zerubbabel from Babylon to Jerusalem in 537 B.C.E. (Ne 12:1-7) A priestly paternal house of the next generation is named "Meraioth," and it is possible that Meremoth was its founder. (Ne 12: 15) The names are rather similar as written in Hebrew characters.

2. Son of Urijah and a prominent priest in the days of Ezra and Nehemiah. When Ezra and a Jewish remnant came to Jerusalem from Babylon in 468 B.C.E., Meremoth was among the priests into whose hands they "proceeded to weigh out the silver and the gold and the utensils in the house" of Jehovah. (Ezr 8:31-34) Meremoth was a descendant of Hakkoz, some of whose descendants could not establish their genealogy. (Ezr 2:61, 62) But that the division of the family to which he belonged could verify its lineage is evident, since Meremoth shared in priestly functions. He also took part in doing repair work on Jerusalem's wall under Nehemiah's supervision.—Ne 3:3, 4, 21.

3. A priest, or the forefather of one of those attesting by seal the "trustworthy arrangement" of Nehemiah's day.—Ne 9:38–10:5.

4. An Israelite among "the sons of Bani" who had accepted foreign wives but sent them away "along with sons" in Ezra's day.—Ezr 10:25, 34, 36, 44.

MERES (Me'res). One of the seven princes whom Ahasuerus consulted when Vashti disobeyed him.—Es 1:14; see MEMUCAN.

MERIBAH (Mer'i·bah) [Quarreling].

1. A place in the vicinity of the Israelite wilderness encampment at Rephidim. It was there that Jehovah provided a miraculous supply of water when Moses struck the rock in Horeb with his rod. Moses then called the site "Massah" (meaning "Testing; Trial") and "Meribah" (meaning "Quarreling"). These names were commemorative of Israel's quarreling with Moses and its testing of God on account of the lack of water.—Ex 17:1-7.

2. The name "Meribah" was later also given to a location near Kadesh, the reason for the name likewise being Israel's quarreling with Moses and Jehovah about the lack of water. (Nu 20:1-13) Unlike the place near Rephidim, where the Israelites encamped less than two months after coming out of Egypt (Ex 16:1; 17:1; 19:1), this Meribah did not bear the name Massah. The Scriptures sometimes distinguish it from the other location by referring to "the waters of Meribah" (Ps 106:32) or "the waters of Meribah at Kadesh." (Nu 27:14; De 32:51) However, at Psalm 81:7 the reference to Jehovah's examining Israel by "the waters of Meribah" may allude to the incident at Meribah near Rephidim.—Compare De 33:8.

Moses and Aaron failed to sanctify Jehovah in connection with the miraculous provision of water at Meribah in the Kadesh area. Therefore they lost the privilege of entering the Promised Land. This event seems to have occurred in the 40th year of Israel's wilderness wanderings.—Nu 20:1, 9-13, 22-28; 33:38, 39.

MERIBATH-KADESH (Mer'i·bath-ka'desh) [Quarreling at Kadesh]. A southern limit of Israel's territory as seen by Ezekiel in vision. (Eze 47:13, 19; 48:28) The name Meribath-kadesh alludes to Israel's quarreling with Jehovah at "the waters of Meribah" while dwelling at Kadesh.—Nu 20:1-13; see KADESH, KADESH-BARNEA; MERIBAH No. 2.

MERIB-BAAL (Mer'ib-ba'al) [possibly, Contender Against Baal; or, Baal Makes a Legal Defense]. Grandson of King Saul, son of Jonathan, and the father of Micah. (1Ch 8:33, 34) This is apparently another name for Mephibosheth. Other persons also had two names, such as Eshbaal, also called Ish-bosheth.—Compare 2Sa 2:8 with 1Ch 8:33.

The name Merib-baal is found in two somewhat different Hebrew forms (*Meriv' ba''al* and *Meri-va''al*) at 1 Chronicles 9:40. The first form is also used at 1 Chronicles 8:34. Indicating similar identity is the fact that Mephibosheth had a boy named Mica and Merib-baal had a son named Micah. (Compare 2Sa 9:12 with 1Ch 9:40.) The forms "Mica" and "Micah" are due merely to a slight variation in the Hebrew spelling of these names.

MERODACH

MERODACH (Mer'o·dach). The Hebrew form for Marduk, the most important Babylonian god, whose downfall was foretold to coincide with Babylon's overthrow.—Jer 50:2.

The Babylonian Kings Merodach-baladan (Isa 39:1) and Evil-merodach (2Ki 25:27) were undoubtedly named after this god. With the rise of Babylon to prominence, because of King Hammurabi's making it the capital of Babylonia, Merodach likewise increased in importance. The attributes of earlier gods came to be assigned to him, and it is thought that the Babylonian priests altered the mythological accounts to make Merodach the slayer of Tiamat and the creator of the world and of man. Babylonian texts identify Marduk (Merodach) as the son of Ea (the god presiding over the watery element), the consort of Sarpanitu, and the father of Nebo.

The kingship over Babylon was closely associated with the image of Merodach at his temple, Esagila, for the rulers of Babylon were not installed by coronation but became kings by taking hold of the hand of Merodach. The ceremony was repeated each year at the New Year's festival. Even during the time that Assyria controlled Babylonia, the kings of Assyria were required to come to the city of Babylon each year for the New Year's festival and legalize their claim to the throne by taking hold of Merodach's hand.

Jeremiah the prophet, with respect to Babylon's fall, foretold that Merodach would "become terrified." This came true in the sense that Merodach proved to be unable to preserve the dignity of the Babylonian World Power, and since the conquerors of Babylon were worshipers of other deities, his future became very uncertain, filled with foreboding.—Jer 50:2; see BEL; GODS AND GODDESSES (Babylonian Deities).

MERODACH-BALADAN

MERODACH-BALADAN (Mer'o·dach-bal'a·dan) [from Babylonian, meaning "Marduk Has Given a Son"]. "The son of Baladan" and king of Babylon who sent letters and a gift to King Hezekiah of Judah following that king's recovery from illness. (Isa 39:1) He is called "Berodach-baladan" at 2 Kings 20:12, but this difference is generally considered to be the result of a scribal error, or else to represent an attempt at transliterating an Akkadian consonant with a sound somewhere between that of "m" and "b."

The name of Merodach-baladan occurs in Assyrian and Babylonian cuneiform inscriptions as "Marduk-apla-iddina." He there appears as the ruler of a Chaldean district known as Bit-Yakin, situated in the marshlands above the head of the Persian Gulf and S of Babylon. He claims royal

Merodach-baladan making a grant of land to an official; King Hezekiah was overly cordial to messengers from Merodach-baladan

descent, giving the name of King Eriba-Marduk of Babylon (considered as of the early part of the eighth century B.C.E.) as his forefather.—*Iraq,* London, 1953, Vol. XV, p. 124.

Tiglath-pileser III, whose rule extended into the reign of King Ahaz of Judah (761-746 B.C.E.), refers to Merodach-baladan as ruler of a Chaldean tribe rendering homage to him when the Assyrians made a campaign into Babylonia.

Sends Delegation to Hezekiah. Merodach-baladan is stated to have entered Babylon and proclaimed himself king at the time of the accession of Sargon II to the Assyrian throne. Merodach-baladan had the support of the Elamites in this action, and although Sargon soon endeavored to dislodge him from Babylon, the Chaldean was able to maintain his position there for a period of about 12 years, according to the Babylonian King List. It may have been during this time that he sent his embassy to King Hezekiah, either in the 14th year of the Judean king (732 B.C.E.) or shortly thereafter. It is suggested by some, including Jewish historian Josephus, that Merodach-baladan's expressions of interest in Hezekiah's health involved more than a formality and that his ulterior motive was to attempt to gain the support of the kingdom of Judah, along with that of Elam, in a coalition against Assyria. At any rate, Hezekiah's action in showing the royal treasure-house and his armory (2Ki 20:13) to the Chaldean's messengers was roundly condemned by the prophet Isaiah as presaging eventual conquest of Judah by Babylon.—Isa 39:2-7.

Defeated by Assyria. Toward the close of his rule of approximately 12 years over Babylon, Merodach-baladan saw his main support from Elam cut off by an Assyrian victory over that kingdom, and thereafter he was attacked and forced to flee from Babylon. Despite losing Babylon to the Assyrians, Merodach-baladan appears to have been able to retain his position as ruler over Bit-Yakin. The Babylonian King List shows a second reign of nine months (Polyhistor says six months) by "Mardukaplaiddin" as king of Babylon during the second year after Sargon's death. This is generally accepted as referring to the same king making a second effort to establish himself on the throne of Babylon. It is to be noted, however, that the Babylonian inscriptions in this case refer to him as "Mardukaplaiddin, a native of Habi," in contrast with "Mardukaplaiddin, [of the] dynasty of the Sea Country," in the case of the earlier reign. (*Ancient Near Eastern Texts,* edited by J. Pritchard, 1974, p. 272) This second reign was very short, as Assyrian King Sennacherib quickly occupied Babylon, and Merodach-baladan had to seek refuge in Elam, where he seems to have ended his ambitious career. Despite Merodach-baladan's failures, in later times the Chaldeans did become the dominant ethnic group in the Babylonian Empire.

MEROM, WATERS OF (Mer'om) [High (Exalted) Place].

It was here that the confederate Canaanite forces under Jabin the king of Hazor encamped before being defeated by Joshua. Probably for the first time the Israelites faced Canaanites equipped with horses and chariots, as may be inferred from Joshua's receiving divine instructions then about burning the chariots and hamstringing the horses.—Jos 11:1-9.

As explained by Y. Aharoni, "The 'waters of Merom' must be the water source of the city Merom beside which the Canaanite forces assembled. Merom is known both from second-millennium Egyptian sources . . . and from Tiglath-pileser III's account of his expedition to

Galilee . . . It is generally accepted to identify Merom with Meirun at the foot of Jebel Jarmaq, but in the absence of a suitable tell at this site, an identification a bit farther north is preferable. Its name is possibly preserved in Jebel Marun and Marun er-Ras, and we may consider its identification with Tell el-Khirbeh, one of the large Canaanite tells in the southern part of Canaanite Upper Galilee. From Hazor both of the suggested identifications are about seven to eight miles as the crow flies."—*The Land of the Bible,* translated and edited by A. Rainey, 1979, pp. 225, 226.

MERONOTHITE (Me·ron'o·thite).

A designation applied to Jehdeiah and Jadon, apparently identifying them as inhabitants of Meronoth. (1Ch 27:30; Ne 3:7) Some scholars believe that Meronoth was located near Gibeah, but its exact location is otherwise unknown. Others tentatively identify it with Beituniya, less than 5 km (3 mi) NNW of Gibeon.

MEROZ (Me'roz).

A place cursed by an angel for not coming "to the assistance of Jehovah." (Jg 5:23) It may be that the inhabitants of Meroz did not aid Jehovah's designated commander Barak in the actual fight against the Canaanites under Sisera. (Jg 5:5-16) Or, if Meroz lay on defeated Sisera's escape route, perhaps its inhabitants failed to detain him. (Jg 4:17) The fact that the Bible account next relates Jael's courageous act in killing Sisera lends some support to the latter view. (Jg 5:24-27) The angel pronouncing the curse possibly was one who fought for Israel.

Meroz' exact location is unknown, although some tentatively place it at Khirbet Marus, about 8 km (5 mi) S of Kedesh in Naphtali.

MESHA (Me'sha).

1. Firstborn son of "Caleb the son of Hezron" of the tribe of Judah. Mesha was the father, or founder, of Ziph.—1Ch 2:18, 42.

2. King of Moab in the time of Kings Jehoshaphat of Judah and Ahab, Ahaziah, and Jehoram of Israel. The Moabites, under subjugation to the northern kingdom of Israel, paid King Ahab a tribute of 100,000 lambs and 100,000 unshorn male sheep, apparently of a breed noted for their quality of wool. Following Ahab's death, Mesha rebelled against Israel's King Ahaziah. But Ahaziah died after a short rule and was succeeded by his brother Jehoram, who secured an alliance with Jehoshaphat of Judah and an unidentified king of Edom, in order to bring Mesha again under subjection. Taking a difficult route S of the Dead Sea, their forces ran out of water. But Elisha the prophet gave assurance that if ditches were dug in the

dried-up torrent valley, Jehovah would fill them with water.—2Ki 1:1; 3:4-19.

This occurred, and the reflection of the early morning sun upon the water made it look like blood to the Moabites, possibly because of red clay in the freshly cut ditches. The illusion deceived them into thinking the allied armies of Israel, Judah, and Edom had turned on one another. It was not unreasonable for them to think this, in view of the fact that they knew of the jealousy between Israel and Judah. Also, the Edomites were no lovers of the men of Judah, who were allied with Israel on this occasion.—2Ki 3:20-23; compare 2Ch 20:10, 11, 24, 25.

Thinking their enemies had slaughtered one another, the Moabites shouted, "So now, to the spoil, O Moab!" and entered the camp of Israel, only to be put to flight. Israel followed up by destroying the Moabite cities, stopping up their springs, and filling their tracts of land with stones, until they got to the city of Kir-hareseth (Kir of Moab).—2Ki 3:23-25.

When King Mesha found himself trapped, he took 700 swordsmen and tried in a counterattack to break through to the king of Edom (perhaps because he thought that there he would meet with the weakest resistance), but he was unable to do so. "Finally he took his firstborn son who was going to reign in place of him and offered him up as a burnt sacrifice upon the wall."—2Ki 3:26, 27.

The majority of commentators agree that Mesha offered up his own son as a sacrifice to his god Chemosh. The few who think otherwise say it was a captured son of the king of Edom that was sacrificed, citing Amos 2:1 as evidence, where reference is made to Moab "burning the bones of the king of Edom for lime." Though grammatically the Hebrew will allow for such an interpretation, this latter suggestion seems contrary to other known facts. For example, it was unheard of for Moabites and Ammonites, Israel's neighbors, to offer up their enemies as sacrifices to their gods, but it was a known practice of their religion to offer their own children as burnt sacrifices to appease the anger of their gods. (De 12:30, 31; Mic 6:6, 7) It is therefore understandable why this Chemosh worshiper, Mesha, faced with imminent danger of defeat, would have resorted to such drastic measures.

The Moabite Stone. The Moabite Stone was discovered at Dhiban (Dibon) in 1868. It is generally accredited to Mesha, and its contents are usually assigned to the period covered by the events recorded in the third chapter of Second Kings. In this famous inscription, Mesha commemorates his breaking Israel's domination, which he says lasted 40 years. There are also various comments made therein about the places Mesha captured (Medeba, Ataroth, Nebo, Jahaz). In boasting of his being very religious, of building cities and a highway, as well as of a victory that he claims over Israel, Mesha gives all the credit to the god Chemosh. Mesha also knew of Israel's God Jehovah, for in the 18th line of this document the Tetragrammaton is found. There Mesha brags: "I took from there the [vessels] of Yahweh, dragging them before Chemosh." (PICTURE, Vol. 1, p. 946) However, his own defeat and the sacrifice of his son are, as one would expect, omitted. *Biblical Archaeology Review* (May/June 1986, p. 57) observes: "Monumental inscriptions on freestanding stones or temple walls were produced for propaganda purposes and for the glorification of the national god and the country's ruler. Hence, it is not surprising that Mesha makes no mention of the military campaign of the kings of Israel, Judah and Edom against his country, of which the Bible gives us a detailed account."

3. [Heb., *Meh·sha'*]. A son of Shaharaim by his wife Hodesh. Mesha became a family head in the tribe of Benjamin.—1Ch 8:1, 8-10.

4. [Heb., *Me·sha'*]. One of the limits of the region inhabited by the descendants of Joktan. (Ge 10:29, 30) The Greek *Septuagint* has translated the name Mesha as *Mas·se*. For this reason "Mesha" is thought to be a variant spelling for "Massa," the name of an Ishmaelite whose descendants appear to have settled in Arabia.—Ge 25: 13, 14.

MESHACH (Me'shach). The Babylonian name given by Nebuchadnezzar's chief court official to Daniel's companion Mishael. The meaning of this new name is uncertain, but it may have included a reference to Aku, a Sumerian god.

Maintains Integrity as a Youth. Meshach (Mishael) was carried captive from Jerusalem to Babylon in 617 B.C.E. along with Jehoiachin and others. Mishael, Azariah, Hananiah, and Daniel were then put through a three-year training course by the Babylonian royalty, at the end of which they proved superior even to the king's counselors. (2Ki 24:1, 6, 8, 12-16; Da 1:1-7, 17-20) During this time these four remained firm in their devotion to God, even refusing to pollute themselves with the king's delicacies.—Da 1:8-16.

There are three probable reasons why they considered the king's delicacies 'polluting': (1) The Babylonians ate animals declared unclean by the Mosaic Law; (2) they would not be careful to see that the animals were properly bled, some perhaps being strangled; (3) the pagans often first sacrificed the animals to their gods, considering the eating of such meat as a part of worship of these gods.—Da 1:8; compare 1Co 10:18-20, 28.

Later, after Daniel had been advanced to a high governmental position in the court of the king, Nebuchadnezzar, at Daniel's request, appointed Meshach, Shadrach, and Abednego over the administration of the jurisdictional district of Babylon.—Da 2:48, 49.

Refuses to Bow to Image. Meshach and his two companions again came to the king's notice because of refusing, in the sight of all the other government personnel, to bow down before the great image Nebuchadnezzar had made. With full faith in Jehovah, they told Nebuchadnezzar that they would not join in serving the king's gods. Whether their God chose to deliver them from the furnace made no difference; they would nonetheless maintain integrity to him rather than compromise for release. (In Heb 11:34, 35 mention is made of those who "stayed the force of fire" and who would not "accept release by some ransom, in order that they might attain a better resurrection.") For their faith Jehovah preserved them by means of his angel. In fact, on their coming out, "the smell of fire itself had not come onto them." Nebuchadnezzar, who had been so enraged that he ordered the furnace to be heated seven times more than customary before throwing the three men into it, now acknowledged their God as a deliverer. Furthermore, he commanded that anyone saying anything wrong against Meshach's God should be dismembered and his house made a public privy.—Da 3:1-30.

MESHECH (Me'shech).

1. One of the sons born after the Flood to Japheth, the son of Noah. (Ge 10:2; 1Ch 1:5) The name evidently extended to his descendants and the land of their settlement. The prophet Ezekiel regularly mentions Meshech along with Tubal, indicating that they were located to the N of Palestine. They are described as exporting slaves and copper to Tyre, as being warlike, and as either allies or subjects of 'Gog of Magog' in his prophesied vicious campaign against "the mountains of Israel." (Eze 27:13; 32:26; 38:2, 3; 39:1, 2; see GOG No. 2.) Meshech is mentioned independently of Tubal at Psalm 120:5, evidently as representing an aggressive, barbarous people.

About a thousand years after the Flood, Assyrian inscriptions begin to mention a people called the Mushku occupying an area in Asia Minor to the W of Assyria. Assyrian Emperors Tiglath-pileser I, Tukulti-Ninurta II, Ashurnasirpal II, and Sargon all mention conflicts with them. The fact that the *Mushku* are frequently mentioned along with the *Tabalu* (evidently the Biblical Tubal) gives reason for believing that the name *Mushku* derives from Meshech. Herodotus (III, 94) later refers to the Moschi and the Tibareni in the same manner.

Many scholars suggest that the *Mushku* are to be related with the Phrygians, who apparently dominated much of western and central Asia Minor about the close of the second millennium B.C.E. King Mita of Muski, referred to by Assyrian Emperor Sargon, is construed by some scholars as being identical with King Midas of Phrygia, described in Greek tradition as ruling in the same period.

2. Meshech appears in the Masoretic text at 1 Chronicles 1:17 as a descendant of Shem, but the corresponding genealogy at Genesis 10:23 reads "Mash."

MESHELEMIAH (Me·shel·e·mi'ah) [Jehovah Makes Peace (Compensates; Repays)]. A Kohathite Levite and ancestral head of a division of Korahites. He "had sons and brothers, capable men, eighteen," who were assigned with him as gatekeepers of the sanctuary during King David's reorganization of the priestly and Levitical services. (1Ch 26:1-3, 9) He is probably identical with the Shelemiah of 1 Chronicles 26:14. His son Zechariah "was the gatekeeper of the entrance of the tent of meeting."—1Ch 9:21.

MESHEZABEL (Me·shez'a·bel).

1. A man of Judah of the family of Zerah and whose "son" Pethahiah "was at the side of the king for every matter of the people."—Ne 11:24.

2. Father of Berechiah and ancestor of the Meshullam who did repair work on the wall of Jerusalem in Nehemiah's day.—Ne 3:4.

3. One of "the heads of the people," or his descendant, who attested by seal the "trustworthy arrangement" of Nehemiah's time.—Ne 9:38; 10:1, 14, 21.

MESHILLEMITH (Me·shil'le·mith) [from a root meaning "make peace; compensate; repay"]. A priest and descendant of Immer. (1Ch 9:10, 12) He is probably the same person as the Meshillemoth of Nehemiah 11:13.

MESHILLEMOTH (Me·shil'le·moth) [from a root meaning "make peace; compensate; repay"].

1. An Ephraimite whose "son" Berechiah was one of the headmen of Ephraim who persuaded

the Israelites of King Pekah's day to release the captives they had taken in a successful military campaign against Judah.—2Ch 28:6-8, 12-15.

2. A priest who descended from Immer and who was the ancestor of certain priests residing in Jerusalem after the Jews returned from Babylonian exile. (Ne 11:10, 13, 14) He is probably identical with the Meshillemith of 1 Chronicles 9:12.

MESHOBAB (Me·sho′bab) [Returned (Brought Back); or, possibly, Unfaithful]. A chieftain of the tribe of Simeon who had a large household and who participated in the seizure of pasturelands from the Hamites and the Meunim near Gedor in the days of King Hezekiah of Judah.—1Ch 4:34-42.

MESHULLAM (Me·shul′lam) [from a root meaning "make peace; compensate; repay"].

1. A family head in the tribe of Benjamin who lived in Jerusalem; son of Elpaal.—1Ch 8:1, 17, 18, 28.

2. A leading Gadite resident of Bashan enrolled genealogically as a son of Abihail during the reigns of Jotham and of Jeroboam II (apparently two different enrollments, for the reigns of these kings did not overlap).—1Ch 5:11, 13, 14, 16, 17.

3. Grandfather or ancestor of King Josiah's secretary Shaphan.—2Ki 22:3.

4. Father or ancestor of High Priest Hilkiah of King Josiah's reign. (1Ch 9:11; Ne 11:11) Meshullam himself had perhaps acted as high priest. Some of his descendants lived in Jerusalem after the Babylonian exile. He is apparently called Shallum at 1 Chronicles 6:12, 13 and Ezra 7:2—See SHALLUM No. 7.

5. A Kohathite Levite, one of several in charge of repairing the temple under King Josiah.—2Ch 34:1, 8, 12.

6. A priest whose descendants (at least three generations after him) lived in Jerusalem after the exile in Babylon.—1Ch 9:2, 3, 10, 12.

7. A Benjamite whose son Sallu was a family head in Jerusalem after the Babylonian exile. (1Ch 9:3, 7, 9) Presumably the same as the Meshullam listed in Nehemiah 11:7.

8. A Benjamite family head who himself lived in Jerusalem after the exile.—1Ch 9:3, 7-9.

9. The first-listed son of Governor Zerubbabel; descendant of King David.—1Ch 3:1, 19.

10. Head of the priestly paternal house of Ezra in the days of Jeshua's successor Joiakim. (Ne 12:12, 13) Possibly the same as No. 18 or 19.

11. Head of the paternal house of priests founded by Ginnethon; during the officiate of Joiakim. (Ne 12:12, 16) Possibly the same as No. 18 or 19.

12. A gatekeeper in the days of Joiakim, Ezra, and Nehemiah.—Ne 12:25, 26.

13. A head one among the people assembled at the river Ahava for the trip to Jerusalem with Ezra in 468 B.C.E. Meshullam was one of several whom Ezra assigned to help gather a number of Levites and Nethinim to make the journey also. (Ezr 8:15-20) Possibly the same as No. 16, 17, 20, or 21.

14. A Levite who perhaps opposed the admonition to send away the foreign wives Ezra found among the Israelites on his return to Jerusalem. However, the text may be read to mean that he opposed only the procedure adopted for carrying it out.—Ezr 10:10-15, ftn.

15. One of the "sons" or descendants of Bani who responded favorably to Ezra's admonition by sending away their foreign wives and sons.—Ezr 10:29, 44.

16. Son of Berechiah who, under direction of Governor Nehemiah, repaired two sections of Jerusalem's wall. (Ne 3:4, 30) Meshullam also gave his daughter in marriage to Jehohanan the son of Tobiah the Ammonite, a marriage union that caused division among the restored Israelites. —Ne 6:17-19; 4:3; see No. 13.

17. Co-rebuilder of the Gate of the Old City in Nehemiah's wall-repair project; son of Besodeiah. —Ne 3:6; see No. 13.

18. One of those who stood at Ezra's left when he read from the Law to the assembled crowd in the seventh month of 455 B.C.E. Meshullam was probably a priest.—Ne 8:2, 4; see Nos. 10 and 11.

19. A priest (or forefather of a priest) who subscribed to the covenant of faithfulness proposed by the Levites.—Ne 9:5, 38; 10:1, 7, 8; see Nos. 10 and 11.

20. A headman of the people whose descendant, if not he himself, also attested to the same contract.—Ne 10:1, 14, 20; see No. 13.

21. Apparently a prince of Judah who marched in one of the processional groups when Jerusalem's rebuilt wall was inaugurated.—Ne 12:32, 33; see No. 13.

MESHULLEMETH (Me·shul′le·meth) [the feminine form of Meshullam]. Daughter of "Haruz from Jotbah" who became the wife of Judean King Manasseh and the mother of King Amon.—2Ki 21:19, 20.

MESOPOTAMIA (Mes·o·po·ta′mi·a) [from Gr. meaning "[Land] Between Rivers"]. The Greek term for the stretch of land located between the Tigris and Euphrates rivers. It apparently corresponds to the Hebrew designation of related meaning, Aram-naharaim. (Ps 60:Sup) In fact, the translators of the Greek *Septuagint* usually rendered "Aram-naharaim" as "Mesopotamia."—See ARAM No. 5.

The application of the term "Mesopotamia" varies both in ancient and modern usage. Basically, in a broad sense, it embraces the entire region that lies between the Tigris and the Euphrates and stretches from the Persian Gulf in the S to the mountains of Turkey and Iran in the N. This would include the alluvial plain of ancient Babylonia extending some 400 km (250 mi) to the S of Baghdad. (See BABYLON No. 2.) In a narrower sense, however, Babylonia is excluded, only the region to the N being termed Mesopotamia. This northern region consists of a low undulating plateau having numerous enclosed basins. It is also a rocky area.

Evidence for the broad usage of the designation in the first century C.E. is found at Acts 7:2, where Stephen spoke of Abraham as residing in "Mesopotamia" while yet at Ur, a city of Babylonia. But it is not possible to establish with certainty whether the Hebrew "Aram-naharaim" likewise included Babylonia. Whenever there is a basis for determining the general geographic location mentioned in the Hebrew Scriptures, the northern area around Haran (Ge 24:2-4, 10) or the northern mountainous region around Pethor (De 23:4; compare Nu 23:7) is included under the designation "Aram-naharaim" (Mesopotamia). Although the extent of the area under the control of Mesopotamian King Cushan-rishathaim (the oppressor of Israel in the time of Judge Othniel) is uncertain, the seat of his government may also have been in the N. (Jg 3:8-10; see CUSHAN-RISHATHAIM.) It was probably from northern Mesopotamia that Ammonite King Hanun hired chariots and horsemen for his fight against King David.—1Ch 19:6, 7.

Among the Jews and proselytes present at Jerusalem for the Festival of Pentecost in 33 C.E., there were inhabitants of Mesopotamia. (Ac 2:1, 2, 9) These could have included residents from the southern part of that land, namely, Babylonia. In this regard it is noteworthy that the historian Josephus reports that "a great number of Jews" were in Babylonia in the first century B.C.E. —*Jewish Antiquities*, XV, 14 (ii, 2).

MESSENGER. One bearing a message, either oral or written, or one sent on an errand. (Ge 32:3-6; Jg 6:34, 35; 11:12-27; 2Sa 5:11; 1Ki 19:2; 2Ki 19:8-14; Lu 7:18-24; 9:52) At times runners served in this capacity. (2Ch 30:6-10; Jer 51:31) For more rapid communication messengers were dispatched on horses. (2Ki 9:17-19; Es 8:10-14; see COURIER.) Messengers of ancient times included heralds who publicly proclaimed royal or state decrees. (Da 3:4-6; 5:29) Messengers might be sent to sue for peace (Isa 33:7), to request military assistance (2Ki 16:7; 17:4), or to demand tribute or the surrender of a city (1Ki 20:1-9; 2Ki 18:17-35). They were accorded freedom of passage to accomplish their mission. A mistreatment of royal messengers sent on a courtesy visit to another nation was serious enough to precipitate war.—2Sa 10:1-7; see AMBASSADOR.

Both the Hebrew and the Greek words for "messenger" may refer to spirit messengers, or angels. (Ps 104:4; Joh 1:51) Whether human or angelic messengers are meant can be determined by the context. At Isaiah 63:9, for example, Jehovah's "personal messenger" is evidently his angel, for this messenger saved the Israelites.—Compare Ex 14:19, 20.

Besides using angelic messengers to convey information to men and women on earth and to accomplish other tasks (see ANGEL), Jehovah has repeatedly employed human messengers. His prophets and priests were his messengers to the nation of Israel. (2Ch 36:15, 16; Hag 1:13; Mal 2:7) The statements of his prophets were certain of fulfillment, for Jehovah is "the One that carries out completely the counsel of his own messengers." —Isa 44:26.

"Messenger of the Covenant." In fulfillment of Malachi 3:1, John the Baptizer appeared as the messenger who prepared the way before Jehovah by getting the Jews ready for the coming of God's chief representative, Jesus Christ.—Mt 11:10, 11; Mr 1:1-4; Lu 7:27, 28.

As the foretold "messenger of the covenant," Jesus Christ came to the temple and cleansed it. (Mt 21:12, 13; Mr 11:15-17; Lu 19:45, 46) He evidently was the messenger of the Abrahamic covenant, for it was on the basis of this covenant that the Jews were the first ones to be granted the opportunity to become Kingdom heirs. This was the covenant to which Peter appealed when calling upon the Jews to repent. It is also noteworthy that John the Baptizer's father, Zechariah, referred to the Abrahamic covenant in connection with Jehovah's raising up 'a horn of salvation in the house of David,' this horn being the Messiah. —Compare Mt 10:5-7; 15:24; 21:31; Lu 1:69-75; Ac 3:12, 19-26.

MESSIAH. From the Hebrew root verb *ma-shach'*, meaning "smear," and so "anoint." (Ex 29:2, 7) Messiah (*ma·shi'ach*) means "anointed" or "anointed one." The Greek equivalent is *Khri·stos'*, or Christ.—Mt 2:4, ftn.

In the Hebrew Scriptures the verbal adjective form *ma·shi'ach* is applied to many men. David was officially appointed to be king by being anointed with oil and so is spoken of as "anointed one" or, literally, "messiah." (2Sa 19:21; 22:51; 23:1; Ps 18:50) Other kings, including Saul and Solomon, are termed "anointed one" or "the anointed of Jehovah." (1Sa 2:10, 35; 12:3, 5; 24:6, 10; 2Sa 1:14, 16; 2Ch 6:42; La 4:20) The term is also applied to the high priest. (Le 4:3, 5, 16; 6:22) The patriarchs Abraham, Isaac, and Jacob are called Jehovah's "anointed ones." (1Ch 16:16, 22, ftn) Persian King Cyrus is termed "anointed one," in that he was appointed by God for a certain assignment.—Isa 45:1; see ANOINTED, ANOINTING.

In the Christian Greek Scriptures the transliterated form *Mes·si'as* occurs in the Greek text at John 1:41, with the explanation, "which means, when translated, Christ." (See also Joh 4:25.) Sometimes the word *Khri·stos'* is used alone with reference to the one who is or who claims to be the Messiah, or the Anointed One. (Mt 2:4; 22:42; Mr 13:21) In most of its appearances, though, *Khri·stos'* is accompanied by the personal name Jesus, as in the expressions "Jesus Christ" or "Christ Jesus," to designate *him* as the Messiah. At times the word is used alone but specifically referring to Jesus with the understanding that Jesus is The Christ, as in the statement, "Christ died for us." —Ro 5:8; Joh 17:3; 1Co 1:1, 2; 16:24; see CHRIST.

Messiah in the Hebrew Scriptures. At Daniel 9:25, 26 the word *ma·shi'ach* applies *exclusively* to the coming Messiah. (See SEVENTY WEEKS.) However, many other texts of the Hebrew Scriptures also point to this coming One, even if not exclusively so. For instance, Psalm 2:2 evidently had first application at the time when Philistine kings tried to unseat anointed King David. But a second application, to the foretold Messiah, is established by Acts 4:25-27, where the text is applied to Jesus Christ. Also, many of the men called "anointed" in various ways prefigured, or pictured, Jesus Christ and the work he would do; among these were David, the high priest of Israel, and Moses (spoken of as "Christ" at Heb 11:23-26).

Prophecies not using "Messiah." Numerous other Hebrew Scripture texts that do not specifically mention "Messiah" were understood by the Jews as prophecies applying to that one. Alfred Edersheim located 456 passages to which the "ancient Synagogue referred as Messianic," and there were 558 references in the most ancient rabbinic writings supporting such applications. (*The Life and Times of Jesus the Messiah,* 1906, Vol. I, p. 163; Vol. II, pp. 710-737) As an example, Genesis 49:10 prophesied that the ruling scepter would belong to the tribe of Judah and that Shiloh would come through that line. The Targum of Onkelos, the Jerusalem Targum, and the Midrash all recognize the expression "Shiloh" as applying to the Messiah.

The Hebrew Scriptures contain many prophecies that provide details about the Messiah's background, time of appearance, activities, treatment by others, and place in God's arrangement. The various indications about the Messiah thus combined to form one grand picture that would help true worshipers to identify him. This would provide a basis for faith in him as the true Leader sent by Jehovah. Though the Jews did not recognize ahead of time all the prophecies that related to the Anointed One, the evidence in the Gospels shows that they had sufficient knowledge by which to recognize the Messiah when he did appear.

Understanding in the First Century C.E. The historical information available reveals a general picture of the extent of understanding about the Messiah prevalent among Jews in the first century of the Common Era. Primarily this information is gleaned from the Gospels.

King and son of David. It was commonly accepted among the Jews that the Messiah would be a king of the line of David. When the astrologers asked about "the one born king of the Jews," Herod the Great knew that they were asking about "the Christ." (Mt 2:2-4) Jesus questioned the Pharisees as to whose descendant the Christ, or Messiah, would be. Though those religious leaders did not believe in Jesus, they knew that the Messiah would be David's son.—Mt 22:41-45.

Born in Bethlehem. Micah 5:2, 4 had indicated that out of Bethlehem would come one to be "ruler in Israel" who would "be great as far as the ends of the earth." This was understood to refer to the Messiah. When Herod the Great asked the chief priests and scribes where the Messiah was to be born, they answered, "In Bethlehem of Judea," and quoted Micah 5:2. (Mt 2:3-6) And even some of the common people knew this.—Joh 7:41, 42.

A prophet who would perform many signs. Through Moses, God had foretold the coming of a great prophet. (De 18:18) In Jesus' day Jews were waiting for this one. (Joh 6:14) The way in which the apostle Peter used Moses' words, at Acts 3:22, 23, indicates he knew they would be accepted as Messianic in nature even by religious opposers, and this gives evidence of widespread understanding of Deuteronomy 18:18. The Samaritan

OUTSTANDING PROPHECIES CONCERNING JESUS AND THEIR FULFILLMENT

Prophecy	Event	Fulfillment
Ge 49:10	Born of the tribe of Judah	Mt 1:2-16; Lu 3:23-33; Heb 7:14
Ps 132:11; Isa 9:7; 11:1, 10	From the family of David the son of Jesse	Mt 1:1, 6-16; 9:27; Ac 13:22, 23; Ro 1:3; 15:8, 12
Mic 5:2	Born in Bethlehem	Lu 2:4-11; Joh 7:42
Isa 7:14	Born of a virgin	Mt 1:18-23; Lu 1:30-35
Jer 31:15	Babes killed after his birth	Mt 2:16-18
Ho 11:1	Called out of Egypt	Mt 2:15
Mal 3:1; 4:5; Isa 40:3	Way prepared before	Mt 3:1-3; 11:10-14; 17:10-13; Lu 1:17, 76; 3:3-6; 7:27; Joh 1:20-23; 3:25-28; Ac 13:24; 19:4
Isa 61:1, 2	Commissioned	Lu 4:18-21
Isa 9:1, 2	Ministry caused people in Naphtali and Zebulun to see great light	Mt 4:13-16
Ps 78:2	Spoke with illustrations	Mt 13:11-13, 31-35
Isa 53:4	Carried our sicknesses	Mt 8:16, 17
Ps 69:9	Zealous for Jehovah's house	Mt 21:12, 13; Joh 2:13-17
Isa 42:1-4	As Jehovah's servant, would not wrangle in streets	Mt 12:14-21
Isa 53:1	Not believed in	Joh 12:37, 38; Ro 10:11, 16
Zec 9:9; Ps 118:26	Entry into Jerusalem on colt of an ass; hailed as king and one coming in Jehovah's name	Mt 21:1-9; Mr 11:7-11; Lu 19:28-38; Joh 12:12-15
Isa 28:16; 53:3; Ps 69:8; 118:22, 23	Rejected but becomes chief cornerstone	Mt 21:42, 45, 46; Ac 3:14; 4:11; 1Pe 2:7
Isa 8:14, 15	Becomes stone of stumbling	Lu 20:17, 18; Ro 9:31-33
Ps 41:9; 109:8	One apostle unfaithful, betrays him	Mt 26:47-50; Joh 13:18, 26-30; Ac 1:16-20
Zec 11:12	Betrayed for 30 pieces of silver	Mt 26:15; 27:3-10; Mr 14:10, 11
Zec 13:7	Disciples scatter	Mt 26:31, 56; Joh 16:32
Ps 2:1, 2	Roman powers and leaders of Israel act together against anointed of Jehovah	Mt 27:1, 2; Mr 15:1, 15; Lu 23:10-12; Ac 4:25-28
Isa 53:8	Tried and condemned	Mt 26:57-68; 27:1, 2, 11-26; Joh 18:12-14, 19-24, 28-40; 19:1-16
Ps 27:12	Use of false witnesses	Mt 26:59-61; Mr 14:56-59
Isa 53:7	Silent before accusers	Mt 27:12-14; Mr 14:61; 15:4, 5; Lu 23:9
Ps 69:4	Hated without cause	Lu 23:13-25; Joh 15:24, 25
Isa 50:6; Mic 5:1	Struck, spit on	Mt 26:67; 27:26, 30; Joh 19:3
Ps 22:16, ftn	Impaled	Mt 27:35; Mr 15:24, 25; Lu 23:33; Joh 19:18, 23; 20:25, 27
Ps 22:18	Lots cast for garments	Mt 27:35; Joh 19:23, 24
Isa 53:12	Numbered with sinners	Mt 26:55, 56; 27:38; Lu 22:37
Ps 22:7, 8	Reviled while on stake	Mt 27:39-43; Mr 15:29-32
Ps 69:21	Given vinegar and gall	Mt 27:34, 48; Mr 15:23, 36
Ps 22:1	Forsaken by God to enemies	Mt 27:46; Mr 15:34
Ps 34:20; Ex 12:46	No bones broken	Joh 19:33, 36
Isa 53:5; Zec 12:10	Pierced	Mt 27:49; Joh 19:34, 37; Re 1:7
Isa 53:5, 8, 11, 12	Dies sacrificial death to carry away sins and open way to righteous standing with God	Mt 20:28; Joh 1:29; Ro 3:24; 4:25; 1Co 15:3; Heb 9:12-15; 1Pe 2:24; 1Jo 2:2
Isa 53:9	Buried with the rich	Mt 27:57-60; Joh 19:38-42
Jon 1:17; 2:10	In grave parts of three days, then resurrected	Mt 12:39, 40; 16:21; 17:23; 27:64; 28:1-7; Ac 10:40; 1Co 15:3-8
Ps 16:8-11, ftn	Raised before corruption	Ac 2:25-31; 13:34-37
Ps 2:7	Jehovah declares him His Son by spirit begetting and by resurrection	Mt 3:16, 17; Mr 1:9-11; Lu 3:21, 22; Ac 13:33; Ro 1:4; Heb 1:5; 5:5

woman by the well also thought the Messiah would be a prophet. (Joh 4:19, 25, 29) People expected the Messiah to perform signs.—Joh 7:31.

Some variety in beliefs. It is evident that even though knowledge about the coming Messiah was common among the Jews, not all persons had the same knowledge or understanding about that one. For instance, though many knew that he would come from Bethlehem, some did not. (Mt 2:3-6; Joh 7:27) Some believed the Prophet to be separate from the Christ. (Joh 1:20, 21; 7:40, 41) Certain prophecies about the Messiah were not understood, even by Jesus' disciples. This was particularly true about those prophecies dealing with the Messiah's rejection, suffering, death, and resurrection. (Isa 53:3, 5, 12; Ps 16:10; Mt 16: 21-23; 17:22, 23; Lu 24:21; Joh 12:34; 20:9) Yet once these things had taken place and the prophecies had been explained, his disciples and even ones who were not yet disciples began to appreciate the prophetic nature of these texts in the Hebrew Scriptures. (Lu 24:45, 46; Ac 2:5, 27, 28, 31, 36, 37; 8:30-35) Since the fact that the Messiah had to suffer and die was not recognized by most Jews, this point was stressed by early Christians when preaching to Jews.—Ac 3:18; 17:1-3; 26: 21-23.

Wrong Expectations. Luke's account indicates that many Jews were anxiously expecting the Messiah to appear at the particular time Jesus was on earth. Simeon and other Jews were "waiting for Israel's consolation" and "Jerusalem's deliverance" when the babe Jesus was brought to the temple. (Lu 2:25, 38) During the ministry of John the Baptizer, the people "were in expectation" about the Christ, or Messiah. (Lu 3:15) Many, though, expected the Messiah to meet their preconceived notions. The prophecies in the Hebrew Scriptures showed the Messiah as coming in two different roles. One was "humble, and riding upon an ass," whereas the other was "with the clouds of the heavens" to annihilate opposers and have all rulerships serve him. (Zec 9:9; Da 7:13) The Jews failed to appreciate the fact that these prophecies related to two distinct appearances of the Messiah, these appearances occurring at widely separated times.

Jewish sources agree with Luke 2:38 that the people at that time were waiting for Jerusalem's deliverance. *The Jewish Encyclopedia* observes: "They yearned for the promised deliverer of the house of David, who would free them from the yoke of the hated foreign usurper, would put an end to the impious Roman rule, and would establish His own reign of peace." (1976, Vol. VIII, p. 508) They tried to make him an earthly king. (Joh 6:15) When he would not fulfill their expectations, they rejected him.

Evidently the expectation that the Messiah would be an earthly king was shared by John the Baptizer and his disciples. John knew Jesus to be the Messiah and the Son of God, having seen him anointed with holy spirit and having heard God's voice of approval. John did not lack faith. (Mt 11:11) So his question, "Are we to expect a different one?" may have meant, 'Are we to expect yet another one who will fulfill all the hopes of the Jews?' Christ in reply pointed to the works he was doing (which things had been foretold in the Hebrew Scriptures). He concluded: "And happy is he who has not stumbled over me." This answer, while implying that faith and discernment would be needed, would satisfy and comfort John, assuring him that Jesus was the One who would fulfill God's promises. (Mt 11:3; Lu 7:18-23) Also, prior to his ascension, Jesus' disciples held the view that he would at that time deliver Israel from Gentile domination and set up the Kingdom (restore the reign of the Davidic line) on earth.—Lu 24:21; Ac 1:6.

False Messiahs. After Jesus' death, the Jews followed many false Messiahs, as Jesus had foretold. (Mt 24:5) "From Josephus it appears that in the first century before the destruction of the Temple [in 70 C.E.] a number of Messiahs arose promising relief from the Roman yoke, and finding ready followers." (*The Jewish Encyclopedia*, Vol. X, p. 251) Then, in 132 C.E., Bar Kokhba (Bar Koziba), one of the most prominent of the pseudomessiahs, was hailed as Messiah-king. In crushing the revolt that he led, Roman soldiers killed thousands of Jews. While such false Messiahs illustrate that many Jews were primarily interested in a political Messiah, they also show that they properly expected a *personal* Messiah, not just a Messianic era or Messianic nation. Some believe Bar Kokhba was a descendant of David, which would have aided his Messianic claim. However, since the genealogical records evidently were destroyed in 70 C.E., later claimants to the office of Messiah could not establish proof that they were of David's family. (The Messiah therefore had to appear before 70 C.E., as Jesus did, in order to prove his claim as the heir of David. This shows that persons still looking for the Messiah's earthly appearance are in error.) Among such later false claimants to messiahship were Moses of Crete, who asserted he would divide the sea between Crete and Palestine, and Serenus, who misled many Jews in Spain. *The Jewish Encyclopedia* lists

28 false Messiahs between the years 132 C.E. and 1744 C.E.—Vol. X, pp. 252-255.

Jesus Was Accepted as the Messiah. The historical evidence found in the Gospels demonstrates that Jesus was indeed the Messiah. Persons in the first century, who were in position to question the witnesses and examine the evidence, accepted the historical information as authentic. They were so sure of its accuracy that they were willing to endure persecution and die on behalf of their faith based on that assured information. The historical Gospel records show that various individuals openly acknowledged that Jesus was the Christ, or Messiah. (Mt 16:16; Joh 1:41, 45, 49; 11:27) Jesus did not say they were incorrect, and on occasion he admitted being the Christ. (Mt 16:17; Joh 4:25, 26) Sometimes Jesus would not say pointedly that he was the Messiah; at times he directed others not to publicize it. (Mr 8:29, 30; 9:9; Joh 10:24, 25) Since Jesus was present where people could hear him and see his works, he wanted them to believe on the solid basis of this evidence, so that their faith would be founded on their own eyewitness view of the fulfillment of the Hebrew Scriptures. (Joh 5:36; 10:24, 25; compare Joh 4:41, 42.) Now the Gospel record of what Jesus was and did has been provided along with the Hebrew Scriptures, which supplied abundant information about what he would do, so that individuals may know and believe that Jesus is indeed the Messiah.—Joh 20:31; see JESUS CHRIST.

METALS.
Seventy-eight of the more than a hundred elements known to man are metals. Gold, silver, copper, iron, and lead are all mentioned specifically in the Scriptures. The first Biblical mention of metals is in Genesis 4:22.

In physical properties metals are opaque, fusible, and ductile; they have a metallic luster and are usually good conductors of heat and electricity. Chemically and physically the metals have certain distinguishing characteristics. For specific information and the Scriptural occurrences, see the above-mentioned metals under their individual names; also the heading REFINE, REFINER.

METALWORKER.
One who casts, hammers, carves, engraves, or otherwise works with metals. (Isa 41:7) The first "forger of every sort of tool of copper and iron" in recorded history was Tubal-cain. (Ge 4:22) Ancient metalworkers made tools, household items, weapons, armor, musical instruments, ornaments, and figurines. Besides fashioning new items, they also did repair work. (2Ch 24:12) Many were specialists in working such metals as gold (Ne 3:8, 31, 32), silver (Jg 17:4; Ac

19:24), or copper (2Ti 4:14). At times they formed a kind of association or guild. (Ne 3:31; Ac 19:24-28) Their trade called for skill in artistic design.

The Israelites may have had knowledge of metalworking prior to their entry into Egypt, or possibly they acquired it there. By the time of the Exodus, they had ability to fashion a molten calf and a copper serpent. (Ex 32:4; Nu 21:9) More impressive, however, was the production of various metal items for the tabernacle service. Bezalel and his assistants were aided by Jehovah's spirit in their metalworking.—Ex 31:2, 3; 35:30-35.

Later, when oppressed by the Philistines, the Israelites were not allowed to have their own metalworkers. This measure prevented them from making weapons. (1Sa 13:19-22) Doubtless for similar reasons Nebuchadnezzar took the metalworkers and other craftsmen captive the first time he assaulted Jerusalem.—2Ki 24:14, 16; Jer 24:1; 29:1, 2.

METHEG-AMMAH
(Meth'eg-am'mah) [Bridle of Ammah (possibly, Cubit)]. A place taken from the Philistines by King David. (2Sa 8:1) Since no site by that name is known, Metheg-ammah may well be a figurative term designating one of the principal Philistine cities. The parallel passage at 1 Chronicles 18:1 says, "Gath and its dependent towns." At 2 Samuel 8:1 the *American Standard Version* evidently took the element "ammah" in Metheg-ammah to be from the Hebrew word for "mother" and translated Metheg-ammah as "the bridle of the mother city." This thought is conveyed by *An American Translation,* which reads "the control of the metropolis" instead of "Metheg-ammah."

METHUSELAH
(Me·thu'se·lah) [possibly, Man of the Missile]. Son of the faithful prophet Enoch; father of Lamech and grandfather of Noah. (Ge 5:21-29; 1Ch 1:1-4; Jude 14, 15) A descendant of Adam through Seth, Methuselah was of the eighth human generation. (Lu 3:37, 38) He enjoyed a life span of 969 years, the longest of Bible record, and one that has become proverbial for longevity. He died in 2370 B.C.E., the year in which the Flood began. But the Scriptures say that Methuselah "died," not that he perished in the Deluge as a result of divine execution.—Ge 5:27; see LIFE SPAN.

METHUSHAEL
(Me·thu'sha·el) [Man of God]. A descendant of Cain through Enoch. Methushael was the son of Mehujael and the father of Lamech (not to be confused with Noah's father Lamech). —Ge 4:17, 18.

MEUNIM (Me·u'nim). On the basis of the name, the Meunim are considered to have been an Arabian people residing in and around Ma'an, a city about 32 km (20 mi) ESE of Petra.

Judean King Uzziah (829-778 B.C.E.), with Jehovah's help, successfully warred against the Meunim. (2Ch 26:1, 7) Perhaps at that time some of the Meunim captives were constituted temple slaves, and therefore, their descendants are later listed among the Nethinim returning from Babylonian exile.—Ezr 2:1, 2, 43, 50; Ne 7:52; compare Ps 68:18.

During Hezekiah's reign (745-717 B.C.E.) a band of Simeonites struck down the tent-dwelling Meunim in the vicinity of Gedor.—1Ch 4:24, 39-41; see AMMONIM.

MEZAHAB (Me'za·hab) [Waters of Gold]. Parent of Matred and ancestor (perhaps, ancestress) of Mehetabel, the wife of Hadar (Hadad), the last named of the kings of Edom.—Ge 36:31, 39; 1Ch 1:50.

MEZOBAITE (Me·zo'ba·ite) [Of (Belonging to) Zobah]. A term alluding to the home of Jaasiel. —1Ch 11:47.

MEZUZAH (me·zu'zah). Anglicized form of the Hebrew word used in the Bible generally to designate a doorjamb or doorpost. *Mezu·zah'* and the plural *mezu·zohth'* appear at Exodus 12:7 (ftn), 22, 23, with reference to the sprinkling of the Passover victim's blood on doorposts, and at Exodus 21:6, regarding a slave who, desiring to remain in his master's service, was brought up against the door or "the doorpost" and had his master pierce his ear with an awl. References are also made to doorposts of the temple constructed by Solomon (1Ki 6:31, 33; 7:5) and of the symbolic temple Ezekiel saw in vision.—Eze 41:21; 45:19; 46:2.

In modern times the Anglicized term "mezuzah" is used to denote a rectangular piece of parchment containing the Hebrew text of Deuteronomy 6:4-9 and Deuteronomy 11:13-21, generally written in 22 lines. The parchment is rolled up and placed in a wooden, metal, or glass case that is affixed in a slanting position on the right-hand doorpost of Orthodox Jewish dwellings, the upper part pointing inward and the lower part outward. The Hebrew word *Shad·dai'* (meaning "Almighty") is written on the back of this parchment and is frequently visible through a glass-covered opening in the container. Sometimes the mezuzah case is artistically decorated. When pious Orthodox Jews enter or leave a house, they touch the mezuzah with the hand and recite the prayer, "May God keep my going out and my coming in from now on and ever more."—Compare Ps 121:8.

The use of the mezuzah is based on a literal interpretation of the command at Deuteronomy 6:9 (ftn) and 11:20.

MIBHAR (Mib'har) [from a root that means "choose"]. Son of Hagri; one of the mighty men of David's military forces. (1Ch 11:26, 38) Some have suggested that there is a discrepancy in the text at 1 Chronicles 11:38 because Bani the Gadite, not Mibhar, is mentioned in a parallel list at 2 Samuel 23:36. They hold that Mibhar is an alteration of the Hebrew for "from Zobah" and that the final words of 1 Chronicles 11:38 resulted because of reading *ben-hagh·ri'* (Mibhar the son of Hagri) for *ba·ni' hag·ga·dhi'* (Bani the Gadite). This remains conjectural.

MIBSAM (Mib'sam) [Perfumed; Balsam Oil; Spicy].

1. One of the sons of Ishmael and founder of a family.—Ge 25:13; 1Ch 1:29.

2. A descendant of Simeon.—1Ch 4:24, 25.

MIBZAR (Mib'zar) [possibly meaning "Fortification"]. One of the sheiks of Edom, or Esau. The name Mibzar perhaps also came to apply both to his descendants and the place they settled.—Ge 36:40, 42; 1Ch 1:53.

MICA (Mi'ca) [shortened form of Michael or Micaiah]. The English names Mica and Micah have resulted from a minor difference in the Hebrew spelling.

1. Son of Mephibosheth (Merib-baal) and grandson of King Saul's son Jonathan. Mica (also called Micah) was the father of Pithon, Melech, Tarea (Tahrea), and Ahaz.—2Sa 9:12; 1Ch 8:33-35; 9:39-41.

2. One of the Levites (or the forefather of one) attesting by seal the "trustworthy arrangement" of Nehemiah's time.—Ne 9:38; 10:1, 9, 11.

3. A Levite descendant of Asaph and the son of Zichri (also identified as Zabdi and Zaccur). Mica was the father of Mattaniah and is also called Micah and Micaiah.—1Ch 9:14, 15; Ne 11:17, 22; 12:35.

MICAH (Mi'cah) [shortened form of Michael or Micaiah].

1. A man of Ephraim. In violation of the eighth of the Ten Commandments (Ex 20:15), Micah took 1,100 silver pieces from his mother. When he confessed and returned them, she said: "I must without fail sanctify the silver to Jehovah from my hand for my son, so as to make a carved image and a molten statue; and now I shall give it back

to you." She then took 200 silver pieces to a silversmith, who made "a carved image and a molten statue" that afterward came to be in Micah's house. Micah, who had "a house of gods," made an ephod and teraphim and empowered one of his sons to act as priest for him. Although this arrangement was ostensibly to honor Jehovah, it was grossly improper, for it violated the commandment forbidding idolatry (Ex 20:4-6) and bypassed Jehovah's tabernacle and his priesthood. (Jg 17:1-6; De 12:1-14) Later, Micah took Jonathan, a descendant of Moses' son Gershom, into his home, hiring this young Levite as his priest. (Jg 18:4, 30) Mistakenly feeling satisfied with this, Micah said: "Now I do know that Jehovah will do me good." (Jg 17:7-13) But Jonathan was not of Aaron's lineage and thus was not even qualified for priestly service, which only added to Micah's error.—Nu 3:10.

In those days, the Danites, searching for territory in which to dwell, sent out five spies, who eventually came to Ephraim "as far as the house of Micah and got to spend the night there." While near Micah's house, they recognized Jonathan's voice, found out what he was doing there, and had him inquire of God so that they might know whether their venture would be successful. The priest told them: "Go in peace. It is before Jehovah that your way is in which you go." (Jg 18:1-6) They subsequently spied out Laish and returned, telling their brothers about it, whereupon the five spies and 600 Danite men girded for warfare headed for that city. En route, as they passed Micah's house, the spies told their brothers about his religious articles and suggested their acquisition. The Danites took these and also convinced the Levite that it would be better for him to be a priest to a tribe and family in Israel than just for one man. They then took him, the ephod, the teraphim, and the carved image and went their way.—Jg 18:7-21.

Shortly thereafter, Micah and a company of men pursued the Danites. Upon catching up with them and being asked what was the matter, Micah said: "My gods that I made you have taken, the priest too, and you go your way, and what do I have anymore?" At that, the sons of Dan warned of possible assault if Micah continued following them and voicing protest. Seeing that the Danites were much stronger than his band, Micah returned home. (Jg 18:22-26) The Danites thereafter struck down and burned Laish, building the city of Dan on its site. Jonathan and his sons became priests to the Danites, who "kept the carved image of Micah, which he had made, set up for themselves all the days that the house of the true God [the tabernacle] continued in Shiloh."—Jg 18:27-31.

2. A Levite of the Kohathite family of Uzziel, of which he was head and his brother Isshiah the second when the Levitical service assignments were distributed by David.—1Ch 23:6, 12, 20; 24:24, 25.

3. Descendant of King Saul; son of Jonathan's son Merib-baal (Mephibosheth). He is also called Mica.—1Ch 8:33-35; 9:39-41; 2Sa 9:12.

4. A Reubenite who was the son of Shimei and father of Reaiah. His descendant Beerah was a chieftain of the tribe of Reuben and was taken into exile by Assyrian King Tilgath-pilneser (Tiglath-pileser III).—1Ch 5:1, 3-6; 2Ki 15:29.

5. Father of Abdon (Achbor). He is also called Micaiah, which is the longer form of his name. —2Ch 34:20; 2Ki 22:12.

6. A Levite and descendant of Asaph. (Ne 11: 15, 17) He is also called Mica and Micaiah.—1Ch 9:15; Ne 11:22; 12:35.

7. Writer of the Bible book bearing his name and a prophet of Jehovah during the reigns of Kings Jotham, Ahaz, and Hezekiah of Judah (777-717 B.C.E.). Micah was a contemporary of the prophets Hosea and Isaiah. The exact duration of his prophetic activity is uncertain. His prophesying apparently closed by the end of Hezekiah's reign, when the composition of the prophet's book was completed.—Mic 1:1; Ho 1:1; Isa 1:1.

Micah was a native of the village of Moresheth, SW of Jerusalem. (Jer 26:18) As a resident of the fertile Shephelah, the prophet was well acquainted with rural living, from which he was inspired to draw meaningful illustrations. (Mic 2:12; 4:12, 13; 7:1, 4, 14) Micah prophesied during very turbulent times when false worship and moral corruption flourished in Israel and Judah, also when King Hezekiah instituted religious reforms. (2Ki 15: 32–20:21; 2Ch 27-32) With good reason, "the word of Jehovah that occurred to Micah" warned that God would make Samaria "a heap of ruins of the field," and it was prophesied that "Zion will be plowed up as a mere field, and Jerusalem herself will become mere heaps of ruins." (Mic 1:1, 6; 3:12) While the devastation of Judah and Jerusalem in 607 B.C.E. occurred many years after Micah's day, he probably lived to see the foretold destruction of Samaria in 740 B.C.E.—2Ki 25:1-21; 17:5, 6.

MICAH, BOOK OF.

A prophetic book of the Hebrew Scriptures containing Jehovah's word through Micah concerning Samaria and Jerusalem. (See MICAH No. 7.) It consists of three basic sections, each beginning with the word "Hear." —Mic 1:2; 3:1; 6:1.

HIGHLIGHTS OF MICAH

A candid statement of the wrongdoing of Israel and of Judah, a forecast of desolation for Samaria and Jerusalem, and promises of restoration

Covers a period leading up to and possibly following the desolation of Samaria in 740 B.C.E.

Wrongdoing of Israel and Judah is contrasted with Jehovah's righteous requirements

Oppressors lie in bed, plotting to seize homes and fields; when day dawns, they carry out their schemes (2:1, 2)

Unsuspecting passersby are robbed; women and children are victimized (2:8, 9)

Those responsible for administering justice exploit the people as though they were animals (3:1-3)

False prophets call out, "Peace!"—but they sanctify war against anyone that "does not put something into their mouths" (3:5)

Judges, priests, and prophets are solely out for gain, yet they claim Jehovah's support (3:9-11)

Loyal ones are virtually nonexistent; princes and judges seek bribes, and not even family members can be trusted (7:1-6)

Jehovah delivered his people from Egypt and guided and protected them; no amount of sacrificing will compensate for their revolt (6:3-7)

He requires that his people exercise justice, love kindness, and walk modestly with him (6:8)

Jehovah's judgments against Israel; Judah, too, will be affected

Jehovah's judgment will result in Samaria's being re-duced to a heap of ruins; the disaster will reach even as far as Judah and Jerusalem (1:3-16)

Calamity will come upon Israel; her fields will be apportioned to others (2:3-5)

Jehovah will strike his people; they will eat but not get filled, they will sow seed but not enjoy any fruitage (6:13-16)

Remnant will be regathered and true worship exalted

The remnant of Israel will be gathered together "like a flock in the pen," with their king before them and Jehovah ahead of them (2:12, 13)

In the final part of the days, the mountain of Jehovah's house will be exalted above the hills and people of many nations will stream to it; they will be taught by Jehovah and learn war no more (4:1-4)

The restored people will walk in Jehovah's name; Zion will be strong before her enemies (4:5-13)

A ruler will be born in Bethlehem who will shepherd in Jehovah's name; under his rulership, the Assyrian will be driven back; the remnant of Jacob will be like refreshing dew and like a mighty lion (5:2-9)

Jehovah will cleanse his people of idolatry and execute vengeance upon disobedient nations (5:10-15)

Rely on Jehovah; the rejoicing of the "woman enemy" will end as Jehovah's repentant people receive his attention and experience wonderful things, filling observing nations with fear; Jehovah will forgive the sins of his people (7:7-20)

Micah's prophetic words regarding Samaria's desolation must have been delivered before that city's destruction in 740 B.C.E., and evidently his oral pronouncements were committed to writing before the close of Hezekiah's reign.

Deplorable moral conditions prevailed among the people of Israel and Judah in Micah's time. The leaders oppressed the people, especially the poor. Judges, priests, and prophets were out for money. Idolatry, fraud, oppression, injustices, and bloodshed abounded. It was precarious to trust even confidential friends and family members.—Mic 1:7; 2:1, 2; 3:1-3, 9-12; 6:12; 7:2-6.

The book of Micah candidly portrays the wrongs of Israel and Judah. While foretelling desolation for Samaria and Jerusalem on account of their transgressions (Mic 1:5-9; 3:9-12), it also contains promises of restoration and divine blessings to follow.—4:1-8; 5:7-9; 7:15-17.

The authenticity of this book is well established. It harmonizes with the rest of the Scriptures in showing Jehovah to be a merciful and loving God, pardoning error and passing over transgression.

(Mic 7:18-20; compare Ex 34:6, 7; Ps 86:5.) From earliest times the Jews accepted this book as authentic. About a century after Micah's time, his words spoken during Hezekiah's reign about the desolation of Jerusalem were quoted by certain older men of Judah when making a point in defense of Jeremiah the prophet. (Jer 26:17-19; compare Mic 3:12.) Centuries afterward, the Jewish chief priests and scribes, on the basis of Micah's prophecy, confidently stated that the Christ was to be born in Bethlehem. (Mt 2:3-6; compare Mic 5:2.) The fulfillment of prophecies respecting Samaria, Jerusalem, and the Messiah, or Christ, stamp this book as being inspired of God. Noteworthy, too, is the fact that Jesus' words about a man's enemies being persons of his household parallel Micah 7:6.—Mt 10:21, 35, 36.

MICAIAH   (Mi·cai′ah) [Who Is Like Jehovah?].

1. Wife of King Rehoboam, daughter of Uriel of Gibeah, and the mother of King Abijah of Judah. She is also called "Maacah."—2Ch 11:18, 20; 13:1, 2.

2. Son of Imlah and a prophet of Jehovah to the northern kingdom of Israel during King Ahab's reign. (1Ki 22:8) While King Jehoshaphat of Judah was visiting Ahab, the Israelite king invited him to join in a military campaign against the Syrians to regain possession of Ramoth-gilead. Before accepting, Jehoshaphat asked that the word of Jehovah be sought. So Ahab summoned 400 prophets and asked them: "Shall I go against Ramoth-gilead in war, or shall I refrain?" They answered in the affirmative, saying that Jehovah would give the city into the king's hand. However, Jehoshaphat wanted more assurance, whereupon Ahab reluctantly sent for Micaiah, the prophet who had always prophesied bad for him. The dispatched messenger urged Micaiah to speak words to Ahab like those of one of the other prophets. At first Micaiah did so, but Ahab placed him under oath to speak "truth in the name of Jehovah." At that, Micaiah said: "I certainly see all the Israelites scattered on the mountains, like sheep that have no shepherd."—1Ki 22:1-17; 2Ch 18:1-16.

Micaiah then proceeded to relate his vision of Jehovah sitting on His heavenly throne and asking assembled spirit creatures: "Who will fool Ahab, that he may go up and fall at Ramoth-gilead?" One of the spirits volunteered to go and become "a deceptive spirit" in the mouth of all of Ahab's prophets. Jehovah replied: "You will fool him, and, what is more, you will come off the winner. Go out and do that way." Micaiah then told Ahab that God had put a deceptive spirit into the mouth of all his prophets, "but Jehovah himself has spoken calamity concerning you." With that the false prophet Zedekiah struck Micaiah upon the cheek and asked mockingly: "Just which way did the spirit of Jehovah pass along from me to speak with you?" Micaiah boldly replied: "Look! You are seeing which way on that day when you will enter the innermost chamber to hide yourself." Ahab then commanded that Micaiah be put in the house of detention, where the prophet would be fed with reduced allowances of bread and water until the king returned in peace. However, Ahab never returned, because during the battle at Ramoth-gilead, "there was a man that bent the bow in his innocence," the arrow struck the Israelite king, and he gradually died. Micaiah's final words to Ahab had been: "If you return at all in peace, Jehovah has not spoken with me." The king's death proved that Micaiah was indeed Jehovah's prophet.—1Ki 22:18-37; 2Ch 18:17-34.

3. One of the princes King Jehoshaphat sent throughout Judah as teachers, along with Levites and priests. They had "the book of Jehovah's law" with them as they taught the people in all the cities of Judah.—2Ch 17:7-9.

4. Father of the Achbor (Abdon) who was sent, along with others, by King Josiah to inquire of Jehovah concerning the words of the newly found book of the Law. He is also called Micah.—2Ki 22:12, 13; 2Ch 34:20, 21.

5. "Son of Gemariah the son of Shaphan." He was present in the dining room of his father, Gemariah, when Baruch publicly read there the roll containing Jehovah's words through Jeremiah against Israel, Judah, and all the nations. After hearing this message, Micaiah reported what he heard to King Jehoiakim's secretary and princes. —Jer 36:2, 9-13.

6. Ancestor of the priest Zechariah, the latter being among those with trumpets at the inaugural ceremony of Jerusalem's rebuilt wall. He is also called Mica.—Ne 11:22; 12:31, 35.

7. A priest among those with trumpets who played in one of the two "thanksgiving choirs" participating in the inaugural march for Jerusalem's rebuilt wall in Nehemiah's day.—Ne 12:40, 41.

MICHAEL (Mi′cha·el) [Who Is Like God?].

1. The only holy angel other than Gabriel named in the Bible, and the only one called "archangel." (Jude 9) The first occurrence of the name is in the tenth chapter of Daniel, where Michael is described as "one of the foremost princes"; he came to the aid of a lesser angel who was opposed by "the prince of the royal realm of Persia." Michael was called "the prince of [Daniel's] people," "the great prince who is standing in behalf of the sons of [Daniel's] people." (Da 10:13, 20, 21; 12:1) This points to Michael as the angel who led the Israelites through the wilderness. (Ex 23:20, 21, 23; 32:34; 33:2) Lending support to this conclusion is the fact that "Michael the archangel had a difference with the Devil and was disputing about Moses' body."—Jude 9.

Scriptural evidence indicates that the name Michael applied to God's Son before he left heaven to become Jesus Christ and also after his return. Michael is the only one said to be "the archangel," meaning "chief angel," or "principal angel." The term occurs in the Bible only in the singular. This seems to imply that there is but one whom God has designated chief, or head, of the angelic host. At 1 Thessalonians 4:16 the voice of the resurrected Lord Jesus Christ is described as being that of an archangel, suggesting that he is, in fact, himself the archangel. This text depicts him as descending from heaven with "a commanding call."

It is only logical, therefore, that the voice expressing this commanding call be described by a word that would not diminish or detract from the great authority that Christ Jesus now has as King of kings and Lord of lords. (Mt 28:18; Re 17:14) If the designation "archangel" applied, not to Jesus Christ, but to other angels, then the reference to "an archangel's voice" would not be appropriate. In that case it would be describing a voice of lesser authority than that of the Son of God.

There are also other correspondencies establishing that Michael is actually the Son of God. Daniel, after making the first reference to Michael (Da 10:13), recorded a prophecy reaching down to "the time of the end" (Da 11:40) and then stated: "And during that time Michael will stand up, the great prince who is standing in behalf of the sons of [Daniel's] people." (Da 12:1) Michael's 'standing up' was to be associated with "a time of distress such as has not been made to occur since there came to be a nation until that time." (Da 12:1) In Daniel's prophecy, 'standing up' frequently refers to the action of a king, either taking up his royal power or acting effectively in his capacity as king. (Da 11:2-4, 7, 16b, 20, 21) This supports the conclusion that Michael is Jesus Christ, since Jesus is Jehovah's appointed King, commissioned to destroy all the nations at Har–Magedon.—Re 11:15; 16:14-16.

The book of Revelation (12:7, 10, 12) specifically mentions Michael in connection with the establishment of God's Kingdom and links this event with trouble for the earth: "And war broke out in heaven: Michael and his angels battled with the dragon, and the dragon and its angels battled. And I heard a loud voice in heaven say: 'Now have come to pass the salvation and the power and the kingdom of our God and the authority of his Christ, because the accuser of our brothers has been hurled down . . . On this account be glad, you heavens and you who reside in them! Woe for the earth and for the sea.'" Jesus Christ is later depicted as leading the heavenly armies in war against the nations of the earth. (Re 19:11-16) This would mean a period of distress for them, which would logically be included in the "time of distress" that is associated with Michael's standing up. (Da 12:1) Since the Son of God is to fight the nations, it is only reasonable that he was the one who with his angels earlier battled against the superhuman dragon, Satan the Devil, and his angels.

In his prehuman existence Jesus was called "the Word." (Joh 1:1) He also had the personal name Michael. By retaining the name Jesus after his resurrection (Ac 9:5), "the Word" shows that he is identical with the Son of God on earth. His resuming his heavenly name Michael and his title (or name) "The Word of God" (Re 19:13) ties him in with his prehuman existence. The very name Michael, asking as it does, "Who Is Like God?" points to the fact that Jehovah God is without like, or equal, and that Michael his archangel is his great Champion or Vindicator.

2. The father of chieftain Sethur of the tribe of Asher who was one of the 12 sent to spy out Canaan.—Nu 13:2, 13.

3. Forefather of Asaph; of the family of Gershom, the son of Levi.—1Ch 6:39, 40, 43.

4. One of the heads of the tribe of Issachar; of the family of Tola.—1Ch 7:1-3.

5. A chieftain of the tribe of Manasseh who deserted to David at Ziklag.—1Ch 12:20.

6. The father of Omri, the head of a paternal house of Issachar during David's reign.—1Ch 27:18.

7. One of the sons of King Jehoshaphat of Judah who, together with his brothers, received costly gifts and fortified cities from their father. However, when his older brother Jehoram became king, Jehoram killed all his six younger brothers, including Michael.—2Ch 21:1-4.

8. A Gadite and descendant of Buz; an ancestor of No. 9, at least five generations removed.—1Ch 5:11, 13, 14.

9. A Gadite, first of seven sons of Abihail, a descendant of No. 8 and a head of a house of Gilead enrolled genealogically during the days of Israelite King Jeroboam II and of Judean King Jotham.—1Ch 5:11-17.

10. A Benjamite; descendant of Shaharaim by his wife Hushim through Elpaal and Beriah.—1Ch 8:1, 8, 11-13, 16.

11. Father of the Zebadiah who went up to Jerusalem from Babylon with Ezra in 468 B.C.E. —Ezr 8:1, 8.

MICHAL (Mi′chal) [probably, Who Is Like God?]. King Saul's younger daughter who became the wife of David. Saul had offered his older daughter Merab to David as a wife but gave her to another man. Michal, however, "was in love with David," and Saul offered her to David if he could produce the foreskins of a hundred Philistines, Saul thinking that David would meet death in attempting to kill that many enemy warriors. David accepted the challenge, presented Saul with 200 Philistine foreskins, and was given Michal as a wife. But, thereafter, "Saul felt still more fear because of David" and became his lasting foe. (1Sa 14:49; 18:17-29) Later, when Saul's hatred for

David reached a peak, Michal helped David escape the king's wrath. During David's long absence, Saul gave her in marriage to Palti the son of Laish from Gallim.—1Sa 19:11-17; 25:44.

When Abner later sought to conclude a covenant with David, David refused to see him unless he brought Michal with him. David, by messenger, presented his demand to Saul's son Ishbosheth, and Michal was taken from her husband Paltiel (Palti) and was returned to David.—2Sa 3:12-16.

Punished for Disrespect to David. When David as king had the ark of the covenant brought to Jerusalem and displayed his joy for Jehovah's worship by dancing exuberantly, "being girded with an ephod of linen," Michal observed him from a window and "began to despise him in her heart." Upon David's return to his household, Michal expressed her feelings sarcastically, revealing a lack of appreciation of the kind of zeal David had displayed for Jehovah's worship and indicating that she felt he had acted in an undignified manner. David then rebuked her and also evidently penalized her by having no further sexual relations with her, so that she died childless.—2Sa 6:14-23.

Rears Her Sister's Children. The account at 2 Samuel 21:8 speaks of "the five sons of Michal the daughter of Saul whom she bore to Adriel," these being among the members of Saul's household whom David gave to the Gibeonites in atonement for Saul's attempt to annihilate them. (2Sa 21:1-10) The apparent conflict between 2 Samuel 21:8 and 2 Samuel 6:23, which shows that Michal died childless, may be resolved by the view taken by some commentators, namely, that these children were the five sons of Michal's sister Merab and that Michal raised them following the early death of their mother.—See MERAB.

MICHMAS(H)

MICHMAS(H) (Mich'mas[h]) [Laid Up [that is, concealed] Place]. A site identified with modern Mukhmas on a hill about 600 m (2,000 ft) above sea level and some 11 km (7 mi) NNE of Jerusalem. It lies N of the Wadi Suweinit (Nahal Mikhmas), considered to be "the ravine pass of Michmash." (1Sa 13:23) Joined by other wadis from the SW and NW, Wadi Suweinit extends from the mountainous region of Ephraim to the Jordan Valley.

Doubtless preparing to free Israel from Philistine control, King Saul selected a force of 3,000 men. Of these, 2,000 encamped with him at Michmash and in the mountainous region of Bethel, and the others took their position with his son

Jonathan at Gibeah. Later, at nearby Geba ("Gibeah," Vg), Jonathan struck down the Philistine "garrison." In retaliation the Philistines rallied a great army, including chariots and horsemen, and apparently forced Saul to retreat from Michmash to Gilgal. Hard pressed by the Philistines, many Israelites hid themselves in caves and hollows; others sought refuge E of the Jordan. This dispersal of the Israelite warriors in the face of the Philistine threat was later presented by Saul as his reason for failing to wait obediently for Samuel to offer sacrifice. Reproved by Samuel for his presumptuous act, Saul, with a reduced force of about 600 men, thereafter came to Jonathan at Geba. (1Sa 13:1-16) According to 1 Samuel 14:2, Saul evidently transferred his camp to Migron near Gibeah.

Jonathan Initiates Rout of Philistines. Because three bands of Philistine pillagers would go out from their camp at Michmash and an outpost of the Philistines would sally forth to "the ravine pass of Michmash," Jonathan decided to end this menace. (1Sa 13:16-23) To do this, he crossed the ravine pass, which (if Wadi Suweinit) forms a deep gorge with nearly vertical cliffs to the E of Geba (Jaba'). Two prominent hills with steep rocky sides rise at a point where the Wadi Suweinit makes a sharp bend. These may be the 'toothlike crags' Bozez and Seneh, their toothlike edges having perhaps been rounded by the erosive forces of some 30 centuries. (1Sa 14:1-7) For a stranger to have made his way through the maze of mounds, knolls, and sharp rocks in the wadi would have been next to impossible. But Jonathan, reared in Benjamite territory, apparently knew it well. While his father's camp was at Michmash and his own at Geba, Jonathan doubtless had repeated opportunities for getting better acquainted with the terrain.

Jonathan and his armor-bearer made their way toward Michmash and then exposed themselves to the view of the Philistine outpost. Catching sight of them, the Philistines called out: "Come on up to us, and we will let you know a thing!" Thereafter, on his hands and feet, Jonathan, followed by his armor-bearer, ascended the steep passage to the Philistine outpost. As a team they struck down some 20 Philistines within a distance of about half the measure of land that a span of bulls can plow in a day.—1Sa 14:8, 11-14, ftn.

A divinely sent earthquake, the effects of which were noted by Saul's watchmen, threw the Philistine camp into turmoil. By the time Saul and his men came on the scene, many of the Philistines had slaughtered one another in confusion and the rest had taken to flight. Saul's army, probably now equipped with Philistine weapons found at the site, pursued the fleeing enemy forces. Joined by Israelites who had gone into hiding and those who had sided with the Philistines, "they kept striking down the Philistines from Michmash to Aijalon." —1Sa 14:15-23, 31.

According to 1 Samuel 13:5, the Philistine forces at Michmash included 30,000 war chariots. This number is far greater than that involved in several other military expeditions (compare Jg 4:13; 2Ch 12:2, 3; 14:9), and it is hard to imagine how so many war chariots could have been used in mountainous terrain. For this reason 30,000 is generally viewed as a scribal error. The Syriac *Peshitta* and the Lagardian edition of the Greek *Septuagint* read 3,000, and numerous Bible translations follow this rendering. (*AT, JB, Mo*) However, even lower figures have been suggested.

Centuries later, the prophecy of Isaiah mentions Michmash as the place where the conquering Assyrian would 'deposit his articles.' (Isa 10:24, 28) After the Israelite return from Babylonian exile in 537 B.C.E., Michmas(h) was apparently reoccupied by Benjamites.—Ezr 2:1, 2, 27; Ne 7:31; 11:31.

MICHMETHATH (Mich·me'thath). A site on the boundary between Ephraim and Manasseh. It is identified with Khirbet Juleijil, a short distance E of Shechem. This agrees with the Biblical statement that Michmethath was "in front of Shechem."—Jos 16:5, 6; 17:7.

MICHRI (Mich'ri) [possibly from a root meaning "sell"]. A Benjamite and an ancestor of Elah who resided in Jerusalem after the Babylonian exile.—1Ch 9:1-3, 7, 8.

MIDDIN (Mid'din). A place in the Judean Wilderness. (Jos 15:20, 61) Middin is perhaps to be identified with Khirbet Abu Tabaq situated in the low-lying plain called el Buqei'a (Biq'at Hureqanya; the Valley of Achor?) near the NW end of the Dead Sea.

MIDIAN (Mid'i·an), **MIDIANITES** (Mid'i·anites) [Of (Belonging to) Midian].

1. One of Abraham's sons by his concubine Keturah; the father of Ephah, Epher, Hanoch, Abida, and Eldaah. (Ge 25:1, 2, 4; 1Ch 1:32, 33) Before his death, Abraham gave presents to Midian and the other sons of his concubines and then sent them to the land of the East.—Ge 25:5, 6.

2. The descendants of Abraham's son Midian are collectively designated as "Midian" and "Midianites." (Nu 31:2, 3) At times the Bible seemingly refers to them as Ishmaelites. (Compare Ge 37:25,

27, 28, 36; 39:1; Jg 8:22, 24.) This may imply that the descendants of Abraham through his sons Ishmael and Midian were much alike in their way of life, and there may have been a further amalgamation through intermarriage among the two peoples. It also appears that at least some of the Kenites were known as Midianites. Since the Kenites are already mentioned as a people before Midian's birth, this may mean that Moses' Kenite brother-in-law Hobab was a Midianite merely from a geographic standpoint.—Ge 15:18, 19; Nu 10:29; Jg 1:16; 4:11; see ISHMAELITE; KENITE.

Being descendants of Abraham, the Midianites likely spoke a language that closely resembled Hebrew. Gideon, for instance, apparently had no difficulty in understanding the Midianites. (Jg 7:13-15; 8:18, 19) There is also a possibility, however, that Gideon learned the tongue of the Midianites, Israel having been under their domination for seven years.—Jg 6:1.

The Midianites were primarily nomadic tent dwellers. (Jg 6:5, 6; Hab 3:7) But in Moses' day they are also reported as residing in cities. (Nu 31:9, 10) At that time they were quite prosperous, having asses and animals of the flock and the herd numbering into the tens of thousands. (Nu 31:32-34) Their riches included gold ornaments having a total weight of more than 191 kg (512 lb t, valued now at over $2,150,000).—Nu 31:50-52.

Apparently both men and women adorned themselves with gold ornaments, including nose rings and earrings. Midianite kings were arrayed in "garments of wool dyed reddish purple," and even their camels had necklaces, evidently with moon-shaped ornaments attached.—Nu 31:50; Jg 8:21, 26.

Doubtless the Midianites acquired much of their wealth through trade and plunder. (Compare Ge 37:28; Jg 6:5, 6.) As early as the time of Joseph, caravans of Midianite merchants traveled to Egypt. It was to such a caravan bound for Egypt and carrying aromatic resins that Joseph was sold by his half brothers.—Ge 37:25, 28.

Probably sometime before Israel's entry into the Promised Land, Edomite King Hadad (son of Bedad) gained the victory over the Midianites in the field of Moab.—Ge 36:35; 1Ch 1:46.

Cause Israel to Sin. Later, the Midianites manifested hostility toward the Israelites. They cooperated with the Moabites in hiring the prophet Balaam to curse Israel. (Nu 22:4-7) When this failed, the Midianites and Moabites, at Balaam's advice, cunningly used their women to induce thousands of Israelite males to become involved in sexual immorality and idolatry in connection with

Baal of Peor. (Nu 25:1-9, 14-18; 31:15, 16; 1Co 10:8; Re 2:14) Thereafter the Israelites, in obedience to divine command, took vengeance upon Midian. The Midianite cities and walled camps in the area were consigned to the fire. Thousands of domestic animals and many gold articles were taken as spoils. With the exception of the virgins, all, including the five kings of Midian—Evi, Rekem, Zur, Hur, and Reba—were put to death. —Nu 31.

Less than three centuries later, the Midianites had recovered from this blow sufficiently to be able to oppress the Israelites for seven years. (Compare Jg 6:1; 11:25, 26.) Along with the Amalekites and "Easterners," these tent-dwelling nomads, with their livestock and innumerable camels, penetrated Israel's land all the way to Gaza, plundering the domestic animals of the Israelites and also consuming their harvests.—Jg 6:2-6.

Crushing Defeat by Gideon. Finally, when Israel called to Jehovah for aid, he raised up Gideon to deliver them. (Jg 6:7-16) The rout that Jehovah effected by means of him was so complete that there is no record of any further harassment from the Midianites. (Jg 8:28) Their princes Oreb and Zeeb were slain, as were their kings Zebah and Zalmunna. (Jg 7:25; 8:5, 21; see GIDEON.) Centuries later the victory over Midian was still alluded to when illustrating the smashing of enemy power.—Isa 9:4; 10:24-26; see also Ps 83:9-11.

In contrast with the earlier enmity of the Midianites, a restoration prophecy pointed to the time when "young male camels of Midian and of Ephah" would bring gifts to Zion.—Isa 60:5, 6, 11-14.

3. The territory occupied by the Midianites was known as "Midian" or "the land of Midian." (1Ki 11:18; Hab 3:7) It is generally agreed that the descendants of Midian established themselves mainly in the NW part of Arabia just E of the Gulf of 'Aqaba. But the extent of their landholdings is uncertain and must have varied in the course of their history. During Moses' lifetime many Midianites were apparently living near Moabite territory and in the vicinity of the region controlled by Amorite King Sihon.—Nu 22:4; 31:8-12; Jos 13:21.

Moses himself spent about 40 years in the land of Midian. There he married Zipporah, one of the seven daughters of Jethro the priest of Midian. (See JETHRO.) By her he had two sons, Gershom and Eliezer. Moses' work as a shepherd for his father-in-law took him to the mountainous area around Horeb, suggesting that he resided in the vicinity of the Gulf of 'Aqaba. However, whether the region around Horeb was then a part of "the land of Midian" cannot be determined. (Ex 2:15-22; 3:1; 4:18-20; 18:1-4; Ac 7:29, 30) It seems that at a later time Edom was at least in part referred to as Midian.—1Ki 11:14-18.

MIDWIFE. The Hebrew term for "midwife" is a feminine participle of the verb *ya·ladh'* (bear; give birth) and thus literally refers to a woman who helps to bear or give birth to a child. (See BIRTH.) A midwife helps the mother during the ordeal of labor, and once the child is born she severs its navel cord and washes the infant. In ancient times she would also rub it with salt and swaddle it with cloth bands.—Eze 16:4.

Close friends or relatives and older women in the community sometimes served in this capacity, but because of the special knowledge, skill, and experience necessary, particularly when the delivery was difficult, midwifery was pursued as a profession by few. In the case of Benjamin's birth, when "it was going hard with [Rachel] in making the delivery," the midwife was able to assure Rachel that she would have the son, though Rachel herself died. (Ge 35:16-19) During the complicated delivery of Tamar's twins, Perez and Zerah, the midwife was alert to identify the one she expected to be the firstborn. She quickly tied a scarlet piece on the extended hand of Zerah. However, the hand was drawn in and his brother emerged first, causing a perineal rupture of the mother.—Ge 38:27-30.

Midwives among the Israelites during their slavery in Egypt found themselves in a very critical and dangerous position. Pharaoh summoned two of them by name, Shiphrah and Puah, and commanded them to put to death every Hebrew male baby as soon as it was born. Probably these two women served as heads of the profession and were responsible to pass the orders of the king on to their associates. However, "the midwives feared the true God, and they did not do as the king of Egypt had spoken to them, but they would preserve the male children alive." For this they were called to account by Pharaoh, who demanded: "Why is it you have done this thing?" Feigning that the matter was beyond their control, they insisted that the Hebrew women were "lively" and gave birth 'before the midwife could come in to them.' (Ex 1:15-19) Because these midwives feared Jehovah and refused to practice infanticide, he blessed and rewarded them with families of their own.—Ex 1:20, 21.

MIGDAL-EL (Mig′dal-el) [Tower of God]. A fortified city in the territory of Naphtali. (Jos 19: 32, 35, 38) One possible identification that has been suggested for Migdal-el is Majadel. This site is on a hill about 17 km (11 mi) ESE of Tyre.

MIGDAL-GAD (Mig′dal-gad) [Tower of Good Fortune]. A Judean city in the Shephelah. (Jos 15:20, 33, 37) It is perhaps to be identified with Khirbet el-Mejdeleh (Horvat Migdal Gad), about 20 km (12 mi) W of Hebron.

MIGDOL (Mig′dol) [Tower].

1. An Egyptian site used as a reference point in describing the location of Israel's last encampment at Pihahiroth before crossing the Red Sea. They were to encamp "before Pihahiroth between Migdol and the sea in view of Baal-zephon." (Ex 14:2; Nu 33:5-8) Scholars generally hold that Migdol is likely an Egyptian pronunciation for the Hebrew *migh·dal′*, meaning "tower," and that it doubtless refers to a military post or watchtower on the Egyptian border. However, there is evidence that there were several such Migdols along the Egyptian border; even today there are three different villages bearing the name Mashtul, the present form of Migdol in Egyptian (of Coptic derivation). (See also No. 2.) Though one of the Amarna Tablets mentions a certain Ma-ag-da-li′, it gives no indication of its location. Since the location of the other sites, Pihahiroth and Baal-zephon, are not presently known, the location of Migdol remains uncertain. Some consider it as likely to have been a site on the height of Jebel 'Ataqah overlooking the northern end of the Gulf of Suez. Though no evidence is known today connecting such a site with the name Migdol, it would obviously be a strategic location for a watchtower or frontier post.

2. The Migdol mentioned by the prophets Jeremiah and Ezekiel some 900 years after the Exodus. While it may be the same as that considered above, most commentators believe that a second Egyptian Migdol is involved.

The prophet Ezekiel foretold a devastation due to come upon Egypt, evidently from Babylon, striking it "from Migdol to Syene and to the boundary of Ethiopia." (Eze 29:10; 30:6) Since Syene is in the extreme S of ancient Egypt, it appears that this Migdol was in the extreme N, thus giving rise to a description similar to the familiar phrase "from Dan down to Beer-sheba" used with reference to Palestine. (Jg 20:1) After Jerusalem's fall in 607 B.C.E., Jewish refugees settled in Migdol, Tahpanhes, Noph (Memphis), and in the land of Pathros. But Migdol and other places were to witness the 'devouring sword' of Babylon's King Nebuchadnezzar.—Jer 44:1; 46: 13, 14.

This Migdol is usually identified with a fortress described in Egyptian hieroglyphic texts as guarding the NE approaches of the country. An itinerary from the Common Era refers to a site called Magdolo near Pelusium, which latter place lay on the Mediterranean Coast at what might be called the entrance into Egypt for those coming from Philistia. Though there is no certainty, some scholars tentatively identify this frontier-fortress called Migdol with Tell el-Heir, about 10 km (6 mi) SSW of Pelusium (Tel el Farame).

MIGRON (Mig′ron) [Threshing Floor]. A location "at the outskirts of Gibeah" where King Saul was encamped when Jonathan and his armor-bearer killed about 20 men from the Philistine outpost near Michmash. (1Sa 13:16, 23; 14:1, 2, 13-16) Tell Miryam, about 1 km (0.6 mi) WSW of Mukhmas (Michmash), is tentatively identified with Migron.

At Isaiah 10:28 Migron is foretold to be one of the cities through which the Assyrians would pass on their way toward Jerusalem. Its being mentioned after Ai (Aiath) and before Michmash appears to locate Migron N, not S, of Michmash. Therefore, a second Migron (Makrun to the NW of Michmash) has been suggested. However, if the Migron of Saul's day was still in existence, it seems unlikely that there would be another town by the same name less than 3 km (2 mi) away. So the prophecy may simply be listing cities to be affected by the Assyrian invasion and that without regard for the order or geographic position of one city in relation to another. (Isa 10:24, 28-32) Thus the Migron of Isaiah 10:28 may be the same as the one mentioned at 1 Samuel 14:2.

MIJAMIN (Mij′a·min) [From the Right Hand].

1. Descendant of Aaron selected by lot to head the sixth division of priestly service in King David's day.—1Ch 24:1, 3, 5, 9.

2. One of the heads of the priests who returned from Babylon with Zerubbabel. (Ne 12:1, 5, 7) He may have founded the paternal house of Miniamin mentioned at Nehemiah 12:17 (where the name of the head of that house appears to have been an inadvertent scribal omission in the Hebrew text).

3. One of "the sons of Parosh" who sent away foreign "wives along with sons" as Ezra counseled —Ezr 10:25, 44.

4. A priest (or possibly the ancestor of a priest listed among those attesting by seal the "trustworthy arrangement" of Nehemiah's time. (Ne 9:38.

10:1, 7, 8) He seems to be identical with the Miniamin of Nehemiah 12:41.

In Hebrew, Mijamin seems to be a contraction of the name Miniamin.

MIKLOTH (Mik′loth).

1. Father of Shimeah (Shimeam); descendant of the Benjamite Jeiel of Gibeon.—1Ch 8:1, 29-32; 9:35-38.

2. Leader appointed for the king's service during the second month in the division commanded by Dodai the Ahohite.—1Ch 27:1, 4.

MIKNEIAH (Mik·ne′iah) [Herds (Livestock) of Jehovah]. One of the Levites who played harps while the Ark was transported from the house of Obed-edom to Jerusalem.—1Ch 15:17, 18, 21.

MIKTAM (mik′tam). A Hebrew word contained in the superscriptions of six psalms ascribed to David. (Ps 16, 56-60) This term may simply mean that the psalms are inscriptions of the episodes that they relate.

MILALAI (Mil′a·lai). A Levite musician who marched in one of the inaugural processions on Jerusalem's rebuilt wall in Nehemiah's day.—Ne 12:31, 36.

MILCAH (Mil′cah).

1. Daughter of Abraham's (Abram's) brother Haran, wife of his brother Nahor (her uncle), and the sister of Lot. (Ge 11:27, 29) Bethuel, one of Milcah's eight children, became father to Rebekah. —Ge 22:20-23; 24:15, 24, 47.

2. One of Zelophehad's five daughters given an inheritance in the territory of Manasseh after their father's death.—Nu 26:33; 27:1-4; 36:10-12; Jos 17:3, 4.

MILCOM (Mil′com) [from a root meaning "king"]. Evidently the same as Molech, god of the Ammonites. It was to Milcom and other deities that King Solomon, when deviating from true worship toward the close of his reign, built high places.—1Ki 11:4, 5, 7, 33; 2Ki 23:13; see MOLECH.

MILDEW. Generally, any of numerous plant diseases caused by fungi. The ruining of crops by mildew was one of the calamities experienced by unfaithful Israel. (De 28:22; 1Ki 8:37-39; 2Ch 6:28-30; Am 4:9; Hag 2:17) It has been suggested that the mildew of the Bible may be black stem rust (*Puccinia graminis*). This serious parasitic disease deprives plants of needed nourishment and water and thus can cause the kernels of grain to dry up. Small rust-colored spots appear on the stems and leaves of attacked cereal plants.

MILDNESS. A *New Testament Wordbook*, by William Barclay, says of the adjective *pra·ys′*: "In classical Greek this is a lovely word. Of things it means 'gentle'. It is used, for instance, of a gentle breeze or a gentle voice. Of persons it means 'mild' or 'gracious'. . . . There is gentleness in *praus* but behind the gentleness there is the strength of steel . . . It is not a spineless gentleness, a sentimental fondness, a passive quietism." (London, 1956, pp. 103, 104) *Vine's Expository Dictionary of Old and New Testament Words* states that the noun form *pra·y′tes* "consists not in a person's 'outward behaviour only; nor yet in his relations to his fellow-men; as little in his mere natural disposition. Rather it is an inwrought grace of the soul; and the exercises of it are first and chiefly towards God. It is that temper of spirit in which we accept His dealings with us as good, and therefore without disputing or resisting; it is closely linked with the word *tapeinophrosune* [humility], and follows directly upon it.'"—1981, Vol. 3, pp. 55, 56.

The word *pra·ys′* is variously translated in Bible versions "meek," "mild," "mild-tempered," and "gentle." (*KJ, AS, NW, NE*) However, as expressed in Barclay's work quoted in the foregoing, *pra·ys′* goes somewhat deeper than gentleness and, when used of persons, means mild, gracious.

Although Jehovah is one who will not tolerate sin and badness, he has lovingly provided the way of approach to himself through the ransom sacrifice and priestly services of Jesus Christ. Jehovah's worshipers and servants can therefore seek his face without any feeling of morbid fear and dread. (Heb 4:16; 10:19-22; 1Jo 4:17, 18) Jesus represented Jehovah God so perfectly that he could say: "He that has seen me has seen the Father also." He also said: "Come to me, all you who are toiling and loaded down, and I will refresh you. Take my yoke upon you and learn from me, for I am mild-tempered [Gr., *pra·ys′*] and lowly in heart, and you will find refreshment for your souls. For my yoke is kindly and my load is light." (Joh 14:9; Mt 11:28-30) Accordingly, Jehovah God is fully approachable by those who love him, and he generates mildness, great confidence, and strength in those appealing to him.

A Trait of Strength. Mildness of temper or of spirit is not an attribute of one weak in character. Jesus Christ said: "I am mild-tempered and lowly in heart." (Mt 11:29; 2Co 10:1) Yet Jesus had the full power of his Father backing him, and he was firm for what is right; he used great freeness of speech and action when such was called for.—Mt 23:13-39; compare 21:5.

The mild-tempered person is such because he

has faith and a source of strength. He is not easily unbalanced or caused to lose his good sense. Lack of mildness of temper is the result of insecurity, frustration, lack of faith and hope, and even desperation. A person who is not mild-tempered is described by the proverb: "As a city broken through, without a wall, is the man that has no restraint for his spirit." (Pr 25:28) He is open and vulnerable to the invasion of any and all improper thoughts, which may motivate him to improper actions.

A Fruit of the Spirit. Mildness is a fruit of God's holy spirit, his active force. (Ga 5:22, 23) God is therefore the Source of mildness, and one must apply to him for his spirit and must cultivate this fruit of the spirit to have genuine mildness of temper. Hence, it is not acquired by the exercise of sheer willpower, but results from drawing close to God.

Lack of mildness results in undue excitability, harshness, lack of self-control, and fights. On the other hand, the Christian is counseled to preserve unity and peace by "lowliness of mind and mildness."—Eph 4:1-3.

Jealousy and contention, if allowed to take root and grow, will lead to disorders of every sort. Mildness, on the other hand, will prevent such conditions from developing among the followers of Christ. Hence, the Bible writer James urges those who are wise and understanding in the congregation to display "fine conduct" in the form of "mildness that belongs to wisdom," "the wisdom from above."—Jas 3:13, 17.

"Mildness," in the Bible, is frequently coupled with "spirit," for example, "mildness of spirit," or "mild spirit." Genuine mildness is, accordingly, something that is more than an outward, transitory or occasional quality; rather, it is a part of one's makeup, or temperament. The apostle Peter points out this fact when he says: "And do not let your adornment be that of the external braiding of the hair and of the putting on of gold ornaments or the wearing of outer garments, but let it be the secret person of the heart in the incorruptible apparel of the quiet and mild spirit, which is of great value in the eyes of God."—1Pe 3:3, 4.

The apostle Paul writes: "Clothe yourselves with . . . mildness," which, superficially read, might seem to indicate that it is somewhat of a veneer for mere outward appearance; but in the same context he admonishes: "Clothe yourselves with the new personality, which through accurate knowledge is being made new according to the image of the One who created it." (Col 3:10, 12; Eph 4:22-24) This shows that mildness is indeed a personality trait, primarily gained as a fruit of God's spirit through accurate knowledge and application thereof, rather than just naturally inherited.

Essential for Those Having Oversight. In his letter of instructions to young Timothy on proper care of the congregation, Paul commanded him as to handling difficult matters, saying: "A slave of the Lord does not need to fight, but needs to be gentle toward all, qualified to teach, keeping himself restrained under evil, instructing with mildness those not favorably disposed; as perhaps God may give them repentance." (2Ti 2:24, 25) Here we see a similarity between mildness and long-suffering. The individual realizes why he has to deal with the difficulty: God has permitted it, and as an overseer he must handle it in the best interests of the individual(s) involved. He must put up with the difficulty until it is settled, without getting overwrought.

Titus, another overseer, residing in Crete, was likewise counseled to remind his Christian brothers "to be reasonable, exhibiting all mildness toward all men." To impress upon Titus the need for mildness, Paul calls attention to the unsurpassed love and mercy of God as manifested through his Son, calling for a forsaking of the old ways of maliciousness and hatred and following the new way leading to everlasting life.—Tit 3:1-7.

Again, Paul addresses those who are spiritually mature ones in the congregation, outlining the responsibility upon them: "Even though a man takes some false step before he is aware of it, you who have spiritual qualifications try to readjust such a man in a spirit of mildness, as you each keep an eye on yourself, for fear you also may be tempted." (Ga 6:1) They should keep in mind how God has dealt with them. Doing so, they should not give the erring man a harsh reprimand but should try to readjust him in a spirit of mildness. This will prove to be far more effective and beneficial to all concerned.

Mildness will accomplish good when dealing with a difficult situation or an angry person, breaking down difficulty, whereas harshness would magnify the bad situation. The proverb says: "An answer, when mild, turns away rage, but a word causing pain makes anger to come up." (Pr 15:1) Mildness can have great force. "By patience a commander is induced, and a mild tongue itself can break a bone."—Pr 25:15.

Essential When Under Discipline. Another fine principle involving mildness or calmness is set forth by Solomon. It concerns the tendency we may have to show a rebellious spirit when corrected or chastised by one in authority. We may get so indignant as to leave our place of proper submission, hastily giving up our assigned position. But Solomon warns: "If the spirit of a ruler should mount up against you, do not leave your own place, for calmness itself allays great sins." (Ec 10:4; compare Tit 3:2.) The proper attitude of calmness and mildness under discipline not only avoids further anger from the authority but also enables us to improve our personality through keeping our temper and our assigned place, or position, and applying the discipline.

This is especially true when the ruler is Jehovah God and when discipline comes through those set in authority by him. (Heb 12:7-11; 13:17) It also applies in our relationship to those permitted by God to wield worldly governing authority. (Ro 13:1-7) Even when such a ruler may make a harsh demand of the Christian as to the reason for the hope he has, the Christian, while firmly putting obedience to God first, should answer "with a mild temper and deep respect."—1Pe 3:15.

MILE.

A measure of distance. (Mt 5:41) In the Scriptures *mi'li·on*, the measure in question, is probably the Roman mile (1,479.5 m; 4,854 ft). At Luke 24:13; John 6:19; 11:18 the word *mi'li·on* does not appear in the Greek text, but the distance figures are given in terms of stadia (1 Roman stadium = 1/8 Roman mi; 185 m; 606.75 ft). In the *New World Translation* the figures for the stadia at Luke 24:13; John 6:19; 11:18 have been converted to statute miles. For example, "sixty stadia" is given as "about seven miles" (11 km).—Lu 24:13.

MILETUS

(Mi·le'tus). A city on the W coast of Asia Minor that is now in ruins. It lies near the mouth of the Maeander (Menderes) River and anciently had four harbors. By the seventh century B.C.E. the Ionians seem to have made Miletus a prosperous commercial center having numerous colonies on the Black Sea and in Egypt. The woolen goods of Miletus became widely known. Indicative of this is the fact that at Ezekiel 27:18 the Greek *Septuagint* lists "wool from Miletus" as an item of Tyre's trade. Miletus was also the home of famous philosophers such as Thales (c. 625-547 B.C.E.), regarded as the founder of Greek geometry, astronomy, and philosophy. In the fifth century B.C.E. the Persians captured and destroyed Miletus for having shared in revolt. Later (in 334 B.C.E.), the rebuilt city fell to Alexander the Great. During Hellenic and Roman times Miletus witnessed considerable architectural activity. An impressive ruin from this period is a large theater built in an open field.

As time passed, the city declined in importance.

This is attributed to the silting up of its harbor facilities by the Maeander River. Ancient Miletus seems to have been situated on a promontory extending from the S side of the Latmian Gulf. But today the ruins of the city lie about 8 km (5 mi) inland, and what was once the gulf is a lake.

Paul Visits. It was to Miletus that the apostle Paul came, in about 56 C.E. Because of wanting to get to Jerusalem by Pentecost if at all possible and not wishing to spend time unnecessarily in Asia Minor, Paul, apparently at Assos, decided to take a vessel that bypassed Ephesus. But he did not neglect the needs of the congregation there. From Miletus, doubtless by means of a messenger, Paul sent for the older men of the Ephesus congregation, about 50 km (30 mi) away. The additional time it took for word to reach them and for them to come to Miletus (perhaps a minimum of three days) apparently was less than might have been involved had Paul gone to Ephesus. Possibly this was because the available ship(s) from Assos putting into port at Ephesus made more breaks in the voyage than did the one(s) stopping at Miletus. Or, circumstances in Ephesus itself might have delayed Paul had he stopped there.—Ac 20:14-17.

In speaking to the older men of the Ephesus congregation, Paul reviewed his own ministry among them, admonished them to pay attention to themselves and to the flock, alerted them to the danger of "oppressive wolves" entering the congregation, and encouraged them to stay awake and to keep in mind his example. Having been told that they would see him no more, these overseers gave way to considerable weeping, "fell upon Paul's neck and tenderly kissed him," and then conducted him to the boat.—Ac 20:18-38.

At an unspecified time after his first imprisonment in Rome, Paul seems to have returned to Miletus. Trophimus, who had earlier accompanied him from Miletus to Jerusalem, became ill, necessitating Paul's leaving him behind.—Compare Ac 20:4; 21:29; 2Ti 4:20.

MILITARY COMMANDER.

The Greek word *khi·li'ar·khos* (chiliarch) means "commander of 1,000 soldiers." With the exception of its use in Revelation, it refers to a Roman military tribune. There were six tribunes in each Roman legion. The legion, however, was not divided into six different commands; rather, each tribune commanded the whole legion one sixth of the time. For each two-month period, two tribunes served on alternate days.—See ARMY (Roman).

Such a military commander was vested with great authority. He nominated and assigned centurions. He presided at courts-martial and could order capital punishment. He had a body of attendants serving as aides. His rank was recognized by his dress: a purple stripe on his toga and a gold ring of distinction. At one time these tribunes were elected by the people; later the Senate and other civil or military personnel were primarily responsible for their appointment. Normally ten years' infantry duty or five years in the cavalry were required. Augustus allowed sons of senators to begin their careers as tribunes. Tiberius reserved the right of appointment to himself.

At the celebration of Herod's birthday these commanders were among the honored guests entertained by the dancer Salome. In the presence of such men of rank, Herod felt compelled to keep his oath and so ordered John the Baptizer beheaded. (Mr 6:21-26) A military commander (chiliarch) accompanied the soldiers who arrested Jesus. —Joh 18:12.

In about 56 C.E., Claudius Lysias was the military commander of the Jerusalem garrison. He was the one who rescued Paul both from the street mob and from the rioting Sanhedrin and who wrote a letter of explanation to Governor Felix when Paul was secretly slipped down to Caesarea. (Ac 21:30–24:22) Military commanders were present in numbers when Paul appeared before Herod Agrippa II.—Ac 25:23.

"Military commanders" are also mentioned in John's vision, in the book of Revelation, as being among those against whom God's judgments are executed.—Re 6:15; 19:18.

MILK. The product of female mammals for nourishment of their young. It is also used as food by mankind in general. (Ge 18:8; Jg 4:19; 5:25) The Hebrew word rendered "milk" usually refers to fresh milk and is generally distinguished from curds, cheese, and butter. (De 32:14; 2Sa 17:29; Job 10:10; Pr 27:27) No distinction is made, however, between milk of cows, sheep, and goats. (Eze 25:4; 1Co 9:7) Sour or curdled milk was often mixed with honey and was regarded as a refreshing drink. David took "ten portions of milk" ("cheese," *Vg*) to "the chief of the thousand" when taking food to his brothers in the army camp. These portions may have been in the form of fresh-milk cheese. *Rotherham* says "ten slices of soft cheese."—1Sa 17:17, 18.

Why did the Law forbid boiling a kid in its mother's milk?

Boiling a kid in its mother's milk was prohibited under the Mosaic Law. (De 14:21) This prohibition is mentioned twice in connection with the giving of one's firstfruits to Jehovah.—Ex 23:19; 34:26.

It has been theorized that this practice had pagan, idolatrous, or magical connections. However, the evidence to support this view is not sound at present.

Another suggestion is that this statute emphasizes that there is a proper and fitting order in matters that should be adhered to. God provided the milk of the mother for the purpose of nourishing her young. To use it to boil her offspring to prepare it to be eaten would be to the kid's harm and the opposite of what God had in mind when making provision for such milk.

A third possibility is that this command was given in order to encourage compassion. This would be in harmony with other commands that prohibited sacrificing an animal if it had not first been with its mother for at least seven days (Le 22:27), slaughtering both an animal and its offspring on the same day (Le 22:28), or taking from a nest both a mother and its eggs or offspring (De 22:6, 7).

In Prophecy. Regarding Immanuel it was foretold: "Due to the abundance of the producing of milk, he will eat butter; because butter and honey are what everyone left remaining in the midst of the land will eat." This circumstance was to result from the devastation of Judah by the Assyrians. On account of this devastation, formerly cultivated land would become choked with weeds. Therefore, those left remaining in the land would have to subsist to a considerable degree on dairy products and wild honey. There being ample pasturage, the animals that had been preserved alive would produce an abundance of milk for the greatly reduced population.—Isa 7:20-25; compare 37:30-33.

Illustrative Use. Often milk is referred to in a figurative or an illustrative way. (Ge 49:12; Ca 5:12; La 4:7) Resources of nations and people are called milk. (Isa 60:16) The Promised Land is repeatedly described as "flowing with milk and honey," denoting abundance, fruitfulness, and prosperity due to Jehovah's blessing. (Ex 3:8; De 6:3; Jos 5:6; Jer 11:5; Eze 20:6; Joe 3:18) The shepherd of The Song of Solomon spoke of his beloved Shulammite as having honey and milk under her tongue, evidently meaning that her tongue gave expression to pleasant words.—Ca 4:11.

Since milk promotes physical growth to maturity, elementary Christian doctrine is likened to "milk" for spiritual babes, which will strengthen them to grow to the point of being able to assimilate "solid food," the deeper spiritual truths. (1Co

3:2; Heb 5:12-14) The apostle Peter, speaking to Christians, says: "As newborn infants, form a longing for the unadulterated milk belonging to the word." For what purpose? That they might keep on growing not merely to maturity but "to *salvation,*" that is, make their calling and choosing sure for themselves. (1Pe 2:2; 2Pe 1:10) At Isaiah 55:1, God calls on spiritually thirsty ones to buy this growth-promoting spiritual "milk," which, through his undeserved kindness, they can obtain "without money and without price."

MILL. A simple apparatus generally consisting of two circular stones (one placed atop the other), between which various edible threshed grains are ground into flour. It was possible to pound grain with a pestle in a mortar, rub it on a stone slab with a stone, or grind it with a hand mill, the method employed in most ancient Palestinian homes. Such devices were used from early patriarchal times, for Abraham's wife Sarah made round cakes from "fine flour." (Ge 18:6) In the wilderness the Israelites ground the divinely provided manna "in hand mills or pounded it in a mortar."—Nu 11:7, 8; see MORTAR, I.

Bread was generally baked every day, and usually each family possessed its own hand mill. The grinding of grain into flour was ordinarily a daily activity of the women in the household. (Mt 24:41; Job 31:10; Ex 11:5; Isa 47:1, 2) They rose early in the morning to prepare the flour needed for the day's bread. The sound of hand mills is referred to in the Bible as a symbol of normal peaceful conditions. Conversely, abandonment and desolation were indicated when "the sound of the hand mill" was absent.—Jer 25:10, 11; Re 18:21, 22; compare Ec 12:3, 4.

Like its modern counterpart in the Middle East, the common hand mill of ancient times consisted of two round stones, the upper grindstone to fit and revolve on the lower one. (De 24:6; Job 41:24) Today, the heavy lower (nether) stone is usually made of basalt and is often about 46 cm (18 in.) in diameter and 5 to 10 cm (2 to 4 in.) thick. A peg fitted into the center of the lower stone serves as a pivot for the upper stone. The grinding surface of the stationary lower stone is convex, allowing the pulverized grain to drift out to the mill's perimeter. The concave lower surface of the upper millstone (the rider) matches the top of the lower stone. A funnellike hole in the center of the upper stone accommodates the peg and also serves as a place to put the grain into the mill. Toward the outer edge of the upper stone there is a hole into which a wooden stick is inserted, this serving as a handle for the upper grindstone.

Two women generally operated this kind of hand mill. (Lu 17:35) They sat facing each other, each placing one hand on the handle to turn the upper stone. With her free hand, one woman fed unground grain in small amounts into the filler hole of the upper stone, while the other gathered the flour as it emerged from the rim of the mill and fell to the tray or the cloth spread beneath the mill.

Since bread was usually baked daily and grain was ground into flour frequently, God's law given to Israel mercifully forbade the seizing of a person's hand mill or its upper grindstone as a pledge. A family's daily bread depended upon the hand mill. Hence, to seize it or its upper grindstone meant seizing "a soul" or "means of life."—De 24:6, ftn.

Larger mills are also mentioned in the Scriptures. Jesus Christ referred to "a millstone such as is turned by an ass" (Mt 18:6), which may have been similar to the one that blind Samson was forced to turn for the Philistines when "he came to be a grinder in the prison house."—Jg 16:21.

During Abimelech's attack on the town of Thebez "a certain woman pitched an upper millstone upon Abimelech's head and broke his skull in pieces." (Jg 9:50, 53; 2Sa 11:21) In Revelation the sudden and final destruction of Babylon the Great is likened to the hurling of "a stone like a great millstone" into the sea.—Re 18:21.

MILLET [Heb., *do'chan*]. The Hebrew word *do'chan* is generally understood to refer to common millet (*Panicum miliaceum*), if not also including other related or similar grasses such as sorghum. Common millet is distinguished by its broad leaves and its bristly, extensively branched panicles, or clusters of seeds. The stalks of the plant are commonly fed to livestock, and its tiny seeds, of which there are many in each panicle, are still used in the Middle East for making bread, usually in combination with other cereals. (Eze 4:9) At Isaiah 28:25, the Hebrew term *soh·rah'* may also denote millet.

MILLO (Mil'lo) [from a root meaning "fill"]. "The house of Millo" ("Beth-millo," *AT, JB, RS*) may have been a fortress or citadel and was perhaps the same as "the tower of Shechem." Apparently the men of "the house of Millo" shared in making Abimelech king. The prophetic words of Gideon's son Jotham pointed to disaster for "the house of Millo" at the hands of Abimelech. This was fulfilled when Abimelech set the vault of the house of El-berith on fire and all those who had sought refuge there perished.—Jg 9:6, 20, 46-49.

MILLSTONE. See MILL.

MINA (mi'na). A unit both of weight and of monetary value. (1Ki 10:17; Ezr 2:69; Ne 7:71) According to the Hebrew text of Ezekiel 45:12, one mina (maneh) equals 60 shekels. The Greek *Septuagint* rendering of the scripture, though, assigns a value of 50 shekels to the mina. (See *RS, Mo.*) Since, when large numbers of shekels are referred to in the Bible, the numbers are divisible by 50, this may indicate that in earlier times a mina consisted of 50 shekels.—Ge 23:15; Ex 30:24; 38:29; Nu 31:52; 1Sa 17:5.

There is archaeological testimony for a mina of 50 shekels. An uninscribed weight of about 4,565 g (12.2 lb t) found at Tell Beit Mirsim, if divided into eight minas of 50 shekels, would yield a shekel of 11.4 grams. This value basically corresponds to that of the average of some 45 inscribed shekel weights found in Palestine. Therefore, in this publication the mina of the Hebrew Scriptures is calculated at 50 shekels or 1/60 talent, that is, 570 g (18.35 oz t). Accordingly, in modern values, the silver mina would equal $110.10 and the gold mina $6,422.50.

There is also a possibility that, as in the case of the cubit, two values were assigned to the mina, one perhaps for a royal mina (compare 2Sa 14:26) and the other for a common mina.—Compare Eze 40:5.

The mina (*mna*) of the Christian Greek Scriptures (Lu 19:13-25) is reckoned at 100 drachmas, this being the value derived from ancient Greek writers. The drachma was worth nearly as much as a denarius. So the mina was a considerable sum. The present-day value would be $65.40; in the first century C.E., it amounted to about a fourth of the wages earned annually by an agricultural worker.

MIND. A faculty of the brain with which we gather information, reason, and draw conclusions. "Mind" is rendered from several related Greek words expressing such attributes of the mind as thinking faculties, intellectual capacity, mental perception, intelligence, reason, thought, intention, remembrance, mental state or view, opinion, and mental inclination, attitude, or powers. Though, at times, in various translations the word "mind" is used, in the same instances other translations employ the above descriptive and specific terms. In the Hebrew text, the words for "remember" and "consider" may be translated in certain places by such expressions as "keep in mind" and "have in mind." In the Hebrew Scriptures, "mind"

appears in some versions as a rendering of the Hebrew words that are, literally and properly, "heart," "soul," and "spirit."—Compare De 4:39, ftn; 2Ki 9:15, *Ro;* Eze 20:32, *JB;* see HEART.

"New in the Force Actuating Your Mind." The inclination of the mind of imperfect man is naturally toward wrong thinking. The Bible terms it the "fleshly frame of mind." (Col 2:18) Christians are reminded that formerly they were enemies of God because their minds had been on the works that were wicked.—Col 1:21.

The mind of the "physical" (literally, "soulical") man, as distinguished from the "spiritual" man, is inclined in the direction of materialistic things. The force that actuates his mind has been formed in him in part by inheritance and in part by the things he has been taught and has experienced. When a matter is presented to him, this force pushes or inclines his mind in a materialistic or fleshly direction. Christians are commanded, therefore, to "be made new in the force [spirit] actuating your mind." (Eph 4:23) By a study of God's Word of truth and by the operation of God's spirit, this actuating force can be changed so that the person's dominant mental attitude is inclined in a right direction. Then, when a matter is presented to the person, the mind will be inclined by this force toward a proper spiritual course. (1Co 2:13-15) Such a person comes to have "the mind of Christ," who was at all times actuated by the proper force, his mental inclination always being spiritual.—1Co 2:16; Ro 15:5.

Mere knowledge or intellectual power is not enough to bring one into God's favor. These things themselves will not make the mind over in the direction of God's will. (Ro 12:2) Jehovah says: "I will make the wisdom of the wise men perish, and the intelligence of the intellectual men I will shove aside." (1Co 1:19) It requires the help of God's spirit to get true understanding (Pr 4:5-7; 1Co 2:11), wisdom, and good sense.—Eph 1:8, 9.

The 'Law of the Mind.' The apostle Paul calls that which directs the operation of this renewed mind the *law of the mind.* It controls the new mind according to "the law of God," and the new mind delights in this law. But "sin's law" operating in fallen flesh fights against the 'law of the mind,' so that there is a constant conflict within the Christian. Can he be victorious? Yes, "thanks to God through Jesus Christ our Lord!" God's undeserved kindness provides, on the basis of Christ's ransom sacrifice, forgiveness for the sins of the flesh and, additionally, the help of holy spirit. The Christian is in a situation different from that of the non-Christian, as Paul sums it up: "So, then, with my mind I myself am a slave to God's law, but with my flesh to sin's law."—Ro 7:21-25; Ga 5:16, 17.

How does the mind win out in the battle? The apostle illuminates the matter further, saying: "Those who are in accord with the flesh set their minds on the things of the flesh, but those in accord with the spirit on the things of the spirit. For the minding of the flesh means death, but the minding of the spirit means life and peace; because the minding of the flesh means enmity with God, for it [fallen, imperfect flesh] is not under subjection to the law of God, nor, in fact, can it be. . . . If, now, the spirit of him that raised up Jesus from the dead dwells in you, he that raised up Christ Jesus from the dead will also make your mortal bodies alive through his spirit that resides in you."—Ro 8:5-11.

The "Meaning" of the Spirit. At Romans 8:26, 27, Paul shows that, when God's servants are praying, they may not always know exactly what they should pray for as they need to. But God knows that they desire his will to be done. He also knows what his servants need. God has in the past caused many inspired prayers to be recorded in his Word, expressing his will or mind for them. He therefore accepts these inspired prayers as being what his people should like to ask and pray for, and accordingly, he fulfills them. God knows the righthearted ones and also knows the meaning of the things that he caused his spirit to speak through the Bible writers. He knows what the "meaning [mind, thought] of the spirit is" when the spirit thus "pleads," or intercedes, for them.

Loving With the Mind. Jehovah foretold the making of a new covenant under which the holy spirit would work to write his laws in the minds and hearts of his people. (Heb 8:10; 10:16) In this way they are able to fulfill that upon which the whole Law and the Prophets hung, namely, to 'love Jehovah your God with your whole heart and with your whole soul and with your whole mind, and your neighbor as yourself.' (Mt 22:37-40; Lu 10:27, 28) A person must love God with his whole heart (the desires, feelings, and emotions of the inner personality), his whole soul (his life and entire being), and his *whole mind* (his intellectual faculties). This latter phrase means that not only must God's servants love with feelings, emotions, and strength but they must also apply their minds vigorously in order to take in knowledge of God and Christ (Joh 17:3), to understand (Mr 12:33; Eph 3:18), to serve God and his purposes, and to share in declaring the good news. They are counseled to 'keep their minds fixed on the things

above' (Col 3:2), to 'brace up their minds for activity,' and to 'keep their senses completely.' (1Pe 1:13) The apostle Peter saw the importance of 'arousing their clear thinking faculties' to keep in mind the things learned. (2Pe 3:1, 2) They must 'keep close in mind the presence of the day of Jehovah.'—2Pe 3:11, 12.

When speaking of miraculous gifts of the spirit as exercised in the early Christian congregation, Paul emphasized the need to use the mind. He said that if he were to pray in a tongue that he could not translate, his mind would be unfruitful. Again, if he were to sing praises in the same manner, how would it help the hearer who did not understand the tongue? Consequently, he said that he would rather speak five words with his mind, in order to instruct others, than ten thousand words in a tongue. He then urged his brothers to become full grown in powers of understanding.—1Co 14:13-20.

Jehovah's servants are commanded to be "fitly united in the *same mind* and in the *same line of thought.*" (1Co 1:10; Php 2:2; 1Pe 3:8) This means, of course, being united where the interests of pure worship are involved—the important things—not in individual tastes or in minor matters that will be resolved as maturity is reached. (Ro 14:2-6, 17) They are to be "of the same mind in the Lord" (Php 4:2), not to be quarreling, but to "think in agreement."—2Co 13:11.

Christians are to strive to know God better, to the extent that he reveals his mind on matters. (Ro 11:33, 34; 16:25, 26) And they are to have the mental attitude of obedience and humility of Jesus Christ; then they will have "the mind of Christ." (1Co 2:15, 16) Peter counsels: "Since Christ suffered in the flesh, you too arm yourselves with the same mental disposition."—1Pe 4:1.

Dullness or Corruptness of Mind. The Israelites at Mount Sinai, because of not having hearts fully turned to Jehovah, were *dull in mental perception,* as were those who continued under the Law after God, through Jesus, had abolished it. (2Co 3:13, 14) They did not see that Jesus was the one pointed to by the Law. (Col 2:17) As to men who did not approve of holding God in accurate knowledge but who worshiped created things, "God gave them up to a disapproved mental state"; they are *in darkness mentally,* doing all manner of unprofitable and unfitting things. (Ro 1:28; Eph 4:17, 18) Corrupt-minded men resisted the truth even in Moses' time, and later such men fought true Christianity, some even claiming to be Christians, yet trying to divide and disrupt congregations. (2Ti 3:8; Php 3:18, 19; 1Ti 6:4, 5) With minds and consciences defiled, nothing is clean to them; therefore they talk profitlessly in an effort to deceive the minds of true Christians by trying to bring them into bondage to ideas of men. (Tit 1:10-16) For this reason it is essential for all Christians, and particularly for those in responsible positions, to be *sound in mind.*—Ro 12:3; 1Ti 3:2; Tit 2:6; 1Pe 4:7.

"The god of this system of things," the Devil, is responsible for *blinding the minds* of unbelievers to the illumination of the good news about the Christ. (2Co 4:4) The danger exists, therefore, that this archenemy of God may seduce Christians by his cunning, to *corrupt their minds* away "from the sincerity and the chastity that are due the Christ." (2Co 11:3) Accordingly, it is necessary that Christians exhibit unity of mind and reasonableness, continuing in prayer, in order that the peace of God "that excels all thought" may guard their mental powers by means of Christ Jesus. —Php 4:2, 5-7.

Healing and Opening Up the Mind. Jesus restored soundness of mind to a man possessed by demons, illustrating his power to do this even to those driven insane by demons.—Mr 5:15; Lu 8:35.

He also can open up the minds of those who have faith to grasp the meaning of the Scriptures. (Lu 24:45) Timid persons or those feeling inferior intellectually can take comfort from the apostle John's words: "We know that the Son of God has come, and he has given us intellectual capacity that we may gain the knowledge of the true one [Jehovah God]."—1Jo 5:20.

Paul showed the Corinthian congregation that he was sound in mind although he appeared in their eyes to be 'out of his mind' (or, 'out of himself') when boasting about his credentials as an apostle, a thing a Christian would not normally do. He explains that he was forced to do this to bring them back to God, to save them from being pulled away. This was because they had looked to false apostles and were being turned in the wrong direction.—2Co 5:13; 11:16-21; 12:11, 12, 19-21; 13:10.

MINE, MINING. Digging beneath the surface of the earth in order to locate metals and precious stones. This is an industry nearly as old as mankind. The Genesis account refers to "Tubalcain, the forger of every sort of tool of copper and iron," who lived in pre-Flood days. (Ge 4:22) Moses, writing about 1513 B.C.E., in describing the river Pishon, mentions the "land of Havilah, where there is gold. And the gold of that land is good."

(Ge 2:11, 12) Whether the gold from Ophir was mined from underground lodes or was placer mined is not known.—1Ki 9:28; Job 28:16.

These metals were probably found to some extent in rather pure forms on or near the surface of the ground. In time, underground or lode mining operations were employed. Shafts were sunk deep along rich ore-bearing veins. About 3,600 years ago Job described how miners had "sunk a shaft far from where people reside." There "in the gloom and deep shadow" they searched, having swung down and precariously dangled to obtain the desired metals.—Job 28:1-11.

Mining was carried on extensively by the Egyptians at the time of the Exodus; the Israelites, upon leaving Egypt, took metals and precious stones, later used in building the tabernacle. (Ex 12:35, 36; 35:22; 39:6-14) Egyptian turquoise mines were located on the Sinai Peninsula some 80 km (50 mi) from Mount Sinai. Remains of Egyptian mining operations have been found along the E coast of the Red Sea.

Moses described the Promised Land into which the Israelites were about to enter as "a land the stones of which are iron and out of the mountains of which you will mine copper."—De 8:9; see COPPER; IRON; REFINE, REFINER.

MINIAMIN (Mi·ni'a·min) [From the Right Hand].

1. One of the Levites serving under Kore in office of trust for the distribution of the holy contribution among their brothers at priests' cities in King Hezekiah's day.—2Ch 31:14, 15.

2. One of the priestly paternal houses existing in the time of High Priest Joiakim. (Ne 12:12, 17) The "Mijamin" of Nehemiah 12:5 may have been its founder.

3. A priest among those with trumpets who participated in the ceremony for the inauguration of Jerusalem's rebuilt wall in Nehemiah's day. (Ne 12:40, 41) He is possibly the priest called "Mijamin" at Nehemiah 10:7.

MINISTER. This term is translated from the Hebrew word *mesha·reth'* and the Greek *di·a'ko·nos.* The Hebrew term is a participle form of the verb *sha·rath',* meaning "wait upon" or "minister to" a superior, and is used in a secular or a religious sense. (Ge 39:4; De 10:8) Concerning the word *di·a'ko·nos,* D. Edmond Hiebert wrote in *Bibliotheca Sacra:* "It has been held that the term is a compound of the preposition [*di·a*], meaning 'through,' and the noun [*ko'nis*], 'dust,' so that the term denotes one who hurries through the dust to carry out his service. But this suggested derivation is not generally accepted today. More probably the verbal root was [di·eʹko], 'to reach from one place to another,' akin to the verb [di·oʹko], 'to hasten after, to pursue.' Then the root idea is one who reaches out with diligence and persistence to render a service on behalf of others."—1983, Vol. 140, p. 153.

In Hebrew and Greek these words and their related forms are applied to both male and female. (2Sa 13:17, 18; 1Ki 1:4, 15; 2Co 3:6; Ro 16:1) Joshua was Moses' minister (or, attendant) "from his young manhood on." (Nu 11:28; Jos 1:1, ftn) Elisha's attendant was called his minister and waiter. (2Ki 4:43; 6:15) Kings and princes had their royal attendants or ministers (2Ch 22:8; Es 2:2; 6:3), some of whom waited on the royal tables.—1Ki 10:4, 5; 2Ch 9:3, 4.

Jehovah's Angelic Ministers. Jehovah God created the angels in their tens of millions, all of whom he has under his control, and whom he doubtless can call by name, as he does the numberless stars. (Ps 147:4) These serve him as his ministers, doing his will in the universe. (Ps 103: 20, 21) The psalmist says of Jehovah that he makes "his angels spirits, his ministers a devouring fire." (Ps 104:4) They are described as "spirits for public service, sent forth to minister for those who are going to inherit salvation." (Heb 1:13, 14) Angels ministered to Jesus Christ in the wilderness, after he had defeated Satan's attempts to cause him to deviate from obedience to Jehovah (Mt 4:11); also an angel appeared, strengthening him when he was praying in Gethsemane. (Lu 22:43) In the prophet Daniel's vision, wherein "someone like a son of man" was given indefinitely lasting rulership over all peoples and languages, millions of angels are shown to be ministering about the throne of the Ancient of Days.—Da 7:9-14.

The Tribe of Levi. After the Israelites were delivered from Egypt, and when the nation was organized under the Law covenant, Jehovah chose the males of the tribe of Levi as his special ministers. (Nu 3:6; 1Ch 16:4) Some of them, the family of Aaron, were priests. (De 17:12; 21:5; 1Ki 8:11; Jer 33:21) The Levites had various duties in their ministry; they were caretakers of the sanctuary with all its utensils, ministers of the singing, and so forth.—Nu 3:7, 8; 1Ch 6:32.

Prophets. In addition to using all the males of the tribe of Levi, Jehovah employed others to minister to his people Israel in a special way. These were the prophets, who served only as individually appointed and commissioned by Jehovah. Some of these were also of the priestly line

of descent, but many were from other tribes of Israel. (See PROPHET.) They were messengers of Jehovah; they were sent to warn the nation when it deviated from the Law, and they sought to turn the kings and the people back to true worship. (2Ch 36:15, 16; Jer 7:25, 26) Their prophecies aided, encouraged, and strengthened righthearted ones, especially during times of spiritual and moral decay, and at times when Israel was threatened by enemies round about.—2Ki 7; Isa 37:21-38.

Their prophecies also pointed to Jesus Christ and the Messianic Kingdom. (Re 19:10) John the Baptizer did an outstanding work, turning "the heart of fathers back toward sons, and the heart of sons back toward fathers" as he prepared the way for Jehovah's representative, the Lord Jesus Christ. (Mal 4:5, 6; Mt 11:13, 14; Lu 1:77-79) The prophets did not minister only to their contemporaries, for the apostle Peter writes to Christians: "It was revealed to them that, not to themselves, but to you, they were ministering the things that have now been announced to you through those who have declared the good news to you with holy spirit sent forth from heaven. Into these very things angels are desiring to peer."—1Pe 1:10-12.

Jesus Christ. Jesus Christ is Jehovah's chief minister (di·aʹko·nos). He "became a minister of those who are circumcised in behalf of God's truthfulness, so as to verify the promises He made to their forefathers," also, "that the nations might glorify God for his mercy." Therefore, "on him nations will rest their hope."—Ro 15:8-12.

Jesus' appointment was from Jehovah himself. When he presented himself for baptism, "the heavens were opened up," the account says, "and he [John the Baptizer] saw descending like a dove God's spirit coming upon him [Jesus]. Look! Also, there was a voice from the heavens that said: 'This is my Son, the beloved, whom I have approved.'" (Mt 3:16, 17) In his prehuman existence Jesus had served Jehovah for untold ages, but here he entered upon a new ministry. Jesus proved he was indeed God's minister, serving both God and his fellowmen. Consequently, in the synagogue of his hometown of Nazareth, Jesus was able to take the scroll of Isaiah and read what is now chapter 61, verses 1, 2: "The spirit of the Sovereign Lord Jehovah is upon me, for the reason that Jehovah has anointed me to tell good news to the meek ones. He has sent me to bind up the brokenhearted, to proclaim liberty to those taken captive and the wide opening of the eyes even to the prisoners; to proclaim the year of goodwill on the part of Jehovah." Then he went on to say to those assembled, "Today this scripture that you just heard is fulfilled."—Lu 4:16-21.

At the time Peter preached to the first Gentile convert, Cornelius, he described Jesus' course during his three and one half years of earthly ministry, calling Cornelius' attention to "Jesus who was from Nazareth, how God anointed him with holy spirit and power, and he went through the land doing good and healing all those oppressed by the Devil; because God was with him." (Ac 10:38) Jesus literally walked throughout his assigned territory in the service of Jehovah and the people. Not only that, but he actually gave up his very soul as a ransom for others. He said: "The Son of man came, not to be ministered to, but to minister and to give his soul a ransom in exchange for many."—Mt 20:28.

Christian Ministers. In his ministerial work Jesus associated with himself many others, apostles and disciples, whom he trained to carry on the same ministerial work. He sent out at first the 12, then 70 others. God's active force was also upon them, enabling them to perform many miracles. (Mt 10:1, 5-15, 27, 40; Lu 10:1-12, 16) But the major work they were to perform was to preach and teach the good news of the Kingdom of God. In fact, the miracles were primarily to give public evidence of their appointment and approval by Jehovah.—Heb 2:3, 4.

Jesus trained his disciples, both by word and by example. He taught not only publicly but also in private homes, taking the good news directly to the people. (Mt 9:10, 28; Lu 7:36; 8:1; 19:1-6) From the accounts given by the writers of the Gospels, it is evident that Jesus' disciples were present in many instances when he gave witness to various kinds of people, for the very conversations are recorded. According to the book of Acts, his disciples followed that example, making calls from house to house to declare the Kingdom message.—Ac 5:42; 20:20; see PREACHER, PREACHING ("From House to House").

Jesus told his disciples what a true minister of God was, saying: "The kings of the nations lord it over them, and those having authority over them are called Benefactors. You, though, are not to be that way. But let him that is the greatest among you become as the youngest, and the one acting as chief as the one ministering. For which one is greater, the one reclining at the table or the one ministering? Is it not the one reclining at the table?" Then, using his own course and conduct as the example, he went on to say: "But I am in your midst as the one ministering." (Lu 22:25-27) On that occasion, he forcefully demonstrated these principles, including that of humility, by washing the feet of the disciples.—Joh 13:5.

Jesus further pointed out to his disciples that true ministers of God do not accept flattering religious titles for themselves, nor do they bestow them on others. "You, do not you be called Rabbi, for one is your teacher, whereas all you are brothers. Moreover, do not call anyone your father on earth, for one is your Father, the heavenly One. Neither be called 'leaders,' for your Leader is one, the Christ. But the greatest one among you must be your minister [or, servant]. Whoever exalts himself will be humbled, and whoever humbles himself will be exalted."—Mt 23:8-12.

The anointed followers of the Lord Jesus Christ are spoken of as 'ministers of the good news,' as Paul was (Col 1:23); they are also "ministers of a new covenant," being in that covenant relationship with Jehovah God, with Christ as Mediator. (2Co 3:6; Heb 9:14, 15) In this way they are ministers of God and of Christ. (2Co 6:4; 11:23) Their qualification comes from God through Jesus Christ, not from any man or organization. The evidence of their ministry is not in some paper or certificate, like a letter of recommendation or authority. Their "letter" of recommendation is found in the persons whom they have taught and trained to be, like them, ministers of Christ. On this matter the apostle Paul says: "Do we, perhaps, like some men, need letters of recommendation to you or from you? You yourselves are our letter, inscribed on our hearts and known and being read by all mankind. For you are shown to be a letter of Christ written by us as ministers, inscribed not with ink but with spirit of a living God, not on stone tablets, but on fleshly tablets, on hearts." (2Co 3:1-3) Here the apostle shows the love and the closeness, the warm affection and care of the Christian minister, for those to whom he ministers, they being 'inscribed on [the minister's] heart.'

Thus, after Christ ascended into heaven, he gave "gifts in men" to the Christian congregation. Among these were apostles, prophets, evangelizers, shepherds, and teachers, given "with a view to the readjustment of the holy ones, for ministerial work, for the building up of the body of the Christ." (Eph 4:7-12) Their qualification as ministers is from God.—2Co 3:4-6.

The Revelation given to the apostle John pictured "a great crowd, which no man was able to number, out of all nations and tribes and peoples and tongues." These are not spoken of as being, like the anointed brothers of Jesus Christ, in the new covenant and therefore as ministers of it; nevertheless, they are shown to have a clean standing before God and "are rendering him sacred service day and night in his temple." They are therefore ministering and can properly be called ministers of God. As both the Revelation vision and Jesus himself showed (by illustration), in the time of Christ's presence on his glorious throne, there would be such persons who would also lovingly minister to the brothers of Jesus Christ, giving them aid, attention, and assistance. —Re 7:9-15; Mt 25:31-40.

Ministerial Servants in the Congregation. After listing requirements for those serving as "overseers" (e·pi'sko·poi) in the congregations, the apostle Paul lists such for those designated as "ministerial servants" (di·a'ko·noi). (1Ti 3:1-10, 12, 13) The Greek word di·a'ko·nos is in places translated simply "minister" (Mt 20:26) and 'servant.' (Mt 22:13) Since all Christians were "ministers" (servants) of God, it is evident that the term di·a'ko·noi here takes on a particular sense, one related to congregational order and structure. Thus, there were two bodies of men filling positions of congregational responsibility: the "overseers," or "older men," and the "ministerial servants." There were generally a number of both overseers and ministerial assistants in each congregation.—Php 1:1; Ac 20:17, 28.

The list of requirements for the ministerial servants as compared with that for the overseers, as well as the designations for the two positions, indicates that the ministerial servants were not assigned the responsibility of teaching or shepherding (a shepherd being an overseer of sheep). Teaching ability was not a prerequisite for their assignment. The designation di·a'ko·nos of itself indicates that these men served as assistants to the body of overseers in the congregation, their basic responsibility being that of caring for matters of a nonpastoral nature so that the overseers might concentrate their time and attention on their teaching and shepherding activity.

An example of the principle governing this arrangement may be found in the action of the apostles when problems arose as to the distribution (literally, the service, di·a·ko·ni'a) of food supplies made daily to those Christians in need at Jerusalem. Stating that it would not be 'pleasing for them to leave the word of God' to concern themselves with administration of material food problems, the apostles instructed the disciples to "search out for yourselves seven certified men from among you, full of spirit and wisdom, that we may appoint them over this necessary business; but we shall devote ourselves to prayer and to the ministry [di·a·ko·ni'ai] of the word." (Ac 6:1-6) This was the principle; but it does not

necessarily hold that the seven men selected were, in this case, not qualified as "older men" (pre·sby'te·roi), for this was not a normal or regular situation but a special problem that had arisen, one of a rather delicate nature due to the feeling that discrimination existed because of nationality. Since it affected the entire Christian congregation, it was a matter calling for "spirit and wisdom," and thus the seven men selected may, in fact, have been in a spiritual sense "older men." But they were now taking on temporarily an assignment of work such as that which "ministerial servants" might normally handle. It was business that was "necessary" but not of the same importance as "the ministry of the word."

The apostles showed their proper evaluation of matters in this action, and it may be expected that the bodies of overseers in the congregations that developed outside of Jerusalem would follow their example in assigning duties to the "ministerial servants." There were doubtless many matters of a more material, routine, or mechanical nature that required attention, perhaps including the purchase of material for copying the Scriptures or even the copying itself.

The qualifications to be met by the ministerial assistants provided standards that would protect the congregation from any legitimate accusation as to its selection of men for particular duties, thus maintaining a right standing with God and a clean reputation among outsiders. (Compare 1Ti 3:10.) The qualifications governed morality, conduct, and spirituality and, where observed, would bring into service men who were sensible, honest, conscientious, and reliable. Those who ministered in a fine manner would acquire for themselves "a fine standing and great freeness of speech in the faith in connection with Christ Jesus."—1Ti 3:13.

Earthly Rulers. God has permitted the governments of this world to operate until his due time to bring them to an end, after which Christ's Kingdom will rule the earth undisputedly. (Da 2:44; Re 19:11-21) During the time of their tolerated rule, they perform many services for the people, such as the building of roads, operation of schools, police and fire departments, and other services. They also have laws to punish thieves, murderers, and other lawbreakers. Therefore, as they perform these services and justly carry out these laws, they are 'ministers' (di·a'ko·noi) of God. If anyone, even a Christian, violates such laws, the punishment he receives at the hands of the government is in an indirect way from God, for God is against all wickedness. Also, if the government protects the Christian from violators of the law, it is acting as a minister of God. It follows that if the ruler misuses his authority and acts against God, he is responsible and must answer to God for it. If such wicked ruler tries to get the Christian to act in violation of God's law, then he is not acting as God's minister and will receive punishment from God.—Ro 13:1-4.

False Ministers. There are men who claim to be ministers of God but who are hypocrites, actually ministers of Satan fighting against God. The apostle Paul had to contend with such ones who were troubling the congregation in Corinth. Of them, he said: "Such men are false apostles, deceitful workers, transforming themselves into apostles of Christ. And no wonder, for Satan himself keeps transforming himself into an angel of light. It is therefore nothing great if his ministers also keep transforming themselves into ministers of righteousness. But their end shall be according to their works."—2Co 11:13-15.

The appearance of such false ministers was foretold many times in the Scriptures. Paul told the overseers of the congregation at Ephesus that after his going away, oppressive wolves would enter in among the congregation and would not treat the flock with tenderness; they would speak twisted things to draw away the disciples after themselves. (Ac 20:29, 30) Paul also warned of such apostate ones in his letters (2Th 2:3-12; 1Ti 4:1-5; 2Ti 3:1-7; 4:3, 4); Peter described them (2Pe 2:1-3); and Jesus Christ himself foretold their existence and destruction (Mt 13:24-30, 36-43). —See MAN OF LAWLESSNESS.

MINISTRY. The work and service performed by a minister, servant, or attendant responsible to a superior authority. In ancient Israel, the Levites served as Jehovah's ministers. Prophets were also used to minister in a special way. (De 10:8; 21:5; see LEVITES; MINISTER; PRIEST.) However, with the coming of Jesus Christ to the earth, a new ministry began. He commissioned his followers to make disciples of people of all the nations. (Mt 28:19, 20) Accordingly, to a world alienated from God, Christians bore a message of reconciliation to God through Christ.—2Co 5:18-20.

Those who responded favorably to "the ministry of the reconciliation" (2Co 5:18) needed to be trained, taught, assisted, and directed in a proper way in order to become and to remain firm in faith, as well as to accomplish the disciple-making work themselves. (Compare 2Ti 4:1, 2; Tit 1:13, 14; 2:1; 3:8.) Therefore, after his ascension to heaven, Christ Jesus, as head of the congregation, gave "gifts in men," apostles, prophets, evangeliz-

ers, shepherds, and teachers, "with a view to the readjustment of the holy ones, for ministerial work, for the building up of the body of the Christ."—Eph 4:7-16; see GIFTS FROM GOD.

Another aspect of the ministry inside the congregation concerned caring materially for needy but deserving brothers. The ministry to which Stephen and six other certified men were appointed involved the distribution of food supplies to Christian widows. (Ac 6:1-6) Later, the congregations in Macedonia and Achaia shared in a ministry of relief for the poor brothers in Judea. (2Co 8:1-4; 9:1, 2, 11-13) When the contribution was finally gathered together and Paul was preparing to take it to Jerusalem, he asked the brothers in Rome to pray along with him that this ministry of relief would be acceptable to the holy ones for whom it was intended.—Ro 15:25, 26, 30, 31.

Some years prior to this, a similar demonstration of love was made by the Christians of Antioch, in Syria, as they shared in a relief ministration for the brothers dwelling in Judea during a time of famine.—Ac 11:28-30.

MINNI (Min'ni). An ancient kingdom that was divinely summoned to fight against Babylon. At that time Minni was allied with the kingdoms of Ararat and Ashkenaz, all under the control of Cyrus.—Jer 51:27-29.

The exact location of this ancient kingdom and its people is uncertain. Some map makers have placed it in the region between Lake Van and the Araxes River, to the NE in eastern Armenia. But most commentators are of the opinion it lay in the general area SE of Lake Van.

If the Mannai or Manneans were inhabitants of Minni, as some scholars say, then according to cuneiform inscriptions Minni was intermittently under subjugation, first by the Assyrians and then by the Median Empire. According to a Babylonian chronicle, in his tenth year of reign (636 B.C.E.) Nabopolassar "captured the Manneans who had come to their (i.e. the Assyrians') aid." (*Assyrian and Babylonian Chronicles*, by A. K. Grayson, 1975, p. 91) But by the time Babylon fell in 539 B.C.E. Minni was dominated by the Medo-Persian Empire.

MINNITH (Min'nith). One of 20 Ammonite cities that Jephthah subdued after making his vow to Jehovah. (Jg 11:30-33) Centuries later "wheat of Minnith" is mentioned as an item of Tyre's trade. (Eze 27:2, 17) The exact location of Minnith is not known. One of a number of possible identifications is Khirbet Hanizeh (Umm el Hanafish), about 6 km (3.5 mi) ENE of Heshbon.

MINT [Gr., *he·dy'o·smon*]. A strongly scented herb, sole mention of which is made in Scripture with reference to the scrupulous care exercised by the scribes and Pharisees in giving the tenth of the mint, while disregarding the weightier matters of the Law. (Mt 23:23; Lu 11:42) Several varieties of mint are found in Palestine and Syria, the horse-mint (*Mentha longifolia*) being the more common. Likely the Greek word *he·dy'o·smon* (literally, sweet-smelling) was not restricted to a particular variety but embraced the various known kinds of mint.

The stems of mint plants are square, with the leaves growing in twos, one on each side of the stem. The small, bluish- or pinkish-white flowers are arranged in clusters, forming either separate whorls or terminal spikes. From ancient times mint has been used in medicine and for flavoring food; this is because of the fragrant oil contained in the plant's leaves and stems.

MIRACLES. Occurrences that excite wonder or astonishment; effects in the physical world that surpass all known human or natural powers and are therefore attributed to supernatural agency. In the Hebrew Scriptures the word *moh·pheth'*, sometimes translated "miracle," also means "portent," "wonder," and "token." (De 28:46; 1Ch 16: 12, ftn) It is often used in conjunction with the Hebrew word *'ohth*, meaning "sign." (De 4:34) In the Greek Scriptures the word *dy'na·mis*, "power," is rendered "powerful works," "ability," "miracle." —Mt 25:15; Lu 6:19; 1Co 12:10, *AT, KJ, NW, RS*.

A miracle, amazing to the eye of the beholder, is something beyond his ability to perform or even to understand fully. It is also a powerful work, requiring greater power or knowledge than he has. But from the viewpoint of the one who is the source of such power, it is not a miracle. He understands it and has the ability to do it. Thus, many acts that God performs are amazing to humans beholding them but are merely the exercise of his power. If a person believes in a deity, particularly in the God of creation, he cannot consistently deny God's power to accomplish things awe-inspiring to the eyes of men.—Ro 1:20; see POWER, POWERFUL WORKS.

Are miracles compatible with natural law?

Through study and observation, researchers have identified various uniform operations of things in the universe and have recognized laws covering such uniformity in natural phenomena. One such is 'the law of gravity.' Scientists admit the complexity and yet the reliability of these laws, and in calling them "laws" imply the existence of One who put such laws into force. Skeptics view a miracle as a violation of laws they accept as natural, irrevocable, inexorable; therefore, they say, a miracle never occurs. It is good to keep in mind that their attitude is that if it is not understandable and explainable to us as far as we discern these laws, it cannot happen.

However, capable scientists are becoming increasingly cautious about saying that a certain thing is *impossible*. Professor John R. Brobeck of the University of Pennsylvania stated: "A scientist is no longer able to say honestly something is impossible. He can only say it is improbable. But he may be able to say something is impossible to explain in terms of our present knowledge. Science cannot say that all properties of matter and all forms of energy are now known. . . . [For a miracle] one thing that needs to be added is a source of energy unknown to us in our biological and physiological sciences. In our Scriptures this source of energy is identified as the power of God." (*Time*, July 4, 1955) Since this statement was made, further scientific development has made it more emphatic.

Scientists do not *fully* understand the properties of heat, light, atomic and nuclear action, electricity, or any of the forms of matter under even normal conditions. Even more deficient is their understanding of these properties under *unusual* or *abnormal* conditions. For example, it is relatively recently that extensive investigations have been made under conditions of extreme cold, but in this brief time, many strange actions of the elements have been observed. Lead, which is not an ideal electrical conductor, when immersed in liquid helium cooled to a temperature of $-271°$ C. ($-456°$ F.) strangely becomes a superconductor and a powerful electromagnet when a bar magnet is placed near it. At such supercold temperature helium itself appears to defy the law of gravity by creeping up the side of a glass beaker and over the edge, draining itself out of the container.—*Matter*, Life Science Library, 1963, pp. 68, 69.

This discovery is one of many that have astounded scientists, seeming to upset their former ideas. How, then, can anyone say that God violated his own laws in performing powerful works that seemed amazing and miraculous to men? Surely the Creator of the physical universe has perfect control of that which he created and can maneuver these things within the framework of the laws he has made inherent in them. (Job 38) He can bring about the condition necessary for the performance of these works; he can speed up, slow down, modify, or neutralize reactions. Or angels, with greater power than man, can do so in carrying out Jehovah's will.—Ex 3:2; Ps 78:44-49.

Certainly the scientist is not superseding or going beyond physical laws when he applies more heat or cold, or more oxygen, and so forth, to speed up or slow down a chemical process. Nevertheless, skeptics challenge the Bible miracles, including the "miracle" of creation. These challengers are asserting, in effect, that they are familiar with all conditions and processes that ever took place. They are insisting that the operations of the Creator must be limited by the narrow confines of their understanding of the laws governing physical things.

This weakness on the part of scientists is acknowledged by a Swedish professor of plasma physics, who pointed out: "No one questions the obedience of the earth's atmosphere to the laws of mechanics and atomic physics. All the same, it may be extremely difficult for us to determine how these laws operate with respect to any given situation involving atmospheric phenomena." (Worlds-Antiworlds, by H. Alfvén, 1966, p. 5) The professor applied this thought to the origin of the universe. God established the physical laws governing the earth, sun, and moon, and within their framework men have been able to do marvelous things. Surely God could bring the laws to play so as to produce a result unexpected by humans; it would present no problem for him to split the Red Sea so that "the waters were a wall" on each side. (Ex 14:22) Though, to man, walking on water is an astounding feat, with what ease it could be accomplished in the power of "the One who is stretching out the heavens just as a fine gauze, who spreads them out like a tent in which to dwell." Further, God is described as creating, and having control of, all the things in the heavens, and it is said that "due to the abundance of dynamic energy, he also being vigorous in power, not one of them is missing."—Isa 40:21, 22, 25, 26.

Since the acknowledgment of the existence of law, such as the law of gravity, presupposes a lawmaker of surpassing, superhuman intelligence and power, why question his ability to do marvelous things? Why try to limit his operation to the infinitesimally narrow scope of man's knowledge and experience? The patriarch Job describes the darkness and foolishness into which God lets these go who thus pit their wisdom against his.—Job 12:16-25; compare Ro 1:18-23.

God's Adherence to His Moral Law. The God of creation is not a whimsical God, unreliably violating his own laws. (Mal 3:6) This fact can be seen in God's adherence to his moral laws, which are in harmony with his physical laws but are higher and grander than they are. In justice he cannot condone unrighteousness. "You are too pure in eyes to see what is bad; and to look on trouble you are not able," says his prophet. (Hab 1:13; Ex 34:7) He expressed his law to Israel: "Soul will be for soul, eye for eye, tooth for tooth, hand for hand, foot for foot." (De 19:21) When he desired to forgive helpless, repentant men for the sin that is the cause of their dying, God had to have a legal basis if he was going to adhere to his law. (Ro 5:12; Ps 49:6-8) He proved to be strict in his adherence to law, going to the point of sacrificing his only-begotten Son as a ransom for the sins of mankind. (Mt 20:28) The apostle Paul points out that, "through the release by the ransom paid by Christ Jesus," Jehovah was able to "exhibit his own righteousness . . . that he might be righteous even when declaring righteous the man that has faith in Jesus." (Ro 3:24, 26) If we appreciate that God, out of respect for his moral laws, did not hold back from sacrificing his beloved Son, certainly we can reason that he would never need to "violate" his physical laws to carry out anything desired within physical creation.

Contrary to Human Experience? Merely to assert that miracles did not take place does not prove that they did not. The truthfulness of any recorded event of history may be challenged by someone living today, because he did not experience it and there are now no living eyewitnesses to testify to it. But that does not change the facts of history. Some object to the accounts about miracles because, they say, they are contrary to human experience, that is, human experience that they acknowledge as true from observation, books, and so forth. If scientists actually took this position in practice, there would be far less research and development of new things and processes on their part. They would not, for instance, continue research on the curing of "incurable" diseases, or on space travel to the planets or even farther into the universe. But they do investigate and sometimes bring mankind into definitely new experiences. What is accomplished today would astonish men of ancient times, and a good share of modern mankind's common daily experiences would be viewed by them as miracles.

Not "Explained Away" by Logic. Some opponents of the Bible account hold that Bible miracles can be scientifically and logically explained as merely natural happenings and that the Bible writers merely attributed these happenings to God's intervention. It is true that such things as earthquakes were employed. (1Sa 14:15, 16; Mt 27:51) But this in itself does not prove that God did not take a hand in these events. Not only were the things powerful works in themselves (for example, the aforementioned earthquakes) but also the *timing* was such as to make the odds overwhelming against any chance happening. For illustration: Some have contended that the manna provided for the Israelites can be found in the desert as a sweet, sticky exudation on tamarisk trees and on bushes. Even if this doubtful contention were true, the provision of it for Israel is still a miracle because of its timing, for it did not appear on the ground on the seventh day of each week. (Ex 16:4, 5, 25-27) Furthermore, whereas it bred worms and stank if kept over until the next day, it did not do so when kept over for food on the Sabbath. (Ex 16:20, 24) It might also be said that the description of this manna as an exudation from trees does not seem to agree fully with the Bible description of the manna. The Bible manna was found *on the ground* and it melted in the hot sun; it could be pounded in a mortar, ground in a mill, boiled, or baked.—Ex 16:19-23; Nu 11:8; see MANNA.

Credibility of the Testimony. The Christian religion is interwoven with the miracle of the resurrection of Jesus Christ. (1Co 15:16-19) The evidence that it took place was not weak but powerful—there were more than 500 eyewitnesses to testify that it did take place.—1Co 15:3-8; Ac 2:32.

The motive of the persons who accepted the miracle of Jesus' resurrection as true must also be considered. Many persons have experienced persecution and death for their beliefs—religious, political, and otherwise. But the Christians who so suffered received no material or political gain. Rather than get power, wealth, and prominence, they often suffered the loss of all these things. They preached Jesus' resurrection but did not use any form of violence to promote their beliefs or to defend themselves. And one reading their arguments can see that they were reasonable persons, not fanatics. They lovingly tried to help their fellowmen.

Characteristics of Bible Miracles. Noteworthy characteristics of the Biblical miracles are their open and public nature, their simplicity, their purpose and motive. Some were performed in private or before small groups (1Ki 17:19-24;

Mr 1:29-31; Ac 9:39-41), but often they were *public,* before thousands or even millions of observers. (Ex 14:21-31; 19:16-19) Jesus' works were open and public—there was no secrecy attached to them; and he healed all who came to him, not failing on the pretext that some lacked sufficient faith.—Mt 8:16; 9:35; 12:15.

Simplicity marked both miraculous cures and control over the elements. (Mr 4:39; 5:25-29; 10:46-52) In contrast to magical feats accomplished with special props, staging, lighting, and ritual, Biblical miracles generally were performed without outward display, frequently in response to a chance encounter, a request, and that on the public street or in an unprepared place.—1Ki 13:3-6; Lu 7:11-15; Ac 28:3-6.

The motive of the individual performing the miracle was not for the selfish prominence of the individual or to make anyone wealthy, but it was primarily to glorify God. (Joh 11:1-4, 15, 40) Miracles were not mysterious acts performed merely to satisfy curiosity and to mystify. They always helped others, sometimes directly in a physical way and always in a spiritual way, turning persons to true worship. Just as "the bearing witness to Jesus is what inspires prophesying ["is the spirit of the prophecy," ftns]," so, too, many of the miracles pointed to Jesus as God's sent one.—Re 19:10.

Bible miracles involved not only animate things but also inanimate ones, such as calming the wind and sea (Mt 8:24-27), stopping and starting rain (1Ki 17:1-7; 18:41-45), and changing water into blood or into wine (Ex 7:19-21; Joh 2:1-11). They also included physical cures of all types, such as "incurable" leprosy (2Ki 5:1-14; Lu 17:11-19) and blindness from birth. (Joh 9:1-7) This great variety of miracles argues for their credibility as backed by the Creator, for it is logical that only the Creator could exercise influence in *all* areas of human experience and over *all forms of matter.*

Purpose in Early Christian Congregation. Miracles served a number of important purposes. Most basic, they helped to establish or confirm the fact that a man was receiving power and support from God. (Ex 4:1-9) Both with Moses and Jesus people drew this correct conclusion. (Ex 4:30, 31; Joh 9:17, 31-33) Through Moses, God had promised a coming prophet. Jesus' miracles helped observers to identify him as that one. (De 18:18; Joh 6:14) When Christianity was young, miracles worked in conjunction with the message to help individuals to see that God was behind Christianity and had turned from the earlier Jewish system of things. (Heb 2:3, 4) In time miraculous gifts

it in the first century would pass away. They were needed only during the infancy of the Christian congregation.—1Co 13:8-11.

In reading the history of the Acts of Apostles, we see that Jehovah's spirit was working mightily, speedily, forming congregations, getting Christianity firmly established. (Ac 4:4; chaps 13, 14, 16-19) In the few short years between 33 and 70 C.E., thousands of believers were gathered in many congregations from Babylon to Rome, and perhaps even farther west. (1Pe 5:13; Ro 1:1, 7; 15:24) It is worthy of note that copies of the Scriptures then were few. Usually only the well-to-do possessed scrolls or books of any sort. In pagan lands there was no knowledge of the Bible or the God of the Bible, Jehovah. Virtually everything had to be done by word of mouth. There were no Bible commentaries, concordances, and encyclopedias readily at hand. So the miraculous gifts of special knowledge, wisdom, speaking in tongues, and discernment of inspired utterances were vital for the congregation then. (1Co 12:4-11, 27-31) But, as the apostle Paul wrote, when those things were no longer needed, they would pass away.

A Different Situation Today. We do not see God performing such miracles by the hands of his Christian servants today, because all needed things are present and available to the literate population of the world, and to help those who cannot read but who will listen, there are mature Christians who have knowledge and wisdom gained by study and experience. It is not necessary for God to perform such miracles at this time to attest to Jesus Christ as God's appointed deliverer, or to provide proof that He is backing up His servants. Even if God were to continue to give his servants the ability to perform miracles, that would not convince everyone, for not even all the eyewitnesses of Jesus' miracles were moved to accept his teachings. (Joh 12:9-11) On the other hand, scoffers are warned by the Bible that there will yet be stupendous acts of God performed in the destruction of the present system of things. —2Pe 3:1-10; Re chaps 18, 19.

In conclusion, it may be said that either those who deny the existence of miracles do not believe there is an invisible God and Creator or they believe that he has not exercised his power in any superhuman way since creation. But their unbelief does not make the Word of God of no effect. (Ro 3:3, 4) The Biblical accounts of God's miracles and the good purpose that they accomplished, always in harmony with the truths and principles found in his Word, instill confidence in God. They give strong assurance that God cares for mankind and that he can and will protect those who serve him. The miracles provide typical patterns, and the record of them builds faith that God will, in the future, intervene in a miraculous way, healing and blessing faithful humankind.—Re 21:4.

MIRIAM (Mirʹi·am) [possibly, Rebellious].

1. Daughter of Amram and his wife Jochebed, both of the tribe of Levi; sister of Moses and Aaron. (Nu 26:59; 1Ch 6:1-3) Though not specifically named in the account, she was undoubtedly the one termed "his sister" who watched to see what would become of the infant Moses as he lay in an ark placed among the reeds of the river Nile. (Ex 2:3, 4) After Pharaoh's daughter discovered the babe, "felt compassion" for it, and recognized that it was "one of the children of the Hebrews," Miriam asked if she should summon a Hebrew woman to nurse the child. Being told to do so by Pharaoh's daughter, "the maiden went and called the child's mother" (Jochebed), who was thereafter employed to care for Moses until he grew up. —Ex 2:5-10.

Leads Israel's Women in Song. Years later, after witnessing Jehovah's triumph over Pharaoh's military forces at the Red Sea and upon hearing the song of Moses and the men of Israel, "Miriam the prophetess" led the women of Israel in joyful tambourine playing and in dancing. Responding to the song led by Moses, Miriam sang: "Sing to Jehovah, for he has become highly exalted. The horse and its rider he has pitched into the sea."—Ex 15:1, 20, 21.

Complains Against Moses. While the Israelites were in the wilderness, Miriam and Aaron began to speak against Moses because of his Cushite wife. Moses' prominence and influence with the people may have created in Miriam and Aaron a jealous desire for more authority, so that they kept saying: "Is it just by Moses alone that Jehovah has spoken? Is it not by us also that he has spoken?" But Jehovah was listening and suddenly instructed Moses, Miriam, and Aaron to go to the tent of meeting. There God reminded the murmurers that their brother Moses was His servant, the one with whom God spoke, not indirectly, but "mouth to mouth." Jehovah next asked Miriam and Aaron: "Why, then, did you not fear to speak against my servant, against Moses?" God's anger got to be hot against them and, as the cloud over the tent moved away, "Miriam was struck with leprosy as white as snow." Aaron made a plea for mercy Moses interceded for her, and Jehovah allowed

Miriam to return to the camp after a humiliating seven-day quarantine.—Nu 12:1-15.

The fact that only Miriam was stricken with leprosy may suggest that she was the instigator of wrong conduct on that occasion. (See AARON.) Her sin in murmuring against Moses may have been greater than Aaron's, possibly even being a case of jealousy of a woman against another woman (since they began to speak against Moses on account of his Cushite wife), with Aaron siding in with his sister rather than his sister-in-law. Since Miriam was viewed as a prophetess, she may have enjoyed being the most prominent woman in Israel. So Miriam perhaps feared that Moses' wife would eclipse her. Regardless of such possibilities, however, and while it was grossly improper for both Miriam and Aaron to murmur against Moses, it was especially wrong for Miriam to do so because of woman's God-assigned place of subjection to the man. (1Co 11:3; 1Ti 2:11-14) Miriam's sinful conduct was later used as a warning example, for at the end of the wilderness trek Moses told the people to comply with priestly instructions regarding leprosy and urged them to remember what Jehovah had done to Miriam when they were coming out of Egypt.—De 24:8, 9.

Miriam died and was buried at Kadesh in the Wilderness of Zin, shortly before Aaron's death. (Nu 20:1, 28) Centuries later, through his prophet Micah, Jehovah called to remembrance the privilege Miriam enjoyed in association with her brothers when Israel came out of Egypt, saying: "For I brought you up out of the land of Egypt, and from the house of slaves I redeemed you; and I proceeded to send before you Moses, Aaron and Miriam."—Mic 6:4.

2. A descendant of Judah.—1Ch 4:1, 17, 18.

MIRMAH
(Mir'mah) [possibly, Deception]. A paternal head of the tribe of Benjamin and son of Shaharaim by his wife Hodesh.—1Ch 8:1, 8-10.

MIRROR.
Ancient hand mirrors (Isa 3:23) were sometimes made of polished stone, though they were generally made of metal, such as bronze or copper, and later of tin, silver, and even gold. It was probably not until the first century C.E. that mirrors of glass were introduced. Since the ancient mirrors were generally made of molten metal, they had to be highly polished in order to have good reflecting surfaces. Pounded pumice stone might be used for this purpose, it being applied periodically thereafter with a sponge that usually hung from the mirror itself. Nevertheless, ancient metal mirrors did not have as fine a reflecting surface as do today's glass mirrors. So the apostle Paul could appropriately write: "At present we see in hazy outline by means of a metal mirror."—1Co 13:12.

Figurative Use. The Scriptures at times refer to mirrors in a figurative, or an illustrative, way. At Job 37:18 the skies are likened to a metal mirror, the burnished face of which gives off a bright reflection. The disciple James used the mirror as figurative of God's word when urging persons to become, not just hearers of the word, but doers of it. (Jas 1:22-25) And the apostle Paul showed that Christians "reflect like mirrors the glory of Jehovah" in their ministry.—2Co 3:18; 4:1.

MISCARRIAGE.
See ABORTION.

MISHAEL
(Mish'a·el) [possibly, Who Is Like God?; or, Who Belongs to God?].

1. A Kohathite Levite and son of Uzziel. (Ex 6:18, 22) After Aaron's sons Nadab and Abihu were executed by Jehovah for offering illegitimate fire, Mishael and his brother Elzaphan carried their bodies outside the camp.—Le 10:1-5.

2. The original name of one of Daniel's three Judean companions who was named "Meshach" by the principal court official of Babylon.—Da 1:6, 7; see MESHACH.

3. One of the men who stood at Ezra's left hand when the copyist read from the book of the Law to the Jews assembled in Jerusalem after the Babylonian exile.—Ne 8:3, 4.

MISHAL
(Mi'shal) [Place of Making Inquiry]. A border city of Asher given to the Gershonite Levites, apparently also called Mashal. Probably Mishal was situated not far from Mount Carmel. (Jos 19:24-26; 21:27, 30; 1Ch 6:74) However, its exact location is unknown.

MISHAM
(Mi'sham). Son of the Benjamite Elpaal. Misham and his brothers built Ono and Lod and its dependent towns.—1Ch 8:1, 11, 12.

MISHMA
(Mish'ma).

1. A son of Ishmael and chieftain of an Arabian clan.—Ge 25:14, 16; 1Ch 1:30, 31.

2. A Simeonite, son of Mibsam and father of Hammuel.—1Ch 4:24-26.

MISHMANNAH
(Mish·man'nah) [Fatness]. One of the valiant Gadite army men who joined David's forces at Ziklag. He is listed fourth among the heads of David's army.—1Ch 12:1, 10, 14.

MISHRAITES
(Mish'ra·ites). One of the four families of Kiriath-jearim from whom descended the Zorathites and the Eshtaolites.—1Ch 2:53.

MISPAR (Mis'par) [possibly, Number]. A leading person among the Jews returning with Zerubbabel from Babylonian exile. (Ezr 2:1, 2) He is called Mispereth at Nehemiah 7:7.

MISPERETH (Mis'pe·reth). One of the prominent leaders among the Jews returning with Zerubbabel from Babylonian exile in 537 B.C.E. (Ne 7:6, 7) In a parallel account his name is spelled "Mispar."—Ezr 2:2.

MISREPHOTH-MAIM (Mis're·photh-ma'im) [Burnings at the Waters]. A point to which the Israelites pursued the armies of northern Canaanite kings allied with Jabin after having defeated them at the waters of Merom. (Jos 11:1-5, 8) When the Promised Land was divided into inheritance portions, the area extending from Lebanon to Misrephoth-maim remained to be conquered. (Jos 13:2, 6) Some tentatively identify Misrephoth-maim with the ruins at Khirbet el-Musheirefeh (Horvat Mashref), about 20 km (12 mi) NNE of Acco ('Akko). This location would have provided the citizens of Misrephoth-maim access to the cities in the Plain of Acco and also the Hula Basin. Perhaps Misrephoth-maim (meaning "Burnings at the Waters") got its name from the warm springs situated about 180 m (590 ft) from the site.

MIST. Particles of water floating in the air; they resemble very light rain. When warm humid air rises from the earth and cools to what is called the dew point, moisture condenses because cool air cannot hold as much water as warm air. If this occurs near the ground, it is called fog; if it takes place higher in the sky, it forms what is called a cloud. (Ps 135:7; Pr 25:14; Jer 10:13; 51:16) Moisture that condenses on cool objects, such as the ground or vegetation (usually at night), is described as dew. (Ex 16:13, 14; Jg 6:36-40; see DEW.) Mist, on the other hand, is composed of airborne particles of moisture that are somewhat larger in size than fog particles, but smaller than raindrops.

The Bible's poetic description of these geophysical processes accords with scientific findings. Elihu tells how Jehovah, the Source of all heat and energy, first causes the moisture to be drawn up from the earth and then allows it to trickle slowly and drip back in the form of rain and mist (Heb., 'edh), as if filtered.—Job 36:27, 28.

In the Genesis account of conditions here on the earth at a certain point during the creative "days" is found the only other occurrence of the Hebrew word 'edh (mist). "Jehovah God had not made it rain upon the earth . . . But a mist would go up from the earth [including the streams, lakes, and seas] and it watered the entire surface of the ground." (Ge 2:5, 6) Translators of ancient versions (*LXX, Vg, Sy*), however, understood the reference to be, not to a mist, but to a fountain, suggesting that watering was accomplished by means of an underground freshwater stream.

Figurative Use. In the city of Paphos on the island of Cyprus, Bar-Jesus (Elymas), a sorcerer and false prophet, opposed Paul when the apostle was speaking to the proconsul Sergius Paulus. Paul told him that Jehovah's hand was upon him and that he would be blind for a period of time. "Instantly a thick mist and darkness fell upon him." Apparently his sight became misty, or foggy, followed quickly by intense darkness. In describing the incident, the physician Luke employed the Greek medical term a·khlys' (thick mist).—Ac 13:4-11.

The apostle Peter, in his warning against the false teachers and would-be corrupters who would quietly slip into the Christian congregation, says: "These are fountains without water, and mists driven by a violent storm, and for them the blackness of darkness has been reserved." Travelers in the Middle East were familiar with the disappointment of approaching a fountain or well with hope of getting refreshing water, only to find it dried up. In Palestine, in the month of August, there are occasional cirrostratus clouds from the W that do not bring rain. A farmer who looked to these wispy, mistlike clouds as a promise of water for his crops would be bitterly disappointed. So with these false teachers, these immoral men, as Peter goes on to say: "For they utter *swelling expressions of no profit,* and by the desires of the flesh and by loose habits they entice those who are just escaping from people who conduct themselves in error. While they are promising them freedom, they themselves are existing as slaves of corruption."—2Pe 2:1, 17-19.

Christians are reminded to take Jehovah into account in all their plans, not bragging about what they will do, but remembering the transitoriness and uncertainty of life in this system of things, that they are like a mist that quickly disappears. —Jas 4:14; see CLOUD.

MITHKAH (Mith'kah) [Sweetness]. One of Israel's wilderness encampments. (Nu 33:28, 29) Its location is not known today. If Mithkah is correctly defined as "Sweetness," the name may allude to the good water of the region.

MITHNITE (Mith'nite). A term applied to Joshaphat, one of the mighty men in David's military forces. It is not known whether "Mithnite" refers to his place of origin or is his family designation.—1Ch 11:26, 43.

MITHREDATH (Mith're·dath) [from Persian, meaning "Gift of Mithra"].

1. The treasurer of Cyrus who, under royal command, turned over some 5,400 temple utensils of gold and silver to the Israelites for return to Jerusalem.—Ezr 1:7, 8, 11.

2. An opposer of the postexilic temple reconstruction who shared with others in writing a letter to Persian King Artaxerxes falsely accusing the Jews.—Ezr 4:7.

MITYLENE (Mit·y·le'ne). The principal city of Lesbos, an island in the Aegean Sea off the W coast of Asia Minor. While en route to Jerusalem in about 56 C.E., the apostle Paul sailed to Mitylene from Assos, a seaport on the mainland of Asia Minor about 45 km (28 mi) to the NNW. (Ac 20:14) The fact that no mention is made of Paul's going ashore may imply that the ship merely anchored at Mitylene, perhaps because the needed N winds had abated. On the following day the ship continued SSW toward Chios.—Ac 20:15.

It is believed that Mitylene originally occupied a small island off the eastern coast of Lesbos. But as the city grew it may have been linked with Lesbos by a causeway and expanded along the coast. This would have created a harbor on the N side and also one on the S side of the causeway. The city was famed as a seat of literary learning and for the architectural beauty of its buildings.

MIXED COMPANY. A group of aliens (strangers) who departed from Egypt with the nation of Israel. (Ex 12:37, 38, ftn; compare Ex 12:43-49.) Some of these people may have been Egyptians or other foreigners who chose to follow the true God and the nation of Israel after witnessing a number of Jehovah's blows against Egypt. Others of this group were likely Egyptians who had married Israelites as well as the offspring of such unions. The Israelitess Shelomith of the tribe of Dan, for example, had an Egyptian husband and at least one son by him.—Le 24:10, 11.

This same group is also called "the mixed crowd [or, the cluster (of people); the rabble]" in Numbers 11:4. Doubtless both their non-Israelite background and the rigors of the wilderness trek prompted a complaining spirit among them that became a source of contention. Their expression of selfish longing spread to the Israelites, so that they too began to weep and say: "How we remember the fish that we used to eat in Egypt for nothing, the cucumbers and the watermelons and the leeks and the onions and the garlic! But now our soul is dried away. Our eyes are on nothing at all except the manna."—Nu 11:4-6.

At Nehemiah 13:3 and Jeremiah 25:20 the expression "mixed company" denotes non-Israelites. The Nehemiah reference pertains to such foreigners as Moabites and Ammonites. (Ne 13:1) That the sons of these foreigners (half-Israelite) may also have been included is suggested by the fact that earlier the Israelites dismissed both their foreign wives and sons.—Ezr 10:44.

MIZPAH (Miz'pah), **MIZPEH** (Miz'peh) [meaning "Watchtower"].

1. A region inhabited by Hivites and situated at the base of Mount Hermon was known as "the land of Mizpah." (Jos 11:3) At least part, if not all, of this area may also have been called "the valley plain of Mizpeh." (Jos 11:8) "The land of Mizpah" possibly was the region around Banyas (Caesarea Philippi) to the S of Mount Hermon or the plain E of Mount Hermon along the Wadi et-Teim.

2. A Judean city in the Shephelah. (Jos 15:33, 38) Its precise location, however, is in question. One suggested identification is Khirbet Safiyeh, about 9 km (5.5 mi) S of ancient Azekah.

3. A city in the territory of Benjamin. (Jos 18:26, 28) Although some suggest Nebi Samwil (c. 8 km [5 mi] NW of Jerusalem) as a possible identification, most favor Tell en-Nasbeh (c. 12 km [7.5 mi] N of Jerusalem) for the ancient site. An interpretation of certain archaeological findings seems to favor Tell en-Nasbeh. For example, jar handles have been found bearing what some scholars consider to be the three Hebrew letters for *m-s-p*, possibly a shortened form of Mizpah.

It was at Mizpah that all the fighting men of Israel assembled and decided to take action against those involved in a mass sex crime committed at Gibeah of Benjamin. When the Benjamites refused to hand over the guilty men of that city, full-scale war erupted. Finally, the tribe of Benjamin was almost annihilated; only 600 able-bodied men escaped. (Jg 20:1-48) Earlier, at Mizpah, the Israelites had sworn that they would not give their daughters in marriage to Benjamites. (Jg 21:1) After the battle, therefore, measures had to be taken to preserve the tribe of Benjamin. One of these was the giving of 400 virgin girls from Jabesh-gilead to the Benjamites. The rest of the population of that city had been destroyed, because none of its inhabitants had come to Mizpah and supported the fight against Benjamin.—Jg 21:5-12.

At a later period the prophet Samuel congregated all Israel and prayed for them. On that occasion the Israelites fasted and confessed their sins. When word about their assembly at Mizpah reached the Philistines, they took advantage of the situation to launch an attack. But Jehovah threw the enemy into confusion, enabling the Israelites to subdue the foe. Apparently to commemorate this God-given victory, Samuel erected a stone between Mizpah and Jeshanah, calling it Ebenezer (meaning "Stone of Help"). Thereafter Samuel continued judging Israel and, as he did so, made a yearly circuit of Bethel, Gilgal, and Mizpah. (1Sa 7:5-16) Later, in 1117 B.C.E., another assembly at Mizpah witnessed Samuel's introducing Saul as Israel's first king.—1Sa 10:17-25.

In the tenth century B.C.E., Mizpah was built up by Judean King Asa with materials from Ramah, a city that Israelite King Baasha had been forced to desert. (1Ki 15:20-22; 2Ch 16:4-6) Some three centuries later, in 607 B.C.E., the victorious Babylonian king Nebuchadnezzar appointed Gedaliah as governor over the Jews remaining in the land of Judah. Gedaliah administered affairs from Mizpah. There the prophet Jeremiah took up residence. Also, surviving army chiefs and other Jews who had been scattered came to Mizpah. Governor Gedaliah, although having been forewarned, failed to exercise caution and was assassinated at Mizpah. Chaldeans and Jews with him there were likewise slaughtered. Thereafter 70 visiting men also met their death. The band of assassins, led by Ishmael the son of Nethaniah, took the rest of the people captive. Overtaken by Johanan the son of Kareah, Ishmael escaped with eight men, but the captives were rescued, later to be taken to Egypt. —2Ki 25:23-26; Jer 40:5–41:18.

Following the Babylonian exile, men of Mizpah and the princes Shallun and Ezer shared in repairing the wall of Jerusalem.—Ne 3:7, 15, 19.

4. A city E of the Jordan in Gilead (Jg 10:17; 11:11, 29), perhaps the same place as the Mizpah mentioned at Hosea 5:1. Mizpah was the home of Jephthah. (Jg 11:34) Some propose a location at or near Khirbet Jal'ad, about 23 km (14 mi) NW of Rabbah ('Amman). But its exact location is uncertain.

5. A city of Moab where David, while outlawed by King Saul, settled his parents. (1Sa 22:3) Mizpeh's precise location cannot be established definitely. Some scholars believe it may be the same place as Kir of Moab. (Isa 15:1) Others have suggested Ruzm el-Mesrife (situated WSW of Madaba [ancient Medeba]) as an identification.

MIZRAIM (Miz'ra·im). Listed second among the sons of Ham. (Ge 10:6) Mizraim was the progenitor of the Egyptian tribes (as well as some non-Egyptian tribes), and the name came to be synonymous with Egypt. (Ge 10:13, 14; 50:11) Thus, the word "Egypt" in English translations actually renders the Hebrew Mits·ra'yim (or Ma·tsohr' in a few cases, 2Ki 19:24; Isa 19:6; 37:25; Mic 7:12). The Amarna Tablets, written in the first half of the second millennium B.C.E., refer to Egypt as Misri, similar to the modern Arabic name for the land (Misr).

Many scholars hold that Mizraim is a dual form representing the duality of Egypt (that is, Upper and Lower Egypt), but this is conjectural. (See EGYPT, EGYPTIAN.) The names of Mizraim's descendants are apparently plural forms: Ludim, Anamim, Lehabim, Naphtuhim, Pathrusim, Casluhim, and Caphtorim. (Ge 10:13, 14; 1Ch 1:11, 12) For this reason it is usually suggested that they represent the names of tribes rather than individual sons. Although this is possible, it should be noted that there are other names that appear to be dual or plural in their construction, such as Ephraim, Appaim, Diblaim, and Meshillemoth (Ge 41:52; 1Ch 2:30, 31; Ho 1:3; 2Ch 28:12), each obviously referring to only one individual.

MIZZAH (Miz'zah). A sheik of Edom; a descendant of Esau through Reuel. (Ge 36:17; 1Ch 1:34-37) Mizzah was Esau's grandson, as he is included among "the sons [or, grandsons] of Basemath, Esau's wife," who was Ishmael's daughter and the mother of Reuel.—Ge 36:2, 3, 10, 13.

MNASON (Mna'son). A native of Cyprus and "an early disciple." Paul and those with him were to be entertained in Mnason's home when the apostle was completing a missionary journey about 56 C.E. Some disciples from Caesarea accompanied Paul's group on the way from Caesarea to Jerusalem, to bring them to Mnason.—Ac 21:15-17.

MOAB (Mo'ab), **MOABITES** (Mo'ab·ites).

1. The son of Lot by his older daughter. Like his half brother Ammon, Moab was conceived after Lot and his daughters left Zoar and began dwelling in a cave of the nearby mountainous region. Moab became the forefather of the Moabites.—Ge 19:30-38.

2. The territory anciently inhabited by the Moabites was called "Moab" and also "the field(s) of Moab." (Ge 36:35; Nu 21:20; Ru 1:2; 1Ch 1:46; 8:8; Ps 60:8) Earlier the Emim had resided in this land but were apparently displaced by the Moabites. (De 2:9-11; compare vss 18-22.) Toward the

close of Israel's wilderness wandering, the territory of Moab appears to have extended from the torrent valley of Zered in the S to the torrent valley of Arnon in the N (a distance of some 50 km [30 mi]), the Dead Sea forming the W boundary and the Arabian Desert an undefined E boundary. (Nu 21:11-13; De 2:8, 9, 13, 18, 19) Rising sharply from the Dead Sea, this region is chiefly a tableland slashed by gorges and has an average elevation of some 900 m (3,000 ft) above the Mediterranean Sea. In ancient times it afforded pasture for vast flocks (2Ki 3:4) and supported vineyards and orchards. (Compare Isa 16:6-10; Jer 48:32, 33.) Grain was also cultivated.—Compare De 23:3, 4.

There was an earlier period when the land of Moab extended N of the Arnon and included "the desert plains of Moab across the Jordan from Jericho." (Nu 22:1) But sometime before the arrival of the Israelites, Amorite King Sihon annexed this region, and the Arnon came to be Moab's N boundary. (Nu 21:26-30; Jg 11:15-18) The Ammonites also suffered defeat at the hands of Sihon and were pushed to the north and east. The territory conquered from both peoples by the Amorites formed a wedge between Moab and Ammon, and thus Moab came to be bounded by Amorite territory on the north and Edomite territory on the south. (Jg 11:13, 21, 22; compare De 2:8, 9, 13, 14, 18.) At its greatest extent the territory of Moab was approximately 100 km (60 mi) from N to S and 40 km (25 mi) from E to W.

Probably because a part of Amorite territory had once belonged to Moab, it continued to be called "the land of Moab." (De 1:5) It was in this former Moabite territory that the Israelites encamped before crossing the Jordan. (Nu 31:12; 33:48-51) There a second census was taken of Israel's able-bodied men from 20 years old upward. (Nu 26:2-4, 63) Also there divine commands and judicial decisions were received about Levite cities, cities of refuge, and inheritance. (Nu 35:1-36:13) There Moses delivered his final discourses and concluded with Israel a covenant urging faithfulness to Jehovah. (De 1:1-5; 29:1) Finally Moses ascended Mount Nebo to view the Promised Land and then died. For 30 days on the desert plains of Moab, Israel mourned Moses' death.—De 32:49, 50; 34:1-6, 8.

Moab's Relationship to Israel. As descendants of Abraham's nephew Lot, the Moabites were related to the Israelites. The languages of both peoples were very similar, as is seen from the inscription on the Moabite Stone. Also, like the Israelites, the Moabites appear to have practiced circumcision. (Jer 9:25, 26) Nevertheless, with few exceptions, such as Ruth and King David's mighty man Ithmah (Ru 1:4, 16, 17; 1Ch 11:26, 46), the Moabites manifested great enmity toward Israel.

Before Israel's entry into the Promised Land. The song of Moses about Jehovah's destroying Egypt's military might in the Red Sea indicated that news of this event would cause "the despots of Moab" to tremble. (Ex 15:14, 15) That the Moabites did become fearful is indicated by their king's denying Israel peaceful passage through his realm about 40 years later. (Jg 11:17) Because of a direct command from God, the Israelites, however, did not attack the Moabites, but upon coming to Moab's southern boundary at the torrent valley of Zered, they skirted the territory of Moab. (Nu 21:11-13; De 2:8, 9; Jg 11:18) Although the Moabites did sell food and water to the Israelites (De 2:26-29), "they did not come to [Israel's] aid with bread and water." (De 23:3, 4) Evidently this means that the Moabites did not receive them hospitably and supply provisions without seeking gain.

Later, after crossing the torrent valley of Arnon, Israel was confronted by the Amorites under King Sihon, who had earlier seized Moabite territory N of the Arnon. Following their God-given victories over this ruler and also King Og of Bashan, the Israelites encamped on the desert plains of Moab. (Nu 21:13, 21-22:1; De 2:24-3:8) The extensive Israelite camp frightened the Moabites and their King Balak, causing them to feel a sickening dread. Although making no claim to the former Moabite territory taken by the Israelites from the Amorites, Balak did fear for his realm. He therefore consulted with the older men of Midian and then sent messengers, older men of both Moab and Midian, to hire the prophet Balaam to come and curse Israel. (Nu 22:2-8; compare Jg 11:25.) In this way Balak 'fought' against the Israelites. (Jos 24:9) Jehovah, however, caused Balaam to bless Israel and even to foretell Israel's ascendancy over Moab. (Nu chaps 23, 24; Jos 24:10; Ne 13:1, 2; Mic 6:5) Next, at Balaam's suggestion, Moabite and Midianite women were used to lure Israelite males into immorality and idolatry in connection with Baal of Peor. Many Israelites succumbed to this temptation, bringing Jehovah's anger and death to 24,000 men. (Nu 25:1-3, 6, 9; 31:9, 15, 16) For failing to aid the Israelites with bread and water and for hiring Balaam to curse Israel, the Moabites were barred from coming into the congregation of Jehovah "even to the tenth generation."—De 23:3, 4; see AMMONITES (Intermarriage With Israelites).

In the time of the Judges. During the period of the Judges, the Moabites appear to have expanded their territory N of the Arnon and, in the reign of their King Eglon, occupied Israelite territory W of the Jordan at least as far as "the city of palm trees," Jericho. (Jg 3:12, 13; compare De 34:3.) Israel's subservience to Moab continued for 18 years until Ehud, a left-handed Benjamite, killed King Eglon while having a private audience with him. Ehud then led the Israelites against Moab, striking down about 10,000 Moabites and subduing them.—Jg 3:14-30.

In this general period, when famine affected Judah, Elimelech, with his wife Naomi and their two sons, Mahlon and Chilion, emigrated to the more fertile land of Moab. There the sons married Moabite women, Ruth and Orpah. After the death of the three men in Moab and improvement of conditions in Israel, Naomi, accompanied by Ruth, returned to Bethlehem. There Boaz, a kinsman of Elimelech, married Ruth, who had abandoned the polytheism of the Moabites and had become a worshiper of Jehovah. Thus Ruth, a Moabitess, became an ancestress of David and therefore also of Jesus Christ.—Ru 1:1-6, 15-17, 22; 4:13, 17.

Also in the time of the Judges, Israel began venerating the deities of the Moabites, doubtless including their god Chemosh. (Jg 10:6; Nu 21:29; Jer 48:46) For adopting such false worship of neighboring peoples, the Israelites lost Jehovah's favor and suffered at the hands of their enemies. (Jg 10:7-10) As late as the time of Samuel, unfaithful Israel experienced harassment from the Moabites.—1Sa 12:9, 10.

During reigns of Saul, David, and Solomon. Difficulties with the Moabites continued for years afterward. Israel's first king, Saul, victoriously warred against them. (1Sa 14:47) Since the Moabites would therefore have regarded Saul as an enemy, understandably the king of Moab was agreeable to having the parents of David, a man whom Saul had outlawed, dwell at Mizpeh in Moab.—1Sa 22:3, 4.

Later, when David himself ruled as king, there also was warfare between Israel and Moab. The Moabites were completely subdued and were made to pay tribute to David. Apparently at the end of the conflict two thirds of Moab's fighting men were put to death. It seems that David had them lie down on the ground in a row and then measured this row to determine the two thirds to be put to death and the one third to be preserved alive. (2Sa 8:2, 11, 12; 1Ch 18:2, 11) Possibly in the course of the same conflict, Benaiah the son of Jehoiada "struck down the two sons of Ariel of

Moab." (2Sa 23:20; 1Ch 11:22) David's decisive victory over the Moabites was a fulfillment of Balaam's prophetic words uttered over 400 years earlier: "A star will certainly step forth out of Jacob, and a scepter will indeed rise out of Israel. And he will certainly break apart the temples of Moab's head and the cranium of all the sons of tumult of war." (Nu 24:17) Also apparently with reference to this victory, the psalmist spoke of God's regarding Moab as his "washing pot."—Ps 60:8; 108:9.

David's son Solomon, however, disregarded God's law and married Moabite women who had not become worshipers of Jehovah. To please them, Solomon built a high place to their god Chemosh. Not until some three centuries later, during Josiah's reign, was this high place made unfit for worship.—1Ki 11:1, 7; 2Ki 23:13.

Until the Judean exile. Sometime after the secession of Israel from Judah, the Moabites appear to have regained territory N of the Arnon. On the black basalt stele known as the Moabite Stone, Moab's King Mesha speaks of Israel's King Omri as taking possession of the region of Medeba. Since the tableland of Medeba was in the territory of Reuben (Jos 13:15, 16), Israel had apparently lost this area to the Moabites so that Omri later had to recapture it.

Evidently Moab remained under Israelite control during the reigns of Kings Omri and Ahab. But following the death of Ahab, Moab's King Mesha, who "paid to the king of Israel a hundred thousand lambs and a hundred thousand unshorn male sheep," revolted. (2Ki 1:1; 3:4, 5) The Moabite Stone memorializes this revolt. (PICTURE, Vol. 1, p. 946) If correctly identified as being the same places mentioned in the Bible, 11 of the cities that King Mesha claims as subject to or captured by or (re)built by him were definitely in Israelite territory N of the Arnon. These cities are Dibon, Ataroth, Aroer, Kiriathaim, Nebo, Baal-meon (Nu 32:34, 37, 38), Medeba, Bamoth-baal, Beth-baal-meon, Jahaz (Jos 13:9, 17-19), and Bezer (Jos 20:8).

Unlike Mesha's propagandistic inscription, the Scriptures report that the Moabites suffered humiliating defeat. Enlisting the aid of King Jehoshaphat of Judah and the king of Edom in putting down the Moabite revolt, Jehoram (who became king of Israel about two years after Ahab's death) marched against Moab from the S, by way of the Wilderness of Edom. But the allied armies and their animals almost perished for lack of water. The prophet Elisha's aid was then sought, and in fulfillment of his prophecy that Jehovah would help on account of Jehoshaphat, the torrent valley became filled with water. The next morning the reflection of the sun upon the water made it look like blood to the Moabites. Wrongly concluding that the allied armies had slaughtered one another, the Moabites abandoned all caution and came to the Israelite camp, only to be put to flight. As the battle progressed, Moabite cities were ruined, good tracts of land were filled with stones, trees were cut down, and springs were stopped up. When King Mesha found himself penned up in the city of Kir-haraseth with the battle going against him, he, with 700 men, unsuccessfully tried to break through to the king of Edom. Finally he took his firstborn son and offered him up as a burnt sacrifice upon the wall. For this or some other reason there "came to be great indignation against Israel" and the siege was abandoned.—2Ki 3:6-27.

As this humiliating defeat did not take place on foreign soil but brought devastation to the land of Moab, reasonably a considerable period of time would have been required for recovery. So it seems likely that it was at an earlier date during Jehoshaphat's reign that Moab combined with the forces of Ammon and the mountainous region of Seir to attack Judah. By Jehovah's intervention the three armies turned on one another and destroyed themselves. (2Ch 20:1, 22-24) Some scholars believe that this event is alluded to at Psalm 83:4-9. —Compare 2Ch 20:14 with Ps 83:Sup.

In subsequent years enmity continued between Moab and Israel. After the death of the prophet Elisha, marauding bands of Moabites regularly invaded Israel. (2Ki 13:20) About two centuries later, in Jehoiakim's time, similar Moabite bands contributed to the ruin of Judah during its final years. (2Ki 24:2) With the destruction of Jerusalem in 607 B.C.E., Jews sought refuge in Moab, returning to Judah when Gedaliah was appointed governor.—Jer 40:11, 12.

After the exile. After an Israelite remnant returned from Babylonian exile in 537 B.C.E., some married Moabite wives. But at Ezra's admonition they dismissed these wives and their children. (Ezr 9:1, 2; 10:10, 11, 44) Years later Nehemiah found a similar situation; many Israelites had taken Moabite wives.—Ne 13:1-3, 23.

Moab in Prophecy. In harmony with its long history of opposition to Israel, Moab is mentioned among the hard-set enemies of Jehovah's people. (Compare Isa 11:14.) Condemned for reproaching Israel and for pride and haughtiness, Moab was finally to become a desolation like Sodom. (Zep 2:8-11; see also Jer 48:29.) Already at the close of the ninth century B.C.E., Amos wrote that Moab would suffer calamity for "burning the bones of

the king of Edom for lime." (Am 2:1-3) While some take this to mean that 2 Kings 3:26, 27 refers to King Mesha's offering up, not his own son, but the firstborn of the king of Edom, this is an unlikely inference. One Jewish tradition, though, does link the event mentioned by Amos with the war waged against Mesha and claims that sometime after this conflict the Moabites dug up the bones of the king of Edom and then burned them for lime. But the Bible record provides no basis for determining the time involved.

Isaiah (chaps 15, 16), apparently around the time of King Ahaz' death and while Assyria dominated in the eighth century B.C.E., referred to one Moabite city after another as being in line for calamity. He concluded with the words: "And now Jehovah has spoken, saying: 'Within three years, according to the years of a hired laborer, the glory of Moab must also be disgraced with much commotion of every sort, and those who remain over will be a trifling few, not mighty.'"—Isa 16:14.

From historical records the fulfillment of the prophecies of Isaiah and Amos cannot be placed precisely in the stream of time. However, there is evidence that Moab did come under the Assyrian yoke. Assyrian King Tiglath-pileser III mentions Salamanu of Moab among those paying tribute to him. Sennacherib claims to have received tribute from Kammusunadbi the king of Moab. And Assyrian monarchs Esar-haddon and Ashurbanipal refer to Moabite Kings Musuri and Kamashaltu as being subject to them. (*Ancient Near Eastern Texts*, edited by J. Pritchard, 1974, pp. 282, 287, 291, 294, 298) There is also archaeological evidence that many places in Moab were depopulated about the eighth century B.C.E.

Jeremiah's prophecy of the seventh century B.C.E. pointed to the time when Jehovah would hold an accounting against Moab (Jer 9:25, 26), doing so by means of the Babylonians under King Nebuchadnezzar. (Jer 25:8, 9, 17-21; 27:1-7) Numerous Moabite cities were to be reduced to a desolation. (Jer 48) Apparently when Judah experienced the execution of Jehovah's judgment by means of the Babylonians, the Moabites said: "Look! The house of Judah is like all the other nations." For thus failing to recognize that the judgment was really God's and that the inhabitants of Judah were his people, the Moabites were to experience disaster and thereby 'come to know Jehovah.'—Eze 25:8-11; compare Eze 24:1, 2.

The Jewish historian Josephus writes that, in the fifth year after desolating Jerusalem, Nebuchadnezzar returned to war against Coele-Syria, Ammon, and Moab and thereafter attacked Egypt.

(*Jewish Antiquities,* X, 181, 182 [ix, 7]) Regarding archaeological confirmation of the desolation of Moab, *The Interpreter's Dictionary of the Bible* observes: "Archaeological exploration has shown that Moab was largely depopulated from *ca.* the beginning of the sixth century, and in many sites from *ca.* the eighth century. From the sixth century on, nomads wandered through the land until political and economic factors made sedentary life possible again in the last centuries B.C."—Edited by G. A. Buttrick, 1962, Vol. 3, p. 418; compare Eze 25:8-11.

Later, in fulfillment of Jeremiah 48:47, Cyrus, the conqueror of Babylon, likely permitted Moabite exiles to return to their homeland.

The accurate fulfillment of the prophecies concerning Moab cannot be denied. Centuries ago the Moabites ceased to exist as a people. (Jer 48:42) Today what are considered to have been such Moabite cities as Nebo, Heshbon, Aroer, Bethgamul, and Baal-meon are represented by ruins. Many other places are now unknown.

The sole explanation for the disappearance of the Moabites as a people is provided by the Bible. Noted the 1959 edition of the *Encyclopædia Britannica* (Vol. 15, p. 629): "Israel remained a great power while Moab disappeared. It is true that Moab was continuously hard pressed by desert hordes; the exposed condition of the land is emphasized by the chains of ruined forts and castles which even the Romans were compelled to construct. But the explanation is to be found within Israel itself, and especially in the work of the prophets."

In view of the disappearance of the Moabites as a people, the inclusion of Moab at Daniel 11:41 among nations in "the time of the end" (Da 11:40) is logically to be regarded in a figurative sense. The Moabites evidently represent hard-set enemies of spiritual Israel.

For information on the Moabite Stone, see ME-SHA No. 2.

MOADIAH   (Mo·a·di'ah) [possibly, Appointed Time (Seasonal Festival; Meeting) of Jah]. A priestly paternal house of which Piltai was the head in the days of Joiakim. (Ne 12:12, 17) It has been suggested that "Moadiah" is a variation of the name "Maadiah" and that Moadiah is the same person as the priest Maadiah who accompanied Zerubbabel to Jerusalem after the Babylonian exile.—Ne 12:1, 5.

MODESTY.   An awareness of one's limitations; also chastity or personal purity. The Hebrew root verb *tsa·na'* is rendered "be modest" in Micah 6:8,

its only occurrence. The related adjective *tsa·nu'a'* (modest) occurs in Proverbs 11:2, where it is contrasted with presumptuousness. Although some modern scholars believe that the sense of this root is "be cautious, careful, judicious," many take it to mean "be modest." For example, *A Hebrew and English Lexicon of the Old Testament* (by Brown, Driver, and Briggs, 1980, p. 857) says that the root conveys the idea of one who is retiring, modest, or humble. "Modesty" is a translation of the Greek *ai·dos'.* (1Ti 2:9) *Ai·dos'* used in a moral sense expresses the thought of reverence, awe, respect for the feeling or opinion of others or for one's own conscience and so expresses shame, self-respect, a sense of honor, sobriety, and moderation. (*A Greek-English Lexicon* by H. Liddell and R. Scott, revised by H. Jones, Oxford, 1968, p. 36) Comparing *ai·dos'* with the more common Greek word for "shame" (*ai·skhy'ne;* 1Co 1:27; Php 3:19), lexicographer Richard Trench says that *ai·dos'* is "the nobler word, and implies the nobler motive: in it is involved an innate moral repugnance to the doing of the dishonorable act, which moral repugnance scarcely or not at all exists in the [*ai·skhy'ne*]." He states that "[*ai·dos'*] would always restrain a good man from an unworthy act, while [*ai·skhy'ne*] might sometimes restrain a bad one." (*Synonyms of the New Testament,* London, 1961, pp. 64, 65) Thus, the conscience is especially involved in the restraining effect implied in *ai·dos'.*

Before God.   With regard to modesty, in the sense of a proper estimate of one's own self, the Scriptures give much counsel. "Wisdom is with the modest ones," says the proverb. This is because the person manifesting modesty avoids the dishonor that accompanies presumptuousness or boastfulness. (Pr 11:2) He is following the course approved by Jehovah and is therefore wise. (Pr 3:5, 6; 8:13, 14) Jehovah loves and grants to such one wisdom. One of the requirements for gaining Jehovah's favor is 'to be modest in walking with him.' (Mic 6:8) This involves a proper appreciation of one's position before God, recognizing one's sinful state as contrasted with Jehovah's greatness, purity, and holiness. It also means that a person should recognize himself as a creature of Jehovah, altogether dependent on Him and subject to His sovereignty. Eve was one who failed to appreciate this. She stepped out for complete independence and self-determination. Modesty would have helped her to dismiss from her mind the thought of becoming "like God, knowing good and bad." (Ge 3:4, 5) The apostle Paul counsels against overconfidence and presumptuousness, saying, "Keep working out your own salvation with fear and trembling."—Php 2:12.

In What to Boast. Boastfulness is the opposite of modesty. The rule is: "May a stranger, and not your own mouth, praise you; may a foreigner, and not your own lips, do so." (Pr 27:2) Jehovah's own words are: "Let not the wise man brag about himself because of his wisdom, and let not the mighty man brag about himself because of his mightiness. Let not the rich man brag about himself because of his riches. But let the one bragging about himself brag about himself because of this very thing, the having of insight and the having of knowledge of me, that I am Jehovah, the One exercising loving-kindness, justice and righteousness in the earth; for in these things I do take delight."—Jer 9:23, 24; compare Pr 12:9; 16:18, 19.

God's Regard for Modest Ones. The apostle Paul shows God's regard for the modest ones and also cites his own conduct in the congregation as exemplary of such modest attitude. He wrote to the Christians at Corinth: "For you behold his calling of you, brothers, that not many wise in a fleshly way were called, not many powerful, not many of noble birth; but God chose the foolish things of the world, that he might put the wise men to shame; and God chose the weak things of the world, that he might put the strong things to shame; and God chose the ignoble things of the world and the things looked down upon, the things that are not, that he might bring to nothing the things that are, in order that no flesh might boast in the sight of God . . . just as it is written: 'He that boasts, let him boast in Jehovah.' And so I, when I came to you, brothers, did not come with an extravagance of speech or of wisdom declaring the sacred secret of God to you. For I decided not to know anything among you except Jesus Christ, and him impaled. And I came to you in weakness and in fear and with much trembling; and my speech and what I preached were not with persuasive words of wisdom but with a demonstration of spirit and power, that your faith might be, not in men's wisdom, but in God's power."—1Co 1:26–2:5.

'Do Not Go Beyond the Things Written.' Later in his letter Paul emphasized the need for modesty on the part of all, just as he himself had displayed modesty, a proper evaluation of himself. The Corinthians had fallen into the trap of boasting in certain men, such as Apollos, and even in Paul himself. Paul corrected them, telling them that they were fleshly, not spiritual, in doing this, and said: "Now, brothers, these things I have transferred so as to apply to myself and Apollos for your good, that in our case you may learn the rule: 'Do not go beyond the things that are written

[that is, do not go beyond the limits that the Scriptures set for humans in their attitude toward one another and toward themselves],' in order that you may not be puffed up individually in favor of the one against the other. For who makes you to differ from another? Indeed, what do you have that you did not receive? If, now, you did indeed receive it, why do you boast as though you did not receive it?" Keeping this in mind will prevent haughtiness and boastfulness in regard to oneself or another as to family descent, race, color or nationality, physical beauty, ability, knowledge, mental brilliance, and so forth.—1Co 4:6, 7.

Jesus Christ's Example. Jesus Christ is the finest example of modesty. He told his disciples that he could not do a single thing of his own initiative, but only what he beheld the Father doing, and that his Father is greater than he is. (Joh 5:19, 30; 14:28) Jesus refused to accept titles not due him. When a ruler called him "Good Teacher," Jesus replied: "Why do you call me good? Nobody is good, except one, God." (Lu 18:18, 19) And he told his disciples that as slaves to Jehovah they should not feel puffed up, either over things accomplished in God's service or because of their worth to God. Rather, they should have the attitude, when they had done all the things assigned to them, that "we are good-for-nothing slaves. What we have done is what we ought to have done."—Lu 17:10.

Additionally, the Lord Jesus Christ, as a perfect man on earth, was superior to his imperfect disciples and also possessed great authority from his Father. Yet, in dealing with his disciples, he was considerate of their limitations. He employed delicacy in training them and propriety of speech toward them. He did not put upon them more than they could bear at the time.—Joh 16:12; compare Mt 11:28-30; 26:40, 41.

In Dress and Other Possessions. In instructing the overseer Timothy as to seeing that proper conduct was observed in the congregation, Paul said: "I desire the women to adorn themselves in well-arranged dress, with modesty and soundness of mind, not with styles of hair braiding and gold or pearls or very expensive garb, but in the way that befits women professing to reverence God, namely, through good works." (1Ti 2:9, 10) Here the apostle does not counsel against neatness and good, pleasing appearance, for he recommends "well-arranged dress." But he shows the impropriety of vanity and ostentatiousness in dress—calling attention to oneself or to one's means of life thereby. Also modesty relating to respect for the feelings of others and to self-respect and a sense of honor is involved. The Christian's manner of dress should not be shocking to decency, to the moral susceptibilities of the congregation, causing offense to some. This counsel as to dress would shed further light on Jehovah's attitude toward the proper view and use of other material possessions that a Christian may have.—See HUMILITY.

MOLADAH (Mo·la′dah) [from a root meaning "give birth; become father to; bear"]. One of the cities in southern Judah allotted to Simeon. Moladah remained in the hands of this tribe at least down till David's reign. (Jos 15:21, 26; 19:1, 2; 1Ch 4:24, 28, 31) After the exile, Judeans resettled the site.—Ne 11:25, 26.

The site of Moladah has not been identified with any certainty.

MOLECH (Mo′lech) [from a root meaning "reign as king" or "king," but with the vowels of bo′sheth, "shame," to denote abhorrence]. A deity particularly associated with the Ammonites (1Ki 11:5, 7, 33); possibly the same as Moloch (Ac 7:43; compare Am 5:26) and Milcom. (1Ki 11:5, 33) At Jeremiah 32:35, Molech is referred to in parallel with Baal, suggesting, if not an identification, at least some connection between the two. Numerous authorities regard "Molech" as a title rather than the name of a specific deity, and therefore, the thought has been advanced that the designation "Molech" may have been applied to more than one god.

It is generally agreed that the Malcam referred to at 2 Samuel 12:30 and 1 Chronicles 20:2 is the idol image of the Ammonite god Milcom, or Molech, although the Hebrew term could be rendered "their king." (Compare KJ; AS.) Earlier in the Biblical account the Ammonite king is referred to by his name Hanun (2Sa 10:1-4); hence, it is reasonable to conclude that the name Hanun rather than Malcam would have appeared in the Scriptural record if the king rather than the idol were intended. Also, it is thought unlikely that a king would have worn a crown weighing about 34 kg (92 lb t). For the same reason it has been suggested that David placed Malcam's crown on his head only temporarily, perhaps to denote his victory over the false god. According to the reading of the Targum, which has been adopted by numerous translators, the crown had only one precious jewel. This has given rise to the view that it was the precious jewel, rather than the crown itself, that came to be on David's head.

Child Sacrifice to Molech. God's law to Israel prescribed the death penalty for anyone, even an alien resident, who would give his offspring to Molech. (Le 20:2-5) Nonetheless, apostate Israelites, both in the kingdom of Judah and in the

ten-tribe kingdom, passed their offspring through the fire.—2Ki 17:17, 18; Eze 23:4, 36-39.

The 'passing through the fire' to Molech has been regarded by some as signifying a purification ritual by means of which children were devoted or dedicated to Molech; others understand this to mean actual sacrificing. That the Canaanites and apostate Israelites did sacrifice their children, there can be no question. (De 12:31; Ps 106:37, 38) King Ahaz of Judah "proceeded to burn up his sons ["son," Sy] in the fire." (2Ch 28:3) The parallel passage, at 2 Kings 16:3, reads: "Even his own son he made pass through the fire." This indicates that 'passing through the fire' is at least sometimes synonymous with sacrificing. Likely, however, the worship of Molech was not always and everywhere the same. For example, King Solomon, under the influence of his foreign wives, built high places to Molech and other deities, but not until the time of Ahaz is mention made of child sacrifice. (1Ki 11:7, 8) Undoubtedly if this abhorrent practice had existed earlier, it would have been denounced along with the other forms of idolatry existing during the reigns of the various kings. For this reason some commentators favor the view that the expression 'to pass through the fire' originally applied to a purification ritual and later came to signify actual sacrifice.

"The passing" to Molech mentioned in the footnote on Leviticus 18:21 evidently refers to devoting or dedicating children to this false god. This text has been variously translated: "You must not dedicate any of your children to the service of Molech." (AT) "Thou shalt not give any of thy seed to make them pass through the fire to Molech." (AS) "Thou shalt not give any of thy seed to be consecrated to the idol Moloch." (Dy) "You must not allow the devoting of any of your offspring to Molech."—NW.

Ahaz and Manasseh are the only Judean kings referred to as making their offspring pass through the fire. However, with the impetus given by these two kings to child sacrifice, the practice apparently became entrenched among the Israelites in general. (2Ki 16:3; 21:6; Jer 7:31; 19:4, 5; 32:35; Eze 20:26) The children, at least at times, were first killed, rather than being burned alive. —Eze 16:20, 21.

King Josiah defiled Topheth, the chief center of Molech worship in Judah, in order to prevent persons from making their offspring pass through the fire. (2Ki 23:10-13) But this did not eradicate the practice for all time. Ezekiel, who began serving as a prophet 16 years after the death of Josiah, mentions it as occurring in his day.—Eze 20:31.

The view has been advanced that the Molech to

whom children were sacrificed had the form of a man but the head of a bull. The image is said to have been heated red hot and the children cast into its outstretched arms, thus to fall into the flaming furnace below. This conception is largely based on the description of the Carthaginian Cronos or Moloch given by the Greek historian Diodorus Siculus of the first century B.C.E.—*Diodorus of Sicily*, XX, 14, 4-6.

Regarding the practice of astrology in connection with worship of Molech, see ASTROLOGERS.

MOLE RAT [Heb., *cho'ledh*]. A rodent measuring 15 to 30 cm (6 to 12 in.) in length. The mole rat (*Spalax ehrenbergi*) resembles a short-legged, tailless, and neckless cylindrical lump of soft, thick fur, generally a yellowish gray-brown color. The head is recognizable by the furless muzzle and two pairs of large protruding teeth. Under the Law, the mole rat was unclean for food.—Le 11:29.

Although numerous translations render *cho'-ledh* as "weasel" (*AS, KJ, RS*), there is a basis for preferring "mole rat." In Arabic, a language related to Hebrew, a very similar word, *khuld,* means "mole rat." Also, *cho'ledh* may be related to a post-Biblical Hebrew term signifying "dig" or "hollow out." This would harmonize with the mole rat's characteristic digging.

Mole rats live in underground communities and dig subterranean sleeping quarters and large storage chambers. These creatures subsist on vegetable matter, primarily on roots and bulbs. Thus they differ from true moles, which feed on insects and earthworms and are not considered native to Palestine.

MOLID (Mo'lid) [from a root meaning "give birth; become father to; bear"]. A man of Judah and descendant of Hezron through Jerahmeel. Molid was the son of Abishur by his wife Abihail.—1Ch 2:4, 5, 9, 25-29.

MOLOCH. See MOLECH.

MOLTEN SEA (Copper Sea). When the temple was constructed during Solomon's reign, a "molten [that is, cast or poured] sea" replaced the portable basin of copper used with the earlier tabernacle. (Ex 30:17-21; 1Ki 7:23, 40, 44) Built by Hiram, a Hebrew-Phoenician, it was evidently called a "sea" because of the large quantity of water it could contain. This vessel, also of copper, was "ten cubits [4.5 m; 14.6 ft] from its one brim to its other brim, circular all around; and its height was five cubits [c. 2.2 m; 7.3 ft], and it took a line of thirty cubits [13.4 m; 44 ft] to circle all around it."—1Ki 7:23.

Circumference. The circumference of 30 cubits is evidently a round figure, for more precisely it would be 31.4 cubits. In this regard, Christopher Wordsworth quotes a certain Rennie as making this interesting observation: "Up to the time of Archimedes [third century B.C.E.], the circumference of a circle was always measured in straight lines by the radius; and Hiram would naturally describe the sea as thirty cubits round, measuring it, as was then invariably the practice, by its radius, or semi-diameter, of five cubits, which being applied six times round the perimeter, or 'brim,' would give the thirty cubits stated. There was evidently no intention in the passage but to give the dimensions of the Sea, in the usual language that every one would understand, measuring the circumference in the way in which all skilled workers, like Hiram, did measure circles at that time. He, of course, must however have known perfectly well, that as the polygonal hexagon thus inscribed by the radius was thirty cubits, the actual curved circumference would be somewhat more." (*Notes* on the *King James Version,* London, 1887) Thus, it appears that the ratio of three to one (that is, the circumference being three times the diameter) was a customary way of stating matters, intended to be understood as only approximate.

Of Copper. The copper sea was decorated with "gourd-shaped ornaments" and had as its base 12 figures of bulls, facing north, south, east, and west in groups of three. The brim of the sea resembled a lily blossom. Since the thickness of this large vessel was "a handbreadth [7.4 cm; 2.9 in.]," it may well have weighed in the neighborhood of 27 metric tons (30 tons). (1Ki 7:24-26) This huge quantity of copper came from the supplies King David had obtained in his conquests in Syria. (1Ch 18:6-8) The casting was done in a clay mold in the region of the Jordan and was indeed a remarkable feat.—1Ki 7:44-46.

Capacity. The account at 1 Kings 7:26 refers to the sea as 'containing two thousand bath measures,' whereas the parallel account at 2 Chronicles 4:5 speaks of it as 'containing three thousand bath measures.' Some claim that the difference is the result of a scribal error in the Chronicles account. However, while the Hebrew verb meaning "contain" in each case is the same, there is a measure of latitude allowable in translating it. Thus some translations render 1 Kings 7:26 to read that the vessel "held" or "would contain" 2,000 bath measures, and translate 2 Chronicles 4:5 to read that it "had a capacity of" or "could hold" or "could contain" 3,000 bath measures. (*AT, JB, NW*) This allows for the understanding that the Kings account sets forth the amount of water customarily stored in the receptacle while the Chronicles account gives the actual capacity of the vessel if filled to the brim.

There is evidence that the bath measure anciently equaled about 22 L (5.8 gal), so that, if kept at two thirds capacity, the sea would normally hold about 44,000 L (11,620 gal) of water. For it to have had the capacity indicated, it must not have had straight sides, but instead, the sides below the rim, or lip, must have been curved, giving the vessel a bulbous shape. A vessel having such a shape and having the dimensions stated earlier could contain up to 66,000 L (17,430 gal). Josephus, Jewish historian of the first century C.E., describes the sea as "in the shape of a hemisphere." He also indicates that the sea's location was between the altar of burnt offering and the temple building, somewhat toward the south. —*Jewish Antiquities*, VIII, 79 (iii, 5); VIII, 86 (iii, 6).

In addition to the copper sea there were ten smaller copper basins resting on carts, and these were evidently filled from the copper sea. (1Ki 7:38, 39) Rabbinic tradition is that the sea was equipped with faucets. The ten basins were used for washing certain sacrifices and likely for other cleansing work, but "the sea was for the priests to wash in it." (2Ch 4:6) Some rabbis have held that the priests completely immersed themselves in the water of the copper sea, while Josephus says it was "for the priests to wash their hands and feet in." (*Jewish Antiquities*, VIII, 87 [iii, 6]) Whatever the procedure, the copper sea is associated with priestly cleansing.

In Prophecy. This may provide a key for understanding the references in the book of Revelation to the "glassy sea" seen before the throne of God in the apostle John's vision. (Re 4:6; 15:2) It was "like crystal," perhaps having transparent sides (compare Re 21:18, 21) so that the contents could be seen. Those standing by it, persons victorious over "the wild beast" and its "image," correspond to those "called and chosen and faithful" ones described at Revelation 17:14; 20:4-6. These serve as "priests of God and of the Christ" and as kings with Christ during his Thousand Year Rule. (Compare 1Pe 2:9.) The position of this priestly class next to the "glassy sea" before God's throne calls to mind the apostle's reference to the Christian congregation's being 'cleansed with the bath of water by means of the word.' (Eph 5:25-27) Jesus also spoke of the cleansing power of the word of God that he proclaimed. (Joh 15:3) The 'mingling of fire' (Re 15:2) with the watery contents of the sea undoubtedly relates to judgments of God, for fire is frequently used in this connection and God himself is described as "a consuming fire" toward those rejecting his divine will.—Heb 12:25, 29.

The symbolism of the "glassy sea" in John's vision thus illustrates Paul's inspired explanation that the earthly tabernacle and temple with their equipment and priestly functions served as patterns of heavenly things. (Compare Heb 8:4, 5; 9:9, 11, 23, 24; 10:1.) As to the significance of the figures of bulls on which the copper sea of Solomon's temple rested, see BULL.

MONEY. A medium of exchange. Anciently, livestock often figured in barter, that is, the exchange of one item for another and evidently the oldest method of making a business transaction. Indicative of this is the fact that the Latin word for money (*pecunia*) is drawn from *pecus*, meaning "cattle." However, livestock (Ge 47:17) and foodstuffs (1Ki 5:10, 11) were not always convenient mediums of exchange. Therefore metals such as gold and silver came to be used. As early as Abraham's time, precious metals served as money. But this was not standard coined money. It consisted of silver and gold, doubtless molded for convenience into bars, rings, bracelets, or other standard shapes having a specific weight. (Compare Ge 24:22; Jos 7:21.) The usual Hebrew term rendered "money" literally means "silver." (Ge 17:12, ftn) Often the metal objects were weighed by the individuals concerned when payment was made.—Ge 23:15, 16; Jer 32:10.

As business transactions involved weighing, understandably designations of weights were also monetary designations. (See WEIGHTS AND MEASURES.) Among the Israelites there were five main divisions: the gerah, half shekel (bekah), shekel, mina (maneh), and talent. (Ex 25:39; 30:13; 38:25, 26; 1Ki 10:17; Eze 45:12; see GERAH; MINA; SHEKEL; TALENT.) Their relationship and comparative modern values in gold and silver are set forth below. (The price of gold and of silver has varied in recent years. In this publication, gold is conservatively calculated at $350.00 per ounce troy and silver at $6.00 per ounce troy; the ancient ratio of gold to silver, however, is considered to have been 13 to 1.)

		Gold		Silver	
1 gerah	= 1/20 shekel	$	6.42	$	.11
1 bekah	= 10 gerahs		64.23		1.10
1 shekel	= 2 bekahs		128.45		2.20
1 mina	= 50 shekels		6,422.50		110.10
1 talent	= 60 minas		385,350.00		6,606.00

The value of the "piece(s) of money" (Heb., *qesi-tah'*) mentioned at Genesis 33:19; Joshua 24:32; and Job 42:11 cannot be definitely established. Likewise the value of the pim is uncertain. It may have been about two thirds of a shekel.—1Sa 13:21; see PIM.

Coins in the Hebrew Scriptures. It is commonly believed that the first coins were struck about 700 B.C.E. The Israelites may have first used coins in their homeland after returning from exile in Babylon. Postexilic Bible books refer to the Persian daric (1Ch 29:7; Ezr 8:27) and drachmas (Heb., *dar·kemoh·nim'*), which are generally equated with the daric. (Ezr 2:69; Ne 7:70-72) The Persian gold daric weighed 8.4 g (0.27 oz t) and is therefore presently evaluated at $94.50. —See DARIC; DRACHMA.

Money in the Christian Scripture Period. The lepton (Jewish), quadrans (Roman), as or assarion (Roman and provincial), denarius (Roman), drachma (Greek), didrachma (Greek), and the stater (Greek; considered by many to be the tetradrachma of Antioch or Tyre) are coins specifically mentioned in the Christian Greek Scriptures. (Mt 5:26; 10:29; 17:24, 27; 20:10; Mr 12:42; Lu 12:6, 59; 15:8; 21:2, *Int;* see DENARIUS; STATER.) The much larger monetary values known as minas and talents were weights, not coins. (Mt 18:24; Lu 19:13-25) The chart that follows shows the relationship between the various monetary units and converts these into approximate modern values.

		Modern Value
1 lepton (copper or bronze)	= ½ quadrans	$ .006
1 quadrans (copper or bronze)	= 2 lepta	.012
1 as (assarion) (copper or bronze)	= 4 quadrantes	.046
1 denarius (silver)	= 16 asses	.74
1 drachma (silver)	=	.65
1 didrachma (silver)	= 2 drachmas	1.31
1 tetradrachma*	= 4 drachmas	2.62
1 mina (silver)	= 100 drachmas	65.40
1 talent (silver)	= 60 minas	3,924.00
1 talent (gold)	=	228,900.00

*Thought to be the same as stater (silver)

Purchasing Power. Modern values for ancient money do not give a true picture of its worth. The Bible, however, provides some indication of purchasing power and this is helpful in understanding ancient values. In the time of Jesus' earthly ministry, agricultural laborers commonly received a denarius for a 12-hour workday. (Mt 20:2) It may be assumed that in the Hebrew Scripture period wages were about the same. If so, a silver shekel would be the equivalent of three days' wages.

The price of a slave was 30 silver shekels (perhaps 90 days' wages). (Ex 21:32; compare Le 27:2-7.) Hosea the prophet purchased a woman for 15 silver pieces and one and a half homers (15 ephahs) of barley. Likely this payment constituted the full price for a slave. If so, an ephah (22 L; 20 dry qt) of barley was then worth one shekel.—Ho 3:2.

In times of scarcity, prices rose sharply. The 80 silver pieces (c. 240 days' wages) that at one time might have bought eight homers (1,760 L; 50 bu) of barley would, in time of siege, only procure the thinly fleshed head of an ass, an animal unfit for food according to the terms of the Mosaic Law.—2Ki 6:25; compare Ho 3:2.

In the first century C.E. two sparrows cost an assarion (45 minutes' wages), and five sparrows could be obtained for double this price. (Mt 10:29; Lu 12:6) The temple contribution of the needy widow that Jesus observed was even less, a mere two lepta (1 quadrans), or 1/64 of a day's wages. Yet Christ Jesus commended her giving as being greater than that of those who had donated much, because she had contributed, not part of her surplus, but "all of what she had, her whole living." (Mr 12:42-44; Lu 21:2-4) The annual temple tax paid by the Jews was two drachmas, or a didrachma (about two days' wages). (Mt 17:24) As a drachma was the equivalent of about a day's wages, a woman might reasonably sweep her whole house and diligently search for a lost drachma coin.—Lu 15:8, 9.

Judas Iscariot betrayed Jesus for 30 pieces of silver, evidently the price of a slave. (Mt 26:14-16, 47-50) No doubt these silver pieces were either shekels or other coins similar in value. But the kind of coin is not specified in the account, except for their being silver.

Money Can Be Both Beneficial and Harmful. Money provides a defense against poverty and its attendant troubles, enabling persons to procure both necessities and luxuries. (Compare Ec 7:12; 10:19.) For this reason the possibility exists of a person's beginning to trust in money as security and to forget his Creator. (Compare De 8:10-14.) "The love of money [literally, fondness of silver] is a root of all sorts of injurious things, and by reaching out for this love some have been led astray from the faith and have stabbed themselves all over with many pains." (1Ti 6:10) For money, persons have perverted justice, prostituted themselves, committed murder, betrayed others, and falsified the truth.—De 16:19; 23:18; 27:25; Eze 22:12; Mt 26:14, 15; 28:11-15.

On the other hand, the proper use of money is approved by God. (Lu 16:1-9) This includes contributing toward the advancement of pure worship and giving material assistance to those in need. (Compare 2Ch 24:4-14; Ro 12:13; 1Jo 3:17, 18; see CONTRIBUTION; GIFTS OF MERCY.) Although much good can thus be done with money, the most valuable things—spiritual food and drink, eternal life itself—can be obtained without it. —Isa 55:1, 2; Re 22:17.

MONEY CHANGER.

One whose function included the exchange of one currency for another and coins of one value for those of another value. For each transaction the money changer received a certain fee. Thus, the Greek word *kol·ly·bi·stes'* (money changer) comes from the term *kol'ly·bos*, a small coin paid as a commission for changing money. The Greek word *ker·ma·ti·stes'* (money broker or coin dealer) in John 2:15 is related to *ker'ma*, rendered 'coin' in the same verse. Other services mentioned in the Jewish Mishnah as being provided by money changers were the safekeeping of money and the payment of wages upon the presentation of drafts.—*Bava Mezia* 3:11; 9:12.

In the time of Jesus' earthly ministry the annual temple tax was two drachmas (a didrachma). (Mt 17:24) As Jews from widely scattered lands came to Jerusalem for the celebration of the Passover and paid this tax then, the services of money changers may have been needed to exchange foreign currency for money that would be acceptable for payment of the temple tax, if not also the purchase of sacrificial animals and other items. According to the Mishnah (*Shekalim* 1:3), on the 15th of Adar, or about a month before Passover, the money changers set up for business in the provinces. But on the 25th of Adar, when Jews and proselytes from many other lands would be arriving at Jerusalem, the money changers established themselves in the temple area.

It was at the temple that Jesus Christ on two occasions overturned the tables of the money changers and condemned them for having made the temple into "a house of merchandise" or "a cave of robbers." (Joh 2:13-16; Mt 21:12, 13; Mr 11:15-17) This may imply that Jesus regarded the fees of the money changers as exorbitant. In this regard it is noteworthy that there were times when great profits were made on the sale of sacrificial animals. The Mishnah tells of a time when the price for a pair of doves was a golden *denar* (25 silver *denars*). This prompted Simeon

the son of Gamaliel to declare: "By this Temple! I will not suffer the night to pass by before they cost but a [silver] *denar*." On that very day the price was drastically reduced.—*Keritot* 1:7 (translated by H. Danby).

MONTH. See CALENDAR.

MONUMENT.

A pillar, a plaque, a building, or other marker set up as a reminder of some person or some special event. A few of such are mentioned in the Bible, though not all of these are referred to as monuments.

Jehovah appeared to Jacob in a night vision, confirming the Abrahamic covenant toward him (1781 B.C.E.). In commemoration, Jacob took the stone he had used as a pillow, set it up to resemble a pillar, and anointed it with oil. He then called the place Bethel. (Ge 28:10-19) Some 20 years later Jacob and Laban, upon concluding a covenant of peace between themselves, set up a pillar, also a heap of stones, in the mountainous region of Gilead, there to serve as a reminder of their agreement. (Ge 31:25, 44-52) When Jehovah brought Israel into the Promised Land (1473 B.C.E.), two monuments were set up at the place where they crossed the Jordan River, one in midstream and the other on the W bank of the river, at Gilgal. These were to be memorial signs commemorating that miraculous crossing, and when their sons thereafter asked what these monuments represented, their fathers were to recount what Jehovah had done in behalf of his people.—Jos 4:4-9, 20-24.

Following his victory over the Amalekites, King Saul erected "a monument [Heb., *yadh*] for himself." (1Sa 15:12) The Hebrew word *yadh*, most often translated "hand," can also mean "monument," as an uplifted hand catches the eye and directs attention in a specific way, so also a monument calls people's attention to certain things.

Absalom's Monument (Heb., *yadh*) was in the form of a pillar like so many others. Absalom erected it on the Low Plain of the King not far from Jerusalem, because, as he said, "I have no son in order to keep my name in remembrance." (2Sa 18:18) However, today nothing is known of that monument or its location beyond what the Bible tells us. It should not be confused with the so-called tomb in the Kidron Valley, which ecclesiastical tradition attributes to Absalom but which belongs to the Greco-Roman period of architecture.—See ABSALOM.

Like Absalom, eunuchs have no hope of a posterity to carry on their names. However, if they are faithful to Jehovah, and not like treasonous

Absalom, Jehovah promises to give them "something better than sons and daughters," namely, to "give to them in my house and within my walls a monument [Heb., *yadh*] and a name . . . A name to time indefinite I shall give them, one that will not be cut off."—Isa 56:4, 5; compare Pr 22:1.

Gravestones were also set up as memory aids, as for example, the one that marked "the burial place of the man of the true God" who foretold what Josiah would do against the altar at Bethel. —2Ki 23:16-18; 1Ki 13:1, 2.

MOON. "The lesser luminary for dominating the night," provided by God as a means for marking "appointed times." (Ge 1:16; Ps 104:19; Jer 31:35; 1Co 15:41) The Hebrew word for "moon" (*ya·re'ach*) is closely related to the Hebrew word *ye'rach,* meaning "lunar month." Since the lunar month always began with the appearing of the new moon (Heb., *cho'dhesh*), the term "new moon" also came to mean "month." (Ge 7:11; Ex 12:2; Isa 66:23) The Greek word *se·le'ne* is rendered "moon," while the Greek word *men* has the idea of a lunar period.—Lu 1:24; Ga 4:10; also Col 2:16, where *ne·o·me·ni'a* (new moon) occurs.

The word *leva·nah',* meaning "white," occurs three times in the Hebrew text poetically describing the white brilliance of the full moon that is particularly evident in Bible lands. (Ca 6:10; Isa 24:23; 30:26) The word *ke·se'* (or *ke'seh*), meaning "full moon," also appears twice.—Ps 81:3; Pr 7:20, *RS.*

Since the average lunation from new moon to new moon is about 29 days, 12 hours, 44 minutes in length, the ancient lunar months had either 29 or 30 days. This may originally have been determined by simple observation of the appearance of the new moon's crescent; but in David's time we find evidence of its being calculated beforehand. (1Sa 20:5, 18, 24-29) Nevertheless, in postexilic times the Mishnah (*Rosh Ha-Shanah* 1:3–2:7) states that the Jewish Sanhedrin met early in the morning on the 30th day of each of seven months in the year to determine the time of the new moon. Watchmen were posted on high vantage points around Jerusalem and carried immediate report to the Jewish court after sighting the new moon. Upon receiving sufficient testimony, the court announced, 'It is consecrated,' officially marking the start of a new month. If cloudy skies or fog caused poor visibility, then the preceding month was declared to have had 30 days, and the new month began on the day following the court assembly. It is also said that further announcement was made by a signal fire lit on the Mount of Olives, which was then repeated on other high points throughout the country. This method was evidently replaced later by the dispatching of messengers to carry the news.

In the fourth century of our Common Era a standardized or continuous calendar was established so that the Jewish months came to have a fixed number of days, with the exception of Heshvan and Chislev as well as the month Adar, which still vary between 29 and 30 days according to certain calculations.

New Moon Observance. Among the Jews each new moon marked the occasion for the blowing of trumpets and the offering up of sacrifices according to the Law covenant. (Nu 10:10; 2Ch 2:4; Ps 81:3; compare Isa 1:13, 14.) The offerings prescribed were, in fact, even greater than those normally offered on the regular Sabbath days. (Nu 28:9-15) While nothing is stated specifically as to the new moon's marking a day of rest, the text at Amos 8:5 indicates a cessation of labor. It was apparently a time of feasting (1Sa 20:5) as well as an opportune time to gather for instruction in God's law.—Eze 46:1-3; 2Ki 4:22, 23; Isa 66:23.

The seventh new moon of each year (corresponding to the first day of the month of Ethanim, or Tishri) was sabbatical, and the Law covenant decreed it to be a time of complete rest. (Le 23:24, 25; Nu 29:1-6) It was the "day of the trumpet blast," but in a greater sense than that of the other new moons. It announced the approach of Atonement Day, held on the tenth day of the same month.—Le 23:27, 28; Nu 29:1, 7-11.

Moon Worship. While guided by the moon as a time indicator in determining their months and festival seasons, the Israelites were to remain free from the practice of moon worship that was prominent in the nations around them. The moon-god Sin was the city god of Ur, the capital of Sumer, the location from which Abraham and his family departed for the Promised Land. Though the inhabitants of Ur were polytheistic, the moon-god Sin, a male deity, was the supreme god to whom their temple and altars were primarily devoted. Abraham and his party traveled from Ur to Haran, which was another major center of moon worship. Abraham's father Terah, who died in Haran, apparently practiced such idolatrous worship. (Ge 11:31, 32) In any case, these circumstances add weight to the significance of Joshua's warning to Israel prior to their entry into the Promised Land, as recorded at Joshua 24:2, 14: "This is what Jehovah the God of Israel has said, 'It was on the other side of the River [Euphrates] that your forefathers dwelt a long time ago, Terah the father of Abraham and the father of Nahor, and they used to serve other gods.' And now fear Jehovah and serve him in faultlessness and in truth, and remove the gods that your forefathers served on the other side of the River and in Egypt, and serve Jehovah."

Job also lived among moon worshipers, and he faithfully rejected their practice of kissing the hand to the moon. (Job 31:26-28) The neighboring Midianites used moon-shaped ornaments, even placing them on their camels. (Jg 8:21, 26) In Egypt, where both Abraham and later the people of Israel resided, moon worship was prominently practiced in honor of the moon-god Thoth, the Egyptian god of measures. Every full moon the Egyptians sacrificed a pig to him. He came to be worshiped in Greece under the title of Hermes Trismegistus (Hermes Thrice Greatest). Moon worship, in fact, extended all the way to the Western Hemisphere, where ancient ziggurat temples dedicated to the moon have been found in Mexico and Central America. In English the second day of the week still derives its name from the Anglo-Saxon worship of the moon, Monday originally meaning "moon-day."

The moon worshipers attributed powers of fertility to the moon and looked to it to make their crops and even their animals grow. In Canaan, where the Israelites finally settled, the worship of the moon was carried on by the Canaanite tribes with the accompaniment of immoral rites and ceremonies. There the moon was sometimes worshiped under the symbol of the goddess Ashtoreth (Astarte). Ashtoreth was said to be the female consort of the male god Baal, and the worship of these two frequently ensnared the Israelites during the period of the Judges. (Jg 2:13; 10:6) King Solomon's foreign wives brought the contamination of moon worship into Judah. Foreign-god priests directed the people of Judah and Jerusalem in making sacrificial smoke to the sun, moon, and stars, a practice that continued until King Josiah's time. (1Ki 11:3-5, 33; 2Ki 23:5, 13, 14) When Jezebel, the daughter of the pagan king Ethbaal who ruled the Sidonians, married King Ahab of Israel, she also brought with her the worship of Baal and, apparently, of the moon-goddess Ashtoreth. (1Ki 16:31) The Israelites again met up with moon worship during their exile in Babylon, where the times of the new moons were considered propitious by the Babylonian astrologers for making forecasts of the future.—Isa 47:12, 13.

God's Word should have served as a protection for the Israelites against such moon worship. It showed the moon to be simply a luminary and a convenient time indicator, devoid of personality.

(Ge 1:14-18) At the time of their approaching Canaan, Jehovah specifically warned the nation of Israel that they should not worship heavenly creations as though they were representations of him. Anyone practicing such worship was to be stoned to death. (De 4:15-19; 17:2-5) By his prophet Jeremiah, God later declared that the bones of deceased idolatrous inhabitants of Jerusalem, including kings, priests, and prophets would be removed from their graves and become as "manure upon the face of the ground."—Jer 8:1, 2.

Some have tried to read into the text at Deuteronomy 33:14 an evidence of pagan influence or a superstitious attitude toward the moon. In the *King James Version* this text speaks of "the precious things put forth by the moon." However, as more modern translations show, the sense of the Hebrew word rendered "moon" here (*yera·chim'*) is actually "months" or "lunar months" and basically refers to the monthly periods in which the fruits ripen.

Similarly, Psalm 121:6 has been held by some to indicate a belief in the idea of illness caused by exposure to the moonlight. By reading the entire psalm, however, it becomes evident that such assumption is unfounded, since the psalm rather expresses in poetic form the assurance of God's protection against calamity under all circumstances and at all times, whether in the sunlit day or the moonlit night.

Still others have taken exception to the term "lunatick" found in the *King James Version* at Matthew 4:24 and Matthew 17:15. This expression comes from the Greek word *se·le·ni·a′zo·mai* and literally means "be moonstruck." In modern translations it is rendered by the word "epileptic." Matthew's use of this common Greek term for an epileptic on these two occasions means, not that he attributed such illness to the moon nor that the Bible so teaches, but simply that he used the word that was evidently, among Greek-speaking people of that time, the currently used name for an epileptic. In this regard, we might note that the term "lunacy" is today primarily a legal term used by the courts to designate a degree of insanity even though they do not attribute such insanity to the effects of the moon. English-speaking Christians today similarly continue to use the name Monday for the second day of the week even though they do not view it as a day sacred to the moon.

In the Common Era. In the days of Christ Jesus and the apostles, moon worship was not in practice among the Jewish people. They did, or course, observe the new moons in accord with the Law covenant. The new moon of each month is still observed by Orthodox Jews as a minor day of atonement for sins committed during the month just ended.

Nisan 14, when the moon was approaching fullness, marked the time of the celebration of the Passover and also the time of the institution by Jesus of the Memorial supper, or the Lord's Evening Meal, commemorating his death.—Mt 26:2, 20, 26-30; 1Co 11:20-26.

Despite the end of the Law covenant, some of the Jewish Christians, as well as others, tended to hold to the practice of the celebration of the new moons as well as of the Sabbath days, and so they needed Paul's corrective counsel as found at Colossians 2:16, 17 and Galatians 4:9-11.

MORDECAI   (Mor′de·cai).

1. One who returned to Jerusalem and Judah in 537 B.C.E. after the 70 years of exile in Babylon. (Ezr 2:1, 2) Mordecai was a prominent Israelite and leader who assisted Zerubbabel and was distinguished in the initial genealogical enrollment of the reestablished community in Judah.—Ne 7:5-7.

2. "The son of Jair the son of Shimei the son of Kish a Benjaminite" (Es 2:5), an older cousin and guardian of Esther. (Es 2:7) Mordecai is portrayed solely in the Bible book of Esther. The book recounts his prominent part in the affairs of the Persian Empire early in the fifth century B.C.E. Evidence points to him as the writer of the book of Esther.

Some doubt the authenticity of the book or that Mordecai was a real person. Their objection, that he would have had to have been at least 120 years old with a beautiful cousin 100 years younger, is based on the erroneous assumption that Esther 2:5, 6 denotes that Mordecai went into Babylonian exile along with King Jeconiah. However, the Bible's purpose in this text is, not to recount Mordecai's history, but to give his lineage. Kish may have been Mordecai's great-grandfather, or even an earlier ancestor who was "taken into exile." Another view, harmonious with Biblical expression, is that Mordecai, though born in exile, was considered to have been taken into exile in 617 B.C.E., since he was in the loins of his ancestors, as yet unborn.—Compare Heb 7:9, 10.

Loyal as Servant to the King.   In the account, Mordecai, although a Jewish exile, was a servant of the king. He heard that Queen Vashti had been deposed by King Ahasuerus of Persia and that all the beautiful young virgins through-

out the empire were being brought together so that from among them a replacement might be found for the queenly office. Mordecai's cousin Esther, a girl "pretty in form and beautiful in appearance," was introduced into the candidacy for queenship, but her Jewish background was not revealed. (Es 2:7, 8) She was selected as queen. Mordecai continued in his duties, "sitting in the king's gate," when information was brought to him that two of the court officials, Bigthan and Teresh, were plotting to lay hands on King Ahasuerus. He warned the king through Esther, and his act of loyalty was recorded in "the book of the affairs of the days."—Es 2:21-23.

Refuses to Bow to Haman.   Subsequent to this, Haman the Agagite was made prime minister by Ahasuerus, who ordered that all in the king's gate prostrate themselves before Haman in his newly exalted position. Mordecai staunchly refused to do so and gave as a reason that he was a Jew. (Es 3:1-4) The fact that Mordecai based his action on this reason proves that it had to do with his relationship, as a dedicated Jew, to his God Jehovah. He recognized that prostrating himself before Haman involved more than falling down to the earth for an exalted personage, as Israelites had done in the past, merely acknowledging such a one's superior position as ruler. (2Sa 14:4; 18:28; 1Ki 1:16) In Haman's case there was good reason why Mordecai did not bow. Haman was probably an Amalekite, and Jehovah had expressed himself as being at war with Amalek "from generation to generation." (Ex 17:16; see HAMAN.) It was a matter of integrity to God and not a political issue on Mordecai's part.

Haman was infuriated, particularly after he realized that Mordecai was a Jew. So great was his hatred that the enjoyment of all his power and privileges was spoiled as long as Mordecai sat at the gate and refused to bow before him. Not limiting his vindictiveness to Mordecai alone, Haman extracted a decree from the king for the destruction of all of Mordecai's people in the realm of Persia.—Es 3:5-12.

Used in Delivering Israel.   In the face of the edict to destroy all the Jews in the empire, Mordecai expressed faith that Esther had been brought to her royal dignity at this very time for deliverance of the Jews. He showed Esther her weighty responsibility and directed her to implore the favor and help of the king. Although it jeopardized her own life, Esther agreed to follow through.—Es 4:7-5:2.

Most timely for Mordecai and the Jews (for it was on the very issue of Mordecai's loyalty to the king), King Ahasuerus' attention was providentially directed, during a sleepless night, to the official book of records of the state. The king was thereby reminded of the fact that Mordecai had not been rewarded for his past service, that is, for uncovering the seditious plot of Bigthan and Teresh. At this the king desired to honor Mordecai grandly—to the mortification of Haman, who was commanded to arrange and announce this honor publicly.—Es 6:1-12.

Esther succeeded in indicting Haman for gross misrepresentation and calumniation of the Jews and for treacherous scheming against the king's own interests as well. The enraged Ahasuerus ordered the death sentence for Haman, and the 22-m-high (73 ft) stake Haman had erected for Mordecai was used to hang Haman's own body. —Es 7:1-10.

Mordecai now replaced Haman as prime minister and received the king's own signet ring for sealing state documents. Esther placed Mordecai over the house of Haman, which the king had turned over to her. Then Mordecai used the king's authorization to issue a counterdecree giving the Jews the legal right to defend themselves. To the Jews it was a light of deliverance and joy. Many in the Persian Empire aligned themselves with the Jews, and when Adar 13, the day for the laws to take force, arrived, the Jews were prepared. Officialdom stood behind them because of Mordecai's high position. In Shushan the fighting was extended for another day. More than 75,000 enemies of the Jews in the Persian Empire were destroyed, including the ten sons of Haman. (Es 8:1–9:18) With Esther's confirmation Mordecai commanded the annual celebration of the festival of the 14th and 15th days of Adar, the "days of Purim," for rejoicing and banqueting and giving gifts to one another and to the poor. The Jews accepted and imposed the festival on their offspring and all those joining themselves to them. As second in the empire, Mordecai was respected by God's dedicated people the Jews and continued working for their welfare.—Es 9:19-22, 27-32; 10:2, 3.

A Man of Faith. Mordecai was a man of faith like those spoken of by the apostle Paul at Hebrews chapter 11, though not mentioned there by name. He displayed courage, decisiveness, integrity, and loyalty to God and his people, and he followed the principle later expressed by Jesus: "Pay back, therefore, Caesar's things to Caesar, but God's things to God." (Mt 22:21) He and Esther were of the tribe of Benjamin, of whom the patriarch Jacob had prophesied: "Benjamin will keep on tearing like a wolf. In the morning he will eat the animal seized and at evening he will divide

spoil." (Ge 49:27) The activity of these Benjamite was in the evening of the nation of Israel, afte their kings were no longer on the throne and the had come under Gentile domination. It is possibl that Mordecai and Esther had the privilege o destroying the last of the hated Amalekites. Mor decai's interest in the welfare of his countrymer indicates that he had faith that from among the children of Israel would come the Seed of Abra ham to bless all families of the earth.—Ge 12:2 22:18.

MOREH (Mo'reh).

1. At least by Abraham's time the big trees o Moreh constituted a well-known landmark nea Shechem and seemingly continued to be such fo centuries afterward. (Ge 12:6; De 11:30; perhap also alluded to at Ge 35:4; Jos 24:25, 26; Jg 9:6. Some scholars link "the big tree of Meonenim with "the big trees of Moreh." (Jg 9:37) "Moreh was perhaps the name of the original owner of the plot near Shechem that had one especially promi nent tree or a clump or grove of big trees.

2. The name of a hill, in the vicinity of which the Midianites were defeated by Gideon. (Jg 7:1 This hill is generally thought to be the bare gray ridge of Jebel Dahi (Giv'at Ha-More), about 8 km (5 mi) N of the suggested site for the well o Harod.

MORESHETH (Mo'resh·eth), **MORESHETH GATH** [Possession of Gath]. Apparently the home of the prophet Micah. (Jer 26:18; Mic 1:1) Tel el-Judeideh (Tel Goded), about 35 km (22 mi) SW of Jerusalem and about 10 km (6 mi) SE of Gath is a possible identification. The composite name Moresheth-gath (Mic 1:14) implies that the city was in some way associated with Gath. Perhaps i was at times dominated by that Philistine city since the Philistines controlled places other thar their five major cities (Gath being one of the five) —1Sa 6:18; 27:5.

Some view Micah 1:14 as a play on the name Moresheth (meaning "Possession"). The Hebrev term for "parting gifts" in this text signifies a person or possession that is temporarily or perma nently given up or sent away. Accordingly, Zior (Mic 1:13) would lose this city, Moresheth itsel constituting the "parting gifts."

MORIAH (Mo·ri'ah). The name of the rocky eminence on which Solomon built a magnificen temple to Jehovah. Earlier, his father David had purchased the site from the Jebusite Araunal (Ornan) in order to erect an altar there, as this was the divinely indicated means for ending a scourge resulting from David's sin in connection with the taking of a census.—2Sa 24:16-25; 1Ch 21:15-28; 2Ch 3:1; see ARAUNAH.

Ancient Jewish tradition links the temple site with the mountain in "the land of Moriah" where Abraham, at God's command, attempted to offer up Isaac. (Ge 22:2; see *Jewish Antiquities*, VII, 329-334 [xiii, 4].) This would make "the land of Moriah" the mountainous region around Jerusalem. It was to "the land of Moriah" that Abraham traveled from the vicinity of Beer-sheba; and on the third day, he saw that divinely designated place from a distance.—Ge 21:33, 34; 22:4, 19.

Some have objected to identifying Mount Moriah with the Temple Mount in Jerusalem, because of its distance from Beer-sheba and its lack of visibility "from a distance." But it was "to the *land* of Moriah" that Abraham was to make a trip. On the first day, Abraham rose early, saddled his ass, split the wood, loaded it on the animal, and then began his trip. (Ge 22:2, 3) It was "on the third day that Abraham raised his eyes and began to see the place [the *land* of Moriah] from a distance." Thus, the second day was the only full day of travel. As to the visibility of Mount Moriah and the traveling distance, *The Illustrated Bible Dictionary* notes: "However, the distance from S Philistia to Jerusalem is *c.* 80 km, which might well have required 3 days to traverse, and in Genesis the place in question is not a 'mount Moriah' but one of several mountains in a land of that name, and the hills on which Jerusalem stands are visible at a distance. There is no need to doubt therefore that Abraham's sacrifice took place on the site of later Jerusalem, if not on the Temple hill." (Edited by J. Douglas, 1980, Vol. 2, p. 1025) Therefore, the trip of some 80 km (50 mi) on foot from Beer-sheba to Mount Moriah would conceivably have taken more than two full days.

Mount Moriah evidently was far enough from the Salem of Abraham's time that the attempted sacrifice of Isaac did not take place in full view of the city's inhabitants. There is no record that these witnessed the incident or tried to interfere. That the site was somewhat isolated centuries later may be deduced from the fact that in David's day there was a threshing floor on Mount Moriah. However, no mention is made of any buildings on the site.—2Ch 3:1.

Today the Islamic shrine known as the Dome of the Rock is situated atop Mount Moriah.—See JERUSALEM (Later Periods).

MORTAR, I.
A vessel having a bowl-shaped interior in which grain, spices, olives, or other substances were pulverized by pounding with a pestle.

Ancient mortar and pestle

Egyptian tomb paintings depict mortars with considerable capacity. These were probably wooden mortars and likely the pestles were made of metal. One tomb painting shows two men at one mortar, alternately raising and dropping metal pestles (club-shaped at both ends), which they gripped at the center with both hands. The painting indicates that after a quantity of material in the mortar had been pounded sufficiently, it was sifted into another container and the coarser remains were returned to the mortar for further pounding.

In the wilderness the Israelites prepared manna for consumption by grinding it in hand mills or pounding it in a mortar (Heb., *medho·khah'*).—Nu 11:7, 8.

The finest olive oil was obtained by beating the olives in a mortar with a pestle. This produced oil from only the olive meat, whereas a press crushed the seeds also. Pure, beaten olive oil was required for burning in the lampstand in the tent of meeting. Beaten oil was also used in connection with the "constant burnt offering" and evidently in the holy anointing oil. Incense beaten into powder was used in the sanctuary.—Ex 27:20, 21; 29:40, 42; 30:23-25, 35, 36.

Since a mortar has a hollow interior, it is suitably used in the Bible to describe the configuration of a specific land area. For instance, according to Judges 15:18, 19, God provided drinking water for Samson by splitting open "a mortar-shaped hollow" (Heb., *makh·tesh'*) in Lehi. Also, a certain section of Jerusalem, the "Maktesh" or

"Mortar-Quarter" (Heb., *Makh·tesh'*, meaning "mortar"), may have been so named to identify a basinlike hollow or depression in that area of the city.—Zep 1:11, ftn.

Grain reduced to flour in a mortar undergoes very severe treatment. Therefore, the Scriptures use this procedure illustratively, saying: "Even if you should pound the foolish one fine with a pestle in a mortar [Heb., *bam·makh·tesh'*], in among cracked grain, his foolishness will not depart from him."—Pr 27:22.

MORTAR, II. A composition that is applied between bricks and stones to cement them together (as in a wall) or that is used as a wall coating. (Le 14:42, 45; 1Ch 29:2; Isa 54:11; Jer 43:9) A weather-resistant mixture (properly termed "mortar") of lime, sand, and water was used in the construction of the finer homes in ancient Palestine. Another type of mortar, used as plaster, was prepared by blending sand, ashes, and lime. Sometimes oil was added to the mixture, or the wall was coated with oil after it was plastered, to produce a nearly waterproof surface. In Egypt (even up to modern times) mortar used for wall plaster has been composed of two parts clay, one part lime, and one part straw and ashes.

Instead of conventional mortar, the builders of the Tower of Babel used bitumen, which "served as mortar for them." (Ge 11:3) The later Babylonians likely obtained their bitumen for mortar from the subterranean fountains near the city of Hit located not far from Babylon on the Euphrates River. According to Herodotus (I, 179), hot asphalt (bitumen) was used as cement, or mortar, when building up the sides of Babylon's moat and when constructing the city's wall.

While the Israelites were slaves in Egypt, the Egyptians "kept making their life bitter with hard slavery at clay mortar and bricks." (Ex 1:14) The mortar was mixed to about the consistency of molasses, usually by trampling it with the feet. Chopped straw was combined with the mortar to increase the cohesiveness of the mixture. Later, in their own land, clay mortar and mud bricks served the Israelites as basic building materials in areas where little good-quality building stone was available.

Mud bricks were not lastingly resistant to wet weather. Therefore, in order to protect a new wall or to save and strengthen a damaged wall, a coat of mortar, or plaster, was sometimes applied. However, if only whitewash or bad mortar containing little or no lime was daubed on such a wall, it could not be expected to withstand severe storms.—Compare Eze 13:11-16.

MOSERAH (Mo·se'rah), **MOSEROTH** (Mo·se'-roth). The place where the Israelites were encamped when Aaron died. (De 10:6) It was evidently near Mount Hor (whereon Aaron died), but its exact location is unknown. (Nu 33:38) The plural form of Moserah, "Moseroth," appears at Numbers 33:30, 31 and apparently refers to an earlier Israelite encampment there.

MOSES (Mo'ses) [Drawn Out [that is, saved out of water]]. "Man of the true God," leader of the nation of Israel, mediator of the Law covenant, prophet, judge, commander, historian, and writer. (Ezr 3:2) Moses was born in 1593 B.C.E., in Egypt, being the son of Amram, the grandson of Kohath, and the great-grandson of Levi. His mother Jochebed was Kohath's sister. Moses was three years younger than his brother Aaron. Miriam their sister was some years older.—Ex 6:16, 18, 20; 2:7.

Early Life in Egypt. Moses, a "divinely beautiful" child, was spared from Pharaoh's genocidal decree commanding the destruction of every newborn Hebrew male. He was hidden by his mother for three months, then placed in a papyrus ark among the reeds by the bank of the Nile River, where Pharaoh's daughter found him. Through the wise action of his mother and sister, Moses came to be nursed and trained by his mother in the employment of the daughter of Pharaoh, who then adopted him as her son. As a member of Pharaoh's household, he was "instructed in all the wisdom of the Egyptians," becoming "powerful in his words and deeds," undoubtedly powerful in both mental and physical capabilities.—Ex 2:1-10; Ac 7:20-22.

In spite of his favored position and the opportunities offered to him in Egypt, Moses' heart was with God's enslaved people. In fact, he hoped to be used by God to bring deliverance to them. In the 40th year of his life, while making observation of the burdens his Hebrew brothers were bearing, he saw an Egyptian striking a Hebrew. In taking up his fellow Israelite's defense, he killed the Egyptian and buried him in the sand. It was at this point that Moses had made the most important decision of his life: "By faith Moses, when grown up, refused to be called the son of the daughter of Pharaoh, choosing to be ill-treated with the people of God rather than to have the temporary enjoyment of sin." Moses thereby gave up the honor and materialism that he might have enjoyed as a member of the household of mighty Pharaoh. —Heb 11:24, 25.

Actually, Moses felt that the time had come that he would be able to give the Hebrews salvation.

But they did not appreciate his efforts, and Moses was forced to flee from Egypt when Pharaoh heard of the slaying of the Egyptian.—Ex 2:11-15; Ac 7:23-29.

Forty Years in Midian. It was a long journey across wilderness territory to Midian, where Moses sought refuge. There, at a well, Moses' courage and readiness to act forcefully to help those suffering injustice again came to the fore. When shepherds drove away the seven daughters of Jethro and their flock, Moses delivered the women and watered the flocks for them. As a result he was invited to Jethro's house, where he entered Jethro's employment as a shepherd for his flocks and eventually married one of Jethro's daughters, Zipporah, who bore him two sons, Gershom and Eliezer.—Ex 2:16-22; 18:2-4.

Training for future service. While it was God's purpose to deliver the Hebrews by the hand of Moses, God's due time had not yet arrived; neither was Moses yet qualified to serve over God's people. He had to undergo another 40 years of training. The qualities of patience, meekness, humility, long-suffering, mildness of temper, self-control, and learning to wait on Jehovah needed to be developed in him to a higher degree, in order for him to be the fitting one to lead God's people. He had to be groomed and prepared to endure the discouragements, disappointments, and hardships he would encounter, and to handle with loving-kindness, calmness, and strength the multitude of problems a great nation would present. He possessed much learning, and his training as a member of Pharaoh's household had doubtless given him dignity, confidence, and poise and had accentuated his ability to organize and command. But the lowly occupation of shepherding in Midian provided the training needed to develop fine qualities that would be even more important for the task ahead of him. Similarly, David underwent rigorous training, even after being anointed by Samuel, and Jesus Christ was tried, tested, and proved, to be perfected as King and High Priest forever. "He [Christ] learned obedience from the things he suffered; and after he had been made perfect he became responsible for everlasting salvation to all those obeying him."—Heb 5:8, 9.

His Appointment as Deliverer. Toward the end of his 40-year sojourn in Midian, Moses was shepherding Jethro's flock near Mount Horeb when he was amazed to see a thornbush flaming with fire but not consumed. As he approached to inspect this great phenomenon, Jehovah's angel spoke out of the flame, revealing that it was now time for God to deliver Israel out of bondage and commissioning Moses to go in His memorial name Jehovah. (Ex 3:1-15) Thus God appointed Moses as His prophet and representative, and Moses could now correctly be called an anointed one, or messiah, or "the Christ" as at Hebrews 11:26. Jehovah, through the angel, provided credentials that Moses could present to the older men of Israel. These were in the form of three miracles as signs. Here, for the first time in the Scriptures, we read of a human empowered to perform miracles.—Ex 4:1-9.

Moses not disqualified because of diffidence. But Moses showed diffidence, arguing that he was unable to speak fluently. Here was a changed Moses, quite different from the one who had, of his own accord, offered himself as Israel's deliverer 40 years earlier. He continued to remonstrate with Jehovah, finally asking Jehovah to excuse him from the task. Although this aroused God's anger, he did not reject Moses but provided Moses' brother Aaron as a mouthpiece. Thus, as Moses was representative for God, so Moses became as "God" to Aaron, who spoke representatively for him. In the ensuing meeting with the older men of Israel and the encounters with Pharaoh, it appears that God gave Moses the instructions and commands and Moses, in turn, relayed them to Aaron, so that Aaron did the actual speaking before Pharaoh (a successor of the Pharaoh from whom Moses had fled 40 years previously). (Ex 2:23; 4:10-17) Later, Jehovah spoke of Aaron as Moses' "prophet," meaning that, as Moses was God's prophet, directed by him, so Aaron should be directed by Moses. Also, Moses was told that he was being made "God to Pharaoh," that is, given divine power and authority over Pharaoh, so that there was now no need to be afraid of the king of Egypt.—Ex 7:1, 2.

Though reproving him, God did not cancel Moses' assignment because of his reluctance to take up the tremendous task as deliverer of Israel. Moses had not demurred because of old age, even though he was 80. Forty years later, at the age of 120 years, Moses still had full vigor and alertness. (De 34:7) During his 40 years in Midian, Moses had had much time to meditate, and he had come to see the mistake he had made in trying to deliver the Hebrews on his own initiative. He now realized his own inadequacy. And after this long time, detached from all public affairs, it was doubtless quite a shock to be suddenly offered this role.

Later the Bible tells us: "The man Moses was by far the meekest of all the men who were upon the surface of the ground." (Nu 12:3) As a meek person, he recognized that he was a mere human, with imperfections and weaknesses. He did not push himself forward as Israel's invincible leader. He expressed, not fear of Pharaoh, but an acute awareness of his own limitations.

Before Pharaoh of Egypt. Moses and Aaron were now key figures in a 'battle of the gods.' In the persons of the magic-practicing priests, the chiefs of whom were apparently named Jannes and Jambres (2Ti 3:8), Pharaoh summoned the power of all the gods of Egypt against the power of Jehovah. The first miracle that Aaron performed before Pharaoh at Moses' direction proved Jehovah's supremacy over the gods of Egypt, even though Pharaoh became more obstinate. (Ex 7:8-13) Later, when the third plague occurred, even the priests were forced to admit, "It is the finger of God!" And they were so severely stricken by the plague of boils that they were altogether unable even to appear before Pharaoh to oppose Moses during that plague.—Ex 8:16-19; 9:10-12.

Plagues do softening and hardening work. Moses and Aaron became the announcers of each of the Ten Plagues. The plagues came as announced, proving Moses' commission as Jehovah's representative. Jehovah's name was declared and much talked about in Egypt, accomplishing both a softening and a hardening toward that name —softening the Israelites and some of the Egyptians; hardening Pharaoh and his advisers and supporters. (Ex 9:16; 11:10; 12:29-39) Instead of believing that they had offended their gods, the Egyptians *knew* that it was Jehovah who was judging their gods. By the time nine plagues had been executed, Moses too had become "very great in the land of Egypt, in the eyes of Pharaoh's servants and in the eyes of the people."—Ex 11:3.

There was a marked change in the men of Israel also. They had at first accepted Moses' credentials, but after experiencing harder working conditions at the order of Pharaoh, they complained against him to the point that Moses in discouragement appealed to Jehovah. (Ex 4:29-31; 5:19-23) The Most High at that time strengthened him by revealing that He was now going to fulfill that for which Abraham, Isaac, and Jacob had looked, namely, the full revealing of the meaning of his name Jehovah in delivering Israel and establishing it as a great nation in the land of promise. (Ex 6:1-8) Even then the men of Israel did not listen to Moses. But now, after the ninth plague, they were solidly behind him, cooperating so that, after the tenth plague, he could organize them and lead them out in an orderly way, "in battle formation." —Ex 13:18.

Courage and faith required to face Pharaoh. It was only in the strength of Jehovah and due to the operation of his spirit upon them that Moses and Aaron proved equal to the task set before them. Picture the court of Pharaoh, the king of the undisputed world power of that time. Here was unparalleled splendor, the haughty Pharaoh, supposed to be a god himself, surrounded by his advisers, military commanders, guards, and slaves. Moreover, there were the religious leaders, the magic-practicing priests, chief among Moses' opposers. These men were, aside from Pharaoh himself, the most powerful men in the realm. All this impressive array was aligned to back up Pharaoh in support of the gods of Egypt. And Moses and Aaron came before Pharaoh, not once, but many times, Pharaoh's heart getting harder each time, because he was determined to keep his valuable Hebrew slaves under his domination. In fact, after announcing the eighth plague, Moses and Aaron were driven out from before Pharaoh, and after the ninth plague they were ordered not to try to see Pharaoh's face again on pain of death. —Ex 10:11, 28.

With these things in mind, it becomes most understandable that Moses repeatedly appealed to Jehovah for assurance and strength. But it must be noted that he never failed to carry out to the letter what Jehovah commanded. He never diminished one word of that which Jehovah gave him to tell Pharaoh, and Moses' leadership was such that, at the time of the tenth plague, "all the sons of Israel did just as Jehovah had commanded Moses and Aaron. They did just so." (Ex 12:50) Moses is held before Christians as an example of outstanding faith. The apostle Paul says of him: "By faith he left Egypt, but not fearing the anger of the king, for he continued steadfast as seeing the One who is invisible."—Heb 11:27.

Before the tenth plague, Moses was privileged to institute the Passover. (Ex 12:1-16) At the Red Sea, Moses had to face further complaints of the people, who appeared trapped and about to be slaughtered. But he expressed the faith of a true leader under Jehovah's mighty hand, assuring Israel that Jehovah would destroy the pursuing Egyptian army. In this crisis he apparently called out to Jehovah, for God said to him: "Why do you keep crying out to me?" Then God commanded Moses to lift up his rod and stretch his hand out over the sea and split it apart. (Ex 14:10-18) Centuries later the apostle Paul said, of Israel's subsequent crossing of the Red Sea: "Our forefathers were all under the cloud and all passed through the sea and all got baptized into Moses by means of the cloud and of the sea." (1Co 10:1, 2) Jehovah did the baptizing. To be delivered from their murderous pursuers, the Jewish forefathers had to unite themselves with Moses as head and follow his leadership as he led them through the sea. The entire congregation of Israel was thus, in effect, immersed into the liberator and leader Moses.

Mediator of the Law Covenant. In the third month after the Exodus from Egypt, Jehovah demonstrated before all Israel the greatness of the authority and responsibility that he placed upon his servant Moses as well as the intimacy of Moses' position with God. Before all Israel, gathered at the foot of Mount Horeb, Jehovah called Moses into the mountain and, by means of an angel, spoke with him. On one occasion Moses was privileged to have what was probably the most awe-inspiring experience of any man prior to the coming of Jesus Christ. High in the mountain, alone, Jehovah gave him a vision of his glory, putting his "palm" over Moses as a screen, allowing Moses to see his "back," evidently the afterglow of this divine manifestation of glory. Then he spoke to Moses personally, as it were.—Ex 19:1-3; 33:18-23; 34:4-6.

Jehovah told Moses: "You are not able to see my face, because no man may see me and yet live." (Ex 33:20) And centuries later, the apostle John wrote: "No man has seen God at any time." (Joh 1:18) The Christian martyr Stephen told the Jews: "This [Moses] is he that came to be among the congregation in the wilderness with the angel that spoke to him on Mount Sinai." (Ac 7:38) So Jehovah was represented on the mountain by an angel. Nevertheless, such was the glory of Jehovah as manifested by Jehovah's angelic representative that the skin of Moses' face emitted rays so that the sons of Israel could not bear to look at him. —Ex 34:29-35; 2Co 3:7, 13.

God constituted Moses mediator of the Law covenant with Israel, an intimate position such as no man has ever held before God except Jesus Christ, the Mediator of the new covenant. With the blood of animal sacrifices Moses sprinkled the book of the covenant, representing Jehovah as one "party," and the people (no doubt the representative older men) as the other "party." He read the book of the covenant to the people, who replied, "All that Jehovah has spoken we are willing to do and be obedient." (Ex 24:3-8; Heb 9:19) In his office of mediator, Moses was privileged to oversee the building of the tabernacle and the making of its utensils, the pattern of which God gave to him, and to install the priesthood in office, anointing the tabernacle and Aaron the high priest with the oil of special composition. Then he took oversight of the first official services of the newly consecrated priesthood.—Ex chaps 25-29; Le chaps 8, 9.

A fitting mediator. Moses went up Mount Horeb several times, remaining on two occasions for periods of 40 days and nights. (Ex 24:18; 34:28) After the first of these occasions he returned with two stone tablets "written on by God's finger," containing "the Ten Words" or Ten Commandments, the basic laws of the Law covenant. (Ex 31:18; De 4:13) On this first occasion Moses showed himself to be fittingly qualified as mediator between Jehovah and Israel and leader of this great nation of perhaps three million or more. When Moses was in the mountain, Jehovah informed him that the people had turned to idolatry and Jehovah said: "Now let me be, that my anger may blaze against them and I may exterminate them, and let me make you into a great nation." Moses' immediate reply revealed that the sanctification of Jehovah's name was the thing of primary importance to him—that he was completely unselfish and did not desire fame for himself. He asked nothing for himself but, rather, showed concern for Jehovah's name that He had recently exalted by the Red Sea miracle, and regard for God's promise to Abraham, Isaac, and Jacob. Jehovah, in approval of Moses' plea, spared the people. Here it is seen that Jehovah regarded Moses as satisfactorily filling his mediatorial role and that He respected the arrangement through which he had appointed Moses to that office. Thus, Jehovah "began to feel regret over the evil that he had spoken of doing to his people"—that is, because of altered circumstances, he changed his attitude regarding bringing evil upon them.—Ex 32:7-14.

Moses' zeal for true worship as he served in behalf of God was displayed when he got down from the mountain. Seeing the idolatrous revelers, he threw the tablets down, breaking them, and called for those who would take Jehovah's side. The tribe of Levi joined Moses, and he commanded them to put to death those engaging in the false worship. This resulted in the slaying of about 3,000 men. Then he returned to Jehovah, acknowledging the people's great sin, and pleaded: "But now if you will pardon their sin,—and if not, wipe me out, please, from your book that you have written." God was not displeased at Moses' mediatorial plea, but answered: "Whoever has sinned against me, I shall wipe him out of my book."—Ex 32:19-33.

Many were the times that Moses represented Jehovah's side of the covenant, commanding true, clean worship and executing judgment on disobedient ones. More than once he also stood between the nation, or individuals thereof, and their destruction at Jehovah's hand.—Nu 12; 14:11-21; 16:20-22, 43-50; 21:7; De 9:18-20.

Unselfishness, Humility, Meekness. Moses' chief interests were in Jehovah's name and His people. Consequently he was not one to seek glory or position. When Jehovah's spirit came upon certain men in the camp and they began to act as prophets, Moses' assistant Joshua wanted to restrain them, evidently because he felt that they were detracting from Moses' glory and authority. But Moses replied: "Are you feeling jealous for me? No, I wish that all of Jehovah's people were prophets, because Jehovah would put his spirit upon them!"—Nu 11:24-29.

Although he was Jehovah's appointed leader of the great nation of Israel, Moses was willing to accept counsel from others, particularly when it would be of value to the nation. Shortly after the Israelites left Egypt, Jethro visited Moses, bringing with him Moses' wife and sons. Jethro observed how hard Moses was working, wearing himself out handling the problems of everyone who came to him. He wisely suggested an orderly arrangement wherein Moses would delegate degrees of responsibility to others, to lighten his load. Moses listened to Jethro's advice, accepted it, and organized the people into thousands, hundreds, fifties, and tens, with a chief over each group as a judge. Only the difficult cases were then brought to Moses. It is noteworthy also that Moses, explaining to Jethro what he was doing, said: "In the event that [the people] have a case arise, it must come to me and I must judge between the one party and the other, and *I must make known the decisions of the true God and his laws.*" In this, Moses indicated that he recognized his duty to judge, not according to his own ideas, but according to Jehovah's decisions and that, moreover, he had the responsibility to help the people to know and recognize God's laws.—Ex 18:5-7, 13-27.

Moses repeatedly pointed to Jehovah, and not himself, as the real Leader. When the people began to complain about food, Moses told them: "Your murmurings are not against us [Moses and Aaron], but against Jehovah." (Ex 16:3, 6-8) Possibly because Miriam felt her prominence might be eclipsed by the presence of Moses' wife, she and Aaron jealously and disrespectfully began to speak against Moses and his authority. The record shows that their speech was all the more contemptible because it is at this point that it says: "The man Moses was by far the meekest of all the men who were upon the surface of the ground." Moses apparently was hesitant to assert himself, meekly enduring the abuse. But Jehovah was incensed at this challenge, which was actually an affront to Jehovah himself. He took up the issue and severely chastised Miriam. Moses' love for his sister moved him to intercede for her, crying out: "O God, please! Heal her, please!"—Nu 12:1-15.

Obedience, Waiting Upon Jehovah. Moses waited upon Jehovah. Though he is called Israel's lawgiver, he recognized that the laws did not originate with him. He was not arbitrary, deciding matters on his own knowledge. In legal cases in which there was no precedent or where he could not discern exactly how to apply the law, he presented the matter to Jehovah to establish a judicial decision. (Le 24:10-16, 23; Nu 15:32-36; 27:1-11) He was careful to carry out instructions. In the intricate work of constructing the tabernacle and making its utensils and the priests' garments, Moses exercised close oversight. The record reads: "And Moses proceeded to do according to all that Jehovah had commanded him. He did just so." (Ex 40:16; compare Nu 17:11.) Repeatedly we find other statements that things were done "just as Jehovah had commanded Moses." (Ex 39:1, 5, 21, 29, 31, 42; 40:19, 21, 23, 25, 27, 29) It is good for Christians that he did so, for the apostle Paul points out that these things constituted "a shadow" and an illustration of heavenly things. —Heb 8:5.

Moses Stumbles. It was while Israel was encamped at Kadesh, probably in the 40th year of their wanderings, that Moses made a serious mistake. A consideration of the incident magnifies in our eyes the fact that Moses not only was in a highly privileged position but also was under very heavy responsibility to Jehovah as leader and mediator for the nation. Because of a water shortage the people began to quarrel bitterly with Moses, putting the blame on him for leading them up out of Egypt into the barren wilderness. Moses had endured much, putting up with the perverseness and insubordination of the Israelites, sharing their hardships, and interceding for them when they sinned, but here he momentarily lost his meekness and mildness of temper. Exasperated and embittered in spirit, Moses and Aaron stood before the people as Jehovah commanded. But instead of calling attention to Jehovah as the Provider, they spoke harshly to the people and directed attention to themselves, Moses saying: "Hear, now, you rebels! Is it from this crag that we shall bring out water for you?" With that, Moses struck the rock and Jehovah caused water to flow forth, sufficient for the multitude and their flocks. But God was displeased with the conduct of Moses and Aaron. They had failed of their primary responsibility, namely, to magnify Jehovah's name. They "acted undutifully" toward Jehovah, and Moses had 'spoken rashly' with his lips.' Later Jehovah decreed: "Because you did not show faith in me to sanctify me before the eyes of the sons of Israel, therefore you will not bring this congregation into the land that I shall certainly give them."—Nu 20:1-13; De 32:50-52; Ps 106:32, 33.

A Writer. Moses was the writer of the Pentateuch, the first five books of the Bible, namely, Genesis, Exodus, Leviticus, Numbers, and Deuteronomy. His writership has been acknowledged by the Jews throughout their history, this section of the Bible being known by them as the Torah, or Law. Jesus and the Christian writers frequently speak of Moses as giving the Law. He is generally credited with writing the book of Job, also Psalm 90 and, possibly, 91.—Mt 8:4; Lu 16:29; 24:27; Ro 10:5; 1Co 9:9; 2Co 3:15; Heb 10:28.

His Death and Burial. Moses' brother Aaron died at the age of 123 years while Israel was encamped at Mount Hor, on the frontier of Edom, in the fifth month of the 40th year of their journey. Moses took Aaron into the mountain, stripped off Aaron's priestly garments, and clothed Aaron's oldest living son and successor, Eleazar, with them. (Nu 20:22-29; 33:37-39) About six months later, Israel arrived at the Plains of Moab. Here Moses, in a series of discourses, explained the Law to the assembled nation, enlarging upon it with adjustments that would be necessary when Israel changed from nomadic camp life to a settled one in their own land. In the 12th month of the 40th year (in the spring of 1473 B.C.E.), he announced to the people that, according to Jehovah's appointment, Joshua would succeed him as leader. Joshua was then commissioned and exhorted to be courageous. (De 31:1-3, 23) Finally, after reciting a song and blessing the people, Moses went up into Mount Nebo according to Jehovah's command, first to view the Promised Land from this mountain vantage point, then to die.—De 32:48-51; 34:1-6.

Moses was 120 years of age at the time of his death. Testifying to his natural strength, the Bible comments: "His eye had not grown dim, and his vital strength had not fled." He was buried by Jehovah in a location never since discovered. (De 34:5-7) Likely, this was to prevent the Israelites from being ensnared into false worship by making a shrine of his grave. Evidently the Devil desired to use Moses' body for some such purpose, for Jude, the Christian disciple and half brother of Jesus Christ, writes: "When Michael the archangel had a difference with the Devil and was disputing about Moses' body, he did not dare to bring a judgment against him in abusive terms, but said: 'May Jehovah rebuke you.'" (Jude 9) Before crossing over into Canaan under the leadership of Josh-

ua, Israel observed a 30-day mourning period for Moses.—De 34:8.

A Prophet Jehovah Knew "Face to Face." When Miriam and Aaron challenged Moses' authority, Jehovah told them: "If there came to be a prophet of yours for Jehovah, it would be in a vision I would make myself known to him. In a dream I would speak to him. Not so my servant Moses! He is being entrusted with all my house. Mouth to mouth I speak to him, thus showing him, and not by riddles; and the appearance of Jehovah is what he beholds. Why, then, did you not fear to speak against my servant, against Moses?" (Nu 12:6-8) The conclusion of the book of Deuteronomy describes Moses' privileged standing with Jehovah: "But there has never yet risen up a prophet in Israel like Moses, whom Jehovah knew face to face, as respects all the signs and the miracles that Jehovah sent him to do in the land of Egypt to Pharaoh and all his servants and all his land, and as regards all the strong hand and all the great awesomeness that Moses exercised before the eyes of all Israel."—De 34:10-12.

According to Jehovah's words, Moses, though he never literally saw the very person of Jehovah, as mentioned in the foregoing, had a more direct, constant, intimate relationship with Jehovah than did any prophet prior to Jesus Christ. Jehovah's statement: "Mouth to mouth I speak to him," revealed that Moses had personal audience with God (by means of angels, who have access to the very presence of God; Mt 18:10). (Nu 12:8) As Israel's mediator, he enjoyed a virtually continuous two-way conversational communication arrangement. He was able at any time to present problems of national importance and to receive God's answer. Jehovah entrusted Moses 'with all His house,' using Moses as his intimate representative in organizing the nation. (Nu 12:7; Heb 3:2, 5) The later prophets simply continued to build on the foundation that had been laid through Moses.

The manner in which Jehovah dealt with Moses was so impressive that it was as if Moses actually had beheld God with his own eyes, instead of merely having a mental vision or a dream in which he heard God speak, which was the usual way in which God communicated with his prophets. Jehovah's dealings with Moses were so real that Moses reacted as if he had seen "the One who is invisible." (Heb 11:27) Evidently the impression made on Moses was similar to the effect of the transfiguration vision on Peter centuries later. The vision was so real to Peter that he began to participate in it, speaking but not realizing what he was saying. (Lu 9:28-36) And the apostle Paul likewise experienced a vision that was so real that he later said of himself: "Whether in the body I do not know, or out of the body I do not know; God knows."—2Co 12:1-4.

No doubt Joshua's extraordinary success in establishing Israel in the Promised Land came, to an extent, by reason of the fine qualities inculcated in him by Moses' training and example. Joshua was Moses' minister "from his young manhood on." (Nu 11:28) Evidently he was army commander under Moses (Ex 17:9, 10) and was close to Moses as his attendant in many experiences.—Ex 24:13; 33:11; De 3:21.

Prefigured Jesus Christ. Jesus Christ made clear that Moses had written about him, for on one occasion he told his opponents: "If you believed Moses you would believe me, for that one wrote about me." (Joh 5:46) "Commencing at Moses and all the Prophets," when in the company of his disciples, Jesus "interpreted to them things pertaining to himself in all the Scriptures."—Lu 24: 27, 44; see also Joh 1:45.

Among the things Moses wrote concerning Christ Jesus are Jehovah's words: "A prophet I shall raise up for them from the midst of their brothers, like you; and I shall indeed put my words in his mouth, and he will certainly speak to them all that I shall command him." (De 18:18, 19) The apostle Peter in quoting this prophecy left no doubt that it referred to Jesus Christ.—Ac 3:19-23.

In the transfiguration scene that Peter, James, and John were permitted to view, Moses and Elijah were seen talking with Jesus. In Moses, the three apostles would see represented the Law covenant, the theocratic arrangement of the congregation, the deliverance of the nation, and its being safely transferred to the Promised Land. Thus the vision indicated that Jesus Christ would do a work like Moses did, but greater; also the visionary appearance of Elijah showed that he would do a work like that of Elijah, but in a larger way. It was there plainly manifested that the Son of God was indeed the 'prophet greater than Moses' and worthy of the title Messiah.—Mt 17:1-3; see TRANSFIGURATION.

In many ways there was pictorial correspondency between these two great prophets, Moses and Jesus Christ. In infancy both escaped the wholesale slaughter ordered by the respective rulers of their time. (Ex 1:22; 2:1-10; Mt 2:13-18) Moses was called out of Egypt with Jehovah's "firstborn," the nation of Israel, Moses being the nation's leader. Jesus was called out of Egypt as God's firstborn Son. (Ex 4:22, 23; Ho 11:1; Mt 2:15, 19-21) Both fasted for 40 days in wilderness places. (Ex 34:28; Mt 4:1, 2) Both came in the name of Jehovah, Jesus' name itself meaning "Jehovah Is Salvation." (Ex 3:13-16; Mt 1:21; Joh 5:43) Jesus, like Moses, 'declared the name of Jehovah.' (De 32:3; Joh 17:6, 26) Both were exceptional in meekness and humility. (Nu 12:3; Mt 11:28-30) Both had the most convincing credentials to show that they were sent by God—astounding miracles of many sorts, Jesus Christ going farther than Moses by raising dead persons to life.—Ex 14:21-31; Ps 78:12-54; Mt 11:5; Mr 5:38-43; Lu 7:11-15, 18-23.

Moses was mediator of the Law covenant between God and the nation of Israel. Jesus was Mediator of the new covenant between God and the "holy nation," the spiritual "Israel of God." (1Pe 2:9; Ga 6:16; Ex 19:3-9; Lu 22:20; Heb 8:6; 9:15) Both served as judges, lawgivers, and leaders. (Ex 18:13; 32:34; Da 9:25; Mal 4:4; Mt 23:10; Joh 5:22, 23; 13:34; 15:10) Moses was entrusted with and proved faithful to his stewardship in the 'house of God,' that is, the nation, or congregation, of Israel. Jesus showed faithfulness over God's house that he as God's Son constructed, namely, the nation, or congregation, of spiritual Israel. (Nu 12:7; Heb 3:2-6) And even in death there was a parallel: God disposed of the bodies of both Moses and Jesus.—De 34:5, 6; Ac 2:31; Jude 9.

Toward the end of Moses' 40-year sojourn in the wilderness, while he was shepherding his father-in-law's flock, God's angel made a miraculous manifestation to him in the flame of a thornbush at the foot of Mount Horeb. Jehovah there commissioned him to deliver His people from Egypt. (Ex 3:1-15) Thus God appointed Moses as His prophet and representative, and Moses could now correctly be called an anointed one, or "Christ." In order to come into that privileged position, Moses had had to give up "the treasures of Egypt" and let himself "be ill-treated with the people of God" and thus suffer reproach. But to Moses such "reproach of the Christ" was riches greater than all of Egypt's wealth.—Heb 11:24-26.

A parallel to this is found in Jesus Christ. According to the angel's announcement at his birth in Bethlehem, he was to become "a Savior, who is Christ the Lord." He became Christ, or Anointed One, after the prophet John baptized him in the Jordan River. (Lu 2:10, 11; 3:21-23; 4:16-21) Thereafter he acknowledged that he was "the Christ," or Messiah. (Mt 16:16, 17; Mr 14:61, 62; Joh 4:25, 26) Jesus Christ also kept his eye on the prize and despised the shame that men heaped upon him, as Moses had done. (Php 2:8, 9; Heb 12:2) It is into this Greater Moses that the Christian congregation is baptized—into Jesus Christ, the foretold Prophet, Liberator, and Leader.—1Co 10:1, 2.

MOSQUITO [Heb., qe'rets]. Any of a great variety of two-winged insects having a round head and long, slender, five-jointed legs. Female mosquitoes are equipped with a strong proboscis that enables them to pierce the skin of man and animals, in order to suck their blood. The Hebrew word rendered "mosquito" (NW) appears as a noun only at Jeremiah 46:20, where it is used to represent the Babylonians under Nebuchadnezzar, the enemy to the north that would come against Egypt, the "pretty heifer."

MOST HIGH. Topmost as to place, or position. The Hebrew word 'el·yohn', used with reference to Jehovah as "Most High," is also applied to other persons or things: The Messianic King, the Greater David, as above the other earthly kings (Ps 89:20, 27), the place above the nations promised to Israel (De 26:18, 19), the topmost basket (Ge 40:17), the upper gate (2Ki 15:35), the upper pool (2Ki 18:17), the upper courtyard (Jer 36:10), the uppermost story (Eze 41:7), the uppermost dining rooms (Eze 42:5), Upper Beth-horon (Jos 16:5), and the upper source of the waters of Gihon (2Ch 32:30). These uses illustrate that 'el·yohn' denotes position rather than power.

When applied to Jehovah, "Most High" emphasizes his supreme position above all others. (Ps 83:18) The title first appears at Genesis 14:18-20 with 'El (God), where Melchizedek is called "priest of the Most High God" and, in that capacity, blesses Abraham as well as the Most High God. "Most High" is used in combination with the divine name Jehovah (Ge 14:22; Ps 7:17) and with the plural of excellence 'Elo·him' (God) (Ps 78:56), and it also appears alone.—De 32:8; Ps 9:2; Isa 14:14.

The plural Aramaic form 'el·yoh·nin' occurs at Daniel 7:18, 22, 25, 27, where it may be translated "Supreme One" (NW), the plural being the plural of excellence, majesty. The Aramaic form in the singular number, 'il·lai' (Most High), is used at Daniel 7:25.

The Greek word hy'psi·stos (Most High), as applying to Jehovah, is employed mainly by Luke, in his Gospel (twice in Gabriel's announcement to Mary about the birth of Jesus) and in the Acts. (Lu 1:32, 35, 76; 6:35; 8:28; Ac 7:48; 16:17) The other occurrences are at Mark 5:7 and Hebrews 7:1.

MOST HOLY. The innermost room of the tabernacle and, later, of the temple; also called the Holy of Holies. (Ex 26:33, ftn; 1Ki 6:16) This compartment in the tabernacle was apparently cubical, each of its three dimensions being ten cubits (4.5 m; 14.6 ft); the dimensions of the Most Holy in the temple built by Solomon were twice those of the tabernacle, so that it was eight times as large in volume.—Ex 26:15, 16, 18, 22, 23; 1Ki 6:16, 17, 20; 2Ch 3:8.

The high priest entered the Most Holy only on the annual Day of Atonement; at no time could any other person go beyond the curtain that hung between this room and the Holy Place. (Le 16:2) In the Most Holy the high priest was surrounded by the colorful embroidered cherubs on the tabernacle's inner covering and on the curtain. (Ex 26:1, 31, 33) In Solomon's temple the walls and ceiling were of cedarwood covered with gold, and cherubs, palm-tree figures, gourd-shaped ornaments, and blossoms were engraved on the walls.—1Ki 6:16-18, 29; 2Ch 3:7, 8.

The Scriptures outline three entries of the high priest into the Most Holy on Atonement Day: First with the golden censer of perfumed incense, fired by coals from off the altar; a second time with the blood of the bull, the sin offering for the priestly tribe; and finally with the blood of the goat, the sin offering for the people. (Le 16:11-15; Heb 9:6, 7, 25) He sprinkled the blood of the animals on the ground before the golden ark of the covenant, on the cover of which were golden cherubs and above which cover Jehovah's presence was symbolized by a cloud. (Ex 25:17-22; Le 16:2, 14, 15) That cloud evidently shone as a bright light, being the sole light for this compartment of the tabernacle, which had no lampstand in it.

While the tabernacle was in the wilderness, above the Most Holy resided a cloud by day and a pillar of fire by night, visible to the entire camp of Israel.—Ex 13:22; 40:38; Nu 9:15; compare Ps 80:1.

No Ark in Later Temples. Just when and under what circumstances the ark of the covenant disappeared is not known. Apparently the Babylonians did not capture it when they pillaged and destroyed the temple in 607 B.C.E., for the Ark is not listed among the temple articles carried off. (2Ki 25:13-17; Ezr 1:7-11) In the second temple, built by Zerubbabel, and in the more elaborate temple of Herod, there was no Ark in the Most Holy. At the time of Jesus' death God expressed his anger by causing the thick, heavy curtain that separated the Most Holy from the Holy Place to be ripped in two from top to bottom. The priests who were carrying on their work in the Holy Place were then able to see into the Most Holy and to have impressed upon them the fact that this compartment contained no Ark representing God's presence with them. This action by God confirmed that the atonement sacrifices offered by the Jewish high priest were now no longer of value and there was no need for the services of the Levitical priesthood anymore.—Mt 27:51; 23:38; Heb 9:1-15.

Symbolic Use. The Most Holy compartment in the tent of meeting, or the tabernacle, contained the ark of the covenant; the cover of that Ark surmounted by two golden cherubs represented God's throne. Therefore the Most Holy was used, figuratively, to represent the dwelling place of Jehovah God, heaven itself. The inspired letter to the Hebrews gives us this interpretation of matters when it compares the entry of Israel's high priest into the Most Holy one day a year, on the Day of Atonement, with the entry of the great High Priest Jesus Christ into what the Most Holy symbolized, once for all time with his sacrifice for sins. It explains: "Into the second compartment [the Most Holy] the high priest alone enters once a year, not without blood, which he offers for himself and for the sins of ignorance of the people. . . . This very tent is an illustration for the appointed time that is now here . . . However, when Christ came as a high priest of the good things that have come to pass, through the greater and more perfect tent not made with hands, that is, not of this creation, he entered, no, not with the blood of goats and of young bulls, but with his own blood, once for all time into the holy place and obtained an everlasting deliverance for us. Therefore it was necessary that the typical representations of the things in the heavens should be cleansed by these means [blood of animal sacrifices sprinkled on them], but the heavenly things themselves with sacrifices that are better than such sacrifices. For Christ entered, not into a holy place made with hands, which is a copy of the reality, but into *heaven itself,* now to appear before the person of God for us."—Heb 9:7-12, 23, 24.

So Jesus Christ as the great High Priest according to the manner of Melchizedek fulfilled what Israel's high priest of the line of Aaron could do only typically when entering into the earthly Most Holy. (Heb 9:24) The spiritual brothers of Christ, joint heirs with him, are strengthened by the words of the same letter to the Hebrews, that "we who have fled to the refuge may have strong encouragement to lay hold on the hope set before us. This hope we have as an anchor for the soul, both sure and firm, and it enters in within the curtain, where a forerunner has entered in our behalf, Jesus, who has become a high priest according to the manner of Melchizedek forever."—Heb 6:18-20.

Again, Paul encouraged these Christians to feel fully free and confident to approach God and to hold fast to their hope without wavering by these further words: "Therefore, brothers, since we have boldness for the way of entry into the holy place by the blood of Jesus, which he inaugurated for us as a new and living way through the curtain, that is, his flesh, and since we have a great priest over the house of God, let us approach with true hearts in the full assurance of faith, having had our hearts sprinkled from a wicked conscience and our bodies bathed with clean water. Let us hold fast the public declaration of our hope without wavering, for he is faithful that promised."—Heb 10:19-23.

MOTH [Heb., '*ash; sas* (clothes moth); Gr., *ses*]. A four-winged insect resembling a butterfly but differing from the latter in that its feelers usually are feathery and not terminated by distinct knobs. When at rest the moth's wings are not held erect, as is often the case with butterflies. Instead, they are either folded back flat over the insect's body or held flat at its sides. Also, moths are generally nocturnal. The insect referred to in Scripture is evidently the webbing clothes moth (*Tineola bisellieila*), particularly in its destructive larval stage. (Job 13:28; Ps 39:11; Isa 50:9; 51:8; Ho 5:12; Mt 6:19, 20; Lu 12:33; compare Jas 5:2.) The ease with which a moth can be crushed was a figure employed by Eliphaz with reference to the frailty of mortal man.—Job 4:17, 19, 20.

Female clothes moths lay their eggs on fabrics of wool or silk or on furs, distributing them so that emerging caterpillars will have ample room and material on which to feed. The caterpillars will not eat until they have first protected themselves with a "house" or case constructed from the available fibers. In this "house" they remain as they feed.—Job 27:18.

MOTHER. Like the Hebrew word '*av* (father), the word '*em* (mother) is probably a mimetic word, one of the first lip sounds of a baby. It is used to designate the immediate mother of an individual, possibly a stepmother (Ge 37:10; compare Ge 30:22-24; 35:16-19), and also an ancestress, since Adam's wife Eve was "the mother of everyone living." (Ge 3:20; 1Ki 15:10) The Greek word for "mother" is *me'ter.* In both Hebrew and Greek, the word for mother is used in a number of figurative ways.

The desire to have a large family was especially strong in the heart of Hebrew women because of

God's promise to make Israel a populous nation and the people through whom the seed of promise would come. (Ge 18:18; 22:18; Ex 19:5, 6) For one to be childless was considered to be one of the greatest of misfortunes.—Ge 30:1.

Under the Law covenant a woman was religiously "unclean" after the birth of a male child for 40 days (7 plus 33), and after the birth of a female child for double this amount of time, or 80 days (14 plus 66). (Le 12:2-5) For the 7 and the 14 days respectively she was unclean to all persons, including her husband, but for the 33 and 66 days respectively she was unclean only as to holy things and things connected with religious services at the sanctuary.

Hebrew mothers breast-fed their children till they were three years old and sometimes up until the age of five years or longer, in the belief that the longer the child was suckled the stronger it would grow. (See WEANING.) Where the mother died or could not provide a sufficient supply of milk, a nurse was employed. Hence, "babes and sucklings" of the Bible could include those old enough to be weaned, old enough to have some knowledge to be able to praise Jehovah and to be trained at the sanctuary.—Mt 21:15, 16; 1Sa 1:23, 24; 2:11.

There was a special closeness between the mother and the children because the mother took immediate care of the children until the time after weaning when the father would begin to guide the child's education more personally. The mother's position in the household was one of recognized importance. She was to be respected even in her very old age. (Ex 20:12; 21:15, 17; Pr 23:22; De 5:16; 21:18-21; 27:16) Of course, her position was always secondary to that of her husband, whom she was to respect and obey. As a child, Jesus kept in subjection to his adoptive father Joseph and his mother Mary.—Lu 2:51, 52.

Where the father had more than one wife, the sons would distinguish their real mother from their father's other wives by using the designation "mother." Full brothers were distinguished from half brothers by the expression "sons of my mother."—Jg 8:19; Ge 43:29.

The mother was required to transmit the instructions and commands of the father to the children and see that these were carried out. (Pr 1:8; 6:20; 31:1) The mother was the manager of her household under her husband's headship. Bearing and rearing children in a right way kept her busy and protected her to a great extent from becoming a gossiper or a meddler in other people's affairs. As long as she continued in the faith, this proved to be a very great safeguard for her. (1Ti 5:9-14; 2:15) A good mother had to prepare food and make cloth as well as articles of clothing for her children and other members of the household, and her husband as well as her sons could well commend and praise such a woman before others. —Pr 31:15, 19, 21, 28.

Figurative Use. The word "mother" is applied at Judges 5:7 in the sense of a woman who assists and cares for others. Paul referred to his gentleness toward those to whom he brought God's truth, his spiritual children, as that of "a nursing mother."—1Th 2:7; see GENTLENESS.

Because of the close spiritual relationship, Christian women are likened to mothers and sisters of their fellow Christians and are to be treated with the same respect and chastity. (Mr 3:35; 1Ti 5: 1, 2) Christian wives who follow the good example of Abraham's wife Sarah are termed her "children."—1Pe 3:6.

Since man's body was made "out of dust from the ground," the earth may figuratively be likened to his "mother." (Ge 2:7; Job 1:21) A city is depicted as a mother, the inhabitants of which are considered her children. In the case of Jerusalem, the city as the seat of government stood for the entire nation, and the people of Israel as individuals were considered her children. (Ga 4:25, 26; Eze 23:4, 25; compare Ps 137:8, 9.) Also, a large city was considered as a mother to her surrounding "dependent towns," or, literally translated, her "daughters." (Eze 16:46, 48, 53, 55; see ftn on vs 46.) Babylon the Great, "the great city," is called "the mother of the harlots and of the disgusting things of the earth."—Re 17:5, 18.

MOUND. A geographic or structural feature of ancient Jerusalem. (2Sa 5:9; 1Ki 9:15, 24; 11:27; 2Ki 12:20; 1Ch 11:8; 2Ch 32:5) At Judges 9:6, 20 the same Hebrew word translated "Mound" (*milloh'*) is rendered "Millo."—See MILLO.

The exact nature of the Mound is today unknown. At 2 Kings 12:20 reference is made to "the house of the Mound," which may indicate that it was a citadellike structure. As to its location, 2 Samuel 5:9 and 2 Chronicles 32:5 associate it with the City of David, indicating that it was either in or at the edge of the City of David.

MOUNT, MOUNTAIN. A landmass projecting conspicuously higher than hills in that area. The distinction between hills and mountains is relative. In an area of low hills a mountain may be only a few hundred feet higher than the surrounding landscape, while in more mountainous regions the lesser summits may also be called hills, even though much higher than an isolated mountain like the 562-m (1,844 ft) Mount Tabor.—Jg 4:6.

The Hebrew word *har* may refer to individual mountains, including Mount Sinai, Mount Gerizim, Mount Ebal, Mount Gilboa, and Mount Zion. (Ex 19:11; De 11:29; 1Sa 31:8; Isa 4:5) It may also refer to mountain ranges like that of Ararat (Ge 8:4) and to entire elevated regions like the mountainous regions of Ephraim (Jos 17:15), Naphtali (Jos 20:7), and Gilead (De 3:12), as well as to those regions anciently occupied by the Amorites and Ammonites. (De 1:7, 20; 2:37) The Aramaic word *tur* (Da 2:35) designates a mountain, as does the Greek word *o'ros*.—See articles on individual mountains by name.

Mountains of Palestine. Palestine on the whole is a rather mountainous land, though it possesses few impressive peaks. West of the Jordan River there are the mountains of Judah in the south, including Mount Moriah, Mount Zion, and the Mount of Olives. (2Ch 3:1; Ps 48:2; Mr 13:3) The central section of this range extends NE to Mount Gilboa (1Sa 31:1) and contains the mountains of Ephraim and Samaria, with the historic peaks of Gerizim and Ebal. (Jos 19:50; De 11:29) To the NNW the Mount Carmel Range juts out into the Mediterranean Sea.—Jer 46:18.

The Valley of Jezreel (Esdraelon) divides the primary range from a second range farther N. This latter range includes Mount Tabor (Jg 4:6) and the coastal chain of Lebanon Mountains.—Jg 3:3; 1Ki 5:6.

East of the Rift Valley are the plateaus of Edom and Moab (2Ch 20:10) and the high cliffs along the eastern side of the Dead Sea, including Mount Nebo from which Moses viewed the Promised Land, as well as the tableland E of the Jordan Valley, which averages about 600 m (2,000 ft) in elevation. (De 3:10; 34:1-3; Jos 13:8, 9; 20:8) This mountainous region continues northward to meet the Anti-Lebanon Range, with its majestic Mount Hermon, the highest peak in the entire Palestinian region.—Ca 4:8.

Value of Mountains. Mountains influence the climate and rainfall; they collect the water and channel it down to the rivers or hold it in underground reservoirs that feed springs in the valleys below. (De 8:7) Their slopes have supported trees (2Ch 2:16, 18), vineyards, and various crops. (Ps 72:16; Pr 27:25; Isa 7:23-25; Jer 31:5) Their higher elevations have served as threshing floors. (Isa 17:13) Mountains have accorded natural protection from invading armies (Ps 125:2); they have offered refuge and storage places in time of danger (Ge 19:17, 30; Jg 6:2; Mt 24:16; compare Re 6:15) and shelter for wildlife. (Ps 50:10, 11; 104:18; Isa 18:6) They have provided sites for cities. (Mt 5:14) Mining operations have yielded useful ores. (De 8:9) Also, valuable building stones have been quarried from mountains.—1Ki 5:15-17.

Jehovah's Possession. All mountains belong to Jehovah God by reason of his being their Former. (Ps 95:4; Am 4:13) However, the words "mountain of Jehovah" or 'of God' often apply in a special way to mountains where Jehovah revealed his presence. These include Mount Sinai or Horeb (Ex 3:1; Nu 10:33) and the mountain associated with Jehovah's sanctuary.—Ps 24:3.

Figurative and Prophetic Use. Sometimes the term "mountain" applies to the soil, vegetation, and trees on the mountain's surface. (Compare Ps 83:14.) Of Jehovah, the psalmist says: "He touches the mountains, and they smoke." (Ps 104:32; 144:5, 6) This may point to the fact that lightning can set mountain forests on fire, thereby causing a mountain to smoke. The effects of a severe storm appear to be described when the Bible speaks of mountains 'melting' or 'flowing away.' (Jg 5:5; Ps 97:5) Heavy rains produce streams and raging torrents that wash the soil away, as if melting it. Similarly, the expression of Jehovah's anger against the nations was foretold to result in such slaughter that the blood of the slain would melt the mountains, that is, wash the soil away. (Isa 34:1-3) For mountains to "drip with sweet wine" means that the vineyards occupying their slopes would produce abundantly.—Joe 3:18; Am 9:13.

At Mount Sinai the revelation of Jehovah's presence was attended by such physical manifestations as lightning, smoke, and fire. Also the mountain trembled. (Ex 19:16-18; 20:18; De 9:15) It appears that this and other physical phenomena provide the basis for figurative expressions found elsewhere in the Bible. (Compare Isa 64:1-3.) The trembling of Mount Sinai evidently is referred to under the figure of 'mountains skipping about like rams.' (Ps 114:4, 6) 'Setting the foundations of mountains ablaze' perhaps alludes to volcanic activity (De 32:22), and the 'foundations of the mountains becoming agitated' refers to their shaking, possibly caused by an earthquake.—Ps 18:7.

Represent governments. In Biblical symbolism mountains can represent kingdoms or ruling governments. (Da 2:35, 44, 45; compare Isa 41:15; Re 17:9-11, 18.) Babylon, by her military conquests, brought other lands to ruin and is, therefore, called a "ruinous mountain." (Jer 51:24, 25) A psalm relating Jehovah's activities against warring men depicts him as being "enveloped with light, more majestic than the mountains of prey." (Ps 76:4) "The mountains of prey" may represent aggressive kingdoms. (Compare Na 2:11-13.) Regarding Jehovah, David said: "You have made my mountain to stand in strength," probably meaning that Jehovah had exalted David's kingdom and firmly established it. (Ps 30:7; compare 2Sa 5:12.) The fact that mountains may represent kingdoms aids one in understanding the significance of what is described at Revelation 8:8 as "something like a great mountain burning with fire." Its resemblance to a burning mountain would suggest that it is associated with a form of rulership having a destructive nature like fire.

The prophecy of Daniel indicated that God's Kingdom, after crushing all other kingdoms, would become a large mountain and fill the whole earth. (Da 2:34, 35, 44, 45) This meant that it would extend its blessed rule over the entire earth. Wrote the psalmist: "Let the mountains carry peace to the people, also the hills, through righteousness." (Ps 72:3) In harmony with this psalm, the blessings that are spoken of in connection with God's mountain, such as Jehovah's banquet for all the peoples, would be experienced on earth.—Isa 25:6; see also Isa 11:9; 65:25.

Associated with worship. Mount Zion became a holy mountain when David brought the sacred Ark to the tent that he had pitched there. (2Sa 6:12, 17) As the Ark was associated with Jehovah's presence and David had evidently acted at divine direction (De 12:5), this meant that Jehovah had chosen Mount Zion as his place of dwelling. With reference to this choosing, David wrote: "The mountainous region of Bashan is a mountain of God [that is, created by God]; the mountainous region of Bashan is a mountain of peaks. Why do you, O you mountains of peaks, keep watching enviously the mountain that God has desired for himself to dwell in? Even Jehovah himself will reside there forever. . . . Jehovah himself has come from Sinai [where he first revealed his presence to the entire nation of Israel] into the holy place." (Ps 68:15-17) The mountainous region of Bashan may be identified with Mount Hauran (Jebel ed Druz), and this mountain range may be meant by the words the "mountain of God" and the "mountain of peaks." Although Mount Hauran towers far above Mount Zion, Jehovah chose the less conspicuous location for his place of dwelling.

After the temple was built on Mount Moriah, the term "Zion" came to include the temple site, and therefore Zion remained God's holy mountain. (Isa 8:18; 18:7; 24:23; Joe 3:17) Since Jehovah's tem-

ple was located at Jerusalem, the city itself was also called his "holy mountain." (Isa 66:20; Da 9:16, 20) It may be with reference to facing the mountains of Jerusalem when praying that the psalmist said: "I shall raise my eyes to the mountains. From where will my help come? My help is from Jehovah."—Ps 121:1, 2; compare Ps 3:4; 1Ki 8:30, 44, 45; Da 6:10.

The prophecy of Isaiah 2:2, 3 and that of Micah 4:1, 2 pointed to the time when "the mountain of the house of Jehovah" would "become firmly established above the top of the mountains" and be "lifted up above the hills," with people of many nations streaming to it. The fact that "the mountain of the house of Jehovah" was to be above mountains and hills would point to the exalted position of true worship, for mountains and hills in ancient times served as sites for idolatrous worship and for sanctuaries of false gods.—De 12:2; Jer 3:6; Eze 18:6, 11, 15; Ho 4:13.

In a typical fulfillment, between 29 and 70 C.E., during the final part of the days of the Jewish system of things, Jehovah's worship was exalted above the lofty elevation that pagan nations gave to their false gods. The King, Jesus Christ, made "a breakthrough" in elevating the true worship, and he was followed, first by a remnant of the nation of Israel and then by people from all nations. (Isa 2:2; Mic 2:13; Ac 10:34, 35) In an antitypical fulfillment, in the final part of the days of this system of things, Jehovah's worship has been elevated heaven high. The King, Jesus Christ, has led the remnant of spiritual Israel to pure worship, and they have been followed by a great crowd out of all nations.—Re 7:9.

Obstacles. At times mountains represent obstacles. For example, the obstacles that stood in the way of Israel's returning from Babylonian exile and those that later prevented progress in the temple rebuilding work were compared to mountains. (Isa 40:1-4; Zec 4:7) Faith can move similar mountainous obstacles and, if it be God's will, even literal mountains.—Mt 17:20; 21:21; Mr 11:23; 1Co 13:2.

Stability, permanence, or loftiness. Stability and permanence are ascribed to the mountains. (Isa 54:10; Hab 3:6; compare Ps 46:2.) Therefore, when the psalmist spoke of Jehovah's righteousness as being like "mountains of God" (Ps 36:6) he may have meant that Jehovah's righteousness is immovable. Or, since mountains are lofty, this may point to the fact that God's righteousness by far transcends that of man. (Compare Isa 55:8, 9.) In connection with the outpouring of the seventh bowl of God's anger, Revelation 16:20 says:

"Mountains were not found." This suggests that not even things as lofty as mountains would escape the outpouring of God's anger.—Compare Jer 4:23-26.

The mountains rejoice and praise Jehovah. When Jehovah turns his favorable attention to his people, this has a good effect upon the land. Cultivated and cared for, mountain slopes cease to have an unkept appearance, as if mourning in a state of desolation or plague. Therefore, figuratively, the mountains "cry out joyfully" and their beauty and productivity praise Jehovah.—Ps 98:8; 148:7-9; compare Isa 44:23; 49:13; 55:12, 13; Eze 36:1-12.

MOUNTAIN OF MEETING.

An expression appearing at Isaiah 14:13, where the king of Babylon is depicted as saying in his heart: "Above the stars of God I shall lift up my throne, and I shall sit down upon the mountain of meeting, in the remotest parts of the north."

Some scholars hold that this "mountain of meeting" was some distant northerly eminence that the Babylonians regarded as the dwelling place of their gods. However, instead of being prophetic of an actual statement that the king of Babylon would make, the words of Isaiah 14:13 reflect what his ambition and attitude would be. (Compare Isa 47:10.) They are part of a proverbial utterance to be lifted up against the king of Babylon by restored Israelites. (Isa 14:1-4) It therefore logically follows that "the mountain of meeting" must be identified in the light of Scripture and not on the basis of what may have been the pagan religious conception held by Babylon's king. Certainly the king of Babylon would have no desire to lift up his throne above the stars of a god whom he worshiped. Also, Isaiah 14:14 clearly shows that the reference is, not to one of the Babylonian gods, but to the Most High. Hence "the mountain of meeting" must be associated with the Most High God.

In Isaiah's time there was only one mountain, Mount Zion (which name came to include the temple site on Mount Moriah), where God representatively met with his people. (Compare Isa 8:18; 18:7; 24:23; Joe 3:17.) It could appropriately be termed "the mountain of meeting" because at the sanctuary there all mature Israelite males were to appear before the face of Jehovah three times each year. (Ex 23:17) Psalm 48:1, 2 further confirms this identification by giving Mount Zion a northerly location, harmonizing with the placement of "the mountain of meeting" in "the remotest parts of the north."

MOUNT OF RUINATION.

Identified in the article OLIVES, MOUNT OF.

MOURNING.

Mourning among Oriental peoples was customarily accompanied by much outward display of grief, and this is reflected in the Biblical accounts of periods of mourning. One entire book of the Bible, Lamentations, is an expression of mourning over the fate of Jerusalem.

Causes of Mourning. Persons mourned to express repentance (Ne 9:1, 2; Jon 3:5-9), or because of the imminence of calamity (Es 4:3; Jer 6:26; Am 5:16, 17) or a disastrous condition already prevailing (Joe 1:5-14). The most common cause of mourning, undoubtedly, was death. The death of a member of the immediate family set in motion a period of mourning (Ge 23:2; 27:41; 37:33-35), while the death of a parent or of an only son are set out as occasions of the deepest grief. (Ps 35:14; Am 8:10; Zec 12:10) The death of a national leader occasioned periods of mourning lasting from 7 to 30 days. (Nu 20:29; De 34:8; 1Sa 31:8, 12, 13) The Egyptians continued to shed tears over the death of Joseph's father Jacob for 70 days, with an additional 7-day period of mourning rites in Canaan.—Ge 50:3-11.

Ways of Expressing Sorrow. Mourning was given expression vocally and by weeping, as well as by disfigurement of the physical appearance and by fasting or otherwise abstaining from normal practices. Wailing or loud and bitter crying might accompany the weeping (2Sa 1:11, 12; Es 4:1), the chest was beaten (Isa 32:11, 12; Na 2:7; Lu 8:52), garments were often ripped apart (Jg 11:35; 2Ki 22:11, 19), dust or ashes might be cast on the head and sackcloth be worn (2Sa 13:19; 2Ki 6:30; Job 2:11, 12), sandals might be removed and the head or face be covered (2Sa 15:30; 19:4), the hair might be pulled out or cut off and the beard shaved (Job 1:20; Ezr 9:3; Jer 41:5), while some persons, following pagan practices, made cuts in their body (Jer 16:6; 47:5). In addition to fasting, the person might abstain from rubbing himself with oil or washing his garments (2Sa 14:2; 19:24; Da 10:2, 3), sometimes sitting on the ground or amid ashes.—2Sa 13:31; Job 2:8; Isa 3:26.

Plaintive elegies at times were composed as songs of mourning. (2Sa 1:17-27; 3:33, 34; 2Ch 35:25) A particular type of song was the *shig·ga·yohn'*, a Hebrew term that occurs in the superscription of Psalm 7; a related term appears in Habakkuk 3:1. This was a dirgelike composition and apparently indicates a highly emotional song with rapid changes of rhythm. It will be noted in both of these references (Ps 7; Hab 3:2-19) that the elements of danger, strong outbursts of appeal or emotion, and subsequent rejoicing in Jehovah are present.

Occasionally, professional mourners were employed at funerals, and musicians played mournful tunes (Jer 9:17, 18; Mt 9:23); these were imitated by little children playing in the marketplaces in the time of Jesus' earthly ministry. (Mt 11:16, 17) The pipe or flute was the preferred instrument for lamentation.—Jer 48:36; Mt 9:23; see Josephus' *Jewish War,* III, 437 (ix, 5).

After a burial the women customarily visited the grave, to weep and mourn. (Joh 11:31) A funeral meal seems to have been served sometime during the mourning period and, in some instances, appears to have been made into a special feast.—Ho 9:4; Jer 16:5, 7.

Prohibitions Involving Mourning. On occasion God's people as a body, or as individuals, were instructed not to mourn over the death of certain ones, such as condemned wrongdoers. (Le 10:1, 2, 6) The prophet Ezekiel was commanded to adopt none of the signs of mourning for his deceased wife, thereby serving as a portent for the Israelites with him in Babylon that they would be so stunned that they would not mourn the divine execution of judgment on Jerusalem for its unfaithfulness. (Eze 24:15-24) Jeremiah received somewhat similar instructions.—Jer 16:5-13.

Certain mourning practices were forbidden under the Mosaic Law, including the inflicting of cuts in the flesh or causing of "baldness on your foreheads" (Le 19:28; De 14:1) and the misuse of tithes in connection with the dead. (De 26:12-14) For certain members of their immediate families the priests could mourn openly, but the high priest was restricted from doing so.—Le 21:1-6, 10-12.

A Time to Mourn. Ecclesiastes 3:1, 4 states that there is "a time to weep and a time to laugh; a time to wail and a time to skip about." In view of all mankind's dying condition, the heart of the wise ones is shown to be "in the house of mourning" rather than in the banquet house. (Ec 7:2, 4; compare Pr 14:13.) Thus, the wise person makes use of his opportunity to express sympathy and give comfort, instead of ignoring such an occasion in favor of seeking pleasure. This helps him to keep in mind his own mortal state and to keep his heart in a right attitude toward his Creator.

Valid motives for mourning are set forth in the Scriptures. In addition to the death of loved ones (Ge 42:38; 44:31), detestable and God-dishonoring practices of false religion are a cause for sighing and groaning (Eze 9:4; compare 1Co 5:2), and grief is rightly expressed because of one's own errors. (Ps 38:4, 6-10) Jehovah urges those who have drawn away from him: "Come back to me with all your hearts, and with fasting and with weeping and with wailing. And rip apart your hearts, and not your garments." (Joe 2:12, 13; compare Jas 4:8, 9.) Elsewhere, also, stress is laid, not on the external expressions of grief or mourning, but on the inner stirrings and pain of heart, marking genuine sadness.—Ps 31:9, 10; Pr 14:10; 15:13; Mr 14:72; Joh 16:6.

Even Jehovah speaks of himself as being "hurt at his heart." (Ge 6:6; compare Isa 63:9.) God's holy spirit can also be 'grieved.' (Eph 4:30) Since that spirit works in God's servants toward the producing of fruits of righteousness (Ga 5:22-24), those who fail to appreciate this divine provision, who resist its working, and who go contrary to its leading are, in effect, "grieving" it.—Compare Isa 63:10; 1Th 5:19.

A Balanced View of Mourning. In the time of Jesus' earthly ministry, mourning was still frequently carried on by the people with much outward expression and accompanying noise and confusion. (Mr 5:38, 39) Though Jesus 'groaned within himself' and wept on a number of occasions (Joh 11:33-35, 38; Lu 19:41; Mr 14:33, 34; Heb 5:7), there is no record of his employing the other more ostentatious expressions already described. (Compare Lu 23:27, 28.) His disciples likewise expressed grief and mourning. (Mt 9:15; Joh 16:20-22; Ac 8:2; 9:39; 20:37, 38; Php 2:27) Paul expressed "great grief and unceasing pain in [his] heart" over his unbelieving relatives according to the flesh. (Ro 9:2, 3) He feared that he might have to mourn over those in the congregation at Corinth who had sinned and had still not repented (2Co 12:21), and he mentioned "with weeping" those who had turned aside to walk "as the enemies of the torture stake of the Christ." (Php 3:17-19) His deep and heartfelt concern for the Christian congregation (2Co 2:1-4) qualified him to instruct others on the need for empathy and sympathy, 'weeping with people who weep.'—Ro 12:15.

However, in view of the weakening effect of mourning and grief (Ps 6:6, 7; Lu 22:45; Ac 21:13; 2Co 2:6, 7), Christian sorrow is shown always to be tempered, balanced, and even overshadowed by hope and strength-giving joy. (Mt 5:4; 1Co 7:29, 30; 2Co 6:10; compare Ne 8:9-12.) Even in his day King David manifested a balanced, sensible, and principled viewpoint as to mourning, so that while the child conceived through his adulterous relationship with Bath-sheba was ill, David fasted and lay on the earth, seeking the true God in the child's behalf. But upon learning of the child's death, David got up, washed, rubbed himself with oil, changed clothes, prayed to Jehovah, and then requested food and began to eat. In explaining his acts to his surprised attendants, he stated: "Now that he has died, why is it I am fasting? Am I able to bring him back again? I am going to him, but, as for him, he will not return to me." (2Sa 12:16, 19-23) Later, however, he needed help from straight-speaking Joab to pull out of his state of deep grief over the death of his son Absalom.—2Sa 18:33; 19:1-8.

Though "all creation keeps on groaning," the sufferings of the Christian are minor compared with the glorious hope ahead (Ro 8:18-22; 1Pe 1:3-7), and the promise of the resurrection enables him not to "sorrow just as the rest also do who have no hope."—1Th 4:13, 14.

Mourning and fasting without obedience to Jehovah's word are of no benefit. (Zec 7:2-7) However, "sadness in a godly way makes for repentance to salvation." Such sadness is the result of a person's seeing a wrongdoing as a sin against God. It moves him to seek God's forgiveness and to turn around from his wrong course. "But the sadness of the world produces death." Although a person may be sad that his wrong was exposed and that this has meant loss to him, he has no desire to gain God's forgiveness. (2Co 7:10, 11) For example, Esau's tears shed selfishly in hope of regaining his forfeited birthright had no effect on Isaac or on God.—Heb 12:16, 17.

Figurative and Prophetic Use. Figuratively, even the land is represented as mourning because of devastations caused by invading armies or by a plague. (Jer 4:27, 28; Joe 1:10-12; contrast Ps 96:11-13.) In its desolation, the land would grow up in weeds and develop a neglected, uncared-for appearance, like that of a person who has not attended to his face, hair, or clothing while in mourning. Similarly, land devastated by a plague upon the crops presents a mournful sight.

"The sign of the Son of man" and Christ's revelation are to cause all the tribes of the earth to "beat themselves in lamentation," or "in grief." (Mt 24:30; Re 1:7) Upon symbolic "Babylon the Great" plagues—death, mourning, and famine—are foretold to come "in one day," causing those who have benefited from her to weep and mourn. (Re 18:2, 7-11, 17-19) By contrast, the New Jerusalem brings in conditions upon earth in which tears, death, mourning, outcry, and pain pass away for all time.—Re 21:2-4.

MOUTH. An organ designed by God to receive and prepare food for the stomach, also, in humans, for speaking. All speech should result in praise to

Him. (Ps 34:1; 51:15; 71:8; 145:21) The psalmist declared that everything that has breath will praise Jehovah; therefore humans must use their mouths to do this if they desire to live. The apostle Paul explains that belief in God and his Son, even believing with the heart, is not enough. It has to be accompanied by public declaration in order to bring salvation.—Ps 150:6; Ro 10:10.

In harmony with his purpose and his right and power as Creator, Jehovah can put the proper words into the mouth of his servant. In the case of his prophets, he did so miraculously, by inspiration. (Ex 4:11, 12, 15; Jer 1:9) In one instance he caused even a dumb animal, an ass, to speak. (Nu 22:28, 30; 2Pe 2:15, 16) Today God's servants can have his words in their mouths, not by inspiration, but from his inspired written Word, which equips them completely for every good work. (2Ti 3:16, 17) They no longer have to wait for Christ to come to provide the good news, nor do they need to go to some other source for what they preach. They have it right before them, ready for them to speak, as they are told: "The word is near you, in your own mouth and in your own heart."—Ro 10:6-9; De 30:11-14.

Can Bring Life or Death. It follows that the proper use of the mouth is vital, and so Jehovah declares it to be. His Word says: "The mouth of the righteous one is a source of life." (Pr 10:11) The mouth, therefore, has to be guarded most carefully (Ps 141:3; Pr 13:3; 21:23), for stupid misuse of it can bring its owner to ruin. (Pr 10:14; 18:7) God holds a person accountable for what he brings forth from his mouth. (Mt 12:36, 37) A person may speak hastily, making a rash vow. (Ec 5:4-6) He may flatter another, to that person's overthrow and his own condemnation. (Pr 26:28) It is especially important to guard one's mouth when before the wicked, because a slight deviation from what God's wisdom directs his servant to say can bring reproach on God's name and may cause that one's death. (Ps 39:1) Jesus gave a fine example of submissiveness to God's will without complaint or any reviling of his wicked opposers.—Isa 53:7; Ac 8:32; 1Pe 2:23.

The Christian must exercise constant vigilance, for he is imperfect; therefore he needs to watch his heart. Jesus said that it is not what goes into the mouth that defiles a man, but what comes forth from the mouth, for "out of the abundance of the heart the mouth speaks." (Mt 12:34; 15:11) Thus one must be careful not to let anything come forth from the mouth without thought, without considering the consequences. This requires that the person use his mind to apply the good things learned from God's Word.—Pr 13:3; 21:23.

Since the power of the mouth is great for good or bad, when Jehovah guides the mouth great results are attained. He made Isaiah's mouth "like a sharp sword" and the words in Jeremiah's mouth "a fire." Jehovah backed up their prophetic words by his power, and they came true. (Isa 49:2; Jer 5:14) On the other hand, it is dangerous to listen to anything that comes out of the mouth of a person known to be an apostate; it can bring a person to ruin.—Pr 11:9.

Figurative Use. God represents himself symbolically as having a mouth. None of his pronouncements are uttered to no purpose, in vain; they will be fulfilled to the smallest detail. (Isa 55:10, 11) Therefore, those who desire life must live by every word proceeding from his mouth. (De 8:3; Mt 4:4) When on earth his Son Jesus Christ conformed his whole life to his Father's words and now has universal authority granted him. As King appointed by Jehovah, he will strike the earth with "the rod of his mouth." (Isa 11:4) The vision of Revelation shows him smiting the nations with a long sword proceeding out of his mouth. (Re 19:15, 21) This figure of speech evidently represents the authority he will exercise in command of all Jehovah's heavenly armies in ordering and supervising the warfare that results in the execution of God's enemies.

"Mouth" is often used synonymously for speech or the power of speech, as can be seen from some of the instances cited above. The rule governing evidence in a case under the Mosaic Law, and also followed in the Christian congregation, is that a person may be found guilty only "at the mouth," that is, on the testimony, of two or three witnesses. (De 17:6; Mt 18:16; compare 2Co 13:1.) A few other examples of similar usage are found at Job 32:5; Psalms 10:7; 55:21; 78:36; Ezekiel 24:27; 29:21; Luke 21:15, ftn; Romans 15:6.

In addition, "mouth" may have reference to the opening of something, such as of a well (Ge 29:2), a bag (Ge 43:12; 44:1, 2), a cave (Jos 10:22), or to an opening in the earth (Nu 16:32), as well as to the ability of the earth to absorb liquids poured onto it (Ge 4:11). Sheol, mankind's common grave, is spoken of as having a wide mouth, so as to receive many dead.—Isa 5:14.

The Palate. The *palate* is the roof of the mouth, which separates the mouth from the nasal cavities; it has a soft part that forms a curtain between the mouth and the pharynx. In the Scriptures, "palate" is, in some cases, used synonymously with "mouth."—Pr 8:7; Ho 8:1, ftn.

Both Job and Elihu make a comparative use of the word when they liken the palate's ability to

discriminate taste to man's judgment as to what is right and wise. (Job 12:11; 34:3) That the palate has a function in tasting is not erroneous, as is sometimes claimed. This can be seen by observing the part played by the palate in swallowing. Food is pressed by the tongue against the palate and spread out as it moves back into the pharynx, which is a cone-shaped tube leading toward the stomach and connecting also with the nasal passages. This brings about better diffusion of the aroma of the food into the nasal passages, which greatly contributes to what is commonly called taste.

MOZA (Mo'za) [A Going Forth].

1. A descendant of Judah and son of Caleb by his concubine Ephah.—1Ch 2:46.

2. A Benjamite and descendant of King Saul. He was the son of Zimri and father of Binea.—1Ch 8:33-37; 9:42, 43.

MOZAH (Mo'zah) [Drained (Pressed; Squeezed) Out]. A Benjamite city. (Jos 18:21, 26) The ancient site is considered to be at or near Qalunyah (Mevasseret Ziyyon), a village about 7 km (4.5 mi) WNW of the Temple Mount in Jerusalem. Jar handles stamped with the name Mozah have been found at Jericho and Tell en-Nasbeh.

MULE [Heb., pe'redh; pir·dah' (she-mule)]. The hybrid offspring of a he-ass and a mare. The mule's body resembles that of the horse, but its short, thick head, long ears, short mane, small feet, and tail terminated by a tuft of long hairs are characteristic of the ass. The mule (*Equus asinus mulus*) combines some of the finer qualities of both parents: the endurance, hardiness, and sure-footedness of the ass, and the strength, vigor, and courage of the horse. The animal is less prone to disease than the horse, displays greater patience when bearing heavy burdens, and enjoys a much longer life span. The hinny, the offspring of a stallion and a she-ass, is smaller than the mule and lacks its strength and beauty. Both sexes of the mule, with rare exceptions, are sterile.

These animals were among the gifts brought to Solomon by kings desiring to hear his wisdom. (1Ki 10:24, 25; 2Ch 9:23, 24) Other mules may have been obtained from traders, such as the Phoenicians. (Eze 27:8, 9, 14) In the time of David, mules were used as mounts by prominent persons. David's own she-mule was assigned for Solomon's use on the occasion of his anointing at Gihon.—2Sa 13:29; 18:9; 1Ki 1:33, 34, 38, 39.

Mules were valued as burden bearers. (2Ki 5:17; 1Ch 12:40) Jehovah, by means of his prophet

Isaiah, indicated that mules would be one of the means of transport for bringing his scattered people to Jerusalem. (Isa 66:20) It is therefore of note that in fulfillment of prophecy those returning from Babylonian exile brought with them 245 mules in addition to other beasts of burden.—Ezr 2:66; Ne 7:68.

Humans are counseled not to make themselves persons without understanding, like a horse or a mule whose spiritedness must be curbed by means of a bridle or a halter.—Ps 32:9.

MUPPIM (Mup'pim). One of the "sons" of Benjamin (Ge 46:21); evidently identical with Shephupham (Nu 26:39), Shephuphan (1Ch 8:5), and Shuppim (1Ch 7:12).

MURDER. The original-language words variously rendered "kill," "murder," and "slay" refer to the taking of a life, the context or other scriptures determining whether the deliberate and unauthorized or unlawful taking of another person's life is involved. For example, in the command, "You must not murder" (Ex 20:13), the Hebrew word for "murder" (ra·tsach') here clearly refers to deliberate and unlawful killing. But at Numbers 35:27 the same term denotes an act that an avenger of blood was authorized to carry out. Therefore, the command, "You must not murder," has to be understood within the framework of the entire Mosaic Law, which authorized the taking of human life under certain circumstances, as in the execution of criminals.

Early History. Almost from the beginning of human history, murder has been known. Through his disobedience, the first man Adam passed sin and death to his offspring, thus, in effect, proving himself to be a murderer. (Ro 5:12; 6:23) It was the Devil who deliberately contributed to this development by inducing Adam's wife Eve to sin, thus himself becoming a manslayer, a murderer, at the beginning of his course as a slanderer of God.—Ge 3:13; Joh 8:44.

Less than 130 years afterward, the first violent murder, a fratricide, occurred. Cain, Adam's firstborn son, motivated by envious hatred, murdered his righteous brother Abel. (Ge 4:1-8, 25; 5:3) For this act Cain was cursed in banishment to become a wanderer and a fugitive in the earth. (Ge 4:11, 12) Not until after the Flood of Noah's day did God authorize humans to administer capital punishment for murder.—Ge 9:6.

Under the Law. Centuries later the Mosaic Law was given to the Israelites, and it included extensive legislation regarding the taking of human life. It differentiated between deliberate and accidental slaying. Factors considered as weighing against a person claiming to be an accidental manslayer were: If he (1) had been a former hater of the slain person (De 19:11, 12; compare Jos 20:5), (2) had lain in wait for the victim (Nu 35:20, 21), or (3) had used an object or implement capable of inflicting a mortal wound (Nu 35:16-18). Even slaves, if killed while being beaten by their masters, were to be avenged. (Ex 21:20) Whereas the death penalty was prescribed for deliberate murderers and a ransom was ruled out in their case, unintentional manslayers could preserve their lives by availing themselves of the safety accorded them in the cities of refuge.—Ex 21:12, 13; Nu 35:30, 31; Jos 20:2, 3; see CITIES OF REFUGE.

Certain deliberate acts that indirectly caused or could have resulted in the death of another person were considered tantamount to deliberate murder. For example, the owner of a goring bull who disregarded previous warnings to keep the animal under guard could be put to death if his bull killed someone. In some cases, however, a ransom could be accepted in place of the life of the owner. Undoubtedly the judges would take circumstances into consideration in such a case. (Ex 21:29, 30) Also, an individual scheming to have another person killed by presenting false testimony was himself to be put to death.—De 19:18-21.

The Law permitted self-defense but restricted an individual's right to fight for his property. Bloodguilt came upon a person who, though catching a thief in the act of breaking into his home, killed the lawbreaker in the daytime. This was evidently because thievery did not carry the death penalty, and the thief could be identified and brought to justice. At night, however, it would be difficult to see what one was doing and to ascertain the intentions of an intruder. Therefore, the person killing an intruder in the dark was considered guiltless.—Ex 22:2, 3.

In the first century C.E. those seeking to kill Jesus were identified as 'children of the Devil,' the first manslayer. (Joh 8:44) The scribes and Pharisees decorated the tombs of righteous ones, claiming that they would not have been sharers in putting the prophets to death. Yet they manifested the same murderous spirit toward the Son of God. —Mt 23:29-32; compare Mt 21:33-45; 22:2-7; Ac 3:14, 15; 7:51, 52.

Hatred Equated With Murder. Murders issue forth from the heart of an individual. (Mt 15:19; Mr 7:21; compare Ro 1:28-32.) Therefore, anyone hating his brother would be a manslayer, a murderer. (1Jo 3:15) Christ Jesus also associated murder with wrong attitudes such as an individual's continuing wrathful with his brother, speaking abusively to him, or wrongly judging and condemning him as a "despicable fool." (Mt 5:21, 22) Such hatred may lead to actual murder. It appears that the words of James (5:6), "You have condemned, you have murdered the righteous one," may be understood in this light. Wicked rich persons who showed hatred for genuine disciples of God's Son and took oppressive action against them did in some instances actually murder these Christians. As treatment accorded to his brothers is considered by Christ Jesus to be meted out to him, these persons had also figuratively murdered him, and James evidently had that in mind. —Compare Jas 2:1-11; Mt 25:40, 45; Ac 3:14, 15.

Although followers of Christ might be persecuted and even murdered for righteousness' sake, they were not to be found suffering for having committed murder or other crimes.—Mt 10:16, 17, 28; 1Pe 4:12-16; Re 21:8; 22:15.

MUSHI (Mu'shi). Grandson of Levi and son of Merari. (Ex 6:16, 19) Mushi became father to three sons and founded a family called the Mushites. —1Ch 23:23; Nu 26:58.

MUSHITES (Mu'shites) [possibly, Of (Belonging to) Moses]. A Levite family that descended from Mushi the son of Merari.—Nu 3:17, 20, 33; 26:58.

MUSIC. One of the gifts of God by which man can render praise and thanksgiving to his Creator as well as give expression to his emotions, his sorrows and joys. Especially has singing been prominent in the worship of Jehovah God, but instrumental music, too, has played a vital role. It has served not only to accompany the vocalists but also to complement their singing. So it is not surprising that references to both vocal and instrumental music abound in the Bible from beginning to end, in association with true worship and otherwise.—Ge 4:21; 31:27; 1Ch 25:1; Re 18:22.

History. The Bible's first reference to music is before the Flood, in the seventh generation following Adam: "[Jubal] proved to be the founder of all those who handle the harp and the pipe." This may describe the invention of the first musical instruments or perhaps even the establishment of some kind of musical profession.—Ge 4:21.

In patriarchal times music seems to have been an integral part of life, judging from Laban's desire to give Jacob and his own daughters a musical farewell. (Ge 31:27) Song and instrumental accompaniment marked the celebration of the deliverance at the Red Sea and the victorious returns from battle of Jephthah, David, and Saul.—Ex 15:20, 21; Jg 11:34; 1Sa 18:6, 7.

On each of the two occasions that were involved in transporting the Ark to Jerusalem, vocalists and instrumentalists were present. (1Ch 13:8; 15:16) In the later years of David's life, Jehovah, through his prophets Nathan and Gad, directed the establishment of the music organization for the sanctuary.—1Ch 23:1-5; 2Ch 29:25, 26.

The music organization begun by David was fully realized at Solomon's temple. The grandeur and magnitude of the music at the dedication of the temple can be appreciated from the fact that the trumpeters alone numbered 120. (2Ch 5:12, 13) But as the nation grew lax in its faithfulness to Jehovah, all features of true worship suffered, including the music. However, when Kings Hezekiah and Josiah instituted their reforms, as well as when the Jews returned from the Babylonian exile, efforts were made to reestablish the arrangement of music that Jehovah had indicated he desired. (2Ch 29:25-28; 35:15; Ezr 3:10) Later, when Nehemiah inaugurated the wall of Jerusalem, the Levite singers, with full instrumental accompaniment, contributed greatly to the joy of the occasion. (Ne 12:27-42) While the Scriptures say nothing more about music in connection with temple worship after Nehemiah's time, other records, such as the Talmud, tell of music being used there until the destruction of Jerusalem in 70 C.E.

How extensive was the musical staff at the temple in Jerusalem?

In conjunction with the preparations for Jehovah's temple, David set aside 4,000 Levites for musical service. (1Ch 23:4, 5) Of these, 288 were "trained in song to Jehovah, all experts." (1Ch 25:7) The whole arrangement was under the direction of three accomplished musicians, Asaph, Heman, and Jeduthun (apparently also named Ethan). Since each of these men was a descendant of one of Levi's three sons, Gershom, Kohath, and Merari, respectively, the three chief Levite families were thus represented in the temple music organization. (1Ch 6:16, 31-33, 39-44; 25:1-6) The sons of these three men totaled 24, all of whom were among the aforementioned 288 skilled musicians. Each son was appointed by lot to be the head of one division of musicians. Under his direction were 11 more "experts," selected from his own sons as well as other Levites. In this manner the 288 ([1 + 11] × 24 = 288) expert Levite musicians, like the priests, were separated into 24 courses. If all the remaining 3,712 'learners' were thus divided, it would average about 155 more men to each of the 24 divisions, meaning there were about 13 Levites in various stages of musical education and training to each expert. (1Ch 25:1-31) Since the trumpeters were priests, they would be in addition to the Levite musicians.—2Ch 5:12; compare Nu 10:8.

Instrumental Music. The Bible gives very little information concerning the shape or construction of the more than a dozen different musical instruments that it mentions. Hence, most scholars draw heavily on what archaeologists have discovered about the instruments used by contemporary surrounding nations. However, this may not always be a reliable guide, since it appears that Israel excelled in music in comparison with her neighbors. Additionally, some have linked various instruments of Scripture to instruments used in modern times in the Middle East, which are supposed to have an ancient background. This, too, is conjectural.

The musical instruments of the Bible may be classified as follows:

String: harp, lute, zither.

Wind: bagpipe, flute, horn, pipe, trumpet, (possibly) nehiloth.

Percussion: cymbals, sistrum, tambourine.

See individual articles on the above instruments for further information.

There is no reason to believe that the musical instruments of Israel were crude in design, construction, or sound production. The Bible notes that the harps and stringed instruments for temple use were of the choicest imported algum wood; the trumpets of silver. (1Ki 10:11, 12; Nu 10:2) Undoubtedly, in the manufacture of the temple instruments, the most skilled craftsmen were employed.

Both the Scriptures and non-Biblical manuscripts dating from before the Common Era testify to the quality of the instruments as well as the competence of the Israelite musicians. The Dead Sea Scrolls state that a number of trumpets were assigned various complicated signals to be executed "as with one mouth." This would require not only skilled musicians but also instruments so constructed that the pitch might be regulated in order to bring them all into tune with one another. Freedom from dissonance is indicated by the inspired account of the music at the inauguration of Solomon's temple: "The [one hundred and twenty] trumpeters and the singers were *as one in causing one sound* to be heard."—2Ch 5:12, 13.

The Bible lists but four instruments as definitely being in the temple orchestra: trumpets, harps, stringed instruments (Heb., *neva·lim'*), and cymbals. While this may not seem to be a complete orchestra by modern standards, it was never intended to be a symphony orchestra, but only to provide accompaniment for the singing at the temple. Such a combination of instruments would serve this purpose excellently.—2Ch 29:25, 26; Ne 12:27, 41, 42.

As to the times when the sacred instruments performed, the Scriptures enumerate the following in connection with the trumpets: "In the day of your rejoicing and in your festal seasons and at the commencements of your months, you must blow on the trumpets over your burnt offerings and your communion sacrifices." (Nu 10:10) After the temple music organization was established, it is likely that the rest of the instruments joined the trumpets on these and other special occasions. This conclusion, as well as the musical procedure followed, seems to be indicated by the order of events described as taking place when sacred services were revived by King Hezekiah after he had cleansed the temple: "At the time that the burnt offering started, the song of Jehovah started and also the trumpets, even under the direction of the instruments of David the king of Israel. And all the congregation were bowing down while the song was resounding and the trumpets were blaring—all this until the burnt offering was finished." (2Ch 29:27, 28) The trumpets' being "under the direction of the instruments of David" seems to denote that the trumpeters played in such a manner as to complement the other instruments rather than to overshadow them. The position of the entire body of musicians was "to the east of the altar."—2Ch 5:12.

Vocal Music. The singers at the temple were Levite males. Nowhere do the Scriptures speak of female vocalists at the temple. One of the Targums (on Ec 2:8) clearly indicates that they were not present in the chorus. The fact that women were prohibited from even entering certain areas of the temple would seem to preclude their occupying any official position there.—2Ch 5:12; Ne 10:39; 12:27-29.

Considerable importance was attached to the singing at the temple. This is evident from the many Scriptural references to the singers as well as from the fact that they were "set free from duty" common to other Levites in order to devote themselves wholly to their service. (1Ch 9:33) Their continuance as a special group of Levites is emphasized by their being listed separately among those returning from Babylon. (Ezr 2:40, 41) Even the authority of the Persian king Artaxerxes (Longimanus) was brought to bear in their behalf, exempting them, along with other special groups, from 'tax, tribute, and toll.' (Ezr 7:24) Later, the king commanded that there was to be "a fixed provision for the singers as each day required." Although Artaxerxes is credited with this order, most likely it was issued by Ezra on the basis of the power granted to him by Artaxerxes. (Ne 11:23; Ezr 7:18-26) Thus, it is understandable that, although the singers were all Levites, the Bible makes reference to them as a special body, speaking of "the singers and the Levites."—Ne 7:1; 13:10.

Apart from temple worship, other singers, men and women, are spoken of in Scripture. Examples of these are the male and female singers maintained by Solomon in his court; also, about 200 singers of both sexes who, in addition to the Levite musicians, returned from Babylon. (Ec 2:8; Ezr 2:65; Ne 7:67) These non-Levite singers, common in Israel, were employed not only to enhance various festive occasions but also to chant dirges in times of sorrow. (2Sa 19:35; 2Ch 35:25; Jer 9:17, 20) The custom of hiring professional musicians at times of joy and of sadness appears to have continued into the time when Jesus was on earth.—Mt 11:16, 17.

Although not as prominent as in the Hebrew Scriptures, music is not ignored or overlooked in the Christian Greek Scriptures. Instrumental music in connection with true worship is mentioned only in a figurative sense in the Greek Scriptures (Re 14:2); yet singing seems to have been quite common among God's servants. Jesus and his apostles sang praises after the Lord's Evening Meal. (Mr 14:26) Luke tells of Paul and Silas singing when in prison, and Paul's encouragement to fellow believers was to sing songs of praise to Jehovah. (Ac 16:25; Eph 5:18, 19; Col 3:16) Paul's statement at 1 Corinthians 14:15 concerning singing appears to indicate that it was a regular feature of Christian worship. In recording his inspired vision, John tells of various heavenly creatures singing to God and Christ.—Re 5:8-10; 14:3; 15:2-4.

Nature of Biblical Music. The Israelites' higher plane of morality and their superior literature, as exemplified by the poetry and prose of the Hebrew Scriptures, suggest that the music of ancient Israel most likely transcended that of her contemporaries. Certainly the inspiration for the music of Israel was far loftier than that of neighboring nations. Of interest is an Assyrian bas-relief in which King Sennacherib is represented as demanding that King Hezekiah pay him as tribute both male and female musicians.—*Ancient Near Eastern Texts,* edited by J. Pritchard, 1974, p. 288.

It has long been held by some that Hebrew music was all melody, without harmony. However, the prominence alone of the harp and other stringed instruments in Israel weighs heavily against this assumption. It is almost inconceivable that a musician would play a multistringed instrument and fail to notice that a combination of certain tones was quite pleasing or that a specific series of notes as in an arpeggio produced a pleasant sound. An informed source on the history of music, Curt Sachs, states: "The deep-rooted prejudice that harmony and polyphony [two or more musical parts or voices combined] have been a prerogative of the medieval and modern West does not hold water." He goes on to say that even among primitive cultures there are many examples of music running in fifths, fourths, thirds as well as in octaves, and that among these peoples, including certain Pygmy tribes, there was a development of overlapping antiphony (alternate singing by two divisions of vocalists) into regular canon singing.

Based on worldwide research Sachs presents the conclusion that "the choruses and orchestras connected with the Temple in Jerusalem suggest a high standard of musical education, skill, and knowledge." He continues: "It is important to realize that the ancient Western Orient had a music quite different from what historians of the nineteenth century conceded it. . . . Though we do not know how that ancient music sounded, we have sufficient evidence of its power, dignity, and mastership."—*The Rise of Music in the Ancient World: East and West,* 1943, pp. 48, 101, 102.

The Scriptures intimate a similar conclusion. For instance, over 30 times the expression "To [For] the director" (*NW; AT*) appears in the superscriptions of the Psalms. (Ps 11, and others) Other translations read "choirmaster" (*Kx; JB; Mo; RS*), "Chief Musician" (*AS; KJ; Le; Ro*), and "Bandmaster" (*Fn*). The Hebrew term seems to refer to one who in some way gave direction to the execution of the song, in arranging it, in rehearsing and training the Levite singers, or in its official performance. Perhaps the chief one of each of the

24 courses of sanctuary musicians is being addressed, or it may have been another one of the accomplished musicians, since the record says that they were "to act as directors." (1Ch 15:21; 25:1, 7-31) In some 20 other Psalms the superscriptions are even more specific in their reference to the "directors": "To the director on stringed instruments," "To the director on the lower octave," and so on. (Ps 4, 12, and others; see SHEMINITH.) Additionally, there are Scriptural references to the "heads of the singers," to the "experts," and to the 'learners.' All of this testifies to a high standard of music.—Ne 12:46; 1Ch 25:7, 8.

Much of the group singing in Israel appears to have been antiphonal, either two half choruses alternating in singing parallel lines, or a soloist and an answering chorus alternating. In the Scriptures this apparently is referred to as "responding." (Ex 15:21; 1Sa 18:6, 7) This type of singing is indicated by the very way some of the psalms are written, such as Psalm 136. The description of the two large thanksgiving choirs in Nehemiah's time and of their part in the inauguration of the wall of Jerusalem implies that they sang in this style. —Ne 12:31, 38, 40-42; see SONG.

Chanting might be said to be halfway between singing and speaking. In pitch it is rather monotonous and repetitious, with the emphasis being on rhythm. While chanting continues to be quite popular in some of the world's leading religions, its use in the Bible appears to be limited to dirges, as in the case of David chanting a dirge over the deaths of his friend Jonathan and of King Saul. (2Sa 1:17; 2Ch 35:25; Eze 27:32; 32:16) Only in a dirge or lamentation would the chanting style be preferable to either the melody of music or the modulation and oral emphasis of pure speech. —See DIRGE.

MUSTACHE. See BEARD.

MUSTARD

[Gr., si'na·pi]. A rapid-growing herb, to the seed or grain of which Jesus referred in an illustration about the Kingdom of the heavens (Mt 13:31, 32; Mr 4:30-32; Lu 13:18, 19; see ILLUSTRATIONS) and in pointing out that even a little faith can accomplish much. (Mt 17:20; Lu 17:6) Several kinds of mustard plants are found growing wild in Palestine, black mustard (Brassica nigra) being the variety commonly cultivated. In rich soil the seed, after a few months, may become treelike, a plant measuring as much as 4.5 m (15 ft) in height, with a central stalk having the thickness of a man's arm. The flowers of mustard plants are yellow and the leaves rather irregularly edged and dark green in color. The pods that develop contain a row of seeds, those of the black mustard being dark brown. In the fall the stems and branches of the plants harden and become rigid, strong enough to support birds such as linnets and finches that feed on the seeds.

While some may argue that a mustard grain is not "the tiniest" of all seeds, orchid seeds being smaller, and that it does not actually become "a tree," it must be borne in mind that Jesus was speaking in terms familiar to his audience. As far as Jesus' listeners were concerned, the mustard grain was indeed among the tiniest seeds planted, and it is noteworthy that the Arabs designate as "trees" plants smaller than the mustard.—Mt 13: 31, 32.

MUTH-LABBEN

(Muth-lab'ben). An expression included in the superscription of one of David's psalms (Ps 9), traditionally said to mean "[concerning] the death of the son." Some commentators suggest that it indicated to the musical director the name or perhaps the opening words of a familiar song that furnished the melody to be used in singing this psalm. One possibility of the word's meaning is advanced by the Targum, in which the superscription of Psalm 9 reads: "On the death of the man who came forth from between the camps," alluding to a champion. The apparent reference here is to Goliath, the Philistine champion whom David defeated in battle between the Israelite and Philistine encampments.—1Sa 17:45-51.

MUZZLE.

A device designed to cover an animal's mouth and prevent it from biting or eating.

Cattle were often used in ancient Palestine when a large quantity of grain was to be threshed. In preparation, the sheaves were untied and distributed over the hard-packed surface of the threshing floor until a thick layer was formed. Then one or more animals trod the grain with their hooves or it was threshed by means of a threshing sledge or other implement they drew over it. The Mosaic Law commanded: "You must not muzzle a bull while it is threshing." (De 25:4) Thus it was not tortured with a desire to eat some of the grain that it was expending its strength to thresh.—Compare Pr 12:10.

The principle involved at Deuteronomy 25:4 can also be applied to human laborers. Paul told Timothy: "Let the older men who preside in a fine way be reckoned worthy of double honor, especially those who work hard in speaking and teaching." Then, confirming his counsel, the apostle quoted the law about not muzzling a bull when it is threshing grain. (1Ti 5:17, 18) Also, as part of Paul's reasoning to show the Corinthians that "the Lord ordained for those proclaiming the good news to live by means of the good news," he quoted Deuteronomy 25:4 and then wrote: "Is it bulls God is caring for? Or is it altogether for our sakes he says it? Really for our sakes it was written, because the man who plows ought to plow in hope and the man who threshes ought to do so in hope of being a partaker."—1Co 9:8-14.

The psalmist David used "muzzle" figuratively when he said that he set one as a guard to his mouth to keep from sinning.—Ps 39:1.

MYRA (My'ra). A major city in the province of Lycia. Situated near the coast of SW Asia Minor, Myra occupied a hill about 3 km (2 mi) inland on the river Andracus. The site is now known as Demre. The ancient name Myra apparently embraced both the city and its excellent harbor.

As a prisoner bound for Rome, the apostle Paul arrived at Myra from Caesarea by way of Sidon. There he and his traveling companions had to transfer to a grain ship from Alexandria that was sailing for Italy. (Ac 27:1-6, 38) Myra was due N of Alexandria and therefore may have been on the regular route of ships from that Egyptian city. Or, it may be that contrary winds (Ac 27:4, 7) forced the Alexandrian vessel to change its course and drop anchor at Myra.

At Acts 21:1 some ancient texts add "and Myra" after "Patara." (See *JB, NE, RS* ftns.) Although this addition would not be out of harmony with the rest of the account, there is insufficient evidence for determining whether the name Myra actually appeared in the original manuscript.

MYRRH. An aromatic gum resin. (Ca 1:13; 4:6, 14; 5:1, 13) Its precise source in ancient times is uncertain. But generally myrrh is the resin obtained from various thorny shrubs or small trees of the genus *Commiphora*, such as *Commiphora myrrha* or *Commiphora abyssinica.* These shrubs thrive in rocky areas, particularly on limestone hills. Their wood and bark have a strong odor. Although the resin exudes by itself from the stem or from the thick and stiff branches of either variety, the flow can be increased by means of incisions. Initially the resin is soft and sticky but, upon dripping to the ground, it hardens.

Myrrh was one of the ingredients for the holy anointing oil. (Ex 30:23-25) Esteemed for its fragrance, it was used to scent garments, beds, and other items. (Compare Ps 45:8; Pr 7:17; Ca 3:6, 7.) The Shulammite maiden of The Song of Solomon appears to have applied liquid myrrh to her body

before retiring for the night. (Ca 5:2, 5) Massages with oil of myrrh were included in the special beauty treatment given to Esther. (Es 2:12) Myrrh was also one of the substances employed in preparing bodies for burial. (Joh 19:39, 40) It was apparently viewed as having sufficient value to be presented as a gift to one born king of the Jews. —Mt 2:1, 2, 11.

MYRTLE [Heb., *hadhas'*]. The myrtle (*Myrtus communis*) grows as either a shrub or a tree and is common in Israel and Lebanon, growing well in stony soil. It is capable of reaching a height of 9 m (30 ft) but is usually found as a shrub 2 to 3 m (7 to 10 ft) high. An evergreen, it is quite bushy in branch structure and has thick, shiny, dark-green leaves; it blossoms with clusters of fragrant white flowers that mature into blue-black berries. Almost the entire plant has a fragrant spicy oil used in perfumes. The berries, though aromatic, are edible. The myrtle is found today particularly in Upper Galilee and the valley of the Jordan, but it also grows in the Jerusalem area, as it evidently did at the time of Zechariah's vision recorded at Zechariah 1:8-11, 16.

Fragrant branches of myrtle were used along with the branches of other trees to cover the temporary outdoor huts or booths used by the Hebrews during the Festival of Booths. (Ne 8:14, 15) In the restoration prophecies the myrtle tree with its fragrance and beauty is foretold to grow in place of the stinging nettle and to spring up even in the wilderness.—Isa 41:19; 55:13.

The Hebrew name of Esther, wife of Persian King Ahasuerus, was Hadassah, which means "Myrtle."—Es 2:7.

MYSIA (Mys'i·a). A region in the NW part of Asia Minor. Its boundaries appear to have fluctuated, but basically Mysia was bounded from W to N by the Aegean Sea, the Hellespont (Dardanelles) and Propontis (Sea of Marmara). Bithynia lay to the E and Lydia to the S. (See Asia.) While on his second missionary journey, Paul, accompanied by Silas and Timothy, endeavored to go to Bithynia, but "the spirit of Jesus did not permit them. So they passed Mysia by and came down to Troas." (Ac 15:40; 16:1-3, 7, 8) Since the seaport of Troas was in Mysia, evidently this means that Paul and his companions, although going through Mysia, omitted it as a field of missionary activity. Other cities of Mysia were Adramyttium (Ac 27:2), Assos (Ac 20:13, 14), and Pergamum.—Re 1:11; see Troas.

MYSTERY. See Sacred Secret.

N

NAAM (Na'am) [Pleasant]. Son of Caleb, Jephunneh's son, of the tribe of Judah.—1Ch 4:1, 15.

NAAMAH (Na'a·mah) [Pleasant].

1. Descendant of Cain; sister of Tubal-cain and the daughter of Lamech by Zillah.—Ge 4: 17-19, 22.

2. Ammonite wife of Solomon and mother of Rehoboam.—1Ki 14:21; 2Ch 12:13.

3. A Judean city in the Shephelah. (Jos 15:20, 33, 41) Its exact location is uncertain.

NAAMAN (Na'a·man) [from a root meaning "be pleasant"].

1. A grandson of Benjamin through his first-born Bela. (1Ch 8:1-4, 7) Having founded a family, the Naamites in the tribe of Benjamin (Nu 26:40), Naaman himself is elsewhere listed as one of the "sons" of Benjamin.—Ge 46:21.

2. A Syrian army chief of the tenth century B.C.E., during the reigns of Jehoram of Israel and Ben-hadad II of Syria. Naaman, 'a great, valiant, mighty man held in esteem,' was the one by whom "Jehovah had given salvation to Syria." (2Ki 5:1) The Bible gives no details as to how or why Naaman was used to bring this salvation to Syria. One possibility is that Naaman headed the Syrian forces that successfully resisted the efforts of Assyrian King Shalmaneser III to overrun Syria. Since, by remaining free, Syria formed a buffer state between Israel and Assyria, this may have served the purpose of slowing down Assyria's aggressive push in the W until Jehovah's due time to allow the northern kingdom to go into exile.

Cured of Leprosy. Naaman was a leper, and while the Syrians did not demand his isolation as Jehovah's law required of lepers in Israel, yet to learn how he might be cured of this loathsome disease was indeed welcome news. Such news came to him through his wife's Israelite slave girl who told of a prophet in Samaria who could cure leprosy. Immediately Naaman set out for Samaria with a letter of introduction from Ben-hadad II. However, Israelite King Jehoram, after receiving him with coolness and suspicion, sent him to Elisha. Elisha did not meet Naaman personally but, instead, had his servant tell Naaman to bathe seven times in the Jordan River. His pride hurt, and apparently feeling he had unceremoniously and fruitlessly been run from one place to another,

Naaman turned away in a rage. Had his attendants not reasoned with him and pointed out the reasonableness of the instructions, Naaman would have returned to his country still a leper. As it turned out, he bathed the seven times in the Jordan and was miraculously cleansed, the only leper whom Elisha was instrumental in curing. —2Ki 5:1-14; Lu 4:27.

Becomes Worshiper of Jehovah. Now filled with gratitude and humble appreciation, the Syrian army chief returned to Elisha, a distance of perhaps 50 km (30 mi), and offered him a most generous gift, which the prophet insistently refused. Naaman then asked for some of the earth of Israel, "the load of a pair of mules," to take home, that upon Israel's soil he might offer sacrifices to Jehovah, vowing that from then on he would worship no other god. Perhaps Naaman had in mind offering sacrifices to Jehovah upon an altar of ground.—2Ki 5:15-17; compare Ex 20:24, 25.

Naaman next requested that Jehovah forgive him when, in the performance of his civil duties, he bowed before the god Rimmon with the king, who evidently was old and infirm and leaned for support upon Naaman. If such was the case, then his bowing would be mechanical, being solely for the purpose of dutifully supporting the king's body and not in personal worship. Elisha believed Naaman's sincere request, replying, "Go in peace." —2Ki 5:18, 19.

After leaving, Naaman was overtaken by Elisha's covetous servant Gehazi, who lyingly made it appear that Elisha had changed his mind and would, after all, accept some gifts. Naaman gladly granted him gifts of silver and garments. But for this greedy and lying act in which he tried, by misusing his office as Elisha's attendant, to profit from the work of Jehovah's spirit, Jehovah punished him by inflicting leprosy on him and on his offspring to time indefinite.—2Ki 5:20-27.

NAAMATHITE (Na'a·ma·thite) [Of (Belonging to) Naamah]. A designation applied to Job's companion Zophar (Job 2:11; 11:1; 20:1; 42:9) and identifying his family or the place of his residence. Djebel-el-Na'ameh in NW Arabia has been presented as a possible location for Zophar's home.

NAAMITES (Na'a·mites) [Of (Belonging to) Naaman]. A family of Israelites descended from Benjamin's grandson Naaman.—Nu 26:38, 40.

NAARAH   (Na'a·rah).

1. [Girl; Young Woman]. A wife of the Judean Ashhur by whom he had four sons.—1Ch 4:1, 5, 6.

2. [from a root meaning "shake off"]. A city on the boundary of Ephraim (Jos 16:5, 7) thought to be the same as Naaran. (1Ch 7:28) Naarah is generally considered to correspond to the *No·o·rath'* of Eusebius' *Onomasticon* (136, 24). Josephus seemingly calls this site Neara. He relates that half of its waters were diverted to irrigate the palms near Archelaus' palace at Jericho. (*Jewish Antiquities*, XVII, 340 [xiii, 1]) It has tentatively been identified with Tell el-Jisr, about 3 km (2 mi) NW of Jericho.

NAARAI   (Na'a·rai) [possibly a shortened form of Neariah, meaning "Boy (Young Man) of Jah"]. Son of Ezbai and a mighty man in David's military forces. (1Ch 11:26, 37) He may be identical with "Paarai the Arbite" mentioned at 2 Samuel 23:35, in what seems to be a parallel list.

NAARAN   (Na'a·ran) [from a root meaning "shake off"]. An Ephraimite border city (1Ch 7:20, 28), apparently the same as Naarah.—Jos 16:5, 7; see NAARAH No. 2.

NABAL   (Na'bal) [Senseless; Stupid]. A wealthy Maonite sheep owner who pastured and sheared his flocks in Carmel of Judah. Nabal was also known as a Calebite, that is, is a descendant of Caleb. Few Bible characters are so contemptuously described as is Nabal. "[He] was harsh and bad in his practices"; "he is too much of a good-for-nothing fellow [son of Belial] to speak to him"; "he repays . . . evil in return for good"; "senselessness is with him."—1Sa 25:2, 3, 17, 21, 25.

David's men had protected Nabal's flocks of 3,000 sheep and 1,000 goats from marauding bands. After showing this kindness and not being guilty of any misappropriation, David requested Nabal to provide some material assistance for him and his men at shearing time, a traditional time of feasting and hospitality. But Nabal "screamed rebukes" at David's messengers and sent them away empty-handed. Nabal's own men feared David's reaction but did not feel free to speak to Nabal about the matter. One of them, however, told Nabal's wife Abigail. As David approached, intending to slay Nabal, Abigail met him with generous gifts of food and drink and persuaded him not to become guilty of shedding her husband's blood. On her return home, she found Nabal "as drunk as could be," so waited until the next morning to tell him of her encounter with David and how near death he had caused them all to come. Thereupon, Nabal's "heart came to be dead inside

him, and he himself became as a stone," perhaps indicating some type of paralysis or else referring to the effect on Nabal's inner emotions. (Compare De 28:28; Ps 102:4; 143:4.) About ten days later Nabal was struck dead by Jehovah. (1Sa 25:2-38) David then took the sensible and courageous Abigail as his wife.—1Sa 25:39-42; 27:3; 30:5; 2Sa 2:2; 3:3.

NABONIDUS   (Nab·o·ni'dus) [from Babylonian meaning "Nebo [a Babylonian god] Is Exalted"]. Last supreme monarch of the Babylonian Empire; father of Belshazzar. On the basis of cuneiform texts he is believed to have ruled some 17 years (556-539 B.C.E.). He was given to literature, art, and religion.

In his own inscriptions Nabonidus claims to be of noble descent. A tablet found near ancient Haran gives evidence that Nabonidus' mother or grandmother was a devotee of the moon-god Sin. (*Ancient Near Eastern Texts*, edited by J. Pritchard, 1974, pp. 311, 312) As king, Nabonidus showed great devotion to the worship of the moon-god, both at Haran and at Ur, where this god occupied a dominant position.—PICTURE, Vol. 2, p. 324.

Cuneiform tablets of the eighth year of Nebuchadnezzar (Nisan 617-Nisan 616 B.C.E.) list a certain Nabu-na'id as the one "who is over the city," and some historians believe this is the same Nabonidus who later became king. However, this would mean that Nabonidus was a very young man when placed in such administrative position and would make him extremely aged at the fall of Babylon, some 77 years later (539 B.C.E.).

Discussing events in the 20th year of Nebuchadnezzar (Nisan 605-Nisan 604 B.C.E.), the Greek historian Herodotus (I, 74) describes a treaty negotiated between the Lydians and the Medes by one "Labynetus the Babylonian" as mediator. (I, 74) Labynetus is considered to be Herodotus' way of writing Nabonidus' name. Later, Herodotus [I, 188] refers to Cyrus the Persian as fighting against the son of Labynetus and Nitocris.

In a book of the Yale Oriental Series entitled *Nabonidus and Belshazzar*, Professor R. P. Dougherty advances the supposition that Nitocris was the daughter of Nebuchadnezzar and that therefore Nabonidus (Labynetus) was Nebuchadnezzar's son-in-law. (1929, p. 63; see also pp. 17, 30.) In turn, the "son" of Nitocris and Nabonidus (Labynetus), mentioned by Herodotus, is thought to be Belshazzar, against whom Cyrus did indeed fight. Although based on much deductive and inductive reasoning, this argument might explain the reason for Nabonidus' ascension to the Babylonian throne. It would also harmonize with the

Biblical fact that Nebuchadnezzar is referred to as the "father" of Nabonidus' son Belshazzar (Da 5:11, 18, 22), the term "father" at times having the meaning of grandfather or ancestor. This view would make Belshazzar a grandson of Nebuchadnezzar.—See, however, BELSHAZZAR.

Nabonidus' ascension to the throne followed the assassination of Labashi-Marduk. Yet, the fact that in one of his inscriptions Nabonidus refers to himself as the "mighty delegate" of Nebuchadnezzar and Neriglissar indicates that he claimed that he gained the throne by legitimate means and was not a usurper.

In a number of prisms Nabonidus associates his firstborn son, Belshazzar, with himself in his prayers to the moon-god. (*Documents From Old Testament Times,* edited by D. W. Thomas, 1962, p. 73) An inscription shows that in his third year, prior to going out on a campaign that resulted in the conquest of Tema in Arabia, Nabonidus appointed Belshazzar to kingship in Babylon. The same text indicates that Nabonidus offended the people of his empire by concentrating worship on the moon-god and by failing to be in Babylon to celebrate the New Year's festival. The document known as the Nabonidus Chronicle states that in the 7th, 9th, 10th, and 11th years of his reign Nabonidus was in the city of Tema, and in each case the statement is made: "The king did not come to Babylon [for the ceremonies of the month of Nisanu]; the (image of the) god Nebo did not come to Babylon, the (image of the) god Bel did not go out (of Esagila in procession), the fest[ival of the New Year was omitted]." (*Ancient Near Eastern Texts,* p. 306) Due to the mutilated condition of the text, the record of the other years is incomplete.

Of the oasis city of Tema it is elsewhere recorded: "He made the town beautiful, built (there) [his palace] like the palace in Su·an·na (Babylon)." (*Ancient Near Eastern Texts,* p. 313) Nabonidus appears to have established his royal residence in Tema, and other texts show that camel caravans carried provisions there from Babylonia. While not relinquishing his position as king of the empire, Nabonidus entrusted the administration of the government of Babylon to Belshazzar. Since Tema was a junction city on the ancient caravan routes along which gold and spices were transported through Arabia, Nabonidus' interest in it may have been motivated by economic reasons or may have been based on factors of military strategy. The suggestion is also advanced that he considered it politically advisable to administer Babylonian affairs through his son. Other factors, such as the healthful climate of Tema and the prominence

of moon worship in Arabia, have likewise been noted as possible motives for Nabonidus' apparent preference for Tema.

There is no available information as to Nabonidus' activities between his 12th year and his final year. Anticipating aggression from the Medes and Persians under Cyrus the Great, Nabonidus had entered into an alliance with the Lydian Empire and Egypt. The Nabonidus Chronicle shows Nabonidus back in Babylon in the year of the Medo-Persian assault, with the New Year's festival being celebrated and the various gods of Babylonia being brought into the city. Regarding Cyrus' advance, the Chronicle states that, following a victory at Opis, he captured Sippar (c. 60 km [37 mi] N of Babylon) and "Nabonidus fled." Then follows the account of the Medo-Persian conquest of Babylon, and it is stated that upon Nabonidus' return there he was taken prisoner. (*Ancient Near Eastern Texts,* p. 306) The writings of Berossus, Babylonian priest of the third century B.C.E., relate that Nabonidus had gone out to engage Cyrus' forces in battle but was defeated. They further tell that Nabonidus took refuge in Borsippa (SSW of Babylon) and that, after Babylon fell, Nabonidus surrendered to Cyrus and was thereafter deported to Carmania (in southern Persia). This account would coincide with the Biblical record at Daniel chapter 5, which shows that Belshazzar was the acting king in Babylon at the time of its overthrow.

As to the absence of any direct mention of Nabonidus in chapter 5 of Daniel, it may be noted that Daniel's description deals with only a very few events prior to the fall of Babylon, and the actual collapse of the empire is set forth in but a few words. However, his rulership is apparently indicated at Daniel 5:7, 16, 29, where Belshazzar offers to make Daniel the *third* ruler in the kingdom, implying that Nabonidus was the first and Belshazzar the second. Thus, Professor Dougherty comments: "The fifth chapter of Daniel may be regarded as comporting with fact in not giving any place to Nabonidus in the narrative, for he seems to have had no share in the events which transpired when Gobryas [at the head of Cyrus' army] entered the city."—*Nabonidus and Belshazzar,* pp. 195, 196; see also pp. 73, 170, 181; see Da 5:1, ftn.

What does the Nabonidus Chronicle actually contain?

Also called "Cyrus-Nabonidus Chronicle" and "The Annalistic Tablet of Cyrus," this is a clay tablet fragment now kept in the British Museum. It primarily depicts the main events of the reign of Nabonidus, the last supreme monarch of Babylon, including a terse account of the fall of Babylon to the troops of Cyrus. Though it was no doubt originally from Babylon and written in Babylonian cuneiform script, scholars who have examined its script style say it may date from some time in the Seleucid period (312-65 B.C.E.), hence two centuries or more after Nabonidus' day. It is considered almost certainly to be a copy of an earlier document. The tone of this chronicle so strongly glorifies Cyrus while presenting Nabonidus in a disparaging way that it is thought to have been the work of a Persian scribe, and in fact, it has been referred to as "Persian propaganda." However, while such may be the case, historians feel that the circumstantial data it contains is nonetheless reliable.

In spite of the brevity of the Nabonidus Chronicle—the tablet measures about 14 cm (5.5 in.) in breadth at the widest point and about the same in length—it remains the most complete cuneiform record of the fall of Babylon available. In the third of its four columns, beginning with line 5, pertinent sections read: "[Seventeenth year:] . . . In the month of Tashritu, when Cyrus attacked the army of Akkad in Opis on the Tigris, the inhabitants of Akkad revolted, but he (Nabonidus) massacred the confused inhabitants. The 14th day, Sippar was seized without battle. Nabonidus fled. The 16th day, Gobryas (Ugbaru), the governor of Gutium and the army of Cyrus entered Babylon without battle. Afterwards Nabonidus was arrested in Babylon when he returned (there). . . . In the month of Arahshamnu, the 3rd day, Cyrus entered Babylon, green twigs were spread in front of him—the state of 'Peace' (sulmu) was imposed upon the city."—*Ancient Near Eastern Texts*, p. 306.

It may be noted that the phrase "Seventeenth year" does not appear on the tablet, that portion of the text being damaged. This phrase is inserted by the translators because they believe that Nabonidus' 17th regnal year was his last. So they assume that the fall of Babylon came in that year of his reign and that, if the tablet were not damaged, those words would appear in the space now damaged. Even if Nabonidus' reign was of greater length than is generally supposed, this would not change the accepted date of 539 B.C.E. as the year of Babylon's fall, for there are other sources pointing to that year. This factor, however, does lessen to some extent the value of the Nabonidus Chronicle.

While the year is missing, the month and day of the city's fall, nevertheless, are on the remaining text. Using these, secular chronologers calculate the 16th day of Tashritu (Tishri) as falling on October 11, Julian calendar, and October 5, Gregorian calendar, in the year 539 B.C.E. Since this date is an accepted one, there being no evidence to the contrary, it is usable as a pivotal date in coordinating secular history with Bible history. —See CHRONOLOGY.

Interestingly, the Chronicle says concerning the night of Babylon's fall: "The army of Cyrus entered Babylon without battle." This likely means without a general conflict and agrees with the prophecy of Jeremiah that 'the mighty men of Babylon would cease to fight.'—Jer 51:30.

Also of interest are the evident references to Belshazzar in the Chronicle. Although Belshazzar is not specifically named, in the light of later portions of the Chronicle (col. II, lines 5, 10, 19, 23), column 1, line 8, is construed by Sidney Smith, in his *Babylonian Historical Texts: Relating to the Capture and Downfall* of *Babylon* (London, 1924, p. 100), as showing that Nabonidus entrusted kingship to Belshazzar, making him coregent. Repeatedly the Chronicle states that the 'crown prince was in Akkad [Babylonia]' while Nabonidus himself was at Tema (in Arabia). However, the fact that Belshazzar is not mentioned by name nor is his death referred to in the Nabonidus Chronicle in no way brings into question the accuracy of the inspired book of Daniel, where the name Belshazzar appears eight times and his death concludes

Nabonidus Chronicle, which tells of the fall of Babylon

the graphic account of Babylon's overthrow narrated in chapter 5. Quite to the contrary, cuneiform experts admit that the Nabonidus Chronicle is extremely brief, and in addition, as shown above, they are of the opinion that it was written to defame Nabonidus, not to give a detailed history. Indeed, as R. P. Dougherty says in his work *Nabonidus and Belshazzar* (p. 200): "The Scriptural account may be interpreted as excelling *because* it employs the name Belshazzar."—Italics ours.

Although column 4 of the Chronicle is badly broken, scholars have concluded from what remains that the subject was a later siege of Babylon by some usurper. The first such siege of Babylon that followed Cyrus is thought to have been the uprising of Nebuchadnezzar III, who claimed to be a son of Nabonidus, Nidintu-Bel. He was defeated in the accession year of Darius I late in 522 B.C.E.

NABOTH (Na'both). A Jezreelite vineyard owner and victim of a wicked plot by Queen Jezebel. Naboth's vineyard in Jezreel was within sight of King Ahab's palace. Naboth declined Ahab's offer to buy the vineyard or to exchange it for a better vineyard somewhere else, because Jehovah had prohibited sale in perpetuity of a family inheritance. (1Ki 21:1-4; Le 25:23-28) Ahab's wife Queen Jezebel, however, schemed to have two witnesses falsely accuse Naboth of blaspheming God and the king. Thereby Naboth and his sons were put to death (2Ki 9:26), enabling Ahab to take possession of the vineyard. Because of this murder, Elijah foretold that the dogs not only would eat up Jezebel but would also lick up Ahab's blood in the same place they licked up Naboth's blood. Ahab's offspring would similarly be cut off. (1Ki 21:5-23) This divine pronouncement was carried out.—1Ki 22:34, 38; 2Ki 9:21, 24-26, 35, 36; 10:1-11.

NACON (Na'con) [possibly, Firmly Established]. According to 2 Samuel 6:6, the name of the threshing floor where Uzzah died for grabbing hold of the ark of the covenant. The parallel account at 1 Chronicles 13:9 says "Chidon," probably indicating that one writer mentioned the name of the place, the other that of its owner, or that one name is an altered form of the other.

NADAB (Na'dab) [Willing; Noble; Generous].

1. The firstborn son of Aaron and Elisheba. (Ex 6:23; 1Ch 6:3) Nadab was born in Egypt and made the great Exodus with Israel. He with his next younger brother Abihu and 70 other Israelites were called with Aaron and Moses up into Sinai, where they saw a vision of Jehovah. (Ex 24:1,

9-11) Nadab and his three brothers were all installed into the priesthood with their father. (Ex 28:1; 40:12-16) Within a month, however, Nadab and Abihu abused their office by offering illegitimate fire. Just what made the fire illegitimate is not stated, but it was probably more than just getting intoxicated (suggested by the immediate prohibition to priests not to drink wine or intoxicating liquor when on duty). However, intoxication may have contributed to their wrongdoing. For their transgression, they were killed by fire from Jehovah and their bodies were disposed of outside the camp. (Le 10:1-11; Nu 26:60, 61) Nadab and Abihu died before they had fathered any sons, leaving their brothers Eleazar and Ithamar to found the two priestly houses.—Nu 3:2, 4; 1Ch 24:1, 2.

2. A descendant of Judah in the line of Jerahmeel; son of Shammai and father to Seled and Appaim.—1Ch 2:3, 25, 26, 28, 30.

3. A son of Jeiel of the tribe of Benjamin.—1Ch 8:1, 29, 30; 9:35, 36.

4. Son of Jeroboam and second king of the northern ten-tribe kingdom of Israel. Nadab ruled for parts of two years, starting in about 976 B.C.E., during which he continued the calf worship instituted by his father. While besieging Gibbethon, a former Levite city (Jos 21:20, 23) taken over by the Philistines, Nadab was assassinated by Baasha, who then killed off all remaining members of Jeroboam's house in order to secure the throne for himself.—1Ki 14:20; 15:25-31.

NAGGAI (Nag'ga-i). Ancestor of Jesus Christ listed in his genealogy as given by Luke.—Lu 3:23, 25.

NAHALAL (Na·hal'al) [Watering Place; Pasture]. A city in Zebulun assigned to the Merarite Levites. (Jos 19:10, 14, 15; 21:34, 35) It was also called Nahalol. Instead of driving out the Canaanites inhabiting this city as divinely instructed, the Zebulunites subjected them to forced labor. (Jg 1:30; 2:2) The site of Nahalal is uncertain.

NAHALIEL (Na·hal'i·el) [Torrent (Torrent Valley) of God]. A place where the Israelites encamped not long before their fight with Amorite King Sihon. (Nu 21:19-24) Eusebius' *Onomasticon* locates it near the Arnon. Nahaliel is therefore commonly linked with one of two wadis, the Wala (a tributary of the Arnon) and the Zarqa Ma'in about 19 km (12 mi) N of the Arnon. A location on either of these wadis would fit the suggested identifications for Mattanah and Bamoth, the two Israelite encampments between which Nahaliel apparently lay.

NAHALOL (Na'ha·lol) [Watering Place; Pasture]. Alternate name for Nahalal, a city in Zebulun.—Jg 1:30.

NAHAM (Na'ham) [Comfort]. Brother-in-law of Hodiah, a descendant of Judah.—1Ch 4:1, 19.

NAHAMANI (Na·ham'a·ni) [from a root meaning "comfort"]. One who returned with Zerubbabel from Babylonian exile.—Ne 7:6, 7.

NAHARAI (Na'ha·rai). A Beerothite (Berothite) and one of Joab's armor-bearers. Naharai was among the mighty men of David's military forces.—2Sa 23:24, 37; 1Ch 11:26, 39.

NAHASH (Na'hash) [Serpent].

1. King of the Ammonites at the time Saul began his reign. Nahash brought his army against Jabesh in Gilead. The account reads: "At that all the men of Jabesh said to Nahash: 'Conclude a covenant with us that we may serve you.' Then Nahash the Ammonite said to them: 'On this condition I shall conclude it with you, on the condition of boring out every right eye of yours, and I must put it as a reproach upon all Israel.' In turn the older men of Jabesh said to him: 'Give us seven days' time, and we will send messengers into all the territory of Israel and, if there is no savior of us, we must then go out to you.'" Israel rallied around Saul, went to Jabesh, and defeated Nahash. Only a few of Nahash's army escaped alive.—1Sa 11:1-11; 12:11, 12.

In a Dead Sea scroll, designated 4QSam[a] and believed to be from the first century B.C.E., the following information is inserted just before 1 Samuel 11:1: "[Na]hash, king of the children of Ammon, sorely oppressed the children of Gad and the children of Reuben, and he gouged out a[ll] their right eyes and struck ter[ror and dread] in Israel. There was not left one among the children of Israel bey[ond the Jordan who]se right eye was no[t put o]ut by Naha[sh king] of the children of Ammon; except that seven thousand men [fled from] the children of [A]mmon and entered [J]abesh-Gilead. About a month later . . ." (*Bible Review*, 1985, Vol. 1, No. 3, p. 28) Basically the same information is given by Josephus.—*Jewish Antiquities*, VI, 68-70 (v, 1).

According to Josephus (*Jewish Antiquities*, VI, 79 [v, 3]), this Nahash was killed in the battle by Saul's forces. If Josephus' information is correct, then the Nahash that extended kindness to David some years later must have been a son and successor to the Nahash defeated by Saul. In such a case, the name Nahash may have been a title bestowed on a series of persons, like the titles "Abimelech," "Pharaoh," and "Jabin." When this second-named Nahash died, David sent ambassadors to his son Hanun, who misunderstood David's honorable intentions and greatly humiliated his representatives. This, in turn, triggered a series of developments that eventually left the Ammonites defeated at the hands of David.—2Sa 10:1-5; 11:1; 12:26-31; 1Ch 19:1-5; 20:1-3.

2. The father of David's sister or half sister Abigail and possibly the father of Zeruiah. He was the grandfather of Abishai, Joab, Asahel, and Amasa. (2Sa 17:25; 1Ch 2:16, 17) Abigail is called "the daughter of Nahash," but she and her sister are not directly called the daughters of Jesse, David's father, though they are referred to as the "sisters" of Jesse's sons, including David. This leaves several possible relationships: (1) That Nahash was a woman, Jesse's wife and the mother of all involved (the name could be given to either sex), but this is not very likely because women were usually introduced into a genealogy only for special reasons, which here seem to be missing. (2) That Nahash was another name for Jesse, as is suggested by early Jewish tradition. The Greek *Septuagint* (Lagardian edition) has "Jesse" instead of Nahash in 2 Samuel 17:25. (3) That Nahash was a former husband of Jesse's wife (a more likely suggestion) and that she bore Nahash two daughters, Abigail and Zeruiah, before marrying Jesse and bearing him several boys.—See ABIGAIL No. 2.

3. A resident of the Ammonite city of Rabbah. His son Shobi showed kindness to David by sending him supplies when he fled to Mahanaim because of Absalom's rebellion. (2Sa 17:27-29) He was possibly an Israelite who went to live in Rabbah after the Ammonites there were defeated by Israel.—2Sa 12:26-31.

NAHATH (Na'hath) [Rest; Quietness].

1. Sheik of Edom, son of Reuel and grandson of Esau and his wife Basemath, Ishmael's daughter.—Ge 36:2-4, 13, 17.

2. A Levite, descendant of Kohath, and ancestor of Samuel. (1Ch 6:16, 22-28) He is apparently also called "Tohu" and "Toah."—1Sa 1:1; 1Ch 6:33-35.

3. A Levite appointed by King Hezekiah as commissioner to assist Conaniah and Shimei with the oversight of "the contribution and the tenth and the holy things" brought to the temple.—2Ch 31:12, 13.

NAHBI (Nah'bi). Son of Vophsi of the tribe of Naphtali. He was one of the 12 men Moses sent to spy out the land of Canaan and was among those returning with a bad report.—Nu 13:1-3, 14, 16, 31-33.

NAHOR   (Na'hor).

1. Father of Terah and grandfather of Abraham. Nahor was a son of Serug and descendant of Shem. He lived 148 years (2177 to 2029 B.C.E.). —Ge 11:22-26; 1Ch 1:24-27; Lu 3:34-36.

2. Son of Terah; grandson of Nahor (No. 1); and brother of Abraham. (Ge 11:26; Jos 24:2) Nahor married Milcah, Lot's sister and the daughter of Nahor's other brother, Haran, hence Nahor's niece. By her he had 8 sons, and by his concubine Reumah he had 4 more sons, totaling 12, some of whom became tribal heads. (Ge 11:27, 29; 22:20-24) Through his son Bethuel, Nahor became grandfather to Laban and Rebekah, and great-grandfather of Leah, Rachel, Jacob (Israel), and Esau.—Ge 24:15, 24, 47; 29:5, 16; 1Ch 1:34.

The Genesis account of Terah and Abraham leaving Ur of the Chaldeans does not include Nahor's name in the list of travelers. (Ge 11:31) It does seem, however, that he may have come later, for Abraham's servant, seeking a wife for Isaac, traveled to Haran, where Terah took up dwelling and where he died, and where Nahor's grandson Laban lived when Jacob went to him. (Ge 11:31, 32; 12:4; 27:43) Abraham's servant came "to the city of Nahor," either to Haran itself or a place close by, perhaps the Nahur frequently mentioned in various Mari tablets of the second millennium B.C.E. (Ge 24:10; 29:4; *The Biblical Archaeologist,* 1948, p. 16) And when Jacob parted company from Laban, Laban called on "the god of Abraham and the god of Nahor" to judge between them. —Ge 31:53; see HARAN No. 4.

NAHSHON   (Nah'shon) [from a root meaning "serpent"]. Wilderness chieftain of the tribe of Judah. Nahshon was the son of Amminadab and among the fifth-listed generation after Judah. (1Ch 2:3-10) His sister was Aaron's wife. (Ex 6:23) Nahshon formed a link in the line of descent that led to David and Jesus, becoming father to Salmon, who married Rahab, and grandfather of Boaz, who, in turn, married Ruth.—1Ch 2:11-15; Ru 4:20; Mt 1:4-6, 16; Lu 3:32.

As chieftain of Judah, the leading tribe of Israel, Nahshon assisted Moses with the first wilderness registration of fighting men. He presented a contribution to the tabernacle service when the altar was inaugurated, and he headed Judah's army of 74,600 that led Israel's line of march.—Nu 1:2-7; 2:3, 4; 7:2, 11, 12-17; 10:14.

NAHUM   (Na'hum) [Comforter [that is, an encourager]].

1. An Israelite prophet of the seventh century B.C.E. and the writer of the book bearing his name. Nahum may have been in Judah at the time he recorded his prophecy. (Na 1:15) His being an Elkoshite evidently means that he was a resident of Elkosh, possibly a city or village of Judah.—Na 1:1; see ELKOSHITE.

2. A postexilic ancestor of Jesus Christ in the line of his earthly mother Mary.—Lu 3:25.

NAHUM, BOOK OF.   This book is a prophetic "pronouncement against Nineveh," the capital of the Assyrian Empire. This Bible book was written by Nahum the Elkoshite. (Na 1:1) The historical fulfillment of that prophetic pronouncement testifies to the authenticity of the book. Sometime after the Egyptian city of No-amon (Thebes) suffered humiliating defeat in the seventh century B.C.E. (3:8-10), the book of Nahum was committed to writing, being completed before Nineveh's foretold destruction came in 632 B.C.E.—See ASSYRIA; NINEVEH.

Harmony With Other Bible Books.   The book of Nahum agrees fully with the rest of the Scriptures in describing Jehovah as "a God exacting exclusive devotion," "slow to anger and great in power," but by no means withholding punishment. (Na 1:2, 3; compare Ex 20:5; 34:6, 7; Job

---

HIGHLIGHTS OF NAHUM

A pronouncement against Nineveh, the capital of Assyria

Written sometime before Nineveh was destroyed in 632 B.C.E.

Jehovah executes vengeance upon his adversaries (1:1-6)

Jehovah requires exclusive devotion; though he is slow to anger, he does not hold back punishment when deserved

No one can stand against the heat of his anger; before him the seas dry up, mountains rock, the hills melt, the earth heaves

Execution of the wicked affords relief for those hoping in Jehovah (1:7-3:19)

Jehovah is a protective stronghold for those relying on him, but he will exterminate the enemy

Good news will be announced to Judah; the "good-for-nothing person" will be cut off, and true worship will be carried on without hindrance

Jehovah will regather his own, but Nineveh will be laid waste, and her war chariots burned

The bloodguilty city is to be plundered as a punishment for her sins; nothing can save her, her warriors have become as women

The stroke inflicted on the king of Assyria has become unhealable

9:4; Ps 62:11.) "Jehovah is good, a stronghold in the day of distress. And he is cognizant of those seeking refuge in him." (Na 1:7; compare Ps 25:8; 46:1; Isa 25:4; Mt 19:17.) These qualities are clearly manifest in his delivering the Israelites from Assyrian oppression and executing vengeance against bloodguilty Nineveh after a considerable period of forbearance.

Noteworthy, too, are the similarities between Nahum chapter 1 and Psalm 97. The words of Isaiah (10:24-27; 30:27-33) regarding Jehovah's judgment against Assyria parallel, to an extent, Nahum chapters 2 and 3.—Also compare Isa 52:7; Na 1:15; Ro 10:15.

Historical Background. Although assured that the conspiracy of Syrian King Rezin and Israelite King Pekah would fail in the attempt to depose him as king (Isa 7:3-7), faithless Ahaz of Judah unwisely appealed to Assyrian King Tiglath-pileser III (Tilgath-pilneser) for aid. Eventually this move "caused him distress, and did not strengthen him," for Judah came under the heavy yoke of Assyria. (2Ch 28:20, 21) Later, Ahaz' son and successor to the throne, Hezekiah, rebelled against Assyrian dominance. (2Ki 18:7) Thereafter the Assyrian monarch Sennacherib invaded Judah and seized one fortified city after another, this resulting in extensive desolation of the land. (Compare Isa 7:20, 23-25; 8:6-8; 36:1, 2.) The next Judean king, Manasseh, was captured by Assyrian army chiefs and taken to Babylon (then under Assyrian control).—2Ch 33:11.

Since Judah had thus suffered long under the heavy hand of Assyria, Nahum's prophecy regarding Nineveh's imminent destruction was good news. As if Assyria had already experienced its downfall, Nahum wrote: "Look! Upon the mountains the feet of one bringing good news, one publishing peace. O Judah, celebrate your festivals. Pay your vows; because no more will any good-for-nothing person pass again through you. In his entirety he will certainly be cut off." (Na 1:15) No longer would there be any interference from the Assyrians; nothing would hinder the Judeans from attending or celebrating the festivals. The deliverance from the Assyrian oppressor would be complete. (Compare Na 1:9.) Also, all other peoples hearing about Nineveh's destruction would "clap their hands," or rejoice, over her calamity, for the city's badness had brought much suffering to them.—3:19.

The military aggressiveness of the Assyrians made Nineveh a "city of bloodshed." (Na 3:1) Cruel and inhuman was the treatment meted out to captives of her wars. Some were burned or skinned alive. Others were blinded or had their noses, ears, or fingers cut off. Frequently, captives were led by cords attached to hooks that pierced the nose or lips. Truly Nineveh deserved to be destroyed for her bloodguiltiness.

NAIL. Ancient nails were quite similar to the larger modern ones, although some kinds had four-sided shanks and a longer taper to the point than those in use today. Apparently, earliest nails were made of bronze, though larger nails of later times were made of iron. David prepared "iron in great quantity for nails for the gates" of the prospective temple. (1Ch 22:3) Ornamental nails have been discovered that were made of bronze overlaid with gold foil, and these are said to date back to about 1300-1200 B.C.E. Concerning nails used in the construction of Solomon's temple it is said: "The weight for the nails was fifty gold shekels [0.6 kg; 1.5 lb t]."—2Ch 3:8, 9.

In 1968, in an excavated tomb located just NE of Jerusalem, the remains were found of a Jew who was executed in the first century by being attached to a torture stake. As shown by subsequent studies, an iron nail 11.5 cm (4.5 in.) long was still piercing the right heel bone. This nail may be similar to the nails employed by the Roman soldiers to impale Jesus Christ. Thomas did not believe that Christ was resurrected until after he saw "the print of the nails" in Jesus' flesh.—Joh 20:24-29.

Figurative Use. Jesus' death on the torture stake resulted in the termination of the Mosaic Law covenant. Referring to its cancellation, Paul pointed out that God took the Law out of the way "by nailing it to the torture stake." (Col 2:13, 14) Solomon likened "those indulging in collections of sentences" to "nails driven in," possibly because they and their good words from Jehovah have a stabilizing and supporting effect upon a hearer. —Ec 12:11.

NAIN (Na'in). A Galilean city where Jesus Christ resurrected the only son of a widow. (Lu 7:11-17) Nain is identified with the village of Nein (Na'im) on the NW side of Jebel Dahi (Giv'at Ha-More; the hill of Moreh?), about 10 km (6 mi) SSE of Nazareth. It is situated in the general area indicated by Jerome and Eusebius for the ancient site. Overlooking the Plain of Jezreel (Esdraelon), Nein lies in an attractive natural setting. Also waters from a spring there support fine groves of olive and fig trees. Today the village is quite small, but ruins in the area show that it was much larger in earlier centuries.—PICTURE, Vol. 2, p. 738.

In 31 C.E., during his first preaching tour of Galilee, Christ Jesus came to Nain from the vicinity of Capernaum. (Lu 7:1-11) A distance of about 35 km (22 mi) separated the two locations. "The gate" may simply have been an opening between the houses by which a road entered Nain, there being no evidence that a wall ever surrounded the city. It was probably at the eastern entrance of Nain that Jesus and his disciples met the funeral procession, which was perhaps headed for the hillside tombs lying to the SE of modern Nein. Moved with pity for the now childless widow, Jesus approached the bier and resurrected the widow's son. News of this miracle spread throughout the region and even reached Judea. The event may also be alluded to by the words "the dead are being raised up," forming part of Jesus' reply to the messengers later sent by the imprisoned John the Baptizer.—Lu 7:11-22.

NAIOTH (Nai'oth). Seemingly a place where certain prophets resided in the time of Samuel. (1Sa 19:18–20:1) It may refer to a certain locality or quarter of the town of Ramah, in the hill country of Ephraim. (See RAMAH No. 5.) Textual critic S. R. Driver corroborates this view, observing: "Probably it is the name of some locality in Ramah, the signification of which is lost to us." —*Notes on the Hebrew Text and the Topography of the Books of Samuel*, Oxford, 1966, p. 159.

NAME. A word or phrase that constitutes a distinctive designation of a person, place, animal, plant, or other object. "Name" can mean a person's reputation or the person himself.

"Every family in heaven and on earth owes its name" to Jehovah God. (Eph 3:14, 15) He established the first human family and permitted Adam and Eve to have children. Therefore, the earthly lines of descent owe their name to him. He is also the Father of his heavenly family. And just as he calls all the countless stars by their names (Ps 147:4), he undoubtedly gave names to the angels.—Jg 13:18.

An interesting example of how something completely new was named involves the miraculously provided manna. When the Israelites first saw it, they exclaimed: "What is it?" (*man hu'?*) (Ex 16:15) It was apparently for this reason that they called it "manna," probably meaning "What is it?" —Ex 16:31.

Scholarly opinions vary as to the origin of certain names, their component roots, and their meaning. For these reasons, the meanings offered for Bible names differ from one reference work to another. In this publication the primary authority for determining the meanings of names is the Bible itself. An example is the meaning of the name Babel. At Genesis 11:9, Moses wrote: "That is why its name was called Babel, because there Jehovah had confused the language of all the earth." Moses here links "Babel" to the root verb *ba·lal'* (confuse), thus indicating that "Babel" means "Confusion."

Bible names variously consist of single elements, phrases, or sentences; those of more than one syllable often have shortened forms. Where the Bible does not specifically state the origin of a name, an effort has been made to determine its root or component parts by using respected modern dictionaries. The dictionary employed to determine the roots of the Hebrew and Aramaic names is entitled *Lexicon in Veteris Testamenti Libros* (by L. Koehler and W. Baumgartner, Leiden, 1958), with its partially completed revision. For Greek names, the ninth edition of *A Greek-English Lexicon* (by H. G. Liddell and R. Scott and revised by H. S. Jones, Oxford, 1968) was the principal dictionary consulted. Renderings found in the *New World Translation of the Holy Scriptures* were then used to assign meanings to these roots. For example, the name Elnathan is made up of the roots *'El* (God) and *na·than'* (give), thus meaning "God Has Given."—Compare Ge 28:4, where *na·than'* is rendered "has given."

Names of Animals and Plants. Jehovah God granted to the first man Adam the privilege of naming the lower creatures. (Ge 2:19) The names given doubtless were descriptive. This is suggested by some of the Hebrew names for animals and even plants. A Hebrew word for "ass" (*chamohr'*) evidently comes from a root meaning "become reddened," referring to the animal's usual color. The Hebrew name for turtledove (*tohr* or *tor*) evidently imitates this bird's plaintive cry of "tur-r-r tur-r-r." "Awakening one" designates the almond tree, apparently because of its being one of the earliest trees to bloom.

Place-Names and Topographical Features. Sometimes men named places after themselves, their offspring, or their ancestors. Murderous Cain built a city and named it after his son Enoch. (Ge 4:17) Nobah began calling the conquered city of Kenath by his own name. (Nu 32:42) The Danites, after capturing Leshem, called that city Dan, this being the name of their forefather.—Jos 19:47; see also De 3:14.

As in the case of altars (Ex 17:14-16), wells (Ge 26:19-22), and springs (Jg 15:19), places were often named on the basis of events that occurred there. Examples of this are Babel (Ge 11:9), Jehovah-jireh (Ge 22:13, 14), Beer-sheba (Ge

26:28-33), Bethel (Ge 28:10-19), Galeed (Ge 31: 44-47), Succoth (Ge 33:17), Abel-mizraim (Ge 50: 11), Massah, Meribah (Ex 17:7), Taberah (Nu 11:3), Kibroth-hattaavah (Nu 11:34), Hormah (Nu 21:3), Gilgal (Jos 5:9), the Low Plain of Achor (Jos 7:26), and Baal-perazim (2Sa 5:20).

There were instances when physical features provided the basis for the names of places, mountains, and rivers. The cities of Geba and Gibeah (both meaning "Hill") doubtless got their names because of occupying hills. Lebanon (meaning "White [Mountain]") may have received its name from the light color of its limestone cliffs and summits or from the circumstance that its upper slopes are covered with snow during a major part of the year. In view of their situation near wells, springs, and meadows, towns and cities often were given names prefixed by "en" (fountain, or, spring), "beer" (well), and "abel" (watercourse).

Other names were derived from such characteristics as size, occupation, and produce. Examples are Bethlehem (meaning "House of Bread"), Bethsaida (House of the Hunter (or, Fisherman)), Gath (Winepress), and Bezer (Unapproachable Place).

Places were also called by the names of animals and plants, many of these names appearing in compound form. Among these were Aijalon (meaning "Place of the Hind; Place of the Stag"), En-gedi (Fountain (Spring) of the Kid), En-eglaim (Fountain (Spring) of Two Calves), Akrabbim (Scorpions), Baal-tamar (Owner of the Palm Tree), and En-Tappuah (Fountain (Spring) of the Apple (Tree)).

"Beth" (meaning "house"), "baal" (owner; master), and "kiriath" (town) frequently formed the initial part of compound names.

Names of Persons. In the earlier period of Biblical history, names were given to children at the time of birth. But later, Hebrew boys were named when they were circumcised on the eighth day. (Lu 1:59; 2:21) Usually either the father or the mother named the infant. (Ge 4:25; 5:29; 16:15; 19:37, 38; 29:32) One notable exception, however, was the son born to Boaz by Ruth. The neighbor ladies of Ruth's mother-in-law Naomi named the boy Obed (meaning "Servant; One Serving"). (Ru 4:13-17) There were also times when parents received divine direction about the name to be given to their children. Among those getting their names in this way were Ishmael (God Hears (Listens)) (Ge 16:11), Isaac (Laughter) (Ge 17:19), Solomon (from a root meaning "peace") (1Ch 22:9), and John (English equivalent of Jehohanan, meaning "Jehovah Has Shown Favor; Jehovah Has Been Gracious") (Lu 1:13).

Especially did names given at divine direction often have prophetic significance. The name of Isaiah's son Maher-shalal-hash-baz (meaning "Hurry, O Spoil! He Has Made Haste to the Plunder; or, Hurrying to the Spoil, He Has Made Haste to the Plunder") showed that the king of Assyria would subjugate Damascus and Samaria. (Isa 8:3, 4) The name of Hosea's son Jezreel (God Will Sow Seed) pointed to a future accounting against the house of Jehu. (Ho 1:4) The names of the two other children borne by Hosea's wife, Lo-ruhamah ([She Was] Not Shown Mercy) and Lo-ammi (Not My People), were indicative of Jehovah's rejecting Israel. (Ho 1:6-10) In the case of the Son of God, the name Jesus (Jehovah Is Salvation) was prophetic of his role as Jehovah's appointed Savior, or means of salvation.—Mt 1:21; Lu 2:30.

The name given to a child often reflected the circumstances associated with its birth or the feelings of the father or the mother. (Ge 29:32–30:13, 17-20, 22-24; 35:18; 41:51, 52; Ex 2:22; 1Sa 1:20; 4:20-22) Eve named her firstborn Cain (meaning "Something Produced"), for, as she said: "I have produced a man with the aid of Jehovah." (Ge 4:1) Regarding him as a replacement for Abel, Eve gave the son born to her after Abel's murder the name Seth (Appointed; Put; Set). (Ge 4:25) Isaac named his younger twin son Jacob (One Seizing the Heel; Supplanter) because at birth this boy was holding on to the heel of Esau his brother. —Ge 25:26; compare the case of Perez at Ge 38: 28, 29.

Sometimes what an infant looked like at birth provided the basis for its name. The firstborn son of Isaac was called Esau (meaning "Hairy") on account of his unusual hairy appearance at birth. —Ge 25:25.

Names given to children were often combined with El (meaning "God") or an abbreviation of the divine name Jehovah. Such names could express the hope of parents, reflect their appreciation for having been blessed with offspring, or make acknowledgment of God. Examples are Jehdeiah (possibly, May Jehovah Feel Glad), Elnathan (God Has Given), Jeberechiah (Jehovah Blesses), Jonathan (Jehovah Has Given), Jehozabad (probably, Jehovah Has Endowed), Eldad (possibly, God Has Loved), Abdiel (Servant of God), Daniel (My Judge Is God), Jehozadak (probably, Jehovah Pronounces Righteous), and Pelatiah (Jehovah Has Provided Escape).

"Ab" (meaning "father"), "ah" (brother), "am" (people), "bath" (daughter), and "ben" (son) were a part of compound names such as Abida (Father Has Known (Me)), Abijah (My Father Is Jehovah),

Ahiezer (My Brother Is a Helper), Ammihud (My People Is Dignity), Amminadab (My People Are Willing (Noble; Generous)), Bath-sheba (Daughter of Plenty; possibly, Daughter [Born on] the Seventh [Day]), and Ben-hanan (Son of the One Showing Favor; Son of the Gracious One). "Melech" (king), "adon" (lord), and "baal" (owner; master) were also combined with other words to form such compound names as Abimelech (My Father Is King), Adonijah (Jehovah Is Lord), and Baal-tamar (Owner of the Palm Tree).

The designations for animals and plants were yet another source of names for people. Some of these names are Deborah (meaning "Bee"), Dorcas or Tabitha (Gazelle), Jonah (Dove), Rachel (Ewe; Female Sheep), Shaphan (Rock Badger), and Tamar (Palm Tree).

As indicated by the repetition of certain names in genealogical lists, it apparently became a common practice to name children after a relative. (See 1Ch 6:9-14, 34-36.) It was for this reason that relatives and acquaintances objected to Elizabeth's wanting to name her newborn son John.—Lu 1:57-61; see GENEALOGY (Repetition of names).

In the first century C.E. it was not uncommon for Jews, especially those living outside Israel or in cities having a mixed population of Jews and Gentiles, to have a Hebrew or an Aramaic name along with a Latin or Greek name. This may be why Dorcas was also called Tabitha and the apostle Paul was also named Saul.

At times names came to be regarded as a reflection of an individual's personality or characteristic tendencies. Esau, with reference to his brother, remarked: "Is that not why his name is called Jacob [One Seizing the Heel; Supplanter], in that he should supplant me these two times? My birthright he has already taken, and here at this time he has taken my blessing!" (Ge 27:36) Abigail observed regarding her husband: "As his name is, so is he. Nabal [Senseless; Stupid] is his name, and senselessness is with him." (1Sa 25:25) No longer considering her name to be appropriate in view of the calamities that had befallen her, Naomi said: "Do not call me Naomi [My Pleasantness]. Call me Mara [Bitter], for the Almighty has made it very bitter for me."—Ru 1:20.

Name changes or new names. Sometimes for a particular purpose names were changed or a person might be given an additional name. While dying, Rachel called her newborn son Ben-oni (meaning "Son of My Mourning"), but her bereaved husband Jacob chose to name him Benjamin (Son of the Right Hand). (Ge 35:16-18) Jehovah changed the name of Abram to Abraham

(Father of a Crowd (Multitude)) and that of Sarai (possibly, Contentious) to Sarah (Princess), both new names being prophetic. (Ge 17:5, 6, 15, 16) Because of his perseverance in grappling with an angel, Jacob was told: "Your name will no longer be called Jacob but Israel [Contender (Perseverer) With God; or, God Contends], for you have contended with God and with men so that you at last prevailed." (Ge 32:28) This change in name was a token of God's blessing and was later confirmed. (Ge 35:10) Evidently, therefore, when the Scriptures prophetically speak of "a new name," the reference is to a name that would appropriately represent its bearer.—Isa 62:2; 65:15; Re 3:12.

At times new names were given to persons elevated to high governmental positions or to those to whom special privileges were extended. Since such names were bestowed by superiors, the name change might also signify that the bearer of the new name was subject to its giver. Subsequent to his becoming Egypt's food administrator, Joseph was called Zaphenath-paneah. (Ge 41:44, 45) Pharaoh Nechoh, when constituting Eliakim as vassal king of Judah, changed his name to Jehoiakim. (2Ki 23:34) Likewise, Nebuchadnezzar, in making Mattaniah his vassal, changed his name to Zedekiah. (2Ki 24:17) Daniel and his three Hebrew companions, Hananiah, Mishael, and Azariah, were given Babylonian names after being selected for special training in Babylon.—Da 1:3-7.

An event in a person's later life sometimes provided the basis for giving a new name to a person. Esau, for example, got his name Edom (meaning "Red") from the red lentil stew for which he sold his birthright.—Ge 25:30-34.

Names of Angels. The Bible contains the personal names of only two angels, Gabriel (meaning "Able-Bodied One of God") and Michael (Who Is Like God?). Perhaps so as not to receive undue honor or veneration, angels at times did not reveal their names to persons to whom they appeared. —Ge 32:29; Jg 13:17, 18.

What is included in knowing the name of God?

The material creation testifies to God's existence, but it does not reveal God's name. (Ps 19:1; Ro 1:20) For an individual to know God's name signifies more than a mere acquaintance with the word. (2Ch 6:33) It means actually knowing the Person—his purposes, activities, and qualities as revealed in his Word. (Compare 1Ki 8:41-43; 9:3, 7; Ne 9:10.) This is illustrated in the case of Moses, a man whom Jehovah 'knew by name,' that is, knew intimately. (Ex 33:12) Moses was privileged to see a manifestation of Jehovah's glory and also to 'hear the name of Jehovah declared.' (Ex 34:5) That declaration was not simply the repetition of the name Jehovah but was a statement about God's attributes and activities. "Jehovah, Jehovah, a God merciful and gracious, slow to anger and abundant in loving-kindness and truth, preserving loving-kindness for thousands, pardoning error and transgression and sin, but by no means will he give exemption from punishment, bringing punishment for the error of fathers upon sons and upon grandsons, upon the third generation and upon the fourth generation." (Ex 34:6, 7) Similarly, the song of Moses, containing the words "for I shall declare the name of Jehovah," recounts God's dealings with Israel and describes his personality. —De 32:3-44.

When Jesus Christ was on earth, he 'made his Father's name manifest' to his disciples. (Joh 17:6, 26) Although having earlier known that name and being familiar with God's activities as recorded in the Hebrew Scriptures, these disciples came to know Jehovah in a far better and grander way through the One who is "in the bosom position with the Father." (Joh 1:18) Christ Jesus perfectly represented his Father, doing the works of his Father and speaking, not of his own originality, but the words of his Father. (Joh 10:37, 38; 12:50; 14:10, 11, 24) That is why Jesus could say, "He that has seen me has seen the Father also."—Joh 14:9.

This clearly shows that the only ones truly knowing God's name are those who are his obedient servants. (Compare 1Jo 4:8; 5:2, 3.) Jehovah's assurance at Psalm 91:14, therefore, applies to such persons: "I shall protect him because he has come to know my name." The name itself is no magical charm, but the One designated by that name can provide protection for his devoted people. Thus the name represents God himself. That is why the proverb says: "The name of Jehovah is a strong tower. Into it the righteous runs and is given protection." (Pr 18:10) This is what persons do who cast their burden on Jehovah. (Ps 55:22) Likewise, to love (Ps 5:11), sing praises to (Ps 7:17), call upon (Ge 12:8), give thanks to (1Ch 16:35), swear by (De 6:13), remember (Ps 119:55), fear (Ps 61:5), search for (Ps 83:16), trust (Ps 33:21), exalt (Ps 34:3), and hope in (Ps 52:9) the name is to do these things with reference to Jehovah himself. To speak abusively of God's name is to blaspheme God.—Le 24:11, 15, 16.

Jehovah is jealous for his name, tolerating no rivalry or unfaithfulness in matters of worship. (Ex 34:14; Eze 5:13) The Israelites were commanded not even to mention the names of other gods. (Ex 23:13) In view of the fact that the names of false gods appear in the Scriptures, evidently the reference concerns mentioning the names of false gods in a worshipful way.

Israel's failure as God's name people to live up to his righteous commands constituted a profanation or defilement of God's name. (Eze 43:8; Am 2:7) Since the Israelites' unfaithfulness resulted in God's punishing them, this also gave opportunity for his name to be spoken of disrespectfully by other nations. (Compare Ps 74:10, 18; Isa 52:5.) Failing to recognize that the chastisement came from Jehovah, these nations wrongly attributed the calamities that befell Israel to the inability of Jehovah to protect his people. To clear his name of such reproach, Jehovah acted for the sake of his name and restored a remnant of Israel to their land.—Eze 36:22-24.

By manifesting himself in special ways, Jehovah caused his name to be remembered. At places where this occurred, altars were erected.—Ex 20:24; compare 2Sa 24:16-18; see JEHOVAH.

The Name of God's Son. Because of remaining faithful to the very death, Jesus Christ was rewarded by his Father, receiving a superior position and "the name that is above every other name." (Php 2:5-11) All those desiring life must recognize what that name stands for (Ac 4:12), including Jesus' position as Judge (Joh 5:22), King (Re 19:16), High Priest (Heb 6:20), Ransomer (Mt 20:28), and Chief Agent of salvation.—Heb 2:10; see JESUS CHRIST.

Christ Jesus as "King of kings and Lord of lords" also is to lead the heavenly armies to wage war in righteousness. As executioner of God's vengeance, he would be displaying powers and qualities completely unknown to those fighting against him. Appropriately, therefore, "he has a name written that no one knows but he himself."—Re 19:11-16.

Various Uses of the Word "Name." A particular name might be "called upon" a person, city, or building. Jacob, when adopting Joseph's sons as his own, stated: "Let my name be called upon them and the name of my fathers, Abraham and Isaac." (Ge 48:16; see also Isa 4:1; 44:5.) Jehovah's name being called on the Israelites indicated that they were his people. (De 28:10; 2Ch 7:14; Isa 43:7; 63:19; Da 9:19) Jehovah also placed his name on Jerusalem and the temple, thereby accepting them as the rightful center of his worship. (2Ki 21:4, 7) Joab chose not to complete the capture of Rabbah in order not to have his name called upon that city, that is, so as not to be credited with its capture.—2Sa 12:28.

A person dying without leaving behind male offspring had his name "taken away," as it were. (Nu 27:4; 2Sa 18:18) Therefore, the arrangement of brother-in-law marriage outlined by the Mosaic Law served to preserve the name of the dead man. (De 25:5, 6) On the other hand, the destruction of a nation, people, or family meant the wiping out of their name.—De 7:24; 9:14; Jos 7:9; 1Sa 24:21; Ps 9:5.

To speak or to act 'in the name of' another denoted doing so as a representative of that one. (Ex 5:23; De 10:8; 18:5, 7, 19-22; 1Sa 17:45; Es 3:12; 8:8, 10) Similarly, to receive a person in the name of someone would indicate a recognition of that one. Therefore, to 'receive a prophet in the name of a prophet' would signify receiving a prophet because of his being such. (Mt 10:41, KJ, NW) And to baptize in "the name of the Father and of the Son and of the holy spirit" would mean in recognition of the Father, the Son, and the holy spirit.—Mt 28:19.

Reputation or Fame. In Scriptural usage, "name" often denotes fame or reputation. (1Ch 14:17, ftn) Bringing a bad name upon someone meant making a false accusation against that person, marring his reputation. (De 22:19) To have one's name 'cast out as wicked' would mean a loss of good reputation. (Lu 6:22) It was to make "a celebrated name" for themselves in defiance of Jehovah that men began building a tower and a city after the Flood. (Ge 11:3, 4) On the other hand, Jehovah promised to make Abram's name great if he would leave his country and relatives to go to another land. (Ge 12:1, 2) Testifying to fulfillment of that promise is the fact that to this day few names of ancient times have become as great as Abraham's, particularly as examples of outstanding faith. Millions still claim to be the heirs of the Abrahamic blessing because of fleshly descent. Similarly, Jehovah made David's name great by blessing him and granting him victories over the enemies of Israel.—1Sa 18:30; 2Sa 7:9.

At birth a person has no reputation, and therefore his name is little more than a label. That is why Ecclesiastes 7:1 says: "A name is better than good oil, and the day of death than the day of one's being born." Not at birth, but during the full course of a person's life does his "name" take on real meaning in the sense of identifying him either as a person practicing righteousness or as one practicing wickedness. (Pr 22:1) By Jesus' faithfulness until death his name became the one name "given among men by which we must get saved,"

and he "inherited a name more excellent" than that of the angels. (Ac 4:12; Heb 1:3, 4) But Solomon, for whom the hope was expressed that his name might become "more splendid" than David's, went into death with the name of a backslider as to true worship. (1Ki 1:47; 11:6, 9-11) "The very name of the wicked ones will rot," or become an odious stench. (Pr 10:7) For this reason a good name "is to be chosen rather than abundant riches."—Pr 22:1.

Names Written in "the Book of Life." It appears that Jehovah God, figuratively speaking, has been writing names in the book of life from "the founding of the world." (Re 17:8) Since Christ Jesus spoke of Abel as living at "the founding of the world," this would indicate that the reference is to the world of ransomable mankind that came into existence after children were born to Adam and Eve. (Lu 11:48-51) Abel's name would evidently be the first one recorded on that symbolic scroll.

The names appearing on the scroll of life, however, are not names of persons who have been predestined to gain God's approval and life. This is evident from the fact that the Scriptures speak of 'blotting out' names from "the book of life." So it appears that only when a person becomes a servant of Jehovah is his name written in "the book of life," and only if he continues faithful is his name retained in that book.—Re 3:5; 17:8; compare Ex 32:32, 33; Lu 10:20; Php 4:3; see also LIFE.

Names Recorded in the Lamb's Scroll. Similarly, the names of persons worshiping the symbolic wild beast have not been recorded in the Lamb's scroll. (Re 13:8) That wild beast received its authority, power, and throne from the dragon, Satan the Devil. Those who worship the wild beast are therefore a part of the 'serpent's seed.' (Re 13:2; compare Joh 8:44; Re 12:9.) Even before children were born to Adam and Eve, Jehovah God indicated that there would be enmity between the 'seed of the woman' and the 'seed of the serpent.' (Ge 3:15) Thus from the founding of the world it had already been determined that no worshiper of the wild beast would have his name written in the Lamb's scroll. Only persons sacred from God's standpoint were to be so privileged. —Re 21:27.

In view of the fact that this scroll belongs to the Lamb, logically the names appearing on it would be those of persons given to him by God. (Re 13:8; Joh 17:9, 24) It is therefore noteworthy that the next reference to the Lamb in the book of Revelation depicts him as standing on Mount Zion with 144,000 persons bought from among mankind. —Re 14:1-5.

NAOMI (Na'o·mi) [My Pleasantness]. Mother-in-law of Ruth, who was an ancestress of David and of Jesus Christ.—Mt 1:5.

Naomi was the wife of Elimelech, an Ephrathite of Bethlehem in Judah, in the days of the Judges. During a severe famine she and her husband and their two sons, Mahlon and Chilion, moved to Moab. There Elimelech died. The sons then married Moabite women, Ruth and Orpah, but about ten years later these sons died childless.—Ru 1:1-5.

The bereaved Naomi decided to return to Judah. Her two widowed daughters-in-law started to accompany her, but Naomi recommended that they return and marry in their own land, for Naomi herself had "grown too old to get to belong to a husband" and could provide no sons as husbands for them. Orpah turned back, but Ruth stuck with Naomi, out of love for Naomi and her God Jehovah.—Ru 1:6-17.

Upon arrival in Bethlehem, Naomi said to the women greeting her: "Do not call me Naomi [My Pleasantness]. Call me Mara [Bitter], for the Almighty has made it very bitter for me." (Ru 1:18-21) Since it was the time of barley harvest, Ruth lovingly went to work gleaning for the support of Naomi and herself, and by chance she lighted upon the field of Boaz. (Ru 2:1-18) When she told Naomi in whose field she was working, Naomi recognized the hand of Jehovah in the matter, inasmuch as Boaz was a near kinsman of Elimelech and therefore one of their repurchasers. She encouraged Ruth to bring this fact to Boaz' attention. (Ru 2:19–3:18) Boaz quickly responded, following the customary legal procedure in repurchasing Elimelech's property from Naomi. Ruth then became the wife of Boaz in Naomi's behalf, in accord with the law of levirate, or brother-in-law, marriage. When a son was born to them, the neighbor ladies gave it the name Obed, saying: "A son has been born to Naomi." Thus Obed became legal heir to the Judean house of Elimelech.—Ru 4:1-22.

NAPHISH (Na'phish) [possibly from a root meaning "soul"]. The 11th listed of Ishmael's 12 sons. (Ge 25:13-16; 1Ch 1:29-31) As chieftain, he also headed an Ishmaelite tribe that took his name and presumably resided in territory bordering on the E or NE frontier of the Promised Land. In the days of Saul, the Israelite tribes of Reuben, Gad, and the half tribe of Manasseh living E of the Jordan successfully made war on the Hagrites and their confederates, including the tribe of Naphish, and captured a great quantity of livestock and people. (1Ch 5:10, 18-22) It is possible, as some

scholars suggest, that these Naphish captives were put to work as Nethinim slaves of the sanctuary and that after the return from Babylonian exile their descendants were called the sons of Nephushesim, or Nephusim.—Ne 7:46, 52; Ezr 2:43, 50.

NAPHTALI (Naph'ta·li) [My Wrestlings].

1. The second son born to Jacob by Rachel's maidservant Bilhah in Paddan-aram. (Ge 35:25, 26; Ex 1:1, 4; 1Ch 2:1, 2) Since Bilhah had substituted for her mistress Rachel, Naphtali, like his older full brother Dan, was considered by barren Rachel as her own son. Although her sister Leah by then already had four sons (Ge 29:32-35), Rachel was elated over her success in getting a second son through her maidservant and exclaimed: "With strenuous wrestlings I have wrestled with my sister. I have also come off winner!" The name given to this son, Naphtali (meaning "My Wrestlings"), appropriately expressed Rachel's feelings at the time of his birth.—Ge 30:2-8.

Later, Naphtali himself became the father of four sons, Jahzeel (Jahziel), Guni, Jezer, and Shillem (Shallum). (Ge 46:24; 1Ch 7:13) When the dying patriarch Jacob related to his sons what would happen to them in "the final part of the days," his statement about Naphtali, though one of the briefest, was favorable.—Ge 49:1, 2, 21.

2. The tribe of Israel named after Naphtali and composed of four tribal families descended from his sons Jahzeel, Guni, Jezer, and Shillem. (Nu 26:48, 49) About a year after the Israelites left Egypt, the fighting men of this tribe from 20 years old upward numbered 53,400. (Nu 1:42, 43) While in the wilderness, the tribe of Naphtali, under the leadership of its chieftain Ahira, encamped N of the tabernacle alongside the tribes of Asher and Dan. As part of the three-tribe division of the camp of Dan, the tribe of Naphtali, along with Dan and Asher, was last in the order of march and occupied the important position of rear guard. —Nu 1:15, 16; 2:25-31; 7:78; 10:25-28.

By the time a second census was taken about four decades after the Exodus from Egypt, the number of able-bodied men in the tribe had dropped to 45,400. (Nu 26:50) Among the men lost to the tribe was Nahbi, one of the ten spies who had brought back a bad report and discouraged the Israelites from entering the Promised Land.—Nu 13:14, 16, 31-33; 14:35-37.

After finally crossing the Jordan and sharing in the conquest of Jericho and Ai under Joshua's leadership, Naphtali was one of the tribes 'standing for the malediction' in front of Mount Ebal. (Jos 6:24, 25; 8:28, 30-35; De 27:13) When the time came for apportioning the land into tribal inheritances, Pedahel, as divinely appointed representative of the tribe of Naphtali, assisted Joshua and Eleazar the priest in this.—Nu 34:16, 17, 28; Jos 19:51.

Land Inheritance. The territory assigned to the tribe of Naphtali was situated in the northern part of the Promised Land. (De 34:1, 2) On the E it was bounded by the Sea of Galilee and the Jordan River. For some distance the territory of Asher extended along the W border. The region assigned to Zebulun bounded Naphtali both on the W and S, and Issachar lay to the S. (Compare Jos 19:32-34.) The reference to Naphtali's boundary reaching to "Judah at the Jordan" (Jos 19:34) evidently does not mean that it extended to the territory of the tribe of Judah, situated a considerable distance S of Naphtali. In this case "Judah" probably refers to the region E of the Jordan occupied by the family of Jair. Although reckoned as a Manassite by reason of his maternal ancestry (Nu 32:41; Jos 13:29, 30), Jair, through his father, was a descendant of Judah. (1Ch 2:5, 21, 22) So the region given to the family of Jair might appropriately be called Judah on the basis of Jair's paternal ancestry.

Included in the territory of Naphtali were 19 fortified cities and their settlements. (Jos 19:35-39) One of these cities, Kedesh, was given to the Levites and assigned a sacred status as a city of refuge. (Jos 20:7, 9) Two other cities, Hammath (Hammoth-dor or Hammon) and Kartan (Kiriathaim), were likewise designated for the Levites. (Jos 19:35; 21:6, 32; 1Ch 6:62, 76) From Beth-shemesh and Beth-anath, two other cities of Naphtali, the Canaanites were not driven out but were subjected to forced labor.—Jg 1:33.

The land once occupied by the tribe of Naphtali, though mountainous (Jos 20:7), is fruitful. Especially fertile are the triangular plain (of Gennesaret) on the NW side of the Sea of Galilee and the Hula region. Moses' blessing directed to Naphtali perhaps alludes to the land inheritance of the tribe. "Naphtali is satisfied with the approval and full of the blessing of Jehovah. Do take possession of the west and south." (De 33:23) "West" may also be rendered "sea" (*AS* ftn) or "lake" (*RS*) and therefore could denote the Sea of Galilee; and "south" perhaps designates the southernmost territory of Naphtali bordering on that sea. There is also a possibility that the text, though alluding to the Sea of Galilee, should read: "The sea and its fish are his possession."—*NW* ftn.

From the Time of Judges to the Exile. In his deathbed prophecy Jacob had referred to Naphtali as "a slender hind." (Ge 49:21) This may

have alluded to the tribe's swiftness and skillfulness in warfare, and the history of the tribe appears to bear this out. Ten thousand men from Naphtali and Zebulun courageously responded to Barak's call to battle against the well-equipped forces under the command of Sisera and, thereafter, were blessed with victory. Barak himself evidently was of the tribe of Naphtali, as Kedesh in Naphtali was apparently his home. (Jg 4:6-15; 5:18) The tribe of Naphtali also gave support to Judge Gideon in the fight against the Midianites. —Jg 6:34, 35; 7:23, 24.

Years later 1,000 chiefs and 37,000 other warriors of the tribe of Naphtali came to Hebron to make David king over all Israel. From as far as Issachar, Zebulun, and Naphtali, food was brought for the feasting done in connection with that event. (1Ch 12:23, 34, 38-40) Under the leadership of King David, the tribe of Naphtali appears to have had a notable part in subduing the enemies of Israel.—Ps 68:Sup, 1, 27.

Some decades after the division of the kingdom of Israel, Naphtali experienced harassment from Syrian King Ben-hadad I. (1Ki 15:20; 2Ch 16:4) About two centuries later, during Pekah's reign, inhabitants of Naphtali were taken into Assyrian exile by Tiglath-pileser III. (2Ki 15:29) Nearly a century after the overthrow of the northern kingdom, Judean King Josiah boldly extended his destruction of appendages of idolatry as far N as the devastated places of Assyrian-dominated Naphtali.—2Ch 34:1-7.

Isaiah's Prophecy. The humiliation suffered at the hands of the Assyrians may well be referred to at Isaiah 9:1: "The obscureness will not be as when the land had stress, as at the former time when one treated with contempt the land of Zebulun and the land of Naphtali." Next Isaiah indicates that at a later time honor would be bestowed on what had been treated with contempt—"the way by the sea, in the region of the Jordan, Galilee of the nations." He continues: "The people that were walking in the darkness have seen a great light. As for those dwelling in the land of deep shadow, light itself has shone upon them." (Isa 9:1, 2) These very words were quoted by Matthew (4:13-17) and applied to Christ Jesus, "the light of the world," and to his activity. (Joh 8:12) Since Jesus made Capernaum in Naphtali's territory "his own city" (Mt 4:13; 9:1), he could in a sense be regarded as belonging to Naphtali. Therefore also Jacob's prophetic words concerning Naphtali, "He is giving words of elegance," could reasonably apply to Jesus. (Ge 49:21) The Son of God truly gave "words of elegance," prompting even officers sent to arrest him to exclaim: "Never has another man spoken like this."—Joh 7:46.

Referred To in Visions. In Ezekiel's vision, Naphtali's land assignment lay between Asher and Manasseh (Eze 48:3, 4), and one of the gates of the city "Jehovah Himself Is There" was named after Naphtali. (Eze 48:34, 35) Also in vision, the apostle John heard that 12,000 had been sealed out of the (spiritual) tribe of Naphtali.—Re 7:4, 6.

NAPHTUHIM (Naph·tu'him). Listed as among the descendants of Mizraim, the son of Ham. (Ge 10:6, 13, 14; 1Ch 1:11, 12) As with the other names in this list, scholars usually take the apparent plural form to indicate a tribe or people. Assuming the name to derive from some geographic relationship, scholars often associate Naphtuhim with an Egyptian phrase meaning "those of the Delta," and on this basis the Naphtuhim are included among the inhabitants of Lower (northern) Egypt. The correctness of these views is not as yet conclusive.

NARCISSUS (Nar·cis'sus). Head of a household in Rome. When Paul wrote his letter to the Romans, he requested that his greetings be given to "those from the household of Narcissus who are in the Lord."—Ro 16:11.

NARD. The precious "perfumed oil" that Mary, the sister of Lazarus, applied to Jesus' head and feet. By reason of its costliness, nard (Gr., nar'dos) was often subjected to adulteration and even counterfeiting. It may be noteworthy, therefore, that both Mark and John use the expression "genuine nard." (Mr 14:3; Joh 12:3) Valuable ointment sealed in a small alabaster container anciently served as a good investment.—Joh 12:5; see SPIKENARD.

NATHAN (Na'than) [[God] Has Given].

1. A descendant of Judah. The son of Attai and father of Zabad. Nathan's grandfather was an Egyptian servant named Jarha.—1Ch 2:3, 34-36.

2. A prophet of Jehovah during David's reign; possibly of the tribe of Levi. When the king revealed to Nathan his desire to build a temple for Jehovah's worship, the prophet replied: "Everything that is in your heart—go, do." (2Sa 7:1-3; 1Ch 17:1, 2) However, that night Jehovah informed Nathan that instead of David's building a temple, Jehovah would build for David a lasting house, and that later on David's descendant would build the house of Jehovah. Thus through Nathan, Jehovah announced to David a covenant for a kingdom "to time indefinite" in David's line.—2Sa 7:4-17; 1Ch 17:3-15.

Nathan was later sent by Jehovah to point out both the magnitude of David's sin against Uriah the Hittite respecting Bath-sheba and the divine penalty imposed because of it. This he did tactfully but forcefully, using an illustration. David was thereby maneuvered into expressing, unwittingly and without personal prejudice, his own judgment on such an act. Nathan then informed him: "You yourself are the man!" and expressed Jehovah's judgment upon David and his house.—2Sa 12:1-18; see also Ps 51:Sup.

In time a second son, named Solomon, was born to David by Bath-sheba. This child Jehovah loved; so he sent his prophet Nathan, who, "for the sake of Jehovah," named the boy Jedidiah, meaning "Beloved of Jah." (2Sa 12:24, 25) During the closing days of David's life when Adonijah attempted to seize the throne, Nathan took appropriate measures to bring the matter to David's attention. Nathan then shared in the anointing and installing of Solomon as king.—1Ki 1:5-40.

It appears that Nathan, together with Gad, advised David on the proper deployment of musical instruments in connection with the sanctuary. (2Ch 29:25) Nathan and Gad were evidently the ones used to record the information contained in the concluding chapters of First Samuel and all of Second Samuel. (1Ch 29:29) "Among the words of Nathan the prophet" were also recorded "the affairs of Solomon."—2Ch 9:29.

This Nathan may have been the father of Azariah and Zabud, both of whom held important positions during the reign of Solomon. Azariah was a princely overseer of the deputies, while Zabud served as a priest and close friend and adviser to the king.—1Ki 4:1, 5.

3. The father of Igal and brother of Joel, two of David's mighty men of war.—2Sa 23:8, 36; 1Ch 11:26, 38.

4. A son of David by his wife Bath-sheba, born to him in Jerusalem. (2Sa 5:13, 14; 1Ch 3:5) The natural lineage of Messiah is traced, from David through Nathan and his descendants down to Jesus, evidently through Jesus' mother Mary. (Lu 3:23, 31) Concerning the time when 'they will look on the One whom they pierced,' the prophecy of Zechariah says there will be a bitter lamentation and wailing throughout the whole land, family by family, and especially for the families of David, Levi, the Shimeites, and "the family of the house of Nathan." (Zec 12:10-14) If the family of Nathan's house here referred to sprang from David's son, this would make it one of the families of David. Therefore the lamentation would affect families *within* families.

5. One of the nine head ones of the exiles encamped at the river Ahava, whom Ezra sent to enlist ministers for the services at the house of God in Jerusalem.—Ezr 8:15-17.

6. A former exile in Babylon, and one of the 13 sons of Binnui who put away their foreign wives in compliance with Ezra's instructions. —Ezr 10:10, 11, 38-42, 44.

NATHANAEL (Na·than′a·el) [from Heb., meaning "God Has Given"]. Presumably the name of Bartholomew, hence one of Jesus' 12 apostles. Bartholomew, meaning "Son of Tolmai," was a patronymic term (that is, a designation derived from his father). The apostle John uses his given name Nathanael, whereas Matthew, Mark, and Luke call him Bartholomew. When doing so they associate Philip and Bartholomew together, in the same way that John links Philip with Nathanael. (Mt 10:3; Mr 3:18; Lu 6:14; Joh 1:45, 46) It was not uncommon for persons to be known by more than one name. For example, "Simon the son of John" also came to be known as Cephas and Peter. (Joh 1:42) Nor was it exceptional for Nathanael to be called Bartholomew, or the "Son of Tolmai," as another man was called simply Bartimaeus, or "Son of Timaeus." (Mr 10:46) The two names, Nathanael and Bartholomew, are used interchangeably by Christian writers of following centuries.

Nathanael was from Cana of Galilee. (Joh 21:2) He began following Jesus early in the Master's ministry. Philip, after responding to Jesus' call "Be my follower," immediately looked up his friend Nathanael and invited him to "come and see" the Messiah. Nathanael asked, "Can anything good come out of Nazareth?" but then responded to the invitation. Jesus, seeing him approach, remarked: "See, an Israelite for a certainty, in whom there is no deceit." Nathanael must have been an exceptional man for Jesus to make a statement like that. Because Jesus said this and stated that he saw Nathanael under a fig tree before Philip called him, Nathanael confessed that Jesus was indeed "the Son of God, . . . King of Israel." Jesus assured him that he would "see things greater than these." —Joh 1:43-51.

As one of the 12, Nathanael was in constant attendance throughout Jesus' ministry, being trained for future service. (Mt 11:1; 19:25-28; 20:17-19, 24-28; Mr 4:10; 11:11; Joh 6:48-67) After Jesus' death and resurrection, Nathanael and others of the apostles went back to their fishing, and it was while they were approaching shore in their boat one morning that Jesus called to them. Nathanael, unlike Peter, stayed in the boat until it got to shore, and then, joining the rest for breakfast, he took in the meaningful conversation between Jesus and Peter. (Joh 21:1-23) He was also present with the other apostles when they met together for prayer and on the day of Pentecost.—Ac 1:13, 14; 2:42.

NATHAN-MELECH (Na′than-mel′ech) [The King Has Given]. A court official of Judah whose dining room was situated in the porticoes of the temple. While taking steps against false worship, King Josiah made the horses that Judean kings had given to the sun "cease from entering the house of Jehovah by the dining room of Nathan-melech."—2Ki 23:11.

NATIONS. In the broad and general sense, a nation is made up of people who are more or less related to one another by blood and who have a common language. Such a national group usually occupies a defined geographic territory and is subject to some form of central governmental control. According to the *Theological Dictionary of the Old Testament*, "Hebrew evidences a tendency for *goy* to describe a people in terms of its political and territorial affiliation, and so to approximate much more closely to our modern term 'nation.' *'am* [people], conversely, always retains a strong emphasis on the element of consanguinity as the basis of union into a people." (Edited by G. J. Botterweck and H. Ringgren, Vol. 2, 1975, p. 427) The Greek terms *e′thnos* (nation) and *la·os′* (people) are used similarly. In the Scriptures the plural forms of *gohy* and *e′thnos* usually refer to Gentile nations.

Origin. The first notice of the forming of separate nations appears in the post-Flood period, in connection with the building of the Tower of Babel. Those sharing in this project were united in their opposition to God's purpose. The principal factor facilitating united action was that "all the earth continued to be of one language and of one set of words." (Ge 11:1-4) Jehovah took notice of this and, by confusing their language, "scattered them from there over all the surface of the earth." —Ge 11:5-9; MAP Vol. 1, p. 329.

Separated now by communication barriers, each linguistic group developed its own culture, art, customs, traits, and religion—each its own ways of doing things. (Le 18:3) Alienated from God, the various peoples contrived many idols of their mythical deities.—De 12:30; 2Ki 17:29, 33.

There were three great branches of these nations stemming from the sons and grandsons of Noah's sons Japheth, Ham, and Shem, and these were reckoned as the founding fathers of the respective nations called by their names. The listing in Genesis, chapter 10, therefore might be termed the oldest tabulation of nations, 70 in number. Fourteen were Japhetic, 30 Hamitic, and 26 Shemitic in origin. (Ge 10:1-8, 13-32; 1Ch 1:4-25) For more information regarding these national groups, see CHART, Vol. 1, p. 329, as well as articles on each of the 70 descendants of Noah.

Many changes, of course, came with the passing of time. Some nations were absorbed by their neighbors or disappeared altogether, because of weakness, disease, or war; others came into existence through new migrations and population increases. The spirit of nationalism at times became very strong among certain groups, and this, coupled with great military exploits, gave ambitious men the necessary thrust to build world empires at the expense of weaker nations.

A Father of Nations. God told Abram to leave Ur and move to a land He would show him, for as He said, "I shall make a great nation out of you." (Ge 12:1-4) Later, God enlarged on his promise, saying, "You will certainly become a father of a crowd of nations. . . . And I will make you very, very fruitful and will make you become nations, and kings will come out of you." (Ge 17:1-6) This promise was fulfilled. Abraham's son Ishmael fathered "twelve chieftains according to their clans" (Ge 25:13-16; 17:20; 21:13, 18), and through the six sons of Keturah, other nations traced their ancestry back to Abraham. (Ge 25:1-4; 1Ch 1:28-33; Ro 4:16-18) From Abraham's son Isaac sprang the Israelites and Edomites. (Ge 25:21-26) In a much larger, spiritual sense Abraham became "a father of many nations," for persons of many national groups, including those of the Christian congregation in Rome, by reason of their faith and obedience could call Abraham their father, "the father of all those having faith."—Ro 4:11, 16-18; see ISRAEL No. 2.

How God Views the Nations. As the Creator and Universal Sovereign, God is within his absolute rights in setting the nations' territorial boundaries (if he chooses to do so), as he did with Ammon, Edom, and Israel. (De 2:17-22; 32:8; 2Ch 20:6, 7; Ac 17:26) The Most High and Lofty One over all the earth is not to be compared in greatness with nations of mankind. (Jer 10:6, 7) Actually the nations are as but a drop from the bucket in his sight. (Isa 40:15, 17) So when such nations rage and mutter against Jehovah, as when they put Jesus to death on a torture stake, He only laughs at them in derision and confounds and destroys their presumptuous counsel against Him.

—Ps 2:1, 2, 4, 5; 33:10; 59:8; Da 4:32b, 34, 35; Ac 4:24-28.

Yet for all of Jehovah's superlative greatness and power, no one can rightly charge him with being unjust in his treatment of national groups. It makes no difference whether God is dealing with a single man or a whole nation, he never compromises his righteous principles. (Job 34:29) If a nation is repentant, as were the people of Nineveh, he blesses them. (Jon 3:5-10) But if they turn to doing bad, even though in a covenant with him, he destroys them. (Jer 18:7-10) When an issue arises, Jehovah sends his prophets with a message of warning. (Jer 1:5, 10; Eze 2:3; 33:7) God is not partial toward any, great or small.—De 10:17; 2Ch 19:7; Ac 10:34, 35.

Therefore, when whole nations refuse to recognize and obey Jehovah, or they cast him out of their minds and hearts, Jehovah executes his judgments upon them. (Ps 79:6; 110:6; 149:7-9) He devotes them to destruction and turns them back to Sheol. (Ps 9:17; Isa 34:1, 2; Jer 10:25) In descriptive language God says that the wicked nations will be turned over to his Son, the one called "Faithful and True . . . The Word of God," to be dashed to pieces.—Ps 2:7-9; Re 19:11-15; compare Re 12:5.

The New Nation of Spiritual Israel. For centuries Jehovah God dealt exclusively with natural Israel, time and again sending his prophets to the nation so that the people might turn from their wayward course. Finally he sent his Son, Christ Jesus, but the majority rejected him. Therefore, Jesus said to the unbelieving chief priests and Pharisees: "The kingdom of God will be taken from you and be given to a nation producing its fruits."—Mt 21:33-43.

The apostle Peter clearly identified that "nation" as one composed of persons who had accepted Christ Jesus. (1Pe 2:4-10) In fact, Peter applied to fellow Christians the very words that had been directed to natural Israel: "You are 'a chosen race, a royal priesthood, a holy nation, a people for special possession.'" (1Pe 2:9; compare Ex 19:5, 6.) All of them recognized God as Ruler and his Son as Lord and Christ. (Ac 2:34, 35; 5:32) They possessed heavenly citizenship (Php 3:20) and were sealed with the holy spirit, which was an advance token of their heavenly inheritance. (2Co 1:22; 5:5; Eph 1:13, 14) Whereas natural Israel was constituted a nation under the Law covenant, the "holy nation" of spirit-begotten Christians became such under the new covenant. (Ex 19:5; Heb 8:6-13) For these reasons it was most appropriate that they be called "a holy nation."

When God's spirit was first poured out upon about 120 disciples of Jesus (all natural Jews) on the day of Pentecost in the year 33 C.E., it became evident that God was dealing with a new spiritual nation. (Ac 1:4, 5, 15; 2:1-4; compare Eph 1:13, 14.) Later, beginning in the year 36 C.E., membership in the new nation was extended to uncircumcised Gentiles, who likewise received God's spirit. —Ac 10:24-48; Eph 2:11-20.

Regarding the preaching of the good news to all nations, see GOOD NEWS.

Gog and Magog.   The Bible book of Revelation (20:7, 8) states that, after Christ's Thousand Year Reign, Satan "will go out to mislead those nations in the four corners of the earth, Gog and Magog." Evidently such nations are the product of rebellion against Christ's administration.—See GOG No. 3.

NATURE.   The basic makeup or constitution of something. It can refer to what a person is by birth, also to hereditary qualities along with general practice. At times it refers to the physical urges of an organism. Translators generally render the Greek words *phy'sis* and *phy·si·kos'* (the adjective form) as "nature" and "natural," respectively.

Men and Animals.   That there is a nature belonging to man different from that of wild beasts, and that even wild beasts are not all of the same nature, is shown by the statement at James 3:7: "For every species [Gr., *phy'sis*, "nature"] of wild beast as well as bird and creeping thing and sea creature is to be tamed and has been tamed by humankind [*phy'sei tei an·thro·pi'nei*, "nature belonging to the man"]." This difference in "nature" reveals the variety in God's creation and is maintained because of the divine law that each produces according to its own kind.—Ge 1:20-28; compare 1Co 15:39.

Divine Nature.   Also, there is a different nature belonging to those in heaven, spirit creatures of God. The apostle Peter speaks to his fellow Christians, spiritual brothers of Jesus Christ, of "the precious and very grand promises, that through these you may become sharers in divine nature [*phy'se·os*]." (2Pe 1:4) That this is a sharing with Christ in his glory as spirit persons, Peter shows in his first letter: "God . . . gave us a new birth [*a·na·gen·ne'sas he·mas'*, "having generated us again"] to a living hope through the resurrection of Jesus Christ from the dead to an incorruptible and undefiled and unfading inheritance. It is reserved in the heavens for you." (1Pe 1:3, 4) "Divine nature" requires a change in nature through death and resurrection, as made plain by the apostle Paul at First Corinthians chapter 15. He explains that the Christian must die and must be resurrected in a different body, a spiritual one, which requires a change.—1Co 15:36, 38, 44, 49, 51.

Inherent Nature.   Paul speaks of his fellow countrymen the Jews, calling them "Jews by nature," that is, born of Jewish parents, of the children of Israel, or Jacob.—Ga 2:15; compare Ro 2:27.

In the illustration of the olive tree, he calls the fleshly Jews the natural (*ka·ta' phy'sin*, "according to nature") branches of the garden olive. He tells the Gentile Christians: "For if you were cut out of the olive tree that is wild by nature and were grafted contrary to nature into the garden olive tree, how much rather will these who are natural be grafted into their own olive tree!" (Ro 11:21-24) The wild olive tree is unfruitful or produces very inferior fruit, but it is common practice in Mediterranean countries to graft branches of cultivated olive trees into the wild olive tree to produce good fruit. However, if the wild olive branch is grafted into the cultivated tree, it produces only the poor fruit of the wild olive tree. Therefore Paul calls this latter grafting "contrary to nature." It serves to emphasize the power of God as well as his undeserved kindness to Gentiles in bringing them in to replace "natural branches." The Jews had been 'cultivated' by Jehovah for centuries, but the Gentiles had been "wild," not having the true religion, not bringing forth fruitage to God. Not naturally, but only by God's power could they be made to bring forth fine fruit. Only Jehovah, therefore, could accomplish this 'grafting' successfully.

Also, in his argument to the Galatians to prevent their enslavement to Judaistic teachings, Paul said: "When you did not know God, then it was that you slaved for those who *by nature* are not gods." These false gods they had worshiped were by their very origin and production not truly gods; it was impossible for them to come into such a status. Not merely did they have no authority to be gods, but they did not have such qualities in their intrinsic nature or makeup.—Ga 4:8.

Conscience.   Certain traits or qualities inhere in mankind from birth, actually having been placed in man from the beginning. The apostle Paul comments on the conscience, or at least a vestige of such, that still persists in fallen man, even though in many cases he has strayed from God and does not have his law. This explains why all nations have established many laws that are in harmony with righteousness and justice, and many individuals follow certain good principles.

Paul says: "For whenever people of the nations that do not have law do *by nature* the things of the law, these people, although not having law, are a law to themselves. They are the very ones who demonstrate the matter of the law to be written in their hearts, while their conscience is bearing witness with them and, between their own thoughts, they are being accused or even excused."—Ro 2:14, 15.

In discussing the matter of headship with the Corinthian congregation, Paul called attention to the rule that a woman should wear a head covering when praying or prophesying before the congregation, as a sign of subjection. In illustration, he says: "Does not *nature itself* teach you that if a man has long hair, it is a dishonor to him; but if a woman has long hair, it is a glory to her? Because her hair is given her instead of a headdress." —1Co 11:14, 15.

Paul's reference to "nature itself" evidently included more than "custom," which he mentions in verse 16 in connection with the use of a head covering by women. Hereditary characteristics also likely had a bearing on what Christians in Corinth viewed as natural. Among Europeans (such as the Greeks), the hair of women, when left uncut, usually becomes considerably longer than that of men. But this is not true of the straight hair of Orientals and Indians or of the woolly hair of Blacks and Melanesians.

In addition to their awareness of hereditary qualities among them, the Christians in Corinth knew that it was the general practice for men to clip their hair to a moderate length. This was common also among Jewish men; so the long uncut hair of Nazirites marked them as men who were not following the general custom. (Nu 6:5) On the other hand, Jewish women usually wore their hair quite long. (Lu 7:38; Joh 11:2) And in the Greek city of Corinth, shaving a woman's head, or clipping her hair very short, was a sign of her being a slave or of her being in disgrace for having been caught in fornication or adultery. —1Co 11:6.

So, when saying that "nature itself" taught them, Paul evidently had in mind various factors that would influence their attitude as to what was natural.

In saying "Does not nature itself teach you . . . ?" Paul was not personifying nature, as though it were a goddess. Rather, God has given man reasoning powers. By observing and reasoning on things as God has made them and the results from using these in various ways, man can learn much as to what is proper. It is really God that teaches, and the man with his mind properly oriented by God's Word can view things in their right perspective and relationship, thereby rightly discerning what is natural or unnatural. By this means the individual can have a trained conscience in this respect and can avoid a conscience that is defiled and that approves unnatural things.—Ro 1:26, 27; Tit 1:15; 1Co 8:7.

Natural Use of Bodies. It is wrong for men and women to use their bodies in any way that is out of harmony with the functions for which God created them. What is *unnatural* in that sense is *sinful*. The Scriptures describe the uncleanness and condemnation coming upon those who practice these things: "That is why God gave them up to disgraceful sexual appetites, for both their females changed the *natural* [*phy·si·ken'*] use of themselves into one *contrary to nature;* and likewise even the males left the *natural* use of the female and became violently inflamed in their lust toward one another, males with males, working what is obscene and receiving in themselves the full recompense, which was due for their error." Such persons lower themselves to a beastlike level. (Ro 1:26, 27; 2Pe 2:12) They go after wrong fleshly things because, like a beast, they lack reasonableness, having no spirituality.—Jude 7, 10.

Birth. Another Greek word often translated "natural" is *ge·ne·sis,* literally meaning "birth" or "origin." James speaks of "a man looking at his *natural* face [literally, the face of the birth of him] in a mirror." (Jas 1:23) James also says that "the tongue is a fire" and that it "sets the wheel of *natural life* [literally, the wheel of the birth] aflame." (Jas 3:5, 6) James may here be alluding to a wheel, such as that on a chariot, that could be set on fire by a hot, glowing axle. Similarly, the tongue can set aflame the whole round of one's life into which he came by birth, making life become like a vicious circle, possibly even resulting in his own destruction as by fire.

NAZARENE

(Naz·a·rene') [probably from Heb. *ne'tser,* "sprout"]. A descriptive epithet applied to Jesus and later to his followers. The names Nazarene and Nazirite are not to be confused, for, though spelled similarly in English, they stem from altogether different Hebrew words with different meanings.—See NAZIRITE.

It was natural and not particularly unusual to speak of Jesus as the Nazarene, since from infancy (less than three years of age) he was raised as the local carpenter's son in the city of Nazareth, a place about 100 km (60 mi) N of Jerusalem. The practice of associating persons with the places from which they came was common in those days.

—2Sa 3:2, 3; 17:27; 23:25-37; Na 1:1; Ac 13:1; 21:29.

Frequently Jesus was referred to, in widely scattered places and by all kinds of persons, as the Nazarene. (Mr 1:23, 24; 10:46, 47; 14:66-69; 16:5, 6; Lu 24:13-19; Joh 18:1-7) Jesus himself accepted and used the name. (Joh 18:5-8; Ac 22:6-8) On the sign that Pilate had placed on the torture stake he wrote in Hebrew, Latin, and Greek: "Jesus the Nazarene the King of the Jews." (Joh 19:19, 20) From Pentecost 33 C.E. forward, the apostles as well as others often spoke of Jesus Christ as the Nazarene or as being from Nazareth.—Ac 2:22; 3:6; 4:10; 6:14; 10:38; 26:9.

Prophetic. Matthew pointed out that the name Nazarene was prophetically foretold as another sign identifying Jesus Christ as the promised Messiah. He called this to the attention of his readers when he told how Joseph brought Mary and her child back from Egypt following Herod's death. "Moreover," Matthew wrote, "being given divine warning in a dream, he [Joseph] withdrew into the territory of Galilee, and came and dwelt in a city named Nazareth, that there might be fulfilled what was spoken through the prophets: 'He will be called a Nazarene.'"—Mt 2:19-23.

Nazareth is not mentioned in the Hebrew Scriptures. Some suppose Matthew had reference to some lost prophetic book or some unwritten tradition, but his expression, "spoken through the prophets," is used by writers of the Christian Greek Scriptures only in reference to the same canonical collection of the Hebrew Scriptures we have today. The key to understanding, apparently, lies in equating Nazarene with ne'tser, mentioned above as meaning sprout.

With this in mind, it is evident that Matthew was referring to what Isaiah (11:1) had said concerning Messiah: "There must go forth a twig out of the stump of Jesse; and out of his roots a sprout [we·ne'tser] will be fruitful." Another Hebrew word, tse'mach, also means sprout and was used by other prophets when referring to the Messiah. Matthew used the plural, saying that "prophets" had mentioned this coming "Sprout." For example, Jeremiah wrote about the "righteous sprout" as an offshoot of David. (Jer 23:5; 33:15) Zechariah describes a king-priest "whose name is Sprout," a prophecy that could apply only to Jesus the Nazarene, the great spiritual Temple-builder. —Zec 3:8; 6:12, 13.

NAZARETH (Naz'a·reth) [probably, Sprout-Town]. A city in Lower Galilee where Jesus lived most of his earthly life, along with his half broth-ers and half sisters. (Lu 2:51, 52; Mt 13:54-56) Both Joseph and Mary were residents of Nazareth when Gabriel announced the approaching birth of Jesus. (Lu 1:26, 27; 2:4, 39) Later, after their return from Egypt, they took up residence in Nazareth again.—Mt 2:19-23; Lu 2:39.

Location. Most scholars identify Nazareth with En Nasira (Nazerat) in Galilee. (PICTURES, Vol. 2, p. 539) If this view is correct, Nazareth was situated in the low mountains just N of the Valley of Jezreel and approximately halfway between the S tip of the Sea of Galilee and the Mediterranean Coast. It was in a mountain basin with hills rising 120 to 150 m (400 to 500 ft) above it. The area was well populated, with a number of cities and towns near Nazareth. Also, it is estimated that one could walk from Nazareth to Ptolemais on the Mediterranean Coast in seven hours, to Tiberias on the Sea of Galilee in five hours, and to Jerusalem in three days.

On one occasion people of Nazareth sought to throw Jesus from "the brow of the mountain upon which their city had been built." (Lu 4:29) That is not to say that Nazareth was on the very brow or edge, but that it was on a mountain having a brow from which they wanted to hurl Jesus. Some have identified it with a rocky cliff some 12 m (40 ft) high located SW of the city.

Prominence of Nazareth. It is difficult to say with certainty just how prominent Nazareth was in the first century. The most common view of commentators is that Nazareth was then a rather secluded, insignificant village. The principal Biblical statement used to support this view is what Nathanael said when he heard that Jesus was from there: "Can anything good come out of Nazareth?" (Joh 1:46) This has been taken by many to mean that Nazareth was looked down upon, even by people of Galilee. (Joh 21:2) Nazareth was near trade routes of the area but not directly on them. It was not mentioned by Josephus, though he referred to nearby Japhia as the largest fortified village of all Galilee, leading to the idea that Nazareth was eclipsed by its neighbor.

On the other hand, Nathanael may simply have been expressing surprise that Philip would claim a man from the neighborhood city of Nazareth in Galilee to be the promised Messiah, for the Scriptures had foretold that that one would come from Bethlehem in Judah. (Mic 5:2) Josephus did not mention many of the settlements in Galilee, so his not mentioning Nazareth might not be particularly significant. It is noteworthy that the Bible does not call Nazareth a village, but always a "city." (Lu 1:26; 2:4, 39) Furthermore, close-by Sepphoris was an important, fortified city having a district court of the Sanhedrin. Nonetheless, whatever its size and prominence, Nazareth was convenient to important trade routes and main cities, and so its inhabitants would have had ready information about the social, religious, and political activities of the time.—Compare Lu 4:23.

Attitude of the People. As Jesus grew up, he progressed "in favor with God and men." (Lu 2:52) He and his half brothers and half sisters were known by the people of Nazareth, and it was his "custom" to attend the local synagogue each week. (Mt 13:55, 56; Lu 4:16) When he was about 30 years of age, Jesus left Nazareth and was baptized by John. (Mr 1:9; Lu 3:23) Some months later, near the start of his Galilean ministry, Jesus returned to Nazareth and in the synagogue read aloud Isaiah 61:1, 2, applying it to himself. The people manifested a lack of faith and attempted to kill him, "but he went through the midst of them and continued on his way," taking up residence in Capernaum.—Lu 4:16-30; Mt 4:13.

Over a year later, Christ again visited Nazareth. (Mt 13:54-58; Mr 6:1-6) Though some have thought this to be the same occasion as in Luke 4:16-30, the order of events in Matthew, Mark, and Luke indicates otherwise, as does the fact that Jesus' activities and the results were somewhat different. His fame may have grown by this time so that a somewhat more hospitable reception was granted him. Though many stumbled over the fact that he was a local man, there is no mention of the people's trying to kill him this time. He performed some powerful works, but not many, because of the people's lack of faith. (Mt 13:57, 58) Jesus then left and began his third circuit of Galilee.—Mr 6:6.

NAZIRITE
(Naz′i·rite) [One Singled Out; Dedicated One; Separated One]. There were two classes of Nazirites: those who volunteered and those who were such by divine appointment. The regulations governing volunteer Nazirites are found in the book of Numbers, chapter 6. Either men or women could take a special vow to Jehovah to live as Nazirites for a period of time. However, if a daughter's father or a wife's husband heard the vow and did not approve, he could cancel it.—Nu 30:1-8.

There were three principal restrictions resting on those taking the Nazirite vow: (1) They were to drink no intoxicating beverage; neither were they to eat any product of the grapevine, whether unripe, ripe, or dried, nor drink any of its juice, whether in the fresh, fermented, or vinegar state. (2) They were not to cut the hair of their heads.

(3) They were not to touch a dead body, even that of the closest relative—father, mother, brother, or sister.—Nu 6:1-7.

Special Vows. The person taking this special vow was "to live as a Nazirite [that is, dedicated, separated] to Jehovah" and not for the plaudits of men due to a showy display of fanatical asceticism. Rather, "all the days of his Naziriteship he is holy to Jehovah."—Nu 6:2, 8; compare Ge 49:26, ftn.

The requirements laid on Nazirites, therefore, had special significance and meaning in the worship of Jehovah. Like the high priest who, because of his holy office, was to touch no dead body, not even that of one of his closest relatives, so too the Nazirite. The high priest and the underpriests, because of the serious responsibility of their offices, were forbidden to drink wine or intoxicating liquor when performing their sacred duties before Jehovah.—Le 10:8-11; 21:10, 11.

Furthermore, the Nazirite "should prove holy by letting the locks of the hair of his head grow," such serving as a crowning sign by which all could quickly recognize his holy Naziriteship. (Nu 6:5) The same Hebrew word na·zir′ was used in regard to the "unpruned" vines during the sacred Sabbath and Jubilee years. (Le 25:5, 11) Interesting too is the fact that the gold plate on the front of the turban of the high priest, engraved with the words "Holiness belongs to Jehovah," was called "the holy sign of dedication [Heb., ne′zer, from the same root as na·zir′]." (Ex 39:30, 31) Likewise, the official headpiece, or diadem, worn by Israel's anointed kings was also called a ne′zer. (2Sa 1:10; 2Ki 11:12; see CROWN; DEDICATION.) In the Christian congregation the apostle says that a woman's long hair is given to her instead of a headdress. It is a natural reminder to her that she is in a position different from the man; she should be mindful of her submissive position under God's arrangement. So such requirements—uncut hair (unnatural for the man), total abstinence from wine as well as the need to be clean and undefiled —impressed on the dedicated Nazirite the importance of self-denial and complete submission to the will of Jehovah.—1Co 11:2-16; see HAIR; HEAD COVERING; NATURE.

Requirements if Nazirite became defiled. A Nazirite would become unclean for seven days if he touched a dead body, even if, because of an accident beyond his control, he inadvertently touched someone that died alongside him. On the seventh day he was to shave the head and purify himself, and the next day he was to take to the priest two turtledoves (or, two young pigeons), one serving as a sin offering, the other serving as a burnt sacrifice; he was also to present a young ram as a guilt offering. Furthermore, the one having taken the vow of Naziriteship must now begin all over again counting the days of the vow as stipulated at the start.—Nu 6:8-12.

Requirements at conclusion of vow. When the specified duration of the vow came to an end, the Nazirite presented himself to the priests before the tent of meeting, bringing along the prescribed sacrifices consisting of a young ram for a burnt offering, a female lamb for a sin offering, and a ram for a communion sacrifice. He also was to bring a basket of unfermented (unleavened) cakes and wafers that were well oiled, together with the proper grain and drink offerings. In addition to these necessary sacrifices, the Nazirite brought such other offerings to the sanctuary as he could afford. (Nu 6:13-17, 21) Next, the Nazirite had his long hair cut off, and it was placed on the fire under the communion sacrifice. Then portions of the offerings were placed in his hands by the officiating priest and waved by the priest as a wave offering before Jehovah.—Nu 6:18-20.

It appears that in time the Jews made it possible for wealthy individuals to provide the necessary sacrifices, as an act of charity, for persons of little means who desired to take the Nazirite vow.

This seemed to be the recognized custom that the apostle Paul took advantage of upon arriving in Jerusalem at the end of his third tour. To allay the false rumors that Paul had been "teaching all the Jews among the nations . . . [not] to walk in the solemn customs" of the Jewish nation, Paul's Christian brothers recommended the following plan. "We have four men with a vow upon themselves," they told Paul. "Take these men along and cleanse yourself ceremonially with them *and take care of their expenses,* that they may have their heads shaved."—Ac 21:20-26.

As to the length of time that one might be a Nazirite, this was optional with the one making the vow. Jewish tradition (not the Bible) said it could not be less than 30 days, for it was thought that anything less than that degraded the solemnity of the vow, making it commonplace.

Lifetime Nazirites. In the case of those appointed as Nazirites by Jehovah for life, being singled out by him for special service, they took no vows and were not bound by a limited period of time (the days of which were recalculated from the beginning if the vow was broken before being completed). For these reasons Jehovah's commandments for them differed somewhat from his requirements for voluntary Nazirites. Samson was

such a God-appointed lifetime Nazirite, having been divinely appointed to be such before his conception. Even with his mother it was not a discretionary matter. Because her son would be a Nazirite, she was commanded by the angel to observe special regulations—not to drink wine or intoxicating liquor or to eat anything unclean during her pregnancy.—Jg 13:2-14; 16:17.

Regarding Samson, the regulation was that "no razor should come upon his head." (Jg 13:5) However, no prohibition was placed on his touching dead bodies. Hence, Samson's killing a lion, or his slaying 30 Philistines and then stripping the corpses of their garments, did not profane his Naziriteship. On still another occasion, with God's approval, he killed a thousand of the enemy "with the jawbone of a male ass—one heap, two heaps!" —Jg 14:6, 19; 15:14-16.

In Samuel's case it was his mother, Hannah, who made a vow, setting apart her yet unconceived child for Jehovah's service as a Nazirite. To God she said in prayer: "If you will without fail . . . give to your slave girl a male offspring, I will give him to Jehovah all the days of his life ["and he shall drink no wine nor strong drink," (1Ki 1:11, *LXX*)], and no razor will come upon his head." (1Sa 1:9-11, 22, 28) John the Baptizer was to "drink no wine and strong drink at all." Few other details concerning his Naziriteship are given except that he, too, by divine appointment, was to be such from the day of his birth.—Lu 1:11-15; compare Mt 3:4; 11:18.

John the Baptizer was among those Nazirites whom Jehovah himself raised up. As he says by the mouth of his prophet Amos: "I kept raising up some of your sons as prophets and some of your young men as Nazirites." However, they were not always accepted or respected, and wayward Israel even tried to break their integrity to Jehovah. (Am 2:11, 12) When the full measure of Israel's sins reached their limits and Jehovah removed typical Israel in 607 B.C.E., the unfaithful Nazirites within Jerusalem did not escape either. Jeremiah describes how the once healthy and strong Nazirites turned black as their skin shriveled up on their bones because of the terrible famine.—La 4:7-9.

NEAH (Ne′ah). A city mentioned in a description of Zebulun's territorial boundaries. (Jos 19:10, 13, 14, 16) Neah's location is uncertain. Some link it with Tell el-Wawiyat, just 1.3 km (0.8 mi) NNW of Rummana, about 10 km (6 mi) N of Nazareth.

NEAPOLIS (Ne·ap′o·lis) [New City]. A city of Greece at the northern end of the Aegean Sea that served as a seaport for Philippi. It is generally linked with modern Kavalla. This city occupies a rocky promontory at the head of the Gulf of Kavalla. Its harbor is situated on the western side, and Kavalla itself lies about 16 km (10 mi) SE of the ruins of Philippi. Latin inscriptions indicate the city's dependence on Philippi in Roman times, and portions of an aqueduct there appear to be of Roman construction. The Roman-built Egnatian Way connected Neapolis and Philippi and ran westward all the way to Durazzo (Durrës) on the Adriatic Sea.

It was at Neapolis that the apostle Paul first entered Europe in response to the call to "step over into Macedonia." From there he went to Philippi, this possibly taking him three or four hours as he crossed the mountain range between the two cities. (Ac 16:9-11) About six years later Paul doubtless passed through Neapolis again.—Ac 20:6.

NEARIAH (Ne·a·ri'ah) [Boy (Young Man) of Jah].

1. A Simeonite, son of Ishi. Neariah and his three brothers headed a force of 500 men that defeated the Amalekites at Mount Seir and thereafter continued to dwell there.—1Ch 4:42, 43.

2. Son of Shemaiah, father of Elioenai, Hizkiah, and Azrikam, and descendant of David.—1Ch 3:1, 22, 23.

NEBAI (Ne'bai) [possibly from a root meaning "thrive; bear fruit"]. One of "the heads of the people" whose descendant, if not he himself, attested by seal the "trustworthy arrangement" of Nehemiah's day.—Ne 9:38; 10:1, 14, 19.

NEBAIOTH (Ne·ba'ioth). The firstborn of Ishmael's 12 sons and founder of one of the prominent Arabian tribes. (Ge 25:13-16; 1Ch 1:29-31) Nebaioth's sister Mahalath (or possibly Basemath) married their cousin Esau. (Ge 28:9; 36:2, 3) The descendants of Nebaioth are not identified as living in any definite locality; they were probably nomads, moving about as Bedouin with their flocks. In the time of Isaiah, "the flocks of Kedar" (Kedar was Nebaioth's brother) and "the rams of Nebaioth" were associated together in a prophecy foretelling how such animals would serve as approved sacrifices on Jehovah's altar.—Isa 60:7.

Some scholars have attempted to equate the descendants of Nebaioth with the Nabataeans of later times, but the evidence in support of such a suggestion is inconclusive.

NEBALLAT (Ne·bal'lat). A place settled by Benjamites after the Babylonian exile. (Ne 11:31, 34) Neballat is generally identified with Beit Nebala (Horvat Nevallat). Situated on a low hill about 6 km (3.5 mi) ENE of modern Lydda (Lod), Beit Nebala overlooks the SE end of the Plain of Sharon.

NEBAT (Ne'bat) [He Has Looked At]. An Ephraimite and father of King Jeroboam I, the first ruler of the ten-tribe kingdom of Israel.—1Ki 11: 26; 2Ki 14:23, 24.

NEBO (Ne'bo).

1. A Moabite city that came under the control of Amorite King Sihon sometime before the Israelites entered the Promised Land. (Compare Nu 21:26; 32:3; Isa 15:2.) Subsequent to Israel's defeating Sihon, the Reubenites rebuilt Nebo. (Nu 32:37, 38) In the latter part of the tenth century B.C.E., however, it appears that the Reubenites (1Ch 5:1, 8) lost the city, for, on the Moabite Stone, King Mesha boasted about having taken it from Israel at the direction of his god Chemosh. Later, both Isaiah (in the eighth century B.C.E.) and Jeremiah (in the seventh century B.C.E.) mentioned Nebo in prophecies directed against Moab. —Isa 15:2; Jer 48:1, 22.

Nebo is commonly identified with Khirbet Mekhayyet (or, Qaryat el Mukhaiyat), situated about 8 km (5 mi) SW of Heshbon. There are ruins of an ancient fortress at this site. Also, large quantities of pottery fragments (thought to date from the 12th to the beginning of the 6th century B.C.E.) have been found.

2. A city, representatives of which returned from Babylonian exile. (Ezr 2:1, 29) In the time of Ezra some of "the sons [probably, inhabitants] of Nebo" dismissed their foreign wives. (Ezr 10:43, 44) Apparently to distinguish this Nebo from No. 1, it is designated as "the other Nebo." (Ne 7:33) Modern Nuba, located about 11 km (7 mi) NW of Hebron, has been presented as a possible identification.

3. Evidently one of the mountains of Abarim. It was from Mount Nebo or from the top of Pisgah (which may have been a part of Nebo or Nebo may have been a part of Pisgah) that Moses viewed the Promised Land, and then he died there. (De 32:48-52; 34:1-4) Mount Nebo is generally identified with Jebel en-Neba (Har Nevo). This mountain has an elevation of more than 820 m (2,700 ft) above sea level and is located about 17 km (11 mi) E of where the Jordan enters the Dead Sea. It is believed that Pisgah may be Ras es-Siyaghah, an eminence just NW of and slightly lower than the peak of Jebel en-Neba. On a clear day the top of Ras es-Siyaghah provides a splendid view of Mounts Hermon, Tabor, Ebal, and Gerizim, the central mountain ridge on which Bethlehem and Hebron are situated, as well as the Jordan Valley and the Dead Sea.

4. A deity whose humiliation at the fall of Babylon was foretold by the prophet Isaiah. (Isa 46:1, 2) Nebo was worshiped both in Babylonia and Assyria. He was identified with the planet Mercury and was regarded as the son of Marduk and Sarpanitu and the consort of Tashmitum. To his worshipers Nebo was a god of wisdom and learning, "the god who possesses intelligence," "he who hears from afar," "he who teaches," and "lord of the tablet stylus."—*The Seven Great Monarchies of the Ancient Eastern World,* by G. Rawlinson, 1885, Vol. I, p. 91; *Ancient Near Eastern Texts,* edited by J. Pritchard, 1974, p. 450.

The prominence of this deity is illustrated by the Babylonian king Nabonidus' referring to Nebo as "the administrator of all the upper and nether world, who lengthens the span of my life" and also as the one "who extends (the length of) my rule." Nabonidus credited Nebo with placing into his hands "the correct scepter, the lawful staff, which (alone) ensures the aggrandizement of the country." (*Ancient Near Eastern Texts,* p. 310) Another indication of the importance of Nebo in Babylonian religion is the fact that a form of the name appears in the names of the Babylonian kings *Nebu*chadnezzar, *Nabo*polassar, and *Nabo*nidus; also in *Neb*uzaradan (2Ki 25:8) and perhaps Abed*nego.*—Da 1:7.

Nebo is prominently associated with the ancient city of Borsippa (modern Birs or Birs-Nimrud) near Babylon. In the spring, every New Year's Day, the image of Nebo was taken in sacred procession from Borsippa to Babylon. Thereafter, when the image was returned to its sanctuary at Borsippa, the image of Marduk (also called by his title Bel [Lord]) was carried partway along with that of Nebo. It was most appropriate, therefore, that the prophecy of Isaiah specifically mentioned the coming disgrace of Bel and Nebo at Babylon's fall.—Isa 46:1, 2.

NEBUCHADNEZZAR (Neb·u·chad·nez′zar), **NEBUCHADREZZAR** (Neb·u·chad·rez′zar) [from Akkadian, meaning "O Nebo, Protect the Heir!"]. Second ruler of the Neo-Babylonian Empire; son of Nabopolassar and father of Awil-Marduk (Evilmerodach), who succeeded him to the throne. Nebuchadnezzar ruled as king for 43 years (624-582 B.C.E.), this period including the "seven times" during which he ate vegetation like a bull. (Da 4:31-33) To distinguish this monarch from the Babylonian ruler by the same name but of a much earlier period (the Isin dynasty), historians refer to him as Nebuchadnezzar II.

Historical notices in cuneiform inscriptions presently available about Nebuchadnezzar somewhat supplement the Bible record. They state that it was in the 19th year of Nabopolassar's reign that he assembled his army, as did his son Nebuchadnezzar, then crown prince. Both armies evidently functioned independently, and after Nabopolassar went back to Babylon within a month's time, Nebuchadnezzar successfully warred in mountainous territory, later returning to Babylon with much spoil. During the 21st year of Nabopolassar's reign, Nebuchadnezzar marched with the Babylonian army to Carchemish, there to fight against the Egyptians. He led his forces to victory. This took place in the fourth year of Judean King Jehoiakim (625 B.C.E.).—Jer 46:2.

The inscriptions further show that news of his father's death brought Nebuchadnezzar back to Babylon, and on the first of Elul (August-September), he ascended the throne. In this his accession year he returned to Hattu, and "in the month Shebat [January-February, 624 B.C.E.] he took the vast booty of Hattu to Babylon." (*Assyrian and Babylonian Chronicles,* by A. K. Grayson, 1975, p. 100) In 624 B.C.E., in the first official year of his kingship, Nebuchadnezzar again led his forces through Hattu; he captured and sacked the Philistine city of Ashkelon. (See ASHKELON.) During his second, third, and fourth years as king he conducted additional campaigns in Hattu, and evidently in the fourth year he made Judean King Jehoiakim his vassal. (2Ki 24:1) Also, in the fourth year Nebuchadnezzar led his forces to Egypt, and in the ensuing conflict both sides sustained heavy losses.

Conquest of Jerusalem. Later, the rebellion of Judean King Jehoiakim against Nebuchadnezzar evidently resulted in a siege being laid against Jerusalem by the Babylonians. It appears that during this siege Jehoiakim died and his son Jehoiachin ascended the throne of Judah. But a mere three months and ten days thereafter the reign of the new king ended when Jehoiachin surrendered to Nebuchadnezzar (in the month of Adar [February-March] during Nebuchadnezzar's seventh regnal year [ending in Nisan 617 B.C.E.], according to the Babylonian Chronicles). A cuneiform inscription (British Museum 21946) states: "The seventh year: In the month Kislev the king of Akkad mustered his army and marched to Hattu. He encamped against the city of Judah and on the second day of the month Adar he captured the city (and) seized (its) king [Jehoiachin]. A king of his own choice [Zedekiah] he appointed in the city (and) taking the vast tribute he brought it into Babylon." (*Assyrian and Babylonian Chronicles,* by A. K. Grayson, 1975, p. 102; PICTURE, Vol. 2, p. 326) Along wih Jehoiachin, Nebuchadnezzar took other members of the royal household, court officials, craftsmen, and warriors into Babylonian exile. It was Jehoiachin's uncle Mattaniah that Nebuchadnezzar made king of Judah, and he changed Mattaniah's name to Zedekiah.—2Ki 24:11-17; 2Ch 36:5-10; see CHRONOLOGY; JEHOIACHIN; JEHOIAKIM.

Sometime later Zedekiah rebelled against Nebuchadnezzar, allying himself with Egypt for military protection. (Eze 17:15; compare Jer 27:11-14.) This brought the Babylonians back to Jerusalem, and on Tebeth (December-January) 10 in the ninth year of Zedekiah's reign, Nebuchadnezzar besieged Jerusalem. (2Ki 24:20; 25:1; 2Ch 36:13) However, news that a military force of Pharaoh was coming out of Egypt caused the Babylonians to lift the siege temporarily. (Jer 37:5) Subsequently Pharaoh's troops were forced to go back to Egypt, and the Babylonians resumed the siege against Jerusalem. (Jer 37:7-10) Finally, in 607 B.C.E., on Tammuz (June-July) 9 in the 11th year of Zedekiah's reign (Nebuchadnezzar's 19th year if counting from his accession year or his 18th regnal year), a breach was made in Jerusalem's wall. Zedekiah and his men fled but were overtaken in the desert plains of Jericho. Since Nebuchadnezzar had retired to Riblah "in the land of Hamath," Zedekiah was brought before him there. Nebuchadnezzar had all of Zedekiah's sons slaughtered, and then he blinded and bound Zedekiah in order to take him as a prisoner to Babylon. The postconquest details, including the burning of the temple and the houses of Jerusalem, the disposition of temple utensils, and the taking of captives, were handled by Nebuzaradan the chief of the bodyguard. Over those not taken captive, Gedaliah, an appointee of Nebuchadnezzar, served as governor.—2Ki 25:1-22; 2Ch 36:17-20; Jer 52:1-27, 29.

His Dream of an Immense Image. The book of Daniel states that it was in "the second year" of Nebuchadnezzar's kingship (probably counting from the destruction of Jerusalem in 607 B.C.E. and therefore actually referring to his 20th regnal year) that Nebuchadnezzar had the dream about the golden-headed image. (Da 2:1) Although the magic-practicing priests, conjurers, and Chaldeans were unable to interpret this dream, the Jewish prophet Daniel did so. This moved Nebuchadnezzar to acknowledge Daniel's God as "a God of gods and a Lord of kings and a Revealer of secrets." He then constituted Daniel "ruler over all the jurisdictional district of Babylon and the chief prefect over all the wise men of Babylon." Nebuchadnezzar also appointed Daniel's three companions, Shadrach, Meshech, and Abednego, to administrative posts.—Da 2.

Later Exiles of Jews. About three years later, in the 23rd year of Nebuchadnezzar's reign, more Jews were taken into exile. (Jer 52:30) This exile probably involved Jews who had fled to lands that were later conquered by the Babylonians. Lending support to this conclusion is the statement of the historian Josephus: "In the fifth year after the sacking of Jerusalem, which was the twenty-third year of the reign of Nebuchadnezzar, Nebuchadnezzar marched against Coele-Syria and, after occupying it, made war both on the Moabites and the Ammanites. Then, after making these nations subject to him, he invaded Egypt in order to subdue it."—*Jewish Antiquities,* X, 181, 182 (ix, 7).

Takes Tyre. It was also sometime after the fall of Jerusalem in 607 B.C.E. that Nebuchadnezzar began the siege against Tyre. During this siege the heads of his soldiers were "made bald" from the chafing of the helmets and their shoulders were "rubbed bare" from carrying materials used in the construction of siegeworks. As Nebuchadnezzar received no "wages" for serving as Jehovah's instrument in executing judgment upon Tyre, He promised to give him the wealth of Egypt. (Eze 26:7-11; 29:17-20; see TYRE.) One fragmentary Babylonian text, dated to Nebuchadnezzar's 37th year (588 B.C.E.), does, in fact, mention a campaign against Egypt. (*Ancient Near Eastern Texts,* edited by J. Pritchard, 1974, p. 308) But it cannot be established whether it relates to the original conquest or a later military action.

Building Projects. Besides attaining numerous military victories and expanding the Babylonian Empire in fulfillment of prophecy (compare Jer 47-49), Nebuchadnezzar engaged in considerable building activity. To satisfy the homesick longings of his Median queen, Nebuchadnezzar reportedly built the Hanging Gardens, rated as one of the seven wonders of the ancient world. Many of the extant cuneiform inscriptions of Nebuchadnezzar tell of his building projects, including his erection of temples, palaces, and walls. An excerpt from one of these inscriptions reads:

"Nebuchadrezzar, King of Babylon, the restorer of Esagila and Ezida, son of Nabopolassar am I. As a protection to Esagila, that no powerful enemy and destroyer might take Babylon, that the line of battle might not approach Imgur-Bel, the wall of Babylon, that which no former king had done [I did]; at the enclosure of Babylon I made an enclosure of a strong wall on the east side. I dug a moat, I reached the level of the water. I then saw that the wall which my father had prepared was too small in its construction. I built with bitumen and brick a mighty wall which, like a mountain, could not be moved and connected it with the wall of my father; I laid its foundations on the breast of the under-world; its top I raised up like a mountain. Along this wall to strengthen it I constructed a third and as the base of a protecting wall I laid a foundation of bricks and built it on the breast of the under-world and laid its foundation. The fortifications of Esagila and Babylon I strengthened and established the name of my reign forever." —*Archaeology and the Bible*, by G. Barton, 1949, pp. 478, 479.

The foregoing harmonizes with Nebuchadnezzar's boast made just before he lost his sanity: "Is not this Babylon the Great, that I myself have built for the royal house with the strength of my might and for the dignity of my majesty?" (Da 4:30) But when, in fulfillment of his divinely sent dream about the chopped-down tree, his reasoning powers were restored, Nebuchadnezzar had to acknowledge that Jehovah is able to humiliate those walking in pride.—Da 4:37; see MADNESS.

Very Religious. The indications are that Nebuchadnezzar was extremely religious, building and beautifying the temples of numerous Babylonian deities. Particularly was he devoted to the worship of Marduk, the chief god of Babylon. To him Nebuchadnezzar gave credit for his military victories. Trophies of war, including the sacred vessels of Jehovah's temple, appear to have been deposited in the temple of Marduk (Merodach). (Ezr 1:7; 5:14) Says an inscription of Nebuchadnezzar: "For thy glory, O exalted MERODACH a house have I made. . . . May it receive within itself the abundant tribute of the Kings of nations and of all peoples!"—*Records of the Past: Assyrian and Egyptian Monuments*, London, 1875, Vol. V, p. 135.

The image of gold set up by Nebuchadnezzar in the Plain of Dura was perhaps dedicated to Marduk and designed to promote religious unity in the empire. Enraged over the refusal of Shadrach, Meshach, and Abednego to worship this image even after being given a second opportunity, Nebuchadnezzar commanded that they be thrown into a fiery furnace heated seven times hotter than usual. However, when these three Hebrews were delivered by Jehovah's angel, Nebuchadnezzar was forced to say that "there does not exist another god that is able to deliver like this one." —Da 3.

Nebuchadnezzar also appears to have relied heavily on divination in planning his military moves. Ezekiel's prophecy, for example, depicts the king of Babylon as employing divination in deciding whether to go against Rabbah of Ammon or against Jerusalem.—Eze 21:18-23.

NEBUSHAZBAN (Neb·u·shaz'ban) [from Akkadian, meaning "O Nebo, Deliver Me!"]. The Rabsaris, chief court official, in the forces of Nebuchadnezzar that destroyed Jerusalem in 607 B.C.E. Nebushazban was one of several princes that directed the release of Jeremiah. (Jer 39:13, 14) Either Nebushazban is referred to by his title or else another man was also called Rabsaris in the group that sat down in the Middle Gate after the Babylonians first broke through Jerusalem's wall. —Jer 39:2, 3.

NEBUZARADAN (Neb·u'zar·ad'an) [from Babylonian, meaning "Nebo Has Given Offspring"]. Chief of the bodyguard and principal figure in Nebuchadnezzar's forces at the actual destruction of Jerusalem in 607 B.C.E. It does not appear that Nebuzaradan was present during the initial siege and breakthrough of Jerusalem, for it was about a month later that he "came to Jerusalem," after King Zedekiah had been brought to Nebuchadnezzar and blinded.—2Ki 25:2-8; Jer 39:2, 3; 52:6-11.

From outside the city, Nebuzaradan directed the Babylonian operations of destroying the city, which began "on the seventh day of the month" (the fifth month, Ab), and which included looting the temple treasures, wrecking the wall, dealing with the captives, and allowing some of the lowly ones to remain. (2Ki 25:8-20; Jer 39:8-10; 43:5, 6; 52:12-26) Three days later, on the tenth day of the month, it appears that Nebuzaradan "came *into* Jerusalem" ("entered Jerusalem," *RS, JB*) and, after an inspection, put a torch to the house of Jehovah and reduced the city to ashes. (Jer 52:12, 13) Josephus observed that it was on the very same day, the *tenth* day of the fifth month, when Solomon's temple was burned, that the temple rebuilt by Herod was also burned, in 70 C.E.—*The Jewish War*, VI, 250 (iv, 5); VI, 268 (iv, 8); see AB.

Nebuzaradan, under orders from Nebuchadnezzar, released Jeremiah and spoke to him kindly, letting him choose what he would do, offering to look after him and granting him some supplies. Nebuzaradan was also spokesman for the king of Babylon in appointing Gedaliah governor over those remaining. (2Ki 25:22; Jer 39:11-14; 40:1-7; 41:10) About five years later, 602 B.C.E., Nebuzaradan took other Jews into exile, apparently those who had fled to surrounding territories.—Jer 52:30.

NECHO(H) (Ne'cho[h]). A pharaoh of Egypt contemporaneous with Judean King Josiah. According to the Greek historian Herodotus (II, 158,

159; IV, 42), Nechos (Necho) was the son of Psam-metichus (Psammetichos, Psamtik I) and succeeded his father as ruler of Egypt. Although beginning construction work on a canal linking the Nile with the Red Sea, he did not complete this project. However, he did send a Phoenician fleet on a voyage around Africa. This journey was successfully completed in three years.

Toward the close of Josiah's 31-year reign (659-629 B.C.E.), Pharaoh Necho was on his way to help the Assyrians at the river Euphrates. At that time Josiah disregarded "the words of Necho from the mouth of God" and was mortally wounded while attempting to turn the Egyptian forces back at Megiddo. About three months later, Pharaoh Necho took Jehoahaz, Josiah's successor to the throne, captive and made 25-year-old Eliakim his vassal, changing the new ruler's name to Jehoiakim. Necho also imposed a heavy fine on the kingdom of Judah. (2Ch 35:20–36:4; 2Ki 23:29-35) At Carchemish, between three and four years later (625 B.C.E.), Necho's forces suffered defeat at the hands of the Babylonians under the command of Nebuchadnezzar.—Jer 46:2.

NECK. The part of a human or an animal that connects the head with the rest of the body. The Hebrew terms for neck evidently emphasize its skeletal structure that can be broken (Ex 13:13; 1Sa 4:18) or the back part of the neck. (Ge 49:8; Jos 10:24) In the Bible the term "neck" is frequently used in a figurative way.

In Hebrew, one fleeing in defeat was literally said to turn his "neck" to the enemy (compare Jos 7:8), that is, the back of his neck. Therefore, to 'have one's hand on the back of the neck' of his enemies was to conquer, or subdue, them. (Ge 49:8; 2Sa 22:41; Ps 18:40) With similar significance, on monuments of Egypt and Assyria, monarchs are represented in battle scenes as treading on the necks of their enemies. Likewise, Joshua ordered his army commanders: "Come forward. Place your feet on the back of the necks of these kings."—Jos 10:24.

A yoke upon the neck indicated servitude, submission, or bondage. (Ge 27:40; Jer 30:8; Ac 15:10) The frequent expressions "stiff-necked" and 'hardened neck' represent a rebellious and obstinate spirit. As a warning to us, the Scriptures say that "a man repeatedly reproved but making his neck hard will suddenly be broken, and that without healing."—Pr 29:1; De 9:6, 13; 31:27; 2Ki 17:14; Ps 75:5; Isa 48:4.

Throat. The Hebrew word for "throat" evidently refers to the front part of the neck where the organs for speaking and swallowing are found.

(Ps 149:6; Jer 2:25) The importance of the discipline and authority of one's parents (and, by implication, the eminent value of God's commandments and laws) is emphasized by the admonition to 'bind them upon the throat,' where beautiful and precious ornaments were worn. (Pr 1:8, 9; 3:1-3; 6:20, 21) Walking with one's throat stretched forth can evidence haughtiness. (Isa 3:16) Of wicked men of lies and bloodshed, the Bible says: "In their mouth there is nothing trustworthy; . . . their throat is an opened burial place."—Ps 5:9; Ro 3:13.

NECKLACE. An ornamental chain or string of beads, gold, silver, coral, jewels, and the like, worn around the neck. Necklaces were anciently worn by women (Ca 1:10; 4:9; compare Eze 16:11) and even by men, especially those of high station. (Ge 41:41, 42; Da 5:7, 16, 17, 29) The Midianites of Gideon's day put necklaces on the necks of their camels, and from these necklaces, apparently, moon-shaped ornaments hung as pendants. (Jg 8:21, 26) Necklace-style chains were at times used for ornamentation, as for the temple pillars Jachin and Boaz.—2Ch 3:15-17.

Of boastful, wicked people it is said that "haughtiness has served as a necklace to them." (Ps 73:3, 6) On the other hand, the discipline of a father and the law of a mother are as a fine necklace to a son's throat.—Pr 1:8, 9.

NEDABIAH (Ned·a·bi'ah) [Jah Is Willing (Noble; Generous)]. Last-named son of King Jeconiah (Jehoiachin), born during Jeconiah's exile in Babylon. (1Ch 3:17, 18; 2Ki 24:15; Jer 29:1, 2, 4, 6) Nedabiah was a descendant of David of the tribe of Judah and an uncle of Zerubbabel, the postexilic governor.—1Ch 3:1, 17-19; Hag 1:1.

NEEDLE. A slender tool with a sharp point at one end and a hole, or eye, at the other; used for sewing with thread (or sometimes with leather strips) and for embroidering. (Ex 28:6; 35:34, 35; Ec 3:7; Lu 5:36) While bone needles and some made of ivory have been discovered at ancient sites, bronze needles were generally used. They are very similar to present-day needles. Bronze needles varying in length from approximately 4 to 14 cm (1.5 to 5.5 in.) have been found in Palestine. Some Egyptian bronze needles were from 8 to 9 cm (3 to 3.5 in.) long.

NEEDLE'S EYE. In an illustration pertaining to entry into the Kingdom, Jesus Christ said: "It is easier for a camel to get through a needle's eye than for a rich man to get into the kingdom of

The Negeb (the south of Judah), though generally a harsh terrain, at one time supported a sizable population

God." (Mt 19:24; Mr 10:25) Some have held the needle's eye to be a small gate through which a camel, if relieved of its load, could pass with difficulty. However, the Greek word for "needle" found at Matthew 19:24 and Mark 10:25 (*rhaphis'*) is drawn from a verb meaning "sew." Also, the Greek word appearing in the parallel passage of Luke 18:25 (*be·lo'ne*) is used to refer to a literal surgical needle. Regarding these Greek terms *Vine's Expository Dictionary of Old and New Testament Words* notes: "The idea of applying 'the needle's eye' to small gates seems to be a modern one; there is no ancient trace of it. The Lord's object in the statement is to express human impossibility and there is no need to endeavour to soften the difficulty by taking the needle to mean anything more than the ordinary instrument." —1981, Vol. 3, p. 106.

As a hyperbole, the illustration emphasized how difficult it would be for rich men not simply to begin serving God but actually to enter into the Kingdom.—1Ti 6:17-19; Lu 13:24.

NEGEB (Neg'eb) [South]. The Hebrew word *ne'ghev* is thought to be derived from a root meaning "be parched" and often denotes the semi-arid area S of the mountains of Judah. From the circumstance that this region lay S of Judah, *ne'ghev* also came to mean "south" and is used with reference to a southern side (Nu 35:5), a southern boundary (Jos 15:4), and a southern gate (Eze 46:9). In some translations a distinction between the geographic designation and the compass direction is not maintained, resulting in confusing renderings. An example of this is Genesis 13:1, where translating *ne'ghev* as "south" (*AS, KJ, Le*)

makes it appear that Abraham went southward out of Egypt, when actually his direction was northward through the Negeb to Bethel. But this difficulty has been eliminated in many modern translations.—*AT, JB, NW, RS.*

Topography. The Negeb of ancient times seems to have embraced an area extending from the district of Beer-sheba in the N to Kadesh-barnea in the S. (Ge 21:14; Nu 13:17, 22; 32:8) The prophet Isaiah described this region as a land of hard conditions, a haunt of lions, leopards, and snakes. (Isa 30:6) In the northern section, occasional springs, wells, and pools are found, and the tamarisk is one of the few trees that thrives there. (Ge 21:33) To the SW of Beer-sheba lie two small areas and one relatively large area of sand dunes. Much of the Negeb is a plateau between 450 and 600 m (1,500 and 2,000 ft) above sea level, with peaks up to 1,050 m (3,440 ft) in elevation. To the S and E of Beer-sheba there are rugged ridges, generally running from E to W.

History. The cisterns, terrace walls, and ruins of many towns that have been found in the Negeb indicate that the area anciently supported a considerable population. Here the patriarchs Abraham and Isaac found pasturage for their large flocks. (Ge 13:1, 2; 20:1; 24:62) And in Abraham's time the Elamite king Chedorlaomer, with his three allies, defeated the inhabitants of the Negeb.—Ge 14:1-7.

Centuries afterward, the Israelite spies sent by Moses entered the Promised Land from the Negeb, which at that time was inhabited by the Amalekites. (Nu 13:17, 22, 29) Under the leadership of Joshua, all the inhabitants of the Negeb were defeated (Jos 10:40; 11:16) and cities in this region became part of the territory of the tribe of Simeon. (Jos 19:1-6) Also, the nomadic Kenites, who were related to Moses through marriage, took up residence in the Negeb. (Jg 1:16; compare 1Sa 15:6, 7.) The Israelites evidently did not maintain control over the area. Over the years there were repeated clashes with the Canaanites of the Negeb and particularly with the Amalekites. (Jg 1:9; 6:3; 1Sa 15:1-9; 30:1-20) From the city of Ziklag, given to him by the Philistine king Achish, David made raids upon the Geshurites, the Girzites, and the Amalekites of the Negeb. (1Sa 27:5-8) Apparently not until David's reign as king, after the defeat of the Edomites, did Israel gain complete control of the Negeb. (2Sa 8:13, 14) The later Judean king Uzziah evidently built towers and hewed out cisterns in this region.—2Ch 26:10.

After the destruction of Jerusalem by the Babylonians, Obadiah foretold that the Israelites would be restored to their land, including the Negeb.—Ob 19, 20.

NEGLECT. This word has the meaning of paying no attention to; disregarding; being remiss in care for or treatment of (someone or something); failure to carry out or perform (orders, duties, and so forth). The word can carry the connotation of willfulness or deliberateness in such failure, or merely of oversight through indifference or carelessness.

One of several Hebrew terms having the meaning "neglect" is the verb *pha·ra'*, which literally means "loosen." (Nu 5:18) It has the sense "go ungroomed" with regard to physical appearance (Le 10:6), "go unrestrained" with regard to conduct (Ex 32:25), and "neglect" or "shun" discipline. (Pr 13:18; 15:32; compare Ex 5:4, where it is rendered "leave off.") Another is the word *'a·zav'*, which literally means "abandon; leave." (De 29: 25; 1Ki 12:8) Thus, Nehemiah encouraged true worshipers not to "neglect" the house of the true God. (Ne 10:39; compare 13:11.) Another Hebrew term to designate neglect literally means "slackness," like that of a loose bow.—Jer 48:10; compare Ps 78:57.

The Greek word *a·me·le'o* (from *a*, "not," and *me'lo*, "care for") contains more definitely the idea of unconcern, not caring, and not so much the thought of unintentional oversight or the overlooking of something. After describing the severe punishment for disobedience to the Mosaic Law, the apostle Paul says: "How shall we escape if we have neglected [Gr., *a·me·le'san·tes*, "having been unconcerned (of)"] a salvation of such greatness in that it began to be spoken through our Lord . . . while God joined in bearing witness?" Here he indicates that it is not the matter of an oversight, but the lack of concern, a 'drifting away' (vs 1), disobedience to the word of God spoken through his only-begotten Son.—Heb 2:1-4, *Int*.

Matthew used a form of this Greek word in relating Jesus' illustration of the marriage feast. Those invited by the king to his son's wedding feast did not come. Why? Not through oversight, but, "unconcerned they went off, one to his own field, another to his commercial business." For this lack of concern they were counted unworthy.—Mt 22:5, 8.

The young man Timothy was given a heavy responsibility as an overseer in Ephesus. Paul admonished him: "Do not be neglecting [or, being careless of] the gift in you that was given you through a prediction and when the body of older men laid their hands upon you." It took much energetic action on Timothy's part to avoid being neglectful. He had to be absorbed in his reading, proper teaching, conduct, exhortation, and example, showing concern by constant, undeviating attention. Otherwise he could lose out by negligence, by lack of real concern for God's favor bestowed upon him.—1Ti 4:11-16, *Int*.

Paul quotes Jehovah's words concerning Israel wherein He spoke of the Law covenant, saying, "which covenant of mine they themselves broke, although I myself had husbandly ownership of them." (Jer 31:32) In place of "had husbandly ownership of them," the *Septuagint* reads: "had stopped caring for them." This doubtless explains why the quotation, at Hebrews 8:9, reads: "Because they did not continue in my covenant, so that I stopped caring [showed no concern] for them." Jehovah was certainly not negligent in the sense of carelessness or oversight; rather, he showed great concern for his covenant people until they disregarded his word and rebelled against him. Only then and on that basis was it that he "stopped caring [Gr., *e·me'le·sa*] for them."

NEHELAM (Ne·hel'am) [Of (Belonging to) Nehelam; or, possibly, The Dreamer]. Perhaps the home of the false prophet Shemaiah. (Jer 29:24, 31, 32) But a location by this name is unknown. Therefore some have suggested that "of Nehelam" may be a family designation and thus translate the phrase "the Nehelamite." (*KJ, NE*) Others believe that Jeremiah was perhaps making a play on the Hebrew word *cha·lam'*, meaning "dream." —Compare Jer 23:25.

NEHEMIAH (Ne·he·mi'ah) [Jah Comforts].

1. One who was possibly a leader among those returning from Babylonian exile with Zerubbabel. —Ezr 2:1, 2; Ne 7:7.

2. Son of Azbuk and prince over half the district of Beth-zur. Since the town of Beth-zur was located in the mountainous region of Judah (Jos 15:21, 48, 58), Nehemiah may have been a Judean. In 455 B.C.E., he shared in repairing the wall of Jerusalem.—Ne 3:16.

3. Son of Hacaliah and brother of Hanani; cupbearer to Persian King Artaxerxes (Longimanus) and, later, governor of the Jews, rebuilder of Jerusalem's wall, and writer of the Bible book bearing his name.—Ne 1:1, 2, 11; 2:1; 5:14, 16.

During the 20th year of King Artaxerxes, in the month Chislev (November-December), Nehemiah, while in Shushan the castle, received visitors, his brother Hanani and other men from Judah. Upon his inquiry, they told him about the bad plight of the Jews and that the wall and gates of Jerusalem were still in ruins. Nehemiah was moved to tears. For days thereafter he mourned, continually fasting and praying. He confessed Israel's sin and, on the basis of God's words to Moses (De 30:1-4), petitioned Jehovah to "make him an object of pity" before King Artaxerxes so that his plan to rebuild Jerusalem's wall might be successful.—Ne 1.

Later, in the month of Nisan (March-April), Nehemiah's prayers were answered. The king noticed that Nehemiah's face was gloomy and asked why. Nehemiah then informed him about the sorry state of affairs in Jerusalem. When asked what he was seeking to secure, Nehemiah, immediately praying to God, requested permission from the king to return and rebuild Jerusalem. The request was granted. Additionally, Nehemiah received letters from the king, entitling him to freedom of passage through the areas under the jurisdiction of governors W of the Euphrates River and also granting timber supplies for the project. With chiefs of the military force and horsemen, he departed for Jerusalem.—Ne 2:1-9.

Jerusalem's Wall Rebuilt. After being in Jerusalem for three days, Nehemiah, unknown to anyone except a few men who were with him, made a nighttime inspection of the city. While the rest were on foot, Nehemiah rode an animal, probably a horse or an ass. When the ruins became so extensive as to obstruct passage, Nehemiah dismounted and continued on foot.—Ne 2:11-16.

Following the completion of his survey, Nehemiah revealed his plan to the Jews, drawing to their attention Jehovah's hand in the matter. Encouraged thereby, they responded: "Let us get up, and we must build." Despite the derisive words of Sanballat the Horonite, Tobiah the Ammonite, and Geshem the Arabian, repair work began on about the fourth of Ab (July-August).—Ne 2:17-20; compare Ne 6:15.

As the work progressed, Sanballat and Tobiah continued to deride and mock the efforts of the Jews to repair the wall of Jerusalem. Nehemiah made this a subject of prayer, "and the people continued to have a heart for working." When the wall reached half its height, Sanballat, Tobiah, and neighboring peoples intensified their opposition to the point of conspiring to fight against Jerusalem. Nehemiah repeatedly received reports to that effect from Jews living near the city. Again Nehemiah manifested prayerful reliance on Jehovah. To meet the tense situation, he armed the workmen, arranged for others to stand guard, and outlined an alarm system. Nehemiah did not even take off his clothes at night, evidently to be ready to fight in the event of an alarm signal from the watch.—Ne 4.

Urgent as the situation was, Nehemiah was not too busy to give due consideration to the outcry of the Jews. Hearing their complaints that they were being oppressed by having to pay interest, he censured the nobles and deputy rulers, arranged a great assembly, and, after exposing this evil, instructed that the situation be rectified.—Ne 5:1-13.

It was after this that the enemies made attempts to stop the rebuilding work. Four times they tried to allure Nehemiah away from his project, but he informed them that he was unable to take time off from the great work that he was doing. Thereafter Sanballat sent an open letter that contained false charges and suggested that they meet for counsel. Nehemiah replied: "Things such as you are saying have not been brought about, but it is out of your own heart that you are inventing them." Trying still another trick, Tobiah and Sanballat hired a Jew to frighten Nehemiah into wrongfully hiding in the temple. Nehemiah, however, did not give way to fear, and the repair work came to a successful completion on the 25th day of Elul (August-September), just 52 days after construction work began. Nevertheless, Tobiah continued to send intimidating letters to Nehemiah.—Ne 6.

With the wall completed, Nehemiah directed his attention to the work of organizing the temple servants. Next he placed two men in command of the city, one of these being his brother Hanani. Nehemiah also gave instructions regarding the opening and the closing of the city gates and the guarding of them.—Ne 7:1-3.

Genealogical Enrollment. At this time Jerusalem's population was quite small. This seemingly was why God put it into Nehemiah's heart to assemble the nobles, deputy rulers, and people to get them enrolled genealogically, for the information procured thereby could have served as a basis for taking steps to increase the population of Jerusalem. Apparently while Nehemiah was giving consideration to this genealogical enrollment, he found the record of those who had returned from Babylonian exile with Zerubbabel.—Ne 7:4-7.

Law Observance Restored. It was probably at Nehemiah's direction that an assembly was held in the public square near the Water Gate. Although Ezra the priest evidently took the lead in giving instruction in the Law, Nehemiah also shared therein. (Ne 8:1-12) Next, the eight-day Festival of Booths was held. Two days later the Israelites convened again. During this assembly a general confession of Israel's sin was made. Thereafter a written confession contract was drawn up. This confession contract or "trustworthy arrangement" was attested by the princes, Levites, and priests. Nehemiah, "the Tirshatha [governor]," was the first to attest it by seal. (Ne 8:13—10:1) All the people agreed to refrain from intermarriage with foreigners, to observe the Sabbaths, and to support the temple service. Next, one person out of every ten was selected by lot to dwell permanently in Jerusalem.—Ne 10:28—11:1.

It was after this that the wall of Jerusalem was inaugurated. For the occasion Nehemiah appointed two large thanksgiving choirs and processions to make a tour of the wall in opposite directions. This was done, and all met at the temple to offer sacrifices. Additionally, men were appointed to be in charge of the contributions for the priests and Levites.—Ne 12:27-47.

About 12 years later, in the 32nd year of Artaxerxes, Nehemiah left Jerusalem. Upon his return, he found deplorable conditions among the Jews. Eliashib the high priest had made a dining hall in the courtyard of the temple for the use of Tobiah, the very man who earlier had viciously opposed the work of Nehemiah. Immediately Nehemiah took action. He threw all of Tobiah's furniture outside the dining hall and instructed that the dining hall be cleansed.

Additionally, Nehemiah took measures to ensure the contributions for the Levites and enforced strict Sabbath observance. He also administered discipline against those who had taken foreign wives, whose sons by these women were not even able to speak the Jewish tongue: "And I began to find fault with them and call down evil upon them and strike some men of them and pull out their hair and make them swear by God: 'You should not give your daughters to their sons, and you should not accept any of their daughters for your sons or yourselves.'"

Nehemiah's 'finding fault' with these men doubtless was his reproving and rebuking them by means of God's law, exposing their wrong action. These men were bringing the restored nation into disfavor with God, after God had kindly repatriated them from Babylon to restore true worship at Jerusalem. Nehemiah 'called down evil upon them,' meaning that he recited the judgments of God's law against such violators. He 'struck' them, probably not personally, but ordered them flogged as an official judicial action. He 'pulled out (a portion of) their hair.' This was a symbol of moral indignation and ignominy before the people. (Compare Ezr 9:3.) Nehemiah then chased away the grandson of High Priest Eliashib, who had become a son-in-law of Sanballat the Horonite.—Ne 13:1-28.

Nehemiah, an Outstanding Example. Nehemiah stands out as a sterling example of faithfulness and devotion. He was unselfish, leaving behind a prominent position as cupbearer in the courtyard of Artaxerxes to undertake the rebuilding of Jerusalem's walls. As there were many enemies, Nehemiah willingly exposed himself to danger in behalf of his people and true worship. Not only did he direct the work of repairing the wall of Jerusalem but he also had an active, personal share in the task. He wasted no time, was courageous and fearless, relied fully on Jehovah, and was discreet in what he did. Zealous for true worship, Nehemiah knew God's law and applied it. He was concerned about building up the faith of his fellow Israelites. He showed himself to be a man who manifested a proper fear of Jehovah God. Though enforcing God's law zealously, he did not domineer over others for selfish benefit but showed concern for the oppressed. Never did he demand the bread due the governor. Instead, he provided food for a considerable number of persons at his own expense. (Ne 5:14-19) Appropriately Nehemiah could pray: "Do remember me, O my God, for good."—Ne 13:31.

NEHEMIAH, BOOK OF.

A book of the Hebrew Scriptures that primarily relates events occurring shortly before and during Nehemiah's governorship in Judah. (Ne 5:14; 13:6, 7) The opening words of this inspired account identify the writer as "Nehemiah the son of Hacaliah" (1:1), and much of it is written in the first person.

Time Covered and Time of Writing. The month of Chislev (November-December) of a certain 20th year is the reference point with which the historical narrative begins. (Ne 1:1) As is evident from Nehemiah 2:1, this 20th year must be that of Artaxerxes' reign. Obviously, the 20th year in this case is not reckoned as starting in Nisan (March-April), for Chislev of the 20th year could not then precede Nisan (mentioned at Ne 2:1) of the same 20th year. So it may be that Nehemiah used his own count of time, reckoning the lunar year as beginning with Tishri (September-October), which month Jews today recognize as the beginning of their civil year. Another possibility is that the reign of the king was reckoned from the actual date that the monarch ascended the throne. This could be so even though the Babylonian scribes continued to reckon the years of the Persian king's reign on their customary basis of a Nisan-to-Nisan count, as their cuneiform tablets show they did.

Reliable historical evidence and the fulfillment of Bible prophecy point to 455 B.C.E. as the year in which Nisan of the 20th year of Artaxerxes' reign fell. (See PERSIA, PERSIANS [The Reigns of Xerxes and of Artaxerxes].) Accordingly, the Chislev preceding Nisan of that 20th year would fall in 456 B.C.E., and the 32nd year of Artaxerxes' reign (the last date mentioned in Nehemiah [13:6]) would include part of 443 B.C.E. Therefore, the book of Nehemiah covers a period from Chislev of 456 B.C.E. until sometime after 443 B.C.E.

It was in the 32nd year of Artaxerxes' reign that Nehemiah left Jerusalem. Upon his return, he found that the Jews were not supporting the priests and Levites, the Sabbath law was being violated, many had married foreign women, and the offspring of the mixed marriages did not even know how to speak the language of the Jews. (Ne 13:10-27) For conditions to have deteriorated to this point indicates that Nehemiah's absence entailed a considerable period. But there is no way to

HIGHLIGHTS OF NEHEMIAH

Events surrounding the rebuilding of the walls of Jerusalem and the subsequent clearing out of wrong practices from among the Jews

Covers a period that begins more than 80 years after the Jews returned from exile in Babylon

Jerusalem's walls are rebuilt in the face of opposition

In Shushan, Nehemiah learns about the ruined state of Jerusalem's wall; he prays for Jehovah's support, then asks the Persian monarch Artaxerxes for permission to go and rebuild the city and its wall; Artaxerxes consents (1:1–2:9)

Arriving in Jerusalem, Nehemiah inspects the ruined walls by night; afterward he reveals to the Jews his purpose to rebuild (2:11-18)

Sanballat, Tobiah, and Geshem—foreigners all—oppose the rebuilding; first they try ridicule, then they conspire to fight against Jerusalem; Nehemiah arms the workers, and they continue building (2:19–4:23)

Plots against Nehemiah himself fail, and the wall is completed in 52 days (6:1-19)

The wall is inaugurated; at the ceremony two thanksgiving choirs and processions march in opposite directions on top of the wall and meet at the temple; there is great rejoicing (12:27-43)

The affairs of Jerusalem are put in order

After the wall is completed, Nehemiah secures Jerusalem with gates and assigns duties to gatekeepers, singers, and Levites; he appoints Hanani and Hananiah to be in charge of the city (7:1-3)

Nehemiah sets out to make a genealogical record of the people; he finds the book of genealogical enrollment of those returning from Babylon with Zerubbabel; priests that cannot establish their genealogy are barred 'until the priest with Urim and Thummim stands up' (7:5-73)

Jerusalem is underpopulated, so one out of every ten of the people is designated by lot to reside in the city (7:4; 11:1, 2)

Efforts are made to improve the spiritual condition of the Jews

Wealthy Jews agree to make restoration to their poor brothers, whom they have wrongly charged interest on loans (5:1-13)

At a public assembly, Ezra reads the Law and certain Levites share in explaining it; the people weep but are encouraged to rejoice because the day is holy; they rejoice, too, because they understand what has been read to them (8:1-12)

The next day, from their reading of the Law, the people learn about celebrating the Festival of Booths; they follow through by observing the feast with great rejoicing (8:13-18)

Next, there is a gathering during which the people confess their national sins and review Jehovah's dealings with Israel; they also make an oath to keep the Law, to refrain from intermarriage with foreigners, and to accept obligations for maintaining the temple and its services (9:1–10:39)

Following the inauguration of the wall, there is another public reading from the Law; when they discern that Ammonites and Moabites should not be allowed into the congregation, they begin to separate "all the mixed company" from Israel (13:1-3)

After a prolonged absence, Nehemiah returns to Jerusalem and finds that things have deteriorated; he cleanses the dining halls, directs that tithes be contributed for the support of the Levites and singers, enforces Sabbath keeping, and reproves those who have married foreign women (13:4-30)

determine just how long after 443 B.C.E. Nehemiah completed the book bearing his name.

Agreement With Other Bible Books. The book of Nehemiah exalts Jehovah God. It reveals him to be the Creator (Ne 9:6; compare Ge 1:1; Ps 146:6; Re 4:11), a God who answers the sincere prayers of his servants (Ne 1:11–2:8; 4:4, 5, 15, 16; 6:16; compare Ps 86:6, 7), and the Defender of his people (Ne 4:14, 20; compare Ex 14:14, 25). He is "a God of acts of forgiveness, gracious and merciful, slow to anger and abundant in loving-kindness" (Ne 9:17; compare Nu 14:18), "the God of the heavens, the God great and fear-inspiring, keeping the covenant and loving-kindness toward those loving him and keeping his commandments."—Ne 1:5; compare De 7:9, 10, 21.

Numerous allusions to the Law are found in the book of Nehemiah. These involve the calamities to result from disobedience and the blessings to come from repentance (Le 26:33; De 30:4; Ne 1:7-9), loans (Le 25:35-38; De 15:7-11; Ne 5:2-11), marriage alliances with foreigners (De 7:3; Ne 10:30), Sabbaths, the release from debts (Ex 20:8; Le 25:4; De 15:1, 2; Ne 10:31), the altar fire (Le 6:13; Ne 10:34), the Festival of Booths (De 31:10-13; Ne 8:14-18), and the entry of Moabites and Ammonites into the congregation of Israel (De 23:3-6; Ne 13:1-3), as well as tithes, firstfruits, and contributions.—Ex 30:16; Nu 18:12-30; Ne 10:32-39.

There is also historical information in this book that is found elsewhere in the Hebrew Scriptures. (Ne 9:7-35; 13:26; compare Ne 13:17, 18 with Jer 17:21-27.) And contemporary history in the account illustrates other Biblical passages. Psalms 123 and 129 find a historical parallel in what was experienced by Nehemiah and the other Jews in connection with their rebuilding of the wall of Jerusalem. (Ne 4:1-5, 9; 6:1-14) Jehovah's causing Artaxerxes to do His will by granting Nehemiah's request to rebuild the wall of Jerusalem historically illustrates Proverbs 21:1: "A king's heart is as streams of water in the hand of Jehovah. Everywhere that he delights to, he turns it."—Ne 2:4-8.

Both the book of Ezra (2:1-67) and the book of Nehemiah (7:6-69) list the number of men from various families or houses who returned from Babylonian exile with Zerubbabel. The accounts harmonize in giving 42,360 as the total number of males among the returned exiles, apart from slaves and singers. (Ezr 2:64; Ne 7:66) However, there are differences in the numbers given for each family or house, and the individual figures in both listings yield a total of far less than 42,360. Many scholars would attribute these variations to

scribal errors. While this aspect cannot be completely ignored, there are other possible explanations for the differences.

It may be that Ezra and Nehemiah based their listings on different sources. For example, Ezra could have used a document listing those who enrolled to return to their homeland, whereas Nehemiah might have copied from a record listing those who actually did return. Since there were priests who were unable to establish their genealogy (Ezr 2:61-63; Ne 7:63-65), it is not unreasonable to conclude that many of the other Israelites faced the same problem. Consequently, the 42,360 men could be the combined total of the number from each family plus many others who were unable to establish their ancestry. Later, however, some may have been able to establish their correct genealogy. This could explain how a fluctuation in numbers might still give the same total.

NEHILOTH (Ne'hi·loth). A transliteration of *nechi·lohth'*, a Hebrew term of uncertain derivation and meaning, occurring only in the superscription of Psalm 5. Nehiloth appears to be a musical expression, and many believe that it refers to a wind instrument, linking it with a Hebrew root related to *cha·lil'* (flute). However, the phrase "for Nehiloth" may designate a melody. The Greek *Septuagint* and the Latin *Vulgate* render the term "[for] her who inherits."

NEHUM (Ne'hum). Apparently an alternate spelling for Rehum, one of the men returning from Babylonian exile with Zerubbabel.—Ezr 2:2; Ne 7:7.

NEHUSHTA (Ne·hush'ta). Daughter of Elnathan of Jerusalem and wife of King Jehoiakim. When the first captives were taken to Babylon in 617 B.C.E. after the three-month rule of her son Jehoiachin, Nehushta was taken along and likely remained there the rest of her life.—2Ki 24:6, 8, 12; Jer 29:2.

NEIEL (Ne·i'el). A city of Asher (Jos 19:24, 27), identified with Khirbet Ya'nin (Horvat Ya'anin), about 15 km (9.5 mi) ESE of Acco.

NEIGHBOR. A person living nearby, whether friend or enemy; or, viewed spiritually, a person who demonstrates to others the love and kindness that the Scriptures command, even though he lives at a distance or is not a relative or an associate. The Hebrew word rendered "neighbor" is *sha·khen'*, which has reference to location, either of cities or of persons, and includes friends and enemies.—Jer 49:18; Ru 4:17; Ps 79:4, 12.

Other associated Hebrew terms that vary slightly in connotation give us a broader view of the relationships expressed in the Hebrew Scriptures. *Re'a'* means "fellow, companion, friend" and can apply to closeness of relationship, but it generally means one's fellowman or fellow countryman, whether he is a close associate, lives nearby or not. In most of its uses in the Scriptures it applies to a fellow member of the commonwealth of Israel or to one residing in Israel. (Ex 20:16; 22:11; De 4:42; Pr 11:9) *'A·mith'* is rendered "associate" and is used often in the sense of one with whom a person has some dealings. (Le 6:2; 19:15, 17; 25:14, 15) *Qa·rohv'*, meaning "near, at hand, related to," has reference to place, time, or persons; it can imply a more intimate relationship than "neighbor" and is thus rendered 'intimate or close acquaintance.' (Ex 32:27; Jos 9:16; Ps 15:3; 38:11; Eze 23:5) No one English word can express fully all these shades of meaning.

Similarly, in the Greek Scriptures there are three words with slightly different flavor that are usually translated "neighbor": *gei'ton,* "one living in the same land" (Lu 14:12; Joh 9:8); *pe·ri'oi·kos,* an adjective meaning "dwelling around," used as a noun (plural) at Luke 1:58; *ple·si'on,* meaning "near," used with the article *ho* (the), literally, "the (one) near." (Ro 13:10; Eph 4:25) Of these Greek words, *Vine's Expository Dictionary of Old and New Testament Words* says: "[These words] have a wider range of meaning than that of the Eng. word neighbour. There were no farmhouses scattered over the agricultural areas of Palestine; the populations, gathered in villages, went to and fro to their toil. Hence domestic life was touched at every point by a wide circle of neighbourhood. The terms for neighbour were therefore of a very comprehensive scope. This may be seen from the chief characteristics of the privileges and duties of neighbourhood as set forth in Scripture, (*a*) its helpfulness, e.g., . . . Luke 10:36; (*b*) its intimacy, e.g., Luke 15:6, 9 . . . Heb. 8:11; (*c*) its sincerity and sanctity, e.g., . . . Rom. 13:10; 15:2; Eph. 4:25; Jas. 4:12."—1981, Vol. 3, p. 107.

Bad Neighbors. However, some living nearby might be evil neighbors, as were the neighbor nations around Israel. When Jerusalem's temple was destroyed by Babylonian hands in 607 B.C.E., these nations, such as Edom, rejoiced, even surrendering fugitive Jews to their enemies. (Ps 137:7; Ob 8-14; Mic 4:11) The psalmist was moved to write: "We have become a reproach to our neighbors [a plural form of *sha·khen'*], a derision and a jeering to those round about us." He prayed: "Repay to our neighbors [a plural form of *sha·khen'*] seven times into their bosom their re-proach with which they have reproached you." Because Jehovah 'dwelt' among Israel, he spoke of the nations that opposed his people as "all my bad neighbors, who are touching the hereditary possession that I caused my people, even Israel, to possess."—Ps 79:4, 12; Jer 12:14; compare Ps 68:16.

Love Toward Neighbor Commanded. The Bible, throughout, instructs one to exercise love, kindness, generosity, and helpfulness toward one's neighbor, whether he be merely a dweller nearby, an associate, a companion, an intimate acquaintance, or a friend. The Law commanded: "With justice you should judge your associate [form of *'a·mith'*]. . . . You must not hate your brother in your heart. You should by all means reprove your associate, that you may not bear sin along with him . . . and you must love your fellow [form of *re'a'*] as yourself." (Le 19:15-18) (In the Greek *Septuagint* the word *re'a'* is here translated by the Greek expression *ho ple·si'on.*) David commends the man who "has not slandered with his tongue. To his companion [form of *re'a'*] he has done nothing bad, and no reproach has he taken up against his intimate acquaintance [form of *qa·rohv'*]." (Ps 15:3) Repeated are the injunctions not to do harm to one's fellowman (*re'a'*), not even to despise him or to desire anything that belongs to him.—Ex 20:16; De 5:21; 27:24; Pr 14:21.

The apostle Paul said: "He that loves his fellowman has fulfilled the law." He then names some of the commandments of the Law and concludes: "and whatever other commandment there is, is summed up in this word, namely, 'You must love your neighbor [*ple·si'on*] as yourself.' Love does not work evil to one's neighbor [*ple·si'on*]; therefore love is the law's fulfillment." (Ro 13:8-10; compare Ga 5:14.) James calls the command to love one's neighbor as oneself "the kingly law." —Jas 2:8.

Second-greatest commandment. To a Jew who asked, "What good must I do in order to get everlasting life?" and who wanted to know which commandments to follow, Jesus named five of the Ten Commandments and added the injunction at Leviticus 19:18 when he said: "You must love your neighbor [*ple·si'on*] as yourself." (Mt 19:16-19) He also classified this injunction as the second most important in the Law—one of the two on which all the Law and the Prophets hung.—Mt 22:35-40; Mr 12:28-31; Lu 10:25-28.

Who is my neighbor? Jesus also deepened the appreciation of his hearers as to the meaning of the word *ple·si'on* when the same man, anxious to prove himself righteous, asked further: "Who really is my neighbor [*ple·si'on*]?" In Jesus' illustration of the merciful Samaritan he made it emphatic that even though one is living at a distance, or is not a relative or an associate, the *real neighbor* is the one who will exercise the love and kindness to another that the Scriptures command.—Lu 10:29-37.

In the Commonwealth of Israel. At Hebrews 8:11 a form of the Greek word *po·liʹtes*, "citizen," appears in most Greek texts; some late manuscripts read *ple·siʹon*. Paul here quotes from the restoration prophecy of Jeremiah 31:34, spoken to those in the commonwealth of Israel: "'And they will no more teach each one his *companion* [form of *reʹaʽ*] and each one his brother, saying, "Know Jehovah!" for they will all of them know me, from the least one of them even to the greatest one of them,' is the utterance of Jehovah." Paul applies it to the spiritual "holy nation," "the Israel of God," saying: "And they will by no means teach each one his *fellow citizen* and each one his brother . . . " Here the flavor of the original languages is kept better by the expression *companion* (for *reʹaʽ*) and *citizen* (for *po·liʹtes*), rather than *neighbor*.—1Pe 2:9; Ga 6:16.

Counsel From Proverbs. While a person is to help his neighbor and to love him, yet he must exercise caution not to make attempts to become the most intimate associate of his neighbor or fellowman—to avoid imposing or presuming upon him. The proverb couches the thought in these terms: "Make your foot rare at the house of your fellowman [form of *reʹaʽ*], that he may not have his sufficiency of you and certainly hate you."—Pr 25:17.

However, faith and trust in a companion, and the advisability of calling on such a person in time of need are counseled in the Proverbs: "Do not leave your own companion or the companion of your father, and do not enter the house of your own brother on the day of your disaster. Better is a neighbor [*sha·khenʹ*] that is near than a brother that is far away." (Pr 27:10) Here the writer seems to be saying that a close family friend is one to be valued and should be looked to for help rather than even so close a relative as a brother, if that brother is far away, because he may not be as ready or at least not in as favorable a position to render help as the family companion.

NEKODA (Ne·koʹda) [Speckled].

1. The forefather of a group of Nethinim who returned from Babylonian exile in 537 B.C.E.—Ezr 2:1, 43, 48; Ne 7:46, 50.

2. The forefather of a group "unable to tell the house of their fathers and their origin." (Ezr 2:59, 60; Ne 7:61, 62) Since the names of Delaiah and

Tobiah associated with Nekoda in these verses do not occur elsewhere in a list of returning exiles, it is assumed that this Nekoda is a person different from No. 1.

NEMUEL (Nemʹu·el).

1. First listed of Simeon's five sons and family head of the Nemuelites. (Nu 26:12-14; 1Ch 4:24) In the list of those who came into Egypt with Jacob he is called Jemuel.—Ge 46:8, 10; Ex 6:15.

2. Son of Eliab and great-grandson of Reuben. His brothers were the rebels Dathan and Abiram, whom the earth swallowed up.—Nu 26:5, 8, 9; De 11:6.

NEMUELITES (Nemʹu·el·ites) [Of (Belonging to) Nemuel]. A family of Simeon descended from Nemuel.—Nu 26:12.

NEPHEG (Neʹpheg).

1. Son of Izhar and brother of Korah and Zichri. Of the tribe of Levi, he was a cousin of Moses and Aaron.—Ex 6:16, 18, 20, 21.

2. One of King David's sons born at Jerusalem. —2Sa 5:13-15; 1Ch 3:5, 7; 14:3-6.

NEPHILIM (Nephʹi·lim) [Fellers; Those Who Cause [Others] to Fall Down]. This is a transliteration of the Hebrew word *nephi·limʹ*, plural in its three occurrences in the Bible. (Ge 6:4; Nu 13:33 [twice]) It evidently stems from the causative form of the Hebrew verb *na·phalʹ* (fall) as found, for example, in 2 Kings 3:19; 19:7.

The Bible account describing Jehovah's displeasure with men in the days of Noah before the Flood relates that "the sons of the true God" took for themselves wives from among the attractive daughters of men. It then mentions the presence of "Nephilim," saying: "The Nephilim proved to be in the earth in those days, and also after that, when the sons of the true God continued to have relations with the daughters of men and they bore sons to them, they were the mighty ones [Heb., *hag·gib·bo·rimʹ*] who were of old, the men of fame."—Ge 6:1-4.

Identity. Bible commentators, considering verse 4, have offered several suggestions as to the identity of these Nephilim. Some have thought that the derivation of the name indicates that the Nephilim had fallen from heaven, that is, that they were 'fallen angels' who mated with women to produce "mighty ones . . . the men of fame." Other scholars, focusing their attention particularly on the statement "and also after that" (vs 4), have said the Nephilim were not the 'fallen angels' or the "mighty ones," since the Nephilim "proved to be in the earth in those days" *before* the sons of

God had relations with women. These latter scholars hold the opinion that the Nephilim were simply wicked men like Cain—robbers, bullies, and tyrants who roamed the earth until they were destroyed by the Flood. Still another group, taking into consideration the context of verse 4, conclude that the Nephilim were not themselves angels, but were the hybrid offspring resulting from materialized angels having intercourse with the daughters of men.

Same as "gib·bo·rim'." Certain Bible translations adjust the location of the phrase "and also after that," placing it near the beginning of verse 4, thus identifying the Nephilim with the "mighty ones," the *gib·bo·rim'*, mentioned in the latter part of the verse. For example: "In those days, as well as afterward, there were giants [Heb., *han·nephi·lim'*] on the earth, who were born to the sons of the gods whenever they had intercourse with the daughters of men; these were the heroes [Heb., *hag·gib·bo·rim'*] who were men of note in days of old."—Ge 6:4, *AT;* see also *Mo, NIV,* and *TEV.*

The Greek *Septuagint* also suggests that both the "Nephilim" and "mighty ones" are identical by using the same word *gi'gan·tes* (giants) to translate both expressions.

Reviewing the account, we see that verses 1 to 3 tell of "the sons of the true God" taking wives and of Jehovah's statement that he was going to end his patience with men after 120 years. Verse 4 then speaks of the Nephilim proving to be in the earth "in those days," evidently the days when Jehovah made the statement. Then it shows that this situation continued "after that, when the sons of the true God continued to have relations with the daughters of men," and describes in more detail the results of the union of "the sons of the true God" with women.

Who were the 'sons of God' that fathered the Nephilim?

Who were "the sons of the true God" that were involved? Were they men who were worshipers of Jehovah (as distinguished from the general run of wicked mankind), as some claim? Evidently not. The Bible implies that their marriage to the daughters of men resulted in whipping up the badness in the earth. Noah and his three sons, along with their wives, were the only ones in God's favor and were the only ones preserved through the Deluge.—Ge 6:9; 8:15, 16; 1Pe 3:20.

Hence, if these "sons of the true God" were merely men, the question arises, Why were their offspring "men of fame" more than those of the wicked, or of faithful Noah? Also, the question might be asked, Why mention their marriage to the daughters of men as something special? Marriage and childbearing had been taking place for more than 1,500 years.

The sons of God mentioned at Genesis 6:2, therefore, must have been angels, spirit "sons of God." This expression is applied to angels at Job 1:6; 38:7. This view is supported by Peter, who speaks of "the spirits in prison, who had once been disobedient when the patience of God was waiting in Noah's days." (1Pe 3:19, 20) Also Jude writes of "the angels that did not keep their original position but forsook their own proper dwelling place." (Jude 6) Angels had the power to materialize in human form, and some angels did so to bring messages from God. (Ge 18:1, 2, 8, 20-22; 19:1-11; Jos 5:13-15) But heaven is the proper *abode* of spirit persons, and the angels there have positions of service under Jehovah. (Da 7:9, 10) To leave this abode to dwell on earth and to forsake their assigned service to have fleshly relations would be rebellion against God's laws, and perversion.

The Bible states that the disobedient angels are now "spirits in prison," having been 'thrown into Tartarus' and "reserved with eternal bonds under dense darkness for the judgment of the great day." This seems to indicate that they are greatly restricted, unable again to materialize as they did prior to the Flood.—1Pe 3:19; 2Pe 2:4; Jude 6.

Increased Wickedness. "The mighty ones who were of old, the men of fame" that were produced by these marriages, were not men of fame with God, for they did not survive the Flood, as did Noah and his family. They were "Nephilim," bullies, tyrants, who no doubt helped to make conditions worse. Their angelic fathers, knowing the construction of the human body and being able to materialize, were not creating life, but lived in these human bodies and, cohabiting with women, brought forth children. Their children, "mighty ones," were therefore unauthorized hybrids. Apparently the Nephilim did not, in turn, have children.

In Mythology. The fame and dread of the Nephilim, it appears, gave rise to many mythologies of heathen people who, after the confusion of languages at Babel, were scattered throughout the earth. Though the historical forms of the Genesis account were greatly distorted and embellished, there was a remarkable resemblance in these ancient mythologies (those of the Greeks being only one example), in which gods and goddesses mated with humans to produce superhuman heroes and fearful demigods having god-man characteristics. —See GREECE, GREEKS (Greek Religion).

A Report Intended to Terrorize. The ten spies who brought back to the Israelites in the wilderness a false report on the land of Canaan declared: "All the people whom we saw in the midst of it are men of extraordinary size. And there we saw the Nephilim, the sons of Anak, who are from the Nephilim; so that we became in our own eyes like grasshoppers, and the same way we became in their eyes." No doubt there were some large men in Canaan, as other scriptures show, but never except in this "bad report," which was carefully couched in language designed to strike terror and cause panic among the Israelites, are they called Nephilim.—Nu 13:31-33; 14:36, 37.

NEPHTOAH (Neph·to′ah). The name associated with a spring on the boundary between Judah and Benjamin. (Jos 15:1, 9; 18:11, 15) This spring is usually identified with the one at Lifta ('En Neftoah), to the E of Kiriath-jearim and about 4 km (2.5 mi) WNW of the Temple Mount in Jerusalem. Although this identification would agree with Joshua 15:9, Joshua 18:15, 16 appears to place "the spring of the waters of Nephtoah" W of Kiriath-jearim. Bible translators have variously handled this seeming discrepancy. Following the reading of the Greek *Septuagint, The Jerusalem Bible* replaces "westward" with "towards Gasin." In the *Revised Standard Version* the text has been changed in harmony with Joshua 15:9 and reads "to Ephron" instead of "westward." Ronald A. Knox translates the Hebrew word *yam′mah* (westward) according to its literal meaning as "seaward" and, in a footnote, explains: "This ought to mean westwards, towards the Mediterranean, but it seems quite clear that at this point the boundary of Benjamin turned eastwards; and the sea is presumably the Dead Sea, its eastward limit."

NEPHUSHESIM (Ne·phush′e·sim), **NEPHUSIM** (Ne·phu′sim). A family head of Nethinim, some of whose descendants returned from Babylonian exile with Zerubbabel, 537 B.C.E. (Ne 7:6, 7, 46, 52; Ezr 2:43, 50) Possibly he was of Ishmaelite ancestry through the Naphish tribe.—Ge 25:13-15; 1Ch 1:29-31; 5:19.

NER [Lamp]. A Benjamite, son of Abiel (Jeiel), father of Abner and Kish, and grandfather of King Saul.—1Sa 14:50, 51; 1Ch 8:33; 9:39; see ABIEL No. 1.

NEREUS (Ne′reus). A brother who, with his sister, was included in Paul's greetings to the Roman congregation. (Ro 16:15) The name is also found on Roman inscriptions listing some of the emperor's household, as well as in legend.

NERGAL (Ner′gal). A Babylonian deity especially worshiped at Cuthah, a city that history says was dedicated to Nergal. The people of Cuth (Cuthah), whom the king of Assyria settled in the territory of Samaria, continued worshiping this deity. (2Ki 17:24, 30, 33) Some scholars suggest that Nergal was originally associated with fire and the heat of the sun and that later he came to be regarded as a god of war and hunting as well as a bringer of pestilence. The appellatives applied to Nergal in religious texts indicate that he was basically viewed as a destroyer. He is called "the raging king," "the violent one," and "the one who burns." Nergal also came to be regarded as the god of the underworld and the consort of Eresh-Kigal. The human-headed and winged lion is thought to have been the emblem of Nergal.

Nergal-sharezer the Rabmag, one of King Nebuchadnezzar's princes, was evidently named after this god.—Jer 39:3, 13.

NERGAL-SHAREZER (Ner′gal-shar·e′zer) [from Akkadian, meaning "May Nergal Protect the King"].

1. A Babylonian prince of Nebuchadnezzar's time.—Jer 39:3.

2. Another important prince in Nebuchadnezzar's forces at the overthrow of Jerusalem, distinguished from No. 1 by the added title Rabmag. It was this Rabmag who assisted in the release of Jeremiah.—Jer 39:3, 13, 14.

Because this name bears such a striking resemblance to that found in Babylonian inscriptions (*Nergal-shar-usur*), some scholars think this prince was Neriglissar (Greek form), believed to be the successor of King Evil-merodach (Awil-Marduk).—*Ancient Near Eastern Texts,* edited by J. Pritchard, 1974, p. 308.

NERI (Ne′ri) [from Heb., a shortened form of Neriah]. A descendant of King David through Nathan in the royal lineage of Jesus. According to Luke, Shealtiel was the son of Neri, yet Matthew says Jeconiah was the father of Shealtiel. (Mt 1:12; Lu 3:27) Perhaps Shealtiel married Neri's daughter, thus becoming his son-in-law. It was not uncommon in Hebrew genealogical listings to speak of a son-in-law as a son. Hence, both accounts are correct.

NERIAH (Ne·ri′ah) [My Lamp Is Jehovah]. Son of Mahseiah, and father of both Baruch, Jeremiah's secretary, and Seraiah, the one who read the denunciation of Babylon to that city.—Jer 32:12; 36:4, 8, 14, 32; 43:3, 6; 45:1; 51:59-64.

NERO. See CAESAR.

NEST

NEST. The place a bird or animal prepares for raising its young; also, a lodging, a retreat, or a snug, comfortable, cozy residence.—Pr 27:8; Isa 10:14; 16:2.

The nests of birds vary greatly in location, size, and construction, but each type suits better than any other the particular use for which it is designed. Locations of different varieties range from the earth or the sand (snakes are also said to have 'nests' on the ground or among rocks; Isa 34:15) to tufts of grass, bushes, rocks, trees, hollow tree trunks, seashore cliffs, mountains, crevices in man's buildings, even suspended over water between reeds. Among building materials used are twigs, leaves, seaweed, wool, cotton, hay, straw, moss, fur, feathers, the down of plants, horsehair, pieces of cloth, and so forth. In general, nests serve as protection from predators, as shelter from storms, and as insulation from heat and cold.

To impress on Job the wisdom of the Creator, Jehovah called attention to the eagle, that "builds its nest high up, that on a crag . . . resides and stays during the night upon the tooth of a crag and an inaccessible place." (Job 39:27, 28) And to illustrate God's loving care for Israel, Moses referred to the eagle that "stirs up its nest," evidently with reference to the manner in which an eagle urges and sometimes shoves the fledgling into the air to teach it to fly. Jehovah similarly brought Israel out of Egypt as a nation. He administered tender care to the young nation throughout the wilderness journey and while they were settling in the Promised Land, just as the eagle watches and cares for the young during their flying lessons.—De 32:11; see EAGLE.

The rock dove also builds its nest high in rocky places. The towering rocks in the vicinity of the Dead Sea provide numerous clefts and caves for its nests. Jeremiah may have had these secluded nests in mind in pronouncing judgment on Moab, who dwelt in this area: "Leave the cities and reside on the crag, you inhabitants of Moab, and become like the dove that makes its nest in the regions of the mouth of the hollow."—Jer 48:28; compare Balaam's utterance at Nu 24:21.

The thick foliage of the strong cedars of Lebanon served as an excellent nesting location for other birds; there was ample year-round shelter and concealment. The psalmist cited this as an example of God's marvelous provisions for the welfare of his creatures.—Ps 104:16, 17.

Under the Law, the Israelites were forbidden to take the eggs or the young from a nest and at the same time kill the mother. This prevented the cruelty of completely wiping out the family at one stroke. The mother was to be spared, to produce more young.—De 22:6, 7.

'Birds Have Roosts.' Certain translations render the Greek word *ka·ta·ske'no·sis* as "nest"; actually it refers to a 'resting-place or roost' where birds settle at night, not a nest for incubating eggs and rearing young. When a certain one of the scribes said to Jesus: "Teacher, I will follow you wherever you are about to go," Jesus replied: "Foxes have dens and birds of heaven have roosts, but the Son of man has nowhere to lay down his head." (Mt 8:19, 20; Lu 9:57, 58) Here Jesus pointed out that to be his follower the man would have to forsake the idea of having the comforts and conveniences commonly enjoyed, and must put his trust completely in Jehovah. This principle is reflected in the model prayer he taught his disciples: "Give us today our bread for this day," and his statement: "Thus, you may be sure, none of you that does not say good-bye to all his belongings can be my disciple."—Mt 6:11; Lu 14:33.

Figurative Usage. In judgment messages against Edom, God used the eagle's high nesting place as a symbol of Edom's literally high location in the mountains, as well as of its haughtiness and presumptuousness.—Jer 49:15-18; Ob 1-4; compare God's declaration against Babylon, at Hab 1:6; 2:6-11.

In prophesying against Jerusalem, Jeremiah referred to the loftiness of Lebanon's trees and the value of its cedarwood, used particularly by kings and rich men in construction of their houses. The palace of Judah's king and the government buildings at Jerusalem had been constructed largely of cedar. Hence Jeremiah spoke of the inhabitants of Jerusalem as those "dwelling in Lebanon, being nested in the cedars." But from this lofty position they were to be brought low.—Jer 22:6, 23.

A 'Compartment.' At Genesis 6:14, the Hebrew word *qin·nim'* ("nests") is translated "rooms" (*KJ*, *RS*), "cabins" (*AT*), and "compartments" (*NW*). Evidently these were relatively small compartments in the ark built by Noah and, similar to birds' nests, served as a protection and shelter through a critical time when men and animals were otherwise helpless.

NET. Generally, a fabric consisting of twine, thread, or rope, and woven into meshes. Nets were used for catching fish (Ec 9:12; Isa 19:8; Mt 4:18-21), birds (Pr 1:17), and other animals (Isa 51:20). Among the main materials used in their construction were flax, palm fiber, and papyrus.

Metal nets, however, served completely different purposes. Nets made from copper were used as ornamentation for the capitals of the temple pillars Jachin and Boaz (see CAPITAL), and a copper net, or network, served as a grating for the altar of sacrifice.—Ex 27:4, 5; 38:4; 1Ki 7:16-18, 41, 42; Jer 52:22, 23.

Figurative Use. "Net" is often used figuratively in the Bible to represent means for ensnaring others—encircling them and taking them captive or bringing calamity upon them. (Job 18:8; 19:6; Ps 66:11; La 1:13; Eze 12:13; 17:20; 19:8; 32:3; Ho 5:1; 7:12; Mic 7:2) The means used by the Chaldeans to conquer nations as they extended their dominion over a wide area is likened to a dragnet. (Hab 1:6, 15-17) Also, flattery and the scheming heart of an immoral woman are compared to nets. (Pr 29:5; Ec 7:26) The psalmist expressed the confidence that Jehovah would deliver him from entangling nets (Ps 25:15; 31:4; 140:5, 12) and that those spreading out such nets would themselves be ensnared thereby.—Ps 9:15; 35:7, 8; 57:6; 141:10.

Concerning the construction and use of various nets, see BIRDCATCHER; DRAGNET; HUNTING AND FISHING.

NETAIM   (Ne·ta′im). A Judean site inhabited by some potters who were in the king's service. (1Ch 4:21-23) Today the location of Netaim is unknown.

NETHANEL   (Ne·than′el) [God Has Given].

1. Chieftain of the tribe of Issachar; son of Zuar. (Nu 1:8, 16) In this office, he supervised the wilderness census for Issachar, presented his gift when the tabernacle altar was inaugurated, and led an army of 54,400.—Nu 2:5, 6; 7:11, 18-23; 10:15.

2. Fourth-named son of Jesse and older brother of King David.—1Ch 2:13-15.

3. A Levite whose son Shemaiah was a secretary during David's reign.—1Ch 24:6.

4. A priest who played a trumpet before the ark of the covenant in the procession that accompanied it to Jerusalem.—1Ch 15:24.

5. A Levite gatekeeper assigned in David's time to the S of the sanctuary where the storehouses were located; fifth son of Obed-edom.—1Ch 26:4, 8, 15.

6. A prince sent by King Jehoshaphat to teach Jehovah's law in the cities of Judah.—2Ch 17:7-9.

7. A chief Levite who contributed animals for sacrifice at Josiah's great Passover celebration. —2Ch 35:9, 18, 19.

8. Head of the priestly paternal house of Jedaiah in the days of Jeshua's successor Joiakim. —Ne 12:12, 21.

9. A priest among those sons of Pashhur who had taken foreign wives but who sent them away at Ezra's urging. (Ezr 10:22, 44) Possibly the same as No. 10.

10. A musician in one of the processions that celebrated the rebuilding of the wall of Jerusalem in Nehemiah's day. (Ne 12:31, 35, 36) Possibly identical with No. 9.

NETHANIAH   (Neth·a·ni′ah) [Jehovah Has Given].

1. Third named of Asaph's four sons chosen by David for musical service at the sanctuary. Of the 24 divisions, Nethaniah headed the fifth.—1Ch 25:1, 2, 12.

2. A Levite of the corps composed of priests, Levites, and princes who were sent out by King Jehoshaphat in the third year of his reign to teach Jehovah's law in the cities of Judah.—2Ch 17:7-9.

3. Son of Shelemiah and father of Jehudi, who read Jeremiah's roll to King Jehoiakim in 625 B.C.E.—Jer 36:14, 21, 23.

4. The son of Elishama and father of Ishmael the murderer of Governor Gedaliah.—2Ki 25:23, 25; Jer 40:8, 14, 15; 41:1-18.

NETHINIM   (Neth′i·nim) [Given Ones]. Non-Israelite temple slaves or ministers. (1Ch 9:2; Ezr 8:17) Representatives of 35 Nethinim families were among those returning from Babylonian exile with Zerubbabel in 537 B.C.E. (Ezr 2:1, 2, 43-54, 58; Ne 7:46-56, 60; the sons of Akkub, Hagab, and Asnah, listed by Ezra, are not mentioned by Nehemiah. They may have been combined under other family names.) Also, in 468 B.C.E., some of the Nethinim accompanied Ezra from Babylon to Jerusalem. (Ezr 7:1-7) Thereafter certain Nethinim shared in repairing Jerusalem's wall. (Ne 3:26) They also joined with the Israelites in a covenant to keep themselves free from marriage alliances with foreigners.—Ne 10:28-30.

Likely many of the Nethinim were descendants of the Gibeonites whom Joshua had constituted "gatherers of wood and drawers of water for the assembly and for Jehovah's altar." (Jos 9:23, 27) Apparently other Nethinim sprang from captives taken by King David and his princes. (Ezr 8:20; compare Ps 68:18.) The Nethinim belonging to the family of Meunim may have been descendants of captives taken by Judean King Uzziah. (2Ch 26:7; Ezr 2:50; Ne 7:52) Still another group, "the sons of Nephusim" (Nephushesim), may have been descendants of Ishmael through Naphish.—Ge 25:13-15; Ezr 2:50; Ne 7:52.

In postexilic times, the Nethinim resided in

Ophel, apparently near the temple area, as well as in other cities. (Ezr 2:70; Ne 3:26, 31; 7:73; 11:3, 21) On account of their temple work, Persian King Artaxerxes exempted them from paying tax, tribute, and toll.—Ezr 7:24.

NETOPHAH (Ne·to′phah) [from a root meaning "drip; drop"], **NETOPHATHITES** (Ne·toph′a·thites). A small village of Judah probably located at Khirbet Bedd Faluh, about 4 km (2.5 mi) SSE of Bethlehem, and its inhabitants. The Bible concerns itself primarily with the inhabitants, who, at first, were apparently related to those who settled in Bethlehem.—1Ch 2:54.

Among the Netophathites were David's mighty men Maharai and Heleb (Heled; Heldai), both of whom became heads of army divisions. (2Sa 23:8, 28, 29; 1Ch 11:26, 30; 27:13, 15) Some Netophathites were left in Judah after the general deportation to Babylon, and they supported Governor Gedaliah. (2Ki 25:23; Jer 40:8) A number of Netophathite descendants of those carried off to Babylon returned with Zerubbabel in 537 B.C.E. (Ezr 2:1, 2, 22; Ne 7:26) Some Levites who lived among the settlements of the Netophathites came to Jerusalem for the inauguration of the rebuilt wall. —1Ch 9:14, 16; Ne 12:27, 28.

NETTLE. Any of a variety of plants with saw-edged leaves that are usually thickly covered with stinging hairs containing an irritating liquid. When touched, the tips of the hairs break off, and the sharp broken ends penetrate the skin, causing the liquid to enter the wound. At least four varieties of nettles are known to exist in Palestine, the most common being the Roman nettle (*Urtica pilulifera*), which can attain a height of 1.8 m (6 ft) and is especially found amid ruins.

The Hebrew terms *cha·rul′* (Pr 24:31; Zep 2:9) and *qim·mohsh′* (Isa 34:13; Ho 9:6) are applied to plants that take over neglected fields and ruins. At Job 30:7, the reference to *cha·rul′* suggests tall plants. Another Hebrew word *sir·padh′* ("brier," *KJ;* "nettle," *Ro;* "stinging nettle," *NW*) is contrasted with myrtle.—Isa 55:13.

At Proverbs 24:31 a form of the word *qim·mohsh′* ("thistles," *AT;* "thorns," *KJ;* "weeds," *NW*) is viewed by some as being in parallel with *cha·rul′*. Therefore some scholars think *qim·mohsh′* denotes weeds generally; others believe that *cha·rul′* may be a generic term applying to brush. The translating of *cha·rul′* as "nettles" in Job 30:7 has also been questioned by some on the basis that people would not voluntarily seek shelter under nettles. In a waterless region, though, people might well avail themselves of the shade of tall

nettles or, because of hunger, be found gathering these plants for food. So the rendering is appropriate.

NEW COVENANT. See COVENANT.

NEW JERUSALEM. An expression that occurs two times, and only in the highly symbolic book of Revelation. (Re 3:12; 21:2) Near the end of that series of visions, and after seeing Babylon the Great destroyed, the apostle John says: "I saw also the holy city, New Jerusalem, coming down out of heaven from God and prepared as a bride adorned for her husband."—Re 21:2.

The Bride of the Lamb. In the light of other scriptures, the identity of New Jerusalem is made certain. She is "as a *bride*." Farther along, John writes: "One of the seven angels . . . spoke with me and said: 'Come here, I will show you the bride, the Lamb's wife.' So he carried me away in the power of the spirit to a great and lofty mountain, and he showed me the holy city Jerusalem coming down out of heaven from God and having the glory of God. Its radiance was like a most precious stone, as a jasper stone shining crystal-clear."—Re 21:9-11.

New Jerusalem is the bride of whom? The Lamb of God, Jesus Christ, who shed his blood sacrificially for mankind. (Joh 1:29; Re 5:6, 12; 7:14; 12:11; 21:14) What is her identity? She is composed of the members of the glorified Christian congregation. The congregation on earth was likened to "a chaste virgin" to be presented to the Christ. (2Co 11:2) Again, the apostle Paul likens the Christian congregation to a wife, with Christ as her Husband and Head.—Eph 5:23-25, 32.

Furthermore, Christ himself addresses the congregation at Revelation 3:12, promising the faithful conqueror that he would have written upon him "the name of my God and the name of the city of my God, the new Jerusalem which descends out of heaven from my God, and that new name of mine." A wife takes her husband's name. Therefore those seen standing with the Lamb upon Mount Zion, numbering 144,000, having the Lamb's name and that of his Father written in their foreheads, are evidently the same group, the bride.—Re 14:1.

Why could "New Jerusalem" not be a city in the Middle East?

New Jerusalem is heavenly, not earthly, for it comes down "out of heaven from God." (Re 21:10) So this city is not one erected by men and consisting of literal streets and buildings constructed in the Middle East on the site of the ancient city of Jerusalem, which was destroyed in 70 C.E. The members of the bride class when on earth are told that their "citizenship exists in the heavens" and that their hope is to receive "an incorruptible and undefiled and unfading inheritance." "It is reserved in the heavens for you," says the apostle Peter.—Php 3:20; 1Pe 1:4.

In 537 B.C.E., Jehovah created "new heavens and a new earth" when the Jewish remnant was restored to Jerusalem from Babylonian exile. (Isa 65:17) Evidently the governorship of Zerubbabel (a descendant of David) aided by High Priest Joshua, at the city of Jerusalem, constituted the "new heavens" then. (Hag 1:1, 14; see HEAVEN [New heavens and new earth].) The New Jerusalem, together with Christ and his throne in this symbolic city, constitutes the "new heavens" that rule over the "new earth," which is human society on earth.

That the New Jerusalem is indeed a heavenly city is further supported by the vision of her that John beheld. Only a symbolic city could have the dimensions and splendor of New Jerusalem. Its base was foursquare, about 555 km (345 mi) on each side, or about 2,220 km (1,379 mi) completely around, that is, 12,000 furlongs. Being a cube, the city was also as high as it was long and wide. No man-made city could ever reach that far into "outer space." Round about was a wall 144 cubits (64 m; 210 ft) high. The wall, itself constructed of jasper, in turn rested on 12 foundation stones, precious stones of great beauty—jasper, sapphire, chalcedony, emerald, sardonyx, sardius, chrysolite, beryl, topaz, chrysoprase, hyacinth, and amethyst. On these 12 foundation stones were engraved the names of the 12 apostles of the Lamb. The city proper within these beautiful walls was no less glorious, for it was described as "pure gold like clear glass," having a broad way of "pure gold, as transparent glass."—Re 21:12-21.

A Pure, Beneficial Rule. Entrance into the New Jerusalem through its magnificent walls was by means of 12 gates, three on a side, each made of a huge pearl. Although these gates were never closed, "anything not sacred and anyone that carries on a disgusting thing and a lie will in no way enter into it; only those written in the Lamb's scroll of life will." A holy and sacred city indeed, yet there was no visible temple of worship, for "Jehovah God the Almighty is its temple, also the Lamb is." And there was "no need of the sun nor of the moon to shine upon it, for the glory of God lighted it up, and its lamp was the Lamb." Its rulership over the nations will be beneficial to them, for "the nations will walk by means of its light."—Re 21:22-27.

NEWT [Heb., *leta·'ah'*]. A small salamander or tailed amphibian, resembling a lizard but scaleless and covered with a soft, moist, thin skin. It is related to the frog and is listed among the unclean creatures of the Mosaic Law. (Le 11:29, 30) The banded newt (*Triturus vittatus*) of Asia Minor and Syria is distinguished by a black band along each side of its body. Born in the water, it lives on land for two or three years after losing its gills, then returns to the water to live out the remainder of its life.

NEZIAH (Ne·zi'ah) [from a root meaning "oversee; excel; endure"]. Forefather of a group of Nethinim who returned with Zerubbabel after the Babylonian exile, 537 B.C.E.—Ezr 2:1, 2, 43, 54; Ne 7:46, 56.

NEZIB (Ne'zib) [from a root meaning "set up; station; erect"]. A Judean site in the Shephelah. (Jos 15:20, 33, 43) It is usually identified with Khirbet Beit Nesib (Horvat Neziv), about 11 km (7 mi) NW of Hebron.

NIBHAZ (Nib'haz). A deity worshiped by the Avvites, whom the king of Assyria settled in the territory of Samaria following the deportation of the Israelites after the fall of the ten-tribe kingdom. (2Ki 17:24-31) Aside from the brief Scriptural reference to Nibhaz, nothing can be said with certainty about the nature or form of this god.

NIBSHAN (Nib'shan). A city in the Judean wilderness. (Jos 15:20, 61, 62) The exact location of Nibshan is unknown. But it is tentatively identified with Khirbet el-Maqari, located on a level ridge about 16 km (10 mi) SE of Jerusalem.

NICANOR (Ni·ca'nor) [probably, Conqueror]. One of the seven men "full of spirit and wisdom" approved by the apostles to look after the daily distribution in the early Jerusalem congregation. —Ac 6:1-6.

NICODEMUS (Nic·o·de'mus) [Conqueror of the People]. A Pharisee and a teacher of Israel, a ruler of the Jews (that is, a member of the Sanhedrin) who is mentioned only in John's Gospel. Nicodemus was impressed with the signs that Jesus performed in Jerusalem at Passover time of 30 C.E. Consequently, he visited Jesus one night and confessed that Jesus must have come from God. (Probably out of fear of the Jews he chose the cover of darkness for this first visit.) It was to Nicodemus that Jesus spoke of being "born again" in order to see the Kingdom of God, of no man's having ascended to heaven, about God's love as being shown by sending the Son to earth, and about the need to exercise faith.—Joh 2:23; 3:1-21.

About two and a half years later, at the Festival of Booths, the Pharisees sent officers to lay hold of Jesus. When the officers returned empty-handed, the Pharisees belittled them for making a report favorable to Jesus, whereupon Nicodemus spoke up, saying: "Our law does not judge a man unless first it has heard from him and come to know what he is doing, does it?" For this the others ridiculed him. (Joh 7:45-52) After Jesus' death, Nicodemus came along with Joseph of Arimathea, that fearful disciple, bringing a heavy roll of myrrh and aloes (c. 100 Roman pounds [33 kg; 72 lb]), a costly offering, with which to prepare Jesus' body for burial. (Joh 19:38-40) There is no Scriptural evidence for or against the traditions that say Nicodemus later became a disciple, was cast out of the Sanhedrin and Jerusalem, died a martyr's death, and so forth.

NICOLAUS (Nic·o·la'us) [Conqueror of the People].

1. One of the seven qualified men whom the congregation recommended to the apostles for appointment as food distributors to ensure just and fair treatment among the early Jerusalem congregation following Pentecost, 33 C.E. Of the seven, Nicolaus is the only one called "a proselyte of Antioch," which suggests that he may have been the only non-Jew of the group, the Greek names of the others being common even among natural Jews.—Ac 6:1-6.

2. "The sect of Nicolaus" (or Nicolaitans) is condemned in two of the seven letters to the congregations in chapters 2 and 3 of Revelation. For hating "the deeds of the sect of Nicolaus," which Christ Jesus himself also hates, "the angel" of the Ephesus congregation was commended. (Re 2:1, 6) In the congregation at Pergamum, however, there were some "holding fast the teaching of the sect of Nicolaus," from which they were urged to turn away and repent.—Re 2:12, 15, 16.

Aside from what is here written in Revelation about the sect of Nicolaus, nothing else is known of it, either of its practices and teachings, which are condemned, or of its origin and development. The connective "so" immediately following the reference to the immoral and idolatrous course the Israelites pursued due to "the teaching of Balaam" (Re 2:14, 15) might indicate some similarity, but Revelation makes a distinction between the two. There is no reason to connect the sect with Nicolaus the Antiochian Christian (No. 1) just because he

is the only person of that name in the Bible, as has also been done by some of the early church writers. Nor is it warranted to say that some apostatized sect took his name to give weight to their wrongdoing. Nicolaus was more probably a Biblically unidentified individual after whom the ungodly movement was named.

NICOPOLIS (Ni·cop'o·lis) [City of Conquest]. A city where the apostle Paul decided to spend the winter during one of his trips and to which he urged Titus to come. (Tit 3:12) The note at the end of Paul's letter to Titus in the *King James Version*, indicating it to have been written "from Nicopolis of Macedonia," is not found in the oldest manuscripts. Evidently Paul did not write his letter from Nicopolis, since Titus 3:12 implies that he was not yet there but had merely decided to winter there.

Of the various ancient cities named Nicopolis, the Nicopolis of Epirus located on a peninsula in NW Greece and about 10 km (6 mi) N of Preveza, seems to fit the Biblical reference best. Being a prominent city, it would have been a good place for Paul to declare the good news, and it was conveniently situated for both Paul (apparently then in Macedonia) and Titus (in Crete). It may be that Paul was arrested in Nicopolis and then taken to Rome for his final imprisonment and execution.

Octavian (Augustus) founded Nicopolis to memorialize his naval victory (of 31 B.C.E.) over Antony and Cleopatra at nearby Actium. The Actian Games instituted by him in honor of the god Apollo also served to commemorate this event. The city itself occupied the site of the Roman encampment, and where his tent had been, Octavian built a temple to the god Neptune. Most of the city's public edifices, according to the historian Josephus, were erected through the interest and financial aid of Herod the Great.—*Jewish Antiquities*, XVI, 147 (v, 3).

NIGER (Ni'ger) [from Lat., meaning "Dark; Black"]. The Latin surname given to Symeon, one of the "prophets and teachers" of the congregation of Antioch, Syria.—Ac 13:1.

NIGHT. The period of darkness from sunset to sunrise was designated by Jehovah God as "Night." (Ge 1:5, 14) Between sunset and the actual darkness there is a short period of evening twilight when the stars begin to be seen. This time was called *ne'sheph* by the Hebrews and evidently is the time meant by the expression "between the two evenings" found at Exodus 12:6. (Pr 7:9) Similarly, at the end of the night's darkness there is a morning twilight leading to the dawn, and this was expressed by the same Hebrew word. Thus, the writer at Psalm 119:147 says: "I have been up early in the morning twilight."

Hebrew Division. The Hebrews divided the night into watches. "When I have remembered you upon my lounge, during the night watches I meditate on you." (Ps 63:6) Since Judges 7:19 speaks of a "middle night watch," it seems evident there were three of them in early times. It appears that each watch covered one third of the time between sundown and sunrise, or about four hours each, depending on the time of the year. The first watch would thus run from about 6:00 p.m. to 10:00 p.m. "The middle night watch" would begin about 10:00 p.m. and run until about 2:00 a.m. This was a strategic time for Gideon to make his surprise attack on the Midianite camp. The third watch was called "the morning watch," lasting from about 2:00 a.m. till sunrise. It was during this morning watch that Jehovah caused the pursuing Egyptian armies to begin to experience grave difficulties in their attempted passage through the Red Sea.—Ex 14:24-28; see also 1Sa 11:11.

Roman Division. At least by the time of the Roman control, the Jews adopted the Greek and Roman practice of four nocturnal watches. Jesus evidently referred to these four divisions when he said: "Therefore keep on the watch, for you do not know when the master of the house is coming, whether late in the day or at midnight or at cockcrowing or early in the morning." (Mr 13:35) The watch "late in the day" ran from sunset until about 9:00 p.m. The second watch, called the "midnight," began about 9:00 p.m. and ended at midnight. (Lu 12:38) The "cockcrowing" covered from midnight till about 3:00 a.m. It was probably during this time that the cockcrowings mentioned at Mark 14:30 occurred. (See COCKCROWING.) Finally, from 3:00 a.m. until sunrise was the fourth watch, "early in the morning."—Mt 14:25; Mr 6:48.

On one occasion mention is made of a specific hour of the 12 hours that make up the nighttime. Acts 23:23 tells us that it was at the "third hour," or about 9:00 p.m., that the military commander ordered the troops to take Paul from Jerusalem on his way to Caesarea.

Whereas the Jews began the new day at sunset, according to Roman custom midnight was the fixed point for ending and beginning the day. This avoided the problem resulting from the lengthening and shortening of the daylight hours due to the seasons (as occurred when starting the day at sunset) and allowed for their dividing the day into two equal 12-hour periods at all times of the year. This is the practice in most nations today.

Figurative Use. The word "night" is at times used in a figurative, or symbolic, sense in the Bible. At John 9:4 Jesus spoke of "the night . . . coming when no man can work." Jesus here referred to the time of his judgment, impalement, and death, when he would be unable to engage in the works of his father.—See Ec 9:10; Job 10:21, 22.

At Romans 13:11, 12, "the night" manifestly refers to a period of darkness caused by God's Adversary, which is due to be ended by Christ Jesus and his reign. (See Eph 6:12, 13; Col 1:13, 14.) At 1 Thessalonians 5:1-11 God's servants who have been enlightened by his truth are contrasted with worldly people who have not. Their way of life manifests that they are "sons of light and sons of day. [They] belong neither to night nor to darkness." (See Joh 8:12; 12:36, 46; 1Pe 2:9; 2Co 6:14.) A similar usage is found at Micah 3:6, where the prophet says to those rejecting true divine guidance: "Therefore you men will have night, so that there will be no vision; and darkness you will have, so as not to practice divination. And the sun will certainly set upon the prophets, and the day must get dark upon them."—Compare Joh 3:19-21.

The night is also used to represent, generally, a time of adversity, since the night with its gloom and obscurity is the time when wild beasts roam, when armies launch surprise attacks, when thieves creep in, and when other acts of evil are committed. (Ps 91:5, 6; 104:20, 21; Isa 21:4, 8, 9; Da 5:25-31; Ob 5) It is in these different figurative senses that we must understand the texts at Revelation 21:2, 25 and 22:5, where we are assured that in the "New Jerusalem" "night will be no more."

NIGHTJAR [Heb., *li·lith'*]. A creature appearing in the description of Edom's utter desolation and of the things inhabiting its ruins. (Isa 34:14) The Hebrew word has been variously translated as "screech owl" (*KJ*), "night-monster" (*AS*), "nightjar" (*NE, NW*), and "night hag" (*RS*), while *The Jerusalem Bible* prefers simply to transliterate the name as "Lilith."

Many scholars endeavor to show that the Hebrew term is a loanword from ancient Sumerian and Akkadian and that it derives from the name of a mythological female demon of the air (*Lilitu*). Professor G. R. Driver, however, considers the Hebrew word (*li·lith'*) to derive from a root word denoting "every kind of twisting motion or twisted object," even as the Hebrew word *la'yil* (or *lai'lah*), meaning "night," suggests a "wrapping itself round or enfolding the earth." Such derivation of *li·lith'*, he suggests, may likely point to the nightjar as both a nocturnal feeding bird and one noted for its rapid twisting and turning flight as it pursues moths, beetles, and other night-flying insects. As quoted by Driver, Tristram, the naturalist, described the nightjar as "becoming very active towards dusk, when they hawk about at great speed and with intricate turnings after their food." —*Palestine Exploration Quarterly*, London, 1959, pp. 55, 56.

The nightjar is almost 30 cm (12 in.) in length with a wingspan of 50 cm (20 in.) or more; its plumage resembles the owl's, being soft and delicately mottled with gray and brown. The soft wing feathers allow for noiseless flight. Its large mouth is evidently the reason for its also being called the goatsucker, an ancient legend holding that the bird sucked the milk of goats.

As to the likelihood of such a bird being found in the arid region of Edom, certain varieties of this bird are known to inhabit waste places. An Egyptian nightjar (*Caprimulgus aegyptius*) lives almost exclusively in the desert, occupying acacia groves and tamarisk bushes and seeking its food in twilight. Another (*Caprimulgus nubicus*) is found in desert fringes between Jericho and the Red Sea, hence in regions like that of Edom.

NILE. The Greek name given to the river, the northern part of whose valley formed the land of ancient Egypt, making that land essentially a river oasis. (MAP, Vol. 1, p. 531) In the Hebrew Scriptures the river is regularly referred to by the term *ye'or'* (sometimes *ye'ohr'*). The word itself means "stream" or "canal" (as at Daniel 12:5 and Isaiah 33:21) or "water-filled gallery" (a shaft made in mining, as at Job 28:10). In one case *ye'or'* is used to refer to the Tigris River (Biblical Hiddekel) of Mesopotamia. (Da 12:5-7; compare 10:4.) All other occurrences, the context indicates, apply to the Nile or, when in the plural form, to the Nile canals. (Ps 78:44; Isa 7:18) The Egyptian name (*jrw*) for the river, at least from the so-called Eighteenth Dynasty on, corresponds closely to the Hebrew.

The Course of the Nile. The Nile is generally ranked as the longest river on earth. Its length of 6,671 km (4,145 mi) is measured from its sources, which take their rise in the lake regions of modern Rwanda and Burundi. These sources flow into Lake Victoria, and from here a river passes over to Lake Mobutu; farther north the stream is known as the White Nile. At Khartoum, the White Nile is joined by the Blue Nile, which cascades down from the mountains of northern Ethiopia. North of Khartoum the river forms the Nile proper, and as such receives the waters of only one more tributary, the Atbara River, its confluence with the Nile occurring about 300 km (190 mi) NE of Khartoum. The Nile then winds its way through the desolate tableland of northern Sudan, passing over six separate beds of hard granite rock that create six cataracts between Khartoum and Aswan (Biblical Syene), the point where Nubia ended and ancient Egypt began. Finally, having lost much of its vol-

Typical scene along the Nile in Egypt

ume because of evaporation by the blazing sun and the demands of Egyptian irrigation, some 2,700 km (1,700 mi) N of Khartoum the Nile's waters empty into the Mediterranean Sea.

The Nile Valley is quite narrow along most of the river's course. Through much of Nubia the river flows through a gorge, bordered on each side by the desert. North of Aswan, in what was Upper Egypt, the valley broadens out, but the rocky cliffs on either side are never much more than about 20 km (12 mi) apart. However, when the river reaches the region just N of modern Cairo it divides into two main branches, now called the Rosetta and the Damietta, after the names of the port cities situated at the mouths of these branches on the Mediterranean coast. This fanning out of the Nile's waters creates the swampy Nile Delta. In ancient times the river had other branches, the classical Greek historians and geographers making mention of from five to seven. These branches and some of the canals have since become silted up and either greatly reduced or eliminated.

Importance of Annual Flooding. A unique characteristic of this major river is the regularity of its rise each year and the consequent flooding of its banks that are lined with agricultural villages. This is produced by the winter and spring rains (as well as the melting of snow from the mountains) in Ethiopia, which convert the Blue Nile into a torrential stream rushing toward its junction with the White Nile, carrying with it rich silt from the Ethiopian highlands. The Atbara River also adds an increased flow to swell the volume of the Nile. Prior to the construction of the Aswan High Dam, this caused the river to begin to rise in Egypt from June onward, cresting in September and thereafter gradually receding. On receding, the waters left behind a deposit of highly fertile soil in the form of a thin layer of mud.

In a virtually rainless land, Egyptian agriculture was totally dependent upon these annual inundations of the lowlands. An insufficient rise had the same effect as drought, bringing famine; while an excessive rise brought damage to the irrigation works (as well as to homes). The concern of the Egyptians for a desirable amount of inundation is seen in the Nilometers (gauges for measuring the river's level) that have been discovered at ancient sites. Without these inundations the never-distant desert would press in from both sides right up to the riverbanks. Yet the Nile's rise and fall has, with few exceptions, been so regular that Egypt throughout its history was noted for its abundant crops and agricultural wealth.

This complete reliance of the Egyptian economy

on the Nile's waters was well illustrated in Pharaoh's dream, the seven fat cows proceeding out of the Nile and feeding on the Nile grass, while the seven thin cows came from the same source. This aptly represented the way good production could be eaten up by poor years resulting from insufficient inundation.—Ge 41:17-21.

The surging of the Nile waters over their banks was used to describe the forward push of marching armies (Jer 46:7, 8; 47:2, 3), while the prophet Amos used the rising and falling of the Nile's waters to represent the agitation due to come upon unfaithful Israel. (Am 8:8; 9:5) Other

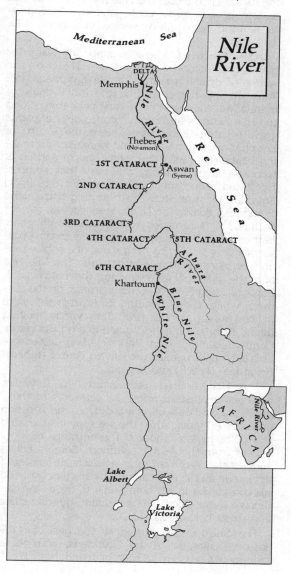

prophets employed the figure of the Nile's drying up to represent the disaster due to come upon Egypt as a result of God's judgment against the nation. The Nile's failure would not only cripple agriculture and the raising of stock but also damage the fishing industry and the production of linen.—Isa 19:1, 5-10; Eze 29:9, 10; Zec 10:11.

To retain some of the floodwaters for later use in irrigation during the growing season, the Egyptians built up earthen embankments to trap the muddy waters in large catch basins. Thus when Jehovah brought the first plague on Egypt, turning its water to blood, the Nile itself, the water in its canals and reedy pools, and the "impounded waters" were all converted into blood.—Ex 7:14-25.

Other Features. Besides supplying water for plants and domestic animals, the Nile was the source of drinking water for the Egyptians. (Ex 7:18, 21, 24) Except during the initial stage of inundation, the water was very palatable. Along the Nile's canals and reedy pools, papyrus plants grew in abundance; these were the source of Egyptian writing material and were used for making boats. (Isa 18:2) The reedy shores and pools were the habitat of many wild birds that fed upon frogs and other small creatures. (Ex 8:5, 9-11) Egyptian pictures show bird hunting being done from small boats. The Nile waters served, too, for bathing; it is recorded that Pharaoh's daughter bathed there. (Ex 2:5) An Egyptian picture presents a very similar bathing scene of a noblewoman with her four female attendants. The Nile was also the principal highway for the entire land. Boats heading N traveled downstream on the current, while those heading S (upstream) were pushed along by the prevailing winds moving inland from the Mediterranean Sea on the north. Commercial ships from Phoenicia and Crete were able to go upstream all the way to Thebes (Biblical No-amon; Na 3:8) and beyond.

The Nile figured prominently in Egyptian defenses against invasion. Its cataracts to the S made the land difficult to attack from the direction of Nubia-Ethiopia, while the swampy land around the Delta region hindered the entrance of large armies from the Asiatic continent. Some scholars suggest that Assyrian King Sennacherib's boast of drying up all the Nile canals with his feet signified his confidence in his being able to overcome defensive water-filled moats around Egyptian cities and strongholds.—2Ki 19:24.

The Nile's cycles served as the basis for the seasonal calendar of the Egyptians, with three four-month seasons: 'Akhet, or Inundation; Peret,

the Coming Forth (evidently of the land as the waters returned to their banks); and Shomu, the Dry season (summer). The period just after the waters were highest was that of the greatest activity; when low water levels prevailed, construction work was programmed to provide a measure of employment.

The symbol of a "great sea monster lying stretched out in the midst of [the] Nile canals," applied to Pharaoh in the book of Ezekiel, is thought to be drawn from the crocodiles that have inhabited the Nile from ancient times. (Eze 29:3-5) Frequent, too, was the hippopotamus, generally identified with the animal designated as "Behemoth" at Job 40:15.

The Egyptians worshiped the Nile as a god of fertility under the name Hapi. This god was depicted as basically male but with large feminine breasts, the head crowned with aquatic plants and a fisherman's girdle around the plump waist. Festivals, with accompanying sacrifices, were held annually in his honor at the beginning of each inundation period. Some scholars suggest that Pharaoh's going out to the Nile, mentioned at Exodus 7:15, relates to some morning devotional act, though it may have been merely for a morning walk or to examine the height of the river.

NILE CANALS. Irrigation canals branching off from the river Nile. (Ex 7:19; 8:5; Ps 78:44) The Hebrew word for Nile canals (ye'o·rim') is the plural form of ye'or' (the river Nile). The Egyptian economy was completely dependent upon the Nile, which provided water for irrigation in a virtually rainless land and regularly flooded the land, leaving behind a deposit of rich silt. The food supply of the nation depended on this arrangement. Thus the turning of these waters into blood resulted in national calamity, even as the drying up of the Nile canals would forebode disaster.—Isa 19:6; see NILE.

NIMRAH (Nim'rah) [possibly from a root meaning "leopard"]. A town E of the Jordan built or rebuilt by the Gadites; a shortened form of Beth-nimrah.—Nu 32:3-5, 34, 36; see BETH-NIMRAH.

NIMRIM (Nim'rim) [possibly, Leopards]. In prophecies directed against Moab, both Isaiah and Jeremiah refer to the "waters of Nimrim." (Isa 15:5-9; Jer 48:34, 35) On the basis of the fertility of the surrounding region, some identify the waters of Nimrim with the Wadi Nimrin, whose waters flow into the Jordan N of the Dead Sea. (See BETH-NIMRAH.) The order in which places are named in the prophecies, however, seems to indicate a location in the S of Moab. Thus many prefer identification with the Wadi en-Numeirah, which flows down into the SE end of the Dead Sea about 17 km (11 mi) WSW of Karak. The prophecies foretell that these waters will become "mere desolations," either in a figurative sense because of the desolating of the land or perhaps because of a damming up of their streams by enemy forces.

NIMROD (Nim'rod). Son of Cush. (1Ch 1:10) The rabbinic writings derived the name Nimrod from the Hebrew verb *ma·radh'*, meaning "rebel." Thus, the Babylonian Talmud (*Erubin* 53a) states: "Why, then, was he called Nimrod? Because he stirred up the whole world to rebel (*himrid*) against His [God's] sovereignty."—*Encyclopedia of Biblical Interpretation,* by Menahem M. Kasher, Vol. II, 1955, p. 79.

Nimrod was the founder and king of the first empire to come into existence after the Flood. He distinguished himself as a mighty hunter "before" in an unfavorable sense; Heb., *liph·neh';* "against" or "in opposition to"; compare Nu 16:2; 1Ch 14:8; 2Ch 14:10) or "in front of" Jehovah. (Ge 10:9, ftn) Although in this case some scholars attach a favorable sense to the Hebrew preposition meaning "in front of," the Jewish Targums, the writings of the historian Josephus, and also the context of Genesis chapter 10 suggest that Nimrod was a mighty hunter in defiance of Jehovah.

The beginning of Nimrod's kingdom included the cities of Babel, Erech, Accad, and Calneh, all in the land of Shinar. (Ge 10:10) Therefore it was likely under his direction that the building of Babel and its tower began. This conclusion is also in agreement with the traditional Jewish view. Wrote Josephus: "[Nimrod] little by little transformed the state of affairs into a tyranny, holding that the only way to detach men from the fear of God was by making them continuously dependent upon his own power. He threatened to have his revenge on God if He wished to inundate the earth again; for he would build a tower higher than the water could reach and avenge the destruction of their forefathers. The people were eager to follow this advice of [Nimrod], deeming it slavery to submit to God; so they set out to build the tower . . . and it rose with a speed beyond all expectation."—*Jewish Antiquities,* I, 114, 115 (iv, 2, 3).

It appears that after the building of the Tower of Babel, Nimrod extended his domain to the territory of Assyria and there built "Nineveh and Rehoboth-Ir and Calah and Resen between Nineveh and Calah: this is the great city." (Ge 10:11, 12; compare Mic 5:6.) Since Assyria evidently derived its name from Shem's son Asshur, Nimrod, as a grandson of Ham, must have invaded Shemite territory. So it would seem that Nimrod made the start in becoming a mighty one or hero, not only as a hunter of animals but also as a warrior, a man of aggression. (Ge 10:8) Observes the *Cyclopædia* by M'Clintock and Strong: "That the mighty hunting was not confined to the chase is apparent from its close connection with the building of eight cities. . . . What Nimrod did in the chase as a hunter was the earlier token of what he achieved as a conqueror. For hunting and heroism were of old specially and naturally associated . . . The Assyrian monuments also picture many feats in hunting, and the word is often employed to denote campaigning. . . . The chase and the battle, which in the same country were connected so closely in aftertimes, may therefore be virtually associated or identified here. The meaning then will be, that Nimrod was the first after the flood to found a kingdom, to unite the fragments of scattered patriarchal rule, and consolidate them under himself as sole head and master; and all this in defiance of Jehovah, for it was the violent intrusion of Hamitic power into a Shemitic territory."—1894, Vol. VII, p. 109.

Concerning deification of Nimrod, see GODS AND GODDESSES (Babylonian Deities).

NIMSHI (Nim'shi). Father of Jehoshaphat (not the king) and grandfather of Jehu. (1Ki 19:16; 2Ki 9:2, 14, 20; 2Ch 22:7) The name has been found inscribed on a fragment of ancient pottery excavated in Samaria.

NINEVEH (Nin'e·veh). A city of Assyria founded by Nimrod, "a mighty hunter in opposition to Jehovah." Together with Rehoboth-Ir, Calah, and Resen it constituted "the great city." (Ge 10:9, 11, 12; Mic 5:6) Much later it became the capital of the Assyrian Empire. As such, Nineveh was a "city of bloodshed" (Na 3:1), for the Assyrians waged many wars of conquest and employed brutal methods in killing captured warriors. Doubtless the military campaigns contributed greatly to the city's wealth. (Na 2:9) The principal deity of Nineveh appears to have been Ishtar, a goddess of love and war.

Archaeological Investigation. Kuyunjik and Nebi Yunus ("Prophet Jonah"), two mounds located on the E bank of the Tigris River opposite Mosul, N Iraq, mark the site of what was once the great city of Nineveh. A modern village, with a cemetery and a mosque, occupies Nebi Yunus. Therefore this mound, which covers a palace of Esarhaddon, has been little investigated. At Kuyunjik, however, excavations have brought to light much that testifies to Nineveh's past glory. The findings include thousands of cuneiform tablets from Ashurbanipal's library and the ruins of the palace of Sennacherib and that of Ashurbanipal. These palaces were impressive structures. Based on his findings, Sir Austen Layard wrote:

"The interior of the Assyrian palace must have been as magnificent as imposing. I have led the reader through its ruins, and he may judge of the impression its halls were calculated to make upon the stranger who in the days of old, entered for the first time the abode of the Assyrian kings. He was ushered in through the portal guarded by the colossal lions or bulls of white alabaster. In the first hall he found himself surrounded by the sculptured records of the empire. Battles, sieges, triumphs, the exploits of the chase, the ceremonies of religion, were portrayed on the walls, sculptured in alabaster, and painted in gorgeous colors. Under each picture were engraved, in characters filled up with bright copper, inscriptions describing the scenes represented. Above the sculptures were painted other events—the king, attended by his eunuchs and warriors, receiving his prisoners, entering into alliances with other monarchs, or performing some sacred duty. These representations were inclosed in colored borders, of elaborate and elegant design. The emblematic tree, winged bulls, and monstrous animals, were conspicuous amongst the ornaments. At the upper end of the hall was the colossal figure of the king in adoration before the supreme deity, or receiving from his eunuch the holy cup. He was attended by warriors bearing his arms, and by the priests or presiding divinities. His robes, and those of his followers, were adorned with groups of figures, animals, and flowers, all painted with brilliant colors.

"The stranger trod upon alabaster slabs, each bearing an inscription, recording the titles, genealogy, and achievements of the great king. Several doorways, formed by gigantic winged lions or bulls, or by the figures of guardian deities, led into other apartments, which again opened into more distant halls. In each were new sculptures. On the walls of some were processions of colossal figures —armed men and eunuchs following the king, warriors laden with spoil, leading prisoners, or bearing presents and offerings to the gods. On the walls of others were portrayed the winged priests, or presiding divinities, standing before the sacred trees.

"The ceilings above him were divided into square compartments, painted with flowers, or

with the figures of animals. Some were inlaid with ivory, each compartment being surrounded b' elegant borders and mouldings. The beams, a well as the sides of the chambers, may have been gilded, or even plated, with gold and silver; and the rarest woods, in which the cedar was conspic uous, were used for the woodwork. Square open ings in the ceilings of the chambers admitted the light of day."—*Nineveh and Its Remains*, 1856 Part II, pp. 207-209.

In the Time of Jonah.   Jehovah's prophet Jo nah, in the ninth century B.C.E., declared impend ing doom for Nineveh because of the wickednes of its inhabitants. However, since the people, in cluding the king, repented, Jehovah spared th city. (Jon 1:1, 2; 3:2, 5-10) At that time Ninevel was a great city, "with a walking distance of three days." (Jon 3:3) Its population numbered mor than 120,000 men. (Jon 4:11) This Biblical descrip tion is not controverted by archaeological evi dence. Observed André Parrot, Curator-in-Chie of the French National Museums:

"Just as today, that part of London which lie within its ancient boundary is very different from what is called 'greater London'—a term which includes the suburbs and denotes a much large area—so it may be that people who lived far awa from Assyria understood by the word 'Ninevel what is now known as 'the Assyrian triangle' . . . which stretches from Khorsabad in the north t Nimrud in the south, and, with an almost unbro ken string of settlements, covers a distance c some twenty-six miles. . . .

"Felix Jones estimated that the population c Nineveh might have numbered 174,000 persons and quite recently, in his excavations at Nimruc M. E. L. Mallowan discovered a stele of Ashurna zirpal on which it is recorded that he invited to banquet the fabulous number of 69,574 guest Mallowan considers that, allowing for foreigners the population of Kalakh (Nimrud) might hav been 65,000. But Nineveh is twice the area c Nimrud, and thus it may be reckoned that th figure in Jonah 4.11 is indirectly confirmed. —*Nineveh and the Old Testament*, 1955, pp. 8 86; see JONAH No. 1; JONAH, BOOK OF.

Its Destruction Fulfills Prophecy.   Althoug repenting at the preaching of Jonah (Mt 12:41; L 11:30, 32), the Ninevites relapsed and again too to their wicked ways. It was some years afte Assyrian King Sennacherib had been murdered a Nineveh in the house of his god Nisroch (2k 19:36, 37; Isa 37:37, 38) that Nahum (1:1; 2:8–3 19) and Zephaniah (2:13-15) foretold the destruc tion of that wicked city. Their prophecies wer fulfilled when the combined forces of Nabopolassar the king of Babylon and of Cyaxares the Mede besieged and captured Nineveh. The city was evidently subjected to burning, for many Assyrian reliefs show damage or stain from fire and accompanying smoke. With reference to Nineveh, a Babylonian chronicle reports: "They carried off the vast booty of the city and the temple (and) turned] the city into a ruin heap." (*Assyrian and Babylonian Chronicles,* by A. Grayson, 1975, p. 94; PICTURE, Vol. 1, p. 958) To this day Nineveh is a desolate waste, and in the spring, flocks graze near or atop the mound of Kuyunjik.

Date of Nineveh's Fall. Though effaced from the extant cuneiform tablet that relates the fall of Nineveh, the date for this event, the 14th year of Nabopolassar, can be supplied from the context. It is also possible to place the destruction of Nineveh in the framework of Bible chronology. According to a Babylonian chronicle, the Egyptians were defeated at Carchemish in the 21st year of Nabopolassar's reign. The Bible shows this to have taken place in the fourth year of Jehoiakim's reign or in 625 B.C.E. (Jer 46:2) Therefore, the capture of Nineveh (about seven years earlier) in the 14th year of Nabopolassar's reign would fall in the year 632 B.C.E.—See ASSYRIA (The fall of the empire).

NISAN (Ni'san). The postexilic name of the first Jewish lunar month of the sacred calendar, corresponding to part of March and part of April. Ne 2:1; Es 3:7) This month, first called "Abib," was originally considered the seventh month and is evidently the month referred to at Genesis 8:4. At the time of the Exodus from Egypt, Jehovah assigned this month to be "the first of the months of the year." (Ex 12:2; 13:4; Nu 33:3) From then on, a distinction existed between a sacred calendar instituted by Jehovah and the previous secular calendar.—See CALENDAR; ABIB.

The weather was often quite cool during this spring month, and in Jerusalem, fires were lit at night to provide warmth. (Joh 18:18) Snow has even fallen in Jerusalem as late as April 6, as it did in 1949. Nisan came at about the close of the rainy season, and the latter or spring rains were counted on to bring the grain to fullness prior to the harvest. (De 11:14; Ho 6:3; Jer 5:24) At this time of the year the Jordan River was normally at flood stage. (Jos 3:15; 1Ch 12:15) The barley harvest began along the coastal plains, and down in the subtropical Jordan Valley the wheat was reaching maturity. (Ru 1:22; 2:23) About this time, harvested flax on Rahab's rooftop in Jericho provided a place for the Israelite spies to hide.—Jos 2:6; 4:19.

Adjusting the Lunar Calendar. God's command required that the Israelites offer up a sheaf of the firstfruits of their harvest on the 16th day of Nisan (Abib) and that, on the 50th day thereafter, they offer up a second grain offering. These offerings corresponded naturally with the barley and wheat harvests, respectively. This precept made essential an adjustment in the calendar of lunar months used by the Israelites. There was need to compensate for the difference of 11¼ days between the full solar year and the shorter lunar year. Otherwise, within the space of three years, the month of Nisan would arrive some 33 days earlier in the season and far ahead of the barley harvest. The Bible record does not specify what method was originally used by the Israelites to accomplish such coordination, but the evidence indicates that a 13th month was added every two or three years to restore the seasons to their proper position in the calendar year. It seems likely that this was determined by simple observation, relating the new moon to the vernal, or spring, equinox of the sun, which comes about March 21 of each year. If the new moon that would ordinarily mark the start of the month of Nisan (Abib) was too distant from the time of the spring equinox, then the month was counted as a 13th or intercalary month, and Nisan began with the following new moon. It was not until the fourth century C.E. that a definitely standardized calendar was adopted by the Jews.

The first of Nisan's festivals was the Passover, originally celebrated in Egypt; it came on the 14th of the month and included the sacrifice of the paschal lamb. (Ex 12:2-14; Le 23:5; De 16:1) The following day was the beginning of the week-long Festival of Unfermented Cakes, running from the 15th to the 21st of the month. On the 16th of Nisan came the offering of the firstfruits of the barley harvest.—Ex 12:15-20; 23:15; 34:18; Le 23:6-11.

Lord's Evening Meal Instituted. Over 15 centuries after the Exodus, on Nisan 14 of the year 33 C.E., Jesus gathered with his 12 apostles in Jerusalem to celebrate the last valid Passover, and then, having dismissed the traitorous Judas, he proceeded to institute the memorial of his death by means of the Lord's Supper, or Evening Meal. (Mt 26:17-30; 1Co 11:23-25) Before Nisan 14 passed, he died as the Lamb of God. On Nisan 16, the day the priest at the temple waved the firstfruits of the barley harvest, Jesus, as the firstfruits of the resurrection, was raised up to life again. —Lu 23:54–24:7; 1Co 15:20.

In obedience to Christ's instructions, "Keep doing this in remembrance of me," the 14th day of

Nisan continues to be observed by his followers till this day as the time for memorializing Christ's death.—Lu 22:19, 20; see LORD'S EVENING MEAL.

NISROCH (Nis'roch). A deity worshiped by Sennacherib the king of Assyria. It was in the temple of Nisroch that Adrammelech and Sharezer murdered their father Sennacherib. (2Ki 19:36, 37; Isa 37:38) A number of scholars suggest identifying Nisroch with the fire-god Nusku, who, it was thought, assisted in bringing defeat to the enemy in warfare and served as messenger of the gods as well as a dispenser of justice. However, certain identification of Nisroch with a known Assyrian deity is not now possible.

NO, NO-AMON (No-a'mon) [from Egyptian, meaning "City of Amon [an Egyptian god]"]. A prominent city and onetime capital of Egypt, located on both banks of the upper Nile about 530 km (330 mi) S of Cairo. The Greeks knew it as Thebes, the name commonly used today.

Some scholars in the past have held that the Hebrew "No" is an incorrect rendering of the Egyptian name. (Jer 46:25) However, Professor T. O. Lambdin points out that "recent investigations in Egypto-Coptic phonology indicate that the Hebrew spelling may well be correct and may reflect an earlier Egyptian pronunciation . . . The problem is further complicated by uncertainty on the part of Egyptologists regarding the precise consonantal reading of the Egyptian word itself." —*The Interpreter's Dictionary of the Bible,* edited by G. A. Buttrick, 1962, Vol. 4, pp. 615, 616.

In ancient Egyptian texts the city is called "the City of Amon." This is because it became the principal center of the worship of the god Amon, who rose from being a minor deity to the position of chief god of the nation, equated by the Greeks with Zeus (Jupiter). (See AMON No. 4.) Here the pharaohs built enormous monuments and temples, covering an extensive area on the E bank of the Nile (at Karnak and Luxor), with other magnificent temples and a huge burial ground on the W bank. The temple of Amon at Karnak is considered the largest columnar structure ever built, some of its massive columns measuring some 3.5 m (12 ft) in diameter.

Becomes Egypt's Capital. Particularly during the period that is termed the "New Kingdom or Empire: Dynasties 18-20," Thebes attained great prominence, becoming the capital of the land. Here, the long distance from the sea and from the land bridge to Asia afforded good protection from that direction. It may be that, because of a very weak and discredited government in Lower Egypt

following the Israelite Exodus, the royalty of Upper Egypt took advantage of the situation and gained the ascendancy. At any rate, there is evidence of considerable reorganization at this time.

Center of priesthood. Even when administrative control shifted to other sites, No-amon (Thebes) continued to be a wealthy and prominent city, the center of the powerful priesthood of Amon, whose chief priest ranked next to Pharaoh himself in power and wealth. But in the seventh century B.C.E., Assyrian aggression spread into Egypt during the rule of Assyrian King Esarhaddon. His son and successor Ashurbanipal renewed the conquest, reaching Thebes and thoroughly sacking the city. It is evidently to this devastation that the prophet Nahum referred when warning Nineveh, Assyria's capital, about destruction of similar magnitude. (Na 3:7-10) No-amon's defenses, stretching across the road from Palestine and on up the Nile, failed, and the riches from her commercial traffic and religious temples became the prize of the ransacking Assyrians.

Brought to Ruin. Yet, by the close of the seventh century or the early part of the sixth century, No-amon had regained a position of some prominence. Jeremiah and Ezekiel foretold a judgment by Jehovah God upon Egypt's chief god Amon of No, and upon Pharaoh and all the Egyptian gods, which judgment would come by the hand of Babylonian King Nebuchadnezzar. (Je 46:25, 26; Eze 30:10, 14, 15) Persian ruler Cambyses dealt another severe blow to No-amon in 525 B.C.E., and the city steadily declined, finally being completely ruined by the Romans under Gaius Cornelius Gallus because of its share in revolt against Roman rule (30/29 B.C.E.). Today only small villages are to be found around the massive ruins of the temples of the impotent god of No.

NOADIAH (No·a·di'ah) [Jah Has Kept Appointment; Jah Has Met by Appointment].

1. Son of Binnui; a Levite who, on the fourth day following Ezra's arrival in Jerusalem 468 B.C.E., helped inventory the silver, gold, and utensils for the temple.—Ezr 8:32, 33.

2. A prophetess who, in 455 B.C.E., was singled out by name as one who tried to stop the rebuilding of Jerusalem's walls by instilling fear in Nehemiah.—Ne 6:14.

NOAH (No'ah).

1. [Heb., *No'ach,* probably, Rest; Consolation]. Son of Lamech and tenth in line from Adam through Seth; born in 2970 B.C.E., 126 years after

Adam's death. When his father Lamech named Noah, he said: "This one will bring us comfort from our work and from the pain of our hands resulting from the ground which Jehovah has cursed."—Ge 5:28-31.

Faultless Among His Contemporaries.

The world in which Noah lived had become degenerate. During this period angels who left their original position and proper dwelling place had married women and produced offspring, "men of fame," whipping up the violence filling the earth (Ge 6:1-4; Jude 6), until "every inclination of the thoughts of [man's] heart was only bad all the time" and the earth became "ruined, because all flesh had ruined its way on the earth." (Ge 6:5, 11, 12) But Noah avoided this corruption and is described by God's Word as "a righteous man. He proved himself faultless among his contemporaries. Noah walked with the true God." (Ge 6:8, 9) Noah could be spoken of as "faultless" because, unlike that ungodly world, he measured up fully to what God required of him.—Compare Ge 6:22; see PERFECTION.

Jehovah Purposes to Destroy That World.

Jehovah set a time limit for the existence of that ungodly world, saying: "My spirit shall not act toward man indefinitely in that he is also flesh. Accordingly his days shall amount to a hundred and twenty years." (Ge 6:3) Evidently these words were spoken to Noah. About 20 years after that, Noah's first son (probably Japheth) was born (2470 B.C.E.), and the record shows that another son, Shem, was born two years later. The time of Ham's birth is not stated, but these three sons were grown and married when the divine instructions were given to Noah to build an ark. Consequently, it is likely that only 40 or 50 years then remained before the Deluge. (Ge 6:13-18) Now, brought into a covenant with Jehovah (Ge 6:18) and assisted by his family, Noah set to work as a builder and "a preacher of righteousness," warning that wicked generation of impending destruction.—2Pe 2:5.

Preservation Through the Flood.

The people did not believe that God would act to destroy a world of wickedness. So it was because Noah possessed strong faith that he, in implicit obedience, did "according to all that God had commanded him. He did just so." (Ge 6:22) It was because of his unswerving faith in Jehovah that the Christian writer of the book of Hebrews included him in that "so great a cloud of witnesses." He wrote: "By faith Noah, after being given divine warning of things not yet beheld, showed godly fear and constructed an ark for the saving of his household; and

through this faith he condemned the world, and he became an heir of the righteousness that is according to faith."—Heb 11:7; 12:1.

Seven days before the floodwaters began to fall, Jehovah instructed Noah to gather the animals into the ark. On the seventh day of that week, "Noah went in, and his sons and his wife and his sons' wives with him, into the ark ahead of the waters of the deluge. . . . After that Jehovah shut the door behind him." On that very day "the flood arrived and destroyed them all."—Ge 7:1-16; Lu 17:27.

With the ark's occupants was preserved the thread of human and animal life. Also, true worship survived, and by means of Noah and his family God carried through the history of creation, along with a system of counting time back to man's creation and the original language (later called Hebrew). Noah kept an accurate log of important events during his stay in the ark.—Ge 7:11, 12, 24; 8:2-6, 10, 12-14.

Post-Flood Blessing and Rainbow Covenant.

After about one year in the ark, Noah and his family came out onto an earth freshly washed clean. The ark had come to rest in the mountains of the Ararat Range. In appreciation for Jehovah's loving-kindness, mercy, and protective hand, Noah constructed an altar and offered up "some of all the clean beasts and of all the clean flying creatures" as a sacrifice to Jehovah. Jehovah was pleased and revealed to Noah that no more would the earth be cursed, nor would God deal everything a blow as he had done. There would always be "seed sowing and harvest, and cold and heat, and summer and winter, and day and night."—Ge 8:18-22.

Jehovah blessed the Flood survivors, commanding them: "Be fruitful and become many and fill the earth." Then he made new decrees for their welfare: (1) He kindly allowed them to add the flesh of animals to their diet; (2) but since the soul is in the blood, the blood was not to be eaten; (3) capital punishment by duly constituted authority was instituted. These laws were to be binding on all mankind, as children of Noah's three sons.—Ge 1:28; 9:1-7; 10:32.

After making these decrees, Jehovah proceeded to say: "And as for me, here I am establishing my covenant with you men and with your offspring after you, and with every living soul that is with you, among fowls, among beasts and among all living creatures of the earth with you . . . Yes, I do establish my covenant with you: No more will all flesh be cut off by waters of a deluge, and no more will there occur a deluge to bring the earth to ruin." The rainbow stands to this day as a "sign," or reminder, of this covenant.—Ge 9:8-17; Isa 54:9.

Noah's Intoxication. Noah lived for 350 years after the Flood. The account reports, candidly and honestly: "Now Noah started off as a farmer and proceeded to plant a vineyard. And he began drinking of the wine and became intoxicated, and so he uncovered himself in the midst of his tent." (Ge 9:20, 21) This does not indicate that Noah was a habitual drunkard. The Bible reports this instance to give the background for the incident that accompanied it, which event had a profound effect on world history. Before the Flood, Noah was not indulging in the "drinking" of that wicked society, which they doubtless carried to extremes of drunken revelry. Such things dulled their sensibilities and were no doubt a factor in their ignoring God's warning, taking no note "until the flood came and swept them all away."—Mt 24:38, 39; Lu 17:27.

While Noah was asleep in his tent Ham, and perhaps also his son Canaan, became implicated in some sort of disrespect for Noah. The account reads: "Finally Noah awoke from his wine and got to know what his youngest son had done to him." Generally Ham is understood to be designated here as Noah's "youngest son." However, in the Bible, the expression sometimes refers to a grandson, who, in this case, was Canaan. Whatever the situation, Canaan's father Ham went telling it to his two brothers instead of himself covering Noah as they did. On learning of the episode, Noah cursed Canaan and blessed Shem's God Jehovah. —Ge 9:20-27.

Nimrod's Rebellion. Noah was the first patriarch of the post-Flood society. (Ge 10:1-32) Nevertheless, during his lifetime false religion again rose up among those under the leadership of Nimrod, as is seen in their rebellious attempt to build "a tower with its top in the heavens" for fear that they might be scattered "over all the surface of the earth." This was in direct opposition to God's command to "fill the earth," and was a rebellion also against Noah's position as God's prophet. Noah died about two years before the birth of Abraham. He therefore got to see Jehovah's judgment on the builders of the Tower of Babel and the scattering of those rebellious ones over the face of the earth. Noah and Shem were not involved in the tower building and consequently would not suffer confusion of their language, but would continue to speak man's original language, which God gave to Adam.—Ge 9:1, 28, 29; 11:1-9.

A Prophetic Pattern. The prophets Isaiah, Ezekiel, and Jesus Christ as well as the apostles Peter and Paul all spoke of God's servant Noah. Noah's days are shown by Jesus and Peter to be prophetic of "the presence of the Son of man" and a future "day of judgment and of destruction of the ungodly men." Jehovah, in sparing Noah and his family when he destroyed that wicked world, was "setting a pattern for ungodly persons of things to come."—2Pe 3:5-7; 2:5, 6; Isa 54:9; Eze 14:14, 20; Mt 24:37-39; Heb 11:7; 1Pe 3:20, 21.

2. [Heb., *No'ah'*]. One of Zelophehad's five daughters, of the tribe of Manasseh. Because Zelophehad died without sons, Jehovah decreed that the daughters should receive their father's tribal possession as an inheritance. This established a legal precedent. Later it was established also that daughters who inherit should become wives of men of their own tribe in order to hold the inheritance, so that it would not circulate from tribe to tribe.—Nu 26:28-33; 27:1-11; 36:6-12; Jos 17:3, 4.

NOB. A city evidently in the territory of Benjamin and close to Jerusalem. While there is some question as to the precise location of Nob, Nehemiah 11:31, 32 and Isaiah 10:28-32 indicate that it was near Anathoth and possibly close to a hill from which one could see Jerusalem. Some tentatively identify it with a spot on Ras el Mushra (Mount Scopus), about 1.5 km (1 mi) NE of the Temple Mount in Jerusalem. That would place it just N of the Mount of Olives.

When David fled from Saul, he went to High Priest Ahimelech, who was at Nob, "the city of the priests," and received from Ahimelech some showbread as food for his men, and Goliath' sword, which was being kept there. Perhaps the tabernacle had been moved to Nob when Shiloh experienced God's adverse judgment. (Compare 1Sa 14:3; Ps 78:60; Jer 7:12-14.) Later, Saul accused Ahimelech of conspiracy, in that he gave assistance to David. At Saul's command, Doeg the Edomite put to death the high priest and 84 other priests. Then Doeg slaughtered the men, women, children, and animals of Nob. Only Abiathar, the son of Ahimelech, escaped.—1Sa 21:1-9; 22:6-23.

Nob was one of the places mentioned in connection with the Assyrians' move toward Jerusalem. (Isa 10:24, 32) Benjamites resettled it after the return from Babylonian exile.—Ne 11:31, 32.

NOBAH (No'bah).

1. [from a root verb meaning "bark"]. An Israelite, probably of the tribe of Manasseh, who captured Kenath and its dependent towns. Thereafter he named the city after himself.—Nu 32:42.

2. A city E of the Jordan, captured by Nobah. (Nu 32:39, 42) Evidently the name Nobah did not stick, because later it is called by its original name, Kenath. (1Ch 2:23) The ruins at Kanaouat, about 90 km (60 mi) SE of Damascus are commonly identified with the ancient site.

3. A place situated E of the Jordan and near Jogbehah in Gad. (Nu 32:34, 35; Jg 8:11) Its precise location is not known today.

NOBLE. See LEADER, NOBLE, PRINCE.

NODAB (No'dab). One of the confederated groups overwhelmingly defeated with Jehovah's help by the tribes of Reuben and Gad and the half tribe of Manasseh. (1Ch 5:18-22) Nothing more is known of this tribe, except the possible preservation of the name in that of the village of Nudebe, in the desert E of Palestine.

NOGAH (No'gah) [from a root meaning "shine"]. Son of King David, born to him in Jerusalem.—1Ch 3:5-7; 14:3-6.

NOHAH (No'hah) [from a root meaning "rest; settle down"]. The fourth-listed son of Benjamin. (1Ch 8:1, 2) Since he is not named among those listed in Genesis chapter 46, he was probably born after the family entered Egypt. Some suppose that Nohah was another name for Shephupham or was his descendant.—Nu 26:39.

NOPH. The usual Hebrew Scripture name for Memphis, an important city of ancient Egypt. —Isa 19:13; Jer 2:16; 44:1; 46:14, 19; Eze 30:13, 16; see MEMPHIS.

NOPHAH (No'phah). According to the Masoretic text, apparently a place in Moab. (Nu 21:29, 30) Such a site is today unknown.

NORTH. In addition to the usual term *tsa-phohn'*, north was also indicated by the direction "left," since the orientation was facing toward the rising sun in the east. (Ge 14:15, ftn) In Scriptural usage, "north" may denote a section of the earth (Ps 107:3; Isa 43:6; Lu 13:29), a northerly direction (Ex 26:20; 1Ki 7:25; Re 21:13), the northern sky (Job 26:7), and various lands or kingdoms (including Assyria [Zep 2:13] and Babylon [Jer 46:10]) that were situated somewhat N and E of the land inhabited by the Israelites. Though Babylon on the Euphrates River actually lay E of Tyre, Ezekiel 26:7 speaks of the king of Babylon as coming against Tyre from the north. Likewise, the calamity that Judah and Jerusalem were to experience from the Babylonians is referred to as coming "out of the north." (Jer 1:14, 15) The reason for this appears to be that, when marching westward, the Babylonian armies took a northerly route and thus avoided passing through the desert. This was, in fact, the customary way, as Babylonian records show.

Since various lands and kingdoms are assigned a northern location, the context and other related scriptures are often helpful in determining what is meant by "north" or "land of the north." For example, Isaiah 21:2, 9 and Daniel 5:28 show that the nations from "the land of the north" mentioned at Jeremiah 50:9 include the Medes, Persians, and Elamites. Apparently the nations attacking Babylon are viewed as a united army or common foe of Babylon, "a congregation." Many of the nations involved were far N of Babylon (Jer 51:27, 28), and much of Media was at least NE of Babylon. The attack, too, evidently came from a northern direction, since Cyrus stopped the flow of the river N of the city.

"The King of the North." Facts of history provide still another basis for determining how "north" is to be understood in some texts. A case in point is "the king of the north" mentioned in Daniel chapter 11. Historical evidence indicates that the "mighty king" of Daniel 11:3 was Alexander the Great. After Alexander's death, the empire was eventually divided among his four generals. One of these generals, Seleucus Nicator, took Mesopotamia and Syria, this making him the ruler of territory situated N of Palestine. Another general, Ptolemy Lagus, gained control of Egypt, to the SW of Palestine. Therefore, with Seleucus Nicator and Ptolemy Lagus the long struggle between "the king of the north" and "the king of the south" began. However, the prophecy concerning "the king of the north" extends from the time of Seleucus Nicator down to "the time of the end." (Da 11:40) Logically, then, the national and political identity of "the king of the north" would change in the course of history. But it would still be possible to determine his identity on the basis of what the prophecy said the "king of the north" would do. —See the book *"Your Will Be Done on Earth,"* 1958, pp. 220-307.

Jehovah's Residence. "North" also appears in the Scriptures with reference to the place where Jehovah resided representatively with the Israelites.—Ps 48:1, 2; Isa 14:13, 14; see MOUNTAIN OF MEETING.

NOSE, NOSTRILS. The part of the face that affords passage for air in respiration and serves as the organ of smell.

When God created Adam, he proceeded to "blow into his nostrils the breath [form of *nesha·mah'*] of life, and the man came to be a living soul." (Ge

2:7) This "breath of life" not only filled the lungs with air but also imparted to the body the life-force that is sustained by breathing. The breath being drawn into the body through the nostrils is essential to life; it sustains the life-force. At the Flood, "everything in which the breath of the force of life was active in its nostrils, namely, all that were on the dry ground, died."—Ge 7:22.

The Hebrew word for nose or nostril ('aph) is frequently used to refer to the entire face. Adam was sentenced to earn his livelihood from the ground 'in the sweat of his face [literally, "nose" or "nostril"].' (Ge 3:19) Lot bowed down with his face (nose) to the ground before the visiting angels. —Ge 19:1.

Sensitivity in Smelling and Tasting. The olfactory area is located in the upper part of the nasal cavity, where the olfactory nerves terminate in hairlike endings; also fine endings of the trigeminal nerve are found in this area. The sense of smell in humans is very acute. According to an article in the *Scientific American* (February 1964, p. 42): "The sense of smell obviously is a chemical sense, and its sensitivity is proverbial; to a chemist the ability of the nose to sort out and characterize substances is almost beyond belief. It deals with complex compounds that might take a chemist months to analyze in the laboratory; the nose identifies them instantly, even in an amount so small (as little as a ten-millionth of a gram) that the most sensitive modern laboratory instruments often cannot detect the substance, let alone analyze and label it."

The nose also plays a large part in taste. There are four primary tastes: sweet, salt, sour, and bitter. These the taste buds in the mouth recognize. But much of the flavor in food is enjoyed because of the sense of smell. For example, a person whose nostrils are stopped up finds difficulty in distinguishing between two kinds of food, as most things then taste more or less flat.

Beauty. Being located so prominently, a well-formed nose contributes greatly to facial beauty. In The Song of Solomon (7:4), the Shulammite girl's nose being likened to "the tower of Lebanon" may have reference to the symmetry of her nose as adding dignity and beauty to her face. God required that Israel's priests, because they were his representatives before the people, be without blemish, one of the requirements being that no priest should have a slit or mutilated nose.—Le 21:18.

Illustrative and Figurative Uses. The word for nose or nostril ('aph) is often used figuratively for anger (because of the violent breathing or snorting of an enraged person). (See ANGER.) It is also employed with reference to Jehovah's action because of his anger (Ps 18:8, 15), or when he exerts his powerful active force.—Ex 14:21; 15:8.

The disgusting idolatry into which Israel fell was a cause for the burning anger of Jehovah against them, which he expressed through the prophet Isaiah, saying: "These are a smoke in my nostrils, a fire burning all day long."—Isa 65:5.

Proverbs 30:32, 33 states: "If you have acted senselessly by lifting yourself up, and if you have fixed your thought upon it, put the hand to the mouth. For the churning of milk is what brings forth butter, and the squeezing of the nose is what brings forth blood, and the squeezing out of anger is what brings forth quarreling." This strongly emphasizes the trouble that can be caused by one who speaks wrongly or who harbors up anger or lets it out unrestrained. Here, in a play on words "anger" is the dual form of the word for "nose."

NOSE RING. An ornamental ring worn on the nose. It was inserted either through the left or the right side of the nose or through the partition separating the nostrils and was especially worn by women. (Ge 24:22, 30, 47; Isa 3:21) Ishmaelite men, however, according to some translations, also wore nose rings.—Jg 8:24-26.

The Hebrew word for "nose ring" (ne'zem) can also be applied to an earring, and in some cases there may have been little difference in the forms of these ornaments. Sometimes the context makes it possible to determine whether a nose ring or an earring is meant.—Compare Ge 24:47 with Ge 35:4; Eze 16:12; see RING.

Though nose rings were generally made of gold, other materials, such as silver, were also used. Nose rings might be ornamented with beads, pieces of coral, or jewels, suspended from them as small pendants. The diameter of nose rings varied from 2.5 to as much as 7.5 cm (1 to 3 in.). Hanging down over the mouth as it did, the nose ring had to be moved when eating.

At Proverbs 11:22 an outwardly beautiful woman who rejects sensibleness is compared to "a gold nose ring in the snout of a pig."

NUMBER, NUMERAL. In ancient Hebrew numbers were spelled out. Sometime after the exile to Babylon, the Jews adopted to some extent the practice of using their alphabetic letters as symbols of numerical figures. However, this usage does not appear even in postexilic Hebrew Bible manuscripts. One of the oldest extant specimens of Hebrew writing is the inscription taken from the Siloam water tunnel (probably from the time of Hezekiah's reign [745-717 B.C.E.]), in which the measurements are written out in full. Spelling out the numbers provides an added measure of accuracy and dependability in the manuscripts of the Hebrew Scriptures, which have been copied many times, for, in copying, a numeral is usually easier to mistake than a word.

In Hebrew, numbers above ten are a combination of words, such as 12 (two and ten) (Ge 14:4), except that 20 is the plural of ten; 30 a plural word derived from three; 40 a plural word derived from four, and so on. One hundred is a separate word; 200 is the dual form. Other "hundreds" are composed of two words, as, 300. The highest number expressed by one Hebrew word is 20,000, the dual form of 10,000 (myriad). Larger numbers are a combination of words. For example, at 1 Chronicles 5:18 the number 44,760 is, literally, forty and four thousand and seven of hundreds and sixty. A million is written as a thousand thousands. (2Ch 14:9) Rebekah's family blessed her, saying: "O you, our sister, may you become thousands times ten thousand [literally, thousands of myriads]." (Rebekah's posterity actually came to number many millions.) (Ge 24:55, 60) In Daniel's vision Jehovah is shown as having "ten thousand times ten thousand [literally, a myriad of myriads]" standing before him.—Da 7:10.

Occasionally numbers are used in an approximate sense, as round numbers, for example, at Psalm 90:10, where the psalmist speaks of man's age limit, and possibly also at 1 Kings 19:18 (7,000 who had not bowed to Baal) and 2 Chronicles 14:9 (the million Ethiopians defeated by Asa).

In the Christian Greek Scriptures numerals are generally expressed in words. The number of "the wild beast" is in words in the Sinaitic and the Alexandrine manuscripts.—Re 13:18.

Bible Usage Not Numerology. Since the Bible is a book of both history and prophecy, the numbers given therein may be either literal or symbolic. The context usually reveals in which sense a number is used. Certain numbers appear often in the Bible in an illustrative, figurative, or symbolic sense, and in such cases an understanding of their significance is vital to an understanding of the text. However, this Bible usage of numbers should not be confused with numerology, in which occult mysticism is attached to figures, their combinations, and numerical totals. Numerology apparently had its origin in ancient Babylon and, along with other forms of divination, comes under divine condemnation.—De 18:10-12.

In the following we will discuss a few of the figurative uses of certain numbers that are used prominently in the Bible.

One. This number, when used figuratively, conveys the thought of singleness, uniqueness, as well as unity and agreement in purpose and action. "Jehovah our God is one Jehovah," said Moses. (De 6:4) He alone is Sovereign. He is unique. He does not share his glory with another, as is the case with pagan trinitarian gods. (Ac 4:24; Re 6:10; Isa 42:8) There is oneness in purpose and activity between Jehovah and Jesus Christ (Joh 10:30) and there should be complete unity of Christ's disciples with God, with his Son, and with one another. (Joh 17:21; Ga 3:28) Such oneness is illustrated in the marriage arrangement.—Ge 2:24; Mt 19:6; Eph 5:28-32.

Two. The number two frequently appears in a legal setting. Agreement in the accounts of two witnesses adds to the force of the testimony. Two witnesses, or even three, were required to establish a matter before the judges. This principle is also followed in the Christian congregation. (De 17:6; 19:15; Mt 18:16; 2Co 13:1; 1Ti 5:19; Heb 10:28) God adhered to this principle in presenting his Son to the people as mankind's Savior. Jesus said: "In your own Law it is written, 'The witness of two men is true.' I am one that bears witness about myself, and the Father who sent me bears witness about me."—Joh 8:17, 18.

Doing something a second time—for example, repetition of a statement or vision, even in only a parallel way—firmly established the matter as sure and true (as in Pharaoh's dream of the cows and the ears of grain; Ge 41:32). Biblical Hebrew poetry is full of thought parallelism, which establishes more firmly in mind the truths stated and at the same time clarifies matters by the variety of wording in the parallelism.—See Ps 2, 44, and others.

In Daniel's prophecy a certain beast's having "two horns" symbolized duality in rulership of the Medo-Persian Empire.—Da 8:20, 21; compare Re 13:11.

Three. While the testifying of two witnesses to the same matter established proof sufficient for legal action, three made the testimony even stronger. The number three, therefore, is used at times to represent intensity, emphasis, or added strength. "A threefold cord cannot quickly be torn in two." (Ec 4:12) Emphasis was achieved in Jesus' threefold questioning of Peter after Peter's three denials of Jesus. (Mt 26:34, 75; Joh 21:15-17) The vision telling Peter to eat of all kinds of animals, including those unclean according to the Law, was intensified by being given to him three times. This doubtless made it easier for Peter to understand, when Cornelius and his household accepted the good news, that God was now turning his attention to uncircumcised people of the nations, considered unclean by the Jews.—Ac 10:1-16, 28-35, 47, 48.

The intensity of Jehovah's holiness and cleanness is emphasized by the declaration of heavenly creatures: "Holy, holy, holy is Jehovah." (Isa 6:3; Re 4:8) Before taking the last earthly king of the line of David off the throne, Jehovah said: "A ruin, a ruin, a ruin I shall make it. As for this also, it will certainly become no one's until he comes who has the legal right, and I must give it to him." Here he emphatically showed there would be no Davidic kings sitting upon the throne at Jerusalem in his name—the throne would be absolutely vacant —until God's time to establish his Messiah in Kingdom power. (Eze 21:27) The intensity of woes to come to those dwelling on earth is forecast by the triple repetition of the declaration "woe."—Re 8:13.

Four. Four is a number sometimes expressing universalness or foursquareness in symmetry and form. It is found three times at Revelation 7:1. Here the "four angels" (all those in charge of "the four winds," ready for complete destruction) stood on earth's "four corners" (they could let loose the winds obliquely or diagonally, and no quarter of the earth would be spared). (Compare Da 8:8; Isa 11:12; Jer 49:36; Zec 2:6; Mt 24:31.) The New Jerusalem is "foursquare," equal in every dimension, being in fact cubical in shape. (Re 21:16) Other figurative expressions using the number four are found at Zechariah 1:18-21; 6:1-3; Revelation 9:14, 15.

Six. This number at times represents imperfection. The number of "the wild beast" is 666 and is called "a man's number," indicating that it has to do with imperfect, fallen man, and it seems to symbolize the imperfection of that which is represented by "the wild beast." The number six being emphasized to a third degree (the six appearing in the position of units, tens, and hundreds) therefore highlights the imperfection and deficiency of that which the beast represents, or pictures.—Re 13:18.

Seven. Seven is used frequently in the Scriptures to signify completeness. At times it has reference to bringing a work toward completion. Or it can refer to the complete cycle of things as established or allowed by God. By completing his work toward the earth in six creative days and resting on the seventh day, Jehovah set the pattern for the whole Sabbath arrangement, from the seven-day week to the Jubilee year that followed the seven-times-seven–year cycle. (Ex 20:10; Le 25:2, 6, 8) The Festival of Unleavened Bread and the Festival of Booths were each seven days long. (Ex 34:18; Le 23:34) Seven appears often in connection with the Levitical rules for offerings (Le 4:6; 16:14, 19; Nu 28:11) and for cleansings.—Le 14:7, 8, 16, 27, 51; 2Ki 5:10.

The "seven congregations" of Revelation, with their characteristics, give a complete picture of *all* the congregations of God on earth.—Re 1:20- 3:22.

The "seven heads" of the "wild beast" (Re 13:1) show the limit to which the beast would be allowed to develop. Although the "scarlet-colored wild beast" is called "an eighth" king, it springs from the seven and does not exist apart from the seven-headed wild beast (Re 17:3, 9-11), as is true also of the "image" of "the wild beast." (Re 13:14) Similarly, the two-horned "wild beast" is actually coexistent with the original "wild beast" whose "mark" it tries to put on all persons.—Re 13:11, 16, 17.

Jehovah was long-suffering with Israel but warned them that if, despite his discipline, they ignored him, he would then chastise them "seven times," thoroughly, for their sins.—Le 26:18, 21, 28.

In historical sections of the Scriptures, seven frequently occurs to denote completeness, or doing a work completely. The Israelites exercised full faith and obedience by marching for seven days around Jericho, encompassing it seven times on the seventh day, after which the city wall collapsed. (Jos 6:2-4, 15) Elijah showed full faith in the efficacy of his prayer to God by commanding his servant up on Mount Carmel to go looking at the sky seven times before a rain cloud appeared. (1Ki 18:42-44) Naaman the leper had to bathe seven times in the Jordan River. He, as a mighty Syrian general, had to display considerable humility to carry out this procedure recommended by the prophet Elisha, but for his obediently doing it, Jehovah cleansed him. (2Ki 5:10, 12) The purity, completeness, perfection, and fineness of Jehovah's sayings are likened with poetic force and intensity to silver refined in a smelting furnace, clarified seven times. (Ps 12:6) Jehovah's mercy is magnified by the statement: "The righteous one may fall even seven times, and he will certainly get up." (Pr 24:16) His deserving all praise is declared by the psalmist: "Seven times in the day I have praised you."—Ps 119:164.

The book of Revelation abounds with symbolic use of the number seven in connection with the things of God and his congregation, and also the things of God's Adversary, Satan the Devil, in his all-out fight to oppose God and his people.—Re 1:4, 12, 16; 5:1, 6; 8:2; 10:3; 12:3; 13:1; 15:1, 7; 17:3, 10; and other texts.

Multiples of seven are used in a similar sense of completeness. Seventy (ten times seven) is employed prophetically in the "seventy weeks" of Daniel's prophecy dealing with Messiah's coming. (Da 9:24-27; see SEVENTY WEEKS.) Jerusalem and Judah lay desolate 70 years, because of disobedience to God, "until the land had paid off [completely] its sabbaths."—2Ch 36:21; Jer 25:11; 29:10; Da 9:2; Zec 1:12; 7:5.

Seventy-seven, a repetition of seven in a number, was equivalent to saying "indefinitely" or "without limit." Jesus counsels Christians to forgive their brothers to that extent. (Mt 18:21, 22) Since God had ruled that anyone killing Cain, the murderer, must "suffer vengeance seven times," Lamech, who apparently killed a man in self-defense, said: "If seven times Cain is to be avenged, then Lamech seventy times and seven." —Ge 4:15, 23, 24.

Eight. The number eight was also used to add *emphasis* to the completeness of something (one more than seven, the number generally used for completeness), thus sometimes representing abundance. Jehovah reassured his people of deliverance from the threat of Assyria, saying that there should be raised up against the Assyrian "seven shepherds, yes, [not merely seven, but] eight dukes of mankind." (Mic 5:5) As a fitting climax to the final festival of the sacred year, the Festival of Booths, the eighth day was to be one of holy convention, solemn assembly, a day of complete rest.—Le 23:36, 39; Nu 29:35.

Ten. Ten is a number denoting fullness, entirety, the aggregate, the sum of all that exists of something. It may be noted also that, where the numbers seven and ten are used together, the seven represents that which is higher or superior and ten represents something of a subordinate nature.

The Ten Plagues poured upon Egypt fully expressed God's judgments upon Egypt—all that were needed to humiliate fully the false gods of Egypt and to break the hold of Egypt upon God's people Israel. The "Ten Words" formed the basic laws of the Law covenant, the approximately 600 other laws merely enlarging on these, elucidating them, and explaining their application. (Ex 20:3-17; 34:28) Jesus used the number ten in several of his illustrations to denote entirety or the full number of something.—Mt 25:1; Lu 15:8; 19:13, 16, 17.

One of the beasts of Daniel's vision and certain beasts described in Revelation had ten horns. These evidently represented all the powers, or "kings," of earth making up the beastly arrangement. (Da 7:7, 20, 24; Re 12:3; 13:1; 17:3, 7, 12) The fullness of the test or period of test that God determines for his servants or allows them to undergo is expressed at Revelation 2:10: "Do not be afraid of the things you are about to suffer. Look! The Devil will keep on throwing some of you into prison that you may be *fully* put to the test, and that you may have tribulation *ten days.*"

Twelve. The patriarch Jacob had 12 sons, who became the foundations of the 12 tribes of Israel. Their offspring were organized by God under the Law covenant as God's nation. Twelve therefore seems to represent a complete, balanced, divinely constituted arrangement. (Ge 35:22; 49:28) Jehovah chose 12 apostles, who form the secondary foundations of the New Jerusalem, built upon Jesus Christ. (Mt 10:2-4; Re 21:14) There are 12 tribes of "the sons of [spiritual] Israel," each tribe consisting of 12,000 members.—Re 7:4-8.

Multiples of 12 are also sometimes significant. David established 24 divisions of the priesthood to serve by turn in the temple later built by Solomon. (1Ch 24:1-18) This assists in identifying the "twenty-four elders" who were seated round about God's throne in white outer garments and who were wearing crowns. (Re 4:4) The footstep followers of Jesus Christ, his spiritual brothers, are promised kingship and priesthood with him in the heavens. These elders could not be only the apostles, who numbered just 12. They therefore evidently represent the entire body of the "royal priesthood," the 144,000 (as represented in the 24 priestly divisions serving at the temple) in their positions in the heavens, as crowned kings and priests.—1Pe 2:9; Re 7:4-8; 20:6.

Forty. In a few instances periods of judgment or punishment seem to be associated with the number 40. (Ge 7:4; Eze 29:11, 12) Nineveh was given 40 days to repent. (Jon 3:4) Another use of the number 40 points out a parallel in the life of Jesus Christ with that of Moses, who typified Christ. Both of these men experienced 40-day periods of fasting.—Ex 24:18; 34:28; De 9:9, 11; Mt 4:1, 2.

NUMBERS, BOOK OF.

The fourth book of the Pentateuch. It derives its English name from the two numberings of the sons of Israel mentioned therein. It relates events that took place in the region of Mount Sinai, in the wilderness during the course of Israel's wandering, and on the

Plains of Moab. The narrative primarily covers a period of 38 years and 9 months, from 1512 to 1473 B.C.E. (Nu 1:1; De 1:3, 4) Although occurring earlier than the events in the surrounding material, the happenings narrated at Numbers 7:1-88 and 9:1-15 provide background information that forms an essential part of the book.

Writership. The writership of the book of Numbers has from ancient times been attributed to Moses. Ample evidence in the book itself confirms this. There is no hint of any other life than that experienced by Israel in Egypt and then in the wilderness. In commenting about the time Hebron was built, the writer used the Egyptian city of Zoan as a reference point. (Nu 13:22) The age of Zoan would reasonably be common knowledge to a man like Moses, who "was instructed in all the wisdom of the Egyptians."—Ac 7:22.

Certain commands recorded in the book of Numbers are unique to the circumstances of a nation on the move. These include the prescribed tribal encampments (Nu 1:52, 53), the order of

---

HIGHLIGHTS OF NUMBERS

A historical narrative that demonstrates how vital it is to obey Jehovah under all circumstances and to respect his representatives

Covers events during most of the time Israel was in the wilderness en route to the Promised Land

The tribes of Israel are registered and organized

About a year after the Exodus from Egypt, all Israelite males 20 years old and over are registered, with the exception of the Levites (1:1-49)

Each three-tribe division is assigned a place to camp and a position in the order of march (2:1-34)

The Levites are set apart to assist the priests; all Levites over a month old are registered; they are taken by Jehovah in exchange for the firstborn of the other tribes (3:1-51)

The male offspring of Kohath, Gershon, and Merari, the three sons of Levi, from 30 to 50 years of age are numbered and given service assignments (4:1-49)

Another census is taken of the Israelites shortly before they enter the Promised Land (26:1-65)

Israelites receive divine commands regarding their worship and their dealings with one another

Requirements are set out for Nazirites (6:1-21)

The Passover is observed; provision is made so that anyone unclean or on a distant journey can observe it a month after Nisan 14 (9:1-14)

Various regulations are given involving the duties and the privileges of priests and Levites, including the preparation of the water for cleansing and its uses (18:1–19:22)

The offerings are listed that must be presented each day, each Sabbath, at the start of each month, during festivals, and during the seventh month (28: 1–29:40)

Jehovah's commands governing vows are recorded (30:1-16)

Guilty ones must confess and compensate the wronged party (5:5-8)

A procedure is established for handling cases when a wife is suspected of secret adultery (5:11-31)

Arrangements are made for six cities of refuge (35:9-34)

Israelites manifest a lack of appreciation for Jehovah's provisions, and they disobey his commands

The people complain about eating manna and long for meat; when Jehovah provides quail, many act with extreme greed and are punished with death (11:4-34)

They believe the bad report of the ten fearful spies and want to return to Egypt; Moses has to intercede for them (13:1–14:19)

When that rebellious generation is sentenced to wander and die in the wilderness, the people attempt to enter the Promised Land without Jehovah's blessing, and they suffer a military defeat (14:26-45)

There is a failure to respect Jehovah's visible representatives

Miriam and Aaron speak out against Moses; Jehovah strikes Miriam with leprosy (12:1-15)

Korah, Dathan, Abiram, On, and 250 chieftains range themselves against Moses and Aaron; Jehovah executes the rebels, and this gives rise to further murmuring; 14,700 more die (16:1-50)

At Kadesh, the Israelites complain bitterly against Moses and Aaron because of a water shortage; when Jehovah miraculously supplies water, Moses and Aaron fail to sanctify Jehovah's name and thus lose the privilege of entering the Promised Land (20:1-13)

The Israelites tire out and speak against Jehovah and Moses; they are plagued by serpents, and many die; Moses intercedes for the people, and anyone bitten can be saved by gazing at a copper serpent (21:4-9)

Jehovah blesses Israel but insists on exclusive devotion as the nation prepares to enter Canaan

Jehovah gives Israel victory over the king of Arad (21:1-3)

Israel defeats Sihon and Og, taking possession of their land (21:21-35)

Balak hires Balaam to curse the Israelites; Jehovah forces him to bless Israel instead (22:2–24:25)

Moabite women lure Israelite men into idolatry and fornication; 24,000 are killed for thus falling into apostasy; Jehovah relents when Phinehas tolerates no rivalry toward Him (25:1-18)

march (2:9, 16, 17, 24, 31), and the trumpet signals for convening the assembly and for breaking camp (10:2-6). Also, the law concerning quarantine is worded to fit camp life. (5:2-4) Various other commands are stated in such a way as to call for a future application when the Israelites would be residing in the Promised Land. Among these are: the use of trumpets for sounding war calls (10:9), the setting aside of 48 cities for the Levites (35:2-8), the action to be taken against idolatry and the inhabitants of Canaan (33:50-56), the selection of six cities of refuge, instructions for handling cases of persons claiming to be accidental manslayers (35:9-33), and laws involving inheritance and marriage of heiresses (27:8-11; 36:5-9).

Additionally, the recording of the Israelite encampments is definitely ascribed to Moses (Nu 33:2), and the concluding words of the book of Numbers also point to him as the writer of the account.—36:13.

Authenticity. The authenticity of the book is established beyond any doubt. Outstanding is its candor. Wrong conduct and defeat are not concealed. (Nu 11:1-5, 10, 32-35; 14:2, 11, 45) Even the transgressions of Moses himself, his brother Aaron, his sister Miriam, and his nephews Nadab and Abihu are exposed. (3:3, 4; 12:1-15; 20:2-13) Repeatedly, happenings recorded in the book are recounted in the Psalms (78:14-41; 95:7-11; 105: 40, 41; 106:13-33; 135:10, 11; 136:16-20). By their allusions to major events and other details in Numbers, Joshua (4:12; 14:2), Jeremiah (2Ki 18:4), Nehemiah (9:19-22), David (Ps 95:7-11), Isaiah (48:21), Ezekiel (20:13-24), Hosea (9:10), Amos (5:25), Micah (6:5), the Christian martyr Stephen (Ac 7:36), the apostles Paul (1Co 10:1-11) and Peter (2Pe 2:15, 16), the disciple Jude (vs 11), and the Son of God (Joh 3:14; Re 2:14) showed that they accepted this record as part of God's inspired Word. There is also Balaam's prophecy regarding the star that would step forth out of Jacob, which had its initial fulfillment when David became king and thereafter subdued the Moabites and Edomites.—Nu 24:15-19; 2Sa 8:2, 13, 14.

Value. The book of Numbers forcefully illustrates the importance of obedience to Jehovah, respect for him and his servants, the need for faith and guarding against ungodly men (Nu 13:25–14: 38; 22:7, 8, 22; 26:9, 10; Heb 3:7–4:11; 2Pe 2:12-16; Jude 11; Re 2:14), not faithlessly putting Jehovah to the test (Nu 21:5, 6; 1Co 10:9), as well as refraining from murmuring (Nu 14:2, 36, 37; 16:1-3, 41; 17:5, 10; 1Co 10:10, 11) and sexual immorality (Nu 25:1-9; 31:16; 1Co 10:6, 8). Jehovah's dealings with Israel give evidence of his great power, mercy, and loving-kindness, as well as his being slow to anger, though not withholding punishment when deserving. (Nu 14:17-20) Further, the position and ministry of Moses (Nu 12:7; Heb 3:2-6), the miraculous provision of water from the rock-mass (Nu 20:7-11; 1Co 10:4), the lifting up of the copper serpent (Nu 21:8, 9; Joh 3:14, 15), and the water of cleansing (Nu 19:2-22; Heb 9:13, 14) provided prophetic pictures that were fulfilled in Christ Jesus.

The account provides background material that illuminates other scriptures. It shows on what basis Judean King Hezekiah was able to arrange the Passover on Ziv (Iyyar) 14, instead of Nisan (Abib) 14. (Nu 9:10, 11; 2Ch 30:15) The full discussion of Naziriteship (Nu 6:2-21) explains why Samson and Samuel were not to have their hair cut (Jg 13:4, 5; 1Sa 1:11) and why John the Baptizer was not to drink intoxicating beverages. (Lu 1:15) For additional examples, compare Numbers 2:18-23 and Psalm 80:2; Numbers 15:38 and Matthew 23:5; Numbers 17:8-10 and Hebrews 9:4; Numbers 18:26 and Hebrews 7:5-9; Numbers 18: 31 and 1 Corinthians 9:13, 14; Numbers 28:9, 10 and Matthew 12:5.

NUN, I. Father of Moses' successor Joshua; son of Elishama of the tribe of Ephraim.—Ex 33:11; Jos 1:1; 1Ch 7:20, 26, 27.

NUN, II [ב; final, ך]. The 14th letter of the Hebrew alphabet. It is one of the five Hebrew letters that have a different form when used as the final letter of a word. In the Hebrew, it is the initial letter in each of the eight verses in Psalm 119:105-112.—See HEBREW, II.

NURSE. Two kinds of nurses were employed in ancient times. The "nursing woman" (Heb., meh·neʹqeth; Ge 24:59; 35:8; Ex 2:7; 2Ki 11:2; 2Ch 22:11; Isa 49:23) served as a mother's substitute for breast-feeding an infant. Deborah was such a nurse to Rebekah but later served as her maid or caretaker, continuing as a family servant even after her mistress' death. (Ge 24:59, 67; 35:8) The other type nurse could be a male (Heb., ʼo·menʹ; Nu 11:12; Isa 49:23 ['caretaker']) or a female (Heb., ʼo·meʹneth; 2Sa 4:4). A person of either sex might care for children, the sick, or older persons. The role of a nurse or caretaker was filled by aged Naomi toward her grandson Obed and by the beautiful virgin Abishag in connection with King David.—Ru 4:13, 16, 17; 1Ki 1:1-4.

At 1 Thessalonians 2:7, Paul likens himself and his companions to "a nursing mother" (Gr., troʹphos), thus emphasizing that they were gentle toward the Macedonian believers.

NUT TREES [Heb., *'eghohz'*]. The Shulammite maiden in The Song of Solomon (6:11) speaks of going down "to the garden of nut trees." The nut trees here referred to may well have been walnut trees (*Juglans regia*). This tree is native to southeastern Europe and western Asia and is presently cultivated in Galilee and on the slopes of Lebanon and Mount Hermon. The Jewish historian Josephus speaks of it as growing in abundance in the area of the Sea of Galilee in the first century C.E. (*The Jewish War,* III, 516, 517 [x, 8]) The walnut is a handsome tree, growing up to 9 m (30 ft) high, with fragrant leaves that provide excellent shade. The wood is close-grained and prized for its beauty by cabinetmakers. The fruit of the tree is encased in a husk containing tannic acid and, when boiled, produces a rich-brown dye. The nutmeats are highly valued for their rich taste and are pressed to produce an oil nearly equal to olive oil in quality.

NYMPHA (Nym'pha) [Bride]. A Christian woman living in or near Laodicea or Colossae in whose home a congregation held meetings, and to whom Paul sent greetings.—Col 4:15.

O

OAR. See SHIP.

OATH. A sworn statement as to the truthfulness of what is said or that a person will or will not do a certain thing; it frequently involves an appeal to a superior, especially to God.

In the Hebrew Scriptures two words are used to denote what we understand as an oath. *Shevu·'ah'* means "an oath or a sworn statement." (Ge 24:8; Le 5:4) The related Hebrew verb *sha·va'*, meaning "swear," or take an oath, comes from the same root as the Hebrew word for "seven." Thus "swear" originally meant "come under the influence of 7 things." (*Theological Dictionary of the New Testament,* edited by G. Friedrich; translator and editor, G. Bromiley, 1970, Vol. V, p. 459) Abraham and Abimelech swore over seven female lambs in making the covenant at the well of Beer-sheba, meaning "Well of the Oath; or, Well of Seven." (Ge 21:27-32; see also Ge 26:28-33.) *Shevu·'ah'* has reference to a sworn statement on the part of a person that he will do or will not do a certain thing. The word itself carries no connotation of a curse upon the one swearing if he fails to fulfill the oath. This is the word used for the oath, or sworn statement, to Abraham by Jehovah, who never fails to fulfill his word and upon whom no curse can come.—Ge 26:3.

The other Hebrew word used is *'a·lah'*, meaning "oath, cursing." (Ge 24:41, ftn) It may also be translated "oath of obligation." (Ge 26:28) A Hebrew and Aramaic lexicon by Koehler and Baumgartner (p. 49) defines the term as a "curse (threat of calamity in case of misdeed), laid on a p[erson] by himself or by others." In ancient Hebrew times it was considered the gravest matter to make an oath. An oath was to be kept, even to the oath taker's hurt. (Ps 15:4; Mt 5:33) A person was held guilty before Jehovah if he spoke thoughtlessly in a sworn statement. (Le 5:4) Violation of an oath would bring the most severe consequences of punishment from God. Among the earliest nations and particularly among the Hebrews an oath was in a sense a religious act, involving God. The use of the term *'a·lah'* by the Hebrews by implication made God a party to the oath and professed a readiness to incur any judgment he might be pleased to inflict in event of the oath maker's infidelity. This term is never used by God with reference to his own oaths.

The corresponding Greek terms are *hor'kos* (oath) and *o·mny'o* (swear), which both occur in James 5:12. The verb *hor·ki'zo* means "put under oath" or "solemnly charge." (Mr 5:7; Ac 19:13) Other terms related to *hor'kos* mean "sworn oath" (Heb 7:20), "put under solemn obligation or oath" (1Th 5:27), "false swearer or oath-breaker" (1Ti 1:10), and "swear without performing or make an oath falsely" (Mt 5:33). The Greek word *a·na·the·ma·ti'zo* is rendered 'bind with a curse' in Acts 23:12, 14, and 21.

Expressions Used in Making Oaths. Often an oath was made by swearing by God or in the name of God. (Ge 14:22; 31:53; De 6:13; Jg 21:7; Jer 12:16) Jehovah swore by himself, or by his own life. (Ge 22:16; Eze 17:16; Zep 2:9) Expressions of a formal nature were sometimes employed by men, such as, "May Jehovah do so to me [or, to you] and add to it if . . . " I (or you) fail to do as sworn. (Ru 1:17; 1Sa 3:17; 2Sa 19:13) The assertion might be made more emphatic by the individual's pronouncing his own name.—1Sa 20:13; 25:22; 2Sa 3:9.

Pagans made similar appeals to their false gods. Jezebel the Baal worshiper appealed, not to Jehovah, but to "gods" ('elo·him', with a plural verb), as did Ben-hadad II, king of Syria. (1Ki 19:2; 20:10) In fact, because such expressions were universally prevalent, idolatry came to be represented in the Bible as a 'swearing by some false god,' or by what was "no God."—Jos 23:7; Jer 5:7; 12:16; Am 8:14.

In a few, very serious cases or when strong emotional feeling attended the solemn declaration, the curses or punishments that would attend failure to fulfill the oath were specifically named. (Nu 5:19-23; Ps 7:4, 5; 137:5, 6) Job, in contending for his uprightness, reviews his life and declares himself willing to undergo the direst punishments if he is found to have violated Jehovah's laws of loyalty, righteousness, justice, and morality. —Job 31.

In the trial resulting from a husband's jealousy, the wife, by answering "Amen! Amen!" to the priest's reading of the oath and the curse, thereby swore an oath as to her innocence.—Nu 5:21, 22.

What amounted practically to an oath was often voiced by affirming not only by Jehovah's name but additionally by the life of the king or of a superior. (1Sa 25:26; 2Sa 15:21; 2Ki 2:2) "As Jehovah lives" was a common assertion adding gravity to one's attestation of determination or of truthfulness of a statement. (Jg 8:19; 1Sa 14:39, 45; 19:6; 20:3, 21; 25:26, 34) A less forceful expression that may not have been intended to be considered an oath but that conveyed a very serious intent and that was given for the assurance of the hearer was a swearing by the life of the person addressed, as in Hannah's words to Eli (1Sa 1:26) and in Uriah's statement to King David.—2Sa 11:11; also 1Sa 17:55.

Forms or Actions Employed. The most frequent gesture used in taking an oath seems to have been the raising of the right hand toward heaven. Jehovah himself is mentioned as uttering an oath in this manner, symbolically. (Ge 14:22; Ex 6:8; De 32:40; Isa 62:8; Eze 20:5) An angel in one of Daniel's visions raised both hands to the heavens in voicing an oath. (Da 12:7) Of false swearers, it is said that their "right hand is a right hand of falsehood."—Ps 144:8.

One requesting an oath from another might ask him to place his hand under his thigh or hip. When Abraham sent his steward to get a wife for Isaac he said to the steward: "Put your hand, please, under my thigh," after doing which the steward swore that he would get the girl from among Abraham's relatives. (Ge 24:2-4, 9) In the same way Jacob exacted an oath from Joseph that

he not bury him in Egypt. (Ge 47:29-31) Regarding the significance of this practice, see ATTITUDES AND GESTURES.

Frequently an oath was connected with the making of a covenant. A common expression in such cases was: "God is a witness between me and you." (Ge 31:44, 50, 53) Such an expression was also made to strengthen a statement of fact or truth. Moses calls on the heavens and the earth as witnesses when discussing Israel's relationship in their oath-bound covenant with Jehovah. (De 4:26) Often a person or persons, a written document, a pillar, or an altar stood as a witness and reminder of an oath or a covenant.—Ge 31:45-52; De 31:26; Jos 22:26-28; 24:22, 24-27; see COVENANT.

Under the Law. Instances in which oaths were required of certain persons under the Mosaic Law were: of a wife in the trial of jealousy (Nu 5:21, 22), of a bailee when property left in his care was missing (Ex 22:10, 11), of the older men of a city in the case of an unsolved murder (De 21:1-9). Voluntary oaths of abstinence were allowed. (Nu 30:3, 4, 10, 11) Servants of God were sometimes adjured by one in authority, and they told the truth. Likewise a Christian under oath would not lie but would tell the whole truth called for, or he may refuse to answer if it jeopardizes the righteous interests of God or of fellow Christians, in which case he must be ready to suffer any consequences that might result from his refusal to testify.—1Ki 22:15-18; Mt 26:63, 64; 27:11-14.

Vows were regarded in Israel as having the strength of an oath, as sacred and to be fulfilled even though they resulted in loss to the vower. God was viewed as watching to see that vows were carried out, and as bringing punishment for failure. (Nu 30:2; De 23:21-23; Jg 11:30, 31, 35, 36, 39; Ec 5:4-6) The vows of wives and unmarried daughters were subject to affirmation or cancellation by the husband or father, but widows and divorced women were bound by their vows. —Nu 30:3-15.

Jesus Christ, in his Sermon on the Mount, corrected the Jews in their practice of light, loose, and indiscriminate making of oaths. It had become common among them to swear by heaven, by the earth, by Jerusalem, and even by their own heads. But since heaven was "God's throne," earth his "footstool," Jerusalem his kingly city, and one's head (or life) was dependent on God, making such oaths was the same as taking oaths in the name of God. It was not to be treated lightly. So Jesus said: "Just let your word Yes mean Yes, your No, No; for what is in excess of these is from the wicked one." —Mt 5:33-37.

Jesus Christ did not hereby prohibit the making of all oaths, for he himself was under the Law of Moses, which required oaths under certain circumstances. In fact, when Jesus himself was on trial he was put under oath by the high priest, yet he did not object to this, but gave an answer. (Mt 26:63, 64) Rather, Jesus was showing that a person should not have two standards. The keeping of one's word, once given, should be viewed as a sacred duty and should be fulfilled just as an oath would be; the person should sincerely mean what he says. He shed further light on the meaning of his words when he exposed the hypocrisy of the scribes and Pharisees by saying to them: "Woe to you, blind guides, who say, 'If anyone swears by the temple, it is nothing; but if anyone swears by the gold of the temple, he is under obligation.' Fools and blind ones! Which, in fact, is greater, the gold or the temple that has sanctified the gold?" He went on to say: "He that swears by heaven is swearing by the throne of God and by him that is sitting on it."—Mt 23:16-22.

By the false reasoning and hairsplitting casuistry of these scribes and Pharisees, as here pointed out by Jesus, they justified themselves in failing to carry out certain oaths, but Jesus showed that such swearing on their part was being dishonest with God and was actually reproaching his name (for the Jews were a people dedicated to Jehovah). Jehovah plainly states that he hates a false oath. —Zec 8:17.

James corroborates Jesus' words. (Jas 5:12) But these statements of Jesus and James against such indiscriminate practices do not prevent the Christian from taking an oath when necessary to assure others of the seriousness of his intentions or of the truthfulness of what he says. For instance, as Jesus illustrated by example before the Jewish high priest, a Christian would not object to taking an oath in court, for he is going to speak the truth whether under oath or not. (Mt 26:63, 64) Even the Christian resolve to serve God is an oath or a swearing to Jehovah, putting the Christian into a sacred relationship. Jesus put swearing and vows in the same category.—Mt 5:33.

Also, the apostle Paul, in order to strengthen his testimony before his readers, makes what is tantamount to an oath at 2 Corinthians 1:23 and Galatians 1:20. He further refers to an oath as a customary and proper way of putting an end to a dispute and calls attention to the fact that God, "when he purposed to demonstrate more abundantly to the heirs of the promise the unchangeableness of his counsel, stepped in with an oath," swearing by himself, since he could not swear by anyone greater. This added to his promise a legal guarantee and gave double assurance by means of "two unchangeable things in which it is impossible for God to lie," namely, God's word of promise and his oath. (Heb 6:13-18) Furthermore, Paul points out that Christ was made High Priest by oath of Jehovah and has been given in pledge of a better covenant. (Heb 7:21, 22) The Scriptures make upwards of 50 references to Jehovah himself as making oaths.

On the night of Jesus' arrest, the apostle Peter three times denied knowing Jesus, finally giving way to cursing and swearing. We read concerning the third denial: "Then [Peter] started to curse and swear: 'I do not know the man [Jesus]!'" (Mt 26:74) Peter was fearfully trying to convince those around him that his denials were truthful. By swearing to the matter, he was taking an oath that his words were true and that a calamity might befall him if they were not.—See also CURSE.

OBADIAH   (O·ba·di′ah) [Servant of Jehovah].

1. A family head in the tribe of Issachar; son of Izrahiah and descendant of Tola.—1Ch 7:1-3.

2. A Zebulunite whose son was a prince of that tribe during David's rule.—1Ch 27:19, 22.

3. A mighty Gadite warrior who crossed the Jordan at flood stage and supported David when he lived as a fugitive from Saul's wrath.—1Ch 12:8, 9, 14, 15.

4. The household steward of King Ahab. Even though King Ahab and Jezebel practiced wickedness, Obadiah greatly feared Jehovah, hiding 100 prophets of Jehovah "by fifties in a cave" when Jezebel had ordered them all slaughtered. During the divinely imposed drought foretold by Elijah, Obadiah's master Ahab divided certain territory with him, and each was searching for grass to feed the livestock when Elijah met up with Obadiah. Elijah had not been seen by Ahab during the drought, a period of some three years. Upon being told to inform Ahab that Elijah had returned, Obadiah, out of great fear, hesitated to go until given assurance that the prophet would not leave, for Ahab would surely kill his servant if this report proved false.—1Ki 18:1-16.

5. A prince sent by Jehoshaphat to teach the law of Jehovah in the cities of Judah.—2Ch 17:7, 9.

6. A distant descendant of Saul and Jonathan in the tribe of Benjamin.—1Ch 8:33-38; 9:44.

7. A Merarite Levite, one of the overseers of the temple repairs that King Josiah ordered to be made.—2Ch 34:8, 12.

8. A prophet of Jehovah and writer of the fourth of the so-called minor prophetic books. (Ob 1) Nothing personal is known of this prophet of the seventh century B.C.E.—See OBADIAH, BOOK OF.

9. A Levite who returned from Babylon and lived in Jerusalem. (1Ch 9:2, 3, 14, 16) He is evidently called Abda at Nehemiah 11:17. Possibly the same as No. 13.

10. A postexilic descendant of David and Zerubbabel.—1Ch 3:5, 9, 10, 19, 21.

11. Head of the paternal house of Joab who led 218 males of this family back to Jerusalem with Ezra in 468 B.C.E.; son of Jehiel.—Ezr 8:1, 9.

12. One of the priests (or his descendant) who subscribed to the covenant of faithfulness made by the returned exiles under Nehemiah's governorship.—Ne 9:38; 10:1, 5, 8.

13. A Levite gatekeeper in the days of Nehemiah and Ezra. (Ne 12:25, 26) Possibly the same as No. 9.

OBADIAH, BOOK OF.

The shortest prophetic book of the Hebrew Scriptures. Written by Obadiah (concerning whom nothing but the name is known), this book contains a proclamation of Jehovah's judgment against Edom, presents the reason for that judgment, and points forward to restoration for "the house of Jacob." The extinction of the Edomites as a people and the restoration of the Israelites to their land confirm the accurate fulfillment of Obadiah's prophecy.—Ob 17, 18; see EDOM, EDOMITES.

The occasion for the prophecy was the 'unbrotherly' treatment that the Edomites rendered to "the sons of Judah" when the latter suffered defeat. The Edomites, through their ancestor Esau, were related to the Israelites. The Edomites rejoiced over Judah's calamity, shared in taking spoil from the Jews, prevented them from escaping out of the land, and even handed them over to the enemy. (Ob 12-14) As is evident from a comparison of Obadiah's prophecy with the words of Jeremiah (25:15-17, 21, 27-29; 49:7-22) and Ezekiel (25:12-14; 35:1-15), this must have happened in connection with the destruction of Jerusalem by the Babylonian armies and would, therefore, place the book's composition about the year 607 B.C.E.

Since many of the things foretold in Obadiah's prophecy were also foretold in the book of Jeremiah, this made the fulfillment of Jehovah's word regarding Edom doubly certain.—Compare Ge 41:32.

OBAL

(O'bal). The 8th listed of Joktan's 13 sons, each of whom founded one of the 70 post-Flood families; descendant of Shem. Exactly where the tribe of Obal settled is uncertain, but similar names occur in Yemenite SW Arabia.—Ge 10:21, 25-30; 1Ch 1:20, 22.

OBED

(O'bed) [Servant; One Serving].

1. A descendant of Judah; the father of Jehu and the son of Ephlal of the family of Jerahmeel. —1Ch 2:3, 25, 37, 38.

2. Father of Jesse, King David's father. Obed was the son of Boaz by his wife Ruth and was an ancestor of Jesus Christ.—Ru 4:13-17, 21, 22; 1Ch 2:12; Mt 1:5; Lu 3:32.

HIGHLIGHTS OF OBADIAH

Jehovah's judgment against Edom and the promise of restoration for Jehovah's people

Written about 607 B.C.E., the year the Babylonians desolated Jerusalem

---

Edom's share in the violence done to the descendants of Jacob

When Jerusalem was conquered and her people were led into captivity, Edom stood off on the side (vss 10, 11)

She should not have rejoiced maliciously over Judah's calamity, sharing in plundering God's people and handing survivors over to the enemy (vss 12-14)

Calamity will come upon Edom

Jehovah calls upon the nations to rise up against her in battle (vs 1)

Despite her seemingly secure position, Edom will be brought down (vss 2-4)

Thieves or harvesters would take only what they wanted and leave something behind; when Edom falls, she will be completely plundered; she will be deceived by those with whom she entered into a covenant, and her wise and mighty ones will suffer destruction (vss 5-9)

The house of Esau will receive the same sort of treatment that it gave to Judah; the house of Esau will cease to exist (vss 15, 18)

The house of Jacob will be restored

Zion will become holy; the house of Jacob will be the fire that consumes the house of Esau like stubble (vss 17, 18)

Jehovah's restored people will take possession of "the things for them to possess," including "the mountainous region of Esau" (vss 19, 20)

The kingship will become Jehovah's (vs 21)

3. One of the mighty men of David's military forces.—1Ch 11:26, 47.

4. A Levite of the family of Korah; the grandson of Obed-edom and the son of Shemaiah. He served as a gatekeeper "at the house of Jehovah."—1Ch 26:1, 4, 7, 12.

5. Father of a certain Azariah, one of "the chiefs of hundreds" who helped High Priest Jehoiada to overthrow Queen Athaliah so that Jehoash could be installed as king.—2Ch 23:1, 12-15, 20; 24:1.

OBED-EDOM (O'bed-e'dom) [meaning "Servant of Edom"].

1. A Gittite at whose home the ark of the covenant was kept for three months after its near upset and the accompanying death of Uzzah. For the duration of its stay there, Obed-edom and his household were blessed by Jehovah, and when David learned of this he took it as an indication that Jehovah favored bringing the sacred chest on to Jerusalem.—2Sa 6:10-12; 1Ch 13:13, 14; 15:25.

Obed-edom was a "Gittite." Normally this term designated a Philistine of Gath, but it can also refer to someone from Gath-rimmon, a Levite city in Dan assigned to the Kohathites. (Jos 21:20, 23, 24) Entrusted as he was with the care of the Ark, he had to be a Levite and hence must have been a Gittite from Gath-rimmon rather than a Philistine Gittite from Gath.

The name Obed-edom is found a number of times among Levite musicians and gatekeepers of the Davidic period. There are at least two such individuals referred to (1Ch 15:21, 24; 16:38), but beyond this it is impossible to determine whether the several other texts refer to either of these, or to still other contemporary individuals. Thus, Obed-edom, the Gittite, may possibly be the same as either No. 2 or No. 3.

2. A musician and gatekeeper in the procession that brought the Ark to Jerusalem. (1Ch 15:18, 21) He was likely the musician who continued to serve before the tent of the Ark in Jerusalem. (1Ch 16:4, 5, 37, 38a) Possibly the same as No. 1.

3. A gatekeeper in the same procession. (1Ch 15:24) He may also have been "the son of Jeduthun." (1Ch 16:38b) Possibly the same as No. 1 or No. 4.

4. A Korahite in the permanent division of gatekeepers who, together with 62 relatives, was assigned to guard the S side of the sanctuary grounds in Jerusalem.—1Ch 26:1, 4-8, 13, 15; see No. 3.

5. Caretaker of the gold, silver, and other articles in the house of Jehovah during the reign of King Amaziah. When Jehoash of Israel invaded Jerusalem sometime between 858 and 844 B.C.E., these goods, and possibly Obed-edom himself, were all taken off to Samaria.—2Ch 25:23, 24.

OBEDIENCE. The submitting to authority, the doing of what is commanded, the complying with what is required, or the abstaining from what is forbidden.

In the Hebrew Scriptures the thought of obedience is expressed by *sha·ma'*, meaning, basically, "hear or listen." Thus, at times *sha·ma'* refers to simple hearing, becoming aware of something through the auditory senses. (Ge 3:10; 21:26; 34:5) But when what is spoken expresses will, desire, instruction, or command, then the sense of the Hebrew term is that of paying heed to or obeying the one speaking. Adam "listened" to his wife's voice, that is, acceded to her desire that he join her in eating the forbidden fruit. (Ge 3:17; compare 21:12.) Joseph refused to "listen" to the importunities of Potiphar's wife. (Ge 39:10) King Saul feared the people and "so obeyed [listened to] their voice," overstepping God's order in doing so. (1Sa 15:24) Jehovah's promise to Abraham concerning a seed was granted because Abraham "listened to," or obeyed, Jehovah's voice, keeping his commands.—Ge 22:18; 26:4, 5; compare Heb 11:8; see EAR.

The same Hebrew term is used with reference to God in 'hearing' or 'listening' to men. Here the English term "obedience" is not suitable, since humans cannot command God but can only petition or supplicate him. Hence, when God told Abraham that "as regards Ishmael I have *heard* you," he was telling Abraham that he had given regard to his request, would act upon it. (Ge 17:20) In a similar way God 'heard' or responded to the appeal of persons in times of difficulty or affliction, answering their pleas where he saw fit to show mercy.—Ge 16:11; 29:33; 21:17; Ex 3:7-9; compare De 1:45.

Similar to *sha·ma'*, one Greek verb expressing the idea of obeying (*hy·pa·kou'o*; noun form *hy·pa·ko·e'*) literally means "hear under," that is, to hear submissively or to attend (as at Ac 12:13). Another term conveying the sense of obedience is *pei'tho*, which means "persuade." (Mt 27:20) In the passive and middle voices it means not only to be persuaded (Lu 16:31), to trust (Mt 27:43), to believe (Ac 17:4) but also to give heed (Ac 5:40), to obey (Ac 5:36, 37). From this term comes the negative form *a·pei·the'o* (meaning to disbelieve [Ac 14:2; 19:9] or disobey [Joh 3:36]), as well as other related terms.

From this it can be seen that obedience, as expressed in the original languages of the Scriptures, depends first upon hearing, that is, receiving information or knowledge (compare Lu 12:47, 48; 1Ti 1:13), and then upon one's submitting to the will or desire of the one who speaks or otherwise expresses such will or desire. Submission, in turn, is dependent upon recognition of that one's authority or right to ask or require the response indicated, as also upon the hearer's desire or willingness to satisfy the will of such one. As indicated by the Greek *pei'tho* and *a·pei·the'o*, belief, trust, and confidence also enter in.

Obedience to God Essential for Life. God has first claim to the obedience of all his creatures. They rightly owe him implicit obedience as their Maker, the Source from whom life derives and on whom life depends. (Ps 95:6-8) Because he is the All-wise and Almighty God, what he says merits the utmost respect and attention. A human father properly expects his word to be carried out by his children, and if a child is slow to respond, the parent may say emphatically, "Did you *hear* me?" Far more so does the heavenly Father rightly require receptive attention and response to his expressions.—Compare De 21:18-21; Pr 4:1; Isa 64:8; 1Pe 1:14.

There is no substitute for obedience, no gaining of God's favor without it. As Samuel told King Saul: "Does Jehovah have as much delight in burnt offerings and sacrifices as in obeying [form of *sha·ma'*] the voice of Jehovah? Look! To obey [literally, to listen] is better than a sacrifice, to pay attention than the fat of rams." (1Sa 15:22) To fail to obey is to reject the word of Jehovah, to demonstrate that one really does not believe, trust, or have faith in that word and its Source. Hence the one failing to obey is no different from the one practicing divination or using idols. (1Sa 15:23; compare Ro 6:16.) Verbal expressions of assent mean nothing if the required action does not follow; the lack of response proves a lack of belief or respect for the source of instructions. (Mt 21:28-32) Those satisfying themselves with only hearing and giving mental acceptance to God's truth, but not *doing* what it calls for, are deceiving themselves with false reasoning and receive no blessing. (Jas 1:22-25) God's Son made clear that even those doing things *similar* to those commanded, but evidently in a wrong way or with a wrong motive, would never gain entrance into the Kingdom but would be completely rejected.—Mt 7:15-23.

Counteracting disobedience due to inborn sin. At the outset God informed man that obedience was basic, a life-and-death matter. (Ge 2:16, 17) The same rule applies to God's spirit sons. (1Pe 3:19, 20; Jude 6; Mt 25:41) The willful disobedience of the perfect man Adam, as the responsible head over Eve and as the male progenitor or life source of the human family, brought sin and death to all his offspring. (Ro 5:12, 19) By nature, then, men are "sons of disobedience" and "children of wrath," meriting God's disfavor because of their violation of his righteous standards. Failure to resist this inherent inclination to disobedience is the course of ultimate destruction.—Eph 2:2, 3; 5:6-11; compare Ga 6:7-9.

Jehovah God has mercifully provided the means for combating sin in the flesh and for gaining forgiveness of wrongdoing resulting from imperfection rather than from willful disobedience. By his holy spirit, God supplies the force for righteousness that enables sinful men to produce good fruitage. (Ga 5:16-24; Tit 3:3-7) Forgiveness for sins comes through faith in Christ's ransom sacrifice, and such faith in itself is a deterrent to wrongdoing and a stimulus to obedience. (1Pe 1:2) Thus Paul refers to "obedience [hearing submissively] by faith." (Ro 16:26; 1:16; compare Ac 6:7.) At Romans 10:16-21 he shows that hearing coupled with faith produces obedience and that the disobeying (disbelieving [from *a·pei·the'o*]) of the Israelites was due to lack of faith. (Compare Heb 3:18, 19.) Since true faith is "the assured expectation of things hoped for" and "the evident demonstration of realities though not beheld," and since it requires believing that God is "and that he becomes the rewarder of those earnestly seeking him," those having faith are moved to obey, having confidence and assurance as to the blessings that obedience will bring.—Heb 11:1, 6.

In harmony with this, God's communication to men is not simply a series of terse commands like those of an unfeeling dictator. God does not desire the kind of obedience one obtains from a beast with a bridle and bit. (Compare Jas 3:3; Ps 32:8, 9.) Not a perfunctory or a begrudging obedience, such as even the demons rendered to Christ and his disciples (Mr 1:27; Lu 10:17, 20), but obedience motivated by an appreciative heart is called for. (Ps 112:1; 119:11, 112; Ro 6:17-19) Jehovah therefore accompanies his expressions of will and purpose with helpful information appealing to one's sense of justice and righteousness, to love and goodness, intelligence, reason, and wisdom. (De 10:12, 13; Lu 1:17; Ro 12:1, 2) Those with the right heart attitude obey out of love. (1Jo 5:2, 3; 2Jo 6) Also, the truthfulness and rightness of the message given through God's servants persuades the hearers to obey, and hence the apostle Peter speaks of "obedience to the truth with unhypocritical brotherly affection as the result."—1Pe 1:22; compare Ro 2:8, 9; Ga 5:7, 8.

Jehovah showed great patience with Israel and speaks of himself as "daily getting up early" and sending his prophets to exhort and admonish them, 'all day long spreading out his hands toward a people that is disobedient and talks back,' but they continued to harden their hearts like emery stone, stubbornly refusing discipline. (Jer 7:23-28; 11:7, 8; Zec 7:12; Ro 10:21) Even after the coming of Messiah, they endeavored to establish their righteousness in their own way, by works of the Law. Their lack of faith and obedience to God's instructions through his Son cost the majority of them a place in the Kingdom government, opening the way for many non-Jews to become part of the chosen nation of spiritual Israel.—Ro 10:1-4; 11:13-23, 30-32.

A healthy fear of God also plays its part in obedience, because one recognizes God's all-powerfulness and that God is not to be trifled with nor can he be mocked, for he renders to each one according to that one's deeds. (Compare Php 2:12, 13; Ga 6:7, 8; Heb 5:7.) Willful disobedience or disregard for God's revealed will brings "a certain fearful expectation of judgment."—Heb 10:26-31.

The Scriptures set forth many encouraging examples of faithful obedience in all manner of circumstances and situations and in the face of all types of opposition. Supreme among these is the example of God's own Son, who "humbled himself and became obedient as far as death, yes, death on a torture stake." (Php 2:8; Heb 5:8) By his obedient course he was justified, proved righteous on his own merit, and hence could provide a perfect sacrifice that would redeem mankind from sin and death.—Ro 5:18-21.

Obedience to Other Superiors. The Son's position as God's appointed King requires that all others obey him. (Da 7:13, 14) He is "Shiloh" of the tribe of Judah, the one 'to whom the obedience of the people belongs' (Ge 49:10), the prophet like Moses to whom every soul must listen or suffer destruction (Ac 3:22, 23), "a leader and commander to the national groups" (Isa 55:3, 4), placed "far above every government and authority and power and lordship" (Eph 1:20, 21), to whom "every knee should bend" in recognition of his God-given authority (Php 2:9-11). He is the High Priest whose instructions lead to healing and life everlasting for those hearing him submissively. (Heb 5:9, 10; Joh 3:36) Since he was God's Chief Spokesman, Jesus could rightly make known that obedience to his sayings constituted the only solid foundation on which persons could build their hopes for the future. (Mt 7:24-27) Obedience is proof of and springs from the love his followers have for him.

(Joh 14:23, 24; 15:10) Because God has made his Son the key figure in the outworking of all his purposes (Ro 16:25-27), life depends upon obedience to "the good news about our Lord Jesus," and this obedience includes making public declaration of one's faith in him.—2Th 1:8; Ro 10:8-10, 16; 1Pe 4:17.

As head of the Christian congregation, Christ Jesus delegates authority to others, as he did to the apostles. (2Co 10:8) These persons convey the instructions of the congregation's Head, and therefore obedience to them is right and necessary (2Co 10:2-6; Php 2:12; 2Th 3:4, 9-15), for such spiritual shepherds are "keeping watch over your souls as those who will render an account." (Heb 13:17; 1Pe 5:2-6; compare 1Ki 3:9.) Willing response and obedience, like that of the Roman and Philippian Christians and like that of Philemon, to whom Paul could say, "I am writing you, knowing you will even do more than the things I say," bring rejoicing to such responsible ones.—Ro 16:19; Php 2:12, 17; Phm 21.

Obedience to parents and husbands. Parents have a God-given natural right to the obedience of their children. (Pr 23:22) Jacob's obedience to his parents was doubtless one of the reasons Jehovah 'loved Jacob but hated Esau.' (Mal 1:2, 3; Ge 28:7) As a child, Jesus showed submission to his earthly parents. (Lu 2:51) The apostle Paul admonishes children to "be obedient to your parents in everything." It must be remembered that his letter was addressed to Christians, and hence "everything" cannot allow for obedience to commands that would result in disobedience to the word of the heavenly Father, Jehovah God, for this could not be "well-pleasing" to the Lord. (Col 3:20; Eph 6:1) Disobedience to parents is not viewed lightly in the Scriptures, and under the Law a continued course of disobedience required the son's being put to death.—De 21:18-21; Pr 30:17; Ro 1:30, 32; 2Ti 3:2.

The headship of the man also calls for obedience of wives to their husbands "in everything," Sarah being cited as an example to be emulated. (Eph 5:21-33; 1Pe 3:1-6) Here, again, it holds true that the headship and authority of the husband is not supreme, but ranks below that of God and Christ —1Co 11:3.

To masters and to governments. Similarly slaves were exhorted to render obedience to their masters "in everything," not with eye-service but as Christ's slaves, with fear of Jehovah. (Co 3:22-25; Eph 6:5-8) Those slaves who must endure suffering could take as their example Christ Jesus, even as could Christian wives under simila circumstances. (1Pe 2:18-25; 3:1) The authority of their masters was relative, not absolute; hence Christian slaves would obey in "everything" that was not in conflict with God's will and commands.

Finally, obedience is due earthly governments, authorities, and rulers (Tit 3:1), since God has allowed them to function and even to render certain services to his people. So it is required that Christians "pay back Caesar's things to Caesar." (Mr 12:14-17) The compelling reason for Christian obedience to Caesar's laws and the payment of taxes is not primarily proper fear of Caesar's "sword" of punishment but is the Christian conscience. (Ro 13:1-7) Since conscience is the decisive factor, Christian submission to human governments obviously is limited to those things not out of harmony with God's law. For this reason, to rulers who ordered them to stop carrying out their God-given commission to preach, the apostles firmly stated: "We must obey God as ruler rather than men."—Ac 5:27-29, 32; 4:18-20.

OBEISANCE.

OBEISANCE. The act of bowing, kneeling, prostrating the body, or making some other gesture to betoken submission; or simply the paying of respect. It adequately translates the Hebrew *hish·ta·chawah'* and the Greek *pro·sky·ne'o* in many cases.

Hish·ta·chawah' means, basically, "bow down." (Ge 18:2) Such bowing might be done as an act of respect or deference toward another human, as to a king (1Sa 24:8; 2Sa 24:20; Ps 45:11), the high priest (1Sa 2:36), a prophet (2Ki 2:15), or other person of authority (Ge 37:9, 10; 42:6; Ru 2:8-10), to an elder relative (Ge 33:1-6; 48:11, 12; Ex 18:7; 1Ki 2:19), or even to strangers as an expression of courteous regard (Ge 19:1, 2). Abraham bowed down to the Canaanite sons of Heth from whom he sought to buy a burial place. (Ge 23:7) Isaac's blessing on Jacob called for national groups and Jacob's own "brothers" to bow down to him. (Ge 27:29; compare 49:8.) When men started to bow down before David's son Absalom, he grabbed them and kissed them, evidently to further his political ambitions by making a show of putting himself on a level with them. (2Sa 15:5, 6) Mordecai refused to prostrate himself before Haman, not because he viewed the practice as wrong in itself, but doubtless because this high Persian official was an accursed Amalekite by descent.—Es 3:1-6.

From the above examples it is clear that this Hebrew term of itself does not necessarily have a religious sense or signify worship. Nevertheless, in a large number of cases it is used in connection with worship, either of the true God (Ex 24:1; Ps 95:6; Isa 27:13; 66:23) or of false gods. (De 4:19; 8:19; 11:16) Persons might bow down in prayer to God (Ex 34:8; Job 1:20, 21) and often prostrated themselves upon receiving some revelation from God or some expression or evidence of his favor, thereby showing their gratitude, reverence, and humble submission to his will.—Ge 24:23-26, 50-52; Ex 4:31; 12:27, 28; 2Ch 7:3; 20:14-19; compare 1Co 14:25; Re 19:1-4.

Bowing down to humans as an act of respect was admissible, but bowing to anyone other than Jehovah as a deity was prohibited by God. (Ex 23:24; 34:14) Similarly, the worshipful bowing down to religious images or to any created thing was positively condemned. (Ex 20:4, 5; Le 26:1; De 4:15-19; Isa 2:8, 9, 20, 21) Thus, in the Hebrew Scriptures, when certain of Jehovah's servants prostrated themselves before angels, they only did so to show they recognized that these were God's representatives, not to render obeisance to them as deities.—Jos 5:13-15; Ge 18:1-3.

Obeisance in the Christian Greek Scriptures. The Greek *pro·sky·ne'o* corresponds closely to the Hebrew *hish·ta·chawah'* as to conveying the thought of both obeisance to creatures and worship to God or a deity. The *manner* of expressing the obeisance is perhaps not so prominent in *pro·sky·ne'o* as in *hish·ta·chawah'*, where the Hebrew term graphically conveys the thought of prostration or bowing down. Scholars derive the Greek term from the verb *ky·ne'o*, "kiss." The usage of the word in the Christian Greek Scriptures (as also in the Greek *Septuagint* translation of the Hebrew Scriptures) shows that persons to whose actions the term is applied prostrated themselves or bowed down.—Mt 2:11; 18:26; 28:9.

As with the Hebrew term, the context must be considered to determine whether *pro·sky·ne'o* refers to obeisance solely in the form of deep respect or obeisance in the form of religious worship. Where reference is directly to God (Joh 4:20-24; 1Co 14:25; Re 4:10) or to false gods and their idols (Ac 7:43; Re 9:20), it is evident that the obeisance goes beyond that acceptably or customarily rendered to men and enters the field of worship. So, too, where the object of the obeisance is left unstated, its being directed to God is understood. (Joh 12:20; Ac 8:27; 24:11; Heb 11:21; Re 11:1) On the other hand, the action of those of "the synagogue of Satan" who are made to "come and do obeisance" before the feet of Christians is clearly not worship.—Re 3:9.

Obeisance to a human king is found in Jesus' illustration at Matthew 18:26. It is evident that this was the kind of obeisance that the astrologers rendered to the child Jesus, "born king of the Jews," that Herod professed interest in expressing, and that the soldiers mockingly rendered to Jesus before his impalement. They clearly did not view Jesus as God or as a deity. (Mt 2:2, 8; Mr 15:19) While some translators use the word "worship" in the majority of cases where *pro·sky·ne′o* describes persons' actions toward Jesus, the evidence does not warrant one's reading too much into this rendering. Rather, the circumstances that evoked the obeisance correspond very closely to those producing obeisance to the earlier prophets and kings. (Compare Mt 8:2; 9:18; 15:25; 20:20 with 1Sa 25:23, 24; 2Sa 14:4-7; 1Ki 1:16; 2Ki 4:36, 37.) The very expressions of those involved often reveal that, while they clearly recognized Jesus as God's representative, they rendered obeisance to him, not as to God or a deity, but as "God's Son," the foretold "Son of man," the Messiah with divine authority. On many occasions their obeisance expressed a gratitude for divine revelation or evidence of favor like that expressed in earlier times. —Mt 14:32, 33; 28:5-10, 16-18; Lu 24:50-52; Joh 9:35, 38.

While earlier prophets and also angels had accepted obeisance, Peter stopped Cornelius from rendering such to him, and the angel or angels of John's vision twice stopped John from doing so, referring to himself as "a fellow slave" and concluding with the exhortation to "worship God [*toi The·oi′ pro·sky′ne·son*]." (Ac 10:25, 26; Re 19:10; 22:8, 9) Evidently Christ's coming had brought in new relationships affecting standards of conduct toward others of God's servants. He taught his disciples that "one is your teacher, whereas all you are brothers . . . your Leader is one, the Christ" (Mt 23:8-12), for it was in him that the prophetic figures and types found their fulfillment, even as the angel told John that "the bearing witness to Jesus is what inspires prophesying." (Re 19:10) Jesus was David's Lord, the greater than Solomon, the prophet greater than Moses. (Lu 20:41-43; Mt 12:42; Ac 3:19-24) The obeisance rendered those men prefigured that due Christ. Peter therefore rightly refused to let Cornelius make too much of him.

So, too, John, by virtue of having been declared righteous or justified by God as an anointed Christian, called to be a heavenly son of God and a member of the Kingdom, was in a different relationship to the angel(s) of Revelation than were the Israelites to the angels that had earlier appeared to them. The angel(s) evidently recognized this change of relationship when rejecting John's obeisance.—Compare 1Co 6:3; see DECLARE RIGHTEOUS.

Obeisance to the glorified Jesus Christ. On the other hand, Christ Jesus has been exalted by his Father to a position second only to God, so that "in the name of Jesus every knee should bend of those in heaven and those on earth and those under the ground, and every tongue should openly acknowledge that Jesus Christ is Lord to the glory of God the Father." (Php 2:9-11; compare Da 7:13, 14, 27.) Hebrews 1:6 also shows that even the angels render obeisance to the resurrected Jesus Christ. Many translations of this text here render *pro·sky·ne′o* as "worship," while some render it by such expressions as "bow before" (*AT; Yg*) and 'pay homage' (*NE*). No matter what English term is used, the original Greek remains the same and the understanding of what it is that the angels render to Christ must accord with the rest of the Scriptures. Jesus himself emphatically stated to Satan that "it is Jehovah your God you must worship [form of *pro·sky·ne′o*], and it is to him alone you must render sacred service." (Mt 4:8-10; Lu 4:7, 8) Similarly, the angel(s) told John to "worship God" (Re 19:10; 22:9), and this injunction came after Jesus' resurrection and exaltation, showing that matters had not changed in this regard. True, Psalm 97, which the apostle evidently quotes at Hebrews 1:6, refers to Jehovah God as the object of the 'bowing down,' and still this text was applied to Christ Jesus. (Ps 97:1, 7) However, the apostle previously had shown that the resurrected Christ is "the reflection of [God's] glory and the exact representation of his very being." (Heb 1:1-3) Hence, if what we understand as "worship" is apparently directed to the Son by angels, it is in reality being directed through him to Jehovah God, the Sovereign Ruler, "the One who made the heaven and the earth and sea and fountains of waters." (Re 14:7; 4:10, 11; 7:11, 12; 11:16, 17; compare 1Ch 29:20; Re 5:13, 14; 21:22.) On the other hand, the renderings "bow before" and 'pay homage' (instead of "worship") are in no way out of harmony with the original language, either the Hebrew of Psalm 97:7 or the Greek of Hebrews 1:6, for such translations convey the basic sense of both *hish·ta·chawah′* and *pro·sky·ne′o*.

OBIL (O′bil). An Ishmaelite caretaker of David's camels.—1Ch 27:30.

OBOTH (O′both). An Israelite encampment between Punon and Iye-abarim. Its location is today unknown.—Nu 21:10, 11; 33:43, 44.

OCHRAN (Och′ran) [from a root meaning "ostracism; trouble"]. An Asherite whose son Pagie was appointed chieftain of the tribe of Asher after the Exodus from Egypt.—Nu 1:13, 16; 2:27; 7:72, 77; 10:26.

ODED (O'ded) [[God] Has Relieved].

1. Father of the prophet Azariah. (2Ch 15:1) Second Chronicles 15:8 describes Oded himself as being a prophet: "As soon as Asa heard these words and the prophecy of Oded the prophet." Some scholars would drop the words "of Oded the prophet" as a copyist's error, but this would not explain why the writer says Asa heard "these words *and* the prophecy." Others would make an addition so as to read, "Asa heard these words and the prophecy of *Azariah the son of* Oded," to agree with the Greek *Septuagint* (Alexandrine Codex), Syriac *Peshitta,* and Latin *Vulgate* (Clementine recension), but this still leaves the above difficulty unexplained. The third solution is to accept the Masoretic text *as it is,* with the understanding that Oded himself gave a prophecy that has not been preserved in the record. Asa heeded the words of Azariah (2Ch 15:2-7) and those of his father Oded.

2. A prophet of Samaria during the overlapping reigns of Pekah of Israel and Ahaz of Judah (761-c. 759 B.C.E.). After Israel and Syria delivered a smashing defeat to Judah, 200,000 captives from the southern kingdom were brought toward Samaria. Oded, however, intercepted the victorious army and warned them of God's wrath if they enslaved their brothers. 'After all,' he explained, 'it was only because of Judah's wickedness that Jehovah permitted you to defeat them. Now do not make servants out of them and bring Jehovah's rage upon yourselves; return the captives!' Four Ephraimite leaders supported Oded, and the captives were cared for and repatriated.—2Ch 28:5-15.

OFFERINGS.

From early times men have presented offerings to God. In the first recorded instance, Adam's oldest son Cain presented the firstfruits of the ground, and Adam's younger son Abel, the firstlings of his flock. Evidently the attitudes and motives of the two brothers were different, for God approved Abel's offering but looked with disfavor on Cain's. (Later, the Law covenant provided for both animal and grain offerings.) Abel must have had faith in God's promise of liberation through the promised Seed and likely realized that blood would have to be shed, someone would have to be 'bruised in the heel,' so that mankind might be uplifted to the perfection that Adam and Eve had lost. (Ge 3:15) Acknowledging himself as a sinner, he was led by faith to present an offering requiring the shedding of blood, thereby accurately foreshadowing the real sacrifice for sins, Jesus Christ.—Ge 4:1-4; Heb 11:4.

In Patriarchal Society. The family head Noah, on coming out of the ark, offered a thanksgiving sacrifice to Jehovah that was "restful" (soothing, tranquilizing), after which Jehovah made the "rainbow" covenant with Noah and his offspring. (Ge 8:18-22; 9:8-16) We read later of the faithful patriarchs' presenting offerings to Jehovah. (Ge 8:20; 31:54) Job, as family head, acted as priest for his family, sacrificing burnt offerings to God in their behalf. (Job 1:5) The most notable and significant of ancient sacrifices was Abraham's attempt to offer up Isaac, at Jehovah's direction. Jehovah, after observing Abraham's faith and obedience, kindly provided a ram as substitute. This act of Abraham foreshadowed Jehovah's offering of his own only-begotten Son, Jesus Christ.—Ge 22:1-14; Heb 11:17-19.

Under the Law. The sacrifices commanded under the Law covenant all pointed forward to Jesus Christ and his sacrifice or to benefits that flow from that sacrifice. (Heb 8:3-5; 9:9; 10:5-10) As Jesus Christ was a perfect man, so all animal sacrifices were to be sound, unblemished specimens. (Le 1:3, 10; 3:1) Both the Israelite and the alien resident who worshiped Jehovah were included in presenting the various offerings.—Nu 15:26, 29.

Burnt offerings. Burnt offerings were presented in their entirety to God; no part of the animal being retained by the worshiper. (Compare Jg 11:30, 31, 39, 40.) They constituted an appeal to Jehovah to accept, or to signify acceptance of, the sin offering that sometimes accompanied them. As a "burnt offering" Jesus Christ gave himself wholly, fully.

Occasions for burnt offerings, and their features:

(1) Regular times offered: Every morning and evening (Ex 29:38-42; Le 6:8-13; Nu 28:3-8); every Sabbath day (Nu 28:9, 10); first day of month (Nu 10:10); Passover and seven days of Festival of Unfermented Cakes (Le 23:6-8; Nu 28:16-19, 24); Day of Atonement (Le 16:3, 5, 29, 30; Nu 29:7-11); Pentecost (Le 23:16-18; Nu 28:26-31); each day of Festival of Booths.—Nu 29:12-39.

(2) Other occasions: At consecration of priesthood (Le 8:18-21; see INSTALLATION); at installation of Levites (Nu 8:6, 11, 12); in connection with making covenants (Ex 24:5; see COVENANT); with communion offerings as well as certain guilt and sin offerings (Le 5:6, 7, 10; 16:3, 5); in performing vows (Nu 15:3, 8); in connection with purifications (Le 12:6-8; 14:2, 30, 31; 15:13-15, 30).

(3) Animals offered and procedure: Bull, ram, male goat, turtledove, or young pigeon. (Le 1:3, 5, 10, 14) If it was an animal, the offerer laid his hand on the animal's head (acknowledging the

offering as his offering, and for him, in his behalf). (Le 1:4) The animal was slaughtered, the blood was sprinkled round about upon the altar of burnt offering (Le 1:5, 11), the animal was skinned and cut up into its parts, its intestines (no offal was burned on altar) and shanks were washed, the head and other body parts were all put on altar (the officiating priest received the skin; Le 7:8). (Le 1:6-9, 12, 13) If it was a bird, the crop and feathers were removed, and the head and body were burned on the altar. (Le 1:14-17)

Communion offerings (or peace offerings). Communion offerings acceptable to Jehovah denoted peace with him. The worshiper and his household partook (in the courtyard of the tabernacle; according to tradition, booths were set up around the inside of the curtain surrounding the courtyard; in the temple, dining rooms were provided). The officiating priest received a portion, and the priests on duty, another portion. Jehovah, in effect, received the pleasing smoke of the burning fat. The blood, representing the life, was given to God as his. Therefore the priests, the worshipers, and Jehovah were as if together at the meal, signifying peaceful relationships. The person partaking while in a state of uncleanness (any of the uncleannesses mentioned in the Law) or who ate the flesh after it had been kept beyond the prescribed time (in the warm climate it would begin to putrefy) was to be cut off from his people. He defiled or desecrated the meal, because of either being unclean himself or eating that which was foul before Jehovah God, showing disrespect for sacred things.—Le 7:16-21; 19:5-8.

The Lord's Evening Meal (Memorial or Last Supper) is a communion meal. (1Co 10:16) Those in "the new covenant by virtue of [Jesus'] blood" share with one another in faith, partaking of the emblems representing Jesus' body and blood. They share also with Jehovah as Author of the arrangement. These are seeking Jehovah's approval and are at peace not only with one another but also with Jehovah through Jesus Christ. In line with the requirement of cleanness for sharers in a communion meal, Paul warns that the Christian should examine himself before the Memorial meal. To treat the occasion or the emblems of wine and unleavened bread lightly or with contempt would be desecration of sacred things, meriting adverse judgment.—1Co 11:25, 27-29; see LORD'S EVENING MEAL.

In the *thanksgiving offering,* which was a communion offering praising God for his provisions and loving-kindnesses, flesh and both leavened and unleavened bread were eaten. The worshiper therefore celebrated the occasion using what might be termed "daily food." (However, no leavened bread was at any time put upon the altar as being offered to God.) And, in this expression of thanks and praise to God, the flesh had to be enjoyed that day, not the next. (In other communion offerings, the flesh could be eaten the second day.) (Le 7:11-15) This brings to mind the prayer Jesus Christ taught his followers: "Give us today our bread for this day."—Mt 6:11.

Occasions for communion offerings, and their features:

(1) Occasions: Making covenants (Ex 24:5); celebrating festal seasons and commencement of months (Nu 10:10; Ex 12:2-14; Le 23:15-19; Nu 29:39), and other occasions.

(2) Purposes: To gain approval of God; entreaty or supplication to God in times of misfortune. (Le 19:5; Jg 20:26; 21:4; 1Sa 13:9; 2Sa 24:25)

(3) Animals used, and procedure: *Male* or *female* cattle, sheep, goats (no birds, since they were not deemed sufficient to constitute a sacrificial meal). (Le 3:1, 6, 12) The offerer laid his hand on the animal's head; the animal was slaughtered; the priest sprinkled its blood round about upon the altar of burnt offering (Le 3:2, 8, 13); the fat (including the fat tail of the sheep) was put upon the altar of burnt offering (Le 3:3-5, 9); the breast went to the priests, the right leg to the officiating priest (Ex 29:26, 28; Le 7:28-36).

(4) Types: Thanksgiving or praise; vow (see Nu 6:13, 14, 17); voluntary.

Sin offerings. These were all for unintentional sin, committed because of weakness of the imperfect flesh, not "with uplifted hand," that is, not openly, proudly, purposely. (Nu 15:30, 31, ftn) Various animal sacrifices, from bull to pigeon, were used, according to the position and circumstances of the one(s) whose sin was being atoned for. It is to be noted that those involved in the sins dealt with in Leviticus chapter 4 were persons who had done "one of the things that Jehovah commands should not be done" and so had become guilty. (Le 4:2, 13, 22, 27) For Atonement Day sin offerings, see ATONEMENT DAY.

Occasions requiring sin offerings, and their features:

(1) For sin of the high priest bringing guilt upon the people (Le 4:3): The high priest brought a bull and laid his hand on the bull's head; the bull was slaughtered; its blood was taken into the Holy Place and sprinkled before the curtain; some of the blood was smeared on the horns of the *altar of incense,* the rest being poured out at the base of the *altar of burnt offering;* the fat (as in commu-

nion offerings) was burned on the altar of burnt offering (Le 4:4-10); and the carcass (including the skin) was burned in a clean place outside the city, where altar ashes were put. (Le 4:11, 12)

(2) For sin of the entire assembly (some sin made by the assembly, of which the leaders were not aware until later) (Le 4:13): The congregation brought a bull; the older men laid their hands on the bull's head; one slaughtered it; the remainder of the procedure was the same as for a sin of the high priest. (Le 4:14-21)

A sin of the high priest committed in his official position and capacity as representative of the entire nation before Jehovah brought guilt upon the entire assembly. This might be an error such as a mistake in judgment, in application of the Law, or in dealing with a question of national importance. For this, and for the sin of the entire assembly, the most valuable of sacrifices, namely, a bull, was required.—Le 4:3, 13-15.

With sin offerings for individuals, the blood was taken no farther than the altar. However, in cases of sin of the high priest and of the entire assembly, the blood was also taken into the Holy Place, the first compartment of the sanctuary, and was sprinkled before the curtain, on the other side of which Jehovah 'resided,' as represented by a miraculous light above the ark of the covenant in the Most Holy. (Only in the sin offerings regularly made on Atonement Day was blood taken into the Most Holy, the second compartment; Le 16.) No priest could eat any portion of offerings from which blood was taken into the Holy Place.—Le 6:30.

(3) Sin of a chieftain: The procedure was similar, except a male goat was used, and blood was *not taken into the Holy Place.* The blood was put on the horns of the *altar of burnt offering;* the rest was poured out at its base; the fat was made to smoke on the altar (Le 4:22-26); the priests evidently received a portion to eat, as in other sin offerings (Le 6:24-26, 29); vessels in which meat was boiled had to be scoured (or broken, if earthenware), so that none of the "most holy thing" would be desecrated, which would happen if any of the sacrifice clung to the vessel and the vessel was later used for ordinary purposes. (Le 6:27, 28)

(4) Sin of an individual Israelite: A female kid of the goats or a female lamb was used; the procedure was the same as for the sin of a chieftain. (Le 4:27-35)

In the following, the sins differ from the foregoing in that the persons involved committed an error and did "not do all [God's] commandments," hence a sin of omission.—Nu 15:22.

(5) For the entire assembly, a kid of the goats was used (Nu 15:22-26); for an individual, a female goat in its first year. (Nu 15:27-29)

In cases where priests were to eat part of the sin offering, it appears that, in partaking, they were considered to be 'answering for the error' of those making the sin offering "so as to make atonement for them before Jehovah," by virtue of their holy office.—Le 10:16-18; 9:3, 15.

Guilt offerings. Guilt offerings were also offerings because of sin, for guilt of any sort involves sin. They were for special sins by which a person had contracted guilt, and they differed slightly from other sin offerings in that they appear to have been to satisfy or restore a right. Either a right of Jehovah or a right of his holy nation had been violated. The guilt offering was to satisfy Jehovah on the right that had been violated, or to restore or recover certain covenant rights for the repentant wrongdoer and to get relief from the penalty for his sin.—Compare Isa 53:10.

In the cases covered in Leviticus 5:1-6, 17-19, the individuals had sinned unwittingly, thoughtlessly, or carelessly, and when the matter was brought to their attention, they desired to right the matter. On the other hand, the sins dealt with at Leviticus 6:1-7 were not unwitting or careless sins but, nevertheless, were sins due to fleshly weaknesses and desires, not deliberate, highhanded, and purposely in rebellion against God. The person had come to be stricken in conscience, so repented voluntarily, confessing his sin, and after making restoration, sought mercy and forgiveness.—Mt 5:23, 24.

These laws highlight the fact that, while the Law was strict for the deliberate, unrepentant sinner, there was room for consideration of motives, circumstances, and attitudes, so that mercy could be extended under the Law, even as is the case in the Christian congregation. (Compare Le 6:1-7; Ex 21:29-31; Nu 35:22-25; 2Co 2:5-11; 7:8-12; 1Ti 1:2-16.) But note that none of these wrongs could be done with impunity; compensation had to be made to the individual harmed, and a guilt offering was to be made to Jehovah. The guilt offerings were, with a few variations, handled in the same way as the sin offerings, the priests getting a portion to eat.—Le 7:1, 5-7.

Occasions requiring guilt offerings, and their features:

(1) A witness to a matter who failed to testify or report after hearing public adjuration; one who had unwittingly become unclean by reason of a dead body or another unclean person; one who rashly or thoughtlessly made an oath to do or not

to do something. (Le 5:1-4): He had to make confession concerning the way in which he had sinned. (Le 5:5) The guilt offerings varied according to financial circumstances. (Le 5:6-10) If it was a grain offering, no oil or frankincense was included because it was a sin offering and was a *required* grain offering, not a voluntary one; a voluntary grain offering was a *joyful* offering of one in good standing with God. (Le 5:11-13)

(2) One who sinned unintentionally against holy things of Jehovah (for example, one who unwittingly appropriated grain set aside as tithe to the sanctuary, and used it for himself or his household [for a common use, profaning the sanctified thing]) (Le 5:15a; compare Le 22:14-16): Compensation plus one fifth was to be given to the sanctuary. (Le 5:16) A ram was presented as a guilt offering. (Le 5:15)

(3) A person who unwittingly did something (probably through negligence) that Jehovah commanded not to be done: A ram "according to the estimated value" was to be offered. (Le 5:17-19)

(4) A person who deceived his associate by taking valuables committed to his care, robbery, defrauding, keeping something found and lying about it (Le 6:2, 3; compare Ex 22:7-13, and note that this does not include testifying falsely *against* one's fellowman, as at De 5:20): First, confession of the wrong was to be made. Then he must make full compensation, plus one fifth, to the injured person. (Le 6:4, 5; Nu 5:6, 7) If the wronged person had died, the nearest male relative got the compensation; if there was no near relative, the priest received it. (Nu 5:8) Then he was to offer a ram for his guilt offering.

Grain offerings. Grain offerings were made along with communion offerings, burnt offerings, and sin offerings, and also as firstfruits; at other times they were made independently. (Ex 29:40-42; Le 23:10-13, 15-18; Nu 15:8, 9, 22-24; 28:9, 10, 20, 26-28; chap 29) These were in recognition of God's bounty in supplying blessings and prosperity. They were often accompanied by oil and incense. Grain offerings could be in the form of fine flour, roasted grain, or ring-shaped cakes or wafers that were baked, griddle cooked, or from the deep-fat kettle. Some of the grain offering was put on the altar of burnt offering, some was eaten by the priests, and in communion offerings the worshiper partook. (Le 6:19-23; 7:11-13; Nu 18:8-11) None of the grain offerings presented on the altar could contain leaven or "honey" (apparently referring to the syrup of figs or juice of fruits) that might ferment.—Le 2:1-16.

Drink offerings. Drink offerings were presented along with most of the other offerings, especially after the Israelites had settled in the Promised Land. (Nu 15:2, 5, 8-10) This consisted of wine ("intoxicating liquor") and was poured out on the altar. (Nu 28:7, 14; compare Ex 30:9; Nu 15:10.) The apostle Paul wrote to the Christians at Philippi: "If I am being poured out like a drink offering upon the sacrifice and public service to which faith has led you, I am glad." Here he used the figure of a drink offering, expressing his willingness to expend himself in behalf of fellow Christians. (Php 2:17) Shortly before his death, he wrote to Timothy: "I am already being poured out like a drink offering, and the due time for my releasing is imminent."—2Ti 4:6.

Wave offerings. In the wave offerings the priest evidently put his hands under the hands of the worshiper, who was holding the sacrifice to be presented, and waved them to and fro; or the thing offered was waved by the priest himself. (Le 23:11a) It seems that Moses, as mediator of the Law covenant, did this for Aaron and his sons when consecrating them to the priesthood. (Le 8:28, 29) This action represented a *presenting* of the sacrificial things to Jehovah. Certain wave offerings went to the priests as their portion.—Ex 29:27.

The presentation of a sheaf (or omer measure) of the firstfruits of the barley harvest on Nisan 16 was a wave offering carried out by the high priest. It was on this date in the year 33 C.E. that Jesus Christ was resurrected, "the firstfruits of those who have fallen asleep in death." (1Co 15:20; Le 23:11b; Joh 20:1) On the day of Pentecost two leavened loaves of the firstfruits of wheat were waved. (Le 23:15-17) This is the day that Jesus, as High Priest in the heavens, was able to present to Jehovah the first of his spiritual brothers of the Christian congregation, taken from among sinful mankind and anointed by the pouring out of the holy spirit.—Ac 2:1-4, 32, 33; compare Jas 1:18.

Sacred portions (heave offerings). The Hebrew word *teru·mah´* is sometimes translated "sacred portion" when referring to the part of the sacrifice that was lifted up, or heaved, off the sacrifice as the portion belonging to the priests. (Ex 29:27, 28; Le 7:14, 32; 10:14, 15) The word is also frequently rendered "contribution," when referring to the things given to the sanctuary, which, with the exception of that which was sacrificed on the altar, also went to the priests for their sustenance.—Nu 18:8-13, 19, 24, 26-29; 31:29; De 12:6, 11.

JEHOVAH'S law given to Israel prohibited the making of images for worship. The true God is a Spirit, and the making of any image to represent Him is grossly inappropriate. In contrast, many images of the gods of other ancient nations have been unearthed. They were nothing more than "the product of the hands of man, wood and stone." (De 4:28) They were "valueless gods," as the Bible says, having neither eyes to see nor ears to hear those who worshiped them. (1Ch 16:26; Ps 115:4-8) Today they are merely museum relics. Nevertheless, they reveal much about the roots of religious beliefs that are widespread today.

Religious triads began in Babylon. This stone tablet portrays a shrine of the Babylonian sun-god Shamash, along with symbols of one such triad: the moon (for the god Sin), the sun (for Shamash), and a star (for Ishtar)

Asshur, the chief god of the Assyrians, is portrayed on this ancient seal as having three heads (above the wings)

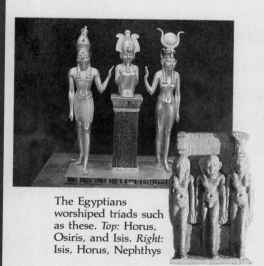

The Egyptians worshiped triads such as these. *Top:* Horus, Osiris, and Isis. *Right:* Isis, Horus, Nephthys

Much like Christendom's Madonna and child, Egypt's mother-son image (Isis and the infant Horus) was venerated

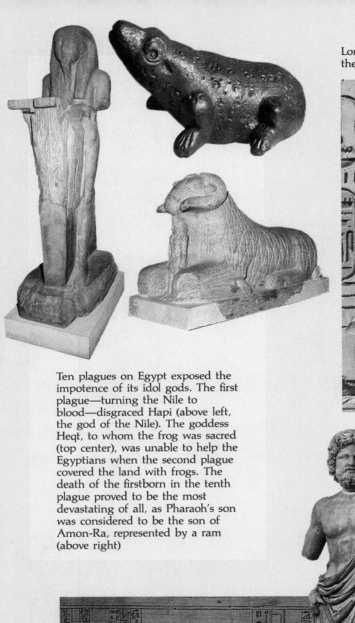

Long before Christianity, the crux ansata, the Egyptian cross, was viewed as sacred

Ten plagues on Egypt exposed the impotence of its idol gods. The first plague—turning the Nile to blood—disgraced Hapi (above left, the god of the Nile). The goddess Heqt, to whom the frog was sacred (top center), was unable to help the Egyptians when the second plague covered the land with frogs. The death of the firstborn in the tenth plague proved to be the most devastating of all, as Pharaoh's son was considered to be the son of Amon-Ra, represented by a ram (above right)

The serpent was featured in worship. Egyptian art (far left) shows two crossed snakes being held by the god at the left, a large snake dominating the picture, and a snake-headed goddess toward the right. The Greek statue of Asclepius (left) also features the serpent. Interestingly, the Bible shows that Satan used a serpent as his mouthpiece (Ge 3:1-15; Re 12:9)

Tyre

THE history of Tyre provides a striking example of the fulfillment of Bible prophecy. First the mainland city fell; then the island city was destroyed. Both events were foretold.

In the days of David and of Solomon, friendly relations had existed between Israel and Tyre. (1Ch 14:1; 1Ki 9:10, 11) But the Tyrians were worshipers of Melkart and Astarte. Tyre was devoted to commerce. As she prospered, she became proud. She became defiant toward Jehovah, and Jehovah's prophets foretold calamity for Tyre.

Nebuchadnezzar II besieged the city. From a military standpoint, after many years it might have seemed futile to continue. But he persevered until Tyre fell at the end of 13 years, thus fulfilling the Bible prophecy that had named him as its conqueror.—Eze 26:7-12.

Later, Zechariah again foretold ruin for Tyre, but this time it was for the island city. To reach it, Alexander the Great scraped up the ruins of the mainland city to construct a causeway; he built huge siege towers. Though Tyre had built its walls 46 m high (150 ft), the prophecy was fulfilled.—Zec 9:3, 4; Eze 26:4, 12.

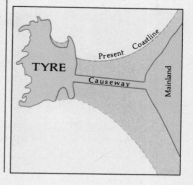

An aerial view of Tyre, with the area around the causeway, which is now considerably filled in

Cedars of Lebanon. Hiram king of Tyre
supplied cedarwood for the construction
of the temple in Jerusalem

Model of a type of trading ship
evidently used by ancient Tyre

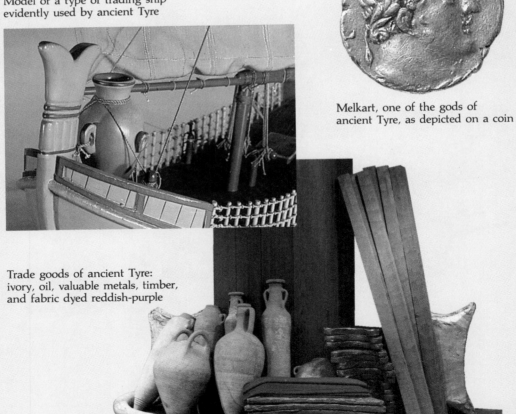

Melkart, one of the gods of
ancient Tyre, as depicted on a coin

Trade goods of ancient Tyre:
ivory, oil, valuable metals, timber,
and fabric dyed reddish-purple

Roman Empire

ROME was depicted in Bible prophecy as a beast that was "fearsome and terrible and unusually strong," with teeth of iron. (Da 7:7) It was this empire that Jehovah permitted to bring Jerusalem to ruin in 70 C.E.

Rome tolerated almost any sort of religious practice, as long as those who held to it would also share in worship of the emperor. Such emperor worship was viewed as an important factor in uniting the empire. So any who refused to share in it were considered to be enemies of the state. Christians did not join in such worship. Thus, although they were honest citizens, Christians often became the objects of vicious persecution. Among those who instigated such persecution were Emperors Nero, Domitian, Marcus Aurelius, and Diocletian. Pontius Pilate, a Roman governor of Judea, when pressured by religious leaders of the Jews, even ordered the execution of Jesus Christ, doing so as an act of political expediency.

PRINCIPAL CITIES

Rome: The western capital of the empire; after 395 C.E., the empire was divided, with emperors in both Rome and Constantinople; the Eastern Empire lasted nearly a thousand years after the Western Empire

Constantinople: Constantine transferred the capital of the empire from Rome to Byzantium, which he renamed to honor himself

Augustus Caesar. Jesus was born during his rule

Tiberius Caesar, as depicted on a coin. The execution of Jesus took place during Tiberius' reign

Claudius Caesar, who banished Jews from Rome

Caesar Nero, before whom the apostle Paul was tried

Vespasian. During his rule Jerusalem and its temple were destroyed

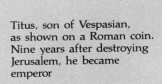

Titus, son of Vespasian, as shown on a Roman coin. Nine years after destroying Jerusalem, he became emperor

Domitian. Official persecution of Christians reached a peak during his rule, evidently resulting in the exile of the apostle John

Ruins of Roman aqueduct at Caesarea. This seaport city, built by Herod the Great, was an official residence of Roman procurators who governed Judea

These columns at the site of ancient Samaria testify to Roman influence there

A picture of the Tower of Antonia. This tower was situated at the northwest corner of Jerusalem's temple court and was used by the Romans to police activities in the temple area

A model of the hippodrome built in Jerusalem, evidently by Herod the Great. In Roman style, there were chariot races here and condemned men were made to fight wild beasts

The Arch of Titus in Rome commemorates the victory of Rome over Jerusalem in 70 C.E.; a relief shows Roman soldiers carrying off sacred vessels from the temple

Ruins of the Colosseum in Rome. Built largely by Jews taken captive in 70 C.E., the Colosseum was the site of the execution of many Christians

An altar devoted to the worship of Caesar. Because Christians would not burn incense to the emperor, they became objects of vicious persecution

THE Bible's record of Jesus' early life is brief but specific. It is not a fanciful story but is historical fact. It involves places that can be visited even now—Bethlehem, Egypt, Nazareth, and Jerusalem. The Bible's dating and explanation of events involves such prominent persons as Caesar Augustus, Governor Quirinius, King Herod the Great, and Archelaus—all of whom are known from secular history.

Above: A recent view of Bethlehem, where Jesus was born. *Below:* A drawing depicting the circumstances under which he was born

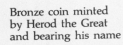

Bronze coin minted by Herod the Great and bearing his name

A bronze coin of Archelaus. When Joseph heard that Archelaus was ruling in Judea, he settled his family outside Archelaus' jurisdiction, up in Nazareth

A model of the palace of Herod the Great, now on display in Jerusalem. It was King Herod who tried to have young Jesus killed

A reconstruction of the temple area as it may have appeared in first-century Jerusalem

At 12 years of age, Jesus was in the temple in Jerusalem, sitting in the midst of the teachers and listening to them and questioning them

En Nasira (Nazerat) in Galilee,
the likely site of ancient Nazareth,
where Jesus grew up

As a young man in
Nazareth, Jesus worked
at carpentry under
the supervision of
his adoptive father

THE ministry of Jesus Christ has deeply influenced the lives of people in every part of the world. Jesus did not allow himself to be distracted from his objective. As he said: "I must declare the good news of the kingdom of God, because for this I was sent forth." —Lu 4:43.

As shown on the accompanying maps, he covered a large territory —mainly on foot. In connection with Jewish festivals, he made regular trips to Jerusalem during his ministry. The journeys specifically mentioned in the Gospels are shown on our maps. From Jerusalem he moved out to cover Judean territory. But he spent most of his time in Galilee, giving the whole province an intensive witness. His ministry also took him to people in the regions of Tyre and Sidon, throughout the cities of the Decapolis, and into Perea. He thoroughly bore witness to the truth, leaving a fine example for his followers. —Joh 18:37; Ac 1:8; Mt 28:19, 20.

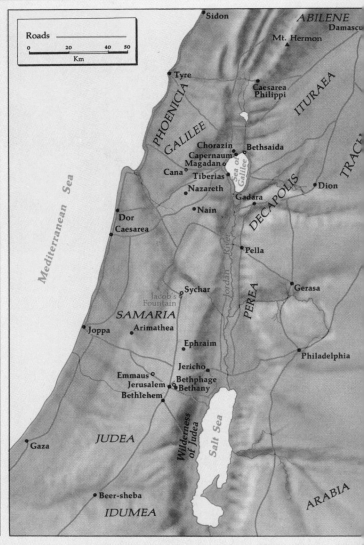

PRINCIPAL LOCATIONS
With Related Scriptures

Bethany	Joh 11:1, 38-44; 12:1-9; Lu 24:50, 51
Bethphage	Mt 21:1-9
Bethsaida	Lu 9:10-17; Mr 8:22-26; Joh 1:44
Caesarea Philippi	Mt 16:13-20
Cana	Joh 2:1-11; 4:46-54
Capernaum	Lu 4:31-41; Mr 2:1-12; Mt 8:5-13; 17:24—18:35
Chorazin	Mt 11:20-22
Decapolis	Mr 5:18-20; 7:31—8:9
Emmaus	Lu 24:13-32
Ephraim	Joh 11:54
Gadara	Mt 8:28-34
Jericho	Lu 18:35—19:27
Jerusalem	Joh 2:13—3:21; 5:1-47; 7:14—10:39; Mt 21:6—26:5; 26:14—28:15
Jordan R.	Mt 3:13-17
Nain	Lu 7:11-17
Nazareth	Lu 4:16-30; Mr 6:1-6
Sidon	Mr 7:24-30
Sychar	Jo 4:5-42
Tyre	Mt 15:21-28
Wilderness	Mt 4:1-11

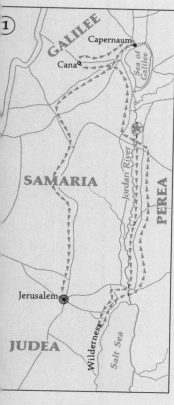

1. GALILEE — Capernaum, Cana, Sea of Galilee, Jordan River, SAMARIA, PEREA, Jerusalem, Wilderness, Salt Sea, JUDEA

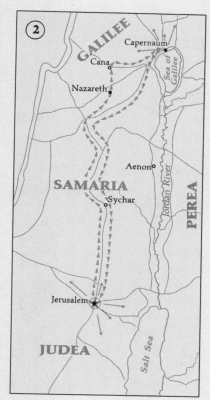

2. GALILEE — Capernaum, Cana, Nazareth, Sea of Galilee, Jordan River, Aenon, SAMARIA, Sychar, PEREA, Jerusalem, Salt Sea, JUDEA

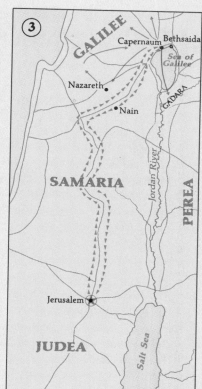

3. GALILEE — Capernaum, Bethsaida, Sea of Galilee, Nazareth, Nain, GADARA, Jordan River, SAMARIA, PEREA, Jerusalem, Salt Sea, JUDEA

4. Sidon, Mt. Hermon, Tyre, GALILEE, Caesarea Philippi, Capernaum, Magadan, Bethsaida, Sea of Galilee, Jordan River, SAMARIA, PEREA, Jerusalem, Bethany, UDEA, Salt Sea

TIME PERIODS COVERED BY MAPS

1: From fall of 29 C.E. through Passover of 30 C.E.

2: After Passover of 30 C.E. through Passover of 31 C.E.

3: After Passover of 31 C.E. until after Passover of 32 C.E.

4: After Passover of 32 C.E. through Festival of Dedication in 32 C.E.

5: After Festival of Dedication in 32 C.E. through Nisan 14, 33 C.E.

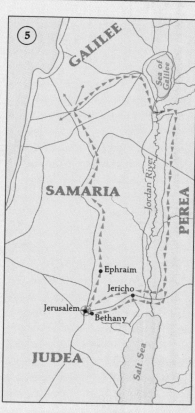

5. GALILEE — Sea of Galilee, Jordan River, SAMARIA, PEREA, Ephraim, Jericho, Jerusalem, Bethany, JUDEA, Salt Sea

First-Century Jerusalem

THE Jerusalem that exists today has changed greatly from what it was in the first century. Nevertheless, on the basis of archaeological research, it has been possible to reconstruct in a tentative way some of the key parts of the city. This can help students to visualize the events that took place there in connection with the ministry of Jesus and that of his apostles.

When in Jerusalem at festival times, Jesus taught in the temple area where the crowds were. (Joh 7:14, 28; 18:20) Following his death and resurrection, his disciples 'filled Jerusalem with their teaching.' (Ac 5:28) From Jerusalem, their witnessing eventually spread to "the most distant part of the earth." —Ac 1:8.

The activity of Jesus and his disciples confronted the nation with an important issue: Would they accept the one whom Jehovah sent as Messiah? Would they recognize their need of the Kingdom of God? Though some put faith in Jesus, most were unresponsive. The nation's faithless actions were climaxed by the impalement of Jesus, which took place with popular support at Jerusalem. As a result, destruction befell the city in 70 C.E., just as Jesus had foretold. —Lu 19:41-44.

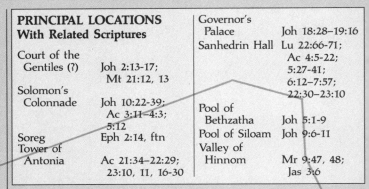

PRINCIPAL LOCATIONS
With Related Scriptures

Court of the Gentiles (?)	Joh 2:13-17; Mt 21:12, 13
Solomon's Colonnade	Joh 10:22-39; Ac 3:11–4:3; 5:12
Soreg	Eph 2:14, ftn
Tower of Antonia	Ac 21:34–22:29; 23:10, 11, 16-30
Governor's Palace	Joh 18:28–19:16
Sanhedrin Hall	Lu 22:66-71; Ac 4:5-22; 5:27-41; 6:12–7:57; 22:30–23:10
Pool of Bethzatha	Joh 5:1-9
Pool of Siloam	Joh 9:6-11
Valley of Hinnom	Mr 9:47, 48; Jas 3:6

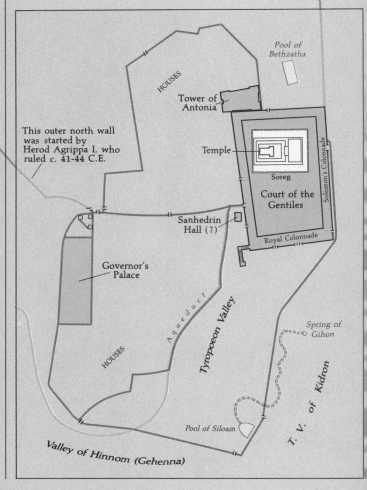

This outer north wall was started by Herod Agrippa I, who ruled c. 41-44 C.E.

Pool of Bethzatha

HOUSES

Tower of Antonia

Temple

Soreg

Solomon's Colonnade

Court of the Gentiles

Royal Colonnade

Sanhedrin Hall (?)

Governor's Palace

HOUSES

Aqueduct

Tyropoeon Valley

Spring of Gihon

Pool of Siloam

T. V. of Kidron

Valley of Hinnom (Gehenna)

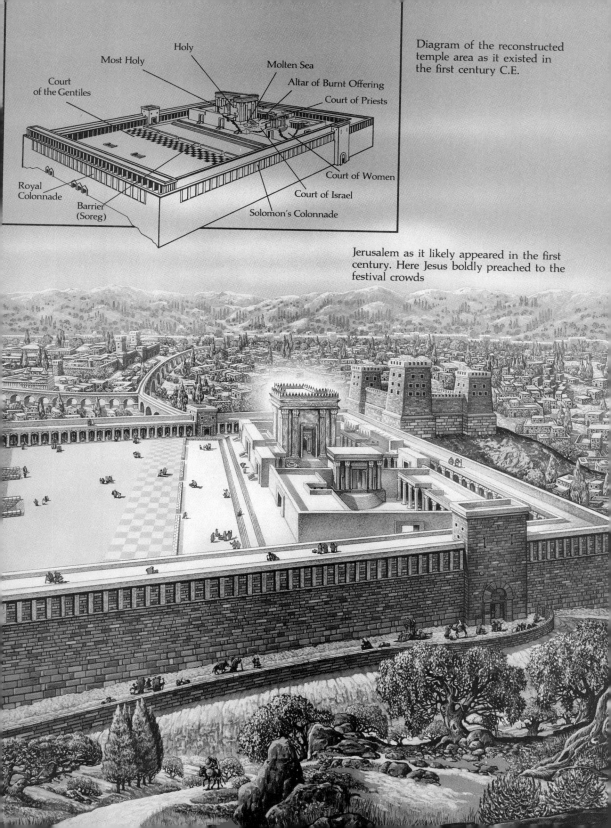

Diagram of the reconstructed temple area as it existed in the first century C.E.

Most Holy

Holy

Molten Sea

Altar of Burnt Offering

Court of the Gentiles

Court of Priests

Royal Colonnade

Court of Women

Barrier (Soreg)

Court of Israel

Solomon's Colonnade

Jerusalem as it likely appeared in the first century. Here Jesus boldly preached to the festival crowds

The Pharisees hired men to trap Jesus on the issue of paying tax to Rome

A denarius bearing the image of Tiberius Caesar

OFFICIAL GARMENT.

The Hebrew word 'ad·de'reth describes that which is "majestic" (Eze 17:8; Zec 11:3) and, in its references to a garment, evidently refers to a wide cloak or robe, perhaps worn over the shoulders and made of skins or of cloth woven from hair or wool.

Evidence that the term describes a hairy garment is seen in the description of Isaac's firstborn Esau. At birth, he "came out red all over like an official garment of hair; so they called his name Esau." (Ge 25:25) His resemblance to an official garment was likely not his reddish color but his hairiness.

When translating 'ad·de'reth, for the official garment used by Elijah and Elisha, the Septuagint uses the Greek word me·lo·te' (meaning sheepskin or any rough woolly skin). (1Ki 19:13) This suggests that the garment was made of skins with the hair left on, similar to the garb worn by certain Bedouin. Paul's description of persecuted servants of God who "went about in sheepskins, in goatskins," may refer to the dress of such prophets of Jehovah. (Heb 11:37) John the Baptizer wore clothing of camel hair, though it is not stated that this was his official garment as a prophet.—Mr 1:6.

However designed, these official garments of hair appear to have been an identifying mark of certain prophets. When King Ahaziah heard the description of "a man possessing a hair garment, with a leather belt girded about his loins," he immediately recognized that it was the prophet Elijah. (2Ki 1:8) This official garment served as the anointing instrument that was thrown upon Elisha when he was 'called' to leave the plow and follow Elijah. (1Ki 19:19-21) Later, at the time Elijah went up in the windstorm, this garment was left for his successor, who soon used it in dividing the Jordan River, just as his master had done. (2Ki 2:3, 8, 13, 14) False prophets, it appears, sometimes wore similar garments of hair to deceive the people into accepting them as reputable prophets of Jehovah, thus making their messages seem more credible.—Zec 13:4.

The term 'ad·de'reth was also used in reference to costly and royal garments, like the one stolen by Achan, "an official garment from Shinar, a good-looking one." (Jos 7:21, 24) Ancient Babylon, or Shinar, was noted for its beautiful robes. The king of Nineveh "put off his official garment," undoubtedly a splendid robe, and clothed himself with sackcloth to show his repentance.—Jon 3:6.

OG.

The powerful Amorite king of Bashan (1Ki 4:19) whom the Israelites defeated before crossing into the Promised Land. Og was one of the giant Rephaim. In fact, his immense iron bier (perhaps a sarcophagus of black basalt) measured 4 by 1.8 m (13.1 by 5.8 ft). (De 3:11, ftn) He and Sihon ruled the Amorites E of the Jordan. (De 3:13; 4:46, 47) The domain of Og extended from Mount Hermon to the Jabbok, territory E of the Jordan that included 60 fortified cities and numerous rural towns. (De 3:3-5, 8-10; Jos 12:4, 5; compare Nu 21:23, 24.) His two principal cities were Edrei and Ashtaroth.—De 1:4; Jos 13:12.

The defeat of Og at the hands of Israel came toward the end of Israel's 40-year wandering, just before they encamped on the Plains of Moab. After defeating Sihon, Israel clashed with Og's forces at Edrei and, in an overwhelming God-given victory, killed off Og and all his army and took possession of his cities and towns. (Nu 21:33–22:1; De 3:1-13) Og's territory became part of Manasseh's inheritance. (Nu 32:33; De 3:13; Jos 13:29-31) The victory brought fright to the inhabitants of Canaan and was a contributing factor prompting Rahab and the Gibeonites to seek peace with Israel so that they too were not exterminated. (Jos 2:10, 11; 9:9, 10) The victory was a great encouragement to Israel and was remembered even many centuries later.—De 31:4; Ne 9:22; Ps 135:10-12; 136:17-22.

OHAD

(O'had). The third-listed son of Simeon. (Ge 46:10; Ex 6:15) His name does not appear as founder of a family in the later registration list. —Nu 26:12-14.

OHEL

(O'hel) [Tent]. A son of Governor Zerubbabel and descendant of David.—1Ch 3:19, 20.

OHOLAH

(O·ho'lah) [Her Tent [of Worship]]. Ezekiel chapter 23 depicts Samaria (representing the ten-tribe kingdom of Israel) as the prostitute Oholah, the older sister of Oholibah, representing Jerusalem (the kingdom of Judah). The fact that the ten-tribe kingdom established its own centers of worship may be alluded to by the name Oholah, "Her Tent [of Worship]." Her spiritual prostitution began in Egypt and continued in the Promised Land. In later times it involved her currying the favor of the Assyrians and engaging in degrading idolatrous practices, including child sacrifice. For her unfaithfulness to him, Jehovah delivered Oholah (the northern kingdom) into the hands of the Assyrians, her lovers.

OHOLIAB

(O·ho'li·ab) [Father's Tent; possibly, Father Is My Tent [that is, protection]]. Chief assistant of Bezalel in constructing the tabernacle; of the tribe of Dan, son of Ahisamach. Oholiab was "a craftsman and embroiderer and weaver in the blue thread and the wool dyed reddish purple and coccus scarlet material and fine linen."—Ex 31:6; 35:34; 36:1, 2; 38:23.

OHOLIBAH (O·hol′i·bah) [My Tent [of Worship] Is in Her]. In Ezekiel chapter 23, Jerusalem's unfaithfulness to Jehovah is portrayed under the allegory of the prostitute Oholibah. The meaning of the name Oholibah seems to allude to the fact that Jehovah's tent, or sanctuary, was in her territory. (Compare OHOLAH.) However, instead of appreciating this and taking to heart the punishment that came upon her sister Oholah (Samaria) for unfaithfulness, Oholibah not only continued the record of infidelity begun in Egypt but conducted herself even worse than her sister. She practiced idolatry on a large scale and became politically involved with the Assyrians and the Babylonians. Consequently her former lovers, the Babylonians, were foretold to come against her and make her "a frightful object."

OHOLIBAMAH (O·hol·i·ba′mah) [Tent of the High Place].

1. A Canaanite wife of Esau. She bore him three sons, Jeush, Jalam, and Korah, all of whom became sheiks of Edom. Oholibamah was a daughter of Anah and granddaughter of Hivite Zibeon.—Ge 36:2, 5-8, 14, 18, 25; see ANAH.

2. The designation of an Edomite sheik; some scholars would apply these listed names to places, believing they should read, "the sheik of Oholibamah," and so forth.—Ge 36:40, 41; 1Ch 1:51, 52.

OIL. The fatty liquid most familiar to the Hebrews was that obtained from olives. Fully ripened black olives gave the most oil, but those yet green, though beginning to change in color, produced the oil of finest quality. After the fruit was carefully removed from the trees, and the twigs and leaves were cleaned from the olives, they were carried to the oil press.

The pulp of the ripe olive berry is about half oil, which varies in grade according to the method of processing the pulp. The very best, called "pure, beaten olive oil," was produced by a simple process before the olives were put into the press. (Le 24:2) First, the olives were placed in a mortar and beaten until they were well bruised, or they were sometimes trodden by foot. (Mic 6:15) Next, the bruised fruit was transferred to strainer baskets in which it "bled" oil until the "virgin" oil was released. The pure, beaten oil was stored in earthenware jars, and the pulp was moved to the olive press.

A common grade of oil was prepared by thoroughly crushing the olives in a mortar or hand mill. After the oil ran off from the pulp, it was allowed to clarify in clay jars or vats.

The lowest grade of oil was that pressed from the pulp refuse in an olive press after the crushing process. The pulverized mass of pulp was packed into baskets and stacked between the two vertical pillars of the olive press. A weighted lever was applied to the stack of baskets to press out the oil, which was then channeled into large reservoirs for clearing. There, the oil would rise to the surface, separating from the bits of pulp and the water below before it was drawn off into large earthenware jars or special cisterns for storage. —Compare 2Ch 32:27, 28; see PRESS.

A Symbol of Prosperity. Great prosperity was signified when reference was made to the 'press vats overflowing with oil.' (Joe 2:24) Suffering Job longed for his previous days of plenty when "the rock kept pouring out streams of oil" for him. (Job 29:1, 2, 6) Jehovah caused "Jacob," or the Israelites, figuratively to suck "oil out of a flinty rock," apparently from olive trees growing in rocky terrain. (De 32:9, 13) Moses declared that Asher would become "one dipping his foot in oil," indicating that this tribe would enjoy material blessings.—De 33:24.

An Important Trade and Food Commodity. Olive oil became an important trade commodity in Palestine because of its abundance there. Yearly, Solomon gave King Hiram of Tyre "twenty cor measures [4,400 L; 1,160 gal] of beaten-out oil" as part of a payment for temple construction materials. (1Ki 5:10, 11) Judah and Israel were once Tyre's "traders" for oil. (Eze 27:2, 17) Perfumed oil and olive oil are also among the items purchased by mystic Babylon the Great from "the traveling merchants" of the earth.—Re 18:11-13.

Olive oil, a high-energy food and one of the most digestible fats, was a principal food in the Israelite diet, probably in many cases taking the place of butter for table use and for cooking purposes. (De 7:13; Jer 41:8; Eze 16:13) It was a common lamp fuel (Mt 25:1-9), and "pure, beaten olive oil" was burned in the lamps of the golden lampstand in the tent of meeting. (Ex 27:20, 21; 25:31, 37) Oil was used in connection with grain offerings presented to Jehovah. (Le 2:1-7) As a cosmetic it was applied to the body after bathing. (Ru 3:3; 2Sa 12:20) It was considered an act of hospitality to grease the head of a guest with oil. (Lu 7:44-46) Oil was also employed to soften and to soothe bruises and wounds (Isa 1:6), sometimes along with wine.—Lu 10:33, 34.

Religious Use and Significance. Jehovah commanded Moses to prepare "a holy anointing oil" that contained olive oil and other ingredients. With it, Moses anointed the tabernacle, the ark of the testimony, the various sanctuary utensils, and its furniture. Moses also used it in anointing Aaron and his sons, to sanctify them as priests to Jehovah. (Ex 30:22-33; Le 8:10-12) Kings were anointed with oil, as when Samuel, anointing Saul, "took the flask of oil and poured it out upon his head." (1Sa 10:1) A horn of oil was used when Solomon was anointed.—1Ki 1:39.

Foretelling the joy-producing effects of Jesus Christ's earthly ministry, it was said that he would give "those mourning over Zion . . . the oil of exultation instead of mourning." (Isa 61:1-3; Lu 4:16-21) It was also prophesied that Jesus would be anointed personally by Jehovah with "the oil of exultation" more than his partners, indicating that he would experience greater joy than his predecessors of the Davidic dynasty.—Ps 45:7; Heb 1: 8, 9; see ANOINTED, ANOINTING.

As the applying of literal oil to one's head is soothing and refreshing, so also is the application of God's Word to a spiritually sick person to soothe, correct, comfort, and heal him. Thus, the older men of the Christian congregation are admonished to pray over such a man, figuratively "greasing him with oil in the name of Jehovah," an essential measure in effecting his spiritual recovery.—Jas 5:13-15; compare Ps 141:5.

OIL TREE

[Heb., 'ets she'men]. The identification of this tree is doubtful. The Hebrew expression indicates a "fatwood" tree, rich in oil or similar substance. It has long been considered to be the oleaster (Elaeagnus angustifolia), which is a small tree or shrub common in Palestine, bearing gray-green leaves similar to those of the olive tree and producing a fruit from which an oil is obtained, much inferior to the oil of the olive. While its wood is hard and fine-grained, making it suitable for carving, it hardly seems to fit the description given of the 'oil tree' at 1 Kings 6:23, 31-33. There it is stated that, in the temple construction, the two cherubs, each standing 4.5 m (14.6 ft) tall, as well as the doors to the Most Holy and the "foursquare" doorposts for the main entrance to the temple, were made of the wood of the 'oil tree.' The oleaster seems much too small a plant to fit these requirements adequately.

The King James Version and Revised Standard Version refer to wood of the olive tree at 1 Kings 6:23, and it is suggested that the cherubs may have been constructed of several pieces joined together, since the olive's short trunk does not provide timbers of great lengths. Still, the fact that the olive tree is alluded to as distinct from the oil tree at Nehemiah 8:15 would seem to rule out this suggestion.

For this reason some scholars recommend the Aleppo pine (Pinus halepensis), which they believe could have been called the oil tree because of its producing tar and turpentine. This lofty pine is one of the most common evergreens in Palestine, and there is evidence to show that the region around Jerusalem once had a sizable forest of it. It grows up to 20 m (66 ft) tall, with smooth gray bark, light-green needles, and reddish-brown cones. Its wood is said to be of a quality approaching that of the cedar. This tree could, therefore, fit the requirements for the temple building; however, in view of the lack of positive evidence, the New World Translation renders the Hebrew expression simply as "oil tree."

Branches of the oil tree, along with those of the olive, myrtle, and palm, were used in Jerusalem at the Festival of Booths. (Ne 8:15) The oil tree is also one of the trees foretold to grace the wilderness, in Isaiah's restoration prophecy.—Isa 41:19.

OINTMENT AND PERFUMES.

The Hebrew terms relating to ointments may apply not only to salvelike preparations that liquefy when rubbed on the skin but also to compounded oil preparations that remain liquid at normal temperatures.—Ex 30:25; Ps 133:2.

In the past as now, ointments were used chiefly as cosmetic and medicinal preparations, their advantage being mainly due to their oil content. The property that fats and oils possess, of absorbing and retaining odors, made it possible for the ointment maker to produce perfumed preparations that were highly prized for their fragrance. (Ca 1:3) The cleansing power and skin-softening characteristic of the oil, plus the fragrance of the additives, made such ointments very useful for the prevention of chafing and skin irritation, and for a body "deodorant" in hot countries where water was often very scarce. Offering guests such a preparation upon their arrival at one's home was certainly an act of hospitality, as noted by what Jesus said when someone greased his feet with perfumed oil.—Lu 7:37-46.

When perfumed ointments of special make were used in preparing a corpse for burial, they no doubt served primarily as disinfectants and deodorants. (2Ch 16:14; Lu 23:56) With such usage in mind, Jesus explained that the anointing he received in the house of Simon the leper, which consisted of very costly perfumed oil the scent of which filled the whole house, was in a figurative sense "for the preparation of me for burial." (Mt 26:6-12; Joh 12:3) Precious perfumes, such as the spikenard used on this occasion, were usually sealed in beautiful alabaster cases or vials.—Mr 14:3; see ALABASTER.

Holy Anointing Oil and Incense. The first ointment mentioned in the Bible was the holy anointing oil used to sanctify the dedicated articles of the tabernacle and its priesthood. (Ex 30:25-30) Personal use of this special ointment was prohibited, under penalty of death. This law shows the sacredness attached to the tabernacle and its personnel.—Ex 30:31-33.

Jehovah gave Moses the formula for the holy anointing oil. Only "the choicest perfumes" were to be used: myrrh, sweet cinnamon, sweet calamus, cassia, and the purest olive oil, and each in specified amounts. (Ex 30:22-24) Likewise, Jehovah gave the formula for the holy incense. It was not just a substance that would smolder and smoke; it was a special perfumed incense. (Ex 30:7; 40:27; Le 16:12; 2Ch 2:4; 13:10, 11) To make it, specific amounts of stacte drops, onycha, perfumed galbanum, and pure frankincense were used, God further describing it as "a spice mixture, the work of an ointment maker, salted, pure, something holy." Some of the incense was finely powdered and was probably sifted to obtain a uniform product, suitable for its special use. Private use was a capital crime.—Ex 30:34-38.

In making both the anointing oil and holy incense, fragrant balsam oil was used. (Ex 25:6; 35:8, 28) It seems reasonable to assume that the perfume agencies used in making the holy ointment were powdered and then cooked in the oil (compare Job 41:31), after which it was allowed to settle before the oil was drawn off and filtered.

Making the anointing oil and perfumed incense was not a matter of trial and error, for at the outset Jehovah said: "In the heart of everyone wise of heart I do put wisdom, that they may indeed make . . . the anointing oil and the perfumed incense for the sanctuary." (Ex 31:6-11; 35:10-15; 37:29; 39:33, 38) Thereafter certain ones of the priests were delegated to be ointment makers for the compounding of these materials and also to take the oversight of the supply of such items. (1Ch 9:30; Nu 4:16) However, when Israel fell away from pure worship, Jehovah ceased to take pleasure in the making or using of these special ointments and incenses.—Isa 1:13.

Economic Value of Ointments and Perfumes. Ointments, perfumes, and incense were not limited to the holy products used in the sanctuary. By Solomon's day there were "all sorts of perfume" and fragrant powders available for scenting houses, garments, beds, and bodies of royalty and others who could afford them. (Es 2:12; Ps 45:8; Pr 7:17; Ca 3:6, 7; 4:10) Nor was the making of these preparations restricted to the Levitical priesthood. Even women were sometimes skilled ointment makers, and in Nehemiah's day there was a trade group to which members of the ointment mixers belonged.—1Sa 8:13; Ne 3:8.

In the ancient world the public interest in perfumed products created commerce and trade not only in such consumer items but also in the raw materials needed to make the same. Besides myrrh especially for ointments, and frankincense for incense, other materials including spikenard, saffron, cane, cinnamon, aloes, cassia, as well as various spices, gums, and aromatic plants, were often transported long distances before reaching the pots and perfumeries of the ointment makers.—Ca 4:14; Re 18:11, 13.

OLDER MAN. The Hebrew word *za·qen'* and the Greek word *pre·sby'te·ros,* both meaning "older man," or "elder," are used not only to refer to persons of advanced age (Ge 18:11; De 28:50; 1Sa 2:22; 1Ti 5:1, 2) or to the older of two persons (Lu 15:25) but also to apply in a special way to those holding a position of authority and responsibility in a community or nation. The latter sense is the predominant one in both the Hebrew and the Christian Greek Scriptures.

The elderly man customarily was held in esteem from ancient times forward, respected for his experience and knowledge and for the wisdom and sound judgment that such may bring. In many nations people submitted themselves to the direction of their older men, either those who were the elder members of family lines or those who were notable for their qualities of knowledge and wisdom. As a result the expression "older man" had a double sense, applying either in a physical sense or as a designation of position or office. The references to the "older men ["dignitaries," *JB*] of the land of Egypt" and to "the older men of Moab and the older men of Midian" do not embrace every aged male of those nations but apply to those serving as a council for directing and guiding national affairs; they were the "princes [Heb., *sa·rim';* "chieftains," *AT*]" of those nations.—Ge 50:7; Nu 22:4, 7, 8, 13-15; Ps 105:17, 21, 22.

In the same way the expressions "older men of Israel," "older men of the assembly," "older men of my people," "older men of the land," are used in this official sense, not applying to every aged man of the nation of Israel. (Nu 16:25; Le 4:15; 1Sa 15:30; 1Ki 20:7, 8) In the relatively few cases where *zeqe·nim'* (older men) appears without some qualifying words, the context must be relied on to determine whether the application is merely to aged males or to those in the official capacity of headmen.

Older Men (Elders) of Israel. Already prior to the Exodus, the Israelites had their "older men," who presented matters to the people, acted as their spokesmen, and reached decisions. When returning to Egypt, Moses was instructed to present his commission to these older men, and these, or at least the principal ones among them, accompanied him when he went in before Pharaoh.—Ex 3:16, 18.

When Moses, as God's representative, presented the Law covenant to the nation, it was the official "older men" who represented the people in entering that covenant relationship with Jehovah. (Ex 19:3-8) Some time later, when the Israelites complained about the conditions in the wilderness, Moses, feeling that the administrative burden of the nation was now too great for him, confessed the problem to Jehovah. Then God commanded Moses: "Gather for me seventy men of the older men of Israel, whom you do know that they are older men of the people and officers of theirs, . . . and I shall have to take away some of the spirit that is upon you and place it upon them, and they will have to help you in carrying the load." (Nu 11:16, 17) These "older men" were appointed theocratically to this service. (Nu 11:24, 25) Jehovah now used them to share the responsibility of leadership and administration with Moses.

In time, the nomadic Israelites conquered the Promised Land and went back to fixed dwellings in towns and cities, as had been their way of life in Egypt. The older men now became responsible for the people on a community level. They acted as a body of overseers for their respective communities, providing judges and officers for the administration of justice and the maintenance of peace, good order, and spiritual health.—De 16:18-20; 25:7-9; Jos 20:4; Ru 4:1-12.

References to "all Israel, its older men and its heads and its judges and its officers" (Jos 23:2; 24:1), "the older men of Israel and all the heads of the tribes, the chieftains of the paternal houses" (2Ch 5:2), do not mean that the "heads," "judges," "officers," and "chieftains" were distinct from the "older men" but, rather, indicate that those named in such a specific way held singular offices within the body of older men.—Compare 2Ki 19:2; Mr 15:1.

Those serving as "older men" on a national level are designated by the expressions "older men of Israel" (1Sa 4:3; 8:4), "older men of the land" (1Ki 20:7), "older men of the assembly" (Jg 21:16), or,

after the division of the kingdom, "older men of Judah and Jerusalem," for the southern kingdom. —2Ki 23:1.

Like many of Israel's kings and priests, the "older men" on the whole proved unfaithful in their responsibility to God and the people. (1Ki 21:8-14; Eze 7:26; 14:1-3) Because of losing God's support, 'boys would become their princes,' and the 'lightly esteemed one would storm against the one to be honored.' (Isa 3:1-5) Thus, the Hebrew Scriptures emphasize that age alone is not sufficient, that "gray-headedness is a crown of beauty" only when "found in the way of righteousness." (Pr 16:31) It is not "those merely abundant in days that prove wise, nor those just old that understand judgment," but those who, along with their experience, are guided by God's spirit and who have gained understanding of his Word.—Job 32:8, 9; Ps 119:100; Pr 3:5-7; Ec 4:13.

Direction by the body of "older men" continued throughout the history of the nation, even during the Babylonian exile and after the restoration to Judah. (Jer 29:1; Ezr 6:7; 10:7, 8, 14) When Jesus was on earth, "older men" (Gr., pre·sby′te·roi) were active in public affairs, both on a community level (Lu 7:3-5) and on a national level. "The assembly of older men" (Gr., pre·sby·te′ri·on) at Jerusalem constituted a major source of opposition to Jesus and his disciples.—Lu 22:66; Ac 22:5.

Elders in Christian Congregation. Viewed against this background, it is not difficult to understand the references to "older men" (pre·sby′te·roi) of the Christian congregation. As in fleshly Israel, so in spiritual Israel, the "older men," or elders, were those responsible for the direction of the congregation.

On the day of Pentecost, the apostles acted as a body, with Peter serving as spokesman by the operation of God's outpoured spirit. (Ac 2:14, 37-42) They were clearly "older men" in the spiritual sense by virtue of their early and intimate association with Jesus and their having been personally commissioned by him to teach. (Mt 28:18-20; Eph 4:11, 12; compare Ac 2:42.) The attitude of those becoming believers shows that they acknowledged that the apostles had governing authority in the new nation under Christ (Ac 2:42; 4:32-37; 5:1-11) and had authority to make appointments to service, either directly as a body or through representatives, the apostle Paul being a notable example. (Ac 6:1-6; 14:19-23) When the issue of circumcision came to the fore, "older men" along with the apostles met in assembly to consider the matter. Their decision was made known to congregations in all places and was accepted as authoritative. (Ac 15:1-31; 16:1-5) Thus, even as some "older men" served Israel on a national basis, so it is evident that these "older men" with the apostles formed a governing body for the entire Christian congregation in all lands. At a later date, Paul went to Jerusalem and met with James and "all the older men," relating to them the results of his work and receiving their counsel on certain matters.—Ac 21:15-26.

In a few cases the term "older men" is used in contrast with younger men or in parallel with older women with no indication of congregational responsibility being involved. In such cases, the term refers simply to men of mature age. (Ac 2:17, 18; 1Ti 5:1, 2) It is also used to refer to "men of old times." (Heb 11:2) However, in most cases in the Christian Greek Scriptures, the "older men" were those responsible for the direction of the congregation. In a few texts the "older men" are called "overseers" (Gr., e·pi'sko·poi; 'bishops,' KJ). Paul used this term in speaking to the "older men" from the one congregation of Ephesus, and he applied it to such ones in his letter to Titus. (Ac 20:17, 28; Tit 1:5, 7) Both terms, therefore, refer to the same position, pre·sby'te·ros indicating the mature qualities of the one so appointed, and e·pi'sko·pos the duties inherent with the appointment.

Regarding the Greek word pre·sby'te·ros, Manuel Guerra y Gomez noted: "The precise translation of the term [pre·sby'te·ros] in almost the majority of the Hellenistic texts, that have survived until now, is that of older man synonym of mature man. Maturity of judgment and guiding criterion is its distinctive note. . . . Whether or not it has a technical sense the term [pre·sby'te·ros] both in the Hellenistic and the Israelite worlds designates, not the ailing elderly, but rather the mature man, suitable by his experience and prudence for the ruling of his family or of his people."—Episcopos y Presbyteros, Burgos, Spain, 1962, pp. 117, 257.

That age, in the physical sense of years lived, was a factor for qualifying to serve as an "older man" in ancient Israel is evident. (1Ki 12:6-13) So, too, the "older men," or overseers, in the Christian congregation were not young men, as is evidenced by the apostle's reference to their having wives and children. (Tit 1:5, 6; 1Ti 3:2, 4, 5) Nevertheless, physical age was not the sole or primary factor, as is seen by the other qualifications set forth (1Ti 3:2-7; Tit 1:6-9), nor is any specific age level stipulated. Timothy, who had to do with appointing "older men," was obviously also recognized as one himself, though relatively young. —1Ti 4:12.

The requirements for the position as an "older man" in the Christian congregation included a high standard of conduct and spirituality. The ability to teach, to exhort, and to reprove played a major part in one's being accredited as an "older man." (1Ti 3:2; Tit 1:9) Paul solemnly charged Timothy to "preach the word, be at it urgently in favorable season, in troublesome season, reprove, reprimand, exhort, with all long-suffering and art of teaching." (2Ti 4:2) As "shepherds," the "older men" are responsible for the spiritual feeding of the flock, as well as for caring for those spiritually ill and for protecting the flock against wolfish elements. (Ac 20:28-35; Jas 5:14, 15; 1Pe 5:2-4) Additionally, Paul, who had himself been zealous in teaching "publicly and from house to house," reminded Timothy of his responsibility to "do the work of an evangelizer, fully accomplish your ministry."—Ac 20:20; 2Ti 4:5.

Each Christian congregation had its body of "older men," or "overseers," these regularly being mentioned in the plural, as at Jerusalem (Ac 11: 30; 15:4, 6; 21:18), at Ephesus (Ac 20:17, 28), at Philippi (Php 1:1). "The body of older men" (Gr., pre·sby·te'ri·on) is mentioned with regard to the 'laying of hands' on Timothy. (1Ti 4:14) "The older men," as the overseers of the congregation, 'presided' over their brothers.—Ro 12:8; 1Th 5:12-15; 1Ti 3:4, 5; 5:17.

Paul and Peter, as "older men" with apostolic authority, at times exercised oversight over other "older men" in certain congregations (compare 1Co 4:18-21; 5:1-5, 9-13; Php 1:1; 2:12; 1Pe 1:1; 5:1-5), as did the apostle John and the disciples James and Jude—all writers of letters to congregations. Paul assigned Timothy and Titus to represent him in certain places. (1Co 4:17; Php 2:19, 20; 1Ti 1:3, 4; 5:1-21; Tit 1:5) In many cases, these men were dealing with newly established congregations of believers; Titus' commission was to "correct the things that were defective [or wanting, lacking]" in the congregations in Crete.

Paul, Barnabas, Titus, and evidently Timothy are recorded as taking part in appointing persons as "older men" in the congregations. (Ac 14:21-23; 1Ti 5:22; Tit 1:5) There is no record of such appointments by the congregations independently. In relating Paul and Barnabas' revisiting of Lystra, Iconium, and Antioch, Acts 14:23 states that "they appointed older men [Gr., khei·ro·to·ne'san·tes] for them in each congregation" ("in each of these churches they appointed elders," JB; "they had appointed elders for them in every church," RS). Regarding the meaning of the Greek verb khei·ro·to·ne'o, the following remark is found in *The Acts of the Apostles,* by F. F. Bruce (1970, p. 286): "Although the etymological sense of [*khei·ro·to·ne'o*] is 'to elect by show of hands', it came to be used in the sense 'designate', 'appoint': cf. the same word with prefix [*pro,* "before"] in x. 41." Liddell and Scott's *Greek-English Lexicon,* after first giving common definitions to *khei·ro·to·ne'o,* says: "later, generally, *appoint, . . . appoint to an office* in the Church." (Revised by H. Jones, Oxford, 1968, p. 1986) Likewise, Parkhurst's *Greek and English Lexicon to the New Testament* (London, 1845, p. 673) says: "With an accusative following, *to appoint* or *constitute to an office,* though without suffrages or votes." The office to which these Christian men were appointed was that of "older man," or elder, without any supporting votes by others stretching forth their hands.

When writing to Timothy, Paul said: "Let the older men who preside in a fine way be reckoned worthy of double honor, especially those who work hard in speaking and teaching." (1Ti 5:17) In view of the following verse (18) and also the preceding discussion of honoring widows in a material way (vss 3-16), this "double honor" evidently included material aid.

Who are the "twenty-four elders" on heavenly thrones?

In the book of Revelation, the term *pre·sby'te·roi* occurs 12 times and is applied to spirit creatures. Their surroundings, dress, and actions give a clue as to their identity.

The apostle John had a vision of Jehovah's throne in heaven, surrounded by 24 lesser thrones upon which were seated 24 elders dressed in white outer garments and having golden crowns upon their heads. (Re 4:1-4) As the vision continued, John saw the 24 elders not only repeatedly falling down in worship before Jehovah's throne but also taking part in the various features of the vision as it progressed. (Re 4:9-11; 5:4-14; 7:9-17; 14:3; 19:4) Especially were they observed joining in the Kingdom proclamation to the effect that Jehovah had taken up his great power and had begun to rule as king.—Re 11:15-18.

In ancient Israel, "older men [elders] of Israel" represented and spoke for the entire nation. (Ex 3:16; 19:7) In the same way "elders" may stand for, or represent, the entire congregation of spiritual Israel. Therefore, the 24 elders seated on thrones about God might well represent the entire body of anointed Christians who, proving faithful till death, receive the promised reward of a heavenly resurrection and thrones near that of Jehovah. (Re 3:21) The number 24 is also significant, for this was the number of the divisions into which King David organized the priests to serve at Jerusalem's temple. The anointed Christians are to be "a royal priesthood."—1Pe 2:9; 1Ch 24:1-19; Lu 1:5-23, 57-66; Re 20:6; see OVERSEER.

OLIVE [Heb., *za'yith;* Gr., *e·lai'a*]. The olive tree was unquestionably one of the most valuable plants in Bible times, of equal importance with the vine and the fig tree. (Jg 9:8-13; 2Ki 5:26; Hab 3:17; Jas 3:12) It appears early in the Bible record; following the Flood it was an olive leaf brought back by a dove that indicated to Noah the recession of the waters.—Ge 8:11.

The olive tree (*Olea europaea*) thrives on mountain slopes of Galilee and Samaria and up in the central highlands, as well as throughout the entire Mediterranean area. (De 28:40; Jg 15:5) It flourishes in rocky, chalky soil, too dry for many other plants, and it can endure frequent droughts. At the time of the Exodus from Egypt, the Israelites were promised that the land into which they would come was one of "oil olives and honey," with "vineyards and olive trees that [they] did not plant." (De 6:11; 8:8; Jos 24:13) Since the olive is a slow-growing tree and may take ten years or more to begin bearing good harvests, the fact that these trees were already growing was a decided advantage for the Israelites. The tree is exceptionally long-lived, producing fruit for hundreds of years, and it is suggested that some of the olive trees in Palestine date back more than 1,000 years.

The olive trees present a refreshing view throughout Palestine, often growing on rocky hillside terraces or carpeting the valley floors. The tree may exceed 6 m (20 ft) in height. The gnarled trunk with its ash-colored bark has a profuse branch system bearing a thick foliage of slender grayish-green leaves. Though not generally thought of by many as being such, the tree is an evergreen. It generally flowers about May and is covered with thousands of pale-yellow blossoms. The ease with which these flowers are blown off is mentioned in the Bible. (Job 15:33) The fruit, or olive berry, is green when immature but ripens into a deep purplish to black color. Harvesting is done in the autumn (October-November), and the ancient method of beating the tree with rods is still frequently employed. (De 24:20; Isa 24:13) In Bible times gleaners gathered the remaining fruit. (Isa 17:6) By nature the tree is an alternately bearing one, that is, its good harvest is followed by a slack one the following year. The fresh fruit contains a bitter substance that is removed by soaking the olives in brine, and the olives are then eaten raw or pickled. Their chief value, however, is in their oil, which composes as much as 30 percent or more (by weight) of the fresh fruit. One good tree, yielding from 38 to 57 L (10 to 15 gal) in a year, thus could provide the proportion of fats needed in the diet of a family of five or six persons. The wood of the tree is very hard and must be seasoned for years to be of value for woodworking.

The olive tree not only lives for centuries but, if cut down, will send up as many as six new shoots from its roots to develop into new trunks, and aged trees also will often perpetuate themselves in this way. New trees are frequently planted by using slips cut from a grown tree. Thus the psalmist's illustration is very apt when likening the blessed man's sons to "slips of olive trees all around your table."—Ps 128:3.

Grafting. Wild olive trees growing on hillsides were often subjected to grafting with cuttings from the cultivated productive trees so that they would produce good fruit. It was quite contrary to the regular procedure, therefore, for wild stock to be grafted into a cultivated tree, inasmuch as the wild stock would continue to bear its own fruit. This heightens the force of Paul's illustration at Romans 11:17-24, in which he likened the Gentile Christians who became part of the 'seed of Abraham' to branches of a wild olive tree grafted into a cultivated tree to replace the unproductive branches that were broken off and that represented the rejected natural Jewish members removed from the symbolic tree for their lack of faith. (Ga 3:28, 29) This act, "contrary to nature," emphasizes God's undeserved kindness toward such Gentile believers, stresses the benefits resulting to them as branches of "a wild olive" in receiving of the "fatness" of the garden olive's roots, and thus removes any basis for boasting on the part of these Gentile Christians.—Compare Mt 3:10; Joh 15:1-10; see GRAFTING.

Groves and Presses. Conditions permitting, nearly every village in Palestine had its olive grove. Its failure, as when damaged by its principal enemy, the caterpillar, constituted a grave disaster for the people. (Am 4:9) King David had valued olive groves in the Shephelah region. (1Ch 27:28) The mountain ridge to the E of Jerusalem about "a sabbath day's journey" distant was noted for its olives in King David's day and, by Zechariah's time, was already called "the mountain of the olive trees." (2Sa 15:30; Zec 14:4; Lu 19:29; 22:39; Ac 1:12) The large number of ancient stone olive presses found throughout Palestine testifies to the extensive cultivation of the tree. The "gardens" of that time were frequently in the nature of an orchard and often contained an olive press. Thus the garden named Gethsemane, to which Jesus retired after his last supper with his disciples, draws its name from an Aramaic term *gath shema·neh'* meaning "an oil press." Olives were also trodden by foot at times.—Mic 6:15.

Figurative Use. The olive tree is used figuratively in the Bible as a symbol of fruitfulness, beauty, and dignity. (Ps 52:8; Jer 11:16; Ho 14:6) Its branches were among those used in the Festival of Booths. (Ne 8:15; Le 23:40) At Zechariah 4:3, 11-14 and Revelation 11:3, 4, olive trees are used as symbols of God's anointed ones and witnesses.

OLIVES, MOUNT OF. A chain of rounded limestone hills located on the eastern side of Jerusalem, "a sabbath day's journey" away, and separated from the city by the Kidron Valley. (Eze

Olive trees thrive in rocky soil, too dry for many other plants

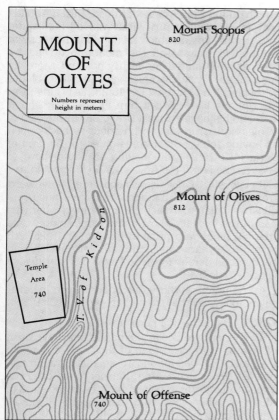

MOUNT OF OLIVES

Numbers represent height in meters

Mount Scopus
820

Mount of Olives
812

T. V. of Kidron

Temple Area
740

Mount of Offense
740

11:23; Zec 14:4; Ac 1:12) This chain includes three major summits. Mount Scopus, the highest and most northerly, rises to about 820 m (2,700 ft) and, hence, higher than the general elevation of Jerusalem. The so-called Mount of Offense, or Mount of Ruination, is the most southerly of the summits and rises to about 740 m (2,430 ft). The central summit, across from the Temple Mount, is about 812 m (2,664 ft) at its highest point and is the one generally referred to in the Bible as the Mount of Olives. Anciently, this ridge was covered with palm, myrtle, oil, and, particularly, olive trees. (Ne 8:15) From the olive trees this range got its name. During the Roman siege of Jerusalem in 70 C.E., however, the Mount of Olives was denuded of its trees.—*The Jewish War*, V, 523 (xii, 4).

Notable events of Bible history are associated with the Mount of Olives. King David, barefoot and weeping, ascended the Mount of Olives as he fled from his rebellious son Absalom. (2Sa 15:14, 30, 32) King Solomon built high places for idolatrous worship there "to the right [south] of the

Mount of Ruination," but King Josiah later made these unfit for worship. (1Ki 11:7; 2Ki 23:13, ftn) In the first century C.E., Jesus Christ often met with his disciples in the garden of Gethsemane, located on or in the vicinity of the Mount of Olives. (Mt 26:30, 36; Joh 18:1, 2) When at Jerusalem, Jesus and his disciples customarily spent the night at Bethany on the E slope of the Mount of Olives, undoubtedly in the home of Martha, Mary, and Lazarus. (Mt 21:17; Mr 11:11; Lu 21:37; Joh 11:1) Apparently from Bethphage, near Bethany, Jesus, seated on the colt of an ass, commenced his triumphal ride over the Mount of Olives to Jerusalem. (Mt 21:1, 2; Mr 11:1; Lu 19:29) And it was on the Mount of Olives that he explained to his disciples what 'the sign of his presence' would be. (Mt 24:3; Mr 13:3) Finally, after his resurrection, Jesus ascended from there into the heavens.—Ac 1:9-12.

OLYMPAS (O·lym'pas). A Christian at Rome to whom the apostle Paul sent greetings.—Ro 16:15.

OMAR (O'mar) [from a root meaning "say"]. Second-listed son of Esau's firstborn Eliphaz; a sheik of Edom.—Ge 36:10, 11, 15; 1Ch 1:36.

OMEGA.   See ALPHA AND OMEGA.

OMEN.   Anything viewed as giving some indication about the future; a situation or occurrence thought of as portending good or evil. (Ge 30:27; Nu 24:1) Looking for omens, as a form of divination, was specifically prohibited by God's law to Israel. (Le 19:26; De 18:10) But apostates like Judean King Manasseh did look for omens. (2Ki 17:17; 21:6) Since this practice is condemned in the Scriptures, evidently faithful Joseph's comment about use of his silver cup to read omens was merely part of a ruse. (Ge 44:5, 15) By making the comment, Joseph represented himself, not as one having faith in Jehovah, but as an administrator of a land where false worship prevailed. He thus gave no hint of having anything in common with his brothers and kept his true identity concealed from them.—See DIVINATION.

OMER (o'mer). A dry measure amounting to one tenth of an ephah. (Ex 16:16, 18, 22, 32, 33, 36) The ephah measure is calculated at 22 L (20 dry qt) on the basis of archaeological evidence concerning the capacity of the corresponding liquid-measure bath. (Compare Eze 45:10, 11.) An omer measure would therefore equal 2.2 L (2 dry qt).

A comparison of the Hebrew text of Exodus 29:40 and Numbers 28:5 reveals that a 'tenth part' means a tenth of an ephah, or an omer. This provides a basis for rendering the Hebrew 'tenth part' as "tenth of an ephah."—Nu 15:4, *AT, NW, Ro, JP.*

OMRI (Om'ri).

1. Fifth listed among the nine sons or descendants of Becher, a son of Benjamin.—1Ch 7:6, 8.

2. Prince of the tribe of Issachar during David's reign; son of Michael.—1Ch 27:18, 22.

3. Sixth king of the northern ten-tribe kingdom of Israel. Nothing of Omri's ancestry is recorded, not even the name of his father or tribe. Omri founded the third dynasty of Israel (those of Jeroboam and Baasha preceded), his son Ahab and grandsons Ahaziah and Jehoram succeeding him, all four totaling some 46 years (c. 951-905 B.C.E.) on the throne. Omri's granddaughter Athaliah ruled six years on the throne of Judah. (2Ki 8:26; 11:1-3; 2Ch 22:2) Jehu, who wiped out the house of Ahab and established the next dynasty of Israel, is called a "son [that is, successor] of Omri" on the Black Obelisk of Shalmaneser III. (*Ancient Near Eastern Texts,* edited by J. Pritchard, 1974, p. 281) In fact, the Assyrians continued calling Israel "the land of Omri" and Israel's kings "the house of Omri" long after his descendants had ceased ruling—a tribute to his power.

Omri came to the throne, not by inheritance, but by the sword. He had been chief of Israel's army under King Elah (and perhaps under his predecessor Baasha) when Zimri, chief of half the chariots, overthrew Elah, took the kingship for himself, and wiped out the house and friends of Baasha. As soon as this was reported to the Israelite army, at the time camped against the Philistines at Gibbethon, "all Israel," doubtless the tribal heads "in the camp," made Omri their king. At once they withdrew from Gibbethon and stormed Zimri's capital Tirzah. Zimri, seeing the hopelessness of his cause, burned down the king's house over himself, tragically ending his seven-day rule. —1Ki 16:8-20.

But a new rival to Omri presented himself —Tibni the son of Ginath. The populace remained divided for about four years, during which time civil war presumably raged until Omri's supporters defeated Tibni's, securing undisputed rule for Omri. Zimri had died in the 27th year of King Asa of Judah (c. 951 B.C.E.). (1Ki 16:15-18) Finally, in the 31st year of Asa (c. 947 B.C.E.), Tibni died in some unstated way, leaving Omri about eight years of sole rule.—1Ki 16:21-23, 29; see CHRONOLOGY.

"Mightiness" is attributed to King Omri. (1Ki 16:27) According to lines 4 through 8 of the Moabite Stone, Omri brought Moab into subjection, which domination Ahab continued. (2Ki 3:4) Midway in his reign, Omri wisely moved his capital away from Tirzah, which he had found so easy to capture. He purchased the mountain owned by Shemer, well suited for fortifying, and there he built a new city, Samaria, which was able to withstand long sieges. (1Ki 16:23, 24) Cuneiform inscriptions likewise call him its founder, and it was also his burial place. (1Ki 16:28) In the course of his reign, Omri met with various setbacks, such as having to surrender some cities to the king of Syria (1Ki 20:34) and having to pay tribute to Assyria, he being the first Israelite king to do so.

Religiously, Omri continued the downward trend of the northern kingdom; he continued Jeroboam's idolatry; in fact, he "kept doing what was bad in the eyes of Jehovah and came to do worse than all who were prior to him." (1Ki 16:25, 26) Some 200 years later, through Micah, Jehovah condemned Israel for following "the statutes of Omri."—Mic 6:16.

4. A Judahite whose descendant lived in Jerusalem following the Babylonian exile.—1Ch 9:3, 4.

ON. The name of a person and a place.

1. [Generative Power; Dynamic Energy]. A son of Peleth; a principal man of the tribe of Reuben. (Nu 16:1) He was among those raising a protest against Moses and Aaron, but his name does not appear among the rebels in their later speeches to Moses or when they were punished by Jehovah with destruction. (Nu 16:2, 3, 12-14, 23-35) This may be due to his playing a very subordinate part in the rebellion, or it may even indicate that he withdrew from it following Moses' initial rebuking of the conspirators.

2. An ancient and renowned city in Egypt, located a short distance NE of Cairo, on the E bank of the Nile and near the point where the river's waters divide to begin the formation of the Delta region. In Egyptian records the city's name was written as *Junu,* while Assyro-Babylonian records mention it as *Ana* or *Unu.* The Egyptian name is thought to mean "City of the Pillar," perhaps referring to the obelisks (tall, tapering columns topped by a pyramid-shaped point) for which the city was famous; or the name may relate to the sacred stone (called the *benben*) connected with the worship of the sun-god Ra (Re). The Greeks called the city Heliopolis, meaning "City of the Sun," because it was the chief center of Egyptian sun worship.

On first appears in the Bible record as the city of the priest Potiphera, whose daughter Asenath was given to Joseph as his wife. (Ge 41:45, 50) The name Potiph*era* itself includes the name of Ra the sun-god.

In course of time the priesthood of On became very wealthy, rivaling the priesthood of Memphis in this respect and being surpassed only by the priesthood of Thebes (Biblical No-amon). Connected with its temple to the sun, a school was operated for training priests and for the teaching of medicine. Greek philosophers and scholars were drawn there to learn the priestly theology, and On became celebrated as a center of Egyptian wisdom.

The prophet Jeremiah was inspired to foretell that King Nebuchadnezzar would overrun Egypt and "break to pieces the pillars of Beth-shemesh, which is in the land of Egypt." (Jer 43:10-13) Beth-shemesh corresponds somewhat to the Greek name Heliopolis and means "House of the Sun." Hence the reference here is likely to the city of On, and "the pillars" that were to be broken may well refer to the many obelisks around the temple of the sun.

Ezekiel's prophecy contains a similar warning. (Eze 30:10, 17) Here the Hebrew vowel pointing of the name varies from that of Genesis so that the name literally is Aven (Heb., 'a'wen). Some scholars suggest that this was done as a play on words, since Aven means "Hurtfulness; Something Hurtful," and On was a center of idolatry.

This may also be the case at Isaiah 19:18, where the Masoretic text refers to one of the "five cities in the land of Egypt speaking the language of Canaan and swearing to Jehovah" as "The City of Tearing Down [Heb., 'Ir ha-He'res]." The Dead Sea Scroll of Isaiah has 'Ir ha-Che'res, meaning "City of the Sun," thus pointing to On (Heliopolis). Here again there may be an intentional play on words, He'res (tearing down) being substituted for Che'res (another Hebrew word for "sun," less common than she'mesh) in view of Jehovah's intention to destroy the idolatrous city of On. The paraphrase of this portion of the verse found in the Aramaic Targums reads: "(City of) the House of the Sun, which is to be destroyed."

Besides the foretold destructive invasion by Nebuchadnezzar, On (Heliopolis) evidently suffered a further blow when Cambyses II conquered Egypt (according to Strabo, Greek geographer who lived near the start of the Common Era). (*Geography*, 17, I, 27) By Strabo's time Heliopolis had lost its position of importance and was partially deserted. Today, the village called Al-Matariya occupies part of the ancient site, and all that remains there of the earlier splendor is a single obelisk of red granite dating from the reign of Sesostris I. Other obelisks from Heliopolis are now to be found in New York, London, and Rome.

ONAM (O'nam) [from a root meaning "generative power; dynamic energy"].

1. Last of the five listed sons of Horite sheik Shobal, and grandson of the Horites' forefather Seir.—Ge 36:20, 21, 23; 1Ch 1:40.

2. A son of Jerahmeel and a link in the Jerahmeelite genealogy in the tribe of Judah; his mother's name was Atarah.—1Ch 2:26, 28.

ONAN (O'nan) [from a root meaning "generative power; dynamic energy"]. A son of Judah, his second by the Canaanite daughter of Shua. (Ge 38:2-4; 1Ch 2:3) After Onan's childless older brother Er was put to death by Jehovah for wrongdoing, Onan was told by Judah to perform brother-in-law marriage with Er's widow Tamar. If a son was produced, he would not be the founder of Onan's family, and the firstborn's inheritance would belong to him as an heir to Er; whereas if no heir came, Onan would get the inheritance for himself. When Onan had relations with Tamar, he "wasted his semen on the earth" instead of giving it to her. This was not an act of masturbation on the part of Onan, for the account says "when he did have relations with his brother's wife" he spilled his semen. Apparently it was a case of "coitus interruptus," in which Onan purposely prevented ejaculation of his semen into Tamar's genital tract. For his disobedience to his father, his covetousness, and his sin against the divine arrangement of marriage, not for self-abuse, Onan, himself also childless, was put to death by Jehovah.—Ge 38:6-10; 46:12; Nu 26:19.

ONESIMUS (O·nes'i·mus) [Profitable]. A runaway slave whom Paul helped to become a Christian. Onesimus had been a servant of Philemon, a Colossian Christian, but had run away from Colossae to Rome. He may even have first robbed his master in order to make the journey. (Col 4:9; Phm 18) It is quite possible that he had met or at least heard of Paul through Philemon; for, though no visit of Paul to Colossae on the missionary tours is specifically mentioned, Paul did travel through the general area and was acquainted with Philemon. (Ac 18:22, 23; Phm 5, 19, 22) At any rate, in some unstated way, Onesimus became associated with Paul in Rome, and he soon became a Christian. (Phm 10) In great contrast with his former uselessness to Philemon as a slave, he now became most useful to Paul as a minister, a "faithful and beloved brother" whom Paul calls "my own tender affections."—Col 4:9; Phm 11, 12.

Nonetheless, Onesimus was still a runaway slave, and the social order of the day obliged Paul to send him back to his owner, though with reluctance in view of how good a companion he had become. The apostle, however, had no way of forcing Onesimus to make the return, so it depended on and resulted from Onesimus' own willingness to go. In dispatching Onesimus, Paul arranged for Tychicus to accompany him and for the two to carry a letter and a report to Colossae. (Col 4:7-9) Additionally, Paul gave Onesimus his letter to Philemon, even though it was late enough in his imprisonment that Paul was expecting release and looking forward to visiting Philemon personally. (Phm 22) This latter letter might be termed one of reintroduction and recommendation for Onesimus, in which Paul assured Philemon of the good Christian ministry and new personality of Onesimus, and in which he pleaded that the reunion be more like that of two Christians than that of a slave and his master. Paul asked that any outstanding debt that Onesimus owed Philemon be charged to the apostle's account. (Phm 12-22) Incidentally, in the letter to the Colossians that Onesimus and Tychicus were carrying, Paul dealt with the Christian principles governing the relationship of slave and master.—Col 3:22–4:1.

ONESIPHORUS (On·e·siph'o·rus) [Profit Bearer].

A Christian referred to in Paul's second letter to Timothy. (2Ti 4:19) In contrast with others in the district of Asia who turned away from Paul, Onesiphorus remained a loyal supporter and, when in Rome, diligently hunted to find Paul in spite of the risk to himself. He was not ashamed of Paul's prison bonds but rendered the apostle good service, as he had done in Ephesus. Paul greatly appreciated this loyalty and prayed that Onesiphorus and his household would receive of Jehovah's mercy.—2Ti 1:15-18.

The fact that Paul sent greetings to the household of Onesiphorus rather than to Onesiphorus himself (2Ti 4:19) does not necessarily indicate that he was no longer alive, though such might be true. He may simply have been away from his family at the time or may even be included in the general greeting sent to his household of believers.

ONION [Heb., ba·tsal'].

A strong-tasting bulbous biennial having slender tubelike leaves. The onion (*Allium cepa*) was one of the items of diet for which the mixed crowd and the Israelites yearned in the wilderness after being liberated from Egypt. (Nu 11:4, 5) In that land of Israel's captivity, onions were extensively cultivated. The Greek historian Herodotus (II, 125) even tells of an inscription that listed onions among the foods provided for the laborers on a certain Egyptian pyramid. In Egypt, onions, usually tied together in a bundle, were offered to the deities, although the priests were not permitted to eat them. The onions of Egypt have been described as soft, and therefore more easily digestible than other varieties, as well as sweet tasting rather than sharp, or acrid.

ONLY-BEGOTTEN.

The Greek word *mo·no·ge·nes'* is defined by lexicographers as "single of its kind, only," or "the only member of a kin or kind." (Thayer's *Greek-English Lexicon of the New Testament,* 1889, p. 417; Liddell and Scott's *Greek-English Lexicon,* Oxford, 1968, p. 1144) The term is used in describing the relation of both sons and daughters to their parents.

The Scriptures speak of "the only-begotten son" of a widow who lived in the city of Nain, of Jairus' "only-begotten daughter," and of a man's "only-begotten" son whom Jesus cured of a demon. (Lu 7:11, 12; 8:41, 42; 9:38) The Greek *Septuagint* uses *mo·no·ge·nes'* when speaking of Jephthah's daughter, concerning whom it is written: "Now she was absolutely the only child. Besides her he had neither son nor daughter."—Jg 11:34.

The apostle John repeatedly describes the Lord Jesus Christ as the only-begotten Son of God. (Joh 1:14; 3:16, 18; 1Jo 4:9) This is not in reference to his human birth or to him as just the *man* Jesus. As the *Lo'gos,* or Word, "this one was in the beginning with God," even "before the world was." (Joh 1:1, 2; 17:5, 24) At that time while in his prehuman state of existence, he is described as the "only-begotten Son" whom his Father sent "into the world."—1Jo 4:9.

He is described as having "a glory such as belongs to an only-begotten son from a father," the one residing "in the bosom position with the Father." (Joh 1:14, 18) It is hard to think of a closer, more confidential, or more loving and tender relationship between a father and his son than this. —See BOSOM POSITION.

The angels of heaven are sons of God even as Adam was a "son of God." (Ge 6:2; Job 1:6; 38:7; Lu 3:38) But the *Lo'gos,* later called Jesus, is "the *only-begotten* Son of God." (Joh 3:18) He is the only one of his kind, the only one whom God himself created directly without the agency or cooperation of any creature. He is the only one whom God his Father used in bringing into existence all other creatures. He is the firstborn and chief one among all other angels (Col 1:15, 16; Heb 1:5, 6), which angels the Scriptures call "godlike ones" or "gods." (Ps 8:4, 5) Therefore, according to some of the oldest and best manuscripts, the Lord Jesus Christ is properly described as "the only-begotten god [Gr., *mo·no·ge·nes' the·os'*]."—Joh 1:18, *NW, Ro, Sp.*

A few translations, in support of the Trinitarian "God the Son" concept, would invert the phrase *mo·no·ge·nes' the·os'* and render it as "God only begotten." But W. J. Hickie in his *Greek-English Lexicon to the New Testament* (1956, p. 123) says it is hard to see why these translators render *mo·no·ge·nes' hui·os'* as "the only begotten Son," but at the same time translate *mo·no·ge·nes' the·os'* as "God only begotten," instead of "the only begotten God."

Paul referred to Isaac as Abraham's "only-begotten son" (Heb 11:17), even though Abraham also fathered Ishmael by Hagar as well as several sons by Keturah. (Ge 16:15; 25:1, 2; 1Ch 1:28, 32) God's covenant, however, was established only through Isaac, Abraham's only son by God's promise, as well as the only son of Sarah. (Ge 17:16-19) Furthermore, at the time Abraham offered up Isaac, he was the only son in his father's household. No sons had yet been born to Keturah, and Ishmael had been gone for some 20 years—no doubt was married and head of his own household.—Ge 22:2.

So from several viewpoints in regard to the promise and the covenant, the things about which Paul was writing to the Hebrews, Isaac was Abraham's only-begotten son. Hence, Paul parallels "the promises" and the "only-begotten son" with "'your seed' . . . through Isaac." (Heb 11:17, 18) Whether Josephus had a similar viewpoint or not, he too spoke of Isaac as Abraham's "only son." —*Jewish Antiquities*, I, 222 (xiii, 1).

ONO

(O'no). A city built either by Benjamite Elpaal or by his "son(s)." (1Ch 8:1, 12) After the Babylonian exile Ono was reoccupied by Benjamites. (Ezr 2:1, 33; Ne 7:6, 37; 11:31, 35) Kafr 'Ana (Ono), about 11 km (7 mi) ESE of Joppa, is identified with the ancient site. This location is just a few kilometers from the suggested sites of ancient Lod and Hadid. "The valley plain of Ono" (Ne 6:2) possibly denotes the wide valley in which Kafr 'Ana lies. This "valley plain" has also been associated with "the valley of the craftsmen [*geh ha·chara·shim'*]." (Ne 11:35) But some scholars understand the Hebrew *geh ha·chara·shim'* to designate another location and transliterate it as a proper name, "Ge-harashim."—*JP;* compare 1Ch 4:14.

ONYCHA

(on'y·cha). An ingredient of the incense designated exclusively for sanctuary use. (Ex 30:34-37) Some believe that onycha may have been derived from the closing valves of certain shellfish. However, since this ingredient was used

for a sacred purpose, others consider it to have been a vegetable product instead of something obtained from an unclean animal.

ONYX.

A semiprecious gemstone, a hard variety of agate; the term also applies to a banded form of chalcedony. The onyx has white layers alternating with black, brown, red, gray, or green. The pale color produced by the combination of the red layers showing through the translucent white layers of this stone evidently reminded the Greeks of the fingernail, which in Greek is *o'nyx.* From early times, onyx has been prized for ornaments, rings, and beads. The varicolored layers made it especially popular for cameo work.

The "land of Havilah" was a prominent source of onyx in early Bible times. (Ge 2:11, 12) Onyx stones were among the valuables contributed for the making of things associated with Israel's tabernacle. (Ex 25:1-3, 7) "The names of the sons of Israel . . . in the order of their births" were engraved upon two onyx stones (six names on each stone) placed upon the shoulder pieces of the high priest's ephod "as memorial stones for the sons of Israel." Another onyx stone was engraved with the name of one of the 12 tribes of Israel and was set in the center position of the fourth row of stones on the high priest's "breastpiece of judgment."—Ex 28:9-12, 15-21; 35:5, 9, 27; 39:6-14.

Later, David personally prepared many valuable things, including onyx stones, for the construction of the prospective temple at Jerusalem. (1Ch 29:2) Onyx was also among the precious stones serving as a figurative "covering" for "the king of Tyre" in the dirge recorded by Ezekiel. (Eze 28:12, 13) Recognizing wisdom's value, Job stated that with "the rare onyx stone" and other precious things one could not buy priceless, godly wisdom.—Job 28:12, 16.

OPHEL

(O'phel) [Mound [that is, bulge, swelling, projection, eminence]]. The Hebrew term *'O'phel* is applied in two ways. Most commonly, it is applied in a topographical sense to a prominent hill or promontory. A form of the term is also applied to the swelling or bulging of body veins known as piles, or hemorrhoids.—De 28:27; 1Sa 5:6, 9, 12; 6:4, 5.

There was a particular hill or eminence located at or near Jerusalem that was called *ha·'O'phel,* or Ophel. The Scriptural indications taken with the comments of Josephus locate Ophel at the SE corner of Moriah. (2Ch 27:3; 33:14; Ne 3:26, 27; 11:21) In the first century C.E., Josephus placed Ophel where the eastern wall "joined the eastern portico of the temple." (*The Jewish War*, V, 145 [iv, 2]) Ophel evidently was the bulge of land extending eastwardly from the SE corner of Jerusalem's temple hill.

Ophel's wall and elevated position over the Kidron Valley gave it a strong defensive position. Nevertheless, Isaiah prophesied that "Ophel," apparently that of Jerusalem, would become a 'bare field.'—Isa 32:14; compare the reference to the tower and "mound" ('O'phel) at Mic 4:8.

Scholars believe that the term 'O'phel at 2 Kings 5:24 refers to some prominent hill or fortified place in the vicinity of Samaria to which Elisha's attendant Gehazi took the riches he obtained from Naaman. This indicates that the word was applied to mounds other than the one in Jerusalem.

OPHIR (O'phir).

1. A descendant of Shem through Arpachshad, Shelah, Eber, and Joktan; the 11th of Joktan's 13 sons. (Ge 10:22-29; 1Ch 1:17-23) Ophir was probably born about 200 years before Abraham, who was a descendant of his paternal uncle Peleg. (Ge 10:25; 11:18-26) As in the case of his brothers, it appears that Ophir also headed one of the Semite tribes that were numbered among the descendants of Noah "according to their families, according to their tongues, in their lands, according to their nations." (Ge 10:31, 32) See No. 2 for possible locations of the land of Ophir in which this tribe eventually settled.

2. A place renowned as a source of much gold of the finest quality. Thus already in Job's time (c. 1600 B.C.E.) "precious ore in the dust" and "pure gold" were spoken of in parallel with the "gold of Ophir." (Job 22:24; 28:15, 16) Psalm 45:9 describes the queenly consort arrayed in precious gold of Ophir, and at Isaiah 13:11, 12, in the pronouncement against Babylon, the relative rarity of Ophir gold is used to symbolize the scarcity of tyrannical men in Babylon after its fall.

David donated 3,000 talents of gold from Ophir for construction of the temple, gold valued at $1,156,050,000. (1Ch 29:1, 2, 4) Later, the trading fleet of David's son Solomon regularly brought back from Ophir 420 talents of gold. (1Ki 9:26-28) The parallel account at 2 Chronicles 8:18 reads 450 talents. Some scholars have suggested that this difference came about when letters of the alphabet served as figures—that an ancient copyist could have mistaken the Hebrew numeral letter *nun* (נ), representing 50, for the letter *kaph* (כ), standing for 20, or vice versa. However, the evidence is that all numbers in the Hebrew Scriptures were spelled out, rather than represented by letters. A more probable explanation, therefore, is that both figures are correct and that the gross amount brought was 450 talents, of which 420 were clear gain.

In 1946, as confirmation of these Biblical accounts about imports of gold from Ophir, a potsherd was unearthed NE of Tel Aviv-Yafo. Thereon was an inscription saying "Ophir gold to *bet horon,* thirty shekels."—*Journal of Near Eastern Studies,* 1951, Vol. X, pp. 265, 266.

In addition to being a source of a vast quantity of gold, the land of Ophir was also a source of the "algum" trees and precious stones imported by Solomon. (1Ki 10:11; 2Ch 9:10) However, when King Jehoshaphat, a hundred years later, attempted an expedition to that land, it ended in disaster, his "Tarshish ships" being wrecked at Ezion-geber at the head of the Gulf of 'Aqaba.—1Ki 22:48; see TARSHISH No. 4.

Location. The precise location of Ophir cannot be determined today with certainty. Of the several suggestions in this regard, three are particularly favored: India, Arabia, and NE Africa —all being within reach of a fleet operating out of Ezion-geber at the head of the eastern arm of the Red Sea. In regard to India, all the goods brought back in the ships of Solomon and Hiram were available there. Josephus, Jerome, and the *Septuagint* could also be marshaled to give some support to Ophir's being in India. On the other hand, those maintaining that Ophir was in the region of NE Africa in the vicinity of Somalia, at the lower extremity of the Red Sea, point out that it would have been a much closer source of supply for all the imported items than India.

However, the weight of opinion appears to support the conclusion that Ophir was a region in SW Arabia in the vicinity of Yemen. Evidence offered for this view is based on the premise that the descendants of Joktan's son Ophir settled in the Arabian Peninsula along with such brother tribes as the descendants of Sheba and Havilah. (Ge 10:28, 29) The account of the visit of the queen of Sheba (likely from southern Arabia) is sandwiched in between two references to Solomon's trade with Ophir.—1Ki 9:26–10:11.

OPHNI (Oph'ni).

A city of Benjamin (Jos 18:21, 24), commonly linked with the Gophna mentioned by Josephus (*The Jewish War,* III, 55 [iii, 5]) and considered to be modern Jifna. This site is about 5 km (3 mi) NNW of Bethel and therefore seemingly N of Benjamite territory. (Jos 18:11-13) For the identification to be correct, it must be assumed either that Ophni was a Benjamite enclave city in Ephraim or that the Benjamite boundary extended northward near Bethel to include this suggested site of Ophni.

OPHRAH (Oph'rah).

1. [Young One [of the Stags]]. A descendant of Judah through Meonothai.—1Ch 4:1, 14.

[2, 3: possibly, Place of Dust]

2. A city of Benjamin. (Jos 18:21, 23) Its relative location may be deduced from the narrative about Israel's encounters with the Philistines during Saul's reign. From their camp at Michmash, bands of Philistine pillagers sallied forth in three different directions. One band turned to the road to Ophrah. Another went westward on the road to Beth-horon, while yet another traveled eastward on "the road to the boundary that looks toward the valley of Zeboim." Since at least part of the Israelite army was encamped at Geba to the S of Michmash, apparently the Philistine band taking the road to Ophrah went northward. Accordingly, this would place Ophrah to the N of Michmash.—1Sa 13:16-18.

Scholars often equate Ophrah with the city called Ephraim (2Sa 13:23; Joh 11:54) and Ephrain (2Ch 13:19), thought to be represented by et-Taiyiba (c. 6 km [3.5 mi] ENE of Bethel).

3. The home of Gideon and the place where Jehovah's angel commissioned him to save Israel out of Midian's palm. (Jg 6:11-32) After his victory over the enemy forces, Gideon made an ephod from the contributed spoils and exhibited it at Ophrah. Subsequently this ephod became an object of idolatrous veneration. (Jg 8:24-27) Later, after Gideon's death and burial at Ophrah, his ambitious son Abimelech "killed his brothers . . . seventy men, upon one stone, but Jotham the youngest . . . was left over." (Jg 8:32; 9:5) Not counting Abimelech, Gideon had 70 sons. (Jg 8:30, 31) Therefore, since Jotham escaped the slaughter, apparently Abimelech killed only 69 sons at Ophrah. Jotham's later words concerning the incident merely appear to point to Abimelech's intention to kill all 70 sons. (Jg 9:18) However, as a Jewish commentary fittingly observes: "It is still correct to speak in round numbers of 'seventy slain.'"—*Soncino Books of the Bible,* edited by A. Cohen, London, 1950 (Joshua and Judges, p. 234).

This Ophrah apparently lay W of the Jordan. It is tentatively identified with el-'Affuleh ('Afula), about 45 km (28 mi) N of Shechem.

OREB (O'reb) [Raven].

1. A prince of Midian. Oreb and Zeeb were in the Midianite army of Kings Zebah and Zalmunna that Gideon and his 300 put to flight. The two princes were captured and put to death by men of Ephraim, and their heads were brought to Gideon. —Jg 7:24, 25; 8:3-5; Ps 83:11.

2. The rock where Midianite prince Oreb was executed and that came to bear his name. Its location is unknown.—Jg 7:25; Isa 10:26.

OREN (O'ren). A son of Jerahmeel in the tribe of Judah.—1Ch 2:25.

ORIENTALS (Ori·en'tals). The populace of those lands viewed by Hebrew writers as "the East." This area was beyond the boundary of Israel not only to the east but also well up to the northeast and to the southeast into Arabia. (Ge 25:6; Jer 49:28) Thus, when Jacob went to Laban's household at Haran, he went "to the land of the Orientals," NE of Canaan.—Ge 29:1.

Job is called "the greatest of all the Orientals [literally, sons of the East]." (Job 1:3, ftn) The forces that oppressed Israel before Gideon rose up and vanquished them were comprised of Amalekites and Midianites in addition to "the Easterners," otherwise unidentified. (Jg 6:3, 33; 7:12; 8:10) The Orientals, noted for their wisdom, were, however, surpassed in this respect by Solomon. (1Ki 4:30) The so-called wise men, or Magi, who visited the young child Jesus were "astrologers from eastern parts."—Mt 2:1, 2, 11.

ORNAMENTS. An adornment, not always essential in itself, but meant to enhance the appearance of something. Ornaments were used especially by women but also by men; they were used to decorate buildings; at times, they were put on animals.

Bible references and the evidence unearthed by archaeologists reveal not only an interest in ornamentation from very ancient times but also great ability and skill in producing ornamentation of high artistic caliber. Artisans did highly decorative work in weaving, in embroidery, in carving wood and ivory, and in metalworking. The remains of palaces in Assyria, Babylon, Persia, and the city of Mari all give evidence of rich decorating, with large murals on interior walls and finely carved bas-reliefs depicting scenes of war, hunting, and palace affairs, to adorn both inner and outer walls. Palace doorways were often guarded by great figures of mighty beasts. The representations of the king and others in the reliefs reveal fine embroidery on their garments. Even the gear of the horses is highly decorated with tassels and engravings. (Compare the necklaces of the Midianites' camels; Jg 8:21, 26.) Tomb paintings provide the principal source of evidence from Egypt, although some artifacts in the form of throne chairs, royal chariots, and other items have survived.

Hebrew and Christian. Early mention is made of jewelry in the form of a gold nose ring and also bracelets given to Rebekah by Abraham's servant. (Ge 24:22, 30, 47, 53) Joseph, upon becoming Pharaoh's prime minister, received a gold necklace and the monarch's own signet ring. (Ge 41:41-43) Such signet rings, or seal rings, were common in all the Bible lands, frequently being worn on a cord around the neck. (Compare Ge 38:18.) They served to affix the signature, or official seal, of the individual to documents and hence, if granted to another person to carry, identified him as a bona fide and authorized representative of the ring's owner.

At the Exodus, the Israelites obtained many silver and gold articles from the Egyptians, and doubtless from these came many of the brooches, earrings, rings, and other items they contributed for the preparation of the tabernacle, even as they had wrongly contributed gold earrings for the forming of an idolatrous calf. (Ex 12:35, 36; 32:1-4; 35:20-24) The tabernacle and its equipment saw much work by artisans skilled in woodworking and working with precious metals and gems as well as weaving and embroidery. (Ex 35:25-35) The later temple by Solomon was even more gloriously adorned. Its cedarwood panels, as well as its doors of oil-tree and juniper wood, were carved with such figures as gourd-shaped ornaments, garlands of blossoms, cherubs, and palm-tree figures and were overlaid with gold; while the two copper pillars in front of the structure had network, chainwork, pomegranates, and lily work adorning their capitals. (1Ki 6:18, 29, 35; 7:15-22) Solomon showed great appreciation for artistic beauty, and his great ivory throne overlaid with gold, with lion figures alongside each arm and 12 more on the six steps before it, was unique in the ancient world.—1Ki 10:16-21.

The Bible lays greater emphasis, however, on spiritual beauty. Parental discipline is "a wreath of attractiveness" to one's head "and a fine necklace" for the throat, "a crown of beauty"; "lips of knowledge are precious vessels" superior to any gold vases of an artisan; "as apples of gold in silver carvings is a word spoken at the right time for it," and "an earring of gold, and an ornament of special gold, is a wise reprover upon the hearing ear." (Pr 1:9; 4:9; 20:15; 25:11, 12) A pretty woman lacking sensibleness is likened to "a gold nose ring in the snout of a pig."—Pr 11:22.

Moderation is encouraged, particularly in the Christian Greek Scriptures. Women were "to adorn themselves in well-arranged dress, with modesty and soundness of mind, not with styles of hair braiding and gold or pearls or very expensive garb, but in the way that befits women professing to reverence God, namely, through good works." (1Ti 2:9, 10) Peter could call upon examples of pre-Christian times in urging that women seek the beauty of "the secret person of the heart in the incorruptible apparel of the quiet and mild spirit, which is of great value in the eyes of God"; he pointed to women such as Sarah who so adorned themselves, "subjecting themselves to their own husbands." (1Pe 3:1-6) Thus, if followed, the Scriptures provide the guide to a proper evaluation of ornamentation and jewelry and good balance in its use.

Ornamentation in Prophecy. Because of his blessing upon Jerusalem, Jehovah likened this capital of Judah to a woman clothed with costly garments, richly ornamented and bejeweled. Her loss of spirituality and her spiritual prostitution with the nations led to her being stripped of her adornments and left as if naked. (Eze 16:2, 10-39) Such stripping came not only in a spiritual way but also literally as her greedy conquerors took the city's wealth, including the bangles, headbands, moon-shaped ornaments, eardrops, bracelets, veils, headdresses, step chains, breastbands, "houses of the soul" (probably referring to perfume receptacles), ornamental humming shells (charms), finger and nose rings that "the daughters of Zion" had worn. (Isa 3:16-26) It would be a time of mourning, for in mourning, ornaments were customarily removed.—Ex 33:4-6.

However, when Jehovah repurchased Zion from Babylonian exile, he would figuratively build her with a sapphire foundation, with battlements of rubies and gates of fiery glowing stones, this because of the peace and righteousness he would bring (Isa 54:7, 8, 11-14), and she would be clothed with bridelike attire and ornaments. (Isa 49:14-18; compare 61:10.) This latter picture resembles somewhat the description of the New Jerusalem with its pearl gates and gemlike foundations, and its being prepared as "a bride adorned for her husband." (Re 21:2, 9-21) Again, it is evident that the ornaments and adornment relate to spiritual qualities and blessings that result from God's approval and favor.

By contrast, Babylon the Great, the symbolic woman committing fornication with the kings of the earth, decks herself with royal garb and ornaments and lives in shameless luxury, but is to be stripped of all her gorgeous finery, made naked, and destroyed. Her beauty is false, and she 'glori-

The osprey, a bird not permitted for use as food under the Mosaic Law

fies herself'; hence her ornamentation does not represent divine blessing and favor but, rather, her own pretenses and the benefits her harlotlike course pays her in the way of power and wealth. —Re 17:3-5, 16; 18:7-20.

See ANKLET; BEADS; BRACELET; BROOCH; EARRING; JEWELS AND PRECIOUS STONES; NECKLACE; NOSE RING; RING.

ORNAN (Or'nan). A Jebusite from whom David bought the threshing floor that later became the site for the temple. (1Ch 21:18-28; 2Ch 3:1) Ornan is also called Araunah.—See ARAUNAH.

ORPAH (Or'pah). The Moabite wife of Chilion, and like Ruth, a daughter-in-law of Naomi. (Compare Ru 1:3-5 with 4:10.) After the husbands of all three died, the childless widows, Naomi, Orpah, and Ruth, began the journey from Moab to Bethlehem. At a certain point Naomi urged her two daughters-in-law to go back to their mothers' homes and marry in Moab, but they both kept saying to Naomi, "No, but with you we shall return to your people." Orpah had dealt kindly with her mother-in-law, for whom she evidently felt considerable affection. (Ru 1:8-10) Her inclination to continue on with Naomi may have been in part the result of having enjoyed life in an Israelite family. But Naomi now stressed the strong probability that for these two Moabite widows to continue with her might mean a life of widowhood in Judah, inasmuch as Naomi had little hope of remarrying so as to bring forth sons, and even should this happen, she was sure that Orpah and Ruth would not want to wait until such sons matured so that they might perform levirate marriage toward these Moabite widows. Orpah's affection and appreciation were not enough to keep her going along in the face of such a possible

future, and after much weeping, she bade farewell to Naomi and Ruth and returned "to her people and her gods."—Ru 1:3-15.

ORPHAN. See FATHERLESS BOY.

OSPREY [Heb., *pe'res*]. One of "the flying creatures" decreed as unclean and not to be eaten, according to the Law covenant. (Le 11:13; De 14:12) Its Hebrew name (*pe'res*) literally means "the breaker." Understanding this to refer to the breaking of bones by a bird of prey, the *King James Version* renders *pe'res* as "ossifrage," a name derived from Latin and meaning "bone-breaker." Others understand the Hebrew name to indicate a bird "tearing its prey" apart, and hence not necessarily denoting a breaker of bones.

The osprey (*Pandion haliaetus*) appears to be related to the hawk but with certain distinct features, including feet with some similarity to those of the owl. The osprey's head and beak resemble those of the hawk, the body and wings are dark brown above and the underparts are white with streaks of brown. Measuring about 65 cm (26 in.) in length, it has a wingspan of nearly 1.8 m (6 ft). The osprey is found throughout the world, living near large bodies of water, where it feeds on fish that swim near the surface. The bird glides almost effortlessly above the water, wheeling gracefully and hovering until it locates its prey. Then it plunges swiftly downward, striking the water forcefully feet first, at times disappearing beneath the surface. It is admirably equipped for this type of attack, having dense compact plumage on its underparts to withstand some of the impact of hitting the water, and long, curved, very sharp claws that extend out from rough toes, enabling the bird to get a firm grip on its slippery prey. Observers say that in flying with the fish to shore to devour it, the osprey always grips the fish so that its head faces forward, thereby reducing air resistance. The osprey is fairly common on the coast and islands of southern Sinai.

Other suggestions for the bird designated by the Hebrew *pe'res* include the sea eagle (*Haliaeetus albicilla*, distinct from the osprey) and the lammergeier (*Gypaetus barbatus*), a vulture known to carry bones and tortoises to some height and then drop them on rocks in order to break them open.

OSTRICH [Heb., *bath hai·ya·'anah'*; *rena·nim'* (plural)]. The first of these Hebrew names is understood to mean either "daughter of the greedy one" or "daughter of the barren ground," terms that may aptly apply to the ostrich. The second name, regarded as indicating a "bird of piercing cries," also fits the ostrich, whose cry is described as a "hoarse, mournful cry which has been likened to the roaring of a lion."—*The Smithsonian Series,* 1944, Vol. 9, p. 105; compare Mic 1:8.

The ostrich (*Struthio camelus*) is the largest living bird known, at times standing over 2 m (7 ft) high at the crown of the head and weighing as much as 140 kg (300 lb). The head is rather small and flat with very large eyes, the flexible neck is about 1 m (3 ft) long, and like the powerful legs, both head and neck are bare of feathers. The body plumage, however, is luxuriant, the long soft wing and tail plumes being much prized in ancient and modern times. The sleek black and white plumage of the male contrasts with the dull grayish-brown color of the female. The ostrich is unique among all birds in having but two toes on each foot, one of them equipped with a clawlike hoof that becomes a dangerous weapon when the bird is forced to defend itself. Its height and keen vision, however, usually enable it to spot its enemies from afar, and the huge bird then warily moves away.

While the ostrich feeds mainly on vegetation, it is also carnivorous, including snakes, lizards, and even small birds in its indiscriminate diet. It is found among the list of 'unclean' birds prohibited by the Mosaic Law. (Le 11:13, 16; De 14:12, 15) Anciently known as the camel bird, the ostrich is able to endure for long periods without water and hence thrives in solitary wastelands. It is used in the Bible, along with jackals and similar creatures, as representative of desert life (Isa 43:20) and to depict the ruinous desolation that became the fate of Edom and Babylon. (Isa 13:21; 34:13; Jer 50:39) Job, rejected and detested, sitting among ashes, and mournfully crying out, considered himself like "a brother to jackals" and "a companion to the daughters of the ostrich."—Job 30:29.

Contrasted With Stork. Jehovah God later drew Job's attention to the ostrich, and the things he pointed out strikingly illustrate some of the unusual features of that bird. (Job 39:13-18) In great contrast to the high-flying, majestically soaring storks with their broad powerful wings, the ostrich is flightless; its wings are incapable of sustaining the bird's weight, and its flat breastbone lacks the "keel" that supports the flying muscles of birds of flight. The ostrich's plumes, though lovely, lack even the tiny hooklike filaments that cling together and give the feathers of flying birds the resistance to air that makes flight possible.—Job 39:13.

Again in contrast to the stork, which builds its big nest firmly in the tops of trees (Ps 104:17),

buildings, or tall rocks, the ostrich merely scoops out a shallow depression in the ground surrounded by a low embankment. Here the female lays the eggs, weighing some 1.5 kg (3 lb) each, and since the ostrich is often polygamous (unlike the stork, which is renowned for its fidelity to one mate), there may be a good number of eggs laid in the nest by the two or three hens. The male ostrich warms the nest eggs during the night and the hen incubates them by day, but she is known to leave the nest for periods during the day when the sun is hot. At such times the eggs, though very thick-shelled, are, nevertheless, vulnerable to damage or despoiling by animals or man.—Job 39:14, 15.

'Treats Sons Roughly.' The statement that the ostrich "does treat her sons roughly, as if not hers" (Job 39:16) and reference to ostriches as being "cruel" with respect to their offspring (La 4:3) have been objected to by some who claim that parent ostriches are quite solicitous in caring for their young. While it is true that the Hebrew term (*rena·nim'*) used at Job 39:13 may grammatically apply to either male or female ostriches, some lexicographers understand it to refer to the female birds. This would seem to be the case in view of the connection with the eggs laid, obviously, by the hen bird. When understood as applying to the female, there is certainly good basis for this poetic expression concerning the 'cruelty' of the bird in the fact that, once the young are hatched, the male "assumes all their care while the hens generally go off together." (*All the Birds of the Bible,* by Alice Parmelee, 1959, p. 207) It is also true that these powerful birds, both male and female, quickly abandon the nest and their young when sensing danger, and even though they may use diversionary tactics to draw enemies away from the nest, this is still 'rough' treatment for the unprotected young. Only the protective coloration given by the Creator is what may save the undefended and abandoned chicks, causing the enemy beasts to overlook them and chase after the fleeing parents. The ostrich may properly be termed "cruel," then, as compared with many other birds and particularly in contrast with the stork, whose affectionate attention and constant concern for its young are proverbial.

'Forgets Wisdom.' The ostrich is said to "forget wisdom" and 'not share in understanding.' (Job 39:17) Modern observers have acknowledged this. The Arabs have a saying "more foolish than an ostrich." (*Soncino Books of the Bible,* edited by A. Cohen, London, 1946, Job, p. 205) The ostrich tends to run in a large curve, which permits its pursuers, if sufficient in number, to surround it. But on a straight course the ostrich's powerful legs enable it to 'laugh at the horse and at its rider.' (Job 39:18) When running, its strides lengthen out to cover as much as 3.5 m (11 ft) at a time, and its pace may reach as high as 70 km/hr (44 mph). The wings, useless for flight, nevertheless help to give lift to the bird's heavy body as it runs.

The ostrich has certain characteristics that are said to stagger scientists, who tend to class the ostrich as among the 'lower or more primitive' of living birds. It has a bladder collecting uric acid, an organ characteristic of mammals but not possessed by any other family of birds. It also possesses eyelashes that protect its eyes from the blowing sand. Thus, though low in intelligence, the powerful, speedy ostrich gives credit to the wisdom of its Creator.

The Arabian ostrich (*Struthio camelus syriacus*), once abundant in Palestine and Arabia, is now extinct. Since 1973, a related African variety has been reintroduced into Israel.

OTHNI (Oth'ni) [shortened form of Othniel]. Son of Shemaiah and grandson of Korahite Obed-edom, appointed as a Levite gatekeeper before the sanctuary. Othni and his brothers were "rulers of the house of their father, . . . capable, mighty men."—1Ch 26:1, 4, 6-8, 15.

OTHNIEL (Oth'ni·el). The first-named judge of Israel after Joshua. Othniel was "the son of Kenaz, Caleb's younger brother." (Jg 1:13; 3:9; Jos 15:17) While this grammatical structure allows for either Othniel or Kenaz to be Caleb's younger brother, to harmonize with other texts Othniel must be viewed as Caleb's nephew, the son of Caleb's brother Kenaz. Thus certain translations read: "Othniel, the son of Caleb's younger brother, Kenaz." (*AT, Mo*) Additionally, Caleb was "the son of Jephunneh," hence not a son of Kenaz as was Othniel.—Nu 32:12; 1Ch 4:15.

Othniel's marriage to Achsah the daughter of Caleb came as a result of his victory over the Canaanite stronghold of Debir. Achsah's father Caleb had promised her to the conqueror of the city. (Jos 15:16-19; Jg 1:11-15) Othniel had a son named Hathath and established a permanent family in the tribe of Judah. Years later a descendant was chosen from this family to head a service group of 24,000 during David's reign.—1Ch 4:13; 27:1, 15.

Israel's first oppression by foreign kings due to disobedience lasted for eight years. When they "began to call to Jehovah for aid," He raised up Othniel to deliver them. With Jehovah's spirit

upon him, Othniel defeated Cushan-rishathaim, "the king of Syria," and took general oversight and rendered judicial decisions among his brothers. —Jg 3:8-11.

OVEN. A chamber that is heated in order to bake or to roast foods. Various types of ovens were used by the Hebrews and others.—PICTURE, Vol. 2, p. 952.

Ovens of considerable size, consisting of a round hole in the ground, have been used in the Middle East up until modern times, some being as much as 1.5 or 1.8 m (5 or 6 ft) deep and almost 1 m (3 ft) in diameter. In an oven of this size, it was possible to roast an entire sheep by suspending it over the hot stones or coals.

The *bowl oven* was used in Biblical days and was probably similar to that employed by Palestinian peasants of modern times. A large clay bowl is placed inverted upon small stones on which the bread rests. The bowl is heated by the burning of fuel heaped over and around it, and the bread is baked.

Every Hebrew home likely had a portable *jar oven*, a type still used in Palestine. It was a large earthenware jar, about 0.9 m (3 ft) high, having an opening at the top and widening toward the bottom. To heat it, fuel such as wood or grass was burned inside, the ashes being removed through a hole provided for that purpose. The top was closed, and when the jar was hot enough, dough was spread around the inside or the outside. Bread baked in this manner was very thin.

A great many *pit ovens* have been unearthed by archaeologists. These were evidently further developments of the jar oven. This type, partly in the ground and partly above ground, was built up of clay and was plastered throughout. It tapered toward the top, and the fuel was burned inside. Monuments and paintings show that the Egyptians placed the dough on the outside of these ovens. For fuel, the Hebrews employing this type might use dry twigs or grass. (Compare Mt 6:30.) Meat could also be roasted in such an oven.

It is interesting that baking ovens now used by peasants in Palestine differ little from those found in ancient ruins or those depicted on Assyrian and Egyptian reliefs and paintings. In ancient Chaldea ovens were located in the courtyards of homes, and today they may be found in small bakehouses in the yards of private dwellings, though ovens may also be grouped together in some part of the village. Large public ovens are still in use.

Household ovens were common among the Israelites and Egyptians in the land of Egypt. Thus, during the second plague, frogs even came up into their ovens and their kneading troughs.—Ex 8:3.

"The Tower of the Bake Ovens" in Jerusalem was repaired under Nehemiah's direction during the restoration of the city's walls. (Ne 3:11; 12:38) This name's origin is uncertain, but it has been suggested that the tower was so named because commercial bakers had their ovens situated in that vicinity.

Illustrative Use. The oven is used in an expression denoting scarcity at Leviticus 26:26, which reads: "When I [Jehovah] have broken for you the rods around which ring-shaped loaves are suspended, ten women will then actually bake your bread in but one oven and give back your bread by weight; and you must eat but you will not be satisfied." Under normal conditions, each woman would need an oven to do her daily baking. However, Leviticus 26:26 pointed to a time when there would be so little food available that one oven would be sufficient to handle all the baking that ten women could do. And Hosea 7:4-7 compares adulterous Israelites to a baker's furnace, apparently because of the wicked desires burning within them.

OVERSEER.

The Hebrew word for overseer, *pa·qidh'*, is drawn from the verb *pa·qadh'*, meaning "turn attention to" (Ge 21:1), "visit" (Jg 15:1), "appoint" (Ge 39:5), or "commission" (Ezr 1:2). Similarly, the Greek word for overseer, *e·pi·sko·pos*, is related to the verb *e·pi·sko·pe'o*, meaning "watch carefully" (Heb 12:15), and to the noun *e·pi·sko·pe'*, meaning "inspection" (Lu 19:44, *Int*; 1Pe 2:12), "office of overseer" (1Ti 3:1), or "office of oversight" (Ac 1:20). The Greek *Septuagint* renders the Hebrew word *pa·qidh'* four times as *e·pi'sko·pos*. (Jg 9:28; Ne 11:9, 14, 22) Therefore, the overseer was one who gave attention to certain matters or persons, visiting, inspecting, and appointing. Protective supervision is a basic idea inherent in the Greek term.

Overseers in the Hebrew Scriptures. Joseph counseled Pharaoh to appoint overseers over the land to lay up stores during the years of plenty against the coming famine. (Ge 41:34-36) Under their respective chieftains, each family line of the Levites had its particular responsibility as regards the oversight of tabernacle duties. (Nu 3:24-26, 30, 31, 35-37) Eleazar, Aaron's son, was made "the chieftain of the chieftains of the Levites" and had general oversight of the tabernacle structure and its utensils. (Nu 3:32; 4:16) The high priest also might appoint overseers for certain sanctuary services. (2Ki 11:18) First Chronicles chapters 23 to 27 shows the numerous and varied positions and arrangements for oversight in effect during David's reign, as regards both the priesthood and the royal court, including economic and military matters.

The prophecy of Isaiah (60:17) sets "overseers" in parallel with "task assigners," since overseers may assign work to others as well as supervise and watch over the interests of those persons or things entrusted to their care. In this prophecy Jehovah foretells the time when he would "appoint peace as your overseers and righteousness as your task assigners," a prophecy initially fulfilled in Israel's restoration from exile but more fully realized in the Christian congregation.

Overseers in the Christian Congregation. The Christian "overseers" (*e·pi'sko·poi*) correspond to those recognized as "older men" (*pre·sby'te·roi*) in the congregation. That both of these terms designate the same position in the congregation can be seen from the instance of Paul's calling "the older men of the congregation" of Ephesus to Miletus to meet with him there. In exhorting these "older men," he states: "Pay attention to yourselves and to all the flock, among which the holy spirit has appointed you overseers [form of *e·pi'sko·poi*], to shepherd the congregation of God." (Ac 20:17, 28) The apostle further makes this clear in writing to Titus, where he discusses the subject of making appointments of "older men in city after city." In evident reference to such ones, he uses the term "overseer" (*e·pi'sko·pos*). (Tit 1:5, 7) Both terms, therefore, refer to the same position, *pre·sby'te·ros* indicating the mature qualities of the one so appointed, and *e·pi'sko·pos* the duties inherent with the appointment.—See OLDER MAN.

There was no set number of overseers for any one congregation. The number of overseers depended upon the number of those qualifying and accredited as "older men" in that congregation. That there were several overseers in the one congregation of Ephesus is evident. Likewise, in writing to the Philippian Christians, Paul referred to the "overseers" there (Php 1:1), indicating that they served as a body, overseeing the affairs of that congregation.

A consideration of the Christian Greek Scriptures indicates that the overseers, or older men, in any one congregation were of equal authority. In his congregational letters, Paul does not single out any one individual as *the* overseer, nor are these letters addressed to any individual as such. The letter to the Philippians was addressed "to all the holy ones in union with Christ Jesus who are in Philippi, along with overseers and ministerial servants." (Php 1:1) In this regard Manuel Guerra y Gomez noted: "Certainly *episcopos* in the protocol of the letter to the Philippians does not suppose a monarchic authority; it is rather a term that names the people of evident plural and collegial structure in charge of the direction and government of the Christian community of the Macedonian city. At the same time the *diaconos,* according to the general meaning of the word, are the helpers, the ministers of the *episcopos* and by the same token were at the service of the believers." —*Episcopos y Presbyteros,* Burgos, Spain, 1962, p. 320.

Qualifications of an overseer, or elder. To attain the office of overseer, the following qualifications must be met: "The overseer should therefore be irreprehensible, a husband of one wife, moderate in habits, sound in mind, orderly, hospitable, qualified to teach, not a drunken brawler, not a smiter, but reasonable, not belligerent, not a lover of money, a man presiding over his own household in a fine manner, having children in subjection with all seriousness; . . . not a newly converted man, . . . he should also have a fine testimony from people on the outside."—1Ti 3:1-7.

Likewise, in his letter to Titus, in discussing the subject of making appointments of elders, Paul said that in order to qualify as such, a man had to be "free from accusation, a husband of one wife, having believing children that were not under a charge of debauchery nor unruly. For an overseer must be free from accusation as God's steward, not self-willed, not prone to wrath, not a drunken brawler, not a smiter, not greedy of dishonest gain, but hospitable, a lover of goodness, sound in mind, righteous, loyal, self-controlled, holding firmly to the faithful word as respects his art of teaching, that he may be able both to exhort by the teaching that is healthful and to reprove those who contradict." (Tit 1:5-9) The differences in this latter list of qualifications evidently take into account the special needs of the congregations in Crete, where Titus was serving.—Tit 1:10-14.

The Supreme Overseer. First Peter 2:25 evidently quotes Isaiah 53:6 as to those who 'like sheep went astray,' and Peter then says: "But now you have returned to the shepherd and overseer of your souls." The reference must be to Jehovah God, since those to whom Peter wrote had not gone astray from Christ Jesus but, rather, *through him* had been led back to Jehovah God, who is the Grand Shepherd of his people. (Ps 23:1; 80:1; Jer 23:3; Eze 34:12) Jehovah is also an overseer, the one who makes inspection. (Ps 17:3) The inspection (Gr., *e·pi·sko·pe'*) could be associated with expression of adverse judgment by him, as in the first century C.E. in the case of Jerusalem, which did not discern the time of her "being inspected [Gr., *e·pi·sko·pes'*]." (Lu 19:44) Or it could bring favorable effect and benefits, as in the case of those glorifying God in the day "for his inspection [Gr., *e·pi·sko·pes'*]."—1Pe 2:12.

"Busybody in Other People's Matters." The apostle Peter warned against becoming "a busybody in other people's matters." (1Pe 4:15) This expression renders the Greek word *al·lo·tri·e·pi'sko·pos,* which literally means "overseer of what is another's." Francisco Zorell defines this word as "one who takes upon himself the duty of minding and correcting other people's matters, the one who imprudently thrusts himself into other people's affairs." —*Lexicon Graecum Novi Testamenti,* Paris, 1961, col. 70.

Overseers, or Older Men		Ministerial Servants
1Ti 3:1-7	Tit 1:5-9	1Ti 3:8-10, 12, 13
irreprehensible	free from accusation	free from accusation
husband of one wife	husband of one wife	husband of one wife
not a drunken brawler	not a drunken brawler	not given to a lot of wine
not a lover of money	not greedy of dishonest gain	not greedy of dishonest gain
presiding over household in fine manner, having children in subjection	having believing children not under charge of debauchery nor unruly	presiding in fine manner over children and own households
not newly converted		tested as to fitness
sound in mind	sound in mind	
hospitable	hospitable	
qualified to teach	holding to the word in the art of teaching, able to exhort and reprove	
not a smiter	not a smiter	
reasonable	not self-willed	
not belligerent	not prone to wrath	

OWL [Heb., *tach·mas';* kohs (little owl); *yan·shuph'* (long-eared owl); *'o'ach* (eagle owl)]. A night bird of prey mentioned several times in the Bible account. Once thought to be related to the hawk family, owls are now generally associated with other night feeders, such as the whippoorwill and the nightjar.

The owl has a short, hooked beak and powerful viselike talons resembling the hawk's, but differs by having a broad head, large eyes and ears, as well as by having a reversible toe on each foot so that, while the other toes point forward, this outer toe can be turned outward or even backward, thereby enabling the bird to get a firm grip on a variety of objects. The large eyes with their expanding irises make the greatest possible use of the dim light at night, and unlike most other birds, the owl's eyes both face forward, enabling it to view an object with both eyes at once. Its soft plumage is in mottled shades of brown, gray, black, and white with an intricate feather pattern and generally gives an impression of exaggerated bulk to the bird's body. According to an article in *Scientific American* (April 1962, p. 78), the owl's wings are ultrasonically quiet; the soft down on the upper surfaces and the feathery fringes on the leading and trailing edges of the wings apparently serve to reduce the turbulence of the air flow. Thus the owl noiselessly swoops through the darkness and silently drops down on its unsuspecting prey, primarily killing rodents, though some also eat smaller birds and insects. The cries of owls range from a shrill screech to a booming hooting sound.

The Hebrew *tach·mas'* denotes a species of owl and is included in the list of 'unclean' birds. (Le 11:13, 16; De 14:15) This Hebrew word, being related to a verb meaning "do violence," is appropriate to the owl, which lives by preying on small rodents and birds. This kind of owl has been identified with the striated scops owl (*Otus brucei*).

Also included among the 'unclean' birds is the Hebrew *kohs*, rendered by some as the "little owl" and designated as *Athene noctua*. (De 14:16, *KJ, NW, RS;* see also *Lexicon in Veteris Testamenti Libros,* by L. Koehler and W. Baumgartner, Leiden, 1958, p. 428) The little owl, about 25 cm (10 in.) in length, is one of the most widely distributed owls in Palestine, found in thickets, olive groves, and desolate ruins. The psalmist in his lonely affliction felt like "a little owl of desolated places." (Ps 102:6) Appropriately, the Arabic name for this variety of owl means the "mother of ruins."

Another bird listed in the Mosaic Law as 'unclean' is the Hebrew *yan·shuph'*, a name thought by some to indicate a "snorting" or "harsh blowing" sound (the Heb. word for "blow" being *na-*

shaph'). Others connect it with the "twilight" (Heb., *ne'sheph*) as indicating simply a nocturnal bird. (Le 11:17; De 14:16) *Lexicon in Veteris Testamenti Libros* (p. 386) identifies this bird as the "long-eared owl" (*Asio otus*). A bird about 38 cm (15 in.) in length, the long-eared owl is so called from the earlike erectile tufts on the sides of its broad head. It frequents wooded and desolate areas and is depicted as one of the creatures to inhabit the ruins of Edom.—Isa 34:11.

The abandoned houses in Babylon's ruins were foretold to be "filled with eagle owls [plural form of *'o'ach*]." (Isa 13:21) These circumstances and the Hebrew name, understood to denote a creature that "howls" with a doleful cry, well fit the eagle owl. Some would identify *'o'ach* with *Bubo bubo aharonii,* a variety of eagle owl inhabiting the desert regions of Palestine. However, the identification as the Egyptian (or dark desert) eagle owl (*Bubo bubo ascalaphus*), found from Morocco to Iraq, harmonizes well with the locale of the prophecy recorded in Isaiah 13. The eagle owl is the largest and most powerful of the owls of these regions. Its cry is a loud, prolonged, powerful hoot. Like other owls, at night its large eyes have a luminescent reddish-yellow glow when reflecting light, and together with its mournful cry, this characteristic doubtless contributed toward its being a symbol of evil portent among superstitious pagan peoples.

Some scholars believe the term *li·lith'*, used at Isaiah 34:14 as among the creatures haunting Edom's ruins, applies to some type of owl. The name is said to be used today "for *Strix,* the tawny owl." (*The Interpreter's Dictionary of the Bible,* edited by G. A. Buttrick, 1962, Vol. 2, p. 252) However, see the article NIGHTJAR.

OZEM (O'zem).

1. Fourth-listed son of Jerahmeel in the tribe of Judah.—1Ch 2:25.

2. The sixth-named son of Jesse and older brother of David; tribe of Judah.—1Ch 2:13, 15.

OZNI (Oz'ni) [possibly a shortened form of Azaniah]. A son of Gad and founder of the tribal family of Oznites numbered in the second wilderness registration of Israel. (Nu 26:15, 16) Ozni is called Ezbon in the first list of Gad's sons, some of whose names are written somewhat differently in Numbers.—Ge 46:16.

OZNITES (Oz'nites) [Of (Belonging to) Ozni]. A family of the tribe of Gad founded by Ozni.—Nu 26:15, 16.

P

PAARAI (Pa′a·rai) [possibly from a root meaning "open wide"]. An Arbite and one of the mighty men of David's military forces. (2Sa 23:8, 35) He may be identical with the Naarai mentioned at 1 Chronicles 11:37, in what appears to be a parallel list.

PADDAN (Pad′dan) [possibly, Plain (Flatland)]. The shortened form of "Paddan-aram" (Ge 35:9; 48:7); apparently the same as "the field of Syria [Aram]." (Ge 28:6, 7; Ho 12:12) Paddan was a region around the city of Haran in northern Mesopotamia. (Ge 28:7, 10; 29:4) Though some consider Paddan and Aram-naharaim to be identical, it seems more likely that Paddan was a part of Aram-naharaim. (Ge 24:10, ftn; 25:20, ftn) This may be deduced from the fact that Aram-naharaim included mountainous territory, something that could not be true of Paddan, if its name is correctly understood to mean "plain," "flatland." —Nu 23:7, ftn; De 23:4, ftn.

The patriarch Abraham resided temporarily at Haran in Paddan. (Ge 12:4; 28:7, 10) Later, from among the offspring of his relatives there, his son Isaac and then his grandson Jacob got their wives. (Ge 22:20-23; 25:20; 28:6) Jacob personally spent 20 years at Paddan in the service of his father-in-law Laban. (Ge 31:17, 18, 36, 41) While there, he became father to Dinah and 11 sons. (Ge 29: 20–30:24) His 12th son, Benjamin, was born in Canaan.—Ge 35:16-18, 22-26; 46:15; 48:7.

PADDAN-ARAM. See PADDAN.

PADON (Pa′don) [from a root meaning "redeem"]. Paternal head of a family of Nethinim. "The sons of Padon" returned with Zerubbabel from Babylonian exile.—Ezr 2:1, 2, 43, 44; Ne 7:46, 47.

PAGIEL (Pa′gi·el) [Encounter With God]. Wilderness chieftain of the tribe of Asher; son of Ochran. (Nu 1:13, 16) He assisted Moses in taking the first census of Israel, presented his offering at the inauguration of the tabernacle altar, and took the military command of his tribe.—Nu 1:4, 5, 13, 17-19; 2:27, 28; 7:11, 72-77; 10:26.

PAHATH-MOAB (Pa′hath-mo′ab) [Governor of Moab]. Founder of a family in Israel. If he was an official over Moab, as his name might imply, it was probably during the time when Moab was under Judah's domination. His holding such a position remains uncertain, however, as nothing is said of him personally in the Scripture record.

Pahath-moab's descendants noted in Ezra and Nehemiah are all postexilic. Some of them comprised the second most numerous family to return with Zerubbabel in 537 B.C.E. (Ezr 2:1, 2, 6; Ne 7:11) By the time of Ezra's return in 468 B.C.E., with more descendants of Pahath-moab accompanying him, some of the first group (or their offspring) had taken foreign wives, but they responded to Ezra's admonition to dismiss them. (Ezr 8:1, 4; 10:30, 44) Another of this family, Hasshub, helped Nehemiah to repair Jerusalem's wall, and a descendant or representative of theirs also attested by seal the agreement of faithfulness that was put forward shortly thereafter.—Ne 3:11; 9:38; 10:1, 14.

PAIN. A sensation of physical discomfort, whether moderate or severe; also acute mental or emotional distress.

Because of exhausting labor in cultivating cursed ground (Ge 3:17-19; 5:29), injurious words (Pr 15:1), the unresponsiveness of others to good (Ro 9:2), disease and other adversities (Job 2:13; 16:6), humans have experienced mental, emotional, and physical pain. Dreadful or frightening situations, whether real or visionary, have likewise given rise to pain.—Ps 55:3, 4; Isa 21:1-3; Jer 4:19, 20; Eze 30:4, 9; see also LABOR PAINS.

'No More Pain.' Although unpleasant, the physical sensation of pain serves a beneficial purpose by alerting a person to danger regarding bodily damage and thereby enables him to take steps to avoid serious injury. The fulfillment of God's promise that "neither will . . . pain be anymore" (Re 21:4), therefore, could not mean that humans would become insensitive to or incapable of experiencing pain. Rather, mental, emotional, and physical pain that has resulted from sin and imperfection (Ro 8:21, 22) will 'be no more' in the sense that its causes (such as disease and death) will be removed. That bodily perfection does not of itself require absolute painlessness is verified by the fact that even the perfect man Jesus experienced physical and emotional pain in connection with his death and the unresponsiveness of those to whom he ministered. (Mt 26:37; Lu 19:41) It was even foretold that he would be "a man meant for pains." (Isa 53:3) By curing those "distressed with various diseases and torments" (Mt 4:24), Jesus bore the pains of others.—Isa 53:4.

Figurative Use. Often the Scriptures refer to pain in a figurative sense. Depending upon the context, it may denote hard work (Pr 5:10) or a wholesome fear and awesome regard for Jehovah God. (1Ch 16:30; Ps 96:9; 114:7) Waters, mountains, and the earth, when in a state of agitation, are described as being in pain. (Ps 77:16; 97:4; Jer 51:29; Hab 3:10) Jehovah viewed unfaithful Judah as having an incurable pain, one threatening death.—Jer 30:15.

Pains, or pangs, can also denote a distressing circumstance. With reference to Jesus Christ, the apostle Peter stated: "God resurrected him by loosing the pangs of death, because it was not possible for him to continue to be held fast by it." (Ac 2:24) Although the dead are not conscious, death is a bitter and distressing circumstance, both in the pain that often precedes it and in the loss of all activity and freedom that its paralyzing grip brings.—Compare Ps 116:3.

PALACE. The royal residence of a sovereign; sometimes the spacious and stately dwelling of a prince or a powerful man of wealth. (Da 4:4; Lu 11:21; see GOVERNOR'S PALACE.) One Hebrew word for palace, heh·khal', often was applied to the temple as the dwelling place of the Sovereign Lord Jehovah. (1Sa 1:9; 1Ki 6:3; Ezr 5:14; Da 5:3) Ancient palaces were frequently castlelike fortresses with battlement walls and massive gates. (Ne 1:1; Es 1:2) The customary spacious courtyards and luxurious private gardens gave regal splendor and beauty to palace grounds.—Es 1:5.

The Bible mentions the palaces of Assyria (Na 1:1; 2:6), Babylon (2Ki 20:18; 2Ch 36:7; Isa 39:7; Da 1:4; 5:5), and Persia (Ezr 4:14; Es 7:7, 8). Those in Babylon were described as "palaces of exquisite delight." (Isa 13:22) One of the grandest palaces of the ancient world was built by Solomon, as is indicated by the impression it made on the queen of Sheba.—1Ki 10:4, 5.

Solomon's palace, erected on Mount Moriah south of the temple, was just one of a number of government structures in this area that, all together, took some 13 years to build. Included in this royal complex of buildings were the House of the Forest of Lebanon, the Porch of Pillars, and the Porch of the Throne. There was also a special house for Pharaoh's daughter, one of Solomon's many wives, besides the king's palace.—1Ki 7:1-8.

The description we have of Solomon's palace is very meager compared with the details of the palatial temple. But the size of the foundation stones indicates that the palace must have been an impressive structure. In length these stones measured eight cubits (3.6 m; 11.7 ft) and ten cubits (4.5 m; 14.6 ft), and they must have been of proportionate size in their width and thickness, weighing many tons. The walls consisted of costly stones carefully sawed to measured specifications on both inside and outside surfaces.—1Ki 7:9-11; compare Ps 144:12.

The psalmist, in the 45th psalm, may have had in mind the decorations and furnishings of Solomon's palace when he made reference to "the grand ivory palace." The apostle Paul applies the words of this psalm to Jesus Christ the heavenly King.—Ps 45:8, 15; compare Ps 45:6, 7 with Heb 1:8, 9; Lu 4:18, 21.

PALAL (Pa'lal) [shortened form of Pelaliah, meaning "Jah Is Arbitrating"]. Repairer of a section of Jerusalem's wall in the days of Nehemiah; son of Uzai.—Ne 3:25.

PALATE. See MOUTH.

PALESTINE. That land situated at the eastern end of the Mediterranean, which was once occupied by the ancient nation of Israel. The name is derived from the Latin Palaestina and the Greek Pa·lai·sti'ne. This latter word, in turn, is drawn from the Hebrew Pele'sheth. In the Hebrew Scriptures Pele'sheth (translated "Philistia") occurs only in reference to the limited coastal territory occupied by the Philistines. (Ex 15:14; Ps 60:8; 83:7; 87:4; 108:9; Isa 14:29, 31; Joe 3:4) Herodotus, however, in the fifth century B.C.E., and later other secular writers (Philo, Ovid, Pliny, Josephus, Jerome) used the Greek and Latin terms to designate all that territory formerly known as "the land of Canaan" or "the land of Israel." (Nu 34:2; 1Sa 13:19) Emperor Vespasian also described this territory as "Palestine" on the coins he struck in commemoration of Jerusalem's fall in 70 C.E. Because Jehovah had promised this land to Abraham and his descendants (Ge 15:18; De 9:27, 28), it was also appropriately called the Promised Land or the Land of Promise. (Heb 11:9) From the Middle Ages on, it has often been called the Holy Land.

In a sense Palestine is the connecting link between the continents of Europe, Asia, and Africa. This placed it in the center of a circle around the rim of which were located the ancient world powers of Egypt, Assyria, Babylon, Persia, Greece, and Rome. (Eze 5:5) Hemmed in by great deserts on the E and S and by the Great Sea, or Mediterranean, on the W, Palestine served as a land bridge between the Nile and Euphrates rivers, over which bridge the caravans on the world trade routes passed. Situated in what has been called the Fertile Crescent, Palestine itself was of particular interest, being a delightful place gifted with its own natural resources and special characteristics.

The term "Palestine" as it is used today refers to a general region. It does not imply precise boundaries. On the S an imaginary line could be drawn from the southern end of the Dead Sea to the SE corner of the Mediterranean, and on the N another line running from the southern slopes of Mount Hermon to a point near the city of Tyre. This area, from N to S, "from Dan to Beer-sheba" (1Sa 3:20; 2Sa 3:10), was about 240 km (150 mi) in length. From the Mediterranean Sea on the W, Palestine extended to the Arabian Desert on the E. All together, the area amounted to approximately 25,500 sq km (9,850 sq mi), less than the size of Belgium, but a little larger than the state of New Hampshire, U.S.A.

Geographic Features. (MAP, Vol. 1, p. 333) For a comprehensive view of its geography, the territory of Palestine may be conveniently divided into four rather parallel regions running from N to S.

First, there was a strip of fertile plain along the coast, a coast that, for the most part, had very little to offer in the way of natural harbors. Dividing this coastal plain in two was the promontory of the imposing Mount Carmel Range, which jutted out almost to the sea. The northern section was known as the Plain of Asher or Phoenicia. The southern portion skirted around sand dunes nestled close to the sea, and it consisted of the Plain of Sharon and the Plain of Philistia, the latter widening out in the S.

The *second* geographic region, next to the maritime plains, contained the principal mountain ranges, which ran N and S like a backbone of the country. In the N were the mountains of Naphtali, also called the Hills of Galilee. They were an extension of the Lebanon ranges, which were noted for their cedar forests and their prominent Mount Hermon, which towered skyward 2,814 m (9,232 ft). The northern mountains of Palestine ranged in altitude from 1,208 m (3,963 ft) at Har Meron in Upper Galilee to 562 m (1,844 ft) for Mount Tabor, made famous in the days of Barak. (Jg 4:12) Below Mount Tabor was a comparatively broad central plain that cut transversely across the country from W to E, separating the northern mountains from those to the S. This valley, where many decisive battles were fought, consisted of two parts, the eastern "low plain of Jezreel," and the western section, "the valley plain of Megiddo." —Jos 17:16; 2Ch 35:22.

To the W and N of the Megiddo valley, which was drained by the Kishon, was the Carmel Range running southeasterly from the coast and joining the mountains of Ephraim, or Samaria, in which the historic peaks of Gerizim and Ebal were located, the latter being over 900 m (3,000 ft) high. (De 11:29) Continuing S, this range was known as "the mountainous region of Judah," for though elevations varied from 600 m (2,000 ft) to over 1,000 m (3,300 ft), the area consisted largely of plateaus, rounded hills, and gentle slopes. (2Ch 27:4; Lu 1:39) Here in this region were such cities as Jerusalem, Bethlehem, and Hebron.

Gradually the Judean Mountains on the S merged into the Negeb, a name thought to be from a root meaning "be parched," a region that

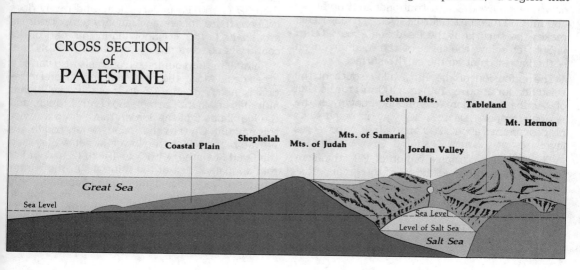

CROSS SECTION of PALESTINE

Lebanon Mts. Tableland Mt. Hermon Mts. of Samaria Jordan Valley Mts. of Judah Shephelah Coastal Plain

Great Sea

Sea Level

Sea Level

Level of Salt Sea

Salt Sea

extended to the torrent valley of Egypt and constituted the southern portion of Palestine. On the northern edge of the Negeb was the oasislike city of Beer-sheba; at the southern extremity, Kadesh-barnea.—Ge 12:9; 20:1; 22:19.

When approaching the mountains of Judah from the W, one comes to the hill section known as the Shephelah, with its several small W-E valleys leading from the coastal plains to the highlands. (Jos 9:1) For the most part these hills were suitable for the grazing of flocks and cattle, the springs in the valleys furnishing the necessary water.

The *third* feature of Palestine's geography was the great Rift Valley, sometimes called the Arabah (De 11:30), which divides the country longitudinally from top to bottom. This deep cleft began in Syria to the N and extended southward all the way to the Red Sea's Gulf of 'Aqaba. What made this central depression of the land all the more spectacular were the parallel mountain ranges and cliffs on either side of it.

When tracing this trenchlike depression from N to S, one quickly drops from the foothills of Mount Hermon to the Hula Basin, where the headwaters of the Jordan once formed a small lake. From there the Jordan, in some 16 km (10 mi), rapidly drops over 270 m (890 ft) to the Sea of Galilee, which is about 210 m (700 ft) below sea level. From Galilee to the Dead Sea, this great rift in the earth's crust is the Jordan Valley proper, and by the Arabs is called the *Ghor,* meaning "depression." It is a "gorge" as much as 19 km (12 mi) wide in places. The Jordan itself is about 45 m (150 ft) below the floor of this valley; and as it slowly snakes its way down to the Dead Sea, it continues to drop about 180 m (600 ft) more. (PICTURE, Vol. 1, p. 334) This makes the surface of the Dead Sea about 400 m (1,300 ft) below the level of the Mediterranean —the lowest point on the earth's surface.

The extension of the Rift Valley south of the Dead Sea for another 160 km (100 mi) to the Gulf of 'Aqaba was more commonly known as the Arabah proper. (De 2:8) Midway it reached its highest point, about 200 m (650 ft) above sea level.

The *fourth* geographic region of Palestine consisted of hills and tablelands E of the great Jordanian rift. (De 2:36, 37; 3:8-10) In the N this arable land extended E of the Sea of Galilee perhaps 100 km (60 mi), while in the S the width was only about 40 km (25 mi) before it became a wilderness, arid steppes that eventually lost themselves in the Arabian Desert. The wider, northern section of this rolling eastern region, above Ramoth-gilead, was called the land of Bashan, about 600 m (2,000 ft) in average altitude; S of Bashan the domelike region of Gilead attained an elevation of 1,000 m (3,300 ft). On its S, Gilead bordered the tableland N of the torrent valley of Arnon, in which area was situated Mount Nebo, over 820 m (2,700 ft) high. This territory, at one time the possession of the Ammonites, was, in turn, bounded S of the torrent valley of Arnon by the land of Moab.—Jos 13:24, 25; Jg 11:12-28.

Geographic Names. The ancient Hebrew names of many cities, mountains, and valleys have been lost, partly due to the occupation of Palestine by the Arabs for much of the time since 638 C.E. But, since Arabic is the living language most closely related to Hebrew, it is possible in some instances to identify with considerable accuracy certain ancient places and sites of major events.

Some common Arabic geographic terms that are helpful in relating places to Biblical sites are given on the following page.

Climatic Conditions. Palestine's climate is as diversified as its topography. In the matter of some 160 km (100 mi), from the Dead Sea to Mount Hermon, the contrasting extremes in altitude produce climatic conditions equivalent to those that are elsewhere spread over thousands of miles in latitude between the Tropics and the Arctic. Mount Hermon is usually snowcapped much of the year, while down along the Dead Sea the thermometer sometimes reaches 50° C. (122° F.). Sea breezes up from the Mediterranean moderate the temperature along the central mountain range. As a result it is seldom hotter than 32° C. (90° F.) in Jerusalem, and rarely does it freeze there. Its average January temperature is around 10° C. (50° F.). Snowfall in that part of the country is not common.—Compare 2Sa 23:20.

Rainfall in this country of contrasts also varies a great deal. Along the coast the annual precipitation is about 38 cm (15 in.), but in the higher altitudes of Mount Carmel, the central range, and the highlands E of the Jordan there is up to twice this amount. On the other hand, desert conditions prevail in the Negeb, the lower Jordan Valley, and the Dead Sea area, with 5 to 10 cm (2 to 4 in.) of rain annually. Most of the rain falls in the winter months of December, January, and February; only 6 or 7 percent in the summer months from June to October. The light "early," or autumn, rain in October and November permits the plowing of soil (baked hard by the summer heat) in preparation for the sowing of winter grains. The "late," or spring, rain comes in March and April.—De 11:14; Joe 2:23; Zec 10:1; Jas 5:7.

One of Palestine's great assets is the abundance of dew, especially through the rainless summer months, for without the heavy dews many of the vineyards and grazing lands would suffer greatly. (Hag 1:10; Zec 8:12) The moisture-laden breezes blowing up from the Mediterranean and down from Mount Hermon account for much of the dew in Palestine. (Ps 133:3) In certain areas the dew at night is so heavy that enough moisture is recovered by the vegetation to compensate for the losses during the heat of the day. (Compare Job 29:19.) Of particular importance is the dew in the Negeb and uplands of Gilead where rainfall is minimal.—See DEW.

Plants and Animals. The tremendous variety of trees, shrubs, and plants found in this small area of the earth has been a source of amazement among botanists, one of whom estimates that there are about 2,600 plant varieties growing there. The diversity in altitude, climate, and soil helps to account for this variety in flora, some plants being at home in the cold alpine, others in the torrid desert, and still others in the alluvial plain or the rocky plateau, each blooming and bearing seed in its season. Within comparatively short distances from one another are found hot-weather palms and cold-weather oaks and pines; willows along the streams and tamarisks in the wilderness. This land is also famous for its cultivated vineyards, olive groves, fig orchards, and fields of wheat, barley, and millet. Other crops include peas, beans, lentils, eggplants, onions, and cucumbers, as well as cotton and flax. Modern visitors to this land are often disappointed unless it is springtime, when the countryside is in full bloom with its flower spectacle. For most of the year, the stony hillsides are barren and bleak. At one time, however, parts of the land were more heavily wooded than at present, lush like "the garden of Jehovah," a veritable botanical garden "flowing with milk and honey," hospitable and inviting.—Ge 13:10; Ex 3:8; Nu 13:23, 24; De 8:7-9.

Animal, bird, and fish life was abundant in parklike Palestine, in the past more so than today. The lion, bear, wild bull, and hippopotamus are no longer present, but other wildlife that may be found include wolves, wild boars, wildcats, jackals, hares, and foxes. Domesticated animals are common—sheep, goats, cows, horses, asses, and camels. It is estimated that there are about 85 different kinds of mammals, 350 kinds of birds, and 75 kinds of reptiles in Israel today.

Resources From the Ground. Besides proving to be a well-watered land capable of producing an abundance of foodstuffs, Palestine's mountains contained useful iron and copper ores. (De 8:9) Gold, silver, tin, and lead had to be imported, but there were large deposits of salt, and in the Jordan Valley there were beds of clay for the brick, pottery, and foundry industries. (1Ki 7:46) Excellent limestone for the building trade was quarried, and there were outcroppings of dark basalt valued for its hardness and fine-grained texture.

PALLU (Pal'lu) [shortened form of Pelaiah, meaning "Jah Has Acted Wonderfully"]. Second-named son of Jacob's firstborn Reuben. (Ge 46:9;

GEOGRAPHIC TERMS		
Arabic	**Hebrew**	**English**
'ain	'en ['enot, pl.]	spring, fountain
beit	bet	house
biq'ah [beqa', pl.]	biq'a(t)	valley plain
bir	be'er	well
birkeh(et)	berekha(t)	pool
burj		tower
darb		road, way
debbeh(et)		sandy height
deir		convent, monastery
	'emeq	low plain
	gay, ge	valley
ghor		depression
	giv'a(t) [giv'ot, pl.]	hill
jebel	har	mountain
kafr	kefar	village
khirbeh(et)	horva(t)	ruin
	ma'ale	ascent
majdel	migdal	tower
	mayan	spring
	mifraz	bay, gulf
mughar	me'arah(t)	cave
nahr		river
naqb		mountain path
nebi		prophet
qal'ah(at)		fortress
qarn	qeren	peak (lit., horn)
qarya(t)	qirya(t)	town
qasr		castle, palace
rameh	rama(t)	plateau
ras	rosh	mountaintop; cape
rujm	rogem	heap of stones, cairn
shatt		shore or bank; river
tal'ah(at)		height
tell [tulul, pl.]	tel	mound
wadi	nahal	torrent valley
	yam	sea

1Ch 5:3) Pallu founded the family of Palluites in the tribe of Reuben. (Ex 6:14; Nu 26:5) He is possibly the same son of Reuben called Peleth at Numbers 16:1.

PALLUITES (Pal′lu·ites) [Of (Belonging to) Pal-lu]. A Reubenite family descended from Pallu. —Nu 26:5.

PALM TREE [Heb., ta·mar′, to′mer (Jg 4:5); Gr., phoi′nix]. The date palm (Phoenix dactylifera), though now found only in certain sections, was once abundant in Palestine and apparently was as characteristic of that area as it was and is of the Nile Valley of Egypt. Following the second destruction of Jerusalem, Roman Emperor Vespasian had numerous coins minted bearing the figure of a weeping woman seated beneath a palm tree with the inscription "Judaea Capta."—PICTURE, Vol. 2, p. 751.

Palms are associated with oases and are a welcome sight to desert travelers, as were the 70 palm trees growing beside the 12 springs of water at Elim, the second stop of the marching Israelites after their crossing the Red Sea. (Ex 15:27; Nu 33:9) The long taproot of the palm enables it to reach down to water sources not available to many plants and thus to thrive amid desert conditions.

In Bible times palms flourished on the coast of the Sea of Galilee (The Jewish War, III, 516, 517 [x, 8]) as well as along the lower reaches of the hot Jordan Valley, and they were particularly abundant around En-gedi (Jewish Antiquities, IX, 7 [i, 2]) and Jericho, called "the city of the palm trees." (De 34:3; Jg 1:16; 3:13; 2Ch 28:15). They also grew in the highlands, as did "Deborah's palm tree" in the mountainous region of Ephraim. (Jg 4:5) That they grew around Jerusalem is evident from the use made of their fronds at the Festival of Booths (Le 23:40; Ne 8:15) and also at the time of Jesus' entry into the city. (Joh 12:12, 13) Tamar, one of Solomon's cities, was named for the palm tree. (1Ki 9:17, 18) The land of Tyre and Sidon also later received the name Phoenicia (from a root meaning "palm tree") from the Greek phoi′nix (Ac 11:19; 15:3), as possibly did the city of Phoenix on the island of Crete.—Ac 27:12.

The tall, stately palm, with its straight, uniform trunk rising up to 30 m (100 ft) and cresting with a plume of long feathery fronds, makes a graceful silhouette of unique beauty. Girls must have been pleased to receive the name Tamar, as did Judah's daughter-in-law (Ge 38:6), Absalom's sister (2Sa 13:1), and also his daughter, who was described as "a woman most beautiful in appearance." (2Sa 14:27) The Shulammite maiden's stature was likened to that of a palm tree and her breasts to its clusters. (Ca 7:7, 8) The spiral arrangement of its wood fibers also makes it a tree of unusual suppleness and strength.

The palm tree comes to full bearing after 10 to 15 years and continues to bear for nearly a hundred years, after which it gradually declines and dies toward the end of the second century. The annual crop of dates grows in immense drooping clusters and is usually harvested by August-September. The Arabs say that the palm tree has as many uses as the year has days. In addition to the many uses for its fruit, the leaves are used for thatching roofs and the sides of houses, as well as for making fences, mats, baskets, and even dishes. Its fibers are used to make ropes and boat rigging. The date seeds, or kernels, are ground up and fed to the camels. Wax, sugar, oil, tannin, and resin are all obtained from the tree, and a potent drink called arrack is distilled from the sap.

Engraved carvings of the palm tree, with its erect form, beauty, and fruitfulness, made an appropriate decoration for the inner walls and the doors of Solomon's temple (1Ki 6:29, 32, 35; 2Ch 3:5) as well as for the sides of the carriages used in the temple service. (1Ki 7:36, 37) Palm trees were seen by Ezekiel as decorating the side pillars of the gates of the visionary temple and also the inner walls and doors of the temple. (Eze 40:16-37; 41:15-26) Being straight and tall as well as fruitful, the palm tree was also a fitting symbol of the 'righteous man' 'planted in the courtyards of Jehovah.'—Ps 92:12, 13.

The use of palm fronds by the crowd of people who hailed Jesus as "the king of Israel" (Joh 12:12, 13) evidently served to symbolize their praise as well as their submission to his regal position. The "great crowd" of Revelation 7:9, 10 are likewise pictured with palm branches in their hands, ascribing salvation to God and to the Lamb.

PALTI (Pal′ti) [shortened form of Paltiel].

1. A Benjamite chieftain selected as one of the 12 spies to preview the land of Canaan in 1512 B.C.E. He was a son of Raphu.—Nu 13:2, 3, 9, 27-33.

2. See PALTIEL No. 2.

PALTIEL (Pal′ti·el) [God Is My Provider of Escape].

1. Representative of Issachar at the time the tribes divided the Promised Land into inheritance portions; son of Azzan.—Nu 34:17, 18, 26.

2. Son of Laish from Gallim. Saul, after outlawing David, took his daughter Michal, David's wife, and gave her in marriage to Palti (Paltiel). (1Sa 25:44) After becoming king, David demanded of Abner and Ish-bosheth that Michal be returned to him. This greatly grieved Paltiel, who followed her, weeping, until Abner ordered him to go home.—2Sa 3:13-16.

PALTITE (Pal'tite) [Of (Belonging to) Beth-pelet; or, Of (Belonging to) the House of Pelet]. A term used with reference to Helez, one of David's mighty men and generally believed to refer to a native of Beth-pelet. (2Sa 23:8, 26) In the corresponding lists at 1 Chronicles 11:27; 27:10, Helez is called "the Pelonite."—See PELONITE.

PAMPHYLIA (Pam·phyl'i·a). A small Roman province on the S coast of Asia Minor visited by Paul on his first missionary tour. Though the size of the province may have varied over the years, Pamphylia is commonly viewed as having been a strip along the coastline some 120 km (75 mi) long and up to 50 km (30 mi) wide. It was bounded by the province of Lycia on the W, the Roman province of Galatia on the N, and the Kingdom of Antiochus on the E. On the coast the climate of Pamphylia was hot and tropical, while it moderated as one moved to the higher elevation of the Taurus Mountains.

The inhabitants are thought to have been a mixture of a native tribe with Greeks, some even suggesting Pamphylia to mean "of mingled tribes or races." (Liddell and Scott's *Greek-English Lexicon*, revised by H. Jones, Oxford, 1968, p. 1295) Evidently Jews or proselytes were in the area, for on Pentecost 33 C.E. persons from Pamphylia were in Jerusalem and were amazed to hear the disciples speaking in their "own language."—Ac 2:6, 10.

A number of principal cities were on or near the coast, such as the seaport town of Attalia, Perga on the Cestrus (Aksu) River, and Side, where coastal pirates sold their booty and a slave market existed. From Paphos on Cyprus, Paul, Barnabas, and John Mark sailed NW across the sea "and arrived at Perga in Pamphylia." It is not definitely known whether they landed at Attalia and traveled on land the few miles to Perga or whether they sailed right to Perga; it is reported that in ancient times the Cestrus was navigable at least as far as Perga. At this point John Mark separated from the others and returned to Jerusalem, but Paul and Barnabas went N through the mountains to Antioch in Pisidia (in the province of Galatia). (Ac 13:13, 14; 15:38; 27:5) That route was notorious for bandits.

(Compare 2Co 11:26.) On the return trip the two Christians traveled through Pamphylia to Perga and preached there. Next they went to the port of Attalia and sailed from there to Antioch in Syria. —Ac 14:24-26.

Pamphylia over the years was ruled by Lydia, Persia, Macedonia, and Rome. Under the Romans it was at various times united as a province with Cilicia (to the E), then with Galatia, and finally with Lycia.—Ac 13:13; 16:6; 27:5.

PAPER. In Bible times, a thin writing material made into sheets from strips obtained from the papyrus plant.—See PAPYRUS.

The Egyptians are credited with being the first manufacturers of papyrus paper for writing purposes, using papyrus plants that then grew along the banks of the Nile River. Some archaeologists would place such paper production as far back as Abraham's time.

Early Christians used papyrus paper for their letters, scrolls, and codices. It also played an important part in the production of Bible manuscripts, until it was replaced by vellum (fine-grained animal skin) in the fourth century C.E. At 2 John 12, the apostle wrote that he would rather convey his message "face to face" than with "paper and ink." Here the word "paper" translates the Greek word *khar'tes,* which is said to mean a sheet of paper made of papyrus.

PAPHOS (Pa'phos). A city on the W coast of the island of Cyprus. Here Paul, after working his way across the island with Barnabas and John Mark, encountered the sorcerer Bar-Jesus (Elymas), who opposed their preaching to Sergius Paulus the proconsul. For this he was miraculously made temporarily blind by Paul. Witnessing this act, Sergius Paulus was converted to Christianity. —Ac 13:6-13.

Two Cypriot cities have borne the name Paphos, "Old Paphos" and "New Paphos." New Paphos, the city referred to in the Acts account, was capital of the senatorial province of Cyprus when Paul visited the island during his first missionary tour. This city is thought to be represented by the ruins at the ancient seaport of Baffo about 1.5 km (1 mi) S of modern Ktima. The natural harbor there, which served as a naval base during Greek and Roman times, was no doubt the point from which Paul and his companions sailed NNW toward Perga in Asia Minor. Moles of the ancient harbor at Baffo still stand, as do the remains of various public and private buildings and a city wall.

Barnabas and Mark no doubt revisited the site around 49 C.E.—Ac 15:36-39.

PAPYRUS (pa·py′rus) [Heb., *go′me*]. A large aquatic plant belonging to the sedge family. It has a tapering three-sided stem, or stock, that grows in shallow water to a height of 2 to 6 m (6.5 to 20 ft) and terminates in a bush, or plume, of fine grasslike panicles. (PICTURE, Vol. 1, p. 544) The papyrus plant was used in the manufacture of various items, including a writing material.

Papyrus (*Cyperus papyrus*) thrives in shallow, stagnant waters or marshes and along the banks of slow-moving rivers, such as the lower Nile, where it once flourished but is now nearly extinct. Bildad asked Job: "Will a papyrus plant grow tall without a swampy place?"—Job 8:11; Isa 35:7.

The plant's stems are buoyant, and to prevent the death of the infant Moses, his mother placed him in "an ark of papyrus" coated with bitumen and pitch and set him adrift on the Nile River. (Ex 2:3) Large vessels for traveling long distances were also made from papyrus. (Isa 18:2) These may have been made of bundles of papyrus stems lashed together. They had narrow ends, but the beams were broad enough to support standing passengers. In 1970, Thor Heyerdahl and a group of associates traveled across thousands of miles of the Atlantic in such a craft.

Use as Writing Material. When the Egyptians prepared papyrus for writing material, they followed a rather simple process. In gathering the stems, they prized the thick pithy part that grew under the surface of the water because it yielded the broadest and whitest raw material. The outer rinds were peeled off, and the remaining pithy cores were cut into convenient lengths of 40 to 45 cm (16 to 18 in.). Next, the cellular pith was sliced into broad, but very thin, strips. The strips were then laid out vertically on a smooth surface and allowed to overlap slightly. After a thin coat of paste was applied, another layer of papyrus strips was placed horizontally over the vertical ones. Mallets were used to beat the layers until they were bonded into a unified sheet. Then after being dried in the sun, the sheets were trimmed to the desired size. Finally, they were smoothed and polished with pumice, shells, or ivory. This process produced a fairly durable, supple, near-white writing material that was available in many sizes and degrees of quality. The side having the horizontal strips was usually chosen for writing, although at times the reverse side was used to finish a writing. The joints of the strips served to guide the writer's hand as he wrote with a reed pen and a writing fluid made from gum, soot, and water.

These papyrus sheets could be pasted along the edges and joined to make a scroll, normally consisting of about 20 sheets. Or they might be folded into leaves to form the booklike codex that became popular among the early Christians. The average scroll measured some 4 to 6 m (14 to 20 ft) in length, though one has been preserved that is 40.5 m (133 ft) long. The Greek word *bi′blos* originally applied to the soft pith of the papyrus plant but was later used with reference to a book. (Mt 1:1; Mr 12:26) The diminutive *bi·bli′on* has the plural *bi·bli′a*, literally meaning "little books," and from this the word "Bible" is derived. (2Ti 4:13, *Int*) A Phoenician city was called Byblos after it became an important center for the papyrus industry.

Papyrus rolls were used widely until the beginning of the second century C.E., when they began to be superseded by the papyrus codex. Later, in the fourth century, the popularity of papyrus waned, and it was replaced extensively by a more durable writing material called vellum.

Papyrus had one major disadvantage as a writing material in that it was not very durable. It deteriorated in a damp environment and, when stored under arid conditions, became very brittle. Until the 18th century C.E., the assumption was that all ancient papyrus manuscripts had perished. However, in the late 19th century, a number of valuable Biblical papyri were brought to light. Discoveries have been made chiefly in Egypt and the region around the Dead Sea, places that afford the ideal dry climate so necessary for the preservation of papyri. Some of the Scriptural papyri found at these locations date back as far as the second or first century B.C.E.

Many of these papyrus manuscript discoveries are designated by the term "papyrus" or "papyri," such as the Nash Papyrus of the first or second century B.C.E., the Papyrus Rylands iii. 458 (second century B.C.E.), and the Chester Beatty Papyrus No. 1 (of the third century C.E.).

PARADISE. A beautiful park, or a parklike garden. The Greek word *pa·ra′dei·sos* occurs three times in the Christian Greek Scriptures. (Lu 23:43; 2Co 12:4; Re 2:7) Greek writers as far back as Xenophon (c. 431-352 B.C.E.) used the word (*pairidaeza*), and Pollux attributed it to Persian sources. (*Cyropaedia*, I, iii, 14; *Anabasis*, I, ii, 7; *Onomasticon*, IX, 13) Some lexicographers would derive the Hebrew word *par·des′* (meaning, basically, a park) from the same source. But since Solomon (of the 11th century B.C.E.) used *par·des* in his writings, whereas existing Persian writings go back only to about the sixth century B.C.E., such derivation of the Hebrew term is only conjectural. (Ec 2:5; Ca 4:13) The remaining use of *par·des'* is at Nehemiah 2:8, where reference is made to a royal wooded park of Persian King Artaxerxes Longimanus, in the fifth century B.C.E.—See PARK.

The three terms (Hebrew *par·des'*, Persian *pairi-daeza,* and Greek *pa·ra'dei·sos*), however, all convey the basic idea of a beautiful park or parklike garden. The first such park was that made by man's Creator, Jehovah God, in Eden. (Ge 2:8, 9, 15) It is called a *gan,* or "garden," in Hebrew but was obviously parklike in size and nature. The Greek *Septuagint* appropriately uses the term *pa·ra'dei·sos* with reference to that garden. (See EDEN No. 1; GARDEN [Garden of Eden].) Because of sin, Adam lost his right to live in that paradise and his opportunity to gain the right to everlasting life, which right was represented in the fruit of a divinely designated tree in the center of the garden. The garden of Eden may have been enclosed in some way, since it was necessary to place angelic guards only at the east side thereof to prevent human entrance.—Ge 3:22-24.

What is the Paradise that Jesus promised to the evildoer who died alongside him?

Luke's account shows that an evildoer, being executed alongside Jesus Christ, spoke words in Jesus' defense and requested that Jesus remember him when he 'got into his kingdom.' Jesus' reply was: "Truly I tell you today, You will be with me in Paradise." (Lu 23:39-43) The punctuation shown in the rendering of these words must, of course, depend on the translator's understanding of the sense of Jesus' words, since no punctuation was used in the original Greek text. Punctuation in the modern style did not become common until about the ninth century C.E. Whereas many translations place a comma before the word "today" and thereby give the impression that the evildoer entered Paradise that same day, there is nothing in the rest of the Scriptures to support this. Jesus himself was dead and in the tomb until the third day and was then resurrected as "the firstfruits" of the resurrection. (Ac 10:40; 1Co 15: 20; Col 1:18) He ascended to heaven 40 days later. —Joh 20:17; Ac 1:1-3, 9.

The evidence is, therefore, that Jesus' use of the word "today" was not to give the time of the evildoer's being in Paradise but, rather, to call attention to the time in which the promise was being made and during which the evildoer had shown a measure of faith in Jesus. It was a day when Jesus had been rejected and condemned by the highest-ranking religious leaders of his own people and was thereafter sentenced to die by Roman authority. He had become an object of scorn and ridicule. So the wrongdoer alongside him had shown a notable quality and commendable heart attitude in not going along with the crowd but, rather, speaking out in Jesus' behalf and expressing belief in his coming Kingship. Recognizing that the emphasis is correctly placed on the time of the promise's being made rather than on the time of its fulfillment, other translations, such as those in English by Rotherham and Lamsa, those in German by Reinhardt and W. Michaelis, as well as the Curetonian Syriac of the fifth century C.E., rendered the text in a form similar to the reading of the *New World Translation,* quoted herein.

As to the identification of the Paradise of which Jesus spoke, it is clearly not synonymous with the heavenly Kingdom of Christ. Earlier that day entry into that heavenly Kingdom had been held out as a prospect for Jesus' faithful disciples but on the basis of their having 'stuck with him in his trials,' something the evildoer had never done, his dying on a stake alongside Jesus being purely for his own criminal acts. (Lu 22:28-30; 23:40, 41) The evildoer obviously had not been "born again," of water and spirit, which Jesus showed was a prerequisite to entry into the Kingdom of the heavens. (Joh 3:3-6) Nor was the evildoer one of the 'conquerors' that the glorified Christ Jesus stated would be with him on his heavenly throne and that have a share in "the first resurrection."—Re 3:11, 12, 21; 12:10, 11; 14:1-4; 20:4-6.

Some reference works present the view that Jesus was referring to a paradise location in Hades or Sheol, supposedly a compartment or division thereof for those approved by God. The claim is made that the Jewish rabbis of that time taught the existence of such a paradise for those who had died and were awaiting a resurrection. Regarding the teachings of the rabbis, Hastings' *Dictionary of the Bible* states: "The Rabbinical theology as it has come down to us exhibits an extraordinary medley of ideas on these questions, and in the case of many of them it is difficult to determine the dates to which they should be assigned. . . . Taking the literature as it is, it might appear that Paradise was regarded by some as on earth itself, by others as forming part of Sheol, by others still as neither on earth nor under earth, but in heaven . . . But there is some doubt as respects, at least, part of this. These various conceptions are found indeed in later Judaism. They appear most precisely and most in detail in the mediæval Cabbalistic Judaism . . . But it is uncertain how far back these things can be carried. The older Jewish theology at least . . . seems to give little or no place to the idea of an intermediate Paradise. It speaks of a *Gehinnom* for the wicked, and a *Gan Eden*, or garden of Eden, for the just. It is questionable whether it goes beyond these conceptions and affirms a Paradise in Sheol."—1905, Vol. III, pp. 669, 670.

Even if they did teach such a thing, it would be most unreasonable to believe that Jesus would propagate such a concept, in view of his condemnation of the non-Biblical religious traditions of the Jewish religious leaders. (Mt 15:3-9) Likely the paradise truly familiar to the Jewish malefactor to whom Jesus spoke was the earthly Paradise described in the first book of the Hebrew Scriptures, the Paradise of Eden. That being so, Jesus' promise would reasonably point to a restoration of such earthly paradisaic condition. His promise to the wrongdoer would therefore give assured hope of a resurrection of such an unrighteous one to an opportunity to life in that restored Paradise. —Compare Ac 24:15; Re 20:12, 13; 21:1-5; Mt 6:10.

A Spiritual Paradise. Throughout many of the prophetic books of the Bible, divine promises are found regarding the restoration of Israel from the lands of its exile to its desolated homeland. God would cause that abandoned land to be tilled and sown, to produce richly, and to abound with humankind and animalkind; the cities would be rebuilt and inhabited, and people would say: "That land yonder which was laid desolate has become like the garden of Eden." (Eze 36:6-11, 29, 30, 33-35; compare Isa 51:3; Jer 31:10-12; Eze 34:25-27.) However, these prophecies also show that paradise conditions related to the *people* themselves, who, by faithfulness to God, could now "sprout" and flourish as "trees of righteousness," enjoying beautiful spiritual prosperity like a "well-watered garden," showered by bounteous blessings from God because of having his favor. (Isa 58:11; 61:3, 11; Jer 31:12; 32:41; compare Ps 1:3; 72:3, 6-8, 16; 85:10-13; Isa 44:3, 4.) The people of Israel had been God's vineyard, his planting, but their badness and apostasy from true worship had caused a figurative 'withering away' of their spiritual field, even before the literal desolation of their land took place.—Compare Ex 15:17; Isa 5:1-8; Jer 2:21.

This undoubtedly provides the key for understanding Paul's description of the vision (evidently had by him, since it forms part of his defense of his own apostleship) referred to at 2 Corinthians 12:1-7. Caught away to "the third heaven" (see

HEAVEN [Third Heaven]), the vision viewer entered "paradise" and heard unutterable words. That this paradise envisioned could refer to a spiritual state among God's people, as in the case of fleshly Israel, can be seen from the fact that the Christian congregation was also God's "field under cultivation," his spiritual vineyard, rooted in Christ Jesus and bearing fruit to God's praise. (1Co 3:9; Joh 15:1-8) As such it had replaced the nation of Israel in God's favor. (Compare Mt 21:33-43.) Paul's vision, nevertheless, must logically have applied to some future time, so as to constitute a 'revelation.' (2Co 12:1) An apostasy was due to set in among the Christian congregation and was already working in Paul's day; it would result in a condition like that of a field oversown with weeds. (Mt 13:24-30, 36-43; Ac 20:29; 2Th 2:3, 7; compare Heb 6:7, 8.) So, Paul's paradise vision would not reasonably apply while such was the case but would evidently relate to the time of "the harvest season" when the genuine Christians would be gathered by the angelic reapers and would enjoy rich blessings and spiritual prosperity from God.

It is evident, however, that the restoration prophecies recorded by the Hebrew prophets include elements that will also find a physical fulfillment in the restored earthly Paradise. There are features, for example, in Isaiah 35:1-7, such as the healing of the blind and the lame, that did not have a literal fulfillment following the restoration from ancient Babylon, nor are they fulfilled in such a manner in the Christian spiritual paradise. It would be inconsistent for God to inspire such prophecies as those of Isaiah 11:6-9, Ezekiel 34:25, and Hosea 2:18, with the intention that they have only a figurative or spiritual meaning, without having a literal fulfillment of these things in the physical experiences of God's servants.

Eating in "the Paradise of God." Revelation 2:7 mentions a "tree of life" in "the paradise of God" and that eating from it would be the privilege of the one "that conquers." Since other promises given in this section of Revelation to such conquering ones clearly relate to their gaining a heavenly inheritance (Re 2:26-28; 3:12, 21), it seems evident that "the paradise of God" in this case is a heavenly one. The word "tree" here translates the Greek word *xy'lon*, which literally means "wood," and could therefore refer to an orchard of trees. In the earthly Paradise of Eden, eating of the tree of life would have meant living forever for man. (Ge 3:22-24) Even the fruit of the other trees of the garden would have been life sustaining for man as long as he continued obedient. So, the partaking of "the tree [or trees] of life" in "the paradise of God" evidently relates to the divine provision for sustained life granted the Christian conquerors, other texts showing that they receive the prize of immortality and incorruptibility along with their heavenly Head and Lord, Christ Jesus.—1Co 15:50-54; 1Pe 1:3, 4.

PARAH (Pa'rah). A city of Benjamin. (Jos 18: 21, 23) Parah is usually identified with Khirbet el-Farah (Horvat 'En Para), about 9 km (5.5 mi) NE of Jerusalem. A nearby spring called 'Ain Farah ('En Perat) furnishes water for the Old City of Jerusalem.

PARALYSIS. Impairment or total loss of muscular power or of sensation in one or more parts of the body. Sometimes called palsy, it results from damage or disorder of the nervous system or from atrophy of muscles, thus either preventing the transmission of nerve impulses or rendering the muscles unable to react to them. Paralysis has many names and forms, some of which types can be fatal. Among its causes are disease (as in the case of diphtheritic paralysis), brain lesions, damage to the spinal cord, or pressure from a tumor.

Paralyzed persons were among those miraculously cured by Jesus Christ. (Mt 4:24) A paralyzed man was brought to Jesus, who cured the sufferer after forgiving his sins. Then, at Christ's bidding, the former paralytic picked up his cot and went home. (Mt 9:2-8; Mr 2:3-12; Lu 5:18-26) On another occasion the manservant of an army officer was laid up with paralysis and was about to die, but Jesus healed him from a distance. (Mt 8:5-13; Lu 7:1-10) This slave was "terribly tormented," or terribly afflicted (Mt 8:6), which may, but does not necessarily, indicate that he was suffering intense pain. Though usually not painful, paralysis may be. Cramplike pains occur in the spine and the extremities in cases of paralysis agitans (parkinsonism, or shaking palsy), and there is agonizing pain in paraplegia dolorosa, a form of paralysis associated with some cases of spinal cord cancer. "Paralytics" are persons afflicted with paralysis.

The evangelist Philip preached, and he performed signs in the city of Samaria, curing many paralyzed persons. (Ac 8:5-8) In Lydda, paralyzed Aeneas, "who had been lying flat on his cot for eight years," was told by Peter: "Aeneas, Jesus Christ heals you. Rise and make up your bed." At that, "he rose immediately."—Ac 9:32-35.

PARAN (Pa'ran). The greater part of that vast wilderness region in which the nation of Israel wandered about for some 38 years before entering the Promised Land. (Nu 10:11, 12; De 2:14) Having no fixed boundaries, Paran occupied the central and northeastern portion of the Sinai Peninsula. On the E was that part of the Rift Valley known as the Arabah and also the Gulf of 'Aqaba, on the S the Wilderness of Sinai, on the SW the Wilderness of Sin, and on the NW and N the Wildernesses of Etham and Shur. Toward the Dead Sea to the NE, Paran blended with, and perhaps included, the Wilderness of Zin and perhaps even reached up to Beer-sheba near the mountains of Judah.—1Sa 25:1, 2.

For the most part Paran was a rough mountainous region of limestone, plateaulike in places, the central section being between 600 and 750 m (2,000 to 2,500 ft) high. (De 33:2; compare Hab 3:3.) It was also included as part of "that great and fear-inspiring wilderness" referred to at Deuteronomy 1:1, 19; 8:15. Except during the brief rainy seasons, the gravel face of this rude country is devoid of green vegetation; springs are few and far between. These factors emphasize how completely the nation of Israel, numbering perhaps 3,000,000 persons, was dependent upon Jehovah for his miraculous provision of food and water during the many years they wandered in the wilderness.—Ex 16:1, 4, 12-15, 35; De 2:7; 8: 15, 16.

Apparently the first reference to this Wilderness of Paran was in the days of Lot when Chedorlaomer and his allies defeated a number of cities in the vicinities of the Dead Sea and Edom as far S as El-paran. (Ge 14:4-6) Later, after Ishmael was dismissed by his father Abraham, he settled down in the Wilderness of Paran and occupied himself mainly with the hunt.—Ge 21:20, 21.

However, the principal references to Paran are in connection with the wanderings of the Israelites. After leaving Mount Sinai, Israel camped at Taberah and Kibroth-hattaavah, then at Hazeroth on the southern edge of Paran, before moving N toward Kadesh-barnea. (Nu 10:12, 33; 11:3, 34, 35; 12:16) Not long after entering Paran, the 12 spies were sent out to investigate Canaan. (Nu 13:3, 26) The bad report given by the majority upon their return resulted in Jehovah's decree that the nation prolong their stay in the wilderness until all the registered ones who had murmured against God had died off. (Nu 13:31-33; 14:20-34) During that 40 years, by far the majority of Israel's campsites, from Egypt to the Promised Land, were in Paran.—Nu 33:1-49.

According to the Greek *Septuagint*, David went into the Wilderness of Maon following the death and burial of Samuel. However, the Masoretic text, Syriac *Peshitta*, and Latin *Vulgate* say he went into the Wilderness of Paran. (1Sa 25:1) When

David became king and made war on Edom, the young Edomite prince Hadad, together with some of his father's servants, made his escape to Egypt. On the way down they were joined by certain men of Paran as they passed through that country.—1Ki 11:15-18.

PARCHMENT. Skins of sheep, goats, or calves prepared for use as writing material. Leather was long used as a writing material among ancient people; the Dead Sea Scroll of Isaiah, copied toward the end of the second century B.C.E., is of leather. Papyrus from Egypt became a more widely used writing material but, according to Pliny, when the ruler of Egypt prohibited the exporting of it about 190 B.C.E., the use of leather parchment was invented in Pergamum. (The English word "parchment" comes from Lat. *pergamena*.) Perhaps this means simply the popularizing of an already-existing method of treating the skins so that both sides could be written on. Scrolls of parchment were much more durable than the less expensive papyrus scrolls.

At 2 Timothy 4:13 the apostle Paul asked Timothy to bring "the scrolls, especially the parchments." (*NW, Ro*) He does not indicate the contents of these requested items, but quite possibly he was asking for portions of the Hebrew Scriptures so that he could study them while imprisoned in Rome. The phrase "especially the parchments" may indicate that both scrolls of papyrus and scrolls of parchment were involved.

Among the early Romans wooden tablets covered with wax were often used for writing matters of a temporary nature. Eventually sheets of leather or parchment were used instead for this purpose. The Latin word *membranae* (skins) was applied to such notebooks of parchment. In the text quoted earlier, Paul employed the Greek equivalent of the word in asking for "the scrolls, especially the parchments [*mem·bra'nas*]." Thus some commentators have suggested that he was requesting scrolls of the Hebrew Scriptures plus notes or letters of some type. So Moffatt translates it, "my books, and particularly my papers," and *The New English Bible* reads, "the books, above all my notebooks." However, whether "the parchments" were in the form of notebooks or papers, or were parchment scrolls (*La; Kx*) cannot be ascertained.

Vellum. Parchments were normally made from sheep, goat, or calf skin. In the third and fourth centuries C.E., there arose a distinction between the coarser and the finer grades of the material, the coarser continuing to be called parchment, but the finer, vellum. The vellum was made from delicate skins of calf (veal) or kid, or of stillborn calves or lambs. It was prepared by scraping the hair from the washed skins, stretching them on a frame, washing and scraping again to remove inequalities, dusting with chalk, and rubbing with pumice. This produced a thin, smooth, almost-white writing material that came to be widely used for important books until the invention of printing, for which paper was better and cheaper. Important Bible manuscripts such as the fourth-century Sinaitic and Vatican No. 1209 as well as the fifth-century Alexandrine manuscripts are of vellum.

PARDON. The Hebrew word *na·sa"*, sometimes translated "pardon," is also used in the Scriptures in the sense of "raise," "lift," "lift up" (Ge 45:19; Ex 6:8; 2Ki 2:16), "take" (Ge 27:3), "take away" (Nu 16:15). A basic meaning of the word, however, is "bear, carry." (Ge 47:30; 1Ki 2:26; Eze 44:12, 13) There is still an allusion to this in instances where *na·sa"* is appropriately translated "pardon." The Scriptures speak of the goat for Azazel as carrying away sin, and it was foretold that the Messiah would bear the error of the people. (Le 16:8, 10, 22; Isa 53:12) By reason of his carrying, or bearing, the error of others, pardon is made possible for them.—See AZAZEL.

Whereas the word *na·sa"* may denote the pardon, or forgiveness, extended by God or by humans (Ge 18:24, 26; 50:17), *sa·lach'* is used exclusively of God's forgiveness, the act by which the sinner is restored to divine favor in answer to his sincere prayer for forgiveness or to another's intercessory prayer.—Nu 14:19, 20; 1Ki 8:30.

When the Hebrew *na·sa"* has the sense of pardon, or forgiveness, the Greek *Septuagint* at times uses the word *a·phi'e·mi*. In its basic sense, *a·phi'e·mi* denotes "let go off." This term can signify "forgive," "pardon." At Romans 4:7, the apostle Paul quoted from Psalm 32:1 (31:1, *LXX*), where the reference is to Jehovah's pardoning "revolt," and he used a form of the word *a·phi'e·mi*, as does the Greek *Septuagint* for the Hebrew *na·sa"*. The term appears elsewhere in the Christian Greek Scriptures and is applied to God's and man's forgiveness of sins, including the cancellation of debts.—Mt 6:12, 14, 15; 18:32, 35.

Jehovah is outstandingly a God who grants pardon to those who seek forgiveness. But he does not withhold punishment from persons who deliberately set themselves in opposition to him and his righteous ways.—Ex 34:6, 7; see FORGIVENESS.

PARK. The word *par·des'* occurs but three times in the Hebrew Scriptures and is considered by some to be derived from the Persian word *pairidaeza*. (However, see PARADISE.) According to

M'Clintock and Strong's *Cyclopædia* (1894, Vol. VII, p. 652), Xenophon used the Persian term as meaning "an extensive plot of ground, enclosed with a strong fence or wall, abounding in trees, shrubs, plants, and garden culture, and in which choice animals were kept in different ways of restraint or freedom, according as they were ferocious or peaceable." The Greek form of the word (*pa·ra'dei·sos*) was used by the translators of the *Septuagint* in all references to the garden of Eden.

Among his great works, Solomon made both "gardens and parks ["orchards," *KJ*; Heb., *phar·de·sim'*]" in which he planted fruit trees of all sorts. (Ec 2:5) He uses the same term in his "superlative song" when he has the shepherd lover describe the Shulammite maiden's skin as "a paradise of pomegranates, with the choicest fruits." (Ca 1:1; 4:12, 13) In postexilic times, Nehemiah 2:7, 8 shows that the Persian king had placed Asaph as "the keeper of the park that belongs to the king" and that application had to be made for permission to fell trees from this park for the reconstruction work in Jerusalem.—See FOREST; GARDEN.

PARMASHTA

PARMASHTA (Par·mash'ta) [from Persian, meaning "The Very First"]. One of Haman's ten sons.—Es 9:9.

PARMENAS

PARMENAS (Par'me·nas). One of the seven recommended to the apostles and appointed by them to ensure a just daily distribution of food supplies in the Jerusalem congregation after Pentecost of 33 C.E.—Ac 6:1-6.

PARNACH

PARNACH (Par'nach). A Zebulunite whose son Elizaphan was the tribal representative in dividing the Promised Land.—Nu 34:17, 18, 25.

PAROSH

PAROSH (Pa'rosh) [Flea]. Founder of a family in Israel. There were 2,172 of his descendants who returned to Jerusalem with Zerubbabel in 537 B.C.E. (Ezr 2:1-3; Ne 7:8) By the time that Ezra arrived in 468 B.C.E., with 150 "sons of Parosh" led by Zechariah, some of their family already in Jerusalem had taken foreign wives, whom they later sent away. (Ezr 8:1, 3; 10:25, 44) Pedaiah, one of the family, repaired a section of Jerusalem's wall. (Ne 3:25) The head of the Parosh family attested to the later covenant agreeing to keep the Law of Jehovah.—Ne 9:38; 10:1, 14.

PARSHANDATHA

PARSHANDATHA (Par·shan·da'tha) [from Persian, possibly meaning "The Investigator"]. One of Haman's ten sons.—Es 9:7.

PARSIN

PARSIN (Par'sin). One of the words mysteriously written on the wall of Belshazzar's palace and read and interpreted by Daniel. (Da 5:25) It is the plural number of "Peres," which means "a half shekel," a division of a shekel. In giving the interpretation, Daniel did not use the plural "Parsin," but used the singular form (Peres). (Da 5:28) Perhaps this was because only Belshazzar was present to hear the prophet explain the prophetic message, although it applied to both rulers of the Babylonian Empire, Belshazzar and Nabonidus.—See PERES.

PARTHIANS

PARTHIANS (Par'thi·ans) [Of (Belonging to) Parthia]. Jews and proselytes from Parthia are listed first among those visitors attending the Festival of Pentecost, 33 C.E., in Jerusalem. God's holy spirit poured out on the group of about 120 Christian disciples enabled them to proclaim the good news in the language or dialect of those Parthians, some of whom doubtless responded favorably, became Christians, and likely spread the message among their own people upon returning to Parthia. (Ac 1:15; 2:1, 4-12, 37-47) The natural Jews from Parthia were part of the Dispersion; the "proselytes" (Ac 2:10) were non-Jews who had become converts to Judaism.

The Parthian Empire originated SE of the Caspian Sea but in time came to extend from the Euphrates as far as India. The Parthians were subject to the Persians from the time of King Cyrus. Later coming under Greek domination, they rebelled against the successors of Alexander the Great and managed to maintain their independence for several centuries, even against Rome. They held Judea for several years before losing it to the Romans. The Parthians were still an independent nation in the first century, and though they practiced the predominant Persian religion, the religions of the Jews and others were tolerated.

PARTRIDGE

PARTRIDGE [Heb., *qo·re'*]. A chickenlike (gallinaceous) bird, stout-bodied, smaller than the pheasant, able to run and dodge with great swiftness, seldom resorting to flight and tiring quickly when it does. Two kinds of partridges found in Palestine are the sand partridge (*Ammoperdix heyi*) and the rock partridge, or chukar (*Alectoris graeca*). The sand partridge is found in deserts and on rocky slopes, while the rock partridge is found principally in the hill country that is covered with sparse vegetation.

The Hebrew name of this bird means "caller." While the partridge does have a ringing call, some believe its Hebrew name is intended to imitate the grating "krrr-ic" sound the bird makes when it is flushed.

The partridge has a delicate flesh and was hunted as food from ancient times, the hunters often using throwing sticks to bring down the bird when it was flushed from cover. Since the partridge seeks escape by running, dodging behind rocks and other obstacles, and seeking out a hiding place in clefts of rocks or similar places of concealment, David, moving from hiding place to hiding place in his endeavor to evade King Saul's relentless pursuit, aptly likened himself to "a partridge upon the mountains."—1Sa 26:20; compare La 3:52.

The text at Jeremiah 17:11, likening the man unjustly amassing wealth to "the partridge that has gathered together [or, possibly, hatched] what it has not laid," has been the subject of much discussion. Whereas certain ancient writers described the partridge as taking eggs from other hens' nests and incubating them, present-day naturalists state that none of the birds classified as partridges have such a practice. However, *Lexicon in Veteris Testamenti Libros* refers to Jewish zoologist Israel Aharoni (1882-1946), a writer of works on Palestinian animal life, as having found "2 layings of 11 eggs each of 2 different females [partridges] in the same nest." (By L. Koehler and W. Baumgartner, Leiden, 1958, p. 851) Thus, the *Encyclopaedia Judaica* (1973, Vol. 13, col. 156) states: "Sometimes two females lay eggs in the same nest, in which case one gains the upper hand and drives the other away; however her small body is unable to keep such a large number of eggs warm, so that eventually the embryos die. It was to this that the proverb [in Jeremiah 17:11] referred when speaking of one who robs another of his possessions without ultimately deriving any benefit."

Jeremiah 17:11 in the *King James Version* reads: "As the partridge sitteth on eggs, and hatcheth them not; so he that getteth riches, and not by right, shall leave them in the midst of his days, and at his end shall be a fool." In support of this alternative interpretation, John Sawyer reasons that "the point is the proverbial vulnerability of the partridge's nest, exposed as it is to marauding predators of many kinds, compared to the vulnerability of the fool who puts his trust in base gain." He goes on to say that the effectiveness of the proverb in Jeremiah 17:11 "does not depend on the treachery of the brooding partridge, but on its vulnerability, compared to the false sense of security of the fool who thinks he can get away with his criminal acquisitiveness . . . unaware of the dangers hanging over him and defenceless when disaster strikes."—*Vetus Testamentum*, Leiden, 1978, pp. 324, 328, 329.

PARUAH (Pa·ru′ah). Father of the Jehoshaphat who served as Solomon's food deputy in the territory of Issachar.—1Ki 4:7, 17.

PASACH (Pa′sach). Family head in the tribe of Asher; son of Japhlet.—1Ch 7:30, 33, 40.

PAS-DAMMIM (Pas-dam′mim). Evidently another name for Ephes-dammim, a place between Socoh and Azekah.—1Sa 17:1; 1Ch 11:13.

PASEAH (Pa·se′ah) [Lame].

1. A descendant of Judah in the line of "Chelub the brother of Shuhah."—1Ch 4:1, 11, 12.

2. Forefather of a family of Nethinim, some of whom returned from the Babylonian exile with Zerubbabel in 537 B.C.E.—Ezr 2:1, 2, 43, 49; Ne 7:51.

3. Father of the Joiada who helped repair the Gate of the Old City in the wall of Jerusalem (455 B.C.E.).—Ne 3:6.

PASHHUR (Pash′hur).

1. Father of the Gedaliah who was one of the princes of Judah responsible for having Jeremiah thrown into a cistern.—Jer 38:1, 4, 6.

2. A prince in the delegation King Zedekiah sent to inquire of Jeremiah concerning the future of Jerusalem. (Jer 21:1, 2) Pashhur also petitioned the king for Jeremiah to be put to death. (Jer 38:1, 4, 6) Pashhur is called in these two passages "the son of Malchijah." The family of priests returning from Babylonian exile contains a similar link in their genealogy, "Pashhur the son of Malchijah." (1Ch 9:12; Ne 11:12) If prince Pashhur was indeed a priest, he may be the one from whom "the sons of Pashhur" (No. 4) draw their name.

3. A priest, "the son [or descendant] of Immer, . . . the leading commissioner in the house of Jehovah." Pashhur, objecting to Jeremiah's prophecies, struck him and put him into the stocks and released him the following day. As a result Jehovah, through Jeremiah, foretold exile and death in Babylon for Pashhur and, accordingly, changed his name from Pashhur to "Fright all around" (Heb., *Ma·ghohr′ mis·sa·viv′*) (Jer 20:1-6), an expression occurring several times in the book of Jeremiah.—Jer 6:25; 20:3, 10; 46:5; 49:29.

4. "The sons of Pashhur" were a paternal house of priests, 1,247 of whom returned from the exile with priest Jeshua in 537 B.C.E. (Ezr 2:1, 2, 36, 38; Ne 7:41) Six of these married foreign wives but sent them away after Ezra arrived in 468 B.C.E.—Ezr 10:22, 44; see No. 2.

5. A priest or the forefather of one who, in the time of Governor Nehemiah, supported the cove-

nant not to take foreign wives.—Ne 9:38; 10:1, 3, 8.

PASSOVER.

Passover (Heb., *pe'sach;* Gr., *pa'-skha*) was instituted the evening preceding the Exodus from Egypt. The first Passover was observed about the time of full moon, on the 14th day of Abib (later called Nisan) in the year 1513 B.C.E. This was thereafter to be celebrated annually. (Ex 12:17-20, 24-27) Abib (Nisan) falls within the months March-April of the Gregorian calendar. Passover was followed by seven days of the Festival of Unfermented Cakes, Nisan 15-21. Passover commemorates the deliverance of the Israelites from Egypt and the 'passing over' of their firstborn when Jehovah destroyed the firstborn of Egypt. Seasonally, it fell at the beginning of the barley harvest.—Ex 12:14, 24-47; Le 23:10.

Passover was a memorial celebration; therefore the Scriptural command was: "And it must occur that when your sons say to you, 'What does this service mean to you?' then you must say, 'It is the sacrifice of the passover to Jehovah, who passed over the houses of the sons of Israel in Egypt when he plagued the Egyptians, but he delivered our houses.'"—Ex 12:26, 27.

Since the Jews reckoned the day as starting after sundown and ending the next day at sundown, Nisan 14 would begin after sundown. It would be in the evening after Nisan 13 concluded that the Passover would be observed. Since the Bible definitely states that Christ is the Passover sacrifice (1Co 5:7) and that he observed the Passover meal the evening before he was put to death, the date of his death would be Nisan 14, not Nisan 15, in order to fulfill accurately the time feature of the type, or shadow, provided in the Law.—Heb 10:1.

Laws Governing Its Observance. Each household was to choose a male sheep or goat that was sound and a year old. It was taken into the house on the 10th day of the month Abib and kept until the 14th, and then it was slaughtered and its blood was splashed with a bunch of hyssop on the doorposts and the upper part of the doorway of the dwelling in which they were to eat it (not on the threshold where the blood would be trampled on).

The lamb (or goat) was slaughtered, skinned, its interior parts cleansed and replaced, and it was roasted whole, well-done, with no bones broken. (2Ch 35:11; Nu 9:12) If the household was too small to consume the whole animal, then it was to be shared with a neighbor household and eaten that same night. Anything left over was to be burned before morning. (Ex 12:10; 34:25) It was eaten with unfermented cakes, "the bread of affliction," and with bitter greens, for their life had been bitter under slavery.—Ex 1:14; 12:1-11, 29, 34; De 16:3.

What is meant by the expression "between the two evenings"?

The Israelites measured their day from sundown to sundown. So Passover day would begin at sundown at the end of the 13th day of Abib (Nisan). The animal was to be slaughtered "between the two evenings." (Ex 12:6) There are differences of opinion as to the exact time meant. According to some scholars, as well as the Karaite Jews and Samaritans, this is the time between sunset and deep twilight. On the other hand, the Pharisees and the Rabbinists considered the first evening to be when the sun began to descend and the second evening to be the real sunset. Due to this latter view the rabbis hold that the lamb was slaughtered in the latter part of the 14th, not at its start, and therefore that the Passover meal was actually eaten on Nisan 15.

On this point Professors Keil and Delitzsch say: "Different opinions have prevailed among the Jews from a very early date as to the precise time intended. Aben Ezra agrees with the Caraites and Samaritans in taking the first evening to be the time when the sun sinks below the horizon, and the second the time of total darkness; in which case, 'between the two evenings' would be from 6 o'clock to 7.20. . . . According to the rabbinical idea, the time when the sun began to descend, viz. from 3 to 5 o'clock, was the first evening, and sunset the second; so that 'between the two evenings' was from 3 to 6 o'clock. Modern expositors have very properly decided in favour of the view held by Aben Ezra and the custom adopted by the Caraites and Samaritans."—*Commentary on the Old Testament,* 1973, Vol. I, The Second Book of Moses, p. 12; see DAY.

From the foregoing, and particularly in view of such texts as Exodus 12:17, 18, Leviticus 23:5-7, and Deuteronomy 16:6, 7, the weight of evidence points to the application of the expression "between the two evenings" to the time between sunset and dark. This would mean that the Passover meal was eaten well after sundown on Nisan 14, for it took considerable time to slaughter, skin, and roast the animal thoroughly. Deuteronomy 16:6 commands: "You should sacrifice the passover in the evening as soon as the sun sets." Jesus and his apostles observed the Passover meal "after evening had fallen." (Mr 14:17; Mt 26:20) Judas went out immediately after the Passover observance, "And it was night." (Joh 13:30) When Jesus observed the Passover with his 12 apostles, there must have been no little conversation; then, too, some time would have been occupied by Jesus in washing the apostles' feet. (Joh 13:2-5) Hence, the institution of the Lord's Evening Meal certainly took place quite late in the evening.—See LORD'S EVENING MEAL.

At the Passover in Egypt, the head of the family was responsible for the slaying of the lamb (or goat) at each home, and all were to stay inside the house to avoid being slain by the angel. The partakers ate in a standing position, their hips girded, staff in hand, sandals on so as to be ready for a long journey over rough ground (whereas they often did their daily work barefoot). At midnight all the firstborn of the Egyptians were slain, but the angel passed over the houses on which the blood had been spattered. (Ex 12:11, 23) Every Egyptian household in which there was a firstborn male was affected, from the house of Pharaoh himself to the firstborn of the prisoner. It was not the head of the house, even though he may have been a firstborn, but was any male firstborn in the household under the head, as well as the male firstborn of animals, that was slain.—Ex 12:29, 30; see FIRSTBORN, FIRSTLING.

The Ten Plagues upon Egypt all proved to be a judgment against the gods of Egypt, especially the tenth, the death of the firstborn. (Ex 12:12) For the ram (male sheep) was sacred to the god Ra, so that splashing the blood of the Passover lamb on the doorways would be blasphemy in the eyes of the Egyptians. Also, the bull was sacred, and the destruction of the firstborn of the bulls would be a blow to the god Osiris. Pharaoh himself was venerated as a son of Ra. The death of Pharaoh's own firstborn would thus show the impotence of both Ra and Pharaoh.

In the Wilderness and the Promised Land. Only one Passover celebration in the wilderness is mentioned. (Nu 9:1-14) The keeping of the Passover during the wilderness journey likely was limited, for two reasons: (1) Jehovah's original instructions were that it must be kept when they reached the Promised Land. (Ex 12:25; 13:5) (2) Those born in the wilderness had not been circumcised (Jos 5:5), whereas all male partakers of Passover had to be circumcised.—Ex 12:45-49.

Record of Passovers Observed. The Hebrew Scriptures give direct accounts of the Passover (1) in Egypt (Ex 12); (2) in the wilderness at Sinai, Nisan 14, 1512 B.C.E. (Nu 9); (3) when they reached the Promised Land, at Gilgal and after the circumcision of the males, 1473 B.C.E. (Jos 5); (4) at the time that Hezekiah restored true worship (2Ch 30); (5) the Passover of Josiah (2Ch 35); and (6) the celebration by Israel after the return from Babylonian exile (Ezr 6). (Also, mention is made of Passovers held in Samuel's day and during the days of the kings, at 2Ch 35:18.) After the Israelites were settled in the land, the Passover festival was observed "in the place that Jehovah will choose to have his name reside," instead of in each home or in the various cities. In time, the chosen place came to be Jerusalem.—De 16:1-8.

Accretions. After Israel had settled in the Promised Land, certain changes were made and various accretions came about in observing the Passover. They no longer partook of the feast in a standing position, or equipped for a journey, for they were then in the land that God had given them. The first-century celebrants customarily ate it while lying on their left side, with the head resting on the left hand. This explains how one of Jesus' disciples could be "reclining in front of Jesus' bosom." (Joh 13:23) Wine was not used at the Passover in Egypt nor was there any command given by Jehovah for its use with the festival. This practice was introduced later on. Jesus did not condemn the use of wine with the meal but he drank wine with his apostles and afterward offered a cup for them to drink as he introduced the Lord's Evening Meal, the Memorial.—Lu 22:15-18, 20.

According to traditional Jewish sources, red wine was used and four cups were handed around, although the service was not restricted to four cups. Psalms 113 to 118 were sung during the meal, concluding with Psalm 118. It is likely that it was one of these psalms that Jesus and his apostles sang in concluding the Lord's Evening Meal —Mt 26:30.

Customs at Passover Time. Great preparations were made in Jerusalem when the festival was due, as it was a requirement of the Law that every male Israelite and every male of the circumcised alien residents observe the Passover. (Nu 9:9-14) This meant that vast numbers would be making the journey to the city for some days in advance. They would come before the Passover in order to cleanse themselves ceremonially. (Joh 11:55) It is said that men were sent out about a month early to prepare the bridges and put the roads in good order for the convenience of the pilgrims. Since contact with a dead body rendered a person unclean, special precautions were taken to protect the traveler. As it was a practice to bury persons in the open field, if they died there, the graves were made conspicuous by being whitened a month ahead. (*The Temple,* by A. Edersheim, 1874, pp. 184, 185) This supplies background for Jesus' words to the scribes and Pharisees, that they resembled "whitewashed graves."—Mt 23:27.

Accommodations were made available in the homes for those coming to Jerusalem for Passover observance. In an Oriental home all the rooms could be slept in, and several persons could be accommodated in one room. Also, the flat roof of the house could be used. Added to this is the fact that numbers of the celebrants obtained accommodations outside the city walls, especially at Bethphage and Bethany, two villages on the slopes of the Mount of Olives.—Mr 11:1; 14:3.

Questions as to Time Order. It was a question of defilement that gave rise to the words: "They themselves did not enter into the governor's palace, that they might not get defiled but might eat the passover." (Joh 18:28) These Jews considered it a defilement to enter into a Gentile dwelling. (Ac 10:28) This statement was made, however, "early in the day," hence after the Passover meal had taken place. It is to be noted that at this time the entire period, including Passover day and the Festival of Unfermented Cakes that followed, was at times referred to as "Passover." In the light of this fact, Alfred Edersheim offers the following explanation: A voluntary peace offering was made on Passover and another, a compulsory one, on the next day, Nisan 15, the first day of the Festival of Unfermented Cakes. It was this second offering that the Jews were afraid they might not be able to eat if they contracted defilement in the judgment hall of Pilate.—*The Temple,* 1874, pp. 186, 187.

"The first day of the unfermented cakes." A question also arises in connection with the statement at Matthew 26:17: "On the first day of the unfermented cakes the disciples came up to Jesus, saying: 'Where do you want us to prepare for you to eat the passover?'"

The expression "the first day" here could be rendered "the day before." Concerning the use of the Greek word here translated "first," a footnote on Matthew 26:17 in the *New World Translation* says: "Or, 'On the day before.' This rendering of the Gr. word [*pro'tos*] followed by the genitive case of the next word agrees with the sense and rendering of a like construction in Joh 1:15, 30, namely, 'he existed before [*pro'tos*] me.'" According to Liddell and Scott's *Greek-English Lexicon,* [*pro'tos*] is sts. [sometimes] used where we should

expect [*pro'te·ros* (meaning 'former, earlier')]." (Revised by H. Jones, Oxford, 1968, p. 1535) At this time, Passover day had come to be generally considered as the first day of the Festival of Unfermented Cakes. So, then, the original Greek, harmonized with Jewish custom, allows for the question to have been asked of Jesus on the day before Passover.

"Preparation." At John 19:14, the apostle John, in the midst of his description of the final part of Jesus' trial before Pilate, says: "Now it was preparation of the passover; it was about the sixth hour [of the daytime, between 11:00 a.m. and noon]." This, of course, was after the time of the Passover meal, which had been eaten the night before. Similar expressions are found at verses 31 and 42. Here the Greek word *pa·ra·skeu·e'* is translated "preparation." This word seems to mark, not the day preceding Nisan 14, but the day preceding the weekly Sabbath, which, in this instance, was "a great one," namely, not only a Sabbath by virtue of being Nisan 15, the first day of the actual Festival of Unfermented Cakes, but also a weekly Sabbath. This is understandable, since, as already stated, "Passover" was sometimes used to refer to the entire festival.—Joh 19:31; see PREPARATION.

Prophetic Significance. The apostle Paul, in urging Christians to live clean lives, attributes pictorial significance to the Passover. He says: "For, indeed, Christ our passover has been sacrificed." (1Co 5:7) Here he likens Christ Jesus to the Passover lamb. John the Baptizer pointed to Jesus, saying: "See, the Lamb of God that takes away the sin of the world!" (Joh 1:29) John may have had in mind the Passover lamb, or he could have been thinking of the male sheep that Abraham offered up instead of his own son Isaac or of the male lamb that was offered up upon God's altar at Jerusalem each morning and evening.—Ge 22:13; Ex 29:38-42.

Certain features of the Passover observance were fulfilled by Jesus. One fulfillment lies in the fact that the blood on the houses in Egypt delivered the firstborn from destruction at the hands of the destroying angel. Paul speaks of anointed Christians as the congregation of the firstborn (Heb 12:23), and of Christ as their deliverer through his blood. (1Th 1:10; Eph 1:7) No bones were to be broken in the Passover lamb. It had been prophesied that none of Jesus' bones would be broken, and this was fulfilled at his death. (Ps 34:20; Joh 19:36) Thus the Passover kept by the Jews for centuries was one of those things in which the Law provided a shadow of the things to come and pointed to Jesus Christ, "the Lamb of God."—Heb 10:1; Joh 1:29.

PASTURE GROUNDS.

Agricultural land, especially that used for grazing animals, around each of the 48 Levite cities scattered in Israel. These lands were never to be sold, though houses in the cities could be sold and came under the Jubilee regulation.—Nu 35:2-5; Le 25:32-34; Jos 21:41, 42.

The area of the pasture grounds was to be "from the wall of the city and out for a thousand cubits [445 m; 1,458 ft] all around." But the next verse adds: "You must measure outside the city on the east side two thousand cubits" and so on in all four directions. (Nu 35:4, 5) Numerous suggestions have been offered to harmonize the two figures. Some have pointed out that the Greek *Septuagint* reads "two thousand" in the first instance instead of "a thousand." However, the Hebrew text as well as the Latin *Vulgate* and the Syriac *Peshitta* read "a thousand." Jewish commentators have offered the possibility that the first thousand cubits (Nu 35:4) were open and used for olive groves and stalls for animals, while the second measurement (Nu 35:5) was for actual grazing or pasture grounds as well as for fields and vineyards, making a total of 3,000 cubits on each side.

However, since this reads into the text thoughts that are not there expressed, another explanation seems more likely. Thus, some commentators believe the measurements to mean that the pastureland was determined by measuring out 1,000 cubits from each of the four sides of the city, east, west, north, and south. As to the 2,000 cubits on

each side, they believe the expression "outside the city" means that these 2,000 cubits were not measured from the city walls outward but were the measurements of each of the four sides of the pasture area as measured along its perimeter. If so, this would mean that the space occupied by "the city in the middle" was not counted in the 2,000 cubits measured. As shown in the diagram below, this would allow for harmonizing the two sets of measurements.

In Ezekiel's temple vision the sanctuary was to have 50 cubits "as pasture ground on each side." (Eze 45:2) The city "Jehovah Himself Is There" that the prophet saw in vision had pasture grounds of 250 cubits on each side. (Eze 48:16, 17, 35) Pasture grounds were mentioned in 1 Chronicles 5:16 in connection with "Sharon," which some believe to have been a region or town E of the Jordan. The Hebrew word translated "pasture ground" in the above instances also appears at Ezekiel 27:28, where it is used in connection with Tyre, the city situated first on the coast and then on an island. In this instance the word has been rendered "coast(s)" (*Mo, JB*), "countryside" (*RS*), "open country" (*NW*), and "rural districts" (*Le*), the prophecy thus perhaps indicating that those along the coast near Tyre would rejoice at her overthrow.

Flocks held an important place in the lives of many Israelites, requiring pasture grounds where sheep and goats could graze. (2Sa 7:8; 1Ch 4:39-41) Lack of pasturage for herds brought hardship. (Ge 47:3, 4) Whereas, abundant grazing land contributed to a time of plenty and peace. (Isa 30:23; Ps 65:12, 13; 23:2) By extension, abandoned pasture ground would indicate complete desolation (Isa 27:10), but restoration to peace and favor would be suggested by pasture grounds being used again. (Isa 65:10; Jer 23:3; 33:12; 50:19; Mic 2:12) As sheep were led by a loving shepherd to pasture grounds where they were safe and had an abundance, so God's people are guided and cared for by Jehovah.—Ps 79:13; 95:7; 100:3; Eze 34:31.

PATARA (Pat′a·ra). The Lycian seaport where the apostle Paul and his associates, likely in 56 C.E., transferred to a boat sailing for Phoenicia. (Ac 21:1, 2) Patara is today identified with ancient ruins at the village of Gelemish on the mountainous SW coast of Asia Minor and lies about 10 km (6 mi) E of the mouth of the Xanthus (Koca) River. It served as a port of call for ships from Italy, Egypt, Syria, and other places, and it was the primary harbor for cities along the Xanthus River valley.

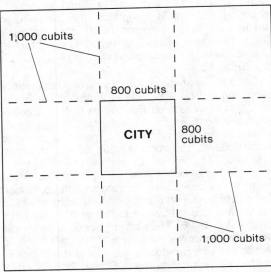

2,800 cubits – 800 cubits [size of city] = 2,000 cubits

At Acts 21:1 certain ancient manuscripts add "and Myra" after Patara. If this addition is correct, then the ship on which Paul sailed from Miletus either passed Patara or put into port there, with the actual transfer to another boat taking place at Myra, not Patara.

PATHROS (Path'ros). Pathros is regularly associated with Egypt (Heb., *Mits·ra'yim*). (Eze 30:13, 14) Most scholars connect the name Pathros with an Egyptian expression meaning "Land of the South" and evidently referring to Upper Egypt. Upper Egypt generally designates the region of the Nile Valley running from a point somewhat S of Memphis on up (south) to Syene (modern Aswan) at the first cataract of the Nile. The text at Isaiah 11:11, which foretells the return of Israelite exiles from 'Egypt (Mizraim), Pathros and Cush,' would seem to corroborate the placing of Pathros somewhere in Upper Egypt, with Cush (Ethiopia) bordering it on the S. An Assyrian inscription of King Esar-haddon gives a similar lineup, referring to "Egypt (*Musur*), Paturisi and Nubia [Kusu, or Cush]."—*Ancient Near Eastern Texts*, edited by J. Pritchard, 1974, p. 290.

Ezekiel 29:14 calls Pathros "the land of their [the Egyptians'] origin." The traditional Egyptian view, as recounted by Herodotus (II, 4, 15, 99), apparently corroborates this, as it makes Upper Egypt, and particularly the region of Thebes, the seat of the first Egyptian kingdom, under a king whom Herodotus calls Menes, a name not found in Egyptian records. Diodorus Siculus (first century B.C.E.) records a similar view. (*Diodorus of Sicily*, I, 45, 1) The Egyptian tradition set forth by these Greek historians may be a feeble echo of the true history presented in the Bible regarding Mizraim (whose name came to stand for Egypt) and his descendants, including Pathrusim.—Ge 10:13, 14.

Following the desolation of Judah by Nebuchadnezzar, a remnant of the Jews fled into Egypt. Among the places listed in which they dwelt are Migdol, Tahpanhes, Noph (all cities of Lower Egypt), and "the land of Pathros." (Jer 44:1) Here they engaged in idolatrous worship, resulting in Jehovah's condemnation of them and the warning of a coming conquest of Egypt by Nebuchadnezzar. (Jer 44:15, 26-30) Papyrus evidence of the fifth century B.C.E. shows a Jewish colony situated all the way at the southern end of ancient Egypt at Elephantine by Syene.

PATHRUSIM (Path·ru'sim) [Of (Belonging to) Pathros]. Listed fifth among the offspring of Mizraim the son of Ham. (Ge 10:6, 13, 14; 1Ch 1:11, 12) The name is apparently the plural form of Pathros. (Eze 29:14) This would indicate that the tribe of Pathrusim settled or became predominant in Upper Egypt.

PATIENCE. See LONG-SUFFERING.

PATMOS (Pat'mos). An island where the apostle John was exiled "for speaking about God and bearing witness to Jesus." (Re 1:9) While there, he received the Revelation. According to ancient tradition, John, having been condemned by Domitian to dwell on the island of Patmos, was released after the death of that ruler (96 C.E.).—*The Ante-Nicene Fathers*, Vol. VIII, p. 562, "Acts of the Holy Apostle and Evangelist John the Theologian."

Situated in the Icarian Sea (a part of the Aegean) about 55 km (34 mi) W of Asia Minor, Patmos lay about 60 km (37 mi) WSW of Miletus and less than 240 km (150 mi) from all seven congregations specifically addressed in Revelation chapters 2 and 3. This small volcanic island has a very irregular coastline and is quite barren and rocky. But today wheat, olives, and grapes are cultivated there. Apparently because of its isolation, Patmos, along with other Aegean islands, served as a penal isle.

PATROBAS (Pat'ro·bas). A Christian of the congregation in Rome whom Paul greets in his letter.—Ro 16:14.

PAU (Pa'u). A place in Edom, where a certain King Hadar (Hadad) evidently had his royal residence. (Ge 36:31, 39; 1Ch 1:43, 50) The location of Pau is now unknown.

PAUL [Little; Small]. An Israelite of the tribe of Benjamin and an apostle of Jesus Christ. (Eph 1:1; Php 3:5) Though perhaps having both the Hebrew name Saul and the Roman name Paul from childhood (Ac 9:17; 2Pe 3:15), this apostle may have chosen to go by his Roman name in view of his commission to declare the good news to the non-Jews.—Ac 9:15; Ga 2:7, 8.

Paul was born in Tarsus, a prominent city of Cilicia. (Ac 21:39; 22:3) His parents were Hebrews and evidently adhered to the Pharisaic branch of Judaism. (Ac 23:6; Php 3:5) He was a Roman citizen from birth (Ac 22:28), his father having perhaps been granted citizenship for services rendered. Paul probably learned the trade of tentmaker from his father. (Ac 18:3) But, at Jerusalem, he received instruction from the learned Pharisee Gamaliel, suggesting that Paul was from a prominent family. (Ac 22:3; 5:34) Languagewise, Paul was versed at least in Greek and Hebrew. (Ac 21:37-40) At the time that Paul traveled as a missionary, he was unmarried. (1Co 7:8) During this general period, if not already earlier, he had a sister and a nephew who resided in Jerusalem.—Ac 23:16-22.

It was the apostle Paul's privilege to write more books, or letters, of the Christian Greek Scriptures than anyone else. He was given supernatural visions (2Co 12:1-5) and, by means of the holy spirit, was enabled to speak numerous foreign tongues.—1Co 14:18.

Persecution, Conversion, Early Ministry.
The Biblical record introduces Saul, or Paul, as the "young man" at whose feet the false witnesses who stoned Christ's disciple Stephen laid their outer garments. (Ac 6:13; 7:58) Paul approved of the murder of Stephen and, because of misdirected zeal for tradition, began a campaign of vicious persecution against Christ's followers. When they were to be executed, he voted against them. At the time of their trial in synagogues, he endeavored to force them to recant. He extended his persecution to cities other than Jerusalem and even procured written authorization from the high priest to search out disciples of Christ as far N as Damascus, in Syria, and to bind them and bring them to Jerusalem, probably for trial by the Sanhedrin.—Ac 8:1, 3; 9:1, 2; 26:10, 11; Ga 1:13, 14.

As Paul neared Damascus, Christ Jesus revealed himself to Paul in a flashing light and commissioned him to be an attendant and a witness of the things he had seen and would yet see. Whereas those with Paul also fell to the ground because of this manifestation and heard the sound of someone speaking, Paul alone understood the words and was blinded, necessitating his being led by the hand to Damascus. (Ac 9:3-8; 22:6-11; 26: 12-18) For three days he neither ate nor drank. Then, while praying in the house of a certain Judas at Damascus, Paul, in vision, saw Christ's disciple Ananias come in and restore his sight. When the vision became reality, Paul was baptized, received holy spirit, partook of food, and gained strength.—Ac 9:9-19.

The record at Acts 9:20-25 describes Paul's spending time with the disciples in Damascus and "immediately" beginning to preach in the synagogues there. It describes his preaching activity up until the time he was forced to leave Damascus because of a plot against his life. On the other hand, Paul's letter to the Galatians speaks of his going off into Arabia after his conversion and then of his returning to Damascus. (Ga 1:15-17) It is not possible to assign the trip into Arabia a definite place in the order of these events.

Paul may have gone into Arabia right after his conversion in order to meditate on God's will for him. In such a case, Luke's use of the word "immediately" would mean that immediately upon his return to Damascus and upon associating with the disciples there, Paul began his preaching. However, at Galatians 1:17 Paul is evidently emphasizing the fact that he did not immediately go up to Jerusalem; that the *only place outside of Damascus* to which he went during that early period was Arabia. So, the trip to Arabia does not necessarily have to have come immediately after his conversion. It may be that Paul first spent some days in Damascus and quickly made public renunciation of his previous course of opposition by expressing his faith in Christ in the synagogues. Thereafter he may have made his trip into Arabia (the actual purpose of which is undisclosed) and upon his return continued his preaching in Damascus, becoming stronger in it to the point that his opposers sought to put him to death. The two accounts are complementary rather than contradictory, and the only question is as to the precise order of events, which simply is not provided.

Arriving at Jerusalem (perhaps in 36 C.E.; the three years mentioned at Galatians 1:18 possibly meaning parts of three years), Paul found that the brothers there did not believe that he was a disciple. However, "Barnabas came to his aid and led him to the apostles," evidently Peter and "James the brother of the Lord." (James, though not one of the 12, could be designated as an apostle because of being such for the Jerusalem congregation.) For 15 days Paul stayed with Cephas (Peter). While at Jerusalem, Paul spoke boldly in the name of Jesus. When the brothers learned that the Greek-speaking Jews were therefore making attempts to kill Paul, "they brought him down to Caesarea and sent him off to Tarsus."—Ac 9:26-30; Ga 1:18-21.

It appears that Paul (about 41 C.E.) was privileged to experience a supernatural vision so real that he did not know whether it was in the body or out of the body that he was caught away to "the third heaven." "The *third* heaven" seems to refer to the superlative degree of the rapture in which he saw the vision.—2Co 12:1-4.

Later, Barnabas brought Saul from Tarsus to assist in the work at Antioch among the Greek-speaking people there. About 46 C.E., after a year's labor at Antioch, Paul and Barnabas were sent by the congregation to Jerusalem with a relief ministration for the brothers there. (Ac 11:22-30) Accompanied by John Mark, they returned to Antioch. (Ac 12:25) Thereafter the holy spirit directed that Paul and Barnabas be set aside for special work.—Ac 13:1, 2.

First Missionary Journey. (MAP, Vol. 2, p. 747) Following the spirit's direction, Paul, in company with Barnabas and with John Mark as their attendant, began his first missionary journey (c. 47-48 C.E.). Embarking from Seleucia, the seaport of Antioch, they sailed to Cyprus. In the synagogues at Salamis, on the E coast of Cyprus, they commenced "publishing the word of God." Traversing the island, they arrived at Paphos on the W coast. There the sorcerer Elymas tried to oppose the witness being given to proconsul Sergius Paulus. Paul then caused Elymas to be struck with temporary blindness. Astounded by what had happened, Sergius Paulus became a believer. —Ac 13:4-12.

From Paphos, Paul and his associates sailed for Asia Minor. On their arrival at Perga in the Roman province of Pamphylia, John Mark left them and returned to Jerusalem. But Paul and Barnabas headed northward to Antioch in Pisidia. Although finding great interest there, they were finally thrown out of the city at the instigation of the Jews. (Ac 13:13-50) Undaunted, they traveled southeastward to Iconium, where the Jews also incited the crowds against them. Learning of an attempt to stone them, Paul and Barnabas fled to Lystra in the region of Lycaonia. After Paul healed a man lame from birth, the populace of Lystra imagined that Paul and Barnabas were incarnate gods. But, later, Jews from Iconium and Pisidian Antioch turned the crowds against Paul so that they stoned him and dragged his body outside the city, believing him to be dead. However, when surrounded by fellow Christians, Paul got up and entered Lystra. The next day he and Barnabas left for Derbe. After making numerous disciples there, they returned to Lystra, Iconium, and Antioch (in Pisidia), strengthening and encouraging the brothers and appointing elders to serve in the congregations established in these places. Later, they preached in Perga and then sailed from the seaport of Attalia for Syrian Antioch.—Ac 13: 51–14:28.

Circumcision Issue. Certain men from Judea came to Antioch (in about 49 C.E.), claiming that non-Jews had to be circumcised in compliance with the Mosaic Law in order to gain salvation. Paul and Barnabas disputed this. Yet Paul, though an apostle, did not take it upon himself to settle the matter on his own authority. Instead, accompanied by Barnabas, Titus, and others, he went to Jerusalem to set the issue before the apostles and older men of the congregation there. The decision then made was that circumcision was not required for Gentile believers but that they should keep free from idolatry, from eating and drinking of blood, and from sexual immorality. Besides providing a letter setting forth this decision, the brothers of the Jerusalem congregation sent Judas and Silas as their representatives to clarify the matter at Antioch. Also, in a discussion with Peter (Cephas), John, and the disciple James, it was agreed that Paul and Barnabas should continue preaching to uncircumcised Gentiles.—Ac 15:1-29; Ga 2:1-10.

Sometime after this, Peter personally came to Syrian Antioch and associated with Gentile Christians. But, when certain Jews from Jerusalem arrived, he, evidently giving way to the fear of men, withdrew from the non-Jews, thereby acting contrary to the spirit's direction that fleshly distinctions did not count with God. Even Barnabas was led astray. Noting this, Paul courageously censured Peter publicly, as his conduct was detrimental to the progress of Christianity.—Ga 2:11-14.

Second Missionary Journey. (MAP, Vol. 2, p. 747) Later, Paul and Barnabas thought about visiting the brothers in the cities where they had preached during their first missionary journey. A dispute about whether to take along John Mark, in view of his having left them the first time, resulted in a split between Paul and Barnabas. Paul therefore chose Silas (Silvanus) and traveled through Syria and into Asia Minor (c. 49-52 C.E.). Evidently at Lystra, Paul arranged for the young man Timothy to accompany him and he also circumcised him. (Ac 15:36–16:3) Though circumcision was not a Christian requirement, had the half Jew Timothy remained in an uncircumcised state, doubtless this would have prejudiced the Jews against Paul's preaching. Therefore, in removing this possible obstacle, Paul acted in agreement with what he later wrote to the Corinthians: "To the Jews I became as a Jew."—1Co 9:20.

One night at Troas on the Aegean Sea, Paul had a vision of a Macedonian man, entreating him: "Step over into Macedonia and help us." Concluding this to be God's will, Paul and his missionary companions, joined by Luke the physician, sailed for Macedonia, in Europe. At Philippi, the chief Macedonian city, Lydia and her household became believers. Paul's causing a girl to lose her powers of prediction by expelling a demon from her led to his being jailed along with Silas. But an earthquake freed them, and the jailer and his household became Christians. At Paul's insistence, on the basis of his Roman citizenship, the civil magistrates came personally to bring the apostle and Silas out of prison. After encouraging the brothers, Paul and his companions traveled through Amphipolis and Apollonia to Thessalonica. A congregation of believers developed there. Jealous

Jews, however, instigated a riot against Paul. For this reason the brothers sent him and Silas to Beroea. Many became believers there also, but trouble caused by Jews from Thessalonica obliged Paul to leave.—Ac 16:8–17:14.

The brothers conducted the apostle to Athens. His preaching in the marketplace there led to his being taken to the Areopagus. His defense moved Dionysius, one of the judges of the court that convened there, and others to embrace Christianity. (Ac 17:15-34) Next Paul went to Corinth, taking up lodging with a Jewish couple, Aquila and Priscilla, and working with them part-time as a tentmaker. From Corinth, Paul apparently wrote his two letters to the Thessalonians. After teaching in Corinth for a year and a half and establishing a congregation, he was accused by the Jews before Gallio. But Gallio dismissed the case. (Ac 18:1-17) Later Paul sailed for Caesarea, first stopping at Ephesus and preaching there. From Caesarea the apostle "went up and greeted the congregation," undoubtedly referring to the congregation at Jerusalem, and then went to Syrian Antioch. (Ac 18:18-22) Possibly earlier from Corinth or perhaps now from Syrian Antioch he wrote his letter to the Galatians.

Third Missionary Journey. (MAP, Vol. 2, p. 747) On his third missionary journey (c. 52-56 C.E.), Paul revisited Ephesus and labored there for some three years. From Ephesus he wrote his first letter to the Corinthians and, it appears, dispatched Titus to assist the Christians there. Following a riot instigated against him by the silversmith Demetrius, Paul left Ephesus and headed for Macedonia. Receiving news from Corinth through Titus, Paul, in Macedonia, composed his second letter to the Corinthians. Before leaving Europe with a contribution from the brothers in Macedonia and Achaia for the needy Christians in Jerusalem, and most probably when he was in Corinth, Paul wrote his letter to the Romans.—Ac 19:1-20:4; Ro 15:25, 26; 2Co 2:12, 13; 7:5-7.

On his way to Jerusalem, Paul discoursed at Troas and raised the accidentally killed Eutychus to life. He also stopped at Miletus, where he met with the overseers of the Ephesus congregation, reviewed his own ministry in the district of Asia, and encouraged them to imitate his example.—Ac 20:6-38.

Arrest. As Paul continued his journey, Christian prophets along the way foretold that bonds awaited him at Jerusalem. (Ac 21:4-14; compare 20:22, 23.) Their prophecies were fulfilled. While Paul was at the temple to cleanse himself ceremonially, Jews from Asia stirred up mob violence

against him, but Roman soldiers rescued the apostle. (Ac 21:26-33) On his way up the stairs to the soldiers' quarters, Paul got permission to address the Jews. As soon as he mentioned his commission to preach to the Gentiles, violence erupted anew. (Ac 21:34–22:22) Inside the soldiers' quarters, Paul was stretched out for whipping in an effort to ascertain the nature of his guilt. The apostle prevented this by calling attention to his Roman citizenship. The next day Paul's case came before the Sanhedrin. Apparently realizing that he would not get a fair hearing, Paul endeavored to create division between the Pharisees and Sadducees by making the resurrection an issue in his case. As he believed in the resurrection and was "a son of Pharisees," Paul identified himself as a Pharisee and thus succeeded in setting the Sadducees, who did not believe in the resurrection, against the Pharisees and vice versa.—Ac 22:23–23:10.

A plot against the prisoner Paul made it necessary to transfer him from Jerusalem to Caesarea. Some days later High Priest Ananias, some of the older men of the Jews, and the orator Tertullus came to Caesarea to present their case against Paul before Governor Felix, accusing Paul of stirring up sedition and trying to profane the temple. The apostle showed that there was no evidence to support their charges against him. But Felix, hoping for a bribe, kept Paul in custody for two years. When Felix was replaced by Festus, the Jews renewed their charges. The case was heard again at Caesarea, and Paul, to prevent a transfer of the trial to Jerusalem, appealed to Caesar. Later, after stating his case before King Herod Agrippa II, Paul and some other prisoners were sent to Rome in about 58 C.E.—Ac 23:12–27:1.

First and Second Imprisonments at Rome. On the way, Paul and those with him experienced shipwreck on the island of Malta. After wintering there, they finally arrived at Rome. (MAP, Vol. 2, p. 750) Paul was permitted to stay in his own hired house, though under soldier guard. Shortly after his arrival, Paul arranged a meeting with the principal men of the Jews. But only some believed. The apostle continued to preach to all those who came to him for two years, from about 59 to 61 C.E. (Ac 27:2-28:31) During this time he also wrote his letters to the Ephesians (4:1; 6:20), Philippians (1:7, 12-14), Colossians (4:18), to Philemon (vs 9), and evidently also to the Hebrews. (PICTURE, Vol. 2, p. 750) It appears that Caesar Nero pronounced Paul innocent and released him. Evidently Paul renewed his missionary activity, in association with Timothy and Titus. After having left Timothy at Ephesus and Titus on Crete, Paul probably from Macedonia, wrote letters to them relative to their duties. (1Ti 1:3; Tit 1:5) Whether the apostle extended his activity to Spain before his final imprisonment at Rome is not known. (Ro 15:24) During that imprisonment (c. 65 C.E.) Paul wrote his second letter to Timothy, wherein he implied that his death was imminent. (2Ti 4:6-8) Likely Paul suffered martyrdom at the hands of Nero shortly thereafter.

An Example Worthy of Imitation. In view of his faithfulness in copying Christ's example, the apostle Paul could say: "Become imitators of me." (1Co 4:16; 11:1; Php 3:17) Paul was alert to follow the leading of God's spirit. (Ac 13:2-5; 16:9, 10) He was no peddler of God's Word, but spoke out of sincerity. (2Co 2:17) Though educated, Paul did not try to impress others with his speech (1Co 2:1-5) nor did he seek to please men. (Ga 1:10) He did not insist on doing what he had the right to do, but adapted himself to the people to whom he preached, exercising care so as not to stumble others.—1Co 9:19-26; 2Co 6:3.

During the course of his ministry, Paul exerted himself zealously, traveling thousands of miles on sea and land, establishing many congregations in Europe and Asia Minor. So he did not need letters of recommendation written with ink but could point to living letters, persons who had become believers through his efforts. (2Co 3:1-3) Yet he humbly acknowledged that he was a slave (Php 1:1), obligated to declare the good news. (1Co 9:16) He did not take any credit to himself, but gave all honor to God as the One responsible for growth (1Co 3:5-9) and the One who had adequately qualified him for the ministry. (2Co 3:5, 6) The apostle highly valued his ministry, glorifying it and recognizing its possession to be an expression of God's mercy and that of his Son. (Ro 11:13; 2Co 4:1; 1Ti 1:12, 13) To Timothy he wrote: "The reason why I was shown mercy was that by means of me as the foremost case Christ Jesus might demonstrate all his long-suffering for a sample of those who are going to rest their faith on him for everlasting life."—1Ti 1:16.

Because of having been a former persecutor of Christians, Paul did not consider himself fit to be called an apostle and acknowledged that he was such only by God's undeserved kindness. Concerned that this undeserved kindness might not have been extended to him in vain, Paul labored in excess of the other apostles. Yet he realized that only by God's undeserved kindness was he able to carry on his ministry. (1Co 15:9, 10) "For all things," said Paul, "I have the strength by virtue of him who imparts power to me." (Php 4:13) He

endured much but did not complain. When comparing his experiences with those of others, he wrote (c. 55 C.E.): "In labors more plentifully, in prisons more plentifully, in blows to an excess, in near-deaths often. By Jews I five times received forty strokes less one, three times I was beaten with rods, once I was stoned, three times I experienced shipwreck, a night and a day I have spent in the deep; in journeys often, in dangers from rivers, in dangers from highwaymen, in dangers from my own race, in dangers from the nations, in dangers in the city, in dangers in the wilderness, in dangers at sea, in dangers among false brothers, in labor and toil, in sleepless nights often, in hunger and thirst, in abstinence from food many times, in cold and nakedness. Besides those things of an external kind, there is what rushes in on me from day to day, the anxiety for all the congregations." (2Co 11:23-28; 6:4-10; 7:5) Besides all of this and more in subsequent years, Paul had to contend with "a thorn in the flesh" (2Co 12:7), possibly an affliction of his eyes or of another sort. —Compare Ac 23:1-5; Ga 4:15; 6:11.

Being imperfect, Paul experienced a continual conflict between his mind and the sinful flesh. (Ro 7:21-24) But he did not give up. He said: "I pummel my body and lead it as a slave, that, after I have preached to others, I myself should not become disapproved somehow." (1Co 9:27) Paul always kept the glorious prize of immortal life in the heavens before him. He viewed all the suffering as nothing in comparison with the glory to be received as a reward for faithfulness. (Ro 8:18; Php 3:6-14) Therefore, evidently not long before his death, Paul could write: "I have fought the fine fight, I have run the course to the finish, I have observed the faith. From this time on there is reserved for me the crown of righteousness."—2Ti 4:7, 8.

As an inspired apostle, Paul had authority to command and give orders, and did so (1Co 14:37; 16:1; Col 4:10; 1Th 4:2, 11; compare 1Ti 4:11), but he preferred to appeal to the brothers on the basis of love, entreating them by "the compassions of God" and by "the mildness and kindness of the Christ." (Ro 12:1; 2Co 6:11-13; 8:8; 10:1; Phm 8, 9) He was gentle and expressed tender affection for them, exhorting and consoling them like a father. (1Th 2:7, 8, 11, 12) While he was entitled to receive material support from the brothers, he chose to work with his hands in order not to be an expensive burden. (Ac 20:33-35; 1Co 9:18; 1Th 2:6, 9) As a result, a close bond of brotherly affection existed between Paul and those to whom he ministered. The overseers of the Ephesus congregation were greatly pained and were moved to tears upon learning that they might see his face no more. (Ac 20:37, 38) Paul was very much concerned about the spiritual welfare of fellow Christians and wanted to do what he could to assist them to make their heavenly calling sure. (Ro 1:11; 15:15, 16; Col 2:1, 2) Constantly he remembered them in his prayers (Ro 1:8, 9; 2Co 13:7; Eph 3:14-19; Php 1:3-5, 9-11; Col 1:3, 9-12; 1Th 1:2, 3; 2Th 1:3) and requested that they also pray for him. (Ro 15:30-32; 2Co 1:11) He drew encouragement from the faith of fellow Christians. (Ro 1:12) On the other hand, Paul was firm for what is right, not hesitating to correct even a fellow apostle when that was necessary for the advancement of the good news.—1Co 5:1-13; Ga 2:11-14.

Was Paul one of the 12 apostles?

Though having strong conviction and proofs as to his own apostleship, Paul never included himself among "the twelve." Prior to Pentecost, as a result of Peter's Scriptural exhortation, the Christian assembly had sought a replacement for unfaithful Judas Iscariot. Two disciples were selected as candidates, perhaps by vote of the male members of the assembly (Peter having addressed himself to the "Men, brothers"; Ac 1:16). Then they prayed to Jehovah God (compare Ac 1:24 with 1Sa 16:7; Ac 15:7, 8) that *He* should designate which of the two he had chosen to replace the unfaithful apostle. Following their prayer, they cast lots and "the lot fell upon Matthias."—Ac 1:15-26; compare Pr 16:33.

There is no reason to doubt that Matthias was God's own choice. True, once converted, Paul became very prominent and his labors exceeded those of all the other apostles. (1Co 15:9, 10) Yet there is nothing to show that Paul was personally predestinated to an apostleship so that God, in effect, refrained from acting on the prayer of the Christian assembly, held open the place vacated by Judas until Paul's conversion, and thus made the appointment of Matthias merely an arbitrary action of the Christian assembly. On the contrary, there is sound evidence that Matthias was a divinely appointed replacement.

At Pentecost the outpouring of holy spirit gave the apostles unique powers; they are the only ones shown to have been able to lay hands on newly baptized ones and communicate to them miraculous gifts of the spirit. (See APOSTLE [Miraculous powers].) If Matthias were not in reality God's choice, his inability to do this would have been apparent to all. The record shows this was not the case. Luke, the writer of Acts, was Paul's traveling companion and associate during certain missions, and the book of Acts therefore undoubtedly reflects and coincides with Paul's own view of matters. That book refers to "the twelve" as appointing the seven men who were to handle the matter of the food distribution problem. This was after Pentecost of 33 C.E. but before Paul's conversion. Hence Matthias is here acknowledged as one of "the twelve," and he shared with the other apostles in laying hands on the seven designates. —Ac 6:1-6.

Whose name then appears among those on the "twelve foundation stones" of the New Jerusalem of John's vision—Matthias' or Paul's? (Re 21:2, 14) One line of reasoning would make it appear that Paul is the more likely one. He contributed so much to the Christian congregation by his ministry and particularly by his writing a large portion of the Christian Greek Scriptures (14 letters being attributed to him). In these respects Paul 'outshone' Matthias, who receives no further direct mention after Acts chapter 1.

But sober consideration makes evident that Paul also 'outshone' many of the original 12 apostles, some of whom are rarely even named outside the apostolic lists. By the time that Paul was converted, the Christian congregation, spiritual Israel, had been established, or founded, and had been growing for perhaps a year or even more. Then, too, Paul's first canonical letter was evidently not written until about 50 C.E. (see THESSALONIANS, LETTERS TO THE) or as much as 17 years after the foundation of the new nation of spiritual Israel on Pentecost of 33 C.E. These facts, plus the evidence submitted earlier in this article, thus clarify the matter. It seems reasonable, therefore, that God's original choice, namely, Matthias, as the one to replace Judas among "the twelve apostles of the Lamb," remained firm and unaffected by the later apostleship of Paul.

What, then, was the purpose of Paul's apostleship? Jesus himself stated that it was for a particular purpose—not as a replacement for Judas —but that Paul might serve as an 'apostle [sent one] to the nations' (Ac 9:4-6, 15), and Paul recognized this as the purpose of his apostleship. (Ga 1:15, 16; 2:7, 8; Ro 1:5; 1Ti 2:7) This being so, his apostleship was not needed to serve as a foundation when spiritual Israel was established on Pentecost, 33 C.E.

PAULUS (Pau′lus) [from Lat., meaning "Little; Small"]. The proconsul of Cyprus when Paul visited there on his first missionary journey, about 47 C.E. Luke is correct in calling him proconsul, since the administration of Cyprus was at that time under the Roman Senate rather than the emperor. (Ac 13:7, 12) Cyprus was formerly an imperial province, but in 22 B.C.E. was placed under control of the Senate by Augustus.—See Proconsul.

At Soli, on the N coast of the island of Cyprus, an inscription was found which includes the words "in the proconsulship of Paulus." The name Lucius Sergius Paullus was found in the Roman world as that of a curator of the Tiber under Claudius Caesar. However, any identification of these persons with the Sergius Paulus mentioned in the Bible is uncertain.—*The Annual of the British School at Athens,* London, 1947, pp. 201-206.

Sergius Paulus resided in Paphos, on the western coast of the island. He was "an intelligent man," and earnestly seeking to hear the word of God, he summoned Barnabas and Paul. As they spoke to the man, Elymas (Bar-Jesus), a Jewish sorcerer, "began opposing them, seeking to turn the proconsul away from the faith." But Paul, filled with holy spirit, told this sorcerer who opposed the good news that he would be struck with temporary blindness. He was. On observing this powerful work of God's spirit, the proconsul became a believer, "as he was astounded at the teaching of Jehovah."—Ac 13:6-12.

PE' [פ; final, ף].

The 17th letter of the Hebrew alphabet. It is one of the five Hebrew letters that have a different form when used as the final letter of a word. The name assigned to the letter means "mouth."

The Hebrew sound corresponds to the English "p," when it has the point (daghesh lene) in it; but without this point it is pronounced like "ph," as in "philosophy." This letter initiates each of the eight verses in the Hebrew text of Psalm 119:129-136. —See Hebrew, II.

PEACE.

Sha·lohm', the Hebrew word rendered "peace," refers to the state of being free from war or disturbance (Jg 4:17; 1Sa 7:14; 1Ki 4:24; 2Ch 15:5; Job 21:9; Ec 3:8); it can convey the idea of health, safety, soundness (Ge 37:14, ftn), welfare (Ge 41:16), friendship (Ps 41:9), and entirety or completeness (Jer 13:19). The Greek word for peace (ei·re'ne) has taken on the same broad connotations as the Hebrew word sha·lohm' and may express the ideas of well-being, salvation, and concord, in addition to the absence of conflict. It occurs in the farewell exclamation "go in peace," which somewhat corresponds to the expression 'may it go well with you.'—Mr 5:34; Lu 7:50; 8:48; Jas 2:16; compare 1Sa 1:17; 20:42; 25:35; 29:7; 2Sa 15:9; 2Ki 5:19.

Since "peace" is not always the exact equivalent for the original-language words, the context must be taken into consideration to determine what is meant. For example, to be 'sent away in peace' could signify being sent away amicably, with no fear of interference from the one granting permission to leave. (Ge 26:29; 44:17; Ex 4:18) To 'return in peace,' as from battle, meant returning unharmed or victoriously. (Ge 28:21; Jos 10:21; Jg 8:9; 11:31; 2Ch 18:26, 27; 19:1) 'Asking concerning the peace' of a person meant inquiring as to how he was getting along. (Ge 29:6, ftn; 43:27, ftn) 'Working for the peace' of someone denoted working for that one's welfare. (De 23:6) For a person to die in peace could mean his dying a tranquil death after having enjoyed a full life or the realization of a cherished hope. (Compare Ge 15:15; Lu 2:29; 1Ki 2:6.) The prophecy concerning Josiah's 'being gathered to his own graveyard in peace' indicated that he would die before the foretold calamity upon Jerusalem. (2Ki 22:20; 2Ch 34:28; compare 2Ki 20:19.) At Isaiah 57:1, 2 the righteous one is depicted as entering into peace at death, thereby escaping calamity.

Acquiring Peace. Jehovah is the God of peace (1Co 14:33; 2Co 13:11; 1Th 5:23; Heb 13:20) and the Source of peace (Nu 6:26; 1Ch 22:9; Ps 4:8; 29:11; 147:14; Isa 45:7; Ro 15:33; 16:20), it being a fruit of his spirit. (Ga 5:22) For this reason true peace can be had only by those who are at peace with God. Serious transgressions put a strain on a person's relationship with God and cause the individual to be disturbed. The psalmist said: "There is no peace in my bones on account of my sin." (Ps 38:3) Those who desire to seek and pursue peace must therefore "turn away from what is bad, and do what is good." (Ps 34:14) Without righteousness, there can be no peace. (Ps 72:3; 85:10; Isa 32:17) That is why the wicked cannot have peace. (Isa 48:22; 57:21; compare Isa 59:2-8.) On the other hand, peace is the possession of those who are fully devoted to Jehovah, love his law (Ps 119:165), and heed his commandments.—Isa 48:18.

When Christ Jesus was on earth, neither the natural Jews nor the non-Jews were at peace with Jehovah God. Having transgressed God's law, the Jews had come under the curse of the Law. (Ga 3:12, 13) As for the non-Jews outside God's covenant, they "had no hope and were without God in the world." (Eph 2:12) However, by means of Christ Jesus both peoples were given the opportunity to come into a peaceful relationship with God. Pointing forward to this was the angelic announcement made to shepherds at Jesus' birth:

"Upon earth peace among men of goodwill."—Lu 2:14.

The peaceful message proclaimed by Jesus and his followers appealed to 'friends of peace,' that is, to persons desiring to be reconciled to God. (Mt 10:13; Lu 10:5, 6; Ac 10:36) At the same time this message caused divisions in households, as some accepted it while others rejected it. (Mt 10:34; Lu 12:51) The majority of the Jews rejected the message and thus failed to discern "the things having to do with peace," evidently including repentance and acceptance of Jesus as the Messiah. (Compare Lu 1:79; 3:3-6; Joh 1:29-34.) Their failure resulted in the destruction of Jerusalem by the Roman armies in 70 C.E.—Lu 19:42-44.

However, even the Jews who did accept "the good news of peace" were sinners and needed to have their transgressions atoned for so as to enjoy peace with Jehovah God. Jesus' death as a ransom sacrifice cared for this need. As had been foretold: "The chastisement meant for our peace was upon him, and because of his wounds there has been a healing for us." (Isa 53:5) Jesus' sacrificial death on the torture stake also provided the basis for canceling the Mosaic Law, which divided the Jews from the non-Jews. Therefore, upon becoming Christians, both peoples could be at peace with God and with one another. The apostle Paul wrote: "[Jesus] is our peace, he who made the two parties one and destroyed the wall in between that fenced them off. By means of his flesh he abolished the enmity, the Law of commandments consisting in decrees, that he might create the two peoples in union with himself into one new man and make peace; and that he might fully reconcile both peoples in one body to God through the torture stake, because he had killed off the enmity by means of himself. And he came and declared the good news of peace to you, the ones far off, and peace to those near, because through him we, both peoples, have the approach to the Father by one spirit."—Eph 2:14-18; compare Ro 2:10, 11; Col 1:20-23.

"The peace of God," that is the calmness and tranquillity that result from a Christian's precious relationship with Jehovah God, guards his heart and mental powers from becoming anxious about his needs. He has the assurance that Jehovah God provides for his servants and answers their prayers. This puts his heart and mind at rest. (Php 4:6, 7) Similarly, the peace that Jesus Christ gave to his disciples, based on their faith in him as God's Son, served to calm their hearts and minds. Although Jesus told them that the time was coming when he would no longer be with them personally, they had no reason to be concerned or to give way to fear. He was not leaving them without help but promised to send them the holy spirit. —Joh 14:26, 27; 16:33; compare Col 3:15.

The peace that Christians enjoyed was not to be taken for granted. They were to be "peaceable"; that is, they were to be peacemakers, going out of their way to establish and to maintain peace. (1Th 5:13) To preserve peace among themselves, they had to exercise care so as not to stumble fellow believers. (Ro 14:13-23) In the Sermon on the Mount, Jesus stated: "Happy are the peaceable [literally, peacemakers], since they will be called 'sons of God.'" (Mt 5:9, ftn; compare Jas 3:18.) Christians were counseled to pursue peace and to do their utmost to be found at peace with God. (2Ti 2:22; Heb 12:14; 1Pe 3:11; 2Pe 3:14) Therefore, they had to fight against the desires of the flesh, as these would cause them to be at enmity with God. (Ro 8:6-8) The fact that remaining in a peaceful relationship with God was necessary for divine approval lends much weight to the oft-repeated prayerful expression 'may you have peace.'—Ro 1:7; 1Co 1:3; 2Co 1:2; Ga 1:3; 6:16; Eph 1:2; 6:23; Php 1:2.

Christians also wanted others to enjoy peace. Therefore, "shod with the equipment of the good news of peace," they carried on their spiritual warfare. (Eph 6:15) Even within the congregation they waged warfare in overturning reasonings that were out of harmony with the knowledge of God, so that these reasonings did not damage their relationship with God. (2Co 10:4, 5) However, it was not a verbal fight or quarrel, not even when correcting those who had deviated from the truth. With reference to handling cases of those who had departed from a right course, the apostle Paul counseled Timothy: "A slave of the Lord does not need to fight, but needs to be gentle toward all, qualified to teach, keeping himself restrained under evil, instructing with mildness those not favorably disposed; as perhaps God may give them repentance leading to an accurate knowledge of truth, and they may come back to their proper senses out from the snare of the Devil, seeing that they have been caught alive by him for the will of that one."—2Ti 2:24-26.

Peaceful Rule. The Son of God, as the one to have 'the princely rule upon his shoulder,' is called the "Prince of Peace." (Isa 9:6, 7) It is, therefore, noteworthy that Christ Jesus, while on earth, showed that his servants should not arm themselves for physical warfare, when saying to Peter: "Return your sword to its place, for all those who take the sword will perish by the sword." (Mt

26:52) Figuratively speaking, those who became Christians "beat their swords into plowshares and their spears into pruning shears." They learned war no more. (Isa 2:4) This and God's past activities, especially in connection with Israel during Solomon's reign, point to the peace that will prevail during Jesus' rule as King. Regarding Solomon's reign, the Bible reports: "Peace itself became his in every region of his, all around. And Judah and Israel continued to dwell in security, everyone under his own vine and under his own fig tree, from Dan to Beer-sheba, all the days of Solomon." (1Ki 4:24, 25; 1Ch 22:9) As is evident from other scriptures (compare Ps 72:7, 8; Mic 4:4; Zec 9:9, 10; Mt 21:4, 5), this served as a pattern of what would take place under the rule of Christ Jesus, the One greater than Solomon, which name comes from a root meaning "peace."—Mt 12:42.

Peace Between Man and Animals. Jehovah God promised to the Israelites, if obedient: "I will put peace in the land, and you will indeed lie down, with no one making you tremble; and I will make the injurious wild beast cease out of the land." (Le 26:6) This meant that the wild animals would stay within the confines of their habitat and not bring harm to the Israelites and their domestic animals. On the other hand, if the Israelites proved to be disobedient, Jehovah would allow their land to be invaded and devastated by foreign armies. As this would result in reducing the population, wild animals would multiply, penetrate formerly inhabited areas, and do injury to the survivors and their domestic animals.—Compare Ex 23:29; Le 26:22; 2Ki 17:5, 6, 24-26.

The peace promised to the Israelites in connection with the wild animals differed from that enjoyed by the first man and woman in the garden of Eden, for Adam and Eve enjoyed full dominion over the animal creation. (Ge 1:28) By contrast, in prophecy, like dominion is attributed only to Christ Jesus. (Ps 8:4-8; Heb 2:5-9) Therefore, it is under the government of Jesus Christ, "a twig out of the stump of Jesse," or God's "servant David," that peace will again prevail between men and the animals. (Isa 11:1, 6-9; 65:25; Eze 34:23-25) These last cited texts have a figurative application, for it is obvious that the peace between animals, such as the wolf and the lamb, there described did not find literal fulfillment in ancient Israel. It was thus foretold that persons of harmful, beastlike disposition would cease their vicious ways and live in peace with their more docile neighbors. However, the prophetic use of the animals figuratively to portray the peaceful conditions to prevail among God's people implies that there will also be peace among literal animals under the rule of Christ Jesus, even as there evidently was in Eden.

PEACOCK [Heb., *tuk·ki·yim'* (plural)]. The brilliantly colored male of the peafowl. It is a large bird of the pheasant family, about the size of a turkey. The peacock (*Pavo muticus* and *Pavo cristatus*) is particularly noted for its magnificent train of iridescent green and gold feathers marked with large "eyespots" of blue. The train can be spread at will to form an impressive semicircular screen, or fan, touching the ground on either side. The peacock shakes the fanned train, producing a rustling sound and causing the feathers to shimmer with their iridescent hues. The neck and breast are also of a beautiful metallic greenish-blue color. Because of its majestic beauty, the bird was greatly prized from ancient times.

In King Solomon's time his fleet of ships of Tarshish made triannual voyages, bringing cargoes of "gold and silver, ivory, and apes and peacocks." (1Ki 10:22) While certain of Solomon's ships made trips to Ophir (evidently in the Red Sea area; 1Ki 9:26-28), 2 Chronicles 9:21 mentions ships "going to Tarshish" (likely in Spain) in connection with the carrying of the above commodities, including peacocks. It is not certain, therefore, from what place or area the peacocks were imported. These beautiful birds are held to be native of SE Asia and are abundant in India and Sri Lanka. Some believe that the Hebrew name (*tuk·ki·yim'*) is to be connected with the Old Tamil name for the peacock, *tokei*. Solomon's fleet could have obtained the peacocks when the ships sailed along their usual route and stopped at some trading center that had contacts with India. Of interest, also, is the statement in *The Animal Kingdom*, by Frederick Drimmer: "For centuries scientists assumed that there were no peacocks in Africa —their known dwelling places were the East Indies and southeastern Asia. The belief of the naturalists was shattered in 1936, when the Congo peacock [*Afropavo congensis*] was discovered in the Belgian Congo."—1954, Vol. II, p. 988.

Some prefer to link the Hebrew word *tuk·ki·yim'* to the Egyptian *ky*, a kind of ape.

PEARL. A smooth, relatively hard, globular, and generally white gem with a soft iridescent luster, which has from ancient times been used for adornment. (1Ti 2:9; Re 17:4; 18:11, 12, 15, 16; 21:2, 21) It is a hardened mass of calcium carbonate that forms inside oysters and certain other mollusks. When a foreign particle (such as a grain of sand or a small parasite) enters the area between the body and the shell of a mollusk, it stimulates the creature's secretion of a calcareous substance called nacre, which hardens into a pearly layer around the irritating intruding material. Successive layers of this shell-like substance are built up around the foreign particle that serves as a nucleus. If the nucleus remains free from the shell because of contractions of the mantle lining the shell, a beautiful pearl is formed in the course of several years.

Pearls of gem quality are taken from the sea pearl oyster, a native of most warm tropical waters, and notably those of the vicinity of Bahrain in the Persian Gulf, and of the Red Sea.

Illustrative Use. The Bible at times alludes to the preciousness of pearls in an illustrative way. With reference to the surpassing value of true wisdom, Job said: "A bagful of wisdom is worth more than one full of pearls." (Job 28:18) In the Sermon on the Mount, Jesus Christ counseled: "Do not give what is holy to dogs, neither throw your pearls before swine, that they may never trample them under their feet and turn around and rip you open." (Mt 7:6) Evidently Jesus meant that, if a person shows that he is like a dog or a swine, with no appreciation for spiritual things, one should not further endeavor to share spiritual thoughts and teachings with him. Such corrupt persons would only trample upon valuable spiritual things and abuse or injure anyone endeavoring to share these with them. Jesus also illustrated the preciousness of the Kingdom of the heavens by speaking of "one pearl" of such high value that a traveling merchant seeking fine pearls "promptly sold all the things he had and bought it." (Mt 13:45, 46) Thereby Jesus showed that an individual appreciating the true worth of gaining the Kingdom of the heavens would be willing to part with everything in order to gain it.—Compare Mt 11:12; Lu 13:23-25; Php 3:8-11.

PEDAHEL (Ped·ah′el) [God Has Redeemed]. A chieftain of Naphtali, appointed by Jehovah to help divide the Promised Land among the tribes; son of Ammihud.—Nu 34:16, 17, 28.

PEDAHZUR (Pe·dah′zur) [The Rock Has Redeemed]. A man in the tribe of Manasseh whose son Gamaliel was appointed chieftain of their tribe after the Exodus.—Nu 1:10, 16; 2:20; 7:54, 59; 10:23.

PEDAIAH (Pe·dai′ah) [meaning "Jehovah Has Redeemed"].

1. Father of Joel; during David's reign he was prince of the half of the tribe of Manasseh dwelling W of the Jordan.—1Ch 27:20, 22.

2. Father of Jehoiakim's mother Zebidah; Pedaiah lived in Rumah.—2Ki 23:36.

3. Third-named son of King Jehoiachin (Jeconiah) born during the Babylonian exile. Pedaiah became father to postexilic Governor Zerubbabel and was therefore a vital link in the line leading to Jesus. (1Ch 3:17-19) Because of some unrecorded circumstance, Zerubbabel is also called the son of Pedaiah's brother Shealtiel. Shealtiel may have adopted Zerubbabel if Pedaiah died when the boy was young; or, if Shealtiel died before fathering a son, Pedaiah may have performed brother-in-law marriage, fathering Zerubbabel in the name of his brother Shealtiel.—Ezr 5:2; Mt 1:12.

4. A Benjamite whose descendant lived in Jerusalem after the Babylonian exile.—Ne 11:4, 7.

5. A descendant of Parosh who helped Nehemiah repair Jerusalem's wall.—Ne 3:25.

6. A postexilic Israelite, probably a priest, who stood at Ezra's left during the reading of Jehovah's Law to the assembled people.—Ne 8:1, 4.

7. A faithful Levite whom Nehemiah, on his second visit to Jerusalem, assigned with Shelemiah the priest and Zadok the copyist to take charge of the contributed tithe.—Ne 13:6, 7, 12, 13.

PEKAH (Pe′kah) [from a root meaning "open"]. King of Israel for a 20-year period beginning in about 778 B.C.E.; contemporaneous with Judean Kings Azariah (Uzziah), Jotham, and Ahaz. Earlier, Pekah had served as adjutant to Israelite King Pekahiah. But in the 52nd year of Uzziah's reign, Pekah the son of Remaliah, with the cooperation of 50 men of Gilead, assassinated Pekahiah and seized the kingship over Israel in Samaria. (2Ki 15:25, 27) During Pekah's reign idolatrous calf worship continued. (2Ki 15:28) This ruler also formed an alliance with Rezin the king of Syria. Toward the close of Judean King Jotham's reign (which began in the second year of Pekah), both Pekah and Rezin caused trouble for Judah.—2Ki 15:32, 37, 38.

After Jotham's son Ahaz began his reign in the 17th year of Pekah, Rezin and Pekah invaded Judah, intending to dethrone that monarch and install a certain son of Tabeel as king. They did not succeed in taking Jerusalem (2Ki 16:1, 5; Isa 7:1-7), but Judah sustained heavy losses. In one day Pekah killed 120,000 valiant men of Judah. The Israelite army also took 200,000 Judeans captive. However, on the advice of the prophet Oded, supported by a number of leading men of Ephraim, these captives were returned to Judah.—2Ch 28:6, 8-15.

Though assured through the prophet Isaiah that the Syro-Israelite combine would fail in deposing him as king (Isa 7:6, 7), faithless Ahaz bribed Assyrian King Tiglath-pileser III to come to his assistance. In response, the Assyrian monarch captured Damascus and put Rezin to death. (2Ki 16:7-9) Apparently also at this time Tiglath-pileser captured the regions of Gilead, Galilee, and Naphtali, as well as a number of cities in northern Israel. (2Ki 15:29) Thereafter Hoshea the son of Elah killed Pekah and became Israel's next king. —2Ki 15:30.

A fragmentary historical text of Tiglath-pileser III reports about his campaign against Israel: "All its inhabitants (and) their possessions I led to Assyria. They overthrew their king Pekah (*Pa-qa-ha*) and I placed Hoshea (*A-ú-si-'*) as king over them."—*Ancient Near Eastern Texts*, edited by J. B. Pritchard, 1974, p. 284.

PEKAHIAH (Pek·a·hi′ah) [Jah Has Opened]. King of Israel in Samaria, son and successor of Menahem. His brief reign of two years (c. 780-779 B.C.E.) was marked by idolatrous calf worship like that introduced by Jeroboam and permitted by Menahem. Pekahiah's adjutant, Pekah, conspired against him, killed him, and began to reign in his place.—2Ki 15:22-26.

PEKOD (Pe′kod). Apparently the name of an area in the vicinity of Babylon. Men of Pekod were to be included among the military forces to execute Jehovah's judgment on unfaithful Jerusalem. (Eze 23:4, 22-26) Later, Pekod itself was to be devoted to destruction.—Jer 50:21.

Pekod is usually identified with the Puqudu of Assyrian inscriptions. The Nimrud Inscription of Tiglath-pileser III indicates that Pekod was added to the Assyrian Empire and lay in the vicinity of Elam. (*Records of the Past: Ancient Monuments of Egypt and Western Asia*, edited by A. Sayce, London, 1891, Vol. V, pp. 120, 121) Therefore, if correctly identified with Puqudu, Pekod would appear to have been located E of the Tigris and N of that river's confluence with the Karkheh.

It has been suggested that at Jeremiah 50:21 the designation "Pekod" (like Merathaim) possibly is a poetic name for Babylon. It is noteworthy that an inscription from the time of Nebuchadnezzar shows that Puqudu was under the control of Babylon. Therefore, when Babylon fell to the Medes and Persians, this must also have affected Pekod.

PELAIAH (Pe·la′iah) [Jah Has Acted Wonderfully].

1. A Levite who assisted Ezra in reading and explaining the Law to the Israelites assembled in Jerusalem's public square. He is probably the same Levite (unless a representative of a family by that name is meant) who attested to the covenant of faithfulness put forward shortly thereafter.—Ne 8:1, 5-8; 9:38; 10:1, 9, 10.

2. One of the last generation of David's descendants mentioned in the Hebrew Scriptures.—1Ch 3:1, 5, 10, 24.

PELALIAH (Pel·a·li′ah) [Jah Is Arbitrating]. A priest whose descendant Adaiah was among those serving at the sanctuary after the return from Babylonian exile.—Ne 11:10, 12.

PELATIAH (Pel·a·ti′ah) [Jehovah Has Provided Escape].

1. One of four Simeonite chieftains who led 500 men against Mount Seir and struck down the remnant of the Amalekites, likely during Hezekiah's reign.—1Ch 4:41-43.

2. Son of Benaiah; a prince of Israel whom Ezekiel saw in vision. Pelatiah, along with Jaazaniah, was "scheming hurtfulness and advising bad counsel" against Jerusalem. Ezekiel was inspired to utter a prophecy against the people of Israel, after which Pelatiah died.—Eze 11:1-13.

3. A distant descendant of David and grandson of Zerubbabel. (1Ch 3:19-21) Possibly the same as No. 4.

4. A family head represented in the signatures to the covenant promising not to take foreign wives.—Ne 9:38; 10:1, 14, 22; see No. 3.

PELEG (Pe′leg) [Division]. A son of Eber and father of Reu in the line from Shem to Abraham, and therefore an early ancestor of Jesus. Peleg lived 239 years (2269-2030 B.C.E.) and founded one of the 70 post-Flood families.—Ge 11:16-19; 1Ch 1:24-27; Lu 3:35.

Peleg was so named, for "in his days the earth was divided." (Ge 10:25; 1Ch 1:19) The text of these passages does not say that this notable division came at Peleg's birth a hundred years after the Deluge, but simply "in his days." If the name was given him at birth, its bestowal was possibly prophetic of the scattering that stemmed from the confusion of languages at the Tower of Babel.—Ge 11:1-9; compare the name Noah (probably meaning "Rest; Consolation"), which also proved to be prophetic, Ge 5:29.

PELET (Pel′et) [Providing of Escape].

1. A son of Jahdai listed in the Calebite division of Judah's genealogy.—1Ch 2:47.

2. One of the ambidextrous Benjamite mighty men who joined David at Ziklag; son of Azmaveth. —1Ch 12:1-3.

PELETH (Pe'leth).

1. A Reubenite whose son On joined Dathan, Abiram, and Korah in their rebellion.—Nu 16:1.

2. A descendant of Judah through Jerahmeel. —1Ch 2:33.

PELETHITES (Pel'e·thites). Loyal fighters for King David; always mentioned with the Cherethites. When David fled from Jerusalem because of Absalom's rebellion (which a major portion of the army supported), the Pelethites went along with David across the Kidron. (2Sa 15:18, 23) They also helped put down the rebellion of Sheba (2Sa 20:7), and later they supported David's choice of Solomon as his successor, instead of siding with Adonijah as Joab did. (1Ki 1:38, 44) The Cherethites and Pelethites were not part of the regular army but were a separate division in the service of King David, for Joab is called the head of the army, but, separately, Benaiah was over the Cherethites and Pelethites. (2Sa 8:18; 20:23; 1Ch 18:17) Since the Pelethites were not mentioned either before or after the reign of David, it may be concluded that they were his personal servants, rather than a permanent group serving the regal office.—Compare 2Sa 8:18 and 23:22, 23.

The lack of any positive identification of the Pelethites has given rise to numerous suggestions, among which are two primary schools of thought: (1) The great similarity in Hebrew between the two names Pelethites and Philistines (פלתי [Pelethite] plus only one additional character gives פלשתי [Philistine]) is the basis for saying that they are of the same background, or perhaps that the Pelethites were a branch of the Philistines. Some object to this suggestion that Philistines comprised David's personal bodyguard, but this possibility should not be wholly discounted. (2) On the other hand, the names Cherethites and Pelethites may perhaps be terms designating duty or ranks of service performed by David's bodyguard, the Cherethites serving as executioners, the Pelethites as runners. Such a division of runners is mentioned during the reigns of Saul and later kings. (1Sa 22:17; 2Ki 11:4; 2Ch 30:6) This second view, however, is less widely held than the first.

PELICAN [Heb., qa·'ath']. The translators of the Greek Septuagint and Latin Vulgate identified the Hebrew word qa·'ath' with the "pelican." It is listed among the birds designated as 'unclean' in the Mosaic Law.—Le 11:13, 18; De 14:11, 12, 17.

The pelican is one of the largest of the flying birds, attaining a length of over 1.5 m (5 ft), with a majestic wingspread of 2.5 m (8 ft) or more. The yellowish beak is long and hooked, and the large elastic pouch beneath is scarcely noticeable when empty. Ponderous on land, the pelicans are strong, graceful fliers and have been known to have their nesting places as much as 100 km (60 mi) from the places of their fishing. They are superb fishers, and their webbed feet enable them to maneuver swiftly in the water.

When the pelican is gorged with food, it often flies away to a lonely place, where it takes a melancholy posture, with its head sunk on its shoulders, so motionless that it might be mistaken from a distance for a white stone. The bird assumes this attitude for hours at a time, thus befitting the melancholy inactivity to which the psalmist refers when he illustrates the poignancy of his grief by writing: "I do resemble the pelican of the wilderness." (Ps 102:6) Here "wilderness" does not necessarily connote a desert, but simply an area away from human habitations, perhaps a swamp. During certain seasons, swamps in the northern Jordan Valley are still the home of pelicans. Three varieties of pelicans are found in Israel. The most common is the eastern white pelican (*Pelecanus onocrotalus*); the Dalmatian pelican (*Pelecanus crispus*) and the pink-backed pelican (*Pelecanus rufescens*) are seen less often.

The pelican shows a distinct preference for uncultivated places, where it will not be disturbed by man. There it nests and hatches its young and retires after fishing. Because of this fondness for lonely, desolate places, this bird is used in the Bible as a symbol of utter desolation. To symbolize Edom's coming desolation, Isaiah foretold that the pelican would take possession of that land. (Isa 34:11) Zephaniah prophesied that pelicans would dwell among the pillar capitals of Nineveh, indicating total ruin and absence of humankind.—Zep 2:13, 14.

PELONITE (Pel'o·nite). A term used with reference to two of David's principal warriors, Helez and Ahijah. (1Ch 11:26, 27, 36; 27:10) Helez is referred to as "the Paltite" in the parallel record at 2 Samuel 23:26, and some lexicographers consider this the preferred rendering of the designation. The name of Ahijah (1Ch 11:36) does not appear, in that form at least, in the corresponding list at 2 Samuel 23:24-39.

PEN.

1. A small enclosure for animals. (Zep 2:6; see SHEEPFOLD.) In Micah's prophecy, regathered and united Israel is likened to "a flock in the pen." (Mic 2:12, *NW; Le*) The Masoretic text here uses the Hebrew word *bots·rah'*, which is elsewhere ren-

dered "Bozrah," the name of a city of Edom and a city of Moab. However, in view of the phraseology of Micah 2:12, some scholars feel that *bots·rah'* also means a "pen" or "fold." (*JP, Mo*) If the word should be vowel pointed slightly differently, it would correspond closely to the Arabic *sirat* (pen).

2. An implement for writing with ink or similar fluid. When ancients wrote on clay, wax, or soft metal they used a stylus (see STYLUS), but writing was also done on parchment or papyrus with pen and ink. (3Jo 13; 2Jo 12) The Greek word translated "pen" (*ka'la·mos*) refers to a reed or cane and can literally be rendered "writing-reed." Among ancient Egyptians the reed pen was made with a flat chisel-shaped head that was cut or sliced so that it would act as a brush. The reeds may have been dried and hardened by leaving them under dung heaps for several months, as has been the practice in recent years. The Greeks and Romans used a reed pen that was pointed and slit, as was later done with quill pens and as has been done even in recent times with pen points.

PENIEL (Pe·ni'el). The place near the ford of the Jabbok where Jacob wrestled with an angel; hence he called the place Peniel because there he 'had seen God face to face.' (Ge 32:22-31) The same as Penuel.—See PENUEL.

PENINNAH (Pe·nin'nah) [Coral]. A wife of El-kanah. Peninnah produced many children, in contrast with Elkanah's other wife, Hannah. Nonetheless, Peninnah was loved less than Hannah, and so she ridiculed Hannah's barrenness, especially at the time of the family's annual visits to the tabernacle.—1Sa 1:1-8.

PENTATEUCH (Pen'ta·teuch). This anglicized Greek word (meaning "five rolls" or "fivefold volume") refers to the first five books of the Bible —Genesis, Exodus, Leviticus, Numbers, and Deuteronomy.

Contents. The Pentateuch is a most important segment of God's written Word, furnishing a solid foundation upon which much that follows firmly rests. Its first book, Genesis, gives us the inspired account of creation and also traces man's history from Eden down through much of the patriarchal era to the death of Joseph ("in the beginning" to 1657 B.C.E.). The second book, Exodus, begins with the death of Joseph and tells of Moses' birth during a time of slavery, of the deliverance of God's people from Egyptian bondage, and of the inauguration of the Law covenant at Sinai; it includes details for the construction of the central structure for worship, namely, the taber-

nacle in the wilderness (historic events from 1657 to 1512 B.C.E.). Leviticus, the third book, covering only about one month's time (1512 B.C.E.), gives invaluable information about the Levitical priesthood, its ordination, and its duties, as well as laws and regulations governing the congregation's obligatory support of Jehovah's worship. The fourth book, Numbers, as its name implies, tells of the censuses taken near the beginning and end of the wilderness journey. It also gives us many details on the 40 years of wandering (down to 1473 B.C.E.) and includes many laws embraced within the framework of the national covenant. The final book, Deuteronomy, covers about two months' time (1473 B.C.E.); it explains portions of the Law covenant and provides many ordinances necessary for the new generation of Israelites who were poised on the Plains of Moab, ready to invade and occupy the Promised Land. The closing chapters tell of the appointment of Joshua as leader and the death of Moses.

Writership. There is no single text saying that Moses wrote the entire Pentateuch, but scattered throughout the material are explicit statements serving the same purpose. (Ex 17:14; 24:4; 34:27; Nu 33:2; De 31:9, 19, 22, 24-26) There are also many sections where the words are directly credited to Moses, beginning with his first recorded conversation (Ex 2:13, 14), continuing to his final blessing on the people (De 33:1-29), and including some of his lengthy speeches (De 1:1; 5:1; 27:1; 29:2; 31:1) and notable songs. (Ex 15:1-19; De 31:30–32:43) The opening verses of 20 out of 27 chapters of Leviticus tell us that what follows are the words of Jehovah spoken to Moses so he, in turn, could inform the people. The same is true in more than 50 instances in the book of Numbers. So, with the exception of the closing verses of Deuteronomy, the evidence within the Pentateuch itself shows that its writership properly belongs to Moses.

Many other passages in the Bible witness to the fact that the Pentateuch was from the hand of Moses. (Jos 1:7; Jg 3:4; 2Ki 18:6; Mal 4:4) Such men as David (1Ki 2:1-3), Daniel (9:11), Ezra (6:18), Nehemiah (8:1), Jesus (Mr 12:26; Lu 16:29; Joh 7:19), Luke (24:27), and John (1:17) make references to this work as that of Moses. More directly to the point, Jesus acknowledged that Moses was the *writer* (Mr 10:3-5; Joh 5:46, 47), as did also the Sadducees.—Mr 12:18, 19.

PENTECOST. A name used in the Christian Greek Scriptures to denote the Festival of Harvest (Ex 23:16) or Festival of Weeks (Ex 34:22), called also "the day of the first ripe fruits." (Nu 28:26)

Instructions for this festival are found at Leviticus 23:15-21; Numbers 28:26-31; Deuteronomy 16:9-12. It was to be celebrated on the 50th day (Pentecost means "Fiftieth [Day]") from Nisan 16, the day that the barley sheaf was offered. (Le 23:15, 16) In the Jewish calendar it falls on Sivan 6. It was after the barley harvest and the beginning of the harvest of wheat, which ripened later than the barley.—Ex 9:31, 32.

The Israelites were not allowed to begin the harvest until the firstfruits of the barley had been presented to Jehovah on Nisan 16. Therefore, in Deuteronomy 16:9, 10 the instructions are: "From when the sickle is first put to the standing grain you will start to count seven weeks. Then you must celebrate the festival of weeks to Jehovah your God." Every male was required to attend, and it is also stated in connection with this festival: "You must rejoice before Jehovah your God, you and your son and your daughter and your man slave and your slave girl and the Levite who is inside your gates and the alien resident and the fatherless boy and the widow, who are in your midst, in the place that Jehovah your God will choose to have his name reside there." (De 16:11) The Passover was a close family observance. The Festival of Harvest, or Pentecost, called for a more open and hospitable liberality, in this sense resembling the Festival of Booths.

The firstfruits of the wheat harvest were to be treated differently from the barley firstfruits. Two tenths of an ephah of fine wheat flour (4.4 L; 4 dry qt) along with leaven was to be baked into two loaves. They were to be "out of your dwelling places," which meant that they were to be loaves like those made for the daily use of the household and not expressly for holy purposes. (Le 23:17) Burnt offerings and a sin offering went along with this, and as a communion offering two male lambs. The priest waved the loaves and the lambs before Jehovah by putting his hands underneath the loaves and the pieces of the lambs and waving them back and forth, signifying that they were presented before Jehovah. After the loaves and the lambs were offered, they became the priest's for him to eat as a communion offering.—Le 23:18-20.

There is a slight difference in description of the other offerings (aside from the communion offering) in the account at Numbers 28:27-30. Instead of seven lambs, one young bull, two rams, and one kid of the goats, as at Leviticus 23:18, 19, it calls for seven lambs, *two* young bulls, *one* ram, and one kid of the goats. Jewish commentators say that the passage in Leviticus refers to the sacrifice

to accompany the wave loaves, and the one in Numbers to the properly appointed sacrifice of the festival, so that both were offered. Supporting this, Josephus, in describing the sacrifices on Pentecost day, first mentions the two lambs of the communion offering, then combines the remaining offerings, enumerating three calves, two rams (evidently a transcriber's error for three), 14 lambs, and two kids. (*Jewish Antiquities,* III, 253 [x, 6]) The day was a holy convention, a sabbath day. —Le 23:21; Nu 28:26.

The Festival of Pentecost came at the end of the barley harvest and was a time of rejoicing, as is indicated by the communion offering that was presented by the congregation and was given to the priest. This offering would also denote peaceful fellowship with Jehovah. At the same time the sin offering reminded the Israelites of sin on their part and was a petition to God for forgiveness and cleansing. The increased burnt offering served as a practical expression of their gratitude for His bountifulness as well as a symbol of their wholeheartedness in carrying out their covenant relationship with God.

Not only was it specially appropriate for Israel to offer thanks to Jehovah on this day but they also were not to forget their poor brothers. After giving instructions on the festival, Jehovah commanded: "And when you people reap the harvest of your land, you must not do completely the edge of your field when you are reaping, and the gleaning of your harvest you must not pick up. You should leave them for the afflicted one and the alien resident. I am Jehovah your God." (Le 23: 22) Thus, the poor would have real incentive for thanking the Lord and enjoying the festival along with all others. There would also be many personal offerings of the firstfruits of the harvest during this festival.

According to rabbinic sources, after the exile the participants in the festival customarily went up to Jerusalem the day previous to its commencement and there prepared everything necessary for its observance. In the evening the blasts of the trumpets announced the approach of the festival day. (Nu 10:10) The altar of burnt sacrifice was cleansed, and the gates of the temple were opened immediately after midnight for the priests and so that the people who brought the sacrifices for burnt offerings and for thanksgiving offerings to the court could have them examined by the priests. Alfred Edersheim comments: "Before the morning sacrifice all burnt- and peace-offerings which the people proposed to bring at the feast had to be examined by the officiating priesthood.

Great as their number was, it must have been a busy time, till the announcement that the morning glow extended to Hebron put an end to all such preparations, by giving the signal for the regular morning sacrifice."—*The Temple,* 1874, p. 228.

After the regular daily morning sacrifice was offered, the festive sacrifices described in Numbers 28:26-30 were brought. Afterward came the offering peculiar to Pentecost—the wave loaves with their accompanying sacrifices. (Le 23:18-20) After the loaves were waved, one of them was taken by the high priest, and the second was divided among all the officiating priests.

Symbolic Significance of the Festival. It was on the day of Pentecost that the holy spirit was poured out by Jesus Christ on the group of about 120 disciples in the upper room at Jerusalem in the year 33 C.E. (Ac 1:13-15) Jesus had been resurrected on Nisan 16, the day of the offering of the barley sheaf by the high priest. He was, in a figurative sense, without leaven, which represents sin. (Heb 7:26) At Pentecost, as the great High Priest, he could present to his Father Jehovah additional spiritual sons, Jesus' footstep followers, who were taken from sinful mankind and who accepted his sacrifice. The approval by God of Jesus' own human sacrifice and of Jesus' presentation of his disciples (although born in sin) to be spiritual sons of God was manifested by the pouring out of God's spirit upon them. The fact that there were *two* loaves of newly ripened grain that were presented to Jehovah at Pentecost indicates that more than one person would be involved in the fulfillment. It may also point to the fact that those who become spirit-begotten followers of Jesus Christ would be taken from two groups on earth: First from the natural circumcised Jews, and later from all the other nations of the world, the Gentiles.—Compare Eph 2:13-18.

The Jews traditionally hold that Pentecost corresponded to the time of the giving of the Law at Sinai, when Israel became a distinguished people. It was early in the third month (Sivan) that the Israelites gathered at Sinai and received the Law. (Ex 19:1) Just as Moses as mediator was used to introduce Israel into the Law covenant, so Jesus Christ as Mediator of spiritual Israel now brought that new nation into the new covenant. The apostle Paul draws a comparison from these two events, saying that Christians are gathered to a far greater assemblage at "a Mount Zion and a city of the living God, heavenly Jerusalem," under new covenant arrangements.—Heb 12:18-24; compare Re 14:1-5.

Jesus had announced the new covenant to his disciples on the evening of his last Passover and, just before his ascension, had instructed them to wait at Jerusalem for the promised holy spirit. Now, as the apostle Peter explained, "because he was exalted to the right hand of God and received the promised holy spirit from the Father, he has poured out this which you see and hear." (Lu 22:20; Ac 2:33) The presence of God's spirit was manifested in that some 120 disciples were miraculously speaking in different tongues. By this means, the multitudes of Jews and proselytes from all parts of the Roman Empire could hear with intelligibility "the magnificent things of God." (Ac 2:7-11) First at this time, by means of Peter, baptism in the name of the Father, Son, and holy spirit was preached, as Jesus had commanded at Matthew 28:19. (Ac 2:21, 36, 38, 39) Having gone into the heavens with the value of his sacrifice, Jesus was able to bring his followers into the new covenant.—Heb 9:15-26.

These followers, then, with the 3,000 added that day (Ac 2:41) and others later, were not the very *first* firstfruits to God, for this was Jesus Christ himself, resurrected on Nisan 16 of 33 C.E. (1Co 15:23), when the barley sheaves were waved. Rather, they were like the firstfruits of the wheat, a second crop, *"certain* firstfruits" to God. (Jas 1:18) They now became God's new nation, God's "chosen race, a royal priesthood, a holy nation, a people for special possession."—1Pe 2:9.

PENUEL   (Pe·nu'el) [Face of God].

1. "Father of Gedor" in the tribe of Judah. (1Ch 4:1, 4) Since Gedor appears as the name of a town in Judah, Penuel may have been its founder or the ancestor of its inhabitants.

2. A family head in the tribe of Benjamin who lived in Jerusalem; son of Shashak.—1Ch 8:1, 25, 28.

3. A city to the S of the Jabbok. In the time of the Judges, Gideon asked the men of Penuel for food in order that his forces might continue to pursue the kings of Midian, but the Penuelites refused, for which reason Gideon later destroyed their tower and killed all their men. (Jg 8:4-9, 17) Nothing more is mentioned of Penuel until King Jeroboam I "built" it again, or at least fortified it. —1Ki 12:25.

Penuel is generally identified with Tulul edh-Dhahab esh-Sherqiyeh, about 6 km (3.5 mi) E of Succoth and near the Jabbok, some 14 km (8.5 mi) or so NE of its confluence with the Jordan. Indications are that it was heavily fortified and strategically positioned so as to control the entrance of the

Jabbok gorge leading westward down to the Jordan.—See PENIEL.

PEOPLE OF THE LAND (EARTH).

This expression (Heb., 'am ha·'a'rets, with its plural forms) occurs 67 times in the Hebrew text. In Jesus' day it was employed by the religious leaders as a term of contempt, but originally this was not the case.

The Hebrew and Aramaic lexicon by Koehler and Baumgartner explains this Hebrew expression to mean "the citizens possessing the full rights." (Lexicon in Veteris Testamenti Libros, Leiden, 1958, p. 711) The Interpreter's Dictionary of the Bible states that the term "in the strict sense includes only the responsible male citizenry, the married men who live on their own land and have full rights and duties, including the duty of serving in the army and of participating in judicial proceedings and . . . festivals." (Edited by G. A. Buttrick, 1962, Vol. 1, p. 106) (Compare Le 20:2-5; 2Ki 15:5; 16:15; Eze 45:16, 22; 46:3, 9.) Thus, originally, the expression was one of respect. It did not apply only to a lowly class or those of the poorer element.

In bargaining for the property rights to the cave of Machpelah, Abraham dealt with the Hittite "people of the land." (Ge 23:7, 13, RS) In these verses both An American Translation and the New World Translation render the Hebrew 'am ha·'a'rets as "natives." Pharaoh, in speaking to Moses and Aaron, referred to the Israelites dwelling in Goshen as "the people of the land." (Ex 5:5) The expression was used in the singular to embrace all the people of Canaan (Nu 14:9), and with the plural of 'am ('am·meh', "peoples") to describe them as forming separate tribes or peoples within that land. (Ne 9:24, 30) It is used in a similar way to refer to the subject peoples within the Persian Empire in Queen Esther's time. (Es 8:17) Sennacherib used the full plural form ('am·meh' ha·'ara·tsohht', "peoples of the lands") as applying to the many peoples or nations conquered by the Assyrian forces.—2Ch 32:13.

Within the nation of Israel, the phrase 'am ha·'a'rets often distinguished the general citizenry from governmental or priestly officials. (2Ki 11:14, 18-20; Jer 1:18; 34:19; 37:2; 44:21; Eze 7:27; Da 9:6; Zec 7:5) However, it is evident that it embraced not merely the poor laboring class but also included persons of means, since Ezekiel, after decrying the injustices committed by greedy prophets, priests, and princes, inveighs against "the people of the land" who have "carried on a scheme of defrauding and have done a tearing away in robbery, and the afflicted one and the poor one they have maltreated, and the alien resident they have defrauded without justice." (Eze 22:25-29) To pay the heavy duties imposed by Pharaoh Nechoh, King Jehoiakim "exacted the silver and the gold from the people of the land" by means of taxation. Thus the 'am ha·'a'rets that struck down the conspirators against King Amon and made Josiah king or that later made Jehoahaz king were no so-called rabble element. (2Ki 23:30, 35; 21:24) When Nebuchadnezzar conquered Judah, 60 men of "the people of the land" were included along with the high court officials who were taken to Riblah and executed, these 60 doubtless being among the more prominent or leading citizens. (2Ki 25:19-21) Of course, the phrase 'am ha·'a'rets did embrace the poor and lowly citizens as well, and the king of Babylon designated a number of such to remain in Judah, as he had done earlier in Jerusalem.—2Ki 24:14; 25:12; Jer 40:7; 52:15, 16.

In postexilic times Ezra and Nehemiah condemned the wrong practice of the returned exiles in mingling with "the peoples of the land(s)," marrying their women, allowing them to carry on commerce within the city on the Sabbath, and learning their detestable practices. (Ezr 9:11; 10:2, 11; Ne 10:28, 31) The expression here referred to the surrounding non-Israelite peoples specified at Ezra 9:1, 2, and the reason for separating from them was not because of any low social or economic position on their part but because of God's law requiring purity of worship.—Ne 10:28-30.

As a Term of Contempt. In course of time, however, the religious leaders of Judah began to use the term to designate those persons, Jewish or non-Jewish, who were unlearned in the Law and more particularly those who were ignorant of or who failed to observe in detail the great body of rabbinic traditions that now developed. (Mt 15:1, 2) The term expressed the contemptuous attitude exemplified in the statement of the Pharisees at John 7:49: "This crowd that does not know the Law are accursed people." Rabbi Joshua said that an 'am ha·'a'rets is: "Anyone who does not put on tefillin [phylacteries]." Other rabbinic statements applying to such nonobservers of Jewish traditions were: "Even if one has learnt Scripture and Mishnah, if he has not ministered to the disciples of the wise, he is an 'am ha-arez." (Babylonian Talmud, Berakhot 47b, translated by M. Simon) "Neither is an ignorant person ['am ha·'a'rets] pious." (Babylonian Talmud, Avot 2:5, translated by J. Israelstam) "The illiterate will not be resurrected." (Babylonian Talmud, Ketubbot 11b, translated by S. Daiches) (Compare Mt

9:11; Lu 15:2; 18:11.) Jesus, however, said that he "came to call . . . sinners," and he showed affection for the people who were "thrown about like sheep without a shepherd."—Mt 9:13, 36.

Thus the sense of 'am ha·'a'rets changed from one of general respect to one of religious opprobrium, much as the Latin term *paganus,* from which the English word "pagan" is derived. Pagan originally meant simply a dweller in a rural community, but since those country people were often the last to be converted, it came to be used by city dwellers as applying to all who did not adopt their professed Christian beliefs. In a similar way the term "heathen" at first meant simply one who lived out on the "heath" or field.

PEOR (Pe'or). In the account of King Balak's efforts to get the prophet Balaam to curse Israel, the third vantage point to which Balaam was conducted is said to be "the top of Peor, which looks toward Jeshimon." (Nu 23:28) From here Balaam could see the tents of Israel spread about on the Plains of Moab below.—Nu 22:1; 24:2.

Some consider Peor to be the abbreviated form of the name Beth-peor. (De 4:46) However, this latter place is evidently a town, included as such in the territorial assignment of Reuben. (Jos 13:15, 16, 20) Others, therefore, consider Peor to be a summit, or peak, and suggest that the town of Beth-peor may have been so named because of being situated on the slopes of such a summit. Both Peor and Beth-peor appear to be connected with the pagan worship of "the Baal of Peor" (Nu 25:1-3, 18; 31:16; Jos 22:17), and it is possible that the height of Peor was a center of such immoral worship.—See BAAL No. 4; BAAL OF PEOR.

Balaam was first taken to Bamoth-baal, then to "the top of Pisgah," and finally to "the top of Peor." (Nu 22:41; 23:14, 28) The direction of movement is from S to N and seems to indicate that Peor was N of Pisgah and Mount Nebo. Based on the testimony of Eusebius and Jerome, of the third and fourth centuries C.E., the summit of Peor is suggested to have been one of the peaks bordering the Wadi Husban.—See BETH-PEOR.

PERAZIM, MOUNT (Pe·ra'zim) [Breakings Through]. A mount seemingly referred to elsewhere as Baal-perazim.—Isa 28:21; see BAAL-PERAZIM.

PERES (Pe'res). Daniel used this Aramaic word when interpreting the handwriting on the wall, "MENE, MENE, TEKEL and PARSIN." (Da 5:25, 28) Dr. Judah Slotki points out that the handwriting means "a maneh, a maneh, a shekel and half

shekels." (*Soncino Books of the Bible,* edited by A. Cohen, London, 1951; see also *Peake's Commentary on the Bible,* edited by M. Black and H. H. Rowley, London, 1964, p. 596.) Since "Peres" is the singular number of "Parsin," it would mean "a half shekel."

In the prophet's interpretation of "Peres," he employed two other Aramaic words spelled with the same three consonants but vocalized differently. "PERES [*Peres'*], your kingdom has been divided [*peri·sath'*] and given to the Medes and the Persians [*u·Pha·ras'*]." Thus the inspired explanation included a double play on the word "Peres" and the root meaning "divide," or "split." The subsequent events of that night proved the accuracy of the interpretation.—See PARSIN.

PERESH (Pe'resh). A son of Machir and Maacah in the tribe of Manasseh.—1Ch 7:14, 16.

PEREZ (Pe'rez) [Rupture; Perineal Rupture]. One of the twin sons of Judah by his daughter-in-law Tamar. At birth, Perez' brother Zerah started to emerge first but withdrew, and Perez came out first, producing a perineal rupture of Tamar. (Ge 38:24-30) Perez retained priority over his brother and is always listed ahead of him, and his house became the more famous of the two. (Ru 4:12) Perez and his own two sons, Hezron and Hamul, are listed among those of Jacob's lineage coming into Egypt, where all three became heads of individual families in Judah. (Ge 46:8, 12) Aside from this, no personal information about him is recorded.

The references to Perez are primarily genealogical, the bulk of Judah's genealogies being traced through Perez. (1Ch 2:4, 5, 9-55; 4:1-20) The families of Perez and his two sons comprised a generous portion of the tribe of Judah at the time of the second wilderness registration. (Nu 26:20-22) Some of Perez' descendants were in the first division of David's monthly militia. (1Ch 27:3) Many sons of Perez returned from the Babylonian exile, and 468 of them resided in Jerusalem. (1Ch 9:3, 4; Ne 11:4, 6) A direct genealogical line from Perez went through Boaz to David and finally to Jesus the Messiah.—Ru 4:18-22; 1Ch 2:4-15; Mt 1:3; Lu 3:33.

PEREZ-UZZAH (Pe'rez-uz'zah) [meaning "Rupture Against Uzzah"]. The name given to the threshing floor of Nacon (Chidon) after Jehovah struck down Uzzah for handling the Ark irreverently when an attempt was made to move it from Kiriath-jearim to the City of David. (2Sa 6:4-10; 1Ch 13:6-11) The exact location of Perez-uzzah is unknown.

PERFECTION

PERFECTION. The thought of perfection is expressed through Hebrew terms drawn from such verbs as *ka·lal'* (perfect [compare Eze 27:4]), *sha·lam'* (come to completion [compare Isa 60:20]), and *ta·mam'* (be completed, come to perfection [compare Ps 102:27; Isa 18:5]). In the Christian Greek Scriptures the words *te'lei·os* (adjective), *te·lei·o'tes* (noun), and *te·lei·o'o* (verb) are used similarly, conveying such ideas as bringing to completeness or full measure (Lu 8:14; 2Co 12:9; Jas 1:4), being full grown, adult, or mature (1Co 14:20; Heb 5:14), having attained the appropriate or appointed end, purpose, or goal (Joh 19:28; Php 3:12).

Importance of Correct Viewpoint. For correct Bible understanding one must not make the common error of thinking that everything called "perfect" is so in an *absolute* sense, that is, to an infinite degree, without limitation. Perfection in this absolute sense distinguishes only the Creator, Jehovah God. Because of this Jesus could say of his Father: "Nobody is good, except one, God." (Mr 10:18) Jehovah is incomparable in his excellence, worthy of all praise, supreme in his superb qualities and powers, so that "his name alone is unreachably high." (Ps 148:1-13; Job 36:3, 4, 26; 37:16, 23, 24; Ps 145:2-10, 21) Moses extolled God's perfection, saying: "For I shall declare the name of Jehovah. Do you attribute greatness to our God! The Rock, perfect is his activity, for all his ways are justice. A God of faithfulness, with whom there is no injustice; righteous and upright is he." (De 32:3, 4) All of God's ways, words, and law are perfect, refined, free from flaw or defect. (Ps 18:30; 19:7; Jas 1:17, 25) There is never any just cause for objection, criticism, or faultfinding regarding Him or his activity; rather, praise is always due Him.—Job 36:22-24.

Other perfection relative. Perfection of any other person or thing, then, is *relative*, not absolute. (Compare Ps 119:96.) That is, a thing is "perfect" according to, or in relation to, the purpose or end for which it is appointed by its designer or producer, or the use to which it is to be put by its receiver or user. The very meaning of perfection requires that there be someone who decides when "completion" has been reached, what the standards of excellence are, what requirements are to be satisfied, and what details are essential. Ultimately, God the Creator is the final Arbiter of perfection, the Standard-Setter, in accord with his own righteous purposes and interests.—Ro 12:2; see JEHOVAH (A God of moral standards).

As an illustration, the planet Earth was one of God's creations, and at the end of six creative 'days' of work toward it, God pronounced the results "very good." (Ge 1:31) It met his supreme standards of excellence, hence it was perfect. Yet he thereafter assigned man to "subdue it," evidently in the sense of cultivating the earth and making the whole planet, and not just Eden, a garden of God.—Ge 1:28; 2:8.

The tent, or tabernacle, built in the wilderness at God's command and according to his specifications served as a type or small-scale prophetic model of a "greater and more perfect tent," Jehovah's heavenly residence into which Christ Jesus entered as High Priest. (Heb 9:11-14, 23, 24) The earthly tent was perfect in that it satisfied God's requirements, served its appointed end. Yet when God's purpose concerning it was accomplished, it ceased to be used and passed out of existence. The perfection of that which it represented was of a far higher type, being heavenly, eternal.

The city of Jerusalem with its hill of Zion was called "the perfection of prettiness." (La 2:15; Ps 50:2) This does not mean that every minute aspect of the city's physical appearance was supremely attractive, but rather, it relates to its use by God, the city's beauty resulting from the splendor that he conferred upon it, making it the capital of his anointed kings and the site of his temple. (Eze 16:14) The wealthy commercial city of Tyre is portrayed as a ship whose builders, those working in behalf of the city's material interests, had 'perfected its prettiness,' filling it with luxury products of many lands.—Eze 27:3-25.

Thus, in each case the context must be considered to determine in what sense or relation perfection is meant.

Perfection of the Mosaic Law. The Law given to Israel through Moses included among its provisions the establishment of a priesthood and the offering of various animal sacrifices. Though from God, and hence perfect, neither the Law, its priesthood, nor the sacrifices brought perfection to those under the Law, as the inspired apostle shows. (Heb 7:11, 19; 10:1) Rather than bring freedom from sin and death, it actually made sin more evident. (Ro 3:20; 7:7-13) All these divine provisions, nevertheless, served the purpose assigned them by God; the Law acted as a "tutor" to lead men to Christ, forming a perfect "shadow of the good things to come." (Ga 3:19-25; Heb 10:1) Hence, when Paul speaks of "an incapability on the part of the Law, while it was weak through the flesh" (Ro 8:3), he is evidently referring to the inability of the fleshly Jewish high priest (who was appointed by the Law to be in charge of the sacrificial arrangements and who entered the

Most Holy on Atonement Day with sacrificial blood) to "save completely" those whom he served, as Hebrews 7:11, 18-28 explains. Although the offering of sacrifices through the Aaronic priesthood maintained a right standing for the people before God, it did not completely or perfectly relieve them of consciousness of sin. The apostle refers to this in saying that the atonement sacrifices could not "make those who approach perfect," that is, as regards their conscience. (Heb 10:1-4; compare Heb 9:9.) The high priest was unable to provide the ransom price needed for a true redemption from sin. Only Christ's enduring priestly service and effective sacrifice do accomplish this. —Heb 9:14; 10:12-22.

The Law was "holy," "good," "fine" (Ro 7:12, 16), and anyone who could fully live up to this perfect Law would prove himself a perfect man, worthy of life. (Le 18:5; Ro 10:5; Ga 3:12) For this very reason the Law brought condemnation, rather than life, not because the Law was not good but because of the imperfect, sinful nature of those under it. (Ro 7:13-16; Ga 3:10-12, 19-22) The perfect Law made their imperfection and sinfulness especially evident. (Ro 3:19, 20; Ga 3:19, 22) The Law in this respect also served to identify Jesus as the Messiah, for he alone was able to keep the Law in every respect, proving himself a perfect man.—Joh 8:46; 2Co 5:21; Heb 7:26.

The Bible's Perfection. The Sacred Scriptures constitute a perfect message from God, refined, pure, and true. (Ps 12:6; 119:140, 160; Pr 30:5; Joh 17:17) Though thousands of years of copying have evidently brought some variations from the original writings, these variations are admittedly very minor, so that, even if our present copies and translations are not absolutely flawless, the divine message conveyed is.

Individuals may find the Bible a more difficult book to read than many, one requiring greater effort and concentration; they may find much they do not understand. Some critical persons may insist that, to be perfect, the Bible should be free of even superficial differences or what appear, according to their standards, to be inconsistencies. None of these things, however, detract from the perfection of the Sacred Scriptures. For the real gauge of its perfection is its measuring up to the standards of excellence set by Jehovah God, its true Author, appointed for it, as well as its being free from falsehood, as the published Word of the God of truth. The apostle Paul points up the perfection of "the holy writings" in saying: "All Scripture is inspired of God and beneficial for teaching,

for reproving, for setting things straight, for disciplining in righteousness, that the man of God may be fully competent, completely equipped for every good work." (2Ti 3:15-17) What the Hebrew Scriptures did for the nation of Israel when they observed them, what the completed Scriptures did for the Christian congregation in the first century, and what the Bible can do for persons in the present, is convincing proof of its qualities as an ideal instrument of God to accomplish his purpose. —Compare 1Co 1:18.

The whole tenor of the Scriptures, including the teachings of God's Son, is to the effect that the gaining of understanding of God's purposes, the doing of his will, and the attaining of salvation to life are dependent primarily upon the individual's heart. (1Sa 16:7; 1Ch 28:9; Pr 4:23; 21:2; Mt 15:8; Lu 8:5-15; Ro 10:10) The Bible is unique in its ability to "discern thoughts and intentions of the heart," revealing what the person really is. (Heb 4:12, 13) It is clear from the Scriptures that God has not made knowledge of himself something to be acquired without effort. (Compare Pr 2:1-14; 8:32-36; Isa 55:6-11; Mt 7:7, 8.) It is also evident that God has caused his purposes to be revealed to humble ones and hidden from haughty ones, because 'to do thus came to be the way approved by him.' (Mt 11:25-27; 13:10-15; 1Co 2:6-16; Jas 4:6) So, the fact that individuals whose hearts do not respond to the Bible's message can find things in the Scriptures that, in their opinion, justify their rejection of its message, its reproof, and its discipline does not show any imperfection on the part of the Bible. Rather, it illustrates the Scriptural points just made and hence demonstrates the perfection of the Bible in the view of its Author, whose view alone is decisive. (Isa 29:13, 14; Joh 9:39; Ac 28:23-27; Ro 1:28) The things relating to God's Word and way that the worldly-wise deem "foolish" or "weak" are proved by time and test to be of superior wisdom and strength compared to the theories, philosophies, and reasonings of human detractors.—1Co 1:22-25; 1Pe 1:24, 25.

Faith remains an essential requirement for the understanding and appreciation of God's perfect Word. The individual may feel that certain details and explanations should be in the Bible, revealing why, in specific cases, God gave approval or disapproval or why he took a particular course of action; the individual also may feel that other details found in the Bible are superfluous. Yet he should realize that if the Bible conformed to human standards or criteria, such as his own, this would not prove it divinely perfect. Exposing the falsity of such an attitude, Jehovah declares the superiority of his thoughts and ways to those of humans, and he assures that his word will "have certain success" in the fulfillment of his purpose. (Isa 55:8-11; Ps 119:89) That is what perfection means, as the definitions in the initial portion of this article show.

Perfection and Free Will. The foregoing information aids in understanding how perfect creatures of God could become disobedient. To view this as incompatible with perfection is to ignore the meaning of the term, substituting a personal concept that goes contrary to fact. God's intelligent creatures are granted free moral agency, the privilege and responsibility of making a personal decision as to the course they will take. (De 30:19, 20; Jos 24:15) It is evident that this was the case with the first human pair, so that their devotion to God could be subject to test. (Ge 2:15-17; 3:2, 3) As their Maker, Jehovah knew what he wanted of them, and from the Scriptures it is clear that he wanted, not an automatic, virtually mechanical obedience, but worship and service that sprang from hearts and minds motivated by genuine love. (Compare De 30:15, 16; 1Ch 28:9; 29:17; Joh 4:23, 24.) If Adam and his wife had *lacked* the ability to choose in this matter, they would not have met God's requirements; they would not have been complete, perfect, according to his standards.

It must be remembered that perfection as it relates to humans is a relative perfection, limited to the human sphere. Though created perfect, Adam could not go beyond the limits assigned him by his Creator; he could not eat dirt, gravel, or wood without suffering ill effects; if he tried to breathe water instead of air, he would drown. Similarly, if he allowed his mind and heart to feed on wrong thoughts, this would lead to entertaining wrong desires and finally bring sin and death. —Jas 1:14, 15; compare Ge 1:29; Mt 4:4.

That the creature's individual will and choice are determining factors readily becomes evident. If we were to insist that a perfect man could not take a wrong course where a moral issue was involved, should we not also logically argue that an *imperfect* creature could not take a *right* course where such moral issue was involved? Yet some imperfect creatures *do* take a right course on moral issues involving obedience to God, even choosing to suffer persecution rather than change from such a course; while at the same time others deliberately engage in doing what they know is wrong. Thus not all wrong actions can be excused by human imperfection. The individual's will and choice are deciding factors. In the same way, it was not human perfection alone that would guar-

antee right action by the first man but, rather, the exercise of his own free will and choice as motivated by love for his God and for what was right.—Pr 4:23.

The first sinner and the king of Tyre. Human sin and imperfection were, of course, preceded by sin and imperfection in the spirit realm, as Jesus' words at John 8:44 and the account in chapter 3 of Genesis reveal. The dirge recorded at Ezekiel 28:12-19, though directed to the human "king of Tyre," evidently parallels the course taken by the spirit son of God who first sinned. The pride of "the king of Tyre," his making himself 'a god,' his being called a "cherub," and the reference to "Eden, the garden of God," certainly correspond to Biblical information concerning Satan the Devil, who became puffed up with pride, is linked to the serpent in Eden, and is called "the god of this system of things."—1Ti 3:6; Ge 3:1-5, 14, 15; Re 12:9; 2Co 4:4.

The anonymous king of Tyre, residing in the city claiming to be "perfect in prettiness," was himself "full of wisdom and perfect [adjective related to Heb. *ka·lal'*] in beauty," and "faultless [Heb., *ta·mim'*]" in his ways from his creation onward until unrighteousness was found in him. (Eze 27:3; 28:12, 15) The first or direct application of the dirge in Ezekiel may be to the line of Tyrian rulers rather than to any one specific king. (Compare the prophecy directed against the anonymous "king of Babylon" at Isa 14:4-20.) In that case, the reference may be to the early course of friendship and cooperation followed by the Tyrian rulership during the reigns of Kings David and Solomon, when Tyre even contributed toward the building of Jehovah's temple on Mount Moriah. At first, therefore, there was no fault to be found in the official Tyrian attitude toward Jehovah's people Israel. (1Ki 5:1-18; 9:10, 11, 14; 2Ch 2:3-16) Later kings, however, departed from this "faultless" course, and Tyre came in for condemnation by God's prophets Joel and Amos, as well as Ezekiel. (Joe 3:4-8; Am 1:9, 10) Aside from the evident similarity of the course of "the king of Tyre" with that of God's principal Adversary, the prophecy illustrates again how "perfection" and "faultlessness" can be used in limited senses.

How could imperfect servants of God be termed "faultless"?

Righteous Noah proved himself "faultless among his contemporaries." (Ge 6:9) Job was "blameless and upright." (Job 1:8) Similar expressions are made regarding other servants of God. Since all were descendants of the sinner Adam and hence sinners, it is clear that such men were "faultless" and "blameless" in the sense of measuring up fully to God's requirements for them, requirements that took into account their imperfection and disability. (Compare Mic 6:8.) Even as a potter would not expect the same quality when molding a vase from common clay as he would when forming one from special refined clay, so Jehovah's requirements take into consideration the weakness of imperfect humans. (Ps 103:10-14; Isa 64:8) Though committing errors and wrongs because of their fleshly imperfection, such faithful men nevertheless manifested "a complete [Heb., sha·lem'] heart" toward Jehovah. (1Ki 11:4; 15:14; 2Ki 20:3; 2Ch 16:9) Thus, within the limits possible for them to attain, their devotion was complete, sound, satisfying the divine requirements in their case. Since God the Judge was pleased with their worship, no human or spirit creature could rightly find fault with their service to Him. —Compare Lu 1:6; Heb 11:4-16; Ro 14:4; see JEHOVAH (Why he can deal with imperfect humans).

The Christian Greek Scriptures recognize the inherent imperfection of mankind descended from Adam. James 3:2 shows that a person would be "a perfect man, able to bridle . . . his whole body," if he could bridle his tongue and not stumble in word; but in this "we all stumble many times." (Compare Jas 3:8.) Nevertheless, certain relative perfections are set forth as attainable by sinful humans. Jesus told his followers: "You must accordingly be perfect, as your heavenly Father is perfect." (Mt 5:48) Here his reference was to the matter of love and generosity. He showed that merely to "love those loving you" constituted an incomplete, defective love; hence his followers should perfect their love or bring it to full measure by loving their enemies also, thereby following God's example. (Mt 5:43-47) Similarly, the young man who questioned Jesus on the way to gain everlasting life was shown that his worship, which already included obedience to the Law's commandments, was still lacking in vital points. If he 'wanted to be perfect' he must bring his worship to full development (compare Lu 8:14; Isa 18:5) by fulfilling these aspects.—Mt 19:21; compare Ro 12:2.

The apostle John shows that God's love is made perfect in Christians who remain in union with Him, observing the word of his Son and loving one another. (1Jo 2:5; 4:11-18) Such perfect love casts out fear, grants "freeness of speech." Here the context shows that John is speaking of "freeness of speech toward God," as in prayer. (1Jo 3:19-22;

compare Heb 4:16; 10:19-22.) The one in whom God's love reaches full expression can approach his heavenly Father in confidence, not feeling condemned in his heart as if hypocritical or disapproved. He knows he is observing God's commandments and that he is doing what pleases his Father, and he is therefore free in his expressions and petitions to Jehovah. He does not feel as if under restriction by God as to what he is privileged to say or to ask for. (Compare Nu 12:10-15; Job 40:1-5; La 3:40-44; 1Pe 3:7.) No morbid fear inhibits him; he does not come to "the day of judgment" conscious of some 'black mark' against him or desirous of hiding certain things. (Compare Heb 10:27, 31.) As a child does not fear to ask his loving parents for anything, so the Christian in whom love is fully developed is sure that "no matter what it is that we ask according to his will, he hears us. Further, if we know he hears us respecting whatever we are asking, we know we are to have the things asked since we have asked them of him."—1Jo 5:14, 15.

Thus, this "perfect love" does not cast out fear of every kind. It does not eliminate the reverential and filial fear of God, born of deep respect for his position, power, and justice. (Ps 111:9, 10; Heb 11:7) Neither does it do away with the normal fear that causes a person, where possible, to avoid danger or to protect his life, nor with the fear caused by sudden alarm.—Compare 1Sa 21:10-15; 2Co 11:32, 33; Job 37:1-5; Hab 3:16, 18.

Also, full unity is achieved through the "perfect bond" of love, causing true Christians to be "perfected into one." (Col 3:14; Joh 17:23) Obviously the perfection of this unity is also relative and does not mean that all differences of personality, such as individual abilities, habits, and conscience, are eliminated. When attained, however, its fullness does lead to unified action, belief, and teaching.—Ro 15:5, 6; 1Co 1:10; Eph 4:3; Php 1:27.

The Perfection of Christ Jesus. Jesus was born as a perfect human—holy, sinless. (Lu 1:30-35; Heb 7:26) His physical perfection, of course, was not infinite but was within the human sphere; he experienced human limitations; he became tired, thirsty, and hungry; he was mortal. (Mr 4:36-39; Joh 4:6, 7; Mt 4:2; Mr 15:37, 44, 45) Jehovah God's purpose was to use his Son as his High Priest in behalf of mankind. Though a perfect man, Jesus had to be 'made perfect' (Gr., te·lei·o'o) for such a position, completely filling the requirements his Father set, being brought to the appointed end or goal. The requirements called for his becoming "like his 'brothers' in all respects," enduring suffering, learning obedience under test, even as his "brothers" or footstep followers would. Thus he would be able to "sympathize with our weaknesses, [as] one who has been tested in all respects like ourselves, but without sin." (Heb 2:10-18; 4:15, 16; 5:7-10) Additionally, following his death as a perfect sacrifice and his resurrection, he would have to receive immortal spirit life in the heavens, thus being "perfected forever" for his priestly office. (Heb 7:15–8:4; 9:11-14, 24) In a similar way, all those who will serve with Christ as underpriests will be 'made perfect,' that is, be brought to the heavenly goal they seek and to which they are called.—Php 3:8-14; Heb 12:22, 23; Re 20:6.

The "Perfecter of our faith." Jesus is called "the Chief Agent [Chief Leader] and Perfecter of our faith." (Heb 12:2) True, long before the coming of Jesus Christ, Abraham's faith was "perfected" by his works of faith and obedience, so that he gained God's approval and became party with God in an oath-bound covenant. (Jas 2:21-23; Ge 22:15-18) But the faith of all those men of faith living prior to Jesus' earthly ministry was incomplete, or imperfect, in the sense of their not understanding the then unfulfilled prophecies regarding him as God's Seed and Messiah. (1Pe 1:10-12) By his birth, ministry, death, and resurrection to heavenly life, these prophecies came to fulfillment, and the faith about Christ had a strengthened foundation, one filled out with historical facts. Thus, faith in this perfected sense "arrived" through Christ Jesus (Ga 3:24, 25), who thereby proved to be the "leader" (*AT*), "pioneer" (*Mo*), or Chief Agent of our faith. He continued to be the Perfecter of the faith of his followers from his heavenly position, by pouring down holy spirit on them at Pentecost and by imparting revelations that progressively filled out and developed their faith.—Ac 2:32, 33; Heb 2:4; Re 1:1, 2; 22:16; Ro 10:17.

"Not Made Perfect Apart From Us." After reviewing the record of faithful men of the pre-Christian period from Abel onward, the apostle says none of these got "the fulfillment of the promise, as God foresaw something better for us, in order that they might not be made perfect apart from us." (Heb 11:39, 40) The "us" here clearly refers to anointed Christians (Heb 1:2; 2:1-4), "partakers of the heavenly calling" (Heb 3:1) for whom Christ "inaugurated . . . a new and living way" into the holy place of God's heavenly presence. (Heb 10:19, 20) That heavenly calling includes service as heavenly priests of God and of Christ during Christ's Thousand Year Reign. "Power of judging" is also granted them. (Re 20:4-6) Logically, then, the heavenly life and privileges

that the called ones receive is the "something better" that God foresaw for such anointed Christians. (Heb 11:40) The revealing of them as they go into action from heaven with Christ to destroy the wicked system, however, is to open the way for bringing liberation from enslavement to corruption for those of creation reaching out for "the glorious freedom of the children of God." (Ro 8:19-22) Hebrews 11:35 shows that faithful men of pre-Christian times maintained integrity under suffering "in order that they might attain a better resurrection," evidently one better than that of the "dead" referred to at the start of the verse, persons who were resurrected only to die again. (Compare 1Ki 17:17-23; 2Ki 4:17-20, 32-37.) For these faithful men of pre-Christian times, therefore, their being "made perfect" must relate to their resurrection, or restoration to life, and thereafter their being "set free from enslavement to corruption" by the services of the priesthood of Christ Jesus and his underpriests during the Millennial Rule.

Mankind's Return to Perfection on Earth. According to the prayer, "Let your will take place, as in heaven, also upon earth," this planet is due to experience the full force and effect of the execution of God's purposes. (Mt 6:10) The wicked system under the control of Satan will be destroyed. All faults and defects will be removed from survivors who continue obediently to demonstrate faith, so that what remains meets God's standards of excellence, completeness, and soundness. That this will include perfection of earthly conditions and of human creatures is evident from Revelation 5:9, 10. There it is stated that persons 'bought for God' (compare Re 14:1, 3) become "a kingdom and priests to our God, and they are to rule as kings over the earth." Under the Law covenant not only did the priests have the duty to represent persons before God in the offering of sacrifices but they also were charged with guarding the physical health of the nation, officiating in the cleansing of those who were defiled, and judging when healing had taken place in cases of leprosy. (Le 13-15) More than this, the priesthood was responsible to aid in the mental and spiritual uplift and health of the people. (De 17:8-13; Mal 2:7) Since the Law had "a shadow of the good things to come," it is to be expected that the heavenly priesthood under Christ Jesus functioning during his Thousand Year Reign (Re 20:4-6) will perform similar work. —Heb 10:1.

That redeemed mankind will experience the removal of tears, mourning, outcry, pain, and death is guaranteed by the prophetic picture at Revelation 21:1-5. Through Adam, sin, and consequent suffering and death, entered the human race (Ro 5:12), and these are certainly among "the former things" due to pass away. Death is the wages of sin, and as "the last enemy, death is to be brought to nothing" through Christ's Kingdom rule. (Ro 6:23; 1Co 15:25, 26, 56) For obedient mankind this means a return to the perfect state enjoyed by man at the beginning of human history in Eden. Thus, humans will be able to enjoy not only perfection as to faith and love but perfection as to sinlessness; they will measure up fully and faultlessly to God's righteous standards for humans. The prophecy at Revelation 21:1-5 likewise relates to the Thousand Year Reign of Christ, since the "New Jerusalem," whose "coming down out of heaven" is linked with the removal of mankind's afflictions, is shown to be Christ's "bride," or glorified congregation, hence those composing the royal priesthood of Christ's Millennial Rule.—Re 21:9, 10; Eph 5:25-32; 1Pe 2:9; Re 20:4-6.

Mankind's perfection will be relative, limited to the human sphere. Yet it will certainly afford those gaining it the ability to enjoy earthly life to the fullest degree possible. "Rejoicing to satisfaction [to the full] is with [Jehovah's] face," and God's 'tenting with mankind' shows that obedient mankind is meant, those toward whom Jehovah's face turns with approval. (Ps 16:11; Re 21:3; compare Ps 15:1-3; 27:4, 5; 61:4; Isa 66:23.) Perfection does not mean an end to variety, however, as persons often assume. The animal kingdom, which is the product of Jehovah's 'perfect activity' (Ge 1:20-24; De 32:4), contains enormous variety. Perfection of the planet Earth is likewise not incompatible with variety, change, or contrast; it allows for the simple and the complex, the plain and the fancy, the sour and the sweet, the rough and the smooth, the meadows and the woods, the mountains and the valleys. It embraces the stimulating freshness of early spring, the warmth of summer with its azure-blue skies, the loveliness of autumn colors, the pure beauty of freshly fallen snow. (Ge 8:22) Perfect humans will thus not be stereotypes of identical personality, talents, and abilities. As the initial definitions have shown, this is not a necessary meaning of perfection.

PERFUME. See OINTMENT AND PERFUMES.

PERGA (Per'ga). A prominent city in the Roman province of Pamphylia. The ruins of ancient Perga are believed to be near the modern village of Murtana, about 13 km (8 mi) inland from the S coast of Asia Minor and some 8 km (5 mi) W of the Cestrus (Aksu) River. It appears that anciently, according to the Greek geographer Strabo, this river was navigable as far N as Perga. (*Geography,*

14, IV, 2) However, nearby Attalia on the coast of Pamphylia seems to have served as Perga's harbor and, in time, even displaced Perga in importance. —Compare Ac 14:24-26.

It was to this city that the apostle Paul and his associates came early in the course of his first missionary journey. (Ac 13:13) Toward its close they 'spoke the word in Perga,' but whether any of the populace accepted Christianity is not known. —Ac 14:24, 25.

PERGAMUM (Per'ga·mum) [Citadel; Acropolis]. A Mysian city in the NW part of Asiatic Turkey (Asia Minor) and the location of one of the seven congregations to which the apostle John addressed letters as recorded in Revelation. (Re 1:11; 2:12-17) The city was about 80 km (50 mi) N of Smyrna (modern Izmir) and about 25 km (15 mi) from the coast of the Aegean Sea. Close to the site of ancient Pergamum lies modern Bergama. Pergamum was originally a fortress on a steep, isolated hill between two rivers. In time the city spread into the valley below, and the hill became the acropolis.

History. There is uncertainty as to the origin of the people of Pergamum, but some evidence points to Achaia in Greece. By 420 B.C.E. the city was striking coins, and in the next century Xenophon mentioned it as a fortified city. After the death of Alexander the Great, it became part of Lysimachus' territory. Lysimachus' lieutenant Philetaerus became ruler of the city and surrounding territory, beginning the reign of the Attalids under whom Pergamum became a wealthy and important city. King Attalus I (241-197 B.C.E.) sided with the Romans against the Macedonians. His successor, Eumenes II, built up an immense library that rivaled the famous library in Alexandria. Supposedly at this time writing parchment (*pergamena charta*) was invented in the city. Also, by this period the kingdom of Pergamum controlled most of W Asia Minor. In 133 B.C.E. Attalus III, on his deathbed, willed Pergamum to Rome, whereupon the city became the capital of the Roman province of Asia. (See ASIA.) Even when it ceased to be the capital, Pergamum continued to hold great importance as an official administrative center.

Religion of Pergamum. Pagan religion was greatly stressed in Pergamum. It seems that Chaldean Magi (astrologers) fled from Babylon to Pergamum, setting up their central college there. Eumenes II built a huge marble altar to the god Zeus to celebrate his defeat of the Gauls. The remains of it have been unearthed and show that it was decorated with an enormous relief depicting gods battling giants. (PICTURE, Vol. 2, p. 945) The sick from all parts of Asia flocked to Pergamum because of its temple of Asclepius, the god of healing and medicine.

An especially noteworthy aspect of religion in Pergamum was its worship of political rulers. The city built a magnificent temple for the worship of Caesar Augustus. Thus it was the first city to have a temple dedicated to the imperial cult. During the days of Emperors Trajan and Severus, two more such temples were constructed there, so that the *Encyclopædia Britannica* calls Pergamum "the chief centre of the imperial cult under the early empire." (1959, Vol. 17, p. 507) Such worship of the Roman emperor doubtless served politically to weld all the various conquered countries of the empire together under a common god; they could each worship their local or national gods, but all must also worship the emperor.

"Where the Throne of Satan Is." In the apostle John's letter to the congregation in Pergamum, he mentioned that the city was "where Satan is dwelling" and that the Christians were thus living "where the throne of Satan is." (Re 2:13) "The phrase has been referred to the complex of pagan cults, . . . but the main allusion is probably to emperor worship. This was where the worship of the divine emperor had been made the touchstone of civic loyalty under Domitian." (*New Bible Dictionary*, edited by J. Douglas, 1985, p. 912) Since the martyrdom of Antipas is mentioned in the same verse as "the throne of Satan," Antipas may have been killed for refusing to worship Caesar.

Perhaps an additional factor bearing on the identification of "where the throne of Satan is" was the prominent worship of Zeus, or Jupiter, the chief god among all the pagan gods and goddesses. Legend said that from the hill where Pergamum was built certain gods had witnessed the birth of Zeus, and the immense altar later located on the acropolis is considered one of the marvels of the age. Persons worshiping Zeus could have other gods but were to view them as subordinate to him. The Christians in Pergamum were commended, though, because they held fast to their exclusive devotion to the true God, Jehovah, and did not deny the faith despite dwelling 'where the throne of Satan was.'

"Teaching of Balaam." However, in the congregation there was the undermining influence of those "holding fast the teaching of Balaam." (Re 2:14) This expression calls to mind the Mesopotamian prophet Balaam, who, after unsuccessful attempts to curse Israel, suggested using pagan

women to draw male Israelites into the lewd worship of false gods. As a consequence of the resulting sexual immorality and idolatry, 24,000 Israelites died. (Nu 25:1-18; 1Co 10:8; see BALAAM.) Evidently some in the Pergamum congregation, those "holding fast the teaching of Balaam," were condoning fornication. (Jude 4, 11; 2Pe 2:14, 15) Pergamum was noted for an elaborate temple of Aphrodite (Venus), the goddess of sexual love, and sensuous religious practices were common.

Some in the congregation had also been influenced by the teaching of "the sect of Nicolaus," and they were urged to repent of that.—Re 2:15, 16.

PERIDA (Pe·ri′da) [Separated]. Forefather of a family of Solomon's servants, some of whom returned to Jerusalem with Zerubbabel. (Ne 7:6, 7, 57) The name is spelled Peruda at Ezra 2:55.

PERIZZITES (Per′iz·zites). One of the tribes that inhabited the land of Canaan before the Israelites occupied it. (Ge 13:3-7; 34:30; Ex 3:8, 17) They are not mentioned in the list of 70 families after the Flood, which names "the families of the Canaanite." (Ge 10:15-18) Their ancestry is unknown.

The Perizzites were one of the tribes whose land God promised to Abraham's seed. (Ge 15:18-21; Ne 9:7, 8) At the time of the Israelite conquest of the Promised Land, Perizzites lived in the mountainous region of Canaan. (Jos 11:3) When the tribe of Judah moved into its assigned territory, it defeated the Perizzites and the Canaanites at Bezek, which appears to have been W of Jerusalem. (Jg 1:4, 5; Jos 24:11) After the land of Canaan was divided by the Israelites, some Perizzites remained in the territory of Ephraim and Manasseh.—Jos 17:15-18.

The Perizzites were one of the seven populous and mighty nations that Jehovah repeatedly commanded Israel to exterminate upon entering the Promised Land. No covenant or marriage alliance was to be made with them, nor was favor to be granted them. (Ex 23:23, 24; 33:2; 34:11-13; De 7:1-3; Jos 3:10) However, the Israelites failed to exterminate them, and as foretold, the Perizzites became a snare to Israel.—De 7:4; 20:17, 18; Jg 3:5, 6.

In Solomon's time some remaining Perizzites were conscripted for forced labor. (1Ki 9:20, 21; 2Ch 8:7, 8) Ezra found that the Jews who had returned from Babylonian exile had entered into marriage alliances with them. However, on his counsel they put away such foreign wives. (Ezr 9:1, 2; 10:11, 12, 44) The Perizzites are not mentioned in later Bible history.

PERSECUTION.

Harassment or injury that is deliberately inflicted on persons because of social status, racial origin, or religious faith and beliefs, the purpose in the latter instance being to stamp out such beliefs and prevent their spread among new converts. The Hebrew verb ra·dhaph' and the Greek di·o'ko, which mean "persecute," can also be rendered "pursue, chase."—Ex 15:9; De 1:44; Ro 14:19; Lu 17:23.

Persecution takes various forms. It may be limited to verbal abuse, ridicule, and insults (2Ch 36:16; Ac 19:9), or it may include economic pressures (Re 13:16, 17), bodily injury (Mt 27:29, 30; Ac 5:40), imprisonment (Lu 21:12; Ac 16:22-24), hatred, and even death. (Mt 24:9; Ac 12:2) It may be promoted by religious authorities (Mr 3:6; Ac 24:1, 27), or it may be carried out by uninformed persons (Ge 21:8, 9; Ga 4:29) and ignorant ones (1Ti 1:13) or by unreasoning, fanatical mobs. (Lu 4:28, 29; Ac 14:19; 17:5) But often these parties are only the agents of more powerful and sinister instigators—unseen wicked spirit forces.—Eph 6:11, 12.

In the original prophecy at Genesis 3:14, 15, Jehovah God foretold enmity between "the serpent" and "the woman" and between their respective 'seeds.' The Bible as a whole bears witness to the fulfillment of this prophecy. Jesus clearly identified the serpent as Satan the Devil and at the same time told those persecuting him that they were 'from their father the Devil,' hence of his "seed." (Joh 8:37-59) The book of Revelation shows that such persecution continues down to the time of Christ's taking power to reign and even thereafter for a period, for when Satan and his angels are cast down to the earth, the dragon 'persecutes the woman, waging war with the remaining ones of her seed who obey God and bear witness to Jesus.' (Re 12:7-17) A prominent agent used throughout history by Satan is the "wild beast," a symbolic figure explained in the article BEASTS, SYMBOLIC (Re 13:1, 7); another is "Babylon the Great," discussed under the article bearing that heading. (Re 17:5, 6) The Satanic enmity toward those seeking to do God's will in righteousness and his use of the above-mentioned agencies can be traced throughout all Biblical periods, as the following history shows.

History.

Religious persecution has a history, according to Jesus, running all the way back to Adam's son Cain. (Ge 4:3-8; Mt 23:34, 35) Cain killed his brother Abel because he was motivated by "the wicked one," Satan the Devil. (1Jo 3:12) The issue involved in Abel's death centered around faithful worship of Jehovah. (Heb 11:4)

Job, a man of God whose name means "Object of Hostility," in time became a target of wicked persecution instigated by Satan. Job's wife and three friends were only tools used wittingly or unwittingly by this archenemy of God and man.—Job 1:8–2:9; 19:22, 28.

From time to time rulers of Judah and Israel inflicted much suffering on God's special representatives. King Saul, for example, made David ('the man agreeable to God's heart'; Ac 13:22) the principal target of his hatred. (1Sa 20:31-33; 23:15, 26; Ps 142:6) During the rule of Ahab and Jezebel, many prophets of Jehovah were forced into hiding as fugitives or were killed. (1Ki 18:13, 14; 19:10) King Manasseh shed innocent blood "in very great quantity." (2Ki 21:16) King Jehoiakim put to death Urijah, "a man prophesying in the name of Jehovah." (Jer 26:20-23) Jeremiah suffered much persecution at the hands of government officials. (Jer 15:15; 17:18; 20:11; 37:15, 16; 38:4-6) Because of the unfaithfulness of his people Israel, Jehovah allowed other nations to persecute them at times, even to the point of taking them into exile.—De 30:7; La 1:3.

There are other instances where violent persecution, legalized by government decree, was turned loose on those maintaining integrity to Jehovah, as when the three Hebrews were thrown into the fiery furnace and when Daniel was cast to the lions. (Da 3:13-20; 6:4-17) During the reign of Persian King Ahasuerus, assault and persecution flared up against the Jews in general, and against Mordecai in particular, at the instance of wicked Haman the Agagite.—Es 3:1-12; 5:14.

Other sources of persecution may be former associates (1Pe 4:4) or friends and neighbors of one's hometown. (Jer 1:1; 11:21) Jesus said that close blood relatives, members of one's own household, would sometimes become rabid persecutors of those believing in him.—Mt 10:21, 35, 36.

The principal human instigators of religious persecution, however, have been the promoters of false religion. This was true in Jeremiah's case. (Jer 26:11) It was also the experience of the apostle Paul. (Ac 13:6-8; 19:23-29) In the case of Jesus we read that "the chief priests and the Pharisees gathered the Sanhedrin together and . . . Caiaphas, who was high priest that year, said to them: '. . . you do not reason out that it is to your benefit for one man to die in behalf of the people and not for the whole nation to be destroyed.' . . . Therefore from that day on they took counsel to kill him [Jesus]." (Joh 11:47-53) Before Jesus finally died on the torture stake, he suffered severe persecution in other ways at the hands of ungodly men—supporters of the religious leaders bent on doing away with him.—Mt 26:67; 27:1, 2, 26-31, 38-44.

Persecution of Christians. With the death of Jesus, persecution of faithful servants of Jehovah would not end. This great Prophet had foretold this when, three days before his impalement, he declared to unfaithful Jerusalem: "I am sending forth to you prophets and wise men and public instructors. Some of them you will kill and impale, and some of them you will scourge in your synagogues and persecute from city to city; that there may come upon you all the righteous blood spilled on earth, from the blood of righteous Abel to the blood of Zechariah son of Barachiah, whom you murdered between the sanctuary and the altar." —Mt 23:34, 35.

Privately, Jesus had also repeatedly warned his disciples, saying, "You will be objects of hatred by all people on account of my name . . . When they persecute you in one city, flee to another." "A slave is not greater than his master. If they have persecuted me, they will persecute you also." "Men will expel you from the synagogue. In fact, the hour is coming when everyone that kills you will imagine he has rendered a sacred service to God."—Mt 10:22, 23; Joh 15:20; 16:2.

Soon after Pentecost 33 C.E., there were arrests, threats, and beatings. (Ac 4:1-3, 21; 5:17, 18) Then Stephen was seized and stoned to death, but not before he bore witness against his persecutors, saying, "Which one of the prophets did your forefathers not persecute? Yes, they killed those who made announcement in advance concerning the coming of the righteous One, whose betrayers and murderers you have now become." (Ac 7:52-60; see also Heb 11:36, 37.) The murder of Stephen was followed by a great siege of persecution led in part by Saul of Tarsus, the results of which scattered the Jerusalem congregation far and wide, but thereby extended the activity of preaching the good news. (Ac 8:1-4; 9:1, 2) Later, Herod Agrippa I had James the brother of John slain with the sword and probably would have done the same thing to Peter had not the angel of Jehovah miraculously rescued him in the dead of night.—Ac 12:1-11.

With his conversion to Christianity, Saul the persecutor became Paul the persecuted, as he says, by Jehovah's undeserved kindness. This occurred when he finally came to appreciate that he was fighting against the Lord himself. (Ac 9:4, 5; 22:4, 7, 8; 26:11, 14, 15; 1Co 15:9; Ga 1:13, 23; Php 3:6) The account of his ministry and travels thereafter tells how Paul, in turn, experienced much persecution at the hands of Christianity's enemies.—Ac 13:50; 2Co 6:3-5; 11:23-25; Ga 5:11; 2Ti 3:10, 11.

Persecution of Christians by the authorities of the Roman Empire from and after the days of Nero is a matter of secular history. (See CHRISTIAN.) The charges varied, but the objectives always seemed to be the same, namely, the suppression of Christianity.

Proper Attitude Toward Persecution. If one keeps God's commandments as a Christian, it is impossible to escape persecution, for "all those desiring to live with godly devotion in association with Christ Jesus will also be persecuted." (2Ti 3:12) Yet true Christians are able to endure all manner of wicked persecution and still maintain a happy attitude free of malice and hatred of the persecutors. This is because they understand the issues involved—the source of the persecution and why it is permitted. Instead of being puzzled and worried over such experiences, they rejoice to share with Christ in the test of loyalty under persecution.—1Pe 4:12-14.

The Christian, however, must be certain that what he suffers is really for a righteous cause. The Bible account and pattern allow for no mixing in politics, plotting of conspiracies, nor any type of criminal activities as the basis for one's being persecuted. Giving particular stress to this, the apostle urges: "Maintain your conduct fine among the nations, that, in the thing in which they are speaking against you as evildoers, they may as a result of your fine works of which they are eyewitnesses glorify God in the day for his inspection." (1Pe 2:11, 12) He followed this up with counsel as to subjection to government officials, to slave owners, to husbands, citing the example of Christ Jesus as the model to be followed. (1Pe 2:13-25; 3:1-6) A Christian could be happy if suffering for the sake of righteousness (1Pe 3:13, 14) but should never suffer "as a murderer or a thief or an evildoer or as a busybody in other people's matters."—1Pe 4:15, 16.

Christians also appreciate the prize awaiting those who endure. Concerning this reward, Jesus declared: "Happy are those who have been persecuted for righteousness' sake, since the kingdom of the heavens belongs to them." (Mt 5:10) Knowledge of the resurrection hope coupled with knowledge of the One who is the Source of that provision strengthens them. It fortifies them to be loyal to God even if threatened by death at the hands of violent persecutors. As a result of their faith in what Jesus' death accomplished, they have been emancipated from the fear of such a violent death. (Heb 2:14, 15) The Christian's mental attitude is important if he is to maintain faithfulness under the pressure of opposition. "Keep this mental attitude in you that was also in Christ Jesus, who . . . became obedient as far as death, yes, death on a torture stake." (Php 2:5-8) "For the joy that was set before [Jesus] he endured a torture stake, despising shame."—Heb 12:2; see also 2Co 12:10; 2Th 1:4; 1Pe 2:21-23.

The Christian's attitude toward the persecutors themselves is also an important factor. Loving one's enemies and blessing those opposed enables a person to endure. (Mt 5:44; Ro 12:14; 1Co 4:12, 13) This too the Christian knows: Anyone forsaking home and relatives for the sake of the Kingdom of heaven is promised a hundredfold more, but "with persecutions" also. (Mr 10:29, 30) It is true that not everyone who hears the good news of the Kingdom will endure the heat of persecution, and some may attempt to sidestep the issues to avoid trouble. (Mt 13:21; Ga 6:12) But it is better to rely on Jehovah's strength, praying as David did for deliverance from the persecutors, knowing he will not leave his servants in the lurch. Then one will be able to say with the apostle: "We are coming off completely victorious through him that loved us."—Ps 7:1; 2Co 4:9, 10; Ro 8:35-37.

PERSIA, PERSIANS.

A land and a people regularly mentioned in association with the Medes, both in the Bible and in secular history. The Medes and Persians evidently were related peoples of the ancient Aryan (Indo-Iranian) tribes, and this would make the Persians descendants of Japheth, perhaps through Madai, the common ancestor of the Medes. (Ge 10:2) In an inscription, Darius the Great calls himself "a Persian, son of a Persian, an Aryan, of Aryan seed."—*History of the Persian Empire,* by A. Olmstead, 1948, p. 231.

Assyrian inscriptions relating to the time of Shalmaneser III (evidently a contemporary of Jehu of Israel) mention an invasion of Media and the receiving of tribute from kings of "Parsua," a region apparently situated to the W of Lake Urmia and bordering on Assyria. Many scholars consider "Parsua" to be the name then applied to the land of the Persians, though others would associate it with the Parthians. At any rate, in later inscriptions the Persians are placed considerably more to the S, being settled in "Parsa" to the SE of Elam in what is now the province of Fars in modern Iran. Anshan, a district or city bordering Elam and possibly once within its domain, was also occupied by the Persians.

Thus, in their earlier history the Persians seem to have held only the southwestern portion of the extensive Iranian plateau, their boundaries being Elam and Media on the NW, Parthia on the N, Carmania on the E, and the Persian Gulf on the S and SW. With the exception of the hot, humid coastlands of the Persian Gulf, the land mainly consisted of the southern portion of the rugged Zagros Mountain range, broken by long and quite fertile valleys having well-wooded slopes. The climate in the valleys is temperate, but on the higher plateau regions the arid, windswept lands experience severe cold in the winter months. Like the Medes, the Persians appear to have done much stock raising, along with necessary agriculture, and Persian King Darius the Great proudly described his native land as "beautiful and rich in horses and men."—*Encyclopædia Britannica,* 1959, Vol. 17, p. 603.

Originally leading a somewhat austere, often nomadic life, the Persians manifested a great love for luxury and luxurious surroundings during the period of the empire. (Compare Es 1:3-7; also the clothing given to Mordecai, 8:15.) Sculptures at Persepolis represent the Persians as dressing with flowing, ankle-length robes, girded at the waist, and wearing low-laced shoes. By contrast, the Medes are depicted as wearing a tight, long-sleeved coat ending near the knee. (PICTURE, Vol. 2, p. 328) Both Persians and Medes apparently made use of trousers; Persian soldiers are shown wearing trousers and sleeved tunics over iron-scaled armor. They were expert horsemen, and the cavalry played an important role in their war strategy.

The Persian language is classed within the Indo-European family and gives evidence of being related to the Indian Sanskrit. At some time in their history the Persians began to make use of the cuneiform style of writing, with, however, a greatly reduced number of signs when compared with the hundreds of signs used in Babylonian and Assyrian cuneiform writing. Whereas during the rule of the Persian Empire some inscriptions are found in Old Persian with translations in Akkadian and in a language generally denominated "Elamite" or "Susian," official documents used in the administration of the imperial territories were recorded primarily in Aramaic as an international language.—Ezr 4:7.

Development of the Medo-Persian Empire.

(MAP, Vol. 2, p. 327) Like the Medes, the Persians seem to have been ruled by several noble families. One of these families produced the Achaemenian dynasty of kings, the royal line from which came the founder of the Persian Empire, Cyrus the Great. Cyrus, who, according to Herodotus and

Xenophon, was born of a Persian father and a Median mother, united the Persians under his leadership. (*Herodotus,* I, 107, 108; *Cyropaedia,* I, ii, 1) Till then the Medes had been dominant over the Persians, but Cyrus gained a swift victory over Median King Astyages and captured his capital city of Ecbatana (550 B.C.E.). (Compare Da 8:3, 20.) The Median Empire thus came under the control of the Persians.

Although the Medes continued subservient to the Persians during the remainder of the Achaemenian dynasty, there can be no doubt as to the dual nature of the empire that resulted. Thus, the book *History of the Persian Empire* (p. 37) says: "The close relationship between Persians and Medes was never forgotten. Plundered Ecbatana remained a favorite royal residence. Medes were honored equally with Persians; they were employed in high office and were chosen to lead Persian armies. Foreigners spoke regularly of the Medes and Persians; when they used a single term, it was 'the Mede.'"

Under Cyrus, the Medo-Persian Empire expanded farther W, reaching to the Aegean Sea as a result of the Persian victory over King Croesus of Lydia and the subjugation of certain Greek coastal cities. His major conquest, however, came in 539 B.C.E. when Cyrus, at the head of a combined force of Medes, Persians, and Elamites, took mighty Babylon, in fulfillment of the Biblical prophecies. (Isa 21:2, 9; 44:26–45:7; Da 5:28) With Babylon's fall came the end of a long period of Semitic supremacy, now superseded by the first dominant world power of Aryan (Japhetic) descent. It also brought the land of Judah (as well as Syria and Phoenicia) within the Medo-Persian domain. By Cyrus' decree, in 537 B.C.E. the exiled Jews were allowed to return to their homeland, which had lain desolate for exactly 70 years. —2Ch 36:20-23; see CYRUS.

Persian capitals. In keeping with the dual nature of the empire, a Mede named Darius became the ruler of the defeated Chaldean kingdom, though likely not independent from Cyrus' suzerainty. (Da 5:31; 9:1; see DARIUS No. 1.) Babylon continued as a royal city of the Medo-Persian Empire, as well as a religious and commercial center. However, the torrid summers there generally seem to have been more than the Persian emperors wanted to endure, so Babylon seldom served as more than a winter location for them. There is archaeological evidence that, following the conquest of Babylon, Cyrus soon returned to Ecbatana (modern Hamadan), situated over 1,900 m (6,200 ft) above sea level at the foot of

Human-headed bulls near the entrance to the city of Persepolis

Mount Alwand, where winters of heavy snow and bitter cold are balanced by delightful summers. It was at Ecbatana that Cyrus' memorandum concerning the reconstruction of Jerusalem's temple was found several years after it had been issued. (Ezr 6:2-5) The earlier Persian capital was at Pasargadae, about 650 km (400 mi) to the SE of Ecbatana, but at about the same altitude. Near Pasargadae, Persian emperors Darius, Xerxes, and Artaxerxes Longimanus later built the royal city of Persepolis, equipping it with a large network of underground tunnels, evidently to supply fresh water. Another capital was Susa (Shushan) located near the Choaspes (Karkheh) River in ancient Elam, occupying a strategic central location between Babylon, Ecbatana, and Persepolis. Here Darius the Great built a magnificent palace that served generally as a winter residence, for, as at Babylon, the summer heat at Susa was extreme. However, as time progressed Susa became more and more the real administrative center of the empire.—See SHUSHAN.

Religion and Law. The Persian rulers, while as capable of cruelty as the Semitic kings of Assyria and Babylonia, initially at least seem to have endeavored to manifest a degree of fairness and legality in their dealings with the conquered peoples. Their religion apparently contained some concept of ethics. Following their chief god Ahura Mazda, a principal deity was Mithra, who became known not only as a god of war but also as the god of contracts, the one whose eyes and ears were ever alert to spy out any violator of an agreement. (See GODS AND GODDESSES.) Greek historian Herodotus (I, 136, 138) wrote of the Persians: "They educate their boys from five to twenty years old, and teach them three things only, riding and archery and truthtelling. . . . They hold lying to be foulest of all." While the history of the Persian rulers shows them to be not above duplicity and intrigue, yet a basic adherence to some tribal creed of 'keeping one's word' may be reflected in their insistence on the inviolability of "the law of the Medes and the Persians." (Da 6:8, 15; Es 1:19; 8:8) Thus, when Cyrus' decree was found some 18 years after its date of issuance, King Darius recognized the legality of the Jews' position as regards the building of the temple and gave orders that full cooperation be extended to them.—Ezr 6:1-12.

Considerable administrative ability is evidenced in the Persian imperial organization. In addition to the king's own privy council, or advisory board, composed of "seven princes of Persia and Media" (Es 1:14; Ezr 7:14), there were satraps appointed over major regions or countries, such as Media, Elam, Parthia, Babylonia, Assyria, Arabia, Armenia, Cappadocia, Lydia, Ionia, and, as the empire expanded, Egypt, Ethiopia, and Libya. These satraps were granted a measure of autonomy in the government of the satrapy, including the administration of judicial and financial affairs within their territory. (See SATRAP.) Within the satrapy there appear to have been subordinate governors of jurisdictional districts (numbering 127 in King Ahasuerus' day), and within the jurisdictional districts there were princes of the particular peoples composing the district's population. (Ezr 8:36; Es 3:12; 8:9) Likely to overcome the disadvantage of the imperial capital's being somewhat in a corner of the far-flung domain, a speedy system of communication was developed by means of a royal mail service employing couriers riding posthorses, thereby connecting the throne with all the jurisdictional districts. (Es 8:10, 14) Royal highways were maintained; one ran from Shushan all the way to Sardis in Asia Minor.

From Cyrus' Death to Darius' Death. The reign of Cyrus the Great ended in 530 B.C.E. when he died while on a warring campaign. His son Cambyses succeeded him to the throne and was successful in conquering Egypt. Though not re-ferred to by the name Cambyses in the Bible, he is evidently the "Ahasuerus" to whom the opposers of the temple work sent false accusations against the Jews, as stated at Ezra 4:6.

The circumstances involving the end of Cambyses' rule are confused. One account, set forth by Darius the Great in his Behistun Inscription, and recounted by Herodotus and others with certain variations, is that Cambyses had his brother Bardiya (called Smerdis by Herodotus) secretly put to death. Then, during Cambyses' absence in Egypt, a Magian named Gaumata (also called Smerdis by Herodotus), posing as Bardiya (Smerdis), usurped the throne and was able to gain recognition as king. While returning from Egypt, Cambyses died, and thus the usurper became secure on the throne. (*Herodotus*, III, 61-67) The other version, favored by some historians, is that Bardiya had not been killed and that he, not some impostor, usurped the throne during Cambyses' absence.

Whatever the case, the reign of Cambyses ended in 522 B.C.E., and the rule that followed lasted seven months, ending also in 522 B.C.E. with the assassination of the usurper (either Bardiya or Gaumata the pseudo Smerdis). Yet during this brief rule apparently a second charge against the Jews was directed to the Persian throne, the king then being designated in the Bible as "Artaxerxes" (perhaps a throne name or title), and this time the accusations were successful in producing a royal ban against further construction on the temple. (Ezr 4:7-23) The temple work then lay idle "until the second year of the reign of Darius the king of Persia."—Ezr 4:24.

Darius I (called Darius Hystaspis or Darius the Great) evidently engineered or instigated the slaying of the one occupying the Persian throne and gained the throne for himself. During his rule the temple work at Jerusalem was renewed with royal approval, and the temple was completed during his sixth year of rule (early in 515 B.C.E.). (Ezr 6:1-15) Darius' reign was one of imperial expansion. He extended Persian dominion as far E as India and as far W as Thrace and Macedonia.

At least by this time the Persian rulers had fulfilled the prophetic symbolisms of Daniel 7:5 and 8:4, where, under the symbols of a bear and also a ram, the Medo-Persian Empire is represented as seizing territories in three principal directions: to the N, the W, and the S. In a campaign against Greece, however, Darius' forces suffered defeat at Marathon in 490 B.C.E. Darius died in 486 B.C.E.—See DARIUS No. 2.

The Reigns of Xerxes and of Artaxerxes. Xerxes, Darius' son, is evidently the king called Ahasuerus in the book of Esther. His actions also fit the description of the fourth Persian king, who would "rouse up everything against the kingdom of Greece." (Da 11:2) Endeavoring to retaliate for the Persian defeat at Marathon, Xerxes launched massive forces against the Greek mainland in 480 B.C.E. Following a costly victory at Thermopylae and the destruction of Athens, his forces met defeat at Salamis and later at Plataea, causing Xerxes to return to Persia.

Xerxes' reign was marked by certain administrative reforms and the completion of much of the construction work his father had initiated at Persepolis. (Compare Es 10:1, 2.) The Greek stories of the end of Xerxes' reign revolve around marital difficulties, disorders in the harem, and a supposed dominance of Xerxes by certain of his courtiers. These accounts may reflect, though in a very confused and twisted way, some of the basic facts of the book of Esther, including the deposing of Queen Vashti and her replacement by Esther, as well as the ascension of Mordecai to a position of great authority in the realm. (Es 2:17; 10:3) According to secular accounts, Xerxes was assassinated by one of his courtiers.

Artaxerxes Longimanus, Xerxes' successor, is notable for his authorization of Ezra's return to Jerusalem with a large contribution for the support of the temple there. This occurred in Artaxerxes' seventh year (468 B.C.E.). (Ezr 7:1-26; 8:24-36) During the 20th year of Artaxerxes (455 B.C.E.), Nehemiah was granted permission to go to Jerusalem to rebuild the city. (Ne 1:3; 2:1, 5-8) Nehemiah later returned for a time to the court of Artaxerxes in that king's 32nd year (443 B.C.E.).—Ne 13:6.

There is some disagreement in historical writings with regard to the reigns of Xerxes and of Artaxerxes. Reference works place Artaxerxes' accession year in 465 B.C.E. Certain documents give to his father, Xerxes, a reign that continued into the 21st year. Xerxes' rule is customarily counted from 486 B.C.E., when Darius, his father, died. His own first regnal year is viewed as having started in 485 B.C.E., and his 21st year and the accession year of Artaxerxes are often said to have been 465 B.C.E. As for Artaxerxes, scholars usually say that his last year of rule began in 424 B.C.E. Some documents present that as year 41 of Artaxerxes' reign. If that were correct, it would mean that his accession year was in 465 B.C.E. and that his first regnal year began in 464 B.C.E.

However, there is strong evidence for calculating the last year of Xerxes and the accession year of Artaxerxes as being 475 B.C.E. This evidence is threefold: from Greek sources, from Persian sources, and from Babylonian sources.

Evidence from Greek sources. An event in Greek history can help us determine when Artaxerxes began ruling. Greek statesman and military hero Themistocles fell into disfavor with his countrymen and fled for safety to Persia. According to Greek historian Thucydides (I, CXXXVII, 3), who has gained fame for his accuracy, at that time Themistocles "sent on a letter to King Artaxerxes son of Xerxes, who had lately come to the throne." *Plutarch's Lives* (Themistocles, XXVII, 1) gives the information that "Thucydides and Charon of Lampsacus relate that Xerxes was dead, and that it was his son Artaxerxes with whom Themistocles had his interview." Charon was a Persian subject who lived through the change of rulership from Xerxes to Artaxerxes. From the testimonies of Thucydides and of Charon of Lampsacus, we can see that when Themistocles arrived in Persia, Artaxerxes had recently begun ruling.

We can establish the time when Artaxerxes began ruling by calculating back from when Themistocles died. Not all reference books give the same date for his death. However, historian Diodorus Siculus (*Diodorus of Sicily*, XI, 54, 1; XI, 58, 3) relates his death in an account of things that happened "when Praxiergus was archon in Athens." Praxiergus was archon in Athens in 471/470 B.C.E. (*Greek and Roman Chronology*, by Alan E. Samuel, Munich, 1972, p. 206) According to Thucydides, Themistocles' arrival in Persia was followed by a year of language study in preparation for an audience with Artaxerxes. Thereafter the king granted him settlement in Persia with many honors. If Themistocles died in 471/470 B.C.E., his settlement in Persia must have been not later than 472 B.C.E. and his arrival a year earlier, in 473 B.C.E. At that time Artaxerxes "had lately come to the throne."

Concerning the time when Xerxes died and Artaxerxes ascended the throne, M. de Koutorga wrote: "We have seen that, according to the chronology of Thucydides, Xerxes died towards the end of the year 475 B.C.E., and that, according to the same historian, Themistocles arrived in Asia Minor shortly after the coming to the throne of Artaxerxes Longimanus."—*Mémoires présentés par divers savants à l'Académie des Inscriptions et Belles-Lettres de l'Institut Impérial de France*, first series, Vol. VI, second part, Paris, 1864, p. 147.

As further support of this, E. Levesque noted the following: "Therefore it is necessary, according to the *Alexandrian Chronicle*, to place Xerxes' death in 475 B.C.E., after eleven years of reign.

The historian Justin, III, 1, confirms this chronicle and the assertions of Thucydides. According to him, at the time of Xerxes' murder, Artaxerxes, his son, was but a child, *puer* [a boy], which is true if Xerxes died in 475. Artaxerxes was then 16 years old, whereas in 465 he would have been twenty-six years old, which would not justify anymore Justin's expression. According to this chronology, since Artaxerxes began to reign in 475, the 20th year of his reign proves to be in 455 and not in 445 as it is said quite commonly."—*Revue apologétique*, Paris, Vol. 68, 1939, p. 94.

If Darius died in 486 B.C.E. and Xerxes died in 475 B.C.E., how could it be explained that some ancient documents allot to Xerxes a reign of 21 years? It is well known that a king and his son might rule together in a double kingship, or coregency. If this was the case with Darius and Xerxes, historians could count the years of Xerxes' reign either from the start of a coregency with his father or from his father's death. If Xerxes ruled 10 years with his father and 11 years by himself, some sources could attribute to him 21 years of rulership, while others might give him 11 years.

There is solid evidence for a coregency of Xerxes with his father Darius. The Greek historian Herodotus (VII, 3) says: "Darius judged his [Xerxes'] plea [for kingship] to be just and declared him king. But to my thinking Xerxes would have been made king even without this advice." This indicates that Xerxes was made king during the reign of his father Darius.

Evidence from Persian sources. A coregency of Xerxes with Darius can be seen especially from Persian bas-reliefs that have come to light. In Persepolis several bas-reliefs have been found that represent Xerxes standing behind his father's throne, dressed in clothing identical to his father's and with his head on the same level. This is unusual, since ordinarily the king's head would be higher than all others. In *A New Inscription of Xerxes From Persepolis* (by Ernst E. Herzfeld, 1932) it is noted that both inscriptions and buildings found in Persepolis imply a coregency of Xerxes with his father Darius. On page 8 of his work Herzfeld wrote: "The peculiar tenor of Xerxes' inscriptions at Persepolis, most of which do not distinguish between his own activity and that of his father, and the relation, just as peculiar, of their buildings, which it is impossible to allocate to either Darius or Xerxes individually, have always implied a kind of coregency of Xerxes. Moreover, two sculptures at Persepolis illustrate that relation." With reference to one of these sculptures, Herzfeld pointed out: "Darius is represented, wearing all the royal attributes, enthroned on a high couch-platform supported by representatives of the various nations of his empire. Behind him in the relief, that is, in reality at his right, stands Xerxes with the same royal attributes, his left hand resting on the high back of the throne. That is a gesture that speaks clearly of more than mere successorship; it means coregency."

As to a date for reliefs depicting Darius and Xerxes in that way, in *Achaemenid Sculpture* (Istanbul, 1974, p. 53), Ann Farkas states that "the reliefs might have been installed in the Treasury sometime during the building of the first addition, 494/493–492/491 B.C.; this certainly would have been the most convenient time to move such unwieldy pieces of stone. But whatever their date of removal to the Treasury, the sculptures were perhaps carved in the 490's."

Evidence from Babylonian sources. Evidence for Xerxes beginning a coregency with his father during the 490's B.C.E. has been found at Babylon. Excavations there have unearthed a palace for Xerxes completed in 496 B.C.E. In this regard, A. T. Olmstead wrote in *History of the Persian Empire* (p. 215): "By October 23, 498, we learn that the house of the king's son [that is, of Darius' son, Xerxes] was in process of erection at Babylon; no doubt this is the Darius palace in the central section that we have already described. Two years later [in 496 B.C.E.], in a business document from near-by Borsippa, we have reference to the 'new palace' as already completed."

Two unusual clay tablets may bear additional testimony to the coregency of Xerxes with Darius. One is a business text about hire of a building in the accession year of Xerxes. The tablet is dated in the first month of the year, Nisan. (*A Catalogue of the Late Babylonian Tablets in the Bodleian Library, Oxford*, by R. Campbell Thompson, London, 1927, p. 13, tablet designated A. 124) Another tablet bears the date "month of Ab(?), accession year of Xerxes." Remarkably, this latter tablet does not attribute to Xerxes the title "king of Babylon, king of lands," which was usual at that time.—*Neubabylonische Rechts- und Verwaltungsurkunden übersetzt und erläutert*, by M. San Nicolò and A. Ungnad, Leipzig, 1934, Vol. I, part 4, p. 544, tablet No. 634, designated VAT 4397.

These two tablets are puzzling. Ordinarily a king's accession year begins after the death of his predecessor. However, there is evidence that Xerxes' predecessor (Darius) lived until the seventh month of his final year, whereas these two documents from the accession year of Xerxes bear dates prior to the seventh month (one has the first month, the other the fifth). Therefore these documents do not relate to an accession period of Xerxes following the death of his father but indicate an accession year during his coregency with Darius. If that accession year was in 496 B.C.E., when the palace at Babylon for Xerxes had been completed, his first year as coregent would begin the following Nisan, in 495 B.C.E., and his 21st and final year would start in 475 B.C.E. In that case, Xerxes' reign included 10 years of rule with Darius (from 496 to 486 B.C.E.) and 11 years of kingship by himself (from 486 to 475 B.C.E.).

On the other hand, historians are unanimous that the first regnal year of Darius II began in spring of 423 B.C.E. One Babylonian tablet indicates that in his accession year Darius II was already on the throne by the 4th day of the 11th month, that is, February 13, 423 B.C.E. (*Babylonian Chronology, 626 B.C.–A.D. 75*, by R. Parker and W. H. Dubberstein, 1971, p. 18) However, two tablets show that Artaxerxes continued to rule after the 11th month, the 4th day, of his 41st year. One is dated to the 11th month, the 17th day, of his 41st year. (p. 18) The other one is dated to the 12th month of his 41st year. (*Old Testament and Semitic Studies*, edited by Harper, Brown, and Moore, 1908, Vol. 1, p. 304, tablet No. 12, designated CBM, 5505) Therefore Artaxerxes was not succeeded in his 41st regnal year but ruled through its entirety. This indicates that Artaxerxes must have ruled more than 41 years and that his first regnal year therefore should not be counted as beginning in 464 B.C.E.

Evidence that Artaxerxes Longimanus ruled beyond his 41st year is found in a business document from Borsippa that is dated to the 50th year of Artaxerxes. (*Catalogue of the Babylonian Tablets in the British Museum*, Vol. VII: Tablets From Sippar 2, by E. Leichty and A. K. Grayson, 1987, p. 153; tablet designated B. M. 65494) One of the tablets connecting the end of Artaxerxes' reign and the beginning of the reign of Darius II has the following date: "51st year, accession year, 12th month, day 20, Darius, king of lands." (*The Babylonian Expedition of the University of Pennsylvania, Series A: Cuneiform Texts*, Vol. VIII, Part I, by Albert T. Clay, 1908, pp. 34, 83, and Plate 57, Tablet No. 127, designated CBM 12803) Since the first regnal year of Darius II was in 423 B.C.E., it means that the 51st year of Artaxerxes was in 424 B.C.E. and his first regnal year was in 474 B.C.E.

Therefore, testimonies from Greek, Persian, and Babylonian sources agree that Artaxerxes' accession year was 475 B.C.E. and his first regnal year

was 474 B.C.E. That places the 20th year of Artaxerxes, when the 70 weeks of Daniel 9:24 begin to count, in 455 B.C.E. If on the basis of Daniel 9:25 we reckon 69 weeks of years (483 years) from 455 B.C.E., we come to a significant year for the arrival of Messiah the Leader.

Counting from 455 B.C.E. to 1 C.E. is a full 455 years. Adding the remaining 28 years (to make up 483 years) brings us to 29 C.E., the exact year when Jesus of Nazareth was baptized in water, anointed with holy spirit, and began his public ministry as Messiah, or Christ.—Lu 3:1, 2, 21, 22.

Down to the Fall and Division of the Empire. Regarding the successors of Artaxerxes Longimanus on the throne of Persia, Diodorus Siculus gives the following information: "In Asia King Xerxes died after a reign of one year, or, as some record, two months; and his brother Sogdianus succeeded to the throne and ruled for seven months. He was slain by Darius, who reigned nineteen years." (*Diodorus of Sicily*, XII, 71, 1) The original name of this Darius (known as Darius II) was Ochus, but he adopted the name Darius upon becoming king. He appears to be the "Darius" referred to at Nehemiah 12:22.

Following Darius II came Artaxerxes II (called Mnemon), during whose reign Egypt revolted and relations with Greece deteriorated. His reign (dated as from 404 to 359 B.C.E.) was followed by that of his son Artaxerxes III (also called Ochus), who is credited with some 21 years of rule (358-338 B.C.E.) and is said to have been the most bloodthirsty of all the Persian rulers. His major feat was the reconquest of Egypt. Secular history then gives a two-year rule for Arses and a five-year rule for Darius III (Codomannus), during whose reign Philip of Macedonia was murdered (336 B.C.E.) and was succeeded by his son Alexander. In 334 B.C.E. Alexander began his attack on the Persian Empire, defeating the Persian forces first at Granicus in the NW corner of Asia Minor and again at Issus at the opposite corner of Asia Minor (333 B.C.E.). Finally, after the Greeks had conquered Phoenicia and Egypt, the Persians' last stand, at Gaugamela in 331 B.C.E., was crushed, and the Persian Empire came to its end.

Following Alexander's death and the subsequent division of the empire, Seleucus Nicator obtained control of the major portion of the Asiatic territories with Persia as its central part. The Seleucid dynasty of kings, thus begun, continued until 64 B.C.E. Seleucus Nicator seems to be the one with whom the prophetic figure of the "king of the north" of Daniel's prophecy first begins to manifest itself, opposing the Ptolemaic line of kings in Egypt, who initially appear to fill the role of the symbolic "king of the south."—Da 11:4-6.

The Seleucid kings were restricted to the western part of their domain by the incursions of the Parthians, who conquered the territory of Persia proper during the third and second centuries B.C.E. They were defeated by the Sassanians in the third century C.E., and the Sassanian rule continued until the Arab conquest in the seventh century.

The prophecy of Ezekiel (27:10) includes Persians among the men of war who served in the military force of wealthy Tyre, and who contributed to its splendor. Persia is also listed among those nations forming part of the hordes directed by the symbolic "Gog of the land of Magog" against Jehovah's covenant people.—Eze 38:2, 4, 5, 8, 9.

PERSIS (Per'sis) [Persian Woman]. A beloved Christian in Rome whom Paul greets and commends for her many Christian works.—Ro 16:12.

PERUDA (Pe·ru'da) [from a root meaning "separate"]. Forefather of a family of Solomon's servants; also called Perida.—Ezr 2:55; Ne 7:57.

PESTILENCE. Any rapidly spreading infectious disease capable of attaining epidemic proportions and of causing death. The Hebrew word for pestilence (de'ver) comes from a root meaning "destroy." (2Ch 22:10) In numerous texts pestilence is related to the execution of divine judgment, as regards both God's name people and their opposers.—Ex 9:15; Nu 14:12; Eze 38:2, 14-16, 22, 23; Am 4:10; see PLAGUE.

Brought by Abandonment of God's Law. The nation of Israel was warned that refusal to keep God's covenant with them would result in his 'sending pestilence into their midst.' (Le 26:14-16, 23-25; De 28:15, 21, 22) Throughout the Scriptures, health, either in a physical or in a spiritual sense, is associated with God's blessing (De 7:12, 15; Ps 103:1-3; Pr 3:1, 2, 7, 8; 4:21, 22; Re 21:1-4), whereas disease is associated with sin and imperfection. (Ex 15:26; De 28:58-61; Isa 53:4, 5; Mt 9:2-6, 12; Joh 5:14) So, while it is true that in certain cases Jehovah God directly and instantaneously brought some affliction on persons, such as the leprosy of Miriam, of Uzziah, and of Gehazi (Nu 12:10; 2Ch 26:16-21; 2Ki 5:25-27), it appears that in many cases the diseases and pestilence that came were the natural and inexorable results of the sinful course followed by persons or nations. They simply reaped what they had sown; their fleshly bodies suffered the effects of their wrong ways. (Ga 6:7, 8) Concerning those who turned to obscene sexual immorality, the apostle says that God "gave them up to uncleanness, that their bodies might be dishonored among them . . . receiving in themselves the full recompense, which was due for their error."—Ro 1:24-27.

Israel affected. Thus, God's warning to Israel in effect told them of the many ailments that a course of disobedience to his will would inevitably produce among them. His Law given to them served as a deterrent to and a protection against disease, because of its high moral and hygienic standards (see DISEASES AND TREATMENT [Accuracy of Scriptural Concepts]), also because of its healthful effect on their mental and emotional state. (Ps 19:7-11; 119:102, 103, 111, 112, 165) Not an occasional infraction of that Law but outright abandonment and rejection of its standards is what Leviticus 26:14-16 describes, and this would certainly make the nation vulnerable to all manner of disease and contagion. History, both past and present, bears testimony to the truthfulness of this.

The nation of Israel fell into gross apostasy, and Ezekiel's prophecy shows the people speaking of themselves as "rotting away" because of their revolts and sins. (Eze 33:10, 11; compare 24:23.) As foretold, the nation experienced "the sword and the famine and the pestilence," this reaching a climax at the time of the Babylonian invasion. (Jer 32:24) The frequent association of pestilence with sword and famine (Jer 21:9; 27:13; Eze 7:15) is in harmony with known facts. Pestilence usually accompanies or follows in the wake of war and its associated food shortages. When an enemy force invades a land, agricultural activities are curtailed, crops are often confiscated or burned. Cities under siege are cut off from outside resources, and famine develops among the populace forced to live amid overcrowded and unsanitary conditions. Under such circumstances, resistance to disease drops and the way is open for the deadly assault of pestilence.

At "the Conclusion of the System of Things." Jesus, when foretelling Jerusalem's destruction and "the conclusion of the system of things," showed that pestilence would be a notable feature among the generation within whose lifetime the "great tribulation" would come. (Mt 24:3, 21; Lu 21:10, 11, 31, 32) Written after Jerusalem's destruction (which was accompanied by grave famine and disease), Revelation 6:1-8 pointed to a future time of sword, famine, and "deadly plague." These would follow the appearance of the crowned rider on a white horse who goes forth to conquer, a figure precisely paralleling the one of Revelation 19:11-16, which clearly applies to the reigning Christ Jesus.

Jehovah's Protection. King Solomon prayed that, when menaced by pestilence, Jehovah's people might pray to Him for relief, spreading out their palms toward the temple, and receive favorable hearing. (1Ki 8:37-40; 2Ch 6:28-31) Jehovah's ability to protect his faithful servant also against spiritual harm, including that of the moral and spiritual "pestilence that walks in the gloom," is comfortingly expressed in Psalm 91.

PETER (Pe'ter) [A Piece of Rock]. This apostle of Jesus Christ is named in five different ways in the Scriptures: by the Hebrew "Symeon," the Greek "Simon" (from a Heb. root meaning "hear; listen"), "Peter" (a Gr. name he alone bears in the Scriptures), its Semitic equivalent "Cephas" (perhaps related to the Heb. ke·phim' [rocks] used at Job 30:6; Jer 4:29), and the combination "Simon Peter."—Ac 15:14; Mt 10:2; 16:16; Joh 1:42.

Peter was the son of John, or Jonah. (Mt 16:17; Joh 1:42) He is first shown residing in Bethsaida (Joh 1:44) but later in Capernaum (Lu 4:31, 38), both places being located on the northern shores of the Sea of Galilee. Peter and his brother Andrew were engaged in the fishing business, evidently associated with James and John, the sons of Zebedee, "who were sharers with Simon." (Lu 5:7, 10; Mt 4:18-22; Mr 1:16-21) Thus, Peter was no lone fisherman but part of an operation of some size. Though the Jewish leaders viewed Peter and John as "men unlettered and ordinary," this does not mean they were illiterate or unschooled. Regarding the word a·gram'ma·tos applied to them, Hastings' *Dictionary of the Bible* (1905, Vol. III, p. 757) says that to a Jew "it meant one who had had no training in the Rabbinic study of Scripture." —Compare Joh 7:14, 15; Ac 4:13.

Peter is shown to be a married man, and at least in later years, his wife apparently accompanied him on his missions (or some of them), as did the wives of others of the apostles. (1Co 9:5) His mother-in-law lived in his home, one he shared with his brother Andrew.—Mr 1:29-31.

Ministry With Jesus. Peter was one of the earliest of Jesus' disciples, being led to Jesus by Andrew, a disciple of John the Baptizer. (Joh 1:35-42) At this time Jesus gave him the name Cephas (Peter) (Joh 1:42; Mr 3:16), and the name was likely prophetic. Jesus, who was able to discern that Nathanael was a man "in whom there is no deceit," could also discern Peter's makeup. Peter, indeed, displayed rocklike qualities, especially after Jesus' death and resurrection, becoming a strengthening influence on his fellow Christians. —Joh 1:47, 48; 2:25; Lu 22:32.

It was sometime later, up in Galilee, that Peter, his brother Andrew, and their associates James and John received Jesus' call to come and be "fishers of men." (Joh 1:35-42; Mt 4:18-22; Mr 1:16-18) Jesus had chosen Peter's boat from which to speak to the multitude on the shore. Afterward Jesus caused a miraculous catch of fish, one that moved Peter, who had at first shown a doubtful attitude, to fall before Jesus in fear. Without hesitation he and his three associates abandoned their business to follow Jesus. (Lu 5:1-11) After about a year's discipleship, Peter was included among those 12 chosen to be "apostles," or 'sent-forth ones.'—Mr 3:13-19.

Of the apostles, Peter, James, and John were several times selected by Jesus to accompany him on special occasions, as in the instances of the transfiguration scene (Mt 17:1, 2; Mr 9:2; Lu 9:28, 29), the raising of the daughter of Jairus (Mr 5:22-24, 35-42), and Jesus' personal trial in the garden of Gethsemane (Mt 26:36-46; Mr 14:32-42). These three, plus Andrew, were those who particularly questioned Jesus about Jerusalem's destruction, Jesus' future presence, and the conclusion of the system of things. (Mr 13:1-3; Mt 24:3) Though Peter is associated with his brother Andrew in the apostolic lists, the record of events more frequently pairs him with John, both before and after Jesus' death and resurrection. (Lu 22:8; Joh 13:24; 20:2; 21:7; Ac 3:1; 8:14; compare Ac 1:13; Ga 2:9.) Whether this was due to natural friendship and affinity or because they were assigned by Jesus to work together (compare Mr 6:7) is not made known.

The Gospel accounts record more of Peter's statements than of any of the other 11. He was clearly of a dynamic nature, not diffident or hesitant. This doubtless caused him to speak up first or to express himself where others remained silent. He raised questions that resulted in Jesus' clarifying and amplifying illustrations. (Mt 15:15; 18:21; 19:27-29; Lu 12:41; Joh 13:36-38; compare Mr 11:21-25.) At times he spoke impulsively, even impetuously. He was the one who felt he had to say something on seeing the vision of the transfiguration. (Mr 9:1-6; Lu 9:33) By his somewhat flustered remark as to the worthwhileness of being there and his offering to build three tents, he apparently was suggesting that the vision (in which Moses and Elijah were now separating from Jesus) should not end but continue on. The night of the final Passover, Peter at first strongly objected to Jesus' washing his feet, and then, on being reproved, wanted him to wash his head and hands also. (Joh 13:5-10) It may be seen, however, that Peter's expressions basically were born of active interest and thought, coupled with strong feeling. That they are included in the Bible record is evidence of their worth, even though at times they reveal certain human weaknesses of the speaker.

Thus, when many disciples stumbled at Jesus' teaching and abandoned him, Peter spoke for all the apostles in affirming their determination to remain with their Lord, the One having "sayings of everlasting life . . . the Holy One of God." (Joh 6:66-69) After the apostles generally had replied to Jesus' question as to what people said about his identity, it was again Peter who expressed the solid conviction: "You are the Christ, the Son of the living God," for which Jesus pronounced Peter blessed, or "happy."—Mt 16:13-17.

Peter's being foremost in speaking was matched by his being most frequently corrected, reproved, or rebuked. Though motivated by compassion, he committed the error of presuming to take Jesus aside and actually rebuke him for foretelling his future sufferings and death as the Messiah. Jesus turned his back on Peter, calling him an opposer, or Satan, who was pitting human reasoning against God's thoughts found in prophecy. (Mt 16:21-23) It may be noted, however, that Jesus 'looked at the other disciples' when doing this, likely indicating that he knew Peter spoke sentiments shared by the others. (Mr 8:32, 33) When Peter presumed to speak for Jesus on the payment of a certain tax, Jesus gently helped him to realize the need for more careful thought before speaking. (Mt 17:24-27) Peter revealed overconfidence and a certain feeling of superiority over the other 11 when declaring that, though they might stumble in connection with Jesus, *he* would never do so, being willing to go to prison or even to die with Jesus. True, all the others joined in making such affirmation, but Peter did so first and "profusely." Jesus then foretold Peter's threefold denial of his Lord.—Mt 26:31-35; Mr 14:30, 31; Lu 22:33, 34.

Peter was not just a man of words but also a man of action, displaying both initiative and courage, as well as a strong attachment for his Lord. When Jesus sought out a lonely place before dawn to pray, Simon was soon out leading a group to 'hunt him down.' (Mr 1:35-37) Again, it was Peter who asked Jesus to command him to walk over the storm-swept waters to meet him, even walking a distance before giving way to doubt and starting to sink.—Mt 14:25-32.

In the garden of Gethsemane on the final night of Jesus' earthly life, Peter, along with James and John, was privileged to accompany Jesus to the area where he engaged in fervent prayer. Peter, like the other apostles, gave way to sleep, induced by tiredness and grief. Doubtless because Peter had so profusely voiced determination to stay by Jesus, it was to him that Jesus particularly addressed himself when he said: "Could you men not so much as watch one hour with me?" (Mt 26:36-45; Lu 22:39-46) Peter failed to "carry on prayer" and suffered the consequences.

The disciples, on seeing the mob about to take Jesus, asked whether they should fight; but Peter, not waiting to find out, acted, cutting off one man's ear with a sword stroke (though the fisherman likely intended to inflict worse damage) and was then reproved by Jesus. (Mt 26:51, 52; Lu 22:49-51; Joh 18:10, 11) Although, like the other disciples, Peter abandoned Jesus, he thereafter followed the arresting mob "at a good distance," apparently torn between fear for his own life and his deep concern as to what would happen to Jesus.—Mt 26:57, 58.

Aided by another disciple, who evidently followed or accompanied him to the high priest's residence, Peter entered right into the courtyard. (Joh 18:15, 16) He did not remain quietly unobtrusive in some dark corner but went up and warmed himself by the fire. The firelight enabled others to recognize him as a companion of Jesus, and his Galilean accent added to their suspicions. Accused, Peter three times denied even knowing Jesus, finally giving way to cursing in the vehemence of his denial. Somewhere in the city a cock crowed a second time, and Jesus "turned and looked upon Peter." Peter now went outside, broke down, and wept bitterly. (Mt 26:69-75; Mr 14:66-72; Lu 22:54-62; Joh 18:17, 18; see COCK-CROWING; OATH.) However, Jesus' earlier supplication on Peter's behalf was answered, and Peter's faith did not give out completely.—Lu 22:31, 32.

Following Jesus' death and resurrection, the women who went to the tomb were told by the angel to carry a message to "his disciples and Peter." (Mr 16:1-7; Mt 28:1-10) Mary Magdalene carried the message to Peter and John, and they began running to the tomb, Peter being outdistanced by John. Whereas John stopped in front of the tomb and only looked inside, Peter went right in, being followed then by John. (Joh 20:1-8) Sometime prior to his appearing to the disciples as a group, Jesus appeared to Peter. This, plus the fact that Peter had been specifically named by the angel, should have assured the repentant Peter that his threefold denial had not forever severed him from association with the Lord.—Lu 24:34; 1Co 15:5.

Prior to Jesus' manifesting himself to the disciples at the Sea of Galilee (Tiberias), energetic Peter had announced he was going fishing, and the others joined him. When John later recognized Jesus on the beach, Peter impulsively swam ashore, leaving the others to bring the boat in, and when Jesus subsequently requested fish, Peter responded by drawing the net in to shore. (Joh 21:1-13) It was on this occasion that Jesus three times questioned Peter (who had three times denied his Lord) as to his love for him, giving Peter the commission to 'shepherd his sheep.' Jesus also foretold the manner of Peter's death, causing Peter, on catching sight of the apostle John, to ask: "Lord, what will this man do?" Once more Jesus corrected Peter's viewpoint, stressing the need to 'be his follower' without concern for what others might do.—Joh 21:15-22.

Later Ministry. Having "returned" from his fall into the snare of fear caused largely by overconfidence (compare Pr 29:25), Peter was now to "strengthen [his] brothers" in fulfillment of Christ's exhortation (Lu 22:32) and to do shepherding work among His sheep. (Joh 21:15-17) In harmony with this, we find Peter taking a prominent part in the activity of the disciples after Jesus' ascension into heaven. Prior to Pentecost of 33 C.E., Peter brought up the matter of a replacement for unfaithful Judas, presenting Scriptural evidence in favor of such action. The assembly carried through on his recommendation. (Ac 1:15-26) Again, on Pentecost, under guidance of holy spirit Peter acted as spokesman for the apostles and made use of the first of the "keys" given him by Jesus, thereby opening up the way for Jews to become members of the Kingdom.—Ac 2:1-41; see KEY.

His prominence in the early Christian congregation did not end at Pentecost. He and John alone of the original apostles are thereafter named in the book of Acts, except for the brief mention of the execution of "James the brother of John," the other member of the group of three apostles who had enjoyed most intimate fellowship with Jesus. (Ac 12:2) Peter seems to have been especially notable for the performance of miracles. (Ac 3:1-26; 5:12-16; compare Ga 2:8.) With the help of the holy spirit, he boldly addressed the Jewish rulers who had him and John arrested (Ac 4:1-21), and on a second occasion he acted as spokesman for all the apostles before the Sanhedrin, firmly declaring their determination to "obey God as ruler" rather than men who opposed God's will. (Ac 5:17-31) Peter must have found particularly great satisfaction in being able to show such a change in attitude from that night when he denied Jesus and also in being able to endure the flogging

meted out by the rulers. (Ac 5:40-42) Prior to his second arrest, Peter had been inspired to expose the hypocrisy of Ananias and Sapphira and pronounce God's judgment upon them.—Ac 5:1-11.

Not long after the martyrdom of Stephen, when Philip (the evangelizer) had aided and baptized a number of believers in Samaria, Peter and John traveled there to enable these believers to receive the holy spirit. There Peter used the second 'key of the kingdom.' Then on their return to Jerusalem, the two apostles "went declaring the good news" to many Samaritan villages. (Ac 8:5-25) Peter evidently went out again on a mission during which, at Lydda, he healed Aeneas, who had been paralyzed for eight years, and he resurrected the woman Dorcas of Joppa. (Ac 9:32-43) From Joppa, Peter was guided to use the third 'key of the kingdom,' traveling to Caesarea to preach to Cornelius and his relatives and friends, resulting in their becoming the first uncircumcised Gentile believers to receive the holy spirit as Kingdom heirs. Upon his return to Jerusalem, Peter had to face opposers of this action, but they acquiesced after he presented the evidence that he had acted at heaven's direction.—Ac 10:1-11:18; compare Mt 16:19.

It may have been about this same year (36 C.E.) that Paul made his first visit to Jerusalem as a Christian convert and apostle. He went to "visit Cephas [Peter]," spending 15 days with him, seeing also James (the half brother of Jesus) but none of the other original apostles.—Ga 1:18, 19; see APOSTLE (Congregational Apostleships).

According to available evidence, it was in 44 C.E. that Herod Agrippa I executed the apostle James and, finding this pleased the Jewish leaders, next arrested Peter. (Ac 12:1-4) 'Intense prayer' was carried on by the congregation for Peter, and Jehovah's angel freed him from prison (and probable death). After relating his miraculous release to those at John Mark's home, Peter asked that a report be made to "James and the brothers," and then Peter "journeyed to another place."—Ac 12:5-17; compare Joh 7:1; 11:53, 54.

He next appears in the Acts account at the assembly of "apostles and the older men" held in Jerusalem to consider the issue of circumcision for Gentile converts, likely in the year 49 C.E. After considerable disputing had gone on, Peter rose and gave testimony as to God's dealings with Gentile believers. That "the entire multitude became silent" gives evidence of the strength of his argument and, likely, also of the respect in which he was held. Peter, like Paul and Barnabas whose testimony followed his, was in effect on the witness stand before the assembly. (Ac 15:1-29) Evidently with reference to that time, Paul speaks of Peter along with James and John as "outstanding men," "the ones who seemed to be pillars" in the congregation.—Ga 2:1, 2, 6-9.

From the record as a whole it is evident that Peter, while certainly very prominent and respected, exercised no primacy over the apostles in the sense of, or on the basis of, appointed rank or office. Thus, when Philip's work in Samaria proved fruitful, the account states that the apostles, apparently acting as a body, "dispatched Peter and John" on the mission to Samaria. (Ac 8:14) Peter did not remain permanently at Jerusalem as though his presence were essential for the proper government of the Christian congregation. (Ac 8:25; 9:32; 12:17; see also OLDER MAN; OVERSEER.) He was active in Antioch, Syria, at the same time that Paul was there, and Paul once found it necessary to reprove Peter (Cephas) "face to face . . . before them all" because of Peter's being ashamed to eat and similarly associate with Gentile Christians because of the presence of certain Jewish Christians who had come from James in Jerusalem.—Ga 2:11-14.

Further information on the question of Peter's position in the Christian congregation is provided under ROCK-MASS. The view that Peter was in Rome and headed the congregation there has only dubious tradition for its support and does not harmonize well with the Scriptural indications. On this point, and with regard to Peter's residing in Babylon and its being the site from which he wrote his two letters, see PETER, LETTERS OF.

PETER, LETTERS OF.

Two inspired letters of the Christian Greek Scriptures composed by the apostle Peter, who identifies himself as the writer in the opening words of each letter. (1Pe 1:1; 2Pe 1:1; compare 2Pe 3:1.) Additional internal evidence unmistakably points to Peter as the writer. He speaks of himself as an eyewitness of the transfiguration of Jesus Christ, a privilege shared only by Peter, James, and John. (2Pe 1:16-18; Mt 17:1-9) And, as is evident from John 21:18, 19, Peter alone could have said: "The putting off of my tabernacle is soon to be, just as also our Lord Jesus Christ signified to me." (2Pe 1:14) The difference in style between the two letters may be attributed to the fact that Peter used Silvanus (Silas) for writing the first letter but apparently did not do so when writing his second letter. (1Pe 5:12) Both were general letters, evidently directed to Jewish and non-Jewish Christians. The first letter is specifically addressed to those in Pontus, Galatia, Cappadocia, Asia, and Bithynia—regions of Asia Minor.—1Pe 1:1; 2:10; 2Pe 1:1; 3:1; compare Ac 2:5, 9, 10.

The letters of Peter agree fully with other Bible books in stressing right conduct and its rewards and also in quoting from them as the authoritative Word of God. Quotations are made from Genesis (18:12; 1Pe 3:6), Exodus (19:5, 6; 1Pe 2:9), Leviticus (11:44; 1Pe 1:16), Psalms (34:12-16; 118:22; 1Pe 3:10-12; 2:7), Proverbs (11:31 [LXX]; 26:11; 1Pe 4:18; 2Pe 2:22), and Isaiah (8:14; 28:16; 40:6-8; 53:5; 1Pe 2:8; 2:6; 1:24, 25; 2:24). Scriptural prophecy is shown to be the product of God's spirit. (2Pe 1:20, 21; compare 2Ti 3:16.) God's promise concerning new heavens and a new earth is repeated. (2Pe 3:13; Isa 65:17; 66:22; Re 21:1) The parallels between 2 Peter (2:4-18; 3:3) and Jude (5-13, 17, 18) evidently indicate that the disciple Jude accepted Peter's second letter as inspired. Noteworthy, too, is the fact that the letters of the apostle Paul are classified by Peter with "the rest of the Scriptures."—2Pe 3:15, 16.

Time of Writing. From the tone of the letters, it appears that they were written prior to the outbreak of Nero's persecution in 64 C.E. The fact that Mark was with Peter would seem to place the time of composition of the first letter between 62 and 64 C.E. (1Pe 5:13) Earlier, during the apostle Paul's first imprisonment at Rome (c. 59-61 C.E.), Mark was there, and when Paul was imprisoned for a second time at Rome (c. 65 C.E.), he requested that Timothy and Mark join him. (Col 4:10; 2Ti 4:11) Likely Peter wrote his second letter not long after his first, or about 64 C.E.

Written From Babylon. According to Peter's own testimony, he composed his first letter while at Babylon. (1Pe 5:13) Possibly also from there he wrote his second letter. Available evidence clearly shows that "Babylon" refers to the city on the Euphrates and not to Rome, as some have claimed. Having been entrusted with 'the good news for those who are circumcised,' Peter could be expected to serve in a center of Judaism, such as Babylon. (Ga 2:8, 9) There was a large Jewish population in Babylon. The Encyclopaedia Judaica (Jerusalem, 1971, Vol. 15, col. 755), when discussing production of the Babylonian Talmud, refers to Judaism's "great academies of Babylon" during the Common Era. Since Peter wrote to "the temporary residents scattered about in [literal] Pontus, Galatia, Cappadocia, Asia, and Bithynia" (1Pe 1:1), it logically follows that the source of the letter, "Babylon," was the literal place by that name. Never does the Bible indicate that Babylon

HIGHLIGHTS OF FIRST PETER

A letter encouraging Christians to be vigilant and to endure faithfully despite trials

Written in Babylon by the apostle Peter using Silvanus as a secretary, about 62-64 C.E.

Christians should act in a manner worthy of their wonderful hope

"The ones chosen" have been given a living hope, an incorruptible inheritance in heaven (1:1-5)

They have faith in Jesus Christ for the salvation of their souls—something that the prophets of old and even the angels were intensely interested in (1:8-12)

Hence, they should brace up their minds for activity; they should shun their former desires, be holy, and conduct themselves with godly fear and brotherly love (1:13-25)

They must form a longing for the 'milk of the word' in order to grow to salvation (2:1-3)

They are a spiritual house, a holy priesthood, built on the foundation of Christ; they must therefore offer spiritual sacrifices acceptable to God (2:4-8)

As a people for special possession, they declare abroad the excellencies of their God and conduct themselves in a manner that honors him (2:9-12)

Relationships with fellow humans should be based on godly principles

Be submissive to human rulers; love the brothers; fear God (2:13-17)

House servants must be in subjection to their masters even when these are unreasonable; Jesus set a good example of patient endurance of evil (2:18-25)

Wives should be subject to their husbands; if the husband is an unbeliever, the wife's fine conduct might win him over (3:1-6)

Husbands are to assign honor to their wives "as to a weaker vessel" (3:7)

All Christians should show fellow feeling toward others, not repaying injury for injury, but pursuing peace (3:8-12)

The end of all things has drawn close, so Christians should be sound in mind and vigilant with a view to prayers, should have intense love for one another and use their gifts to honor God (4:7-11)

Elders should be eager to shepherd the flock of God; young men must remain in subjection to older men; all should manifest lowliness of mind (5:1-5)

Faithful endurance of suffering results in blessings

Christians can rejoice even under grievous trials, since the quality of their faith will be made manifest (1:6, 7)

They should not suffer because of wrongdoing; if they suffer for righteousness' sake, they should glorify God and not feel shame; it is a time of judgment (3:13-17; 4:15-19)

Christ suffered and died in the flesh to lead us to God; hence, we no longer live according to fleshly desires —even if fleshly people abuse us because we are different (3:18–4:6)

If a Christian endures trials faithfully, he will share in great rejoicing at Jesus' revelation as well as be assured that he has God's spirit right now (4:12-14)

Let each one humble himself under God's hand and throw his anxiety upon Him; let him take his stand against Satan, with confidence that God himself will make His servants strong (5:6-10)

---

specifically refers to Rome, nor does it state that Peter was ever in Rome.

The first to claim that Peter was martyred at Rome is Dionysius, bishop of Corinth in the latter half of the second century. Earlier, Clement of Rome, though mentioning Paul and Peter together, makes Paul's preaching in both the E *and* the W a distinguishing feature of that apostle, implying that Peter was never in the W. As the vicious persecution of Christians by the Roman government (under Nero) had seemingly not yet begun, there would have been no reason for Peter to veil the identity of Rome by the use of another name. When Paul wrote to the Romans, sending greetings by name to many in Rome, he omitted Peter. Had Peter been a leading overseer there, this would have been an unlikely omission. Also, Peter's name is not included among those sending greetings in Paul's letters written from Rome —Ephesians, Philippians, Colossians, 2 Timothy, Philemon, Hebrews.

First Peter. The Christians to whom the apostle Peter addressed his first letter were experiencing severe trials. (1Pe 1:6) Additionally, "the end of all things" had drawn close—evidently the end of the Jewish system of things foretold by Jesus. (Compare Mr 13:1-4; 1Th 2:14-16; Heb 9:26.) It was, therefore, a time for them to be "vigilant with a view to prayers." (1Pe 4:7; compare Mt 26:40-45.) They also needed encouragement to endure faithfully, the very encouragement provided by the apostle.

Repeatedly, Peter reminded fellow Christians of the blessings they enjoyed. Because of God's mercy, they had received a new birth to a living hope, giving them reason for rejoicing. (1Pe 1:3-9) They had been bought with Christ's precious blood. (1Pe 1:18, 19) Through the baptismal arrangement, they had received a good conscience and would continue to enjoy such by living in harmony with what their water baptism symbolized. (1Pe 3:21–4:6) As living stones, they were being built on Christ Jesus to become a spiritual house or temple. They were "a chosen race, a royal priesthood, a holy nation, a people for special possession."—1Pe 2:4-10.

In view of what God and his Son had done in their behalf, Christians, as Peter showed, had reason to endure sufferings and to maintain fine conduct. They were to expect sufferings, for "even Christ died once for all time concerning sins, a righteous person for unrighteous ones." (1Pe 3:17, 18) Sharing in the sufferings of Christ was in itself a reason for rejoicing, as it would result in being overjoyed at the revelation of Christ's glory. To be reproached for the name of Christ constituted an evidence that a person had God's spirit. (1Pe 4:12-14) The trials themselves resulted in faith of tested quality, which was needed for salvation. (1Pe 1:6-9) Moreover, by faithfully enduring, they would continue to experience God's care. He would make them firm and strong.—1Pe 5:6-10.

However, as Peter emphasized, Christians were never to suffer because of being lawbreakers. (1Pe 4:15-19) Theirs was to be exemplary conduct, which would serve to silence ignorant talk against them. (1Pe 2:12, 15, 16) This involved every aspect of a Christian's life—his relationship to governmental authority, to masters, to family members, and to Christian brothers. (1Pe 2:13–3:9) It called for right use of the organs of speech, holding a good conscience (1Pe 3:10-22), and remaining free from the defiling practices of the nations. (1Pe 4:1-3) Inside the congregation, older men serving as shepherds were not to lord it over the sheep, but were to do their work willingly and eagerly. The younger men were to be in subjection to the older men. (1Pe 5:1-5) All Christians were to be hospitable, seek to build one another up, have intense love for one another, and gird themselves with lowliness of mind.—1Pe 4:7-11; 5:5.

Second Peter. The purpose of Peter's second letter was to assist Christians to make their calling and choosing sure and to avoid being led astray by false teachers and ungodly men within the congregation itself. (2Pe 1:10, 11; 3:14-18) Christians are urged to have faith, virtue, knowledge, self-control, endurance, godly devotion, brotherly affection, and love (2Pe 1:5-11), and they are admonished to pay attention to the inspired "prophetic word." (2Pe 1:16-21) Examples of past executions of Jehovah's judgments against ungodly persons are cited to show that those abandoning the path of righteousness will not escape God's wrath. (2Pe 2:1-22) Despite what ridiculers might say in "the last days," the coming of Jehovah's day, a day for the execution of ungodly men, is just as certain as what befell the world of Noah's day. Also, God's promise of new heavens and a new earth is sure and should inspire diligent efforts to be found unblemished from God's standpoint.—2Pe 3:1-18.

HIGHLIGHTS OF SECOND PETER

A letter encouraging Christians to exert themselves and to cling to the prophetic word; it contains powerful warnings against apostasy

Written perhaps from Babylon about 64 C.E.

Christians must exert themselves and trust in the prophetic word

God has freely given all things that concern life and godly devotion; in response Christians must exert themselves to develop faith, virtue, knowledge, self-control, endurance, godly devotion, brotherly affection, and love—qualities that will make them active and fruitful (1:1-15)

Christians must pay attention to the divinely inspired prophetic word; when Peter saw Jesus transfigured and heard God speak in the mountain, the prophetic word was made more sure (1:16-21)

Guard against false teachers and other corrupt persons; Jehovah's day is coming

False teachers will infiltrate the congregation, bringing in destructive sects (2:1-3)

Jehovah is sure to judge these apostates, just as he judged the disobedient angels, the ungodly world in Noah's day, and the cities of Sodom and Gomorrah (2:4-10)

Such false teachers despise authority, stain the good name of Christians by excesses and immorality, entice the weak, and promise freedom while they themselves are slaves of corruption (2:10-19)

These are worse off now than when they did not know about Jesus Christ (2:20-22)

Beware of ridiculers in the last days who will mock the message about Jesus' promised presence; they forget that the God who purposes to destroy this system of things already destroyed the world before the Flood (3:1-7)

Do not confuse God's patience with slowness—he is patient because he wants men to repent; nevertheless, this system of things will be destroyed in Jehovah's day, and a righteous new heavens and earth will replace it (3:8-13)

Christians must do their utmost to be "spotless and unblemished and in peace"; then they will not be misled by false teachers but will grow in undeserved kindness and knowledge of Christ (3:14-18)

PETHAHIAH
(Peth·a·hi′ah) [Jah Has Opened [the Womb]].

1. The paternal house selected for the 19th of the 24 rotating priestly divisions that David organized.—1Ch 24:5-7, 16.

2. One of the Levites whom Ezra encouraged to dismiss their foreign wives. (Ezr 10:23, 44) Possibly the same as No. 3.

3. One of the Levites who joined in proposing the "trustworthy arrangement" to the returned exiles in which they reviewed the history of God's dealings with their nation, confessed their sin, and agreed to renew true worship. (Ne 9:5-38) Possibly the same as No. 2.

4. A postexilic go-between for the restored exiles and the Persian king; son of Meshezabel and descendant of Zerah in the tribe of Judah.—Ne 11:24.

PETHOR
(Pe′thor). The home of Balaam, the prophet who attempted to curse Israel. Pethor was situated "by the River," apparently the Euphrates, in "Aram-naharaim" (Masoretic text) or "Mesopotamia" (LXX). (Nu 22:5; 23:7; De 23:4, ftn) It is generally identified with the "Pitru" of Assyrian inscriptions. Pitru lay on the Sajur River, a western tributary of the Euphrates to the S of Carchemish. However, only if the region designated "Aram-naharaim" or "Mesopotamia" extended W of the Euphrates in this area would such location on the Sajur fit the Biblical description.

PETHUEL
(Pe·thu′el). Father of the prophet Joel.—Joe 1:1.

PEULLETHAI
(Pe·ul′le·thai) [from a root meaning "wages"]. The eighth of Obed-edom's sons, listed as a gatekeeper.—1Ch 26:1, 4, 5, 15.

PHANUEL
(Phan′u·el) [from Heb. "Penuel," meaning "Face of God"]. A descendant of Asher, whose daughter Anna was a prophetess at the temple in Jerusalem when Joseph and Mary brought Jesus there.—Lu 2:36.

PHARAOH.
A title given to the kings of Egypt. It is derived from an Egyptian word for "Great House." In the earliest documents of Egypt, the word apparently designated the royal palace and in course of time came to apply to the head of government, the king. Scholars hold that this latter application came about the middle of the second millennium B.C.E. If so, this would mean that Moses used the term as applied in his day (1593-1473 B.C.E.) when recording the account of Abraham's visit to Egypt. (Ge 12:14-20) On the other hand, it is entirely possible that the title was so applied in Abraham's day (2018-1843 B.C.E.), if not in official documents, then at least in common usage. The first document in which the title is connected with the king's personal name comes from the reign of Shishak, who ruled contemporaneously with Solomon and Rehoboam. In the Bible the title is similarly linked with the name in the cases of Pharaoh Nechoh (2Ki 23:29) and Pharaoh Hophra (Jer 44:30), of the late seventh and early sixth centuries B.C.E. By this time Egyptian documents were also inserting the title in the cartouches especially reserved for writing the royal name.

The pharaohs named in the Bible are Shishak, So, Tirhakah, Nechoh, and Hophra, each of these being considered under separate articles in this work. There is some question as to whether Zerah the Ethiopian was a ruler of Egypt or not. Other pharaohs are left anonymous. Because of the confused state of Egyptian chronology (see CHRONOLOGY [Egyptian Chronology]; EGYPT, EGYPTIAN [History]), it is not possible to connect these pharaohs to those of secular history with certainty. These anonymous pharaohs include: The one who tried to take Abraham's wife Sarah (Ge 12:15-20); the pharaoh who promoted Joseph's rise to authority (Ge 41:39-46); the pharaoh (or pharaohs) of the period of oppression of the Israelites prior to Moses' return from Midian (Ex chaps 1, 2); the pharaoh ruling during the Ten Plagues and at the time of the Exodus (Ex 5-14); the father of Bithiah, wife of Mered of the tribe of Judah (1Ch 4:18); the pharaoh who gave asylum to Hadad of Edom in David's time (1Ki 11:18-22); the father of Solomon's Egyptian wife (1Ki 3:1); and the pharaoh who struck down Gaza during the days of Jeremiah the prophet (Jer 47:1).

The Egyptians viewed the ruling pharaoh as a god, the son of the sun-god Ra, and not merely as a representative of the gods. He was thought to be the incarnation of the falcon-headed god Horus the successor of Osiris. Among the pompous titles accorded him were "the sun of the two worlds," "Lord of the Crown," "the mighty god," "offspring of Ra," "the eternal," and many, many others. (History of Ancient Egypt, by G. Rawlinson, 1880, Vol. I, pp. 373, 374; History of the World, by J. Ridpath, 1901, Vol. I, p. 72) Fastened to the front of his crown was an image of the sacred uraeus, or cobra, which supposedly spat out fire and destruction upon his enemies. The image of the pharaoh was often placed in temples among those of the other gods. There are even Egyptian pictures of the reigning pharaoh worshiping his own image. As god, Pharaoh's word was law, and he ruled not according to a law code but by decree. Nevertheless, history shows that his supposedly absolute power was considerably limited by other forces within the empire, including the priesthood, the nobility, and the military. These points help in understanding how difficult Moses' assignment was in appearing before Pharaoh and presenting Jehovah's requests and warnings.—Compare Ex 5:1, 2; 10:27, 28.

There is nothing to indicate that the daughter of Pharaoh given to Solomon in marriage abandoned her false worship. (1Ki 3:1; 11:1-6) Such marriages were often employed by ancient kings (as also by modern ones) as a means for strengthening their relations with other kingdoms. The record does not show whether the initial proposal for the alliance came from Solomon or from Pharaoh. (See ALLIANCE.) Solomon's likening the Shulammite maiden to a mare in the chariots of Pharaoh reflects the fame of Egypt's chariots at that time. —Ca 1:9; compare 1Ki 10:29.

Isaiah's prophecy, written in the eighth century B.C.E., describes a confused, disconcerted state as existing or due to exist within Egypt and on the part of Pharaoh's counselors. (Isa 19:11-17) Secular history shows internal friction and disruption within Egypt from Isaiah's time on into the following century. Though, contrary to Jehovah's word, unfaithful Judah at times turned to Egypt for military assistance, boastful pharaohs proved to be like a 'crushed reed' providing no solid support. —Isa 30:2-5; 31:1-3; Eze 29:2-9; compare Isa 36:4, 6.

PHARISEES

PHARISEES (Phar′i·sees). A prominent religious sect of Judaism existing in the first century C.E. According to some scholars, the name literally means "Separated Ones; Separatists," referring perhaps to avoidance of ceremonial uncleanness or to separation from Gentiles. Just when the Pharisees had their beginning is not precisely known. The writings of the Jewish historian Josephus indicate that in the time of John Hyrcanus I (latter half of the second century B.C.E.) the Pharisees already formed an influential body. Wrote Josephus: "And so great is their influence with the masses that even when they speak against a king or high priest, they immediately gain credence." —Jewish Antiquities, XIII, 288 (x, 5).

Josephus also provides details concerning the beliefs of the Pharisees. He observes: "They believe that souls have power to survive death and that there are rewards and punishments under the earth for those who have led lives of virtue or vice: eternal imprisonment is the lot of evil souls, while the good souls receive an easy passage to a new life." (Jewish Antiquities, XVIII, 14 [i, 3]) "Every soul, they maintain, is imperishable, but

the soul of the good alone passes into another body, while the souls of the wicked suffer eternal punishment." Regarding their ideas about fate or providence, Josephus reports: "[They] attribute everything to Fate and to God; they hold that to act rightly or otherwise rests, indeed, for the most part with men, but that in each action Fate co-operates."—The Jewish War, II, 162, 163 (viii, 14).

The Christian Greek Scriptures reveal that the Pharisees fasted twice each week, tithed scrupulously (Mt 9:14; Mr 2:18; Lu 5:33; 11:42; 18:11, 12), and did not agree with the Sadducees in saying that "there is neither resurrection nor angel nor spirit." (Ac 23:8) They prided themselves on being righteous (actually, self-righteous) and looked down on the common people. (Lu 18:11, 12; Joh 7:47-49) To impress others with their righteousness, the Pharisees broadened the scripture-containing cases that they wore as safeguards and they enlarged the fringes of their garments. (Mt 23:5) They loved money (Lu 16:14) and desired prominence and flattering titles. (Mt 23:6, 7; Lu 11:43) The Pharisees were so biased in their application of the Law that they made it burdensome for the people, insisting that it be observed according to their concepts and traditions. (Mt 23:4) They completely lost sight of the important matters, namely, justice, mercy, faithfulness, and love of God. (Mt 23:23; Lu 11:41-44) The Pharisees went to great lengths in making proselytes.—Mt 23:15.

The main issues over which they contended with Christ Jesus involved Sabbath observance (Mt 12:1, 2; Mr 2:23, 24; Lu 6:1, 2), adherence to tradition (Mt 15:1, 2; Mr 7:1-5), and association with sinners and tax collectors (Mt 9:11; Mr 2:16; Lu 5:30). The Pharisees apparently thought that defilement resulted from association with persons who did not observe the Law according to their view of it. (Lu 7:36-39) Therefore, when Christ Jesus associated and even ate with sinners and tax collectors, this prompted them to object. (Lu 15:1, 2) The Pharisees found fault with Jesus and his disciples because of their not practicing the traditional washing of hands. (Mt 15:1, 2; Mr 7:1-5; Lu 11:37, 38) But Jesus exposed their wrong reasoning and showed them to be violators of God's law on account of their adherence to man-made traditions. (Mt 15:3-11; Mr 7:6-15; Lu 11:39-44) Rather than rejoicing and glorifying God in connection with the miraculous cures performed by Christ Jesus on the Sabbath, the Pharisees were filled with rage over what they deemed a violation of the Sabbath law and therefore plotted to kill Jesus. (Mt 12:9-14; Mr 3:1-6; Lu 6:7-11; 14:1-6) To a blind man whom Jesus had cured on the Sabbath they said concerning Jesus: "This is not a man from God, because he does not observe the Sabbath."—Joh 9:16.

The attitude the Pharisees displayed showed that they were not righteous and clean inside. (Mt 5:20; 23:26) Like the rest of the Jews, they were in need of repentance. (Compare Mt 3:7, 8; Lu 7:30.) But the majority of them preferred to remain spiritually blind (Joh 9:40) and intensified their opposition to the Son of God. (Mt 21:45, 46; Joh 7:32; 11:43-53, 57) There were Pharisees who falsely accused Jesus of expelling demons by means of the ruler of the demons (Mt 9:34; 12:24) and of being a false witness. (Joh 8:13) Certain Pharisees tried to intimidate the Son of God (Lu 13:31), demanded that he display a sign to them (Mt 12:38; 16:1; Mr 8:11), endeavored to trap him in his speech (Mt 22:15; Mr 12:13; Lu 11:53, 54), and otherwise tried to test him by questionings (Mt 19:3; 22:34-36; Mr 10:2; Lu 17:20). Jesus finally silenced their questionings by asking them how it would be possible for David's lord also to be David's son. (Mt 22:41-46) The mob that later seized Jesus in the garden of Gethsemane included Pharisees (Joh 18:3-5, 12, 13), and Pharisees were among those who requested that Pilate secure Jesus' tomb so that the body could not be stolen.—Mt 27:62-64.

During the earthly ministry of Christ Jesus, the Pharisees exerted such great influence that prominent persons were afraid to confess him openly. (Joh 12:42, 43) One of such fearful ones evidently was Nicodemus, himself a Pharisee. (Joh 3:1, 2; 7:47-52; 19:39) There may also have been Pharisees who did not manifest bitter opposition or who later became Christians. For example, the Pharisee Gamaliel counseled against interfering with the work of Christians (Ac 5:34-39), and the Pharisee Saul (Paul) of Tarsus became an apostle of Jesus Christ.—Ac 26:5; Php 3:5.

PHARPAR (Phar'par). One of the two "rivers of Damascus" that Naaman considered superior to "all the waters of Israel." (2Ki 5:12) The fact that Naaman mentioned the Pharpar second may indicate that it was the smaller stream. This river is usually linked with the Nahr el-'A'waj. Besides the Nahr Barada (identified with the Abanah), it is the only independent stream in the Damascus area. But the volume of the 'A'waj is about one quarter that of the Barada. The smaller streams that unite to form the 'A'waj take their rise on the eastern slopes of Mount Hermon and merge about 30 km (19 mi) SW of Damascus. From this point the river winds its way through a deep rocky channel until finally losing itself in a swamp to the SE of Damascus. The airline distance spanned by this river (including its sources) is about 64 km (40 mi).

The major objection raised to the above identification is that the 'A'waj is not actually a 'river of Damascus,' since it flows about 15 km (9.5 mi) and more to the S of that city. For this reason some favor identifying the Pharpar with the Nahr Taura, a branch of the Nahr Barada. However, Naaman's reference to Damascus could have included the Plain of Damascus through which the Nahr el-'A'waj courses.

PHICOL (Phi'col). Army chief of Philistine King Abimelech. Phicol accompanied Abimelech when covenants were concluded with both Abraham and Isaac. (Ge 21:22, 32; 26:26, 31) As these two meetings were more than 75 years apart, "Phicol" might well be a title or name used for whoever held this office rather than the name of one man in the position for so long. For similar reasons his king's name may also have been a title.

PHILADELPHIA [Brotherly Affection]. A city in W Asia Minor having a Christian congregation to which one of the seven letters contained in Revelation was written. (Re 1:11; 3:7-13) The Lydian city of Philadelphia was situated on a hilly plateau S of the Cogamis River, about 45 km (28 mi) SE of Sardis and 80 km (50 mi) NW of Laodicea. It was built in the second century B.C.E. by Eumenes II, king of Pergamum, or his brother Attalus II (Philadelphus), after whom the city was named. The city lay at the head of a broad valley leading through Sardis to Smyrna (modern Izmir) on the seacoast. Roads connected it with the coast, Pergamum to the N, and Laodicea to the SE. The city served as a doorway to the heart of Phrygia.

Philadelphia was the prosperous center of a wine-producing section, and its chief deity was Dionysus the god of wine. The area was subject to repeated earthquakes, one of which destroyed Philadelphia in 17 C.E. With financial aid from Rome, the city was rebuilt and adopted the name Neocaesarea (New Caesarea) and, at a later period, Flavia. The site is now occupied by modern Alasehir. The ancient city was a center from which Hellenism spread in Asia Minor.

Evidently there were Jews there, Revelation 3:9 mentioning "those from the synagogue of Satan who say they are Jews." Perhaps these worked against the faithful Christians in the city by trying to win back Christians who were Jews by birth or to persuade them to retain or take up again certain practices of the Mosaic Law. The attempt was unsuccessful. Jesus commended the Christians for their endurance. He encouraged them to "keep on holding fast."—Re 3:9-11.

For Philadelphia of the Decapolis, see RABBAH No. 1.

PHILEMON (Phi·le'mon) [Loving]. A Christian slave owner associated with the congregation at Colossae. His house in this city of southwestern Asia Minor served as a meeting place for the congregation there. Philemon proved himself to be a source of refreshment to fellow Christians and an example in faith and love. The apostle Paul regarded him as a beloved fellow worker. (Phm 1, 2, 5-7; compare Col 4:9 with Phm 10-12.) Paul's desire to lodge with Philemon reflects favorably on this man's hospitality.—Phm 22; compare Ac 16:14, 15.

Apphia and Archippus seem to have been members of Philemon's household, as they are also addressed in Paul's personal letter to Philemon. Apphia was perhaps Philemon's wife, and Archippus may have been his son.—Phm 2.

It appears that Philemon became a Christian through Paul's efforts. (Phm 19) However, since Paul had done no preaching in Colossae itself (Col 2:1), Philemon may have become acquainted with Christianity as a result of the apostle's two-year activity in Ephesus, when "all those inhabiting the district of Asia [which embraced Colossae] heard the word of the Lord."—Ac 19:10.

Sometime before receiving Paul's letter, Philemon had been deserted by his slave Onesimus. This runaway slave possibly even stole funds from his master to finance the voyage to Rome, where he later met Paul and became a Christian.—Phm 10, 11, 18, 19; see SLAVE.

PHILEMON, LETTER TO. A letter written by the apostle Paul with his own hand and addressed primarily to Philemon. (Phm 1, 2, 19) It must have been composed sometime after the start of Paul's first imprisonment at Rome (probably c. 60-61 C.E.), for the apostle entertained the hope of being "set at liberty."—Vs 22; see ONESIMUS; PHILEMON.

The apostle's purpose in writing this letter was to encourage Philemon to accept his runaway slave Onesimus back kindly. Instead of using his apostolic authority to command him to do so, Paul appealed on the basis of love and personal friendship. (Phm 8, 9, 17) Knowing Philemon as a man of faith and love, Paul was confident that he would receive his formerly useless, but now Christian, slave back as he would the apostle himself. (Vss 10, 11, 21) This is especially noteworthy,

---

HIGHLIGHTS OF PHILEMON

A letter encouraging that love and mercy be shown to a runaway slave who had become a Christian

Written about 60-61 C.E. while Paul was a prisoner in Rome

Commendation of Philemon for his love and faith (vss 1-7)

Paul addresses Philemon as a beloved one and a fellow worker

Reports of Philemon's love and faith move Paul to thank God and bring the apostle much joy and comfort

Paul sends back Onesimus as "more than a slave" (vss 8-25)

The imprisoned Paul appeals on the basis of love on behalf of the runaway slave Onesimus, who has become a Christian through his association with Paul

As Onesimus is useful in ministering to him, Paul would like to keep him; the apostle is sending him back, though, since he does not want to do anything without Philemon's consent

Paul urges Philemon to receive Onesimus as a brother, as if he were the apostle himself, and Paul expresses confidence in Philemon's doing even more than is being requested

---

since Philemon had the legal right to mete out severe punishment to Onesimus.

Besides providing an actual example illustrating the beauty of Christian kindness, forgiveness, and mercy, the letter tells us something about the early Christians. They assembled in private homes, called one another "brother" and "sister" (Phm 1, 2, 20), prayed for one another (vss 4, 22), and were encouraged by the faith and love manifested by fellow believers (vss 4-7).

PHILETUS (Phi·le'tus) [Beloved; Worthy of Love]. A first-century apostate from Christianity whom Paul mentions with Hymenaeus; Paul describes Philetus and Hymenaeus as false teachers concerning the resurrection and as subverters of the faith.—2Ti 2:17, 18.

PHILIP (Phil'ip) [meaning, "Fond of Horses; Horse-Loving"].

1. One of the earliest disciples among the 12 apostles of Jesus Christ. In the Gospel accounts of Matthew, Mark, and Luke, Philip is mentioned by name solely in the lists of the apostles. (Mt 10:3; Mr 3:18; Lu 6:14) John's account alone gives some detailed information about him.

Philip was from the same hometown as Peter and Andrew, namely, Bethsaida, on the N shore of the Sea of Galilee. Upon hearing Jesus' invitation, "Be my follower," Philip did much as Andrew had done the day before. Andrew had searched out his brother Simon (Peter) and brought him to Jesus, and Philip now did this with Nathanael (Bartholomew), saying: "We have found the one of whom Moses, in the Law, and the Prophets wrote, Jesus, the son of Joseph, from Nazareth. . . . Come and see." (Joh 1:40, 41, 43-49) The statement that "Jesus found Philip" may indicate some prior acquaintance between them, as do Philip's words to Nathanael, inasmuch as Philip gave Jesus' name, his family, and his residence. Whether any connection other than friendship existed between Philip and Nathanael (Bartholomew) is not stated, but in Biblical lists they are usually placed together, Acts 1:13 being the exception.

On the occasion of Jesus' triumphal entry into Jerusalem five days before Passover of 33 C.E. (Mr 11:7-11), some Greeks wanted to see Jesus. They requested Philip to introduce them, possibly being attracted to the apostle because of his Greek name, or perhaps simply because he happened to be the one who was available to ask. At any rate, Philip evidently did not feel qualified to answer the request of these Greeks (perhaps proselytes). He first conferred with Andrew, with whom he is elsewhere mentioned (Joh 6:7, 8) and who perhaps had more confidential relations with Jesus. (Compare Mr 13:3.) Together they presented the petition, not the petitioners, to Jesus for his consideration. (Joh 12:20-22) This circumspect, somewhat cautious, attitude is reflected in Philip's response to Jesus' question about feeding the multitude and even in his request (made after the rather blunt questions of Peter and Thomas) when he said: "Show us the Father, and it is enough for us." (Joh 6:5-7; 13:36, 37; 14:5-9) His tactful manner stands in contrast to Peter's directness and bluntness, and thus the brief accounts involving Philip reveal something of the variety of personality to be found among Jesus' chosen apostles.

Because of his close association with Nathanael (Bartholomew) and with the sons of Zebedee, Philip may have been one of the two unidentified disciples who were on the shore of the Sea of Galilee when the resurrected Jesus appeared. —Joh 21:2.

2. A first-century evangelizer and missionary. Together with Stephen, Philip was among the seven "certified men . . . full of spirit and wisdom" chosen for the impartial daily distribution of food among the Greek- and Hebrew-speaking Christian widows in Jerusalem. (Ac 6:1-6) The account of Philip's activity (as also that of Stephen) after

this special service ended confirms the high spiritual quality of the men forming this chosen administrative body, for Philip did a work similar to that later effected by the apostle Paul, though more limited in scope.

When the persecution scattered all except the apostles, who remained in Jerusalem, Philip went to Samaria; there he declared the good news of the Kingdom and, with the miraculous power of holy spirit, cast out demons and cured the paralyzed and lame. Overjoyed, multitudes accepted the message and were baptized, including a certain Simon who had been practicing the magical arts. (Ac 8:4-13) So when the apostles "heard that Samaria had accepted the word of God, they dispatched Peter and John to them," that these baptized believers might receive the free gift of the holy spirit.—Ac 8:14-17.

Philip was then led by Jehovah's spirit to meet the Ethiopian eunuch on the road to Gaza, and there, in a short time, this "man in power under Candace queen of the Ethiopians" put faith in Jesus and asked Philip to baptize him. (Ac 8:26-38) From there he made his way to Ashdod and on to Caesarea, "declaring the good news to all the cities" along the way. (Ac 8:39, 40) These brief accounts illustrate the work of an "evangelizer." —Ac 21:8.

It was in this international crossroads of Caesarea some 20 years later that Philip was found still active in the ministry, still known for having been "one of the seven men" selected by the apostles. As reported by Luke, when he and Paul stayed in Philip's home for a time, about the year 56 C.E., "this man [Philip] had four daughters, virgins, that prophesied." (Ac 21:8-10) That the four daughters were of sufficient age to engage in prophetic speaking may mean that Philip was already a married man at the time of his earlier activity.

3. Husband of Herodias and father of Salome. He was living in Rome at the time his wife adulterously left him to become the wife of his half brother Herod Antipas. (Mt 14:3, 4; Mr 6:17, 18; Lu 3:19, 20) Philip was a son of Herod the Great by his third wife, Mariamne II the daughter of the high priest Simon. He was, therefore, half Jew and half Idumean.—See HEROD No. 5.

4. The district ruler of Ituraea and Trachonitis at the time John the Baptizer began his ministry in "the fifteenth year of the reign of Tiberius Caesar," 29 C.E. (Lu 3:1-3) Philip was a son of Herod the Great by Cleopatra of Jerusalem and was, therefore, half brother of Herod Antipas, Archelaus, and Philip No. 3.—See HEROD No. 6.

PHILIPPI (Phi·lip′pi). At the time of the apostle Paul's second missionary tour, this city was "the principal [or, first] city of the district of Macedonia," though apparently not its capital. It was located in the eastern part of the district, at the N end of the Aegean Sea, not far from the district of Thrace. Paul, coming by boat from Troas, landed at Philippi's seaport town, Neapolis, and traveled about 15 km (9.5 mi) NW along the *Via Egnatia,* or Egnatian Way, the great commercial and military road from Asia to Rome, which ran through a mountain pass some 500 m (1,600 ft) above sea level and down into the Philippian Plain.—Ac 16: 11, 12.

The city was situated on a hill rising out of the plain, near the river Gangites. On the S was an extensive marsh. Philippi's acropolis was on a large rock formation in the NE part of the city. Excavations of the ruins indicate that the Egnatian Way ran through the middle of the city and that alongside it there was a fair-sized forum. Amphipolis, to which Paul traveled after leaving Philippi, was apparently the capital of the district; it lay about 50 km (30 mi) SW of Philippi. From Amphipolis, Paul went S approximately 50 km (30 mi) to Apollonia and from there to Thessalonica some 60 km (37 mi) W, where he stayed for about three weeks before heading SW through Beroea to take a boat for Athens.

History. Philippi was originally called Crenides (Krenides). Philip II of Macedon (father of Alexander the Great) took the city from the Thracians about the middle of the fourth century B.C.E. and named it after himself. There were rich gold mines in the area, and gold coins were issued in Philip's name. About 168 B.C.E. the Roman consul Lucius Aemilius Paulus defeated Perseus, the last of the Macedonian kings, and took Philippi and the surrounding territory. In 146 B.C.E. all Macedonia was formed into a single Roman province. The battle in which Octavian and Mark Antony defeated the armies of Brutus and Gaius Cassius Longinus, assassins of Julius Caesar, took place on the Plain of Philippi (in 42 B.C.E.). Afterward, as a memorial of his great victory, Augustus made Philippi a Roman "colony." (Ac 16:12) Some years later, when Octavian was made Caesar Augustus by the Roman senate, he called the town *Colonia Augusta Julia Philippensis.*

Its designation as a Roman colony granted the city freedom from taxes along with other privileges, possibly including a secondary form of Roman citizenship for its inhabitants. The citizens therefore had a stronger attachment to and sentiment toward Rome than would otherwise have been the case. This may explain why the masters of the girl from whom the apostle Paul exercised a demon of divination stressed the point before the magistrates by saying, in their accusation against Paul and Silas, "We are *Romans.*" (Ac 16:16-24) It also would be very understandable to the Philippian Christians when Paul later wrote exhorting them to be "behaving as citizens" worthy of the good news of the Christ, and reminding them that "our citizenship exists in the heavens," for worldly, Roman citizenship would be highly prized in Philippi, even something about which to boast.—Php 1:27; 3:20, *Int.*

Paul's Visit. Philippi was privileged to be the first city in Europe to hear Paul preach the good news, in about 50 C.E., during his second missionary tour. He went there in obedience to a night vision at Troas in Asia Minor, in which a Macedonian man entreated him: "Step over into Macedonia and help us." (Ac 16:8-10) Paul and his companions, evidently including their chronicler Luke, stayed there for several days, and on the Sabbath they "went forth outside the gate beside a river," where, Luke recounts, "we were thinking there was a place of prayer." Some think that there was no synagogue in Philippi, because of the city's military character—that the Jews there may have been forbidden to assemble inside the city for worship. In any case, Paul spoke to the women assembled there and found one, Lydia by name, a worshiper of God, who "opened her heart wide to pay attention to the things being spoken by Paul." She and her household were baptized, and her appreciation and hospitality were so great that "she just made [Paul and his companions] come" to stay at her house.—Ac 16:11-15.

But now, after answering the call to come into Macedonia, Paul was faced with persecution in this very first city, this time not from Jewish sources, as had been the case in Galatia. The magistrates of the city acted on false accusations made by the owners of a demonized girl. They had lost their income because she was no longer able to carry on the practice of prediction, from which they had made much gain. Paul and Silas were beaten with rods, they were thrown into prison, and their feet were made fast in stocks.—Ac 16:16-24.

In the middle of the night, however, as they, in the hearing of the other prisoners, were praying and praising God with song, a miracle occurred. An earthquake broke the prisoners' bonds and threw the doors open. The jailer, knowing that he would face the death penalty for loss of the prisoners committed to him, was about to kill himself when Paul called out: "Do not hurt yourself, for we are all here!" The jailer and his household then listened to Paul and Silas, took care of their stripe wounds, and became baptized believers.—Ac 16:25-34; PICTURE, Vol. 2, p. 749.

The next morning, perhaps hearing of the miraculous occurrence, the city magistrates ordered the jailer to release Paul. But Paul was concerned with vindicating, defending, and legally establishing the good news more than with immediate release. He was not going to submit to any secret "back-door" release in order to save face for the magistrates. He called attention to his own Roman citizenship and the fact that they had *publicly* beaten him and Silas, uncondemned. No, indeed! they must openly acknowledge that they, and not the Christians, had acted unlawfully. On hearing that Paul and Silas were Romans, the magistrates were struck with fear and, coming down personally, "entreated them," brought them out, and requested that they leave the city.—Ac 16:35-40.

Nevertheless, Paul had established a fine congregation in Philippi, one that was always dear to his heart. Their love for him was manifested by their anxious care and provision for him, even when he was elsewhere. (Php 4:16) Paul visited Philippi again during his third missionary tour and, possibly, a third time, after his release from his first imprisonment in Rome.—Ac 20:1, 2, 6; Php 1:19; 2:24.

PHILIPPIANS, LETTER TO THE.

A book of the Christian Greek Scriptures written by the apostle Paul to the congregation in the city of Philippi in the province of Macedonia, a congregation that Paul had established about 50 C.E., in the course of his second missionary tour.

When and Where Written. The letter's internal evidence indicates it was written during Paul's first imprisonment in Rome. In it he speaks of "all the Praetorian Guard" as knowing the reason for his being in bonds, and he sends greetings from "those of the household of Caesar." (Php 1:13; 4:22) Paul's first imprisonment in Rome is generally considered to have taken place about 59-61 C.E. Several events occurred between Paul's arrival in Rome and his decision to write to the Philippians. Epaphroditus had made the trip from Philippi, had worked to assist Paul, and had fallen very sick. The Philippians, some 1,000 km (600 mi) distant, had received news of his sickness. Now Epaphroditus had recovered, and Paul

---

HIGHLIGHTS OF PHILIPPIANS

A letter reflecting the special bond of love that existed between Paul and the Christians in Philippi

Written by Paul about 60-61 C.E. while in prison in Rome

Paul's love for the brothers and his appreciation for their generosity

Paul thanks God for the Philippians' contribution to the furtherance of the good news. Out of deep affection for them, he prays that their love increase and that they make sure of the more important things (1:3-11)

Paul is concerned about the Philippians' welfare; he hopes to send them Timothy, whom he highly recommends; he is confident that he himself will also visit them shortly (2:19-24)

To reassure the brothers regarding Epaphroditus, whom the Philippians had heard was very sick, Paul is sending them this loyal servant whom they had assigned to minister to Paul (2:25-30)

Although Paul is self-sufficient in all circumstances thanks to the strength granted to him from above, he highly commends the Philippians for their generosity (4:10-19)

Results of Paul's imprisonment

Paul's imprisonment has led to the advancement of the good news; his situation is well known among the Praetorian Guard, and most of the brothers are showing more courage to speak the word of God fearlessly (1:12-14)

Some are preaching with a good motive, others with a bad motive—either way, Christ is being publicized; whether Paul lives or dies, he will magnify Christ; but he feels he will live so as to minister to the Philippians (1:15-26)

Upbuilding counsel regarding attitude and conduct

Behave in a manner worthy of the good news, not being frightened by enemies; opponents will be destroyed, whereas believers will gain salvation (1:27-30)

Display the same mental attitude as Christ by manifesting humility and not being self-seeking (2:1-11)

As blameless children, shine as illuminators among a twisted generation, "keeping a tight grip on the word of life" (2:12-16)

Guard against those promoting circumcision; a Christian's confidence is in Christ, not in fleshly circumcision (3:1-3)

Paul has the highest standing when it comes to fleshly qualifications, yet he considers all of this as refuse on account of "the excelling value of the knowledge of Christ"; he is pursuing down toward the prize and urges others to do likewise (3:4-21)

Continue rejoicing in the Lord; manifest reasonableness and commit anxieties to God in prayer; fill the mind with wholesome thoughts (4:4-9)

was sending him back with the letter. So the letter was written about 60 or 61 C.E.

Background and Reasons for Writing. The Philippian congregation had shown great love and regard for Paul. Shortly after his visit to them, the congregation had generously sent him material provisions during his stay of several weeks in nearby Thessalonica. (Php 4:15, 16) Later, when the brothers in Jerusalem entered into a period of intense persecution and were in need of material help, the Christians in Philippi, themselves very poor and undergoing a great test of affliction, had nevertheless demonstrated a readiness to contribute even beyond their ability. Paul so much appreciated their fine attitude that he cited them as an example to the other congregations. (2Co 8:1-6) They were also very active and busy in preaching the good news, so they apparently had not been closely in touch with Paul for a time. But now, in his need in prison bonds, they not only sent material gifts so that Paul had an abundance but also dispatched their personal envoy Epaphroditus, a man valuable to them. This zealous brother courageously gave assistance to Paul, even endangering his own life. Consequently, Paul commends him highly to the congregation.—Php 2:25-30; 4:18.

Paul expresses confidence that, in harmony with their prayers, he will be released from this imprisonment and will be able to visit them again. (Php 1:19; 2:24) He knows that for him to continue to live is to be useful to them, though he looks longingly forward to the time when Christ will receive him home to himself. (Php 1:21-25; compare Joh 14:3.) In the meantime, he hopes to send Timothy, who, more than anyone else available, will genuinely have their interests at heart.—Php 2:19-23.

The letter breathes love. Paul never withheld commendation where due, nor did he shrink back from giving necessary reproof, but in this case encouragement was the thing needed. The congregation had their opponents, "workers of injury," who wanted to boast in fleshly connections and in circumcision of the flesh, but it appears that the brothers were not seriously affected or upset. (Php 3:2) So Paul did not have to present strong argument and reproof as, for example, in his letters to the congregations in Galatia and Corinth. The only hint of correction was his exhortation to unity on the part of Euodia and Syntyche. Throughout the letter he encourages the Philippian congregation to continue in their fine course —seeking greater discernment and getting a sure grip on the Word of life, a stronger faith, and hope in the prize to come.

There are many fine principles expressed in the letter that provide guidance and encouragement to all Christians. Some of them are:

Chapter and verse	Principle
1:9, 10	Make sure of the more important things so as not to stumble others over any matter
1:15-18	We can rejoice even when the enemies of the truth speak about it contentiously, for this only serves to publicize the truth
1:19	Prayer by God's servants is effectual
1:27, 28	Christians' unity and courage in the presence of their opponents is a proof from God that he will deliver his servants and destroy his enemies
2:5-11	Humility brings exaltation from God
2:27	God can be thanked for his mercy when one of his faithful servants recovers from an illness
3:16	To what extent the Christian has made progress, he should continue walking orderly in this same routine in order to receive the prize
3:20	Christians should look to the heavens, where their citizenship exists, not to earthly connections
4:6, 7	Do not be anxious; in every situation submit your petitions to God, and he will give peace that guards your heart and mental powers
4:8	Consider at all times the right and praiseworthy things

PHILISTIA (Phi·lis'ti·a), **PHILISTINES** (Phi·lis'tines). Covering an area from a point near Joppa in the N down to Gaza in the S, Philistia stretched for about 80 km (50 mi) along the Mediterranean Sea (Ex 23:31) and extended some 24 km (15 mi) inland. "The sea of the Philistines" evidently refers to the part of the Mediterranean that bordered the coast of Philistia. The sand dunes along the coast penetrate the land for a considerable distance, sometimes for as much as 6 km (3.5 mi). Apart from this, the region is fertile and supports grain, olive groves, and fruit trees.

During a major part of the Hebrew Scripture period, the Philistines occupied the coastal plain and were among Israel's avowed enemies. (Isa 9:12; 11:14) An uncircumcised (2Sa 1:20), polytheistic people (Jg 16:23; 2Ki 1:2; see BAAL-ZEBUB; DAGON), the Philistines superstitiously consulted their priests and diviners to make decisions. (1Sa 6:2; compare Isa 2:6.) And their warriors, when going into battle, carried idols of their gods. (2Sa 5:21) Within their land, known as Philistia (Ex 15:14; Ps 60:8; 87:4; 108:9; Isa 14:29, 31), lay the cities of Gaza, Ashkelon, Ashdod, Ekron, and Gath. For centuries each of these cities was ruled over by an axis lord.—Jos 13:3; 1Sa 29:7; see AXIS LORDS.

History. The island of Crete (usually held to be identical with Caphtor), though not necessarily the original home of the Philistines, was the place from which they migrated to the coast of Canaan. (Jer 47:4; Am 9:7; see CAPHTOR; CRETE.) Just when this migration began is uncertain. However, as early as the time of Abraham and his son Isaac, Philistines resided at Gerar in southern Canaan. They had a king, Abimelech, and an army under the command of a certain Phicol.—Ge 20:1, 2; 21:32-34; 26:1-18; see ABIMELECH Nos. 1 and 2.

Some object to the Genesis references to Philistine residence in Canaan, arguing that the Philistines did not settle there until the 12th century B.C.E. But this objection does not rest on a solid basis. The *New Bible Dictionary* edited by J. Douglas (1985, p. 933) observes: "Since the Philistines are not named in extra-biblical inscriptions until the 12th century BC, and the archaeological remains associated with them do not appear before this time, many commentators reject references to them in the patriarchal period as anachronistic." However, in showing why such a position is not sound, mention is made of the evidence of a major expansion of Aegean trade reaching back to about the 20th century B.C.E. It is pointed out that a particular group's not being prominent enough to be mentioned in the inscriptions of other nations does not prove that the group did not exist. The conclusion reached in that *New Bible Dictionary* is: "There is no reason why small groups of Philistines could not have been among the early Aegean traders, not prominent enough to be noticed by the larger states."

When Israel left Egypt in 1513 B.C.E., Jehovah chose not to lead the Israelites by way of Philistia (the most direct route from Egypt to the Promised Land), lest they become discouraged because of immediate warfare and decide to return to Egypt. (Ex 13:17) The Philistines likely would not view the approach of millions of Israelites as mere international traffic, which normally flowed through their land. They were then a settled people, whereas the Sinai region to which Jehovah directed Israel had largely nomadic tribes and many unsettled regions into which Israel could enter without provoking immediate conflict.

At the time aged Joshua apportioned the land W of the Jordan, the Philistine territories were still untouched by the conquest. (Jos 13:2, 3) Later, however, the men of Judah did capture three of the main Philistine cities, Gaza, Ashkelon, and Ekron. But this was only a partial victory, for Judah "could not dispossess the inhabitants of the low plain, because they had war chariots with iron scythes."—Jg 1:18, 19.

In the time of Judges. For years thereafter, the continuance of the Philistines and other peoples in Canaan served to test Israel's obedience to Jehovah. (Jg 3:3, 4) Time and again they failed the test by adopting false worship. Therefore Jehovah abandoned the Israelites to their enemies, including the Philistines. (Jg 10:6-8) But when they cried to him for aid, he mercifully raised up judges to deliver them. (Jg 2:18) One of these judges, Shamgar, struck down 600 Philistines using a mere cattle goad. (Jg 3:31) Years later, as had been foretold before his birth, Samson took "the lead in saving Israel out of the hand of the Philistines." (Jg 13:1-5) Evidence of the extent of Philistine control early in Samson's judgeship can be seen in that, to avoid trouble, men of Judah on one occasion even delivered up Samson to them.—Jg 15:9-14.

The prophet Samuel witnessed oppression from the Philistines and also shared in defeating them. While he was serving at the tabernacle in Shiloh during the final part of High Priest Eli's judgeship, the Philistines struck down about 4,000 Israelites in the area of Aphek and Ebenezer. The Israelites then had the sacred Ark brought to the battlefield, thinking that this would bring them victory. The Philistines intensified their efforts. Thirty thousand Israelites were slain, and the Ark was captured. (1Sa 4:1-11) The Philistines took the Ark to the temple of their god Dagon at Ashdod. Twice the image of this god fell on its face. The second time the idol itself was broken. (1Sa 5:1-5) The Ark was then passed from one Philistine city to another. Wherever it went, there came to be panic and pestilence. (1Sa 5:6-12) Finally, seven months after the capture, the Ark was returned to Israel. —1Sa 6:1-21.

Some 20 years later (1Sa 7:2), the Philistines marched against the Israelites who were, at Samuel's direction, assembled at Mizpah for worship. This time Jehovah threw the Philistines into confusion, enabling his people to subdue them. Later, "the cities that the Philistines had taken from Israel kept coming back to Israel from Ekron to Gath."—1Sa 7:5-14.

Saul's reign until subjugation by David. However, this did not end Israel's difficulties with the Philistines. (1Sa 9:16; 14:47) Apparently before Saul's reign they had established garrisons in Israelite territory. (Compare 1Sa 10:5; 13:1-3.) The Philistines were strong enough to prohibit the Israelites from having their own smiths, thereby keeping them disarmed. This also forced the Israelites to go to them to have their agricultural implements sharpened. (1Sa 13:19-22) The situation was so severe that even Hebrews sided with the Philistines against fellow Israelites. (1Sa 14:21) Nevertheless, with Jehovah's help, Saul's first major campaign against the Philistines resulted in Israel's striking them down from Michmash to Aijalon.—1Sa 13:1–14:31; see MICHMAS(H).

Later, upon recovering from this defeat, the Philistines assembled their forces to fight against Israel. The two armies took their position on opposite sides of the Low Plain of Elah, in Judah. Morning and evening, for 40 days, the warrior Goliath emerged from the Philistine camp, challenging Israel to supply a man to fight him in single combat. (1Sa 17:1-10, 16) This challenge was answered by the shepherd David, who struck Goliath to the earth with a stone from his sling and used Goliath's own sword to put him to death. (1Sa 17:48-51) The Israelites then pursued the fleeing Philistines, striking them down as far as the cities of Gath and Ekron.—1Sa 17:52, 53.

Thereafter David continued waging successful warfare against the Philistines. When he would return from battle, the women, in celebration of the victory, would say: "Saul has struck down his thousands, and David his tens of thousands." (1Sa 18:5-7; see also 1Sa 18:25-27, 30; 19:8.) This caused Saul to become jealous of David, finally resulting in David's having to run for his life. He fled to the Philistine city of Gath. (1Sa 18:8, 9; 20:33; 21:10) There the servants of King Achish appear to have sought David's death. But by disguising his sanity, he was able to leave the city unharmed. (1Sa 21:10-15) Sometime thereafter David, though still pursued by Saul, saved the Judean city of Keilah from Philistine pillagers. (1Sa 23:1-12) A later Philistine raid in Israelite territory forced Saul to turn back temporarily from chasing David.—1Sa 23:27, 28; 24:1, 2.

Because of continually being hunted by Saul, David again decided to take refuge in Philistine territory. Received favorably by King Achish of Gath, David was given the city of Ziklag. (1Sa 27:1-6) A year or two later, when the Philistines were preparing to fight against Saul's forces, King Achish, believing that David had become "a stench among his people Israel," invited him to go along. But the other Philistine axis lords did not trust David, and at their insistence, he and his men returned to Philistia. In the ensuing conflict with Israel, the Philistines gained a decisive victory and Saul and three of his sons perished.—1Sa 27:12; 28:1-5; 29:1-11; 31:1-13; 1Ch 10:1-10, 13; 12:19.

When David was finally anointed as king over all Israel, the Philistines invaded the Low Plain of Rephaim (SW of Jerusalem) but suffered humiliating defeat. (2Sa 5:17-21; 1Ch 14:8-12) A later Philistine offensive likewise ended in victory for Israel. (2Sa 5:22-25; 1Ch 14:13-16) During his reign David fought numerous other battles with the Philistines and succeeded in subduing them. On one occasion, however, he nearly lost his life. —2Sa 8:1; 21:15-22; 1Ch 18:1; 20:4-8.

From Solomon's reign onward. For years after that there is no record of warfare with the Philistines. David's son Solomon enjoyed a peaceful reign (1037-998 B.C.E.), and his dominions extended as far as the Philistine city of Gaza.—1Ki 4: 21-25; 2Ch 9:26.

Some 20 years after the ten-tribe kingdom came into existence, the Philistines occupied Gibbethon, a city in Dan. While trying to take the city, Israel's King Nadab was killed by Baasha, who subsequently began to reign as king. (Jos 19:40, 44; 1Ki 15:27, 28) Gibbethon was still under Philistine control some 24 years later when Omri, army chief of Israel, encamped against it.—1Ki 16: 15-17.

While Jehoshaphat reigned (936-c. 911 B.C.E.), the Philistines were evidently subject to him, for they brought gifts and tribute. (2Ch 17:11) But, during the rule of his son Jehoram, the Philistines and Arabs invaded Judah and carried away considerable spoil from Jerusalem. They also took captive Jehoram's wives and sons—all except the youngest, Jehoahaz. (2Ch 21:16, 17) Decades later Judean King Uzziah successfully warred against the Philistines, capturing Gath, Jabneh, and Ashdod. He even built cities in Philistine territory. (2Ch 26:6-8) However, the reign of Uzziah's grandson Ahaz saw the Philistines capture, and take up residence in, a number of Israelite cities all the way from the Negeb up to the northern border of the kingdom of Judah. (2Ch 28:18) Ahaz' son Hezekiah, in fulfillment of a prophecy uttered by Isaiah (14:28, 29), struck down the Philistines clear to Gaza.—2Ki 18:8.

Prophetic References. The prophecy of Joel indicated that because of their selling "the sons of Judah" and "the sons of Jerusalem" to "the sons of the Greeks," the Philistines would experience like treatment. (Joe 3:4-8) Since the words of the prophet Joel appear to have been recorded in the ninth century B.C.E., the defeats of the Philistines at the hands of Uzziah (2Ch 26:6-8) and Hezekiah (2Ki 18:8) could have been included in the fulfillment of this prophecy.

However, a larger fulfillment evidently came after the Israelites returned from Babylonian exile. Notes commentator C. F. Keil: "Alexander the Great and his successors set many of the Jewish prisoners of war in their lands at liberty (compare the promise of King Demetrius to Jonathan, 'I will send away in freedom such of the Judæans as have been made prisoners, and reduced to slavery in our land,' Josephus, *Ant.* xiii. 2, 3), and portions of the Philistian and Phœnician lands were for a time under Jewish sway." (*Commentary on the Old Testament,* 1973, Vol. X, Joel, p. 224) (Compare Ob 19, 20.) Noteworthy, too, is the fact that Alexander the Great took the Philistine city of Gaza. Many of the inhabitants were slain, and the survivors were sold into slavery. A number of other prophecies likewise pointed to the execution of Jehovah's vengeance upon the Philistines.—Isa 14:31; Jer 25:9, 20; 47:1-7; Eze 25:15, 16; Am 1:6-8; Zep 2:5; Zec 9:5-7; for details see ASHDOD; ASHKELON; EKRON; GATH; GAZA No. 1.

At Ezekiel 16:27, "the daughters of the Philistines" are depicted as being humiliated on account of Jerusalem's loose conduct. (Eze 16:2) The reason for this appears to be that Jerusalem's unfaithfulness to her God Jehovah was without parallel, for the Philistines and other peoples had held fast to the worship of their false gods.—Compare Jer 2:10, 11.

PHILOLOGUS (Phi·lol′o·gus) [Fond of Words (Learning)]. A Christian whom Paul greets in his letter to the Romans. (Ro 16:15) The same name is found on inscriptions associated with the household of Caesar.

PHILOSOPHY. The Greek word *phi·lo·so·phi′a* means, literally, "love of wisdom." In modern usage the term relates to human endeavors to understand and interpret through reason and speculation the whole of human experience, including the underlying causes and principles of reality.

The Greek words for "philosophy" and "philosopher" each occur only once in the Christian Greek Scriptures. (Col 2:8; Ac 17:18) Evidently when Paul wrote to the congregation at Colossae in Asia Minor, some there were in danger of being affected by "the philosophy and empty deception according to the tradition of men." Greek philosophies were then quite prominent. But the context of Colossians 2:8 shows that of special concern to Paul were Judaizers who were trying to bring Christians back to observing the Mosaic Law with its required circumcision, festival days, and abstinence from eating certain foods. (Col 2:11, 16, 17) Paul was not opposed to knowledge, for he prayed that Christians be filled with it. But, as he showed, one must appreciate the role of Jesus Christ in the outworking of God's purpose in order to obtain true wisdom and accurate knowledge. (Col 1:9, 10; 2:2, 3) The Colossians were to look out lest perhaps someone with persuasive arguments carry them off as prey through a human way of thinking or outlook. Such a philosophy would be part of "the elementary things [*stoi·khei′a*] of the world," that is, the principles or basic components and motivating factors of the world, "and not according to Christ."—Col 2:4, 8.

When in Athens Paul had an encounter with "the Epicurean and the Stoic philosophers." (Ac 17:18) They termed the apostle a "chatterer," using the Greek word *sper·mo·lo′gos,* which literally applies to a bird that picks up seeds. The word also carries the thought of one who picks up scraps of knowledge and repeats such without order or method. Those philosophers disdained Paul and his message. Basically the Epicurean philosophy was that the obtaining of pleasure, particularly mental pleasure, was the chief good in life (1Co 15:32); though it acknowledged gods, it explained these as being beyond human experience and concern. The philosophy of the Stoics stressed fate or natural destiny; one should be of high virtue but strive for indifference to pain or pleasure. Neither Epicureans nor Stoics believed in the resurrection. In his speech before such men, Paul highlighted the relationship and accountability of the individual to the Creator and connected therewith Christ's resurrection and the "guarantee" this provided men. To Greeks asking for "wisdom" the message about Christ was "foolishness" (1Co 1:22, 23), and when Paul mentioned the resurrection, many of his hearers began to mock, although some became believers.—Ac 17:22-33.

In his inspired letters Paul emphasized a number of times that the wisdom and falsely called knowledge of the world is foolishness with God and is to be avoided by Christians.—1Co 1:18-31; 2:6-8, 13; 3:18-20; 1Ti 6:20.

PHINEHAS (Phin′e·has).

1. Son of Eleazar and grandson of Aaron. His mother was a daughter of Putiel, and his son's name was Abishua. (Ex 6:25; 1Ch 6:4) It was young Phinehas' quick action that halted the scourge from Jehovah after 24,000 Israelites had died on the Plains of Moab because of fornication and because they attached themselves to the Baal of Peor. When he spotted Zimri taking the Midianitess Cozbi into his tent, he pierced them both through with a lance, "the woman through her genital parts." This zeal in "tolerating no rivalry at

all" toward Jehovah was "counted to him as righteousness," and God made a covenant for the priesthood to remain in his line "to time indefinite."—Nu 25:1-3, 6-15; Ps 106:30, 31.

During his lifetime Phinehas served in various capacities. He was the priestly representative in the army that executed Jehovah's vengeance upon Midian. (Nu 31:3, 6) When it was thought that three tribes were forsaking Jehovah's worship, he headed a group of investigators. (Jos 22:9-33) He was chief of the tabernacle gatekeepers. (1Ch 9:20) After the burial of his father in the Hill of Phinehas, he served in the office of high priest. (Jos 24:33; Jg 20:27, 28) His name is prominent in several postexilic genealogies.—1Ch 6:4, 50; Ezr 7:5; 8:2.

2. The younger of the two "good-for-nothing" sons of priest Eli. (1Sa 1:3; 2:12) While serving as priests, he and his brother Hophni cohabited with women at the sanctuary and "treated the offering of Jehovah with disrespect." (1Sa 2:13-17, 22) When feebly reprimanded by their father, they refused to hear. For their wickedness God pronounced judgment against them. This was fulfilled when they were both killed on the same day in battle with the Philistines. (1Sa 2:23-25, 34; 3:13; 4:11) News about the capture of the Ark and the deaths of her father-in-law and her husband was too much for Phinehas' wife. She was thrown into shock and died giving birth to Ichabod.—1Sa 4:17-21.

3. A Levite, whose son Eleazar helped inventory the temple treasures in the time of Ezra, 468 B.C.E.—Ezr 8:33, 34.

PHLEGON (Phle′gon) [Burning]. One of the Roman Christians whom Paul greets in his letter. —Ro 16:14.

PHOEBE (Phoe′be) [Pure; Bright; Radiant]. A Christian sister of the first-century congregation in Cenchreae. Paul, in his letter to the Christians at Rome, 'recommends' this sister to them and calls on them to render her any needed assistance as one who "proved to be a defender of many, yes, of me myself." (Ro 16:1, 2) It may be that Phoebe delivered Paul's letter in Rome or else accompanied the one who did.

Paul refers to Phoebe as "a minister of the congregation that is in Cenchreae." This raises the question as to the sense in which the term *di·a′ko·nos* (minister) is here used. Some translators view the term in an official sense and hence render it "deaconess" (*RS, JB*). But the Scriptures make no provision for female ministerial servants. Goodspeed's translation views the term in a general

sense and translates it "helper." However, Paul's reference is evidently to something having to do with the spreading of the good news, the Christian ministry, and he was speaking of Phoebe as a female minister who was associated with the congregation in Cenchreae.—Compare Ac 2:17, 18.

Phoebe served as "a defender of many." The term translated "defender" (*pro·sta′tis*) has the basic sense of "protectress" or "succorer," so that it implies not mere cordiality but a coming to the aid of others who are in need. It may also be rendered "patroness." Phoebe's freedom to travel and to render notable service in the congregation may indicate that she was a widow and possibly a woman of some material wealth. So, she may have been in position to use influence in the community in behalf of Christians who were being wrongly accused, defending them in this way; or she may have provided refuge for them in time of danger, serving as a protectress. The record gives no details.

PHOENICIA (Phoe·ni′cia) [from a root meaning "palm tree"]. That strip of coastland along the eastern shore of the Mediterranean between Syria and Israel that was bounded on the E by the Lebanon Mountains. It roughly corresponded to the modern country of Lebanon. For many years the principal city of ancient Phoenicia was Sidon, but later it was eclipsed in importance by Tyre, a city founded by a colony from Sidon.—See SIDON, SIDONIANS; TYRE.

Geographic Features. The coastal plains of this long, narrow country were interrupted in a few places by the foothills of the mountains that reached down to the sea. The plains were well watered by a number of streams originating in the mountain range that formed the natural boundary along the eastern frontier. Here were several peaks over 3,000 m (10,000 ft) high, the highest over 3,350 m (11,000 ft), peaks that were snow-capped a good part of the year. Extensive forests and orchards of various types at one time covered much of the land—cedar and pine as well as oak, beech, mulberry, fig, olive, and date palm.

Origin and Name. The history of the Phoenicians begins after the Flood with Noah's grandson Canaan, a son of Ham. Canaan became the progenitor of 11 tribes, one of these, the Sidonians, being the descendants of Canaan's firstborn, Sidon. (Ge 10:15-18; 1Ch 1:13-16) The Sidonians were therefore Canaanites. (Jos 13:4-6; Jg 10:12) They themselves, and others too, called their land Canaan. On a coin of the time of Antiochus Epiphanes the Syrophoenician city of Laodicea is described as "a mother city of Canaan."

However, in time the Greeks preferred to call these Canaanite Sidonians by yet another term, Phoenicians. So it was that Canaanite, Sidonian, and Phoenician were names sometimes used interchangeably for the same people. In Isaiah's prophecy, for example, Phoenicia is termed "Canaan."—Isa 23:11; *JP; RS; NW*, ftn.

Land of Seafaring Traders. The Phoenicians were among the great seafaring peoples of the ancient world. Their ships were very seaworthy for their size. They were high both at the bow and at the stern, of wide beam, and could be powered by both sails and oars. (Eze 27:3-7) Phoenician vessels handled much of the commerce on the Mediterranean. In the 11th century B.C.E., Solomon employed Phoenician "servants of Hiram" to accompany his ships going to Tarshish (Spain). (2Ch 9:21) Phoenician sailors were also used aboard Solomon's fleet sent from Ezion-geber to Ophir. (1Ki 9:26-28; 10:11) In the seventh century B.C.E., Phoenician vessels were still sailing to Tarshish and bringing back silver, iron, tin, and lead. —Eze 27:12.

Arts and Crafts. Phoenician metalworkers were skilled in casting, hammering, and engraving objects of gold and silver. Other artisans specialized in carving wood and ivory, fashioning glassware, weaving wool and linen, and dyeing cloth. Phoenicia was especially noted for her purple-dye industry. Royal or Tyrian purple robes commanded the highest prices, for many thousands of murex, shellfish, each yielding but a single drop of dye, were needed for a few yards of cloth. The dye varied in hue, depending on where along the shores of the Mediterranean the shellfish were found, and this fact, plus the special skills of the Phoenician dye masters who often used a double- or triple-dyeing process, resulted in many varieties of costly fabrics that were sought after by those of rank and nobility.—Eze 27:2, 7, 24.

In the time of David and Solomon, the Phoenicians were famous as cutters of building stones and as woodsmen skilled in bringing down the stately trees of their forests.—2Sa 5:11; 1Ki 5:1, 6-10, 18; 9:11; 1Ch 14:1.

Religion. As Canaanites, the Phoenicians practiced a very base religion centered around the fertility god Baal; it involved sodomy, bestiality, and ceremonial prostitution, as well as abhorrent rites of child sacrifice. (See PICTURE, Vol. 1, p. 739; CANAAN, CANAANITE No. 2 [Conquest of Canaan by Israel].) The Phoenician city of Baalbek (c. 65 km [40 mi] NE of Beirut) became one of the great centers of polytheistic worship in the ancient world; in Roman times great temples to various gods and goddesses were erected there, the ruins of which can be seen today.

In the spring of 31 C.E., certain residents of Phoenicia demonstrated faith by traveling inland to Galilee to listen to Jesus and to be cured of their ailments. (Mr 3:7-10; Lu 6:17) A year or so later, Jesus visited the coastal plains of Phoenicia and was so impressed by the faith of a Syrophoenician woman living there that he miraculously cured her demon-possessed daughter.—Mt 15:21-28; Mr 7:24-31.

When persecution broke out in Judea following the martyrdom of Stephen, some Christians fled to Phoenicia. There, for some time, they proclaimed the good news only to Jews. But following the conversion of Cornelius, congregations that had a mixture of Jews and non-Jews began to spring up along the Phoenician coast as well as in other parts of the Roman Empire. The apostle Paul visited some of these congregations in Phoenicia during the course of his travels; the last recorded visit with believers there was at Sidon when he was on his way to Rome as a prisoner in about 58 C.E. —Ac 11:19; 15:3; 21:1-7; 27:1-3.

PHOENIX (Phoe′nix) [from a root meaning "palm tree"]. "A harbor of Crete." (Ac 27:12) The grain boat on which Paul was traveling as a prisoner to Rome attempted to sail from Fair Havens to Phoenix for winter anchorage. Seized by a storm, it was subsequently wrecked on the island of Malta.—Ac 27:13–28:1.

As to the location of Phoenix, the Acts narrative indicates only that it was W of Fair Havens, on the S side of Crete, and that it provided safe winter anchorage. Two sites have therefore been proposed. One is Loutro, on the E side of a cape, about 65 km (40 mi) W of Fair Havens, and the other Phineka, on the opposite side of this cape. The literal Greek text describes the harbor at Phoenix as "looking down [ka·ta′] the southwest wind and down [ka·ta′] the northwest wind." Scholars favoring Loutro interpret this to mean looking "along" or "toward" (ka·ta′) the direction in which the SW and NW winds are blowing. (Ac 27:12, ftn) By this understanding the harbor is said to open 'toward the NE and the SE' (*RS, NW*), a description that could fit the large semicircular entrance to the harbor at Loutro. Phineka, because of its structure, is not used as a harbor today, though geologic changes in the vicinity may have affected its formation. However, Phineka does have two inlets, one *facing* SW and the other NW. Thus, those favoring this site understand the expression "looking down" to mean facing the direction from which the winds *originate* rather than that in which they blow.

PHRYGIA (Phryg′i·a). A country or region in central Asia Minor. The geographic boundaries of Phrygia fluctuated greatly over the years, so it is difficult to define the area encompassed unless one refers to a specific period. In the first century "Phrygia" was an inland area in the Roman provinces of Galatia and Asia, covering the plateau country N of the Taurus Range, from the Halys River on the E to the upper valleys of the Hermus and Maeander rivers on the W. The apostle Paul traveled through portions of Phrygia on at least two of his trips.—Ac 16:6; 18:23; 19:1.

It is commonly believed that the Phrygians spread S from Greece toward the close of the second millennium B.C.E. and gained control of much of central and western Asia Minor N of the Taurus Mountains, from the Halys River to the Aegean Sea. Archaeological evidence points to Gordium as their capital and King Midas as one of their prominent rulers. A noteworthy aspect of the religion of the people of early Phrygia is the worship of a mother-goddess (Rhea Cybele).

The western part of Phrygia came under the control of the Attalid kings of Pergamum. This kingdom became the Roman province of Asia, but the SE portion is often referred to as Asian Phrygia. (See ASIA.) The king of Galatia ruled the more easterly section of Phrygia, and it eventually formed a part of the Roman province of Galatia. This eastern section is sometimes termed Galatian Phrygia; it was N of Pisidia and NW of Lycaonia. Depending on the point of view of the writer and the time period involved, Antioch and Iconium might be called Phrygian cities, though often Antioch is connected with Pisidia, and Iconium with Lycaonia.—Ac 13:14; see ANTIOCH No. 2; ICONIUM.

The population of Phrygia included many Jews, their presence having been encouraged by the Seleucid rulers in Syria. According to Josephus, Antiochus III (223-187 B.C.E.) transported "two thousand Jewish families with their effects from Mesopotamia and Babylonia" to Lydia and Phrygia in order to stabilize conditions among the seditious people there. (*Jewish Antiquities*, XII, 149 [iii, 4]) And Jews evidently continued to be numerous in Asia Minor under the Romans. On Pentecost 33 C.E. there were present in Jerusalem Jews from "the district of Asia, and Phrygia and Pamphylia."—Ac 2:9, 10.

On his second missionary tour, Paul and his companions, coming NW through Cilicia and Lycaonia, "went through Phrygia and the country of Galatia, because they were forbidden by the holy spirit to speak the word in the district of Asia." (Ac 15:41; 16:1-6) So they had entered the eastern part of old Phrygia (which by Paul's time was Galatian Phrygia), but instead of continuing W through the province of Asia (containing Asian Phrygia), they went N toward the province of Bithynia and then W to Troas.

Paul's third tour took him through Galatian Phrygia and Asian Phrygia. He left Antioch in Pisidia and "went from place to place through the country of Galatia and Phrygia." (Ac 18:23) The account also says that he "went through the inland parts and came down to Ephesus" on the Aegean Coast. (Ac 19:1) It seems that he did not travel the main road to Ephesus, passing down the Lycus River valley and by the Phrygian cities of Laodicea, Colossae, and Hierapolis (Col 2:1; 4:13), but, instead, took a more direct route somewhat to the N.—See COLOSSAE.

PHYGELUS (Phy·gel′us). One from the district of Asia who "turned away from" Paul.—2Ti 1:15; see ASIA.

PHYLACTERY. See SCRIPTURE-CONTAINING CASE.

PHYSICIAN. See DISEASES AND TREATMENT.

PIBESETH (Pi·be′seth) [from Egyptian, meaning "House of [the goddess] Bastet"]. A city mentioned along with On (Heliopolis) at Ezekiel 30:17 in a prophecy directed against Egypt. The *Septuagint* rendering of the text identifies Pibeseth with Bubastis, an ancient city of the Delta region, the remains of which are at Tell Basta, about 70 km (43 mi) NNE of Cairo, near the modern city of Zagazig. The name of the ancient city as it appears on Egyptian inscriptions shows a clear similarity to the Hebrew Pibeseth.

Pibeseth, or Bubastis, was the seat of the worship of the goddess Bastet, or Bast, a feline goddess often represented with the head of a cat. The presence of a large burial ground for cats near the city testifies to the prominence of her worship there. An annual festival was held in honor of Bastet, drawing thousands of adherents from all parts of the land.

While Pibeseth was the capital of the 18th nome (district) of Lower Egypt, it reached its greatest political prominence with the line of Libyan rulers over Egypt begun by Pharaoh Shishak, a contemporary of Solomon and Rehoboam. (1Ki 11:40; 14:25, 26) Pibeseth was a royal city of Shishak. Ezekiel's prophecy relates to the Babylonian conquest of Egypt when Pibeseth would be overrun. The Persians later destroyed the city, and today only ruins remain on the ancient site.

PIG. See SWINE.

PIGEON

PIGEON [Heb., *yoh·nah'*, *goh·zal'* (young pigeon or fledgling); Gr., *pe·ri·ste·ra'*]. As noted under the heading DOVE, the same Hebrew word (*yoh·nah'*) is applied to both the dove and the pigeon. Similarly, in English the distinction between the two birds is not sharply defined, although the name pigeon is usually applied to the larger types and especially to those that are domesticated and thus nonmigrating. Like the dove, the pigeon is a stout-bodied, short-legged bird with smooth and compact plumage.

As a rule, Bible translations render the Hebrew *yoh·nah'* as "pigeon" only in texts involving sacrifices, in which "turtledoves" (Heb., *to·rim'*) are also regularly mentioned. The expression "young pigeon(s)" (*NW, KJ, RS*) in Hebrew is literally "son(s) of a (or the) pigeon." Along with turtledoves, pigeons were acceptable for sacrificial use in burnt offerings (Le 1:14); a pair could be presented by those too poor to afford a female lamb or kid for a guilt offering (Le 5:5-7); a pigeon (or else a turtledove) as a sin offering was to accompany the offering of a young ram in a woman's purification rites following delivery of a child unless she lacked the ability to present the ram, in which case "two young pigeons" were acceptable (Le 12:6-8) (as was the case in Mary's purification following the birth of Jesus; Lu 2:22-24); and a pair of either pigeons or turtledoves was to be included in the purification offerings of a person who had recovered from a running discharge (Le 15:13, 14, 28, 29). They were also acceptable in connection with the Nazirite's cleansing from defilement.—Nu 6:10.

While many families among the Jews doubtless had their own pigeons, the expression, "Now if he does not have the means for two turtledoves or two young pigeons," evidently indicates that they were often purchased for sacrificial purposes.—Le 5:11.

The Hebrew term *goh·zal'*, used in the account of Abraham's offering when "Jehovah concluded with Abram a covenant," is understood to refer to "a young pigeon." (Ge 15:9, 18) This is because of the constant association of the pigeon with the turtledove in sacrifices prescribed in the Law later given to Israel. The same Hebrew word is rendered "fledgling" in Deuteronomy 32:11. A pigeon doubtless formed part of the earlier sacrifice by Noah, since that sacrifice included "some . . . of all the clean flying creatures."—Ge 8:20.

The provision of the Law in making optional the use of either young pigeons or turtledoves was a helpful arrangement for the Jews, inasmuch as most turtledoves migrated from the land of Israel during the winter months, while the nonmigratory pigeons were available the year round.

The pigeon is a strong, swift flier, able to reach speeds of over 80 km/hr (50 mph). Its homing instinct caused it to be used for carrying messages from early times. Unlike human navigators who must use chronometers and sextants to determine their position, homing pigeons almost instantly know—by sensing the earth's magnetic field and from the position of the sun—which direction to fly, even though released in strange territory hundreds of kilometers from their homesite. They automatically allow for the movement of the sun across the sky so that the angle of their flight does not err.

As common as chickens in many parts of the earth, pigeons differ from domestic fowl not only in their flying ability but also in their structure and in the fact that they are monogamous. Different from the rooster, the faithful male pigeon aids the female in building the nest and in incubating the eggs. Pigeons differ from all other birds in their distinct manner of feeding their young with "pigeon's milk," a curdlike substance produced within the parents' crop. Young pigeons, called squabs, are commonly used as food in many lands.

PIHAHIROTH

PIHAHIROTH (Pi·ha·hi'roth). The last camping site of the Israelites before crossing the Red Sea. (Nu 33:7, 8) After having encamped at "Etham at the edge of the wilderness" (Ex 13:20), Moses received instructions from Jehovah God to "turn back and encamp before Pihahiroth between Migdol and the sea in view of Baal-zephon." (Ex 14:1, 2) If the sites of Migdol and Baal-zephon were known today, the identification of Pihahiroth would not be difficult. This is not the case, however, and attempts at linking their names, as well as that of Pihahiroth, with certain localities along Egypt's eastern frontier have been varied and quite inconclusive. For this reason certain other geographic requirements contained in the account itself seem to present the soundest basis for obtaining some idea of the location of Pihahiroth.

Pihahiroth was near the Red Sea at some point where the only route of escape from the advancing Egyptian forces was through the sea itself. The sea at that point must have been of sufficient depth to allow for the waters to be "split apart" to form a passage through "the midst of the sea," with the waters forming a "wall" on both sides. (Ex 14:16, 21, 22) No site N of the Gulf of Suez could adequately provide these requirements. It is true that many modern scholars favor the theory of a crossing in the shallow Bitter Lakes region, which begins about 25 km (16 mi) N of Suez. This view, however, is accompanied either by a denial of the miraculous nature of the crossing (claiming that the crossing was only through a marsh or swamp) or by the idea that the northern end of the Red Sea anciently ran up into the Bitter Lakes region and that the waters there were of much greater depth at that time, whereas archaeological evidence is that there has been very little change in the water level from ancient times.

For this reason the suggestion advanced by earlier scholars (of the past century) still seems to be that which meets best the requirements of the Bible history. Pihahiroth is evidently a site on the narrow plain running along the southeastern foot of Jebel 'Ataqah about 20 km (12 mi) SW of Suez. It is suggested that the crossing started from the promontory called Ras 'Ataqah and led across the seabed to the vicinity of the oasis 'Ayun Musa' on the opposite shore. The seabed in this section descends quite gradually from either shore because of shoals that run out 3 km (2 mi) from either side. The maximum depth of water near the middle of this trajectory is about 15 m (50 ft). The distance from shore to shore is about 10 km (6 mi) allowing ample space for the possibly three million Israelites to be traversing the seabed while, at the same time, the military forces of Pharaoh were also making their way through the miraculously provided passage in an effort to overtake the Israelite host.—See EXODUS (Route of the Exodus).

This view coincides generally with the tradition handed down by Josephus, Jewish historian of the first century C.E., that the Israelites prior to the crossing were 'confined between inaccessible cliffs and the sea.' (*Jewish Antiquities,* II, 324 [xv, 3]) A 'turning back' of the Israelite nation from Etham to the place described above would also harmonize well with Jehovah's forecast that Pharaoh would say of them, "They are wandering in confusion in the land. The wilderness has closed in upon them." (Ex 14:3) This would hardly be true of locations N of Suez. The location of Pihahiroth in the vicinity of Jebel 'Ataqah would likewise allow for Pharaoh's forces to advance rapidly on the fleeing Israelites by a regularly traveled route from Memphis (the likely capital of Egypt at that time) to the Sinai Peninsula.—Ex 14:4-9.

While satisfying the geographic requirements, such location of Pihahiroth must be viewed as only tentative, dependent on possible future confirmation.

PILATE. Roman governor of Judea during Jesus' earthly ministry. (Lu 3:1) After Herod the Great's son Archelaus was removed from being king over Judea, provincial governors were appointed by the emperor to rule the province, Pilate evidently being the fifth of these. Tiberius appointed him in 26 C.E., and his rule lasted ten years.

Little is known of Pontius Pilate's personal history. The only period of his life to receive historical notice is his Judean governorship. The one inscription known bearing his name was found in 1961 at Caesarea. It also refers to the "Tiberieum," a building Pilate dedicated in honor of Tiberius.

As the emperor's representative, the governor exercised full control of the province. He could impose the death sentence, and according to those endorsing the view that the Sanhedrin could pass the death sentence, the governor's ratification had to be obtained by that Jewish court for such sentence by them to be valid. (Compare Mt 26:65, 66; Joh 18:31.) As the official residence of the Roman ruler was at Caesarea (compare Ac 23:23, 24), the main body of Roman troops was stationed there, with a smaller force garrisoned at Jerusalem. Customarily, however, the governor resided at Jerusalem during festival seasons (such as at Passover time) and brought up military reinforcements with him. Pilate's wife was with him in Judea (Mt 27:19), this being possible because of an earlier

Inscription discovered at Caesarea in 1961 naming Pontius Pilate

change in Roman governmental policy concerning governors in dangerous assignments.

Pilate's tenure of office was not a peaceful one. According to the Jewish historian Josephus, Pilate made a bad start as to his relations with his Jewish subjects. He sent Roman soldiers bearing standards with images of the emperor on them into Jerusalem at night. This move provoked great resentment; a delegation of Jews traveled to Caesarea to protest the presence of the standards and call for their removal. After five days of discussion, Pilate sought to frighten the petitioners with the threat of execution by his soldiers, but their determined refusal to yield caused him to accede to their request.—*Jewish Antiquities*, XVIII, 55-59 (iii, 1).

Philo, a Jewish writer of the first century C.E. in Alexandria, Egypt, describes a somewhat similar act by Pilate evoking protest, this time involving gold shields bearing the names of Pilate and Tiberius, which shields Pilate placed in his quarters at Jerusalem. A Jewish appeal went to the emperor at Rome, and Pilate was ordered to remove the shields to Caesarea.—*The Embassy to Gaius*, XXXVIII, 299-305.

Josephus lists yet another disturbance. To construct an aqueduct to bring water into Jerusalem from a distance of about 40 km (25 mi), Pilate used money from the temple treasury at Jerusalem. Large crowds clamored against this act when Pilate made a visit to the city. Pilate sent disguised soldiers to mix in with the multitude and, at a signal, to attack them, resulting in Jews' being injured and some being killed. (*Jewish Antiquities*, XVIII, 60-62 [iii, 2]; *The Jewish War*, II, 175-177 [ix, 4]) Apparently the project was carried through to completion. This latter conflict is often suggested as the occasion when Pilate 'mixed the blood of Galileans with their sacrifices,' as recorded at Luke 13:1. From this expression it appears that these Galileans were slain right in the temple area. There is no way of determining if this incident relates to that described by Josephus or is a separate occasion. However, since the Galileans were subjects of Herod Antipas, the district ruler of Galilee, this slaughter may have been at least a factor contributing to the enmity that existed between Pilate and Herod up until the time of Jesus' trial.—Lu 23:6-12.

Trial of Jesus. On Nisan 14, 33 C.E., at dawn, Jesus was brought by the Jewish leaders to Pilate. As they would not enter the Gentile ruler's premises, Pilate went out to them and inquired as to the charge against Jesus. The charges were that Jesus was subversive, was advocating nonpayment of taxes, and was saying he was a king, thus rivaling Caesar. Told to take Jesus and judge him themselves, his accusers replied that it was not lawful for them to execute anyone. Pilate then took Jesus into the palace and questioned him concerning the charges. (PICTURE, Vol. 2, p. 741) Returning to the accusers, Pilate announced that he found no fault in the accused. The accusations continued, and upon learning that Jesus was from Galilee, Pilate sent him to Herod Antipas. Herod, displeased because Jesus refused to perform some sign, subjected him to mistreatment and ridicule and returned him to Pilate.

The Jewish leaders and the people were again summoned, and Pilate renewed his efforts to avoid sentencing an innocent man to death, asking the crowd if they wanted Jesus released in accord with the custom of freeing a prisoner at each Passover festival. Instead, the crowd, incited by their religious leaders, clamored for the release of Barabbas, a thief, murderer, and seditionist. Repeated attempts by Pilate to free the accused brought only an increase in the shouting for Jesus' impalement. Fearing a riot and seeking to placate the crowd, Pilate acceded to their wishes, washing his hands with water as though cleansing them from bloodguilt. Sometime prior to this, Pilate's wife had advised him of her troublesome dream concerning "that righteous man."—Mt 27:19.

Pilate now had Jesus whipped, and the soldiers placed a crown of thorns on Jesus' head and dressed him with royal robes. Again Pilate appeared before the crowd, renewed his disavowal of finding any guilt in Jesus, and had Jesus come out before them with his robes and crown of thorns. At Pilate's cry, "Look! The man!" the leaders of the people renewed their demand for impalement, now revealing for the first time their charge of blasphemy. Their reference to Jesus as making himself God's son added to Pilate's apprehension, and he took Jesus inside for further questioning. Final efforts at releasing him brought the warning by the Jewish opposers that Pilate was becoming vulnerable to the charge of opposing Caesar. Hearing this threat, Pilate, bringing Jesus forth, now seated himself on the judgment seat. Pilate's cry, "See! Your king!" only revived the clamor for impalement and brought the declaration: "We have no king but Caesar." Pilate then handed Jesus over to them to be impaled.—Mt 27:1-31; Mr 15:1-15; Lu 23:1-25; Joh 18:28-40; 19:1-16.

Jewish writers, such as Philo, paint Pilate as an inflexible, self-willed man. (*The Embassy to*

Gaius, XXXVIII, 301) However, it may be that the actions of the Jews themselves were largely responsible for the strong measures the governor had taken against them. At any rate the Gospel accounts give some accurate insight into the man's makeup. His approach to matters was typical of the Roman ruler, his speech terse and blunt. Outwardly expressing the skeptical attitude of the cynic, as in saying "What is truth?" he, nevertheless, showed fear, likely a superstitious fear, upon hearing that he was dealing with one who claimed to be God's son. Though obviously not the condescending type, he displayed the politician's lack of integrity. He was concerned primarily with his position, what his superiors would say if they heard of further disturbances in his province, fearful of appearing to be overly lenient toward those accused of sedition. Pilate recognized Jesus' innocence and the envy that motivated his accusers. Yet he gave in to the crowd and turned an innocent victim over for them to slaughter rather than risk damage to his political career.

As part of "the superior authorities," Pilate exercised power by divine tolerance. (Ro 13:1) He bore responsibility for his decision, responsibility that water could not wash away. His wife's dream was evidently of divine origin, even as were the earthquake, the unusual darkness, and the rending of the curtain that took place on that day. (Mt 27:19, 45, 51-54; Lu 23:44, 45) Her dream should have warned Pilate that this was no ordinary trial, no ordinary defendant. Yet, as Jesus said, the one delivering him to Pilate 'bore the greater guilt of sin.' (Joh 19:10, 11) Judas, who originally betrayed Jesus, was called "the son of destruction." (Joh 17:12) Those Pharisees who were guilty of complicity in the plot against Jesus' life were described as 'subjects for Gehenna.' (Mt 23:15, 33; compare Joh 8:37-44.) And particularly the high priest, who headed the Sanhedrin, was responsible before God for handing over God's Son to this Gentile ruler for sentencing to death. (Mt 26:63-66) Pilate's guilt did not equal theirs; yet his act was extremely reprehensible.

Pilate's distaste for the promoters of the crime evidently was reflected in the sign he had placed over the impaled Jesus, identifying him as "the King of the Jews," as well as his curt refusal to change it, saying: "What I have written I have written." (Joh 19:19-22) When Joseph of Arimathea requested the dead body, Pilate, after first displaying the thoroughness of a Roman official by making sure Jesus was dead, granted the request. (Mr 15:43-45) The concern of the chief priests and Pharisees over the possibility of theft of the body brought the terse reply: "You have a guard.

Go make it as secure as you know how."—Mt 27:62-65.

Removal and Death.   Josephus reports that Pilate's later removal from office resulted from complaints lodged by the Samaritans with Pilate's immediate superior, the governor of Syria, Vitellius. The complaint was about Pilate's slaughter of a number of Samaritans who were deluded by an impostor into assembling at Mount Gerizim in hopes of uncovering sacred treasures supposedly hidden there by Moses. Vitellius ordered Pilate to Rome to appear before Tiberius, and he put Marcellus in his place. Tiberius died in 37 C.E. while Pilate was still on his way to Rome. (*Jewish Antiquities,* XVIII, 85-87 [iv, 1]; XVIII, 88, 89 [iv, 2]) History gives no reliable data as to the ultimate results of his trial. The historian Eusebius of the late third and early fourth centuries claims that Pilate was obliged to commit suicide during the reign of Tiberius' successor Gaius (Caligula).—*The Ecclesiastical History,* II, VII, 1.

PILDASH   (Pil′dash). Sixth named of the eight sons of Abraham's brother Nahor by his wife Milcah.—Ge 22:21-23; 11:29.

PILES.   Hemorrhoids; swellings of veins at the anus, frequently accompanied by bleeding. In this often painful disorder, there are vascular tumors beneath the mucous membrane of the rectum, either within the external sphincter (internal hemorrhoids) or on its outer side (external hemorrhoids), or both.

Piles were among the disorders that Jehovah warned the Israelites they would suffer for disobedience. (De 28:15, 27) He afflicted the Philistines of Ashdod and its territories, Gath and Ekron, with piles while the sacred Ark was in their possession. —1Sa 5:6-12.

The Hebrew word rendered "piles" (*Harkavy; NW*), "hemorrhoids" (*Le*), "tumors" (*AS; RS*), and "plague-boils" (*AT*), as at 1 Samuel 5:6, is ′* opha·lim*′, denoting rounded swellings or eminences, hemorrhoids, or tumors at the anus. At 1 Samuel 6:11, 17 in the Masoretic text, the swellings afflicting the Philistines are referred to as *techo·rim*′, meaning "tumors." In all six Scriptural occurrences of ′*opha·lim*′ (piles), the Jewish Masoretes pointed this word with the vowels for *techo·rim*′ (tumors) and showed this latter term in the margin as the word to be read instead of ′*opha·lim*′.

The five Philistine axis lords returned the Ark to Israel with a guilt offering to Jehovah, consisting partly of five golden images of the piles, that is, representations of these swellings. (1Sa 6:4, 5, 11, 17) In a somewhat similar manner, certain ancient peoples (particularly the Greeks and the Romans) invoked their deities for cures by presenting to them replicas of afflicted body parts, or they presented models thereof in gratitude for supposed cures.

Since jerboas (mouselike jumping rodents) were bringing the land to ruin (1Sa 6:5), some scholars believe the Philistines were afflicted with bubonic plague, a highly fatal infectious disease marked by such symptoms as fever, chills, prostration, and painful enlargement of the lymphatic glands, or buboes. This plague is transmitted chiefly through bites by fleas that have bitten infected rats or other rodents that are dying or dead.

"A death-dealing confusion" occurred when the Ark was in Ekron, where "the men that did not die had been struck with piles." (1Sa 5:10-12) Both pile and jerboa images are mentioned at 1 Samuel 6:4, where the Philistine priests and diviners are quoted as saying, "every one of you and your axis lords have the same scourge." But this may mean only that the entire nation, the axis lords and people alike, had suffered a common calamity, "the same scourge," not necessarily that the rodents and the piles were associated in one epidemic disease or plague. The Bible seems to indicate only that the jerboas destroyed vegetation throughout Philistia, thus ruining the land, and does not specifically state that they were carriers of infection to the Philistines stricken by Jehovah.

PILHA (Pil'ha) [Millstone]. A family head of Israel or a representative of a family of that name attesting the postexilic "trustworthy arrangement."—Ne 9:38; 10:1, 14, 24.

PILLAR. An upright structural support or column, or something resembling or comparable to such a supporting column.

Some ancient peoples of the Middle East set up sacred pillars in connection with their false religion; quite likely these involved phallic symbolism. The Israelites, upon entering the Promised Land, were to destroy such sacred pillars, and they were forbidden to set up pillars of that sort. (De 7:5; 16:22) However, at times they took up heathen religion and used sacred pillars.—1Ki 14: 23; 2Ki 3:2; see SACRED PILLAR.

Quite apart from the improper use of pillars hated by God, the Hebrew Scriptures mention the setting up of pillars or stones of a commemorative nature. Such pillars were neither objects of idolatrous worship nor symbolic of sex organs. They served to recall historic acts or events.

On two occasions Jacob set up stone pillars at Bethel. Both instances involved taking note of Je-

hovah's dealing with Jacob in a special way at that place. (Ge 28:18, 19, 22; 31:13; 35:14, 15) The pillar Jacob stationed over Rachel's grave was no doubt stone and still existed in Moses' day. (Ge 35:19, 20) When the Israelites accepted the laws Moses had received from God, Moses built an altar and "twelve pillars corresponding with the twelve tribes of Israel." (Ex 24:4) Joshua gave similar instruction involving stones to represent the tribes, though the account does not call them pillars. These were to serve as a memorial to Israel and would give occasion for fathers to explain to their sons what the twelve stones meant.—Jos 4:1-9, 20-24.

A covenant or a victory could be marked by setting up a stone, often a pillar. (Ge 31:44-53; Jos 24:26; 1Sa 7:10-12) After his victory over the Amalekites, King Saul 'erected a monument for himself at Carmel.' (1Sa 15:12) The Hebrew word here translated "monument" is usually rendered "hand," but it is also used at 2 Samuel 18:18 in connection with the "pillar" Absalom raised up called "Absalom's Monument" (*NW, AT, RS*), so evidently Saul erected a victory monument or pillar.—Compare Isa 56:5; see ABSALOM.

The idea of a pillar as a commemorative monument may be involved in the prophecy at Isaiah 19:19. Written in the eighth century B.C.E., it dealt with circumstances after the destruction of Jerusalem in 607 B.C.E. Some of the Jews who were left in their land by the Babylonians fled to Egypt and dwelt in Egyptian cities, as foretold in Isaiah 19:18. (Jer 43:4-7; 44:1) Thus the promise that there would be "a pillar to Jehovah" beside Egypt's boundary has been understood by many commentators to mean that Jehovah would be taken note of or commemorated in Egypt, whether there was a literal pillar or not.—Compare Isa 19:20-22.

Structural Pillars. Biblical references and archaeological discoveries show pillars of wood, stone, and brick being used in the Middle East as structural supports. Often the roof beams or upper stories of a building were held up by vertical columns. (Pr 9:1; Jg 16:25, 29; 1Ki 7:2) The wood or brick pillars might rest on stone bases. Solomon's House of the Forest of Lebanon contained rows of cedarwood pillars supporting the beams and upper chambers. Apparently the fact that the cedar was from Lebanon or the resemblance of the pillars to a forest resulted in the building's name. The nearby Porch of Pillars was obviously also noted for its abundant pillars, though the record does not give their number or material. (1Ki 7:1-6; compare Eze 40:16, 48, 49.) Marble pillars were used in the courtyard of Ahasuerus' palace. —Es 1:6.

The most noteworthy pillars in Solomon's temple were two huge copper pillars named Jachin and Boaz in front of the porch. (1Ki 7:15; 2Ki 25:17; Jer 52:21; see CAPITAL.) The *New Bible Dictionary* edited by J. Douglas (1985, p. 941) suggests that the king stood by one of these pillars on ceremonial occasions, but that cannot be confirmed, for the Bible merely says the king was "standing by his pillar at the entry." (2Ch 23:13; 2Ki 11:14; 23:3) He could have been standing at a gate of the inner court or some other elevated place for addressing the people.

Smaller pillars were used in the tabernacle, four of acacia wood to support the curtain between the Holy and Most Holy and five to hold up the screen at the entrance. (Ex 26:32-37) Sixty other pillars supported the linen hangings around the courtyard and the screen at the gate of the courtyard. —Ex 27:9-16.

Small, ornamental pillars of silver apparently supported the canopy of Solomon's litter.—Ca 3:9, 10.

Figurative Use. The material and function of structural pillars made them fitting symbols of sturdy support. They would illustrate that which securely upholds. The Christian congregation could be called "a pillar and support of the truth," for it upholds the truth in contrast to religious error. (1Ti 3:15) James, Cephas, and John were spoken of as 'seeming to be pillars' in the early congregation; they were solidly fixed and strong supporters of it. (Ga 2:9) Christians who conquer will be made pillars in "the temple" of God, gaining a permanent position in the spiritual structure. (Re 3:12) The idea of the sturdiness of a pillar is found in the allusions to pillars in describing the feet of a strong angel. (Re 10:1) The legs of the shepherd lover of the Shulammite girl were like "pillars of marble," being beautiful as well as strong.—Ca 5:15.

How long did the miraculous pillars of cloud and of fire remain with the camp of Israel?

Jehovah miraculously guided the Israelites out of Egypt and through the wilderness, "going ahead of them in the daytime in a pillar of cloud . . . and in the nighttime in a pillar of fire to give them light to go." (Ex 13:21) This was, not two pillars, but one "pillar of fire and cloud" that would normally appear as a cloud in the daytime and as fire at night. (Ex 14:24) When the Egyptians pursued the Israelites, the pillar moved to the rear, perhaps spreading out like a wall. (Ps 105:38, 39) It caused darkness on the Egyptian side but shed light on the Israelite side. (Ex 14:19, 20) When the tabernacle was set up, the pillar above it served as a sign that Jehovah was in his holy place. (Ex 40:35) The pillar represented Jehovah, and he spoke out of it. (Nu 14:14; 12:5; Ps 99:7) The last historical notice of the pillar was just before Israel entered the Promised Land. (De 31:15) When they were settled in their land the guiding pillar was not needed as it had been during their wandering. —Compare Ex 40:38; Isa 4:5.

PILLORY (pil'lo·ry). A device for confining the neck and arms; used to punish offenders by exposing them to public ridicule. At Jeremiah 29:26, "pillory" is translated from the Hebrew word *tsi·noq'*.

From exile in Babylon, the false prophet Shemaiah wrote to the priests in Jerusalem, urging that Jeremiah be rebuked and put in the pillory.

PILTAI (Pil'tai) [shortened form of Pelatiah, meaning "Jehovah Has Provided Escape"]. Postexilic head of the priestly paternal house of Moadiah in the days of Jeshua's successor Joiakim. —Ne 12:12, 17.

PIM. The price that the Philistines charged the Israelites for sharpening various metal implements. (1Sa 13:20, 21) The pim apparently was a weight. Several stone weights found in Palestinian excavations bear the consonants of "pim" in ancient Hebrew characters; these vary from 7.18 to 8.13 g (0.231 to 0.261 oz t). On this basis the pim would be approximately two thirds of a shekel.

PINON (Pi'non). One of the sheiks of Esau (Edom). (Ge 36:40-43; 1Ch 1:51, 52) Some think these names are listings of places or settlements rather than of individuals or that the names came to apply to the particular regions or cities ruled by the sheiks.—See TIMNA No. 3.

PIPE. A tubular wind instrument (Ge 4:21); also a long tube used to convey liquids.—Zec 4:2.

The exact identification of the musical instrument termed in Hebrew *'u·ghav'* is uncertain, since the Bible does not describe it; however, modern Bible translations generally render the Hebrew word "pipe." (Job 21:12; 30:31; Ps 150:4; AS, Da, NW, RS) The pipe is thus the first wind instrument (likely, woodwind) mentioned in the Scriptures. Jubal, the seventh generation from Adam, is identified as "the founder [literally, father] of all those who handle . . . the pipe [or, flute]." (Ge 4:21, ftn) This possibly indicates the establishment of a profession, either of craftsmen making the instruments or of those playing them.

Although the 'u·ghav' was never listed as one of the temple instruments, some scholars believe that this name became a general term, designating any woodwind. Originally, though, it may have been a specific instrument, perhaps the flute or possibly a series of multitoned pipes all closed at one end and blown across the open ends. The instrument in Nebuchadnezzar's orchestra specified by the Aramaic word *mash·roh·qi'* ("pipe," Da 3:5, 7, 10, 15; *AT, Da, Mo, NW, RS*) may correspond to the Hebrew 'u·ghav'.

PIRAM (Pi'ram) [Zebra]. The Amorite king of Jarmuth at the time Israel entered the Promised Land. Piram joined with four other Amorite kings in a conspiracy against the Gibeonites, who had made peace with Joshua. In the battle that followed, Piram and the other kings took refuge in a cave at Makkedah, which the Israelites sealed up until the fighting was over. Piram and the others were then slain, hung on stakes until evening, and entombed in the same cave.—Jos 10:1-27.

PIRATHON (Pir'a·thon), **PIRATHONITE** (Pir'-a·thon·ite) [Of (Belonging to) Pirathon]. Pirathon was a town of Ephraim "in the mountain of the Amalekite." Evidently an inhabitant of Pirathon was known as a "Pirathonite," as were Hillel and, later, Benaiah, one of David's mighty men. Hillel's son Judge Abdon was buried there. (Jg 12:13, 15; 2Sa 23:8, 30; 1Ch 11:31; 27:14) Far'ata, about 10 km (6 mi) W of the suggested location for Shechem, has been suggested as a possible identification.

PISGAH (Pis'gah). An elevated place in the northern section of the Abarim mountain range immediately E of the Dead Sea. The exact location is unknown. Bible references are not in conflict with its suggested identity with Ras es-Siyaghah, a headland located about 16 km (10 mi) E of where the Jordan empties into the Dead Sea. Ras es-Siyaghah is a little NW of Jebel en-Neba, the summit traditionally known as Mount Nebo (Har Nevo).

The physical features of these two elevations are in agreement with the Bible's brief description. Ras es-Siyaghah is about 100 m (330 ft) lower in elevation than Jebel en-Neba and is separated from the latter by a slight depression, or saddle. Though slightly lower than its neighbor summit, Ras es-Siyaghah is closer to Jericho and affords an unobstructed view of the Dead Sea some 1,000 m (3,300 ft) below, as well as a splen-

did view of the Jordan Valley, of the central range on which Hebron, Bethlehem and Jerusalem are situated, and of Mount Hermon over 160 km (100 mi) to the N.

The first mention of this place is in connection with the campsites along the line of Israel's march toward the Promised Land. (Nu 21:20) It was located in the southern part of that territory taken in the conquest of the Amorites after their king, Sihon, refused to let the Israelites pass through the land. (De 4:46, 49; Jos 12:1-3) Later, Balak the king of Moab took Balaam "to the field of Zophim, to the top of Pisgah," in a vain attempt to have the Israelites cursed.—Nu 23:14.

Pisgah, however, is best remembered in connection with Moses' extensive view of the Promised Land shortly before his death. (De 3:27; 34:1-3) Pisgah was designated as part of Reuben's tribal territory.—De 3:16, 17; Jos 13:15, 20.

Wherever the name Pisgah occurs in the Bible, it is always qualified by such expressions as "the head of," "the top of," or "the slopes of" Pisgah. As a consequence it is frequently referred to as *Mount* Pisgah, though not so in the Scriptures.

PISHON (Pi'shon) [possibly, More Scattered]. One of the four rivers branching out from the "river issuing out of Eden" and thereafter encircling the entire land of Havilah, a land stated to be the source of gold, bdellium gum, and onyx stone. (Ge 2:10-12) The identification of the Pishon River is conjectural, suggestions ranging from certain rivers in Armenia all the way to the Ganges River of India.

In the article EDEN No. 1, we mentioned the possibility that the global Flood obliterated the evidence for positive identification of the Pishon and Gihon rivers today. This, of course, does not eliminate the possibility that these rivers were still in existence and known in Moses' day when the book of Genesis was recorded. His reference to the "land of Havilah" is not likely to be understood as meaning that a region was so named prior to the Flood, even as is the case with his reference to the "land of Cush." (Ge 2:13) Rather, Moses' references to these lands are evidently to places so named in post-Flood times and serve as geographic points commonly known in his day. In addition to whatever changes the Flood wrought, the ability of earthquakes to change the course of rivers or to wipe sections of them out must also be given consideration. Such could have occurred in post-Flood times; Armenia, the probable location of Eden, is in an earthquake belt.—See HAVILAH No. 1.

PISIDIA (Pi·sid'i·a). An interior region of southern Asia Minor. It was a mountainous section, taking in the western portion of the Taurus Range, lying N of Pamphylia and S of Galatian Phrygia, with Caria and Lycia on the W and Lycaonia on the E. The region is believed to have been about 190 km (120 mi) from E to W and about 80 km (50 mi) in breadth. It had many lofty ridges cut by valleys and mountain rivers; there were forests and pasturelands.

The people of Pisidia were wild and warlike, forming tribal bands of robbers. These mountaineers were difficult to control and slow to be affected by Hellenic or Roman culture. The Romans assigned Galatian King Amyntas the task of subjugating them, but he died before accomplishing it. Pisidia became part of the Roman province of Galatia in 25 B.C.E., and in 6 B.C.E. colonies in the area were garrisoned to hold the people in check. These colonies were directed from Antioch, a city near the border between Pisidia and Phrygia. (See ANTIOCH No. 2.) In 74 C.E. the southern part of Pisidia was combined with Pamphylia and Lycia into a Roman province. The northern section remained part of the province of Galatia until, in postapostolic times, it was included in a new province bearing the name Pisidia.

The apostle Paul passed through Pisidia on his first missionary tour, traveling from coastal Pamphylia over the mountains to Pisidian Antioch. (Ac 13:13, 14) He also passed through Pisidia on the return trip. (Ac 14:21, 24) The bandits and rushing mountain rivers of the area might well have been a basis for Paul's statement that he had been in "dangers from rivers, in dangers from highwaymen."—2Co 11:26.

PISPAH (Pis'pah). A leading Asherite; son of Jether.—1Ch 7:38, 40.

PISTACHIO NUT [Heb., bot·nah']. The fruit of the Pistacia vera tree. This deciduous tree thrives in dry areas and seldom reaches a height in excess of 9 m (30 ft). The nuts measure 1.5 to 2 cm (0.6 to 0.8 in.) in length and grow in large clusters. The thin, but hard, light-colored shell of ripe pistachio nuts is covered with a somewhat wrinkly husk. Each nut contains one yellow-green kernel surrounded by thin reddish skin. The kernel has a mild, sweet flavor and is commonly eaten raw or fried. Sometimes kernels are pressed for oil, and ground kernels are used for confectionery items.

Pistachio nuts were among "the finest products of the land" of Canaan that were brought as a gift by Jacob's sons to one who was a ruler in Egypt.

(Ge 43:11) Even in modern times large quantities of pistachio nuts have been exported from parts of the Middle East.

The city of Betonim, situated E of the Jordan in the territory of Gad, appears to have been named after pistachio nuts.—Jos 13:24, 26.

PIT. A deep or sunken place, either natural or artificial. The pits of bitumen into which the kings of Sodom and Gomorrah fell were evidently natural sunken places in the area (Ge 14:10); whereas the pit into which Joseph's brothers threw him was evidently a man-made waterpit. (Ge 37:20-29) The two principal Hebrew words for pit are bohr (also meaning "waterpit" or "cistern") and sha'chath.

The Hebrew word she'ohl' is translated "pit" three times in the King James Version. (Nu 16:30, 33; Job 17:16) However, Sheol actually refers to the common grave of mankind rather than to an individual grave. In Job 17:13-16 we find Sheol and the pit (Heb., sha'chath) used in parallel by Job as places of darkness and dust. Similarly, David's prayer to God at Psalm 30:3 says: "O Jehovah, you have brought up my soul from Sheol itself; you have kept me alive, that I should not go down into the pit." In Psalm 88:3-5 reference is made to Sheol, the pit, and the burial place in that order.—See also Job 33:18-30; Ps 30:3, 9; 49:7-10, 15; 88:6; 143:7; Pr 1:12; Isa 14:9-15; 38:17, 18; 51:14; see GRAVE; SHEOL.

Jonah also used the word for "pit" in a figurative sense when he compared the inside of the fish to "the belly of Sheol" as well as to "the pit." (Jon 2:2, 6) Such association of the pit with death and the grave was quite natural in view of the ancient custom of using or excavating a pit as a grave site.

Pits were evidently used as a means of trapping or ensnaring an enemy or for catching animals, and so are used in a figurative sense to stand for dangerous situations or intrigues besetting God's servants. (Ps 7:15; 40:2; 57:6; Pr 26:27; 28:10; Jer 18:20, 22) Sometimes the pits were netted to enmesh the victim caught in them. (Ps 35:7, 8) According to the Law, if a domestic animal fell into an excavated pit and died, the owner of the pit was required to make compensation to the owner of the animal.—Ex 21:33, 34.

A prostitute and "the mouth of strange women" are spoken of as "a deep pit." This is because a prostitute, often by persuasive speech, ensnares men to have relations with her.—Pr 22:14; 23:27.

The cisterns used by the Hebrews and other Orientals to store water were basically excavated pits. These were often shaped like a bottle; the mouth was generally narrow, only 0.3 m (1 ft) or so wide for the first meter (3 ft) down, and then the lower part widened out into a bulbous-shaped cavity.—See CISTERN.

The Greek word *phre'ar*, "pit," in the expression at Revelation 9:1, 2, "pit of the abyss," is the same word that John uses in his Gospel account to describe "the well" at Jacob's fountain where Jesus met the Samaritan woman. (Joh 4:11, 12) *Phre'ar* in its simplest meaning refers to such a well or pit dug in the earth; it may, however, be used in referring to any pit or abyss, including the unfathomable one from which the locusts of the Revelation ascend. (Re 9:3; see ABYSS.) The Greek word *bo'thy.nos,* rendered "pit," may also mean "ditch." (Mt 12:11; 15:14, ftn; Lu 6:39) Peter, in 2 Peter 2:4, speaks of the demon angels as confined to "pits [Gr., *sei.rois'*] of dense darkness."—See TARTARUS.

See also LIONS' PIT.

PITCH. The sticky, liquid form of bitumen, a dark-colored hydrocarbon similar to what is generally called tar. (See BITUMEN.) It is translated from the Hebrew word *ze'pheth.*

Mineral pitch is highly flammable and, unless kept well supplied with air, gives off great quantities of smoke when burning. Filling Edom's torrents with pitch and causing the land to become "burning pitch" with smoke ascending to time indefinite would be a fitting picture of devastating destruction. (Isa 34:9, 10) This description also helps to identify the substance, for Edom was near the Dead Sea, and even today bitumen is occasionally washed up on its shores, evidently coming from deposits now covered by the sea.

According to Exodus 2:3 the papyrus ark in which Moses was concealed was coated with both "bitumen and pitch." Jewish commentator Rashi suggested that this meant bitumen on the inside and pitch on the outside. Or it could mean a mixture of two different consistencies of the same basic substance. For instance, in *The Land and the Book,* W. M. Thomson suggests that Exodus 2:3 "reveals the process by which they prepared the bitumen. The mineral, as found in this country, melts readily enough by itself; but then, when cold, it is as brittle as glass. It must be mixed with tar while melting, and in that way it forms a hard, glassy wax, perfectly impervious to water." (Revised by J. Grande, 1910, p. 200) The Greek *Septuagint* uses the single term *a.sphal.to'pis.sa,* a mixture of asphalt and pitch. In parts of the Middle East, mineral pitch has been used even in recent times as a coating for certain sailing vessels.

PITHOM (Pi'thom) [from Egyptian, meaning "House [Temple] of Atum"]. One of two storage cities built by the enslaved Israelites in Egypt, the other being Raamses. (Ex 1:11) No positive identification of the site has been made. Archaeologists have apparently been influenced in their conclusions by the popular view that the Pharaoh of the Israelite oppression was Ramses II, a view that is not soundly founded.—See RAAMSES, RAMESES.

PITHON (Pi'thon). A descendant of King Saul through Jonathan and Merib-baal (Mephibosheth).—1Ch 8:33-35; 9:39-41.

PITY. A tender feeling toward persons in a state of suffering or in need, or toward anything that may have been treated in a harsh manner. The plural noun *ra.chamim'* denotes "pity," "mercies," or "inward emotions." (Ge 43:14, 30; 1Ch 21:13; Ps 40:11; see MERCY.) In Greek, the verb *splag.khni'zo.mai* means "be moved with pity or compassion," "have or feel pity." This term is drawn from the noun *splag'khna,* literally meaning "intestines." (Ac 1:18) Since strong emotions can have an effect on the abdominal area of the body, the Greek noun *splag'khna* is often used to denote "tender affections," or "tender compassions."—See AFFECTION.

Jehovah God set the example in manifesting pity for those in distress, and he can move men to show this loving feeling. That is why King Solomon could appropriately pray that Jehovah would make the Israelites objects of pity before their captors if they became captives because of unfaithfulness. (1Ki 8:50) As to the answer to this prayerful request, the inspired psalmist wrote: "He would grant them to be objects of pity before all those holding them captive." (Ps 106:46) Thus in time Jehovah restored a repentant remnant to its land. (Jer 33:26; Ezr 1:1-4) And in harmony with Jehovah's will, King Artaxerxes granted Nehemiah permission to rebuild the city of Jerusalem.—Ne 1:11–2:6.

Jesus Christ perfectly reflected the personality of his Father in the display of pity. He "felt pity" for the crowds, even when his privacy was interrupted, "because they were skinned and thrown about like sheep without a shepherd." (Mt 9:36; Mr 6:34) The sight of persons who were bereaved or who had leprosy or who were blind moved Jesus to feel pity, so that he brought them miraculous relief. (Mt 14:14; 20:30-34; Mr 1:40, 41; Lu 7:12, 13) And it was pity for the people who had been with him for three days with nothing to eat that prompted the Son of God miraculously to provide food for them.—Mt 15:32-38; Mr 8:2-9.

Disciples of Jesus Christ can imitate his example and that of his Father by responding willingly and gladly in rendering aid to those in distress and in welcoming all who sincerely repent of sin and make a wholehearted return to Jehovah. (Mt 18:21-35; Lu 10:30-37; 15:11-32) Thus they can rest assured of the Almighty's continued mercy toward them.—Mt 5:7.

PLAGUE.

The Hebrew words that are rendered "plague" or "scourge" have the literal meanings "touching," "smiting," "blow," "defeat," and "death." Jehovah God dealt blows as a punishment for rebellious murmuring (Nu 16:41-50), refusal to comply with his will (Zec 14:12, 15, 18), the profane use of something sacred (1Sa 5:1–6:4), touching his anointed ones (Ge 12:17; Ps 105:15), and unfaithfulness or violations of his law (Le 26:21; Nu 14:36, 37; 31:16; De 28:59-61; 1Ch 21:17, 22; 2Ch 21:12-15). Such blows might be administered by angelic or by human means. (2Sa 24:17; Jer 19:1-8; 25:8, 9; 49:17; 50:13, 14) Prayers of intercession by Jehovah's servants or sincere prayers by repentant ones were required for the removal of plagues sent by God.—Ge 20:17, 18; 1Ki 8:37, 38; 2Ch 6:28, 29.

A plague could also result from the natural outworking of a person's sin. (Pr 6:32, 33) It could be an affliction, such as "the plague of leprosy" (Le 13:2), or an adversity resulting from time and circumstance.—Ps 38:11; 73:5, 14.

The plagues Jehovah visited upon Egypt in the time of Moses were manifestations of his great power and caused his name to be declared among the nations. (Ex 9:14, 16) For generations afterward their effects were talked about by other peoples. (Jos 2:9-11; 9:9; 1Sa 4:8; 6:6) Also, these plagues proved that the gods of Egypt were powerless.—Ex 12:12; Nu 33:4; see GODS AND GODDESSES (The Ten Plagues); MOSES (Before Pharaoh of Egypt).

The plagues (Gr., *ple·gai'*, literally, "blows or strokes") mentioned in the book of Revelation evidently are expressions of God's anger and symbolically point to the result or effect of his judicial decisions.—Re 9:18, 20; 11:6; 15:1, 6, 8; 16:9, 21; 18:4, 8; 21:9; 22:18.

PLAIN.

Relatively level land, in contrast to hilly or mountainous country. The Hebrew Scriptures are quite explicit in their use of different words to identify or describe various types of land.

The Hebrew term *'ara·vah'* is used both as a name for a specific area and as a word descriptive of a certain type of land. (See ARABAH.) When used without the definite article, *'ara·vah'* indicates a desert plain or steppe, such as those of Moab and Jericho. (Nu 22:1; 35:1; Jos 5:10; 13:32; Jer 52:8) Though there might be rivers to provide some water for the area, *'ara·vah'* generally emphasizes that the plain is an arid one. Thus it would be quite a reversal for the fertile, watered Plain of Sharon to become like the desert plain (Isa 33:9), or for torrents of water to come to the desert plain.—Isa 35:1, 6; 51:3.

The word *biq·'ah'* indicated a wide plain bounded by mountains. It comes from a verb meaning "split" and can be accurately rendered "valley plain." Even today the broad valley plain between the Anti-Lebanon Range and the Lebanon Mountains is known as the Beqa'. (Jos 11:17) Often in the Scriptures *biq·'ah'*, or "valley plain," is set in contrast to mountains or hills (De 8:7; 11:11; Ps 104:8; Isa 41:18) or to rugged or rough ground. (Isa 40:4) The related Aramaic word appearing at Daniel 3:1 is frequently translated just "plain," referring to the place where Nebuchadnezzar erected the gold image.

A long low plain, or valley, was designated in Hebrew *'e'meq*. The word signifies "a long broad sweep between parallel ranges of hills of less extent than the preceding term [*biq·'ah*], . . . [*'e'meq*] having the idea of lowness and breadth rather than precipitateness or confinement." (M'Clintock and Strong's *Cyclopædia*, 1881, Vol. X, p. 703) The Hebrew word is applied to many different localities, such as "the low plain of Achor," "the low plain of Aijalon," and "the low plain of Rephaim."—Jos 7:24; 10:12; 1Ch 11:15.

PLANE TREE

[Heb., *'er·mohn'*]. A tree of stately appearance, growing to a height of some 20 m (70 ft), with wide spreading branches and broad dark-green, vinelike leaves affording splendid shade. The girth of the trunk is often 3 to 4 m (10 to 13 ft). The plane tree (*Platanus orientalis*) annually peels off its outer bark in strips or sections, exposing smooth whitish inner bark beneath.

The name of this tree in Hebrew possibly comes from the verb *'a·rah'*, meaning "lay bare; uncover." (Zep 2:14; Isa 22:6) At Genesis 30:37, 38, Jacob is described as placing staffs from this tree, along with those of other trees, before the flocks of Laban at Haran in Syria. The staffs were peeled, "laying bare," or revealing, "white places."

The tree was one worthy of comparison with, but not actually being a match for, the majestic cedar of Lebanon, which Ezekiel used as a figure of Pharaoh and all his crowd.—Eze 31:8.

Plane trees are found along the rivers and streams throughout Syria and in the region of ancient Assyria, as well as to a lesser degree in Palestine and Lebanon.

PLASTER. A coating for walls and partitions that was commonly made of clay mixed with straw. At times the mixture included lime, ashes, pulverized pottery fragments, or pounded shells or limestone.—Le 14:42; Eze 13:10-16; Da 5:5; see MORTAR, II.

PLEDGE. An object of personal property, such as a ring or garment, surrendered by a debtor to his creditor as a guarantee of the future repayment of a loan. The regulations of the Mosaic Law concerning pledges protected the interests of impoverished and defenseless members of the nation. They showed that God appreciated the difficulties of the poor and widows. The two Hebrew verbs *cha·val'* and *'a·vat'*, and their related nouns, have to do with a pledge.

If a poor man gave his outer garment as a pledge, or security on a loan, the creditor was not to keep it overnight. (Ex 22:26, 27; De 24:12, 13) A poor person would likely use his outer garment for covering at night; if he were deprived of it, he might suffer from the cold. For a person to ignore this law would mark him as greedy and heartless. (Job 22:6; 24:9) Yet, during Israel's apostasy, some persons not only seized garments from the poor as pledges but used them during their idolatrous feasts.—Am 2:8.

Not returning "a pledged thing" was listed in Ezekiel 18:10-13 along with robbing and shedding blood as things combining to prove an unrepentant sinner worthy of death. On the other hand, a wicked man who abandoned his sins by, among other things, returning "the very thing pledged" would "positively keep living." (Eze 33:14-16) It was also forbidden to take a hand mill or its upper grindstone as a pledge, for bread was usually baked daily, and to take the implements necessary for grinding the grain would mean seizing "a soul," or life.—De 24:6.

Widows were especially protected, since often they would not have anyone to defend or assist them. The Law forbade seizing a widow's garment as a pledge at all.—De 24:17; compare Job 24:3.

Also, one could not enter a man's house to take a pledged item from him. The debtor was to bring the pledge out to his creditor. (De 24:10, 11) In this way the inviolability of the man's home was upheld, and he could maintain self-respect, which would hardly be so if his creditor felt at liberty to enter the man's home without invitation. Thus, in addition to compassion and generosity (De 15:8), the laws about pledges encouraged respect for the person and rights of others.

Illustrative Use. Deuteronomy 15:6 gave as a sign of God's blessing the fact that the Jews would have sufficient means to "lend on pledge to many nations."

If a person "despised the word," by failing to repay a loan, he would forfeit what he put up as a pledge; in like manner a person would experience loss if he failed to obey God's commandment.—Pr 13:13.

In the Hebrew Scriptures advice is repeatedly given against going surety for a stranger, thereby promising to pay that person's debt if he failed to do so. (Pr 11:15; 22:26, 27; see SURETY.) Thus, Proverbs 20:16 speaks of 'taking the garment' of the one going surety for a stranger. This is in direct contrast to the sympathetic consideration to be shown the poor man who is obliged to become debtor to another because of his own misfortune. The one going surety for a stranger is not simply unfortunate but is stupid; the proverb evidently says to 'let him suffer the consequences.' The latter part of the verse calls for 'seizing a pledge' in "the instance of a foreign woman." The man entering into relationship with such a woman may become impoverished (compare Pr 5:3, 8-10), and so he may have to pledge his remaining possessions as security for his debts. The proverb apparently says that he merits no pity, inasmuch as he acted contrary to all sound advice in having dealings with the "foreign woman."

PLOW. See FARMING IMPLEMENTS.

PLOWING. Conclusions as to the type of plow used by Hebrew farmers in Biblical times are dependent on ancient pictures of plows used in neighboring lands and on plows used in recent times by some Arab farmers. Some plows consisted of a simple pointed piece of wood, perhaps metal-tipped, attached to a beam and pulled by an animal or animals. Using such a type, plowing likely only cut the surface of the soil without turning it over. Of course, lack of direct evidence precludes ruling out the possibility that more substantial plows were used in Israel.

With soil baked hard by the hot summer sun, the practice was to hold up plowing until the autumn or winter rains softened the soil. The soil was then plowed and the seed sown. Colder days or times of uncertain weather or threatening clouds would not deter a manly person from work in the plowing season, but a lazy farmer would seize upon such as excuse to avoid work. His neighbors would have no reason to sympathize with him when he had no harvest because of his laziness at plowing time. (Pr 20:4; Ec 11:4) Even in plowing time, though, Israelite farmers were to keep the Sabbath.—Ex 34:21.

A bull and an ass were not to be yoked to the same plow, doubtless because of the inequality of their strength and pace. (De 22:10) Often a pair of cattle pulled the plow. (Lu 14:19; Job 1:14) A number of men, each with a pair, or span, of cattle, might work together, plowing parallel rows one behind the other. In Elisha's case, as related at 1 Kings 19:19, he was the 12th and last so he could stop without disrupting others following him. He left the field and used his wood plowing instruments as firewood in offering the bulls as a sacrifice. (1Ki 19:21) In *The Land and the Book* (revised by J. Grande, 1910, p. 121), W. M. Thomson reports that one man could easily sow the area plowed by a group of men.

Illustrative Use. The familiar work of plowing often was used as the basis for an illustration. When Philistines convinced Samson's wife to obtain from him the answer to his riddle, Samson said they had 'plowed with his young cow,' that is, used for their service one who should have been serving him. (Jg 14:15-18) A rocky crag is no place for plowing, and as Amos shows, it was equally irrational for Israel's leaders to corrupt justice and practice unrighteousness and yet expect to derive benefit from such a course. (Am 6:12, 13) Hosea 10:11 evidently uses plowing (a much harder work for a heifer than threshing was) to represent laborious or slavish labor, likely imposed by foreign oppressors, that was due to come on apostate Judah. What Judah and Israel needed, according to Jeremiah 4:3, 4 and Hosea 10:12, 13, was a change in their way of life, preparing, softening, and cleansing their hearts (compare Lu 8:5-15) as by plowing and removing thorns, so that, instead of wasting their efforts and labor in wrong practices that bring only a bad harvest, they might instead reap divine blessings.

The description of the orderly, purposeful, and judicious methods of the farmer in plowing, harrowing, sowing, and threshing are used at Isaiah 28:23-29 to illustrate the ways of Jehovah, who is "wonderful in counsel, who has done greatly in effectual working." Even as plowing and harrowing are limited, being merely preparatory to sowing, so, too, Jehovah does not forever discipline or punish his people, but he disciplines primarily to soften them and make them amenable to receiving his counsel and guidance, which produce blessings. (Compare Heb 12:4-11.) Even as the hardness of the soil governs the extent or intensity of the plowing, so the type of grain determines the force and weight of the instruments used for threshing to eliminate the chaff, all of this illustrating God's wisdom in cleansing his people and getting rid of whatever is undesirable, varying his treatment according to existing needs and circumstances.—Compare Isa 21:10; 1:25.

A city "plowed up as a mere field" meant a city completely overturned and laid waste. (Jer 26: 18; Mic 3:12) Israel's speaking of those who had 'plowed upon my very back, lengthening their furrows,' evidently describes the nation's sufferings under its many enemies who relentlessly and cruelly overran and mistreated them, as Israel made its back "just like the earth . . . for those crossing over." (Ps 129:1-3; Isa 51:23; compare Ps 66:12.) In the restoration prophecy at Amos 9:13-15, Jehovah's blessing is shown to make the soil so productive that the harvest is still going on when the time comes to plow for the next season. —Compare Le 26:5.

Even as Jesus had said that his disciples should accept food, drink, and lodging from those they served, since "the worker is worthy of his wages," so the apostle Paul upheld the right of those laboring in Christian ministry to receive material support from others, just as the man who plows does so with the legitimate hope of being a partaker of the harvest to which his labor contributed. Yet Paul personally and willingly preferred not to avail himself of the right to refrain from secular work, so as to furnish "the good news without cost" to those to whom he ministered.—Lu 10:7; 1Co 9:3-10, 15, 17, 18.

Jesus Christ referred to the work of plowing to emphasize the importance of wholehearted discipleship. When a man expressed his desire to be a disciple but stipulated the condition of being permitted first to say good-bye to his household, Jesus replied: "No man that has put his hand to a plow and looks at the things behind is well fitted for the kingdom of God." (Lu 9:61, 62) If a plowman allowed himself to be distracted from the work at hand, he would make crooked furrows. Similarly, the person who is invited to Christian discipleship but permits himself to be turned aside from carrying out the attendant responsibilities would become unfit for God's Kingdom. As the Son of God exemplified in his own case, even the most intimate family ties are subordinate to faithfulness in the accomplishment of the divine will. —Mr 3:31-35; 10:29, 30.

PLUMMET. A plumb line; a cord to the end of which was fastened a metal, stone, or clay weight that kept the line straight and made it possible to build walls and other structures that were straight and perpendicular to the horizon. The weight itself is sometimes called the plumb bob, or plummet. Carpenters, masons, and other craftsmen of ancient times used the plummet.

In connection with the rebuilding of the temple in Jerusalem, Zerubbabel is represented as having in hand a plummet, literally, "the stone [or, weight], the tin," according to the Masoretic text. (Zec 4:9, 10) As foretold, not only was the temple's foundation laid by Zerubbabel but under his supervision the work was carried to completion. —Ezr 3:8-10; 6:14, 15.

In vision, Amos beheld Jehovah stationed on a wall made with a plummet, and thus one that was originally straight, perpendicular. Jehovah was seen holding a plummet, and the prophet was told that God was setting a plummet in the midst of His people. As Israel did not meet the test of straightness in a spiritual way, not acting in accord with God's requirements, Jehovah would mete out justice and "no more do any further excusing of it." Israel's high places would be laid desolate, her sanctuaries would be devastated, and God would "rise up against the house of Jeroboam with a sword." (Am 7:7-9) True to these words, Israel was devastated and Samaria destroyed by the Assyrians in 740 B.C.E.

POCHERETH-HAZZEBAIM (Po'che·reth-haz-ze·ba'im). Head of a family whose descendants were among "the sons of the servants of Solomon" returning from the exile under the leadership of Zerubbabel.—Ezr 2:1, 2, 55, 57; Ne 7:59.

POISON. See VENOM.

POISONOUS PLANT. While some have suggested equating the Hebrew word *ro'sh* (or, *rohsh*) with hemlock, colocynth, or the poppy, no certain identification of the plant is possible. The Hebrew term at times refers to (1) a bitter and poisonous plant (La 3:5, 19), (2) poison or "venom" (De 32:33; Job 20:16), and (3) when used in connection with water, poisonous water (Jer 8:14; 9:15; 23:15). It appears in an illustrative sense with reference to a perversion of justice (Ho 10:4; Am 6:12) and to those who apostatize.—De 29:18; compare Ac 8:23; Heb 12:15.

Concerning the Messiah, it was foretold that he would be given "a poisonous plant" for food. (Ps 69:21) This occurred when Jesus Christ, before his impalement, was offered wine mixed with gall but, upon tasting it, refused the stupefying drink that was probably intended to alleviate his sufferings. In recording the fulfillment of this prophecy, Matthew (27:34) employed the Greek word *kho·le'* (gall), the same term found in the Greek *Septuagint* at Psalm 69:21. However, Mark's Gospel account mentions myrrh (Mr 15:23), and this has given rise to the view that in this case the "poisonous plant" or "gall" was "myrrh." Another possibility is that the drugged drink contained both gall and myrrh.

POLYGAMY. See MARRIAGE.

POMEGRANATE [Heb., *rim·mohn'*]. A fruit that, when ripe, is of a maroon color, shaped like an apple, with a rosette or crown extending around the bottom. Within the hard rind it is crowded with small capsules full of juice, each containing a small pink or red seed.

The pomegranate tree (*Punica granatum*), also denoted by the Hebrew word *rim·mohn'*, grows throughout the Middle East. It seldom passes 4.5 m (15 ft) in height. The spreading branches are numerous and have dark-green leaves that are shaped like the head of a lance and that produce blossoms with coral-red to scarlet flowers.—PICTURE, Vol. 1, p. 742.

Pomegranate juice makes a refreshing drink (Ca 8:2), a syrup called grenadine is produced from the seeds, and the blossoms are used in the preparation of an astringent medicine used as a remedy for dysentery. The Shulammite maiden's veiled temples were compared to "a segment of pomegranate" and her skin to "a paradise of pomegranates."—Ca 4:3, 13; 6:7.

By means of Moses, Jehovah promised the nation of Israel that He would bring them into a land of wheat, barley, vines, figs, pomegranates, olives, and honey. (De 8:7-9) Prior to this the spies who went into the land had returned with grapes, figs, and pomegranates. (Nu 13:2, 23) The Israelites had known the pomegranate in Egypt, as their complaint at Numbers 20:5 indicates.

The sleeveless coat of High Priest Aaron's garments had on its hem a series of pomegranates made of blue thread, reddish-purple wool, and scarlet material twisted together and alternating with golden bells. (Ex 28:33, 34; 39:24-26) Later, when the temple was constructed, the capitals of the two copper pillars in front of the porch of the house were decorated with chains of pomegranate figures.—1Ki 7:18, 20, 42; 2Ki 25:17; 2Ch 3:16; 4:13; Jer 52:22, 23.

The pomegranate was extensively cultivated in Bible times, and the place-names of Rimmon, En-rimmon, and Gath-rimmon doubtless were derived from the abundance of these trees in their area. (Jos 15:32; 19:45; Ne 11:29) The pomegranate tree was much prized and thus is often associated with other important fruit producers such as the vine and the fig tree.—Ca 7:12, 13; Joe 1:12; Hag 2:19.

PONTIUS. See PILATE.

PONTUS (Pon'tus) [Sea]. A district of northern Asia Minor along the Euxine Sea (Black Sea). The name evidently was applied in pre-Christian times to that part of northern Asia Minor bordering Pontus Euxinus, as the sea was sometimes called. Pontus ran from the lower course of the Halys River on the W (near Bithynia) eastward along the coast toward the SE limit of the sea. Along the fertile coastline the climate is warm in the summer and mild in the winter. The interior forms the NE corner of the central plateau, broken by many river valleys, and in these grain was grown. The mountain slopes were forested and produced timber for shipbuilding. Along the coast the influence of Greek colonies was felt, but the people of the interior had close ties to Armenia to the E.

After being under Persian influence for a time, the separate kingdom of Pontus was set up in the fourth century B.C.E. There was a succession of kings called Mithradates, and close ties with Rome developed. However, Mithradates VI Eupator challenged Roman power and expanded his kingdom greatly. After a series of wars, the Romans under Pompey defeated him about 66 B.C.E. Much of Pontus was then united with Bithynia to the W into a combined province called Bithynia and Pontus. But the eastern section was added to the province of Galatia (Galatian Pontus). Later, some of this eastern part was given to Polemon (c. 36 B.C.E.) to form part of the Kingdom of Polemon. (MAP, Vol. 1, p. 195) Thus in the first century C.E. the term "Pontus" referred either to the entire geographic area along the coast or to that part found in the combined province of Bithynia and Pontus or even to the eastern section that had become part of Galatia and the Kingdom of Polemon.

The first-century Jewish writer Philo said that Jews had spread to every part of Pontus. Jews from Pontus were present in Jerusalem on Pentecost 33 C.E. (Ac 2:9) Possibly some of these Jews of Pontus who heard Peter's speech became Christians and returned to their home territory. Some 30 years later, Peter addressed his first canonical letter (c. 62-64 C.E.) to "temporary residents scattered about in Pontus" and other parts of Asia Minor. (1Pe 1:1) Since he mentioned "older men" who were to shepherd the flock, Christian congregations likely existed in Pontus. (1Pe 5:1, 2) The Jew named Aquila who was a native of Pontus traveled to Rome and then to Corinth, where he met the apostle Paul.—Ac 18:1, 2.

POOL. A large open reservoir for collecting and storing water. Artificial pools were dug out of the soil or hewn out of rock. At times they were located inside the cities and linked to springs by means of conduits. This ensured the inhabitants a supply of water even in time of siege. Some pools were enlargements or adaptations of such existing natural features as caves.

Among the various pools mentioned in the Scriptures are those of Gibeon (2Sa 2:13; see GIBEON, GIBEONITES), Hebron (2Sa 4:12), Heshbon (Ca 7:4; see BATH-RABBIM), Samaria (1Ki 22:38), and Jerusalem. It has been suggested that the pools made by the congregator (King Solomon) for irrigation purposes are perhaps to be identified with reservoirs found S of Bethlehem. (Ec 2:6) Water from nearby springs was stored in these reservoirs.

Pools of Jerusalem. The general location of the ancient Pool of Siloam (Joh 9:7) is thought to be the present Birket Silwan, just SW of the City of David. Likely this is also the approximate location of King Hezekiah's pool adjoining the conduit that he constructed to bring the waters of the spring of Gihon into Jerusalem.—2Ki 20:20; 2Ch 32:30.

The Biblical references to the "old pool" (Isa 22:11), "upper pool" (2Ki 18:17; Isa 7:3; 36:2), and "lower pool" (Isa 22:9) give no indication about their exact position in relation to the city of Jerusalem. Scholars generally believe that the "lower pool" (perhaps the same as "the Pool of the Canal" mentioned at Ne 3:15) may be identified with Birket el-Hamra at the southern end of the Tyropoeon Valley. But opinions vary considerably regarding the placement of the "upper pool."—See POOL OF THE CANAL.

"The King's Pool" was evidently located between the Gate of the Ash-heaps and the Fountain Gate. (Ne 2:13-15) It may be the same pool that is mentioned at Nehemiah 3:16.

Concerning the Pool of Bethzatha, see BETHZATHA.

Reedy Pools. Whereas the Hebrew term *bere·khah'* means "pool" (such as an artificial pool), the word *'agham'* signifies "reedy pool," likely a natural collection of water in a depression. (Ex 7:19; 8:5; Ps 107:35; 114:8; Isa 35:7; 41:18) The prophecy that God would make Babylon "reedy pools of water" graphically indicated how desolate she would become.—Isa 14:23.

POOL OF THE CANAL. A pool or reservoir of water, apparently S of the City of David where the Valley of Hinnom and the Central (Tyropoeon) Valley meet. (Ne 3:15) It seems that this pool was also termed "the lower pool."—Isa 22:9.

The Masoretic text at Nehemiah 3:15 designates this "the Pool of Shelah." Some scholars believe that "Shelah" should be emended to "Shiloah," meaning "Sender" and applying to a canal, or channel, that delivers water to a pool. (Isa 8:6) Thus, while some Bible versions leave "Shelah" untranslated, *The Jerusalem Bible* renders the expression "the conduit cistern," and the *New World Translation* reads "the Pool of the Canal."

Remains have been found of a channel, or canal, that ran S from the Gihon spring, following the contour of the Kidron's bank and terminating in an ancient reservoir now called Birket el-Hamra. Sections of the canal were covered with stone slabs, but it appears that there were openings so that water could be drawn off to irrigate parts of the valley. The gradual slope of this canal may be referred to in the words "the waters of the Shiloah that are going gently." (Isa 8:6) The location of Birket el-Hamra fits Nehemiah's placement of the Pool of the Canal, near the King's Garden and the Stairway going down from the S end of the City of David.

POOR. Lacking material possessions or the necessities of life; at times, inferior in quality; also, pitiable because of spiritual deficiency.

The problem of poverty is an ancient one. Down through the centuries the needy generally have outnumbered those having much. When accepting an act of generosity, Jesus recognized the hard fact that poverty would persist among humans living in imperfection, saying to his disciples: "For you always have the poor with you, and whenever you want to you can always do them good, but me you do not have always." (Mr 14:7) The Bible presents a balanced view of the problem, expressing compassion for those suffering under oppressive conditions, while also reproving those who, in effect, 'eat their own flesh' because of indolence. (Ec 4:1, 5; Pr 6:6-11) It stresses spiritual prosperity over material prosperity (1Ti 6:17-19); hence, the apostle wrote: "For we have brought nothing into the world, and neither can we carry anything out. So, having sustenance and covering, we shall be content with these things." (1Ti 6:7, 8) But the Scriptures do not portray material poverty as a virtue in itself, and they warn of the temptation to steal, which extreme poverty may bring.—Pr 6:30, 31; 30:8, 9; contrast Eph 4:28.

The Poor in Israel. It was not Jehovah's purpose that any of the Israelites suffer poverty. The nation was given an inheritance of land. (Nu 34:2-12) All Israelite families, with the exception of the Levites, who received a tenth of the produce of the land for their service at the sanctuary, shared in that inheritance and therefore had a means of supporting themselves. (Nu 18:20, 21) Landholdings were secure. Laws of inheritance ensured that the land would continue to be held by the family or tribe to which it belonged. (Nu 27:7-11; 36:6-9; De 21:15-17; see INHERITANCE.) It could not be sold in perpetuity. (Le 25:23) In the Jubilee year all hereditary lands that had been sold were restored to their rightful owners. (Le 25:13) Thus even if a man squandered his substance, the inheritance could not be forever lost to his posterity.

Faithful adherence to God's law would largely have prevented poverty among the Israelites. (De 15:4, 5) However, if disobedient, they would not have Jehovah's blessing, and this would lead to impoverishment due to such calamities as invasions by enemy armies and severe drought. (De 28:22-25; compare Jg 6:1-6; 1Ki 17:1; 18:17, 18; Jas 5:17, 18.) Individuals, because of being lazy (Pr 6:10, 11; 10:4; 19:15; 20:13; 24:30-34), drunkards, gluttons (Pr 23:21), or pleasure-seekers (Pr 21:17), could bring poverty on themselves and their families. Then, too, unforeseen circumstances might arise that could plunge persons into poverty. Death could leave behind orphans and widows. Accidents and sickness could temporarily or permanently hinder a person from performing necessary work. For these reasons Jehovah could say to Israel: "Someone poor will never cease to be in the midst of the land."—De 15:11.

The Law, however, did much to make it easier for the poor to cope with their situation. During the harvest they had the right to glean in the fields, orchards, and vineyards and, therefore, did not have to beg for bread or resort to stealing. (Le 19:9, 10; 23:22; De 24:19-21) A needy Israelite could borrow money without having to pay interest, and a spirit of generosity was to be shown toward him. (Ex 22:25; Le 25:35-37; De 15:7-10; see DEBT, DEBTOR.) To build up his financial resources, he could sell his land or sell himself into slavery, on a temporary basis. (Le 25:25-28, 39-54) So as not to put a hardship on the poor, the Law permitted them to present less valuable offerings at the sanctuary.—Le 12:8; 14:21, 22; 27:8.

God's law prescribed equal justice for rich and poor alike, not favoring either one because of his position. (Ex 23:3, 6; Le 19:15) But as the nation of Israel lapsed into unfaithfulness, the poor suffered much oppression.—Isa 10:1, 2; Jer 2:34.

In the First Century C.E. It appears that considerable poverty prevailed among the Jews in the first century C.E. Foreign domination from the time of the Babylonian exile had doubtless interfered with the application of the Mosaic Law which protected hereditary possessions. (Compare Ne 9:36, 37.) The religious leaders, especially the Pharisees, were more concerned about tradition than instilling genuine love of neighbor and proper regard for aged and needy parents. (Mt 15:5, 6; 23:23; compare Lu 10:29-32.) The money-loving Pharisees had little interest in those who were poor.—Lu 16:14.

Christ Jesus, though, 'felt pity for the crowds, because they were skinned and thrown about like sheep without a shepherd.' (Mt 9:36) His declaring the good news to the poor and oppressed stood in such marked contrast with the attitude of the religious leaders of Judaism that it constituted one of the proofs that he was indeed the Messiah. (Mt 11:5; Lu 4:18; 7:22) To responsive ones it also opened up the glorious privilege of inheriting the heavenly Kingdom.—Mt 5:3; Lu 6:20.

Being in a covenant relationship with God, the Jews were under obligation to assist needy fellow Israelites. (Pr 14:21; 28:27; Isa 58:6, 7; Eze 18:7-9) Appreciating this, Zacchaeus, upon accepting Jesus as the Messiah, exclaimed: "Look! The half of my belongings, Lord, I am giving to the poor." (Lu 19:8) For the same reason, Christ Jesus could say: "When you spread a feast, invite poor people, crippled, lame, blind; and you will be happy, because they have nothing with which to repay you." (Lu 14:13, 14) On another occasion he encouraged a rich young ruler: "Sell all the things you have and distribute to poor people, and you will have treasure in the heavens; and come be my follower." (Lu 18:22) The fact that this man was unwilling to part with his possessions to aid others showed that he had no real concern for the oppressed and thus did not have the qualities required for being a disciple of Jesus.—Lu 18:23.

Jesus' encouragement to assist the poor was in line with what he himself had done. As God's Son in the heavens, he had had everything. But "though he was rich he became poor." As a poor man on earth, he was able to redeem the human race, making available the greatest of riches, that is, the prospect for his followers to become sons of God. (2Co 8:9) Additionally, other great spiritual riches became available to them.—Compare 2Co 6:10; Re 2:9; 3:17, 18.

Also, while on earth, Jesus personally took an interest in the materially poor. He and his apostles had a common fund from which they gave to needy Israelites. (Mt 26:9-11; Mr 14:5-7; Joh 12:5-8; 13:29) The same loving concern for the poor was manifested in later years by Christians as they provided material assistance for their poor brothers. (Ro 15:26; Ga 2:10) But some did forget,

making it necessary for the disciple James to reprimand them for bestowing favoritism on the rich and looking down on the poor.—Jas 2:2-9.

Of course, only those who were deserving received material assistance. By no means was laziness encouraged. As the apostle Paul wrote to the Thessalonians: "If anyone does not want to work, neither let him eat."—2Th 3:10; see BEGGAR, BEGGING; GIFTS OF MERCY.

POPLARS [Heb., 'ara·vim' (plural)]. The Hebrew name for this tree corresponds to the Arabic *gharab*, which continues to be used for the Euphrates poplar. Thus, although the poplar and willow are of the same family of trees, and both common to the Middle East, modern lexicographers favor the poplar tree (*Populus euphratica*) in translation.—See Koehler and Baumgartner's *Lexicon in Veteris Testamenti Libros*, Leiden, 1958, p. 733; Brown, Driver, and Briggs' *Hebrew and English Lexicon of the Old Testament*, 1980, p. 788; *The New Westminster Dictionary of the Bible*, edited by H. Gehman, 1970, p. 998.

The poplar tree is very common along the banks of the Euphrates (while the willow is comparatively rare there) and thus fits well the reference at Psalm 137:1, 2, which describes the weeping Jewish exiles as hanging their harps on the poplar trees. The small, crisp, heart-shaped leaves of the Euphrates poplar (also called aspen) are carried on flattened stems that hang obliquely from the main stalk, and this results in their swaying back and forth at the slightest breeze, a motion that might suggest the emotional swaying of persons weeping in grief.

Euphrates poplars are also found along the banks of rivers and streams in Syria and Palestine, and particularly in the Jordan River valley. There, along with tamarisk trees, they often form dense thickets, while elsewhere they may grow to a height of from 9 to 14 m (30 to 45 ft). In all the Scriptural references, these poplar trees are associated with watercourses or 'torrent valleys.' They were included among the trees whose boughs were used at the Festival of Booths (Le 23:40); they provided cover for the mighty "Behemoth" (hippopotamus) along the river (Job 40:15, 22); and the ease with which they sprout along well-watered places is used at Isaiah 44:3, 4 to describe the rapid growth and increase resulting from Jehovah's outpoured blessings and spirit.

POPLARS, TORRENT VALLEY OF. At Isaiah 15:7 the prophet describes the escaping Moabites as fleeing with their goods across "the torrent valley of the poplars." If their flight was to the S, as it seems likely to have been, this torrent valley would appear to refer to "the torrent valley of Zered" (Nu 21:12; De 2:13), which acted as the frontier boundary between Moab and Edom to the S. The torrent valley of Zered is generally identified with the Wadi el-Hasa', which flows into the S end of the Dead Sea. In its lower course it passes through a small plain that is somewhat swampy in places and could thus be a suitable place for poplars to have grown.—See ZERED, TORRENT VALLEY OF.

PORATHA (Po·ra'tha). One of the ten sons of Haman.—Es 9:8, 10.

PORCH. In the Hebrew Scriptures the word for porch, 'eh·lam' (or 'u·lam'), is not used in regard to an architectural portion of individual homes, private houses. Whether Israelite homes had a porch of some sort is difficult to determine. But the archaeological remains of some houses in Megiddo indicate that they were built around a courtyard and that "one ground floor room served as an entrance vestibule." (*The Biblical Archaeologist,* May 1968, pp. 46, 48) In the Scriptures 'eh·lam' is applied to two of the public buildings Solomon constructed, the front part of Solomon's temple, and to certain parts of the gateways and temple that Ezekiel was shown in vision.

Porch of Pillars. One of the official buildings Solomon constructed in the temple area sometime after he completed the temple was the Porch of Pillars. (1Ki 7:1, 6) Since mention of the Porch of Pillars is made between comments about the House of the Forest of Lebanon and comments about the Porch of the Throne, it is quite possible that the Porch of Pillars was S of the temple and between these other two official buildings. Thus, one coming from the S might pass through or around the House of the Forest of Lebanon and then enter the Porch of Pillars, walking through it into the Porch of the Throne.

The building was 50 cubits (22.3 m; 72.9 ft) long and 30 cubits (13.4 m; 43.7 ft) wide. Its very name suggests that it was made up of rows of impressive pillars. First Kings 7:6 mentions another porch in front with pillars and a canopy. Perhaps this means that one first came to a porch having an extending canopy supported by pillars. Then this porch merged right into the Porch of Pillars proper. If the dimensions given apply just to the Porch of Pillars, then the size of the canopied portion is not given.

This building may have served as a grand entranceway to the Porch of the Throne and as a place where the king conducted the ordinary business of the kingdom and received some visitors.

Porch of the Throne. Another building that Solomon constructed after the temple was completed was the Porch of the Throne. (1Ki 7:1, 7) "The porch of judgment" referred to in the text seems to be synonymous with "the Porch of the Throne." So "the Porch of the Throne" evidently was where Solomon placed his ornate ivory and gold throne and did judging.—1Ki 10:18-20.

The entire description of this building is: "He made the porch of judgment; and they covered it in with cedarwood from the floor to the rafters." (1Ki 7:7) The Masoretic text actually says, "from floor to floor," leading some to believe that there was cedar from the floor of this building to the floor of the Porch of Pillars mentioned in the preceding verse. However, the Syriac *Peshitta* reads "from floor to ceiling," and the Latin *Vulgate* says "from floor to top." So, certain translators believe that the cedar was some sort of splendid paneling from the floor of the Porch to its rafters or ceiling. (*NW, RS, JB, Ro*) Though other architectural details are lacking, this would suggest a building not having open pillars on a side or sides, as may have been the case with the House of the Forest of Lebanon and the Porch of Pillars.

Since the Porch of the Throne is listed right after the Porch of Pillars, it is possible that this latter building served as a grand entrance to the Porch of the Throne. A person coming from the S may have had to walk through the Porch of Pillars to enter the porch of judgment.

Solomon's Temple. While the primary portions of the temple were the Holy and Most Holy compartments, in front of the Holy (toward the E) there was a massive porch that served as an entranceway to the temple. The porch was 20 cubits (8.9 m; 29.2 ft) long (running along the width of the temple) and 10 cubits (4.5 m; 14.6 ft) deep. (1Ki 6:3) It was 120 cubits (53.4 m; 175 ft) high. Second Chronicles 3:4 presents the height of the porch in the context of other measurements for the house, measurements that are generally accepted and that harmonize with those in First Kings. (Compare 2Ch 3:3, 4 with 1Ki 6:2, 3, 17, 20.) Thus the porch would have appeared as a tall, evidently rectangular, tower that extended high above the rest of the temple building. In front of it stood two massive copper pillars named Jachin and Boaz. (1Ki 7:15-22; 2Ch 3:15-17) The porch also had doors (King Ahaz closed these up, but his son Hezekiah later opened and repaired them). (2Ch 28:24; 29:3, 7) Especially in the morning when the sun rising in the E shone directly on it, the lofty temple porch must have been a most impressive sight.

Ezekiel's Temple Vision. Quite a number of porches are mentioned in the vision Ezekiel had of a temple sanctuary. The temple building itself had a porch in front (toward the E), as did Solomon's temple. However, this porch was 20 cubits (10.4 m; 34 ft) in length and 11 cubits (5.7 m; 18.7 ft) in width; the height is not stated. (These measurements are based on the long cubit of about 51.8 cm [20.4 in.]; see Eze 40:5, ftn.) This porch had pillars as well as side pillars, and there was a wood canopy, probably near the top. (Eze 40:48, 49; 41:25, 26) Each of the three elaborate outer gateways (approaching from the E, S, and N) incorporated a porch with windows of narrowing frames. Apparently, one ascending the stairs into the gateway passed three guard chambers on each side and then, by crossing a threshold, came into the porch before entering the outer courtyard. (Eze 40:6-17) Each of the three inner gateways also had a porch, perhaps just as one ascended the steps and entered the gate. The porch in the gateway approached from the N contained four tables for slaughtering the whole burnt offering. —Eze 40:35-42.

PORCIUS FESTUS. See FESTUS.

PORCUPINE

[Heb., *qip·podh'*]. A large rodent distinguished by its protective spines or quills. There is considerable dispute as to the exact meaning of the Hebrew word *qip·podh'*, variously rendered "bittern" (*KJ, Da*), "bustard" (*NE*), "hedgehog" (*AT, Le*), and "porcupine(s)" (*AS, NW*). (Isa 14:23; 34:11; Zep 2:14) In the light of Hebrew etymology, G. R. Driver rejects the rendering "bittern" and suggests that the Hebrew *qip·podh'* may apply both to the porcupine and to a bird. But he recommends "ruffed bustard" as a likely translation for *qip·podh'* in the above texts. (*Palestine Exploration Quarterly,* London, 1955, p. 137) Koehler and Baumgartner prefer "hedgehog" at Isaiah 14:23; 34:11, but "short-eared owl" at Zephaniah 2:14. (*Lexicon in Veteris Testamenti Libros,* Leiden, 1958, p. 845) That one Hebrew word may apply to two entirely different animals is illustrated by the term *tin·she'meth,* which denotes both a flying creature, "the swan," and a swarming creature, "the chameleon."—Le 11:18, 30.

Despite the uncertainty, however, there is good basis for consistently translating *qip·podh'* as either "porcupine" or "hedgehog," rather than "bittern." Both older and modern lexicons generally list "hedgehog" or "porcupine" as defining *qip·podh'* in all cases. These renderings have the support of the Greek *Septuagint* and the Latin *Vulgate,* as well as of Hebrew etymology and related languages such as Aramaic, Arabic, and Ethiopic.

On the basis of inferences drawn from Isaiah 14:23 and Zephaniah 2:14 regarding the desolation of Babylon and Nineveh, some raise the objection that the porcupine (or the hedgehog) could not be the animal intended, since this creature does not frequent reedy pools of water, nor can it sing or climb to the top of columns. However, according to Isaiah 14:23, not the reedy pools but Babylon was to become the possession of porcupines. One explorer of Babylon's ruins reported finding "*quantities* of porcupine quills." Similarly, the reference to a voice "singing in the window" at desolated Nineveh can apply to any bird that might perch in a deserted window or even to the sound of the wind and need not apply to the porcupine. (Zep 2:14) As to the porcupine's 'spending the night among the pillar capitals [the top portion of the pillars],' it must be remembered that the picture drawn is of a city in ruins. Hence, it is certainly possible that the pillars are here regarded as fallen to the ground.

PORPHYRY

(por'phy·ry). A kind of stone, usually dark red, purple, or sometimes green, containing feldspar crystals. Together with marble and pearl, it was used as pavement in the Persian palace at Shushan in the days of King Ahasuerus. —Es 1:6.

PORTENT.

Something that presages future situations or events; also, a marvel.

The Hebrew word *moh·pheth'* generally carries the idea of a "miracle," as in the miracles performed through Moses and Aaron in Egypt. However, in some cases the term is definitely used in the sense of a "portent," as with regard to the prophet or dreamer who offers a sign or portent (to be fulfilled in the future) to lend support to his prophecy.—De 13:1-3.

The portent (*moh·pheth'*) might be a miraculous act manifesting divine power, as when the altar of Jeroboam was ripped apart by God, portending the still future and greater execution of his adverse judgment regarding that altar and those serving at it. (1Ki 13:1-5; compare the fulfillment some 300 years later at 2Ki 23:16-20.) Or it might be just an unusual action performed by someone, as when Isaiah went naked and barefoot to portend the circumstances due to come on Egypt and Ethiopia at the hands of the king of Assyria (Isa 20:3-6), or when Ezekiel made a hole in the wall (likely the wall of his residence) and took out his luggage through it as a portent of the exile facing Judah.—Eze 12:5-11; compare 24:18-27.

Since a portent is a sign pointing to future things or circumstances, one writer may employ the word *moh·pheth'* (portent, or miracle) while another uses *'ohth* (sign) to describe the same thing. (Compare 2Ch 32:24 with 2Ki 20:8, 9.) A "sign" may serve as a guide or indicator for the present, as well as for the future, whereas a "portent" relates primarily to the future. The designating of something as a "sign" stresses that it has *significance*, whether for the present or the future. Its being called a "portent" stresses its significance as relating to the future.

Thus, when referring to Joel 2:30, which foretold "portents [plural of the Hebrew *moh·pheth'*] in the heavens and on the earth," the apostle Peter spoke of "portents [plural of the Gr. *te'ras*] in heaven above and signs [plural of *se·mei'on*] on earth." (Ac 2:14, 19) In the Christian Greek Scriptures *te'ras* is consistently used in combination with *se·mei'on* ("sign"), both terms being used in the plural form.—Ac 7:36; 14:3; 15:12; 2Co 12:12.

Basically, *te'ras* refers to any act or thing exciting wonderment, hence it is properly translated "wonders" in some cases. (Mt 24:24; Joh 4:48) Where the future is more clearly involved, "portent" is more appropriate. Serving as credentials that Jesus was God's "Sent One" were the "powerful works and portents and signs that God did through him." (Ac 2:22) The miraculous cures and resurrections he performed not only excited wonderment but also portended what he would do on a greater scale in the future. (Joh 6:54; compare Joh 1:50, 51; 5:20, 28.) Some acts were portents of his future activity as God's High Priest, forgiving sins and acting as Judge. (Mt 9:2-8; Joh 5:1-24) Others served as evidence of his future authority and power to act against Satan and his demons, abyssing them. (Mt 12:22-29; Lu 8:27-33; compare Re 20:1-3.) All such acts pointed forward to his Messianic Rule as Anointed King of God's Kingdom.

Similarly, Jesus' disciples, as witnesses of his teachings and resurrection, were backed up by God with "signs as well as portents and various powerful works." (Heb 2:3, 4; Ac 2:43; 5:12) These gave evidence of God's dealings with the newly formed Christian congregation and portended his future use of that congregation to carry out his will and purpose.—Compare Joh 14:12.

As false prophets arose in Israel, so the foretold apostasy in the Christian congregation would produce a "man of lawlessness" whose presence would be evidenced by "the operation of Satan with every powerful work and lying signs and portents." (2Th 2:3-12) Thus, the evidence marshaled to support the apostate movement would not be weak or puny but would manifest Satan's

might. The portents would be lying ones, however, either fraudulent on their face or deceptive as to the conclusions to which they would lead. Appearing to manifest God's benevolence and blessing, they would in reality divert persons from the source and path of life.—Compare 2Co 11:3, 12-15; see MIRACLES; POWER, POWERFUL WORKS; SIGN.

POT. See COOKING, COOKING UTENSILS.

POTIPHAR (Pot'i·phar) [from Egyptian, a shortened form of Potiphera]. An Egyptian court official and chief of Pharaoh's bodyguard. He was Joseph's master for a time and, it appears, was a man of wealth. (Ge 37:36; 39:4) Potiphar purchased Joseph from the traveling Midianite merchants and, observing what a good servant Joseph was, eventually put him in charge of his whole house and field, which establishment Jehovah blessed on Joseph's account.—Ge 37:36; 39:1-6.

Potiphar's wife was not as faithful to him as was his servant Joseph. She repeatedly endeavored to seduce Joseph and, one day when no other men were around, grabbed hold of him, but Joseph still refused and ran out. When Potiphar came home, he heard only his wife's frustrated barrage of false accusations. Potiphar angrily had Joseph thrown into prison.—Ge 39:7-20.

This prison seems to have been connected with Potiphar's house or at least came under his jurisdiction as "chief of the bodyguard." Thus, the record speaks of Pharaoh's chief cupbearer and chief baker being thrown into this same jail, "the jail of the house of the chief of the bodyguard," "the jail of [Joseph's] master's house." (Ge 39:1; 40:1-7) However, it seems unlikely that Potiphar is to be equated with "the chief officer of the prison house" who "gave over into Joseph's hand all the prisoners who were in the prison house." (Ge 39:21-23) This officer was probably a subordinate of Potiphar.

Potiphar's title "court official" translates the Hebrew word *sa·ris'*, "eunuch," which in its broader usage meant a chamberlain, courtier, or trusted officer of the throne. The "court official [*sa·ris'*] that had a command over the men of war" when Jerusalem fell in 607 B.C.E. was no doubt a high government official, not a castrated person lacking masculinity. (2Ki 25:19) So, also, Potiphar was a military man, chief of the bodyguard, as well as a married man, facts that indicate that he was not a eunuch in the more common sense.

POTIPHERA (Pot·i'phe·ra) [from Egyptian, meaning "He Whom Ra Has Given"]. Joseph's father-in-law, whose daughter Asenath bore Manasseh and Ephraim. (Ge 41:45, 50; 46:20) Potiphera was the priest, likely of the sun-god Ra, officiating at On, a center of Egyptian sun worship. In the Cairo Museum there is a stele, a funeral pillar, procured in 1935, that has on it the name "Putiphar."—*Annales du service des antiquités de l'Égypte,* Cairo, 1939, Vol. XXXIX, pp. 273-276.

POTSHERD.

A shard or broken piece of pottery; a fragment of earthenware. The Hebrew word *che'res,* though sometimes applying to an earthenware vessel or earthenware flask that is unbroken (Nu 5:17; Jer 19:1), is possibly related to an Arabic word meaning "scrape" or "scratch" and can thus denote something rough, like a potsherd. When Satan struck Job with "a malignant boil" from the crown of his head to the sole of his foot, Job "proceeded to take for himself a fragment of earthenware with which to scrape himself." (Job 2:7, 8) And concerning Leviathan it is stated: "As pointed earthenware fragments are its underparts."—Job 41:1, 30.

The Greek word *o'stra·kon* (appearing in *LXX* at Job 2:8) was applied by the Greeks to potsherds on which they recorded votes.

Archaeological Discoveries. Potsherds, or pieces of pottery, are the most numerous items found by archaeologists during excavations of ancient sites. In the past, a broken piece of pottery might be used for such things as raking ashes or dipping water. (Isa 30:14) But especially were potsherds employed as inexpensive writing materials in Egypt, Mesopotamia, and elsewhere in the ancient Middle East. For instance, earthenware fragments were used for the well-known Lachish Letters, which repeatedly contain the divine name, Jehovah, in Tetragrammaton form (YHWH). In Egypt, archaeologists have found numerous pieces of limestone and earthenware fragments on which there appear drawings and inscriptions written in ink (generally in cursive hieroglyphic script), many said to date from about the 16th to the 11th centuries B.C.E. and some thus possibly reaching back to the days of Moses and of Israel's bondage in Egypt. Certain of these inscribed fragments consist of stories, poems, hymns, and the like, some of which were probably written as school lessons. Earthenware fragments apparently were used as writing material by people generally much as memo pads and other pieces of paper are today, to record accounts, sales, marriage contracts, lawsuits, and many other matters.

More than 60 ostraca inscribed with ink in Paleo-Hebrew script were discovered in the ruins of the royal palace in Samaria. They seem to be records of vineyard production, many possibly dating from the time of Jeroboam II. They give names of places and persons, the latter including some compound forms involving the use of the names Baal, El, and Jehovah.

Greek ostraca found in Egypt include various types of documents but principally tax receipts. They give some insight into the Greek language as spoken by the common people of that land during Ptolemaic, Roman, and Byzantine times, and so they are of some use in studies of the Koine used by writers of the Christian Greek Scriptures. Twenty Greek ostraca found in Upper Egypt were inscribed with portions of the four Gospels, these probably dating from the seventh century C.E.

Used in Illustrations. Potsherds are also used with figurative associations in the Scriptures. David, distressed and surrounded by enemies, said in a psalm prophetic of the Messiah's sufferings: "My power has dried up just like a fragment of earthenware." (Ps 22:11-15) As articles made of clay were baked they would become very dry, and their brittleness became evident when a vessel was reduced to fragments.

Glazing methods were evidently common in King Solomon's day, for Proverbs 26:23 states: "As a silver glazing overlaid upon a fragment of earthenware are fervent lips along with a bad heart." Like "silver glazing" that would hide the earthenware it covered, "fervent lips" could conceal "a bad heart" when there was only a pretense of friendship.

Oholibah (Jerusalem) was warned by Jehovah that she would be filled with drunkenness and grief, drinking the cup her sister Oholah (Samaria) had drunk. Judah would drink this figurative cup to the limit, God's judgments being fully executed upon her. Thus, through Ezekiel, God said: "You will have to drink it and drain it out, and its earthenware fragments you will gnaw."—Eze 23:4, 32-34.

The utter folly of man's complaining about God and finding fault with the divine way of doing things is shown in the words: "Woe to the one that has contended with his Former, as an earthenware fragment with the other earthenware fragments of the ground! Should the clay say to its former: 'What do you make?' And your achievement say: 'He has no hands'?"—Isa 45:9, 13.

POTTER.

The maker of earthenware pots, dishes, and other vessels. The Hebrew word for potter (*yoh·tser'*) literally means "former" or "one forming" (Jer 18:4, ftn), while the Greek term (ke·ra·meus') comes from a root meaning "mix," perhaps referring to the need to mix water with the soil or clay to prepare it for use. Since very early times potters have fashioned clay into vessels and baked these, thus producing hardened utensils that would not soften when wet. The potter might work alone, but he sometimes had assistants, frequently apprentices. Among the Hebrews a group of royal potters seems to have existed at one time.—1Ch 4:21-23.

A typical method of making pottery began with such steps as washing the clay and purifying it of foreign matter, weathering it, and trampling the moistened clay by foot to make it pasty and malleable. (Isa 41:25) Next the clay was kneaded by hand and then placed on the potter's wheel.

The early potter's wheel was generally made of stone (though sometimes of wood) and was, basically, a flat disk centered on a vertical axle and made to rotate horizontally. Heavy material at its edge gave the disk stability and momentum as it was turned by hand. The later addition of a larger, heavier lower wheel (on the same shaft as the top wheel and also revolving horizontally) enabled the seated potter to rotate the wheels by foot.

Having "thrown" or placed the shapeless clay on the wheel, the potter used his hands to form a vessel as the wheel was turned. (Jer 18:3, 4) The utensil might next be dried somewhat in the sun and again put on the wheel, where the potter might employ pebbles, shells, or some implement to smooth and burnish it and to impart a design to its surface. Methods varied, but he could give it a rope pattern, for instance, by pressing a twisted cord against the still-moist article. Vessels were often painted decoratively. Others were glazed (Pr 26:23) and then fired, or baked, in the nearby pottery kiln. Or, colored "slip" (potter's clay in a semiliquid state) might be applied for decorative purposes, after which the article was again fired in the kiln.

The potter made articles ranging from large jars (La 4:2) to lamps, ovens, and toys such as dolls and animal figures. Bowls, cups, flasks, and other vessels were among his products. (Le 15:12; 2Sa 17:28; Jer 19:1; Lu 22:10) He also produced cooking pots and some griddles. Earthenware items were sometimes stamped to show where they were made. The potter frequently stamped his own "trademark" on a pot handle.

Sometimes the potter used an open mold, into which the clay was pressed to pick up details. In later times lamps were often made in that way, in two pieces that were joined when the clay had dried to about a leathery hardness. Occasionally

things were molded by hand without using the wheel. Usually, however, the potter used the wheel.

Broken pieces of pottery are often discovered at archaeological sites, sometimes in great numbers. (See POTSHERD.) The kinds of pottery found are viewed by archaeologists as aids in identifying different cultures as well as in estimating the period of occupation represented by various layers at such sites. They have also endeavored to estimate population density of a particular place in ancient times on the basis of the quantity of such fragments discovered there.

The potter's authority over the clay is used illustratively to show Jehovah's sovereignty over individuals and nations. (Isa 29:15, 16; 64:8) To God the house of Israel was "as the clay in the hand of the potter," He being the Great Potter. (Jer 18:1-10) Man is in no position to contend with God, just as clay would not be expected to challenge the one shaping it. (Isa 45:9) As an earthenware vessel can be smashed, so Jehovah can bring devastating calamity upon a people in punishment for wrongdoing.—Jer 19:1-11.

Concerning the Messianic King's exercise of God-given authority against the nations, it was foretold: "You will break them with an iron scepter, as though a potter's vessel you will dash them to pieces."—Ps 2:9; compare Da 2:44; Re 2:26, 27; 12:5.

From a single lump of clay the potter could make a vessel for an honorable use and another for a dishonorable, a common, or an ordinary use. Similarly, Jehovah has authority to mold individuals as he pleases and has tolerated wicked ones, "vessels of wrath made fit for destruction," but this has worked to the benefit of "vessels of mercy," persons making up spiritual Israel.—Ro 9:14-26.

POTTER'S FIELD. After remorseful Judas threw into the temple the betrayal price of 30 pieces of silver (if shekels, $66), the chief priests used the money to buy "the potter's field to bury strangers." (Mt 27:3-10) The field came to be known as Akeldama, or "Field of Blood." (Ac 1:18, 19; see AKELDAMA.) Since the fourth century C.E. this field has been identified with a location on the S slope of the Hinnom Valley, just before it joins the Kidron Valley.

The expression "the potter's field" does not specifically indicate whether the field was one simply owned by a potter or was called that because, at some point in its history, it was an area where potters pursued their craft. The latter, though, seems probable if the traditional site is correct. It would be near the Gate of the Potsherds (or "Gate of the Potters," according to J. Simons in his footnote in *Jerusalem in the Old Testament,* Leiden, 1952, p. 230), mentioned in Jeremiah 19:1, 2. (Compare Jer 18:2.) Even in recent times the necessary raw material, clay, has been available in the vicinity. Also, making pottery required a good water supply, and the site was close to the spring at En-rogel and the Pool of Siloam as well as near such water as might be in the Hinnom Valley in the winter.

POUND [Gr., *li'tra*]. A weight mentioned only at John 12:3 (ftn) and 19:39 (ftn). The Greek term is usually equated with the Roman pound (Lat., *libra*). Thus it was about 327 g (11.5 oz). Some versions render the Greek word *mna* as "pound" (Lu 19:18, *KJ, Dy, JB, We*), but it is more appropriately rendered "mina." (*Da, Fn, NW, Ro*) Whereas "pound" is used in the Bible just as a weight or measurement, "mina" is a monetary weight indicating a specific value of gold or silver.

POWER, POWERFUL WORKS. Power is the ability to perform acts, the capacity to accomplish things, to do work; also, authority or influence as a result of endowments or position. The Hebrew word *ko'ach* is translated "power"; *gevu·rah', "mightiness"; and *'oz,* "strength." The Greek *dy'na·mis* is translated both "power" and "powerful works," as the context makes appropriate.

At the close of the sixth creative "day," God began "resting from all his work that [he had] created for the purpose of making." (Ge 2:2, 3) He rested from *these creative* works, but his power has since not become dormant or remained quiescent. Over 4,000 years after the completion of earthly creation, his Son stated: "My Father has kept working until now, and I keep working." (Joh 5:17) Not only as regards the spirit realm has Jehovah been active; the Bible record pulsates with his expressions of power and his mighty acts toward humankind. Though at times he has "kept quiet . . . exercising self-control," whenever his due time came to act he has taken vigorous action with "full might."—Isa 42:13, 14; compare Ps 80:2; Isa 63:15.

"Work" indicates purposeful activity. Jehovah's acts are not isolated, unrelated, or erratic expressions of energy but are coordinated, purposeful acts with a definite end in view. Although his power sustains the universe and the living creatures in it (Ps 136:25; 148:2-6; Mt 5:45), Jehovah is not like an impersonal power plant; his acts prove he is a personal and purposeful God. He is also a historical God, as he has perceptively intervened in human affairs at definite dates of history, at specified places, and with regard to particular persons or peoples. As the "living and true God" (1Th 1:9; Jos 3:10; Jer 10:10), he has shown himself aware of all that is taking place in the universe, reacting according to what has occurred, as well as taking the initiative in furthering his purpose.

In every case, his varied expressions of power have been in harmony with his righteousness (Ps 98:1, 2; 111:2, 3, 7; Isa 5:16); they all bring enlightenment to his creatures. They show on the one hand that fear of him "is fitting," for he is a God "exacting exclusive devotion" and "a consuming fire" against those practicing wickedness, making it "a fearful thing to fall into the hands of the living God." (Jer 10:6, 7; Ex 20:5; Heb 10:26-31; 12:28, 29) He is not to be trifled with. —Ex 8:29.

On the other hand, his use of power is even more wonderfully manifest in rewarding righteous-hearted persons sincerely seeking him, strengthening them to do assigned tasks and needful work (Ps 84:5-7; Isa 40:29-31) as well as to endure under stress (Ps 46:1; Isa 25:4), providing for and sustaining them (Ps 145:14-16), protecting, saving, and liberating them in times of danger and aggression. (Ps 20:6, 7) "His eyes are roving about through all the earth to show his strength in behalf of those whose heart is complete toward him." (2Ch 16:9) Those who come to know him find his name to be "a strong tower" to which they can turn. (Pr 18:10; Ps 91:1-8) Knowledge of his mighty acts gives assurance that he hears the prayers of his trusting servants and is able to answer, if necessary, with "fear-inspiring things in righteousness." (Ps 65:2, 5) In a figurative sense, he is "near" and hence can be swift in responding.—Ps 145:18, 19; Jude 24, 25.

Power Manifest in Creation. Humans see evidence of power in all physical creation, in the immense and countless stellar bodies (compare Job 38:31-33) as well as in all earthly things. The very soil is spoken of as having power (Ge 4:12), producing food that gives strength (1Sa 28:22), and power is seen in all living things—plants, animals, and man. In modern times the tremendous power potential in even the minute atomic elements forming all matter has also become well known. Scientists sometimes call matter organized energy.

Throughout the Scriptures the power and "dynamic energy" of God as the Maker of heaven and earth are repeatedly highlighted. (Isa 40:25, 26; Jer 10:12; 32:17) The very term for "God" in Hebrew ('El) probably has the root meaning of "mighty" or "powerful." (Compare the use of the term at Ge 31:29 in the expression "the power ['el] of my hand.")

Need for Special Demonstrations of Power. The first man knew Jehovah God as his Creator, his only Parent and Life-Giver. God endowed man with a measure of power, intellectual and physical, and gave him work to perform. (Ge 1:26-28; 2:15) Such exercise of power must harmonize with his Creator's will and hence be governed by other qualities divinely granted, such as wisdom, justice, and love.

The rebellion in Eden presented a challenge to God's sovereignty. Primarily a moral issue, it nevertheless has caused God to exercise his power in special ways. (See JEHOVAH [The supreme issue a moral one].) The rebellion was instigated by a spirit son of God who thereby became God's opposer or resister (Heb., sa·tan'). Jehovah reacted to the situation, judging the rebels. His expulsion of the human pair from Eden and the stationing of his loyal spirit creatures at the garden's entrance was a demonstration of divine power. (Ge 3:4, 5, 19, 22-24) Jehovah's word proved to be, not impotent, weak, or wavering, but full of power, irresistible as to fulfillment. (Compare Jer 23:29.) As the Sovereign God, he proved ready and able to back up his word with the full weight of his authority.

Fixing his purpose, Jehovah has consistently worked toward its realization. (Ge 3:15; Eph 1:8-11) In his due time he would end all earthly rebellion, cause the original spirit rebel and those allied with him to be crushed as one crushes the head of a serpent. (Compare Ro 16:20.) While allowing his spirit Adversary to continue for a time and to endeavor to prove successful his challenge, Jehovah would not abdicate his sovereign position. Exercising rightful authority, he would reward or punish when and as he saw fit, judging men according to their deeds. (Ex 34:6, 7; Jer 32:17-19) Additionally, he would use his power to attest the credentials of those whom he designated as his representatives on earth. By revealing his power, he would put the seal of genuineness on messages they delivered.

This has been a divine kindness. Thereby Jehovah has given men proof that he, and no other, is the true God; he has given proof of his worthiness to receive the fear, respect, trust, praise, and love of his intelligent creatures. (Ps 31:24; 86:16, 17; Isa 41:10-13) Over the centuries, Jehovah has repeatedly assured his servants that his power has

not waned, his "hand" has not 'grown short,' and his "ear" has not become too heavy to hear. (Nu 11:23; Isa 40:28; 50:2; 59:1) More important, these expressions of power have contributed toward the sanctifying and vindicating of Jehovah's own name. His use of power exalts him, it does not debase him, does not sully his reputation; rather, by it he makes "a beautiful name" for himself. —Job 36:22, 23; 37:23, 24; Isa 63:12-14.

Prior to and at the Global Flood. In the pre-Flood period, men had ample evidence of God's power. They knew the way back into Eden was impassable, blocked by powerful spirit creatures. God showed he was alive to what was going on, approving Abel's sacrifice, expressing judgment upon his murderous brother Cain, yet warning men against executing Cain. —Ge 3:24; 4:2-15.

Some 1,400 years later, the earth became filled with wickedness and violence. (Ge 6:1-5, 11, 12) God expressed displeasure at this situation. After sounding a warning through his servant Noah, he forcefully demonstrated by means of a global Flood that he would not allow wicked men to ruin the earth. He did not use his power to force them to worship him but, through Noah's work as "a preacher of righteousness," gave them opportunity to change. At the same time he showed his ability to liberate righteous-hearted persons from evil circumstances. (2Pe 2:4, 5, 9) Even as his judgment came upon the wicked suddenly and his destruction of them did not 'slumber' but wiped them out within a 40-day period, so he would act in similar ways in the future. —2Pe 2:3; Ge 7:17-23; Mt 24:37-39.

Challenge of False Gods in Post-Flood Era. Both the Scriptures and ancient secular records reveal men's deviation from worship of the true God in the post-Flood period. There is strong evidence that Nimrod, who "displayed himself [as] a mighty hunter in opposition to Jehovah," played a major role in this; and there is evidence pointing to Babel (Babylon) as the major site where false worship developed. (Ge 10:8-12; 11:1-4, 9; see BABEL; BABYLON No. 1; GODS AND GODDESSES.) The tower project proposed at Babel was a demonstration of human power and ability, independent of God, unauthorized by him. It was to bring reputation and fame to its builders, not to God. And, as God realized, this would be only the beginning. It could lead to a series of ambitious power projects taking men on a course farther and farther away from the true God, in defiance of him and his purpose for the planet and for the human race. Again, God stepped in, throwing the project into confusion by acting upon human powers of speech, causing the peoples to disperse throughout the globe.—Ge 11:5-9.

"Nature gods" contrasted with the true God.

Ancient documents from Babylon and from points of mankind's migration show that the worship of "nature gods" (such as the Babylonian sun-god Shamash, the Egyptian rain and thunder god Thoth, and the Canaanite fertility god Baal) became very prominent in those early times. The "nature gods" were associated in men's minds with periodic or cyclic manifestations of power, such as the daily beaming forth of the sun's rays, the seasonal results of solstices and equinoxes (producing summer and winter, spring and fall), the winds and storms, the falling of rain and its effect on earth's fertility in seedtime and harvest, and similar evidences of power. These forces are impersonal. So men had to fill in the blank, providing personality for their gods by their own imagination. The personalities they conjured up for their gods were generally capricious; they lacked any definite purpose, were morally debased, and were unworthy of worship and service.

Yet the visible heavens and earth give clear proof of a superior Source of power that produced all these forces in an interrelated, coordinated arrangement, one giving undeniable evidence of intelligent purpose. To that Source the acclamation goes: "You are worthy, Jehovah, even our God, to receive the glory and the honor and the power, because you created all things, and because of your will they existed and were created." (Re 4:11) Jehovah is not a God governed by or limited to celestial or earthly cycles. Nor are his expressions of power capricious, erratic, or inconsistent. In each case they reveal something about his personality, his standards, his purpose. The *Theological Dictionary of the New Testament*, edited by G. Kittel, in treating the view of God contained in the Hebrew Scriptures, thus observes that "the important and predominant feature is not force or power but the will which this power must execute and therefore serve. This is everywhere the decisive feature."—Translated and edited by G. Bromiley, 1971, Vol. II, p. 291.

The worship of such "nature gods" by the Israelites was apostasy, a suppression of truth in favor of a lie, an unreasoning course of worshiping the creation rather than the One who created it; this is what the apostle states at Romans 1:18-25. Though invisible, Jehovah God had made his qualities manifest among men, for as Paul says, these are "clearly seen from the world's creation onward, because they are perceived by the things made, even his eternal power and Godship, so that they are inexcusable."

God's control of natural forces distinctive.

To prove himself the true God, Jehovah might reasonably be expected to demonstrate his control over the created forces, doing so in a way that would be distinctly connected with his name. (Ps 135:5, 6) Since the sun, moon, planets, and stars follow their regular courses, since the earthly atmospheric conditions (producing wind, rain, and other effects) obey the laws governing them, since locusts swarm and birds migrate, then these and many other normal functions would not suffice to sanctify God's name in the face of opposition and false worship.

Nevertheless, Jehovah God could cause the natural creation and elements to testify to his Godship by using them to fulfill specific purposes beyond their ordinary function, often at a specifically designated time. Even when the events, such as a drought, a rainstorm, or a similar weather condition, were not unique in themselves, their coming in fulfillment of Jehovah's prophecy made them distinctive. (Compare 1Ki 17:1; 18:1, 2, 41-45.) In most cases, though, the events were extraordinary in themselves, either because of their magnitude or intensity (Ex 9:24) or because they occurred in an unusual, even unheard of, way or at an abnormal time.—Ex 34:10; 1Sa 12:16-18.

Similarly, the birth of a child was ordinary. But the birth of a child to a woman who had been sterile all her life and who had passed the age of childbirth (as in the case of Sarah) was extraordinary. (Ge 18:10, 11; 21:1, 2) It gave evidence of God's intervention. Death, too, was a common occurrence. But when the death came at a predicted time or in a preannounced way with the causative factor otherwise unknown, this was extraordinary, pointing to divine action. (1Sa 2:34; 2Ki 7:1, 2, 20; Jer 28:16, 17) All these things proved Jehovah to be the true God, and the "nature gods" to be "valueless gods."—Ps 96:5.

Jehovah Proves Himself God to Abraham.

Abraham and his favored descendants Isaac and Jacob came to know God as Almighty in power. (Ex 6:3) As their "shield," he protected them and their families from the mighty ones of earth. (Ge 12:14-20; 14:13-20; 15:1; 20:1-18; 26:26-29; Ps 105:7-15) The birth of Isaac to aged parents demonstrated that nothing is "too extraordinary for Jehovah." (Ge 18:14; 21:1-3) God prospered his servants; he carried them through times of famine. (Ge 12:10; 13:1, 2; 26:1-6, 12, 16; 31:4-13) As "the Judge of all the earth," Jehovah executed sentence on the infamous cities of Sodom and

Gomorrah, while preserving the life of faithful Lot and his daughters, doing so out of consideration for Abraham, his friend. (Ge 18:25; 19:27-29; Jas 2:23) With good reason these men had strong faith not only that God is alive but also that he is the powerful "rewarder of those earnestly seeking him." (Heb 11:6) Abraham, when called upon to sacrifice his beloved son, had sound basis for trusting in God's ability to raise up Isaac even from the dead.—Heb 11:17-19; Ge 17:7, 8.

Proves to Be God to Israel. To the nation of Israel down in Egypt, Jehovah promised: "I shall indeed prove to be God to you; and you will certainly know that I am Jehovah your God." (Ex 6:6, 7) Pharaoh trusted in the power of Egypt's gods and goddesses to counteract the workings of Jehovah. God purposely allowed Pharaoh to continue in his defiant course for a time. This extension of matters was so that Jehovah might 'show his power and have his name declared in all the earth.' (Ex 9:13-16; 7:3-5) It permitted the multiplying of God's "signs" and "miracles" (Ps 105:27), the bringing of ten plagues demonstrating the Creator's control over water, sunlight, insects, animals, and human bodies.—Ex 7-12.

In this, Jehovah proved distinct from the "nature gods." These plagues, including darkness, storm, hail, swarms of locusts, and similar events, were predicted and came precisely as indicated. They were not mere coincidences or random occurrences. Advance warnings enabled those who heeded them to escape certain plagues. (Ex 9:18-21; 12:1-13) God could be selective as to the plagues' effect, causing some to leave a specific area exempt, thereby identifying who were his approved servants. (Ex 8:22, 23; 9:3-7, 26) He could start and stop the plagues at will. (Ex 8:8-11; 9:29) Though Pharaoh's magic-practicing priests appeared to duplicate the first two plagues (perhaps even trying to credit them to their Egyptian deities), their secret arts soon failed them, and they were obliged to acknowledge "the finger of God" in the execution of the third plague. (Ex 7:22; 8:6, 7, 16-19) They could not reverse the plagues and were themselves affected.—Ex 9:11.

Jehovah 'proved himself God to Israel' and 'near to them' by reclaiming them with "an outstretched arm and with great judgments." (Ex 6:6, 7; De 4:7) Following the destruction of Pharaoh's hosts in the Red Sea, the people of Israel "began to fear Jehovah and to put faith in Jehovah and in Moses his servant."—Ex 14:31.

Establishing the Law covenant. Before establishing the Law covenant with Israel, Jehovah performed miracles, providing water and food for the millions now in the desert region of Sinai and giving victory over attackers. (Ex 15:22-25; 16:11-15; 17:5-16) At the place previously appointed, Mount Sinai, Jehovah gave an awe-inspiring demonstration of his control over the created earthly forces. (Ex 19:16-19; compare Heb 12:18-21.) The nation had every reason to recognize the divine Source of the covenant and accept its terms with deep respect. (De 4:32-36, 39) Jehovah's remarkable use of Moses also gave real basis for people to accept with conviction the Pentateuch, the initial part of the Sacred Scriptures written by Moses' hand, as divinely inspired. (Compare De 34:10-12; Jos 1:7, 8.) When the authority of the Aaronic priesthood was questioned, Jehovah gave further visible confirmation. —Nu chaps 16, 17.

Conquest of Canaan. The conquest of seven nations of Canaan, "more populous and mighty" than Israel (De 7:1, 2), gave added testimony to Jehovah's Godship. (Jos 23:3, 8-11) His fame paved the way (Ex 9:16; Jer 32:20, 21), and 'dread and the fear' of Israel as his people weakened their opposers. (De 11:25; Ex 15:14-17) Those opposing were all the more reprehensible therefore, for they had evidence that these were the people of the true God; to fight them was to fight against God. Some Canaanites wisely recognized Jehovah's superiority over their idol gods, as had others earlier, and sought his favor.—Jos 2:1, 9-13.

Sun and moon stand still. In acting on behalf of the besieged Gibeonites, Canaanites who put faith in him, Jehovah extended Israel's onslaught against the besieging forces by causing the sun and moon to hold their positions in relation to the viewpoint of those at the battle scene, postponing sunset for almost a day's time. (Jos 10:1-14) While this could mean a stopping of earth's rotation, it could have been accomplished by other means, such as a refraction of solar and lunar light rays to produce the same effect. Whatever the method employed, it demonstrated again that "everything that Jehovah delighted to do he has done in the heavens and in the earth, in the seas and all the watery deeps." (Ps 135:6) As the apostle Paul later wrote: "Every house is constructed by someone, but he that constructed all things is God." (Heb 3:4) Jehovah does as he pleases with his own building, utilizing it as it suits him, even as does the man who builds a house.—Compare 2Ki 20:8-11.

During the next four centuries, throughout the period of the Judges, Jehovah continued to support the Israelites when they were loyal to Him and to withdraw his support when they turned to other gods.—Jg 6:11-22, 36-40; 4:14-16; 5:31; 14:3, 4, 6, 19; 15:14; 16:15-21, 23-30.

Under the Israelite monarchy. During the 510 years of the Israelite monarchy, Jehovah's mighty "arm" and protecting "hand" frequently kept powerful aggressors at bay, confused and disrupted their forces, and sent them fleeing back to their home territories. These nations worshiped not only "nature gods" but gods (and goddesses) of war. In some cases the head of the country was himself viewed as a god. Since they insisted on warring against his people, Jehovah showed himself again as "a manly person of war," a 'glorious King, mighty in battle.' (Ex 15:3; Ps 24:7-10; Isa 59:17-19) In effect, he met them on all types of terrain, employed war strategy that outwitted their boastful generals, and overcame warriors of many nations as well as their special war equipment. (2Sa 5:22-25; 10:18; 1Ki 20:23-30; 2Ch 14:9-12) He could cause their secret battle plans to be known to his people as accurately as if electronic listening devices were planted in their palaces. (2Ki 6:8-12) At times he strengthened his people to do the fighting; at other times he gained victories without their striking a blow. (2Ki 7:6, 7; 2Ch 20:15, 17, 22, 24, 29) In all of this, Jehovah shamed the war gods of the nations, exposed them as failures, frauds.—Isa 41:21-24; Jer 10:10-15; 43:10-13.

In exile and restoration. Though Jehovah allowed the nation to go into exile, the northern kingdom being conquered by Assyria and the kingdom of Judah desolated by Babylon, he kept alive the Davidic line in fulfillment of his covenant with David for an everlasting kingdom. (Ps 89:3, 4, 35-37) During the period of exile, he also kept alive the faith of his people, using Daniel and others in marvelous ways, performing miraculous acts that caused even world rulers humbly to acknowledge his power. (Da 3:19-29; 4:34-37; 6:16-23) By the fall of mighty Babylon, Jehovah again demonstrated his unique Godship, exposed the unreality of the pagan gods, and put them to shame. His people were witnesses of this. (Isa 41:21-29; 43:10-15; 46:1, 2, 5-7) He maneuvered the kings of Persia in behalf of Israel, effecting the release of his people and their return to their homeland, enabling them to rebuild the temple and later the city of Jerusalem. (Ezr 1:1-4; 7:6, 27, 28; Ne 1:11; 2:1-8) Ezra rightly felt ashamed to ask the Persian king for military protection of his company, though they carried cargo with a total value evidently in excess of $43,000,000. Jehovah guarded them during their journey to Jerusalem in answer to their prayer.—Ezr 8:21-27.

In the interim between the closing of the Hebrew Scripture part of the Bible and the birth of God's Son on earth, God's power must have been active in order to guarantee the preservation of the nation of Israel, its capital city Jerusalem, the neighboring town of Bethlehem, the temple with its priesthood, and other features of the Jewish system. For all of these would have to be there for the fulfillment of prophecy in Christ Jesus and his activity. History relates attempts at replacing the Jewish system of things completely by process of Hellenization, that is, by converting it to the Grecian way of worship. But this ultimately failed.—See GREECE, GREEKS (Effect of Hellenization on the Jews).

"Christ the Power of God." From Jesus' miraculous birth forward, God's power was displayed toward and through him as never before. Like the psalmist, he became "just like a miracle to many people." (Ps 71:7) Jesus and his disciples, like Isaiah and his children, were "as signs and as miracles in Israel from Jehovah of armies," portending the future and revealing God's purpose. (Isa 8:18; Heb 2:13; compare Lu 2:10-14.) In Jesus, God's powerful workings during thousands of years now found fulfillment, came to fruition. Rightly the apostle could speak of Jesus as "the power of God and the wisdom of God."—1Co 1:24.

Jesus proved to be the long-awaited Messiah, Jehovah's Anointed One, foretold to manifest the 'spirit of mightiness.' (Isa 11:1-5) As such, it could be expected that he would have powerful testimony to support that fact. (Mic 5:2-5; compare Joh 7:31.) Already by means of Jesus' birth from a virgin Jewess, God had begun testifying on his Son's behalf. (Lu 1:35-37) This birth was not simply a spectacular display of divine power but served very definite purposes. It provided a perfect human, a 'second Adam,' one who could sanctify his Father's name, erase the reproach the first human son had brought on that name, and thereby give the lie to Satan's challenge; moreover, the perfect Jesus would provide a legal basis for ransoming obedient mankind from the grip of Kings Sin and Death. (1Co 15:45-47; Heb 2:14, 15; Ro 5:18-21; see RANSOM.) And this perfect descendant of David would be the heir to an everlasting Kingdom.—Lu 1:31-33.

Jesus' anointing by God's spirit was accompanied by divine power. (Ac 10:38) Moses was "powerful in his words and deeds." As 'the prophet greater than Moses,' Jesus had credentials that were proportionately greater. (De 34:10-12; Ac 7:22; Lu 24:19; Joh 6:14) Rightly he 'taught with authority.' (Mt 7:28, 29) Thus, even as God gave cause for faith in Moses, Joshua, and others, he now gave sound basis for faith in his Son. (Mt 11:2-6; Joh 6:29) Jesus took no credit for himself, constantly acknowledging God as the Source of his powerful works. (Joh 5:19, 26; 7:28, 29; 9:3, 4; 14:10) Honest persons recognized "the majestic power of God" manifested through him.—Lu 9:43; 19:37; Joh 3:2; 9:28-33; compare Lu 1:68; 7:16.

What did the miracles of Jesus portend?

What Jesus did gave proof of God's interest in mankind, evidence of what God would eventually do for all loving righteousness. Jesus' powerful works were largely related to mankind's problems, first and most basic among which is that of sin, with all its damaging effects. Sickness and death are concomitants of sin, and Jesus' ability to heal sickness of all kinds (Mt 8:14, 15; Lu 6:19; 17:11-14; 8:43-48) and even to resurrect the dead (Mt 9:23-25; Lu 7:14, 15; Joh 11:39-44) gave proof that he was God's appointed means for freeing mankind from sin and its penalty. (Compare Mr 2:5-12.) Far superior to the manna Israel ate in the wilderness, Jesus was "the true bread from heaven," "the bread of life." (Joh 6:31-35, 48-51) He brought, not literal water from a rock, but "living water," the 'water of life.'—Joh 7:37, 38; Re 22:17; compare Joh 4:13, 14.

His powerful works were also portents of other blessings due to come by his kingly rule. Whereas Elisha had fed 100 men with only 20 loaves and some grain, Jesus fed thousands with far less. (2Ki 4:42-44; Mt 14:19-21; 15:32-38) Moses and Elisha had made bitter or poisoned water sweet. Jesus converted ordinary water into fine wine to contribute to the relaxing enjoyment of a marriage feast. (Ex 15:22-25; 2Ki 2:21, 22; Joh 2:1-11) His rule therefore would certainly bring freedom from hunger to all of his subjects, bring a pleasant 'banquet for all peoples.' (Isa 25:6) His ability to make men's work abundantly productive, as with regard to his disciples' fishing efforts, assured that, under his Kingdom's blessing, men would not be reduced to barely eking out a living at a mere subsistence level.—Lu 5:4-9; compare Joh 21:3-7.

More important, these things were all related to spiritual matters. As Jesus brought spiritual sight, speech, and health to the spiritually blind, dumb, and ailing, he also brought and assured the enjoyment of spiritual food and drink in abundance and guaranteed the productiveness of his disciples'

ministry. (Compare Lu 5:10, 11; Joh 6:35, 36.) His miraculously satisfying people's physical needs on certain occasions was primarily to strengthen faith. Such things were never the end in themselves. (Compare Joh 6:25-27.) The Kingdom and God's righteousness, not food and drink, were to be sought first. (Mt 6:31-33) Jesus set the example in this by his refusal to change stones into bread for himself.—Mt 4:1-3.

Spiritual liberation. The nation of Israel had known mighty warriors, but God's power through his Son was aimed at greater enemies than mere human militarists. Jesus was the Liberator (Lu 1:69-74) providing the way to freedom from the chief source of oppression, Satan and his demons. (Heb 2:14, 15) Not only did Jesus personally free many from demonic obsession (Lu 4:33-36) but by his liberating words of truth he opened wide the gates to freedom for those wishing to cast off the oppressive burdens and slavery that false religion had imposed on them. (Mt 23:4; Lu 4:18; Joh 8:31, 32) By his own faithful, integrity-keeping course he conquered, not just a city or an empire, but "the world."—Joh 14:30; 16:33.

Relative importance of miraculous acts. Although Jesus laid principal stress on the truths he proclaimed, he nevertheless showed the relative importance of his powerful works, regularly calling attention to them as authenticating his commission and message. Their importance lay particularly in their fulfillment of prophecy. (Joh 5:36-39, 46, 47; 10:24-27, 31-38; 14:11; 20:27-29) Those seeing such works came under special responsibility. (Mt 11:20-24; Joh 15:24) As Peter later told the crowds at Pentecost, Jesus was "a man publicly shown by God to you through powerful works and portents and signs that God did through him in your midst, just as you yourselves know." (Ac 2:22) These evidences of divine power showed that God's Kingdom had "overtaken" them.—Mt 12:28, 31, 32.

By God's significant use of his Son, the 'reasonings of many hearts were uncovered.' (Lu 2:34, 35) They were seeing 'the arm of Jehovah' manifested, but many, the majority, preferred to read some other meaning into the events beheld or to allow selfish interests to keep them from acting in harmony with the 'sign' seen. (Joh 12:37-43; 11:45-48) Many wanted personal benefits from God's power but were not sincerely hungering for truth and righteousness. Their hearts were not moved by the compassion and kindness that motivated so many of Jesus' powerful works (compare Lu 1:78; Mt 9:35, 36; 15:32-37; 20:34; Mt 1:40, 41; Lu 7:11-15; with Lu 14:1-6; Mr 3:1-6).

which compassion reflected that of his Father. —Mr 5:18, 19.

Responsible use of power. Jesus' use of power was always responsible, never done for mere display. The cursing of the barren fig tree evidently had symbolic meaning. (Mr 11:12-14; compare Mt 7:19, 20; 21:42, 43; Lu 13:6-9.) Jesus refused to engage in purposeless theatrics as suggested by Satan. When he walked over water, it was because he was going somewhere with no transportation at hand at that late hour, something quite different from jumping off a temple battlement like a potential suicide. (Mt 4:5-7; Mr 6:45-50) The wrongly motivated curiosity of Herod was left unsatisfied when Jesus refused to put on any performance for him. (Lu 23:8) Jesus earlier refused to cause "a sign from heaven" at the request of Pharisees and Sadducees, evidently because they sought such, not to strengthen their faith in the fulfillment of God's Word, but to obviate the need of such faith. Their motive was bad.—Mt 16:1-4; compare 15:1-6; 22:23, 29.

Similarly, the lack of faith in Nazareth kept him from performing many powerful works there, certainly not because his source of power was insufficient but because the circumstances did not warrant it, did not allow for it. Divine power was not to be wasted on unreceptive skeptics. (Mr 6:1-6; compare Mt 10:14; Lu 16:29-31.) That the faith of others was not an absolute essential for Jesus to perform miraculous acts can be seen in his healing the severed ear of the high priest's slave, part of the crowd that came to arrest Jesus.—Lu 22:50, 51.

The resurrection of Jesus Christ from the dead to spirit life was the greatest demonstration ever of God's power. Without it, Christian faith would be "in vain," his followers would be "of all men most to be pitied." (1Co 15:12-19) It was the act most consistently recounted by Jesus' disciples and the greatest single factor in strengthening faith. Distance had not hindered Jesus' exercise of power when on earth (Mt 8:5-13; Joh 4:46-53), and now, from his heavenly position, Jesus anointed his followers with God's spirit on Pentecost, enabling them to do powerful works in his absence. He thereby authenticated their testimony concerning his resurrection (Ac 4:33; Heb 2:3, 4) and also gave proof that these were God's approved people, his congregation.—Ac 2:1-4, 14-36, 43; 3:11-18.

The death of his Son as a human had not shortened Jehovah's hand, as the many miracles, signs, and portents performed by the apostles and others testified. (Ac 4:29, 30; 6:8; 14:3; 19:11, 12) The powerful works they performed were like those of their Master, healing the lame (Ac 3:1-9; 14:8-10) and ill (Ac 5:12-16; 28:7-9), raising the dead (Ac 9:36-41; 20:9-11), casting out demons (Ac 8:6, 7; 16:16-18), doing so without seeking personal benefit or honor for themselves. (Ac 3:12; 8:9-24; 13:15-17) Through them God expressed judgments against wrongdoers, even as he had done through the earlier prophets, fostering due respect toward himself and his representatives. (Ac 5:1-11; 13:8-12) New abilities were granted them, such as the ability to speak in foreign languages and interpret them. This, too, was for "a beneficial purpose," for they were soon to extend the preaching work beyond Israel, telling Jehovah's wonderful works among the nations.—1Co 12:4-11; Ps 96:3, 7.

Jehovah God did other powerful things as well, opening up 'doors' of opportunity for them to preach in certain territories, protecting them against those who would shut down their ministerial work, directing their activity, doing so in ways generally unobserved by the public.—Ac 5:17-20; 8:26-29, 39, 40; 9:1-8; 10:19-22, 44-48; 12:6-11; 13:2; 16:6-10, 25-33; 18:9, 10; 1Co 16:8, 9.

It was foretold that miraculous abilities granted by the spirit to the apostles, and passed on by them to others, would last only during the 'infancy' of the Christian congregation, thereafter ending. (1Co 13:8-11; see GIFTS FROM GOD [Gifts of the Spirit].) M'Clintock and Strong's *Cyclopædia* (Vol. VI, p. 320) says that it is "an uncontested statement that during the first hundred years after the death of the apostles we hear little or nothing of the working of miracles by the early Christians." Nevertheless, Jesus and his apostles warned of future deceptive powerful works that would be done by apostates and also by a symbolic wild beast, enemies of God.—Mt 7:21-23; 24:23-25; 2Th 2:9, 10; Re 13:11-13; see BEASTS, SYMBOLIC.

The expressions of God's power reach a high point in the establishment of his Kingdom by Christ Jesus and the judgment acts that result from that event.

See FILL HAND WITH POWER.

PRAETORIAN GUARD. A special group of Roman soldiers, originally organized by Augustus as an imperial bodyguard for the emperor. It consisted of nine (later increased to ten) cohorts of 1,000 men each. They were all Italian volunteers; their pay was double or triple that of a soldier in the legions. Tiberius concentrated this corps d'elite in Rome by constructing fortified barracks N of the walls of the city. Though cohorts might be

Model of a member of the Praetorian Guard

under guard in the praetorian palace of Herod."
—Ac 23:35.

In view of this usage, some have suggested that
prai·to'ri·on at Philippians 1:13 applied to Nero's
palace on Palatine Hill or to a judgment hall where
Paul's case might be heard. However, the *Cyclopædia* by M'Clintock and Strong (Vol. VIII, p. 469)
points out: "It was not the imperial palace, . . . for
this was never called *prætorium* in Rome; nor was
it the judgment-hall, for no such building stood in
Rome, and the name *prætoria* was not until much
later applied to the courts of justice." When first
imprisoned in Rome, Paul was "permitted to stay
by himself with the soldier guarding him." (Ac
28:16) So his prison bonds would have become
public knowledge in association with Christ
among the soldiers of the Praetorian Guard, and
especially so if his guard was changed daily. As a
consequence, many translators understand *prai-
to'ri·on* at Philippians 1:13 to signify the Praetorian Guard and not some building or judicial body.
—*RS, NW, AS, TC.*

The *Textus Receptus* includes at Acts 28:16: "the
centurion delivered the prisoners to the captain of
the guard." (*KJ*) This latter officer has been explained by some to have been Sextus Afranius
Burrus, the prefect of the Praetorian Guard under
Nero until 62 C.E. Darby even renders it: "the
centurion delivered up the prisoners to the præto-
rian prefect." However, Darby's version puts this
material in brackets as an instance where there
are variations in the manuscripts. Other modern
versions omit the phrase altogether since it is not
in ancient manuscripts such as the Sinaitic, Alexandrine, and Vatican No. 1209.—*RS, AT, NW, JB.*

PRAISE. An expression of commendation, of
admiration, even of worship when the praise is
directed to God. The Hebrew verb *ha·lal'* and the
Greek *ai·ne'o* are rendered "praise." (Ps 113:1; Isa
38:18; Ro 15:11; see HALLEL; HALLELUJAH.) The
Greek noun *hy'mnos*, from which the English
word "hymn" is drawn, conveys the thought of
praise or a song of praise directed to God.—Mr 14:
26, ftn.

To praise God's name means to praise the Most
High himself. (Ps 69:30) He is deserving of the
greatest praise, for he is "good," or the ultimate in
moral excellence, the Creator, the Helper of those
in distress, the Sustainer and Deliverer of his
people. (Ps 135:3; 150:2; 1Ch 16:25, 26) Never will
he share this praise with lifeless images that can
provide no aid to their worshipers.—Isa 42:8.

Praise had an important place in Israel's worship of Jehovah. Because of being completely sur-

sent to foreign lands, three were always stationed
in Rome, one being in barracks adjacent to the
emperor's palace. Since the Praetorian Guard were
basically the only permanent troops in Italy, they
came to constitute a powerful political force in
supporting or overthrowing an emperor. Eventually the size and makeup of the Praetorian Guard
changed, men from the provinces even being admitted. It was finally abolished by Emperor Constantine in 312 C.E.

In the Gospels and Acts, the Latinism *prai·to'ri-
on* is used with regard to a palace or residence.
The tent of an army commander had been known
as *praetorium,* and so, in time, the term was
applied to the residence of a provincial governor.
Thus Pilate interrogated Jesus in the *praetorium,*
or "governor's palace." (Joh 18:28, 33; 19:9; see
GOVERNOR'S PALACE.) Evidently there, judgments
were rendered and troops were barracked. (Mt
27:27; Mr 15:16) At Caesarea, Paul was "kept

rounded by praise, the Almighty is referred to as "inhabiting the praises of Israel." (Ps 22:3) It was King David who organized the priests and Levites for praising Jehovah with song and instrumental music. The organized arrangement begun by David continued in effect at the temple built by Solomon, and for years thereafter priests and Levites led the rendering of praise, using inspired compositions that have been preserved to this day in the book of Psalms.—1Ch 16:4-6; 23:2-5; 2Ch 8:14; see MUSIC.

Jehovah's faithful servants permitted nothing to interfere with their rendering the praise to which he has the exclusive claim. The prophet Daniel did not stop praising Jehovah when it was decreed unlawful and the one doing it could be punished by being thrown into a lions' pit. (Da 6:7-10) Jesus Christ, by doing nothing of his own originality, set the superlative example in praising his Father. The whole life and ministry of God's Son, including the miracles he performed, brought praise to his Father.—Lu 18:43; Joh 7:17, 18.

Among first-century Christians, the inspired psalms continued to be used in praising Jehovah. Additionally, there appear to have been Christian compositions—"praises to God," or hymns, and "spiritual songs," or songs dealing with spiritual matters. (Eph 5:19; Col 3:16) Christian praise, however, is not limited to song. It finds expression in one's life and in one's active concern for the spiritual and material welfare of others.—Heb 13:15, 16.

Praise Directed to Humans. Self-praise is an evidence of pride and is not upbuilding to the hearers. It is unloving, because it is an exalting of oneself above others. (1Co 13:4) If there is to be praise, it should come spontaneously from impartial observers who have nothing to gain by their commendation.—Pr 27:2.

Though coming from others, praise can still be a test to its recipient. It may foster feelings of superiority or pride and thus lead to a person's downfall. But when accepted in the right spirit, praise may affect an individual in a positive way. He may humbly acknowledge his indebtedness to Jehovah God and be encouraged to conduct himself so as not to fall short of his praiseworthy moral standing. The inspired proverb points to the effect that praise can have in revealing what a person actually is: "The refining pot is for silver, and the furnace is for gold; and an individual is according to his praise."—Pr 27:21; compare NE.

No greater praise or commendation can any human receive than to be acknowledged as approved by God. Such praise will be given at the revelation of the Lord Jesus Christ in glory. (1Co 4:5; 1Pe 1:7) This praise is dependent, not on fleshly distinctions, but on whether a person has lived in a way befitting a servant of Jehovah. (Ro 2:28, 29; see JEW[ESS].) Meanwhile, men in high governmental station and others may praise true Christians for being law abiding and upright. (Ro 13:3) When it is clear to observers that the reason for the fine conduct of Christians is that they are devoted servants of Jehovah, praise goes to Jehovah and to his Son, whose loyal disciples they are.

PRAYER. Worshipful address to the true God, or to false gods. Mere speech to God is not necessarily prayer, as is seen in the judgment in Eden and in the case of Cain. (Ge 3:8-13; 4:9-14) Prayer involves devotion, trust, respect, and a sense of dependence on the one to whom the prayer is directed. The various Hebrew and Greek words relating to prayer convey such ideas as to ask, make request, petition, entreat, supplicate, plead, beseech, beg, implore favor, seek, inquire of, as well as to praise, thank, and bless.

Petitions and supplications, of course, can be made to men, and the original-language words are sometimes so used (Ge 44:18; 50:17; Ac 25:11), but "prayer," used in a *religious* sense, does not apply to such cases. One might "beseech" or "implore" another person to do something, but in so doing he would not view this individual as his God. He would not, for example, silently petition such one, nor do so when the individual was not visibly present, as one does in prayer to God.

The "Hearer of Prayer." The entire Scriptural record testifies that Jehovah is the One to whom prayer should be directed (Ps 5:1, 2; Mt 6:9), that he is the "Hearer of prayer" (Ps 65:2; 66:19) and has power to act in behalf of the petitioners. (Mr 11:24; Eph 3:20) To pray to false gods and their idol images is exposed as stupidity, for the idols do not have the ability either to hear or to act, and the gods they represent are unworthy of comparison with the true God. (Jg 10:11-16; Ps 115:4, 6; Isa 45:20; 46:1, 2, 6, 7) The contest concerning godship between Baal and Jehovah, held on Mount Carmel, demonstrated the foolishness of prayer to false deities.—1Ki 18:21-39; compare Jg 6:28-32.

Though some claim that prayer may properly be addressed to others, such as to God's Son, the evidence is emphatically to the contrary. True, there are rare instances in which words are addressed to Jesus Christ in heaven. Stephen, when about to die, appealed to Jesus, saying, "Lord Jesus, receive my spirit." (Ac 7:59) However, the context reveals a circumstance giving basis for this exceptional expression. Stephen at that very time had a vision of "Jesus standing at God's right hand," and evidently reacting as if he were in Jesus' personal presence, he felt free to speak this plea to the one whom he recognized as the head of the Christian congregation. (Ac 7:55, 56; Col 1:18) Similarly, the apostle John, at the conclusion of the Revelation, says, "Amen! Come, Lord Jesus." (Re 22:20) But again the context shows that, in a vision (Re 1:10; 4:1, 2), John had been hearing Jesus speak of his future coming and thus John responded with the above expression of his desire for that coming. (Re 22:16, 20) In both cases, that of Stephen and that of John, the situation differs little from that of the conversation John had with a heavenly person in this Revelation vision. (Re 7:13, 14; compare Ac 22:6-22.) There is nothing to indicate that Christian disciples so expressed themselves under other circumstances to Jesus after his ascension to heaven. Thus, the apostle Paul writes: "In *everything* by prayer and supplication along with thanksgiving let your petitions be made known *to God.*"—Php 4:6.

The article APPROACH TO GOD considers the position of Christ Jesus as the one *through* whom prayer is directed. Through Jesus' blood, offered to God in sacrifice, "we have boldness for the way of entry into the holy place," that is, boldness to approach God's presence in prayer, approaching "with true hearts in the full assurance of faith." (Heb 10:19-22) Jesus Christ is therefore the one and only "way" of reconciliation with God and approach to God in prayer.—Joh 14:6; 15:16; 16: 23, 24; 1Co 1:2; Eph 2:18; see JESUS CHRIST (His Vital Place in God's Purpose).

Those Whom God Hears. People "of all flesh" may come to the "Hearer of prayer," Jehovah God. (Ps 65:2; Ac 15:17) Even during the period that Israel was God's "private property," his covenant people, foreigners could approach Jehovah in prayer by recognizing Israel as God's appointed instrument and the temple at Jerusalem as his chosen place for sacrifice. (De 9:29; 2Ch 6:32, 33; compare Isa 19:22.) Later, by Christ's death, the distinction between Jew and Gentile was forever removed. (Eph 2:11-16) At the home of the Italian Cornelius, Peter recognized that "God is not partial, but in every nation the man that fears him and works righteousness is acceptable to him." (Ac 10:34, 35) The determining factor, then, is the heart of the individual and what his heart is moving him to do. (Ps 119:145; La 3:41) Those who observe God's commandments and do "the things that are pleasing in his eyes" have the assurance that his "ears" are also open to them. —1Jo 3:22; Ps 10:17; Pr 15:8; 1Pe 3:12.

Conversely, those who disregard God's Word and law, shedding blood and practicing other wickedness, do not receive a favorable hearing from God; their prayers are "detestable" to him. (Pr 15:29; 28:9; Isa 1:15; Mic 3:4) The very prayer of such ones can "become a sin." (Ps 109:3-7) King Saul, by his presumptuous, rebellious course, lost God's favor, and "although Saul would inquire of Jehovah, Jehovah never answered him, either by dreams or by the Urim or by the prophets." (1Sa 28:6) Jesus said that hypocritical persons who sought to draw attention to their piety by praying received their "reward in full"—from men, but not from God. (Mt 6:5) The pious-appearing Pharisees made long prayers, boasted of their superior morality, yet were condemned by God for their hypocritical course. (Mr 12:40; Lu 18:10-14) Though they drew near with their mouths, their hearts were far from God and his Word of truth.—Mt 15:3-9; compare Isa 58:1-9.

The individual must have faith in God and in his being "the rewarder of those earnestly seeking him" (Heb 11:6), approaching in "the full assurance of faith." (Heb 10:22, 38, 39) Recognition of one's own sinful state is essential, and when serious sins have been committed, the individual must 'soften the face of Jehovah' (1Sa 13:12; Da 9:13) by first softening his own heart in sincere repentance, humility, and contrition. (2Ch 34:26-28; Ps 51:16, 17; 119:58) Then God may let himself be entreated and may grant forgiveness and a favorable hearing (2Ki 13:4; 2Ch 7:13, 14; 33:10-13; Jas 4:8-10); no longer will one feel that God has 'blocked approach to himself with a cloud mass, that prayer may not pass through.' (La 3:40-44) Though a person may not be cut off completely from receiving audience with God, his prayers can be "hindered" if he fails to follow God's counsel. (1Pe 3:7) Those seeking forgiveness must be forgiving toward others.—Mt 6:14, 15; Mr 11:25; Lu 11:4.

What are proper matters about which to pray?

Basically prayers involve confession (2Ch 30: 22), petitions or requests (Heb 5:7), expressions of praise and thanksgiving (Ps 34:1; 92:1), and vows (1Sa 1:11; Ec 5:2-6). The prayer given by Jesus to his disciples was evidently a model, or a basic pattern, because later prayers by Jesus himself, as well as by his disciples, did not rigidly adhere to the specific words of his model prayer. (Mt 6:9-13) In its initial words, this prayer concentrates on the prime issue, calling for the sanctification of God's name, which began to be reproached by the rebellion in Eden, as well as for the realization of the divine will by means of the promised Kingdom, which government is headed by the prophesied Seed, the Messiah. (Ge 3:15; see JEHOVAH [Name to Be Sanctified and Vindicated].) Such prayer requires that the one praying be definitely on God's side in the issue.

Jesus' parable at Luke 19:11-27 shows what the 'coming of the Kingdom' means—its coming to execute judgment, to destroy all opposers, and to bring relief and reward to those hoping in it. (Compare Re 16:14-16; 19:11-21.) The following expression, "let your will take place, as in heaven, also upon earth," thus refers primarily, not to the doing of God's will by humans, but, rather, to God's own acting in fulfillment of his will toward the earth and its inhabitants, manifesting his power to realize his declared purpose. The person praying, of course, also expresses thereby his own preference for, and submission to, that will. (Mt 6:10; compare Mt 26:39.) The request for daily bread, forgiveness, protection against temptation, and deliverance from the wicked one all relate to the petitioner's desire to continue living in God's favor. He expresses this desire for all others of like faith, not for himself alone.—Compare Col 4:12.

These matters in this model prayer are of fundamental importance to all men of faith and express needs they all have in common. The Scriptural account shows that there are, on the other hand, many other matters that may affect individuals to a greater or lesser degree or that result from particular circumstances or occasions and that are also proper subjects for prayer. Though not specifically mentioned in Jesus' model prayer, they are, nevertheless, related to the matters there presented. Personal prayers, then, may embrace virtually every facet of life.—Joh 16:23, 24; Php 4:6; 1Pe 5:7.

Thus, all rightly seek increased knowledge, understanding, and wisdom (Ps 119:33, 34; Jas 1:5); yet some may need such in special ways. They may call on God for guidance in matters of judicial decisions, as did Moses (Ex 18:19, 26; compare Nu 9:6-9; 27:1-11; De 17:8-13), or in the appointment of persons to special responsibility among God's people. (Nu 27:15-18; Lu 6:12, 13; Ac 1:24, 25; 6:5, 6) They may seek strength and wisdom to carry out certain assignments or to face up to particular trials or dangers. (Ge 32:9-12; Lu 3:21; Mt 26:36-44) Their reasons for blessing God and thanking him may vary according to their own personal experiences.—1Co 7:7; 12:6, 7; 1Th 5:18.

At 1 Timothy 2:1, 2, the apostle speaks of prayers being made "concerning all sorts of men, concerning kings and all those who are in high station." On his final night with his disciples, Jesus, in prayer, said that he did not make request concerning the world, but concerning those whom God had given him, and that these were not of the world but were hated by the world. (Joh 17:9, 14) It therefore appears that Christian prayers regarding officials of the world are not without limitation. The apostle's further words indicate that such prayers are ultimately in favor of God's people, "in order that *we* may go on leading a calm and quiet life with full godly devotion and seriousness." (1Ti 2:2) Earlier examples illustrate this: Nehemiah prayed that God would 'give him pity' before King Artaxerxes (Ne 1:11; compare Ge 43: 14), and Jehovah instructed the Israelites to "seek the peace of the city [Babylon]" in which they would be exiled, praying on its behalf, since "in its peace there will prove to be peace for you yourselves." (Jer 29:7) Similarly, Christians prayed concerning the threats of the rulers in their day (Ac 4:23-30), and undoubtedly their prayers in behalf of imprisoned Peter also involved the officials with authority to release him. (Ac 12:5) In harmony with Christ's counsel, they prayed for those persecuting them.—Mt 5:44; compare Ac 26:28, 29; Ro 10:1-3.

Giving thanks for God's provisions, such as food, was done from early times. (De 8:10-18; note also Mt 14:19; Ac 27:35; 1Co 10:30, 31.) Appreciation for God's goodness, however, is to be shown in "everything," not only for material blessings. —1Th 5:17, 18; Eph 5:19, 20.

In the final analysis, it is knowledge of God's will that governs the contents of a person's prayers, for the supplicant must realize that, if his request is to be granted, it must please God. Knowing that the wicked and those disregarding God's Word have no favor with Him, the supplicant obviously cannot request that which runs counter to righteousness and to God's revealed will, including the teachings of God's Son and his inspired disciples. (Joh 15:7, 16) Thus, statements regarding the asking of "anything" (Joh 16:23) are not to be taken out of context. "Anything" clearly does not embrace things the individual knows, or has reason to believe, are not pleasing to God. John states: "This is the confidence that we have toward him, that, no matter what it is that we ask *according to his will,* he hears us." (1Jo 5:14; compare Jas 4:15.) Jesus told his disciples: "If two of you on earth agree concerning *anything of importance* that they should request, it will take place for them due to my Father in heaven." (Mt 18:19) While material things, such as food, are proper subjects of prayer, materialistic desires and ambitions are not, as such texts as Matthew 6:19-34 and 1 John 2:15-17 show. Nor can one rightly pray for those whom God condemns.—Jer 7:16; 11:14.

Romans 8:26, 27 shows that the Christian, under certain circumstances, will not know just what to pray for; but his unuttered 'groanings' are nonetheless understood by God. The apostle shows that this is by means of God's spirit, or active force. It should be remembered that it was by his spirit that God inspired the Scriptures. (2Ti 3:16, 17; 2Pe 1:21) These contained prophecies and included events that prefigured the circumstances that would come upon his servants in later times and showed the way in which God would guide his servants and bring them the help they needed. (Ro 15:4; 1Pe 1:6-12) It may not be until after the needed help has been received that the Christian realizes that what he *might* have prayed for (but did not know how to) was already set forth in God's spirit-inspired Word.—Compare 1Co 2:9, 10.

The Answering of Prayers. Although God anciently carried on a measure of two-way communication with certain individuals, this was not common, for the most part being restricted to special representatives, such as Abraham and Moses. (Ge 15:1-5; Ex 3:11-15; compare Ex 20:19.) Even then, with the exception of when he spoke to or about his Son while on earth, God's words were evidently transmitted through angels. (Compare Ex 3:2, 4; Ga 3:19.) Messages delivered personally by materialized angels were likewise uncommon, as is evidenced by the disturbed effect they generally produced on the receivers. (Jg 6:22; Lu 1:11, 12, 26-30) The answering of prayers in the majority of cases, therefore, was through prophets or by the granting of, or the refusal to grant, the request. Jehovah's answers to prayers often had a clearly recognizable effect, as when he delivered his servants from their enemies (2Ch 20:1-12, 21-24) or when he provided for their physical needs in times of dire scarcity. (Ex 15:22-25) But undoubtedly the most frequent answer was not so easily discernible, since it related to giving moral strength and enlightenment, enabling the person to hold to a righteous course and carry out divinely assigned work. (2Ti 4:17) Particularly for the Christian the answer to prayers involved matters mainly spiritual, not as spectacular as some powerful acts of God in earlier times, but equally vital. —Mt 9:36-38; Col 1:9; Heb 13:18; Jas 5:13.

Acceptable prayer must be made to the right person, Jehovah God; on right matters, those in harmony with God's declared purposes; in the right manner, through God's appointed way, Christ Jesus; and with a right motive and a clean heart. (Compare Jas 4:3-6.) Along with all of this, there is need for persistence. Jesus said to 'keep on asking, seeking, and knocking,' not giving up. (Lu 11:5-10; 18:1-7) He raised the question as to whether, at his future 'arrival,' he would find faith in the power of prayer on earth. (Lu 18:8) The seeming delay on God's part in answering some prayers is not due to any inability nor to a lack of willingness, as the Scriptures make clear. (Mt 7:9-11; Jas 1:5, 17) In some cases the answer must await God's 'timetable.' (Lu 18:7; 1Pe 5:6; 2Pe 3:9; Re 6:9-11) Primarily, however, it is evident that God allows his petitioners to demonstrate the depth of their concern, the intensity of their desire, the genuineness of their motive. (Ps 55:17; 88:1, 13; Ro 1:9-11) At times they must be like Jacob in his wrestling a long time in order to obtain a blessing.—Ge 32:24-26.

Similarly, while Jehovah God cannot be pressured by numbers into acting, he evidently takes note of the extent of concern shown among his servants as a body, taking action when they collectively show deep concern and united interest. (Compare Ex 2:23-25.) Where apathy or a measure of it exists, God may withhold action. In the reconstruction of Jerusalem's temple, a project for some time not well supported (Ezr 4:4-7, 23, 24; Hag 1:2-12), there were interruptions and delay, whereas later, in Nehemiah's reconstruction of the city walls, accomplished with prayer and good support, the work was done in just 52 days. (Ne 2:17-20; 4:4-23; 6:15) Writing the Corinthian congregation, Paul speaks of God's deliverance of him from danger of death, and he states: "You also can help along by your supplication for us, in order that thanks may be given by many in our behalf for what is kindly given to us due to many prayerful faces." (2Co 1:8-11; compare Php 1:12-20.) The power of intercessory prayer is regularly stressed, whether by an individual or a collective group. It was in regard to 'praying for one another' that James said: "A righteous man's supplication, when it is at work, has much force."—Jas 5:14-20; compare Ge 20:7, 17; 2Th 3:1, 2; Heb 13:18, 19.

Also notable is the frequent 'pleading' of one's case before Jehovah, the Sovereign Ruler. The petitioner presents reasons why he believes the request to be right, evidence of his having a right and unselfish motive, and reasoning to show that there are other factors outweighing his own interests or considerations. These might be that the honor of God's own name or the good of his people is involved, or they may include the effect on others as a result of God's action or refusal to act. Appeals may be made to God's justice, his loving-kindness, his being a God of mercy. (Compare Ge 18:22-33; 19:18-20; Ex 32:11-14; 2Ki 20:1-5; Ezr 8:21-23.) Christ Jesus also 'pleads' for his faithful followers.—Ro 8:33, 34.

The entire book of Psalms consists of prayers and songs of praise to God, its contents illustrating what prayer should be. Among many notable prayers are those by Jacob (Ge 32:9-12), Moses (De 9:25-29), Job (Job 1:21), Hannah (1Sa 2:1-10), David (2Sa 7:18-29; 1Ch 29:10-19), Solomon (1Ki 3:6-9; 8:22-61), Asa (2Ch 14:11), Jehoshaphat (2Ch 20:5-12), Elijah (1Ki 18:36, 37), Jonah (Jon 2:1-9), Hezekiah (2Ki 19:15-19), Jeremiah (Jer 20:7-12; the book of Lamentations), Daniel (Da 9:3-21), Ezra (Ezr 9:6-15), Nehemiah (Ne 1:4-11), certain Levites (Ne 9:5-38), Habakkuk (Hab 3:1-19), Jesus (Joh 17:1-26; Mr 14:36), and Jesus' disciples (Ac 4:24-30).—See ATTITUDES AND GESTURES; INCENSE (Significance).

PREACHER, PREACHING.

The Biblical concept of "preaching" is best ascertained from an examination of the sense of the original Hebrew and Greek terms. The Greek ke·rys′so, which is commonly rendered "preach," means, basically, 'make proclamation as a herald, to be a herald, officiate as herald, proclaim (as conqueror).' The related noun is ke′ryx and means 'herald, public messenger, envoy, crier (who made proclamation and kept order in assemblies, etc.).' Another related noun is ke′ryg·ma, which means 'that which is cried by a herald, proclamation, announcement (of victory in games), mandate, summons.' (A Greek-English Lexicon, by H. Liddell and R. Scott, revised by H. Jones, Oxford, 1968, p. 949) Ke·rys′so thus does not convey the thought of the delivery of a sermon to a closed group of disciples but, rather, of an open, public proclamation. This is illustrated by its use to describe the "strong angel proclaiming [ke·rys′son·ta] with a loud voice: 'Who is worthy to open the scroll and loose its seals?'"—Re 5:2; compare also Mt 10:27.

The word eu·ag·ge·li′zo·mai means "declare good news." (Mt 11:5) Related words are di·ag·gel′lo, "declare abroad; give notice" (Lu 9:60; Ac 21:26; Ro 9:17) and ka·tag·gel′lo, "publish; talk about; proclaim; publicize." (Ac 13:5; Ro 1:8; 1Co 11:26; Col 1:28) The principal difference between ke·rys′so and eu·ag·ge·li′zo·mai is that the former stresses the manner of the proclamation, that it is a public, authorized pronouncement, and the latter stresses the content thereof, the declaring or bringing of the eu·ag·ge′li·on, the good news or gospel.

Ke·rys′so corresponds in some measure to the Hebrew ba·sar′, meaning "bear news; announce; act as a news bearer." (1Sa 4:17; 2Sa 1:20; 1Ch 16:23) Ba·sar′, however, does not imply official capacity to the same extent.

Preaching in the Hebrew Scriptures. Noah is the first person designated as "a preacher" (2Pe 2:5), although Enoch's earlier prophesying may have been made known by preaching. (Jude 14, 15) Noah's preaching righteousness prior to the Flood evidently included a call for repentance and a warning of coming destruction, as is evidenced by Jesus' reference to the people's 'failing to take note.' (Mt 24:38, 39) Noah's divinely authorized public proclamation, therefore, was not primarily a bringing of good news.

Following the Flood, many men, such as Abraham, served as prophets, speaking forth divine revelations. (Ps 105:9, 13-15) However, prior to the establishing of Israel in the Promised Land, regular or vocational preaching does not seem to have been done in a public way. The early patriarchs were under no instructions to act as heralds. During the period of the kingdom rule in Israel, prophets did act as public spokesmen proclaiming God's decrees, judgments, and summonses in public places. (Isa 58:1; Jer 26:2) Jonah's proclamation to Nineveh fits well the thought conveyed by ke′ryg·ma, and it is so described. (Compare Jon 3:1-4; Mt 12:41.) The prophets' ministry, however, generally was much broader than that of a herald or preacher, and in some cases they employed others to act as their spokesmen. (2Ki 5:10; 9:1-3; Jer 36:4-6) Some of their messages and visions were written rather than orally proclaimed (Jer 29:1, 30, 31; 30:1, 2; Da chaps 7-12); many were given in private audience, and the prophets also used symbolic acts to convey ideas.—See PROPHECY; PROPHET.

Admonition, warnings, and judgments were proclaimed, and so was good news—of victories, deliverance, and blessings—as well as praises to Jehovah God. (1Ch 16:23; Isa 41:27; 52:7; the Hebrew ba·sar′ is used in these texts.) At times women cried out or sang the news of battles won or of coming relief.—Ps 68:11; Isa 40:9; compare 1Sa 18:6, 7.

The Hebrew Scriptures also pointed forward to the preaching work that would be done by Christ Jesus and the Christian congregation. Jesus quoted Isaiah 61:1, 2 as foretelling his divine commission and his authorization to preach. (Lu 4:16-21) In fulfillment of Psalm 40:9 (the preceding verses being applied to Jesus by the apostle Paul at Heb 10:5-10), Jesus "told the good news [form of ba·sar'] of righteousness in the big congregation." The apostle Paul quoted Isaiah 52:7 (concerning the messenger bringing the news of Zion's release from its captive state) and related it to the public preaching work of Christians.—Ro 10:11-15.

In the Christian Greek Scriptures. Though active primarily in the wilderness regions, John the Baptizer did the work of a preacher or public messenger, heralding the approach of the Messiah and God's Kingdom to the Jews who came out to him and summoning them to repentance. (Mt 3:1-3, 11, 12; Mr 1:1-4; Lu 3:7-9) At the same time John served as a prophet, a teacher (with disciples), and an evangelizer. (Lu 1:76, 77; 3:18; 11:1; Joh 1:35) He was "a representative of God" and His witness.—Joh 1:6, 7.

Jesus did not remain in the wilderness region of Judea after his 40-day fast there, nor did he isolate himself as in a monastic life. He recognized that his divine commission called for a preaching work, and he carried it on publicly, in cities and villages, in the temple area, synagogues, marketplaces and streets, as well as in the countryside. (Mr 1:39; 6:56; Lu 8:1; 13:26; Joh 18:20) Like John, he did more than preach. His teaching receives even greater emphasis than his preaching. Teaching (di·da'sko) differs from preaching in that the teacher does more than proclaim; he instructs, explains, shows things by argument, and offers proofs. The work of Jesus' disciples, both before and after his death, was thus to be a combination of preaching and teaching.—Mt 4:23; 11:1; 28:18-20.

The theme of Jesus' preaching was: 'Repent, for the kingdom of the heavens has drawn near.' (Mt 4:17) Like an official herald, he was alerting his listeners to his Sovereign God's activity, to a time of opportunity and decision. (Mr 1:14, 15) As foretold by Isaiah, not only did he bring good news and comfort for the meek, brokenhearted, and mourning ones, as well as proclaim release to captives, but he also declared "the day of vengeance on the part of our God." (Isa 61:2) He boldly announced God's purposes, decrees, appointments, and judgments before rulers and people.

Following Jesus' Death. After his death, and particularly from Pentecost of 33 C.E. onward, Jesus' disciples carried on the preaching work, first among the Jews and eventually to all the nations. Anointed by holy spirit, they recognized and repeatedly informed their listeners that they were authorized heralds (Ac 2:14-18; 10:40-42; 13:47; 14:3; compare Ro 10:15), even as Jesus had stressed that he was 'sent by God' (Lu 9:48; Joh 5:36, 37; 6:38; 8:18, 26, 42), who gave him "a commandment as to what to tell and what to speak." (Joh 12:49) Therefore, when ordered to cease their preaching, the disciples' reply was: "Whether it is righteous in the sight of God to listen to you rather than to God, judge for yourselves. But as for us, we cannot stop speaking about the things we have seen and heard." "We must obey God as ruler rather than men." (Ac 4:19, 20; 5:29, 32, 42) This preaching activity was an essential part of their worship, a means of praising God, a requisite to the gaining of salvation. (Ro 10:9, 10; 1Co 9:16; Heb 13:15; compare Lu 12:8.) As such, it was to be shared in by all disciples, men and women, down till "the conclusion of the system of things."—Mt 28:18-20; Lu 24:46-49; Ac 2:17; compare Ac 18:26; 21:9; Ro 16:3.

These early Christian preachers were not highly educated men by worldly standards. The Sanhedrin perceived the apostles Peter and John to be "men unlettered and ordinary." (Ac 4:13) Concerning Jesus himself, "the Jews fell to wondering, saying: 'How does this man have a knowledge of letters, when he has not studied at the schools?'" (Joh 7:15) Secular historians noted the same points. "Celsus, the first writer against Christianity, makes it a matter of mockery, that labourers, shoemakers, farmers, the most uninformed and clownish of men, should be zealous preachers of the Gospel." (*The History of the Christian Religion and Church, During the Three First Centuries,* by Augustus Neander; translated from the German by Henry John Rose, 1848, p. 41) Paul explained it in this way: "For you behold his calling of you, brothers, that not many wise in a fleshly way were called, not many powerful, not many of noble birth; but God chose the foolish things of the world, that he might put the wise men to shame." —1Co 1:26, 27.

However, although not highly educated in worldly schools, the early Christian preachers were not untrained. Jesus gave extensive training to the 12 apostles before he sent them out to preach. (Mt 10) This training was not just the giving of instructions, but it was a practical training.—Lu 8:1.

The theme of Christian preaching continued to be "the kingdom of God." (Ac 20:25; 28:31) However, their proclamation contained added features as compared with that made prior to Christ's death. "The sacred secret" of God's purpose had been revealed through Christ; his sacrificial death had become a vital factor in true faith (1Co 15:12-14); his exalted position as God's assigned King and Judge must be known, recognized, and submitted to by all who would gain divine favor and life. (2Co 4:5) Thus, the disciples are often spoken of as 'preaching Christ Jesus.' (Ac 8:5; 9:20; 19:13; 1Co 1:23) An examination of their preaching makes clear that their 'preaching Christ' was not done so as to isolate him in the minds of their listeners as though he were somehow independent or detached from God's Kingdom arrangement and overall purpose. Rather, they proclaimed what Jehovah God had done for and through his Son, how God's purposes were being fulfilled and would be fulfilled in Jesus. (2Co 1:19-21) Thus, all such preaching was to God's own praise and glory, "through Jesus Christ."—Ro 16:25-27.

Their preaching was not performed simply as a duty, nor did their heralding consist merely of speaking out a message in a formal way. It sprang from heartfelt faith and was done with the desire to honor God and with the loving hope of bringing salvation to others. (Ro 10:9-14; 1Co 9:27; 2Co 4:13) Therefore the preachers were willing to be treated as foolish by the worldly wise or be persecuted as heretics by the Jews. (1Co 1:21-24; Ga 5:11) For this reason, too, their preaching was accompanied by the use of reasoning and persuasion to help the hearers to believe and exercise faith. (Ac 17:2; 28:23; 1Co 15:11) Paul speaks of himself as being appointed "a preacher and apostle and teacher." (2Ti 1:11) These Christians were not salaried heralds but were dedicated worshipers giving of themselves, giving their time and their strength to the preaching activity.—1Th 2:9.

Since all who became disciples also became preachers of the Word, the good news spread rapidly, and by the time Paul wrote his letter to the Colossians (c. 60-61 C.E. or about 27 years after Christ's death), he could speak of the good news "which was preached in all creation that is under heaven." (Col 1:23) Hence, Christ's prophecy of the 'preaching of the good news in all the nations' saw a certain fulfillment prior to the destruction of Jerusalem and its temple in 70 C.E. (Mt 24:14; Mr 13:10; MAP, Vol. 2, p. 744) Jesus' own words, as well as the book of Revelation, written after that destruction, point to a greater fulfillment of this prophecy at the time of Christ's beginning to exercise Kingdom rule and preliminary to the destruction of all adversaries of that Kingdom, a logical time for a great heralding work to be accomplished.—Re 12:7-12, 17; 14:6, 7; 19:5, 6; 22:17.

What results should Christian preachers expect for their efforts? Paul's experience was that "some began to believe the things said; others would not

believe." (Ac 28:24) Real Christian preaching, based on God's Word, requires a response of some kind. It is vigorous, dynamic, and above all, it presents an issue on which people must take sides. Some become active opposers of the Kingdom message. (Ac 13:50; 18:5, 6) Others listen for a time, but eventually they turn back for various reasons. (Joh 6:65, 66) Still others accept the good news and act upon it.—Ac 17:11; Lu 8:15.

"From House to House."   Jesus went right to the people with the Kingdom message, teaching them publicly and in their homes. (Mt 5:1; 9:10, 28, 35) When he sent out his early disciples to preach, he directed them: "Into whatever city or village you enter, search out who in it is deserving." (Mt 10:7, 11-14) Such 'searching out' would reasonably include going to the people's homes, where "deserving" persons would heed the message and the disciples would find lodging for the night.—Lu 9:1-6.

On a later occasion Jesus "designated seventy others and sent them forth by twos in advance of him into every city and place to which he himself was going to come." These were not just to preach in public places but were also to contact people at their homes. Jesus instructed them: "Wherever you enter into a house say first, 'May this house have peace.'"—Lu 10:1-7.

In the days following Pentecost 33 C.E., Jesus' disciples continued bringing the good news right to the homes of the people. Though ordered to "stop speaking," the inspired record says that "every day in the temple and *from house to house* they continued without letup teaching and declaring the good news about the Christ, Jesus." (Ac 5: 40-42; compare *Dy, NIV.*) The expression "from house to house" translates the Greek *kat' oi'kon,* literally, "according to house"; the sense of the Greek preposition *ka·ta'* is distributive ("from house to house") and not merely adverbial ('at home'). (See *NW* ftn.) This method of reaching people—going directly to their homes—brought outstanding results. "The number of the disciples kept multiplying in Jerusalem very much."—Ac 6:7; compare 4:16, 17 and 5:28.

The apostle Paul told the elders of Ephesus: "From the first day that I stepped into the district of Asia . . . I did not hold back from telling you any of the things that were profitable nor from teaching you publicly and from house to house. But I thoroughly bore witness both to Jews and to Greeks about repentance toward God and faith in our Lord Jesus." (Ac 20:18-21; compare *KJ, Dy, AS, RS, Mo, NIV, La.*) Paul was here speaking of his efforts to preach to these men when they were yet unbelievers, persons needing to know "about repentance toward God and faith in our Lord Jesus." Thus, from the start of his missionary service in Asia, Paul searched "from house to house" for spiritually inclined persons. Finding such ones, he doubtless returned to their homes to teach them further and, as these became believers, to strengthen them in the faith. Dr. A. T. Robertson, in his book *Word Pictures in the New Testament,* comments as follows on Acts 20:20: "By (according to) houses. It is worth noting that this greatest of all preachers preached from house to house and did not make his visits mere social calls."—1930, Vol. III, pp. 349, 350.

Preaching Within the Congregation. Most preaching activity recorded in the Christian Greek Scriptures relates to the proclamation done outside the congregation. However, Paul's exhortation to Timothy to "preach the word, be at it urgently in favorable season, in troublesome season," includes preaching within the congregation, as done by a general overseer. (2Ti 4:2) Paul's letter to Timothy is a pastoral letter, that is, it was directed to one who was doing pastoral work among the Christians and provides counsel on such superintending ministry. Previous to this exhortation to "preach the word," Paul warned Timothy of the apostasy beginning to manifest itself, which was to develop to serious proportions. (2Ti 2:16-19; 3:1-7) Following up his exhortation to Timothy to hold to and not be sidetracked from "the *word*" in his preaching, Paul shows the need for the urgency, saying, "for there will be a period of time when they will not put up with the healthful teaching" but, rather, will seek teachers who teach according to their own desires and so will "turn their ears away from the truth," hence describing, not outsiders, but those within the congregation. (2Ti 4:3, 4) Timothy, therefore, was not to lose his spiritual balance but was to be constant in boldly declaring God's Word (not human philosophies or useless speculations) to the brothers, even though this might bring him trouble and suffering from those wrongly inclined within the congregations. (Compare 1Ti 6:3-5, 20, 21; 2Ti 1:6-8, 13; 2:1-3, 14, 15, 23-26; 3:14-17; 4:5.) By so doing, he would act as a deterrent to the apostasy and be free of responsibility for bloodguilt, even as Paul had been.—Ac 20:25-32.

What was the objective of Jesus' preaching "to the spirits in prison"?

At 1 Peter 3:19, 20, after describing Jesus' resurrection to spirit life, the apostle says: "In this state also he went his way and preached to the spirits in prison, who had once been disobedient when the patience of God was waiting in Noah's days, while the ark was being constructed." Commenting on this text, *Vine's Expository Dictionary of Old and New Testament Words* says: "In I Pet. 3:19 the probable reference is, not to glad tidings (which there is no real evidence that Noah preached, nor is there evidence that the spirits of antediluvian people are actually 'in prison'), but to the act of Christ after His resurrection in proclaiming His victory to fallen angelic spirits." (1981, Vol. 3, p. 201) As has been noted, *ke·rys′so* refers to a proclamation that may be not only of something good but also of something bad, as when Jonah proclaimed Nineveh's coming destruction. The only imprisoned spirits referred to in the Scriptures are those angels of Noah's day who were 'delivered into pits of dense darkness' (2Pe 2:4, 5) and "reserved with eternal bonds under dense darkness for the judgment of the great day." (Jude 6) Therefore the preaching by the resurrected Jesus to such unrighteous angels could only have been a preaching of judgment. It may be noted that the book of Revelation transmitted in vision to John by Christ Jesus toward the close of the first century C.E. contains much about Satan the Devil and his demons as well as their ultimate destruction, hence, a preaching of judgment. (Re 12-20) Peter's use of the past tense ("preached") indicates that such preaching had been done prior to the writing of his first letter.

PREFECT. An official lower than a satrap in the Babylonian government. The title is used at Daniel 2:48 in conjunction with "wise men of Babylon." It seems that these "wise men" were classed as to their official functions. Daniel was appointed chief prefect over all "the wise men of Babylon." —Da 3:2, 3, 27.

Under the rule of King Darius the Mede, the royal officials entered before Darius "as a throng," indicating that a goodly number were involved, and said that all the officials, including the prefects, recommended the making of a law limiting petitions to the king only, for 30 days. Daniel continued to petition Jehovah, and Jehovah delivered him; the conspirators themselves suffered death in the lions' pit.—Da 6:6, 7, 24.

PREGNANCY. The condition of having conceived and having the unborn offspring within the mother's body.

By his command to Adam and Eve, "Be fruitful and become many and fill the earth," Jehovah indicated that pregnancy was to be part of the woman's normal role. (Ge 1:28) With the introduction of imperfection into the human family, God explained that the pain of pregnancy would be increased. (Ge 3:16; see LABOR PAINS.) The Hebrew word ha·rah' means "conceive, become pregnant." (1Ch 4:17; 7:23) The equivalent thought in Greek was most often expressed by the idiom "have in [the] belly," which meant "be with child," or be pregnant.—Mt 1:18, 23.

Among the Jews, children, and especially male children, were viewed as a blessing (Ps 127:3; 128:3; Ge 29:32-35; 30:5, 6), and barrenness as a shame and a reproach. (Lu 1:24, 25; Ge 25:21; 30:1) Consequently, pregnancy was something a married woman desired. (1Sa 1:2, 11, 20) When once a child had been conceived, the developing embryo or fetus was considered a soul. Action that resulted in killing a developing child in the womb was handled according to the rule "soul for soul." (Ex 21:22, 23) It was a horrendous act for an enemy to rip up or split open a pregnant woman. —Ho 13:16; Am 1:13; 2Ki 8:12; 15:16.

Pregnancy would include pain at its termination (Ps 48:6; 1Th 5:3), but that temporary grief would end with the birth of the child, and so pregnancy would normally come to a happy and satisfying conclusion.—Joh 16:21, 22.

"Woe to the Pregnant Women." When responding to the apostles' question about the conclusion of the system of things, Jesus spoke about fleeing from Judea and said: "Woe to the pregnant women and those suckling a baby in those days!" (Mt 24:19; Mr 13:17; Lu 21:23) The fulfillment and truthfulness of those words became apparent in the events prior to and during the destruction of Jerusalem in 70 C.E. Though reasonable activity and movement is usually possible for a woman during her pregnancy (Lu 1:39, 56; 2:5), extended flight on foot over mountainous country would be hard on her, and especially if her time for delivery was close. Extreme adversity befell pregnant women and those suckling babies when Roman forces laid siege to Jerusalem. Famine prevailed. During pregnancy it is important for a woman to have proper nourishment. If, for example, she does not get sufficient calcium, she might lose her teeth, as the body takes calcium to form the bones of the developing baby. Furthermore a woman's maternal protective instinct would increase her suffering as she saw infants starving and dying, all the while knowing that she would soon bring a child into such conditions. Josephus wrote about some starving men in besieged Jerusalem: "There was no compassion for hoary hairs or infancy: children were actually lifted up with the fragments to which they clung and dashed to the ground."—*The Jewish War*, V, 433 (x, 3); compare Lu 23:29.

Figurative Use. The period of pregnancy culminating in the birth of a child is used several times in a figurative sense. Israel lost God's favor because her unfaithful people 'conceived trouble and brought to birth what is hurtful.' (Isa 59:2-8; compare Ps 7:14.) The process began with their allowing "hurtful thoughts" and wrong desires to impregnate their minds and hearts and, in effect, incubate there, with the inevitable result that "hurtful works" came to birth.—Compare Jas 1: 14, 15.

Elsewhere Isaiah depicts Israel as a woman crying out in labor pains and saying to God: "So we have become because of you, O Jehovah. We have become pregnant, we have had labor pains; as it were, we have given birth to wind. No real salvation do we accomplish as regards the land, and no inhabitants for the productive land proceed to fall in birth ["come to life," *JP*]." (Isa 26:17, 18) This may refer to the fact that, despite God's blessings (compare Isa 26:15) and his having set before Israel the opportunity to become "a kingdom of priests and a holy nation" (Ex 19:6), Israel had not yet seen realized the long-awaited fulfillment of the promise regarding the Seed through whom blessings would flow. (Ge 22:15-18) Israel's own efforts at salvation had produced nothing, unreality; as a nation it could not bring about the freedom "from enslavement to corruption" for which all creation "keeps on groaning together and being in pain together." (Ro 8:19-22; compare 10:3; 11:7.) With the Babylonian conquest, the land "faded away" because of its pollution through the violation of God's covenant, and 'the inhabitants of the land decreased in number.'—Isa 24:4-6.

In contrast, by bringing back his people from exile, Jehovah made Jerusalem like a woman who had been made pregnant by her husband and who brought forth numerous children.—Isa 54:1-8.

The apostle Paul quotes this prophecy of Isaiah chapter 54 and applies it to "the Jerusalem above [which] is free, and she is our mother." (Ga 4:26, 27) This evidently provides the key for understanding the vision recorded at Revelation 12:1-5, in which a pregnant heavenly "woman" gives birth to "a son, a male, who is to shepherd all the nations with an iron rod." The shepherding of the nations with an iron rod is directly connected with the Messianic Kingdom of God, and hence the vision must relate to the producing of that Kingdom, so that, following the defeat of Satan's attack on the newborn "child," the ensuing cry goes forth: "Now have come to pass the salvation and the power and the kingdom of our God and the authority of his Christ." (Re 12:10) The anguish of the pregnant heavenly "woman" preceding the birth calls to mind Paul's expression at Galatians 4:19, "childbirth pains" there apparently representing stirring interest and fervent desire to see full development of matters reached (in Paul's case, the full development of the Galatian believers as Christians).

PREPARATION. A name applied to the day preceding the weekly Sabbath, during which the Jews prepared for the Sabbath.

When Jehovah began to provide manna in the wilderness he directed that a double portion be collected on the sixth day, since the people were not to gather manna on the Sabbath, or seventh day. So, in preparation for the weekly Sabbath, the Jews collected and baked or boiled extra manna. (Ex 16:5, 22-27) In time "the day before the sabbath" came to be termed "Preparation," as Mark explained. (Mr 15:42) (Somewhat similarly, in German *Samstag* [Saturday] is also called *Sonnabend* [literally, "Sun evening"] or "evening before Sunday [*Sonntag*].") The Jewish Preparation day would end at sundown of what is today called Friday, at which time the Sabbath would commence, the Jewish day running from evening to evening.

On Preparation the people prepared meals for the next day, the Sabbath, and completed any other pressing work that could not wait until after the Sabbath. (Ex 20:10) The Law stipulated that the body of a man executed and hung on a stake "should not stay all night on the stake." (De 21:22, 23; compare Jos 8:29; 10:26, 27.) Since Jesus and those impaled with him were on stakes on the afternoon of Preparation, it was important to the Jews that their deaths be hastened if necessary so that they could be buried before sunset. This was especially so since the day soon to begin at sundown was a regular Sabbath (the seventh day of the week) and also a Sabbath because of being Nisan 15 (Le 23:5-7), hence it was a "great" Sabbath. (Joh 19:31, 42; Mr 15:42, 43; Lu 23:54) Josephus quoted a decree of Caesar Augustus that said the Jews "need not give bond (to appear in court) on the Sabbath or on the day of preparation for it (Sabbath Eve) after the ninth hour," indicating that they began to prepare for the Sabbath at the ninth hour on Friday.—*Jewish Antiquities,* XVI, 163 (vi, 2).

Regarding the morning of Jesus' trial and appearance before Pilate, which was in the morning period of Nisan 14 (the Passover day having begun the evening before), John 19:14 says: "Now it was

preparation of the passover." (*NW, KJ, Da*) Some commentators have understood this to mean "preparation *for* the passover," and certain translations so render the verse. (*AT, We, CC*) This, though, suggests that the Passover had not yet been celebrated, whereas the Gospel accounts explicitly show that Jesus and the apostles had celebrated it the night before. (Lu 22:15; Mt 26:18-20; Mr 14:14-17) Christ perfectly carried out the regulations of the Law, including the requirement to celebrate the Passover on Nisan 14. (Ex 12:6; Le 23:5; see PASSOVER.) The day of Jesus' trial and death could be viewed as the "preparation *of* the passover" in the sense that it was the preparation for the seven-day Festival of Unfermented Cakes that began the next day. Because of their closeness on the calendar, the entire festival itself was often included in the term "Passover." And the day after Nisan 14 was always a Sabbath; additionally, in 33 C.E., Nisan 15 fell on the regular Sabbath, making the day a "great" or double Sabbath.

PRESENCE. The Greek word from which "presence" is translated is *pa·rou·si′a,* formed from *pa·ra′* (alongside) and *ou·si′a* (being; derived from *ei·mi′,* meaning "be"). Hence, *pa·rou·si′a* means, literally, "being alongside," that is, a "presence." It is used 24 times in the Christian Greek Scriptures, frequently with regard to the presence of Christ in connection with his Messianic Kingdom.—Mt 24:3; see *NW* appendix, pp. 1576, 1577.

Many translations vary their renderings of this word. While translating *pa·rou·si′a* as "presence" in some texts, they more frequently render it as "coming." This has been the basis for the expression "second coming" or "second advent" (*adventus* ["advent" or "coming"] being the Latin *Vulgate* translation of *pa·rou·si′a* at Mt 24:3) with regard to Christ Jesus. While Jesus' presence of necessity implies his arrival at the place where he is present, the translation of *pa·rou·si′a* by "coming" places all the emphasis on the arrival and obscures the subsequent presence that follows the arrival. Though allowing for both "arrival" and "presence" as translations of *pa·rou·si′a,* lexicographers generally acknowledge that the *presence* of the person is the principal idea conveyed by the word.

Vine's Expository Dictionary of Old and New Testament Words (1981, Vol. 1, pp. 208, 209) states: "PAROUSIA . . . denotes both an arrival and a consequent presence with. For instance, in a papyrus letter [written in Greek] a lady speaks of the necessity of her *parousia* in a place in order to attend to matters relating to her property there. . . . When used of the return of Christ, at the Rapture of the Church, it signifies, not merely His momentary coming for His saints, but His presence with them from that moment until His revelation and manifestation to the world." Liddell and Scott's *Greek-English Lexicon* (revised by H. Jones, Oxford, 1968, p. 1343) shows that *pa·rou·si'a* is used at times in secular Greek literature to refer to the *"visit* of a royal or official personage."

Secular Greek writings are, of course, helpful in determining the sense of this Greek term. However, even more effective is the use given the word in the Bible itself. At Philippians 2:12, for example, Paul speaks of the Philippian Christians as obeying "not during my presence [*pa·rou·si'ai*] only, but now much more readily during my absence [*a·pou·si'ai*]." So, too, at 2 Corinthians 10:10, 11, after referring to those who said that "his letters are weighty and forceful, but his presence [*pa·rou·si'a*] in person is weak and his speech contemptible," Paul adds, "Let such a man take this into account, that what we are in our word by letters when absent [*a·pon'tes*], such we shall also be in action when present [*pa·ron'tes*]." (Compare also Php 1:24-27.) Thus, the contrast is between presence and absence, not between an arrival (or coming) and departure.

In view of this, J. B. Rotherham's *Emphasised Bible* states in its appendix (p. 271): "In this edition the word *parousia* is uniformly rendered 'presence' ('coming,' as a representative of *this* word, being set aside). . . . The sense of 'presence' is so plainly [shown] by the contrast with 'absence' . . . that the question naturally arises, —Why not always so render it?"

That Jesus' *pa·rou·si'a* is not simply a momentary coming followed by a rapid departure but is, rather, a presence covering a period of time is also indicated by his words recorded at Matthew 24:37-39 and Luke 17:26-30. Here "the days of Noah" are compared to "the presence of the Son of man" ("the days of the Son of man," in Luke's account). Jesus, therefore, does not limit the comparison just to the coming of the Deluge as a final climax during Noah's days, though he shows that his own "presence" or "days" will see a similar climax. Since "the days of Noah" actually covered a period of years, there is basis for believing that the foretold "presence [or "days"] of the Son of man" would likewise cover a period of some years, being climaxed by the destruction of those not giving heed to the opportunity afforded them to seek deliverance.

Nature of Christ's "Parousia." A *pa·rou·si'a*, or presence, can, of course, be visible, and in six occurrences of the word the reference is to the visible, human presence of men, such as Stephanas, Fortunatus, Achaicus, Titus, and Paul. (1Co 16:17; 2Co 7:6, 7; 10:10; Php 1:26; 2:12) That a *pa·rou·si'a* can also be invisible is indicated by Paul's use of the related verb form (*pa·rei·mi*) when speaking of being "present in spirit" though absent in body. (1Co 5:3) So, too, Jewish historian Josephus, writing in Greek, refers to God's *pa·rou·si'a* at Mount Sinai, his invisible presence being evidenced by the thunders and lightning.—*Jewish Antiquities,* III, 80 (v, 2).

The Scripturalness of an invisible presence is also borne out by Jehovah God's saying to Moses regarding the ark of the covenant in the Most Holy of the tabernacle: "And I will present myself to you there and speak with you from above the cover." (Ex 25:22) God's presence was not in a visible form, since the Scriptures are clear that "no man has seen God at any time"—neither Moses nor the high priest who entered the Most Holy. (Joh 1:18; Ex 33:20) When King Solomon inaugurated the temple at Jerusalem, the cloud of "the glory of Jehovah" filled the house. Solomon spoke of Jehovah as 'residing in the temple.' Nevertheless, Solomon himself stated: "But will God truly dwell upon the earth? Look! The heavens, yes, the heaven of the heavens, themselves cannot contain you; how much less, then, this house that I have built!" However, God's eyes would be opened continually toward that house and prayers that were made there would be heard by him "at the place of [his] dwelling, in the heavens."—1Ki 8:10-13, 27-30; compare Ac 7:45-50.

These accounts illustrate God's power to 'be present' on earth in a spiritual (hence, invisible) way while He yet remains in heaven. His presence might in some cases be by means of an angelic representative who acted and spoke for God, even saying, "I am the God of your father," as did the angel in the flaming bush who spoke to Moses. (Ex 3:2-8; compare Ex 23:20; 32:34.) So, too, Jehovah told Moses that he was "coming" to him at Mount Sinai and would "come down" there (Ex 19:9, 11, 18, 20), yet the apostolic writings show that it was actually by his angels that God was there present and delivered to Moses his covenant.—Ga 3:19; Heb 2:2; see FACE.

Since Jehovah's resurrected Son Jesus Christ was granted 'all authority in heaven and on the earth,' and is "the exact representation of [God's] very being," it follows that he should also be able to be invisibly present in a similar manner. (Mt 28:18; Heb 1:2, 3) In this regard we may note that, even when on earth, Jesus Christ was able to effect healings of persons from a distance, just as though he were there personally present.—Mt 8:5-13; Joh 4:46-53.

It is also clear that Jehovah God has placed angels subject to his glorified Son's command. (1Pe 3:22) Texts relating to Jesus' presence regularly describe him as 'accompanied' by angelic hosts or as 'sending them forth.' (Mt 13:37-41, 47-49; 16: 27; 24:31; Mr 8:38; 2Th 1:7) This does not mean, however, that his foretold presence in Kingdom power and glory consists solely of using angelic messengers or deputies on earthly missions, for this was being done already back in the first century C.E. in connection with the apostles and others. (Ac 5:19; 8:26; 10:3, 7, 22; 12:7-11, 23; 27:23) Jesus' parables and other texts show that his presence is like that of a master returning to his household and that of a man receiving kingship who returns to take control of his domain, and that Jesus' presence means a personal inspection and judgment followed by the active expression or execution of that judgment and the giving of reward to those found approved. (Mt 24:43-51; 25:14-45; Lu 19:11-27; compare Mt 19:28, 29.) Since Jesus' kingship includes the whole earth, his presence is a global one (compare Mt 24:23-27, 30) and Paul's inspired words at 1 Corinthians 15:24-28, as well as references to Christ's reign in Revelation (5:8-10; 7:17; 19:11-16; 20:1-6; 21:1-4, 9, 10, 22-27), imply that Christ's presence is the time for him to direct his full attention to the whole earth and its population, bringing the full force of his kingly power to bear so as to accomplish his Father's will for the earth and its inhabitants.—Compare Mt 6:9, 10.

Some, on the basis of texts speaking of Jesus' being seen "coming in clouds with great power and glory" (Mr 13:26; Re 1:7), conclude that his presence must be a visible one. Yet, as shown under the heading CLOUD (Illustrative Usage), the use of clouds in connection with other divine manifestations suggests invisibility rather than visibility. So, too, 'seeing' can refer to figurative sight, perception with the mind and heart. (Isa 44:18; Jer 5:21; Eze 12:2, 3; Mt 13:13-16; Eph 1:17, 18) To deny this would be to deny that the opposite of sight, namely, blindness, could be used in a figurative or spiritual, rather than literal, sense. Yet Jesus clearly used both sight and blindness in such a figurative or spiritual sense. (Joh 9:39-41; Re 3:14-18; compare also 2Co 4:4; 2Pe 1:9.) Job, being spoken to by Jehovah "out of the windstorm" (likely accompanied by clouds), afterward said: "In heresay I have heard about you, but now my own eye does see you." (Job 38:1; 42:5) This, too, must have been by perception of mind and heart rather than the literal eye, in view of the clear Scriptural teaching that "no man has seen God at any time."—Joh 1:18; 5:37; 6:46; 1Jo 4:12.

Evidence weighing against Jesus' presence as being a visible one (in the sense of Jesus' appearing in a bodily form that could be seen by human eyes) is found in Jesus' own statement that by his death he would sacrifice his flesh in behalf of the life of the world (Joh 6:51) and in the apostle Paul's declaration that the resurrected Jesus "dwells in unapproachable light, whom not one of men has seen or can see." (1Ti 6:14-16) Jesus therefore could tell his disciples that "a little longer and the world will behold me no more." True, his disciples would behold him, not only because he would appear to them after his resurrection but also because in due time they would be resurrected to join him in the heavens and 'behold the glory that his Father had given him.' (Joh 14:19; 17:24) But the world in general would not behold him because after his resurrection to life as a spirit creature (1Pe 3:18), Jesus restricted his appearances to his disciples. His ascension to heaven was also seen only by them, not by the world, and the angels present assured the disciples that Jesus' return would be in "the same manner" (Gr., tro'pos, not mor·phe', "form"), hence without public display, discerned only by his faithful followers. —Ac 1:1-11.

A bad condition of heart coupled with wrong expectations regarding Christ's presence no doubt contributes to the attitude of ridiculers. It was foretold that, in "the last days," they would scoff, saying: "Where is this promised presence of his? Why, from the day our forefathers fell asleep in death, all things are continuing exactly as from creation's beginning."—2Pe 3:2-4; compare 1:16.

Clearly, men will be aware of what is taking place at "the revelation" (Gr., a·po·ka'ly·psis) of Jesus Christ "with his powerful angels in a flaming fire, as he brings vengeance upon those who do not know God and those who do not obey the good news about our Lord Jesus." (2Th 1:7-9) This, however, still allows for an invisible presence that goes undiscerned by all but the faithful prior to that revelation. We may recall that Jesus, when paralleling his presence with "the days of Noah," states that in Noah's time the people "took no note" until watery destruction came upon them, and "so the presence of the Son of man will be."—Mt 24:37-39.

Events marking his presence. Jesus had promised to be with his followers in their meeting together (Mt 18:20), and he also assured them that he would be 'with them' in their discipling work "all the days until the conclusion of the system of things." (Mt 28:19, 20) The *pa·rou·si'a* of Matthew 24:3 and related texts, of course, must signify something beyond this. It clearly relates to a special presence, one involving and affecting all earth's inhabitants and inseparably connected with Jesus' expression of full authority as King anointed by God.

Among the events marking Jesus' presence in Kingdom power are: The resurrection of those of his followers who have died, these being joint heirs with him to the heavenly Kingdom (1Co 15:23; Ro 8:17); his gathering together and bringing into union with himself other followers who are living at the time of his presence (Mt 24:31; 2Th 2:1); his 'bringing to nothing' the apostate "man of lawlessness," this being accomplished "by the manifestation [*e·pi·pha·nei'ai*] of his [Jesus'] presence" (2Th 2:3-8; see MAN OF LAWLESSNESS); the destruction of all those who give no heed to the opportunity for deliverance (Mt 24:37-39); and, of necessity, the introduction of his Thousand Year Reign (Re 20:1-6). See also the article TRANSFIGURATION for information on the way in which observers of that vision of Christ in Kingdom glory were enabled to acquaint others with "the power and presence of our Lord Jesus Christ."—2Pe 1:16-18.

Conditions accompanying his presence. The book of Revelation presents in symbolic expression much information relating to Christ's presence and his manifestation and revelation. The symbolic picture of the crowned rider on the white horse depicted in Revelation 6:1, 2 corresponds to that of the rider of Revelation 19:11-16, who is the "King of kings and Lord of lords," Christ Jesus. Revelation chapter 6 shows that when Christ rides forth as conquering King he does not immediately bring about removal of wickedness from the earth, but rather, his ride is accompanied by war that takes "peace away from the earth," as well as by food scarcity and deadly plague. (Re 6:3-8) This, in turn, parallels features found in Christ's prophecy at Matthew 24, Mark 13, and Luke 21. It therefore appears that Jesus' prophecy found in the Gospel accounts, which clearly involves the destruction of Jerusalem and its temple (occurring in 70 C.E.), also has an application to the time of Christ's presence, thereby supplying a "sign" that allows for determining when that presence is taking place and when "deliverance is getting near."—Mt 24:3, 32, 33; Lu 21:28-31.

Other references to Christ's presence generally present encouragement to faithfulness and endurance until and during that time.—1Th 2:19; 3:12, 13; 5:23; Jas 5:7, 8; 1Jo 2:28.

The Presence of the Day of Jehovah. In his second letter Peter exhorts his brothers to be "awaiting and keeping close in mind the presence of the day of Jehovah," demonstrating this by the way they live. (2Pe 3:11, 12) They must be careful to keep Jehovah's day of judgment constantly in mind, realizing that it is close at hand. In that "day of Jehovah," the governmental "heavens" of this wicked world will be destroyed as by fire and the "elements" that go with it will not be able to hold together but will melt because of the intense heat. The present system under the control of Satan will come to its end.

Since Jehovah God acts by and through his Son and appointed King, Christ Jesus (Joh 3:35; compare 1Co 15:23, 24), it follows that there is a relationship between this promised "presence" of Jehovah and the "presence" of Christ Jesus. Logically, those who scoff at the proclamation of the one will scoff at the proclamation of the other. Again the attitude of the people prior to the Deluge is used as a corresponding example.—2Pe 3:5-7; compare Mt 24:37-39.

The Lawless One's Presence. At 2 Thessalonians 2:9-12 the apostle describes "the lawless one's presence" as being "according to the operation of Satan with every powerful work and lying signs and portents and with every unrighteous deception." This, too, illustrates the point that *pa·rou·si'a* means more than a momentary coming, or arrival, for a period of time of some length is required for the effecting of all these works, signs, portents, and this deception.

PRESENTS. See GIFTS, PRESENTS.

PRESS. An apparatus used to apply pressure to fruit so that liquid is forced out. Since the harvest of olives came after that of grapes, the same presses were often used for extracting both grape juice and olive oil, although there was also a pillar type of press used for olives.

Common presses usually consisted of two shallow sinklike cavities cut out of natural limestone, the one on a higher level connected by a small channel to the lower one. (Nu 18:27, 30; 2Ki 6:27) The grapes or olives were trodden or crushed in the upper basin (*gath*, Ne 13:15), allowing the juices to flow by gravity into the lower vat (*ye'qev*, Jg 7:25; Pr 3:10; Joe 2:24; Hag 2:16). In Joel 3:13 both terms occur: "Come, descend, for the winepress [*gath*] has become full. The press vats [*ha·yeqa·vim'*, plural of *ye'qev*] actually overflow." Apparently the term *ye'qev* was also used in reference to single-basin presses, in which both the treading of the grapes and the collecting of the juice took place. (Job 24:11; Isa 5:2; 16:10; Jer 48:33) The bottoms of these presses were more on an incline than the conventional two-basin type, to allow for the collecting of the juice at the lower end. If the press was long and narrow, like a trough, it was called pu·rah'. (Isa 63:3; Hag 2:16) The Christian Greek Scriptures also speak of the winepress (le·nos', Mt 21:33), as well as the "vat for the winepress" (hy·po·le'ni·on, Mr 12:1).

One such winepress was found, the upper basin of which measured 2.4 m (8 ft) square and 38 cm (15 in.) deep. The smaller vat, some 0.6 m (2 ft) lower in elevation, into which the juice ran, was 1.2 m (4 ft) square and 0.9 m (3 ft) deep. Such a winepress served Gideon as a place in which to thresh his wheat.—Jg 6:11.

Crushing the fruit in these presses was usually done by bare feet or by heavy stones. From two to seven or more treaders worked as a team in the press. It was therefore noteworthy that Isaiah said the Great Treader, Jehovah, will tread the wine trough *alone.* (Isa 63:3) Above the heads of the treaders was a crossbeam from which ropes extended for the men to hold on to for support. The splashing of "the blood of grapes" stained the upper garments of the treaders. (Ge 49:11; Isa 63:2) Although it meant plenty of hard work, the crushing season was usually a time of rejoicing; joyful shouting and singing helped to keep rhythm in the treading. (Jg 9:27; Jer 25:30; 48:33) The expression "upon the Gittith" (rendered "winepresses" in the Greek *Septuagint* and the Latin *Vulgate*) appearing in the superscription of three Psalms (8, 81, 84) may indicate that they were songs associated with the vintage.

Figurative Use. There are a number of Scriptural instances where the winepress is referred to in a figurative sense. (Isa 63:2, 3; La 1:15) In the day of Jehovah when crowds are assembled in the low plain of decision, the command goes forth: "Thrust in a sickle, for harvest has grown ripe. Come, descend, for the winepress has become full. The press vats actually overflow; for their badness has become abundant." (Joe 3:13, 14) Similarly, John saw in vision "the vine of the earth" hurled "into the great winepress of the anger of God," there trodden until the "blood came out of the winepress as high up as the bridles of the horses." The one called "Faithful and True," "The Word of God," is the one who treads this winepress of the "anger of the wrath of God the Almighty."—Re 14:19, 20; 19:11-16.

PRESUMPTUOUSNESS. The taking upon oneself of more than what right or propriety warrants, or without authority; impertinent boldness in conduct or thought; the taking of undue liberties; the undertaking of something in rash defiance. The word is related to haughtiness, arrogance, pride, and forwardness. Its antonyms are meekness and modesty.

Pride and Anger Bring Presumptuousness. The Hebrew word za·dhohn', rendered "presumptuousness," is derived from the verb zidh, meaning "boil up, become heated." (Ge 25:29; Ex 21:14) The heat of anger or pride can cause one to act rashly, to become unwarrantedly bold, and to overstep one's rights. The proverb says: "Presumptuous, self-assuming braggart is the name of the one who is acting in a fury of presumptuousness." (Pr 21:24) At Deuteronomy 1:43 the verb form is used in describing the action of the people of Israel in disobeying God's command and running ahead without authorization. Moses said to them: "So I spoke to you, and you did not listen but began to behave rebelliously against Jehovah's order and *to get all heated up,* and you tried to go up into the mountain." Another Hebrew word, 'a·phal', is employed in the account of the same incident at Numbers 14:40-44: "Moses said: '. . . Do not go up, because Jehovah is not in your midst . . . ' However, they *presumed* to go up to the top of the mountain," where they met defeat at the hands of the inhabitants. They were 'swelled up' with false confidence.—Compare Hab 2:4.

The fact that anger can bring destructive presumptuousness and gross violation of God's law is also shown in God's command to Israel: "In case a man *becomes heated* [form of zidh] against his fellow to the point of killing him with craftiness, you are to take him even from being at my altar to die."—Ex 21:14.

To Be Carefully Guarded Against. King David, who was granted many favors and great authority by God, realized that, nonetheless, he could be guilty of presumptuousness. He prayed: "Mistakes—who can discern? From concealed sins pronounce me innocent. Also from presumptuous acts hold your servant back; do not let them dominate me. In that case I shall be complete, and I shall have remained innocent from much transgression." (Ps 19:12, 13) The danger is great, therefore, and something to be closely guarded against. A presumptuous act is a much more serious sin than a mistake. Whether one is in a high position or a low one, the taking of liberties is a detestable thing in God's sight. Uzziah, though a mighty king who had experienced God's blessings, was struck with leprosy for presumptuously taking priestly duties into his own hands. (2Ch

26:16-21) Presumptuousness prompted King Saul into rebellion against Jehovah. Not willing to wait for Samuel's arrival, Saul took it upon himself to offer sacrifice. (1Sa 13:8-14) He also used his own judgment in sparing Amalekite King Agag and the best of the spoil, when Jehovah's command had been to devote the Amalekites to destruction. For his presumptuous course Saul was rejected as king.—1Sa 15:8, 9, 11, 18, 19.

A notable example of presumption on the part of a nonroyal Israelite is that of Uzzah. The ark of the covenant was being transported to Jerusalem in a cattle-drawn cart, contrary to the divinely outlined procedure. When the cattle nearly caused an upset, Uzzah reached out and grabbed hold of the Ark to steady it. For this irreverent presumption Jehovah struck him, and he died.—2Sa 6:6, 7.

A person not sure of what action he should take on a matter, or not certain if it is within his authority to do a certain thing, should by all means first consult others who have knowledge and discernment. The Scriptures counsel: "By presumptuousness one only causes a struggle, but with those consulting together there is wisdom." (Pr 13:10) Presumptuousness leads to disastrous results; modesty will save a person. The wise man says: "Has presumptuousness come? Then dishonor will come; but wisdom is with the modest ones."—Pr 11:2.

Disrespect for God's Sovereignty. When a person acts presumptuously toward God he is showing disrespect for Jehovah's sovereignty and Godship. Those claiming to be his servants and misrepresenting him are most reprehensible. Of the false prophets, Jehovah said: "The prophet who *presumes* to speak in my name a word that I have not commanded him to speak . . . that prophet must die. . . . When the prophet speaks in the name of Jehovah and the word does not occur or come true, . . . with *presumptuousness* the prophet spoke it."—De 18:20-22.

Also, disrespect for Jehovah is shown by disrespect for his appointed servants, which can be caused by presumptuousness. In Israel, difficult cases were brought to 'the place Jehovah chose' (which, from David's day onward, was Jerusalem). Anyone who flouted the judgment rendered was to be put to death, for in standing up against God's representatives he was acting in defiance of God. The law read: "In accordance with the law that they will point out to you, and according to the judicial decision that they will say to you, you should do. . . . And the man who will *behave with presumptuousness* in not listening to the priest who is standing to minister there to Jehovah your

God or to the judge, that man must die; and you must clear out what is bad from Israel. And all the people will hear and become afraid, and they will not act presumptuously anymore." (De 17:8-13; compare Nu 15:30.) The apostle Peter speaks of some who show great disrespect for God and his anointed servants, describing them as "daring [from Greek *tol·me·tes'*, "presumptuous," *KJ*], self-willed, they do not tremble at glorious ones but speak abusively." Such men, Peter says, "suffer destruction in their own course of destruction."—2Pe 2:10, 12.

Presuming on fleshly connections can be a snare. John the Baptizer discerned the Jews' thinking when they approached him. He warned them: "Do not presume to say to yourselves, 'As a father we have Abraham.' For I say to you that God is able to raise up children to Abraham from these stones." (Mt 3:9) The Greek word here rendered "presume" is *do·xe·te*, from *do·ke'o*, which, basically, means "think; form an opinion (right or wrong)."

Presumptuousness to End. Ancient Babylon was a prototype of presumptuousness against God, for which God's everlasting enmity was against her. The prophet Jeremiah said to her: "'Look! I am against you, O Presumptuousness,' is the utterance of the Sovereign Lord. . . . Presumptuousness will certainly stumble and fall." (Jer 50:29, 31, 32) Symbolic Babylon the Great has proved to be God's bitter and most presumptuous enemy on earth; she makes the inhabitants of the earth drunk "with the wine of her fornication" and is responsible for "the blood of prophets and of holy ones and of all those who have been slaughtered on the earth." For this she will suffer everlasting destruction. (Re 17:2, 5; 18:7, 8, 20, 24) This is in harmony with Jehovah's promise to bring an end to all Babylonish presumptuousness: "I shall actually cause the pride of the presumptuous ones to cease, and the haughtiness of the tyrants I shall abase."—Isa 13:11.

PRIDE. Inordinate self-esteem; an unreasonable feeling of superiority as to one's talents, beauty, wealth, rank, and so forth; disdainful behavior or treatment; insolence or arrogance of demeanor; haughty bearing. Pride can, more rarely, have the good connotation of a sense of delight or elation arising from some act or possession. Some synonyms of pride are egotism, arrogance, haughtiness.

The Hebrew verb *ga·'ah'* literally means "grow tall; get high" and is the root of a number of Hebrew words conveying the idea of pride. These related forms are rendered "haughtiness," "self-exaltation," and, in both good and bad senses, "eminence," and "superiority."—Job 8:11; Eze 47:5; Isa 9:9; Pr 8:13; Ps 68:34; Am 8:7.

The Greek word *kau·kha'o·mai*, meaning "boast, take pride, exult," likewise is used in both a good and a bad sense, the usage being determined by the context.—1Co 1:29; Ro 2:17; 5:2.

Pride Is Deceptive and Destructive. The proud person may not recognize that he is proud and may attribute his actions to other causes in order to avoid facing the fact of his pride. Each person should examine himself and his motives thoroughly to determine whether he has this bad trait. The apostle Paul shows the need for the right motive, and the knowledge a person should have of himself in this respect, when he says: "If I give all my belongings to feed others, and if I hand over my body, that I may boast [*kau·khe'so·mai*], but do not have love, I am not profited at all." —1Co 13:3.

Pride should therefore be rooted out of one's personality for one's own benefit. More important, it must be done if a person hopes to please God. One must even come to hate it, for God's Word says: "The fear of Jehovah means the hating of bad. Self-exaltation and pride and the bad way and the perverse mouth I have hated."—Pr 8:13.

The individual who does not get rid of his pride will suffer. "Pride is before a crash, and a haughty spirit before stumbling" (Pr 16:18), and "the house of the self-exalted ones Jehovah will tear down." (Pr 15:25) There are a number of examples of the crash that proud individuals, dynasties, and nations have suffered.—Le 26:18, 19; 2Ch 26:16; Isa 13:19; Jer 13:9; Eze 30:6, 18; 32:12; Da 5:22, 23, 30.

Pride is deceptive. The apostle Paul counsels: "If anyone thinks he is something when he is nothing, he is deceiving his own mind." (Ga 6:3) The proud person seems to be taking the way most beneficial or profitable for him, but he is leaving God out of account. (Compare Jer 49:16; Re 3:17.) The Bible says: "Better is it to be lowly in spirit with the meek ones than to divide spoil with the self-exalted ones."—Pr 16:19.

Boasting. The Greek verb *kau·kha'o·mai* (boast) is used frequently in the sense of selfish pride. The Bible shows that no man has any ground for boasting in himself or his accomplishments. In the Christian congregation at Corinth, some were puffed up with pride in themselves or in other men, bringing about divisions in the congregation. They were thinking in a fleshly way, looking to men instead of to Christ. (1Co 1:10-13; 3:3, 4) These men were not interested in the congregation's spiritual welfare, but they wanted to boast in outward appearances, not really wanting to help fellow Christians develop good hearts before God. (2Co 5:12) Consequently, the apostle Paul severely reproved the congregation, showing that there was no room for them to be boasting in anyone but Jehovah God and what he had done for them. (1Co 1:28, 29; 4:6, 7) The rule was: "He that boasts, let him boast in Jehovah."—1Co 1:31; 2Co 10:17.

Jesus' half brother James went even further in condemning those who boasted about certain worldly projects they were intending to carry out, telling them: "You take pride in your self-assuming brags. All such taking of pride is *wicked.*"—Jas 4:13-16; compare Pr 27:1.

A Good Connotation. The Hebrew word *ga-'ah'*, the Greek word *kau·kha'o·mai*, and their related forms are also used in a favorable sense with reference to pride or delight that arises from an action or possession. The psalmist spoke of Israel as "the pride of Jacob, whom [Jehovah] has loved." (Ps 47:4) In a restoration prophecy Isaiah said that the fruitage of the land would be "something to be proud of." (Isa 4:2) The apostle told the Thessalonian congregation that, as a result of their faith, love, and endurance, "we ourselves take pride in you among the congregations of God." (2Th 1:3, 4) Christians are proud that Jehovah is their God, that they have come to know him, and that he has recognized them. They follow the principle: "Let the one bragging about himself brag about himself because of this very thing, the having of insight and the having of knowledge of me, that I am Jehovah, the One exercising loving-kindness, justice and righteousness in the earth."—Jer 9:24; compare Lu 10:20.

PRIEST. Among true worshipers of Jehovah before the formation of the Christian congregation, priests officially represented God to the people they served, instructing them about God and his laws. In turn, they represented the people before God, offering sacrifices as well as interceding and pleading for the people. Hebrews 5:1 explains: "Every high priest taken from among men is appointed in behalf of men over the things pertaining to God, that he may offer gifts and sacrifices for sins." The Hebrew term translated "priest" is *ko·hen'*; the Greek, *hi·e·reus'*.

In Early Times. In patriarchal times the family head served as priest for his family, the duty passing to the firstborn son in the event of the father's death. Thus, in very early times we find Noah representing his family in a priestly capacity. (Ge 8:20, 21) The family head Abraham had a large household with which he traveled from place to place, building altars and making sacrifices to

Jehovah at his various places of encampment. (Ge 14:14; 12:7, 8; 13:4) God said of Abraham: "I have become acquainted with him in order that he may command his sons and his household after him so that they shall keep Jehovah's way to do righteousness and judgment." (Ge 18:19) Isaac and Jacob followed the same pattern (Ge 26:25; 31:54; 35:1-7, 14), and Job, a non-Israelite but likely a distant relative of Abraham, regularly offered sacrifices to Jehovah in behalf of his children, saying: "Maybe my sons have sinned and have cursed God in their heart." (Job 1:4, 5; see also 42:8.) However, the Bible does not specifically call these men *ko·hen'* or *hi·e·reus'*. On the other hand, Jethro, the family head and the father-in-law of Moses, is called a "priest [*ko·hen'*] of Midian."—Ex 2:16; 3:1; 18:1.

Melchizedek king of Salem was a priest (*ko·hen'*) extraordinary. The Bible gives no record of his ancestry, his birth, or his death. His priesthood was not by inheritance, and he had no predecessors or successors in office. Melchizedek held both the office of king and of priest. His priesthood was greater than the Levitical priesthood, for Levi, in effect, paid tithes to Melchizedek, since he was still in the loins of Abraham when Abraham offered tithes to Melchizedek and was blessed by him. (Ge 14:18-20; Heb 7:4-10) In these things Melchizedek foreshadowed Jesus Christ, the "priest forever according to the manner of Melchizedek."—Heb 7:17.

Evidently the family heads acted as priests among the offspring of Jacob (Israel) until the Levitical priesthood was established by God. Hence, when God led the people to Mount Sinai he commanded: "Let the priests also who regularly come near to Jehovah sanctify themselves, that Jehovah may not break out upon them." (Ex 19: 22) This was before the Levitical priesthood was established. But Aaron, though not yet designated as priest, was allowed to go partially up the mountain with Moses. This circumstance harmonized with the later appointment of Aaron and his posterity as priests. (Ex 19:24) Seen in retrospect, this was an early indication that God had in mind a superseding of the old arrangement (of family-head priesthood) by means of a priesthood of Aaron's house.

Under the Law Covenant. When the Israelites were in slavery in Egypt, Jehovah sanctified to himself every firstborn son of Israel at the time that he destroyed Egypt's firstborn in the tenth plague. (Ex 12:29; Nu 3:13) These firstborn ones accordingly belonged to Jehovah, to be used exclusively in special service to him. God could have designated all of these firstborn males of Israel as the priests and caretakers of the sanctuary. Instead, it suited his purpose to take male members of the tribe of Levi for this service. For this reason he permitted the nation to substitute the Levite males for the firstborn males of the other 12 tribes (the offspring of Joseph's sons Ephraim and Manasseh being counted as two tribes). In a census there proved to be 273 more firstborn non-Levite sons from a month old and upward than there were Levite males, so God required a ransom price of five shekels ($11) for each of the 273, the money being turned over to Aaron and his sons. (Nu 3:11-16, 40-51) Prior to this transaction Jehovah had already set apart the male members of the family of Aaron of the tribe of Levi as constituting the priesthood of Israel.—Nu 1:1; 3:6-10.

For a long period of time Israel had the exclusive opportunity to supply the members of "a kingdom of priests and a holy nation." (Ex 19:6) But that opportunity ceased to be exclusively theirs because of the national rejection of God's Son. —Compare Mt 21:43; 1Pe 2:7-10.

Initially, Israel's King was Jehovah. Later Jehovah directed that the kingship be vested in the line of David. Jehovah was still their invisible King but used the Davidic line as his representatives, as to secular rulership. As such, these earthly kings were said to sit on "Jehovah's throne." (1Ch 29:23) But the priesthood was still kept separate, in the line of Aaron. Therefore to that nation alone belonged both the kingdom and the priesthood of Jehovah God with its "sacred service."—Ro 9:3, 4.

Inauguration of the priesthood. The appointment of a priest must come from God; a man does not take the office of his own accord. (Heb 5:4) Accordingly, Jehovah himself appointed Aaron and his house to the priesthood "to time indefinite," separating them from the family of the Kohathites, one of the three main divisions of the tribe of Levi. (Ex 6:16; 28:43) First, however, Moses the Levite, as mediator of the Law covenant, represented God in the sanctification of Aaron and his sons and the filling of their hands with power to serve as priests, the procedure being described at Exodus chapter 29 and Leviticus chapter 8. Their installation apparently occupied the seven-day period of Nisan 1-7, 1512 B.C.E. (See INSTALLATION.) The newly installed priesthood began their services toward Israel the next day, Nisan 8.

Qualifications. Jehovah laid down the qualifications for those of Aaron's family line who would serve at God's altar. To be a priest, a man had be physically sound and of normal appea·

Otherwise he could not approach the altar with offerings and he could not come near to the curtain between the Holy and Most Holy compartments of the tabernacle. Such a one was entitled, however, to receive support from the tithe and could partake of "the holy things" provided as food for the priesthood.—Le 21:16-23.

The age for entering upon the priesthood is not specifically stated, although the census of the Kohathites, taken at Mount Sinai, included those from 30 to 50 years old. (Nu 4:3) The service of the Levites at the sanctuary began at age 25 (reduced in King David's time to 20). (Nu 8:24; 1Ch 23:24) Retirement of nonpriestly Levites from obligatory service at the sanctuary was at 50 years, but there was no retirement provided for priests.—Nu 8:25, 26; see RETIREMENT.

Maintenance. The tribe of Levi was not given a block of land as an inheritance, but they were 'scattered in Israel,' receiving 48 cities in which to live with their families and cattle. Thirteen of these cities went to the priests. (Ge 49:5, 7; Jos 21:1-11) One of the cities of refuge, Hebron, was a priestly city. (Jos 21:13) The Levites received no region as a tribal inheritance because, as Jehovah said, "I am your share and your inheritance in the midst of the sons of Israel." (Nu 18:20) The Levites did the assigned work of their ministry and maintained their houses and the pasture grounds of the cities allotted to them. They would also care for other land that the Israelites might devote to sanctuary use. (Le 27:21, 28) Jehovah provided for the Levites by arranging for them to receive a tithe of all the produce of the land from the other 12 tribes. (Nu 18:21-24) Of this tithe, or tenth, the Levites were, in turn, to give a tenth of the very best as a tithe to the priesthood. (Nu 18:25-29; Ne 10:38, 39) The priesthood would thereby receive 1 percent of the national produce, enabling them to devote all their time to their assigned service of God.

This provision for the priesthood, though abundant, was in contrast to the luxury and financial power attained by the priesthood of pagan nations. In Egypt, for example, the priests *owned* portions of the land (Ge 47:22, 26) and by crafty maneuvering eventually were the richest and most powerful men in Egypt. James H. Breasted, in *A History of the Ancient Egyptians* (1908, pp. 355, 356, 431, 432), records that during the so-called Twentieth Dynasty the Pharaoh was reduced to a mere puppet. The priesthood had possession of the Nubian gold country and the great province of the Upper Nile. The high priest was the most important fiscal officer of the state, next to the chief treasurer himself. He commanded all the armies and held the treasury in his hands. He is represented more prominently in the monuments than the Pharaoh.

It was only when Israel became lax in their worship and negligent in paying their tithes that the priesthood suffered, along with nonpriestly Levites, who had to look for other work to provide for themselves and their families. In turn, this bad attitude toward the sanctuary and its maintenance caused the nation to suffer still further for lack of spirituality and knowledge of Jehovah. —Ne 13:10-13; see also Mal 3:8-10.

The priesthood received: (1) The regular tithe. (2) The redemption money for a firstborn male child or beast. In the case of a firstborn bull, male lamb, or goat, they received the flesh for food. (Nu 18:14-19) (3) The redemption money for men and things sanctified as holy and also the things devoted to Jehovah. (Le 27) (4) Certain parts of the various offerings brought by the people, as well as the showbread. (Le 6:25, 26, 29; 7:6-10; Nu 18:8-14) (5) Benefit from the offerings of the best of the first ripe fruits of grain, wine, and oil. (Ex 23:19; Le 2:14-16; 22:10 ["stranger" in the latter text means one not a priest]; De 14:22-27; 26:1-10) Except for certain specified portions that only the priests could eat (Le 6:29), their sons and daughters and, in some cases, the priest's household—even slaves—could lawfully share. (Le 10: 14; 22:10-13) (6) No doubt a share in the third-year tithe for the Levites and the poor. (De 14: 28, 29; 26:12) (7) The booty taken in war.—Nu 31:26-30.

Dress. In performing their official duties, the priests served barefoot, in harmony with the fact that the sanctuary was holy ground. (Compare Ex 3:5.) In the instructions for making the special garments for the priests, sandals were not mentioned. (Ex 28:1-43) They wore linen drawers extending from the hips to the thighs for moral propriety, "to cover the naked flesh . . . that they [might] not incur error and certainly die." (Ex 28:42, 43) Over this they wore a fine linen robe tied about the body by a linen sash. Their headgear was "wrapped" upon them. (Le 8:13; Ex 28: 40; 39:27-29) This headdress seems to have been somewhat different from the turban of the high priest, which may have been sewn into a wraparound form and set on the high priest's head. (Le 8:9) It appears that it was in later times that the underpriests on occasion wore ephods of linen, though these were not richly embroidered as was the ephod of the high priest.—Compare 1Sa 2:18.

Regulations and functions. The priests were required to maintain personal fleshly cleanliness and high moral standards. When entering the tent of meeting and before presenting an offering at the altar, they were to wash their hands and feet at the basin in the courtyard "that they [might] not die." (Ex 30:17-21; 40:30-32) With similar warning they were commanded not to drink wine or intoxicating liquor when serving at the sanctuary. (Le 10:8-11) They could not defile themselves by touching a corpse or mourning for the dead; this would make them temporarily unclean for service. The underpriests (but not the high priest) might do so, however, for one in very close family relationship: mother, father, son, daughter, brother, or virgin sister who was close to (apparently, living with or near) him; also the wife was possibly included as one close to him. (Le 21:1-4) Any priest who became unclean, by leprosy, by a running discharge, or by a corpse or other unclean thing, could not eat of the holy things or perform sanctuary service until cleansed, otherwise he must die.—Le 22:1-9.

The priests were commanded not to shave their heads or the extremities of their beards, or to make cuttings in themselves, practices common among pagan priests. (Le 21:5, 6; 19:28; 1Ki 18:28) While the high priest could marry only a virgin girl, the underpriests could marry a widow, but not a divorced woman or a prostitute. (Le 21:7, 8; compare Le 21:10, 13, 14.) Evidently, all the members of the high priest's family were to uphold the high standard of morality and the dignity due the priest's office. Thus, a priest's daughter who became a prostitute was to be put to death, being burned afterward as something detestable to God.—Le 21:9.

When in the wilderness, at the time of moving camp, it was the duty of Aaron and his sons to cover the holy furniture and utensils in the tent of meeting before the other Kohathites were allowed to come in to carry them, so that the Kohathites would not die. Likewise they uncovered and set up these things in the tent at the new location. (Nu 4:5-15) On the march, the priests carried the ark of the covenant.—Jos 3:3, 13, 15, 17; 1Ki 8:3-6.

The priests were responsible for blowing the holy trumpets, thus giving definite leadership to the people, whether in the matter of setting up or breaking camp, assembling, engaging in battle, or celebrating some festival to Jehovah. (Nu 10:1-10) The priests and Levites were exempt from military conscription, though they did serve as blowers of the trumpets and singers before the army.—Nu 1:47-49; 2:33; Jos 6:4; 2Ch 13:12.

When the priests were on assignment at the sanctuary, their duties included the slaughtering of sacrifices brought by the people, sprinkling the blood on the altar, cutting up the sacrifices, keeping the altar fire burning, cooking the meat, and accepting all other offerings, such as the grain offerings. They were to take care of matters dealing with uncleannesses contracted by individuals, as well as their special vows, and so forth. (Le chaps 1-7; 12:6; chaps 13-15; Nu 6:1-21; Lu 2:22-24) They took care of the morning and evening burnt offerings and all other sacrifices regularly made at the sanctuary except those that it was the high priest's duty to offer; they burned incense on the golden altar. (Ex 29:38-42; Nu 28:1-10; 2Ch 13:10, 11) They trimmed the lamps and kept them supplied with oil (Ex 27:20, 21) and took care of the holy oil and the incense. (Nu 4:16) They blessed the people at the solemn assemblies in the manner outlined at Numbers 6:22-27. But no other priest could be in the sanctuary when the high priest went into the Most Holy to make atonement.—Le 16:17.

The priests were primarily the ones privileged to explain God's law, and they played a major role in Israel's judiciary. In the cities allotted to them the priests were available to assist the judges, and they also served with the judges in extraordinarily difficult cases beyond the ability of local courts to decide. (De 17:8, 9) They were required to be on hand along with the older men of the city in cases of unsolved murder, to assure that the proper procedure was followed to remove bloodguilt from the city. (De 21:1, 2, 5) If a jealous husband charged his wife with secret adultery, she had to be brought to the sanctuary, where the priest carried out the prescribed ceremony in which Jehovah's knowledge of the truth of the woman's innocence or guilt was appealed to for His direct judgment. (Nu 5:11-31) In all cases, judgment rendered by the priests or appointed judges was to be respected; deliberate disrespect or disobedience brought the death penalty.—Nu 15:30; De 17:10-13.

The priests were teachers of the Law to the people, reading and explaining it to those coming to the sanctuary to worship. Also, when not on assigned duty, they would have wide opportunity for such teaching, whether in the area of the sanctuary or in other parts of the land. (De 33:10; 2Ch 15:3; 17:7-9; Mal 2:7) Upon returning to Jerusalem from Babylon, Ezra the priest, assisted by other priests along with the Levites, gathered the people and spent hours reading and explaining the Law to them.—Ne 8:1-15.

The priestly administration served as a safeguard to the nation in religious cleanness as a physical health. The priest was to judge between the clean and the unclean in cases of leprosy of a man, a garment, or a house. He saw to it that the legal quarantine regulations were carried out. He also officiated in the cleansing of those who had been defiled by a dead body or were unclean from morbid discharges, and so forth.—Le 13-15.

How were the assignments of temple service for the priests in Israel determined?

Of the 24 divisions, or courses, of the priests established by King David, 16 were made up from the house of Eleazar and 8 from the house of Ithamar. (1Ch 24:1-19) However, at least initially, priests from only four of the divisions returned from the Babylonian exile. (Ezr 2:36-39) Some suggest that, in order to continue the former organizational arrangement, the four families returning were divided so that there were again 24 courses. Alfred Edersheim, in The Temple (1874, p. 63), suggests that this was accomplished by each family's drawing five lots for those who had not returned, thereby forming from their groups 20 more courses to which they gave the original names. John the Baptizer's father Zechariah was a priest of the eighth division, that of Abijah. However, if the above view represents the true case, he may not have been a descendant of Abijah—he may have merely belonged to the division which carried his name. (1Ch 24:10; Lu 1:5) Absence of full information does not allow for firm conclusions on these points.

In the temple service the priests were organized under various officers. Lots were drawn in assigning certain services. Each of the 24 divisions served one week at a time, being on assigned duty twice a year. Evidently the entire priesthood served at festival seasons when thousands of sacrifices were offered by the people, as they did at the temple dedication. (1Ch 24:1-18, 31; 2Ch 5:11; compare 2Ch 29:31-35; 30:23-25; 35:10-19.) A priest might serve at other times as long as he did not interfere with the allotted services of the priests on assigned duty. According to rabbinic traditions, in the time of Jesus' earthly life, the priests were numerous, so that the service of the week was subdivided among the various families making up the division, each family serving one or more days according to their number.

Probably considered the most honorable of the daily services was the burning of incense on the golden altar. This was done after the sacrifice was offered. During the burning of incense, the people would be gathered outside the sanctuary in prayer. Rabbinic tradition is that lots were drawn for this service but that one who had previously officiated was not allowed to participate unless all present had performed the service before. (The Temple, pp. 135, 137, 138) If this is so, a priest would usually have the honor only once in a lifetime. It was this service that Zechariah was performing when the angel Gabriel appeared to him to announce that Zechariah and his wife Elizabeth would have a son. When Zechariah came out of the sanctuary, the crowd gathered there could discern by his appearance and his inability to speak that Zechariah had seen a supernatural sight in the sanctuary; thus the event became public knowledge.—Lu 1:8-23.

Each Sabbath day, it appears, the priests had the privilege of changing the showbread. It was also on the Sabbath that the priestly division for that week completed its service and the new course began duty for the following week. These and other necessary duties were performed by the priests without constituting a breaking of the Sabbath.—Mt 12:2-5; compare 1Sa 21:6; 2Ki 11:5-7; 2Ch 23:8.

Loyalty. When the ten tribes broke away from the kingdom under Rehoboam and established the northern kingdom under Jeroboam, the tribe of Levi remained loyal and stuck with the two-tribe kingdom of Judah and Benjamin. Jeroboam appointed non-Levite men to be priests serving in the worship of golden calves, and he drove out the priests of Jehovah, the sons of Aaron. (1Ki 12:31, 32; 13:33; 2Ch 11:14; 13:9) Later on in Judah, although many of the priests became unfaithful to God, the priesthood at times exercised strong influence to keep Israel faithful to Jehovah. (2Ch 23:1, 16; 24:2, 16; 26:17-20; 34:14, 15; Zec 3:1; 6:11) By the time of the ministry of Jesus and the apostles, the high priesthood had become very corrupt, but there were many priests with good hearts toward Jehovah, as is evidenced by the fact that not long after Jesus' death "a great crowd of priests began to be obedient to the faith." —Ac 6:7.

Other applications of "priest." Moses was called a priest, at Psalm 99:6, because of his mediatorship and his being designated to perform the sanctification service at the sanctuary, in which Aaron and his sons were inducted into the priesthood. Moses interceded for Israel, calling upon Jehovah's name. (Nu 14:13-20) The word "priest" was also used occasionally to denote a "lieutenant" or "chief minister or official." In the list of the chief officers serving under King David the record reads: "As for the sons of David, they became priests."—2Sa 8:18; compare 2Sa 20:26; 1Ki 4:5; 1Ch 18:17.

The Christian Priesthood. Jehovah had promised that if Israel kept his covenant they would become to Him "a kingdom of priests and a holy nation." (Ex 19:6) However, the priesthood of Aaron's line was to continue only until the coming of the greater priesthood that it foreshadowed. (Heb 8:4, 5) It would endure until the ending of the Law covenant and the inauguration of the new covenant. (Heb 7:11-14; 8:6, 7, 13) The offer was first made exclusively to Israel to become Jehovah's priests serving in God's promised Kingdom arrangement; in time this offer was extended to the Gentiles.—Ac 10:34, 35; 15:14; Ro 10:21.

Only a remnant of the Jews accepted Christ, the nation thereby failing to provide the members of the *real* kingdom of priests and the holy nation. (Ro 11:7, 20) Because of Israel's unfaithfulness God had forewarned them of this by his prophet Hosea centuries before, saying: "Because the knowledge is what you yourself have rejected, I shall also reject you from serving as a priest to me; and because you keep forgetting the law of your God, I shall forget your sons, even I." (Ho 4:6) Correspondingly, Jesus told the Jewish leaders: "The kingdom of God will be taken from you and be given to a nation producing its fruits." (Mt 21:43) Nevertheless, Jesus Christ, being under the Law while on earth, recognized the Aaronic priesthood as being in force, and he directed ones whom he cured of leprosy to go to the priest and make the required offering.—Mt 8:4; Mr 1:44; Lu 17:14.

On Pentecost day of the year 33 C.E., the Law covenant came to an end and the "better covenant," the new covenant, was inaugurated. (Heb 8:6-9) On that day God made manifest this change by the outpouring of holy spirit. The apostle Peter then explained to the Jews present from many nations that their only salvation now lay in repentance and acceptance of Jesus Christ. (Ac 2; Heb 2:1-4) Later, Peter spoke of the Jewish builders rejecting Jesus Christ as the cornerstone and then said to Christians: "But you are 'a chosen race, a royal priesthood, a holy nation, a people for special possession.'"—1Pe 2:7-9.

Peter explained also that the new priesthood is "a spiritual house for the purpose of a holy priesthood, to offer up spiritual sacrifices acceptable to God through Jesus Christ." (1Pe 2:5) Jesus Christ is their great High Priest, and they, like Aaron's sons, make up the underpriesthood. (Heb 3:1; 8:1) Yet, different from the Aaronic priesthood, which had no part in kingship, kingship and priesthood

are combined in this "royal priesthood" of Christ and his joint heirs. In the Bible book of Revelation the apostle John speaks of the followers of Jesus Christ as "loosed . . . from our sins by means of his own blood" and says that he "made us to be a kingdom, priests to his God and Father."—Re 1:5, 6.

This last book of the Bible also reveals the number composing the body of underpriests. Those whom Jesus Christ made "to be a kingdom and priests to our God" are shown as singing a new song in which they say that they were bought by Christ's blood. (Re 5:9, 10) Further on, the ones singing the new song are enumerated as 144,000 persons "bought from among mankind as firstfruits to God and to the Lamb." (Re 14:1-5) Finally this underpriesthood is shown as being resurrected to heaven and joining Jesus Christ in his rule, becoming "priests of God and of the Christ" and ruling "as kings" with Christ during his Thousand Year Reign.—Re 20:4, 6.

By comparing the priesthood of Israel, as well as its functions and benefits to the people of that nation (Heb 8:5), we can get some idea of the benefits and blessings to be received by the people of earth from the perfect and everlasting priesthood of Jesus Christ and his body of underpriests during their joint reign over the earth for a thousand years. They will have the privilege of teaching the people the law of God (Mal 2:7), accomplishing complete forgiveness of sins on the basis of the ransom sacrifice of the great High Priest (administering the benefits of Christ's sacrifice) and bringing about the healing of all infirmities (Mr 2:9-12; Heb 9:12-14; 10:1-4, 10), distinguishing between what is clean and what is unclean in God's sight and removing all uncleanness (Le 13-15), judging the people in righteousness, and seeing that Jehovah's righteous law is enforced throughout the earth (De 17:8-13).

Just as the ancient tent of meeting in the wilderness was God's place of dwelling with men, a sanctuary where they could approach him, so during the thousand years God's tent will again be with mankind in a much closer, more lasting and beneficial way, as he deals with them representatively through his great High Priest, Jesus Christ, and the 144,000 who serve with Christ as underpriests in the great spiritual temple that was foreshadowed by that sacred tabernacle. (Ex 25:8; Heb 4:14; Re 1:6; 21:3) With such a royal priesthood the people will certainly be happy, as was Israel when the kingdom and priesthood were faithful to God, during which time "Judah and Israel were many, like the grains of sand that are by the sea for multitude, eating and drinking and rejoicing" and dwelling "in security, everyone under his own vine and under his own fig tree." —1Ki 4:20, 25.

Pagan Priests. The ancient nations had priests through whom they made approach to their gods. These men were reverenced by the people and always wielded great influence, generally being among the ruling class, or being close advisers to the rulers. The priesthood was the most educated class and generally held the people in ignorance. In this way they were able to prey on the superstition of the people and their fear of the unknown. In Egypt, for example, the people were led to worship the Nile River as a god, viewing their priests as possessing divine control over its seasonal overflow, on which their crops depended.

This encouragement of superstitious ignorance was in direct contrast to Israel's priests, who constantly read and taught the Law to the entire nation. Each man was to know God and his law. (De 6:1-3) The people themselves were able to read and write, being commanded by Jehovah to read and teach his law to their children.—De 6:4-9.

Not the pattern for Israel's priesthood. In spite of these facts, there are some who claim that the priesthood of Israel and the formulation of many of its regulations were patterned after those of Egypt. They argue that Moses, the mediator of the Law covenant, was deeply influenced by his life in Egypt, his training in the court of Pharaoh, and his instruction "in all the wisdom of the Egyptians." (Ac 7:22) Their line of argument, however, ignores the fact that Moses, though used to deliver the Law to Israel, was in no sense the lawmaker. Israel's Lawgiver was Jehovah God (Isa 33:22), who used angels to transmit the Law by the hand of the mediator Moses.—Ga 3:19.

Every detail of Israel's worship was outlined by God. The plans for the tent of meeting were given to Moses (Ex 26:30), and it is written that he was commanded: "See that you make all things after their pattern that was shown to you in the mountain." (Heb 8:5; Ex 25:40) All the service at the sanctuary was of Jehovah's origination and direction. The record repeatedly assures us of this by saying that Moses and the sons of Israel "kept doing according to all that Jehovah had commanded Moses. They did just so." "According to all that Jehovah had commanded Moses, that was the way the sons of Israel did all the service. And Moses got to see all the work, and, look! they had done it just as Jehovah had commanded. That was

the way they had done." "And Moses proceeded to do according to all that Jehovah had commanded him. He did just so."—Ex 39:32, 42, 43; 40:16.

According to Egyptologists, some things in the dress of the Egyptian priests was similar to that of the priests of Israel, such as their use of linen; there was a shaving of the bodies of the Egyptian priests, as with the Levites (though the priests of Israel did not; Nu 8:7); there were washings. But do these few similarities prove that they had the same origin, or that one came from the other? Similar materials and methods are used worldwide in making clothing, houses, and buildings and in performing daily duties, such as washing, but there is great divergence also in style and methods. We do not say that one came from the other, or that the dress or the act has the same religious or symbolic significance.

In most features of their dress and functions there was no similarity whatsoever between the Israelite and the Egyptian priests. For example, while the Israelite priests served barefoot, the Egyptian priests wore sandals. The robes of the Egyptian priests were entirely different in design, and their dress and appurtenances bore symbols of the worship of their false gods. They shaved their heads, which Israel's priests did not do (Le 21:5), and used wigs or wore headgear totally unlike that of Israel's priests, according to inscriptions found on monuments in Egypt. Furthermore, Jehovah made it clear that Israel was not to adopt any of the practices of Egypt or the other nations, either in worship or in judicial practice. —Le 18:1-4; De 6:14; 7:1-6.

The argument made by supporters of the theory that Israel's priesthood borrowed from Egypt has, therefore, no foundation. We must remember that the idea of sacrifice and priesthood came originally from God and, from the beginning, was expressed by faithful men such as Abel and Noah; in patriarchal society it was carried out by Abraham and others. All nations therefore had an inheritance of this knowledge, though it was distorted into many forms because they forsook the true God and pure worship. Having the inborn desire to worship but lacking the guidance of Jehovah, the pagan nations developed many unrighteous and even degrading rites, all of which brought them into opposition to true worship.

Disgusting practices of pagan priests. The Egyptian priests of Moses' day opposed Moses before Pharaoh, trying to discredit Moses and his God Jehovah by the practice of magic. (Ex 7:11-13, 22; 8:7; 2Ti 3:8) But they were forced to bow in defeat and humiliation. (Ex 8:18, 19; 9:11) The worshipers of Molech of Ammon sacrificed their sons and daughters by burning them in the fire. (1Ki 11:5; 2Ki 23:10; Le 18:21; 20:2-5) Baal worshipers of the Canaanites followed the same detestable practice, also performing self-laceration and lewd, disgusting, immoral rites. (Nu 25:1-3; 1Ki 18:25-28; Jer 19:5) The priests of the Philistine god Dagon and the Babylonian priests of Marduk, Bel, and Ishtar practiced magic and divination. (1Sa 6:2-9; Eze 21:21; Da 2:2, 27; 4:7, 9) All of them worshiped images made of wood, stone, and metal. Even King Jeroboam of the ten-tribe kingdom of Israel set up priests to direct the worship of golden calves and "goat-shaped demons" to prevent the people from engaging in true worship at Jerusalem.—2Ch 11:15; 13:9; see also MICAH No. 1.

Unauthorized priesthoods condemned by God. Jehovah was unalterably opposed to all these forms and practices, which actually constituted the worship of demons. (1Co 10:20; De 18:9-13; Isa 8:19; Re 22:15) Whenever these gods or the priesthood representing them came into open defiance of Jehovah they were humiliated. (1Sa 5:1-5; Da 2:2, 7-12, 29, 30; 5:15) Often their priests and prophets suffered death. (1Ki 18:40; 2Ki 10:19, 25-28; 11:18; 2Ch 23:17) And since Jehovah recognized no priesthood aside from that of the house of Aaron during the existence of the Law covenant, it follows that what Aaron's office foreshadowed, namely, the priesthood of Jesus Christ, who is also the greater High Priest according to the manner of Melchizedek, is the only way of approach to Jehovah. (Ac 4:12; Heb 4:14; 1Jo 2:1, 2) Any priesthood that opposes this God-ordained King-Priest and his underpriesthood is to be avoided by true worshipers of God.—De 18:18, 19; Ac 3:22, 23; Re 18:4, 24.

See HIGH PRIEST.

PRIESTS' CITIES.

Locations in the Promised Land that were set aside as places of residence for the Aaronic priests and their families. Of the 48 cities given to the tribe of Levi by Israel's other tribes, 13 were assigned to the Kohathite priests of Aaron's family. (Jos 21:1-42; 1Ch 6:54-81) The tribes of Judah and Simeon gave them nine cities and four were given by the tribe of Benjamin. Thus, "all the cities of the sons of Aaron, the priests, were thirteen cities and their pasture grounds." (Jos 21:4, 9-19) These cities were Hebron (a city of refuge), Libnah, Jattir, Eshtemoa, Holon (apparently Hilen), Debir, Ain (Ashan), Juttah, Beth-shemesh, Gibeon, Geba, Anathoth, and Almon (Alemeth), all except Juttah and Gibeon again being named at 1 Chronicles 6:54-60.

David sent word to priests in their various cities to gather together when he was about to bring the ark of Jehovah to Jerusalem. (1Ch 13:1-5) And specific reference is made to the appointment of men to distribute contributed portions to their priestly brothers residing in priests' cities during King Hezekiah's reign.—2Ch 31:11-19.

PRINCE.

See LEADER, NOBLE, PRINCE.

PRISCA

(Pris′ca) [Old Woman]; **PRISCILLA** (Pris·cil′la) [Little Old Woman]. The shorter form of the name is found in Paul's writings, the longer form in Luke's. Such a variation was common in Roman names.

Priscilla was the wife of Aquila, with whom she is always mentioned. The two showed fine Christian works and hospitality not only to individuals but also to the congregation by having congregation meetings in their home in both Rome and Ephesus.

Because of Emperor Claudius' decree, Aquila and his wife left Rome and went to Corinth in about 50 C.E. Not long after their arrival Paul joined them in tentmaking. (Ac 18:2, 3) They traveled on with Paul to Ephesus, remained there for a time, and were instrumental in 'expounding the way of God more correctly' to the eloquent Apollos. (Ac 18:18, 19, 24-28; 1Co 16:19) Returning to Rome for a time (Ro 16:3-5), they later traveled back to Ephesus. (2Ti 4:19; 1Ti 1:3) Their personal contact with Paul extended from about 50 C.E. to Paul's death, some 15 years later, during which association they "risked their own necks" for the apostle's soul.—Ro 16:3, 4; see AQUILA.

PRISON.

A place of confinement for one being held for trial or for one found guilty of lawbreaking. Various original-language expressions referring to a prison, or jail, have the following meanings: "house of roundness" (Ge 39:20; compare ftn), "house of the cistern" (Ex 12:29, ftn), "house of detention" (1Ki 22:27), "house of custody" (Ge 42:19; Jer 52:11), "house of the prisoners or those bound" (Jg 16:21; Ec 4:14), "house of the stocks" (2Ch 16:10), "place of bonds" (Mt 11:2), "place of guarding" (Mt 14:10), and "place of custody or observation" (Ac 5:18).

Among various ancient peoples, including the Egyptians, Philistines, Assyrians, Babylonians, and Persians, imprisonment was a form of legal punishment. (Ge 39:20; Jg 16:25; 2Ki 17:4; Ezr 7:26; Jer 52:31-33) Prisoners might be bound with fetters and forced to work at hard labor, such as grinding. (Jg 16:21; 2Ki 17:4; Ps 105:17, 18; Jer 52:11) In Egypt, a trusted prisoner (as was Joseph) might be placed in charge of other inmates and assigned to wait upon those who had held prominent positions before their confinement.—Ge 39: 21–40:4.

Prisons date back at least to the 18th century B.C.E., for it was then that Joseph was wrongly confined to the jail that was connected to "the house of the chief of the bodyguard." (Ge 39:20; 40:3; 41:10) This Egyptian jail apparently had a dungeon, or hole shaped like a cistern, where some prisoners were kept.—Ge 40:15; 41:14; compare Isa 24:22.

The Mosaic Law did not provide for prisons as a form of punishment. Since justice was to be executed swiftly (Jos 7:20, 22-25), only in cases requiring divine clarification do we read in the Pentateuch of individuals being committed into custody. (Le 24:12; Nu 15:34) Eventually, however, places of imprisonment came to be used by the Israelites. The prophet Jeremiah, for example, was held in "the house of fetters, in the house of Jehonathan." This place of confinement had "vaulted rooms," perhaps dungeon cells. Conditions were so bad there that Jeremiah feared for his life. (Jer 37:15-20) Subsequently he was transferred to "the Courtyard of the Guard," where he got a daily allowance of bread, could receive visitors, and was able to conduct business transactions.—Jer 32:2, 8, 12; 37:21; see also 1Ki 22:27; 2Ch 16:10; Heb 11:36.

In the first century C.E., according to Roman custom, the jailers or guards were held personally accountable for prisoners. (Ac 12:19) Therefore, the jailer in Philippi, believing that his prisoners had escaped, was ready to commit suicide. (Ac 16:27) For security measures guards were often stationed at prison doors, and prisoners might have their feet put in stocks or have their hands chained to those guarding them. (Ac 5:23; 12:6-10; 16:22-24) Some prisoners were allowed visitors.—Mt 25:36; Ac 23:35; 24:23, 27; 28:16-31; see BOND; JAILER.

As foretold by Christ Jesus, many of his followers experienced imprisonment. (Lu 21:12; Ac 26: 10; Ro 16:7; Col 4:10; Heb 10:34; 13:3) The apostle John, in exile on the isle of Patmos, wrote that imprisonment would continue to be a form of persecution of Christians.—Re 2:10.

Figurative Use. In a figurative sense, "prison" can refer to a land of exile (as was Babylon) or to a state of spiritual bondage or confinement. (Isa 42:6, 7; 48:20; 49:5, 8, 9; 61:1; Mt 12:15-21; Lu 4:17-21; 2Co 6:1, 2) Though the spirit creatures who were disobedient in Noah's day do not have physical bodies that can be held by material restraints, they have been limited in their activities and are in a state of dense darkness with reference to Jehovah God, as if in a prison. (1Pe 3:19; Jude 6; see TARTARUS.) Also, the abyss in which Satan will be shut up for a thousand years is a "prison," a place of deathlike restraint or confinement.—Re 20:1-3, 7.

PROCESSION. See TRIUMPHAL PROCESSION.

PROCHORUS (Proch'o·rus) [possibly from a Gr. root meaning "go (or, dance) before in a chorus"]. One of the seven certified men full of spirit and wisdom appointed to assure equal treatment in the daily distribution of food in the first-century Christian congregation at Jerusalem.—Ac 6:1-6.

PROCONSUL. Principal local administrator of a province that was under the supervision of the Roman Senate.

In 27 B.C.E., Emperor Augustus of Rome took charge of all provinces requiring the presence of military forces, leaving ten others as senatorial provinces. The administration of the latter was carried out through proconsuls. The proconsuls were of two classes: Ex-consuls (those who had already attained the rank of consul), who were sent to the provinces of Asia and Africa (where a legionary force was maintained), and ex-praetors, sent to the other senatorial provinces.

It was the proconsul's responsibility to direct the civil affairs of the province, make judicial decisions, and maintain law and order. His jurisdiction was supreme in the province, although his actions were subject to review by the Roman senate. The collection of revenues was under a quaestor. The proconsul did not wear military dress or carry a sword.

The proconsul Sergius Paulus is mentioned at Acts 13:7, 12 as one who became a Christian. He was the proconsul of Cyprus. At Acts 18:12, Gallio is mentioned as being proconsul of the province of Achaia. Luke is accurate in using the term "proconsul" in these cases, for Achaia was a senatorial province from 27 B.C.E. to 15 C.E., and again after 44 C.E.; and Cyprus became a senatorial province in 22 B.C.E. A coin from Cyprus has been found with the head and title of Claudius (in Latin) on the obverse side and "Under Arminius Proclus, Proconsul of the Cyprians" (in Greek) on the reverse side.

PROPHECY. An inspired message; a revelation of divine will and purpose or the proclamation thereof. Prophecy may be an inspired moral teaching, an expression of a divine command or judgment, or a declaration of something to come. As shown under PROPHET, prediction, or foretelling, is not the basic thought conveyed by the root verbs in the original languages (Heb., na·va"; Gr., pro·phe·teu'o); yet it forms an outstanding feature of Bible prophecy.

Illustrating the sense of the original words are these examples: When Ezekiel in a vision was told to "prophesy to the wind," he simply expressed God's command to the wind. (Eze 37:9, 10) When individuals at Jesus' trial covered him, slapped him, and then said, "Prophesy to us, you Christ. Who is it that struck you?" they were not calling for prediction but for Jesus to identify the slappers by divine revelation. (Mt 26:67, 68; Lu 22:63, 64) The Samaritan woman at the well recognized Jesus as "a prophet" because he revealed things about her past that he could not have known except by divine power. (Joh 4:17-19; compare Lu 7:39.) So, too, such Scriptural portions as Jesus' Sermon on the Mount and his denunciation of the scribes and Pharisees (Mt 23:1-36) may properly be defined as prophecy, for these were an inspired 'telling forth' of God's mind on matters, even as were the pronouncements by Isaiah, Jeremiah, and other earlier prophets.—Compare Isa 65:13-16 and Lu 6:20-25.

Examples of foretelling, or prediction, are, of course, very numerous throughout the entire Bible, some earlier examples being found at Genesis 3:14-19; 9:24-27; 27:27-40; 49:1-28; Deuteronomy 18:15-19.

The Source of all true prophecy is Jehovah God. He transmits it by means of his holy spirit or, occasionally, by spirit-directed angelic messengers. (2Pe 1:20, 21; Heb 2:1, 2) The Hebrew prophecies frequently begin, "Hear the word of Jehovah" (Isa 1:10; Jer 2:4), and by the expression "the word" is often meant an inspired message, or prophecy.—Isa 44:26; Jer 21:1; Eze 33:30-33; compare Isa 24:3.

In what way did 'the bearing witness to Jesus inspire prophesying'?

In the apostle John's vision he was told by an angel that "the bearing witness to Jesus is what inspires [literally, "is the spirit of"] prophesying." (Re 19:10) The apostle Paul calls Christ "the sacred secret of God" and says that "carefully concealed in him are all the treasures of wisdom and of knowledge." (Col 2:2, 3) This is because Jehovah God assigned to his Son the key role in the outworking of God's grand purpose to sanctify His name and restore earth and its inhabitants to their proper place in His arrangement of things, doing this by means of "an administration at the full limit of the appointed times, namely, to gather all things together again in the Christ, the things in the heavens and the things on the earth." (Eph 1:9, 10; compare 1Co 15:24, 25.) Since the fulfillment of God's great purpose is all bound up in Jesus (compare Col 1:19, 20), then all prophecy, that is, all inspired messages from God proclaimed by his servants, pointed toward his Son. Thus, as Revelation 19:10 states, the entire "spirit" (the whole inclination, intent, and purpose) of prophecy was to bear witness to Jesus, the one Jehovah would make "the way and the truth and the life." (Joh 14:6) This would be true not only of prophecy that preceded Jesus' earthly ministry but also of prophecy subsequent thereto.—Ac 2:16-36.

At the very time rebellion arose in Eden, Jehovah God started off this "witness to Jesus" by his prophecy regarding the "seed" that would eventually 'crush the head of the serpent,' God's Adversary. (Ge 3:15) The Abrahamic covenant was prophetic of that Seed, of its blessing all the families of earth, and of its victory over the Adversary and his "seed." (Ge 22:16-18; compare Ga 3:16.) It was foretold that the promised Seed, called "Shiloh" (meaning "He Whose It Is; He To Whom It Belongs"), would come from the tribe of Judah. (Ge 49:10) By means of the nation of Israel, Jehovah revealed his purpose to have "a kingdom of priests and a holy nation." (Ex 19:6; compare 1Pe 2:9, 10.) The sacrifices of the Law given to Israel foreshadowed the sacrifice of God's Son, and its priesthood pictures his royal heavenly priesthood (with associate priests) during his Thousand Year Reign. (Heb 9:23, 24; 10:1; Re 5:9, 10; 20:6) Consequently the Law became a "tutor leading to Christ."—Ga 3:23, 24.

Of events marking the history of the nation of Israel, the apostle says: "Now these things went on befalling them as examples [or, "for a typical purpose"], and they were written for a warning to us [followers of Christ Jesus] upon whom the ends of the systems of things have arrived." (1Co 10:11) David, the nation's most prominent king, became a prophetic figure of God's Son, and God's covenant with David for an everlasting kingdom was inherited by Jesus Christ. (Isa 9:6, 7; Eze 34:23, 24; Lu 1:32; Ac 13:32-37; Re 22:6) The various battles fought by faithful kings (usually guided and encouraged by God's prophets) prefigured the war to be waged by God's Son against enemies of his Kingdom, and the victories God gave them thus prefigured Christ's victory over all of Satan's forces, bringing deliverance to God's people.—Ps 110:1-5; Mic 5:2-6; Ac 4:24-28; Re 16:14, 16; 19:11-21.

Many of the prophecies during this period described the reign of God's Anointed One (Messiah, or Christ) and the blessings of his rule. Other Messianic prophecies pointed to persecution of God's Servant and his suffering. (Compare Isa 11:1-10; 53:1-12; Ac 8:29-35.) As the apostle Peter states, the ancient prophets themselves kept "investigating what particular season or what sort of season the spirit in them was indicating concerning Christ [Messiah] when it was bearing witness beforehand about the sufferings for Christ and about the glories to follow these." It was revealed to them that these things were to have a future fulfillment beyond their own time.—1Pe 1:10-12; compare Da 9:24-27; 12:1-10.

Since Christ Jesus is the One in whom all these prophecies see realization, marking them all as true, it can be seen how "the truth came to be through Jesus Christ." "For no matter how many the promises of God are, they have become Yes by means of him." (Joh 1:17; 2Co 1:20; compare Lu 18:31; 24:25, 26, 44-46.) Peter could rightly say of Jesus that 'all the prophets bear witness to him.'—Ac 3:20-24; 10:43; compare 28:23.

Purpose and Time of Fulfillment. Prophecy, whether prediction, simply inspired instruction, or reproof, served for the benefit of both those initially hearing it and those in all future periods who would put faith in God's promises. For the original receivers, the prophecies assured them that the passing of years or centuries had not caused God to waver in his purpose, that he was holding firm to his covenant terms and promises. (Compare Ps 77:5-9; Isa 44:21; 49:14-16; Jer 50:5.) Daniel's prophecy, for example, provided information that constituted an invaluable link between the close of the writing of the Hebrew or pre-Christian Scriptures and Messiah's coming. Its forecast of world events, including the rise and fall of successive world powers, gave assurance to Jews living during the centuries of Persian, Greek, and Roman dominance (as well as to Christians thereafter) that there was no "blind spot" in God's forevision, that their own times were indeed foreseen and that Jehovah's sovereign purpose was still certain of fulfillment. It protected them against putting faith and hope in such passing world regimes with their transient power of control and enabled those faithful ones to direct their course with wisdom.—Compare Da 8:20-26; 11:1-20.

The fact that many prophecies were fulfilled in their own times convinced sincere ones of God's power to carry out his purpose despite all opposition. It was proof of his unique Godship that he, and he alone, could foretell such events and bring them to pass. (Isa 41:21-26; 46:9-11) These prophecies also enabled them to become better acquainted with God, understanding more clearly his will and the moral standards by which he acts and judges, so that they might harmonize their lives with these.—Isa 1:18-20; 55:8-11.

A large number of prophecies had their initial application or fulfillment on the contemporary people, many prophecies expressing God's judgment on fleshly Israel and surrounding nations and foretelling Israel and Judah's overthrow and subsequent restoration. Yet these prophecies did not lose their value for later generations, as for the Christian congregation, either in the first century C.E. or in our own time. The apostle says: "For all the things that were written aforetime were written for our instruction, that through our endurance and through the comfort from the Scriptures we might have hope." (Ro 15:4) Since God is unchangeable in his moral standards and purpose (Mal 3:6; Heb 6:17, 18), his dealings with Israel shed light on how he will deal with similar situations at any given time. Hence Jesus and his disciples were warranted in using prophetic statements applying centuries earlier as also applicable in their day. (Mt 15:7, 8; Ac 28:25-27) Other prophecies were clearly predictive, some relating specifically and uniquely to Jesus' earthly ministry and subsequent events. (Isa 53; Da 9:24-27) For those living at the time of Messiah's appearance, the prophecies supplied the means for identifying him and authenticating his commission and message.—See MESSIAH.

After Jesus' departure from earth, the Hebrew Scriptures and their prophecies supplemented Jesus' teachings in supplying the vital background against which his Christian followers could view succeeding events, fit them in, and learn their meaning and significance. This gave validity and strength to their preaching and teaching, and it gave them confidence and courage as they faced opposition. (Ac 2:14-36; 3:12-26; 4:7-12, 24-30; 7:48-50; 13:40, 41, 47) They found in the early inspired revelations a great body of moral instruction to draw on for "teaching, for reproving, for setting things straight, for disciplining in righteousness." (2Ti 3:16, 17; Ro 9:6-33; 1Co 9:8-10; 10:1-22) Peter, who had had the prophecies confirmed by his seeing the transfiguration vision, said: "Consequently we have the prophetic word made more sure; and you are doing well in paying attention to it as to a lamp shining in a dark place." (2Pe 1:16-19; Mt 16:28–17:9) So, the pre-Christian prophecy supplemented Jesus' instruction and was God's means to guide the Christian congregation in important decisions, as in regard to Gentile believers.—Ac 15:12-21; Ro 15:7-12.

Prophecies also served to warn, advising when urgent action was needed. A forceful example of this is Jesus' warning of Jerusalem's coming destruction and the situation that would signal the time for his followers to flee from her to a place of safety. (Lu 19:41-44; 21:7-21) Similar prophetic warnings apply to Christ's presence.—Compare Mt 24:36-42.

By the outpouring of the holy spirit at Pentecost, Christians were granted such miraculous gifts as prophesying and the ability to speak in tongues they had not studied. In some (but not necessarily all) cases, the gift of prophesying produced predictions, as those of Agabus (Ac 11:27, 28; 21:8-11), enabling the Christian congregation or individuals thereof to gird for certain emergencies or trials. The canonical letters of the apostles and disciples also contain inspired forecasts of the future; these warned of the coming apostasy, told the form it would take, warned of God's judgment and the future execution thereof, and revealed doctrinal truths not before understood or amplified and clarified those already given. (Ac 20:29, 30; 1Co 15:22-28, 51-57; 1Th 4:15-18; 2Th 2:3-12; 1Ti 4:1-3; 2Ti 3:1-13; 4:3, 4; compare Jude 17-21.) The book of Revelation is filled with prophetic information enabling persons to be warned, so they can discern "the signs of the times" (Mt 16:3) and take urgent action.—Re 1:1-3; 6:1-17; 12:7-17; 13:11-18; 17:1-12; 18:1-8.

However, in Paul's first letter to the Corinthians he shows that the miraculous gifts, including that of inspired prophesying, were due to be done away with. (1Co 13:2, 8-10) The evidence is that with the death of the apostles these gifts ceased to be transmitted and thereafter passed off the Christian scene, having served their purpose. By that time, of course, the Bible canon was complete.

Jesus' illustrations, or parables, were similar in form to some of the allegorical pronouncements of the earlier prophets. (Compare Eze 17:1-18; 19:1-14; Mt 7:24-27; 21:33-44.) Almost all of them had some fulfillment in that time. Some basically set forth moral principles. (Mt 18:21-35; Lu 18:9-14) Others had time features that extended down to Jesus' presence and "the conclusion of the system of things."—Mt 13:24-30, 36-43; 25:1-46.

Multiple fulfillment. The use made of prophecy by Jesus and his disciples shows that a predictive prophecy may have more than one fulfillment, as when Paul referred to Habakkuk's prophecy, originally fulfilled in Babylon's desolation of Judah, and applied it in his day. (Hab 1:5, 6; Ac 13:40, 41) Jesus showed that Daniel's proph-

ecy concerning "the disgusting thing that is causing desolation" was due for fulfillment in the generation then living; yet Daniel's prophecy also connects "the disgusting thing" causing desolation with the "time of the end." (Da 9:27; 11:31-35; Mt 24:15, 16) Biblical evidence shows that when Michael 'stands up,' this signifies that Jesus Christ takes action as king on behalf of Jehovah's servants. (Da 12:1; see MICHAEL No. 1.) Jesus' own prophecy regarding the conclusion of the system of things likewise includes mention of his coming in Kingdom power, which did not take place in the first century C.E. (Mt 24:29, 30; Lu 21:25-32) This indicates a dual fulfillment. Hence, in discussing the matter of double fulfillment of prophecy, M'Clintock and Strong's *Cyclopædia* (1894, Vol. VIII, p. 635) comments: "This view of the fulfilment of prophecy seems necessary for the explanation of our Lord's prediction on the Mount, relating at once to the fall of Jerusalem and to the end of the Christian dispensation."

Forms of Prophecy. In addition to direct statements issued through his prophets (perhaps accompanied by symbolic acts [1Ki 11:29-31] or in allegorical form), Jehovah used other forms. *Prophetic characters* prefigured the Messiah, Christ Jesus. Besides David, already mentioned, these included the priest-king Melchizedek (Heb 7:15-17), the prophet Moses (Ac 3:20-22), and others. It should be noted that, with regard to prophetic characters, the individual is not to be viewed as typical or prophetic in every aspect. Thus Jonah's three days in the belly of the great fish prefigured Jesus' time in Sheol; but Jonah's reluctance to accept his assignment and other aspects did not prefigure the course of God's Son. Jesus spoke of himself as "something more than Solomon," for Jesus' wisdom and the peace of his Kingdom rule are like that of Solomon but superior to it. However, Jesus does not become spiritually delinquent as Solomon did.—Mt 12:39-42.

Prophetic dramas were also used by God, details from the lives of individuals and nations being recorded as a pattern of future events in the outworking of Jehovah's purpose. Paul speaks of such "a symbolic drama" involving Abraham's two sons by Sarah and the slave girl Hagar. He shows that the two women "mean" two covenant relationships. They did not personally typify, or picture, such covenants. But in the prophetic drama those women corresponded to symbolic women who produced children under those covenants. Thus Hagar corresponded to earthly Jerusalem, which failed to accept the Deliverer to whom the Law covenant pointed and clung to that Law even after God had terminated it; earthly Jerusalem and its children were thus in slavery to the Law. On the other hand, Sarah, the free woman, corresponded to "the Jerusalem above," God's heavenly wifelike organization, which produces sons in accord with what was foretold in the Abrahamic covenant. (Ga 4:21-31; compare Joh 8:31-36.) The Flood of Noah's day and the conditions precedent to it were prophetic of conditions at the time of Christ's future presence and of the result to those rejecting God's way.—Mt 24:36-39; compare 1Co 10:1-11.

Places were used prophetically, the city of Jerusalem on Mount Zion at times being used to represent a heavenly organization that is the "mother" of spirit-anointed Christians. (Ga 4:26) "New Jerusalem" symbolized Christ's heavenly "bride," made up of members of the glorified Christian congregation. (Re 21:2, 9-14; compare Eph 5:23-27, 32, 33; Re 14:1-4.) However, Jerusalem, because of the general unfaithfulness of its inhabitants, may be used in an unfavorable way as well. (Ga 4:25; compare Eze 16:1-3, 8-15; see JERUSALEM [The City's Significance].) Other places obviously used with prophetic significance are Sodom, Egypt, Megiddo, Babylon, and the Valley of Hinnom, or Gehenna.—Re 11:8; 16:16; 18:2; Mt 23:33.

A *prophetic pattern,* involving objects and procedures, is found in the case of the tabernacle. The apostle shows that its equipment, functions, and sacrifices were a pattern of heavenly realities, "a typical representation and a shadow of the heavenly things."—Heb 8:5; 9:23, 24.

Testing Prophecy and Its Interpretation. In view of the activity of false prophets, John warned against believing every "inspired expression," which is basically what prophecies are. Instead, he admonished Christians to "test the inspired expressions to see whether they originate with God." (1Jo 4:1) John cites one doctrine as a means for determining divine origin of the inspired expression, namely, Christ's having come in the flesh. Obviously, however, he was not saying that this was the sole criterion but evidently was citing an example of something currently, perhaps predominantly, in dispute then. (1Jo 4:2, 3) A vital factor is the prophecy's harmony with God's revealed word and will (De 13:1-5; 18:20-22), and this harmony could not be partial but must be complete for the prophecy or an interpretation of prophecy to be correct. (See PROPHET [Distinguishing the True From the False].) In the first-century Christian congregation some were granted the gift of "discernment of inspired utterances" (1Co 12:10), making possible the au-

thentication of prophecies. Though this miraculous ability also ceased, it is reasonable that correct understanding of prophecy would still be made available by God through the congregation, particularly in the foretold "time of the end," not miraculously, but as the result of their diligent investigation and study and comparison of prophecy with circumstances and events taking place. —Compare Da 12:4, 9, 10; Mt 24:15, 16; 1Co 2:12-14; 1Jo 4:6; see INTERPRETATION.

PROPHET. One through whom divine will and purpose are made known. (Lu 1:70; Ac 3:18-21) Although the etymology of the Hebrew term for a prophet (*na·vi'*) is uncertain, the use of this distinctive term shows that true prophets were no ordinary announcers but were spokesmen for God, 'men of God' with inspired messages. (1Ki 12:22; 2Ki 4:9; 23:17) They stood in God's "intimate group," and he revealed his "confidential matter" to them.—Jer 23:18; Am 3:7; 1Ki 17:1; see SEER.

The Greek *pro·phe'tes* literally means "a speaker out [Gr., *pro,* "before" or "in front of," and *phe·mi',* "say"]" and thus describes a proclaimer, one who makes known messages attributed to a divine source. (Compare Tit 1:12.) Though this includes the thought of a predictor of the future, the *fundamental* meaning of the word is not that of prediction. (Compare Jg 6:7-10.) Nonetheless, living in harmony with God's will requires that the individual know what Jehovah's revealed purposes for the future are so that he may bring his ways, desires, and goals into line with the divine will. Hence, in the great majority of cases, the Biblical prophets did convey messages that were, directly or indirectly, related to the future.

Prophetic Office in the Hebrew Scriptures. The first human spokesman for God obviously was Adam, who initially conveyed God's instructions to his wife Eve and to that extent fulfilled the role of prophet. Those instructions had to do not only with the present (for them) but also with the future, outlining God's purpose for earth and mankind and the course humans must take to enjoy a blessed future. (Ge 1:26-30; 2:15-17, 23, 24; 3:1-3) The first faithful human prophet mentioned was Enoch, and his message did contain direct prediction. (Jude 14, 15) Lamech and his son Noah both proclaimed inspired revelations of God's purpose and will.—Ge 5:28, 29; 9:24-27; 2Pe 2:5.

The word *na·vi'* itself is first applied to Abraham. (Ge 20:7) Abraham was not notable for foretelling the future, certainly not in a public way. Yet God had given him a message, a prophetic promise. Abraham must have felt agitated, impelled to 'speak forth' about this, particularly to his family, explaining why he was leaving Ur and what God's promise to him was. (Ge 12:1-3; 13:14-17; 22:15-18) In a similar way, Isaac and Jacob, the inheritors of the promise, were "prophets" having intimate communication with God. (Ps 105:9-15) Additionally, they gave predictive blessings to their sons. (Ge 27:27-29, 39, 40; 49:1-28) With the exception of Job and Elihu, who were evidently used by God prior to the Exodus to reveal divine truths, all true prophets were thereafter drawn from Jacob's descendants (the Israelites) down till the first century of the Common Era.

With Moses, the role of the prophet comes into sharper focus. The prophet's position as spokesman for God is emphasized by Jehovah's assignment of Aaron as a "prophet" or "mouth" to Moses, while Moses 'served as God to Aaron.' (Ex 4:16; 7:1, 2) Moses foretold many events that saw early fulfillment, such as the Ten Plagues. However, he served even more impressively as prophet, or spokesman for God, in the delivering of the Law covenant at Sinai and in instructing the nation in God's will. Though the Law covenant was of immense immediate value to the Israelites as a moral code and guide, it, too, pointed forward to the future and 'better things to come.' (Ga 3:23-25; Heb 8:6; 9:23, 24; 10:1) Moses' intimate, often two-way, communication with God, and the greatly increased understanding of Jehovah's will and purpose he was used to convey, made his prophetic position outstanding. (Ex 6:2-8; De 34: 10) His brother and sister, Aaron and Miriam, also rendered prophetic service in the sense of being transmitters of divine messages or counsel (though not necessarily predictions), as did 70 older men of the nation.—Ex 15:20; Nu 11:25; 12: 1-8.

Aside from the anonymous man of Judges 6:8, the only person specifically mentioned in the book of Judges as rendering prophetic service was Deborah the prophetess. (Jg 4:4-7; 5:7) However, the absence of the term *na·vi'* does not of itself mean that others did not serve in this capacity. By Samuel's time, "word from Jehovah had become rare . . . ; there was no vision being spread abroad." From boyhood Samuel served as God's spokesman, and the fulfillment of the divine messages caused all to recognize him as "one accredited for the position of prophet to Jehovah."—1Sa 3:1-14, 18-21.

With the establishment of the monarchy, an almost continuous line of prophets appears. (Compare Ac 3:24.) Gad began prophesying prior to Samuel's death. (1Sa 22:5; 25:1) And he and the prophet Nathan were prominent during David's reign. (2Sa 7:2-17; 12:7-15; 24:11-14, 18) As did other prophets later, they served as royal advisers and historians. (1Ch 29:29; 2Ch 9:29; 29:25; 12: 15; 25:15, 16) David himself was used to deliver certain divine revelations and is called "a prophet" by the apostle Peter. (Ac 2:25-31, 34) The divided kingdom saw faithful prophets active in the northern and southern kingdoms. Some were used to prophesy to the leaders and people of both kingdoms. Among exilic and postexilic prophets were Daniel, Haggai, Zechariah, and Malachi.

The prophets played a vital role in maintaining true worship. Their activity served as a check on the kings of Israel and Judah, for they boldly reproved erring rulers (2Sa 12:1-12) and declared God's judgments against those who practiced wickedness. (1Ki 14:1-16; 16:1-7, 12) When the priesthood deviated and suffered corruption, the prophets were Jehovah's means for strengthening the faith of a righteous remnant and for pointing the way back to God's favor for those who had strayed. Like Moses, the prophets on many occasions acted as intercessors, praying to God in behalf of king and people. (De 9:18-29; 1Ki 13:6; 2Ki 19:1-4; compare Jer 7:16; 14:11, 12.) They were especially active in times of crisis or great need. They gave hope for the future, as at times their messages foretold the blessings of Messiah's government. In this way they benefited not only those then living but future generations down to our day. (1Pe 1:10-12) Yet, in doing this they endured great reproach, mockings, and even physical mistreatment. (2Ch 36:15, 16; Jer 7:25, 26; Heb 11:32-38) Those receiving them favorably, however, were blessed with spiritual and other benefits.—1Ki 17:8-24; 2Ki 4:8-37; compare Mt 10:41.

Means of Appointment and Inspiration. The office of prophet was not received because of line of descent; however, several prophets were Levites, such as Samuel, Zechariah the son of Jehoiada, Jeremiah, and Ezekiel, and some prophets' descendants also became prophets. (1Ki 16:7; 2Ch 16:7; Zec 1:1) Nor was it a profession entered on one's own initiative. Prophets were selected by God and appointed by means of holy spirit (Nu 11:24-29; Eze 1:1-3; Am 7:14, 15), by which means they also knew what to proclaim. (Ac 28: 25; 2Pe 1:21) Some showed great reluctance initially. (Ex 3:11; 4:10-17; Jer 1:4-10) In Elisha's case, his divine appointment came through his predecessor, Elijah, and was symbolized by Elijah's throwing his mantle, or official garment, over Elisha.—1Ki 19:19-21.

Though appointed by Jehovah's spirit, it does not appear that the prophets spoke continually under inspiration. Rather, God's spirit 'came upon them' at certain times, revealing the messages to be announced. (Eze 11:4, 5; Mic 3:8) This had a stirring effect upon them, impelling them to speak. (1Sa 10:10; Jer 20:9; Am 3:8) Not only did they do things that were out of the ordinary but also their expression and manner doubtless reflected intensity and feeling that were truly extraordinary. This may explain in part what is meant by individuals' "behaving like prophets." (1Sa 10:6-11; 19:20-24; Jer 29:24-32; compare Ac 2:4, 12-17; 6:15; 7:55.) Their total concentration and zealous boldness in their mission might cause their behavior to appear strange, even irrational, to others, just as a prophet so appeared to military chiefs when Jehu was anointed. Yet, on realizing that the man was a prophet, the chiefs accepted his message with full seriousness. (2Ki 9:1-13; compare Ac 26:24, 25.) When Saul, in pursuit of David, was caused to 'behave like a prophet,' he stripped off his garments and lay "naked all that day and all that night," during which time David evidently escaped. (1Sa 19:18–20:1) This does not mean that prophets frequently went naked, for the Biblical record shows the contrary. In the two other cases recorded, the prophet went naked for a purpose, to represent some facet of his prophecy. (Isa 20:2-4; Mic 1:8-11) The reason for Saul's nakedness—whether to show him as a mere man, divested of his royal garments, impotent against Jehovah's own regal authority and power, or for some other purpose—is not stated.

Jehovah used various methods to inspire the prophets: *verbal communication* through angels (Ex 3:2-4; compare Lu 1:11-17; Heb 1:1, 2; 2:1, 2), *visions* that impressed God's message on the conscious mind (Isa 1:1; Hab 1:1), *dreams* or *night visions* given while the prophet slept (Da 7:1), and messages conveyed while the person was in a *trance* (Ac 10:10, 11; 22:17-21). On occasion, music might contribute to the prophet's receiving the divine communication. (1Sa 10:5; 2Ki 3:15) Similarly, the proclamation of the inspired message was effected in diverse manners. (Heb 1:1) Generally the prophet spoke it, both in public places and in sparsely populated regions. (Jer 7:1, 2; 36:4-13; Mt 3:3) But he might dramatize the message by use of symbols or symbolic acts, as in Ezekiel's portraying the siege of Jerusalem by use of a brick, or in Hosea's marriage to Gomer.—Eze 4:1-3; Ho 1:2, 3; compare 1Ki 11:30-39; 2Ki 13:14-19; Jer 19:1, 10, 11; see DREAM; INSPIRATION; VISION.

Distinguishing the True From the False. In some cases, such as that of Moses, Elijah, Elisha, and Jesus, God's prophets performed miraculous works that attested to the genuineness of their message and office. Not all, however, are recorded as performing such powerful works. The three essentials for establishing the credentials of a true prophet, as given through Moses, were: The true prophet would speak in Jehovah's name; the things foretold would come to pass (De 18:20-22); and his prophesying must promote true worship, being in harmony with God's revealed word and commandments (De 13:1-4). The last requirement was probably the most vital and decisive, for an individual might hypocritically use God's name, and by coincidence, his prediction might see fulfillment. But the true prophet was not solely or even primarily a prognosticator, as has been shown. Rather, he was an advocate of righteousness, and his message dealt primarily with moral standards and their application. He expressed God's mind on matters. (Isa 1:10-20; Mic 6:1-12) Hence, it was not necessary to wait perhaps for years or generations to determine whether the prophet was true or false by fulfillment of a prediction. If his message contradicted God's revealed will and standards, he was false. Thus, a prophet who foretold peace for Israel or Judah, at a time when the people were engaging in disobedience to God's Word and Law, of necessity was false.—Jer 6:13, 14; 14:11-16.

Jesus' later warning concerning false prophets paralleled that of Moses. Though using his name, and giving "signs and wonders to lead astray," their fruits would prove them "workers of lawlessness."—Mt 7:15-23; Mr 13:21-23; compare 2Pe 2:1-3; 1Jo 4:1-3.

The true prophet never foretold simply to satisfy human curiosity. Every prediction related to God's will, purpose, standards, or judgment. (1Ki 11:29-39; Isa 7:3-9) Often the future events foretold were the consequence of existing conditions; as the people sowed, so they would reap. The false prophets lulled the people and their leaders with soothing assurances that, despite their unrighteous course, God was still with them to protect and prosper them. (Jer 23:16-20; 28:1-14; Eze 13:1-16; compare Lu 6:26.) They imitated the true prophets, employing symbolic language and actions. (1Ki 22:11; Jer 28:10-14) While some were outright frauds, many were evidently prophets who became delinquent or apostate. (Compare 1Ki 18:19; 22:5-7; Isa 28:7; Jer 23:11-15.) Some were women, false prophetesses. (Eze 13:17-23; compare Re 2:20.) A "spirit of uncleanness" replaced

God's spirit. All such false prophets were to be put to death.—Zec 13:2, 3; De 13:5.

As to those measuring up to the divine standards, the fulfillment of certain "short-range" prophecies, some being accomplished in just a day or a year, gave basis for confidence that their prophecies relating to a more distant future would also see fulfillment.—1Ki 13:1-5; 14:12, 17; 2Ki 4:16, 17; 7:1, 2, 16-20.

"Sons of the Prophets." As *Gesenius' Hebrew Grammar* explains (Oxford, 1952, p. 418), the Hebrew *ben* (son of) or *beneh'* (sons of) may denote "membership of a guild or society (or of a tribe, or any definite class)." (Compare Ne 3:8, where "a member of the ointment mixers" is literally "a son of the ointment mixers.") "The sons of the prophets" may thus describe a school of instruction for those called to this vocation or simply a cooperative association of prophets. Such prophetic groups are mentioned as being at Bethel, Jericho, and Gilgal. (2Ki 2:3, 5; 4:38; compare 1Sa 10:5, 10.) Samuel presided over a group at Ramah (1Sa 19:19, 20), and Elisha seems to have held a similar position in his day. (2Ki 4:38; 6:1-3; compare 1Ki 18:13.) The record mentions their building their own dwelling place and the use of a borrowed tool, which may indicate that they lived simply. Though often sharing quarters and food in common, they might receive individual assignments to go out on prophetic missions.—1Ki 20:35-42; 2Ki 4:1, 2, 39; 6:1-17; 9:1, 2.

Prophets in the Christian Greek Scriptures. The Greek word *pro·phe'tes* corresponds to the Hebrew *na·vi'*. The priest Zechariah, father of John the Baptizer, acted as prophet in revealing God's purpose concerning his son, John, who would be "called a prophet of the Most High." (Lu 1:76) John's simple mode of life and his message were reminiscent of earlier Hebrew prophets. He was widely recognized as a prophet; even Herod felt some restraint because of him. (Mr 1:4-6; Mt 21:26; Mr 6:20) Jesus said John was "far more than a prophet."—Mt 11:7-10; compare Lu 1:16, 17; Joh 3:27-30.

Jesus, the Messiah, was "The Prophet," the long-awaited one foretold by Moses. (Joh 1:19-21, 25-27; 6:14; 7:40; De 18:18, 19; Ac 3:19-26) His ability to perform powerful works and to discern matters in a way beyond the ordinary caused others to recognize him as a prophet. (Lu 7:14-16; Joh 4:16-19; compare 2Ki 6:12.) More than all others he was one in God's "intimate group." (Jer 23:18; Joh 1:18; 5:36; 8:42) He regularly quoted earlier prophets as testifying to his divine commission and office. (Mt 12:39, 40; 21:42; Lu 4:18-21; 7:27; 24:25-27, 44; Joh 15:25) He foretold

the manner of his own betrayal and death, that as a prophet he would die at Jerusalem, "the killer of the prophets," that his disciples would abandon him, that Peter would deny him three times, that he would be resurrected on the third day—many of these prophecies being based on earlier prophecies in the Hebrew Scriptures. (Lu 13:33, 34; Mt 20:17-19; 26:20-25, 31-34) Beyond this, he foretold the destruction of Jerusalem and its temple. (Lu 19:41-44; 21:5-24) The precise fulfillment of all of these things within the life of those hearing him gave solid basis for faith and conviction as to the fulfillment of his prophecies relating to his presence.—Compare Mt 24; Mr 13; Lu 21.

Pentecost, 33 C.E., saw the foretold outpouring of God's spirit on the disciples at Jerusalem, causing them to 'prophesy and see visions.' They did this by declaring "the magnificent things of God," and by inspired revelation of knowledge about God's Son and what this meant for their listeners. (Ac 2:11-40) Again it should be remembered that prophesying does not mean solely or necessarily predicting the future. The apostle Paul stated that "he that prophesies upbuilds and encourages and consoles men by his speech," and he held prophesying forth as a proper and particularly desirable goal for all Christians to strive after. Whereas speaking foreign tongues was a sign for unbelievers, prophesying was for believers. Yet even the unbeliever attending a Christian meeting would benefit by prophesying, being reproved and closely examined by it so that "the secrets of his heart become manifest." (1Co 14:1-6, 22-25) This, too, indicates that Christian prophesying did not consist mainly of prediction but instead often dealt with things relating to the present, though clearly proceeding from a source beyond the ordinary, being inspired by God. Paul counseled on the need for good order and self-control in congregational prophesying, so that all could learn and be encouraged.—1Co 14:29-33.

There were, of course, certain ones particularly selected, or gifted, to serve as prophets. (1Co 12:4-11, 27-29) Paul himself had the gift of prophesying, yet he is primarily known as an apostle. (Compare Ac 20:22-25; 27:21-26, 31, 34; 1Co 13:2; 14:6.) Those especially designated as prophets, such as Agabus, Judas, and Silas, appear to have been outstanding spokesmen for the Christian congregation, second only to the apostles. (1Co 12:28; Eph 4:11) Like the apostles, they not only served locally but also traveled to different points, gave discourses, and also foretold certain future events. (Ac 11:27, 28; 13:1; 15:22, 30-33; 21:10, 11) As earlier, some Christian women received the gift of prophesying, though always subject to the headship of the male members of the congregation.—Ac 21:9; 1Co 11:3-5.

PROPHETESS.

A woman who prophesies or carries on the work of a prophet. As shown under the headings PROPHET and PROPHECY, prophesying basically means the inspired telling forth of messages from God, the revealing of the divine will. Prediction of future events might or might not be involved. Even as there were both true and false prophets, so some prophetesses were used by Jehovah and were moved by his spirit while others were false prophetesses, disapproved by Him.

Miriam is the first woman designated a prophetess in the Bible. God evidently conveyed some message or messages through her, perhaps in inspired singing. (Ex 15:20, 21) Thus, she and Aaron are recorded as saying to Moses: "Is it not by us also that [Jehovah] has spoken?" (Nu 12:2) Jehovah himself, through the prophet Micah, spoke of having sent "Moses, Aaron and Miriam" before the Israelites when bringing them up out of Egypt. (Mic 6:4) Though Miriam was privileged to be used as an instrument of divine communication, her relationship as such toward God was inferior to that of her brother Moses. When she failed to keep her proper place, she suffered severe chastisement from God.—Nu 12:1-15.

In the period of the Judges, Deborah served as a source of information from Jehovah, making known his judgments on certain matters and conveying his instruction, as in his commands to Barak. (Jg 4:4-7, 14-16) Thus, during a period of national weakness and apostasy, she served figuratively as "a mother in Israel." (Jg 5:6-8) Huldah the prophetess served in a similar manner, in King Josiah's day, making known God's judgment toward the nation and its king.—2Ki 22:14-20; 2Ch 34:22-28.

Isaiah refers to his wife as "the prophetess." (Isa 8:3) Though some commentators suggest that she was such only in the sense of being married to a prophet, this conjecture has no Scriptural evidence to back it up. It appears more likely that she had received a prophetic assignment of some sort from Jehovah, as had earlier prophetesses.

Nehemiah speaks unfavorably of the prophetess Noadiah, who, along with "the rest of the prophets," tried to instill fear in Nehemiah and so obstruct the rebuilding of Jerusalem's walls. (Ne 6:14) Though she acted in opposition to God's will, this does not necessarily mean that she had not held a valid standing as a prophetess prior thereto.

Jehovah spoke to Ezekiel of Israelite women who were "acting as prophetesses out of their own heart." This implies that these prophetesses had no divine commission from God but were merely imitations, self-made prophetesses. (Eze 13:17-19) By their ensnaring and hoodwinking practices and propaganda they were 'hunting souls,' condemning the righteous and condoning the wicked, but Jehovah would deliver his people out of their hand.—Eze 13:20-23.

In the first century C.E., while the Jews were still Jehovah's covenant people, the aged Anna served as a prophetess. She "was never missing from the temple, rendering sacred service night and day with fastings and supplications." By "speaking about the child [Jesus] to all those waiting for Jerusalem's deliverance," she acted as a prophetess in the basic sense of 'telling forth' a revelation of God's purpose.—Lu 2:36-38.

Prophesying was among the miraculous gifts of the spirit that were granted to the newly formed Christian congregation. Certain Christian women, such as Philip's four virgin daughters, prophesied under the impulse of God's holy spirit. (Ac 21:9; 1Co 12:4, 10) This was in fulfillment of Joel 2:28, 29, which foretold that "your sons and your daughters will certainly prophesy." (Ac 2:14-18) Such gift, however, did not remove a woman from subjection to the headship of her husband or to that of men within the Christian congregation; in symbol of her subjection she was to wear a head covering when prophesying (1Co 11:3-6) and was not to act as a teacher within the congregation. —1Ti 2:11-15; 1Co 14:31-35.

A Jezebel-like woman in the congregation of Thyatira claimed to have prophetic powers but followed the course of ancient false prophetesses and received the condemnation of Christ Jesus in his message to John at Revelation 2:20-23. She improperly acted as a teacher and misled members of the congregation into wrong practices.

PROPITIATORY COVER.

The cover of the ark of the covenant, before which the high priest spattered blood of sin offerings on Atonement Day.

Bible translations render the Hebrew term *kap-po'reth* variously as "mercy seat" (KJ, RS, Yg), "propitiatory" (AT, Dy), "cover" (Le), "ark-cover" (JP), or "cover," "propitiatory cover" (NW). The Hebrew term is from a root verb meaning "cover," "cover over (sin)."

As Jehovah instructed Moses, the craftsman Bezalel made a cover of pure gold for the sacred chest or ark of the covenant, 2.5 cubits (111 cm; 44 in.) long and 1.5 cubits (67 cm; 26 in.) wide. It was surmounted by two golden cherubs, one at each end of the cover, their wings spread upward, screening the cover. The cherubs' faces were toward the cover. The Ark was placed in the Most Holy compartment of the tabernacle.—Ex 25:17-21; 37:1, 6-9.

On the Day of Atonement (*yohm hak·kip·pu-rim'*, meaning "day of the coverings or propitiations" [Le 23:27, 28]), the high priest entered the Most Holy and spattered some of the bull's blood before the cover (at its front, or east side) and then did the same with the blood of the goat. (Le 16:14, 15) Thus the gold cover of the Ark played a special role in the typical propitiation (covering) of sins.

From between the cherubs on the propitiatory cover, God spoke when he desired to communicate with Moses or with the high priest. (Ex 25:22; Nu 7:89; compare Le 10:8-10; Nu 27:18-21.) Jehovah said that he would appear in a cloud over the cover of the Ark. This cloud apparently glowed or shone, lighting up the Most Holy compartment. —Le 16:2; compare Ps 80:1.

In 1 Chronicles 28:11 the Most Holy, the innermost compartment of the temple, is referred to as "the house of the *kap·po'reth.*" In this instance the Hebrew word is evidently not used simply as designating a lid, or cover, for a chest, but is employed with regard to the special function of the cover in the propitiation of sins. Accordingly, the expression is rendered "the house of the atonement" (*Yg*), "the house of propitiation" (*AT*), "the house of the propitiatory cover" (*NW*).

Symbolic. At Hebrews 9:5 the Greek word *hi·la·ste'ri·on*, "propitiatory," is used for the cover of the Ark. In the type, or pattern, God's presence was represented between the two cherubs over the propitiatory cover. (Le 16:2; Ex 25:22) The inspired writer of the book of Hebrews points out that these things were symbolic. As the high priest on the Day of Atonement entered the Most Holy with sacrificial blood, so Christ took the value of his sacrifice, not before a literal propitiatory cover, but before the very presence of Jehovah God in heaven.—Le 16:15; Heb 9:11-14, 24-28.

PROSELYTE.

A convert, that is, one who embraced Judaism, getting circumcised, if a male. (Mt 23:15, ftn) The Greek word *pro·se'ly·tos* (proselyte) is used in both the *Septuagint* and the Christian Greek Scriptures.

For more than 19 centuries Jehovah dealt with a special, select people, the family of Abraham and his seed, primarily the nation of Israel. Yet it was possible for a non-Hebrew or a non-Israelite who desired to serve Jehovah according to the requirements of true worship to do so. However, he would have to convert to true religion, that is, become a proselyte. The Mosaic Law made specific provisions for a person of non-Israelite origin dwelling in Israel. Such an "alien resident" could become a full worshiper of Jehovah, being circumcised, if a male, in acknowledgment of his acceptance of true worship. (Ex 12:48, 49) A proselyte was responsible to obey all of the Law, and he was to be treated by natural Jews as a brother. (Le 19:33, 34; 24:22; Ga 5:3; see ALIEN RESIDENT.) The Hebrew word *ger,* rendered "alien resident" ("stranger," *KJ*), does not always signify such a religious convert (Ge 15:13; Ex 2:22; Jer 14:8), but in more than 70 instances where the translators of the *Septuagint* possibly believed that it did, they rendered it by the Greek *pro·se'ly·tos.*

Throughout Israelite history non-Jews became proselytes, in effect saying about the Jews what Moabitess Ruth said to Naomi: "Your people will be my people, and your God my God." (Ru 1:16; Jos 6:25; Mt 1:5) Solomon's prayer at the inauguration of the temple reflected God's open and generous spirit toward those of many nations who might want to serve Him as proselytes. (1Ki 8:41-43) Non-Jews mentioned by name who evidently became proselytes included Doeg the Edomite (1Sa 21:7), Uriah the Hittite (2Sa 11:3, 11), and Ebed-melech the Ethiopian (Jer 38:7-13). When the Jews in Mordecai's time received permission to stand and defend themselves, "many of the peoples of the land were declaring themselves Jews." (Es 8:17) The *Septuagint* reads: "And many of the Gentiles were circumcised, and became Jews."—Bagster.

Active in Proselytizing. As a result of the Babylonian exile Judaism became widespread. Jews of the Dispersion came into contact with pagans of many nations. The establishment of synagogues and the availability of the Hebrew Scriptures in the Greek language made it easier for persons throughout the Roman world to learn of the Jewish religion. Ancient writers such as Horace and Seneca testified that numerous persons in various lands joined themselves to the Jews, thus becoming proselytes. Josephus reported that Jews in Syrian Antioch "were constantly attracting to their religious ceremonies multitudes of Greeks, and these they had in some measure incorporated with themselves." (*The Jewish War*, VII, 45, [iii, 3]) *The Interpreter's Dictionary of the Bible* points out that "the Jews in Rome exhibited such an aggressive spirit of proselytism that they were charged with seeking to infect the Romans with their cult, and the government expelled the chief propagandists from the city in 139 B.C." (Edited by G. Buttrick, 1962, Vol. 3, p. 925) This charge, of course, may have been unfounded or exaggerated, perhaps being politically motivated or due to some racial or religious prejudice. Nevertheless, Jesus himself said about the hypocritical scribes and Pharisees: "You traverse sea and dry land to make one proselyte, and when he becomes one you make him a subject for Gehenna twice as much so as yourselves."—Mt 23:15.

Proselytizing by force. Not all the Jewish proselytes were won over by peaceful means. Historian Josephus related that, when John Hyrcanus I conquered the Idumeans, which was in about 125 B.C.E., he told the people that they could stay in their country only if they submitted to circumcision, thus forcing them to become proselytes. (*Jewish Antiquities,* XIII, 257, 258 [ix, 1]) Aristobulus, the son of John Hyrcanus, did the same with the Ituraeans. (XIII, 318 [xi, 3]) Later, Jews under Alexander Jannaeus demolished Pella because the inhabitants refused to become proselytes. (XIII, 397 [xv, 4]) Political considerations, rather than missionary zeal, were undoubtedly the basis for such deeds.

Proselytes Became Christians. The record in the Christian Greek Scriptures indicates that some of the circumcised Jewish proselytes were sincere in their worship of Jehovah. The crowd from many lands who heard Peter on the day of Pentecost 33 C.E. and became Christians was made up of "both Jews and proselytes." (Ac 2:10) The proselytes from other lands had journeyed to Jerusalem in obedience to Jehovah's law. Similarly, the Ethiopian eunuch whom Philip baptized had gone to Jerusalem to worship and was reading God's Word as he traveled homeward. (Ac 8:27-38) He must have been a eunuch in the sense of "court official," for had he been castrated he could not have become a proselyte. (De 23:1; see ETHIOPIA, ETHIOPIAN.) In the early days of the Christian congregation "Nicolaus, a proselyte of Antioch," was appointed to special duties in connection with the distribution of food, being a man "full of spirit and wisdom."—Ac 6:2-6.

Good news spread among the Gentiles. Until 36 C.E. the Christian message was directed solely to Jews, to Gentiles who had become circumcised Jewish proselytes, and to Samaritans. The Italian Cornelius is described as "a devout man and one fearing God . . . [who] made many gifts of mercy to the people and made supplication to God continually." But he was not a Jewish proselyte, for he was an uncircumcised Gentile. (Ac 10:1, 2; compare Lu 7:2-10.) When once the door was opened to the Gentiles, active Christian missionary work expanded. Nevertheless, Paul often preached first to the Jews and proselytes in cities to which he traveled. Paul had great love for his Jewish brothers and a desire that they might be saved. (Ro 9:3;

10:1) Moreover, the Jews and proselytes were the logical ones to approach first, for they knew of Jehovah and his laws and were looking for the Messiah. Their background enabled those among them with good hearts to recognize Jesus Christ as the fulfillment of their hopes. These could form a strong nucleus for a congregation and could, in turn, teach the Gentiles, who knew nothing about Jehovah and his Word.

PROSTITUTE. A person, usually a woman, given to indiscriminate lewdness; specifically, a woman who offers herself indiscriminately for sexual intercourse for hire; a harlot. The Hebrew word for prostitute is *zoh·nah'*, while its Greek equivalent is *por'ne.*—See HARLOT.

Under the Law. The law that God gave to Israel commanded: "Do not profane your daughter by making her a prostitute, in order that the land may not commit prostitution and the land actually be filled with loose morals." (Le 19:29) Adultery was prohibited by the seventh commandment (Ex 20:14; De 5:18); the penalty was death for both parties. (Le 20:10) The girl found guilty of having married under the false pretense of virginity was to be put to death. (De 22:13-21) The engaged girl who committed fornication with another man was considered the same as an adulterous wife, and she was put to death. (De 22:23, 24) The single girl who committed fornication was to be married to the man who seduced her unless the father refused to permit the marriage.—Ex 22:16, 17; De 22:28, 29.

For these and other reasons, prostitutes in Israel were, doubtless with few exceptions, foreign women. The Proverbs repeatedly warn against the "strange woman" and the "foreign woman" who would entice a man to commit immorality. —Pr 2:16; 5:20; 7:5; 22:14; 23:27.

A priest was forbidden by the Law to marry a prostitute, and the daughter of a priest who committed prostitution was to be put to death and afterward burned in the fire. (Le 21:7, 9, 14) The 'hire of a prostitute' was not to be received as a contribution at Jehovah's sanctuary, because prostitutes were detestable in Jehovah's sight.—De 23:18.

It was the case of two prostitutes, handled in a wise and understanding way, that greatly strengthened the faith of the people in Solomon as the fitting successor of David to the throne of Israel. Probably the case had been one upon which the judges of the lower court could not decide, and it was referred, therefore, to the king. (De 1:17; 17:8-11; 1Sa 8:20) These women may have been prostitutes, not in a commercial sense, but women who had committed fornication, either Jewish women or, quite possibly, women of foreign descent.—1Ki 3:16-28.

Temple Prostitutes. Temple prostitutes constituted a prominent feature of false religion. The historian Herodotus (I, 199) reports the "foulest Babylonian custom is that which compels every woman of the land once in her life to sit in the temple of Aphrodite and have intercourse with some stranger." Temple prostitutes were also connected with the worship of Baal, Ashtoreth, and other gods and goddesses worshiped in Canaan and elsewhere.

Male temple prostitutes were also a part of degenerate worship.—1Ki 14:23, 24; 15:12; 22:46.

'The Way to Death.' King Solomon, in the seventh chapter of Proverbs, describes a scene that he observed, illustrating the workings of the prostitute and the results to those who are ensnared by her. He speaks of a young man passing along the street near a prostitute's house, at the approach of night. Solomon describes the young man as "in want of heart," lacking discernment or good sense. (See HEART.) The woman, dressed in the immodest manner of a prostitute, is lying in wait and approaches him. She has smooth lips and fair speech, but her actual disposition is boisterous and stubborn; she is cunning of heart. This prostitute puts on a display of being righteous by saying that she had made communion sacrifices that very day (implying that there would be food on which to feast, inasmuch as the offerer regularly took part of the communion sacrifice for himself and his family).—Pr 7:6-21.

Now that the young man is enticed to this point, Solomon shows, he is irresistibly drawn into sin with her, throwing all good sense to the wind, going ahead 'like a bull to the slaughter,' as a man who is in fetters and cannot escape the discipline he will get. "Until," says Solomon, "an arrow cleaves open his liver," that is, until he gets the wound that causes death, both spiritually and physically, for not only has he exposed his body to death-dealing sexually transmitted disease (in advanced cases of syphilis, bacterial organisms overwhelm the liver), but also "he has not known that it involves his very soul." His entire being and his life are seriously affected, and he has sinned seriously against God. Solomon concludes his account saying: "The ways to Sheol her house is; they are descending to the interior rooms of death."—Pr 7:22, 23, 27; compare Pr 2:16-19; 5:3-14.

'Destroys valuable things.' The proverb says: "A man that is loving wisdom makes his father rejoice, but he that is having companionship with prostitutes destroys valuable things." (Pr 29:3) First of all, he destroys his relationship with God, the most valuable possession; then he brings reproach upon his family and destroys family relationships. As another proverb warns, such a man 'gives to others his dignity and his years to what is cruel; strangers take their fill of his power, and the things he got by pain come to be in the house of a foreigner.'—Pr 5:9, 10.

The wise man therefore counsels: "Do not desire her [the foreign woman's] prettiness in your heart, . . . because in behalf of a woman prostitute one comes down to a round loaf of bread; but as regards another man's wife, she hunts even for a precious soul." (Pr 6:24-26) This may mean that a man in Israel, by his association with a prostitute, squandered his substance and was reduced to poverty (compare 1Sa 2:36; Lu 15:30), but the man who committed adultery with another man's wife was losing his soul (under the Law death was the penalty for adultery). Or, the entire passage may be referring to the adulterous wife as a prostitute.

The concluding verses of the chapter (Pr 6:29-35) say: "[As to] anyone having relations with the wife of his fellowman, no one touching her will remain unpunishable. People do not despise a thief just because he commits thievery to fill his soul when he is hungry. But, when found, he will make it good with seven times as much; all the valuables of his house he will give. Anyone committing adultery with a woman is in want of heart; he that does it is bringing his own soul to ruin. A plague and dishonor he will find, and his reproach itself will not be wiped out. For the rage of an able-bodied man is jealousy, and he will not show compassion in the day of vengeance. He will have no consideration for any sort of ransom, neither will he show willingness, no matter how large you make the present."

The meaning of Proverbs 6:30-35 may be that men do not look down greatly on a thief who steals to satisfy hunger; they understand his action to an extent. Nevertheless, if caught, he is made to restore with 'interest' what he stole (this was especially so under the Law [Ex 22:1, 3, 4]; "seven times" may be used in the proverb to indicate that he is made to pay the penalty to the fullest extent). But the adulterer can make no restitution for his sin; his reproach, which is great, remains, and in no way can he ransom or buy himself off from the punishment he deserves.

If a Christian who is a member of the spiritual body of Christ has relations with a prostitute or commits fornication, he is taking a member of the

Christ away and making it the member of a harlot, joining himself to a prostitute as one body. He is thereby sinning against his own body as regards its being 'a member of Christ.'—1Co 6:15-18.

Must Forsake Such Practice to Be Saved. There is hope for those who are prostitutes if they turn away from the detestable practice and exercise faith in the ransom sacrifice of Jesus Christ. The apostle wrote to the Christians at Corinth, reminding them that some of them were fornicators and adulterers but that they had forsaken that course and had been washed clean and declared righteous in the name of the Lord Jesus Christ. (1Co 6:9-11) Many of the harlots in Israel showed themselves to have better hearts than the religious leaders. These women, viewed with scorn by the scribes and Pharisees, humbly accepted the preaching of John the Baptizer, and Jesus used them as an example to the religious leaders, saying: "Truly I say to you that the tax collectors and the harlots are going ahead of you into the kingdom of God."—Mt 21:31, 32.

Rahab. Rahab is an example of a prostitute who expressed faith in God and was counted righteous. (Jas 2:25) Men sent by Joshua to spy out Jericho lodged at Rahab's house. (Jos 2:1) It would not be reasonable to assume that they did so for immoral purposes. As to their motive, Professors C. F. Keil and F. Delitzsch, in *Commentary on the Old Testament* remark: "Their entering the house of such a person would not excite so much suspicion. Moreover, the situation of her house against or upon the town wall was one which facilitated escape. But the Lord so guided the course of the spies, that they found in this sinner the very person who was the most suitable for their purpose, and upon whose heart the tidings of the miracles wrought by the living God on behalf of Israel had made such an impression, that she not only informed the spies of the despondency of the Canaanites, but, with believing trust in the power of the God of Israel, concealed the spies from all the inquiries of her countrymen, though at the greatest risk to herself." (1973, Vol. II, Joshua, p. 34) In view of God's statement that Israel was to drive out the Canaanites because of their immoral practices and in view also of God's blessing on the conquest of Jericho and upon Rahab herself, it would be entirely unreasonable to assume that the spies committed immorality with Rahab or that she continued her practice of prostitution afterward.—Le 18:24-30.

In regard to Jephthah's being the son of a prostitute woman (Jg 11:1), and Samson's lodging in the house of a prostitute in the city of Gaza (Jg 16:1), see JEPHTHAH; SAMSON.

Figurative Use. A person, a nation, or a congregation of persons dedicated to God who make alliances with the world or who turn to the worship of false gods are called in the Bible "prostitutes." Such was the nation of Israel. Israel was seduced into having "immoral intercourse" with foreign gods and, just as an unfaithful wife would seek out other men, she looked to foreign nations for security and salvation from her enemies instead of looking to her "husbandly owner," Jehovah God. (Isa 54:5, 6) Moreover, Jerusalem became so debased in her unfaithfulness that she went beyond the usual custom of prostitutes, as the prophet Ezekiel was inspired to say: "To all prostitutes they are accustomed to give a present, but you—you have given your presents to all those passionately loving you, and you offer a bribe to them to come in to you from all around in your acts of prostitution." (Eze 16:33, 34) Both the ten-tribe kingdom of Israel and the two-tribe kingdom of Judah were denounced as prostitutes in this symbolic manner.—Eze 23:1-49.

The most notorious example of spiritual prostitution is "Babylon the Great, the mother of the harlots and of the disgusting things of the earth."—Re 17:5; see BABYLON THE GREAT.

PROSTRATE. See ATTITUDES AND GESTURES.

PROVERBIAL SAYING. The Hebrew term translated "proverbial saying" or "proverbial utterance" (*ma·shal'*) is generally thought to be derived from a root word meaning "be like" or "be comparable" (Ps 49:12), and indeed, many proverbial sayings employ likenesses or comparisons. Some scholars relate the expression "proverbial saying" to the Hebrew verb meaning "rule"; so it could be construed at times to be a saying of a ruler, an expression that carries power, or one that indicates superiority in mental action. Consistent with this view is the fact that King Solomon, who was known for his wisdom, could speak 3,000 proverbs and recorded many of these proverbial sayings. —1Ki 4:32.

Among the Israelites there were popular or frequently used expressions that were full of meaning because of the circumstances that surrounded them. Generally, these proverbial sayings were concisely stated. (1Sa 10:12) Not all of them expressed proper viewpoints, however, and there were some with which Jehovah specifically took issue.—Eze 12:22, 23; 18:2, 3.

Some sayings became common expressions of

ridicule or contempt for certain people. (Hab 2:6) In such cases even the object of the scorn, whether a person or something inanimate, was said to be "a proverbial saying." Thus the Israelites were warned that if they failed to listen to Jehovah and obey his commandments, both they and their temple would become a proverbial saying among the nations. (De 28:15, 37; 1Ki 9:7; 2Ch 7:20) The attitude expressed toward a nation that became a proverbial saying is well indicated in the Bible in the accompanying expressions, which show that Israel would become a reproach, an object of derision, of jeering, of humiliation, and of taunts. (Ps 44:13-15; Jer 24:9) Individuals who became proverbial sayings thereby became the subject of the songs of drinkers of intoxicating liquor and someone in whose face others would spit. (Ps 69:11, 12; Job 17:6) Clearly, one who became a proverbial saying was reduced to a very low state.

Not all proverbial sayings were expressed in one or two short, pithy sentences. In Isaiah chapter 14 is recorded a more extensive one, portraying vividly and with apt comparisons the disastrous effects of the pride of the king of Babylon. With biting sarcasm it heaps ridicule on the one who thought of himself as the "shining one, son of the dawn."

When the likeness or comparison embodied in a proverbial saying was at first somewhat obscure or puzzling, it might also be called a riddle. (Ps 78:2) That was true of the one that Ezekiel was inspired to tell Israel in which he likened the course of the nation in relation to Babylon and Egypt to a vine planted by one eagle that later reached out hungrily to another.—Eze 17:2-18.

Some proverbial utterances, such as those of Job, were set out in poetic style. (Job 27:1; 29:1) The ideas that Job was inspired to express were not put down in the concise style characteristic of most proverbs but were developed into highly instructive poems filled with figurative speech.

God also caused Balaam to make a series of proverbial utterances, and these, too, are put down in the form of poetry. (Nu 23:7, 18; 24:3, 15, 20, 21, 23) Far from expressing any scorn for Israel in these proverbial utterances, Balaam "blessed them to the limit," though he did prophesy woe for other peoples. (Nu 23:11) The proverbial aspect here is not because of any popular repetition of what Balaam said nor because his statements were concise expressions of wisdom. Rather, these are termed proverbial utterances because of the power and rich meaning of what was said, along with his use of a variety of likenesses or comparisons in some of his statements.

PROVERBS, BOOK OF. A book consisting of a compilation of proverbs or wise sayings from a number of other collections. The book itself sets forth its objective: "For one to know wisdom and discipline, to discern the sayings of understanding, to receive the discipline that gives insight, righteousness and judgment and uprightness, to give to the inexperienced ones shrewdness, to a young man knowledge and thinking ability." (Pr 1:2-4) "The purpose is that you may walk in the way of good people and that the paths of the righteous ones you may keep."—2:20.

The introductions to three of the book's sections attribute the proverbs contained in them to Solomon. (Pr 1:1; 10:1; 25:1) This agrees with the fact that Solomon "could speak three thousand proverbs." (1Ki 4:32) There can be little question that many, if not all, of the proverbs in these sections were recorded during Solomon's reign. With reference to himself, Solomon stated: "The congregator had become wise, he also taught the people knowledge continually, and he pondered and made a thorough search, that he might arrange many proverbs in order. The congregator sought to find the delightful words and the writing of correct words of truth."—Ec 12:9, 10.

However, various arguments have been advanced against crediting most of the proverbs to Solomon. Certain proverbs (Pr 16:14; 19:12; 20:2; 25:3) have been cited as being derogatory to monarchs and therefore not from the time of Solomon. Upon closer examination, though, it is found that, instead of being derogatory, these proverbs exalt kings, showing that they should be accorded due fear because of their power. (Compare 24:21.) Those who claim that a polygamist like Solomon would not have spoken of husband-wife relationships in such a way as to imply monogamy (5:15-19; 18:22; 19:13, 14) lose sight of the fact that polygamy was not advocated but simply tolerated and regulated by the Law. And it may well be that the Jews generally practiced monogamy. Likewise such critics forget that Proverbs is inspired of God and is not simply the opinions of Solomon. Nevertheless, from his observations and his own experiences Solomon may very well have come to appreciate the wisdom of God's original standard for marriage, monogamy.—Compare Ec 2:8; 7:27-29.

The proverbs not attributed to Solomon had their origin in the sayings of other wise men and one woman. (Pr 22:17; 30:1; 31:1; see AGUR; LEMUEL.) Just when all these proverbs were put into final form is not precisely known. The last time indicator appearing in the book itself is a reference to Hezekiah's reign. (25:1) So there is a basis for believing that the proverbs were compiled in book form by the time of that ruler's death in c. 717 B.C.E. The repetition of certain proverbs suggests that the book was compiled from various separate collections.—Compare 10:1 and 15:20; 10:2 and 11:4; 14:20 and 19:4; 16:2 and 21:2.

Style and Arrangement. The book of Proverbs is written in Hebrew poetic style, which consists of thought rhythm, employing parallelisms, the ideas of which are either similar (Pr 11:25; 16:18; 18:15) or contrasting. (10:7, 30; 12:25; 13:25; 15:8) Its first section (1:1–9:18) consists of short discourses addressed by a father to a son or sons. This serves as an introduction to the short, pithy sayings found in the remaining sections of the book. The last 22 verses of the book are written in acrostic, or alphabetic, style, a form of composition also employed by David for a number of his psalms.—Ps 9, 10, 25, 34, 37, 145.

Inspired of God. The writers of the Christian Greek Scriptures testify to the fact that the book of Proverbs is part of God's inspired Word. The apostle Peter (1Pe 4:18; 2Pe 2:22; Pr 11:31 [*LXX*]; 26:11) and the disciple James (Jas 4:6; Pr 3:34, *LXX*) referred to it, as did the apostle Paul when writing to the Corinthians (2Co 8:21; Pr 3:4, *LXX*), the Romans (Ro 12:16, 20; Pr 3:7; 25:21, 22), and the Hebrews (Heb 12:5, 6; Pr 3:11, 12). Additionally, numerous parallel thoughts may be found in the Christian Greek Scriptures.—Compare Pr 3:7 with Ro 12:16; Pr 3:12 with Re 3:19; Pr 24:21 with 1Pe 2:17; Pr 25:6, 7 with Lu 14:7-11.

To Know Jehovah Is the Way of Life. The book of Proverbs speaks much about knowledge in conjunction with discernment, wisdom, understanding, and thinking ability. The knowledge that it strives to impart and encourage is, therefore, more than mere head knowledge, an array of facts or learning. Proverbs points out that any true knowledge has as its starting point an appreciation of one's relationship to Jehovah. In fact, at chapter 1, verse 7, the theme of the book is set forth: "The fear of Jehovah is the beginning of knowledge."

Of course, the most important knowledge that one can acquire is about God himself. "The knowledge of the Most Holy One is what understanding is," says Proverbs 9:10. This knowledge goes beyond the mere fact of God's existence and his creatorship, even beyond the knowledge of many facts about his dealings. To "know" him denotes a deep appreciation of his fine qualities and his great name, and a close relationship with him.

Jesus Christ said to Jews who had knowledge about God: "No one fully knows the Son but the Father, neither does anyone fully know the Father but the Son and anyone to whom the Son is willing to reveal him." (Mt 11:27) A knowledge of Jehovah's qualities will deepen one's proper fear of God, and it will bring the realization that Jehovah is deserving of all worship and service and that to know and obey him is the way of life. "The fear of Jehovah is a well of life, to turn away from the snares of death," and, "The fear of Jehovah tends toward life."—Pr 14:27; 19:23.

Jehovah the Creator. Jehovah, in matchless wisdom, is the Creator of all things and the Decreer of the laws governing these things; so he deserves the worship of all creatures. (Pr 3:19, 20) He made the hearing ear and the seeing eye, both literally and in a moral sense. Accordingly, one must look to Him in order to see and hear with true understanding. And a person must realize his accountability to the One who sees and hears all. —20:12.

Righteousness. The book exalts Jehovah as the center of all things and the One in whom all righteous principles find their origin. For example: "The just indicator and scales belong to Jehovah; all the stone weights of the bag are his work." (Pr 16:11) His will as the Lawgiver is that honesty and justice rule in all transactions. (11:1; 20:10) By fearing him, one learns to love what He loves and to hate what He hates and thereby make one's way of life straight, for "the fear of Jehovah means the hating of bad." (8:13) Proverbs reveals that Jehovah especially hates lofty eyes, a false tongue, hands shedding innocent blood, a heart fabricating hurtful schemes, feet in a hurry to run to badness, a false and lying witness, and one causing contentions among brothers. (6:16-19; 12:22; 16:5) One who truly *hates* these things is well on the way to life.

Additionally, the book of Proverbs illuminates the way of the righteous by showing what Jehovah approves. "The ones blameless in their way are a *pleasure* to him," as also are the prayers of such ones. (Pr 11:20; 15:8, 29) "One that is good gets approval from Jehovah." (12:2) "The one pursuing righteousness he loves."—15:9.

Judgment and direction. One knowing Jehovah realizes through knowledge and experience that, as Proverbs 21:30 says, "there is no wisdom, nor any discernment, nor any counsel in opposition to Jehovah." Therefore, though he may hear other plans or have them in his own heart, the sensible person will direct his way of life in harmony with the counsel of Jehovah, knowing that contrary counsel, no matter how seemingly wise or plausible, cannot stand against the word of Jehovah.—Pr 19:21; compare Jos 23:14; Mt 5:18.

Inspired King Solomon said: "Trust in Jehovah with all your heart . . . In all your ways take notice of him, and he himself will make your paths straight." (Pr 3:5, 6) A man's heart chooses the way he desires to go, but even when he chooses the correct way, to succeed he must look to Jehovah to direct his steps.—16:3, 9; 20:24; Jer 10:23.

Having chosen the path of life, the individual should recognize Jehovah's keen interest in him. Proverbs reminds us that Jehovah's eyes "are in every place, keeping watch upon the bad ones and the good ones." (Pr 15:3) "For the ways of man are in front of the eyes of Jehovah, and he is contemplating all his tracks." (5:21) Not only what he appears to be outwardly but also his *heart* is examined by Jehovah. (17:3) "Jehovah is making an estimate of hearts" (21:2), and He weighs the true value of the thinking, motivation, and inmost desires of the person.

The judgments of Jehovah are shown to be altogether, in every respect, right and for the good of those who seek uprightness. In due time God

---

HIGHLIGHTS OF PROVERBS

A book consisting of sections in the form of discourses as well as collections of wise sayings regarding practical matters of life

Though attributed chiefly to King Solomon, Proverbs was not compiled in its entirety until Hezekiah's reign

The excelling value of wisdom

Wisdom, along with understanding, is the prime thing (4:5-8; 16:16)

Essentials for gaining wisdom (2:1-9; 13:20)

Benefits that come from wisdom, such as security, protection, honor, and a longer, happier life (2:10-21; 3:13-26, 35; 9:10-12; 24:3-6, 13, 14)

Wisdom personified was Jehovah's coworker (8:22-31)

The bitter consequences for failing to act wisely (1:24-32; 2:22; 6:12-15)

Proper attitude toward Jehovah

Trust in Jehovah (3:5, 6; 16:20; 18:10; 29:25)

Fear him and shun badness (3:7; 10:27; 14:26, 27; 16:6; 19:23)

Honor him, supporting true worship (3:9, 10)

Accept his discipline as an expression of love (3:11, 12)

Show appreciation for his word (3:1-4; 30:5, 6)

Find out what Jehovah hates and act in harmony with this knowledge (6:16-19; 11:20; 12:22; 16:5; 17:15; 28:9)

If we please Jehovah, he will care for us, protect us, and hear our prayers (10:3, 9, 30; 15:29; 16:3)

Fine counsel governing family life

A capable wife is a blessing from Jehovah (12:4; 14:1; 18:22; 31:10-31)

Parents should give their children training and discipline (13:1, 24; 22:6, 15; 23:13, 14; 29:15, 17)

Children should deeply respect their parents (1:8, 9; 4:1-4; 6:20-22; 10:1; 23:22-26; 30:17)

Love and peace are very desirable in the home (15:16, 17; 17:1; 19:13; 21:9, 19)

Resist immorality and thus avoid much pain and suffering (5:3-23; 6:23-35; 7:4-27; 9:13-18)

Traits that should be cultivated, and those that should be avoided

Cultivate loving consideration for the poor and afflicted (3:27, 28; 14:21, 31; 19:17; 21:13; 28:27)

Be generous, avoid greed (11:24-26)

Cultivate diligence; do not be lazy (6:6-11; 10:26; 13:4; 20:4; 24:30-34; 26:13-16)

Modesty and humility bring honor; presumptuousness and pride lead to humiliation (11:2; 16:18, 19; 25:6, 7; 29:23)

Have self-control in the matter of anger (14:29; 16:32; 25:28; 29:11)

Avoid a malicious spirit or a desire for revenge (20:22; 24:17, 18, 28, 29; 25:21, 22)

Practice righteousness in everything (10:2; 11:18, 19; 14:32; 21:3, 21)

Practical guidelines for daily living

Respond properly to discipline, reproof, counsel (13:18; 15:10; 19:20; 27:5, 6)

Be a true friend (17:17; 18:24; 19:4; 27:9, 10)

Be discreet in accepting hospitality (23:1-3, 6-8; 25:17)

Materialism is vain (11:28; 23:4, 5; 28:20, 22)

Hard work brings blessings (12:11; 28:19)

Cultivate honest business practices (11:1; 16:11; 20:10, 23)

Beware of going surety for others, especially for strangers (6:1-5; 11:15; 22:26, 27)

Shun unwholesome speech; be sure your speech is upbuilding (10:18-21, 31, 32; 11:13; 12:17-19; 15:1, 2, 4, 28; 16:24; 18:8)

Flattery is treacherous (28:23; 29:5)

Avoid quarrels (3:30; 17:14; 20:3; 26:17)

Shun bad associations (1:10-19; 4:14-19; 22:24, 25)

Learn to deal wisely with ridiculers as well as with foolish ones (9:7, 8; 19:25; 22:10; 26:4, 5)

Avoid the pitfalls of strong drink (20:1; 23:29-35; 31:4-7)

Do not envy the wicked (3:31-34; 23:17, 18; 24:19, 20)

will clear the wicked out of the land, their death being the price of freedom for the righteous ones. Accordingly, the proverb states: "The wicked is a ransom for the righteous one; and the one dealing treacherously takes the place of the upright ones." (Pr 21:18) Among such wicked ones are the proud, who are detestable to Jehovah. They "will not be free from punishment." (16:5) "The house of the self-exalted ones Jehovah will tear down." (15:25) He will "rob of soul" those robbing the lowly. —22:22, 23.

By observing these dealings of Jehovah the right-minded man makes his paths straight. (Compare Pr 4:26.) He sees that allowing partiality through bribery (17:23) or influence of personality (18:5) causes one to pervert judgment. 'Pronouncing the wicked righteous and the righteous wicked' would make him detestable in Jehovah's eyes. (17:15) He also learns not to be prejudiced but to hear fully both sides of a matter before judging it.—18:13.

Security with happiness. To the one who guards practical wisdom and thinking ability that he receives from Jehovah, the book of Proverbs says: "Jehovah himself will prove to be, in effect, your confidence, and he will certainly keep your foot against capture." (Pr 3:21, 26; 10:29; 14:26) If one fears Jehovah, "in that case there will exist a future." (23:17, 18) Moreover, not only is there a future hope but there is also happiness and security for the present time. (3:25, 26) "When Jehovah takes pleasure in the ways of a man he causes even his enemies themselves to be at peace with him." (16:7) God will not let the righteous one go hungry. (10:3) If a person honors God with the valuable things he possesses, his "stores of supply will be filled with plenty." (3:9, 10) He adds days to such a man's life.—10:27.

One 'taking refuge' in Jehovah's name (understanding and acknowledging that name for all that it represents) will find it to be like a strong tower, a place to which, in ancient times, people fled for safety from the enemy.—Pr 18:10; 29:25.

Humility before Jehovah brings "riches and glory and life." (Pr 22:4) Mercy and truth are what he desires; these are more valuable than sacrifice. Those who turn from bad, who fear Jehovah, and who serve him in this manner will not receive his adverse judgment. (Pr 16:6; compare 1Sa 15:22.) By knowing Jehovah's ways, one can follow "the entire course of what is good."—Pr 2:9.

Aimed at the Heart. To achieve its purpose, the book of Proverbs aims at the *heart*. More than 75 times it refers to the heart as receiving knowledge, understanding, wisdom, and discernment;

as being responsible for words and actions; or as being affected by circumstances and conditions. The heart is to be applied to discernment (Pr 2:2); the heart is to observe right commandments (3:1); these are to be written "upon the tablet of [the] heart." (3:3) "More than all else" the heart is to be safeguarded. (4:23) It is with all the heart that one is to trust in Jehovah.—3:5; See HEART.

Discipline and the heart. Proverbs puts a high value on discipline in various forms. (Pr 3:11, 12) It says: "Anyone shunning discipline is rejecting his own soul, but the one listening to reproof is acquiring heart." (15:32) So reproof reaches to and adjusts the heart, helping one to acquire good sense or discernment. "For want of heart [lack of discernment] the foolish themselves keep dying." (10:21) Because it is the heart that must be reached in training children, we are informed: "Foolishness is tied up with the heart of a boy; the rod of discipline is what will remove it far from him."—22:15.

The Spirit and the Soul. Proverbs is not a book of statements of mere men's wisdom, of how to please or influence men. Rather, Proverbs goes deep, into the heart as affecting thinking and motivation, into the spirit or mental inclination, and into the soul as comprising every fiber of one's being and personality. (Heb 4:12) Even though a man may think he is right, or may justify himself in his actions, 'all the ways of a man being pure in his own eyes,' Proverbs 16:2 reminds us that "Jehovah is making an estimate of spirits" and so knows what one's disposition is. Might or power is highly prized in the world, but "he that is slow to anger is better than a mighty man, and he that is controlling his spirit than the one capturing a city."—Pr 16:32.

Getting the knowledge and wisdom of this divinely provided book will greatly help a person to find happiness in this present life and will put him on the pathway to everlasting life. Since "he that is acquiring heart is loving his own soul," the inspired counsel and discipline therein, if followed will add "length of days and years of life" and "will prove to be life to your soul." (Pr 19:8; 3:2, 13-18 21-26) "Jehovah will not cause the soul of the righteous one to go hungry." (10:3) "He that is keeping the commandment is keeping his soul," Solomon admonishes.—19:16.

Relations With Others. Proverbs describes the true servant of God as one who uses his tongue for good (Pr 10:20, 21, 31, 32), not speaking falsely nor even hurting others by thoughtless words. (12:6, 8, 17-19; 18:6-8, 21) If provoked, he turns away the rage of his opponent by a mild answer. (15:1; 25:15) He does not enjoy disputes or quarrels, and he exercises self-control against outbursts of anger, knowing that he might commit irreparable foolishness. (Pr 14:17, 29; 15:18; compare Col 3:8.) In fact, he will avoid companionship with those letting anger control them and who display fits of rage, for he knows that they would bring him into a snare.—Pr 22:24, 25; compare 13:20; 14:7; 1Co 15:33.

Render good, not evil. The inspired Proverbs urge one to take the initiative to do good toward others. Not only is he to act with good toward those 'dwelling in security' with him, who have rendered no bad to him (Pr 3:27-30), but he is also urged to return good for bad. (25:21, 22) He is to watch his heart closely, that he does not have inner rejoicing at calamity that comes to one whom he despises or to one who hates him. —17:5; 24:17, 18.

Gossip and slander. Much is said in the book of Proverbs about the trouble, grief, and damage brought by gossiping, as well as the gravity of the guilt resting on the talebearer. The 'choice morsel' of a slanderer is "swallowed greedily" by its hearer and is not taken lightly but makes a lasting impression, going down "into the innermost parts of the belly." Therefore it causes trouble, and the speaker cannot 'wash his hands' of guilt. Though such a person may appear very gracious and may disguise his true heart condition, God will see to it that the hate and badness that is actually within him is "uncovered in the congregation." He will fall into the pit he has dug for someone else.—Pr 26:22-28.

Family relationships. In the Proverbs marital fidelity is strictly counseled. One should find delight in 'the wife of his youth' and not be seeking satisfaction elsewhere. (Pr 5:15-23) Adultery will bring ruin and death to its practicers. (5:3-14; 6:23-35) A good wife is "a crown" and a blessing to her husband. But if a wife acts shamefully, she is "as rottenness in [her husband's] bones." (12:4) And it is a misery to a man even to live with a wife that is contentious. (25:24; 19:13; 21:19; 27: 15, 16) Outwardly pretty and charming though she may be, she is like "a gold nose ring in the snout of a pig." (11:22; 31:30) A foolish woman actually tears down her own house. (14:1) The fine value of the good wife—her industriousness, trustworthiness, and management of the household in faithfulness and submission to her husband—is fully described in Proverbs chapter 31.

Parents are shown to be fully responsible for their children, and discipline is emphasized as essential. (Pr 19:18; 22:6, 15; 23:13, 14; 29:15, 17)

The father's responsibility is highlighted, but the child must respect both father and mother if he wants life from Jehovah.—19:26; 20:20; 23:22; 30:17.

Animal care. Even concern for domestic animals is considered in the Proverbs. "The righteous one is caring for the soul of his domestic animal." (Pr 12:10) "You ought to know positively the appearance of your flock."—27:23.

Government stability and fidelity. The Proverbs express principles of good government. Men of high station, such as kings, should search matters through (Pr 25:2), manifest loving-kindness and trueness (20:28), and deal justly with their subjects (29:4; 31:9), including the lowly ones (29:14). Their counselors cannot be wicked men if the rulership is to be firmly established by righteousness. (25:4, 5) A leader must be a man of discernment and a hater of unjust profit.—28:16.

Whereas 'righteousness exalts a nation' (Pr 14: 34), transgression results in unstable government. (28:2) Revolution also brings great instability, and it is counseled against at Proverbs 24:21, 22: "My son, fear Jehovah and the king. With those who are for a change, do not intermeddle. For their disaster will arise so suddenly, that who is aware of the extinction of those who are for a change?"

Useful for Counsel. Since the Proverbs cover a wide range of human endeavor, they can provide a basis for giving much practical counsel and admonition, as they did for the writers of the Christian Greek Scriptures. "The heart of the righteous one meditates so as to answer." (Pr 15:28) However, it is not wise to counsel ridiculers. "He that is correcting the ridiculer is taking to himself dishonor, and he that is giving a reproof to someone wicked—a defect in him. Do not reprove a ridiculer, that he may not hate you. Give a reproof to a wise person and he will love you." (Pr 9:7, 8; 15:12; compare Mt 7:6.) Not all persons are ridiculers, and hence those in a position to counsel others should do so, as is highlighted by the words: "The very lips of the righteous one keep pasturing many."—Pr 10:21.

PROVINCE. The Greek term *e·par·khei´a*, rendered "province," refers to the sphere of authority of a Roman administrator. When Rome expanded its conquests beyond the Italian peninsula, the territory or geographic limits of the rule of a governor came to be called a province.

In 27 B.C.E. the first Roman emperor, Augustus, arranged the 22 then-existing provinces into two categories. The ten more peaceful ones that did not require the constant presence of Roman legions became senatorial provinces. The chief

Roman official of this type of province was the proconsul. (Ac 18:12; see PROCONSUL.) The remaining provinces were constituted imperial provinces, being directly responsible to the emperor and administered by a governor and, in larger ones, a military commander called a legate. Imperial provinces were often near the frontier or for some other reason required legions to be stationed in them; by closely controlling these provinces the emperor kept the army under his authority. After 27 B.C.E. new provinces formed from conquered territories became imperial provinces. A province might be subdivided into smaller administrative sections or districts.

The status of a province could shift between senatorial and imperial. (See CYPRUS.) Also, the boundaries of a province were sometimes adjusted. As a result, a particular city or area might be in a certain province at one time and later in an adjacent one, or even in a newly formed province. For examples of this, see CAPPADOCIA; CILICIA; PAMPHYLIA; PISIDIA.

With the banishment of Archelaus (Mt 2:22), son of Herod the Great, Judea came under the rule of Roman governors. The governor of the province was to some degree responsible to the legate of the larger province of Syria.

When Paul was delivered to Felix at Caesarea, the governor "inquired from what province he [Paul] was, and ascertained that he was from Cilicia." (Ac 23:34) Tarsus, Paul's birthplace, was in the Roman province of Cilicia.—Ac 22:3.

The governor of an imperial province was appointed by the emperor for no set period of office, unlike the proconsul of a senatorial province, who normally served for only one year. Felix was replaced as governor of the imperial province of Judea by Festus.—Ac 25:1.

See also JURISDICTIONAL DISTRICT.

PRUNING SHEARS. See FARMING IMPLEMENTS.

PSALMS, BOOK OF. A book seemingly consisting of five collections of sacred songs—(1) Ps 1-41; (2) 42-72; (3) 73-89; (4) 90-106; (5) 107-150 —each collection ending with a blessing pronounced on Jehovah. According to their place in the book, the individual psalms were evidently known by number from ancient times. For example, what is now called "the second psalm" was also designated as such in the first century C.E. —Ac 13:33.

Style. The poetry of the book of Psalms consists of parallel thoughts or expressions. (See HEBREW, II [Hebrew Poetry].) Distinctive are the

acrostic, or alphabetic, psalms. (Ps 9, 10, 25, 34, 37, 111, 112, 119, 145) In these psalms the initial verse or verses of the first stanza begin with the Hebrew letter 'a'leph, the next verse(s) with behth, and so on through all or nearly all the letters of the Hebrew alphabet. This arrangement may have served as a memory aid. For the terminology found in the book of Psalms, see ALAMOTH; ASCENTS; GITTITH; HIGGAION; MAHALATH, II; MASKIL; MIKTAM; MUTH-LABBEN; NEHILOTH; SELAH; SHEMINITH.

Superscriptions. The headings, or superscriptions, found at the beginning of many psalms identify the writer, furnish background material, provide musical instructions, or indicate the use or purpose of the psalm. (See the superscriptions of Ps 3, 4, 5, 6, 7, 30, 38, 60, 92, 102.) At times the superscriptions provide the needed information for locating other scriptures that illuminate a particular psalm. (Compare Ps 51 with 2Sa 11:2-15; 12:1-14.) Since other poetic parts of the Bible are often introduced similarly (Ex 15:1; De 31:30; 33:1; Jg 5:1; compare 2Sa 22:1 with the superscription of Ps 18), this suggests that the superscriptions originated with either the writers or the collectors of the psalms. Lending support to this is the fact that as far back as the writing of the Dead Sea Psalms Scroll (dated between 30 and 50 C.E.), the superscriptions were part of the main text.

Writers. Of the 150 psalms, the superscriptions attribute 73 to David, 11 to the sons of Korah (one of these [Ps 88] also mentioning Heman), 12 to Asaph (evidently denoting the house of Asaph; see ASAPH No. 1), one to Moses, one to Solomon, and one to Ethan the Ezrahite. Additionally, Psalm 72 is "regarding Solomon" and apparently was written by David. (See Ps 72:20.) From Acts 4:25 and Hebrews 4:7 it is evident that Psalms 2 and 95 were written by David. Psalms 10, 43, 71, and 91 appear to be continuations of Psalms 9, 42, 70, and 90 respectively. Therefore, Psalms 10 and 71 may be attributed to David, Psalm 43 to the sons of Korah, and Psalm 91 to Moses. There are indications that Psalm 119 may have been written by young prince Hezekiah (Note Ps 119:9, 10, 23, 46, 99, 100.) This leaves over 40 psalms without a specific composer named or indicated.

The individual psalms were written over a period of about 1,000 years, from the time of Moses until after the return from Babylonian exile.—Ps 90:Sup; 126:1, 2; 137:1, 8.

Compilation. Since David composed many of them and organized the Levite musicians into 24 service groups, it is reasonable to conclude that he started a collection of these songs to be used at the sanctuary. (2Sa 23:1; 1Ch 25:1-31; 2Ch 29:25-30) Thereafter other collections must have been made, as may be deduced from the repetition found in the book. (Compare Ps 14 with 53; 40:13-17 with 70; 57:7-11 with 108:1-5.) Numerous scholars believe that Ezra was responsible for arranging the book of Psalms into final form.

HIGHLIGHTS OF PSALMS

A compilation of 150 sacred songs, many of which are based on the personal experiences of David and other servants of Jehovah

Composed over a period of some 1,000 years, starting with the time of Moses and extending beyond the return from Babylonian exile

Expressions of thanks and praise to Jehovah

Because of the greatness of his name (99:3; 113; 148:13, 14)

For his grand creative works (33:1-9; 148:1-12)

Since he is the Great Shepherd (23)

On account of his answering prayers (21:1-7; 28; 116; 118:21)

Because of who he is (50; 95:1-7; 96:4-13; 97; 150)

For deliverances from enemies and from distressing circumstances (18; 30; 107; 140; 149)

On account of his righteous judgments (67:3, 4; 98)

Because of his personal qualities (57:9-11; 92; 100; 108:1-4; 117; 138:1, 2)

For his bounteous provisions (37:25; 67:5-7; 145:15, 16)

Prompted by his past dealings with his people (66; 81; 105; 106; 126; l36:10-24; 147)

Petitions for God's mercy and help

For deliverance from enemies (3-5; 7; 12; 13; 17; 31; 59)

To have sins forgiven (19:12, 13; 25:7, 11; 32; 51:1, 2, 7-15; 130)

For guidance in conduct (119:124, 125; 143:8, 10)

To be sustained in sickness and distress (41:1-4)

For favor when experiencing affliction (6:2, 9; 9:13, 14; 123)

Prophecies fulfilled in the Messiah

He was from the royal line of David (89:3, 4, 29, 36, 37; 132:11)

Zeal for Jehovah's house consumed him (69:9)

He spoke with illustrations (78:2)

He was betrayed by an intimate associate (41:9; 55:12-14)

The manner of his execution was indicated (22:16, ftn)

He was reproached and reviled (22:6-8; 69:9)

Lots were cast over clothing (22:18)

He was given vinegar to drink (69:21)

None of his bones were broken (34:20)

He was raised from Sheol (16:10)

The stone rejected by the builders became head of the corner (118:22)

He ascended on high, provided gifts in the form of men (68:18)

He was glorified and given dominion over everything (8:5-8)

He received kingship (2:6; 110)

He will destroy nations that oppose him (2:8, 9; 45:3-5)

He has a royal marriage; he will appoint princes in the earth (45:2, 6-17)

His rule over the earth will be just and compassionate (72)

Basic Bible doctrines appearing in the book of Psalms

The identity and qualities of the true God (78:38, 39; 83:18; 86:15; 90:1-4; 102:24-27; 103; 139)

Jehovah's sovereignty (11:4-7; 24:1; 29; 44; 47; 48; 76; 93)

Sanctification of God's name (79; 83)

All men are sinners (14:1-3; 51:5; 53:1-3)

The folly of idolatry (115:4-8; 135:15-18)

The condition of the dead (6:5; 88:10-12; 115:17; 146:4)

The earth will be a lasting home for the righteous (37:9-11, 29; 104:5; 115:16)

Inspired advice to help us gain Jehovah's approval

Fear Jehovah and obey his commands (112:1-4; 128)

Cultivate a high esteem for God's utterances, his law (1:2; 19:7-11; 119)

Trust in Jehovah (9:10; 115:9-11; 125; 146:5-7)

Patiently wait on him to act (42; 43)

Pursue peace and righteousness (34:14, 15)

Keenly appreciate being with God's people, being in His house (84; 122; 133)

Avoid bad associations (1:1; 26:4, 5; 101:3-8)

Teach children about Jehovah's dealings (78:3-8)

Speak the truth; avoid slander and false oaths (15:2, 3; 24:3-5; 34:13)

Keep your word, even when it proves to be bad for you (15:4)

Avoid the misuse of money (15:5)

Generosity brings blessings to the giver (112:5-10)

Praise Jehovah publicly (26:7, 12; 40:9)

There is evidence that the contents of the book of Psalms were fixed at an early date. The order and content of the book in the Greek *Septuagint* basically agree with the Hebrew text. Reasonably, therefore, the book of Psalms must have been complete in the third century B.C.E., when work on this Greek translation began. A fragment of the Hebrew text that was in use in the third quarter of the first century C.E. containing Psalm 150:1-6 is immediately followed by a blank column. This appears to indicate that this ancient Hebrew manuscript ended the book of Psalms there and thus likewise corresponded to the Masoretic text.

Accurate Preservation of Text. The Dead Sea Psalms Scroll provides evidence of the accurate preservation of the Hebrew text. Although about 900 years older than the generally accepted Masoretic text, the contents of this scroll (41 canonical psalms, whole or in part) basically correspond to the text on which most translations are based. Noted Professor J. A. Sanders: "Most of [the variants] are orthographic and important only to those scholars who are interested in clues to the pronunciation of Hebrew in antiquity, and such matters. . . . Some variants commend themselves immediately as improvements of the text, especially those that offer a clearer Hebrew text but make little or no difference in translation or interpretation."—*The Dead Sea Psalms Scroll,* 1967, p. 15.

Inspired of God. That the book of Psalms is part of God's inspired Word there can be no question. It is in complete harmony with the rest of the Scriptures. Comparable thoughts are often found elsewhere in the Bible. (Compare Ps 1 with Jer 17:5-8; Ps 49:12 with Ec 3:19 and 2Pe 2:12; Ps 49:17 with Lu 12:20, 21.) Also, many are the quotations from the Psalms found in the Christian Greek Scriptures.—Ps 5:9 (Ro 3:13); 8:6 (1Co 15:27; Eph 1:22); 10:7 (Ro 3:14); 14:1-3; 53:1-3 (Ro 3:10-12); 19:4 (Ro 10:18); 24:1 (1Co 10:26); 32:1, 2 (Ro 4:7, 8); 36:1 (Ro 3:18); 44:22 (Ro 8:36); 50:14 (Mt 5:33); 51:4 (Ro 3:4); 56:4, 11; 118:6 (Heb 13:6); 62:12 (Ro 2:6); 69:22, 23 (Ro 11:9, 10); 78:24 (Joh 6:31); 94:11 (1Co 3:20); 95:7-11 (Heb 3:7-11, 15; 4:3-7); 102:25-27 (Heb 1:10-12); 104:4 (Heb 1:7); 112:9 (2Co 9:9); 116:10 (2Co 4:13); 144:3 (Heb 2:6), and others.

With reference to himself David wrote: "The spirit of Jehovah it was that spoke by me, and his word was upon my tongue." (2Sa 23:2) Such inspiration is confirmed by the apostle Peter (Ac 1:15, 16), by the writer of the letter to the Hebrews (Heb 3:7, 8; 4:7), and by other first-century Christians (Ac 4:23-25). Most outstanding is the testimony of the Son of God. (Lu 20:41-44) After his resurrection, he said to his disciples: "These are my words which I spoke to you while I was yet with you, that all the things written in the law of Moses and in the Prophets and Psalms [the first book of the Hagiographa, or Holy Writings, and hence designating this entire section] about me must be fulfilled."—Lu 24:44.

Messiah's experiences and activities foretold. An examination of the Christian Greek Scriptures reveals that much was foretold in the Psalms concerning the activities and experiences of the Messiah, as the following examples will demonstrate.

When presenting himself for baptism, Jesus signified that he had come to do his Father's "will" in connection with the sacrifice of his own "prepared" body and with reference to the doing away of animal sacrifices offered according to the Law, as written at Psalm 40:6-8. (Heb 10:5-10) Jehovah accepted Jesus' presentation of himself, pouring out his spirit upon him and acknowledging him as his Son, as foretold at Psalm 2:7. (Mr 1:9-11; Heb 1:5; 5:5) Also, as had been foretold at Psalm 8:4-6, the man Jesus was "a little lower than angels."—Heb 2:6-8.

During the course of his ministry, he gathered and trained disciples. These he was not ashamed to call his "brothers," as had been written at Psalm 22:22. (Heb 2:11, 12; compare Mt 12:46-50; Joh 20:17.) In accord with what had been foretold in the Psalms, Jesus spoke with illustrations (Ps 78:2; Mt 13:35), manifested zeal for Jehovah's house by cleansing it of commercialism, and did not please himself. (Ps 69:9; Joh 2:13-17; Ro 15:3) Yet he was hated without cause. (Ps 35:19; 69:4; Joh 15:25) The ministry of Christ Jesus in behalf of circumcised Jews served to verify the promises made to their forefathers and, later, moved people of the nations to glorify and praise Jehovah. This too had been foretold.—Ps 18:49; 117:1; Ro 15:9, 11.

When Jesus rode into Jerusalem on the colt of an ass, crowds hailed him with the words of Psalm 118:26. (Mt 21:9) When the chief priests and scribes objected to what boys at the temple were saying in acknowledging Jesus as "the Son of David," Jesus silenced the religious opposers by quoting Psalm 8:2.—Mt 21:15, 16.

The book of Psalms pointed forward to Jesus' betrayal by an intimate associate (Ps 41:9; Joh 13:18), for whom, as foretold, replacement would be made. (Ps 69:25; 109:8; Ac 1:20) Even the ranging up against Jesus by rulers (Herod and Pontius Pilate) with men of nations (such as the Roman soldiers) and with peoples of Israel ha-been foretold (Ps 2:1, 2; Ac 4:24-28), as had his rejection by Jewish religious builders. (Ps 118:22, 23; Mt 21:42; Mr 12:10, 11; Ac 4:11) And false witnesses testified against him, as Psalm 27:12 foretold.—Mt 26:59-61.

Upon arriving at the place of impalement, Jesus was offered wine mixed with gall. (Ps 69:21; Mt 27:34) Prophetically alluding to the impalement itself, the psalmist wrote: "Dogs have surrounded me; the assembly of evildoers themselves have enclosed me. Like a lion they are at my hands and my feet." (Ps 22:16) Roman soldiers distributed Jesus' garments by casting lots. (Ps 22:18; Mt 27:35; Lu 23:34; Joh 19:24) His religious enemies mocked him in the words recorded by the psalmist. (Ps 22:8; Mt 27:41-43) Suffering from intense thirst, Jesus asked for a drink. (Ps 22:15; Joh 19:28) Again he was offered sour wine. (Ps 69:21; Mt 27:48; Joh 19:29, 30) Just before his death, Jesus, quoting Psalm 22:1, cried out: "My God, my God, why have you forsaken me?" (Mt 27:46; Mr 15:34) Breathing his last, he drew on Psalm 31:5 as he said: "Father, into your hands I entrust my spirit." (Lu 23:46) As the psalmist had further foretold, none of his bones were broken.—Ps 34: 20; Joh 19:33, 36.

Though laid in a tomb, Jesus was not forsaken in Hades nor did his flesh see corruption, but he was raised from the dead. (Ps 16:8-10; Ac 2:25-31; 13:35-37) Upon his ascension to heaven, he was seated at God's right hand, waiting until his enemies would be placed as a stool for his feet. (Ps 110:1; Ac 2:34, 35) He also became a priest according to the manner of Melchizedek (Ps 110:4; Heb 5:6, 10; 6:20; 7:17, 21) and gave gifts in the form of men. (Ps 68:18; Eph 4:8-11) All these details were prophesied in the Psalms. Jesus' coming in the role of God's executioner to dash the nations to pieces is yet future. (Ps 2:9; Re 2:27; 19:14, 15) Thereafter Christ as King will bring lasting blessings to his loyal subjects. Though originally written regarding Solomon, the description of his rulership at Psalm 72 applies to an even greater degree to the Messiah. Testifying to this fact is the prophecy of Zechariah (9:9, 10), which echoes Psalm 72:8 and is applied to Christ Jesus. —Mt 21:5.

For other fulfillments of the book of Psalms, compare Psalm 45 with Hebrews 1:8, 9; Revelation 19:7-9, 11-15; 21:2, 9-11.

More Than Beautiful Poetry. Besides pointing to future events, the Psalms contain much from which an individual can draw encouragement and that can serve as a guide for him. The Psalms are more than beautiful poetry. They de-

pict life as it actually is—the joys, sorrows, fears, and disappointments. Throughout, there is evidence of the psalmists' intimate relationship with Jehovah God. And God's activities and qualities are sharply brought into focus, motivating expressions of praise and thanks.

Real happiness is shown to stem from avoiding association with wicked ones (Ps 1:1, 2), finding delight in Jehovah's law (Ps 1:1, 2), taking refuge in his anointed one (2:11, 12), trusting in Jehovah (40:4), acting with consideration toward the lowly ones (41:1, 2), receiving correction from Jehovah (94: 12, 13), obeying his commands (112:1; 119:1, 2), and having him as God and Helper (146:5, 6).

Reliance on Jehovah is admonished. "Throw your burden upon Jehovah himself, and he himself will sustain you. Never will he allow the righteous one to totter." (Ps 55:22; 37:5) Such reliance rules out the fear of men.—56:4, 11.

Waiting for God (Ps 42:5, 11; 43:5) as well as right speech and action are encouraged for one to gain divine approval. (1:1-6; 15:1-5; 24:3-5; 34: 13, 14; 37:3, 4, 8, 27; 39:1; 100:2) Stress is placed on the value of good association. (18:25, 26; 26: 4, 5) And counsel is given not to envy the prosperity or success of wicked persons, for they will perish.—37:1, 2, 7-11.

The Psalms indicate that God's servants can properly pray for such things as salvation or deliverance (Ps 3:7, 8; 6:4; 35:1-8; 71:1-6), favor (4:1; 9:13), guidance (5:8; 19:12-14; 25:4, 5; 27:11; 43:3), protection (17:8), forgiveness of sins (25:7, 11, 18; 32:5, 6; 41:4; 51:1-9), a pure heart, a new and steadfast spirit (51:10), and the glorification of God's name (115:1). They can also pray to be examined, refined (26:2), and judged (35:24; 43:1), as well as to be taught goodness, sensibleness, knowledge, and God's regulations.—119:66, 68, 73, 124, 125, 135.

Highlight God's activities and qualities. The Psalms enhance appreciation for Jehovah God, whose existence only the senseless one would deny. (Ps 14:1; 19:7-11; 53:1) Jehovah is revealed as "a lover of righteousness and justice" (33:5), "a refuge and strength, a help that is readily to be found during distresses." (46:1) He is a righteous Judge (7:11; 9:4, 8), the Creator (8:3; 19:1; 33:6), King (10:16; 24:8-10), Shepherd (23:1-6), and Teacher (25:9, 12), the Provider for both man and the animals (34:10; 147:9), the Savior or Deliverer (35:10; 37:39, 40; 40:17; 54:7), and the Source of life (36:9) and of comfort (86:17), blessing, and strength.—29:11.

Jehovah does not "forget the outcry of the afflicted ones" (Ps 9:12; 10:14) but answers the prayers of his servants (3:4; 30:1, 2; 34:4, 6, 17, 18), rewarding and protecting them. (3:3, 5, 6; 4:3, 8; 9:9, 10; 10:17, 18; 18:2, 20-24; 33:18-20; 34:22; see 34:7 concerning angelic protection.) He hates wickedness and takes action against wrongdoers.—5:4-6, 9, 10; 9:5, 6, 17, 18; 21:8-12; 99:8.

Jehovah is shown to be fear inspiring (Ps 76:7) and great (77:13), yet humble (18:35); he is holy (99:5) and abundant in goodness (31:19) and power. (147:5) He is "merciful and gracious, slow to anger and abundant in loving-kindness and trueness." (86:15) His understanding is beyond recounting (147:5), and his creative works bespeak his wisdom. (104:24) He counts the number of stars and calls all of them by name. (147:4) He is able to see even the human embryo. (139:16) He can heal all maladies. (103:3) He can cause wars to cease by wrecking the war equipment of the enemy. (46:9) He has been actively involved in many events of history in furtherance of his righteous purpose. (44:1-3; 78:1-72; 81:5-7; 105:8-45; 106:7-46; 114:1-8; 135:8-12; 136:4-26) Truly such a God deserves to be given praise and thanks. (92:1; 96:1-4; 146–150) To trust in men (60:11; 62:9), riches (49:6-12, 17), or idols (115:4-8; 135:15-18) would be foolishness.

Discuss value of God's word. The Psalms also teach appreciation for God's word. The sayings of Jehovah are shown to be pure (Ps 12:6) and refined. (18:30) His law is precious (119:72) and is truth. (119:142) Lasting benefits result from observing his perfect law, trustworthy reminders, upright orders, clean commandments, and righteous judicial decisions. (19:7-11) God's word serves to illuminate an individual's path (119:105), and his commandments make one wise, give insight and understanding.—119:98-100, 104.

Clarify and supplement other scriptures. At times the book of Psalms clarifies or supplements other parts of the Bible. It shows that 'afflicting one's soul,' as was done by the Israelites on Atonement Day (Le 16:29; 23:27; Nu 29:7), pertains to fasting. (Ps 35:13) The psalmist alone tells of the severe treatment accorded, at least initially, to Joseph while imprisoned in Egypt: "With fetters they afflicted his feet, into irons his soul came." (105:18) From the Psalms we learn that "deputations of angels" were involved in bringing the plagues upon Egypt (78:44-51) and that, in the wilderness, the miraculously provided water "went through the waterless regions as a river" (105:41), thus providing an ample and readily accessible water supply for the nation of Israel and their many domestic animals. The Psalms furnish evidence that Pharaoh himself died in the Red Sea. —136:15.

The Psalms indicate that the Israelites experienced reverses and great hardship prior to the defeat of the Edomites in the Valley of Salt. (Ps 60:Sup, 1, 3, 9) This suggests that the Edomites invaded Judah while the nation was warring in the N with the forces of Aram-naharaim and Aram-Zobah.

Psalm 101 reveals David's manner of administering affairs of state. As his servants, David selected only faithful persons. He could not put up with arrogant individuals and did not tolerate slander. Daily he was concerned about bringing wicked ones to justice.

PTOLEMAIS (Ptol·e·ma'is) [City of [Named for] Ptolemy]. Later name of Acco. The apostle Paul stopped at this seaport city near Mount Carmel on his way to Jerusalem about 56 C.E.—Ac 21:7; see Acco.

PUAH (Pu'ah). This name represents two similar Hebrew names that differ in gender and meaning but that are spelled alike in both their Greek and English translations.

1. [*Pu·'ah'*]. Second son of Issachar.—1Ch 7:1; see Puvah.

2. [*Pu·'ah'*]. A Hebrew midwife who, together with midwife Shiphrah, was commanded by Pharaoh to kill all male babies born to the Hebrews. However, because she feared God, she preserved the baby boys alive and was blessed by Jehovah with a family of her own.—Ex 1:15-21.

3. [*Pu·'ah'*]. Father of Judge Tola and son of Dodo; tribe of Issachar.—Jg 10:1.

PUBLIC INSTRUCTOR. One who has been educated in a particular field of knowledge and who teaches others publicly. The expression "public instructor" is translated from the Greek word *gram·ma·teus'. The New English Bible* renders this "teacher"; *Knox* uses the expressions "scholar" and 'man of learning.' A footnote in the *New World Translation* reads: "learned person." (Mt 13:52, ftn; Mt 23:34) The same Greek word is usually rendered "scribe"; but to make clear that it is not the Jewish religious group known as the scribes to which reference is being made, the expression "public instructor" is used in the *New World Translation* when the passage refers to Jesus' own disciples.

When Jesus was on earth, the scribes (*gram·ma·teis'*) were men versed in the Law and teachers of the people, but they had become corrupted by traditions of men and pagan doctrines. The term "scribes" was used toward them more as a title designating them as a class, rather than having to do with their original copyist duties.

Jesus came to bear witness to the truth. To get the good news of the Kingdom preached, he prepared his disciples to be teachers, public instructors, respecting the Kingdom of God. He magnified their office and the importance of listening to their teaching when he spoke of them as public instructors; he likened each of them to a learned man having a veritable treasure store from which to draw. (Mt 13:52) These he sent forth to Israel, but Israel's own scribes did not discern the treasures that God, through these men, was holding out to them. On the contrary, they opposed the public instruction and took part in scourging, persecuting, and killing Jesus and his associate public instructors, thereby proving themselves to be false instructors. Nevertheless, many persons of Israel and of the nations were taught by Jesus' instructed ones, and in turn, they themselves became public instructors in God's Word.—Mt 23:34; 28:19, 20.

Under the Law, the Levites were charged with seeing that the people received public instruction. (Le 10:11; De 17:10, 11; 2Ch 17:7-9) Moses the Levite, as mediator of the Law covenant, and later, Joshua of the tribe of Ephraim, as leader of the nation, were public instructors of God's people. (De 4:1; 34:9; Jos 8:35) Likewise, the judges and the faithful kings gave instructions in the Law when they heard and judged cases and when they presided on occasions having to do with worship.—1Ki 8:1-61; 2Ki 23:2.

An outstanding example of a public instructor is the priest Ezra, who, with Nehemiah's support, conducted a program of public instruction for the Israelites repatriated from Babylon. He read the Law and organized the Levites for the performance of their duties of "explaining the law to the people," "putting of meaning into it," and "giving understanding in the reading," thereby "instructing the people."—Ne 8:1-9.

PUBLIC READING.
Reading aloud for a group of persons to hear. In the Jewish synagogues there was a public reading of a portion of the Law on the Sabbath. Similarly, at meetings of the Christian congregation, there was public reading of the inspired Scriptures.

The Greek word a·na·gi·no'sko, which basically means "well know" (2Co 1:13), is rendered "read" or "read aloud" and is used with reference to both private and public reading of the Scriptures. (Mt 12:3; Lu 4:16; Ac 8:28; 13:27) The noun form a·na'gno·sis is rendered "public reading."—Ac 13:15; 1Ti 4:13.

Public reading was an important means that Jehovah used to instruct and educate his covenant people concerning his purposes and requirements. Such reading is first mentioned at Exodus 24:7, where Moses read from "the book of the covenant" in the ears of all the people. The Israelites were thereby enabled to enter intelligently into an agreement with Jehovah to keep the Law. Relatively few copies of Scripture were available in the days of ancient Israel; so the Levite priests were commanded: "You will read this law in front of all Israel in their hearing." Moses ordered them to read the Law to all the people together, young and old, male and female, Israelite and alien resident, in every Sabbath year at the Festival of Booths.—De 31:9-12.

After Israel entered the Promised Land, Joshua read aloud to the people "all the words of the law, the blessing and the malediction." (Jos 8:33-35) King Jehoshaphat dispatched princes, Levites, and priests to teach in the cities of Judah (2Ch 17:7-9), which teaching no doubt included public reading. Centuries later Josiah read in the hearing of all the people "the book of Jehovah's law by the hand of Moses" that Hilkiah the priest found during temple repair work, doubtless the original book of the Law written by Moses. (2Ki 23:2; 2Ch 34:14) The result was a national purge of demon worship. After the return from exile, Ezra, with Governor Nehemiah's support, read the Law to the people from daybreak until noon. Along with the reading, an explanation, or the sense, was given.—Ne 8:3, 8; see HEBREW, II (When Did Hebrew Begin to Wane?).

In the Synagogues. It was Jesus' custom to do public reading in the synagogue on the Sabbath; then he aided his listeners by explaining what he had read. (Lu 4:16) This had been done for many years. "For from ancient times Moses has had in city after city those who preach him, because he is read aloud in the synagogues on every sabbath." (Ac 15:21) Such public reading of the Law and Prophets was the synagogue custom and, according to rabbinic sources, followed this program: First, the Shema, or what amounted to the Jewish confession of faith, taken from Deuteronomy 6:4-9; 11:13-21 and Numbers 15:37-41, was read. Next came the reading of a portion of the Torah or Law, the Pentateuch, which in most cases was covered in one year. Finally, excerpts from the Prophets or haftarahs were read, along with appropriate exposition. At the conclusion of the public reading, a discourse or exhortation was given. After such a public reading in a synagogue in Antioch in Pisidia, Paul was invited to speak and gave a discourse or exhortation and encouragement to those assembled.—Ac 13:15.

In the Christian Congregation. In the first century, few possessed copies of the many scrolls of the Bible, making public reading essential. The apostle Paul commanded public reading of his letters at the meetings of the Christian congregations and ordered them to be exchanged with his letters to other congregations so that these also might be read. (Col 4:16; 1Th 5:27) Paul counseled the young Christian overseer Timothy to apply himself to "public reading, to exhortation, to teaching."—1Ti 4:13.

Public reading should be done with fluency. (Hab 2:2) Since public reading is for the education of others, a public reader must thoroughly discern what he is reading and have a clear understanding of the writer's intention, being careful in reading to avoid giving the wrong idea or impression to the listeners. According to Revelation 1:3, those who read that prophecy aloud, as well as those who hear the words and observe them, will be happy.

PUBLIUS (Pub′li·us) [from Lat., meaning "Popular"]. A wealthy land-owning resident of Malta who kindly entertained Paul and those with him for three days after their shipwreck on the island. Paul, in turn, healed Publius' father of fever and dysentery.—Ac 28:7, 8.

Publius was "the principal man of the island." In this instance such a designation appears to denote an official title comparable to governor, probably denoting the leading Roman officer on the island.

PUDENS (Pu′dens) [from Lat., meaning "Modest"]. A companion of Paul near the close of the apostle's life. He sent greetings to Timothy.—2Ti 4:21.

PUL.

1. The name given a king of Assyria at 2 Kings 15:19 and 1 Chronicles 5:26. During the reign of Menahem, king of Israel, Pul entered Palestine and received tribute from Menahem. The identity of Pul was long an open question. However, most scholars now conclude that Pul and Tiglath-pileser III of Assyria were the same, since the name Pulu (Pul) is found in the dynastic tablet known as the Babylonian King List A, whereas in the corresponding location in the "Synchronistic Chronicle" the name Tukultiapilesharra (Tiglath-pileser) is listed. (*Ancient Near Eastern Texts,* edited by J. Pritchard, 1974, pp. 272, 273) Perhaps "Pul" was his personal name or the name he was known by in Babylon, while Tiglath-pileser (Tiglath-pilneser) was the name he assumed when he became king of Assyria. With this understanding, 1 Chronicles 5:26 may be read to refer

to the same individual in saying, "Pul the king of Assyria even . . . Tilgath-pilneser the king of Assyria."—See TIGLATH-PILESER (III).

2. A country or people listed only in Isaiah 66:19, along with Tarshish (apparently southern Spain) and Lud (in N Africa). Evidently all three places were noted for their skilled archers. The exact location of Pul is unknown. The Greek *Septuagint* reads "Phud" or "Put" at Isaiah 66:19 instead of "Pul," and Put (identified with the Libyans in Africa) and Lud are linked in other texts. (Eze 27:10; Jer 46:9; see PUT.) However, the Masoretic text's reading of "Pul" is supported by the Dead Sea Scroll of Isaiah and the Syriac *Peshitta.* Some scholars have suggested that "Pul" was the island Philae in the Nile.

PUNISHMENT. See CRIME AND PUNISHMENT.

PUNITES (Pu′nites) [Of (Belonging to) Puvah or Puah]. The family descendants of Issachar's second son, Puvah.—Nu 26:23.

PUNON (Pu′non). A campsite between Zalmonah and Oboth that Israel reached sometime after leaving Mount Hor (Jebel Madurah [?]). (Nu 33:41-43) Its location has not been determined with certainty, but it is generally identified with Feinan, about 30 km (19 mi) SE of 'Ain Husb.

PUPIL. The opening in the colored iris of the eye. It appears black because behind the pupil is the dark interior of the eye. The pupil changes in size as the iris adjusts to existing light conditions. Light enters the clear cornea, passes through the pupil and into the eye's lens.

The Hebrew word *'i·shohn'* (De 32:10; Pr 7:2) when used with *'a′yin* (eye), literally means "little man of the eye"; similarly, *bath* (daughter) is used at Lamentations 2:18 with the idea "daughter of the eye," both expressions referring to the pupil. The two are combined for emphasis at Psalm 17:8 (*'i·shohn' bath 'a′yin*), literally, "little man, daughter of the eye" ("pupil of the eyeball," *NW*). The reference is evidently to the tiny image of oneself that can be seen reflected in that part of another's eye.

The eye is extremely tender and sensitive; even a small hair or speck of dust between the lid and eyeball is quickly noticed. The transparent part of the eye (the cornea) covering the pupil must be guarded and cared for, because if this portion is scarred by injury or becomes cloudy through disease, distorted vision or blindness can result. With force and yet with delicacy of expression the Bible uses "the pupil of your eyes" in speaking of that which is to be guarded with utmost care. God' law is to be so treated. (Pr 7:2) Mentioning God's fatherly care of Israel, Deuteronomy 32:10 says that He safeguarded the nation "as the pupil of his eye." David prayed that he would be protected and cared for by God as "the pupil of the eyeball." (Ps 17:8) He wanted Jehovah to be quick to act in his behalf when under enemy attack. (Compare Zec 2:8; where the Hebrew ba·vah', "eyeball," is used.)—See EYE.

Disciple. "Pupil" also means one who learns or takes instruction, a disciple. Thus some Bible versions use it to render the Greek ma·the·tes', as at Luke 6:40 (NE, TEV, NW, AT). On this meaning, see DISCIPLE.

PUR. A non-Hebrew word found at Esther 3:7 and 9:24, 26; it means "lot" (Heb., goh·ral'; see LOT, I). This is the singular form, the plural being "Purim." (Es 9:26, 28-32) "Pur" is linked with an Akkadian word, puru, meaning "lot." It is the source of the name of the Jewish festival Purim. —See PURIM.

PURAH (Pu'rah). The attendant, probably armor-bearer, of Gideon who went with him during the night to spy on the Midianite camp.—Jg 7:9-15.

PURCHASE. Something acquired as a result of giving in exchange items of value—money, goods, services, or even a life.

As early as Abraham's day people were formally buying and selling goods, properties, or services, using a medium of exchange such as money, much the same as today. Abraham "purchased with money" male slaves. (Ge 17:12, 13) Upon Sarah's death Abraham formally purchased a family burial plot from Ephron, one of the sons of Heth. (Ge 23:3-20; 49:29-32) The details of that first Scripturally recorded legal contract of history are interesting.

In a true display of courtesy Abraham bowed down when making his offer. Not the field, but only the cave "which is at the extremity of [Ephron's] field" is what Abraham wanted to buy. Ephron made a counteroffer. Whether he was feigning Oriental liberality by saying he would give the property to Abraham (Ge 23:7-11), or as some think, he was merely expressing willingness to part with it, that is 'give it up' for a price, is not certain. What is certain is his insistence that both the cave and the field be included in the deal. Final agreement was reached, the price named, the bargain made, and the money carefully weighed out, "four hundred silver shekels current with the merchants." (c. $880) (Ge 23:16) In those days money was not minted into coins but was

weighed on scales. Thus "the field and the cave that was in it and all the trees that were in the field, which were within all its boundaries round about, became confirmed to Abraham as his purchased property." All this legal transaction took place in the presence of both parties and witnesses, yes, "before the eyes of the sons of Heth among all those entering the gate of his city." (Ge 23:17, 18) Similarly, Jacob later purchased a tract of land from the Shechemites.—Ge 33:18, 19.

During a seven-year famine, Joseph, as the prime minister of Egypt, sold grain at first for money, and when that was exhausted, for payment he accepted their domestic animals, next the land, and finally the people themselves.—Ge 42:2-25; 47:13-23.

The Law of Moses strictly forbade buying and selling on the Sabbath, as it also prohibited unfair business dealings. During Israel's apostasy these laws were often violated.—Le 25:14-17; Ne 10:31; 13:15-18; Am 8:4-6.

When King David wanted to purchase the threshing floor of Araunah (Ornan), the man graciously tried to give it to the king. However, David insisted on paying a sum of 50 silver shekels ($110) for the immediate altar site plus the necessary sacrificial materials. Later, it appears, more of the surrounding property was added to include an area large enough for the whole temple site, the purchase price being 600 gold shekels by weight (c. $77,070). (2Sa 24:21-24; 1Ch 21:22-25) During the reigns of both Kings Jehoash and Josiah, purchases of materials and labor for the repair of the temple were made.—2Ki 12:9-12; 22:3-7.

Jeremiah purchased a field in his hometown of Anathoth, describing the legal transaction this way: "I wrote in a deed and affixed the seal and took witnesses as I went weighing the money in the scales."—Jer 32:9-16, 25, 44.

In the Christian Greek Scriptures there are also a number of references made to purchasing goods and materials—foodstuffs, oil, garments, pearls, fields, houses, gold, eyesalve, merchandise in general, animals, and even humans. (Mt 13:44-46; 25:8-10; 27:7; Mr 6:37; Joh 4:8; 13:29; Ac 1:18; 4:34-37; 5:1-3; Re 3:18; 13:17; 18:11-13; see BANK, BANKER.) Believing Jews were by purchase released from the curse of the Law through Christ, who became a curse instead of them when he, although innocent, was hanged upon a stake. (Ga 3:13; 4:5) "With the blood of his own Son," Jehovah purchased the entire "congregation of God." —Ac 20:28.

PURIFICATION. See CLEAN, CLEANNESS.

PURIM (Pu'rim). The festival celebrated on the 14th and 15th of Adar, the last month of the Jewish year, corresponding to late February and early March; also called the Festival of Lots. (Es 9:21) The name comes from the act of Haman in casting pur (lot) to determine the auspicious day to carry out an extermination plot against the Jews. Being an Agagite, perhaps a royal Amalekite, and a worshiper of pagan deities, he was resorting to this as "a species of divination." (Es 3:7, *Le*, ftn; see DIVINATION; LOT, I; PUR.) In King Ahasuerus' (Xerxes I) 12th year, on Nisan 13, apparently in the spring of 484 B.C.E., the official extermination decree that Haman had induced the king to approve was prepared for all the Persian provinces, commanding the destruction of the Jews.

Commemoration of Deliverance. The festival commemorates the Jews' deliverance from destruction through Haman's plot. Consequently, the name Purim was probably given by the Jews in irony. (Es 9:24-26) It is also called in the Apocryphal book of Maccabees "Mordecai's day," since Mordecai played an important part in the events pertaining to the festival. (2 Maccabees 15:36, *AT*) Through the efforts of Queen Esther, at the risk of her life and as directed by her older cousin Mordecai, the Jews were delivered. Esther fasted for three days before seeking an audience with the king to invite him to a banquet, and then to a second banquet where her petition could be presented. (Es 4:6–5:8) The petition was favorably heard, and since the original decree could not be changed on account of the unchangeable law of the Medes and Persians (Da 6:8), another decree was issued on the 23rd day of Sivan. This document granted the Jews the right to defend themselves and enabled them to prepare. It was written by Mordecai and translated into many languages for various districts of the Persian Empire. The Jews fought—with the help of the princes, satraps, and governors—and turned the tables on the anti-Jewish enemies. A great slaughter took place on Adar 13, not of the Jews, but of their enemies. It continued in the royal city of Shushan through the 14th. On the 14th day of Adar the Jews in the jurisdictional districts rested, and those in Shushan on the 15th day, with banqueting and rejoicing.—Es 8:3–9:19.

To commemorate this deliverance, Mordecai imposed upon the Jews the obligation to observe Adar 14 and 15 each year with 'banqueting and rejoicing and sending portions to one another and gifts to the poor people.' (Es 9:20-22) Later, another letter was written with the confirmation of Esther the queen commanding this festival. It was to be held in each generation, in each family, jurisdictional district, and city at the appointed time each year.—Es 9:28-31; see ESTHER, BOOK OF.

The festival is celebrated by the Jews to this day in a detailed way, with many additions. One of the traditional enlargements that came in the process of time was the setting aside of the 13th day of Adar as a day of fasting, called the Fast of Esther. Trade or labor is not prohibited during this festival.

A Question on John 5:1. There is no direct mention of the Festival of Purim in the Christian Greek Scriptures. Some have claimed that there is a reference to it at John 5:1: "After these things there was a festival of the Jews, and Jesus went up to Jerusalem." However, the application of this verse to the Festival of Purim is unsubstantiated. Certain manuscripts have the definite article, reading: "the festival of the Jews." (See *NW* ftn.) This would indicate that it must have been one of the three solemn seasonal festivals listed at Deuteronomy 16:16, especially when we note that Jesus went up to Jerusalem, which he would not be required to do to keep the Festival of Purim. Purim was connected more with the local synagogue and the local area than with the temple; the festival was to be kept in the city of one's residence. It is also improbable that Jesus would travel on foot all the way to Jerusalem and then leave again for Galilee, with Passover only a month away. Furthermore, if one adopts the view that John 5:1 refers to Purim and John 6:4 to Passover a month later, it would crowd an impossible number of events into this short space of time, for it would include the ministry of Jesus in Capernaum, travels in Galilee, and a return to Capernaum and to Judea and Jerusalem. (See JESUS CHRIST [Chart of Main Events of Jesus' Earthly Life].) There is reason to believe, then, that the "festival of the Jews" at John 5:1 was actually the Passover festival of 31 C.E.—See JESUS CHRIST (Evidence for three-and-a-half-year ministry).

Purpose. While it is said by some commentators that the Festival of Purim as celebrated by the Jews in the present day has more of a secular than a religious nature and is sometimes accompanied by excesses, this was not so at the time of its institution and early celebration. Both Mordecai and Esther were servants of the true God Jehovah, and the festival was established to honor Him. The deliverance of the Jews at that time can be attributed to Jehovah God, because the issue arose by reason of Mordecai's integrity in his course of exclusive worship of Jehovah. Haman was probably an Amalekite, whose nation Jehovah had specifically cursed and condemned to destruction. Mordecai respected God's decree and refused to bow to Haman. (Es 3:2, 5; Ex 17:14-16) Also, the words of Mordecai to Esther (Es 4:14) indicate that he looked to a higher power for deliverance for the Jews, and Esther's fasting before entering the king's presence with her original petition, a banquet invitation, indicated her appeal to God for help.—Es 4:16.

PURPLE. See Colors; Dyes, Dyeing.

PURSE. A bag or pouch used by both men and women to carry gold, silver, copper, coined money, or other items. Women sometimes had ornamental purses, or handbags, possibly of a long, round shape. (Isa 3:16, 22; 46:6; Mt 10:9) Early purses were made of leather, of woven rushes, or of cotton. Since they were in the form of bags, they were drawn together and secured at the neck by means of leather straps or other cords.—See Bag.

Also in use was the girdle purse (literally, 'girdle'; Gr., zo'ne; Mt 10:9; Mr 6:8), perhaps a type of money belt. Either the girdle had a hollow space in which money could be carried, or if the girdle was made of cloth and worn in folds, the money was kept in its folds.

Jesus, when sending out his 70 disciples in preaching work, evidently in Judea, told them not to provide themselves with purses, indicating that Jehovah God would provide for them through fellow Israelites, among whom hospitality was a custom. (Lu 10:1, 4, 7) Shortly before his death, however, Jesus advised the apostles to carry purses, for he knew that his disciples would soon be scattered and persecuted. Because of official opposition, even persons favoring their message might be afraid to assist them. Also, they would soon be carrying the Kingdom message to Gentile lands. All of this would require that Jesus' followers be prepared to care for themselves materially. —Lu 22:35, 36.

Highlighting the excelling value of spiritual things, Jesus urged his followers to make lasting purses for themselves, acquiring heavenly treasure.—Lu 12:33.

PUT. A "son" of Ham. (Ge 10:6; 1Ch 1:8) Although Put is mentioned elsewhere in the Bible, none of his individual offspring are named. Often his descendants lent military support to Egypt. (Jer 46:9; Eze 30:4-6; Na 3:9) They served as mercenaries in the armies of Tyre and contributed to that city's greatness. (Eze 27:3, 10) It was also foretold that Put would be among the forces of Gog of Magog.—Eze 38:5.

Available evidence points to a connection between Put and the Libyans of N Africa. In three of its occurrences, "Put" is rendered "Libyans" or "Libya" by the Greek *Septuagint* and the Latin *Vulgate*. (Jer 46:9; Eze 27:10; 38:5) The Hebrew "Put" also corresponds closely to the *put[i]ja* (usually considered to be Libya) of Old Persian inscriptions. However, Nahum 3:9 seems to indicate that Put and the *Lu·vim'* (Libyans) are separate peoples. But this in itself would not rule out identifying Put with the Libyans. The term "Libyans" was perhaps more comprehensive than the Hebrew designation *Lu·vim'*, as may be deduced from the reference made by Herodotus (II, 32) to "Libyans, many tribes of them."

The identification of Put with the "Punt" of Egyptian inscriptions is not generally accepted today for phonetic reasons.

PUTEOLI (Pu·te'o·li). In the first century C.E., a chief port SE of Rome. Paul arrived at Puteoli on his way to stand before Caesar in Rome about the year 59 C.E. (Ac 28:13) With the help of a S wind, his ship arrived "on the second day" at Puteoli from Rhegium, a place some 320 km (200 mi) to the SSE.

Christian brothers of Puteoli entreated Paul and those accompanying him to spend a week with them. (Ac 28:14) This indicates he enjoyed some freedom, though a prisoner. Earlier, while in custody at Caesarea and Sidon, Paul had similarly benefited from limited freedom.—Ac 24:23; 27:3.

Puteoli is generally identified with modern Pozzuoli, on the bay of the same name, about 10 km (6 mi) WSW of Naples. Extensive ruins of an ancient mole still are visible. Josephus calls the site by its older name, Dicaearchia, and says a Jewish colony was located there.—*Jewish Antiquities*, XVII, 328 (xii, 1).

PUTHITES (Pu'thites). A family that lived in Kiriath-jearim; descendants of Judah through Shobal.—1Ch 2:52, 53.

PUTIEL (Pu'ti·el). Father-in-law of Aaron's son Eleazar and grandfather of Phinehas.—Ex 6:25.

PUVAH (Pu'vah). A son of Issachar whose family descendants were called Punites. (Ge 46: 13; Nu 26:23) His name is spelled Puah at 1 Chronicles 7:1.

PYRRHUS (Pyr'rhus)[Fiery-Colored; Fiery Red]. A Beroean whose son Sopater accompanied Paul through Macedonia on part of his third missionary journey.—Ac 20:3, 4.

Q

QOHPH [ק]. The 19th letter of the Hebrew alphabet. In translating Hebrew names where it occurs, *qohph* is usually represented in English by "c" or "k," as in "Cainan" and "Kish." The sound is stronger than that of the letter *kaph* [כ] and is pronounced farther back in the throat, as a strong English "q" formed at the back of the palate. In the Hebrew, it is the initial letter in each of the eight verses in Psalm 119:145-152.

QUAIL [Heb., *selaw'*]. A small, plump-bodied bird, about 18 cm (7 in.) in length, that spends most of its time on the ground. Its flesh is very edible, and it is reported that by 1920 Egypt was exporting some three million quail annually to foreign markets, though this exportation has since decreased.

The birds described in the Bible are evidently the common migratory quail (*Coturnix coturnix*), which move northward from within Africa in the spring, arrive in Egypt about March, thereafter pass through Arabia and Palestine, and return at the approach of winter. They travel in large flocks, making their migration in stages and often flying during the night. Their wings allow for speedy flight but not for very long distances. Because of the heaviness of their bodies in relation to their wing strength, they sometimes arrive at their destination in a state of exhaustion. Quail, therefore, fly with the wind and customarily fly at rather low altitudes. Colonel Richard Meinertzhagen relates that in Port Said, Egypt, men at times use butterfly nets to catch quail as the birds fly down the streets at dawn.—*Birds of Arabia*, Edinburgh, 1954, p. 569.

The first reference to quail in the Biblical account (Ex 16:13) is with reference to events in the spring (Ex 16:1), and so the birds would have been flying north. The Israelites were in the Wilderness of Sin on the Sinai Peninsula, complaining about their food supplies. In response, Jehovah assured Moses that "between the two evenings" they would eat meat and in the morning would be satisfied with bread. (Ex 16:12) That evening "the quails began to come up and cover the camp," while in the morning the manna appeared on the earth. (Ex 16:13-15; Ps 105:40) Again, evidently in the spring (Nu 10:11, 33), about one year later, the grumblings of the Israelites over their limited diet of manna caused Jehovah to foretell that they would eat meat "up to a month of days" until it

became revolting to them. (Nu 11:4, 18-23) God then caused a wind, likely from the E or SE, to drive quail from the sea and caused them to "fall above the camp," abundant "like the sand grains" over a wide area for several miles around the camp's perimeter.—Nu 11:31; Ps 78:25-28.

The expression "about two cubits [c. 1 m; 3 ft] above the surface of the earth" has been explained in different ways. (Nu 11:31) Some consider that the quail actually fell to the ground and that in some places they were piled up to that height. Others, objecting that such action would undoubtedly result in a large portion of them dying and hence becoming unfit for eating by the Israelites, understand the text to mean that the quail flew at that low altitude over the ground, thereby making it quite easy for the Israelites to knock them to the ground and capture them. Expressing a similar idea, the Greek *Septuagint* reads: "all around the camp, about two cubits from the earth"; and the Latin *Vulgate* says: "all around the camp, and they were flying in the air at an altitude of two cubits above the earth."

The Israelites spent a day and a half gathering the quail; "the one collecting least gathered ten homers [2,200 L; 62 bu]." (Nu 11:32) In view of the "six hundred thousand men on foot," mentioned by Moses (Nu 11:21), the number of quail collected must have been many millions; hence it was no simple catch resulting from ordinary migration but, rather, a powerful demonstration of divine power. The quantity collected was too great for eating then; hence the greedy Israelites "kept spreading them extensively all around the camp for themselves." (Nu 11:32) This may have been for the purpose of drying out the meat of the slaughtered quail in order to preserve as many of them as possible for future consumption. Such action would be similar to the ancient Egyptian practice, described by Herodotus (II, 77), of salting fish and then putting it in the sun to dry out.

QUARANTINE. See DISEASES AND TREATMENT.

QUARREL. A dispute (De 17:8), controversy (Jer 25:31), or case at law (Jer 11:20).

The Scriptures counsel against becoming involved in quarrels, or disputes, without cause. (Pr 3:30) Says the proverb: "As one grabbing hold of the ears of a dog is anyone passing by that is becoming furious at the quarrel that is not his." (Pr 26:17) The speech of stupid ones readily leads them into quarrels, and foolish ones do not exercise the needed restraint to avoid quarreling. (Pr 18:6; 20:3) Since "the squeezing out of anger" results in quarreling (Pr 30:33), slowness to anger has the opposite effect.—Pr 15:18.

Quarreling destroys a peaceful atmosphere (Pr 17:1) and may cause even the meekest of persons to lose self-control. For example, Israel's quarreling about there being no water at Kadesh prompted Moses and Aaron to act rashly, thereby losing the privilege of entering the Promised Land. Israel's unjustified quarreling with Jehovah's representatives actually constituted a quarrel with Jehovah. (Nu 20:2, 3, 10-13; 27:14; Ps 106:32) Those who become similarly involved in quarreling or violent controversies with God's servants are in a very serious position, one that can lead to death.—Compare Isa 41:8, 11, 12; 54:17.

Because of the detrimental effect of quarreling, the proverb counsels: "Before the quarrel has burst forth, take your leave." (Pr 17:14) Abram (Abraham) set a good example in this regard. Concerned that there be no disputes between his herdsmen and those of his nephew Lot, Abram suggested that they separate. Unselfishly he gave Lot the opportunity to choose the area where he would pasture his animals. (Ge 13:7-11) On the other hand, unfaithful Israelites in the time of Isaiah did not act like their forefather Abraham. Of them, it is said: "For quarreling and struggle you would fast." Even during the fast they were engaged in quarreling.—Isa 58:4.

The Mosaic Law covered cases of quarreling resulting in bodily injury. It prescribed paying compensation to the injured party for time lost from work.—Ex 21:18, 19.

Murmuring. Murmuring discourages and tears down. The Israelites, not long out of Egypt, murmured against Jehovah, finding fault with the leadership that he provided by his servants Moses and Aaron. (Ex 16:2, 7) Later their complaints so discouraged Moses that he asked to die. (Nu 11:13-15) Murmuring can be a deadly danger to the murmurer. Jehovah counted the things said by murmurers about Moses as actually being a rebellious complaint against His own divine leadership. (Nu 14:26-30) Many lost their lives as a result of faultfinding.

Accordingly, the Christian Greek Scriptures draw on the ancient examples to warn of the destructiveness of murmuring, or complaining. (1Co 10:10, 11) Jude tells of those who 'disregard lordship and speak abusively of glorious ones,' describing such ones as "murmurers, complainers about their lot in life, proceeding according to

their own desires, and their mouths speak swelling things, while they are admiring personalities for the sake of their own benefit."—Jude 8, 16.

Jesus condemned the faultfinding attitude when he said: "Stop judging that you may not be judged. Why, then, do you look at the straw in your brother's eye, but do not consider the rafter in your own eye? . . . Hypocrite! First extract the rafter from your own eye, and then you will see clearly how to extract the straw from your brother's eye."—Mt 7:1, 3-5; compare Ro 2:1.

QUARRY. An open-pit excavation from which various types of stone are cut. Limestone and marble, lying near the surface, are thus quarried. A large area near the present Damascus Gate of Jerusalem is believed to have been an ancient quarry. The first reference to such a place is at Joshua 7:4, 5, where it is reported that about 3,000 Israelites fled from Ai as far as Shebarim, meaning "Quarries." When Solomon prepared to build the temple, he commanded that great foundation stones be quarried from the mountains of Lebanon, and tens of thousands of men were conscripted for the work. (1Ki 5:13-18; 6:7) When it was necessary to repair the temple in the days of Jehoash, hewers of stone were hired for the work. (2Ki 12:11, 12) The tomb where Jesus was buried was one quarried out of rock.—Mt 27:59, 60; Mr 15:46.

Using an eloquent metaphor, Jehovah, by the mouth of Isaiah, calls to mind the quarry and its operation. (Isa 51:1) As indicated in the succeeding verse, "the rock" was apparently Abraham, as the human source of the nation, and "the hollow of the pit" was Sarah, whose pitlike womb bore Israel's ancestor Isaac. (Isa 51:2) However, since the birth of Isaac was by divine power and a miraculous act, the metaphoric quarrying may also have a higher spiritual application. Thus, Deuteronomy 32:18 refers to Jehovah as "The Rock who fathered" Israel, and the "One bringing you forth [the same verb used of Sarah at Isa 51:2] with childbirth pains."

Sometimes the product of the quarry was called by the same name. Hence the Hebrew word *pesilim'*, rendered "quarries" at Judges 3:19, 26, is elsewhere translated "graven images." (De 7:5; Ps 78:58; Isa 10:10) For this reason some have suggested that it may have been at a grove of such pagan gods, the product of the quarry, that Ehud turned back to pay Eglon a personal visit. Most translators, however, prefer the rendering "quarries."

Old quarries where partially finished work was abandoned have shed some light on the ancient methods of quarrying. Narrow channels were cut deep in the rock. Into these, dry wood was driven, where it was then made to swell with water until the rock split along its cleavage lines. In Roman times, stones weighing as much as five or ten tons were quarried some distance from the building sites. These were then moved on rollers or on sledges, the power being supplied by great armies of slave labor.

QUART. After the opening of "the third seal," as referred to at Revelation 6:5, 6, both a *khoi'nix* of wheat and three *khoi'ni·kes* of barley are said to sell for a denarius. Generally, scholars believe the size of the *khoi'nix* to be slightly more than a liter or a little less than a U.S. dry quart. Since a denarius was a day's wage in John's time (Mt 20:1-12), the selling of grains at such prices would indicate famine conditions.

QUARTERMASTER. Possibly the officer in charge of rations and supplies for the troops. A literal translation of the Hebrew *sar menu·chah'* is "prince of the resting-place" and may mean the one in charge of the king's living quarters when on a campaign or journey. Seraiah as quartermaster for King Zedekiah of Judah accompanied him on the trip to Babylon in the fourth year of Zedekiah's reign, carrying with him Jeremiah's written prophecy against Babylon. After reading it aloud in that city, Seraiah pitched it, tied to a stone, into the Euphrates, as a symbol of Babylon's future fall, never to rise again.—Jer 51:59-64.

QUARTUS (Quar'tus) [from Latin, meaning "Fourth"]. One living in Corinth whose greetings Paul included in his letter to the Romans, about 56 C.E. (Ro 16:23) Having a Roman name and knowing the brothers in Rome, he may have formerly been of that congregation.

QUEEN. In the modern sense, a title given either to a wife of a king or to a female monarch. In the Bible the title most often refers to women outside the kingdoms of Israel and Judah. The Hebrew word most nearly expressing the idea of queen as it is understood today is *mal·kah'*. But it was rare in the Orient for a woman to possess ruling authority. The queen of Sheba may have been one with such power. (1Ki 10:1; Mt 12:42) In the Christian Greek Scriptures, "queen" is translated from the word *ba·si'lis·sa*, the feminine form of the word for "king." The title is applied to Queen Candace of Ethiopia.—Ac 8:27.

In the Hebrew Scriptures *mal·kah'* is more often used with reference to a queen consort, or the leading wife of a king of a foreign power. Vashti,

as the chief wife of King Ahasuerus of Persia, was a consort queen rather than a ruling one. She was replaced by the Jewess Esther, making Esther consort queen, and while Esther had royal dignity, she was not an associate ruler (Es 1:9, 12, 19; 2:17, 22; 4:11); any authority she might have had was by the king's grant.—Compare Es 8:1-8, 10; 9:29-32.

Israel. The Hebrew word *gevi·rah'*, translated "queen" in some versions, means, more correctly, "lady" or "mistress." In the instances where the title is used, it seems to apply mainly to the mother or grandmother of the king, such women being given royal respect, for example, Jezebel the mother of King Jehoram of Israel. (2Ki 10:13) When Solomon's mother approached him with a request, he bowed to her and had a throne set for her at his right. (1Ki 2:19) The "lady" could be deposed by the king, as was Maacah the grandmother of King Asa of Judah, whom he removed from being "lady" because she had made a horrible idol to the sacred pole.—1Ki 15:13.

No woman could legally become head of state in the kingdoms of Israel and Judah. (De 17:14, 15) However, after the death of her son Ahaziah king of Judah, Athaliah, who was the daughter of wicked King Ahab of Israel and his wife Jezebel, destroyed all the kingdom heirs except Ahaziah's son Jehoash, whom Ahaziah's sister Jehosheba had hidden. Athaliah then reigned illegally for six years, until executed on orders from High Priest Jehoiada.—2Ki 11:1-3, 13-16.

Babylon. In Babylon the throne was confined to kings. At Daniel 5:10, the "queen" (Aramaic *mal·kah'*) was apparently, not the wife, but the mother of Belshazzar, as is indicated by her familiarity with events regarding Nebuchadnezzar, Belshazzar's grandfather. As the queen mother, she possessed a certain amount of royal dignity and was greatly respected by all, including Belshazzar.

Egypt. Early Egyptian heads of state were men. "Queens" were actually consorts. Tahpenes the wife of Pharaoh is called "lady" at 1 Kings 11:19. Hatshepsut ruled as queen only because she refused to surrender her regency when the heir, Thutmose III, became of age. After her death Thutmose III obliterated or destroyed all her monuments. Later, however, during the time of Ptolemaic (Macedonian) reign over Egypt, there were ruling queens.

In False Worship. The apostate Israelites of Jeremiah's day forsook Jehovah, their real King, and idolatrously made cakes, drink offerings, and sacrificial smoke to the "queen [Heb., *mele'kheth* of the heavens."—Jer 7:18; 44:17, 18; see QUEEN OF THE HEAVENS.

Babylon the Great is shown, at Revelation 18:7, to be saying boastfully, "I sit a queen [Gr., ba·si'lis·sa]," sitting on "peoples and crowds and nations and tongues." (Re 17:15) She maintains her control through her immoral relations with earthly rulers, even as did many queens of the past.—Re 17:1-5; 18:3, 9; see BABYLON THE GREAT.

"Queenly Consort" in Heaven. Since Hebrews 1:8, 9 applies Psalm 45:6, 7 to Christ Jesus, it seems likely that "the king's daughter" of Psalm 45:13 is prophetic of his bride class. This would make "the queenly consort" (Heb., she·ghal') mentioned in Psalm 45:9 the wife of the Great King, Jehovah. It is not upon this "queenly consort" but upon Jesus Christ and his 144,000 associates redeemed from the earth that Jehovah confers authority to rule as kings.—Re 20:4, 6; Da 7:13, 14, 27.

QUEEN OF THE HEAVENS.
The title of a goddess worshiped by apostate Israelites in the days of Jeremiah.—Jer 44:17-19.

Although the women were primarily involved, apparently the entire family participated in some way in worshiping the "queen of the heavens." The women baked sacrificial cakes, the sons collected the firewood, and the fathers lit the fires. (Jer 7:18) That the worship of this goddess had a strong hold on the Jews is reflected by the fact that those who had fled down to Egypt after the murder of Governor Gedaliah attributed their calamity to their neglecting to make sacrificial smoke and drink offerings to the "queen of the heavens." The prophet Jeremiah, though, forcefully pointed out the wrongness of their view.—Jer 44:15-30.

The Scriptures do not specifically identify the "queen of the heavens." It has been suggested that this goddess is to be identified with the Sumerian fertility goddess Inanna, Babylonian Ishtar. The name Inanna literally means "Queen of Heaven." The corresponding Babylonian goddess Ishtar was qualified in the Akkadian texts by the epithets "queen of the heavens" and "queen of the heavens and of the stars."

It appears that Ishtar worship spread to other countries. In one of the Amarna Tablets, Tushratta, writing to Amenophis III, mentions "Ishtar, mistress of heaven." In Egypt, an inscription of King Horemheb, believed to have reigned in the 14th century B.C.E., mentions "Astarte [Ishtar] lady of heaven." A fragment of a stele found at Memphis from the reign of Merneptah, Egyptian king believed to have reigned in the 13th century B.C.E., represents Astarte with the inscription: "Astarte, lady of heaven." In the Persian period, at Syene (modern Aswan), Astarte was surnamed "the queen of the heavens."

The worship of the "queen of the heavens" was practiced as late as the fourth century C.E. In about 375 C.E., in his treatise Panarion (79, 1, 7), Epiphanius states: "Some women decorate a sort of chariot or a four-cornered bench and, after stretching over it a piece of linen, on a certain feast day of the year they place in front of it a loaf for some days and offer it up in the name of Mary. Then all the women partake of this loaf." Epiphanius (79, 8, 1, 2) connected these practices with the worship of the "queen of the heavens" presented in Jeremiah and quotes Jeremiah 7:18 and 44:25.—Epiphanius, edited by Karl Holl, Leipzig, 1933, Vol. 3, pp. 476, 482, 483.

QUIRINIUS
(Qui·rin'i·us). Roman governor of Syria at the time of the "registration" ordered by Caesar Augustus that resulted in Jesus' birth taking place in Bethlehem. (Lu 2:1, 2) His full name was Publius Sulpicius Quirinius.

In the Chronographus Anni CCCLIIII, a list of Roman consuls, the name of Quirinius appears in 12 B.C.E. along with that of Messala. (Chronica Minora, edited by T. Mommsen, Munich, 1981, Vol. I, p. 56) Roman historian Tacitus briefly recounts Quirinius' history, saying: "[He] sprang from the municipality of Lanuvium—had no connection; but as an intrepid soldier and an active servant he won a consulate under the deified Augustus, and, a little later, by capturing the Homonadensian strongholds beyond the Cilician frontier, earned the insignia of triumph . . . , adviser to Gaius Caesar during his command in Armenia." (The Annals, III, XLVIII) His death took place in 21 C.E.

Not mentioned by Tacitus is Quirinius' relationship to Syria. Jewish historian Josephus relates Quirinius' assignment to Syria as governor in connection with the simultaneous assignment of Coponius as the Roman ruler of Judea. He states: "Quirinius, a Roman senator who had proceeded through all the magistracies to the consulship and a man who was extremely distinguished in other respects, arrived in Syria, dispatched by Caesar to be governor of the nation and to make an assessment of their property. Coponius, a man of equestrian rank, was sent along with him to rule over the Jews with full authority." Josephus goes on to relate that Quirinius came into Judea, to which his authority was extended, and ordered a taxation there. This brought much resentment and an unsuccessful attempt at revolt, led by "Judas, a

Gaulanite." (*Jewish Antiquities*, XVIII, 1, 2, 3, 4 [i, 1]) This is evidently the revolt referred to by Luke at Acts 5:37. According to Josephus' account it took place in "the thirty-seventh year after Caesar's defeat of Antony at Actium." (*Jewish Antiquities*, XVIII, 26 [ii, 1]) That would indicate that Quirinius was governor of Syria in 6 C.E.

For a long time this was the only governorship of Syria by Quirinius for which secular history supplied confirmation. However, in the year 1764 an inscription known as the *Lapis Tiburtinus* was found in Rome, which, though not giving the name, contains information that most scholars acknowledge could apply only to Quirinius. (*Corpus Inscriptionum Latinarum*, edited by H. Dessau, Berlin, 1887, Vol. 14, p. 397, No. 3613) It contains the statement that on going to Syria he became governor (or, legate) for 'the second time.' On the basis of inscriptions found in Antioch containing Quirinius' name, many historians acknowledge that Quirinius was also governor of Syria in the B.C.E. period.

There is uncertainty on their part, however, as to where Quirinius fits among the secularly recorded governors of Syria. Josephus lists Quintilius Varus as governor of Syria at the time of, and subsequent to, the death of Herod the Great. (*Jewish Antiquities*, XVII, 89 [v, 2]; XVII, 221 [ix, 3]) Tacitus also refers to Varus as being governor at the time of Herod's death. (*The Histories*, V, IX) Josephus states that Varus' predecessor was Saturninus (C. Sentius Saturninus).

Many scholars, in view of the evidence of an earlier governorship by Quirinius, suggest the years 3-2 B.C.E. for his governorship. While these dates would harmonize satisfactorily with the Biblical record, the *basis* on which these scholars select them is in error. That is, they list Quirinius as governor during those years because they place his rule *after* that of Varus and hence *after* the death of Herod the Great, for which they use the popular but erroneous date of 4 B.C.E. (See CHRONOLOGY; HEROD No. 1 [Date of His Death].) (For the same reason, that is, their use of the unproved date 4 B.C.E. for Herod's death, they give Varus' governorship as from 6 to 4 B.C.E.; the length of his rule, however, is conjectural, for Josephus does not specify the date of its beginning or of its end.) The best evidence points to 2 B.C.E. for the birth of Jesus. Hence Quirinius' governorship must have included this year or part thereof.

Some scholars call attention to the fact that the term used by Luke, and usually translated "governor," is he·ge·mon'. This Greek term is used to describe Roman legates, procurators, and proconsuls, and it means, basically, a "leader" or "high executive officer." Some, therefore, suggest that, at the time of what Luke refers to as the *"first registration,"* Quirinius served in Syria in the capacity of a special legate of the emperor exercising extraordinary powers. A factor that may also aid in understanding the matter is Josephus' clear reference to a dual rulership of Syria, since in his account he speaks of two persons, Saturninus and Volumnius, serving simultaneously as "governors of Syria." (*Jewish Antiquities*, XVI, 277, 280 [ix, 1]; XVI, 344 [x, 8]) Thus, if Josephus is correct in his listing of Saturninus and Varus as successive presidents of Syria, it is possible that Quirinius served simultaneously either with Saturninus (as Volumnius had done) or with Varus prior to Herod's death (which likely occurred in 1 B.C.E.). *The New Schaff-Herzog Encyclopedia of Religious Knowledge* presents this view: "Quirinius stood in exactly the same relation to Varus, the governor of Syria, as at a later time Vespasian did to Mucianus. Vespasian conducted the war in Palestine while Mucianus was governor of Syria; and Vespasian was *legatus Augusti,* holding precisely the same title and technical rank as Mucianus."—1957, Vol. IX, pp. 375, 376.

An inscription found in Venice (*Lapis Venetus*) refers to a census conducted by Quirinius in Syria. However, it provides no means for determining whether this was in his earlier or his later governorship.—*Corpus Inscriptionum Latinarum*, edited by T. Mommsen, O. Hirschfeld, and A. Domaszewski, 1902, Vol. 3, p. 1222, No. 6687.

Luke's proved accuracy in historical matters gives sound reason for accepting as factual his reference to Quirinius as governor of Syria around the time of Jesus' birth. It may be remembered that Josephus, virtually the only other source of information, was not born until 37 C.E., hence nearly four decades after Jesus' birth. Luke, on the other hand, was already a physician traveling with the apostle Paul by about 49 C.E. when Josephus was but a boy of 12. Of the two, Luke, even on ordinary grounds, is the more likely source for reliable information on the matter of the Syrian governorship just prior to Jesus' birth. Justin Martyr, a Palestinian of the second century C.E., cited the Roman records as proof of Luke's accuracy as regards Quirinius' governorship at the time of Jesus' birth. (*A Catholic Commentary on Holy Scripture,* edited by B. Orchard, 1953, p. 943) There is no evidence that Luke's account was ever challenged by early historians, even by early critics such as Celsus.

QUIVER. See ARMS, ARMOR.

R

RAAMAH (Ra'a·mah). A son of Ham's first-born, Cush, and brother of Nimrod. Raamah and his two sons Sheba and Dedan founded three of the 70 post-Flood families. (Ge 10:6-8; 1Ch 1:9) Many centuries later the tribal descendants of Raamah, Dedan, and Sheba all carried on trade with Tyre. (Eze 27:20, 22) Just where the tribe springing from Raamah resided is uncertain, but the city of Raamah near Ma'in in SW Arabia is likely.

RAAMIAH (Ra·a·mi'ah) [Jehovah Has Thundered; Uproar of Jehovah]. One who returned to Jerusalem with Zerubbabel. The name is an alternate form of Reelaiah.—Ne 7:7; Ezr 2:2.

RAAMSES (Ra·am'ses), **RAMESES** (Ram'e·ses) [from Egyptian, meaning "Ra [the sun-god] Has Begotten Him"]. When Jacob's family moved into Egypt they were assigned to live in "the land of Rameses." (Ge 47:11) Since elsewhere they are spoken of as residing in the land of Goshen, it appears that Rameses was either a district within Goshen or was another name for Goshen. (Ge 47:6) Later, the Israelites were enslaved and put to building cities "as storage places for Pharaoh, namely, Pithom and Raamses [the vowel pointing here differs slightly from that of "Rameses"]." (Ex 1:11) Many scholars suggest that Raamses was so named for the district of Rameses in which they assume it was located.

When the Exodus from Egypt began, Rameses is given as the starting point. Most scholars assume that the city is here meant, perhaps being the rendezvous site where the Israelites gathered from various parts of Goshen. But Rameses may here refer to a district, and it may be that the Israelites pulled away from all parts of the district, converging on Succoth as the place of rendezvous. —Ex 12:37; Nu 33:3-5.

The exact location of this starting point, if a city rather than a district is meant, is very uncertain. Modern scholars identify Rameses with the city called Per-Ramses (House of Ramses) in Egyptian records, placed by some at San el-Hagar in the NE corner of the Delta, and by others at Qantir, about 18 km (11 mi) to the south. But this identification rests on the theory that Ramses II was the Pharaoh of the Exodus. This theory, in turn, is based on inscriptions of Ramses II giving his claim to having built the city bearing his name (Per-Ramses), using slave labor. There is little reason, however, to believe that Ramses II was the ruler at the time of the Exodus, since his rule is not likely to have been much earlier than the 13th century B.C.E., or between 200 and 300 years after the Exodus (1513 B.C.E.). The Biblical Raamses began to be built before Moses' birth, hence over 80 years before the Exodus. (Ex 1:11, 15, 16, 22; 2:1-3) Furthermore, it is held that Per-Ramses was the capital city in the time of Ramses II, whereas the Biblical Raamses was only a 'storage place.' It is generally accepted that Ramses II was guilty of taking credit for certain achievements of his predecessors, and this raises the possibility that, at best, he only rebuilt or enlarged Per-Ramses. Finally, the name Rameses was clearly in use as far back as the time of Joseph (in the 18th century B.C.E.); so there is no reason to assume that its application (in the form Raamses) as the name of a city was exclusive with the time of Ramses II. (Ge 47:11) Its very meaning, too, makes it likely that it was popular among the Egyptians from early times. By the reign of Ramses II there were a number of towns that bore that name. D. B. Redford says: "Biblical Raamses and the capital *Pr R'-mś-św* [Per-Ramses], apart from the personal name, seem to have nothing in common. In the complete lack of corroborative evidence it is absolutely essential to exercise caution in equating the two."—*Vetus Testamentum,* Leiden, 1963, p. 410.

Because of the lack of reliable information, it can only be said that Rameses was likely not far from the Egyptian capital of the time of the Exodus. This would allow for Moses to have been at Pharaoh's palace on the night of the tenth plague and, before the next day's end, to begin leading the people of Israel on their march out of Egypt. (Ex 12:31-42; Nu 33:1-5) If the capital was then at Memphis, a city holding that position for many centuries, this would explain the Jewish tradition that the Exodus march (with Rameses as its starting point) began from the neighborhood of Memphis.—Compare *Jewish Antiquities,* II, 315 (xv, 1), which refers to Letopolis, a location near Memphis.

RABBAH (Rab'bah) [Many; Abundant].

1. A city in the SW extremity of the ancient kingdom of Ammon after its loss of territory to the Amorites. Rabbah is the only city of the Ammonite kingdom that is named in the Biblical record, so it is assumed to have been the capital. It lay about 37 km (23 mi) E of the Jordan. The city was on a

Ruins at 'Amman, the location of ancient Rabbah of Ammon and later of Philadelphia in the Decapolis

tributary of the upper Jabbok and was thus in position to benefit from the rich fertility of that region. Also, it was an important link in the trade route between Damascus and Arabia.

"Rabbah of the sons of Ammon" (*Rab·bath′ beneh′ 'Am·mohn′*) is first mentioned in the Bible as being the location of the iron bier of Og, king of Bashan. (De 3:11) When the Israelites came to the Promised Land, the tribe of Gad received Amorite land (formerly, it seems, held by Ammon) "as far as Aroer, which is in front of [perhaps to the NE of] Rabbah."—Jos 13:25.

Captured by David. The city is mentioned again in connection with war resulting from the abuse of David's messengers by King Hanun of Ammon. (2Sa 10:1-19; 1Ch 19:1-19) Joab and his troops fought Syrians hired by the Ammonites, while the Israelites under Abishai went up against the Ammonites "at the entrance of the city," evidently Rabbah. (1Ch 19:9) When the Syrians were defeated, the Ammonites retreated into the city. The next spring Joab and his army besieged Rabbah. It was during this campaign that David in Jerusalem sinned with Bath-sheba. The king sent her husband Uriah the Hittite back to battle, and according to David's instructions, Uriah was put in the front lines. When some Ammonites sallied forth from Rabbah, the battle brought Uriah close enough to be killed by an archer on the wall.—2Sa 11:1-25; 1Ch 20:1.

In time Joab succeeded in his fight against Rabbah to the point of capturing "the city of waters." (2Sa 12:27) Since Joab then informed David of the situation so that the king would come and complete the conquest and thus get credit for capturing Rabbah, it seems that Joab captured only a portion of the city. The expression "city of waters" may refer to a part on the riverbank, as distinguished from some other part of the city, or it may mean that he secured control of the city's principal water supply.—2Sa 12:26-28.

David came and completed the capture of Rabbah, and "the spoil of the city that he brought out was very much." (2Sa 12:29-31; 1Ch 20:2-4) Eventually the Ammonites became independent again. In the ninth century B.C.E., Amos foretold judgment against the Ammonites and he specifically mentioned that Rabbah would be burned. (Am 1:13, 14) Both Jeremiah and Ezekiel also delivered messages against Rabbah. As shown under AMMONITES, these prophecies were evidently fulfilled in Nebuchadnezzar's time.—Jer 49:2, 3; Eze 21:19-23; 25:5.

In the third century B.C.E., Ptolemy Philadelphus rebuilt Rabbah and renamed the city Philadelphia. It was later included among the cities of the Decapolis and apparently was quite prosperous and strong. The modern city of 'Amman is located here, and there are considerable ancient ruins, including a huge amphitheater, but these date mainly from Roman times.

2. One of the cities given to the tribe of Judah in its territorial allotment. Its exact location is unknown. In Joshua 15:60 it is listed with Kiriathjearim, which was in the hill country of Judah 13 km (8 mi) WNW of Jerusalem.

RABBI. The designation "Rabbi" was used in a de facto sense as "teacher." (Joh 1:38) But among the Jews, shortly before the birth of Jesus, it came to be used also as a form of address and as a title of respect and honor meaning "my great one; my excellent one." The title was demanded by some of the learned men, scribes, teachers of the Law. They delighted to be called "Rabbi" as an honorary title. Jesus Christ condemned such title-seeking and forbade his followers to be called "Rabbi," as he was their teacher.—Mt 23:6-8.

In the Bible the term "Rabbi" is used only in the Christian Greek Scriptures. It is employed 12 times in connection with Jesus, in the de facto sense of "Teacher": twice by Peter (Mr 9:5; 11:21), once by two disciples of John (Joh 1:38), once by Nathanael (Joh 1:49), once by Nicodemus (Joh 3:2), three times by disciples of Jesus whose names are not specified (Joh 4:31; 9:2; 11:8), once by the crowds (Joh 6:25), and two times by Judas (one instance is repeated) (Mt 26:25, 49; Mr 14: 45). Jesus is addressed by Mary Magdalene as *Rabboni* (My Teacher), also by a blind man whom he healed. The personal pronoun "my" is a suffix here, but because of usage it seems to have lost its significance, as in *Monsieur*, originally meaning "my lord." (Joh 20:16; Mr 10:51) John the Baptizer is once addressed as Rabbi. —Joh 3:26.

RABBITH

(Rab′bith) [Multitude; Abundance]. According to the Masoretic text, a site on Issachar's boundary. (Jos 19:17, 18, 20) It is thought to be the same as Daberath, identified with Khirbet Dabura (Horvat Devora). (Jos 19:12) Supporting this view is the fact that Vatican Manuscript No. 1209, of the fourth century C.E., has *Da·bi·ron* in place of "Rabbith."—See DABERATH.

RABBONI

(Rab·bo′ni). A Semitic word meaning "My Teacher." (Mr 10:51) It may be that *Rabboni* was a more respectful form than "Rabbi," which title of address means "Teacher," or that it conveyed more personal warmth. (Joh 1:38) However, when John wrote, perhaps the first person suffix (i) on this word had lost its special significance in the title, since John translates it as meaning merely "Teacher."—Joh 20:16.

RABMAG

(Rab′mag). The title of a major official of the Babylonian Empire at the time that Jerusalem was destroyed in 607 B.C.E. The title has been identified on excavated inscriptions. Nergal-sharezer the Rabmag was one of the men in the special tribunal of high Babylonian princes who sat in judgment in Jerusalem's Middle Gate after the city fell to Nebuchadnezzar and who is mentioned in connection with Jeremiah's being released to go to Gedaliah.—Jer 39:3, 13, 14.

RABSARIS

(Rab′sa·ris) [Chief Court Official]. The title of the chief court official in the Assyrian and Babylonian governments. The Rabsaris was one of the committee of three high Assyrian dignitaries that was sent by the king of Assyria to demand the surrender of Jerusalem in King Hezekiah's time.—2Ki 18:17.

The Rabsaris was one of the Babylonian officials taking control of Jerusalem for Nebuchadnezzar when the city fell in 607 B.C.E., and Nebushazban is named as the Rabsaris in connection with Jeremiah's being directed to dwell with Gedaliah. (Jer 39:3, 13, 14; 40:1-5) Excavations have unearthed inscriptions bearing the title.—*Bulletin of the Israel Exploration Society,* Jerusalem, 1967, Vol. XXXI, p. 77; *Le palais royal d'Ugarit,* III, Paris, 1955, No. 16:162, p. 126.

RABSHAKEH

(Rab′sha·keh) [from Akkadian, probably meaning "Chief Cupbearer"]. The title of a major Assyrian official. (2Ki 18:17) A building inscription of the Assyrian king Tiglath-Pileser III says: "I sent an officer of mine, the *rabsaq,* to Tyre." Also, from a tablet in the British Museum an inscription of King Ashurbanipal reads: "I ordered to add to my former (battle-) forces (in Egypt) the *rabsaq* -officer."—*Ancient Near Eastern Texts,* edited by J. Pritchard, 1974, pp. 282, 296.

While Sennacherib, the king of Assyria, was laying siege to the Judean fortress of Lachish, he sent a heavy military force to Jerusalem under the Tartan, the commander-in-chief, along with two other high officials, the Rabsaris and the Rabshakeh. (2Ki 18:17; the entire account appears also at Isa chaps 36, 37.) Of these three superior Assyrian officials, Rabshakeh was the chief spokesman in an effort to force King Hezekiah to capitulate in surrender. (2Ki 18:19-25) The three stood by the conduit of the upper pool. This Rabshakeh, whose personal name is not revealed, was a fluent speaker in Hebrew as well as Syrian. He called out in Hebrew to King Hezekiah, but three of Hezekiah's officials came out to meet him. King Hezekiah's officers asked Rabshakeh to speak to them in the Syrian language rather than in the Jews' language because the common people on the wall were listening. (2Ki 18:26, 27) But the situation suited Rabshakeh's purpose as a propagandist. He wanted the people to hear, with a view to demoralizing their ranks. By words calculated to induce terror, by false promises and lies, by reproach, and by ridicule of Jehovah, Rabshakeh spoke even more loudly in Hebrew, submitting arguments to the people to turn traitor to King Hezekiah by surrendering to the Assyrian army. (2Ki 18:28-35)

Nevertheless, the people of Jerusalem remained loyal to Hezekiah.—2Ki 18:36.

The taunting words of Rabshakeh were taken by Hezekiah to Jehovah in prayer, and a delegation was sent to the prophet Isaiah to receive Jehovah's reply. (2Ki 18:37; 19:1-7) In the meantime Rabshakeh was quickly called away when he heard that the king of Assyria had pulled away from Lachish and was fighting against Libnah. Keeping up his propaganda campaign against Hezekiah from a distance, Sennacherib sent messengers to Jerusalem with letters of continued taunt and strong threat to bring Hezekiah to surrender. (2Ki 19:8-13) King Hezekiah took the letters to the temple of Jerusalem and spread them before Jehovah along with his urgent prayer for help. (2Ki 19:14-19) Jehovah gave his answer through the prophet Isaiah that the king of Assyria "will not come into this city nor will he shoot an arrow there nor confront it with a shield nor cast up a siege rampart against it. By the way by which he proceeded to come, he will return, and into this city he will not come, is the utterance of Jehovah." (2Ki 19:32, 33) That night the angel of Jehovah struck down in death 185,000 soldiers of the Assyrians. This unexpected mighty blow caused Sennacherib, the king of Assyria, to withdraw immediately and return to Nineveh, Assyria's capital, where Sennacherib was assassinated sometime later. (2Ki 19:35-37) As a blasphemous taunter of the living God Jehovah, Rabshakeh's efforts came to nothing.

RACAL (Ra'cal). One of the places to which David sent spoils from his war with the Amalekites. (1Sa 30:18, 26, 29) The Greek *Septuagint* has "Carmel" instead of Racal, and some scholars believe this represents the original reading.

RACE(S). See BIBLE (Races and Languages); GAMES; MAN.

RACHEL (Ra'chel) [Ewe; Female Sheep]. A daughter of Laban, younger sister of Leah, and Jacob's first cousin and preferred wife. (Ge 29:10, 16, 30) Jacob fled from his murderous brother Esau in 1781 B.C.E., traveling to Haran in Paddan-aram, in "the land of the Orientals." (Ge 28:5; 29:1) Rachel, a girl "beautiful in form and beautiful of countenance," served as a shepherdess for her father; she met Jacob at a well near Haran. Jacob was received into his uncle's household and one month later agreed to serve Laban seven years in order to marry Rachel, with whom he was now in love. His love did not weaken during the seven years, and so these "proved to be like some few days" to him. On the wedding night,

however, his uncle substituted the older daughter Leah, who evidently cooperated in carrying out the deceit. The following morning when Jacob accused him of trickery, Laban appealed to local custom as an excuse for his conduct. Jacob agreed to carry out a full marriage week with Leah before receiving Rachel and thereafter to work another seven years for Laban.—Ge 29:4-28.

Rachel did not disappoint Jacob as his wife, and Jacob showed her more love than Leah. Jehovah now favored Leah in her disadvantaged position, blessing her with four sons, while Rachel remained barren. (Ge 29:29-35) Rachel displayed jealousy of her sister as well as despair over her own infertility, a condition then viewed as a great reproach among women. Her fretful impatience angered even her loving husband. To compensate for her own barrenness, she gave Jacob her maidservant for procreation purposes (as Sarah had done earlier with her slave Hagar), and the two children born as a result were considered Rachel's. Leah's maid and Leah herself produced a total of four more sons before Rachel's hope was finally realized and she brought forth her own first son, Joseph.—Ge 30:1-24.

Jacob was now ready to depart from Haran, but his father-in-law prevailed upon him to remain longer, and it was six years later that, at God's direction, Jacob pulled away. Because of Laban's double-dealing methods, Jacob did not advise him of his departure, and both Leah and Rachel were in agreement with their husband in this. Before leaving, Rachel stole her father's "teraphim," evidently some type of idol images. When Laban later caught up with the group and made known the theft (apparently his major concern), Jacob, unaware of Rachel's guilt, showed his disapproval of the act itself, decreeing death for the offender if that one was found in his entourage. Laban's search led into Rachel's tent, but she avoided exposure, claiming to be indisposed because of her menstrual period, while remaining seated on the saddle basket containing the teraphim.—Ge 30:25-30; 31:4-35, 38.

At his meeting with his brother Esau, Jacob showed his continued preference for Rachel by putting her and her only son last in the order of travel, doubtless viewing this as the safest position in the event of attack by Esau. (Ge 33:1-3, 7) After dwelling for a time in Succoth, then in Shechem, and finally in Bethel, Jacob headed farther south. Somewhere between Bethel and Bethlehem, Rachel gave birth to her second child, Benjamin, but died in childbearing and was buried there, Jacob erecting a pillar to mark the grave. —Ge 33:17, 18; 35:1, 16-20.

The few details recorded can give only an incomplete picture of Rachel's personality. She was a worshiper of Jehovah (Ge 30:22-24), but she showed human failings, her theft of the teraphim and her shrewdness in avoiding detection perhaps being at least partly attributable to her family background. Whatever her weaknesses, she was dearly loved by Jacob, who, even in old age, viewed her as having been his true wife and prized her children over all his others. (Ge 44:20, 27-29) His words to Joseph shortly before dying, though simple, nevertheless convey the depth of Jacob's affection for her. (Ge 48:1-7) She and Leah are spoken of as having "built the house of Israel [Jacob]."—Ru 4:11.

Archaeological discoveries may shed some light on Rachel's appropriation of her father's "teraphim." (Ge 31:19) Cuneiform tablets found at Nuzi in N Mesopotamia, believed to date from about the middle of the second millennium B.C.E., reveal that some ancient peoples viewed the possession of household gods as representing legal title to inheritance of family property. (*Ancient Near Eastern Texts*, edited by J. Pritchard, 1974, pp. 219, 220) Some suggest that Rachel may have felt that Jacob had the right to a share in the inheritance in Laban's property as an adopted son and that she may have taken the teraphim to ensure this or even to gain advantage over Laban's sons. Or she may have viewed the possession of these as a means of blocking any legal attempt by her father to claim some of the wealth Jacob had gained while in his service. (Compare Ge 30:43; 31:1, 2, 14-16.) These possibilities, of course, depend upon the existence of such a custom among Laban's people and upon the teraphim's actually being such household gods.

Rachel's grave site "in the territory of Benjamin at Zelzah" was still known in Samuel's time, some six centuries later. (1Sa 10:2) The traditional location of the grave lies about 1.5 km (1 mi) N of Bethlehem. This, however, would place it in the territory of Judah, not Benjamin. Therefore others suggest a location farther N, but any attempt at being precise is useless today.

Centuries after Rachel's death, why did the Bible tell of her weeping over her sons in the future?

At Jeremiah 31:15 Rachel is depicted as weeping over her sons who have been carried into the land of the enemy, her lamentation being heard in Ramah (N of Jerusalem in the territory of Benjamin). (See RAMAH No. 1.) Since Ephraim, whose tribal descendants are often used collectively to stand for the northern kingdom of Israel, is mentioned several times in the context (Jer 31:6, 9, 18, 20), some scholars believe this prophecy relates to the exiling of the people of the northern kingdom by the Assyrians. (2Ki 17:1-6; 18:9-11) On the other hand, it might relate to the eventual exiling of both those of Israel and of Judah (the latter by Babylon). In the first case, the figure of Rachel would be very appropriate since she was the maternal ancestor of Ephraim (through Joseph), the most prominent tribe of the northern kingdom. In the second case, Rachel's being the mother not only of Joseph but also of Benjamin, whose tribe formed part of the southern kingdom of Judah, would make her a fitting symbol of the mothers of *all* Israel, their bringing forth sons now seeming to have been in vain. Jehovah's comforting promise, however, was that the exiles would "certainly return from the land of the enemy."—Jer 31:16.

This text was quoted by Matthew in connection with the slaughter of infants in Bethlehem at Herod's order. (Mt 2:16-18) Since Rachel's grave was at least relatively near Bethlehem (though apparently not at the traditional site), this figure of Rachel weeping was appropriate to express the grief of the mothers of the slain children. But even more so was this quotation of Jeremiah's prophecy appropriate in view of the similarity of the situation. The Israelites were subject to a foreign power. Their sons had again been taken away. This time, however, "the land of the enemy" into which they had gone was obviously not a political region as in the earlier case. It was the grave, the region ruled over by 'King Death' (compare Ps 49:14; Re 6:8), death being called "the last enemy" to be destroyed. (Ro 5:14, 21; 1Co 15:26) Any return from such "exile" would, of course, be by means of a resurrection from the dead.

RADDAI (Rad'dai). Jesse's fifth-named son; an older brother of David in the tribe of Judah.—1Ch 2:13-15.

RAHAB (Ra'hab).

1. [Heb., *Ra·chav'*, possibly, Wide; Spacious]. A prostitute of Jericho who became a worshiper of Jehovah. In the spring of 1473 B.C.E., two Israelite spies came into Jericho and took up lodging at Rahab's home. (Jos 2:1) The duration of their stay there is not stated, but Jericho was not so big that it would take a long time to spy it out.

That Rahab really was a harlot, or prostitute, in the common sense of the word has been denied in some circles, especially among Jewish traditionalists, but this does not seem to have support in fact.

The Hebrew word zoh·nah' always has to do with an illicit relationship, either sexual or as a figure of spiritual unfaithfulness, and in each instance where it denotes a prostitute, it is so translated. It is not rendered "hostess," "innkeeper," or the like. Besides, among the Canaanites harlotry was not a business of ill repute.

Rahab's two guests were recognized as Israelites by others, who reported the matter to the king. However, Rahab quickly hid the men among flax stalks that were drying on the roof so that when the authorities got there to pick the men up she was able to direct them elsewhere without arousing their suspicions. In all of this, Rahab demonstrated greater devotion to the God of Israel than to her own condemned community.—Jos 2:2-7.

At what point Rahab had become aware of the spies' purpose there and Israel's intentions concerning Jericho is uncertain. But she now confessed to them the great fear and dread existing in the city because of reports about Jehovah's saving acts for Israel over the past 40 years or more. She asked the spies to swear to her for the preservation of herself and her whole family—father, mother, and all the rest. To this they agreed, provided she gather all the family into her house, hang a scarlet cord from the window, and remain silent concerning their visit, all of which she promised to do. Further protecting the spies, she enabled them to escape through a window (the house being on the city wall) and told them how they could avoid the search party that had headed for the Jordan at the fords.—Jos 2:8-22.

The spies reported back to Joshua all that had happened. (Jos 2:23, 24) Then when Jericho's wall fell down, Rahab's house, "on a side of the wall," was not destroyed. (Jos 2:15; 6:22) On Joshua's orders that Rahab's household be spared, the same two spies brought her out to safety. After a period of separation from Israel's camp, Rahab and her family were permitted to dwell among the Israelites. (Jos 6:17, 23, 25) This former prostitute then became the wife of Salmon and the mother of Boaz in the royal ancestry of the Davidic kings; she is one of the four women named in Matthew's genealogy of Jesus. (Ru 4:20-22; Mt 1:5, 6) She is also an outstanding example of one who, though not an Israelite, by works proved her complete faith in Jehovah. "By faith," Paul tells us, "Rahab the harlot did not perish with those who acted disobediently, because she received the spies in a peaceable way." "Was not also Rahab the harlot declared righteous by works, after she had received the messengers hospitably and sent them out by another way?" asks James.—Heb 11:30, 31; Jas 2:25.

2. [Heb., Ra'hav, from a root meaning "storm with importunities"]. A symbolic expression first used in Job (9:13; 26:12), where it is translated "stormer." (NW) In the second of these passages, the context and parallel construction connect it with a great sea monster. Similarly, Isaiah 51:9 links Rahab with a sea monster: "Are you not the one that broke Rahab to pieces, that pierced the sea monster?"

Rahab, a "sea monster," came to symbolize Egypt and her Pharaoh who opposed Moses and Israel. Isaiah 51:9, 10 alludes to Jehovah's delivering Israel from Egypt: "Are you not the one that dried up the sea, the waters of the vast deep? The one that made the depths of the sea a way for the repurchased ones to go across?" At Isaiah 30:7 "Rahab" is again connected with Egypt. Psalm 87:4 mentions "Rahab" where Egypt appropriately fits, as the first in a list of Israel's enemies, along with Babylon, Philistia, Tyre, and Cush. The Targums use "the Egyptians" in this verse, and at Psalm 89:10 they paraphrase "Rahab" in such a way as to link the term with Egypt's arrogant Pharaoh whom Jehovah humiliated.

RAHAM (Ra'ham) [Vulture]. A son of Shema in the Calebite branch of Judah's genealogy.—1Ch 2:4, 5, 9, 42-44.

RAIN. A vital part of the cycle by which water that rises into the atmosphere as vapor from land and water surfaces of the globe later condenses and falls to the ground, thus providing moisture necessary for plant and animal life. The Bible mentions rain in connection with this wisely arranged and dependable cycle.—Job 36:27, 28; Ec 1:7; Isa 55:10.

In addition to the general words for rain, a number of Hebrew and Greek terms referring to rain have the various meanings "downpour; pouring rain" (1Ki 18:41; Eze 1:28), "steady rain" (Pr 27:15), "spring or early rain" and "autumn or late rain" (De 11:14; Jas 5:7), "gentle rain" (De 32:2), "rainstorm" (Isa 4:6), and "copious showers" (Ps 65:10).

At an early point in the history of the preparation of the earth, "God had not made it rain upon the earth," but "a mist would go up from the earth and it watered the entire surface of the ground." The time referred to is evidently early on the third creative "day," before vegetation appeared. (Ge 2:5, 6; 1:9-13; see MIST.) The first instance in the Biblical record when rain is specifically mentioned as falling is in the account of the Flood. Then "the floodgates of the heavens were opened," and "the downpour upon the earth went on for forty days and forty nights."—Ge 7:11, 12; 8:2.

Formation. Among the questions that Jehovah put to Job, emphasizing man's limited understanding of the forces and laws of creation and the earth, was: "Does there exist a father for the rain?" (Job 38:28) Though meteorologists have studied extensively the formation of rain, what have emerged are, as *The World Book Encyclopedia* says, "theories." (1987, Vol. 16, pp. 123, 124) As warm air containing water vapor rises and cools, moisture condenses into tiny water droplets. One theory holds that as the larger droplets fall through a cloud, they collide with smaller droplets and combine with them, until they become too heavy for the air to support. Another theory proposes that ice crystals form in cloud tops where the temperature is below the freezing point and change to rain as they fall through warmer air.

Jehovah as a Source. Jehovah was no mere "rain god" for Israel. He was not like Baal, whom the Canaanites thought brought the rainy season with his awakening to life. Faithful Israelites recognized that Jehovah, not Baal, could withhold the precious rain. This was clearly illustrated when Jehovah brought a drought in Israel when Baal worship there was at its peak, in the time of the prophet Elijah.—1Ki 17:1, 7; Jas 5:17, 18.

It is Jehovah who prepared rain for the earth. (Ps 147:8; Isa 30:23) He "has divided a channel for the flood," perhaps referring to the way in which God causes clouds to channel rain down over certain parts of the globe. (Job 38:25-27; compare Ps 135:7; Jer 10:13.) His ability to control rain in harmony with his purpose is one of the things that distinguished Jehovah from the lifeless idol gods worshiped by the nations surrounding Israel. (Jer 14:22) In the Promised Land the Israelites had even more reason to appreciate that than when they were in Egypt, where rain was very infrequent.—De 11:10, 11.

In preaching to the Greeks in Lystra, Paul and Barnabas explained that the rains served as a witness about "the living God" and a demonstration of his goodness. (Ac 14:14-17) The benefits of rain are felt not just by the good and righteous but by all people; so, Jesus pointed out, God's love in this regard should serve as a pattern for humans. —Mt 5:43-48.

Rainfall in the Promised Land. A distinct feature of the climate of the Promised Land is its variety as to rainfall. Two chief factors determining the amount of rain are proximity to the sea and the land's elevation. The plains along the Mediterranean receive considerable rain during the rainy season, with the amount decreasing as one goes from N to S. The rainfall tends to be greater in the hills and mountains because the moisture carried eastward from the sea condenses more heavily there. The Jordan Valley lies in a "rain shadow," for the air traveling over the mountains has by then given up much of its moisture, and the air is warmed as it moves into the valley. Yet, when this air meets the elevated plateau E of the Jordan, clouds again form, resulting in some rainfall. This makes a strip of land E of the Jordan suitable for grazing or limited agriculture. Farther E is the desert, where the rain is too light and irregular to be useful for raising crops or for grazing herds.

Seasons. The two primary seasons in the Promised Land, summer and winter, can rather accurately be viewed as the dry season and the rainy season. (Compare Ps 32:4; Ca 2:11, ftn.) From about mid-April to mid-October very little rain falls. Rain is rare in this period during which the harvest takes place. Proverbs 26:1 shows that rain at harvesttime was considered quite out of place. (Compare 1Sa 12:17-19.) During the rainy season the rain is not constant; it alternates with clear days. Since this is also the cold period, exposure to the rain is very chilling. (Ezr 10:9, 13) Therefore, a comfortable shelter is most appreciated.—Isa 4:6; 25:4; 32:2; Job 24:8.

Autumn and spring rain. The Bible mentions "the autumn [early or former] rain and the spring [latter] rain," which were promised by God as a blessing upon the faithful Israelites. (De 11:14, ftn; Jer 5:24; Joe 2:23, 24) The farmer patiently awaited the rains of these periods between the summer and winter. (Jas 5:7; compare Job 29:23.) The early, or autumn, rain (beginning about mid-October) was anxiously anticipated to relieve the heat and dryness of summer. It was necessary before planting could begin, for the rain softened the ground and allowed the farmer to plow his land. Similarly, the late, or spring, rain about mid-April) was required to water the growing crops so that they would mature, and particularly so that the grain would ripen.—Zec 10:1; Am 4:7; Ca 2:11-13.

Figurative Use. When God blessed Israel with rains in their appointed time, an abundance resulted. Hence, Hosea could promise that Jehovah would "come in like a pouring rain," "like a spring rain that saturates the earth," for those who sought to know him. (Ho 6:3) God's instructions were to "drip as the rain" and his sayings as "gentle rains upon grass and as copious showers upon vegetation." (De 32:2) They would be able to sink in slowly but be sufficient to provide full refreshment, as showers on vegetation. Similarly, a source of refreshment and plenty was depicted in likening the regathered remnant of Jacob to "copious showers upon vegetation."—Mic 5:7.

The reign of God's king described in Psalm 72 would be marked by prosperity and blessing. Consequently, he was represented as descending "like the rain upon the mown grass, like copious showers that wet the earth" and produce fresh vegetation. (Ps 72:1, 6; compare 2Sa 23:3, 4.) The goodwill of a king was likened to "the cloud of spring rain," for it gave evidence of pleasant conditions to come, just as rain-bearing clouds assured the water necessary for the crops to come to fruition.—Pr 16:15.

However, the falling rain does not always result in vegetation that is a blessing to the human cultivator; the watered earth may produce thorns and thistles. Paul used this as an example, comparing the rain-watered ground to Christians who have "tasted the heavenly free gift, and who have become partakers of holy spirit." If they do not produce the fruits of the spirit but fall away from the truth, they are due to be burned, like a field producing only thorns.—Heb 6:4-8.

In John's vision in Revelation he saw "two witnesses" with "the authority to shut up heaven that no rain should fall during the days of their prophesying." (Re 11:3-6) These "witnesses" representing God as 'prophets,' or spokesmen, would not pronounce God's favor or blessing on the plans and works of wicked men on earth. Like Elijah, who announced a three-and-a-half-year drought on Israel because of their practice of Baal worship promoted by King Ahab and his wife Jezebel, so these "two witnesses" figuratively "shut up heaven" so that no refreshing "rain" from God would come to bring prosperity to such efforts of men. —1Ki 17:1–18:45; Lu 4:25, 26; Jas 5:17, 18.

RAINBOW. A semicircular bow, or arc, exhibiting a spectrum of colors; a visible sign of Jehovah's covenant promise that 'no more would all flesh be cut off by waters of a deluge, and no more would there occur a deluge to bring the earth to ruin.' (Ge 9:11-16) There is no separate Hebrew word for rainbow, so the normal word in the Bible (with which to shoot arrows) is used in the Bible. —Eze 1:28.

Complicated theories and formulas are used to explain the formation of a rainbow. Basically, it seems that as white light enters a raindrop it is refracted and dispersed into different colors, the drop acting like a tiny prism. Each color strikes the inner surface of the drop and is reflected back at a different and specific angle. Thus an observer sees a bow with all seven colors of the spectrum (from the inside of the arc outward: violet, indigo, blue, green, yellow, orange, and red), though these may blend so that only four or five are clear. Sometimes a larger and less distinct "secondary" bow is formed with the colors reversed. Scientists are still studying the rainbow. Carl B. Boyer observes: "Within a raindrop the interaction of light energy with matter is so intimate that one is led directly to quantum mechanics and the theory of relativity. . . . Although much is known about the production of the rainbow, little has been learned about its perception."—*The Rainbow, From Myth to Mathematics*, 1959, pp. 320, 321.

The first Biblical reference to a rainbow is in the account of the covenant God made with Noah and his offspring after the Flood survivors came out of the ark. (Ge 9:8-17; Isa 54:9, 10) This splendid sight of itself would have been reassuring and an indication of peace to Noah and his family.

Many opinions have been offered as to whether this was the first time humans saw a rainbow. Some commentators have held that rainbows had been seen before and that God's 'giving' the rainbow at this time was really a 'giving' of special meaning or significance to a previously existing phenomenon. Many of those holding this view believe that the Flood was only local or did not substantially change the atmosphere.

Nevertheless, this is the first mention of a rainbow, and if a rainbow had been seen earlier, there would have been no real force in God's making it an outstanding sign of his covenant. It would have been commonplace, and not a significant marker of a change, of something new.

The Bible does not describe the degree of clarity of the atmosphere just prior to the Flood. But apparently atmospheric conditions were such that, until a change came about when "the floodgates of the heavens were opened" (Ge 7:11), no others before Noah and his family had seen a rainbow. Even today, atmospheric conditions affect whether a rainbow can be seen or not.

The glory, beauty, and peacefulness of a rainbow that appears after a storm are drawn upon in Biblical descriptions of God and his throne. In Ezekiel's vision of God, the prophet saw "something like the appearance of the bow that occurs in a cloud mass on the day of a pouring rain." This emphasized "the glory of Jehovah." (Eze 1:28) Similarly, John saw Jehovah's throne of splendor, and 'round about it there was a rainbow like an emerald in appearance.' The restful emerald-green color of the rainbow would have suggested composure and serenity to John, and appropriately so since Jehovah is the master of every situation, a glorious Ruler. (Re 4:3) John also saw an angel with 'a rainbow upon his head' (Re 10:1), which may suggest that he was a special representative of "the God of peace."—Php 4:9.

RAKKATH (Rak′kath). A fortified city of Naphtali. (Jos 19:32, 35) It is identified with Khirbet el-Quneitireh (Tel Raqqat), located on the Sea of Galilee a short distance N of Tiberias.

RAKKON (Rak′kon). A city listed when describing the border of Dan. (Jos 19:40, 41, 46) It is tentatively identified by some with Tell er-Reqqeit, a short distance N of Tel Aviv-Yafo, on the shore of the Mediterranean Sea.

RAM [High].

1. A descendant of Judah through Perez and Hezron; he lived while Israel was in Egypt. Though Ram was apparently not the first son of Hezron, Ram's genealogy, leading to the Davidic line, is listed first among the three sons of Hezron. (1Ch 2:4, 5, 9-17, 25) Having Nahshon, Boaz, and David among his descendants, Ram was an ancestor of Jesus. (Nu 1:7; Ru 4:18-22; Mt 1:3, 4) His name is spelled Arni (Aram in some manuscripts) in Luke's ancestry of Jesus.—Lu 3:33.

2. The firstborn son of Jerahmeel and nephew of No. 1. He fathered three sons.—1Ch 2:9, 25, 27.

3. Founder of Elihu's family.—Job 32:2.

RAMAH (Ra′mah) [Height]. The Hebrew word signifies a height or a high place. (Eze 16:24) It was used as a proper name for a number of locations in Israel.

1. A city in the territory of Benjamin. In Joshua 18:25 it is listed between Gibeon and Beeroth. Apparently it was near Bethel, which city was in the S of Ephraim's territory. (Jg 4:5) A Levite traveling N past Jerusalem came to Gibeah, with Ramah evidently just beyond. (Jg 19:11-15; Ho 5:8) And it was in the neighborhood of Geba. (Isa 10:29) These references combine with testimony of Eusebius in identifying Ramah in Benjamin with the locality of modern er-Ram, which is about 8 km (5 mi) N of Jerusalem, 3 km (2 mi) N of Gibeah, 5 km (3 mi) E of Gibeon, and 3 km (2 mi) W of Geba. The city is on an elevation, as the name implies.

During the divided kingdom, Ramah came in for considerable attention, located, as it was, near the border between Israel and Judah and the N-S road of the hill country. King Baasha of Israel began to expand or fortify Ramah in Benjamin while warring against Asa. (1Ki 15:16, 17; 2Ch 16:1) But when the king of Syria attacked Israel from the N, Baasha's attention was diverted and Asa took Ramah as well as the building materials Baasha had been using there, using these to build up neighboring Geba and Mizpah. (1Ki 15:20-22; 2Ch 16:4-6) It appears that, when Jerusalem was destroyed in 607 B.C.E., the Jews taken captive were assembled in Ramah before being moved to Babylon. (Jer 40:1) After the exile Ramah was repopulated.—Ezr 2:1, 26; Ne 7:30; 11:33.

Some scholars have concluded that such an assembling of Jews at Ramah before taking them into exile (perhaps accompanied by the slaughtering of some there) was referred to with the words: "In Ramah a voice is being heard, lamentation and bitter weeping; Rachel weeping over her sons. She has refused to be comforted over her sons, because they are no more." (Jer 31:15) Jacob's wife Rachel had so desired children as to consider herself "dead" without them. (Ge 30:1) So now Rachel might be spoken of figuratively as weeping over the loss of the Jews in death or captivity. Or, since Rachel was the mother of Benjamin, Jeremiah's words may represent her as weeping particularly over the Benjamite inhabitants of Ramah. Jeremiah went on to explain that hope existed, for the exiles would return. (Jer 31:16) At Matthew 2:18, the prophetic words in Jeremiah 31:15 are quoted as applying also to the time when Herod had young children of Bethlehem slaughtered.—See RACHEL.

2. An enclave city of the tribe of Simeon in the Negeb. (Jos 19:1, 8) It was the same as Baalath-beer and was known as "Ramah of the south." It is tentatively identified with Khirbet Ghazzah (Horvat 'Uza), about 30 km (19 mi) E of Beer-sheba. —See BAALATH-BEER.

3. An unidentified city in the territory of Asher listed only in Joshua 19:24, 29. It is difficult from the text to determine exactly where in Asher's inheritance the city was located, though it seems to have been N toward Tyre.

4. A fortified city in Naphtali's territory. (Jos 19:32, 36) It is tentatively identified with Khirbet Zeitun er-Rameh (also known as Khirbet Jul) just E of er-Rameh (Rama) and about 30 km (19 mi) E of the seaport city of 'Akko (Acco). But the single reference to it in Joshua does not allow for positive identification of its location.

5. The hometown of the prophet Samuel and his parents. In 1 Samuel 1:1, Samuel's father Elkanah is described as a "man of Ramathaim-zophim of the mountainous region of Ephraim." Throughout the rest of the account the shortened form "Ramah" is used. (1Sa 1:19) Perhaps the longer name is first used to distinguish this Ramah from other places of the same name, such as Ramah in Benjamin. *An American Translation* reads: "man of Ramah, a Zuphite." This rendering of the Masoretic text would indicate that Elkanah was either a descendant of Zuph (Zophai) or from the district of Zuph.—1Ch 6:27, 28, 34, 35; 1Sa 9:5.

An ancient tradition presented by Eusebius identifies Ramah with the location of modern Rentis (Rantis), in the hills of Ephraim about 35 km (22 mi) NW of Jerusalem. This would be the same place as the Arimathea (Gr. form of Heb. *Ra·mah'*) mentioned in the Christian Greek Scriptures.—Lu 23:50-53.

Elkanah made his home in Ramah, where Samuel evidently was born, but each year he traveled to Shiloh to sacrifice. (1Sa 1:3, 19; 2:11) Though Samuel lived with Eli the priest at Shiloh for some time, eventually he took up residence at Ramah and used it as a base from which he traveled in a circuit judging Israel. (1Sa 3:19-21; 7:15-17; 8:4; 15:24-35; 16:4, 13; 19:18-24) When Samuel died he was buried at his house in Ramah, "his own city."—1Sa 25:1; 28:3.

6. A shortened form for Ramoth-gilead.—2Ki 8:28, 29; 2Ch 22:5, 6; see RAMOTH-GILEAD.

RAMATHAIM-ZOPHIM (Ra·math·a'im-zo'-phim). The home of Elkanah, father of Samuel, in the mountainous region of Ephraim.—1Sa 1:1; see RAMAH No. 5.

RAMATHITE (Ra'math·ite) [Of (Belonging to) Ramah]. A designation for Shimei, the vineyard keeper of King David. (1Ch 27:27) It indicates that he was from one of the several towns named Ramah, but there is no way of determining which one.

RAMATH-LEHI (Ra'math-le'hi) [Lofty Place of the Jawbone]. The name Samson gave the site in Judah where he struck down a thousand Philistines with the moist jawbone of an ass.—Jg 15:16-18; see LEHI.

RAMATH-MIZPEH (Ra'math-miz'peh) [Lofty Place of the Watchtower]. One of the cities E of the Jordan given to the tribe of Gad. (Jos 13:24, 26) Evidently Ramath-mizpeh was near Betonim.

RAMESES. See RAAMSES, RAMESES.

RAMIAH (Ra·mi'ah) [possibly, Jah Is High (Exalted)]. An Israelite, one of "the sons of Parosh" who sent away their foreign wives and sons at the encouragement of Ezra.—Ezr 10:10, 11, 25, 44.

RAMOTH (Ra'moth) [probably, Lofty Places; from a root meaning "rise"].

1. A Levite city in the territory of Issachar. (1Ch 6:71-73) It is apparently the same as Remeth and Jarmuth (No. 2). (Jos 19:17, 21; 21:27-29) Ramoth is tentatively identified with Kokab el-Hawa (Kokhav ha-Yarden), on a tableland about 10 km (6 mi) N of Beth-shean.

2. "Ramoth of the south" at 1 Samuel 30:27 apparently refers to the "Baalath-beer, Ramah of the south" mentioned at Joshua 19:8. Its location was evidently in the Negeb.—See RAMAH No. 2.

3. A city in Gilead, east of the Jordan River. (Jos 20:8) In time it came to be called Ramoth-gilead.—See RAMOTH-GILEAD.

RAMOTH-GILEAD (Ra'moth-gil'e·ad) [probably, Lofty Places of Gilead]. A strategic city in the territory of Gad, E of the Jordan. The city was also called by the shortened form Ramah. (2Ki 8:28, 29; 2Ch 22:5, 6) It was one of the Levite cities on that side of the river (1Ch 6:80), and it was selected as one of the cities of refuge. (De 4:43; Jos 20:8; 21:38) Solomon appointed a deputy in Ramoth-gilead to care for providing food for the king from cities in Gilead and Bashan.—1Ki 4:7, 13.

When, after the division of the kingdom, Syria made attacks on Israel, Ramoth-gilead played an important part in Israelite history, evidently being sort of a key to the territory E of the Jordan. At some point the Syrians took the city. Despite the promise of Ben-hadad II to return the Israelite cities that had been taken earlier, apparently Ramoth-gilead was not returned. (1Ki 20:34) Hence, Ahab of Israel attempted to recover it, with the aid of King Jehoshaphat of Judah. This effort, which Micaiah counseled against, resulted in Ahab's death.—1Ki 22:13-38.

Ahab's son Jehoram, along with Ahaziah of Judah, also fought the Syrians at Ramoth-gilead. Second Kings 9:14 says: "Jehoram himself had happened to be keeping guard at Ramoth-gilead . . . because of Hazael the king of Syria." So it may be that Jehoram had taken the city earlier and was defending it (not attacking it) when Ahaziah joined him in the fight against Hazael. In the fighting, Jehoram was wounded and he retired to Jezreel to recover.—2Ki 8:25-29; 9:14, 15; 2Ch 22:5-8.

At Ramoth-gilead, Elisha's attendant anointed Jehu, the military chief, to be the next king.—2Ki 9:1-14.

The exact location of Ramoth-gilead is uncertain. One of many suggested locations is Tell Ramith, about 45 km (28 mi) SE of the southern tip of the Sea of Galilee. The name of this tell could have been derived from the name Ramoth-gilead. It is on a hill overlooking a plain, which agrees with the probable meaning of Ramoth (Lofty Places; from a root meaning "rise"). The location would have been appropriate for a deputy responsible for Gilead and Bashan.—1Ki 4:13.

RAMPART.
A mound of earth or stones, or even a wall, raised as a fortification around a place.

The siege rampart (Heb., so·le·lah') was a mound of earth (and sometimes stones) cast up by an army to form an inclined plane for bringing battering rams and other siege equipment against a fortified city. (2Sa 20:15) The Assyrian king Sennacherib cast up a siege rampart against Lachish. Excavations at Lachish show that this rampart consisted mainly of stones bound together by a large quantity of mortar. However, Sennacherib was not able to cast up a siege rampart against Jerusalem.—2Ki 19:32.

Siege ramparts were to be thrown up by Nebuchadnezzar the king of Babylon against Jerusalem and against Tyre. (Jer 6:6; Eze 21:22; 26:7, 8) The siege against Jerusalem was illustrated prophetically when Ezekiel was directed to engrave a model of Jerusalem on a brick and build a siege rampart against it.—Eze 4:1, 2.

The rampart (Heb., ma·tsohr') mentioned at Zechariah 9:3, 4 apparently has reference to the strong fortifications of Tyre, which consisted of high walls constructed of large blocks of stone. The city of Babylon was unusually strong, having an inner rampart and an outer rampart, both of them made of bricks.—See BABYLON No. 1.

In some instances the rampart (Heb., chehl) that a city had as a part of its fortifications was built from the earth dug up when a moat was excavated around the city. The rampart rising from the moat at Hazor was about 15 m (50 ft) high. This made the top of the rampart nearly 30 m (100 ft) from the bottom of the moat. The city of Jerusalem had its own fortifications, including a rampart.—Ps 122:7; 48:13; see FORTIFICATIONS.

Divine help or "salvation" may serve as a sure protection, comparable to walls and a rampart. Thus, with apparent reference to Jerusalem, Isaiah 26:1 says what Jehovah God would do for the city: "He sets salvation itself for walls and rampart."

RANSOM.
A price paid to buy back or to bring about release from some obligation or undesirable circumstance. The basic idea of "ransom" is a price that covers (as in payment for damages or to satisfy justice), while "redemption" emphasizes the releasing accomplished as a result of the ransom paid. The most significant ransom price is the shed blood of Jesus Christ, which made deliverance from sin and death possible for the offspring of Adam.

In the various Hebrew and Greek terms translated "ransom" and "redeem," the inherent similarity lies in the idea of a price, or thing of value, given to effect the ransom, or redemption. The thought of exchange, as well as that of correspondency, equivalence, or substitution, is common in all. That is, one thing is given for another, satisfying the demands of justice and resulting in a balancing of matters.—See RECONCILIATION.

A Price That Covers. The Hebrew noun ko'-pher comes from the verb ka·phar', meaning, basically, "cover," as in Noah's covering the ark with tar. (Ge 6:14) Ka·phar', however, is used almost entirely to describe the satisfying of justice through the covering of or atoning for sins. The noun ko'pher refers to the thing given to accomplish this, the ransom price. (Ps 65:3; 78:38; 79:8, 9) A covering corresponds to the thing it covers, either in its form (as in a material lid, such as the "cover [kap·po'reth]" of the ark of the covenant; Ex 25:17-22), or in its value (as in a payment to cover the damages caused by an injury).

As a means for balancing justice and setting matters straight with his people Israel, Jehovah, in the Law covenant, designated various sacrifices and offerings to atone for, or cover, sins, including those of the priests and the Levites (Ex 29:33-37; Le 16:6, 11), of other individuals, or of the nation as a whole (Le 1:4; 4:20, 26, 31, 35), as well as to purify the altar and tabernacle, making atonement because of the sins of the people surrounding these. (Le 16:16-20) In effect, the life of the animal sacrificed went in place of the life of the sinner, its blood making atonement on God's altar, that is, to the extent that it could. (Le 17:11; compare Heb 9:13, 14.) The "day of atonement [yohm hak·kip·pu·rim']" could just as properly be referred to as the "day of the ransoms." (Le 23:26-28) These sacrifices were required if the nation and its worship were to have and maintain the acceptance and approval of the righteous God.

Well illustrating the sense of a redeeming exchange is the law regarding a bull known to gore.

If the owner allowed the bull to go loose so that it killed someone, the owner was to be put to death, paying for the life of the slain person with his own life. However, since he did not deliberately or directly kill another, if the judges viewed it proper to impose upon him a "ransom [ko'pher]" instead, then he must pay that redemption price. The sum assessed and paid was viewed as taking the place of his own life and compensating for the life lost. (Ex 21:28-32; compare De 19:21.) On the other hand, no ransom could be accepted for the deliberate murderer; only his own life could cover the death of the victim. (Nu 35:31-33) Evidently because a census involved lives, at the time such was taken each male over 20 had to have a ransom (ko'pher) of half a shekel ($1.10) given for his soul to Jehovah, the same price applying whether the individual was rich or poor.—Ex 30:11-16.

Since any imbalance of justice is displeasing to God, as well as among humans, the ransom, or covering, could have the additional effect of averting or quelling anger. (Compare Jer 18:23; also Ge 32:20, where "appease" translates ka·phar'.) The husband enraged at the man committing adultery with his wife, however, refuses any "ransom [ko'-pher]." (Pr 6:35) The term may also be used with regard to those who *should* execute justice but who instead accept a bribe or gift as "hush money [ko'pher]" to cover over the wrongdoing in their sight.—1Sa 12:3; Am 5:12.

The Redemption, or Releasing. The Hebrew verb pa·dhah' means "redeem," and the related noun pidh·yohn' means "redemption price." (Ex 21:30) These terms evidently emphasize the *releasing* accomplished by the redemption price, while ka·phar' places stress on the *quality* or *content* of the price and its *efficacy* in balancing the scales of justice. The releasing, or redeeming (pa·dhah'), may be from slavery (Le 19:20; De 7:8), from other distressing or oppressive conditions (2Sa 4:9; Job 6:23; Ps 55:18), or from death and the grave. (Job 33:28; Ps 49:15) Frequent reference is made to Jehovah's redeeming the nation of Israel from Egypt to be his "private property" (De 9:26; Ps 78:42) and to his redeeming them from Assyrian and Babylonian exile many centuries later. (Isa 35:10; 51:11; Jer 31:11, 12; Zec 10:8-10) Here, too, the redemption involved a price, an exchange. In redeeming Israel from Egypt, Jehovah evidently caused the price to be paid by Egypt. Israel was, in effect, God's "firstborn," and Jehovah warned Pharaoh that his stubborn refusal to release Israel would cause the life of Pharaoh's firstborn and the firstborn of all Egypt, human and animals, to be exacted. (Ex 4:21-23; 11:4-8) Similarly, in return for Cyrus' overthrow of Bab-

ylon and his liberation of the Jews from their exiled state, Jehovah gave "Egypt as a ransom [form of ko'pher] for [his people], Ethiopia and Seba" in their place. The Persian Empire thus later conquered those regions, and so 'national groups were given in place of the Israelites' souls.' (Isa 43:1-4) These exchanges are in harmony with the inspired declaration that the "wicked is [or serves as] a ransom [ko'pher] for the righteous one; and the one dealing treacherously takes the place of the upright ones."—Pr 21:18.

Another Hebrew term associated with redemption is ga·'al', and this conveys primarily the thought of reclaiming, recovering, or repurchasing. (Jer 32:7, 8) Its similarity to pa·dhah' is seen by its parallel use with that term at Hosea 13:14: "From the hand of Sheol I shall redeem [form of pa·dhah'] them; from death I shall recover [form of ga·'al'] them." (Compare Ps 69:18.) Ga·'al' gives emphasis to the right of reclaiming or repurchasing, either by a near kinsman of a person whose property or whose very person needed to be repurchased or reclaimed, or by the original owner or seller himself. A near kinsman, called a go·'el', was thus "a repurchaser" (Ru 2:20; 3:9, 13) or, in cases where a murder was involved, a "blood avenger."—Nu 35:12.

The Law provided that in the case of a poor Israelite whose circumstances forced him to sell his hereditary lands, his city house, or even to sell himself into servitude, "a repurchaser closely related to him," or go·'el', had the right to "buy back [ga·'al'] what his brother sold," or the seller could do so himself if funds became available to him. (Le 25:23-27, 29-34, 47-49; compare Ru 4:1-15.) If a man should make a vow offering to God of a house or a field and then desire to buy it back, he had to pay the valuation placed on the property plus a fifth in addition to that estimated value. (Le 27:14-19) However, no exchange could be made for anything "devoted to destruction."—Le 27:28, 29.

In the case of murder, the murderer was not allowed sanctuary in the appointed cities of refuge but, after the judicial hearing, was turned over by the judges to the "avenger [go·'el'] of blood," a near kinsman of the victim, who then put the murderer to death. Since no "ransom [ko'pher]" was allowed for the murderer and since the near kinsman with right of repurchase could not reclaim or recover the life of his dead relative, he rightfully claimed the life of the one who had taken his relative's life by murder.—Nu 35:9-32; De 19:1-13.

Not Always a Tangible Price. As has been shown, Jehovah "redeemed" (pa·dhah') or 're-claimed' (ga·'al') Israel from Egypt. (Ex 6:6; Isa

51:10, 11) Later, because the Israelites kept "selling themselves to do what was bad" (2Ki 17:16, 17), Jehovah on several occasions 'sold them into the hands of their enemies.' (De 32:30; Jg 2:14; 3:8; 10:7; 1Sa 12:9) Their repentance caused him to buy them back, or reclaim them, out of distress or exile (Ps 107:2, 3; Isa 35:9, 10; Mic 4:10), thereby performing the work of a Go·el', a Repurchaser related to them inasmuch as he had espoused the nation to himself. (Isa 43:1, 14; 48:20; 49:26; 50:1, 2; 54:5-7) In 'selling' them, Jehovah was not paid some material compensation by the pagan nations. His payment was the satisfaction of his justice and the fulfillment of his purpose to have them corrected and disciplined for their rebellion and disrespect.—Compare Isa 48:17, 18.

God's 'repurchasing' likewise need not involve the payment of something tangible. When Jehovah repurchased the Israelites exiled in Babylon, Cyrus willingly liberated them, without tangible compensation. However, when redeeming his people from oppressor nations that had acted with malice against Israel, Jehovah exacted the price from the oppressors themselves, making them pay with their own lives. (Compare Ps 106:10, 11; Isa 41:11-14; 49:26.) When his people were sold to pagan nations, they received "nothing" from their enslavers in the way of true benefit or relief, and Jehovah therefore needed to make no payment to their captors to balance matters out. Instead, he effected the repurchase through the power of "his holy arm."—Isa 52:3-10; Ps 77:14, 15.

Jehovah's role of Go·el' thus embraced the avenging of wrongs done to his servants and resulted in the sanctifying and vindicating of his own name against those who used Israel's distress as an excuse to reproach him. (Ps 78:35; Isa 59:15-20; 63:3-6, 9) As the Great Kinsman and Redeemer of both the nation and its individuals, he conducted their "legal case" to effect justice. —Ps 119:153, 154; Jer 50:33, 34; La 3:58-60; compare Pr 23:10, 11.

Though living before and outside the nation of Israel, the disease-stricken Job said: "I myself well know that my redeemer is alive, and that, coming after me, he will rise up over the dust." (Job 19:25; compare Ps 69:18; 103:4.) Following God's own example, Israel's king was to act as a redeemer in behalf of the lowly and poor ones of the nation. —Ps 72:1, 2, 14.

Christ Jesus' Role as Ransomer. The foregoing information lays the basis for understanding the ransom provided for humankind through God's Son, Christ Jesus. Mankind's need for a ransom came about through the rebellion in Eden. Adam sold himself to do evil for the selfish pleasure of keeping continued company with his wife, now a sinful transgressor, so he shared the same condemned standing with her before God. He thereby sold himself and his descendants into slavery to sin and to death, the price that God's justice required. (Ro 5:12-19; compare Ro 7:14-25.) Having possessed human perfection, Adam lost this valuable possession for himself and all his offspring.

The Law, which had "a shadow of the good things to come," provided for animal sacrifices as a covering for sin. This, however, was only a symbolic or token covering, since such animals were inferior to man; hence, it was "not possible for the blood of bulls and of goats [actually] to take sins away," as the apostle points out. (Heb 10:1-4) Those pictorial animal sacrifices had to be without blemish, perfect specimens. (Le 22:21) The real ransom sacrifice, a human actually capable of removing sins, must therefore also be perfect, free from blemish. He would have to correspond to the perfect Adam and possess human perfection, if he were to pay the price of redemption that would release Adam's offspring from the debt, disability, and enslavement into which their first father Adam had sold them. (Compare Ro 7:14; Ps 51:5.) Only thereby could he satisfy God's perfect justice that requires like for like, a 'soul for a soul.'—Ex 21:23-25; De 19:21.

The strictness of God's justice made it impossible for mankind itself to provide its own redeemer. (Ps 49:6-9) However, this results in the magnifying of God's own love and mercy in that he met his own requirements at tremendous cost to himself, giving the life of his own Son to provide the redemption price. (Ro 5:6-8) This required his Son's becoming human to correspond to the perfect Adam. God accomplished this by transferring his Son's life from heaven to the womb of the Jewish virgin Mary. (Lu 1:26-37; Joh 1:14) Since Jesus did not owe his life to any human father descended from the sinner Adam, and since God's holy spirit 'overshadowed' Mary, evidently from the time she conceived until the time of Jesus' birth, Jesus was born free from any inheritance of sin or imperfection, being, as it were, "an unblemished and spotless lamb," whose blood could prove to be an acceptable sacrifice. (Lu 1:35; Joh 1:29; 1Pe 1:18, 19) He maintained that sinless state throughout his life and thus did not disqualify himself. (Heb 4:15; 7:26; 1Pe 2:22) As a 'sharer of blood and flesh,' he was a near kinsman of mankind and he had the thing of value, his own perfect life maintained pure through tests of integrity, with which to repurchase mankind, emancipate them.—Heb 2:14, 15.

The Christian Greek Scriptures make clear that the release from sin and death is indeed by the paying of a price. Christians are said to be "bought with a price" (1Co 6:20; 7:23), having an "owner that bought them" (2Pe 2:1), and Jesus is presented as the Lamb who 'was slaughtered and with his blood bought persons for God out of every tribe, tongue, and nation.' (Re 5:9) In these texts the verb a·go·ra'zo is used, meaning simply "buy at the market [a·go·ra']." The related e·xa·go·ra'zo (release by purchase) is used by Paul in showing that Christ released "by purchase those under law" through his death on the stake. (Ga 4:5; 3:13) But the thought of redemption or ransoming is more frequently and more fully expressed by the Greek ly'tron and related terms.

Ly'tron (from the verb ly'o, meaning "loose") was especially used by Greek writers to refer to a price paid to ransom prisoners of war or to release those under bond or in slavery. (Compare Heb 11:35.) In its two Scriptural occurrences it describes Christ's giving "his soul a ransom in exchange for many." (Mt 20:28; Mr 10:45) The related word an·ti'ly·tron appears at 1 Timothy 2:6. Parkhurst's *Greek and English Lexicon to the New Testament* says it means: *"a ransom, price of redemption,* or rather *a correspondent ransom."* He quotes Hyperius as saying: "It properly signifies *a price* by which captives are *redeemed* from the enemy; and that kind of *exchange* in which the *life of one is redeemed by the life of another."* He concludes by saying: "So Aristotle uses the verb [an·ti·ly·tro'o] for *redeeming life by life."* (London, 1845, p. 47) Thus Christ "gave himself a corresponding ransom for all." (1Ti 2:5, 6) Other related words are ly·tro'o·mai, "loose by ransom" (Tit 2:14; 1Pe 1:18, 19), and a·po·ly'tro·sis, "a releasing by ransom." (Eph 1:7, 14; Col 1:14) The similarity of the usage of these words with that of the Hebrew terms considered is evident. They describe, not an ordinary purchase or releasing, but a redeeming or ransoming, a deliverance effected by payment of a corresponding price.

Though available to all, Christ's ransom sacrifice is not accepted by all, and "the wrath of God remains" upon those not accepting it, as it also comes upon those who first accept and then turn away from that provision. (Joh 3:36; Heb 10:26-29; contrast Ro 6:9, 10.) They gain no deliverance from the enslavement to Kings Sin and Death. (Ro 5:21) Under the Law the deliberate

murderer could not be ransomed. Adam, by his willful course, brought death on all mankind, hence was a murderer. (Ro 5:12) Thus, the sacrificed life of Jesus is not acceptable to God as a ransom for the sinner Adam.

But God is pleased to approve the application of the ransom to redeem those of Adam's offspring who avail themselves of such a release. As Paul states, "as through the disobedience of the one man many were constituted sinners, likewise also through the obedience of the one person many will be constituted righteous." (Ro 5:18, 19) At the time of Adam's sin and his being sentenced to death, his offspring or race were all unborn in his loins and so all died with him. (Compare Heb 7:4-10.) Jesus as a perfect man, "the last Adam" (1Co 15:45), had a race or offspring unborn in his loins, and when he died innocently as a perfect human sacrifice this potential human race died with him. He had willingly abstained from producing a family of his own by natural procreation. Instead, Jesus uses the authority granted by Jehovah on the basis of his ransom to give life to all those who accept this provision.—1Co 15:45; compare Ro 5:15-17.

Thus, Jesus was indeed "a corresponding ransom," not for the redemption of the one sinner, Adam, but for the redemption of all mankind descended from Adam. He repurchased them so that they could become his family, doing this by presenting the full value of his ransom sacrifice to the God of absolute justice in heaven. (Heb 9:24) He thereby gains a Bride, a heavenly congregation formed of his followers. (Compare Eph 5:23-27; Re 1:5, 6; 5:9, 10; 14:3, 4.) Messianic prophecies also show he will have "offspring" as an "Eternal Father." (Isa 53:10-12; 9:6, 7) To be such, his ransom must embrace more than those of his "Bride." In addition to those "bought from among mankind as *firstfruits"* to form that heavenly congregation, therefore, others are to benefit from his ransom sacrifice and gain everlasting life through the removal of their sins and accompanying imperfection. (Re 14:4; 1Jo 2:1, 2) Since those of the heavenly congregation serve with Christ as priests and "kings over the earth," such other recipients of the ransom benefits must be earthly subjects of Christ's Kingdom, and as children of an "Eternal Father" they attain everlasting life. (Re 5:10; 20:6; 21:2-4, 9, 10; 22:17; compare Ps 103:2-5.) The entire arrangement manifests Jehovah's wisdom and his righteousness in perfectly balancing the scales of justice while showing undeserved kindness and forgiving sins.—Ro 3:21-26.

GALILEE, located in northern Palestine, was a prosperous and well populated province in Bible times. To this day its geographic features are inviting—the deep blue Sea of Galilee, the rugged northern terrain, and the fertile plains. (Picture below) Here in this picturesque region, Jesus spent most of his earthly life, being raised in the Galilean city of Nazareth.—Mt 2:21-23; Lu 2:51, 52.

Farming, sheepherding, and fishing were common occupations among the Galileans, and this is reflected in many of Jesus' parables. A hardworking, industrious people, the common Galileans were looked down upon by the Pharisees and chief priests at Jerusalem. Their distinct accent made the Galileans easily recognizable to their fellow Jews.—Mt 26:73.

Galilee was the scene of some of the outstanding events of Jesus' ministry. On a mountainside near Capernaum, Jesus gave his famous Sermon on the Mount. (Mt 5:1, 2) Here in Galilee, he miraculously healed many persons. —Mr 1:32-34; 6:53-56; Joh 4:46-54.

How were Jesus' preaching and miracles received in Galilee? When he preached in his hometown, Nazareth, the people at first 'marveled at the winsome words proceeding out of his mouth.' But after Jesus compared them to the Israelites in the days of Elijah and Elisha, they sought to kill him. (Lu 4:22-30) The Galileans in general, though, were very responsive to Jesus' ministry. Thus, it was from Galileans that his early disciples were drawn, and all of his apostles (with the possible exception of Judas Iscariot) were Galilean. (Mt 4:18-22; Lu 6:12-16) The crowd of about 120 disciples that received the holy spirit on the day of Pentecost 33 C.E. were Galileans. —Ac 1:15; 2:1-7.

Map based on satellite photo of Galilee

Nain as it appears now.
Jesus brought great joy to a widow
here when he resurrected her son
(Lu 7:11-17)

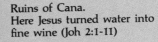

Ruins of Cana.
Here Jesus turned water into
fine wine (Joh 2:1-11)

Ruins of Capernaum on the
northwest shore of the Sea of Galilee.
From this area Jesus selected
fishermen and a tax collector
as apostles (Mt 4:18-22; 9:9)

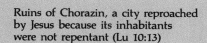

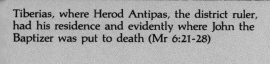

Ruins of Chorazin, a city reproached
by Jesus because its inhabitants
were not repentant (Lu 10:13)

Tiberias, where Herod Antipas, the district ruler,
had his residence and evidently where John the
Baptizer was put to death (Mr 6:21-28)

The fruitful Plain of Gennesaret,
where Jesus performed many miraculous cures
(Mt 14:34-36)

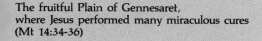

Around the Sea of Galilee

SURROUNDED by hills in northern Palestine lies the freshwater inland lake called the Sea of Galilee, Sea of Tiberias, or Lake of Gennesaret. (Picture below) Set like a jewel in a deep basin, the lake is located some 210 m (700 ft) below sea level. It is about 21 km (13 mi) long and about 12 km (7.5 mi) wide. Both on and around this lake many outstanding events of Jesus' ministry took place.

Several times Jesus spoke from a boat to crowds assembled on the shores of the sea. (Mr 4:1, 2) Capernaum, a city on the northern shore, came to be known as Jesus' "own city," even though he traveled much of the time. (Mt 9:1; Mr 2:1) Jesus walked on the waters of this sea and appeared near it after his resurrection.—Joh 6:1, 16-21; 21:1, 4-19.

LOCATIONS ON MAP
With Related Scriptures

Bethsaida	Mr 8:22-26; Lu 9:10-17; 10:13
Capernaum	Lu 4:31-41; Mt 9:1-13; 11:23
Chorazin	Mt 11:20-22
Gadara	Mt 8:28-34
Magadan	Mt 15:39–16:4
Plain of Gennesaret	Mt 14:34-36
Sea of Galilee	Mt 14:24-34; Mr 4:35-41; Lu 5:1-11
Tiberias	Mt 14:1-11

Events Leading Up to the Death of Christ

EVENTS leading up to Jesus' death took place in and around Jerusalem. Here the Son of God was presented to the nation as its King. As he approached the city, a multitude of the disciples cried out: "Blessed is the One coming as the King in Jehovah's name!" (Lu 19:37, 38) But the religious leaders of the nation rejected him and falsely charged that he was inciting the people to revolt. When the Roman governor, Pontius Pilate, pointedly asked Jesus whether he was a king, Jesus replied: "My kingdom is no part of this world." (Picture below) When Pilate himself presented Jesus to the Jews, saying: "See! Your king!" the chief priests answered: "We have no king but Caesar." —Joh 18:33-38; 19:14, 15.

Above: Inscribed stone bearing the name of Pontius Pilate, in Latin; discovered in 1961

When and Where Events Took Place

NISAN 9
Bethany
To Jerusalem
Joh 12:2-9
Lu 19:29-44

NISAN 10
Jerusalem, temple
Mr 11:15-18

NISAN 11
Jerusalem, temple
Mt 21:23–24:2;
Lu 21:1-4

Mount of Olives,
east of Jerusalem
Mt 24:3–25:46

NISAN 12
Jerusalem
Lu 22:1-6

NISAN 13
Near and
in Jerusalem
Lu 22:7-13

NISAN 14
Jerusalem
Joh 13:1–17:26;
Mt 26:26-29

Garden of
Gethsemane,
east of Jerusalem
Mt 26:36-56

Jerusalem, house
of Caiaphas
Joh 18:13, 24;
Mt 26:57-75

Jerusalem,
Sanhedrin hall
Lu 22:66-71

Jerusalem,
governor's palace
Joh 18:28–19:16

Golgotha,
outside Jerusalem
Lu 23:33-46

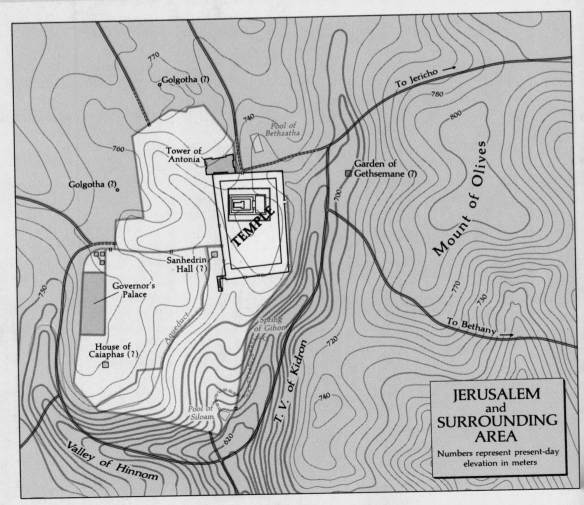

JERUSALEM and SURROUNDING AREA

Numbers represent present-day elevation in meters

Nisan 9: As Christ entered Jerusalem, he was hailed as King

Nisan 10: He threw out of the temple those who were using it for commerce

Nisan 11: He foretold the end of the old system and the time of his presence as King in heavenly glory

Nisan 14: Before he was impaled, he instituted the Memorial of his death

BEFORE ascending to heaven in 33 C.E., Jesus Christ gave his followers this parting commission: "You will be witnesses of me both in Jerusalem and in all Judea and Samaria and to the most distant part of the earth." (Ac 1:8) They proved true to their commission.

Ten days later, at Pentecost, holy spirit came upon about 120 disciples waiting in Jerusalem, and they proceeded to speak "about the magnificent things of God." (Ac 2:1-4, 11) On that same day, about 3,000 were baptized. (Ac 2:37-41) Within a short time, the disciples 'filled Jerusalem with their teaching.' (Ac 5:27, 28, 40-42) With what result? "The number of the disciples kept multiplying in Jerusalem very much."—Ac 6:7.

From Jerusalem, the witnessing work spread out. As a result of opposition to their witnessing in Jerusalem, the disciples were scattered throughout Judea and Samaria. Again, the result was increase.—Ac 8:1, 4, 14-17.

In 36 C.E. the apostle Peter brought the good news to Caesarea, where Cornelius and his household, the first uncircumcised Gentile converts, were baptized. (Ac 10) Following that, systematic witnessing among non-Jews apparently began in Syrian Antioch. As a result, "a great number that became believers turned to the Lord." (Ac 11:20, 21) Since then, the witnessing work has expanded to other nations and has literally reached "to the most distant part of the earth."

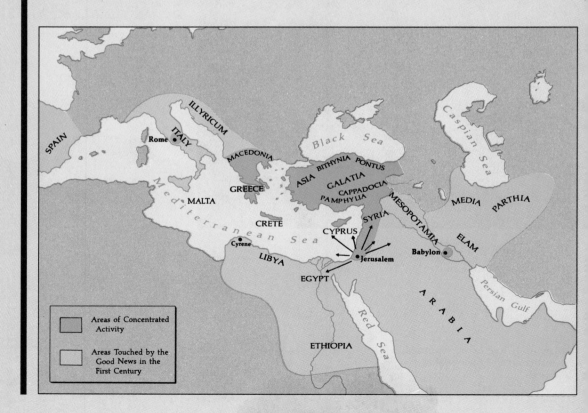

Areas of Concentrated Activity

Areas Touched by the Good News in the First Century

Model of the first-century temple showing
Solomon's Colonnade to the east.
The apostles carried on an intensive
ministry in this area (Ac 3:11; 5:12)

Roman ruins in Samaria.
The district of Samaria was
the first region outside of
Judea to receive the
Christian good news (Ac 8:1-5)

The seaport city of Joppa. Here the apostle Peter was given
a vision directing him to preach to uncircumcised Gentiles (Ac 10:9-29)

COMMISSIONED by Jesus to be an apostle to the nations, Paul zealously carried out his assignment. (Ro 11: 13) His first missionary trip took him through Cyprus and into Asia Minor. He was thrown out of cities by angry mobs, even stoned and left for dead. But he returned to strengthen those who had become disciples.

On his second trip, he reached into Macedonia and Greece. Here he was able to give a witness at the Areopagus in Athens, as illustrated below.

On Paul's third trip, he preached for some three years in Ephesus, a crossroads of the Roman world. Then he went on to Macedonia and Greece to build up the congregations there.

When being held prisoner by the Roman government, Paul used his time well to write inspired letters that are part of the Bible today.

First trip: Ac 13:1–14:28
Second trip: Ac 15:36–18:22
Third trip: Ac 18:23–21:19

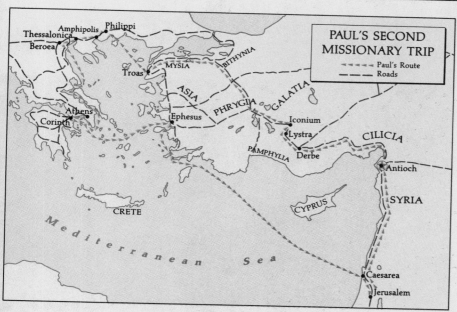

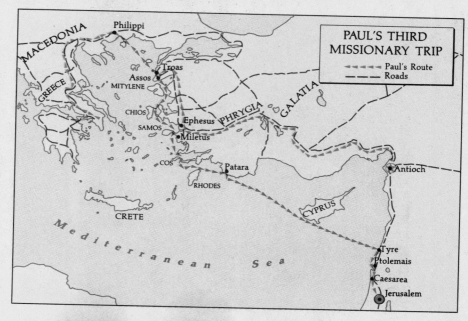

Damascus, the street called Straight. After his conversion, blinded Saul was led to a home on this street (Ac 9:3-16)

Theater in Ephesus where worshipers of Artemis (inset) rioted in protest against Paul's ministry (Ac 19:29-41)

Ruins of Antioch in Pisidia. After Paul had witnessed effectively in the synagogue here, he was thrown out of the city by an angry mob (Ac 13:14-50)

Ruins of an ancient prison in Philippi. Paul was beaten and imprisoned in this city, but the jailer and his household became Christians (Ac 16:19-34)

Wall of ancient Thessalonica. After Paul had reasoned from the Scriptures with the people here, an angry mob threw the city into an uproar (Ac 17:1-9)

Ruins of ancient Corinth (below), with Acrocorinthus in the background. Paul endeavored to fortify Christians here in Corinth against the immoral way of life that surrounded them

Athenian Acropolis as it now appears (right). In the right foreground is the Areopagus, where Paul spoke

Paul was kept
under guard in a
house in Rome for
two years; during
that time he wrote
five inspired letters
to fellow Christians

To Rome as a prisoner:
Ac 23:11–28:31

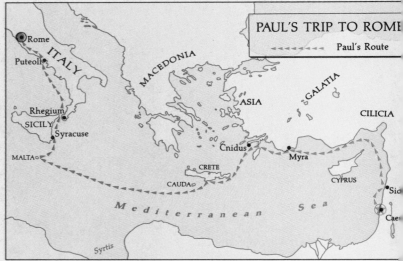

PAUL'S TRIP TO ROME

⊲⊲⊲⊲⊲⊲ Paul's Route

Rome

Puteoli

ITALY

MACEDONIA

ASIA

GALATIA

CILICIA

Rhegium

SICILY

Syracuse

Cnidus

Myra

MALTA

CRETE

CYPRUS

CAUDA

Sid

Cae

M e d i t e r r a n e a n   S e a

Syrtis

SHORTLY before his death in 33 C.E., Jesus called Jerusalem "the killer of the prophets and stoner of those sent forth to her." The city as a whole followed the pattern of its past and rejected the Son of God.—Mt 23:37.

Jesus foretold what would happen: "The days will come upon you when your enemies will build around you a fortification with pointed stakes." (Lu 19:41-44) He also said: "When you see Jerusalem surrounded by encamped armies, then . . . let those in Judea begin fleeing to the mountains."—Lu 21:20, 21.

In 66 C.E., following a Jewish revolt, Roman armies under Cestius Gallus came against Jerusalem. But, as Josephus notes, Gallus "suddenly recalled his troops, . . . and, contrary to all calculation, retired from the city." This afforded Christians the opportunity to

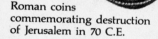

Roman coins commemorating destruction of Jerusalem in 70 C.E.

flee from Jerusalem, which they did. Soon the Roman armies under Titus returned. This time they built "a fortification with pointed stakes," an encircling fence 7.2 km (4.5 mi) long. After a siege of about five months, the city was thoroughly destroyed and the temple reduced to ruins. Three years later, in 73 C.E., the Roman armies captured the last Jewish stronghold, the mountaintop fortress of Masada. (See below.)

Jerusalem's destruction emphasizes the importance of paying attention to Bible prophecy.

Arch of Titus in Rome showing
Roman soldiers with temple loot

Roman conquest and
destruction of Jerusalem, 70 C.E.

RAPE. Rape is defined as unlawful sexual intercourse without the woman's consent, effected by force, duress, intimidation, or deception as to the nature of the act.

Jehovah warned of the consequences that would come upon Israel if the people disobeyed his law. He foretold that, besides suffering sicknesses and calamities, they would fall into the hands of their enemies, and he said: "You will become engaged to a woman, but another man will rape [form of *sha·ghal'*] her." (De 28:30) This took place when, because of their disobedience, Jehovah removed his protection from the nation, and the pagan enemies overran their cities. (Compare Zec 14:2.) Babylon was also foretold to suffer such treatment, which occurred when it fell to the Medes and Persians. (Isa 13:1, 16) According to the Law, such would not happen to nations subjugated by Israel, for the soldiers were forbidden to have sexual relations during a military campaign.—1Sa 21:5; 2Sa 11:6-11.

A case of multiple rape in the city of Gibeah of Benjamin in the days of the Judges set off a chain of events in retribution, which resulted in nearly wiping out the tribe of Benjamin. Good-for-nothing men in the city, perverted in sex desires, demanded to have sex relations with a Levite visitor. Instead of submitting, he gave them his concubine who had previously committed fornication against him. The men abused her all night until she died. The Hebrew term *'a·nah'*, rendered "rape" in this account, also has the meanings "afflict," "humiliate," and "oppress."—Jg chaps 19, 20.

King David's son Amnon forcibly violated his half sister Tamar, for which Tamar's brother Absalom brought about his death. (2Sa 13:1-18) When the scheming Haman the Agagite was exposed before the Persian king Ahasuerus for his treachery against the Jews, and especially against Ahasuerus' queen, Esther, the king was enraged. Knowing that he could expect no mercy from the king, Haman in desperation fell down upon the couch where Esther was lying, pleading with her. When the king reentered the room, he saw Haman there and cried out: "Is there also to be a raping of the queen, with me in the house?" Immediately he sentenced Haman to death. The sentence was carried out, and evidently afterward Haman was hanged on the stake that had been erected by Haman for the hanging of Esther's cousin Mordecai. (Es 7:1-10) In the record of the king's statement (Es 7:8) the Hebrew word *ka·vash'* is used; it means "subdue, subject" (Ge 1:28; Jer 34:16) but can also mean "rape."

Under the Law, if an engaged girl committed fornication with another man, both she and the man were to be put to death. But if the girl screamed for help, this was taken as proof of her innocence. The man was put to death for his sin in which he forced her, and the girl was exonerated. —De 22:23-27.

RAPHA (Ra'pha) [from a root meaning "heal"]. A son of Benjamin, called his fifth at 1 Chronicles 8:1, 2. His name is absent from the list of those who went into Egypt (Ge 46:21) and from the listing of Benjamin's tribal families. (Nu 26:38-40) This may indicate that, regardless of where Rapha was born, he died soon with no descendants, or else they were absorbed into a different family.

RAPHAH (Ra'phah) [shortened form of Rephaiah, meaning "Jah Has Healed"]. A descendant of Benjamin through Saul; also called Rephaiah. —1Ch 8:33-37; 9:43.

RAPHU (Ra'phu) [from a root meaning "heal"]. A Benjamite whose son Palti was one of the 12 to spy out the land of Canaan in 1512 B.C.E.—Nu 13:9, 16.

RAVEN [Heb., *'o·rev'*; Gr., *ko'rax*]. The first bird specifically named in the Bible. (Ge 8:7) The largest of the crowlike birds, the raven measures about 0.6 m (2 ft) in length and may have a wingspan of some 0.9 m (3 ft). Its glossy plumage is notable for its jet-black color (Ca 5:11) with iridescent steel-blue and purple hues, the underparts at times having a touch of green. It has an extremely wide range of diet, eating anything from nuts, berries, and grains to rodents, reptiles, fish, and young birds. Though it will attack the young and weak among small animals, it is primarily a scavenger. When eating carrion it has the habit of eating the eyes and other soft parts of the victim before tearing at the abdomen with its sturdy beak. (Pr 30:17) It is a powerful flier, flapping its wings in strong, steady beats, or soaring effortlessly in wide circles while it scans the area below for food. Its continuous search for food takes it over an unusually large area.

By naturalists, the crafty raven is considered to be one of the most adaptable and resourceful of all birds. In view of this as well as its flying strength and ability to survive on a wide variety of food, including carrion, the raven was an apt candidate for being the first creature to be sent outside the ark by Noah at the time the waters of the Flood had begun to recede. The text indicates that the raven thereafter remained outside the ark, using it only as a resting-place.—Ge 8:5-7.

The raven was declared unclean in the Law covenant (Le 11:13, 15; De 14:12, 14), and the phrase "according to its kind" is understood to embrace the crow and other apparently related crowlike birds such as the rook, the jackdaw, and the chough, all of which are to be found in Palestine.

The raven, unlike the crow, is usually a bird of the wilderness, often inhabiting mountainous regions and even deserts. It was among the creatures envisioned by Isaiah as inhabiting the "emptiness and the stones of wasteness" of ruined Edom. (Isa 34:11) The raven also has the practice of storing surplus food in rock crevices or burying it beneath leaves. These birds were thus an apt selection when God used them miraculously to carry in bread and meat twice daily to Elijah while the prophet was concealed in the torrent valley of Cherith.—1Ki 17:2-6.

Ravens nest on cliffs or rocky headlands, as well as in tall trees; they mate for life and are devoted parents. Jehovah God, the true Provider for all His creatures, directed Job's attention to Himself by the question: "Who prepares for the raven its food when its own young ones cry to God for help, when they keep wandering about because there is nothing to eat?" (Job 38:41) The psalmist also showed that the food brought by the wide-ranging parent birds to satisfy the raucous cries of their hungry young is due to the Creator's kindly provisions (Ps 147:7-9), while Jesus referred to the ravens in a similar way to assure his followers that the One caring for such birds of the air would surely provide for the needs of His human servants.—Lu 12:24; compare Ps 104:27, 28; Mt 6:26.

Evidently because of its impressive size, its somber colors, and its mournful croak, pagan peoples anciently viewed the raven as a bird of ill omen and a portent of death. Among the Greeks, the bold, often impudent raven was viewed as a prophetic bird, perhaps because of its reputation for cunning and sagacity. It was held to be sacred to the god Apollo and to an oracular order of priests, some of whom dressed in black.

A prince of Midian in Judge Gideon's day bore the name Oreb, meaning "Raven."—Jg 7:25.

RAZOR. A sharp instrument used to remove hair. The two Hebrew words for razor come from a root meaning "lay bare." (Isa 3:17) Specimens of this instrument found in Egypt are of bronze. These finds harmonize with the Bible record that razors were used there from very early times. —Ge 41:14.

Although the men of Israel wore beards and moderately long hair, a razor was apparently used for trimming; mention is made also of having the hair "shorn" (*KJ*), or "clipped short" (*NW*), at Acts 18:18. (See also 2Sa 19:24; Eze 44:20.) The Levites shaved all their flesh with a razor in connection with their installation into service at the tent of meeting in the wilderness. (Nu 8:7) A person under a Nazirite vow was not to use a razor on his head until the completion of the period of his vow. (Nu 6:5, 18; Jg 13:5; 16:17; Ac 21:23, 24) Samuel, a Levite, was devoted by his mother before his birth to the service of the tent of meeting. A razor was never to be used on the hair of his head.—1Sa 1:11.

Jehovah forewarned Judah that the Assyrian would be used as a "razor" by Jehovah to "shave the head and the hair of the feet" and to "sweep away even the beard itself," evidently picturing the devastation of much of the land of Judah and the carrying away of the captured population. —Isa 7:20.

That swords could be made razor sharp is shown by God's command to Ezekiel to use a sword as a barber's razor to cut off his hair and beard, and then to strike one third of the hair with the sword, pictorial of the destruction by the sword to come on a portion of Jerusalem's populace. (Eze 5:1, 2, 12) This also reveals that barbering was an early profession.

Because of the cutting damage a tongue used deceitfully can do, it is likened to a razor.—Ps 52:2.

READING. Learning from what a person sees in writing; uttering aloud what is written.

From early times men were interested in reading. King Ashurbanipal of Assyria, who established a library of 22,000 clay tablets and texts, claimed: "I had my joy in the reading of inscriptions on stone from the time before the flood." (*Light From the Ancient Past,* by J. Finegan, 1959, pp. 216, 217) This may refer to some traditional accounts regarding the global Flood or else to Assyrian records predating some local flood. The only writings regarding a flood found in the ruins of Ashurbanipal's palace were those of the Babylonian flood account, containing much mythology. Whether any genuine accounts or writings actually from before the global Flood were possessed by the pagan Assyrians cannot be determined now.

The origin of reading would, of course, be associated with the origin of writing. As to available evidence concerning this, see WRITING.

It is noteworthy that, in the Bible record of events of the 16th century B.C.E. in the days of Moses, there is specific reference to reading and writing. (Ex 17:14) The nation of Israel was encouraged to read and write. (De 6:6-9) Joshua, Moses' successor, as leader of Israel, was under command to engage in the reading of the Scriptures "day and night," regularly, in order to be successful in the assignment that God had given him. To impress Joshua with the importance of God's Word, and doubtless as a memory aid, he was to read "in an undertone."—Jos 1:8.

The kings of Israel were under divine command to write for themselves copies of God's law and to read it daily. (De 17:18, 19; see MEDITATION.) Their failure to heed this command contributed to the neglect of true worship in the land, resulting in the demoralization of the people, which led to the destruction of Jerusalem in 607 B.C.E.

Jesus had access to all the inspired scrolls of the Hebrew Scriptures in the synagogues, where, in one recorded instance, he read publicly and applied the text to himself. (Lu 4:16-21) Also, when tested three times by Satan, Jesus' reply was in all three occurrences, "It is written." (Mt 4:4, 7, 10) Obviously, he was well acquainted with the Scriptures.

The apostles, who were secondary foundation stones of a holy temple, the Christian congregation, found that reading the Scriptures was essential for their ministry. They quoted from and referred to the Hebrew Scriptures hundreds of times in their writings and advocated the reading of them by others. (Ac 17:11) The Jewish rulers perceived that Peter and John were unlettered and ordinary. (Ac 4:13) But this did not mean that they could not read and write, as the letters written by these apostles testify that they could. They were, however, not educated in the higher learning of the Hebrew schools, at the feet of the scribes. For similar reasons the Jews were astonished that Jesus had knowledge, although, as they said, "he has not studied at the schools." (Joh 7:15) That reading was widespread in that time is indicated by the account concerning the Ethiopian eunuch, a proselyte, who was reading the prophet Isaiah, and who by reason of this was approached by Philip. The eunuch was rewarded for his concern for God's Word by receiving the privilege of becoming a follower of Christ.—Ac 8:27-38.

The languages of the part of the Bible written before the first century were Hebrew and Aramaic. In the third century B.C.E., the Hebrew Scriptures were translated into Greek, which had become the international language. The Christian Scriptures were all originally written in Greek, with the exception of Matthew's Gospel. This made the reading of the Bible possible for most of the literate people in the Roman Empire, and particularly was it available to both Jews in Palestine and those of the Dispersion.

The popular demand for the Bible has reflected its readability and value, since it has far outstripped all other books in publication and circulation and is at this writing translated, either entirely or in part, in more than 1,800 languages and dialects, in billions of copies. It is reportedly available to 97 percent of earth's population in their own tongue.

The Bible enumerates many benefits derived from reading the Scriptures, among them being humility (De 17:19, 20), happiness (Re 1:3), and a discerning of the fulfilling of Bible prophecy (Hab 2:2, 3). It warns its readers to be selective as to reading material: Not all books upbuild and refresh the mind.—Ec 12:12.

The help of God's spirit is necessary for real discernment and understanding of God's Word. (1Co 2:9-16) To get understanding and other benefits, a person must approach the reading of God's Word with an open mind, throwing aside all prejudice and preconceived opinions; otherwise his understanding will be veiled, as was the case with the Jews who rejected the good news preached by Jesus. (2Co 3:14-16) Superficial reading is not enough. The reader must put his heart into it, be absorbed in study of the material, meditate deeply upon it, and seek to benefit from it personally.—Pr 15:28; 1Ti 4:13-16; Mt 24:15; see PUBLIC READING.

REAIAH   (Re·a'iah) [Jah Has Seen].

1. A son of Shobal and descendant of Judah. (1Ch 4:1, 2) It may be that Haroeh at 1 Chronicles 2:52 is the same person. The spelling in Hebrew is quite similar.

2. A Reubenite, presumably an ancestor of persons taken into exile by Tiglath-pileser III.—1Ch 5:5, 6.

3. Forefather of some of the Nethinim who returned to Jerusalem after the Babylonian exile. —Ezr 2:1, 43, 47; Ne 7:6, 46, 50.

REAPER, REAPING.

Harvesting of grain in ancient times was accomplished by cutting the grain with a sickle (De 16:9; Mr 4:29), or sometimes by uprooting it from the earth. In the latter case, the complete stalk was reaped by pulling the roots from the soil, which was important in arid lands where straw was scarce and grain did not grow very tall.

The ancient sickle was fashioned from wood or bone and had flint inserts that served as a cutting edge. Later, the more familiar curved metal blade was used. The reaper would grasp the stalks with one hand and cut them with the other.

The Israelites were commanded not to reap the edges of their fields. Instead, they were to leave a little grain standing "for the afflicted one and the alien resident." (Le 19:9, 10) After the grain was reaped, it was gathered, bound in sheaves, and piled in heaps, perhaps on the threshing floor. —Ge 37:6, 7; Ru 3:6, 7.

Figurative Use. Reaping is often used figuratively in the Scriptures to illustrate the end result of one's works, whether good or bad. The divine principle is that "whatever a man is sowing, this he will also reap." Paul showed that, whereas the one sowing with a view to the flesh reaps corruption therefrom, "he who is sowing with a view to the spirit will reap everlasting life from the spirit," and he assured Galatian Christians that they would reap if they did not tire out. (Ga 6:7-9; Pr 22:8; Ho 8:1, 7) In encouraging Christian generosity toward needy fellow believers in Judea, the apostle told the Corinthians: "He that sows sparingly will also reap sparingly; and he that sows bountifully will also reap bountifully."—2Co 9:5-7.

Jesus Christ dispatched his disciples to "reap," implying that they were to gather responsive ones as his disciples. (Joh 4:35-38) According to Jesus' illustration of the symbolic "wheat" and "weeds," at "the conclusion of the system of things," the Son of man sends out his angelic reapers to "collect out from his kingdom all things that cause stumbling and persons who are doing lawlessness." These "weeds" ("the sons of the wicked one") are pitched into a figurative fiery furnace, whereas "the wheat" ("the sons of the kingdom") are preserved and "will shine as brightly as the sun in the kingdom of their Father."—Mt 13:24-30, 36-43.

That the glorified and enthroned Jesus Christ directs this reaping and separating work is shown by John's vision in Revelation, where Christ is pictured as someone "like a son of man, with a golden crown on his head and a sharp sickle in his hand." In response to the angelic cry, "Put your sickle in and reap, because the hour has come to reap, for the harvest of the earth is thoroughly ripe," John beheld that he "thrust in his sickle on the earth, and the earth was reaped." The apostle observed that thereafter "the vine of the earth" was gathered and hurled into "the great winepress of the anger of God."—Re 14:14-20; compare Re 19:11-16.

REASONABLENESS. The Greek word *e·pi·ei·kes'*, which is translated "reasonableness," has been defined as meaning "seemly, fitting; hence, equitable, fair, moderate, forbearing, not insisting on the letter of the law; it expresses that consider-

ateness that looks 'humanely and reasonably at the facts of a case.'"—*Vine's Expository Dictionary of Old and New Testament Words,* 1981, Vol. 2, pp. 144, 145.

Reasonableness is a distinctive feature of heavenly wisdom. (Jas 3:17) It is a quality that a man who is appointed as an overseer in a Christian congregation must have. (1Ti 3:2, 3) He would have to be reasonable with himself, in dealing with others, and in his view of problems. Also, Christians generally are encouraged to be reasonable. The apostle Paul counseled the Philippians: "Let your reasonableness ["yieldingness," *Int*] become known to all men." (Php 4:5) And Titus was instructed to remind the Christians of Crete "to be reasonable [literally, yielding]." (Tit 3:1, 2, ftn) This was especially fitting, since the inhabitants of Crete as a whole had the reputation of being liars, injurious wild beasts, and unemployed gluttons. —Tit 1:12.

At 1 Peter 2:18 house servants are admonished to "be in subjection to their owners with all due fear, not only to the good and reasonable, but also to those hard to please."

REBA (Re'ba) [possibly, Fourth [Part]]. One of the five kings of Midian slain in the avenging of Midian's immoral seduction of Israel. (Nu 31:2, 8) At the time, the five were presumably vassals of the Amorites and hence are also called "the dukes of Sihon."—Jos 13:21.

REBEKAH (Re·bek'ah) [possibly, Cow]. Daughter of Bethuel the son of Nahor, and therefore grandniece of Abraham. Her brother's name was Laban.—Ge 22:20-23.

In 1878 B.C.E., when Abraham sent his household manager, likely Eliezer, in search of a suitable wife for his son Isaac (now 40 years old), he came to "the city of Nahor" in the upper Mesopotamian valley. There at a well, this servant prayed that Jehovah's choice would be the damsel who not only would give him a drink when asked but also would volunteer to water his ten camels. (Ge 24:1-14) While he was praying, Rebekah came to the well with a water jar. When he asked her for a sip of water, she graciously gave him a drink and then "quickly emptied her jar into the drinking trough and ran yet again and again to the well to draw water, and kept drawing for all his camels. All the while the man was gazing at her in wonder, keeping silent to know whether Jehovah had made his trip successful or not." Rebekah proved to be kind, hospitable, modest in her manner, and industrious; besides this, "the young woman was very attractive in appearance."—Ge 24:14-21.

Abraham's servant, recognizing that his prayer had been answered, bestowed upon Rebekah a gold nose ring and two beautiful gold bracelets (worth c. $1,350 in modern-day values). These she showed to her family—her mother and her brother Laban—who, in turn, extended the hospitality of their home to the visitor and the attendants with him. (Ge 24:22-32) But before he would eat, the man stated his business. Laban and his father Bethuel gave their consent for Rebekah to marry Isaac; gifts, consisting of precious articles of gold and silver and exquisite garments, were given to Rebekah and her family, and then they all ate together. (Ge 24:33-54) This transaction constituted an honorable marriage contract, not between Rebekah and Isaac, but between their parents, according to the custom of the time. Rebekah was in this way betrothed to Isaac and was from then on, in effect, his wife.

With Rebekah's consent, the caravan took off the next morning for the long journey to the Negeb near Beer-lahai-roi, where Isaac was living at the time. Before she left, Rebekah's family blessed her, saying: "May you become thousands times ten thousand, and let your seed take possession of the gate of those who hate it." Her nurse Deborah and other lady attendants accompanied Rebekah, none of whom, it appears, ever returned to their homeland.—Ge 24:55-62; 35:8.

Upon reaching their destination, Rebekah put on a headcloth at the approach of her bridegroom Isaac, and after Abraham's servant had recounted all the events of his mission, relating how Jehovah had directed the choice, Isaac brought Rebekah into his mother's tent to become his wife. Isaac dearly loved Rebekah, and in her he "found comfort after the loss of his mother" Sarah, who had died three years earlier.—Ge 24:63-67.

Like Sarah, Rebekah for a long time remained barren. After some 19 years, during which time Isaac persistently appealed to Jehovah, she conceived and then bore the twins Esau and Jacob. So distressing was her pregnancy, as the two struggled with each other in her womb, that Rebekah wondered, "Just why am I alive?" In response, Jehovah assured her that she would become the mother of two great nations and that "the older will serve the younger." (Ge 25:20-26) This, Paul says, was to demonstrate that the choice of the 'seed of promise' depended entirely on God.—Ro 9:6-13.

Also like Sarah, Rebekah disguised her identity on one occasion, passing herself off as her husband's sister. This was when a famine in the land forced her family to take up residence for a time in Philistine territory ruled over by King Abimelech. Rebekah must have been well along in years, yet because of her great beauty Isaac, the designated heir of the Abrahamic covenant, was presumed to be in danger of being killed if it was known he was her husband.—Ge 26:1-11.

When Isaac had grown old and was preparing to bless Esau his firstborn, Rebekah took immediate steps to secure the desired blessing for Jacob. (Ge 25:28-34; 27:1-5) Whether Rebekah knew of Jacob's legal right to the birthright through purchase is not stated, but she was well aware of what Jehovah had told her, namely, that the older would serve the younger. So she took action to see that Jacob would secure his father's blessing. The outcome was in harmony with Jehovah's purpose. —Ge 27:6-29; see JACOB.

Later, when Rebekah learned of Esau's plans to kill Jacob, she influenced Isaac to send Jacob to her homeland in search of a wife for himself. It had grieved both her and Isaac very much that Esau had taken two wives from among the hated Canaanites.—Ge 26:34, 35; 27:41-46; 28:1-5; 29:10-12.

Just when Rebekah died is not stated, but it may have been before Jacob returned home from Mesopotamia. (Ge 35:27) She was buried in the family cave of Machpelah along with Abraham and Sarah, where later Isaac, Leah, and Jacob were interred.—Ge 49:29-31; 50:13.

REBELLIOUSNESS.

Disobedience or resistance to and defiance of a superior authority. Pride, selfishness, outside pressures, disagreement with the judgment of a superior, and a desire to get out from under subjection or oppression, either real or imagined, have been among the leading causes for rebellion.

Early History. Rebellion against God had its start in the invisible realm. By means of a serpent, a spirit creature, who later became known as Satan the Devil, endeavored to get the first woman Eve to rebel against her Creator. He made rebellion attractive, presenting it as a course that would lead to enlightenment. Eve gave in to the selfish ambition to "be like God," in the sense of determining for herself what was good and what was bad instead of abiding by God's judgment on this matter. (See TREES [Figurative Use].) Imagining herself to be deprived of something that she had now come to view as rightfully belonging to her, Eve chose to transgress God's command. Later her husband Adam yielded to her pressure and joined in this rebellion. He did so, not because he was deceived into thinking that the serpent was speaking the truth, but evidently because he self-ishly chose the companionship of his sinful wife in preference to the approval of God.—Ge 3:1-6; 1Ti 2:14.

For centuries afterward it appears that the majority of mankind did not want to submit themselves to God. From the time of Abel's death until the birth of Noah, a period of more than 926 years, only Enoch is specifically mentioned as one who walked with God. (Ge 5:22) Rebelliousness also continued to spread in the heavenly realm. In Noah's day, angels, desiring sensual pleasure, disobediently forsook their heavenly posts, materialized human bodies, married women, and fathered offspring.—Ge 6:4; 1Pe 3:19, 20; 2Pe 2:4, 5; Jude 6.

By Noah's time the spirit of rebelliousness had so saturated mankind that Jehovah God saw fit to destroy the human race by means of a flood. Only Noah and his immediate family, eight persons all together, were found worthy of preservation.—Ge 6:5-8; 7:13, 23.

In Israel. Years later Jehovah God began to deal exclusively with the nation of Israel. Yet throughout Israel's history there were numerous cases of rebellion against Jehovah and against his representatives, on a national, group, or individual level. In certain cases those who rebelled were not constantly rebellious persons. For example, Moses and Aaron faithfully served Jehovah God for many years. However, when subjected to the pressure of quarreling Israelites on one occasion, they lost self-control and rebelliously failed to give glory to God for a miraculous provision of water. (Nu 20:12, 24; 27:13, 14) But the nation as a whole was so persistent in its rebellious course that Ezekiel 44:6 applies the name "Rebelliousness" to the house of Israel, as if the nation of Israel came to personify rebelliousness.

Jehovah God did not leave such rebelliousness unpunished. (1Sa 12:15; 15:23; 1Ki 13:21, 22, 26; Ps 5:10; Isa 1:20; 63:10; Jer 4:16-18; Eze 20:21; Ho 13:16) His law demanded the death penalty for those persisting in rebellion against parents. (De 21:18-21) Divine execution came upon proud and ambitious Korah, Dathan, Abiram, and those associated with them in the rebellion against Moses and Aaron, God's appointed representatives. When the Israelites disputed the rightness of this execution and manifested a rebellious spirit toward Moses and Aaron, 14,700 more perished by a scourge from Jehovah. (Nu 16:1-3, 25-50) Often Jehovah let other nations serve as instruments to inflict punishment upon the Israelites when they yielded to the pressure to be like the surrounding nations and rebelliously abandoned true worship. —Jg 2:3, 11-16; 3:4, 5; Ne 9:26, 27.

King Zedekiah's covenant-breaking rebellion. At the time King Nebuchadnezzar made Judean King Zedekiah a vassal king, he had Zedekiah make a covenant in Jehovah's name. Therefore, when Zedekiah rebelled against Nebuchadnezzar, wanting to be free from subjection to a foreign power, he also rebelled against Jehovah, in whose name he had obligated himself to be a loyal vassal king. Because of this rebellion, Jehovah decreed that Zedekiah would die as a captive in Babylon. —2Ki 24:17-20; 2Ch 36:11-21; Eze 17:12-18.

Among Christians. Christians have also had to contend with rebellious persons. The apostle Paul foretold an apostasy, or rebellion, among professed Christians (2Th 2:3), and already in his time, apostates existed. (1Ti 1:19, 20; 2Ti 2:16-19) The disciple Jude wrote about those who spoke abusively of "glorious ones" in the Christian congregation. As the destruction of such rebellious ones was certain, Jude referred to that destruction as if it had already taken place, saying: "[They] have perished in the rebellious talk of Korah!" —Jude 8, 11; see APOSTASY.

Subjection to governmental authority proper. Instead of rebelling, those desiring to gain God's approval as Christ's followers are called upon to be obedient to those taking the lead inside the congregation (Heb 13:17) and to governmental authorities outside the congregation. (Tit 3:1, 2) Rebellion against secular governmental authority constitutes a rebellion against God, for these authorities exist by God's permission and it is his will that Christians be subject to them as long as what they require does not conflict with his law. —Ro 13:1-7; Ac 5:29.

REBUKE. The idea of sharply expressing disapproval or of checking by words or actions is commonly conveyed by the Hebrew verb *ga·ʽar′.* (Ge 37:10) Another Hebrew verb rendered "rebuke" literally means "humiliate" (Job 11:3); one Hebrew noun rendered "rebuke" literally means "a reproving." (2Ki 19:3) In Greek, the sense of "rebuke" is conveyed by *e·pi·ti·ma′o,* which may also mean "strictly charge," "sternly tell," "reprimand." —Mt 12:16; Lu 18:39; 2Ti 4:2.

One sense of rebuke not limited to persons is "to check," "to put a stop to something." Jehovah's rebuking sown seed denotes his preventing a good harvest. (Mal 2:3) His rebuking devouring insects means his putting an end to their causing serious harm to crops. (Mal 3:11) The psalmist, speaking of the enemies of God's people under the figure of animals, appealed to the Most High to check their power to do injury: "Rebuke the wild beast of the reeds, the assembly of bulls." (Ps 68:30) Jesus Christ rebuked the wind and a fever.—Mr 4:39; Lu 4:39.

At times "rebuke" conveys the thought of "threat." Thus, the words "rebuke of your face" may indicate that the countenance has taken on a threatening demeanor.—Ps 80:16.

The effect of a rebuke may call attention to Jehovah's great power. A notable example was the parting of the Red Sea.—Ps 106:9.

Valid or Unjustified. A rebuke may be either valid or unjustified. Because a dream related by Joseph contained thoughts that seemed to violate the natural sense of fitness as regards the parent-child relationship, his father Jacob rebuked him. (Ge 37:10) When Jesus Christ told his disciples that suffering and an executional death awaited him, Peter rebuked him with the words: "Be kind to yourself, Lord; you will not have this destiny at all." (Mt 16:22) Since Peter was wrong, Jesus rightly rebuked him in very strong terms: "Get behind me, Satan, because you think, not God's thoughts, but those of men."—Mr 8:33.

Beneficial. Though a rebuke from a wise person may hurt, the inspired counsel is: "Better is it to hear the rebuke of someone wise than to be the man hearing the song of the stupid ones." (Ec 7:5) The rebuke from a wise man, when accepted in the right spirit and acted on, can bring about improvement in a person's conduct. The sensible person is more deeply affected by a simple rebuke than is a senseless person who receives 100 strokes for a misdeed. (Pr 17:10) Congregational rebuke in the form of disfellowshipping may bring a wrongdoer to his senses, as it appears to have done in the case of an incestuous man at Corinth.—2Co 2:6, 7; 1Co 5:1-5.

RECAH

(Re'cah). Apparently the name of a Judean site. It is mentioned along with genealogical information for the tribe of Judah.—1Ch 4:12.

RECHAB

(Re'chab) [Charioteer].

1. A Benjamite son of Rimmon the Beerothite. Rechab and his brother Baanah, both captains of marauding bands, murdered Ish-bosheth, the son and successor of Saul, and presented his head to David, expecting to win favor, but David had them both executed for their wicked deed against a righteous man.—2Sa 4:2, 5-12.

2. A Kenite father or ancestor of Jehu's companion Jehonadab and forefather of the Rechabites.—1Ch 2:55; 2Ki 10:15, 23; Jer 35:6, 8, 14, 16, 18, 19; see RECHABITES.

3. Father or ancestor of the Malchijah who helped Nehemiah repair a gate of Jerusalem's wall. (Ne 3:14) If he is the same Rechab as No. 2, Malchijah's presence confirms the fulfillment of Jehovah's promise to the Rechabites as found at Jeremiah 35:19.

RECHABITES

(Re'cha·bites) [Of (Belonging to) Rechab]. Descendants of Rechab the Kenite through Jehonadab.—Jer 35:6; 1Ch 2:55.

During Jehonadab's time it seems that at least some of the Rechabites lived in the northern kingdom, for it was there that Jehonadab joined Jehu (king, c. 904-877 B.C.E.) in opposing Baal worship and "all who were left over of Ahab's in Samaria." (2Ki 10:15-17) Jehonadab laid a command on his family (whether before or after the experience with Jehu is not stated) to live in tents, not sowing seed, not planting vineyards, and not drinking wine, because they were alien residents in the land.—Jer 35:6-10.

In the final part of Jehoiakim's reign (628-618 B.C.E.) a number of Rechabites dwelt in Judah. When Nebuchadnezzar came against the land, the Rechabites entered Jerusalem for protection from the Chaldeans and Syrians. At Jehovah's order, Jeremiah brought Jaazaniah their leader and all the Rechabites to a dining room in the temple. (Jer 35:1-4) That they could all fit in one of the temple's dining rooms suggests that they were not very numerous. Jeremiah, as God had directed, put cups of wine before them and said: "Drink wine." Out of respect for the command of their ancestor they refused to do so, and they explained that they had recently left their usual habitat to move into the city only because of the invading armies.—Jer 35:5-11.

Jehovah was pleased with the respectful obedience they showed. Their unswerving obedience to an earthly father stood in contrast to the disobedience of the Judeans to their Creator. (Jer 35:12-16) God gave the Rechabites the rewarding promise: "There will not be cut off from Jonadab the son of Rechab a man to stand before me always."—Jer 35:19.

During Nehemiah's governorship after the exile, "Malchijah the son of Rechab" repaired the Gate of the Ash-heaps. If this Rechab is the same one who was the father or ancestor of Jehonadab, it shows that Rechabites survived the exile and returned to the land. (Ne 3:14) At 1 Chronicles 2:55 Hammath is listed as "the father of the house of Rechab." It is uncertain whether Hammath was an ancestor of the Rechabites or was a town from which they came.

RECONCILIATION.

To reconcile means to bring back into harmony or cause to be friendly again; also to adjust or settle, as in reconciling differences. In Greek, the words related to reconciliation are derived from the verb *al·las'so*, which, basically, means "change, alter."—Ac 6:14; Ga 4:20, *Int*.

Thus, the compound form *ka·tal·las'so*, while meaning, basically, "exchange," came to have the meaning "reconcile." (Ro 5:10) Paul used this verb when speaking of a woman's 'making up again' with her husband, from whom she had separated. (1Co 7:11) The related *di·al·las'so·mai* appears at Matthew 5:24 in Jesus' instructions that a person should first 'make his peace' with his brother before presenting an offering on the altar.

Reconciliation to God. In Paul's letter to the Romans and in several other letters, he uses *ka·tal·las'so* and *a·po·ka·tal·las'so* (an intensified form) in dealing with man's being reconciled to God by means of the sacrifice of Christ Jesus.

Such reconciliation to God is necessary because an alienation has existed, a separation, a lack of harmony and of friendly relations, more than that, a state of enmity. This came through the first man Adam's sin and the resultant sinfulness and imperfection inherited by all his descendants. (Ro 5:12; compare Isa 43:27.) The apostle could therefore say that "the minding of the flesh means enmity with God, for it is not under subjection to the law of God, nor, in fact, can it be [due to its inherited imperfect, sinful nature]. So those who are in harmony with the flesh cannot please God." (Ro 8:7, 8) Enmity exists because God's perfect standards do not allow for his approving or condoning wrongdoing. (Ps 5:4; 89:14) Of his Son, who reflected his Father's perfect qualities, it is written: "You loved righteousness, and you hated lawlessness." (Heb 1:9) Hence, even though "God is love" and even though "God loved the world [of mankind] so much that he gave his only-begotten Son" on mankind's behalf, the fact remains that mankind as a whole has been in a state of enmity toward God and that God's love toward the world of mankind was love toward enemies, a love guided by principle (Gr., *a·ga'pe*) rather than affection or friendship (Gr., *phi·li'a*).—1Jo 4:16; Joh 3:16; compare Jas 4:4.

Since God's standard is one of perfect righteousness, he cannot countenance, or view with favor, sin, which is the violation of his express will. He is "gracious and merciful" and "rich in mercy" (Ps 145:8, 9; Eph 2:4); but he does not disregard justice in order to display mercy. As correctly observed in M'Clintock and Strong's *Cyclopædia*

(1894, Vol. VIII, p. 958), the relation between God and sinful man is thus "a legal one, as that of a sovereign, in his judicial capacity, and a criminal who has violated his laws and risen up against his authority, and who is therefore treated as an enemy." This is the situation into which mankind was brought because of the inheritance of sin from their first father, Adam.

The basis for reconciliation. It is only by and through the ransom sacrifice of Christ Jesus that full reconciliation to God is possible; he is "the way," and no one comes to the Father except through him. (Joh 14:6) His death served as "a propitiatory sacrifice [Gr., *hi·la·smon'*] for our sins." (1Jo 2:2; 4:10) The word *hi·la·smos'* signifies a "means of appeasing," an "atonement." Clearly, the sacrifice of Jesus Christ was not a "means of appeasing" in the sense of soothing hurt feelings on the part of God, mollifying him, for the death of his beloved Son certainly would produce no such effect. Rather, that sacrifice appeased, or satisfied, the demands of God's perfect justice by providing the just and righteous basis for pardoning sin, so that God "might be righteous even when declaring righteous the man [the hereditarily sinful man] that has faith in Jesus." (Ro 3:24-26) By supplying the means for expiating (making complete satisfaction for) man's sins and unlawful acts, Christ's sacrifice made it *propitious* (favorable) for man's seeking and receiving a restoration to right relations with the Sovereign God.—Eph 1:7; Heb 2:17; see RANSOM.

Thus, through Christ, God made it possible to "reconcile again to himself all other things by making peace through the blood he [Jesus] shed on the torture stake," and thereby persons once "alienated and enemies" because of having their minds on wicked works could now be "reconciled by means of that one's fleshly body through his death, in order to present [them] holy and unblemished and open to no accusation before him." (Col 1:19-22) Jehovah God could now 'declare righteous' those whom he selected to become his spiritual sons; they would not be subject to any accusation, since they were now persons fully reconciled to, and at peace with, God.—Compare Ac 13:38, 39; Ro 5:9, 10; 8:33.

What, then, can we say of men who served God in times before Christ's death? This would include men such as Abel, who "had witness borne to him that he was righteous, God bearing witness respecting his gifts"; Enoch, who "had the witness that he had pleased God well"; Abraham, who "came to be called 'Jehovah's friend'"; Moses, Joshua, Samuel, David, Daniel, John the Baptizer, and Christ's disciples (to whom Jesus said prior to his death, "the Father himself has affection for you"). (Heb 11:4, 5; Jas 2:23; Da 9:23; Joh 16:27) Jehovah dealt with all of these and blessed them. How, then, would such ones need any reconciling by means of Christ's death?

These persons obviously enjoyed a measure of reconciliation to God. Nevertheless, they, even as the rest of the world of mankind, were still sinners by inheritance and had acknowledged themselves as such by the animal sacrifices they offered. (Ro 3:9, 22, 23; Heb 10:1, 2) True, some men have been more overt or gross in their sinning than others, even being openly rebellious; but sin is sin, whatever the degree or extent. Since all are sinners, all men descended from Adam have, without exception, needed the reconciliation with God that his Son's sacrifice made possible.

God's relative friendship toward men such as those considered earlier was on the basis of the faith they showed, faith that embraced the belief that God would in his due time provide the means for relieving them completely of their sinful state. (Compare Heb 11:1, 2, 39, 40; Joh 1:29; 8:56; Ac 2:29-31.) Hence, the measure of reconciliation they enjoyed was contingent upon God's future provision of the ransom. As shown under the heading DECLARE RIGHTEOUS, God "counted," "reckoned" or credited, their faith as righteousness, and on that basis, with the absolute certainty of his own provision of a ransom in view, Jehovah could provisionally have friendly relations with them without violating his standards of perfect justice. (Ro 4:3, 9, 10, *NW* and *KJ;* also compare 3:25, 26; 4:17.) Nevertheless, the proper demands of his justice must eventually be satisfied, so that the "crediting" would be covered by actual payment of the required ransom price. All of this exalts the importance of Christ's position in God's arrangement and demonstrates that, apart from Christ Jesus, men have no righteousness that could qualify them for a standing before God.—Compare Isa 64:6; Ro 7:18, 21-25; 1Co 1:30, 31; 1Jo 1:8-10.

Steps necessary for attaining reconciliation. Since God is the offended party whose law has been and is being violated, it is man who must become reconciled to God, not God to man. (Ps 51:1-4) Man does not meet God on equal terms, nor is God's stand as to what is right subject to change, emendation, or modification. (Isa 55:6-11; Mal 3:6; compare Jas 1:17.) His conditions for reconciliation are therefore nonnegotiable, not subject to question or compromise. (Compare Job 40:1, 2, 6-8; Isa 40:13, 14.) While many translations render Isaiah 1:18 to read, "Come now, and

let us reason together, says the LORD" (*KJ; AT; JP; RS*), a more appropriate and consistent translation is: "'Come, now, you people, and let us set matters straight ["let us settle the dispute," *Ro*] between us,' says Jehovah." The fault producing the disharmony lies entirely with man, not with God. —Compare Eze 18:25, 29-32.

This does not prevent God from mercifully taking the initiative in opening the way for reconciliation. He did so through his Son. The apostle writes: "For, indeed, Christ, while we were yet weak, died for ungodly men at the appointed time. For hardly will anyone die for a righteous man; indeed, for the good man, perhaps, someone even dares to die. But God recommends his own love [a·ga′pen] to us in that, while we were yet sinners, Christ died for us. Much more, therefore, since we have been declared righteous now by his blood, shall we be saved through him from wrath. For if, when we were enemies, we became reconciled to God through the death of his Son, much more, now that we have become reconciled, we shall be saved by his life. And not only that, but we are also exulting in God through our Lord Jesus Christ, through whom we have now received the reconciliation." (Ro 5:6-11) Jesus, who "did not know sin," was made to "be sin for us," dying as a human sin offering, to relieve persons of the charge and penalty of sin. Relieved of the charge of sin, such ones could thus appear righteous in God's eyes, hence "become God's righteousness by means of him [Jesus]."—2Co 5:18, 21.

God additionally displays his mercy and love by sending out ambassadors to sinful mankind. In ancient times ambassadors were sent out primarily in times of hostility (compare Lu 19:14), not peace, their mission frequently being to see if war could be averted or to arrange terms for peace where a state of war prevailed. (Isa 33:7; Lu 14:31, 32; see AMBASSADOR.) God sends his Christian ambassadors to men to enable them to learn his terms for reconciliation and to avail themselves of such. As the apostle writes: "We are therefore ambassadors substituting for Christ, as though God were making entreaty through us. As substitutes for Christ we beg: 'Become reconciled to God.'" (2Co 5:20) Such entreaty does not signify any weakening of God's position nor of his opposition to wrongdoing; it is, instead, a merciful urging to the offenders to seek peace and escape the inevitable consequence of God's righteous anger toward all who persist in going contrary to his holy will, destruction being the certain end of such. (Compare Eze 33:11.) Even Christians must be careful "not to accept the undeserved kindness of God and miss its purpose" by failing to seek continually God's favor and goodwill during the "acceptable time" and the "day of salvation" God mercifully provides, as Paul's following words show.—2Co 6:1, 2.

Recognizing the need for reconciliation and accepting God's provision for reconciliation, namely, the sacrifice of God's Son, the individual must then repent of his sinful course and convert, or turn around, from following the way of the sinful world of mankind. By appealing to God on the basis of Christ's ransom, forgiveness of sins and reconciliation can be obtained, bringing "seasons of refreshing . . . from the person of Jehovah" (Ac 3:18, 19) as well as peace of mind and heart. (Php 4:6, 7) No longer an enemy under the wrath of God, one has, in effect, "passed over from death to life." (Joh 3:16; 5:24) Thereafter the individual must retain God's goodwill by 'calling upon him in trueness,' 'continuing in the faith, and not being shifted away from the hope of the good news.'—Ps 145: 18; Php 4:9; Col 1:22, 23.

In what sense has God 'reconciled a world to himself'?

The apostle Paul speaks of God "by means of Christ reconciling a world to himself, not reckoning to them their trespasses." (2Co 5:19) This should not be misread as meaning that all persons are automatically reconciled to God by Jesus' sacrifice, inasmuch as the apostle immediately goes on to describe the ambassadorial work of entreating men to "become reconciled to God." (2Co 5:20) In reality, the means was provided whereby all those of the world of mankind *willing to respond* could gain reconciliation. Hence, Jesus came "to give his soul a ransom in exchange for many," and "he that exercises faith in the Son has everlasting life; he that disobeys the Son will not see life, but the wrath of God remains upon him."—Mt 20:28; Joh 3:36; compare Ro 5:18, 19; 2Th 1:7, 8.

Nevertheless, Jehovah God purposed to "gather all things together again in the Christ, the things in the heavens and the things on the earth." (Eph 1:10) Though a destruction of those who refuse to "set matters straight" (Isa 1:18) with Jehovah God is required, the result will be a universe in total harmony with God, and mankind will again rejoice in God's friendship and enjoy the full flow of his blessings as at the start in Eden.—Re 21:1-4.

Jehovah God terminated his covenant relationship with Israel as a nation because of its unfaithfulness and its national rejection of his Son. (Mt 21:42, 43; Heb 8:7-13) Evidently the apostle refers to this when saying that 'the casting of them away meant reconciliation for the world' (Ro 11:15), for as the context shows, the way was thereby opened for the world outside the Jewish community or congregation. That is, the non-Jewish nations now had opportunity to be joined with a faithful Jewish remnant in the new covenant as God's new nation, spiritual Israel.—Compare Ro 11:5, 7, 11, 12, 15, 25.

As God's covenant people, his "special property" (Ex 19:5, 6; 1Ki 8:53; Ps 135:4), the Jewish people had enjoyed a measure of reconciliation to God, though still in need of full reconciliation by means of the foretold Redeemer, the Messiah. (Isa 53:5-7, 11, 12; Da 9:24-26) The non-Jewish nations, on the other hand, were "alienated from the state of Israel and strangers to the covenants of the promise, and . . . had no hope and were without God in the world," for they had no recognized standing with him. (Eph 2:11, 12) In harmony with the sacred secret regarding the Seed, God nevertheless purposed to bring blessings for persons of "all nations of the earth." (Ge 22:15-18) The means for doing this, Christ Jesus' sacrifice, therefore opened the way for those of the alienated non-Jewish nations to "come to be near by the blood of the Christ." (Eph 2:13) Not only this, but that sacrifice also removed the division between Jew and non-Jew, for it fulfilled the Law covenant and took it out of the way, thereby allowing Christ to "fully reconcile both peoples in one body to God through the torture stake, because he had killed off the enmity [the division produced by the Law covenant] by means of himself." Jew and non-Jew now would have the one approach to God through Christ Jesus, and in course of time, non-Jews were brought into the new covenant as Kingdom heirs with Christ.—Eph 2:14-22; Ro 8:16, 17; Heb 9:15.

RECORDER. A highly responsible officer in the royal court of Israel. The title is translated from a form of the Hebrew word *za·khar'* (remember) and literally means "remembrancer." (2Sa 8: 16, ftn) His duties are not described in the Bible, but it appears that he was the official chronicler of the kingdom, furnishing the king with information on developments in the realm and also reminding him of important matters for his attention, supplying advice on them.

On occasion the recorder represented the king on important national matters. Joah the son of Asaph was one of the officials of King Hezekiah who went out to speak to the Assyrian Rabshakeh when that one threatened Jerusalem. (2Ki 18:18, 37) Another recorder, Joah the son of Joahaz, officiated in connection with the repairing of the temple. (2Ch 34:8) A recorder is named also in the courts of David and Solomon.—2Sa 8:16; 20:24; 1Ki 4:3; see CITY RECORDER.

RE-CREATION. See CREATION; TRIBE.

RED. See COLORS.

REDEMPTION. See RANSOM.

RED SEA.
The body of water that separates northeastern Africa from the Arabian Peninsula; it includes the two arms known as the Gulf of Suez and the Gulf of 'Aqaba. The Red Sea, as the term is now used, measures some 2,250 km (1,400 mi) in length, has a maximum width of about 354 km (220 mi) and an average depth of approximately 610 m (2,000 ft). It is part of the great geologic fault known as the Rift Valley. Because of a fast rate of evaporation, the waters of this sea are quite salty. Strong winds, rapid changes in wind direction, and the presence of large reefs make it hazardous for boats to navigate the Red Sea. Along the eastern coast there are high mountain ranges, whereas rocky tablelands and low hills occupy the western coast.

There is good reason for understanding that the original-language expressions rendered "Red Sea" apply to the Red Sea in general or to either one of its northern arms. (Ex 10:19; 13:18; Nu 33:10, 11; Jg 11:16; Ac 7:36) It was the waters of the Red Sea that Jehovah miraculously divided to let the Israelites pass through on dry land, but he drowned Pharaoh and his military forces who came in pursuit. (Ex 14:21–15:22; De 11:4; Jos 2:10; 4:23; 24:6; Ne 9:9; Ps 106:7, 9, 22; 136:13, 15) The Biblical passages relating this incident use the Hebrew expression yam (sea) or yam-suph' (sea of reeds or rushes). On the basis of the literal meaning of yam-suph', certain scholars have argued that the Israelites crossed a mere swampy place, such as the Bitter Lakes region, and not the Red Sea (principally the western arm, the Gulf of Suez, where others believe the crossing likely occurred). However, it should be noted that the waters were sufficient to cover Pharaoh's military forces. (Ex 14:28, 29) This would have been impossible in a mere swamp. Also, Acts 7:36 and Hebrews 11:29 rule out a mere swampy place, for these texts mention the same incident and use the Greek expression e·ry·thra' tha·las·sa, meaning "Red Sea." (See EXODUS.) The historian Herodotus (fifth century B.C.E.) used the same Greek expression to refer, not to a swamp or an insignificant body of water, but to "the Indian Ocean, in which the Red Sea" is located.—A Greek-English Lexicon, by H. G. Liddell and R. Scott, revised by H. Jones, Oxford, 1968, p. 693; see PIHAHIROTH.

In a pronouncement of doom for Edom, the outcry resulting from Edom's calamity is described as being heard at the Red Sea. (Jer 49:21) This is understandable, since Edomite territory in its southern extremity bordered on the Red Sea (1Ki 9:26), that is, the sea's northeastern arm, the Gulf of 'Aqaba. Israel's boundary also extended to this point.—Ex 23:31.

REED
[Heb., qa·neh'; Gr., ka'la·mos]. These terms evidently embrace numerous reedlike plants commonly growing in wet places. (Job 40:21; Ps 68: 30; Isa 19:6; 35:7; see CALAMUS, CANE.) Some scholars believe that in many cases the "reed" intended is Arundo donax. This plant is common in Egypt, Palestine, and Syria. Its stem, terminating in a large plume of white flowers, has a diameter of 5 to 8 cm (2 to 3 in.) at the base and grows to a height of 2.5 to 5.5 m (8 to 18 ft). The leaves measure from 30 to 90 cm (1 to 3 ft) in length. The common reed (Phragmites australis) is also found in swamps and on the banks of rivers in Israel. It is a leafy grass 1.5 to 5 m (5 to 16 ft) high and has fluffy flower clusters atop its stiff, smooth stems.

In mockery, Roman soldiers placed a reed, representative of a royal scepter, in Jesus' right hand and later hit him with it. Also, a reed was used to convey a sponge soaked with sour wine to the impaled Jesus.—Mt 27:29, 30, 48; Joh 19:29; see HYSSOP.

The reed was also used for measuring. The book of Ezekiel (40:5) indicates that a measuring reed was 6 cubits long. So a reed based on the common cubit measured 2.67 m (8.75 ft), and one based on the long cubit measured 3.11 m (10.2 ft).—Re 11:1; 21:15, 16; see WEIGHTS AND MEASURES.

Figurative Use. "Reed" is used in the Bible to represent instability and frailty. (1Ki 14:15; Eze 29:6, 7) Egypt was compared to a crushed reed, the sharp, pointed slivers of which would penetrate the palm of anyone leaning upon it. (2Ki 18:21; Isa 36:6) Concerning John the Baptizer, Jesus said: "What did you go out into the wilderness to behold? A reed being tossed by a wind?" (Mt 11:7) These words may have been intended to show that John the Baptizer was not a person who was wavering or vacillating but one who was firm, stable, and upright. At Matthew 12:20 (Isa 42:3), the "bruised reed" seems to represent oppressed people like the man with the withered hand whom Jesus healed on the Sabbath.—Mt 12:10-14; see Mt 23:4; Mr 6:34.

REELAIAH
(Re·el·ai'ah). One whose name occurs with those of such prominent men as Zerubbabel and Jeshua at the beginning of the list of

those returning from Babylon to Jerusalem in 537 B.C.E. (Ezr 2:1, 2) The name is spelled Raamiah (meaning, "Jehovah Has Thundered; Uproar of Jehovah") at Nehemiah 7:7.

REFINE, REFINER. To separate and purify metals, and the craftsman who does it. By repeated melting in clay refining pots called crucibles, the slag and impurities were removed from the desired metal. (Ps 12:6; Pr 17:3; 27:21) Remnants of slag dumps have been found in the region around ancient Succoth, where some of Solomon's mining and smelting operations were located. Sometimes impurities were burned off; at other times refiner's lye (see LAUNDRYMAN) was used to consolidate the scummy dross so it could be skimmed off the surface. (Isa 1:25; Mal 3:2) The refiner sat in front of his furnace and supplied the charcoal fire with a forced draft by means of bellows.—Jer 6:29; Mal 3:3.

Gold frequently has silver with it in varying amounts. How these were separated in Bible times is not known, but a distinction in the methods of treating the two seems to be noted in Proverbs 17:3 and 27:21: "The refining pot is for silver and the furnace for gold." Nitric acid was evidently not discovered until the ninth century C.E.; so, previously gold was purified by other means. For example, if lead was present with the gold, the impurities could be fluxed off as a slag while the gold would be held by the lead. Then by slowly boiling off the lead (an operation known as cupelling) pure gold would remain behind. This process requires considerable skill, for if the temperature is too high or the boiling off too rapid, the gold is carried away with the lead. The operator learns to judge and control the refining by the color of the molten metal. (Compare Ps 12:6; Jer 6:28-30; Eze 22:18-22.) The use of lye in the refining of silver is alluded to in the Scriptures.—Mal 3:2, 3.

If the copper-bearing ore was an oxide or a carbonate, mixing the crushed ore with charcoal and burning it freed the copper in the metallic state. However, if the copper ore was a sulfide, preliminary roasting was necessary first to burn off the sulfur as sulfur dioxide and at the same time convert the copper sulfide to copper oxide. Then it could be reduced with charcoal to obtain the free metal.

Extraction of iron was more difficult, because of the tremendous heat required. Iron melts at 1,535° C. (2,795° F.) The ancients, however, built smelting furnaces equipped with bellows to give a forced draft similar to present-day blast furnaces. (De 4:20; Jer 6:29; Eze 22:20-22) There are no details as to Hebrew iron furnaces, but they may

have been similar to those known to have existed in ancient India. Made of clay, pear-shaped, about 1.2 m (4 ft) in diameter at the bottom, narrowing to 0.3 m (1 ft) at the top, they had goatskin bellows equipped with nozzles attached to clay tubes that supplied air to the bottom of the furnace. Charged with charcoal, the fire was started and the ore was added. Another layer of charcoal was then added on top, and the forced heat was continued for three or four hours. With the run completed, the front of the furnace was broken down to remove the bloom of metal.

It is a simple matter to win lead from its common ore, galena, that is, lead sulfide. First the ore is roasted with an injection of air to convert the lead sulfide to lead oxide; the sulfur combines with oxygen and forms the gas sulfur dioxide. The lead oxide is then mixed with charcoal and charged into a blast furnace; then the carbon dioxide is driven off, leaving the liquid lead behind in the crucible.

Figurative Use. Jehovah himself is referred to as a refiner. His Word is highly refined. (2Sa 22:31; Ps 18:30; 119:140; Pr 30:5) This tried and tested Word is one means by which God purifies his people in removing all sinful dross of uncleanness. (Ps 17:3; 26:2; 105:19; Da 12:9, 10; Mal 3:3) Fiery trials also refine the faithful. (Isa 48:10; Da 11:35; Zec 13:9; compare 1Pe 1:6, 7.) The wicked, on the other hand, are judged as nothing more than scummy dross, fit only for the worthless slag heap.—Ps 119:119; Pr 25:4, 5; Eze 22:18-20.

REFUGE. See CITIES OF REFUGE.

REGEM (Re′gem). First-named son of Jahdai in the Calebite branch of Judah's genealogy.—1Ch 2:3, 42, 47.

REGEM-MELECH (Re′gem-mel′ech). One of two leading men sent by the people of postexilic Bethel to "soften the face of Jehovah" and to inquire about continuing the customary fasting. This was more than two years before the rebuilt temple was completed.—Zec 7:1-3; Ezr 6:15.

REGISTRATION. An enrollment, usually by name and lineage according to tribe and household. It involved more than a simple census or count of heads. The national registrations referred to in the Bible served various purposes, such as taxation, assignments of military service, or (for those Levites included) appointments to duties at the sanctuary.

At Sinai. At Jehovah's command the first registration took place during the encampment at Sinai in the second month of the second year following the Exodus from Egypt. To assist Moses in this undertaking, a chieftain was selected out of each tribe to take the responsibility and oversight of the registration in his tribe. Not only were all males listed who were 20 years old and upward —eligible for service in the army—but the Law also placed on the registered ones a head tax of half a shekel ($1.10) for the service of the tabernacle. (Ex 30:11-16; Nu 1:1-16, 18, 19) The total number listed amounted to 603,550, excluding the Levites, who would have no inheritance in the land. These paid no tabernacle tax and were not required to serve in the army.—Nu 1:44-47; 2:32, 33; 18:20, 24.

The record in the book of Numbers shows that a count was also made of the number of firstborn males from the 12 tribes, and of all the Levite males, from a month old and upward. (Nu 3:14, 15) This was because Jehovah had bought the firstborn ones as his when he saved them from the destruction of the firstborn in Egypt. Now he desired to use the Levites as his specially sanctified ones for sanctuary service. The Levites were therefore to be given to Jehovah by Israel to redeem the firstborn of the other tribes. The count showed that there were 22,000 male Levites and 22,273 non-Levite firstborn. (Nu 3:11-13, 39-43) To redeem the 273 firstborn in excess of the Levites, a five-shekel ($11) payment to the sanctuary was required for each.—Nu 3:44-51.

Also the Kohathites, Gershonites, and Merarites between 30 and 50 years of age were numbered. These were given special assignments of service at the sanctuary.—Nu 4:34-49.

On the Plains of Moab. A second recorded registration is the one taken on the Plains of Moab, after the scourge because of Israel's sin in connection with Baal of Peor. It was found then that the number of men 20 years old and upward was 601,730, a decrease of 1,820 from the census taken nearly 39 years earlier. (Nu 26:1, 2, 51) The count of Levites from a month old and upward was 23,000, or 1,000 more than the first census.—Nu 26:57, 62.

David's Calamitous Registration. A registration taken toward the end of King David's reign is also recorded, one that brought calamity. The account at 2 Samuel 24:1 reads: "And again the anger of Jehovah came to be hot against Israel, when one incited David against them, saying: 'Go, take a count of Israel and Judah.'" The "one" who did the inciting is not there identified. Was it some human counselor? Was it Satan? Or even God? First Chronicles 21:1 helps to answer the question, saying: "Satan proceeded to stand up against Isra-

el and to incite David to number Israel." That rendering in the *New World Translation* agrees with the Hebrew text and with translations into Greek, Syriac, and Latin. It is also consistent with the renderings in other translations.—*AT, NE, RS, JB, Mo.*

However, as the footnote at 1 Chronicles 21:1 points out, the Hebrew word *sa·tan'* can also be rendered "a resister." Byington translates it "a Satan"; Young's translation reads, "an adversary." So it is possible that the "one" moving David to decide on the calamitous course was a bad human counselor.

Interestingly, a footnote at 2 Samuel 24:1 shows that this text could be rendered: "And again the anger of Jehovah came to be hot against Israel, when *he* incited David against them." The translation in *The Bible in Basic English* reads: "Again the wrath of the Lord was burning against Israel, and moving David against them, he said, Go, take the number of Israel and Judah." Hence, some commentators consider that the "one" or "he" who incited David to take the census was Jehovah. His 'anger against Israel,' according to this view, predated the census and was due to their recent rebellions against Jehovah and his appointed king, David, when they followed first ambitious Absalom and then the good-for-nothing Sheba, the son of Bichri, in opposition to David. (2Sa 15:10-12; 20:1, 2) Such a viewpoint could be harmonized with the view that Satan or some bad human counselor incited David if the incitement is viewed as something that Jehovah purposely allowed, as by removing his protection or restraining hand. —Compare 1Ki 22:21-23; 1Sa 16:14; see FORE-KNOWLEDGE, FOREORDINATION (Concerning individuals).

On David's part, there may have been wrong motive due to pride and trust in the numbers of his army, hence a failing to manifest full reliance on Jehovah. In any case, it is clear that on this occasion David's chief concern was not that of glorifying God.

Objected to by Joab. When ordered to take the registration, David's general Joab objected, saying, "May Jehovah your God even add to the people a hundred times as many as they are while the very eyes of my lord the king are seeing it. But as for my lord the king, why has he found delight in this thing?" (2Sa 24:3) Joab's words imply that the national strength did not depend on numbers but on Jehovah, who could supply numbers if that was his will. Joab, at David's insistence, took the census, but unwillingly, the report stating: "Levi and Benjamin he did not register in among them, because the king's word had been detestable to Joab" (Levi not being counted, in accord with the law at Numbers 1:47-49). Joab either stopped before registering Benjamin or delayed the progress of the registration, and David came to his senses and called a halt to it before Joab had completed it. (1Ch 21:6) Joab may have avoided Benjamin because he did not want to stir up this tribe that was the tribe of Saul, which had fought David's army under Joab before uniting with the other tribes under David. (2Sa 2:12-17) No doubt because the making of the count was wrong, it was not entered into "the account of the affairs of the days of King David."—1Ch 27:24.

The count revealed that Israel had 1,100,000 men and Judah had 470,000, according to the record at 1 Chronicles 21:5. The report at 2 Samuel 24:9 says 800,000 men of Israel and 500,000 men of Judah. Some believe that a scribal error exists. But it is unwise to ascribe error to the record when the circumstances, methods of counting, and so forth, are not fully understood. The two accounts may have reckoned the number from different viewpoints. For example, it is possible that members of the standing army and/or their officers were counted or omitted. And different methods of reckoning may have caused a variation in the listing of certain men, as to whether they were under Judah or Israel. We find what may be such an instance at 1 Chronicles 27. Here 12 divisions of the army are listed, naming all the tribes except Gad and Asher, and naming Levi and the two half tribes of Manasseh. This may have been because the fighting men of Gad and Asher were combined under other heads at the time, or for other reasons not stated.

Jehovah's judgment. Jehovah's prophet Gad was sent to David, giving David, the authorizer of the census, a choice of one of three forms of punishment: a famine for three years, the sword of Israel's enemies overtaking Israel for three months, or a pestilence for three days. David, leaning on God's mercy rather than man's, chose "to fall into the hand of Jehovah"; in the pestilence that followed, 70,000 persons died.—1Ch 21:10-14.

Here another variation is found between the Samuel and Chronicles accounts. Whereas 2 Samuel 24:13 says seven years of famine, 1 Chronicles 21:12 says three. (The Greek *Septuagint* reads "three" in the Samuel account.) One proffered explanation is that the seven years referred to at Second Samuel would, in part, be an extension of the three years of famine that came because of the sin of Saul and his house against the Gibeonites.

(2Sa 21:1, 2) The current year (the registration took 9 months and 20 days [2Sa 24:8]) would be the fourth, and three years to come would make seven. Although the difference may have been due to a copyist's error, it may be said again that a full knowledge of all the facts and circumstances should be had before one reaches such a conclusion.

For the Temple Service. Sometime later David, who was now quite old, had the Levites numbered for future temple service, with Jehovah's apparent approval. This count revealed that there were 38,000 Levites 30 years of age and upward, all able-bodied men. They were listed as follows: 24,000 supervisors, 6,000 officers and judges, 4,000 gatekeepers, and 4,000 musicians.—1Ch 23:1-5.

In connection with the building of the temple we read: "Then Solomon took a count of all the men that were alien residents, who were in the land of Israel, after the census that David his father had taken of them; and there came to be found a hundred and fifty-three thousand six hundred. So he made seventy thousand of them burden bearers and eighty thousand cutters in the mountain and three thousand six hundred overseers for keeping the people in service."—2Ch 2:17, 18.

Later Registrations. There were other registrations carried out by succeeding kings of Israel and Judah. In the days of King Amaziah the men in Judah and Benjamin from 20 years upward numbered 300,000. (2Ch 25:5) In King Uzziah's registration the army forces were 307,500 men, with 2,600 of the heads of the paternal houses over them.—2Ch 26:11-13.

The returning exiles under Zerubbabel, in 537 B.C.E., were also enumerated. They included 42,360 males, also 7,337 slaves and 200 singers (the Masoretic text of Nehemiah says 245 singers). —Ezr 2:64, 65; Ne 7:66, 67; see NEHEMIAH, BOOK OF.

At the Time of Jesus' Birth. Two registrations are mentioned in the Christian Greek Scriptures as taking place after Judea came under subjection to Rome. Such were not merely to ascertain population figures but, rather, were mainly for purposes of taxation and conscription of men for military service. Concerning the first of these we read: "Now in those days [c. 2 B.C.E.] a decree went forth from Caesar Augustus for all the inhabited earth to be registered; (this first registration took place when Quirinius was governor of Syria;) and all people went traveling to be registered, each one to his own city." (Lu 2:1-3)

This edict of the emperor proved providential, for it compelled Joseph and Mary to journey from the city of Nazareth to Bethlehem in spite of the fact that Mary was then heavy with child; thus Jesus was born in the city of David in fulfillment of prophecy.—Lu 2:4-7; Mic 5:2.

Two registrations under Quirinius. Bible critics have said that the only census taken while Publius Sulpicius Quirinius was governor of Syria was about 6 C.E., which event sparked a rebellion by Judas the Galilean and the Zealots. (Ac 5:37) This was really the second registration under Quirinius, for inscriptions discovered at and near Antioch revealed that some years earlier Quirinius had served as the emperor's legate in Syria. (*The Bearing of Recent Discovery on the Trustworthiness of the New Testament,* by W. Ramsay, 1979, pp. 285, 291) Concerning this, the *Dictionnaire du Nouveau Testament* in Crampon's French Bible (1939 ed., p. 360) says: "The scholarly researches of Zumpt (*Commentat. epigraph.*, II, 86-104; *De Syria romana provincia*, 97-98) and of Mommsen (*Res gestæ divi Augusti*) place beyond doubt that Quirinius was twice governor of Syria." Many scholars locate the time of Quirinius' first governorship as somewhere between the years 4 and 1 B.C.E., probably from 3 to 2 B.C.E. Their method of arriving at these dates, however, is not solid, and the actual period of this governorship remains indefinite. (See QUIRINIUS.) His second governorship, however, included 6 C.E., according to details reported by Josephus.—*Jewish Antiquities,* XVIII, 26 (ii, 1).

So historian and Bible writer Luke was correct when he said concerning the registration at the time of Jesus' birth: "This *first* registration took place when Quirinius was governor of Syria," distinguishing it from the *second,* which occurred later under the same Quirinius and to which Gamaliel makes reference as reported by Luke at Acts 5:37.

REGRET.   See REPENTANCE.

REHABIAH   (Re·ha·bi'ah) [Jehovah Has Widened (Made Spacious)]. Grandson of Moses, only son of Eliezer, and founder of a family of Levites that still existed when David was king.—1Ch 23: 15, 17; 24:21; 26:25.

REHOB   (Re'hob) [Public Square; Broad Place].

1. Father of Hadadezer the king of Zobah against whom David warred victoriously.—2Sa 8:3-12.

2. One of the Levites or the forefather of one attesting by seal a covenant in the time of Nehemiah and Ezra.—Ne 10:1, 9, 11.

3. A place or city mentioned in the exploration of Canaan by the 12 Hebrew spies sent out by Moses. (Nu 13:21) It is probably the same place as "Rehob" and "Beth-rehob" mentioned at 2 Samuel 10:6, 8.—See BETH-REHOB.

4. The name of at least one and perhaps two cities in the territory of Asher. (Jos 19:24, 28, 30) While some scholars consider both references to denote the same city, other related texts appear to indicate separate sites. Thus, Judges 1:31, 32 says that "Asher did not drive out the inhabitants of . . . Rehob," so that the Asherites were obliged to dwell among the Canaanites of the land, whereas Joshua 21:27, 31 and 1 Chronicles 6:71, 75 state that Rehob was given to the sons of Gershom as a Levite city. Those favoring but one site consider these texts to mean that the task of evicting the Canaanites from Rehob was hindered originally but was accomplished at a later time, thus allowing for its occupation by the Levites. Those favoring two sites suggest one town as remaining in Canaanite hands, the other as among those initially captured by Asher and given to the Levites. For the two sites, some suggest an identification with Khirbet el-'Amri, about 4 km (2.5 mi) NE of Achzib, for the Rehob of Joshua 19:28; and for that of the other texts, they suggest Tell el-Bir el-Gharbi (Tel Bira), about 10 km (6 mi) ESE of Acco. This latter site is the one preferred by those who consider the name to refer to but one town.

REHOBOAM   (Re·ho·bo'am) [Widen (Make Spacious) the People]. Son of Solomon by his Ammonite wife Naamah. He succeeded his father to the throne in 997 B.C.E. at the age of 41 and reigned for 17 years. (1Ki 14:21; 1Ch 3:10; 2Ch 9:31) Rehoboam had the distinction of being, at least briefly, the last king of the united monarchy and then the first ruler of the southern two-tribe kingdom of Judah and Benjamin, for shortly after he was crowned king at Shechem by all Israel, the united kingdom of David and Solomon was divided. Ten tribes withdrew their support from Rehoboam and made Jeroboam their king, even as Jehovah by the prophet Ahijah had foretold.—1Ki 11:29-31; 12:1; 2Ch 10:1.

This separation took place after a delegation of the people, with Jeroboam as their spokesman, pleaded with Rehoboam to remove some of the oppressive measures laid upon them by Solomon. Rehoboam took the matter under advisement. First he consulted the older men, who counseled him to heed the cry of the people and reduce their burdens, thereby he would prove himself a wise king, one who would be loved by his people. But Rehoboam spurned this mature advice and sought the counsel of young men with whom he had grown up. They told the king he should in effect make his little finger as thick as his father's hips, increasing their yoke burden and chastising them with scourges instead of whips.—1Ki 12:2-15; 2Ch 10:3-15; 13:6, 7.

This arrogant, high-handed attitude adopted by Rehoboam completely alienated the majority of the people. The only tribes continuing to support the house of David were Judah and Benjamin, while the priests and Levites of both kingdoms, as well as isolated individuals of the ten tribes, also gave support.—1Ki 12:16, 17; 2Ch 10:16, 17; 11: 13, 14, 16.

Subsequently, when King Rehoboam and Ado-ram (Hadoram), who was over the conscripted forced laborers, entered the territory of the secessionists, Adoram was stoned to death but the king managed to escape with his life. (1Ki 12:18; 2Ch 10:18) Rehoboam then mustered an army of 180,-000 from among Judah and Benjamin, determined that the ten tribes would be forcibly brought under his subjection. But Jehovah through the prophet Shemaiah forbade them to fight against their brothers, since God himself had decreed the division of the kingdom. Though open warfare on the battlefield was thus avoided, hostilities between the two factions continued all the days of Rehoboam.—1Ki 12:19-24; 15:6; 2Ch 10:19; 11:1-4.

For a time Rehoboam walked quite closely to the laws of Jehovah, and early in his reign he built and fortified a number of cities, some of which he stocked with food supplies. (2Ch 11:5-12, 17) However, when his kingship was firmly established he abandoned Jehovah's worship and led Judah in the practice of detestable sex worship, perhaps because of Ammonite influence on his mother's side of the family. (1Ki 14:22-24; 2Ch 12:1) This, in turn, provoked Jehovah's anger, and in expression of it he raised up the king of Egypt, Shishak, who, together with his allies, overran the land and captured a number of cities in Judah in the fifth year of Rehoboam's reign. Had it not been that Rehoboam and his princes humbled themselves in repentance, not even Jerusalem would have escaped. As it was, the treasures of the temple and the king's house, including the gold shields that Solomon had made, were taken by Shishak as his booty. Rehoboam then replaced these shields with copper ones.—1Ki 14:25-28; 2Ch 12:2-12.

During his lifetime Rehoboam married 18 wives, including Mahalath a granddaughter of David, and Maacah the granddaughter of David's son

Absalom. Maacah was his favorite wife and the mother of Abijah (Abijam), one of his 28 sons and the heir apparent to the throne. Other members of Rehoboam's family included 60 concubines and 60 daughters.—2Ch 11:18-22.

Before his death at the age of 58, and the ascension of Abijah to the throne in 980 B.C.E., Rehoboam distributed many gifts among his other sons, presumably to prevent any revolt against Abijah after his death. (1Ki 14:31; 2Ch 11:23; 12:16) On the whole, Rehoboam's life is best summed up in this commentary: "He did what was bad, for he had not firmly established his heart to search for Jehovah."—2Ch 12:14.

REHOBOTH (Re·ho'both) [Broad Places].

1. The name that Isaac gave to a well he dug. (Ge 26:22) Some scholars have tentatively identified Rehoboth with Ruheibeh (Horvat Rehovot [ba-Negev]), about 35 km (22 mi) SW of Beer-sheba. The names bear certain similarities. In naming the well, Isaac said that now God had given ample room. He and his shepherds could be fruitful without interfering with, or getting interference from, others.

2. A city of unknown location from which came Shaul, an early Edomite king. (Ge 36:31, 37; 1Ch 1:43, 48) In both references to it, the place is called "Rehoboth by the River." Generally in the Bible the designation "the River" means the Euphrates. (Ps 72:8; 2Ch 9:26; compare Ex 23:31 and De 11:24.) Thus some geographers have suggested either of two sites near the junction of the Khabur and Euphrates rivers. This would mean, however, that Shaul was from a city far outside of Edomite territory. Certain modern geographers, however, believe that in these two instances "the River" refers to a river in Edom or near one of its borders, such as the Zered (Wadi el-Hasa') running into the southern end of the Dead Sea. Geographer J. Simons proposes a site about 37 km (23 mi) SE of the tip of the Dead Sea.

REHOBOTH-IR (Re·ho'both-Ir) [Broad Places (or, Public Squares) of the City]. Possibly a suburb of ancient Nineveh. It was built by Nimrod. The exact location is not now known.—Ge 10:10, 11.

REHSH [ר] (or, as commonly Anglicized, resh). The 20th letter of the Hebrew alphabet. Because of the similarity in form between rehsh [ר] and da'-leth [ד], the two were sometimes confused by copyists.

In the Hebrew, this letter appears as the initial letter in each of the eight verses of Psalm 119:153-160.

REHUM (Re'hum).

1. One of those listed at the head of the register of exiles who returned from Babylon to Jerusalem with Zerubbabel and Jeshua. (Ezr 2:1, 2) His name is spelled Nehum at Nehemiah 7:7.

2. A priest listed among those who returned with Zerubbabel. (Ne 12:1, 3) A simple transposition of Hebrew characters would make him the one called Harim in Nehemiah 12:15 and elsewhere.—See HARIM No. 1.

3. "The chief government official" (of the Persian Empire) who presumably resided in Samaria and who took the lead in writing a letter to King Artaxerxes that falsely accused the Jews concerning their intentions in rebuilding Jerusalem. The imperial reply ordered Rehum and his compatriots to go to Jerusalem and forcibly put a stop to the Jews' rebuilding work. (Ezr 4:8-24) Haggai and Zechariah, however, not long thereafter stirred up the Jews to resume their rebuilding, which was finally sanctioned by the Persian review of Cyrus' original decree.—Ezr 5:1–6:13.

4. A Levite son of Bani who helped repair Jerusalem's wall.—Ne 3:17.

5. The head of a postexilic family whose representative, if not he himself, attested to the covenant of faithfulness during Nehemiah's governorship.—Ne 10:1, 14, 25.

REI (Re'i) [Companion; Friend].

One of David's mighty men who refused to join Adonijah's conspiracy.—1Ki 1:8.

REKEM (Re'kem) [possibly, Weaver].

1. A king of Midian, one of five such who were slain when Midian was punished for having seduced Israel with immorality. The five, presumably vassals of the Amorites, were also called "dukes of Sihon."—Nu 31:8; Jos 13:21.

2. A descendant of Manasseh.—1Ch 7:14, 16.

3. A descendant of Judah through Hezron's son Caleb.—1Ch 2:4, 5, 9, 42-44.

4. A city in Benjamin's territory allotment, the location of which is unknown.—Jos 18:21, 27, 28.

RELIEF.

Material aid for those who, because of old age, famine, or other adversity, do not have sufficient of life's necessities.

A distinguishing feature of God's faithful servants has been their willingness to assist needy persons. (Job 29:16; 31:19-22; Jas 1:27) In the first century the Jerusalem congregation arranged for distribution of food to needy Christian widows, and later, seven qualified men were appointed to see to it that no deserving widows were overlooked in the daily distribution. (Ac 6:1-6) Years afterward, in his letter to Timothy, the apostle Paul pointed out that the congregation's relief to widows should be limited to those not less than 60 years of age. Such widows were to be persons having a record of good works in the advancement of Christianity. (1Ti 5:9, 10) However, it was the primary obligation of children and grandchildren, not of the congregation, to care for aged parents and grandparents. As Paul wrote: "If any widow has children or grandchildren, let these learn first to practice godly devotion in their own household and to keep paying a due compensation to their parents and grandparents, for this is acceptable in God's sight."—1Ti 5:4, 16.

There were times when Christian congregations shared in relief measures in behalf of their brothers in other places. Thus, when the prophet Agabus foretold that a great famine would occur, the disciples in the congregation of Syrian Antioch "determined, each of them according as anyone could afford it, to send a relief ministration to the brothers dwelling in Judea." (Ac 11:28, 29) Other organized relief measures for needy brothers in Judea were likewise strictly voluntary.—Ro 15:25-27; 1Co 16:1-3; 2Co 9:5, 7.

REMALIAH (Rem·a·li'ah).

Father of Israelite King Pekah.—2Ki 15:25; 2Ch 28:6; Isa 7:4, 5.

REMETH (Re'meth).

A boundary city of Issachar. (Jos 19:17, 18, 21) It appears to be the same as JARMUTH No. 2 and RAMOTH No. 1.

REMNANT.

Ones left over of a family, nation, tribe, or kind; the survivors of a slaughter or destruction or of some epoch-making event; those remaining faithful to God out of a nation or body of people who have fallen away.

Noah and his family were a remnant of the world of mankind that preceded the Flood. The verb sha·'ar', "remain," is used to describe them as the only ones who kept on surviving. (Ge 7:23) Later, in Egypt, Joseph told his brothers: "Consequently God sent me ahead of you in order to place a remnant [that is, survivors to preserve posterity and family line; compare 2Sa 14:7] for you men in the earth and to keep you alive by a great escape."—Ge 45:4, 7, ftn.

A Remnant of Israel Returns From Exile. The most frequent references in the Bible to a remnant are concerning those who were God's people. Through his prophets God warned Israel of punishment for their disobedience, but he also gave comfort by foretelling that a remnant would be preserved, would return to Jerusalem and rebuild it, and would prosper and bear fruitage. —Isa 1:9; 11:11, 16; 37:31, 32; Jer 23:3; 31:7-9.

After King Nebuchadnezzar of Babylon had carried captives off with King Jehoiachin of Judah in 617 B.C.E., Jehovah gave the prophet Jeremiah a vision. Good figs in the vision represented the exiles of Judah who were taken to Babylon and whom Jehovah would in time restore to their land. Bad figs represented King Zedekiah, his princes, and others like them that were not then taken into exile (actually the larger number of Jerusalem's and Judah's inhabitants) as well as those living in Egypt. In 607 B.C.E. nearly all those in Judah were killed or exiled at the final destruction of Jerusalem by Nebuchadnezzar. And later the ones in Egypt, including those who fled there after 607 B.C.E., suffered when Nebuchadnezzar made a military excursion into that land.—Jer 24:1-10; 44:14; 46:13-17; La 1:1-6.

Jehovah promised the faithful remnant, those who repented of their sins for which he let them go into exile, that he would collect them together as a flock in a pen. (Mic 2:12) This he did in 537 B.C.E., with the return of a remnant of the Jews under Zerubbabel. (Ezr 2:1, 2) They were formerly "limping," but Jehovah gathered them, and (even though they were under Persian domination) because of having Governor Zerubbabel over them and because true worship was reestablished at the temple, God was again their real King. (Mic 4:6, 7) They would become like "dew from Jehovah," which brings refreshment and prosperity, and they would be courageous and strong like "a lion among the beasts of a forest." (Mic 5:7-9) This latter prophecy apparently had a fulfillment during the Maccabean period, resulting in the preservation of the Jews in their land and the preservation of the temple, until the Messiah's coming.

The name of the prophet Isaiah's son Shear-jashub incorporated the noun she'ar' (verb, sha-'ar') and meant "A Mere Remnant (Those Remaining Over) Will Return." The name was a sign that Jerusalem would fall and its inhabitants would go into exile but that God would have mercy and bring back a remnant to the land.—Isa 7:3.

No Remnant Left to Babylon. Babylon was used by God to punish his people, but she went beyond what was necessary and took delight in oppressing and mistreating them and intended to hold them in exile forever. This was actually because Babylon was the chief exponent of false worship and hated Jehovah and his worship. For these reasons God declared: "I will cut off from Babylon name and remnant and progeny and posterity." (Isa 14:22) Eventually, Babylon became a complete and permanent desolation, with no remnant to return to rebuild her.

A Remnant of Israel Accepts Christ. When Jesus Christ came to the nation of Israel the majority rejected him. Only a remnant expressed faith and became followers of him. The apostle Paul applies certain prophecies of Isaiah (10:22, 23; 1:9) to this Jewish remnant when he writes: "Moreover, Isaiah cries out concerning Israel: 'Although the number of the sons of Israel may be as the sand of the sea, it is the remnant that will be saved. For Jehovah will make an accounting on the earth, concluding it and cutting it short.' Also, just as Isaiah had said aforetime: 'Unless Jehovah of hosts had left a seed to us, we should have become just like Sodom, and we should have been made just like Gomorrah.'" (Ro 9:27-29) Again Paul uses the example of the 7,000 left in Elijah's time who had not bowed to Baal, and he says: "In this way, therefore, at the present season also a remnant has turned up according to a choosing due to undeserved kindness."—Ro 11:5.

The Spiritual Remnant. In Revelation (12) John recorded his vision of a woman in heaven, and a dragon, and concluded that part of the vision, saying: "And the dragon grew wrathful at the woman, and went off to wage war with the remaining ones [loi·pon'] of her seed, who observe the commandments of God and have the work of bearing witness to Jesus." These "remaining ones" who have "the work of bearing witness to Jesus" are the last ones on earth of the brothers of Jesus Christ, living on earth after the hurling of the Devil down to the earth and the announcement: "Now have come to pass the salvation and the power and the kingdom of our God and the authority of his Christ." The Devil, the dragon, wars against this remnant of Christ's spiritual brothers by means of the 'wild beasts' and "the image of the wild beast," described in Revelation chapter 13. But the remnant are victorious, as Revelation chapter 14 discloses.—See SEED.

REPENTANCE. The verb "repent" means "change one's mind with regard to past (or intended) action, or conduct, on account of regret or dissatisfaction," or "feel regret, contrition, or compunction, for what one has done or omitted to do." In many texts this is the thought of the Hebrew na·cham'. Na·cham' can mean "feel regret, keep a period of mourning, repent" (Ex 13:17; Ge 38:12; Job 42:6), as well as "comfort oneself" (2Sa 13:39; Eze 5:13), "relieve oneself (as of one's enemies)." (Isa 1:24) Whether regret or comfort, it can be seen that a change of mind or feeling is involved.

In Greek, two verbs are used in connection with repentance: me·ta·no·e'o and me·ta·me'lo·mai. The first is composed of me·ta', meaning "after," and *no·e'o* (related to *nous,* the mind, disposition, or moral consciousness), meaning "perceive, discern, mentally grasp, or be aware." Hence, *me·ta·no·e'o* literally means *after*knowing (in contrast to *fore*-knowing) and signifies a change in one's mind, attitude, or purpose. *Me·ta·me'lo·mai,* on the other hand, comes from *me'lo,* meaning "care for or have interest in." The prefix *me·ta'* (after) gives the verb the sense of 'regretting' (Mt 21:30; 2Co 7:8), or 'repenting.'

Thus, *me·ta·no·e'o* stresses the changed *viewpoint* or *disposition,* a rejecting of the past or intended course or action as undesirable (Re 2:5; 3:3), while *me·ta·me'lo·mai* lays emphasis on the *feeling* of regret experienced by the person. (Mt 21:30) As the *Theological Dictionary of the New Testament* (edited by G. Kittel, Vol. IV, p. 629) comments: "When, therefore, the N[ew] T[estament] separates the meanings of [these terms], it displays a clear awareness of the unchangeable substance of both concepts. In contrast, Hellenistic usage often effaced the boundary between the two words."—Translated by G. Bromiley, 1969.

Of course, a changed viewpoint often brings with it a changed feeling, or the feeling of regret may precede and lead to a definite change in viewpoint or will. (1Sa 24:5-7) So the two terms, though having distinct meanings, are closely related.

Human Repentance for Sins. The cause making repentance necessary is sin, failure to meet God's righteous requirements. (1Jo 5:17) Since all mankind was sold into sin by Adam, all of his descendants have had need of repentance. (Ps 51:5; Ro 3:23; 5:12) As shown in the article REC-ONCILIATION, repentance (followed by conversion) is a prerequisite for man's being reconciled to God.

Repentance may be with regard to one's whole life course, a course that has been contrary to God's purpose and will and, instead, has been in harmony with the world under the control of God's Adversary. (1Pe 4:3; 1Jo 2:15-17; 5:19) Or it may be with regard to a particular aspect of one's life, a wrong practice marring and staining an otherwise acceptable course; it may be for just a single act of wrongdoing or even a wrong tendency, inclination, or attitude. (Ps 141:3, 4; Pr 6:16-19; Jas 2:9; 4:13-17; 1Jo 2:1) The range of faults may therefore be very broad or quite specific.

Similarly, the extent to which the person deviates from righteousness may be major or minor, and logically the degree of regret ought to be commensurate with the degree of deviation. The

Israelites went "deep in their revolt" against Jehovah and were "rotting away" in their transgressions. (Isa 31:6; 64:5, 6; Eze 33:10) On the other hand, the apostle Paul speaks of the "man [who] takes some false step before he is aware of it," and counsels that those with spiritual qualifications "try to readjust such a man in a spirit of mildness." (Ga 6:1) Since Jehovah mercifully considers the fleshly weakness of his servants, they need not be in a constant state of remorse due to their errors resulting from inherent imperfection. (Ps 103:8-14; 130:3) If they are conscientiously walking in God's ways, they may be joyful.—Php 4:4-6; 1Jo 3:19-22.

Repentance may be on the part of those who already have enjoyed a favorable relationship with God but who have strayed away and suffered the loss of God's favor and blessing. (1Pe 2:25) Israel was in a covenant with God—they were "a holy people" chosen from among all the nations (De 7:6; Ex 19:5, 6); Christians also came into a righteous standing before God through the new covenant mediated by Christ. (1Co 11:25; 1Pe 2:9, 10) In the case of such ones who strayed, repentance led to the restoration of their right relationship with God and the consequent benefits and blessings of that relationship. (Jer 15:19-21; Jas 4:8-10) For those who have not previously enjoyed such a relationship with God, such as the pagan peoples of the non-Israelite nations during the time God's covenant was in force with Israel (Eph 2:11, 12) and also those persons of whatever race or nationality who are outside the Christian congregation, repentance is a primary and essential step toward being brought into a right standing before God, with life everlasting in view.—Ac 11:18; 17:30; 20:21.

Repentance may be on a collective basis as well as an individual basis. Thus, Jonah's preaching caused the entire city of Nineveh, from the king down to "the least one of them," to repent, for in God's eyes they were all sharers in the wrong. (Jon 3:5-9; compare Jer 18:7, 8.) The entire congregation of returned Israelites, under Ezra's prompting, acknowledged community guilt before God, expressing repentance through their princely representatives. (Ezr 10:7-14; compare 2Ch 29:1, 10; 30:1-15; 31:1, 2.) The congregation at Corinth expressed repentance over having tolerated in their midst a practicer of gross wrongdoing. (Compare 2Co 7:8-11; 1Co 5:1-5.) Even the prophets Jeremiah and Daniel did not completely exempt themselves of guilt when confessing the wrongdoing of Judah that led to her overthrow. —La 3:40-42; Da 9:4, 5.

What true repentance requires. Repentance involves both mind and heart. The wrongness of the course or act must be recognized, and this requires an acknowledgment that God's standards and will are righteous. Ignorance or forgetfulness of his will and standards is a barrier to repentance. (2Ki 22:10, 11, 18, 19; Jon 1:1, 2; 4:11; Ro 10:2, 3) For this reason Jehovah mercifully has sent prophets and preachers to call persons to repentance. (Jer 7:13; 25:4-6; Mr 1:14, 15; 6:12; Lu 24:27) By means of the publishing of the good news through the Christian congregation, and particularly from the time of the conversion of Cornelius forward, God has been "telling mankind that they should all everywhere repent." (Ac 17: 22, 23, 29-31; 13:38, 39) God's Word—whether written or spoken—is the means for 'persuading' them, convincing them of the rightness of God's way and the wrongness of their own ways. (Compare Lu 16:30, 31; 1Co 14:24, 25; Heb 4:12, 13.) God's law is "perfect, bringing back the soul."—Ps 19:7.

King David speaks of 'teaching transgressors God's ways so that they may turn back to him' (Ps 51:13), these sinners doubtless being fellow Israelites. Timothy was instructed not to fight when dealing with Christians in the congregations he served, but to 'instruct with mildness those not favorably disposed' as God might give them "repentance leading to an accurate knowledge of truth, and they may come back to their proper senses out from the snare of the Devil." (2Ti 2:23-26) Hence, the call to repentance may be given inside the congregation of God's people, as well as outside of it.

The person must see that he has sinned *against God.* (Ps 51:3, 4; Jer 3:25) This may be quite evident where open or direct blasphemy, vocal misuse of God's name, or worship of other gods, as by use of idol images, is involved. (Ex 20:2-7) But even in what one might consider a "private matter" or something between himself and another human, wrongs committed must be recognized as sins against God, a treating of Jehovah with disrespect. (Compare 2Sa 12:7-14; Ps 51:4; Lu 15:21.) Even wrongs committed in ignorance or by mistake are to be recognized as making one guilty before the Sovereign Ruler, Jehovah God.—Compare Le 5:17-19; Ps 51:5, 6; 119:67; 1Ti 1:13-16.

The work of the prophets was largely one of convincing Israel of its sin (Isa 58:1, 2; Mic 3:8-11), whether this was idolatry (Eze 14:6), injustice, oppression of one's fellowman (Jer 34:14-16; Isa 1:16, 17), immorality (Jer 5:7-9), or failing to trust in Jehovah God and, instead, trusting in men and the military might of nations (1Sa 12:19-21; Jer 2:35-37; Ho 12:6; 14:1-3). The message of John the Baptizer and that of Jesus Christ were calls to repentance on the part of the Jews. (Mt 3:1, 2, 7, 8; 4:17) John and Jesus stripped away from the people and their religious leaders the cloak of self-righteousness and of observance of manmade traditions and hypocrisy, exposing the sinful state of the nation.—Lu 3:7, 8; Mt 15:1-9; 23:1-39; Joh 8:31-47; 9:40, 41.

Getting the sense with the heart. For repentance, then, there must initially be a hearing and seeing with understanding, due to a receptive heart. (Compare Isa 6:9, 10; Mt 13:13-15; Ac 28: 26, 27.) Not only does the mind perceive and grasp what the ear hears and the eye sees, but more important, those repenting "get the sense of it ["the thought," Joh 12:40] with their hearts." (Mt 13:15; Ac 28:27) There is, therefore, not merely an intellectual recognition of the wrongness of their ways but a heart appreciation of this fact. With those already having knowledge of God, it may be a case of their 'calling back to their heart' such knowledge of him and his commandments (De 4:39; compare Pr 24:32; Isa 44:18-20) so that they can "come to their senses." (1Ki 8:47) With the right heart motivation they can 'make their mind over, proving to themselves the good, acceptable, and perfect will of God.'—Ro 12:2.

If there is faith and love for God in the person's heart, there will be sincere regret, sadness over the wrong course. Appreciation for God's goodness and greatness will make transgressors feel keen remorse at having brought reproach on his name. (Compare Job 42:1-6.) Love for neighbor will also make them rue the harm they have done to others, the bad example set, perhaps the way in which they have sullied the reputation of God's people among outsiders. They seek forgiveness because they desire to honor God's name and to work for the good of their neighbor. (1Ki 8:33, 34; Ps 25:7-11; 51:11-15; Da 9:18, 19) Repentantly they feel "broken at heart," "crushed and lowly in spirit" (Ps 34:18; 51:17; Isa 57:15), they are "contrite in spirit and trembling at [God's] word," which calls for repentance (Isa 66:2), and in effect, they "come quivering to Jehovah and to his goodness." (Ho 3:5) When David acted foolishly in the matter of a census, his "heart began to beat him." —2Sa 24:10.

There must therefore be a definite rejection of the bad course, a heartfelt hating of it, repugnance for it (Ps 97:10; 101:3; 119:104; Ro 12:9; compare Heb 1:9; Jude 23), for "the fear of Jehovah means the hating of bad," including self-exaltation, pride, the bad way, and the perverse mouth. (Pr 8:13; 4:24) Along with this, there must be a loving of righteousness and the firm determination to adhere to a righteous course from then on. Without both this hatred of bad and love of righteousness, there will be no genuine force to the repentance, no following through with true conversion. Thus, King Rehoboam humbled himself under the expression of Jehovah's anger, but afterward Rehoboam "did what was bad, for he had not firmly established his heart to search for Jehovah."—2Ch 12:12-14; compare Ho 6:4-6.

Sadness in a godly way, not that of the world. The apostle Paul, in his second letter to the Corinthians, refers to the "sadness in a godly way" that they expressed as a result of the reproof given them in his first letter. (2Co 7:8-13) He had 'regretted' (*me·ta·me'lo·mai*) having to write them so sternly and causing them pain, but he ceased to feel any regret upon seeing that the sadness his rebuke produced was of a godly sort, leading to earnest repentance (*me·ta'noi·a*) for their wrong attitude and course. He knew that the pain he had caused them was working to their good and would cause them "no damage." The sadness leading to repentance was not something they should regret either, for it kept them on the way of salvation; it saved them from backsliding or apostasy and gave them hope of life everlasting. He contrasts this sadness with "the sadness of the world [that] produces death." Such does not stem from faith and love of God and righteousness. The world's sadness, born of failure, disappointment, loss, punishment for wrongdoing, and shame (compare Pr 5:3-14, 22, 23; 25:8-10), is often accompanied by or produces bitterness, resentment, envy; and it leads to no lasting benefit, no improvement, no genuine hope. (Compare Pr 1:24-32; 1Th 4:13, 14.) Worldly sadness mourns the unpleasant consequences of sin, but it does not mourn the sin itself and the reproach it brings on God's name. —Isa 65:13-15; Jer 6:13-15, 22-26; Re 18:9-11, 15, 17-19; contrast Eze 9:4.

Cain's case illustrates this, he being the first one called on by God to repent. Cain was divinely warned to "turn to doing good" so that sin should not win out over him. Rather than repent of his murderous hatred, he let it motivate him to kill his brother. Questioned by God, he gave a devious reply, and only when sentence was pronounced on him did he express any regret—regret over the severity of the punishment, not over the wrong committed. (Ge 4:5-14) He thus showed that he "originated with the wicked one."—1Jo 3:12.

Worldly sadness was also displayed by Esau when he learned that his brother Jacob had received the blessing of firstborn (a right Esau had

callously sold to Jacob). (Ge 25:29-34) Esau cried out "in an extremely loud and bitter manner," with tears seeking "repentance" (*me·ta·noi'a*)—not his own, but "a change of mind" on the part of his father. (Ge 27:34; Heb 12:17, *Int*) He regretted his loss, not the materialistic attitude that caused him to 'despise the birthright.'—Ge 25:34.

Judas, after having betrayed Jesus, "felt remorse [form of *me·ta·me'lo·mai*]," tried to return the bribe he had bargained for, and thereafter committed suicide by hanging. (Mt 27:3-5) The enormity of his crime and, likely, the awful certainty of divine judgment against him evidently overwhelmed him. (Compare Heb 10:26, 27, 31; Jas 2:19.) He felt the remorse of guilt, despair, even desperation, but there is nothing to show he expressed the godly sadness that leads to repentance (*me·ta·noi'a*). He sought out, not God, but the Jewish leaders to confess his sin to them, returning the money evidently with the mistaken idea that he could thereby to some extent undo his crime. (Compare Jas 5:3, 4; Eze 7:19.) To the crime of treason and contributing to the death of an innocent man, he added that of self-murder. His course is in contrast with that of Peter, whose bitter weeping after having denied his Lord was due to heartfelt repentance, which led to his being restored.—Mt 26:75; compare Lu 22:31, 32.

Regret, remorse, and tears, then, are not a certain measure of genuine repentance; the heart *motive* is determinative. Hosea voices Jehovah's denunciation of Israel, for in their distress "they did not call to [him] for aid with their heart, although they kept howling on their beds. On account of their grain and sweet wine they kept loafing about . . . And they proceeded to return, not to anything higher." Their groaning for relief in time of calamity was selfishly motivated, and if granted relief, they did not use the opportunity to improve their relationship with God by closer adherence to his high standards (compare Isa 55:8-11); they were like "a loose bow" that never hits the mark. (Ho 7:14-16; compare Ps 78:57; Jas 4:3.) Fasting, weeping, and wailing were proper —but only if the repentant ones 'ripped apart their hearts' and not simply their garments.—Joe 2:12, 13; see FAST; MOURNING.

Confession of wrongdoing. The repentant person, then, humbles himself and seeks God's face (2Ch 7:13, 14; 33:10-13; Jas 4:6-10), supplicating his forgiveness. (Mt 6:12) He is not like the self-righteous Pharisee of Jesus' illustration but is like the tax collector whom Jesus portrayed as beating his breast and saying, "O God, be gracious to me a sinner." (Lu 18:9-14) The apostle John states: "If we make the statement: 'We have no sin,' we are misleading ourselves and the truth is not in us. If we confess our sins, he is faithful and righteous so as to forgive us our sins and to cleanse us from all unrighteousness." (1Jo 1:8, 9) "He that is covering over his transgressions will not succeed, but he that is confessing and leaving them will be shown mercy."—Pr 28:13; compare Ps 32:3-5; Jos 7:19-26; 1Ti 5:24.

Daniel's prayer at Daniel 9:15-19 is a model of sincere confession, expressing prime concern for Jehovah's name and basing its appeal "not according to our righteous acts . . . but according to your many mercies." Compare, also, the humble expression of the prodigal son. (Lu 15:17-21) Sincerely repentant ones 'raise their heart along with their palms to God,' confessing their transgression and seeking forgiveness.—La 3:40-42.

Confessing sins to one another. The disciple James counsels: "Openly confess your sins to one another and pray for one another, that you may get healed." (Jas 5:16) Such confession is not because any human serves as "helper ["advocate," RS]" for man with God, since Christ alone fills that role by virtue of his propitiatory sacrifice. (1Jo 2:1, 2) Humans, of themselves, cannot actually right the wrong toward God, on their own behalf or on behalf of others, being unable to provide the needed atonement. (Ps 49:7, 8) However, Christians can help one another, and their prayers on behalf of their brothers, while not having an effect on God's application of justice (since Christ's ransom alone serves to bring remission of sins), do count with God in petitioning his giving needed help and strength to the one who has sinned and is seeking aid.—See PRAYER (The Answering of Prayers).

Conversion—A Turning Back. Repentance marks a halt in the person's wrong course, the rejection of that wrong way, and the determination to take a right course. If genuine, it will therefore be followed by "conversion." (Ac 15:3) Both in Hebrew and in Greek the verbs relating to conversion (Heb., *shuv;* Gr., *stre'pho; e·pi·stre'pho*) mean simply "turn back, turn around, or return." (Ge 18:10; Pr 15:1; Jer 18:4; Joh 21:20; Ac 15:36) Used in a *spiritual* sense, this can refer to either a turning away from God (hence turning back to a sinful course [Nu 14:43; De 30:17]) or a turning to God from a wrong way.—1Ki 8:33.

Conversion implies more than a mere attitude or verbal expression; it involves the "works that befit repentance." (Ac 26:20; Mt 3:8) It is an active 'seeking,' 'searching,' 'inquiring' for Jehovah with all one's heart and soul. (De 4:29; 1Ki 8:48; Jer 29:12-14) This, of necessity, means seeking God's

favor by 'listening to his voice' as expressed in his Word (De 4:30; 30:2, 8), 'showing insight into his trueness' through better understanding and appreciation of his ways and will (Da 9:13), observing and 'doing' his commandments (Ne 1:9; De 30:10; 2Ki 23:24, 25), "keeping loving-kindness and justice" and 'hoping in God constantly' (Ho 12:6), abandoning the use of religious images or the idolizing of creatures so as to "direct [one's] heart unswervingly to Jehovah and serve him alone" (1Sa 7:3; Ac 14:11-15; 1Th 1:9, 10), and walking in his ways and not in the way of the nations (Le 20:23) or in one's own way (Isa 55:6-8). Prayers, sacrifices, fastings, and observance of sacred festivals are meaningless and are of no value with God unless they are accompanied by good works, justice, the elimination of oppression and violence, the exercise of mercy.—Isa 1:10-19; 58:3-7; Jer 18:11.

This calls for "a new heart and a new spirit" (Eze 18:31); one's changed thinking, motivation, and aim in life produce a new frame of mind, disposition, and moral force. For the one whose life course changes, the result is a "new personality which was created according to God's will in true righteousness and loyalty" (Eph 4:17-24), free from immorality, covetousness, as well as violent speech and conduct. (Col 3:5-10; contrast Ho 5:4-6.) For such ones God causes the spirit of wisdom to "bubble forth," making his words known to them.—Pr 1:23; compare 2Ti 2:25.

Thus genuine repentance has real impact, generates force, moves the person to "turn around." (Ac 3:19) Hence Jesus could say to those in Laodicea: "Be *zealous* and repent." (Re 3:19; compare Re 2:5; 3:2, 3.) There is evidence of 'great earnestness, clearing of oneself, godly fear, longing, and righting of the wrong.' (2Co 7:10, 11) Absence of concern for rectifying wrongs committed shows lack of true repentance.—Compare Eze 33:14, 15; Lu 19:8.

The expression "newly converted man," "recent convert" (*RS*), in Greek (*ne·o'phy·tos*) literally means "newly planted" or "newly grown." (1Ti 3:6) Such a man was not to be assigned ministerial duties in a congregation lest he become "puffed up with pride and fall into the judgment passed upon the Devil."

What are the "dead works" from which Christians must repent?

Hebrews 6:1, 2 shows that "primary doctrine" includes "repentance from dead works, and faith toward God," followed by the teaching on baptisms, the laying on of hands, the resurrection, and everlasting judgment. The "dead works" (an expression appearing elsewhere only at Heb 9:14) evidently mean not merely sinful works of wrongdoing, works of the fallen flesh that lead one to death (Ro 8:6; Ga 6:8), but all works that in themselves are spiritually dead, vain, fruitless.

This would include works of self-justification, efforts by men to establish their own righteousness apart from Christ Jesus and his ransom sacrifice. Thus, the formal observance of the Law by the Jewish religious leaders and others constituted "dead works" because it lacked the vital ingredient of *faith*. (Ro 9:30-33; 10:2-4) This caused them to stumble at Christ Jesus, God's "Chief Agent . . . to give repentance to Israel and forgiveness of sins," instead of repenting. (Ac 5:31-33; 10:43; 20:21) So, too, would the observance of the Law, as though it were still in force, become "dead works" after Christ Jesus had fulfilled it. (Ga 2:16) Similarly, all works done that might otherwise be of value become "dead works" if the motivation is not that of love, love of God and love of neighbor. (1Co 13:1-3) Love, in turn, must be "in deed and truth," harmonizing with God's will and ways communicated to us through his Word. (1Jo 3:18; 5:2, 3; Mt 7:21-23; 15:6-9; Heb 4:12) The one turning in faith to God through Christ Jesus repents from all works rightly classed as "dead works," and thereafter avoids them, his conscience thereby becoming cleansed.—Heb 9:14.

Baptism (immersion in water), except in the case of Jesus, was a divinely provided symbol associated with repentance, both on the part of those among the Jewish nation (which had failed to keep God's covenant while it was in force) and on the part of people of the nations who 'turned around' to render sacred service to God.—Mt 3:11; Ac 2:38; 10:45-48; 13:23, 24; 19:4; see BAPTISM.

Unrepentant. Lack of genuine repentance led to exile for Israel and Judah, two destructions of Jerusalem, and finally, complete rejection of the nation by God. When reproved, they did not really return to God but kept "going back into the popular course, like a horse that is dashing into the battle." (Jer 8:4-6; 2Ki 17:12-23; 2Ch 36:11-21; Lu 19:41-44; Mt 21:33-43; 23:37, 38) Because in their heart they did not want to repent and 'turn back,' what they heard and saw brought no understanding and knowledge; a "veil" lay on their hearts. (Isa 6:9, 10; 2Co 3:12-18; 4:3, 4) Unfaithful religious leaders and prophets, as well as false prophetesses, contributed to this, strengthening the people in their wrongdoing. (Jer 23:14; Eze 13:17, 22, 23; Mt 23:13, 15) Christian prophecies foretold that future divine action reproving men and calling them to repentance would be similarly rejected by many. It foretold that the things they would suffer would only harden and embitter them to the point of blaspheming God, even though it would be their own rejection of his righteous ways that would form the root and generative cause of all their troubles and plagues. (Re 9:20, 21; 16:9, 11) Such ones 'store up wrath for themselves on the day of revealing God's judgment.'—Ro 2:5.

Beyond repentance. Those 'practicing sin willfully' after having received the accurate knowledge of the truth have gone beyond the point of repentance, for they have rejected the very purpose for which God's Son died and so have joined the ranks of those who sentenced him to death, in effect, 'impaling the Son of God afresh for themselves and exposing him to public shame.' (Heb 6:4-8; 10:26-29) This, then, is unforgivable sin. (Mr 3:28, 29) It would have been better for such "not to have accurately known the path of righteousness than after knowing it accurately to turn away from the holy commandment delivered to them."—2Pe 2:20-22.

Since Adam and Eve were perfect creatures, and since God's command to them was explicit and understood by both, it is evident that their sinning was willful and was not excusable on the basis of any human weakness or imperfection. Hence, God's words to them afterward offer no invitation to repentance. (Ge 3:16-24) So, too, with the spirit creature who had induced them into rebellion. His end and the end of other angelic creatures who joined him is everlasting destruction. (Ge 3:14, 15; Mt 25:41) Judas, though imperfect, had lived in intimate association with God's own Son and yet turned traitor; Jesus himself referred to him as "the son of destruction." (Joh 17:12) The apostate "man of lawlessness" is also called "the son of destruction." (2Th 2:3; see ANTICHRIST; APOSTASY; MAN OF LAWLESSNESS.) All those classed as figurative "goats" at the time of Jesus' kingly judgment of mankind likewise "depart into everlasting cutting-off," no invitation to repentance being extended to them.—Mt 25:33, 41-46.

Resurrection Affords Opportunity. By contrast, the people of Sodom and Gomorrah as well as those of Canaanite Tyre and Sidon are spoken of by Jesus as finding "Judgment Day" more endurable than would the people of certain Jewish cities. (Mt 10:14, 15; 11:20-24) Those of pagan Nineveh are similarly spoken of. (Mt 12:41) This of itself implies that people from all such places, including the Jewish cities mentioned, will be resurrected and have opportunity to manifest humble repentance and "turn around" in conversion to God through Christ. Those failing to do so will receive everlasting destruction. (Compare Re 20:11-15; see JUDGMENT DAY.) Those, however, who follow a course like many scribes and Pharisees, who willfully and knowingly fought the manifestation of God's spirit through Christ, will receive no resurrection, and so they cannot "flee from the judgment of Gehenna."—Mt 23:13, 33; Mr 3:22-30.

Thief on the stake. The thief on the stake who showed a measure of faith in Jesus, impaled alongside, was given the promise of being in Paradise. (Lu 23:39-43; see PARADISE.) While some have endeavored to read into this promise the idea that the thief was thereby guaranteed life everlasting, the evidence of the many scriptures already considered does not allow this. Though he admitted the wrongness of his criminal activity in contrast with Jesus' innocence (Lu 23:41), there is nothing to show that the thief had come to 'hate badness and love righteousness'; in his dying state he obviously was in no position to 'turn around' and produce the "works that befit repentance"; he had not been baptized. (Ac 3:19; 26:20) It therefore appears that upon his resurrection from the dead he will be given the opportunity to take this course.—Compare Re 20:12, 13.

How can God, who is perfect, "feel regret"?

In the majority of cases where the Hebrew *na-cham'* is used in the sense of "feeling regret," the reference is to Jehovah God. Genesis 6:6, 7 states that "Jehovah felt regrets that he had made men in the earth, and he felt hurt at his heart," their wickedness being so great that God determined he would wipe them off the surface of the ground by means of the global Flood. This cannot mean that God felt regret in the sense of having made a mistake in his work of creation, for "perfect is his activity." (De 32:4, 5) Regret is the opposite of pleasurable satisfaction and rejoicing. Hence, it must be that God regretted that after he had created mankind, their conduct became so evil that he now found himself obliged (and justly so) to destroy all mankind with the exception of Noah and his family. For God 'takes no delight in the death of the wicked.'—Eze 33:11.

M'Clintock and Strong's *Cyclopædia* comments: "God himself is said to repent [*na·cham'*, feel regret]; but this can only be understood of his altering his conduct towards his creatures, either in

the bestowing of good or infliction of evil—which change in the divine conduct is founded on a change in his creatures; and thus, speaking after the manner of men, God is said to repent." (1894, Vol. VIII, p. 1042) God's righteous *standards* remain constant, stable, unchanging, free from fluctuation. (Mal 3:6; Jas 1:17) No circumstance can cause him to change his mind about these, to turn from them, or to abandon them. However, the attitude and reactions of his intelligent creatures toward those perfect standards and toward God's application of them can be good or bad. If good, this is pleasing to God; if bad, it causes regret. Moreover, the creature's attitude can change from good to bad or bad to good, and since God does not change his standards to accommodate them, his pleasure (and accompanying blessings) can accordingly change to regret (and accompanying discipline or punishment) or vice versa. His judgments and decisions, then, are totally free from caprice, fickleness, unreliability, or error; hence he is free from all erratic or eccentric conduct.—Eze 18:21-30; 33:7-20.

A potter may begin to make one type of vessel and then change to another style if the vessel is "spoiled by the potter's hand." (Jer 18:3, 4) By this example Jehovah illustrates, *not* that he is like a human potter in 'spoiling by his hand,' but rather, that he has divine *authority* over mankind, authority to adjust his dealings with them according to the way they respond or fail to respond to his righteousness and mercy. (Compare Isa 45:9; Ro 9:19-21.) He can thus "feel regret over the calamity that [he] had thought to execute" upon a nation, or "feel regret over the good that [he] said to [himself] to do for its good," all depending upon the reaction of the nation to his prior dealings with it. (Jer 18:5-10) Thus, it is not that the Great Potter, Jehovah, errs, but rather, that the human "clay" undergoes a "metamorphosis" (change of form or composition) as to its heart condition, producing regret, or a change of feeling, on Jehovah's part.

This is true of individuals as well as of nations, and the very fact that Jehovah God speaks of his 'feeling regret' over certain of his servants, such as King Saul, who turned away from righteousness, shows that God does not predestinate the future of such individuals. (See FOREKNOWLEDGE, FOREORDINATION.) God's regret over Saul's deviation does not mean that God's choice of him as king had been erroneous and was to be regretted on that ground. God must rather have felt regret because Saul, as a free moral agent, had not made good use of the splendid privilege and opportunity God had afforded him, and because Saul's change called for a change in God's dealings with him.—1Sa 15:10, 11, 26.

The prophet Samuel, in declaring God's adverse decision regarding Saul, stated that "the Excellency of Israel will not prove false, and He will not feel regrets, for He is not an earthling man so as to feel regrets." (1Sa 15:28, 29) Earthling men frequently prove untrue to their word, fail to make good their promises, or do not live up to the terms of their agreements; being imperfect, they commit errors in judgment, causing them regret. This is never the case with God.—Ps 132:11; Isa 45:23, 24; 55:10, 11.

God's covenant made between God and "all flesh" after the Flood, for example, unconditionally guaranteed that God would never again bring a flood of waters over all the earth. (Ge 9:8-17) There is, then, no possibility of God's changing with regard to that covenant or 'regretting it.' Similarly, in his covenant with Abraham, God "stepped in with an oath" as "a legal guarantee" so as to "demonstrate more abundantly to the heirs of the promise the unchangeableness of his counsel," his promise and his oath being "two unchangeable things in which it is impossible for God to lie." (Heb 6:13-18) God's sworn covenant with his Son for a priesthood like that of Melchizedek was likewise something over which God would "feel no regret."—Heb 7:20, 21; Ps 110:4; compare Ro 11:29.

However, in stating a promise or making a covenant, God may set out requirements, conditions to be met by those with whom the promise or covenant is made. He promised Israel that they would become his "special property" and "a kingdom of priests and a holy nation," *if* they would strictly obey his voice and keep his covenant. (Ex 19:5, 6) God held true to his side of the covenant, but Israel failed; they violated that covenant time and again. (Mal 3:6, 7; compare Ne 9:16-19, 26-31.) So, when God finally annulled that covenant he did so with complete justice, the responsibility for the nonfulfillment of his promise resting entirely with the offending Israelites.—Mt 21:43; Heb 8:7-9.

In the same way God can "feel regret" and 'turn back' from carrying out some punishment when his warning of such action produces a change in attitude and conduct on the part of the offenders. (De 13:17; Ps 90:13) They have returned to him and he 'returns' to them. (Zec 8:3; Mal 3:7) Instead of being 'pained,' he now rejoices, for he finds no delight in bringing death to sinners. (Lu 15:10; Eze 18:32) While never shifting away from his righteous standards, God extends help so persons can return to him; they are encouraged to do so. He kindly invites them to return, 'spreading out his hands' and saying by means of his representatives, "Turn back, please, . . . that I may not cause calamity to you," "Do not do, please, this detestable sort of thing that I have hated." (Isa 65:1, 2; Jer 25:5, 6; 44:4, 5) He gives ample time for change (Ne 9:30; compare Re 2:20-23) and shows great patience and forbearance, since "he does not desire any to be destroyed but desires all to attain to repentance." (2Pe 3:8, 9; Ro 2:4, 5) On occasion he kindly saw to it that his message was accompanied by powerful works, or miracles, that established the divine commission of his messengers and helped strengthen faith in those hearing. (Ac 9:32-35) When his message receives no response, he employs discipline; he withdraws his favor and protection, thereby allowing the unrepentant ones to undergo privations, famine, suffering of oppression from their enemies. This may bring them to their senses, may restore their proper fear of God, or may cause them to realize that their course was stupid and that their set of values was wrong. —2Ch 33:10-13; Ne 9:28, 29; Am 4:6-11.

However, his patience has its limits, and when these are reached he gets "tired of feeling regret"; then his decision to render punishment is unchangeable. (Jer 15:6, 7; 23:19, 20; Le 26:14-33) He is no longer merely "thinking" or "forming" against such ones a calamity (Jer 18:11; 26:3-6) but has reached an irreversible decision.—2Ki 23:24-27; Isa 43:13; Jer 4:28; Zep 3:8; Re 11:17, 18.

God's willingness to forgive repentant ones, as well as his mercifully opening the way to such forgiveness even in the face of repeated offenses, sets the example for all of his servants.—Mt 18:21, 22; Mr 3:28; Lu 17:3, 4; 1Jo 1:9; see FORGIVENESS.

REPHAEL (Reph'a·el) [God Has Healed]. A son of Obed-edom's firstborn Shemaiah. He was assigned with his brothers as a gatekeeper caring for the storehouses on the S of the sanctuary.—1Ch 26:4, 7, 8, 15.

REPHAH (Re'phah). An Ephraimite ancestor of Joshua.—1Ch 7:22-27.

REPHAIAH (Re·pha'iah) [Jah Has Healed].

1. Second-named son of Tola and head of a paternal house in the tribe of Issachar.—1Ch 7:1, 2.

2. A Benjamite descendant of King Saul and of Jonathan. (1Ch 9:39-43) He is called Raphah at 1 Chronicles 8:37.

3. One of the four sons of Ishi who, likely during Hezekiah's reign, led 500 Simeonites against the Amalekites who had escaped into Mount Seir. The Simeonites then took over this territory. —1Ch 4:41-43.

4. A postexilic descendant of David.—1Ch 3:5, 9, 10, 21.

5. An official in Jerusalem who helped on Nehemiah's project of repairing Jerusalem's wall; son of Hur.—Ne 3:9.

REPHAIM (Reph'a·im). A tall people or tribe. There is uncertainty as to the meaning and origin of the name. Likely, they were called Rephaim because of being descendants of a man named Raphah. At 2 Samuel 21:16 *ha·Ra·phah'* (literally, the Raphah) seems to employ the father's name to stand for the entire giant race.

At some early period the Rephaim evidently dwelt E of the Dead Sea. The Moabites, who dispossessed them, referred to the Rephaim as Emim ("Frightful Things"). The Ammonites called them Zamzummim (possibly from a root meaning "have in mind; scheme"). (De 2:10, 11, 19, 20) When King Chedorlaomer of Elam came W to fight five rebellious kings near the Dead Sea (taking Lot captive), he defeated the Rephaim in Ashteroth-karnaim. (Ge 14:1, 5) This locates the Rephaim at that time in Bashan, E of the Jordan. Shortly thereafter God said that he would give Abraham's descendants the Promised Land, which included territory where the Rephaim lived.—Ge 15:18-20.

More than 400 years later, just before Israel entered Canaan, "the land of the Rephaim" was still identified with Bashan. There the Israelites defeated Og the king of Bashan (De 3:3, 11, 13; Jos 12:4; 13:12), who alone "remained of what was left of the Rephaim." It is uncertain whether this means that he was the last king of the Rephaim or that he was the last of the Rephaim in that section, for Rephaim were shortly found W of the Jordan.

In the Promised Land the Israelites had problems with the Rephaim, for some of them persisted in the forests of the mountainous region of Ephraim. The sons of Joseph were afraid to drive them away. (Jos 17:14-18) When David was fighting the Philistines, he and his servants struck down four men "born to the Rephaim in Gath." One of them was described as "a man of extraordinary size whose fingers and toes were in sixes, twenty-four." The description of their armor indicates that they were all men of great stature. One of these was "Lahmi the brother of Goliath the Gittite." (1Ch 20:4-8) This Goliath, whom David killed, was in height six cubits and a span (2.9 m;

9.5 ft). (1Sa 17:4-7) The account at 2 Samuel 21:16-22 reads "Goliath," instead of "the brother of Goliath," as at 1 Chronicles 20:5, which may indicate that there were two Goliaths.—See GOLIATH.

The Hebrew *repha·im'* is used in another sense in the Bible. Sometimes it clearly applies, not to a specific people, but to those who are dead. Linking the word to a root meaning "drop down, relax," some scholars conclude that it means "sunken, powerless ones." In texts where it has this sense, the *New World Translation* renders it "those impotent in death," and many other translations use renderings such as "dead things," "deceased," and "dead."—Job 26:5; Ps 88:10; Pr 2:18; 9:18; 21:16; Isa 14:9; 26:14, 19.

REPHAIM, LOW PLAIN OF. A broad plain or valley near Jerusalem. Presumably it got its name from the tall people named the Rephaim who must have lived there at one time. It is listed as a boundary between the territories of Judah and Benjamin. (Jos 15:1, 8; 18:11, 16) At its northern end was a mountain or a ridge that faced the Valley of Hinnom. The traditional identification for the Low Plain of Rephaim is the plain of the Baqa' to the SW of the Temple Mount. It descends for about 1.5 km (1 mi) and then narrows into the Wadi el Werd (Nahal Refa'im).

The plain's fertility (Isa 17:5) as well as its proximity to Jerusalem and Bethlehem would have made it desirable to the Philistines. (2Sa 23:13, 14; 1Ch 11:15-19) After David had been anointed as king over Israel, the Philistines made raids in the Low Plain of Rephaim. David followed God's directions, however, and was victorious over them.—2Sa 5:17-25; 1Ch 14:8-17; see BAAL-PERAZIM.

REPHAN (Re'phan). An astral deity mentioned by Stephen in his defense before the Sanhedrin. (Ac 7:43) Stephen likely quoted from the Greek *Septuagint* the words of Amos 5:26, 27, to show that Israel's exile resulted from their worship of foreign deities, such as Rephan (Kaiwan). The translators of the *Septuagint* rendered "Kaiwan" as *Rhai·phan'*, but in Stephen's quotation the designation *Rhom·pha'* appears in the Westcott and Hort Greek text. In a note on Acts 7:43, F. J. A. Hort remarked: "In the LXX of Am v 26 the form used is [*Rhai·phan'*] or [*Rhe·phan'*], which is similar to *Repa* or *Repha*, one of the names of the Egyptian Saturn (Seb)."—*The New Testament in the Original Greek,* by Westcott and Hort, Graz, 1974, Vol. II, appendix, p. 92; see ASTROLOGERS (Molech and Astrology in Israel); KAIWAN.

REPHIDIM

REPHIDIM (Reph'i·dim) [from a root meaning "spread out"; or, "refresh"]. One of the places where the Israelites encamped on their journey from the Red Sea to Mount Sinai. Upon leaving the Wilderness of Sin, they encamped at Dophkah, then Alush, and finally Rephidim. (Ex 17:1; Nu 33:12-14) Lacking water at Rephidim, the people complained and quarreled with Moses. At God's direction Moses took some of the older men to "the rock in Horeb" (evidently the mountainous region of Horeb, not Mount Horeb) and struck a rock with his rod. Water flowed, apparently reaching to the people camped in Rephidim.—Ex 17:2-7.

The Amalekites attacked the Israelites in Rephidim, but with Joshua leading in the fighting, God's people vanquished the attackers. (Ex 17:8-16) The placement of the account in the record indicates that it was while the Israelites were at Rephidim that Moses' father-in-law brought Zipporah and her two sons to Moses and suggested that he select chiefs to aid in judging the people.—Ex 18:1-27.

The exact location of Rephidim is uncertain. The various locations offered by geographers have been determined in accord with their understanding as to the route the Israelites traveled from the Wilderness of Sin to Mount Sinai. Many modern geographers identify Rephidim with a site in Wadi Refayied, not far to the NW of the traditional location of Mount Sinai. Adjacent to the wadi is a hill of the same name, on which Moses might have stood with arms elevated during the battle with the Amalekites.

REPROACH

REPROACH. Defamation, disgrace, or scorn, whether for just cause or not. Commonly translated from the Greek noun o·nei·di·smos' (and o'nei·dos) and the Hebrew noun cher·pah'.—Compare Ge 30:23; Ps 69:9; Lu 1:25; Ro 15:3.

Causes for reproach could, of course, vary according to circumstances. For an Israelite male to be uncircumcised during the period of the Law covenant would be cause for reproach. (Compare Jg 14:3.) Thus when all the males born during the wilderness journey were finally circumcised just after the crossing of the Jordan, Jehovah stated: "Today I have rolled away the reproach of Egypt from off you." (Jos 5:2-9) Since the evidence indicates that the Egyptians practiced circumcision, this may mean that now the Egyptians would have no basis for reproaching Israel because so many of its males were uncircumcised (Jer 9:25, 26; see CIRCUMCISION.) On the other hand, circumcision was "a sign of the covenant" between Jehovah and Abraham's seed. (Ge 17:9-11) Now, by this circumcision of the new generation that had grown up in the wilderness (the older generation having died there), circumcision could point to a reaffirming of their covenant relationship with God. The 40 years of wandering having ended, God was also showing them his favor; he had introduced them into the Promised Land and would now enable them to conquer it. Therefore any past Egyptian taunts, or reproach, because of what may have seemed to the Egyptians to be inability of Jehovah to bring Israel into a land of their own were now proved false. Christians under the new covenant, whether Jew or Gentile, were not subject to reproach for uncircumcision. —Ro 2:25-29; 3:28-30; 4:9-12; 1Co 7:18, 19.

For Hebrew women, continuous singleness or widowhood (Isa 4:1; 54:4), also barrenness (Ge 30:23; Lu 1:25), was viewed as a reproach. God's promise concerning the Abrahamic seed and its becoming like "the grains of sand that are on the seashore" doubtless contributed to this feeling. (Ge 22:15-18; compare 24:59, 60.) By contrast, the apostle Paul commended singleness on the part of both men and women where the motive was service to God with undivided attention, and he said of the widow that "she is happier if she remains as she is, according to my opinion."—1Co 7:25-28, 32-40; compare Mt 19:10-12.

Wrongs such as idolatry, adultery, thievery, and other types of immorality, however, were constant in being cause for reproach, as was all disloyalty to God.—2Sa 13:13; Pr 6:32, 33; Ro 1:18-32; 2:17-24.

Those seeking God's approval cannot be defaming others. Concerning one who would be a guest in God's tent, the psalmist declared: "To his companion he has done nothing bad, and no reproach has he taken up against his intimate acquaintance," that is, he does not spread defamatory information about his intimate acquaintance. (Ps 15:1, 3) One who defrauds the lowly one or holds him in derision actually reproaches God (Pr 14:31; 17:5), as do those who level reproach against God's servants. (Ps 74:18-23) Ultimately such reproaching leads to calamity for those engaging in it.—Zep 2:8-10.

Jehovah Silences Reproach of His People. When the Israelites engaged in false worship or in unrighteous practices, they reproached Jehovah God, because they made the worship of Jehovah appear no better than that of the nations around them. (Isa 65:7) For their unfaithfulness God permitted calamity to befall them, causing them to become an object of reproach among the nations. (Eze 5:14, 15) Not appreciating that the judgment was from God, other nations attributed it to his inability to save Israel, so additional reproach was brought upon Jehovah. Therefore, in restoring the Israelites on the basis of their repentance, Jehovah cleared his name of such reproach.—Eze 36:15, 20, 21, 30-36.

Whenever situations arise that make it appear that God has seemingly forsaken his people, others conclude that he is not protecting or blessing them and so they heap reproach upon them. (Ps 31:9-11; 42:10; 74:10, 11; 79:4, 5; 102:8, 9; Joe 2:17-19) But eventually Jehovah demonstrates his saving acts and thereby silences those who reproach.—Ne 1:3; 2:17; 4:4; 6:16.

Bearing Reproach for Sake of Christ. Also, in carrying out their commission, Jehovah's servants have been reproached by those to whom they were sent. This was the experience of Jeremiah (Jer 6:10; 15:15-18; 20:8), of Christ Jesus (Mt 27:44; Mr 15:32; Ro 15:3), and of his followers (Heb 10:33). An individual who is reproached for the sake of Christ has reason for rejoicing, because his continued faithfulness under such reproach leads to a great reward in the heavens (Mt 5:11; Lu 6:22, 23) and constitutes a proof of his having God's spirit. (1Pe 4:14) Therefore, reproach should not be feared. To those knowing righteousness, Jehovah said: "Do not be afraid of the reproach of mortal men, and do not be struck with terror just because of their abusive words."—Isa 51:7.

Although knowing the great reproach that would come upon him, Jesus voluntarily submitted to the doing of his Father's will to the point of dying a shameful death on a torture stake. (Isa 53:3-7; Joh 10:17, 18; Heb 12:2; 13:12, 13) To render good to others, he did not seek to please himself but was willing to take reproach from persons who by word and deed reproached Jehovah God. The apostle Paul pointed to this when highlighting the right attitude toward spiritually weak ones: "We, though, who are strong ought to bear the weaknesses of those not strong, and not to be pleasing ourselves. Let each of us please his neighbor in what is good for his upbuilding. For even the Christ did not please himself; but just as it is written: 'The reproaches of those who were reproaching you have fallen upon me.'" (Ro 15:1-3) In the previous chapter (Ro 14), Paul had discussed the weaknesses of some Christians who had conscientious scruples regarding certain foods or the observance of a certain day; he had shown the need to avoid being a cause for stumbling such ones and the need to build them up. This would likely mean that those strong in understanding, faith, and conscience would have to restrict them-

selves in the exercise of their rights, and this might be somewhat unpleasant to them. Nevertheless, they must "bear" (the verb here allowing both the sense of "carry" and "put up with or endure" [compare Ga 6:2; Re 2:2]) whatever burdens such weaknesses might cause them, imitating Christ. (Compare Mt 17:17-20; also Moses' expression at Nu 11:10-15.) Additionally, they should not simply forge ahead in their own pursuit of God's favor, blessings, and rewards, while pushing aside these spiritually weak ones as an encumbrance or allowing them to be lopped off by the Adversary because of lack of consideration and help from these strong ones.—Compare 1Co 9:19-23; 10:23-33.

Avoid Bringing Reproach by Wrongdoing. While expecting reproach for righteousness' sake, a Christian should never "suffer as a murderer or a thief or an evildoer or as a busybody in other people's matters." (1Pe 4:15, 16) One of the qualifications for an overseer in the Christian congregation is that he "have a fine testimony from people on the outside, in order that he might not fall into reproach." This would prevent bringing dishonor to the position and would avoid the spread of unfavorable talk about true Christians because of the conduct of one of the prominent members of the congregation.—1Ti 3:7.

REPROOF. That which is designed to convince others of their having erred, in order to move them to acknowledge their mistakes and correct these. Unlike reproof, a rebuke may be a censure without any laying bare of fault by the presentation of evidence. (See REBUKE.) The Hebrew verb *ya·khach'* (reprove) is a legal term also rendered 'call to account' (Isa 37:4), "set matters straight" (Isa 1:18), and "render judgment" (Isa 2:4). The corresponding Greek term is *e·leg'kho.* Both terms often convey the idea of convicting one of sin and summoning that one to repentance. Regarding the use of *e·leg'kho* in the Greek *Septuagint* to translate many occurrences of *ya·khach',* the *Theological Dictionary of the New Testament* states: "It denotes the disciplining and educating of man by God as a result of His judicial activity. This embraces all aspects of education from the conviction of the sinner to chastisement and punishment, from the instruction of the righteous by severe tests to his direction by teaching and admonition." —Edited by G. Kittel, 1964, Vol. II, p. 473.

When Needed. In God's law to Israel, persons transgressed against were urged: "You must not hate your brother in your heart. You should by all means reprove your associate, that you may not bear sin along with him." (Le 19:17) Feelings of resentment against the erring brother were not to be allowed to fester. He was to be reproved with a view to recovering him from sin. Failure to discharge this moral responsibility could contribute toward further sin, and the person who held back from reproving his associate would share responsibility for such sin.—Compare Mt 18:15.

At times, elders representative of the congregation must reprove serious wrongdoers, even doing so in the presence of others who have knowledge of the sinful course. Such reproof is not reserved only for those who show a receptiveness to it. Elders are also called on to "reprove those who contradict" and to 'reprove with severity' those who are "unruly" and "profitless talkers."—1Ti 5:20; Tit 1:9, 10, 13.

Although reproof can benefit those who receive it, the efforts of the reprover are not always appreciated. Thus Proverbs 9:7, 8 warns: "He that is correcting the ridiculer is taking to himself dishonor, and he that is giving a reproof to someone wicked—a defect in him. Do not reprove a ridiculer, that he may not hate you. Give a reproof to a wise person and he will love you."

Proper Attitude. Since the Scriptures are inspired of God, all reproof solidly based on them is really reproof from him. (2Ti 3:16) Jehovah's reproof is an expression of love, not to be abhorred or rejected. (Pr 3:11, 12) As head of the Christian congregation, Jesus Christ, in affection for its members, sees to it that needed reproof is given through spiritually qualified men. (Re 3:14, 19) Wise ones appreciate that "the reproofs of discipline are the way of life."—Pr 6:23.

The sinful human tendency is to resent reproof and the human servant through whom it may be given. But yielding to this tendency degrades one to the level of an unreasoning beast lacking moral discrimination; as the inspired proverb expresses it: "A hater of reproof is unreasoning." (Pr 12:1) In contrast, the psalmist David, who was himself repeatedly reproved, wrote: "Should the righteous one strike me, it would be a loving-kindness; and should he reprove me, it would be oil upon the head, which my head would not want to refuse."—Ps 141:5.

REPTILES. A reptile is a cold-blooded, vertebrate, air-breathing animal. The Hebrew term for reptiles comes from the verb za·chal', meaning "glide." As stated at Deuteronomy 32:24, among the things that would bring trouble upon idolatrous Israel was "the venom of reptiles of the dust," evidently referring there to poisonous snakes. (Compare Jer 8:17.) At Micah 7:17, the nations that are overwhelmed by God's power are spoken of as coming out of their defensive positions like excited reptiles.

In addition to serpents, other reptiles mentioned in the Bible are the chameleon, the gecko and other lizards.—See comments under their individual names.

REPURCHASE, REPURCHASER. The Hebrew verb ga·'al', appearing first in Genesis 48:16 ('recover'), also has the meaning of "repurchase or redeem," that is, to recover, redeem, or buy back the person, property, or inheritance of the next of kin; it was also used with reference to a blood avenger. (Ps 74:2; Isa 43:1) The next of kin having the obligation of being a repurchaser (Heb., go·'el') evidently fell in this order: (1) brother, (2) uncle, (3) son of an uncle, (4) any other male blood relative of the family.—Le 25:48, 49; compare the order in Nu 27:5-11; see AVENGER OF BLOOD.

Under the Mosaic Law, if an Israelite, because of economic circumstances, had sold himself into slavery, the repurchaser could buy him back out of slavery. (Le 25:47-54) Or, if he had sold his land inheritance, his repurchaser could buy back the property, and he could return to his possession. (Le 25:25-27) However, no thing "devoted," "devoted to destruction," not even a man's life, could be repurchased.—Le 27:21, 28, 29; see DEVOTED THING.

An example of the transaction of repurchase by a go·'el' is found in the book of Ruth. When Ruth reported that she had gleaned in the field of Boaz, her mother-in-law Naomi exclaimed: "The man is related to us. He is one of our repurchasers." (Ru 2:20) Boaz accepted this obligation and concluded a covenant of repurchase before judges and witnesses, but only after another relative more closely related than Boaz had turned down this privilege.—Ru 3:9, 12, 13; 4:1-17.

Jehovah as Repurchaser. By the sacrifice of his only-begotten Son, Jehovah as Repurchaser provided for the recovery of mankind from sin and death and the power of the grave. This Son had to come to earth, becoming "like his 'brothers' in all respects," partaking of blood and flesh, thereby being a near relative of mankind. (Heb 2:11-17) The apostle Paul writes to Christians: "By means of him we have the release by ransom through the blood of that one."—Eph 1:7; compare Re 5:9; 14:3, 4; for further details see RANSOM.

RESEN (Re'sen). A city in Assyria built by Nimrod between Nineveh and Calah. Its location is otherwise unknown.—Ge 10:10-12.

RESHEPH (Re'sheph). An Ephraimite; one of Joshua's ancestors.—1Ch 7:22-27.

RESIDENT. See ALIEN RESIDENT.

RESINOUS TREE [Heb., *go'pher*]. A tree whose wood Noah used in the construction of the ark but which cannot be identified with any degree of certainty. (Ge 6:14) The *King James Version* simply transliterates the Hebrew name. On the basis of the similarity between the Hebrew name and the Hebrew term for "tar" ("pitch," *KJ*; Heb., *ko'pher*) some have related it to the resinous trees of the pine family, particularly to the cypress, which is a very durable tree, extremely resistant to decay.—See CYPRESS.

RESPECT. The giving of particular attention or deference to one judged worthy of esteem; a recognition and due regard for a thing or, especially, for another person, his qualities, achievements, office, position, or authority. To manifest respect is to "honor." Various original-language words convey the thought of according to others honor, respect, or wholesome fear.—See FEAR; HONOR.

Toward Jehovah and His Representatives. By reason of his being Creator, Jehovah God is worthy of the greatest honor from all his intelligent creatures. (Re 4:11) Such honor calls for individuals to render faithful obedience to him, obedience based on love for him and an appreciation for what he has done in their behalf. (Mal 1:6; 1Jo 5:3) It also includes the use of one's valuable things on behalf of true worship.—Pr 3:9.

One who appropriates to himself that which belongs to the Creator shows disrespect for sacred things. This was done by Hophni and Phinehas, the sons of High Priest Eli. They seized the best of every offering made to Jehovah. And Eli, by failing to take firm measures against his sons for this, honored them more than Jehovah.—1Sa 2:12-17, 27-29.

Whereas the honor given by men to Jehovah God is manifested by faithful obedience to him and furthering the interests of his worship, God honors humans by blessing and rewarding them. (1Sa 2:30) Thus King David, who served Jehovah faithfully and desired to build a temple for housing the sacred ark of the covenant, was honored or rewarded with a covenant for a kingdom.—2Sa 7:1-16; 1Ch 17:1-14.

As Jehovah's spokesmen, the prophets, especially God's Son Jesus Christ, were deserving of respect. But instead of being accorded such by the Israelites, they were abused verbally and physically, even to the point of being put to death. Israel's disrespect for Jehovah's representatives reached its climax in their killing his Son. For this reason Jehovah used the Roman armies to execute his vengeance upon unfaithful Jerusalem in 70 C.E.—Mt 21:33-44; Mr 12:1-9; Lu 20:9-16; compare Joh 5:23.

In the Christian congregation. Those entrusted with special responsibilities as teachers in the Christian congregation deserved the support and cooperation of fellow believers. (Heb 13:7, 17) They were "worthy of double honor," including voluntary material assistance for their hard work in behalf of the congregation.—1Ti 5:17, 18; see OLDER MAN.

However, all Christians were entitled to honor from fellow believers. The apostle Paul counseled: "In showing honor to one another take the lead." (Ro 12:10) As the individual Christian knows his own weaknesses and failings better than fellow believers do, it is only right that he put others ahead of himself, honoring or highly valuing them on account of their faithful work. (Php 2:1-4) Needy and deserving widows were honored by receiving material assistance from the congregation.—1Ti 5:3, 9, 10.

Among family members. A wife is rightly to manifest wholesome fear, or deep respect, for her husband as head of the family. (Eph 5:33) This harmonizes with the preeminence given to man in God's arrangement. Man, not woman, was created first, and he is "God's image and glory." (1Co 11:7-9; 1Ti 2:11-13) Sarah was a notable example of a woman who had deep respect for her husband. Her respect came from the heart, for Sarah referred to her husband as "lord," not merely for others to hear but even "inside herself."—1Pe 3:1, 2, 5, 6; compare Ge 18:12.

On the other hand, husbands are admonished: "Continue dwelling in like manner with [your wives] according to knowledge, assigning them honor as to a weaker vessel, the feminine one, since you are also heirs with them of the undeserved favor of life." (1Pe 3:7) Thus spirit-anointed Christian husbands were to take into consideration that their wives had an equal standing as joint heirs with Christ (compare Ro 8:17; Ga 3:28) and should be treated in an honorable way in recognition of the fact that they have less strength than men.

In relation to their children, parents are God's representatives, authorized to train, discipline, and direct them. Parents are therefore entitled to honor, or respect. (Ex 20:12; Eph 6:1-3; Heb 12:9) This would not be limited to a child's obedience and his manifesting a high regard for his parents. When necessary, it would include lovingly caring for parents in later life. (Compare Mt 15:4-6.) In the Christian congregation, one who failed to provide for an aged and needy parent was regarded as being worse than a person without faith. (1Ti 5:8) As the apostle Paul pointed out to Timothy, the congregation was not to take on the burden of caring for widows who had children or grandchildren that were able to render material assistance. —1Ti 5:4.

Toward Rulers and Others. Honor, or respect, is also due men in high governmental station. A Christian shows such respect, not to gain some favor, but because it is God's will. Personally these men may be corrupt. (Compare Lu 18:2-6; Ac 24:24-27.) But respect is rendered to them out of regard for the position of responsibility for which their office stands. (Ro 13:1, 2, 7; 1Pe 2:13, 14) Similarly, slaves were to consider their owners worthy of full honor, doing their assigned work and not giving cause for bringing reproach upon God's name.—1Ti 6:1.

When others demanded that a Christian give a reason for his hope, he was to do so "with a mild temper and deep respect [literally, fear]." Though questions might be propounded in an insulting manner, the Christian would present his reasons with calmness and gentleness, not responding in an irritated, angry, or resentful way. Though not cowed because of fear of men, the Christian would manifest deep respect, or a wholesome fear, as if in the presence of Jehovah God and the Lord Jesus Christ. (1Pe 3:14, 15, ftn) In this regard he could take as an example the angels, who, though greater in strength and power, do not present accusations in abusive terms.—2Pe 2:11.

RESTORATION.

A bringing back to a former condition. Outstandingly, in the Scriptures, in connection with the return of Christ, mention is made of "times of restoration [form of Gr., a·po·ka·ta'sta·sis] of all things of which God spoke through the mouth of his holy prophets."—Ac 3:20, 21.

The *King James Version* here renders a·po·ka·ta'sta·sis as "restitution." The Greek word itself comes from a·po', meaning "back" or "again," and ka·thi'ste·mi, literally meaning "set down." The corresponding verb form is translated 'restore' in Acts 1:6. The *Theological Dictionary of the New Testament,* edited by G. Kittel, states that the basic meaning of the term is "restitution to an earlier state" or "restoration." (Translated by G. Bromiley, 1964, Vol. I, p. 389) It was used by Jewish historian Josephus in referring to the return of the Jews from exile. In papyrus writings it is used of the repair of certain buildings, the restoration of estates to rightful owners, and a balancing of accounts.

The text itself does not specify what the things to be restored are, hence the "all things" must be ascertained by the study of God's message spoken through his prophets.

RESURRECTION.

The Greek word a·na'sta·sis literally means "raising up; standing up." It is used frequently in the Christian Greek Scriptures with reference to the resurrection of the dead. The Hebrew Scriptures at Hosea 13:14, quoted by the apostle Paul (1Co 15:54, 55), speak of the abolition of death and the rendering powerless of Sheol (Heb., she'ohl'; Gr., hai'des). She'ohl' is rendered in various versions as "grave" and "pit." The dead are spoken of as going there. (Ge 37:35; 1Ki 2:6; Ec 9:10) Its usage in the Scriptures, along with the usage of its Greek equivalent hai'des in the Christian Greek Scriptures, shows that it refers, not to an individual grave, but to the common grave of mankind, gravedom. (Eze 32:21-32; Re 20:13; see HADES; SHEOL.) To render Sheol powerless would mean to loosen its hold on those in it, which would imply the emptying of gravedom. This, of course, would require a resurrection, a raising up from the lifeless condition of death or out of the grave for those there.

Through Jesus Christ. The foregoing shows that the teaching of resurrection appears in the Hebrew Scriptures. Nevertheless, it remained for Jesus Christ to "shed light upon life and incorruption through the good news." (2Ti 1:10) Jesus said: "I am the way and the truth and the life. No one comes to the Father except through me." (Joh 14:6) Just how *everlasting life* would come, and more than that, *incorruption* for some, was brought to light through the good news about Jesus Christ. The apostle affirms that the resurrection is a sure hope, arguing: "Now if Christ is being preached that he has been raised up from the dead, how is it some among you say there is no resurrection of the dead? If, indeed, there is no resurrection of the dead, neither has Christ been raised up. But if Christ has not been raised up, our preaching is certainly in vain, and our faith is in vain. Moreover, we are also found false witnesses of God, because we have borne witness against God that he raised up the Christ, but whom he did not raise up if the dead are really not to be raised up. . . . Further, if Christ has not been raised up, your faith is useless; you are yet in your sins. . . . However, now Christ has been raised up from the dead, the firstfruits of those who have fallen asleep in death. For since death is through a man, *resurrection of the dead is also through a man.*"—1Co 15:12-21.

Christ himself when on earth performed resurrections. (Lu 7:11-15; 8:49-56; Joh 11:38-44) Only through Jesus Christ can resurrection, with everlasting life thereafter, be possible.—Joh 5:26.

A Sure Purpose of God. Jesus Christ pointed out to the Sadducees, a sect that did not believe in resurrection, that the writings of Moses in the Hebrew Scriptures, which they possessed and claimed to believe, prove there is a resurrection; Jesus reasoned that when Jehovah said He was "the God of Abraham and the God of Isaac and the God of Jacob" (who were actually dead), He counted those men as alive because of the resurrection that He, "the God, not of the dead, but of the living," purposed to give them. God, because of his power, "makes the dead alive and calls the things that are not as though they were." Paul includes this fact when speaking of Abraham's faith.—Mt 22:23, 31-33; Ro 4:17.

God's ability to resurrect. For the One with the ability and power to create man in His own image, with a perfect body and with the potential for full expression of the marvelous characteristics implanted in the human personality, it would pose no insurmountable problem to resurrect an individual. If scientific principles established by God can be used by scientists to preserve and later reconstruct a visible and audible scene by means of videotape, how easy it is for the great Universal Sovereign and Creator to resurrect a person by repatterning the same personality in a newly formed body. Concerning the revitalizing of Sarah to have a child in her old age, the angel said: "Is anything too extraordinary for Jehovah?"—Ge 18:14; Jer 32:17, 27.

How the Need for Resurrection Arose. In the beginning a resurrection was not necessary. It was not a part of God's original purpose for mankind, because death was not the natural, purposed thing for humans. Rather, God indicated that he purposed the earth to be full of *living* humans, not a deteriorating, dying race. His work was perfect, hence without flaw, imperfection, or sickness. (De 32:4) Jehovah blessed the first human pair, telling them to multiply and fill the earth. (Ge 1:28) Such blessing certainly did not include sickness and death; God set no limited life span for man, but he told Adam that disobedience is what would cause death. This implies that man would otherwise live forever. Disobedience would incur God's disfavor and remove his blessing, bringing a curse.—Ge 2:17; 3:17-19.

Consequently, death was introduced into the human race by the transgression of Adam. (Ro 5:12) Because of their father's sinfulness and resultant imperfection, Adam's offspring could not get a heritage of everlasting life from him; in fact, not even a *hope* of living forever. "Neither can a rotten tree produce fine fruit," said Jesus. (Mt 7:17, 18; Job 14:1, 2) The resurrection was brought in, or *added*, to overcome this disability for those of Adam's children who would desire to be obedient to God.

Purpose of the Resurrection. The resurrection shows forth not only Jehovah's unlimited power and wisdom but also his love and his mercy and vindicates him as the Preserver of those who serve him. (1Sa 2:6) Having resurrection power, he can go to the extent of showing that his servants will be faithful to him to the very death. He can answer Satan's accusation that asserted that "skin in behalf of skin, and everything that a man has he will give in behalf of his soul." (Job 2:4) Jehovah can let Satan go the full limit, even to killing some in a vain effort to support his false accusations. (Mt 24:9; Re 2:10; 6:11) The fact that Jehovah's servants are willing to give up life itself in his service proves their service is, not for selfish considerations, but out of love. (Re 12:11) It also proves that they acknowledge Him as the Almighty, the Universal Sovereign, and the God of love, who is able to resurrect them. It proves they render exclusive devotion to Jehovah for his wonderful qualities and not for selfish material reasons. (Consider some of the exclamations of his servants, as recorded at Ro 11:33-36; Re 4:11; 7:12.) The resurrection also is a means by which Jehovah sees that his purpose toward the earth, as stated to Adam, is carried out.—Ge 1:28.

Essential to man's happiness. The resurrection of the dead, an undeserved kindness on God's part, is essential to mankind's happiness and to the undoing of all the harm, suffering, and oppression that have come upon the human race. These things have befallen man as a result of his imperfection and sickness, the wars he has waged, the murders committed, and the inhumanities practiced by wicked people at the instance of Satan the Devil. We cannot be completely happy if we do not believe in a resurrection. The apostle Paul expressed the feeling in these words: "If in this life only we have hoped in Christ, we are of all men most to be pitied."—1Co 15:19.

How Early Was Resurrection Hope Given? After Adam had sinned and had brought death upon himself and thereby introduced death for those who would be his posterity, God, in addressing the serpent, said: "And I shall put enmity between you and the woman and between your seed and her seed. He will bruise you in the head and you will bruise him in the heel."—Ge 3:15.

One originally causing death to be removed.
Jesus said to the religious Jews who opposed him: "You are from your father the Devil, and you wish to do the desires of your father. That one was a manslayer when he began, and he did not stand fast in the truth, because truth is not in him." (Joh 8:44) This is evidence that it was the Devil who spoke through the instrumentality of the serpent, and that this one was a manslayer from the beginning of his lying, devilish course. In the vision that Christ later gave to John, he revealed that Satan the Devil is also called "the original serpent." (Re 12:9) Satan got his hold on mankind, gaining influence over Adam's children, by inducing their father Adam to rebel against God. So in the first prophecy, of Genesis 3:15, Jehovah gave hope that this Serpent would be put out of the way. (Compare Ro 16:20.) Not only is Satan's head to be crushed but also all of his works are to be broken up, destroyed, or undone. (1Jo 3:8; *NW, KJ, AT*) The fulfillment of this prophecy would of necessity require the undoing of the death introduced by Adam, including bringing back by a resurrection those of Adam's offspring who go into Sheol (Hades) as a result of his sin, the effects of which they inherit.—1Co 15:26.

Hope of freedom entails resurrection. The apostle Paul describes the situation that God permitted to exist following man's fall into sin and His end purpose in doing so: "For the creation was subjected to futility [being born in sin and with death facing all], not by its own will [the children of Adam were brought into the world facing this situation, though they themselves had no control over what Adam had done, and by no choice of their own] but through him [God, in his wisdom] that subjected it, on the basis of hope that the creation itself also will be set free from enslavement to corruption and have the glorious freedom of the children of God." (Ro 8:20, 21; Ps 51:5) In order to experience the fulfillment of this hope of glorious freedom, those who have died would have to have a resurrection; they would have to be freed from death and the grave. Thus, by his promise of the "seed" that would crush the serpent's head, God set a marvelous hope before mankind.—See SEED.

Abraham's basis for faith. The evidence in the Bible record reveals that when Abraham attempted to offer up his son Isaac he had faith in God's ability and purpose to raise the dead. And as stated at Hebrews 11:17-19, he did receive Isaac back from the dead "in an illustrative way." (Ge 22:1-3, 10-13) Abraham had a basis for faith in a resurrection because of God's promise of the "seed." (Ge 3:15) Also, he and Sarah had already

experienced something comparable to a resurrection in the revitalizing of their reproductive powers. (Ge 18:9-11; 21:1, 2, 12; Ro 4:19-21) Job expressed similar faith, saying, in his intense suffering: "O that in Sheol you would conceal me, . . . that you would set a time limit for me and remember me! If an able-bodied man dies can he live again? . . . You will call, and I myself shall answer you. For the work of your hands you will have a yearning."—Job 14:13-15.

Resurrections before ransom was given. Resurrections were performed by or through the prophets Elijah and Elisha. (1Ki 17:17-24; 2Ki 4:32-37; 13:20, 21) However, these resurrected persons died again, as did those resurrected by Jesus when he was on earth as well as those resurrected by the apostles. This reveals that resurrection is not to *everlasting* life in every case.

Because of having been resurrected by his friend Jesus, Lazarus was likely alive Pentecost 33 C.E., when the holy spirit was poured out and the first ones of the heavenly calling (Heb 3:1) were anointed and spirit begotten. (Ac 2:1-4, 33, 38) Lazarus' resurrection was similar to those performed by Elijah and Elisha. But it probably opened up to Lazarus the opportunity of receiving a resurrection like Christ's, which he otherwise would not have had. What a remarkable act of love on Jesus' part!—Joh 11:38-44.

"A better resurrection." There were those faithful persons of old times of whom Paul speaks: "Women received their dead by resurrection; but other men were tortured because they would not accept release by some ransom, in order that they might attain a better resurrection." (Heb 11:35) These men exhibited faith in the resurrection hope, knowing that life *at that time* was not the all-important thing. The resurrection they and others will have through Christ comes *after* his resurrection and appearance in heaven before his Father with the value of his ransom sacrifice. At that time he repurchased the life right of the human race, becoming the potential "Eternal Father." (Heb 9:11, 12, 24; Isa 9:6) He is "a life-giving spirit." (1Co 15:45) He has "the keys of death and of Hades [Sheol]." (Re 1:18) With the authority now to give *everlasting* life, at God's due time he performs "a better resurrection," since those experiencing it can live forever; none of such unavoidably need to die again. If obedient, they will continue living.

Heavenly Resurrection. Jesus Christ is called "the firstborn from the dead." (Col 1:18) He was the first ever to be resurrected to everlasting life. And his resurrection was "in the spirit," to life in heaven. (1Pe 3:18) Moreover, he was raised to a higher form of life and a higher position than that which he had held in the heavens prior to coming to earth. He was granted immortality and incorruption, which no creature in the flesh can have, and was made "higher than the heavens," second only to Jehovah God in the universe. (Heb 7:26; 1Ti 6:14-16; Php 2:9-11; Ac 2:34; 1Co 15:27) His resurrection was performed by Jehovah God himself.—Ac 3:15; 5:30; Ro 4:24; 10:9.

However, for 40 days after his resurrection Jesus appeared to his disciples on different occasions in various fleshly bodies, just as angels had appeared to men of ancient times. Like those angels, he had the power to construct and to disintegrate those fleshly bodies at will, for the purpose of proving visibly that he had been resurrected. (Mt 28:8-10, 16-20; Lu 24:13-32, 36-43; Joh 20:14-29; Ge 18:1, 2; 19:1; Jos 5:13-15; Jg 6:11, 12; 13:3, 13) His many appearances, and particularly his manifesting himself to more than 500 persons at one time, provide strong testimony to the truth of his resurrection. (1Co 15:3-8) His resurrection, so well attested, furnishes "a guarantee to all men" regarding the certainty of a future day of reckoning or judgment.—Ac 17:31.

Resurrection of Christ's "brothers." Those who are "called and chosen and faithful," Christ's footstep followers, his "brothers," who are spiritually begotten as "God's children," are promised a resurrection like his. (Re 17:14; Ro 6:5; 8:15, 16; Heb 2:11) The apostle Peter writes to fellow Christians: "Blessed be the God and Father of our Lord Jesus Christ, for according to his great mercy he gave us a new birth to a living hope through the resurrection of Jesus Christ from the dead, to an incorruptible and undefiled and unfading inheritance. It is reserved in the heavens for you."—1Pe 1:3, 4.

Peter also describes the hope such ones possess as "precious and very grand promises, that through these you may become sharers in divine nature." (2Pe 1:4) They must undergo a change of nature, giving up human nature to obtain "divine" nature, thus sharing with Christ in his glory. They must die a death like Christ's—maintaining integrity and giving up human life forever—and then they receive immortal, incorruptible bodies like Christ's by a resurrection. (Ro 6:3-5; 1Co 15:50-57; 2Co 5:1-3) The apostle Paul explains that it is not the *body* that is resurrected, but rather, he likens their experience to the planting and sprouting of a seed, in that "God gives it a body just as it has pleased him." (1Co 15:35-40) It is the *soul,* the

person, that is resurrected, with a body to suit the environment into which God resurrects him.

In the case of Jesus Christ, he gave up his human life as a ransom sacrifice for the benefit of mankind. The 40th Psalm is applied to him by the inspired writer of the book of Hebrews, who represents Jesus as saying, when he came "into the world" as God's Messiah: "Sacrifice and offering you did not want, but you prepared a *body* for me." (Heb 10:5) Jesus himself said: "For a fact, the bread that I shall give is my flesh in behalf of the life of the world." (Joh 6:51) It follows that Christ could not take his body back again in the resurrection, thereby taking back the sacrifice offered to God for mankind. Besides, Christ was no longer to abide on earth. His "home" is in the heavens with his Father, who is not flesh, but spirit. (Joh 14:3; 4:24) Jesus Christ therefore received a glorious immortal, incorruptible body, for "he is the reflection of [Jehovah's] glory and the exact representation of his very being, and he sustains all things by the word of his power; and after he had made a purification for our sins he sat down on the right hand of the Majesty in lofty places. So he has become better than the angels [who are themselves mighty spirit persons], to the extent that he has inherited a name more excellent than theirs."—Heb 1:3, 4; 10:12, 13.

Christ's faithful brothers, who join him in the heavens, give up human life. The apostle Paul shows that they have to have new bodies repatterned, or refashioned, for their new environment. "As for us, our citizenship exists in the heavens, from which place also we are eagerly waiting for a savior, the Lord Jesus Christ, who will *refashion* our humiliated body to be conformed to his glorious body according to the operation of the power that he has."—Php 3:20, 21.

Time of the heavenly resurrection. The heavenly resurrection of Christ's joint heirs begins after Jesus Christ returns in heavenly glory, to give first attention to his spiritual brothers. Christ himself is called "the firstfruits of those who have fallen asleep in death." Paul then says that each one will be resurrected in his own rank, "Christ the firstfruits, afterward those who belong to the Christ during his presence." (1Co 15:20, 23) These as "the house of God," have been under judgment during their Christian life course, beginning with the first of their number at Pentecost. (1Pe 4:17) They are *"certain* [literally, some] firstfruits." (Jas 1:18, *Int;* Re 14:4) Jesus Christ can be compared to the barley firstfruits offered by the Israelites on Nisan 16 ("Christ the firstfruits"), and his spiritual brothers as "firstfruits" ("certain firstfruits") can be compared to the wheat firstfruits offered on Pentecost day, the 50th day from Nisan 16.—Le 23:4-12, 15-20.

These have been under judgment, so at Christ's return it is time to give the reward to them, his faithful anointed ones, just as he promised his 11 faithful apostles on the evening before his death: "I am going my way to prepare a place for you. Also, . . . I am coming again and will receive you home to myself, that where I am you also may be."—Joh 14:2, 3; Lu 19:12-23; compare 2Ti 4:1, 8; Re 11:17, 18.

"The Lamb's marriage." These as a body are called his (prospective) "bride" (Re 21:9); they are promised to him in marriage, and they must be resurrected to the heavens in order to take part in "the marriage of the Lamb." (2Co 11:2; Re 19:7, 8) The apostle Paul looked forward to receiving his heavenly resurrection. (2Ti 4:8) When Christ's "presence" takes place, there are some of his spiritual brothers yet alive on earth, "invited to the evening meal of the Lamb's marriage," but those of their number who have died are given first attention by a resurrection. (Re 19:9) This is explained at 1 Thessalonians 4:15, 16: "For this is what we tell you by Jehovah's word, that we the living who survive to the presence of the Lord shall in no way precede those who have fallen asleep in death; because the Lord himself will descend from heaven with a commanding call, with an archangel's voice and with God's trumpet, and those who are dead in union with Christ will rise first."

Paul then adds: "Afterward we the living who are surviving will, together with them, be caught away in clouds to meet the Lord in the air; and thus we shall always be with the Lord." (1Th 4:17) Thus, at the time that they finish their earthly course faithfully in death, the remaining ones who have the invitation to "the evening meal of the Lamb's marriage" are immediately resurrected to join their fellow members of the bride class in heaven. They do not "fall asleep in death" in the sense of waiting in a long sleep, as did the apostles but, on dying, are "changed, in a moment, in the twinkling of an eye, during the last trumpet. For the trumpet will sound, and the dead will be raised up incorruptible, and we shall be changed." 1Co 15:51, 52) Evidently, though, "the marriage of the Lamb" does not take place until after judgment has been executed upon "Babylon the Great." (Re 18) After describing the destruction of his "great harlot," Revelation 19:7 says: "Let us rejoice and be overjoyed, and let us give him the glory, because the marriage of the Lamb has arrived and his wife has prepared herself." When all

the 144,000 have been finally approved and "sealed" as faithful ones and have been resurrected to the heavens, the marriage can proceed.

First resurrection. Revelation 20:5, 6 refers to the resurrection of those who will reign with Christ as "the first resurrection." The apostle Paul speaks of this first resurrection also as "the earlier resurrection from the dead [literally, the out-resurrection the out of dead (ones)]." (Php 3:11, *NW, Ro, Int*) On the expression Paul uses here, Robertson's *Word Pictures in the New Testament* (1931, Vol. IV, p. 454) says: "Apparently Paul is thinking here only of the resurrection of believers out from the dead and so double *ex* [out] (*ten exanastasin ten ek nekron*). Paul is not denying a general resurrection by this language, but emphasizing that of believers." Charles Ellicott's *Commentaries* (1865, Vol. II, p. 87) remarks on Philippians 3:11: "'The resurrection from the dead;' i.e., as the context suggests, the *first* resurrection (Rev. xx. 5), when, at the Lord's coming the dead in Him shall rise first (1 Thessalon. iv. 16), and the quick be caught up to meet Him in the clouds (1 Thess. iv. 17); compare Luke xx. 35. The first resurrection will include only true believers, and will apparently precede the second, that of nonbelievers and disbelievers, in point of time . . . Any reference here to a merely ethical resurrection (Cocceius) is wholly out of the question." One of the basic meanings of the word *e·xa·na'sta·sis* is getting up from bed in the morning; thus it can well represent a resurrection occurring early, otherwise called "the first resurrection." Rotherham's translation of Philippians 3:11 reads: "If by any means I may advance to the earlier resurrection which is from among the dead."

Earthly Resurrection. While Jesus was hanging on a stake, one of the evildoers alongside him, observing that Jesus was not deserving of punishment, requested: "Jesus, remember me when you get into your kingdom." Jesus replied: "Truly I tell you today, You will be with me in Paradise." (Lu 23:42, 43) In effect, Jesus said: 'On this dark day, when my claim to a kingdom is to outward appearances highly unlikely, you express faith. Indeed, when I do get into my kingdom, I will remember you.' (See PARADISE.) This would require a resurrection for the evildoer. This man was not a faithful follower of Jesus Christ. He had been engaged in wrongdoing, lawbreaking meriting the death penalty. (Lu 23:40, 41) Therefore, he could not hope to be one of those receiving the first resurrection. Additionally, he died 40 days before Jesus ascended into heaven and hence before Pentecost, which was 10 days after that ascension, when God through Jesus anointed the first members of those who will receive the heavenly resurrection.—Ac 1:3; 2:1-4, 33.

The evildoer, Jesus said, would be in Paradise. The word means "a park or pleasure ground." The *Septuagint* rendered the Hebrew word for "garden" (*gan*), as at Genesis 2:8, by the Greek word *pa·ra′dei·sos.* The paradise in which the evildoer will be would not be "the paradise of God" promised to "him that conquers," at Revelation 2:7, for the evildoer was not a conqueror of the world with Jesus Christ. (Joh 16:33) The evildoer would therefore not be in the heavenly Kingdom as a member of it (Lu 22:28-30) but would be a subject of the Kingdom when those of "the first resurrection" would, as kings of God and Christ, sit on thrones, ruling with Christ for a thousand years. —Re 20:4, 6.

"The righteous and the unrighteous." The apostle Paul said to a group of Jews who also entertained the hope of a resurrection that "there is going to be a resurrection of both the righteous and the unrighteous."—Ac 24:15.

The Bible makes it plain who are "the righteous." First of all, those who are to receive a heavenly resurrection are declared righteous.—Ro 8:28-30.

Then the Bible calls faithful men of old such as Abraham righteous. (Ge 15:6; Jas 2:21) Many of these men are listed at Hebrews chapter 11, and of them the writer says: "And yet all these, although they had witness borne to them through their faith, did not get the fulfillment of the promise, as God foresaw something better for us [spirit-begotten, anointed Christians like Paul], in order that they might not be made perfect apart from us." (Heb 11:39, 40) So, the perfecting of them will take place after that of the ones having part in "the first resurrection."

Then there is the "great crowd" described in Revelation chapter 7, who are not members of the 144,000 "sealed" ones, and who consequently do not have "the token" of the spirit as being spirit-begotten. (Eph 1:13, 14; 2Co 5:5) They are described as coming "out of the great tribulation" as survivors of it; this would seem to locate the gathering of this group in the last days shortly before that tribulation. These are righteous through faith, being clothed in white robes washed in the blood of the Lamb. (Re 7:1, 9-17) As a class, they will not need to be resurrected, but faithful ones of that group who die before the great tribulation will be resurrected in God's due time.

Also, there are many "unrighteous" persons buried in Sheol (Hades), mankind's common grave, or in "the sea," watery graves. The judgment of these along with "the righteous" resurrected on earth is described in Revelation 20:12, 13: "And I saw the dead, the great and the small, standing before the throne, and scrolls were opened. But another scroll was opened; it is the scroll of life. And the dead were judged out of those things written in the scrolls according to their deeds. And the sea gave up those dead in it, and death and Hades gave up those dead in them, and they were judged individually according to their deeds."

Time of the earthly resurrection. We note that this judgment is placed in the Bible in the account of events occurring during Christ's Thousand Year Reign with his associate kings and priests. These, the apostle Paul said, "will judge the world." (1Co 6:2) "The great and the small," persons from all walks of life, will be there, to be judged impartially. They are "judged out of those things written in the scrolls" that will be opened then. This could not mean the record of their past lives nor a set of rules that judges them on the basis of their past lives. For since "the wages sin pays is death," these by their death have received the wages of their sin in the past. (Ro 6:7, 23) Now they are resurrected that they might demonstrate their attitude toward God and whether they wish to take hold of the ransom sacrifice of Jesus Christ that was given for all. (Mt 20:28; Joh 3:16) Though their past sins are not accounted to them, they need the ransom to lift them up to perfection. They must make their minds over from their former way of life and thought in harmony with God's will and regulations for the earth and its population. Accordingly, "the scrolls" evidently set forth the will and law of God for them during that Judgment Day, their faith and their obedience to these things being the basis for judgment and for writing their names indelibly, at last, into "the scroll of life."

Resurrection to Life and to Judgment. Jesus gave the comforting assurance to mankind: "The hour is coming, and it is now, when the dead will hear the voice of the Son of God and those who have given heed will live. . . . Do not marvel at this, because the hour is coming in which all those in the memorial tombs will hear his voice and come out, those who did good things to a resurrection of life, those who practiced vile things to a resurrection of judgment."—Joh 5:25-29.

A judgment of condemnation. In Jesus' words here, the word "judgment" translates the Greek word *kri′sis*. According to Parkhurst, the meanings of this word in the Christian Greek

Scriptures are as follows: "I. *Judgment*. . . . II. *Judgment, justice.* Mat. xxiii. 23. Comp. xii. 20. . . . III. *Judgment of condemnation, condemnation, damnation.* Mark iii. 29. John v. 24, 29. . . . IV. *The cause* or *ground of condemnation* or *punishment.* John iii. 19. V. *A particular court of justice* among the Jews, . . . Mat. v. 21, 22."—*A Greek and English Lexicon to the New Testament,* London, 1845, p. 342.

If Jesus, in speaking of judgment, meant a trial the result of which might be life, then there would be no contrast between this and the "resurrection of life." Therefore, the context indicates that Jesus meant by "judgment" a condemnatory judgment.

"The dead" that heard Jesus speak on earth. In considering Jesus' words, we note that when Jesus spoke, some of "the dead" were hearing his voice. Peter used similar language when he said: "In fact, for this purpose the good news was declared also *to the dead,* that they might be judged as to the flesh from the standpoint of men but might live as to the spirit from the standpoint of God." (1Pe 4:6) This is so because those hearing Christ were 'dead in trespasses and sins' before hearing but would begin to 'live' spiritually because of faith in the good news.—Eph 2:1; compare Mt 8:22; 1Ti 5:6.

John 5:29 refers to end of judgment period. But a very important thing to notice, something that helps to determine the time feature of Jesus' words concerning the 'resurrection of life and the resurrection of judgment,' is what he said earlier in the same context, in speaking of those living then who were spiritually dead (as explained under the subheading 'Passing Over From Death to Life'): "The hour is coming, and it is now, when the dead will hear the voice of the Son of God and those who *have given heed* [literally, word for word, "the (ones) having heard"] will live." (Joh 5:25, *Int*) This indicates that he was not speaking merely of someone audibly hearing his voice but, rather, of the ones "having heard," namely, those who, after hearing, accept as true what they hear. The terms "hear" and "listen" are used very frequently in the Bible with the meaning of "give heed" or "obey." (See OBEDIENCE.) Those who prove to be obedient will live. (Compare the use of the same Greek term [*a·kou'o*], "hear or listen," at Joh 6:60; 8:43, 47; 10:3, 27.) They are judged, not on what they did *before* hearing his voice, but on what they do *after* hearing it.

Jesus was therefore evidently taking a similar position in time in speaking of "those who did good things" and "those who practiced vile things," namely, a position at the end of the period of judgment, as looking back in retrospect or in review of the actions of these resurrected persons *after* they had opportunity to obey or disobey the "things written in the scrolls." Only at the end of the judgment period would it be demonstrated who had done good or bad. The outcome to "those who did good things" (according to "those things written in the scrolls") would be the reward of life; to "those who practiced vile things," a judgment of condemnation. The resurrection would have turned out to be either to life or to condemnation.

The practice of stating things as viewed from the standpoint of the outcome, or stating them as already accomplished, considering them in retrospect, is common in the Bible. For God is "the One telling from the beginning the finale, and from long ago the things that have not been done." (Isa 46:10) Jude adopts this same viewpoint when he speaks of corrupt men who slipped into the congregation, saying of them: "Too bad for them, because they have gone in the path of Cain, and have rushed into the erroneous course of Balaam for reward, and *have perished* [literally, they destroyed themselves] in the rebellious talk of Korah!" (Jude 11) Some of the prophecies use similar language.—Compare Isa 40:1, 2; 46:1; Jer 48:1-4.

Consequently the viewpoint taken at John 5:29 is not identical with that at Acts 24:15 in which Paul speaks of the resurrection of "the righteous and the unrighteous." Paul is plainly referring to those who have had a righteous or unrighteous standing before God *during this life,* and who will be resurrected. They are "those in the memorial tombs." (Joh 5:28; see MEMORIAL TOMB.) At John 5:29, Jesus views such persons *after* their coming out of the memorial tombs and *after* they, by their course of action during the reign of Jesus Christ and his associate kings and priests, have proved themselves either obedient, with eternal "life" as their reward, or disobedient, and so deserving "judgment [condemnation]" from God.

Soul Recovered From Sheol. King David of Israel wrote: "I foresaw the Lord always before my face; for he is on my right hand, that I should not be moved . . . moreover also my flesh shall rest in hope: because thou wilt not leave my soul in hell [Sheol], neither wilt thou suffer thine Holy One to see corruption." (Ps 15:8-10, *LXX,* Bagster [16:8-11, *NW*]) On the day of Pentecost, 33 C.E., the apostle Peter applied this psalm to Jesus Christ, in declaring to the Jews the truth of Christ's resurrection. (Ac 2:25-31) The Scriptures, both the Hebrew and the Greek, therefore show that it was the "soul" of Jesus Christ that was resurrected. Jesus Christ was 'put to death in the flesh, but made alive in the spirit.' (1Pe 3:18) "Flesh and blood cannot inherit God's kingdom," said the apostle Paul. (1Co 15:50) This would also exclude flesh and bones. Flesh and bones do not have life unless they have blood, for the blood contains the "soul" or is that which is necessary for the life of the creature of flesh.—Ge 9:4.

Throughout the Scriptures it is evident that there is no "immaterial soul" separate and distinct from the body. The soul dies when the body dies. Even of Jesus Christ it is written that "he poured out his soul to the very death." His soul was in Sheol. He had no existence as a soul or person during that time. (Isa 53:12; Ac 2:27; compare Eze 18:4; see SOUL.) Consequently, in the resurrection there is no joining again of soul and body. However, whether spiritual or earthly, the individual must have a body or organism, for all persons, heavenly or earthly, possess bodies. To be again a person, one who has died would have to have a body, either a physical or a spiritual body. The Bible says: "If there is a physical body, there is also a spiritual one."—1Co 15:44.

But is the old body reassembled in the resurrection? or is it a precise replica of the former body, made exactly as it was when the person died? The Scriptures answer in the negative when they deal with the resurrection of Christ's anointed brothers to life in the heavens: "Nevertheless, someone will say: 'How are the dead to be raised up? Yes, with what sort of body are they coming?' You unreasonable person! What you sow is not made alive unless first it dies; and as for what you sow, you sow, not the body that will develop, but a bare grain, it may be, of wheat or any one of the rest; but God gives it a body just as it has pleased him, and to each of the seeds its own body."—1Co 15:35-38.

The heavenly ones receive a spiritual body, for it pleases God for them to have bodies suitable for their heavenly environment. But those whom Jehovah pleases to raise to an earthly resurrection, what body does he give them? It could not be the same body, of exactly the same atoms. If a man dies and is buried, by process of decay his body is reconverted into organic chemicals that are absorbed by vegetation. Persons may eat that vegetation. The elements, the atoms of that original person, now are in many persons. In the resurrection it is obvious that the same atoms cannot be in the original person and in all the others at the same time.

Neither is the resurrected body necessarily one constructed to be the exact duplicate of the body at the moment of death. If a person has had his body mutilated before death, will he return in the same way? That would be unreasonable, for he might not be in a condition even to hear and to do "those things written in the scrolls." (Re 20:12) Say a person died from having the blood drained from his body. Would he return without blood? No, for he could not live in an earthly body without blood. (Le 17:11, 14) Rather, he would be given a body as it pleases God. Since God's will and pleasure are that the resurrected person must obey the "things written in the scrolls," it would have to be a sound body, possessing all its faculties. (Even though Lazarus' body was already partially decomposed, Jesus resurrected Lazarus in a whole, sound body. [Joh 11:39]) In this way the individual could properly and justly be held responsible for his deeds during the judgment period. Yet the individual would not be perfect when brought back, for he must exercise faith in Christ's ransom and must have the priestly ministrations of Christ and his "royal priesthood."—1Pe 2:9; Re 5:10; 20:6.

'Passing Over From Death to Life.' Jesus spoke of those who 'have everlasting life' because they hear his words with faith and obedience and then believe on the Father who sent him. He said about each one of such: "He does not come into judgment but has passed over from death to life. Most truly I say to you, The hour is coming, and it is now, when the dead will hear the voice of the Son of God and those who have given heed will live."—Joh 5:24, 25.

Those who have 'passed over from death to life now' would not be those who had literally died and were in actual graves. At the time when Jesus spoke, all mankind were under the condemnation of death before God the Judge of all. So the ones Jesus referred to were evidently persons on earth who had been dead in a spiritual sense. Jesus must have referred to such spiritually dead ones when he said to the Jewish son who wanted to go home first to bury his father: "Keep following me and let the dead bury their dead."—Mt 8:21, 22.

Those who become Christians with true belief were once among the spiritually dead people of the world. The apostle Paul reminded the congregation of this fact, saying: "It is you God made alive though you were dead in your trespasses and sins, in which you at one time walked according to the system of things of this world . . . But God, who is rich in mercy, for his great love with which he loved us, made us alive together with the Christ, even when we were dead in trespasses—by undeserved kindness you have been saved—and he raised us up together and seated us together in the heavenly places in union with Christ Jesus."—Eph 2:1, 2, 4-6.

Thus, because of their no longer walking in trespasses and sins against God, and because of their faith in Christ, Jehovah lifted his condemnation from them. He raised them up out of spiritual death and gave them hope of everlasting life. (1Pe 4:3-6) The apostle John describes this transfer from deadness in trespasses and sins to spiritual life in these words: "Do not marvel, brothers, that the world hates you. We know we have passed over from death to life, because we love the brothers."—1Jo 3:13, 14.

An Undeserved Kindness of God. The provision of a resurrection for humankind is indeed an undeserved kindness of Jehovah God, for he was not obligated to provide a resurrection. Love for the world of mankind moved him to give his only-begotten Son so that millions, yes, even thousands of millions who have died without a real knowledge of God might have opportunity to know and love him, and so that those who love and serve him can have this hope and encouragement to faithful endurance, even as far as death. (Joh 3:16) The apostle Paul comforts fellow Christians with the resurrection hope, writing to the congregation at Thessalonica about those of the congregation who had died and who had hope of a heavenly resurrection: "Moreover, brothers, we do not want you to be ignorant concerning those who are sleeping in death; that you may not sorrow just as the rest also do who have no hope. For if our faith is that Jesus died and rose again, so, too, those who have fallen asleep in death through Jesus God will bring with him."—1Th 4:13, 14.

Likewise, for those faithful to God who died with hope of life on earth under God's Messianic Kingdom, and also for others who have not come to know God, Christians should not sorrow as the rest do who have no hope. When Sheol (Hades) is opened, those in there will come out. The Bible mentions many who have gone there, including the people of ancient Egypt, Assyria, Elam, Meshech, Tubal, Edom, and Sidon. (Eze 32:18-31) Jesus himself said that the people of Tyre, Sidon, and Sodom would be on hand for Judgment Day, some of the pagans being more likely to repent than many to whom Jesus himself preached in Bethsaida, Chorazin, and Capernaum.—Mt 11:20-24; Lu 10:11-15.

Ransom applied to all for whom it was given. The greatness and expansiveness of God's love and undeserved kindness in giving his Son that 'whoever should believe in him might have life' would not limit the application of the ransom to only those whom God chooses for the heavenly calling. (Joh 3:16) In fact, the ransom sacrifice of Jesus Christ would not be completely applied if it left off with those who become members of the Kingdom of heaven. It would fall short of accomplishing the full purpose for which God provided it, because God's purpose was that the Kingdom have earthly subjects. Jesus Christ is High Priest not only over the underpriests with him but also for the world of mankind who will live when his associates also rule as kings and priests with him. (Re 20:4, 6) He has "been tested in all respects like ourselves [his spiritual brothers], but without sin." Therefore he can sympathize with the weaknesses of persons who are conscientiously trying to serve God; and his associate kings and priests have been tested in the same way. (Heb 4:15, 16; 1Pe 4:12, 13) On behalf of whom could they be priests if not on behalf of mankind, including those resurrected, during the Thousand Year Reign and judgment period?

Servants of God have anxiously looked forward to the day when the resurrection will complete its work. In the outworking of his purposes, God has set exactly the proper time for it, in which his wisdom and long-suffering will be fully vindicated. (Ec 3:1-8) He and his Son, being both able and willing to perform the resurrection, will complete it in that set time.

Jehovah joyfully anticipates the resurrection. Jehovah and his Son must anticipate the full carrying out of that work with great joy. Jesus showed this willingness and desire when a leper entreated him: "'If you just want to, you can make me clean.' At that [Jesus] was moved with pity, and he stretched out his hand and touched him, and said to him: 'I want to. Be made clean.' And immediately the leprosy vanished from him, and he became clean." This touching incident demonstrating Christ's loving-kindness for mankind was recorded by three of the Gospel writers. (Mr 1:40-42; Mt 8:2, 3; Lu 5:12, 13) And of Jehovah's love and willingness to help mankind, we call again to mind the words of faithful Job: "If an able-bodied man dies can he live again? . . . You will call, and I myself shall answer you. For the work of your hands you will have *a yearning*."—Job 14:14, 15.

Some Not Resurrected. While it is true that Christ's ransom sacrifice was given for mankind in general, Jesus indicated that its actual application nevertheless would be limited when he said: "Just as the Son of man came, not to be ministered to, but to minister and to give his soul a ransom in exchange for *many*." (Mt 20:28) Jehovah God has the right to refuse to accept a ransom for anyone he deems unworthy. Christ's ransom covers the sins an individual has because of being a child of sinful Adam, but a person can add to that by his own deliberate, willful course of sin, and he can thus die for such sin that is beyond coverage by the ransom.

Sin against the holy spirit. Jesus Christ said that one who sinned against the holy spirit would not be forgiven in the present system of things nor in that to come. (Mt 12:31, 32) A person whom God judged as having sinned against the holy spirit in the present system of things would therefore not profit by a resurrection, since his sins would never be forgiven, making resurrection useless for him. Jesus uttered judgment against Judas Iscariot in calling him "the son of destruction." The ransom would not apply to him, and his destruction already being a judicially established judgment, he would not receive a resurrection. —Joh 17:12.

To his opposers, the Jewish religious leaders, Jesus said: "How are you to flee from the judgment of Gehenna [a symbol of everlasting destruction]?" (Mt 23:33; see GEHENNA.) His words indicate that these persons, if they did not take action to turn to God before their death, would have a final adverse judgment entered against them. If so, a resurrection would accomplish nothing for them. This would also appear to be true of "the man of lawlessness."—2Th 2:3, 8; see MAN OF LAWLESSNESS.

Paul speaks of those who have known the truth, have been partakers of holy spirit, and then have fallen away, as falling into a condition in which it is impossible "to revive them again to repentance, because they impale the Son of God afresh for themselves and expose him to public shame." The ransom could no longer help them; hence they would receive no resurrection. The apostle goes on to liken such ones to a field that produces only thorns and thistles and is therefore rejected and ends up being burned. This illustrates the future before them: complete annihilation.—Heb 6:4-8.

Again, Paul says of those who "practice sin willfully after having received the accurate knowledge of the truth, [that] there is no longer any sacrifice for sins left, but there is a certain fearful expectation of judgment and there is a fiery jealousy that is going to consume those in opposition." He then illustrates: "Any man that has disregarded the law of Moses dies without compassion, upon the testimony of two or three. Of how much more severe a punishment, do you think, will the man be counted worthy who has trampled upon

the Son of God and who has esteemed as of ordinary value the blood of the covenant by which he was sanctified, and who has outraged the spirit of undeserved kindness with contempt? . . . It is a fearful thing to fall into the hands of the living God." The judgment is *more severe* in that such ones are not merely killed and buried in Sheol, as were violators of the Law of Moses. These go into Gehenna, from which there is no resurrection. —Heb 10:26-31.

Peter writes to his brothers, pointing out that they, as "the house of God," are under judgment, and he then quotes from Proverbs 11:31 (LXX) warning them of the danger of disobedience. He here implies that their present judgment could end with a judgment of everlasting destruction for them, just as Paul had written.—1Pe 4:17, 18.

The apostle Paul also tells of some who will "undergo the judicial punishment of everlasting destruction from before the Lord and from the glory of his strength, at the time he comes to be glorified in connection with his holy ones." (2Th 1:9, 10) These would therefore not survive into the Thousand Year Reign of Christ, and since their destruction is "everlasting," they would receive no resurrection.

Resurrection During 1,000 Years. A very liberal estimate of the number of persons that have ever lived on earth is 20 billion (20,000,000,000). Many students of the subject calculate that not nearly so many have lived. Not *all* of these, as it has been shown in the foregoing discussion, will receive a resurrection, but even assuming that they did, there would be no problem as to living space and food for them. The land surface of the earth at present is about 148,000,000 sq km (57,000,000 sq mi), or about 14,800,000,000 ha (36,500,000,000 acres). Even allowing half of that to be set aside for other uses, there would be more than a third of a hectare (almost 1 acre) for each person. As to earth's potential food production, a third of a hectare will actually provide much more than enough food for one person, especially when, as God has demonstrated in the case of the nation of Israel, there is abundance of food as a result of God's blessing.—1Ki 4:20; Eze 34:27.

On the question of the earth's food-producing power, the United Nations Food and Agriculture Organization maintains that, with only moderate improvements in agricultural methods, in even the developing areas the earth could easily feed up to nine times the population that scientists have estimated for the year 2000.—*Land, Food and People,* Rome, 1984, pp. 16, 17.

How, though, could the thousands of millions be

adequately cared for, in view of the fact that most of them did not in the past know God and must learn to conform to his laws for them? First, the Bible states that the kingdom of the world becomes "the kingdom of our Lord and of his Christ, and he [rules] as king forever and ever." (Re 11:15) And the Bible principle is that "when there are judgments from you [Jehovah] for the earth, righteousness is what the inhabitants of the productive land will certainly learn." (Isa 26:9) In his due time, when it is necessary to make it known to his servants, God will reveal how he purposes to take care of this work.—Am 3:7.

How would it be possible in 1,000 years to resurrect and educate the billions now in the grave?

Nevertheless, an illustration reveals what a simple, practical thing Jehovah has in mind for mankind. Not to prophesy, but merely for the purpose of illustration, let us assume that those who compose the "great crowd" of righteous persons who "come out of the great tribulation" on this system of things alive (Re 7:9, 14) number 3,000,000 (about $\frac{1}{1666}$ of earth's present population). Then if, after allowing, say, 100 years spent in their training and in 'subduing' a portion of the earth (Ge 1: 28), God purposes to bring back three percent of this number, this would mean that each newly arrived person would be looked after by 33 trained ones. Since a yearly increase of three percent, compounded, doubles the number about every 24 years, the entire 20 billion (20,000,000,000) could be resurrected before 300 years of Christ's Thousand Year Reign had elapsed, giving ample time for training and judging the resurrected ones without disrupting harmony and order on earth. Thus God, with his almighty power and wisdom, is able to bring his purpose to a glorious conclusion fully within the framework of the laws and arrangements he has made for mankind from the beginning, with the added undeserved kindness of the resurrection.—Ro 11:33-36.

RETIREMENT.
Withdrawal from one's employment or from certain aspects of it.

In assigning the Levites (not of the priestly family of Aaron) to serve at the tent of meeting under the direction of the priests, Jehovah made loving provisions for their welfare. He commanded Moses: "This is what applies to the Levites: From twenty-five years old upward he will come to enter into the company in the service of the tent of meeting. But after the age of fifty years he will

retire from the service company and serve no longer. And he must minister to his brothers in the tent of meeting in taking care of the obligation, but he must render no service." —Nu 8:23-26; 1Ch 23:3.

At Numbers chapter 4 the service organization of the Levites is described. There it is stated that they were to be registered from the ages of 30 to 50.

It was heavy manual labor to set up, take down, and transport the tent of meeting. The 96 socket pedestals of silver for the panel frames weighed a talent (c. 34 kg; 92 lb t) each; there were also four pedestals for the pillars between the Holy and Most Holy compartments, of probably the same weight, and five copper pedestals for the pillars at the tabernacle entrance. (Ex 26:19, 21, 25, 32, 37; 38:27) The 48 panel frames (4.5 m [14.6 ft] long; 67 cm [26 in.] wide) were made of acacia, a fine-grained, heavy wood, which was gold plated. (Ex 26:15-25, 29) There were gold-plated bars running lengthwise on each side and across the back of the tabernacle. (Ex 26:26-29) All these items would be heavy. Additionally, there was the considerable weight of the coverings of sealskin, ram skin, goat hair, and linen, as well as the linen screen around the courtyard, with its poles, socket pedestals, tent pins, and so forth. So the handling of the tabernacle involved real muscular work. (Ex 26:1-14; 27:9-19) Six wagons were provided for hauling these items, but the table of showbread, the golden lampstand, and the copper-covered altar of sacrifice were carried. (The priests, not the nonpriestly Levites, carried the ark of the covenant.)—Nu 7:7-9; Ex 25:10-40; 27:1-8; Nu 4:9, 10; Jos 3:15.

Another purpose of the retirement arrangement was apparently to give all the Levites the opportunity to have assignments of service at the sanctuary, because only a limited number were needed, especially during the time the tent of meeting or tabernacle was in use. There was no retirement provided for the priests, the Levites of the family of Aaron.

Evidently there was a five-year period from the ages of 25 to 30 years in which the Levite was serving in what may be termed "training." It may have been that these younger ones were not used for the heavy duties, which were reserved for those 30 years and older—full-grown men. (See AGE.) Later, after the Ark was permanently located on Mount Zion (and especially with the temple construction just ahead), the heavy work of carrying the sanctuary would no longer exist. David therefore arranged for the Levites to begin serving at the age of 20. Doubtless this was done because at the temple more would be needed to care for the greatly enlarged services there.—1Ch 23:24-27.

The Levites who retired at the age of 50 did not retire from all service. They could still serve voluntarily and "minister to [their] brothers in the tent of meeting in taking care of the obligation." (Nu 8:26) Probably they served as counselors and assisted in caring for some of the lighter work included in the obligation of the Levites, but they were spared the heavier work. And they were still teachers of the Law to the people. (De 33:8-10; 2Ch 35:3) Those of their number who lived in the cities of refuge were helpful to those taking refuge there.

The Christian Ministry. Those who become spiritual "brothers" of Jesus Christ and footstep followers of his are termed "a royal priesthood." (Heb 2:10-12; 1Pe 2:9) For these, there is no provision for retirement. The apostle Paul was active in his ministry while in prison and continued steady ministerial activity until he was put to death. (Ac 28:30, 31; 2Ti 4:6, 7) Peter was active to the end of his life. (2Pe 1:13-15) John wrote his Gospel and three canonical letters at an extremely old age, in about 98 C.E.

The "great crowd," who were seen by John after the vision of the 144,000 "sealed" ones, are said to be "rendering [God] sacred service day and night," or continually. There is therefore no retirement from God's service for any Christian.—Re 7:4, 9, 15.

RETRIBUTION. The dispensing or receiving of reward or punishment according to the just deserts of the individual or the group; that given or exacted in recompense, especially for evil.

Variants of, or words drawn from, the Hebrew root verbs *sha·lam'* and *ga·mal'* are translated "reward," "recompense," "retribution," "due treatment," "repay," "pay back," and so forth. The Greek *a·po·di'do·mi, an·ti·mi·sthi'a, mi·stha·po·do·si'a,* and related words are similarly translated.

To the Nations That Oppressed Israel. In the song Moses gave to Israel on the Plains of Moab just before his death, he described Jehovah as one who 'pays back vengeance' to His adversaries and who 'renders retribution' to those that intensely hate Him. (De 32:35, 41; Heb 10:30) The vengeance and the retribution are executed by God in complete self-control, in full harmony with his justice and never without abundant cause. For example, he punished Israel for disobedience, sometimes using pagan nations such as Assyria and Babylon as his instruments. (De 28:15-68; 2Ki

17:7-23; 2Ch 21:14-20) But, on their part, these pagan nations acted out of hatred for Jehovah and his true worship, and they went too far in exulting over Israel's defeat and in oppressing Israel. Consequently God uttered judgments of retribution upon them.—Isa 10:12; 34:1, 2, 8; Jer 51:6, 56; Ob 8-16; Zec 1:15.

Babylon in particular suffered retribution for her age-old enmity against Jehovah and his people. Downfall and complete desolation were prophesied against her. She was overthrown by Cyrus the Persian in 539 B.C.E. but continued to exist as a city for centuries, finally falling into utter desolation, never to be rebuilt. (Jer chaps 50, 51) Symbolic Babylon the Great is to suffer like retribution, being thrown down "never [to be] found again."—Re 18:2, 6, 20, 21; see BABYLON THE GREAT.

Under the Law. God's law to Israel given through Moses was one of exact retribution, although mercy was extended to the unwitting and repentant sinner. (Le 5:4-6, 17-19; 6:1-7; Nu 35:22-29) But the law of retribution applied fully to the deliberate and unrepentant violator. (Nu 15:30) In cases in which a man acted as a false witness, giving lying testimony against a fellowman before the judges, he was to receive retribution, the exact punishment that he would have caused the innocent man to receive. Jehovah said: "And your eye should not feel sorry: soul will be for soul, eye for eye, tooth for tooth, hand for hand, foot for foot."—De 19:16-21.

On the Jewish Nation in the First Century. The Jewish nation manifested a selfish viewpoint in accepting God's undeserved kindnesses and favors to them. Jehovah allowed this selfish course and attitude to bring retribution upon them. They went about trying to establish their own righteousness instead of subjecting themselves to the righteousness of God. (Ro 10:1-3) As a result, the majority of the nation stumbled over Jesus Christ and rejected him, sharing bloodguilt in connection with his death, thereby bringing destruction to their city and temple and ruin to their nation. (Mt 27:25; Da 9:26) The apostle Paul quotes from the Psalms (69:22) and applies it to them when he writes: "Also, David says: 'Let their table become for them a snare and a trap and a stumbling block and a retribution.'"—Ro 11:9.

On Disobedient Christians. The apostle Paul refers back to retributive justice under the Law in emphasizing the seriousness of Christians' obeying the Son of God: "For if the word spoken through angels proved to be firm, and every transgression and disobedient act received a retribution [literally, paying back of reward] in harmony with justice; how shall we escape if we have neglected a salvation of such greatness in that it began to be spoken through our Lord and was verified for us by those who heard him?" (Heb 2:2, 3, ftn; compare Heb 10:28-31.) The judgment of destruction upon the apostate "man of lawlessness" furnishes an example of such retribution. —2Th 2:3, 9, 10; see MAN OF LAWLESSNESS.

REU (Re'u) [Companion; Friend]. Son of Peleg and father of Serug; a link in the genealogy between Shem and Abraham. (1Ch 1:24-27) Reu, who lived 239 years (2239-2000 B.C.E.), was also an ancestor of Jesus Christ.—Ge 11:18-21; Lu 3:35.

REUBEN   (Reu'ben) [See, a Son!].

1. The firstborn of Jacob's 12 sons. His mother was Jacob's less favored wife, Leah, who named her boy Reuben, "because," to quote her, "Jehovah has looked upon my wretchedness, in that now my husband will begin to love me." (Ge 29:30-32; 35:23; 46:8; Ex 1:1, 2; 1Ch 2:1) As a result of Jehovah's continued favor on his mother, Reuben and his five full brothers (Simeon, Levi, Judah, Issachar, and Zebulun) constituted half of the original tribal heads of Israel; the other six (Joseph, Benjamin, Dan, Naphtali, Gad, and Asher) were Reuben's half brothers.—Ge 35:23-26.

Some of Reuben's good qualities displayed themselves when he persuaded his nine brothers to throw Joseph into a dry well instead of killing him, Reuben intending to return secretly and deliver Joseph out of the well. (Ge 37:18-30) More than 20 years later when these same brothers reasoned that the spy charges against them down in Egypt were due to their mistreatment of Joseph, Reuben reminded the others that he had not shared in their plot on Joseph's life. (Ge 42:9-14, 21, 22) Again, when Jacob refused to let Benjamin accompany his brothers on their second trip to Egypt, it was Reuben who offered his own two sons as surety, saying: "You may put [them] to death if I do not bring [Benjamin] back to you." —Ge 42:37.

As the firstborn son of Jacob, Reuben naturally had the rights of the firstborn son of the family. As such, he was entitled to two portions in the estate that his father Jacob left behind. At the time just before Jacob's death, when he blessed his sons, the question was, Would Reuben come into these rights of the firstborn? Also, the patriarch Jacob, as head of the family, had acted as Jehovah's priest for the whole family and had offered up sacrifices at the family altar and had led in prayer and in giving religious instruction.

As father, he had also acted as the governor of the whole family and of all its servants, its livestock, and its properties. Would these responsibilities devolve upon Reuben?

Jacob dealt with Reuben first, saying: "Reuben, you are my firstborn, my vigor and the beginning of my generative power, the excellence of dignity and the excellence of strength. With reckless license like waters, do not you excel, because you have gone up to your father's bed. At that time you profaned my lounge. He went up to it!"—Ge 49:3, 4.

Jacob recalled a disqualification for Reuben that affected his future privileges. Reuben had disgraced his father. He had committed incestuous immorality with his father's concubine, Bilhah, the maidservant of Jacob's beloved wife Rachel. This was shortly after Rachel died following her giving birth to Benjamin. The Bible record does not explain whether firstborn Reuben violated the maidservant Bilhah to prevent her from taking Rachel's place in Jacob's affection, thus becoming more favored than Reuben's mother Leah, or whether Reuben acted out of sheer lust for Bilhah. It simply says: "And it came about while Israel was tabernacling in that land that once Reuben went and lay down with Bilhah his father's concubine, and Israel got to hear of it." (Ge 35:22) The Greek *Septuagint* adds: "And it appeared evil in his sight."—Ge 35:21, *LXX*, Thomson.

Reuben was not disowned and cast out for this. It was years later, when he blessed his sons, that Jacob said to Reuben, by divine inspiration: "Do not you excel." Thus Reuben was stripped of privileges that would otherwise have been his as a firstborn son. This was because he acted with "reckless license like waters." He proved himself either unstable like waters or turbulent and headlong like waters bursting a dam or raging down a torrent valley. Reuben should have exercised self-control. He should have shown a son's respect for his father's dignity and for the honor of the two sons of Bilhah, his father's concubine.

2. The name Reuben also stands for the tribe made up of Reuben's descendants as well as for the land of their inheritance. Reuben's tribe stemmed from his four sons, Hanoch, Pallu, Hezron, and Carmi, the family heads of the Reubenites.—Ge 46:8, 9; Ex 6:14; 1Ch 5:3.

A year after the Exodus from Egypt, Elizur, the son of Shedeur, was selected as chieftain to represent the entire tribe of Reuben. (Nu 1:1, 4, 5; 10:18) The tribe of Reuben was consistently one of the less numerous among the 12. A census taken in the second year of the wilderness experience enumerated 46,500 Reubenites fit for military service, 20 years old and upward. About 39 years later this force, now 43,730, was somewhat less.—Nu 1:2, 3, 20, 21; 26:5-7.

In the camp of Israel the Reubenites, flanked by the descendants of Simeon and Gad, were situated on the S side of the tabernacle. When on the march this three-tribe division headed by Reuben followed the three-tribe division of Judah, Issachar, and Zebulun. (Nu 2:10-16; 10:14-20) This was also the order in which the tribes made their presentation offerings on the day the tabernacle was inaugurated.—Nu 7:1, 2, 10-47.

When Korah the Levite rebelled against Moses, three Reubenites—On, the son of Peleth, along with Dathan and Abiram, sons of Eliab—joined in the revolt, charging Moses with trying "to play the prince" over them and with failing to bring them into "a land flowing with milk and honey." Nemuel, the brother of Dathan and Abiram, apparently took no part in the revolt. (Nu 16:1, 12-14; 26:8, 9) Jehovah showed that the revolt was actually disrespect against him; he caused the earth to open up and swallow the rebels and their families alive, together with all their belongings.—Nu 16:23-33; De 11:6; see ABIRAM No. 1.

Territory Assignments. Shortly before Israel entered the Promised Land the tribes of Reuben and Gad requested that they be given territory E of the Jordan. The land had been acquired through the victory over the two kings Sihon and Og. They reasoned that it was ideal for them because they had large flocks and herds. Moses granted this request to them (and half the tribe of Manasseh) on one condition, that the fighting forces of these tribes also cross over the Jordan and assist the other tribes in the conquest of Canaan, a condition that the two and a half tribes willingly met.—Nu 32:1-38; Jos 1:12-18; 4:12, 13; 12:6; 13:8-10.

Reuben's territorial inheritance was thus settled even before the Israelites crossed the Jordan, Moses himself giving the southern portion of Sihon's conquered kingdom to this tribe. It extended from the torrent valley of Arnon, a natural boundary that separated this territory from Moab on the S, to just N of the Dead Sea; the land N of Reuben was given to the Gadites. (Nu 34:13-15; De 3:12, 16; 29:8; Jos 13:15-23; 18:7) The territory of the Ammonites formed the E boundary, with the Dead Sea and Jordan River on the west. (Jos 15:1, 6; 18:11, 17) One of the six cities of refuge, Bezer, lay in Reuben's territory. This and other Reubenite cities were set aside for the use of the Levites.—De 4:41-43; Jos 20:8; 21:7, 36; 1Ch 6:63, 78, 79.

Moses directed that, once the Israelites reached the heart of Canaan, the tribe of Reuben, together with Gad, Asher, Zebulun, Dan, and Naphtali, was to be represented on Mount Ebal for the reading of the maledictions and curses, with the rest of the tribes represented on Mount Gerizim for the pronouncing of blessings. (De 27:11-13) After Moses made these arrangements he blessed Reuben along with the rest of the tribes. To the Reubenites, Moses said: "Let Reuben live and not die off, and let his men not become few."—De 33:1, 6.

At the end of Joshua's campaign in Canaan he called together the armed forces of Reuben, Gad, and half of the tribe of Manasseh and, after commending them on keeping their promises to Moses, sent them home with his blessing. (Jos 22:1-8) When they reached the Jordan, they erected a huge altar on the western bank, which action, being at first misinterpreted by the other tribes, nearly resulted in a rupture of relations, even civil war. But when it was explained that the altar was not for sacrifices, but was for a witness of faithfulness between the tribes on both sides of the Jordan, the altar was given a name, likely "Witness," for, as they said, "It is a witness between us that Jehovah is the true God."—Jos 22:9-34.

Later History. Many years later, when Barak and Deborah sang a great victory song, they recalled that the Reubenites had failed to join them in the battle against Sisera. As a result, "among the divisions of Reuben great were the searchings of the heart." (Jg 5:15, 16) In the days of Saul, the Reubenites joined forces with their neighbors and gained a great victory over the Hagrites and their allies, "for it was to God that they called for aid in the war, and he let himself be entreated in their favor because they trusted in him." (1Ch 5:10, 18-22) The Reubenites then shared in the occupation of Hagrite territory apparently down to the Assyrian subjugation of Israel in the eighth century B.C.E., when the Reubenites were among the first taken into exile. (1Ch 5:6, 22b, 26) Individual Reubenites, and the tribe as a whole, are mentioned in connection with David's history, both before and after he became king.—1Ch 11:26, 42; 12:37, 38; 26:32; 27:16.

In Prophecy. In the symbolic books of Ezekiel and Revelation, Reuben is mentioned in significant order along with the other tribes. For example, in vision Ezekiel saw in the middle of the tribes "the holy contribution" of land containing Jehovah's temple, the city called Jehovah-Shammah, meaning "Jehovah Himself Is There," and territory belonging to the priests, Levites, and the chieftain. Immediately adjacent to this holy strip on the north was Judah, with Reuben bordering next to Judah on the north. (Eze 48:6-22, 35) Also, the gate named Reuben on the N side of the holy city, Jehovah-Shammah, was next to that named Judah. (Eze 48:31) Similarly, in John's vision of the sealing of the 12 tribes of spiritual Israel, Reuben is named second, after the tribe of Judah.—Re 7:4, 5.

REUEL (Reu′el) [Companion (Friend) of God].

1. Second-named son of Esau, by Ishmael's daughter Basemath. Reuel's own four sons became Edomite sheiks.—Ge 36:2-4, 10, 13, 17; 1Ch 1:35, 37.

2. Moses' father-in-law, a priest of Midian. (Ex 2:16-21; Nu 10:29) Elsewhere called Jethro.—See JETHRO.

3. A Gadite whose son Eliasaph was tribal chieftain during the wilderness march. (Nu 2:14) The name is spelled Deuel in its other occurrences. —See DEUEL.

4. Ancestor of a Benjamite who lived in Jerusalem after the Babylonian exile.—1Ch 9:3, 7, 8.

REUMAH (Reu′mah). Concubine of Abraham's brother Nahor. She gave birth to four sons. —Ge 22:20, 24.

REVELATION. The Greek word (a·po·ka′ly·psis) thus translated denotes "an uncovering" or "a disclosure" and is often used regarding revelations of spiritual matters or of God's will and purposes. (Lu 2:32; 1Co 14:6, 26; 2Co 12:1, 7; Ga 1:12; 2:2; Eph 1:17; Re 1:1; Int) The operation of God's spirit makes such revelations possible. Concerning the revelation of "the sacred secret," the apostle Paul wrote: "In other generations this secret was not made known to the sons of men as it has now been revealed to his holy apostles and prophets by spirit, namely, that people of the nations should be joint heirs and fellow members of the body and partakers with us of the promise in union with Christ Jesus through the good news."—Eph 3:1-6; Ro 16:25.

The book of Acts forcefully confirms that this revelation of the sacred secret resulted from the operation of God's spirit. It had been at the spirit's direction that Peter, Paul, and Barnabas preached to non-Jews. Believing non-Jews, "people of the nations," received holy spirit while in an uncircumcised state, thereby becoming a people for God's name. (Ac 10:9-48; 13:2-4) The prophet Amos, under inspiration, had foretold this and, in the first century C.E., the fulfillment of his prophecy became evident through the operation of God's spirit.—Ac 15:7-20; compare Am 9:11, 12, LXX.

The Bible also speaks of "the revealing of God's righteous judgment" (Ro 2:5), "the revealing of the sons of God" (Ro 8:19), and "the revelation of Jesus Christ" and "of his glory." (1Pe 1:13; 4:13) A consideration of the context and related texts aids in determining when such revealings, or revelations, occur. In each case, the revealing, or revelation, is a time for causing righteous persons to enter into particular rewards and blessings or for bringing destruction upon wicked ones.

Of the Sons of God. In his letter to the Romans, the apostle Paul identified God's "sons" as those having received a spirit of adoption. Being joint heirs with Christ, these sons of God will be glorified. (Ro 8:14-18) The Lord Jesus Christ will refashion their humiliated body to conform to his glorious body (Php 3:20, 21), and they will reign with him as kings. (2Ti 2:12) So "the revealing of the sons of God" points to the time when it will become evident that they have indeed been glorified and are reigning with Christ Jesus. The glory that will be revealed in them will be so grand that it will make all their former suffering on earth seem like nothing. (Ro 8:18, 19) This revealing is attended by grand blessings, for the apostle Paul writes: "The creation itself also will be set free from enslavement to corruption and have the glorious freedom of the children of God."—Ro 8:21.

Of God's Righteous Judgment. At Romans 2:5 "the revealing of God's righteous judgment" is associated with 'the day of God's wrath.' Therefore, God's righteous judgment is revealed when 'he renders to each one according to his works,' everlasting life to those enduring in work that is fine and destruction to those obeying unrighteousness.—Ro 2:6-8.

Of Jesus Christ. "The revelation of Jesus Christ" and "of his glory" is a time for rewarding his faithful followers and executing vengeance upon the ungodly. He is thus revealed as a glorious King, empowered to reward and to punish. The Scriptures show that spirit-anointed Christians who faithfully endured suffering would be "overjoyed" during the revelation of Christ's glory. (1Pe 4:13) The tested quality of their faith would be found a cause for praise and glory and honor at the revelation of Jesus Christ, and these Christians would become recipients of undeserved kindness. (1Pe 1:7, 13) On the other hand, those who do not know God and who do not obey the good news about the Lord Jesus would be destroyed everlastingly, thereby bringing relief to those who have suffered tribulation at their hands.—2Th 1:6-10.

REVELATION TO JOHN.

The last book of the Bible as arranged in most translations, though not the last written. It is also called the Apocalypse of John the Apostle.

Writer, and When and Where Written. The apostle John names himself as the writer of the book and designates the place of writing as the island of Patmos, where John was in exile at the time for being a preacher of God's Word and a witness of Jesus Christ. (Re 1:1, 9) The time of writing was possibly about 96 C.E.

Style and Appropriateness. The book is in letter form, detailing a series of visions set forth in a proper order in regular progression, finally coming to the climactic vision. It supplies a fitting conclusion to the entire Bible.

The book seems to proceed on the basis of series of sevens. Seven seals open into the blowing of seven trumpets, then into seven plagues. There are seven lampstands, seven stars, seven thunders, and many other things by sevens, evidently because the number seven here represents completeness, and the book deals with the completion of the sacred secret of God.—Re 10:7; see SACRED SECRET.

Author and Channel. Jehovah God the Almighty is the book's author, and the channel of information is Jesus Christ, who sent it to John and presented it to him by means of his angel. (Re 1:1) The spirit of God is represented as being sevenfold, hence acting in its fullest capacity to convey this disclosure. John was given divine command to write.—1:4, 11.

Purpose. While some of the things seen by John in the vision may seem terrifying—the beasts, the woes, the plagues—the book was written, not to terrify, but to comfort and encourage those who read it with faith. It can lead the reader to blessings. In fact, the writer of the book states at the outset: "Happy ["blessed," *KJ*] is he who reads aloud and those who hear the words of this prophecy, and who observe the things written in it." (Re 1:3) John also says that the book is for the purpose of showing God's slaves the things that "must shortly take place."—1:1, 2.

Bears Witness to Jesus. In Revelation 19:10, the angel tells John: "The bearing witness to Jesus is what inspires prophesying [literally, "is the spirit of the prophecy"]." That is, the intent and purpose of all prophecy is to point to Jesus Christ. This does not mean that Jehovah God is bypassed or ignored. Earlier in verse 10 the angel had told John, who fell down before him: "Worship God," and the apostle Paul had said that "God exalted [Christ] to a superior position and kindly gave him the name that is above every other name, so that in the name of Jesus every knee should bend of those in heaven and those on earth and those under the ground, and every tongue should openly acknowledge that Jesus Christ is Lord *to the glory of God the Father.*" Magnifying Jesus Christ, therefore, and getting acquainted with the knowledge of him result in a better knowledge of God and His purposes, thereby giving the glory to God above all.—Php 2:9-11; see PROPHECY.

The reason why prophecy bears witness to Jesus is that Jesus is the one through whom God accomplishes his purposes in sanctifying his name, destroying wickedness, and blessing mankind. "Carefully concealed in him [Christ] are all the treasures of wisdom and of knowledge." (Col 2:3) He is the Seed of promise, the One in whom the sacred secret is revealed. From the very beginning of God's dealings with men following Adam's rebellion, God has caused Christ to be foretold and foreshadowed and has pointed men to the Kingdom of God in the hands of his Son.—Ge 3:15; 22:18; Ga 3:16; 2Sa 7:12-16; Ps 2:6-12; 110:1-7; Eze 21:27; Acts 2:29, 36; 3:19-26; 1Ti 3:16.

In simple language, what is the meaning of "Revelation"?

The opening chapter of the book concluding the Bible introduces us to the One over all, the Originator of the Revelation message, Jehovah God the Almighty, "the Alpha and the Omega." It gives a vision of the Channel of the communication, Jesus Christ, showing him as having died but now being alive, in great power in heaven. The sharers with him in his tribulation and in the Kingdom are next brought into view, and Christ's interest in them and loving-kindness toward them are displayed in his messages to "the angels" of the seven congregations.—Re 1-3.

Then by the spirit of inspiration John is ushered into the heavens to begin seeing "the things that must take place." He is given a vision of the throne of God and its surroundings, and he describes the One sitting upon it as glorious, supreme, throning in perfect sereneness and composure.—Re 4.

The glorious position of "the Lamb" of God, Jesus Christ, is portrayed as that of the one second only to Jehovah God, the only one in heaven and earth qualified to approach God to open up the revelation of God's purpose. Attention is given to a warrior-king (apparently also Jesus) riding forth "conquering and to complete his conquest." The result to earth, especially to God's enemies, when this king begins his ride is shown and so is God's purpose to avenge the blood of his people upon his enemies.—Re 5, 6.

How God views his servants on earth who have been chosen by him to share in the heavenly Kingdom is shown in his holding up destructive action until these servants are 'sealed in their foreheads.' The full number of sealed ones is revealed to be 144,000. Others not sealed, and unlimited as to number, who become servants of God and escape the destructiveness of "the great tribulation" are then shown. The judgments of God against various sections of his enemies on earth, as well as the fight that these enemies wage against his people, are related. This leads up to the efforts of the archenemy, the dragon Satan the Devil, to thwart God's purpose to bring forth the "son, a male, who is to shepherd all the nations with an iron rod." Next, wild beasts are seen, symbolizing instrumentalities that this archenemy uses to fight the remaining ones of the seed of the woman and to prevent the completion of the sealing work.—Re 7-13; see BEASTS, SYMBOLIC.

All these attempts of Satan utterly fail. The 144,000 are seen victorious, standing with the Lamb upon Mount Zion, displaying the name of the Father and of the Lamb on their foreheads, and singing as if a new song before the heavenly ones. After these and a "great crowd" of earthly associates are all gathered in "the harvest of the earth," the time has arrived for the great "vine of the earth" to be trodden out in the winepress. —Re 14.

With another symbolism, God's final judgments are portrayed. Seven angels are provided with seven bowls of God's anger. They go forth to carry out this final work. One of the chief foes of God and of the "bride" of Christ comes in for attention, namely, "Babylon the Great, the mother of the harlots," "the great city that has a kingdom over the kings of the earth." Her alliance with the seven-headed beast collapses, the beast becoming enraged with her, eating her flesh, and burning her with fire. The mourning of those who made gain by their dealings with her is great, but heaven rejoices.—Re 15-18.

Babylon the Great, as "the mother of the harlots," would logically make every attempt to seduce the "bride" of Christ to become unfaithful to her promised husband (2Co 11:2, 3; Eph 5:25-27) and thereby make her another harlot. Hence, the heavenly rejoicing is accentuated because Babylon the Great's corrupting efforts have been frustrated. The great harlot is now out of the way, and the bride has gained the victory. She has prepared herself for her espoused One. Therefore it is time for the Lamb's marriage to take place. All those invited to the marriage rejoice. Jehovah now begins a new epoch in his reign, the great harlot having disappeared as a rival to pure worship. —Re 19:1-10.

But God's other enemies must come in for execution of judgment. The Bridegroom goes forth to complete his conquest, to rid the earth of all foes, political and otherwise. The destruction is thorough. Finally, the Devil, having experienced the defeat of all of his agents and instruments, is himself bound for the thousand years of Christ's reign. The vision passes over this Millennial Reign for the moment to detail a judgment that comes at the end of the thousand years; the Devil is temporarily loosed, then, together with all those joining his attack on "the camp of the holy ones and the beloved city," he is completely annihilated.—Re 19:11–20:10.

Turning back to events during the thousand years, the vision depicts the resurrection and judgment that take place under the rule of Christ and his bride, the New Jerusalem. The beauty and grandeur of this heavenly "city" is described, with the healing, life-giving benefits it brings to mankind.—Re 20:11–22:5.

In conclusion, Jehovah God speaks of 'coming quickly with reward according to each one's work.' As "the faithful and true witness," Jesus bears testimony to the completion of the sacred secret concerning the kingdom, saying: "I am the root and the offspring of David, and the bright morning star." He is David's permanent heir, the eternal one in the Kingdom covenant and the one foretold at Numbers 24:17. All efforts by Satan, the wild beast, and Babylon the Great (Re 12:1-10; 17:3-14) have therefore been unable to prevent this "star" from rising out of the house of David to sit down on the throne in the heavens forever. —Re 22:6-16.

The spirit, the active force of God, along with "the bride," extend the invitation to all hearing to take of life's water free. With a final warning not to add to or take from the words of the prophecy, and a declaration of the nearness of his coming, Jesus closes the revelation; and John responds, "Amen! Come, Lord Jesus."—Re 22:17-21.

The book of Revelation is of great importance in that it provides spiritual strength and insight for God's people. It highlights God's interest in the congregations of his people and the close and loving care that Jesus Christ exercises toward them as the Fine Shepherd. Jesus knows exactly

HIGHLIGHTS OF REVELATION

A disclosure of God's view of conditions as well as a foreview of what he permits and what he will accomplish through Christ during "the Lord's day"

A series of visions recorded by the apostle John in about 96 C.E.

The glorified Christ gives loving counsel to fellow Kingdom heirs (1:1–3:22)

The Ephesus congregation has endured but has left its first love

The spiritually rich Smyrna congregation is encouraged to remain faithful in the face of tribulation

The Pergamum congregation has held fast to Christ's name under persecution but has tolerated sectarianism

The Thyatira congregation has a record of increased activity, but it has tolerated a Jezebel influence

The Sardis congregation is dead spiritually; it must wake up

The Philadelphia congregation, which has kept Christ's word, is urged to keep holding fast what it has

The Laodicea congregation is lukewarm; let it obtain from Christ what is needed for spiritual healing

A vision of Jehovah's heavenly presence (4:1–5:14)

Jehovah is seen in awesome splendor on his throne, surrounded by 24 elders and four living creatures; he holds a scroll sealed with seven seals

The Lamb is declared worthy to take the scroll and open it

The Lamb opens six seals of the scroll (6:1–17)

As he opens the first seal, a rider on a white horse receives a crown and goes forth conquering and to complete his conquest

The opening of the next three seals introduces three more horsemen, bringing war, famine, and death to mankind

The fifth seal is opened; those martyred for Christ cry for their blood to be avenged; each is given a white robe

At the opening of the sixth seal, a great earthquake heralds the day of the wrath of God and of the Lamb

The four winds of the earth are held back (7:1–17)

John hears that the four winds will be held back until the slaves of God are sealed; the number of those sealed is 144,000

Then, John sees a great, unnumbered crowd out of all nations; these come out of the great tribulation

The seventh seal is opened (8:1–11:14)

There is a half-hour silence; fire from the altar is hurled to the earth; seven angels prepare to blow trumpets

The first four trumpet blasts herald plagues on the earth, the sea, the freshwater sources, as well as on the sun, moon, and stars

The fifth trumpet calls forth a plague of locusts, and the sixth unleashes a terrifying cavalry attack

John eats a little scroll and learns he must prophesy some more

He measures the sanctuary; two witnesses prophecy in sackcloth, are killed, and are raised again

The seventh trumpet: the Kingdom is born (11:15–12:17)

The seventh trumpet sounds and the Kingdom of Jehovah and the authority of his Christ are announced

A woman gives birth to a male child in heaven

The dragon tries to devour the child; there is war in heaven; Michael casts the dragon and its angels down to earth

The dragon wages war on the remnant of the woman's seed

The wild beast from the sea (13:1–18)

A wild beast with seven heads and ten horns comes out of the sea

The dragon gives the beast its authority, and a beast with two horns like a lamb makes an image to it; many are forced to worship the wild beast and accept its mark

Jehovah's faithful servants in action (14:1–20)

The 144,000 on Mount Zion sing a new song

Angels flying in midheaven declare vital messages

Someone like a son of man reaps the harvest of the earth

An angel treads the winepress of God, with much bloodshed

Jehovah, from his heavenly sanctuary, commands seven angels to pour out the seven bowls of his anger (15:1–16:21)

The first six bowls are poured out into the earth, the sea, and freshwater sources, upon the sun, the throne of the wild beast, and the Euphrates

God's servants must stay awake, as demonic propaganda gathers human kings to Har–Magedon

The seventh bowl is poured out upon the air with devastating results

Visions of the end of Babylon the Great (17:1–18:24)

Babylon the Great, drunk with the blood of the holy ones, sits on a scarlet beast having seven heads and ten horns; the ten horns turn on her and devastate her

Her fall is announced; God's people must get out of her

Her final destruction is mourned by many on earth

The marriage of the Lamb (19:1–10)

Heavenly voices praise Jah for the destruction of Babylon

A thunderous chorus of praise heralds the marriage of the Lamb

King of kings triumphant over the nations (19: 11-21)

The Word of God goes to war against the nations; the wild beast and the false prophet are hurled into the lake of fire; all of God's enemies are killed off; animals eat their fleshy parts

Satan abyssed; Christ rules for 1,000 years (20: 1–21:8)

Satan is abyssed for 1,000 years

Jesus' fellow rulers judge with him for 1,000 years, after which, Satan is released; he sets out to mislead mankind again, but finally he and all who follow him are destroyed

All those in death, Hades, and the sea are raised and judged before the One seated on the great white throne; death and Hades are cast into the lake of fire

John sees a new heaven and a new earth

The New Jerusalem (21:9–22:21)

The glorious New Jerusalem comes down from heaven, illuminating the nations; a river of water of life flows through it, with trees for healing on each bank

Revelation closes with final messages from Jehovah and Jesus; the spirit and the bride invite anyone thirsting to take life's water free

what conditions prevail and what must be done. This is especially manifest in the first three chapters of the book.

Some persons view Revelation as being so highly symbolic that it cannot be understood, or they view it as being impractical. But Jehovah God wants his people to understand, and he caused the Bible to be written to be understood and to provide guidance for them. The key to understanding Revelation is the same as the key to understanding other parts of the Bible. The apostle Paul points to that key. After explaining that God reveals the hidden wisdom through his spirit, Paul says: "These things we also speak, not with words taught by human wisdom, but with those taught by the spirit, as we combine spiritual matters with spiritual words." (1Co 2:8-13) If we search the Scriptures (and in some cases the customs and practices of those days), we find in them many of the things used as symbolisms in Revelation. By comparing these Scripture texts, we can often understand what the Revelation symbol means. It should be noted, however, that a term or expression may refer to or symbolize different things, according to the context in which it appears.

REVELRY. The Greek word *ko'mos*, translated "revelry," occurs three times in the Christian Greek Scriptures and always in a bad or unfavorable sense. Joseph Thayer's *Greek-English Lexicon of the New Testament* points out that in ancient Greek writings it applied to "a nocturnal and riotous procession of half-drunken and frolicsome fellows who after supper parade through the streets with torches and music in honor of Bacchus or some other deity [or a victor in the games], and sing and play before the houses of their male and female friends." (1889, p. 367) Such licentious and intemperate conduct, with street processions that were similar to modern carnival celebrations in certain lands, were common in Greek cities of the apostles' time. So warning counsel on this was appropriate and beneficial for true worshipers.

Revelries are definitely not for Christians; they are condemned by God's Word. Before they became Christians, some of those to whom Peter wrote his letter, residents in Greek-influenced provinces in Asia Minor (1Pe 1:1), "proceeded in deeds of loose conduct, lusts, excesses with wine, *revelries,* drinking matches, and illegal idolatries." But upon becoming Christians, they ceased such things. (1Pe 4:3, 4) With its gross sensuality and dissolution, a revelry was a 'work belonging to darkness' in which Christians would not walk. —Ro 13:12-14.

The Bible does not rule out joy and merriment. Man is told to rejoice in his Creator, the husband to rejoice in his wife, the laborer in the work of his hands, and the farmer in the fruit of his toil. (Ps 32:11; Pr 5:18; Ec 3:22; De 26:10, 11) Food and drink can accompany and contribute to rejoicing (Ec 9:7; Ps 104:15), yet moderation should prevail. (Pr 23:20; 1Ti 3:2, 11; 1Co 10:31) Carrying merrymaking to the point of intoxication, along with scenes of disorder and sensuality, is revelry. Paul included revelries among "the works of the flesh," the practicers of which would "not inherit God's kingdom."—Ga 5:19-21.

REVILING. Subjecting a person to insulting speech, heaping abuse upon him.

For Israelites to revile or call down evil upon their parents was an offense punishable by death. (Ex 21:17; Mt 15:4; Mr 7:10) Like verbal abuse, physical abuse of parents originated from the same evil disposition and, therefore, carried the same penalty. (Ex 21:15) Since parents were Jehovah's representatives in relation to their children, a son who reviled his parents was, in effect, reviling God.—Compare Ex 20:12.

Due respect was also to be shown to those who were rulers in Israel. That is why the apostle Paul, although having been treated unjustly, apologized for having unknowingly addressed the high priest with words that were regarded by others as abusive.—Ex 22:28; Ac 23:1-5.

Deliberate reviling had no place among first-century Christians. (1Co 6:9, 10; 1Pe 3:8, 9) One guilty of habitually and intentionally vilifying others was to be expelled from the congregation.—1Co 5:11-13.

Being seemingly insignificant and unpopular in the world on account of their activity and message, followers of Jesus Christ were often the objects of reviling. (Compare Joh 9:28, 29; 17:14; 1Co 1:18; 4:11-13.) But they were not to retaliate by reviling opposers. In this respect Christ Jesus had set the example for them. (1Pe 2:21, 23) Accused of being a man given to wine, a glutton, an agent of the Devil, a Sabbath breaker, and a blasphemer of God, Christ Jesus did not retaliate by reviling his accusers. (Mt 11:19; 26:65; Lu 11:15; Joh 9:16) When false charges were leveled against him in the presence of Pilate, Jesus remained silent. (Mt 27:12-14) A Christian's imitating the example of Jesus could have a good effect on some opposers, causing them to recognize that their abusive words were without any basis. This realization could even lead them to become glorifiers of God.—Compare Ro 12:17-21; 1Pe 2:12.

Christians had to exercise care that they conducted themselves in a fine manner so as not to give needless occasion for opposers to revile. This is a point the apostle Paul made in connection with younger widows in the congregation. Since they were prone to gossip and meddle in other people's affairs, he encouraged them to marry and become occupied with raising children and managing a household. Being busy wives, they would not be giving inducement for any opposer to revile Christians as gossipers and meddlers in other people's affairs.—1Ti 5:13, 14.

Some who did not accompany Jesus Christ when he was on earth showed by their actions that they were 'on his side' and would not quickly be joining opposers in reviling him. This was the situation with a certain man who expelled demons on the basis of Jesus' name, evidently having been empowered by God to do so. John and others concluded that this man should be stopped, as he was not accompanying them. But Jesus said: "Do not try to prevent him, for there is no one that will do a powerful work on the basis of my name that will quickly be able to revile [literally, speak badly of] me." (Mr 9:38-40) At the time Jesus made this statement the Jewish congregation still had divine recognition and the establishment of the Christian congregation was yet future. (Compare Mt 16:18; 18:15-17.) Also, Jesus did not require that all believers follow him bodily. (Mr 5:18-20) There-

fore, the performance of powerful works by a Jew, one of God's covenant people, on the basis of Jesus' name would have been a proof that this man had divine favor. However, as soon as the Christian congregation was established, individuals desiring God's favor had to be associated with it as faithful followers of Jesus Christ. (Compare Ac 2:40, 41.) The mere performance of powerful works on the basis of Jesus' name would no longer be an evidence of a person's being on the side of Jesus Christ, nor would it guarantee that such a one would not be guilty of reviling God's Son.—Mt 7:21-23; see ABUSIVE SPEECH; BLASPHEMY.

REZEPH (Re′zeph). A place cited in Sennacherib's message to King Hezekiah boasting that Assyrian kings had ruined various "nations." (2Ki 19:8-12; Isa 37:12) Rezeph's exact location is not known, several places having had this name. One such site, thought by some to have been part of an ancient district, is identified with modern Rusa′feh, located W of the Euphrates about 145 km (90 mi) S of modern Haran. It is thus in the vicinity of the suggested site of Gozan, with which Rezeph is mentioned.

REZIN (Re′zin).

1. King of Syria who reigned in Damascus during parts of the reigns of King Jotham (777-762 B.C.E.) of Judah and his son King Ahaz (whose reign ended in 746 B.C.E.).

Evidently near the end of Jotham's reign, Rezin joined with Pekah the king of Israel in warring against Judah. (2Ki 15:36-38) During the warfare, which continued into the reign of Ahaz, the Syrians, evidently under Rezin, captured many Judeans and took them to Damascus. (2Ch 28:5) Also, Rezin wrested from Judah the city of Elath on the Gulf of ′Aqaba, clearing out the Jews and restoring the city to the Edomites. (2Ki 16:6) The combined Syro-Israelite forces laid siege to Jerusalem, intending to make "the son of Tabeel" its king, but they were unable to capture the city. (2Ki 15:5; Isa 7:1, 6) The situation greatly frightened Ahaz, despite Isaiah's assurance that Rezin of Syria and Pekah of Israel need cause no fear. (Isa 7:3-12; 8:6, 7) Ahaz turned to Assyria for help, bribing Tiglath-pileser III to attack Syria.—2Ki 16:7, 8; 2Ch 28:16, 20.

Tiglath-pileser III warred against Damascus, capturing it and putting Rezin to death. Syria thus came under Assyrian domination.—2Ki 16:9.

2. The father of a certain family of Nethinim, some of whom returned to Jerusalem from Babylon in 537 B.C.E.—Ezr 2:1, 43, 48; Ne 7:6, 46, 50.

REZON (Re'zon) [probably, High Official]. A resister of King Solomon. This son of Eliada had been in the service of Hadadezer the king of Zobah, from whom David took over Damascus. Rezon abandoned Hadadezer, however, and organized a marauder band. At some undisclosed time Rezon himself took up reigning over Syria from Damascus, and especially from the time of Solomon's apostasy to the end of his reign, Rezon gave vent to his abhorrence of Israel. (1Ki 11:23-25; 1Ch 18:3-6) If, as some suggest, he was the person called Hezion at 1 Kings 15:18, this would make him founder of the Syrian dynasty that had extensive dealings with Israel.

RHEGIUM (Rhe'gi·um). A city in southern Italy today called Reggio or Reggio di Calabria. The ship on which the apostle Paul was traveling as a prisoner made a stop at Rhegium when he was on his way to appear before Caesar in Rome, about the year 59 C.E.

Rhegium is situated on the Strait of Messina, which separates Italy and Sicily. Just N of Rhegium the ship on which Paul was traveling would have had to navigate past the promontory Scylla on the Italian side of the strait and the whirlpool Charybdis on the Sicilian side, both considered hazardous by ancient mariners. A day after their arrival at Rhegium a S wind sprang up and this moved them safely through the strait and NNW to Puteoli.—Ac 28:13.

RHESA (Rhe'sa). Son, that is, descendant, of Zerubbabel and ancestor of Jesus Christ.—Lu 3:23, 27.

RHODA (Rho'da) [possibly, Rose]. A member of the Christian congregation in Jerusalem at the time of the apostle Peter's miraculous release from prison in about 44 C.E. Rhoda was a servant girl, presumably in the household of Mark's mother Mary. At least she was one of those who spent the night there praying for Peter. Answering a knock at the door of the gateway, and recognizing Peter's voice, Rhoda was so overcome with joy that, instead of letting him in, she ran back inside to tell the others. "You are mad," they said, but she continued insisting. All the while Peter kept knocking until they finally let him in.—Ac 12:3, 5, 12-16.

RHODES [Rose]. An island off the SW corner of Turkey and one of the largest in the Aegean Sea, measuring about 75 km long by 35 km wide (47 by 22 mi). Its capital city also is called Rhodes. A ship on which Paul was traveling came from Cos to Rhodes near the close of the apostle's third missionary journey in about 56 C.E.—Ac 21:1.

Rhodes, because of its strategic location and good harbors, was prominent as a trading center early in its history. However, it appears that in time the city of Rhodes itself became more noted as a cultural center.

The Colossus of Rhodes, a bronze statue of the sun-god Helios, stood near the harbor of the city of Rhodes. Considered one of the "seven wonders" of the ancient world, it is said to have been some 70 cubits (31 m; 102 ft) high. Though it was not standing in Paul's day, having been toppled by an earthquake in the third century B.C.E., enormous fragments of the Colossus did exist well into the Common Era. The idea that the statue straddled the entrance to the harbor with ships sailing between its legs cannot be verified.

RIB. In the human body there are 24 of these long, slender, curved bones enclosing the chest cavity. Arranged in 12 pairs, they form a cage protecting the heart and lungs. Blood is produced in the marrow of the rib bones.

In the creation of woman, God did not make her separate and distinct from man by forming her from the dust of the ground, as he had done in the creation of Adam. He took a rib from Adam's side, and from it He built for Adam a perfect counterpart, the woman Eve. (Ge 2:21, 22) Adam, nevertheless, remained a perfect man, now united as 'bone of bone and flesh of flesh' with his wife. (Ge 2:23; De 32:4) Moreover, this did not disturb the reproductive cells of Adam so as to affect his children, boys or girls, in their rib structure. The human male and female both have 24 ribs.

It is of interest to note that a rib that has been removed will grow again, replacing itself, as long as the periosteum (the membrane of connective tissue that covers the bone) is allowed to remain. Whether Jehovah God followed this procedure or not the record does not state; however, as man's Creator, God was certainly aware of this unusual quality of the rib bones.

The word "rib" is found again in the Bible in Daniel's account of a vision that God gave to him during the rule of King Belshazzar of Babylon. A first beast representing the dynastic line of rulers of Babylon appeared, followed by a beast like a bear, which pictured the next 'king,' or line of world rulers, namely, those of Medo-Persia. This bearlike beast had three ribs in its mouth. These ribs may denote that the 'king' symbolized by the bear pushed its conquests in three directions, as Medo-Persia did. Since the number three is used in the Scriptures as a symbol of intensity or emphasis, the three ribs may also emphasize the greed of this symbolic bear for territorial conquests.—Da 7:5, 17; see BEASTS, SYMBOLIC.

RIBAI (Ri'bai) [possibly a shortened form of Jeribai, meaning "May He Contend; He Has Conducted [Our] Legal Case"]. A Benjamite of Gibeah whose son Ittai (Ithai) was one of David's "thirty" famous warriors.—2Sa 23:24, 29; 1Ch 11:31.

RIBLAH (Rib'lah).

1. An unidentified location on the eastern boundary of "the land of Canaan."—Nu 34:2, 10, 11.

2. A town N of Israel "in the land of Hamath." (Jer 52:9) The site generally accepted for Riblah is that of the ruins near modern Ribleh on the E bank of the Orontes River, about 60 km (37 mi) NE of Baalbek, in the valley between the Lebanon and Anti-Lebanon mountains. Evidently Pharaoh Nechoh encamped at Riblah after defeating King Josiah, about 629 B.C.E. He was at that time marching N to fight against the Babylonians, who by then dominated Assyria. Jehoahaz succeeded Josiah, but after three months Nechoh replaced Jehoahaz with Eliakim (Jehoiakim). Nechoh had Jehoahaz brought to him at Riblah before taking this king captive to Egypt. (2Ki 23:29-34) Riblah was a strategic location for a military camp. It dominated a N-S trade and military route between Egypt and the Euphrates. Water was readily available, and food and fuel could be obtained from the surrounding valley and forests.

The same military advantages served the Babylonians at a later time. At some point after beginning the siege of Jerusalem in late 609 B.C.E., Nebuchadnezzar apparently set up a camp at Riblah to direct military operations from there. This put him in position to strike Damascus or to return speedily to Babylon if necessary. When Zedekiah was captured in 607 B.C.E., he was brought to Nebuchadnezzar at Riblah, as were certain other important men of the city shortly thereafter.—2Ki 25:1, 5-7, 18-21; Jer 39:5; 52:9-11, 26, 27.

Many scholars conclude that the "Diblah" at Ezekiel 6:14 should read "Riblah," referring to the Riblah on the Orontes.—See DIBLAH.

RICHES.   Abundance of material possessions; also spiritual qualities, privileges of service, and divine approval.

Throughout the Scriptures the emphasis is placed, not on the possession of material riches, but on a good standing with Jehovah God, a standing that is maintained by a person's continuing to do the divine will by faith. Christ Jesus encouraged others to be "rich toward God" (Lu 12:21) and to store up "treasures in heaven." (Mt 6:20; Lu 12:33) An individual's record of fine works would be like riches deposited with the Creator in heaven, assuring lasting blessings for the one concerned. Persons who became spirit-anointed followers of Jesus Christ could look forward to "the glorious riches" of a heavenly inheritance (Eph 1:18), and during their 'alien residence' on earth, they would be rich or abound in faith, love, goodness, and other godlike qualities. —Compare Ga 5:22, 23; Jas 2:5; 1Pe 2:11, 12; 2Pe 1:5-8.

The Wealthy Patriarchs.   Faithful servants of Jehovah God, such as the patriarchs Abraham and Job, were not given the commission to assist persons outside their households to adopt true worship. For this reason their time appears to have been mainly filled with caring for the physical and spiritual needs of their respective households. Jehovah blessed the diligent efforts of these servants of his so that they came to have much livestock, many servants, and much gold and silver.—Ge 12:16; 13:2; 14:14; 30:43; 32:10; Job 1:2, 3; 42:10-12.

Though wealthy, these men were not materialists. They appreciated that their material prosperity was due to Jehovah's blessing upon them, and they were not greedy for riches. Abraham, after defeating four allied kings and recovering all the goods that they had seized from Sodom, could have greatly increased his wealth. But he turned down the offer of the king of Sodom to take the recovered goods, saying: "I do lift up my hand in an oath to Jehovah the Most High God, Producer of heaven and earth, that, from a thread to a sandal lace, no, I shall take nothing from anything that is yours, in order that you may not say, 'It was I who made Abram rich.' Nothing for me!" (Ge 14:22-24) When Job lost all his livestock and his children, he exclaimed: "Jehovah himself has given, and Jehovah himself has taken away. Let the name of Jehovah continue to be blessed."—Job 1:21.

Abraham, Job, and others showed that they could be trusted with riches. They were industrious and used their material possessions properly. Job, for example, was ever ready to help the poor and afflicted. (Job 29:12-16) In view of their right attitude, there was good reason for Jehovah God to protect his servants from being defrauded by selfish and greedy men.—Ge 31:5-12; Job 1:10; Ps 105:14.

Israel, if Obedient, Was to Prosper.   As in the case of the faithful patriarchs, the material prosperity of the Israelites depended on their maintaining a proper relationship with Jehovah God. Moses strictly counseled them to remember that it was Jehovah their God who gave them power to make wealth. (De 8:18) Yes, Jehovah was the One who gave an inheritance of land to that nation in covenant relationship with him. (Nu 34:2-12) He could also see to it that they received the rain in its season and did not experience loss through crop failures or invasions by enemy forces.—Le 26:4-7.

It was God's purpose that Israel, if obedient, would be a prosperous nation. Said Moses: "Jehovah will open up to you his good storehouse, the heavens, to give the rain on your land in its season and to bless every deed of your hand; and you will certainly lend to many nations, while you yourself will not borrow. And Jehovah will indeed put you at the head and not at the tail; and you must come to be only on top, and you will not come to be on the bottom, because you keep obeying the commandments of Jehovah your God." (De 28:12, 13) The prosperity of the nation would have brought honor to Jehovah, constituting a powerful proof to surrounding nations that he was the "Enricher" (1Sa 2:7) of his people and that the Law he had given to them was beyond compare in securing the welfare of all concerned.

That Israel's prosperity did move other peoples to glorify Jehovah is illustrated in the case of King Solomon. At the start of his kingship, he, when given the opportunity to request what he wanted from Jehovah, did not ask for great riches but requested wisdom and knowledge to judge the nation. Jehovah granted Solomon his request and also gave him "wealth and riches and honor." (2Ch 1:7-12; 9:22-27) As a result, reports of Solomon's wisdom and wealth came to be associated with the name of Jehovah. Having heard about Solomon in connection with Jehovah, the queen of Sheba, for instance, came from a distant land to see whether the reports about his wisdom and prosperity were true. (1Ki 10:1, 2) What she saw prompted her to acknowledge Jehovah's love for Israel. She said: "True has the word proved to be that I heard in my own land about your matters and about your wisdom. And I did not put faith in the words until I had come that my own eyes might see; and, look! I had not been told the half. You have surpassed in *wisdom* and *prosperity* the things heard to which I listened. Happy are your men; happy are these servants of yours who are standing before you constantly, listening to your wisdom! May Jehovah your God come to be blessed, who has taken delight in you by putting you upon the throne of Israel; because Jehovah loves Israel to time indefinite, so that he appointed you as king to render judicial decision and righteousness."—1Ki 10:6-9.

As a prosperous nation, the Israelites were able to enjoy food and drink (1Ki 4:20; Ec 5:18, 19), and their riches served to protect them from the problems of poverty. (Pr 10:15; Ec 7:12) However, although it was in harmony with Jehovah's purpose that the Israelites enjoy prosperity from their hard work (compare Pr 6:6-11; 20:13; 24:33, 34), he also saw to it that they were warned concerning the danger of forgetting him as the Source of their wealth and beginning to trust in their riches. (De 8:7-17; Ps 49:6-9; Pr 11:4; 18:10, 11; Jer 9:23, 24) They were reminded that riches were but temporary (Pr 23:4, 5), could not be given to God as a ransom to deliver one from death (Ps 49:6, 7), and were of no value to the dead (Ps 49:16, 17; Ec 5:15). They were shown that attaching undue importance to riches would lead to fraudulent practices and Jehovah's disfavor. (Pr 28:20; compare Jer 5:26-28; 17:9-11.) They were also encouraged to "honor Jehovah with [their] valuable things."—Pr 3:9.

Of course, the prosperity of the nation did not mean that every individual was wealthy or that those who had little were necessarily under divine disapproval. Unforeseen occurrences might plunge individuals into poverty. (Ec 9:11, 12) Death could leave behind orphans and widows. Accidents and sickness could temporarily or permanently hinder a person from performing necessary work. Hence the Israelites were encouraged to be generous with their riches in giving aid to the poor and afflicted in their midst.—Le 25:35; De 15:7, 8; Ps 112:5, 9; Pr 19:17; see GIFTS OF MERCY; POOR.

Riches Among the Followers of Christ Jesus. Unlike the patriarchs and the nation of Israel, the followers of Jesus Christ had the commission to "make disciples of people of all the nations." (Mt 28:19, 20) Fulfilling that commission required time and effort that might otherwise have been properly used in secular pursuits. Therefore, a person who continued to cling to his wealth instead of unburdening himself sufficiently to be able to use his time and resources to fulfill that commission could not be a disciple of Jesus, with the prospect of gaining life in the heavens. That is why the Son of God said: "How difficult a thing it will be for those having money to make their way into the kingdom of God! It is easier, in fact, for a camel to get through the eye of a sewing needle than for a rich man to get into the kingdom of God." (Lu 18:24, 25) These words were prompted by the reaction of a rich young ruler upon being told by Jesus: "Sell all the things you have and distribute to poor people, and you will have treasure in the heavens; and come be my follower."

(Lu 18:22, 23) That rich young ruler was under obligation to help needy fellow Israelites. (Pr 14: 21; 28:27; Isa 58:6, 7; Eze 18:7-9) But his unwillingness to part with his material possessions, using these to assist others, and to devote himself to being a follower of Jesus Christ blocked his gaining entrance into the Kingdom of the heavens.

Christ's followers, however, were not to reduce themselves to a state of poverty and then depend upon others for support. Rather, they were to work hard so they would be able to care for their families and also have "something to distribute to someone in need." (Eph 4:28; 1Th 4:10-12; 2Th 3:10-12; 1Ti 5:8) They were to be content with sustenance and covering, not striving to become rich. Any who made material pursuits of prime concern were in danger of becoming involved in dishonest practices and losing their faith because of neglecting spiritual things. This did happen to some, as is shown by Paul's words to Timothy: "Those who are determined to be rich fall into temptation and a snare and many senseless and hurtful desires, which plunge men into destruction and ruin. For the love of money is a root of all sorts of injurious things, and by reaching out for this love some have been led astray from the faith and have stabbed themselves all over with many pains."—1Ti 6:9, 10.

Of course, what Jesus said to the rich young ruler does not mean that a Christian cannot have material riches. In the first century C.E., for instance, wealthy Christians were associated with the congregation at Ephesus. The apostle Paul did not instruct Timothy to advise these rich brothers specifically to divest themselves of all material things, but he wrote: "Give orders to those who are rich in the present system of things not to be high-minded, and to rest their hope, not on uncertain riches, but on God, who furnishes us all things richly for our enjoyment; to work at good, to be rich in fine works, to be liberal, ready to share, safely treasuring up for themselves a fine foundation for the future, in order that they may get a firm hold on the real life." (1Ti 6:17-19) Thus these wealthy Christians had to watch their attitude, keeping riches in their proper place and using them generously to aid others.

Mammon. The original-language term *ma-mo·nas'* (or, its Anglicized form "mammon") is generally understood to denote money or riches. (Mt 6:24; Lu 16:9, 11, 13; compare *AS, KJ, NW*.) There is no evidence that the expression was ever the name of a specific deity. Jesus used the term when showing that a person cannot be a slave to God if Riches is his master. (Mt 6:24) He urged his

hearers: "Make friends for yourselves by means of the unrighteous riches, so that, when such fail, they may receive you into the everlasting dwelling places." (Lu 16:9) Since the possession or desire for material riches can lead to lawless acts, they may for this reason have been designated as "unrighteous riches," in contrast with spiritual riches. Also, material riches, particularly money, actually belong to and are under the control of "Caesar," who issues money and assigns a particular value to it. Such riches are transitory, and loss may be experienced as a result of economic conditions or other circumstances. Hence, the person having such riches should not put his trust in them, nor should he use them as the world in general does for selfish purposes, such as the amassing of still greater wealth. (1Co 7:31) Rather, he should be alert and diligent to make friends of the possessors of the everlasting dwelling places.

The possessors of "the everlasting dwelling places" are Jehovah God and his Son Christ Jesus. (Compare Joh 6:37-40, 44.) Persons who do not use their "unrighteous riches" in a proper way (as in assisting those in need and in furthering "the good news"; Ga 2:10; Php 4:15) could never be friends of God and of his Son, Christ Jesus. Their unfaithfulness in the use of unrighteous riches would show that they are unfit to be entrusted with spiritual riches. (Lu 16:10-12) Such persons could never be fine stewards of God's undeserved kindness, dispensing spiritual riches to others. —1Pe 4:10, 11.

RIDDLE. A saying that is puzzling. The Hebrew word for riddle may also be rendered 'ambiguous saying' or 'perplexing question.' (Compare Da 8:23, ftn.) Riddles are contrasted with plain speech that can be readily understood. (Nu 12:8) The word is sometimes used as an expression parallel to "proverbial saying," because a riddle may well be a statement that is full of meaning but set out in obscure language. (Ps 49:4) The same Hebrew word that is rendered "riddles" is also, in a different context, translated "perplexing questions." (2Ch 9:1) Formulating a riddle, which often involves an obscure but accurate analogy, requires a keen mind, and solving such a riddle calls for ability to see things in relation to one another; so the Bible refers to riddles as the product of wise persons and as something that can be fathomed by a man of understanding.—Pr 1:5, 6.

The Bible itself contains riddles involving Jehovah's purposes. (Ps 78:2-4) They are statements that may at first perplex the reader; they may be intentionally obscure, employing meaningful comparisons that were not meant to be understood by persons at the time they were first written. For example, in Zechariah 3:8 Jehovah refers prophetically to "my servant Sprout," but he does not there explain that this one is a sprout, or an offspring, of the royal line of David and that actually such one is God's own Son then in the heavens who would be born to a virgin descendant of King David. And Revelation 13:18 says that "the number of the wild beast" is said to be "six hundred and sixty-six," but it does not there explain the significance of that number.

At times riddles were used, not to mystify the ones who heard them, but apparently to arouse interest and to make the message conveyed more vivid. Such was the case with the riddle of the two eagles and the vine, propounded to the house of Israel by the prophet Ezekiel. (Eze 17:1-8) Immediately after he had presented the riddle, Ezekiel was instructed by Jehovah to ask the people if they understood it and then to explain it to them.

Some riddles were set forth for men to guess, and often they were presented in verse, as was the case with the one Samson propounded to the Philistines. When he said: "Out of the eater something to eat came forth, and out of the strong something sweet came forth," he deliberately employed comparisons that would not be readily perceived. (Jg 14:12-18) His riddle was based on an experience he had personally had shortly before this when he scraped honey out of the carcass of a lion, where it had been deposited by a swarm of bees.—Jg 14:8, 9.

RIDICULE.

The act of belittling or exposing to contempt, derision, or mockery. There are a number of Hebrew and Greek words that express varying degrees of ridicule, the choice of word depending on circumstances. We therefore read in the Bible of persons that mock, deride, sneer, scoff, jeer, laugh at, or make fun of others.

Ridiculers are, in general, detestable to others. (Pr 24:9) If such do not accept reproof, they will experience disaster. (Pr 1:22-27) And how despicable are those who deride the poor, or their own parents! (Pr 17:5; 30:17) Ridiculers often refuse to listen to rebuke (Pr 13:1) and do not love those reproving them. (Pr 9:7, 8; 15:12) Nevertheless, they should be disciplined for the benefit of others. (Pr 9:12; 19:25, 29; 21:11) Instead of keeping company with such unholy ones, it is better to drive them away; much happier are those who refuse to sit with ungodly ridiculers.—Ps 1:1; Pr 22:10.

Ridicule Against God's Servants. Unjustified ridicule of every sort is suffered by faithful servants of Jehovah. Job was falsely accused of deriding others (Job 11:3), whereas, in reality, he was the one derided, mocked, and made a laughingstock for his course of integrity. (Job 12:4; 17:2; 21:3) David was derided and mocked. (Ps 22:7; 35:16) Likewise, Elisha (2Ki 2:23), Nehemiah and those associated with him (Ne 2:19; 4:1), and many others "received their trial by mockings" (Heb 11:36). When King Hezekiah of Judah sent runners throughout cities of Ephraim and Manasseh, urging them to come to Jerusalem and celebrate the Passover, many individuals mocked and derided the messengers. (2Ch 30:1, 10) This, in fact, was the way apostates of both houses of Israel treated God's prophets and messengers until the rage of Jehovah swept them all away.—2Ch 36:15, 16.

Ridiculing Jesus and his disciples. As God's Servant and Prophet, Jesus Christ was sneered at, laughed at, made fun of, treated insolently, even spit upon, during his ministry on earth. (Mr 5:40; Lu 16:14; 18:32) The Jewish priests and rulers were especially hateful in their derision. (Mt 27:41; Mr 15:29-31; Lu 23:11, 35) The Roman soldiers joined in the mockery when he was delivered up to them.—Mt 27:27-31; Mr 15:20; Lu 22:63; 23:36.

The disciples of Jesus Christ were likewise mocked by the uninformed and by unbelievers. (Ac 2:13; 17:32) The apostle Paul, speaking of the derision suffered by his fellow disciples at the hands of the Jews, points back to the prophetic picture of ancient times, in which Isaac, at the age of about five years, was derided by his 19-year-old half brother Ishmael, who, in jealousy, was "poking fun" at ("mocking," KJ, Yg) Isaac. (Ge 21:9) Paul gives the prophetic application, saying: "Now we, brothers, are children belonging to the promise the same as Isaac was. But just as then the one born in the manner of flesh began persecuting the one born in the manner of spirit [God having intervened to bring about Isaac's birth], so also now." (Ga 4:28, 29) Later Paul writes: "In fact, all those desiring to live with godly devotion in association with Christ Jesus will also be persecuted." —2Ti 3:12.

Enduring ridicule with the proper viewpoint. Jesus Christ knew all along that he would face ridicule and that it would culminate in his being put to death. But he recognized that the reproaches were actually against Jehovah, whom he represented, and this was all the more painful to him, for he 'always did the things pleasing to his Father' (Joh 8:29), and he was more concerned with the sanctification of his Father's name than with anything else. (Mt 6:9) Accordingly, "when he was being reviled, he did not go reviling in return. When he was suffering, he did not go threatening, but kept on committing himself to the one who judges righteously." The apostle Peter expresses this point when writing to Christians, particularly to slaves, exhorting them not to let such treatment incite them to retaliate; for Christ is their example, "a model," Peter says, "for [them] to follow his steps closely."—1Pe 2:18-23; Ro 12:17-21.

At one point in his career, Jeremiah the prophet of God said, "I became an object of laughter all day long; everyone is holding me in derision." Momentarily he weakened and considered stopping his prophetic work because of the unceasing reproach and jeering. But he recognized that it was "for the word of Jehovah" that the derision came, and God's word in his heart proved to be like a burning fire that he could not endure to hold in. For his faithfulness Jehovah was with him "like a terrible mighty one," and Jeremiah was strengthened to keep on loyally.—Jer 20:7-11.

Job was a man righteously maintaining his integrity through great ridicule. But he developed the wrong viewpoint and made a mistake, for which he was corrected. Elihu said of him: "What able-bodied man is like Job, who drinks up derision like water?" (Job 34:7) Job became too concerned with his own justification rather than God's, and he tended to magnify his own righteousness more than God's. (Job 35:2; 36:24) In receiving the severe ridicule of his three "companions," Job tended to count it directed toward himself rather than toward God. In this he was like a person who gives himself up to derision and ridicule and delights in it, taking it in as though he were drinking water with enjoyment. God later explained to Job that these ridiculers were actually (in the final analysis) speaking untruth against *God.* (Job 42:7) Similarly, Jehovah told the prophet Samuel when Israel demanded a king: "It is not you whom they have rejected, but it is I whom they have rejected from being king over them." (1Sa 8:7) And Jesus said to his disciples: "You will be objects of hatred by all the nations [not on your own account, but] on account of *my name.*" (Mt 24:9) Keeping these things in mind will enable the Christian to endure ridicule in the right spirit and will qualify him to receive a reward for his endurance.—Lu 6:22, 23.

Justifiable Ridicule. Ridicule may be deserved and well justified. A person who does not exercise foresight or who neglects good counsel may take a foolish course that makes him the object of ridicule. Jesus gave an example of such a man, who started to build a tower without first counting the cost. (Lu 14:28-30) Jehovah set Israel "as a reproach to [her] neighbors, a derision and jeering to those all around" her, justly so, because of her own waywardness and disobedience to God, even to the point of bringing reproach upon God's name among the nations. (Ps 44:13; 79:4; 80:6; Eze 22:4, 5; 23:32; 36:4, 21, 22) The prophet Elijah appropriately mocked the priests of Baal for their defiance of Jehovah. (1Ki 18:26, 27) After Sennacherib had taunted and spoken of Jehovah abusively before King Hezekiah and the people of Jerusalem, the tables were turned; ridicule, derision, reproach, and ignominious defeat fell upon this haughty Assyrian king and his army. (2Ki 19:20, 21; Isa 37:21, 22) In a similar manner Moab became an object of ridicule. (Jer 48:25-27, 39) The nations of earth have gone to the extreme in ridiculing God, but Jehovah laughs at them and holds them in derision for their impudent resistance to his universal sovereignty, as they reap the bad fruitage of their course.—Ps 2:2-4; 59:8; Pr 1:26; 3:34.

Ridiculers in "the Last Days." One of the signs marking "the last days" would be "ridiculers [literally, players in sport (of mocking)] with their ridicule, proceeding according to their own desires ["own desires for ungodly things"; Jude 17, 18] and saying: 'Where is this promised presence of his? Why, from the day our forefathers fell asleep in death, all things are continuing exactly as from creation's beginning.'" (2Pe 3:3, 4) Obviously, such ones do not heed the advice of Isaiah 28:21, 22, warning of the grave danger of scoffing at Jehovah.

"God Is Not One to Be Mocked." The apostle Paul warns of the serious danger that attends an attempt to mock God, that is, the danger that comes to one who thinks that the principles of God's administration can be treated with contempt or can successfully be evaded. He writes to the Galatian Christians: "For if anyone thinks he is something when he is nothing, he is deceiving his own mind. . . . Do not be misled: God is not one to be mocked. For whatever a man is sowing, this he will also reap; because he who is sowing with a view to his flesh will reap corruption from his flesh, but he who is sowing with a view to the spirit will reap everlasting life from the spirit."—Ga 6:3-8.

Here the apostle shows that a person should not deceive himself with a false estimate of his own worth, thereby ignoring God and his Word. He should clean up his life to walk by the spirit as the Word directs. If a person does not do this, but instead goes on sowing with a view to fleshly desires, he is 'accepting the undeserved kindness of God and missing its purpose' and is treating God's instruction as contemptible. (2Co 6:1) He may deceive himself into thinking that he is safe. Nevertheless, God knows his heart and will judge him accordingly.

RIGHTEOUSNESS.

The Hebrew *tse'dheq* and *tsedha·qah'* as well as the Greek *di·kai·o·sy'ne* have the thought of "rectitude," "uprightness," indicating a *standard* or *norm* determining what is upright. "Righteousness" is frequently used in connection with a judge, or with judgment, giving the term a somewhat legal flavor (hence, the original-language terms are at times translated "justice"). (Ps 35:24; 72:2; 96:13; Isa 11:4; Re 19:11) In the Mosaic Law, at Leviticus 19:36, *tse'dheq* is used four times in connection with business transactions: "You should prove to have *accurate* ["just," AT, KJ, Le] scales, *accurate* weights, an *accurate* ephah and an *accurate* hin."

God Sets the Standard. Greek scholar Kenneth S. Wuest says: "God is the objective standard which determines the content of meaning of *dikaios* [righteous], and at the same time keeps that content of meaning constant and unchanging, since He is the unchanging One." He then quotes Cremer as saying: "Righteousness in the biblical sense is a condition of rightness the standard of which is God, which is estimated according to the divine standard, which shows itself in behavior conformable to God, and has to do above all things with its relation to God, and with the walk before Him. It is, and it is called *dikaiosune theou* (righteousness of God) (Rom. 3:21, 1:17), righteousness as it belongs to God, and is of value before Him, Godlike righteousness, see Eph. 4:24; with this righteousness thus defined, the gospel (Rom. 1:17) comes into the world of nations which had been wont to measure by a different standard."—*Studies in the Vocabulary of the Greek New Testament*, 1946, p. 37.

Luke shows the sense of one's being righteous in saying of the priest Zechariah and his wife Elizabeth (the parents of John the Baptizer): "They both were righteous before God because of walking blamelessly in accord with all the commandments and legal requirements of Jehovah." (Lu 1:6) Righteousness is measured by conformity to God's will and his commands. His specific commands may vary from one time to another and from one person to another—his command to Noah to build an ark has never been repeated nor does his command regarding circumcision apply to Christians. Nevertheless, God's personal standards, his personality, and what he *is,* as ex-

pressed in his words and ways, remain ever constant and hence provide a perfect standard, 'rocklike' in firmness and stability, with which to measure the conduct of all his creatures.—De 32:4; Job 34:10; Ps 92:15; Eze 18:25-31; 33:17-20.

Goodness and Righteousness. The apostle Paul seems to make a distinction between goodness and righteousness when, speaking of Christ's sacrificial death, he says: "For hardly will anyone die for a righteous man; indeed, for the good man, perhaps, someone even dares to die. But God recommends his own love to us in that, while we were yet sinners, Christ died for us." (Ro 5:7, 8) A man can be termed "righteous" if he fulfills his proper obligations, is just, impartial, honest, not guilty of wrongdoing or immorality, hence one known for integrity of conduct and uprightness. Paul's statement, however, implies a certain superiority in "the good" man. To be "good," the individual could not, of course, be unrighteous or unjust; yet other qualities distinguish him from the man primarily known for his righteousness. The use of the Greek term shows that the person noteworthy for, or distinguished by, goodness is one who is benevolent (disposed to do good or bring benefit to others) and beneficent (actively expressing such goodness). He is not merely concerned with doing what justice requires but goes beyond this, being motivated by wholesome consideration for others and the desire to benefit and help them.—Compare Mt 12:35; 20:10-15; Lu 6:9, 33, 35, 36; Joh 7:12; Ac 14:17; Ro 12:20, 21; 1Th 5:15.

Thus, Paul evidently is showing that, while the man noted for being "righteous" may win the respect, even the admiration, of others, he may not appeal to their heart so strongly as to impel anyone to die for him. However, the man outstanding for his goodness, who is warm, helpful, considerate, merciful, actively beneficial, wins affection; and his goodness may appeal to the heart sufficiently that, for such a one, a person might be willing to die.

It may be noted that, in the Scriptures, that which is "good" is contrasted with that which is "vile" (Joh 5:29; Ro 9:11; 2Co 5:10), "wicked" (Mt 5:45; Ro 12:9), "evil" (Ro 16:19), and, of course, "bad" (1Pe 3:11; 3Jo 11). The "righteous" one, on the other hand, is contrasted with the "sinner" (the unrighteous person). (Mr 2:17; Lu 15:7) Just as a person may be a sinner (because he fails to meet righteous standards) and yet not necessarily be termed or classed as "vile," "wicked," or "evil," so, too, one may be a "righteous" person and yet not necessarily be termed or classed as a "good" person, in the sense described earlier.

Joseph of Arimathea was known as being both "good and righteous," these terms, of course, always being used in a relative sense when applying to imperfect humans. (Lu 23:50; compare Mt 19:16, 17; Mr 10:17, 18; see GOODNESS [Jehovah's Goodness].) The commandments of God's law to Israel were "holy [being from God] and righteous [being perfect in justice] and good [being beneficial in *every respect* for those observing them]." —Ro 7:12; compare Eph 5:9.

Jehovah, the Righteous One. The Hebrew words *tse'dheq* and *tsedha·qah'* and the Greek *di·kai·o·sy'ne* appear frequently with reference to the rightness of God's ways: as Sovereign (Job 37:23; Ps 71:19; 89:14), in administering and executing judgment and justice (Ps 9:8; 85:11; Isa 26:9; 2Co 3:9), in the punishing of his professed people (Isa 10:22), in vindication of himself in judgment (Ps 51:4; Ro 3:4, 5), and in vindication of his people (Mic 7:9).

Jehovah himself is called "the abiding place of righteousness." (Jer 50:7) He is therefore the Righteous One, and all righteousness on the part of his creatures comes from their relationship with him. Jehovah abides by his own standard of righteousness without deviation. Therefore, his creatures can have the utmost confidence in him. Of him it is written: "Righteousness and judgment are the established place of your throne."—Ps 89:14.

Righteous while exercising mercy. Jehovah's righteousness, justice, holiness, and purity are such that no sin can be condoned by him. (Ps 5:4; Isa 6:3, 5; Hab 1:13; 1Pe 1:15) Consequently he could not forgive the sins of mankind without satisfying justice—in effect, without a legal basis. But through his undeserved kindness he made this just arrangement by providing his Son as a sacrificial offering, a propitiation, or a covering for sins. In this way he can righteously exercise mercy toward sinners who accept this arrangement. Paul expresses the matter in the following manner: "But now apart from law God's righteousness has been made manifest, . . . yes, God's righteousness through the faith in Jesus Christ . . . For all have sinned and fall short of the glory of God, and it is as a free gift that they are being declared righteous by his undeserved kindness through the release by the ransom paid by Christ Jesus. . . . that he [God] *might be righteous even when declaring righteous the man* [the inherently sinful man] that has faith in Jesus."—Ro 3:21-26; see DECLARE RIGHTEOUS.

Seek God's Righteousness. Jesus admonished his hearers: "Keep on, then, seeking first the kingdom and [God's] righteousness, and all these other things will be added to you." (Mt 6:33) A person needs to keep seeking the Kingdom; he must desire that government and be loyal to it. But he cannot forget that it is the Kingdom of *God;* he must conform to God's will, to God's standard of right and wrong in conduct, and he must continually 'make his mind over' so that every facet of his life is in accord with God's righteousness. (Ro 12:2) He must "put on the new personality which was created according to God's will in true righteousness and loyalty."—Eph 4:23, 24.

The Jews thought that they were safe and would receive God's Kingdom by seeking to establish their own righteousness, but they did not subject themselves to the righteousness of God. (Ro 10:1-3) That is why Jesus said to his disciples: "For I say to you that if your righteousness does not abound more than that of the scribes and Pharisees, you will by no means enter into the kingdom of the heavens." These men had a form of righteousness in their obedience to certain of the requirements of the Law and to their added traditions. But they had actually made the word of God invalid because of their tradition, and they rejected Christ, the way provided by God through whom they could have obtained real righteousness.—Mt 5:17-20; 15:3-9; Ro 10:4.

Righteousness not by one's own works. Consequently, it is clear that imperfect men could never attain true righteousness—they could not measure up to the righteousness of God—either by dependence on works of the Mosaic Law or by their own works of self-righteousness. (Ro 3:10; 9:30-32; Ga 2:21; 3:21; Tit 3:5) The men whom God called "righteous" were men who had exercised faith in God and who did not trust in their own works but backed up that faith by works in harmony with his righteous standard.—Ge 15:6; Ro 4:3-9; Jas 2:18-24.

The Law was righteous. This is not to say that the Law given through Moses did not contain God's standard of righteousness. It did. The apostle argues: "Wherefore, on its part, the Law is holy, and the commandment is holy and righteous and good." (Ro 7:12; De 4:8) It served God's purpose in making transgressions manifest and being a tutor to lead the Jews of honest heart to Christ, as well as having a shadow of the good things to come. (Ga 3:19, 24; Heb 10:1) But it could not bring real, complete righteousness to those under it. All of them were sinners; they could not keep the Law perfectly; and their high priest was unable to remove their sins by his sacrifices and services. Therefore, only through acceptance of God's provision of his Son could they attain righteousness.

(Ro 8:3, 4; Heb 7:18-28) Those accepting Christ were declared righteous, not as something earned, but as a *gift*, and Christ became to them "wisdom from God, also righteousness and sanctification and release by ransom." Accordingly, real righteousness can come only through Christ. This exalts Jehovah, giving him, and not man or self-works, the credit as the Source of all righteousness, "that it may be just as it is written: 'He that boasts, let him boast in Jehovah.'"—1Co 1:30, 31; Ro 5:17.

Benefits of Righteousness. God loves the righteous and cares for them. David wrote: "A young man I used to be, I have also grown old, and yet I have not seen anyone righteous left entirely, nor his offspring looking for bread." (Ps 37:25) Solomon said: "Jehovah will not cause the soul of the righteous one to go hungry, but the craving of the wicked ones he will push away." (Pr 10:3) God is to judge the inhabited earth in righteousness by Jesus Christ, and he will create "new heavens and a new earth" in which righteousness is to dwell. (Ac 17:31; 2Pe 3:13) Eventual possession of the earth is promised to the righteous; the wicked are to be cleared out of the earth as "a ransom" for the righteous, for as long as the wicked are in control, the righteous cannot have peace. And the possessions of the wicked will go to the righteous, as the proverb states: "The wealth of the sinner is something treasured up for the righteous one."—Pr 13:22; 21:18.

The person who perseveres in righteousness is assured of God's goodwill and the approval of righthearted men now and for all time to come, for "the remembrance of the righteous one is due for a blessing [and will be "to time indefinite"], but the very name of the wicked ones will rot."—Pr 10:7; Ps 112:6.

Respect and Heed Righteous Ones. It is the course of wisdom to respect those whom Jehovah counts righteous and to follow their counsel and reproof, which will bring good to those accepting it. David received reproof from Jehovah through righteous men, God's servants and prophets, and he said: "Should the righteous one strike me, it would be a loving-kindness; and should he reprove me, it would be oil upon the head, which my head would not want to refuse."—Ps 141:5.

"The Breastplate of Righteousness." Because the Bible tells us, "More than all else that is to be guarded, safeguard your heart, for out of it are the sources of life," Christians need to have on "the breastplate of righteousness." (Pr 4:23; Eph 6:14) As a protection against his heart turning bad, it is essential that a person follow God's righteousness since the heart of fallen, sinful man is treacherous and desperate. (Jer 17:9) The heart needs much discipline and training. The Christian can be assured of this course only by sticking close to the Scriptures, which, the apostle Paul says, are "beneficial for teaching, for reproving, for setting things straight, for disciplining in righteousness, that the man of God may be fully competent, completely equipped for every good work." He should accept gratefully the discipline that is received from righteous men who make such use of God's Word.—2Ti 3:16, 17.

RIMMON (Rim′mon) [Pomegranate Tree].

1. The Benjamite father of Baanah and Rechab, the murderers of Saul's son Ish-bosheth; from Beeroth N of Gibeah.—2Sa 4:2, 5-7, 9.

2. A city of the tribe of Simeon in the area surrounded by the tribe of Judah. (Jos 19:1, 2, 7; "Remmon," *KJ*) It is listed after the city of Ain, and apparently En-rimmon at Nehemiah 11:29 is a combined form to designate the twin cities. It is mentioned as a southern point in Zechariah 14:10. The ruins of a place called Khirbet Umm er-Ramamin (Horvat Ramalya), about 14 km (8.5 mi) N of Beer-sheba, are thought to be the ancient site.

3. A Levite enclave city of the Merari family on the E border of the land of Zebulun (Jos 19:10, 13); evidently called "Dimnah" at Joshua 21:35 and "Rimmono" at 1 Chronicles 6:77. It is identified with Rummana (Rimmon), about 10 km (6 mi) N of Nazareth.

4. A craglike eminence to which 600 men of the tribe of Benjamin retreated as survivors of the battle near Gibeah, in which all Israel rose up against the Benjamites to avenge the rape and murder of the concubine of a Levite. (Jg 20:45-47) They remained there until approached by peace envoys. (Jg 21:13) Located about 6 km (3.5 mi) E of Bethel and 18 km (11 mi) NNE of Jerusalem, the former stronghold today is known as Rammun, where a small village is located. There is a cone-shaped limestone mountain there, protected on three sides by ravines and containing numerous caves.

5. A Syrian god. The Syrian army chief Naaman, after being cured of his leprosy, acknowledged Jehovah as the true God but expressed concern over his having to accompany the king of Syria into the temple of Rimmon and there bow down with the king before the idol of Rimmon, as the king would be leaning upon Naaman's arm.—2Ki 5:15-18.

Rimmon is generally identified with Ramman (meaning "Roarer, Thunderer"), a god known to have been venerated in Assyria and Babylonia. It has been suggested that the worship of Rimmon (Ramman) was brought westward from Assyria by some of the tribes that later settled around Damascus. A number of scholars regard Rimmon (Ramman) as but a title of the storm-god Hadad (Adad). The fact that Tab*rimmon* and Ben-*hadad* were names of Syrian kings suggests a basis for equating Rimmon with Hadad, since these kings likely bore the name or title of their chief god. —1Ki 15:18.

The Rimmon venerated in Syria undoubtedly had much in common with Ramman. To the Assyrians, the latter was primarily a god of storm and thunder. Although regarded as the giver of rain and hence the provider of water for wells and fields, Ramman is associated more prominently with the destructive aspects of rain and lightning. On the Assyrian monuments Ramman is portrayed repeatedly as a god of war. He was regarded as such also in Babylonia, where Ramman, the moon-god Sin, and the sun-god Shamash constituted one of numerous triads.

RIMMONO (Rim′mo·no). Apparently another name for the site called Dimnah at Joshua 21:35 and Rimmon at Joshua 19:13.—1Ch 6:77; see DIMNAH; RIMMON No. 3.

RIMMON-PEREZ (Rim′mon-pe′rez) [Pomegranate Tree of Perez]. One of Israel's wilderness camping sites, mentioned between Rithmah and Libnah. (Nu 33:19, 20) The location has not been definitely determined, though certain geographers suggest Neqb el-Biyar, about 25 km (16 mi) WSW of the northern end of the Gulf of 'Aqaba.

RING. A circular band. Ring-shaped ornaments of various kinds, worn by both men and women, were common among the Hebrews, Egyptians, Assyrians, Babylonians, Greeks, Romans, and other peoples of antiquity. These were worn on the nose, the ears, and the fingers. (See EARRING; NOSE RING.) Materials used included gold, silver, brass, bronze, glass, iron, and ivory; some rings were set with stones. Egyptians particularly favored rings bearing images of the scarab beetle, which was to them a symbol of eternal life. Among the many pieces of jewelry recovered from the tomb of Egyptian Pharaoh Tutankhamen was a ring with a triple band that bore three scarabs, one of lapis lazuli and two of gold. Some rings of the Romans were engraved with mythological designs or even representations of their ancestors or friends.

In Jesus' illustration of the prodigal son, he represented the forgiving father as ordering that a ring be put on the hand of the returning prodigal. (Lu 15:22) This act showed the favor and affection of the father as well as the dignity, honor, and status accorded this restored son. Jesus' half brother James counseled Christians against showing favoritism to those splendidly clothed and wearing gold rings on their fingers (indicating wealth and social status). (Jas 2:1-9) In similar vein, the apostle Peter, while not condemning the wearing of such ornaments, pointed out that spiritual adornment is far more important.—1Pe 3:1-5.

Signet Rings. Hebrew words used to designate a ring, signet ring, or seal ring come from roots meaning "sink down" (Jer 38:6) and "seal." (1Ki 21:8) These terms may be linked with a chief use of some ancient rings, that is, to make an impression on clay or wax by being 'sunk' or pressed into it. Rings of this kind were of gold, silver, or bronze; some were set with an engraved stone bearing the owner's name or symbol. Such rings were mounted in set fashion or were of the swivel or roller type. Some were hung, probably from the neck, on an ornamental cord.—Ge 38: 18, 25.

The signet ring of a ruler or official was a symbol of his authority. (Ge 41:41, 42) Official documents or things not to be tampered with or altered were sealed with them, similar to the manner in which official seals or signatures are used in modern times.—Es 3:10-13; 8:2, 8-12; Da 6:16, 17.

Figurative Use. In ancient times a signet ring seems to have become proverbial of a valued object or person. Jeremiah's prophecy indicated that Judean King Coniah (Jehoiachin) would not be spared calamity even if he were a 'seal ring on Jehovah's right hand.' Jehoiachin was dethroned after a very brief rule. (Jer 22:24; 2Ki 24:8-15) Also, Jehovah said with respect to faithful Zerubbabel: "I shall take you, . . . and I shall certainly set you as a seal ring, because you are the one whom I have chosen." (Hag 2:23) Zerubbabel, who was serving Jehovah in an official capacity in connection with the rebuilding of the temple in Jerusalem, was precious to Jehovah, like a signet ring on God's own hand. Zerubbabel had fearlessly obeyed Jehovah's encouragement through the prophets Haggai and Zechariah and had taken up the temple-building work in spite of a ban by a misinformed king of Persia. (Ezr 4:24–5:2) Jehovah would continue to use Zerubbabel to fulfill His declared purpose, and no human ruler would be able to remove him from that honored service.

RING-SHAPED CAKE. See CAKE.

RINGWORM. A contagious skin disease characterized by ring-shaped patches. The word occurs in the *New World Translation* at Leviticus 21:20 and 22:22, translating the Hebrew word *yal·le'pheth.* Caused by fungi, ringworm is found on animals and man. In humans ringworm may attack not only the body's hairy parts, especially the scalp of children and the beard of adults, but also the nonhairy sections of the body. The latter form develops as a round, rose-colored spot usually having very small blisters around its edge. As the patch expands, the center clears up, giving the afflicted area its usual ringlike appearance.

Though *yal·le'pheth* has been rendered by other skin-disease terms, Jewish tradition connects it with Egyptian herpes or lichen. For *yal·le'pheth* the Greek *Septuagint* translators used *lei·khen',* which can refer to ringworm. Thus Hebrew scholars L. Koehler and W. Baumgartner suggest "ringworm, herpes."—*Lexicon in Veteris Testamenti Libros,* Leiden, 1958, p. 383.

A man of priestly descent who had ringworm was disqualified from presenting offerings to Jehovah. (Le 21:20, 21) And animals afflicted with it were not to be offered in sacrifice to God.—Le 22:22.

RINNAH (Rin'nah) [Joyful Cry; Entreating Cry]. One of "the sons" of Shimon listed among the descendants of Judah.—1Ch 4:1, 20.

RIPHATH (Ri'phath). A son of Gomer and grandson of Japheth. (Ge 10:2, 3; 1Ch 1:6) At 1 Chronicles 1:6 the Masoretic Hebrew text has "Diphath"; however, the Greek *Septuagint,* the Latin *Vulgate,* and some 30 Hebrew manuscripts have "Riphath." The difference in spelling is perhaps the result of a copyist's writing the Hebrew *da'leth* (ד) instead of the Hebrew *rehsh* (ר), the letters being very similar in appearance.

Riphath is listed among those from whom the various nations and peoples were spread about in the earth following the global Flood. (Ge 10:32) The only historical reference regarding his descendants is that of Josephus, of the first century C.E., who claims that the early inhabitants of Paphlagonia (along the S side of the Black Sea in northwestern Asia Minor) were anciently called Ripheans. Some scholars would also connect the name with that of the river called the Rhebas in that general area, while others favor a relationship with the district of Rhebantia in the region of the Bosporus, farther to the W. The limited mention of Riphath in the Bible record and the lack of reference to the name in available ancient secular history allows for no certain identification.

RIPPING OF GARMENTS. A common sign of grief among the Jews, as well as among other Orientals, particularly upon hearing of the death of a near relative. In many cases such ripping consisted of a rending of the garment in front just sufficient to lay open the breast, thus not necessarily a complete ripping of the garment so as to make it unfit for wearing.

The first instance of this practice recorded in the Bible is that of Reuben, Jacob's eldest son, who, upon returning and not finding Joseph in the waterpit, ripped his garments apart, saying: "The child is gone! And I—where am I really to go?" As the firstborn, Reuben was particularly responsible for his younger brother. His father Jacob when told of the supposed death of his son likewise ripped his mantles apart and put on sackcloth in mourning (Ge 37:29, 30, 34), and down in Egypt Joseph's half brothers showed their grief by ripping their garments apart, when Benjamin was made to appear as a thief.—Ge 44:13.

In contrast, when Aaron's two older sons, Nadab and Abihu, were destroyed by Jehovah for their wicked act, Moses instructed their father Aaron and the two surviving sons: "Do not let your heads go ungroomed, and you must not tear your garments, that you may not die." (Le 10:6) On other occasions, however, the lesser priests of the Aaronic line were permitted to display such evidence of grief in the case of the death of near relatives, but the high priest was not permitted to let his hair go ungroomed or tear his garments. —Le 21:1-4, 10, 11.

Many other instances of such expression of grief are found: that of Job, who ripped his sleeveless coat apart when advised of the death of his children (Job 1:20); his three pretended friends who, when they first saw him in his diseased state, put on a demonstration of grief by weeping, ripping their garments, and throwing dust into the air (Job 2:12); Joshua, after the defeat at Ai (Jos 7:6); the young man announcing King Saul's death (2Sa 1:2); David, when given the false notice of the murder by Absalom of all his other sons (2Sa 13:30, 31); and King Hezekiah and his servants, who ripped apart their garments upon hearing the words spoken by Assyrian Rabshakeh against Jehovah and Jerusalem (Isa 37:1; 36:22). Queen Athaliah, seeing her usurpation of the throne coming to an end, also "ripped her garments apart and began crying: 'Conspiracy! Conspiracy!'"—2Ki 11:14.

In the twilight of the history of the kingdom of Judah, the insensibility of the hardened hearts of

King Jehoiakim and his princes is noted in the fact that when Jeremiah's prophecy, which warned of Jehovah's judgments, had been read to them, they felt no dread and did not "rip their garments apart."—Jer 36:24.

However, showing that such outward demonstration might be hypocritical or at least insincere and that it had no value unless the person's grief was genuine, Jehovah spoke to the people of Judah through the prophet Joel and said to them: "Rip apart your hearts, and not your garments; and come back to Jehovah your God."—Joe 2:13.

Later, High Priest Caiaphas affected great indignation and outrage by ripping his garments over Jesus' admission that he was the Son of God. (Mt 26:65) By contrast, Paul and Barnabas, as Christian followers of Jesus, showed sincere dismay and anguish by ripping their outer garments apart when they saw that the people of Lystra were about to worship them as gods.—Ac 14:8-18.

The Law required a leper to wear a torn garment (Le 13:45), perhaps because of the Hebrew association of leprosy with death, reflected in such accounts as Miriam's being referred to as "like someone dead" after being struck with the dread disease. (Nu 12:12) So the leprous one was obligated to wear distinguishing garb, in effect mourning for himself as among the 'living dead.'

Symbolic Use. Clothing was also torn on occasion for symbolic reasons, as when Ahijah the prophet ripped the garment he was wearing into 12 pieces and told Jeroboam to take 10 of them, thereby representing the division of Solomon's kingdom. (1Ki 11:29-39) Similarly Samuel illustrated Jehovah's rejection of Saul's house by his reference to Samuel's sleeveless coat that had been ripped from Saul's grasp.—1Sa 15:26-28.

RISSAH (Ris'sah) [possibly, Sprinkling]. An Israelite wilderness campsite mentioned between Libnah and Kehelathah. (Nu 33:21, 22) Rissah's location is not certain, though some have connected it with Kuntilla (Gerasa), about 55 km (34 mi) NNW of the northern end of the Gulf of 'Aqaba.

RITHMAH (Rith'mah) [Broom Tree]. One of Israel's encampments in the wilderness. (Nu 33: 18, 19) Its site is now unknown.

RIVER. The Hebrew term *na·har'* refers to a river, that is, a considerable body of water that flows fairly constantly in a natural channel. In contrast, a wadi, or torrent valley (Heb., *na'chal*), is often dry but at times carries a turbulent flow of water. Among the main rivers mentioned in the Bible are the Hiddekel (Tigris), Euphrates, Jordan,

Abanah, and Pharpar. (Ge 2:14; 2Ki 5:10, 12) The Nile, though not designated by that name, is referred to as *ye'or'* (sometimes *ye'ohr'*), which is understood to mean also a stream or canal (Isa 33:21) or a water-filled shaft or gallery. (Job 28: 10) The context makes it apparent when the terms *ye'or'* or *ye'ohr'* designate the Nile; therefore, the name Nile appears in Bible translations.—Ge 41: 17,18.

"The river of Egypt" (Ge 15:18) may be the same as "the torrent valley of Egypt."—Nu 34:5; see SHIHOR.

The Euphrates is often simply called "the River." (Jos 24:2, 3; Ezr 8:36; Isa 7:20; 27:12; Mic 7:12) Being the longest and most important river of SW Asia, the Euphrates was "the great river" to the Hebrews. (Ge 15:18) Therefore, its being referred to as "the River" resulted in no ambiguity.

King David, with the help of Jehovah, was able to extend the boundaries of the Promised Land as far as the Euphrates. (1Ch 18:3-8) Concerning his son Solomon, it was stated: "He will have subjects from sea to sea and from the River [Euphrates] to the ends of the earth." (Ps 72:8) In Zechariah's prophecy these words are repeated and point forward to the earth-wide rulership of the Messiah. —Zec 9:9, 10; compare Da 2:44; Mt 21:4, 5.

The first river mentioned in the Bible is the one that apparently had its source in Eden and watered the garden that Jehovah provided as a home for Adam and Eve. This river broke up into four headwaters, which, in turn, resulted in rivers, the Pishon, the Gihon, the Hiddekel, and the Euphrates. The regions (Havilah, Cush, and Assyria) referred to in connection with these four rivers existed in the post-Flood period. (Ge 2:10-14) So it appears that the writer of the account, Moses, used terms familiar in his day to indicate the location of Eden's garden. For this reason it cannot be established with certainty whether what is said about the courses of the Pishon, Gihon, and Hiddekel applies to the post-Flood period or to the pre-Flood period. If the description relates to the time before the Flood, the Flood itself may well have contributed to changing the courses of these rivers. If to the post-Flood period, other natural phenomena, such as earthquakes, may since have altered their courses, hindering the identification of some.

Figurative Use. Rivers served as a barrier to the progress of enemy forces and played a vital role in the defense of certain cities, such as Babylon. Jerusalem, however, had no river as a natural means of defense. Nevertheless, Jehovah God was described as being the source of a mighty river of protection to that city. Enemies that might come against Jerusalem like a hostile galley fleet would experience disaster.—Isa 33:21, 22; see GALLEY.

The disastrous flooding of a river is used to represent the invasion of enemy forces.—Isa 8:7.

Water is necessary for life, and Jehovah is referred to as the Source of living water. (Jer 2:13) But apostate Israelites turned their attention to Egypt and to Assyria. That is why Jehovah, through his prophet Jeremiah, said: "What concern should you have for the way of Egypt in order to drink the waters of Shihor? And what concern should you have for the way of Assyria in order to drink the waters of the River? . . . Know, then, and see that your leaving Jehovah your God is something bad and bitter." (Jer 2:18, 19) Evidently the waters from human sources that are looked to as being vital to one's existence are also referred to at Revelation 8:10 and 16:4.

Regarding the "river of water of life" (Re 22:1), see LIFE (River of Water of Life).

RIVER OF EGYPT. Jehovah promised that Abraham's seed would be given the land "from the river of Egypt" to the Euphrates River. (Ge 15:18) Commentators generally understand "the river of Egypt" to refer to "the torrent valley of Egypt" now identified with Wadi el-'Arish of the Sinai Peninsula, which empties into the Mediterranean Sea about 150 km (90 mi) E of Port Said. (See EGYPT, TORRENT VALLEY OF.) At 1 Chronicles 13:5 certain translations read "river [shi·chohr'] of Egypt" (NW, La, AT), and this reference also may be to Wadi el-'Arish. However, another possibility is that both texts refer to a branch of the Nile. —See SHIHOR.

RIZIA (Ri·zi'a) [from a root meaning "take pleasure; approve"]. A warrior and family head in the tribe of Asher; son of Ulla.—1Ch 7:39, 40.

RIZPAH (Riz'pah) [Heated Stone; or, Glowing Coal]. A concubine of King Saul; daughter of Aiah. (2Sa 3:7; 21:11) After Saul's death, his son Ishbosheth alienated General Abner by calling him to account for having relations with Rizpah, an act he construed as intimating seizure of the throne. As a consequence, Abner defected to David.—2Sa 3:7-21.

Rizpah had given birth to two sons by Saul, Armoni and Mephibosheth. Long after Saul's death, David took these two sons of Rizpah along with five other descendants of Saul and handed them over to the Gibeonites, to be slain, in order to remove bloodguilt from the land. The seven were exposed on a mountain, where Rizpah

guarded their bodies from the birds and wild beasts "from the start of harvest until water poured down upon them from the heavens." (2Sa 21:1-10) This indefinite period of time may have been five or six months, unless, as some suggest, there was an exceptional, out-of-season downpour. Such a heavy rain before October would have been most unusual. (1Sa 12:17, 18; Pr 26:1) David finally heard of the matter and relieved Rizpah of her vigil by having the bodies buried. —2Sa 21:11-14.

ROAD. See HIGHWAY, ROAD.

ROBE. See DRESS.

ROCK. The Scriptures as written in Hebrew distinguish between a rock or a large piece of rock (tsur) and a crag (se'la'). Both terms are used literally and figuratively in the Scriptures. The two are found in parallel at 2 Samuel 22:2, 3 and Psalm 18:2: "Jehovah is my crag . . . My God is my rock."

The Bible preserves the names of certain crags and rocks. For example, the Midianite prince Oreb was killed by Gideon's men at a rock called Oreb, evidently so named because of this incident. (Jg 7:25; Isa 10:26) Mention is made of the crag of Etam, where Samson lived for a time (Jg 15:8), and the toothlike crags of Bozez and Seneh, where Jonathan and his armor-bearer attacked an outpost of the Philistines. (1Sa 14:4, 5) It was at Meribah, in the vicinity of Kadesh (there was another Meribah near Rephidim in the mountainous region of Horeb [Ex 17:7]), that Moses and Aaron were aggravated to the point of failing to sanctify Jehovah in bringing water out of the crag for the assembly.—Nu 20:11-13; Ps 106:32, 33; see MASSAH; MERIBAH Nos. 1 and 2.

Figurative Use. In a figurative sense "rock" describes the qualities of Jehovah as the Father of Israel (De 32:18), as a stronghold (2Sa 22:32, 33; Isa 17:10), as the secure height and refuge of his people (Ps 62:7; 94:22), and as their salvation (De 32:15; Ps 95:1). Some have looked to false gods as their "rock." (De 32:37) There are other examples in which "rock" symbolizes in a general way a place of safety, protection, security, and refuge. (Isa 2:10, 19, 21) In Isaiah 8:14 Christ Jesus is alluded to as "a rock" over which "both the houses of Israel" stumbled.—Compare Mt 21:42-44.

In Jesus' illustration of the sower, the Greek adjective pe·tro'des (related to the noun pe'tros) is used to describe the rocky places upon which some of the seed fell. (Mt 13:3-5, 20) Pe'tros is used as a proper name, "Peter." (Joh 1:42) On the meaning of this term *Vine's Expository Dictionary of Old and New Testament Words* (1981, Vol. 4, p. 76) remarks: *"Petros* denotes a piece of a rock, a detached stone or boulder, in contrast to *petra,* a mass of rock." *Word Studies in the New Testament* says about *pe'tros:* "In classical Greek the word means a *piece of rock,* as in Homer, of Ajax throwing a *stone* at Hector, . . . or of Patroclus grasping and hiding in his hand a jagged *stone."*—By M. Vincent, 1957, Vol. I, p. 91.

The Greek word *tra·khys',* which means "rough" (Lu 3:5), refers to jagged, uneven reefy rocks at Acts 27:29.

Another Greek word, *spi·las',* evidently has reference to a rock or reef that is hidden beneath the water. It is used by Jude to illustrate certain men who had slipped into the Christian congregation with corrupt motives. As hidden rocks were a menace to ships, so these men constituted a real danger to others in the congregation. He says of such men: "These are the rocks hidden below water in your love feasts while they feast with you."—Jude 12.

For a discussion of Matthew 16:18, see ROCK-MASS.

ROCK BADGER [Heb., *sha·phan'*]. The Hebrew word is also rendered "hyrax" (*JB,* ftn) and "coney." (*KJ*) The rock badger somewhat resembles a large rabbit but has short, rounded ears, short legs, and virtually no tail. Its feet are furnished with elastic underpads. The rock badger dwells in rocky areas, where it finds holes and crevices to which it can quickly retire at the least sign of danger. Although very shy by nature, this creature can inflict savage bites with its incisors when cornered in a hole. The animal is a vegetarian. The variety referred to in the Bible is evidently that known as *Procavia syriaca.*

Some have taken issue with its classification in Scripture as a creature that chews the cud but does not split the hoof. (Le 11:5; De 14:7) However, zoologist Hubert Hendrichs, in observing rock badgers at the Hellabrunn Zoological Gardens near Munich, Germany, noticed that these creatures made peculiar chewing and swallowing movements. He found that rock badgers actually do chew the cud from 25 to 50 minutes a day, usually during the night. The German newspaper *Stuttgarter Zeitung* of March 12, 1966, commented on the discovery: "Although this fact was previously unknown to accepted zoology, it is not new. In the eleventh chapter of Leviticus . . . you can find it."

The claim has also been made that the hoofed toes of the rock badger are doubly cloven. However, it could hardly be said that the rock badger's front feet, each having four toes terminating in hooflike endings, and the hind feet, each equipped with three toes and a corresponding number of miniature hoofs or nails, resemble the foot member of a 'splitter of the hoof' such as a cow.

The Scriptures speak of the instinctive wisdom of this little creature. Although not "mighty," the rock badger makes up for its seeming defenselessness by dwelling in inaccessible rocky places.—Ps 104:18; Pr 30:26.

ROCK-MASS. This translates the Greek word *pe'tra* (feminine gender), which designates a mass of rock (Mt 7:24, 25; 27:51, 60; Lu 6:48; 8:6, 13; Re 6:15, 16) and therefore differs from *pe'tros* (masculine gender and employed as a proper name, Peter), meaning "piece of rock." This distinction makes it clear that, when saying to Peter, "You are Peter, and on this rock-mass I will build my congregation," Jesus was not using synonymous terms. (Mt 16:18) Even in the Aramaic (Syriac) version the distinction is apparent from a difference in the gender of the particle preceding the word *ki'pha',* used for both "Peter" and "rock." The masculine verbal pronoun (*hu*) precedes "Peter," but "rock" is preceded by the feminine demonstrative adjective (*hade'*).

That the apostles did not understand Jesus' statement to signify that Peter was the rock-mass is evident from the fact that they later disputed about who seemed to be the greatest among them. (Mr 9:33-35; Lu 22:24-26) There would have been no basis for such disputing had Peter been given the primacy as the rock-mass on which the congregation was to be built. The Scriptures clearly show that as foundation stones, all the apostles are equal. All of them, including Peter, rest upon Christ Jesus as the foundation cornerstone. (Eph 2:19-22; Re 21:2, 9-14) Peter himself identified the rock-mass (*pe'tra*) on which the congregation is built as being Christ Jesus. (1Pe 2:4-8) Similarly, the apostle Paul wrote: "For they [the Israelites] used to drink from the spiritual rock-mass that followed them, and that rock-mass meant the Christ." (1Co 10:4) On at least two occasions and in two different locations the Israelites received a miraculous provision of water from a rock-mass. (Ex 17:5-7; Nu 20:1-11) Therefore, the rock-mass as a source of water, in effect, followed them. The rock-mass itself was evidently a pictorial, or symbolic, type of Christ Jesus, who said to the Jews: "If anyone is thirsty, let him come to me and drink."—Joh 7:37.

It is also of interest that Augustine (354-430 C.E.), usually referred to as "Saint Augustine," at one time believed that Peter was the rock-mass but later changed his view. Lange's *Commentary on the Holy Scriptures* (Mt 16:18, ftn, p. 296) quotes Augustine as saying: "The rock is not so named from Peter, but Peter from the rock (*non enim a Petro petra, sed Petrus a petra*), even as Christ is not so called after the Christian, but the Christian after Christ. For the reason why the Lord says, 'On this rock I will build my church,' is that Peter had said: 'Thou art the Christ, the Son of the living God.' On this rock, which thou hast confessed, says he, I will build my church. For Christ was the rock (*petra enim erat Christus*), upon which also Peter himself was built; for other foundation can no man lay, than that is laid, which is Jesus Christ."—Translated and edited by P. Schaff, 1976.

ROD, STAFF.

The Hebrew words *she'vet* and *mat·teh'* are frequently translated "rod" and "staff." *She'vet* has the meaning of a staff, stick, or rod (for support) and is also rendered "crook" (as a shepherd's crook or staff). (Le 27:32) Possibly because tribal chieftains carried a staff, or scepter, *she'vet* and *mat·teh'* both also designated a "tribe" and are so translated. (Ex 31:2; De 18:1; 29:18) The shaft of a spear or like weapon was designated by the Hebrew words *she'vet* or *'ets* (literally, tree).—2Sa 18:14; 21:19.

Another term, *maq·qel'*, is rendered 'staff' and 'stave' (Ge 30:37; 1Sa 17:43), and *mish·'e'neth* is translated "staff" or "support."—Jg 6:21; 2Ki 18:21.

The Greek word for "rod" is *rha'bdos*, sometimes translated "staff." (Re 19:15; Mt 10:10) Another word, *xy'lon*, is rendered "staff" in some translations. It literally means "wood" or something made of wood. This word is translated "clubs" at Matthew 26:47, 55 and in parallel passages.

Uses. Rods or staffs were used for support (Ex 12:11; Zec 8:4; Heb 11:21); for defense or protection (2Sa 23:21; Mt 10:10); to punish children, slaves, or others (Ex 21:20 ["stick," *NW*]; Pr 10:13; 23:13, 14; Ac 16:22); in threshing (Isa 28:27 [both *mat·teh'* and *she'vet* appear in this verse, translated "rod" and "staff," respectively, *NW*]; compare Jg 6:11; Ru 2:17); and for reaping olives (De 24:20; Isa 24:13). Also, shepherds used the crook in leading the flock, to manage and help them. As to selecting animals to be given to the sanctuary as a tithe, the Law said, "As for every tenth part of the herd and flock, everything that passes under the crook [whatever falls under the shepherd's care], the tenth head should become something holy to Jehovah. He should not examine whether

it is good or bad, neither should he exchange it." (Le 27:32, 33) It is said that the shepherd stood at the gate of the sheepfold as the sheep were coming out with a piece of cloth soaked in dye fastened to the end of his staff; this he touched to every tenth sheep and set aside the ones thus marked as the tithe.—Compare Jer 33:13.

As a Symbol of Authority. One's staff was considered a valuable personal possession, and some staffs were doubtless identifiable as belonging to the individual. Judah gave Tamar his staff and his signet ring as security until he should send her a kid of the goats in payment for his relations with her. (Ge 38:18, 25) Chieftains carried a rod as a symbol of authority. Therefore the Bible often uses the rod to symbolize the authority one has or the authority vested in him by another. Moses' rod became a symbol of his authority and commission from God when he appeared before the older men of Israel, also when he appeared before Pharaoh and the magic-practicing priests of Egypt. (Ex 4:29-31; 7:9-12) In the latter case the rod is said to be Aaron's, but it was evidently Moses' rod used by Aaron as Moses' spokesman, as a comparison of Exodus 7:15, 17 indicates.

After this, Moses' rod was used many times as a symbol that he was appointed and backed up by Jehovah with authority as the nation's leader. (Ex 8:5; 9:23; 10:13; Nu 20:11) When the authority of Moses and Aaron was challenged, out of all the rods for the leaders of the 12 tribes, it was the rod of Aaron, representing the house of Levi, that God caused to bud and produce ripe almonds. This thoroughly proved that Aaron, hence, also his house, was designated by God to hold the office and authority of the priesthood. This rod was thereafter kept for some time in the ark of the covenant.—Nu 17:1-11; Ex 29:9; Heb 9:4.

The psalmist wrote: "The utterance of Jehovah to my Lord is: 'Sit at my right hand until I place your enemies as a stool for your feet.' The rod of your strength Jehovah will send out of Zion, saying: 'Go subduing in the midst of your enemies.'" (Ps 110:1, 2) The apostle Paul applies this text to Jesus Christ, who has, as it were, the 'rod of Jehovah's strength,' going forth as Jehovah's representative with full authority to execute judgment on his enemies. (Heb 10:12, 13) Jesus Christ, the "twig out of the stump of Jesse," "must strike the earth with the rod of his mouth; and with the spirit of his lips he will put the wicked one to death." (Isa 11:1, 4) He speaks with the authority and exercises the power that Jehovah has given him to punish the wicked. It is said that he will rule the nations, not as a shepherd peacefully

ROD, STAFF

leading the flock with his staff, but with an *iron rod.*—Re 2:27; 12:5; 19:15.

The oppressive rod, or staff of rule or authority, that the enemies of Israel wielded over her is referred to at Isaiah 9:4; 14:5. God used the nations around Israel, such as Assyria, to execute punishment on Israel for her sins, and in this action those nations were as a rod of punishment, or chastisement, under God's authority or allowance. Yet these nations acted, not out of love for Jehovah or hate for the sins of Israel, but out of animosity toward both God and Israel, and they went beyond their commission and enjoyed heaping additional afflictions upon Israel. Besides that, these powers, especially Assyria and Babylon, lifted themselves up in haughtiness against Jehovah God himself. God said of Assyria by means of his prophet Isaiah: "Aha, the Assyrian, the rod for my anger," but he also described Assyria's haughtiness, saying: "Will the ax enhance itself over the one chopping with it, or the saw magnify itself over the one moving it back and forth, as though the staff moved back and forth the ones raising it on high, as though the rod raised on high the one who is not wood?" Then He foretold punishment to come upon the nation of Assyria for thus thinking that it was greater than the One using it and for lifting itself up against Him.—Isa 10:5, 15.

When Jehovah made a covenant for the kingdom with David, he said of the line of kings of David's dynasty: "I myself shall become his father, and he himself will become my son. When he does wrong, I will also reprove him with the rod of men and with the strokes of the sons of Adam." (2Sa 7:14) Here the rod of discipline that Jehovah as a Father would use was the authority of the governments of the world, such as Babylon. This nation was used to overturn the kingdom of God in the hands of the kings of David's line, until 'he should come whose legal right it is.' (Eze 21:27) In 70 C.E., the Roman armies under General Titus were a "rod" to execute punishment on unfaithful Jerusalem.—Da 9:26, 27.

Wrong use of the rod. The governments and judges of earthly nations often used their rod of authority in an unrighteous way, even fighting against God and his people. When Jesus Christ was brought before the Jewish high court and before the Roman governor Pilate, he was afflicted, mocked, spit upon, beaten, and finally killed. The Jewish leaders first used their authority against Jesus and then made the "rod" heavier by turning him over to the Roman government for execution. The prophet Micah foretold such affliction in these words: "With the rod they will strike upon the cheek the judge of Israel." (Mic 5:1) After Jesus' death and resurrection, the Jewish rulers used their authority to persecute Jesus' followers, and in many instances Rome and the other governments of earth likewise used their rod of authority in a wrong way. For this they would be brought to account by God.—Joh 19:8-11; 2Th 1:6-9.

Parental authority. "Rod" is used also to symbolize the authority of parents over their children. The book of Proverbs makes many references to this authority, the term symbolizing all forms of discipline used, including the literal rod used for chastisement. The parent is actually responsible before God to exercise this rod, controlling the child. If the parent fails in this, he will bring ruination and death to his child and disgrace and God's disapproval to himself also. (Pr 10:1; 15:20; 17:25; 19:13) "Foolishness is tied up with the heart of a boy; the rod of discipline is what will remove it far from him." "Do not hold back discipline from the mere boy. In case you beat him with the rod, he will not die. With the rod you yourself should beat him, that you may deliver his very soul from Sheol itself." (Pr 22:15; 23:13, 14) In fact, "the one holding back his rod is hating his son, but the one loving him is he that does look for him with discipline."—Pr 13:24; 19:18; 29:15; 1Sa 2:27-36.

Jehovah God, as the 'Father of the spiritual lives' of Christians, does not spare the "rod" toward his children. The inspired Christian writer of the letter to the Hebrews said: "God is dealing with you as with sons. For what son is he that a father does not discipline? . . . But he does so for our profit that we may partake of his holiness." (Heb 12:7, 9, 10) In administering discipline to the Christian congregation, Jehovah placed authority in the hands of faithful men, particularly the apostles. This authority was to 'build up the brothers and not to tear them down.' (2Co 10:1-11) It included the right to discipline wrongdoers. When the congregation at Corinth deviated from righteousness and began to look to men rather than to Christ, Paul wrote to correct them and said: "What do you want? Shall I come to you with a rod, or with love and mildness of spirit?"—1Co 4:21.

The staff of leadership, shepherding. The shepherd used his staff or crook in directing, defending, and helping his flock. Jehovah and his Son Jesus Christ provide similar shepherding for God's flock of people. Jehovah often spoke of Israel, in covenant relationship with him, as his flock. David wrote: "Jehovah is my Shepherd. . . . He leads me in the tracks of righteousness for his name's sake. Even though I walk in the valley of deep shadow, I fear nothing bad. For you are with me; your rod and your staff are the things that comfort me." (Ps 23:1-4) Micah prayed: "Shepherd your people with your staff, the flock of your inheritance."—Mic 7:14; compare Joh 10:11, 14; Heb 13:20; 1Pe 2:25; 5:4.

RODANIM (Ro'da·nim). Listed as one of Javan's four sons at 1 Chronicles 1:7. There is uncertainty as to the correct spelling of the name, since the Masoretic text at 1 Chronicles 1:7 has "Rodanim," whereas many Hebrew manuscripts and the Latin *Vulgate* here read "Dodanim." "Dodanim" also appears in the Masoretic text at Genesis 10:4, where, however, the Greek *Septuagint* and the Samaritan *Pentateuch* read "Rodanim." In Hebrew the letter "r" (ר) and the letter "d" (ד) are very similar and hence could be confused by a copyist. (Thus "Riphath" in Ge 10:3 appears as "Diphath" at 1Ch 1:6 in the Masoretic text.) Most translations present both names. Many lexicographers consider "Rodanim" to be the preferred reading. Commentators that accept this reading consider it likely that the people descending from this son of Javan populated the island of Rhodes and the neighboring islands of the Aegean Sea.

ROEBUCK [Heb., *yach·mur'*]. The male of the roe deer, a small variety resembling a gazelle. The roebuck (*Capreolus capreolus*) stands over 0.6 m (2 ft) high at the shoulder and measures about 1.2 m (4 ft) in length. Only the males have antlers, and these are shed each year. The roebuck's summer coat is reddish brown, and this may have been the basis for its Hebrew name *yach·mur'*, considered to be derived from a root meaning "be red." This animal is not generally gregarious. Small groups of three or four, the buck, the doe, and a fawn or two, may be seen feeding together. The roebuck has one mate for life.

Being a chewer of the cud and a splitter of the hoof, the roebuck was acceptable for food according to the terms of the Mosaic Law. (De 14:5, 6) The flesh of this creature was one of the meats regularly provided for King Solomon's table.—1Ki 4:22, 23.

ROGELIM (Ro·ge'lim). A town in Gilead and home of David's friend Barzillai. (2Sa 17:27-29; 19:31, 32) Some geographers tentatively place Rogelim at Bersinya, about 7 km (4.5 mi) WSW of Irbid. Wadi er-Rejeileh, near there, possibly preserves the name Rogelim.

ROHGAH (Roh'gah). Second-listed son of Shemer in the genealogy of Asher.—1Ch 7:30, 34.

ROLL. See SCROLL, ROLL.

ROMAMTI-EZER (Ro·mam'ti-e'zer). A son of Heman selected by lot during David's reign to head the last of the 24 Levitical groups of musicians at the sanctuary.—1Ch 25:1, 4, 5, 9, 31.

ROMAN. Originally, and in the restrictive sense, one who lived in the city of Rome, Italy. (Ac 2:10; Ro 1:7) With the expansion of the empire the name took on broader meanings. Sometimes "the Romans" referred to the imperial authority that ruled; "Roman procedure" meant that authority's methods of rule. (Joh 11:48; Ac 25:16; 28:17) At other times a "Roman" simply meant anyone having Roman citizenship, regardless of his nationality or place of birth.—Ac 16:21.

In the latter case one could become a Roman by purchasing citizenship, as in the instance of the military commander Claudius Lysias. Or one might be born a Roman, that is, be a Roman citizen from birth. The apostle Paul was such a one, for although he was a Jew by nationality, and born in the Cilician city of Tarsus hundreds of miles from Italy, from birth he was a Roman.—Ac 21:39; 22:3, 25-28; 23:26, 27; see CITIZEN, CITIZENSHIP.

Being a Roman citizen carried with it many privileges and protections. After Macedonia was conquered in 167 B.C.E., Roman citizens for the most part were exempted from paying taxes. The *Lex Valeria* and the *Lex Porcia*, enacted at various times between 509 and 195 B.C.E., exempted Roman citizens from scourging. The *Lex Valeria* provided such exemption when the citizen appealed to the people; the *Lex Porcia*, without such appeal. At a later date, appeals were made direct to the emperor. If certain capital offenses were involved, citizens could request to be sent to Rome, there to stand trial before the emperor himself. (Ac 25:11, 12) For anyone to violate the Valerian or Porcian laws was a very serious matter, as was demonstrated twice in connection with Paul.—Ac 16:37-40; 22:25-29.

ROMANS, LETTER TO THE. A book of the Christian Greek Scriptures written by the apostle Paul to Christians in Rome. Paul's writership has never been seriously challenged, and the book's authenticity as a part of the sacred canon has been almost universally acknowledged by Bible scholars, with the exception of some who could not fit it in with their own doctrinal beliefs. Actually, the letter is in full harmony with the rest of the inspired Scriptures. In fact, Paul quotes copiously from the Hebrew Scriptures and makes numerous other references to them, so that the letter can be said to be most solidly based on the Hebrew Scriptures and the teachings of Christ.

HIGHLIGHTS OF ROMANS

A letter explaining that righteousness comes, not as a result of ancestry or through works of the Mosaic Law, but through faith in Jesus Christ and as a result of God's undeserved kindness

Written about 56 C.E., some 20 years after the first Gentiles became Christians

---

Righteousness is through faith in Christ and as a result of God's undeserved kindness (1:1–11:36)

Faith is essential for salvation; the scripture says, "The righteous one—by means of faith he will live"

The Jews, although highly favored by God, have not been able to attain to righteousness by means of the Law

Jews as well as non-Jews are under sin; "there is not a righteous man, not even one"

By God's undeserved kindness both Jews and non-Jews can be declared righteous as a free gift through faith, just as Abraham was counted righteous as a result of faith—even before he was circumcised

Men inherit sin and death from one man, Adam; through one man, Jesus, many sinners are declared righteous

This does not give a license to sin; any remaining slaves to sin are not slaves of righteousness

Those formerly under the Law are "made dead to the Law" through Christ's body; they must walk in harmony with the spirit, putting sinful practices of the body to death

The Law served the purpose of making sins manifest; only through Christ, though, is there salvation from sin

God calls those who come to be in union with Christ and declares them righteous; His spirit bears witness that they are His sons

Fleshly Israel received the promises but most of them try to attain righteousness by the Law, hence, only a remnant of them are saved; a public declaration of faith in Christ is necessary for salvation

The illustration of the olive tree shows how, because of the lack of faith of fleshly Israel, non-Israelites were grafted in so that the true Israel might be saved

Attitude regarding superior authorities, self, other persons (12:1–15:13)

Present your body as an acceptable sacrifice to God, make your mind over, use your gifts in God's service, be loving and aglow with the spirit, endure, and keep conquering the evil with the good

Be in subjection to the superior authorities

Love one another; walk decently, not planning ahead for fleshly desires

Do not judge others in matters of conscience, nor abuse your Christian freedom and so stumble those with weak consciences

Be guided by Christ's example in not pleasing self; be willing to bear others' weaknesses, doing what is good for their upbuilding

Paul's loving interest in the congregation at Rome (15:14–16:27)

Paul's reason for writing is to fulfill his commission as an apostle to the Gentiles and in order that these Gentiles might be an acceptable offering to God

No longer having territory where the good news had not already been proclaimed, Paul wants to fulfill his longing to visit Rome and from there to go to Spain, after first traveling to Jerusalem with a contribution from the brothers in Macedonia and Achaia for the holy ones

Paul greets numerous believers by name, encouraging the brothers to avoid those causing divisions and also to be wise regarding what is good

---

Time and Place of Writing. The letter was written about 56 C.E., from Corinth. Tertius was evidently Paul's secretary, writing at Paul's dictation. (Ro 16:22) Phoebe, who lived at Cenchreae, the seaport town of Corinth about 11 km (7 mi) away, was possibly the carrier of the letter. (Ro 16:1) Paul had not yet been to Rome, as is evident from his remarks in chapter 1, verses 9 to 15. The evidence also points to the fact that Peter had never been there.—See PETER, LETTERS OF.

Establishment of the Congregation at Rome. The congregation may have been established by some of the Jews and proselytes from Rome who had visited Jerusalem on Pentecost 33 C.E., had witnessed the miraculous outpouring of holy spirit, and had heard the speech of Peter and the other Christians gathered there. (Ac 2) Or others who converted to Christianity later on may have taken

the good news about the Christ to Rome, for, since this great city was the center of the Roman Empire, many moved there in time, and many were the travelers and businessmen visiting there. Paul sends respectful greetings to Andronicus and Junias, his 'relatives and fellow captives,' who were "men of note among the apostles," and who had been in the service of Christ longer than Paul had. These men may well have had a share in establishing the Christian congregation in Rome. (Ro 16:7) At the time Paul wrote, the congregation had evidently been in existence for some time and was vigorous enough that its faith was being talked about throughout the whole world.—Ro 1:8.

Purpose of the Letter. It becomes clear in reading the letter that it was written to a Christian congregation composed of both Jews and Gentiles. There were many Jews in Rome at the time; they returned after the death of Emperor Claudius, who had banished them sometime earlier. Although Paul had not been in Rome to experience personally the problems the congregation faced, he may have been informed of the congregation's condition and affairs by his good friends and fellow workers Priscilla and Aquila, and possibly by others Paul had met. His greetings in chapter 16 indicate that he knew a good many of the members of the congregation personally.

In Paul's letters he attacked specific problems and dealt with matters he considered most vital to those to whom he wrote. As to Jewish opposition, Paul had already written to the Galatian congregations in refutation, but that letter dealt more specifically with efforts made by Jews who professed Christianity but were "Judaizers," insisting that Gentile converts be circumcised and otherwise be required to observe certain regulations of the Mosaic Law. In the Roman congregation there did not seem to be such a concerted effort in this direction, but there were apparently jealousies and feelings of superiority on the part of both Jews and Gentiles.

The letter, therefore, was not merely a general letter written to the Roman congregation with no specific aim toward them, as some suppose, but it evidently dealt with the things they needed under the circumstances. The Roman congregation would be able to grasp the full meaning and force of the apostle's counsel, for they were doubtless wrestling with the very questions he answered. It is obvious that his purpose was to settle the differences in viewpoint between Jewish and Gentile Christians and to bring them toward complete unity as one man in Christ Jesus. However, in writing as he did, Paul illuminates and enriches our minds in the knowledge of God, and he exalts the righteousness and undeserved kindness of God and the position of Christ toward the Christian congregation and all mankind.

Earnestness and Warmth of Feeling. Commenting on the authenticity of the letter to the Romans, Dr. William Paley, English Bible scholar, said: "In a real St. Paul writing to real converts, it is what anxiety to bring them over to his persuasion would naturally produce; but there is an earnestness and a personality, if I may so call it, in the manner, which a cold forgery, I apprehend, would neither have conceived nor supported." —Horæ Paulinæ, 1790, p. 50.

Paul very straightforwardly and directly outlined the position of the Jews and showed that Jews and Gentiles are on the same level before God. This required him to say some things that might have been considered an occasion for offense by Jews. But Paul's love for his countrymen and his warmth of feeling for them was shown in the delicateness with which he handled these matters. When he said things that might sound derogatory of the Law, or of the Jews, he tactfully followed up with a softening statement.

For example, when he said: "He is not a Jew who is one on the outside, nor is circumcision that which is on the outside upon the flesh," he added: "What, then, is the superiority of the Jew, or what is the benefit of the circumcision? A great deal in every way. First of all, because they were entrusted with the sacred pronouncements of God." (Ro 2:28; 3:1, 2) After saying: "A man is declared righteous by faith apart from works of law," he quickly continued: "Do we, then, abolish law by means of our faith? Never may that happen! On the contrary, we establish law." (3:28, 31) Following his statement: "But now we have been discharged from the Law," he asked: "Is the Law sin? Never may that become so! Really I would not have come to know sin if it had not been for the Law." (7:6, 7) And in chapter 9, verses 1 to 3, he made the strongest possible expression of affection for his fleshly brothers the Jews: "I am telling the truth in Christ; I am not lying, since my conscience bears witness with me in holy spirit, that I have great grief and unceasing pain in my heart. For I could wish that I myself were separated as the cursed one from the Christ in behalf of my brothers, my relatives according to the flesh." —Compare also Ro 9:30-32 with 10:1, 2; and 10: 20, 21 with 11:1-4.

By a study of the book we find, therefore, that it is not a desultory, or aimless, discussion but that it is a discourse with a purpose and a theme, and that no one part can be fully understood without a study of the entire book and a knowledge of its purpose. Paul stresses the undeserved kindness of God through Christ, and he emphasizes that it is only by this undeserved kindness on God's part, coupled with faith on the part of the believer, that men are declared righteous; he notes that neither Jew nor Gentile has any basis for boasting or for lifting himself above the other. He strictly warns the Gentile Christians that they should not become lofty-minded because they profited from the Jews' failure to accept Christ, since the Jews' fall allowed Gentiles to have the opportunity of membership in Christ's "body." He says: "See, therefore, God's kindness and severity. Toward those who fell there is severity, but toward you there is God's kindness, provided you remain in his kindness; otherwise, you also will be lopped off."—Ro 11:22.

ROME

ROME. The once-small city in Latium that became the government seat of the greatest world empire in ancient Bible times; today, it is the capital of Italy. Rome is located inland about 25 km (16 mi) up the Tiber River, on both banks, about halfway down the W side of the 1,100-km-long (700 mi) Italian peninsula.

Just when Rome was founded, and by whom, is shrouded in legend and mythology. Tradition says it was in 753 B.C.E. by a certain Romulus, its first king, but there are graves and other evidence indicating it was inhabited at a much earlier time.

The first known settlements were built on seven hills on the E side of the Tiber River. According to tradition the Palatine hill was the site of the oldest settlement. The other six hills located around Palatine (beginning in the N and turning clockwise) were Quirinal, Viminal, Esquiline, Caelian, Aventine, and Capitoline. In time the marshy valleys between the hills were drained, and in these valuable areas dwellings, forums, and circuses were built. According to Pliny the Elder, in 73 C.E. the walls surrounding the city were some 21 km (13 mi) long. In time the hills and valleys to the W side of the Tiber were annexed, including the more than 40 ha (100 acres) occupied today by the Vatican. Before the great fire of Nero's time, according to conservative estimates, the population of the city was well over a million people.

Rome's Political Image. Over the centuries Rome experimented with many types of political rule. Some institutions were adaptations from other nations; some were innovations of her own. In his *Pocket History of the World*, H. G. Wells observed: "This new Roman power which arose to dominate the western world in the second and first centuries B.C. was in several respects a different thing from any of the great empires that had hitherto prevailed in the civilised world." (1943, p. 149) Rome's political complexion kept changing as various styles of rule came and went. These included coalitions of patriarchal chieftains, kingships, governments concentrated in the hands of a few families of noble birth, dictatorships, and different forms of republican rule in which the power conferred on the senators, consuls, and triumvirates (three-man governmental coalitions) varied, with typical party struggles between classes and factions. In the latter years of the empire there was a series of emperors. As is common with human governments, Rome's political history was mottled with hatred, jealousy, intrigue, and murder, with many plots and counterplots generated from internal friction and external wars.

Domination of the world by Rome was a gradual development. First, her influence spread over the entire Italian Peninsula and eventually around the Mediterranean and far beyond. The name of the city became practically synonymous with that of the empire.

In international affairs Rome reached the zenith of her glory under the Caesars. Heading this list was Julius Caesar, appointed dictator for ten years in 46 B.C.E. but murdered by conspirators in 44 B.C.E. After an interval in which a triumvirate attempted to hold the reins of power, Octavian finally became the sole ruler of the Roman Empire (31 B.C.E.–14 C.E.). In 27 B.C.E. he succeeded in becoming emperor, having himself proclaimed "Augustus." It was during the rule of Augustus that Jesus was born in 2 B.C.E. (Lu 2:1-7) The successor to Augustus, Tiberius (14-37 C.E.), was ruling during Jesus' ministry. (Lu 3:1, 2, 21-23) Next came Gaius (Caligula) (37-41 C.E.) and Claudius (41-54 C.E.), the latter issuing a decree expelling the Jews from Rome. (Ac 18:1, 2) Nero's rule followed (54-68 C.E.), and it was to him that Paul appealed his case.—Ac 25:11, 12, 21; PICTURES, Vol. 2, p. 534.

Roman emperors in the order of succession after Nero (through the first century) were Galba (68-69 C.E.); Otho and Vitellius (69 C.E.); Vespasian (69-79 C.E.), during whose reign Jerusalem was destroyed; Titus (79-81 C.E.), who previously had directed the successful assault on Jerusalem; Domitian (81-96 C.E.), under whose rule, tradition says, John was exiled to the penal island of Patmos; Nerva (96-98 C.E.); and Trajan (98-117 C.E.). It was under Trajan that the empire reached its greatest limits, the boundaries by then extending far out in all directions—to the Rhine and the North Sea, the Danube, the Euphrates, the cataracts of the Nile, the great African Desert, and the Atlantic on the W.—MAP, Vol. 2, p. 533.

During the declining years of the Roman Empire, Constantine the Great was emperor (306-337 C.E.). After seizing control, he transferred the capital to Byzantium (Constantinople). In the next century Rome fell, in 476 C.E., and the German warlord Odoacer became its first "barbarian" king.

City Life and Conditions. Administration of city government was divided into 14 districts under Augustus, with a magistrate chosen annually by lot to govern each district. Seven fire-fighting brigades called *vigiles* were organized, each responsible for two of the districts. Just outside the NE city limits was stationed a special force of about 10,000, known as the Praetorian, or Imperial, Guard, for the protection of the emperor. There were also three "urban cohorts," a kind of city police force, to maintain law and order in Rome.

The wealthy and influential often lived in palatial homes on the hills; their homes were maintained by large households of servants and slaves, sometimes numbering into the hundreds. Down in the valleys the common people were crowded together in enormous insulae, or tenement houses, several stories high, limited in height by Augustus to 21 m (70 ft). These tenement blocks were separated by narrow, crooked, dirty streets filled with the customary traffic and corruption prevalent in big cities.

It was in these poor sections that the historic fire of 64 C.E. resulted in the greatest suffering and loss of life. Tacitus describes the plight of "shrieking and terrified women; fugitives stricken or immature in years." (*The Annals*, XV, XXXVIII) Only 4 out of the 14 districts of Rome were spared.

There were very few persons in Rome who could be called middle class; the wealth rested with a small minority. When Paul first reached Rome, perhaps half the population were slaves, brought there as prisoners of war, as condemned criminals, or as children sold by parents, slaves with no legal rights. The greater part of the free half of the population were paupers who practically lived off government subsidies.

Two things, food and entertainment, were provided by the state to keep these poor people from rioting, hence the satirical phrase, *panem et circenses* (bread and circuses), implying that this was all that was needed to satisfy the poor of Rome. From 58 B.C.E. on, grain was generally distributed free as well as water, which was brought many miles into the city by aqueducts. Wine was a cheap commodity. For the enjoyment of those so inclined, there were libraries available. For the entertainment of the general populace, there were public baths and gymnasiums, as well as the theaters and circuses. The theatrical performances consisted of Greek and Roman plays, dances, and pantomimes. In the great amphitheaters and circuses exciting games were held, chiefly spectacular chariot races and desperate gladiatorial contests in which men and beasts fought to the death. The Circus Maximus had a capacity of more than 150,000 persons. Admission to the games was free.

The high cost of these government expenses was not borne by the populace of Rome, for after the conquest of Macedonia in 167 B.C.E., Roman citizens were tax free. Instead, the provinces were heavily taxed, both directly and indirectly.—Mt 22:17-21.

Foreign Influence. In many ways Rome proved to be a great melting pot of races, languages, cultures, and ideas. Out of the forge of Roman politics the code of Roman law gradually emerged—laws that defined the rights and limitations of governments, courts, and magistrates and that provided legal devices such as citizenship for the protection of human rights. (Ac 25:16) Citizenship was extended to Rome's confederate cities and to various colonies of the empire. It carried with it many advantages. (Ac 16:37-39; 22:25, 26) If not obtained by birth, it could be purchased. (Ac 22:28) In this and other ways, Rome sought to Romanize the territories she won and thus to strengthen her position as mistress of the empire.

One of the best examples of outside influence on Rome is found in her ruins of past architectural glories. Everywhere, the visitor to this museum city sees how she borrowed from the Greeks and others. The so-called Roman arch, which she used to great advantage, was not her own engineering discovery. Rome's successes as a builder were also due in large measure to her use of a primitive form of concrete as mortar and as a major ingredient in making artificial stones.

The building program of Rome began in earnest in the last century of the republic and was thereafter given special impetus by the emperors. Augustus said he found Rome a city of bricks but left it a city of marble. For the most part, the marble was a veneer over the structural brick or concrete. There was a second rebuilding of the city, after the conflagration of 64 C.E. Among the more notable Roman structures were the forums, temples, palaces, amphitheaters, baths, aqueducts, sewers, and monuments. The great Colosseum and some monuments, like Titus' archway depicting the fall of Jerusalem, either are still standing or are partly standing. (PICTURES, Vol. 2, p. 536) The Romans also made a name for themselves as builders of roads and bridges throughout the empire.

There was such an influx of foreigners that the Romans complained Rome was no longer Roman. Gravitating from all quarters of the empire, they brought with them their trades, customs, traditions, and religions. Whereas Latin was the official language, the international language was Common Greek (Koine). That is why the apostle Paul wrote his letter to the Romans in Greek. Greek influence had its impact on the literature and methods of education too. Boys, and sometimes girls, were formally educated according to the Athenian system, being schooled in Greek literature and oratory, and the sons of those who could afford it were sent to one of the schools of philosophy in Athens.

Religion. Rome also became the recipient of every form of false worship. As historian John Lord described it: "Superstition culminated at Rome, for there were seen the priests and devotees of all the countries that it governed,—'the dark-skinned daughters of Isis, with drum and timbrel and wanton mien; devotees of the Persian Mithras; emasculated Asiatics; priests of Cybele, with their wild dances and discordant cries; worshippers of the great goddess Diana; barbarian captives with the rites of Teuton priests; Syrians, Jews, Chaldæan astrologers, and Thessalian sorcerers.'"—*Beacon Lights of History*, 1912, Vol. III, pp. 366, 367.

Devotion to these religions, and indulgence in their wanton sex orgies, opened the door to total abandonment of moral virtue and righteousness among Romans of both low and high rank. According to Tacitus, among the latter, Messalina, the adulterous, murderous wife of Emperor Claudius, is an example.—*The Annals*, XI, I-XXXIV.

Outstanding among the religions of Rome was emperor worship. The Roman ruler was deified. Emperor worship was recognized especially in the provinces, temples being built in which they sacrificed to him as to a god. (PICTURE, Vol. 2, p. 536) In *A History of Rome*, George Botsford says: "The worship of the emperor was to be the most vital force in the religion of the Roman world till the adoption of Christianity." An inscription found in Asia Minor says of the emperor: "He is the paternal Zeus and the saviour of the whole race of man, who fulfils all prayers, even more than we ask. For land and sea enjoy peace; cities flourish; everywhere are harmony and prosperity and happiness." This cult proved to be a chief instrument of persecution for Christians, concerning whom this writer says: "Their refusal to worship the *Genius*, or guardian spirit, of the emperor was naturally construed as impiety and treason."—1905, pp. 214, 215, 263.

The Appian Way, over which Paul traveled en route to Rome

Christianity Comes to Rome. On the day of Pentecost, 33 C.E., there were "sojourners from Rome, both Jews and proselytes," present to witness the results of the outpouring of the holy spirit, and some of them were no doubt among the 3,000 baptized on that occasion. (Ac 2:1, 10, 41) Upon returning to Rome, they doubtless preached, resulting in the formation of a very strong, active Christian congregation whose faith the apostle Paul mentioned as being "talked about throughout the whole world." (Ro 1:7, 8) Both Tacitus (*The Annals,* XV, XLIV) and Suetonius (*The Lives of the Caesars,* Nero, XVI, 2) referred to the Christians in Rome.

Paul wrote to the Christian congregation in Rome about 56 C.E., and about three years later he arrived in Rome as a prisoner. Although he had entertained desires of visiting there sooner and under different circumstances (Ac 19:21; Ro 1:15; 15:22-24), he was able, even though a prisoner, to give a thorough witness by having people come to his house. For two years, under these conditions, he continued "preaching the kingdom of God to them and teaching the things concerning the Lord Jesus Christ with the greatest freeness of speech, without hindrance." (Ac 28:14-31) Even the emperor's Praetorian Guard became acquainted with the Kingdom message. (Php 1:12, 13) So, as it had been foretold of him, Paul 'gave a thorough witness even in Rome.'—Ac 23:11.

During this two-year detention in Rome Paul found time to write letters, those to the Ephesians, Philippians, Colossians, and Philemon. Evidently about the same time, Mark wrote his Gospel account in Rome. Shortly before or immediately after Paul's release, he penned his letter to the Hebrews in about 61 C.E. (Heb 13:23, 24) It was during his second imprisonment in Rome, in about 65 C.E., that Onesiphorus visited him and that Paul wrote his second letter to Timothy.—2Ti 1:15-17.

Though Paul, Luke, Mark, Timothy, and other first-century Christians visited Rome (Php 1:1; Col 4:10, 14), there is no evidence that Peter was ever in Rome, as some traditions would have it. The stories about Peter's martyrdom in Rome are strictly traditional, with no solid historical support.—See PETER, LETTERS OF.

The city of Rome developed a very bad reputation for its persecution of Christians, particularly during the reigns of Nero and Domitian. These persecutions were attributed to two causes: (1) the great evangelizing zeal of Christians to convert others, and (2) Christians' uncompromising stand in giving to God the things that are God's rather than giving them to Caesar.—Mr 12:17.

ROOF CHAMBER. See HOUSE.

ROSH.

1. A son of Benjamin listed among those who went into Egypt in 1728 B.C.E. with Jacob's household or who were born shortly thereafter. (Ge 46:21, 26; see BENJAMIN No. 1.) The omission of his name from later lists of Benjamite families may indicate that he died childless or that his sons merged with a different tribal family.

2. A name found in some translations of Ezekiel 38:2 and 39:1 (*AS, JB, Le, LXX, Mo, Yg, Ro*), viewed by some scholars as designating a barbarous people called Rosh, who are said to have lived in Russia along the Volga River north of the Taurus Mountains. In view of the meaning of the term and its application to Gog, however, it is appropriately translated as part of a title rather than a geographic name: thus, "head chieftain" (*NW*); "chief prince" (*KJ, Dy, Fn, JP, RS*); "great prince" (*AT*); "prince of the head" and "head prince" (*Vg*); "leader and head" (*Sy*); "head great one" (Targums).

RUBY. A precious, transparent, rich-red gemstone that is a variety of corundum. It is composed of aluminum oxide containing minute traces of chromium and iron oxide that impart the red color. It is very rare, slightly inferior to the diamond in hardness, and when of excellent quality and large size, it may exceed a diamond of the same size in value. Colors range from rose to the highly appraised deep bluish red often identified as "pigeon blood" red. "Ruby," as used in the *New World Translation,* is translated from two Hebrew words ('o'dhem; kadh·kodh') that evidently both denote bright redness or extreme redness.

The first stone in the first row of gems on High Priest Aaron's "breastpiece of judgment" was a ruby, and engraved upon it was the name of one of the 12 tribes of Israel. (Ex 28:2, 15, 17, 21; 39:10) The "covering" of the king of Tyre consisted of the ruby and other precious stones. (Eze 28: 12, 13) Edom was Tyre's "merchant" for precious rubies. Commercial Tyre eagerly traded its stores for these and other goods. (Eze 27:2, 16) When Jehovah, the husbandly owner of Zion, comforted her and described her forthcoming beauty, he said, in part: "I will make your battlements of rubies, and your gates of fiery glowing stones." —Isa 54:5, 6, 11, 12.

RUDDER. A key part of a ship's steering apparatus. Ancient sailing vessels had various styles and numbers of rudders. Some had a single steering oar. Usually, however, Greek and Roman ships had two steering paddles at the stern, each probably capable of being operated independently through a rowlock (something like an open porthole). When the vessel was anchored, the rudder oars were held out of the water by lashings or rudder bands.

"Rudder oars" ("steering-paddles," *NE*) were used to guide the vessel on which Paul was sailing en route to Rome and which was wrecked on Malta. The anchors were cut away, and before the foresail was hoisted, the lashings were loosened, freeing the rudder oars to aid the sailors in directing the ship toward the beach.—Ac 27:40.

James (3:4, 5) shows the tremendous power the tongue has in controlling the direction of one's whole body by comparing it to the relatively small rudder ("rudder-oar," *Int*) of a large ship.

RUE [Gr., *pe'ga·non*]. The common variety of rue (*Ruta graveolens*) is a strong-scented shrubby perennial with hairy stems that attains a height of about 1 m (3 ft). It has gray-green leaves and bears clusters of yellow flowers. During the days of Jesus' earthly ministry rue may have been cultivated in Palestine for use in medicine and as a flavoring for food.

This plant is mentioned only at Luke 11:42, with reference to the scrupulous tithing of the Pharisees. Instead of "rue," the parallel account at Matthew 23:23 mentions "dill," as does a third-century manuscript (P[45]) at Luke 11:42.

RUFUS (Ru'fus) [Red].

1. Son of the Simon who was compelled to help carry Jesus' torture stake; brother of a certain Alexander.—Mr 15:21; Lu 23:26.

2. A Christian in Rome, "the chosen one in the Lord," whom Paul greets in his letter. With endearment Paul also greets Rufus' mother as "his mother and mine."—Ro 16:13.

RUINATION, MOUNT OF. See the subject OLIVES, MOUNT OF.

RULER. A person who exercises authority or control; a sovereign. The Hebrew verb *ma·shal'* has the meaning "rule, dominate"; the Greek term *ar'khon* is translated "ruler."—See CITY RULERS.

The supreme Ruler is Jehovah God, who exercises absolute sovereign authority over the universe, visible and invisible, by virtue of being the Creator and Life-Giver.—Da 4:17, 25, 35; 1Ti 1:17.

The kings of the line of David on the throne of Israel ruled as representatives of Jehovah, their real, invisible King. They were, therefore, said to be God's anointed, sitting on "Jehovah's throne." (1Ch 29:23) When Jesus Christ "the Son of David" appeared (Mt 21:9; Lu 20:41), he was anointed, not with oil, but with holy spirit, to rule on a heavenly throne. (Ac 2:34-36) Under Jehovah, Jesus and his fellow heirs of the Kingdom constitute the government of the universe.—Re 14:1, 4; 20:4, 6; 22:5.

Satan the Devil and his demons are also rulers. He is spoken of as "the ruler of this world" and "the ruler of the authority of the air." (Joh 12:31; 14:30; Eph 2:2) That all the governments of this world are under his power is indicated by his offering them to Jesus Christ at the price of an act of worship. (Mt 4:8, 9) Satan gives these governments their authority. (Re 13:2) Within his organization the demons also exercise ruling power. They are referred to as "the world rulers of this darkness" who have exercised authority over the world powers of history, as, for example, the invisible 'princes' over Persia and Greece. (Eph 6:12; Da 10:13, 20) Their ruler is, of course, the Devil himself.—Mt 12:24.

In the days of Jesus' earthly ministry, Palestine was under the dual rule of the Roman Empire and the Jewish rulers, the chief body of the latter being the Great Sanhedrin, a council of 70 elders to which the Roman government granted limited authority over Jewish affairs. It is to the Jewish rulers that reference is made at John 7:26, 48; Nicodemus was one of these. (Joh 3:1) A presiding officer of the synagogue was called an *ar'khon*. (Compare Mt 9:18 and Mr 5:22.) The Law commanded respect for rulers. (Ac 23:5) However, the Jewish rulers became corrupt and are mentioned as the ones on whom the chief blame rested for Jesus Christ's death.—Lu 23:13, 35; 24:20; Ac 3:17; 13:27, 28.

Ar'khon is also applied to civil magistrates and government officials in general. (Ac 16:19, 20; Ro 13:3) The Hebrew word *segha·nim'*, translated "rulers" (*KJ*), "deputies" (*Ro*), "deputy rulers" (*NW*), is used with reference to subordinate Jewish rulers under the Persian Empire (Ne 2:16; 5:7), also of ones holding authority under the kings of Media, Assyria, and Babylon.—Jer 51:28; Eze 23: 12, 23; see DEPUTY.

Rulers can bring prosperity and happiness, or poverty and suffering, to their subjects. (Pr 28:15; 29:2) David quotes Jehovah God as saying: "When one ruling over mankind is righteous, ruling in the fear of God, then it is as the light of morning, when the sun shines forth, a morning without clouds." (2Sa 23:3, 4) Such a ruler is Jesus Christ the Prince of Peace.—Isa 9:6, 7.

RUMAH (Ru′mah) [Height; Exalted Place]. Home of Zebidah (and her father Pedaiah), a wife of King Josiah of Judah and the mother of Jehoiakim. (2Ki 23:34, 36) Its location is uncertain. It is tentatively identified with Khirbet er-Rumeh, which bears a similar name. Today called Horvat Ruma, it is situated about 10 km (6 mi) N of Nazareth. But some connect Rumah with the Biblical town of Arumah, mentioned at Judges 9:41 and thought to have been located near Shechem. —See ARUMAH.

RUNNERS. Swift foot couriers or servants of a prominent person who ran before his chariot. The word is translated from the participial form of the Hebrew word *ruts,* meaning "run." It is rendered "footmen," "guard," and "post" in some translations. But there is another word for "footmen" or "men on foot," namely *ragh·li′,* or, more fully, *′ish ragh·li′.*

"Runners" can refer to any swift messengers or fleet-footed persons, such as Asahel the brother of Joab, and Ahimaaz the son of Zadok. (2Sa 2:18; 18:19, 23, 27) Elijah on one occasion ran perhaps at least 30 km (19 mi), to arrive from Carmel at Jezreel ahead of King Ahab's chariot. This was because "the very hand of Jehovah proved to be upon Elijah."—1Ki 18:46.

In an official sense, runners were fleet-footed men selected to run before the king's chariot. When Absalom and, later, Adonijah conspired to usurp the kingship, each employed 50 runners before his chariot to add prestige and dignity to his scheme. (2Sa 15:1; 1Ki 1:5) Runners served as the king's personal force, somewhat like a modern-day bodyguard. (1Sa 22:17; 2Ki 10:25) They served as guards at the entrance to the king's house and accompanied the king from his house to the temple. (1Ki 14:27, 28; 2Ki 11:6-8, 11; 2Ch 12:10) They carried messages for the king. (2Ch 30:6) In the days of Persian King Ahasuerus, foot couriers were apparently replaced by men riding fast post-horses.—Es 3:13, 15; 8:10, 14.

Illustrative Use. In the Christian Greek Scriptures, there are a few references to running simply in haste. (Mt 28:8; Mr 9:15, 25; 10:17; Joh 20:2) However, running is used illustratively by the apostle Paul. He wrote to the congregation at Corinth: "Do you not know that the runners in a race all run, but only one receives the prize? Run in such a way that you may attain it. Moreover, every man taking part in a contest exercises self-control in all things. Now they, of course, do it that they may get a corruptible crown, but we an incorruptible one. Therefore, the way I am running is not uncertainly; the way I am directing my blows is so as not to be striking the air; but I pummel my body and lead it as a slave, that, after I have preached to others, I myself should not become disapproved somehow."—1Co 9:24-27.

Contestants in the Greek games were strenuously trained, and discipline was rigid; diet and behavior were closely observed. The rules of the race were strictly enforced by the judges. If a runner came in first but had violated the rules, his running was in vain; as the apostle expressed it: "Moreover, if anyone contends even in the games, he is not crowned unless he has contended according to the rules." (2Ti 2:5) Runners directed their eyes toward the prize located at the finish line. Paul 'ran' in this single-minded, wholehearted way. (Ga 2:2; Php 2:16; 3:14) Near the end of his life he was able to say: "I have fought the fine fight, I have run the course to the finish, I have observed the faith. From this time on there is reserved for me the crown of righteousness."—2Ti 4:7, 8.

In discussing God's dealings in connection with his choosing of those making up spiritual Israel, Paul explained that Israel according to the flesh counted on their fleshly relationship to Abraham. (Ro 9:6, 7, 30-32) They thought they were the chosen ones and 'ran,' or pursued righteousness, but in the wrong way. Trying to establish their righteousness by their own works, they did not subject themselves to the righteousness of God. (Ro 10:1-3) Paul directs attention to God's justice in rejecting fleshly Israel as a nation and forming a spiritual Israel. In connection with that discussion, he makes the statement that "it depends, not upon the one wishing nor upon the one running, but upon God, who has mercy."—Ro 9:15, 16.

RUSH [Heb., *′agh·mohn′*]. Any of a variety of grasslike plants commonly growing in marshes. The true rushes have round, frequently hollow, stems with three rows of grasslike leaves, and small brownish or greenish flowers. The designation *′agh·mohn′* may have included the various kinds of true rushes as well as the rushlike plants of the sedge family.

Anciently, rushes were employed in starting the fire in a furnace. (Job 41:20) At Job 41:2 "rush" may refer to a cord of twisted rushes or to one spun from their fibers.

The other Scriptural references to *′agh·mohn′* are illustrative. Jehovah took no delight in renegade Israel's fasting, attended by bowing their heads ceremonially like a rush. (Isa 58:5) At Isaiah 9:14, "rush" seems to refer to the false prophets (the "tail") who merely spoke what the leaders of the nation of Israel (the "head," or "shoot") wanted to hear.—Isa 9:15; see also 19:15, where "rush" appears to denote the Egyptians in general.

RUST. The reddish, porous, brittle coating formed on iron especially when chemically attacked by moist air; by extension, the coating produced on any of various other metals by corrosion. Iron rusts, copper and silver are said to corrode, even gold can be attacked by certain acids or elements. The Hebrew word *chel·'ah'*, translated "rust" (*NW; RS*) or "scum" (*KJ*), is drawn from a word meaning "be sick" (2Ch 16: 12); hence with reference to metal, it denotes rust. (Eze 24:6, 11, 12) The Greek word *bro'sis* means "an eating" (Mt 6:19, 20), while *i·os'* means both "poison" (Ro 3:13; Jas 3:8) and "rust."—Jas 5:3.

Ezekiel compared Jerusalem to a widemouthed copper cooking pot "the rust of which is in it." This rust represented the uncleanness, loose conduct, and bloodshed for which Jerusalem was responsible. The command was given, after cooking flesh in the pot, to "stand it empty upon its coals in order that it may get hot; and its copper must become heated up, and its uncleanness must be liquefied in the midst of it. Let its rust get consumed [and its copper may burn, that its filthiness may be melted in it, its rust consumed; *RS*]."—Eze 24:3-12.

Jesus Christ said, in his Sermon on the Mount: "Stop storing up for yourselves treasures upon the earth, where moth and rust [*bro'sis*] consume, and where thieves break in and steal. Rather, store up for yourselves treasures in heaven, where neither moth nor rust consumes, and where thieves do not break in and steal." (Mt 6:19, 20) Material wealth hoarded up is put to no beneficial use; idle, it may rust and eventually be of no use even to its owner. In fact, as James warns rich men who trust in material wealth: "Your riches have rotted . . . Your gold and silver are rusted away, and their rust [*i·os'*] will be as a witness against you and will eat your fleshy parts. Something like fire is what you have stored up in the last days. Look! The wages due the workers who harvested your fields but which are held up by you, keep crying out, and the calls for help on the part of the reapers have entered into the ears of Jehovah of armies." (Jas 5:2-4) Instead of using their riches in the right way, they unrighteously hold them back. The longer this is done, and the greater the corrosion and rust gathered, the greater the witness is against them before the judgment throne of God. The opposite of such failure to use material wealth was recommended by Jesus when he said: "Make friends for yourselves by means of the unrigh-

teous riches, so that, when such fail, they may receive you into the everlasting dwelling places." —Lu 16:9.

RUTH. A Moabitess who married Mahlon after the death of his father Elimelech and while Mahlon, his mother Naomi, and his brother Chilion were living in Moab. A famine had caused the family to leave their native Bethlehem in Judah. Ruth's brother-in-law Chilion was married to the Moabitess Orpah. Eventually the two brothers died, leaving behind childless widows. Learning that Jehovah's favor was again manifest in Israel, Naomi, accompanied by her two daughters-in-law, proceeded to return to Judah.—Ru 1:1-7; 4:9, 10.

Her Loyal Love. Whereas Orpah finally returned to her people at Naomi's recommendation, Ruth stuck with her mother-in-law. Deep love for Naomi and a sincere desire to serve Jehovah in association with his people enabled Ruth to leave her parents and her native land, with little prospect of finding the security that marriage might bring. (Ru 1:8-17; 2:11) Her love for her mother-in-law was such that, later, others were able to say that she was better to Naomi than seven sons. —Ru 4:15.

Arriving in Bethlehem at the commencement of the barley harvest, Ruth, in behalf of Naomi and herself, went out to the field to procure food. By chance she lighted on the field belonging to Boaz, a relative of Elimelech, and requested the overseer of the harvesters for permission to glean. Her diligence in gleaning must have been outstanding, as is evident from the fact that the overseer commented about her work to Boaz.—Ru 1:22–2:7.

When Boaz extended kindnesses to her, Ruth responded with appreciation and humbly acknowledged being less than one of his maidservants. At mealtime he provided roasted grain for her in such abundance that she had some left over to give to Naomi. (Ru 2:8-14, 18) Though Boaz arranged matters to make it easier for her to glean, Ruth did not quit early but continued to glean until the evening, "after which she beat out what she had gleaned, and it came to be about an ephah [22 L; 20 dry qt] of barley." Having been requested by Boaz to continue gleaning in his field, Ruth did so during the remainder of the barley harvest, as well as the wheat harvest.—Ru 2:15-23.

Requests That Boaz Act as a Repurchaser. Desiring to find "a resting-place," or home, for her daughter-in-law, Naomi instructed Ruth to request Boaz to repurchase her. Accordingly, Ruth went down to Boaz' threshing floor. After Boaz lay down, Ruth quietly approached, uncovered him at his feet, and lay down herself. At midnight, trembling, he awoke and bent forward. Not recognizing her in the dark, he asked: "Who are you?" She replied, "I am Ruth your slave girl, and you must spread out your skirt over your slave girl, for you are a repurchaser."—Ru 3:1-9.

Ruth's actions, in compliance with Naomi's instructions, must have been in line with the customary procedure followed by women when claiming the right to brother-in-law marriage. In Lange's *Commentary on the Holy Scriptures*, Paulus Cassel makes this observation regarding Ruth 3:9: "Undoubtedly this symbolical method of claiming the most delicate of all rights, presupposes manners of patriarchal simplicity and virtue. The confidence of the woman reposes itself on the honor of the man. The method, however, was one which could not easily be brought into operation. For every foreknowledge or pre-intimation of it would have torn the veil of silence and secrecy from the modesty of the claimant. But when it was once put into operation, the petition preferred could not be denied without disgrace either to the woman or the man. Hence, we may be sure that Naomi did not send her daughter-in-law on this errand without the fullest confidence that it would prove successful. For it is certain that to all other difficulties, this peculiar one was added in the present case: namely, that Boaz, as Ruth herself says, was indeed *a goel* [a repurchaser], but not *the goel*. The answer of Boaz, also, suggests the surmise that such a claim was not wholly unexpected by him. Not that he had an understanding with Naomi, in consequence of which he was alone

on the threshing-floor; for the fact that he was startled out of his sleep, shows that the night visit was altogether unlooked for. But the thought that at some time the claim of Ruth to the rights of blood-relationship might be addressed to himself, may not have been strange to him. Even this conjecture, however, of what might possibly or probably take place, could not be used to relieve Ruth of the necessity of manifesting her own free will by means of the symbolical proceeding." —Translated and edited by P. Schaff, 1976, p. 42.

That Boaz viewed Ruth's actions as being completely virtuous is evident from his reaction: "Blessed may you be of Jehovah, my daughter. You have expressed your loving-kindness better in the last instance than in the first instance, in not going after the young fellows whether lowly or rich." Ruth unselfishly chose Boaz, a much older man, because of his being a repurchaser, in order to raise up a name for her deceased husband and her mother-in-law. As it would have been a natural thing for a young woman like Ruth to prefer a younger man, Boaz viewed this as an even better expression of her loving-kindness than her choosing to stick with her aged mother-in-law.—Ru 3:10.

Doubtless Ruth's voice must have reflected some anxiety, prompting Boaz to reassure her: "Now, my daughter, do not be afraid. All that you say I shall do for you, for everyone in the gate of my people is aware that you are an excellent woman." The hour being late, Boaz instructed Ruth to lie down. However, both of them got up while it was still dark, evidently to avoid starting any rumor that would cast a bad reflection on

HIGHLIGHTS OF RUTH

A narrative showing how the God-fearing Moabitess Ruth was blessed by Jehovah by becoming part of the unbroken Messianic line leading to King David

Setting is during the time of the Judges; writing was likely completed about 1090 B.C.E.

Ruth decides to stay with Naomi and her God, Jehovah (1:1-22)

Childless and widowed, Ruth and Orpah accompany their mother-in-law Naomi, widow of Elimelech, as she departs from Moab to return to Judah

Dissuaded by Naomi's words regarding the bleak prospects for remarriage, Orpah turns back

Ruth is undeterred; she declares that Naomi's people will be her people and Naomi's God her God

Finally, Ruth and Naomi arrive in Bethlehem

Ruth gleans in the field of Boaz (2:1–3:18)

By chance, Ruth begins gleaning in the field of Boaz, a

kinsman of Elimelech, and gains his favorable attention

Ruth continues gleaning in Boaz' field until the end of the barley and wheat harvests

Then, following Naomi's instructions, Ruth requests Boaz to act as a repurchaser; Boaz is willing, but there is a man more closely related to Naomi than he is

Boaz, as repurchaser, marries Ruth (4:1-22)

Before ten elders of Bethlehem, Boaz offers the closer relative the opportunity to repurchase the field of Elimelech and to raise up offspring for the dead man by performing brother-in-law marriage with Ruth

When the relative declines, Boaz acts as repurchaser

The union of Boaz and Ruth is blessed with the birth of a son, Obed, the grandfather of King David

either one of them. Boaz also gave Ruth six measures of barley. This may have signified that, just as six working days were followed by a day of rest, Ruth's day of rest was at hand, for he would see to it that she would have "a resting-place."—Ru 3:1, 11-15, 17, 18.

Upon Ruth's arrival, Naomi, perhaps not recognizing the woman seeking admittance in the dark, asked: "Who are you, my daughter?" Or, it may be that this question pertained to Ruth's possible new identity in relationship to her repurchaser.—Ru 3:16.

Later, when the nearer relative refused to perform brother-in-law marriage, Boaz promptly did so. Thus Ruth became the mother of Boaz' son Obed and an ancestress of King David and also of Jesus Christ.—Ru 4:1-21; Mt 1:5, 16.

RUTH, BOOK OF. This Bible book takes its name from one of its principal characters, Ruth the Moabitess. The narrative shows how Ruth became an ancestress of David by undergoing brother-in-law marriage with Boaz in behalf of her mother-in-law Naomi. The appreciation, loyalty, and the trust in Jehovah that were manifested by Boaz, Naomi, and Ruth permeate the account. —Ru 1:8, 9, 16, 17; 2:4, 10-13, 19, 20; 3:9-13; 4:10.

With the exception of the genealogical listing (Ru 4:18-22), the events related in the book of Ruth cover a period of about 11 years in the time of the Judges, though it is not stated exactly when it was during this period that they occurred.—Ru 1:1, 4, 22; 2:23; 4:13.

Jewish tradition credits Samuel with the writership of the book, and this would not disagree with internal evidence. The fact that the account concludes with David's genealogy suggests that the writer knew about God's purpose respecting David. This would fit Samuel, for he was the one who anointed David to be king. Therefore, it would also have been appropriate for Samuel to make a record of David's ancestral background.—1Sa 16: 1, 13.

Authenticity and Value. That the book of Ruth is historical is confirmed by Matthew's genealogy of Jesus Christ, which lists Boaz, Ruth, and Obed in the line of descent. (Mt 1:5; compare Ru 4:18-22; 1Ch 2:5, 9-15.) Moreover, it is inconceivable that a Hebrew writer would have deliberately invented a *foreign* maternal ancestry for David, the first king in the royal line of Judah.

The historical record provides background material that illustrates and illuminates other parts of the Bible. The application of the laws involving gleaning (Le 19:9, 10; De 24:19-22; Ru 2:1, 3, 7, 15-17, 23) and brother-in-law marriage (De 25:5-10; Ru 3:7-13; 4:1-13) are vividly portrayed. There is evidence of Jehovah's guidance in the preservation of the line of descent leading to the Messiah and also in the choice of individuals for that line. Israelite women who were married to a man of the tribe of Judah had the possible prospect of contributing to Messiah's earthly line of descent. (Ge 49:10) The fact that Ruth, a Moabitess, was so favored illustrates the principle stated by the apostle Paul: "It depends, not upon the one wishing nor upon the one running, but upon God, who has mercy." (Ro 9:16) Ruth had chosen Jehovah as her God and Israel as her people, and in his great mercy, Jehovah granted to her "a perfect wage" in permitting her to become a link in the most important line of descent.—Ru 2:12; 4:13-17.

S

SABBATH DAY. A day set apart by God for rest from regular labors; the Sabbath was given by Jehovah as a sign between him and the sons of Israel. (Ex 31:16, 17) The Hebrew expression *yohm hash·shab·bath'* is drawn from the verb *sha·vath'*, meaning "rest, cease." (Ge 2:2; 8:22) In Greek, *he he·me'ra tou sab·ba'tou* means "sabbath day."

The history of a weekly 24-hour sabbath observance begins with the nation of Israel in the wilderness in the second month after their Exodus from Egypt in 1513 B.C.E. (Ex 16:1) Jehovah had told Moses that the miraculous provision of the manna would be double on the sixth day. When this proved true, the chieftains of the assembly reported the matter to Moses and then the arrangement for the weekly Sabbath was announced. (Ex 16:22, 23) That Israel was obligated from that time forward is shown by Jehovah's words at Exodus 16:28, 29.

The weekly Sabbath was made an integral part of a system of sabbaths when the Law covenant was formally inaugurated at Mount Sinai a short time later. (Ex 19:1; 20:8-10; 24:5-8) This sabbatical system was composed of many types of sabbaths: the 7th day, the 7th year, the 50th year (Jubilee year), Nisan 14 (Passover), Nisan 15, Nisan 21, Sivan 6 (Pentecost), Ethanim 1, Ethanim 10 (Atonement Day), Ethanim 15, and Ethanim 22.

That the Sabbath was not enjoined upon any of God's servants until after the Exodus is evident from the testimony of Deuteronomy 5:2, 3 and Exodus 31:16, 17: "It was not with our forefathers that Jehovah concluded this covenant, but with us." "The sons of Israel must keep the sabbath . . . during their generations. . . . Between me and the sons of Israel it is a sign to time indefinite." If Israel had already been observing the Sabbath, it could not have served as a reminder of their deliverance from Egypt by Jehovah, as shown at Deuteronomy 5:15. The fact that some of the Israelites went out to pick up manna on the seventh day, in spite of direct instruction to the contrary, indicates that Sabbath observance was something new. (Ex 16:11-30) That there was uncertainty in handling the case of the first recorded Sabbath breaker after the Law had been given at Sinai also shows that the Sabbath had only recently been instituted. (Nu 15:32-36) While in Egypt the Israelites, being slaves, could not have kept the Sabbath even if they had been under such law at the time. Pharaoh complained that Moses was interfering even when he asked for a three-day period to make a sacrifice to God. How much more so if the Israelites had tried to rest one day out of every seven. (Ex 5:1-5) While it is true that the patriarchs apparently measured time in a week of seven days, there is no evidence that any distinction was made as to the seventh day. Seven was prominent, however, as a number that often denoted completeness. (Ge 4:15, 23, 24; 21:28-32) The Hebrew word "swear" (sha·va′) is evidently from the same root as the word meaning "seven."

The Sabbath was celebrated as a sacred day (De 5:12), a day of rest and rejoicing for all—Israelites, servants, alien residents, and animals—ceasing from all labors. (Isa 58:13, 14; Ho 2:11; Ex 20:10; 34:21; De 5:12-15; Jer 17:21, 24) A special burnt offering, along with grain and drink offerings, was made, in addition to the regular daily "constant burnt offering." (Nu 28:9, 10) The showbread was renewed in the sanctuary, and a new division of priests took up their duties. (Le 24:5-9; 1Ch 9:32; 2Ch 23:4) Priestly duties were not curtailed on the Sabbath (Mt 12:5), and infants were even circumcised on the Sabbath if that happened to be their eighth day of life. In later times the Jews had a

saying, "There is no sabbath in the sanctuary," meaning that the priestly duties went right on.—Joh 7:22; Le 12:2, 3; The Temple, by A. Edersheim, 1874, p. 152.

According to rabbinic sources, in the time when Jesus was on earth three trumpet blasts at about the ninth hour, or three o'clock, on Friday afternoon announced the Sabbath day's approach. At this, all work and business were to cease, the Sabbath lamp was lit, and festive garments were put on. Then three more blasts indicated that Sabbath had actually begun. The outgoing division of priests offered the morning sacrifice on the Sabbath and the incoming division offered the evening sacrifice, both spending Sabbath in the sanctuary. Each one of the divisions would give to the high priest half of its portion of the bread. It was eaten during the Sabbath in the temple itself by the priests who were in a state of cleanness. The heads of the families of the incoming divisions determined by lot which of the families were to serve on each special day of their week of ministry and who were to discharge the priestly functions on the Sabbath.—Le 24:8, 9; Mr 2:26, 27; The Temple, pp. 151, 152, 156-158.

There was a distinction in requirements for the regular weekly Sabbath and the Sabbaths or "holy conventions" that were connected with the festivals. (Le 23:2) Generally speaking, the weekly Sabbath was more restrictive; no work, laborious or otherwise, could be done (except in the sanctuary). Even gathering wood or lighting a fire was prohibited. (Nu 15:32-36; Ex 35:3) Travel was also restricted, this apparently being based on Exodus 16:29. The Day of Atonement was likewise a time of rest from all sorts of work. (Le 16:29-31; 23:28-31) However, on the holy convention days of the festivals no laborious work, trade, or business activities could be engaged in, but cooking, festival preparations, and so forth, were allowed.—Ex 12:16; Le 23:7, 8, 21, 35, 36.

Sometimes two legal Sabbaths would fall on the same 24-hour period, and this was called a "great" Sabbath, such as when Nisan 15 (a sabbath day) coincided with the regular Sabbath.—Joh 19:31.

Benefits and Importance of the Sabbath. The desisting from all labor and observing other God-given Sabbath requirements not only gave rest to the body but, more important, provided opportunity for the individual to demonstrate his faith and obedience through Sabbath observance. It gave parents the opportunity to inculcate God's laws and commandments in the minds and hearts of their children. (De 6:4-9) The Sabbath was customarily occupied with taking in knowledge of

God and attending to spiritual needs, as is indicated by the reply of the Shunammite woman's husband when she requested permission to go to see Elisha, the man of God: "Why are you going to him today? It is not a new moon nor a sabbath." (2Ki 4:22, 23) And the Levites who were scattered throughout the land doubtless took advantage of the Sabbath to teach the Law to the people of Israel.—De 33:8, 10; Le 10:11.

It was important for individual Israelites to remember to keep the Sabbath because violation was regarded as rebellion against Jehovah and was punished by death. (Ex 31:14, 15; Nu 15:32-36) The same principle applied to the nation. Their observing the entire sabbath system, days and years, in a wholehearted way was a vital factor to their continued existence as a nation on their God-given land. Their failure to honor the Sabbath laws contributed largely to their downfall and the desolation of the land of Judah for 70 years to make up for the Sabbaths violated. —Le 26:31-35; 2Ch 36:20, 21.

Rabbinic Sabbath Restrictions. The Sabbath was originally intended to be a joyous, spiritually upbuilding time. But in their zeal to distinguish themselves from the Gentiles as much as possible, the Jewish religious leaders, especially after the return from Babylonian exile, gradually made it a burdensome thing by greatly increasing the Sabbath restrictions to 39, with innumerable lesser restrictions. These, when compiled, filled two large volumes. For example, catching a flea was forbidden as hunting. A sufferer could not be given relief unless death threatened. A bone could not be set, nor a sprain bandaged. The true purpose of the Sabbath was made void by these Jewish religious leaders, for they made the people slaves to tradition, instead of having the Sabbath serve men to the honor of God. (Mt 15: 3, 6; 23:2-4; Mr 2:27) When Jesus' disciples picked grain and rubbed it in their hands to eat, they evidently were accused on two counts, namely, harvesting and threshing on the Sabbath. (Lu 6: 1, 2) The rabbis had a saying: "The sins of everyone who strictly observes every law of the Sabbath, though he be an idol worshiper, are forgiven."

Not Enjoined on Christians. Jesus, being a Jew under the Law, observed the Sabbath as God's Word (not the Pharisees) directed. He knew it was lawful to do fine things on the Sabbath. (Mt 12:12) However, the inspired Christian writings state that "Christ is the end of the Law" (Ro 10:4), which results in Christians' being "discharged from the Law." (Ro 7:6) Neither Jesus nor his disciples made any distinction between so-called moral and cere-

monial laws. They quoted from the other parts of the Law as well as from the Ten Commandments and considered all of it equally binding on those under the Law. (Mt 5:21-48; 22:37-40; Ro 13:8-10; Jas 2:10, 11) The Scriptures plainly state that Christ's sacrifice "abolished . . . the Law of commandments consisting in decrees" and that God "blotted out the handwritten document against us, which consisted of decrees . . . and He has taken it out of the way by nailing it to the torture stake." It was the complete Mosaic Law that was "abolished," "blotted out," taken "out of the way." (Eph 2:13-15; Col 2:13, 14) Consequently, the whole *system* of Sabbaths, be they days or years, was brought to its end with the rest of the Law by the sacrifice of Christ Jesus. This explains why Christians can esteem "one day as all others," whether it be a sabbath or any other day, with no fear of judgment by another. (Ro 14:4-6; Col 2:16) Paul made the following expression concerning those scrupulously observing "days and months and seasons and years": "I fear for you, that somehow I have toiled to no purpose respecting you." —Ga 4:10, 11.

After Jesus' death, his apostles at no time commanded Sabbath observance. The Sabbath was not included as a Christian requirement at Acts 15:28, 29, or later. Nor did they institute a new sabbath, a "day of the Lord." Even though Jesus was resurrected on the day now called Sunday, nowhere does the Bible indicate that this day of his resurrection should be commemorated as a "new" sabbath or in any other way. First Corinthians 16:2 and Acts 20:7 have been appealed to by some as a basis for observing Sunday as a sabbath. However, the former text merely indicates that Paul instructed Christians to lay aside in their homes for their needy brothers at Jerusalem a certain amount each first day of the week. The money was not to be turned in at their place of meeting but was to be retained until Paul's arrival. As for the latter text, it was only logical that Paul would meet with the brothers in Troas on the first day of the week, since he was leaving the very next day.

From the foregoing it is clear that literal observance of Sabbath days and years was not a part of first-century Christianity. It was not until 321 C.E. that Constantine decreed Sunday (Latin: *dies Solis,* an old title associated with astrology and sun worship, not *Sabbatum* [Sabbath] or *dies Domini* [Lord's day]) to be a day of rest for all but the farmers.

Entering Into God's Rest. According to Genesis 2:2, 3, following the sixth creative day, or period, God "proceeded to rest on the seventh day," desisting from creative works with respect to the earth, as described in Genesis chapter 1.

The apostle Paul shows in Hebrews, chapters 3 and 4, that the Jews in the wilderness failed to enter into God's rest, or sabbath, because of disobedience and lack of faith. (Heb 3:18, 19; Ps 95: 7-11; Nu 14:28-35) Those who did enter the Promised Land under Joshua experienced a rest, but not the full rest to be enjoyed under the Messiah. It was only typical, or a shadow of the reality. (Jos 21:44; Heb 4:8; 10:1) However, Paul explains, "there remains a sabbath resting for the people of God." (Heb 4:9) Those who are obedient and exercise faith in Christ thereby enjoy "a sabbath resting" from their "own works," works by means of which they formerly sought to prove themselves righteous. (Compare Ro 10:3.) Thus Paul shows that God's sabbath, or rest, was still continuing in his day and Christians were entering into it, indicating that God's rest day is thousands of years long.—Heb 4:3, 6, 10.

"Lord of the Sabbath." While on earth, Jesus Christ referred to himself as "Lord of the sabbath." (Mt 12:8) The literal Sabbath day, which was meant to bring the Israelites relief from their labors, was "a shadow of the things to come, but the reality belongs to the Christ." (Col 2:16, 17) In connection with those "things to come," there is a sabbath of which Jesus is to be the Lord. As Lord of lords, Christ will rule all the earth for a thousand years. (Re 19:16; 20:6) During his earthly ministry, Jesus performed some of his most outstanding miraculous works on the Sabbath. (Lu 13: 10-13; Joh 5:5-9; 9:1-14) This evidently shows the kind of relief that he will bring as he raises mankind to spiritual and physical perfection during his coming Millennial Rule, which thus will be like a period of sabbath rest for the earth and mankind. —Re 21:1-4.

SABBATH DAY'S JOURNEY. See JOURNEY.

SABBATH YEAR.

The seventh in each cycle of seven years; during this year, in ancient Israel the land was allowed to rest, lying uncultivated, and fellow Hebrews were not pressed for payment of debts.

Counting from 1473 B.C.E., the year that Israel entered the Promised Land, a sabbath year was to be celebrated "at the end of every seven years," actually on every seventh year. (De 15:1, 2, 12; compare De 14:28.) The Sabbath year evidently began with the trumpet blast on Ethanim (Tishri) 10, the Day of Atonement. However, some hold that, while the Jubilee year started with the Day of Atonement, the Sabbath year started with Tishri 1.

There was to be no cultivating of the land, sowing, or pruning, nor any gathering in of the crops grown, but what grew of itself was left in the field, open to the owner of the field as well as to his slaves, the hired laborers, and the alien residents to eat. This was a merciful provision for the poor and, additionally, for the domestic animals and wild beasts, as these would also have access to the produce of the land during the Sabbath year.—Le 25:1-7.

The Sabbath year was called "the year of the release [*hash·shemit·tah'*]." (De 15:9; 31:10) During that year the land enjoyed a complete rest, or release, lying uncultivated. (Ex 23:11) There was also to be a rest, or a release, on debts incurred. It was "a release to Jehovah," in honor of him. Though others view it differently, some commentators hold that the debts were not actually canceled, but, rather, that a creditor was not to press a fellow Hebrew for payment of a debt, for there would be no income for the farmer during that year; though the lender could press a foreigner for payment. (De 15:1-3) Some rabbis hold the view that debts for loans of charity to help a poor brother were canceled, but that debts incurred in business dealings were in a different category. It is said by them that, in the first century of the Common Era, Hillel instituted a procedure whereby the lender could go before the court and secure his debt against forfeiture by making a certain declaration.—*The Pentateuch and Haftorahs*, edited by J. Hertz, London, 1972, pp. 811, 812.

This year of release, or rest from being pressed for payment of debts, did not apply to the release of slaves, many of whom would be in slavery because of indebtedness. Rather, the Hebrew slave was released in the seventh year of his servitude or on the Jubilee, whichever came first. —De 15:12; Le 25:10, 54.

It required faith to keep the Sabbath years as part of Jehovah's covenant with Israel, but observing the covenant fully would result in great blessings. (Le 26:3-13) God promised to provide enough during the sixth year's harvest to supply food for parts of three years, from the sixth until the harvest in the eighth year. Because no crops could be sown in the seventh year, no harvest could be gathered until the eighth year. (Compare Le 25:20-22.) When Israel entered the Promised Land under Joshua, six years were occupied in subduing the nations in Canaan and allotting land inheritances. Of course, during that time Israel could sow few, if any, crops, but there was some food from Canaanite crops. (De 6:10, 11) The seventh year was a sabbath, so that they had to

SABEANS

demonstrate faith and obedience by waiting until the harvest of the eighth year, and by God's blessing they survived.

Every year of release, during the Festival of Booths, all the people were to assemble, men and women, little ones and the alien residents, to hear the Law read.—De 31:10-13.

The land would have enjoyed 121 Sabbath years besides 17 Jubilee years prior to the exile if Israel had kept the Law properly. But the Sabbath years were only partially kept. When the people went into exile in Babylon, the land remained desolate for 70 years "until the land had paid off its sabbaths." (2Ch 36:20, 21; Le 26:34, 35, 43) Nowhere do the Scriptures state that the Jews had failed to keep exactly 70 Sabbath years; but Jehovah let 70 years of enforced desolation of the land make up for all the Sabbath years that had not been kept.

SABEANS (Sa·be′ans).

1. The designation of a band of raiders who attacked the property of Job of the land of Uz. These Sabeans took Job's cattle and she-asses and slaughtered his attendants. (Job 1:14, 15) Job also mentions "the traveling company of Sabeans," at Job 6:19.

It is difficult to identify with certainty these Sabeans, since they might have been descendants of a number of different men named Sheba. Abraham's son Jokshan had a son named Sheba (Ge 25:1-3), and the possibility of the Sabean raiders' being from this line cannot be ruled out. However, scholars more commonly suggest that the Sabeans came through the Sheba who descended from Ham through Cush (Ge 10:6, 7) or Sheba the son of Joktan in Shem's line.—Ge 10:21-29.

2. A tall people linked in Isaiah 45:14 with laborers of Egypt and merchants of Ethiopia as ones who would recognize Jehovah and his people. Isaiah 43:3 also associates Egypt and Ethiopia but, instead of "Sabeans," uses "Seba," indicating that the men of Seba were called Sabeans.—See SEBA No. 2.

3. The descendants of Sheba (whether of the line of Shem or of Ham is uncertain) who evidently formed a kingdom near the tip of the Arabian Peninsula. Likely the queen of Sheba who visited Solomon was from this land. (1Ki 10:1) Secular sources often refer to this kingdom as Sabean, and the Bible may do likewise.—See SHEBA No. 6.

Certain translations read "Sabeans" at Ezekiel 23:42 (KJ, Yg, Da), so interpreting the marginal reading in the Hebrew Bible. However, the main text reads "drunkards," and that is how modern translations frequently render the verse.—Ro, NW, AS, RS.

SABTAH (Sab′tah). A son of Cush and brother of Nimrod; progenitor of one of the 70 post-Flood families. (Ge 10:7, 8, 32; 1Ch 1:9, 10) Sabtah's descendants apparently settled in southern Arabia, perhaps in one of the places later bearing a name similar to his. Sabota, the ancient capital of Hadhramaut, has been suggested, and Ptolemy mentions a town called Saptha near the Persian Gulf, but any connection of these places with Sabtah remains uncertain.

SABTECA (Sab′te·ca). Fifth-named son of Cush and father of one of the 70 post-Flood families. (Ge 10:7, 32; 1Ch 1:9) His descendants likely settled in southern Arabia or perhaps Ethiopia, the exact location being unknown.

SACAR (Sa′car) [Wages].

1. Hararite father of David's warrior Ahiam. (1Ch 11:26, 35) Sacar is called Sharar at 2 Samuel 23:33.

2. The fourth son of Obed-edom and one of the gatekeepers during David's reign.—1Ch 26:1, 4.

SACHIA (Sa·chi′a). The head of a paternal house in the tribe of Benjamin; son of Shaharaim by his wife Hodesh.—1Ch 8:1, 8-10.

SACK. See BAG.

SACKCLOTH. A coarse cloth used in making sacks, or bags, such as those for containing grain. It was usually woven from goat's hair of a dark color. (Re 6:12; Isa 50:3) The Hebrew word for sackcloth (saq) is used also to designate the bags made from it.—Ge 42:25; Jos 9:4.

It was the traditional garment of mourning, and we first read of its use when Jacob mourned over the supposed death of his son Joseph, girding sackcloth upon his hips. (Ge 37:34; 2Sa 3:31) In some cases the mourners used it as a seat or used it to sleep on. (2Sa 21:10; Isa 58:5; Joe 1:13) The servants of Ben-hadad, in pleading for the life of their king before Ahab, went with sackcloth on their loins and ropes on their heads. (1Ki 20:31, 32) It was worn next to the skin at times, with other clothing on top (Job 16:15; Isa 32:11; 1Ki 21:27; 2Ki 6:30), while in other cases it may possibly have been simply "girded on" over undergarments.—Eze 7:18; Joe 1:8.

As a result of Jonah's preaching, the king of Nineveh issued a decree that not only all the people of the city should follow his example of putting on sackcloth but even the 'domestic animals' should be covered with it.—Jon 3:6-8.

The Hebrew prophets were occasionally wearers of sackcloth. They did this in harmony with the warning messages and calls to repentance they were commissioned to deliver, or when they prayed with expressions of repentance in behalf of the people. (Isa 20:2; Da 9:3; compare Re 11:3.) It was worn by the king and the people in times of great crisis or upon receiving calamitous news. —2Ki 19:1; Isa 15:3; 22:12.

SACRED PILLAR.

The Hebrew term so translated basically refers to something set up or stationed. It was evidently a phallic symbol of Baal or, at times, of other false gods. (Ex 23:24; 2Ki 3:2; 10:27) At various sites in the Middle East, upright stone pillars with no apparent structural function have been found. Their being discovered along with artifacts of a religious nature suggests that they were sacred pillars. Some of these are unhewn and measure 1.8 m (6 ft) or more in height.

Before entering the Promised Land, the Israelites were commanded not to erect any sacred pillars and were instructed to break down or shatter the already existing sacred pillars of the Canaanites. (Ex 34:13; Le 26:1; De 12:3; 16:22) The manner in which these were to be destroyed indicates that they were probably made of stone. At 2 Kings 10:26, however, mention is made of burning sacred pillars, suggesting that some were made of wood. In this case, though, the reference may be to the sacred pole, or Asherah.—See SACRED POLE.

Israel disregarded God's clear warnings given through Moses. The territory of the kingdom of Judah and that of the ten-tribe kingdom became filled with sacred pillars. (1Ki 14:22, 23; 2Ki 17:10) However, faithful Judean kings, like Asa, Hezekiah, and Josiah, broke the sacred pillars (2Ki 18:4; 23:14; 2Ch 14:3), and when Jehu eradicated Baal worship from the ten-tribe kingdom, the sacred pillar of Baal was pulled down.—2Ki 10:27, 28.

SACRED POLE.

The Hebrew word 'asheˈrah' (pl., 'asheˈrim') is thought to refer to (1) a sacred pole representing Asherah, a Canaanite goddess of fertility (Jg 6:25, 26), and (2) the goddess Asherah herself. (2Ki 13:6, ftn) However, it is not always possible to determine whether a particular scripture is to be understood as referring to the idolatrous object or to the goddess. A number of modern Bible translations, though, have rendered the original-language word as "sacred pole(s) [or post]" but transliterated it when the reference is apparently to the goddess. (AT, JB) Others have not endeavored to make a distinction but have simply transliterated the Hebrew word (RS) or have consistently translated it "sacred pole(s)." (NW) In the older translations of the Bible, the Hebrew word has usually been rendered as "grove(s)." (KJ, Le) But this rendering is inappropriate in such texts as Judges 3:7 and 2 Kings 23:6 (KJ), which speak of serving "groves" and bringing out the "grove" from the temple at Jerusalem.

The Sacred Poles. The sacred poles apparently stood upright and were made of wood, or at least contained wood, the Israelites being commanded to cut them down and to burn them. (Ex 34:13; De 12:3) They may have simply been uncarved poles, perhaps even trees in some instances, for God's people were instructed: "You must not plant for yourself any sort of tree as a sacred pole."—De 16:21.

Both Israel and Judah disregarded God's express command not to set up sacred pillars and sacred poles; they placed them upon "every high hill and under every luxuriant tree" alongside the altars used for sacrifice. It has been suggested that the poles represented the female principle, whereas the pillars represented the male principle. These appendages of idolatry, likely phallic symbols, were associated with grossly immoral sex orgies, as is indicated by the reference to male prostitutes being in the land as early as Rehoboam's reign. (1Ki 14:22-24; 2Ki 17:10) Only seldom did kings such as Hezekiah (and Josiah) come along, who "removed the high places and broke the sacred pillars to pieces and cut down the sacred pole."—2Ki 18:4; 2Ch 34:7.

Asherah. The Ras Shamra texts identify this goddess as the wife of the god El, the "Creator of Creatures," and refer to her as "Lady Asherah of the Sea" and "Progenitress of the Gods," this also making her apparently the mother of Baal. However, there apparently was considerable overlapping in the roles of the three prominent goddesses of Baalism (Anath, Asherah, and Ashtoreth), as may be observed in extra-Biblical sources as well as in the Scriptural record. While Ashtoreth appears to have figured as the wife of Baal, Asherah may also have been so viewed.

During the period of the Judges, it is noted that the apostate Israelites "went serving the Baals and the sacred poles [the Asherim]." (Jg 3:7, ftn; compare 2:13.) The mention of these deities in the plural may indicate that each locality had its Baal and Asherah. (Jg 6:25) Jezebel, the Sidonian wife of Ahab the king of Israel, entertained at her table 450 prophets of Baal and 400 prophets of the sacred pole, or Asherah.—1Ki 18:19.

The degraded worship of Asherah came to be practiced in the very temple of Jehovah. King Manasseh even placed there a carved image of the sacred pole, evidently a representation of the goddess Asherah. (2Ki 21:7) Manasseh was disciplined by being taken captive to Babylon and, upon his returning to Jerusalem, showed he had profited from that discipline and cleansed Jehovah's house of idolatrous appendages. However, his son Amon resumed the degrading worship of Baal and Asherah, with its accompanying ceremonial prostitution. (2Ch 33:11-13, 15, 21-23) This made it necessary for righteous King Josiah, who succeeded Amon to the throne, to pull down "the houses of the male temple prostitutes that were in the house of Jehovah, where the women were weaving tent shrines for the sacred pole."—2Ki 23:4-7.

SACRED PRONOUNCEMENTS.

This expression occurs only four times in the Christian Greek Scriptures, and it translates the Greek word lo'gi·on (meaning "little word"), a diminutive of lo'gos (word). Originally lo'gi·on meant only a brief sacred utterance, but in time it came to signify any divine communication or oracle. Certain English versions render lo'gi·on simply as 'oracle.' (AS, KJ, RS) Wuest's translation uses "divine utterances" at Acts 7:38 and Romans 3:2.

Stephen spoke of the Law given to Moses on Mount Sinai as "living sacred pronouncements." (Ac 7:38) The apostle Paul referred to the entire Hebrew Scriptures and evidently also to all the inspired Christian Scriptures written up to that time, saying: "What, then, is the superiority of the Jew, or what is the benefit of the circumcision? A great deal in every way. First of all, because they were entrusted with the sacred pronouncements of God." (Ro 3:1, 2) Therefore, the writing of this body of inspired Scriptures was committed to Jews, writing "as they were borne along by holy spirit."—2Pe 1:20, 21.

In the letter to the Hebrews the apostle Paul includes as "sacred pronouncements" the teachings delivered to mankind by the Lord Jesus Christ, his apostles, and other inspired Christian writers. (Heb 5:12; compare Heb 6:1, 2.) Peter also reflects this broad scope in speaking to the followers of Christ, at 1 Peter 4:11: "If anyone speaks, let him speak as it were the sacred pronouncements of God." He also classifies writings of the apostle Paul as of equal authority with "the rest of the Scriptures."—2Pe 3:15, 16.

The Greek Septuagint frequently uses the word lo'gi·on, as in translating Psalm 12:6 (11:6, LXX): "The sayings of Jehovah are pure sayings." Bagster's English translation of the Septuagint reads, at this verse: "The oracles of the Lord are pure oracles."

SACRED SECRET.

Something that originates with God, is withheld until his own time, and is revealed only to those to whom he chooses to make it known.

The Greek word my·ste'ri·on, translated "sacred secret," has reference primarily to that which is known by those who are initiated. In the ancient mystery religions that flourished in the time of the early Christian congregation, those who wished to take part in the mystery celebrations had to undergo initiation; the uninitiated were denied both access to the so-called sacred actions and to knowledge of them. Those initiated into them were bound by a vow of silence, not to reveal the secrets. However, there was also a secular, "everyday" use of the word, such as for a private secret, a secret between friends, family secrets. The apostle Paul uses the passive of my·e'o in this latter sense when he says: "I have learned the secret [literally, I have been initiated into secrets] of both how to be full and how to hunger, both how to have an abundance and how to suffer want."—Php 4:12.

Different From Mystery Religions. Concerning the Greek my·ste'ri·on, Vine's Expository Dictionary of Old and New Testament Words explains: "In the [New Testament] it denotes, not the mysterious (as with the Eng. word), but that which, being outside the range of unassisted natural apprehension, can be made known only by Divine revelation, and is made known in a manner and at a time appointed by God, and to those only who are illumined by His Spirit. In the ordinary sense a mystery implies knowledge withheld; its Scriptural significance is truth revealed. Hence the terms especially associated with the subject are 'made known,' 'manifested,' 'revealed,' 'preached,' 'understand,' 'dispensation.'"—1981, Vol. 3, p. 97.

The sacred secrets of God and other "mysteries" of the Bible, such as that of Babylon the Great, are therefore things, not to be kept secret forever, but to be revealed by Jehovah God in his own time to those who look to him and to whom he chooses to reveal them. The apostle Paul discusses this aspect of matters at 1 Corinthians 2:6-16. There he speaks of the "sacred secret" of God as "hidden wisdom," revealed through God's spirit to his Christian servants. It is something that the spirit of the world or the human wisdom of physical men cannot fathom but that is spoken and understood by those 'combining spiritual matters with spiritual words.' Jesus Christ earlier pointed out to his disciples: "To you the sacred secret [Gr., my·ste'ri·on] of the kingdom of God has been given, but to those outside all things occur in illustrations, in order that, though looking, they may look and yet not see, and, though hearing, they may hear and yet not get the sense of it, nor ever turn back and forgiveness be given them."—Mr 4:11, 12; Mt 13:11-13; Lu 8:10.

The great difference between the sacred secret of God and the secrets of mystery religions is, first of all, in content: God's secret is good news and is not a lie or man-made deception. (Joh 8:31, 32, 44; Col 1:5; 1Jo 2:27) Second, those who are chosen to understand the sacred secret of God are bound, not to keep it secret, but to give it the widest possible proclamation and publication. This is revealed, as noted in the foregoing, by the Bible use of terms such as "preached," "made known," "manifested," and also "declaring," 'speaking,' in connection with "the sacred secret of the good news." True Christians exercised the greatest vigor in telling this good news containing the understanding of the sacred secret to "all creation that is under heaven." (1Co 2:1; Eph 6:19; Col 1:23; 4: 3, 4) God determines who are not deserving and withholds understanding from such ones. God is not partial when he does this; it is because of "the insensibility of their hearts" that God does not open up to them the understanding of his sacred secret.—Eph 4:17, 18.

Centers Around Christ.   Since "the bearing witness to Jesus is what inspires prophesying," "the sacred secret of God" must center around Christ. (Re 19:10; Col 2:2) All "the sacred secrets" of God have to do with his Messianic Kingdom. (Mt 13:11) The apostle Paul writes to fellow Christians: "Carefully concealed in him are all the treasures of wisdom and of knowledge," and "it is in him that all the fullness of the divine quality dwells bodily." —Col 2:2, 3, 9.

Paul spoke of himself as having a stewardship of "sacred secrets of God." (1Co 4:1) He speaks of the comprehension he has "in the sacred secret of the Christ." (Eph 3:1-4) He explains that this sacred secret is hidden wisdom foreordained by God before the systems of things. (1Co 2:7) The declaration of the mystery, or "the sacred secret of God," began with Jehovah's own prophecy at Genesis 3:15. For centuries men of faith looked forward to the "seed" of promise to deliver mankind from sin and death, but it was not clearly understood just who the "seed" would be and just how this "seed" would come and bring deliverance. It was not until Christ came and "shed light upon life and incorruption through the good news" that this was made clear. (2Ti 1:10) Then the knowledge of the mystery of the 'seed of the woman' began to be understood.

The Messianic Kingdom.   In Paul's writings he gives a full view of the revelation of the sacred secret of the Christ. At Ephesians 1:9-11 he speaks of God's making known "the sacred secret" of his will, and says: "It is according to his good pleasure which he purposed in himself for an administration at the full limit of the appointed times, namely, to gather all things together again in the Christ, the things in the heavens and the things on the earth. Yes, in him, in union with whom we were also assigned as heirs, in that we were foreordained according to the purpose of him who operates all things according to the way his will counsels." This "sacred secret" involves a government, the Messianic Kingdom of God. "The things in the heavens," to which Paul refers, are the prospective heirs of that heavenly Kingdom with Christ. "The things on the earth" will be its earthly subjects. Jesus pointed out to his disciples that the sacred secret had to do with the Kingdom when he said to them: "To you the sacred secret of the kingdom of God has been given."—Mr 4:11.

Includes the Congregation.   There are many features in the knowledge of the sacred secret. The apostle gave further details when he explained that the sacred secret includes the congregation, of which Christ is Head. (Eph 5:32; Col 1:18; Re 1:20) These are his joint heirs, with whom he shares the Kingdom. (Lu 22:29, 30) They are taken from among both Jews and Gentiles. (Ro 11:25; Eph 3:3-6; Col 1:26, 27) This feature of "the sacred secret" could not be made clearly known until Peter was directed to visit the Gentile Cornelius and saw this Gentile household receive the gifts of the holy spirit, in 36 C.E. (Ac 10:34, 44-48) In writing to Gentile Christians, Paul told them: "You were . . . without Christ, . . . strangers to the covenants of the promise, and you had no hope and were without God in the world. But now in union with Christ Jesus you who were once far off have come to be near by the blood of the Christ." (Eph 2:11-13) Through God's dealings with the congregation, "the governments and the authorities in the heavenly places" would come to know "the greatly diversified wisdom of God." —Eph 3:10.

This congregation is shown in vision in the Revelation to John to be composed of 144,000 persons "bought from among mankind as firstfruits to God and to the Lamb." They are standing with the Lamb, Jesus Christ, on Mount Zion, the place where the "city of the living God, heavenly Jerusalem," is located. In ancient earthly Jerusalem was situated "Jehovah's throne," with kings of the line of David seated on it; also the temple of Jehovah was there. In heavenly Jerusalem Jesus

Christ is enthroned, and his loyal spirit-anointed followers share his Kingdom rule. (Re 14:1, 4; Heb 12:22; 1Ch 29:23; 1Pe 2:4-6) The resurrection of such ones to immortality and incorruption during the time of Christ's presence is one of the features of God's dealings with the congregation, "a sacred secret" in itself.—1Co 15:51-54.

The Sacred Secret of Godly Devotion. Paul wrote to Timothy: "I am writing you these things, . . . that you may know how you ought to conduct yourself in God's household, which is the congregation of the living God, a pillar and support of the truth. Indeed, the sacred secret of this godly devotion is admittedly great: 'He [Jesus Christ] was made manifest in flesh, was declared righteous in spirit, appeared to angels, was preached about among nations, was believed upon in the world, was received up in glory.'"—1Ti 3:14-16.

"The congregation of the living God" had the truth, and it knew accurately the mystery, or "the sacred secret," of true godly devotion, and the congregation had not only the *form* but also the *power* of such godly devotion. (Contrast 2Ti 3:5.) Hence, it could be the "pillar and support of the truth" in the midst of a world of error and false religion, the 'mysteries' sacred to Satan and those he has blinded. (2Co 4:4) Jesus Christ himself is the One whose godly devotion was foretold and described in the inspired Hebrew Scriptures. For centuries, ever since the challenge was launched against God's sovereignty, with the integrity of man being brought into question, it was a mystery, or "sacred secret," whether complete, unswerving, unblemished godly devotion could be fully maintained by anyone upon whom the Devil would bring pressure. Who, if anyone, would be able to hold up under the test and come through wholly clean, without sin, and untarnished in exclusive devotion to Jehovah? Related to this was the question concerning who would be the 'seed of the woman' that would bruise the Serpent's head. This would be fully revealed when Christ "was made manifest in flesh, was declared righteous in spirit, appeared to angels, was preached about among nations, was believed upon in the world, was received up in glory." (1Ti 3:16; 6:16) This was admittedly a great thing. The great question of godly devotion centered around the one person, Jesus Christ. What greatness there was to Christ's course of godly devotion! How it benefits mankind and vindicates and exalts Jehovah's name!—See GODLY DEVOTION.

Comes to a Finish. In the apostle John's vision, he was told: "In the days of the sounding of the seventh angel, when he is about to blow his trumpet, the sacred secret of God according to the good news which he declared to his own slaves the prophets is indeed brought to a finish." (Re 10:7) This finishing of the sacred secret is closely connected with the seventh angel's blowing of his trumpet, upon the blowing of which the announcement is made in heaven: "The kingdom of the world did become the kingdom of our Lord and of his Christ, and he will rule as king forever and ever." (Re 11:15) Accordingly, the sacred secret of God is finished at the time that Jehovah begins his Kingdom by means of his Messiah, or Christ. Jesus Christ spoke much to his disciples, God's "slaves," about the Kingdom of God and said that the "good news of the kingdom" would continue to be preached right up to the end (Gr., te'los) of "the system of things." After 'the sacred secret of God is brought to a finish,' the "good news" to be preached would therefore include what the voices in heaven announced: "The kingdom of the world did become the kingdom of our Lord and of his Christ."—Mt 24:3, 14.

For the 'mystery of lawlessness' (2Th 2:7), see MAN OF LAWLESSNESS. For "Mystery: 'Babylon the Great'" (Re 17:5), see BABYLON THE GREAT.

SACRED SERVICE. Ministry, or work, that is sacred, being directly related to one's worship of God.

The Hebrew term 'a·vadh' basically means "serve" (Ge 14:4; 15:13; 29:15) or "labor" (Ex 34: 21) and is also rendered "cultivate." (Ge 4:12; De 28:39) When used with reference to service rendered to Jehovah or to false deities, 'a·vadh' implies worship, or sacred service. (Ex 10:26; De 11:16) Similarly, the Greek verb la·treu'o denotes serving. It is used in regard to serving God (Mt 4:10; Lu 1:74; 2:37; 4:8; Ac 7:7; Ro 1:9; Php 3:3; 2Ti 1:3; Heb 9:14; 12:28; Re 7:15; 22:3), as was done at the sanctuary or temple (Heb 8:5; 9:9; 10:2; 13:10), and also in connection with false worship, rendering service to created things. (Ac 7:42; Ro 1:25) In the Christian Greek Scriptures the noun la·trei'a appears solely with reference to serving God. (Joh 16:2; Ro 9:4; 12:1; Heb 9:1, 6) It differs from the Greek di·a·ko·ni'a, which also means "ministry, service," but which is used in connection with common, ordinary, mundane things—things that are not sacred.

The only One to whom worship, or sacred service, can be rightly directed is Jehovah God. (Mt 4:10; Lu 4:8) On account of their special covenant relationship with Jehovah God, the privilege of rendering sacred service as spirit-begotten sons of God and members of "a royal priesthood" should have gone to the Jews. But the majority lost out because of their failure to exercise faith in Christ Jesus. (Ro 9:3-5, 30-33; 1Pe 2:4-10) Many, like the Pharisee Saul before his becoming a Christian, imagined that they were actually rendering sacred service to God by persecuting Christ's followers.—Joh 16:2; Ac 26:9-11; Ga 1:13, 14.

SACRIFICE. See OFFERINGS; RANSOM.

SADDLE. A seat fastened across the back of an animal for a rider. Numerous Biblical references mention saddling asses (Ge 22:3; Nu 22:21; 2Sa 17:23; 19:26; 1Ki 2:40; 13:13, 27; 2Ki 4:24), but no description is provided of the saddles. From the evidence of ancient monuments, it appears that early saddles for horses were little more than a cloth or leather padding. The Hebrew verb "saddle" basically means "bind," indicating that the saddles were strapped to the animal. One ancient relief depicts a boxlike saddle strapped to the back of a one-humped camel. Nothing definite can be said about "the woman's saddle basket of the camel" mentioned at Genesis 31:34. The Hebrew expression *kar hag·ga·mal'* has been variously rendered "camel-bag" (*NE*), "camel's litter" (*JB*), and "camel's saddle" (*AT*).

Under the Law, anyone touching a saddle upon which one with a running discharge had been riding became unclean, as did a person touching an article on which a menstruating woman had been sitting.—Le 15:9, 19-23.

SADDUCEES (Sad'du·cees). A prominent religious sect of Judaism associated with the priesthood. (Ac 5:17) They did not believe in either resurrection or angels.—Ac 23:8.

The precise time for the emergence of the Sadducees as a religious sect is not known. First historical mention of them by name appears in the writings of Josephus, which indicate that they opposed the Pharisees in the latter half of the second century B.C.E. (*Jewish Antiquities,* XIII, 293 [x, 6]) Josephus also provides information about their teachings. However, there is a question as to whether his presentation is completely factual. Unlike the Pharisees, says Josephus, the Sadducees denied the workings of fate, maintaining that an individual, by his own actions, was solely responsible for what befell him. (*Jewish Antiquities,* XIII, 172, 173 [v, 9]) They rejected the many oral traditions observed by the Pharisees and also Pharisaic belief in the immortality of the soul and in punishments or rewards after death. In their dealings with one another, the Sadducees were somewhat rough. They were said to be disputatious. According to Josephus, their teachings appealed to the wealthy.—*Jewish Antiquities,*

XIII, 298 (x, 6); XVIII, 16, 17 (i, 4); *The Jewish War,* II, 162-166 (viii, 14).

As pointed out by John the Baptizer, the Sadducees needed to produce fruits befitting repentance. This was because they, like the Pharisees, had failed to keep God's law. (Mt 3:7, 8) Christ Jesus himself compared their corrupting teaching to leaven.—Mt 16:6, 11, 12.

With reference to their religious beliefs, Acts 23:8 states: "Sadducees say there is neither resurrection nor angel nor spirit, but the Pharisees publicly declare them all." It was in connection with the resurrection and brother-in-law marriage that a group of Sadducees attempted to stump Christ Jesus. But he silenced them. By referring to the writings of Moses, which the Sadducees professed to accept, Jesus disproved their contention that there is no resurrection. (Mt 22:23-34; Mr 12:18-27; Lu 20:27-40) Later, the apostle Paul, when before the Sanhedrin, divided that highest Jewish court by playing the Pharisees against the Sadducees. This was possible because of the religious differences existing between them. —Ac 23:6-10.

Although religiously divided, Sadducees joined Pharisees in trying to tempt Jesus by asking him for a sign (Mt 16:1), and both groups were united in their opposition to him. Biblical evidence indicates that the Sadducees took a leading part in seeking Jesus' death. Sadducees were members of the Sanhedrin, which court plotted against Jesus and, later, condemned him to death. Included in the court were Caiaphas, the Sadducee and high priest, and evidently also other prominent priests. (Mt 26:59-66; Joh 11:47-53; Ac 5:17, 21) Therefore, whenever the Christian Greek Scriptures speak of certain action as being taken by the chief priests, Sadducees were evidently involved. (Mt 21:45, 46; 26:3, 4, 62-64; 28:11, 12; Joh 7:32) Sadducees appear to have taken the lead in trying to stop the spread of Christianity after Jesus' death and resurrection.—Ac 4:1-23; 5:17-42; 9:14.

SAFFRON [Heb., *kar·kom'*]. The Hebrew word, appearing only in The Song of Solomon (4:14), has usually been identified with the saffron-yielding crocus (*Crocus sativus*), a fall-blooming bulbous plant with grasslike leaves and purple flowers that is much like the common spring crocus. To produce just 28 g (1 oz) of saffron, a deep orange-colored substance composed of the dried styles and stigmas of the flowers, about 4,000 blossoms are needed. When the flowers open, or shortly thereafter, the stigma and upper part of the style are removed and then dried. Saffron is used in coloring and flavoring foods and was formerly employed more extensively than now for dyeing cloth a yellow hue. It was also used medicinally and as a perfume.

The Hebrew term *chavats·tse'leth*, variously rendered "crocus," "lily," "rose," and "saffron" (compare *AT, KJ, Le, NW, Yg*), likely refers to a bulbous plant. (Ca 2:1, ftn; Isa 35:1, ftn) According to the Hebrew lexicographer Gesenius, *chavats·tse'leth* probably contains a root meaning "bulb," and he considered "meadow saffron" to be the more exact equivalent of the original-language word. (*A Hebrew and English Lexicon of the Old Testament*, translated by E. Robinson, 1836, p. 317) A Hebrew and Aramaic lexicon by Koehler and Baumgartner associates the word *chavats·tse'leth* with an Akkadian term meaning "stalk" and defines it as "asphodel," a plant of the lily family.—*Hebräisches und Aramäisches Lexicon zum Alten Testament*, Leiden, 1967, p. 275.

SAKKUTH (Sak'kuth). Possibly an astral deity, as suggested by the fact that "Sakkuth" is put in a parallelism with the phrase "the star of your god." (Am 5:26) This name was purposely vocalized in the Hebrew Masoretic text to correspond to *shiqquts'*, meaning "disgusting thing." Perhaps Sakkuth is to be identified with "Sakkut," this being the Babylonian designation for Saturn (a star-god). However, in the Greek *Septuagint* the expression "Sakkuth your king" reads "the tent of Moloch," and Stephen, who probably quoted the *Septuagint*, also used the words "the tent of Moloch." (Ac 7:43) This suggests that "Sakkuth" may have been a portable shrine, a tent or booth, in which the idol image of Moloch was housed.—See ASTROLOGERS (Molech and Astrology in Israel).

SALAMIS (Sal'a·mis). An important city of Cyprus. Paul, Barnabas, and John Mark 'published the word of God' there near the start of Paul's first missionary tour in about 47 C.E. How long they stayed in the city is not stated. Apparently there was a large Jewish population in Salamis, as it had more than one synagogue.—Ac 13:2-5.

Salamis is usually identified with the ruins found some 5 km (3 mi) N of the modern city of Famagusta. This would place it at the E end of a large fertile plain, just N of the river Pedias (Pediaeus). Salamis would thus be some 200 km (120 mi) WSW across the Mediterranean Sea from Seleucia, where Paul had left Syria. Though the Bible does not specifically say that the ship on which Paul traveled anchored in a harbor at Salamis, the city once had a good harbor that is now silted up.

It appears that Salamis was connected by at least one road with Paphos, at the other end of the island. This could have facilitated travel for Paul and his associates as they preached through "the whole island as far as Paphos."—Ac 13:4-6.

Barnabas and John Mark likely visited Salamis again in about 49 C.E.—Ac 15:36-39.

SALECAH (Sal'e·cah). A city at the eastern limit of Bashan, and part of the domain of Og. Taken by Israel under Moses, Salecah came to be inhabited by Gadites. (De 3:8, 10; Jos 12:4, 5; 13:8, 11; 1Ch 5:11) It is usually identified with Salkhad, situated on a southern extension of Jebel ed Druz (Jebel Hauran), some 100 km (60 mi) ESE of the southern end of the Sea of Galilee.

SALEM (Sa'lem) [Peace]. An ancient city where Melchizedek was king and priest. (Ge 14:18) The Hebrew spelling of "Salem" suggests a dual form and, therefore, the word may be defined as "Twofold Peace." That the name means "Peace" is confirmed by the inspired words of Hebrews 7:2.

Ancient Jewish tradition identifies Salem with Jerusalem, and Scriptural evidence supports this. Abraham met the king of Sodom and Melchizedek in "the king's Low Plain." Since King David's son Absalom centuries later erected a monument there, this low plain must have been near Jerusalem, the capital of the kingdom. (Ge 14:17, 18; 2Sa 18:18) The word "Salem" is, in fact, incorporated in the name "Jeru*salem*," and the psalmist used it in parallel with "Zion." (Ps 76:2) Also, it would have been fitting for Melchizedek to be king and priest in the very place where later the kings of the Davidic line and the Levitical priesthood served and where Jesus Christ, the one chosen to be a king and priest "according to the manner of Melchizedek," was offered in sacrifice.—Heb 3:1; 7:1-3, 15-17.

SALIM (Sa'lim). A place mentioned at John 3:23 to help locate Aenon, where John the Baptizer immersed persons. Hence, Salim must have been well known at the time. Today its situation is uncertain, but Tell Ridgha (Tel Shalem), about 12 km (7 mi) S of Beth-shean, has been suggested as a possible identification.—See AENON.

SALLAI (Sal·la'i).

1. A name in the list of Benjamites who lived in Jerusalem following the Babylonian exile.—Ne 11:4, 7, 8.

2. A priestly paternal house in the days of High Priest Jeshua's successor Joiakim. (Ne 12:12, 20) Presumably the name is spelled Sallu in Nehemiah 12:7.

SALLU (Sal'lu).

1. A postexilic Benjamite resident of Jerusalem; son of Meshullam.—1Ch 9:3, 7; Ne 11:7.

2. A priestly family head who returned to Jerusalem with Zerubbabel. (Ne 12:1, 7) At Nehemiah 12:20, in the list of later paternal houses, the name Sallai appears at the corresponding place.

SALMA (Sal'ma).

1. Descendant of Judah and ancestor of David. (1Ch 2:3-5, 9-15) He is also called Salmon.—Ru 4:12, 18-22; Lu 3:32; see SALMON.

2. Forefather of those who settled in places such as Bethlehem, Netophah, and Atroth-beth-joab. (1Ch 2:51, 54) Salma was a son of Hur in the Calebite branch of Judah's genealogy.—1Ch 2:4, 5, 9, 18, 19, 50, 51.

SALMAI (Sal'mai).
One of the Nethinim whose descendants returned to Jerusalem in 537 B.C.E.—Ezr 2:1, 2, 43, 46; Ne 7:48.

SALMON (Sal'mon).
The son of Judah's chieftain Nahshon, likely born during the 40-year wilderness trek. Salmon married Rahab of Jericho, by whom he fathered Boaz. He was, therefore, a link in the genealogical line leading to David and Jesus. (Nu 2:3; Ru 4:20-22; Mt 1:4, 5; Lu 3:32) In 1 Chronicles 2:11 he is called Salma. However, this descendant of Ram, Salmon, whose progeny lived in Bethlehem, should not be confused with the Salma mentioned in 1 Chronicles 2:51, 54 as "the father" or builder of Bethlehem, for the latter was a descendant of Ram's brother Caleb.—Compare 1Ch 2:9, 18.

SALMONE (Sal·mo'ne).
A promontory of Crete, generally identified with Cape Sidero at the E end of the island. Paul sailed past Salmone in about 58 C.E. on his way to Rome for trial. However, strong winds apparently did not permit the vessel, en route from Cnidus, to sail N of Crete past the southern tip of Greece and on to Rome. Forced southward, the craft passed Salmone and thereafter had some protection from the wind while sailing along Crete's southern shores.—Ac 27:7.

SALOME (Sa·lo'me) [probably from a Heb. root meaning "peace"].

1. A comparison of Matthew 27:56 with Mark 15:40 may indicate that Salome was the mother of the sons of Zebedee—James and John, who were apostles of Jesus Christ. The former text names two of the Marys, namely, Mary Magdalene and Mary the mother of James (the Less) and of Joses; and with these it also mentions the mother of the sons of Zebedee as being present at Jesus' impalement; while the latter text names the woman with the two Marys as Salome.

It is conjectured on similar grounds that Salome was also the fleshly sister of Mary, the mother of Jesus. This has been suggested because the scripture at John 19:25 names the same two Marys, Mary Magdalene and "the wife of Clopas" (generally understood to be the mother of James the Less and of Joses), and also says: "By the torture stake of Jesus, however, there were standing his mother and the sister of his mother." If this text (aside from mentioning Jesus' mother) is speaking of the same three persons mentioned by Matthew and Mark, it would indicate that Salome was the sister of Jesus' mother. On the other hand, Matthew 27:55 and Mark 15:40, 41 state that there were many other women present who had accompanied Jesus, and therefore Salome may have been among them.

Salome was a disciple of the Lord Jesus Christ, among the women accompanying him and ministering to him from their belongings, as Matthew, Mark, and Luke (8:3) imply.

If her identification as the mother of Zebedee's sons is accurate, she was the one who approached Jesus with the request that her sons be granted seats on the right and the left of Jesus in his Kingdom. Matthew depicts the mother as making the request, while Mark shows James and John doing the asking. Apparently the boys had the desire and induced their mother to make the request. This is supported by Matthew's report that, on hearing about the request, the other disciples became indignant, not at the mother, but at the two brothers.—Mt 20:20-24; Mr 10:35-41.

At the break of dawn on the third day after Jesus' death, Salome was among the women who went to Jesus' tomb to rub his body with spices, only to find the stone rolled away and, inside the tomb, an angel who announced to them: "He was raised up, he is not here. See! The place where they laid him."—Mr 16:1-8.

2. A daughter of Herod Philip and only child of her mother Herodias. In time Herod Antipas married Salome's mother, having adulterously taken her from his half brother Philip. Shortly before Passover 32 C.E., Antipas held an evening meal in Tiberias in celebration of his birthday. He invited the princess Salome, now his stepdaughter, to dance before the group, which consisted of "his top-ranking men and the military commanders and the foremost ones of Galilee." So delighted was Herod at Salome's performance that he

promised her anything she requested—up to half his kingdom. Upon her wicked mother's advice, Salome asked for the head of John the Baptizer. Herod, though grieved, "out of regard for his oaths and for those reclining with him commanded it to be given; and he sent and had John beheaded in the prison. And his head was brought on a platter and given to the maiden, and she brought it to her mother."—Mt 14:1-11; Mr 6:17-28.

Though her name is not given in the Scriptures, it is preserved in the writings of Josephus. He also tells of her childless marriage to the district ruler Philip, another half brother of Herod Antipas. After Philip's death, Josephus' account says, she married her cousin Aristobulus and bore him three sons.

SALT. The white crystalline compound of sodium chloride (NaCl), known as common salt. There are in the earth vast underground deposits of rock salt, some hundreds of meters thick. The oceans of the world contain about 3.5 percent salts, mostly sodium chloride. This may seem to be very little, yet a cubic kilometer of seawater holds nearly 27 million metric tons of salt. The Dead Sea (Salt Sea) in Palestine is about nine times as salty. (Ge 14:3) Salt was readily available to the Israelites. Evaporation of the Dead Sea waters furnished an ample supply, although of poor quality. There were salt-bearing hills near the southern end of the Dead Sea, not far from where Lot's wife became a pillar of salt. (Ge 19:26; Zep 2:9) Supplies of salt in northern Palestine may have come, at least partly, from the Phoenicians, who, it is said, obtained it by evaporation from the Mediterranean.

Notwithstanding such virtually inexhaustible supplies, salt has not always been readily available to man. Wars and revolutions have been fought for it. In ancient China salt was second to gold in value. Wives and children have been sold into slavery just for common salt. Caesar's soldiers received money to buy salt, the sum being called a *salarium,* from which comes the English word "salary."—Compare Ezr 4:14.

The Bible takes note of salt as an essential part of man's diet, as a seasoning for food. (Job 6:6) Under the Mosaic Law anything offered on the altar to Jehovah had to be salted, not because of flavor, but doubtless because salt represented freedom from corruption or decay. (Le 2:11, 13; Eze 43:24) Large quantities of salt evidently were stored on the temple grounds for this purpose. Ezra saw to it that plenty was on hand for the sacrifices. (Ezr 6:9; 7:21, 22) It is reported that

Antiochus III (c. 198 B.C.E.) gave 375 medimni (c. 200 kl; 562 bu) of salt to the temple service.

Certain healing, medicinal, and antiseptic values are attributed to salt. Newborn babies were sometimes rubbed with salt at birth. (Eze 16:4) In limited quantities salt is beneficial on certain acid soils or when mixed with manure, but if allowed to accumulate in the soil, it kills vegetation and the land becomes barren and unfruitful, as was the case with the once-fertile Euphrates Valley. A city condemned to total destruction was sometimes deliberately sown with salt, this act expressing the desire that the place be perpetually barren and sterile.—De 29:22, 23; Jg 9:45; Job 39:5, 6; Jer 17:6.

Figurative Use. Salt is often used in the Bible figuratively. Jesus told his disciples: "You are the salt of the earth," a preserving influence on others, preventing spiritual putrefaction and moral decay. The good news they carried would preserve life. However, he went on to say to them: "But if the salt loses its strength, how will its saltness be restored? It is no longer usable for anything but to be thrown outside to be trampled on by men." (Mt 5:13; Mr 9:50; Lu 14:34, 35) One Bible commentator remarks on Matthew 5:13: "The salt used in this country [United States] is a chemical compound—muriate of soda—and if the *saltness* were lost, or it were to lose its *savour,* there would be nothing remaining. It enters into the very *nature* of the substance. In eastern countries, however, the salt used was impure, mingled with vegetable and earthy substances; so that it might lose the whole of its saltness, and a considerable quantity of earthy matter remain. This was good for nothing, except that it was used, as it is said, to place in paths, or walks, as we use gravel. This kind of salt is common still in that country. It is found in the earth in veins or layers, and when exposed to the sun and rain, loses its saltness entirely."—*Barnes' Notes on the New Testament,* 1974.

Because salt prevented decay, it became a symbol of stability and permanence. Often when covenants were made, the parties ate together—eating salt together—denoting perpetual loyalty and fidelity to one another in the covenant relationship. "A covenant of salt" therefore was considered very binding. (Nu 18:19) Accordingly, Judean King Abijah's statement that Jehovah had made "a covenant of salt" with David and his sons meant that the covenant with David's line for the kingship would stand forever. Jesus Christ the "son of David" and "the root of David" proves to be the one holding the Kingdom and administering its affairs forever.—2Ch 13:4, 5; Ps 18:50; Mt 1:1; Re 5:5; Isa 9:6, 7.

Jesus said: "For everyone must be salted with fire." The context here points to a salting with the fire of Gehenna in the case of all who stumble into a life of sin or who are responsible for so stumbling others.—Mr 9:42-49.

Using the term to convey a different sense, Jesus thereafter said: "Have salt in yourselves, and keep peace between one another." (Mr 9:50) The apostle Paul used it in a similar way, saying: "Let your utterance be always with graciousness, seasoned with salt, so as to know how you ought to give an answer to each one." (Col 4:6) One's conduct and speech should always be in good taste, considerate, wholesome, and tend toward preserving the lives of others.

SALT, CITY OF.

A Judean city in the wilderness. (Jos 15:61, 62) It is identified with Khirbet Qumran (Horvat Qumeran), about 20 km (13 mi) E of Jerusalem, by the NW shore of the Dead Sea.

SALT, VALLEY OF.

A valley where, on two occasions, the Israelites defeated the Edomites. (2Sa 8:13; 2Ki 14:7) Its precise location is uncertain, but scholars have generally recommended either of two locations, one near Beer-sheba and the other to the S of the Salt Sea.

East from Beer-sheba in the Negeb is a valley the Arabic name of which (Wadi el-Milh) means Valley of Salt. The location is one where Judeans from the N and Edomites coming from the SE might conceivably meet in combat. However, some scholars, preferring a location in Edom's territory, identify the Scriptural Valley of Salt with a plain SSW of the Salt Sea. At present, the lowland S of the Salt Sea is quite marshy and hardly a location that would be chosen for a battle. But, since the level of the Salt Sea has risen, the plain may have been more firm at the time the battles occurred, or the fighting could have begun in a portion of the valley where the ground was not marshy. After the second conflict, 10,000 Edomites were hurled to their deaths from a crag, but the location of that crag is not stated. —2Ch 25:11, 12.

In the first battle, David and Joab (evidently with Abishai in charge of at least some of the troops) struck down 18,000 Edomites in the Valley of Salt. (2Sa 8:13; 1Ki 11:15; 1Ch 18:12; Ps 60:Sup) Later, King Amaziah (858-830 B.C.E.) attacked and slaughtered 10,000 Edomites in the same valley, following this with the execution of 10,000 Edomites who were captured, as well as the seizing of the Edomite stronghold Sela.—2Ki 14:7; 2Ch 25:11, 12; see EDOM, EDOMITES.

SALT HERB

[Heb., mal·lu'ach]. This term is mentioned only once in Scripture as a food eaten by those of little account. (Job 30:4) The original-language word is considered to be derived from a root meaning "salt," and it has also been translated "salt-wort" (AS, AT, Da), "cress" (Fn), "grass" (Dy), and "mallow(s)" (KJ, Le, RS). The rendering "mallows" appears to have resulted from the similarity between the Hebrew word mal·lu'ach and the Greek word mo·lo'khe, which is believed to be related to the English designation "mallow." However, at Job 30:4 the translators of the Greek Septuagint did not use mo·lo'khe but ha'li·ma ("salt herbs," LXX, Bagster), and ha'li·ma, like mal·lu'ach, is thought to refer either to the salty taste of the plant or to the region where it grows.

The plant most frequently suggested as corresponding to the mal·lu'ach of the Bible is sea purslane or shrubby orache (Atriplex halimus). Ordinarily this bushy shrub grows 1 to 2 m (3 to 6.5 ft) high. The plant has small, thick, sour-tasting leaves, and in the spring, it bears tiny purple flowers. It grows in saline soil.

SALT SEA.

One of the Biblical designations for the large lake or sea now generally known as the Dead Sea. The Salt Sea (Yam ha-Melah) forms the southern termination of the Jordan River.

Name. The first and most frequent designation of this sea in the Bible, "Salt Sea," is quite appropriate, since it is the saltiest body of water on the earth. (Ge 14:3; Nu 34:3, 12; Jos 15:2, 5) It is also called the sea of the Arabah (De 4:49; 2Ki 14:25), being in the huge rift of which the Arabah is a part. Sometimes, though, the name "Salt Sea" is added after "sea of the Arabah" as if to explain exactly which body of water is meant by the later name. (De 3:17; Jos 3:16; 12:3) The Salt Sea was on the E boundary of the Promised Land and was termed "the eastern sea," thus distinguishing it from "the western [Mediterranean] sea." (Eze 47: 18; Joe 2:20; Zec 14:8) Josephus, who was aware that large pieces of bitumen, or asphalt, occasionally surface in this sea, called it Lake Asphaltitis. (The Jewish War, I, 657 [xxxiii, 5]; IV, 479 [viii, 4]) Evidently it was not until the second century C.E. that it came to be called the Dead Sea. The Arabic name is Bahr Lut, "Sea of Lot."

Physical Description. The Salt Sea is oblong, about 15 km (9 mi) wide and about 75 km (47 mi) long, the length varying somewhat according to the season. Its outline is interrupted by a large peninsula called the Lisan (the tongue) reaching out from the SE side. This peninsula now divides the sea into two sections, although a channel is maintained between the two parts. The portion embayed S of the Lisan is quite shallow,

Limestone cliffs that border the Salt Sea

while the main part of the sea in the N reaches a depth of about 400 m (1,300 ft). The surface of the water is about 400 m (1,300 ft) below the level of the Mediterranean Sea, making it the lowest spot on earth.

The E shore (N of the Lisan) consists mainly of sandstone cliffs that rise steeply to the plateau of Moab. Several gorges, the most prominent being the Arnon, cut through these barren hills and empty water into the sea. To the E and S of the peninsula lies a plain that is well watered with streams. The S end of the sea is a flat salt marsh. On the W side of the sea the limestone cliffs are not as precipitous as those on the E. These Judean hills are more terraced and receding, but very desolate, since no permanent streams cut through to the sea. The beach and slopes near the shore allow travel along the W side. On a high mesa opposite the Lisan is Masada, the fortress that Herod strengthened and where, in 73 C.E., the Romans defeated the last of the Jews who were holding out against the Roman army. Farther N is the oasis En-gedi. At the N end, the Jordan empties into the sea, mixing its fresh water with the extremely salty water of the sea.

Water. The water of the sea is unique in that it is about nine times as salty as the oceans. The Salt Sea has no outlet, so most of the water coming into it evaporates in the intense heat, leaving behind more mineral salts. The salt concentration is such that no fish, even saltwater varieties, are able to live; the few fish in the brackish water where fresh water mixes with the salt water are killed if they are swept into the sea proper. This adds meaning to Ezekiel's description of a torrent flowing from Jehovah's temple into "the eastern sea" and healing the upper portion so that it abounded in fish like the Mediterranean Sea and could support a flourishing fishing industry. (Eze 47:8-10, 18) The high density of the water causes objects to float easily, and it contributes to a smooth surface because the water is not ruffled by light breezes.

Sodom and Gomorrah. It is generally believed that Sodom and Gomorrah were located near the southern end of the Salt Sea. The kings of these cities were among those who battled in "the Low Plain of Siddim, that is, the Salt Sea," and the way this is phrased suggests that the Low Plain of Siddim came to be covered by the Salt Sea. (Ge 14:3) The region of Sodom and Gomorrah where Lot settled was 'well watered, like the garden of Jehovah.' (Ge 13:10-12) Even today, in the plain along the SE shore, vegetation is abundant, and wheat, barley, dates, and vines can be grown there. The large amounts of bitumen and salt, especially in this southern section, also match the Biblical account of Sodom and Gomorrah.—Ge 14:10; 19:24-26.

SALU (Sa'lu). A Simeonite whose son Zimri was executed for immorality on the Plains of Moab.—Nu 25:14.

SALVATION. See RANSOM; SAVIOR.

SAMARIA (Sa·mar'i·a) [Belonging to the Clan Shemer].

1. The city that King Omri began to build about the middle of the tenth century B.C.E.; it served as the capital of the northern kingdom of Israel for more than 200 years. Omri purchased the mountain, on top of which this city was built, from Shemer, for two talents of silver, a price equal to $13,212. (1Ki 16:23, 24) The mountain as well as the city continued to be called after the name of this former owner.—Am 4:1; 6:1.

Location. Samaria is identified with ruins called Shomeron adjacent to the Arab village Sabastiya, about 55 km (34 mi) N of Jerusalem, and 11 km (7 mi) NW of Shechem. It was in Manasseh's territory. When Samaria was described as "the head" of Ephraim, the reference was to its position as the capital of the ten-tribe kingdom, Ephraim being the dominant tribe of that kingdom. (Isa 7:9) Samaria was near to, if not the same location as, "Shamir in the mountainous region of Ephraim," the home of Judge Tola, who served during the period of the Judges.—Jg 10:1, 2.

The rather flat top of the Samarian hill, about 2 km (1 mi) across from E to W, was an ideal location for a city. The abrupt rise of about 90 m (300 ft) from the plain below made the location easy to defend. The view too was magnificent, for to the N, E, and S were higher peaks, while to the W the land gently sloped down from an altitude of 463 m (1,519 ft) to the blue Mediterranean, 34 km (21 mi) away.

Much of Samaria's history is bound up with the wayward record of the 14 kings of Israel from Omri to Hoshea.—1Ki 16:28, 29; 22:51, 52; 2Ki 3:1, 2; 10:35, 36; 13:1, 10; 14:23; 15:8, 13, 14, 17, 23, 25, 27; 17:1.

During Time of Ahab. After the death of Omri, his son Ahab continued the city's building program during his 22-year reign. This included the construction of a Baal temple, the setting up a Baal altar, and the erection of "the sacred pole" of worship—all evidence, in this newly created city, of the Canaanite religion sponsored by Ahab's Phoenician wife Jezebel. (1Ki 16:28-33; 18:18, 19; 2Ki 13:6) Ahab also embellished Samaria with a beautiful "house of ivory" that was possibly furnished with "couches of ivory" similar to those referred to by the prophet Amos a hundred years later. (1Ki 22:39; Am 3:12, 15; 6:1, 4) Archaeologists have found more than 500 fragments of ivory, many artistically carved, in the ruins of Samaria.

During the latter part of Ahab's reign, the Syrian king Ben-hadad II laid siege to Samaria, vowing he would strip it so completely that there would not be sufficient dust to fill the hands of those in his army. However, the Israelites were given the victory in order that Ahab should know that Jehovah is God Almighty. (1Ki 20:1-21) In a second encounter less than a year later, when Ben-hadad was forced to surrender, Ahab let him go on the promise that cities would be returned to Israel and 'streets in Damascus would be assigned' to Ahab the same as Ben-hadad's father had assigned himself streets in Samaria. (1Ki 20:26-34) These "streets" evidently had been for the establishment of bazaars, or markets, to promote the commerical interests of Ben-hadad's father. Nevertheless, Ahab returned to Samaria sad and dejected, for, since he had spared Ben-hadad's life, Jehovah told him he would forfeit his own.—1Ki 20:35-43.

This forfeiture came about in the third year after that when Ahab invited Judean King Jehoshaphat to help him recover Ramoth-gilead from Syria. The two kings formally held court at the entrance of Samaria and, after ignoring Jehovah's prophet and listening to the deceptive counsel of false prophets, set out for the battle. (1Ki 22:1-28; 2Ch 18:2, 9) Ahab disguised himself, but he was struck by an arrow, though the enemy archer had not recognized him as the king. Ahab bled to death in his chariot. He was returned to his capital for burial, and the chariot was washed out alongside the pool of Samaria. (1Ki 22:29-38) This pool may be the rather shallow but large rectangular one discovered there by archaeologists.

The final accounting with the house of Ahab was at the hands of Jehu, whom Jehovah anointed for this work of execution. (2Ki 9:6-10) After killing Ahab's son Jehoram, Ahab's grandson Ahaziah, and Ahab's widow Jezebel (2Ki 9:22-37), Jehu next, in an exchange of letters with the princes and older men residing at Samaria, arranged for the beheading of Ahab's 70 remaining sons. "Know, then," Jehu declared, "that nothing of Jehovah's word will fall unfulfilled to the earth that Jehovah has spoken against the house of Ahab; and Jehovah himself has done what he spoke by means of his servant Elijah." —2Ki 10:1-12, 17.

Other pronouncements of Jehovah by his prophets Elijah and Elisha, and the events connected with them, occurred in Samaria and its vicinity. For example, Ahab's son Ahaziah fell through the grating in his palace roof chamber in Samaria (2Ki 1:2-17), the Syrian leper Naaman came to Samaria seeking a cure (2Ki 5:1-14), and the Syrian military force, sent out to capture Elisha, was mentally blinded and led to Samaria, where the men were fed and sent home (2Ki 6:13-23). During the reign of Ahab's son Jehoram, the Syrians besieged Samaria, causing such a famine that some persons ate their own children. But then, in fulfillment of Elisha's prophecy, the famine was broken in one night when Jehovah caused the Syrians to flee in panic and leave behind their foodstuffs.—2Ki 6:24-29; 7:1-20.

Rival of Jerusalem. From time to time the rivalry and animosity between Samaria and Jerusalem, the respective capitals of the northern and southern kingdoms, burst into open warfare. On one occasion the king of Judah, when about to attack Edom, sent 100,000 mercenaries of Israel back home on orders from Jehovah. And even though paid 100 silver talents ($660,600), these Israelites were so enraged that they raided and plundered Judean towns "from Samaria clear to Beth-horon." (2Ch 25:5-13) The king of Judah, flushed with victory over Edom, then picked a quarrel with the king of Samaria, a quarrel that was not settled until all the gold and silver from the house of Jehovah and the king's treasury in Jerusalem had been carried off to Samaria. (2Ki 14:8-14; 2Ch 25:17-24) Years later, however, after a defeat of King Ahaz of Judah, in order to escape Jehovah's anger, the men of Israel returned certain captives and booty that had been taken to Samaria.—2Ch 28:5-15.

The city of Samaria was eventually destroyed for its idolatry, moral corruption, and continued disregard for God's laws and principles. (2Ki 17:7-18) Repeatedly Jehovah warned her rulers and their subjects by the mouths of such prophets as Isaiah (8:4; 9:9), Hosea (7:1; 8:5, 6; 10:5, 7; 13:16), Amos (3:9; 8:14), Micah (1:1, 5, 6), as well as Elijah and Elisha (1Ki 20:13, 28, 35-42; 22:8). Later on, after her destruction, other prophets

Roman ruins at ancient Samaria

referred to Samaria as a warning example to those who would reject Jehovah's instructions. —2Ki 21:10-13; Jer 23:13; Eze 16:46, 51, 53, 55; 23:4, 33.

Later History. In 742 B.C.E. Shalmaneser V, king of Assyria, laid siege to Samaria, but the city was able to hold out for nearly three years. When it finally fell in 740 B.C.E., many of the leading inhabitants were deported into exile and settled in Mesopotamia and Media. Whether credit for the ultimate capture of the city goes to Shalmaneser V or to his successor Sargon II is still not a settled question.—2Ki 17:1-6, 22, 23; 18:9-12; see SARGON.

With the fall of Samaria to the Assyrians, the Bible's detailed history of the city ends. Thereafter, mention of the city is often, though not always (2Ki 23:18; Ac 8:5), made by way of a reminder of what becomes of those who rebel against Jehovah. (2Ki 18:34; 21:13; Isa 10:9-11; 36:19) The Bible relates that after the destruction of Jerusalem and the subsequent assassination of Gedaliah, 80 men from Shechem, Shiloh, and Samaria came down toward Mizpah and encountered Ishmael the assassin. Ishmael slaughtered many of these men, sparing some of them who promised to show him where they had treasures of wheat, barley, and oil hidden.—Jer 41:1-9.

Secular records relate some of Samaria's history from and after the days of Alexander the Great.

In Roman times its splendor was due to the building program of Herod the Great, who renamed the city Sebaste (a feminine Greek form for the Latin name Augustus), in honor of Augustus, the first emperor. Today the Arabic name Sabastiya preserves the name Herod gave it. It is therefore not surprising that excavations at this site have uncovered the remains of a number of different periods in its history; some of these remains are from the days of Israel's kings.

2. The territory of the ten-tribe northern kingdom of Israel. The name of its capital city, Samaria, was sometimes applied to this entire area. For example, when Ahab was called "the king of Samaria," it was not with the restricted meaning of being king of the city only, but in the broader sense as king of the ten tribes. (1Ki 21:1) So, too, "the cities of Samaria" referred to those scattered throughout the ten tribes, not to towns clustered around the capital. (2Ki 23:19; this same expression recorded at 1Ki 13:32 as if used before the city Samaria was built, if not prophetic, may have been introduced by the compiler of the Kings account.) The famine "in Samaria" in the days of Ahab was extensive throughout the whole kingdom of Samaria and, in fact, even took in Phoenicia, extending at least from the torrent valley of Cherith, E of the Jordan, to Zarephath on the Mediterranean. (1Ki 17:1-12; 18:2, 5, 6) Similarly, the restoration promise regarding "the mountains of Samaria" must have embraced the whole of the realm of Samaria.—Jer 31:5.

Tiglath-pileser III seems to have been the first to uproot Israelites from Samaria's territory, some prominent Reubenites, Gadites, and Manassites from E of the Jordan being among those moved to Assyria. (1Ch 5:6, 26) When the northern kingdom finally fell, more were taken into exile. (2Ki 17:6) But this time the king of Assyria replaced these Israelites with people from other parts of his realm, a transplanting policy continued by Esar-haddon and Asenappar (Ashurbanipal).—2Ki 17:24; Ezr 4:2, 10.

Lions began to multiply in the land, probably because the land, or a large part of it, had lain waste for a time. (Compare Ex 23:29.) The settlers doubtless felt, superstitiously, that it was because they did not understand how to worship the god of the land. Therefore the king of Assyria sent back a calf-worshiping Israelite priest from exile. He taught the settlers about Jehovah, but in the same manner as Jeroboam had done, so that they learned something about Jehovah but actually continued to worship their own false gods. —2Ki 17:24-41.

3. The Roman district through which Jesus occasionally traveled and into which the apostles later brought the message of Christianity. Its boundaries are not definitely known today, but, generally, it lay between Galilee in the N and Judea in the S, and it extended W from the Jordan to the coastal plains of the Mediterranean. For the most part the district embraced the territories once belonging to the tribe of Ephraim and half the tribe of Manasseh (W of the Jordan).

From time to time, on his way to and from Jerusalem, Jesus passed through Samaria, situated as it was between the districts of Judea and Galilee. (Lu 17:11; Joh 4:3-6) But for the most part he refrained from preaching in this territory, even telling the 12 whom he sent out to avoid Samaritan cities and, instead, to "go continually to the lost sheep of the house of Israel," that is, the Jews.—Mt 10:5, 6.

However, this restriction covered only a limited time, for just before his ascension to heaven, Jesus told his disciples they should carry the good news not only to Samaria but to the most distant part of the earth. (Ac 1:8, 9) So it was that when persecution broke out in Jerusalem the disciples, Philip in particular, took up the ministry in Samaria. Peter and John were later sent there, resulting in further expansion of Christianity.—Ac 8:1-17, 25; 9:31; 15:3.

SAMARITAN (Sa·mar'i·tan) [probably, Of (Belonging to) Samaria]. The term "Samaritans" first appeared in Scripture after the conquest of the ten-tribe kingdom of Samaria in 740 B.C.E.; it was applied to those who lived in the northern kingdom before that conquest as distinct from the foreigners later brought in from other parts of the Assyrian Empire. (2Ki 17:29) It appears that the Assyrians did not remove all the Israelite inhabitants, for the account at 2 Chronicles 34:6-9 (compare 2Ki 23:19, 20) implies that during King Josiah's reign there were Israelites still in the land. In time, "Samaritans" came to mean the descendants of those left in Samaria and those brought in by the Assyrians. Therefore some were undoubtedly the products of mixed marriages. At a still later period, the name carried more of a religious, rather than a racial or political, connotation. "Samaritan" referred to one who belonged to the religious sect that flourished in the vicinity of ancient Shechem and Samaria and who held to certain tenets distinctly different from Judaism. —Joh 4:9.

The Samaritan Religion. The development of the Samaritan religion was due to a number of factors, not the least of which stemmed from

Jeroboam's efforts at alienating the ten tribes from Jehovah's worship as centered in Jerusalem. For about 250 years after the nation had split into two kingdoms, the God-ordained Levitical priests were replaced by a man-appointed priesthood, which, in turn, led the kingdom of Israel in the practice of demoralizing idolatry. (1Ki 12:28-33; 2Ki 17:7-17; 2Ch 11:13-15; 13:8, 9) Then came the fall of the northern kingdom. The pagan immigrants brought in from Babylon, Cuthah, Avva, Hamath, and Sepharvaim were worshipers of many deities—Succoth-benoth, Nergal, Ashima, Nibhaz, Tartak, Adrammelech, and Anammelech. Although they learned something about Jehovah through instruction by a priest of the Jeroboam priesthood, yet, as Samaria had done with the golden calves, they continued to worship their false gods, generation after generation. (2Ki 17:24-41) Josiah's extensive efforts to rid these northern communities of their idol worship, nearly a hundred years after Samaria fell, had no more lasting effect than similar reforms made by him in the southern kingdom of Judah.—2Ki 23:4-20; 2Ch 34:6, 7.

In 537 B.C.E. a remnant of the 12 tribes returned from Babylonian exile prepared to rebuild Jehovah's temple in Jerusalem. (Ezr 1:3; 2:1, 70) It was then that the "Samaritans," who were already in the land when the Israelites arrived and who were described as "adversaries of Judah and Benjamin," approached Zerubbabel and the older men, saying, "Let us build along with you; for, just like you, we search for your God and to him we are sacrificing since the days of Esarhaddon the king of Assyria, who brought us up here." (Ezr 4:1, 2) This claim of devotion to Jehovah, however, proved to be only lip service, for when Zerubbabel declined their offer, the Samaritans did everything they could to prevent the building of the temple. After all their concerted efforts at harassment and intimidation had failed, they then made false accusations in a letter to the Persian emperor and succeeded in getting a government decree issued that put a stop to the construction for a number of years.—Ezr 4:3-24.

In the middle of the fifth century B.C.E., when Nehemiah began repairing Jerusalem's walls, Sanballat (governor of Samaria, according to one of the Elephantine Papyri) made several strenuous but unsuccessful efforts to stop the project. (Ne 2:19, 20; 4:1-12; 6:1-15) Later, after an extended absence, Nehemiah returned to Jerusalem to find that the grandson of High Priest Eliashib had married Sanballat's daughter. Immediately, Nehemiah "chased him away."—Ne 13:6, 7, 28.

The erection of the Samaritan temple on Mount Gerizim, perhaps in the fourth century B.C.E., in competition to the one in Jerusalem is considered by some to mark the final separation of the Jews and Samaritans, although some think the severance in relations came more than a century later. When Jesus began his ministry, the breach between the two had not been healed, although the Gerizim temple had been destroyed about a century and a half earlier. (Joh 4:9) The Samaritans were still worshiping on Mount Gerizim (Joh 4:20-23), and the Jews had little respect for them. (Joh 8:48) This existing scornful attitude permitted Jesus to make a strong point in his illustration of the neighborly Samaritan.—Lu 10:29-37.

Samaritan Pentateuch. From early times, the Scriptures of the Samaritans have consisted of only the first five books of the Bible, and these only in their own recension, written in their own characters and known as the Samaritan Pentateuch. The rest of the Hebrew Scriptures, with the possible exception of the book of Joshua, they rejected. The Samaritan Pentateuch differs from the Masoretic text in some 6,000 instances, most of which are minor. However, some are major, as, for example, the reading of Deuteronomy 27:4, where Gerizim is substituted for Ebal, the place where the laws of Moses were to be inscribed on whitewashed stones. (De 27:8) The obvious reason for this change was to give credence to their belief that Gerizim is the holy mountain of God.

But their acceptance of the Pentateuch, by and large, gave the Samaritans the basis for believing that a prophet greater than Moses would come. (De 18:18, 19) In the first century Samaritans were looking for the coming of Christ the Messiah, and some of them recognized him; others rejected him. (Lu 17:16-19; Joh 4:9-43; Lu 9:52-56) Later, through the preaching of the early Christians, many Samaritans gladly embraced Christianity. —Ac 8:1-17, 25; 9:31; 15:3.

SAMEKH [ס] (sa′mekh). The 15th letter of the Hebrew alphabet. Sa′mekh represents the sound that the Ephraimites used when endeavoring to pronounce the word "shibboleth," which begins with the letter shin (שׁ) rather than with sa′mekh. (Jg 12:6; see also SIN, SHIN.) In the Hebrew, sa′mekh is the initial letter in each of the eight verses of Psalm 119:113-120.

SAMGAR-NEBO (Sam′gar-ne′bo). The name or title of one of the Babylonian princes who entered Jerusalem right after a breach was made in its walls in the summer of 607 B.C.E.—Jer 39:3.

SAMLAH (Sam'lah). The fifth-named king of Edom who reigned before a king ruled Israel. Samlah was from Masrekah.—Ge 36:31-37; 1Ch 1:47, 48.

SAMOS (Sa'mos) [Height]. An island in the Aegean Sea near the W coast of Asia Minor. Paul apparently stopped briefly at Samos on the return from his third missionary tour.—Ac 20:15.

A strait about 1.5 km (1 mi) long separates this mountainous island from the Asian promontory named Samsun Dagi. Samos was SW of Ephesus and NW of Miletus. It is about 43 km (27 mi) in length and 23 km (14 mi) in width. At the time of Paul's missionary journeys, it was a free state. Its major city and port was also named Samos. The island was celebrated for the cult of Hera (Juno, the Roman goddess of marriage and childbirth) and had a temple to her that vied in splendor and celebrity with the temple of Artemis at Ephesus.

According to the Scriptural account, the ship Paul was on when returning to Jerusalem stopped at Chios, sailed some 105 km (65 mi) down the coast of Asia Minor and 'touched at Samos, and on the following day arrived at Miletus.' (Ac 20:15) Certain manuscripts add an expression that leads to the rendering "we touched at Samos and, after stopping at Trogyllium, made Miletus the next day." (*JB*) This has been understood to mean that the ship did not remain in port at Samos but, instead, crossed the strait and anchored in the protection of the high promontory. However, the oldest and most reliable manuscripts omit the expression about "Trogyllium," and it was rejected by Westcott and Hort as well as Nestle and Aland in preparing their master texts. The ship Paul was on evidently docked briefly at Samos and then traveled on to Miletus.

SAMOTHRACE (Sam'o·thrace) [possibly, Samos of Thrace]. A mountainous island located in the NE Aegean Sea, having a city of the same name on its N side. Likely in the spring of 50 C.E., during Paul's second missionary journey, the ship on which he was traveling came "with a straight run" to the island of Samothrace from Troas in NW Asia Minor. There is, however, no indication that he went ashore. (Ac 16:11) The modern-day island (Samothraki) lacks a good harbor, though it offers a number of places for safe anchorage.

SAMSON (Sam'son) [from a root meaning 'sun']. One of Israel's outstanding judges; son of Manoah, a Danite from Zorah. Prior to Samson's birth an angel appeared to his mother and announced that she would bear a son who was to be a Nazirite from birth and "take the lead in saving Israel out of the hand of the Philistines." (Jg 13:1-5, 24; 16:17) As future leader in the fight against the Philistines, Samson would have to come near the dead bodies of persons slain in battle. Therefore, the very nature of his commission showed that he did not come under the law prescribing that Nazirites not touch dead bodies. (Nu 6:2-9) It should also be noted that this law applied to persons who *voluntarily* took a vow of Naziriteship; but in Samson's case, the requirements that applied were those specifically stated to his mother by Jehovah's angel.

When old enough to marry, Samson requested that his parents get a certain Philistine woman from Timnah for him as a wife. This was in harmony with the direction of God's spirit, as it was to provide occasion for Samson to fight against the Philistines. (Jg 13:25–14:4) Subsequently, near Timnah, a maned young lion confronted Samson. Empowered by God's spirit, he tore the animal in two with his bare hands. He then continued on his way to Timnah and there spoke with the Philistine woman whom he wanted as a wife.—Jg 14:5-7.

Sometime later Samson, accompanied by his parents, went to Timnah to bring his betrothed home. On the way there he turned aside from the road to look at the corpse of the lion that he had killed earlier and found a swarm of bees and honey inside. Samson ate some of the honey and, upon rejoining his parents, offered honey to them. At the wedding banquet he made this incident an object of a riddle and propounded it to 30 Philistine groomsmen. Further developments centering around this riddle provided the occasion for Samson to kill 30 Philistines at Ashkelon.—Jg 14:8-19.

When the father of his betrothed gave her to another man and did not permit Samson to see her, Samson was furnished with yet another opportunity to act against the Philistines. Using 300 foxes, he set the grainfields, vineyards, and olive groves of the Philistines on fire. The enraged Philistines therefore burned Samson's betrothed and her father, because the Philistines' loss had resulted from his treatment of Samson. By this act the Philistines once more gave Samson reason for avenging himself upon them. He slew many of them, "piling legs upon thighs."—Jg 14:20–15:8.

Seeking revenge against Samson, the Philistines came to Lehi. Three thousand fearful men of Judah then prevailed upon Samson at the crag Etam to surrender, thereafter binding him with two new ropes and leading him to the Philistines. Exultantly, the Philistines prepared to receive

Samson. But "Jehovah's spirit became operative upon him, and the ropes that were upon his arms came to be like linen threads that have been scorched with fire, so that his fetters melted off his hands." Taking the moist jawbone of a male ass, Samson struck down a thousand men, after which he ascribed this victory to Jehovah. On that occasion Jehovah, in answer to Samson's request, miraculously provided water to relieve his thirst. —Jg 15:9-19.

Another time Samson went to the home of a prostitute in the Philistine city of Gaza. Hearing of this, the Philistines laid in wait for him, intending to kill him in the morning. But at midnight Samson got up and ripped the city gate and its side posts and bar from the wall of Gaza, and he carried them "up to the top of the mountain that is in front of Hebron." (Jg 16:1-3; see GAZA.) This was a great humiliation for the Philistines, as it left Gaza weak and unprotected from intruders. The fact that Samson was able to accomplish this amazing feat indicates that he still had God's spirit. This would argue against his having gone to the house of the prostitute for immoral purposes. In Lange's *Commentary on the Holy Scriptures* (Jg 16:1, p. 212), commentator Paulus Cassel says on this point: "Samson did not come to Gaza for the purpose of visiting a harlot: for it is said that 'he went, thither, and saw there a [prostitute].' But when he wished to remain there [at Gaza] over night, there was nothing for him, the national enemy, but to abide with the [prostitute]. . . . His stay is spoken of in language not different from that employed with reference to the abode of the spies in the house of Rahab. The words, 'he saw her,' only indicate that when he saw a woman of her class, he knew where he could find shelter for the night." (Translated and edited by P. Schaff, 1976) It should also be noted that the account reads "Samson kept lying till midnight" and not 'Samson kept lying *with her* till midnight.'

By going into enemy territory, Samson demonstrated his fearlessness. It may well be that he went to Gaza to 'look for an opportunity against the Philistines,' as had been the case earlier when he sought a wife among them. (Jg 14:4) If so, Samson apparently intended to turn any effort directed against him into an occasion for inflicting injury upon the Philistines.

Betrayed by Delilah. It was after this that Samson fell in love with Delilah. (See DELILAH.) For material gain she sought to learn the secret of Samson's strength. Three times he gave her misleading answers. But, because of her persistent pestering, he finally gave in and revealed to her that his strength lay in his being a Nazirite from birth. She then got in touch with the Philistines to get the reward for turning him over to them. While Samson was sleeping on her knees, Delilah had his hair shaved off. Upon awakening, he no longer had Jehovah's spirit, for he had allowed himself to get into a position that led to the termination of his Naziriteship. Not the hair itself but what it stood for, that is, Samson's special relationship with Jehovah as a Nazirite, was the source of his strength. With the end of that relationship, Samson was no different from any other man. Therefore, the Philistines were able to blind him, bind him with copper fetters, and put him to work as a grinder in the prison house.—Jg 16:4-21.

While Samson languished in prison, the Philistines arranged for a great sacrifice to their god Dagon, to whom they attributed their success in having captured Samson. Great throngs, including all the axis lords, were assembled in the house used for Dagon worship. On the roof alone there were 3,000 men and women. The merry Philistines had Samson, whose hair had meanwhile grown luxuriantly, brought out of prison to provide amusement for them. Upon his arrival, Samson asked the boy who was leading him to let him feel the pillars that supported the structure. He then prayed to Jehovah: "Remember me, please, and strengthen me, please, just this once, O you the true God, and let me avenge myself upon the Philistines with vengeance for one of my two eyes." (Jg 16:22-28) It may be that he prayed to avenge himself for only one of his eyes because of recognizing that the loss of them had come about partly through his own failure. Or, it may be that he felt it would be impossible to avenge himself completely as Jehovah's representative.

Samson braced himself against the two supporting pillars and "bent himself with power," causing the house to collapse. This resulted in his own death and that of more Philistines than he had killed in his entire lifetime. Relatives buried him "between Zorah and Eshtaol in the burial place of Manoah his father." Thus Samson died faithful to Jehovah after having judged Israel for 20 years. Therefore his name rightly appears among men who, through faith, were made powerful.—Jg 15:20; 16:29-31; Heb 11:32-34.

SAMUEL (Sam'u·el) [Name of God]. A prominent prophet (Ac 3:24; 13:20), traditionally credited with the writership of the Bible books of Judges, Ruth, and part of First Samuel. (Compare 1Sa 10:25; 1Ch 29:29.) His father Elkanah was

Levite of the nonpriestly Kohathites. (1Ch 6:27, 28, 33-38) Samuel came to have three full brothers and two full sisters.—1Sa 2:21.

Promised to the service of Jehovah as a Nazirite by his mother Hannah before conception (1Sa 1:11), Samuel was taken to the tabernacle at Shiloh upon being weaned (perhaps at the age of at least three years; compare 2Ch 31:16) and was left there in the charge of High Priest Eli. (1Sa 1:24-28) Thus Samuel, having a linen ephod girded on, 'ministered to Jehovah' as a boy. Annually his mother visited him and brought him a new sleeveless coat. (1Sa 2:18, 19) As he grew, Samuel became "more likable both from Jehovah's standpoint and from that of men."—1Sa 2:26.

Becomes Prophet at an Early Age. At night Samuel slept in "the temple of Jehovah, where the ark of God was," and his first assignment in the morning appears to have been to open "the doors of Jehovah's house." (1Sa 3:3, 15) Evidently the words "where the ark of God was" apply to the tabernacle area and are not to be understood as signifying that Samuel slept in the Most Holy. As a nonpriestly Kohathite Levite he was not entitled to see the Ark or any of the other sacred furnishings inside the sanctuary. (Nu 4:17-20) The only part of the house of Jehovah to which Samuel had access was the tabernacle courtyard. Therefore, he must have opened the doors leading into the courtyard, and it must have been there that he slept. During the period that the tabernacle was permanently located at Shiloh, various structures were likely erected, and one of these could have served as Samuel's sleeping place.

One night, after having retired, Samuel heard a voice calling him by name. Imagining the speaker to be High Priest Eli, he ran to see him. After this occurred three times, Eli discerned that Jehovah was calling Samuel and Eli instructed him accordingly. Jehovah then made known to Samuel his judgment against Eli's house. Fearful, Samuel did not volunteer any information concerning the word of Jehovah until requested to do so by Eli. Thus began Samuel's prophetic work, and all Israel eventually became aware that he was indeed Jehovah's prophet.—1Sa 3:2-21.

Leads Israel in True Worship. Over 20 years later, at Samuel's exhortation, the Israelites abandoned idolatrous worship and began serving Jehovah alone. Subsequently, Samuel had the Israelites assemble at Mizpah. Taking advantage of the situation, the Philistines invaded. Becoming fearful, the sons of Israel requested that Samuel call to Jehovah for aid. He did so and also offered up a sucking lamb in sacrifice. (1Sa 7:2-9) Of course, as a nonpriestly Kohathite Levite, Samuel was not authorized to officiate at the sanctuary altar (Nu 18:2, 3, 6, 7), and there is no record that he ever did so. However, as Jehovah's representative and prophet, he could sacrifice at other places in compliance with divine direction, as did Gideon (Jg 6:25-28) and Elijah. (1Ki 18:36-38) Jehovah answered Samuel's prayer, throwing the Philistines into confusion and thereby enabling the Israelites to gain a decisive victory. To commemorate this, Samuel set up a stone between Mizpah and Jeshanah and called it Ebenezer (meaning "Stone of Help"). (1Sa 7:10-12) Doubtless from the spoils of this and other wars, Samuel set aside things as holy to maintain the tabernacle.—1Ch 26:27, 28.

The days of Samuel brought additional reverses for the Philistines (1Sa 7:13, 14) and proved to be a period marked by outstanding Passover celebrations. (2Ch 35:18) Samuel also seems to have worked out some arrangement for the Levite gatekeepers, and his arrangement may have served as a basis for the organization put into operation by David. (1Ch 9:22) From his home at Ramah in the mountainous region of Ephraim, Samuel annually made a circuit of Bethel, Gilgal, and Mizpah, judging Israel at all these places. (1Sa 7:15-17) Never did he abuse his position. His record was without blame. (1Sa 12:2-5) But his sons, Joel and Abijah, perverted justice.—1Sa 8:2, 3.

Anoints Saul as King. The unfaithfulness of Samuel's sons, coupled with the threat of warfare with the Ammonites, prompted the older men of Israel to request that Samuel appoint a king over them. (1Sa 8:4, 5; 12:12) Jehovah's answer to Samuel's prayer concerning this was that, though the request of the people showed lack of faith in Jehovah's kingship, nevertheless, the prophet should accede to it and advise them what the rightful due of the king involved. Though informed by Samuel that the monarchy would result in the loss of certain liberties, the people still insisted on having a king. After Samuel dismissed the men of Israel, Jehovah directed matters so that Samuel anointed the Benjamite Saul as king. (1Sa 8:6–10:1) Thereafter Samuel arranged for the Israelites to assemble at Mizpah, and there Saul was designated by lot as king. (1Sa 10:17-24) Again Samuel spoke about the rightful due of the kingship, and he also made a written record of it. —1Sa 10:25.

Following Saul's victory over the Ammonites, Samuel directed that the Israelites come to Gilgal to confirm the kingship anew. On that occasion

Samuel reviewed his own record, as well as Israel's past history, and showed that obedience to Jehovah by the king and the people was needed to maintain divine approval. To impress upon them the seriousness of having rejected Jehovah as King, Samuel prayed for an unseasonal thunderstorm. Jehovah's answering that petition motivated the people to acknowledge their serious transgression.—1Sa 11:14–12:25.

On two occasions thereafter Samuel had to censure Saul for disobedience to divine direction. In the first instance, Samuel announced that Saul's kingship would not last because he had presumptuously gone ahead in making a sacrifice instead of waiting as he had been commanded. (1Sa 13:10-14) Rejection by Jehovah of Saul himself as king was the second condemnatory message that Samuel delivered to Saul for disobediently pre-

---

HIGHLIGHTS OF FIRST SAMUEL

Record of the beginning of kingship in Israel, emphasizing obedience to Jehovah

Written by Samuel, Nathan, and Gad; First Samuel covers the time from the birth of Samuel to the death of Israel's first king, Saul.

Jehovah raises up Samuel as prophet in Israel (1:1–7:17)

Samuel is born as an answer to his mother Hannah's prayer; after he is weaned, he is presented for sanctuary service in fulfillment of Hannah's vow

Jehovah speaks to Samuel, pronouncing judgment against Eli's house because his sons Hophni and Phinehas act wickedly and Eli does not rebuke them

As Samuel grows up he is recognized as Jehovah's prophet

Jehovah's word against Eli begins to be fulfilled: Philistines capture the Ark and slay Eli's sons; Eli dies on hearing the news

Years later, Samuel urges the Israelites to abandon idolatry and serve Jehovah alone; Jehovah gives them victory over the Philistines

Saul becomes Israel's first king (8:1–15:35)

The Israelite elders approach aged Samuel, requesting a human king; Jehovah tells him to listen to their voice

Jehovah directs Samuel to anoint Saul, a Benjaminite, as king

Samuel presents Saul to an assembly of Israelites at Mizpah; not everyone accepts him

Saul defeats the Ammonites; his kingship is reconfirmed at Gilgal; Samuel admonishes the people to remain obedient to Jehovah

Faced with Philistine aggression, Saul fails to obey Jehovah and wait for Samuel's arrival, offering sacrifices himself; Samuel tells him that because of this his kingdom will not last

Saul defeats the Amalekites, but he disobediently preserves alive King Agag and the best of the animals; Samuel tells Saul he is rejected by Jehovah as king and that obedience is more important than sacrifice

David comes to prominence, and this angers Saul (16:1–20:42)

Samuel anoints David, and Jehovah's spirit leaves Saul; David becomes a harpist for Saul to soothe him when disturbed

David kills the Philistine champion Goliath, and a deep friendship develops between David and Saul's son Jonathan

Placed over Saul's warriors, David gains repeated victories and is celebrated in song more than Saul; Saul becomes jealous

Twice Saul's attempts to kill David fail, as does his scheme to have David die at the hands of the Philistines while procuring the bride-price for Saul's daughter Michal

Despite his promise to Jonathan, Saul for a third time tries to kill David, and David flees to Samuel at Ramah

Jonathan unsuccessfully tries to intercede for David with his father; he warns David, and he and David make a covenant

David's life as a fugitive (21:1–27:12)

At Nob, High Priest Ahimelech gives David food and Goliath's sword; David then flees to Gath, where he escapes harm by acting insane

He takes refuge in the cave of Adullam and then in the forest of Hereth; Saul has Ahimelech and everyone in Nob killed; Ahimelech's son Abiathar survives and comes to David

David saves Keilah from Philistines, but afterward he leaves the city to avoid being surrendered to Saul

The men of Ziph reveal David's whereabouts; he narrowly escapes capture

David has the opportunity to kill Saul but spares his life

Samuel dies

Abigail's wise intervention prevents David from shedding blood in the heat of anger

David spares Saul's life a second time and takes refuge in Philistine territory

The end of Saul's reign (28:1–31:13)

Saul assembles an army against Philistine invaders

Jehovah will not answer Saul's inquiries because of his disobedience, so Saul consults a spirit medium at En-dor

In battle with Philistines, Saul is severely wounded and commits suicide; his sons Jonathan, Abinadab, and Malchi-shua are slain

serving alive King Agag and the best of the Amalekite flock and herd. In response to Saul's plea, Samuel appeared with him before the older men of Israel and the people. After that Samuel commanded that Agag be brought to him and then "went hacking [him] to pieces before Jehovah in Gilgal."—1Sa 15:10-33.

Anoints David. When the two men parted, they had no further association. Samuel, however, went into mourning for Saul. But Jehovah God interrupted his mourning, commissioning him to go to Bethlehem to anoint one of the sons of Jesse as Israel's future king. To avoid any suspicion on Saul's part that might result in Samuel's death, Jehovah directed that Samuel take along a cow for sacrifice. Perhaps fearing that Samuel had come to reprove or punish some wrongdoing, the older men of Bethlehem trembled. But he assured them that his coming meant peace and then arranged for Jesse and his sons to share in a sacrificial meal. Impressed by the appearance of Jesse's firstborn Eliab, Samuel reasoned that this son must surely be Jehovah's choice for the kingship. But neither Eliab nor any of the other six sons of Jesse present had been chosen by Jehovah. Therefore, at Samuel's insistence, the youngest son, David, was called from pasturing the sheep, and then at Jehovah's direction Samuel anointed David in the midst of his brothers.—1Sa 15:34–16:13.

Later, after King Saul had made several attempts on his life, David fled to Samuel at Ramah. The two men then went to Naioth, and David remained there until Saul personally came to look for him. (1Sa 19:18–20:1) During the time David was still under restriction because of Saul, "Samuel died; and all Israel proceeded to collect together and bewail him and bury him at his house in Ramah." (1Sa 25:1) Thus Samuel died as an approved servant of Jehovah God after a lifetime of faithful service. (Ps 99:6; Jer 15:1; Heb 11:32) He had demonstrated persistence in fulfilling his commission (1Sa 16:6, 11), devotion to true worship (1Sa 7:3-6), honesty in his dealings (1Sa 12:3), and courage and firmness in announcing and upholding Jehovah's judgments and decisions (1Sa 10:24; 13:13; 15:32, 33).

Regarding the account of Saul's request for the spirit medium at En-dor to bring up Samuel for him, see SAUL No. 1.

SAMUEL, BOOKS OF. Two books of the Hebrew Scriptures that apparently were not divided in the original Hebrew canon. Indicative of this is a note in the Masora showing that words in First Samuel, chapter 28 (one of the concluding chapters of First Samuel), were in the middle of the book.

Writers and Time Covered. Ancient Jewish tradition credits Samuel with the writership of the first part of the book, and Nathan and Gad with the remaining portion. That these three prophets did write is confirmed at 1 Chronicles 29:29. The book itself reports: "Samuel spoke to the people about the rightful due of the kingship and wrote it in a book and deposited it before Jehovah." (1Sa 10:25) However, on the basis of 1 Samuel 27:6, where there is reference to "the kings of Judah," numerous scholars place the final compiling of the books of Samuel sometime after the ten-tribe kingdom of Israel came into existence. If the expression "the kings of Judah" denotes only Judean kings of the *two-tribe kingdom*, this would show that the writings of Samuel, Nathan, and Gad must have been put into final form by someone else. On the other hand, if "the kings of Judah" simply means kings from the *tribe* of Judah, these words could have been recorded by Nathan, since he lived under the rulership of two Judean kings, David and Solomon.—1Ki 1:32-34; 2Ch 9:29.

The fact that Hannah and an unnamed "man of God" used the expressions "king" and "anointed one" years before a king actually ruled over Israel does not support the argument of some that these passages date from a period later than indicated in the book. (1Sa 2:10, 35) The idea of a future king was by no means foreign to the Hebrews. God's promise concerning Sarah, the ancestress of the Israelites, was that "kings of peoples" would come from her. (Ge 17:16) Also, Jacob's deathbed prophecy (Ge 49:10), the prophetic words of Balaam (Nu 24:17), and the Mosaic Law (De 17:14-18) pointed to the time when the Israelites would have a king.

The historical narrative contained in the two books of Samuel commences with the time of High Priest Eli and concludes with events from David's reign. It therefore covers a period of approximately 140 years (c. 1180-c. 1040 B.C.E.). As David's death is not mentioned in the record, the account (possibly with the exception of editorial additions) was probably completed about 1040 B.C.E.

Authenticity. The authenticity of the account contained in the books of Samuel is well established. Christ Jesus himself, when refuting an objection raised by the Pharisees, cited the incident recorded at 1 Samuel 21:3-6 about David's receiving showbread from Ahimelech the priest. (Mt 12:1-4) In the synagogue of Antioch in Pisidia, the apostle Paul quoted from 1 Samuel 13:14 as he briefly reviewed events from Israel's history. (Ac 13:20-22) This apostle, in his letter to the Romans, used words from David's psalm, which passage is found at both 2 Samuel 22:50 and Psalm 18:49, to prove that Christ's ministry to the Jews verified God's promises and gave a basis for non-Jews to "glorify God for his mercy." (Ro 15:8, 9) Jehovah's words to David at 2 Samuel 7:14 are quoted and applied to Christ Jesus in Hebrews 1:5, thus showing that David served as a prophetic type of the Messiah.

Outstanding, too, is the candor of the record. It exposes the wrongs of the priestly house of Eli (1Sa 2:12-17, 22-25), the corruption of Samuel's sons (1Sa 8:1-3), and the sins and family difficul-ties of King David (2Sa 11:2-15; 13:1-22; 15:13, 14; 24:10).

Another evidence of the authenticity of the account is the fulfillment of prophecies. These relate to Israel's request for a king (De 17:14; 1Sa 8:5), Jehovah's rejection of Eli's house (1Sa 2:31; 3:12-14; 1Ki 2:27), and the continuance of the kingship in David's line (2Sa 7:16; Jer 33:17; Eze 21:25-27; Mt 1:1; Lu 1:32, 33).

The record is in complete harmony with the rest of the Scriptures. This is especially noticeable when examining the psalms, many of which are illuminated by what is contained in the books of Samuel. King Saul's sending messengers to watch David's house in order to kill him provides the background for Psalm 59. (1Sa 19:11) David's experiences at Gath, where he disguised his sanity

---

HIGHLIGHTS OF SECOND SAMUEL

Record of David's kingship—the blessings he experienced, as well as the discipline he received when he sinned

Originally part of one scroll with First Samuel; the portion in Second Samuel was completed by Gad and Nathan by the end of David's life in about 1040 B.C.E.

David becomes king and rules from Hebron (1:1–4:12)

David mourns the death of Saul and Jonathan; he takes up residence at Hebron and is anointed king by the men of Judah

Abner makes Saul's son Ish-bosheth king over the rest of Israel; fighting breaks out between the rival kingdoms

Abner defects to David but is killed by Joab

Ish-bosheth is murdered; David orders the execution of the assassins

David rules as king over all the tribes of Israel (5:1–10:19)

David is anointed as king over all Israel; he captures the stronghold of Zion and makes Jerusalem his capital city

The Philistines invade twice but are defeated each time

David attempts to bring the Ark to Jerusalem; the attempt is abandoned when Uzzah dies trying to steady it from falling

His second attempt succeeds when the Ark is transported in the proper way

David expresses to Nathan his desire to build a temple for Jehovah; Jehovah concludes a covenant with him for a kingdom

David sins with Bath-sheba; calamity comes on him out of his own house (11:1–20:26)

The Israelites go to war against Ammon; David commits adultery with Bath-sheba, whose husband Uriah is serving in the army; when efforts to conceal his sin fail, David arranges for Uriah to die in battle and marries the widowed Bath-sheba

With skillful use of an illustration, Nathan reproves David for his sin and announces Jehovah's judgment: Calamity will come out of his own house, his own wives will be violated, the son from Bath-sheba will die

The child dies; Bath-sheba, pregnant again, gives birth to Solomon

David's son Amnon rapes his half sister Tamar; David's son Absalom, Tamar's full brother, avenges her by having Amnon killed; then he flees to Geshur

Absalom, having gained David's full pardon, starts scheming against his father; finally he has himself proclaimed king at Hebron

David and his supporters flee Jerusalem to escape from Absalom and his partisans; in Jerusalem, Absalom has relations with ten of David's concubines; Absalom's forces pursue David and suffer defeat; Absalom himself is killed contrary to David's specific orders

David is restored as king; the Benjaminite Sheba revolts, and David gives command of the army to Amasa to put down the rebellion; Joab kills Amasa and takes charge; Sheba is killed

Closing events of David's reign (21:1–24:25)

David hands over seven sons of Saul to Gibeonites for execution so that the bloodguilt of Saul's house toward them can be avenged

David composes songs of praise to Jehovah, acknowledging him as the source of inspiration

David sins in ordering a census, resulting in death for about 70,000 from pestilence

David buys the threshing floor of Araunah the Jebusite as the site of an altar for Jehovah

to escape death, are alluded to in Psalms 34 and 56. (1Sa 21:10-15; evidently the name Abimelech appearing in the superscription of Psalm 34 is to be viewed as a title for King Achish.) Psalm 142 may reflect David's thoughts while hiding from Saul in the cave of Adullam (1Sa 22:1) or in the cave in the Wilderness of En-gedi. (1Sa 24:1, 3) This is perhaps also the case with Psalm 57. However, a comparison of Psalm 57:6 with 1 Samuel 24:2-4 seems to favor the cave in the Wilderness of En-gedi, for there Saul, as it were, fell into the pit he had excavated for David. Psalm 52 pertains to Doeg's informing Saul about David's dealings with Ahimelech. (1Sa 22:9, 10) The action of the Ziphites in revealing David's whereabouts to King Saul furnished the basis for Psalm 54. (1Sa 23:19) Psalm 2 seems to allude to the attempts made by the Philistines to unseat David as king after his capture of the stronghold of Zion. (2Sa 5:17-25) Trouble with the Edomites during the war with Hadadezer is the setting for Psalm 60. (2Sa 8:3, 13, 14) Psalm 51 is a prayer of David, beseeching forgiveness for his sin with Bath-sheba. (2Sa 11:2-15; 12:1-14) David's flight from Absalom provides the basis for Psalm 3. (2Sa 15:12-17, 30) Possibly Psalm 7 finds its historical setting in Shimei's cursing David. (2Sa 16:5-8) Psalm 30 may allude to events in connection with David's erection of an altar on the threshing floor of Araunah. Psalm 18 parallels 2 Samuel 22 and pertains to Jehovah's delivering David from Saul and other enemies.

Sections Missing in the Greek "Septuagint." First Samuel 17:12-31, 55–18:6a does not appear in the Greek *Septuagint* as contained in Vatican Manuscript No. 1209. Numerous scholars have, therefore, concluded that the omissions are later additions to the Hebrew text. Arguing against this view, C. F. Keil and F. Delitzsch comment: "The notion, that the sections in question are interpolations that have crept into the text, cannot be sustained on the mere authority of the Septuagint version; since the arbitrary manner in which the translators of this version made omissions or additions at pleasure is obvious to any one."—*Commentary on the Old Testament*, 1973, Vol. II, 1 Samuel, p. 177, ftn.

If it could be definitely established that actual discrepancies exist between the omitted sections and the rest of the book, the authenticity of 1 Samuel 17:12-31, 55–18:6a would reasonably be in question. A comparison of 1 Samuel 16:18-23 and 1 Samuel 17:55-58 reveals what appears to be a contradiction, for in the latter passage Saul is depicted as asking about the identity of his own court musician and armor-bearer, David. How-

ever, it should be noted that David's earlier being described as "a valiant, mighty man and a man of war" could have been based on his courageous acts in single-handedly killing a lion and a bear to rescue his father's sheep. (1Sa 16:18; 17:34-36) Also, the Scriptures do not state that David actually served in battle as Saul's armor-bearer before he killed Goliath. Saul's request to Jesse was: "Let David, please, keep attending upon me, for he has found favor in my eyes." (1Sa 16:22) This request does not preclude the possibility that Saul later permitted David to return to Bethlehem so that, when war broke out with the Philistines, David was then shepherding his father's flock.

Regarding Saul's question, "Whose son is the boy, Abner?" the aforementioned commentary observes (p. 178, ftn.): "Even if Abner had not troubled himself about the lineage of Saul's harpist, Saul himself could not well have forgotten that David was a son of the Bethlehemite Jesse. But there was much more implied in Saul's question. It was not the name of David's father alone that he wanted to discover, but what kind of man the father of a youth who possessed the courage to accomplish so marvellous a heroic deed really was; and the question was put not merely in order that he might grant him an exemption of his house from taxes as the reward promised for the conquest of Goliath (ver. 25), but also in all probability that he might attach such a man to his court, since he inferred from the courage and bravery of the son the existence of similar qualities in the father. It is true that David merely replied, 'The son of thy servant Jesse of Bethlehem;' but it is very evident from the expression in ch. xviii. 1, 'when he had made an end of speaking unto Saul,' that Saul conversed with him still further about his family affairs, since the very words imply a lengthened conversation." (For other instances where "who" involves more than mere knowledge of a person's name, see Ex 5:2; 1Sa 25:10.)

So there is sound reason for viewing 1 Samuel 17:12-31, 55–18:6a as part of the original text.

SANBALLAT (San·bal′lat) [from Akkadian, meaning "Sin [the moon-god] Has Made Well"]. A Horonite (meaning a resident of Beth-horon or of Horonaim) who opposed Nehemiah's efforts to repair the wall of Jerusalem. (Ne 2:10) He is thought to be the Sanballat mentioned in a papyrus found at Elephantine, Egypt, which identifies a man of that name as the governor of Samaria and the father of Delaiah and Shelemiah.

Sanballat, along with Tobiah and Geshem, derided the Jews and accused them of rebelling against the king of Persia. (Ne 2:19; 4:1) As the repair work progressed, he and other opposers conspired to fight against Jerusalem. But whatever efforts they made in this regard were ineffective, for the Jews relied on Jehovah and kept a guard posted. (Ne 4:7-9) After the gaps in the wall of Jerusalem were filled, Sanballat and others repeatedly tried to lure Nehemiah away from the city. When this failed, he and Tobiah hired a Jew to frighten Nehemiah into wrongfully hiding in the temple. But they did not succeed.—Ne 6:1-14.

Later, upon his return after an absence from Jerusalem, Nehemiah found that a grandson of High Priest Eliashib had become a son-in-law of Sanballat. Nehemiah therefore chased this grandson away.—Ne 13:6, 7, 28.

SANCTIFICATION.

The act or process of making holy, separating, or setting apart for the service or use of Jehovah God; the state of being holy, sanctified, or purified. "Sanctification" draws attention to the *action* whereby holiness is produced, made manifest, or maintained. (See HOLINESS.) Words drawn from the Hebrew verb *qa-dhash'* and words related to the Greek adjective *ha'gi·os* are rendered "holy," "sanctified," "made sacred," and "set apart."

A better understanding of the subject can be gained by a consideration of the usage of the words in the original languages. They are applied in the Scriptures to (1) Jehovah God, (2) Jesus Christ, (3) angels, (4) men and animals, (5) things, (6) periods of time or occasions, and (7) land possessions. Sometimes the Hebrew word for "sanctify" was used in the sense of preparing or making oneself ready or in fit condition. Jehovah commanded Moses to say to the complaining Israelites: "Sanctify yourselves for tomorrow, as you will certainly eat meat." (Nu 11:18) Before Israel crossed the Jordan River, Joshua ordered: "Sanctify yourselves, for tomorrow Jehovah will do wonderful things in your midst." (Jos 3:5) In all cases the term has a religious, spiritual, and moral sense. It can denote the getting away from anything that displeases Jehovah or appears bad in his eyes, including physical uncleanness. God said to Moses: "Go to the people, and you must sanctify them today and tomorrow, and they must wash their mantles. . . . because on the third day Jehovah will come down before the eyes of all the people upon Mount Sinai." (Ex 19:10, 11) The word is used to mean *purifying* or *cleansing,* as at 2 Samuel 11:4, which reads: "She was sanctifying herself from her uncleanness."

Jehovah told Israel that they should be separate from the nations of the world and clean from their practices; he gave Israel laws to keep them set apart, including the laws defining what was clean and what was unclean for eating. Then he gave them the reason: "For I am Jehovah your God; and you must sanctify yourselves and you must prove yourselves holy, because I am holy." —Le 11:44.

Jehovah God. Jehovah God is holy and absolutely clean. As the Creator and Universal Sovereign, he has the right to the exclusive worship of all of his creatures. Therefore he says that he will demonstrate his holiness, acting to sanctify himself and his name before the eyes of all creation: "I shall certainly magnify myself and sanctify myself and make myself known before the eyes of many nations; and they will have to know that I am Jehovah." (Eze 38:23) Those who desire his favor, and life, must "sanctify" him and his name, that is, they must hold that name in its proper place as separate from and higher than all others. (Le 22:32; Isa 8:13; 29:23) Jesus taught his followers to pray as the foremost thing: "Our Father in the heavens, let your name be sanctified [or "be held sacred; be treated as holy"]."—Mt 6:9 ftn.

Jesus Christ. Jehovah God selected his only-begotten Son and sent him to earth to do a special work in behalf of God's name and to give his life as a ransom for humankind. But he was not received and respected by the Jewish nation as that sent one; rather, they denied his sonship and his position with his Father. He replied to them: "Do you say to me *whom the Father sanctified* and dispatched into the world, 'You blaspheme,' because I said, I am God's Son?"—Joh 10:36.

The apostle Peter writes to Christians, telling them to "sanctify the Christ as Lord in your hearts." He shows that one who does this will stay away from what is bad and will do good. The people of the nations hold in their hearts an awe and a fear of men and of other things. But the Christian should set Christ in the right place in his affections and motivations. This would mean recognizing Christ's position as God's Chief Agent of life, the Messianic King, God's High Priest, and the one who gave his life as a ransom. He should also keep Christ's example of good conduct before him and hold a good conscience in connection with his own conduct as a Christian. If a person, even a ruler, should harshly demand a reason for his hope, the Christian who thus sanctifies Christ in his heart will make a good defense, yet with mild temper and deep respect.—1Pe 3:10-16.

Angels. The angels of God are called by Jesus "holy" angels, sanctified, set apart for Jehovah's holy use. (Mr 8:38; Lu 9:26; compare Ps 103:20.) They appear in the sacred presence of Jehovah, beholding his face.—Mt 18:10; Lu 1:19.

Men and Animals. In times past God has chosen certain persons whom he desired to use for his exclusive service, and he sanctified them. When he determined to use the males of the tribe of Levi to take care of the sacred tabernacle and its services, he said to Moses: "As for me, look! I do take the Levites from among the sons of Israel in place of all the firstborn opening the womb of the sons of Israel; and the Levites must become mine. For every firstborn is mine. In the day that I struck every firstborn in the land of Egypt I sanctified to myself every firstborn in Israel from man to beast. They should become mine. I am Jehovah." In order to release the firstborn of the other 11 tribes, the Israelites were required to give in exchange all the males of the tribe of Levi. Then they had to give five shekels ($11) to the sanctuary for every male firstborn above the total number of male Levites. This released the firstborn ones from being set apart for Jehovah's exclusive service.—Nu 3:12, 13, 46-48.

After this, all male firstborn ones opening the womb were considered to be sanctified but were presented at the temple and redeemed by a payment of five shekels ($11). (Ex 13:2; Le 12:1-4; Nu 18:15, 16) Those under Nazirite vows were sanctified for the period of their vow. (Nu 6:1-8) The firstborn of domestic animals were also sanctified, to be sacrificed or, in some cases, to be redeemed. —De 15:19; see FIRSTBORN, FIRSTLING.

The priesthood. Jehovah also purposed to set aside an exclusive family within the tribe of Levi to serve as his priests of sacrifice, namely, Aaron and his sons and their male descendants. (Ex 28:1-3, 41) They were then sanctified with fitting sacrifices in a symbolic series of acts described in Exodus chapter 29. Jehovah's everlasting High Priest, Jesus Christ, and his fellow priests, or underpriests, namely those who follow Christ's footsteps and whom God anoints to be members of Christ's body, are also sanctified.—2Th 2:13; Re 1:6; 5:10.

The Process of Sanctification. There is a certain process or procedure that the one to be sanctified as a footstep follower of Christ must undergo. Using the word *sanctify* in the sense of *purify* or *cleanse* from sin in God's sight, the apostle Paul wrote: "For if the blood of goats and of bulls and the ashes of a heifer sprinkled on those who have been defiled sanctifies to the extent of cleanness of the flesh, how much more will the blood of the Christ, who through an everlasting spirit offered himself without blemish to God, cleanse our consciences from dead works that we may render sacred service to the living God?"—Heb 9:13, 14.

"The blood of the Christ" signifies the value of his perfect human life; and it is this that washes away the guilt of sin of the person believing in him. Hence it *really* (not just typically [compare Heb 10:1-4]) sanctifies to the purifying of the believer's flesh, from God's standpoint, so that the believer has a clean conscience. Also, God declares such believer righteous and makes him suitable to be one of the underpriests of Jesus Christ. (Ro 8:1, 30) Such ones are called *ha'gi·oi*, "holy ones," "saints" (*KJ*), or persons sanctified to God.—Eph 2:19; Col 1:12; compare Ac 20:32, which refers to "sanctified ones [*tois he·gi·a·sme'nois*]."

So the procedure for those who are to become joint heirs with Christ is, first, that they are drawn by Jehovah God to Jesus Christ by faith in the truth of God's Word. (Joh 6:44; 17:17; 2Th 2:13) Accepted by Jehovah, they are "washed clean, . . . sanctified, . . . declared righteous in the name of our Lord Jesus Christ and with the spirit of our God." (1Co 6:11) Christ thus becomes to them 'wisdom, righteousness, and sanctification and release by ransom.' (1Co 1:30) Of these, the apostle Paul said: "For both he [Christ] who is sanctifying and those who are being sanctified all stem from one, and for this cause he is not ashamed to call them 'brothers.'" (Heb 2:11) They become 'sons of God' and "brothers" of God's Chief Son by spirit begetting.—Ro 8:14-17; Joh 3:5, 8.

Must be maintained. The process of sanctification is not all on one side. Sanctification must be maintained, and in this the believer has a part. He can lose his sanctification or he can hold on to it.

Christ Jesus has set the pattern for those who are sanctified. (Joh 13:15) He said in prayer to God: "I am sanctifying myself in their behalf, that they also may be sanctified by means of truth." (Joh 17:19) Jesus kept himself blameless and maintained his status of being set apart for the purpose of sanctifying his followers. They must maintain their sanctification down to the end of their earthly course. To do this, they must keep clear of dishonorable things and of persons who practice dishonorable things, so as to be "a vessel for an honorable purpose, *sanctified,* useful to his owner, prepared for every good work." (2Ti 2:20, 21) They must realize that it is with Christ's own blood that they are bought, and that it is by God's will that they "have been sanctified through the offering of the body of Jesus Christ once for all time." (Heb 10:10) They are counseled to "pursue . . . the sanctification without which no man will see the Lord."—Heb 12:14.

Though they are still in the imperfect flesh, which tends toward sin, the sanctified ones can be successful. In warning of the danger of losing one's sanctification, Paul reminds the sanctified ones that it was "the blood of the [new] covenant by which [they were] sanctified." (Heb 10:29; Lu 22:20) As Mediator of the new covenant, Christ assists them to carry out the terms of the covenant by obedience and clean behavior so that they keep their sanctification. "It is by one sacrificial offering that he has made those who are being sanctified perfect perpetually." (Heb 10:14) As Mediator and High Priest, Christ "is able also to save completely those who are approaching God through him." (Heb 7:25) But if they return to a practice of sin, there is not a second sacrifice, only the expectation of judgment and destruction. —Heb 10:26, 27.

Accordingly, the sanctified ones are not called so they can continue as they did before being sanctified, or so they can go back to such a course. The apostle exhorts: "For this is what God wills, the sanctifying of you, that you abstain from fornication; that each one of you should know how to get possession of his own vessel in sanctification and honor." "For God called us, not with allowance for uncleanness, but in connection with sanctification."—1Th 4:3, 4, 7.

God's Word and spirit. God's Word plays a great part in sanctification, and it must be followed closely for sanctification to be maintained. (Ac 20:32) To the believer and sanctified one, God also sends his holy spirit, which is a strong force working in him for cleanness. It helps the sanctified one to be obedient, keeping him in a clean way of life. (1Pe 1:2) Guidance by God's spirit makes it possible for the offering of such ones to be sanctified, clean, acceptable to God. (Ro 15:16) Any uncleanness is a disregarding of God's spirit and tends to 'grieve' it. (Eph 4:30; 1Th 4:8; 5:19) It can go so far as to lead to blasphemy against the holy spirit, which will not be forgiven.—Mt 12:31, 32; Lu 12:8-10.

Sanctification of Places. The place where Jehovah dwells or any place where he dwells representatively is a sanctified or holy place, a sanctuary. The tabernacle in the wilderness and the temples later built by Solomon and Zerubbabel (and rebuilt and enlarged by Herod the Great) were designated as miq·dash' or qo'dhesh, 'set apart' or 'holy' places. Being located in the midst of a sinful people, these places had to be purified (in a typical, or pictorial, way) of defilement periodically by sprinkling with the blood of sacrificial animals.—Le 16:16.

Jerusalem. Likewise Jerusalem, the city of the grand King (Ps 48:1, 2; 135:21), and the site on which it stood were considered sanctified. (Isa 48:1, 2; 52:1; Ne 11:1; Da 9:24) Correspondingly, New Jerusalem, the heavenly city, is a sanctuary into which only sanctified persons, and none who practice any form of uncleanness (such as spiritism, fornication, murder, idolatry, and lying) are allowed to enter.—Re 21:2; 22:14, 15, 19.

The garden of Eden, a sanctuary. Jehovah appeared, representatively, in the garden of Eden to converse with and instruct Adam and Eve; it was a clean, sinless, perfect place, where man was at peace with God. (Ge 1:28; 2:8, 9; 3:8, 9; De 32:4) Therefore Adam and Eve were driven out of it when they rebelled. This paradise was a place set apart or sanctified by God for clean, righteous persons to occupy. Now that Adam and Eve were sinners, they were driven out so that they could not partake of the tree of life and thus, despite being sinners, live forever.—Ge 3:22-24.

The burning bush and Mount Sinai. When Jehovah commissioned Moses to go back down into Egypt to deliver His people from slavery, sending Moses in His own memorial name Jehovah (Ex 3:15, 16), God dispatched his angel, who appeared to Moses in a burning bush. When Moses approached, the angel, appearing representatively for Jehovah, commanded Moses to remove his sandals because, he said, "the place where you are standing is holy [qo'dhesh] ground."—Ex 3:1-5.

Later, when the people were gathered at the foot of Mount Sinai, at the time the Law covenant was given, Jehovah gave Moses the command: "Set bounds for the mountain and make it sacred, because Jehovah was there, representatively by his angels. (Ex 19:23; Ga 3:19) Anyone who went beyond the boundaries would be put to death, for no unauthorized persons can approach Jehovah's presence. (Ex 19:12, 13) However, Moses as God's appointed mediator could draw nearer. In this Moses prophetically foreshadowed Jesus Christ, the great Mediator for anointed Christians as they approach heavenly Mount Zion.—Heb 12:22-24.

Cities of refuge and army camps. Certain cities in Israel were set aside for the special purpose of providing a place of refuge for the unintentional manslayer. They were sanctified, or given "sacred status."—Jos 20:7-9.

The army camps of Israel were places that were sanctified, for God 'walked about within the camp.' Therefore moral, spiritual, and physical cleanness had to be maintained.—De 23:9-14; 2Sa 11:6-11.

Sanctification of Things. Since the tabernacle and the temple were sanctified buildings, the things in them likewise had to be holy, sanctified. The ark of the covenant, the altar of incense, the table of showbread, the lampstand, the altar of burnt offering, the basin, all the utensils, the incense and the anointing oil, even the priests' garments, were sanctified items. They were to be handled and transported only by sanctified persons—the priests and Levites. (Ex 30:25, 32, 35; 40:10, 11; Le 8:10, 11, 15, 30; Nu 4:1-33; 7:1) The priests serving at the tabernacle rendered "sacred service in a typical representation and a shadow of the heavenly things; just as Moses, when about to make the tent in completion, was given the divine command: For says he: 'See that you make all things after their pattern that was shown to you in the mountain.'"—Heb 8:4, 5.

Sacrifices and food. The sacrifices and offerings were sanctified by reason of being offered upon the sanctified altar in the manner prescribed. (Mt 23:19) The portion that the priests received was holy and could not be eaten by those outside the priestly households, and even the priests could not eat such things while in an "unclean" state. (Le 2:3; 7:6, 32-34; 22:1-13) The showbread was likewise holy, sanctified.—1Sa 21:4; Mr 2:26.

Just as the food provided by Jehovah for his priesthood was sanctified, so the food provided by him for his Christian servants is likewise sanctified, as all things partaken of or engaged in by his sanctified servants should be. The apostle Paul warns against conscienceless men who put on a display of sanctification that is false, "forbidding to marry, commanding to abstain from foods which God created to be partaken of with thanksgiving by those who have faith and accurately know the truth. The reason for this is that every creation of God is fine, and nothing is to be rejected if it is received with thanksgiving, for it is sanctified through God's word and prayer over it." (1Ti 4:1-5) If God's Word declares a thing clean, it is clean, and the Christian, by giving thanks for it in prayer, accepts it as sanctified, and God counts him clean in eating.

Tithes. The tithe of the grain, fruit, and flocks that the Israelites set aside was considered sanctified and could be used for no other purpose.

(Le 27:30, 32) Accordingly no one can misuse a sanctified thing or harm or speak evil against any of God's sanctified persons, including the anointed brothers of Christ, and be guiltless before God. Jesus showed the Jews this when they accused him of blasphemy. (Joh 10:36) The apostle Peter warned of destruction that is to come upon wicked men whom he describes as "daring, self-willed, [who] do not tremble at glorious ones [whom Jehovah has sanctified] but speak abusively."—2Pe 2:9-12; compare Jude 8.

Periods of Time or Occasions. The Bible record tells us what God did when he completed his creative work toward the earth: "By the seventh day God came to the completion of his work . . . , and he proceeded to rest . . . And God proceeded to bless the seventh day and make it sacred." (Ge 2:2, 3) This "day" was therefore to be employed by men as a "day" of sacred service and obedience to Jehovah. It was not to be defiled by self-works on the part of man. Adam and Eve therefore violated that "day" when they set out on a program of self-determination, to do as they pleased in the earth, independent of their Sovereign, Jehovah. God's 'rest day' still continues, according to the record at Hebrews 3:11, 13; 4:1-11. Since God sanctified the "day," setting it aside to his purpose, this "day" will see that purpose toward the earth fully accomplished in righteousness.—Compare Isa 55:10, 11.

Sabbath days and special feast days were sanctified, as were other periods, such as the Jubilee year.—Ex 31:14; Le 23:3, 7, 8, 21, 24, 27, 35, 36; 25:10.

Sanctifying of Land. In Israel, a man might sanctify a part of his inheritance to God. He would do this by setting it aside so that the produce of the land would go to the sanctuary, or he could pay over to the sanctuary the value of the land (that is, its crops) according to the estimation of the priest. If he decided to buy it back, he was required to add one fifth to the valuation of the field (governed by the number of crops until the Jubilee year) as estimated by the priest. Of course, the field would be returned to its owner at the Jubilee.—Le 27:16-19.

The next verses apparently speak of the owner who does not repurchase the field but sells it to another man, and the law is that the field then becomes the permanent possession of the sanctuary at the time of the Jubilee. Concerning this law, at Leviticus 27:20, 21, Cook's *Commentary* says: "[The words] may refer to a case in which a man might have fraudulently sold his interest in a field and appropriated the price after having vowed it to the Sanctuary." Or they may refer to a case in which a man retained the use of the field and fulfilled his vow for a while by paying as a yearly rent a due proportion of the redemption money but then later parted with his interest to another for the sake of acquiring some ready money. Such a field was considered "devoted," because he treated that which was sanctified to the sanctuary as his own, disrespecting its sancti- ty by making merchandise of it.

The principle may have been similar to the law at Deuteronomy 22:9: "You must not sow your vineyard with two sorts of seed, for fear that the full produce of the seed that you might sow and the product of the vineyard may be forfeited to the sanctuary." Such forfeit would result from the violation of the law stated earlier at Leviticus 19:19.

The distinction between things "sanctified" and things "devoted" was that the "devoted" thing could not be redeemed. (See BAN.) Houses were handled in the same manner. (Le 27:14, 15) How- ever, if a man sanctified a field that he had bought from someone else's hereditary posses- sion, the field returned at Jubilee to the original owner.—Le 27:22-24.

In Marriage. The apostle Paul tells the mar- ried Christian: "The unbelieving husband is sanc- tified in relation to his wife, and the unbelieving wife is sanctified in relation to the brother; other- wise, your children would really be unclean, but now they are holy." Through Jehovah's regard for the Christian, his (or her) marriage relationship with his unbelieving mate is not considered to be defiling. The cleanness of the sanctified one does not sanctify the mate as one of God's holy ones, but the relationship is clean, honorable. The un- believing mate has a fine opportunity to receive benefits from observing the Christian course of the believer and may himself be saved. (1Co 7:14-17) Because of the 'merit' of the believer, the young children of the union are considered holy, under divine care and protection—not unclean as are children who do not have even one believing parent.—See HOLINESS (Holiness Blessed by Jeho- vah).

SANCTUARY.   A place set apart for the wor- ship of God or of gods, a holy place; a divine habitation. (1Ch 22:19; Isa 16:12; Eze 28:18; Am 7:9, 13) A "sanctuary" need not necessarily be a special building, for the one at Shechem referred to at Joshua 24:25, 26 may simply have been the site where Abraham had centuries earlier erected an altar. (Ge 12:6, 7) However, frequently the expression "sanctuary" designates either the tab- ernacle (Ex 25:8, 9) or the temple at Jerusalem. (1Ch 28:10; 2Ch 36:17; Eze 24:21) As applied to the tabernacle, "sanctuary" could mean the entire tent and its courtyard (Ex 25:8, 9; Le 21:12, 23), the furniture and utensils of the sanctuary (Nu 10:21; compare Nu 3:30, 31), or it could refer to the Most Holy (Le 16:16, 17, 20, 33).

As a holy place, God's sanctuary was to be kept undefiled. (Nu 19:20; Eze 5:11) The Israel- ites should, therefore, "stand in awe" of that spe- cial place where God dwelt representatively. (Le 19:30; 26:2) When they were removed from the Promised Land into exile, they no longer had a material sanctuary. But Jehovah promised that he himself would, as it were, become "a sanctuary" for them.—Eze 11:16.

The Greek term na·os' is used in a broad sense to stand for the entire temple complex (Joh 2:20) or for the central edifice, with its Holy and Most Holy compartments separated by the curtain. (Mt 27:51) When Zechariah, for instance, went "into the sanctuary" to offer incense, he entered the Holy, for it was there that the altar of incense was located.—Lu 1:9-11.

God's dwelling place in the heavens is a sanctu- ary, or a holy place. It is in this heavenly sanctu- ary that the apostle John, in vision, saw the ark of the covenant after the blowing of the 'seventh trumpet.' (Re 11:15, 19) Thereafter he observed angels emerging from this sanctuary and, in con- nection with the outpouring of "the seven bowls" of God's anger, heard a "loud voice" issuing forth from it.—Re 14:15, 17; 15:5, 6, 8; 16:1, 17.

Regarding the earthly courtyard of God's great spiritual temple, the apostle John was told in vision: "Get up and measure the temple sanctuary of God and the altar and those worshiping in it. But as for the courtyard that is outside the temple sanctuary, cast it clear out and do not measure it, because it has been given to the nations, and they will trample the holy city underfoot for forty-two months." (Re 11:1, 2) The temple here referred to could not be the one at Jerusalem, for that struc- ture had been destroyed nearly three decades earlier. Being earthly, the nations could only be "given" a courtyard that was likewise on earth. So it must represent a condition enjoyed by Jesus' anointed followers while here on earth. Whereas it would be impossible for the nations to trample upon a location in the heavens, they could treat disgracefully those persons who had been begot- ten by God's spirit to be his sons and who were in line to receive a heavenly inheritance with Christ. (Re 3:12) Similarly, Daniel's prophecy regarding the throwing down of "the established place of the sanctuary" (Da 8:11) and the profaning of the sanctuary (Da 11:31) appears to point to events in connection with those serving as underpriests in God's great spiritual temple.

The members of the Christian congregation, Christ's body, constitute a temple, or sanctuary, that God inhabits by spirit.—1Co 3:17; Eph 2: 21, 22; 1Pe 2:5, 9; see TEMPLE (The Anointed Christians—A Spiritual Temple).

SAND. A loose granular material that consists of particles smaller than gravel but coarser than silt. Jehovah God, in his great wisdom, has "set the sand as the boundary for the sea, an indefinitely lasting regulation that it cannot pass over." Jer 5:22) Unlike solid rock, sand yields and thus absorbs the impact of the waves that pound against it. The force of the raging waves is diffused and dissipated, so that the sea is kept in check.

In blessing the tribes of Zebulun and Issachar, Moses said that they would "suck the abounding wealth of the seas and the hidden hoards of the sand." (De 33:18, 19) This may mean that they would be blessed with the riches of sea and land.

Time and again the "sand of the sea" is used in the Bible to designate innumerableness or great abundance. (Ge 22:17; 32:12; 41:49; Jos 11:4; Ps 78:27; 139:17, 18; Jer 15:8; Heb 11:12) But the number in question is not astronomically great in each case. To the beholder, however, the number of persons or things involved is so great that it cannot be ascertained. For example, one part of the Philistine forces that came against Israel in the days of King Saul is described as "people like the grains of sand that are upon the seashore for multitude." (1Sa 13:5) The number of those that would be misled by Satan following his release from the abyss, as seen by John in vision, was said to be "as the sand of the sea," that is, the number was great enough that John could not determine how many there would be.—Re 20:8.

Describing the magnitude of his vexation, faithful Job declared: "It is heavier even than the sands of the seas." (Job 6:3) On the average, just 1 cu m (1.3 cu yd) of wet sand weighs 1,900 kg (4,200 lb). Though a load of sand is a heavy burden, the vexation of a foolish person is even heavier to the one having to bear it. This is alluded to at Proverbs 27:3: "The heaviness of a stone and a load of sand—but the vexation by someone foolish is heavier than both of them."

SANDAL. A flat sole of leather, wood, or other fibrous material strapped to the foot by laces that are usually leather thongs passing between the big toe and second toe, around the heel, and over the top of the foot. In some cases the strap may have gone as high as around the ankle.

Egyptian sandals usually turned up at the toe. Some Assyrian sandals consisted only of a casement for the heel and side of the foot, fastened over the foot by thongs and having no sole for the front part of the foot. The Romans wore sandals and are said also to have worn shoes similar to modern ones. The aristocracy and royalty of the Assyrians, Romans, and others wore more elaborate sandals or bootlike shoes. Some Bedouin around Mount Sinai wear sandals made of a species of dugong (a seallike sea animal). Jehovah speaks figuratively of shoeing Jerusalem with "sealskin" (Heb., *ta'chash*).—Eze 16:10.

The priests in Israel are said to have served at the tabernacle and the temple barefoot. (Compare Ex 3:5; Jos 5:15; Ac 7:33.) But to go about outdoors barefoot was a sign of grief or humiliation. —2Sa 15:30; Isa 20:2-5; contrast the command to Ezekiel (24:17, 23).

On a long journey it was a custom to carry an extra pair of sandals, as the soles might become worn out or the laces broken. Jesus, in sending out the apostles, and also 70 disciples, commanded them not to take two pairs but to rely on the hospitality of those who accepted the good news. —Mt 10:5, 9, 10; Mr 6:7-9; Lu 10:1, 4.

Figurative Use. Under the Law a widow took the sandal off one who refused to perform brother-in-law marriage with her, and his name was called, reproachfully, "The house of the one who had his sandal drawn off." (De 25:9, 10) The transfer of property or of right of repurchase was represented by handing one's sandal to another. —Ru 4:7-10; see BROTHER-IN-LAW MARRIAGE.

By the expression "over Edom I shall throw my sandal" (Ps 60:8; 108:9) Jehovah may have meant that Edom would be brought under subjection. It possibly had reference to the custom of indicating the taking of possession by throwing one's sandal on a piece of land. Or, it could have indicated contempt for Edom, since Moab is called "my washing pot" in the same text. In the Middle East today, throwing the sandal is a gesture of contempt.

David instructed Solomon to punish Joab, who had "put the blood of war . . . in his sandals" during peacetime—a figurative statement representing Joab's bloodguilt for killing Generals Abner and Amasa. (1Ki 2:5, 6) This, together with the fact that one putting on his sandals was about to undertake some business away from his house (or wherever he was staying; compare Ac 12:8), illuminates the apostle Paul's admonition to Christians that they have their feet "shod with the equipment of the good news of peace."—Eph 6:14, 15.

To untie another's sandal laces or to carry his sandals was considered a menial task such as was often done by slaves. John used this simile to denote his inferiority to Christ.—Mt 3:11; Mr 1:7.

SAND LIZARD [Heb., *cho'met*]. There is some uncertainty about the unclean 'swarming creature' designated by the Hebrew term *cho'met*. (Le 11:30, 31) The renderings of the Greek *Septuagint* and the Latin *Vulgate* point to a kind of lizard, and the word has been variously translated "sand lizard" (*AS, JP, NW, RS*), "chameleon" (*AT*), and "snail" (*KJ*). It is possibly a skink.—See LIZARD.

SANHEDRIN. See COURT, JUDICIAL.

SANSANNAH (San·san'nah) [possibly, Fruit Stalk of Dates]. A town in the southern portion of the territory of the tribe of Judah. (Jos 15:21, 31) It is identified with Khirbet esh-Shamsaniyat (Horvat Sansanna), about 12 km (7.5 mi) NNE of Beer-sheba. A comparison of Joshua 15:31 with parallel lists of cities at Joshua 19:5 and 1 Chronicles 4:31 indicates that it may be the same as Hazar-susah (or Hazar-susim).—See HAZAR-SUSAH.

SAPH. One of four giantlike Rephaim who fought with the Philistines against Israel, only to be put to death by David's mighty men. Saph, or Sippai, was slain by Sibbecai.—2Sa 21:18, 22; 1Ch 20:4.

SAPPHIRA (Sap·phi'ra) [from Aramaic, and meaning "Beautiful"]. The wife of Ananias. With her husband she entered a conspiracy that resulted in their death. They sold a field of their possession and hypocritically pretended to bring the full value obtained to the apostles, as other Christians in Jerusalem were doing to meet the emergency that developed after Pentecost of 33 C.E.

The sin of Ananias and Sapphira was, not that they did not give the entire amount of the price of the possession sold, but that they lyingly *claimed* to do so, evidently to receive plaudits of men rather than to honor God and do good toward his congregation. Their deception was exposed by Peter, under the inspiration of holy spirit. He said: "Ananias, why has Satan emboldened you to play false to the holy spirit and to hold back secretly some of the price of the field? As long as it remained with you did it not remain yours, and after it was sold did it not continue in your con-

trol? Why was it that you purposed such a deed as this in your heart? You have played false, not to men, but to God." On hearing Peter's words, Ananias fell down and expired.

After about three hours Sapphira came in and repeated the lie. Peter then asked her: "Why was it agreed upon between you two to make a test of the spirit of Jehovah?" Sapphira likewise fell down and expired. This incident served as discipline for the congregation, causing them to have great fear, and doubtless great respect and appreciation for the fact that Jehovah indeed dwelt in the congregation by spirit.—Ac 4:34, 35; 5:1-11; 1Co 3:16, 17; Eph 2:22; compare 1Ti 1:20.

SAPPHIRE. A transparent or translucent precious stone; a variety of corundum. Although sapphires occur in many colors, the deep-blue shades are most highly esteemed. The sapphires referred to in the Bible were apparently blue.

A sapphire was one of the stones in the high priest's "breastpiece of judgment."—Ex 28:15-18; 39:11.

Job, who lived in about the 17th century B.C.E. described the efforts of men in digging deep into the earth to mine gold and precious jewels, and he mentions the sapphire as being among the rare stones so located. But, says Job, valuable as sapphire is and difficult as it is to obtain, wisdom is far superior and cannot be paid for with such stones.—Job 28:4-6, 12, 16.

Figurative Use. The lustrous beauty, as well as the pleasurable, captivating, and enthralling effect caused by viewing precious gems, was used figuratively in connection with visions of God's glory. After the Law covenant was instituted, Moses, Aaron, Nadab, Abihu, and 70 of the older men of Israel received a vision of Jehovah, and beneath his feet "there was what seemed like a work of sapphire flagstones and like the very heavens for purity." (Ex 24:8-11) In visions of the glory of Jehovah, Ezekiel twice beheld "the likeness of a throne" that was "like sapphire stone." —Eze 1:1, 26-28; 10:1-4.

When Jehovah, as Zion's husbandly Owner, spoke of her restoration and beautification, he said: "I will lay your foundation with sapphires." (Isa 54:5, 11) Similarly, the apostle John's vision of the heavenly New Jerusalem revealed that sapphire was part of its foundations.—Re 21:2, 19.

SARAH (Sar'ah) [Princess], **SARAI** (Sar'ai) [possibly, Contentious]. Half sister and wife of Abraham and mother of Isaac. (Ge 11:29; 20:12; Isa 51:2) Her original name was Sarai. (Ge 17:15

She was ten years younger than Abraham (Ge 17:17) and married him while they were living in the Chaldean city of Ur. (Ge 11:28, 29) She continued barren until her reproductive powers were miraculously revived after she had already stopped menstruating.—Ge 18:11; Ro 4:19; Heb 11:11.

Sarah may have been in her 60's when she left Ur with Abraham and took up residence in Haran. At the age of 65 she accompanied her husband from Haran to the land of Canaan. (Ge 12: 4, 5) There they spent time at Shechem and in the mountainous region E of Bethel, as well as in various other places, before famine forced them to go to Egypt.—Ge 12:6-10.

Though advanced in years, Sarah was very beautiful in appearance. Therefore, Abraham had earlier requested that, whenever necessary in the course of their travels, Sarah identify him as her brother, lest others kill him and then take her. (Ge 20:13) In Egypt this resulted in Sarah's being taken into the household of Pharaoh on the recommendation of his princes. But divine intervention prevented Pharaoh from violating her. Thereafter he returned Sarah to Abraham, requesting that they leave the land. He also provided safe conduct for Abraham and his possessions. —Ge 12:11-20.

It is noteworthy that an ancient papyrus tells of a Pharaoh who commissioned armed men to seize an attractive woman and kill her husband. Thus Abraham's fear that he might be killed on account of Sarah was not unfounded. Instead of endangering his life in an unsuccessful attempt to save the honor of his wife in an alien land, Abraham followed what appeared to him to be the safest course. It should be remembered that Abraham was the owner of his wife. Sarah was happy to serve Jehovah and Abraham in this way. Never do the Scriptures censure Abraham for having done this.

Ten years after having originally entered Canaan, 75-year-old Sarah requested that Abraham have relations with her Egyptian maidservant Hagar in order to have children from her. (Ge 16:1-3) The resultant difficulties made it apparent that this was not Jehovah's way of fulfilling the promise previously made to Abraham concerning the "seed." (Ge 15:1-16) Becoming aware of her pregnancy, Hagar began despising her mistress. When Sarah voiced complaint, Abraham granted his wife full authority to deal with Hagar as her maidservant. Humiliated by Sarah, Hagar ran away from her mistress but returned in obedience to divine direction, after which she gave birth to Ishmael.—Ge 16:4-16.

About 13 years after Ishmael's birth, on the occasion of Abraham's being divinely commanded to circumcise all the males of his household, Abraham was also instructed to call his wife, no longer by the name "Sarai," but "Sarah," meaning "Princess." Regarding Sarah, God said: "I will bless her and also give you a son from her; and I will bless her and she shall become nations; kings of peoples will come from her." (Ge 17:9-27) Not long thereafter, at Mamre, one of three angelic visitors reaffirmed that Sarah would give birth to a son. Overhearing this, "Sarah began to laugh inside herself, saying: 'After I am worn out, shall I really have pleasure, my lord being old besides?'" Reproved for laughing, Sarah fearfully denied having done so. (Ge 18:1-15; Ro 9:9) Since Sarah is cited at Hebrews 11:11 as an example of faith, evidently her laughter was not an expression of complete unbelief but merely indicated that the thought of having a son in her old age apparently struck her as somewhat humorous. Sarah's acknowledgment (inside herself) of Abraham as her lord was indicative of her obedience and subjection to her husbandly head, and her example is recommended to Christian wives. —1Pe 3:5, 6.

Sarah and her husband began residing at Gerar. As previously, Abraham referred to his wife as his sister. The king of Gerar, Abimelech, then took Sarah. Again Jehovah's intervention saved her from being violated. Upon returning Sarah to Abraham, Abimelech gave livestock and male and female servants to Abraham, perhaps in compensation for having temporarily deprived him of his wife. Additionally he gave Abraham a thousand pieces of silver (c. $2,200). These silver pieces were to serve as evidence that Sarah was cleared of all reproach against her as a moral woman.—Ge 20.

At the age of 90, Sarah had the joy of giving birth to Isaac. She then exclaimed: "God has prepared laughter for me: everybody hearing of it will laugh at me." Such laughter would evidently be prompted by delight and amazement over the birth of the child. Sarah nursed her son for about five years. When Isaac was finally weaned, Abraham spread a big feast. On that occasion Sarah observed Hagar's son Ishmael, now about 19 years old, "poking fun," or playing with Isaac in a mocking way. Apparently fearing for the future of her son Isaac, Sarah requested that Abraham dismiss Hagar and Ishmael. Abraham did so, subsequent to his receiving divine approval for this action.—Ge 21:1-14.

About 32 years later Sarah died, at the age of 127 years, and Abraham buried her "in the cave of the field of Machpelah."—Ge 23:1, 19, 20.

Figures in a Symbolic Drama. In writing to the Galatians, the apostle Paul showed that Abraham's wife Sarah represented "the Jerusalem above," the mother of spirit-anointed Christians, the spiritual "seed" of Abraham. Like Sarah, "the Jerusalem above," God's symbolic woman, has never been in slavery, and therefore, her children are also free. For an individual to become a free child of "the Jerusalem above," having "her freedom," he must be emancipated from the bondage of sin by the Son of God. (Ga 4:22-31; 5:1, ftn) As Christ Jesus told the natural descendants of Abraham: "Most truly I say to you, Every doer of sin is a slave of sin. Moreover, the slave does not remain in the household forever; the son remains forever. Therefore if the Son sets you free, you will be actually free."—Joh 8:34-36; see FREE WOMAN; HAGAR.

SARAPH (Sa'raph) [from a root meaning "burn"]. A descendant of Shelah of the tribe of Judah, one who took a Moabite wife (or wives) for himself. (*JB, NW*) Perhaps, according to alternate readings, Saraph ruled in (or for) Moab.—1Ch 4:21, 22, *AS, AT, KJ, Mo, Ro, RS*.

SARDIS (Sar'dis). The ancient capital of Lydia (in western Asia Minor) and a center of the worship of an Asiatic goddess, linked either with Artemis or with Cybele. Situated S of the Gediz (formerly Hermus) River, Sardis lay about 50 km (30 mi) S of Thyatira (now Akhisar) and about 75 km (47 mi) E of Smyrna (now Izmir). The acropolis of the city occupied an almost inaccessible rocky crag. Although a mountain range limited communication with areas in the S, Sardis commanded the E-W trade route. Its commercial activity and trade, the great fertility of surrounding land, and the manufacture of woolen cloth and carpets contributed much toward making Sardis wealthy and important. At one time Sardis may have had a population of about 50,000 persons.

In the sixth century B.C.E., Cyrus the Great defeated the last Lydian king, Croesus, and for over 200 years thereafter Sardis served as the capital for the western part of the Persian Empire. In 334 B.C.E. the city surrendered without resistance to Alexander the Great. Later it came under the rule of Pergamum and then Rome. A great earthquake nearly leveled Sardis in 17 C.E., but the city was rebuilt with generous aid from Rome.

The Jewish historian Josephus indicates that in the first century B.C.E. there was a large Jewish community in Sardis. (*Jewish Antiquities*, XIV, 259 [x, 24]) By the latter part of the first century

C.E., the Christian congregation that had been established at Sardis needed to "wake up" spiritually. However, there were also persons associated with this congregation who had not 'defiled their outer garments.'—Re 3:1-6.

Prominent ruins at the ancient site of Sardis include those of the temple of the Ephesian Artemis (or Cybele), a Roman theater and stadium, and an ancient synagogue.—PICTURE, Vol. 2, p. 946.

SARDIUS (sar'di·us). A translucent, reddish-brown variety of the mineral chalcedony used as a gemstone. According to Pliny the Elder, it was named after the city of Sardis in Lydia, where it was first introduced to that part of the world. However, it has been suggested that the name originated with the Persian word *sered*, meaning "yellowish-red," and accompanied the stone from its source in Persia. Sardius has also been called "sard," "sardine," and "sardoine." Its beauty, its toughness, the ease with which it can be engraved, and the fact that it can be highly polished made it a most popular stone among artisans. The Hebrews possibly obtained their sardius stones from the Arabian Peninsula.

The sardius is referred to at Revelation 4:3, where the One seated upon his heavenly throne of splendor "is, in appearance, like . . . a precious red-colored stone ["a sardius," ftn]." "The holy city, New Jerusalem," is described as having a wall with foundations that "were adorned with every sort of precious stone," the sixth being sardius.—Re 21:2, 19, 20.

SARDONYX (sar'do·nyx). An ornamental stone that is a variety of agate, a kind of chalcedony. It is an onyx composed of two or more layers of milk-white chalcedony and transparent red sard. However, the contrasting layer is sometimes golden or brown. The red layer showing through the white one appeared much like the color of a fingernail to the Greeks, which was probably why they applied to it the Greek word *o'nyx* (meaning "fingernail"). Sardonyx is found in various places, including Palestine and Arabia.

The stone is mentioned once in the Bible, at Revelation 21:2, 19, 20, where the fifth foundation stone of "the holy city, New Jerusalem," is a sardonyx stone.

SARGON (Sar'gon) [from old Akkadian and Assyrian, meaning "The King Is Legitimate"]. The successor of Shalmaneser V as king of Assyria. Historians refer to him as Sargon II. An earlier king, not of Assyria, but of Babylon is designated as Sargon I.

Nimrud Prism, which boasts of conquests by Sargon; but some of those conquests may actually have been made by his predecessor

Sargon is mentioned by name but once in the Bible record. (Isa 20:1) In the early 1800's the Biblical reference to him was often discounted by critics as of no historical value. However, from 1843 onward archaeological excavations uncovered the ruins of his palace at Khorsabad and the inscribed records of his royal annals.—PICTURE, Vol. 1, pp. 955, 960.

In his annals Sargon made the claim: "I besieged and conquered Samaria (*Sa-me-ri-na*)." (*Ancient Near Eastern Texts,* edited by James B. Pritchard, 1974, p. 284) However, that appears to be simply a boastful claim by Sargon or those who sought to glorify him, in which the accomplishment of the preceding ruler was claimed for the new monarch. A Babylonian chronicle, which may be more neutral, states concerning Shalmaneser V: "He ravaged Samaria." (*Assyrian and Babylonian Chronicles,* by A. K. Grayson, 1975, p. 73) The Bible, at 2 Kings 18:9, states simply that Shalmaneser 'laid siege' to Samaria and that "they got to capture it." Compare 2 Kings 17:1-6, which says that Shalmaneser the king of Assyria imposed tribute on Hoshea, the king of Samaria, and then states that later "the king of Assyria captured Samaria."

Inscriptions relating to Sargon illustrate the folly of placing great confidence in the ancient secular records, even to the point of equating them in value with the Biblical record. Following Sargon's accession to the throne, the Babylonians under Merodach-baladan revolted, with the support of Elam. Sargon warred against them at Der but was evidently unable to smash the revolt. Sargon's inscriptions show him claiming a complete victory in the battle, yet the Babylonian Chronicle states that the Elamites defeated the Assyrians, and a text of Merodach-baladan boasts that he 'overthrew the Assyrian hosts and smashed their weapons.' The book *Ancient Iraq* observes: "Amusing detail: Merodach-Baladan's inscription was found at Nimrud, where Sargon had taken it from Uruk . . . , replacing it in that city with a clay cylinder bearing his own and, of course, radically different version of the event. This shows that political propaganda and 'cold war' methods are not the privilege of our epoch."—By G. Roux, 1964, p. 258.

Sargon was more successful against a coalition formed by the kings of Hamath and Damascus and other allies, gaining the victory over them in a battle at Karkar on the Orontes River. Second Kings 17:24, 30 lists people from Hamath among those whom "the king of Assyria" settled in the cities of Samaria in place of the exiled Israelites.

According to Sargon's records, in his fifth year he attacked and conquered Carchemish, a city of commercial and military importance on the upper Euphrates River. The standard Assyrian procedure of deportation of the city's inhabitants and of their replacement by foreign elements followed. In Isaiah's warning concerning the Assyrian menace (Isa 10:5-11), Carchemish, along with Hamath and other cities, is cited as an example of the crushing power of Assyria. Later, Sargon reports settling Arab tribes as colonists in Samaria. —*Ancient Near Eastern Texts,* pp. 285, 286.

Assyrian records relate that the king of Ashdod, Azuri, engaged in rebellious conspiracy against the Assyrian yoke and that Sargon removed him, putting Azuri's younger brother in his place. Another revolt followed, and Sargon launched an attack against Philistia and "besieged and conquered the cities Ashdod, Gath . . . (and) Asdudimmu." (*Ancient Near Eastern Texts,* p. 286) It is apparently at this point that the Bible record mentions Sargon directly by name at Isaiah 20:1.

Following this, Sargon forced Merodach-baladan out of Babylon and conquered the city. Sargon's name is listed on an inscription as king of Babylon for a period of five years.

Sargon's aggressive reign brought the Assyrian Empire to a new peak of power and produced the

SARID

last great Assyrian dynasty. Historians would credit Sargon with a rule of 17 years. Since he is supposed to have begun his rule at or shortly after the fall of Samaria in Hezekiah's sixth year (2Ki 18:10), and since his son and successor to the throne, Sennacherib, invaded Judah in Hezekiah's 14th year (2Ki 18:13), a 17-year rule for Sargon could be possible only if Sennacherib were a coregent at the time of his attacking Judah. It seems equally likely that the historians' figure is in error. They certainly cannot rely on the eponym lists to establish these reigns, as is shown in the article CHRONOLOGY. The general unreliability of the Assyrian scribes and their practice of "adjusting" the different editions of the annals to suit the ruler's ego are also discussed there.

During his reign Sargon erected a new capital city about 20 km (12 mi) NE of Nineveh, near the present-day village of Khorsabad. On a virgin site he laid out the city called Dur Sharrukin (what might be called Sargonsburg) and built a 200-room royal palace on a raised platform some 15 m (50 ft) high and covering an area of about 0.8 ha (2 acres). Colossal human-headed, winged bulls guarded the palace entrance, one pair being about 5 m (16 ft) high. The walls were adorned with frescoes as well as carved reliefs depicting his campaigns and feats, the total wall space occupied by these reliefs equaling an overall distance of about 2.5 km (1.5 mi). In one of his inscriptions Sargon says: "For me, Sargon, who dwells in this palace, may he [that is, the god Asshur] decree as my destiny long life, health of body, joy of heart, brightness of soul." (*Ancient Iraq*, p. 262) Yet the records indicate that a year or so after the palace inauguration Sargon was killed, the manner of his death not being certain. His son Sennacherib replaced him.

SARID (Sa′rid). A city on the border of Zebulun. (Jos 19:10, 12) It is identified with Tell Shadud, some 10 km (6 mi) NNE of Megiddo.

SARSECHIM (Sar′se·chim) [possibly, Chief of the Slaves]. A Babylonian prince who was among the first to enter Jerusalem after the army broke through the walls in the summer of 607 B.C.E. (Jer 39:2, 3) His position and duties are not stated, though "Sarsechim" may have been a title, and its meaning may indicate his work.

SATAN [Resister]. In many places in the Hebrew Scriptures, the word *sa·tan′* appears without the definite article. Used in this way, it applies in its first appearance to the angel that stood in the road to *resist* Balaam as he set out with the objective of cursing the Israelites. (Nu 22:22, 32)

In other instances it refers to individuals as resisters of other men. (1Sa 29:4; 2Sa 19:21, 22; 1Ki 5:4; 11:14, 23, 25) But it is used with the definite article *ha* to refer to Satan the Devil, the chief Adversary of God. (Job 1:6, ftn; 2:1-7; Zec 3:1, 2) In the Greek Scriptures the word *sa·ta·nas′* applies to Satan the Devil in nearly all of its occurrences and is usually accompanied by the definite article *ho*.

Origin. The Scriptures indicate that the creature known as Satan did not always have that name. Rather, this descriptive name was given to him because of his taking a course of opposition and resistance to God. The name he had before this is not given. God is the only Creator, and 'his activity is perfect,' with no injustice or unrighteousness. (De 32:4) Therefore, the one becoming Satan was, when created, a perfect, righteous creature of God. He is a spirit person, for he appeared in heaven in the presence of God. (Job chaps 1, 2; Re 12:9) Jesus Christ said of him: "That one was a manslayer when he began, and he did not stand fast in the truth, because truth is not in him." (Joh 8:44; 1Jo 3:8) Jesus here shows that Satan was once in the truth, but forsook it. Beginning with his first overt act in turning Adam and Eve away from God, he was a manslayer, for he thereby brought about the death of Adam and Eve, which, in turn, brought sin and death to their offspring. (Ro 5:12) Throughout the Scriptures the qualities and actions attributed to him could be attributed only to a person, not to an abstract principle of evil. It is clear that the Jews, and Jesus and his disciples, knew that Satan existed as a *person*.

So, from a righteous, perfect start, this spirit person deviated into sin and degradation. The process bringing this about is described by James when he writes: "Each one is tried by being drawn out and enticed by his own desire. Then the desire, when it has become fertile, gives birth to sin; in turn, sin, when it has been accomplished, brings forth death." (Jas 1:14, 15) In the course that Satan took, there seems to be, in some respects, a parallel with that of the king of Tyre as described in Ezekiel 28:11-19.—See PERFECTION (The first sinner and the king of Tyre).

The Scriptural account, therefore, makes it plain that it was Satan who spoke through the medium of a serpent, seducing Eve into disobedience to God's command. In turn, Eve induced Adam to take the same rebellious course. (Ge 3:1-7; 2Co 11:3) As a consequence of Satan's use of the serpent, the Bible gives Satan the title "Serpent," which came to signify "deceiver"; he also became "the Tempter" (Mt 4:3) and a liar, "the father of the lie."—Joh 8:44; Re 12:9.

Issue of Sovereignty Raised. When Satan approached Eve (through the speech of the serpent), he actually challenged the rightfulness and righteousness of Jehovah's sovereignty. He intimated that God was unrightfully withholding something from the woman; he also declared that God was a liar in saying that she would die if she ate the forbidden fruit. Additionally, Satan made her believe she would be free and independent of God, becoming like God. By this means this wicked spirit creature raised himself higher than God in Eve's eyes, and Satan became her god, even though Eve, at the time, apparently did not know the identity of the one misleading her. By his action he brought man and woman under his leadership and control, standing up as a rival god in opposition to Jehovah.—Ge 3:1-7.

The Bible, in lifting the veil to give a glimpse into heavenly affairs, reveals that Satan later as a rival god appeared before Jehovah in heaven, challenging Jehovah to His face, saying that he could turn God's servant Job, and by implication any servant of God, away from Him. He charged God, in effect, with unrighteously giving Job everything, along with full protection, so that he, Satan, could not test Job and show what was really in his heart, which, Satan intimated, was bad. He implied that Job served God primarily for selfish considerations. Satan made this point of his argument clear when he said: "Skin in behalf of skin, and everything that a man has he will give in behalf of his soul. For a change, thrust out your hand, please, and touch as far as his bone and his flesh and see whether he will not curse you to your very face."—Job 1:6-12; 2:1-7; see SOVEREIGNTY.

In this special case, Jehovah allowed Satan to bring calamity upon Job by not interfering when Satan brought about a raid from Sabean marauders as well as destruction of flocks and shepherds by what Job's messenger called "the very fire of God" from the heavens; whether this was lightning or other fire is not stated. Satan also brought a raid by three bands of Chaldeans, as well as a windstorm. These things caused the death of all of Job's children and destroyed his property. Finally, Satan inflicted a loathsome disease upon Job himself.—Job 1:13-19; 2:7, 8.

These things reveal the might and power of the spirit creature Satan, as well as his vicious, murderous attitude.

It is important to note, however, that Satan recognized his impotence in the face of God's express command, for he did not challenge God's power and authority when God restricted him from taking Job's life.—Job 2:6.

Continued Opposition to God. By his challenge of God and his charging God's servants with lack of integrity, Satan lived up to his title "Devil," meaning "Slanderer," which title he deserved for having slandered Jehovah God in the garden of Eden.

Joined by other wicked demons. Before the Flood of Noah's day, it appears that other angels of God left their proper habitation in the heavens, as well as their assigned positions there. Materializing human bodies, they came to dwell on earth, marrying women and producing offspring called Nephilim. (Ge 6:1-4; 1Pe 3:19, 20; 2Pe 2:4; Jude 6; see NEPHILIM; SON[S] OF GOD.) These angels, having left God's service, came under the control of Satan. Hence Satan is called "the ruler of the demons." In one instance, when Jesus expelled demons from a man, the Pharisees accused him of doing so by the power of "Beelzebub, the ruler of the demons." That they had reference to Satan is shown by Jesus' answer: "If Satan expels Satan, he has become divided against himself."—Mt 12:22-27.

The apostle Paul associates Satan with "the wicked spirit forces in the heavenly places," and he speaks of them as "the world rulers of this darkness." (Eph 6:11, 12) As a governing force in the invisible realm immediately about the earth, Satan is "the ruler of the authority of the air." (Eph 2:2) In Revelation he is shown to be the one "misleading the entire inhabited earth." (Re 12:9) The apostle John said that "the whole world is lying in the power of the wicked one." (1Jo 5:19) He is therefore "the ruler of this world." (Joh 12:31) That is why James wrote that "the friendship with the world is enmity with God."—Jas 4:4.

His Fight to Destroy the "Seed." Satan made early efforts to block the promise of the "seed" to come through Abraham. (Ge 12:7) He evidently tried to get Sarah contaminated so that she would be unfit to bear the seed; but God protected her. (Ge 20:1-18) He did everything possible to destroy the ones whom God chose as Abraham's seed, the nation of Israel, by inducing them to sin and by bringing other nations against them, as Bible history shows throughout. A high point in Satan's ambitious attempts in his fight against God, and what appeared to Satan to be success, was reached when the king of the Third World Power of Bible history, Babylon, took Jerusalem, overturning the rulership of King Zedekiah of the line of David, and destroyed the temple of Jehovah, desolating Jerusalem and Judah.—Eze 21:25-27.

As an instrument of Satan, the ruling dynasty of Babylon, initially headed by Nebuchadnezzar, held Israel in exile for 68 years, until Babylon's overthrow. Babylon had no intention of ever releasing its captives and so reflected Satan's own boastful, ambitious attempts as a rival god opposed to the Universal Sovereign Jehovah. The Babylonian kings, worshiping their idol god Marduk, the goddess Ishtar, and a host of others, were actually worshipers of the demons and, as part of the world alienated from Jehovah, were under Satan's domination.—Ps 96:5; 1Co 10:20; Eph 2:12; Col 1:21.

Satan filled the king of Babylon with the ambition to have complete domination over the earth, even over "Jehovah's throne" (1Ch 29:23) and "the stars of God," the kings of the line of David sitting on the throne at Mount Moriah (by extension, Zion). This "king," that is, the dynasty of Babylon, 'lifted himself up' in his own heart and was in his own eyes and in the eyes of his admirers a "shining one," a "son of the dawn." (In some translations the Latin *Vulgate* term "Lucifer" is retained. It is, however, merely the translation of the Hebrew word *heh·lel'*, "shining one." *Heh·lel'* is not a name or a title but, rather, a term describing the boastful position taken by Babylon's dynasty of kings of the line of Nebuchadnezzar.) (Isa 14:4-21) Since Babylon was a tool of Satan, its "king" reflected Satan's own ambitious desire. Again, Jehovah came to the salvation of his people by restoring them to their land, until the real Seed of promise should come.—Ezr 1:1-6.

Efforts to cause Jesus to stumble. Satan, no doubt identifying Jesus as the Son of God and the one who was prophesied to bruise him in the head (Ge 3:15), did everything he could to destroy Jesus. But, when announcing the conception of Jesus to Mary, the angel Gabriel told her: "Holy spirit will come upon you, and power of the Most High will overshadow you. For that reason also what is born will be called holy, God's Son." (Lu 1:35) Jehovah safeguarded his Son. The efforts to destroy Jesus when an infant were unsuccessful. (Mt 2:1-15) God continued to protect Jesus during his youth. After his baptism, Satan approached Jesus in the wilderness with three different strong temptations, thoroughly testing him on the issue of devotion to Jehovah. In one of his appeals Satan showed Jesus all the kingdoms of the world, claiming them to be his own. Jesus did not contradict this claim. Nonetheless, Jesus re-

fused to contemplate even for the briefest instant of time any "shortcut" to kingship, nor did he consider for an instant the doing of anything merely to please himself. His immediate reply to Satan was, "Go away, Satan! For it is written, 'It is Jehovah your God you must worship, and it is to him alone you must render sacred service.'" At this, "the Devil . . . retired from him until another convenient time." (Mt 4:1-11; Lu 4:13) This illustrates the truth of James' words later written: "Oppose the Devil, and he will flee from you." —Jas 4:7.

Jesus was ever alert to the danger of Satan's machinations and to the fact that Satan desired to cause his destruction by getting him to entertain a thought contrary to Jehovah's will. This was demonstrated when Peter, on one occasion, though with good intentions, was actually throwing temptation in his way. Jesus had spoken of the suffering and death he was to undergo. "At this Peter took him aside and commenced rebuking him, saying: 'Be kind to yourself, Lord; you will not have this destiny at all.' But, turning his back, he said to Peter: 'Get behind me, *Satan!* You are a stumbling block to me, because you think, not God's thoughts, but those of men.'"—Mt 16:21-23.

Throughout Jesus' ministry he was in danger; Satan used human agents to oppose Jesus, trying either to cause him to stumble or to kill him. At one time the people were about to seize Jesus to make him king. But he would not consider such a thing; he would accept kingship only in God's time and way. (Joh 6:15) On another occasion those of his own hometown attempted to kill him. (Lu 4:22-30) He was constantly harassed by those whom Satan used to try to trap him. (Mt 22:15) But in all of Satan's efforts, he failed to cause Jesus to sin in the slightest thought or deed. Satan was thoroughly proved to be a liar, and he failed in his challenge of God's sovereignty and the integrity of God's servants. As Jesus said, shortly before his death: "Now there is a judging of this world; now the ruler of this world will be cast out" —completely discredited. (Joh 12:31) Satan had a grip on all mankind through sin. But, knowing that Satan would soon bring about his death, Jesus, after celebrating his last Passover with his disciples, could say: "The ruler of the world is coming. And *he has no hold on me.*"—Joh 14:30.

A few hours later, Satan succeeded in having Jesus put to death, first getting control of one of Jesus' apostles, then using the Jewish leaders and the Roman World Power to execute Jesus in a painful and ignominious manner. (Lu 22:3; Joh

13:26, 27; chaps 18, 19) Here Satan acted as "the one having the means to cause death, that is, the Devil." (Heb 2:14; Lu 22:53) But in this Satan failed to promote his cause; he only unwillingly fulfilled prophecy, which required that Jesus die as a sacrifice. The death of Jesus in blamelessness provided the ransom price for humankind, and by his death (and subsequent resurrection by God) Jesus could now help sinful humankind to escape from the grip of Satan, for, as it is written, Jesus became blood and flesh "that through his death he might bring to nothing the one having the means to cause death, that is, the Devil; and that he might emancipate all those who for fear of death were subject to slavery all through their lives."—Heb 2:14, 15.

Continues to fight Christians. After Jesus' death and resurrection, Satan continued to wage a bitter fight against Christ's followers. The accounts in the book of Acts and in the letters of the Christian Greek Scriptures furnish numerous proofs of this. Paul said that he had been given "a thorn in the flesh, an angel of Satan, to keep slapping" him. (2Co 12:7) And as in the case with Eve, Satan disguised his real nature and purposes by "transforming himself into an angel of light," and he had agents, ministers who "also keep transforming themselves into ministers of righteousness." (2Co 11:14, 15) Examples of these were the false apostles who fought against Paul (2Co 11:13) and those in Ephesus 'who said they themselves were Jews, and yet they were not but were a synagogue of Satan.' (Re 2:9) Satan never ceased in making accusations "day and night" against Christians, challenging their integrity, as he did Job's. (Re 12:10; Lu 22:31) But Christians have "a helper with the Father, Jesus Christ, a righteous one," who appears before the person of God in their behalf.—1Jo 2:1.

His Abyssing and Final Destruction. At the time of Satan's act in causing Eve and then Adam to rebel against God, God said to the serpent (actually speaking to Satan, since a mere beast could not understand the issues involved): "Dust is what you will eat all the days of your life. And I shall put enmity between you and the woman and between your seed and her seed. He will bruise you in the head and you will bruise him in the heel." (Ge 3:14, 15) Here God made it known that Satan, cast outside God's holy organization, would have no life-sustaining hope but would 'eat dust,' as it were, until he died. The 'seed' eventually was to bruise him in the head, which would signify a death wound. When Christ was on earth, the demons identified him as the

One who was to hurl them into the "abyss," evidently a condition of restraint that in the parallel account is spoken of as "torment."—Mt 8:29; Lu 8:30, 31; see TORMENT.

In the book of Revelation, we find described the last days of Satan and his end. Revelation reports that at the time of Christ's taking Kingdom power, Satan is hurled down out of heaven to the earth, no longer having access to the heavens, as he did in the days of Job and for centuries thereafter. (Re 12:7-12) After this defeat Satan has only a "short period of time," during which he makes war with "the remaining ones of [the woman's] seed, who observe the commandments of God and have the work of bearing witness to Jesus." In his efforts to devour the remaining ones of the woman's seed, he is called "the dragon," a swallower or crusher. (Re 12:16, 17; compare Jer 51:34, where Jeremiah speaks for Jerusalem and Judah, saying: "Nebuchadrezzar the king of Babylon . . . has swallowed me down like a big snake [or, "a dragon," ftn].") In the earlier description of his fight against the woman and his efforts to devour her man child, he is pictured as "a great fiery-colored dragon."—Re 12:3.

Revelation's 20th chapter describes Satan's being bound and abyssed for a thousand years, at the hands of a great angel—doubtless Jesus Christ, who has the key of the abyss and who is the "seed" to bruise Satan's head.—Compare Re 1:18; see ABYSS.

Satan's final effort culminates in permanent defeat. The prophecy says that he is to be let loose for "a little while" as soon as Christ's Thousand Year Reign is ended and that he will lead rebellious persons in another attack upon God's sovereignty; but he is hurled (along with his demons) into the lake of fire and sulfur, everlasting destruction.—Re 20:1-3, 7-10; compare Mt 25:41; see LAKE OF FIRE.

What is meant by 'handing a person over to Satan for destruction of the flesh'?

In instructing the congregation at Corinth as to the action to take toward a member of the congregation who had wickedly been committing incest with the wife of his father, the apostle Paul wrote: "Hand such a man over to Satan for the destruction of the flesh." (1Co 5:5) This was a command to expel the man from the congregation, cutting off all fellowship with him. (1Co 5:13) Turning him over to Satan would put him out of the congregation and into the world over which Satan is the god and ruler. Like "a little leaven" in "the whole lump" of dough, this man was "the flesh," or fleshly element inside the congregation; and by removing this incestuous man, the spiritually minded congregation would destroy "the flesh" from the midst of it. (1Co 5: 6, 7) Similarly, Paul handed Hymenaeus and Alexander over to Satan, because they had thrust aside faith and a good conscience and had experienced shipwreck concerning their faith.—1Ti 1:20.

Later, the incestuous man in Corinth apparently repented from his wrongdoing and cleaned up, prompting the apostle Paul to recommend his being received back into the congregation. In exhorting them to forgiveness, he gave as one of the reasons, "that we may not be overreached by Satan, for we are not ignorant of his designs." (2Co 2:11) In the first instance, Satan had brought the congregation into a bad condition in which they had to be reproved by the apostle, for they were too lenient, in fact, were letting the wicked man carry on his practice without regard for the reproach it brought, being "puffed up" in allowing it. (1Co 5:2) But on the other hand, if they now swung to the other extreme and refused forgiveness to the repentant one, Satan would be overreaching them in another direction, namely, that he could take advantage of their becoming hard and unforgiving. Through God's Word, Christians are enlightened to realize Satan's existence, his power, his designs and purposes, and his manner of operation, so that they can fight this spiritual foe with the spiritual weapons God provides. —Eph 6:13-17.

SATRAP

SATRAP (sa′trap). A viceroy, or governor of a province, in the Babylonian and Persian empires appointed by the king as a chief ruler of a jurisdictional district. Daniel mentioned satraps as serving under Nebuchadnezzar in the Babylonian Empire. (Da 3:1-3) After the Medes and Persians conquered Babylon, Darius the Mede set up 120 satraps over his entire kingdom. (Da 6:1) Ezra had dealings with satraps in the time of King Artaxerxes of Persia. (Ezr 8:36) In the days of Esther and Mordecai, the satraps supervised 127 jurisdictional districts under the Persian king Ahasuerus. (Es 1:1) Being the king's official representatives, they were responsible to him and had quite free access to his presence. Consequently, they wielded considerable influence and power as civil and political chiefs. They collected taxes and remitted to the royal court the stipulated tribute.

Daniel, as one of the three high officials under Darius over the 120 satraps, distinguished himself above all of them to the point that the king was intending to elevate him over all the kingdom. Because they were envious, the officials and the satraps schemed to get Daniel thrown into a lions' pit. The Bible does not state how many of the satraps personally appeared before the king with the accusation. But Jehovah proved to be with Daniel, sending his angel to shut the mouths of the lions. Then Darius had these official slanderers of Daniel, with their wives and their sons, thrown into the pit to be killed by the lions.—Da 6:1-24.

The book *History of the Persian Empire* says of the satrapal organization under Cyrus the Persian: "Each [province] was ruled by a satrap whose title meant literally 'protector of the Kingdom.' As successor to a former king, ruling a truly enormous territory, he was in point of fact himself a monarch and was surrounded by a miniature court. Not only did he carry on the civil administration but he was also commander of the satrapal levies. When his office became hereditary, the threat to the central authority could not be ignored. To meet this threat, certain checks were instituted; his secretary, his chief financial official, and the general in charge of the garrison stationed in the citadel of each of the satrapal capitals were under the direct orders of, and reported directly to, the great king in person. Still more effective control was exercised by the 'king's eye' (or 'king's ear' or 'king's messenger'), [an official] who every year made a careful inspection of each province."—By A. T. Olmstead, 1948, p. 59.

SAUL

SAUL [Asked [of God]; Inquired [of God]].

1. A Benjamite descended from Jeiel (presumably also called Abiel) through Ner and Kish (1Ch 8:29-33; 9:35-39; see ABIEL No. 1); the first divinely selected king of Israel. (1Sa 9:15, 16; 10:1) Saul came from a wealthy family. A handsome man, standing head and shoulders taller than all others of his nation, he possessed great physical strength and agility. (1Sa 9:1, 2; 2Sa 1:23) The name of his wife was Ahinoam. Saul fathered at least seven sons, Jonathan, Ishvi, Malchi-shua, Abinadab, Ish-bosheth (Eshbaal), Armoni, and Mephibosheth, as well as two daughters, Merab and Michal. Abner, evidently King Saul's uncle (see ABNER), served as chief of the Israelite army. —1Sa 14:49, 50; 2Sa 2:8; 21:8; 1Ch 8:33.

The young man Saul lived during a turbulent time of Israel's history. Philistine oppression had reduced the nation to a helpless state militarily (1Sa 9:16; 13:19, 20), and the Ammonites under

King Nahash threatened aggression. (1Sa 12:12) Whereas Samuel had faithfully judged Israel, his sons were perverters of justice. (1Sa 8:1-3) Viewing the situation from a human standpoint and, therefore, losing sight of Jehovah's ability to protect his people, the older men of Israel approached Samuel with the request that he appoint a king over them.—1Sa 8:4, 5.

Anointed as King. Thereafter Jehovah guided matters to provide the occasion for anointing Saul as king. With his attendant, Saul looked for the lost she-asses of his father. Since the search proved to be fruitless, he decided to return home. But his attendant suggested that they seek the assistance of the "man of God" known to be in a nearby city. This led to Saul's meeting Samuel. (1Sa 9:3-19) In his first conversation with Samuel, Saul showed himself to be a modest man. (1Sa 9:20, 21) After eating a sacrificial meal with Saul, Samuel continued speaking with him. The next morning Samuel anointed Saul as king. To confirm that God was with Saul, Samuel gave him three prophetic signs, all of which were fulfilled that day.—1Sa 9:22–10:16.

Later, at Mizpah, when chosen as king by lot (1Sa 10:20, 21, *JB; NE*), Saul bashfully hid among the luggage. Found, he was presented as king, and the people approvingly shouted: "Let the king live!" Escorted by valiant men, Saul returned to Gibeah. Though good-for-nothing men spoke disparagingly of him and despised him, Saul remained silent.—1Sa 10:17-27.

Early Victories. About a month later (according to the reading of the Greek *Septuagint* and Dead Sea Scroll 4QSamᵃ in 1Sa 10:27b) Ammonite King Nahash demanded the surrender of Jabesh in Gilead. (See NAHASH.) When messengers brought news of this to Saul, God's spirit became operative upon him. He quickly rallied an army of 330,000 men and led it to victory. This resulted in a strengthening of Saul's position as king, the people even requesting that those who had spoken against him be put to death. But Saul, appreciating that Jehovah had granted the victory, did not consent to this. Subsequently, at Gilgal, Saul's kingship was confirmed anew.—1Sa 11:1-15.

Next Saul undertook steps to break the power of the Philistines over Israel. He chose 3,000 Israelites, placing 2,000 under himself and the remainder under his son Jonathan. Evidently acting at his father's direction, "Jonathan struck down the garrison of the Philistines that was in Geba." In retaliation, the Philistines assembled a mighty force and began camping at Michmash.—1Sa 13: 3, 5.

Sins Presumptuously. Meanwhile Saul had withdrawn from Michmash to Gilgal in the Jordan Valley. There he waited seven days for Samuel. But Samuel did not come at the appointed time. Fearing that the enemy would sweep down upon him when he had not secured Jehovah's help and that further delay would result in losing his army, Saul 'compelled himself' to offer up the burnt sacrifice. Samuel, on arriving, condemned Saul's 'foolish act' as sinful. Evidently, Saul's sin consisted of his presumptuously going ahead with the sacrifice and not obeying Jehovah's commandment, which had been given through his representative Samuel, to wait for Samuel to offer up the sacrifice. (Compare 1Sa 10:8.) As a consequence of this act, Saul's kingdom was not to last. —1Sa 13:1-14.

In the progress of the campaign against the Philistines, Saul pronounced a curse upon anyone partaking of food before vengeance was executed on the enemy. This rash oath led to adverse consequences. The Israelites tired, and though they triumphed over the Philistines, their victory was not as great as it might have been. Famished, they did not take time to drain the blood from the animals they afterward slaughtered, thereby violating God's law concerning the sanctity of blood. Not having heard his father's oath, Jonathan ate some honey. Saul, therefore, pronounced the death sentence upon him. But the people redeemed Jonathan, for he had been instrumental in Israel's gaining the victory.—1Sa 14:1-45.

Rejected by God. Throughout Saul's reign there were repeated battles against the Philistines and other peoples, including the Moabites, Ammonites, Edomites, and Amalekites. (1Sa 14: 47, 48, 52) In the war against the Amalekites, Saul transgressed Jehovah's command by sparing the best of their flock and herd as well as their king, Agag. When asked why he had not obeyed Jehovah's voice, Saul disclaimed guilt and shifted the blame onto the people. Only after Samuel emphasized the serious nature of the sin and said that, because of it, Jehovah was rejecting him as king did Saul acknowledge that his error was the result of his fearing the people. After Saul pleaded with Samuel to honor him in front of the older men and in front of Israel by accompanying him, Samuel did appear with him before them. Then Samuel himself proceeded to put Agag to death. After that, Samuel parted from Saul and they had no further association.—1Sa 15:1-35.

It was after this and after the anointing of David as Israel's future king that Jehovah's spirit left Saul. From then on "a bad spirit from Jehovah terrorized him." Having withdrawn his spirit from Saul, Jehovah made it possible for a bad spirit to gain possession of him, depriving Saul of his peace of mind and stirring up his feelings, thoughts, and imaginations in a wrong way. Saul's failure to obey Jehovah indicated a bad inclination of mind and heart, against which God's spirit offered Saul no protection or resistive force. However, since Jehovah had permitted the "bad spirit" to replace his spirit and terrorize Saul, it could be termed a "bad spirit from Jehovah," so that Saul's servants spoke of it as "God's bad spirit." On the recommendation of one of his attendants, Saul requested that David be his court musician to calm him when he was troubled by the "bad spirit."—1Sa 16:14-23; 17:15.

Relationships With David. Thereafter the Philistines threatened Israel's security. While they were camped on one side of the Low Plain of Elah and King Saul's forces were camped on the opposite side, Goliath, morning and evening, for 40 days, emerged from the Philistine camp, challenging Israel to furnish a man to fight him in single combat. King Saul promised to enrich and to form a marriage alliance with any Israelite who might strike down Goliath. Also, the house of the victor's father was to be "set free," probably from the payment of taxes and compulsory service. (Compare 1Sa 8:11-17.) When David arrived on the scene with food supplies for his brothers and certain portions for the chief of the thousand (possibly the commander under whom David's brothers served), his questionings apparently suggested his willingness to answer the challenge. This led to his being brought to Saul and to his subsequent victory over Goliath.—1Sa 17:1-58.

Develops enmity for David. Saul thereafter placed David over the men of war. This eventually resulted in David's being celebrated in song more than the king himself. Saul, therefore, came to view David with suspicion and envious hatred. On one occasion, as David was playing on the harp, Saul 'began behaving like a prophet.' Not that Saul began to utter prophecies, but he evidently manifested extraordinary feeling and a physical disturbance like that of a prophet just prior to prophesying or when prophesying. While in that unusual, disturbed state, Saul twice hurled a spear at David. Failing in his attempts to pin David to the wall, Saul later agreed to give his daughter Michal in marriage to David upon the presentation of a hundred foreskins of the Philistines. Saul's intent in making this offer was that David would die at their hands. The scheme failed, David presenting, not 100, but 200 fore-

skins to form a marriage alliance with Saul. The king's fear of and hatred for David therefore intensified. To his son Jonathan and to all of his servants, Saul spoke about his desire to put David to death. When Jonathan interceded, Saul promised not to kill David. Nevertheless, David was forced to flee for his life, as Saul hurled a spear at him for the third time. Saul even had messengers watch David's house and commanded that he be put to death in the morning.—1Sa 18:1-19:11.

That night David made his escape through a window of his house and ran to Ramah, where Samuel resided. With Samuel he then took up dwelling in Naioth. When news of this reached Saul, he sent messengers to seize David. But upon arriving, they "began behaving like prophets." Evidently God's spirit operated upon them in such a way that they completely forgot the purpose of their mission. When this also happened to two other groups of messengers dispatched by him, Saul personally went to Ramah. He likewise came under the control of God's spirit, and that for a prolonged period, this evidently providing David sufficient time to flee.—1Sa 19:12-20:1; see PROPHET (Means of Appointment and Inspiration).

David spares Saul's life as God's anointed. After these unsuccessful attempts on David's life, Jonathan, for a second time, spoke out in behalf of David. But Saul became so enraged that he hurled a spear at his own son. (1Sa 20:1-33) From that time onward Saul relentlessly pursued David. Learning that High Priest Ahimelech had assisted David, Saul ordered that he and his associate priests be executed. (1Sa 22:6-19) Later, he planned to attack the Judean city of Keilah because David was residing there but abandoned the plan when David escaped. Saul continued the chase, hunting for him in wilderness regions. A Philistine raid, however, brought his pursuit to a temporary halt and enabled David to seek refuge in the Wilderness of En-gedi. On two occasions thereafter Saul came into a position that would have allowed David to kill him. But David refused to put out his hand against Jehovah's anointed one. The second time Saul, learning of David's restraint, even promised not to do injury to David. But this was an insincere expression, for it was only when he learned that David had run away to the Philistine city of Gath that he abandoned the chase.—1Sa 23:10-24:22; 26:1-27:1, 4.

Saul turns to spiritism. About a year or two later (1Sa 29:3), the Philistines came against Saul. Without Jehovah's spirit and guidance, and abandoned to a disapproved mental state, he turned to spiritism, a transgression worthy of death. (Le 20:6) Disguised, Saul went to see a spirit medium at En-dor, requesting that she bring up the dead Samuel for him. From her description of what she saw, Saul concluded that it was Samuel. However, it should be noted that Jehovah had not answered Saul's inquiries and obviously did not do so by means of a practice condemned by His law as warranting the death penalty. (Le 20:27) There-fore, what the woman said must have been of demonic origin. The message gave no comfort to Saul but filled him with fear.—1Sa 28:4-25; see SPIRITISM.

Saul's death. In the ensuing conflict with the Philistines, Saul was severely wounded at Mount Gilboa and three of his sons were slain. As his armor-bearer refused to put him to death, Saul fell upon his own sword. (1Sa 31:1-7) About three days later a young Amalekite came to David, boasting that he had put the wounded king to death. This was evidently a lie, designed to gain David's favor. David, however, commanded that the man be executed on the basis of the claim, because Saul had been Jehovah's anointed one. —2Sa 1:1-15.

Meanwhile the Philistines had fastened the corpses of Saul and his three sons on the wall of Beth-shan. Courageous men of Jabesh-gilead, however, retrieved the bodies, burned them, and then buried the bones.—1Sa 31:8-13.

Years later, during David's reign, the bloodguilt that had been incurred by Saul and his house in connection with the Gibeonites was avenged when seven of his descendants were slain.—2Sa 21:1-9.

2. A Benjamite of the city of Tarsus in Asia Minor who persecuted Christ's followers but later became an apostle of Jesus Christ. (Ac 9:1, 4, 17; 11:25; 21:39; Php 3:5) In all of his letters he referred to himself by his Latin name Paul.—See PAUL.

SAVIOR.

One who preserves or delivers from danger or destruction. Jehovah is identified as the principal Savior, the only Source of deliverance. (Isa 43:11; 45:21) He was the Savior and Deliverer of Israel, time and again. (Ps 106:8, 10, 21; Isa 43:3; 45:15; Jer 14:8) He saved not only the nation but also individuals who served him. (2Sa 22:1-3) Often his salvation was through men raised up by him as saviors. (Ne 9:27) During the period of the Judges, these special saviors were divinely selected and empowered to deliver Israel from foreign oppression. (Jg 2:16; 3:9, 15) While the judge lived, he served to keep Israel in the right way, and this brought them relief from their enemies. (Jg 2:18) When Jesus was on earth, Jehovah was his Savior, supporting and strength-ening him to maintain integrity through his strenuous trials.—Heb 5:7; Ps 28:8.

Along with his role as Savior, Jehovah is also the "Repurchaser." (Isa 49:26; 60:16) In the past he redeemed his people Israel from captivity. In delivering Christians from sin's bondage, he does the repurchasing through his Son Jesus Christ (1Jo 4:14), Jehovah's provision for salvation, who is therefore exalted as "Chief Agent and Savior." (Ac 5:31) Accordingly, Jesus Christ can rightly be called "our Savior," even though he performs the salvation as the agent of Jehovah. (Tit 1:4; 2Pe 1:11) The name Jesus, given to God's Son by angelic direction, means "Jehovah Is Salvation," for, said the angel, "he will save his people from their sins." (Mt 1:21; Lu 1:31) This name points out that Jehovah is the Source of salvation, ac-complished *through* Jesus. For this reason we find the Father and the Son spoken of together in connection with salvation.—Tit 2:11-13; 3:4-6.

Salvation is provided by Jehovah through Jesus Christ for "all sorts of men." (1Ti 4:10) He saves them from sin and death (Ro 8:2), from Babylon the Great (Re 18:2, 4), from this world under Satan's control (Joh 17:16; Col 1:13), and from destruction and everlasting death (Re 7:14-17; 21:3, 4). "A great crowd" is shown at Revelation 7:9, 10 attributing salvation to God and to the Lamb.

The ransom sacrifice is the basis for salvation, and as King and everlasting High Priest, Christ Jesus has the authority and power "to save com-pletely those who are approaching God through him." (Heb 7:23-25; Re 19:16) He is "a savior of this body," the congregation of his anointed fol-lowers, and also of all who exercise faith in him. —Eph 5:23; 1Jo 4:14; Joh 3:16, 17.

SAW.

A cutting tool with a notched or toothed blade and one or two handles. Early saws did not cut in both directions; some were designed to cut when pulled toward the user; others, when pushed away. Egyptian saws were generally made of bronze and usually had teeth that slant-ed in the direction of the handle. Such a saw would cut when drawn toward the person using it. The blade was either inserted in the handle or fastened to it by means of thongs. Two-handled saws having iron blades were in use among the Assyrians. Hebrew carpenters employed the saw to cut wood, and their masons used saws capable of cutting stone.—Isa 10:15; 1Ki 7:9.

David put captive Ammonites to work at such tasks as sawing stones. (2Sa 12:29-31) Their tools included "axes," or, literally, "stone saws," according to the Masoretic text at 1 Chronicles 20:3. In some cases it appears that copper-bladed saws with stone teeth were used to cut stone. But apparently an abrasive such as emery powder was sometimes put under the cutting edge of a saw having a copper or a bronze blade so as to facilitate the cutting of stone.

Persecution of faithful pre-Christian witnesses of Jehovah was so severe at times that some were killed by being "sawn asunder." (Heb 11:37, 38) According to tradition, wicked King Manasseh had Isaiah put to death in that extremely painful manner, though the Scriptures do not say so.

SCALES.
A number of Hebrew and Greek words are appropriately rendered "scales"; the expression has various meanings.

Animal Scales. Flattened, rigid plates forming part of the outer body covering of many fishes and reptiles. The Law ruled as ceremonially clean for food "everything that has fins and scales in the waters." Water animals lacking such could not be eaten; they were "a loathsome thing." (Le 11:9, 10, 12; De 14:9, 10) Thus scales (Heb., qas·qas·sim', plural of qas·qe'seth) were one of the easily recognizable signs as to whether a certain fish could be eaten. Though there are four types of fish scales, most common are ctenoid scales (with a comblike edge) and cycloid scales (with a rounded border). These are arranged in overlapping rows, forming a thin, light, and flexible covering.

The same Hebrew word is used in Ezekiel 29:4, where the Egyptian Pharaoh is symbolically described as what seems to be a crocodile. The entire body of a crocodile is covered with strong plates of horn set in its leathery skin. Job 41:15-17 apparently also refers to the scales (AS, NW, MR) of the crocodile, in this case using the Hebrew word that is often translated "shield."—See LEVIATHAN.

Scales for Weighing. A device for weighing objects. The ancients were acquainted with the simple beam scale, or balance. It consisted of a horizontal bar, or beam, pivoted at the center on a peg or cord, and from each end of the beam hung a pan or hook. The object to be weighed was put in one pan (or hung on one hook, as with a small bag of money), and the known weights were put on the other side. (Jer 32:10; Isa 46:6; Ge 23:15, 16; Eze 5:1; see MONEY.) During a famine, even food might be measured carefully on a balance. The rider of the black horse described at Revelation 6:5 held a pair of scales "for measuring bread by weight, to personify . . . bad times, when provisions became cruelly expensive."—*The Expositor's Greek Testament*, edited by W. Nicoll, 1967, Vol. V, p. 390.

Jehovah commanded honesty and accuracy in using scales (Le 19:35, 36), for a cheating pair of scales was detestable to him. (Pr 11:1; 16:11; Eze 45:10) Scales could be made inaccurate by having the arms of unequal length, or they could be rendered less sensitive by having the arms relatively short or by making the beam thicker and heavier. At times Israelites used scales fraudulently (Ho 12:7; Am 8:5), and they multiplied the deception by using inaccurate weights, one set for buying and another for selling.—Pr 20:23.

Weighing scales were spoken of figuratively, as when Job mentioned 'weighing his adversity on scales.' (Job 6:2) The littleness of earthling men was emphasized by saying that they are lighter than an exhalation on the scales (Ps 62:9), and the nations were compared to an insignificant film of dust on the scales from the standpoint of Jehovah, who could, as it were, weigh all the hills in the scales. (Isa 40:12, 15) Scales were sometimes used to represent accurate measurement in judgment.—Job 31:6; Da 5:27.

Scales of Armor. A coat of mail might have had scales (Heb., qas·qas·sim', plural of qas·qe'seth) attached to it. These were small metal plates that overlapped and provided a relatively flexible armor plate.—1Sa 17:5; see ARMS, ARMOR (Coat of Mail).

Scales on Paul's Eyes. When Paul was cured of the blindness resulting from Jesus' appearing to him, "what looked like scales" fell from his eyes. (Ac 9:18) Some scholars take the view that nothing actually fell from Paul's eyes but that this is simply figurative language meaning that Paul regained his sight. However, numerous modern translations indicate that something really fell from Paul's eyes.—AT, NW, RS, Sd, We.

SCARECROW.
An object such as a pole or pile of stones, usually in a form suggesting a human figure, arranged in a field in such a way as to frighten away birds or other animals. Jeremiah likened the idols of the nations to "a scarecrow [Heb., to'mer] of a cucumber field." (Jer 10:5) The word to'mer is elsewhere rendered "palm tree." (Jg 4:5) Truly the idols of the nations amounted to no more than a scarecrow, a falsity.—AT, Mo, NE, NW, RS.

SCARLET.
See COLORS.

SCENTED WOOD.
Among the luxury items that traders brought to symbolic "Babylon the Great" were articles in "scented wood," or in

thyine wood." (Re 17:5; 18:11, 12, ftn) Such wood, likely from N Africa, was prized by the ancient Romans for the making of very costly furniture. The most costly wood was that from the lower part of the trunk, because of the variety in the grain and the broadness of the sections obtainable. The wood was fragrant, hard, and took a high polish; and because of wavy or spiral lines in the grain, some of the tables came to be called "tiger tables" or "panther tables." Among the Greeks the balsamic wood was used in temple worship, and its name is derived from the Greek term for making burnt offerings.

The tree producing this scented wood is understood to be the sandarac tree (*Tetraclinus articulata*), a coniferous tree native to N Africa and of the cypress family, growing to a height of 4.5 to 7.5 m (15 to 25 ft). Its wood has a rich reddish-brown hue and is finely marked.

SCEPTER. A baton or rod carried by a ruler as an emblem of royal authority. At times "scepter" is used in a figurative sense to represent kings (Eze 19:10, 11, 14) or authority (Zec 10:11), especially royal authority.

In ancient Persia, unless the monarch held out the golden scepter, anyone who appeared uninvited before the king was put to death.—Es 4:11; 5:2; 8:4.

Jacob's prophetic words that 'the scepter would not turn aside from Judah' indicated that the kingship would come to be the possession of the tribe of Judah and would remain such until Shiloh came. (Ge 49:10; see COMMANDER'S STAFF.) Centuries later the Babylonians, acting as Jehovah's executional "sword," destroyed the kingdom of Judah and took its king captive. This is alluded to by Jehovah's words through Ezekiel: "A sword, a sword! It has been sharpened, and it is also polished. . . . Is it rejecting the scepter of my own son, as it does every tree? . . . For an extermination has been made, and what of it if it is rejecting also the scepter?" (Eze 21:9, 10, 13) Thus the "sword" treated the Judean "scepter" of the Davidic dynasty like every tree (to be chopped down) or like other kings or kingdoms that it brought to ruin.

Psalm 2, a prophecy that Peter applied to Jesus Christ (Ac 4:25-27), showed that Jehovah's anointed one would use an iron scepter to break the nations to pieces. (Ps 2:2, 6, 9; compare Re 2:5; 19:15.) As Jesus Christ always uses his royal authority in the right way, his scepter is one of uprightness.—Ps 45:6, 7; Heb 1:8, 9.

Psalm 125:3 states that "the scepter of wickedness will not keep resting upon the lot of the righteous ones." These words give assurance that the righteous will not always be oppressed by those who exercise authority in a wicked way.

SCEVA (Sce'va). A Jewish "chief priest." His seven sons were among "certain ones of the roving Jews who practiced the casting out of demons." In one instance, in the city of Ephesus, they tried to exorcise a demon by saying, "I solemnly charge you by Jesus whom Paul preaches." The wicked spirit responded by saying: "I know Jesus and I am acquainted with Paul; but who are you?" The man obsessed by the spirit then leaped upon Sceva's seven sons and drove them out of the house naked and wounded. This resulted in magnifying the name of the Lord and caused many to give heed to the good news that Paul was preaching.—Ac 19:13-20.

No Jewish priest named Sceva is elsewhere mentioned, unless Sceva was a Latin name for a priest otherwise known by a Hebrew name.

SCHOOL. An institution that provides instruction. The word "school" is derived from the Greek *skho·le'*, which means, basically, "leisure"; then, that for which leisure is employed—discussion, lecture, study, learning.

The Creator placed the responsibility upon parents to teach their offspring the true meaning of life, physical life as well as spiritual life. In ancient Israel, he also set aside the tribe of Levi to provide religious education.—See EDUCATION.

At a later time, places of advanced religious schooling developed among the Jews. For example, Saul (Paul) had studied at the feet of Gamaliel. The Jews challenged the qualifications of anyone claiming to instruct in God's law if he had not studied at their schools.—Ac 22:3; Joh 7:15.

When he was in Ephesus, Paul gave talks in the synagogue for a period of three months, since synagogues were places of instruction. But when some strongly opposed the good news, Paul withdrew the disciples to the school auditorium of Tyrannus, where he gave talks daily for two years. No details are provided as to the purpose for which that school had been established, but Paul was evidently welcome to use the facilities, perhaps for a number of hours each day.—Ac 19:8-10, ftn.

Meeting places of the Christian congregation served as schools where the scrolls of the Hebrew Scriptures as well as the writings of the apostles and their associates could be considered. Few Christians could possess all the Hebrew scrolls or copies of all the Christian letters. The meetings provided an opportunity for thorough examination and discussion of these. (Col 4:16) Poor Christians who did not possess other writing material likely wrote down Bible texts for personal study and use on ostraca, that is, pieces of broken pottery. As they heard the Scriptures read or had access to the scrolls at the meeting, they could copy them in ink on the pottery fragments. At the same time schooling at home for the entire family continued as a vital part of Christian education. (Eph 6:4; 1Co 14:35) No separate arrangement for children, as with the modern-day "Sunday school," was anywhere authorized or practiced by the Jews or by the Christian apostles.

SCORPION [Heb., 'aq·rav'; Gr., skor·pi'os]. A small animal (an arachnid, not included by biologists as among insects) classified in the same group as spiders. But, unlike other arachnids, the female scorpion gives birth to living offspring instead of depositing eggs.

The scorpion is equipped with eight walking legs; a long, narrow, segmented tail terminating in a curved, poisonous stinger; and a pair of pincers resembling those of a lobster and studded with hypersensitive hairs. The tail is usually carried upward and curved forward over the creature's back and waves in all directions. The scorpion uses its stinger in defense and also to procure its prey. The victim is seized by the nippers and then, if necessary, stung to death. A nocturnal animal, the scorpion spends the day hidden under stones, in cracks and crevices of buildings, and even under mats and beds, coming out at night to feed on spiders and insects.

Of the over 600 varieties of scorpions, generally ranging in size from less than 2.5 cm (1 in.) to 20 cm (8 in.), about a dozen types have been encountered in Palestine and Syria. Although the scorpion's sting is usually not fatal to humans, there are several varieties with venom proportionately more potent than that of many dangerous desert vipers. The most poisonous of the kinds found in Israel is the yellow Buthus quinquestriatus. The great pain caused by a scorpion's sting is noted at Revelation 9:3, 5, 10, where symbolic locusts are described as having "the same authority as the scorpions of the earth" and as having the capability of tormenting men just as "a scorpion when it strikes a man."

Scorpions were common in the Wilderness of Judah and the Sinai Peninsula with its "fear-inspiring wilderness." (De 8:15) An ascent on the SE frontier of Judah, located SW of the southern end of the Dead Sea, was even called Akrabbim

(meaning "Scorpions").—Nu 34:4; Jos 15:3; Jg 1:36.

At 1 Kings 12:11, 14 and 2 Chronicles 10:11, 14, the Hebrew term 'aq·rab·bim', which is rendered "scourges," literally means "scorpions." The instrument of punishment alluded to may have been a scourge equipped with sharp points.

In illustrating that his heavenly Father would give holy spirit to those asking him, Jesus Christ pointed out that a human father would not hand his son a scorpion if he requested an egg. (Lu 11:12, 13) To the 70 disciples he sent out, Jesus gave authority over injurious things, represented by serpents and scorpions.—Lu 10:19; compare Eze 2:6.

SCOURGE. See BEATING; PLAGUE.

SCRIBE. A secretary or a copyist of the Scriptures; later, a person educated in the Law. The Hebrew word so·pher', which comes from a root meaning "count," is translated "secretary," "scribe," "copyist"; and the Greek word gram·ma·teus' is rendered "scribe" and "public instructor." The term implies one who has learning. The tribe of Zebulun had those who possessed "the equipment of a scribe" for numbering and enrolling troops. (Jg 5:14; compare 2Ki 25:19; 2Ch 26:11.) There were scribes, or secretaries, in connection with the temple. (2Ki 22:3) King Jehoash's secretary worked together with the high priest in counting money contributed and then gave it to those paying wages to the workers repairing the temple. (2Ki 12:10-12) Baruch wrote at the prophet Jeremiah's dictation. (Jer 36:32) Secretaries of King Ahasuerus of Persia worked under the direction of Haman in writing out the decree for the destruction of the Jews, and under Mordecai when the counterdecree was sent out.—Es 3:12; 8:9.

The Egyptian scribe was usually a man of the lower class but intelligent. He was well schooled. He carried his equipment, consisting of a palette with hollow places to hold ink of different colors, a water jug, and a reed-brush case. He was acquainted with the legal and business forms in use. For filling out such forms, taking dictation, and so forth, he received a fee.

In Babylon the scribe held a professional position. His services were practically indispensable, as the law required that business transactions be in writing, duly signed by the contracting parties and witnessed. The secretary would sit near the city gate, where most of the business was carried on, with his stylus and lump of clay, ready to sell his services whenever required. The scribes recorded business transactions, wrote letters, prepared documents, cared for temple records, and performed other clerical duties.

The Hebrew scribes acted as public notaries, prepared bills of divorce, and recorded other transactions. At least in later times they had no fixed fee, so one could bargain with them beforehand. Usually one of the parties to a transaction paid the fee, but sometimes both shared. Ezekiel, in his vision, saw a man with a recorder's inkhorn doing a marking work.—Eze 9:3, 4.

Scripture Copyists. It was in the days of Ezra the priest that the scribes (soh·pherim', "Sopherim") first began to come into prominence as a distinct group. They were copyists of the Hebrew Scriptures, very careful in their work and regarding mistakes with terror. As time went on they became extremely meticulous, going so far as to count not only the words copied but the letters also. Until centuries after Christ was on earth, the written Hebrew consisted only of consonants, and the omission or addition of a single letter often would have changed one word into another. If they detected the slightest error, the miswriting of a single letter, that entire section of the roll was rejected as unfit for synagogue use. Thereupon that section was cut out and replaced by a new and faultless one. They read aloud each word before writing. To write even a single word from memory was regarded as gross sin. Absurdities of practice crept in. It is said that the religious scribes prayerfully wiped their pen before writing the word 'Elo·him' (God) or 'Adho·nai' (Sovereign Lord).

But, despite this extreme care to avoid inadvertent errors, in process of time the Sopherim began to take liberties in making textual changes. In 134 passages the Sopherim changed the primitive Hebrew text to read 'Adho·nai' instead of YHWH. In other passages 'Elo·him' was the word used as a substitute. Many of the changes were made by the Sopherim because of superstition in connection with the divine name and to avoid anthropomorphisms, that is, attributing human attributes to God. (See JEHOVAH [Superstition hides the name].) The Masoretes, the name by which copyists came to be known centuries after Jesus' days on earth, took note of the alterations made by the earlier Sopherim, recording them in the margin or at the end of the Hebrew text. These marginal notes came to be known as the Masorah. In 15 passages in the Hebrew text, certain letters or words were marked by the Sopherim with extraordinary points, or dots. The meaning of these extraordinary points is disputed.

In standard Hebrew manuscripts the Masorah, that is, the small writing in the margins of the page or at the end of the text, contains a note opposite a number of Hebrew passages that reads: "This is one of the eighteen Emendations of the Sopherim," or similar words. These emendations were made evidently because the original passages in the Hebrew text appeared to show irreverence for Jehovah God or disrespect for his earthly representatives. However well intentioned, this was an unjustified alteration of God's Word. For a list of occurrences of emendations by the Sopherim, see the appendix of the *New World Translation*, page 1569.

Scribes as Teachers of the Law. At first the priests served as scribes. (Ezr 7:1-6) But great stress was laid on the need for every Jew to have a knowledge of the Law. Therefore those who studied and gained a great deal of knowledge were looked up to, and these scholars eventually formed an independent group, many not being priests. By the time Jesus came to earth the word "scribes," therefore, designated a class of men learned in the Law. They made the systematic study of the Law and its exposition their professional occupation. They were evidently among the teachers of the Law, the ones versed in the Law. (Lu 5:17; 11:45) They were generally associated with the religious sect of the Pharisees, for this body recognized the interpretations or "traditions" of the scribes that had developed in course of time into a bewildering maze of minute, technical regulations. The expression 'scribes of the Pharisees' appears several times in the Scriptures. (Mr 2:16; Lu 5:30; Ac 23:9) This may indicate that some scribes were Sadducees, who believed only in the *written* Law. The scribes of the Pharisees zealously defended the Law, but additionally upheld the traditions that had been developed, and they held sway over the thought of the people to an even greater extent than the priests. Primarily, the scribes were in Jerusalem, but they also were to be found all over Palestine and in other lands among the Jews of the Dispersion. —Mt 15:1; Mr 3:22; compare Lu 5:17.

The scribes were looked up to by the people and were called "Rabbi" (Gr., rhab·bei', "My great one; My excellent one"; from Heb., rav, meaning "many," "great"; a title of respect with which teachers were addressed) a title applied to Christ several places in the Scriptures. At John 1:38 it is interpreted as meaning "Teacher." Jesus was, in fact, the teacher of his disciples, but he forbade them, at Matthew 23:8, to covet that designation or to apply it to themselves as a title, as was done by the scribes. (Mt 23:2, 6, 7) The scribes of the Jews along with the Pharisees were strongly condemned by Jesus because they had added to the Law and had provided loopholes by which to circumvent the Law, so that he said to them: "You have made the word of God invalid because of your tradition." He cited an instance of this: They would permit one who should have helped his father or mother to avoid doing so—by claiming that the substance or possession he had with which he could help his parents was a gift dedicated to God.—Mt 15:1-9; Mr 7:10-13; see CORBAN.

Jesus declared that the scribes, like the Pharisees, had added many things, making the Law burdensome for the people to follow, loading the people down. Furthermore, as a class, they had no genuine love for the people nor did they desire to help them, being unwilling to use a finger to lighten the people's burdens. They loved the plaudits of men and high-sounding titles. Their religion was a front, a ritual, and they were hypocrites. Jesus showed how difficult their attitude and practices had made it for them to come into God's favor, saying to them: "Serpents, offspring of vipers, how are you to flee from the judgment of Gehenna?" (Mt 23:1-33) The scribes were heavily responsible, for they knew the Law. Yet they took away the key of knowledge. They were not content with refusing to acknowledge Jesus, of whom their copies of the Scriptures testified, but they added to their reprehensibility by fighting bitterly to keep anyone else from acknowledging him, yes, from listening to Jesus.—Lu 11:52; Mt 23:13; Joh 5:39; 1Th 2:14-16.

In their office, not only were the scribes as "rabbis" responsible for theoretic development of the Law and the teaching of the Law but they also had judicial authority, expressing sentence in courts of justice. There were scribes on the Jewish high court, the Sanhedrin. (Mt 26:57; Mr 15:1) They were not to receive any pay for judging, because the Law prohibited presents or bribes. Some rabbis may have had inherited wealth; almost all practiced a trade, of which they were proud, in that they were capable of supporting themselves aside from their rabbinic office. While they could not properly receive anything for work as judges, they may have expected and received pay for teaching the Law. This may be inferred from the words Jesus spoke when he warned the crowds about the greed of the scribes, also when he spoke of the hired man who did not care for the sheep. (Mr 12:37-40; Joh 10:12, 13) Peter warned Christian shepherds against making gain of their positions.—1Pe 5:2, 3.

Copyists of the Christian Greek Scriptures. In the apostle Paul's letter to the Colossians, he orders that the letter be read in the congregation of the Laodiceans in exchange for the one to Laodicea. (Col 4:16) No doubt all the congregations desired to read all the congregational letters of the apostles and their fellow members of the Christian governing body, and so copies were made for later consultation and to give them wider circulation. The ancient collections of Paul's letters (copies of the originals) stand as evidence that there was considerable copying and publication of them.

The Bible translator Jerome of the fourth century and Origen of the third century C.E. say that Matthew wrote his Gospel in Hebrew. It was directed primarily to Jews. But there were many Hellenized Jews among the Dispersion; so it may be that it was Matthew himself who later translated his Gospel into Greek. Mark wrote his Gospel mainly with Gentile readers in view, as is indicated by his explanations of Jewish customs and teachings, by his translations of certain expressions that would not be understood by Roman readers, and by other explanations. Both Matthew's and Mark's Gospels were intended for wide circulation, and of necessity, many copies would be made and distributed.

Christian copyists were not often professional, but having respect and high regard for the value of the inspired Christian writings, they copied them carefully. Typical of the work of these early Christian copyists is the oldest extant fragment of any of the Christian Greek Scriptures, the Papyrus Rylands No. 457. With writing on both sides, it consists of but some 100 letters (characters) of Greek and has been dated as early as the first half of the second century C.E. (PICTURE, Vol. 1, p. 323) While it has an informal air about it and makes no pretensions to be fine writing, it is a careful piece of work. Interestingly, this fragment is from a codex that most likely contained all of John's Gospel, or some 66 leaves, about 132 pages in all.

Bearing more extensive witness, but at later dates, are the Chester Beatty Biblical Papyri. These consist of portions of 11 Greek codices, produced between the second and fourth centuries C.E. They contain parts of 9 Hebrew and 15 Christian Bible books. These are quite representative in that a variety of writing styles is found in them. One codex is said to be "the work of a good professional scribe." Of another it is said: "The writing is very correct, and though without calligraphic pretensions, is the work of a competent scribe." And of still another, "The hand is rough, but generally correct."—*The Chester Beatty Biblical Papyri: Descriptions and Texts of Twelve Manuscripts on Papyrus of the Greek Bible,* by Frederic Kenyon, London, 1933, Fasciculus I, General Introduction, p. 14; 1933, Fasciculus II, The Gospels and Acts, Text, p. ix; 1936, Fasciculus III, Revelation, Preface.

More important than these characteristics, however, is their subject matter. In the main they corroborate those fourth-century vellum manuscripts termed the "Neutrals," which are rated most highly by textual scholars Westcott and Hort; among these are the Vatican No. 1209 and the Sinaiticus. Further, they contain none of the striking interpolations that are found in certain vellum manuscripts that have been termed, perhaps mistakenly, "Western."

There are extant thousands of manuscripts dating from especially the fourth century C.E. forward. That the copyists used extreme care is seen by scholars who have carefully studied and compared these manuscripts. Some of these scholars have made recensions or collations based on these comparisons. Such recensions form the basic texts for our modern translations. Scholars Westcott and Hort stated that "the amount of what can in any sense be called substantial variation is but a small fraction of the whole residuary variation, and can hardly form more than a thousandth part of the entire text." (*New Testament in the Original Greek,* Graz, 1974, Vol. II, p. 2) Sir Frederic Kenyon stated concerning the Chester Beatty Papyri: "The first and most important conclusion derived from the examination of them is the satisfactory one that they confirm the essential soundness of the existing texts. No striking or fundamental variation is shown either in the Old or the New Testament. There are no important omissions or additions of passages, and no variations which affect vital facts or doctrines. The variations of text affect minor matters, such as the order of words or the precise words used." —Fasciculus I, General Introduction, p. 15.

For several reasons, little remains of the earliest copyists' work today. Many of their copies of the Scriptures were destroyed during the time that Rome persecuted the Christians. Wear through use took its toll. Also, the hot, humid climate in some locations caused rapid deterioration. Additionally, as the professional scribes of the fourth century C.E. replaced papyrus manuscripts with vellum copies, there seemed to be no need of preserving the old papyrus copies.

The ink used by copyists in writing was a mixture of soot and gum made in a cake form and mixed in water for use. The pen consisted of a reed. The tip, when softened with water, resembled a brush. Writing was done on leather and papyrus in scrolls or rolls; later in codex form on sheets which, if bound, often had a wooden cover.

SCRIPTURE. As used in the Christian Greek Scriptures, the Greek word *gra·phe'* ("a writing") refers only to the sacred writings in God's Word the Bible. There were other documents used by the writers of both the Hebrew and the Greek Scriptures, such as official public genealogical records, histories, and so forth, but these were not regarded as inspired or on an equal level with the writings recognized as canonical. Even the apostles may have written other letters to certain congregations. For example, Paul's statement at 1 Corinthians 5:9: "In my letter I wrote you," implies that he wrote a previous letter to the Corinthians, one that is not now existent. Such writings evidently were not preserved by God's holy spirit for the Christian congregation because they were essential only to those to whom they were addressed.

The Greek word *gram'ma,* denoting a letter, or character of the alphabet, is drawn from the verb *gra'pho.* Used in the sense of "document," it is at times rendered "scripture" in some translations, "writing" in others. At John 5:47 and 2 Timothy 3: 15, the word is used with reference to inspired "writings" of the Hebrew Scriptures.—See CHRISTIAN GREEK SCRIPTURES; HEBREW SCRIPTURES.

Appealed To by Christ and Apostles. Jesus Christ and the writers of the Christian Scriptures often used the word *gra·phe'* in appealing to the writings of Moses and the prophets as their authority for their teaching or for their work, on the grounds that these writings were inspired by God. Frequently these Hebrew writings as a whole were designated "Scriptures." (Mt 21:42; Mr 14:49; Joh 5:39; Ac 17:11; 18:24, 28) Sometimes the singular form "Scripture" was used where a certain text was cited, referring to it as part of the entire body of writings in the Hebrew Scriptures. (Ro 9:17; Ga 3:8) Again, reference was made to a single text as a "scripture," with the sense of its being an authoritative statement. (Mr 12:10; Lu 4:21; Joh 19:24, 36, 37) At 2 Timothy 3:16 and 2 Peter 1:20, Paul and Peter appear to refer to both the inspired Hebrew and Greek writings as "Scripture." Peter classifies Paul's writings as part of the "Scriptures" at 2 Peter 3:15, 16.

The expression "prophetic scriptures" (Ro 16: 26) may have reference to the prophetic character of all the Hebrew Scriptures.—Compare Re 19:10.

Personified. Since the Scriptures were recognized as inspired by God, as his Word, the voice of God—God speaking, in effect—they were sometimes personified as though speaking with divine authority (just as God's holy spirit, or active force, was personified by Jesus, and was said to teach and to bear witness [Joh 14:26; 15:26]). (Joh 7:42; 19:37; Ro 4:3; 9:17) For the same reason the Scriptures are spoken of as though they possess the quality of foresight and the active power of preaching.—Ga 3:8; compare Mt 11:13; Ga 3:22.

Essential for Christians. Since Jesus Christ constantly appealed to the Hebrew Scriptures to support his teaching, it is important for his followers not to deviate from them. The apostle Paul emphasizes their value and essential nature when he says: "All Scripture is inspired of God and beneficial for teaching, for reproving, for setting things straight, for disciplining in righteousness, that the man of God may be fully competent, completely equipped for every good work."—2Ti 3:16, 17.

SCRIPTURE-CONTAINING CASE.

A relatively small case containing four portions of the Law (Ex 13:1-10, 11-16; De 6:4-9; 11:13-21) and worn by Jewish men on their forehead and left arm. Concerning the practice of wearing such cases, or phylacteries, *The Jewish Encyclopedia* (1976, Vol. X, p. 21) observes: "The laws governing the wearing of phylacteries were derived by the Rabbis from four Biblical passages (Deut. vi. 8, xi. 18; Ex. xiii. 9, 16). While these passages were interpreted literally by most commentators, . . . the Rabbis held that the general law only was expressed in the Bible, the application and elaboration of it being entirely matters of tradition and inference."

Christ Jesus censured the scribes and Pharisees for 'broadening the scripture-containing cases that they wore as safeguards.' (Mt 23:5) By enlarging these cases, they apparently wanted to give others the impression that they were very zealous and conscientious about the Law. Jesus' words indicate that the religious leaders viewed these cases as safeguards, or charms. The Greek word *phy·lak·te'ri·on*, in fact, primarily means an outpost, fortification, or safeguard.—See FRONTLET BAND.

SCROLL, ROLL.

The common book form during the period of Bible writing. The Scriptures were written and often copied on rolls or scrolls of leather, parchment, or papyrus. (Jer 36:1, 2, 28, 32; Joh 20:30; Ga 3:10; 2Ti 4:13; Re 22:18, 19) A scroll was made by gluing together pieces of such materials to form a long sheet, which was then rolled around a stick. For a very long scroll, a stick was used at each end and the scroll was rolled on both sticks toward the center. When about to read such a roll, a person unrolled it with one hand while rolling it up with the other until he located the desired place. After reading, he again rolled up the scroll.—For details as to material, size, and so forth, see BOOK.

Bears Witness to Jesus. Jesus Christ came to earth to do God's will, as foretold within the Hebrew Scriptures, in "the roll of the book." (Ps 40:7, 8; Heb 10:7-9) In the synagogue at Nazareth, Jesus opened the scroll of Isaiah and read the prophetic words about his anointing by Jehovah's spirit to preach. Christ then rolled up the scroll, handed it to the attendant, sat down, and explained to all present: "Today this scripture that you just heard is fulfilled." (Lu 4:16-21; Isa 61:1, 2) In fact, since "the bearing witness to Jesus is what inspires prophesying," all the scrolls of all the Scriptures and the public proclamation of the good news contained in the scrolls of the Christian Scriptures concerns Jesus Christ's position and work in Jehovah's purpose.—Re 19:10.

At the conclusion of John's Gospel account, he said: "There are, in fact, many other things also which Jesus did, which, if ever they were written in full detail, I suppose, the world itself could not contain the scrolls written." (Joh 21:25) John in his Gospel did not try to write it all, but he wrote only what was sufficient to establish his main point, namely, that Jesus Christ was the Son of God and His Messiah. Indeed, there is enough in John's "scroll," as well as the other inspired Scriptures, to prove to the fullest satisfaction that "Jesus is the Christ the Son of God."—Joh 20:30, 31.

Symbolic Use. There are several instances of symbolic use of the word "scroll" in the Bible. Ezekiel and Zechariah each saw a scroll with writing on both sides. Since only one side of a scroll was commonly used, writing on both sides may refer to the weightiness, extent, and seriousness of the judgments written in these scrolls. (Eze 2:9–3:3; Zec 5:1-4) In the vision of Revelation, the one on the throne held in his right hand a scroll having seven seals, preventing detection of what was written until God's Lamb opened them. (Re 5:1, 12; 6:1, 12-14) Later in the vision John himself was presented a scroll and was commanded to eat it. It tasted sweet to John but made his belly bitter. Since the scroll was open and not sealed, it was something that was to be understood. It was "sweet" to John to get the message contained therein but apparently had bitter things for him to prophesy, as he was told to do. (Re 10:1-11) Ezekiel had a similar experience with the scroll presented to him in which there were "dirges and moaning and wailing." —Eze 2:10.

"The scroll of life of the Lamb." Idolatrous worshipers of the symbolic "wild beast" are not God's choice for the associates of the Lamb. Hence, "the name of not one of them stands written in the scroll of life of the Lamb who was slaughtered," and "from the founding of the world" of mankind it was determined that this would be the case.—Re 13:1-8; 21:27.

Scrolls of judgment and of life. John also observed that "scrolls were opened" and resurrected ones were "judged out of those things written in the scrolls according to their deeds." These scrolls apparently contain Jehovah's laws and instructions setting forth the divine will for humans during that judgment period, and it is their deeds of obedience in faith or of disobedience to what is written in the scrolls that reveal whether their names are worthy of having their names written or retained in Jehovah's "scroll of life." —Re 20:11-15; see LIFE.

'Rolled up like a book scroll.' At Isaiah 34:4, the prophet speaks judgment against the nations, saying: "And the heavens must be rolled up, just like a book scroll." Evidently he here refers to the rolling up and putting away of a scroll after one has finished reading it. So the expression is a symbol of the putting away or doing away with that which is no longer of any use or value.

SCYTHIAN
(Scyth′i·an). A fierce, nomadic people generally associated with the region N and NE of the Black Sea. Evidence suggests that they extended their roaming to western Siberia near the border of Mongolia. In the first century C.E. the word "Scythian" implied the worst of uncivilized people. However, even such persons could become Christians and have an equal standing with other believers as members of Christ's body. Wrote the apostle Paul: "There is neither Greek nor Jew, circumcision nor uncircumcision, foreigner, Scythian, slave, freeman, but Christ is all things and in all."—Col 3:11; see CUTTINGS.

SEA.
The collective waters of the earth as distinguished from land; or a large body of salt or fresh water, usually meaning a body smaller than an ocean and partially or wholly enclosed by land. Water covers over 70 percent of the earth's surface.

Jehovah the Creator and Controller. The Bible repeatedly acknowledges Jehovah as the Creator of the seas, which were formed as distinct from the dry land on the third creative day. (Ge 1:9, 10, 13; Ne 9:6; Ac 4:24; 14:15; Re 14:7) It also comments on his ability to extend his power over the sea and to control it. (Job 26:12; Ps 65:7; 89:9; Jer 31:35) When his Son was on earth he was given authority by his Father to command the sea, with effectiveness. (Mt 8:23-27; Mr 4:36-41; Joh 6:17-20) God's control of the seas is demonstrated by the way the coasts and the tides keep the sea within its set limits, barricaded, as it were, by doors. (Job 38:8-11; Ps 33:7; Pr 8:29; Jer 5:22; see SAND.) This accomplishment in connection with the sea, as well as its role in the earth's water cycle (Ec 1:7; Am 5:8), makes the sea an example of Jehovah's wonderful works. (Ps 104:24, 25) Poetically speaking, even the seas join in praising their Creator.—Ps 96:11; 98:7.

Seas in the Area of Israel. Of the seas in the area of Israel, the most prominent was "the Great [Mediterranean] Sea," also called "the western sea" or simply "the Sea." (Jos 1:4; De 11:24; Nu 34:5) Others were the Red Sea, or the Egyptian Sea (Ex 10:19; Isa 11:15); the Salt (Dead) Sea, the Sea of the Arabah, or "the eastern sea" (De 3:17; Eze 47:18); and the Sea of Galilee, the Sea of Chinnereth, or the Sea of Tiberias. (Mt 4:18; Nu 34:11; Joh 6:1; see GALILEE, SEA OF; GREAT SEA; RED SEA; SALT SEA.) In Biblical references the particular body of water intended by the expression "the sea" often has to be determined from the context. (Ex 14:2 [compare 13:18]; Mr 2:13 [compare vs 1].) Sometimes the Hebrew term is applied to rivers.—Jer 51:36 (speaking of the Euphrates); Isa 19:5 (the Nile).

The Abyss. According to Parkhurst's Greek and English Lexicon to the New Testament (London, 1845, p. 2), the Greek word a′bys·sos, meaning "very or exceedingly deep" and often translated "abyss," is sometimes used with reference to or in making a comparison to the sea because of the sea's great, seemingly fathomless, depth. (Ro 10:6, 7; compare De 30:12, 13.) In the symbols of Revelation, "the wild beast that ascends out of the abyss" (Re 11:7) is said, at Revelation 13:1, to ascend out of "the sea."—See ABYSS.

Origin of Sea Life. The Genesis account reports that sea life and flying creatures were the first animal life on earth. It reads: "And God went on to say: 'Let the waters swarm forth a swarm of living souls and let flying creatures fly over the earth upon the face of the expanse of the heavens.' And God proceeded to create the great sea monsters and every living soul that moves about, which the waters swarmed forth according to their kinds, and every winged flying creature according to its kind. And God got to see that it was good. With that God blessed them, saying: 'Be fruitful and become many and fill the waters in the sea basins, and let the flying creatures become many in the earth.' And there came to be evening and there came to be morning, a fifth day."—Ge 1:20-23.

In saying "Let the waters swarm," God was not leaving the emergence of life to the seas themselves, to bring forth some primeval form from which all other animals evolved. For the account also says that "God proceeded to create [marine creatures] . . . according to their kinds." Also in the record of the 'sixth day' and the creation of land animals, God is represented as saying: "Let the earth put forth living souls according to their kinds." God did not command the sea to put forth living things for the land, or let these things evolve from the sea, but "God proceeded to make" each kind to suit the habitat each was to occupy. —Ge 1:24, 25.

Illustrative Use. While the Promised Land was to extend "from the Red Sea to the sea of the Philistines [the Mediterranean Sea] and from the wilderness to the River [Euphrates]," the description of the dominion of the coming Messianic King as being "from sea to sea and from the River to the ends of the earth" would apparently refer to the entire globe. (Ex 23:31; Zec 9:9, 10; compare Da 2:34, 35, 44, 45.) This is indicated by Matthew and John in their application of the prophecy of Zechariah, in which prophecy Zechariah quotes Psalm 72:8.—Mt 21:4-9; Joh 12:12-16.

Overflowing armies. Jeremiah described the sound of the attackers of Babylon as being "like the sea that is boisterous." (Jer 50:42) Hence, when he foretold that "the sea" would come up over Babylon, he evidently meant the flood of conquering troops under the Medes and Persians. —Jer 51:42; compare Da 9:26.

Masses alienated from God. Isaiah likened the wicked people of earth, the masses alienated from God, to "the sea that is being tossed, when it is unable to calm down, the waters of which keep tossing up seaweed and mire." (Isa 57:20) At Revelation 17:1, 15 the "waters" on which Babylon the Great "sits" are said to mean "peoples and crowds and nations and tongues." Isaiah further prophesied to God's "woman" Zion: "Because to you the wealthiness of the sea will direct itself; the very resources of the nations will come to you." (Isa 59:20; 60:1, 5) This seems to mean the turning of many persons from among the multitudes of earth toward God's symbolic "woman."

Daniel described four "beasts" that came up "out of the sea" and revealed these to be symbolic of political kings or kingdoms. (Da 7:2, 3, 17, 23) Similarly, John spoke of a "wild beast ascending out of the sea," that is, out of that vast portion of mankind that is estranged from God; and his mention, in symbolic language, of a political organization with this beast out of "the sea." (Re 13:1, 2) He also saw in vision the time when there would be "a new heaven and a new earth" and when "the sea," that is, the turbulent masses of people alienated from God, would be no more.—Re 21:1.

Persons lacking faith. A person who lacks faith, having doubts when he prays to God, is likened by the disciple James to "a wave of the sea driven by the wind and blown about." He does not recognize or appreciate God's fine qualities of generosity and loving-kindness. "Let not that man suppose that he will receive anything from Jehovah; he is an indecisive man, unsteady in all his ways," James declares.—Jas 1:5-8.

Immoral men. James' brother Jude warns his fellow Christians of the great danger from wicked men who slip into the congregation with the purpose of bringing in moral defilement. He calls them "wild waves of the sea that foam up their own causes for shame." (Jude 4-13) Jude may have had in mind an earlier expression of Isaiah (57:20) and may be figuratively describing such ones' passionate, reckless disregard for God's laws and their rushing against the divinely constituted moral barriers in their degraded, lustful course. As Cook's *Commentary* on Jude 13 remarks: "They cast forth to public view the mire and dirt of their excesses . . . So these men foam out their own acts of shame, and cast them forth for all men to see, and so to blame the Church for the ill-deeds of these professors." Another commentator says: "What they impart is as unsubstantial and valueless as the foam of the ocean waves, and the result is in fact a proclamation of their own shame."—*Barnes' Notes on the New Testament,* 1974; compare Peter's description of such men at 2Pe 2:10-22.

SEAH (se'ah). A dry measure that, according to rabbinic sources, is equal to one third of an ephah. (Ge 18:6; 1Sa 25:18; 1Ki 18:32; 2Ki 7:1, 16, 18) Since, on the basis of archaeological evidence regarding the capacity of the corresponding liquid bath measure (compare Eze 45:11), the ephah measure is reckoned at 22 L (20 dry qt), the seah measure would equal 7.33 L (6.66 dry qt).

SEAL. An object used to make an impression (usually on clay or wax) that indicated ownership, authenticity, or agreement. Ancient seals consisted of a piece of hard material (stone, ivory, or wood) having engraved letters or designs in reverse. They were made in various shapes, including cones, squares, cylinders, scarabs, and animal heads. (Regarding signet or seal rings, see RING.) Those in the form of a cylinder commonly measured between 2 and 4 cm (0.75 to 1.5 in.) in length. When a cylinder that was engraved on its curved surface was rolled on moist clay, it produced a continuous impression in relief. Often cylinder seals were pierced through from end to end and thus could be suspended from a cord.

Religious symbols, as well as plants, animals, and simple scenes, are among the things depicted on Egyptian and Mesopotamian seals. The

Ancient cylinder seal, along with the clay impression; it depicts worshipers flanking a tree, with water birds below

Babylonian "Temptation" Seal (British Museum) shows a tree with a man seated on one side and a woman on the other, and behind the woman is an erect serpent. Often seals gave the owner's name and his position. For example, one seal found in Palestine reads, "Belonging to Shema, the minister of Jeroboam."—*The Biblical World*, edited by C. Pfeiffer, 1966, p. 515.

Seal impressions could indicate ownership or authenticity and could prevent tampering with documents or other things that were sealed, including bags, doors, and tombs. (Job 14:17; Da 6:17; Mt 27:66) When the prophet Jeremiah purchased a field, the copy of the deed bearing the signatures of witnesses was sealed, but a second copy was left open. Perhaps the sealing was done by folding the deed closed, tying it with a cord, and then putting a lump of wax or other soft substance on the cord and impressing the soft material with a seal. If later any question would arise about the accuracy of the open copy, the deed that had been sealed before witnesses could

be produced. (Jer 32:10-14, 44) A person entrusted with the king's seal could issue official decrees, the seal impression stamping the decrees as authentic. (1Ki 21:8; Es 3:10, 12; 8:2, 8, 10) Affixing one's seal to a document could signify an acceptance of the terms contained therein. (Ne 9:38; 10:1) Numerous ancient jar handles with seal impressions on them have been found. Some of these seal impressions identified the owner of the jars and their contents; others gave an indication of the quantity or quality of the contents.

Figurative Use. The actual uses for seals provide the basis for a number of figurative expressions found in the Bible. It was foretold that the Messiah would "imprint a seal upon vision and prophet." This is because, by fulfilling the prophecies, the Messiah would stamp them as authentic and inspired of God. (Da 9:24; compare Joh 3:33.) In the sense of a mark of possession, or ownership, Abraham received circumcision as a "seal" of the righteousness that he had. (Ro 4:11) Since the apostle Paul had helped many Corinthian Christians to become believers, they served as a seal confirming the genuineness of his apostleship. (1Co 9:1, 2) First-century Christians are spoken of as being "sealed" by means of holy spirit, which is an advance token of their heavenly inheritance. (Eph 1:13, 14; 4:30) The seal signifies their being God's possession (2Co 1:21, 22) and shows that they are truly in line for heavenly life. The book of Revelation shows the number finally sealed to be 144,000.—Re 7:2-4; 9:4.

The Bible speaks of something that is closed, hidden, or secret as being sealed. Prophetic messages were "sealed" during the time they were not understood. (Da 12:4, 9; Re 5:1; 22:10; compare Isa 8:16; 29:11.) And Jehovah is said to 'put a seal around stars,' evidently meaning that he hides them from view by means of clouds.—Job 9:7.

SEALSKIN. There is uncertainty as to the particular kind of skin referred to as *ta'chash;* this Hebrew word is used in describing the outer cover of the tabernacle and a wrapping for the furnishings and utensils of the sanctuary for transport. *Ta'chash* or *techa·shim'* (plural) usually appears alongside *'ohr* or *'oh·rohth'* (skin, skins). (Ex 25:5; 26:14; 35:7, 23; 36:19; 39:34; Nu 4:6-14, 25; Eze 16:10) The translators of the Greek *Septuagint* seem to have understood the Hebrew word to denote, not an animal, but the color blue. (Compare Nu 4:14, ftn.) However, the almost unanimous opinion of Jewish commentators is that *ta'chash* refers to an animal. This view was also endorsed by the Hebrew lexicographer Gesenius, who considered the *Septuagint* reading to be simply conjecture, a rendering having the support neither of etymology nor of related languages. He understood *ta'chash* to mean either the seal or the badger, basing his conclusions on the context, the authority of the Talmudists, a comparison of the Hebrew word with similar words in other languages, and Hebrew etymology.

Bible translators have variously rendered *'ohr* (*'oh·rohth'*) *ta'chash* (*techa·shim'*) as "badgers' skin(s)" (*KJ*), "goatskin(s)" (*RS*), "porpoise skin(s)" (*AT*), "sealskin(s)" (*AS*), "leather" (*Mo*), "fine leather" (*JB*), "violet skins" (*Dy*), and "tahash leather" (*NW*, Ex 25:5, ftn, but "sealskins" in main text). The rendering "badgers' skin(s)" is not generally favored by scholars, since it is thought unlikely that the Israelites would have been able to procure enough badger skins, either in Egypt or in the wilderness, for covering the tabernacle. There are also scholars who consider neither "badgers' skin(s)" nor "sealskin(s)" nor "porpoise skin(s)" to be correct, in view of the fact that badgers, seals, porpoises or dolphins, dugongs, and similar creatures were evidently unclean for food. (Le 11:12, 27) They therefore find it hard to conceive that the skin of an "unclean" animal would have been used for something so sacred as the construction of the tabernacle and as a protective covering for the furnishings and utensils of the sanctuary. Those taking this view suggest that *ta'chash* may designate the skin of a clean animal, possibly of a kind of antelope, sheep, or goat.

Usable, Though Seal Classed as Unclean. The fact that seals were evidently unclean for food would not necessarily rule out using their skins as a covering for the tabernacle. For instance, whereas the lion and the eagle were "unclean" (Le 11:13, 27), the heavenly cherubs seen by Ezekiel in vision were depicted with four faces, including that of a lion and of an eagle. (Eze 1:5, 10; 10:14) Also, the copper carriages that Solomon made for temple use were adorned with representations of lions, and this undoubtedly according to the plans given to David by divine inspiration. (1Ki 7:27-29; 1Ch 28:11-19) The Israelites used "unclean" animals, such as asses, for mounts, it even being foretold that the Messiah would ride into Jerusalem upon an ass. (Zec 9:9; Mt 21:4, 5) Although John the Baptizer had a most sacred commission to "go in advance before Jehovah to make his ways ready," he wore clothing made from the hair of an "unclean" animal. (Lu 1:76; Mt 3:4; Le 11:4) All of this tends to indicate that the distinction between clean and unclean was simply dietary, though at times it was also used with reference to sacrifice, and did not require that the Israelites regard "unclean" animals with general abhorrence. (Le 11:46, 47) Also, these, like the "clean" animals, were created by God and were therefore good, not loathsome in themselves.—Ge 1:21, 25.

How Obtainable by Israelites. If the *ta'-chash* of the Bible does designate a kind of seal, then a question may arise as to how it was possible for the Israelites to obtain sealskins. While seals are generally associated with Arctic and Antarctic regions, some seals favor warmer climates. Today a few monk seals still inhabit part of the Mediterranean Sea, as well as other warmer waters. Over the centuries man has greatly reduced the number of seals, and in Bible times these animals may have been abundant in the Mediterranean and in the Red Sea. As late as 1832 an English edition of Calmet's *Dictionary of the Holy Bible* (p. 139) observed: "On many of the small islands of the Red sea, around the peninsula of Sinai, are found seals."—See also *The Tabernacle's Typical Teaching*, by A. J. Pollock, London, p. 47.

The ancient Egyptians engaged in commerce on the Red Sea and, of course, received goods from many of the Mediterranean regions. So the Egyptians would have had access to sealskins. Hence, when the Israelites left Egypt, they might have taken with them the sealskins they already had, along with others obtained when the Egyptians gave into their hands an abundance of valuable things.—Ex 12:35, 36.

SEA MONSTER. This generally translates the Hebrew word *tan·nin'* (*tan·nim'*, "sea monster" at Eze 29:3 and "marine monster" at Eze 32:2). This term is rendered "big snake" when not mentioned in connection with the sea or water (Jer 51:34) or when a reference to snakes is definitely indicated by the context. (Ex 7:9, 12; compare Ex 4:2, 3.) Undoubtedly *tan·nin'* includes a variety of large marine animals (Ge 1:21; Ps 148:7), but this term is usually employed in a figurative sense. The destruction of Pharaoh and his hosts appears to be alluded to by the phrase: "You [Jehovah] broke the heads of the sea monsters in the waters." (Ps 74:13) At Isaiah 51:9, "sea monster" appears in parallel with Rahab (Egypt; compare Isa 30:7) and hence may denote Egypt, or the reference may be to Pharaoh, as in Ezekiel 29:3 and 32:2. Faithful Job asked whether he himself was "a sea monster" that had to have a guard set over him. —Job 7:12; see LEVIATHAN.

SEASONS. A season is a period during which a specific type of agricultural work is normal or a certain kind of weather prevails; a suitable or appointed time for something.

As the earth revolves around the sun, the tilt of the earth's axis at an angle to the plane of the ecliptic produces a cycle of weather seasons. As markers of the passing of time, the heavenly bodies serve as indicators of seasons. (Ge 1:14) Genesis 8:22 says that the earth's seasons will "never cease." For a correlation of the months of the Jewish and Gregorian calendars and the festival, weather, and agricultural seasons, see CALENDAR.

Closely connected with the agricultural seasons were the annual "festival seasons" when the festivals established by the Mosaic Law were celebrated. (1Ch 23:31; 2Ch 31:3) Hence, when Paul counseled some Jewish Christians who were "scrupulously observing days and months and seasons," he meant the festival seasons that were a part of the Law, not simply weather or agricultural seasons.—Ga 4:10.

"Season" can therefore refer to a fixed or an appointed time or a period possessed of certain characteristics. (Ac 3:19, ftn; Ro 8:18; Ga 6:9) In time what constituted healthful teaching and proper conduct were made very clear to Christians. Accordingly, it was the "season" to be awake. (Ro 13:11-14) The "times or seasons," or periods when Jehovah's will in certain matters would take place, were of real interest to his worshipers (Ac 1:7), who understood them as they were progressively revealed.—1Th 5:1.

In regard to the dwelling of nations on the earth, God "decreed the appointed times" (Ac 17:26; "fixed the epochs of their history," NE) in that he determined when certain changes should occur, such as when the divinely appointed time came to uproot the Canaanite inhabitants of the Promised Land.—Ge 15:13-21; Jer 25:8-11; Da 2:21; 7:12; see APPOINTED TIMES OF THE NATIONS.

SEAT. See JUDGMENT SEAT.

SEBA (Se′ba).

1. One of the five sons of Cush.—Ge 10:7; 1Ch 1:9.

2. A people of E Africa. At Isaiah 43:3 Seba is linked with Egypt and Ethiopia (Cush), in being given as a ransom in place of Jacob. In a similar listing, Isaiah 45:14 has "Sabeans" in place of "Seba," indicating that the people of Seba were called Sabeans. These verses suggest that Seba bordered on or was included in Ethiopia. This is supported by Josephus, who says that "Saba" ap-

plied to the city of Meroë on the Nile and to the large section (Isle of Meroë) between the Nile, Blue Nile, and Atbara rivers. (*Jewish Antiquities,* II, 249, [x, 2]) The reference to these Sabeans as "tall men" (Isa 45:14) is borne out by Herodotus (III, 20), who speaks of the Ethiopians as "the tallest and fairest of all men."—See CUSH Nos. 1 and 2.

Meroë was long an important trading place. Among the distant places mentioned in Psalm 72 in describing the dominion and influence of the one Jehovah would appoint as King, Seba and Sheba are named as places whose kings would present a gift.—Ps 72:10; Joe 3:8.

SEBAM (Se′bam). Apparently an alternate name for Sibmah.—Nu 32:3, 38; see SIBMAH.

SECACAH (Se·ca′cah) [from a root meaning "cover; screen over"]. A city of Judah in the wilderness. (Jos 15:20, 61) Secacah is often identified with Khirbet es-Samrah, on a hill about 6 km (3.5 mi) W of the northern part of the Dead Sea. This is in the heart of el Buqei′a (Biq′at Hureqan-ya), a barren plateau, in the northern section of the Judean Wilderness.

SECRET. See SACRED SECRET.

SECRETARY. Usually an appointed official skilled at writing and keeping records. The Hebrew word so·pher′ can also be rendered "scribe" and "copyist."

At least at times in Israel there was a trusted court official of high rank called "the secretary of the king" or "the secretary." (2Ch 24:11; 2Ki 19:2) He was not simply a scribe who was employed in making documents, nor was he merely a copyist of the Law. (Jg 5:14; Ne 13:13; compare 2Sa 8:15-18; 20:23-26; see COPYIST; SCRIBE.) On occasion the secretary of the king handled financial matters (2Ki 12:10, 11) and spoke as a representative of the king, in a capacity similar to that of a 'foreign secretary.' (Isa 36:2-4, 22; 37:2, 3) Under Solomon's rule two of the "princes" are named as secretaries.—1Ki 4:2, 3; compare 2Ch 26:11; 34:13.

In addition to "the secretary of the king," the Bible mentions "the secretary of the chief of the army" (2Ki 25:19; Jer 52:25) and "the secretary of the Levites." (1Ch 24:6) Baruch was a scribal secretary for Jeremiah.—Jer 36:32.

SECRETARY'S INKHORN. At Ezekiel 9:2, 3, 11 the man in linen responsible to mark individuals on the forehead is described as having "a secretary's inkhorn at his hips," such evidently being held in place by the girdle about his waist.

This secretary's inkhorn may have been similar to those used at one time in ancient Egypt. The Egyptian 'scribe kit' was a long, narrow case made out of wood and had a compartment or slots for reed pens. On the outer face, near the top, it had at least one recess for a small cake of dried ink. The scribe could prepare to write by applying the moistened end of his pen to the ink. Inscriptions show that Syrian scribes used a similar 'scribal kit.'

SECT. The Greek word (*hai're·sis*, from which comes the English word "heresy") thus translated means "choice" (Le 22:18, *LXX*) or "that which is chosen," hence "a body of men separating themselves from others and following their own tenets [*a sect* or *party*]." (Thayer's *Greek-English Lexicon of the New Testament*, 1889, p. 16) This term is applied to the adherents of the two prominent branches of Judaism, the Pharisees and Sadducees. (Ac 5:17; 15:5; 26:5) Non-Christians also called Christianity a "sect" or "the sect of the Nazarenes," possibly viewing it as a break-off from Judaism.—Ac 24:5, 14; 28:22.

The founder of Christianity, Jesus Christ, prayed that unity might prevail among his followers (Joh 17:21), and the apostles were vitally interested in preserving the oneness of the Christian congregation. (1Co 1:10; Jude 17-19) Disunity in belief could give rise to fierce disputing, dissension, and even enmity. (Compare Ac 23:7-10.) So sects were to be avoided, being among the works of the flesh. (Ga 5:19-21) Christians were warned against becoming promoters of sects or being led astray by false teachers. (Ac 20:28; 2Ti 2:17, 18; 2Pe 2:1) In his letter to Titus, the apostle Paul directed that, after being admonished twice, a man who continued promoting a sect be rejected, evidently meaning that he be expelled from the congregation. (Tit 3:10) Those who refused to become involved in creating divisions within the congregation or in supporting a particular faction would distinguish themselves by their faithful course and give evidence of having God's approval. This is apparently what Paul meant when telling the Corinthians: "There must also be sects among you, that the persons approved may also become manifest among you." —1Co 11:19.

SECU (Se'cu). Apparently the name of a site with a great cistern where Saul inquired as to the whereabouts of David and Samuel. (1Sa 19:21, 22) Secu was near Ramah, but its exact location is now unknown. Instead of the proper name "Secu," some scholars, following certain Greek and Latin manuscripts, prefer such expressions as

"the threshing-floor on the bare hill [height]." —*JB, AT*.

SECUNDUS (Se·cun'dus) [from Lat., meaning "Second"]. A Thessalonian Christian who accompanied Paul through Macedonia into Asia Minor on the return leg of the apostle's third missionary journey, probably in the spring of 56 C.E. How far Secundus went with Paul is not stated.—Ac 20:3-5.

SEDITION. The Greek word *sta'sis*, which basically means "standing" (Heb 9:8), came to have the meaning "a standing [off]" or "sedition." (Mr 15:7; Lu 23:19, 25, *Int*) It can also be rendered "dissension" (Ac 15:2), and sometimes it embraces the idea of violence.—Ac 23:7, 10.

It was a capital offense under Roman law to engage in sedition or to promote or take part in a riot. Thus the city recorder was alerting the riotous mob in Ephesus of their peril when he said: "We are really in danger of being charged with sedition over today's affair, no single cause existing that will permit us to render a reason for this disorderly mob." (Ac 19:40) And Tertullus' accusation before Roman Governor Felix that Paul was "stirring up seditions among all the Jews" was a very serious one. If found guilty, Paul would have been punished with death.—Ac 24:5.

SEED. The Hebrew *ze'ra'* and the Greek *sper'ma*, both translated "seed," appear many times in the Scriptures, with the following uses or applications: (a) agricultural and botanical, (b) physiological, and (c) figurative for "offspring."

Agricultural, Botanical. Israel's economy was primarily agricultural, hence much is said about sowing, planting, and harvesting, and "seed" is mentioned frequently, the first instance being in the record of earth's third creative day. Jehovah commanded: "Let the earth cause grass to shoot forth, vegetation bearing seed, fruit trees yielding fruit according to their kinds, the seed of which is in it, upon the earth." (Ge 1:11, 12, 29) Here the Creator revealed his purpose to clothe the earth with vegetation by reproduction through seed, keeping the various created kinds separate, so that each brings forth "according to its kind" through its own distinctive seed.

Physiological. The Hebrew term *ze'ra'* is used in a physiological sense at Leviticus 15:16-18; 18:20, with reference to an emission of semen. At Leviticus 12:2 the causative form of the verb *za·ra'* (sow) is rendered in many translations by the English expressions "conceive" or "conceive seed." At Numbers 5:28 a passive form of *za·ra'* appears with *ze'ra'* and is rendered "made pregnant with semen" (*NW*), "sown with seed" (*Yg*), "conceive seed" (*KJ*).

Figurative Use. In the majority of instances in which the word *ze'ra'* appears in the Bible, it is used with reference to offspring, or posterity. Animal offspring are designated by this term at Genesis 7:3. Human offspring of Noah are referred to at Genesis 9:9; those of the woman Hagar at Genesis 16:10. God commanded Abram and his natural "seed" to be circumcised as a sign of the covenant God was making with them.—Ge 17:7-11.

The Greek word *sper'ma* is used in the same applications as the Hebrew *ze'ra'*. (Compare Mt 13:24; 1Co 15:38; Heb 11:11; Joh 7:42.) Jesus Christ used the related word *spo'ros* (thing sown) to symbolize the word of God.—Lu 8:11.

A Sacred Secret. At the time God judged Adam and Eve, he spoke a prophecy that gave hope to their offspring, saying to the serpent: "I shall put enmity between you and the woman and between your seed and her seed. He will bruise you in the head and you will bruise him in the heel." (Ge 3:15) From the beginning, the identity of the promised "seed" was a sacred secret of God.

This prophetic statement revealed that there would be a deliverer who would destroy the one really represented by the serpent, namely, the great serpent and enemy of God, Satan the Devil. (Re 12:9) It also indicated that the Devil would have a "seed." It would require time for the two seeds to be brought forth and for enmity to develop between them.

The seed of the Serpent. We note that when the Bible speaks of "seed" in a symbolic sense, it does not refer to literal children, or offspring, but to those who follow the pattern of their symbolic "father," those having his spirit or disposition. Adam and Eve's first son Cain is an example of one of the Serpent's offspring. The apostle John writes enlighteningly on this point: "The children of God and the children of the Devil are evident by this fact: Everyone who does not carry on righteousness does not originate with God, neither does he who does not love his brother. For this is the message which you have heard from the beginning, that we should have love for one another; not like Cain, who *originated with the wicked one* and slaughtered his brother. And for the sake of what did he slaughter him? Because his own works were wicked, but those of his brother were righteous."—1Jo 3:10-12; compare Joh 8:44.

Thus the seed of the Serpent throughout the centuries consisted of those who had the spirit of the Devil, who hated God and fought God's people, and it included particularly the religious persons who claimed to serve God but who were actually false, hypocrites. Jesus identified the Jewish religious leaders of his day as a part of the Serpent's seed, saying to them: "Serpents, offspring [Gr., *gen·ne'ma·ta,* "generated ones"] of vipers, how are you to flee from the judgment of Gehenna?"—Mt 23:33, *Int.*

There was a gradual revelation of features of God's secret concerning the promised "seed" of the woman. The questions to be answered were: Would the seed be heavenly or earthly? If spiritual or heavenly, would it nevertheless run an earthly course? Would the seed be *one* or *many*? How would it destroy the Serpent and liberate mankind?

As has already been shown, the serpent to whom Jehovah was directing his words recorded at Genesis 3:15 was not the animal on the ground. Obviously, it could not understand an issue such as was involved here, a challenge of Jehovah's sovereignty. Therefore, as later developments revealed, God was speaking to an intelligent individual, his archenemy Satan the Devil. The book of Job enlightens us on this matter, as there we find Satan presenting his accusation against Job's integrity to Jehovah in order to support his challenge against God's sovereignty. (Job 1:6-12; 2:1-5) The "father," then, of the seed of the serpent would be, not a literal animal serpent, but an angelic, spirit "father," Satan the Devil.

'Seed of the woman' spiritual. Accordingly, regardless of how faithful men of old may have viewed the matter, it becomes clear, in the light of the Christian Scriptures, that the promised 'seed of the woman' would have to be more than human in order to 'bruise in the head' this spiritual enemy, this angelic person, the Devil. The "seed" would have to be a mighty spirit person. How would he be provided, and who would be his 'mother,' the "woman"?

The next recorded mention of the promised "seed" came over 2,000 years later, to faithful Abraham. Abraham was of the line of Shem, and in an earlier prophecy Noah had spoken of Jehovah as "Shem's God." (Ge 9:26) This indicated God's favor on Shem. In Abraham's time the "seed" of promise was foretold to come through Abraham. (Ge 15:5; 22:15-18) Priest Melchizedek's blessing on Abraham gave additional confirmation of this. (Ge 14:18-20) While God's statement to Abraham revealed that Abraham would

SEED

have offspring, it also disclosed that the ancestral line of the prophetically promised "seed" of deliverance would indeed run an earthly course.

One person foretold. In speaking of the offspring of Abraham and others, the Hebrew and Greek terms used are in the singular form, usually referring to such offspring in a collective sense. There seems to be one strong reason why the collective term ze'ra', "seed," rather than the strictly plural word ba·nim', "sons" (singular ben), was used so often with respect to Abraham's posterity. The apostle Paul points to this fact in explaining that when God spoke of the blessings to come through Abraham's seed, he had primary reference to one person, namely, Christ. Paul says: "Now the promises were spoken to Abraham and to his seed. It [or, He] says, not: 'And to seeds [Gr., sper'ma·sin],' as in the case of many such, but as in the case of one: 'And to your seed [Gr., sper'ma·ti'],' who is Christ."—Ga 3:16, ftn.

Some scholars have objected to Paul's statement regarding the singular and plural use of "seed." They point out that in Hebrew the word for "seed" (ze'ra'), when used for posterity, never changes its form, in this use resembling the English word "sheep." Also, the accompanying verbs and adjectives do not in themselves indicate the singularity or plurality intended by the word for "seed." While this is so, there is another factor that demonstrates that Paul's explanation was accurate grammatically as well as doctrinally. Explaining this factor, M'Clintock and Strong's Cyclopædia (1894, Vol. IX, p. 506) states: "In connection with pronouns, the construction is entirely different from both the preceding [that is, the verbs and adjectives used with the word "seed"]. A singular pronoun [used with ze'ra'] marks an individual, an only one, or one out of many; while a plural pronoun represents all the descendants. This rule is followed invariably by the Sept[uagint] . . . Peter understood this construction, for we find him inferring a singular seed from Gen. xxii, 17, 18, when speaking to native Jews in the city of Jerusalem before Paul's conversion (Acts iii, 26), as David had set the example a thousand years before (Psa. lxxii, 17)."

Additionally this reference work says: "The distinction made by Paul is not between one seed and another, but between the one seed and the many; and if we consider him quoting the same passage with Peter [cited earlier], his argument is fairly sustained by the pronoun 'his [not their] enemies.' Seed with a pronoun singular is exactly equivalent to son."

Using an English illustration, the expression "my offspring" could refer to one or to many. But if after such expression the offspring should be referred to as "he," it would be apparent that a single child or descendant was meant.

The promise to Abraham that all the families of the earth would bless themselves in his "seed" could not have included all of Abraham's offspring as his "seed," since the offspring of his son Ishmael and also those of his sons by Keturah were not used to bless humankind. The seed of blessing was through Isaac. "It is by means of Isaac that what will be called your seed will be," said Jehovah. (Ge 21:12; Heb 11:18) This promise was subsequently narrowed down yet more when, of Isaac's two sons Jacob and Esau, Jacob was specially blessed. (Ge 25:23, 31-34; 27:18-29, 37; 28:14) Further, Jacob limited the matter by showing that the gathering of the people would be to Shiloh (meaning "He Whose It Is; He To Whom It Belongs") of the tribe of Judah. (Ge 49:10) Then, of all Judah, the coming seed was restricted to the line of David. (2Sa 7:12-16) This narrowing down was noted by the Jews in the first century C.E., who actually looked for one person to come as the Messiah or Christ, as deliverer (Joh 1:25; 7:41, 42), even though they also thought that they, as Abraham's offspring, or seed, would be the favored people and, as such, God's children.—Joh 8:39-41.

An enlargement. After Jehovah's angel prevented Abraham from actually sacrificing his son Isaac, the angel called out to Abraham: "'By myself I do swear,' is the utterance of Jehovah, 'that by reason of the fact that you have done this thing and you have not withheld your son, your only one, I shall surely bless you and I shall surely multiply your seed like the stars of the heavens and like the grains of sand that are on the seashore; and your seed will take possession of the gate of his enemies. And by means of your seed all nations of the earth will certainly bless themselves.'"—Ge 22:16-18.

If this promise of God was to have fulfillment in a spiritual seed, then it would indicate that others would be added to the one primary seed. And the apostle Paul explains that this is true. He argues that Abraham was given the inheritance by promise and not by law. The Law was merely added to make transgressions manifest "until the seed should arrive." (Ga 3:19) It follows, then, that the promise was sure to all his seed, "not only to that which adheres to the Law, but also to that which adheres to the faith of Abraham." (Ro 4:16) The words of Jesus Christ to Jews who opposed him: "If you are Abraham's children, do the works of Abraham," indicate that, not those descending through the flesh, but those having the faith of Abraham are accounted by God as Abraham's seed. (Joh 8:39) The apostle makes it very specific when he says: "Moreover, if you belong to Christ, you are really Abraham's seed, heirs with reference to a promise."—Ga 3:29; Ro 9:7, 8.

Consequently, God's promise, "I shall surely multiply your seed like the stars of the heavens and like the grains of sand that are on the seashore," has a spiritual fulfillment and means that others, who "belong to Christ," are added as part of Abraham's seed. (Ge 22:17; Mr 9:41; 1Co 15:23) God did not disclose the number but left it as indeterminate to man as is the number of the stars and the grains of sand. Not until about 96 C.E., in the Revelation to the apostle John, did He reveal that spiritual Israel, those "sealed" with God's spirit, which is a token of their heavenly inheritance, numbers 144,000 persons.—Eph 1:13, 14; Re 7:4-8; 2Co 1:22; 5:5.

These 144,000 are shown standing with the Lamb upon Mount Zion. "These were bought from among mankind as firstfruits to God and to the Lamb." (Re 14:1, 4) Jesus Christ gave his life for them, "assisting Abraham's seed" as their great High Priest. (Heb 2:14-18) God the Father kindly gives his Son this congregation, this "bride." (Joh 10:27-29; 2Co 11:2; Eph 5:21-32; Re 19:7, 8; 21:2, 12) They become kings and priests, and with them Jesus shares the glory and Kingdom that the Father has given him. (Lu 22:28-30; Re 20:4-6) In fact, the sacred secret concerning the Seed is only one feature of the great sacred secret of God's Kingdom by his Messiah.—Eph 1:9, 10; see SACRED SECRET.

Paul illustrates this action of God by speaking of Abraham, his free wife (Sarah), and Isaac the son by promise. He likens Sarah to "the Jerusalem above," "our mother [that is, mother of spirit-begotten Christians]." Isaac is likened to these Christians as the offspring or sons of this "mother."—Ga 4:22-31.

Arrival of the "seed." Jesus, as has been established, is the primary "seed." However, he was not the 'seed of the woman' (that is, of "the Jerusalem above") at the time of his human birth. True, he was of the natural seed of Abraham, through his mother Mary; he was of the tribe of Judah; and both naturally through Mary and legally through his adoptive father Joseph, he was of the line of David. (Mt 1:1, 16; Lu 3:23, 31, 33, 34) So Jesus qualified according to the prophetic promises.

But it was not until Jesus was begotten by the spirit, thus becoming a *spiritual* son of God, that he became the 'seed of the woman' and the Seed that was to bless all nations. This occurred at the time of his baptism by John in the Jordan River, 29 C.E. Jesus was then about 30 years of age. The holy spirit, coming upon Jesus, manifested itself to John in the form of a dove, and God himself acknowledged Jesus as his Son at that time.—Mt 3:13-17; Lu 3:21-23; Joh 3:3.

The addition of the associate "seed," the Christian congregation, began to take place at the time of the outpouring of holy spirit on the day of Pentecost 33 C.E. Jesus had ascended into heaven, into the presence of his Father, and had sent forth the holy spirit to these first followers of his, including the 12 apostles. (Ac 2:1-4, 32, 33) Acting as the High Priest according to the manner of Melchizedek, he here rendered great 'assistance' to the secondary seed of Abraham.—Heb 2:16.

Enmity between the two seeds. The great serpent Satan the Devil has produced "seed" that has manifested the bitterest enmity toward those who have served God with faith like Abraham, as the Bible record abundantly testifies. Satan has tried to block or hinder the development of the woman's seed. (Compare Mt 13:24-30.) This enmity reached its height, however, in the persecution of the spiritual seed, particularly in that displayed toward Jesus Christ. (Ac 3:13-15) Paul refers to the prophetic drama to illustrate, saying: "Just as then the one born in the manner of flesh [Ishmael] began persecuting the one born in the manner of spirit [Isaac], so also now." (Ga 4:29) And a later report, in reality a prophecy, describes the Kingdom's establishment in heaven and the Devil's being hurled out of heaven down to the earth, with only a short time to continue his enmity. It concludes: "And the dragon grew wrathful at the woman, and went off to wage war with the remaining ones of her seed, who observe the commandments of God and have the work of bearing witness to Jesus." (Re 12:7-13, 17) This war against the remnant of the woman's seed ends when 'Satan is crushed under their feet.'—Ro 16:20.

Blessing all families of the earth. Jesus Christ, the Seed, has already brought great blessings to honesthearted persons through his teachings and through the guidance he has given his congregation since Pentecost. But with the beginning of his Thousand Year Reign, his spiritual "brothers," resurrected and sharing his Kingdom rule, will also be underpriests with him. (Re 20:4-6) During the time when "the dead, the great and the small," stand before the throne to be judged, those who exercise faith and obedience will "bless themselves," taking hold of life by means of Abraham's seed. (Re 20:11-13; Ge 22:18) This will mean everlasting life and happiness for them.—Joh 17:3; compare Re 21:1-4.

Resurrection of the "seed." In explaining the resurrection of the Seed, Jesus Christ, the apostle Peter writes that he was 'put to death in the flesh, but was made alive in the spirit.' (1Pe 3:18) His fellow apostle Paul, in dealing with the subject of the resurrection of Christ's associates, draws upon an agricultural illustration. He argues: "What you sow is not made alive unless first it dies; and as for what you sow, you sow, not the body that will develop, but a bare grain, it may be, of wheat or any one of the rest; but God gives it a body just as it has pleased him, and to each of the seeds its own body. . . . So also is the resurrection of the dead. It is sown in corruption, it is raised up in incorruption. It is sown in dishonor, it is raised up in glory. . . . It is sown a physical body, it is raised up a spiritual body." (1Co 15:36-44) Those composing the 'seed of the woman,' "Abraham's seed," therefore die, giving up earthly bodies of corruptible flesh, and are resurrected with glorious incorruptible bodies.

Incorruptible reproductive seed. The apostle Peter speaks to his spiritual brothers concerning their being given "a new birth to a living hope through the resurrection of Jesus Christ from the dead, to an incorruptible and undefiled and unfading inheritance." He says, "It is reserved in the heavens for you." He calls to their attention that it was not with corruptible things such as silver and gold that they were delivered, but with the blood of Christ. After this he says: "For you have been given a new birth, not by corruptible, but by incorruptible reproductive seed, through the word of the living and enduring God." Here the word "seed" is the Greek word *spo·ra'*, which denotes seed sown, hence in position to be reproductive.—1Pe 1:3, 4, 18, 19, 23.

In this manner Peter reminds his brothers of their relationship as sons, not to a human father who dies and who can transmit neither incorruptibility nor everlasting life to them, but to "the living and enduring God." The incorruptible seed with which they are given this new birth is God's holy spirit, his active force, working in conjunction with God's enduring Word, which is itself spirit inspired. The apostle John likewise says of such spirit-begotten ones: "Everyone who has been born from God does not carry on sin, because His reproductive seed remains in such one, and he cannot practice sin, because he has been born from God."—1Jo 3:9.

This spirit in them operates to generate a new birth as God's sons. It is a force for cleanness, and it produces the fruitage of the spirit, not the corrupt works of the flesh. The person having this reproductive seed in himself will therefore not make a practice of the works of the flesh. The apostle Paul comments on this matter: "For God called us, not with allowance for uncleanness, but in connection with sanctification. So, then, the man that shows disregard is disregarding, not man, but God, who puts his holy spirit in you."—1Th 4:7, 8.

However, one of these spirit-begotten ones who constantly resists the spirit or 'grieves' it, that is, 'saddens' it or 'hurts' it, will eventually cause God to withdraw his spirit. (Eph 4:30, *Int;* compare Isa 63:10.) A person might go so far as to commit blasphemy against the spirit, which would be calamitous for him. (Mt 12:31, 32; Lu 12:10) Therefore Peter and John stress the need to maintain holiness and the love of God, to love one's brothers from the heart, and to display submission to the guidance of the spirit of God, thereby proving oneself a true, loyal son of God.—1Pe 1:14-16, 22; 1Jo 2:18, 19; 3:10, 14.

SEER. Evidently a man enabled by God to discern the divine will, one having such insight; one whose eyes had been unveiled, as it were, to see or understand things that were not open to men in general. The Hebrew word *ro·'eh'*, translated "seer," is drawn from a root word meaning "see," literally or figuratively. The seer was a man consulted by others for wise counsel on problems encountered. (1Sa 9:5-10) The Bible names Samuel (1Sa 9:9, 11, 18, 19; 1Ch 9:22; 29:29), Zadok (2Sa 15:27), and Hanani (2Ch 16:7, 10) as seers.

The designations "seer," "prophet," and "visionary" are closely related in the Scriptures. The distinction between the terms may be that "seer" may relate to discernment, "visionary" to the manner in which the divine will was made known, and "prophet" more to the speaking forth or the proclamation of the divine will. Samuel, Nathan, and Gad are all called prophets (1Sa 3:20; 2Sa 7:2; 24:11), but 1 Chronicles 29:29 indicates a distinction between the three terms when it says, "among the words of Samuel the seer and among the words of Nathan the prophet and among the words of Gad the visionary."

First Samuel 9:9 states: "The prophet of today used to be called a seer in former times." This may have been because toward the close of the days of the Judges and during the reigns of the kings of Israel (which began in the days of Samuel) the prophet as a public proclaimer of God's will came to be more prominent. Samuel is commonly called the first of the line of men called "the prophets."—Ac 3:24; 13:20; see PROPHET.

SEGUB   (Se′gub) [High Up; Protected].

1. Son of Hezron and father of Jair in the tribe of Judah.—1Ch 2:21, 22.

2. The youngest son of Hiel the Bethelite. In fulfillment of Joshua's curse, Segub lost his life when his father rebuilt Jericho during the reign of King Ahab.—Jos 6:26; 1Ki 16:34.

SEIR   (Se′ir) [from a root meaning "bristle up," possibly referring to wooded hills; or, possibly meaning "Bristle Up (Shudder) in Horror"].

1. A "Horite" whose seven "sons" were sheiks in the land of Seir prior to its being occupied by Esau (Edom). (Ge 36:20, 21, 29, 30; 1Ch 1:38; compare Ge 14:4-6.) Seir may have lived in the mountainous region S of the Dead Sea, and this area was perhaps named after him. Whether the seven "sons" of Seir were immediate offspring or included later descendants is uncertain.—See ANAH; DISHON.

2. The mountainous region between the Dead Sea and the Gulf of 'Aqaba. (Ge 36:8, 30; De 2:1, 8) In Abraham's time Horites inhabited Seir. (Ge 14:6) Later, Abraham's grandson Esau established interests in Seir, while his twin brother Jacob resided at Paddan-aram. (Ge 32:3) But it seems that Esau did not complete the move to Seir until sometime after Jacob returned to Canaan. (Ge 36:6-9) Finally Esau's descendants, the Edomites, dispossessed the Horites (De 2:4, 5, 12; Jos 24:4), and the land came to be called Edom. However, the older name Seir was also applied to the descendants of Esau and to the area where they lived. (Nu 24:18; compare 2Ki 14:7; 2Ch 25:11.) It appears that during the reign of King Hezekiah men of the tribe of Simeon went to Mount Seir, and after they annihilated the remnant of the Amalekites, Simeonites began residing there. (1Ch 4:41-43) For details about the geography and history of Seir, see EDOM, EDOMITES.

3. A mountain between Baalah (Kiriath-jearim) and Chesalon on the N border of Judah's territory. (Jos 15:10) Seir is commonly identified with the ridge about 15 km (9.5 mi) W of Jerusalem, on the southern side of which lies the village of Shoresh.

SEIRAH   (Se·i′rah) [from a root meaning "bristle up," possibly referring to wooded hills]. The place to which Ehud escaped after assassinating Moabite King Eglon. Its exact location, some place in the mountainous region of Ephraim, is not known today.—Jg 3:26, 27.

SELA   (Se′la) [Crag].

1. A location on the boundary of Amorite territory after the Israelites took possession of the Promised Land. (Jg 1:36) The site is unknown today. Some would identify this Sela with the one in Edom (2Ki 14:7), but there is no evidence that Amorite territory ever extended so far S into the region controlled by the Edomites.

2. A major Edomite city that was captured by Judean King Amaziah and renamed Joktheel. (2Ki 14:7) Sela may have been the unnamed "fortified city" referred to at Psalm 108:10.

This city is identified by some with Um el-Biyara, a rocky acropolis lying about 100 km (60 mi) NNE of the northern tip of the Gulf of 'Aqaba. This site is located in the western corner of the plain where the Nabataean city of Petra was later built. Accessible by means of a narrow, twisting gorge and surrounded by precipitous sandstone cliffs, this plain is well protected. The impressive ruins of Petra, including temples, tombs, and dwellings hewn out of the rock, were no part of the ancient Edomite city of Sela. Scholars have recently favored identifying Sela with es-Sela', about 4 km (2.5 mi) NNW of Bozrah.

3. A place mentioned in a pronouncement against Moab. (Isa 15:1; 16:1) There is uncertainty as to whether or not it is the same site as No. 2.

SELAH   (Se′lah). A transliterated Hebrew expression found frequently in the Psalms and also appearing in Habakkuk chapter 3. Although it is generally thought to be a technical term for music or recitation, its exact significance is unknown. It is held by some to mean a "pause, suspension, or holding back," either of the singing of the psalm for a musical interlude or of both singing and instrumental music for silent meditation. In either event, the pause was doubtless used to make the fact or sentiment just expressed more impressive, to allow the full import of the last utterance to sink in. The Greek *Septuagint* rendering of Selah is *di·a′psal·ma*, defined as "a musical interlude." Selah always appears at the end of a clause and generally at the end of a strophe, every occurrence being in a song containing some kind of musical direction or expression. In Psalm 9:16 it is accompanied by "Higgaion," there understood by some to be associated with the music of the harp.

SELED   (Se′led) [possibly from a root meaning "leap [for joy]"]. A son of Nadab in the Jerahmeelite division of Judah's genealogy. Seled died without sons.—1Ch 2:25, 30.

SELEUCIA (Se·leu'cia). A fortified Mediterranean port town serving Syrian Antioch and located about 20 km (12 mi) SW of that city. The two sites were connected by road; and the navigable Orontes River, which flowed past Antioch, emptied into the Mediterranean Sea a short distance S of Seleucia. Accompanied by Barnabas, Paul sailed from Seleucia at the start of his first missionary journey, in about 47 C.E. (Ac 13:4) Though thereafter unnamed in the Acts account, Seleucia likely figured in events narrated therein. (Ac 14:26; 15:30-41) To distinguish this city from other similarly named sites in the ancient Middle East, it is sometimes called Seleucia Pieria. It was just N of modern-day Süveydiye, or Samandag, in Turkey. Silt from the Orontes has converted ancient Seleucia's harbor into a marsh.

SELF-CONTROL. Keeping in check, restraining, or controlling one's person, actions, speech, or thoughts. (Ge 43:31; Es 5:10; Ps 119:101; Pr 10:19; Jer 14:10; Ac 24:25) The Hebrew and Greek terms involving self-control literally denote having power or control over oneself. Self-control is a 'fruit of God's spirit' (Ga 5:22, 23); and Jehovah, though possessing unlimited powers, has exercised it at all times. Instead of taking immediate action against wrongdoers, he has allowed time to pass so that they might have the opportunity to turn from their bad ways and thereby gain his favor.—Jer 18:7-10; 2Pe 3:9.

However, once it was firmly established that those to whom time for repentance had been extended would not avail themselves of his mercy, Jehovah rightly ceased to refrain from executing his judgment. A case in point involves the desolaters of Jerusalem. Failing to recognize that Jehovah allowed them to gain control of Israel to discipline the Israelites for unfaithfulness, these desolaters treated them without mercy and carried the discipline farther than God's judgment had required. (Compare Isa 47:6, 7; Zec 1:15.) Jehovah had foreknown this and, through the prophet Isaiah, indicated that the time would come when he would no longer hold back from punishing the desolaters: "I have kept quiet for a long time. I continued silent. I kept exercising self-control. Like a woman giving birth I am going to groan, pant, and gasp at the same time. I shall devastate mountains and hills, and all their vegetation I shall dry up."—Isa 42:14, 15.

Christ Jesus also exercised self-control. The apostle Peter, when calling to the attention of house servants the need to be in subjection to their owners, wrote: "In fact, to this course you were called, because even Christ suffered for you, leaving you a model for you to follow his steps closely. . . . When he was being reviled, he did not go reviling in return. When he was suffering, he did not go threatening, but kept on committing himself to the one who judges righteously."—1Pe 2:21-23.

In "the last days" lack of self-control was to be one of the characteristics marking those who would not be practicing true Christianity. (2Ti 3:1-7) However, since Christians are to be imitators of God and of his Son (1Co 11:1; Eph 5:1), they should strive to cultivate self-control in all things. (1Co 9:25) The apostle Peter stated: "Supply to your faith virtue, to your virtue knowledge, to your knowledge self-control, to your self-control endurance, to your endurance godly devotion, to your godly devotion brotherly affection, to your brotherly affection love. For if these things exist in you and overflow, they will prevent you from being either inactive or unfruitful regarding the accurate knowledge of our Lord Jesus Christ." —2Pe 1:5-8.

The quality of self-control should especially be in evidence among those serving as overseers in Christian congregations. (Tit 1:8) If overseers are to deal effectively with problems inside the congregation, they must maintain self-control in word and deed. The apostle Paul counseled Timothy: "Further, turn down foolish and ignorant questionings, knowing they produce fights. But a slave of the Lord does not need to fight, but needs to be gentle toward all, qualified to teach, keeping himself restrained under evil, instructing with mildness those not favorably disposed."—2Ti 2:23-25.

Failure to exercise self-control in a given situation can tarnish a long record of faithful service and plunge one into all kinds of difficulties. An illustration of this is what happened to King David. Though loyal to true worship and having love for the righteous principles of God's law (compare Ps 101), David committed adultery with Bath-sheba, and this led to his having her husband Uriah placed in a battle position where death was a near certainty. As a consequence, for years afterward, David was plagued with severe difficulties within his family. (2Sa 12:8-12) His case also demonstrates the wisdom of avoiding situations that can lead to a loss of self-control. Whereas he could have left the rooftop of his palace, David evidently kept on looking at Bath-sheba as she bathed herself and so came to have a passion for her.—2Sa 11:2-4.

Similarly, it would not be good for a person lacking self-control to remain single when he could enter into an honorable marriage and thereby protect himself against committing fornication. In this regard, the apostle Paul wrote: "If they do not have self-control, let them marry, for it is better to marry than to be inflamed with passion."—1Co 7:9, 32-38.

SELF-WILL. The Greek term rendered "self-willed" (Tit 1:7; 2Pe 2:10, *AS, KJ, NW*) literally means "self-pleasing" and "denotes one who, dominated by self-interest, and inconsiderate of others, arrogantly asserts his own will." (*Vine's Expository Dictionary of Old and New Testament Words,* 1981, Vol. 3, p. 342) Self-will is therefore a quality that is out of harmony with the spirit of Christianity. Especially should it not be reflected by Christian overseers. (Tit 1:5, 7) The apostle Peter described individuals who had departed from proper Christian conduct as being "daring" and "self-willed."—2Pe 2:10.

SEMACHIAH (Sem·a·chi'ah) [Jehovah Has Supported]. A Levite grandson of Obed-edom assigned as a gatekeeper to the S of the sanctuary during David's reign. Semachiah and his fleshly brothers are commended for their capabilities. —1Ch 26:1, 4, 6-8, 15.

SEMEIN (Sem'e·in). A descendant of David and ancestor of Jesus' mother Mary.—Lu 3:26.

SENAAH (Se·na'ah). Over 3,000 "sons of Senaah" returned from exile in Babylon with Zerubbabel in 537 B.C.E. (Ezr 2:1, 2, 35; Ne 7:38) Senaah may be the same as Hassenaah, a name having the Hebrew definite article *ha(s).*—Ne 3:3.

Many of the names in the lists of Ezra 2 and Nehemiah 7 are apparently places rather than people, and Senaah is accordingly thought by some to be a place a little N of Jericho, where Eusebius and Jerome mention a tower "Magdalsenna." (*Onomasticon,* 154, 16, 17) It is tentatively identified with Khirbet al Beiyudat (Horvat el-Beidat), about 11 km (7 mi) NNE of Jericho.

SENEH (Se'neh). "A toothlike crag" facing Geba and lying to the S of another crag called by the name Bozez, both crags being situated between the towns of Michmash and Geba and figuring in the account of Jonathan's attack on the Philistines. (1Sa 14:4, 5, 13) No positive location can now be assigned to these crags, but they are generally considered to have formed part of the nearly vertical cliffs along the Wadi Suweinit (Nahal Mikhmas), which runs between Michmash and Geba.—See BOZEZ.

SENIR (Se'nir). The Amorite name for Mount Hermon. (De 3:9) Since 1 Chronicles 5:23 mentions "Senir and Mount Hermon," the name Senir may also have been used to denote a part of the Hermon, or Anti-Lebanon, Range. Senir was a source of juniper timbers (Eze 27:5) and a haunt of lions and leopards. (Ca 4:8) One Assyrian inscription describes Senir (Sa-ni-ru) as "a mountain, facing the Lebanon."—*Ancient Near Eastern Texts,* edited by J. Pritchard, 1974, p. 280; see HERMON.

SENNACHERIB (Sen·nach'er·ib) [from Akkadian, meaning "Sin [the moon-god] Has Taken the Place of Brothers to Me"]. Son of Sargon II; king of Assyria. He inherited from his father an empire of great strength but was obliged to spend most of his reign subduing revolts, particularly as regards the city of Babylon.

Sennacherib appears to have been serving as a governor or general in the northern region of Assyria during his father's reign. After his succession to the throne, this region evidently caused him little trouble, his difficulties coming chiefly from the S and the W. The Chaldean Merodach-baladan (Isa 39:1) abandoned his refuge in Elam, into which Sennacherib's father Sargon had driven him, and now proclaimed himself king of Babylon. Sennacherib marched against him and his Elamite allies, defeating them at Kish. Merodach-baladan, however, escaped, going into hiding for another three years. Sennacherib entered Babylon and set Bel-ibni on the throne as viceroy. Other punitive expeditions were thereafter effected to keep in check the peoples in the hill countries surrounding Assyria.

Then, in what Sennacherib refers to as his "third campaign," he moved against "Hatti," a term evidently referring at that time to Phoenicia and Palestine. (*Ancient Near Eastern Texts,* edited by J. Pritchard, 1974, p. 287) This area was in a state of general rebellion against the Assyrian yoke. Among those who had rejected such domination was King Hezekiah of Judah (2Ki 18:7), though there is no evidence to show that he was in coalition with the other kingdoms in revolt.

In Hezekiah's 14th year (732 B.C.E.) Sennacherib's forces swept westward, capturing Sidon, Achzib, Acco, and other cities on the Phoenician coast, and then they headed south. Frightened kingdoms, including those of Moab, Edom, and Ashdod, are listed as now sending out tribute to express submission. Recalcitrant Ashkelon was taken by force along with the nearby towns of Joppa and Beth-dagon. An Assyrian inscription accuses the people and nobles of the Philistine city of Ekron of having handed their king Padi over to Hezekiah, who, according to Sennacherib, "held him in prison, unlawfully." (*Ancient Near Eastern Texts*, p. 287; compare 2Ki 18:8.) The inhabitants of Ekron are described as having petitioned Egypt and Ethiopia for help to stave off or thwart the Assyrian attack.

The Bible record indicates that at about this point Sennacherib attacked Judah, laying siege to and capturing many of its fortified cities and towns. Hezekiah now sent word to the Assyrian at Lachish offering to pay the sum of tribute Sennacherib might impose. (2Ki 18:13, 14) Sennacherib's capture of Lachish is presented in a frieze showing him seated on a throne before the vanquished city, accepting the spoils of that city brought to him while some of the captives are being tortured.

The Bible account does not indicate whether King Padi, if in reality a captive of Hezekiah, was now released, but it does show that Hezekiah paid the tribute demanded by Sennacherib of 300 silver talents (c. $1,982,000) and 30 gold talents (c. $11,560,000). (2Ki 18:14-16) Now, however, Sennacherib sent a committee of three officers to call upon the king and people of Jerusalem to make a capitulation to him and, eventually, submit to being sent off into exile. The Assyrian message was particularly disdainful of Hezekiah's reliance on Jehovah. Through his spokesman, Sennacherib boasted that Jehovah would prove to be as impotent as were the gods of the lands that had already fallen before the Assyrian might.—2Ki 18:17-35.

The Assyrian committee returned to Sennacherib, who was now fighting against Libnah, as it was being heard "respecting Tirhakah the king of Ethiopia: 'Here he has come out to fight against you.'" (2Ki 19:8, 9) Sennacherib's inscriptions speak of a battle at Eltekeh (c. 15 km [9.5 mi] NNW of Ekron) in which he claims to have defeated an Egyptian army and the forces of "the king of Ethiopia." He then describes his conquest of Ekron and his restoration of the freed Padi to the throne there.—*Ancient Near Eastern Texts*, pp. 287, 288.

Jehovah Defeats Sennacherib's Army. As for Jerusalem, though Sennacherib sent threatening letters warning Hezekiah that he had not desisted from his determination to take the Judean capital (Isa 37:9-20), the record shows that the Assyrians did not so much as "shoot an arrow there, . . . nor cast up a siege rampart against it." Jehovah, whom Sennacherib had taunted, sent out an angel who, in one night, struck down "a hundred and eighty-five thousand in the camp of the Assyrians," sending Sennacherib back "with shame of face to his own land."—Isa 37:33-37; 2Ch 32:21.

Sennacherib's inscriptions make no mention of the disaster suffered by his forces. But, as Professor Jack Finegan comments: "In view of the general note of boasting which pervades the inscriptions of the Assyrian kings, . . . it is hardly to be expected that Sennacherib would record such a defeat." (*Light From the Ancient Past*, 1959, p. 213) It is interesting, nevertheless, to note the version that Sennacherib presents of the matter, as found inscribed on what is known as the Sennacherib Prism preserved in the Oriental Institute at the University of Chicago. In part he says: "As to Hezekiah, the Jew, he did not submit to my yoke, I laid siege to 46 of his strong cities, walled forts and to the countless small villages in their vicinity, and conquered (them) by means of well-stamped (earth-)ramps, and battering-rams brought (thus) near (to the walls) (combined with) the attack by foot soldiers, (using) mines, breeches as well as sapper work. I drove out (of them) 200,150 people, young and old, male and female, horses, mules, donkeys, camels, big and small cattle beyond counting, and considered (them) booty. Himself [Hezekiah] I made a prisoner in Jerusalem, his royal residence, like a bird in a cage. . . . His towns which I had plundered, I took away from his country and gave them (over) to Mitinti, king of Ashdod, Padi, king of Ekron, and Sillibel, king of Gaza. . . . Hezekiah himself . . . did send me, later, to Nineveh, my lordly city, together with 30 talents of gold, 800 talents of silver, precious stones, antimony, large cuts of red stone, couches (inlaid) with ivory, *nimedu* -chairs (inlaid) with ivory, elephant-hides, ebony-wood, boxwood (and) all kinds of valuable treasures, his (own) daughters, concubines, male and female musicians. In order to deliver the tribute and to do obeisance as a slave he sent his (personal) messenger."—*Ancient Near Eastern Texts*, p. 288.

This boastful version inflates the number of silver talents sent from 300 to 800, and doubtless it does so with other details of the tribute paid; but in other regards it remarkably confirms the Bible record and shows that Sennacherib made no claim that he captured Jerusalem. It should be noted, however, that Sennacherib presents the matter of Hezekiah's paying tribute as having come *after* the Assyrian's threat of a siege against Jerusalem, whereas the Bible account shows it was paid *before*. As to the likely reason for this inversion of matters, note the observation made in *Funk and Wagnalls New Standard Bible Dictionary* (1936, p. 829): "The close of this campaign of

S[ennacherib] is veiled in obscurity. What he did after the capture of Ekron . . . is still a mystery. In his annals, S[ennacherib] locates at this point his punishment of Hezekiah, his raiding of the country of Judah, and his disposition of the territory and cities of Judah. This order of events looks like a screen to cover up something which he does not wish to mention." The Bible record shows that Sennacherib hurried back to Nineveh after the divinely wrought disaster to his troops, and so Sennacherib's inverted account conveniently has Hezekiah's tribute being paid to him through a special messenger *at Nineveh*. It is certainly significant that ancient inscriptions and records show no further campaign by Sennacherib to Palestine, although historians claim that his reign continued for another 20 years.

The Jewish historian of the first century C.E., Josephus, claims to quote the Babylonian Berossus (considered to be of the third century B.C.E.) as recording the event thus: "When Senacheirimos returned to Jerusalem from his war with Egypt, he found there the force under Rapsakes in danger from a plague, for God had visited a pestilential sickness upon his army, and on the first night of the siege one hundred and eighty-five thousand men had perished with their commanders and officers." (*Jewish Antiquities*, X, 21 [i, 5]) Some commentators attempt to explain the disaster by referring to an account written by Herodotus (II, 141) in the fifth century B.C.E. in which he claims that "one night a multitude of fieldmice swarmed over the Assyrian camp and devoured their quivers and their bows and the handles of their shields," thus leaving them unable to carry out an invasion of Egypt. This account obviously does not coincide with the Biblical record, nor does Herodotus' description of the Assyrian campaign harmonize with the Assyrian inscriptions. Nevertheless, the accounts by Berossus and Herodotus do reflect the fact that Sennacherib's forces met up with sudden and calamitous difficulty in this campaign.

Sennacherib's troubles had not ended, however, and following his return to Assyria he had to quell another revolt in Babylon, provoked by Merodach-baladan. This time Sennacherib placed his own son, Ashurnadinshumi, as king in Babylon. Six years later Sennacherib embarked on a campaign against the Elamites, but they soon retaliated by invading Mesopotamia. They captured Ashurnadinshumi and placed their own king on the throne of Babylon. Several years of struggle for control of the region followed, until finally the enraged Sennacherib took vengeance on Babylon by leveling it to the ground, an unparalleled act in view of Babylon's position as the "Holy City" of all Mesopotamia. The remaining years of Sennacherib's reign were apparently without major incident.

Sennacherib's death is considered to have come some 20 years after his campaign against Jerusalem. This figure is dependent on Assyrian and Babylonian records, their reliability being subject to question. At any rate, it should be noted that the Bible account does not state that Sennacherib's death occurred immediately upon his return to Nineveh. "Later on he entered the house of his god" Nisroch, and his sons, Adrammelech and Sharezer, "struck him down with the sword," escaping to the land of Ararat. (2Ch 32:21; Isa 37:37, 38) An inscription of his son and successor, Esar-haddon, confirms this.—*Ancient Records of Assyria and Babylonia,* by D. Luckenbill, 1927, Vol. II, pp. 200, 201; see ESAR-HADDON.

Building Works. The Assyrian Empire thus saw no particular expansion under Sennacherib. He did, however, carry out an ambitious building project in Nineveh, which he had restored to its position as the capital city. The vast palace he erected there was a complex of halls, courts, and rooms of state covering an area 450 m (1,500 ft) long by 210 m (690 ft) wide. He brought in water from 48 km (30 mi) away, constructing a causeway over the Gomel River, known as the Jerwan Aqueduct. Its waters contributed to the irrigation of gardens and parks, as well as to the filling of the city's encircling moat, thereby strengthening the city's defenses.

SEORIM (Se·o′rim). Head of the fourth of the 24 priestly service divisions selected by lot during David's reign.—1Ch 24:5, 8.

SEPHAR (Se′phar). One limit of the territory in which descendants of Joktan resided. The Bible says: "And their place of dwelling came to extend from Mesha as far as Sephar, the mountainous region of the East." (Ge 10:29, 30) One suggested location is Zafar (once the capital of the Himyarite kings) in Yemen, about 160 km (100 mi) NE of the southern end of the Red Sea. Another is a coastal city in Mahra, on the Arabian Sea. But the exact location of ancient Sephar remains uncertain.

SEPHARAD (Se·phar′ad). A place from which Jerusalem's exiles were due to return. (Ob 20) Its exact location is unknown, but of several suggestions a likely possibility is Saparda, mentioned in certain Assyrian annals as a territory of Media. The Assyrians once exiled people of Israel's northern kingdom to "cities of the Medes." —2Ki 17:5, 6.

SEPHARVAIM

SEPHARVAIM (Seph·ar·va'im). A city from which the king of Assyria brought people to dwell in Samaria after the Israelites had been taken into exile. (2Ki 17:24) Earlier, Sepharvaim and its king appear to have experienced defeat at the hands of the Assyrians. (2Ki 19:13; Isa 37:13) Being mentioned along with places in Syria and Babylonia, Sepharvaim was perhaps in one of these areas.

SEPHARVITES (Se'phar·vites) [Of (Belonging to) Sepharvaim]. People of the city of Sepharvaim. After 740 B.C.E., at least some of the inhabitants of Sepharvaim were taken by the Assyrians as colonists to Samaria. The Sepharvites brought with them their false religion, which included the sacrificing of their sons to the gods Adrammelech and Anammelech.—2Ki 17:24, 31-33; 18:34; Isa 36:19.

SERAH (Se'rah). A daughter of Asher among "the souls of the house of Jacob who came into Egypt."—Ge 46:7, 17, 27; Nu 26:46; 1Ch 7:30.

SERAIAH (Se·rai'ah) [Jehovah Has Contended (Persevered)].

1. A son of Kenaz in the tribe of Judah, brother of Judge Othniel, and nephew of Caleb the spy. Seraiah's descendants through his son Joab became craftsmen.—1Ch 4:13, 14.

2. The secretary in King David's administration. (2Sa 8:15, 17) Unless there were several changes in the personnel of this office, he is elsewhere called Sheva (2Sa 20:25), Shavsha (1Ch 18:16), and Shisha, whose two sons later cared for like duties under Solomon. (1Ki 4:3) The names of most of the other governmental officials are the same in the three Davidic lists.

3. A son of Asiel in the tribe of Simeon whose descendants, contemporary with Hezekiah, joined the force that struck down Hamites and Meunim occupying an area and used the land for grazing. —1Ch 4:24, 35, 38-41.

4. One of the three whom King Jehoiakim, late in 624 B.C.E., sent to fetch Jeremiah and Baruch because of the prophecy against Jerusalem and Judah that Baruch had recorded at Jeremiah's dictation. Seraiah was the son of Azriel.—Jer 36:9, 26.

5. The quartermaster of King Zedekiah; son of Neriah and brother of Baruch. (Jer 32:12; 51:59) In the fourth year of Zedekiah, 614 B.C.E., Seraiah accompanied Zedekiah to Babylon. Jeremiah had given him a scroll containing prophetic denunciations of Babylon, instructing him to read it alongside the Euphrates River, then tie a stone to the scroll and pitch it into the river, thus illustrating the permanence of Babylon's fall. (Jer 51:59-64) Seraiah likely passed on to the Israelite exiles already there some of the thoughts from the prophecy. It is of interest that archaeologists have found a seal bearing the inscription "Belonging to Seraiah (ben) Neriah."—*Israel Exploration Journal*, Jerusalem, 1978, Vol. 28, p. 56.

6. The chief priest when Babylon destroyed Jerusalem in 607 B.C.E. Though Seraiah was slain at Nebuchadnezzar's order, his son Jehozadak was spared and taken captive to Babylon. (2Ki 25:18-21; Jer 52:24-27) Through Seraiah's son Jehozadak, the high-priestly line from Aaron continued; Jehozadak's son Jeshua held this office at the time of the Jews' release and return. (1Ch 6:14, 15; Ezr 3:2) Seraiah is also called the father of Ezra, but in view of the 139 years between Seraiah's death and Ezra's return, there were probably at least two unnamed generations in between them, a type of omission common in Biblical genealogies.—Ezr 7:1.

7. One of the military chiefs remaining in Judah after the general deportation to Babylon; son of Tanhumeth. Seraiah and the others of his rank supported Gedaliah's appointment as governor, warned him of Ishmael's threat on his life, and later endeavored to avenge his death. Fearing the Babylonians, however, Seraiah and the other chiefs led the remaining Jews into Egypt.—2Ki 25:23, 26; Jer 40:8, 13-16; 41:11-18; 43:4-7.

8. One of those apparent leaders listed with Zerubbabel as returning from exile in 537 B.C.E. (Ezr 2:1, 2) He is called Azariah in the parallel list at Nehemiah 7:7.

9. A priest who returned from exile with Zerubbabel. In the following generation, Meraiah represented his paternal house. (Ne 12:1, 12) The Seraiah included among the signers of the covenant in the days of Ezra and Nehemiah may also have been a representative of the same family, or another priest of this name. (Ne 10:1, 2, 8) Seraiah, again possibly one of this paternal house or a priest of the same name, lived in Jerusalem after the walls were rebuilt.—Ne 11:1, 10, 11.

SERAPHS. Spirit creatures stationed about Jehovah's throne in the heavens. (Isa 6:2, 6) The Hebrew word *sera·phim'* is a plural noun derived from the verb *sa·raph'*, meaning "burn." (Le 4:12) Thus the Hebrew term *sera·phim'* literally means "burning ones." Elsewhere the noun occurs in singular (Heb., *sa·raph'*) or plural and refers to earthly creatures. In this usage the meaning is variously "poisonous," "fiery (inflammation-causing)," and "fiery snake."—Nu 21:6, 8, ftns.

The prophet Isaiah describes his vision for us,

saying: "In the year that King Uzziah died I, however, got to see Jehovah, sitting on a throne lofty and lifted up, and his skirts were filling the temple. Seraphs were standing above him. Each one had six wings. With two he kept his face covered, and with two he kept his feet covered, and with two he would fly about. And this one called to that one and said: 'Holy, holy, holy is Jehovah of armies. The fullness of all the earth is his glory.' . . . And I proceeded to say: 'Woe to me! For I am as good as brought to silence, because a man unclean in lips I am, and in among a people unclean in lips I am dwelling; for my eyes have seen the King, Jehovah of armies, himself!' At that, one of the seraphs flew to me, and in his hand there was a glowing coal that he had taken with tongs off the altar. And he proceeded to touch my mouth and to say: 'Look! This has touched your lips, and your error has departed and your sin itself is atoned for.'"—Isa 6:1-7.

No description is given of the Divine Person. However, the skirts of his majestic garment are said to have filled the temple, leaving no place for anyone to stand. His throne did not rest upon the ground but, besides being "lofty," was "lifted up." The seraphs' "standing" may mean "hovering," by means of one of their sets of wings, just as the cloud was 'standing' or hovering by the entrance of Jehovah's tent in the wilderness. (De 31:15) Professor Franz Delitzsch comments on the position of the seraphs: "The seraphim would not indeed tower above the head of Him that sat upon the throne, but they hovered above the robe belonging to Him with which the hall was filled." (*Commentary on the Old Testament,* 1973, Vol. VII, Part 1, p. 191) The Latin *Vulgate,* instead of saying "seraphs were standing above him," says they were standing above "it."—Isa 6:1, 2.

Of High Rank. These mighty heavenly creatures are angels, evidently of very high position in God's arrangement, since they are shown in attendance at God's throne. The cherubs seen in Ezekiel's vision corresponded to runners that accompanied the celestial chariot of God. (Eze 10:9-13) This idea of positions of rank or authority in the heavens is in harmony with Colossians 1:16, which speaks of things "in the heavens and upon the earth, the things visible and the things invisible, no matter whether they are thrones or lordships or governments or authorities."

Their Function and Duty. The number of seraphs is not mentioned, but they were calling to one another, evidently meaning that some were on each side of the throne and were declaring Jehovah's holiness and glory in antiphonal song,

one (or one group) repeating after the other or responding to the other with a part of the declaration: "Holy, holy, holy is Jehovah of armies. The fullness of all the earth is his glory." (Compare the reading of the Law and the people's answering, at De 27:11-26.) With humility and modesty in the presence of the Supreme One, they covered their faces with one of their three sets of wings, and being in a holy location, they covered their feet with another set, in due respect for the heavenly King.—Isa 6:2, 3.

The cry of the seraphs concerning God's holiness shows that they have to do with seeing that his holiness is declared and that his glory is acknowledged in all parts of the universe, including the earth. One of the seraphs touched Isaiah's lips to cleanse away his sin and his error by means of a glowing coal from off the altar. This may indicate that their work is in some way associated with cleansing away sin from among God's people, such cleansing being based on the sacrifice of Jesus Christ on God's altar.—Isa 6:3, 6, 7.

Their Visionary Form. The description of the seraphs as having feet, wings, and so forth, must be understood to be symbolic, their likeness to the form of earthly creatures being only representative of abilities they have or of functions they perform, just as God often speaks symbolically of himself as having eyes, ears, and other human features. Showing that no man knows the form of God, the apostle John says: "Beloved ones, now we are children of God, but as yet it has not been made manifest what we shall be. We do know that whenever he is made manifest we shall be like him, because we shall see him just as he is."—1Jo 3:2.

SERED (Se'red). First-named son of Zebulun and founder of the Seredites, a Zebulunite tribal family.—Ge 46:14; Nu 26:26, 27.

SEREDITES (Ser'e·dites) [Of (Belonging to) Sered]. Zebulunite family founded by Sered.—Nu 26:26.

SERPENT, SNAKE [Heb., *na·chash', tan·nin', tse'pha', tsiph·'oh·ni';* Gr., *o'phis*]. A long, scaly, limbless reptile. Serpents travel on their belly or rib cage, and because of the nearness of their head to the ground, their flickering tongue appears to be licking the dust. (Ge 3:14) Over 30 kinds of snakes are found in Israel.

The Hebrew word *na·chash'* is evidently a generic, or general, term applying to all snakes or serpentlike creatures, and it is often used along with other Hebrew words that denote a particular kind of snake. (Ps 58:4; 140:3; Pr 23:32) Thus the tribe of Dan is likened first simply to "a serpent [na·chash´]" and then specifically to "a horned snake [shephi·phon´]" lying by the roadside and striking out at Israel's enemies. (Ge 49:17) This Hebrew term corresponds to the Greek o´phis, which is also generic. While many snakes in Israel today are of the nonvenomous types, Biblical references to snakes are mainly with regard to those that are dangerous or venomous.

The Hebrew words tse´pha´ and tsiph·oh·ni´ are understood by lexicographers to refer to poisonous snakes, the Hebrew pronunciation perhaps representing in sound the hissing noise made by such snakes when they are approached. Both may refer to some variety of viper, but identification is uncertain. The King James Version incorrectly translated these words as referring to the mythical "cockatrice," at Isaiah 11:8; 14:29; 59:5; and Jeremiah 8:17.

In the account about the converting of Moses' rod into a snake (Ex 7:9-13), the Hebrew word tan·nin´ is used, evidently referring to a "big snake" in view of the use of the word in other texts as describing a monstrous creature of the sea. (Ge 1:21; Job 7:12; Ps 74:13; 148:7; Isa 27:1; 51:9) Other texts where the term clearly applies to venomous snakes are Deuteronomy 32:33 and Psalm 91:13, where cobras are also mentioned. A fountain in postexilic Jerusalem was known as "the Fountain of the Big Snake."—Ne 2:13.

The well-known characteristics of a serpent are referred to in various texts: its gliding motion (Job 26:13), its bite and its hiding place in stone walls (Ec 10:8, 11; Am 5:19), also its being cautious (Ge 3:1). This latter characteristic was used by Jesus as an example in admonishing his disciples as to their conduct when among wolfish opposers.—Mt 10:16.

Such 'caution' is referred to by an eminent British zoologist, H. W. Parker, in his book Snakes: A Natural History (1977, p. 49): "Even when the last line of defence has been reached, the counterattack in its initial stages may be more simulated than real; frequent lunges are made with apparent ferocity, but they fall short of the objective and sometimes the mouth is not even opened. It is also not unusual at this stage for the snake to uncoil itself stealthily to be ready for a speedy withdrawal and flight if the enemy recoils. But when an all-out attack finally develops, it follows the pattern usually employed in securing prey, though with increased ferocity; species that would normally bite and then release their victim, or merely hold it, bite repeatedly or worry their molester."

Figurative Use. The serpent is used figuratively in many texts: The lies of the wicked are likened to its venom (Ps 58:3, 4), the sharp tongue of evil schemers to that of the serpent (Ps 140:3), and wine in excess is said to bite as serpents do (Pr 23:32). The freedom from violence and hurt amid Jehovah's restored people is illustrated by the 'serpent's food being dust.'—Isa 65:25.

The symbolic figure of the serpent, or snake, is also used in God's pronouncements of judgment upon certain nations, such as Philistia (Isa 14:29) and unfaithful Judah (Jer 8:17), as well as Egypt, whose voice is likened to that of a serpent, doubtless referring either to a hissing retreat in defeat or to the lowness of her national voice because of the disaster she suffers. (Jer 46:22) This latter reference was probably also an expression designed to expose as futile the practice of the Egyptian pharaohs of wearing the uraeus, a representation of the sacred snake on the front of their headdress, as a sign of protection by the serpent-goddess Uatchit. At Micah 7:17 all the nations opposing God's people are foretold to be obliged to "lick up dust like the serpents."—See also Am 9:3.

At Jeremiah 51:34 the inhabitress of Zion likens King Nebuchadnezzar to a "big snake" that has swallowed her down.

Satan the Devil. At Revelation 12:9 and 20:2 God's principal opposer, Satan, is referred to as "the original serpent," evidently because of his employing the literal serpent in Eden as his means of communication with the woman. (Ge 3:1-15) As "the original serpent," he is also the progenitor in a spiritual sense of other opposers; hence Jesus' classification of such ones as "serpents, offspring of vipers."—Mt 23:33; compare Joh 8:44; 1Jo 3:12.

In false religion. The serpent was a frequent symbol among pagan religions and was often an object of adoration. (PICTURES, Vol. 2, p. 530) In Mesopotamia, Canaan, and Egypt the serpent was the symbol of fecundity and of sex goddesses; two serpents intertwined were used to denote fertility through sexual union, and because of the repeated shedding of the serpent's skin, it was used as a symbol of continuing life.

King Hezekiah acted to eradicate any serpent worship from among his subjects by crushing to pieces the copper serpent that had been used in Moses' time during an attack by venomous snakes in the wilderness.—Nu 21:6-9; 2Ki 18:4; see COPPER SERPENT; FIERY SNAKE.

SERUG (Se´rug). A descendant of Shem, son of Reu, and great-grandfather of Abraham, therefore an ancestor of Jesus. Serug lived 230 years

(2207-1977 B.C.E.) and had a number of children, becoming father to Nahor at the age of 30.—Ge 11:10, 20-23; 1Ch 1:24-27; Lu 3:35.

SERVICE. See COMPULSORY SERVICE; SACRED SERVICE.

SETH [Appointed; Put; Set]. The son of Adam and Eve born when Adam was 130 years old. Eve named him Seth because, as she said, "God has appointed another seed in place of Abel, because Cain killed him." Seth may not have been the third child of Adam and Eve. According to Genesis 5:4, Adam had "sons and *daughters*," some of whom may have been born before Seth. Seth is worthy of note because Noah, and through him the present-day race of mankind, descended from him, not from the murderous Cain. At the age of 105 years Seth became father to Enosh. Seth died at the age of 912 years (3896-2984 B.C.E.).—Ge 4:17, 25, 26; 5:3-8; 1Ch 1:1-4; Lu 3:38.

SETHUR (Se'thur) [from a root meaning "hide; conceal"]. The Asherite chieftain appointed with representatives of the other tribes to spy out Canaan; son of Michael.—Nu 13:2, 3, 13.

SETTLER. See ALIEN RESIDENT.

SEVEN. See NUMBER, NUMERAL.

SEVENTY WEEKS. A prophetic time period referred to at Daniel 9:24-27 during which Jerusalem would be rebuilt and Messiah would appear and then be cut off; following that period the city as well as the holy place would be made desolate.

In the first year of Darius "the son of Ahasuerus of the seed of the Medes," the prophet Daniel discerned from the prophecy of Jeremiah that the time for the release of the Jews from Babylon and their return to Jerusalem was near. Daniel then diligently sought Jehovah in prayer, in harmony with Jeremiah's words: "'And you will certainly call me and come and pray to me, and I will listen to you. And you will actually seek me and find me, for you will search for me with all your heart. And I will let myself be found by you,' is the utterance of Jehovah. . . . 'And I will bring you back to the place from which I caused you to go into exile.'"—Jer 29:10-14; Da 9:1-4.

While Daniel was praying, Jehovah sent his angel Gabriel with a prophecy that nearly all Bible commentators accept as Messianic, though there are many variations in their understanding of it. Gabriel said:

"There are seventy weeks that have been determined upon your people and upon your holy city, in order to terminate the transgression, and to finish off sin, and to make atonement for error, and to bring in righteousness for times indefinite, and to imprint a seal upon vision and prophet, and to anoint the Holy of Holies. And you should know and have the insight that from the going forth of the word to restore and to rebuild Jerusalem until Messiah the Leader, there will be seven weeks, also sixty-two weeks. She will return and be actually rebuilt, with a public square and moat, but in the straits of the times. And after the sixty-two weeks Messiah will be cut off, with nothing for himself. And the city and the holy place the people of a leader that is coming will bring to their ruin. And the end of it will be by the flood. And until the end there will be war; what is decided upon is desolations. And he must keep the covenant in force for the many for one week; and at the half of the week he will cause sacrifice and gift offering to cease. And upon the wing of disgusting things there will be the one causing desolation; and until an extermination, the very thing decided upon will go pouring out also upon the one lying desolate."—Da 9:24-27.

A Messianic Prophecy. It is quite evident that this prophecy is a "jewel" in the matter of identifying the Messiah. It is of the utmost importance to determine the time of the beginning of the 70 weeks, as well as their length. If these were literal weeks of seven days each, either the prophecy failed to be fulfilled, which is an impossibility (Isa 55:10, 11; Heb 6:18), or else the Messiah came more than 24 centuries ago, in the days of the Persian Empire, and was not identified. In the latter case, the other scores of qualifications specified in the Bible for the Messiah were not met or fulfilled. So it is evident that the 70 weeks were symbolic of a much longer time. Certainly the events described in the prophecy were of such a nature that they could not have occurred in a literal 70 weeks, or a little more than a year and four months. The majority of Bible scholars agree that the "weeks" of the prophecy are weeks of years. Some translations read "seventy weeks of years" (*AT, Mo, RS*); the *Tanakh*, a new Bible translation published in 1985 by the Jewish Publication Society, also includes this rendering in a footnote.—See Da 9:24, ftn.

When did the prophetic "seventy weeks" actually begin?

As to the beginning of the 70 weeks, Nehemiah was granted permission by King Artaxerxes of Persia, in the 20th year of his rule, in the month of Nisan, to rebuild the wall and the city of Jerusalem. (Ne 2:1, 5, 7, 8) In his calculations as to the reign of Artaxerxes, Nehemiah apparently used a calendar year that began with the month Tishri (September-October), as does the Jews' present civil calendar, and ended with the month Elul (August-September) as the 12th month. Whether this was his own reckoning or the manner of reckoning employed for certain purposes in Persia is not known.

Some may object to the above statement and may point to Nehemiah 7:73, where Nehemiah speaks of Israel as being gathered in their cities in the *seventh* month—the monthly order here being based on a Nisan-to-Nisan year. But Nehemiah was here copying from "the book of genealogical enrollment of those who came up at the first" with Zerubbabel, in 537 B.C.E. (Ne 7:5) Again, Nehemiah describes the celebration of the Festival of Booths in his time as taking place in the *seventh* month. (Ne 8:9, 13-18) This was only fitting because the account says that they found what Jehovah commanded "written in the law," and in that law, at Leviticus 23:39-43, it says that the Festival of Booths was to be in "the seventh month" (that is, of the sacred calendar, running from Nisan to Nisan).

However, as evidence indicating that Nehemiah may have used a fall-to-fall year in referring to certain events, we can compare Nehemiah 1:1-3 with 2:1-8. In the first passage he tells of receiving the bad news about Jerusalem's condition, in Chislev (third month in the civil calendar and ninth in the sacred calendar) in Artaxerxes' 20th year. In the second, he presents his request to the king that he be permitted to go and rebuild Jerusalem, and he is granted permission in the month Nisan (seventh in the civil calendar and first in the sacred), but *still in the 20th year of Artaxerxes.* So Nehemiah was obviously not counting the years of Artaxerxes' reign on a Nisan-to-Nisan basis.

To establish the time for the 20th year of Artaxerxes, we go back to the end of the reign of his father and predecessor Xerxes, who died in the latter part of 475 B.C.E. Artaxerxes' accession year thus began in 475 B.C.E., and his first regnal year would be counted from 474 B.C.E., as other historical evidence indicates. The 20th year of Artaxerxes' rule would accordingly be 455 B.C.E. —See PERSIA, PERSIANS (The Reigns of Xerxes and of Artaxerxes).

"The Going Forth of the Word." The prophecy says there would be 69 weeks of years "from the going forth of the word to restore and to rebuild Jerusalem until Messiah the Leader." (Da 9:25) Secular history, along with the Bible, gives evidence that Jesus came to John and was baptized, thereby becoming the Anointed One, Messiah the Leader, in the early autumn of the year 29 C.E. (See JESUS CHRIST [Time of Birth, Length of Ministry].) Calculating back from this vantage point in history, we can determine that the 69 weeks of years began in 455 B.C.E. In that year the significant "going forth of the word to restore and to rebuild Jerusalem" took place.

In Nisan (March-April) of the 20th year of Artaxerxes' rule (455 B.C.E.), Nehemiah petitioned the king: "If your servant seems good before you, . . . send me to Judah, to *the city* of the burial places of my forefathers, that *I may rebuild it.*" (Ne 2:1, 5) The king granted permission, and Nehemiah made the long journey from Shushan to Jerusalem. On about the fourth of Ab (July-August), after making a night inspection of the walls, Nehemiah gave the command to the Jews: "Come and let us *rebuild the wall of Jerusalem,* that we may no longer continue to be a reproach." (Ne 2:11-18) Thus, "the going forth of the word" to rebuild Jerusalem, as authorized by Artaxerxes, was put into effect by Nehemiah in Jerusalem that same year. This clearly establishes 455 B.C.E. as the year from which the 70 weeks would begin to count.

The repair work on the walls was completed on the 25th day of Elul (August-September), in just 52 days. (Ne 6:15) After the rebuilding of the walls, the repairing of the rest of Jerusalem went forward. As to the first seven "weeks" (49 years), Nehemiah, with the help of Ezra and, afterward, others who may have succeeded them, worked, "in the straits of the times," with difficulty from within, among the Jews themselves, and from without, on the part of the Samaritans and others. (Da 9:25) The book of Malachi, written after 443 B.C.E., decries the bad state into which the Jewish priesthood had by then fallen. Nehemiah's return to Jerusalem following a visit to Artaxerxes (compare Ne 5:14; 13:6, 7) is thought to have taken place after this. Just how long after 455 B.C.E. he personally continued his efforts in building Jerusalem, the Bible does not reveal. However, the work was evidently completed within 49 years (seven weeks of years) to the extent necessary, and Jerusalem and its temple remained for the Messiah's coming.—See MALACHI, BOOK OF (Time of Composition).

Messiah's Arrival After 'Sixty-Nine Weeks.' As to the following "sixty-two weeks" (Da 9:25), these, being part of the 70 and named second in order, would continue from the conclusion of the "seven weeks." Therefore, the time "from the going forth of the word" to rebuild Jerusalem until "Messiah the Leader" would be 7 plus 62 "weeks," or 69 "weeks"—483 years—from the year 455 B.C.E. to 29 C.E. As mentioned above, in the autumn of that year, 29 C.E., Jesus was baptized in water, was anointed with holy spirit, and began his ministry as "Messiah the Leader."—Lu 3:1, 2, 21, 22.

Thus, centuries in advance Daniel's prophecy pinpointed the exact year of the Messiah's arrival. Perhaps the Jews in the first century C.E. had made calculations on the basis of Daniel's prophecy and were therefore on the alert for Messiah's appearance. The Bible reports: "Now as the people were in expectation and all were reasoning in their hearts about John: 'May he perhaps be the Christ?'" (Lu 3:15) Although they were expecting the Messiah, they evidently could not pinpoint the exact month, week, or day of his arrival. Therefore, they wondered whether John was the Christ, even though John evidently began his ministry in the spring of 29 C.E., about six months before Jesus presented himself for baptism.

"Cut off" at the half of the week. Gabriel further said to Daniel: "After the sixty-two weeks Messiah will be cut off, with nothing for himself." (Da 9:26) It was sometime after the end of the 'seven plus sixty-two weeks,' actually about three and a half years afterward, that Christ was cut off in death on a torture stake, giving up all that he had, as a ransom for mankind. (Isa 53:8) Evidence indicates that the first half of the "week" was spent by Jesus in the ministry. On one occasion, likely in the fall of 32 C.E., he gave an illustration, apparently speaking of the Jewish nation as a fig tree (compare Mt 17:15-20; 21:18, 19, 43) that had borne no fruit for "three years." The vine-dresser said to the owner of the vineyard: "Master, let it alone also this year, until I dig around it and put on manure; and if then it produces fruit in the future, well and good; but if not, you shall cut it down." (Lu 13:6-9) He may have referred here to the time period of his own ministry to that

unresponsive nation, which at that point had continued for about three years and was to continue into a fourth year.

Covenant in force "for one week." Daniel 9:27 states: "And he must keep the covenant in force for the many for one week [or seven years]; and at the half of the week he will cause sacrifice and gift offering to cease." The "covenant" could not be the *Law* covenant, for Christ's sacrifice, three and a half years after the 70th "week" began, resulted in its removal by God: "He has taken it [the Law] out of the way by nailing it to the torture stake." (Col 2:14) Also, "Christ by purchase released us from the curse of the Law . . . The purpose was that the blessing of Abraham might come to be by means of Jesus Christ for the nations." (Ga 3:13, 14) God, through Christ, did extend the blessings of the *Abrahamic* covenant to the natural offspring of Abraham, excluding the Gentiles until the gospel was taken to them through Peter's preaching to the Italian Cornelius. (Ac 3:25, 26; 10:1-48) This conversion of Cornelius and his household occurred after the conversion of Saul of Tarsus, which is generally considered to have taken place in about 34 C.E.; after this the congregation enjoyed a period of peace, being built up. (Ac 9:1-16, 31) It appears, then, that the bringing of Cornelius into the Christian congregation took place about the autumn of 36 C.E., which would be the end of the 70th "week," 490 years from 455 B.C.E.

Sacrifices and offerings 'caused to cease.' The expression 'cause to cease,' used with reference to sacrifice and gift offering, means, literally, "cause or make to sabbath, to rest, to desist from working." The "sacrifice and gift offering" that are 'caused to cease,' according to Daniel 9:27, could not be Jesus' ransom sacrifice, nor would they logically be any spiritual sacrifice by his footstep followers. They must refer to the sacrifices and gift offerings that were offered by the Jews at the temple in Jerusalem according to Moses' Law.

"The half of the week" would be at the middle of seven years, or after three and a half years within that "week" of years. Since the 70th "week"

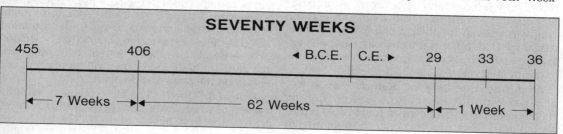

SEVENTY WEEKS

| 455 | 406 | ◄ B.C.E. | C.E. ► | 29 | 33 | 36 |

◄— 7 Weeks —►◄————————— 62 Weeks ————————►◄— 1 Week —►

began about the *fall* of 29 C.E. at Jesus' baptism and anointing to be Christ, half of that week (three and a half years) would extend to the *spring* of 33 C.E., or Passover time (Nisan 14) of that year. This day appears to have been April 1, 33 C.E., according to the Gregorian calendar. (See LORD'S EVENING MEAL [Time of Its Institution].) The apostle Paul tells us that Jesus 'came to do the will of God,' which was to 'do away with what is first [the sacrifices and offerings according to the Law] that he may establish what is second.' This he did by offering as a sacrifice his own body.—Heb 10:1-10.

Although the Jewish priests continued to offer sacrifices at the temple in Jerusalem until its destruction in 70 C.E., the sacrifices for sin ceased having acceptance and validity with God. Just before Jesus' death he said to Jerusalem: "Your house is abandoned to you." (Mt 23:38) Christ "offered one sacrifice for sins perpetually . . . For it is by one sacrificial offering that he has made those who are being sanctified perfect perpetually." "Now where there is forgiveness [of sins and lawless deeds], there is no longer an offering for sin." (Heb 10:12-14, 18) The apostle Paul points out that Jeremiah's prophecy spoke of a new covenant, the former covenant (Law covenant) being thereby made obsolete and growing old, "near to vanishing away."—Heb 8:7-13.

Transgression and sin terminated. Jesus' being cut off in death, his resurrection, and his appearance in heaven resulted in 'terminating transgression and finishing off sin as well as in making atonement for error.' (Da 9:24) The Law covenant had exposed the Jews as sinners, condemned them as such, and brought upon them the curse as covenant breakers. But where sin "abounded" as exposed or made evident by the Mosaic Law, God's mercy and favor abounded much more through his Messiah. (Ro 5:20) By Messiah's sacrifice, transgression and sin of the repentant sinners can be canceled and the penalty thereof be lifted.

Everlasting righteousness brought in. The value of Christ's death on the stake provided a reconciliation for repentant believers. A propitiatory covering was drawn over their sins, and the way was opened for their being "declared righteous" by God. Such righteousness will be everlasting and will procure everlasting life for the ones declared righteous.—Ro 3:21-25.

Anointing the Holy of Holies. Jesus was anointed with holy spirit at the time of baptism, the holy spirit coming down on him visibly represented in the form of a dove. But the anointing of "the Holy of Holies" refers to more than the anointing of the Messiah, because this expression does not refer to an individual person. "The Holy of Holies" or "the Most Holy" is the expression used to refer to the true sanctuary of Jehovah God. (Da 9:24; Ex 26:33, 34; 1Ki 6:16; 7:50) Therefore, the anointing of "the Holy of Holies" mentioned in the book of Daniel must relate to "the greater and more perfect tent not made with hands," into which Jesus Christ as the great High Priest entered "with his own blood." (Heb 9:11, 12) When Jesus presented the value of his human sacrifice to his Father, heaven itself had the appearance of the spiritual reality represented by the Most Holy of the tabernacle and of the later temple. So God's heavenly abode had indeed been anointed, or set apart, as "the Holy of Holies" in the great spiritual temple arrangement that came into being at the time of Jesus' being anointed with holy spirit in 29 C.E.—Mt 3:16; Lu 4:18-21; Ac 10:37, 38; Heb 9:24.

'Imprinting a seal upon vision and prophet.' All this work accomplished by the Messiah—his sacrifice, his resurrection, his appearance with the value of his sacrifice before the heavenly Father, and the other things occurring during the 70th week—'imprints a seal upon vision and prophet,' showing these to be true and from God. It stamps them with the seal of divine backing, as being from one divine source and not from erring man. It seals up the vision as being restricted to Messiah because it finds its fulfillment in him and God's work through him. (Re 19:10) Its interpretation is found in him, and we cannot look to anyone else for its fulfillment. Nothing else will unseal its meaning.—Da 9:24.

Desolations to the city and the holy place. It was after the 70 "weeks," but as a direct result of the Jews' rejection of Christ during the 70th "week," that the events of the latter parts of Daniel 9:26 and 27 were fulfilled. History records that Titus the son of Emperor Vespasian of Rome was the leader of the Roman forces that came against Jerusalem. These armies actually entered into Jerusalem and the temple itself, like a flood, and desolated the city and its temple. This standing of pagan armies in the holy place made them a "disgusting thing." (Mt 24:15) All efforts made prior to Jerusalem's end to quiet the situation failed because God's decree was: "What is decided upon is desolations," and "until an extermination, the very thing decided upon will go pouring out also upon the one lying desolate."

A Jewish View. The Masoretic text, with its system of vowel points, was prepared in the latter half of the first millennium C.E. Evidently because of their rejection of Jesus Christ as the Messiah, the Masoretes accented the Hebrew text at Daniel 9:25 with an 'ath·nach', or "stop," after "seven weeks," thereby dividing it off from the "sixty-two weeks"; in this way the 62 weeks of the prophecy, namely, 434 years, appear to apply to the time of rebuilding ancient Jerusalem. The translation by Isaac Leeser reads: "Know therefore and comprehend, that from the going forth of the word to restore and to build Jerusalem unto the anointed the prince will be seven weeks: [the stop is represented here by a colon] and *during* sixty and two weeks will it be again built with streets and ditches (around it), even in the pressure of the times." The translation of the Jewish Publication Society of America reads similarly: "shall be seven weeks; and *for* threescore and two weeks, it shall be built again." In these two versions the words "during" and "for," respectively, appear in the English translation, evidently to support the translators' interpretation.

Professor E. B. Pusey, in a footnote on one of his lectures delivered at the University of Oxford, remarks on the Masoretic accenting: "The Jews put the main stop of the verse under שִׁבְעָה [seven], meaning to separate the two numbers, 7 and 62. This they must have done dishonestly, למען המינים (as Rashi [a prominent Jewish Rabbi of the 11th and 12th centuries C.E.] says in rejecting literal expositions which favored the Christians) 'on account of the heretics,' i.e. Christians. For the latter clause, so divided off, could only mean, 'and *during threescore and two weeks* street and wall shall be being restored and builded,' i.e. that Jerusalem should be 434 years in rebuilding, which would be senseless."—*Daniel the Prophet,* 1885, p. 190.

As to Daniel 9:26 (*Le*), which reads, in part, "And after the sixty and two weeks will an anointed one be cut off without a successor to follow him," the Jewish commentators apply the 62 weeks to a period up to the Maccabean age, and the term "anointed one" to King Agrippa II, who lived at the time of Jerusalem's destruction, 70 C.E. Or some say this was a high priest, Onias, who was deposed by Antiochus Epiphanes in 175 B.C.E. Their applications of the prophecy to either of these men would rob it of any real significance or import, and the discrepancy in the dating would make the 62 weeks no accurate time prophecy at all.—See *Soncino Books of the Bible* (commentary on Da 9:25, 26), edited by A. Cohen, London, 1951.

In an attempt to justify their view, these Jewish scholars say that the "seven weeks" are, not 7 times 7, or 49 years, but 70 years; yet they count the 62 weeks as 7 times 62 years. This, they claim, referred to the period of Babylonian exile. They make Cyrus or Zerubbabel or High Priest Jeshua the "anointed one" in this verse (Da 9:25), with the "anointed one" in Daniel 9:26 being another person.

It may be noted, in this connection, that the *Septuagint* translation, made by Jewish scholars in the first three centuries B.C.E., reads, at Daniel 9:25, "From the going forth of the command for the answer and for the building of Jerusalem until Christ the prince *there shall be* seven weeks, and sixty-two weeks: and then *the time* shall return, and the street shall be built, and the wall." (*LXX,* Bagster) Thomson's *Septuagint* reads, in part: "seven weeks, and sixty-two weeks. They shall indeed return and a street shall be built and a wall."

Most English translations do not follow the Masoretic punctuation here. They either have a comma after the expression "seven weeks" or in the wording indicate that the 62 weeks follow the 7 as part of the 70, and do not denote that the 62 weeks apply to the period of rebuilding Jerusalem. (Compare Da 9:25 in *KJ, AT, Dy, NW, Ro, Yg.*) An editorial note by James Strong in Lange's *Commentary on the Holy Scriptures* (Da 9:25, ftn, p. 198) says: "The only justification of this translation, which separates the two periods of seven weeks and sixty-two weeks, assigning the former as the *terminus ad quem* of the Anointed Prince, and the latter as the time of rebuilding, lies in the Masoretic interpunction, which places the Athnac [stop] between them. . . . and the rendering in question involves a harsh construction of the second member, being without a preposition. It is better, therefore, and simpler, to adhere to the Authorized Version, which follows all the older translations."—Translated and edited by P. Schaff, 1976.

Numerous other views, some Messianic and some non-Messianic, have been set forth as to the meaning of the prophecy. Some attempt to change the order of the time periods of the prophecy, while others make them run simultaneously or deny that they have any actual time fulfillment. Also many efforts have been made to fit the events mentioned into the Maccabean period or even into the final time of the end. But those presenting such views become hopelessly entangled, and their attempts to extricate themselves result in absurdity or in an outright denial that the prophecy is inspired or true. Of the latter ideas particularly, which raise more problems than they solve, the aforementioned scholar, E. B. Pusey, remarks: "These were the impossible problems for unbelief to solve; it had to solve them for itself, which was, so far, easier; for nothing is impossible for unbelief to believe, except what God reveals."—P. 206.

SEWING. Fastening together by stitches of some sort. From earliest times sewing, including embroidery, has played a prominent part in mankind's activities. (Ex 26:1; 35:35; Job 16:15; Ec 3:7; Eze 13:18) The first man and woman, Adam and Eve, "sewed fig leaves together and made loin coverings." (Ge 3:7) This may simply mean that they fastened the large fig leaves together, using twigs of the fig tree to do so.

When explaining why his disciples did not fast as did the Pharisees and John's disciples, Christ Jesus pointed out that sewing a piece of unshrunk cloth on an old garment would worsen the tear. (Mr 2:18, 21) When washed, the patch would shrink and, in the process, pull away from the old garment, ripping it. This illustration should have helped those hearing Jesus' words to see that it was now time for them to become his followers and that it was wrong for them to try to impose their practices on Jesus' disciples. John himself had earlier explained that his work was preparatory for Christ's coming and, therefore, was of a temporary nature.—Joh 3:27-30.

SHAALABBIN. See SHAALBIM.

SHAALBIM (Sha·al'bim). A city whose Amorite inhabitants were subjected to forced labor by the house of Joseph. (Jg 1:35) Later, Shaalbim was included in one of the districts annually providing Solomon's household with food. (1Ki 4:7-9) It is generally understood to be the same as Shaalabbin, a border city of Dan. (Jos 19:40-42) There is only the difference of the final consonant in the Hebrew spelling of the two names. Shaalbon may be an alternate name for Shaalbim. —2Sa 23:32; 1Ch 11:33.

Shaalbim is identified with the abandoned village of Selbit (Tel Sha'alvim), which appears to preserve the Biblical name. It is situated about 25 km (16 mi) WNW of Jerusalem and relatively near the suggested sites of other places mentioned with Shaalbim in the Scriptures.

SHAALBONITE (Sha·al'bo·nite). The designation of Eliahba, one of David's warriors, presumably indicating one from the city of Shaalbim. —2Sa 23:8, 32; 1Ch 11:26, 33.

SHAALIM (Sha·a'lim) [Handfuls; Hollows of the Hand]. A "land" Saul passed through when searching for the lost she-asses belonging to his father Kish. (1Sa 9:3, 4) Because of the difficulty of determining Saul's exact route, the situation of Shaalim is not definitely known. Some scholars have equated "the land of Shaalim" with "the land of Shual" in 1 Samuel 13:17. At any rate, a location in Ephraim seems best suited to the context.

SHAAPH (Sha'aph).

1. A son of Caleb (the son of Hezron) by his concubine Maacah. Shaaph was the founder or "father" of those who settled Madmannah.—1Ch 2:9, 42, 48, 49.

2. Last named of the six sons of Jahdai listed among the descendants of Caleb the son of Hezron in the tribe of Judah.—1Ch 2:9, 42, 47.

SHAARAIM (Sha'a·ra'im) [Double Gate].

1. A city of Judah in the Shephelah. (Jos 15:20, 33, 36) After David's defeat of Goliath and because of the Israelite pursuit, the Philistine dead were scattered from 'Shaaraim as far as Gath and Ekron.' (1Sa 17:52) Shaaraim was in the vicinity of "the low plain of Elah" (the es-Sant ['Emeq ha-'Ela]) and Azekah (Tell Zakariyeh [Tel 'Azeqa]). (Jos 15:35; 1Sa 17:1, 2) A specific identification has not been made.

2. A city of Simeon. (1Ch 4:24, 31) It is apparently the same as Shilhim (Jos 15:32) and Sharuhen. (Jos 19:6) It is tentatively identified with Tell el-Far'ah (Tel Sharuhen), about 35 km (22 mi) W of Beer-sheba.

SHAASHGAZ (Sha·ash'gaz). The guardian of the concubines of King Ahasuerus; his eunuch in charge of the second house of women.—Es 2:14.

SHABBETHAI (Shab'be·thai) [[Born on the] Sabbath]. A postexilic Levite. The text at Ezra 10:15 reads: "However, Jonathan the son of Asahel and Jahzeiah the son of Tikvah themselves stood up against this, and Meshullam and Shabbethai the Levites were the ones that helped them." This verse may be read to mean that Shabbethai helped those who opposed Ezra's proposal that those who had taken foreign wives dismiss them. Or it could mean that he joined in opposing the procedure recommended by the congregation for resolving the matter. Another possible rendering would indicate that he helped those who acted representatively in dealing with the situation on behalf of the people. This latter view would perhaps find support if the Shabbethai mentioned here is the same person who is named at Nehemiah 8:5-7; 11:1, 2, 15, 16 as assisting Ezra at the public reading of the Law and who lived in Jerusalem after the wall was rebuilt.

SHACKLES.   See BOND.

SHADOW.   A place of shade, whether provided by a crag (Isa 32:2), a cloud (Isa 25:5), a booth (Isa 4:6), a tree (Ca 2:3; Eze 17:23; Ho 4:13), or another kind of plant (Jon 4:5, 6). It may afford welcome protection from the hot sun. Therefore, one is figuratively said to come under the "shadow" of that which serves as or is looked to for protection, covering, security, or refuge. Thus, with reference to the strangers he had taken into his home, Lot said to the men of Sodom: "Only to these men do not do a thing, because that is why they have come under the shadow of my roof." (Ge 19:8) And Jehovah, by means of his prophet Isaiah, pronounced woe upon those taking refuge in "the shadow of Egypt," that is, looking to Egypt for protection. (Isa 30:1-3; see also La 4:20; Eze 31:6, 12, 17.) Especially is Jehovah described as providing protective shade or shadow to his people (Ps 91:1; 121:5; Isa 25:4) or giving them shadowlike protection under his "hand" or his "wings." (Ps 17:8; 36:7; 57:1; 63:7; Isa 49:2; 51:16) On the other hand, "deep shadow" is associated with gloom, danger, even the grave—"the land of darkness."—Job 10:21, 22; 24:17; 38:17; Ps 23:4.

The way in which a shadow changes in size and finally is no more as a result of the sun's progress is used as a simile of man's being short-lived or transient. (1Ch 29:15; Job 8:9; 14:1, 2; Ps 102:11; 144:4; Ec 6:12; 8:13) For an individual's days to be "like a shadow that has declined" signifies that his death is near. (Ps 102:11; 109:23) Whereas shadows cast by the sun are always changing in size and direction as the earth rotates, Jehovah is unchangeable. As the disciple James wrote: "With him there is not a variation of the turning of the shadow."—Jas 1:17.

The shadow, or dark image, that an object casts on a surface is not substantial, not the real thing. Yet it can give an idea of the general shape or design of the reality that casts it. In this connection Paul explained that the Law, including its festivals, tabernacle, and sacrifices, had a shadow that represented greater things to come. He wrote: "The reality belongs to the Christ."—Col 2:16, 17; Heb 8:5; 9:23-28; 10:1.

Regarding the miraculous reversing of the shadow mentioned at 2 Kings 20:9-11 and Isaiah 38:8, see SUN.

SHADRACH   (Sha'drach). The Babylonian name of a Jewish exile elevated to a high position in the government of Babylon. Shadrach, Me-

shach, and Abednego—the three companions of Daniel—are always mentioned together, and Shadrach is always listed first, perhaps because their corresponding Hebrew names—Hananiah, Mishael, and Azariah—always appear in alphabetical order according to the Hebrew characters. The Babylonian names were given to them after they had been taken to Babylon. There they received training, since they had been observed to be without blemish, good-looking and intelligent youths. By the end of three years' study, Shadrach, Meshach, and Abednego were found to be ten times better than the wise men of Babylon. Certainly they had Jehovah's blessing, which in turn, no doubt, was partly due to their steadfast refusal to pollute themselves with the Babylonian delicacies. (Da 1:3-20) Their next-recorded appointment was to the administration of the jurisdictional district of Babylon. (Da 2:49) They temporarily lost the king's favor when they refused to bow to his great image, but after Jehovah brought them out of the fiery furnace unharmed, they were restored to their former position.—Da 3:1-30.

SHAGEE   (Sha'gee). A Hararite whose son Jonathan was one of David's mighty men. (1Ch 11:26, 34) The parallel passage at 2 Samuel 23:32, 33 reads, "Jonathan, Shammah the Hararite." It is usually agreed that the words "son of" have somehow been lost, which, if supplied, would make the text read "Jonathan [the son of] Shammah the Hararite," Shammah apparently being an alternative name for Shagee.

SHAHARAIM   (Sha·ha·ra'im) [[Born at] Dawn]. A Benjamite who lived in Moab for a time and whose three named wives bore him many sons, some of whom became family heads.—1Ch 8:8-11.

SHAHAZUMAH   (Sha·ha·zu'mah) [Majestic Place]. An unidentified boundary site of Issachar. (Jos 19:17, 22) It is located somewhere between Beth-shemesh and Mount Tabor.

SHALISHAH   (Shal'i·shah). A "land" or district Saul journeyed through while searching for his father's she-asses (1Sa 9:3, 4), likely the area in which Baal-shalishah was located. (2Ki 4:42) This latter site is identified with Kafr Thulth, about 20 km (12 mi) NW of Gilgal.—See BAAL-SHALISHAH.

SHALLECHETH   (Shal'lech·eth). A gate situated to the W of the sanctuary at Jerusalem. —1Ch 26:16.

SHALLUM (Shal'lum) [from a root meaning "make peace; compensate; repay"].

1. Last-named son of Naphtali. (1Ch 7:13) Spelled Shillem in other texts.

2. Son of Shaul, grandson of Simeon, and father of Mibsam.—1Ch 4:24, 25.

3. Son of Sismai and father of Jekamiah in the Jerahmeelite genealogical division in Judah. —1Ch 2:4, 5, 9, 25, 40, 41.

4. A head gatekeeper of the sanctuary who at one time was stationed at the king's gate to the E; a descendant of Korah. Though the name appears mainly in lists of those returning from Babylon and living in Jerusalem (1Ch 9:2, 3, 17-19, 31, 34; Ezr 2:1, 42; Ne 7:45), references such as to "the dining room of Maaseiah the son of Shallum the doorkeeper" in Jeremiah's time (Jer 35:4) might indicate that the name appearing in the postexilic lists refers to a paternal house, or family, of gatekeepers descended from an earlier Shallum. Added assurance that this is so would be given if he is the same as the Shelemiah and Meshelemiah mentioned in 1 Chronicles 26:1, 2, 9, 14 as the gatekeeper E of the sanctuary during David's reign.

5. Sixteenth king of the ten-tribe kingdom; son of Jabesh. In a conspiracy Shallum killed Zechariah, the last of Jehu's ruling descendants, and became king in Samaria for one lunar month in about 791 B.C.E., only to be murdered by Menahem.—2Ki 15:8, 10-15.

6. An Ephraimite whose son Jehizkiah was one of the tribal leaders who objected to making captives of their brothers from Judah.—2Ch 28:12, 13.

7. A descendant of Aaron in the high-priestly line. Shallum's son or descendant Hilkiah officiated during Josiah's reign. (1Ch 6:12, 13; 2Ch 34:9) Ezra also descended from him. (Ezr 7:1, 2) He is elsewhere called Meshullam.—1Ch 9:11; Ne 11:11; see MESHULLAM No. 4.

8. Husband of Huldah, the prophetess whom King Josiah's delegation visited; son of Tikvah. He was presumably "the caretaker of the garments," either for the priests or the king. (2Ki 22:14; 2Ch 34:22) Possibly the same as No. 10.

9. A son of Josiah; king of Judah for three months before being exiled by Pharaoh Nechoh. (1Ch 3:15; 2Ki 23:30-34; Jer 22:11, 12) He is elsewhere called Jehoahaz.—See JEHOAHAZ No. 3.

10. Jeremiah's paternal uncle. In 608 B.C.E. Jeremiah bought a field from Shallum's son Hanamel. (Jer 32:1, 7-9) The time period would allow for him to be the same as No. 8.

11. One of the gatekeepers who agreed to dismiss their foreign wives and sons after Ezra returned to Jerusalem. (Ezr 10:24, 44) He is likely related in some way to No. 4.

12. One of the sons of Binnui who also dismissed their foreign wives and sons.—Ezr 10:38-42, 44.

13. A prince of half the district of Jerusalem who, with his daughters, joined in doing repair work on Jerusalem's wall; a son or descendant of Hallohesh.—Ne 3:12.

SHALLUN (Shal'lun) [Free From Care; Unworried; Unconcerned]. A prince of the district of Mizpah; son of Colhozeh. Shallun helped Nehemiah to rebuild a section of Jerusalem's wall and repaired the Fountain Gate.—Ne 3:15.

SHALMAN (Shal'man) [from a root meaning "make peace; compensate; repay"]. The despoiler of the house of Arbel whom Hosea mentions when prophesying against the faithless northern kingdom of Israel. Though neither Shalman nor Arbel are otherwise mentioned in the Bible, Hosea's incidental but emphatic reference to them suggests that the incident was fresh in the mind of his audience.—Ho 10:14.

A building inscription of Tiglath-pileser III refers to a prince of Moab named Salamanu, but there is no historical basis for connecting him with a despoiling in Israel.—*Ancient Near Eastern Texts*, edited by J. Pritchard, 1974, p. 282.

Shalman is therefore most generally thought to be a shortened form of "Shalmaneser," the name of five Assyrian kings. Shalmaneser V emerges as the most likely person here referred to, for toward the end of Hosea's period of prophesying, Shalmaneser V invaded Israel and laid siege to Samaria.

SHALMANESER (Shal·man·e'ser) [from Akkadian, meaning "Shulman [an Assyrian god] Is Superior"]. Five different Assyrian monarchs bore this name; however, only two of them appear to have had direct contact with Israel: Shalmaneser III and Shalmaneser V. Only the latter is actually mentioned in the Bible account.

1. Shalmaneser III succeeded his father Ashurnasirpal II to the Assyrian throne. In one inscription he speaks of himself as "the king of the world, the king without rival, the 'Great Dragon,' the (only) power within the (four) rims (of the earth)." (*Ancient Near Eastern Texts*, edited by J. Pritchard, 1974, p. 276) He is considered to have ruled for about 35 years. Thirty-one of those years appear to have been employed in warring campaigns to maintain and extend Assyrian dominion. Shalmaneser III made repeated thrusts to the W against the Aramaean kingdoms in Syria.

His Inscription Supposedly Involving Ahab.
In the Monolith Inscription of Shalmaneser III, a description is given of the battle of Karkar (near Hamath in the Orontes Valley), fought in the sixth year of Shalmaneser's reign. The Assyrians there battled an enemy coalition of 12 kings, primarily Syrians. However, in the list appears one called *A-ha-ab-bu* ^mat^*Sir-'i-la-a-a*. This name is regularly translated as "Ahab the Israelite" in modern reference works. (See *Ancient Near Eastern Texts*, p. 279.) The participation of Ahab in the battle as an ally of the Syrians is popularly viewed as an accepted fact. Yet, the Bible makes no mention of such event, and despite the apparent similarity in the names, there are serious reasons for doubting the identification of *A-ha-ab-bu* ^mat^*Sir-'i-la-a-a* with Ahab of Israel. The *Encyclopædia Biblica* (London, 1899, Vol. I, col. 91) says "The name of Ahabbu Sir'lai, which, *as most scholars are now agreed*, can only mean Ahab of Israel (or, as Hommel thinks, of Jezreel)." (Italics ours.) This shows that the identification was not always as generally accepted as today, and it shows as well that the translation of ^mat^*Sir-'i-la-a-a* as "Israelite" has also been subject to doubt. It may be noted that ^mat^*Sir-'i-la-a-a* is not the term used elsewhere in Assyrian inscriptions to refer to the northern kingdom of Israel. In other Assyrian inscriptions of the time, that land is referred to either by the name of its capital Samaria (*Sa-me-ri-na* in the inscriptions) or as *Bit Hu-um-ri-ia* (Omri-land), an expression still used a century after the death of Omri.—*Ancient Near Eastern Texts*, pp. 284, 285.

Shalmaneser's inscriptions show that in his 18th year of rule, or *12 years* after the battle of Karkar, he fought against Hazael of Damascus and also that: "At that time I received the tribute of the inhabitants of Tyre, Sidon, and of Jehu, son of Omri." (*Ancient Near Eastern Texts*, p. 280) Thus, the identification of *A-ha-ab-bu* with King Ahab would create a contradiction of the Bible chronology, which shows that between Ahab's death and Jehu's reign there intervened a period of approximately *14 years*, covering the reigns of Ahaziah and Jehoram. (1Ki 22:51; 2Ki 3:1) Though most commentators would place Ahab's supposed joining of the Syrian alliance toward the close of his reign, this still does not fit the Bible's chronological framework. Recognizing this problem, scholars Kamphausen and Kittel offered the suggestion that Ahab's name has been confused with that of Jehoram in the Assyrian records. (Hastings' *Dictionary of the Bible*, 1904, Vol. I, p. 53) There is, however, no record in the Bible of any such participation by Jehoram in the battle of Karkar.

It is also difficult to explain why Ahab would unite with the hard-set enemies of Israel in such a coalition. Thus, *The Encyclopedia Americana* (1956, Vol. I, p. 269) says, "We find [Ahab] strangely allied with his old enemy Benhadad against Shalmaneser (q.v.) of Assyria, though one would suppose he would gladly have seen Benhadad crushed, and Assyria was no immediate danger." Ahab had just fought two wars with the Syrians, and though there was a brief period of nonaggression between Israel and Syria, in the third year of that period Ahab fought a final conflict with them, losing his life. (1Ki 22:1-4, 34-37) The efforts made at explaining his entry into the Syrian combine, either as a willing ally or under compulsion, are not convincing.

Finally, the large force attributed to *A-ha-ab-bu* in Shalmaneser's inscription does not ring true with the Biblical indications of Israel's war equipment. *A-ha-ab-bu* is listed as bringing "2,000 chariots" with him, more than any of the other kings in the alliance. Recognizing the difficulty here, the advocates of *A-ha-ab-bu's* identification with King Ahab only compound the problem by suggesting a further strange union of Judean, Tyrian, Edomite, and even Moabite contingents with Ahab's forces to fill out the needed number of chariots. (*Encyclopædia Biblica*, Vol. I, col. 92; *The Encyclopædia Britannica*, 1910, Vol. I, p. 429) It may be noted that in his reign even powerful King Solomon had only 1,400 chariots.—1Ki 10:26.

In view of all the above points, it appears entirely possible that the translation of *A-ha-ab-bu* ^mat^*Sir-'i-la-a-a* as "Ahab the Israelite" is not the correct rendering and that the decipherers of the inscription were perhaps overly eager to see in the name an association with a known figure of history. It may be noted that in the same inscription reference is made to "Musri," and although this term is elsewhere used to refer to Egypt, the translators here reject such connection as illogical and suggest that the name "refers probably to a country in southern Asia Minor." (*Ancient Near Eastern Texts*, p. 279, ftn. 9) There seem to be equally good reasons for viewing the connection of ^mat^*Sir-'i-la-a-a* with Israel as illogical. Time may prove this to be the case.

The principal leaders in the Syrian coalition

that Shalmaneser III faced at Karkar appear to have been King Adad-idri of Damascus and King Irhuleni of Hamath. Shalmaneser claimed to have gained a great victory in the battle, but the results were evidently not sufficiently decisive to allow for further Assyrian advance in the W. Thus, additional battles against Adad-idri of Damascus are listed during succeeding years.

Inscriptions Concerning Hazael and Jehu. In fulfillment of Jehovah's prophecy through Elisha, Hazael, the chamberlain of King Ben-hadad of Damascus, killed his master and became king, probably toward the close of the reign of King Jehoram (c. 917-905 B.C.E.). (2Ki 8:7-15) An inscription of Shalmaneser III confirms this, stating: "Hadadezer [Adad-'idri, evidently Ben-hadad II of Damascus] (himself) perished. Hazael, a commoner (lit.: son of nobody), seized the throne." Conflicts with Hazael are mentioned in Shalmaneser's 18th and 21st years, with the Assyrian gaining victories but never being able to take Damascus. —Ancient Near Eastern Texts, p. 280.

The name of King Jehu of Israel (c. 904-877 B.C.E.) also appears on the Black Obelisk of Shalmaneser (now at the British Museum) accompanying a relief depicting what appears to be an ambassador of Jehu kneeling before the Assyrian king and bringing him presents. The inscription states: "The tribute of Jehu (Ia-ú-a), son of Omri (Hu-um-ri) [meaning a successor of Omri]; I received from him silver, gold, a golden saplu-bowl, a golden vase with pointed bottom, golden tumblers, golden buckets, tin, a staff for a king." (Ancient Near Eastern Texts, p. 281) This tribute is not mentioned in the Bible account concerning Jehu, and while such action may quite possibly have been taken by the Israelite king in view of the conditions described at 2 Kings 10:31-33, it should never be assumed that the egotistical Assyrian monarchs were beyond the expressing of gross misrepresentations, both in their inscriptions and in their engraved reliefs.

2. Shalmaneser V was the successor of Tiglath-pileser III. As far as secular records are concerned,

his reign is obscure. He is apparently listed as king over Babylon for five years under the name Ululaia. (Ancient Near Eastern Texts, p. 272, ftn. 4) Josephus also quotes Menander of Tyre as describing a siege of that city by Shalmaneser V. (Jewish Antiquities, IX, 283-288 [xiv, 2]) Aside from this, the Bible is the prime source of information regarding this king.

Domination of Israel. During the reign of King Hoshea of Israel (c. 758-740 B.C.E.), Shalmaneser V advanced into Palestine and Hoshea became his vassal under an imposition of annual tribute. (2Ki 17:1-3) However, at a later time Hoshea failed to pay the tribute and was found to be conspiring with King So of Egypt. (See So.) For this, Shalmaneser placed Hoshea under detention and thereafter laid siege against Samaria for three years, after which the well-fortified city finally fell, and the Israelites were led into exile. —2Ki 17:4-6; 18:9-12; compare Ho 7:11; Eze 23:4-10.

The Bible record does not specifically name the Assyrian king that finally captured Samaria. —See SARGON.

With the fall of Samaria in 740 B.C.E., the 257-year rule of the ten-tribe kingdom of Israel ended.

SHAMA (Sha'ma) [possibly a shortened form of Shemaiah, meaning "Jehovah Has Heard (Listened)"]. One of David's mighty men; brother of Jeiel and son of Hotham the Aroerite.—1Ch 11: 26, 44.

Obelisk of Shalmaneser showing Jehu (or more likely his emissary) paying tribute to the Assyrian king

SHAMGAR (Sham'gar). A deliverer of Israel between the judgeships of Ehud and Barak. Only one heroic deed of Shamgar is recorded, the slaying of 600 Philistines with a cattle goad, but he is accredited thereby with 'saving Israel.' (Jg 3:31) According to Josephus, Shamgar died in his first year of judgeship. (*Jewish Antiquities*, V, 197 [iv, 3]) His being a "son of Anath" may refer to the Naphtalite city of Beth-anath.—Jg 1:33.

SHAMHUTH (Sham'huth). Izrahite chieftain for the fifth month in David's rotational service reorganization.—1Ch 27:8; see SHAMMAH No. 4.

SHAMIR (Sha'mir).

1. A Levite who was the son of Micah.—1Ch 24:20, 24.

2. A city in the mountainous region of Judah. (Jos 15:20, 48) The ancient name appears to be preserved at Khirbet Somerah, though the actual site is thought to have been at nearby el-Bireh, about 20 km (12 mi) SW of Hebron.

3. Residence and burial site of Judge Tola in the mountainous region of Ephraim. (Jg 10:1, 2) Shamir may have been situated at or near the later location of Samaria. This view is supported somewhat by the Codex Alexandrinus (*LXX*), which reads *Sa·ma·rei'ai* (Samaria) in Judges 10:1.

SHAMMA (Sham'ma). A leading member of the tribe of Asher; son or descendant of Zophah. —1Ch 7:36, 37, 40.

SHAMMAH (Sham'mah).

1. An Edomite sheik; grandson of Esau through Reuel.—Ge 36:10, 13, 17; 1Ch 1:37.

2. An older brother of King David, also called Shimea(h) and Shimei. (1Ch 2:13; 2Sa 13:3; 21: 21) As the third son of Jesse, Shammah was the third possible choice rejected from being anointed as king by Samuel. (1Sa 16:6-9) He was in Saul's army that was being taunted by Goliath when David brought provisions. (1Sa 17:13, 14, 20, 23) One of Shammah's sons, Jonathan, killed a Philistine giant. (2Sa 21:20, 21; 1Ch 20:6, 7) Some suggest that Shammah's son Jonathan was also called Jehonadab and was the wily adviser of Amnon.—2Sa 13:3, 32.

3. One of David's top three warriors; son of Agee the Hararite. On one occasion, Shammah defended a whole field against the Philistines, striking down many of them. (2Sa 23:11, 12) He and the other two principal mighty men made their way in to the cistern of Bethlehem (at the time held by the Philistines), to get water for David, which he refused to drink. (2Sa 23:13-17) Comparison of the similar lists at 1 Chronicles 11:33, 34 and 2 Samuel 23:32, 33 (where in the latter text the generally suggested reading is "Jonathan the son of Shammah the Hararite") would indicate that Shagee is an alternative name for Shammah, and that Shammah had a son Jonathan who also became a distinguished warrior of David.

4. One of David's 30 mighty men; a Harodite. (2Sa 23:8, 25) Varied spellings of his name seemingly occur at 1 Chronicles 11:27 (Shammoth) and 1 Chronicles 27:8 (Shamhuth), which latter text identifies him as head of the fifth monthly service division.

SHAMMAI (Sham'mai) [from a root meaning "hear; listen"].

1. A man in the Jerahmeelite branch of Judah's genealogy; son of Onam and father of Nadab and Abishur.—1Ch 2:4, 5, 9, 26, 28, 32.

2. A man in the Calebite branch of Judah's genealogy; son of Rekem and father of Maon. —1Ch 2:4, 5, 9, 42-45.

3. The name of a person in the tribe of Judah. —1Ch 4:17.

SHAMMOTH (Sham'moth). One of David's mighty men; a Harorite.—1Ch 11:26, 27; see SHAMMAH No. 4.

SHAMMUA (Sham·mu'a) [a shortened form of Shemaiah, meaning "Jehovah Has Heard (Listened)"].

1. The chieftain representing the tribe of Reuben whom Moses sent into the Promised Land as a spy; son of Zaccur. He joined nine other spies in discouraging the Israelites from having faith that Jehovah would clear Canaan of their enemies. —Nu 13:2-4, 28, 29.

2. A son of David among those borne by Bathsheba, therefore a full brother of King Solomon. (2Sa 5:13, 14; 1Ch 14:3, 4) He is once called Shimea.—1Ch 3:5.

3. A Levite of the line of Jeduthun whose son or descendant Abda lived in Jerusalem after the Babylonian exile. (Ne 11:17) He is called Shemaiah at 1 Chronicles 9:16.

4. A priest heading the paternal house of Bilgah in the days of Jeshua's successor Joiakim. —Ne 12:12, 18.

SHAMSHERAI (Sham'she·rai). The head of a forefather's house that lived in Jerusalem; son of Jeroham in the tribe of Benjamin.—1Ch 8:1, 26-28.

SHANK. The lower part of the leg, between the knee and the ankle. In each appearance of the word in the Bible, the limb of an animal is referred to, usually with reference to animals prepared for sacrifice. (Le 1:9, 13; 4:11, 12; 8:21; 9:14) The Hebrew term rendered "shanks" is once used for the "leaper legs" of winged swarming creatures. (Le 11:21) At Amos 3:12, Jehovah's prophet uses the figure of a shepherd snatching two shanks away from the mouth of a lion (evidently to exonerate himself from responsibility for the loss of one of his herd). Here the prophet graphically portrays the destruction coming upon Samaria, particularly the leaders thereof. There would be very few who would escape the lionlike devouring by Samaria's enemies.

SHAPHAM (Sha'pham). The second in charge of the tribe of Gad in Bashan sometime prior to the reign of Jeroboam II in the ninth century B.C.E.—1Ch 5:11, 12, 17.

SHAPHAN (Sha'phan) [Rock Badger]. Son of Azaliah and a royal secretary. King Josiah, in 642 B.C.E., sent Shaphan and two other officials to High Priest Hilkiah with instructions for temple repairs. On this occasion Hilkiah turned over to Shaphan "the very book of the law," likely even the original, that had recently been found in the temple. No sooner had Shaphan read a portion of the Law to Josiah than he and his son Ahikam, along with others, were dispatched by Josiah as a delegation to inquire concerning Jehovah's purpose for Judah. They went to the prophetess Huldah and reported back to the king Jehovah's prophecy that destruction would come, but not during Josiah's reign.—2Ki 22:3-20; 2Ch 34:8-28.

Shaphan's sons Ahikam (Jer 26:24), Elasah (Jer 29:1-3), and Gemariah (Jer 36:10-12, 25) apparently were also adherents to true worship. His son Jaazaniah was not, however. (Eze 8:10, 11) Shaphan's grandson Gedaliah was the God-fearing governor appointed after Jerusalem's fall. —2Ki 25:22; Jer 39:14.

SHAPHAT (Sha'phat) [a shortened form of Shephatiah, meaning "Jehovah Has Judged"].

1. A chieftain representing the tribe of Simeon as one of the spies who spent 40 days in the Promised Land; son of Hori.—Nu 13:2, 5, 25; see SPIES.

2. One of King David's herdsmen; son of Adlai. The flocks Shaphat cared for were in the low plains.—1Ch 27:29.

3. Father of the prophet Elisha.—1Ki 19:16, 19; 2Ki 3:11; 6:31.

4. A descendant of Gad who lived in Bashan. —1Ch 5:11, 12.

5. One of King David's post-exilic descendants. —1Ch 3:22.

SHAPHIR (Sha'phir) [Elegant; Polished; Agreeable]. A place, evidently in Judah, the inhabitants of which were included in Micah's prophecy of judgment that was due to come upon Judah and Jerusalem. (Mic 1:11) In this section of the prophecy, Micah makes a frequent play on words in his usage of the place-names. (See BETH-EZEL.) A tentative identification of Shaphir is with Khirbet el-Kaum, about 15 km (9.5 mi) W of Hebron.

SHARAI (Sha'rai). One of those sons of Binnui who, after the exile, dismissed their foreign wives.—Ezr 10:38, 40, 44.

SHARAR (Sha'rar). Hararite father of David's warrior Ahiam. (2Sa 23:33) He is called Sacar at 1 Chronicles 11:35.

SHAREZER (Shar·e'zer).

1. A son of Assyrian King Sennacherib. Sometime after his father's defeat by Jehovah, Sharezer and his brother Adrammelech killed their father with the sword while he was bowing down to his idol god, after which they fled to the land of Ararat. (2Ki 19:7, 35-37; Isa 37:38) Their brother Esar-haddon, Sennacherib's successor, claims, in an inscription, to have pursued his father's murderers.—See ESAR-HADDON.

2. The first named of two representatives of postexilic Bethel sent, about two years before the temple rebuilding was completed, to 'soften Jehovah's face' and inquire about the propriety of fasting.—Zec 7:1-3; Ezr 6:15.

SHARON (Shar'on).

1. The maritime plain between the Plain of Dor (S of Carmel) and the Plain of Philistia. From its northern border formed by the Crocodile River (Nahr ez-Zerqa), Sharon extends southward for about 60 km (40 mi) to the area of Joppa and varies in width from about 16 to 19 km (10 to 12 mi). Extensive sand dunes are found along the coast. Crossed by highways, the area anciently was of considerable military and commercial importance.

Sharon was noted for its fertility (compare Isa 35:2), being a well-watered region through which several streams flowed. Flocks and herds grazed there. (1Ch 27:29; compare Isa 65:10.) Great oak forests once occupied the northern part of Sharon, whereas the southern part, as today, likely was more extensively cultivated. It appears that much of the region was desolated during the Assyrian invasion in the eighth century B.C.E.—Isa 33:9.

In The Song of Solomon the Shulammite is depicted as describing herself as "a mere saffron of the coastal plain," evidently meaning just a common flower among the many growing in Sharon.—Ca 2:1.

2. According to 1 Chronicles 5:16, the tribe of Gad dwelt in "Gilead, in Bashan and in its dependent towns and in all the pasture grounds of Sharon." Some scholars think that this means that Gadites grazed their flocks in the coastal plains of Sharon. However, Gad received territory E of the Jordan, and both Gilead and Bashan are on that side. Thus many conclude that there was also a region in Gad's territory called Sharon.

SHARONITE (Shar'on·ite) [Of (Belonging to) Sharon]. A person from the Plain of Sharon. Shitrai, the man in charge of David's herds in Sharon, was called a Sharonite.—1Ch 27:29, 31.

SHARUHEN (Sha·ru'hen). A city of Simeon. (Jos 19:1, 6) It also appears to be called Shilhim (Jos 15:32) and Shaaraim. (1Ch 4:31) Scholars generally believe it to be Tell el-Far'ah (Tel Sharuhen), about 35 km (22 mi) W of Beer-sheba.

SHASHAI (Sha'shai). One of the postexilic sons of Binnui who took foreign wives for themselves but, in response to Ezra's urging, sent them away.—Ezr 10:10, 11, 38, 40, 44.

SHASHAK (Sha'shak). A Benjamite whose 11 sons are listed among the headmen who lived in Jerusalem.—1Ch 8:14, 22-25, 28.

SHAUL (Sha'ul) [Asked [of God]; Inquired [of God].

1. Sixth-named king of ancient Edom; successor of Samlah and predecessor of Baal-hanan. Shaul was from "Rehoboth by the River."—Ge 36:31, 37, 38; 1Ch 1:48, 49.

2. Last-named son of Simeon, born of a Canaanite woman. (Ge 46:10; 1Ch 4:24) Shaul founded the family of the Shaulites numbered among the Simeonites.—Ex 6:15; Nu 26:12, 13.

3. A Levite descendant of Kohath.—1Ch 6:22-24.

SHAULITES (Sha·u'lites) [Of (Belonging to) Shaul]. A Simeonite family founded by Shaul. —Nu 26:12, 13.

SHAVEH, LOW PLAIN OF (Sha'veh). "The king's Low Plain," where Abraham, victorious over Chedorlaomer and his allies, was met by the king of Sodom and received a blessing from Melchizedek, king of Salem. (Ge 14:17-24) Centuries later, Absalom erected his monument in "the Low Plain of the King," apparently the same place and likely near Jerusalem. (2Sa 18:18) Josephus indicated that Absalom's Monument was set up "two stades [370 m; 1,214 ft] distant from Jerusalem." (*Jewish Antiquities,* VII, 243 [x, 3]) However, the exact location of the Low Plain of Shaveh cannot now be ascertained.

SHAVEH-KIRIATHAIM (Sha'veh-kir·i·a·tha'-im) [Smoothed-Out Place of Kiriathaim]. Scene of Chedorlaomer's victory over the Emim. (Ge 14:5) It was apparently the plain near or surrounding the city of Kiriathaim, E of the Jordan and later built or rebuilt by the Reubenites. (Nu 32:37; Jos 13:15, 19) Geographers tentatively place Kiriathaim near Quraiyat, about 10 km (6 mi) NW of Dibon.

SHAVING.   See BALDNESS; BEARD.

SHAVSHA (Shav'sha). A secretary of King David.—1Ch 18:16; see SERAIAH No. 2.

SHEAL (She'al). One of several in the family of Bani whom Ezra induced to dismiss their foreign wives and sons.—Ezr 10:10, 11, 29, 44.

SHEALTIEL (She·al'ti·el) [Asked (Inquired) of God]. A descendant of King David and ancestor of Jesus in the tribe of Judah. Shealtiel is called the son both of Jehoiachin (Jeconiah) and of Neri. Both Shealtiel and his brother Pedaiah are called the father of postexilic Governor Zerubbabel.

As to Shealtiel's father: Shealtiel is listed first among the sons born to Jehoiachin during his exile. (1Ch 3:17; Mt 1:12) If Shealtiel married an unnamed daughter of Neri through whom Luke traces Jesus' genealogy, Shealtiel might be referred to by Luke as being "of Neri" in the sense that he was Neri's son-in-law. This would be the same as Luke's later referring to Joseph, who took Mary (apparently Heli's daughter) in marriage, as being "of Heli."—Lu 3:23, 27.

As to Zerubbabel's father: Pedaiah is once so identified (1Ch 3:19), but Pedaiah's brother Shealtiel (1Ch 3:17, 18) is so termed in all other instances. (Ezr 3:2, 8; 5:2; Ne 12:1; Hag 1:1, 12, 14; 2:2, 23; Mt 1:12; Lu 3:27) If Pedaiah died when his son Zerubbabel was a boy, Pedaiah's oldest brother Shealtiel might have raised Zerubbabel as his own son. Or, if Shealtiel died childless and Pedaiah performed levirate marriage on his behalf, the son of Pedaiah by Shealtiel's wife would have been the legal heir of Shealtiel.

SHEARIAH (She·a·ri'ah). A descendant of Saul and Jonathan; one of Azel's six sons.—1Ch 8:33-38; 9:44.

SHEAR-JASHUB (She'ar-ja'shub) [A Mere Remnant (Those Remaining Over) Will Return]. The first son of Isaiah. Shear-jashub went along when Isaiah delivered a prophetic message to King Ahaz at the time of Israelite King Pekah's invasion of Judah. (Isa 7:1, 3) Isaiah and his sons were to serve as signs and miracles from Jehovah in Israel; hence Shear-jashub's name foretold that 'a mere remnant would return' from Babylonian exile.—Isa 8:18; 10:21.

SHEBA (She'ba).

1. The first-listed son of Raamah the son of Cush.—Ge 10:7; 1Ch 1:9.

2. A son of Joktan of the line of Shem (Ge 10:21-30; 1Ch 1:17-23); progenitor of one of the 13 Arabian tribes. It may be that men of this nomadic tribe were the marauding "Sabeans" who made the raid described in Job 1:14, 15.

3. One of the two sons of Jokshan, the son of Abraham by Keturah. (Ge 25:1-3; 1Ch 1:32) While Abraham was still alive he sent his offspring through Keturah "eastward, to the land of the East." (Ge 25:6) So it seems that this Sheba settled somewhere in Arabia.

4. The son of Bichri a Benjamite, one who lost his life in a revolt against David. (2Sa 20:1, 2) At the time David was returning to Jerusalem after Absalom's rebellion, Sheba, "a good-for-nothing man," detected the ill-feeling of ten of the tribes toward the men of Judah, David's tribe. (2Sa 19:40-43) Sheba fanned the flames of this bitterness, saying that the other tribes had no "share in David" and urging: "Every one to his gods." The men of Judah stuck to the king, but "all the men of Israel" deserted David to follow Sheba. One motive behind this rebellion may have been to bring back to the tribe of Benjamin some of the prominence it had when Saul was king.

David told his general, Amasa, to collect the men of Judah for battle within three days in order to put down Sheba's uprising. When Amasa did not appear on time, the king sent Abishai after fleeing Sheba (though it appears that Abishai's brother Joab actually took charge during the chase). Sheba and his supporting relatives fled all the way N to Abel-beth-maacah, a fortified city of Naphtali. The pursuers laid siege to the city and began to undermine the wall. Then a wise woman of the city spoke with Joab, requesting peace. Joab replied that the army would withdraw if the city delivered up the rebel Sheba. On hearing this, the people of the city cut off Sheba's head and pitched it over the city wall to Joab.—2Sa 20:1-8, 13-22.

5. A Gadite living in Bashan, a descendant of Abihail.—1Ch 5:11, 13.

6. A wealthy kingdom, in all probability located in SW Arabia. It was especially known for its gold, perfumes, and incense. (1Ki 10:1, 2; Isa 60:6; Jer 6:20; Eze 27:22) The origin of these people of Sheba, or Sabeans, as they are frequently designated in secular sources, cannot be established with certainty. There were two Shebas in the line of Shem (SHEBA Nos. 2 and 3) who evidently settled in Arabia. However, some modern scholars believe that the people of this kingdom were Semitic, of the line of Joktan, descendants of Shem through Eber. (Ge 10:26-28) Sheba's own name and those of some of his brothers are connected with locations in S Arabia.—See HAVILAH No. 3; HAZARMAVETH.

The kingdom of Sheba was located, according to some sources, in the eastern portion of what is today the Yemen Arab Republic. Its capital was evidently Marib, on the E side of the mountain range and about 100 km (60 mi) E of San'a.

Before nautical improvements made navigation in the Red Sea less hazardous, trade from S Arabia and possibly E Africa and India was largely accomplished by means of camel caravans through Arabia. Sheba dominated the caravan routes and became renowned for its traders of frankincense, myrrh, gold, precious stones, and ivory. The Bible indicates that these traders reached as far as Tyre. (Eze 27:2, 22-24; Ps 72:15; Isa 60:6) A clay stamp unearthed at Bethel provides material confirmation of commerce between Palestine and S Arabia. Discoveries from excavations at Marib suggest that the Sabeans were a relatively peaceful, commercially minded people. At their capital they had a huge temple to the moon-god.

Queen of Sheba. Sometime after Solomon had completed many building works, he was visited by "the queen of Sheba," who had heard "the report about Solomon in connection with the name of Jehovah." This queen, unnamed in the Bible, went to Jerusalem with "a very impressive train, camels carrying balsam oil and very much gold and precious stones." (1Ki 10:1, 2) The mode of her travel and the type of gifts she brought indicate that she was from the kingdom of Sheba in SW Arabia. This is also indicated by Jesus' comment that she was "the queen of the south" and that she "came from the ends of the earth." (Mt 12:42) From the standpoint of persons in Jerusalem, she had truly come from a distant part of the then-known world. (Ps 72:10; Joe 3:8

SHEBNA(H)

Marib is about 1,900 km (1,200 mi) from Ezion-geber, which is on the N shore of the Red Sea.

Jesus said of the queen of Sheba that she came "to hear the wisdom of Solomon." (Lu 11:31) She was impressed by what Solomon said, by what she saw of the prosperity of his kingdom, and by his wise organization of his staff. She pronounced the king's servants happy for being able to hear his wisdom, and she blessed Jehovah for putting him on the throne. (1Ki 10:2-9; 2Ch 9:1-9) The queen gave Solomon 120 talents of gold (valued now at $46,242,000) as well as balsam oil and precious stones. Solomon gave her gifts that apparently exceeded the value of the treasures she brought, and then she returned to her own land. —2Ch 9:12, AT, Mo.

Christ stated that this woman would rise up in the judgment and condemn the men of the first-century generation. (Mt 12:42; Lu 11:31) She had made an arduous trip to hear Solomon's wisdom, but the unbelieving Jews, who claimed to be servants of Jehovah, had present in Jesus something more than Solomon and did not pay attention to him.

7. Apparently one of the enclave cities given to the tribe of Simeon in the S part of the territory of Judah. (Jos 19:2) The name, though, does not appear in the parallel list in 1 Chronicles 4:28-32 or among the accounts of cities at first assigned to Judah. (Jos 15:26) Since Joshua 19:2-6 gives the sum as 13 cities, but actually seems to list 14 cities, some scholars have suggested that Sheba and Beer-sheba were two parts of the same city, Sheba being the older. If it was a separate location, it may have been the same as Shema, named in the list at Joshua 15:26-32.

SHEBANIAH (Sheb·a·ni′ah).

1. A priest who played a trumpet in the procession that accompanied the ark of the covenant to Jerusalem in David's day.—1Ch 15:3, 24.

2. A priestly paternal house that Joseph represented in the days of High Priest Jeshua's successor Joiakim. (Ne 12:12, 14) In a generally similar list of priests who returned with Zerubbabel in 537 B.C.E., the name Shecaniah appears in the place of Shebaniah. (Ne 12:1-7) During Nehemiah's governorship, a member of the same family or some individual priest of the same name attested to the national covenant then made.—Ne 10:1, 4, 8.

3. One of the Levites or a representative of a Levitical family of the same name, contemporaneous with Ezra and Nehemiah, who led the Jews in a prayer of confession, after which they proposed and sealed a covenant of faithfulness.—Ne 9:4, 5, 38; 10:1, 9, 10.

4. Another Levite who attested to the same trustworthy arrangement, in either his own name or that of a forefather.—Ne 9:38; 10:9, 12.

SHEBARIM (Sheb′a·rim) [Quarries]. The place to which men of Ai chased the Israelites, when they were unable to stand before the enemy after Achan's sin. (Jos 7:5) The site is unknown, except that it was near Ai. Certain translators prefer to render the Hebrew term as "stone-works" or "stone-quarries" rather than as "Shebarim." —BE; Le.

SHEBAT (She′bat). The postexilic name of the 11th Jewish lunar month of the sacred calendar, but the fifth of the secular calendar. (Zec 1:7; De 1:3; 1Ch 27:14) It corresponds to part of January and part of February. The meaning of the name is uncertain.

This midwinter month comes somewhat after the peak of the heavy rains but is still a time of major rainfall. Average temperatures run about 7° C. (45° F.) in Jerusalem and about ten degrees higher along the Mediterranean Coast. The pink and white flowers of the almond tree are the first to brighten up the winter scenery and herald the approach of spring.

Shebat was not marked by any festival seasons in the Bible record.

SHEBER (She′ber) [possibly, Fracture; Breakdown; Crash]. A son of Caleb by Maacah his concubine; of the tribe of Judah.—1Ch 2:48.

SHEBNA(H) (Sheb′na[h]) [possibly a shortened form of Shebaniah]. An officer of King Hezekiah. At one time Shebna was the "steward . . . over the house," presumably of Hezekiah—an influential position. Jehovah, however, directed Isaiah to denounce Shebna, prophesying that he would be 'pushed away from his position,' apparently because of his pride and glory-seeking, shown by building himself a conspicuous sepulcher. His robe, sash, and dominion, together with "the key of the house of David," were given instead to 'God's servant Eliakim.'—Isa 22:15-24.

Shebna was not stripped of all privileges, however, for when Sennacherib threatened Jerusalem in 732 B.C.E. and Eliakim had become steward, Shebna was the royal secretary sent with Eliakim and the recorder to speak with Rabshakeh. With clothes ripped apart, they reported back to Hezekiah what had been said, and they were then sent to Isaiah to inquire of Jehovah.—2Ki 18:18–19:7; Isa 36:3–37:7.

SHEBUEL (Sheb'u·el) [He Returned to God; Captive of God]. The two men named Shebuel are both alternately referred to as Shubael.

1. A Levitical son or descendant of Moses' son Gershom. (1Ch 23:15, 16) Shebuel's (Shubael's) paternal house was enrolled when David reorganized the Levitical services (1Ch 24:20, 30b, 31), being given duties that included caring for the stores.—1Ch 26:24.

2. One of the sons of Heman and an expert musician selected by lot to head the 13th division of sanctuary musicians.—1Ch 25:4, 6, 9, 20.

SHECANIAH (Shec·a·ni'ah) [Residence of Jehovah].

1. A descendant of Aaron whose paternal house was selected by lot as 10th of the 24 priestly divisions that David organized.—1Ch 24:1-3, 7, 11.

2. One of those entrusted with equal distribution of the tithes and other contributions in the priests' cities during Hezekiah's reign.—2Ch 31: 12, 15.

3. A priest who returned to Jerusalem with Zerubbabel.—Ne 12:1, 3, 7; see SHEBANIAH No. 2.

4. A paternal house represented among the group that returned with Ezra in 468 B.C.E.—Ezr 8:1, 3.

5. Head of the paternal house of Zattu, 300 males of which returned with Ezra; son of Jahaziel.—Ezr 8:1, 5.

6. "The son of Jehiel of the sons of Elam" who suggested to Ezra the covenant by which those in restored Judah having foreign wives volunteered to send them away.—Ezr 10:2-4.

7. Father of the Shemaiah who did repair work on Jerusalem's wall.—Ne 3:29.

8. Father-in-law of Tobiah the Ammonite; son of Arah.—Ne 4:3; 6:17, 18.

9. A descendant of David who lived after the Babylonian exile.—1Ch 3:5, 9, 10, 21, 22.

SHECHEM (She'chem) [Shoulder [of Land]].

1. Son of Hivite chieftain Hamor. (Ge 33:19; Jos 24:32) After Jacob settled near the city of Shechem (see No. 4), his daughter Dinah began associating with females of that city. The man Shechem, described as being "the most honorable of the whole house of his father," saw Dinah and "lay down with her and violated her." Then he fell in love with Dinah and wanted to marry her. But Jacob's sons were enraged about the affair and, "with deceit," said that they could make marriage arrangements only with circumcised men. This was agreeable to Shechem and his father Hamor,

and they convinced the Shechemites to get circumcised. However, before the males of Shechem could recover from being circumcised, Jacob's sons Simeon and Levi attacked the city, killing Hamor, Shechem, and all the other men.—Ge 34:1-31.

2. A son of Gilead of the tribe of Manasseh. Shechem became the family head of the Shechemites, who are not to be confused with the Canaanite inhabitants of Shechem.—Nu 26:28, 30, 31; Jos 17:2.

3. A son of Shemida of the tribe of Manasseh. —1Ch 7:19.

4. An ancient city linked with Nablus or, more precisely, with nearby Tell Balata. (Ps 60:6; 108:7; PICTURE, Vol. 1, p. 530) Situated at the E end of the narrow valley running between Mount Gerizim and Mount Ebal, Tell Balata lies about 48 km (30 mi) N of Jerusalem. A good supply of water is available, and just E of the site there is a fertile plain. Anciently Shechem commanded the E-W and N-S roads traversing central Palestine. (Compare Jg 21:19.) Lacking the military advantage of being built on a mountain, the city depended on its fortifications for security.—Jg 9:35.

When Abram (Abraham) first entered the Promised Land, he traveled as far as "the site of Shechem" and encamped near the big trees of Moreh, where he later built an altar. (Ge 12:6-9) Nearly two centuries afterward Jacob, upon returning from Paddan-aram, pitched camp in front of Shechem and purchased some land there. In reaction to their sister Dinah's being violated by Shechem the son of Hamor, the sons of Jacob —Simeon and Levi—killed the men of the city. (Ge 33:18–34:31) At God's direction Jacob left Shechem but, before doing so, took all the foreign gods and earrings in the possession of his household and buried them under the big tree close by Shechem. (Ge 35:1-4) Later, Jacob's sons pastured their flocks near the city, being able to do so safely, doubtless because the "terror of God," which had kept the neighboring peoples from pursuing Jacob, still exercised some effect on them.—Ge 35:5; 37:12-17.

When Jacob's descendants, the Israelites, entered the Promised Land after the sojourn of more than two centuries in Egypt, they buried Joseph's bones "in Shechem in the tract of the field that Jacob had acquired from the sons of Hamor." (Jos 24:32) However, in his defense before the Jews, Stephen said that Joseph was buried "in the tomb that Abraham had bought . . . from the sons of Hamor in Shechem." (Ac 7:16) Perhaps Stephen's statement was an elliptic one. If the ellipsis was filled in, Stephen's statement could read: 'Jacob went down into Egypt. And he deceased; and so did our forefathers, and they were transferred to Shechem and were laid in the tomb that Abraham had bought for a price with silver money [and in that bought] from the sons of Hamor in Shechem.' (Ac 7:15, 16) There is also a possibility that, since Jacob was Abraham's grandson, the purchase could have been ascribed to Abraham as the patriarchal head. This would be using the name of the forefather as applying to and being used for the descendants, in the same manner as the names Israel (Jacob) and others were later used.—Compare Ho 11:1, 3, 12; Mt 2:15-18.

Among the tribal allotments in the Promised Land, Shechem seems to have been within Manasseh's territory, being about 3 km (2 mi) NW of the border town of Michmethath. (Jos 17:7) Since Shechem is described as being "in the mountainous region of Ephraim," it may have been an Ephraimite enclave city in Manassite territory. (Jos 16:9; 1Ch 6:67) The city was thereafter assigned with other Ephraimite cities to the Levites and given sacred status as a city of refuge. (Jos 21:20, 21) Just before his death, Joshua assembled all the tribes of Israel at Shechem, encouraging them to serve Jehovah.—Jos 24:1-29.

Although the Israelites had covenanted at Shechem to uphold true worship, the inhabitants of that city began worshiping Baal-berith. (Jg 8:33; 9:4) They also supported the efforts of Abimelech (the son of Judge Gideon and his Shechemite concubine) to become king. But, in time, they revolted against King Abimelech. In crushing the revolt, Abimelech destroyed the city and sowed it with salt, this perhaps being symbolic of desiring lasting desolation.—Jg 8:31-33; 9:1-49; compare Ps 107:33, 34; see ABIMELECH No. 4; BAAL-BERITH.

Later Shechem was rebuilt. That it became an important city is suggested by the fact that Rehoboam was installed as king there. (1Ki 12:1) After the division of the kingdom, Jeroboam, first king of the northern kingdom, had building work done at Shechem and apparently ruled from there for a time. (1Ki 12:25) Centuries later, in 607 B.C.E., after the destruction of Jerusalem by the Babylonians, men from Shechem came to Jerusalem for worship.—Jer 41:5.

SHECHEMITES (She'chem·ites) [Of (Belonging to) Shechem]. The descendants of Manasseh through Shechem.—Nu 26:29, 31.

SHEDEUR (Shed'e·ur) [possibly, Light of the Almighty]. A Reubenite whose son Elizur was appointed by Jehovah to be chieftain of their tribe in the wilderness.—Nu 1:5; 2:10; 7:30, 35; 10:18.

SHEEP. One of the principal animals of pastoral life. (Ge 24:35; 26:14) Sheep are ruminants, or cud chewers. As is the case today, the predominant variety of ancient Palestine may have been the broad-tailed sheep, distinguished by its prominent fatty tail, generally weighing about 4.5 kg (10 lb) or more. (Compare Ex 29:22; Le 3:9.) Generally sheep were white in color (Ca 6:6), though there were also dark-brown and parti-colored ones. (Ge 30:32) In a pastoral society men of great wealth, such as Job, had thousands of sheep. (Job 1:3, 16; 42:12) The Israelites probably kept some lambs as pets.—2Sa 12:3; Jer 11:19.

Without a shepherd, domestic sheep are helpless and fearful. They get lost and scattered and are at the complete mercy of their enemies. (Nu 27:16, 17; Jer 23:4; Eze 34:5, 6, 8; Mic 5:8) Sheep allow themselves to be led, and they faithfully follow their shepherd. They can learn to recognize his voice and to respond to him alone. (Joh 10:2-5) Illustrating this is a passage from *Researches in Greece and the Levant,* by J. Hartley (London, 1831, pp. 321, 322):

"Having had my attention directed last night to the words [in] John x. 3 . . . I asked my man if it was usual in Greece to give names to the sheep. He informed me that it was, and that the sheep obeyed the shepherd when he called them by their names. This morning I had an opportunity of verifying the truth of this remark. Passing by a flock of sheep, I asked the shepherd the same question which I had put to my servant, and he gave me the same answer. I then bade him to call one of his sheep. He did so, and it instantly left its pasturage and its companions, and ran up to the hand of the shepherd, with signs of pleasure, and with a prompt obedience which I had never before observed in any other animal. It is also true of the sheep in this country, that *a stranger will they not follow, but will flee from him* . . . The shepherd told me, that many of his sheep are still wild; that they had not yet learned their names; but that, by teaching, they would all learn them." —See SHEPHERD.

Areas anciently suited to the raising of sheep included the Negeb (1Sa 15:7, 9), Haran (Ge 29:2-4), the land of Midian (Ex 2:16), the mountainous region of Judah, where the city of Carmel was located (1Sa 25:2), the land of Uz (Job 1:1, 3), as well as Bashan and Gilead (De 32:14; Mic 7:14).

Sheep provided the Hebrews and other peoples with numerous products. From the horns of the ram, containers and sounding horns were made. (Jos 6:4-6, 8, 13; 1Sa 16:1) Sheepskins sometimes served as clothing (Heb 11:37), and ram skins that had been dyed red were used in the construction of the tabernacle. (Ex 26:14) Sheep's wool furnished the fiber for what was probably the most common material for clothing. (Job 31:20; Pr 27:26) Sheep served as an important item of trade (Eze 27:21), and they were even used to pay tribute. (2Ki 3:4; 2Ch 17:11) Both the milk and the meat of sheep were items of diet. (De 14:4; 32:14; 2Sa 17:29; Isa 7:21, 22) Mutton and lamb were enjoyed regularly by kings, governors, and others.—1Sa 8:17; 1Ki 4:22, 23; Ne 5:18; Am 6:4.

The meat was prepared by boiling or roasting. For the Passover, a year-old ram or a male goat was roasted whole after the skin was removed and the internal organs were cleaned. (Ex 12:5, 9) When a sheep was prepared by boiling, the animal was first skinned and then disjointed. At times the bones were cracked open to free the marrow. Both the flesh and the bones were boiled in a large vessel. (Eze 24:3-6, 10; Mic 3:1-3) Once the meat was cooked, it was removed from the pot, and the remaining broth was served separately. (Compare Jg 6:19.) Serving lamb to a guest was a gesture of hospitality.—2Sa 12:4.

The time for shearing the sheep was looked forward to with anticipation, as it was much like a harvest. Feasting and rejoicing attended the event.—1Sa 25:2, 11, 36; 2Sa 13:23, 24, 28.

The Mosaic Law prohibited eating the fat of sheep (Le 7:23-25), as well as slaughtering a sheep and its young one on the same day. (Le 22:28) It also included provisions for handling matters involving straying sheep and loss, maiming, or theft of sheep. (Ex 22:1, 4, 9-13; De 22:1, 2) Israel's obedience to God's laws determined whether their flocks and herds would be blessed or cursed.—De 7:12, 13; 28:2, 4, 15, 18, 31, 51.

Sheep have from earliest times been offered in sacrifice. (Ge 4:2, 4; 22:7, 8, 13; Job 42:8) Under the Law, all firstborn male lambs were to be sacrificed, but not until at least eight days old. To redeem a firstborn male ass, a sheep was to be offered. (Ex 34:19, 20; Le 22:27) Rams were presented as guilt offerings (Le 5:15, 16, 18; 6:6), burnt offerings (Le 9:3; 16:3; 23:12), and communion sacrifices (Le 9:4); and a ram served as an installation offering for the Aaronic priesthood. (Ex 29:22; Le 8:22-28) Daily, two year-old rams constituted the constant burnt offering. (Ex 29:38-42) At the start of the months and in connection with the annual festivals, aside from the constant burnt offering, rams and male lambs were sacrificed. (Nu 28:11, 17-19, 26, 27; 29:1-38) The ram was such a prominent feature of Israel's

offerings that the prophet Samuel used "fat of rams" in parallel with "sacrifice." (1Sa 15:22) However, at times female lambs could be presented as communion sacrifices (Le 3:6), sin offerings (Le 4:32; Nu 6:14), and guilt offerings (Le 5:6).

Prophetic and Figurative Use. In the Scriptures, "sheep" often denote the defenseless, innocent, and, at times, abused people of Jehovah. (2Sa 24:17; Ps 44:11, 22; 95:7; 119:176; Mt 10:6, 16; Joh 21:16, 17; Ro 8:36) Under unfaithful shepherds or leaders, the Israelites as God's sheep suffered greatly. Through his prophet Ezekiel, Jehovah presents a most pathetic picture of neglect: "The flock itself you do not feed. The sickened ones you have not strengthened, and the ailing one you have not healed, and the broken one you have not bandaged, and the dispersed one you have not brought back, and the lost one you have not sought to find, but with harshness you have had them in subjection, even with tyranny. And they were gradually scattered because of there being no shepherd, so that they became food for every wild beast of the field." (Eze 34:3-5) By contrast, Jesus' sheep, both the "little flock" and the "other sheep," who follow his lead, are well cared for. (Lu 12:32; Joh 10:4, 14, 16; Re 7:16, 17) Jesus compared those doing good toward the least of his brothers to sheep, whereas those refusing to do so he likened to goats.—Mt 25:31-45.

"Rams" sometimes represent persons, particularly oppressive leaders of a nation who are destined for destruction. (Jer 51:40; Eze 39:18) At Ezekiel 34:17-22, the rams, the he-goats, and the plump sheep stand for the unfaithful leaders of Israel who appropriated the best for themselves and then befouled what was left for the lean and sick sheep, that is, the people who were oppressed, exploited, and shoved about.

Jesus Christ was prophetically spoken of as sheep brought to the slaughtering and as a ewe that remains mute before her shearers. (Isa 53:7; Ac 8:32, 35; compare 1Pe 2:23.) Because of Jesus' sacrificial role, John the Baptizer identified Jesus as "the Lamb of God that takes away the sin of the world," and in the book of Revelation the Son of God is repeatedly called "the Lamb."—Joh 1:29; Re 5:6; 6:16; 7:14, 17; 14:1; 17:14; 19:7.

The Medo-Persian World Power was depicted under the figure of a ram with two horns of unequal height. The taller horn evidently signified the ascendancy of the Persian kings. (Da 8:3-7, 20) At Revelation 13:11, the wild beast out of the earth is shown as having two horns like

Shepherd's hut with stone-enclosed sheepfold

lamb, suggestive of a pretense of inoffensiveness. Similarly, Jesus spoke of false prophets as wolves in sheep's covering, hence dangerous, although appearing to be harmless.—Mt 7:15.

The trembling of Mount Sinai at the time of Jehovah's giving the Law to Israel (Ex 19:18) seems to be alluded to under the figure of 'mountains skipping about like rams.'—Ps 114:4-6; compare Ps 29:5, 6; 68:8.

Wild Sheep. The Hebrew word *te'oh'* has been variously translated "wild bull" (*KJ*), "antelope" (*AS*), and "gazelle" (*Ro*). However, *Lexicon in Veteris Testamenti Libros,* by Koehler and Baumgartner (Leiden, 1958, p. 1016), gives "wild sheep" as a possible rendering, and it is thus translated at Deuteronomy 14:5 and Isaiah 51:20.

Wild sheep are distinguished from domestic sheep by their outer coat, which is of coarse hair rather than wool. The variety of wild sheep that is now geographically closest to Palestine is the Armenian wild sheep (*Ovis gmelini*), found in the mountain ridges of Asia Minor and eastern Iran. The ram of this variety measures less than 0.9 m (3 ft) high at the shoulder.

SHEEPFOLD. The enclosure into which the sheep were usually brought for the night to protect them from thieves and predatory animals. Although caves and other natural shelters were also used, often sheepfolds were permanent pens having stone walls (Nu 32:16; 1Sa 24:3; Zep 2:6) and an entranceway. (Joh 10:1) As in more recent times, the branches of thorny plants may have covered the tops of the stone walls. There may also have been low, flat buildings on the protected side of the enclosure, where the sheep were sheltered in severe weather. Whereas the flocks of several shepherds might be kept in the same sheepfold, there was no danger of confusion. The sheep responded only to the voice of their respective shepherds. A doorkeeper served at the entranceway of the sheepfold and opened to the shepherds in the morning.—Joh 10:2-4.

SHEEP GATE. See GATE, GATEWAY.

SHEERAH (She'e·rah) [from a root meaning "remain over"]. A daughter of Ephraim or of his son Beriah. She is mentioned as building or founding lower and upper Beth-horon and Uzzen-sheerah, though this may have been done by some of her descendants.—1Ch 7:22-24.

SHEHARIAH (She·ha·ri'ah) [Jah Has Looked For]. Head of a Benjamite family living in Jerusalem; son or descendant of Jeroham.—1Ch 8:1, 26-28.

SHEIK. A title usually given to the Edomite and Horite tribal chiefs, the sons of Esau and the sons of Seir the Horite. (Ex 15:15) In Hebrew the designation is *'al·luph',* meaning "chief," "leader of a thousand." (See Ge 36:15, ftn.) The ancient Edomite and Horite designation corresponds to the title "sheik" as used for tribal leaders among modern Bedouin. In some Bible translations such titles as "chief," "chieftain," and "duke" are used instead of "sheik."

Seven sheiks of the Horites are listed, all "sons of Seir." (Ge 36:20, 21, 29, 30) The sheiks of Edom were evidently 14 in number: seven grandsons from Esau's firstborn Eliphaz the son of his wife Adah, four grandsons from his son Reuel the son of his wife Basemath, and three of his sons by his wife Oholibamah. (Ge 36:15-19) There is a question, however, whether the sheik Korah who is included among the sons of Eliphaz should be counted. If the inclusion of the sheik Korah is a scribal error, as some believe, this would mean that there were only 13 sheiks of Edom. (Ge 36: 16, ftn) The clans that developed from the sheiks came to bear their names as clan names.

At Genesis 36:40-43 and 1 Chronicles 1:51-54 a different listing is given of the "sheiks of Esau [Edom]." These may be later sheiks than those listed earlier. Some commentators, however, believe the names to be those, not of persons, but of the cities or regions where the various sheikdoms were centered. Following this view, the translation of the Jewish Publication Society reads: "the chief of Timna, the chief of Alvah," and so forth.

SHEKEL (shek'el).

The basic Hebrew unit of weight (1Sa 17:5, 7; Eze 4:10; Am 8:5) and of monetary value. Based on the average of some 45 inscribed shekel weights, the shekel may be reckoned at 11.4 g (0.403 oz avdp; 0.367 oz t). One shekel equaled 20 gerahs (Nu 3:47; 18:16), and there is evidence that 50 shekels equaled one mina. (See MINA.) Calculated in modern values, a shekel of silver would be worth $2.20, and a shekel of gold, $128.45.

The shekel is often referred to in connection with silver or gold. (1Ch 21:25; Ne 5:15) Before coins were used, pieces of silver (and, less frequently, gold) were used for money, the weight being checked at the time the transaction was made. (Ge 23:15, 16; Jos 7:21) Things pertaining to the tabernacle were sometimes stated in terms of shekels "by the shekel of the holy place." (Ex 30:13; Le 5:15; 27:2-7, 25) This may have been to emphasize that the weight should be precise or, perhaps, that it should conform to a standard weight kept at the tabernacle.

It is generally thought that the "silver pieces" often mentioned in the Hebrew Scriptures were silver shekels, the standard monetary unit. (Jg 16:5; 1Ki 10:29; Ho 3:2) This is borne out by the Septuagint (in which the Greek word for "silver pieces" at Genesis 20:16 is the same as the Greek word for "shekels" at Genesis 23:15, 16) as well as by the Targums. According to Jeremiah 32:9, the prophet paid "seven shekels and ten silver pieces" for a field. Perhaps this was simply a legal formula meaning 17 silver shekels (AS, Da, NE, RS), or possibly, it meant seven gold shekels and ten silver shekels.

Second Samuel 14:26 may indicate that there was a "royal" shekel different from the common shekel, or the reference may be to a standard weight kept at the royal palace.

SHELAH (She'lah).

1. [Heb., She'lach, possibly, Missile]. Son of Arpachshad and grandson of Shem, who was born in 2333 B.C.E. and died in 1900 B.C.E., at the age of 433. Shelah and one of his sons, Eber, each founded one of the 70 post-Flood families; through Eber ran the genealogical line that led from Shem to Abraham and finally to Jesus.—Ge 10:22, 24; 11:12-15; 1Ch 1:18, 24; Lu 3:35.

2. [Heb., She·lah', possibly, Petition]. The third son of Judah by his Canaanite wife. (1Ch 2:3) Tamar should have been given in levirate marriage to Shelah but was not. (Ge 38:1-5, 11-14, 26) Shelah's descendants, some of whom, with their places of settlement, are listed by name, formed the tribal family of Shelanites. Some of these returned from Babylonian exile.—Nu 26:20; 1Ch 4:21-23; 9:5; Ne 11:5.

SHELANITES (She·la'nites) [Of (Belonging to) Shelah].

A family of Judah founded by Shelah. (Nu 26:20) Some scholars believe that "Shelanite" (instead of the Masoretic text's "Shilonite") should appear at Nehemiah 11:5, in the listing of those who lived in Jerusalem after the exile.

SHELEMIAH (Shel·e·mi'ah) [Jehovah Is Recompense; or, Communion Sacrifice of Jehovah].

1. A Levitical gatekeeper assigned by lot to the E of the sanctuary during David's reign.—1Ch 26:14; see MESHELEMIAH.

2. Grandfather of Jehoiakim's officer Jehudi, son of Cushi.—Jer 36:14.

3. Father of Zedekiah's messenger Jehucal (Jucal).—Jer 37:3; 38:1.

4. Father of Irijah, the officer in charge of Jerusalem's Gate of Benjamin; son of Hananiah.—Je 37:13.

5. One of the messengers of King Jehoiakim sent to bring Jeremiah and Baruch before him; son of Abdeel.—Jer 36:26.

6, 7. Two men listed among the sons or descendants of Binnui who, on Ezra's return to Jerusalem in 468 B.C.E., sent away their foreign wives.—Ezr 10:38, 39, 41, 44.

8. Father of the Hananiah who helped repair Jerusalem's wall.—Ne 3:30.

9. A priest, and one of those whom Nehemiah, on his second visit to Jerusalem, entrusted with the stores and with the distribution of the tithe to their proper recipients.—Ne 13:6, 7, 12, 13.

SHELEPH (She'leph).

The second-named son of Joktan; founder of one of the early post-Flood families. (Ge 10:26; 1Ch 1:20) Arabian equivalents of this name are found in Sabean inscriptions (dated before the seventh century B.C.E.

that speak of a Yemenite district of *Salaf* or *Salif*. Another form of the name may have survived in *Sulaf*, a place about 100 km (60 mi) N of San'a, the capital of Yemen Arab Republic. These similarities, however, only suggest in a general way where Sheleph's descendants settled.

SHELESH (She'lesh) [Third; Three Parts]. An Asherite son of Helem; head of a family and an outstanding warrior.—1Ch 7:30, 35, 40.

SHELOMI (She·lo'mi) [from a root meaning "peace"]. An Asherite whose chieftain son was appointed to help divide the Promised Land among Israel's tribes.—Nu 34:17, 18, 27.

SHELOMITH (She·lo'mith) [from a root that means "peace"].

1. A Danite daughter of Dibri whose son by an Egyptian was put to death in the wilderness for abusing Jehovah's name.—Le 24:10-14, 23.

2. A Kohathite Levite of the family of Izhar; also called Shelomoth.—1Ch 23:12, 18; 24:22.

3. A Levite descendant of Moses' son Eliezer; also called Shelomoth.—1Ch 26:25-28.

4. Son of Judean King Rehoboam by his favorite wife Maacah; brother of King Abijah.—2Ch 11:20-23; 12:16.

5. Daughter of Governor Zerubbabel.—1Ch 3:19.

6. Son of Josiphiah and head of the paternal house of Bani. Shelomith, accompanied by 160 males, came to Jerusalem with Ezra.—Ezr 8:1, 10.

SHELOMOTH (She·lo'moth) [from a root that means "peace"].

1. Head of a paternal house among the descendants of Levi's son Gershon.—1Ch 23:6, 7, 9.

2. A Kohathite Levite of the family of Izhar; also known as Shelomith.—1Ch 23:12, 18; 24:22.

3. A Levite descendant of Moses through his son Eliezer. David placed Shelomoth and his brothers in charge of the treasures of holy things, including sanctified war spoil taken by the Israelites. (1Ch 26:25-28) He was also called Shelomith.

SHELUMIEL (She·lu'mi·el) [Peace of God]. A Simeonite chieftain. Shelumiel assisted with the national census that was taken about a year after the Exodus from Egypt. He was chieftain of the army of Simeon; also, he presented his offering when the tabernacle altar was inaugurated.—Nu 1:4, 6; 2:12; 7:36-41; 10:19.

SHEM [Name; Fame]. One of Noah's three sons; from these "all the earth's population spread abroad" following the global Flood.—Ge 6:10; 9:18, 19.

Although the three sons are consistently listed as "Shem, Ham and Japheth," there is some uncertainty as to their relative positions according to age. The fact that Shem is mentioned first is of itself no definite indication that Shem was Noah's firstborn, since Shem's own firstborn son (Arpachshad) is listed third in the genealogical records. (Ge 10:22; 1Ch 1:17) In the original Hebrew, Genesis 10:21 allows for more than one possible translation, some translations referring to Shem as "the brother of Japheth the oldest ["elder," *KJ*]," while others call him the "elder ["older," *AT*] brother of Japheth." (*AS, Dy, RS, JB, Ro*) The ancient versions likewise differ—the *Septuagint*, the translation by Symmachus, and the Targum of Onkelos present Japheth as the older, while the Samaritan *Pentateuch*, the Latin *Vulgate*, and the Syriac versions place Shem as the older brother of Japheth. The weight of evidence found in the rest of the Bible record, however, indicates that Shem likely was Noah's second son, younger than Japheth.

The record shows that Noah began to father sons after reaching 500 years of age (2470 B.C.E.), the Deluge occurring in his 600th year. (Ge 5:32; 7:6) Already married at the time of the Deluge (Ge 6:18), Shem is stated to have fathered his first son, Arpachshad, two years after the Deluge (2368 B.C.E.) when he, Shem, was 100 years old. (Ge 11:10) This would mean that Shem was born when Noah was 502 years of age (2468 B.C.E.); and since Ham appears to be referred to as the "youngest son" (Ge 9:24), Japheth would logically be the first son born to Noah, when he was 500 years of age.

Following the birth of Arpachshad, other sons (and also daughters) were born to Shem, including Elam, Asshur, Lud, and Aram. (Ge 10:22; 11:11) After Aram, the parallel account at 1 Chronicles 1:17 also lists "Uz and Hul and Gether and Mash," but at Genesis 10:23 these are shown to be sons of Aram. Biblical and other historical evidence indicates that Shem was thus the progenitor of the Semitic peoples: the Elamites, the Assyrians, the early Chaldeans, the Hebrews, the Aramaeans (or Syrians), various Arabian tribes, and perhaps the Lydians of Asia Minor. This would mean that the population descended from Shem was concentrated principally in the southwestern corner of the Asiatic continent, extending throughout most of the Fertile Crescent and occupying a considerable portion of the Arabian Peninsula.—See articles under the names of the individual sons of Shem.

When Shem and his brother Japheth covered

over their father's nakedness at the time of Noah's being overcome by wine, they showed not only filial respect but also respect for the one whom God had used to effect their preservation during the Flood. (Ge 9:20-23) Thereafter, in the blessing Noah pronounced, indication was given that the line of Shem would be particularly favored by God and would contribute to the sanctification of God's name, Noah referring to Jehovah as "Shem's God." (Ge 9:26) It was from Shem, through his son Arpachshad, that Abraham descended, and to him was given the promise concerning the Seed in whom all the families of the earth would receive a blessing. (1Ch 1:24-27; Ge 12:1-3; 22:15-18) Noah's prediction concerning Canaan's becoming "a slave" to Shem was fulfilled by the Semitic subjugation of the Canaanites as a result of the Israelite conquest of the land of Canaan.—Ge 9:26.

Shem lived 500 years after fathering Arpachshad, dying at the age of 600 years. (Ge 11:10, 11) His death thus occurred some 13 years after the death of Sarah (1881 B.C.E.) and ten years after the marriage of Isaac and Rebekah (1878 B.C.E.). In view of this, it has been suggested that Shem may have been Melchizedek (meaning "King of Righteousness"), the king-priest to whom Abraham paid tithes. (Ge 14:18-20) The Bible record does not say this, however, and the apostle Paul shows that no available genealogical record or other vital statistics were left concerning Melchizedek, so that he became an apt type of Christ Jesus, who is King-Priest perpetually.—Heb 7: 1-3.

SHEMA   (She′ma).
[1-4: Melodious Sound]

1. A son of Hebron and father of Raham in the line of Judah's descendants through Caleb.—1Ch 2:42-44.

2. A descendant of Reuben.—1Ch 5:3, 8.

3. Head of a Benjamite household that settled in Aijalon and one of those who chased away the inhabitants of Gath. (1Ch 8:12, 13) Probably the same as Shimei in 1 Chronicles 8:21, there identified as a father of nine sons.—1Ch 8:19-21.

4. One of the six who stood on Ezra's right when he read the Law to the assembled people; probably a priest.—Ne 8:4.

5. A city within Judah's southern territory (Jos 15:21, 26), perhaps the same as Simeon's enclave city Sheba. (Jos 19:1, 2) Some suggest that it was the same as Jeshua and identify it with Tell es-Sa′weh (Tel Yeshu′a), about 15 km (9.5 mi) ENE of Beer-sheba.

SHEMAAH   (She·ma′ah) [from a root meaning "hear; listen"]. A Benjamite of Gibeah whose two sons Ahi-ezer and Joash defected from Saul to David at Ziklag.—1Ch 12:1-3.

SHEMAIAH   (She·mai′ah) [meaning "Jehovah Has Heard (Listened)"].

1. A Simeonite whose distant descendant joined the expedition that seized grazing territory from Canaanites in the days of Hezekiah.—1Ch 4:24, 37-41.

2. A son of Joel in the tribe of Reuben.—1Ch 5:3, 4.

3. Chief of the Levitical house of Elizaphan. Shemaiah and 200 of his brothers, having sanctified themselves, were in the procession that brought the ark of the covenant to Jerusalem —1Ch 15:4, 8, 11-16.

4. Secretary of the Levites who recorded the 24 priestly divisions organized according to David's instruction; son of Nethanel.—1Ch 24:6.

5. Firstborn son of Obed-edom, a Levite. Shemaiah and his sons were all enrolled as gatekeepers assigned to the sanctuary storehouses.—1Ch 26:1, 4, 6, 7, 12, 13, 15.

6. A prophet of Jehovah during the reign of Solomon's son Rehoboam. Following the revolt of the ten northern tribes in 997 B.C.E., Shemaiah pronounced Jehovah's words forbidding an attempt by Rehoboam to reconquer them. (1Ki 12:21-24; 2Ch 11:1-4) In Rehoboam's fifth year (993 B.C.E.), Egyptian King Shishak invaded Judah, and Shemaiah informed Rehoboam and his princes that Jehovah had abandoned them since they had abandoned Him. However, because Rehoboam and the princes humbled themselves, Jehovah lessened the destructiveness of the invasion. (2Ch 12:1-12) Shemaiah also penned one of the written records of Rehoboam's reign.—2Ch 12:15.

7. One of the Levites sent by King Jehoshaphat in his third year (934 B.C.E.) to teach the Law in the cities of Judah.—2Ch 17:7-9.

8. A Levite descendant of Jeduthun commissioned by Hezekiah in his first year of rule (745 B.C.E.) to help cleanse the temple. Shemaiah and the other Levites took the unclean things down to the Kidron Valley. (2Ch 29:12, 14-16) Possibly the same person as No. 9.

9. One of the Levites who distributed the tithes and other contributions in the cities of the priests during Hezekiah's reign. (2Ch 31:6, 12, 14, 15) Possibly the same as No. 8.

10. One of the Levite chieftains who made

generous contribution of animal victims for Josiah's great Passover celebration.—2Ch 35:1, 9.

11. Father of Urijah, a prophet contemporary with Jeremiah; from Kiriath-jearim.—Jer 26:20.

12. Father of Delaiah, a Judean prince during the reign of Jehoiakim.—Jer 36:12.

13. A false prophet of the town of Nehelam and opponent of Jeremiah, taken captive to Babylon with Jehoiachin in 617 B.C.E. From there he wrote back to the priest Zephaniah and associate priests in Jerusalem, condemning Jeremiah for foretelling a long exile and for urging the exiles to settle down in Babylonia. Shemaiah contended that Jeremiah should be put in stocks. Jehovah, however, prophesied that because Shemaiah attempted to make the Jews trust in falsehood and he spoke outright revolt, neither he nor his offspring would be among the returning exiles.—Jer 29:24-32.

14. A priest, and likely the founder of a priestly family, who returned to Jerusalem with Zerubbabel in 537 B.C.E. In the following generation, Jehonathan headed Shemaiah's paternal house. (Ne 12:1, 6, 7, 12, 18) Their representative, or some other priest of the same name, attested to the national covenant during Nehemiah's governorship.—Ne 10:1, 8.

15. A Levite descended from Jeduthun whose son or descendant Obadiah lived in Jerusalem after the exile.—1Ch 9:16, 34.

16. A Levite of the descendants of Merari who also lived in Jerusalem sometime after the Babylonian exile; son of Hasshub.—1Ch 9:14, 34; Ne 11:15.

17. A leader of the sons of Adonikam who accompanied Ezra to Jerusalem in 468 B.C.E. He is possibly one of those whom Ezra had dispatched to request ministers for the sanctuary, resulting in the gathering of some Levites and Nethinim for the journey.—Ezr 8:1, 13, 16-20.

18. One of the priests whom Ezra, on arriving in Jerusalem, encouraged to send away the foreign wives they had taken; son of Harim.—Ezr 10:10, 11, 21, 44.

19. One of the Israelites, son of another Harim, who had also taken foreign wives but who sent them away.—Ezr 10:25, 31, 44.

20. One of those who helped repair Jerusalem's wall; son of Shecaniah, and a gatekeeper, therefore probably a Levite.—Ne 3:29.

21. The false prophet hired by Tobiah and Sanballat to tell Nehemiah of a supposed threat on his life, in this way trying to frighten Nehemiah, who was not a priest, into committing a sin by hiding in the temple. Son of Delaiah.—Ne 6:10-13.

22. Presumably a prince of Judah in the thanksgiving choir that marched to the right around Jerusalem atop the rebuilt wall at its inauguration.—Ne 12:31-34.

23. A priest of the family of Asaph whose descendant marched in the same procession, evidently as a trumpeter.—Ne 12:31, 35.

24. A priestly musician in the same procession; apparently a relative of No. 23.—Ne 12:31, 36.

25. A priest who apparently played the trumpet when the two thanksgiving choirs met at the house of Jehovah on the occasion of the wall's inauguration.—Ne 12:40-42.

26. A distant descendant of David. (1Ch 3:9, 10, 22) Some scholars think that the words "and the sons of Shemaiah," in the middle of verse 22 (which is followed by only five names), should be omitted as a scribal error, thus crediting Shecaniah with six sons. However, other scholars suggest that Shemaiah and his five sons were reckoned as the six descendants of Shecaniah.

SHEMARIAH (Shem·a·ri'ah) [meaning "Jehovah Has Guarded"].

1. One of the ambidextrous Benjamite warriors who joined David while he was a fugitive at Ziklag.—1Ch 12:1, 2, 5.

2. A son of King Rehoboam, hence a great-grandson of David.—2Ch 11:18, 19.

3. One of the sons of Harim who dismissed their foreign wives and sons when Ezra came back to Jerusalem.—Ezr 10:31, 32, 44.

4. One of the sons of Binnui who had also taken foreign wives but sent them away.—Ezr 10:38, 41, 44.

SHEMEBER (Shem·e'ber). The king of Zeboiim whom Chedorlaomer and his allies defeated in the Low Plain of Siddim.—Ge 14:1-11.

SHEMED (She'med). A head of a forefather's house in Benjamin; son or descendant of Elpaal.—1Ch 8:1, 12, 13.

SHEMER (She'mer) [possibly from a root meaning "guard"].

1. A descendant of Asher, perhaps his great-grandson. Four sons of Shemer are named. (1Ch 7:30, 34) Shemer is spelled Shomer in 1 Chronicles 7:32.

2. A Merarite Levite, ancestor of Ethan.—1Ch 6:44-47.

3. The owner of the hill of Samaria; possibly a tribe rather than an individual, for "Samaria" means "Belonging to the Clan Shemer." Israelite King Omri bought the mountain for two talents of silver ($13,212) and began ruling from there in about 945 B.C.E.—1Ki 16:23, 24.

SHEMIDA (She·mi'da). A son of Gilead and great-grandson of Manasseh. From Shemida's four sons grew a tribal family, the Shemidaites, that was numbered in the second wilderness census and received a territory allotment in the Promised Land.—Nu 26:2, 29-32; Jos 17:2; 1Ch 7:19.

SHEMIDAITES (She·mi'da·ites) [Of (Belonging to) Shemida]. A family of Manasseh founded by Shemida.—Nu 26:29, 32.

SHEMINITH (Shem'i·nith). Although the literal meaning of this musical term is "the eighth," its exact significance is uncertain. It may refer to a particular musical register, or mode, a lower one, and if any musical instruments were associated with the term, they would probably be those used to play the bass tones of the musical scale.

At 1 Chronicles 15:21, harps are spoken of as being "tuned to Sheminith ["possibly referring to the eighth key or a lower octave," *NW* ftn; "probably the bass octave," *Da* ftn z]." Consistently, the superscriptions of Psalms 6 and 12 (both psalms being of somber character) read: "To the director (on stringed instruments) on the lower octave [*shemi·nith'*]," which may indicate that these songs would be accompanied by music in a lower range and sung accordingly.—See ALAMOTH.

SHEMIRAMOTH (She·mir'a·moth).

1. A Levite musician who accompanied the ark of the covenant from Obed-edom's house to Jerusalem and was afterward stationed to play before its tent.—1Ch 15:17, 18, 20, 25; 16:1, 4, 5.

2. One of the Levites whom Jehoshaphat sent out to teach the Law to the people in 934 B.C.E. —2Ch 17:7-9.

SHEMUEL (She·mu'el) [Name of God]. The same Hebrew name is also translated "Samuel."

1. Head of a forefather's house; son or descendant of Issachar's son Tola.—1Ch 7:1, 2.

2. Simeon's tribal representative to the delegation that divided the Promised Land into tribal allotments; son of Ammihud.—Nu 34:17, 18, 20.

SHENAZZAR (She·naz'zar) [from Akkadian, meaning "Sin [the moon-god], Protect!"]. Fourth-named son of Jehoiachin (Jeconiah), born during his exile in Babylon.—1Ch 3:17, 18; see SHESHBAZZAR.

SHEOL (She'ol). The common grave of mankind, gravedom; not an individual burial place or grave (Heb., *qe'ver,* Jg 16:31; *qevu·rah',* Ge 35: 20), nor an individual tomb (Heb., *ga·dhish',* Job 21:32).

While several derivations for the Hebrew word *she'ohl'* have been offered, apparently it is derived from the Hebrew verb *sha·al',* meaning "ask; request." Regarding Sheol, in *A Compendious Hebrew Lexicon,* Samuel Pike stated that it is "the common receptacle or region of the dead; so called from the insatiability of the grave, which is as it were always asking or craving more." (Cambridge, 1811, p. 148) This would indicate that Sheol is the place (not a condition) that asks for or demands all without distinction, as it receives the dead of mankind within it.—Ge 37:35, ftn; Pr 30:15, 16.

The Hebrew word *she'ohl'* occurs 65 times in the Masoretic text. In the *King James Version,* it is translated 31 times as "hell," 31 times as "grave," and 3 times as "pit." The Catholic *Douay Version* rendered the word 63 times as "hell," once as "pit," and once as "death." In addition, at Isaiah 7:11 the Hebrew text originally read *she'ohl',* and it was rendered as "Hades" in the ancient Greek versions of Aquila, Symmachus, and Theodotion, and as "hell" in the *Douay Version.*—See *NW* ftn.

There is no English word that conveys the precise sense of the Hebrew word *she'ohl'.* Commenting on the use of the word "hell" in Bible translation, *Collier's Encyclopedia* (1986, Vol. 12, p. 28) says: "Since Sheol in Old Testament times referred simply to the abode of the dead and suggested no moral distinctions, the word 'hell,' as understood today, is not a happy translation. More recent versions transliterate the word into English as 'Sheol.'"—*RS, AT, NW.*

Regarding Sheol, the *Encyclopædia Britannica* (1971, Vol. 11, p. 276) noted: "Sheol was located somewhere 'under' the earth. . . . The state of the dead was one of neither pain nor pleasure. Neither reward for the righteous nor punishment for the wicked was associated with Sheol. The good and the bad alike, tyrants and saints, kings and orphans, Israelites and gentiles—all slept together without awareness of one another."

While the Greek teaching of the immortality of the human soul infiltrated Jewish religious thinking in later centuries, the Bible record shows that Sheol refers to mankind's common grave as a place where there is no consciousness. (Ec 9: 4-6, 10) Those in Sheol neither praise God nor mention him. (Ps 6:4, 5; Isa 38:17-19) Yet it cannot be said that it simply represents 'a condition of being separated from God,' since the Scriptures render such a teaching untenable by showing that Sheol is "in front of" him, and that God is in effect "there." (Pr 15:11; Ps 139:7, 8; Am 9:1, 2) For this reason Job, longing to be relieved of his suffering, prayed that he might go to Sheol and later be remembered by Jehovah and be called out from Sheol.—Job 14:12-15.

Throughout the inspired Scriptures, Sheol is continually associated with death and not life. (1Sa 2:6; 2Sa 22:6; Ps 18:4, 5; 49:7-10, 14, 15; 88:2-6; 89:48; Isa 28:15-18; also compare Ps 116:3, 7-10 with 2Co 4:13, 14.) It is spoken of as "the land of darkness" (Job 10:21) and a place of silence. (Ps 115:17) Abel apparently was the first one to go to Sheol, and since then countless millions of human dead have joined him in the dust of the ground.

On the day of Pentecost 33 C.E., the apostle Peter quoted from Psalm 16:10 and applied it to Christ Jesus. Luke, in quoting Peter's words, used the Greek word *hai'des,* thereby showing that Sheol and Hades refer to the same thing, mankind's common grave. (Ac 2:25-27, 29-32) During the Thousand Year Reign of Jesus Christ, Sheol, or Hades, is emptied and destroyed, through a resurrection of all of those in it.—Re 20:13, 14; see GRAVE; HADES; HELL.

Jonah and Sheol. In the account about Jonah, it is stated that "Jonah prayed to Jehovah his God from the inward parts of the fish and said: 'Out of my distress I called out to Jehovah, and he proceeded to answer me. Out of the belly of Sheol I cried for help. You heard my voice.'" (Jon 2:1, 2) Therefore, Jonah was comparing the inside of the fish to Sheol. He was as good as dead inside the fish, but Jehovah brought up his life from the pit, or Sheol, by preserving him alive and having him disgorged.—Jon 2:6; compare Ps 30:3.

Jesus compared Jonah's being in the belly of the fish with what would happen in his own case, saying: "For just as Jonah was in the belly of the huge fish three days and three nights, so the Son of man will be in the heart of the earth three days and three nights." (Mt 12:40) Although Jesus did not here use the word "Sheol" (Hades), the apostle Peter did use the word "Hades" when referring to Jesus' death and resurrection.—Ac 2:27.

Regarding the word "Sheol," Brynmor F. Price and Eugene A. Nida noted: "The word occurs often in the Psalms and in the book of Job to refer to the place to which all dead people go. It is represented as a dark place, in which there is no activity worthy of the name. There are no moral distinctions there, so 'hell' (KJV) is not a suitable translation, since that suggests a contrast with 'heaven' as the dwelling-place of the righteous after death. In a sense, 'the grave' in a generic sense is a near equivalent, except that Sheol is more a mass grave in which all the dead dwell together. . . . The use of this particular imagery may have been considered suitable here [in Jonah 2:2] in view of Jonah's imprisonment in the interior of the fish."—*A Translators Handbook on the Book of Jonah,* 1978, p. 37.

SHEPHAM (She'pham). A site on the eastern border of the Promised Land, apparently no great distance from Riblah. (Nu 34:10, 11) Its location is now unknown.

SHEPHATIAH (Sheph·a·ti'ah) [Jehovah Has Judged].

1. One of the Benjamite warriors who defected from Saul to David at Ziklag; a Hariphite.—1Ch 12:1, 2, 5.

2. The fifth son born to David while he was ruling in Hebron (1077-1070 B.C.E.). Shephatiah's mother was Abital.—2Sa 3:2, 4; 1Ch 3:1, 3.

3. Prince of the tribe of Simeon during David's reign; son of Maacah.—1Ch 27:16, 22.

4. A son of Jehoshaphat given many gifts and fortified cities by his father, later slain by his oldest brother Jehoram.—2Ch 21:2-4.

5. One of the princes of Judah who, on securing King Zedekiah's permission to kill Jeremiah, had him thrown into a cistern; son of Mattan.—Jer 38:1-6, 10.

6. Founder of a family in Israel of which 372 males returned to Jerusalem with Zerubbabel in 537 B.C.E., and 80 more, headed by Zebadiah, with Ezra in 468 B.C.E.—Ezr 2:1, 2, 4; 8:1, 8; Ne 7:9.

7. A family of "the sons of the servants of Solomon" who also returned from Babylon with Zerubbabel.—Ezr 2:1, 2, 55, 57; Ne 7:59.

8. A Benjamite, one of whose descendants is listed as living in Jerusalem after the Babylonian exile.—1Ch 9:7, 8.

9. A descendant of Judah through Perez and ancestor of one who lived in Jerusalem during Nehemiah's governorship.—Ne 11:1, 2, 4.

SHEPHELAH (She·phe'lah) [Lowland]. A designation usually applied to the region of low hills between Palestine's central mountain range and the coastal plains of Philistia. (De 1:7; Jos 9:1; 10:40; 11:2; 12:8; Jg 1:9; 2Ch 28:18; Ob 19; Zec 7:7) The Shephelah was one of the regions of the territory assigned to Judah. (Jos 15:33-44)

Though attaining an altitude of about 450 m (1,500 ft), it is a "lowland" (compare Jer 17:26; 32:44; 33:13 where *shephe·lah'* appears in the Hebrew text) when compared with the much higher central mountain range. "The Shephelah" was bordered by the Negeb on the S (Jg 1:9) and "the mountainous region of Israel" (beyond the Low Plain of Aijalon) on the N.—Jos 11:16.

The valleys that divide the rolling foothills of this region served as natural routes for E-W travel. The Shephelah is fertile, and a temperate climate prevails there. Anciently the region was noted for its many sycamore trees and olive groves. It also provided pasturage for flocks and herds.—1Ki 10:27; 1Ch 27:28; 2Ch 1:15; 9:27; 26:10.

The Shephelah associated with "the mountainous region of Israel" (Jos 11:16) is perhaps the hilly region between the mountains of Samaria and the Plain of Sharon. This area is narrower and less distinct than the Judean Shephelah. There is no basis for viewing the distinction between Judah and Israel in the 11th chapter of Joshua (see vs 21) as an anachronism. A footnote in a commentary by C. F. Keil and F. Delitzsch observes: "The distinction . . . may be explained without difficulty even from the circumstances of Joshua's own time. Judah and the double tribe of Joseph (Ephraim and Manasseh) received their inheritance by lot before any of the others. But whilst the tribe of Judah proceeded into the territory allotted to them in the south, all the other tribes still remained in Gilgal; and even at a later period, when Ephraim and Manasseh were in their possessions, all Israel, with the exception of Judah, were still encamped at Shiloh. Moreover, the two parts of the nation were now separated by the territory which was afterwards assigned to the tribe of Benjamin, but had no owner at this time; and in addition to this, the altar, tabernacle, and ark of the covenant were in the midst of Joseph and the other tribes that were still assembled at Shiloh."—*Commentary on the Old Testament*, 1973, Vol. II, Joshua, pp. 124, 125.

SHEPHER, MOUNT (She'pher). A mountain on the Sinai Peninsula at which Israel had a campsite.—Nu 33:23, 24.

SHEPHERD. A person who tends, feeds, and guards sheep or flocks of both sheep and goats. (Ge 30:35, 36; Mt 25:32; see SHEEP.) The occupation of shepherds dates back to Adam's son Abel. (Ge 4:2) Although looked upon honorably elsewhere, in agricultural Egypt shepherds were viewed with disdain.—Ge 46:34.

Often the owner, his children (both sons and daughters), or another relative cared for the flock. (Ge 29:9; 30:31; 1Sa 16:11) Among the wealthy, as in Nabal's case, servants worked as shepherds, and there may have been a chief or principal shepherd over the others. (1Sa 21:7; 25:7, 14-17) When the owner or members of his family shepherded the animals, the flock usually fared well. But a hired man did not always have the same personal interest in the flock, which therefore suffered at times.—Joh 10:12, 13.

The shepherd's equipment might include a tent (Isa 38:12), a garment in which he could wrap himself (Jer 43:12), a rod and a sling for defense, a bag for keeping provisions of food (1Sa 17:40; Ps 23:4), and a long curved staff or crook used in guiding the flock (Le 27:32; Mic 7:14).

Nomadic shepherds, like Abraham, dwelt in tents and moved about from one location to another to find pasturage for their flocks. (Ge 13:2, 3, 18) However, at times the owner of the animals remained at a certain location, his home or base camp, whereas his servants or some family members traveled with the flock.—Ge 37:12-17; 1Sa 25:2, 3, 7, 15, 16.

Do sheep really know the voice of their particular shepherd?

The flocks of several shepherds were sometimes penned in the same sheepfold for the night, with a doorkeeper to watch over them. When the shepherds arrived in the morning, they called to their flock, and the sheep responded to their shepherd and to him only. Walking ahead of the flock, the shepherd led it to pasture. (Joh 10:1-5) From personal observations in Syria and Palestine in the nineteenth century, W. M. Thomson wrote: "[The sheep] are so tame and so trained that they *follow* their keeper with the utmost docility. He leads them forth from the fold, or from their houses in the villages, just where he pleases. As there are many flocks in such a place as this, each one takes a different path; and it is his business to find pasture for them. It is necessary, therefore, that they should be taught to follow, and not to stray away into the unfenced fields of corn which lie so temptingly on either side. Any one that thus wanders is sure to get into trouble. The shepherd calls sharply from time to time to remind them of his presence. They know his voice, and follow on; but if a stranger call, they stop short, lift up their heads in alarm, and, if it is repeated, they turn and flee, because they know not the voice of a stranger. This is not the fanciful costume of parable; it is simple fact. I have made the experiment repeatedly. The shepherd goes before, not merely to point out the way but to see that it is practicable and safe."—*The Land and the Book,* revised by J. Grande, 1910, p. 179.

Similarly, J. L. Porter, in *The Giant Cities of Bashan and Syria's Holy Places,* observes: "The shepherds led their flocks forth from the gates of the city. They were in full view, and we watched them and listened to them with no little interest. Thousands of sheep and goats were there, grouped in dense, confused masses. The shepherds stood together until all came out. Then they separated, each shepherd taking a different path, and uttering as he advanced a shrill peculiar call. The sheep heard them. At first the masses swayed and moved, as if shaken by some internal convulsion; then points struck out in the direction taken by the shepherds; these became longer and longer until the confused masses were resolved into long, living streams, flowing after their leaders."—1868, p. 45.

In the evening the shepherd brought the animals back to the sheepfold, where he stationed himself at the door and counted the sheep as they passed beneath his crook or his hands.—Le 27:32; Jer 33:13; see SHEEPFOLD.

A Rigorous Life. The shepherd's life was not an easy one. He was exposed to both heat and cold, as well as to sleepless nights. (Ge 31:40; Lu 2:8) With personal danger to himself, he protected the flock from predators, such as lions, wolves, and bears, as well as from thieves. (Ge 31:39; 1Sa 17:34-36; Isa 31:4; Am 3:12; Joh 10:10-12) The shepherd had to keep the flock from scattering (1Ki 22:17), look for lost sheep (Lu 15:4), carry feeble or weary lambs in his bosom (Isa 40:11), and care for the sick and injured—bandaging broken limbs and rubbing injuries with olive oil. (Ps 23:5; Eze 34:3, 4; Zec 11:16) He had to exercise care when shepherding ewes giving suck. (Ge 33:13) Daily, generally around noon, the shepherd watered the flock. (Ge 29:3, 7, 8) If the animals were watered at wells, gutters in the ground or troughs had to be filled with water. (Ex 2:16-19; compare Ge 24:20.) At the wells there sometimes were unpleasant encounters with other shepherds.—Ge 26:20, 21.

The shepherd was entitled to a share of the flock's produce (1Co 9:7), and often his wages were paid in animals (Ge 30:28, 31-33; 31:41), although sometimes also in money. (Zec 11:7, 12) He might have to make compensation for losses (Ge 31:39), but under the Law covenant no compensation was required for an animal torn by a wild beast.—Ex 22:13.

What has been said concerning the shepherd can generally be applied to the herdsman. However, the occupation of herdsman was not restricted to tending sheep and goats. There were also herders of cattle, asses, camels, and swine. —Ge 12:16; 13:7, 8; Mt 8:32, 33.

Figurative and Illustrative. Jehovah is a Shepherd who lovingly cares for his sheep, that is, his people. (Ps 23:1-6; 80:1; Jer 31:10; Eze 34:11-16; 1Pe 2:25) His Son Jesus Christ is "the great shepherd" (Heb 13:20) and "the chief shepherd," under whose direction the overseers in Christian congregations shepherd the flock of God, willingly, unselfishly, and eagerly. (1Pe 5:2-4) Jesus referred to himself as "the fine shepherd," one who really has compassion for "the sheep" and demonstrated this by surrendering his soul in their behalf. (Joh 10:11; see Mt 9:36.) But as foretold, the striking of "the fine shepherd" caused the flock to scatter.—Zec 13:7; Mt 26:31.

In the Bible, the term "shepherds" at times denotes the rulers and leaders of the Israelites, both faithful and unfaithful. (Isa 63:11; Jer 23:1-4; 50:6; Eze 34:2-10; compare Nu 27:16-18; Ps 78:70-72.) Similarly, the term "shepherds" applies to leaders of other nations. (Jer 25:34-36; 49:19; Na 3:18; compare Isa 44:28.) At Jeremiah 6:3, "the shepherds" seem to represent the commanders of invading armies. The presence of shepherds with their flocks figures in a picture of restoration (Jer 33:12), whereas Babylon's desolation was foretold to be so complete that 'not even a shepherd would make his flock lie down there.' —Isa 13:20.

At Revelation 12:5, the 'shepherding' of the nations with an iron rod means their destruction. —Compare Ps 2:9.

SHEPHERD'S BAG. See BAG; FOOD POUCH.

SHEPHO (She′pho). A son of the Horite sheik Shobal who lived in Edom.—Ge 36:20, 21, 23; 1Ch 1:40.

SHEPHUPHAM (She·phu′pham), **SHEPHUPHAN** (She·phu′phan). A Benjamite who founded the tribal family of Shuphamites. (Nu 26:38, 39; 1Ch 8:5) Elsewhere called Muppim (Ge 46:21) and Shuppim.—1Ch 7:12.

SHEREBIAH (She·re·bi′ah) [possibly meaning "Jah [Has Sent] Parching Heat"].

1. A prominent Levite who returned to Jerusalem with Zerubbabel in 537 B.C.E.—Ne 12:1, 8.

2. A Levite descended from Mahli; "a man of discretion" who was summoned to join Ezra on his journey to Jerusalem in 468 B.C.E. (Ezr 8:17,

18) He is probably the same person as the 'chief of the priests' mentioned in Ezra 8:24, one of those entrusted with transporting to Jerusalem the valuable things contributed for temple use. —Ezr 8:25-30.

3. A Levite who assisted Ezra with reading and explaining the Law to the people assembled in Jerusalem after the wall was rebuilt in 455 B.C.E. (Ne 8:2, 7, 8) Later the same month, they again convened and Sherebiah joined in proposing "a trustworthy arrangement," which the nation ratified, promising to remain faithful to Jehovah. (Ne 9:1, 4, 5, 38) This Sherebiah may have been the same Levite as No. 2, personally attesting to the covenant, or he may have been a representative of some family by that name, perhaps descended from No. 1.—Ne 10:1, 9, 12; 12:24.

SHERESH (She′resh) [Root]. A descendant of Manasseh and son of Machir by his wife Maacah. —1Ch 7:14, 16.

SHESHACH (She′shach). Probably a symbolic name for Babylon. (Jer 25:26; 51:41) One suggestion is that Sheshach means "Copper-Gated," and this would fit Babylon. Still another view is that "Sheshach" stood for *SiskuKI* of an old Babylonian royal register. *Sisku* or *Siska* may have been a district of ancient Babylon. Jewish tradition, however, has it that Sheshach is a cipher for the Hebrew name Babel (or, Babylon), by the device known as athbash. According to this cryptographic system, the true name is disguised by replacing the last letter of the Hebrew alphabet (*taw*) with the first (*'a'leph*), and the second-last letter (*shin*) with the second (*behth*), and so on. Consequently, in "Babel" each *behth* (b) would be changed to *shin* (sh), and the *la'medh* (l) to *kaph* (kh), thus becoming *She·shakh'*. The name Sheshach may also imply humiliation, for which Babylon was due.—Jer 25:26, ftn; *Soncino Books of the Bible*, edited by A. Cohen, London, 1949.

SHESHAI (She′shai). Brother of Ahiman and Talmai.—Nu 13:22; Jos 15:14; Jg 1:10; see AHIMAN No. 1.

SHESHAN (She′shan). A descendant of Judah through Jerahmeel. Sheshan had no sons and so gave his daughter (probably Ahlai) in marriage to his slave Jarha in order to continue his line of descent.—1Ch 2:31, 34, 35.

SHESHBAZZAR (Shesh·baz′zar). An appointee of King Cyrus over the first exiles returning from Babylon. As he led the Jews back, Sheshbazzar brought with him the gold and silver utensils that Nebuchadnezzar had looted from the temple. On arrival in Jerusalem, he laid the foundations of the second temple.—Ezr 1:7-11; 5:14-16.

Opinion is somewhat divided as to whether Sheshbazzar was the same person as Governor Zerubbabel or was some other individual. Shenazzar the son of King Jehoiachin mentioned at 1 Chronicles 3:18 is suggested by some in view of the resemblance between the two names, as well as Sheshbazzar's title "prince of Judah" appearing in some versions of Ezra 1:8. (*AS, RS*) This theory is very weak, however, for the resemblance in names is not great, and Zerubbabel, a grandson of Jehoiachin, had just as much claim to the title "prince ["chieftain," *NW*] of Judah" as an offspring of the first generation.

Some modern scholars, in attempting to identify Sheshbazzar and Zerubbabel as separate individuals, say that Cyrus first appointed Sheshbazzar as governor but that later Sheshbazzar was succeeded by Zerubbabel during the reign of Darius, and therefore the building of the temple is credited to Zerubbabel.

A greater likelihood, it appears, is that Sheshbazzar is the same as Zerubbabel, and the majority of scholars and reference works so connect the names. Note these points of comparison: In general, what is attributed to Sheshbazzar in the two passages where he is mentioned by name is elsewhere in effect credited to Zerubbabel. Both are called by the title "governor." (Ezr 1:11; 2:1, 2; 5:2, 14, 16; Hag 1:1, 14; 2:2, 21; Zec 4:9) Zerubbabel is acknowledged as leader of the returning exiles; the name "Sheshbazzar" is not even found in this list.—Ezr 2:2; 3:1, 2.

The name Sheshbazzar seems to have been an official or Babylonian name given to Zerubbabel, as Daniel and others were given official court names. (Da 1:7) "Sheshbazzar" is more typically Chaldean than "Zerubbabel." In Ezra 5:14-16 an official letter is quoted, and in Ezra chapter 1 the official edict of Cyrus has just been quoted, perhaps giving rise to the use of such a possible official name in these passages.

SHETHAR (She′thar). One of the seven princes of Persia and Media consulted by King Ahasuerus when Queen Vashti refused to obey him.—Es 1:13-15.

SHETHAR-BOZENAI (She′thar-boz′e·nai) An official, perhaps a secretary, associated with Tattenai the Persian governor "beyond the River" during the reign of Darius I (Hystaspis). (Ezr 5:3 6; 6:6, 13) Shethar-bozenai came with Tattenai and others to Jerusalem to register their objec tions to the Jews' rebuilding the temple, which work Artaxerxes had banned. However, the Jews kept working in spite of the complaints while a report was made to Darius. Tattenai and Shethar-bozenai and his colleagues wrote to the king reporting on the activities in Jerusalem and stating that the temple builders had referred to an order of authorization that had been put through by Cyrus the king. They asked that the matter be investigated. Darius' reply acknowledged Cyrus' unchangeable decree and not only ordered Shethar-bozenai and his comrades to 'keep their distance' from Jerusalem but also demanded, under severe penalty, that material support be provided from the royal treasury for the Jews so that their temple building and services could continue. Shethar-bozenai and his associates did as commanded.—Ezr 4:23–6:13.

SHEVA (She'va).

1. [from a root meaning "make equal; smooth out"]. Father of Machbenah and Gibea. As these are names of towns, however, Sheva was perhaps the father of those who settled there or was himself the founder of these towns. Sheva's father Caleb (Chelubai) headed one of the three major divisions of Judah's descendants through Hezron. —1Ch 2:9, 48-50.

2. David's secretary.—2Sa 20:25; see SERAIAH No. 2.

SHIBAH (Shi'bah) [Oath; or, Seven].
A well that Isaac's servants dug, or redug, at Beer-sheba. (Ge 26:32, 33; compare 26:18.) They reported finding water there after concluding a covenant of peace with Abimelech the king of Gerar; hence, Isaac named the well "Shibah" (referring to an oath or statement sworn to by seven things). (Ge 26:26-33) Abraham had similarly made a covenant with Abimelech (either this Philistine king or another having the same name or title). On that occasion Abimelech accepted seven female lambs from the patriarch in evidence of Abraham's title to a controversial well, perhaps the same one that Isaac later named "Shibah." By using "Shibah" (another form of the name Sheba), Isaac also apparently was preserving the name "Beer-sheba," originally given to this place by Abraham.—Ge 21:22-32; see BEER-SHEBA.

SHIBBOLETH (Shib'bo·leth).
The password used by the men of Gilead to identify Ephraimites who tried to flee across the Jordan. It means "ear of grain" or "flowing stream." Escaping Ephraimites, during their conflict with Jephthah, gave themselves away to the Gileadite sentries at the

fords of the Jordan by mispronouncing the initial "sh" sound of this password. They would say "Sibboleth." (Jg 12:4-6) Thus, it is evident that some variation of pronunciation existed among the tribes, even as in later times the Galileans had a manner of speech distinct from the Judeans. —Compare Mt 26:73; Lu 22:59.

SHIELD. See ARMS, ARMOR.

SHIHOR (Shi'hor) [from Egyptian, meaning "Pond of Horus"].
Evidently the easternmost branch of the Nile River in the Delta region. Shihor, in its four occurrences in the Hebrew text, is always associated with Egypt. (Jos 13:3, "branch of the Nile"; 1Ch 13:5, "river"; Isa 23:3; Jer 2:18) While some commentators would equate it with "the torrent valley of Egypt" (Nu 34:5), usually identified with the Wadi el-'Arish, SW of Gaza, Jeremiah 2:18 and Isaiah 23:3 appear to link it more closely with Egypt and the Nile than was the case with this latter torrent valley, or wadi. Particularly the Isaiah text with its reference to "the seed of Shihor" would seem to apply to a regularly flowing stream (na·har') rather than to a seasonal one (na'chal). For these reasons the Shihor, at least in these two texts, is more often identified with the easternmost arm of the Nile (after it divides into several branches upon reaching the Delta region). This position might allow for its being referred to as "in front of [that is, on the E of or to the E of] Egypt," as at Joshua 13:3.

This latter text, however, forms part of the description of the land that was yet to be conquered by the Israelites after the initial campaigns under Joshua, extending as far N as "the entering in of Hamath." (Jos 13:1-6) Those arguing for an identification with the Wadi el-'Arish point out that elsewhere the boundaries of Israel's inheritance are given as from "the torrent valley of Egypt" up to "the entering in of Hamath." (Nu 34:2, 5, 7, 8) At Joshua 13:3, some translations (RS, NW), however, consider the reference to the Shihor ("branch of the Nile," NW) to be part of a parenthetical expression giving a historical note as to how far to the SW the land of the Canaanites at one time had extended. On this basis, instead of describing the territory to be conquered, the text could simply be showing that the Canaanites once resided as far as the easternmost border of Egypt proper.

Similarly, a correspondency is noted between the reference to David's congregating the people of Israel from Shihor ("the river of Egypt," NW) to Hamath (when endeavoring to bring the ark of the covenant up to Jerusalem) and the congregating of the people in Solomon's day from "the entering in of Hamath down to the torrent valley of Egypt." (1Ch 13:5; 1Ki 8:65) The explanation for this may be that in the latter case (Solomon's time) the account gives the practical boundaries of Israelite residence. The region between the Wadi el-'Arish and the eastern arm of the Nile is basically desert territory and scrubland, so this wadi, or torrent valley, fittingly marked the limit of territory suitable for Israelite inhabitation, whereas in the former case (David's) the description may be that of the entire region of Israelite activity, the region effectively dominated by David, which indeed ran to the border of Egypt.

Even prior to David, King Saul had pursued the Amalekites as far as Shur, "which is in front of Egypt" (1Sa 15:7), and the dominion Solomon received through David is stated to have reached to "the boundary of Egypt." (1Ki 4:21) So, even though the territory actually distributed to the Israelite tribes did not extend beyond "the torrent valley of Egypt," this would not appear to argue against the identification of the Shihor with a "branch of the Nile" at Joshua 13:3 and "the river of Egypt" at 1 Chronicles 13:5.

The word "Shihor" does not occur at Genesis 15:18, where Jehovah promised Abraham the land from "the river of Egypt to the great river, the river Euphrates." So, here also, there is a question as to whether "the river [form of *na·har'*] of Egypt" refers to some part of the Nile or to "the torrent valley [*na'chal*] of Egypt" (the Wadi el-'Arish). The answer would depend upon whether Jehovah here described the actual area distributed as a tribal inheritance or referred to the whole region dominated by the Israelite kingdom at its greatest extent. If the former, then this text would likely apply to the Wadi el-'Arish; if the latter, then to the Shihor.—See EGYPT, TORRENT VALLEY OF.

SHIHOR-LIBNATH (Shi'hor-lib'nath). Eusebius and Jerome believed Shihor-libnath originally constituted the name of two sites, Shihor *and* Labanath. However, it is apparently a river on Asher's boundary. (Jos 19:24-26) Some geographers connect the Shihor-libnath with the Nahr ez-Zerqa (Nahal Tanninim), which flows into the Mediterranean Sea about 10 km (6 mi) S of Dor.

SHIKKERON (Shik'ke·ron). A site on the boundary of Judah. (Jos 15:1, 11) Some tentatively identify it with Tell el-Ful, about 5 km (3 mi) NW of Ekron (Khirbet el-Muqanna' [Tel Miqne]), with which it is mentioned in the Joshua account.

SHILHI (Shil'hi). Father of Azubah, who was Asa's wife and the mother of Jehoshaphat.—1Ki 22:41-43; 2Ch 20:31.

SHILHIM (Shil'him). A city in the southern part of Judah. (Jos 15:21, 32) It seems to be the same as Sharuhen, listed among the cities in Judah's territory belonging to Simeon. (Jos 19: 1, 6) The list at 1 Chronicles 4:31 appears to call the same city Shaaraim. Tell el-Far'ah (Tel Sharuhen), about 35 km (22 mi) W of Beer-sheba, is tentatively identified with it.

SHILLEM (Shil'lem) [from a root meaning "make peace; compensate; repay"]. Last named of Naphtali's four sons listed among "the names of Israel's sons who came into Egypt." (Ge 46:8, 24) He founded the tribal family of Shillemites. (Nu 26:49, 50) At 1 Chronicles 7:13 his name is spelled Shallum in the Masoretic text, though Shillem is found in seven Hebrew manuscripts.

SHILOAH (Shi·lo'ah) [Sender]. It appears that the name Shiloah designated a conduit or canal at Jerusalem. One ancient canal ran from the mouth of the cave of the Gihon Spring down the Kidron Valley and around the end of the SE hill to a pool at the junction of the Hinnom and Tyropoeon valleys. The canal's gradient of about 4 or 5 mm per meter (less than 0.2 in. per yard) produced a slow gentle flow, a feature that would fit "the waters of the Shiloah that are going gently." The reference to these "waters of the Shiloah" at Isaiah 8:6 is figurative and represents the source of real salvation and security.

SHILOH (Shi'loh) [He Whose It Is; He to Whom It Belongs].

1. In pronouncing a blessing upon Judah, the dying patriarch Jacob said: "The scepter will not turn aside from Judah, neither the commander's staff from between his feet, until Shiloh comes; and to him the obedience of the peoples will belong." (Ge 49:10) Beginning with the rule of the Judean David, power to command (the commander's staff) and regal sovereignty (the scepter) were the possessions of the tribe of Judah. This was to continue until the coming of Shiloh, indicating that the royal line of Judah would terminate in Shiloh as the permanent heir. Similarly, before the overthrow of the kingdom of Judah, Jehovah indicated to the last Judean king Zedekiah, that rulership would be given to one having the legal right. (Eze 21:26, 27) This would evidently be Shiloh, as the name "Shiloh" is understood to signify "He Whose It Is; He to Whom It Belongs."

Shiloh; its desolate condition was used by Jeremiah as a vivid example

In the centuries that followed, Jesus Christ is the only descendant of David to whom kingship was promised. Before the birth of Jesus, the angel Gabriel said to Mary: "Jehovah God will give him the throne of David his father, and he will rule as king over the house of Jacob forever, and there will be no end of his kingdom." (Lu 1:32, 33) Therefore, Shiloh must be Jesus Christ, "the Lion that is of the tribe of Judah."—Re 5:5; compare Isa 11:10; Ro 15:12.

Concerning the ancient Jewish view of Genesis 49:10, a *Commentary* edited by F. C. Cook (p. 233) notes: "All Jewish antiquity referred the prophecy to Messiah. Thus the Targum of Onkelos has 'until the Messiah come, whose is the kingdom;' the Jerusalem Targum, 'until the time that the king Messiah shall come, whose is the kingdom.' . . . So the Babylonian Talmud ('Sanhedrim,' cap. II. fol. 982), 'What is Messiah's name? His name is Shiloh, for it is written, Until Shiloh come.'"

2. A city located in the territory of Ephraim and "north of Bethel, toward the east of the highway that goes up from Bethel to Shechem and toward the south of Lebonah." (Jg 21:19) The suggested identification for Shiloh is Khirbet Seilun (Shillo), about 15 km (9.5 mi) NNE of Bethel. The site fits the Biblical description. It occupies a hill and, with the exception of a valley on the SW, is surrounded by higher hills.

After the tabernacle was set up at Shiloh (Jos 18:1), the apportioning of the land to the Israelites was completed from there. (Jos 18:1–21:42)

Following the division of the land, the tribes E of the Jordan erected an altar by that river. Viewing this as an act of apostasy, the other tribes assembled at Shiloh to fight against them. However, when it was explained that the altar was to be a memorial of faithfulness to Jehovah, peaceful relations were maintained.—Jos 22:10-34.

At a later time, 12,000 valiant Israelite warriors undertook punitive action against the inhabitants of Jabesh-gilead for failing to join in the fight against the Benjamites. However, 400 virgins of Jabesh-gilead were brought to Shiloh and later given to the Benjamites. The Benjamites were also instructed to get other wives from the daughters of Shiloh, carrying them off by force as the women participated in the circle dances associated with the yearly festival to Jehovah held at Shiloh.—Jg 21:8-23.

During most, if not all, of the period covered by the book of Judges, the tabernacle remained at Shiloh. (Jg 18:31; 1Sa 1:3, 9, 24; 2:14; 3:21; 1Ki 2:27) Shortly before High Priest Eli's death, the Israelites, while fighting the Philistines, removed the Ark from the tabernacle and transferred it to the battlefield, trusting in its presence to give them victory. However, Jehovah allowed the Philistines to capture the Ark. As it was never returned to Shiloh, this signified that Jehovah had forsaken Shiloh, since the Ark represented his presence. (1Sa 4:2-11) The forsaking of Shiloh is alluded to by the psalmist (Ps 78:60, 61; compare 1Sa 4:21, 22) and is used in Jeremiah's prophecy to illustrate what Jehovah was going to do to the temple at Jerusalem.—Jer 7:12, 14; 26:6, 9.

In the tenth century B.C.E., the prophet Ahijah lived at Shiloh. (1Ki 12:15; 14:2, 4) After the assassination of Gedaliah, in 607 B.C.E., certain men from Shiloh (either from the city or the region) came to Jerusalem to sacrifice.—Jer 41:5.

SHILONITE (Shi'lo·nite) [Of (Belonging to) Shiloh].

1. An alternate form (used in the plural) for the name of the family that sprang from Judah's third son Shelah.—1Ch 9:5; Ge 46:12; see SHELAH No. 2; SHELANITES.

2. An inhabitant of Shiloh, a town of quite some prominence in Israel's history. The designation is applied in Scripture only to the prophet Ahijah from Shiloh.—1Ki 11:29; 12:15; 15:29; 2Ch 9:29; 10:15.

SHILSHAH (Shil'shah) [Third; Three Parts]. A valiant, mighty chieftain in the tribe of Asher; son or descendant of Zophah.—1Ch 7:36, 37, 40.

SHIMEA (Shim'e·a) [possibly a shortened form of Shemaiah, meaning "Jehovah Has Heard (Listened)"].

1. A Merarite Levite.—1Ch 6:29, 30.

2. Ancestor of temple musician Asaph in the Levitical family of Gershon (Gershom).—1Ch 6:39, 43; Ex 6:16.

3. The third son of Jesse, hence an older brother of David.—1Ch 2:13, 15; 20:7; see SHAMMAH No. 2.

4. A son borne by Bath-sheba to David. (1Ch 3:5) He is elsewhere called Shammua.—2Sa 5:14; 1Ch 14:4.

SHIMEAH (Shim'e·ah) [possibly a shortened form of Shemaiah, meaning "Jehovah Has Heard (Listened)"].

1. Son of Mikloth, a Benjamite related to King Saul's ancestors; also called Shimeam.—1Ch 8:32; 9:35-39.

2. Another name for David's brother Shammah.—1Sa 16:9; 2Sa 13:3, 32; see SHAMMAH No. 2.

SHIMEAM (Shim'e·am). Son of Mikloth, who, it appears, lived in Jerusalem. This Benjamite was related to King Saul's ancestors. (1Ch 9:35-39) He is called Shimeah at 1 Chronicles 8:32.

SHIMEATH (Shim'e·ath) [from a root meaning "hear; listen"]. An Ammonite woman whose son was one of the assassins of Judah's King Jehoash.—2Ki 12:20, 21; 2Ch 24:25, 26.

SHIMEATHITES (Shim'e·ath·ites). A Kenite family of scribes living at Jabez. What connection they have in the genealogies of Judah is unknown.—1Ch 2:55.

SHIMEI (Shim'e·i) [possibly a shortened form of Shemaiah, meaning "Jehovah Has Heard (Listened)"].

1. Second-named son of Gershon (Gershom); grandson of Levi. (Ex 6:16, 17; Nu 3:17, 18; 1Ch 6:16, 17) Several Shimeite families of Levites descended from him.—Nu 3:21-26; 1Ch 23:7, 10, 11; Zec 12:13.

2. A Reubenite whose descendant Beerah, a chieftain, was taken into exile by Assyrian King Tilgath-pilneser (Tiglath-pileser III).—1Ch 5:1, 4-6.

3. A Merarite Levite.—1Ch 6:29.

4. A Gershonite Levite; ancestor of Asaph.—1Ch 6:39, 42.

5. A Benjamite whose nine sons (or descendants) were heads of forefathers' houses living in Jerusalem. (1Ch 8:1, 19-21, 28) He is apparently called Shema in 1 Chronicles 8:13, there identified as a family head in Aijalon.

6. A Simeonite, the son of Zaccur; he had 16 sons and 6 daughters.—1Ch 4:24-27.

7. One of David's brothers.—2Sa 21:21; see SHAMMAH No. 2.

8. A descendant of Gershon through Ladan. During David's reign, three sons (or descendants) of Shimei were heads of Levite families.—1Ch 23:8, 9.

9. Head of the tenth division of Levite musicians; son of Jeduthun.—1Ch 25:1, 3, 17.

10. Caretaker of David's vineyards; a Ramathite.—1Ch 27:27.

11. A loyal supporter of King David who refused to join Adonijah's conspiracy. (1Ki 1:8) He is presumably the same Shimei appointed as King Solomon's food deputy in Benjamin's territory; son of Ela.—1Ki 4:7, 18.

12. A Benjamite from the village of Bahurim. Shimei, the son of Gera, of a family in King Saul's house, harbored a grudge against David for years after Saul's death and the removal of the kingship from his house. Shimei found an occasion to vent his long-contained wrath when David and his party fled from Jerusalem on account of Absalom's rebellion. Just a little E of the Mount of Olives, Shimei walked along throwing stones and dust down at them and cursing David. Abishai asked David's permission to kill Shimei, but David refused, hoping that perhaps Jehovah would turn Shimei's curse into a blessing.—2Sa 16:5-13.

On David's return, with the situation reversed, Shimei and a thousand other Benjamites were the first to meet him, Shimei bowing before him and making expression of repentance for his sins. Again Abishai wanted to kill him, but again David did not allow it, this time swearing that he would not put Shimei to death. (2Sa 19:15-23) However, before his death David told Solomon to "bring his gray hairs down to Sheol with blood."—1Ki 2:8, 9.

At the start of his reign, Solomon called Shimei and ordered him to move to Jerusalem and not to leave the city; if he ever left the city, he would be put to death. Shimei agreed to these terms, but three years later he left the city to recover two of his slaves who had fled to Gath. On learning of this violation, Solomon called Shimei to account for breaking his oath to Jehovah and ordered Benaiah to execute him.—1Ki 2:36-46.

13. A Levite descendant of Heman who sanctified himself and helped dispose of the unclean objects removed from the temple at the beginning of Hezekiah's reign. (2Ch 29:12, 14-16) Probably the same as No. 14.

14. The Levite second in charge of storing the generous contributions and tithes brought to the temple during Hezekiah's reign. (2Ch 31:11-13) Probably identical with No. 13.

15. Ancestor of Mordecai; tribe of Benjamin. —Es 2:5.

16. Brother of Governor Zerubbabel; descendant of David in the tribe of Judah.—1Ch 3:19.

17. One of the Levites who dismissed their foreign wives and sons when reprimanded by Ezra for having made foreign marriage alliances. —Ezr 10:10, 11, 23, 44.

18, 19. Two Israelites, sons of Hashum and Binnui respectively, who also sent away their foreign wives and sons.—Ezr 10:33, 38, 44.

SHIMEITES (Shim′e·ites) [Of (Belonging to) Shimei]. Descendants of Shimei, the son of Gershon and the grandson of Levi. (Ex 6:16, 17) When the first census in the wilderness was taken, the Shimeites and the Libnites ("the families of the Gershonites") had registered ones totaling 7,500. (Nu 3:20b-22) The Shimeites were encamped with the Libnites "behind the tabernacle," that is, to the W. As Gershonites, their Levitical duties included transporting, erecting, and maintaining the tabernacle and its coverings, as well as the hangings of the courtyard, the screens (both to the entrance of the courtyard and to the tent), and the tent cords.—Ex 26:1, 7, 14, 36; 27: 9, 16; Nu 3:23-26.

Shimei had four sons—Jahath, Zina, Jeush, and Beriah. But since the last two did not have many sons, they joined together to become "a paternal house for one official class." This is mentioned in the time of David when it appears that the assigned tabernacle service of the Shimeites was divided among these three families. (1Ch 23:6, 7, 10, 11) Zechariah's prophecy especially included the family of the Shimeites among those who wail bitterly over "the One whom they pierced," a prophecy relating to Jesus.—Zec 12:10-13; Joh 19:37.

SHIMEON (Shim′e·on) [from a root meaning "hear; listen"]. One of the eight sons of Harim whom Ezra encouraged to dismiss their pagan wives and sons.—Ezr 10:10, 11, 31, 32, 44.

SHIMON (Shi′mon). Father of four sons in the tribe of Judah.—1Ch 4:20.

SHIMRATH (Shim′rath) [from a root meaning "guard"]. A Benjamite family head in Jerusalem; one of the nine sons of Shimei.—1Ch 8: 19-21, 28.

SHIMRI (Shim′ri) [from a root that means "guard"].

1. Simeonite ancestor of one of the chieftains who expanded the tribe's territory in the days of Hezekiah.—1Ch 4:24, 37-41.

2. Father of David's mighty man Jediael and probably also of "Joha his brother the Tizite." —1Ch 11:26, 45.

3. A Merarite son of Hosah included among the Levite gatekeepers selected by lot to the assignment W of the sanctuary. Though Shimri was not Hosah's firstborn, his father appointed him head of the paternal house.—1Ch 26:10, 12, 13, 16.

4. One of the Levites who helped dispose of the unclean objects that Hezekiah had cleared out of the temple; descendant of Elizaphan.—2Ch 29:12-16.

SHIMRITH (Shim′rith). A Moabitess whose son Jehozabad was one of the assassins of King Jehoash of Judah. (2Ch 24:25, 26) The name appears in the masculine gender at 2 Kings 12:21. —See SHOMER No. 2.

SHIMRON (Shim′ron).

1. [Thornbush]. A son of Issachar. (Ge 46:13; 1Ch 7:1) He was among "Israel's sons who came into Egypt." His descendants, the Shimronites, formed one of the families of Issachar.—Ge 46:8; Nu 26:23, 24.

2. [From a root meaning "guard"]. A town whose king joined the confederation of northern Canaanites that Joshua defeated at the waters of Merom. (Jos 11:1, 5, 8; 12:20; see SHIMRON-MERON.) Shimron was included in the tribal allotment of Zebulun. (Jos 19:10, 15) It is identified with Khirbet Sammuniyeh (Tel Shimron), about 8 km (5 mi) W of Nazareth.

SHIMRONITES (Shim′ron·ites) [Of (Belonging to) Shimron]. Descendants of Issachar's son Shimron. At the time of the second wilderness census, the registered ones of this family, together with those of the three other families making up this tribe, numbered 64,300.—Nu 26:23-25.

SHIMRON-MERON

SHIMRON-MERON (Shim'ron-me'ron). A town, the domain of a king defeated by Joshua. (Jos 12:7, 8, 20) It is perhaps the full name of the town Shimron, or possibly it is a reference to the fact that the king of Shimron was one of those defeated at the waters of Merom. (Jos 11:1, 5, 7, 8) Some manuscripts separate the names as being two towns, Shimron and Meron, but no place called Meron is elsewhere alluded to.

SHIMSHAI (Shim'shai) [from a root meaning "sun"]. A scribe in the administration of Rehum, the chief government official of the Persian province "beyond the River," which included Jerusalem. Shimshai joined in writing a letter to the Persian ruler Artaxerxes in an effort to stop the Jews from their rebuilding work in Jerusalem. Artaxerxes put through an order to stop the work, which was resumed during the reign of his successor, King Darius Hystaspis (Darius I of Persia).—Ezr 4:8-24.

SHIN. See SIN, SHIN.

SHINAB (Shi'nab) [from Akkadian, meaning "Sin [the moon-god] Is His Father"]. King of Admah; one of five monarchs in the southern Dead Sea area whose rebellion against vassalage to Chedorlaomer was unsuccessful.—Ge 14:1-10.

SHINAR (Shi'nar). The original name of the area between the Tigris and Euphrates rivers later called Babylonia. It was there that Nimrod assumed kingship over Babel, Erech, Accad, and Calneh, and where construction of the temple-tower of Babel was aborted. (Ge 10:9, 10; 11:2-8) Later, the king of Shinar, Amraphel, was one of the confederates who took Abraham's nephew Lot captive. (Ge 14:1, 9, 12) This territory was still called by its original name in the days of Joshua. (Jos 7:21) It is referred to by the prophets Isaiah, Daniel, and Zechariah.—Isa 11:11; Da 1:2; Zec 5:11; see BABEL; BABYLON No. 2.

SHINING ONE. A descriptive designation applied to the "king of Babylon." (Isa 14:4, 12) The Hebrew expression thus translated (*NW, Ro, Yg*) comes from a root meaning "shine." (Job 29:3) The rendering "Lucifer" (*KJ, Da*) is derived from the Latin *Vulgate.*

The "shining one" is represented as saying in his heart: "Above the stars of God I shall lift up my throne, and I shall sit down upon the mountain of meeting." (Isa 14:13) Biblical evidence points to Mount Zion as the "mountain of meeting." (See MOUNTAIN OF MEETING.) Hence, since stars can refer to kings (Nu 24:17; Re 22:16), "the stars of God" must be the kings of the Davidic line who ruled from Mount Zion. The "king of Babylon" (the dynasty of Babylonian kings), reflecting the attitude of Satan the god of this system of things, indicated his ambition to lift up his throne "above the stars of God" by desiring to make the kings of the line of David mere vassals and then finally to dethrone them. Like stars that shed light, the "king of Babylon" shone brightly in the ancient world and could be termed "shining one."

SHION (Shi'on) [from a root meaning "crash in ruins"]. A city of Issachar. (Jos 19:17, 19) 'Ayun esh-Sha'in, a short distance E of Nazareth, may preserve the name Shion and has been tentatively identified with it.

SHIP. A relatively large seagoing vessel. The Bible generally makes only incidental mention of ships, shipping, and ship's gear, but it does afford some clues as to ships of Biblical times. Other descriptions of ancient ships are derived from historical annals of various nations or from pictorial representations of merchant ships, marine battles, and so forth.

Egyptian. Papyrus reeds, woven and lashed together, provided material for a wide variety of Egyptian boats. They ranged in size from small riverboats that could hold one or just a few hunters or fishermen, and that could be swiftly paddled along the Nile, to the large sailing vessel with upturned prow and the sturdiness to ply the open seas. The Ethiopians and the Babylonians likewise used reed vessels; Babylon also possessed a large fleet of galley ships.

A relief at Medinet Habu depicts Egyptian vessels that had a mast with a sail and a crow's nest atop the mast. They were also powered by oars, with a large paddle at the stern for a rudder. The prow is fashioned in the figure of a lioness' head having the body of an Asian person in its mouth.

Large ships with rectangular sails and more than 20 oars, probably having a center keel, made long journeys across the Mediterranean Sea. That ships already were plying the seas in the time of Moses is shown by Jehovah's warning on the Plains of Moab that, if disobedient, the Israelites would be brought "back to Egypt by ships," there to be offered on the slave market.—De 28:68.

Phoenician. In picturing the city of Tyre as a pretty ship, the prophet Ezekiel (27:3-7) gave details that evidently provide a description of a Phoenician ship. It had planks of durable juniper, a single mast of cedar from Lebanon, and oars of "massive trees" from Bashan, probably oak. The prow, likely high and curved, was made of cypress wood inlaid with ivory. The sail was of colored Egyptian linen, and the deck covering (perhaps an awning above the deck to provide shade) was of dyed wool. The ship's seams were caulked. (Eze 27:27) The Phoenicians were skilled sailors, carrying on extensive trade in the Mediterranean area, even going as far as Tarshish (probably Spain). It is believed by some that in time the term "Tarshish ships," or "ships of Tarshish," came to signify the type of ship used by the Phoenicians in trading with that distant point, that is, a seaworthy vessel able to make a long voyage. (1Ki 22:48; Ps 48:7; Isa 2:16; Eze 27:25) Possibly Jonah fled on a ship of this type. It had a deck, allowing space in the hold for cargo and passengers.—Jon 1:3, 5.

One of Sennacherib's sculptures portrays a Phoenician ship with a superstructure deck, a double bank of oars, a sail, and a screen around the upper deck on which shields were hung. The prow of this fighting ship was long and pointed.

Hebrew Ships. When settled in the Promised Land, Dan was spoken of as dwelling for a time in ships (Jg 5:17), possibly referring to its assigned territory by the Philistine coast. (Jos 19:40, 41, 46) The territory of Asher was along the seacoast and included the cities of Tyre and Sidon (though there is no evidence that these cities were ever taken by Asher). The tribes of Manasseh, Ephraim, and Judah had territory along the Mediterranean Coast, so that they, too, were quite familiar with ships. (Jos 15:1, 4; 16:8; 17:7, 10) Manasseh, Issachar, and Naphtali also held land on or near the Sea of Galilee.

While Israel had apparently used boats from early times, Solomon was evidently the first ruler in Israel to put emphasis on commercial shipping. With the help of Hiram, he built a fleet of cargo ships that sailed from Ezion-geber to Ophir. (1Ki 9:26-28; 10:22; 2Ch 8:17, 18; 9:21) These vessels were jointly manned by Israelites and experienced seamen from Tyre. Every three years the ships would come in with cargoes of gold, silver, ivory, apes, and peacocks.—1Ki 9:27; 10:22.

King Jehoshaphat of Judah later entered into partnership with wicked King Ahaziah of Israel in building ships at Ezion-geber to send to Ophir for gold; but Jehovah warned him of His disapproval of the alliance. Accordingly, the ships were wrecked at Ezion-geber, and Jehoshaphat apparently rejected a request by Ahaziah to give the project a second try.—1Ki 22:48, 49; 2Ch 20:36, 37.

During the First Century C.E. In the first century C.E., numerous merchant ships of various types plied the waters of the Mediterranean.

Some of them were coastal vessels, such as the boat from Adramyttium in which Paul, as a prisoner, sailed from Caesarea to Myra. (Ac 21:1-6; 27:2-5) However, the merchant ship that Paul boarded at Myra was a large ship carrying a cargo of wheat and a crew and passengers totaling 276 persons. (Ac 27:37, 38) Josephus reports that he once sailed on a ship carrying 600.—*The Life*, 15 (3).

Paul had done much traveling in ships; he had experienced three shipwrecks prior to this journey. (2Co 11:25) The one he was on this time was a sailing ship that had a mainsail and foresail and was steered by two large oars located in the stern. Such ships often had a figurehead representing certain gods or goddesses. (The ship that Paul boarded afterward had the figurehead "Sons of Zeus.") (Ac 28:11) A small boat, or skiff, was pulled behind the ship. It was used to get to shore when the ship was anchored near a coast. To prevent its being swamped or crushed, the skiff was hauled up during storms. In this voyage of Paul's, the violence of the storm that arose caused the sailors to undergird the ship (this was apparently the passing of ropes or chains under the hull from one side to the other to hold the ship together), lower the gear (evidently the sails), dump the cargo of wheat overboard, throw away the tackling, and lash up the rudder oars (to prevent their being damaged).—Ac 27:6-19, 40.

The Sea of Galilee. The Gospels frequently mention the presence of boats on the Sea of Galilee. Evidently these were mainly used for fishing with nets (Mt 4:18-22; Lu 5:2; Joh 21:2-6), though fishing with hooks was also done. (Mt 17:27) Jesus sometimes used a boat as a convenient spot from which to preach to crowds on the nearby shore (Mt 13:2; Lu 5:3), and he and his apostles used them often for transportation. (Mt 9:1; 15:39; Mr 5:21) Such a boat was powered by oars or a small sail. (Mr 6:48; Lu 8:22) Though the Bible does not describe these fishing boats, some of them were large enough to accommodate 13 persons or more.—Mr 8:10; Joh 21:2, 3; see GALLEY; MARINER.

Anchors. The first anchors, as far as is known, were of stone and were let down from the bow of the ship. Later wooden anchors of hook form, weighted with stone or metal, were used in the Mediterranean. Some had lead arms. A specimen discovered near Cyrene weighs about 545 kg (1,200 lb). Eventually, anchors made entirely of metal were used, some were of the familiar form and others were double fluked. The sailors of the ship in which Paul was sailing cast out four anchors from the boat's stern (the practice sometimes followed when riding out a gale). (Ac 27:29, 30, 40) A sounding lead was used to determine the depth of the water.—Ac 27:28.

The apostle Paul uses the term "anchor" figuratively when he speaks to his spiritual brothers in Christ, calling the hope set before them "an anchor for the soul."—Heb 6:19; compare Eph 4:13, 14; Jas 1:6-8.

SHIPHI (Shi'phi) [from a root that means "abound"]. A Simeonite whose son was one of the tribal chieftains who extended their pasture grounds during Hezekiah's reign.—1Ch 4:24, 37-41.

SHIPHMITE (Shiph'mite) [possibly, Of (Belonging to) Shepham]. The designation for Zabdi, David's manager of the wine supply. (1Ch 27: 27) It could indicate that Zabdi came from either Siphmoth (1Sa 30:28) or Shepham.—Nu 34: 10, 11.

SHIPHRAH (Shiph'rah) [Agreeable; Polished; Elegant]. The Greek *Septuagint* reads Sepphora in both Exodus 1:15 and 2:21; the Masoretic text, however, reads Shiphrah and Zipporah respectively. The Aramaic form of the name is Sapphira.

Shiphrah was one of the Hebrew midwives who, together with Puah, was commanded by Pharaoh to kill all the Hebrew male babies immediately at birth. Being a God-fearing woman, however, and having respect for the sanctity of human life (Ge 9:6), she preserved the boy babies alive and was blessed by Jehovah with a family of her own.—Ex 1:15-21; see MIDWIFE.

SHIPHTAN (Shiph'tan) [from a root meaning "judge"]. Father of Kemuel, the chieftain representing Ephraim when the Promised Land was divided among the tribes of Israel.—Nu 34:17, 18, 24.

SHISHA (Shi'sha). Father of Solomon's secretaries Elihoreph and Ahijah.—1Ki 4:3; see SERAIAH No. 2.

SHISHAK (Shi'shak). An Egyptian king that is known as Sheshonk (I) from Egyptian records. Shishak, regarded as the founder of the "Libyan dynasty," is generally credited with a rule of about 21 years. His son Osorkon I succeeded him to the throne.

When Jeroboam fled to Egypt to escape the wrath of King Solomon, Shishak ruled there. (1Ki 11:40) Some years later, in the fifth year of Solomon's successor Rehoboam (993 B.C.E.), Shishak invaded Judah with a mighty force of chariots and horsemen. He captured fortified cities in Judah and then came to Jerusalem. But Jehovah did not allow him to bring Jerusalem to ruin, for Rehoboam and the princes of Judah humbled themselves upon receiving a message from the prophet Shemaiah. Shishak, however, did strip the city of its treasures.—2Ch 12:1-12.

There is archaeological evidence concerning Shishak's invading the area of Palestine. A fragment of a stele found at Megiddo mentions Sheshonk (Shishak), possibly indicating that the stele was erected there to commemorate his victory. (*Ancient Near Eastern Texts*, edited by J. Pritchard, 1974, pp. 263, 264) Also, a relief on a temple wall at Karnak (the N part of the ancient Egyptian city of Thebes) lists numerous cities or villages that Shishak conquered. (PICTURE, Vol. 1, p. 952; *Supplements to Vetus Testamentum*, Leiden, 1957, Vol. IV, pp. 59, 60) A considerable number of the places that can be identified with Biblical sites were located in the territory of the ten-tribe kingdom. This would indicate that the purpose of Shishak's campaign was, not to assist the ten-tribe kingdom, but to gain control of the important trade routes and thereby extend Egypt's power and influence.

SHITRAI (Shit'rai) [Officer]. A native of Sharon placed over the herds of David that grazed there.—1Ch 27:29.

SHITTIM (Shit'tim) [Acacia [Trees]].

1. A location on the desert plains of Moab to which the encampment of the Israelites extended from Beth-jeshimoth. (Nu 25:1; 33:49; Jos 2:1) Evidently "Shittim" is a shortened form of the name Abel-shittim (Watercourse of the Acacia [Trees]). Some have identified it with Tell el-Kefrein, a low hill about 8 km (5 mi) NE of Beth-jeshimoth (Tell el-'Azeimeh, near the NE corner of the Dead Sea). However, Tell el-Hammam, a larger site occupying a strategic position and lying 2.5 km (1.5 mi) E of Tell el-Kefrein, is preferred.

By means of his prophet Micah, Jehovah reminded the Israelites of what he had done in their behalf: "O my people, remember, please, what Balak the king of Moab counseled, and what Balaam the son of Beor answered him. From Shittim it was, all the way to Gilgal, to the intent that the righteous acts of Jehovah might be known." (Mic 6:5) While Israel was encamped on the Plains of Moab, which included Shittim, Jehovah frustrated Balak's attempt to have Balaam curse the Israelites; he blocked the Moabite effort to bring ruin to his people. He enabled Israel to defeat the Midianites, who, along with the Moabites, had shared in getting many Israelites to become involved in immorality and idolatry. Jehovah brought Israel across the Jordan by a miracle, and at Gilgal he "rolled away the reproach of Egypt."—Nu 22:4-25:8; 31:3-11, 48-50; Jos 3:1, 14-17; 5:9.

2. If it designates a particular torrent valley, "the torrent valley of the Acacia Trees" (Shittim) may be the lower course of the torrent valley of Kidron.—Joe 3:18.

SHIZA (Shi'za). Reubenite father of David's warrior Adina.—1Ch 11:26, 42.

SHOA (Sho'a). A people or an area named along with Pekod and Koa as providing military forces that Jehovah would bring against unfaithful Jerusalem.—Eze 23:4, 22, 23.

SHOBAB (Sho'bab) [from a root meaning "return; bring back"].

1. A son of Caleb the brother of Jerahmeel; tribe of Judah.—1Ch 2:9, 18.

2. A son of David and Bath-sheba.—2Sa 5:14; 1Ch 3:5; 14:4.

SHOBACH (Sho'bach). Army chief of Syrian King Hadadezer. In directing an army of Syrians hired by the Ammonites to fight against David, Shobach lost the battle and his life along with 40,700 of his men. (2Sa 10:15-19) His name is spelled Shophach at 1 Chronicles 19:16, 18.

SHOBAI (Sho'bai). A Levite founder of a family of temple gatekeepers. Some of his descendants returned from Babylonian exile with Zerubbabel.—Ezr 2:1, 2, 40, 42; Ne 7:45.

SHOBAL (Sho'bal).

1. A Horite sheik, son of Seir, and himself the father of five sons.—Ge 36:20, 23, 29; 1Ch 1:38, 40.

2. A son of Hur descended from Caleb of the tribe of Judah. A number of descendants are credited to Shobal, including the inhabitants of Kiriath-jearim and other towns.—1Ch 2:50, 52, 53; 4:1, 2.

SHOBEK (Sho'bek). An Israelite or the head of a family represented in the attestations to the "trustworthy arrangement" put forward during Nehemiah's governorship.—Ne 9:38; 10:1, 14, 24.

SHOBI (Sho'bi). A loyal subject of King David. Shobi and two others brought much-needed supplies to David when Absalom's rebellion caused the king and his party to flee Jerusalem. (2Sa 17:27-29) Shobi was "the son of Nahash from Rabbah of the sons of Ammon."—See NAHASH No. 3.

SHOHAM (Sho'ham) [Onyx]. A Merarite Levite involved in David's reorganization of the Levitical services; son of Jaaziah.—1Ch 24:27, 31.

SHOMER (Sho'mer) [from a root that means "guard"].

1. A descendant of Asher whose four sons were chieftains and family heads. His name is also spelled Shemer.—1Ch 7:30, 32, 34, 40.

2. Jehozabad, one of the assassins of Judah's King Jehoash, is identified as a son of both Shomer and "Shimrith the Moabitess." (2Ki 12:21; 2Ch 24:26) Shomer is a masculine word in Hebrew; Shimrith is feminine. Some view Shomer as the father of Jehozabad and Shimrith as his mother. However, Shomer may have been the father of Shimrith. If this is the case, Jehozabad was the grandson of Shomer, the term "son" often meaning descendant.

SHOPHACH (Sho'phach). Alternate form of the name Shobach.—1Ch 19:16, 18; see SHOBACH.

SHOULDER. The part of the body of man or beast that protrudes to the sides below the neck; by extension, a rounded or sloping part of a hill; also capacity for bearing burdens or responsibility.

Anciently, as today, it was customary to carry loads on the shoulders. (Ge 21:14; Ex 12:34) The ark of the covenant was to be carried, not on a wagon, but on the shoulders of the Levites. (1Ch 15:15; Jos 3:14, 15; 2Sa 6:3, 6-9, 13) A heavy load on the shoulders could denote oppression or slavery. (Ps 81:5, 6; Isa 10:27; 14:25; Mt 23:4) The tribe of Issachar was foretold to "bend down his shoulder to bear burdens." (Ge 49:14, 15) In Israel's history this tribe was willing to take responsibility and do hard work. It supplied many courageous fighters for Judge Barak and, later, provided Judge Tola; also, in the time of David, this tribe furnished many wise and valiant men.—Jg 5:13, 15; 10:1, 2; 1Ch 7:1-5; 12:23, 32.

An authority or responsibility was said to rest on one's shoulder. Isaiah's prophecy foretold that the princely rule would come to be on the shoulder of Jesus Christ. (Isa 9:6) Isaiah told unfaithful Shebna that Eliakim would take his place as steward over the king's house, God putting "the key of the house of David" upon his shoulder. Since a key in such cases represented responsibility and authority, this prophecy may relate to Christ's receiving the authority of the Kingdom as represented in the Davidic covenant. (Isa 22:15, 20-22; Lu 1:31-33; compare also Re 3:7.) It is interesting to note also that the breastpiece of judgment hung from the shoulder pieces of the high priest's garments, evidently picturing certain authorities that would depend on or rest upon the shoulders of the great High Priest, Jesus Christ.—Ex 28:6, 7, 12, 22-28; see HIGH PRIEST.

After blessing Joseph's sons, Ephraim and Manasseh, Jacob said to Joseph: "I do give you one shoulder [of land] more than to your brothers," thereby designating Joseph as the possessor of firstborn rights. (Ge 48:22; compare De 21:17; 1Ch 5:1, 2.) Moses said of Benjamin, when he blessed the sons of Israel: "Let the beloved one of Jehovah reside in security by him, . . . and he must reside between his shoulders." (De 33:12) This seems to refer to the fact that the kings of the line of David would have their seat of government in Benjamin's territory. The same Hebrew word used here for "shoulder" is translated "side" or "slope" at Joshua 15:8 (AT, Mo, NW), speaking of a slope of the hill on which Jerusalem then stood.—See other examples at Ex 27:14, 15; Nu 34:11; Jos 15:10; 1Ki 6:8; Eze 25:9.

"Giving a stubborn shoulder" represents resistance against God's counsel and law (Ne 9:29; Zec 7:11), while serving "shoulder to shoulder" indicates unity of action.—Zep 3:9.

The officiating priest was given the shoulder of a ram of the Nazirite's sacrifice at the completion of his vow, this constituting a part of the priest's portion.—Nu 6:19, 20; see also De 18:3.

SHOVEL. A long-handled scooping implement. Shovels made of copper were employed at the tabernacle for clearing away the ashes from the altar of burnt offering. (Ex 27:1-3; 38:3; Nu 4:14) Serving the same purpose were the copper shovels the Hebrew-Phoenician workman Hiram made for use at the temple built by Solomon. (1Ki 7:13, 14, 40, 45) These were among the temple utensils that the Babylonians carried away in 607 B.C.E.—2Ki 25:8, 14; Jer 52:18.

Shovels, perhaps made of wood, were used to winnow grain. (Isa 30:24) The broad winnowing shovel was employed at a threshing floor to scoop up threshed grain and throw it into the air against the wind, which blew away the refuse, such as chaff, and allowed the grain to fall to the threshing floor. John the Baptizer prophetically described the Messiah as having in hand a figurative winnowing shovel, with which he would separate symbolic "wheat" from "chaff."—Mt 3:1, 12; see WINNOWING.

SHOWBREAD. Twelve cakes of bread that were placed on a table in the Holy compartment of the tabernacle or temple and that were re-

placed with fresh ones each Sabbath. (Ex 35:13; 39:36; 1Ki 7:48; 2Ch 13:11; Ne 10:32, 33) The literal Hebrew designation for the showbread is the "bread of the face." The word for "face" sometimes denotes "presence" (2Ki 13:23), and so the showbread was in front of Jehovah's face as an offering before him constantly. (Ex 25:30, ftn) The showbread is also referred to as "layer bread" (2Ch 2:4), "loaves of presentation" (Mr 2:26), and simply "the loaves" (Heb 9:2).

The Kohathites were responsible to bake the showbread "sabbath by sabbath," as well as to transport it when the tabernacle was moved. (Nu 4:7; 1Ch 9:32) Each of the 12 ring-shaped cakes was made of two omers (0.2 ephah; equal to 4.4 L or 4 dry qt) of fine flour, and according to Josephus, no leaven was used. (Jewish Antiquities, III, 142 [vi, 6]) On the Sabbath the old loaves were removed from the table of showbread on the N side of the Holy (Ex 26:35) and replaced with 12 fresh ones. The cakes were stacked in two piles consisting of six loaves or layers each. Pure frankincense was put on each stack. Jewish tradition has it that the frankincense was put in golden vessels and not directly on the cakes. When the showbread was removed on the Sabbath, the frankincense is said to have been burned on the altar.—Le 24:5-8.

The old loaves were something most holy, having been in the Holy before Jehovah for a week, and were to be eaten by the Aaronic priests in a holy place, evidently somewhere in the sanctuary precincts. (Le 24:9) There is only one recorded instance in Biblical history regarding the use of the old loaves by non-Aaronites. When David was fleeing from Saul, he requested bread for himself and his men from Ahimelech the high priest. As Ahimelech had no "ordinary bread," he gave David loaves of showbread that had been replaced. But the high priest, believing that David was on a mission for the king, did this only after being assured that David and his men were ceremonially clean. (1Sa 21:1-6) Jesus Christ referred to this incident when the Pharisees objected to his disciples' plucking ears of grain on the Sabbath.—Mt 12:3-7; Lu 6:1-4.

SHREWMICE [Heb., chaphar·pa·rohth']. Small, mouselike animals covered with fine, short fur. The original-language term is thought to be derived from a root signifying "dig" (Ge 26:15), and therefore a number of scholars have suggested that it may denote any of a variety of burrowing animals, including rats, mice, mole rats, jerboas, and the like. However, according to Koehler and Baumgartner, chaphar·pa·rohth' designates "shrewmice."—*Lexicon in Veteris Testamenti Libros*, Leiden, 1958, p. 322.

These creatures have long, slender snouts, tiny eyes, and rounded ears with a rather crumpled appearance. Of enormous appetite, shrewmice can devour more than their own weight in food in a day. They subsist largely on insects and worms, although also feeding on small animals their own size and larger, such as mice. The kind of shrew-mouse mentioned in Isaiah 2:20 is identified by I. Aharoni as *Crocidura religiosa.*—*Osiris*, Brugge, 1938, Vol. 5, p. 463.

SHUA (Shu'a).

1. Canaanite father of Judah's wife; grandfather of Er, Onan, and Shelah.—Ge 38:2-5, 12; 1Ch 2:3.

2. Daughter of Heber of the tribe of Asher. —1Ch 7:30, 32.

SHUAH (Shu'ah). The sixth- and last-named son of Abraham by his second wife Keturah. (1Ch 1:32) Shuah and his five brothers received gifts from Abraham and were sent out of his household toward the E. (Ge 25:1, 2, 5, 6) Shuah's descendants, the Shuhites, are thought by some to have lived along the Euphrates between two of its tributaries, the Balikh and Khabur. The only Shuhite named in the Bible is Job's companion Bildad.—Job 2:11.

SHUAL (Shu'al) [Fox].

1. Son of Zophah; a headman in the tribe of Asher.—1Ch 7:36, 40.

2. A region associated with Ophrah, presumably to the N of Michmash. The Philistines who encamped at Michmash made raids in the direction of Shual. (1Sa 13:16, 17) No exact location is known.

SHUBAEL (Shu'ba·el) [God Has Taken Captive].

1. Descendant of Levi through Moses' son Gershom. Another form of the name is Shebuel. —1Ch 24:20; 26:24; see SHEBUEL No. 1.

2. Son of Heman, also called Shebuel.—1Ch 25:4, 20; see SHEBUEL No. 2.

SHUHAH (Shu'hah) [Pit]. Brother of Chelub in the tribe of Judah.—1Ch 4:11.

SHUHAM (Shu'ham), **SHUHAMITES** (Shu'-ham·ites) [Of (Belonging to) Shuham]. The only son of Dan mentioned in the Bible. He was forefather of the Shuhamites, which is the only tribal family enrolled for Dan and which numbered

64,400 at the end of the 40-year wilderness wandering. (Nu 26:42, 43) He is called Hushim at Genesis 46:23.

SHUHITE (Shu'hite) [meaning "Of (Belonging to) Shuah"]. Evidently a descendant of Shuah, a son of Abraham by his wife Keturah. (Ge 25:2; 1Ch 1:32) Job's companion Bildad is the only Shuhite named in the Scriptures.—Job 2:11; 8:1; 18:1; 25:1; 42:9.

SHULAMMITE (Shu'lam·mite). The designation for the beautiful country girl who is the principal character of The Song of Solomon (6:13). Likely this title portrays her as from the city of Shunem (modern Sulam). (Compare 1Ki 1:3.) Lending support to this view is the fact that the Greek *Septuagint* (Vatican Manuscript No. 1209) calls the girl the "Sunamite." Also, the ecclesiastical writer Eusebius of the fourth century C.E. referred to Shunem as Shulem.—*Onomasticon*, 158, 11.

SHUMATHITES (Shu'math·ites). One of the families of Kiriath-jearim, likely descendants of Judah through Caleb and Shobal.—1Ch 2:19, 50, 52, 53.

SHUNAMMITE (Shu'nam·mite) [Of (Belonging to) Shunem]. An inhabitant of Shunem. Abishag, the nurse of David in his old age, is called a "Shunammite."—1Ki 1:3, 4, 15; 2:17, 21, 22; see ABISHAG.

A prominent woman of Shunem who showed hospitality to the prophet Elisha, regularly offering him food and lodging, is left unnamed. For her kindness, she was rewarded with a son. When, several years later, the boy died, the Shunammite woman rode about 30 km (19 mi), and upon finding Elisha at Mount Carmel, she expressed her bitter grief, saying: "Did I ask for a son through my lord? Did I not say, 'You must not lead me to a false hope'?" Returning with her, the prophet prayed to Jehovah, and the boy was restored to life.—2Ki 4:8-37.

Upon Elisha's warning her of a coming famine, the Shunammite woman, apparently now a widow, together with her household, took up living among the Philistines for seven years. At the end of this time she returned, only to find her property confiscated. When the king learned of her past dealings with Elisha, all her belongings were returned.—2Ki 8:1-6.

SHUNEM (Shu'nem). A city in the territory of Issachar (Jos 19:17, 18) and not far from Jezreel and Mount Gilboa. (1Sa 28:4) Shunem is identified with modern Sulam (Shunem), which is on the SW slope of Jebel Dahi (Giv'at ha-More) and overlooks the Low Plain of Jezreel. The place lies about 5 km (3 mi) N of the abandoned village of Zer'in (Tel Yizre'el) and some 8 km (5 mi) N of the western end of Mount Gilboa.

It was at Shunem that the Philistines encamped before the battle that resulted in the death of King Saul. (1Sa 28:4) From Shunem came the beautiful Abishag ("the Shunammite") who cared for aged King David (1Ki 1:3, 4), and later, the prophet Elisha often lodged in the home of a hospitable couple there.—2Ki 4:8.

SHUNI (Shu'ni), **SHUNITES** (Shu'nites) [Of (Belonging to) Shuni]. Shuni was the third named of Gad's seven sons. He accompanied Jacob into Egypt in 1728 B.C.E., and when his own offspring expanded in numbers, they formed the tribal family of the Shunites.—Ge 46:8, 16; Nu 26:15.

SHUPHAMITES (Shu'pham·ites). Benjamite descendants of Shephupham, a variant spelling of Shuppim and Shephuphan.—Nu 26:38, 39; 1Ch 7:12; 8:5; see SHUPPIM No. 1.

SHUPPIM (Shup'pim).

1. A descendant of Benjamin, perhaps through Bela and Ir(i). (1Ch 7:6, 7, 12) The introduction of Shuppim into the genealogies of Manasseh in 1 Chronicles 7:15 may indicate some unusual intertribal relationship. In Genesis 46:21 Shuppim is called Muppim, possibly because of the similarity of the letters in the ancient Hebrew alphabet represented in English by *sh* and *m*. The name is also spelled Shephupha(m, n), and it identifies the individual as founder of a Benjamite tribal family of Shuphamites.—Nu 26:39; 1Ch 8:5.

2. A gatekeeper appointed to the W of the sanctuary. (1Ch 26:16) Since the last three characters of his name in Hebrew (*Shup·pim'*) are identical to the last three characters of the previous term (*behth ha·'asup·pim'*), scholars suspect that it is a dittograph (an unintentional scribal repetition), therefore, in this verse, not the name of a person.—Compare 1Ch 26:10, 11.

SHUR [Wall]. A geographic name that has variously been said to be a city, a series of border forts, a region, or a mountain range. It is described as "in front of Egypt," that is, on the E border of or to the E of Egypt. The context locates Shur in the NW portion of the Sinai Peninsula. (Ge 25:18) After Israel crossed the Red Sea, Moses led them from the shores of the sea into "the wilderness of Shur."—Ex 15:22.

Earlier, it was at a fountain "on the way to Shur" that Jehovah's angel spoke to Abraham's Egyptian slave girl Hagar (who was likely fleeing back to Egypt). (Ge 16:7) Later, Abraham moved from the region of Hebron (Ge 13:18) and took up dwelling between Kadesh (Kadesh-barnea, S of Beer-sheba in the Negeb region) and Shur, though also residing for a time at Gerar, a Philistine town considerably N of Kadesh. (Ge 20:1) The rangings of the desert-dwelling Ishmaelites took them as far as "Havilah near Shur." (Ge 25:18) King Saul successfully waged war against the Amalekites as far as Shur, but in David's time the Amalekites, along with the Geshurites and the Girzites, were still inhabiting a similar area.—1Sa 15:7; 27:8.

Some of these texts seem to point more to a particular place than to just a general region. If this is the case, then the expression "wilderness of Shur," used only once, might mean the wilderness in the proximity of a city or site named Shur.—Ex 15:22; compare the reference to the "wilderness of Damascus" at 1Ki 19:15, or to that of Ziph, 1Sa 23:14.

The meaning of the name (Wall) has prompted some to endeavor to identify Shur with the ancient defense wall along the Isthmus of Suez that Egyptian inscriptions indicate was built very early in that nation's history. Others think the term applies to a series of Egyptian fortresses along Egypt's eastern frontier facing the Sinai Peninsula. Exodus 15:22, however, points to a location on the E side of the Red Sea, hence, to a place outside Egypt rather than within its boundaries. For this reason, the suggestion is also advanced that the name Shur (Wall) identifies the NW part of the mountain chain that covers a large portion of the Sinai Peninsula. Seen from the Egyptian side of the Gulf of Suez, the white cliffs of this long range have the appearance of a wall, or barrier. There may have been a place or town called Shur on, or at the foot of, the range, perhaps the last Arabian town before crossing Egypt's frontier. Definite identification, however, awaits further evidence.

SHUSHAN (Shu'shan). An ancient city, the ruins of which lie between the Karkheh River and the Ab-i-Diz River on the E bank of the Sha'ur about 350 km (220 mi) E of Babylon. There are four major mounds on the site. The modern village Shush lies below the slopes of the acropolis, the most important of the mounds. Shushan or a fortified part of the city, "Shushan the castle," was the setting for one of the visions of the prophet Daniel (Da 8:2), the scene for the events narrated in the book of Esther (Es 1:2, 5, 6; 2:3, 5, 8, 21

3:2, 15; 8:14; 9:12-15), and the place where Nehemiah served as cupbearer during the reign of Artaxerxes (Longimanus, the son of Xerxes I). —Ne 1:1; 2:1; see CASTLE; ELAM No. 1; PERSIA, PERSIANS (Persian capitals).

There is evidence that Shushan (also called Susa; Ezr 4:9) was the capital of ancient Elam. In the seventh century B.C.E., King Asenappar (Ashurbanipal) of Assyria conquered Shushan and transported inhabitants of the city to Samaria. (Ezr 4:9, 10) Under Persian domination, Shushan was a royal city. In the fourth century B.C.E., Shushan fell to Alexander the Great and eventually witnessed decline. Today only a mound of ruins occupies the site.

Archaeologists have uncovered the ruins of a palace, thought to be the one begun by Persian King Darius I and completed by his son Xerxes I (believed to be Ahasuerus, the husband of Esther). The panels of colored glazed bricks and the stone capitals give some indication of its former glory. An inscription of Darius I about the erection of the palace reads: "This is the *hadish* palace which at Susa I built. From afar its ornamentation was brought. Deep down the earth was dug, until rock bottom I reached. When the excavation was made, gravel was packed down, one part sixty feet, the other thirty feet in depth. On that gravel a palace I built. And that the earth was dug down and the gravel packed and the mud brick formed in molds, that the Babylonians did. The cedar timber was brought from a mountain named Lebanon; the Assyrians brought it to Babylon, and from Babylon the Carians and Ionians brought it to Susa. Teakwood was brought from Gandara and from Carmania. The gold which was used here was brought from Sardis and from Bactria. The stone—lapis lazuli and carnelian— was brought from Sogdiana. The turquoise was brought from Chorasmia. The silver and copper were brought from Egypt. The ornamentation with which the wall was adorned was brought from Ionia. The ivory was brought from Ethiopia, from India, and from Arachosia. The stone pillars were brought from a place named Abiradush in Elam. The artisans who dressed the stone were Ionians and Sardians. The goldsmiths who wrought the gold were Medes and Egyptians. Those who worked the inlays were Sardians and Egyptians. Those who worked the baked brick (with figures) were Babylonians. The men who adorned the wall were Medes and Egyptians. At Susa here a splendid work was ordered; very splendid did it turn out."—*History of the Persian Empire,* by A. T. Olmstead, 1948, p. 168; see ARCHAEOLOGY (Persia).

SHUTHELAH (Shu′the·lah).

1. A son of Ephraim and forefather of the tribal family of Shuthelahites. (1Ch 7:20; Nu 26: 35-37) Shuthelah is not mentioned in the Masoretic text of Genesis 46:20, but a form of his name is among the several names here added in the Greek *Septuagint.*

2. An Ephraimite descendant of No. 1.—1Ch 7:20, 21.

SHUTHELAHITES (Shu′thel·a′hites) [Of (Belonging to) Shuthelah]. The family descendants of Shuthelah; included among the registered ones in the tribe of Ephraim at the time of the second census in the wilderness.—Nu 26:35, 37.

SIA (Si′a), **SIAHA** (Si′a·ha). One of the Nethinim whose descendants returned from Babylonian exile with Zerubbabel in 537 B.C.E.—Ezr 2:1, 2, 43, 44; Ne 7:47.

SIBBECAI (Sib′be·cai). One of David's mighty men, a Hushathite. (1Ch 11:26, 29) Sibbecai, in a war with the Philistines at Gob, slew Saph (Sippai), one of the giantlike Rephaim, thereby subduing the enemy. (2Sa 21:18; 1Ch 20:4) When David organized the monthly rotational service of the nation's forces, Sibbecai was placed in charge of the eighth division. (1Ch 27:1, 11) He is apparently called Mebunnai at 2 Samuel 23:27.

SIBBOLETH. See SHIBBOLETH.

SIBMAH (Sib′mah). A town E of the Jordan, taken by Israel from Amorite King Sihon and assigned to the Reubenites, who desired it because of surrounding pasturelands. Apparently it was also called Sebam. (Nu 32:2-5, 37, 38; Jos 13:15, 19, 21) Originally a city of the Moabites (compare Nu 21:25, 26), it reverted to them at an undisclosed time. It was noted for its vineyards and summer fruitage. (Isa 16:8, 9, 13, 14; Jer 48:32, 46, 47) The exact location of Sibmah (Sebam) is now unknown, though it is mentioned with Heshbon and Nebo (Nu 32:3), and Jerome's commentary on Isaiah 16:8 says that it was only about 500 paces from Heshbon. However, some tentatively identify it with Qurn el-Kibsh, about 5 km (3 mi) WSW of Heshbon (modern Hisban).

SIBRAIM (Sib′ra·im). A northern boundary site listed in Ezekiel's vision of Israel's territorial inheritance. (Eze 47:15-17) Its location is not known, though some seek to place it in the Hums area, S of Hamath in Syria. It may be the same as Sepharvaim.

SICKLE. See FARMING IMPLEMENTS.

SICKNESS. See DISEASES AND TREATMENT.

SIDDIM, LOW PLAIN OF (Sid'dim). A valley linked in Scripture with the Salt (Dead) Sea. (Ge 14:3) There, in Abraham's day, the rebellious kings of Sodom, Gomorrah, Admah, Zeboiim, and Zoar battled with Elamite King Chedorlaomer and his three allies. Defeated, the kings of Sodom and Gomorrah fled, only to have some of their troops fall into the "pits upon pits of bitumen" that filled the area.—Ge 14:4, 8-10.

Some believe that the Low Plain of Siddim is the baylike section of the Dead Sea S of the Lisan Peninsula. They believe that it once was a fertile valley and was apparently later submerged, perhaps because of earthquake activity or because of topographical changes resulting from God's destruction of Sodom, Gomorrah, and the entire District. (Ge 19:24, 25) From time to time, pieces of bituminous matter still rise to the surface of the shallow waters there.—See SALT SEA.

SIDON (Si'don), SIDONIANS (Si·do'ni·ans). Canaan's firstborn son Sidon was the progenitor of the Sidonians. The seaport town of Sidon was named after their forefather, and for many years it was the principal city of the Phoenicians, as the Greeks called the Sidonians. Today the city is known as Saida.

A colony of Sidonians also settled about 35 km (22 mi) S of Sidon and called the place Tyre. In time Tyre surpassed Sidon in many respects, but she never completely lost her identity as a Sidonian settlement. The king of Tyre was sometimes called "the king of the Sidonians" (1Ki 16:31), and frequently Tyre and Sidon are mentioned together in prophecy. (Jer 25:22; 27:3; 47:4; Joe 3:4; Zec 9:2) Between the two cities was Zarephath, "which belongs to Sidon" and where Elijah was fed by a widow during a prolonged famine.—1Ki 17:9; Lu 4:25, 26.

Originally Sidon was considered the N limit of the Canaanite nations. (Ge 10:19) After Joshua's conquest of the kings of northern Canaan (who had been pursued as far N as "populous Sidon"), the land was divided among the nine and a half tribes that had as yet received no allotment. At that time land under Sidon's control was yet remaining to be taken. (Jos 11:8; 13:2, 6, 7; Nu 32:33) Asher received the coastal plains immediately S of Sidon, and as had been prophesied, Zebulun's territory lay with 'his remote side toward Sidon,' that is, in the N part of the Promised Land. (Jos 19:24, 28; Ge 49:13) The Asherites, however, instead of driving the Sidonians out of their God-assigned territory, were content to settle down among them. (Jg 1:31, 32; 3:1, 3) During the period of the Judges, the tribe of Dan annexed Laish, possibly a Sidonian colony, and renamed it Dan. The conquest was accomplished with apparent ease, for the people were "quiet and unsuspecting," hence unprepared for the attack. (Jg 18:7, 27-29) Sidon is also mentioned in connection with the census taken in David's day.—2Sa 24:6.

A port city favored with two of the few harbors on the Phoenician coast, Sidon became a great trading center where overland caravans met and exchanged their wares for goods brought in vessels plying the shipping lanes of the Mediterranean. Among the Sidonians were wealthy merchants, skilled sailors, and hardy rowers. (Isa 23:2; compare Eze 27:8, 9.) Sidonians were also famous for their craftsmanship in the manufacture of glass and in their weaving and dyeing of cloth. They were also noted for their ability as loggers and lumbermen.—1Ki 5:6; 1Ch 22:4; Ezr 3:7.

Sidonian Religion and Its Consequence. Religiously, the Sidonians were depraved; lewd sex orgies in connection with the goddess Ashtoreth were a prominent part of their worship. The Israelites, allowing the Sidonians to remain among them, were eventually ensnared into worshiping their false gods. (Jg 10:6, 7, 11-13) Some of the foreign wives that Solomon married were Sidonians, and these caused the king to go after the disgusting fertility goddess Ashtoreth. (1Ki 11:1, 4-6; 2Ki 23:13) King Ahab also did what was bad in Jehovah's eyes by marrying Jezebel, the daughter of a Sidonian king. Jezebel, in turn, zealously promoted false worship in Israel.—1Ki 16:29-33; 18:18, 19.

The Sidonians were made to drink of Jehovah's wrath, first by hearing the pronouncements of his prophets, and later by the destruction meted out at the hands of the Babylonians and others. (Isa 23:4, 12; Jer 25:17, 22; 27:1-8; 47:4; Eze 28:20-24; 32:30; Joe 3:4-8; Zec 9:1-4) Secular history reports that the empires of Babylon, Persia, Greece, and Rome each in turn dominated Sidon.

Sidonian History During First Century C.E. But, despite the Sidonians' corrupt manner of worship, they were not as reprehensible as wayward Israel. Hence, Jesus said it would be more tolerable on Judgment Day for the people of Sidon than for those Jews of Chorazin and Bethsaida who rejected Jesus as Messiah. (Mt 11:20-22; Lu 10:13, 14) Sometime later, when Jesus was traveling through the district around Sidon, a Phoenician woman showed faith in him. (Mt 15:21-28; Mr 7:24-31) However, the 'crowds' that Jesus had cured previously, among whom were some from around Tyre and Sidon, were no doubt in the majority Jews or proselytes. (Mr 3:7, 8; Lu 6:17) On his first trip to Rome as a prisoner, Paul was permitted to visit with the brothers in Sidon.—Ac 27:1, 3.

For reasons not stated by history, Herod Agrippa I was in "a fighting mood" against the Sidonians, who were supplied with food from the king. When a day was set for reconciling matters and the Sidonians were applauding Herod as speaking with "a god's voice, and not a man's," Jehovah's angel struck him so that he was soon eaten up with worms.—Ac 12:20-23.

SIGN. An object, act, situation, or unusual display that has significance as an indicator of something else, present or future. The sign (Heb., 'ohth; Gr., se·mei'on) might be an evidence of authenticity or of authority, a warning of danger, or an indicator as to the wise course to follow.

Among the many signs that Jehovah has provided for human guidance, the first mentioned as such are the heavenly luminaries, the sun and the moon. (Ge 1:14) They are time indicators as well as visible signs of God's existence and qualities. (Ps 19:1-4; Ro 1:19, 20) Evidently because of looking to these luminaries as well as to the stars for omens, as by astrology, the nations have been "struck with terror," as stated at Jeremiah 10:2.

Purposes of Signs. Jehovah gave signs as an assurance of truthfulness and dependability of his words. (Jer 44:29; 1Sa 2:31-34; 10:7, 9; 2Ki 20:8-11) They demonstrated God's backing of Moses or other servants (Ex 3:11, 12; compare Jg 6:17, 20-22), of an apostle (2Co 12:12), of the Christian congregation (1Co 14:22).

Signs were not essential to prove God's backing, as is seen in the case of John the Baptizer. (Joh 10:41; Mt 11:9-11) Also, a false prophet might perform a sign, but he could be identified as false by the means Jehovah provided.—De 13:1-5; 18:20-22; Isa 44:25; Mr 13:22; 2Th 2:9; Re 13:13, 14; 19:20.

Certain signs are reminders, remembrancers, memorials. (Ge 9:12-14; 17:11; Ro 4:11) The Sabbaths and the Passover constituted memorial signs for the Jews. (Ex 13:3-9; 31:13; Eze 20:12, 20) A sign of a literal or symbolic nature could serve as an identification.—Nu 2:2; Ex 12:13.

A Sign Demanded of Jesus. During Jesus' ministry he performed numerous signs that helped many to believe in him. (Joh 2:23) But the signs did not produce faith in hardhearted ones. (Lu 2:34; Joh 11:47, 53; 12:37; compare Nu 14: 11, 22.) When on two occasions religious leaders asked Jesus to display to them a sign from heaven,

they likely were demanding that he perform, as proof that he was the Messiah, the sign foretold at Daniel 7:13, 14, namely, the "son of man" appearing with the clouds of the heavens to take his Kingdom power. But it was not God's time for that prophecy to be fulfilled, and Christ would not perform a showy display merely to gratify their selfish demand. (Mt 12:38; 16:1) Rather, he told them that the only sign that would be given them was "the sign of Jonah the prophet." (Mt 12:39-41; 16:4) After about three days in the belly of a huge fish, Jonah had gone and preached to Nineveh. Jonah thereby became a "sign" to the capital of Assyria. Jesus' generation had "the sign of Jonah" when Christ spent parts of three days in the grave and was resurrected after which his disciples proclaimed the evidence of that event. In this, Christ was a sign to that generation, but even that did not convince most of the Jews.—Lu 11:30; 1Co 1:22.

Sign of Christ's Presence. Shortly before Jesus' death his apostles asked him: "What will be the sign of your presence and of the conclusion of the system of things?" (Mt 24:3; Mr 13:4; Lu 21:7) There were distinct differences between this question and the requests for a sign that the religious leaders had made. While right there, able to see him and his works, those leaders would not accept him as Messiah and King-Designate. (Joh 19:15) Once they asked for a sign "to tempt him" (Lu 11:16); also some may have been infected with idle curiosity about Jesus' signs, as was Herod. (Lu 23:8) Quite the opposite, the disciples who asked about the sign of Christ's presence already accepted him as Messiah and King. (Mt 16:16) But Jesus had said that the Kingdom was "not coming with striking observableness." (Lu 17:20) Consequently (though the apostles mistakenly believed that the Kingdom would be established on earth; Ac 1:6), at the arrival of the Kingdom they did not want to be like the Jewish leaders—blind to Jesus' presence. Accordingly, they asked, not for a miraculous sign to be performed right there, but what the future identifying sign would be.

In response Jesus described a composite "sign," one made up of many evidences, including wars, earthquakes, persecution of Christians, and a preaching about the Kingdom. (Mt 24:4-14, 32, 33) The destruction of Jerusalem and its temple was under consideration when the disciples asked Jesus for the "sign" (Lu 21:5-7), and his reply gave prophecies that applied to Jerusalem and Judea, which were fulfilled during their lifetime. (Lu 21: 20; Mt 24:15) But his answer also dealt with the establishment of the Kingdom of God and its effects on *all* mankind.—Lu 21:31, 35.

"Sign of the Son of man." On that same occasion Jesus said to his disciples: "And then the sign of the Son of man will appear in heaven, and then all the tribes of the earth will beat themselves in lamentation, and they will see the Son of man coming on the clouds of heaven with power and great glory." (Mt 24:30; Lu 21:27) Just before this comment he had spoken of the prophet Daniel. (Mt 24:15; Da 9:27; 11:31) And from the expression Jesus here used it is evident that he was now referring back to Daniel 7:13, 14, where the vision depicted "with the clouds of the heavens someone like a son of man" gaining access to "the Ancient of Days" and receiving a 'kingdom that will not be brought to ruin.' This linked "the sign of the Son of man" with the time when Jesus would be exercising Kingdom power. Jesus applied the expression "Son of man" and the prophecy at Daniel 7:13, 14 to himself.—Mt 26:63, 64; Mr 14:61, 62.

About 96 C.E., 26 years after the destruction of Jerusalem, John wrote about things that would take place in the future, and he saw in vision Jesus Christ "coming with the clouds, and every eye will see him, and those who pierced him." (Re 1:1, 7) Hence, both this statement about something that was to take place after 96 C.E. and what Christ said about "the sign of the Son of man" referred to Jesus as coming in the clouds and as being seen by all people. (See CLOUD.) It should be noted, however, that while the Greek verb ho·ra'o, "see," used at Matthew 24:30 and Revelation 1:7, can mean literally to "see an object, behold," it can also be used metaphorically, of mental sight, to "discern, perceive."—*A Greek-English Lexicon,* by H. Liddell and R. Scott, revised by H. Jones, 1968, p. 1245, col. 1.

For a comparison of "miracles," "portents," and "signs," see MIRACLES; PORTENT.

SIGNAL.
The Hebrew word *nes* appears to denote a stationary pole or stake occupying an elevated site; it is used both literally and figuratively. Hence, it does not denote a signal for sending messages, such as "a smoke signal" (Jg 20:38, 40) or "a fire signal" (Jer 6:1), for which other Hebrew words are used. Rather, such a pole could serve as a rallying point to which people or armies could assemble themselves. (Isa 5:26; 13:2; 18:3; 30:17; 31:9; Jer 4:6, 21; 50:2; 51:12, 27; compare Ps 60:4, ftn.) For example: When the Israelites on one occasion complained about manna and the lack of water, Jehovah punished them by sending poisonous serpents among them. After the Israelites manifested repentance, Jehovah instructed Moses to fashion a serpent and to place it upon a signal pole (*nes*). "Moses at once made a serpent of

copper and placed it upon the signal pole; and it did occur that if a serpent had bitten a man and he gazed at the copper serpent, he then kept alive." (Nu 21:5-9) Evidently this signal pole stood in a fixed location and was doubtless on an elevated place so that it was visible to the Israelites who had been bitten by serpents.

Similarly, in 537 B.C.E., Jerusalem, whose rebuilding had been foretold, became the signal that beckoned the Jewish remnant to leave the lands to which they had been dispersed and to return to the then desolated Jerusalem to rebuild the temple. (Isa 11:11, 12; compare Isa 49:22; 62:10, 11.) The prophecy, however, is not limited to this sixth-century application. Isaiah 11:10 reads: "And it must occur in that day that there will be the root of Jesse that will be standing up as a signal for the peoples." The apostle Paul applied these words to Christ Jesus, the one who would rule nations. (Ro 15:8, 12) Also, Jesus spoke of himself as 'the root of David' the son of Jesse. (Re 22:16) Accordingly, the signal is Christ Jesus as reigning King standing on heavenly Mount Zion. —Compare Heb 12:22; Re 14:1.

SIGNATURE.
A person's identifying mark. The word "signature" is a translation of the Hebrew word *taw*, the name of the last letter of the Hebrew alphabet. (*Taw* is also rendered "mark"; Eze 9:4 [compare ftn], 6.) A signature may have been, at times, the impression of one's signet ring or cylinder seal, or it may have been a written mark peculiar to the user or a mark selected by him as an identification.

In protesting his innocence before his three "companions" who were charging that sins against God were the cause for his suffering, Job presented evidence and argument as to his blamelessness. He called upon God to hear his case and give him an answer, saying: "O that I had someone listening to me, that according to my signature the Almighty himself would answer me! Or that the individual in the case at law with me had written a document itself!" (Job 31:35) Job here expressed willingness to present his case before God, affixing his own signature to it in attestation.

SIHON
(Si'hon). An Amorite king at the time Israel approached the Promised Land. Sihon's kingdom at one time extended from the torrent valley of Jabbok, where it bordered King Og's domain, down at least to the torrent valley of Arnon, and from the Jordan River eastward toward the desert. His capital city was Heshbon, E of the northern end of the Dead Sea. (Nu 21:23, 24; Jos 12:2, 3) Sihon had seized the land of Moab N of

the Arnon, and apparently he dominated Midian, for the chieftains of Midian are called "the dukes of Sihon." (Nu 21:26-30; Jos 13:21) When Israel sent messengers asking Sihon's permission to pass through his kingdom on the king's road and promising not to steal anything from the Amorites, Sihon denied permission and gathered his army to block Israel. At Jahaz he was defeated and killed. —Nu 21:21-24; De 1:3, 4; 2:24-35; 3:2, 6.

The significance of Israel's victory over Sihon can be seen from the fact that it is mentioned many times in Israelite history, alongside the defeat of the Egyptians at the Red Sea. Moses, Jephthah, a psalmist, and the postexilic Levites sometimes used it as an encouraging example of Jehovah's victories in behalf of his faithful people. (Nu 21:34; De 31:4; Jg 11:19-22; Ne 9:5, 22; Ps 135:9-12; 136:18, 19) Reports of it prompted Rahab and the Gibeonites to make peace with Israel. (Jos 2:10; 9:9, 10) Sihon's land was divided among the tribes of Reuben and Gad.—Nu 21:25, 31, 32; De 29:7, 8; Jos 13:8-10, 15-28.

SILAS (Si′las), SILVANUS (Sil·va′nus) [from Lat., meaning "Forest; Woods"].

A leading member of the first-century Christian congregation in Jerusalem, a prophet, and a companion of Paul on his second missionary journey. He was apparently a Roman citizen. (Ac 15:22, 26, 27, 32, 40; 16:19, 25, 37, 38) Likely the name Silvanus, found in the letters of Paul and Peter, was the Latinized form of the Greek name Silas, used by Luke in Acts.

The congregation at Jerusalem chose Silas to accompany Barnabas and Paul back to Antioch, Syria, to carry to the congregation there the decision regarding circumcision.—Ac 15:22, 30-32.

Whether Silas remained in the vicinity of Antioch or returned to Jerusalem is uncertain. Some manuscripts contain Acts 15:34, which reads: "But it seemed good to Silas to remain there further." But the most prominent manuscripts omit this verse. (See NW ftn.) At any rate Silas was in Antioch at the start of Paul's second missionary tour. Beginning there, he and Paul traveled N and W through Syria, then Cilicia and other regions of Asia Minor. Timothy joined them at Lystra and Luke at Troas.

Being invited into Macedonia in a dream given to Paul, they first stayed in Philippi. In the marketplace there, Silas and Paul were beaten with rods by order of the civil magistrates and were put in prison stocks, but during the night, while they were praying and singing songs, an earthquake loosened their prison bonds and the prison doors were opened. The jailer was much frightened and, listening to Paul and Silas, became a Christian, caring for their injuries suffered from the beating. —Ac 15:41–16:40.

Their ministry found success in Thessalonica and Beroea, where Silas and Timothy remained behind temporarily while Paul went on to Athens and Corinth. (Ac 17:1, 10, 14-16; 18:1) When Silas and Timothy finally caught up with Paul in Corinth, they continued to assist Paul. While there they joined with Paul in writing the two letters to the Thessalonians. (1Th 1:1; 2Th 1:1) Silas is not mentioned again in the historical narrative of Paul's travels.

Some years later, around 62-64 C.E., Peter wrote his first letter from Babylon "through Silvanus," evidently meaning that Silvanus acted as Peter's secretary. He was there described as "a faithful brother," and he was likely the Silvanus earlier associated with Paul.—1Pe 5:12.

SILK.

The strongest of natural fibers, used since Bible times to make beautiful, lightweight cloth. Silk is produced by caterpillars of various species and especially by the Chinese silkworm, which feeds on mulberry leaves and emits a fluid that hardens into fine threads to form a cocoon. Silken fabric, considered by archaeologists to have been woven over 2,000 years ago, has been found in tombs of a Phoenician cemetery near Sabrata, Libya.

Silkworm culture appears to have had its start in China and to have spread from there to other lands, such as India. The Greeks described things made of silk as si·ri·kos′, thus linking silk with the "Seres" (generally identified as the Chinese). Silk is listed in Scripture among the costly articles of merchandise bought by "Babylon the Great."—Re 18:2, 11, 12.

Some Bible translations use "silk" for the Hebrew word me′shi at Ezekiel 16:10, 13. (AS, AT, KJ, JP, Le, Mo, Ro, RS) According to rabbinic tradition, me′shi denotes silk; however, there is uncertainty. Accordingly, the New World Translation, with the support of modern lexicographers, renders it "costly material."

SILLA (Sil′la).

Name of an otherwise unknown site at ancient Jerusalem. King Jehoash was assassinated "at the house of the Mound, on the way that goes down to Silla."—2Ki 12:20.

SILOAM (Si·lo′am) [from Heb., meaning "Sent; Sent Forth"].

A pool in Jerusalem where Jesus Christ had a blind man wash in order to receive sight. (Joh 9:6, 7, 11) Little is known about this pool as it then existed, though its general location apparently is marked by the present Birket

Silwan, just SW of the City of David. Likely this is also the approximate site of King Hezekiah's "pool" or reservoir adjoining the conduit he constructed to carry the waters of Gihon.—2Ki 20:20; 2Ch 32:30.

For the Siloam inscription, see HEZEKIAH; also PICTURE, Vol. 1, p. 960.

In the days of Jesus' earthly ministry, evidently it was common knowledge that "the tower in Siloam" had collapsed, killing 18 persons. It has been suggested that this tower was situated on the Ophel Ridge, but its actual location in Jerusalem is unknown.—Lu 13:4.

SILVANUS. See SILAS, SILVANUS.

SILVER.
A valuable white metallic element that takes a high polish. Since silver is seldom found in the native state, the base ore has to be smelted and purified to release the silver and separate it from the gangue, dross, and scummy foreign matter, as well as to free it from other metals such as lead. (Ps 12:6; Pr 27:21; Eze 22:20-22; Mal 3:3) At times, the Hebrew term for silver (ke'seph) is rendered "money" and the Greek term for silver (ar·gy'ri·on) is rendered "silver money" or "silver pieces."—Ge 17:12, ftn; Mt 25: 18; 26:15; see MONEY.

Refined silver had two principal uses. (1) It was used as a measure of wealth and a medium of exchange. Abraham, using this medium of exchange, bought a family burial plot. (Ge 13:2; 23:15-18) Payment was made by weight, since coinage was not devised until centuries later. (2) Objects of beauty and ornamentation were fashioned of this metal from the days of the patriarchs. (Ge 24:53; 44:2; Ex 11:2; 12:35) Silver was employed for Israel's two trumpets (Nu 10:2), in the construction of the tabernacle (Ex 26:19, 21, 25, 32; 27:10, 11, 17), and in Solomon's temple (1Ch 28:15-17). It was also used in making idols. —Ex 20:23; Ho 13:2; Hab 2:19; Ac 19:24.

Silver was treasured by all nations of the past. (2Sa 8:10, 11; 2Ch 9:14) Under Solomon's rule, not only silver but also gold became so abundant in Jerusalem that silver was counted "as nothing at all," "like the stones." (1Ki 10:21, 27; 2Ch 9:20; compare Da 2:32.) Once every three years ships brought cargoes of silver from Tarshish (apparently Spain, which is still a producer of silver).—1Ki 10:22; 2Ch 9:21; Jer 10:9; Eze 27:12.

In contrast with the transient value of silver, and to be more highly estimated, are the wisdom, discipline, and understanding that come from Jehovah. (Pr 3:13, 14; 8:10, 19; 16:16) Also, the Scriptures use silver in a number of symbolic senses.—Ec 12:6; Isa 60:17; Da 2:32; 1Co 3:12.

SIMEON
(Sim'e·on) [Hearing].

1. The second of Jacob's 12 sons; so named because, as his mother Leah said, "Jehovah has *listened,* in that I was hated and so he gave me also this one."—Ge 29:32, 33; 35:23-26; 48:5; Ex 1:1-4; 1Ch 2:1, 2.

When his father Jacob was encamped near Shechem, Simeon, together with his next younger brother Levi, displayed a vengeful anger that was unreasonably harsh and cruel. Arbitrarily, without their father's knowledge or consent, they set about avenging the honor of their younger sister Dinah by slaughtering the Shechemites, bringing ostracism upon Jacob's whole family.—Ge 34:1-31.

Simeon was later involved in wrongdoing when he and his brothers planned to kill Joseph. (Ge 37:12-28, 36) Whether Simeon, as second oldest, was or was not the ringleader in this plot on Joseph's life is not stated. Years later, when Joseph as food administrator of Egypt was testing out his brothers, Simeon was selected by Joseph to be bound and imprisoned until the other brothers brought Benjamin down to Egypt.—Ge 42:14-24, 34-36; 43:15, 23.

Shortly before Jacob's death, when blessing his sons, Jacob recalled with disapproval the violence of Simeon and Levi in connection with the Shechemites many years earlier, saying: "Instruments of violence are their slaughter weapons. Into their intimate group do not come, O my soul. With their congregation do not become united, O my disposition, because in their anger they killed men, and in their arbitrariness they hamstrung bulls. Cursed be their anger, because it is cruel, and their fury, because it acts harshly. Let me parcel them out in Jacob, but let me scatter them in Israel." (Ge 49:5-7) Jacob thus removed any hope Simeon may have entertained of receiving the birthright forfeited by his older brother Reuben. Simeon had six sons, one from a Canaanite woman. As prophesied, Simeon's tribal allotment was not united with Levi's, but these two were 'scattered'; even internally, Simeon's portion was divided up as enclave cities in Judah's territory. —Ge 46:10; Ex 6:15; 1Ch 4:24; Jos 19:1.

2. The tribe of Israel stemming from the families of Simeon's six sons: Jemuel, Jamin, Ohad, Jachin, Zohar, and Shaul. (Ge 46:10; Ex 6:15) During Israel's wilderness journey, Simeon encamped with Reuben and Gad on the S of the tabernacle, the three-tribe division being headed by Reuben. On the march, this same tribal arrangement was maintained, with Shelumiel serving as Simeon's chieftain, both of the camp and of the army.—Nu 1:4, 6; 2:10-15; 10:18-20.

[Continued on page 961]

Congregations of Revelation

TOWARD the end of the first century C.E., the resurrected Jesus Christ in a very touching way showed keen interest in his anointed followers still on earth. How? By directing the aged apostle John to write letters to "the seven congregations that (were) in the district of Asia." (Re 1:1-4) Those letters contained much needed encouragement, counsel, and warning.

Today, only ruins are found on the sites of most of the cities where those congregations were located. Yet, these give evidence that what was written deals with real places, actual situations, and people who truly lived. Of even greater interest, however, is the fact that these messages pointed to conditions that would exist at a future time in the Christian congregation.

Ruins of Ephesus. Some Christians in this materialistic city lost the love for Jehovah that they had at first

Reconstructed altar to Zeus from Pergamum. Christians in Pergamum were tested in regard to giving worship exclusively to Jehovah

Smyrna (now called Izmir). Early Christians here, though thrown into prison, were urged not to be afraid. Those in Philadelphia (at the head of a long valley that led west to Smyrna), though they had already endured, were also urged to keep holding fast what they had

Thyatira (now called Akhisar). Some early Christians in Thyatira, although sharing in good works, foolishly got involved in immoral conduct

Sardis. Not all Christians here were truly alive spiritually

Laodicea. Christians in this city were reproved for being lukewarm, like the water that reached the city through its aqueduct

JERUSALEM—once the center of true worship of Jehovah God, but no longer the city bearing God's name. Jerusalem lost its privileged position after it apostatized from the teachings of God's Word and rejected the Messiah, Jesus. (Lu 13:34, 35) To this day, however, Jerusalem is of keen interest to lovers of the Bible because events of universal importance took place there.

An aerial view of the city from the south (such as the one on this page) shows features of Jerusalem in relation to one another. Mount Moriah, where the temple was located, is in the background. In the foreground is Mount Zion, bounded by the torrent valley of Kidron on the east and the Tyropoeon Valley on the west. The City of David was built on Mount Zion.

Standing on the Mount of Olives to the east of Jerusalem, a person can look across the Kidron Valley and see the site where the temple once stood. Now it is dominated by a Muslim shrine known as the Dome of the Rock. Jesus was "sitting on the Mount of Olives with the temple in view" when he gave his famous prophecy about "the conclusion of the system of things."—Mr 13:3; Mt 24:3.

The temple site as seen from the
Mount of Olives. In the foreground are
the burial places of Jews who believed that
someday the Messiah would appear here

At the Holyland Hotel in
Jerusalem is this model of what many
believe represents the appearance
of first-century Jerusalem

The Garden Tomb (right) and the
Church of the Holy Sepulchre (below).
Each is claimed by some to be
the site of Jesus' burial

Damascus Gate, Jerusalem

Street scene in the
old part of Jerusalem

The Pool of Siloam, fed by the
spring of Gihon through Hezekiah's Tunnel

The Valley of Hinnom, which lay to
the south and southwest of ancient Jerusalem,
was called Gehenna in the first century

Aerial view across Jerusalem toward the east shows the Dead Sea in the distance

Traditional location of the garden of Gethsemane

Bethany, as it now appears

Warren's Shaft, through which water from the spring of Gihon could have been drawn by buckets. It may have been through such a shaft that David's men gained access to the Jebusite stronghold on Zion (2Sa 5:8)

Recent archaeological excavations on the north side of the ancient City of David

Western Wall of Jerusalem, including massive stones from the first century. Many Jews come here to pray

Everyday Life in Ancient Israel

WHAT was everyday life like back in Bible times? What sort of homes did ordinary people have? What kinds of work did they do? What were their customs? Your having some knowledge of these things can aid you in visualizing Bible accounts. At times, that background information is also the key to understanding the meaning of scriptures.

Most houses, like this one in Jerusalem, had flat roofs on which people might visit, walk in the cool evening, or even sleep (Lu 17:31)

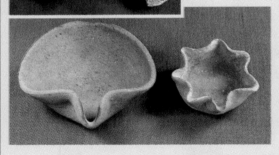

Ancient lamps, made of earthenware, in which oil was burned (Mt 25:1-4)

A household oven of the sort that was common among the Israelites (Le 26:26)

Hebrew men and women often carried loads on their shoulder (Ge 24:15; Nu 7:9)

Vessels were of many sizes and shapes, usually earthenware, sometimes made of stone (1Ki 17:12)

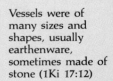

Threshing, sometimes done with the hooves of animals, separated grain from the chaff (1Ti 5:18)

Winnowing involved tossing the grain so that the wind would carry away the chaff (Jer 51:2)

A millstone that was likely used to crush olives so that the oil could be extracted (Nu 18:27)

Hand mill, used to grind grain into flour (Mt 24:41)

Sheepherding was
a common occupation
in Bible times (Lu 15:4)

Donkeys, or asses, were
frequently used as beasts
of burden (1Ch 12:40)

Wells were, and
still are, a common
source of water in
this land (Ge 29:10)

Goats were used to illustrate undesirable qualities and wicked persons (Zec 10:3; Mt 25:33), but goats offered in sacrifice were also used to foreshadow the sacrifice of Christ (Heb 9:12)

Using a vivid illustration, Jesus said that it would be easier for a camel to go through the eye of a sewing needle than for a rich man to get into the Kingdom (Lu 18:25)

The wild ass avoids places inhabited by humans. Among such creatures Nebuchadnezzar dwelt during his seven years of madness (Da 5:21)

Gazelles were used as symbols of beauty (Ca 2:9) and of speed (1Ch 12:8)

DETAILED
MAPS

Great Sea

Lod (Lydda) Hadid
Gimzo
Lower
Beth-
horon
Elteke(h)   Uzzen-sheerah
Jabneel   Shaalbim
            Baalah   Gezer   Aijalon
                        Gibbethon   Em
Gederoth   Shikkeron   C
            of Sorek   Seir   Kiri
Gederah   Makaz   jear
                                Timnah   Ashnah   (Baa
Ekron   Zorah Eshtaol Chesalon
Ashdod   Beth-shemesh   Lehi
                    Makkedah   En-gannim
                          Zanoah
            Gath   Jarmuth
                        Azekah   Tappuah Timnah   Elt
                        Low Plain of Elah Soco(h)
Ashkelon   Holon   Gibeah
                    Achzib
                    (Cozeba)   Adullam
            Libnah   Moresheth   Gilo   Gedo
            Ether   Keilah   Giloh   M
                    Mizpah   Nebo
            Elkosh   Ir-nahash   Beth-zur
Zaanan   Maresha(h)   Nezib   Halhul
(Zenan)   Lahmam   Beth-and
            Lachish   Ashnah   Iphtah   Mamre
Eglon   Migdal-gad   Beth-tappuah Hebron
                    Bozkath   Shaphir   Cave of Machpelah
            Chitlish   Adoraim
Gaza   Dilean   Aphekah
                    Etam   Zanoah
                    Beth-ezel   Juttah
                        Dumah Debir   Ca
                    Shamir   Arab
Gerar   Ziklag   Anab Goshen
                                Socoh   Eshtemoa
                    Ain (En-rimmon; Rimmon)
                        Madmannah   Jattir Anim
                    Sansannah
Sharuhen (Shaaraim; Shilhim)
                        Kabzeel
                        (Jekabzeel) Jeshua
                                    (Shema)
                    Beer-sheba
                    Hazar-shual   Jagur
                                    Arad
                                    [Canaanite]
                        Aroer

Chephar-ammoni
Senaah
Rabbah
(Philadelphia)
Ephraim(n)
(Ophrah)
Rimmon
Bethel
(Luz)
Ai
Avvim
Beth-nimrah
Mizpah
Naarah
Gilgal
Abel-keramim
Migron
Michmas(h)
Jericho
Geba
Bozez
Shittim
Minnith
Ramah
Azmaveth
Parah
Beth-haran(m)
Elealeh
eon
Gibeah
Adummim
Beth-arabah
Heshbon
Gallim
Almon
Anathoth
Beth-hoglah
Beth-peor
Bezer
Nephtoah
Bahurim
Beth-jeshimoth
erusalem
En-shemesh
Pisgah
n-rogel
Bethany (Ananiah)
Mt. Nebo
nahath
Nebo
Middin
City of Salt
Bamoth-baal
Secacah
Medeba
Bethlehem
Low Plain
Nibshan
of Achor
Baal-meon
Netophah
Suph
Tekoa
Almon-diblathaim

Salt

Sea

Zereth-shahar
Mattanah
Ataroth

Dibon

Beth-gamul
En-gedi
Aroer

V. of Arnon

Eglaim
Dimon
Rabbath-moab

(Baal; Baalath-beer)

Kir of Moab (Kir-hareseth; Kir-heres)

Nimrim

Jordan
River

The maps on these facing pages show the area north of what is on the preceding page spread and adjoining it

Jotbah
Cana
Neah
Rumah
Dimn
(Rimm
Hannathon
Hali
Beten
Gath-hepher
Harosheth
Bethlehem
Idalah
Nazareth
D
(R
Shimron
Mareal
Japhia
Che
(Chislo
Dabbesheth
Jokneam
Sarid
Mt.
Low Plain of Jezreel
Mor
Ophrah
Shunem
Dor
Megiddo
Carmel
Kedesh
Jez
Well of Hare
Caesarea
Hadadrimmon
Taanach
Binding House of the Shepher
En-gannim
Ibleam
Arubboth
Dothan
Hepher
Socoh
Th
Samaria
Mt. Ebal
Jacob's Fountain
Sychar
Shechem
Pirathon
Mt. Gerizim
Michmethath
Taanath
Baal-shalishah
Jar
Arumah
Rakkon
Tappuah
Gath-rimmon
Aphek (Antipatris)
Lebonah
Ebenezer
Shiloh
Joppa
Zeredah
Bene-berak
Gilgal
Ono
Jehud
Arimathea
(Ramah)
Beth-dagon
Timnath-serah
Jeshanah
Neballat
Baal-hazor

Great Sea

T. v. of Kishon

Magadan o

Rakkath •

Sea of Galilee

Madon o

Tiberias •

Aphek o

Hammath •

Adami-nekeb •

abor
eleph

Lassharon •

Jabneel •

Golan •

Ashtaroth •

Lakkum o

En-haddah •

Beth-shemesh o

or

N a h a l   Y a r m u k

Edrei •

Hapharaim •

Ramoth •

Debir o

House of Arbel o

Beth-shittah o

River

Rogelim o

Ham •

Beth-shean •

Ramoth-gilead o

Salim o

Aenon o

Abel-meholah •

Jordan

•

Tabbath o

Zaphon o

adi Far ah

Succoth •

Mahanaim •

Penuel
(Peniel) •

T. V. of J a b b o k

Mizpah o

Zarethan
(Zeredah) o

Adam •

Jogbehah •

Betonim o

This map, which adjoins the preceding ones, shows the area farthest to the north

Great Sea

Sidon

Luz

Baal-gad

Zarephath

Ijon

Helbah

Tyre

Abel-beth-maacah
Dan
(Laish; Leshem)
Caesarea Philippi

Migdal-el

Kanah
Beth-anath

Janoah

Hammon

Kedesh

Misrephoth-maim

Yiron
Merom
Edrei

Achzib
Abdon

Meroz
Hazor

Beth-emek

Ramah

Ptolemais
Acco

Chorazin
Bethsaida
Neiel
Capernaum
Hukkok
Cabul
Chinnereth
Sea of Galilee
Aphek

Reduction in Tribal Population. At the time of the first census, taken a year after the Exodus from Egypt, the tribe of Simeon numbered 59,300 able-bodied men 20 years old and upward who were fit for military service. (Nu 1:1-3, 22, 23) However, about 39 years later, the second census revealed that the tribe had suffered great losses, there being only 22,200 in the same category. This amounted to a decrease of more than 62 percent, far greater than that experienced by any other tribe.—Nu 26:1, 2, 12-14.

Moses did not mention Simeon by name in his farewell blessing of Israel. This is not to say the tribe was not blessed, for it was included at the end in the general blessing. (De 33:6-24, 29) Simeon was named first among the tribes assigned to stand on Mount Gerizim in connection with the blessings to be pronounced.—De 27:11, 12.

Simeon's reduced size was no doubt considered when it came to assigning individual territories in the Promised Land; the tribe was not given a self-contained, unbroken portion but, rather, cities entirely enclosed within Judah's territory. In this way Jacob's deathbed prophecy uttered more than 200 years earlier was fulfilled. (Nu 34:16-20; Jos 19:1-9; compare Ge 49:5-7.) Simeon shared with Judah in wresting this territory out of the hands of the Canaanites. (Jg 1:1-3, 17) Enclave cities were also set aside in Simeon's inheritance for the tribe of Levi.—Jos 21:4, 9, 10; 1Ch 6:64, 65.

Mention in Later Bible History. The Simeonites were mentioned from time to time in the later history of Israel—in the time of David (1Ch 4:24-31; 12:23, 25; 27:16), in the days of Asa (2Ch 15:8, 9), and in Josiah's time (2Ch 34:1-3, 6, 7). This latter reference to Josiah's reforms shows that, though geographically in Judah's territory, Simeon had politically and religiously cast in its lot with the northern kingdom. It appears that in the days of Hezekiah 500 Simeonites struck down a remnant of the Amalekites and took up dwelling in their place.—1Ch 4:41-43.

In the prophetic books of Ezekiel and Revelation, Simeon's name occurs along with others of the tribes of Israel. The strip of territory assigned to Simeon in Ezekiel's envisioned layout of the Promised Land lay between those of Benjamin and Issachar, S of "the holy contribution." But the gate assigned to Simeon on the S of the holy city was with those named after Issachar and Zebulun. (Eze 48:21-25, 28, 33) In the vision of the 144,000 sealed ones in Revelation chapter 7, Simeon is the seventh tribe listed.—Re 7:7.

3. The righteous, reverent old man who entered the temple on the very day that Joseph and Mary brought in the child Jesus. It had been divinely revealed to Simeon that before his death he would see the Christ. He therefore took the baby up in his arms, blessed Jehovah, and with holy spirit upon him, declared to the child's mother: "This one is laid for the fall and the rising again of many in Israel." Simeon also prophesied that Mary would be greatly grieved, as if run through with a sword, over the agonizing death of this son of hers.—Lu 2:22, 25-35.

SIMEONITES (Sim'e·on·ites) [Of (Belonging to) Simeon]. The descendants of Jacob's second son Simeon. After about 40 years of wandering in the wilderness, the male population among the Simeonites who were 20 years old and upward and who were qualified for military service numbered only 22,200, constituting the smallest of the 12 tribes. They were divided into five principal families—the Nemuelites, Jaminites, Jachinites, Zerahites, and Shaulites. (Nu 25:14; 26:1, 2, 12-14; Jos 21:4; 1Ch 27:16) If there were any descendants of a sixth son, Ohad, when this second census was taken, they were probably too few in number to be listed as a separate family of their own.—Ge 46:10; Ex 6:15.

SIMON (Si'mon) [from a Heb. root meaning "hear; listen"].

1. Simon Iscariot, father of Jesus' betrayer Judas.—Joh 6:71; 13:2, 26.

2. Another name for the apostle Peter.—Mr 3:16; see PETER.

3. An apostle of Jesus Christ, distinguished from Simon Peter by the term "Cananaean." (Mt 10:4; Mr 3:18) While it is possible that Simon once belonged to the Zealots, a Jewish party opposed to the Romans, it may instead have been due to his religious zeal that he was called "the zealous one," or "the zealot."—Lu 6:15, ftn; Ac 1:13.

4. A younger half brother of Jesus. (Mt 13:55; Mr 6:3) Though he was still an unbeliever prior to the Festival of Tabernacles in 32 C.E. (Joh 7:2-8), he may have become a disciple later. Jesus' fleshly brothers were among the crowd of about 120 disciples in Jerusalem during the season of Pentecost 33 C.E., although Simon is not specifically named as being present.—Ac 1:14, 15.

5. A Pharisee at whose house Jesus dined. It was there that a sinful woman showed him great kindness and respect, greasing his feet with perfumed oil.—Lu 7:36-50.

6. A resident of Bethany, spoken of as a "leper" (perhaps one cured by Jesus), in whose house Christ and his disciples, as well as the resurrected Lazarus and his sisters Mary and Martha, had a meal. There Mary anointed Jesus with costly perfumed oil.—Mt 26:6-13; Mr 14:3-9; Joh 12:2-8.

7. A native of Cyrene and the father of Alexander and Rufus. As a passerby who was coming from the country, Simon was pressed into service to help carry Jesus' torture stake.—Mt 27:32; Mr 15:21; Lu 23:26; see CYRENE, CYRENIAN.

8. A magician in the city of Samaria who so amazed the nation with his magical arts that the people said of him: "This man is the Power of God, which can be called Great." Because of Philip's ministry, Simon "became a believer" and was baptized. Later, when the believers received the holy spirit as a result of the apostles Peter and John laying their hands upon them, Simon displayed a wrong motive, offering money for the authority needed so that those upon whom he laid his hands would receive holy spirit. Peter strongly rebuked him, telling Simon that his heart was not straight in God's sight and urging him to repent and pray for forgiveness. In response, Simon asked these apostles to make supplication to Jehovah in his behalf.—Ac 8:9-24.

9. A tanner of Joppa in whose house by the sea the apostle Peter was entertained for quite a few days in 36 C.E.—Ac 9:43; 10:6, 17, 32.

SIN, I. Anything not in harmony with, hence contrary to, God's personality, standards, ways, and will; anything marring one's relationship with God. It may be in word (Job 2:10; Ps 39:1), in deed (doing wrong acts [Le 20:20; 2Co 12:21] or failing to do what should be done [Nu 9:13; Jas 4:17]), or in mind or heart attitude (Pr 21:4; compare also Ro 3:9-18; 2Pe 2:12-15). Lack of faith in God is a major sin, showing, as it does, distrust of him or lack of confidence in his ability to perform. (Heb 3:12, 13, 18, 19) A consideration of the use of the original-language terms and examples associated with them illustrates this.

The common Hebrew term translated "sin" is *chat·ta'th'*; in Greek the usual word is *ha·mar·ti'a*. In both languages the verb forms (Heb., *cha·ta"*; Gr., *ha·mar·ta'no*) mean "miss," in the sense of missing or not reaching a goal, way, mark, or right point. At Judges 20:16 *cha·ta"* is used, with a negative, to describe the Benjamites who were 'slingers of stones to a hairbreadth and would not miss.' Greek writers often used *ha·mar·ta'no* with regard to a spearman missing his target. Both of these words were used to mean missing or failing to reach not merely physical objects or goals (Job 5:24) but also moral or intellectual goals or marks. Proverbs 8:35, 36 says the one finding godly wisdom finds life, but the 'one missing [from Heb., *cha·ta"*] wisdom is doing violence to his soul,' leading to death. In the Scriptures both the Hebrew and Greek terms refer mainly to sinning

on the part of God's intelligent creatures, their missing the mark with regard to their Creator.

Man's Place in God's Purpose. Man was created in "God's image." (Ge 1:26, 27) He, like all other created things, existed and was created because of God's will. (Re 4:11) God's assigning work to him showed that man was to serve God's purpose on earth. (Ge 1:28; 2:8, 15) According to the inspired apostle, man was created to be both "God's image and glory" (1Co 11:7), hence to reflect the qualities of his Creator, conducting himself so as to reflect the glory of God. As God's earthly son, man should resemble, or be like, his heavenly Father. To be otherwise would be to contradict and reproach the divine parenthood of God.—Compare Mal 1:6.

Jesus showed this when encouraging his disciples to manifest goodness and love in a way surpassing that done by "sinners," persons known to practice sinful acts. He stated that only by following God's example in mercy and love could his disciples 'prove themselves sons of their Father who is in the heavens.' (Mt 5:43-48; Lu 6:32-36) Paul ties in God's glory with the matter of human sin in saying that "all have sinned and *fall short of the glory of God.*" (Ro 3:23; compare Ro 1:21-23; Ho 4:7.) At 2 Corinthians 3:16-18; 4:1-6 the apostle shows that those turning from sin to Jehovah "with unveiled faces reflect like mirrors the glory of Jehovah, [and] are transformed into the same image from glory to glory," because the glorious good news about the Christ, who is the image of God, shines through to them. (Compare also 1Co 10:31.) The apostle Peter quotes from the Hebrew Scriptures in stating God's express will for his earthly servants, saying: "In accord with the holy one who called you, do you also become holy yourselves in all your conduct, because it is written: 'You must be holy, because I am holy.'"—1Pe 1:15, 16; Le 19:2; De 18:13.

Sin, therefore, mars man's reflection of God's likeness and glory; it makes man unholy, that is, unclean, impure, tarnished in a spiritual and moral sense.—Compare Isa 6:5-7; Ps 51:1, 2; Eze 37:23; see HOLINESS.

All these texts, then, stress God's original purpose that man should be in harmony with God's personality, be like his Creator, similar to the way a human father who loves his son desires the son to be like him as to outlook on life, standards of conduct, qualities of heart. (Compare Pr 3:11, 12; 23:15, 16, 26; Eph 5:1; Heb 12:4-6, 9-11.) This, of necessity, requires man's obedience and submission to the divine will, whether that will is conveyed in the form of an express commandment or not. Sin, thus, involves a moral *failure*, a missing of the mark, in all these aspects.

The Introduction of Sin.

Sin occurred first in the spirit realm before its introduction on earth. For unknown ages full harmony with God prevailed in the universe. Disruption came through a spirit creature referred to simply as the Resister, Adversary (Heb., *Sa·tan'*; Gr., *Sa·ta·nas'*; Job 1:6; Ro 16:20), the principal False Accuser or Slanderer (Gr., *Di·a'bo·los*) of God. (Heb 2:14; Re 12:9) Hence, the apostle John says: "He who carries on sin originates with the Devil, because the Devil has been sinning from the beginning."—1Jo 3:8.

By "the beginning" John clearly means the beginning of Satan's career of opposition, even as "beginning" is used to refer to the start of the discipleship of Christians at 1 John 2:7; 3:11. John's words show that, once having introduced sin, Satan continued his sinful course. Hence, any person that "makes sin his business or practice" reveals himself to be a 'child' of the Adversary, spiritual offspring reflecting the qualities of his "father."—*The Expositor's Greek Testament*, edited by W. R. Nicoll, 1967, Vol. V, p. 185; Joh 8:44; 1Jo 3:10-12.

Since cultivation of wrong desire to the point of fertility precedes the 'birth of sin' (Jas 1:14, 15), the spirit creature who turned opposer had already begun to deviate from righteousness, had experienced disaffection toward God, prior to the actual *manifestation* of sin.

Revolt in Eden.

God's will as expressed to Adam and his wife was primarily positive, setting forth things they were to do. (Ge 1:26-29; 2:15) One prohibitive command was given to Adam, that forbidding eating of (or even touching) the tree of the knowledge of good and bad. (Ge 2:16, 17; 3:2, 3) God's test of man's obedience and devotion is notable for the respect it showed for man's dignity. By it God attributed nothing bad to Adam; he did not use as a test the prohibition of, for example, bestiality, murder, or some similar vile or base act, thereby implying that God felt Adam might have some despicable inclinations residing within him. Eating was normal, proper, and Adam had been told to "eat to satisfaction" of what God had given him. (Ge 2:16) But God now tested Adam by restricting his eating of the fruit of this one tree, God thus causing the eating of that fruit to symbolize that the eater comes to a knowledge that enables him to decide for himself what is "good" or what is "bad" for man. Thus, God neither imposed a hardship on the man nor did He attribute to Adam anything beneath his dignity as a human son of God.

The woman was the first human sinner. Her temptation by God's Adversary, who employed a serpent as a medium of communication (see PERFECTION [The first sinner and the king of Tyre]), was not through an open appeal to immorality of a sensual nature. Rather, it paraded as an appeal to the desire for supposed intellectual elevation and freedom. After first getting Eve to restate God's law, which she evidently had received through her husband, the Tempter then made an assault on God's truthfulness and goodness. He asserted that eating fruit from the prescribed tree would result, not in death, but in enlightenment and godlike ability to determine for oneself whether a thing was good or bad. This statement reveals that the Tempter was by now thoroughly alienated in heart from his Creator, his words constituting open contradiction plus veiled slander of God. He did not accuse God of unknowing error but of deliberate misrepresentation of matters, saying, "For God knows . . . " The gravity of sin, the detestable nature of such disaffection, is seen in the means to which this spirit son stooped to achieve his ends, becoming a deceitful liar and an ambition-driven murderer, since he obviously knew the fatal consequences of what he now suggested to his human listener.—Ge 3:1-5; Joh 8:44.

As the account reveals, improper desire began to work in the woman. Instead of reacting in utter disgust and righteous indignation on hearing the righteousness of God's law thus called into question, she now came to look upon the tree as desirable. She coveted what rightly belonged to Jehovah God as her Sovereign—his ability and prerogative to determine what is good and what is bad for his creatures. Hence, she was now starting to conform herself to the ways, standards, and will of the opposer, who contradicted her Creator as well as her God-appointed head, her husband. (1Co 11:3) Putting trust in the Tempter's words, she let herself be seduced, ate of the fruit, and thus revealed the sin that had been born in her heart and mind.—Ge 3:6; 2Co 11:3; compare Jas 1:14, 15; Mt 5:27, 28.

Adam later partook of the fruit when it was offered to him by his wife. The apostle shows that the man's sinning differed from that of his wife in that Adam was not deceived by the Tempter's propaganda, hence he put no stock in the claim that eating the fruit from the tree could be done with impunity. (1Ti 2:14) Adam's eating, therefore, must have been due to desire for his wife, and he 'listened to her voice' rather than to that of his God. (Ge 3:6, 17) He thus conformed to her ways and will, and through her, to those of God's Adversary. He therefore 'missed the mark,' failed to act in God's image and likeness, did not reflect God's glory, and, in fact, insulted his heavenly Father.

Effects of Sin. Sin put man out of harmony with his Creator. It thereby damaged not only his relations with God but also his relations with the rest of God's creation, including damage to man's own self, to his mind, heart, and body. It brought consequences of enormous evil upon the human race.

The conduct of the human pair immediately revealed this disharmony. Their covering portions of their divinely made bodies and thereafter their attempting to hide themselves from God were clear evidences of the alienation that had taken place within their minds and hearts. (Ge 3:7, 8) Sin thus caused them to feel guilt, anxiety, insecurity, shame. This illustrates the point made by the apostle at Romans 2:15, that God's law was 'written on man's heart'; hence a violation of that law now produced an internal upheaval within man, his conscience accusing him of wrongdoing. In effect, man had a built-in lie detector that made impossible his concealing his sinful state from his Creator; and God, responding to the man's excuse for his changed attitude toward his heavenly Father, promptly inquired: "From the tree from which I commanded you not to eat have you eaten?"—Ge 3:9-11.

To be true to himself, as well as for the good of the rest of his universal family, Jehovah God could not countenance such a sinful course, on the part of either his human creatures or the spirit son turned rebel. Maintaining his holiness, he justly imposed the sentence of death on them all. The human pair were then expelled from God's garden in Eden, hence cut off from access to that other tree designated by God as "the tree of life."—Ge 3:14-24.

Results to mankind as a whole. Romans 5:12 states that "through one man sin entered into the world and death through sin, and thus death spread to all men because they had all sinned." (Compare 1Jo 1:8-10.) Some have explained this as meaning that all of Adam's future offspring shared in Adam's initial act of sin because, as their family head, he represented them and thereby made them, in effect, participants with him in his sin. The apostle, however, speaks of death as 'spreading' to all men, which implies a progressive rather than a simultaneous effect on Adam's descendants.

Additionally, the apostle goes on to speak of death as ruling as king "from Adam down to Moses, *even over those who had not sinned after the likeness of the transgression by Adam.*" (Ro 5:14) Adam's sin is rightly called a "transgression" since it was an overstepping of a stated law, an express command of God to him. Also, when Adam sinned, it was of his own free choice, as a perfect human who was free from disabilities. Clearly, his offspring have never enjoyed that state of perfection. So, these factors seem out of harmony with the view that 'when Adam sinned, all of his as yet unborn descendants sinned with him.' For all of Adam's descendants to be held accountable as participants in Adam's personal sin would require some expression of *will* on their part as to having him as their family head. Yet none of them in reality willed to be born of him, their birth into the Adamic line resulting from the fleshly will of their parents.—Joh 1:13.

The evidence, then, points to a passing on of sin from Adam to succeeding generations as a result of the recognized law of heredity. This is evidently what the psalmist refers to in saying: "With error I was brought forth with birth pains, and in sin my mother conceived me." (Ps 51:5) Sin, along with its consequences, entered and spread to all the human race not merely because Adam was the family *head* of the race but because he, not Eve, was its *progenitor,* or human life source. From him, as well as from Eve, his offspring would inescapably inherit not merely physical characteristics but also personality traits, including the inclination toward sin.—Compare 1Co 15:22, 48, 49.

Paul's words also point to this conclusion when he says that "just as through the disobedience of the one man [Adam] many were constituted sinners, likewise also through the obedience of the one person [Christ Jesus] many will be constituted righteous." (Ro 5:19) Those to be "constituted righteous" by Christ's obedience were not all immediately so constituted at the moment of his presenting his ransom sacrifice to God, but they progressively come under the benefits of that sacrifice as they come to exercise faith in that provision and become reconciled to God. (Joh 3:36; Ac 3:19) So, too, progressive generations of Adam's descendants have been constituted sinners as they have been conceived by their innately sinful parents in Adam's line.

Sin's power and wages. "The wages sin pays is death" (Ro 6:23), and by being born in Adam's line all men have come under "the law of sin and of death." (Ro 8:2; 1Co 15:21, 22) Sin, with death, has "ruled as king" over mankind, enslaving them, this slavery being one into which they were sold by Adam. (Ro 5:17, 21; 6:6, 17; 7:14; Joh 8:34) These statements show that sin is viewed not only as the actual commission or omission of certain acts but also as a *law* or *governing principle* or *force* operating in them, namely, the inborn inclination toward wrongdoing that they inherit from Adam. Their Adamic inheritance has therefore produced 'weakness of the flesh,' imperfection. (Ro 6:19) Sin's "law" continually works in their fleshly members, in effect trying to control their course, to make them its subjects, out of harmony with God.—Ro 7:15, 17, 18, 20-23; Eph 2:1-3.

"King" sin may give its 'orders' in different ways to different persons and at different times. Thus, God, noting the anger of Adam's first son Cain against his brother Abel, warned Cain that he should turn to doing good, for, he said: "There is sin crouching at the entrance, and for you is its craving; and will you, for your part, get the mastery over it?" Cain, however, let the sin of envy and hatred master him, leading him to murder.—Ge 4:3-8; compare 1Sa 15:23.

Sickness, pain, and aging. Since death in humans is generally associated with disease or the aging process, it follows that these are concomitants of sin. Under the Mosaic Law covenant with Israel, the laws governing sacrifices for sin included atonement for those who had suffered from the plague of leprosy. (Le 14:2, 19) Those touching a human corpse or even entering the tent where a person had died became unclean and required ceremonial purification. (Nu 19:11-19; compare Nu 31:19, 20.) Jesus, too, associated illness with sin (Mt 9:2-7; Joh 5:5-15), although he showed that specific afflictions are not necessarily the result of any specific sinful acts. (Joh 9:2, 3) Other texts show the beneficial effects of righteousness (a course opposite from sinning) on one's health. (Pr 3:7, 8; 4:20-22; 14:30) During Christ's reign, the elimination of death, which rules with sin (Ro 5:21), will be accompanied by the end of pain.—1Co 15:25, 26; Re 21:4.

Sin and Law. The apostle John writes that "everyone who practices sin is also practicing lawlessness, and so sin is lawlessness" (1Jo 3:4); also that "all unrighteousness is sin." (1Jo 5:17) The apostle Paul, on the other hand, speaks of "those who sinned without law." He further states that "until the Law [given through Moses] sin was in the world, but sin is not charged against anyone when there is no law. Nevertheless, death ruled as king from Adam down to Moses, even

over those who had not sinned after the likeness of the transgression by Adam." (Ro 2:12; 5:13, 14) Paul's words are to be understood in context; his earlier statements in this letter to the Romans show that he was comparing those under the Law covenant with those outside that covenant, hence not under its law code, while he demonstrated that both classes were sinful.—Ro 3:9.

During the approximately 2,500 years between Adam's deflection and the giving of the Law covenant in 1513 B.C.E., God had not given mankind any comprehensive code or systematically arranged law that specifically defined sin in all its ramifications and forms. True, he had given certain decrees, such as those given to Noah following the global Flood (Ge 9:1-7) as well as the covenant of circumcision given to Abraham and his household, including his foreign slaves. (Ge 17:9-14) But concerning Israel the psalmist could say that God "is telling his word to Jacob, his regulations and his judicial decisions to Israel. He has not done that way to any other nation; and as for his judicial decisions, they have not known them." (Ps 147:19, 20; compare Ex 19:5, 6; De 4:8; 7:6, 11.) Of the Law covenant given Israel it could be said, "The man that has done the righteousness of the Law will live by it," for perfect adherence to and compliance with that Law could be accomplished only by a sinless man, as was the case with Christ Jesus. (Ro 10:5; Mt 5:17; Joh 8:46; Heb 4:15; 7:26; 1Pe 2:22) This was true of no other law given from the time of Adam to the giving of the Law covenant.

'Doing by nature the things of the law.' This did not mean that, since there was no comprehensive law code against which to measure their conduct, men during that period between Adam and Moses were free from sin. At Romans 2:14, 15, Paul states: "For whenever people of the nations that do not have law do by nature the things of the law, these people, although not having law, are a law to themselves. They are the very ones who demonstrate the matter of the law to be written in their hearts, while their conscience is bearing witness with them and, between their own thoughts, they are being accused or even excused." Having been originally made in God's image and likeness, man has a moral nature, which produces the faculty of conscience. Even imperfect, sinful men retain a measure of this, as Paul's words indicate. (See CONSCIENCE.) Since law is basically a 'rule of conduct,' this moral nature operates in their hearts as a law. However, set over against this law of their moral nature is another inherited law, the 'law of sin,'

which wars against righteous tendencies, making slaves of those who do not resist its dominance. —Ro 6:12; 7:22, 23.

This moral nature and associated conscience can be seen even in Cain's case. Although God had given no law regarding homicide, by the evasive way Cain responded to God's inquiry, he showed that his conscience condemned him after he murdered Abel. (Ge 4:8, 9) Joseph the Hebrew showed God's 'law in his heart' when he responded to the seductive request of Potiphar's wife, saying: "How could I commit this great badness and actually sin against God?" Though God had not specifically condemned adultery, yet Joseph recognized it as wrong, violating God's will for humans as expressed in Eden.—Ge 39:7-9; compare Ge 2:24.

Thus, during the patriarchal period from Abraham through the 12 sons of Jacob, the Scriptures show men of many races and nations speaking of "sin" (chat·ta·th'), such as sins against an employer (Ge 31:36), against the ruler to whom one is subject (Ge 40:1; 41:9), against a relative (Ge 42:22; 43:9; 50:17), or simply against a fellow human (Ge 20:9). In any case, the one using the term acknowledged thereby a certain relationship with the person against whom the sin was or might be committed and recognized an accompanying responsibility to respect that one's interests or his will and authority, as in the case of a ruler, and not go contrary to them. They thereby showed evidence of moral nature. With the passing of time, nonetheless, sin's mastery over those not serving God grew, so that Paul could speak of the people of the nations as walking in "darkness mentally, and alienated from the life that belongs to God . . . past all moral sense." —Eph 4:17-19.

How the Law made sin "abound." While man's measure of conscience gave him a certain natural sense of right and wrong, God, by making the Law covenant with Israel, now specifically identified sin in its multiple aspects. The mouth of any person descended from God's friends Abraham, Isaac, and Jacob who might voice the claim that he was innocent from sin was thereby "stopped and all the world [became] liable to God for punishment." This was so because the imperfect flesh they inherited from Adam made it impossible for them to be declared righteous before God by works of law, "for by law is the accurate knowledge of sin." (Ro 3:19, 20; Ga 2:16) The Law spelled out clearly what the full range and scope of sin was, so that, in effect, it caused trespassing and sin to "abound," in that so many

acts and even attitudes were now identified as sinful. (Ro 5:20; 7:7, 8; Ga 3:19; compare Ps 40:12.) Its sacrifices continually served to remind those under the Law of their sinful state. (Heb 10:1-4, 11) The Law by these means acted as a tutor to lead them to Christ, that they "might be declared righteous due to faith."—Ga 3:22-25.

How could sin 'receive an inducement' through God's commandment to Israel?

In pointing out that the Mosaic Law is not the means for humans to gain a righteous standing before Jehovah God, the apostle Paul wrote: "When we were in accord with the flesh, the sinful passions that were excited by the Law were at work in our members that we should bring forth fruit to death. . . . What, then, shall we say? Is the Law sin? Never may that become so! Really I would not have come to know sin if it had not been for the Law; and, for example, I would not have known covetousness if the Law had not said: 'You must not covet.' But sin, receiving an inducement through the commandment, worked out in me covetousness of every sort, for apart from law sin was dead."—Ro 7:5-8.

Without the Law, the apostle Paul would not have known or discerned the full range or scope of sin, for example, the sinfulness of covetousness. As the apostle notes, the Law "excited" sinful passion, and the commandment against coveting provided an "inducement" for sin. This is to be understood in the light of Paul's statement that "apart from law sin was dead." As long as sin had not been defined specifically, a person could not be accused of committing sins that were not legally identified as such. Before the Law came, Paul and others of his nation lived uncondemned for sins that were not specified. With the introduction of the Law, however, Paul and his fellow countrymen were designated as sinners under condemnation of death. The Law made them more conscious of being sinners. This does not mean that the Mosaic Law prompted them to sin, but it exposed them as sinners. Thus sin received an inducement through the Law and worked out sin in Paul and his people. The Law provided the basis for condemning more people as sinners and on many more legal counts.

The answer to the question "Is the Law sin?" is therefore definitely 'No!' (Ro 7:7) The Law did not 'miss the mark' by failing the purpose for which God gave it but, rather, scored a 'bull's-eye,' not only in being good and beneficial as a protective guide but also in legally establishing that all persons, the Israelites not excepted, were sinners in need of redemption by God. It also pointed the Israelites to Christ as the needed Redeemer.

Errors, Transgressions, Trespasses. The Scriptures frequently link "error" (Heb., *'a·won'*), "transgression" (Heb., *pe'sha'*; Gr., *pa·ra'ba·sis*), "trespass" (Gr., *pa·ra'pto·ma*), and other such terms with "sin" (Heb., *chat·ta'th'*; Gr., *ha·mar·ti'a*). All such related terms present specific aspects of sin, forms that it takes.

Errors, mistakes, and foolishness. Thus, *'a·won'* basically relates to erring, acting crookedly or wrongly. The Hebrew term refers to a moral error or wrong, a distortion of what is right. (Job 10:6, 14, 15) Those not submitting to God's will obviously are not guided by his perfect wisdom and justice, hence are bound to err. (Compare Isa 59:1-3; Jer 14:10; Php 2:15.) Doubtless because sin causes man to be off balance, distorting what is upright (Job 33:27; Hab 1:4), *'a·won'* is the Hebrew term most frequently linked with or used in parallel with *chat·ta'th'* (sin, missing the mark). (Ex 34:9; De 19:15; Ne 4:5; Ps 32:5; 85:2; Isa 27:9) This imbalance produces confusion and disharmony within man and difficulties in his dealings with God and with the rest of God's creation.

The "error" (*'a·won'*) may be intentional or unintentional, either a conscious deviation from what is right or an unknowing act, a "mistake" (*shegha·ghah'*), which, nevertheless, brings the person into error and guilt before God. (Le 4:13-35; 5:1-6, 14-19; Nu 15:22-29; Ps 19:12, 13) If intentional, then, of course, the error is of far graver consequence than if by mistake. (Nu 15:30, 31; compare La 4:6, 13, 22.) Error is contrary to truth, and those willfully sinning pervert the truth, a course which only brings forth grosser sin. (Compare Isa 5:18-23.) The apostle Paul speaks of "the deceptive power of sin," which has a hardening effect on human hearts. (Heb 3:13-15; compare Ex 9:27, 34, 35.) The same writer, in quoting from Jeremiah 31:34, where the Hebrew original spoke of Israel's "error" and "sin," wrote *ha·mar·ti'a* (sin) and *a·di·ki'a* (unrighteousness) at Hebrews 8:12, and *ha·mar·ti'a* and *a·no·mi'a* (lawlessness) at Hebrews 10:17.

Proverbs 24:9 states that "the loose conduct of foolishness is sin," and Hebrew terms conveying the idea of foolishness are often used in connection with sinning, the sinner at times repentantly acknowledging, "I have acted foolishly." (1Sa 26:21; 2Sa 24:10, 17) Undisciplined by God, the sinner gets tangled up in his errors and foolishly goes astray.—Pr 5:22, 23; compare 19:3.

Transgression, an "overstepping" Sin may take the form of a "transgression." The Greek *pa·ra'ba·sis* (transgression) refers basically to an "overstepping," that is, going beyond certain limits or boundaries, especially as in breaking a law. Matthew uses the verb form (*pa·ra·bai'no*) in recounting the question of the Pharisees and scribes as to why Jesus' disciples 'overstepped the tradition of men of former times,' and Jesus' counterquestion as to why these opposers 'overstepped the commandment of God because of their tradition,' by which they made God's word invalid. (Mt 15:1-6) It also can mean a "stepping aside," as in Judas' 'deviating' from his ministry and apostleship. (Ac 1:25) In some Greek texts the same verb is used when referring to one who *"goes beyond, and does not abide in the doctrine of the Anointed one."*—2Jo 9, *ED*.

In the Hebrew Scriptures there are similar references to sinning by persons who "overstepped," 'sidestepped,' "bypassed," or 'passed beyond' (Heb., *'a·var'*) God's covenant or specific orders. —Nu 14:41; De 17:2, 3; Jos 7:11, 15; 1Sa 15:24; Isa 24:5; Jer 34:18.

The apostle Paul shows the special connection of *pa·ra'ba·sis* with violation of established law in saying that "where there is no law, neither is there any transgression." (Ro 4:15) Hence, in the absence of law the sinner would not be called a "transgressor." Consistently, Paul and the other Christian writers use *pa·ra'ba·sis* (and *pa·ra·ba'tes*, "transgressor") in the context of law. (Compare Ro 2:23-27; Ga 2:16, 18; 3:19; Jas 2:9, 11.) Adam, having received a direct command from God, was therefore guilty of "transgression" of stated law. His wife, though deceived, was also guilty of transgression of that law. (1Ti 2:14) The Law covenant spoken to Moses by angels was added to the Abrahamic covenant "to make transgressions manifest," that 'all things together might be delivered up to the custody of sin,' legally convicting all of Adam's descendants, Israel included, of sin, and demonstrating that all clearly needed forgiveness and salvation through faith in Christ Jesus. (Ga 3:19-22) Thus, if Paul had put himself back under the Mosaic Law, he would have made himself a "transgressor" again of that Law, subject to its condemnation, and would thereby have shoved aside the undeserved kindness of God that provided release from that condemnation.—Ga 2:18-21; compare 3:1-4, 10.

The Hebrew *pe'sha'* carries the idea of transgression (Ps 51:3; Isa 43:25-27; Jer 33:8) as well as that of "revolt," which is a turning away from, or rejection of, the law or authority of another.

(1Sa 24:11; Job 13:23, 24; 34:37; Isa 59:12, 13) Willful transgression, then, amounts to rebellion against God's paternal rule and authority. It sets the will of the creature against that of the Creator, and so he indulges in revolt against God's sovereignty, His supreme rulership.

Trespass. The Greek *pa·ra'pto·ma* means, literally, "a fall beside," hence a false step (Ro 11:11, 12) or blunder, a "trespass." (Eph 1:7; Col 2:13) Adam's sin in eating the forbidden fruit was a "transgression" in that he overstepped God's law; it was a "trespass" in that he fell or made a false step instead of standing or walking upright in harmony with God's righteous requirements and in support of His authority. The many statutes and requirements of the Law covenant in effect opened the way for many such trespasses because of the imperfection of those subject to it (Ro 5:20); the nation of Israel as a whole blundered as to keeping that covenant. (Ro 11:11, 12) Since all the various statutes of that Law were part of one covenant, the person making "a false step" in one point thereby became an offender and "transgressor" against the covenant as a whole and hence against all its statutes.—Jas 2:10, 11.

"Sinners." Since "there is no man that does not sin" (2Ch 6:36), all of Adam's descendants can properly be termed "sinners" by nature. But in the Scriptures "sinners" usually applies in a more specific way, designating those who practice sin or who have a reputation of sinning. Their sins have become public knowledge. (Lu 7:37-39) The Amalekites, whom Jehovah ordered Saul to destroy, are called "sinners" (1Sa 15:18); the psalmist prayed that God would not take away his soul "along with sinners," his following words identifying such as "bloodguilty men, in whose hands there is loose conduct, and whose right hand is full of bribery." (Ps 26:9, 10; compare Pr 1:10-19.) Jesus was condemned by religious leaders for associating with "tax collectors and sinners," and tax collectors were viewed by the Jews as a generally disreputable class. (Mt 9:10, 11) Jesus referred to them along with harlots as preceding the Jewish religious leaders in entry into the Kingdom. (Mt 21:31, 32) Zacchaeus, a tax collector and a "sinner" in the eyes of many, acknowledged that he had illegally extorted money from others.—Lu 19:7, 8.

Hence, when Jesus said "there will be more joy in heaven over one sinner that repents than over ninety-nine righteous ones who have no need of repentance," he was evidently using these terms in a *relative* sense (see RIGHTEOUSNESS [Goodness and Righteousness]), for all men are by nature sinners and none are righteous in the absolute sense.—Lu 15:7, 10; compare Lu 5:32; 13:2; see DECLARE RIGHTEOUS.

Comparative Gravity of Wrongdoing. Although sin is sin, and in any case could justly make the guilty one worthy of sin's "wages," death, the Scriptures show that God views mankind's wrongdoing as varying in degrees of gravity. Thus, the men of Sodom were "gross sinners against Jehovah," and their sin was "very heavy." (Ge 13:13; 18:20; compare 2Ti 3:6, 7.) The Israelites' making a golden calf was also called "a great sin" (Ex 32:30, 31), and Jeroboam's calf worship similarly caused those of the northern kingdom "to sin with a great sin." (2Ki 17:16, 21) Judah's sin became "like that of Sodom," making the kingdom of Judah abhorrent in God's eyes. (Isa 1:4, 10; 3:9; La 1:8; 4:6) Such a course of disregard for God's will can make even one's very prayer become a sin. (Ps 109:7, 8, 14) Since sin is an affront to God's own person, he is not indifferent to it; as its gravity increases, his indignation and wrath are understandably increased. (Ro 1:18; De 29:22-28; Job 42:7; Ps 21:8, 9) His wrath, however, is not solely due to the involvement of his own person but is likewise stirred by the injury and injustice done to humans and particularly to his faithful servants.—Isa 10:1-4; Mal 2:13-16; 2Th 1:6-10.

Human weakness and ignorance. Jehovah takes into account the weakness of imperfect men descended from Adam, so that those sincerely seeking Him can say, "He has not done to us even according to our sins; nor according to our errors has he brought upon us what we deserve." The Scriptures show the wonderful mercy and lovingkindness that God has displayed in his patient dealings with men of flesh. (Ps 103:2, 3, 10-18) He also takes into account ignorance as a contributory factor in sins (1Ti 1:13; compare Lu 12:47, 48), provided such ignorance is not willful. Those who willfully reject the knowledge and wisdom God offers, 'taking pleasure in unrighteousness,' are not excused. (2Th 2:9-12; Pr 1:22-33; Ho 4:6-8) Some are temporarily misled from the truth but, with help, turn back (Jas 5:19, 20), while others 'shut their eyes to the light and forget their earlier cleansing from sins.'—2Pe 1:9.

What is unforgivable sin?

Knowledge brings greater responsibility. Pilate's sin was not as great as that of the Jewish religious leaders who turned Jesus over to the governor, nor that of Judas, who betrayed his

Lord. (Joh 19:11; 17:12) Jesus told Pharisees of his day that if they were blind, they would have no sin, evidently meaning that their sins could be forgiven by God on the basis of their ignorance; however, because they denied being in ignorance, 'their sin remained.' (Joh 9:39-41) Jesus said they had "no excuse for their sin" because they were witnesses of the powerful words and works proceeding from him as the result of God's spirit on him. (Joh 15:22-24; Lu 4:18) Those who, either in word or by their course of action, willfully and knowingly blasphemed God's spirit thus manifested would be "guilty of everlasting sin," with no forgiveness possible. (Mt 12:31, 32; Mr 3: 28-30; compare Joh 15:26; 16:7, 8.) This could be the case with some who came to be Christians and then deliberately turned from God's pure worship. Hebrews 10:26, 27 states that "if we practice sin willfully after having received the accurate knowledge of the truth, there is no longer any sacrifice for sins left, but there is a certain fearful expectation of judgment and there is a fiery jealousy that is going to consume those in opposition."

At 1 John 5:16, 17, John evidently refers to willful, knowing sin in speaking of "a sin that does incur death" as contrasted with one that does not. (Compare Nu 15:30.) Where the evidence indicates such willful, knowing sin, the Christian would not pray for the one so offending. God, of course, is the final Judge as to the heart attitude of the sinner.—Compare Jer 7:16; Mt 5:44; Ac 7:60.

Single sin versus practice of sin. John also makes a distinction between a single sin and the practice of sinning as is shown by a comparison of 1 John 2:1 and 3:4-8 as rendered in the *New World Translation*. As to the correctness of the rendering "everyone who practices sin [*poi·on' ten ha·mar·ti'an*]" (1Jo 3:4), Robertson's *Word Pictures in the New Testament* (1933, Vol. VI, p. 221) says: "The present active participle (*poion*) means the habit of doing sin." As to 1 John 3:6, where the phrase *oukh ha·mar·ta'nei* is used in the Greek text, the same scholar comments (p. 222): "Linear present . . . active indicative of *hamartano,* 'does not keep on sinning.'" Thus, the faithful Christian may at some time lapse or fall into sin because of weakness or being misled, but he "does not carry on sin," continuing to walk in it.—1Jo 3:9, 10; compare 1Co 15:33, 34; 1Ti 5:20.

Sharing in the sins of others. A person can become guilty of sin before God by his willing association with wrongdoers, by his approval of their wrongdoing, or by his covering over their conduct so that the elders do not know about it and take appropriate action. (Compare Ps 50:18, 21; 1Ti 5:22.) Those who stay in the symbolic city "Babylon the Great" therefore also "receive part of her plagues." (Re 18:2, 4-8) A Christian associating with or even saying "a greeting" to one who abandons the teaching of the Christ becomes "a sharer in his wicked works."—2Jo 9-11; compare Tit 3:10, 11.

Timothy was warned by Paul against being "a sharer in the sins of others." (1Ti 5:22) Paul's preceding words as to 'never laying hands hastily upon any man' must refer to the authority granted Timothy to appoint overseers in congregations. He was not to appoint a newly converted man, for such a one might get puffed up with pride; if Timothy failed to heed this counsel, he would reasonably bear a measure of the responsibility for whatever wrongs such a one might commit.—1Ti 3:6.

An entire nation could become guilty of sin before God on the basis of the above principles.—Pr 14:34.

Sins Against Men, God, and Christ. As shown earlier, the Hebrew Scriptures record references to sin by men of different nations during the patriarchal period. Mainly these related to sins against other humans.

Since God alone is the standard of righteousness and goodness, sins committed against humans are not failures to conform to such persons' 'image and likeness,' but they are a failure to respect or care for their rightful and proper interests, thus committing offense against them, causing them unjust damage. (Jg 11:12, 13, 27; 1Sa 19:4, 5; 20:1; 26:21; Jer 37:18; 2Co 11:7) Jesus set forth the guiding principles for a person to follow if certain serious sins were committed against him. (Mt 18:15-17) Even though one's brother sinned against him 77 times or 7 times in a single day, such an offender was to be forgiven if, upon being rebuked, he showed repentance. (Mt 18:21, 22; Lu 17:3, 4; compare 1Pe 4:8.) Peter speaks of house servants being slapped for sins committed against their owners. (1Pe 2:18-20) One can sin against constituted authority by failing to show it due respect. Paul declared himself innocent of any sin "against the Law of the Jews [or] against the temple [or] against Caesar."—Ac 25:8.

Sins against humans, nevertheless, are also sins against the Creator, to whom men must make an accounting. (Ro 14:10, 12; Eph 6:5-9; Heb 13:17) God, who held Abimelech back from having relations with Sarah, told the Philistine king, "I was also holding you back from sinning *against me.*"

(Ge 20:1-7) Joseph likewise recognized that adultery was a sin against the Creator of male and female and against the Former of the marriage union (Ge 39:7-9), as did King David. (2Sa 12:13; Ps 51:4) Such sins as robbery, defrauding, or embezzlement of another's property are classified in the Law as 'unfaithful behavior toward Jehovah.' (Le 6:2-4; Nu 5:6-8) Those hardening their hearts and being closefisted toward their poor brothers and those withholding men's wages were subject to divine reproof. (De 15:7-10; 24:14, 15; compare Pr 14:31; Am 5:12.) Samuel declared it unthinkable, on his part, "to sin against Jehovah by ceasing to pray" on behalf of his fellow Israelites and at their request.—1Sa 12:19-23.

Similarly, James 2:1-9 condemns as sin the showing of favoritism or the making of class distinctions among Christians. Paul says that those paying no heed to the weak consciences of their brothers and thus causing such to stumble are "sinning against Christ," God's Son who gave his own lifeblood for his followers.—1Co 8:10-13.

Thus, while all sins in reality are sins against God, Jehovah views some sins as more directly against his own person, sins such as idolatry (Ex 20:2-5; 2Ki 22:17), faithlessness (Ro 14:22, 23; Heb 10:37, 38; 12:1), disrespect for sacred things (Nu 18:22, 23), and all forms of false worship (Ho 8:11-14). This is doubtless why the high priest Eli told his sons, who disrespected God's tabernacle and service: "If a man should sin against a man, God will arbitrate for him [compare 1Ki 8:31, 32]; but if it is against Jehovah that a man should sin, who is there to pray for him?"—1Sa 2:22-25; compare vss. 12-17.

Sinning against one's own body. In warning against fornication (sex relations outside of Scripturally approved marriage), Paul states that "every other sin that a man may commit is outside his body, but he that practices fornication is sinning against his own body." (1Co 6:18; see FORNICATION.) The context shows that Paul had been emphasizing that Christians were to be united with their Lord and Head, Christ Jesus. (1Co 6:13-15) The fornicator wrongly and sinfully becomes one flesh with another, who is often a harlot. (1Co 6:16-18) Since no other sin can thus separate the body of the Christian from union with Christ and make it "one" with another, this is evidently why all other sins are here viewed as 'outside one's body.' Fornication can also result in incurable damage to the fornicator's own body.

Sins by Angels. Since God's spirit sons are also to reflect God's glory and bring praise to him, carrying out his will (Ps 148:1, 2; 103:20, 21), they can sin in the same *basic* sense as humans.

Second Peter 2:4 shows that some of God's spirit sons did sin, being "delivered [into] pits of dense darkness to be reserved for judgment." First Peter 3:19, 20 evidently refers to the same situation in speaking of "the spirits in prison, who had once been disobedient when the patience of God was waiting in Noah's days." And Jude 6 indicates that the 'missing of the mark,' or sinning, by such spirit creatures was because they "did not keep their original position but forsook their own proper dwelling place," that proper dwelling place logically referring to the heavens of God's presence.

Since Jesus Christ's sacrifice contains no provision for covering the sins of spirit creatures, there is no reason to believe that the sins of those disobedient angels were forgivable. (Heb 2:14-17) Like Adam, they were perfect creatures with no inborn weakness to be considered as an extenuating factor in judging their wrongdoing.

Remission of Sins. As shown in the article DECLARE RIGHTEOUS (How "counted" righteous), Jehovah God in effect 'credits' righteousness to the account of those living according to faith. In so doing, God correspondingly 'covers over,' 'wipes out,' or 'blots out' the sins that would otherwise be charged against the account of such faithful ones. (Compare Ps 32:1, 2; Isa 44:22; Ac 3:19.) Jesus, thus, likened "trespasses" and "sins" to 'debts.' (Compare Mt 6:14; 18:21-35; Lu 11:4.) Though their sins were as scarlet, Jehovah 'washes away' the stain that makes them unholy. (Isa 1:18; Ac 22:16) The means by which God can thus express his tender mercy and lovingkindness while yet maintaining his perfect justice and righteousness is considered under RANSOM; RECONCILIATION; REPENTANCE; and related articles.

Avoidance of Sin. Love of God and of neighbor is a principal means for avoiding sin, which is lawlessness, for love is an outstanding quality of God; he made love the foundation of his Law to Israel. (Mt 22:37-40; Ro 13:8-11) In this way Christians can be, not alienated from God, but in joyful union with him and his Son. (1Jo 1:3; 3:1-11, 24; 4:16) Such are open to the guidance of God's holy spirit and can "live as to the spirit from the standpoint of God," desisting from sins (1Pe 4:1-6) and producing the righteous fruitage of God's spirit in place of the wicked fruitage of the sinful flesh. (Ga 5:16-26) They can thus gain freedom from sin's mastery.—Ro 6:12-22.

Having faith in God's sure reward for righteousness (Heb 11:1, 6), one can resist the call of sin to share its temporary enjoyment. (Heb 11:24-26) Since "God is not one to be mocked," a person knows the inescapability of the rule that "whatever a man is sowing, this he will also reap," and he is protected against the deceitfulness of sin. (Ga 6:7, 8) He realizes that sins cannot remain forever hidden (1Ti 5:24) and that "although a sinner may be doing bad a hundred times and continuing a long time as he pleases," yet it will "turn out well with those fearing the true God," but not with the wicked one who is not in fear of God. (Ec 8:11-13; compare Nu 32:23; Pr 23:17, 18.) Any material riches the wicked have gained will buy them no protection from God (Zep 1:17, 18), and indeed, in time the sinner's wealth will prove to be "something treasured up for the righteous one." (Pr 13:21, 22; Ec 2:26) Those who pursue righteousness by faith can avoid carrying the "heavy load" that sin brings, the loss of peace of mind and heart, the weakness of spiritual sickness.—Ps 38:3-6, 18; 41:4.

Knowledge of God's word is the basis for such faith and the means of fortifying it. (Ps 119:11; compare Ps 106:7.) The person who moves hastily without first seeking knowledge as to his path will 'miss the mark,' sinning. (Pr 19:2, ftn) Realizing that "one sinner can destroy much good" causes the righteous person to seek to act with genuine wisdom. (Compare Ec 9:18; 10:1-4.) It is the wise course to avoid association with those practicing false worship and immorally inclined persons, for these entrap one in sin and spoil useful habits.—Ex 23:33; Ne 13:25, 26; Ps 26: 9-11; Pr 1:10-19; Ec 7:26; 1Co 15:33, 34.

There are, of course, many things that can be done or not done, or that can be done one way or another, without any condemnation of sin. (Compare 1Co 7:27, 28.) God did not hem man in with multitudinous instructions governing minute details as to how things were to be done. Clearly, man was to use his intelligence, and he was also given ample latitude to display his individual personality and preferences. The Law covenant contained many statutes; yet even this did not rob men of their freedom of personal expression. Christianity, with its strong emphasis on love of God and neighbor as the guiding rule, similarly allows men the widest possible freedom that persons with righteously inclined hearts could desire. —Compare Mt 22:37-40; Ro 8:21; see FREEDOM; JEHOVAH (A God of moral standards).

SIN, II.

A name applying to a wilderness and a city.

1. A wilderness region to which the Israelites, approximately one month after their Exodus from Egypt, transferred after leaving Elim and a campsite by the Red Sea. After this wilderness, there were several more campsites, including Dophkah, Alush, and Rephidim, before they came to Sinai. (Ex 16:1; 17:1; Nu 33:9-15) It was in the Wilderness of Sin that murmuring and complaints arose in the camp because of the lack of meat. Here Jehovah caused a flock of quail to "cover the camp," and here the Israelites ate manna for the first time. It was also at this point that the Sabbath law was put into effect.—Ex 16:2-30.

The exact location of the Wilderness of Sin is uncertain, though it is obviously along the SW border of the Sinai Peninsula. Geographers generally favor the sandy tract known as Debbet er-Ramleh, lying along the foot of the Sinai Plateau. This desert plain is also near the suggested site of Dophkah.

2. Sin was among the cities of Egypt due to feel the sword brought on that land by the hand of Babylonian King Nebuchadnezzar. (Eze 30:6, 10, 15, 16) It is called the "fortress of Egypt." Some authorities today accept the identification Pelusium found in the Latin *Vulgate*. Pelusium was an ancient fortress city situated in a key defense position against invasion from the Asiatic continent. Its location is generally accepted to coincide with present-day Tel el Farame, a site about 32 km (20 mi) SE of Port Said on the Mediterranean seacoast. Caravans or armies coming down the Philistine coast thus found this fortress guarding the entrance to Egypt. Assyrian King Ashurbanipal refers to it in his annals. Today the ancient site is surrounded by sand and marshes.

SIN [ש], SHIN [ש].

The 21st letter in the Hebrew alphabet. This letter was used to represent two sounds, and in later periods, these were distinguished by the use of a diacritical mark. A dot placed over the left-hand "horn" [ש] gave the pronunciation "s," while a dot placed over the right-hand "horn" [ש] gave the pronunciation "sh."

In the Hebrew, each of the eight verses of Psalm 119:161-168 begins with this letter.

SINAI

(Si'nai).

1. A mountain in Arabia (Ga 4:25), apparently also called Horeb. (Compare Ex 3:2, 12; 19:1, 2, 10, 11; see HOREB.) In the vicinity of Mount Sinai the Israelites and a vast mixed company, with numerous flocks and herds, encamped for nearly a year. (Ex 12:37, 38; 19:1; Nu 10:11, 12) Besides accommodating so great a camp, numbering perhaps over three million persons, the area around Mount Sinai also furnished sufficient water and pasturage for the domestic animals. At least one torrent descended from the mountain. (De 9:21) Evidently at the base of Mount Sinai there was an

area large enough for the Israelites to assemble and to observe the phenomena on the mountaintop. In fact, they could withdraw and stand at a distance. Even from the camp itself the top of Mount Sinai was visible.—Ex 19:17, 18; 20:18; 24:17; compare De 5:30.

Identification. The exact location of Mount Sinai, or Horeb, is uncertain. Tradition links it with a red granite ridge centrally situated in the southern part of the Sinai Peninsula between the two northern arms of the Red Sea. This ridge measures about 3 km (2 mi) from NW to SE and has two peaks, Ras Safsafa and Jebel Musa. The area in which this ridge lies is well watered by several streams. In front of the northern peak (Ras Safsafa) lies the Plain of er-Raha, having an approximate length of 3 km (2 mi) and extending about 1 km (0.6 mi) in width.—PICTURE, Vol. 1, p. 540.

Based on his observations at the site in the 19th century, A. P. Stanley writes: "That such a plain should exist at all in front of such a cliff is so remarkable a coincidence with the sacred narrative, as to furnish a strong internal argument, not merely of its identity with the scene, but of the scene itself having been described by an eyewitness." Commenting on the descent of Moses and Joshua from Mount Sinai, he states: "Any one coming down from one of the secluded basins behind the Ras Sa[f]safeh, through the oblique gullies which flank it on the north and south, would hear the sounds borne through the silence from the plain, but would not see the plain itself till he emerged from the Wady El-Deir or the Wady Leja; and when he did so, he would be immediately under the precipitous cliff of Sa[f]safeh." Stanley further observes that Moses' throwing the dust of the golden calf into "the torrent that was descending from the mountain" (De 9:21) would also fit this area, saying: "This would be perfectly possible in the Wady Er-Raheh, into which issues the brook of the Wady Leja, descending, it is true, from Mount St. Catherine, but still in sufficiently close connection with the Gebel Mousa [Jebel Musa] to justify the expression, 'coming down out of the mount.'"—*Sinai and Palestine,* 1885, pp. 107-109.

The traditional view is that Mount Sinai may be identified with the loftier southern peak (Jebel Musa, meaning "Mountain of Moses"). However, numerous scholars concur with Stanley's view that the northern peak, Ras Safsafa, is more likely, there being no extensive plain in front of Jebel Musa.

Events. Near Mount Sinai, or Horeb, Jehovah's angel appeared to Moses in the burning thornbush and commissioned him to lead the enslaved Israelites out of Egypt. (Ex 3:1-10; Ac 7:30) Probably about a year later the liberated nation arrived at Mount Sinai. (Ex 19:2) Here Moses ascended the mountain, evidently to receive further instruction from Jehovah, since it had already been revealed to him at the burning thornbush that 'on this mountain they would serve the true God.'—Ex 3:12; 19:3.

Moses was then directed to tell the people that their strict obedience to Jehovah's word and covenant would result in their becoming a kingdom of priests and a holy nation. (Ex 19:5, 6) The older men, as representatives of the entire nation, agreed to do this. Jehovah then instructed Moses to sanctify the people so that they might meet him on the third day thereafter. Bounds were set around the mountain, because anyone touching it, whether man or beast, was to die. —Ex 19:10-15.

On the morning of the third day, "thunders and lightnings began occurring, and a heavy cloud upon the mountain and a very loud sound of a horn." The people in the camp trembled. Moses then brought them from the camp to the base of the mountain to meet the true God. Mount Sinai rocked and smoked all over. (Ex 19:16-19; Ps 68:8) At God's invitation Moses went up the mountain and again was instructed to impress upon the people that they must not try to ascend. Even the "priests" (not the Levites, but apparently Israelite males who, like the patriarchs, served in priestly capacity for their households according to natural right and custom) could not go beyond the set bounds.—Ex 19:20-24.

After Moses descended from Mount Sinai, the Israelites heard the "Ten Words" from the midst of the fire and the cloud. (Ex 19:19–20:18; De 5:6-22) Jehovah here spoke to them through an angelic representative, as is made clear at Acts 7:38, Hebrews 2:2, and Galatians 3:19. Frightened by the awesome display of lightning and smoke, and by the sound of the horn and thunders, the people, through their representatives, requested that God no longer speak with them in this manner but that he do so through Moses. Jehovah then instructed Moses to tell them to return to their tents. The spectacle at Mount Sinai was intended to instill in the Israelites a wholesome fear of God so that they might continue observing his commandments. (Ex 20:19, 20; De 5:23-30) After this, perhaps accompanied by Aaron (compare Ex 19:24), Moses went near the dark cloud mass on Mount Sinai to hear Jehovah's further commands and judicial decisions.—Ex 20: 21; 21:1.

When Moses came down from Mount Sinai he related Jehovah's words to the people, and they again expressed their willingness to be obedient. Thereafter he wrote down the words of God and early the next morning built an altar and erected 12 pillars at the foot of the mountain. Burnt sacrifices and communion sacrifices were offered, and with the blood of the sacrificial victims the Law covenant was inaugurated.—Ex 24:3-8; Heb 9:16-22.

Having come into a covenant relationship with Jehovah, the Israelites, through their representatives, were able to draw near to Mount Sinai. Moses, Aaron, Nadab, Abihu, and 70 of the older men of Israel approached the mountain and saw a magnificent vision of God's glory. (Ex 24:9-11) Afterward Moses, accompanied by Joshua, ascended the mountain, this time to receive further commands and the stone tablets containing the "Ten Words." Not until the seventh day, however, was Moses invited to enter the cloud. It seems that Joshua continued to wait for Moses on the mountain, at a point where he could neither see nor hear anything that occurred in the Israelite camp. (Ex 24:12-18) However, whether Joshua, like Moses, did not eat or drink for the entire 40-day period is not stated. As Moses and Joshua at the end of this period descended Mount Sinai they could hear the festive singing in the Israelite camp. From the foot of Mount Sinai, Moses caught sight of the golden calf and the festivities. Immediately he threw down the two stone tablets, shattering them at the foot of the mountain.—Ex 32:15-19; Heb 12:18-21.

Later, Moses was instructed to make two stone tablets like those he had shattered and again ascend Mount Sinai, in order to have the "Ten Words" recorded thereon. (Ex 34:1-3; De 10:1-4) Moses spent another 40 days on the mountain without eating or drinking. To make this possible, he doubtless received divine assistance.—Ex 34: 28; apparently this is the same 40-day period as that mentioned at De 9:18; compare Ex 34:4, 5, 8; De 10:10.

From the time that the tabernacle, or tent of meeting, was erected and the cloud began to cover it, divine communication no longer came directly from Mount Sinai but from the tent of meeting set up in its vicinity.—Ex 40:34, 35; Le 1:1; 25:1; Nu 1:1; 9:1.

Centuries later the prophet Elijah spent 40 days at Horeb, or Sinai, "the mountain of the true God." —1Ki 19:8.

2. "Sinai" also designates the wilderness adjacent to the mountain by the same name. (Le 7:38) The exact geographic limits of the Wilderness of Sinai cannot be determined from the Bible record. It was apparently located near Rephidim. (Ex 19:2; compare Ex 17:1-6.) It was to the Wilderness of Sinai that Moses' father-in-law Jethro brought Moses' wife Zipporah and his two sons Gershom and Eliezer, for them to be reunited with Moses. (Ex 18:1-7) Among other noteworthy events occurring in the Wilderness of Sinai were: Israel's succumbing to calf worship during Moses' absence (Ex 32:1-8), the execution of 3,000 men who undoubtedly had a major part in calf worship (Ex 32:26-28), Israel's outward expression of repentance by stripping themselves of their ornaments (Ex 33:6), the construction of the tabernacle and its furnishings and the making of the priestly garments (Ex 36:8–39:43), the installation of the priesthood and the beginning of its services at the tabernacle (Le 8:4–9:24; Nu 28:6), the execution of Aaron's sons Nadab and Abihu by fire from Jehovah for offering illegitimate fire (Le 10:1-3), the first registration of Israelite males for the army (Nu 1:1-3), and the initial celebration of the Passover outside Egypt (Nu 9:1-5).

SINEW. A tendon of the body. Man is said to be woven together with bones and sinews.—Job 10:11; see also Job 40:15-18.

During Jacob's grappling with an angel, the angel touched the socket of Jacob's thigh joint, causing it to get out of place. The account written later by Moses says: "That is why the sons of Israel are not accustomed to eat the sinew of the thigh nerve, which is on the socket of the thigh joint, down to this [Moses'] day, because he touched the socket of Jacob's thigh joint by the sinew of the thigh nerve." (Ge 32:32) Many Jews still adhere to this custom, removing the sciatic nerve together with arteries and tendons before eating the animal. This precept is considered by some Jewish commentators a reminder of God's providence to Israel as exemplified in the experience of the patriarch Jacob, father of the 12 tribes.

Figurative Use. In a figurative sense the Israelites were said to have a neck as "an iron sinew," meaning that they were rigid, stubborn, stiff-necked. (Isa 48:4; compare Ex 32:9.) God's spiritual revival of his people was pictured by the bringing together of bones and the putting of flesh and sinews upon them.—Eze 37:6-8.

SINGERS, SINGING. See MUSIC.

SINGLENESS. The state of being unmarried. In the beginning, after creating the man Adam, "Jehovah God went on to say: 'It is not good for the man to continue by himself. I am going to make a helper for him, as a complement of him.'" (Ge 2:18, 21-24) Thereafter, marriage was the normal way of life among mankind, and exceptions were rare and were for special reasons. —See MARRIAGE.

One such special case was that of Jeremiah. He was under divine command to remain single and not to father children, since there were desperate circumstances coming on that nation in which children would be ruthlessly slaughtered by a cruel conqueror. (Jer 16:1-4) Jephthah's daughter was another exception. Out of respect for her father's vow, she willingly remained single in full-time service at Jehovah's house.—Jg 11:34-40.

The apostle Paul discussed the benefits of singleness, provided one is not under excessive pressure, not "inflamed with passion" and therefore in danger of committing fornication. The course of singleness is "better" in that it allows one to serve God "without distraction." (1Co 7:1, 2, 8, 9, 29-38; 9:5) Whether the four daughters of Philip the evangelizer married later in life is not stated, but at the time Luke wrote his account they were mentioned as "virgins, that prophesied."—Ac 21:8, 9.

Christ Jesus, like Jeremiah, remained unmarried. In conversation with his disciples about the question of whether singleness was to be preferred over the state of marriage, Jesus said, "Not all men make room for the saying, but only those who have the gift . . . and there are eunuchs that have made themselves eunuchs on account of the kingdom of the heavens. Let him that can make room for it make room for it."—Mt 19:10-12.

Singleness, then, is a gift having as its basic advantage the freedom afforded the possessor. Jesus here used figurative language. Men "make room for it," not by literal self-emasculation, but in their hearts, by willingly resolving to keep themselves physically in the unmarried state, whether for a lifetime or for a more limited period of time, maintaining this status by self-control.

The teaching and practice of compulsory celibacy by certain religious sects, however, finds no support in Scripture. On the contrary, it is written, "In later periods of time some will fall away from the faith, . . . forbidding to marry." (1Ti 4:1-3) Notably, many or most of the apostles were married men. (1Co 9:5) What keeps those with the gift of singleness from marrying need not be a vow of celibacy but their desire and ability to apply themselves to the service of God in the single state.

SINIM, LAND OF (Si'nim). A country from which, it was foretold, scattered Israelites would come when the time arrived for them to dwell in and rehabilitate their homeland. (Isa 49:12) Reference to the N and W in the same verse suggests that Sinim was S or E of the land of Israel. Instead of "Sinim," the Greek *Septuagint* reads "land of the Persians," which could include Elam, called Si-nim in Old Akkadian. (Compare Isa 11:11.) The Targums and the Latin *Vulgate*, on the other hand, read "[land] to the south." Certain scholars have suggested identification with Syene (Eze 30:6) in the southern extremity of Egypt. But Sinim's location is uncertain.

SINITE (Si'nite). A branch of Canaan's descendants, and one of the 70 post-Flood families. (Ge 10:15, 17; 1Ch 1:15) Several Lebanese locations of similar name are noted in various ancient writings, but the exact place where the Sinites settled remains uncertain.

SIN OFFERING. See OFFERINGS.

SION (Si'on) [Excellency]. Another, perhaps older, name for Mount Hermon. (De 4:48) Sion (not Zion), like the Amorite name Senir, may have designated a particular part of Mount Hermon. —Compare De 3:9; 1Ch 5:23; Ca 4:8; see HERMON.

SIPHMOTH (Siph'moth). A Judean city to which David sent "a gift blessing" of the spoils of his victory over the Amalekites. While a fugitive, he and his men had free access to the city. (1Sa 30:26-31) Its location is today unknown.—Compare 1Ch 27:27; see SHIPHMITE.

SIPPAI (Sip'pai). Equivalent name of Saph, a man among those born of the Rephaim. He was struck down by Sibbecai.—1Ch 20:4; 2Sa 21:18.

SIRAH, CISTERN OF (Si'rah). Abner was at the cistern of Sirah when Joab's messengers had him return to Hebron, where he was subsequently murdered. (2Sa 3:26, 27) Sirah may correspond to 'Ain Sarah, a spring or well about 2.5 km (1.5 mi) NW of Hebron. Josephus claims that Sirah, which he calls Besera, was 20 furlongs (c. 4 km; 2.5 mi) from Hebron.—*Jewish Antiquities*, VII, 34 (i, 5).

SIRION (Sir'i-on). The old Sidonian name for Mount Hermon, called Senir by the Amorites. (De 3:9) The name Sirion appears in the Ugaritic texts found at Ras Shamra on the coast of northern Syria, thus corroborating the Bible's exactness. Like Senir, Sirion perhaps also designates a particular part of Mount Hermon. (Compare 1Ch 5:23.) At Psalm 29:6 Sirion and Lebanon are mentioned together. For this reason it has been suggested that Sirion perhaps refers to the Anti-Lebanon Range.—See HERMON.

SISERA (Sis′e·ra).

1. Army chief under Canaanite King Jabin. Sisera, who lived at Harosheth rather than at Jabin's city Hazor, is more prominent in the account than King Jabin. Sometime after Judge Ehud had overthrown Moabite domination, Sisera and Jabin came to oppress Israel for 20 years. —Jg 4:1-3; 1Sa 12:9.

On hearing that Deborah and Barak had mustered the Israelites to fight against him, Sisera collected his forces, including his 900 iron-scythed chariots, and confronted Israel at the torrent valley of Kishon. But Jehovah fought against Sisera and threw his whole army into confusion, resulting in their total defeat.—Jg 4:7, 12-16, 23; 5:20, 21; Ps 83:9.

His chariots bogged down (compare Jg 5:21), and Sisera fled on foot, coming to the tent of Jael, the wife of Heber the Kenite, who was at peace with Jabin. She invited him inside. Exhausted from the battle and the flight, the weary Sisera, depending on the safety of Jael's tent, decided to rest. Jael gave Sisera some milk to drink, and he asked her to stand guard. When he had fallen into a sound sleep, she stealthily went up to him and drove a tent pin through his temples into the earth. When Barak arrived, Jael presented to him the fallen enemy. (Jg 4:9, 17-22; 5:25-27) Sisera's mother and her household waited in vain for him to return with great spoil.—Jg 5:28-30.

2. Forefather of a family of Nethinim that returned to Jerusalem with Zerubbabel in 537 B.C.E. (Ezr 2:1, 2, 43, 53; Ne 7:55) War captives were included among the Nethinim, and while some may have been taken at the time Sisera (No. 1) was defeated and may have become temple servants, there is no reason to conclude that the Nethinim who returned from Babylon were descendants of the Sisera of Barak's time.

SISMAI (Sis′mai). A descendant of Judah through Jerahmeel and Sheshan; son of Eleasah and father of Shullam. (1Ch 2:3-5, 25, 34, 40) Sismai possibly lived during the period of the Judges.

SISTER.

In the Scriptures the term is applied to full sisters and to half sisters, those having the same father but different mothers (Ge 34:1, 27; 1Ch 3:1-9), or the same mother but different fathers, as in the case of the sisters of Jesus.—Mt 13:55, 56; Mr 6:3.

Adam's sons obviously married their sisters, since all humankind sprang from Adam and Eve. (Ge 3:20; 5:4) Adam's wife Eve, as 'bone of his bones and flesh of his flesh,' was even more closely related than a sister. (Ge 2:22-24) There was no stigma attached to marriage to sisters or half sisters. The account reports that more than 2,000 years later, Abraham married Sarah his half sister. (Ge 20:2, 12) The Mosaic Law, some 430 years later, however, forbade such unions as incestuous. (Le 18:9, 11; 20:17) Doubtless, as the human race deteriorated from Adam's original perfection, it became detrimental for closely related persons to marry.

"Sister" in its broader usage included fellow countrywomen of a nation. (Nu 25:17, 18) Nations or cities that had a close relationship or that carried on similar moral practices were likened to sisters.—Jer 3:7-10; Eze 16:46, 48, 49, 55; 23: 32, 33.

The Hebrew word for sister (′a·chohth′) is translated "the other" when describing the placing of objects in relationship to corresponding pieces in the tabernacle and in Ezekiel's visions. —Ex 26:3, 5, 6, 17; Eze 1:9, 23; 3:13.

In the Christian Congregation. Jesus taught that spiritual relationships take priority over fleshly ones. Those women who did his Father's will were 'sisters' held in higher regard than mere fleshly relations. (Mt 12:50; Mr 3:34, 35) One willing to sever earthly ties, if necessary, for the sake of the Kingdom, will have a "hundredfold" of "sisters" and other 'family' relations now, plus "everlasting life" in the future. (Mt 19:29; Mr 10:29, 30; Lu 14:26) Women in the Christian congregation are called sisters, in a spiritual sense.—Ro 16:1; 1Co 7:15; 9:5; Jas 2:15.

Figurative Use. Closeness to wisdom is encouraged by the wise writer Solomon when he stresses the importance of Jehovah's commandments. "Say to wisdom: 'You are my sister'; and may you call understanding itself 'Kinswoman.'" —Pr 7:4.

SISTRUM.

The Hebrew word mena·an′im′ (sistrums) occurs but once in Scripture and seems to be derived from a root meaning "quiver," that is, move back and forth. (2Sa 6:5) Since the sistrum is characteristically played in this manner, being, as it were, a musical rattle, many lexicographers and music historians favor this rendering, one that has also been adopted by a number of Bible translators.—Da; NW; Ro; Vg.

The sistrum generally consisted of a small oval metal frame attached to a handle. The complete instrument varied from about 20 to 46 cm (8 to 18 in.) in length, according to extant ancient specimens as well as Egyptian and other monumental representations. The frame loosely held a small number of metal crossbars that, when shaken, produced sharp, ringing sounds. The horizontal bars may have been of differing lengths so as to produce a series of tones. Another type of sistrum was equipped with rings on the bars, and these rings jingled when agitated. Although its single Biblical appearance is in the description of a great celebration, traditional Jewish sources state that the sistrum was played on sad occasions as well.

SITHRI (Sith′ri) [[Jehovah] Is My Hiding Place; [Jehovah] Is My Place of Concealment]. A Levite living during the Israelite slavery in Egypt; son of Uzziel and cousin of Moses.—Ex 6:18, 20, 22.

SITNAH (Sit′nah) [Accusation]. A well that Isaac's servants dug in the vicinity of Gerar and Rehoboth. It was named Sitnah because of their dispute over it with the shepherds of Gerar. (Ge 26:19-22) It was perhaps somewhere in Wadi Ruheibe (Nahal Shunera), about 30 km (19 mi) SW of Beer-sheba. But Sitnah's exact location is not known.

SIVAN (Si′van). The postexilic name of the third Jewish lunar month of the sacred calendar, but the ninth of the secular calendar. (Es 8:9; 1Ch 27:5; 2Ch 31:7) It corresponds to part of May and part of June. The meaning of the name is uncertain.

Sivan comes at the end of the spring when the intense heat of summer is approaching. This was the time of the wheat harvest and also the early part of the dry season, which would continue until about mid-October or the lunar month Bul. (Ex 34:22; Pr 26:1) This was doubtless the month when the prophet Samuel prayed to Jehovah and an unseasonal rainstorm occurred, causing great fear among the people. (1Sa 12:16-19) By now the "early figs" that came on the trees toward the close of the winter months were fully ripe. (Isa 28:4; Jer 24:2) In the coastal area of the Mediterranean, apples were also in season.—Ca 2:3; compare Joe 1:10-12.

The Festival of Weeks, or Pentecost, was celebrated on the sixth day of Sivan, accompanied by the offering of the firstfruits of the wheat harvest, on the 50th day after the offering of the firstfruits of the barley harvest. (Ex 34:22; Le 23:15-21) It was on this sixth day of Sivan, in the year 33 C.E., that the holy spirit was poured out on the group of about 120 disciples assembled in the upper room at Jerusalem. From the crowds gathered at the city for the feast came the 3,000 persons who were baptized on that day.—Ac 1:15; 2:1-42.

It was in the month of Sivan that King Asa celebrated a grand feast following his reform activity in eradicating false religion from Judah, Jerusalem, and other areas. (2Ch 15:8-10) The swift couriers sent by King Ahasuerus to deliver the message granting the Jews the right to defend themselves on the 13th day of Adar were dispatched almost nine months earlier, on the 23rd day of Sivan, to the 127 jurisdictional districts of the Persian Empire extending from India to Ethiopia.—Es 8:9-14.

SIX. See NUMBER, NUMERAL.

SKIN. The external layer of the body of a human or an animal. The skin is classified as an organ of the body, and indeed it performs many functions for the body's well-being, including protection, regulation of body temperature, and removal of certain waste materials.

The Bible mentions skin afflictions (Le 13:1-46; 21:20; De 28:27) and certain deteriorating effects of disease and starvation upon the skin.—Job 7:5; 30:30; La 4:8; 5:10.

According to the Law, skins of animals used for certain sin offerings were burned outside the camp of Israel, or outside the gate of Jerusalem. (Ex 29:14; Le 4:11, 12; 8:17; 9:11; 16:27; Heb 13:11) The priest received the skin of an animal presented by an Israelite for a burnt offering.—Le 7:8.

Jehovah provided skin garments for Adam and Eve to cover their nakedness, after they had sinned. (Ge 3:21) Undressed skins were used for garments by some, notably some of the prophets (2Ki 1:8; Mt 3:4), including some false prophets. (Zec 13:4) Animal skins also served for sandals (Eze 16:3, 10); to make bags (1Sa 17:40) and skin bottles for water, milk, and wine (Ge 21:14; Jos 9:13; Jg 4:19; Mt 9:17); as drumheads; and possibly as a sounding base for the ne′vel or "stringed instrument." (Isa 5:12) Skins were used as coverings for the tabernacle.—Ex 25:2, 5; 26:14; 35:7, 23; 36:19.

Skin of sheep, goats, or calves was also employed as a writing material.—See PARCHMENT.

Figurative Use. Concerning Job, Satan said to Jehovah: "Skin in behalf of skin, and everything that a man has he will give in behalf of his soul." (Job 2:4) The Devil thereby challenged man's integrity, claiming that Job would curse God if his own physical well-being was impaired.

Job himself said: "I escape with the skin of my teeth." (Job 19:20) Other readings of the above scripture have been proposed by translators, but these require adjustments in the Hebrew text. It does not seem to be necessary to endeavor to explain Job's statement in the light of discoveries that scientists have made in recent times with the aid of microscopes. It seems that Job was simply saying that he had escaped with nothing or with next to nothing. He had escaped with the skin of his teeth, that is, with the "skin" of what apparently has no skin.

SKULL PLACE. See GOLGOTHA.

SKY. "Sky [Heb., sha'chaq]," as used by the Bible writers, may mean the expanse of atmosphere that surrounds the earth in which clouds float (Isa 45:8), or it may mean the apparent vault or dome over the earth that is blue in the daytime and star-studded at night. (Ps 89:37) In most cases the writer evidently is merely referring to what is high above man without specifying which aspect of the "sky" is involved.—Ps 57:10; 108:4.

The fine dust particles in the atmosphere, the molecules of water vapor, and, to some extent, the molecules of other gases in the atmosphere, such as oxygen, nitrogen, and carbon dioxide, scatter the rays of light, the blue rays being most diffused, which gives the clear sky its characteristic blue color. Fine dust particles also play a large part in producing clouds, the water vapor collecting around these particles.

The Hebrew word sha'chaq (sky) is also translated "film of dust," "cloud," "cloudy sky"; it is apparently from a root meaning "pound fine." (2Sa 22:43) Jehovah speaks of himself as the one who "beat out the skies hard like a molten mirror." (Job 37:18) The particles forming the atmosphere are indeed compressed under the pull of gravity, and their outer limits are within set boundaries, gravity preventing their escape from the earth. (Ge 1:6-8) They do reflect the sunlight in a manner comparable to a mirror. Because of this the sky looks bright, whereas without an atmosphere an observer on the earth would see only blackness in the sky, with the heavenly bodies glowing brilliantly on a black background, as is the case with the atmosphereless moon. Astronauts can observe the earth's atmosphere from outer space as an illuminated, glowing halo.

Jehovah used figurative language in warning Israel that, for disobedience, the skies overhead would become copper and the earth beneath, iron, and powder and dust would be the rain of their land. Doubtless under such conditions of lack of rain the "shut up," cloudless skies would become reddish, copper, in color, because increased dust particles in the atmosphere tend to diffuse the blue light to the point that the red waves are more prominent, just as the setting sun appears red because of the greater depth or thickness of atmosphere that the sun's rays must traverse.—De 28:23, 24; compare 1Ki 8:35, where "heaven" is used as referring to the expanse.

Another Hebrew word occasionally rendered "skies" is sha·ma'yim (heavens). (De 28:23) Similarly, the Greek ou·ra·nos', literally "heaven," is also translated "sky."

When Jesus ascended toward heaven, a cloud caught him away from the disciples' vision. As they gazed into the sky, angels appeared and said: "Men of Galilee, why do you stand looking into the sky? This Jesus who was received up from you into the sky will come thus in the same manner as you have beheld him going into the sky." (Ac 1:9-11, ftn) The angels, in effect, told the disciples that there was no point in their gazing into the sky, expecting him to appear to their vision there. For the cloud had caught him up, and he had become invisible. But he would come back in like manner, invisibly, unobserved by the physical eyes.

Occasionally, "sky" is used in parallel with "heaven."—See HEAVEN.

SLANDER. See GOSSIP, SLANDER.

SLAP. See ATTITUDES AND GESTURES.

SLAVE. The original-language words rendered "slave" or "servant" are not limited in their application to persons owned by others. The Hebrew word 'e'vedh can refer to persons owned by fellowmen. (Ge 12:16; Ex 20:17) Or the term can designate subjects of a king (2Sa 11:21; 2Ch 10:7), subjugated peoples who paid tribute (2Sa 8:2, 6), and persons in royal service, including cupbearers, bakers, seamen, military officers, advisers, and the like, whether owned by fellowmen or not (Ge 40:20; 1Sa 29:3; 1Ki 9:27; 2Ch 8:18; 9:10; 32:9). In respectful address, a Hebrew, instead of using the first person pronoun, would at times speak of himself as a servant ('e'vedh) of the one to whom he was talking. (Ge 33:5, 14; 42:10, 11, 13; 1Sa 20:7, 8) 'E'vedh was used in referring to servants, or worshipers, of Jehovah generally (1Ki 8:36; 2Ki 10:23) and, more specifically, to special representatives of God, such as Moses. (Jos 1:1, 2; 24:29; 2Ki 21:10) Though not a worshiper of Jehovah, one who performed a

service that was in harmony with the divine will could be spoken of as God's servant, an example being King Nebuchadnezzar.—Jer 27:6.

The Greek term *dou'los* corresponds to the Hebrew word *'e'vedh*. It is used with reference to persons owned by fellowmen (Mt 8:9; 10:24, 25; 13:27); devoted servants of God and of his Son Jesus Christ, whether human (Ac 2:18; 4:29; Ro 1:1; Ga 1:10) or angelic (Re 19:10, where the word *syn'dou·los* [fellow slave] appears); and, in a figurative sense, to persons in slavery to sin (Joh 8:34; Ro 6:16-20) or corruption (2Pe 2:19).

The Hebrew word *na''ar*, like the Greek term *pais*, basically means a boy or a youth and can also designate a servant or an attendant. (1Sa 1:24; 4:21; 30:17; 2Ki 5:20; Mt 2:16; 8:6; 17:18; 21:15; Ac 20:12) The Greek term *oi·ke'tes* denotes a house servant or slave (Lu 16:13), and a female slave or servant is designated by the Greek word *pai·di'ske.* (Lu 12:45) The participial form of the Hebrew root *sha·rath'* may be rendered by such terms as "minister" (Ex 33:11) or "waiter." (2Sa 13:18) The Greek word *hy·pe·re'tes* may be translated "attendant," "court attendant," or "house attendant." (Mt 26:58; Mr 14:54, 65; Joh 18:36) The Greek term *the·ra'pon* occurs solely at Hebrews 3:5 and means subordinate or attendant.

Before the Common Era. War, poverty, and crime were the basic factors that reduced persons to a state of servitude. Captives of war were often constituted slaves by their captors or were sold into slavery by them. (Compare 2Ki 5:2; Joe 3:6.) In Israelite society a person who became poor could sell himself or his children into slavery to care for his indebtedness. (Ex 21:7; Le 25:39, 47; 2Ki 4:1) One guilty of thievery but unable to make compensation was sold for the things he stole, evidently regaining his freedom at the time all claims against him were cared for.—Ex 22:3.

At times slaves held a position of great trust and honor in a household. The patriarch Abraham's aged servant (likely Eliezer) managed all of his master's possessions. (Ge 24:2; 15:2, 3) Abraham's descendant Joseph, as a slave in Egypt, came to be in charge of everything belonging to Potiphar, a court official of Pharaoh. (Ge 39:1, 5, 6) In Israel, there was a possibility of a slave's becoming wealthy and redeeming himself.—Le 25:49.

Regarding conscription of workers, see COMPULSORY SERVICE; FORCED LABOR.

Laws governing slave-master relationships. Among the Israelites the status of the Hebrew slave differed from that of a slave who was a foreigner, alien resident, or settler. Whereas the non-Hebrew remained the property of the owner and could be passed on from father to son (Le 25:44-46), the Hebrew slave was to be released in the seventh year of his servitude or in the Jubilee year, depending upon which came first. During the time of his servitude the Hebrew slave was to be treated as a hired laborer. (Ex 21:2; Le 25:10; De 15:12) A Hebrew who sold himself into slavery to an alien resident, to a member of an alien resident's family, or to a settler could be repurchased at any time, either by himself or by one having the right of repurchase. The redemption price was based on the number of years remaining until the Jubilee year or until the seventh year of servitude. (Le 25:47-52; De 15:12) When granting a Hebrew slave his freedom, the master was to give him a gift to assist him in getting a good start as a freedman. (De 15:13-15) If a slave had come in with a wife, the wife went out with him. However, if the master had given him a wife (evidently a foreign woman who would not be entitled to freedom in the seventh year of servitude), she and any children by her remained the property of the master. In such a case the Hebrew slave could choose to remain with his master. His ear would then be pierced with an awl to indicate that he would continue in servitude to time indefinite.—Ex 21:2-6; De 15:16, 17.

Female Hebrew slaves. Certain special regulations applied to a female Hebrew slave. She could be taken as a concubine by the master or designated as a wife for his son. When designated as a wife for the master's son, the Hebrewess was to be treated with the due right of daughters. Even if the son took another wife, there was to be no diminishing of her sustenance, clothing, and marriage due. A failure on the son's part in this respect entitled the woman to her freedom without the payment of a redemption price. If the master sought to have a Hebrewess redeemed, he was not permitted to accomplish this by selling her to foreigners.—Ex 21:7-11.

Protections and privileges. The Law protected slaves from brutalities. A slave was to be set at liberty if mistreatment by the master resulted in the loss of a tooth or an eye. As the usual value for a slave was 30 shekels (compare Ex 21:32), his liberation would have meant considerable loss to the master and, therefore, would have served as a strong deterrent against abuse. Although a master could beat his slave, the slave, depending upon the decision of the judges, was to be avenged if he died under his master's beating. However, if the slave lingered on for a day or two before dying—this indicating that the master had not intended to kill the slave but to discipline him —he was not to be avenged. (Ex 21:20, 21, 26, 27; Le 24:17) Also, it would appear that for the master to have been considered free of guilt the beating could not have been administered with a lethal instrument, as that would have signified intent to kill. (Compare Nu 35:16-18.) Therefore, if a slave lingered on for a day or two, there would be reasonable question as to whether the death resulted from the chastisement. A beating with a rod, for example, would not normally be fatal, as is shown by the statement at Proverbs 23:13: "Do not hold back discipline from the mere boy. In case you beat him with the rod, he will not die."

Certain privileges were granted to slaves by the terms of the Law. As all male slaves were circumcised (Ex 12:44; compare Ge 17:12), they could eat the Passover, and slaves of the priest could eat holy things. (Ex 12:43, 44; Le 22:10, 11) Slaves were exempted from working on the Sabbath. (Ex 20:10; De 5:14) During the Sabbath year they were entitled to eat of the growth from spilled kernels and from the unpruned vine. (Le 25:5, 6) They were to share in the rejoicing associated with the sacrificing at the sanctuary and the celebration of the festivals.—De 12:12; 16:11, 14.

First-Century Christian Position. In the Roman Empire slaves were very numerous, with individuals owning hundreds and even thousands of slaves. The institution of slavery had the protection of the imperial government. First-century Christians did not take a stand against governmental authority in this matter and advocate a slaves' revolt. They respected the legal right of others, including fellow Christians, to own slaves. That is why the apostle Paul sent back the runaway slave Onesimus. Because he had become a Christian, Onesimus willingly returned to his master, subjecting himself as a slave to a fellow Christian. (Phm 10-17) The apostle Paul also admonished Christian slaves not to take improper advantage of their relationship with believing masters. He said: "Let those having believing owners not look down on them, because they are brothers. On the contrary, let them the more readily be slaves, because those receiving the benefit of their good service are believers and beloved." (1Ti 6:2) For a slave to have a Christian master was a blessing, as his owner was under obligation to deal righteously and fairly with him. —Eph 6:9; Col 4:1.

The acceptance of Christianity by those in servitude placed upon them the responsibility of being better slaves, "not talking back, not committing theft, but exhibiting good fidelity." (Tit 2:9, 10) Even if their masters treated them unjustly, they were not to render inferior service. By suffering for righteousness' sake, they imitated the example of Jesus Christ. (1Pe 2:18-25) "You slaves," wrote the apostle Paul, "be obedient in everything to those who are your masters in a fleshly sense, not with acts of eye-service, as men pleasers, but with sincerity of heart, with fear of Jehovah. Whatever you are doing, work at it whole-souled as to Jehovah, and not to men." (Col 3:22, 23; Eph 6:5-8) Such fine conduct toward their masters prevented bringing reproach upon the name of God, as no one could blame Christianity for producing lazy, good-for-nothing slaves.—1Ti 6:1.

Of course, a slave's 'obedience in everything' could not include disobeying God's law, as that would have meant fearing men rather than God. Wrongdoing by slaves, even when committed at the direction of a superior, would not have 'adorned the teaching of their Savior, God,' but would have misrepresented and disgraced this teaching. (Tit 2:10) Thus, their Christian conscience would govern.

In the Christian congregation all persons, regardless of their social status, enjoyed the same standing. All were anointed by the same spirit and thus shared in the same hope as members of one body. (1Co 12:12, 13; Ga 3:28; Col 3:11) While more limited in what he could do in spreading the good news, the Christian slave was not to worry about this. If granted the opportunity to gain freedom, however, he would take advantage of it and thereby enlarge his sphere of Christian activity.—1Co 7:21-23.

Enslavement to Sin. At the time the first man Adam disobeyed God's law, he surrendered perfect control of himself and yielded to the selfish desire to continue sharing association with his sinful wife and pleasing her. Adam's surrendering himself to his sinful desire made this desire and its end product, sin, his master. (Compare Ro 6:16; Jas 1:14, 15; see SIN, I.) He thus sold himself under sin. As all of his offspring were yet in his loins, Adam also sold them under sin. That is why the apostle Paul wrote: "I am fleshly, sold under sin." (Ro 7:14) For this reason there was no way for any of Adam's descendants to make themselves righteous, not even by trying to keep the Mosaic Law. As the apostle Paul put it: "The commandment which was to life, this I found to be to death." (Ro 7:10) The inability of humans to keep the Law perfectly showed that they were slaves to sin and deserving of death, not life.—See DEATH.

Only by availing themselves of the deliverance made possible through Jesus Christ could individuals be emancipated or gain freedom from this enslavement. (Compare Joh 8:31-34; Ro 7:21-25; Ga 4:1-7; Heb 2:14-16; see RANSOM.) Having been bought with the precious blood of Jesus, Christians are slaves, or servants, of Jehovah God and of his Son, obligated to keep their commands. —1Co 7:22, 23; 1Pe 1:18, 19; Re 19:1, 2, 5; see FREEDMAN, FREEMAN; FREEDOM.

See also FAITHFUL AND DISCREET SLAVE.

SLEDGE. See FARMING IMPLEMENTS.

SLEEP. A period of rest marked by the cessation of conscious activity. It is vital for the maintenance of human life and health. Being fully aware of the importance of rest, Jesus Christ was concerned about his disciples' having time to rest up a bit. (Mr 6:31) Jesus' example shows that, even in human perfection, rest and sleep are necessary.—Compare Mr 4:38.

Hard work (Ec 5:12), a clear conscience (compare Ps 32:3-5), and freedom from undue anxiety as well as trust in Jehovah (Ps 3:5; 4:8; Pr 3:24-26) contribute much toward making an individual's sleep pleasurable and refreshing. Content with life's necessities (compare 1Ti 6:8), the servant of God does not have to spend long hours in arduous toil to the point of sacrificing necessary sleep and still derive no real benefit from his work.—Compare Ps 127:1, 2.

Of course, there are times when God's servants experience sleepless nights. If not due to sickness or other adverse or trialsome circumstances, their sleeplessness may stem from concern for fellow believers and the advancement of true worship. (2Co 6:3-5; 11:23, 27; compare Ps 132:3-5, where the reference is, not to actual sleep, but to rest, cessation from activity.) However, they do not need to worry needlessly about material possessions and lose sleep as a result. (Ec 5:12; compare Mt 6:25-34.) On the other hand, wrongdoing serves to make wicked persons content. "They do not sleep unless they do badness, and their sleep has been snatched away unless they cause someone to stumble."—Pr 4:16.

While sleep is important, a person should not become a lover of sleep. (Pr 20:13) "Laziness causes a deep sleep to fall," making an individual inactive when he should be accomplishing something. (Pr 19:15) For a person to prefer to sleep or to be inactive when he should be working is to choose a course that eventually leads to poverty. —Pr 6:9-11; 10:5; 24:33, 34.

Unlike men, Jehovah God does not become drowsy and require sleep. His servants, therefore, can rest assured that he can at all times supply needed help. (Ps 121:3, 4) Only when, for his own good reasons, he delays or refrains from taking action, as in relation to those professing to be his people but proving to be unfaithful, is Jehovah likened to one who is asleep.—Ps 44:23; 78:65.

Spiritual Wakefulness. When encouraging Christians at Rome not to be asleep or inactive and insensible to their responsibilities, the apostle Paul wrote: "It is already the hour for you to awake from sleep, for now our salvation is nearer than at the time when we became believers. The night is well along; the day has drawn near. Let us therefore put off the works belonging to darkness and let us put on the weapons of the light. As in the daytime let us walk decently, not in revelries and drunken bouts, not in illicit intercourse and loose conduct, not in strife and jealousy." (Ro 13:11-13; compare Eph 5:6-14; 1Th 5:6-8; Re 16:15.) Those who engage in wrong practices or advance false teachings are asleep as to righteousness and need to wake up if they are to gain God's approval.

Death Compared With Sleep. There is evidence that people sleep in cycles. Each cycle is made up of a deep sleep followed by a lighter sleep. During periods of deep sleep it is very difficult to awaken a person. He is completely unaware of his surroundings and the things that may be occurring about him. There is no conscious activity. Similarly, the dead are "conscious of nothing at all." (Ec 9:5, 10; Ps 146:4) Therefore death, whether that of a man or of an animal, is like sleep. (Ps 13:3; Joh 11:11-14; Ac 7:60; 1Co 7:39; 15:51; 1Th 4:13) The psalmist wrote: "From your rebuke, O God of Jacob, both the charioteer and the horse have fallen fast asleep." (Ps 76:6; compare Isa 43:17.) Were it not for God's purpose to awaken persons from the sleep of death, they would never wake up.—Compare Job 14:10-15; Jer 51:39, 57; see RESURRECTION.

However, "death" and "sleep" may also be contrasted. Concerning a dead girl, Christ Jesus said: "The little girl did not die, but she is sleeping." (Mt 9:24; Mr 5:39; Lu 8:52) As he was going to resurrect her from death, Jesus may have meant that the girl had not ceased forever to exist but would be as one awakened from her sleep. Also, this girl had not been buried, nor had her body had time to begin decaying, as had the body of Lazarus. (Joh 11:39, 43, 44) On the basis of the authority granted to him by his Father, Jesus could say this just as does his Father, "who makes the dead alive and calls the things that are not as though they were."—Ro 4:17; compare Mt 22:32.

It should be noted that the term "asleep" is applied in the Scriptures to those dying because of the death passed on from Adam. Those suffering the "second death" are not spoken of as asleep. Rather, they are shown to be completely annihilated, out of existence, burned up as by an unquenchable fire.—Re 20:14, 15; compare Heb 10:26-31, where a contrast is made between the death of those who violated the Mosaic Law and the much more severe punishment meted out to Christians who turn to a willful practice of sin; Heb 6:4-8.

SLING. See ARMS, ARMOR.

SLINGER. A person who hurls missiles from a sling. The sling was usually a relatively short strap that was doubled over and whirled around. From it a missile, such as a stone, was propelled at high speed by releasing one end of the strap.

In early times, slingers of stones formed an important part of a military force. The tribe of Benjamin had 700 picked men, every one of whom was "a slinger of stones to a hairbreadth and would not miss." (Jg 20:15, 16) The Targums say that the Cherethites and the Pelethites among David's warriors were adept slingers. Slingmen were an important part of King Uzziah's military force. (2Ch 26:13, 14) Sennacherib employed a corps of slingers in the Assyrian army, as monuments attest. The fighting forces of the Egyptians, Syrians, Persians, Sicilians, and others also had similar divisions. In the Roman army, slingers were among the *auxilia*. As late as the first century C.E., Josephus relates that Jewish slingers pitted their skill against Roman forces.—*Jewish Antiquities*, XVII, 259 (x, 2); *The Jewish War*, II, 422, 423 (xvii, 5); IV, 14, 15 (i, 3).

In ancient armies the slingers usually made up only one division of the foot soldiers. Archers, as a complement of the slingers, and a smaller number of spearmen completed the infantry. When called forward to begin an engagement or to stall an enemy advance, the slingers passed from the rear of the ranks through corridors among the soldiers. At other times they fired from behind, over the heads of the spearmen. Slingers were especially effective fighters when attacking walled cities. Their missiles, hurled from the ground, could pick the enemy off the walls or reach targets inside the city. (2Ki 3:25) When siege engines and assault towers were developed, slingers took advantage of the elevated positions their platforms afforded.

An advantage of the slinger over the armor-clad swordsman or spearman was his effectiveness from a distance. It is claimed that their range of effectiveness was up to 122 m (400 ft) with stones, and even farther with lead pellets.

David's Use of the Sling. Much time and training was required to become a skilled and experienced slinger. Young shepherd boys attending and protecting flocks against beasts of prey developed the needed skill. The shepherd-boy David felt much better equipped with his sling than with the heavy armor of Saul. But he doubtless would have been unable to stand before Goliath without faith in Jehovah and strength from Him. The outcome of the fight depended, not on superiority of weapons or upon skill, but upon Jehovah, who supported David. As David called out to Goliath: "I am coming to you with the name of Jehovah of armies, . . . whom you have taunted. . . . And all this congregation will know that neither with sword nor with spear does Jehovah save, because to Jehovah belongs the battle." It was a stone from David's sling, no doubt guided and given unusual force by Jehovah, that sank into Goliath's forehead, striking him down so that David could "definitely put him to death" by Goliath's own sword.—1Sa 17:38-51.

SMOKE. The visible soot-producing mixture of carbon particles and gases from burning organic materials; also vapor or a cloud resembling smoke. Aside from the mention of literal smoke (Heb., 'a·shan'; Gr., ka·pnos') in numerous instances, there are a number of figurative uses of the word, and there is figurative meaning to the appearance of smoke itself.

Jehovah's Presence, and His Anger. Jehovah has manifested his presence by a cloud of "smoke," sometimes accompanied by fire. (Ex 19: 18; 20:18; Isa 4:5) He symbolized his presence in this way at the visionary temples seen by Isaiah the prophet and by John the apostle.—Isa 6:1-6; Re 15:8; see CLOUD.

Smoke is also associated with Jehovah's burning anger. (De 29:20) On the other hand, those in Israel who had fallen away to the worship of false gods were said to be "a smoke" in God's nostrils, signifying that they provoked his great anger. —Isa 65:5.

A Warning or Portent. Smoke signals were used in warfare to communicate messages between cities or divisions of an army. (Jg 20:38-40) It was also an evidence that something was being destroyed by fire, as, for example, smoke rising from a distant city. (Ge 19:28; Jos 8:20, 21) Or it could metaphorically refer to an army on its way to accomplish destruction, which often included the burning of conquered cities. —Isa 14:31.

Consequently, a rising column or cloud of smoke came to be used symbolically as a token of woe to come or of destruction. (Re 9:2-4; compare Joe 2:30, 31; Ac 2:19, 20; Re 9:17, 18.) The psalmist says of the wicked: "In smoke they must come to their end." (Ps 37:20) Smoke also symbolized the *evidence* of destruction. (Re 18:9, 18) Smoke that keeps ascending "to time indefinite" therefore is evidently an expression denoting complete and everlasting annihilation, as in Isaiah's prophecy against Edom: "to time indefinite its smoke will keep ascending." (Isa 34:5, 10) Edom as a nation was wiped out and remains desolate to this day, and the evidence of this fact stands in the Bible account and in the records of secular history. Similarly, the everlasting destruction of Babylon the Great is foretold at Revelation 18:8, and a like judgment is entered against those who worship "the wild beast" and its image, at Revelation 14:9-11.

Other Illustrative Uses. Just as smoke normally dissipates quickly and disappears, so it sometimes figuratively denotes that which is transitory. It is used with regard to: God's enemies (Ps 68:2), idol worshipers (Ho 13:3), and the shortened life of the afflicted one (Ps 102:3).

"As vinegar to the teeth and as smoke to the eyes, so the lazy man is to those sending him forth," says the proverb. Just as smoke causes the eyes to sting and smart, so the one who employs a lazy man does so to the injury of his own purposes.—Pr 10:26.

The psalmist, waiting for Jehovah to comfort him, says: "I have become like a skin bottle in the smoke." (Ps 119:83) Skin bottles, such as those used in the Middle East, hanging on the wall when not in use, became dried up and shriveled from the smoke of the house. So the psalmist had become at the hands of those persecuting him.

Jehovah, in describing his creations to Job, calls attention to Leviathan, saying: "Out of [its] nostrils smoke goes forth, like a furnace set aflame even with rushes." (Job 41:20) Many Bible scholars believe that God here had reference to the crocodile, which, when coming up out of the water, breathes out a thick, steamy vapor with a thundering sound.

Sacrificial Smoke. Another Hebrew word, *qa·tar'*, has reference to making sacrificial smoke, whether that of incense or of another sacrifice on the altar. (1Ch 6:49; Jer 44:15) Such sacrificial smoke was viewed as a pleasing odor ascending to the One to whom it was offered.—Ge 8:20, 21; Le 26:31; Eph 5:2.

SMYRNA (Smyr'na) [Myrrh]. An ancient city on the W coast of Asia Minor; now called Izmir. (PICTURE, Vol. 2, p. 946) Early settled by the Greeks, it was destroyed about 580 B.C.E. by Lydian King Alyattes. More than two centuries later, Alexander the Great planned to rebuild it as a Greek city, this being done by his successors on another site. Smyrna thereafter became an important commercial city. When it became part of the Roman province of Asia, Smyrna, with its fine public buildings, was noted for its beauty. It had a temple of Tiberius Caesar and therefore promoted emperor worship.

Smyrna was the second of the seven Christian congregations in Asia Minor to which the glorified Jesus Christ directed the apostle John to write a message. (Re 1:11) The congregation was said to be poor materially but rich spiritually. It was tested by tribulation, evidently persecution, and was blasphemed by some who called themselves Jews, but who were actually "a synagogue of Satan." However, despite their poverty and tribulation, Christians of the congregation in Smyrna were encouraged not to fear the things they would yet suffer but to be "faithful even to death" in order to receive "the crown of life."—Re 2:8-11.

SNAIL [Heb., *shab·belul'*]. Any of a variety of slow-moving mollusks, generally distinguished by their spiral or conical shells into which they can withdraw for protection. Numerous varieties of snails have been encountered in Palestine, but on account of the dry climate, there are few slugs, that is, snails having no visible shell. Both slugs and snails secrete a slimy substance that protects them from abrasive injury as they crawl along. Many believe that the snail's slimy trail is alluded to by the phrase "a snail melting away." (Ps 58:8) Another suggestion is that the reference is to the drying up of the snail in its shell when exposed for some time to the sun.

SNAKE. See ARROW SNAKE; FIERY SNAKE; SERPENT, SNAKE.

SNARE. See TRAP.

SNOW. White crystals of frozen water that form from water vapor in the atmosphere. Each descending snow crystal washes out the atmosphere and carries with it compounds of elements such as sulfur and nitrogen, thus contributing to soil fertility while supplying moisture. (Isa 55:10, 11) Snow can be a source of clean water for washing. (Job 9:30) Though either rare or unknown in certain areas of Palestine, it sometimes falls during January and February in hill country, as at Jerusalem. (Compare 2Sa 23:20; 1Ch 11:22.) During most of the year there is snow in the heights and ravines of the Lebanon Range; lofty Mount Hermon is snowcapped nearly all year long. (Jer 18:14) Psalm 68:14 refers to snow in Zalmon, which is part of Mount Hauran (Jebel ed Druz), located E of the Jordan.

Jehovah, the Producer of snow, can also control it. (Job 37:6; Ps 147:16) To serve His purpose, God has stored snow and hail "for the day of fight and war."—Job 38:22, 23.

Illustrative Use. Snow is used in Scriptural similes to help convey the idea of whiteness. (Ex 4:6; Nu 12:10; 2Ki 5:27; Da 7:9; Mt 28:3; Re 1:14) Sometimes it is associated with purity. (Isa 1:18; La 4:7) For example, David begged God to purify him from sin, washing him so that he might become "whiter even than snow."—Ps 51:7.

Job's three companions, being no source of true comfort to him, were likened to a winter torrent, swollen by melting ice and snow in the mountains but running dry in the heat of summer. (Job 6:15-17) Sheol is said to snatch away sinners as drought and heat do snow waters. (Job 24:19) Just as snow is unnatural and would harm crops in summer, so "glory is not fitting for a stupid one." (Pr 26:1) However, a faithful envoy, one who would fulfill his commission to the satisfaction of those sending him, is likened to a drink that is cooled with snow from the mountains and that brings refreshment on a hot day of harvest. —Pr 25:13.

SNUFFERS.
Golden implements used in connection with the lamps on the branches of the lampstand(s) in Israel's tabernacle and temple. (Ex 25:37, 38; 37:23; Nu 4:9; 1Ki 7:48, 49; 2Ch 4:19-21) The snuffers are designated by the dual Hebrew word mel·qa·cha'yim, derived from a root meaning "take." Use of the dual form suggests a device possibly having two parts. Accordingly, at Isaiah 6:6 mel·qa·cha'yim denotes the "tongs" with which a seraph removed a glowing coal from the altar.

A distinction is drawn between the lampstand "snuffers" and "the extinguishers" in use at the temple. (1Ki 7:49, 50; 2Ch 4:21, 22) Though not described in Scripture, the snuffers may have been tongs used to hold the burnt lampwicks, while the extinguishers may have been scissorlike utensils employed to cut off the burnt part of the wicks. At the tabernacle, these trimmings, held by means of the snuffers, were deposited in fire holders, apparently containers for holding such pieces until their disposal.—Ex 37:23.

SO.
An Egyptian king contemporary with Hoshea, the last king of the ten-tribe kingdom of Israel. When Hoshea conspired with So against Shalmaneser V and stopped paying tribute to Assyria, Hoshea was imprisoned. (2Ki 17:3, 4) Attempts to identify So with secularly known Egyptian rulers of this general period (such as Osorkon IV or Shabaka) are very uncertain, particularly in view of the uncertainty of Egyptian chronology.—See CHRONOLOGY.

SOBERNESS.
The Greek words ne'pho (verb) and ne·pha'li·os (adjective) basically refer to being free from the influence of intoxicants. However, they are used in the Scriptures mainly in a figurative sense. They carry the idea of being sober, moderate in habits, vigilant, watchful, or keeping the senses. A related word, e·kne'pho, meaning, primarily, "sober up," is used in the Greek Septuagint at Genesis 9:24: "Noah recovered [awoke] from the wine." Also, the Greek term is used in the same version at Joel 1:5, where the prophet calls to the spiritual "drunkards" of Israel to 'wake up,' and at Habakkuk 2:19, where woe is foretold to the worshipers of idols who say to pieces of wood and stone, "Awake!"

In enumerating the qualifications for those who would be appointed as overseers in the Christian congregations, the apostle Paul states that the overseer should be "moderate in habits" (Gr., ne·pha'li·os). This would include freedom from overindulgence in wine, as it is also stated that he is not to be "a drunken brawler." The word ne·pha'li·os would show that the man would have good sense and exercise moderation in other things, such as speech and conduct, besides being habitually temperate in the use of liquor.—1Ti 3:2, 3.

Women in the congregation are given like counsel, to be "serious, not slanderous, moderate in habits, faithful in all things." (1Ti 3:11) The aged men and women are similarly counseled, the older women setting an example "that they may recall the young women to their senses," to be good wives and mothers, in subjection to their husbands.—Tit 2:2-5.

In correcting the congregation at Corinth, which had been influenced by certain men who were advocating wrong doctrine, Paul said: "Bad associations spoil useful habits. Wake up to soberness [form of e·kne'pho] in a righteous way and do not practice sin, for some are without knowledge of God. I am speaking to move you to shame." (1Co 15:33, 34) They should wake up from the stupor of wrong doctrine, which was misleading some and causing spiritual sickness and even death. (1Co 11:30) In a similar vein he had written previously to the Thessalonians, who had been troubled by persons advocating things not taught by the apostles. He said, concerning "Jehovah's day," that that day would come suddenly but it would not overtake true, faithful Christians as it would thieves. Consequently, they should not be sleepy but be sure they were alert; they should "stay awake and *keep* [*their*] *senses* [literally, be sober]."—1Th 5:2-6, 8.

Paul also warned Timothy of the apostasy to come, with its danger to the integrity of those Christians who wished to remain true. Timothy, especially, as an overseer, had to be on guard to *"keep* [*his*] *senses* [be sober-minded] in all things," to "suffer evil, do the work of an evangelizer, fully accomplish [his] ministry." (2Ti 4:3-5) In keeping his senses, Timothy was to realize that Paul would not be on the scene much longer (2Ti 4:6-8), and Timothy himself would eventually pass off the scene, so he must commit the things learned to faithful men, who, in turn, would be adequately qualified to teach others. (2Ti 2:2) Thus the congregation would be built up as a bulwark against the apostasy to come, being "a pillar and support of the truth."—1Ti 3:15.

The apostle Peter likewise, knowing that he and his fellow apostles would not be on hand much longer (2Pe 1:14), able to act as a restraint to the apostate movement instigated by the Devil, counseled Christians to hold fast to their salvation through Christ, *'keeping their senses* completely [literally, being sober perfectly], setting their hope upon the undeserved kindness that was to be brought to them at the revelation of Jesus Christ.' (1Pe 1:13) Knowing the seriousness of the times, with growing persecution from the world, they should be sound in mind, watchful, vigilant, and should not neglect serious prayer, to obtain the strength they would need for endurance. (1Pe 4:7) He warned them to keep their senses, because the Devil was like a roaring lion seeking to devour, and they had to take a solid stand against the Devil. This required soberness, seriousness, self-control.—1Pe 5:8, 9.

SOCO(H) (So′co[h]) [possibly, Branch [of a Tree]].

1. A Judean city in the Shephelah, seemingly referred to as both Soco and Socoh. (Jos 15:20, 33, 35) The Philistines collected their army together at Socoh and then camped at nearby Ephes-dammim before Goliath's encounter with David. (1Sa 17:1) Years later this Soco was apparently among the cities that Rehoboam strengthened. (2Ch 11:5-7; however, this passage may apply to No. 2.) Nevertheless, Soco, along with its dependent towns, was captured by the Philistines more than 200 years later, during King Ahaz' rule. (2Ch 28:16-18) It is identified with the ruins at Khirbet ′Abbad (Horvat Sokho), in the Low Plain of Elah about 4 km (2.5 mi) ESE of Azekah, although Khirbet Shuweikeh, a short distance to the E, seems to preserve the Biblical name.

2. Socoh, a city in the mountainous region of Judah. (Jos 15:20, 48) It is often identified with a Khirbet Shuweikeh, about 17 km (11 mi) SW of Hebron. This is a different Khirbet Shuweikeh from the one mentioned in No. 1.

3. Socoh, a place under the administration of one of Solomon's deputies. (1Ki 4:7, 10) The suggested identification of it with Khirbet Shuweiket er-Ras, about 15 km (9.5 mi) WNW of Samaria, seems to fit the account, since the proposed sites of both Arubboth and Hepher (mentioned with Socoh in the Kings account) are nearby.

4. In the genealogy of Judah, Heber is called "the father of Soco." (1Ch 4:18) Soco could be a personal name of Heber's descendant, or the text could indicate that Heber was the founder of the city of Soco or its population. Assuming that this latter situation was the case, it is not possible to determine whether the reference is to Soco(h) No. 1 or No. 2.

SODI (So′di) [from a root meaning "intimate group"]. A Zebulunite whose son Gaddiel represented his tribe in spying out the Promised Land. —Nu 13:2, 10.

SODOM (Sod′om). A city situated along the SE boundary of Canaan. (Ge 10:19; 13:12) Often mentioned along with Gomorrah, Sodom seems to have been the most prominent of five cities, all of which were apparently located at the Low Plain of Siddim. (Ge 14:2, 3) Many scholars believe that the original sites of Sodom and the other "cities of the District" now lie submerged beneath the waters of the Dead Sea, though some others recently have claimed that the ruins of the cities may be identified with sites along wadis to the E and SE of the Dead Sea.—Ge 13:12; see SALT SEA.

When Abraham and Lot decided to move farther apart, to avoid disputes among their herdsmen, Lot went eastward into the well-watered District of the Jordan and pitched his tent near Sodom. There he found that "the men of Sodom were bad and were gross sinners against Jehovah," much to Lot's distress. (Ge 13:5-13; 2Pe 2:7, 8) Sometime later, after a 12-year subjection to Chedorlaomer, king of Elam, the inhabitants of Sodom and the other four cities rebelled. In the following year, Chedorlaomer and his allies defeated Bera, the king of Sodom, and his confederates. Besides seizing possessions and foodstuffs, the victors took Lot and others captive.—Ge 14:1-12.

Abraham's forces overtook Chedorlaomer and recovered the captives and booty, including Lot and his household. The king of Sodom insisted that Abraham keep the recovered material goods, but Abraham refused, lest Bera should say, "It was I who made Abram rich."—Ge 14:13-24.

Everlasting Destruction. Sodom, however, persisted in a course in defiance of Jehovah, becoming known for such immoral practices as homosexuality. "The cry of complaint about Sodom and Gomorrah," Jehovah declared, "yes, it is loud, and their sin, yes, it is very heavy." God therefore sent his angels to destroy Sodom, with the assurance to Abraham that if ten righteous persons could be found in the place, the whole city would be spared.—Ge 18:16, 20-33.

The city showed it deserved destruction, for a vile mob of residents of Sodom, including boys and old men, surrounded Lot's house, attempting to rape his angelic guests. The next day, after Lot, along with his wife and two daughters, left the city, Sodom and Gomorrah were destroyed by sulfur and fire. (Ge 19:1-29; Lu 17:28, 29) Thereafter Sodom and Gomorrah became a proverbial figure of utter destruction from God Almighty (De 29:23; Isa 1:9; 13:19; Jer 49:18; 50:40; La 4:6; Am 4:11; Zep 2:9; Ro 9:29) and of extreme wickedness.—De 32:32; Isa 1:10; 3:9; Jer 23:14; Eze 16:46-56; see GOMORRAH.

Jude mentions that "Sodom and Gomorrah . . . are placed before us as a warning example by undergoing the judicial punishment of everlasting fire." This would not conflict with Jesus' statement about a Jewish city that would reject the good news: "It will be more endurable for the land of Sodom and Gomorrah on Judgment Day than for that city." Sodom and Gomorrah were everlastingly destroyed as *cities,* but this would not preclude a resurrection for *people* of those cities. —Jude 7; Mt 10:15; compare Lu 11:32; 2Pe 2:6.

"In a Spiritual Sense." Revelation 11:3, 8 says that the corpses of God's "two witnesses" lay in the broad way of the great city 'called in a spiritual sense Sodom and Egypt.' Isaiah's prophecy (1:8-10) likens Zion or Jerusalem to Sodom and calls her rulers "dictators of Sodom." However, about 96 C.E. when John was given the Revelation vision of events to occur in the future, the typical city of Jerusalem had been destroyed long before, in 70 C.E. The reference therefore must be to a "great city" or organization, an antitypical Jerusalem, pictured by unfaithful Jerusalem of old.

SOLDIER. A person who serves in an army. In the Hebrew Scriptures military personnel are often precisely designated according to the specific function they served: cavalrymen (Ex 14:9), runners (1Sa 22:17), slingers (2Ki 3:25), men handling the lance and shield (2Ch 25:5), shooters (2Ch 35:23), archers (Job 16:13), or bowmen (Isa 21:17). The Greek word for "soldier" is *stra·ti·o'tes.* —See ARMY.

During the time of Roman domination of Judea, soldiers were a common sight there. The fact that an army officer at Capernaum could say: "For I . . . [have] soldiers under me," indicates that soldiers were stationed there under his command. (Mt 8:5-9) Roman troops were stationed in the Tower of Antonia in Jerusalem, serving as a point of control over the Jews. The military commander there when Paul made his last visit to Jerusalem rescued him from a mob, and again the next day from the rioting Pharisees and Sadducees. (Ac 21:30-35; 22:23, 24; 23:10) When a plot against Paul's life was revealed, the commander supplied an escort of 70 horsemen, 200 soldiers, and 200 spearmen to take Paul as far as Antipatris, the horsemen going on with him from there to Caesarea.—Ac 23:12-33.

Jewish Soldiers. There were also Jewish soldiers, among them being those who approached John the Baptizer with the question, "What shall we do?" These were possibly engaged in a type of police inspection, especially in connection with the customs or collection of the tax.—Lu 3:12-14.

Jesus' Execution and Burial. Roman soldiers were used in the execution of Jesus, inasmuch as he was turned over to the Roman governor, charged with sedition against Rome. These soldiers submitted him to great indignities, mocking him, spitting upon him, and striking him before leading him off for impaling. (Mt 27:27-36; Joh 18:3, 12; 19:32-34) They divided his outer garments among themselves and cast lots for his inner garment. Four soldiers were evidently employed in the detachment that impaled Jesus. (Joh 19:23, 24) The army officer having oversight of the execution, observing the phenomena that occurred and the circumstances under which Jesus died, said: "Certainly this man was God's Son." (Mr 15:33-39) Roman soldiers were also placed as guards at Jesus' tomb. (Mt 27:62-66) If these guards had been Jewish temple police, the Jews would not have had to ask Pilate about the matter. Likewise, the chief priests promised to set matters right with the governor if he heard of the disappearance of Jesus' body.—Mt 28:14.

The First Gentile Christian. About three and a half years later, it was a Roman soldier, a centurion, who sent two of his house servants and "a devout soldier" to invite Peter to Caesarea. At Peter's preaching, Cornelius and his household, doubtless including the "devout soldier" in his service, received the outpouring of holy spirit and became the first members of the Christian congregation taken from among the Gentiles.—Ac 10:1, 7, 44-48.

Peter's Deliverance. The apostle Peter was later arrested by order of Herod Agrippa I and was imprisoned under four shifts of four soldiers each. On each shift two soldier guards watched the prison door while two personally guarded Peter, who was chained to them, one on each side. An angel appeared in the night, releasing Peter from his chains and freeing him from the prison. This created a stir among the soldiers, and Herod, after examining those guards who were responsible, had them "led off to punishment," probably to be put to death according to the Roman custom. —Ac 12:4-10, 18, 19.

Kindness Shown to Paul. When the apostle Paul was taken by ship to Rome because of his appeal to Caesar, he was placed in the custody of a detachment of soldiers under the command of an army officer named Julius of the band of Augustus. This man treated Paul with kindness and permitted him to go to his friends and enjoy their care. At first he evidently did not accept Paul as having God's guidance, and therefore he gave more heed to the ship's owner and to the pilot. But after a great tempest drove the ship along and tossed it violently for days, when Paul related a vision he had in which the lives of all on the ship were guaranteed, the officer and his men listened to Paul. When the boat began to break up near Malta the soldiers prepared to kill all the prisoners, but the officer Julius, desiring to bring Paul safely through, restrained them. (Ac 27:1, 3, 9-11, 20-26, 30, 31, 39-44) In Rome, Paul was permitted to live in his own hired house with a soldier guarding him.—Ac 28:16, 30.

Symbolic Use. In defending his apostleship in his letter to the congregation at Corinth, Paul wrote: "Who is it that ever serves as a soldier at his own expense?" (1Co 9:7) Although Paul had not accepted material help from the Corinthians, he here argued that, as a soldier in the service of his Master Christ, he certainly had authority to do so. Paul also considered as soldiers of Christ those who worked in cooperation with him in the

preaching of the good news, calling them 'fellow soldiers.'—Php 2:25; Phm 2.

To Timothy, who was charged with a heavy responsibility by Paul, the apostle wrote: "As a fine soldier of Christ Jesus take your part in suffering evil. No man serving as a soldier involves himself in the commercial businesses of life, in order that he may gain the approval of the one who enrolled him as a soldier." (2Ti 2:3, 4) A good soldier expects hardships, and he knows the need to be ready to serve at all times and to endure under the most trying conditions. As long as he is in a war he does not look for comfort and that which pleases him. His time and energy are at the command of his superior. Moreover, a soldier gives up business, farm, trade, or vocation in order to serve. He does not get involved in other things that would take his mind and energy away from the all-important fight in which he is engaged. Otherwise, it would likely cost him his life or it would cost the lives of those depending on him. According to historians, Roman soldiers were not allowed to engage in any trade and were forbidden to act as tutors or as curators to an estate so that they would not be diverted from their purpose as soldiers. Even under the Mosaic Law, the newly married man, or the man with a house he had not dedicated or a vineyard from which he had not received fruit, was exempt from military service. And a man who was fearful would certainly make a bad soldier and would break down the morale of his fellow soldiers; therefore such a man was exempt under the Law. (De 20:5-8) So Christians, both Jewish and Gentile, would readily get the force of Paul's illustration.

In a letter to the Ephesians, Paul outlined clearly that the fight of the Christian soldier is not against blood and flesh but is against "the wicked spirit forces in the heavenly places." Therefore the armor necessary for this fight could not be obtained from worldly sources, but it had to be the armor from Jehovah God, who brings victory under his army Commander, Jesus Christ.—Eph 6:11-17.

SOLOMON (Sol'o·mon) [from a root meaning "peace"]. Son of King David of the line of Judah; king of Israel from 1037 to 998 B.C.E. The Bible record, after reporting the death of the son born to David through his illicit relations with Bath-sheba, continues: "And David began to comfort Bath-sheba his wife. Further, he came in to her and lay down with her. In time she bore a son, and his name came to be called Solomon. And Jehovah himself did love him. So he sent by means of Nathan the prophet and called his name Jedidiah, for the sake of Jehovah." (2Sa 12:24, 25) Solomon later had three full brothers, sons of David and Bath-sheba: Shimea, Shobab, and Nathan.—1Ch 3:5.

Jehovah's Promise to David. Jehovah had declared to David, before Solomon's birth, that a son would be born to him and that his name would be Solomon, and that this one would build a house to His name. The name Jedidiah (meaning "Beloved of Jah") seems to have been given as an indication to David that Jehovah had now blessed his marriage to Bath-sheba and that the fruitage thereby produced was approved by him. But this was not the name by which the child was commonly known. Undoubtedly the name Solomon (from a root meaning "peace") applied in connection with the covenant that Jehovah made with David, in which he said that David, being a man who had shed much blood in warfare, would not build the house for Jehovah, as David had it in his heart to do. (1Ch 22:6-10) Not that David's warfare was wrong. But Jehovah's typical kingdom was essentially of a peaceful nature and objective; its wars were to clean out wickedness and those opposing Jehovah's sovereignty, to extend Israel's dominion to the boundaries that God had outlined, and to establish righteousness and peace. These objectives the wars of David accomplished for Israel. Solomon's rule was essentially a reign of peace.

Adonijah's Attempt to Take the Throne. After his birth Solomon next appears in the Scriptural record in the time of David's old age. David, doubtless on account of Jehovah's promise, had previously sworn to Bath-sheba that Solomon would succeed him on the throne. This was known to the prophet Nathan. (1Ki 1:11-13, 17) Whether Solomon's half brother Adonijah knew of this oath or intent of David is not stated. In any case, Adonijah made an attempt to gain the throne in a manner similar to that employed by Absalom. Perhaps because of the king's feebleness and because Adonijah had the support of Joab the army chief and of Abiathar the priest, he had confidence that he would be successful. It was nonetheless a treasonable action, an effort to seize the throne while David was still alive and without the approval of David or of Jehovah. Also, Adonijah revealed his underhandedness when he arranged for a sacrifice at En-rogel, where he intended to be acclaimed as king, but invited only the king's other sons and men of Judah, the king's servants, leaving out Solomon, Nathan the prophet, Zadok the priest, and the mighty men who had fought closely with David, including Benaiah

their leader. This indicates that Adonijah counted Solomon as a rival and an obstacle to his ambitions.—1Ki 1:5-10.

Solomon Enthroned. The prophet Nathan, ever faithful to Jehovah and to David, was on the alert. First sending Bath-sheba with instructions to inform the king of the plot, he then came in himself, asking David if this proclaiming of Adonijah as king had been authorized by him. David acted quickly and decisively, calling for Zadok the priest and Nathan to take Solomon to Gihon under the protection of Benaiah and his men. They were to put Solomon on the king's own she-mule (denoting a high honor to the one riding, in this case, that he was successor to the kingship). (Compare Es 6:8, 9.) David's instructions were followed out, and Solomon was anointed and acclaimed as king. —1Ki 1:11-40.

On hearing the sound of the music at Gihon, not so very far away, and the shouting of the people: "Let King Solomon live," Adonijah and his fellow conspirators fled in fear and confusion. Solomon gave a foregleam of the peace that would mark his rulership by refusing to mar his ascension to the throne by taking revenge. Had matters been reversed, Solomon would very likely have lost his life. Adonijah fled to the sanctuary for asylum, so Solomon sent word there and had Adonijah brought before him. Informing Adonijah that he would continue to live unless bad should be found in him, Solomon then dismissed him to his house. —1Ki 1:41-53.

David's Charge to Solomon. David, before dying, gave Solomon the solemn charge to "keep the obligation to Jehovah your God by walking in his ways, by keeping his statutes, his commandments and his judicial decisions and his testimonies." He further instructed him not to let Joab and Shimei 'go down into Sheol in peace'; also to show loving-kindness toward the sons of Barzillai the Gileadite. (1Ki 2:1-9) Probably it was prior to this that David had given instructions to Solomon regarding the building of the temple, passing on to him the architectural plan "that had come to be with him by inspiration." (1Ch 28:11, 12, 19) David gave command to the princes of Israel there present to help Solomon his son and to join in building the sanctuary of Jehovah. On this occasion the people anointed Solomon again as king and Zadok as priest. (1Ch 22:6-19; chap 28; 29:1-22) God's blessing on Solomon is shown early in his reign, as he began to sit upon "Jehovah's throne as king in place of David his father and to make a success" of the kingship and to develop strength in it.—1Ch 29:23; 2Ch 1:1.

SOLOMON

Adonijah's Seditious Request. It was not long until Solomon had to act to carry out David's instructions concerning Joab. This was prompted by the action of Adonijah, who still manifested ambition despite the mercy that Solomon had shown him. Adonijah approached Solomon's mother with the words: "You yourself well know that the kingship was to have become mine, and it was toward me that all Israel had set their face for me to become king; but the kingship turned and came to be my brother's, for it was from Jehovah that it became his." Here Adonijah acknowledged that Jehovah was behind the enthroning of Solomon, yet his request that followed these words was a further crafty bid for usurpation of the kingship. He said to Bath-sheba: "Please, say to Solomon the king . . . that he should give me Abishag the Shunammite as a wife." Adonijah may have felt that he had a strong enough following, together with the support of Joab and Abiathar, that, by taking David's nurse, considered to have been David's concubine, though David had had no relations with her, he could start an uprising that might overthrow Solomon. By custom the wives and concubines of a king could only become those of his legal successor, so the taking of such wives was considered a claim to the throne. (Compare 2Sa 16:21, 22.) When Bath-sheba, not discerning Adonijah's duplicity, transmitted his request to Solomon, Solomon interpreted it immediately as a bid for the kingship and forthwith sent Benaiah to put Adonijah to death.—1Ki 2:13-25.

Abiathar deposed; Joab put to death. Then Solomon gave attention to those who had conspired with Adonijah. Abiathar was dismissed from the priesthood in fulfillment of Jehovah's word spoken against the house of Eli (1Sa 2:30-36), but he was not killed, because he had carried the Ark before David and had suffered affliction with him. Zadok replaced Abiathar. In the meantime, Joab, having heard of Solomon's action, fled to grab hold of the horns of the altar, but there he was slain by Benaiah at Solomon's order.—1Ki 2:26-35.

Shimei executed. Solomon also placed Shimei on oath to observe certain restrictions, for this man had called down evil on his father David. When Shimei, about three years later, violated this restriction, Solomon had him put to death. Thus David's injunction to Solomon was fully carried out.—1Ki 2:36-46.

Solomon's Wise Request. In the early part of Solomon's reign the people were sacrificing on many "high places," because there was no house of Jehovah, though the tabernacle was at Gibeon and the ark of the covenant was in a tent on Zion. Although Jehovah had said that his name was to be placed upon Jerusalem, he evidently tolerated this practice until the temple should be built. (1Ki 3:2, 3) At Gibeon, known as "the great high place," Solomon offered a thousand burnt sacrifices. Here Jehovah appeared to him in a dream, saying: "Request what I should give you." Instead of asking for riches, glory, and victory, Solomon requested a wise, understanding, and obedient heart in order to be able to judge Israel. Solomon's humble request so pleased Jehovah that he gave him not only what he had asked for but also riches and glory "so that there will not have happened to be any among the kings like you, all your days." Jehovah, however, added the admonition: "And if you will walk in my ways by keeping my regulations and my commandments, just as David your father walked, I will also lengthen your days."—1Ki 3:4-14.

Shortly afterward, when two prostitutes presented a difficult problem of parental identity, Solomon demonstrated that God had indeed endowed him with judicial wisdom. This greatly strengthened Solomon's authority in the eyes of the people.—1Ki 3:16-28.

Building Projects. (PICTURES, Vol. 1, pp. 748, 750, 751) In the fourth year of his reign, in the second month of the year (the month Ziv [April-May]), in 1034 B.C.E., Solomon began to build the house of Jehovah on Mount Moriah. (1Ki 6:1) The building of the temple was peacefully quiet; the stones were fitted before being brought to the site, so that no sound of hammers or axes or of any tools of iron was heard. (1Ki 6:7) King Hiram of Tyre cooperated in supplying timbers of cedar and juniper trees in exchange for wheat and oil. (1Ki 5:10-12; 2Ch 2:11-16) He also furnished workmen, including an expert craftsman named Hiram, the son of a Tyrian man and a Hebrew woman. (1Ki 7:13, 14) Solomon conscripted for forced labor 30,000 men, sending them to Lebanon in shifts of 10,000 a month. Each group returned to their homes for two-month periods. Besides these, there were 70,000 burden bearers and 80,000 cutters. These last-named groups were non-Israelites.—1Ki 5:13-18; 2Ch 2:17, 18.

Inauguration of the temple. The tremendous building project occupied seven and a half years, being concluded in the eighth month, Bul, in 1027 B.C.E. (1Ki 6:37, 38) It appears that it took some time afterward to bring in the utensils and to get everything arranged, for it was in the seventh month, Ethanim, at the time of the Festival of Booths, that the sanctification and inauguration of the temple were carried out by Solomon. (1Ki 8:2; 2Ch 7:8-10) Therefore it must have taken place in the seventh month of 1026 B.C.E., 11 months after completing the building, rather than a month before the structure was completed (in 1027 B.C.E.), as some have thought.

Another view adopted by some is that the inauguration services were in Solomon's 24th year (1014 B.C.E.), after he had also built his own house and other government buildings, which occupied 13 more years, or 20 years of building work in all. This view is supported by the Greek *Septuagint,* which interpolates certain words not found in the Masoretic text, at 1 Kings 8:1 (3 Kings 8:1 in *LXX,* Bagster) reading: "And it came to pass when Solomon had finished building the house of the Lord and his own house after twenty years, then king Solomon assembled all the elders of Israel in Sion, to bring the ark of the covenant of the Lord out of the city of David, this is Sion, in the month of Athanin." However, a comparison of the accounts in Kings and Chronicles indicates that this is an incorrect conclusion.

The record in 1 Kings chapters 6 to 8 describes the temple construction and its completion; next it mentions Solomon's 13-year government building program; and then, after speaking again at length of the temple construction and the bringing in of the "things made holy by David his father," the account proceeds to describe the inauguration. This seems to indicate that the description of the government building program (1Ki 7:1-8) was inserted parenthetically, as it were, to round out and complete the discussion about the building operations. But the record at 2 Chronicles 5:1-3 appears to indicate more directly that the inauguration took place as soon as the temple and its furnishings were ready, for it reads: "Finally all the work that Solomon had to do for the house of Jehovah was at its completion, and Solomon began to bring in the things made holy by David his father; and the silver and the gold and all the utensils he put in the treasures of the house of the true God. It was then that Solomon proceeded to congregate the older men of Israel and all the heads of the tribes." After detailing the installation of the ark of the covenant in the temple by the priests, who carried it from the City of David up to the temple hill, the account then goes on to describe the inauguration.—2Ch 5:4-14; chaps 6, 7.

Some have questioned the view just mentioned that the inauguration took place in the year after the temple was completed, because of 1 Kings 9:1-9, which speaks of Jehovah as appearing to Solomon after "the house of the king" was constructed, saying that he had heard Solomon's prayer. (Compare 2Ch 7:11-22.) This was in his 24th year, after his 20-year building work. Was God 12 years in answering Solomon's prayer given at the inauguration of the temple? No, for at that inauguration, at the close of Solomon's prayer, "the fire itself came down from the heavens and proceeded to consume the burnt offering and the sacrifices, and Jehovah's glory itself filled the house." This was a powerful manifestation of Jehovah's hearing of the prayer, an answer by *action,* and was acknowledged as such by the people. (2Ch 7:1-3) God's later appearance to Solomon showed that he had not forgotten that prayer offered 12 years previously, and now he was answering it *verbally* by assuring Solomon of his response to it. God, at this second appearance, also gave Solomon added admonition to continue faithful as had David his father.

Solomon's prayer. In Solomon's prayer at the temple inauguration he referred to Jehovah as the God above all, a God of loving-kindness and loyalty, the Fulfiller of his promises. Though the temple was a house for Jehovah, Solomon realized that "the heavens, yes, the heaven of the heavens, themselves" could not contain Him. He is the Hearer and Answerer of prayer, the God of justice, rewarding the righteous and repaying the wicked, but forgiving the sinner who repents and returns to Him. He is not a 'nature god,' but does exercise control over the elements, over animal life, even over the nations of earth. He is not a mere national God of the Hebrews but is the God of all men who seek him. In his prayer Solomon manifested the desire to see Jehovah's name made great in all the earth; Solomon expressed his own love for righteousness and justice, love for God's people Israel and for the foreigner who would seek Jehovah.—1Ki 8:22-53; 2Ch 6:12-42.

At the inauguration all the priests officiated; on this occasion there was no need to observe the divisions that David had arranged. (2Ch 5:11) The need for the services of all can be seen in that, besides the grain offerings presented, 22,000 cattle and 120,000 sheep were offered as burnt offerings and communion sacrifices during that festal seven-day period, which was concluded by a solemn assembly on the eighth day. So large was the number of sacrifices that the great copper altar proved too small; to accommodate them, Solomon had to sanctify a portion of the courtyard for this purpose.—1Ki 8:63, 64; 2Ch 7:5, 7.

Solomon later set the divisions of the priests

over their services and the Levites in their posts of duty as these had been outlined by David. The temple now became the place where all the Israelites were to gather for their seasonal festivals and their sacrifices to Jehovah.

Government buildings. During the 13 years after completing the temple, Solomon built a new royal palace on Mount Moriah, immediately to the S of the temple, so that it was near the temple's outer courtyard, but on lower ground. Near this he built the Porch of the Throne, the Porch of Pillars, and the House of the Forest of Lebanon. All these buildings were on the descending terrain between the summit of the temple hill and the low spur of the City of David. He also built a house for his Egyptian wife; she was not allowed to "dwell in the house of David the king of Israel, for," as Solomon said, "the places to which the ark of Jehovah has come are something holy."—1Ki 7:1-8; 3:1; 9:24; 11:1; 2Ch 8:11.

Nationwide building. After completing his governmental building projects, Solomon set out on a nationwide construction program. He used as forced labor the offspring of Canaanites whom Israel had not devoted to destruction in their conquest of Canaan, but he did not reduce any Israelite to this slave status. (1Ki 9:20-22; 2Ch 8:7-10) He built up and fortified Gezer (which Pharaoh had taken from the Canaanites and presented as a gift to his daughter, Solomon's wife), as well as Upper and Lower Beth-horon, Baalath, and Tamar; he also constructed storage cities, chariot cities, and cities for horsemen. The entire realm, including the territory E of the Jordan, benefited from his building works. He further fortified the Mound, which David had built. He "closed up the gap of the City of David." (1Ki 11:27) This may have reference to his building or extending "Jerusalem's wall all around." (1Ki 3:1) He strongly fortified Hazor and Megiddo; archaeologists have discovered portions of strong walls and fortified gates that they believe to be the remains of Solomon's works in these cities, now in ruins.—1Ki 9:15-19; 2Ch 8:1-6.

His Riches and Glory. Solomon engaged extensively in trade. His fleet, in cooperation with Hiram's, brought in great quantities of gold from Ophir, as well as "algum" timbers and precious stones. (1Ki 9:26-28; 10:11; 2Ch 8:17, 18; 9:10, 11) Horses and chariots were imported from Egypt, and traders from all over the world of that time brought their goods in abundance. Solomon's annual revenue of gold came to be 666 talents (c. $256,643,000), aside from silver and gold and other items brought in by merchants.

(1Ki 10:14, 15; 2Ch 9:13, 14) Additionally, "all the kings of the earth" brought gifts yearly from their lands: gold and silver articles, balsam oil, armor, horses, mules, and other riches. (1Ki 10:24, 25, 28, 29; 2Ch 9:23-28) Even apes and peacocks were imported in ships of Tarshish. (1Ki 10:22; 2Ch 9:21) Solomon came to have 4,000 stalls of horses and chariots (1Ki 10:26 says 1,400 chariots) and 12,000 steeds (or, possibly, horsemen). —2Ch 9:25.

There was no king in all the earth who possessed the riches of Solomon. (1Ki 10:23; 2Ch 9:22) The approach to his throne exceeded in magnificence anything in other kingdoms. The throne itself was of ivory overlaid with fine gold. It had a round canopy behind it; six steps led up to it, with six lions on each side, and two lions stood beside the throne's armrests. (1Ki 10:18-20; 2Ch 9:17-19) For his drinking vessels only gold was used; it is specifically stated that "there was nothing of silver; it was considered as nothing at all in the days of Solomon." (2Ch 9:20) There were harps and stringed instruments in Solomon's house and in the temple that were made from algum timbers such as had never been seen before in Judah.—1Ki 10:12; 2Ch 9:11.

His household food supply. The daily food for Solomon's royal household amounted to "thirty cor measures [6,600 L; 188 bu] of fine flour and sixty cor measures [13,200 L; 375 bu] of flour, ten fat cattle and twenty pastured cattle and a hundred sheep, besides some stags and gazelles and roebucks and fattened cuckoos." (1Ki 4:22, 23) Twelve deputies supervised the supplying of food, one deputy for each month of the year. They each had supervision of a portion of the land; for this purpose it was not divided according to the tribal boundaries but according to agricultural growing regions. Included in the supplies was provender for Solomon's many horses.—1Ki 4:1-19, 27, 28.

Queen of Sheba visits Solomon. One of the most distinguished visitors that came from a foreign land to view the glory and riches of Solomon was the queen of Sheba. Solomon's fame had reached "all the people of the earth" so that she made the trip from her faraway domain "to test him with perplexing questions." She spoke to him "all that happened to be close to her heart," and "there proved to be no matter hidden from the king that he did not tell her."—1Ki 10:1-3, 24; 2Ch 9:1, 2.

After the queen also observed the splendor of the temple and of Solomon's house, his table and drinking service along with the attire of his waiters, and the regular burnt sacrifices at the temple, "there proved to be no more spirit in her," so she exclaimed, "Look! I had not been told the half. You have surpassed in wisdom and prosperity the things heard to which I listened." Then she proceeded to pronounce happy the servants who served such a king. By all this she was led to give praise to Jehovah, to bless Jehovah God, who expressed his love to Israel by appointing Solomon as king to render judicial decision and righteousness.—1Ki 10:4-9; 2Ch 9:3-8.

Then she bestowed upon Solomon the magnificent gift of 120 talents of gold ($46,242,000) and a great number of precious stones and balsam oil in unusually great quantity. Solomon, in turn, gave the queen whatever she asked, apart from his own generous-hearted bounty, possibly more than she had brought to him.—1Ki 10:10, 13; 2Ch 9:9, 12.

Prosperity of his rule. Jehovah blessed Solomon with wisdom, glory, and riches as long as he remained firm for true worship, and the nation of Israel likewise enjoyed God's favor. David had been used to subdue Israel's enemies and to establish the kingdom firmly to its outer boundaries. The account reports: "As for Solomon, he proved to be ruler over all the kingdoms from the River [Euphrates] to the land of the Philistines and to the boundary of Egypt. They were bringing gifts and serving Solomon all the days of his life." (1Ki 4:21) During Solomon's reign there was peace, and "Judah and Israel were many, like the grains of sand that are by the sea for multitude, eating and drinking and rejoicing." "And Judah and Israel continued to dwell in security, everyone under his own vine and under his own fig tree, from Dan to Beer-sheba, all the days of Solomon."—1Ki 4:20, 25; Map, Vol. 1, p. 748.

Solomon's Wisdom. "And God continued giving Solomon wisdom and understanding in very great measure and a broadness of heart, like the sand that is upon the seashore. And Solomon's wisdom was vaster than the wisdom of all the Orientals and than all the wisdom of Egypt." Then other men of unusual wisdom are named: Ethan the Ezrahite (apparently a singer of David's time and the writer of Psalm 89) and three other wise men of Israel. Solomon was wiser than these; in fact, "his fame came to be in all the nations all around. And he could speak three thousand proverbs, and his songs came to be a thousand and five." The range of his knowledge covered the plants and animals of earth, and his proverbs, along with his writings in the books of Ecclesiastes and The Song of Solomon, reveal that he had a deep knowledge of human nature. (1Ki 4:29-34) From Ecclesiastes we learn that he did much meditation in order to find "the delightful words and the writing of correct words of truth." (Ec 12:10) He experienced many things, going out among the lowly and the high ones, keenly observant of their life, their work, their hopes and aims, and the vicissitudes of mankind. He exalted the knowledge of God and his law, and he emphasized above all things that 'the fear of Jehovah is the beginning of knowledge and wisdom' and that the whole obligation of man is to "fear the true God and keep his commandments."—Pr 1:7; 9:10; Ec 12:13; see ECCLESIASTES.

His Deviation From Righteousness. As long as Solomon remained true to the worship of Jehovah, he prospered. Evidently his proverbs were uttered, and the books of Ecclesiastes and The Song of Solomon, as well as at least one of the Psalms (Ps 127), were written during his period of faithful service to God. However, Solomon began to disregard God's law. We read: "And King Solomon himself loved many foreign wives along with the daughter of Pharaoh, Moabite, Ammonite, Edomite, Sidonian and Hittite women, from the nations of whom Jehovah had said to the sons of Israel: 'You must not go in among them, and they themselves should not come in among you; truly they will incline your heart to follow their gods.' It was to them that Solomon clung to love them. And he came to have seven hundred wives, princesses, and three hundred concubines; and his wives gradually inclined his heart. And it came about in the time of Solomon's growing old that his wives themselves had inclined his heart to follow other gods; and his heart did not prove to be complete with Jehovah his God like the heart of David his father. And Solomon began going after Ashtoreth the goddess of the Sidonians and after Milcom the disgusting thing of the Ammonites. And Solomon began to do what was bad in the eyes of Jehovah, and he did not follow Jehovah fully like David his father. It was then that Solomon proceeded to build a high place to Chemosh the disgusting thing of Moab on the mountain that was in front of Jerusalem, and to Molech the disgusting thing of the sons of Ammon. And that was the way he did for all his foreign wives who were making sacrificial smoke and sacrificing to their gods."—1Ki 11:1-8.

While this took place "in the time of Solomon's growing old," we need not assume that his deviation was because of senility, for Solomon was relatively young when taking the throne, and the length of his reign was 40 years. (1Ch 29:1; 2Ch 9:30) The account does not say that Solomon completely forsook the worship at the temple and the offering of sacrifices there. He apparently attempted to practice a sort of interfaith, in order to please his foreign wives. For this, "Jehovah came to be incensed at Solomon, because his heart had inclined away from Jehovah the God of Israel, the one appearing to him twice." Jehovah informed Solomon that, as a consequence, He would rip part of the kingdom away from him, but not in Solomon's day, out of respect for David and for the sake of Jerusalem. But he would do it in the days of Solomon's son, leaving that son with only one tribe (besides Judah), which tribe proved to be Benjamin.—1Ki 11:9-13.

Resisters of Solomon. From that time on, Jehovah began to raise up resisters to Solomon, primarily Jeroboam of the tribe of Ephraim, who finally pulled ten tribes away from being loyal to the throne in Rehoboam's time, and who established the northern kingdom that came to be called Israel. As a young man, Jeroboam, because of his industriousness, had been placed by Solomon over all the compulsory service of the house of Joseph. Also giving trouble to Solomon were Hadad the Edomite and Rezon, an enemy of David who became king of Syria.—1Ki 11:14-40; 12:12-15.

King Solomon's drawing away from God had its bad effect on Solomon's rule. It became oppressive, doubtless due to the drain on the economy because of the high cost of his government, which must have been increasing to excess. There was also discontent among those he had conscripted for forced labor and, no doubt, also among their Israelite overseers. Having turned away from following God with a complete heart, Solomon would no longer receive Jehovah's blessing and prosperity or the continued wisdom to govern in righteousness and justice and to solve the problems arising. As Solomon himself had stated: "When the righteous become many, the people rejoice; but when anyone wicked bears rule, the people sigh."—Pr 29:2.

That this situation came about is made clear by the record of what took place shortly after Solomon's death, when Rehoboam ruled. Through the prophet Ahijah, God had sent a message to Jeroboam, telling Jeroboam that God would give him ten tribes and that if he would keep His statutes, God would build him a lasting house, just as he had done for David. After this, Solomon sought to kill Jeroboam, who fled to Egypt, where a successor of the father of Solomon's Egyptian wife now ruled. Jeroboam remained there until Solomon's death. Then he led the people in a complaint to Rehoboam and finally in rebellion.—1Ki 11:26-40; 12:12-20.

Though Solomon had inclined his heart away from Jehovah, he "lay down with his forefathers, and was buried in the City of David his father." —1Ki 11:43; 2Ch 9:31.

Jesus, a Legal Heir of Solomon. Matthew traces the descendants of Solomon down to Joseph, the adoptive father of Jesus, thus demonstrating that Jesus had the legal right to the throne of David through the kingly line. (Mt 1:7, 16) Luke traces Jesus' lineage to Heli (apparently the father of Mary) through Nathan, who was another son of David and Bath-sheba and therefore Solomon's full brother. (Lu 3:23, 31) Both lines of descent merge in Zerubbabel and Shealtiel and again branch out into two lines of descent. (Mt 1:13; Lu 3:27) Mary the mother of Jesus was a descendant through Nathan, and Joseph his adoptive father descended through Solomon, so that Jesus was both the natural and legal descendant of David, with full right to the throne.—See GENEALOGY OF JESUS CHRIST.

Need to Guard the Heart. As long as Solomon maintained an "obedient heart," with which he was concerned at the beginning, he had Jehovah's favor and he prospered. But his bad outcome demonstrates that knowledge, great ability, or power, riches, and fame are not the most important things, and that to turn away from Jehovah is to forsake wisdom. Solomon's own counsel proved true: "More than all else that is to be guarded, safeguard your heart, for out of it are the sources of life." (1Ki 3:9; Pr 4:23) His case illustrates the treacherousness and desperateness of the heart of sinful man, but more, it shows that the best of hearts can be enticed if constant vigilance is not kept. Loving what Jehovah loves and hating what he hates, constantly seeking his guidance and the doing of what pleases him, are a sure protection.—Jer 17:9; Pr 8:13; Heb 1:9; Joh 8:29.

Messianic Prophecies. There are many similarities between the reign of Solomon and that of the great King Jesus Christ, as prophesied in the Scriptures. In many respects Solomon's rule, as long as he was obedient to Jehovah, is a small-scale pattern of the Messianic Kingdom. Jesus Christ, "something more than Solomon," came as a man of peace, and he appears to have carried out a spiritual building work especially related to the restoration of true worship among his anointed followers in Jehovah's great spiritual temple. (Mt 12:42; 2Co 6:16; Joh 14:27; 16:33; Ro 14:17; Jas 3:18) Solomon was of the line of David, as was Jesus. Solomon's name (from a root meaning "peace") fits the glorified Jesus Christ as the

"Prince of Peace." (Isa 9:6) His name Jedidiah (meaning "Beloved of Jah") harmonizes with God's own statement about his Son at the time of Jesus' baptism: "This is my Son, *the beloved,* whom I have approved."—Mt 3:17.

Psalm 72 is a prayerful expression in behalf of the rule of Solomon: "Let the mountains carry peace to the people . . . In his days the righteous one will sprout, and the abundance of peace until the moon is no more. And he will have subjects from sea to sea [apparently the Mediterranean and the Red Sea (Ex 23:31)] and from the River [Euphrates] to the ends of the earth."—Ps 72:3-8.

On Psalm 72:7 ("until the moon is no more"), Cook's *Commentary* says: "This passage is important as shewing that the idea of a King whose reign should last to the end of time was distinctly present to the Psalmist's mind. It determines the Messianic character of the whole composition." And on verse 8, he remarks: "The kingdom was to be universal, extending to the ends of the earth. The extension of the Israelitish realm under David and Solomon was sufficient to suggest the hope, and might be regarded by the Psalmist as a pledge of its realization, but taken in connection with the preceding verses this declaration is strictly Messianic."

The prophet Micah, in a prophecy almost universally accepted as Messianic, drew on the circumstance described in Solomon's reign, that "Judah and Israel continued to dwell in security, everyone under his own vine and under his own fig tree, . . . all the days of Solomon." (1Ki 4:25; Mic 4:4) Zechariah's prophecy (Zec 9:9, 10) quotes Psalm 72:8, and Matthew applies Zechariah's prophecy to Jesus Christ.—Mt 21:4, 5.

SON. The Hebrew word *ben* and the Greek word *hui·os'*, both meaning "son," are often used in a sense broader than merely to designate one's immediate male offspring. "Son" may mean adopted son (Ex 2:10; Joh 1:45), a descendant such as a grandson or great-grandson (Ex 1:7; 2Ch 35:14; Jer 35:16; Mt 12:23), or a son-in-law. —Compare 1Ch 3:17 and Lu 3:27 (Shealtiel was evidently the son of Jeconiah and the son-in-law of Neri); Lu 3:23, "Joseph, son of Heli," evidently the son-in-law (in this phrase *hui·os'*, "son," does not appear in the Greek text, but is understood).

Men were often identified or distinguished by their father's name or that of a more distant forefather, as, (David) "the son of Jesse." (1Sa 22:7, 9) The Hebrew and Aramaic words *ben* and *bar*, "son," were frequently attached as prefixes to the father's name, giving the son a surname, as Bar-Jesus (meaning "Son of Jesus"). (Ac 13:6)

Some versions leave the prefix untranslated; others translate it in most cases; some give the translation in the margin. Or the prefix may be attached to the name because of the circumstances surrounding the birth of the child, as Ben-ammi, meaning "Son of My People [that is, relatives]," and not the son of foreigners; or Ben-oni, meaning "Son of My Mourning," Benjamin being so named by his dying mother Rachel.—Ge 19:38; 35:18.

Additionally, the word "sons" frequently serves a descriptive purpose, as: Orientals (literally, "sons of the East" [1Ki 4:30; Job · 1:3, ftn]); "anointed ones" (literally, "sons of the oil" [Zec 4:14, ftn]); members ("sons") of occupational classes, as, "sons of the prophets" (1Ki 20:35) or, "a member ["son"] of the ointment mixers" (Ne 3:8); returned exiles ("sons of the Exile") (Ezr 10:7, 16, ftn); good-for-nothing men, scoundrels ("sons of belial") (Jg 19:22, ftn). Those who pursue a certain course of conduct, or who manifest a certain characteristic, are designated by such expressions as "sons of the Most High," "sons of light and sons of day," "sons of the kingdom," "sons of the wicked one," "son of the Devil," "sons of disobedience." (Lu 6:35; 1Th 5:5; Mt 13:38; Ac 13:10; Eph 2:2) So, too, with the judgment or outcome that corresponds to the characteristic, as, "a subject for Gehenna" (literally, a son of Gehenna); "the son of destruction." (Mt 23:15; Joh 17:12; 2Th 2:3) Isaiah, who prophesied God's chastisement of Israel called the nation "my threshed ones and the son of my threshing floor."—Isa 21:10.

Angels, created by God, are sons of God. (Job 1:6; 38:7) Adam as a creation of God was a son of God. (Lu 3:38) Those judges and rulers in Israel against whom God's word came were called "sons of the Most High," doubtless because they held office in Israel as representing the divine rule, though they had transgressed. (Ps 82:6) Those whom God selects to be joint heirs with his Son Jesus Christ are called "God's sons."—Ro 8:14-17.

Desire for Male Offspring. In ancient times married couples strongly desired a male offspring. (Ge 4:1, 25; 29:32-35) As the psalmist expressed it: "Sons are an inheritance from Jehovah . . . Happy is the able-bodied man that has filled his quiver with them." (Ps 127:3-5) With sons the line of descent was made certain, the name of the forefathers was preserved among posterity, and the hereditary possession of land remained in the family. (Nu 27:8) Israelite women desired to have sons, perhaps entertaining hope that one of their sons might prove to be the "seed" through whom blessings from God would come to mankind, as promised to Abraham. (Ge 22:18; 1Sa 1:5-11) In due time the angel Gabriel announced to Mary, a virgin girl of the tribe of Judah, that she was a "highly favored one," adding: "You will conceive in your womb and give birth to a son, and you are to call his name Jesus. This one will be great and will be called Son of the Most High; and Jehovah God will give him the throne of David his father."—Lu 1:28, 31, 32.

SONG.   A composition including music and words; a poetic composition. (See MUSIC.) About one tenth of the entire Bible is song, the foremost examples being the Psalms, The Song of Solomon, and Lamentations. While the Scriptures do refer to secular songs, songs of contempt and of seduction, the majority of the Bible's some 300 references to the subject relate to the worship of Jehovah God. In the main, singing is associated with joy, as when the disciple James wrote: "Is there anyone in good spirits? Let him sing psalms [songs of praise to God]." (Jas 5:13) Songs expressing sorrow might more properly be termed dirges.—Am 8:10; see DIRGE.

The first song recorded in the Bible was that sung by Moses and the men of Israel, to which Miriam and the women responded, upon their deliverance at the Red Sea. (Ex 15:1-21) Among others are Moses' farewell song, Deborah and Barak's victory song, and David's dirge lamenting the death of Saul and David's dear friend Jonathan. (De 31:30; 32:1-43; Jg 5:1-31; 2Sa 1:17-27) Additional compositions of David include at least 73 of the Psalms. The Bible also refers to "the song of Jehovah," mentioned in connection with Hezekiah's restoration of pure worship, as well as the 'song of Moses and the Lamb.'—2Ch 29:27; Re 15:3, 4.

References to "a new song" appear not only in the Psalms but also in the writings of Isaiah and the apostle John. (Ps 33:3; 40:3; 96:1; 98:1; 144:9; 149:1; Isa 42:10; Re 5:9; 14:3) An examination of the context surrounding most occurrences of the expression "new song" reveals that such is sung because of a new development in Jehovah's exercise of his universal sovereignty. As joyfully proclaimed in Psalm 96:10: "Jehovah himself has become king." The new developments in Jehovah's extension of his kingship, as well as what these signify for heaven and earth, appear to be the subject of this "new song."—Ps 96:11-13; 98:9; Isa 42:10, 13.

SONG OF SOLOMON, THE.   A poetic book of the Hebrew Scriptures that tells of the unswerving love of a Shulammite girl (a country girl from Shunem, or Shulem) for a shepherd boy and King Solomon's unsuccessful attempt to capture her love. The opening words of the Hebrew text designate this poem as the "song of songs," that is, a "superlative song," the most beautiful, the most excellent song. (See *NW* ftn on title.) It is but one song and not a collection of songs.

At the outset Solomon is identified as the writer. (Ca 1:1) Internal evidence agrees with this, for it reveals the writer to have been one who was well acquainted with God's creation, as was Solomon. (1Ki 4:29-33) Repeatedly plants, animals, precious stones, and metals figure in the vivid imagery of the book. (Ca 1:12-14, 17; 2:1, 3, 7, 9, 12-15; 4:8, 13, 14; 5:11-15; 7:2, 3, 7, 8, 11-13) The writer, as would be expected from a king like Solomon, was very familiar with the land inhabited by the Israelites—the coastal plain; the low plains (2:1); the mountain ranges of Lebanon, Hermon, Anti-Lebanon, and Carmel (4:8; 7:5); the vineyards of En-gedi (1:14); and "the pools in Heshbon, by the gate of Bath-rabbim" (7:4).

The poem was composed when Solomon had 60 queens and 80 concubines. (Ca 6:8) This points to the earlier part of his 40-year reign (1037-998 B.C.E.), since Solomon finally came to have 700 wives and 300 concubines.—1Ki 11:3.

The expressions of endearment contained in The Song of Solomon may seem very unusual to the Western reader. But it should be remembered that the setting for this song is an Oriental one of about 3,000 years ago.

Persons Involved.   The central figure of The Song of Solomon is the Shulammite. Other persons mentioned in the poem are her shepherd lover (Ca 1:7) and her mother and brothers (1:6; 8:2), King Solomon (3:11), the "daughters of Jerusalem" (the ladies of Solomon's court), and the "daughters of Zion" (women residents of Jerusalem) (3:5, 11). The individuals can be differentiated by what they say of themselves or by what is said to them. In the Hebrew text, grammatical forms often imply gender (masculine or feminine) as well as number (singular or plural), thereby facilitating identification of the characters. To make this distinction evident in the English language it is often necessary to add clarifying words to convey fully the meaning of the original. Thus at The Song of Solomon 1:5 the Hebrew reads literally: "Black I and comely." However, the Hebrew words for "black" and "comely" are in the feminine gender. Therefore the *New World Translation* reads: "A black *girl* I am, but comely."

The Drama.   The Shulammite met the shepherd at the place of his birth. (Ca 8:5b) Jealous for the chastity of their sister, the brothers of the

HIGHLIGHTS OF THE SONG OF SOLOMON

The unswerving love of a Shulammite maiden for a shepherd boy in spite of King Solomon's attempts to win her for himself

Written by Solomon, evidently quite early in his reign

The Shulammite maiden in Solomon's camp (1:1–3:5)

She longs for the love of her dear one, a shepherd, and wants him to take her away from the royal surroundings

To the women of the court, she explains that the reason for her dark complexion is exposure to the sun while working in her brothers' vineyards

Solomon promises her gold and silver ornaments, but she insists that she will keep loving her dear one

Her shepherd appears and praises the Shulammite girl's beauty, likening her to a lily among weeds

The Shulammite tells the women of the court that her shepherd is like an apple tree whose shade she passionately desires; she puts them under oath not to arouse in her a love for Solomon; she remembers when her lover invited her to accompany him; however, her brothers told her that the vineyards must be protected from the little foxes

At night, she dreams about looking for her lover and finding him

Tested in the city of Jerusalem (3:6–8:4)

Solomon's magnificent entourage begins its return to Jerusalem

The shepherd again gets in touch with the Shulammite (now veiled) and speaks of her beauty, likening her to a barred garden filled with aromatic plants

She invites him to enter this garden and enjoy its fruits

To the women of the court, the Shulammite relates her bad dream: Her lover arrived while she was in bed; he departed before she could open the door; she searched for him fruitlessly in the city and was mistreated by the city watchmen

The daughters of Jerusalem ask about her dear one, and she replies by giving a glowing description of him

Solomon now expresses his love for the Shulammite, saying she is more beautiful than his 60 queens and 80 concubines

The Shulammite is unmoved, pointing out that she is only here because an errand of service brought her near his camp

Solomon vividly describes her beauty, but the Shulammite resists his skillful speech, insisting that she belongs to her dear one

The Shulammite returns, her loyalty proved (8:5–14)

The Shulammite returns home, leaning upon her dear one

Earlier, her brothers wondered whether she would be constant like a wall, or fickle like a swinging door that admits anyone

The Shulammite has turned down all that Solomon could offer, proving her exclusive devotion to her dear one; her love is as strong as death, and its blazings as the flame of Jah

---

Shulammite tried to protect her from temptation. Therefore, when she wanted to accept her lover's invitation to join him in viewing the beauties of early spring (2:8-14), they became angry with her and, taking advantage of the seasonal need, appointed her to guard the vineyards against the depredations of the little foxes. (1:6; 2:15) Exposed to the sun's rays, the Shulammite lost the fairness of her skin.—1:5, 6.

Later, while on her way to the garden of nut trees, she unintentionally came upon the encampment of King Solomon. (Ca 6:11, 12) Either seen there by the king himself or noticed by someone else and then recommended to him, the Shulammite was brought to Solomon's camp. King Solomon made known his admiration for her. But she felt no attraction for him and voiced a longing for her shepherd lover. (1:2-4, 7) The "daughters of Jerusalem" therefore recommended that she leave the camp and find her lover. (1:8) Solomon, however, was unwilling to let her go and began praising her beauty, promising to fashion circlets of gold and studs of silver for her. (1:9-11) The Shulammite then informed the king that the object of her love was someone else. —1:12-14.

Thereafter the Shulammite's shepherd lover came to Solomon's camp and voiced his affection for her. She, too, assured him of her love. (Ca 1:15–2:2) When speaking to the "daughters of Jerusalem," the Shulammite compared her lover to a fruit tree among the trees of the forest and solemnly charged them by what was beautiful and graceful not to try to arouse unwanted love in her. (2:3-7) Always, even during the night hours, she continued to long for her shepherd lover, and she reminded the "daughters of Jerusalem" that they were under oath not to attempt to awaken love in her until it felt inclined.—2:16–3:5.

Returning to Jerusalem, Solomon took the Shulammite along. Seeing them approaching the city, several "daughters of Zion" commented about the appearance of the procession. (Ca 3:6-11) At Jerusalem, the shepherd lover, having followed the procession, got in touch with the Shulammite and praised her beauty, thereby assuring her of his love. (4:1-5) The Shulammite voiced her desire to leave the city (4:6), and he continued expressing his admiration for her. (4:7-16a) "Let my dear one come into his garden and eat its choicest fruits," she said. (4:16b) His response to this invitation was: "I have come into my garden, O my sister, my bride." (5:1a) Women of Jerusalem encouraged them, saying: "Eat, O companions! Drink and become drunk with expressions of endearment!"—5:1b.

When the Shulammite, after having a bad dream, related it to the "daughters of Jerusalem" and told them that she was lovesick (Ca 5:2-8), they wanted to know what was so special about her dear one. At that the Shulammite proceeded to describe her lover in glowing terms. (5:10-16) Asked by them where he was, she informed them that he was shepherding among the gardens. (6:1-3) Once again Solomon confronted the Shulammite with expressions of praise. (6:4-10) Told that she had not sought his company (6:11, 12), Solomon appealed to her to come back. (6:13a) This prompted her to ask: "What do you people behold in the Shulammite?" (6:13b) Solomon used this as an opening to express further admiration for her. (7:1-9) But the Shulammite remained changeless in her love and called upon the "daughters of Jerusalem" not to awaken love in her when it did not feel inclined to come forth spontaneously.—7:10–8:4.

Apparently Solomon then allowed the Shulammite to return to her home. Seeing her approaching, her brothers asked: "Who is this woman coming up from the wilderness, leaning upon her dear one?" (Ca 8:5a) The brothers of the Shulammite had not realized that their sister had such constancy in love. In earlier years one brother had said concerning her: "We have a little sister that does not have any breasts. What shall we do for our sister on the day that she will be spoken for?" (8:8) Another brother replied: "If she should be a wall, we shall build upon her a battlement of silver; but if she should be a door, we shall block her up with a cedar plank." (8:9) However, since the Shulammite had successfully resisted all enticements, being satisfied with her own vineyard and remaining loyal in her affection for her lover (8:6, 7, 11, 12), she could properly say: "I am a wall, and my breasts are like towers. In this case I have become in his eyes like her that is finding peace."—8:10.

The song concludes with an expression of her shepherd lover's desire to hear her voice (Ca 8:13), and with the expression of her desire that he come leaping, crossing the mountains that separated them.—8:14.

Value. The Song of Solomon illustrates the beauty of enduring and constant love. Such unswerving love is reflected in the relationship of Christ Jesus and his bride. (Eph 5:25-32) Thus The Song of Solomon can serve to encourage those professing to be of Christ's bride to remain faithful to their heavenly bridegroom.—Compare 2Co 11:2.

SON(S) OF GOD.

The expression "Son of God" primarily identifies Christ Jesus. Others referred to as "son(s) of God" include intelligent spirit creatures produced by God, the man Adam before he sinned, and humans with whom God has dealt on the basis of covenant relationship.

"Sons of the True God." The first mention of "sons of the true God" is at Genesis 6:2-4. There such sons are spoken of as 'beginning to notice the daughters of men, that they were good-looking; and they went taking wives for themselves, namely, all whom they chose,' this prior to the global Flood.

Many commentators hold that these 'sons of God' were themselves human, being in reality men of the line of Seth. They base their argument on the fact that Seth's line was that through which godly Noah came, whereas the other lines from Adam, that of Cain and those of any other sons born to Adam (Ge 5:3, 4), were destroyed at the Flood. So, they say that the taking as wives "the daughters of men" by "the sons of the true God" means that Sethites began to marry into the line of wicked Cain.

There is, however, nothing to show that God made any such distinction between family lines at this point. Corroborating Scriptural evidence is lacking to support the view that intermarriage between the lines of Seth and Cain is what is here meant, or that such marriages were responsible for the birth of "mighty ones" as mentioned in verse 4. It is true that the expression "sons of men [or "of mankind"]" (which those favoring the earlier mentioned view would contrast with the expression 'sons of God') is frequently used in an unfavorable sense, but this is not consistently so. —Compare Ps 4:2; 57:4; Pr 8:22, 30, 31; Jer 32:18, 19; Da 10:16.

Angelic sons of God. On the other hand, there is an explanation that finds corroborating evidence in the Scriptures. The expression "sons of the true God" next occurs at Job 1:6, and here the reference is obviously to spirit sons of God assembled in God's presence, among whom Satan, who had been "roving about in the earth," also appeared. (Job 1:7; see also 2:1, 2.) Again at Job 38:4-7 "the sons of God" who 'shouted in applause' when God 'laid the cornerstone' of the earth clearly were angelic sons and not humans descended from Adam (as yet not even created). So, too, at Psalm 89:6 "the sons of God" are definitely heavenly creatures, not earthlings. —See GOD (Hebrew Terms).

The identification of "the sons of the true God" at Genesis 6:2-4 with angelic creatures is objected to by those holding the previously mentioned view because they say the context relates entirely to *human* wickedness. This objection is not valid, however, since the wrongful interjection of spirit creatures in human affairs most certainly could contribute to or accelerate the growth of human wickedness. Wicked spirit creatures during Jesus' time on earth, though not then materializing in visible form, were responsible for wrong human conduct of an extreme nature. (See DEMON; DEMON POSSESSION.) The mention of a mixing into human affairs by angelic sons of God could reasonably appear in the Genesis account precisely because of its explaining to a considerable degree the gravity of the situation that had developed on earth prior to the Flood.

Supporting this are the apostle Peter's references to "the spirits in prison, who had once been disobedient when the patience of God was waiting in Noah's days" (1Pe 3:19, 20), and to "the angels that sinned," mentioned in connection with the "ancient world" of Noah's time (2Pe 2:4, 5), as well as Jude's statement concerning "the angels that did not keep their original position but forsook their own proper dwelling place." (Jude 6) If it is denied that "the sons of the true God" of Genesis 6:2-4 were spirit creatures, then these statements by the Christian writers become enigmatic, with nothing to explain the manner in which this angelic disobedience took place, or its actual relation to Noah's time.

Angels definitely did materialize human bodies on occasion, even eating and drinking with men. (Ge 18:1-22; 19:1-3) Jesus' statement concerning resurrected men and women not marrying or being given in marriage but being like the "angels in heaven" shows that marriages between such heavenly creatures do not exist, no male and female distinction being indicated among them. (Mt 22:30) But this does not say that such angelic creatures could not materialize human forms and enter marriage relations with human women. It should be noted that Jude's reference to angels as

not keeping their original position and to them as forsaking their "proper dwelling place" (certainly here referring to an abandoning of the spirit realm) is immediately followed by the statement: "So too Sodom and Gomorrah and the cities about them, after they *in the same manner as the foregoing ones* had committed fornication excessively and *gone out after flesh for unnatural use,* are placed before us as a warning example." (Jude 6, 7) Thus, the combined weight of the Scriptural evidence points to angelic deviation, the performance of acts contrary to their spirit nature, occurring in the days of Noah. There seems to be no valid reason, then, for doubting that the 'sons of God' of Genesis 6:2-4 were angelic sons.—See NEPHILIM.

First Human Son and His Descendants. Adam was the first human "son of God" by virtue of his creation by God. (Ge 2:7; Lu 3:38) When he was condemned to death as a willful sinner and was evicted from God's sanctuary in Eden, he was, in effect, disowned by God and lost his filial relationship with his heavenly Father.—Ge 3:17-24.

Those descended from him have been born with inherited sinful tendencies. (See SIN, I.) Since they were born of one rejected by God, Adam's descendants could not claim the relationship of being a son of God simply on the basis of birth. This is demonstrated by the apostle John's words at John 1:12, 13. He shows that those who received Christ Jesus, exercising faith in his name, were given "authority to become God's children, . . . [being] born, not from blood or from a fleshly will or from man's will, but from God." Sonship in relation to God, therefore, is not viewed as something automatically received by all of Adam's descendants at birth. This and other texts show that, since Adam's fall into sin, it has required some special recognition by God for men to be designated as his "sons." This is illustrated in his dealings with Israel.

"Israel Is My Son." To Pharaoh, who considered himself a god and a son of the Egyptian god Ra, Jehovah spoke of Israel as "my son, my firstborn," and called on the Egyptian ruler to "send my son away that he may serve me." (Ex 4:22, 23) Thus the entire nation of Israel was viewed by God as his "son" because of being his chosen people, a "special property, out of all the peoples." (De 14:1, 2) Not only because Jehovah is the Source of all life but more specifically because God had, in harmony with the Abrahamic covenant, produced this people, he is called their "Creator," their "Former," and their "Father," the one by whose name they were called. (Compare Ps 95:6, 7; 100:3; Isa 43:1-7, 15; 45:11, 12, 18, 19; 63:16.) He had 'helped them even from the belly,' evidently referring to the very beginning of their development as a people, and he 'formed' them by his dealings with them and by the Law covenant, giving shape to the national characteristics and structure. (Isa 44:1, 2, 21; compare God's expressions to Jerusalem at Eze 16:1-14; also Paul's expressions at Ga 4:19 and 1Th 2:11, 12.) Jehovah protected, carried, corrected, and provided for them as a father would for his son. (De 1:30, 31; 8:5-9; compare Isa 49:14, 15.) As "a son," the nation should have served to the praise of its Father. (Isa 43:21; Mal 1:6) Otherwise Israel would belie its sonship (De 32:4-6, 18-20; Isa 1:2, 3; 30:1, 2, 9), even as some of the Israelites acted in disreputable ways and were called "sons of belial" (literal Hebrew expression rendered "good-for-nothing men" at De 13:13 and other texts; compare 2Co 6:15). They became "renegade sons."—Jer 3:14, 22; compare 4:22.

It was in this national sense, and due to their covenant relationship, that God dealt with the Israelites as sons. This is seen by the fact that God simultaneously refers to himself not only as their "Maker" but also as their "Repurchaser" and even as their "husbandly owner," this latter expression placing Israel in the relationship of a wife to him. (Isa 54:5, 6; compare Isa 63:8; Jer 3:14.) It was evidently with their covenant relationship in mind, and recognizing God as responsible for the formation of the nation, that the Israelites addressed themselves to Jehovah as "our Father."—Isa 63:16-19; compare Jer 3:18-20; Ho 1:10, 11.

The tribe of Ephraim became the most prominent tribe of the northern kingdom of ten tribes, its name often standing for that entire kingdom. Because Jehovah chose to have Ephraim receive the firstborn son's blessing from his grandfather Jacob instead of Manasseh, the real firstborn son of Joseph, Jehovah rightly spoke of the tribe of Ephraim as "my firstborn."—Jer 31:9, 20; Ho 11:1-8, 12; compare Ge 48:13-20.

Individual Israelite 'sons.' God also designated certain individuals within Israel as his 'sons,' in a special sense. Psalm 2, attributed to David at Acts 4:24-26, evidently applies to him initially when speaking of God's "son." (Ps 2:1, 2, 7-12) The psalm was later fulfilled in Christ Jesus, as the context in Acts shows. Since the context in the psalm shows that God is speaking, not to a baby, but to a grown man, in saying, "You are my son; I, today, I have become your father," it follows that David's entry into such sonship resulted

from God's special selection of him for the kingship and from God's fatherly dealings with him. (Compare Ps 89:3, 19-27.) In a similar way Jehovah said of David's son Solomon, "I myself shall become his father, and he himself will become my son."—2Sa 7:12-14; 1Ch 22:10; 28:6.

Loss of sonship. When Jesus was on earth the Jews still claimed God as their "Father." But Jesus bluntly told certain opposing ones that they were 'of their father the Devil,' for they listened to and did the will and works of God's Adversary; hence they showed they were "not from God." (Joh 8:41, 44, 47) This again shows that sonship with God on the part of any of Adam's descendants requires not simply some natural fleshly descent but primarily God's provision of a spiritual relationship with Him, and that such relationship, in turn, requires that the "sons" keep faith with God by manifesting his qualities, being obedient to his will, and faithfully serving his purpose and interests.

Christian Sons of God. As John 1:11, 12 makes evident, only some of the nation of Israel, those showing faith in Christ Jesus, were granted "authority to become God's children." Christ's ransom sacrifice brought this Jewish "remnant" (Ro 9:27; 11:5) out from under the Law covenant, which, though good and perfect, nevertheless condemned them as sinners, as slaves in the custody of sin; Christ thus freed them that they might "receive the adoption as sons" and become heirs through God.—Ga 4:1-7; compare Ga 3:19-26.

People of the nations, previously "without God in the world" (Eph 2:12), also became reconciled to God through faith in Christ and came into the relationship of sons.—Ro 9:8, 25, 26; Ga 3:26-29.

As did Israel, these Christians form a covenant people, being brought into the "new covenant" made valid by the application of Christ's shed blood. (Lu 22:20; Heb 9:15) However, God deals *individually* with Christians in accepting them into this covenant. Because they hear the good news and exercise faith, they are called to be joint heirs with God's Son (Ro 8:17; Heb 3:1), are "declared righteous" by God on the basis of their faith in the ransom (Ro 5:1, 2), and thus are 'brought forth by the word of truth' (Jas 1:18), being "born again" as baptized Christians, begotten or produced by God's spirit as his sons, due to enjoy spirit life in the heavens (Joh 3:3; 1Pe 1:3, 4). They have received, not a spirit of slavery such as resulted from Adam's trespass, but "a spirit of adoption as sons, by which spirit [they] cry out: 'Abba, Father!'" the term *"Abba"* being an intimate and endearing form of address. (Ro 8:14-17; see ABBA; ADOPTION [A Christian significance].) Thanks to Christ's superior mediatorship and priesthood and God's undeserved kindness expressed through him, the sonship of these spirit-begotten Christians is a more intimate relationship with God than that enjoyed by fleshly Israel.—Heb 4:14-16; 7:19-25; 12:18-24.

Maintaining sonship. Their "new birth" to this living hope (1Pe 1:3) does not of itself guarantee their continued sonship. They must be "led by God's spirit," not by their sinful flesh, and they must be willing to suffer as Christ did. (Ro 8:12-14, 17) They must be "imitators of God, as beloved children" (Eph 5:1), reflecting his divine qualities of peace, love, mercy, kindness (Mt 5:9, 44, 45; Lu 6:35, 36), being "blameless and innocent" of the things characterizing the "crooked and twisted generation" among whom they live (Php 2:15), purifying themselves of unrighteous practices (1Jo 3:1-4, 9, 10), being obedient to God's commandments, and accepting his discipline (1Jo 5:1-3; Heb 12:5-7).

Attaining full adoption as sons. Although called to be God's children, while in the flesh they have only a "token of what is to come." (2Co 1:22; 5:1-5; Eph 1:5, 13, 14) That is why the apostle, though speaking of himself and his fellow Christians as already "God's sons," could nevertheless say that "we ourselves also who have the firstfruits, namely, the spirit, yes, we ourselves groan within ourselves, while we are earnestly waiting for adoption as sons, the release from our bodies by ransom." (Ro 8:14, 23) Thus, after conquering the world by faithfulness until death, they receive the full realization of their sonship by being resurrected as spirit sons of God and "brothers" of God's Chief Son, Christ Jesus.—Heb 2:10-17; Re 21:7; compare Re 2:7, 11, 26, 27; 3:12, 21.

Those who are God's spiritual children, called to this heavenly calling, know they are such, for God's 'spirit itself bears witness with their spirit that they are God's children.' (Ro 8:16) This evidently means that their spirit acted as an impelling force in their lives, moving them to respond positively to the expressions of God's spirit through his inspired Word in speaking about such heavenly hope and also to his dealings with them by that spirit. Thus they have the assurance that they are indeed God's spiritual children and heirs.

Glorious Freedom of the Children of God. The apostle speaks of "the glory that is going to be revealed in us" and also of "the eager expectation of the creation . . . waiting for the revealing of the sons of God." (Ro 8:18, 19) Since the glory of these sons is heavenly, it is clear that such "revealing" of their glory must be preceded by their resurrection to heavenly life. (Compare Ro 8:23.) However, 2 Thessalonians 1:6-10 indicates that this is not all that is involved; it speaks of "the revelation of the Lord Jesus" as bringing judicial punishment on those judged adversely by God, doing so "at the time he comes to be glorified in connection with his holy ones."—See REVELATION.

Since Paul says that "the creation" is waiting for this revealing, and will then be "set free from enslavement to corruption and have the glorious freedom of the children of God," it is apparent that others aside from these heavenly "sons of God" receive benefit from their revelation in glory. (Ro 8:19-23) The Greek term rendered "creation" can refer to any creature, human or animal, or to creation in general. Paul refers to it here as being in "eager expectation," as "waiting," as "subjected to futility, [though] not by its own will," as being "set free from enslavement to corruption [in order to] have the glorious freedom of the children of God," and as "groaning together" even as the Christian "sons" groan within themselves; these expressions all point conclusively to the *human* creation, the human family, hence not to creation in general, including animals, vegetation, and other creations, both animate and inanimate. (Compare Col 1:23.) This must mean, then, that the revelation of the sons of God in glory opens the way for others of the human family to enter into a relationship of actual sonship with God and to enjoy the freedom that accompanies such relationship.—See DECLARE RIGHTEOUS (Other Righteous Ones); GREAT CROWD.

Since Christ Jesus is the one foretold to become the "Eternal Father" (Isa 9:6) and since the Christian "sons of God" become his "brothers" (Ro 8:29), it follows that there must be others of the human family who gain life through Christ Jesus and who are, not his joint heirs and associate kings and priests, but his subjects over whom he reigns.—Compare Mt 25:34-40; Heb 2:10-12; Re 5:9, 10; 7:9, 10, 14-17; 20:4-9; 21:1-4.

It may be noted also that James (1:18) speaks of these spirit-begotten "sons of God" as being "certain firstfruits" of God's creatures, an expression similar to that used of the "hundred and forty-four thousand" who are "bought from among mankind" as described at Revelation 14:1-4. "Firstfruits" implies that other fruits follow, and hence the "creation" of Romans 8:19-22 evidently applies to such 'after fruits' or 'secondary fruits' of mankind who, through faith in Christ Jesus, gain eventual sonship in God's universal family.

In speaking of the future "system of things" and "the resurrection from the dead" to life in that system, Jesus said that these become "God's children by being children of the resurrection."—Lu 20:34-36.

From all the foregoing information it can be seen that 'sonship' of humans in relation to God is viewed from several different aspects. In each case, then, the sonship must be viewed in context to determine what it embraces and the exact nature of the filial relationship.

Christ Jesus, the Son of God. The Gospel account by John particularly emphasizes Jesus' prehuman existence as "the Word" and explains that "the Word became flesh and resided among us, and we had a view of his glory, a glory such as belongs to an only-begotten son from a father." (Joh 1:1-3, 14) That his sonship did not begin with his human birth is seen from Jesus' own statements, as when he said, "What things I have seen with my Father I speak" (Joh 8:38, 42; compare Joh 17:5, 24), as well as from other clear statements of his inspired apostles.—Ro 8:3; Ga 4:4; 1Jo 4:9-11, 14.

"Only-begotten." Some commentators object to the translation of the Greek word *mo·no·ge·nes'* by the English "only-begotten." They point out that the latter portion of the word (*ge·nes'*) does not come from *gen·na'o* (beget) but from *ge'nos* (kind), hence the term refers to the 'only one of a class or kind.' Thus many translations speak of Jesus as the "only Son" (*RS; AT; JB*) rather than the "only-begotten son" of God. (Joh 1:14; 3:16, 18; 1Jo 4:9) However, while the individual components do not include the verbal sense of being born, the usage of the term definitely does embrace the idea of descent or birth, for the Greek word *ge'nos* means "family stock; kinsfolk; offspring; race." It is translated "race" in 1 Peter 2:9. The Latin *Vulgate* by Jerome renders *mo·no·ge·nes'* as *unigenitus,* meaning "only-begotten" or "only." This relationship of the term to birth or descent is recognized by numerous lexicographers.

Edward Robinson's *Greek and English Lexicon of the New Testament* (1885, p. 471) gives the definition of *mo·no·ge·nes'* as: "only born, only begotten, i.e. an only child." The *Greek-English Lexicon of the New Testament* by W. Hickie (1956, p. 123) also gives: "only begotten." The *Theological Dictionary of the New Testament,* edited by G. Kittel, states: "The μονο- [*mo·no-*] does not denote the source but the nature of derivation. Hence μονογενής [*mo·no·ge·nes'*] means 'of

sole descent,' i.e., without brothers or sisters. This gives us the sense of only-begotten. The ref. is to the only child of one's parents, primarily in relation to them. . . . But the word can also be used more generally without ref. to derivation in the sense of 'unique,' 'unparalleled,' 'incomparable,' though one should not confuse the refs. to class or species and to manner."—Translator and editor, G. Bromiley, 1969, Vol. IV, p. 738.

As to the use of the term in the Christian Greek Scriptures or "New Testament," this latter work (pp. 739-741) says: "It means 'only-begotten.' . . . In [John] 3:16, 18; 1 Jn. 4:9; [John] 1:18 the relation of Jesus is not just compared to that of an only child to its father. It *is* the relation of the only-begotten to the Father. . . . In Jn. 1:14, 18; 3:16, 18; 1 Jn. 4:9 μονογενής denotes more than the uniqueness or incomparability of Jesus. In all these verses He is expressly called the Son, and He is regarded as such in 1:14. In Jn. μονογενής denotes the origin of Jesus. He is μονογενής as the only-begotten."

In view of these statements and in view of the plain evidence of the Scriptures themselves, there is no reason for objecting to translations showing that Jesus is not merely God's unique or incomparable Son but also his "only-begotten Son," hence descended from God in the sense of being produced by God. This is confirmed by apostolic references to this Son as "the firstborn of all creation" and as "the One born [form of *gen·na'o*] from God" (Col 1:15; 1Jo 5:18), while Jesus himself states that he is "the beginning of the creation by God."—Re 3:14.

Jesus is God's "firstborn" (Col 1:15) as God's first creation, called "the Word" in his prehuman existence. (Joh 1:1) The word "beginning" in John 1:1 cannot refer to the "beginning" of God the Creator, for he is eternal, having no beginning. (Ps 90:2) It must therefore refer to the beginning of creation, when the Word was brought forth by God as his firstborn Son. The term "beginning" is used in various other texts similarly to describe the start of some period or career or course, such as the "beginning" of the Christian career of those to whom John wrote his first letter (1Jo 2:7; 3:11), the "beginning" of Satan's rebellious course (1Jo 3:8), or the "beginning" of Judas' deflection from righteousness. (Joh 6:64; see JUDAS No. 4 [Became Corrupt].) Jesus is the "only-begotten Son" (Joh 3:16) in that he is the only one of God's sons, spirit or human, created solely by God, for all others were created through, or "by means of," that firstborn Son.—Col 1:16, 17; see JESUS CHRIST (Prehuman Existence); ONLY-BEGOTTEN.

Spirit begettal, return to heavenly sonship.
Jesus, of course, continued to be God's Son when born as a human, even as he had been in his prehuman existence. His birth was not the result of conception by the seed, or sperm, of any human male descended from Adam, but was by action of God's holy spirit. (Mt 1:20, 25; Lu 1:30-35; compare Mt 22:42-45.) Jesus recognized his sonship in relation to God, at the age of 12 years saying to his earthly parents, "Did you not know that I must be in the house of my Father?" They did not grasp the sense of this, perhaps thinking that by "Father" he was referring to God only in the sense that the term was used by Israelites in general, as considered earlier.—Lu 2:48-50.

However, about 30 years after his birth as a human, when he was immersed by John the Baptizer, God's spirit came upon Jesus and God spoke, saying: "You are my Son, the beloved; I have approved you." (Lu 3:21-23; Mt 3:16, 17) Evidently Jesus, the man, was then "born again" to be a spiritual Son with the hope of returning to life in heaven, and he was anointed by spirit to be God's appointed king and high priest. (Joh 3:3-6; compare 17:4, 5; see JESUS CHRIST [His Baptism].) A similar expression was made by God at the transfiguration on the mount, in which vision Jesus was seen in Kingdom glory. (Compare Mt 16:28 and 17:1-5.) With regard to Jesus' resurrection from the dead, Paul applied part of Psalm 2 to that occasion, quoting God's words, "You are my son, I have become your Father this day," and he also applied words from God's covenant with David, namely: "I myself shall become his father, and he himself will become my son." (Ps 2:7; 2Sa 7:14; Ac 13:33; Heb 1:5; compare Heb 5:5.) By his resurrection from the dead to spirit life, Jesus was "declared God's Son" (Ro 1:4), "declared righteous in spirit."—1Ti 3:16.

Thus, it is seen that, even as David as a grown man could 'become God's son' in a special sense, so, too, Christ Jesus also 'became God's Son' in a special way, at the time of his baptism and at his resurrection, and also, evidently, at the time of his entrance into full Kingdom glory.

False charge of blasphemy. Because of Jesus' references to God as his Father, certain opposing Jews leveled the charge of blasphemy against him, saying, "You, although being a man, make yourself a god." (Joh 10:33) Most translations here say "God"; Torrey's translation lowercases the word as "god," while the interlinear reading of *The Emphatic Diaglott* says "a god." Support for the rendering "a god" is found princi-

pally in Jesus' own answer, in which he quoted from Psalm 82:1-7. As can be seen, this text did not refer to persons as being called "God," but "gods" and "sons of the Most High."

According to the context, those whom Jehovah called "gods" and "sons of the Most High" in this psalm were Israelite judges who had been practicing injustice, requiring that Jehovah himself now judge 'in the middle of such gods.' (Ps 82:1-6, 8) Since Jehovah applied these terms to those men, Jesus was certainly guilty of no blasphemy in saying, "I am God's Son." Whereas the works of those judicial "gods" belied their being "sons of the Most High," Jesus' works consistently proved him to be in union, in harmonious accord and relationship, with his Father.—Joh 10:34-38.

SON OF MAN. In Hebrew this is mainly a translation of the expression *ben-'a·dham'*. Instead of referring to the person, Adam, *'a·dham'* is here used generically for "mankind" so that the expression *ben-'a·dham'* means, in essence, "a son of mankind, a human, an earthling son." (Ps 80:17; 146:3; Jer 49:18, 33) The phrase is often employed in parallel with other Hebrew terms for "man," namely, *'ish,* meaning "a male person" (compare Nu 23:19; Job 35:8; Jer 50:40) and *'enohsh',* "a mortal man." (Compare Ps 8:4; Isa 51:12; 56:2.) At Psalm 144:3 the "son of mortal man" is *ben-'enohsh',* while the Aramaic equivalent (*bar 'enash'*) appears at Daniel 7:13.

In Greek the expression is *hui·os' tou an·thro'pou,* the latter part of the phrase representing the Greek generic word for "man" (*an'thropos*).—Mt 16:27.

In the Hebrew Scriptures the most frequent occurrence of the expression is in the book of Ezekiel, where over 90 times God addresses the prophet as "son of man." (Eze 2:1, 3, 6, 8) The designation as so used apparently serves to emphasize that the prophet is simply an earthling, thus heightening the contrast between the human spokesman and the Source of his message, the Most High God. The same designation is applied to the prophet Daniel at Daniel 8:17.

Christ Jesus, "the Son of Man." In the Gospel accounts the expression is found nearly 80 times, applying in every case to Jesus Christ, being used by him to refer to himself. (Mt 8:20; 9:6; 10:23) The occurrences outside the Gospel accounts are at Acts 7:56; Hebrews 2:6; and Revelation 1:13; 14:14.

Jesus' application of this expression to himself clearly showed that God's Son was now indeed a human, having 'become flesh' (Joh 1:14), having 'come to be out of a woman' through his conception and birth to the Jewish virgin Mary. (Ga 4:4; Lu 1:34-36) Hence he had not simply materialized a human body as angels had previously done; he was not an incarnation but was actually a 'son of mankind' through his human mother.—Compare 1Jo 4:2, 3; 2Jo 7; see FLESH.

For this reason the apostle Paul could apply Psalm 8 as prophetic of Jesus Christ. In his letter to the Hebrews (2:5-9), Paul quoted the verses reading: "What is mortal man ['enohsh'] that you keep him in mind, and the son of earthling man [ben-'a·dham'] that you take care of him? You also proceeded to make him a little less than godlike ones ["a little lower than angels," at Hebrews 2:7], and with glory and splendor you then crowned him. You make him dominate over the works of your hands; everything you have put under his feet." (Ps 8:4-6; compare Ps 144:3.) Paul shows that, to fulfill this prophetic psalm, Jesus indeed was made "a little lower than angels," becoming actually a mortal "son of earthling man," that he might die as such and thereby "taste death for every man," thereafter being crowned with glory and splendor by his Father, who resurrected him.—Heb 2:8, 9; compare Heb 2:14; Php 2:5-9.

The designation "Son of man," therefore, also serves to identify Jesus Christ as the great Kinsman of mankind, having the power to redeem them from bondage to sin and death, as well as to identify him as the great Avenger of blood.—Le 25:48, 49; Nu 35:1-29; see AVENGER OF BLOOD; RANSOM; REPURCHASE, REPURCHASER.

Thus, Jesus' being called the "Son of David" (Mt 1:1; 9:27) emphasizes his being the heir of the Kingdom covenant to be fulfilled in David's line; his being called the "Son of man" calls attention to his being of the human race by virtue of his fleshly birth; his being called the "Son of God" stresses his being of divine origin, not descended from the sinner Adam or inheriting imperfection from him but having a fully righteous standing with God.—Mt 16:13-17.

What is "the sign of the Son of man"?

However, there is evidently another major reason for Jesus' frequent use of the expression "Son of man" as applying to himself. This is with regard to the fulfillment of the prophecy recorded at Daniel 7:13, 14. In vision, Daniel saw "someone like a son of man" coming with the clouds of the heavens, gaining access to "the Ancient of Days," and being granted "rulership and dignity and kingdom, that the peoples, national groups and languages should all serve even him," his Kingdom being an enduring one.

Because the angelic interpretation of the vision in Daniel 7:18, 22, and 27 speaks of "the holy ones of the Supreme One" as taking possession of this Kingdom, many commentators have endeavored to show that the "son of man" is here a 'corporate personality,' that is, 'the saints of God in their corporate aspect, regarded collectively as a people,' 'the glorified and ideal people of Israel.' This reasoning, however, proves superficial in the light of the Christian Greek Scriptures. It fails to consider that Christ Jesus, God's anointed King, made a 'covenant for a kingdom' with his followers that they might share with him in his Kingdom, and that, while they are to rule as kings and priests, it is under his headship and by his grant of authority. (Lu 22:28-30; Re 5:9, 10; 20:4-6) Thus, they receive ruling authority over the nations only because he has first received such authority from the Sovereign God.—Re 2:26, 27; 3:21.

The correct understanding is made more evident by Jesus' own statements. Regarding "the sign of the Son of man," he stated that "they will see the Son of man coming on the clouds of heaven with power and great glory." (Mt 24:30) This was clearly a reference to Daniel's prophecy. So, likewise, was his answer to the high priest's interrogation, saying: "I am [the Christ, the Son of God]; and you persons will see the Son of man sitting at the right hand of power and coming with the clouds of heaven."—Mr 14:61, 62; Mt 26:63, 64.

Therefore the prophecy of the coming of the Son of man into the presence of the Ancient of Days, Jehovah God, clearly applies to an individual, the Messiah, Jesus Christ. The evidence is that it was so understood by the Jewish people. Rabbinic writings applied the prophecy to the Messiah. (Soncino Books of the Bible, edited by A. Cohen, 1951, commentary on Da 7:13) It was doubtless due to wanting some literal fulfillment of this prophecy that the Pharisees and Sadducees asked Jesus to "display to them a sign from heaven." (Mt 16:1; Mr 8:11) After Jesus had died as a man and had been resurrected to spirit life, Stephen had a vision in which "the heavens opened up" and he saw "the Son of man standing at God's right hand." (Ac 7:56) This shows that Jesus Christ, although sacrificing his human nature as a ransom for mankind, rightly retains the Messianic designation "Son of man" in his heavenly position.

The first part of Jesus' statement to the high priest about the coming of the Son of man spoke of him as "sitting at the right hand of power." This is evidently an allusion to the prophetic Psalm 110, Jesus Christ having earlier shown that this psalm applied to him. (Mt 22:42-45) This psalm, as well as the apostle's application of it at Hebrews 10:12, 13, reveals that there would be a waiting period for Jesus Christ before his Father would send him forth to "go subduing in the midst of [his] enemies." It therefore appears that the fulfillment of the prophecy of Daniel 7:13, 14 comes, not at the time of Jesus' resurrection and ascension to heaven, but at the time of his being authorized by God to take action against all opposers in vigorous expression of his kingly authority. The 'coming of the Son of man to the Ancient of Days,' then, apparently corresponds in time to the situation presented at Revelation 12:5-10, when the symbolic man-child is brought forth and caught up to God's throne. Then war breaks out in heaven, and the cry goes up: "Now have come to pass the salvation and the power and the kingdom of our God *and the authority of his Christ.*"

Further prophetic visions in Revelation (17: 12-14; 19:11-21) show the exercise of full regnal power by the Messianic King over "peoples, national groups and languages" (Da 7:14), and hence the one "like a son of man" at Revelation 14:14 undoubtedly also represents Jesus Christ, as does the one so described at Revelation 1:13. —Compare Re 14:14-20; 19:15; and 1:13-18; see KINGDOM OF GOD ("Kingdom of Our Lord and of His Christ").

As to the 'Son of man's coming on the clouds' and being seen by "every eye" (Mt 24:30; Re 1:7), see CLOUD (Illustrative Usage); EYE; PRESENCE.

SOPATER
(Sop'a·ter) [probably, Save the Father]. A Beroean Christian associated with Paul in Greece at the time of Paul's third missionary journey. Sopater was a son of Pyrrhus and may be the same person as Sosipater in Rome, to whom Paul sent greetings.—Ac 20:2-6; Ro 16:21.

SOPHERETH
(So·phe'reth) [from a root meaning "count; number"]. Apparently an ancestor of a family ("the sons of Sophereth") among "the sons of the servants of Solomon" who returned from the Babylonian exile. (Ezr 2:55; Ne 7:57) Ezra puts a definite article in front of *So·phe'reth,* making it *Has·so·phe'reth,* possibly meaning "the scribe." Some suggest that the sons of Sophereth were a staff of scribes or copyists. The meanings of some of the other names in the list might allow for reference to an occupation, while others do not.

SORCERER.
See MAGIC AND SORCERY.

SOREK, TORRENT VALLEY OF
(So'rek). Location of the home of Delilah, where Samson was seduced to reveal the secret of his strength, leading to his capture, blinding, and imprisonment by the Philistines. (Jg 16:4-21) It is identified with the Wadi es-Sarar (Nahal Soreq), which cuts westward across the Shephelah toward the Mediterranean Sea. The name Sorek, which means "Choice Red Vine," seems to be preserved in Khirbet Suriq, about 25 km (16 mi) W of Jerusalem, situated on the N side of the wadi and opposite Beth-shemesh. Much of this region, as today, was probably suited for vineyards (a possible reason for its name). The Philistine wagon that returned the ark of the covenant to the Israelites evidently followed the torrent valley of Sorek from Ekron on the road to Beth-shemesh. —1Sa 5:10; 6:10-12.

SORREL.
Any of a number of plants of the buckwheat family having a sour taste because of the presence of oxalic acid in their juicy leaves and stems. The radical leaves of garden sorrel (*Rumex acetosa*) grow in a cluster. Shaped like an arrow at the base, the somewhat oval leaves measure about 10 cm (4 in.) in length. The flower stalks may attain a height of about 0.6 m (2 ft) or more. Anciently, the Israelites mixed sorrel with the fodder for their cattle and asses.—Isa 30:24.

SOSIPATER
(So·sip'a·ter) [Saving the Father]. A companion of Paul when in Corinth, whom the apostle described as 'my relative,' and whose greetings are sent from Corinth in Paul's letter to the Romans. (Ro 16:21) He is possibly the same person as Sopater, mentioned at Acts 20:4 as associated with Paul in Greece.

SOSTHENES
(Sos'the·nes) [from roots meaning "save" and "strength"]. The presiding officer of the Corinthian synagogue during Paul's visit in Corinth; possibly the successor of Crispus, who became a Christian. When Proconsul Gallio declined to hear the Jews' charges against Paul's religious teaching, the crowd took Sosthenes and beat him. Certain manuscripts say the crowd was composed of anti-Jewish "Greeks"; others read "Jews." Both, however, are interpolations, since the three oldest manuscripts do not tell us which partisan group attacked Sosthenes.—Ac 18:8, 12-17.

It is possible that this bad experience suffered by Sosthenes led to his conversion to Christianity and later association with Paul at Ephesus, for in the salutations at the outset of his first letter to the Corinthians, Paul includes those of a certain Sosthenes (a not-too-common Greek name), speaking of him as "our brother."—1Co 1:1.

SOTAI (So'tai). One of Solomon's servants whose offspring returned to Jerusalem with Zerubbabel in 537 B.C.E.—Ezr 2:55; Ne 7:57.

SOUL. The original-language terms (Heb., *ne'-phesh* [נֶפֶשׁ]; Gr., *psy·khe'* [ψυχή]) as used in the Scriptures show "soul" to be a person, an animal, or the life that a person or an animal enjoys.

The connotations that the English "soul" commonly carries in the minds of most persons are not in agreement with the meaning of the Hebrew and Greek words as used by the inspired Bible writers. This fact has steadily gained wider acknowledgment. Back in 1897, in the *Journal of Biblical Literature* (Vol. XVI, p. 30), Professor C. A. Briggs, as a result of detailed analysis of the use of *ne'phesh*, observed: "Soul in English usage at the present time conveys usually a very different meaning from נפש [*ne'phesh*] in Hebrew, and it is easy for the incautious reader to misinterpret."

More recently, when The Jewish Publication Society of America issued a new translation of the Torah, or first five books of the Bible, the editor-in-chief, H. M. Orlinsky of Hebrew Union College, stated that the word "soul" had been virtually eliminated from this translation because, "the Hebrew word in question here is 'Nefesh.'" He added: "Other translators have interpreted it to mean 'soul,' which is completely inaccurate. The Bible does not say we have a soul. 'Nefesh' is the person himself, his need for food, the very blood in his veins, his being."—*The New York Times*, October 12, 1962.

What is the origin of the teaching that the human soul is invisible and immortal?

The difficulty lies in the fact that the meanings popularly attached to the English word "soul" stem primarily, not from the Hebrew or Christian Greek Scriptures, but from ancient Greek philosophy, actually pagan religious thought. Greek philosopher Plato, for example, quotes Socrates as saying: "The soul, . . . if it departs pure, dragging with it nothing of the body, . . . goes away into that which is like itself, into the invisible, divine, immortal, and wise, and when it arrives there it is happy, freed from error and folly and fear . . . and all the other human ills, and . . . lives in truth through all after time with the gods."—*Phaedo*, 80, D, E; 81, A.

In direct contrast with the Greek teaching of the *psy·khe'* (soul) as being immaterial, intangi-

ble, invisible, and immortal, the Scriptures show that both *psy·khe'* and *ne'phesh*, as used with reference to earthly creatures, refer to that which is material, tangible, visible, and mortal.

The *New Catholic Encyclopedia* says: "*Nepes* [*ne'phesh*] is a term of far greater extension than our 'soul,' signifying life (Ex 21.23; Dt 19.21) and its various vital manifestations: breathing (Gn 35.18; Jb 41.13[21]), blood [Gn 9.4; Dt 12.23; Ps 140(141).8], desire (2 Sm 3.21; Prv 23.2). The soul in the O[ld] T[estament] means not a part of man, but the whole man—man as a living being. Similarly, in the N[ew] T[estament] it signifies human life: the life of an individual, conscious subject (Mt 2.20; 6.25; Lk 12.22-23; 14.26; Jn 10.11, 15, 17; 13.37)."—1967, Vol. XIII, p. 467.

The Roman Catholic translation, *The New American Bible*, in its "Glossary of Biblical Theology Terms" (pp. 27, 28), says: "In the New Testament, to 'save one's soul' (*Mk 8:35*) does not mean to save some 'spiritual' part of man, as opposed to his 'body' (in the Platonic sense) but the whole person with emphasis on the fact that the person is living, desiring, loving and willing, etc., in addition to being concrete and physical."—Edition published by P. J. Kenedy & Sons, New York, 1970.

Ne'phesh evidently comes from a root meaning "breathe" and in a literal sense *ne'phesh* could be rendered as "a breather." Koehler and Baumgartner's *Lexicon in Veteris Testamenti Libros* (Leiden, 1958, p. 627) defines it as: "the breathing substance, making man a[nd] animal living beings Gn 1, 20, the soul (strictly distinct from the greek notion of soul) the seat of which is the blood Gn 9, 4f Lv 17, 11 Dt 12, 23: (249 X) . . . soul = living being, individual, person."

As for the Greek word *psy·khe'*, Greek-English lexicons give such definitions as *"life,"* and "the *conscious self* or *personality* as centre of emotions, desires, and affections," "a living being," and they show that even in non-Biblical Greek works the term was used "of animals." Of course, such sources, treating as they do primarily of classical Greek writings, include all the meanings that the pagan Greek philosophers gave to the word, including that of *"departed spirit,"* "the immaterial and immortal *soul,"* "the *spirit* of the universe," and "the immaterial principle of movement and life." Evidently because some of the pagan philosophers taught that the soul emerged from the body at death, the term *psy·khe'* was also applied to the *"butterfly* or *moth,"* which creatures go through a metamorphosis, changing from caterpillar to winged creature.—Liddell and Scott's *Greek-English Lexicon*, revised by H. Jones, 1968, pp. 2026, 2027; Donnegan's *New Greek and English Lexicon*, 1836, p. 1404.

The ancient Greek writers applied *psy·khe'* in various ways and were not consistent, their personal and religious philosophies influencing their use of the term. Of Plato, to whose philosophy the common ideas about the English "soul" may be attributed (as is generally acknowledged), it is stated: "While he sometimes speaks of one of [the alleged] three parts of the soul, the 'intelligible,' as necessarily immortal, while the other two parts are mortal, he also speaks as if there were two souls in one body, one immortal and divine, the other mortal."—*The Evangelical Quarterly*, London, 1931, Vol. III, p. 121, "Thoughts on the Tripartite Theory of Human Nature," by A. McCaig.

In view of such inconsistency in non-Biblical writings, it is essential to let the Scriptures speak for themselves, showing what the inspired writers meant by their use of the term *psy·khe'*, as well as by *ne'phesh*. *Ne'phesh* occurs 754 times in the Masoretic text of the Hebrew Scriptures, while *psy·khe'* appears by itself 102 times in the Westcott and Hort text of the Christian Greek Scriptures, giving a total of 856 occurrences. (See *NW* appendix, p. 1573.) This frequency of occurrence makes possible a clear concept of the sense that these terms conveyed to the minds of the inspired Bible writers and the sense their writings should convey to our mind. An examination shows that, while the sense of these terms is broad, with different shades of meaning, among the Bible writers there was no inconsistency, confusion, or disharmony as to man's nature, as existed among the Grecian philosophers of the so-called Classical Period.

Earth's First Souls. The initial occurrences of *ne'phesh* are found at Genesis 1:20-23. On the fifth creative "day" God said: "'Let the waters swarm forth a swarm of living souls [*ne'phesh*] and let flying creatures fly over the earth . . .' And God proceeded to create the great sea monsters and every living soul [*ne'phesh*] that moves about, which the waters swarmed forth according to their kinds, and every winged flying creature according to its kind." Similarly on the sixth creative "day" *ne'phesh* is applied to the "domestic animal and moving animal and wild beast of the earth" as "living souls."—Ge 1:24.

After man's creation, God's instruction to him again used the term *ne'phesh* with regard to the animal creation, "everything moving upon the earth in which there is life as a soul [literally, in which there is living soul (*ne'phesh*)]." (Ge 1:30)

Other examples of animals being so designated are found at Genesis 2:19; 9:10-16; Leviticus 11:10, 46; 24:18; Numbers 31:28; Ezekiel 47:9. Notably, the Christian Greek Scriptures coincide in applying the Greek *psy·khe'* to animals, as at Revelation 8:9; 16:3, where it is used of creatures in the sea.

Thus, the Scriptures clearly show that *ne'phesh* and *psy·khe'* are used to designate the animal creation lower than man. The same terms apply to man.

The Human Soul. Precisely the same Hebrew phrase used of the animal creation, namely, *ne'phesh chai·yah'* (living soul), is applied to Adam, when, after God formed man out of dust from the ground and blew into his nostrils the breath of life, "the man came to be a living soul." (Ge 2:7) Man was distinct from the animal creation, but that distinction was not because he was a *ne'phesh* (soul) and they were not. Rather, the record shows that it was because man alone was created "in God's image." (Ge 1:26, 27) He was created with moral qualities like those of God, with power and wisdom far superior to the animals; hence he could have in subjection all the lower forms of creature life. (Ge 1:26, 28) Man's organism was more complex, as well as more versatile, than that of the animals. (Compare 1Co 15:39.) Likewise, Adam had, but lost, the prospect of eternal life; this is never stated with regard to the creatures lower than man.—Ge 2:15-17; 3:22-24.

It is true that the account says that 'God proceeded to blow into the man's nostrils the breath [form of *nesha·mah'*] of life,' whereas this is not stated in the account of the animal creation. Clearly, however, the account of the creation of man is much more detailed than that of the creation of animals. Moreover, Genesis 7:21-23, in describing the Flood's destruction of "all flesh" outside the ark, lists the animal creatures along with mankind and says: "Everything in which the breath [form of *nesha·mah'*] of the force of life was active in its nostrils, namely, all that were on the dry ground, died." Obviously, the breath of life of the animal creatures also originally came from the Creator, Jehovah God.

So, too, the "spirit" (Heb., *ru'ach;* Gr., *pneu'ma*), or life-force, of man is not distinct from the life-force in animals, as is shown by Ecclesiastes 3:19-21, which states that "they all have but one spirit [*u·ru'ach*]."

Soul—A Living Creature. As stated, man "came to be a living soul"; hence man *was* a soul, he did not *have* a soul as something immaterial, invisible, and intangible residing inside him. The apostle Paul shows that the Christian teaching did not differ from the earlier Hebrew teaching, for he quotes Genesis 2:7 in saying: "It is even so written: 'The first man Adam became a living soul [psy·khen' zo'san].' . . . The first man is out of the earth and made of dust."—1Co 15:45-47.

The Genesis account shows that a living soul results from the combination of the earthly body with the breath of life. The expression "breath of the force of life [literally, breath of the spirit, or active force (ru'ach), of life]" (Ge 7:22) indicates that it is by breathing air (with its oxygen) that the life-force, or "spirit," in all creatures, man and animals, is sustained. This life-force is found in every cell of the creature's body, as is discussed under LIFE; SPIRIT.

Since the term ne'phesh refers to the creature itself, we should expect to find the normal physical functions or characteristics of fleshly creatures attributed to it. This is exactly the case. Ne'phesh (soul) is spoken of as eating flesh, fat, blood, or similar material things (Le 7:18, 20, 25, 27; 17:10, 12, 15; De 23:24); being hungry for or craving food and drink (De 12:15, 20, 21; Ps 107:9; Pr 19:15; 27:7; Isa 29:8; 32:6; Mic 7:1); being made fat (Pr 11:25); fasting (Ps 35:13); touching unclean things, such as a dead body (Le 5:2; 7:21; 17:15; 22:6; Nu 19:13); being 'seized as a pledge' or being 'kidnapped' (De 24:6, 7); doing work (Le 23:30); being refreshed by cold water when tired (Pr 25:25); being purchased (Le 22:11; Eze 27:13); being given as a vow offering (Le 27:2); being put in irons (Ps 105:18); being sleepless (Ps 119:28); and struggling for breath (Jer 15:9).

It may be noted that in many texts reference is made to "my soul," "his [or her] soul," "your soul," and so forth. This is because ne'phesh and psy·khe' can mean one's own self as a soul. The sense of the term can therefore often be expressed in English by use of personal pronouns. Thus Lexicon in Veteris Testamenti Libros (p. 627) shows that "my ne'phesh" means "I" (Ge 27:4, 25; Isa 1:14); "your [singular] ne'phesh" means "thou" or "you" (Ge 27:19, 31; Isa 43:4; 51:23); "his ne'-phesh" means "he, himself" (Nu 30:2; Isa 53:10); "her ne'phesh" means "she, herself" (Nu 30:5-12), and so forth.

The Greek term psy·khe' is used similarly. Vine's Expository Dictionary of Old and New Testament Words (1981, Vol. 4, p. 54) says it may be used as "the equivalent of the personal pronoun, used for emphasis and effect:—1st person, John 10:24 ('us'); Heb. 10:38; cp. [compare] Gen. 12:13; Num. 23:10; Jud. 16:30; Ps. 120:2 ('me'); 2nd person, 2 Cor. 12:15; Heb. 13:17," and so forth.

Represents life as a creature. Both ne'phesh and psy·khe' are also used to mean life—not merely as an abstract force or principle—but life as a creature, human or animal.

Thus when Rachel was giving birth to Benjamin, her ne'phesh ("soul," or life as a creature) went out from her and she died. (Ge 35:16-19) She ceased to be a living creature. Similarly, when the prophet Elijah performed a miracle regarding the dead son of the widow of Zarephath, the child's ne'phesh ("soul," or life as a creature) came back into him and "he came to life," was again a living creature.—1Ki 17:17-23.

Because the creature's life is so inseparably connected with and dependent on blood (shed blood standing for the life of the person or creature [Ge 4:10; 2Ki 9:26; Ps 9:12; Isa 26:21]), the Scriptures speak of the ne'phesh (soul) as being "in the blood." (Ge 9:4; Le 17:11, 14; De 12:23) This is, obviously, not meant literally, inasmuch as the Scriptures also speak of the "blood of your souls" (Ge 9:5; compare Jer 2:34) and the many references already considered could not reasonably be applied solely to the blood or its life-supporting qualities.

Ne'phesh (soul) is not used with reference to the creation of vegetable life on the third creative "day" (Ge 1:11-13) or thereafter, since vegetation is bloodless.

Examples of the use of the Greek psy·khe' to mean "life as a creature" may be found at Matthew 6:25; 10:39; 16:25, 26; Luke 12:20; John 10:11, 15; 13:37, 38; 15:13; Acts 20:10. Since God's servants have the hope of a resurrection in the event of death, they have the hope of living again as "souls," or living creatures. For that reason Jesus could say that "whoever loses his soul [his life as a creature] for the sake of me and the good news will save it. Really, of what benefit is it for a man to gain the whole world and to forfeit his soul? What, really, would a man give in exchange for his soul?" (Mr 8:35-37) Similarly, he stated: "He that is fond of his soul destroys it, but he that hates his soul in this world will safeguard it for everlasting life." (Joh 12:25) These texts, and others like them, show the correct understanding of Jesus' words at Matthew 10:28: "Do not become fearful of those who kill the body but cannot kill the soul; but rather be in fear of him that can destroy both soul and body in Gehenna." While men can kill the body, they cannot kill the person for all time, inasmuch as he lives in God's purpose (compare Lu 20:37, 38) and God can and will restore such faithful one to life as a creature by means of a resurrection. For God's servants, the loss of their "soul," or life as a creature, is only temporary, not permanent.—Compare Re 12:11.

Mortal and destructible. On the other hand, Matthew 10:28 states that God "can destroy both soul [*psy·khen'*] and body in Gehenna." This shows that *psy·khe'* does not refer to something immortal or indestructible. There is, in fact, not one case in the entire Scriptures, Hebrew and Greek, in which the words *ne'phesh* or *psy·khe'* are modified by terms such as immortal, indestructible, imperishable, deathless, or the like. (See IMMORTALITY; INCORRUPTION.) On the other hand, there are scores of texts in the Hebrew and Greek Scriptures that speak of the *ne'phesh* or *psy·khe'* (soul) as mortal and subject to death (Ge 19:19, 20; Nu 23:10; Jos 2:13, 14; Jg 5:18; 16:16, 30; 1Ki 20:31, 32; Ps 22:29; Eze 18:4, 20; Mt 2:20; 26:38; Mr 3:4; Heb 10:39; Jas 5:20); as dying, being "cut off" or destroyed (Ge 17:14; Ex 12:15; Le 7:20; 23:29; Jos 10:28-39; Ps 78:50; Eze 13:19; 22:27; Ac 3:23; Re 8:9; 16:3), whether by sword (Jos 10:37; Eze 33:6) or by suffocation (Job 7:15), or being in danger of death due to drowning (Jon 2:5); and also as going down into the pit or into Sheol (Job 33:22; Ps 89:48) or being delivered therefrom (Ps 16:10; 30:3; 49:15; Pr 23:14).

Dead soul. The expression 'deceased or dead soul' also appears a number of times, meaning simply "a dead person."—Le 19:28; 21:1, 11; 22:4; Nu 5:2; 6:6; Hag 2:13; compare Nu 19:11, 13.

Desire. At times the word *ne'phesh* is used to express the desire of the individual, one that fills him and then occupies him in achieving its goal. Proverbs 13:2, for example, says of those dealing treacherously that 'their very soul is violence,' that is, that they are 'all out' for violence, in effect, become violence personified. (Compare Ge 34:3, ftn; Ps 27:12; 35:25; 41:2.) Israel's false shepherds are called "dogs strong in soul[ful desire]," who have known no satisfaction.—Isa 56:11, 12; compare Pr 23:1-3; Hab 2:5.

Serving With One's Whole Soul. The "soul" basically means the entire person, as has been shown. Yet certain texts exhort us to seek for, love, and serve God with 'all our heart *and* all our soul' (De 4:29; 11:13, 18), while Deuteronomy 6:5 says: "You must love Jehovah your God with all your heart and all your soul and all your vital force." Jesus said it was necessary to serve with one's whole soul and strength and, additionally, "with your whole mind." (Mr 12:30; Lu 10:27) The question arises as to why these other things are mentioned with the soul, since it embraces them all. To illustrate the probable meaning: A person might sell himself (his soul) into slavery to another, thereby becoming the possession of his owner and master. Yet he might not serve his master wholeheartedly, with full motivation and desire to please him, and thus he might not use his full strength or his full mental capacity to advance his master's interests. (Compare Eph 6:5; Col 3:22.) Hence these other facets are evidently mentioned to focus attention on them so that we do not fail to remember and consider them in our service to God, to whom we belong, and to his Son, whose life was the ransom price that bought us. "Whole-souled" service to God involves the entire person, no bodily part, function, capacity, or desire being left out.—Compare Mt 5:28-30; Lu 21:34-36; Eph 6:6-9; Php 3:19; Col 3:23, 24.

Soul and Spirit Are Distinct. The "spirit" (Heb., *ru'ach*; Gr., *pneu'ma*) should not be confused with the "soul" (Heb., *ne'phesh*; Gr., *psy·khe'*), for they refer to different things. Thus, Hebrews 4:12 speaks of the Word of God as 'piercing even to the dividing of soul and spirit, and of joints and their marrow.' (Compare also Php 1:27; 1Th 5:23.) As has been shown, the soul (*ne'phesh*; *psy·khe'*) is the creature itself. The spirit (*ru'ach*; *pneu'ma*) generally refers to the life-force of the living creature or soul, though the original-language terms may also have other meanings.

Illustrating further the distinction between the Greek *psy·khe'* and *pneu'ma* is the apostle Paul's discussion, in his first letter to the Corinthians, of the resurrection of Christians to spirit life. Here he contrasts "that which is physical [*psy·khi·kon'*, literally, soulical]" with "that which is spiritual [*pneu·ma·ti·kon'*]." Thus, he shows that Christians until the time of their death have a "soulical" body, even as did the first man Adam; whereas, in their resurrection such anointed Christians receive a spiritual body like that of the glorified Jesus Christ. (1Co 15:42-49) Jude makes a somewhat similar comparison in speaking of "animalistic men [*psy·khi·koi'*, literally, soulical (men)], not having spirituality [literally, not having spirit (*pneu'ma*)]."—Jude 19.

God as Having Soul. In view of the foregoing, it appears that the scriptures in which God speaks of "my soul" (Le 26:11, 30; Ps 24:4; Isa 42:1) are yet another instance of an anthropomorphic usage, that is, the attributing of physical and human characteristics to God to facilitate understanding, as when God is spoken of as having eyes, hands, and so forth. By speaking of 'my *ne'phesh*,' Jehovah clearly means "myself" or "my person." "God is a Spirit [*Pneu'ma*]."—Joh 4:24; see JEHOVAH (Descriptions of his presence).

SOURDOUGH.

SOURDOUGH. A piece of dough that is set aside for a day or longer and allowed to sour or ferment. The Hebrew term *se'or'* denotes such sourdough and means "fermented or leavened mass." Sourdough readily leavens new mixtures to which it is added.

The Israelites used sourdough in making leavened bread. The lump of dough preserved from a former baking was generally dissolved in water in the kneading trough prior to the adding of the flour, or it might be put in the flour and then kneaded along with it. The latter seems to be the method referred to by Jesus Christ when he said: "The kingdom of the heavens is like leaven, which a woman took and hid in three large measures of flour, until the whole mass was fermented." (Mt 13:33; Lu 13:20, 21) Though there is no direct evidence, it has been suggested that the Jews also used wine dregs as yeast.

Israel's grain offerings presented by fire to Jehovah were not to be made with sourdough. (Le 2:11) Also, the Israelites were expressly commanded not to have sourdough (here an apparent symbol of corruption and sin) in their homes or within the boundaries of their territory during the seven-day Festival of Unleavened Bread. (Ex 12:15; 13:7; De 16:4) Anyone eating something leavened during that time was to be "cut off from the assembly of Israel."—Ex 12:19.

In ancient Egypt it was also customary, when baking, to set aside some dough, to be used for leavening fresh dough. Even today, when the kneading of dough has been completed, some people of Cyprus, for instance, put aside a piece of dough in a warm place. After 36 to 48 hours it can be used to ferment an entire lump of new dough.

Paul may have had sourdough in mind when he urged the Corinthians: "Clear away the old leaven [Gr., *zy'men*], that you may be a new lump, according as you are free from ferment."—1Co 5:7; see LEAVEN.

SOUTH.

SOUTH. See NEGEB.

SOVEREIGNTY.

SOVEREIGNTY. Supremacy in rule or power; the dominion or rule of a lord, king, emperor, or the like; the power that, in the final analysis, determines the government of a state.

In the Hebrew Scriptures the word *'Adho·nai'* appears frequently, and the expression *'Adho·nai' Yehwih'* 285 times. *'Adho·nai'* is a plural form of *'a·dhohn'*, meaning "lord; master." The plural form *'adho·nim'* may be applied to men in simple plurality, as "lords," or "masters." But the term *'Adho·nai'* without an additional suffix is always used in the Scriptures with reference to God, the plural being employed to denote excellence or majesty. It is most frequently rendered "Lord" by translators. When it appears with the name of God (*'Adho·nai' Yehwih'*), as, for example, at Psalm 73:28, the expression is translated "Lord GOD" (*AT, KJ, RS*); "Lord God" (*Dy* [72:28]); "Lord, my Master" (*Kx* [72:28]); "Lord Jehovah" (*Yg*); "Sovereign Lord Jehovah" (*NW*). In Psalms 47:9; 138:5; 150:2, Moffatt uses the word "sovereign," but not to translate *'Adho·nai'*.

The Greek word *de·spo'tes* means one who possesses supreme authority, or absolute ownership and uncontrolled power. (*Vine's Expository Dictionary of Old and New Testament Words,* 1981, Vol. 3, pp. 18, 46) It is translated "lord," "master," "owner," and when used in direct address to God is rendered "Lord" (*KJ, Yg,* and others), "Ruler of all" (*Kx*), "Sovereign Lord" (*NW*), at Luke 2:29, Acts 4:24, and Revelation 6:10. In the last text, Knox, *The New English Bible, Moffatt,* and the *Revised Standard Version* read "Sovereign Lord"; Young's translation and the *Kingdom Interlinear* read "master."

So, while the Hebrew and Greek texts do not have a separate qualifying word for "sovereign," the flavor is contained in the words *'Adho·nai'* and *de·spo'tes* when they are used in the Scriptures as applying to Jehovah God, the qualification denoting the excellence of his lordship.

Jehovah's Sovereignty. Jehovah God is the Sovereign of the universe ("sovereign of the world," Ps 47:9, *Mo*) by reason of his Creatorship, his Godship, and his supremacy as the Almighty. (Ge 17:1; Ex 6:3; Re 16:14) He is the Owner of all things and the Source of all authority and power, the Supreme Ruler in government. (Ps 24:1; Isa 40:21-23; Re 4:11; 11:15) The psalmist sang of him: "Jehovah himself has firmly established his throne in the very heavens, and over everything his own kingship has held domination." (Ps 103:19; 145:13) Jesus' disciples prayed, addressing God: "Sovereign Lord, you are the One who made the heaven and the earth." (Ac 4:24, *NW; Mo*) To the nation of Israel, God himself constituted all three branches of government, the judicial, the legislative, and the executive. The prophet Isaiah said: "Jehovah is our Judge, Jehovah is our Statute-giver, Jehovah is our King; he himself will save us." (Isa 33:22) Moses gives a notable description of God as Sovereign at Deuteronomy 10:17.

In his sovereign position Jehovah has the right and authority to delegate ruling responsibilities.

David was made king of Israel, and the Scriptures speak of 'the kingdom of David' as though it was *his* kingdom. But David acknowledged Jehovah as the great Sovereign Ruler, saying: "Yours, O Jehovah, are the greatness and the mightiness and the beauty and the excellency and the dignity; for everything in the heavens and in the earth is yours. Yours is the kingdom, O Jehovah, the One also lifting yourself up as head over all."—1Ch 29:11.

Earthly Rulers. The rulers of the nations of earth exercise their limited rulership by the toleration or permission of the Sovereign Lord Jehovah. That the political governments do not receive their authority from God, that is, that they are not acting by reason of any grant of authority or power from him, is shown at Revelation 13:1, 2, where the seven-headed, ten-horned wild beast is said to get "its power and its throne and great authority" from the Dragon, Satan the Devil.—Re 12:9; see BEASTS, SYMBOLIC.

So, while God has allowed various rulerships of men to come and go, one of their mighty kings, after having had demonstrated, in his own experience, the fact of Jehovah's sovereignty, was moved to say: "His rulership is a rulership to time indefinite and his kingdom is for generation after generation. And all the inhabitants of the earth are being considered as merely nothing, and he is doing according to his own will among the army of the heavens and the inhabitants of the earth. And there exists no one that can check his hand or that can say to him, 'What have you been doing?' "—Da 4:34, 35.

Accordingly, as long as it is God's will to permit man-made governments to rule, the apostle Paul's injunction to Christians will apply: "Let every soul be in subjection to the superior authorities, for there is no authority except by God; the existing authorities stand placed in their relative positions by God." The apostle then goes on to point out that when such governments act to punish one who does what is bad, the 'superior authority' or ruler (even though not a faithful worshiper of God) is acting indirectly as a minister of God in this particular capacity, expressing wrath upon the one practicing what is bad.—Ro 13:1-6.

As to such authorities' being "placed in their relative positions by God," the Scriptures indicate that this does not mean that God formed these governments or that he backs them up. Rather, he has maneuvered them to suit his good purpose, with relation to his will concerning his servants in the earth. Moses said: "When the Most High gave the nations an inheritance, when he parted the sons of Adam from one another, he proceeded to fix the boundary of the peoples with regard for the number of the sons of Israel."—De 32:8.

God's Son as King. Following the overthrow of the last king to sit on "Jehovah's throne" in Jerusalem (1Ch 29:23), the prophet Daniel was given a vision describing the future appointment of God's own Son to serve as King. Jehovah's position stands out clearly when he, as the Ancient of Days, grants rulership to his Son. The account states: "I kept on beholding in the visions of the night, and, see there! with the clouds of the heavens someone like a son of man happened to be coming; and to the Ancient of Days he gained access, and they brought him up close even before that One. And to him there were given rulership and dignity and kingdom, that the peoples, national groups and languages should all serve even him. His rulership is an indefinitely lasting rulership that will not pass away, and his kingdom one that will not be brought to ruin." (Da 7:13, 14) A comparison of this text with Matthew 26:63, 64 leaves no doubt that the "son of man" in Daniel's vision is Jesus Christ. He gains access to Jehovah's presence and is given rulership. —Compare Ps 2:8, 9; Mt 28:18.

Jehovah's Sovereignty Challenged. Wickedness has been in existence for nearly all the years that Bible chronology indicates man has been on the earth. All mankind have been dying, and sins and transgressions against God have multiplied. (Ro 5:12, 15, 16) Since the Bible indicates that God gave man a perfect start, the questions have arisen: How did sin, imperfection, and wickedness get their start? And why has the Almighty God allowed these things to remain for centuries? The answers lie in a challenge against God's sovereignty that brought forth a paramount issue involving mankind.

What God wants in those who serve him. Jehovah God, by his words and acts, has, over the centuries, proved that he is a God of love and undeserved kindness, exercising perfect justice and judgment, and extending mercy to those seeking to serve him. (Ex 34:6, 7; Ps 89:14; see MERCY; RIGHTEOUSNESS.) Even to the ungrateful and wicked he has expressed kindness. (Mt 5:45; Lu 6:35; Ro 5:8) He delights in the fact that his sovereignty is administered in love.—Jer 9:24.

Accordingly, the kind of persons he desires in his universe are persons who serve him because of love for him and for his fine qualities. They must love God first and their neighbor second. (Mt 22:37-39) They must love Jehovah's sovereignty; they must desire it and prefer it over any other. (Ps 84:10) They must be persons that, even if it were possible for them to become independent, would choose His sovereignty because they know that his rulership is far wiser, more righteous, and better than any other. (Isa 55:8-11; Jer 10:23; Ro 7:18) Such persons serve God not merely because of fear of his almightiness nor for selfish reasons but out of love of his righteousness, justice, and wisdom and because of having the knowledge of Jehovah's greatness and lovingkindness. (Ps 97:10; 119:104, 128, 163) They exclaim with the apostle Paul: "O the depth of God's riches and wisdom and knowledge! How unsearchable his judgments are and past tracing out his ways are! For 'who has come to know Jehovah's mind, or who has become his counselor?' Or, 'Who has first given to him, so that it must be repaid to him?' Because from him and by him and for him are all things. To him be the glory forever. Amen."—Ro 11:33-36.

Such ones come to *know* God, and really knowing him means to love him and stick to his sovereignty. The apostle John writes: "Everyone remaining in union with him does not practice sin; no one that practices sin has either seen him or come to know him." And, "He that does not love has not come to know God, because God is love." (1Jo 3:6; 4:8) Jesus knew his Father better than anyone else. He said: "All things have been delivered to me by my Father, and no one fully knows the Son but the Father, neither does anyone fully know the Father but the Son and anyone to whom the Son is willing to reveal him."—Mt 11:27.

A failure to develop love and appreciation. Consequently, when the challenge was hurled against Jehovah's sovereignty, it came from one who, although enjoying the benefits of God's sovereignty, did not appreciate and develop the knowledge of God and thereby deepen his love for him. This one was a spirit creature of God, an angel. When the human pair Adam and Eve were put on earth, this one saw an opportunity to set out on an attack on God's sovereignty. First, he would make an attempt (which proved successful) to turn Eve, then Adam, away from subjection to God's sovereignty. He hoped to establish a rival sovereignty.

As for Eve, the person approached first, she certainly had not appreciated her Creator and God, and she had not taken advantage of her opportunity to *know* him. She listened to the voice of an inferior, ostensibly the serpent, actually the rebellious angel. The Bible does not allude to any surprise on her part at hearing the serpent talk. It does say that the serpent was "the most cautious of all the wild beasts of the field that Jehovah God had made." (Ge 3:1) Whether it ate of the forbidden fruit of "the tree of the knowledge of good and bad" and then appeared to be made wise, able to speak, is not stated. The rebellious angel, using the serpent to speak to her, presented (as she supposed) the opportunity to become independent, "to be like God, knowing good and bad," and succeeded in convincing her that she would not die.—Ge 2:17; 3:4, 5; 2Co 11:3.

Adam, who also showed no appreciation and love for his Creator and Provider when faced with rebellion in his household, and who showed no loyalty to stand up for his God when put to the test, succumbed to Eve's persuasiveness. He evidently lost faith in God and His ability to provide all good things for His loyal servant. (Compare what Jehovah said to David after his sin with Bath-sheba, at 2Sa 12:7-9.) Adam also seemed to be taking offense against Jehovah, as is indicated by his reply when questioned about his wrong act: "The *woman* whom *you* gave to be with me, she gave me fruit from the tree and so I ate." (Ge 3:12) He did not believe the Serpent's lie that he would not die, as Eve had, but both Adam and Eve deliberately went in a course of self-determination, rebellion against God.—1Ti 2:14.

Adam could not say, "I am being tried by God." Rather, this principle went into operation: "Each one is tried by being drawn out and enticed by his own desire. Then the desire, when it has become fertile, gives birth to sin; in turn, sin, when it has been accomplished, brings forth death." (Jas 1:13-15) Thus, the three rebels—the angel, Eve, and Adam—used the freedom of will with which God had endowed them, to turn from sinlessness to a course of willful sin.—See PERFECTION; SIN, I.

The point at issue. What was here challenged? Who was reproached and defamed by this challenge of the angel who was later called Satan the Devil, which challenge Adam supported by his rebellious act? Was it the *fact* of Jehovah's *supremacy,* the existence of his *sovereignty?* Was God's sovereignty in danger? No, for Jehovah has supreme authority and power, and no one in heaven or earth can take this out of his hand. (Ro 9:19) The challenge therefore must have been of the *rightfulness, deservedness, and righteousness* of God's sovereignty—whether his sovereignty was exercised in a worthy way, righteously, and for the best interests of his subjects or not. An indication of this is the approach to Eve: "Is it really so that God said you must not eat from every tree of the garden?" Here the Serpent intimated that such a thing was unbelievable—that God was unduly restrictive, withholding something that was the rightful due of the human pair. —Ge 3:1.

What was "the tree of the knowledge of good and bad"?

By taking of the fruit of "the tree of the knowledge of good and bad," Adam and Eve expressed their rebellion. The Creator, as Universal Sovereign, was acting wholly within his right in making the law regarding the tree, for Adam, being a created person, and not sovereign, had limitations, and he needed to acknowledge this fact. For universal peace and harmony, it would devolve upon all reasoning creatures to acknowledge and support the Creator's sovereignty. Adam would demonstrate his recognition of this by refraining from eating the fruit of that tree. As father-to-be of an earth full of people, he must prove obedient and loyal, even in the smallest thing. The principle involved was: "The person faithful in what is least is faithful also in much, and the person unrighteous in what is least is unrighteous also in much." (Lu 16:10) Adam had the capability for such perfect obedience. There was evidently nothing bad intrinsically in the fruit of the tree itself. (The thing forbidden was not sex relations, for God had commanded the pair to "fill the earth." [Ge 1:28] It was the fruit of an actual tree, as the Bible says.) What was represented by the tree is well expressed in a footnote on Genesis 2:17, in *The Jerusalem Bible* (1966):

"This knowledge is a privilege which God reserves to himself and which man, by sinning, is to lay hands on, 3:5, 22. Hence it does not mean omniscience, which fallen man does not possess; nor is it moral discrimination, for unfallen man already had it and God could not refuse it to a rational being. It is the power of deciding for himself what is good and what is evil and of acting accordingly, a claim to complete moral independence by which man refuses to recognise his status as a created being. The first sin was an attack on God's sovereignty, a sin of pride."

God's servants charged with selfishness. A further expression of the issue is found in Satan's statement to God about his faithful servant Job. Satan said: "Is it for nothing that Job has feared God? Have not you yourself put up a hedge about him and about his house and about everything that he has all around? The work of his hands you have blessed, and his livestock itself has spread abroad in the earth. But, for a change, thrust out your hand, please, and touch everything he has and see whether he will not curse you to your very face." Again, he charged: "Skin in behalf of skin, and everything that a man has he will give in behalf of his soul." (Job 1:9-11; 2:4) Satan therewith charged Job with being not in harmony with God at heart, as serving God obediently only because of selfish considerations, for gain. Satan thereby slandered God as to his sovereignty, and God's servants as to integrity to that sovereignty. He said, in effect, that no man could be put on earth who would maintain integrity to Jehovah's sovereignty if he, Satan, was allowed to put him to the test.

Jehovah permitted the issue to be joined. Not, however, because he was unsure of the righteousness of his own sovereignty. He needed nothing proved to himself. It was out of love for his intelligent creatures that he allowed time for the testing out of the matter. He permitted men to undergo a test by Satan, before all the universe. And he gave his creatures the privilege of proving the Devil a liar, and of removing the slander not only from God's name but also from their own. Satan, in his egotistic attitude, was 'given up to a disapproved mental state.' In his approach to Eve, he had evidently been contradictory in his own reasoning. (Ro 1:28) For he was charging God with unfair, unrighteous exercise of sovereignty and, at the same time, was evidently counting on God's fairness: He seemed to think that God would consider Himself obliged to let him live on if he proved his charge concerning the unfaithfulness of God's creatures.

Settlement of the issue, a vital need. The settling of the issue was actually a matter vital to all who live, as respects their relationship to God's sovereignty. For, once settled, such an issue would never need to be tried again. It seems apparent that Jehovah desired that full knowledge of all the questions connected with this issue be thoroughly made known and understood. The action that God took engenders confidence in his unchangeableness, it enhances his sovereignty, and it makes that sovereignty even more desirable and firmly established in the minds of all who choose it.—Compare Mal 3:6.

A moral issue. The question, then, is not one of might, of raw strength; it is primarily a *moral* issue. However, because of God's invisibility and because Satan has exerted every effort to blind men's minds, Jehovah's power or even his existence has at times been questioned. (1Jo 5:19; Re 12:9) Men have mistaken the reason for God's patience and kindness and have themselves become more rebellious. (Ec 8:11; 2Pe 3:9) Because of this, it has taken faith, along with suffering, to serve God with integrity. (Heb 11:6, 35-38) Nevertheless, Jehovah purposes to make his sovereignty known to all. In Egypt he said to Pharaoh: "In fact, for this cause I have kept you in existence, for the sake of showing you my power and in order to have my name declared in all the earth." (Ex 9:16) Likewise God has allowed a time for this world and its god, Satan the Devil, to exist and develop in their wickedness, and He has set a time for their destruction. (2Co 4:4; 2Pe 3:7) The prophetic prayer of the psalmist was: "That people may know that you, whose name is Jehovah, you alone are the Most High over all the earth." (Ps 83:18) Jehovah himself has sworn: "To me every knee will bend down, every tongue will swear, saying, 'Surely in Jehovah there are full righteousness and strength.'"—Isa 45:23, 24.

How far the issue reached. How far-reaching was the issue? Since man had been induced to sin, and since an angel had sinned, the question reached up to and included God's heavenly creatures, even God's only-begotten Son, the one closest to Jehovah God. This One, who always did the things pleasing to his Father, would be most anxious to serve for the vindication of God's name and sovereignty. (Joh 8:29; Heb 1:9) God selected him for this assignment, sending him to the earth, where he was born as a male child through the virgin Mary. (Lu 1:35) He was perfect, and he maintained that perfection and blamelessness throughout his life, even to a disgraceful death. (Heb 7:26) Before his death he said: "Now there is a judging of this world; now the ruler of this world will be cast out." Also: "The ruler of the world is coming. And he has no hold on me." (Joh 12:31; 14:30) Satan could get no hold so as to break Christ's integrity, and he was judged as having failed, ready to be cast out. Jesus "conquered the world."—Joh 16:33.

Jesus Christ, God's Vindicator. So Jesus Christ, in a totally perfect way, proved the Devil a liar, completely settling the question, Will any man be faithful to God under whatever test or trial may be brought against him? Jesus therefore was appointed by the Sovereign God as the Executor of His purposes, the one to be used to destroy wickedness, including the Devil, from the universe. This authority he will exercise, and 'every knee will bend and every tongue openly acknowledge that Jesus Christ is Lord *to the glory of God the Father.*'—Php 2:5-11; Heb 2:14; 1Jo 3:8.

In the dominion granted the Son, he rules in his Father's name, 'bringing to nothing' all government and all authority and power that stand against Jehovah's sovereignty. The apostle Paul reveals that Jesus Christ then offers the greatest tribute to Jehovah's sovereignty, for, "when all things will have been subjected to him, then the Son himself will also subject himself to the One who subjected all things to him, that God may be all things to everyone."—1Co 15:24-28.

The book of Revelation shows that after the end of Christ's Thousand Year Reign, in which he puts down all authority that attempts to rival Jehovah's sovereignty, the Devil will be loosed for a short time. He will try to revive the issue, but no long grant of time will be given for that which is already settled. Satan and those following him will be completely annihilated.—Re 20:7-10.

Other vindicators. Though Christ's faithfulness thoroughly proved God's side of the issue, others are permitted to share in this. (Pr 27:11) The effects of Christ's integrity-keeping course, including his sacrificial death, are pointed out by the apostle: "Through one act of justification the result to men of all sorts is a declaring of them righteous for life." (Ro 5:18) Christ has been made the Head of a congregational "body" (Col 1:18), the members of which share in his death of integrity, and he is glad to have them share with him as joint heirs, as associate kings in his Kingdom rule. (Lu 22:28-30; Ro 6:3-5; 8:17; Re 20: 4, 6) Faithful men of old, looking forward to God's provision, maintained integrity, though imperfect in body. (Heb 11:13-16) And the many others who eventually bend the knee in acknowledgment will likewise do so in heartfelt recognition of God's righteous, worthy sovereignty. As the psalmist sang prophetically: "Every breathing thing—let it praise Jah. Praise Jah, you people!" —Ps 150:6.

SOW.   See SWINE.

SOWER, SOWING. The ancient method of sowing seed, or scattering it on the earth for growth, was generally by "broadcasting." The sower carried grain seed in a fold of his garment or in a container. He dispersed the seed before him with his hand in a long sweeping motion that extended from the seed supply to the opposite side. In Israel the sowing season extended from about October until the first part of March, depending on the kind of grain sown.

Jehovah's Blessing. Jehovah is the One providing the seed and the growing process, as well as the sunshine and rain, by which the field produces many times the quantity that is planted. (2Sa 23:3, 4; Isa 55:10) All mankind, whether righteous or wicked, thus receive benefits from the Creator.—Mt 5:45; Ac 14:15-17.

However, Jehovah God does not generally exercise specific control over the factors that make growth possible. Thus wicked persons at times may enjoy a bountiful harvest, whereas righteous ones, because of experiencing unfavorable conditions, may have a crop failure.—Compare Job 21:7-24.

On the other hand, when it suits his purpose, Jehovah can bless the sower and bring him abundant crops, or he can cause a scarcity of fruitage, depending upon the sower's faithfulness and obedience to Him. For example, Jehovah purposed to make Israel a great and numerous nation in the Promised Land, so he blessed his obedient servants bountifully. When Isaac was sojourning in Canaan, even though he was harassed by the natives of the land, Jehovah blessed him so that his sowing resulted in a harvest of up to a hundred measures from one measure sown.—Ge 26:12.

The spiritual condition of Israel determined the kind of harvest they received. Jehovah said to them before they entered the Promised Land: "If you continue walking in my statutes and keeping my commandments and you do carry them out, . . . your threshing will certainly reach to your grape gathering, and the grape gathering will reach to the sowing of seed." The crops would be so bountiful that the harvest would not be finished before the time to sow the next crop. (Compare Am 9:13.) On the other hand, God warned: "If you will not listen to me nor do all these commandments, . . . you will simply sow your seed for nothing, as your enemies will certainly eat it up." And he added, "your earth will not give its yield." (Le 26:3-5, 14-16, 20; compare Hag 1:6.) Later, in the prophet Jeremiah's day, Jehovah's warning proved true. Describing their bad condition, Jehovah then said: "They have sown wheat, but thorns are what they have reaped."—Jer 12:13.

Israel's Law Governing Sowing. In the Law given through Moses, God commanded that the land was to be sown for six years, but no sowing or harvesting was to be done during the seventh year (Sabbath year) nor on the Jubilee year. (Ex 23:10, 11; Le 25:3, 4, 11) This served to test their faith and it gave them more time for pursuit of spiritual things; it also was good for the soil.

Since the land was Jehovah's, it was, in a sense, holy, and his people were holy. Therefore care had to be taken to prevent any kind of defilement. If the dead body of an unclean animal, for example, a rat or a lizard, fell upon seed that was wet, it was unclean for use, whereas if the seed was dry, it was clean. This was no doubt because the wetness would tend to spread the uncleanness throughout the seed.—Le 11:31, 37, 38.

Also, the mixing of different seeds in sowing was not permitted, though seeds of different kinds could be sown, each kind in separate places in the same field. (Le 19:19; Isa 28:25) This may have been to keep the Israelites mindful of their separateness and distinctness as God's people, under his Kingship. If an Israelite violated this law, mixing two sorts of seeds, the entire produce of his field or vineyard became as something "devoted." It was therefore forfeited to the sanctuary.—De 22:9; compare Le 27:28; Nu 18:14.

Illustrative Use. Illustrating Jehovah's care for and blessing on the remnant that returned from Babylon, the psalmist wrote: "Those sowing seed with tears will reap even with a joyful cry. The one that without fail goes forth, even weeping, carrying along a bagful of seed, will without fail come in with a joyful cry, carrying along his sheaves." (Ps 126:1, 5, 6) Those returning from Babylon were very happy at their release, but they may have wept when sowing seed in the desolate ground that had been unworked for 70 years. Nevertheless, Jehovah had gathered them back for his name's sake, and those who went ahead with the sowing and reconstruction work enjoyed fruitage from their labor. For a while, when the temple construction was stopped, Jehovah withheld the land's fruitage, but through the prophets Haggai and Zechariah the people again were stirred to activity and again received God's favor.—Hag 1:6, 9-11; 2:15-19.

Jehovah uses the sowing and growing process to illustrate the sure effectiveness of his word. —Isa 55:10, 11.

Diligence and generosity. Solomon set forth a principle in connection with generosity and doing one's work industriously when he wrote: "He that is watching the wind will not sow seed; and he that is looking at the clouds will not reap." A person who holds back, waiting for a time to come when everything seems to him fully and exactly favorable for the work God has set before him, or who is looking for an excuse to avoid the work, will not receive anything from God. Rather, Solomon recommends diligence, for, he says in verse 5, it is God who "does all things" and man does not understand all of God's ways of working. Accordingly, he advises: "In the morning sow your seed and until the evening do not let your hand rest; for you are not knowing where this will have success, either here or there, or whether both of them will alike be good."—Ec 11:4-6.

The apostle Paul seems to be thinking similarly when he encourages the Christians at Corinth in their generosity in connection with the relief ministration for the brothers at Jerusalem, who had suffered hardships and had lost many of their possessions through persecution leveled against them by the Jews. Paul said: "He that sows sparingly will also reap sparingly; and he that sows bountifully will also reap bountifully. . . . God, moreover, is able to make all his undeserved kindness abound toward you, that, while you always have full self-sufficiency in everything, you may have plenty for every good work. . . . Now he that abundantly supplies seed to the sower and bread for eating will supply and multiply the seed for you to sow and will increase the products of your righteousness." Then Paul points out the good that results in addition to God's favor and bounty in a material way, namely, that such generosity results in thanks to God and glorification of God, along with the love and prayers of those being helped, in behalf of those extending help. There is also an increase of love in the congregation.—2Co 9:6-14.

Preaching the good news. Jesus Christ likened the sowing of seed to preaching the word, the good news of the Kingdom. He was the Sower of the Kingdom truths, and John the Baptizer had also worked as a sower. Jesus' disciples were sent out to reap in the fields that had been sown and were white for harvesting. Therefore he said to them: "Already the reaper is receiving wages and gathering fruit for everlasting life, so that the sower and the reaper may rejoice together. . . . One is the sower and another the reaper. I dispatched you to reap what you have spent no labor on. Others have labored [in sowing], and you have entered into the benefit of their labor [by reaping]."—Joh 4:35-38.

Again, Jesus likened the preaching work to sowing, in the illustration of the sower. In this parable the seed sown is "the word of the kingdom." Jesus pointed out that the conditions under which the seed is sown can affect the sprouting and growing of the seed in the hearts of men. —Mt 13:1-9, 18-23; Lu 8:5-15.

The wheat and the weeds. In another illustration Jesus likened himself to a sower of fine seed, and the seed to "sons of the kingdom."

Another sower, an enemy who sows weeds in the field, is the Devil. Here Jesus was evidently foretelling an apostasy to come, when, in and among the Christian congregation, there would be men falsely claiming to be servants of God and attempting to defile the congregation and to draw away the disciples.—Mt 13:24-30, 36-43; compare Ac 20:29; 2Co 11:12-15; 2Th 2:3-9; 1Ti 4:1; 2Ti 4:3, 4; 2Pe 2:1-3.

'Sowing with a view to the flesh.' The apostle Paul, after enumerating the fruits of the spirit and the works of the flesh, and admonishing each one to prove his own work, said: "Do not be misled: God is not one to be mocked. For whatever a man is sowing, this he will also reap; because he who is sowing with a view to his flesh will reap corruption from his flesh, but he who is sowing with a view to the spirit will reap everlasting life from the spirit."—Ga 5:19-23; 6:4, 7, 8.

An example of sowing to the flesh, with its results, was cited by Paul at Romans 1:24-27. Other examples were the incestuous person in the Corinthian congregation, practicing unclean fleshly things; also Hymenaeus and Alexander, who were promoting unclean teaching and blasphemy, and who were handed over to Satan "for the destruction of the flesh," that is, to clear such fleshly element out of the congregation.—1Co 5:1, 5; 1Ti 1:20; 2Ti 2:17, 18.

Instructing, caring for, the congregation. When writing to the congregation at Corinth, Paul compared his instructing and helping the congregation to sowing, and he explained to them that, doing so, he had authority to receive material things from them to assist him in carrying on his ministry. But he did not do this, so as not to offer any hindrance to the good news.—1Co 9:11, 12.

Just as a farmer sows seed in peace, so the good news is sown in peace, not with wrangling, strife, tumult, and the use of force. And the men doing the sowing are men of peace, not quarrelsome, belligerent, or riotous. Therefore peaceful conditions must exist in the Christian congregation for their sowing to produce fruitage of righteousness. —Jas 3:18.

The resurrection. When discussing the spiritual resurrection, Paul likened the burial of the physical body to the sowing of a seed, stating: "Nevertheless, someone will say: 'How are the dead to be raised up? Yes, with what sort of body are they coming?' You unreasonable person! What you sow is not made alive unless first it dies; and as for what you sow, you sow, not the body that will develop, but a bare grain, it may be, of wheat or any one of the rest; but God gives it a body just as it has pleased him, and to each of the seeds its own body. . . . And there are heavenly bodies, and earthly bodies . . . So also is the resurrection of the dead. It is sown in corruption, it is raised up in incorruption. . . . It is sown a physical body, it is raised up a spiritual body. . . . For this which is corruptible must put on incorruption, and this which is mortal must put on immortality."—1Co 15:35-53.

Those who are chosen by God to be joint heirs with his Son, and to receive incorruption and immortality, must die and give up the body of flesh in order to obtain a heavenly body by resurrection. This is similar to the way a seed that has been planted "dies," disintegrates, and is of an entirely different form and appearance from the plant that results.

For a discussion of the sowing mentioned at Isaiah 28:24, with its illustrative significance, see PLOWING.

SPAIN.

A country situated on the Iberian Peninsula in SW Europe. After visiting the Roman Christians, the apostle Paul hoped to be escorted partway there by his fellow believers in Rome. (Ro 15:23, 24, 28) Whether the apostle ever reached Spain is not certain. However, Clement of Rome stated (c. 95 C.E.) that Paul came "to the extreme limit of the W[est]," which could have included Spain. (*The Ante-Nicene Fathers,* Vol. I, p. 6, "The First Epistle of Clement to the Corinthians," chap. V) If he reached that land, the visit probably occurred between Paul's release from his first imprisonment in Rome (c. 61 C.E.) and his imprisonment there once again in about 65 C.E. At that time Spain was under Roman rule. Some identify Tarshish with the southern part of Spain. —See TARSHISH No. 4.

SPAN.

A linear measure approximately corresponding to the distance between the end of the thumb and the end of the little finger when the hand is spread out. (Ex 28:16; 39:9; 1Sa 17:4; Eze 43:13) Two spans equal one cubit; and three handbreadths, one span. There is evidence that the cubit commonly used by the Israelites was 44.5 cm (17.5 in.) in length. (See CUBIT.) Accordingly, the span would be 22.2 cm (8.75 in.) in length.

When highlighting Jehovah's greatness, the prophet Isaiah asked: "Who has . . . taken the proportions of the heavens themselves with a mere span?"—Isa 40:12.

"Span" also translates the Hebrew term *tse'-medh* and refers to a "pair" or "couple" of animals yoked together.—See ACRE.

SPARROW

[Gr., *strou·thi'on*]. The Greek word *strou·thi'on* is a diminutive form meaning any small bird, but was used especially as applying to sparrows. A variety of common house sparrow (*Passer domesticus biblicus*) is abundant in Israel. Small brown and gray birds, the sparrows are noisy and gregarious, chirping and twittering, fluttering from their perch on a housetop, tree, or bush to the ground and back again. Their diet consists chiefly of seeds, insects, and worms. The Spanish sparrow (*Passer hispaniolensis*) is also common, especially in the northern and central areas of Israel.

The only direct references to sparrows in the Bible are found in a statement that Jesus made during his third Galilean tour and evidently restated about a year thereafter in his later Judean ministry. Pointing out that "two sparrows sell for a coin of small value [literally, an assarion, worth less than one cent]" or, if bought in quantities of five, "for two coins of small value," Jesus stated that, though these small birds were counted as of such little worth, "yet not one of them will fall to the ground without your Father's knowledge," "Not one of them goes forgotten before God." He then encouraged his disciples to be free from fear, assuring them, "You are worth more than many sparrows."—Mt 10:29-31; Lu 12:6, 7.

Both anciently and modernly, sparrows have been sold in the markets of the Middle East. As an item of food, they were plucked and spitted on wooden skewers and roasted (like shish kebabs). An ancient inscription of Emperor Diocletian's tariff law (301 C.E.) shows that of all the birds used for food, sparrows were the cheapest. —*Light From the Ancient East,* by A. Deissmann, 1965, pp. 273, 274.

Although the sparrow appears in the Hebrew Scriptures in the *King James Version* (Ps 84:3; 102:7) and in other translations, the Hebrew term so rendered (*tsip·pohr'*) is evidently a generic term referring to small birds in general and not specifically identifying the sparrow.

SPEAR.

See ARMS, ARMOR.

SPEARMEN.

Soldiers armed with spears. They anciently constituted a section of the light infantry, and they were backed up by archers and slingers. Charioteers and cavalrymen often carried spears. Spearmen were a part of the Roman occupational forces in Palestine, 200 of whom were included in secretly escorting Paul out of Jerusalem.—Ac 23:23.

SPEECH.

See ABUSIVE SPEECH.

SPELL. See CHARM.

SPELT [Heb., *kus·se'meth*]. An inferior kind of wheat, the kernels of which are not readily separated from the chaff. Spelt (*Triticum spelta*) was anciently cultivated in Egypt (Ex 9:32), where, according to the Greek historian Herodotus (II, 36), it was made into bread. (See Eze 4:9.) The Israelites seem to have planted it as a border around their fields to serve as a kind of fence. —Isa 28:25.

SPICE. Any of a variety of fragrant plant products, including aloe, balsam, calamus, cassia, cinnamon, frankincense, galbanum, labdanum, myrrh, and stacte. Although condiments such as cumin, mint, dill, and salt are mentioned in the Bible, the original-language words translated "spice" and "spices" are not applied to food seasonings.

Spices were employed in making the holy anointing oil and the incense designated exclusively for sanctuary use. (Ex 30:23-25, 34-37) They were also used in preparing the dead for burial, myrrh and aloes being specifically mentioned in Jesus' case. (Joh 19:39, 40; see also Mr 16:1; Lu 23:56; 24:1.) In connection with the burial of King Asa of Judah, there was an extraordinarily great funeral burning—not a cremation, but a burning of spices. (2Ch 16:14) Anciently spices were added to wines to increase their "headiness."—Ca 8:2.

The garden spice referred to in The Song of Solomon (5:1, 13; 6:2) may denote fragrant herbs generally or, as suggested by some scholars, balsam (*Commiphora opobalsamum*). The "Indian spice" of Revelation 18:13 is literally "amomum," an aromatic shrub of the ginger family.

SPIDER [Heb., *'ak·ka·vish'*]. A small, eight-legged, wingless animal that, according to strict biologic definition, is not an insect but an arachnid.

Most spiders spin webs to catch their prey. Spiders generally have three pairs of spinnerets, or spinning organs, located on the rear underside of the abdomen. These are linked with the silk glands inside the creature's body by means of many minute tubes. To spin its thread, the spider presses its spinning organs against an object and forces out some liquid silk. Moving away from the object, it draws out the liquid, which, in turn, hardens in the air. By keeping its spinnerets together, the spider can produce one thick thread. A band of fine threads results when the spinning organs are held apart.

The web, differing according to the variety of spider making it, is beautiful in symmetry and complex in design. At equidistant intervals on the silken strands are drops of glue, likewise made by the spider. After having laid a line between two spokes and smeared it with glue, the spider pulls down the thread and then lets it snap back. This results in the equidistant spacing of the tiny glue droplets. The sticky thread serves to trap the spider's prey.

In its two occurrences in Scripture, the spider figures in illustrative settings. Bildad, in speaking to Job, referred to an apostate as one who trusts in or leans upon a "spider's house," or web, something that would be too frail to keep him standing. (Job 8:14, 15) The hurtful and violent works of unfaithful Israelites are likened to the weaving of a spider's web. However, such unfaithful ones could not cover themselves with their works, any more than a cobweb would be suitable for a garment.—Isa 59:5, 6.

SPIES. Persons who obtain information by making secret observations. From Israel's encampment in the Wilderness of Paran, in 1512 B.C.E., Moses sent 12 chieftains (representing all the tribes except Levi) to search out the land of Canaan. This was permitted by Jehovah at the request of the Israelites, who said: "Do let us send men ahead of us that they may search out the land for us and bring us back word concerning the way by which we should go up and the cities to which we will come." (De 1:22, 23) Probably separating, perhaps in twos, they traveled through the land as far N as "the entering in of Hamath" and W toward the sea. (Nu 13:21; see HAMATH.) On returning, though all agreed that the land was indeed "flowing with milk and honey," ten of the spies gave a faithless report that put fear into the Israelites. Only Joshua and Caleb encouraged them to go on into the land and take it. For Israel's lack of faith in being influenced by the bad report, God decreed that all the men who were 20 years of age and older should die in the wilderness during an extended period of 40 years of wandering. Joshua and Caleb were excepted, and the tribe of Levi was not included.—Nu 13:1-33; 14:6-38; De 1:24-40.

Joshua sent two spies across the Jordan to spy out Jericho in 1473 B.C.E. Rahab the harlot assisted the spies and was delivered along with her household when Jericho fell. (Jos 2:1-24; 6:1, 22-25; Heb 11:31) Other instances of spying are mentioned at Judges 1:22-26; 18:1-10, 14, 17; 1 Samuel 26:4. David's messengers to King Hanun of Ammon were charged with being spies and were mistreated. (2Sa 10:1-7) Absalom sent spies throughout Israel, not so much to gain information for his conspiracy against David as to stir up support for his subversive cause.—2Sa 15:10-12.

The apostle Paul wrote about his visit to Jerusalem with Barnabas and Titus, mentioning that at the time there were "false brothers brought in quietly, who sneaked in to spy upon our freedom which we have in union with Christ Jesus."—Ga 2:1-5.

SPIKENARD [Heb., *nerd;* Gr., *nar'dos*]. A small aromatic plant (*Nardostachys jatamansi*) found in the Himalaya Mountains. The stems and roots of this plant are generally considered the source of the nard or spikenard mentioned in Scripture. (Ca 1:12; 4:13, 14; Mr 14:3) The spikenard plant is distinguished by its clusters of blackish, hairy stems, about 5 cm (2 in.) long, that branch out from the top of the root. The leaves sprout from the upper portion of the plant, which is terminated by heads of pink flowers.

To preserve its fragrance, nard, a light, fragrant, reddish-colored liquid, was sealed in cases of alabaster, a soft, usually whitish, marblelike stone named after Alabastron, Egypt, where vessels of this material were manufactured. The pound of perfumed oil, "genuine nard," poured by Mary from an alabaster case upon the head and feet of Jesus Christ, 'in view of his burial,' was evaluated at 300 denarii, the equivalent of about a year's wages. (Mr 14:3-9; Joh 12:3-8; Mt 20:2) The fact that this perfumed oil was so expensive suggests that its source may have been distant India.

SPINNING. The process of drawing out and twisting together plant or animal fibers, such as flax, cotton, wool, and goat's hair, into thread or yarn. Spun threads were used for weaving, sewing, embroidering, or the making of rope.

Among the Hebrews and others the distaff and spindle were employed in this process. It is said concerning the capable wife: "Her hands she has thrust out to the distaff, and her own hands take hold of the spindle." (Pr 31:19) The distaff was a stick on which the cleansed and combed or carded (Isa 19:9) fibers were loosely wound. Methods varied, but one way was to hold the distaff in the left hand. The fibers were drawn from it to some length and attached to the spindle. This was a shorter stick with a hook at one end to hold the fibers and a whorl (a disc of heavy material such as stone) near the other end. Using the right hand, the spinner twirled the hanging spindle, thus twisting the fibers into thread. This spun thread was next wound around the shank of the spindle and fastened. Then the operation was repeated until all the fibers on the distaff had been made into one long thread.

Both men and women of ancient Egypt spun thread, but among the Hebrews the spinning seems to have been done primarily by women. Israelite women were privileged to spin and contribute materials when the tabernacle was to be constructed.—Ex 35:25, 26.

Jesus Christ referred to spinning when he urged his disciples, not to be unduly anxious about clothing, but to trust in God to clothe them. Jesus said: "Mark well how the lilies grow; they neither toil nor spin; but I tell you, Not even Solomon in all his glory was arrayed as one of these."—Lu 12:27, 28; Mt 6:28-30.

SPIRIT. The Greek *pneu'ma* (spirit) comes from *pne'o,* meaning "breathe or blow," and the Hebrew *ru'ach* (spirit) is believed to come from a root having the same meaning. *Ru'ach* and *pneu'ma,* then, basically mean "breath" but have extended meanings beyond that basic sense. (Compare Hab 2:19; Re 13:15.) They can also mean *wind;* the *vital force* in living creatures; *one's spirit; spirit persons,* including God and his angelic creatures; and *God's active force,* or *holy spirit.* (Compare Koehler and Baumgartner's *Lexicon in Veteris Testamenti Libros,* Leiden, 1958, pp. 877-879; Brown, Driver, and Briggs' *Hebrew and English Lexicon of the Old Testament,* 1980, pp. 924-926; *Theological Dictionary of the New Testament,* edited by G. Friedrich, translated by G. Bromiley, 1971, Vol. VI, pp. 332-451.) All these meanings have something in common: They all refer to that which is invisible to human sight and which gives evidence of force in motion. Such invisible force is capable of producing visible effects.

Another Hebrew word, *nesha·mah'* (Ge 2:7), also means "breath," but it is more limited in range of meaning than *ru'ach.* The Greek *pno·e'* seems to have a similar limited sense (Ac 17:25) and was used by the *Septuagint* translators to render *nesha·mah'.*

Wind. Consider first the sense that is perhaps easiest to grasp. The context in many cases shows *ru'ach* to mean "wind," as the "east wind" (Ex 10:13), "the four winds." (Zec 2:6) The mention of such things as clouds, storm, the blowing of chaff or things of similar nature appearing in the context often makes evident this sense. (Nu 11:31; 1Ki 18:45; 19:11; Job 21:18) Because the four winds are used to mean the four directions —east, west, north, and south—*ru'ach* at times may be rendered as 'direction' or 'side.'—1Ch 9:24; Jer 49:36; 52:23; Eze 42:16-20.

Job 41:15, 16 says of Leviathan's closely fitting scales that "not even air [*weru'ach*] can come in between them." Here again *ru'ach* represents air *in motion,* not merely air in a quiescent or motionless state. Thus the thought of an *invisible force* is present, the basic characteristic of the Hebrew *ru'ach.*

Evidently the only case in the Christian Greek Scriptures in which *pneu'ma* is used in the sense of "wind" is at John 3:8.

Man cannot exercise control over the wind; he cannot guide, direct, restrain, or possess it. Because of this, "wind [*ru'ach*]" frequently stands for that which is uncontrollable or unattainable by man—elusive, transitory, in vain, of no genuine benefit. (Compare Job 6:26; 7:7; 8:2; 16:3; Pr 11:29; 27:15, 16; 30:4; Ec 1:14, 17; 2:11; Isa 26:18; 41:29.) For a full discussion of this aspect, see WIND.

Spirit Persons. God is invisible to human eyes (Ex 33:20; Joh 1:18; 1Ti 1:17), and he is alive and exercises unsurpassed force throughout the universe. (2Co 3:3; Isa 40:25-31) Christ Jesus states: "God is a Spirit [*Pneu'ma*]." The apostle writes: "Now Jehovah is the Spirit." (Joh 4:24; 2Co 3:17, 18) The temple built on Christ as foundation cornerstone is "a place for God to inhabit by spirit."—Eph 2:22.

This does not mean that God is an impersonal, bodiless force like the wind. The Scriptures unmistakably testify to his personality; he also has location so that Christ could speak of 'going to his Father,' this in order that he might "appear before the person of God [literally, "face of God"] for us." —Joh 16:28; Heb 9:24; compare 1Ki 8:43; Ps 11:4; 113:5, 6; see JEHOVAH (The Person Identified by the Name).

The expression "my spirit" (*ru·chi'*) used by God at Genesis 6:3 may mean "I the Spirit," even as his use of "my soul" (*naph·shi'*) has the sense of "I the person," or "my person." (Isa 1:14; see SOUL [God as Having Soul].) He thereby contrasts his heavenly spiritual position with that of earthly, fleshly man.

God's Son. God's "only-begotten son," the Word, was a spirit person like his Father, hence "existing in God's form" (Php 2:5-8), but later "became flesh," residing among mankind as the man Jesus. (Joh 1:1, 14) Completing his earthly course, he was "put to death in the flesh, but [was] made alive in the spirit." (1Pe 3:18) His Father resurrected him, granted his Son's request to be glorified alongside the Father with the glory he had had in his prehuman state (Joh 17:4, 5), and God made him "a life-giving spirit." (1Co 15:45) The Son thus became again invisible to human sight, dwelling "in unapproachable light, whom not one of men has seen or can see."—1Ti 6:14-16.

Other spirit creatures. Angels are designated by the terms *ru'ach* and *pneu'ma* in a number of texts. (1Ki 22:21, 22; Eze 3:12, 14; 8:3; 11:1, 24; 43:5; Ac 23:8, 9; 1Pe 3:19, 20) In the Christian Greek Scriptures, the majority of such references are to wicked spirit creatures, demons.—Mt 8:16; 10:1; 12:43-45; Mr 1:23-27; 3:11, 12, 30.

Psalm 104:4 states that God makes "his angels spirits, his ministers a devouring fire." Some translations would render this: "Who makest the winds thy messengers, fire and flame thy ministers," or similarly. (*RS, JP, AT, JB*) Such translation of the Hebrew text is not inadmissible (compare Ps 148:8); however, the apostle Paul's quotation of the text (Heb 1:7) coincides with that of the Greek *Septuagint* and harmonizes with the rendering first given. (In the Greek text of Hebrews 1:7, the definite article [*tous*] is used before "angels," not before "spirits [*pneu'ma·ta*]," making the angels the proper subject of the clause.) *Barnes' Notes on the New Testament* (1974) says: "It is to be presumed that [Paul], who had been trained in the knowledge of the Hebrew language, would have had a better opportunity of knowing its [referring to Psalm 104:4] fair construction than we can; and it is morally certain, that he would employ the passage *in an argument* as it was commonly understood by those to whom he wrote—that is, to those who were familiar with the Hebrew language and literature." —Compare Heb 1:14.

God's angels, though capable of materializing human form and appearing to men, are not by nature material or fleshly, hence are invisible. They are actively alive and able to exert great force, and the terms *ru'ach* and *pneu'ma* therefore aptly describe them.

Ephesians 6:12 speaks of Christians wrestling, "not against blood and flesh, but against the governments, against the authorities, against the world rulers of this darkness, against the wicked spirit forces in the heavenly places." The latter part of the text in Greek literally reads: "Toward the spiritual (things) [Gr., *pneu·ma·ti·ka'*] of the wickedness in the heavenly [places]." Most modern translations recognize that the reference here is not simply to something abstract, "spiritual wickedness" (*KJ*), but refers to wickedness carried out by spirit *persons*. Thus, we have such renderings as: "the spirit-forces of evil on high" (*AT*), "the spiritual hosts of wickedness in the heavenly places" (*RS*), "the spiritual army of evil in the heavens" (*JB*), "the superhuman forces of evil in the heavens" (*NE*).

God's Active Force; Holy Spirit. By far the majority of occurrences of *ru'ach* and *pneu'ma* relate to God's spirit, his active force, his holy spirit.

Not a person. Not until the fourth century C.E. did the teaching that the holy spirit was a person and part of the "Godhead" become official church dogma. Early church "fathers" did not so teach; Justin Martyr of the second century C.E. taught that the holy spirit was an 'influence or mode of operation of the Deity'; Hippolytus likewise ascribed no personality to the holy spirit. The Scriptures themselves unite to show that God's holy spirit is not a person but is God's *active force* by which he accomplishes his purpose and executes his will.

It may first be noted that the words "in heaven, the Father, the Word, and the Holy Ghost: and these three are one" (*KJ*) found in older translations at 1 John 5:7 are actually spurious additions to the original text. A footnote in *The Jerusalem Bible,* a Catholic translation, says that these words are "not in any of the early Greek MSS [manuscripts], or any of the early translations, or in the best MSS of the Vulg[ate] itself." *A Textual Commentary on the Greek New Testament,* by Bruce Metzger (1975, pp. 716-718), traces in detail the history of the spurious passage. It states that the passage is first found in a treatise entitled *Liber Apologeticus,* of the fourth century, and that it appears in Old Latin and Vulgate manuscripts of the Scriptures, beginning in the sixth century. Modern translations as a whole, both Catholic and Protestant, do not include them in the main body of the text, because of recognizing their spurious nature.—*RS, NE, NAB.*

Personification does not prove personality. It is true that Jesus spoke of the holy spirit as a "helper" and spoke of such helper as 'teaching,' 'bearing witness,' 'giving evidence,' 'guiding,' 'speaking,' 'hearing,' and 'receiving.' In so doing, the original Greek shows Jesus at times applying the personal pronoun "he" to that "helper" (paraclete). (Compare Joh 14:16, 17, 26; 15:26; 16:7-15.) However, it is not unusual in the Scriptures for something that is not actually a person to be personalized or personified. Wisdom is personified in the book of Proverbs (1:20-33; 8:1-36); and feminine pronominal forms are used of it in the original Hebrew, as also in many English translations. (*KJ, RS, JP, AT*) Wisdom is also personified at Matthew 11:19 and Luke 7:35, where it is depicted as having both "works" and "children." The apostle Paul personalized sin and death and also undeserved kindness as "kings." (Ro 5:14, 17, 21; 6:12) He speaks of sin as "receiving an inducement," 'working out covetousness,' 'seducing,' and 'killing.' (Ro 7:8-11) Yet it is obvious that Paul did not mean that sin was actually a person.

So, likewise with John's account of Jesus' words regarding the holy spirit, his remarks must be taken in context. Jesus personalized the holy spirit when speaking of that spirit as a "helper" (which in Greek is the masculine substantive *pa·ra'kle·tos*). Properly, therefore, John presents Jesus' words as referring to that "helper" aspect of the spirit with masculine personal pronouns. On the other hand, in the same context, when the Greek *pneu'ma* is used, John employs a neuter pronoun to refer to the holy spirit, *pneu'ma* itself being neuter. Hence, we have in John's use of the masculine personal pronoun in association with *pa·ra'kle·tos* an example of conformity to grammatical rules, not an expression of doctrine.—Joh 14:16, 17; 16:7, 8.

Lacks personal identification. Since God himself is a Spirit and is holy and since all his faithful angelic sons are spirits and are holy, it is evident that if the "holy spirit" were a person, there should reasonably be given some means in the Scriptures to distinguish and identify such spirit *person* from all these other 'holy spirits.' It would be expected that, at the very least, the definite article would be used with it in all cases where it is not called "God's holy spirit" or is not modified by some similar expression. This would at least distinguish it as THE Holy Spirit. But, on the contrary, in a large number of cases the expression "holy spirit" appears in the original Greek without the article, thus indicating its lack of personality.—Compare Ac 6:3, 5; 7:55; 8:15, 17, 19; 9:17; 11:24; 13:9, 52; 19:2; Ro 9:1; 14:17; 15:13, 16, 19; 1Co 12:3; Heb 2:4; 6:4; 2Pe 1:21; Jude 20, *Int* and other interlinear translations.

How baptized in its "name." At Matthew 28:19 reference is made to "the name of the Father and of the Son and of the holy spirit." A "name" can mean something other than a personal name. When, in English, we say, "in the name of the law," or "in the name of common sense," we have no reference to a person as such. By "name" in these expressions we mean 'what the law stands for or its authority' and 'what common sense represents or calls for.' The Greek term for "name" (o'no·ma) also can have this sense. Thus, while some translations (*KJ, AS*) follow the Greek text at Matthew 10:41 literally and say that the one that "receiveth a prophet *in the name of* a prophet, shall receive a prophet's reward; and he that receiveth a righteous man *in the name of* a righteous man, shall receive a righteous man's reward," more modern translations say, "receives a prophet *because he is* a prophet" and "receives a righteous man *because he is* a righteous man," or similar. (*RS, AT, JB, NW*) Thus, Robertson's *Word Pictures in the New Testament* (1930, Vol. I, p. 245) says on Matthew 28:19: "The use of name (*onoma*) here is a common one in the Septuagint and the papyri for power or authority." Hence baptism 'in the name of the holy spirit' implies recognition of that spirit as having its source in God and as exercising its function according to the divine will.

Other evidence of its impersonal nature. Further evidence against the idea of personality as regards the holy spirit is the way it is used in association with other impersonal things, such as water and fire (Mt 3:11; Mr 1:8); and Christians are spoken of as being baptized "in holy spirit." (Ac 1:5; 11:16) Persons are urged to become "filled with spirit" instead of with wine. (Eph 5:18) So, too, persons are spoken of as being 'filled' with it along with such qualities as wisdom and faith (Ac 6:3, 5; 11:24) or joy (Ac 13:52); and holy spirit is inserted, or sandwiched in, with a number of such qualities at 2 Corinthians 6:6. It is most unlikely that such expressions would be made if the holy spirit were a divine person. As to the spirit's 'bearing witness' (Ac 5:32; 20:23), it may be noted that the same thing is said of the water and the blood at 1 John 5:6-8. While some texts refer to the spirit as 'witnessing,' 'speaking,' or 'saying' things, other texts make clear that it spoke through persons, having no personal voice of its own. (Compare Heb 3:7; 10:15-17; Ps 95:7; Jer 31:33, 34; Ac 19:2-6; 21:4; 28:25.) It may thus be compared to radio waves that can transmit a message from a person speaking into a microphone and cause his voice to be heard by persons a distance away, in effect, 'speaking' the message by a radio loudspeaker. God, by his spirit, transmits his messages and communicates his will to the minds and hearts of his servants on earth, who, in turn, may convey that message to yet others.

Distinguished from "power." Ru'ach and pneu'ma, therefore, when used with reference to God's holy spirit, refer to God's invisible active force by which he accomplishes his divine purpose and will. It is "holy" because it is from Him, not of an earthly source, and is free from all corruption as "the spirit of holiness." (Ro 1:4) It is not Jehovah's "power," for this English word more correctly translates other terms in the original languages (Heb., ko'ach; Gr., dy'na·mis). Ru'ach and pneu'ma are used in close association or even in parallel with these terms signifying "power," which shows that there is an inherent connection between them and yet a definite distinction. (Mic 3:8; Zec 4:6; Lu 1:17, 35; Ac 10:38) "Power" is basically the ability or capacity to act or do things and it can be latent, dormant, or inactively resident in someone or something. "Force," on the other hand, more specifically describes energy *projected* and *exerted* on persons or things, and may be defined as "an influence that produces or tends to produce motion, or change of motion." "Power" might be likened to the energy stored in a battery, while "force" could be compared to the electric current flowing from such battery. "Force," then, more accurately represents the sense of the Hebrew and Greek terms as relating to God's spirit, and this is borne out by a consideration of the Scriptures.

Its Use in Creation. Jehovah God accomplished the creation of the material universe by means of his spirit, or active force. Regarding the planet Earth in its early formative stages, the record states that "God's active force [or "spirit" (ru'ach)] was moving to and fro over the surface of the waters." (Ge 1:2) Psalm 33:6 says: "By the word of Jehovah the heavens themselves were made, and by the spirit of his mouth all their army." Like a powerful breath, God's spirit can be sent forth to exert power even though there is no bodily contact with that which is acted upon. (Compare Ex 15:8, 10.) Where a human craftsman would use the force of his hands and fingers to produce things, God uses his spirit. Hence that spirit is also spoken of as God's "hand" or "fingers."—Compare Ps 8:3; 19:1; Mt 12:28 with Lu 11:20.

Modern science speaks of matter as organized energy, like bundles of energy, and recognizes that "matter can be changed into energy and energy into matter." (*The World Book Encyclopedia*, 1987, Vol. 13, p. 246) The immensity of the universe that man has thus far been able to discern with his telescopes gives some slight concept of the inexhaustible source of energy to be found in Jehovah God. As the prophet wrote: "Who has taken the proportions of the spirit of Jehovah?"—Isa 40:12, 13, 25, 26.

Source of animate life, reproductive powers. Not only inanimate creation but also all animate creation owes its existence and life to the operation of Jehovah's spirit that produced the original living creatures through whom all living creatures today have come to exist. (Compare Job 33:4; see section of this article under "Breath; Breath of Life; Life-Force.") Jehovah used his holy spirit to revive the reproductive powers of Abraham and Sarah, and therefore Isaac could be spoken of as "born in the manner of spirit." (Ga 4:28, 29) By his spirit God also transferred his Son's life from heaven to earth, causing conception in the womb of the virgin Jewess Mary.—Mt 1:18, 20; Lu 1:35.

Spirit Used on Behalf of God's Servants. A principal operation of God's spirit involves its ability to inform, to illuminate, to reveal things. Therefore David could pray: "Teach me to do your will, for you are my God. Your spirit is good; may it lead me in the land of uprightness." (Ps 143:10) Much earlier, Joseph had given the interpretation of Pharaoh's prophetic dreams, being enabled to do so by God's help. The Egyptian ruler recognized the operation of God's spirit in him. (Ge 41:16, 25-39) This illuminating power of the spirit is particularly notable in prophecy. Prophecy, as the apostle shows, did not spring from human interpretation of circumstances and events; it was not the result of some innate ability of the prophets to explain the meaning and significance of these or to forecast the shape of coming events. Rather, such men were "borne along by holy spirit"—conveyed, moved, and guided by God's active force. (2Pe 1:20, 21; 2Sa 23:2; Zec 7:12; Lu 1:67; 2:25-35; Ac 1:16; 28:25; see PROPHECY; PROPHET.) So, too, all the inspired Scriptures were "inspired of God," which translates the Greek the·o'pneu·stos, meaning, literally, "God-breathed." (2Ti 3:16) The spirit operated in various manners in communicating with such men and guiding them, in some cases causing them to see visions or dreams (Eze 37:1; Joe 2:28, 29; Re 4:1, 2; 17:3; 21:10), but in all cases operating on their minds and hearts to motivate and guide them according to God's purpose.—Da 7:1; Ac 16:9, 10; Re 1:10, 11; see INSPIRATION.

God's spirit, then, not only brings revelation and understanding of God's will but also energizes his servants to accomplish things in accord with that will. That spirit acts as a driving force that moves and impels them, even as Mark says the spirit "impelled" Jesus to go into the wilderness after his baptism. (Mr 1:12; compare Lu 4:1.) It can be like a "fire" within them, causing them to be "aglow" with that force (1Th 5:19; Ac 18:25; Ro 12:11), in a sense 'building up steam' or pressure in them to do certain work. (Compare Job 32:8, 18-20; 2Ti 1:6, 7.) They receive the "power of the

spirit," or "power through his spirit." (Lu 2:27; Eph 3:16; compare Mic 3:8.) Yet it is not merely some unconscious, blind impulse, for their minds and hearts are affected as well so that they can intelligently cooperate with the active force given them. Thus the apostle could say of those who had received the gift of prophecy in the Christian congregation that the "gifts of the spirit of the prophets are to be controlled by the prophets," so that good order might be maintained.—1Co 14:31-33.

Variety of operations. Even as an electric current can be used to accomplish a tremendous variety of things, so God's spirit is used to commission and enable persons to do a wide variety of things. (Isa 48:16; 61:1-3) As Paul wrote of the miraculous gifts of the spirit in his day: "Now there are varieties of gifts, but there is the same spirit; and there are varieties of ministries, and yet there is the same Lord; and there are varieties of operations, and yet it is the same God who performs all the operations in all persons. But the manifestation of the spirit is given to each one for a beneficial purpose."—1Co 12:4-7.

The spirit has qualifying force or capacity; it can qualify persons for a work or for an office. Though Bezalel and Oholiab may have had knowledge of crafts before their appointment in connection with the making of the tabernacle equipment and priestly garments, God's spirit 'filled them with wisdom, understanding, and knowledge' so that the work could be done in the way purposed. It heightened whatever natural abilities and acquired knowledge they already had, and it enabled them to teach others. (Ex 31:1-11; 35:30-35) The architectural plans for the later temple were given to David by inspiration, that is, through the operation of God's spirit, thus enabling David to undertake extensive preparatory work for the project.—1Ch 28:12.

God's spirit acted on and through Moses in prophesying and performing miraculous acts, as well as in leading the nation and acting as judge for it, thereby foreshadowing the future role of Christ Jesus. (Isa 63:11-13; Ac 3:20-23) However, Moses as an imperfect human found the load of responsibility heavy, and God 'took away some of the spirit that was on Moses and placed it upon 70 older men' so that they might help in carrying the load. (Nu 11:11-17, 24-30) The spirit also became operative on David from the time of his anointing by Samuel onward, guiding and preparing him for his future kingship.—1Sa 16:13.

Joshua became "full of the spirit of wisdom" as Moses' successor. But the spirit did not produce in him the ability to prophesy and perform miraculous works to the extent that it had in Moses. (De 34:9-12) However, it enabled Joshua to lead Israel in the military campaign that brought about the conquest of Canaan. Similarly, Jehovah's spirit "enveloped" other men, 'impelling' them as fighters on behalf of God's people, fighters such as Othniel, Gideon, Jephthah, and Samson.—Jg 3:9, 10; 6:34; 11:29; 13:24, 25; 14:5, 6, 19; 15:14.

The spirit of God energized men to speak his message of truth boldly and courageously before opposers and at the risk of their lives.—Mic 3:8.

Its being 'poured out' on his people is evidence of his favor, and it results in blessings and makes them prosper.—Eze 39:29; Isa 44:3, 4.

Judging and executing judgment. By his spirit God exercises judgment on men and nations; he also carries out his judgment decrees —punishing or destroying. (Isa 30:27, 28; 59:18, 19) In such cases, *ru'ach* may be fittingly rendered "blast," as when Jehovah speaks of causing "a blast [*ru'ach*] of windstorms to burst forth" in his rage. (Eze 13:11, 13; compare Isa 25:4; 27:8.) God's spirit can reach everywhere, acting for or against those who receive his attention.—Ps 139:7-12.

At Revelation 1:4 "the seven spirits" of God are mentioned as before his throne, and thereafter seven messages are given, each concluding with an admonition to "hear what the spirit says to the congregations." (Re 2:7, 11, 17, 29; 3:6, 13, 22) These messages contain heart-searching pronouncements of judgment and promises of reward for faithfulness. God's Son is shown as having these "seven spirits of God" (Re 3:1); and they are spoken of as being "seven lamps of fire" (Re 4:5), and also as seven eyes of the lamb that is slaughtered, "which eyes mean the seven spirits of God that have been sent forth into the whole earth." (Re 5:6) Seven being used as representative of completeness in other prophetic texts (see NUMBER, NUMERAL), it appears that these seven spirits symbolize the full active capacity of observation, discernment, or detection of the glorified Jesus Christ, the Lamb of God, enabling him to inspect all the earth.

God's Word is the spirit's "sword" (Eph 6:17), revealing what a person really is, exposing hidden qualities or heart attitudes and causing him either to soften his heart and conform to God's will expressed by that Word or to harden his heart in rebellion. (Compare Heb 4:11-13; Isa 6:9, 10; 66:2, 5.) God's Word therefore plays a forceful part in predicting adverse judgment, and since God's word or message must be carried out, the fulfillment of that word produces an action like that of fire on straw and like that of a forge hammer in smashing the crag. (Jer 23:28, 29) Christ Jesus, as God's principal Spokesman, as "The Word of God," declares the divine judgment messages and is authorized to order the execution of such judgments upon those judged. This is doubtless what is meant by references to his doing away with God's enemies "by the spirit [activating force] of his mouth."—Compare 2Th 2:8; Isa 11:3, 4; Re 19:13-16, 21.

God's spirit acts as "helper" for congregation. As he promised, Jesus upon ascending to heaven requested of his Father the holy spirit, or active force of God, and was granted the authority to employ this spirit. He 'poured it out' on his faithful disciples on the day of Pentecost, continuing to do so thereafter for those turning to God through his Son. (Joh 14:16, 17, 26; 15:26; 16:7; Ac 1:4, 5; 2:1-4, 14-18, 32, 33, 38) As they had been baptized in water, now they were all "baptized into one body" by that one spirit, immersed in it, as it were, somewhat like a piece of iron can be immersed in a magnetic field and thereby be imbued with magnetic force. (1Co 12:12, 13; compare Mr 1:8; Ac 1:5.) Though God's spirit had operated on the disciples before, as evidenced by their being able to cast out demons (compare Mt 12:28; Mr 3:14, 15), it now operated on them in a heightened and more extensive manner and in new ways not previously experienced.—Compare Joh 7:39.

As the Messianic King, Christ Jesus has the "spirit of wisdom and of understanding, the spirit of counsel and of mightiness, the spirit of knowledge and of the fear of Jehovah." (Isa 11:1, 2; 42:1-4; Mt 12:18-21) This force for righteousness is manifest in his use of God's active force, or spirit, in directing the Christian congregation on earth, Jesus being, by God's appointment, its Head, Owner, and Lord. (Col 1:18; Jude 4) As a "helper," that spirit now gave them increased understanding of God's will and purpose and opened up God's prophetic Word to them. (1Co 2:10-16; Col 1:9, 10; Heb 9:8-10) They were energized to serve as witnesses in all the earth (Lu 24:49; Ac 1:8; Eph 3:5, 6); they were granted miraculous 'gifts of the spirit,' enabling them to speak in foreign languages, prophesy, heal, and perform other activities that would both facilitate their proclamation of the good news and serve as evidence of their divine commission and backing. —Ro 15:18, 19; 1Co 12:4-11; 14:1, 2, 12-16; compare Isa 59:21; see GIFTS FROM GOD (Gifts of the Spirit).

As the congregation's Overseer, Jesus used the spirit in a governmental way—guiding in the selection of men for special missions and for serving in the oversight, teaching, and "readjustment" of the congregation. (Ac 13:2-4; 20:28; Eph 4:11, 12) He moved them, as well as restricted them, indicating where to concentrate their ministerial efforts (Ac 16:6-10; 20:22), and made them effective as writers of 'letters of Christ, inscribed with the spirit of God on fleshly tablets, human hearts.' (2Co 3:2, 3; 1Th 1:5) As promised, the spirit refreshed their memories, stimulated their mental powers, and emboldened them in bearing witness even before rulers.—Compare Mt 10:18-20; Joh 14:26; Ac 4:5-8, 13, 31; 6:8-10.

As "living stones," they were being formed into a spiritual temple based on Christ, one through which "spiritual sacrifices" would be made (1Pe 2:4-6; Ro 15:15, 16) and spiritual songs sung (Eph 5:18, 19) and in which God would reside by spirit. (1Co 3:16; 6:19, 20; Eph 2:20-22; compare Hag 2:5.) God's spirit is a unifying force of enormous strength, and as long as such Christians allowed it free course among them, it joined them peacefully together in bonds of love and devotion to God, his Son, and one another. (Eph 4:3-6; 1Jo 3:23, 24; 4:12, 13; compare 1Ch 12:18.) The gift of the spirit did not equip them for mechanical types of activity, as it had Bezalel and others who manufactured and produced material structures and equipment, but it fitted them for spiritual works of teaching, guiding, shepherding, and counseling. The spiritual temple they formed was to be adorned with the beautiful fruits of God's spirit, and that fruitage of "love, joy, peace, longsuffering, kindness, goodness, faith," and similar qualities was proof positive that God's spirit was operating in and among them. (Ga 5:22, 23; compare Lu 10:21; Ro 14:17.) This was the basic and primary factor producing good order and effective guidance among them. (Ga 5:24-26; 6:1; Ac 6:1-7; compare Eze 36:26, 27.) They submitted themselves to the 'law of the spirit,' an effective force for righteousness working to keep out the practices of the innately sinful flesh. (Ro 8:2; Ga 5:16-21; Jude 19-21) Their confidence was in God's spirit operating on them, not in fleshly abilities or background.—1Co 2:1-5; Eph 3:14-17; Php 3:1-8.

When questions arose, the holy spirit was a helper in arriving at a decision, as in the question of circumcision, decided by the body, or council, of apostles and older men at Jerusalem. Peter told of the spirit's being granted to uncircumcised people of the nations; Paul and Barnabas related the spirit's operations in their ministry among such persons; and James, his memory of the Scriptures doubtless aided by holy spirit, called attention to the inspired prophecy of Amos foretelling that God's name would be called on people of the nations. Thus all the thrust or drive of God's holy spirit pointed in one direction, and hence, in recognition of this, when writing the letter conveying their decision, this body or council said: "For the holy spirit and we ourselves have favored adding no further burden to you, except these necessary things."—Ac 15:1-29.

Anoints, begets, gives 'spiritual life.' As God had anointed Jesus with his holy spirit at the time of Jesus' baptism (Mr 1:10; Lu 3:22; 4:18; Ac 10:38), so he now anointed Jesus' disciples. This anointing with the spirit was a "token" to them of the heavenly inheritance to which they were now called (2Co 1:21, 22; 5:1, 5; Eph 1:13, 14), and it bore witness to them that they had been 'begotten,' or brought forth, by God to be his sons with the promise of spirit life in the heavens. (Joh 3:5-8; Ro 8:14-17, 23; Tit 3:5; Heb 6:4, 5) They were made clean, sanctified, and declared righteous "in the name of our Lord Jesus Christ and with the spirit of our God," by which spirit Jesus had been qualified to provide the ransom sacrifice and become God's high priest.—1Co 6:11; 2Th 2:13; Heb 9:14; 1Pe 1:1, 2.

Because of this heavenly calling and inheritance, Jesus' spirit-anointed followers had a spiritual life, though yet living as imperfect, fleshly creatures. This is evidently what the apostle refers to when contrasting earthly fathers with Jehovah God, "the Father of our spiritual life [literally, "Father of the spirits"]." (Heb 12:9; compare verse 23.) As joint heirs with Christ, who are due to be raised up from death in a spiritual body bearing his heavenly image, they should live on earth as "one spirit" in union with him as their Head, not letting the desires or immoral tendencies of their flesh be the force controlling them, such a thing even resulting perhaps in their becoming "one flesh" with a harlot.—1Co 6:15-18; 15:44-49; Ro 8:5-17.

Gaining and retaining God's spirit. The holy spirit is God's "free gift," which he gladly grants to those who sincerely seek and request it. (Ac 2:38; Lu 11:9-13) A right heart is the key factor (Ac 15:8), but knowledge and conformity to God's requirements are also essential factors. (Compare Ac 5:32; 19:2-6.) Once received, the Christian should not 'grieve' God's spirit by disregarding it (Eph 4:30; compare Isa 63:10), taking a course contrary to its leading, fixing the heart on goals other than that to which it points and impels, rejecting the inspired Word of God and its counsel and application to oneself. (Ac 7:51-53; 1Th 4:8; compare Isa 30:1, 2.) By hypocrisy one can "play false" to that holy spirit by which Christ directs the congregation, and those who "make a test" of its power in this way follow a disastrous course. (Ac 5:1-11; contrast Ro 9:1.) Deliberate opposition to and rebellion against the evident manifestation of God's spirit can mean blasphemy against that spirit, a sin that is unforgivable.—Mt 12:31, 32; Mr 3:29, 30; compare Heb 10:26-31.

Breath; Breath of Life; Life-Force. The account of the creation of man states that God formed man from the dust of the ground and proceeded to "blow [form of *na·phach'*] into his nostrils the breath [form of *nesha·mah'*] of life, and the man came to be a living soul [*ne'phesh*]." (Ge 2:7; see SOUL.) *Ne'phesh* may be translated literally as "a breather," that is, "a breathing creature," either human or animal. *Nesha·mah'* is, in fact, used to mean "breathing thing [or creature]" and as such is used as a virtual synonym of *ne'phesh*, "soul." (Compare De 20:16; Jos 10:39, 40; 11:11; 1Ki 15:29.) The record at Genesis 2:7 uses *nesha·mah'* in describing God's causing Adam's body to have life so that the man became "a living soul." Other texts, however, show that more was involved than simple breathing of air, that is, more than the mere introduction of air into the lungs and its expulsion therefrom. Thus, at Genesis 7:22, in describing the destruction of human and animal life outside the ark at the time of the Flood, we read: "Everything in which the breath [form of *nesha·mah'*] of the force [or, "spirit" (*ru'ach*)] of life was active in its nostrils, namely, all that were on the dry ground, died." *Nesha·mah'*, "breath," is thus directly associated or linked with *ru'ach*, which here describes the spirit, or life-force, that is active in all living creatures—human and animal souls.

As the *Theological Dictionary of the New Testament* (Vol. VI, p. 336) states: "Breath may be discerned only in movement [as in the movement of the chest or the expanding of the nostrils], and it is also a sign, condition and agent of life, which seems to be esp[ecially] tied up with breathing." Hence, the *nesha·mah'*, or "breath," is both the product of the *ru'ach*, or life-force, and also a principal means of sustaining that life-force in living creatures. It is known from scientific studies, for example, that life is present in every single cell of the body's one hundred trillion cells and that, while thousands of millions of cells die each minute, constant reproduction of new living cells goes on. The life-force active in all the living cells is dependent upon the oxygen that breath-

ing brings into the body, which oxygen is transported to all the cells by the bloodstream. Without oxygen some cells begin to die after several minutes, others after a longer period. While a person can go without breathing for a few minutes and still survive, without the *life-force* in his cells he is dead beyond all human ability to revive him. The Hebrew Scriptures, inspired by man's Designer and Creator, evidently use *ru'ach* to denote this vital force that is the very principle of life, and *nesha·mah'* to represent the breathing that sustains it.

Because breathing is so inseparably connected with life, *nesha·mah'* and *ru'ach* are used in clear parallel in various texts. Job voiced his determination to avoid unrighteousness "while my breath [form of *nesha·mah'*] is yet whole within me, and the spirit [*weru'ach*] of God is in my nostrils." (Job 27:3-5) Elihu said: "If that one's spirit [form of *ru'ach*] and breath [form of *nesha·mah'*] he [God] gathers to himself, all flesh will expire [that is, "breathe out"] together, and earthling man himself will return to the very dust." (Job 34:14, 15) Similarly, Psalm 104:29 says of earth's creatures, human and animal: "If you [God] take away their spirit, they expire, and back to their dust they go." At Isaiah 42:5 Jehovah is spoken of as "the One laying out the earth and its produce, the One giving breath to the people on it, and spirit to those walking in it." The breath (*nesha·mah'*) sustains their existence; the spirit (*ru'ach*) energizes and is the life-force that enables man to be an animated creature, to move, walk, be actively alive. (Compare Ac 17:28.) He is not like the lifeless, breathless, inanimate idols of human fabrication.—Ps 135:15, 17; Jer 10:14; 51:17; Hab 2:19.

While *nesha·mah'* (breath) and *ru'ach* (spirit; active force; life-force) are sometimes used in a parallel sense, they are not identical. True, the "spirit," or *ru'ach*, is at times spoken of as though it were the respiration (*nesha·mah'*) itself, but this seems to be simply because breathing is the prime visible evidence of the life-force in one's body.—Job 9:18; 19:17; 27:3.

Thus at Ezekiel 37:1-10 the symbolic vision of the valley of dry bones is presented, the bones coming together, becoming covered with sinews, flesh, and skin, but "as regards breath [*weru'ach*], there was none in them." Ezekiel was told to prophesy to "the wind [*ha·ru'ach*]," saying, "From the four winds [form of *ru'ach*] come in, O wind, and blow upon these killed people, that they may come to life." The reference to the *four* winds shows that wind is the appropriate rendering for ru'ach in this case. However, when such "wind," which is simply air in motion, entered the nostrils of the dead persons of the vision, it became "breath," which is also air in motion. Thus, the rendering of ru'ach as "breath" at this point of the account (vs 10) is also more appropriate than "spirit" or "life-force." Ezekiel also would be able to see the bodies begin to breathe, even though he could not see the life-force, or spirit, energizing their bodies. As verses 11-14 show, this vision was symbolic of a spiritual (not physical) revivification of the people of Israel who were for a time in a spiritually dead state due to their Babylonian exile. Since they were already physically alive and breathing, it is logical to render ru'ach as "spirit" in verse 14, where God states that he will put 'his spirit' in his people so that they would become alive, spiritually speaking.

A similar symbolic vision is given at Revelation chapter 11. The picture is presented of "two witnesses" who are killed and whose corpses are allowed to lie on the street for three and a half days. Then "spirit [or breath, pneu'ma] of life from God entered into them, and they stood upon their feet." (Re 11:1-11) This vision again draws on a physical reality to illustrate a spiritual revivification. It also shows that the Greek pneu'ma, like the Hebrew ru'ach, may represent the life-giving force from God that animates the human soul or person. As James 2:26 states: "The body without spirit [pneu'ma·tos] is dead."—Int.

Therefore, when God created man in Eden and blew into his nostrils "the breath [form of nesha·mah'] of life," it is evident that, in addition to filling the man's lungs with air, God caused the life-force, or spirit (ru'ach), to vitalize all the cells in Adam's body.—Ge 2:7; compare Ps 104:30; Ac 17:25.

This life-force is passed on from parents to offspring through conception. Since Jehovah was the original Source of this life-force for man, and the Author of the procreation process, one's life can properly be attributed to Him, though received not directly but indirectly through one's parents.—Compare Job 10:9-12; Ps 139:13-16; Ec 11:5.

Life-force, or spirit, is impersonal. As noted, the Scriptures refer to the ru'ach, or life-force, as being not only in humans but also in animals. (Ge 6:17; 7:15, 22) Ecclesiastes 3:18-22 shows that man dies in the same manner as the beasts, for "they all have but one spirit [weru'ach], so that there is no superiority of the man over the beast," that is, as to the life-force common to both. This being so, it is clear that the "spirit," or life-force

(ru'ach), as used in this sense is impersonal. As an illustration, one might compare it to another invisible force, electricity, which may be used to make various types of machines operate—causing stoves to produce heat, fans to produce wind, computers to solve problems, television sets to produce figures, voices and other sounds—yet which electric current never takes on any of the characteristics of the machines in which it functions or is active.

Thus, Psalm 146:3, 4 says that when man's "spirit [form of ru'ach] goes out, he goes back to his ground; in that day his thoughts do perish." The spirit, or life-force, that was active in man's body cells does not retain any of the characteristics of those cells, such as the brain cells and their part in the thinking process. If the spirit, or life-force (ru'ach; pneu'ma), were not impersonal, then it would mean that the children of certain Israelite women who were resurrected by the prophets Elijah and Elisha were actually in conscious existence somewhere in the period during which they were dead. So, too, with Lazarus, who was resurrected some four days after his death. (1Ki 17:17-23; 2Ki 4:32-37; Joh 11:38-44) If such had been the case, it is reasonable that they would have remembered such conscious existence during that period and upon being resurrected would have described it, told about it. There is nothing to indicate that any of them did so. Hence, the personality of the dead individual is not perpetuated in the life-force, or spirit, that stops functioning in the deceased person's body cells.

Ecclesiastes 12:7 states that at death the person's body returns to the dust, "and the spirit itself returns to the true God who gave it." The person himself was never in heaven with God; what "returns" to God is therefore the vital force that enabled the person to live.

In view of the impersonal nature of the life-force, or spirit, found in man (as also in the animal creation), it is evident that David's statement at Psalm 31:5, quoted by Jesus at the time of his death (Lu 23:46), "Into your hand I entrust my spirit," meant that God was being called upon to guard, or care for, that one's life-force. (Compare Ac 7:59.) That there be an actual and literal transmission of some force from this planet to the heavenly presence of God is not necessarily required. Even as the fragrant scent of animal sacrifices was spoken of as being 'smelled' by God (Ge 8:20, 21), whereas such scent undoubtedly remained within earth's atmosphere, so, too, God could 'gather in,' or could accept as entrusted to him, the spirit or life-force in a figurative sense, that is, without any literal transmission of vital force from earth. (Job 34:14; Lu 23:46) A person's entrusting his spirit evidently means, then, that he places his hope in God for a future restoration of such life-force to himself through a resurrection.—Compare Nu 16:22; 27:16; Job 12:10; Ps 104:29, 30.

Impelling Mental Inclination. *Ru'ach* and *pneu'ma* are both used to designate the force that causes a person to display a certain attitude, disposition, or emotion or to take a certain action or course. While that force within the person is itself invisible, it produces visible effects. This use of the Hebrew and Greek terms rendered "spirit" and basically related to breath or to air in motion is paralleled to a considerable degree by English expressions. Thus, we speak of a person as 'putting on airs,' or of manifesting an 'air of calmness' or of 'having a bad spirit.' We speak of 'breaking a person's spirit,' in the sense of discouraging and disheartening him. As applying to a group of persons and the dominant force activating them, we may talk of 'getting into the spirit of an occasion,' or we may refer to the 'mob spirit' that infects them. Metaphorically we may refer to an 'atmosphere of discontent' or to 'winds of change and revolution blowing through a nation.' By all of these we refer to this invisible activating force working in persons, moving them to speak and act as they do.

Similarly, we read of Isaac and Rebekah's "bitterness of spirit" resulting from Esau's marriage to Hittite women (Ge 26:34, 35) and of the sadness of spirit that overwhelmed Ahab, robbing him of his appetite. (1Ki 21:5) A "spirit of jealousy" could move a man to view his wife with suspicion, even to bring charges against her of adultery.—Nu 5:14, 30.

The basic sense of a force that moves and gives "drive" or "thrust" to one's actions and speech is also seen in the reference to Joshua as "a man in whom there is spirit" (Nu 27:18), and to Caleb as demonstrating "a different spirit" from that of the majority of the Israelites who had become demoralized by the bad report of ten spies. (Nu 14:24) Elijah was a man of much drive and force in his zealous service to God, and Elisha sought a two-part share in Elijah's spirit as his successor. (2Ki 2:9, 15) John the Baptizer demonstrated the same vigorous drive and energetic zeal that Elijah had shown, and this resulted in John's having a powerful effect on his listeners; hence he could be said to have gone forth "with Elijah's spirit and power." (Lu 1:17) By contrast, Solomon's wealth and wisdom had such an overwhelming and breathtaking effect on the queen of Sheba that "there proved to be no more spirit in her." (1Ki 10:4, 5) In this same fundamental sense one's spirit may be "stirred up" or "roused" (1Ch 5:26; Ezr 1:1, 5; Hag 1:14; compare Ec 10:4), become "agitated" or "irritated" (Ge 41:8; Da 2:1, 3; Ac 17:16), be "calmed down" (Jg 8:3), be 'distressed,' be made to 'faint' (Job 7:11; Ps 142:2, 3; compare Joh 11:33; 13:21), be 'revived' or "refreshed" (Ge 45:27, 28; Isa 57:15, 16; 1Co 16:17, 18; 2Co 7:13; compare 2Co 2:13).

Heart and spirit. The heart is frequently tied in with the spirit, indicating a definite relationship. Since the figurative heart is shown to have the capacity for thinking and motivation, and to be intimately related with emotions and affection (see HEART), it undoubtedly has a major share in the development of the spirit (the dominant mental inclination) that one shows. Exodus 35:21 places heart and spirit in parallel in saying that "everyone whose heart impelled him, . . . everyone whose spirit incited him," brought contributions for the tabernacle construction. Conversely, on learning of Jehovah's powerful works on behalf of Israel, the Canaanites 'hearts began to melt and no spirit arose among them,' that is, there was no urge to initiate action against the Israelite forces. (Jos 2:11; 5:1; compare Eze 21:7.) References are also made to 'pain of heart and breakdown of spirit' (Isa 65:14) or similar expressions. (Compare Ps 34:18; 143:4, 7; Pr 15:13.) Evidently because of the powerful effect of the activating force on the mind, Paul admonishes: "You should be made new in the force actuating [form of *pneu'ma*] your mind, and should put on the new personality which was created according to God's will in true righteousness and loyalty." —Eph 4:23, 24.

The vital necessity to control one's spirit is strongly emphasized. "As a city broken through, without a wall, is the man that has no restraint for his spirit." (Pr 25:28) Under provocation a person may act as the stupid one who impatiently 'lets all his spirit out,' whereas the wise one "keeps it calm to the last." (Pr 29:11; compare 14:29, 30.) Moses allowed himself to become unduly provoked when the Israelites "embittered his spirit" on one occasion, and he "began to speak rashly with his lips," to his own loss. (Ps 106:32, 33) Thus, "he that is slow to anger is better than a mighty man, and he that is controlling his spirit than the one capturing a city." (Pr 16:32) Humility is essential for this (Pr 16:18, 19; Ec 7:8, 9), and the one "humble in spirit will take hold of glory." (Pr 29:23) Knowledge and discernment keep a man "cool of spirit," in control of his tongue. (Pr 17:27; 15:4) Jehovah makes "an estimate of spirits" and judges those who fail to 'guard themselves respecting their spirit.'—Pr 16:2; Mal 2:14-16.

Spirit shown by a body of persons. As an individual may show a certain spirit, so too a group or body of people may manifest a certain spirit, a dominant mental inclination. (Ga 6:18; 1Th 5:23) The Christian congregation was to be united in spirit, reflecting the spirit of their Head, Christ Jesus.—2Co 11:4; Php 1:27; compare 2Co 12:18; Php 2:19-21.

Paul refers to "the spirit of the world" in contrast with God's spirit. (1Co 2:12) Under the control of God's Adversary (1Jo 5:19), the world shows a spirit of catering to the desires of the fallen flesh, of selfishness, bringing enmity toward God. (Eph 2:1-3; Jas 4:5) Like unfaithful Israel, the world's unclean motivation promotes fornication, either physical or spiritual, with idolatry.—Ho 4:12, 13; 5:4; Zec 13:2; compare 2Co 7:1.

SPIRITISM. The belief or doctrine that the spirits of the human dead, surviving the death of the physical body, can and do communicate with the living, especially through a person (a medium) particularly susceptible to their influence. Both the Bible and secular history reveal that spiritism existed from very early times. Egypt's religion was permeated with it. (Isa 19:3) And the religion of Babylon (which city was also the chief religious center for Assyria) was spiritistic.—Isa 47:12, 13.

The Greek word for "spiritism" is *phar·ma·ki'a*. *Vine's Expository Dictionary of Old and New Testament Words* (1981, Vol. 4, pp. 51, 52) says of the word: "(Eng., pharmacy etc.) primarily signified the use of medicine, drugs, spells; then, poisoning; then, sorcery, Gal. 5:20, R.V., 'sorcery' (A.V., 'witchcraft'), mentioned as one of 'the works of the flesh.' See also Rev. 9:21; 18:23. In the Sept[u-agint], Ex. 7:11, 22; 8:7, 18; Isa. 47:9, 12. In sorcery, the use of drugs, whether simple or potent, was generally accompanied by incantations and appeals to occult powers, with the provision of various charms, amulets, etc., professedly designed to keep the applicant or patient from the attention and power of demons, but actually to impress the applicant with the mysterious resources and powers of the sorcerer."

Its Source. A major feature of spiritism is claimed communication with the dead. Since the dead "are conscious of nothing at all," communication with such dead persons is actually impos-

sible. (Ec 9:5) God's law to Israel forbade anyone's inquiring of the dead and made the practice of spiritism a capital offense. (Le 19:31; 20:6, 27; De 18:9-12; compare Isa 8:19.) And in the Christian Greek Scriptures the statement is made that those who practice spiritism "will not inherit God's kingdom." (Ga 5:20, 21; Re 21:8) It, therefore, logically follows that any claimed communication with dead persons, if not a deliberate lie on the part of the claimant, must be from an evil source, a source that stands in opposition to Jehovah God.

The Bible clearly indicates that wicked spirits, demons, are this evil source. (See DEMON; DEMON POSSESSION.) A case in point is "a certain servant girl" in the city of Philippi. She used to furnish her masters with much gain by practicing "the art of prediction," one of the things related to spiritism. (De 18:11) The account plainly says that the source of her predictions was, not God, but "a demon of divination," a wicked spirit. Hence, when the apostle Paul expelled the wicked spirit, this girl lost her powers of prediction. (Ac 16:16-19) Regarding the Greek expression *pneu'-ma py'tho·na*, here rendered "a demon of divination," *Vine's Expository Dictionary of Old and New Testament Words* (Vol. 1, p. 328) says: "Python, in Greek mythology was the name of the Pythian serpent or dragon, dwelling in Pytho, at the foot of mount Parnassus, guarding the oracle of Delphi, and slain by Apollo. Thence the name was transferred to Apollo himself. Later the word was applied to diviners or soothsayers, regarded as inspired by Apollo. Since demons are the agents inspiring idolatry, I Cor. 10:20, the young woman in Acts 16:16 was possesed by a demon instigating the cult of Apollo, and thus had 'a spirit of divination.'"

In Israel. Even though God had legislated strictly against spiritism, spirit mediums appeared from time to time in the land of Israel. These were probably foreigners who came into the land or some of those who had been spared from destruction by the Israelites. King Saul removed them from the land during his reign, but evidently toward the end of his rule some spirit mediums again began their practice. Saul demonstrated how far he had removed himself from God when he went to consult the "mistress of spirit mediumship in En-dor."—1Sa 28:3, 7-10.

King Saul's visit to a medium. When Saul went to the medium, Jehovah's spirit had for some time been removed from him, and in fact, God would not answer his inquiries by means of dreams or by the Urim (used by the high priest) or by the prophets. (1Sa 28:6) God would have no more to do with him; and God's prophet Samuel had not seen Saul for a long period of time, from before David's being anointed to be king. So it would be unreasonable to think that Samuel, even if still alive, would now come to give Saul advice. And God would certainly not cause Samuel, whom he had not sent to Saul before his death, to come back from the dead to talk to Saul.—1Sa 15:35.

That Jehovah would in no way approve of or cooperate with Saul's action is shown by his later statement through Isaiah: "And in case they should say to you people: 'Apply to the spiritistic mediums or to those having a spirit of prediction who are chirping and making utterances in low tones,' is it not to its God that any people should apply? Should there be application to dead persons in behalf of living persons? To the law and to the attestation!"—Isa 8:19, 20.

Therefore, when the account reads: "When the woman saw 'Samuel' she began crying out at the top of her voice," it obviously recounts the event *as viewed by the medium,* who was deceived by the spirit that impersonated Samuel. (1Sa 28:12) As for Saul himself, the principle stated by the apostle Paul applied: "Just as they did not approve of holding God in accurate knowledge, God gave them up to a disapproved mental state, to do the things not fitting . . . Although these know full well the righteous decree of God, that those practicing such things are deserving of death, they not only keep on doing them but also consent with those practicing them."—Ro 1:28-32.

The *Commentary on the Old Testament,* by C. F. Keil and F. Delitzsch (1973, Vol. II, First Samuel, p. 265), refers to the Greek *Septuagint* at 1 Chronicles 10:13, which has added the words "and Samuel the prophet answered him." (Bagster) The *Commentary* supports the view that is implied by these uninspired words in the *Septuagint,* but it adds: "Nevertheless the fathers, reformers, and earlier Christian theologians, with very few exceptions, assumed that there was not a real appearance of Samuel, but only an imaginary one. According to the explanation given by Ephraem Syrus, an apparent image of Samuel was presented to the eye of Saul through demoniacal arts. Luther and Calvin adopted the same view, and the earlier Protestant theologians followed them in regarding the apparition as nothing but a diabolical spectre, a phantasm, or diabolical spectre in the form of Samuel, and Samuel's announcement as nothing but a diabolical revelation made by divine permission, in which truth is mixed with falsehood."

In a footnote (First Samuel, pp. 265, 266), this *Commentary* says: "Thus Luther says . . . 'The raising of Samuel by a soothsayer or witch, in 1 Sam. xxviii. 11, 12, was certainly merely a spectre of the devil; not only because the Scriptures state that it was effected by a woman who was full of devils (for who could believe that the souls of believers, who are in the hand of God, . . . were under the power of the devil, and of simple men?), but also because it was evidently in opposition to the command of God that Saul and the woman inquired of the dead. The Holy Ghost cannot do anything against this himself, nor can He help those who act in opposition to it.' Calvin also regards the apparition as only a spectre . . . : 'It is certain,' he says, 'that it was not really Samuel, for God would never have allowed His prophets to be subjected to such diabolical conjuring. For here is a sorceress calling up the dead from the grave. Does any one imagine that God wished His prophet to be exposed to such ignominy; as if the devil had power over the bodies and souls of the saints which are in His keeping? The souls of the saints are said to rest . . . in God, waiting for their happy resurrection. Besides, are we to believe that Samuel took his cloak with him into the grave? For all these reasons, it appears evident that the apparition was nothing more than a spectre, and that the senses of the woman herself were so deceived, that she thought she saw Samuel, whereas it really was not he.' The earlier orthodox theologians also disputed the reality of the appearance of the departed Samuel on just the same grounds."

Jesus' Power Over the Demons. When Jesus was on earth, he proved that he was the Messiah, God's Anointed One, by expelling the demons from possessed persons. This he did without special ritual or séance or any form of magic. He simply commanded the demons to come out, and they obeyed his voice. Even though unwillingly, the demons were forced to recognize his authority (Mt 8:29-34; Mr 5:7-13; Lu 8:28-33), just as Satan recognized Jehovah's authority when Jehovah permitted him to afflict Job for a test but commanded Satan not to kill Job. (Job 2:6, 7) Also, Jesus performed this work without cost.—Mt 8:16, 28-32; Mr 1:34; 3:11, 12; Lu 4:41.

Refutes Pharisees' false charge. After one of such cures by Jesus, his enemies, the Pharisees, charged: "This fellow does not expel the demons except by means of Beelzebub, the ruler of the demons." But, says the account: "Knowing their thoughts, he said to them: 'Every kingdom divided against itself comes to desolation, and every city or house divided against itself will not stand. In the same way, if Satan expels Satan, he has become divided against himself; how, then, will his kingdom stand? Moreover, if I expel the demons by means of Beelzebub, by means of whom do your sons expel them? This is why they will be judges of you.'"—Mt 12:22-27.

The Pharisees were forced to concede that superhuman power was needed to expel the demons. Yet they wanted to keep the people from believing in Jesus. Therefore they attributed his power to the Devil. Jesus then enforced the consequences of their argument by showing what the logical outcome of such an argument would mean. He answered that if he were an agent of the Devil, undoing what Satan did, then Satan was indeed working against himself (which no human king would do) and would soon fall. Moreover, he called attention to their "sons," or disciples, who also claimed to expel demons. If the Pharisees' argument was true, that the one expelling demons did so by the power of Satan, then their own disciples were acting under this power, a thing that the Pharisees were, of course, unwilling to acknowledge. Jesus said that therefore their own "sons" were judges condemning them and their argument. Then Jesus said: "But if it is by means of God's spirit that I expel the demons, the kingdom of God has really overtaken you." —Mt 12:28.

Jesus followed up his argument by pointing out that no one could enter a strong man's (Satan's) house and seize his goods unless he had the power to bind the strong man. The false charge on the part of the Pharisees prompted the warning about sin against the holy spirit, since it was by God's spirit that Jesus expelled the demons, and in speaking against this work, the Pharisees were not merely expressing hatred of Jesus but were speaking against the evident demonstration of God's holy spirit.—Mt 12:29-32.

What Jesus Christ said about expelling demons should not be understood to signify that the "sons" of the Pharisees and all others who claimed to cast out demons were necessarily God's instruments. Jesus mentioned persons who would ask: "Lord, Lord, did we not prophesy in your name, and expel demons in your name, and perform many powerful works in your name?" But his reply to them would be: "I never knew you! Get away from me, you workers of lawlessness." (Mt 7:22, 23) Not being true disciples of Jesus Christ, such workers of lawlessness would be children of the Devil. (Compare Joh 8:44; 1Jo 3:10.) So, any

claimed expelling of demons on their part would be, not as instruments of God, but as agents of the Devil. In using persons as exorcists, even doing so in Jesus' name (compare the attempt of the seven sons of Sceva at Ac 19:13-16), Satan would not be divided against himself. Rather, by this seemingly good work of undoing the case of demon obsession, Satan would be transforming himself into "an angel of light," thereby advancing his power and influence over the deceived. —2Co 11:14.

"He that is not against us is for us." On one occasion the apostle John said to Jesus: "Teacher, we saw a certain man expelling demons by the use of your name and we tried to prevent him, because he was not accompanying us." This man was evidently successful in expelling demons, for Jesus said: "There is no one that will do a powerful work on the basis of my name that will quickly be able to revile me." Therefore Jesus ordered that they not try to prevent him, "for he that is not against us is for us." (Mr 9:38-40) Not all who believed in Jesus personally accompanied him and his apostles in their ministry. During this time the Law covenant was in force, by God's will, and God through Jesus Christ had not yet inaugurated the new covenant and the beginning of the Christian congregation of called ones. Only from Pentecost of 33 C.E. onward, after Jesus by his sacrifice had brought about the removal of the Law, was it necessary for anyone serving in the name of Christ to associate with this congregation, the members of which were baptized into Christ. (Ac 2:38-42, 47; Ro 6:3) Then, instead of dealing with the fleshly nation of Israel as he had done until that time, God recognized the Christian congregation as his "holy nation."—1Pe 2:9; 1Co 12:13.

A Work of the Flesh. While it might be thought by the practicers of spiritism that it is a 'spiritual practice,' God's Word calls it, not a work of the spirit or part of its fruitage, but a work of the flesh. Note the detestable things with which it is classified: "fornication, uncleanness, loose conduct, idolatry, practice of spiritism [literally, druggery], enmities, strife, jealousy, fits of anger, contentions, divisions, sects, envies, drunken bouts, revelries, and things like these." It appeals to the desires of the sinful flesh, not to the things of the spirit, and the apostle warns that "those who practice such things will not inherit God's kingdom."—Ga 5:19-21, Int.

Will bring its practicers eternal destruction. As for Babylon the Great, which is to be hurled into the sea, never to be found again, one of the sins charged against her is stated in the Revelation: "By your spiritistic practice all the nations were misled." (Re 18:23) Concerning the everlasting destruction of those who practice spiritism, the Revelation says: "As for the cowards and those without faith and those who are disgusting in their filth and murderers and fornicators and those practicing spiritism [literally, druggers] and idolaters and all the liars, their portion will be in the lake that burns with fire and sulphur. This means the second death."—Re 21:8, *Int.*

Magical Art, a Related Practice. Related to spiritism is magical art. In Ephesus many believed the preaching of Paul, and "quite a number of those who practiced magical arts brought their books together and burned them up before everybody." (Ac 19:19) The Greek word for "magical arts" is *pe·ri'er·ga,* "curiosities," literally, "things that are around work," and thus superfluous, that is, the arts of those who pry into forbidden things, with the aid of evil spirits.—*Int; Vine's Expository Dictionary of Old and New Testament Words,* Vol. 1, p. 261.

A Prophecy Against Jerusalem. In a pronouncement against Jerusalem for her unfaithfulness, Jehovah said: "And you must become low so that you will speak from the very earth, and as from the dust your saying will sound low. And like a spirit medium your voice must become even from the earth, and from the dust your own saying will chirp." (Isa 29:4) This pointed to the time when enemies would come up against Jerusalem and reduce her to a very low state, crushed to the earth, as it were. Accordingly, what utterance Jerusalem's inhabitants made would come from low down in their abasement. It would be as if a spirit medium were talking in such a way as to make it appear that a soft, dull, low, hushed, and weak sound were coming from the dust of the earth. However, as Isaiah 29:5-8 shows, Jerusalem was to be delivered.

SPIT. Saliva ejected from one's mouth. Spitting upon a person or in his face was an act of extreme contempt, enmity, or indignation, bringing humiliation upon the victim. (Nu 12:14) Job, in his adversity, was the object of such a display of detestation. (Job 17:6; 30:10) As a public humiliation of a man in Israel who refused to perform brother-in-law marriage under the Mosaic Law, the rejected widow was to draw the man's sandal off his foot and spit in his face in the presence of the older men of his city.—De 25:7-10.

Jesus Christ was spit upon during his appearance before the Sanhedrin (Mt 26:59-68; Mr 14:

65) and by the Roman soldiers after his trial by Pilate. (Mt 27:27-30; Mr 15:19) Jesus had predicted that he would experience such contemptuous treatment (Mr 10:32-34; Lu 18:31, 32), and it fulfilled the prophetic words: "My face I did not conceal from humiliating things and spit."—Isa 50:6.

In contrast, on three occasions of Bible record, Jesus Christ used his saliva when miraculously healing persons. (Mr 7:31-37; 8:22-26; Joh 9:1-7) Since the results Jesus effected were miraculous and Jesus' miracles were performed under the power of God's spirit, Christ's use of his own saliva in these cases was not the mere effective application of a natural healing agent.

SPOIL. Plunder or booty taken from a defeated enemy as customarily belonging to the victors in war or, less frequently, that seized by bandits or robbers. (Lu 11:21, 22) Though spoil was taken by Israel in its victories, the acquiring of spoil was not the motive for their battles, but it constituted a part of Jehovah's reward to them for carrying out his will, as his executioners.

Abraham, when he rescued Lot from Chedorlaomer's forces, refused to accept from the king of Sodom any of the spoil for himself, so that no one could say that he, not Jehovah, had made Abraham rich.—Ge 14:1-24; Heb 7:4.

Division of Spoil. When vengeance was taken upon the Midianites for their causing the sin and destruction of many of Israel (Nu 25), much spoil was taken. This was divided so that the 12,000 fighting men received half, and those remaining home, the other half. Then one part out of 500 from the fighting men's share went to the priests, and one part out of 50 of the other half to the Levites. The soldiers voluntarily gave much spoil of gold, particularly in the form of jewelry and ornaments, to the sanctuary in appreciation for Jehovah's protection in the fight, in which they did not lose one man.—Nu 31:3-5, 21-54.

This formula may not have been followed exactly in later cases, but it seems to have established a general basis for division of spoil. (1Sa 30:16-20, 22-25; Ps 68:12) Later, under the kingdom, a portion of the spoil was set aside for the king or for the sanctuary.—2Sa 8:7, 8, 11, 12; 2Ki 14:14; 1Ch 18:7, 11.

In the Conquest of Canaan. Cities of the seven nations of Canaan were to be devoted to destruction; all the inhabitants were to be killed; only cattle and other items could be taken. (De 20:16-18; 7:1, 2; Jos 11:14) Jericho, as the firstfruits of the conquest of Canaan, was an exception; only the metals were kept and devoted to the sanctuary. (Jos 6:21, 24) Rahab's household was spared because of her faith. (Jos 6:25) In cities belonging to people of other nations, if they had to be taken by warfare, the virgin women and the children were saved. (De 20:10-15) All spoil in the form of goods or other items had to be cleansed: If of fabric, skin, or wood, it was to be washed; if metal, it was to be processed with fire. —Nu 31:20-23.

Apostate Cities. Israelite cities that turned apostate were to be completely annihilated with all their inhabitants, the spoil was to be burned in the public square, and the city was to be left "a heap of ruins to time indefinite."—De 13:12-17.

Christ Despoils Satan's House. When on earth, Jesus Christ despoiled or 'plundered' the house of Satan by delivering those held in bondage to the demons, curing the afflictions the demons had brought upon them. (Mt 12:22-29) Also, "when he ascended on high he carried away captives; he gave gifts in men." These he took away from Satan's control as gifts for the building up of his congregation.—Eph 4:8, 11, 12.

False Religious Spoilers. Christ declared the scribes and Pharisees to be, like robbers, "full of plunder," evidently acquired by extortion from widows and other defenseless persons; and also because they kept the people in religious bondage by taking away "the key of knowledge." (Mt 23:25; Lu 11:52) The religious leaders of the Jews were likewise prominent in causing the plundering of the possessions of Christians.—Heb 10:34.

SPONGE. The absorbent, tough, elastic skeleton of certain aquatic animals found in abundance in the waters of the eastern Mediterranean Sea and elsewhere. Sponges were probably obtained (in the past as today) by divers who removed them by hand from underwater rocks. After the living animal died and decayed within its skeleton, the sponge was washed thoroughly until only the skeleton remained.

The sponge's ability to absorb and release liquids made it commercially important in ancient times. While Jesus Christ was on the torture stake he was offered some sour wine contained in a sponge that was at the end of a reed.—Mt 27:48; Mr 15:36; Joh 19:29.

SPRING. See FOUNTAIN, SPRING.

SPROUT. See BRANCH, SPROUT.

STACHYS (Sta'chys) [Head of Grain]. One in the Christian congregation at Rome in about 56 C.E. whom Paul speaks of as "my beloved" and to whom he sends his greetings.—Ro 16:9.

STACTE. Stacte drops (Heb., *na·taph'*) were one of the ingredients of the incense limited to sacred use. (Ex 30:34) The related verb form means "drip." (Jg 5:4) The Greek *Septuagint* rendered this word *sta·kte'*, meaning "oil of myrrh," from the Greek verb *sta'zo*, "drip." Thus the Hebrew and Greek terms indicate that this was a balsam that drips from resinous trees. The Latin *Vulgate* rendered the word *stacte*.

The specific tree yielding stacte is uncertain. Among the sources that have been suggested are the Oriental sweet gum tree (*Liquidambar orientalis*) and the mastic pistacia bush (*Pistacia lentiscus*).

STAFF. See COMMANDER'S STAFF; ROD, STAFF.

STAG [Heb., *'ai·yal'*]. An adult male deer. The red deer (*Cervus elaphus*), the fallow deer (*Dama mesopotamica*), and the roe deer (*Capreolus capreolus*) are three varieties of deer that were once native to Palestine.

Being a chewer of the cud and a splitter of the hoof, the stag, according to the Law, was acceptable for food if, as in the case of other creatures, its blood was poured out upon the ground. (De 12:15, 16, 22, 23; 14:4-6; 15:22, 23) The flesh of the stag was included among the meats provided for King Solomon's table.—1Ki 4:22, 23.

Other Scriptural references to the stag are illustrative. The Shulammite compared her shepherd lover to a young stag and made allusion to the swiftness of this animal. (Ca 2:9, 17; 8:14) The stag's ability to climb steep places with ease is used to illustrate the complete cure of lame persons. (Isa 35:6; compare Heb 12:12, 13.) When faced with the Babylonian siege, Zion's princes were like stags too weak from lack of food to run. —La 1:6.

STAKE. See TORTURE STAKE.

STALL. See MANGER, STALL.

STAR. The Hebrew word *koh·khav'* as well as the Greek *a·ster'* and *a'stron* are applied in a general sense to any luminous body in space, except the sun and moon, for which other names are used.

Vastness of Universe. The galaxy within which Earth is located, commonly called the Milky Way, is believed to measure some 100,000 light-years across and to contain over 100,000,000,000 stars like our sun. The closest star to Earth, one of the Alpha Centauri group, is over 40,000,000,000,000 km (25,000,000,000,000 mi) away. Yet this immensity seems relatively small in view of the estimate that there are 100,-000,000,000 galaxies throughout universal space. About 10,000,000,000 of these are within the range of modern telescopes.

The vastness of the stellar creation adds infinite force and meaning to the Creator's statement at Isaiah 40:26: "Raise your eyes high up and see. Who has created these things? It is the One who is bringing forth the army of them even by number, all of whom he calls even by name. Due to the abundance of dynamic energy, he also being vigorous in power, not one of them is missing." (Compare Ps 147:4.) The reverent psalmist was led to say: "When I see your heavens, the works of your fingers, the moon and the stars that you have prepared, what is mortal man that you keep him in mind, and the son of earthling man that you take care of him?"—Ps 8:3, 4.

Age. The fact that rays from remote stars and galaxies millions of light-years distant now reach giant telescopes on earth indicates that the creation of these astral bodies occurred millions of years in the past, since otherwise these rays would not yet have reached our planet. Such creation is evidently included in the initial statement at Genesis 1:1: "In the beginning God created the heavens and the earth." Verse 16 does not contradict this in saying that during the fourth creative "day," or period, "God proceeded to make . . . the stars." The word "make" (Heb., 'a·sah') does not mean the same as the word "create" (Heb., ba·ra').—See CREATION.

Number of Stars. In addressing man, God used the stars to denote a countless number, comparable to the grains of sand on the seashore. (Ge 22:17; 15:5; Ex 32:13; compare Ne 9:23; Na 3:15, 16; Heb 11:12.) Since the stars clearly discernible to the unaided eye number only a few thousand, this comparison was viewed by many in the past as out of balance. Yet today the evidence shows that the number of stars does indeed compare to all the grains of sand in all the earth.

It is of interest to note that, while Moses spoke of Israel as having seen a certain fulfillment of this Abrahamic promise, the censuses taken of the population, as recorded in the Bible, never did include the total number in the nation. (De 1:10; 10:22; 28:62) David is mentioned later as specifically refraining from taking the number of those "from twenty years of age and under, because Jehovah had promised to make Israel as many as the stars of the heavens." (1Ch 27:23) Such concept of the innumerableness of these heavenly bodies distinguishes the Bible writings as unique when compared with contemporary views of ancient peoples.

Orderly Arrangement. Additionally, the orderliness of the arrangement of these celestial bodies is emphasized in various texts, references being made to "statutes," "regulations," and "orbits" ("courses," RS). (Jer 31:35-37; Jg 5:20; compare Jude 13.) The tremendous forces that determine the relative positions of certain stars according to physical laws are indicated by God's questions to Job: "Can you tie fast the bonds of the Kimah constellation, or can you loosen the very cords of the Kesil constellation? Can you bring forth the Mazzaroth constellation in its appointed time? . . . Have you come to know the statutes of the heavens, or could you put its authority in the earth?" (Job 38:31-33; see ASH CONSTELLATION; KESIL CONSTELLATION; KIMAH CONSTELLATION; MAZZAROTH CONSTELLATION.) Thus, the *New Bible Dictionary* states: "We assert, then, that the Bible consistently assumes a universe which is fully rational, and vast in size, in contrast to the typical contemporary world-view, in which the universe was not rational, and no larger than could actually be proved by the unaided senses." —Edited by J. Douglas, 1985, p. 1144.

The apostle Paul's expression concerning the difference between individual stars can be appreciated even more in the light of modern astronomy, which shows the contrast existing as to color, size, amount of light produced, temperature, and even the relative density of the stars.—1Co 15: 40, 41.

Star Worship. While star worship was rampant among the ancient nations of the Middle East, the Scriptural view held by God's faithful servants was that such astral bodies were simply material bodies subject to divine laws and control, not dominating man but serving as luminaries and time indicators. (Ge 1:14-18; Ps 136:3, 7-9; 148:3) In warning Israel against making any representation of the true God Jehovah, Moses commanded them not to be seduced into worship of sun, moon, and stars, "which Jehovah your God has apportioned to all the peoples under the whole heavens." (De 4:15-20; compare 2Ki 17:16; 21:5; 23:5; Zep 1:4, 5.) Pagan nations identified their particular gods with certain stars and thus took a nationalistic view of those stellar bodies. Sakkuth and Kaiwan, mentioned at Amos 5:26 as gods worshiped by apostate Israel, are considered to be Babylonian names for the planet Saturn, called Rephan in Stephen's quotation of this text. (Ac 7:42, 43) Star worship was especially prominent in Babylon but was proved worthless at the time of her destruction.—Isa 47:12-15.

"Star" Seen After Jesus' Birth. The "astrologers from eastern parts," hence from the neighborhood of Babylon, whose visit to King Herod after the birth of Jesus resulted in the slaughter of all the male infants in Bethlehem, were obviously not servants or worshipers of the true God. (Mt 2:1-18; see ASTROLOGERS.) As to the "star" (Gr., a·ster´) seen by them, many suggestions have been given as to its having been a comet, a meteor, a supernova, or, more popularly, a conjunction of planets. None of such bodies could logically have 'come to a stop above where the young child was,' thereby identifying the one house in the village of Bethlehem where the child was found. It is also notable that only these pagan astrologers "saw" the star. Their condemned practice of astrology and the adverse results of their visit, placing in danger the life of the future Messiah, certainly allow for, and even make advisable, the consideration of their having been directed by a source *adverse* to God's purposes as relating to the promised Messiah. It is certainly reasonable to ask if the one who "keeps transforming himself into an angel of light," whose operation is "with every powerful work and lying signs and portents," who was able to make a serpent appear to speak, and who was referred to by Jesus as "a manslayer when he began," could not also cause astrologers to 'see' a starlike object that guided them first, not to Bethlehem, but to Jerusalem, where resided a mortal enemy of the promised Messiah.—2Co 11:3, 14; 2Th 2:9; Ge 3:1-4; Joh 8:44.

Figurative Use. Stars are used in the Bible in a figurative sense and in metaphors or similes to represent persons, as in Joseph's dream in which his parents were represented by the sun and moon, and his 11 brothers by 11 stars. (Ge 37:9, 10) Job 38:7 parallels "the morning stars" that joyfully cried out at earth's founding with the angelic "sons of God." The resurrected and exalted Jesus spoke of himself as "the bright morning star" and promised to give "the morning star" to his conquering followers, evidently indicating a sharing with him in his heavenly position and glory. (Re 22:16; 2:26, 28; compare 2Ti 2:12; Re 20:6.) The seven "angels" of the congregations, to whom written messages are delivered, are symbolized by seven stars in the right hand of Christ. (Re 1:16, 20; 2:1; 3:1) "The angel of the abyss" called Abaddon is also represented by a star.—Re 9:1, 11; see ABADDON.

In the proverbial saying of Isaiah chapter 14, the boastful and ambitious king of Babylon (that is, the Babylonian dynasty of kings represented by Nebuchadnezzar), called the "shining one" (Heb., heh·lel´; "Lucifer," *KJ*), is presented as seeking to lift up his throne "above the stars of God." (Isa 14:4, 12, 13; see SHINING ONE.) The metaphor of a "star" is used in referring prophetically to the Davidic kings of Judah (Nu 24:17), and Bible history shows that the Babylonian dynasty for a time did rise above these Judean kings by conquest of Jerusalem. A similar prophecy in Daniel chapter 8 describes the small "horn" of some future power as trampling down certain stars of "the army of the heavens" and moving against the Prince of the army and his sanctuary (Da 8:9-13); while at Daniel chapter 12, by simile, those persons "having insight" and bringing others to righteousness are pictured as shining "like the stars" in "the time of the end." (Da 12:3, 9, 10) By contrast, immoral deviators from truth are compared to "stars with no set course."—Jude 13.

The darkening of the stars, along with the sun and moon, is a frequent figure used in prophetic warnings of disaster brought as a result of God's judgment. (Isa 13:10; Eze 32:7; Re 6:12, 13; 8:12; compare Job 9:6, 7.) The dimming of such luminaries is also used in the description of the fading years of the aged person at Ecclesiastes 12:1, 2. Elsewhere stars are spoken of as falling or being cast down to earth. (Mt 24:29; Re 8:10; 9:1; 12:4) "Signs" in sun, moon, and stars are foretold as evidence of the time of the end.—Lu 21:25.

"Daystar." The expression "daystar" (Gr., pho·spho´ros) occurs once, at 2 Peter 1:19, and is similar in meaning to "morning star." Such stars at certain seasons of the year are the last stars to rise on the eastern horizon before the sun appears and thus are heralds of the dawn of a new day. Peter's previous reference to the vision of Jesus' transfiguration in magnificent glory suggests a relation to his entering into kingly power as "the root and the offspring of David, and the bright morning star [a·ster´]."—Re 22:16; 2:26-28.

'Stars Fought Against Sisera.' The account at Judges 5:20 has occasioned discussion with regard to the phrase, "From heaven did the stars fight, from their orbits they fought against Sisera." Some view it as merely a poetical reference to divine assistance. (Compare Jg 4:15; Ps 18:9.) Other suggestions include the falling of showers of meteorites, or the dependence of Sisera on astrological predictions, which proved false. Since the Bible record does not detail the manner in which the stars "fought," it appears sufficient to regard the statement as showing some divine action of a miraculous nature taken on behalf of Israel's army.

STATER. A silver coin with which the temple tax was paid for Jesus and his apostle Peter. Equivalent to four drachmas, it amounted to about four days' wages at that time. (Mt 17:24, 27) Many scholars view it as the tetradrachma minted at Antioch, Syria, or at Tyre. The Tyrian tetradrachma, approximately the size of the United States half-dollar, bore the head of the god Melkart on the obverse side, an eagle perched on a ship's rudder on the reverse side, and an inscription reading "Tyre the Holy and Invincible." A likeness of Emperor Augustus appeared on the tetradrachma of Antioch.

STATUTE. A formally established and recorded rule, or law—divine or human. (Ge 26:5; Ps 89:30-32; Da 6:15) The Bible reveals Jehovah God to be the supreme Statute-Giver.—Isa 33:22; see LAW; LAWGIVER.

STATUTE-GIVER. See LAWGIVER.

STEALING. See THIEF.

STEPHANAS (Steph'a·nas) [from a root that means "crown; wreath"]. One of the mature members of the congregation at Corinth, the capital of the Roman province of Achaia in southern Greece. Paul personally baptized Stephanas' household as the "firstfruits" of his ministry in that province. (1Co 1:16; 16:15) Some five years later, about 55 C.E., Stephanas, together with two other brothers from Corinth, visited Paul in Ephesus, and it may have been through them that Paul learned of the distressing conditions about which he wrote in his first canonical letter to the Corinthians. (1Co 1:11; 5:1; 11:18) Also, it may have been by their hands that this letter was delivered to Corinth.—1Co 16:17.

STEPHEN (Ste'phen) [from a root meaning "crown; wreath"]. The first Christian martyr. Though his name is Greek, he was one of the faithful Jewish remnant that accepted and followed the Messiah.—Ac 7:2.

His Appointment to a Special Ministry. Stephen's name first appears in the Bible record in connection with the appointment of men to special service responsibilities in the Christian congregation at Jerusalem. The account reads: "Now in these days, when the disciples were increasing, a murmuring arose on the part of the Greek-speaking Jews against the Hebrew-speaking Jews, because their widows were being overlooked in the daily distribution." The apostles saw the need for special attention to this matter, and they instructed the congregation: "So, brothers, search out for yourselves seven certified men

from among you, full of spirit and wisdom, that we may appoint them over this necessary business." These qualified men were then selected and were appointed by the apostles.—Ac 6:1-6.

Stephen therefore received an appointment to a ministry in a special way. He and the six others appointed over "this necessary business," the distribution of food supplies, may have already been older men, or overseers. These men were men "full of spirit and wisdom," which this particular emergency required, for it was not only the mechanical distribution of food supplies (possibly in the form of grains and other staples) but also a matter of administration. The duties may have called for these men to handle buying, keeping of records, and so forth. So, although such work, if on a lesser scale or under other circumstances, might have been such as would be handled by a di·a'ko·nos, a "ministerial servant," not by an overseer, or older man, the situation here was a sensitive one, difficulty and differences already existing in the congregation. Therefore it required men of notable judgment, discretion, understanding, and experience. Stephen's defense before the Sanhedrin indicates his qualifications.

While taking care of these appointed ministerial duties, Stephen vigorously continued his Christian preaching. The chronicler Luke reports that "Stephen, full of graciousness and power," and "performing great portents and signs among the people," was bitterly opposed by Jews of the so-called Synagogue of the Freedmen and others from Asia and Africa. But Stephen spoke with such wisdom and spirit that they could not hold their own against him. As had been done in Jesus' case, enemies secretly secured false witnesses to accuse Stephen of blasphemy before the Sanhedrin.—See FREEDMAN, FREEMAN.

His Defense Before the Sanhedrin. Stephen boldly recounted God's dealings with the Hebrews from the time of their forefather Abraham, and he concluded with powerful accusations against his own audience of religious leaders. As they were cut to the heart by the truth of the accusations and began to gnash their teeth at him, Stephen was favored by God with a vision of God's glory and of Jesus standing at God's right hand. At his description of the vision, the assembly shouted and rushed upon him with one accord and threw him outside the city. Then, laying their garments at the feet of Saul, they stoned Stephen to death. Just before 'falling asleep in death,' Stephen prayed: "Jehovah, do not charge this sin against them." Certain reverent men came and gave him a burial and lamented his death. Great persecution then broke out against the Christians, scattering them (though the apostles remained in Jerusalem) and resulting in the spreading of the good news.—Ac 6:8–8:2; 11:19; 22:20.

Stephen's account delivered before the Sanhedrin includes a number of facts concerning Jewish history that are not found in the Hebrew Scriptures: Moses' Egyptian education, his age of 40 when he fled Egypt, the 40-year duration of his stay in Midian before returning to Egypt, and the role of angels in giving the Mosaic Law.—Ac 7:22, 23, 30, 32, 38.

Stephen was the first to bear witness that he had seen, in a special vision, Jesus returned to heaven and at the right hand of God, as prophesied at Psalm 110:1.—Ac 7:55, 56.

STEWARD.

One placed in charge of the household or certain property belonging to another. The Hebrew word so·khen' is rendered "steward" (Isa 22:15); mo·shel', which means "one managing," likewise refers to a steward. (Ge 24:2, ftn) The Greek oi·ko·no'mos (steward) can also be translated "house manager."—Lu 12:42, ftn.

A steward might be a freeman or a trusted slave. The 'unrighteous steward' to whom Jesus referred in one of his illustrations seems to be pictured as a freeman. (Lu 16:1, 2, 4) Kings, and many other persons of wealth or distinction, had a steward, and men varied as to the degree of authority they gave to their stewards. The Greek word e·pi'tro·pos, "man in charge," is closely related in meaning, since a steward often had oversight of the house as well as the other servants and the property, and at times over business affairs.—Ga 4:1-3; Lu 16:1-3.

Abraham had a faithful servant, Eliezer of Damascus, as man in charge of his extensive belongings, which consisted of great wealth of livestock and, at one time, many slaves, although Abraham held no land possessions other than a burial plot. (Ge 13:2; 14:14; 15:2; 23:17-20; Ac 7:4, 5) Joseph, as a slave in Egypt, came to be in charge of Potiphar's house. (Ge 39:1-4, 8, 9) Later, he too had a steward. (Ge 44:4) King Elah of Israel had a man over his household in Tirzah. This was likely a custom also of the other ancient kings. (1Ki 16:9) Shebna was steward over the king's house in the days of King Hezekiah of Judah, but he was unfaithful and was replaced by Eliakim the son of Hilkiah.—Isa 22:15, 20, 21.

In the Christian Greek Scriptures we find that Herod Antipas had a man in charge of his house; this man's wife ministered from her belongings to Jesus. (Lu 8:3) Jesus, in an illustration, referred to a man in charge of the vineyard laborers who paid them at the end of the day.—Mt 20:8.

The responsibilities and administrative duties of a steward suitably describe the ministry entrusted by Jehovah God to the Christian. Jesus describes his body of faithful anointed ones on earth as "the faithful and discreet slave," but as a slave they also serve as a steward for him, having had committed to them in these last days "all his belongings"—including the preaching of "this good news of the kingdom" throughout the earth, teaching those who wish to hear, and serving as God's instrument to gather into association with the congregation the international "great crowd" that would survive the great tribulation. (Mt 24: 14, 45; Lu 12:42-44; Re 7:9-14) Overseers in the Christian congregation are "stewards," and faithfulness is strictly required of them. (Tit 1:7; 1Co 4:1, 2) Paul, as an apostle, especially as the apostle to the Gentiles, had a special stewardship entrusted to him. (1Co 9:17; Eph 3:1, 2) Peter points out to all Christians, overseers and others, that they are stewards of God's undeserved kindness expressed in various ways, and he shows that each has a sphere, or a place, in God's arrangement in which he can carry out a faithful stewardship.—1Pe 4:10.

STOCKS.

An ancient instrument of confinement and punishment, consisting of a wooden frame in which a seated victim's feet were locked (2Ch 16:10; Jer 20:2, 3), often while he was exposed to public gaze and ridicule. Roman stocks had several holes so that, if desired, the legs could be widely separated, adding to the torture. Stocks for confining the feet are called sadh in Hebrew (Job 13:27; 33:11), and since they are made of wood, they are designated by the Greek term xy'lon (wood). While imprisoned at Philippi, Paul and Silas were confined in stocks that held their feet.—Ac 16:24.

Elsewhere in the Hebrew Scriptures another word, mah·pe'kheth, is rendered "stocks." Since it carried the thought of turning, it appears that the person so confined was forced into a bent or distorted bodily posture. This device may have held the feet, hands, and neck, or perhaps it could have been used with other means for holding the neck and arms. The stocks and the pillory might have been combined to hold the legs as well as the neck and arms. (Jer 29:26, NE, NW) None of such instruments were prescribed by the Law given by God to Israel, nor did the Law provide for prisons.

STOICS

(Sto'ics). Philosophers whom Paul encountered when he was preaching in the marketplace at Athens. Though their views changed somewhat with the passing of time, basically the Stoics held that matter and force (the latter sometimes being called providence, reason, or God) were the elemental principles in the universe. To the Stoics all things, even vices and virtues, were material. Not believing in God as a Person, they thought that all things were part of an impersonal deity and that the human soul emanated from such source. Thinking the soul survived death of the body, some Stoics believed it would eventually be destroyed with the universe; others, that ultimately it would be reabsorbed by this deity. The Stoics maintained that to attain the highest goal, happiness, man should use his reason to understand and conform to the laws governing the universe. To them pursuing a life of virtue therefore meant 'following nature.' The truly wise man, in their estimation, was indifferent to pain or pleasure, independent of riches or poverty and the like. Fate, they thought, governed human affairs, and if problems seemed overwhelming, suicide was considered unobjectionable.

Zeno of Citium, Cyprus, after associating with the Cynics for a time, established this separate school of philosophy about 300 B.C.E. His disciples got the name Stoics from the Stoa Poikile, the painted porch in Athens where he taught for some 58 years. Stoic philosophy was further developed particularly by Cleanthes and Chrysippus and was widely accepted among the Greeks and Romans, its adherents including Seneca, Epictetus, and the Roman emperor Marcus Aurelius. It flourished until about 300 C.E.

Like the Epicureans, the Stoics did not believe in the resurrection as taught by Christians. So, when Paul declared the good news about Jesus and the resurrection, they called him a "chatterer" and said he seemed to be "a publisher of foreign deities." Later, having been led to the Areopagus, Paul cited writings of the Stoics Aratus of Cilicia (in his *Phænomena*) and Cleanthes (in *Hymn to Zeus*), saying: "For by [God] we have life and move and exist, even as certain ones of the poets among you have said, 'For we are also his progeny.'"—Ac 17:17-19, 22, 28.

STOMACH. An enlarged part of the alimentary canal in humans and animals. In some animals the stomach includes four compartments. Under the Law, a person who sacrificed a victim had to give the stomach (Heb., *qe·vah'*) to the priest. (De 18:3) In the Christian Greek Scriptures, the apostle Paul recommended that Timothy use a little wine for the sake of his stomach (Gr., *sto'ma·khos*).—1Ti 5:23.

In some instances where the Hebrew words translated "belly" and "inward parts" are used, they apparently include the stomach. (Pr 13:25; Jon 1:17) The same is true in the usage of "belly" in the Christian Greek Scriptures, as, for example, at Romans 16:18 and 1 Corinthians 6:13.—See BELLY.

STONE. A material widely used in building. Its durable nature has been of great aid to archaeologists in gaining some knowledge of the past. Temples, palaces, monuments, and other structures of stone were erected by the Egyptians, Assyrians, and other nations. On many of these structures are pictorial representations and inscriptions relating events, describing victories, and depicting customs, which throw light on their history as well as on their everyday life. The Hebrews used stone widely in buildings (Le 14:40, 41), walls (Ne 4:3; Pr 24:31), altars (Ex 20:25), millstones (Jg 9:53), water vessels (Joh 2:6), weights (Pr 16:11), for covering wells, caves, and tombs (Ge 29:8; Jos 10:18; Joh 11:38), as well as for many other purposes. However, the Hebrews did not erect monuments with pictorial bas-reliefs, as did the pagan nations; consequently little is known about their appearance, the exact styles of their clothing, and so forth. But the Bible provides a richer history of Israel, their manner of life, and their personalities than do the stone remains of any of the other nations.

Stonecutting was a highly developed craft. (2Sa 5:11; 1Ki 5:18) The stones for the temple of Solomon at Jerusalem were cut at the quarry so that they fitted together at the temple site without further shaping.—1Ki 6:7.

Figurative Use. Anointed Christians on earth are likened to a temple, Jesus Christ being its "foundation cornerstone." (See CORNERSTONE.) Upon this "foundation cornerstone," the spirit-begotten followers of Christ "as living stones are being built up a spiritual house." The Jewish religious leaders, as national "builders," rejected Jesus as "the chief cornerstone," stumbling over this stone because they were disobedient to God's Word.—Eph 2:19-22; 1Pe 2:4-8; Mt 21:42; Mr 12:10; Lu 20:17; Ro 9:32, 33.

God's Kingdom is likened to a stone "cut out not by hands," a stone that will crush and put an end to all other kingdoms. This Kingdom will itself stand "to times indefinite."—Da 2:34, 44, 45.

At Revelation 2:17, the glorified Christ Jesus promises concerning the Christian conqueror: "I will give him a white pebble ["stone," *KJ*], and upon the pebble a new name written which no one knows except the one receiving it." The word "pebble" here translates the Greek word *pse'phon*. The apostle Paul uses the word when he recounts his former persecution of Christians, saying: "I cast my vote [*pse'phon;* literally, (voting) pebble] against them." (Ac 26:10) Pebbles were used in courts of justice in rendering judgment or voicing an opinion of either innocence or guilt. White pebbles were used for pronouncing innocence, acquittal; black ones for pronouncing guilt, condemnation. The white pebble given to the conqueror therefore appears to mean Jesus' judgment of him as innocent, pure, clean, passing Christ's approval as a disciple.

See JEWELS AND PRECIOUS STONES; ROCK-MASS.

STONECUTTER. A hewer of stone; one who cuts, carves, or dresses stones to be used for building purposes. (2Ki 12:11, 12; 2Ch 24:12) King David made alien residents in Israel stone hewers "to hew squared stones" (cutting them to the proper size) for the prospective temple of Jehovah.—1Ch 22:2, 15; compare 1Ki 6:7; see QUARRY.

STONE PAVEMENT. A paved place at Jerusalem where Roman Governor Pontius Pilate sat on the judgment seat when Jesus Christ was before him for trial. (Joh 19:13) The site was called, in Hebrew, "*Gabbatha*," a word of uncertain derivation and possibly meaning "hill," "height," or "open space." The Greek name for it, *Li·tho'stro·ton* (Stone Pavement), may indicate a tessellated pavement, one of ornamental mosaic work.

"The Stone Pavement" where Jesus appeared before Pilate was in some way associated with "the governor's palace." (Jo 19:1-13) It may have been an open area in front of the palace of Herod the Great; some scholars favor identification with a site near or a central court within the Tower of Antonia, NW of the temple grounds. But the exact site of The Stone Pavement remains unknown. —See ANTONIA, TOWER OF; GOVERNOR'S PALACE.

STONING. Under the Law, a wrongdoer deserving capital punishment usually was pelted to death with stones. (Le 20:2) This was to 'clear out what was bad from their midst.' All Israel would hear of the punishment, and fear of such wrongdoing would be instilled in their hearts. (De 13:5, 10, 11; 22:22-24) In stoning an evildoer, they showed that they were zealous for true worship, anxious to see that no reproach came upon God's name, and desirous of maintaining a clean congregation.

Before a wrongdoer could be stoned, at least two witnesses had to give harmonious testimony against him, and thereafter they cast the first stones. (Le 24:14; De 17:6, 7) The prospect of being the executioner made a person think searchingly in giving evidence and doubtless was a deterrent to false testimony, which, if discovered, would cost the lying witness his own life. —De 19:18-20.

Stoning no doubt usually took place outside the city. (Nu 15:35, 36; 1Ki 21:13; contrast De 22:21.) Thereafter, as a warning, the corpse might be impaled on a stake, but not beyond sunset. It was buried that same day.—De 21:21-23.

Jesus spoke of Jerusalem as "the killer of the prophets and stoner of those sent forth to her." (Mt 23:37; compare Heb 11:37.) Christ himself was threatened with stoning. (Joh 8:59; 10:31-39; 11:8) Stephen was killed in this manner. (Ac 7:58-60) At Lystra fanatical Jews "stoned Paul and dragged him outside the city, imagining he was dead."—Ac 14:19; compare 2Co 11:25.

For offenses carrying the penalty of stoning, see CRIME AND PUNISHMENT.

STORAGE CITIES. Cities especially designed as government storage centers. Reserves of provisions such as grain, as well as other things, were preserved in warehouses and granaries built at these locations.

Under Egyptian oppression, the Israelites were compelled to build "cities as storage places for Pharaoh, namely, Pithom and Raamses." (Ex 1:11) Storage cities were also built by Solomon. (1Ki 9:17-19; 2Ch 8:4-6) Later, as King Jehoshaphat prospered, "he went on building fortified places and storage cities in Judah."—2Ch 17:12; see STOREHOUSE.

STORAX [Heb., *liv·neh'*]. The name of this tree in Hebrew means "white," and the related Arabic word *lubna* is applied to the storax tree (*Styrax officinalis*). The storax grows as a tall shrub or small tree, seldom exceeding 6 m (20 ft) in height. It is plentiful in Syria, where Jacob made use of its staffs (Ge 30:37), and throughout Palestine, often growing on dry hillsides and rocky places, where its shade would be appreciated. (Ho 4:13) Its oval-shaped leaves, growing on long flexible twigs, are green on top but woolly white underneath. The showy flowers with their white petals and delightful fragrance are very similar to orange blossoms.

STOREHOUSE. A warehouse or building in which foodstuffs—wine, and oil—as well as even precious metals or stones and other articles are stored. A granary is a structure used to store threshed grain. Barns, towers, and other storage facilities were common in ancient times (1Ch 27:25; 2Ch 32:27, 28; Joe 1:17; Hag 2:19), and certain cities served principally as storage centers.—Ex 1:11.

Storehouses were needed in conjunction with the sanctuary to take care of the tithes and contributions from the fields, orchards, and vineyards given by Israel to the Levites. (Mal 3:10) Certain Levites were put in charge of the stores and they distributed such provisions to their brothers.—1Ch 26:15, 17; Ne 12:44; 13:12, 13.

In ancient Egypt granaries varied in structure, one type resembling the present-day silo. It had a door at the top for depositing grain (by ascending a ladder) and small sliding doors at ground level for its removal. Underground granaries have also long been used in the Middle East, these evidently being preferred in sparsely populated areas because they are concealed from marauders.

Illustrative Use. Jesus Christ, in urging his disciples not to be anxious about material needs, but to seek only their "bread for this day," reminded them that God feeds the birds though they do not gather things into storehouses or barns. (Mt 6:11, 25, 26; Lu 12:22, 24) To show that life does not result from the things one possesses, Jesus gave an illustration of a rich man who considered replacing his storehouses with bigger ones to hold his many goods, only to face death; his material riches therefore were of no benefit to him.—Lu 12:13-21.

Instead of encouraging us to look to earthly goods and accordingly build up a great store of them, the wise writer of Proverbs says: "Honor Jehovah with your valuable things . . . Then your stores of supply will be filled with plenty." (Pr 3:9, 10) This was exemplified in the experience of the nation of Israel, which, when obediently serving Jehovah and bringing full tithes to the sanctuary, was blessed with abundance. (De 28:1, 8; 1Ki 4:20; 2Ch 31:4-10; Mal 3:10) Apparently King David uses contrast at Psalm 144:11-15 to show who are the really happy people. In view of the context (see vss 11, 12), it seems likely that he is depicting those who trust in their hoard of material things as boasting in their wealth by saying: "Our garners [are] full, furnishing products of one sort after another . . . Happy is the people for whom it is just like that!" But David's next words, "Happy is the people whose God is Jehovah!" apparently are intended to show the true Source of happiness in contrast with material wealth.

Figurative Use. John the Baptizer warned the Pharisees and Sadducees of their dangerous situation, likening truly repentant ones to wheat to be gathered, but comparing those leaders to chaff. He said to them: "The one coming after me . . . will gather his wheat into the storehouse, but the chaff he will burn up with fire that cannot be put out." (Mt 3:7-12; Lu 3:16, 17) Jesus foretold a "harvest," which he equated with "a conclusion of a system of things" and in which angelic "reapers" would gather symbolic "weeds" to be burned, whereas "the wheat" would be gathered into God's "storehouse," the restored Christian congregation, where they would have God's favor and protection.—Mt 13:24-30, 36-43.

Jehovah speaks of things around which he has put boundaries by means of created forces, or natural laws, as well as of things he has reserved under his control for special purposes, as being in "storehouses." The sea is said to be 'gathered like a dam, put in storehouses.' (Ps 33:7) Also of other natural phenomena that he has at times used against his enemies, he asked Job: "Have you entered into the storehouses of the snow, or do you see even the storehouses of the hail, which I have kept back for the time of distress, for the day of fight and war?" (Job 38:22, 23; compare Jos 10:8-11; Jg 5:20, 21; Ps 105:32; 135:7.) Even the armies of the Medes and Persians under King Cyrus were included by Jehovah among "the weapons of his denunciation" brought out of his "storehouse" against Babylon.—Jer 50:25, 26.

STORK [Heb., chasi·dhah′]. The name of this bird is the feminine form of the Hebrew word for "loyal one; one of loving-kindness." (Compare 1Sa 2:8; Ps 18:25, ftn.) This description fits the stork well, as it is noted for its tender care of its young and its faithfulness to its lifelong mate.

The stork is a large, long-legged wading bird similar to the ibis and heron. The white stork (*Ciconia ciconia*) has white plumage except for the flight feathers of its wings, which are a glossy black. An adult stork may stand as much as 1.2 m (4 ft) high, measuring nearly 1.2 m (4 ft) in body length, with a magnificent wingspan that may extend up to 2 m (6.5 ft). Its long red bill, broad at the base and sharply pointed, is used by the stork in probing in the mud for frogs, fish, or small reptiles. In addition to small water creatures, it feeds on grasshoppers and locusts and also may resort to carrion and offal. The stork was included in the list of unclean creatures, which, according to the Law covenant, the Israelites were prohibited from eating.—Le 11:19; De 14:18.

When reprimanding the apostate people of Judah who failed to discern the time of Jehovah's judgment, the prophet Jeremiah called their attention to the stork and other birds that 'well know their appointed times.' (Jer 8:7) The stork regularly migrates through Palestine and Syria from its winter quarters in Africa, appearing in large flocks during March and April. Of the two kinds of storks found in Israel, the white stork and the black stork (*Ciconia nigra*), the former only occasionally remains to breed in that region, usually making its nest in trees but also on man-made structures. The black stork, so named for its black head, neck, and back, is more common in the Hula and Bet She'an valleys and it seeks trees, where available, to build its nest. The psalmist referred to the storks nesting in the tall juniper trees.—Ps 104:17.

Contrasting the flightless ostrich with the high-flying stork, Jehovah asked Job: "Has the wing of the female ostrich flapped joyously, or has she the pinions of a stork and the plumage?" (Job 39:13) The stork's pinions are of great breadth and power, the secondary and tertiary feathers being almost as long as the primaries, giving an immense surface to the wing and enabling the stork to be a bird of lofty and long-continued flight. A stork in flight soaring on its powerful wings, with its neck extended and its long legs stretched out straight behind it, makes an imposing sight. The two women seen in Zechariah's vision (Zec 5:6-11) carrying an ephah measure containing the woman called "Wickedness" are described as having "wings like the wings of the stork." The reference to the 'wind in their wings' (vs 9) harmonizes also with the rushing sound produced by the air passing through the stork's pinions. The primary feathers are fingered out in flight so that slots are formed at the ends of the wings, thereby controlling the airflow over the top of the wings and improving their lifting power.

STRAIGHT.

A street in Damascus, Syria. (Ac 9:10, 11; PICTURE, Vol. 2, p. 748) During the Roman period, it was a major thoroughfare approximately 1.5 km (1 mi) long and about 30 m (100 ft) wide. Then divided by colonnades into three sections, its center lane was used by pedestrians and the two outside lanes were for mounted and vehicular traffic moving in opposite directions. Still bearing an Arabic equivalent of the former name (Darb al-Mustaqim), but no longer completely straight, it runs W from the city's East Gate. On this ancient street, at the house of a man named Judas, Saul of Tarsus stayed for a time after the glorified Jesus Christ appeared to him. In a vision, Jesus directed the disciple Ananias to this home on "the street called Straight" to restore Saul's sight.—Ac 9:3-12, 17-19.

STRANGER.   See ALIEN RESIDENT.

STRAW.

The dried stalks of grains such as wheat and barley; in the Bible, particularly the fragments remaining after the completion of the threshing operation. Anciently straw, either by itself or mixed with other provender, was used as fodder for domestic animals. (Ge 24:25, 32; Jg 19:19; 1Ki 4:28; Isa 11:7; 65:25) Straw was also employed in the manufacture of bricks. (Ex 5:7-18; see BRICK.) It appears in illustrative settings with reference to the destruction of the wicked (Job 21:18) and the subjugation and humiliation of Moab. (Isa 25:10-12) Mighty Leviathan is depicted as accounting iron like mere straw.—Job 41:1, 27.

STREET.

A public way in a city or town. The common Hebrew term for street (*chuts*) basically means "outside." (Isa 42:2, ftn) In ancient towns and cities of Bible lands it appears that most streets were unpaved. (Ps 18:42; Isa 10:6; La 2:21) However, channels for water drainage from the streets have been discovered in Jericho and Gezer.

Generally, streets were narrow and winding. But there were also "broad ways." (Lu 14:21; compare Re 21:21.) Nineveh's streets were wide enough to accommodate chariots. (Na 2:4) Babylon and Damascus had broad avenues or processional ways, and some streets bore names. During the Roman period, "the street called Straight" in Damascus was a three-lane thoroughfare about 30 m (100 ft) wide.—Ac 9:11; see STRAIGHT.

An open area, the public square, likely near a city gate, might serve as a place to transact business or meet for instruction. (Ge 23:10-18; Ne 8:1-3; Jer 5:1) There children played (Zec 8:4, 5); the streets in general were usually filled with sounds of activity. (Job 18:17; Jer 33:10, 11; contrast Isa 15:3; 24:11.) They were places of commercial enterprise, shops of a certain kind sometimes being grouped together, as on "the street of the bakers" in Jerusalem. (Jer 37:21) The "streets" that Ben-hadad offered to be assigned to Ahab in Damascus were evidently for the establishment of bazaars, or markets, to promote Ahab's commercial interests in that Syrian capital. (1Ki 20:34) At night the streets of some cities apparently were under the vigilant eyes of watchmen.—Ca 3:1-3.

The streets also were places where news was announced. (2Sa 1:20; Jer 11:6) There Jesus Christ taught, and cured the ailing, though not wrangling and crying aloud in the broad ways, which would have caused a public sensation, magnifying his own name and drawing attention away from Jehovah God and the Kingdom good news. (Lu 8:1; Mt 12:13-19; Isa 42:1, 2) Jesus, therefore, was not like the hypocrites whom he condemned for praying "on the corners of the broad ways to be visible to men."—Mt 6:5.

STRIFE. Wrangling, quarreling, contending with another because of enmity. One Hebrew verb rendered "engage in strife" is also rendered "stir up" and "excite oneself." Among the causes for strife alluded to in the Scriptures are hatred (Pr 10:12), rage (Pr 15:18; 29:22), intrigues (Pr 16:28), ridicule (Pr 22:10), heavy drinking (Pr 23:29, 30), slander (Pr 26:20), arrogance or pride, and lack of right teaching (Pr 28:25; 1Ti 6:4). Strife destroys peace and happiness. Its unpleasant and repelling effect on other persons is repeatedly highlighted in the book of Proverbs. (Pr 19:13; 21:9, 19; 25:24; 27:15) Contentions between those who at one time enjoyed a brotherly relationship may present an almost insurmountable barrier to reconciliation. "A brother who is transgressed against is more than a strong town; and there are contentions that are like the bar of a dwelling tower."—Pr 18:19.

As one of the works of the flesh that is hated by Jehovah (Ga 5:19, 20; compare Pr 6:19; Ro 1:28, 29, 32; Jas 3:14-16), strife or contention has no place in the Christian congregation. (Ro 13:13; 1Co 3:3; 2Co 12:20; Php 2:3; Tit 3:9) One of the qualifications for a Christian overseer is that he be a nonbelligerent man. (1Ti 3:1, 3) Therefore, persons persisting in contention or strife are among those to receive God's adverse judgment. —Ro 2:6, 8.

In the first century C.E., the apostle Paul had to contend with persons who were given to strife. Some were declaring the good news out of contentiousness, probably with a view to making themselves prominent and undermining Paul's authority and influence. But Paul did not permit this to take away his joy in seeing that Christ was being publicized.—Php 1:15-18.

STRINGED INSTRUMENT. There is uncertainty about the instrument(s) designated by the various original-language words rendered "stringed instrument." The *ne'vel* is usually mentioned together with the *kin·nohr'* (harp), indicating that these instruments are distinctly different. The *ne'vel*, a portable instrument made from wood (1Ki 10:12), was used to play both sacred and secular music. (2Sa 6:5; 2Ch 5:12; Ne 12:27; Isa 5:12; 14:4, 11) Evidently various stringed instruments were employed, for the Bible mentions

min·nim' ("strings"; Ps 150:4), *keli' ne'vel* ('instrument of the string type' or "stringed sort"; 1Ch 16:5; Ps 71:22), *ne'vel 'a·sohr'* ("an instrument of ten strings," *'a·sohr'* being linked with a word meaning "ten"; Ps 33:2; 144:9), *neghi·nohth'* (related to a verb meaning "play a stringed instrument"; superscriptions of Ps 4, 6, 54, 55, 61, 67, 76), and *pesan·te·rin'* (understood to mean a "stringed instrument" of triangular shape; Da 3:5, 7, 10, 15).—See HARP.

STRONG DRINK. See the article WINE AND STRONG DRINK.

STUBBLE. In Biblical usage, stubble appears to refer to the remnants of grain stalks remaining in the field after the harvest. Stubble is what the Israelites had to gather when Egypt's Pharaoh deprived them of the regular provision of straw for making bricks.—Ex 5:10-12.

Stubble repeatedly figures in illustrative settings, allusions being made to the fact that it is light and frail (Job 13:25; 41:1, 28, 29), is easily blown away by the wind (Isa 40:24; 41:2; Jer 13:24), and burns readily and noisily (Isa 5:24; Joe 2:5; Ob 18; Na 1:10). The wicked, the enemies of Jehovah, as well as schemes that were bound to fail, are compared to stubble. (Ex 15:7; Ps 83:13; Mal 4:1; Isa 33:11) The apostle Paul, in discussing Christian building work, listed stubble as the least valuable material, one that would not withstand the fire test.—1Co 3:12, 13.

STUBBORNNESS. The basic meaning of the various original-language words that convey the idea of stubbornness is hardness or strength, especially in a bad sense. Often a deliberate refusal to comply with God's will or commands is involved. (Ps 78:8; 81:12; Isa 1:23; 65:2; Jer 3:17; 5:23; 7:23-26; 11:8; 18:12; Ho 4:16; Ac 7:51) That disaster comes to those who persist in a stubborn course is repeatedly highlighted in the Scriptures. (De 29:19, 20; Ne 9:29, 30; Pr 28:14; Isa 30:1; Jer 6:28-30; 9:13-16; 13:10; 16:12, 13; Da 5:20; Ho 9:15; Zec 7:12; Ro 2:5) For instance, God's law to Israel prescribed that a stubborn and rebellious son be stoned to death.—De 21:18, 20.

In his dealings with humankind, Jehovah God has patiently allowed individuals and nations, although deserving of death, to continue in existence. (Ge 15:16; 2Pe 3:9) Whereas some have responded favorably to this by putting themselves in line for receiving mercy (Jos 2:8-14; 6:22, 23; 9:3-15), others have hardened themselves to an even greater degree against Jehovah and against his people. (De 2:30-33; Jos 11:19, 20) Since Jehovah does not prevent persons from becoming stubborn, he is spoken of as 'letting them become obstinate' or 'making their hearts hard.' When he finally does execute vengeance upon the stubborn ones, this results in a demonstration of his great power and causes his name to be declared.—Compare Ex 4:21; Joh 12:40; Ro 9:14-18.

A case in point is what God did in connection with the Pharaoh who refused to let the Israelites leave Egypt. Jehovah brought ten devastating plagues upon the land of Egypt. Each time that Pharaoh hardened his heart after a certain plague ended, Jehovah used this as an opportunity to demonstrate his great power still further by other miracles. (Ex 7:3-5, 14–11:10) Therefore, some of the Egyptians came to realize that Jehovah is a God who has to be obeyed. For example, when the seventh plague was announced, even some of Pharaoh's servants saw to it that their own servants and livestock were safely sheltered before the destructive hailstorm began. (Ex 9:20, 21) Finally, when Pharaoh, after having released the Israelites, again made his heart obstinate and mustered his forces to wreak vengeance upon them (Ex 14:8, 9; 15:9), Jehovah destroyed him and his army in the Red Sea. (Ex 14:27, 28; Ps 136:15) For years afterward, God's name was declared among the nations as they talked about what Jehovah did to the Egyptians on account of their stubbornness.—Ex 18:10, 11; Jos 2:10, 11; 9:9; 1Sa 6:6.

Since Jehovah gives advance warning of his judgment against stubborn ones, the execution of that judgment cannot be attributed to other causes or to a different source. Said Jehovah, through the prophet Isaiah, to obstinate Israelites: "Due to my knowing that you are hard and that your neck is an iron sinew and your forehead is copper, I also kept telling you from that time. Before it could come in, I caused you to hear it, that you might not say, 'My own idol has done them, and my own carved image and my own molten image have commanded them.'"—Isa 48:4, 5; compare Jer 44:16-23.

STYLUS.
A writing instrument used in making impressions on materials such as clay or wax. (Ps 45:1; Isa 8:1; Jer 8:8) The stylus used for cuneiform writing had either a square or a wedge-shaped tip and was commonly made of reed or hardwood.

A stylus or chisel of metal or some other hard material was needed to cut or carve letters into stone or metal. The patriarch Job declared: "O that now my words were written down! O that in a book they were even inscribed! With an iron stylus and with lead, forever in the rock O that they were hewn!" (Job 19:23, 24) Apparently it was Job's desire that his words be cut into rock and the inscribed letters filled with lead to make them more enduring. Centuries later, Jehovah spoke of Judah's sins as being written down with an iron stylus, that is, indelibly recorded.—Jer 17:1.

SUAH
(Su'ah). Of the tribe of Asher, the first-listed son of Zophah. He was one of the paternal heads among some 26,000 select, valiant, and mighty men of Israel's army.—1Ch 7:30, 36, 40.

SUBMISSIVENESS.
Willingness to be in subjection, to yield, or to submit—to superiors, to law, or to a particular arrangement of things. Included are the subjection of Jesus Christ to his Father (1Co 15:27, 28), the Christian congregation to Jesus (Eph 5:24) and to God (Heb 12:9; Jas 4:7), individual Christians to those taking the lead in the congregation (1Co 16:15, 16; Heb 13:17, ftn; 1Pe 5:5), Christian women to the arrangement in the congregation regarding teaching (1Ti 2:11), slaves to their owners (Tit 2:9; 1Pe 2:18), wives to their husbands (Eph 5:22; Col 3:18; Tit 2:5; 1Pe 3:1, 5), children to their parents (1Ti 3:4; compare Lu 2:51; Eph 6:1), and the ruled to the rulers or the superior authorities (Ro 13:1, 5; Tit 3:1; 1Pe 2:13).—See HEADSHIP; OBEDIENCE; SUPERIOR AUTHORITIES.

The submissiveness, or subjection, that a Christian displays toward humans involves conscience and is governed by his relationship to God. Therefore, when submissiveness would lead to compromise or a violation of divine law, God rather than men must be obeyed. (Ac 5:29) Thus, Paul and Barnabas "did not yield by way of submission" to the false brothers who, contrary to God's revealed purpose, advocated circumcision and adherence to the Mosaic Law as requirements for gaining salvation.—Ga 2:3-5; compare Ac 15:1, 24-29.

At 2 Corinthians 9:13 contributions made in behalf of needy fellow Christians are shown to be an evidence of an individual's submissiveness to the good news, it being a Christian obligation to assist needy fellow believers.—Jas 1:26, 27; 2:14-17.

SUCATHITES
(Su'cath·ites). A Kenite family of scribes who lived at Jabez.—1Ch 2:55.

SUCCOTH
(Suc'coth) [Booths].
1. A place where, after his meeting with Esau, Jacob built himself a house and made booths, or

covered stalls, for his herd; hence the name Succoth. (Ge 33:16, 17) The statement that his next stopping place, Shechem, was "in the land of Canaan" implies that Succoth was not in Canaan proper.—Ge 33:18.

Other references also indicate a location E of the Jordan River, since they likely refer to the same place. Thus, Succoth is named as one of the cities in the inheritance of the tribe of Gad, E of the Jordan. (Jos 13:24, 25, 27) Gideon, pursuing remnants of Midianite forces, crossed the Jordan and came to Succoth, where the city princes refused his request for food for his troops, as did the men at nearby Penuel. On his return trip, Gideon obtained the names of 77 princes and elders of Succoth (indicating that it was a city of considerable size) and punished them for their failure to support his God-directed military action. (Jg 8:4-16) When the temple was built by Solomon, the copper items were cast in the District of the Jordan, between Succoth and Zarethan.—1Ki 7:46.

On the basis of these references, Succoth is generally identified with a site at or near Tell Deir 'Alla (today called Sukkot), about 5 km (3 mi) E of the Jordan River and just a little N of the Jabbok at the point where it issues forth from the hills. The nearby Tell el-Ekshas may perpetuate the original name, for it is the Arabic equivalent of the Hebrew Succoth. Tell Deir 'Alla overlooks a fertile plain that may be "the low plain of Succoth" spoken of at Psalms 60:6; 108:7.

2. The first stopping point mentioned in the Israelite march toward the Red Sea. (Ex 12:37) Since the location of Rameses, the starting point of the march, and that of Etham, the camping site after Succoth, are both unknown today, the location of Succoth is also uncertain. (Ex 13:20) At best, it can be said that Succoth was evidently about a day's journey (32 to 48 km; 20 to 30 mi) away from the Wilderness of Etham, which is believed to extend along the northwestern side of the Sinai Peninsula.

SUCCOTH-BENOTH (Suc′coth-be′noth)
[Booths of Benoth]. A deity worshiped by the Babylonians whom the king of Assyria brought into the cities of Samaria after his taking the Israelites of the ten-tribe kingdom into exile. (2Ki 17:30) Some scholars suggest that the name "Succoth-benoth" is a Hebraized form of Sarpanitu, the consort of Merodach (Marduk). Others favor an identification with Merodach, or Marduk, on the basis that the name "Succoth-benoth" may be Sakut(h)ban′wat(h), meaning "the Counselor,

Creator of the Land." This title is understood to apply to Merodach, who was viewed by the Babylonians as the creator of the world.

SUKKIIM (Suk′ki·im). A component force of the army of Egyptian King Shishak, who invaded Judah during Rehoboam's reign. (2Ch 12:2, 3) Some scholars believe the Sukkiim are referred to on certain ancient Egyptian texts and that they were of Libyan origin.

SULFUR. A yellow nonmetallic element occurring free or combined with other elements in sulfide and sulfate compounds. Its melting point is unusually low, 113° C. (235° F.). It readily burns with a pale blue flame, at the same time forming sulfur dioxide, which has a pungent odor.

The first historical reference to sulfur tells how destruction rained down on the wicked cities of Sodom and Gomorrah in the form of fire and sulfur. (Ge 19:24; Lu 17:29) On the basis of geologic evidence, some suggest that this catastrophic execution from Jehovah was possibly in the form of a volcanic eruption in the southern region of the Dead Sea, accounting for the prevalence of sulfur in that area today.

It is believed that a high-temperature incinerator or crematory for the ancient city of Jerusalem was developed by adding sulfur to the constantly burning fires in the Valley of Hinnom (Gehenna) just outside the walls.

Ever since the fiery judgment on Sodom and Gomorrah in 1919 B.C.E., the highly flammable nature of sulfur has been referred to in the Scriptures. (Isa 30:33; 34:9; Re 9:17, 18) It is a symbol of total desolation. (De 29:22, 23; Job 18:15) "Fire and sulphur" are associated together when utter destruction is depicted. (Ps 11:6; Eze 38:22; Re 14:9-11) We are told that the Devil will be "hurled into the lake of fire and sulphur," a fitting description of complete annihilation, "the second death." —Re 19:20; 20:10; 21:8.

SUN. The greater of earth's two heavenly luminaries; the earth's principal created source of energy, without which life on earth would be impossible. The sun (Heb., she′mesh; Gr., he′li-os), together with the moon, also serves man as a timepiece for measuring the seasons, days, and years. (Ge 1:14-18) The sun is a gift from "the Father of the celestial lights," who makes it shine upon all alike, the wicked and the good. (Jas 1:17; Jer 31:35; Mt 5:45) Certainly the sun can be said to praise its magnificent Creator.—Ps 148:3.

The sun is a star about 1,392,000 km (865,-000 mi) in diameter, more than a hundred times the diameter of the earth, and more than a million times the volume of the earth. Its average distance from the earth is over 149,600,000 km (93,000,000 mi). The surface temperature of the sun is said to be about 6,000° C. (11,000° F.). But because of its great distance from the earth only about one two-billionth (one two-thousand-millionth) of its radiant energy reaches the earth, an amount, however, fully sufficient to provide ideal climatic conditions that make vegetable and animal life on earth possible.—De 33:14; 2Sa 23:4.

Jehovah and Christ More Brilliant. The surpassing brilliance and glory of Jehovah, the sun's Creator, is indicated by the fact that his resurrected Son, in a partial revelation to Saul, presented a light "beyond the brilliance of the sun." (Ac 26:13) In the holy city, New Jerusalem, there will be no need for the sun as light, for "the glory of God" will light it up and "its lamp" will be the Lamb.—Re 21:2, 23; 22:5.

God's Power Over the Sunlight. The day Jesus was fastened to a torture stake, from the sixth hour (11:00 a.m. to 12 noon) until the ninth hour (2:00 to 3:00 p.m.) a darkness fell over all the land. (Mt 27:45; Mr 15:33) Luke's account adds that the darkness fell "because the sunlight failed." (Lu 23:44, 45) This could not have been due to an eclipse of the sun by the moon, as some think, for the darkness occurred at Passover time, which was always the time of *full* moon. It is about two weeks later that the moon is *new,* that is, in the same direction as the sun from the earth (the time when solar eclipses occur).

Long before this occasion, Jehovah had demonstrated his ability to shut out the sunlight. This was when the Israelites were down in Egypt. During the ninth plague thick darkness enveloped the Egyptians with darkness that could "be felt." It lasted for three days, longer than any eclipse of the sun by the moon. Also, in the nearby land of Goshen, the Israelites at the same time enjoyed light.—Ex 10:21-23.

In answering his disciples' question as to his presence and the conclusion of the system of things, Jesus predicted unusual darkening of the sun.—Mt 24:3, 29; Mr 13:24; Lu 21:25; compare Isa 13:10; Joe 2:10, 31; 3:15; Ac 2:20; see HEAVEN (Darkening of the Heavens).

Time and Direction. Time was often designated by references to the sun's position. (Ge 15:12, 17; 32:31; De 16:6; Jos 8:29; Jg 9:33; 1Sa 11:9; Ps 113:3) Direction was similarly indicated. (De 11:30; Jos 12:1) "Under the sun" was used to mean "anywhere (or everywhere) on earth." (Ec 5:18; 9:11) "Under the eyes" of the sun or "in front

of the sun" meant "in the open, for all to see." —2Sa 12:11, 12.

Figurative Use. Jehovah God is called "a sun and a shield," not that he is a nature god, but that he is the Source of light, life, and energy. (Ps 84:11) He is also spoken of as a shade to his people, so that "the sun itself will not strike" them. Here that which brings calamity is likened to the sun's heat. (Ps 121:6, 7) Persecution (Mt 13:5, 6, 20, 21) and divine anger are sometimes represented by the scorching heat of the sun.—Re 7:16.

Jehovah likened rebellious Jerusalem to a woman who had borne seven sons, describing the judgment coming upon her by the figurative expression, "Her sun has set while it is yet day," that is, before the evening of her life was reached she would experience calamity. This was fulfilled when Babylon destroyed Jerusalem. (Jer 15:9) In similar vein, Micah prophesied against the prophets misleading Israel: "The sun will certainly set upon the prophets, and the day must get dark upon them." (Mic 3:6; compare Am 8:9.) Jehovah's Kingdom rule is pictured as so bright that it can be said, in comparison: "The full moon has become abashed, and the glowing sun has become ashamed." (Isa 24:23) Jesus said that, at the conclusion of the system of things, "the righteous ones will shine as brightly as the sun in the kingdom of their Father."—Mt 13:39, 43; compare Da 12:3; see LIGHT.

Sun Worship. During King Josiah's cleansing work, "he put out of business the foreign-god priests, whom the kings of Judah had put in that they might make sacrificial smoke . . . to the sun and to the moon." "Further, he caused the horses that the kings of Judah had given to the sun to cease from entering the house of Jehovah . . . and the chariots of the sun he burned in the fire." (2Ki 23:5, 11) Later, the prophet Ezekiel, down in Babylon, was given a vision of Jehovah's temple at Jerusalem. There he saw about 25 men between the porch and the altar, "bowing down to the east, to the sun." (Eze 8:16) Such disgusting practices brought Jerusalem to ruin in 607 B.C.E., when Jehovah's instrument Nebuchadnezzar destroyed the city and the temple.—Jer 52:12-14.

Shadow That Went Ten Steps Back. The use of sundials extends back beyond the eighth century B.C.E. in both Babylon and Egypt. However, the Hebrew word *ma·'alohth',* translated "dial" at 2 Kings 20:11 and Isaiah 38:8, in the *King James Version,* literally means "steps" (*NW*) or "degrees," as is indicated in the *King James Version* marginal readings on these verses. This word is also used in the superscriptions of the 15 'Songs of the Ascents,' Psalms 120 to 134.

In the scriptures mentioned, at 2 Kings 20:8-11 and Isaiah 38:4-8, the account is related of the portent God gave sick King Hezekiah in answer to Isaiah's prayer. It consisted of causing a shadow that had gradually fallen to reverse its direction and go back up ten steps. This could refer to the steps, or degrees, of a dial for measuring time, and it is not impossible that Hezekiah's father possessed such a sundial, even obtaining it from Babylon. However, the Jewish historian Josephus in discussing the account speaks of these steps of Ahaz as being "in the house," apparently indicating that they formed part of a stairway. (*Jewish Antiquities*, X, 29 [ii, 1]) There may have been a column placed alongside the stairs to receive the sun's rays and cause a shadow to extend gradually along the steps and serve as a measurement of time.

The miracle performed could have involved the relationship between earth and sun, and if so, it could have been similar to the miracle recorded at Joshua 10:12-14. (See POWER, POWERFUL WORKS [Sun and moon stand still].) It appears that this portent had far-reaching effects, inasmuch as 2 Chronicles 32:24, 31 shows that messengers were sent from Babylon to Jerusalem to inquire about it.

SUNRISING, SUNSET. The time when the sun appears to rise above the horizon, and the time when it disappears from view below the horizon. These times were pivotal points in the daily life of people in the Biblical period. For most persons, the dawn opened the curtain on the day's activity and the dusk drew it closed again. As the psalmist wrote: "The sun . . . sets. You cause darkness, that it may become night; in it all the wild animals of the forest move forth. The maned young lions are roaring for the prey and for seeking their food from God himself. The sun begins to shine—they withdraw and they lie down in their own hiding places. Man goes forth to his activity and to his service until evening. How many your works are, O Jehovah! All of them in wisdom you have made. The earth is full of your productions."—Ps 104:19-24.

The rising of the sun marked the start of the natural daylight period and, when Jesus Christ was on earth, the start of the counting of the "twelve hours of daylight." (Mr 16:2; Joh 11:9) Many, of course, were up before dawn, like the diligent woman of Proverbs 31:15. Jesus, too, is mentioned as rising before the sun was up, to spend time in prayer. (Mr 1:35) When sunrise came the large city gates swung open, men went out to their fields or to the vineyards, women lined up at the wells for water, people filled the marketplaces, and fishermen pulled for shore to sell the night's catch, after which they would clean and mend their nets.

The day's normal activities and labor went on until sundown. At its approach the men returned from their fields, their masters paid them their wages for the day, women carried their night's supply of water home, the city gates swung shut, and the watchmen began the first of the four night watches, while throughout the city oil lamps began to flicker in the homes. (Jg 19:14-16; Mt 20:8-12; De 24:15; Ge 24:11; Ne 13:19; Mr 13:35) For many, however, work went on after the evening meal, as industrious men and women did weaving or engaged in other indoor crafts. (Pr 31:18, 19; 2Th 3:8) At times Jesus and his apostles also continued their ministry and its related activity on into the night.—Mt 14:23-25; Mr 1: 32-34; 4:35-39; Lu 6:12; 2Co 6:4, 5.

While sunset marked the close of the daylight period, for the Jews it marked the start of the new calendar day, which officially began at sunset, being counted from evening to evening. (Le 23: 32; compare Mr 1:21, 32, which shows that the day, in this case a sabbath, ended in the evening.) It was, therefore, at sunset that Nisan 14 began and the time came for slaughtering the lamb and eating the Passover.—Ex 12:6-10; De 16:6; Mt 26:20; see PASSOVER.

Because the day ended at sundown, the Law required that certain things be done then. A garment taken in pledge had to be returned to its owner "at the setting of the sun." (Ex 22:26; De 24:13) At that time, too, wages were to be paid to hired laborers (De 24:15), a dead body hanging on a stake had to be removed and buried (De 21:22, 23; Jos 8:29; 10:26, 27), and a person who had been ceremonially unclean had to bathe himself and, following sunset, would be considered clean again (Le 22:6, 7; De 23:11). The fact that sunset closed one day and initiated a new one added meaning to the apostle's exhortation: "Let the sun not set with you in a provoked state."—Eph 4:26.

The rising or shining of the sun is occasionally used in a figurative way. At 2 Samuel 23:3, 4 the reign of a righteous ruler who fears God is said to be as refreshing as "the light of morning, when the sun shines forth, a morning without clouds." (Compare Mal 4:2; Mt 17:2; Re 1:16.) On behalf of God's servants the request is made to Jehovah: "Let your lovers be as when the sun goes forth in its mightiness."—Jg 5:31; Mt 13:43; Ps 110:3; Da 12:3; contrast with Mic 3:5, 6; Joh 3:19, 20.

The terms "sunrising" and "sunset" are also used in a geographic sense, meaning from E to W. (Ex 27:13; Jos 1:4; Ps 107:3; Re 16:12) This is the sense of Psalm 113:3: "From the rising of the sun until its setting Jehovah's name is to be praised." (See also Mal 1:11; Isa 45:6.) 'From sunrise to sunset' may also mean all day long.

SUPERIOR AUTHORITIES.

An expression at Romans 13:1 designating human governmental authorities. That scripture has been variously rendered: "Let every soul be in subjection to the superior authorities, for there is no authority except by God; the existing authorities stand placed in their relative positions by God." (*NW*) "Let every subject be obedient to the ruling authorities, for there is no authority not under God's control, and under His control the existing authorities have been constituted." (*We*) "Everyone must obey the state authorities, for no authority exists without God's permission, and the existing authorities have been put there by God."—*TEV*.

Jehovah God, though not originating them (compare Mt 4:8, 9; 1Jo 5:19; Re 13:1, 2), has allowed man's governmental authorities to come into existence, and they continue to exist by his permission. However, when he chooses to do so, Jehovah can remove, direct, or control such authorities in order to accomplish his will. The prophet Daniel declared regarding Jehovah: "He is changing times and seasons, removing kings and setting up kings." (Da 2:21) And Proverbs 21:1 says: "A king's heart is as streams of water in the hand of Jehovah. Everywhere that he delights to, he turns it."—Compare Ne 2:3-6; Es 6:1-11.

Reasons for Christian Subjection. There being no reason for Christians to set themselves in opposition to an arrangement that God has permitted, they have good reason to be in subjection to the superior authorities. Governmental rulers, though they may be corrupt personally, would not normally punish others for doing good, that is, for adhering to the law of the land. But a person who engages in thievery, murder, or other lawless acts could expect an adverse judgment from the ruling authority. One guilty of deliberate murder, for instance, might be executed for his crime. Since Jehovah God authorized capital punishment for murderers after the Flood (Ge 9:6), the human authority, by executing the lawbreaker, would be acting as "God's minister, an avenger to express wrath upon the one practicing what is bad."—Ro 13:2-4; Tit 3:1; 1Pe 2:11-17.

Christian subjection to the superior authorities is not based merely on their ability to punish evildoers. With a Christian, it becomes a matter of conscience. He is submissive to human authorities because he recognizes that this is in harmony with God's will. (Ro 13:5; 1Pe 2:13-15) Therefore, subjection to the superior authorities—to worldly political authorities—could never be absolute. It would be impossible for a Christian to preserve a good conscience and do the divine will if he broke God's law because that is what the political authority demanded. For this reason, subjection to superior authorities must always be viewed in the light of the apostles' statement to the Jewish Sanhedrin: "We must obey God as ruler rather than men."—Ac 5:29.

Since the governmental authorities render valuable services to ensure the safety, security, and welfare of their subjects, they are entitled to taxes and tribute in compensation for their services. The governmental authorities can be termed "God's public servants" in the sense that they provide beneficial services. (Ro 13:6, 7) At times such services have directly assisted God's servants, as when King Cyrus made it possible for the Jews to return to Judah and Jerusalem and rebuild the temple. (2Ch 36:22, 23; Ezr 1:1-4) Often the benefits are those shared by all from the proper functioning of the authorities. These would include the maintenance of a legal system to which persons can appeal for justice, protection from criminals and from illegal mobs, and so forth.—Php 1:7; Ac 21:30-32; 23:12-32.

Of course, a ruler who misuses his authority is accountable to God. Wrote the apostle Paul: "Do not avenge yourselves, beloved, but yield place to the wrath; for it is written: 'Vengeance is mine; I will repay, says Jehovah.'"—Ro 12:19; Ec 5:8.

SUPH

[possibly, Reeds]. One of the locations mentioned to indicate where Moses spoke to the Israelites in the 40th year of their wilderness wandering. (De 1:1, ftn) Instead of "Suph," the Greek *Septuagint* (Bagster) and the Latin *Vulgate* read "the Red Sea," perhaps because it was thought that the Hebrew word *yam* (meaning "sea") had been dropped, leaving *Suph* as an abbreviation for *yam-suph'* (Red Sea). In such a case, the reference would be to that part of the sea called the Gulf of 'Aqaba. However, taken as it stands, the Hebrew Masoretic text says that Moses spoke to Israel "on the desert plains in front of Suph." And verse 5 adds that this was "in the region of the Jordan in the land of Moab." Therefore, though its exact site is unknown, Suph apparently was a place E of the Jordan. It is tentatively identified with Khirbet Sufa, about 6 km (3.5 mi) SSE of Madaba.

SUPHAH (Su'phah). As ordinarily rendered, a region or valley, probably in the vicinity of the Arnon. (Nu 21:14) This Hebrew word has been translated by such terms as "hurricane" (*Ro*) and "storm" (*AS* ftn). However, most modern translations indicate that it was a region or valley, saying that Vaheb was located "by Suphah" (*JB*) or "in Suphah."—*AT, JP, NW, RS.*

SURETY. Security for the fulfillment of an obligation; a pledge, guaranty, or bond; one who has made himself responsible for another. The psalmist appealed to Jehovah to act as his "surety," protecting him from defrauders.—Ps 119:122.

The customary mode of becoming surety for another remained unchanged for centuries. The patriarch Job made the following reference to it: "Please, do put my security with yourself. Who else is there that will shake hands with me in pledge?" (Job 17:3) Proverbs 17:18 is helpful in determining the procedure followed: "A man that is wanting in heart shakes hands, going full surety before his companion." Evidently a person became surety for another when, in the presence of witnesses, he struck, clasped, or shook the hand of the creditor of the transaction and promised to assume the obligations of the debtor if he should fail to make payment. In the Orient this act of striking or touching hands meant that a bargain or covenant was sealed. (Pr 11:21) Apparently in this way Jehu confirmed Jehonadab's affirmative reply to the question, "Is your heart upright with me, just as my own heart is with your heart?" For he said to Jehonadab: "If it is, do give me your hand."—2Ki 10:15.

Employing other means, Judah gave his seal ring, cord, and rod as security to Tamar until he should send her a kid of the goats as payment for sex relations. (Ge 38:17-20) Reuben offered surety to Jacob for Benjamin, when proposing to take him to Egypt, saying: "My own two sons you may put to death if I do not bring him back to you." Jacob refused. Later, Judah successfully offered himself as surety for Benjamin: "I shall be the one to be surety for him. Out of my hand you may exact the penalty for him." When it appeared that Benjamin would become a slave in Egypt, Judah stood ready to take his place as slave, since he was surety for the boy. This was the legal basis of his plea to Joseph: "For your slave became surety for the boy when away from his father . . . So now, please, let your slave stay instead of the boy as a slave to my master."—Ge 42:37, 38; 43:8, 9; 44:32, 33.

Pledges given as security by a debtor to his creditor were closely regulated by the Law. As commerce increased in Israel, so did suretyship in mercantile affairs. The proverbs warned that this was a dangerous, foolish practice, especially when one could not afford it without risking the loss of essential items of living.—Pr 6:1-5; 11:15; 22:26, 27; see PLEDGE.

SUSA. See SHUSHAN.

SUSANNA (Su·san'na). One of the many faithful women, who, out of their own belongings, cared for the needs of Jesus and his 12 apostles during Jesus' Galilean ministry of 31 C.E.—Lu 8:1-3.

SUSI (Su'si) [from a root meaning "horse"]. Father of Gaddi, who represented the tribe of Manasseh in spying out the Promised Land.—Nu 13:2, 11.

SWALLOW [Heb., *derohr'*]. The Hebrew word *derohr'* is identical in form with a Hebrew word translated "liberty" (Le 25:10; Isa 61:1), and some commentators feel the name describes the graceful free-flying swallow with its uninhibited movement.

Swallows frequently build their cuplike nests (formed of mud pellets) on houses or other buildings, often under the eaves. They at one time nested in the temple structure in Jerusalem, as they do today in similar buildings throughout Israel. Later, sharp golden spikes protruded from the summit of Herod's temple in order to prevent birds from settling on the building.—*The Jewish War*, by F. Josephus, V, 224 (v, 6).

The psalmist, in proclaiming his yearning for the courtyards of Jehovah's house, makes reference to the swallow's finding a nest for herself in which to place her young—yes, right in the temple, evidently somewhere around Jehovah's "grand altar." (Ps 84:1-3) As a nonpriestly Levite, the psalmist served at the temple only one week every six months, but he knew that the swallow had a more permanent dwelling there. Thus he expressed his longing to be in the courtyards of Jehovah's tabernacle as much as possible.

The other reference to the swallow occurs at Proverbs 26:2, where it states that even "as a bird has cause for fleeing and just as a swallow for flying, so a malediction itself does not come without real cause." (*NW*) Some translations render the Hebrew instead as a "curse that is causeless [and] does not alight" (*RS;* see also *AS, Ro*) and so consider the text to mean that such a causeless curse does not come to fulfillment or "alight" but, rather, is like the restless flight of the swallow as it continues almost tirelessly on the wing in pursuit of its insect prey. In the surrounding verses the writer is discussing the fool and his ways, and thus in the rendering first cited (*NW*) the sense may be instead that, even as the flying of the birds when fleeing from danger or searching for food has a real cause, so, too, if a fool's course brings a malediction upon him, it was not without there being real cause; his foolish course was responsible.—Compare Pr 26:3; also 1:22-32.

The common or barn swallow (*Hirundo rustica*) is abundant in Palestine. One variety spends the year there, whereas others arrive from southern Africa in March and depart at the approach of winter. Many pass through during migration in the spring and fall. Small, with long powerful wings and, usually, a forked tail, the swallow is a bird of unusually graceful and speedy flight, able to cover long distances in migration. The plumage often has a rich iridescent hue; its song is a pleasant combination of soft twittering and warbling.

SWAN
[Heb., *tin·she'meth*]. A large, graceful water bird with a long, slender curving neck. Some swans may weigh as much as 18 kg (40 lb) and may have a wingspan of about 2.5 m (8 ft).

The Hebrew name (*tin·she'meth*), appearing in the list of unclean flying creatures (Le 11:13, 18; De 14:12, 16), is from a root meaning "pant." (Isa 42:14) It may describe the swan with its loud hissing sound, made when the bird is excited or angered, and is so rendered in a number of translations (*KJ, Da, Le, NW, Ro, Yg*). This identification dates back at least to the Latin *Vulgate*, in which Jerome rendered the Hebrew *tin·she'meth* (at Le 11:18) by the Latin word *cycnus* (swan). The earlier Greek *Septuagint* here reads "purple-colored bird" (Gr., *por·phy·ri'on*), evidently the purple gallinule (*Porphyrio porphyrio*). However, both of these ancient versions translate *tin·she'meth* as "ibis" at Deuteronomy 14:16, thus showing their uncertainty.

The swan, though found in Palestine, is not common there in modern times. Because of this, and also because the swan is primarily a vegetarian, many modern translators prefer to identify the *tin·she'meth* with the "water hen" (*RS, Mo*), "eagle-owl" (*AT*), "ibis" (*JB*), or other birds known to be either carnivorous or scavengers. However, the rarity of the appearance of swans in Palestine in modern times is not a certain evidence that they were not more common there in ancient times. Likewise, it must be recognized that the view that the classification of certain birds as

unclean depended upon their being either raptorial or scavengers is only a deduction and is not directly stated in the Bible.

In addition to its usual diet of seeds, roots of water plants, and worms, the swan is known to feed on shellfish.

SWARMING THING
[Heb., *she'rets*]. The root word from which this term is drawn means to "swarm" or "teem." (Ge 8:17; Ex 8:3) The noun appears to apply to small creatures to be found in large numbers. (Ex 8:3; Ps 105:30; compare Ex 1:7.) It first occurs at Genesis 1:20 with the initial appearance of living souls on the fifth creative day when the waters began to swarm with living souls. The Flood destroyed earthly 'swarming things' outside the ark.—Ge 7:21.

The law regarding clean and unclean things shows that the term may apply to aquatic creatures (Le 11:10); winged creatures, including bats and insects (Le 11:19-23; De 14:19); land creatures, including rodents, lizards, chameleons (Le 11:29-31); as well as creatures traveling on their "belly" and multilegged creatures (Le 11:41-44). Many, but not all, of these were "unclean" as food under the Law.

SWEARING.
See OATH.

SWEAT.
Perspiration; bodily moisture or liquid excreted by the sudoriferous (sweat) glands and flowing through pores in the skin. Exertion (as during laborious work), emotion (such as anxiety), heat, and so forth, are generally the causes of sweat.

After sinning, Adam had to eke out an existence from cursed ground outside the garden of Eden, doing so through sweat-producing toil amid thorns and thistles. Jehovah told him, in part: "In the sweat of your face you will eat bread until you return to the ground, for out of it you were taken."—Ge 3:17-19.

During Ezekiel's temple vision, Jehovah stated that the priests ministering there were to wear linen garments and that "no wool should come up on them." They were not to gird themselves with wool or anything 'causing sweat.' Perhaps this was to avoid any uncleanness that sweat would produce, or because perspiration would make their service unpleasant rather than joyful, sweat being suggestive of toil or drudgery, as in Adam's case.—Eze 44:15-18.

Jesus in Gethsemane. Concerning Jesus Christ when in Gethsemane on the final night of his earthly life, Luke 22:44 states: "But getting into an agony he continued praying more earnestly; and his sweat became as drops of blood falling to the ground." The writer does not say that Jesus' sweat was actually mingled with his blood. He may only have been drawing a comparison, perhaps indicating that Christ's perspiration formed like drops of blood or describing how the dripping of Jesus' sweat resembled a drop-by-drop flowing of blood from a wound. On the other hand, Jesus' blood may have exuded through his skin, being mixed with his sweat. Bloody sweat has reportedly occurred in certain cases of extreme mental stress. Blood or elements thereof will seep through unruptured walls of blood vessels in a condition called diapedesis, and in hematidrosis there is an excreting of perspiration tinged with blood pigment or blood, or of bodily fluid mingled with blood, thus resulting in the 'sweating of blood.' These, of course, are only suggestions as to what possibly took place in Jesus' case.

Luke 22:43, 44 is omitted in the Vatican Manuscript No. 1209, the Alexandrine Manuscript, the Syriac Sinaitic codex, and in the corrected reading of the Sinaitic Manuscript. However, these verses do appear in the original Sinaitic Manuscript, the Codex Bezae, the Latin *Vulgate,* the Curetonian Syriac, and the Syriac *Peshitta.*

SWIFT [Heb., *sis*]. One of the fastest of all flying birds, regularly attaining speeds of over 100 km/hr (60 mph) and capable of bursts of speed probably of 200 km/hr (120 mph) or more. It uses its long, thin scythelike wings energetically and with seeming tirelessness as it swoops and darts after insect prey, which it engulfs while on the wing. Of the four varieties of swifts to be seen in Israel, the Alpine swift (*Apus melba*) is the largest and is distinguished by its white underparts. It is the first of the migrating swifts to appear in Palestine at the approach of spring, followed shortly thereafter by long streams of common swifts (*Apus apus*). Their nests are built in dark places, often under the eaves of roofs, and sometimes inside hollow trees or on the sides of cliffs, and are formed of straw and feathers cemented together with the sticky saliva that the bird's glands produce. The swift's feet are evidently not structurally designed to allow for walking or perching, so the bird obtains all its food and nest materials while in flight and even drinks by skimming over the surface of the water; it rests by clinging to vertical surfaces. The swift's cry has a somewhat wailing, melancholy note.

That the Hebrew *sis* identifies the swift is indicated by the use of the same name in Arabic for that bird. The name is suggested by some scholars to indicate a rushing sound; but others consider the name to represent the shrill *si-si-si* cry of the swift.

Hezekiah, upon recovering from illness, said in a thoughtful composition that he 'kept chirping like the swift,' evidently in a melancholy way, and the prophet Jeremiah used the migratory swift as an example when rebuking the people of Judah for not discerning the time of God's judgment. —Isa 38:14; Jer 8:7.

SWIMMER. A person who can propel himself through water by the use of his arms and legs. The ability to swim was common among the ancients. (Eze 47:5; Ac 27:42, 43) In an early Egyptian text, a father mentions that his children took swimming lessons, and Assyrian reliefs depict warriors as swimming, often with the aid of inflated skins.

Ability to swim was a must for fishermen. When using a dragnet, they would occasionally dive into the water and pull a portion of the weighted edge under the rest of the net to form a bottom. Although apparently a good swimmer (Joh 21:7, 8), the fisherman Peter began to sink and called for Jesus Christ to save him at the time Peter walked on the water. This was likely the result of the unusually rough water, coupled with Peter's personal fear.—Mt 14:27-31.

In a prophecy against Moab, Isaiah alluded to the actions of a swimmer, saying: "The hand of Jehovah will settle down on this mountain, and Moab must be trodden down in its place as when a straw heap is trodden down in a manure place. And he must slap out [literally, stretch out] his hands in the midst of it as when a swimmer slaps them out to swim, and he must abase its haughtiness with the tricky movements of his hands." (Isa 25:10, 11) This rendering, as well as the one in the Greek *Septuagint,* suggests that Jehovah stretches out his hands against Moab to deliver destructive blows. Another reading, however, makes Moab the one doing the swimming. The *American Translation,* for example, states: "The hand of the LORD will rest on this mountain, but Moab will be trampled down where he stands, as straw is trampled down in the water of a dungpit; and though he spread out his hands in the midst of it, as a swimmer spreads out his hands to swim, his pride will be laid low despite all the tricks of his hands."

SWINE [Gr., *khoi′ros; hys* (sow); Heb., *chazir′* (pig; boar)]. The collective designation for the ordinary pig (*Sus domestica*); a medium-sized, cloven-hoofed, short-legged mammal having a thick-skinned, stocky body usually covered with coarse bristles. The pig's snout is blunt, and its neck and tail are short. Not being a cud chewer, the pig was ruled unacceptable for food or sacrifice by the terms of the Mosaic Law.—Le 11:7; De 14:8.

While Jehovah's ban on eating pork was not necessarily based on health considerations, there were and still are hazards connected with the use of this meat for food. Since pigs are indiscriminate in their feeding habits, even eating carrion and offal, they tend to be infested with various parasitic organisms, including those responsible for diseases such as trichinosis and ascariasis.

The Israelites generally seem to have viewed swine as especially loathsome. Hence the ultimate degree in disgusting worship is conveyed by the words: "The one offering up a gift—the blood of a pig!" (Isa 66:3) To the Israelites, few things could have been more inappropriate than a pig with a gold nose ring in its snout. And it is to this that Proverbs 11:22 compares an outwardly beautiful woman who is not sensible.

Although apostate Israelites ate pork (Isa 65:4; 66:17), the Apocryphal books of First Maccabees (1:65, Dy) and Second Maccabees (6:18, 19; 7:1, 2, Dy) show that during the foreign domination of Palestine by the Syrian king Antiochus IV Epiphanes and his vicious campaign to stamp out the worship of Jehovah, there were many Jews who refused to eat the flesh of swine, preferring to die for violating the decree of the king rather than to violate the law of God.

Whereas some other nations did not eat pork, to the Greeks it was a delicacy. Hence, likely as a result of Hellenistic influence, by the time of Jesus Christ's earthly ministry, there were apparently quite a number of pigs in Palestine, particularly in the Decapolis region. In the country of the Gadarenes there was at least one herd of about 2,000 pigs. When Jesus permitted the demons that he had expelled to enter this large herd, every last one of the animals rushed over a precipice and drowned in the sea.—Mt 8:28-32; Mr 5:11-13.

The Cast-Out Demons Who Entered Swine.
No fault can be found with Jesus for allowing the demons to enter the swine, especially since certain unstated factors may very well have been involved, such as whether the owners of the swine were Jews, thus being guilty of disrespect for the Law. It was, of course, not required that Jesus exercise foreknowledge as to what the demons would do once they entered the unclean animals. And the demons may have wanted to take possession of the swine in order to derive therefrom some unnatural sadistic pleasure. Also, it might reasonably be argued that a man is worth more than a herd of swine. (Mt 12:12) Furthermore, all animals actually belong to Jehovah by reason of his Creatorship, and thus Jesus as God's representative had every right to permit the demons to take possession of the herd of swine. (Ps 50:10; Joh 7:29) The demons' entering the swine manifested their ouster from the men in a very forceful way, thus also making very apparent to observers the harm that came to creatures of flesh that became demon possessed. It demonstrated for such human observers both Jesus' power over the demons and demonic power over fleshly creatures. All of this may have suited Jesus' purpose and may explain why he allowed the unclean spirits to enter the swine.

Illustrative Use.   The inability of swine to recognize the value of pearls was employed by Jesus in illustrating the unwisdom of sharing spiritual things with those having no appreciation whatever of spiritual thoughts and teachings. (Mt 7:6) And in Jesus' illustration of the prodigal son, the degradation to which a young man had sunk was accentuated by his having to hire himself out as a swineherd, a most despicable occupation for a Jew, and by his willingness even to eat the food of these animals.—Lu 15:15, 16.

The apostle Peter compared Christians who revert to their former course of life to a sow that returns to its wallow after having been washed. (2Pe 2:22) However, it is evident that, as relates to the pig, this illustration is not intended to apply beyond the surface appearance of things. Actually, the pig, under natural conditions, is no dirtier than other animals, although it indulges in wallowing in the mud from time to time in order to cool off in the heat of the summer and to remove external parasites from its hide.

SWORD.   See ARMS, ARMOR.

SYCAMORE   [Heb., shiq·mah′]. This tree mentioned in the Hebrew Scriptures has no relation to the North American sycamore, which is a type of plane tree. It is evidently the same as the "fig-mulberry" tree of Luke 19:4. This tree (Ficus sycomorus) has fruit like that of the common fig, but its foliage resembles that of the mulberry. It grows to a height of 10 to 15 m (33 to 50 ft), is strong, and may live for several hundred years. Unlike the common fig, the sycamore (fig-mulberry) is an evergreen. While its heart-shaped leaves are smaller than those of the fig tree, the foliage is thick and wide-spreading, and the tree provides good shade. It was frequently planted along roadsides for that reason. The short, stout trunk soon branches out with its lower limbs close to the ground, and this made it a convenient tree along the roadside for a small man like Zacchaeus to climb in order to get a view of Jesus.—Lu 19:2-4.

The figs grow in abundant clusters and are smaller than those of the common fig tree and are inferior to them. It is the present practice of Egyptian and Cypriot growers of the sycamore (fig-mulberry) trees to pierce the premature fruit with a nail or other sharp instrument in order to make the fruit edible. The wounding, or piercing, of sycamore figs at an early ripening stage induces a sharp increase in the emanation of ethylene gas, which accelerates the growth and ripening of the fruit considerably (three to eight times). This is important since otherwise the fruit will not fully develop and will stay hard or it will be spoiled by parasitic wasps that penetrate the fruit and inhabit it for reproduction. This sheds some light on the occupation of the prophet Amos, who describes himself as "a herdsman and a *nipper* of figs of sycamore trees."—Am 7:14.

In addition to growing in the Jordan Valley (Lu 19:1, 4) and around Tekoa (Am 1:1; 7:14), the sycamore trees were especially abundant in the lowlands of the Shephelah (1Ki 10:27; 2Ch 1:15; 9:27), and though their fruit was not of the quality of the common fig tree, King David considered it of sufficient value to place the Shephelah groves under the care of an administrative chief. (1Ch 27:28) The sycamore (fig-mulberry) trees were evidently abundant in Egypt at the time of the Ten Plagues, and they continue to provide a source of food there today. (Ps 78:47) The wood is somewhat soft and porous and quite inferior to that of the cedar, but it was very durable and much used in building. (Isa 9:10) Mummy cases made of sycamore wood have been found in Egyptian tombs and are still in good condition after some 3,000 years.

SYCHAR (Sy'char). A city of Samaria and the site of Jacob's fountain. It was "near the field that Jacob gave to Joseph his son" in the vicinity of Shechem. (Joh 4:5, 6; compare Jos 24:32.) The Syriac Sinaitic codex has "Sychem" instead of "Sychar." However, the best Greek manuscripts support the reading "Sychar." Certain early non-Biblical writers distinguish between Shechem and Sychar; others do not. Recent excavations have led some to identify Sychar tentatively with the village of 'Askar, 0.7 km (0.4 mi) NNE of Jacob's fountain and about 1 km (0.6 mi) NE of Shechem.

SYENE (Sy·e'ne). A city apparently situated at the southern extremity of ancient Egypt. (Eze 29:10; 30:6) The city may have served as a market or trading post. It is identified with Aswan, situated on the E bank of the Nile near the island Elephantine and about 690 km (430 mi) S of Cairo.

SYMEON (Sym'e·on) [from a Heb. root meaning "hear; listen"].

1. An ancestor of Jesus' mother Mary.—Lu 3:30.

2. The form of the name of Simon (Peter) used once by James at the Jerusalem council.—Ac 15:14.

3. One of the prophets and teachers of the congregation in Antioch, Syria, who laid their hands on Barnabas and Paul after the holy spirit had designated these two for missionary work. Symeon's Latin surname was Niger.—Ac 13:1-3.

SYNAGOGUE. In the Greek *Septuagint* the two words *ek·kle·si'a*, meaning "assembly" or "congregation," and *sy·na·go·ge'* (a bringing together) are used interchangeably. The word "synagogue" eventually took on the meaning of the place or building where the assembly was held. However, it did not completely lose its original meaning, for the Great Synagogue was not a large building but an assembly of noted scholars, credited with settling the Hebrew Scripture canon for the Palestinian Jews. It is said to have had its beginning in the days of Ezra or of Nehemiah and to have continued until the time of the Great Sanhedrin, about the third century B.C.E. James uses the word in the sense of a Christian meeting or public gathering.—Jas 2:2.

In Revelation 2:9; 3:9, "synagogue" applies to an assembly under the domination of Satan. Also, we read of the "Synagogue of the Freedmen." —Ac 6:9; see FREEDMAN, FREEMAN.

It is not known just when synagogues were instituted, but it seems to have been during the 70-year Babylonian exile when there was no temple in existence, or shortly following the return from exile, after Ezra the priest had so strongly stressed the need for knowledge of the Law.

In the days of Jesus Christ's earthly ministry, each town of any size in Palestine had its own synagogue, and the larger cities had more than one. Jerusalem had many. There is even an instance in the Scriptures of a synagogue that was built for the Jews by a Roman army officer. (Lu 7:2, 5, 9) One of the finest synagogue ruins yet discovered has been excavated at Tell Hum (Kefar Nahum), the likely site of ancient Capernaum.

The edifice originally had two stories. Dates given by scholars for this synagogue vary from the late second century C.E. to the early fifth century C.E. The structure itself was built on the site of an earlier synagogue dating back to the first century C.E. The earlier synagogue, which was partially excavated recently, was 24.2 m (79.4 ft) long and 18.5 m (60.7 ft) wide.

One feature of ancient synagogues was a repository for Scripture rolls. Evidently the oldest custom was to keep the scrolls either outside the main building or in a separate room, for safety's sake. Eventually they came to be kept in a portable ark, or chest, that was put in position during worship. In later synagogues, the ark became an architectural feature of the building itself, being built into or onto one of the walls. Adjacent to the ark and facing the congregation was seating for the presiding officers of the synagogue and any distinguished guests. (Mt 23:6) The reading of the Law was done from an elevated platform, traditionally located in the center of the synagogue. Around the three sides was seating space or benches for the audience, possibly including a separate section for women. It seems that the orientation of the building was considered important, an effort being made to have the worshipers face Jerusalem.—Compare Da 6:10.

Program of Worship. The synagogue served as a place for instruction, not sacrifice. Sacrifices were made only at the temple. Synagogue exercises appear to have consisted of praise, prayer, recital and reading of the Scriptures, as well as exposition and exhortation or preaching. The giving of praise featured the Psalms. Prayers, while taken from the Scriptures to an extent, in time came to be long and ritualistic and were often recited for pretext or show.—Mr 12:40; Lu 20:47.

One element of synagogue worship was the reciting of the Shema, or what amounted to the Jewish confession of faith. It received its name from the first word of the first scripture used, "Listen [*Shema*ʽ], O Israel: Jehovah our God is one Jehovah." (De 6:4) The most important part of the service was the reading of the Torah or Pentateuch, which took place on Mondays, Thursdays, and each Sabbath. In many synagogues, the Law was scheduled to be read entirely in the course of one year; in others the program took three years. It was because of the emphasis on the reading of the Torah that the disciple James could well observe to the members of the governing body at Jerusalem: "From ancient times Moses has had in city after city those who preach him, because he is read aloud in the synagogues on every sabbath." (Ac 15:21) The Mishnah (*Me-*

gillah 4:1, 2) also refers to the practice of reading excerpts of the prophets, known as the haftarahs, each with its exposition. When Jesus entered the synagogue of his hometown Nazareth, he was handed one of the scrolls that contained the haftarahs to be read, after which he made an exposition upon it, as was the custom.—Lu 4:17-21.

After the reading of the Torah and the haftarahs, together with their exposition, came preaching or exhortation. We read that Jesus taught and preached in the synagogues throughout the whole of Galilee. Likewise Luke records that it was "after the public reading of the Law and of the Prophets" that Paul and Barnabas were invited to speak, to preach.—Mt 4:23; Ac 13: 15, 16.

Paul's Preaching. Following Pentecost of 33 C.E. and the establishment of the Christian congregation, the apostles, particularly Paul, did much preaching in the synagogues. When entering a city, Paul usually went first to the synagogue and preached there, giving the Jews the first opportunity of hearing the good news of the Kingdom, afterward going to the Gentiles. In some cases he spent considerable time, preaching for several Sabbaths, in the synagogue. In Ephesus he taught in the synagogue for three months, and after opposition arose, he withdrew the disciples who believed and used the school auditorium of Tyrannus for about two years.—Ac 13:14; 17:1, 2, 10, 17; 18:4, 19; 19:8-10.

Paul was not using the Jewish synagogues as places of meeting for a Christian congregation. Neither was he having Sunday meetings, for he was using the Jewish Sabbath, which was Saturday, to preach to the Jews because of their being gathered together on that day.

Christian Similarities. It was not difficult for the first Jewish Christians to conduct orderly, educational Bible study meetings, for they had the basic pattern in the synagogues with which they were familiar. We find many similarities. In the Jewish synagogue, as also in the Christian congregation, there was no set-apart priesthood or clergyman who did virtually all the talking. In the synagogue, sharing in the reading and in the exposition was open to any devout Jew. In the Christian congregation, all were to make public declaration and to incite to love and fine works, but in an orderly way. (Heb 10:23-25) In the Jewish synagogue, women did not teach or exercise authority over men; neither did they do so in the Christian assembly. First Corinthians chapter 14 gives instructions for the meetings of the Christian congregation, and it can be seen that they were very similar to synagogue procedure. —1Co 14:31-35; 1Ti 2:11, 12.

Synagogues had presiding officers and overseers, as did the early Christian congregations. (Mr 5:22; Lu 13:14; Ac 20:28; Ro 12:8) Synagogues had attendants or assistants, and so did the Christians in their form of worship. There was one called the sent one or messenger of the synagogue. While finding no counterpart in the historical record of the early Christian congregation, a similar designation, "angel," appears in the messages that Jesus Christ sent to the seven congregations in Asia Minor.—Lu 4:20; 1Ti 3:8-10; Re 2:1, 8, 12, 18; 3:1, 7, 14.

Among other respects in which the synagogue served as a precursor of the Christian assemblies are the following: The local synagogues recognized the authority of the Sanhedrin at Jerusalem, even as Christian congregations recognized the authority of the governing body at Jerusalem, as Acts chapter 15 so clearly shows. In neither were collections taken, and yet in both provision was made for contributions for the assembly and its ministers and for the poor.—2Co 9:1-5.

Both also served as courts. The synagogue was the place where minor cases involving Jews were heard and disposed of; and so also the apostle Paul argues that Christians should let the mature ones in the congregation judge matters involving Christians rather than go to worldly courts to settle such differences. (1Co 6:1-3) While the synagogue arrangement made provision for the administering of stripes, in the Christian congregation such punishment was limited to rebukes. Similar to the arrangement for Jews in the synagogue, in the Christian congregation the severest measure that could be taken against the one professing to be a Christian was that of expelling him, disfellowshipping or excommunicating him, from the Christian congregation.—1Co 5:1-8, 11-13; see CONGREGATION; EXPELLING.

Jesus foretold that his followers would be scourged in the synagogues (Mt 10:17; 23:34; Mr 13:9) and that they would be put out, expelled. (Joh 16:2) Some of the rulers among the Jews believed in Jesus, but for fear of being expelled from the Jewish congregation, they would not confess him. (Joh 12:42) For giving testimony in behalf of Jesus, a man Jesus had healed from congenital blindness was thrown out by the Jews. —Joh 9:1, 34.

SYNTYCHE (Syn'ty·che) [With Fortune (Success)]. A Christian woman at Philippi whom Paul commended for her integrity and whom he exhorted to "be of the same mind in the Lord" with a Christian sister named Euodia. (Php 4:2, 3) The apostle gave this counsel apparently because of some disagreement between these two, a conclusion supported by several modern translations. —AB, JB, NE, Ph, TEV.

SYRACUSE (Syr'a·cuse). A city with a fine harbor, on the SE coast of the island of Sicily, today called Siracusa (Italian). According to Thucydides, a Greek colony was established at Syracuse in the eighth century B.C.E.

The apostle Paul stayed at Syracuse for three days toward the close of his trip to Rome, in about 59 C.E. The layover there may have been necessary because the ship had to wait for suitable sailing wind. (Ac 28:12) From Syracuse, Paul's ship went "around" and came to Rhegium, on the southern tip of Italy. The exact meaning of this expression is not known. Possibly the vessel took a somewhat curved route, away from the coast, in order to get sufficient wind to fill its sails. Or, maybe it "made a circuit—following the coast—" to reach Rhegium.—Ac 28:13, AB.

SYRIA. That region bounded on the E by Mesopotamia, on the W by the Lebanon Mountains, on the N by the Taurus Mountains, on the S by Palestine and the Arabian Desert. The region is called Aram in the Hebrew Scriptures. These boundaries are only general, since Syrian influence and domination within this area were rather fluid and unstable most of the time.

In Patriarchal Times. Of patriarchal times our only Biblical records of the Syrians concern events around Haran involving the lives of Rebekah's family, her father Bethuel and brother Laban both being described as Syrians, or literally, Aramaeans. (Ge 25:20; 28:5; 31:20, 24) Jacob was described as "a perishing Syrian" because he had resided 20 years in the area around Haran. There he married Laban's two daughters and fathered sons and daughters; he also experienced affliction in Laban's service. Additionally, Jacob's mother was a Syrian.—De 26:5; Ge 31:40-42; Ho 12:12.

Period of the Judges. During the period of the Judges when the Israelites fell away from Jehovah's worship, the Syrian king Cushanrishathaim subjugated them for a period of eight years. (Jg 3:7-10) On another occasion, Syria's influence proved strong enough to cause Israel to worship her gods along with other pagan deities. —Jg 10:6.

Period of Kings of Israel and of Judah. From and after the birth of Israel's monarchy, Syria became aggressively active militarily, and throughout the entire history of the northern kingdom, hostilities between the two prevailed. Israel's first king, Saul, went to war with the Syrian kings of Zobah. (1Sa 14:47) David, upon becoming king, inflicted heavy losses on the army of Syrian King Hadadezer. At the same time much gold, silver, and copper were taken and sanctified to Jehovah. David also set up garrisons in Damascus and compelled the Syrians to pay tribute. (2Sa 8:3-12; 1Ch 18:3-8) Later, more than 30,000 Syrian mercenaries who were hired by the Ammonites, instead of fighting, took flight before the Israelites. After Syrian reinforcements were brought up, however, a battle with Israel ensued and the Syrians suffered great losses, causing them to sue for peace.—2Sa 10:6-19; 1Ch 19:6-19.

Following this, a certain Syrian rebel named Rezon, who had fled from Hadadezer, made himself king at Damascus and became a resister of Israel all the days of Solomon. (1Ki 11:23-25) With these developments Damascus became the most prominent Syrian city and was long recognized as "the head of Syria," toward which Jehovah's pronouncements against that nation were directed. —Isa 7:8; 17:1-3; Am 1:5.

After division of Israel's kingdom. Bible history of the Syrians following the death of Solomon and the dividing of his kingdom tells, in the main, of their successes and reverses in their relations with the Israelites of both the northern and the southern kingdoms. Particular events are mentioned as occurring during the reigns of Asa (1Ki 15:18-20; 2Ch 16:2-4, 7), Ahab (1Ki 20:1-34; 22:3, 4, 29-35; 2Ch 18:10, 28-34), Jehoram of Israel (2Ki 6:24–7:16; 8:28, 29; 9:14b, 15; 2Ch 22:5, 6), Jehoash of Judah (2Ki 12:17, 18; 2Ch 24:23, 24), Jehoahaz (2Ki 13:3-7, 22), Jehoash of Israel (2Ki 13:14-19, 24, 25), Jotham (2Ki 15:37, 38), Ahaz (2Ki 16:5-9; 2Ch 28:5; Isa 7:1-8; 9:12), and Jehoiakim (2Ki 24:2). It was most unusual, worthy of special mention, when there were 'three years without war between Syria and Israel.'—1Ki 22:1.

Jehovah's prophet Elisha had certain contacts with the Syrians; for example, he cured the Syrian army chief Naaman of leprosy (2Ki 5:1-20), and he disclosed to Hazael that he would be king of Syria in place of his master Ben-hadad II. (2Ki 8:7-15) On another occasion when a detachment of Syrians surrounded Dothan to take Elisha captive, the prophet first asked God to strike them with a form of blindness, and then he led them to Samaria, where their vision was restored; then he had them fed and sent home. (2Ki 6:8-23) For further details on these experiences of the Syrians with the prophet, see the article ELISHA.

The Syrians were Semites, closely related to and associated with the Israelites. Yet in the eighth century B.C.E. there was sufficient difference between their languages that the common Jew did not understand Aramaic. (2Ki 18:26-28; Isa 36:11, 12; see ARAMAIC [The Language].) Also religiously, there were vast differences between the polytheistic Syrians and the Jews, and it was only when the latter apostatized that worship of the Syrian gods was allowed in the land of Israel. —Jg 10:6; 2Ki 16:10-16; 2Ch 28:22, 23.

In the First Century C.E. Syria of apostolic times meant the Roman province that Pompey annexed to the empire in 64 B.C.E. This province embraced much of the old territory of Syria. The governor of Syria also had supervision of the whole of Palestine. At the time of Jesus' birth Syria was ruled over by Governor Quirinius, the legate of Emperor Augustus, whose residence was in the capital of the province and third-largest city of the Roman Empire, Antioch, on the Orontes River. (Lu 2:1, 2) Jesus restricted his ministry to Palestine proper, but reports of his wonderful miracles reached out "into all Syria." —Mt 4:24.

When the Christians in Jerusalem were scattered because of the persecution following the stoning of Stephen, some of them carried the good news to Syria's capital, Antioch. First the Jews there heard the message, and later those of other national groups did. Barnabas and Paul were both instrumental in building up the congregation of Antioch. It was first in this Syrian city that "the disciples were by divine providence called Christians."—Ac 11:19-26; Ga 1:21.

About the year 46 C.E., when a great famine occurred during the reign of Emperor Claudius, the Christians in and around Antioch sent a relief ministration by Barnabas and Paul to their brothers in Jerusalem. (Ac 11:27-30) The letter regarding circumcision sent out by the apostles and older men in Jerusalem was addressed particularly to the congregations in Antioch, Syria, and Cilicia (a neighboring region). (Ac 15:23) During the years when Paul traveled extensively as a missionary, he used Antioch of Syria as his home base.—Ac 15:40, 41; 18:18; 20:3; 21:3; Ga 2:11.

SYROPHOENICIAN (Syʹro·phoeʹniʹcian). The designation applied in Mark 7:26 to a non-Israelite woman from the regions of Tyre and Sidon. Being a combination of "Syrian" and "Phoenician," the expression "Syrophoenician" probably had its origin in the circumstance that Phoenicia was part of the Roman province of Syria. The Syrophoenician woman is also called Khaʹna·naiʹa

(literally, Canaanite; translated "Phoenician" in *NW*), for the early inhabitants of Phoenicia descended from Canaan, and in time, "Canaan" came to refer primarily to Phoenicia. (Mt 15:22, ftn) Her being termed "Grecian" likely means that she was of Greek descent.—Mr 7:26.

Not long after Passover of 32 C.E., this Syrophoenician woman approached Jesus Christ, repeatedly requesting that he expel a demon from her daughter. At first Jesus declined, saying: "It is not right to take the bread of the children and throw it to little dogs." To the Jews dogs were unclean animals. But, in likening the non-Jews to "little dogs," which might be kept in a home, and not to wild dogs of the street, Jesus softened the comparison. Nevertheless, what Jesus said apparently served to test the woman. Humbly, she acknowledged: "Yes, Lord; but really the little dogs do eat of the crumbs falling from the table of their masters." Her words reflected great faith, and therefore, her daughter was healed.—Mt 15:21-28; Mr 7:24-30.

SYRTIS (Syr′tis) [from a root meaning "drag"]. The Greek name of two gulfs located within the large indentation on the coast of northern Africa. The western gulf (between Tunis and Tripoli) was called Syrtis Minor (now the Gulf of Gabès). Just to the E was Syrtis Major, the modern Gulf of Sidra. Ancient sailors dreaded both gulfs because of their treacherous sandbanks, which were constantly being shifted by the tides. Regarding vessels that became involved in the shoals, Strabo, a geographer of the first century C.E., reported, "The safe escape of a boat is rare."—*Geography*, 17, III, 20.

When the apostle Paul was being taken to Rome as a prisoner, the ship on which he traveled was seized S of Crete by a northeasterly gale. The crew, therefore, feared that the ship would be run aground on the "Syrtis," evidently the quicksands or sandbanks of the Gulf of Sidra.—Ac 27:14-17.

SYSTEMS OF THINGS. The phrase "system of things" expresses the sense of the Greek term *ai·on′* in more than 30 of its occurrences in the Christian Greek Scriptures.

On the meaning of *ai·on′*, R. C. Trench states: "Like [*ko′smos*, world] it [*ai·on′*] has a primary and physical, and then, superinduced on this, a secondary and ethical, sense. In its primary [sense], it signifies time, short or long, in its unbroken duration; . . . but essentially time as the condition under which all created things exist, and the measure of their existence . . . Thus signifying time, it comes presently to signify all which exists

in the world under conditions of time; . . . and then, more ethically, the course and current of this world's affairs." In support of this latter sense, he quotes German scholar C. L. W. Grimm as giving the definition: "The totality of that which manifests itself outwardly in the course of time."—*Synonyms of the New Testament*, London, 1961, pp. 202, 203.

The basic sense of *ai·on′*, therefore, is "age," or "period of existence," and in Scripture it often denotes a long space of time (Ac 3:21; 15:18), including an endless period of time, that is, forever, eternity. (Mr 3:29; 11:14; Heb 13:8) For these senses, see AGE. Here, however, we consider the sense of the term dealt with in the latter part of the definition quoted in the preceding paragraph.

As an aid in understanding this sense, we may recall certain uses of the terms "age," "era," and "epoch" in English. We may speak of an age, era, or epoch in the sense of a period of time in history characterized by a distinctive development or course of events or distinguished by some prominent figure or typical feature or features. We may speak of the "Age of Exploration," referring to the time of Columbus, Magellan, Cook, and other maritime explorers, or to the "Feudal Age," the "Dark Ages," the "Victorian Era," or, more recently, the "Space Age." In each case what is prominent is not so much the time period itself but the distinguishing or characteristic *feature* or *features* of that time period. Those features provide the determining factors, or lines, marking the beginning, duration, and end of the period. Without them, the period would be just time, not a particular epoch, era, or age.

Thus, Liddell and Scott's *Greek-English Lexicon* lists as one definition of *ai·on′*: "space of time clearly defined and marked out, *epoch, age*." (Revised by H. Jones, Oxford, 1968, p. 45) And *Vine's Expository Dictionary of Old and New Testament Words* (1981, Vol. 1, p. 41) says: "an age, era . . . [it] signifies a period of indefinite duration, or time viewed in relation to what takes place in the period."

For this reason, where the distinguishing features of a period rather than the time itself are the more prominent thought in a particular text, *ai·on′* may appropriately be rendered as "system of things" or "state." The advisability of doing this is illustrated at Galatians 1:4, where the apostle writes: "He gave himself for our sins that he might deliver us from the present wicked system of things [form of *ai·on′*] according to the will of our God and Father." Many translations here render *ai·on′* as "age," but it is evident that Christ's ransom sacrifice did not serve to deliver Christians from an age or space of time, for they continued living in the same age as the rest of mankind. However, they were delivered from the *state* or *system of things* existing during that time period and characterizing it.—Compare Tit 2:11-14.

The apostle wrote to the Christians at Rome: "Quit being fashioned after this system of things, but be transformed by making your mind over." (Ro 12:2) It was not the time period itself that set the fashion, pattern, or model for people of that time, but it was the standards, practices, manners, customs, ways, outlook, styles, and other features characterizing that time period. At Ephesians 2:1, 2 the apostle speaks of those to whom he writes as having been "dead in your trespasses and sins, in which you at one time walked according to the system of things ["following the way," *JB;* "following the course," *RS*] of this world." In commenting on this text, *The Expositor's Greek Testament* (Vol. III, p. 283) shows that time is not the sole or prime factor here expressed by *ai·on'.* In support of the rendering of *ai·on'* by "course," it says: "That word conveys the three ideas of *tenor, development,* and *limited continuance.* This course of a world which is evil is itself evil, and to live in accordance with it is to live in trespasses and sins."—Edited by W. Nicoll, 1967.

Ages, States, Systems of Things. There are various systems of things, or prevailing states of affairs, that have existed or will exist. Those brought about by God through his Son are, obviously, righteous systems of things.

For example, by means of the Law covenant God introduced what some might call the Israelite or Jewish Epoch. However, here again what distinguished this period of history (as regards God's relations with mankind) was the state of affairs and the characteristic features brought about by the Law covenant. Those features included a priesthood; a system of sacrifices and dietary regulations as well as of tabernacle and temple worship with festivals and sabbaths, all of which formed prophetic types and shadows; and also a national system that came to involve a human king. However, when God foretold a new covenant (Jer 31:31-34), the old covenant became in a sense obsolete, even though God permitted it to continue in operation for a period of centuries thereafter. (Heb 8:13) Then, in 33 C.E., God brought the Law covenant to its end by his nailing it, in effect, to his Son's torture stake.—Col 2:13-17.

Evidently for this reason, Hebrews 9:26 says of Christ that he "manifested himself once for all time at the conclusion of the systems of things to put sin away through the sacrifice of himself." Nevertheless, the distinguishing features of that age or epoch did not come to their *complete* end until 70 C.E., when Jerusalem and its temple were destroyed and the Jewish people were scattered. This disaster—although the last Judean stronghold (at Masada) fell to the Romans three years later, or in 73 C.E.—permanently ended the Jewish priesthood, sacrifices, and temple worship as prescribed in the Law; it also ended the Jewish national arrangement as established by God. This is undoubtedly why the apostle, many years after Christ's death, but prior to the Roman devastation of Jerusalem, could relate certain past Israelite history and say: "Now these things went on befalling them as examples, and they were written for a warning to us *upon whom the ends of the systems of things have arrived.*"—1Co 10:11; compare Mt 24:3; 1Pe 4:7.

By means of his ransom sacrifice and the new covenant that it validated, Jesus Christ was used by God to bring in a different system of things, one primarily involving the congregation of anointed Christians. (Heb 8:7-13) This marked the opening of a new epoch, characterized by the realities foreshadowed by the Law covenant. It brought in a ministry of reconciliation, intensified operations of God's holy spirit, worship through a spiritual temple with spiritual sacrifices (1Pe 2:5) instead of a literal temple and animal sacrifices; and it brought in revelations of God's purpose and a relationship with God that meant a new way of life for those in the new covenant. All of these were features characterizing that system of things introduced by Christ.

Unrighteous Age, or System of Things. When Paul wrote Timothy about those who were "rich in the present system of things," undoubtedly he was not referring to the Jewish system of things, or epoch, for in his ministry Timothy dealt not only with Jewish Christians but also with many Gentile Christians, and the wealth of any of these Gentile Christians would not likely be bound up with the Jewish system of things. (1Ti 6:17) Similarly, when referring to Demas as one who had forsaken him "because he loved the present system of things," Paul evidently did not mean that Demas had loved the Jewish system of things but, rather, that he loved the prevailing state of affairs in the world in general and the worldly way of life.—2Ti 4:10; compare Mt 13:22.

The worldly *ai·on',* or system of things, had

been in existence even before the introducing of the Law covenant. It continued contemporaneously with the *ai·on'* of that covenant, and it endured beyond the end of the *ai·on'*, or state of affairs, that the Law covenant had introduced. The worldly *ai·on'* evidently began sometime after the Flood, when an unrighteous way of life developed, one characterized by sin and rebellion against God and his will. Hence, Paul could also speak of "the god of this system of things" as blinding the minds of unbelievers, an evident reference to Satan the Devil. (2Co 4:4; compare Joh 12:31.) Primarily, Satan's dominion and influence have molded the worldly *ai·on'* and given it its distinctive features and spirit. (Compare Eph 2:1, 2.) Commenting on Romans 12:2, *The Expositor's Greek Testament* (Vol. II, p. 688) says: "Even apparent or superficial conformity to a system controlled by such a spirit, much more an actual accommodation to its ways, would be fatal to the Christian life." Such worldly *ai·on'* was to continue long after the apostle's day.

For example, at Matthew 13:37-43, in explaining the parable of the sower, Jesus said that "the field is the world [*ko'smos*]; . . . The harvest is a conclusion of a system of things [form of *ai·on'*] . . . Therefore, just as the weeds are collected and burned with fire, so it will be in the conclusion of the system of things." Some translations, such as the *King James Version*, use "world" to translate both *ko'smos* and *ai·on'* in these verses. It is clear, however, that the farmer in the illustration does not burn up the "field," representing the "world," but only the "weeds." Hence, what comes to an end, or 'concludes,' is not the "world" (*ko'smos*) but the "system of things" (*ai·on'*). George Campbell's translation renders these portions: "The field is the world . . . the harvest is the conclusion of this state . . . so shall it be at the conclusion of this state."—*The Four Gospels*, London, 1834.

Jesus showed that the wheat represented true anointed Christians, genuine disciples, whereas the weeds represented imitation Christians. Thus, the conclusion of the system of things, here depicted as the harvesttime, would not refer to the conclusion of the Jewish system of things, in this case, nor to the conclusion of the "state" in which "wheat" and "weeds" grew together undisturbed, but must refer to the end of the same system of things as later referred to by the apostle, that is, "the present system of things" marked by Satanic domination. (1Ti 6:17) So, too, with the additional illustration given by Jesus regarding the dragnet and the separation of the fish, depicting "how it will be in the conclusion of the system of things: the angels will go out and separate the wicked

from among the righteous." (Mt 13:47-50) These expressions by Jesus were doubtless in the disciples' minds when sometime later they asked the question as to 'the sign of his presence and of the conclusion of the system of things.' (Mt 24:3) Jesus' promise to be with his disciples in their discipling work right down to the conclusion of the system of things also must refer to the conclusion of the state of affairs resulting from domination by Satan.—Mt 28:19, 20.

Other examples of texts where *ai·on'* refers to such wicked system of things include Luke 16:8; 1 Corinthians 1:20; 2:6, 8; 3:18; Ephesians 1:21.

The Coming System of Things. At Matthew 12:32 Jesus is quoted as saying that anyone speaking against the holy spirit will not be forgiven in this "system of things nor in that to come." This might be read as a reference to the Jewish system of things and the then future system of things that Christ would bring in by means of the new covenant. However, the evidence indicates that he referred instead to the present wicked system of things and to a system of things that would be introduced at the conclusion of that wicked system of things. He referred to that same future state in promising that those leaving home and family for the sake of God's Kingdom would get "many times more in this period of time [form of *kai·ros'*, meaning "appointed time"], and in the coming system of things [form of *ai·on'*] everlasting life." (Lu 18:29, 30) That coming system of things would also mark the period of time in which persons would receive a resurrection with the opportunity of being counted as among God's children. (Lu 20:34, 35) The plural form of *ai·on'* is used at Ephesians 2:7 in referring to the "coming systems of things" in which the anointed Christians are to experience a surpassingly rich demonstration of God's undeserved kindness toward them "in union with Christ Jesus." (Compare Eph 1:18-23; Heb 6:4, 5.) This indicates that there will be systems of things, or states, *within* the overall "coming system of things," even as the system of things under the Law covenant embraced interrelated, contemporaneous systems, as has already been shown.

God 'Puts in Order' the "Systems of Things." Hebrews 11:3 states: "By faith we perceive that the systems of things [plural of *ai·on'*] were put in order by God's word, so that what is beheld has come to be out of things that do not appear." Many consider the text at Hebrews 1:2 to be parallel in its use of the plural form of *ai·on'*; it says that Jehovah spoke through his Son, Jesus Christ, "whom he appointed heir of all things, and through whom he made the systems of things." The particular meaning of the Greek word *ai·on'* in these two verses has been variously understood.

One way to understand them is to view the Greek term as referring to the distinguishing or characteristic features of a time period. In Hebrews chapter 11, the inspired writer is discussing how, by faith, "the men of old times had witness borne to them." (Vs 2) Then, in his succeeding words, he presents examples of faithful men in the pre-Flood era, in the patriarchal epoch, and in the period of Israel's covenant relationship with God. During all these distinct periods, and by means of the developments caused, formed, and accomplished in them, God was working out his purpose to eliminate rebellion and provide the way for reconciliation with himself on the part of deserving humans by means of successive "systems of things." So those men of old had to have, and did have, faith that the invisible God was indeed directing matters in an orderly manner. They believed that he was the unseen Producer of the various systems of things and that the goal they sought, "the fulfillment of the promise," was an absolute certainty in God's due time. In faith, they looked forward to the further outworking of God's purpose, which included the system of things produced by the new covenant based on Jesus' sacrifice.—Heb 11: 39, 40; 12:1, 18-28.

Another way to understand the use of *ai·on'* in Hebrews 1:2 and 11:3 is that it is an equivalent of the Greek term *ko'smos* in the sense of the world or universe, the totality of created things including the sun, moon, stars, and the earth itself. This view is evidently supported by the statement in Hebrews 11:3 that "what is beheld has come to be out of things that do not appear." This verse could also be taken as a reference to the Genesis creation account, which could logically precede Paul's references to Abel (vs 4), Enoch (vss 5, 6), and Noah (vs 7). Thus, Paul may have been expanding upon his definition of faith by referring to the existence of the universe consisting of sun, moon, and stars as clear evidence that there is a Creator. —Compare Ro 1:20.

In the Hebrew Scriptures. The Hebrew term *che'ledh* is similar in meaning to *ai·on'*, referring in some texts to "life's duration" (Job 11:17; Ps 39:5; 89:47), but in other cases the *features* of the time period appear to be the main thing signified, allowing for rendering it "system of things." (Ps 17:13, 14; 49:1) Some translations use the word "world" to render this term in these latter texts, but this rendering more or less bypasses the sense implied, namely, that of continuing time.

T

TAANACH (Ta'a·nach). An enclave city of Manasseh in the territory of Issachar (Jos 17:11; 1Ch 7:29) that was assigned to the Kohathite Levites. (Jos 21:20, 25) Under the command of Joshua, the Israelites defeated the king of Taanach. (Jos 12:7, 21) But the Manassites failed to drive out the Canaanites from this and other cities. Eventually, however, these Canaanites were put to forced labor. (Jg 1:27, 28) In the time of Judge Barak the forces of Jabin the king of Hazor, led by his army chief Sisera, were defeated at Taanach. (Jg 5:19) During Solomon's reign the city was in the district assigned to Baana, one of the 12 deputies in charge of supplying food for the royal table. (1Ki 4:7, 12) Archaeological evidence from Taanach and the relief on a temple wall at Karnak indicate that the city was taken by Pharaoh Shishak when he invaded Palestine in the fifth year of the reign of Solomon's son and successor Rehoboam.—2Ch 12:2-4.

Taanach is identified with Tell Ta'anakh, about 8 km (5 mi) SSE of Megiddo and on the south edge of the Plain of Jezreel ('Emeq Yizre'el). The site occupied an important position on at least two trade routes, one leading to the Plain of Acco and the other to the Plain of Sharon.

TAANATH-SHILOH (Ta'a·nath-shi'loh). A site on Ephraim's border. (Jos 16:5, 6) It is identified with Khirbet Ta'na el-Fauqa, about 10 km (6 mi) ESE of Shechem.

TABBAOTH (Tab·ba'oth) [Signet Rings]. Forefather of a family of Nethinim. Some of his descendants returned to Jerusalem with Zerubbabel.—Ezr 2:1, 2, 43; Ne 7:46.

TABBATH (Tab'bath). After being attacked by Gideon's forces, the enemy Midianites fled "as far as the outskirts of Abel-meholah by Tabbath." (Jg 7:12, 19-22) Tabbath is tentatively identified with Ras Abu Tabat, about 5 km (3 mi) E of the Jordan River and 10 km (6 mi) N of Succoth. Abel-meholah apparently was W of the Jordan and is spoken of as "by ["opposite," *JB*] Tabbath." —See ABEL-MEHOLAH.

TABEEL (Tab'e·el) [Good Is God].

1. Father of a man whom the kings of Israel and Syria intended to place on the throne in Jerusalem if they captured Judah's capital. The name of the son is not given. The incident occurred during the period when the reigns of Ahaz and Pekah overlapped (between about 762 and 759 B.C.E.).—Isa 7:5, 6.

2. Joint author of an Aramaic letter sent to Persian King Artaxerxes opposing the Jews' reconstruction work in Jerusalem and resulting in a halt of temple rebuilding.—Ezr 4:7, 24.

TABERAH (Tab'e·rah) [Burning [that is, a conflagration; blaze]]. An Israelite encampment in the Wilderness of Sinai, the precise location of which is unknown. On account of Israel's complaining there, God sent a fire that consumed some of the people at the extremity of the camp. But when Moses supplicated Jehovah, the blaze "sank down" or was extinguished. This incident gave rise to the name "Taberah."—Nu 11:1-3; De 9:22.

TABERNACLE. A transportable tent of worship used by Israel; at times also called "the tent of meeting." (Ex 39:32, 40; see TENT OF MEETING.) In Hebrew it is called *mish·kan'* (residence; dwelling; tabernacle), *'o'hel* (tent), and *miq·dash'* (sanctuary). In Greek it is referred to as *ske·ne'*, which means "tent; booth; residence; dwelling place."—See HOLY PLACE.

The tabernacle was a central feature of Jehovah's arrangement for approach to him by the nation of Israel. It consisted of two compartments. (PICTURE, Vol. 1, p. 538) The first, the Holy, contained a golden lampstand, the golden altar of incense, the table of showbread, and golden utensils; and the innermost compartment, the Most Holy, contained the ark of the covenant, surmounted by two golden cherubs.—See ARK OF THE COVENANT; MOST HOLY.

When Inaugurated. The tabernacle, or "tent of meeting" (called "the temple of Jehovah" at 1Sa 1:9 and "the house of Jehovah" at 1Sa 1:24), was constructed in the wilderness at Mount Sinai in 1512 B.C.E. It was completely set up, with its furniture and utensils installed, on the first day of the first month, Abib or Nisan. (Ex 40) The priesthood was installed at Jehovah's direction by the mediator Moses on that day, and the full installation services occupied seven days. On the eighth day the priests began to carry out their official functions.—Le chaps 8, 9; see INSTALLATION.

Design. Jehovah had spoken to Moses in the mountain, giving him the complete pattern for the tabernacle, commanding him: "See that you make all things after their pattern that was shown to you in the mountain." It served in providing "a shadow of the heavenly things" and therefore had to be accurate to the least detail. (Heb 8:5) Jehovah inspired Bezalel and Oholiab, so that the work, which others including both men and women shared in, could be done perfectly, according to the instructions Moses gave. The result was: "According to all that Jehovah had commanded Moses, that was the way the sons of Israel did all the service." (Ex 39:42; 35:25, 26; 36:1, 4) The materials were provided through voluntary contributions from the people. (Ex 36:3, 6, 7) Doubtless the gold, silver, and copper, as well as the yarns, fabrics, and skins, came as contributions largely from that which the Israelites had taken out of Egypt. (Ex 12:34-36; see SEALSKIN.) Acacia wood was available in the wilderness.—See ACACIA.

The calculations in this article are based on a cubit of 44.5 cm (17.5 in.). However, the long cubit of about 51.8 cm (20.4 in.) may have been used.—Compare 2Ch 3:3; Eze 40:5.

Coverings and screens. The entire framework of the structure was covered first by a linen covering embroidered with colorful figures of cherubs. The covering was in two large sections of five cloths each, the sections being joined by loops of blue thread that fastened over gold hooks. Each cloth was only 28 cubits (12.5 m; 40.8 ft) long, which would be at least one cubit (44.5 cm; 17.5 in.) short of reaching the ground on each side of the structure.—Ex 26:1-6.

On top of the linen covering went a goat's hair cover, made in two sections, one of six cloths and one of five. Each of the 11 cloths was 30 cubits (13.4 m; 43.7 ft) long. Over this was put the covering of ram skins dyed red and, finally, one of sealskins, apparently reaching to the ground and evidently provided with ropes so that the covering could be fastened at the ground by tent pins. —Ex 26:7-14.

Another curtain placed inside between the Holy and Most Holy was embroidered with cherubs (Ex 36:35), and the screen to the entrance on the E was of colorful wool and linen material.—Ex 36:37.

Dimensions. The Bible describes the tabernacle (evidently inside measurements) as being 30 cubits (13.4 m; 43.7 ft) long and 10 cubits (4.5 m; 14.6 ft) in height. (Compare Ex 26:16-18.) It was also evidently 10 cubits in width. (Compare Ex 26:22-24.) The width may be figured as follows: The rear or W wall was constructed of six panel frames of one and one half cubits each (totaling 9 cubits) and two panel frames called corner posts, which evidently were positioned so that each added one half cubit to the inside dimension. The Jewish scholar Rashi (1040-1105 C.E.), commenting on Exodus 26:23, noted: "All the eight boards were set in a row, only that *the entire width of* these two [the corner posts] did not show in the interior of the Tabernacle, but only a half cubit on the one side and a half cubit on the other side could be seen in the interior, thus making up the breadth to ten cubits. The *remaining* cubit of one *board* and the *remaining* cubit of the other *board* came against the cubit thickness of the boards of the Tabernacle on the north and the south sides, so that the outside should be even."—*Pentateuch With Targum Onkelos, Haphtaroth and Rashi's Commentary, Exodus,* translated by M. Rosenbaum and A. M. Silbermann, p. 144; italics by the translators.

The Most Holy compartment was apparently a cube 10 cubits on a side—even as the Most Holy of Solomon's temple built later was cubical, each dimension being 20 cubits (8.9 m; 29.2 ft). (1Ki 6:20) The Holy compartment was twice as long as it was wide. As to the length of the Holy of the tabernacle, these points are significant: Each of the two sections of the linen covering was 20 cubits wide. (Ex 26:1-5) Thus, one section (20 cubits) would stretch from the entrance to the place where hooks joined it to the other section. The junction apparently was above the pillars supporting the curtain to the Most Holy. Then the other half of the covering (20 cubits) served to cover the Most Holy (10 cubits) and also the rear or W side of the tabernacle (10 cubits).

Panel frames. The walls were of acacia wood, gold overlaid, evidently in the form of panel frames (similar to window frames), instead of solid boards. (Ex 26:15-18) This view seems to be logical, for two reasons: (1) Solid acacia boards of the size described would be unnecessarily heavy, and (2) the cherubs embroidered on the curtain that went over the boards would be hidden except for those seen on the ceiling of the structure, inside. (Ex 26:1) So it appears that each panel frame was constructed in such a way that the priests in the tabernacle could see the cherubs embroidered on the linen covering. Some modern scholars also hold the view that the panel-frame construction rather than a solid-board design was used. Thus, although the Hebrew word *qe'resh* is rendered "board" in older versions, several modern translations render the word "frame" or "panel frame."—Ex 26:15-29, *AT, JB, Mo, NW, RS.*

There were 20 panel frames on the N side and 20 on the S side. (Ex 26:18, 20) Each frame was 10 cubits (4.5 m; 14.6 ft) high and one and one half cubits (67 cm; 26 in.) wide and of unspecified depth. On the rear or W end there were six panel frames and at the back corners two frames called "corner posts."—Ex 26:22-24.

In connection with the panel frames, the Bible mentions "rings." The rings were no doubt fastened to the frames to accommodate the bars, three rows of which were passed through the rings to tie the structure together. Evidently the top and bottom rows consisted of two bars each, for only the bar at the center is described as "running through from end to end." These bars were of wood overlaid with gold.—Ex 26:26-29.

Pillars and foundation. Five pillars overlaid with gold were at the front, or entrance, and four such pillars supported the curtain dividing the Holy from the Most Holy. (Ex 26:32, 37) The foundation for the entire structure consisted of 100 pedestals that had sockets to receive tenons that were on the bottom of the 48 panel frames (two pedestals to a panel frame; four pedestals served for the four pillars dividing the Holy and Most Holy). These pedestals were all of silver (Ex 26:19-25, 32), each pedestal weighing a talent (c. 34 kg; 92 lb t). (Ex 38:27) Additionally, there were five copper pedestals for the pillars at the entrance. (Ex 26:37) Considering the weight of silver, these pedestals evidently would not be very thick, but would be more in the nature of heavy plates.

The courtyard. The courtyard surrounding the tabernacle was 100 by 50 cubits (44.5 by 22.2 m; 146 by 73 ft). The fencelike curtain around it was 5 cubits (2.2 m; 7.3 ft) high. Twenty pillars of copper were the supports for each side, and ten for each end of the area. The screen to the entranceway on the E was made of linen and colored material and was 20 cubits (8.9 m; 29 ft) across.—Ex 38:9-20.

Estimated cost. The value of the gold and silver used for the tabernacle would be in the neighborhood of $12,000,000, and the cost of the entire tabernacle possibly more than $13,000,000, judged at present-day values.—Ex 38:24-29.

Possible additions. It appears that in time chambers were built for the use of the priests in the courtyard of the tabernacle, probably at the sides of the structure. (1Sa 3:3) Also, booths may have been erected in the courtyard, so that some of those making communion offerings, along with their families, could eat the sacrifices there.

Its Location in Israel's Camp. (DIAGRAM, Vol. 1, p. 538) The tabernacle was the center of the camp of Israel. Nearest it, but at a respectful distance, possibly 2,000 cubits (890 m; 2,920 ft), were encamped the families of the tribe of Levi, the caretakers of the structure. (Compare Jos 3:4.) On the E was the priestly family of Aaron, on the S the Kohathites (from which Aaron's family had been selected for the priesthood [Ex 6:18-20]), on the W the Gershonites, and on the N the Merarites. (Nu 3:23, 29, 35, 38) Farther away were the other 12 tribes: Judah, Issachar, and Zebulun on the E; Reuben, Simeon, and Gad on the S; Ephraim, Manasseh, and Benjamin on the W; and Dan, Asher, and Naphtali on the N. (Nu 2:1-31) From any part of the camp the tabernacle could always be easily located, because of the cloud by day and the fire by night, which stood over the Most Holy where the ark of the covenant was situated.—Ex 40:36-38.

How Transported. In moving the tabernacle and its furniture and utensils, the priests covered the utensils of the holy place; and then the Kohathites carried the covered ark of the covenant, table of showbread, lampstand, and altars. They transported these things on their shoulders, walking. (Nu 4:4-15; 7:9) The Gershonites, having two wagons, transported the tent cloths (except the curtain to the Most Holy, which was placed over the Ark [Nu 4:5]), the tabernacle coverings, courtyard hangings, screens, related tent cords, and certain service utensils. (Nu 4:24-26; 7:7) The Merarites, with four wagons, took care of the very heavy items, including the panel frames and the pillars, socket pedestals and related tent pins, and cords of both the tabernacle and the courtyard.—Nu 4:29-32; 7:8.

History. After Israel crossed the Jordan River into the Promised Land, the tabernacle was set up at Gilgal. (Jos 4:19) It was relocated at Shiloh during the time of dividing the land (Jos 18:1), where it remained for years (1Sa 1:3, 24) before being moved to Nob. (1Sa 21:1-6) Later it was at Gibeon. (1Ch 21:29) When the ark of the covenant was moved to Zion by David, it had not been in the tabernacle for many years. But until the temple was built by Solomon, sacrifices were still offered at the tabernacle in Gibeon, it being called "the great high place." (1Ki 3:4) After the construction of the temple, Solomon had the tabernacle brought up to Jerusalem and apparently stored there.—1Ki 8:4; 2Ch 5:5.

Figurative Use. The apostle Paul throws light upon the pictorial significance of the tabernacle. In a context discussing the pattern made by the tabernacle and the services carried on therein, he speaks of Jesus Christ as "a public servant of the holy place and of the true tent, which Jehovah put up, and not man." (Heb 8:2) Farther on he says: "Christ came as a high priest of the good things that have come to pass, through the greater and more perfect tent not made with hands, that is, not of this creation." (Heb 9:11) The tent in the wilderness was an arrangement set up by God's command for approach to him in true worship, an arrangement for typical removal of sins. Being an illustration (Heb 9:9), it would foreshadow the arrangement that God established in which the great High Priest Jesus Christ could serve, appearing in heaven before his Father with the value of his sacrifice, which can actually remove sins. (Heb 9:24-26; see TEMPLE.) Through this arrangement faithful men can have real approach to God. (Heb 4:16) The heavenly "tent of the witness" or tabernacle was seen by the apostle John in vision.—Re 15:5.

The apostle Peter, being a spirit-begotten son of God with the hope of heavenly life in association with Christ Jesus, spoke of his fleshly body as a "tabernacle." It was a 'dwelling place,' but was only temporary, since Peter knew his death was near and his resurrection would be not in the flesh but in the spirit.—2Pe 1:13-15; 1Jo 3:2; 1Co 15:35-38, 42-44.

For the various articles of furniture and equipment used in the tabernacle, see articles under individual names.

TABITHA. See DORCAS.

TABLELAND. The Hebrew term *mi·shohr'*, rendered "tableland," is derived from a root meaning "be straight, right." This Hebrew word may refer to "level land" in contrast to mountainous or hilly country (1Ki 20:23, 25; Isa 40:4; 42:16; Zec 4:7) and can mean "uprightness" (Ps 27:11; 45:6; 67:4; 143:10; Isa 11:4) or designate a situation free from obstacles. (Ps 26:12) At times *mi·shohr'* applies to the tableland situated E of the Dead Sea between Heshbon in the N and the torrent valley of Arnon in the S.—De 3:10; Jos 13:9, 15-17; 20:8.

TABOR (Ta'bor).

1. An outstanding mountain in the territory of Issachar on its northern boundary. (Jos 19:17, 22) In Arabic it is called Jebel et-Tur; in Hebrew, Har Tavor. It is situated about 20 km (12 mi) W of the

southern end of the Sea of Galilee and about 8 km (5 mi) ESE of the city of Nazareth.

Isolated from other mountains, Tabor rises abruptly from the Valley of Jezreel to an altitude of about 562 m (1,844 ft) above sea level. From the WNW it looks like a truncated cone, and from the SW like the segment of a sphere. From its summit, a rather flat elliptic area about 0.4 km (0.25 mi) wide from N to S and twice as long from E to W, it affords a magnificent view in all directions. The impressive prominence of this mountain probably explains why the psalmist mentions Tabor and Mount Hermon together as outstanding examples of the Creator's majestic craftsmanship. (Ps 89:12) Jehovah also used the striking massiveness of Tabor—standing alone in the Valley of Jezreel—to illustrate the impressiveness of Nebuchadnezzar upon his entering Egypt with a mighty military force.—Jer 46:13, 18.

Tabor was made particularly famous when Barak, at God's direction, assembled 10,000 men from the tribes of Naphtali and Zebulun against Sisera and his army, which included 900 chariots with "iron scythes." At the given signal Barak and his forces hurried down the slopes of Tabor, and after Jehovah had thrown the Canaanites into confusion, the Israelites won a decisive victory over the fleeing forces of Sisera.—Jg 4:4-16.

Some years later Tabor witnessed the killing of Gideon's brothers by Zebah and Zalmunna, the kings of Midian. (Jg 8:18, 19) By the middle of the eighth century B.C.E., the unfaithful priestly and regal houses of Israel were "as a net spread over Tabor," possibly using that mountain W of the Jordan as a center for idolatry to snare the Israelites; Mizpah may have been so used E of the Jordan.—Ho 5:1.

The summit of Tabor provided a commanding position and a most suitable location for a fortified city. The ruins show that such a city flourished there before and after the first century C.E. This fact gives reason to question the tradition that Tabor was the location of Jesus' transfiguration, for the accounts say that Jesus and his three companions were in the mountain "by themselves," "to themselves alone." Mount Hermon is more likely that "lofty mountain," and it is near Caesarea Philippi at the headwaters of the Jordan, where Jesus had been shortly before the transfiguration.—Mt 17:1, 2; Mr 8:27; 9:2.

2. One of the cities in the territory of Zebulun given to the Levitical sons of Merari. Today its location is unknown.—1Ch 6:1, 77.

3. "The big tree of Tabor" was presumably in Benjamin's territory. It was a landmark that Samuel referred to in his instructions to Saul after Saul's anointing, where he was to meet three men en route to Bethel. The site is unknown today.—1Sa 10:1-3.

TABRIMMON (Tab-rim′mon) [Good Is Rimmon [the Assyrian storm-god]]. Father of Syrian King Ben-hadad I; son of Hezion.—1Ki 15:18.

TADMOR (Tad′mor). A wilderness location where Solomon did building work sometime after 1017 B.C.E. (2Ch 8:1, 4) Tadmor is commonly identified with the city known to the Greeks and Romans as Palmyra. Its ruins lie in an oasis on the northern edge of the Syrian Desert about 210 km (130 mi) NE of Damascus. A

Mount Tabor rises abruptly from the Valley of Jezreel

nearby village is still called Tudmur by the Arabs. If correctly identified with Palmyra, Tadmor may have served as a garrison city for defending the distant northern border of Solomon's kingdom and also as an important caravan stop.—See TA-MAR No. 4.

TAHAN (Ta'han), **TAHANITES** (Ta'han·ites) [Of (Belonging to) Tahan]. Tahan was the founder of an Ephraimite tribal family, the Tahanites. (Nu 26:35) It is not certain whether he is the same Tahan mentioned at 1 Chronicles 7:25.

TAHASH (Ta'hash) [Sealskin]. A son of Abraham's brother Nahor by his concubine Reumah. —Ge 22:23, 24.

TAHATH (Ta'hath) [from a root meaning "lower; under"].

1. A descendant of Ephraim through Shuthelah.—1Ch 7:20.

2. Another Ephraimite, related to No. 1.—1Ch 7:20.

3. A Kohathite Levite; forefather of Samuel and Heman.—1Ch 6:22, 24, 33, 37, 38.

4. A wilderness campsite of Israel; its location is unknown.—Nu 33:26, 27.

TAHCHEMONITE (Tah·che'mo·nite). A designation for one of David's mighty men, Joshebbasshebeth. (2Sa 23:8) Spelled Hachmonite at 1 Chronicles 11:11, it indicates a descendant of Hachmoni.

TAHPANES (Tah'pan·es), also **TAHPANHES** (Tah'pan·hes), **TEHAPHNEHES** (Te·haph'ne·hes). A city in Egypt regularly mentioned with other cities of northern (Lower) Egypt, such as Noph (Memphis), On (Heliopolis), and Pibeseth (Bubastis).

During the last years of the Judean kingdom, the prophet Jeremiah consistently warned his people against political alliances with Egypt or reliance on Egypt for help against the rising power of Babylon. Noph (Memphis), the Egyptian capital, and Tahpanhes are spoken of as "feeding on [Judah and Jerusalem] at the crown of the head" as a result of the apostasy of the Jews. Any support from Egypt was doubtless obtained at a high cost to the royal leaders of Judah; but they would become ashamed of Egypt, even as they had become ashamed of Assyria.—Jer 2:1, 2, 14-19, 36.

Remnant Flee There. Following the Babylonian conquest of Judah in 607 B.C.E. and the subsequent assassination of Gedaliah, the remnant of Jews went down to Egypt, taking the prophet Jeremiah with them. The first place mentioned at which they arrived (or settled) in Egypt is Tahpanhes. (Jer 43:5-7) This would evidently locate Tahpanhes in the eastern Delta region, that is, the NE corner of Lower Egypt. Some of the refugees settled in Tahpanhes. (Jer 44:1, 7, 8) On arrival at Tahpanhes, Jeremiah enacted a prophetic scene directed by Jehovah, placing stones in the mortar of "the terrace of bricks that is at the entrance of the house of Pharaoh in Tahpanhes" in the presence of the other Jews. Then he made the proclamation that Nebuchadnezzar would come and place his throne and extend his state tent right over those very stones.—Jer 43:8-13; compare 46:13, 14.

In faraway Babylon (in the 27th year of the first exile, that is, 591 B.C.E.), the prophet Ezekiel also foretold that Nebuchadnezzar would conquer Egypt and "in Tehaphnehes the day will actually grow dark," for Jehovah would there break the yoke bars and the pride of Egypt's strength. This statement and Ezekiel's reference to the "dependent towns" of Tahpanhes indicate that the city was one of importance and size.—Eze 29:19; 30:1, 2, 10-18.

Suggested Origin of Name. Some translators understand the name Tahpanhes to mean (in Egyptian) "the Fortress of Penhase," Penhase being a general from the southern city of Thebes who overcame rebellious elements in the Delta region of Egypt, apparently in the latter part of the second millennium B.C.E.

The Greek *Septuagint* renders Tahpanhes as *Taph'nas*, and it is generally believed that this name coincides with that of an important fortified city on Egypt's eastern border called Daphnae by the Greek writers of the classical period. For this reason some geographers identify Tahpanhes with Tell Defneh, nearly 50 km (30 mi) SSW of Port Said and about 45 km (28 mi) WSW of Pelusium, the suggested site of Sin.

TAHPENES (Tah'pe·nes). Wife of the Egyptian Pharaoh contemporary with David and Solomon. Tahpenes' sister was given in marriage to Hadad, a resister of Solomon. Tahpenes raised Genubath, the child of this marriage, with her own children in the house of Pharaoh.—1Ki 11:19, 20.

TAHREA (Tahr'e·a). A 'son' of Micah and descendant of King Saul. (1Ch 9:39-41) He is called "Tarea" at 1 Chronicles 8:35.

TAHTIM-HODSHI (Tah'tim-hod'shi). This was a "land" on the route of the census takers sent out by David. (2Sa 24:4-6) The exact location of

Tahtim-hodshi is not known. However, it is mentioned between Gilead and Dan-jaan, placing it in the northern part of the Promised Land. The Lagardian edition of the Greek *Septuagint* says "land of the Hittites toward Kadesh," a similar reading being used by some modern translations. —JB, NE, RS.

TALENT. The largest of the Hebrew units of weight and of monetary value. (Ex 38:29; 2Sa 12:30; 1Ki 10:10; 2Ki 23:33; 1Ch 29:7; 2Ch 36:3; Ezr 8:26) Calculated on the basis of its equaling 60 minas or 3,000 shekels (Ex 38:25, 26; see MINA), a talent weighed 34.2 kg (75.5 lb avdp; 91.75 lb t; 1101 oz t). In modern values a talent of silver would be reckoned at $6,606.00 and a talent of gold at $385,350.00.

Since a mina equaled 100 Greek drachmas in the first century C.E., a talent of 60 minas weighed 20.4 kg (44.8 lb avdp; 54.5 lb t; 654 oz t), less than in Hebrew Scripture times. Accordingly, in modern values, a first-century silver talent would be worth $3,924.00, and a gold talent $228,900.00.

Reckoned according to the Greek standard, the symbolic hailstones weighing about one talent (20.4 kg; 44.8 lb), as referred to at Revelation 16:21, would be a devastating plague.

TALITHA CUMI (Tal'i·tha cu'mi). The Semitic expression used by Jesus Christ at the time he resurrected Jairus' daughter. It means, "Maiden, I say to you, Get up!" (Mr 5:41) The transliterations of this expression vary in Greek manuscripts. While it is often referred to as Aramaic, at least the latter part of the phrase (*"cumi"*) could be either Hebrew or Aramaic, according to *Vine's Expository Dictionary of Old and New Testament Words* (1981, Vol. 4, p. 109). Lexicographer Gesenius derives *"talitha"* from the Hebrew word for lamb (ta·leh').—*A Hebrew and English Lexicon of the Old Testament,* by Brown, Driver, and Briggs, 1980, p. 378.

TALMAI (Tal'mai).

1. Brother of Ahiman and Sheshai, sons of Anak. (Nu 13:22; Jos 15:14; Jg 1:10; see AHIMAN No. 1.) Some scholars think that the name *Tanmahu,* found in a hieroglyphic inscription depicting a tall, light-complexioned man, is the Egyptian equivalent for Talmai. This Canaanite name also occurs in the Ras Shamra texts of the period of the Judges.

2. A son of Ammihud; king of Geshur. (2Sa 13:37) Talmai's daughter Maacah bore Absalom to David. (2Sa 3:3; 1Ch 3:2) After having Amnon

killed for violating his sister Tamar, Absalom fled to his grandfather Talmai.—2Sa 13:28, 29, 37, 38.

TALMON (Tal'mon). Head of a postexilic Levitical family of gatekeepers. After having returned from Babylon with Zerubbabel, he 'and his brothers' were chosen to live in Jerusalem.—1Ch 9:3, 17; Ezr 2:42; Ne 7:45; 11:1, 19; 12:25.

TAMAR (Ta'mar) [Palm Tree].

1. Daughter-in-law of Jacob's son Judah. Tamar married Judah's first son Er, but Jehovah put Er to death for his wickedness, leaving Tamar a widow. She was then given Onan, but Jehovah put him to death for failure to perform brother-in-law marriage, and Tamar still remained a childless widow. Judah procrastinated in giving her his third son. Tamar concealed her identity and disguised herself as a prostitute in order to get Judah himself to have relations with her, cleverly taking his seal ring, cord, and rod as security. When Judah learned that Tamar was pregnant, he at first commanded that she be burned after being stoned. (Compare Jos 7:15, 25.) But on learning that through her maneuvering to get an heir he had become the father, Judah exclaimed, "She is more righteous than I am." In the difficult birth that followed, Tamar produced twins, Perez and Zerah. (Ge 38:6-30) The Messianic lineage is traced through her son Perez.—Ru 4:12, 18-22; 1Ch 2:4; Mt 1:3.

2. A beautiful daughter of King David and full sister of Absalom. (1Ch 3:9; 2Sa 13:1) Her oldest half brother Amnon became infatuated with her and through craftiness succeeded in violating her, though she resisted him. Absalom consoled her, kept her in his house, and two years later avenged Tamar by having Amnon murdered. —2Sa 13:1-33.

3. Daughter of Absalom, likely named after her aunt (No. 2). (2Sa 14:27) Like her father, she was very attractive in appearance. She may have married Uriel, which would have made her the mother of Rehoboam's favored wife Maacah. —2Ch 11:20, 21; 13:1, 2.

4. One of several cities built (possibly rebuilt or fortified) by King Solomon. (1Ki 9:17-19) Tamar is mentioned at 1 Kings 9:18 as being "in the land," evidently indicating that it was found in Israelite territory. Yohanan Aharoni identifies Tamar with 'Ain Husb ('En Hazeva), about 30 km (20 mi) SSW of the Dead Sea. The basis for his identification is a comparison of the boundary descriptions of Canaan found in Numbers 34:3-6; Joshua 15:1-4; and Ezekiel 47:19; 48:28.

Although the parallel text at 2 Chronicles 8:4

reads "Tadmor," it evidently refers to a different city, one that is commonly identified with Palmyra.—See TADMOR.

TAMARISK

TAMARISK [Hebrew, *'e'shel*]. The tamarisk grows as a tree or shrub. Though its trunk is gnarled, the branches are often wandlike, giving the tree a feathery appearance. The evergreen leaves are tiny, scalelike, and pressed close to the branches, so they lose very little moisture by transpiration, enabling the trees to live in desert regions and even on sand dunes. In spring the tree blossoms with spikes of tiny pink or white flowers, which give welcome color to otherwise barren regions. Salt-loving tamarisks will often grow very near the ocean and on salt marshes. Abundant tamarisks along the banks of the Jordan form junglelike thickets that are the habitat of wild animals, and in Bible times they may have helped compose "the proud thickets along the Jordan" where lions once found cover.—Jer 49:19; Zec 11:3.

Though the tamarisk is generally of relatively low height, one kind of tamarisk tree (*Tamarix aphylla*) sometimes grows to a height of 18 m (60 ft). Abraham is recorded as having planted a tamarisk at Beer-sheba (Ge 21:33), King Saul sat in the shade of a tamarisk at Gibeah (1Sa 22:6), and his bones and those of his sons were buried under a large tamarisk tree in Jabesh-gilead. —1Sa 31:13; compare 1Ch 10:12, where the Hebrew word for "big tree" (*'e·lah'*) is used.

Dr. Joseph Weitz, a noted authority on reforestation in Israel, said: "The first tree Abraham put in the soil of Beersheba was a tamarisk. Following his lead, four years ago we put out two million in the same area. Abraham was right. The tamarisk is one of the few trees we have found that thrives in the south where yearly rainfall is less than six inches."—*The Reader's Digest,* March 1954, p. 30.

Another type of tamarisk (*Tamarix mannifera*), when pierced by a scale insect, exudes drops of honeylike sap that are gathered and sold to pilgrims in some places as "manna." This has no relation, however, to the manna provided for Israel in the wilderness, since such true manna was miraculously provided and gathered from the ground.—Ex 16:13-15.

TAMBOURINE

TAMBOURINE. A percussion instrument used since patriarchal times. The Hebrew word *toph* has also been translated "timbrel," "tambour," and "tabret." (Ge 31:27, *Kx, Da, AS*) All these renderings essentially are descriptive of the same instrument—a small hand drum of animal skin or parchment stretched on one or both sides of a wooden or metal frame, likely about 25 cm (10 in.) in diameter. In view of its festive use, some models may have had pieces of metal, perhaps jingles, attached to the sides and could have been played like a modern tambourine. Other types probably had more the appearance and use of a tom-tom, being beaten with both hands.

Although the tambourine is not mentioned in connection with temple worship, it was used by both men and women in praising Jehovah and on other joyful occasions such as feasts and weddings. (1Sa 10:5; 2Sa 6:5; Ps 150:4; Isa 5:12) Women especially would accompany themselves with tambourines in singing and dancing. (Ex 15:20; Jg 11:34; 1Sa 18:6) The tambourine is also associated with the prospective gladness of Israel when the time of her restoration would arrive.—Jer 31:4.

TAMMUZ, I

TAMMUZ, I (Tamm'uz). A deity over whom apostate Hebrew women in Jerusalem were seen weeping in the sixth year of the prophet Ezekiel's exile (612 B.C.E.).—Eze 8:1, 3, 14.

In Sumerian texts, Tammuz is called Dumuzi and is identified as the consort or lover of the fertility goddess Inanna (Babylonian Ishtar). It has been suggested that Tammuz was originally a king who was deified after his death. Sumerian texts believed to date from the 18th century B.C.E. show that the kings of Sumer were identified with Dumuzi.

Regarding the identification of Tammuz, D. Wolkstein and S. N. Kramer

Tamarisk trees are able to live in very dry areas

remarked: "There were quite a number of 'dying gods' in ancient Sumer, but the best known is Dumuzi, the biblical Tammuz, whom the women of Jerusalem were still mourning in the days of the prophet Ezekiel. Originally, the god Dumuzi was a mortal Sumerian ruler, whose life and death had made a profound impression on the Sumerian thinkers and mythographers." (*Inanna, Queen of Heaven and Earth,* New York, 1983, p. 124) In addition, O. R. Gurney wrote: "Dumuzi was originally a man, a king of Erech . . . The humanity of Dumuzi is, moreover, confirmed by the mythological passage in which he says to Inanna 'I will lead you to the house of my god'. This is not the way in which a god would speak."—*Journal of Semitic Studies,* Vol. 7, 1962, pp. 150-152.

TAMMUZ, II (Tam′muz).
The postexilic name given to the fourth Jewish lunar month of the sacred calendar, but the tenth of the secular calendar. Thus, in the Targum of Jonathan the expression "the tenth month" at Genesis 8:5 is rendered "the month Tammuz." Tammuz was the name of a Babylonian deity. (Eze 8:14) The Bible record does not apply this name to the fourth month but merely refers to the month by its numerical order. (Eze 1:1) The name does appear, however, in the Jewish Mishnah (*Ta′anit* 4:6) and other postexilic works. The use of the pagan name Tammuz as applying to the fourth month, as well as the use of the other postexilic names, may have been only a matter of convenience among the Jews. It should be remembered that they were then a subjugated people, obliged to deal with and report to the foreign powers dominating them, and in view of this it is no strange thing if they utilized the names of the months employed by these foreign powers. The Gregorian calendar used today has months named after the gods Janus and Mars, and the goddess Juno, as well as for Julius and Augustus Caesar, yet it continues to be used by Christians who are subject to "the superior authorities."—Ro 13:1.

This month, Tammuz, corresponded to part of June and part of July and, therefore, came in the growing heat of summer. By now the grapevines were beginning to yield their first ripe fruit.—Nu 13:20.

It was on the ninth day of this fourth month (Tammuz) that Nebuchadnezzar breached the walls of Jerusalem in 607 B.C.E. after an 18-month siege. (2Ki 25:3, 4; Jer 39:2; 52:6, 7) During the 70 years of exile that followed, the Jews customarily fasted on the ninth day of the fourth month in memory of this blow against Jerusalem. (Zec 8:19) However, following the sec-

ond destruction of Jerusalem, in the year 70 C.E., the fast was observed on the 17th day of the fourth month, the day the walls of the temple were breached by Roman General Titus. There were no festivals appointed by Jehovah for this month.

TANHUMETH (Tan·hu′meth) [from a root meaning "comfort"].
The Netophathite father of Seraiah, a military leader of the Jews left in Jerusalem after the deportation to Babylon.—2Ki 25:23; Jer 40:8.

TANNER.
A person skilled in the tanning profession, the craft of converting animal hides into leather that can then be used to make articles of various kinds. (2Ki 1:8; Mt 3:4) Doubtless the tanning operation was performed in the past as it has been recently in the Middle East—in a one- or two-room tannery, housing tools and vats for preparing the hides. The basic process of preparing leather involved (1) loosening the hair, usually with a lime solution; (2) removing the hair, bits of flesh, and fat adhering to the hide; and (3) tanning the hide with a liquor made from such things as the bark of sumac or of oak, or from other kinds of plants.

Peter spent "quite a few days . . . in Joppa with a certain Simon, a tanner," whose house was by the sea.—Ac 9:43; 10:32.

TAPHATH (Ta′phath).
A daughter of King Solomon and wife of one of his 12 deputies.—1Ki 4:7, 11.

TAPPUAH (Tap′pu·ah) [Apple (Tree)].
1. One of Hebron's four sons and a descendant of Caleb. (1Ch 2:42, 43) Some suggest that his name is to be connected with Beth-tappuah, a town near Hebron.—See BETH-TAPPUAH.

2. A town in the Shephelah region assigned to the tribe of Judah. (Jos 15:20, 33, 34) It is thus distinct from Beth-tappuah in the Hebron area. Horvat Bet Natif within the abandoned village of Beit Nattif, about 20 km (12 mi) W of Bethlehem, is tentatively identified as the site.

3. A town on the boundary between Ephraim and Manasseh. (Jos 16:8) The surrounding area, "the land of Tappuah," was allotted to Manasseh, but the city to Ephraim. (Jos 17:8) En-Tappuah (Jos 17:7) evidently refers to a nearby spring (Heb., ′A′yin, or En, meaning "fountain [spring]," when used as a prefix) and may have been a more complete name used for the city of Tappuah.

"The king of Tappuah" is mentioned among the rulers vanquished by Joshua in the conquest of Canaan (Jos 12:17), and "Tappuah" here probably refers to the Ephraimite city. Ephraimite Tappuah is identified with Tell Sheikh Abu Zarad (Tel 'Abu Zarad), about 13 km (8 mi) SSW of Shechem and just below the town of Yasuf.

TAR. See BITUMEN.

TARALAH (Tar′a·lah). A Benjamite city, the location of which is today unknown. It is listed, however, with other cities situated in the mountainous region N of Jerusalem.—Jos 18:25-28.

TAREA (Ta·re′a). A descendant of King Saul through Jonathan; also called Tahrea.—1Ch 8: 33-35; 9:39-41.

TARSHISH (Tar′shish) [from a root meaning "shatter"].

1. One of Javan's four sons born after the Flood. (Ge 10:4; 1Ch 1:7) He is included among the 70 family heads from whom the nations were "spread about in the earth." (Ge 10:32) As in the case of Javan's other sons, the name Tarshish came to apply to a people and a region.

2. A descendant of Benjamin and son of Bilhan. —1Ch 7:6, 10.

3. One of seven princely counselors of King Ahasuerus who considered the case of rebellious Queen Vashti.—Es 1:12-15.

4. A region initially populated by offspring of Tarshish, a son of Javan and grandson of Japheth. There are some indications of the direction in which the descendants of Tarshish migrated during the centuries following the Flood.

The prophet Jonah (c. 844 B.C.E.), commissioned by Jehovah to go to Nineveh in Assyria, tried to escape his assignment by going to the Mediterranean seaport of Joppa (Tel Aviv-Yafo) and buying passage on "a ship going to Tarshish." (Jon 1:1-3; 4:2) Thus, Tarshish must obviously have been in or on the Mediterranean in the opposite direction from Nineveh, and evidently it was better reached by sea than by land. "The heart of the open sea" is mentioned in connection with "the ships of Tarshish," at Ezekiel 27:25, 26. —Compare Ps 48:7; Jon 2:3.

An inscription of Assyrian Emperor Esarhaddon (of the seventh century B.C.E.) boasts of his victories over Tyre and Egypt, and it claims that all the kings of the islands from Cyprus "as far as Tarsisi" paid him tribute. (*Ancient Near Eastern Texts*, edited by J. Pritchard, 1974, p. 290) Since Cyprus is in the eastern Mediterranean, this reference would also indicate a location in the western Mediterranean. Some scholars identify Tarshish with Sardinia, an island in the western Mediterranean.

Possibly Identified With Spain. Most scholars associate Tarshish with Spain, based on ancient references to a place or region in Spain called Tartessus by Greek and Roman writers. While Greek geographer Strabo (of the first century B.C.E.) placed a city called Tartessus in the region around the Guadalquivir River in Andalusia (*Geography*, 3, II, 11), the name Tartessis appears to have applied generally to the southern part of the Iberian Peninsula.

Many reference works give great emphasis to Phoenician colonization of the Spanish coastlands and refer to Tartessus as a Phoenician colony, but there appears to be no solid basis for such theory. Thus, the *Encyclopædia Britannica* (1959, Vol. 21, p. 114) states: "Neither the Phoenicians nor the Carthaginians left any very permanent mark upon the land, while the Greeks influenced it profoundly. Ships from Tyre and Sidon may have traded beyond the straits and in Cádiz at least as early as the 9th century B.C.; yet modern archaeology, which has located and excavated Greek, Iberian and Roman towns, has not laid bare a single Phoenician settlement or found more important Phoenician remains than the odds and ends of trinkets and jewels and similar articles of barter. The inference is clear that, except perhaps at Cádiz, the Phoenicians built no towns, but had mere trading posts and points of call." History also shows that when the Phoenicians and Greeks began trading with Spain the land was already populated and the native inhabitants brought forth the silver, iron, tin, and lead that the traders sought.

There appears to be good reason for believing, then, that descendants of Javan (Ionians) through his son Tarshish eventually spread into and became prominent in the Iberian Peninsula. Such suggested location of Tarshish at least harmonizes satisfactorily with the other Biblical references.

Trade Relations With Solomon. Phoenician trading with Tarshish is clearly borne out by the record of King Solomon's time (some 13 centuries after the Flood), when maritime commerce also began to be engaged in by the nation of Israel. Solomon had a fleet of ships in the Red Sea area manned in part by experienced seamen provided by Phoenician King Hiram of Tyre, and trafficking especially with the gold-rich land of Ophir. (1Ki 9:26-28) Reference is thereafter made to "a fleet of ships of Tarshish" that Solomon had on the sea "along with Hiram's fleet of ships," and these ships are stated to have made voyages once every three years for the importation of gold, silver, ivory, apes, and peacocks. (1Ki 10:22) It is generally believed that the term "ships of Tarshish" in course of time came to stand for a *type* of ship, as one lexicon puts it: "large, sea-going vessels, *fit to ply to Tarshish.*" (*A Hebrew and English Lexicon of the Old Testament,* by Brown, Driver, and Briggs, 1980, p. 1077) In a similar way, the name Indiamen originally was derived from the name applied to large British ships engaged in trade with India and in time came to apply to ships of that type no matter what their origin or destination. Thus 1 Kings 22:48 shows that King Jehoshaphat (936-911 B.C.E.) "made Tarshish ships to go *to Ophir* for gold."

The Chronicles account, however, states that Solomon's ships used for the triannual voyages "were going to Tarshish" (2Ch 9:21); also that Jehoshaphat's ships were designed "to go to Tarshish" and, when wrecked, "did not retain strength to go to Tarshish." (2Ch 20:36, 37) This would indicate that Ophir was not the only port of call of the Israelite "ships of Tarshish," but that they also navigated Mediterranean waters. This, of course, poses a problem, since the launching site of at least some of these vessels is shown to have been Ezion-geber on the Gulf of ʽAqaba. (1Ki 9:26) For the ships to reach the Mediterranean Sea, they would either have to traverse a canal from the Red Sea to the Nile River and then into the Mediterranean or else circumnavigate the continent of Africa. While it is by no means possible to determine now the details of navigational routes (including canals) available or employed in Solomon's and in Jehoshaphat's time, there is likewise no need to view the record of their maritime projects as unfeasible.

In Prophecy. Tarshish appears to have been a major market for the merchant city of Tyre, perhaps her source of greatest riches during part of her history. From ancient times Spain has had mines working the rich deposits of silver, iron, tin, and other metals found there. (Compare Jer 10:9; Eze 27:3, 12.) Thus Isaiah's prophetic pronouncement of Tyre's overthrow depicts the ships of Tarshish as 'howling' upon reaching Kittim (Cyprus, perhaps their last port of call on the eastern run) and receiving the news that the wealthy port of Tyre has been despoiled.—Isa 23: 1, 10, 14.

Other prophecies foretell God's sending some of his people to Tarshish, there to proclaim his glory (Isa 66:19), and of "ships of Tarshish" bringing Zion's sons from far away. (Isa 60:9) "The kings of Tarshish and of the islands" are to pay tribute to the one Jehovah designates as king. (Ps 72:10) On the other hand, at Ezekiel 38:13 "the merchants of Tarshish" are represented along with other trading peoples as expressing selfish interest in Gog of Magog's proposed plunder of Jehovah's regathered ones. As included among other things symbolizing self-exaltation, haughtiness, and loftiness, the ships of Tarshish are to be brought low, and only Jehovah is to be exalted in "the day belonging to Jehovah of armies."—Isa 2:11-16.

TARSUS (Tarʹsus). The principal city and capital of the Roman province of Cilicia; birthplace of the apostle Paul. (Ac 9:11; 22:3) Ruins of the ancient town remain in the modern settlement of the same name, situated about 16 km (10 mi) from the mouth of the Cydnus River, which empties into the eastern Mediterranean about 130 km (80 mi) N of the eastern tip of Cyprus.

No one knows when Tarsus was first settled or by whom, for it is a city of great antiquity. First mentioned in secular history as being captured by the Assyrians (it was never a strongly fortified city), Tarsus was thereafter in servitude and paid tribute much of the time to the successive powers of Assyria, Persia, Greece, then to the Seleucid kings, and finally to Rome.

Tarsus was situated in a fertile coastal area where flax was raised, and this, in turn, supported flourishing industries such as the weaving of linens and the making of tents. Fabrics woven of goat's hair and called *cilicium* also found special use in the making of tents. A more important factor, however, contributing to Tarsus' fame and wealth was its excellent harbor strategically located along a prime E-W overland trade route. Running eastward, it led to Syria and Babylon; leading to the northern and western sections of Asia Minor, this route threaded itself through the Cilician Gates, a narrow gorge in the Taurus Mountains about 50 km (30 mi) to the N of the city.

During its history a number of noted personalities visited Tarsus, including Julius Caesar, Mark Antony, and Cleopatra, as well as several emperors. Cicero was the city's governor from 51 to 50 B.C.E. Tarsus was also famous as a seat of learning in the first century C.E., and according to the Greek geographer Strabo, as such it outranked even Athens and Alexandria.—*Geography,* 14, v, 13.

So, for these several reasons, Paul could well describe Tarsus as "no obscure city." He said this when informing a military commander that he was a citizen of Tarsus, not an Egyptian.—Ac 21:37-39.

From time to time in the course of his ministry, Paul returned to his hometown of Tarsus (Ac

9:29, 30; 11:25, 26), and no doubt he passed through there on some of his missionary journeys.—Ac 15:23, 41; 18:22, 23.

TARTAK (Tar′tak). A deity worshiped by the Avvites, whom the king of Assyria settled in the territory of Samaria after he took the Israelites of the ten-tribe kingdom into exile. (2Ki 17:31) According to the Babylonian Talmud, Tartak had the form of an ass. (*Sanhedrin* 63*b*) Based on the conclusion that the name Tartak may be comparable to the Pahlavi (Persian) word *tar-thakh* (intense darkness, hero of darkness), it has been suggested that Tartak may have been a demon of the lower regions. Aside from the brief reference to Tartak in the Scriptures, however, nothing can be stated with any certainty concerning the nature of this deity.

TARTAN (Tar′tan). Assyrian writings indicate that the title Tartan applied to an officer of high rank, probably second only to the king. Concerning the order of the titles in Assyrian eponym lists, James B. Pritchard, editor of *Ancient Near Eastern Texts* (1974, p. 274), comments: "Later on, the position of the official within the hierarchy was decisive for the sequence, the highest official (*tartanu*) following the king immediately, while important palace officers . . . and the governors of the foremost provinces took their turn in well-established order." (See CHRONOLOGY [Eponym (limmu) lists].) An inscription by Assyrian King Ashurbanipal, now in the British Museum, reads, in part: "I became very angry on account of these happenings, my soul was aflame. I called the *turtan* -official, the governors, and also their assistants and gave immediately the order."—*Ancient Near Eastern Texts*, p. 296.

King Sennacherib sent the Tartan along with other officials, including the Rabshakeh, the king's chief cupbearer who acted as spokesman, to deliver an ultimatum of capitulation to Jerusalem. The Tartan is listed first, possibly because his was the superior position. (2Ki 18:17, 28-35) A Tartan was sent by King Sargon II of Assyria to besiege the city of Ashdod, in the days of Isaiah the prophet.—Isa 20:1.

TARTARUS (Tar′ta·rus). A prisonlike, abased condition into which God cast disobedient angels in Noah's day.

This word is found but once in the inspired Scriptures, at 2 Peter 2:4. The apostle writes: "God did not hold back from punishing the angels that sinned, but, by throwing them into Tartarus, delivered them to pits of dense darkness to be reserved for judgment." The expression "throwing them into Tartarus" is from the Greek verb *tar·ta·ro′o* and so includes within itself the word "Tartarus."

A parallel text is found at Jude 6: "And the angels that did not keep their original position but forsook their own proper dwelling place he has reserved with eternal bonds under dense darkness for the judgment of the great day." Showing when it was that these angels "forsook their own proper dwelling place," Peter speaks of "the spirits in prison, who had once been disobedient when the patience of God was waiting in Noah's days, while the ark was being constructed." (1Pe 3:19, 20) This directly links the matter to the account at Genesis 6:1-4 concerning "the sons of the true God" who abandoned their heavenly abode to cohabit with women in pre-Flood times and produced children by them, such offspring being designated as Nephilim.—See NEPHILIM; SON(S) OF GOD.

From these texts it is evident that Tartarus is a *condition* rather than a particular location, inasmuch as Peter, on the one hand, speaks of these disobedient spirits as being in "pits of dense darkness," while Paul speaks of them as being in "heavenly places" from which they exercise a rule of darkness as wicked spirit forces. (2Pe 2:4; Eph 6:10-12) The dense darkness similarly is not literally a lack of light but results from their being cut off from illumination by God as renegades and outcasts from his family, with only a dark outlook as to their eternal destiny.

Tartarus is, therefore, not the same as the Hebrew Sheol or the Greek Hades, both of which refer to the common earthly grave of mankind. This is evident from the fact that, while the apostle Peter shows that Jesus Christ preached to these "spirits in prison," he also shows that Jesus did so, not during the three days while buried in Hades (Sheol), but *after* his resurrection out of Hades.—1Pe 3:18-20.

Likewise the abased condition represented by Tartarus should not be confused with "the abyss" into which Satan and his demons are eventually to be cast for the thousand years of Christ's rule. (Re 20:1-3) Apparently the disobedient angels were cast into Tartarus in "Noah's days" (1Pe 3:20), but some 2,000 years later we find them entreating Jesus "not to order them to go away into the abyss."—Lu 8:26-31; see ABYSS.

The word "Tartarus" is also used in pre-Christian heathen mythologies. In Homer's *Iliad* this mythological Tartarus is represented as an underground prison 'as far below Hades as earth is below heaven.' In it were imprisoned the lesser gods, Cronus and the other Titan spirits. As we have seen, the Tartarus of the Bible is not a place but a condition and, therefore, is not the same as this Tartarus of Greek mythology. However, it is worth noting that the mythological Tartarus was presented not as a place for humans but as a place for superhuman creatures. So, in that regard there is a similarity, since the Scriptural Tartarus is clearly not for the detention of human souls (compare Mt 11:23) but is only for wicked superhuman spirits who are rebels against God.

The condition of utter debasement represented by Tartarus is a precursor of the abyssing that Satan and his demons are to experience prior to the start of the Thousand Year Reign of Christ. This, in turn, is to be followed after the end of the thousand years by their utter destruction in "the second death."—Mt 25:41; Re 20:1-3, 7-10, 14.

TATTENAI (Tat'te·nai). The governor of the Persian province "beyond the River" during the reign of Darius I (Hystaspis). When the Jews again started to rebuild the temple in Darius' second year (520 B.C.E.), Tattenai and his colleagues came to Jerusalem to conduct an inquiry. The Jews appealed to Cyrus' original decree; so Tattenai wrote to Darius asking if such a decree had been issued, as the Jews contended. The answer received confirmed Cyrus' decree and the validity of the temple work, and it warned Tattenai not to interfere but to render material assistance to the Jews. This, Tattenai proceeded to do. —Ezr 4:24–6:13.

TATTOO. A permanent mark or design on the skin made by cutting the skin to produce scars or by inserting coloring matter under the skin. The Israelites were forbidden to engage in this practice, one that was common among some other ancient peoples. (Le 19:28) For example, there were times when the Egyptians tattooed the names or symbols of their deities on their breast or arms. By complying with Jehovah's law not to disfigure their bodies, the Israelites would have stood out as different from other nations. (De 14:1, 2) The prohibition would also have impressed upon them a proper respect for the human body as God's creation, to be used in honoring him.—Ps 100:3; 139:13-16; Ro 12:1.

TAW [ת]. The 22nd and last letter of the Hebrew alphabet. The name of the letter literally means "mark." (Compare Eze 9:4, ftn.) In the Hebrew, it is the initial letter in each of the eight verses of Psalm 119:169-176.

TAXATION. An assessment (of money, of goods, or of labor) imposed by an authority on persons or property. Forms of taxation have long been employed to support the services of government, public officials, and also priests. The taxes that were imposed anciently included the tithe, tribute, toll, head or poll tax, and tax on consumer items, exports, imports, and goods taken through a country by merchants.

Taxes for Maintaining Jehovah's Sanctuary. The service of the sanctuary was maintained through taxation. Obligatory tithing provided the major source of maintenance for the Aaronic priests and Levites, and on at least one occasion, they received a share of the war booty in accordance with a tax stipulated by Jehovah. (Nu 18:26-29; 31:26-47; see TITHE.) Jehovah also instructed Moses that after he took a census, each person registered was to give a half shekel ($1.10) as "Jehovah's contribution," it serving in behalf of the tent of meeting. (Ex 30:12-16) It appears that it became customary for the Jews to give a fixed amount every year, even though a census was not taken annually. Jehoash, for example, called for "the sacred tax ordered by Moses." (2Ch 24: 6, 9) The Jews of Nehemiah's time obligated themselves to pay a third of a shekel (c. 75 cents) yearly for the service of the temple.—Ne 10:32.

In the time of Jesus' earthly ministry, the Jews paid two drachmas to the temple. When asked whether Jesus complied with this taxation, Peter replied in the affirmative. Later, in discussing the matter, Jesus pointed out that kings do not tax their sons, the sons being part of the royal household for whom tax is collected. However, though being the only-begotten Son of the One worshiped at the temple, Jesus, to avoid giving occasion for stumbling others, saw to it that the tax was paid.—Mt 17:24-27.

Taxes Imposed by Rulers. With the establishment of kingship in Israel, taxes, including a tenth of the flock and of the produce, were imposed to support the king, his household, and the various governmental officials and servants. (1Sa 8:11-17; 1Ki 4:6-19) By the end of the reign of Solomon, conscription for forced labor and the support of the government had become so burdensome to the people that they requested Solomon's son and successor, Rehoboam, to lighten 'the hard service and the heavy yoke.' Rehoboam's refusal to do so prompted ten tribes to revolt.—1Ki 12:3-19; see COMPULSORY SERVICE; FORCED LABOR.

Upon coming under foreign domination, the Israelites had to submit to still other forms of taxation. For instance, when Pharaoh Nechoh made Jehoiakim his vassal and imposed a heavy fine or tribute on Judah, Jehoiakim raised the necessary funds by having his subjects pay a certain sum "according to each one's individual tax rate."—2Ki 23:31-35.

During the Persian period, the Jews (with the exception of the priests and others serving at the sanctuary, who were exempted by Artaxerxes Longimanus) had to pay tax (Aramaic, *mid·dah'* or *min·dah'*), tribute (*beloh'*), and toll (*halakh'*). (Ezr 4:13, 20; 7:24) *Mid·dah'* is thought to designate personal tax on individuals; *beloh'*, a tax on consumer items, excise; and *halakh'*, toll paid by travelers at road stations or river fords. The *mid·dah'* (translated "tribute" in *AS, KJ, NW* at Ne 5:4) must have been quite high, for many of the Jews had to borrow money to pay it. Besides having to care for the taxes levied by the Persians, the Jews normally also had to pay for the support of the governor.—Ne 5:14, 15.

In the first century C.E., the Jews very much resented the payment of taxes, not only on account of the corruption prevalent among tax collectors but also because this forced them to acknowledge their subjection to Rome. (See TAX COLLECTOR.) However, both Jesus Christ and the apostle Paul showed that it was proper to pay taxes to "Caesar," or "the superior authorities." (Mt 22:17-21; Ro 13:1, 7; see CAESAR [God and Caesar].) Among the various kinds of taxes mentioned in the Christian Greek Scriptures is *te'los* (an indirect tax, duty, or tribute; Mt 17:25; Ro 13:7). Also referred to are *ken'sos* (a head or poll tax; Mt 17:25; 22:17, 19; Mr 12:14) and *pho'ros* (a broader term thought to designate a tax levied upon houses, lands, and persons; Lu 20:22; 23:2).

TAX COLLECTOR. In the Roman Empire, poll and land taxes were collected by imperial officers as part of their official function. But the authority to collect taxes on exports, imports, and goods taken through a country by merchants was purchased at public auction. Thus the right to collect such taxes went to the highest bidders. When they collected taxes, they made a profit from tax receipts that exceeded the amount of their bid. These men, known as publicans, farmed out to subcontractors the right to collect taxes in certain portions of their territory. The subcontractors, in turn, were in charge of other men who personally collected the taxes. Zacchaeus, for example, appears to have been the chief over the tax collectors in and around Jericho. (Lu 19:1, 2) And Matthew, whom Jesus called to be an apos-

tle, was one who did the actual work of collecting taxes, apparently having his tax office in or near Capernaum.—Mt 10:3; Mr 2:1, 14.

Thus, in Palestine many Jewish tax collectors were active. They were held in low esteem by their fellow countrymen, since they often exacted more than the tax rate. (Mt 5:46; Lu 3:12, 13; 19:7, 8) The other Jews generally avoided voluntary association with tax collectors and classified them with persons known to be sinners, including harlots. (Mt 9:11; 11:19; 21:32; Mr 2:15; Lu 5:30; 7:34) They also resented tax collectors because of their being in the service of a foreign power, Rome, and in close contact with "unclean" Gentiles. Hence, to treat a "brother" who proved to be an unrepentant wrongdoer like "a tax collector" meant having no voluntary association with him. —Mt 18:15-17.

Christ Jesus did not condone the corruption prevalent among tax collectors. Though criticized for doing so, he was willing to help spiritually those who manifested a desire to hear him. (Mt 9:9-13; Lu 15:1-7) In one of his illustrations, Jesus showed that the tax collector who humbly recognized himself as a sinner and repented was more righteous than the Pharisee who proudly viewed himself as righteous. (Lu 18:9-14) And humble, repentant tax collectors (like Matthew and Zacchaeus) came in line for membership in the Kingdom of the heavens.—Mt 21:31, 32.

TEACHER, TEACHING. A teacher is one who imparts information or skill to others by word or by example. An effective teacher usually provides explanation or supporting evidence or he employs some other method intended to help hearers to accept and remember what they hear.

Jehovah God, the Creator, is the Grand Instructor, or Teacher, of his servants. (1Ki 8:36; Ps 27:11; 86:11; 119:102; Isa 30:20; 54:13) The creative works themselves teach that an all-wise God exists, and they provide a field for investigation and observation that to the present day has only been partially tapped. (Job 12:7-9) Additionally, by means of special revelations, Jehovah God has taught humans his name, purposes, and laws. (Compare Ex 4:12, 15; 24:12; 34:5-7.) Such revelations are found in God's Word, the Bible, and serve as a basis for correct teaching regarding his will. (Ro 15:4; 2Ti 3:14-17) God's spirit also functions as a teacher.—Joh 14:26.

Teaching Among the Israelites. In Israel, parents had the God-given responsibility of teaching their children. (De 4:9; 6:7, 20, 21; 11:19-21; Ps 78:1-4) For the nation as a whole, prophets, Levites, especially the priests, and other wise men served as teachers.—Compare 2Ch 35:3; Jer 18:18; see EDUCATION.

Prophets. The prophets taught the people about Jehovah's attributes and purposes, exposed the wrongdoing of the Israelites, and outlined the right course for them to take. Often prophets imparted their teaching orally, later committing it to writing. (Compare 1Sa 12:23-25; Isa 7:3, 4; 22:15, 16; Jer 2:2.) Their teaching methods included the use of questions (Jer 18:13, 14; Am 3:3-8; Hag 2:11-14), illustrations (2Sa 12:1-7; Isa 10:15; Jer 18:3-10), riddles (Eze 17:2), and symbolic acts (1Ki 11:30-32; Jer 13:4-11; 19:1-12; 27:2; 28:10-14; Eze 4:1–5:4).

Priests and Levites. It was the responsibility of the priests and Levites to teach God's law to the nation of Israel. (Le 10:11; 14:57; 2Ch 15:3; 35:3) This was accomplished in various ways. Every Sabbath year, during the Festival of Booths, the entire Law was read to all the people—men, women, children, and alien residents. (De 31:9-13) At times, by getting responses from the people, the Levites would impress the divine laws upon the listeners. (Compare De 27:14-26.) Besides reading the Law, the priests and Levites doubtless explained its significance. (Compare Ne 8:8.) And the judicial decisions rendered by them taught principles of divine justice.—De 17:8-13; 1Ch 26:29; 2Ch 19:8-11.

Scribes. In the time of Jesus' earthly ministry, the scribes were prominent as teachers of the Law. But they did not come to grips with the real problems and needs of the people. Like the Pharisees, the scribes placed greater emphasis on technical regulations and traditions than on mercy, justice, and faithfulness. They made the Law burdensome to the people. (Mt 23:2-4, 23, 24; Lu 11:45, 46) Their teaching was not as effective as it could have been, for they assumed a superior attitude toward the common people and did not prove themselves to be examples worthy of imitation.—Compare Mt 23:3, 6, 7; Joh 7:48, 49; see SCRIBE.

What made the teaching done by Jesus outstandingly effective?

Although the religious leaders of Judaism evidently were not sincere in addressing him as "Teacher [Gr., Di·da'ska·los]," Jesus Christ was recognized as such by both believers and unbelievers. (Mt 8:19; 9:11; 12:38; 19:16; 22:16, 24, 36; Joh 3:2) Officers sent to arrest him were so impressed with his teaching that they returned empty-handed, saying: "Never has another man spoken like this." (Joh 7:46) Jesus taught "as a person having authority, and not as [the] scribes." (Mt 7:29) The Source of his teaching was God (Joh 7:16; 8:28), and Jesus conveyed information with simplicity, irrefutable logic, thought-provoking questions, striking figures of speech, and meaningful illustrations drawn from things familiar to his listeners. (Mt 6:25-30; 7:3-5, 24-27; see ILLUSTRATIONS.) Jesus also used object lessons, on one occasion washing the feet of his disciples in order to teach them that they should serve one another. —Joh 13:2-16.

Jesus' knowledge was enhanced by his having had an intimate relationship with his Father and God before coming to the earth. Therefore he knew God as no other man did, and this enabled him to provide authoritative teaching concerning his Father. As Jesus himself said: "No one fully knows the Son but the Father, neither does anyone fully know the Father but the Son and anyone to whom the Son is willing to reveal him."—Mt 11:27; Joh 1:18.

Jesus was also thoroughly acquainted with God's written Word. When asked which commandment was the greatest in the Law, without hesitation he summed up the entire Law in two commandments, quoting from Deuteronomy (6:5) and Leviticus (19:18). (Mt 22:36-40) During the course of his ministry, he is known to have referred to or expressed thoughts that parallel passages from about half of the books of the Hebrew Scriptures—Genesis (2:24; Mt 19:5; Mr 10:7, 8), Exodus (3:6; Mt 22:32; Lu 20:37), Leviticus (14:2-32; Mt 8:4), Numbers (30:2; Mt 5:33), Deuteronomy (5:16; Mt 15:4; Mr 7:10), First Samuel (21:4-6; Mt 12:3, 4), First Kings (17:9; Lu 4:26), Job (42:2; Mt 19:26), Psalms (8:2; 110:1; Mt 21:16; 22:44), Proverbs (24:12; Mt 16:27), Isaiah (6:9, 10; Mt 13:14, 15; Joh 12:40), Jeremiah (7:11; Mt 21:13; Mr 11:17; Lu 19:45, 46), Lamentations (2:1; Mt 5:35), Daniel (9:27; Mt 24:15), Hosea (6:6; Mt 9:13), Jonah (1:17; Mt 12:40), Micah (7:6; Mt 10:21, 35, 36), Zechariah (13:7; Mt 26:31), and Malachi (3:1; Mt 11:10).

Additionally, Jesus' perfect example lent real force to what he taught. (Joh 13:15) He was not like the scribes and Pharisees, concerning whom Jesus said: "All the things they tell you, do and observe, but do not do according to their deeds, for they say but do not perform."—Mt 23:3.

Other aspects that made Jesus' teaching authoritative and effective were his understanding of man and his loving concern for others. His keen discernment was enhanced by miraculous knowledge of the background and reasoning of others. (Mt 12:25; Lu 6:8; Joh 1:48; 4:18; 6:61, 64; 13:11) "He himself knew what was in man." (Joh 2:25) His heart went out to the people to such an extent that he sacrificed needed rest to teach them. On one occasion Jesus and his disciples took a boat and headed for an isolated spot to rest up a bit. "But people saw them going and many got to know it, and from all the cities they ran there together on foot and got ahead of them. Well, on getting out, he saw a great crowd, but he was moved with pity for them, because they were as sheep without a shepherd. And he started to teach them many things."—Mr 6:31-34.

Jesus treated his listeners with understanding. When his disciples did not get the point of an illustration, he patiently explained it to them. (Mt 13:10-23) Aware of their limitations, he did not give them too much information. (Joh 16:4, 12) When needed, Jesus repeated practically identical information. (Mr 9:35; 10:43, 44) In answering questions, Jesus often fortified his reply by means of illustrations or object lessons, thereby leaving a deep impression on the minds of the listeners and stirring up their thinking faculties.—Mt 18:1-5, 21-35; Lu 10:29-37.

God's Spirit Teaches. During the three and a half years of his earthly ministry, Jesus trained his apostles to continue the work he had started. As imperfect humans, they could not possibly remember every detail of his teaching. But Jesus promised them: "The helper, the holy spirit, which the Father will send in my name, that one will teach you all things and bring back to your minds all the things I told you." (Joh 14:26) This meant that God's spirit would teach them whatever they needed to know to accomplish their ministry. Particularly would it open up to their understanding what they had previously heard but not understood. As a remembrancer, the holy spirit would bring back to their minds things that Jesus had said while with them. And, as a teacher, it would show them the correct application of his words.—Compare Joh 2:19-22; see TRUTH ("The Spirit of the Truth").

When brought before public assemblies, kings, and other men in high governmental station, Jesus' disciples could confidently rely on God's spirit as a remembrancer and teacher. Like a friend, it would bring back to their minds things to say and it would help them to make appropriate applications. This would result in giving a good witness and would also silence opposers. (Mt 10:18-20; Mr 13:11; Lu 12:11, 12; 21:13-15) That is why Peter and John were able to speak boldly when questioned by the highest Jewish court, the Sanhedrin, about their having healed a man lame from birth. Their outspokenness was something completely unexpected from 'unlettered and ordinary men.' It caused the members of the Sanhedrin to wonder. And Peter's words, coupled with the presence of the cured man, left these learned men with "nothing to say in rebuttal."—Ac 4:5-14.

Since all of God's Word was written under inspiration (2Ti 3:16), it alone contains the spirit's teaching. Therefore, teaching that conflicts with God's Word is not to be given any attention by Christians. As the apostle John wrote: "You do not need anyone to be teaching you; but, as the anointing from him is teaching you about all things, and is true and is no lie, and just as it has taught you, remain in union with him." (1Jo 2:27) Those to whom John directed these words were spirit-begotten Christians. They had come to know both Jehovah God and his Son, Christ Jesus. They were fully acquainted with God's truth. So they did not need persons as teachers who denied the Father and the Son. Such teachers would only mislead them from what they knew to be the truth as taught by God's spirit and plainly set forth in the Sacred Writings. (1Jo 2:18-26) For this reason Christians were not to receive apostate teachers into their homes or even to say a greeting to them.—2Jo 9-11.

Making and Teaching Disciples. After his resurrection Jesus Christ commissioned his followers to make disciples, baptizing them and teaching them all the things he had commanded. (Mt 28:19, 20) This extensive teaching work had its beginning on the day of Pentecost in 33 C.E., when about 3,000 Jews and proselytes accepted Jesus as the promised Messiah and were baptized. The teaching of these new disciples did not end with the apostle Peter's discourse that led to their becoming followers of Christ Jesus. There was much more for them to learn. For this reason those who had come to Jerusalem from distant places to be present for the Festival of Pentecost extended their stay in order to be able to devote themselves to the apostles' teaching. Day after day they would assemble in the temple area, evidently to listen to the apostles. Other Jews and proselytes also got to hear the good news there, and the number of believing men eventually increased to about 5,000. (Ac 2:14–4:4) Besides teaching publicly at the temple, the apostles also declared the good news about Jesus Christ from house to house.—Ac 5:42; see PREACHER, PREACH-ING ("From House to House").

Later, the scattering of the believers through persecution and the beginning of the preaching among the non-Jews extended the disciple-making work to distant places. (Ac 8:4-12; 11:1-26) As in Jerusalem, however, often public preaching and teaching was employed to locate interested ones, after which those who became disciples continued to be taught. In Ephesus, for example, the apostle Paul taught publicly in the synagogue. After opposition arose, he separated the disciples from the unbelieving Jews, delivering discourses to them in the school auditorium of Tyrannus. (Ac 19:8-10) Paul also taught disciples in their homes and he searched out other interested persons by teaching from house to house. As he reminded the older men of the Ephesus congregation: "I did not hold back from telling you any of the things that were profitable nor from teaching you publicly and from house to house."—Ac 20:20, 21; compare Ac 18:6, 7 regarding Paul's activity in Corinth; see DISCIPLE.

Teachers in the Christian Congregation. Through the activity of the apostle Paul and others, Christian congregations were established in many places, and these continued to enjoy increases. Qualified teachers were needed to assist all associated with these congregations to "attain to the oneness in the faith and in the accurate knowledge of the Son of God, to a full-grown man, to the measure of stature that belongs to the fullness of the Christ." (Eph 4:11-13) This placed a weighty responsibility on those serving as teachers, one that had a direct bearing upon the lives of fellow Christians. The position of teachers was of such importance that it is listed third, right after apostles and prophets, in the placement of members in the congregation. (1Co 12:28) It was not a position filled by Christians generally (1Co 12:29), and it was never filled by women. Wrote the apostle Paul: "I do not permit a woman to teach, or to exercise authority over a man." (1Ti 2:12) Overseers, or older men, appointed to their positions by holy spirit served in this capacity. —Ac 20:17, 25-30; 1Ti 3:1, 2; 5:17.

These older men had to be examples worthy of imitation and accurate in their teaching, always adhering to the inspired Word of God. As qualified teachers, they served as a bulwark against the falling away from true belief, being ever alert to correct those who had fallen victim to wrong teaching and taking action against those promoting sects.—1Ti 4:6, 7, 16; 6:2b-6; 2Ti 2:2, 14-26; 3:14-17; Tit 1:10, 11; 2:1, 6, 7; 3:9-11; compare Re 2:14, 15, 20-24.

The older men (Gr., pre·sby′te·roi) who worked hard in teaching fellow Christians were deserving of respect, consideration (compare Heb 13:17), and even voluntary material assistance. This is what the apostle Paul meant when he wrote: "Moreover, let anyone who is being orally taught [literally, being sounded down to] the word share in all good things with the one who gives such oral teaching." (Ga 6:6, ftn) "Let the older men who preside in a fine way be reckoned worthy of double honor, especially those who work hard in speaking and teaching. For the scripture says: 'You must not muzzle a bull when it threshes out the grain'; also: 'The workman is worthy of his wages.'"—1Ti 5:17, 18.

Men who unselfishly sought to be overseers, qualified to teach others in the congregation, were "desirous of a fine work." (1Ti 3:1) Obviously, therefore, it was not to discourage such men from becoming qualified to teach that the disciple James wrote: "Not many of you should become teachers, my brothers, knowing that we shall receive heavier judgment." (Jas 3:1) Rather, these words emphasized the heavy responsibility that as a result comes upon teachers in the congregation. Evidently some had set themselves up as teachers, although not being appointed or qualifying as such. The persons whom James had in mind were probably much like those of whom Paul wrote to Timothy: "Certain ones have been turned aside into idle talk, wanting to be teachers of law, but not perceiving either the things they are saying or the things about which they are making strong assertions." (1Ti 1:6, 7) Evidently such men desired the prominence that came with being a teacher of fellow believers. But James placed matters in the right perspective by showing that more would be required of teachers in the congregation. They would have to render a more serious account than Christians generally. (Compare Ro 14:12.) Yet like others, they too would stumble in word.—Jas 3:2.

How all Christians should be teachers. While relatively few served as teachers in the congregation itself, the desirable goal for all Christians was to have the ability to teach their beliefs to others, at least privately. This point was made clear to Hebrew Christians: "Although you ought to be teachers in view of the time, you again need someone to teach you from the beginning the elementary things of the sacred pronouncements of God." As the Jews had been the first to receive the good news about the Christ, they really should have been, not spiritual babes, but examples in Christian maturity and ability to teach others. (Heb 5:12–6:2) Thus the inspired writer is here evidently speaking of teaching in a general sense, rather than in an appointed capacity. Somewhat similar, therefore, is his reference to the Jew who, on the basis of his knowledge, becomes "a corrector of the unreasonable ones, a teacher of babes." (Ro 2:17-20) Paul shows, however, that in such teaching also one's life course must harmonize with what is taught if the teaching is to bring honor to God.—Ro 2:21-24.

Christians could also learn from one another. Younger women, for instance, could be taught by aged women about such matters as 'loving their husbands, loving their children, being sound in mind, chaste, workers at home, good, subjecting themselves to their own husbands, so that the word of God may not be spoken of abusively.' Such teaching in private was effective when backed up by a good example.—Tit 2:3-5; compare 2Ti 1:5; 3:14, 15.

TEBAH (Te′bah) [Slaughter]. First-named son of Abraham's brother Nahor by his concubine Reumah. (Ge 22:23, 24) His descendants may be connected with the town of Betah (Tibhath). —2Sa 8:8; 1Ch 18:8; see BETAH.

TEBALIAH (Teb·a·li′ah) [possibly, Good for Jehovah]. A Merarite Levite, the third-listed son of Hosah, and a gatekeeper in the time of David. —1Ch 26:1, 10, 11, 16.

TEBETH (Te′beth). The postexilic name of the tenth Jewish lunar month of the sacred calendar, but the fourth of the secular calendar. (Es 2:16) It corresponds to part of December and part of January. It is generally referred to simply as "the tenth month."—1Ch 27:13.

The name Tebeth is believed to have come from an Akkadian root meaning "sink" or "sink down," and this may have reference to the muddy conditions that prevail during this winter month when rainfall is at its peak. The winter rains are often torrential, like the one that ended the three-and-a-half-year drought in Elijah's day or the kind that Jesus described in his illustration of the house, the sand foundation of which was washed away by the lashing rain. (1Ki 18:45; Mt 7:24-27) According to *The Geography of the Bible* by Denis Baly (1957, p. 50), the latter part of December brings frequent frosts in the hill country and occasional snow flurries in Jerusalem. (2Sa 23:20) Though it is unusual, there have been times when roads were temporarily blocked by heavy snowfall. It may have been during this month, Tebeth, that a heavy snowfall hindered the Syrian army commander Tryphon when on his way to Jerusa-

lem. (*Jewish Antiquities,* XIII, 208 [vi, 6]; 1 Maccabees 13:22) The month Tebeth was evidently neither a month for traveling nor a month in which shepherds would spend the night in the fields. For these and other reasons it could not have been the month in which Jesus was born.

It was on the tenth day of Tebeth in 609 B.C.E. that Nebuchadnezzar began his siege against the city of Jerusalem. (2Ki 25:1; Jer 39:1; 52:4; Eze 24:1, 2) Possibly in memory of this event the Jews observed "the fast of the tenth month." —Zec 8:19.

TEETH. Hard, bony appendages in the mouth that are used for the chewing of food and, in the case of animals, also as weapons.

Job, the faithful servant of God, barely escaping death in his sufferings, said: "I escape with the *skin of my teeth.*" (Job 19:20) It seems that Job was simply saying that he had escaped with nothing or with next to nothing. He had escaped with the skin of his teeth, that is, with the "skin" of what apparently has no skin.

Grinding or gnashing of the teeth is frequently used to denote rage (Job 16:9; Ac 7:54) or anguish and despair. (Mt 8:12; 13:42, 50; 22:13; 24:51; 25:30) Such gnashing may be accompanied by bitter words and violent action against the object of anger.

At Amos 4:6 the expression *"cleanness of teeth"* is paralleled with "want of bread," representing famine conditions.

Teeth also symbolize destructive power of a nation or a people. (Da 7:5, 7, 19; Joe 1:6; Re 9:8) David likens the wicked enemies of the righteous to ferocious lions, and he petitions God to strike them in the jaw and to *break their teeth.* This would render them powerless to do harm. (Ps 3:7; 58:6) The false prophets of Israel are pictured as greedy and voracious, "biting with their teeth," and sanctifying war against anyone who does not feed them.—Mic 3:5; compare Eze 34:2, 3; Mt 7:15; Ac 20:29.

In the days before Jerusalem's destruction, a common saying of the people was: "The fathers were the ones that ate the unripe grape, but it was the *teeth* of the sons that *got set on edge.*" (Jer 31:29; Eze 18:2-4) By this means they tried to excuse themselves of the blame for the adverse conditions brought upon the nation because of its wickedness, saying that what they were experiencing was as a result of what their fathers had done.

TEHAPHNEHES. See TAHPANES, TAHPANHES, TEHAPHNEHES.

TEHINNAH (Te·hin′nah) [Request for Favor]. Descendant of Chelub in the genealogies of Judah. He is also identified as the father of Ir-nahash, probably meaning that he was the founder of such a community.—1Ch 4:11, 12.

TEHTH [ט]. The ninth letter of the Hebrew alphabet. The sound represented by the letter corresponds to an emphatic English "t," produced by pressing the tongue strongly against the palate. Its sound differs from that of the letter *taw* [ת] primarily because of its lack of aspiration after the "t" sound. In the original Hebrew, it appears at the beginning of each verse of Psalm 119:65-72.

TEKEL. See MENE.

TEKOA (Te·ko′a). A town in the territory of Judah that is commonly identified with Khirbet ′et-Tuqu′, some 16 km (10 mi) S of Jerusalem and lying at an elevation of about 820 m (2,700 ft). To the E stretches the Wilderness of Judah, of which "the wilderness of Tekoa" (where the Ammonites, Moabites, and the forces from Mount Seir suffered a crushing defeat during Jehoshaphat's reign) was apparently a part. (2Ch 20:20, 24) King Rehoboam, David's grandson, rebuilt and fortified Tekoa, and for centuries thereafter the city evidently served as an outpost in the Judean defense system. (2Ch 11:5, 6; compare Jer 6:1.) It was the home of Ikkesh, the father of Ira, one of David's mighty men. (1Ch 11:26, 28) From there came the wise woman who, at the direction of Joab, appealed to King David in behalf of Absalom. (2Sa 14:1-21) And there, in the ninth century B.C.E., the prophet Amos raised sheep.—Am 1:1.

Some may conclude that the Tekoa mentioned in the Judean genealogical records (1Ch 2:3, 24; 4:5) was a son of Ashhur. However, Tekoa is not listed in 1 Chronicles 4:5-7 among the seven sons of Ashhur's two wives, suggesting that Ashhur, rather than being the father of a son named Tekoa, may have been the founder of the town or of its population.

TEKOITE (Te·ko′ite) [Of (Belonging to) Tekoa]. An inhabitant of Tekoa. (2Ch 11:6; Jer 6:1) The term is applied to Ikkesh, the father of David's warrior Ira (2Sa 23:26; 1Ch 11:28; 27:9); likewise to a wise woman who, at the behest of Joab, feigned widowhood before David in a scheme to accomplish Absalom's return from banishment. (2Sa 14:2, 4, 9) After the return from Babylonian exile, Tekoites were among those who shared in repairing Jerusalem's walls, though their "majestic ones" ("nobles," *AT*) took no part in the work. —Ne 3:5, 27.

TEL-ABIB (Tel-a′bib) [Mound of Green Ears]. A place by the river Chebar in the land of the Chaldeans where Ezekiel and other Jews were exiled. Its exact location is unknown.—Eze 1:1-3; 3:15; see CHEBAR.

TELAH (Te′lah). An Ephraimite ancestor of Joshua the son of Nun.—1Ch 7:20, 25-27.

TELAIM (Te·la′im). A site, apparently in Judah, where Saul numbered his forces before striking the Amalekites. (1Sa 15:1-4) Telaim appears to be the same as Telem, listed with southern Judean cities. (Jos 15:21, 24) It is also probably to be connected with "Telam."—1Sa 27:8.

TELAM (Te′lam). Twelve manuscripts of the Greek *Septuagint* say that Tela(m) was one of the limits of the dwellings of the Geshurites, Girzites, and Amalekites in David's day. (1Sa 27:8) This would appear to connect Telam with Telaim, referred to at 1 Samuel 15:4, and Telem in southern Judah. (Jos 15:21, 24) At 1 Samuel 27:8, the Hebrew Masoretic text reads "from long ago," which differs from the expression "from Telam" by only two Hebrew consonants.

TEL-ASSAR (Tel-as′sar). A place inhabited by "the sons of Eden" mentioned along with Gozan, Haran, and Rezeph—sites in northern Mesopotamia. (2Ki 19:12; Isa 37:12) Sennacherib boasted, through his messengers, that the gods worshiped by the people of these places had been unable to deliver them from the power of his forefathers. Because of the reference to "the sons of Eden," Tel-assar is generally associated with the small kingdom of Bit-adini along the Upper Euphrates. Assyrian monarchs Tiglath-pileser III and Esarhaddon both refer to a Til-Ashuri, but its location is considered to have been near the Assyrian border of Elam. Hence, identification of Tel-assar remains uncertain.

TELEM (Te′lem).

1. A gatekeeper among those dismissing their foreign wives in the days of Ezra.—Ezr 10:16, 17, 24.

2. A city in the southern part of Judah. (Jos 15:21, 24) It is possibly the same as Telaim.

TEL-HARSHA (Tel-har′sha). A Babylonian site from which certain persons unable to establish their genealogy as Israelites came to Judah with the exiles in 537 B.C.E. (Ezr 2:1, 59; Ne 7:6, 61) Otherwise the site is unknown.

TEL-MELAH (Tel-me′lah) [Mound of Salt]. One of the Babylonian places from which individuals unable to tell their genealogy came to Judah in 537 B.C.E.—Ezr 2:1, 59; Ne 7:6, 61.

TEMA (Te'ma).

1. One of the sons of Ishmael.—Ge 25:13-15; 1Ch 1:29, 30.

2. Probably the same as modern Taima, an oasis located about 400 km (250 mi) SE of Ezion-geber, where two major caravan routes crossed. (Job 6:19) Tema, along with nearby Dedan, is mentioned in the prophecies of Isaiah (21:13, 14) and Jeremiah (25:15-23). In this latter prophecy Tema was specifically named as among the places whose inhabitants would be compelled to drink of Jehovah's "cup of the wine of rage." Babylonian King Nabonidus apparently established a second capital in Tema, leaving Belshazzar at Babylon in charge during his absence.

TEMAH (Te'mah). Forefather of a family of Nethinim who returned from Babylon to Jerusalem with Zerubbabel.—Ezr 2:1, 2, 43, 53; Ne 7:55.

TEMAN (Te'man) [Right Side; South].

1. A descendant of Esau through his firstborn Eliphaz (Ge 36:10, 11; 1Ch 1:35, 36); an Edomite sheik.—Ge 36:15, 16, 34, 42.

2. A place identified by some scholars with Tawilan, about 5 km (3 mi) E of Petra. It was evidently an Edomite city or district (the land of the Temanites), where the descendants of Teman resided. (Ge 36:34; Jer 49:7, 20; Eze 25:13; Am 1:11, 12; Ob 9) The place became noted as a center of wisdom. (Jer 49:7) In the book of Habakkuk, God is spoken of as coming from "Teman, even a Holy One from Mount Paran." This may refer to Jehovah's shining forth in glory, his splendor reflecting from the mountains as he brought his newly formed nation past Edom en route to the Promised Land.—Hab 3:3, 4; compare De 33:2.

TEMANITE (Te'man·ite) [Of (Belonging to) Teman]. A term generally understood to refer to a native of Teman in Edom. An early Edomite king, Husham, came from "the land of the Temanites," and Eliphaz, one of Job's three companions, was a Temanite. (Ge 36:31-34; Job 2:11; 4:1; 42:7) That Eliphaz came from Teman in Edom is suggested by the understanding that the land of Uz, where Job lived, was near Edom. Some scholars, however, believe that there is a possibility that the Eliphaz named in the book of Job was, not from Teman, but from Tema, a place identified with an oasis on the Arabian Peninsula about 400 km (250 mi) SE of Ezion-geber.—Job 6:19.

TEMENI (Te'me·ni) [from a root meaning "right side; south"]. A son of Ashhur by his wife Naarah; of the tribe of Judah.—1Ch 4:1, 5, 6.

TEMPLE. A divine habitation, sacred place or sanctuary, either physical or spiritual, that is employed for worship. The Hebrew word heh·khal', translated "temple," also means "palace." The Greek hi·e·ron' and na·os' are both rendered "temple" and may refer to the entire temple complex or to its central edifice; na·os', meaning "sanctuary" or "divine habitation (dwelling)," at times refers specifically to the sacred inner rooms of the temple.—See HOLY PLACE.

Solomon's Temple. King David entertained a strong desire to build a house for Jehovah, to contain the ark of the covenant, which was "dwelling in the middle of tent cloths." Jehovah was pleased with David's proposal but told him that, because he had shed much blood in warfare, his son (Solomon) would be privileged to do the building. This was not to say that God did not approve David's wars fought in behalf of Jehovah's name and His people. But the temple was to be built in peace by a man of peace.—2Sa 7:1-16; 1Ki 5:3-5; 8:17; 1Ch 17:1-14; 22:6-10.

Cost. Later David purchased the threshing floor of Ornan (Araunah) the Jebusite on Mount Moriah as the temple site. (2Sa 24:24, 25; 1Ch 21:24, 25) He amassed 100,000 talents of gold, 1,000,000 talents of silver, and copper and iron in great abundance, besides contributing from his personal fortune 3,000 talents of gold and 7,000 talents of silver. He also received as contributions from the princes, gold worth 5,000 talents and 10,000 darics and silver worth 10,000 talents, as well as much iron and copper. (1Ch 22:14; 29:3-7) This total, amounting to 108,000 talents and 10,000 darics of gold and 1,017,000 talents of silver, would be worth $48,337,047,000 at current values. His son Solomon did not spend the entire amount in building the temple; the remainder he put in the temple treasury.—1Ki 7:51; 2Ch 5:1.

Workmen. King Solomon began building the temple for Jehovah in the fourth year of his reign (1034 B.C.E.), in the second month, Ziv, following the architectural plan that David had received by inspiration. (1Ki 6:1; 1Ch 28:11-19) The work continued over a seven-year period. (1Ki 6:37, 38) In exchange for wheat, barley, oil, and wine, Hiram king of Tyre supplied timbers from Lebanon along with skilled workers in wood and stone, and one special expert, also named Hiram, whose father was a Tyrian and his mother an Israelitess of the tribe of Naphtali. This man was a fine workman in gold, silver, copper, iron, wood, stones, and fabrics.—1Ki 5:8-11, 18; 7:13, 14, 40, 45; 2Ch 2:13-16.

In organizing the work, Solomon conscripted 30,000 men out of Israel, sending them to Lebanon in shifts of 10,000 for a month, with a two-month stay at home between shifts. (1Ki 5:13, 14) As burden bearers, he conscripted 70,000 from among the "alien residents" in the land, and as cutters, 80,000. (1Ki 5:15; 9:20, 21; 2Ch 2:2) As foremen over the work, Solomon appointed 550 men and apparently 3,300 as assistants. (1Ki 5:16; 9:22, 23) It appears that, of these, 250 were Israelites and 3,600 were "alien residents" in Israel.—2Ch 2:17, 18.

Length of "cubit" used. In the following discussion of the measurements of the three temples —built by Solomon, Zerubbabel, and Herod—we shall calculate them on the basis of the cubit of 44.5 cm (17.5 in.). However, it is possible that they used the longer cubit of about 51.8 cm (20.4 in.).—Compare 2Ch 3:3 (which mentions a "length in cubits by the former measurement," this perhaps being a longer measure than the cubit that came to be commonly in use) and Eze 40:5; see CUBIT.

Plan and materials. The temple, a most magnificent structure, followed the general plan of the tabernacle. However, the inside dimensions of the Holy and Most Holy were greater than those of the tabernacle. The Holy was 40 cubits (17.8 m; 58.3 ft) long, 20 cubits (8.9 m; 29.2 ft) wide, and evidently 30 cubits (13.4 in.; 43.7 ft) high. (1Ki 6:2) The Most Holy was a cube 20 cubits on a side. (1Ki 6:20; 2Ch 3:8) Additionally, there were roof chambers over the Most Holy that were approximately 10 cubits (4.5 m; 14.6 ft) high. (1Ch 28:11) There was also a side structure around the temple on three sides, containing storage chambers, and so forth.—1Ki 6:4-6, 10.

Materials used were primarily stone and wood. The floors of these rooms were overlaid with juniper wood; the inside walls were of cedar engraved with carvings of cherubs, palm trees, and blossoms; the walls and ceiling were entirely overlaid with gold. (1Ki 6:15, 18, 21, 22, 29) The doors of the Holy (at the temple entrance) were made of juniper—carved and overlaid with gold foil. (1Ki 6:34, 35) Doors of oil-tree wood, likewise carved and overlaid with gold, provided entrance between the Holy and Most Holy. Whatever their exact position, these doors did not fully replace the curtain arrangement that had been in effect in the tabernacle. (Compare 2Ch 3:14.) Two gigantic cherubs of oil-tree wood, gold overlaid, occupied the Most Holy. Under these the ark of the covenant was placed.—1Ki 6:23-28, 31-33; 8:6; see CHERUB No. 1.

All the utensils of the Holy were of gold: the altar of incense, the ten tables of showbread, and the ten lampstands, together with their appurtenances. Beside the entrance to the Holy (the first compartment) stood two copper pillars, called "Jachin" and "Boaz." (1Ki 7:15-22, 48-50; 1Ch 28:16; 2Ch 4:8; see BOAZ, II.) The inner courtyard was constructed of fine stone and cedarwood. (1Ki 6:36) The courtyard furnishings, the altar of sacrifice, the great "molten sea," ten carriages for water basins, and other utensils were of copper. (1Ki 7:23-47) Dining rooms were provided around the perimeter of the courtyards.—1Ch 28:12.

An outstanding feature of the construction of this temple was the fact that all the stone was cut at the quarry, so that it fit perfectly at the temple site. "As for hammers and axes or any tools of iron, they were not heard in the house while it was being built." (1Ki 6:7) The work was completed in seven and a half years (from spring 1034 B.C.E. to fall [Bul, the eighth month] 1027 B.C.E.).—1Ki 6:1, 38.

Inauguration. In the seventh month, Ethanim, apparently in the 12th year of Solomon's reign (1026 B.C.E.), Solomon congregated the men of Israel to Jerusalem for the temple inauguration and the Festival of Booths. The tabernacle with its holy furniture was brought up, and the ark of the covenant was placed in the Most Holy. (See MOST HOLY.) At this Jehovah's cloud filled the temple. Solomon then blessed Jehovah and the congregation of Israel and, standing on a special platform before the copper altar of sacrifice (see ALTAR), offered a long prayer praising Jehovah and asking for his loving-kindness and mercy in behalf of those who turned toward Him to fear and to serve Him, both the Israelite and the foreigner. A grand sacrifice of 22,000 cattle and 120,000 sheep was offered. The inauguration occupied 7 days, and the Festival of Booths 7 days, after which, on the 23rd day of the month, Solomon sent the people home joyful and thankful for Jehovah's goodness and bountifulness.—1Ki 8; 2Ch 5:1–7:10; see SOLOMON (Inauguration of the temple).

History. This temple existed until 607 B.C.E., when it was destroyed by the Babylonian army under King Nebuchadnezzar. (2Ki 25:9; 2Ch 36:19; Jer 52:13) Because of the falling away of Israel to false religion, God permitted the nations to harass Judah and Jerusalem, at times stripping the temple of its treasures. The temple also suffered periods of neglect. King Shishak of Egypt robbed it of its treasures (993 B.C.E.) in the days of Rehoboam the son of Solomon, only about 33 years after its inauguration. (1Ki 14:25, 26; 2Ch

12:9) King Asa (977-937 B.C.E.) had respect for Jehovah's house, but to protect Jerusalem he foolishly bribed King Ben-hadad I of Syria, with silver and gold from the treasures of the temple, to break his covenant with Baasha king of Israel. —1Ki 15:18, 19; 2Ch 15:17, 18; 16:2, 3.

After a period of turbulence and neglect of the temple, King Jehoash of Judah (898-859 B.C.E.) oversaw its repair. (2Ki 12:4-12; 2Ch 24:4-14) In the days of his son Amaziah, Jehoash king of Israel robbed it. (2Ki 14:13, 14) King Jotham (777-762 B.C.E.) did some construction work on the temple area, building "the upper gate." (2Ki 15: 32, 35; 2Ch 27:1, 3) King Ahaz of Judah (761-746 B.C.E.) not only sent the treasures of the temple to Tiglath-pileser III, king of Assyria, as a bribe but he also polluted the temple by building an altar patterned after one in Damascus and by replacing the copper altar of the temple with it. (2Ki 16:5-16) Finally he closed the doors of Jehovah's house.—2Ch 28:24.

Ahaz' son Hezekiah (745-717 B.C.E.) did what he could to undo the bad works of his father. At the very beginning of his reign, he reopened the temple and had it cleaned up. (2Ch 29:3, 15, 16) However, later on, for fear of Sennacherib king of Assyria, he cut off the doors and the doorposts of the temple that he himself had caused to be overlaid with gold and sent them to Sennacherib. —2Ki 18:15, 16.

But when Hezekiah died, the temple entered a half century of desecration and disrepair. His son Manasseh (716-662 B.C.E.) went beyond any of Judah's previous kings in wickedness, setting up altars "to all the army of the heavens in two courtyards of the house of Jehovah." (2Ki 21:1-5; 2Ch 33:1-4) By the time of Manasseh's grandson Josiah (659-629 B.C.E.), the formerly magnificent edifice was in a state of disrepair. Evidently it was in a disorganized or cluttered condition, for High Priest Hilkiah's finding the book of the Law (likely an original scroll written by Moses) was an exciting discovery. (2Ki 22:3-13; 2Ch 34:8-21) After the temple's repair and cleansing, the greatest Passover since the days of Samuel the prophet was celebrated. (2Ki 23:21-23; 2Ch 35:17-19) This was during the ministry of the prophet Jeremiah. (Jer 1:1-3) From this time until the temple's destruction, it remained open and in use by the priesthood, though many of the priests were corrupt.

The Temple Built by Zerubbabel. As foretold by Jehovah's prophet Isaiah, God raised up Cyrus king of Persia as a liberator of Israel from the power of Babylon. (Isa 45:1) Jehovah also stirred up his own people under the leadership of Zerubbabel of the tribe of Judah to return to Jerusalem. This they did in 537 B.C.E., after 70 years of desolation, as Jeremiah had foretold, for the purpose of rebuilding the temple. (Ezr 1:1-6; 2:1, 2; Jer 29:10) This structure, though not nearly so glorious as Solomon's temple, endured longer, standing for nearly 500 years, from 515 B.C.E. to very late in the first century B.C.E. (The temple built by Solomon had served about 420 years, from 1027 to 607 B.C.E.)

In Cyrus' decree he ordered: "As for anyone that is left from all the places where he is residing as an alien, let the men of his place assist him with silver and with gold and with goods and with domestic animals along with the voluntary offering for the house of the true God, which was in Jerusalem." (Ezr 1:1-4) Cyrus also returned 5,400 vessels of gold and silver that Nebuchadnezzar had taken from Solomon's temple.—Ezr 1:7-11.

In the seventh month (Ethanim, or Tishri) of the year 537 B.C.E., the altar was set up; and in the following year, the foundation of the new temple was laid. As Solomon had done, the builders hired Sidonians and Tyrians to bring cedar timbers from Lebanon. (Ezr 3:7) Opposition, particularly from the Samaritans, disheartened the builders, and after about 15 years those opposers even incited the king of Persia to ban the work. —Ezr 4.

The Jews had stopped their temple building work and had turned to other pursuits, so Jehovah sent his prophets Haggai and Zechariah to stir them to renew their efforts in the second year of Darius I (520 B.C.E.), and thereafter a decree was made upholding Cyrus' original order and commanding that moneys be provided from the royal treasury, to supply what the builders and priests needed. (Ezr 5:1, 2; 6:1-12) The building work was carried on, and the house of Jehovah was completed on the third day of Adar in the sixth year of Darius (probably March 5 of 515 B.C.E.), after which the Jews inaugurated the rebuilt temple and held the Passover.—Ezr 6:13-22.

Little is known about the details of the architectural plan of this second temple. Cyrus' decree authorized the building of a structure "its height being sixty cubits [c. 27 m; 88 ft], its width sixty cubits, with three layers of stones rolled into place and one layer of timbers." The length is not stated. (Ezr 6:3, 4) It had dining rooms and storerooms (Ne 13:4, 5), and undoubtedly it had roof chambers, and possibly other buildings were associated with it, along the same lines as Solomon's temple.

This second temple did not contain the ark of the covenant, which seems to have disappeared before Nebuchadnezzar captured and looted Solomon's temple in 607 B.C.E. According to the account in the Apocryphal book of First Maccabees (1:21-24, 57; 4:38, 44-51), there was one lampstand instead of the ten that were in Solomon's; the golden altar, the table of showbread, and the vessels are mentioned, as is the altar of burnt offering, which, instead of being of copper as was the altar in Solomon's temple, is there described as being of stone. This altar, after being defiled by King Antiochus Epiphanes (in 168 B.C.E.), was rebuilt with new stones under the direction of Judas Maccabaeus.

The Temple Rebuilt by Herod. This temple is not described in any detail in the Scriptures. The primary source is Josephus, who personally saw the structure and who reports on its construction in *The Jewish War* and *Jewish Antiquities.* The Jewish Mishnah supplies some information, and a little is gained from archaeology. Therefore the description set forth here is from these sources, which in some instances may be open to question.—PICTURE, Vol. 2, p. 543.

In *The Jewish War* (I, 401 [xxi, 1]), Josephus says that Herod rebuilt the temple in the 15th year of his reign, but in *Jewish Antiquities* (XV, 380 [xi, 1]), he says it was in the 18th year. This latter date is generally accepted by scholars, although the beginning of Herod's reign, or how Josephus calculated it, is not established with certainty. The sanctuary itself took 18 months to build, but the courtyards, and so forth, were under construction for eight years. When certain Jews approached Jesus Christ in 30 C.E., saying, "This temple was built in forty-six years" (Joh 2:20), these Jews were apparently talking about the work that continued on the complex of courts and buildings up until then. The work was not finished until about six years before the destruction of the temple in 70 C.E.

Because of hatred and distrust of Herod, the Jews would not permit him to rebuild the temple, as he proposed, until he had everything prepared for the new building. For the same reason they did not consider this temple as a third one, but only as a rebuilt one, speaking only of the first and second temples (Solomon's and Zerubbabel's).

As to Josephus' measurements, Smith's *Dictionary of the Bible* (1889, Vol. IV, p. 3203) says:

"His horizontal dimensions are so minutely accurate that we almost suspect he had before his eyes, when writing, some ground-plan of the building prepared in the quartermaster-general's department of Titus's army. They form a strange contrast with his dimensions in height, which, with scarcely an exception, can be shown to be exaggerated, generally doubled. As the buildings were all thrown down during the siege, it was impossible to convict him of error in respect to elevations."

Colonnades and gates. Josephus writes that Herod doubled the size of the temple area, building up the sides of Mount Moriah with great stone walls and leveling off an area on the top of the mountain. (*The Jewish War*, I, 401 [xxi, 1]; *Jewish Antiquities*, XV, 391-402 [xi, 3]) The Mishnah (*Middot* 2:1) says the Temple Mount measured 500 cubits (223 m; 729 ft) square. On the outer edge of the area were colonnades. The temple faced the E, as did the previous ones. Along this side was the colonnade of Solomon, consisting of three columns of marble pillars. On one occasion, in the wintertime, Jesus was approached here by certain Jews asking if he was the Christ. (Joh 10:22-24) In the N and W were also colonnades, dwarfed by the Royal Colonnade on the S, consisting of four rows of Corinthian pillars, 162 in all, with three aisles. The pillars' circumferences were so great that it took three men with outstretched arms to reach around one of them, and they stood much higher than those of the other colonnades.

There were evidently eight gates leading into the temple area: four on the W side, two on the S, and one each on the E and N. (See GATE, GATEWAY [Temple Gates].) Because of these gates, the first court, the Court of the Gentiles, also served as a thoroughfare, travelers preferring to go through it instead of outside around the temple area.

Court of the Gentiles. The colonnades surrounded the large area named the Court of the Gentiles, so called because Gentiles were permitted to enter it. It was from it that Jesus, on two occasions, once near the beginning and once at the close of his earthly ministry, expelled those who had made the house of his Father a house of merchandise.—Joh 2:13-17; Mt 21:12, 13; Mr 11:15-18.

There were several courts through which a person passed as he proceeded to the central building, the sanctuary itself. Each succeeding court was of a higher degree of sanctity. Passing through the Court of the Gentiles, one encountered a wall three cubits (1.3 m; 4.4 ft) high, with openings through which to pass. On its top were large stones bearing a warning in Greek and Latin. The Greek inscription read (according to one translation): "Let no foreigner enter inside of the barrier and the fence around the sanctuary. Whosoever is caught will be responsible for his death which will ensue." (*The New Westminster Dictionary of the Bible,* edited by H. Gehman, 1970, p. 932) On the occasion when the apostle Paul was mobbed in the temple, it was because the Jews rumored that he had brought a Gentile within the forbidden area. We are reminded of this wall, though Paul was using the term "wall" symbolically, when we read that Christ "destroyed the wall" that fenced off Jew from Gentile.—Eph 2:14, ftn; Ac 21:20-32.

Court of Women. The Court of Women was 14 steps higher. Here women could enter for worship. Among other things, the Court of Women contained treasure chests, near one of which Jesus stood when he commended the widow for

A notice from Jerusalem's temple courtyard warning Gentiles not to approach closer

giving her all. (Lu 21:1-4) In this court were also several buildings.

Court of Israel and Court of Priests. Fifteen large semicircular steps led up to the Court of Israel, which could be entered by men who were ceremonially clean. Against the outside wall of this court were storage chambers.

Then came the Court of Priests, which corresponded to the courtyard of the tabernacle. In it was the altar, built of unhewn stones. According to the Mishnah, it was 32 cubits (14.2 m; 46.7 ft) square at the base. (*Middot* 3:1) Josephus gives a higher figure. (*The Jewish War,* V, 225 [v, 6]; see ALTAR [Postexilic Altars].) The priests reached the altar by an inclined plane. A "laver" was also in use, according to the Mishnah. (*Middot* 3:6) Around this court also were various buildings.

The temple building. As previously, the temple proper consisted primarily of two compartments, the Holy and the Most Holy. The floor of this building was 12 steps above the Court of Priests. Even as with Solomon's temple, chambers were built on the sides of this building and there was an upper chamber. The entrance was closed by golden doors, each 55 cubits (24.5 m; 80.2 ft) high and 16 cubits (7.1 m; 23.3 ft) broad. The front of the building was wider than the back, having wings or "shoulders" that extended out 20 cubits (8.9 m; 29.2 ft) on each side. The inside of the Holy was 40 cubits (17.8 m; 58.3 ft) long and 20 cubits wide. In the Holy were the lampstand, the table of showbread, and the altar of incense—all of gold.

The entrance to the Most Holy was a beautifully ornamented thick curtain, or veil. At the time of Jesus' death, this curtain was torn in two from top to bottom, exposing the Most Holy as containing no ark of the covenant. In place of the Ark was a stone slab upon which the high priest sprinkled the blood on the Day of Atonement. (Mt 27:51; Heb 6:19; 10:20) This room was 20 cubits long and 20 cubits wide.

The Jews used the temple area as a citadel, or fortress, during the Roman siege of Jerusalem in 70 C.E. They themselves set fire to the colonnades, but a Roman soldier, contrary to the wishes of the Roman commander Titus, fired the temple itself, thereby fulfilling Jesus' words regarding the temple buildings: "By no means will a stone be left here upon a stone and not be thrown down."—Mt 24:2; *The Jewish War,* VI, 252-266 (iv, 5-7); VII, 3, 4 (i, 1).

Jehovah's Great Spiritual Temple. The tabernacle constructed by Moses and the temples built by Solomon, Zerubbabel, and Herod were only typical, or pictorial. This was shown by the apostle Paul when he wrote that the tabernacle, the basic features of which were included in the later temples, was "a typical representation and a shadow of the heavenly things." (Heb 8:1-5; see also 1Ki 8:27; Isa 66:1; Ac 7:48; 17:24.) The Christian Greek Scriptures disclose the reality represented by the type. These Scriptures show that the tabernacle and the temples built by Solomon, Zerubbabel, and Herod, along with their features, represented a greater, spiritual temple of Jehovah, "the true tent, which Jehovah put up, and not man." (Heb 8:2) As revealed by its various features, that spiritual temple is the arrangement for approaching Jehovah in worship on the basis of the propitiatory sacrifice of Jesus Christ. —Heb 9:2-10, 23.

The inspired letter to the Hebrews states that in this spiritual temple the Most Holy is "heaven itself," the area where the person of God is. (Heb 9:24) Since only the Most Holy is "heaven itself," then the Holy and the priestly courtyard, as well as their features, must pertain to things on earth, those things having to do with Jesus Christ during his ministry on earth and his followers who are "partakers of the heavenly calling."—Heb 3:1.

The curtain was a barrier separating the Holy from the Most Holy; in Jesus' case it represented "his flesh," which he had to lay down in sacrifice, giving it up forever, to be able to enter heaven, the antitypical Most Holy. (Heb 10:20) Anointed Christians must also pass the fleshly barrier that separates them from access to God's presence in heaven. Consistently, the Holy represents their condition as spirit-begotten sons of God, with heavenly life in view, and they will attain to that heavenly reward when their fleshly bodies are laid aside in death.—1Co 15:50; Heb 2:10.

While still in the antitypical Holy, these who have been anointed with holy spirit and who serve as underpriests with Christ are able to enjoy spiritual enlightenment, as from the lampstand; to eat spiritual food, as from the table of showbread; and to offer up prayer, praise, and service to God, as if presenting sweet-smelling incense at the golden altar of incense. The Holy of the typical temple was screened off from the view of outsiders, and similarly, how a person knows that he is a spirit-begotten son of God and what he experiences as such cannot be fully appreciated by those who are not.—Re 14:3.

In the ancient temple courtyard was the altar for offering sacrifices. This foreshadowed God's provision, according to his will, for a perfect human sacrifice to ransom the offspring of Adam.

(Heb 10:1-10; 13:10-12; Ps 40:6-8) In the spiritual temple the courtyard itself must pertain to a condition related to that sacrifice. In the case of Jesus, it was his being a perfect human that made the sacrifice of his life acceptable. In the case of his anointed followers, all of these are declared righteous on the basis of their faith in Christ's sacrifice, and thus they are viewed by God as sinless while in the flesh.—Ro 3:24-26; 5:1, 9; 8:1.

The features of "the true tent," God's great spiritual temple, already existed in the first century C.E. This is indicated by the fact that, with reference to the tabernacle constructed by Moses, Paul wrote that it was "an illustration for the appointed time that is now here," that is, for something that existed when Paul was writing. (Heb 9:9) That temple certainly existed when Jesus presented the value of his sacrifice in its Most Holy, in heaven itself. It must actually have come into existence in 29 C.E., when Jesus was anointed with holy spirit to serve as Jehovah's great High Priest.—Heb 4:14; 9:11, 12.

Jesus Christ promises the spirit-begotten Christians that the one who conquers, who endures faithfully to the end, will be made "a pillar in the temple of my God, and he will by no means go out from it anymore." (Re 3:12) So, such a one is granted a permanent place in "heaven itself," the antitypical Most Holy.

Revelation 7:9-15 reveals "a great crowd" of other worshipers of Jehovah sharing in pure worship at the spiritual temple. Those making up this "great crowd" are not described in terms that identify them as underpriests. So they must be understood to be standing in what was represented by the courtyard of the Gentiles, a special feature of the temple as rebuilt by Herod. The ones who make up this "great crowd" are said to have "washed their robes and made them white in the blood of the Lamb." Because of their faith in the sacrifice of Christ, they are credited with a righteous standing that makes possible their preservation through "the great tribulation," so they are said to "come out of" it as survivors.

At Isaiah 2:1-4 and Micah 4:1-4, reference is made to a 'lifting up' of "the mountain of the house of Jehovah" in "the final part of the days," and it is foretold that there would be a gathering of people of "all the nations" to that "house of Jehovah." Since there has been no physical temple of Jehovah in Jerusalem since 70 C.E., this must refer, not to some physical structure, but to an elevating of true worship in the lives of Jehovah's people during "the final part of the days" and a great gathering of people of all nations to share in worship at Jehovah's great spiritual temple.

Detailed description of a temple of Jehovah is also found at Ezekiel chapters 40-47, but it is not a temple that was ever built on Mount Moriah in Jerusalem, nor would it fit there. So, it must be another illustration of God's great spiritual temple. In this instance, however, the focus of attention is the time after the attack by Gog of Magog. (Eze chaps 38, 39) Special consideration is given in the account to the provisions that emanate from the temple and to the fact that precautions are taken to keep out all who are unworthy to be among the worshipers in its courtyards.

Ezekiel's temple vision. In 593 B.C.E., in the 14th year after the destruction of Jerusalem and Solomon's temple therein, the priest-prophet Ezekiel, transported in vision to a high mountaintop, beheld a great temple of Jehovah. (Eze 40:1, 2) To humiliate and bring about repentance of the exiled Jews, also doubtless to comfort faithful ones, Ezekiel was instructed to relate everything he saw to "the house of Israel." (Eze 40:4; 43:10, 11) The vision gave careful attention to the details of measurement. The units of measure used were the "reed" (the long reed, 3.11 m; 10.2 ft) and the "cubit" (the long cubit, 51.8 cm; 20.4 in.). (Eze 40: 5, ftn) This attention to measurement has led some to believe that this visionary temple was to serve as a model for the temple later constructed by Zerubbabel in the postexilic period. There is, however, no conclusive substantiation of this assumption.

The entire temple area was evidently a square 500 cubits to a side. It contained an outer courtyard, an elevated inner courtyard, the temple with its altar, various dining rooms, and a building to the W, or rear, of the temple. Providing access to the temple's outer and inner courtyards were six huge gateways, three for the outer courtyard and three for the inner courtyard. These faced N, E, and S, each inner gate being directly behind (in line with) its corresponding outer gate. (Eze 40:6, 20, 23, 24, 27) Inside the outer wall was the lower pavement. It was 50 cubits (25.9 m; 85 ft) wide, the same as the length of the gateways. (Eze 40:18, 21) Thirty dining rooms, likely places for the people to eat their communion sacrifices, were located there. (Eze 40:17) At each of the four corners of this outer courtyard were locations where the peoples' portions of their sacrifices were cooked by the priests, according to the Law's requirement; then they were apparently consumed in the provided dining rooms. (Eze 46:21-24) The remainder of the outer courtyard between the lower pavement and the gates to the inner courtyard was apparently 100 cubits in width.—Eze 40:19, 23, 27.

The priests' dining rooms were separated from the people's, being placed closer to the temple. Two of these, along with two dining rooms for the temple singers, were in the inner courtyard beside the massive inner gateways. (Eze 40:38, 44-46) The priests also had dining-room blocks, to the N and S of the sanctuary itself. (Eze 42:1-12) These dining rooms, in addition to their most evident purpose, were places for the priests to change the linen garments used in temple service prior to their entering the outer courtyard. (Eze 42:13, 14; 44:19) Also in that area, to the rear of the dining-room blocks, were the boiling and baking places of the priests, intended for the same basic purpose as those in the outer courtyard, but these for only the priests.—Eze 46:19, 20.

Progressing across the outer courtyard and through the inner gateway, one entered the inner courtyard. The edge of the inner courtyard was 150 cubits (77.7 m; 255 ft) from the edge of the outer courtyard on the E, N, and S. The inner courtyard was 200 cubits (103.6 m; 340 ft) wide. (Ezekiel 40:47 says the inner courtyard was 100 cubits square. This evidently refers to just the area in front of the temple and into which the inner gateways led.) Prominent in the inner courtyard was the altar.—Eze 43:13-17; see ALTAR (Altar of Ezekiel's Temple).

The sanctuary's first room, 40 cubits (20.7 m; 68 ft) long and 20 cubits (10.4 m; 34 ft) wide, was entered by a doorway having two 2-leaved doors. (Eze 41:23, 24) Therein was "the table that is before Jehovah," a wooden altar.—Eze 41:21, 22.

The outer walls of the sanctuary had side chambers four cubits (2 m; 6.8 ft) wide incorporated into and against them. Rising three stories, they covered the western, northern, and southern walls, 30 chambers to a story. (Eze 41:5, 6) To ascend the three stories, winding passages, seemingly circular staircases, were provided on the N and S. (Eze 41:7) To the rear, or W, of the temple, lying apparently lengthwise N to S, was a structure called *bin·yan'*, a 'building to the west.' (Eze 41:12) Although some scholars have attempted to identify this building with the temple or sanctuary itself, there appears no basis for such an identification in the book of Ezekiel; the 'building to the west,' for one thing, was of different shape and dimensions from those of the sanctuary. This structure doubtless served some function in connection with the services carried on at the sanctuary. There may have been a similar building or buildings W of Solomon's temple.—Compare 2Ki 23:11 and 1Ch 26:18.

The Most Holy was of the same shape as that of Solomon's temple, being 20 cubits square. In the vision, Ezekiel saw Jehovah's glory come from the E, filling the temple. Jehovah described this temple as "the place of my throne."—Eze 43:1-7.

Ezekiel describes a wall 500 reeds (1,555 m; 5,100 ft) on each side, around the temple. This has been understood by some scholars to be a wall at a distance of about 600 m (2,000 ft) from the courtyard, a space surrounded by the wall "to make a division between what is holy and what is profane."—Eze 42:16-20.

Ezekiel also beheld a stream of water flowing "from under the threshold of the House eastward" and south of the altar, growing into a deep and mighty torrent as it flowed down through the Arabah into the north end of the Salt Sea. Here it healed the salt waters so that they became filled with fish.—Eze 47:1-12.

Anointed Christians—A Spiritual Temple. Anointed Christians on earth are likened to a number of things, including a temple. This comparison is fitting because God's spirit dwells within the congregation of anointed ones. Paul wrote to the Christians in Ephesus "in union with Christ Jesus," those who are "sealed with the promised holy spirit," saying: "You have been built up upon the foundation of the apostles and prophets, while Christ Jesus himself is the foundation cornerstone. In union with him the whole building, being harmoniously joined together, is growing into a holy temple for Jehovah. In union with him you, too, are being built up together into a place for God to inhabit by spirit." (Eph 1:1, 13; 2:20-22) These "sealed" ones, laid upon Christ as Foundation, are shown to number 144,000. (Re 7:4; 14:1) The apostle Peter speaks of these as "living stones" being "built up a spiritual house for the purpose of a holy priesthood."—1Pe 2:5.

Since these underpriests are "God's building," he will not let this spiritual temple suffer defilement. Paul emphasizes the holiness of this spiritual temple, and the danger to one who attempts to defile it, when he writes: "Do you not know that you people are God's temple, and that the spirit of God dwells in you? If anyone destroys the temple of God, God will destroy him; for the temple of God is holy, which temple you people are."—1Co 3:9, 16, 17; see also 2Co 6:16.

Jehovah God and the Lamb 'Are Its Temple.' When John sees New Jerusalem coming down from heaven, he remarks: "And I did not see a temple in it, for Jehovah God the Almighty is its temple, also the Lamb is." (Re 21:2, 22) Since the members of New Jerusalem will have direct access to the face of Jehovah himself, they will not need a temple through which to approach God. (1Jo 3:2; Re 22:3, 4) Those who make up New Jerusalem will render sacred service to God directly under the high priesthood of the Lamb, Jesus Christ. For this reason the Lamb shares with Jehovah in being, in effect, the temple of the New Jerusalem.

An Impostor. The apostle Paul, in warning of the apostasy to come, spoke of "the man of lawlessness" as setting himself up "so that he sits down in the temple of The God, publicly showing himself to be a god." (2Th 2:3, 4) This "man of lawlessness" is an apostate, a false teacher, so he actually seats himself only in what he falsely claims to be that temple.—See MAN OF LAWLESSNESS.

An Illustrative Use. On one occasion, when the Jews demanded a sign from Jesus, he replied: "Break down this temple, and in three days I will raise it up." The Jews thought he was speaking of the temple building, but the apostle John explains: "He was talking about the temple of his body." When he was resurrected by his Father Jehovah on the third day of his death, the disciples recalled and understood this saying and believed it. (Joh 2:18-22; Mt 27:40) He was resurrected, but not in his fleshly body, which was given as a ransom sacrifice; yet that fleshly body did not go into corruption, but was disposed of by God, just as a sacrifice was consumed on the altar. Jesus, when resurrected, was the same person, the same personality, in a new body made for his new dwelling place, the spiritual heavens.—Lu 24:1-7; 1Pe 3:18; Mt 20:28; Ac 2:31; Heb 13:8.

TEN. See NUMBER, NUMERAL.

TEN COMMANDMENTS. See TEN WORDS.

TENT. A collapsible shelter made of cloth or skin and supported by poles. Tents were one of the earliest types of man-made dwellings (Ge 4:20; 9:21) and were commonly used by nomadic peoples in the Middle East.—Ge 9:27; Ps 83:6.

Some details of the design and use of tents are available from the Bible. This is supplemented by knowledge of tents used by Arabs in more recent years, since it seems that these do not differ substantially from those of the Biblical period. Many scholars believe that the earliest tents were of animal skins. (Ge 3:21; Ex 26:14) Among modern-day Bedouin, tents made of blackish goat-hair cloth are customary. (Compare Ex 36: 14; Ca 1:5.) Strips of this material are sewn together, the overall size of the rectangular tent depending on the wealth of the owner and the number of occupants. The tent is supported by a number of poles about 1.5 to 2 m (5 to 7 ft) long, the highest being near the middle; it is held fast against wind by cords fastened to tent pins. (Jg 4:21) For privacy and protection from the wind, cloths are hung along the sides of the tent, but these can be raised or removed for ventilation.

It appears that in Bible times larger tents were usually divided into at least two compartments by means of hanging tent cloths. The "tent of Sarah" mentioned at Genesis 24:67 may refer to her compartment or to a tent that she alone occupied, for some wealthy men had a number of tents, and women sometimes were assigned their own tents. (Ge 13:5; 31:33) Probably mats were used on the ground inside the tent.

Tents were a distinctive feature of nomadic life, contrasting with the houses of those having a more settled life. Thus, Abraham is described as 'dwelling in tents' while he was "awaiting the city having real foundations." (Heb 11:9, 10) It seems that during their stay in Egypt, the Israelites mainly lived in houses, not tents. (Ex 12:7) But upon leaving Egypt, they reverted to tents (Ex 16:16) and used them throughout the 40 years in the wilderness. (Le 14:8; Nu 16:26) During this period two particular tents were especially important, "the tabernacle" and Moses' tent.—Ex 25:8, 9; 26:1; 33:7; see TABERNACLE; TENT OF MEETING.

Even after the Israelites conquered the Promised Land, tents were still used at times by shepherds or agricultural workers in the field. (Ca 1:8) Zechariah 12:7 likely refers to such ones, as they would be the first to be affected and in need of protection if an enemy nation came against the land to attack the city of Jerusalem. Also, tents were used by military commanders and armies when on distant expeditions.—1Sa 17:54; 2Ki 7:7; compare Da 11:45.

The long contact of the Israelites with tents undoubtedly gave rise to the poetic use of "tent" to refer to any habitation, even if it was a normal house.—Ex 12:23, 30; 1Sa 13:2; 1Ki 12:16; Ps 78:51.

Figurative Uses. This familiarity with tents is also reflected in the Bible's many figurative references to tents. Regarding the time he was approaching death, Hezekiah wrote: "My own habitation has been pulled out and removed from me like the tent of shepherds." (Isa 38:12) As a tent occupying a spot could quickly be taken down and removed, the poles taken out and the pegs pulled up, so Hezekiah's place in the land of

the living seemed transitory and easily removed. Eliphaz likened death to pulling out the tent cord, which would make a tent collapse.—Job 4:21.

Somewhat similarly, Paul used the metaphor of a tent when speaking of the human bodies of spirit-begotten Christians. A collapsible tent is a more fragile and temporary dwelling than a normal house. Though existing on earth in a mortal body of flesh, the Christians who have the spirit as a token of the heavenly life to come look forward to "a building from God," a heavenly body that is everlasting, incorruptible.—1Co 15:50-53; 2Co 5:1-5; compare 2Pe 1:13, 14.

In portraying the destruction to come upon the Jews, Jeremiah used the figure of a tent. (Jer 4:20) He likened the desolated nation to a woman whose tent was down, with its cords cut. Adding to the pathetic condition, her sons were in exile, so there was no one remaining who could help her with the work of raising and stretching the tent. (Jer 10:20) When the Babylonians destroyed Jerusalem, the city as a former collection of dwellings could be described as "the tent of the daughter of Zion" into which God had poured his rage. —La 2:4.

A "tent" also served in another figurative way in a number of instances. The tent of an individual was a place of rest and protection from the elements. (Ge 18:1) In view of the customs regarding hospitality, visitors had reason to believe that they would be cared for and respected when welcomed into someone's tent. Consequently, when Revelation 7:15 says about the great crowd that God "will spread his tent over them," it suggests protective care and security. (Ps 61:3, 4) Isaiah speaks of the preparations that God's wife, Zion, is to make for the sons she will produce. She is told to "make the place of your tent more spacious." (Isa 54:2) Thus, she enlarges the protective place for her children.

At Revelation 21:1-3, God projected John's vision into the Thousand Year Reign of Christ and said: "Look! The tent of God is with mankind, and he will reside with them [or, tent with them]." In a way foreshadowed by the tent, or tabernacle, in the wilderness, God will dwell, not personally, but *representatively* with mankind as he deals with them through "the Lamb of God," who is also the great High Priest.—Ex 25:8; 33:20; Joh 1:29; Heb 4:14.

TENTH PART.   See TITHE.

TENTMAKER.   One who makes or repairs tents. Acts 18:3 designates the trade of Paul, Aquila, and Priscilla by the Greek term *ske·no·poi·os'*. Various opinions have been offered as to the exact type of craftsman indicated by this word (whether a tentmaker, weaver of tapestry, or ropemaker); however, numerous scholars acknowledge that "there seems no reason to depart from the translation 'tent-makers.'"—*The Expositor's Greek Testament,* edited by W. Nicoll, 1967, Vol. II, p. 385.

When Paul first visited Corinth he stayed with Aquila and Priscilla "on account of being of the same trade." (Ac 18:1-3) The apostle Paul was from Tarsus in Cilicia, an area famous for its goat-hair cloth named *cilicium* from which tents were made. (Ac 21:39) Among the Jews of the first century C.E., it was considered honorable to teach a lad a trade even if he was to receive a higher education. So Paul likely gained experience in the manufacture of tents while still a youth. Tentmaking may also have been the type of work the apostle did in Thessalonica (1Th 2:9; 2Th 3:8) and other places. (Ac 20:34, 35; 1Co 4:11, 12) The work was not easy, for it is reported that the *cilicium* tended to be stiff and rough, consequently difficult to cut and sew.

TENT OF MEETING. An expression applied both to the tent of Moses (Ex 33:7) and to the sacred tabernacle erected in the wilderness. (Ex 39:32, 40; 40:2, 6, 7, 22, 24, 26, 29, 30, 32, 34, 35) For a time until the erection of the tabernacle, the tent of Moses served as a temporary sanctuary. This was because the cloud, representing Jehovah's presence, stationed itself "at" (likely, in front of) the entrance of this tent whenever Moses entered, and Jehovah communicated with Moses there. It was called the "tent of meeting," evidently because the people had to go there to inquire of Jehovah and thus, in effect, they met Jehovah there. (Ex 33:7-11) Apparently for the same reason the sacred tabernacle was termed the "tent of meeting."—See TABERNACLE.

TENT OF THE TESTIMONY. See TABERNACLE.

TEN WORDS. This translation of the Hebrew expression *'ase'reth had·deva·rim',* found only in the Pentateuch, designates the ten basic laws of the Law covenant; commonly called the Ten Commandments. (Ex 34:28; De 4:13; 10:4) This special code of laws is also spoken of as the "Words" (De 5:22) and as "the words of the covenant." (Ex 34:28) The Greek *Septuagint* (Ex 34:28; De 10:4) reads *de'ka* (ten) *lo'gous* (words), from which combination the word "Decalogue" is derived.

Source of Tablets. The Ten Words were first orally given at Mount Sinai by the angel of Jehovah. (Ex 20:1; 31:18; De 5:22; 9:10; Ac 7:38, 53;

see also Ga 3:19; Heb 2:2.) Moses then ascended the mountain to receive the Ten Words in written form on two stone tablets, along with other commandments and instructions. During his extended 40-day stay, the people grew restless and made a molten calf to worship. Descending the mountain, Moses saw this spectacle of idolatry and threw down "the tablets [that] were the workmanship of God," the very tablets upon which the Ten Words had been written, and shattered them.—Ex 24:12; 31:18–32:19; De 9:8-17; compare Lu 11:20.

Jehovah later told Moses: "Carve out for yourself two tablets of stone like the first ones, and I must write upon the tablets the words that appeared on the first tablets, which you shattered." (Ex 34:1-4) And so after another 40 days spent in the mountain, a duplicate copy of the Ten Words was obtained. These were kept by Moses in an ark of acacia wood. (De 10:1-5) The two tablets were called "the tablets of the covenant." (De 9:9, 11, 15) Evidently this is why the gold-overlaid ark later made by Bezalel, in which the tablets were eventually kept, was called "the ark of the covenant." (Jos 3:6, 11; 8:33; Jg 20:27; Heb 9:4) This legislation of the Ten Words was also called "the testimony" (Ex 25:16, 21; 40:20) and the "tablets of the Testimony" (Ex 31:18; 34:29), hence the expressions "the ark of the testimony" (Ex 25:22; Nu 4:5), and also "the tabernacle of the Testimony," that is, the tent where the Ark was housed. —Ex 38:21.

Concerning the first set of tablets, it is stated that they not only were made by Jehovah but were also "written on by God's finger," evidently denoting God's spirit. (Ex 31:18; De 4:13; 5:22; 9:10) Likewise, the second set of tablets, although carved out by Moses, were written upon by Jehovah. When, at Exodus 34:27, Moses was told, "Write down for yourself these words," reference was not to the Ten Words themselves, but, rather, as on a previous occasion (Ex 24:3, 4), he was to write down some of the other details pertaining to the covenant regulations. Hence, the pronoun "he" in Exodus 34:28b refers to Jehovah when it says: "And he [Jehovah, not Moses] proceeded to write upon the tablets the words of the covenant, the Ten Words." Verse 1 shows this to be so. Later, when recalling these events, Moses confirms that it was Jehovah who duplicated the tablets.—De 10:1-4.

Contents of the Commandments. By way of an introduction to these Ten Words is the forthright statement in the first person: "I am Jehovah your God, who have brought you out of the land of Egypt, out of the house of slaves." (Ex 20:2) This not only states who is speaking to whom but shows why the Decalogue was especially given to the Jews at that time. It was not given to Abraham.—De 5:2, 3.

The *first* commandment, "You must not have any other gods against my face," put Jehovah first. (Ex 20:3) It involved his lofty office and unique position as God Almighty, the Most High, the Supreme Sovereign. This commandment indicated that the Israelites were not to have any other gods as rivals to Jehovah.

The *second* commandment was a natural follow-up of the first in that it forbade idolatry in any shape or form as an open affront to Jehovah's glory and Personage. 'You must not make a carved image or a form like anything in the heavens, on the earth, or in the waters under the earth, nor are you to bow down to or serve them.' This prohibition is underscored with the declaration: "Because I Jehovah your God am a God exacting exclusive devotion."—Ex 20:4-6.

The *third* commandment, in its proper and logical sequence, declared: "You must not take up the name of Jehovah your God in a worthless way." (Ex 20:7) This harmonizes with the prominence attached to Jehovah's name throughout the Hebrew Scriptures (6,973 times in *NW;* see JEHOVAH [Importance of the Name]). Within just these few verses of the Ten Words (Ex 20:2-17), the name occurs eight times. The phrase "not take up" has the thought of "not pronounce" or "not lift up (carry)." To do this to God's name in "a worthless way" would be to lift up that name to a falsehood, or "in vain." The Israelites who were privileged to bear Jehovah's name as his witnesses and who became apostate were in effect taking up and carrying about Jehovah's name in a worthless way.—Isa 43:10; Eze 36:20, 21.

The *fourth* commandment stated: "Remembering the sabbath day to hold it sacred, you are to render service and you must do all your work six days. But the seventh day is a sabbath to Jehovah your God. You must not do any work, you nor your son nor your daughter, your slave man nor your slave girl nor your domestic animal nor your alien resident who is inside your gates." (Ex 20:8-10) By their holding this day as holy to Jehovah, all, even the slaves and the domestic animals, would have the benefit of refreshing rest. The Sabbath day also provided opportunity to concentrate on spiritual matters without distraction.

The *fifth* commandment, "Honor your father and your mother," may be viewed as linking together the first four, which define man's duties toward God, and the remaining commandments, which set forth man's obligations toward fellow creatures. For since parents serve as God's representatives, by keeping the fifth command one is honoring and obeying both the Creator and those creatures upon whom God has conferred authority. This command was the only one of the ten with a promise attached: "in order that your days may prove long upon the ground that Jehovah your God is giving you."—Ex 20:12; De 5:16; Eph 6:2, 3.

The next commandments in the code were stated very tersely: the *sixth,* "You must not murder"; the *seventh,* "You must not commit adultery"; the *eighth,* "You must not steal." (Ex 20:13-15) This is the way these laws are listed in the Masoretic text—from laws dealing with crimes causing the greatest harm to one's neighbor to the one causing the least, in that order. In some Greek manuscripts (Codex Alexandrinus, Codex Ambrosianus) the order is 'murder, theft, adultery'; Philo (*The Decalogue,* XII, 51) has "adultery, murder, theft"; the Codex Vaticanus, 'adultery, theft, murder.' Going next from deeds to words, the *ninth* says: "You must not testify falsely as a witness against your fellowman."—Ex 20:16.

The *tenth* commandment (Ex 20:17) was unique in that it forbade covetousness, that is, wrong desire for the property and possessions, including the wife, belonging to a fellowman. No human lawmakers originated such a law, for, indeed, there would be no way humanly possible of enforcing it. Jehovah, on the other hand, by this tenth commandment made each one directly accountable to Him as the one who sees and knows all the secret thoughts of a person's heart.—1Sa 16:7; Pr 21:2; Jer 17:10.

Other Listings of These Laws. The above division of the Ten Words as found at Exodus 20:2-17 is a natural one. It is the same as given by Josephus, Jewish historian of the first century C.E. (*Jewish Antiquities,* III, 91, 92 [v, 5]), and by the Jewish philosopher Philo, also of the first century C.E., in *The Decalogue* (XII, 51). Others, however, including Augustine, combined the two laws against foreign gods and images (Ex 20:3-6; De 5:7-10) into one commandment, and then, in order to recover a tenth, divided Exodus 20:17 (De 5:21) into two commandments, thus making a ninth against coveting a man's wife, and a tenth against coveting his house, and so forth. Augustine sought to support his theoretical division on the later parallel listing of the Decalogue at Deuteronomy 5:6-21, where two different Hebrew words in verse 21 are found ("Neither must you *desire* [form of Heb. *cha·madh'*] . . . Neither must you *selfishly crave* [form of Heb. *'a·wah'*]"), rather than on the earlier text in Exodus 20:17, where just the one verb (desire) occurs twice.

There are other minor differences in the wording between the parallel enumerations of the Ten Commandments in Exodus and Deuteronomy, but these in no way affect the force or the meaning of the laws. Whereas, in the former listing, the Ten Words are stated in formal legislative style, its later repetition is more narrative in form, for on the latter occasion Moses was merely rehearsing God's commandment in the way of a reminder. The Ten Words also appear elsewhere in still other variations, for they were often quoted or cited along with other instructions by Bible writers of both the Hebrew and Christian Greek Scriptures.—Ex 31:14; 34:14, 17, 21; Le 19:3, 11, 12; De 4:15-19; 6:14, 15; Mt 5:27; 15:4; Lu 18:20; Ro 13:9; Eph 6:2, 3.

The Ten Words were God-given, hence comprise a perfect law code. When a man "versed in the Law" asked Jesus Christ, "Teacher, which is the greatest commandment in the Law?", Jesus quoted a command that, in effect, epitomized the first four (or possibly five) of the Ten Commandments, saying: "You must love Jehovah your God with your whole heart and with your whole soul and with your whole mind." The rest of the Decalogue, Jesus then summed up in the few words of another command: "You must love your neighbor as yourself."—Mt 22:35-40; De 6:5; Le 19:18.

Christians Not Under Decalogue. Jesus was born under the Law, and he kept it perfectly, finally giving up his life as a ransom for mankind. (Ga 4:4; 1Jo 2:2) Furthermore, by his death on the torture stake, he freed those under the Law (including the basic Ten Words or Commandments) "by becoming a curse instead" of them. His death provided the 'blotting out of the handwritten document,' it being nailed to the torture stake.—Ga 3:13; Col 2:13, 14.

Nevertheless, a study of the Law with its Ten Words is essential for Christians, for it reveals God's viewpoint of matters, and it had "a shadow of the good things to come," of the reality that belongs to the Christ. (Heb 10:1; Col 2:17; Ga 6:2) Christians are "not without law toward God but under law toward Christ." (1Co 9:21) But they are not condemned as sinners by that law, for the undeserved kindness of God through Christ provides forgiveness for their errors due to fleshly weakness.—Ro 3:23, 24.

TERAH (Te'rah) [possibly from Babylonian, meaning "Ibex"].

1. Abraham's father, the eighth generation from Shem. (Lu 3:34; Ge 11:10-24; 1Ch 1:24-26) Terah, through his sons Abraham, Nahor, and Haran, became a forefather of numerous tribes. (Ge 11:27; 22:20-24; 25:1-4, 13-15; 1Ch 1:28-42; 2:1, 2) Terah began having children at 70. While Abraham is listed first, this appears to be because he is the most famous of Terah's sons rather than the firstborn. When Terah died at 205, Abraham was only 75, so Terah must have been 130 when Abraham was born. (Ge 11:26, 32; 12:4) Sarah was Abraham's half sister, likely a daughter of Terah by a different wife. (Ge 20:12) Terah's firstborn was most likely Haran, whose daughter was old enough to marry Terah's other son Nahor. —Ge 11:29.

Terah lived in Ur of the Chaldeans, and there his family grew up. (Ge 11:28) According to Joshua 24:2, Terah at one time worshiped gods other than Jehovah, perhaps the moon-god Sin, the favored deity of Ur. Nonetheless, when Jehovah called Abraham to leave Ur, Terah as family head went along to Haran where they all lived until after his death about 1943 B.C.E.—Ge 11:31, 32; Ac 7:2-4.

2. One of the campsites during Israel's wilderness wandering; its location is unknown.—Nu 33:27, 28.

TERAPHIM. Family gods or idols. (Ge 31:30, 34) Although in the plural, the designation "teraphim" can also apply to a single idol. At least some of these idols may have been the size and shape of a man. (1Sa 19:13, 16) Others must have been much smaller, able to fit inside a woman's saddle basket. (Ge 31:34) The teraphim were, on occasion, consulted for omens.—Eze 21:21; Zec 10:2.

The findings of archaeologists in Mesopotamia and adjacent areas indicate that the possession of the teraphim images had a bearing on who would receive the family inheritance. According to one tablet found at Nuzi, the possession of the household gods could under certain circumstances entitle a son-in-law to appear in court and claim the estate of his deceased father-in-law. (*Ancient Near Eastern Texts*, edited by J. Pritchard, 1974, pp. 219, 220, and ftn 51) Perhaps Rachel, with this in mind, reasoned that she was justified in taking the teraphim because of her father's deceptive dealings with her husband Jacob. (Compare Ge 31:14-16.) The importance of the teraphim with respect to inheritance rights would also explain why Laban was so anxious to recover them, even to the point of taking his brothers with him and pursuing Jacob for a distance of seven days' journey. (Ge 31:19-30) Of course, what Rachel had done was completely unknown to Jacob (Ge 31:32), and there is no indication that he ever attempted to use the teraphim to gain the inheritance from Laban's sons. Jacob had nothing to do with idols. At the latest, the teraphim would have been disposed of when Jacob hid all the foreign gods turned over to him by his household under the big tree that was close to Shechem. —Ge 35:1-4.

In Israel the idolatrous use of teraphim existed in the days of the Judges as well as the kings. (Jg 17:5; 18:14, 17, 20; Ho 3:4) It is not likely, though, that the teraphim served for purposes of inheritance in Israel, in view of God's express command against the making of images. (Ex 20:4) Also, the prophet Samuel spoke of teraphim in parallel with uncanny power, comparing the use of both to pushing ahead presumptuously (1Sa 15:23), and the teraphim were among the appendages of idolatry cleared out of Judah and Jerusalem by faithful King Josiah. (2Ki 23:24) Hence, the fact that Michal, the wife of David, had a teraphim image among her possessions suggests that her heart was not complete with Jehovah and that David either did not know about her having the teraphim image or else tolerated it because she was the daughter of King Saul.—1Sa 19:12, 13.

TERESH (Te'resh). One of two doorkeepers in the Persian palace who conspired against King Ahasuerus. Upon learning of the plot, Mordecai informed Queen Esther who, in turn, revealed it to the king. Teresh and his accomplice were hanged on a stake, and the incident was entered in the royal records.—Es 2:21-23; 6:1, 2.

TERTIUS (Ter'tius) [from Lat., meaning "Third"]. The writer or transcriber of Paul's letter to the Romans, and the only one of Paul's "secretaries" identified by name. Tertius inserts his own personal greetings to the Romans.—Ro 16:22.

TERTULLUS (Ter·tul'lus) [from Lat., diminutive of Tertius]. A public speaker who presented the Jews' case against Paul before Governor Felix in Caesarea. Of what Luke recorded, much of Tertullus' statement personally praises Felix, with only a very brief accusation against Paul, attempting to implicate him with the frequent seditions against Rome. (Ac 24:1-8) Nothing definite is known as to Tertullus' nationality, whether Jewish or Roman.

TESTICLES. Male genital glands. God's law to Israel barred from the priesthood a man having his testicles broken, as one of several disqualifying physical defects. (Le 21:17-21, 23) This high standard for the priesthood was in harmony with the holiness of the office of the priests as representatives of Jehovah's holiness before Israel. It likewise accords with the fact that Israel's priesthood symbolized the heavenly priesthood of Christ and his congregation of underpriests, among whom there is found no blemish. (Heb 7:26; Eph 5:27; Re 14:1, 5; 20:6) Furthermore, God wanted priests who could have children to succeed them. The Law provided, however, that such a defective person could eat of the holy things provided for the sustenance of the priesthood.—Le 21:21, 22.

For similar reasons an animal having its testicles squeezed, crushed, cut off, or pulled off could not be offered up as a sacrifice. (Le 22:24; compare Mal 1:6-8; 1Pe 1:19.) On this account the Israelites did not castrate their animals, for the Law required that all domestic animals slaughtered for food be brought to the sanctuary to be killed and eaten as a communion offering. The same law applied in the Promised Land for those who did not live far off from Jerusalem.—Le 17:3-5; De 12:20-25.

The Law further read: "No man castrated by crushing the testicles or having his male member cut off may come into the congregation of Jehovah." (De 23:1) Such 'castration' did not relate to congenital defects or to an accidental condition. (Compare Le 21:17-21; De 25:11, 12.) Evidently, therefore, it had to do with deliberate emasculation for immoral purposes, such as homosexuality. Such a one was to be kept out of the congregation, not being allowed to associate with it, thereby protecting its purity.

The respect that Jehovah has for man's right to have children by his wife, and for the reproductive powers He has placed in man and woman, was emphasized by the Law. Brother-in-law marriage provided for the continuance of a man's family line, name, and inheritance. (De 25:5-10) Immediately following the statement of this arrangement, the Law went on to say that if two men were struggling together and the wife of one of them grabbed the other man by his private parts in order to assist her husband (an act that could destroy the reproductive powers of the man), her hand was to be amputated. (De 25:11, 12) So the law of like for like did not here apply. (De 19:21) God did not require the destruction of her reproductive organs or those of her husband.

In this way the marriage could still be fruitful, her husband's family line being carried on through it.

In the case of the Christian congregation, persons who have been castrated are not barred from entry, for the Law has been set aside on the basis of Christ's sacrifice. (Col 2:13, 14) Nevertheless, the laws above quoted illustrate God's regard for the reproductive organs and strongly indicate that an operation that would destroy a person's procreative powers simply because he had no appreciation for that gift from God would be wrong.

Genital Organ. The Hebrew word for "flesh" (ba·sar´) is used in the Scriptures at Leviticus 15:2, 3 with reference to the man's genital organ, the penis, as separate from the testicles.—See CLEAN, CLEANNESS; compare Isa 57:8, ftn.

The male genital organ was an object of sex worship by pagans in ancient times, as it is today in some countries. Reference may be made at Ezekiel 8:17 (NW, ftn) to such worship as infecting the apostate Israelites in Ezekiel's day.

THADDAEUS
(Thad·dae´us). An apostle of Jesus Christ. (Mt 10:2, 3; Mr 3:18) He appears to be called elsewhere "Judas the son of James."—Lu 6:16; Joh 14:22; Ac 1:13; see JUDAS No. 3.

THEATER.
A structure (referred to by the Greeks as the´a·tron) where dramatic performances, tragedies, comedies, dances, musical presentations, and spectacles were staged. The theater was often the scene of immoral presentations, shunned by faithful Christians. (Eph 5:3-5) But it also served as a place of public assembly for other purposes.

It was to the theater in Ephesus that Paul's traveling companions were brought when Demetrius the silversmith stirred up a riot against these Christian missionaries. Though the apostle was willing to go before the people assembled in the theater, the disciples and some friendly commissioners of festivals and games dissuaded him. —Ac 19:23-31.

Theaters were constructed in Greece from about the fifth century B.C.E. onward, and in time they were built in various principal cities. Most Greek theaters were constructed in semicircular fashion on a hillside of concave formation. The seats might have been made of wood or stone. Aisles separated them into sections, and they were lined up in tiers on the hill's gradual incline. At the center was the or·khe´stra (a dancing or chorus area), behind which there was a raised stage backed by a ske·ne´, or background.

Ruins of theaters have been found in such places as Ephesus, Athens, and Corinth. The large theater excavated at Ephesus had 66 rows of seats and could hold an audience of about 25,000 persons. The acoustics were, and still are, so good that even a low voice from the stage can be heard in the topmost row with ease.

The Romans frequently constructed theaters as individual buildings dependent upon no natural sloping ground formation. Sometimes their theaters had a roof over the stage and a portion of the seating area. Another type, the Roman amphitheater, was a roofless circular or oval structure that enclosed a large center space or arena, from which the seats radiated in tiers. The partially standing Colosseum in Rome, finished in 80 C.E., is a noted Roman amphitheater. Herod the Great constructed theaters in various cities, including Damascus and Caesarea. Josephus said that Herod "built a theatre in Jerusalem, and after that a very large amphitheatre in the plain." —*Jewish Antiquities*, XV, 268 (viii, 1).

The Greek word the´a·tron can denote either the place where a show is presented or the "theatrical spectacle" itself. Paul wrote: "For it seems to me that God has put us the apostles last on exhibition as men appointed to death, because we have become a theatrical spectacle [the´a·tron] to the world, and to angels, and to men." (1Co 4:9) Paul thus alluded to the customary closing event of Roman gladiatorial contests in the amphitheater arena when certain participants were brought out unclad and defenseless, being subjected to butchery and certain death.

The Greeks and Romans customarily led criminals condemned to death through the theater, where they were subjected to ridicule by the assembled throngs. Paul wrote to the Hebrew Christians, apparently referring to this practice. Though there is no record to the effect that these Christians had been subjected to that treatment, they had endured sufferings that were comparable. The apostle urged them: "Keep on remembering the former days in which, after you were enlightened, you endured a great contest under sufferings, sometimes while you were being exposed as in a theater both to reproaches and tribulations, and sometimes while you became sharers with those who were having such an experience."—Heb 10:32, 33.

THEBEZ
(The´bez). A city having a strong tower. When Abimelech had taken Thebez and was attempting to assault the tower where the populace had sought refuge, a woman pitched an upper millstone upon him from atop the wall. His skull shattered by the blow, Abimelech had his

attendant put him to death so that no one could say, "It was a woman that killed him."—Jg 9:50-54; 2Sa 11:21.

Thebez is tentatively connected with modern Tubas, about 15 km (9.5 mi) NNE of Shechem, although no suitable remains have been found.

THEOPHILUS (The·oph'i·lus) [Loved by God; Friend of God]. The person to whom Luke addressed both his Gospel and the Acts of Apostles. (Lu 1:3, 4; Ac 1:1) His being called "most excellent" may indicate a high position of some kind, or it may simply be an expression of high esteem. Theophilus apparently was a Christian, having been orally taught about Jesus Christ and his ministry. Luke's written statement served to assure him of the certainty of what he had learned previously by word of mouth.

THESSALONIANS, LETTERS TO THE.
Two inspired letters of the Christian Greek Scriptures, perhaps the first to be composed by the apostle Paul, who identifies himself as the writer of both. (1Th 1:1; 2:18; 2Th 1:1; 3:17) At the time these letters were committed to writing, Silvanus (Silas) and Timothy were with Paul. (1Th 1:1; 2Th 1:1) This points to Corinth as the place from which the letters were sent, as there is no record that all three men labored together again after their stay at Corinth in the course of Paul's second missionary journey. (Ac 18:5) Since the apostle's 18-month activity in Corinth appears to have begun in the autumn of 50 C.E., likely it was at about this time that the first letter was written to the Thessalonians. (Ac 18:11; see CHRONOLOGY [The later apostolic period].) The second letter must have followed not long thereafter, probably about 51 C.E.

In all outstanding catalogs of the second, third, and fourth centuries C.E., both letters are listed as canonical. They also harmonize fully with the rest of the Scriptures in admonishing God's servants to maintain fine conduct at all times. Noteworthy, too, is the emphasis placed on prayer in these letters. Paul, along with his fellow workers, always remembered the Thessalonians in prayer (1Th 1:2; 2:13; 2Th 1:3, 11; 2:13), and the apostle encouraged them: "Pray incessantly. In connection with everything give thanks." (1Th 5:17, 18) "Brothers, continue in prayer for us."—1Th 5:25; 2Th 3:1.

HIGHLIGHTS OF FIRST THESSALONIANS

Encouragement and counsel to a relatively new congregation

Written by Paul about 50 C.E., a few months after he had left Thessalonica because of mob violence

Commendation for the congregation (1:1-10)

Paul warmly commends the Thessalonians for their faithful work and endurance

The Thessalonians have become an example to other believers in accepting the word under tribulation and with the joy that God's spirit produces

Everywhere it is being reported how they abandoned idolatry and turned to slaving for the living God and to waiting for Jesus

Paul's example when among them (2:1-12)

After suffering insolent treatment at Philippi, Paul drew strength from God and preached boldly to the Thessalonians

Paul shunned flattery, covetousness, and glory-seeking

He avoided becoming a burden to the brothers, but instead treated them gently as a nursing mother would and exhorted them as a loving father

Encouragement to remain firm in the face of persecution (2:13-3:13)

The brothers in Thessalonica, after accepting the message proclaimed to them as the word of God, were persecuted by their fellow countrymen; the same things have happened in Judea, where Christians are suffering at the hands of Jews

Paul has greatly desired to see the Thessalonians; when he could no longer bear the lack of news about them, he sent Timothy, and Timothy has just returned with good news about their spiritual condition

Paul prays for their continued increase

Admonition regarding attitude and conduct (4:1-5:28)

Walk more fully in the course pleasing to God; abstain from fornication

Love the brothers to an even greater degree; work with your hands so that even people outside can see that you walk decently

Comfort one another with the hope that at Christ's presence spirit-begotten believers who have died will be raised first and united with Christ; afterward those still living will join him and the resurrected ones

Jehovah's day is coming as a thief—when they say: "Peace and security!" sudden destruction will come; in view of this, remain spiritually awake, protected by faith and love as a breastplate and by the hope of salvation as a helmet

Have deep regard for those presiding in the congregation; be peaceable, pursue what is good, always rejoice, render thanksgiving, make sure of all things, hold fast to what is fine, and abstain from wickedness

HIGHLIGHTS OF SECOND THESSALONIANS

A letter to correct a wrong view regarding Christ's presence and to offer counsel on how to treat disorderly persons

Written by Paul shortly after his first letter to the Thessalonians

---

Relief to come at the revelation of Christ (1:1-12)

The Thessalonians are commended for their endurance and faith while experiencing persecutions and distress

Relief will come at Christ's revelation; then Jesus Christ, accompanied by powerful angels, will destroy those not obeying the good news and will be glorified in connection with his holy ones

Paul prays that the Thessalonians will be counted worthy so that the Lord Jesus' name will be glorified in them

Man of lawlessness to be revealed before the presence of Christ (2:1-17)

The Thessalonians are admonished not to be unsettled or excited by any message suggesting that Jehovah's day is already upon them

The apostasy has to come first, and the man of lawlessness has to be revealed; he will lift himself up over every object of reverence and display himself to be a god

When he that acts as a restraint is removed, the lawless one will be revealed, he whose presence is marked by lying signs and every unrighteous deception in order to deceive those who are perishing

Jesus Christ will bring him to nothing at the manifestation of his presence

How to deal with disorderly persons (3:1-18)

Withdraw from disorderly ones, those meddling in what does not concern them, those disregarding the order: "If anyone does not want to work, neither let him eat"

Mark such ones as persons with whom there is to be no fraternizing, but admonish them as brothers so that they may change their ways

Background for First Thessalonians. Practically from the beginning the congregation to which First Thessalonians was addressed experienced persecution. After arriving at Thessalonica, Paul preached in the synagogue there for three Sabbaths. A considerable number of persons became believers, and a congregation was established. Fanatical Jews, however, stirred up mob violence. Not finding Paul and Silas at the home of Jason, the mob dragged Jason and certain other brothers before the city rulers, accusing them of sedition. Only upon giving "sufficient security" were Jason and the others released. This prompted the brothers to send Paul and Silas to Beroea by night, evidently for the sake of the congregation and the safety of the two men.—Ac 17:1-10.

Thereafter, besides continued persecution (1Th 2:14), the congregation seemingly experienced great sorrow over losing one(s) of their number in death. (4:13) Aware of the pressure that was being brought to bear against the new congregation and very much concerned about its effect, Paul dispatched Timothy to comfort and strengthen the Thessalonians. Earlier the apostle had tried to visit them twice, but 'Satan cut across his path.' —2:17–3:3.

Receiving Timothy's encouraging report about the faithfulness and love of the Thessalonians, Paul rejoiced. (1Th 3:6-10) However, they needed further encouragement and admonition to resist weaknesses of the flesh. For this reason Paul, besides commending the Thessalonians for their faithful endurance (1:2-10; 2:14; 3:6-10) and comforting them with the resurrection hope (4:13-18), exhorted them to continue following a course approved by God and to do so more fully. (4:1, 2) The apostle, among other things, counseled them to abstain from fornication (4:3-8), love one another in fuller measure, work with their hands (4:9-12), stay awake spiritually (5:6-10), have regard for those working hard among them, "admonish the disorderly, speak consolingly to the depressed souls, support the weak, be long-suffering toward all," and "abstain from every form of wickedness" (5:11-22).

Background for Second Thessalonians. The faith of the Christians at Thessalonica was growing exceedingly, their love for one another was increasing, and they were continuing to endure persecution and tribulation faithfully. Therefore, the apostle Paul, as in his first letter, commended them and encouraged them to continue standing firm.—2Th 1:3-12; 2:13-17.

Some in the congregation, however, were wrongly contending that the presence of Jesus Christ was imminent. Possibly even a letter wrongly attributed to Paul was interpreted as indicating that "the day of Jehovah is here." (2Th 2:1, 2) This may have been why the apostle made a point of the genuineness of his second letter, saying: "Here is my greeting, Paul's, in my own hand, which is a sign in every letter; this is the way I write." (3:17) Not wanting the brothers to be seduced into accepting erroneous teaching, Paul showed that other events had to precede the coming of Jehovah's day. He wrote: "It will not come unless the apostasy comes first and the man of lawlessness gets revealed."—2:3.

A problem that had already existed earlier in the congregation still needed attention. In his first letter to the Thessalonians, Paul had told them: "We exhort you, brothers, . . . to make it your aim to live quietly and to mind your own business and work with your hands, just as we ordered you; so that you may be walking decently as regards people outside and not be needing anything." (1Th 4:10-12) There were those in the congregation who had not taken this admonition to heart. Hence Paul ordered such persons to work with quietness and eat food they had themselves earned, adding: "But if anyone is not obedient to our word through this letter, keep this one marked, stop associating with him, that he may become ashamed. And yet do not be considering him as an enemy, but continue admonishing him as a brother."—2Th 3:10-15.

THESSALONICA (Thes·sa·lo·ni′ca). The principal seaport of Macedonia where Paul established a Christian congregation about the year 50 C.E.; now the city is called Salonika (or, Thessaloniki). (PICTURE, Vol. 2, p. 749) Originally, a nearby town named Therme, meaning "Hot Spring," was one of the some 26 towns destroyed by Cassander, who then built Thessalonica in 316 or 315 B.C.E. He named it after his wife, the sister of Alexander the Great. This new city was situated on the W side of the Chalcidice Peninsula, on the Thermaicus Sinus (now called the Gulf of Salonika), at the junction between the road running N to the Danube and the main road (the paved Via Egnatia built by the Romans) that extended for hundreds of miles across Macedonia to the Adriatic Sea.

Macedonia was divided into four districts before the middle of the second century B.C.E., with Thessalonica the capital of the second. A few years later when Macedonia became a Roman province, Thessalonica was made the administrative seat of its provincial government. So, when the apostle Paul and Silas arrived there, about 120 km (75 mi) W of Philippi, they found it to be a thriving metropolis of quite some importance.

For three Sabbaths, Paul preached in Thessalonica's synagogue. As a result, some Jews and a great multitude of Greek proselytes became believers and associated themselves with Paul and Silas; among them were "not a few of the principal women." (Ac 17:1-4) How long Paul remained there is not disclosed, though it was long enough for him and his companion to obtain work so they could support themselves. Although as an apostle Paul had the authority to receive material help from those to whom he ministered spiritual things, he set the example that 'a person should eat food he himself earns.' (1Co 9:4-18; 1Th 2:9; 2Th 3:7-12) This was probably done partly because of the tendency toward idleness that some there had. During his stay there Paul received from the brothers in Philippi two different gifts supplying things he needed.—Php 4:16.

In time those Thessalonian Jews that rejected Paul's message rounded up a mob of idlers from the marketplace and assaulted the house of Jason where Paul was staying. But when they learned that the object of their search was not there, they dragged Jason and other believers off to the city rulers, that is, "the politarchs," according to the literal Greek. (Ac 17:5-9; *Int*) It is of special interest that inscriptions from that period have been found in and about Thessalonica that refer to certain of their local officials as politarchs.

For safety's sake, Paul and Silas were sent away at night to Beroea by the Thessalonian brothers. There Paul found the Beroeans 'more noble-minded than those in Thessalonica, in that they not only received the word with great eagerness but also carefully examined the Scriptures daily as to whether what the apostle said was so.' Soon, however, trouble developed when opposing Jews arrived from Thessalonica and stirred up a mob, making it again necessary for Paul to slip away secretly.—Ac 17:10-15.

In less than a year after leaving Thessalonica, Paul, by now down in Corinth, wrote his first letter to the Thessalonians. He had sent Timothy to comfort and encourage them and had received Timothy's good report. In the letter he commended them for their fine example "to all the believers in Macedonia and in Achaia" and urged them not to be discouraged because of the persecution. (1Th 1:1-8; 3:1-13; 4:1) This letter may well have been the first of Paul's canonical writings and, with the probable exception of Matthew's Gospel, the first book of the Christian Greek Scriptures to be put into writing. Shortly thereafter Paul wrote a second letter to the Thessalonians, that they might not be turned aside by false teachers. —2Th 1:1; 2:1-3.

Over the years Paul no doubt revisited Thessalonica on occasions when passing through Macedonia in the course of his travels. (Ac 20:1-3; 1Ti 1:3) And certain Thessalonians who are mentioned by name, Aristarchus and Secundus, were traveling companions of Paul. (Ac 20:4; 27:2) Demas, who forsook Paul in Rome, went to Thessalonica, possibly his hometown.—2Ti 4:10.

THEUDAS (Theu'das). A rebel who started an insurrection with a following of about 400 men sometime before 6 C.E. By using this Theudas as his first example of a movement that caused no more trouble after its leader was put to death, the Pharisee Gamaliel persuaded the Sanhedrin not to bother the youthful Christian congregation so soon after Jesus' death.—Ac 5:34-40.

THIEF. One who deliberately takes that which belongs to another without permission, especially one who practices fraud and deception or who steals secretly. The ways of thieves were much the same in the past as today. They came to steal usually at night (Job 24:14; Jer 49:9; Mt 24:43; Lu 12:39; Joh 10:10; 1Th 5:2-5; 2Pe 3:10; Re 3:3; 16:15), and one of their common entrances was through a window. (Joe 2:9) On the other hand, robbers and highwaymen lay in wait and fell upon their victims in lonely areas, where it was virtually impossible to get help. Often they did not hesitate to use violence or to threaten and endanger the lives of those whose valuables they seized.—Jg 9:25; Lu 10:30, 36; 2Co 11:26.

The original-language terms rendered "rob" and "robber" can also refer to withholding from another what is rightfully his, or getting things from others by fraudulent means or by appropriating to one's own use that which one was obligated to give to others. By failing to pay tithes for the support of true worship at the temple, the Jews of Malachi's time were 'robbing God.' (Mal 3:8, 9) Proverbs 28:24 speaks of a man robbing his father or his mother, evidently meaning depriving his parents in some way of what was rightfully theirs. Jesus Christ condemned the money changers for having made the temple into "a cave of robbers." This suggests that the money changers were charging exorbitant fees for their services.—Mt 21:12, 13.

In his second letter to the Corinthians, the apostle Paul wrote: "Other congregations I robbed by accepting provisions in order to minister to you." (2Co 11:8) There was nothing fraudulent about Paul's receiving provisions from others. But evidently he spoke as though he had robbed those congregations in the sense of having used what he had received from them to supply his needs while laboring, not with them, but in behalf of the Corinthians.

In some cases, stealing may refer to the justified act of taking what one has a right to take, the emphasis being on the *stealthy manner* in which the act is executed. For example, Israelites 'stole' the body of Saul from the public square of Beth-shan. (2Sa 21:12) The aunt of young Jehoash saved his life by 'stealing him away from among his brothers,' who were killed by wicked Athaliah.—2Ki 11:1, 2; 2Ch 22:11.

Condemned by God. Most of the Biblical references to stealing, however, pertain to the unlawful taking of what belongs to someone else. Jehovah's law to Israel explicitly stated: "You must not steal." (Ex 20:15; Le 19:11, 13; De 5:19; Mt 19:18) A thief had to make twofold, fourfold, or as much as fivefold compensation, depending upon what the Law outlined. If he could not do so, he was sold into slavery, evidently regaining his freedom upon making full compensation. (Ex 22:1-12) In addition to making compensation, the disgraced thief (Jer 2:26) was to bring a guilt offering and have the priest make atonement for his sins.—Le 6:2-7.

Eventually the nation of Israel came to disregard these laws, and as a consequence, Jehovah allowed robbers and thieves from within and from without to plague the nation. (De 28:29, 31; Eze 7:22) Fraudulent practices, especially the oppression of poor and needy persons, became common.—Isa 1:23; 3:14; Jer 7:9-11; 21:12; 22:3; Eze 22:29; Mic 2:2.

While the thief who steals for hunger's sake may not be as reprehensible as one who, like Achan and Judas Iscariot, steals out of greed and because of a bad heart (Jos 7:11, 20, 21; Pr 6:30; Mt 15:19; Joh 12:4-6), those desiring God's approval cannot be guilty of thievery. (Isa 61:8; Ro 2:21) Although Christians are not under the Mosaic Law, they are under command to love their fellowman. "Love does not work evil to one's neighbor"; therefore, thievery has no place among Christians. (Ro 13:9, 10; Mt 22:39; Jas 2:8) Any thief wanting to live under God's Kingdom rule must repent of his former course of conduct and learn to do hard work for a living. (1Co 6:10; Eph 4:28; 1Pe 4:15) And the genuinely repentant ex-thief can rest assured of Jehovah's forgiveness.—Eze 33:14-16.

A Hebrew idiom literally meaning "steal the heart" has the sense "outwit."—Ge 31:20, 26, ftn; compare 2Sa 15:6.

THIGH. That part of the leg that extends from the hip to the knee. Since it is on a person's side, the Hebrew word also may refer to the side of something, as "the side" of the tabernacle, or of an altar.—Ex 40:24; 2Ki 16:14.

The sword was worn at the side, on the thigh. (Ex 32:27; Jg 3:16, 21; Ca 3:8; Ps 45:3) In Revelation 19:11-21, Christ Jesus is portrayed as riding a white war mount into the battle against "the wild beast" and the kings of the earth with their armies. His title "King of kings and Lord of lords" is plainly announced in writing on his outer garment at the thigh, where usually the sword of authority is worn.

The drawers of the priests in Israel extended from the hips and to the thighs, that is, to where the thighs ended, so that their nakedness was well covered when they served at the sanctuary and Jehovah's altar. Otherwise, they would die. —Ex 28:42, 43.

When swearing an oath, a custom occasionally followed was for the swearer to put his hand under the thigh of the person to whom it was sworn. (Ge 24:2-4, 9; 47:29-31) As to the significance of this, see ATTITUDES AND GESTURES (Swearing). The practice of slapping the thigh denoted grief, sorrow, or remorse.—Jer 31:19; Eze 21:12.

Reproductive Organs. The thigh being in the general area of the body in which the reproductive organs are located, offspring are said to 'issue out of the upper thigh.' (Ge 46:26; Ex 1:5; Jg 8:30) This sheds light on the nature of the punishment to come upon a woman found guilty of secret adultery.

In case a husband suspected his wife of unfaithfulness, he was to bring her to the priest. The priest made the woman stand before Jehovah, took some holy water (evidently pure, fresh water), sprinkled into it some dust from the tabernacle floor, and washed or wiped into it the cursings he had written down. After swearing to her innocence, she was required to drink the water. If guilty, her 'thigh fell away' and her belly swelled. If she was innocent, no harm would come upon her.—Nu 5:12-31.

What was meant by the 'falling away of the thigh' of an adulterous woman?

The thigh is apparently used as an inoffensive substitution in this passage to refer to the sexual organs. (Compare Ge 46:26.) Logically the punishment affected those organs that were involved in committing the wrong. (Compare Mr 9:43-47.) The expression "fall away" is understood to mean "waste away" (*The Holy Bible*, translated by the Catholic Biblical Association of America), "shrink" (*Da*) or "shrivel" (*Mo*), and may suggest that the sex organs atrophied and that there was a loss of fertility and ability to conceive. The fact that the innocent wife was to be made pregnant by her husband would seem to indicate that future pregnancy would be denied the adulterous woman.

(Nu 5:28) Moreover, the belly of the guilty wife would swell because of the curse, but not as a result of the blessing of pregnancy.

This was by no means a trial by ordeal that sometimes required a virtual miracle to survive, such as those practiced in the Dark Ages. There was nothing in the water itself to cause the affliction. However, it was holy water and had in it holy ground or dust and the writing of the cursings washed off in it. Therefore, it contained powerful symbolisms, and it was drunk before Jehovah and with a solemn oath to him. There was no uncertainty as to the outcome of matters. If the woman was guilty, Jehovah caused the drink to have miraculous potency to produce the deserved results. Adultery carried the death penalty, but in this instance there were not the required two witnesses. (Nu 35:30; De 19:15) Also, usually in this case the identity of the guilty man, who would likewise be worthy of death, had not been revealed.

THINKING ABILITY. The Hebrew term *mezim·mah'* is used to designate thinking ability, or the ability to give wise and thoughtful consideration to a matter, based on thorough knowledge (Pr 5:2; 8:12); the schemes, devices, and foolish ideas of wicked men (Ps 10:2, 4; 21:11; 37:7; 139:19, 20; Pr 12:2; 24:8; Jer 11:15); or the purposeful 'ideas' of Jehovah God or of his "heart" (Job 42:2; Jer 23:20; 30:24; 51:11).

One of the aims of the Proverbs is to give to a young man knowledge and thinking ability. (Pr 1:1-4) The information contained in the Proverbs enables an individual to formulate wholesome thoughts and ideas that can give purposeful direction to his life. Thinking ability safeguards him from following a wrong course and associating with those who would influence him toward bad, as it helps him to see what such action would lead to. This results in blessing for the individual. Wisdom and thinking ability safeguard him from engaging in activities leading to calamity and thus prove to be life to his soul. He enjoys security, not needing to fear that justice might catch up with him for having become guilty of wrongdoing.—Pr 3:21-25.

However, the one who truly exercises thinking ability may also become an object of hatred. This could be the thought expressed at Proverbs 14:17: "The man of thinking abilities is hated." Often persons who are not thinkers themselves look unfavorably upon those who utilize their mental faculties. Also, in principle, those who exercise their minds in doing God's will are hated. As Jesus Christ said: "Because you are no part of the world, but I have chosen you out of the world, on this account the world hates you." (Joh 15:19) Of course, the original-language term for "thinking abilities" at Proverbs 14:17 can embrace malicious thinking. Therefore, the text may also mean that a man who devises evil is hated, and some translations read accordingly: "And a man of wicked devices is hated."—*JP, Ro.*

THISTLE [Heb., *dar·dar'*; Gr. *tri'bo·los*]. Any of a variety of plants having prickly, irregular-edged leaves, tough stems, and bearing round or cylindrical heads that produce soft and silky purple, yellow, or white flowers. Adam, and later his descendants, had to contend with troublesome thistles when cultivating the cursed ground. (Ge 3:17, 18) Since their seeds are scattered by the wind, thistles readily gain a foothold in neglected and desolated areas. (See Ho 10:8.) Jesus Christ referred to thistles in illustrating that people, just like plants, are recognized by their fruits. (Mt 7:16) In Palestine it is not uncommon to see a number of star thistles being driven along as a rolling mass by fall winds, a feature perhaps alluded to at Psalm 83:13 and Isaiah 17:13.

THOMAS (Thom'as) [from Aramaic, meaning "Twin"]. This apostle of Jesus Christ was called "The Twin," or Didymous. (Mt 10:3; Mr 3:18; Lu 6:15; Joh 11:16, ftn) He appears to have been somewhat impetuous in expressing his feelings or in voicing his doubts. However, upon having his doubts removed, Thomas did not hesitate to make acknowledgment of his belief.

When Jesus proposed returning to Judea that he might awaken Lazarus from death, Thomas declared: "Let us also go, that we may die with him." (Joh 11:16) Since the Judeans had shortly before this time sought to stone Jesus (Joh 11:7, 8), Thomas perhaps had in mind encouraging the other disciples to accompany Jesus even though this might result in their joining Lazarus or Jesus in death.

Thomas showed a doubting attitude in response to Jesus' comment about going away to prepare a place for the apostles, saying: "Lord, we do not know where you are going. How do we know the way?" (Joh 14:2-6) Similarly, after hearing about Jesus' resurrection, Thomas stated: "Unless I see in his hands the print of the nails and stick my finger into the print of the nails and stick my hand into his side, I will certainly not believe." Eight days later Thomas had the opportunity to do this when Jesus again appeared to the disciples. But whether Thomas actually did feel the wounds on this occasion is not stated. He was nevertheless convinced and exclaimed: "My

Lord and my God!" Christ then mildly reproved him, saying: "Happy are those who do not see and yet believe."—Joh 20:24-29.

THORN. Any of numerous thorny or prickly plants. Over 70 varieties of thorny plants have been reported as growing in Israel, among them being the thorny burnet, the thorny caper, the acanthus, the boxthorn, and hawthorns. Although thorns proved to be troublesome to man, they were not altogether useless. Thorny plants were employed as hedges (Ho 2:6) and for fuel (Ec 7:6), and they served as food for asses, camels, and goats. In more recent times, as may have been the case anciently, the boxthorn and the bramble in particular have been used for hedges, and the thorny burnet has been cut up as fuel for limekilns.—Isa 33:12.

The effects of the cursed ground, with its thorns and thistles, were keenly felt by the descendants of Adam (Ge 3:17, 18), so that Noah's father Lamech spoke of "the pain of our hands resulting from the ground which Jehovah has cursed." (Ge 5:29) After the Flood, Jehovah blessed Noah and his sons, stating that his purpose for them was to fill the earth. (Ge 9:1) God's curse on the ground was apparently lifted. (Ge 13:10) However, Jehovah did not, as in perfect Adam's case, tell Noah and his family to 'subdue the earth.' (Compare Ge 1:28 with Ge 8:21–9:2.) This suggests that imperfect man, without divine guidance, could never subdue the earth in the way God had originally purposed. Man would continue experiencing difficulties in cultivating the soil, including having to fight such troublesome plants as thorns and thistles. Undoubtedly man's mismanagement of earth's resources has increased his problems in this regard.

In the Promised Land, "a land flowing with milk and honey" (Ex 3:8), the Israelites had to work to keep the land free of thorns and other weeds, as these quickly take over neglected or desolated land. (Isa 5:6; 7:23-25; 34:13) Eventually, through disobedience to Jehovah, Israel brought spiritual ruin to the nation, God's "inheritance," and this was reflected both figuratively and literally in their laboring in vain, sowing wheat but reaping thorns.—Jer 12:7, 13.

As highlighted by Jesus' illustration concerning the sower, thorns threaten the growth of cultivated crops. (Mt 13:7; Lu 8:7) So before a field covered with thorns and thistles was cultivated, these troublesome plants were removed, generally by burning the field over. (Heb 6:8) Thorns also presented somewhat of a fire hazard. Especially at harvesttime, when the thorns alongside the

THORNBUSH

standing grain are dry, they readily catch fire, and an entire field can be consumed as the fire spreads from the thorns to the standing grain. —Ex 22:6.

In mockery, Roman soldiers braided a crown of thorns and placed it on Jesus' head. (Mr 15:17; Joh 19:2) While the particular plant in question has been linked by many with *Paliurus spina-christi*, a shrub growing to a height of 6 m (20 ft) and having flexible branches with stiff thorns, no certain identification is possible.

Figurative Use. Frequently "thorns" are mentioned in a figurative, or an illustrative, sense. The Assyrians, although interwoven like thorns, were to be consumed as fully dry stubble. (Na 1:10) Thorns are used to denote people, even rulers, whose actions being bad, are in line for adverse judgment. (2Ki 14:9, 10; Isa 9:18, 19; 10:17-19) Wicked opposers of Jehovah's servant are depicted as being extinguished like a fire of thornbushes. (Ps 118:10, 12) Jesus Christ referred to thorns when illustrating the truth that individuals are known by their fruits.—Mt 7:16.

Thorns designate persons and things that cause injury and are troublesome. (Nu 33:55; Pr 22:5; Eze 28:24) Paul's "thorn in the flesh" (2Co 12:7) may have been an affliction of his eyes or another part of his body (see Ac 23:1-5; Ga 4:15; 6:11) or perhaps the false apostles and other disturbers who challenged Paul's apostleship and work. (See 2Co 11:5, 6, 12-15; Ga 1:6-9; 5:12; 6:17.) Jehovah, through his prophet Jeremiah, compared the hearts of the men of Judah and the inhabitants of Jerusalem to ground covered with thorns, that is, with untruth, injustice, and unrighteousness. (Jer 4:1-4; compare Ho 10:12, 13.) Fittingly the replacement of thorns by trees represents the restoration of divine favor.—Isa 55:13; see BRAMBLE; BRIER; BUSH; LOTUS TREE; WEEDS.

THORNBUSH. See BUSH.

THREE TAVERNS. A resting-place attested to in ancient writings, situated on the Appian Way, the well-known highway that ran from Rome to Brundusium by way of Capua. The place perhaps got its name from three inns where travelers could stop to rest and refresh themselves. The site of Three Taverns is 58 km (36 mi) SE of Rome. The Marketplace of Appius was about 15 km (9.5 mi) farther down the Appian Way. A few Roman ruins are all that remain today at the site. Having heard about Paul's coming, part of the delegation of the Christians from Rome waited at Three Taverns while the rest traveled as far as the Marketplace of Appius.—Ac 28:13-15.

THRESHING. The process of releasing grain from its stalk and chaff. If gleaners had a small amount to thresh, or if the grain was of small size like cumin, or if the threshing was done secretly during dangerous times, a rod or flail was used to beat the grain by hand, either on the ground or in a winepress.—Jg 6:11; Ru 2:17; Isa 28:27.

The threshing floor, however, was the location of normal threshing operations. Usually situated on a higher elevation exposed to the wind, it consisted of a flat circular area, up to 15 m (50 ft) in diameter, made either of stone or hard-packed earth. Threshing floors not privately owned were often clustered together near a village for communal use. The sheaves of barley or wheat, the principal grains of Palestine, were spread out on the floor (today generally to a depth of 30 to 46 cm [12 to 18 in.]). The treading by bulls or other animals, as they constantly circled the floor, gradually broke down the straw and freed the grain from the chaff. The animals were not muzzled while treading the grain.—De 25:4; Ho 10:11; 1Co 9:9, 10.

Threshing instruments pulled by animals speeded up the process and were more thorough than animal hooves alone. (Isa 41:15; Am 1:3) Models used in more modern times are either broad flat heavy sledges with sharp teeth of stone or of iron on their underside or frames that pull heavy cylindrical rollers fitted with knives to cut and break down the grain stalks. Such sledges and roller devices covered an additional swath each round, and the added weight of the driver riding on top increased the effectiveness.—Compare Isa 28:28.

After the grain had been thoroughly threshed, and turned over several times in the process, it was winnowed.—See WINNOWING.

Because of providing an open, level space, threshing floors were often used for other purposes. The mourning rites for Jacob were held on the threshing floor of Atad near the Jordan. (Ge 50:10, 11) At Jehovah's direction, David purchased the threshing floor of Araunah (Ornan), built there an altar, and made a sacrifice to Jehovah. (2Sa 24:16-25; 1Ch 21:15-28) Later this threshing floor became the site of Solomon's temple. (2Ch 3:1) When Jehoshaphat and Ahab conferred about warring against Syria, their thrones were set up on a threshing floor at the entrance of the gate of Samaria.—1Ki 22:10.

Figurative Use. In a figurative sense, the treatment the stalks of grain receive on the threshing floor is a very fitting symbol of how Jehovah's enemies will be beaten and cut to pieces. (Isa 41:15; Jer 51:33; Mic 4:12, 13; Hab 3:12) Threshing also illustrates the crushing treatment men sometimes mete out to others. (2Ki 13:7) Or the separation of wheat from chaff may depict the separation of the righteous from the wicked by Jehovah's judgment. (Mt 3:12) In yet another sense, a long and bountiful threshing denotes prosperity and Jehovah's blessing.—Le 26:5; Joe 2:24.

THROAT. See NECK.

THRONE.

The Hebrew term *kis·se'* basically means "seat" (1Sa 4:13), "chair" (2Ki 4:10), or a seat of special importance such as a "throne" (1Ki 22:10). Its application is not limited to the seats of ruling monarchs (1Ki 2:19; Ne 3:7; Es 3:1; Eze 26:16), nor does it strictly refer to a seat with a high back and armrests. Eli, for instance, while at the gate of Shiloh, fell backward from his *kis·se'*, evidently a backless seat. (1Sa 4:13, 18) The Greek term *thro'nos* generally refers to a high stool, with back, arms, and a footstool.

Isaiah 14:9 intimates that thrones were universally used by monarchs, the Bible specifically mentioning the thrones of Egypt (Ge 41:40; Ex 11:5; 12:29), Assyria (Jon 3:6), Babylon (Isa 14:4, 13; Da 5:20), Persia (Es 1:2; 5:1), and Moab (Jg 3:17, 20). Archaeologists believe that they have found thrones used by rulers or their associates of all these powers, except Moab. An ivory panel, thought to depict a Canaanite throne and footstool, was found at Megiddo. Generally, these non-Israelite thrones have backs and armrests, being richly carved or ornamented. One extant Egyptian throne was made of wood overlaid with gold, while an Assyrian one was of wrought iron with ivory carvings. The throne seems customarily to have been placed on a dais, or raised platform, and in most cases a footstool was present.

The only throne of a ruler of Israel described in detail is the one Solomon made. (1Ki 10:18-20; 2Ch 9:17-19) It appears to have been located in "the Porch of the Throne," one of the buildings that stood on Mount Moriah in Jerusalem. (1Ki 7:7) It was 'a great ivory throne overlaid with refined gold with a round canopy behind it and armrests.' Although ivory could have been the basic material in this royal chair, the construction technique generally followed at the temple would seem to indicate that it was made of wood, overlaid with refined gold and richly ornamented with inlaid panels of ivory. To the observer, such a throne would appear to be made entirely of ivory and gold. After mentioning six steps leading to the throne, the record continues: "Two lions were standing beside the armrests. And there were twelve lions standing there upon the six steps, on this side and on that side." (2Ch 9:17-19) The symbolism of the lion denoting ruling authority is appropriate. (Ge 49:9, 10; Re 5:5) The 12 lions appear to have corresponded to the 12 tribes of Israel, possibly symbolizing their subjection to and support of the ruler on this throne. Attached in some way to the throne was a footstool of gold. By its description this ivory-and-gold throne—in its lofty, canopied position with the majestic lions in front—transcends any throne of that time period, whether discovered by archaeologists, depicted on the monuments, or described in the inscriptions. As the chronicler truthfully observed: "No other kingdom had any made just like it."—2Ch 9:19.

Figurative Usage. "Throne" figuratively signifies a seat of ruling authority (1Ki 2:12; 16:11) or the kingly authority and sovereignty itself (Ge 41:40; 1Ch 17:14; Ps 89:44); a reigning government or royal administration (2Sa 14:9); sovereign control over a territory (2Sa 3:10); and a position of honor (1Sa 2:7, 8; 2Ki 25:28).

What is "Jehovah's throne"?

Jehovah, whom even "the heaven of the heavens" cannot contain, does not have to sit on a literal throne or chair. (1Ki 8:27) He does, however, picture his royal authority and sovereignty by the symbol of a throne. Certain ones of God's servants were privileged to see a vision of his throne. (1Ki 22:19; Isa 6:1; Eze 1:26-28; Da 7:9; Re 4:1-3) The Psalms describe Jehovah's throne, his majesty or power, his position as Supreme Judge, as being established on righteousness and justice "from long ago."—Ps 89:14; 93:2; 97:2.

Jehovah extended his throne to earth in a typical, specific way in his dealings with the sons of Israel. Since the one ruling in Israel was to be "a king whom Jehovah your God will choose," who would rule in Jehovah's name over Jehovah's people and according to Jehovah's law, his throne was really "Jehovah's throne."—De 17:14-18; 1Ch 29:23.

Besides his kingly identity with the royal line of Judah, Jehovah was enthroned in Israel in another sense as well. As Jeremiah expressed it: "There is the glorious throne on high from the start; it is the place of our sanctuary." (Jer 17:12) Jehovah was spoken of as "sitting upon the cherubs" that were on the propitiatory cover of the ark of the testimony in the sanctuary. (Ex 25:22; 1Sa 4:4)

The divine presence was symbolized by a cloud that reportedly produced a miraculous light that later Jewish writers called the *Shekhi·nah'*. (Le 16:2) While Jeremiah foretold the absence of the ark of the covenant when Israel would be restored from Babylon, this would not mean that Jehovah no longer purposed to be enthroned at his center of worship. As He said: "In that time they will call Jerusalem the throne of Jehovah." (Jer 3:16, 17) Ezekiel's restoration prophecies are in agreement, for in his vision of Jehovah's temple in which no ark of the covenant was seen, he was told: "Son of man, this [temple] is the place of my throne." —Eze 43:7.

Jehovah covenanted that the throne of David's seed should "itself become one lasting to time indefinite." (1Ch 17:11-14) In announcing the fulfillment of this promise, the angel Gabriel said to Mary: "Jehovah God will give [Jesus] the throne of David his father, and he will rule as king over the house of Jacob forever, and there will be no end of his kingdom." (Lu 1:32, 33) Not only would there be an inheritance of an earthly dominion on Jesus' part but he would share Jehovah's throne, which is universal. (Re 3:21; Isa 66:1) In turn, Jesus promised to share his throne of kingly authority with all those who, like his faithful apostles, were in the new covenant with his Father, and who would conquer the world as Jesus had done. This would be granted to them in "the re-creation," during Jesus' presence.—Mt 19:28; Lu 22:20, 28-30; Re 3:21.

In harmony with Jehovah's prophecy through Zechariah that the man named "Sprout," the builder of the future temple for Jehovah, "must become a priest upon his throne," Paul records concerning Jesus: "We have such a high priest as [Melchizedek, a king-priest], and he has sat down at the right hand of the throne of the Majesty in the heavens." (Zec 6:11-13; Heb 8:1) In addition to Christ Jesus, John saw the whole spiritual house or sanctuary of God, the faithful Christian congregation, enthroned as king-priests to rule for a thousand years.—Re 20:4, 6; 1Pe 2:5.

As foretold in Psalm 45:6, and applied by Paul in Hebrews 1:8, Jesus' throne, his office or authority as sovereign, has its source in Jehovah: "God is your throne forever." On the other hand, the Devil, too, provides basis or authority for his organizations to rule, as emphasized in Revelation 13:1, 2, with respect to the 'wild beast that came out of the sea': "The dragon gave to the beast its power and its throne and great authority." When Satan offered similar power and authority to Jesus Christ, his price was stated: "If you do an act

of worship before me, it will all be yours." (Lu 4:5-7) Correspondingly, the grant of a throne or authority to "the wild beast" must have been on the condition of its serving Satan.

In discussing Jesus' position as God's Master Worker, Paul mentions that through Christ "thrones" were created. The term appears to refer to positions of official authority, both visible and invisible, within God's administrative arrangement.—Col 1:16.

THUMB. The finger on the human hand that can be moved against each of the other fingers. Humans can grasp things and perform many delicate operations that would be impossible if they did not have opposable thumbs. Anciently, a captive was sometimes incapacitated for military service by having his thumbs and big toes cut off. —Jg 1:6, 7.

The Hebrew word *bo'hen* is used to designate both the thumb and the big toe; the appendage that *bo'hen* has reference to in any given text is indicated by the accompanying expressions 'of the hand' and 'of the foot.' Whenever the thumb is mentioned in the Scriptures, the big toe is referred to in the same text.—Ex 29:20; Le 14:14, 17, 25, 28.

During the installation of Aaron and his sons as priests, a ram was killed, and Moses put some of its blood on the lobe of Aaron's right ear, the thumb of his right hand, and the big toe of his right foot. Then he did the same to each of Aaron's sons. (Le 8:23, 24) The blood on the right thumb figuratively represented that they should carry out their priestly duties with the best of their ability.

THUMMIM. See URIM AND THUMMIM.

THUNDER. The loud sound that follows a flash of lightning. It is due to the sudden expansion of air that has been heated by such electrical discharge, causing the air to move violently away from the lightning's path and then back again behind it.—Job 28:26; 38:25.

The Hebrew verb *ra·am'* (meaning "thunder") is at times mentioned in connection with Jehovah (1Sa 2:10; 2Sa 22:14; Ps 18:13), the One who has on occasion employed thunder to accomplish his will. For example, in the time of Samuel, Jehovah threw the Philistines into confusion by means of thunder (Heb., *ra·am*). (1Sa 7:10; compare Isa 29:6.) Another Hebrew word, *qohl*, sometimes translated "thunder" (1Sa 12:17, 18, ftn) basically means "sound" (Ex 32:18, 19) or "voice."—De 21: 18; 1Ki 19:12.

The awesome sound of thunder is associated with Jehovah's voice. (Job 37:4, 5; 40:9; Ps 29:3-9) When certain Jews heard Jehovah speak from heaven to Jesus, there was a difference of opinion whether the sound was thunder or the voice of an angel. (Joh 12:28, 29; compare Re 6:1; 14:2; 19:6.) The sound of thunder often being an advance indication of an approaching storm, "thunders" can designate divine warnings, as at Revelation 8:5; 10:3, 4; 16:18.

To the Jews at the foot of Mount Sinai, the thunder that they heard was a manifestation of God's presence. (Ex 19:16; compare Re 4:5; 11: 19.) Either this event or God's leading Israel by means of a pillar of cloud (a place of thunder) may be alluded to by the psalmist's words: "I [Jehovah] began to answer you in the concealed place of thunder."—Ps 81:7.

THUNDER, SONS OF. See BOANERGES.

THYATIRA (Thy·a·ti'ra). The city rebuilt early in the third century B.C.E. by the former general of Alexander the Great, Seleucus Nicator. It was situated about 60 km (40 mi) inland from the Aegean Sea along a tributary of the Gediz (ancient Hermus River) in western Asia Minor. Thyatira's Christian congregation received a message written by the hand of the apostle John at the dictation of the Lord Jesus Christ.—Re 1:11.

Thyatira today is called Akhisar and is located about 250 km (155 mi) SSW of Istanbul and about 375 km (233 mi) E of Athens. (PICTURE, Vol. 2, p. 946) This city was never a great metropolis or a center of special political significance or importance; but it was a wealthy industrial center, noted for its numerous crafts, including weaving, dyeing, brassworking, tanning, and pottery making. Its dye business is frequently mentioned in inscriptions. Dyemakers of Thyatira used madder root as a source for their celebrated scarlet or purple color, known in later times as Turkey red.

Lydia, converted to Christianity during Paul's first visit to Philippi in Macedonia, was a "seller of purple, of the city of Thyatira." She may have been an overseas representative of Thyatiran manufacturers, a businesswoman of some means who owned a house spacious enough to entertain Paul and his companions during their stay in Philippi.—Ac 16:12-15.

When and by whom Christianity was first introduced to the Thyatirans is not known. There is no record that Paul or other evangelists ever visited the city or that Lydia returned there. Possibly the message reached there during the two years (c. 53-55 C.E.) that Paul was active in Ephesus about 115 km (70 mi) SW of Thyatira, for during that time "all those inhabiting the district of Asia heard the word of the Lord, both Jews and Greeks." (Ac 19:10) What is known is that some 40 years later there was a rather vigorous congregation of Christians in Thyatira.—Re 1:10, 11.

Christ's Message to Thyatira Congregation. This congregation, the fourth of the seven to receive its message, was commended for the love, faith, and endurance it had shown. Its ministry was also approved; its "deeds of late are more than those formerly." But, though the congregation had these commendable qualities, a very bad condition had also been allowed to develop and remain within this congregation. In this regard the Lord's condemnation declared: "You tolerate that woman Jezebel, who calls herself a prophetess, and she teaches and misleads my slaves to commit fornication and to eat things sacrificed to idols." This "woman" was probably given the name Jezebel because her wicked conduct resembled that of Ahab's wife, and because of her callous refusal to repent. It seems, however, that only a minority of the Thyatira congregation approved this Jezebel influence, since the message went on to speak "to the rest of you who are in Thyatira, all those who do not have this teaching, the very ones who did not get to know the 'deep things of Satan.'"—Re 2:18-29.

TIBERIAS (Ti·be'ri·as).

1. A city built by Herod Antipas about 21 C.E. and named after Tiberius Caesar, emperor of the Roman Empire at the time. It is still called Tiberias (Teverya) and is situated about 25 km (15 mi) ENE of Nazareth, on a comparatively narrow strip along the western shore of the Sea of Galilee, 210 m (690 ft) below the level of the Mediterranean. Tiberias was about 15 km (9.5 mi) around the sea from Capernaum and 9 km (5.5 mi) above where the Jordan leaves that body of water. Here Herod as the tetrarch made his residence. Nearby, to the S of the city, were famous warm springs. The city is mentioned only once in the Scriptures.—Joh 6:23; PICTURE, Vol. 2, p. 739.

2. The Sea of Galilee (Yam Kinneret) was sometimes called Tiberias, after the city by that name located on its western shore.—Joh 6:1; 21:1.

TIBERIUS (Ti·be'ri·us). The second emperor of Rome. He was born in 42 B.C.E. as the son of Tiberius Claudius Nero and Livia Drusilla. But when his mother married Augustus in 38 B.C.E., Tiberius became the adopted son of the emperor. At the age of 31, upon the insistence of his

stepfather, he divorced his wife Vipsania Agrippina and married Julia, the daughter of Augustus.

Augustus chose Tiberius as his successor only after others whom he preferred above Tiberius had all died. On August 17, 14 C.E. (Gregorian calendar), Augustus died; on September 15, Tiberius allowed the Senate to name him emperor. John started baptizing "in the fifteenth year of the reign of Tiberius Caesar." If the years were counted from the death of Augustus, the 15th year ran from August 28 C.E. to August 29 C.E. If counted from when he was formally proclaimed emperor, the year would run from September 28 C.E. to September 29 C.E.—Lu 3:1-3.

Tiberius lived until March 37 C.E. and hence was emperor for the entire period of Jesus' ministry. It was therefore Tiberius' image that was on the tax coin brought to Jesus when he said, "Pay back Caesar's things to Caesar." (Mr 12:14-17; Mt 22:17-21; Lu 20:22-25) Tiberius extended the law of *laesa majestas* (injured majesty) to include, in addition to seditious acts, merely libelous words against the emperor, and presumably on the strength of this law the Jews pressured Pontius Pilate to have Jesus killed. (Joh 19:12-16) Tiberius later called Pilate to Rome because of Jewish complaints against his administration, but Tiberius died and Caligula succeeded him before Pilate arrived.

As an emperor, Tiberius had both virtues and vices. He restrained spending on luxuries and so had funds to use generously to build up the empire's prosperity as well as reserves to assist recovery from disasters and bad times. Tiberius viewed himself as a man not a god, declined many honorary titles, and generally directed emperor worship to Augustus rather than to himself.

His vices exceeded his virtues, however. He was extremely suspicious and hypocritical in his dealings with others, and his reign abounded with ordered killings, many of his former friends being numbered among the victims. He consulted astrologers. At his villa on Capri where he spent the last ten years of his life, he indulged his perverted lusts in a most debased manner with men kept for unnatural purposes.

Tiberius was despised not only by such individuals as his schoolteacher Theodorus the Gadarene and his stepfather Augustus, but also by his subjects in general. After his death, the Senate refused to deify him. For these reasons and others too, Bible scholars see in Tiberius a fulfillment of prophecy that says "one who is to be despised" would arise as "the king of the north."—Da 11:15, 21.

TIBHATH (Tib′hath) [Slaughter]. A city N of Palestine from which David took a great quantity of copper after striking down Hadadezer, king of Zobah, at Hamath, about 230 km (140 mi) NNE of Dan. (1Ch 18:3, 8) In the parallel description of David's campaign at 2 Samuel 8:8, Tibhath is apparently called Betah. (See BETAH.) Some suggest that Tibhath may have been named for Nahor's son Tebah. (Ge 22:24) In harmony with its being part of the Aramaean kingdom of Zobah, the location of Tibhath was probably in the valley lying between the Lebanon and Anti-Lebanon mountains. Traces of ancient copperworks have been found in Lebanon, in harmony with the Biblical account.

TIBNI (Tib′ni). A contender for the kingship of the ten-tribe kingdom of Israel following the seven-day rule of Israel's fifth king Zimri in about 951 B.C.E. The populace was divided over whether Tibni or Omri should now be king. Four years later, during which time civil war presumably raged, the issue was finally settled; Tibni lost to Omri's supporters and met death. He was a son of Ginath.—1Ki 16:15, 21-23.

TIDAL (Ti′dal). The king of Goiim and an ally or vassal of Elamite King Chedorlaomer when they and two other monarchs subjugated five kings near the Dead Sea. Following 12 years of domination, the five defeated kings staged a rebellion. Tidal, Chedorlaomer, and the others came W to put it down, and in doing so took spoil and captives, including Abraham's nephew Lot. Abraham pursued the oppressors and recovered the prisoners and pillaged goods, but there is no indication that Tidal or those kings with him were captured or slain.—Ge 14:1-17.

TIGLATH-PILESER (III) (Tig′lath-pil·e′ser). A powerful king of Assyria (whose name is also spelled Tilgath-pilneser) and the first such to be mentioned by name in the Bible record. Though some consider Tiglath-pileser III to have been of royal blood and others classify him as a usurper of the throne, his origin and the manner of his attaining the kingship are in reality unknown. His reign, however, marked an era of reorganization, growing expansion and strength that brought the Assyrian Empire to new heights. He is considered to have been the first Assyrian monarch to establish as a definite policy the mass deportation and transplantation of conquered peoples. As many as 154,000 persons are stated to have been forcibly shifted around within the realm of conquered lands in one year. The apparent purpose behind such harsh policy was to break the spirit of the national groups and weaken or eliminate any unity of action in attempts to throw off the Assyrian yoke.

This king first appears in the Bible account as "Pul." (2Ki 15:19) First Chronicles 5:26 also states that God "stirred up the spirit of Pul the king of Assyria even the spirit of Tilgath-pilneser the king of Assyria, so that he took into exile" peoples of certain tribes of Israel. The ancient secular records apply both names to the same individual, the name "Pulu" appearing in what is known as "The Babylonian King List A," while "The Synchronistic Chronicle" lists "Tukultiapilesharra" (Tiglath-pileser). (*Ancient Near Eastern Texts,* edited by J. Pritchard, 1974, pp. 272, 273) It is also of note that, in the Hebrew, the above-quoted scripture uses the verb "took" in the singular rather than in the plural. It is commonly suggested that "Pul" was the monarch's personal name and that he assumed the name "Tiglath-pileser" (the name of an earlier and famous Assyrian king) upon ascending the throne.

It appears that during the early part of his reign, Tiglath-pileser III was occupied in hammering out stronger borders for the empire in the S, E, and N. The menacing shadow of Assyria, however, soon loomed large over the lands of Syria and Palestine to the W.

The Assyrian inscriptions prominently mention Azriau of Ia-ú-da-a-a (Judah) in connection with a campaign by Tiglath-pileser III in Syria. (*Ancient Near Eastern Texts,* pp. 282, 283) This would seem to be a reference to King Azariah of Judah, more commonly known as Uzziah (829-778 B.C.E.), but the matter is a debated one, because some hold that the small kingdom of Sam'al in Syria was on occasion also called Judah. The likelihood of such a pagan king having a name including the name of Jah (the abbreviated form of Jehovah) and living at the same time as the Judean king of the same name seems slight; however, the Bible does not mention Tiglath-pileser III in connection with Azariah (Uzziah), and the Assyrian records are considerably mutilated.

During the reign of King Menahem of Israel (c. 790-781 B.C.E.), Tiglath-pileser III (Pul) advanced into Palestine, and Menahem sought the Assyrian's favor by paying him tribute to the amount of "a thousand talents of silver" ($6,606,-000 in current values). Temporarily appeased, Tiglath-pileser withdrew his forces. (2Ki 15:19, 20) The Assyrian documents refer to *Me-ni-hi-im-me* (Menahem), along with Rezon (Rezin) of Damascus and Hiram of Tyre, as tributary to Tiglath-pileser.

Subsequently, in the time of King Ahaz of Judah (761-746 B.C.E.), King Pekah of Israel formed a confederation with King Rezin of Damascus and attacked Judah. (2Ki 16:5, 6; Isa 7:1, 2) Though assured by the prophet Isaiah that within a short time the two conspiring kingdoms would be wiped off the scene, King Ahaz chose to send a bribe to Tiglath-pileser to come to his rescue. (2Ki 16:7, 8; Isa 7:7-16; 8:9-13) An Assyrian inscription describes the tribute paid by *Ia-u-ha-zi* (Jehoahaz, or Ahaz) of Judah and other kings of that area as follows: "gold, silver, tin, iron, antimony, linen garments with multicolored trimmings, garments of their native (industries) (being made of) dark purple wool . . . all kinds of costly objects be they products of the sea or of the continent, the (choice) products of their regions, the treasures of (their) kings, horses, mules (trained for) the yoke." (*Ancient Near Eastern Texts,* p. 282) The aggressive Assyrian responded to Ahaz' urging by invading Israel, capturing several northern cities, and overrunning the regions of Gilead, Galilee, and Naphtali, carrying many off into exile. (2Ki 15:29; 1Ch 5:6, 26) Damascus was attacked and fell to the Assyrian forces, and its King Rezin was slain. Here at Damascus, Tiglath-pileser III received the visit of King Ahaz of Judah, coming either to express gratitude or submission to Assyria.—2Ki 16:9-12.

Isaiah had been inspired to foretell that Jehovah would use the king of Assyria like "a hired razor" to "shave" the kingdom of Judah. (Isa 7:17, 20) Whether the "hired razor" referred specifically to Tiglath-pileser III, whom Ahaz bribed, or not, the record does show that he caused great distress to the Judean king and that Ahaz' bribe proved to be "of no assistance to him." (2Ch 28:20, 21) This may have marked the initial phase of the "flood" of Assyrian invasion of Judah, which eventually was to 'reach up to the very neck of the kingdom,' as it clearly did in Hezekiah's time. —Isa 8:5-8; 2Ki 18:13, 14.

Tiglath-pileser III, in his inscriptions, says concerning the northern kingdom of Israel: "They overthrew their king Pekah (*Pa-qa-ha*) and I placed Hoshea (*A-ú-si-'*) as king over them. I received from them 10 talents of gold [$3,853,-500], 1,000(?) talents of silver [$6,606,000] as their [tri]bute and brought them to Assyria." (*Ancient Near Eastern Texts,* p. 284) Thus the Assyrian king assumes credit for the assumption of the kingship of Israel by Hoshea following his conspiratorial assassination of Hoshea's predecessor, Pekah (c. 758 B.C.E.).—2Ki 15:30.

In ancient Assyrian records Tiglath-pileser III is assigned a reign of 18 years. Biblical references, however, seem to indicate that his kingship was of longer duration, inasmuch as references to him appear from the time of Menahem down to that of Hoshea. But the Hebrew Scriptures do not set forth all the details needed for one to state positively that the Assyrian records are in error in this case. This is so for several reasons: There is some uncertainty regarding the manner in which the reigns of the Israelite kings are to be fitted into a chronological framework. It is also worth noting that the period prior to the time generally assigned for the start of Tiglath-pileser's reign is one of relative obscurity as far as the ancient records are concerned and is considered to have been a time of great decline for the Assyrians. Thus the French scholar, Georges Roux, in his book *Ancient Iraq,* states that "for thirty-six years . . . Assyria was practically paralysed." As for Ashurnirari V, considered to have been the predecessor of Tiglath-pileser III, the same author observes: "He hardly dared leave his palace and was probably killed in a revolution which broke out in Kalhu and put upon the throne his younger brother [?], Tiglath-pileser III." (1964, p. 251) In view of this it seems entirely possible that Tiglath-pileser may have exercised the power of kingship for a longer period of time than commonly credited to him, even perhaps as a coregent.

At 2 Chronicles 28:16 Ahaz is spoken of as sending "to the *kings* of Assyria for *them* to help him." While the plural "kings," occurring in the Hebrew Masoretic text, appears in the singular ("king") in the *Septuagint* and in other ancient manuscripts, there are modern translations that favor the Hebrew plural. (*JP, NW*) Some scholars view the plural here as merely indicating the sum of majesty and greatness ascribed to the one monarch (Tiglath-pileser III) as the "king of kings." Yet attention is also called to the boastful claim of the Assyrian monarch recorded at Isaiah 10:8: "Are not my princes at the same time kings?" It is thus possible that the reference to "Pul the king of Assyria" (2Ki 15:19) may also be applied in the sense of his being the ruler of an Assyrian province prior to becoming head of the entire empire.

Upon his death Tiglath-pileser III was succeeded by Shalmaneser V. More details might be known concerning this king were it not for the fact that a still later king, Esar-haddon, caused Tiglath-pileser's inscriptions to be mutilated, a rare affront elsewhere unknown in Assyrian history.

TIKVAH (Tik'vah) [Hope].

1. Father-in-law of Huldah the prophetess; son of Harhas. (2Ki 22:14) The name is spelled Tokhath according to the Masoretic text at 2 Chronicles 34:22.

2. Father of a certain Jahzeiah who lived in the time of Ezra.—Ezr 10:10, 11, 15; see JAHZEIAH.

TILGATH-PILNESER. See TIGLATH-PILESER (III).

TILON (Ti'lon). A son of Shimon in the tribe of Judah.—1Ch 4:20.

TIMAEUS (Ti·mae'us) [Honored]. Father of Bartimaeus the blind beggar healed by Jesus. —Mr 10:46.

TIME(S). See ACCEPTABLE TIME; APPOINTED TIMES OF THE NATIONS; CALENDAR.

TIME INDEFINITE. The Hebrew word *'oh·lam'* carries the thought of indefinite or uncertain time. Lexicographer Gesenius defines it as meaning "*hidden time,* i.e. obscure and long, of which the beginning or end is uncertain or indefinite." (*A Hebrew and English Lexicon of the Old Testament,* translated by E. Robinson, 1836, p. 746) Accordingly, expressions such as "time indefinite" (Ps 25:6), "indefinitely lasting" (Hab 3:6), "of old" (Ge 6:4), "a long time ago," "of long ago" (Jos 24:2; Pr 22:28; 23:10), and "long-lasting" (Ec 12:5) appropriately convey the thought of the original-language term.

The word *'oh·lam'* is at times associated with that which is everlasting. (1Ki 2:45, ftn) The prophet Isaiah wrote: "Jehovah, the Creator of the extremities of the earth, is a God to time indefinite." (Isa 40:28) Jehovah is "from time indefinite to time indefinite." (Ps 90:2) Since Jehovah is immortal and does not die, he will continue to be God for all eternity. (Hab 1:12; 1Ti 1:17) However, the Hebrew expression *'oh·lam'* does not *in itself* mean "forever." It often refers to things that have an end, but the period of such things' existence can be said to be 'to time indefinite' because the time of their end is not then *specified.* For example, the 'indefinitely lasting' Law covenant came to an end with Jesus' death and the bringing in of a new covenant. (Ex 31:16, 17; Ro 10:4; Ga 5:18; Col 2:16, 17; Heb 9:15) And the 'indefinitely lasting' Aaronic priesthood similarly came to an end.—Ex 40:15; Heb 7:11-24; 10:1.

Another Hebrew term, *'adh,* denotes unlimited future time, everlastingness, or eternity. (1Ch 28:9; Ps 19:9; Isa 9:6; 45:17; Hab 3:6) At times, as at Psalm 45:6, the words *'oh·lam'* and *'adh* appear together and may be rendered "age-during, and for ever" (*Yg*), "age-abiding and beyond" (*Ro*), and "time indefinite, even forever" (*NW*). Concerning the earth, the psalmist declared: "It will not be made to totter to time indefinite, or forever."—Ps 104:5.

The Hebrew term *ne'tsach* can also denote everlastingness. Among the ways it may be rendered are "forever" (Job 4:20; 14:20), "perpetually" (Isa 57:16), and "always" (Ps 9:18). Sometimes *ne'tsach* and *'oh·lam'* occur in parallel (Ps 49:8, 9), or the terms *ne'tsach* and *'adh* appear together. (Am 1:11) All three words are found at Psalm 9:5, 6: "You have rebuked nations . . . Their name you have wiped out to time indefinite [*le'oh·lam'*], even forever [*wa·'edh'*]. O you enemy, your desolations have come to their perpetual [*la·ne'tsach*] finish."

In the Christian Greek Scriptures, the word *ai·on'* may denote a time period of indefinite or indeterminate length, a period of remote, but not endless, time. For example, at Luke 1:70 and Acts 3:21 *ai·on'* can be rendered "of old," "of old time," "in ancient times." (*RS, NW, AT*) Often, however, the context suggests that *ai·on'* is to be understood to refer to a time period of undefined length because of such period being endless in duration. (Lu 1:55; Joh 6:50, 51; 12:34; 1Jo 2:17) Similarly, the adjective *ai·o'ni·os* (drawn from *ai·on'*) can, as is evident from the context, signify both "long lasting" (Ro 16:25; 2Ti 1:9; Tit 1:2) and "everlasting." (Mt 18:8; 19:16, 29) Another Greek adjective, *a·i'di·os,* specifically means "eternal" or "everlasting."—Ro 1:20; Jude 6, *NW, RS, AT;* for a further consideration of *ai·on'*, see AGE; SYSTEMS OF THINGS.

TIME OF THE END.

An expression found six times in the book of Daniel. It refers to a time period marking the conclusion of a system of things and culminating in its destruction. The prophet Daniel was given a preview of events to occur in the distant future. Thereafter he was told: "And as for you, O Daniel, make secret the words and seal up the book, until the time of the end. Many will rove about, and the true knowledge will become abundant."—Da 12:4.

Concerning this text, commentator Thomas Scott, in the first half of the 19th century, observed: "The angel, by way of conclusion, intimated to Daniel, that this prophecy would remain obscure, and as 'a sealed book,' of which little would be understood, 'till the time of the end' . . . The fact has evidenced this to be the case: immense difficulties have always been acknowledged in many of Daniel's prophecies, and they have been 'as words shut up' even from believers in general. . . . In these latter ages many have bestowed great pains, in searching into history, to illustrate those parts of these prophecies which are already accomplished; and by comparing them with other scriptures, to form some judgment of what yet remains to be fulfilled: and thus much light has been thrown on them. As they shall gradually be more and more accomplished, they will be better understood: and future generations will be far more surprised and instructed by them, than we are." (Scott's *Explanatory Notes,* 1832) The lack of understanding concerning Daniel's prophecies in the early part of the 19th century indicated that this foretold "time of the end" was yet future, since those "having insight," God's true servants, were to understand the prophecy in "the time of the end."—Da 12:9, 10.

The expression "time of the end" is also used in association with particular developments in connection with human government. Daniel 11:40 reads: "In the time of the end the king of the south will engage with [the king of the north] in a pushing, and against him the king of the north will storm with chariots and with horsemen and with many ships." Thereafter the prophecy discusses the actions of the "king of the north" and indicates that he will come to his end. (Da 11:41-45) Thus "the time of the end" here is evidently to be understood as a period culminated by the destruction of "the king of the north." Lending confirmation to this is the fact that "the king of the north" is earlier portrayed as persecuting God's servants, those "having insight," until "the time of the end," that is, until his time of the end.—Da 11:33-35.

Another feature associated with "the time of the end" is the standing up of "a king fierce in countenance" that would range himself against "the Prince of princes," finally to be broken or destroyed. This "king" was to stand up in the final part of the kingdoms that sprang from the four parts into which the Grecian Empire was to be divided. (Da 8:8-25) Since "the king of the north" and "the king of the south" came from the same source, it logically follows that the "king fierce in countenance" corresponds to one of these 'kings' in his "time of the end."

The expression "time of the end" does not mean an 'end of time' but denotes a period of time that culminates in the *end or destruction, not of all things, but of the things mentioned in the prophecy.* That time itself will not end is made clear in the Scriptures. For example, the psalmist said concerning the earth: "It will not be made to totter to time indefinite, or forever." (Ps 104:5) Since the earth will continue to exist, it necessarily follows that time, as an earthly "dimension" or measurement, will not cease. While it is true that Revelation 10:6 may be rendered "there should be time no longer," the context indicates that this means *no further grant of time;* thus, a specific or allotted period of time terminates. (*KJ*) Other translations, therefore, read: "There should be no more delay." (*AT, RS*) "There will be no delay any longer." (*NW*) Commenting on this text, A. T. Robertson observes: "This does not mean that *chronos* (time) . . . will cease to exist, but only that there will be no more delay in the fulfillment of the seventh trumpet (verse 7), in answer to the question, 'How long?' (6:10)."—*Word Pictures in the New Testament,* 1933, Vol. VI, p. 372.

TIMNA   (Tim′na).

1. Concubine of Esau's son Eliphaz and mother of Amalek. (Ge 36:10-12) In the genealogy at 1 Chronicles 1:36, there are first enumerated five sons of Esau's son Eliphaz. Next are added, "Timna and Amalek." Professor C. F. Keil remarks on this: "The addition of the two names *Timna* and *Amalek* in the Chronicle thus appears to be merely an abbreviation, which the author might well allow himself, as the posterity of Esau were known to his readers from Genesis. The name Timna, too, by its form (a feminine formation), must have guarded against the idea of some modern exegetes that Timna was also a son of Eliphaz." (*Commentary on the Old Testament,* 1973, Vol. III, First Chronicles, p. 53) Thus, Eliphaz' six sons were listed, but with the notation that one of them, Amalek, was of Eliphaz' concubine, Timna. It must be remembered that Amalek became a nation that hated God's people and concerning whom Jehovah said: "Jehovah will have war with Amalek from generation to generation." (Ex 17:8-16) Thus the accounts, both in Genesis and in Chronicles, give this detail concerning the origin of Amalek. This Timna is possibly the same as No. 2.

2. A daughter of Seir the Horite, therefore sister of Lotan and Seir's other sons. (Ge 36:20-22; 1Ch 1:39) Possibly identical with No. 1.

3. The first name found in the list of 11 "sheiks of Esau," or Edom. (Ge 36:40-43; 1Ch 1:51-54) In the view of many translators, Timna and the other names listed are personal names. (*AS, KJ, JB, NW, RS*) However, it is generally acknowledged that the expression "according to their families, according to their *places,* by their names" indicates that a tribe or an area is meant. Some versions therefore prefer expressions such as "the chief *of* Timna." (*JP, AT*) In fact, at Genesis 36:41, in the same list, a woman's name, Oholibamah, appears, allowing for the name Timna to be that of a woman. Eusebius and Jerome identified Timna with an Edomite site called "Thamna," which stood in their day. (*Onomasticon,* 96, 24-27) However, the location of any such region named for Timna is currently unknown.

TIMNAH   (Tim′nah).

1. A location at the boundary of Judah and Dan. (Jos 15:1, 10; 19:40-43) Some have identified it with a place preserving some similarity to the ancient name, Khirbet Tibnah, about 6 km (3.5 mi) W of Beth-shemesh, but no archaeological remains earlier than Roman times have been found on the site. Many favor Tell el-Batashi (Tel Batash), about 7 km (4.5 mi) WNW of Beth-shemesh, situated on the S bank of the torrent valley of Sorek.

Samson selected a Philistine woman of Timnah for marriage when "looking for an opportunity against the Philistines," who then ruled over Israel. En route to the city, he killed a lion barehanded at the vineyards of Timnah. (Jg 14:1-6) In the time of King Ahaz, the Philistines captured Timnah and its dependent towns.—2Ch 28:16-19.

2. A city in the mountainous region of Judah. Scholars identify this Timnah with Khirbet et-Tabbana (Horvat Tibnah), about 3 km (2 mi) NW of Gibeah (El Jab'a). (Jos 15:20, 48, 57) Apparently, near this Timnah, Judah planned to shear his sheep, and at Enaim (which was on the road to Timnah) he had relations with Tamar, mistaking her for a harlot.—Ge 38:12-18.

TIMNATH-HERES   (Tim′nath-he′res). Location of Joshua's inheritance and later burial in the mountainous region of Ephraim, N of Mount Gaash. (Jg 2:8, 9) It is called Timnath-serah elsewhere.

TIMNATH-SERAH   (Tim′nath-se′rah). The city given to Joshua as his inheritance in the mountainous region of Ephraim. He requested Timnath-serah, and the sons of Israel gave it to him "at the order of Jehovah." Joshua built up the city and was later buried there. (Jos 19:49, 50; 24:30) Judges 2:9 reads "Timnath-heres" instead of "Timnath-serah" in both the Hebrew Masoretic text and the Greek *Septuagint.* The reason for this difference in names is unknown.

Some identify Timnath-serah with Khirbet Tibnah, about 30 km (19 mi) SW of Shechem. Situated on the western edge of the mountainous region, Khirbet Tibnah overlooks the coastal plain. Mount Gaash, S of Timnath-serah (Timnathheres) (Jos 24:30; Jg 2:9), cannot now be located definitely.

TIMNITE (Tim′nite) [Of (Belonging to) Timnah]. A person of Timnah; in its only occurrence the term is applied to Samson's father-in-law. —Jg 15:6.

TIMON (Ti′mon) [from a root meaning "honor"]. One of the seven men "full of spirit and wisdom" appointed by the apostles to care for "the daily distribution" in the infant Christian congregation. In spite of his Greek name, he was likely a Jew by birth.—Ac 6:1-6.

TIMOTHY (Tim′o·thy) [One Who Honors God]. Son of a Jewess, Eunice, and a Greek father (not named in the Scriptures). While very young, Timothy was taught "the holy writings" by his mother and probably also by his grandmother Lois. (Ac 16:1; 2Ti 1:5; 3:15) It is not known precisely when Timothy embraced Christianity. However, perhaps late in 49 or early in 50 C.E., when the apostle Paul arrived at Lystra (apparently Timothy's home) in the course of his second missionary journey, the disciple Timothy (perhaps in his late teens or early twenties) "was well reported on by the brothers in Lystra and Iconium."—Ac 16:2.

It may have been at this time that, as a result of the operation of God's spirit, certain prophecies or predictions were voiced concerning Timothy. After the holy spirit had in this way indicated the future of Timothy, the older men of the congregation joined the apostle Paul in laying their hands upon Timothy, thereby setting him apart for a particular service in connection with the Christian congregation. (1Ti 1:18; 4:14; 2Ti 1:6; compare Ac 13:3.) Paul chose Timothy as a traveling companion and, to avoid giving Jews an occasion for stumbling, circumcised him.—Ac 16:3.

Travels With Paul. With Paul, Timothy shared in Christian activities in Philippi, Thessalonica, and Beroea. (Ac 16:11–17:10) When opposition that was stirred up by fanatical Jews made it necessary for Paul to depart from Beroea, the apostle left Silas and Timothy behind to care for the new group of believers there. (Ac 17:13-15) It appears that Paul thereafter sent word to Beroea, advising Timothy to visit the brothers at Thessalonica, encouraging them to remain faithful despite tribulation. (1Th 3:1-3; see ATHENS [Paul's Activity in Athens].) Apparently rejoining Paul at Corinth, Timothy brought good news about the faithfulness and love of the Thessalonian Chris-

tians. (Ac 18:5; 1Th 3:6) In the letter Paul then sent to the Thessalonians, he included the names of Silvanus (Silas) and Timothy in the salutation, as he also did in his second letter to them.—1Th 1:1; 2Th 1:1.

During Paul's third missionary journey (c. 52-56 C.E.), Timothy again traveled with the apostle. (Compare Ac 20:4.) While at Ephesus (1Co 16:8), Paul, in his first letter to the Corinthians, wrote: "I am sending Timothy to you, as he is my beloved and faithful child in the Lord; and he will put you in mind of my methods in connection with Christ Jesus, just as I am teaching everywhere in every congregation." (1Co 4:17) Toward the close of this letter, though, Paul implied that Timothy might not get to Corinth: "If Timothy arrives, see that he becomes free of fear among you, for he is performing the work of Jehovah, even as I am." (1Co 16:10) If Timothy did indeed visit Corinth, this must have been before he and Erastus left Ephesus for Macedonia, since Timothy and Paul were together in Macedonia when the second letter to the Corinthians (based on the report of Titus, not of Timothy) was written. (Ac 19:22; 2Co 1:1; 2:13; 7:5-7) Perhaps Timothy's intended visit did not materialize. This is suggested by the fact that, in his second letter to the Corinthians, Paul makes no mention of Timothy's being there other than in association with himself. (2Co 1:19) Later, at the time Paul wrote to the Romans, apparently from Corinth (the home of Gaius), Timothy was with him. —Compare Ro 16:21, 23; 1Co 1:14.

Timothy's name is included in the salutation of letters written by Paul to the Philippians (1:1), Colossians (1:1), and Philemon (vs 1) during the apostle's first imprisonment at Rome. It appears that Timothy personally endured imprisonment at Rome sometime within the period between the writing of the letter to the Philippians and the one to the Hebrews.—Php 2:19; Heb 13:23.

Responsibilities and Qualifications. After Paul's release from prison, Timothy again shared with the apostle in the ministry, remaining in Ephesus at his direction. (1Ti 1:1-3) At this time (c. 61-64 C.E.) Timothy may have been in his 30's and had authority in the appointment of overseers and ministerial servants in the congregation. (1Ti 5:22) He was fully capable of handling these weighty responsibilities, having proved himself by laboring in close association with the apostle Paul for 11 years or more. Regarding him, Paul could say: "I have no one else of a disposition like his who will genuinely care for the things pertaining to you. . . . You know the proof he gave of himself, that like a child with a father he slaved with me in furtherance of the good news." (Php 2:20-22) And to Timothy he wrote: "I never leave off remembering you in my supplications, night and day longing to see you, as I remember your tears, that I may get filled with joy. For I recollect the faith which is in you without any hypocrisy." —2Ti 1:3-5.

Although having to contend with frequent illness because of stomach trouble (1Ti 5:23), Timothy willingly expended himself in behalf of others. His fine qualities endeared him to the apostle Paul, who very much desired Timothy's association when facing imminent death. (2Ti 4:6-9) Being relatively young, Timothy may have been diffident and hesitant about asserting his authority. (Compare 1Ti 4:11-14; 2Ti 1:6, 7; 2:1.) This shows that Timothy was not a proud man but appreciated his limitations.

TIMOTHY, LETTERS TO.

Two inspired letters of the Christian Greek Scriptures addressed to Timothy by the apostle Paul, who identifies himself as the writer in the opening words of each letter. (1Ti 1:1; 2Ti 1:1) The first letter was evidently written from Macedonia. A basis for assigning an approximate date for the composition of this letter is found in the first chapter, verse 3, which reads: "Just as I encouraged you to stay in Ephesus when I was about to go my way into Macedonia, so I do now." There is no mention of this in the book of Acts, which covers a period from the time of Jesus' ascension to heaven in 33 C.E. until the second year of Paul's imprisonment in Rome, about 61 C.E. Accordingly, it seems that it was sometime after his being released that Paul encouraged Timothy to stay in Ephesus, and then Paul apparently departed for Macedonia. This would place the time for the writing of First Timothy between the date of the apostle's release from his first imprisonment at Rome and his final imprisonment there, or about 61-64 C.E. The second letter was composed at Rome during Paul's final imprisonment (likely c. 65 C.E.) and not long before his death.—2Ti 1:8, 17; 4:6-9.

Authenticity. The authenticity of First and Second Timothy is well established. All outstanding ancient catalogs, starting with the Muratorian Fragment of the second century C.E., list both letters as canonical. Most important, these letters are in complete agreement with the rest of the Scriptures and quote from them. They contain quotations from or allusions to Numbers (16:5; 2Ti 2:19), Deuteronomy (19:15; 25:4; 1Ti 5:18, 19), Isaiah (26:13; 2Ti 2:19), and the words of

Jesus Christ (Mt 10:10; Lu 10:7; 1Ti 5:18). Noteworthy are the frequent references to faith (1Ti 1:2, 4, 5, 14, 19; 2:7, 15; 3:9, 13; 4:1, 6, 12; 5:8, 12; 6:10, 11, 12, 21; 2Ti 1:5, 13; 2:18, 22; 3:8, 10, 15; 4:7), as well as the emphasis on right doctrine (1Ti 1:3, 4; 4:1-3, 6, 7; 6:3, 4, 20, 21; 2Ti 1:13; 3:14, 15; 4:3, 5), conduct (1Ti 2:8-11, 15; 3:2-13; 4:12; 5:1-21; 6:1, 2, 11-14; 2Ti 2:22), prayer (1Ti 2:1, 2, 8; 4:5; 5:5; 2Ti 1:3), and faithful endurance through suffering (2Ti 1:8, 12; 2:3, 8-13).

Background for First Timothy. In about 56 C.E., when meeting at Miletus with the older men of the Ephesus congregation, the apostle Paul said to them: "I know that after my going away oppressive wolves will enter in among you and will not treat the flock with tenderness, and from among you yourselves men will rise and speak twisted things to draw away disciples after themselves." (Ac 20:29, 30) Within a few years the situation regarding the teaching of false doctrines did become so serious that Paul encouraged Timothy to stay in Ephesus, that he "might command certain ones not to teach different doctrine, nor to pay attention to false stories and to genealogies." (1Ti 1:3, 4) Timothy, therefore, had to wage spiritual warfare inside the Christian congregation to preserve its purity and to help its members to remain in the faith. (1:18, 19) His applying the things mentioned in the apostle's letter would serve to protect members of the congregation from falling away.

For the congregation to prosper, prayer could not be overlooked. So that Christians might go on leading a calm and quiet life, without interference, it was proper for them to pray concerning kings and men in high governmental station. Regarding those representing the congregation in prayer, Paul wrote: "I desire that in every place the men carry on prayer, lifting up loyal hands, apart from wrath and debates." This meant approaching God in a pure way, without any feelings of animosity or anger toward others.—1Ti 2:1-8.

Timothy also had to be alert that women kept their God-assigned place (1Ti 2:9-15), that only qualified men served as overseers and ministerial servants because such would serve as a strong bulwark against apostasy (3:1-13; 5:22), that deserving widows received assistance from the congregation (5:3-16), that due consideration was given to the older men presiding in a fine manner (5:17-19), that slaves conducted themselves aright toward their owners (6:1, 2), that all were content with what they had instead of seeking to be rich (6:6-10), and that the rich did not rest their hopes on material things, being instead rich in fine works and manifesting generosity (6: 17-19). Timothy himself had to be "an example to the faithful ones in speaking, in conduct, in love, in faith, in chasteness" and also had to be concerned about continuing to make advancement. —4:12, 15, 16; 6:11-14.

Background for Second Timothy. In 64 C.E. a great fire ravaged Rome, destroying about a fourth of the city. Rumor had it that Caesar Nero was responsible for it. To protect himself, Nero placed the blame upon the Christians. This appears to have prompted a wave of violent governmental persecution. It was likely about this time (c. 65 C.E.) that the apostle Paul was again imprisoned at Rome. Though forsaken by many, suffering in chains, and facing imminent death

(2Ti 1:15, 16; 4:6-8), the apostle wrote an encouraging letter to Timothy, one that prepared his younger fellow worker to resist apostate elements inside the congregation and to stand firm in the face of persecution. (2:3-7, 14-26; 3:14–4:5) By learning about Paul's circumstances, Timothy would have been able to draw encouragement from the apostle's good example of faithful endurance under great tribulation.—2:8-13.

Fearless in the strength of Jehovah, Paul exhorted Timothy: "Stir up like a fire the gift of God which is in you through the laying of my hands upon you. For God gave us not a spirit of cowardice, but that of power and of love and of soundness of mind. Therefore do not become ashamed of the witness about our Lord, neither of me a

---

HIGHLIGHTS OF FIRST TIMOTHY

Counsel to a Christian elder regarding his responsibilities

Written by the apostle Paul evidently sometime after his release from his first imprisonment in Rome

---

Counsel for Timothy's own spiritual well-being

Wage spiritual warfare, maintaining faith and a good conscience (1:18, 19)

Your concern should be, not with bodily training, but with godly devotion; do not let others look down on your youth but rather be a good example and make advancement (4:7b-16)

Do not appoint someone hastily to a position, so as to avoid being a sharer in sins of others (5:22)

Warnings against corrupting influences in the congregation

Command certain ones not to teach different doctrines, nor to pay attention to false stories and genealogies (1:3, 4)

Certain ones have deviated from love and unhypocritical faith; they want to be teachers of law but lack understanding of its intent (1:5-11)

In later periods of time there will be a falling away from the faith (4:1-5)

Counteract wrong influences; be nourished with words of faith; reject false stories (4:6, 7a)

False teaching breeds envy, strife, abusive speeches, suspicions, violent disputes, and the use of what is godly for selfish gain (6:3-5)

Flee from bad fruitage resulting from love of money; fight the fine fight of the faith and resist false doctrine (6:11, 12, 20, 21)

Qualifications for those appointed to serve as overseers and ministerial servants

Overseer's qualifications include his being irreprehensible; having only one wife; being sound in mind, orderly, hospitable, qualified to teach, self-controlled as to drink and temper, reasonable; not loving money;

presiding well over his household; not being a new convert; and having a good reputation outside the congregation (3:1-7)

Ministerial servants must be serious, not double-tongued, not heavy drinkers, nor greedy of dishonest gain, first tested as to fitness, free from accusation, presiding well over their households (3:8-10, 12, 13)

Instructions regarding various congregation needs

Prayers should be offered for all sorts of men—including rulers, to the end that Christians may live peaceably with godly devotion; it is God's will that all sorts of men should be saved (2:1-4)

There is only one God and one mediator, Jesus Christ, so men offering prayers should lift up "loyal hands, apart from wrath and debates" (2:5-8)

Women should dress in a modest, becoming manner, reflecting reverence for God; they may not teach in the congregation or exercise authority over a man (2:9-15)

Only widows aged 60 and over who have a fine reputation and no living children or grandchildren should be included on the list of those to receive material help from the congregation (5:3-16)

Elders working hard in speaking and teaching should be viewed as deserving of "double honor" (5:17, 18)

Do not accept an accusation against an older man unless there are two or three witnesses; practicers of sin must be reproved before all onlookers (5:19-21)

Slaves should be exemplary in subjection to their owners, especially if their masters are fellow believers (6:1, 2)

All should be content if they have sustenance and covering; the love of money is a root of injurious things, and those determined to be rich come to spiritual harm (6:6-10)

Wealthy ones must not be arrogant, trusting in riches; rather, they should be ready to share generously with needy ones (6:17-19)

HIGHLIGHTS OF SECOND TIMOTHY

Encouragement and counsel to help Timothy remain firm in the difficult times ahead

The last inspired letter written by Paul, during his second imprisonment in Rome

---

Encouragement for Timothy to keep making progress

"Stir up like a fire the gift of God" that you received; do not be ashamed of the witness about Christ or of Paul as a prisoner; take your part in suffering for the good news (1:6-8)

Guard the pattern of healthful words (1:13, 14)

Like a soldier, be single-minded; like an athlete in the games, contend according to the rules; be like the hardworking farmer; endure faithfully (2:3-13)

Do your utmost to present yourself approved to God, handling the word of truth aright (2:15)

Flee from desires of youth, but pursue godly qualities in company with those who call on the Lord out of a clean heart (2:22)

Counsel to help Timothy stand firm against false teachers

Avoid fights about words and talk that violates what is holy; with mildness, try to recover those ensnared by the Devil (2:16-26)

In the last days there will be critical times hard to deal with because of the wicked attitudes of people; they will be lovers of money and of pleasures rather than lovers of God; shun such people (3:1-7)

These corrupted men will go on resisting the truth; but stick to what you have accepted as true because you learned it from people you knew well and from the inspired Scriptures (3:8-17)

Persevere in preaching the word, evangelizing, fully accomplishing your ministry—even though times are coming when men will not want to listen to healthful doctrine but will prefer having their ears tickled by teachers of their own choosing (4:1-5)

Paul's circumstances as a prisoner

Paul was appointed an apostle of Jesus Christ; he is now suffering because of this but is not ashamed (1:11, 12)

As a prisoner in chains, he was virtually abandoned by all from the district of Asia, but Onesiphorus diligently searched for him and brought him refreshment (1:15-18)

Recognizing his death to be imminent, Paul confidently looks forward to the day when Jesus Christ will give the crown of righteousness to him as well as to all others who have loved his manifestation (4:6-8)

No one took his side in his first defense; nevertheless, Paul was strengthened by the Lord Jesus Christ; he is confident that the Lord will save him for His heavenly Kingdom (4:16-18)

---

prisoner for his sake, but take your part in suffering evil for the good news according to the power of God."—2Ti 1:6-8.

TIN. A faintly bluish white metal that is very malleable. Of the six products of the ancient metallurgist's furnace, tin had the lowest melting point of all, only 232° C. (449° F.). (Eze 22:18, 20) The original Hebrew word *bedhil'* means "that which is separated or divided," that is, from precious metals by smelting; it is also translated "waste products."—Isa 1:25.

The first reference to tin, soon after the Exodus, includes it among the valuable spoils of war taken from the Midianites. (Nu 31:2, 22) There were no tin mines in Palestine; the heavy dark oxide of tin called cassiterite came from river sands in Tarshish and from England. (Eze 27:12) Tin, it appears, was used to make plummets, for at Zechariah 4:10 (which speaks of "the plummet") the Masoretic text reads, "the stone [or, weight], the tin." In Amos 7:7, 8 the Hebrew word translated "plummet" may mean tin or lead. Tin's greatest usefulness, however, was as a hardening agent; copper alloyed with 2 to 18 percent tin has been found in ancient specimens of bronze.

TIPHSAH (Tiph'sah).

1. A place at the extreme N of Solomon's kingdom. (1Ki 4:24) Some tentatively identify it with Dibseh on the Euphrates River, about 90 km (56 mi) ESE of Aleppo and about the same distance from the confluence of the Euphrates and Balikh rivers.

2. A place, apparently in the vicinity of Tirzah, that was struck down by Israel's King Menahem (c. 790-781 B.C.E.). (2Ki 15:16) Its exact location is not known. Khirbet Tafsah, about 10 km (6 mi) WSW of ancient Shechem, bears a similar name but appears to be too far from the assumed site of Tirzah to be the location of this Tiphsah.

TIRAS (Ti'ras). One of the seven sons of Japheth. (Ge 10:2; 1Ch 1:5) The people who descended from Japheth's sons were later "spread about in their lands, each according to its tongue." —Ge 10:5.

Generally, scholars of the present day consider Tiras to be identified with the *Tyr·se·noi'* of classical Greek writers, also called *Tyr·rhe·noi'*. The *Tyr·se·noi'* were a seafaring people of the islands and coastlands of the Aegean Sea.

TIRATHITES (Ti′rath·ites). A Kenite family of scribes living at Jabez.—1Ch 2:55.

TIRHAKAH (Tir·ha′kah). Usually identified as Pharaoh Taharqa, although the dates generally assigned by modern historians to Taharqa's rule do not fit Biblical chronology. (For evidence favoring Biblical chronology over the secular, see CHRONOLOGY [Bible Chronology and Secular History].) During Hezekiah's reign, while Assyrian King Sennacherib was fighting against Libnah, news came that Tirhakah, the Ethiopian king of Egypt, was on his way to fight the Assyrians. (2Ki 19:8, 9; Isa 37:8, 9) An Assyrian inscription, though not mentioning Tirhakah, indicates that Sennacherib defeated the forces that came from Egypt and captured "the charioteers of the king of Ethiopia." The next Assyrian king, Esar-haddon, boasted about his conquest of Egypt, saying: "Its king, Tirhakah, I wounded five times with arrowshots and ruled over his entire country." During the reign of Esar-haddon's son and successor Ashurbanipal, Tirhakah revolted against submission to Assyria. But, according to Ashurbanipal, "the terror of the (sacred) weapon of Ashur, my lord, overcame Tirhakah where he had taken refuge and he was never heard of again."—*Ancient Near Eastern Texts,* edited by J. Pritchard, 1974, pp. 287, 288, 290, 295.

TIRHANAH (Tir′ha·nah). Child of Caleb by his concubine Maacah; of the tribe of Judah. —1Ch 2:3, 48.

TIRIA (Tir′i·a). A 'son' of Jehallelel in the genealogies of Judah.—1Ch 4:1, 16.

TIRSHATHA (Tir·sha′tha). The Persian title for the governor of a jurisdictional district. In the five times it is used, it is preceded by the Hebrew definite article *ha,* making it in English "*the* Tirshatha."

The officials mentioned in the Bible by the title "Tirshatha" ruled over Judah, one of the Persian provinces. Zerubbabel was evidently the Tirshatha mentioned in Ezra 2:63 and Nehemiah 7:65, 70. Later when Nehemiah became governor he was the Tirshatha and is referred to as such at Nehemiah 8:9 and 10:1.

TIRZAH (Tir′zah) [from a root meaning "take pleasure; approve"].

1. One of the five daughters of the Manassite Zelophehad; a contemporary of Moses and Joshua.—Nu 26:29, 33; 27:1-7; 36:11, 12; Jos 17:3, 4.

2. A city in Samaria. Archaeological evidence seems to favor identifying it with Tell el-Far′ah, about 10 km (6 mi) NNE of Shechem.

Under the command of Joshua, the Israelites defeated the king of Tirzah. (Jos 12:7, 24) Centuries later, Jeroboam, the first king of the northern kingdom, transferred his residence to Tirzah. (Compare 1Ki 12:25; 14:17.) Tirzah evidently continued to be the capital of the northern kingdom during the reigns of Jeroboam's son Nadab (1Ki 15:25-28) and his successors Baasha, Elah, and Zimri. (1Ki 15:33; 16:5, 6, 8, 15) The last of these kings, Zimri, committed suicide at Tirzah when Omri captured the city. (1Ki 16:17-20) After reigning in Tirzah for six years, Omri built Samaria and made that city his capital. (1Ki 16:23, 24, 29) More than 150 years later, Menahem, a resident of Tirzah, killed Shallum and became king in Samaria.—2Ki 15:14, 17.

TISHBITE (Tish′bite). Evidently an inhabitant of Tishbeh, apparently a village E of the Jordan, in the land of Gilead. The term "Tishbite" is applied to Elijah in each of its six occurrences. —1Ki 17:1; 21:17, 28; 2Ki 1:3, 8; 9:36.

TISHRI. See ETHANIM.

TITHE. A tenth part, or 10 percent, given or paid as a tribute, especially for religious purposes.

The Bible tells of two instances prior to the setting up of the Law covenant in which a tenth part of possessions was paid to God or to his representative. The first of these was on the occasion when Abraham gave Melchizedek one tenth of the spoils of his victory over Chedorlaomer and his allies. (Ge 14:18-20) The apostle Paul cites this incident as proof that Christ's priesthood according to the manner of Melchizedek is superior to that of Levi, since Levi, being in the loins of Abraham, paid tithes, in effect, to Melchizedek. (Heb 7:4-10) The second case concerned Jacob, who vowed at Bethel to give one tenth of his substance to God.—Ge 28:20-22.

These two accounts, however, are merely instances of voluntarily giving one tenth. There is no record to the effect that Abraham or Jacob commanded their descendants to follow such examples, thereby establishing a religious practice, custom, or law. It would have been superfluous for Jacob, if already under a compulsory obligation to pay tithes, to vow to do so, as he did. It is therefore evident that the tithing arrangement was not a custom or a law among the early Hebrews. It was instituted with the inauguration of the Law covenant, not before.

Mosaic Tithing Laws. Jehovah gave Israel tithing laws for definite purposes, apparently involving the use of *two* tenths of their annual income, except during the Sabbath years, when no tithe was paid, since no income was anticipated. (Le 25:1-12) However, some scholars believe there was only one tithe. Such tithes were in addition to the firstfruits they were under obligation to offer to Jehovah.—Ex 23:19; 34:26.

The first tithe, consisting of one tenth of the produce of the land and fruit trees and (evidently of the *increase*) of the herds and flocks, was brought to the sanctuary and given to the Levites, since they had no inheritance in the land but were devoted to the service of the sanctuary. (Le 27:30-32; Nu 18:21, 24) The Levites, in turn, gave a tenth of what they received to the Aaronic priesthood for their support.—Nu 18:25-29.

Evidently the grain was threshed and the fruit of the vine and of the olive tree was converted into wine and oil before tithing. (Nu 18:27, 30; Ne 10:37) If an Israelite wished to give money instead of this produce, he could do so, provided he added an additional fifth to the valuation. (Le 27:31) But it was different with the flock and the herd. As the animals came out of the pen one by one through a gate, the owner stood by the gate with a rod and marked every tenth one as the tithe, without examination or selection.—Le 27: 32, 33.

It seems there was an additional tithe, a second tenth, set aside each year for purposes other than the direct support of the Levitical priesthood, though the Levites shared in it. Normally it was used and enjoyed in large measure by the Israelite family when assembling together at the national festivals. In cases where the distance to Jerusalem was too great for the convenient transport of this tithe, then the produce was converted into money and this, in turn, was used in Jerusalem for the household's sustenance and enjoyment during the holy convention there. (De 12:4-7, 11, 17, 18; 14:22-27) Then, at the end of every third and sixth years of the seven-year sabbatical cycle, this tithe, instead of being used to defray expenses at the national assemblies, was set aside for the Levites, alien residents, widows, and fatherless boys in the local community.—De 14:28, 29; 26:12.

These tithing laws binding on Israel were not excessive. Nor should it be overlooked that God promised to prosper Israel by opening "the floodgates of the heavens" if his tithing laws were obeyed. (Mal 3:10; De 28:1, 2, 11-14) When the people became negligent as to tithing, the priesthood suffered, for the priests and Levites were forced to spend their time in secular work and consequently neglected their ministerial services.

(Ne 13:10) Such unfaithfulness tended to bring about a decline in true worship. Sadly, when the ten tribes fell away to calf worship, they used the tithe to support that false religion. (Am 4:4, 5) On the other hand, when Israel was faithful to Jehovah and was under the rule of righteous administrators, tithing for the Levites was restored, and true to Jehovah's promise, there were no shortages.—2Ch 31:4-12; Ne 10:37, 38; 12:44; 13: 11-13.

Under the Law there was no stated penalty to be applied to a person failing to tithe. Jehovah placed all under a strong moral obligation to provide the tithe; at the end of the three-year tithing cycle, they were required to confess before him that the tithe had been paid in full. (De 26:12-15) Anything wrongfully withheld was viewed as something stolen from God.—Mal 3:7-9.

By the first century C.E., the Jewish religious leaders, particularly among the scribes and Pharisees, were making a sanctimonious show of tithing and other outward works, in a form of worship, but their hearts were far removed from God. (Mt 15:1-9) Jesus reproved them for their selfish, hypocritical attitude, calling attention to their being meticulous to give a tenth even of "the mint and the dill and the cumin"—something they should have done—yet at the same time disregarding "the weightier matters of the Law, namely, justice and mercy and faithfulness." (Mt 23:23; Lu 11:42) By way of illustration, Jesus contrasted the Pharisee who boastfully felt self-righteous because of his own works of fasting and tithing, with the tax collector who, though considered as nothing by the Pharisee, humbled himself, confessed his sins to God, and begged for divine mercy.—Lu 18:9-14.

No Tithing for Christians. At no time were first-century Christians commanded to pay tithes. The primary purpose of the tithing arrangement under the Law had been to support Israel's temple and priesthood; consequently the obligation to pay tithes would cease when that Mosaic Law covenant came to an end as fulfilled, through Christ's death on the torture stake. (Eph 2:15; Col 2:13, 14) It is true that Levitical priests continued serving at the temple in Jerusalem until it was destroyed in 70 C.E., but Christians from and after 33 C.E. became part of a new spiritual priesthood that was not supported by tithes.—Ro 6:14; Heb 7:12; 1Pe 2:9.

As Christians, they were encouraged to give support to the Christian ministry both by their own ministerial activity and by material contributions. Instead of giving fixed, specified amounts to defray congregational expenses, they were to contribute "according to what a person has," giving "as he has resolved in his heart, not grudgingly or under compulsion, for God loves a cheerful giver." (2Co 8:12; 9:7) They were encouraged to follow the principle: "Let the older men who preside in a fine way be reckoned worthy of double honor, especially those who work hard in speaking and teaching. For the scripture says: 'You must not muzzle a bull when it threshes out the grain'; also: 'The workman is worthy of his wages.'" (1Ti 5:17, 18) However, the apostle Paul set an example in seeking to avoid bringing an undue financial burden on the congregation. —Ac 18:3; 1Th 2:9.

TITIUS JUSTUS.   See Justus.

TITUS   (Ti'tus). A Greek Christian who labored with the apostle Paul. At the time the circumcision issue arose at Antioch (c. 49 C.E.), it appears that Titus accompanied Paul and Barnabas to Jerusalem. (Ac 15:1, 2; Ga 2:1-3) About 55 C.E., Titus ministered unselfishly to the Corinthian congregation, having been sent to Corinth by the apostle Paul to assist in the collection for the needy brothers in Judea and perhaps also to note the reaction of the congregation to Paul's first

letter to them. (2Co 2:13; 8:1-6; 12:17, 18) When Titus thereafter met the apostle in Macedonia, he was able to give a good report about the Corinthian congregation, one that brought comfort and joy to Paul. Titus himself had developed great affection for the Corinthian Christians because of their obedience and because their commendable attitude had proved to be a source of encouragement and joy to him.—2Co 7:6, 7, 13-15.

Since Titus had initiated matters in connection with the contribution, Paul desired that he complete the task and commended Titus to the Corinthian congregation as "a sharer with me and a fellow worker for your interests." Being sincerely interested in the welfare of the Corinthians, and encouraged by the apostle to do so, Titus willingly departed for Corinth.—2Co 8:6, 16, 17, 23.

After Paul was released from his first imprisonment at Rome, Titus and Timothy apparently worked with him in the ministry. While in Crete (evidently sometime between 61 and 64 C.E.), Paul left Titus there to 'correct the things that were defective and to make appointments of older men in city after city.' (Tit 1:4, 5) This was apparently a temporary assignment, for Paul requested that Titus do his utmost to join him at Nicopolis.—Tit 3:12.

HIGHLIGHTS OF TITUS

Counsel to an elder regarding the handling of situations in a most difficult assignment

Written by the apostle Paul evidently after his first imprisonment in Rome

Appointment of overseers and handling of serious problems

Titus is commissioned to correct things that are defective and to appoint overseers in various cities of Crete (1:5)

A man who is appointed to be an overseer should be free from accusation, exemplary both in his person and in his family life, hospitable, balanced, and self-controlled; he must properly represent the truth in his teaching and thus be able to exhort and to reprove those who contradict (1:6-9)

Unruly men in the congregations must be silenced, especially those adhering to the circumcision, who have subverted entire households; severe reproof must be given so that all may be healthy in the faith (1:10-16)

Foolish questionings, genealogies, and conflicts over the Law must be avoided; reject a promoter of a sect after he has been admonished twice (3:9-11)

Healthful counsel to all kinds of Christians

Aged men are encouraged to be exemplary in modera-

tion, seriousness, soundness of mind, faith, love, and endurance (2:1, 2)

Aged women are likewise urged to be exemplary; they should be teachers of good, in order that they may help younger women to have the right view of their responsibilities as wives and mothers so as not to bring reproach on the word of God (2:3-5)

Younger men are exhorted to have a sound mind (2:6-8)

Slaves should be in subjection to their owners in a manner that will adorn the teaching of God (2:9, 10)

God's undeserved kindness should motivate Christians to repudiate ungodliness and live with soundness of mind in this system of things, while they wait patiently for the glorious manifestation of God and of Jesus Christ (2:11-15)

Show proper submission to rulers, shun belligerency, and cultivate reasonableness and mildness (3:1, 2)

Paul and his fellow Christians, too, at one time carried on badness; but by God's undeserved kindness they were saved and now have the sure hope of everlasting life; constantly stress these facts in order to encourage believers to keep their minds on fine works (3:3-8)

Sometime during Paul's second imprisonment at Rome (c. 65 C.E.), Titus, likely at the apostle's direction or with his approval, left for Dalmatia. —2Ti 4:10; see DALMATIA.

TITUS, LETTER TO.

A letter written by the apostle Paul to Titus, a fellow worker whom Paul had left behind in Crete to 'correct the things that were defective and to make appointments of older men' in the various congregations there. (Tit 1:1, 4, 5) The letter's authenticity is attested by all outstanding ancient catalogs of the Christian Greek Scriptures, starting with the Muratorian Fragment of the second century C.E.

Time and Place of Writing. As no record exists that Paul engaged in Christian activity on the island of Crete before his first imprisonment at Rome, he must have been there with Titus sometime between his release and his final imprisonment. Thus the time for the letter's composition would be between about 61 and 64 C.E. Macedonia may have been the place from which the letter was sent; it was apparently there in the same general period that Paul wrote First Timothy.—1Ti 1:3.

The Letter's Purpose. The letter evidently was to serve as a guide for Titus and gave him apostolic backing for the performance of his duties in connection with the Cretan congregations. His assignment was not an easy one, for he had to contend with rebellious persons. As Paul wrote: "There are many unruly men, profitless talkers, and deceivers of the mind, especially those men who adhere to the circumcision. It is necessary to shut the mouths of these, as these very men keep on subverting entire households by teaching things they ought not for the sake of dishonest gain." (Tit 1:10, 11) Also, lying, gluttony, and laziness were common among the Cretans, and apparently some of the Christians reflected these bad traits. For this reason Titus had to reprove them with severity and show what was required of Christians, whether young or old, male or female, slave or free. Personally he had to be an example in fine works and show uncorruptness in teaching.—1:12–3:2.

TIZITE

(Ti'zite). Designation of David's warrior Joha. (1Ch 11:26, 45) The name is probably derived from a place now unknown.

TOAH

(To'ah). A Kohathite Levite ancestor of the prophet Samuel and Heman the singer. (1Ch 6:33, 34, 38) He is probably called Nahath in 1 Chronicles 6:26 and Tohu at 1 Samuel 1:1.

TOB.

A "land" to which Jephthah fled from his half brothers. In Tob he gathered a force of men before his half brothers asked him to be their commander in fighting against the Ammonites. (Jg 11:3-11) There is possibly another Biblical reference to Tob if the name Ishtob is rather to be translated "men of Tob" at 2 Samuel 10:6-8. (See *AS, JP, RS, NW* ftn.) Tob's location is not definitely known. However, it is often identified with the region centering around Taiyiba, about 60 km (37 mi) ESE of the Sea of Galilee.

TOB-ADONIJAH

(Tob-ad·o·ni'jah) [Good Is the Lord Jah]. One of the Levites whom Jehoshaphat, in the third year of his reign, sent out to teach Jehovah's law in the cities of Judah. (2Ch 17:7-9) Reference to Adonijah and Tobijah in the same verse leads some scholars to believe this name is a scribal dittograph, that is, an inadvertent repetition.

TOBIAH

(To·bi'ah) [Good Is Jah].

1. Forefather of some returned exiles who were unable to establish their Israelite genealogy. —Ezr 2:1, 59, 60; Ne 7:61, 62.

2. An opponent of Nehemiah. Tobiah was "the servant," likely some official under the Persian king. (Ne 2:19) Both he and his son Jehohanan married Jewish women, and Tobiah was also related to High Priest Eliashib. This put Tobiah in a position of advantage for undermining Nehemiah's authority, in that many Jews looked up to and spoke highly of Tobiah.—Ne 6:17-19; 13:4; compare 3:4; 7:6, 7, 10.

When Nehemiah arrived in Jerusalem, Tobiah and his associates were displeased with Israel's brightening prospect. (Ne 2:9, 10) At first they merely derided and mocked the Jews (Ne 2:19; 4:3), but when the wall rebuilding made progress, they became very angry. However, various conspiracies—to kill off the Jews (Ne 4:7-9, 11, 14, 15), and an attempt to get Nehemiah to violate the sanctity of the temple (Ne 6:1, 10-13)—all failed. Even after the walls were completed, Tobiah, through correspondence with his sympathizers in Jerusalem, attempted to intimidate Nehemiah. (Ne 6:16-19) Properly, therefore, Nehemiah asked Jehovah to remember the many wicked deeds of Tobiah and his confederates. (Ne 6:14) On Nehemiah's second arrival from Babylon, when he found a dining room in the temple court reserved for Tobiah, he promptly threw Tobiah's things out.—Ne 13:4-9.

TOBIJAH

(To·bi'jah) [Good Is Jehovah].

1. One of the Levites whom Jehoshaphat dispatched to teach Jehovah's law in the cities of Judah in 934 B.C.E.—2Ch 17:7-9.

2. One of the returned Jewish exiles from whom gold and silver were taken to make a crown for High Priest Jeshua.—Zec 6:10, 11, 14.

TOCHEN (To'chen) [Fixed Amount]. A city of Simeon. (1Ch 4:24, 32) It appears to be called Ether at Joshua 19:7.—See ETHER.

TOE. One of the terminal members of the human foot. The Hebrew and Aramaic words used in the Bible for finger refer also, at times, to the toe. (2Sa 21:20; 1Ch 20:6; Da 2:41, 42) In other places the Hebrew word for "thumb" is used also for "toe."—Ex 29:20; Le 8:23, 24; 14:14, 17, 25, 28.

The toes, being important for balance and direction to the body in walking, are referred to in the Scriptures with literal and figurative significance. A custom occasionally practiced to incapacitate a captured enemy for battle was to cut off his thumbs and big toes.—Jg 1:6, 7.

At the installation of the priesthood in Israel, Moses took some blood of the ram of the installation and put it on the right ear, the right thumb, and the right big toe of Aaron and each of his sons. (Le 8:23, 24) The blood of the sacrifice on the prominent member of the right foot meant that they must point their course and walk unswervingly with the best of their ability in the sacrificial duties of the priesthood. Jesus Christ the great High Priest fulfilled this prophetic type when on earth (Mt 16:21-23), and his underpriests, his spirit-begotten brothers, must follow his steps closely.—Heb 7:26; 1Pe 2:5, 8; Re 20:6.

TOGARMAH (To·gar'mah).

1. A son of Gomer the son of Japheth, hence a great-grandson of Noah.—Ge 10:1-3; 1Ch 1:4-6.

2. Descendants of Gomer's son Togarmah and the region they occupied. In Ezekiel's dirge concerning Tyre, Togarmah is mentioned as the source of "horses and steeds and mules," for which Tyre traded certain goods. (Eze 27:2, 14) The same prophet lists Togarmah among Gog of Magog's allies and gives its situation as among the peoples of "the remotest parts of the north."—Eze 38:6.

Many commentators connect Togarmah with the Armenians. The Armenians themselves traditionally claim to be descended from "Haik, son of *Thorgom.*" Ancient Greek writers speak of the Armenians as famed for their horses and mules.

TOHU (To'hu). An ancestor of Samuel. (1Sa 1:1) He is apparently called "Nahath" and "Toah" in Chronicles.—1Ch 6:16, 22-28, 34.

TOI (To'i), **TOU** (To'u). King of Hamath. On learning that David had defeated their mutual enemy Hadadezer the king of Zobah, Toi immedi-

ately sent his son with congratulations and gifts. These David sanctified along with his battle spoil. —2Sa 8:9-12; 1Ch 18:9-11.

TOLA (To'la) [Crimson (Scarlet) Cloth].

1. First-named son of Issachar who accompanied Jacob's household into Egypt in 1728 B.C.E. (Ge 46:8, 13) Tola's sons and some of his grandsons founded populous tribal families in Issachar, collectively known as Tolaites.—Nu 26:23; 1Ch 7:1-4.

2. A judge of Israel; the son of Puah. Tola was a descendant of Issachar, but he lived and was later buried in the mountainous region of Ephraim. No experiences from his 23-year judgeship are recorded.—Jg 10:1, 2.

TOLAD (To'lad). Apparently the alternative name of Eltolad, a Simeonite city.—1Ch 4:24, 29, 31; Jos 15:30; 19:1, 4; see ELTOLAD.

TOLAITES (To'la·ites) [Of (Belonging to) Tola]. A family in the tribe of Issachar founded by Tola. —Nu 26:23; see TOLA No. 1.

TOMB. See MEMORIAL TOMB.

TONGUE. An organ of the body playing a prominent role in tasting and in speech. What is commonly called taste results from reactions of the taste buds *plus* the aroma detected by the sense of smell. More important, the tongue is also essential to speech, because articulation of words requires active maneuvering on its part, which it does with dexterity and remarkable speed.—See MOUTH (The Palate).

In Bible usage, "tongue" often stands for "language." (Ge 10:5; De 28:49; Isa 28:11; Ac 2:4; 19:6; 1Co 12:10; see LANGUAGE.) Or, at times, it refers to a people speaking a certain language. —Isa 66:18; Re 5:9; 7:9; 13:7.

Jesus' half brother James vividly describes the power exercised by the tongue and the need for the Christian to exercise great care to use it properly. He points out that failure to bridle the tongue can be a factor in causing one's worship to be futile. (Jas 1:26) He likens the tongue to a fire that can destroy a forest. The unbridled tongue can be influenced by destructive forces and can bring about such a great quantity or extent of unrighteousness that it can contaminate the individual's entire life. It can be poisonous, spiritually, to oneself and to others. It cannot be tamed by man's own efforts; nor can any imperfect human be completely exempt from 'stumbling in word.' (Jas 3:2-8) But the taming of this unruly organ of the imperfect human flesh is not impossible for the Christian, for by Jehovah's undeserved kindness through Christ a person can bridle his tongue and can make over his personality.—Jas 3:10-18; 1Pe 3:10; Col 3:9, 10; compare Ps 34:13; 39:1.

In harmony with James' description of the tongue, the writer of Proverbs says that the calmness of the tongue can be "a tree of life." On the other hand, a distortion in it can mean "a breaking down in the spirit"; death and life are in its power. (Pr 15:4; 18:21) "A mild tongue itself can break a bone," in that a person hard as bone may be softened by a mild answer and break down in his hardness and opposition. (Pr 25:15) In fact, the tongue can heal in a spiritual way if it speaks the words of God. (Pr 12:18) "From Jehovah is the answer of the tongue," for only he can provide spiritually correct words that result in healing. (Pr 16:1) The Scriptures foretold the spiritual healing from Jesus' ministry as he spoke God's words, 'binding up the brokenhearted.'—Isa 61:1.

Jehovah emphasizes how he views the badness of the false tongue, listing it as one of the seven things that he hates, placing it alongside "hands that are shedding innocent blood." (Pr 6:16-19) David describes the wicked as attempting to destroy God's servant with a 'tongue sharpened just like a sword,' but he points out that actually God will see to it that they themselves are wounded, for "their tongue is against their own selves." (Ps 64:3, 7, 8) Jehovah promises his people: "Any tongue at all that will rise up against you in the judgment you will condemn." (Isa 54:17) This is comforting to God's servants, who stick to his law even though those considered wise in the world may speak great things and say: "With our tongue we shall prevail." (Ps 12:3-5) They may "keep sticking out the tongue" and striking with the tongue (Isa 57:4; Jer 18:18), but their failure is certain.—Pr 10:31.

Jehovah promised to make tongues that formerly were stammering "quick in speaking clear things" and to cause speechless tongues to "cry out in gladness." (Isa 32:4; 35:6) When Jesus was on earth, he healed literally speechless persons, or those with some speech impediment. (Mr 7:33-37) The time will come when every tongue will speak right things, for Jehovah declares that every tongue will swear to him. The apostle Paul reveals that this will be done through Jesus Christ, when he says that every tongue will "openly acknowledge that Jesus Christ is Lord to the glory of God the Father."—Php 2:11; Isa 45: 23; Ro 14:11.

Jehovah symbolically describes himself as having a tongue that he will use in his anger, "like a devouring fire." (Isa 30:27) At Pentecost, when Jesus Christ poured out holy spirit on some 120 disciples gathered in a room in Jerusalem, that spirit was made manifest audibly by their speaking in different tongues and visibly by a tongue as if of fire sitting upon each one of them.—Ac 2:3, 4.

TONGUES, SPEAKING IN. See GIFTS FROM GOD ("Tongues").

TOPAZ. The variety used for gemstones is a hard, transparent, crystalline mineral composed of aluminum fluosilicate. It is harder than quartz and is often found in cavities of granitic rocks. Topaz may be colorless, but it also occurs in a great range of colors that include white, yellow, light brown, pinkish red, and sometimes pale green or blue. The most popular shade is wineyellow. The name topaz is from the Greek word to·pa'zi·on, which alludes to the Topaz Island situated in the Red Sea where the Greeks obtained the topazes familiar to Pliny the Elder and to other early writers. The book of Job links topaz with Cush, a region that bordered the Red Sea.

A topaz was among the precious stones on "the breastpiece of judgment" worn by High Priest Aaron. It was set as the middle stone in the first row of gems, and engraved upon it was the name of one of Israel's 12 tribes. (Ex 28:2, 15, 17, 21; 39:10) The foundations of "the holy city, New Jerusalem, coming down out of heaven from God . . . were adorned with every sort of precious stone," the ninth foundation being topaz.—Re 21:2, 19, 20.

TOPHEL (To'phel). A site mentioned with others as an aid in locating the place where Moses addressed the Israelites shortly before his death. —De 1:1.

TOPHETH (To'pheth). A place outside Jerusalem where, for a considerable period, apostate Israelites, including Ahaz and Manasseh, engaged in child sacrifice. Finally, King Josiah made it unfit for worship. (2Ki 23:10; 2Ch 28:3; 33:6; Jer 7:31-33; 19:3-14; 32:35) Topheth probably occupied a section of the eastern part of the Valley of Hinnom near the Gate of the Potsherds.—Jer 19:2, 6, 14; see HINNOM, VALLEY OF.

Commenting on 2 Kings 23:10, the Jewish commentator David Kimhi (1160?-1235?) offers this possible explanation concerning Topheth: "The name of the place where they caused their sons to pass through [the fire] to Molech. The name of the place was Topheth, and they said it was called thus because at the time of worship they would dance and strike tambourines [Heb., *tup·pim'*] so that the father would not hear his son's cries when they were causing him to pass through the fire, and that his heart might not become agitated over him and he take him from their hand. And this place was a valley that belonged to a man named Hinnom, and it was called 'Valley of Hinnom' and 'Valley of the Son of Hinnom' . . . . And Josiah defiled that place, reducing it to an unclean place, to cast there carcasses and all uncleanness, that it might never again come up into the heart of a man to cause his son and his daughter to pass through in the fire to Molech."—*Biblia Rabbinica*, Jerusalem, 1972.

At Isaiah 30:32, 33 it is stated that the punishment that Jehovah will bring against Assyria "will certainly prove to be with tambourines [Heb., *betup·pim'*] and with harps . . . . For his Topheth is set in order from recent times . . . . Fire and wood are in abundance. The breath of Jehovah, like a torrent of sulphur, is burning against it." Here Topheth is used figuratively as a place of burning with fire, to represent the destruction that was to come upon Assyria.

TORCH. A light usually carried in the hand and often consisting either of a burning stick of resinous wood or of a stick wrapped with an absorbent material that has been soaked with oil and ignited.—Ge 15:17; Jg 7:16, 20; 15:4; Isa 62:1; Eze 1:13; Da 10:6; Na 2:4; Joh 18:3.

TORMENT. The Greek word *ba·sa·ni'zo* (and related terms) occurs over 20 times in the Christian Greek Scriptures. It basically meant "test by the proving stone [*ba'sa·nos*]" and, by extension, "examine or question by applying torture." Lexicographers point out that in the Christian Greek Scriptures it is used with the sense of 'vexing with grievous pains; being harassed, distressed.'—Mt 8:29; Lu 8:28; Re 12:2.

The Bible used *ba·sa·ni'zo* in a number of instances. For example, a manservant afflicted with paralysis was "terribly tormented" (*NW*) or "racked with pain" (*NE*) by it. (Mt 8:6; compare 4:24.) Also, Lot "used to torment his soul" (*Ro*) or "was vexed" (*Mo, RS*) by the lawless deeds of the people of Sodom. (2Pe 2:8) The word is even used in regard to the difficult progress of a boat.—Mt 14:24; Mr 6:48.

The Greek noun *ba·sa·ni·stes'* occurring at Matthew 18:34 is rendered "jailers" in some translations (*AT, Fn, NW*; compare Mt 18:30) and "tor-

mentors" or "torturers" in others. (*AS, KJ, JB*) Torture was sometimes used in prisons to obtain information (compare Ac 22:24, 29, which shows that this was done, although *ba·sa·ni'zo* is not used here), so *ba·sa·ni·stes'* came to be applied to jailers. Regarding its use at Matthew 18:34, *The International Standard Bible Encyclopaedia* observed: "Probably the imprisonment itself was regarded as 'torment' (as it doubtless was), and the 'tormentors' need mean nothing more than jailers." (Edited by J. Orr, 1960, Vol. V, p. 2999) Thus, the mentioning in Revelation 20:10 of ones who will be "tormented day and night forever and ever" evidently indicates that they will be in a condition of restraint. That a condition of restraint can be spoken of as "torment" is indicated by the parallel accounts at Matthew 8:29 and Luke 8:31.—See LAKE OF FIRE.

Some commentators have pointed to Biblical instances of the word "torment" to support the teaching of eternal suffering in fire. However, as just indicated, there is Scriptural reason to believe that Revelation 20:10 does not have that sense. In fact, verse 14 shows that "the lake of fire" in which the torment occurs, actually means "the second death." And though Jesus spoke of a certain rich man as "existing in torments" (Lu 16:23, 28), as the article LAZARUS (No. 2) shows, Jesus was not describing the literal experience of a real person but, rather, was setting forth an illustration. Revelation provides a number of other instances where "torment" clearly has an illustrative or symbolic sense, as is evident from context. —Re 9:5; 11:10; 18:7, 10.

TORRENT VALLEY. The Hebrew word *na'chal* may denote either the valley through which a stream flows (Ge 26:19; 2Ki 3:16; Job 30:6; Ca 6:11) or the stream itself. (1Ki 17:4; Ps 110:7) Regarding the word *na'chal*, A. P. Stanley, in his book *Sinai and Palestine* (1885, p. 590), observes: "No English word is exactly equivalent, but perhaps 'torrent-bed' most nearly expresses it." A Hebrew and Aramaic lexicon by Koehler and Baumgartner lists "torrent-valley" as one of its definitions. (*Lexicon in Veteris Testamenti Libros*, Leiden, 1958, p. 607) The term "wadi" (Arabic) is also used to designate a torrent valley.—Ge 32: 23, ftn.

The Promised Land is described as "a land of torrent valleys of water, springs and watery deeps issuing forth in the valley plain and in the mountainous region." (De 8:7) Some of the streams are fed by springs and are therefore perennial, whereas others are torrents during the rainy season but dry up completely during the rainless season. (1Ki 17:7; 18:5) Faithful Job compared the treacherous dealings of his brothers toward him to a winter torrent that dries up in the summer.—Job 6:15.

Among the torrent valleys mentioned in the Bible are those of the Arabah (Am 6:14), Arnon (De 2:36), Besor (1Sa 30:9), Cherith (1Ki 17:3), Egypt (Jos 15:4), Eshcol (Nu 13:23), Gerar (Ge 26:17), Jabbok (De 2:37), Kanah (Jos 16:8), Kidron (2Sa 15:23), Kishon (Jg 4:7), Sorek (Jg 16:4), and Zered (De 2:13; see the torrent valleys under their respective names). Other torrent valleys that are not mentioned but are principal tributaries of the Jordan are the Yarmuk and the Far-'ah.

TORTURE STAKE.

An instrument such as that on which Jesus Christ met death by impalement. (Mt 27:32-40; Mr 15:21-30; Lu 23:26; Joh 19:17-19, 25) In classical Greek the word (*stau·ros'*) rendered "torture stake" in the *New World Translation* primarily denotes an upright stake, or pole, and there is no evidence that the writers of the Christian Greek Scriptures used it to designate a stake with a crossbeam.—See IMPALEMENT; *Int*, pp. 1149-1151.

The book *The Non-Christian Cross*, by John Denham Parsons, states: "There is not a single sentence in any of the numerous writings forming the New Testament, which, in the original Greek, bears even indirect evidence to the effect that the stauros used in the case of Jesus was other than an ordinary stauros; much less to the effect that it consisted, not of one piece of timber, but of two pieces nailed together in the form of a cross. . . . it is not a little misleading upon the part of our

teachers to translate the word stauros as 'cross' when rendering the Greek documents of the Church into our native tongue, and to support that action by putting 'cross' in our lexicons as the meaning of stauros without carefully explaining that that was at any rate not the primary meaning of the word in the days of the Apostles, did not become its primary signification till long afterwards, and became so then, if at all, only because, despite the absence of corroborative evidence, it was for some reason or other assumed that the particular stauros upon which Jesus was

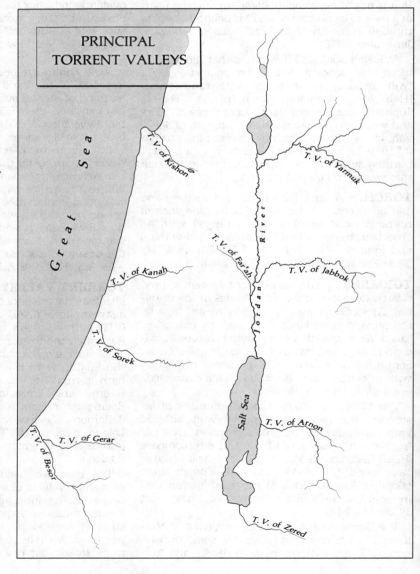

PRINCIPAL TORRENT VALLEYS

Great Sea

T. V. of Kishon

T. V. of Yarmuk

Jordan River

T. V. of Far·ah

T. V. of Jabbok

T. V. of Kanah

T. V. of Sorek

Salt Sea

T. V. of Arnon

T. V. of Gerar

T. V. of Besor

T. V. of Zered

executed had that particular shape."—London, 1896, pp. 23, 24.

Why Jesus Had to Die on a Stake. At the time Jehovah God gave his law to the Israelites, they obligated themselves to abide by its terms. (Ex 24:3) However, as descendants of sinner Adam, they were unable to do so perfectly. For this reason they came under the curse of the Law. To remove this special curse from them, Jesus had to be hanged on a stake like an accursed criminal. Concerning this the apostle Paul wrote: "All those who depend upon works of law are under a curse; for it is written: 'Cursed is every one that does not continue in all the things written in the scroll of the Law in order to do them.' . . . Christ by purchase released us from the curse of the Law by becoming a curse instead of us, because it is written: 'Accursed is every man hanged upon a stake.'"—Ga 3:10-13.

Figurative Use. "Torture stake" sometimes stands for the sufferings, shame, or torture experienced because of being a follower of Jesus Christ. As Jesus said: "Whoever does not accept his torture stake and follow after me is not worthy of me." (Mt 10:38; 16:24; Mr 8:34; Lu 9:23; 14:27) The expression "torture stake" is also used in such a way as to represent Jesus' death upon the stake, which made possible redemption from sin and reconciliation with God.—1Co 1:17, 18.

Jesus' death on the torture stake was the basis for removing the Law, which had separated the Jews from the non-Jews. Therefore, by accepting the reconciliation made possible by Jesus' death, both Jews and non-Jews could become "one body to God through the torture stake." (Eph 2:11-16; Col 1:20; 2:13, 14) This proved to be a stumbling block for many Jews, since they insisted that circumcision and adherence to the Mosaic Law were essential for gaining God's approval. That is why the apostle Paul wrote: "Brothers, if I am still preaching circumcision, why am I still being persecuted? Then, indeed, the stumbling block of the torture stake has been abolished." (Ga 5:11) "All those who want to make a pleasing appearance in the flesh are the ones that try to compel you to get circumcised, only that they may not be persecuted for the torture stake of the Christ, Jesus. Never may it occur that I should boast, except in the torture stake of our Lord Jesus Christ, through whom the world has been impaled to me and I to the world." (Ga 6:12, 14) For confessing Jesus' death on the torture stake as the sole basis for gaining salvation, Paul was persecuted by the Jews. As a consequence of this confession, to the apostle the world was as something impaled, condemned, or dead, whereas the world viewed him with hatred, as a criminal impaled on a stake.

Persons who embraced Christianity but who afterward turned to an immoral way of life proved themselves to be "enemies of the torture stake of the Christ." (Php 3:18, 19) Their actions demonstrated that they had no appreciation for the benefits resulting from Jesus' death on the torture stake. They "trampled upon the Son of God" and 'esteemed as of ordinary value the blood of the covenant by which they were sanctified.'—Heb 10:29.

TOU. See Toi.

TOW. The original Hebrew word thus translated is understood to designate coarse, short fibers of flax. Tow will burn readily. When Delilah bound Samson with moist sinews, he easily tore them in two, "just as a twisted thread of tow is torn in two when it smells fire." (Jg 16:8, 9) Jehovah decreed that among his ancient people the wicked and their works would perish together, saying: "The vigorous man will certainly become tow, and the product of his activity a spark; and both of them will certainly go up in flames at the same time, with no one to do the extinguishing."—Isa 1:24, 31.

TOWER. A building (or a part of a structure) that is usually higher than its diameter and tall in relation to its surroundings. The history of tower building goes back to the time shortly after the Flood when men on the Plains of Shinar declared: "Come on! Let us build ourselves a city and also a tower with its top in the heavens." (Ge 11:2-4) That tower is thought to have been styled along the oblique pyramid lines of the religious ziggurats discovered in that part of the earth.—See BABEL; ARCHAEOLOGY (Babylonia).

Simple towers were built in vineyards as vantage points for watchmen in guarding the vines against thieves and animals.—Isa 5:1, 2; Mt 21:33; Mr 12:1.

For military defense, towers were built into the walls of cities, usually with more prominent ones at the corners and flanking the gates. (2Ch 26:9; 32:5; Eze 26:4, 9; Zep 1:16; 3:6) In some instances towers served as a chain of outposts along a frontier, or as places of refuge in isolated areas for shepherds and others.—2Ch 26:10; 27:4; see FORTIFICATIONS; WATCHTOWER.

Often a tower inside the city served as a citadel. The towers of Shechem, Thebez, and Penuel were such structures. (Jg 8:9, 17; 9:46-54) Ruins of other city towers have also been found in Jericho, Beth-shan, Lachish, Megiddo, Mizpah, and Samaria.

The Hebrew term *migh·dal'*, meaning "tower" (Eze 29:10; 30:6), forms part of the name of certain places, such as Migdal-gad (meaning "Tower of Good Fortune") and Migdal-el (meaning "Tower of God").—Jos 15:37; 19:38.

"Siege towers" on occasion were built by the attacking armies when assaulting fortified cities. These served as elevated firing positions for archers or throwers. Also, some assault towers contained battering rams and provided protection for those operating the rams.—Isa 23:13.

Jerusalem's Towers. The *Tower of the Bake Ovens* was located on the NW side of the city near or at the Corner Gate. (Ne 3:11; 12:38) Why it was so named is not certain, but quite possibly commercial bakers were present in that vicinity. It may have been one of the towers built by Uzziah, who reigned in Jerusalem from 829 to 778 B.C.E. (2Ch 26:9) Along the N wall of the city were two other important towers: The *Tower of Hananel* was restored and sanctified in Nehemiah's day. (Ne 3:1; 12:39; Jer 31:38; Zec 14:10) Close by it and to the E near the Sheep Gate was the *Tower of Meah.* Why it was called Meah, meaning "Hundred," is not known.—Ne 3:1; 12:39.

Along the E wall S of the temple area was what is referred to as "the protruding tower," and still farther S, somewhere in the vicinity of David's palace, was a tower associated with the King's House near the Courtyard of the Guard. (Ne 3:25-27) Some think that this latter tower was the one referred to in The Song of Solomon as "the *tower of David,* built in courses of stone, upon which are hung a thousand shields, all the circular shields of the mighty men." (Ca 4:4) This tower should not be confused with the more modern so-called Tower of David, which incorporates the tower of Phasael, partly destroyed by Titus in 70 C.E. This Phasael tower was one of the three built by Herod the Great for the protection of his new palace erected near the site of the ancient Corner Gate on the W side of the city.

The *Tower in Siloam* was probably in the vicinity of the pool by that name in the SE sector of Jerusalem. Jesus mentioned that this tower collapsed, killing 18 men, an event that must have been fresh in the memory of his audience.—Lu 13:4; see also ANTONIA, TOWER OF.

Figurative Use. Those who look in faith and obedience to Jehovah have great security, as David sang: "You [Jehovah] have proved to be a refuge for me, a strong tower in the face of the enemy." (Ps 61:3) Those who recognize what his name stands for, and who trust in and faithfully

represent that name, have nothing to fear, for: "The name of Jehovah is a strong tower. Into it the righteous runs and is given protection."—Pr 18:10; compare 1Sa 17:45-47.

TOWER OF BABEL. See BABEL.

TOWN. See CITY; DEPENDENT TOWNS.

TRACHONITIS (Trach·o·ni'tis) [from a Gr. root meaning "rough," probably a rough area]. That region which, together with Ituraea, was under the administration of Philip, a Roman district ruler during the ministries of John the Baptizer and Jesus. (Lu 3:1) The northern limits of Trachonitis were some 40 km (25 mi) SE of Damascus in the northeastern part of Bashan. In size, it embraced a pear-shaped area of about 900 sq km (350 sq mi).

For the most part, exposed lava deposits with their deep fissures and holes cover the central portion of this country, leaving little land suitable for the cultivation of anything other than vineyards. It is a wild, inhospitable, and foreboding country, known today by the Arabic name *el Leja* (meaning "the Refuge"), for it affords a suitable hideout for fugitives from justice.

Judging from the ruins of its ancient cities, at one time the population of Trachonitis was much greater than at present. The absence of wood in the construction of these cities indicates that even in ancient times the country was probably as devoid of timber as it is today. Sufficient rainfall and the presence of springs make the raising of sheep and goats possible.

Trachonitis is mentioned only once in the Bible, though Strabo and Josephus make several references to this region. From such secular sources it is learned that Roman Emperor Augustus included Trachonitis in the kingdom territory given to Herod the Great. Upon Herod's death, his son Philip received Trachonitis as part of his tetrarchy over which he ruled down to his death.

TRADITION. Information, doctrines, or practices that have been handed down from parents to children or that have become the established way of thinking or acting. The Greek word *pa·ra'do·sis* means, literally, "a thing given beside" and hence "that which is transmitted by word of mouth or in writing." (1Co 11:2, *Int*) The word as used in the Christian Greek Scriptures is applied to traditions that were proper or acceptable aspects of true worship, as well as to those that were in error or were followed or viewed in a way that made them harmful and objectionable.

Over the centuries the Jews acquired many traditions. These included ways of dress and handling social matters such as weddings and burials. (Joh 2:1, 2; 19:40) Also, some aspects of Jewish worship in the first century C.E. were customary or traditional, like using wine in the Passover meal and celebrating the rededication of the temple. (Lu 22:14-18; Joh 10:22) Jesus and his apostles did not object to such, though they knew that those things were not required by the Law. When the synagogue became a common place of Jewish worship, it was custom or tradition to worship there each Sabbath. Luke says that Jesus also attended, "according to his custom."—Lu 4:16.

Disapproved Traditions. The Jewish religious leaders, though, had added to the written Word many verbal traditions that they viewed as indispensable to true worship. Paul (Saul), as a Pharisee before his conversion to Christianity, was unusually zealous to follow the traditions of Judaism. These would, of course, include the unobjectionable ones as well as the bad ones. But by following the "commands of men as doctrines," he was led to be a persecutor of Christians. (Mt 15:9) For instance, they 'did not eat unless they washed their hands up to the elbow, holding fast the tradition of the men of former times.' (Mr 7:3) Among those men, this practice was not for hygienic purposes, but it was a ceremonious ritual that supposedly had religious merit. (See WASHING OF HANDS.) Christ showed that they had no basis for criticizing his disciples for not following that and other unnecessary "commands of men." (Mt 15:1, 2, 7-11; Mr 7:4-8; Isa 29:13) Furthermore, by their tradition regarding "corban" (a gift dedicated to God) the religious leaders had made God's Word invalid, overstepping the commandment of God.—Ex 20:12; 21:17; Mt 15:3-6; Mr 7:9-15; see CORBAN.

Neither Jesus nor his disciples ever quoted oral Jewish tradition to support their teachings but, rather, appealed to the written Word of God. (Mt 4:4-10; Ro 15:4; 2Ti 3:15-17) Once the Christian congregation was established, observance of the unscriptural Jewish traditions amounted to a "fruitless form of conduct" that Jewish persons had 'received by tradition from their forefathers [Gr., pa·tro·pa·ra·do'tou, "given along from fathers"].' (1Pe 1:18) Upon becoming Christians, those Jews abandoned such traditions. When some false teachers in Colossae urged taking up that form of worship, Paul warned against "the philosophy and empty deception according to the tradition of men." Evidently he meant, especially, the traditions of Judaism.—Col 2:8, 13-17.

Christian Traditions. Viewing tradition in the sense of guidelines handed down orally or by example, the information that the apostle Paul received directly from Jesus could properly be passed on to the Christian congregations as acceptable Christian tradition. This was so, for example, regarding the celebration of the Lord's Evening Meal. (1Co 11:2, 23) The teachings and example set by the apostles constituted valid tradition. Thus, Paul, who had personally toiled with his hands so as not to be a financial burden on his brothers (Ac 18:3; 20:34; 1Co 9:15; 1Th 2:9), could urge the Thessalonian Christians "to withdraw from every brother walking disorderly and not according to the tradition [pa·ra'do·sin]" they had received. One who would not work was plainly not following the fine example or tradition of the apostles.—2Th 3:6-11.

The "traditions" that are necessary for worship of God that is clean and undefiled were in time included as part of the inspired Scriptures. Hence, the traditions or precepts that were transmitted by Jesus and the apostles and that were vital for life were not left in oral form to be distorted by the passage of time but were accurately recorded in the Bible for the benefit of Christians living at later periods.—Joh 20:30, 31; Re 22:18.

TRAITOR. One who betrays another's trust, is false to a duty, or acts treasonously against his country or ruler. The most infamous traitor of the Bible was "Judas Iscariot, who turned traitor." (Lu 6:16) The Greek noun pro·do'tes ("betrayer; traitor," from a verb meaning "give forth or over; betray") aptly describes Judas, for after being selected as an apostle, he became a greedy, practicing thief (Joh 12:6) and finally betrayed Jesus to the authorities for a comparatively small sum. (Mt 26:14-16, 25, 48, 49) His was not merely a temporary abandoning of Christ by fleeing from what appeared to be a dangerous situation (Mr 14:50) but was a deliberate betrayal of Jesus to those seeking his death.

The Jewish religious leaders were correctly termed "betrayers and murderers," for they employed traitorous Judas, personally turned their fellow countryman Christ over to the Romans, and then, in an outrage of justice, opposed the declaration of Jesus' innocence and demanded his death.—Joh 18:28–19:16; Ac 3:13-15; 7:52.

Another outstanding example of a traitor listed in the Bible was Ahithophel. Though having been King David's trusted counselor, he joined Absalom's insurrection. (2Sa 15:12, 31; 16:20-23; compare Ps 55:20, 21.) God thwarted the traitorous adviser's counsel, leading to Ahithophel's death by suicide. (2Sa 17:23) Evidently David had other experiences with persons who turned against him. A number of modern Bible translations render the plural Hebrew participial form of *ba-ghadh'* (meaning "deal treacherously") as "traitors" at Psalm 59:5: "Do not show favor to any hurtful traitors." (*JB, NE, NW, Mo*) The superscription of the psalm suggests that it relates to the time when Saul sent men to watch David's house in order to kill him. (1Sa 19:11-18) So the "traitors" mentioned at Psalm 59:5 may have been associates of David who had deserted him or who were willing to betray him in that hour of trial. Or, since the preceding words call on God to turn his attention to "all the nations," the term "traitors" may have referred to all opposers of God's will, whether inside or outside Israel.

The prophecy in 2 Timothy 3:1-5 about conditions to exist in "the last days" indicates that there would be many betrayers, or traitors (Gr., *pro-do'tai*). Christians were advised to "turn away" from such, as befits persons striving to be loyal and honest in all things.—1Th 2:10; Heb 13:18.

TRANCE.   See VISION.

TRANSFIGURATION.   A miraculous event witnessed by Peter, James, and John, in which Jesus' "face shone as the sun, and his outer garments became brilliant as the light." (Mt 17:1-9; Mr 9:2-10; Lu 9:28-36) Mark says that on this occasion Jesus' outer garments became "far whiter than any clothes cleaner on earth could whiten them," and Luke states that "the appearance of his face became different." The transfiguration occurred on a mountain sometime after Passover of 32 C.E., quite a while before Jesus' final trip to Jerusalem. It probably took place at night, for the apostles "were weighed down with sleep." (Lu 9:32) At night the event would be more vivid, and they did spend the night on the mountain, for it was not until the next day that they descended. (Lu 9:37) Just how long the transfiguration lasted, however, the Bible does not say.

Prior to ascending the mountain, Christ had asked all of his disciples: "Who are men saying that I am?" whereupon Peter replied: "You are the Christ." At that Jesus told them that he would die and be resurrected (Mr 8:27-31), though he also promised that some of his disciples would "not taste death at all" until they had first seen "the Son of man coming in his kingdom," or "the kingdom of God already come in power." (Mt 16:28; Mr 9:1) This promise was fulfilled "six days later" (or "eight" according to Luke, who apparently

includes the day of the promise and that of the fulfillment) when Peter, James, and John accompanied Jesus into "a lofty mountain" (Mt 17:1; Mr 9:2; Lu 9:28) where, while praying, Jesus was transfigured before them.

Location of the Transfiguration.   Just before the transfiguration, Jesus and his disciples were in the region of Caesarea Philippi, the present-day village of Banyas. (Mr 8:27) It is unlikely that Christ and the apostles departed from this vicinity or region when going to the "lofty mountain." (Mr 9:2) Mount Tabor has been viewed as the traditional site from about the fourth century C.E., but lying about 70 km (40 mi) SSW of Caesarea Philippi, it seems an improbable location.—See TABOR No. 1.

Mount Hermon, on the other hand, is only about 25 km (15 mi) NE of Caesarea Philippi. It rises to a height of 2,814 m (9,232 ft) above sea level and would therefore be "a lofty mountain." (Mt 17:1) Hence, the transfiguration may have taken place on some spur of Mount Hermon. This is the view of many modern scholars, though the Bible's silence on the matter leaves the exact location uncertain.

What is the significance of the transfiguration?

During Jesus' transfiguration, Moses and Elijah also appeared "with glory." (Lu 9:30, 31; Mt 17:3; Mr 9:4) It had been foretold that Jehovah would raise up a prophet like Moses, and that promise was fulfilled in Christ. (De 18:15-19; Ac 3:19-23) There were many similarities between Moses and Jesus, such as: Babes were killed at their births, though they themselves were spared (Ex 1:20–2:10; Mt 2:7-23); they both experienced fasts of 40 days' duration (Ex 24:18; 34:28; De 9:18, 25; Mt 4:1, 2); both were raised up by God in the interests of true worship and to effect deliverance (Ex 3:1-10; Ac 7:30-37; 3:19-23); they were each privileged by God to mediate a covenant with his people (Ex 24:3-8; Heb 8:3-6; 9:15); both were used by Jehovah to magnify his name (Ex 9:13-16; Joh 12:28-30; 17:5, 6, 25, 26).

It was also foretold that Jehovah would send Elijah the prophet, among whose works was that of turning persons of Israel to true repentance. While Jesus was on earth, John the Baptizer did a work of that kind and served as the Messiah's forerunner, fulfilling Malachi 4:5, 6. (Mt 11:11-15; Lu 1:11-17) But, since the transfiguration occurred after the death of John the Baptizer, Elijah's appearance in it indicates that a work of restoration of true worship and vindication of Jehovah's name would be associated with the establishment of God's Kingdom in the hands of Christ.

During the transfiguration, Jesus, Moses, and Elijah talked about Christ's "departure [a form of the Greek word *e'xo·dos*] that he was destined to fulfill at Jerusalem." (Lu 9:31) This *e'xo·dos*, exodus or departure, evidently involved both Christ's death and his subsequent resurrection to spirit life.

Some critics have endeavored to class the transfiguration as simply a dream. However, Peter, James, and John would not logically all have had exactly the same dream. Jesus himself called what took place a "vision" (Mt 17:9), but not a mere illusion. Christ was actually there, though Moses and Elijah, who were dead, were not literally present. They were represented in vision. The Greek word used for "vision" at Matthew 17:9 is *ho'ra·ma*, also rendered "sight." (Ac 7:31) It does not imply unreality, as though the observers were laboring under a delusion. Nor were they insensible to what occurred, for they were fully awake when witnessing the transfiguration. With their literal eyes and ears they actually saw and heard what took place at that time.—Lu 9:32.

As Moses and Elijah were being separated from Jesus, Peter, "not realizing what he was saying," suggested the erecting of three tents, one each for Jesus, Moses, and Elijah. (Lu 9:33) But as the apostle spoke, a cloud formed (Lu 9:34), evidently (as at the tent of meeting in the wilderness) symbolizing Jehovah's presence there on the mountain of the transfiguration. (Ex 40:34-38) From out of the cloud there came Jehovah's voice, saying: "This is my Son, the one that has been chosen. Listen to him." (Lu 9:35) Years later, with reference to the transfiguration, Peter identified the heavenly voice as that of "God the Father." (2Pe 1:17, 18) In the transfiguration, evidently Moses and Elijah represented the Law and the Prophets, both of which pointed toward and were fulfilled in Christ. Whereas in the past God had spoken through prophets, he now indicated that he would do so through his Son.—Ga 3:24; Heb 1:1-3.

The apostle Peter viewed the transfiguration as a marvelous confirmation of the prophetic word, and by having been an eyewitness of Christ's magnificence, he was able to acquaint his readers "with the power and presence of our Lord Jesus Christ." (2Pe 1:16, 19) The apostle had experienced the fulfillment of Christ's promise that

some of his followers would "not taste death at all until first they see the kingdom of God already come in power." (Mr 9:1) The apostle John may also have alluded to the transfiguration at John 1:14.

Jesus told his three apostles: "Tell the vision to no one until the Son of man is raised up from the dead." (Mt 17:9) They did refrain from then reporting what they saw to anyone, apparently even to the other apostles. (Lu 9:36) While descending the mountain, the three apostles discussed among themselves what Jesus meant by "this rising from the dead." (Mr 9:10) One current Jewish religious teaching was that Elijah must appear before the resurrection of the dead that would inaugurate the Messiah's reign. So, the apostles inquired: "Why, then, do the scribes say that Elijah must come first?" Jesus assured them that Elijah had come, and they perceived that he spoke of John the Baptizer.—Mt 17:10-13.

The transfiguration, it seems, served to fortify Christ for his sufferings and death, while it also comforted his followers and strengthened their faith. It showed that Jesus had God's approval, and it was a foreview of his future glory and Kingdom power. It presaged the presence of Christ, when his kingly authority would be complete.

TRANSGRESSION. See SIN.

TRANSLATOR. See INTERPRETATION.

TRANSPORTATION. A means of conveyance from one place to another. Ancient modes and vehicles of transport varied with the circumstances of travelers and their destination or the places to which articles were taken.

The camel's ability to subsist on the common plants of the desert and to go without water for prolonged periods made it an ideal animal for travel in arid regions. Camels served both as mounts and for transporting merchandise from place to place. (Ge 37:25-28; Jg 6:3-5; 7:12; 1Ki 10:2) Other animals employed as mounts or beasts of burden were the ass (Jos 15:18; Jg 5:10; 10:4; 12:14; 1Sa 25:42; Isa 30:6), the mule (1Ki 1:33), and the horse (1Ki 4:26; Ac 23:23, 24, 31-33). Ships were used extensively. (2Ch 9:21; Eze 27:9; Jon 1:3; Ac 20:13-15; 27:1-44) Wagons were employed to transport both goods and persons. (Ge 46:5; Nu 7:1-9) Chariots or litters, at times richly decorated, served as a regular means of transport for royalty or men of high station. (2Ki 10:15; Ca 3:6-10; Ac 8:26-31) And the common people usually traveled on foot.

—Lu 24:13-15; see CHARIOT; COMMUNICATION; HIGHWAY, ROAD; LITTER; SHIP; WAGON.

TRAP. A means or device for catching an animal, usually having a snare or spring that, when triggered, seizes, imprisons, or kills the animal. As a rule, it is hidden, camouflaged, or disguised in some manner so as to deceive the victim; bait is often used. A number of different Hebrew words are rendered variously as "trap," 'snare,' and 'net.' (Ps 141:9, 10) Though the Bible does not provide detailed descriptions of the kinds of animal traps and snares used in ancient times, passages such as Job 18:8-10; Psalm 10:9; 140:5; and Jeremiah 18:22 give a general idea of how some of these were employed. For information regarding their construction and use, see BIRDCATCHER; HUNTING AND FISHING.

Figurative or Illustrative Use. As they bring captivity, harm, or death to animals caught in them, snares and traps can represent causes of loss of freedom, or calamity, ruin, or death. Thus, after Moses announced the coming of a severe locust plague on Egypt, Pharaoh's servants asked: "How long will this man prove to be as a snare to us?" (Ex 10:7) The previous plagues had all come at the announcement of Moses, and therefore, he had proved to be as a snare, that is, a cause of calamity or ruin to the Egyptians. So that they would not fall into the trap of idolatry, Jehovah repeatedly warned the Israelites about allowing the Canaanites to remain in the Promised Land. (Ex 23:32, 33; 34:12; De 7:16, 25; Jos 23:13) Idolatry was a trap, or an insidious cause of calamity, for the Israelites in that it resulted in their losing Jehovah's favor and protection and led to oppression and restraint at the hands of their enemies. It was also deceptive, was baited with the pretense of bringing benefits and pleasures. (Jg 2:2, 3, 11-16; 8:27) Similarly, King Saul used his daughter Michal in a scheme, saying: "I shall give her to [David] that she may serve as a snare to him." (1Sa 18:21) Saul secretly hoped that David would lose his life in the venturesome exploit needed to obtain a hundred foreskins of the Philistines to give to the king instead of "marriage money."—1Sa 18:25.

Another feature of traps alluded to in figurative terms is the speed with which they can operate, catching one unawares. The fall of Babylon to the Medes and Persians, for example, came so suddenly and unexpectedly that it was as if Jehovah had sprung a snare or trap on her.—Jer 50:24; compare Lu 21:34, 35.

An individual must carefully examine and be cautious about what he vows or guarantees to do

so that he does not find himself trapped in a situation from which escape may be difficult or virtually impossible. (Pr 6:1-3; 20:25) Companionship with a person given to fits of anger can cause one to become just like him. This is a snare, for it leads to entanglement in quarrels, ruinous complications, and sin. (Pr 22:24, 25; compare 1Co 15:33.) On the other hand, fear of God and striving to keep His way aids the wise one to avoid being enticed into wrongdoing (such as involvement with prostitutes) that might become a trap leading to death.—Pr 13:14; 14:27; compare 5:3-8; 7:21-23.

In the first century C.E., some Christians, attracted by the allurement of riches, fell into a snare that brought spiritual ruin. (1Ti 6:9, 10) Others are said to have fallen into "the snare of the Devil." Evidently this means that they had been misled and had deviated from the truth and thus had become victims of the Adversary. Timothy was urged to instruct such persons with mildness so that they might come to their senses and repent, thereby getting free from the Devil's snare.—2Ti 2:23-26; compare 1Ti 1:3, 4; Tit 3:9.

Though it is common for schemers to try to trap an innocent person, Jehovah can reverse things and "rain down upon the wicked ones traps, fire and sulphur." (Ps 11:6) He can trap them, cutting off all means of escape, and then execute judgment upon them.—Compare 1Th 5:1-3.

TREASURY. A place, usually a building or a room, where money or other valuables are kept for security. Numbers 31:54 indicates that at an early period "the tent of meeting" served, in a sense, as a sacred treasury holding contributed gold. The valuable things from Jericho that 'belonged to Jehovah' were given "to the treasure of Jehovah's house," suggesting that a treasury of some sort was established in connection with the tabernacle. (Jos 6:17, 24) Levites were appointed over the treasures that were contributed and over that which came as spoil made holy to God. (1Ch 26:20-28) The temple Solomon constructed also had a treasury, where gold and silver, as well as the costly utensils of the temple, were kept.—1Ki 7:51; 2Ch 5:1.

Under the monarchy in Israel, there was in addition a royal treasury. (2Ki 20:13; 24:13; 2Ch 32:27, 28; Jer 38:11) Over the years the valuables of the royal treasury as well as the treasury of the house of Jehovah were repeatedly taken by enemies as plunder or were used to buy off or bribe pagan nations.—1Ki 14:26; 15:18; 2Ki 12:18; 14: 14; 16:8; 18:15; 24:13.

Concerning the Babylonian treasury, Daniel 1:2 says that Nebuchadnezzar brought the valuable utensils of Jehovah's house into "the treasure-house of his god." One Babylonian inscription represents Nebuchadnezzar as saying about the temple of Merodach: "I stored up inside silver and gold and precious stones . . . and placed there the *treasure house* of my kingdom." (Compare Ezr 1:8.) The Babylonians may have had secondary treasuries in different parts of the empire. (Da 3:2) The Persians had such an arrangement, with the more localized treasuries holding some of the money collected as taxes by the satraps. (Ezr 7:20, 21) At least the main Persian treasuries also served as royal archives, containing important records in addition to gold and other valuables. —Ezr 6:1, 2; Es 3:9.

Christian Greek Scriptures. When Jesus was on earth, a portion of the temple in Jerusalem was termed "the treasury." (Joh 8:20) This apparently was located in the area called the Court of the Women. According to rabbinic sources, in this temple rebuilt by Herod there were 13 treasury chests around the wall in this court. (The Mishnah, *Shekalim* 2:1; 6:1, 5) These were shaped like trumpets, with small openings at the top, and the people would deposit in them various contributions and offerings. (Mr 12:41) The priests refused to put into this sacred treasury the silver pieces Judas threw into the temple, "because," they said, "they are the price of blood." (Mt 27:6) It is believed that this temple also contained a major treasury where the money from the treasury chests was brought.

TREES [Heb., *'ets*; Gr., *den'dron*]. The great variation in the climate of Palestine and neighboring lands made possible a very diversified growth of trees, from the cedars of Lebanon to the date palms of Jericho and the broom trees of the desert. Some 30 different types of trees are mentioned in the Bible, and these are considered in this publication under the particular name of the tree.

The problem of identifying the particular tree indicated by the original Hebrew or Greek word is frequently a difficult one, and in a number of cases, the identification is only tentative. Such identification depends upon the extent of description given in the actual Bible record as to the characteristics of the tree (at times indicated by the meaning of the root word from which the name is derived) and by comparison of such de-

scription with the trees now known to grow in Bible lands, particularly in the regions indicated in the Bible text, when these are so mentioned. Additional help comes from a study of cognate words (that is, words that by their form give evidence of being related and having proceeded from the same original root or source) in other languages, such as Arabic and Aramaic. In some cases it seems the wiser course simply to transliterate the name, as, for example, in the case of the algum tree.

As Harold and Alma Moldenke point out in their book *Plants of the Bible* (1952, pp. 5, 6), many of the trees now found in Palestine may not have been growing there in Bible times, since, as they state, "floras change, especially in regions like Palestine and Egypt where man, notorious for his aptitude in upsetting the delicately adjusted balances in nature, has been most active" for thousands of years. They further state: "Many plants which grew in abundance in the Holy Land or surrounding countries in Biblical days are now no longer found there or else grow in far smaller numbers." Some types have been exterminated or greatly diminished by excessive cultivation of the land or by devastation of timberlands due to the invading forces of Assyria, Babylon, on down to Rome. (Jer 6:6; Lu 19:43) The destruction of trees and forests has allowed the topsoil to wash away and has resulted in barrenness and desolation in many areas.

As early as in Abraham's day, trees were listed in a contract for the transfer of property.—Ge 23:15-18.

In the Law. Later Jehovah God brought Israel into Canaan, a land containing "trees for food in abundance." He promised to provide the needed rain if Israel obeyed him, and he required that a tenth of the fruits be set aside for the use of the sanctuary and the priesthood. (Ne 9:25; Le 26:3, 4; 27:30) On invading the land, the Israelites were instructed not to destroy the fruit-bearing trees when attacking the cities, although centuries later the kings of Judah and Israel were authorized by God to devastate the 'good trees' of the kingdom of Moab. The reason appears to be that Moab was outside the Promised Land. It was punitive warfare against Moab, and the Israelite action was a protection against Moabite revolt or retaliation. (De 20:19, 20; 2Ki 3:19, 25; compare Jer 6:6.) On planting a tree, the owner was not to eat of its fruit during the first three years, and in the fourth year its fruitage was to be devoted to sanctuary use. (Le 19:23-25; compare De 26:2.) Thereafter the annual first ripe fruits were likewise so dedicated.—Ne 10:35-37.

TRESPASS

Figurative Use. In the garden of Eden, God employed two trees for symbolic purposes: "the tree of life" and "the tree of the knowledge of good and bad." Failure to respect God's decree concerning the latter brought man's fall.—Ge 2:9, 16, 17; 3:1-24.

The significance of "the tree of the knowledge of good and bad" and of the restriction placed on its fruit has often been incorrectly viewed as relating to the sexual act between the first human pair. This view is contradicted by God's plain command to them as male and female to "be fruitful and become many and fill the earth." (Ge 1:28) Rather, by standing for "the knowledge of good and bad" and by God's pronouncement decreeing it to be out-of-bounds for the human pair, the tree became a symbol of God's right to determine or set the standards for man as to what is "good" (approved by God) and what is "bad" (condemned by God). It thus constituted a test of man's respect for his Creator's position and his willingness to remain within the area of freedom decreed by God, an area that was by no means cramped and that allowed for the greatest enjoyment of human life. Therefore, to violate the boundaries of the prohibited area by eating of "the tree of the knowledge of good and bad" would be an invasion of or a revolt against God's domain and authority.—See SOVEREIGNTY.

Trees were also used to symbolize individuals, rulers, and kingdoms, as in the prophecy likening the fall of Pharaoh and his crowd to the cutting down of a lofty cedar (Eze 31), as well as in Daniel's prophecy regarding the mighty tree representing dominion "in the kingdom of mankind." (Da 4:10-26) The righteous man is likened to a tree planted by streams of water (Ps 1:3), whose foliage is luxuriant and whose fruit continues to grow even in drought.—Jer 17:8.

The promise that the days of God's restored people will be like those of a tree (Isa 65:22) is made more meaningful by the fact that some trees of Palestine live for centuries, even up to a thousand years or more. In Ezekiel's vision a stream flowing from the visionary temple was lined with fruitful trees of healing foliage, and a similar vision is presented in the book of Revelation. (Eze 47:7, 12; Re 22:2, 14) The expression "tree of life" is used with regard to true wisdom, the fruitage of the righteous, the realization of a thing desired, and calmness of the tongue; it is also associated with the crown of life. (Pr 3:18; 11:30; 13:12; 15:4; Re 2:7, 10) Trees are mentioned in association with the fruitful, peaceful, and joyful conditions resulting from Jehovah's kingship and the restoration of his people.—1Ch 16:33; Ps 96:12; 148:9; Isa 55:12; Eze 34:27; 36:30.

Jesus used trees in some of his illustrations stressing the need for fruitfulness in true righteousness, as John the Baptizer had done before him. (Mt 3:10; 7:15-20) Since fruit trees were taxed in Palestine in that time, an unproductive tree (as good as dead) was an undesirable burden to the owner and, hence, a tree to be chopped down and destroyed. (Lu 13:6-9) At Jude 12, immoral persons who infiltrate the Christian congregation are likened to fruitless trees in autumn time that have died twice. Their being described as 'twice dead' may be an emphatic way of expressing that they are completely dead. Or, it could signify that they are dead from two viewpoints. They are (1) barren or fruitless and (2) literally dead, possessing no vitality.

The Hebrew word for tree is also used with regard to the stake or post on which a body was hung. (Ge 40:19; De 21:22, 23; Jos 8:29; Es 2:23) In applying Deuteronomy 21:23, the apostle Paul used the Greek word *xy'lon* (wood).—Ga 3:13; see TORTURE STAKE; individual trees by name.

TRESPASS. See SIN.

TRIAL. See LEGAL CASE.

TRIBE. A group of people, comprising a number of families or clans, who are united by race or custom under the same leaders.

The Hebrew words often rendered "tribe" (*mat·teh'* and *she'vet*) both mean "rod" or "staff." (Ex 7:12; Pr 13:24) Apparently these words came to signify "tribe" in the sense of a group of persons led by a chief or chieftains carrying a scepter or staff. (Compare Nu 17:2-6.) In most cases where the context shows that either word has the thought of "tribe," it is used in regard to one of the tribes of Israel, such as "the tribe [*mat·teh'*] of Gad" or "the tribe [*she'vet*] of the Levites." (Jos 13:24, 33) However, the 'tribe that God redeemed as his inheritance,' mentioned at Psalm 74:2, evidently refers to the entire nation of Israel, speaking of it as a "tribe" or people distinct from other nations and peoples. And the term "tribe" at Numbers 4:18 seems to be used in a more restrictive sense, as applied to the Kohathites who were a subdivision of the tribe of Levi. The Egyptian "tribes" of Isaiah 19:13 must apply to certain categories of people, whether according to region, caste, or something else.

The Greek term *phy·le'* (rendered "tribe") refers to a group of people united by common descent and also to a subdivision thereof, that is, a clan or tribe. The word is often used in the Christian Greek Scriptures in regard to the tribes of the nation of Israel. (Ac 13:21; Ro 11:1; Php 3:5; Heb 7:13, 14; Re 5:5) In expressions like "out of every tribe and tongue and people and nation," "tribe" seems to mean a group of people related by common descent. (Re 5:9) Such expressions, then, are exhaustive, referring to all people, whether viewed according to tribes of interrelated individuals, language groups, large segments of mankind, or political divisions. (Re 7:9; 11:9; 13:7; 14:6) Also, *phy·le'* appears in the expression "all the tribes of the earth" at Revelation 1:7, which evidently means all people on earth, for the verse also says "every eye will see him."—Compare Mt 24:30.

Tribes of Israel. The tribal arrangement in Israel was based on descent from the 12 sons of Jacob. (Ge 29:32–30:24; 35:16-18) These "twelve family heads [Gr., *do·de·ka pa·tri·ar'khas*]" produced "the twelve tribes of Israel." (Ge 49:1-28; Ac 7:8) However, Jacob blessed Joseph's two sons, Manasseh the older and Ephraim the younger, and said: "Ephraim and Manasseh will become mine like [his actual sons] Reuben and Simeon." (Ge 48:5, 13-20) When the various tribes received their land inheritance in the Promised Land (Jos 13-19), there was no "tribe" of Joseph. Instead, "the sons of Joseph," Manasseh and Ephraim, were counted as distinct tribes in Israel. (See BOUNDARY; MAP, Vol. 1, p. 744.) As Jehovah had arranged, though, this did not increase the tribes of Israel receiving an inheritance to 13, because the Levites got no land inheritance. Jehovah had chosen "the tribe of Levi" (Nu 1:49) in place of the firstborn of the other tribes to minister at the sanctuary. (Ex 13:1, 2; Nu 3:6-13, 41; De 10:8, 9; 18:1; see LEVITES.) Consequently, there were 12 non-Levite tribes in Israel.—Jos 3:12, 13; Jg 19:29; 1Ki 11:30-32; Ac 26:7.

When Moses blessed the tribes (De 33:6-24), Simeon was not mentioned by name, perhaps because the tribe was greatly reduced in size and its land portion was to be enclosed in the territory of Judah. In Ezekiel's vision of the holy contribution and the 12 tribes, the tribes listed are the same as those who received a land inheritance as given in the book of Joshua. (Eze 48:1-8, 23-28) The tribe of Levi was located within "the holy contribution" in Ezekiel's vision.—Eze 48:9-14, 22.

Tribal structure. Much of the organization of the Israelites revolved around the tribal structure. Both their order of marching and encampment in the wilderness were according to tribes. (Nu 2:1-31; 10:5, 6, 13-28) The land inheritance was apportioned on the basis of tribes, and special laws were given so that the land would not circulate from tribe to tribe.—Nu 36:7-9; Jos 19:51.

The dividing up of the nation according to family heads was further carried out within each tribe. Though the tribe was the basic and most important division of the nation, each tribe was subdivided into large "families" (with "family" used in a broad sense) based on descent from paternal heads. (Nu 3:20, 24; 34:14) Within each "family" there were many individual households. This arrangement, patterned after the tribal structure, is well illustrated in Joshua 7:16-18 and 1 Samuel 9:21; 10:20, 21.

Tribes of Spiritual Israel. Revelation 7:4-8 divides the 144,000 members of spiritual Israel into 12 'tribes' of 12,000 each. (See ISRAEL OF GOD.) The list differs slightly from the lists of Jacob's sons (including Levi) who were the tribal heads of natural Israel. (Ge 49:28) The following may be the reason for the difference:

Jacob's firstborn son Reuben lost his right as firstborn by his misconduct. (Ge 49:3, 4; 1Ch 5:1, 2) Joseph (the firstborn son of Jacob through his second, but favorite, wife Rachel) gained the privileges of firstborn son, including the right to have two parts, or portions, in Israel. (Ge 48:21, 22) In the Revelation list "Joseph" evidently stands for Ephraim. And Manasseh represents Joseph's second portion in spiritual Israel. The tribe of Levi is listed; to make room for Levi without increasing the number of tribes, no tribe of Dan is included in Revelation 7:4-8, but apparently not because of any unsuitability on Dan's part. The inclusion of Levi would also serve to show that there is no special priestly tribe in spiritual Israel, the entire spiritual nation being "a royal priesthood."—1Pe 2:9.

"Judging the Twelve Tribes of Israel." Jesus told the apostles that in "the re-creation" they would "sit upon twelve thrones, judging the twelve tribes of Israel." (Mt 19:28; see CREATION [Re-Creation].) And he expressed a similar thought when he made a covenant with his faithful apostles for a Kingdom. (Lu 22:28-30) It is not reasonable that Jesus meant that they would judge the 12 tribes of spiritual Israel later mentioned in Revelation, for the apostles were to be part of that group. (Eph 2:19-22; Re 3:21) Those "called to be holy ones" are said to judge, not themselves, but "the world." (1Co 1:1, 2; 6:2) Those reigning with Christ form a kingdom of priests. (1Pe 2:9; Re 5:10) Consequently, "the twelve tribes of Israel" mentioned at Matthew 19:28 and Luke 22:30 evidently represent "the world" of mankind who are outside that royal priestly class and whom those sitting on heavenly thrones will judge.—Re 20:4.

TRIBULATION.

The Greek word *thli'psis*, usually rendered "tribulation," basically means distress, affliction, or suffering resulting from the pressures of circumstances. It is used with reference to the affliction associated with childbirth (Joh 16:21), persecution (Mt 24:9; Ac 11:19; 20: 23; 2Co 1:8; Heb 10:33; Re 1:9), imprisonment (Re 2:10), poverty and other adversities common to orphans and widows (Jas 1:27), famine (Ac 7:11), and punishment for wrongdoing (Ro 2:9; Re 2:22). The "tribulation" mentioned at 2 Corinthians 2:4 apparently refers to the distress felt by the apostle Paul because of the wrong conduct of the Christians at Corinth and because he had to correct them with severity.

Marriage Brings Tribulation in the Flesh. When recommending singleness as the better course, the apostle Paul observed: "But even if you did marry, you would commit no sin. . . . However, those who do will have tribulation in their flesh." (1Co 7:28) Marriage is attended by certain anxieties and cares for husband, wife, and children. (1Co 7:32-35) Sickness can bring burdens and stresses on the family. For Christians, persecution may arise; families may even be driven from their homes. Fathers may find it hard to provide life's necessities for their households. Parents or children may be separated by imprisonment, suffer torture at the hands of persecutors, or even lose their lives.

Faithfulness Under Tribulation. Tribulation in the form of persecution can have a weakening effect upon the faith of an individual. Christ Jesus, in his illustration of the sower, indicated that certain persons would actually be stumbled on account of tribulation or persecution. (Mt 13: 21; Mr 4:17) Being aware of this danger, the apostle Paul was very much concerned about the newly formed congregation at Thessalonica. Those associated with that congregation had embraced Christianity under much tribulation (1Th 1:6; compare Ac 17:1, 5-10) and continued to experience such. The apostle therefore sent Timothy to strengthen and comfort them, "that no one might be swayed by these tribulations." (1Th 3:1-3, 5) When Timothy brought back news that the Thessalonians had remained firm in the faith, Paul was greatly comforted. (1Th 3:6, 7) Doubtless the apostle's efforts in preparing them to

expect tribulation also helped the Thessalonians to continue to be faithful servants of God.—1Th 3:4; compare Joh 16:33; Ac 14:22.

Although tribulation is unpleasant, the Christian can exult while enduring it, since he knows that faithfulness is approved by God and will ultimately lead to the realization of his grand hope. (Ro 5:3-5; 12:12) The tribulation itself is but momentary and light in comparison with the everlasting glory to be received for remaining faithful. (2Co 4:17, 18) The Christian can also rest assured that God's loyal love will never waver, whatever tribulation may come upon the faithful believer.—Ro 8:35-39.

In writing to the Corinthians, the apostle Paul pointed to yet other factors that would help the Christian to endure tribulation. He stated: "Blessed be the God . . . of all comfort, who comforts us in all our tribulation, that we may be able to comfort those in any sort of tribulation through the comfort with which we ourselves are being comforted by God. . . . Now whether we are in tribulation, it is for your comfort and salvation; or whether we are being comforted, it is for your comfort that operates to make you endure the same sufferings that we also suffer." (2Co 1:3-6) The precious promises of God, the help of his holy spirit, and his answering the prayers of those experiencing tribulation are a source of comfort to Christians. On the basis of their own experience, they can encourage and comfort still others; their example of faithfulness and expressions of conviction inspire fellow Christians likewise to remain faithful.

Paul himself appreciated the comfort given to him by fellow believers as he endured tribulations. He commended the Philippian Christians for this: "You acted well in becoming sharers with me in my tribulation." (Php 4:14) Being genuinely interested in Paul, who was imprisoned at Rome, they helped him to bear his tribulation by assisting him materially.—Php 4:15-20.

There are times, however, when certain persons become fearful on account of the tribulation experienced by others. With this in mind, Paul encouraged the Ephesian Christians: "I ask you not to give up on account of these tribulations of mine in your behalf, for these mean glory for you." (Eph 3:13) The persecutions or tribulations experienced by Paul resulted from his ministering to the Ephesians and others. For this reason he could speak of them as tribulations 'in their behalf.' His faithful endurance under such tribulations meant "glory" for the Ephesian Christians, since it demonstrated that what they had as

Christians (including God's sure promises and their precious relationship with Jehovah God and his Son Christ Jesus) was worth enduring for. (Compare Col 1:24.) If Paul, as an apostle, had given up, it would have meant disgrace for the congregation. Others could have been stumbled. —Compare 2Co 6:3, 4.

The "Great Tribulation." When answering the question of his disciples concerning the sign of his presence and the conclusion of the system of things, Jesus mentioned a "great tribulation such as has not occurred since the world's beginning until now, no, nor will occur again." (Mt 24:3, 21) As a comparison of Matthew 24:15-22 with Luke 21:20-24 reveals, this had initial reference to a tribulation to come upon Jerusalem. The fulfillment came in 70 C.E., when the city was besieged by the Roman armies under General Titus. This resulted in severe famine conditions and much loss of life. The Jewish historian Josephus relates that 1,100,000 Jews died or were killed, whereas 97,000 survived and were taken into captivity. (*The Jewish War,* VI, 420 [ix, 3]) Such a "great tribulation" has not occurred again or been repeated upon Jerusalem.

Jesus also referred to this tribulation in connection with his coming in glory: "Immediately after the tribulation of those days the sun will be darkened, and the moon will not give its light, and the stars will fall from heaven, and the powers of the heavens will be shaken. And then the sign of the Son of man will appear in heaven, and then all the tribes of the earth will beat themselves in lamentation, and they will see the Son of man coming on the clouds of heaven with power and great glory. And he will send forth his angels with a great trumpet sound, and they will gather his chosen ones together from the four winds, from one extremity of the heavens to their other extremity." (Mt 24:29-31) The term "immediately" in this passage does not rule out the possibility of a lapse of a considerable period between the tribulation upon Jerusalem in 70 C.E. and the events that were to follow. Writes Greek scholar A. T. Robertson: "This word, common in Mark's Gospel as *euthus,* gives trouble if one stresses the time element. The problem is how much time intervenes between 'the tribulation of those days' and the vivid symbolism of verse 29. The use of *en tachei* [shortly] in Rev. 1:1 should make one pause before he decides. Here we have a prophetic panorama like that with foreshortened perspective. The apocalyptic pictures in verse 29 [of Matthew 24] also call for sobriety of judgment. . . . Literalism is not appropriate in this apocalyptic

eschatology."—*Word Pictures in the New Testament,* 1930, Vol. I, pp. 192, 193.

Others have made like observations concerning the use of the Greek word rendered "immediately" at Matthew 24:29. A footnote on this text in *The Westminster Version of the Sacred Scriptures* reads: "'Straightway' [immediately] is probably here 'a term of prophecy, not of history', and so does not imply immediate sequence, which indeed in any case is not always to be pressed . . . Similar terms are common in apocalyptic literature to introduce a new scene in a rapidly changing series of visions: *cf.* Apoc. xi. 14: xxii. 12." *Matthew Henry's Commentary on the Whole Bible* states: "It is usual, in the prophetical style, to speak of things great and certain as near and just at hand, only to express the greatness and certainty of them. . . . *A thousand years are,* in God's sight, *but as one day,* 2 Pet. iii. 8."—1976, Vol. III, p. 205.

Biblical evidence indicates that the tribulation upon Jerusalem in 70 C.E. pointed forward to a far greater tribulation. About three decades after Jerusalem's destruction, the apostle John, with reference to a great crowd of persons from all nations, tribes, and peoples, was told: "These are the ones that come out of the great tribulation." (Re 7:13, 14) Earlier, the apostle John had seen "four angels" holding back destructive winds so that the sealing of the 144,000 slaves of God might be completed. This sealing evidently links up with the 'gathering of the chosen ones' that Jesus foretold would follow the tribulation upon earthly Jerusalem. (Mt 24:31) Accordingly, the "great tribulation" must come after the chosen ones have been gathered and their sealing is completed and when the four angels release the four winds to blow upon the earth, sea, and trees. (Re 7:1-4) The fact that a great crowd 'comes out of the great tribulation' shows that they survive it. This is confirmed by a similar expression at Acts 7:9, 10: "God was with [Joseph], and he delivered him out of all his tribulations." Joseph's being delivered out of all his tribulations meant not only that he was enabled to endure them but also that he survived the afflictions he experienced.

It is noteworthy that the apostle Paul referred to the execution of God's judgment upon the ungodly as tribulation. He wrote: "This takes into account that it is righteous on God's part to repay tribulation to those who make tribulation for you, but, to you who suffer tribulation, relief along with us at the revelation of the Lord Jesus from heaven with his powerful angels in a flaming fire, as he brings vengeance upon those who do not know God and those who do not obey the good news about our Lord Jesus." (2Th 1:6-8) The book of Revelation shows that "Babylon the Great" and "the wild beast" have brought tribulation upon God's holy ones. (Re 13:3-10; 17:5, 6) It therefore logically follows that the tribulation to come upon "Babylon the Great" and "the wild beast" is included in the "great tribulation."—Re 18:20; 19:11-21.

TRIBUNAL. A court or forum of justice. The word appears in some Bible translations at 1 Corinthians 4:3, where Paul says: "Now to me it is a very trivial matter that I should be examined by you or by a human tribunal [Gr., *an·thro·pi'nes he·me'ras*]." The Greek expression literally means "human day" and is understood to refer to a set day, or day set by a human judge for a trial or for rendering judgment.

Paul acknowledged that men such as Apollos, Cephas, and himself in a sense belonged to or were servants of the Corinthian congregation. (1Co 3:21, 22) Yet some in that congregation were criticizing and judging Paul, which attitude grew out of their sectarianism, their fleshliness rather than spirituality, their looking to men instead of to Christ. (1Co 9:1-4) Paul ably defended his ministry (1Co 9:5-27), setting forth the general rule or view that a Christian should not be primarily concerned about the judgment of men, whether by the Corinthians or by some human court on a set day. Rather, Paul was concerned about the future day of judgment or evaluation by God (through Jesus). He was the one who had given Paul the stewardship to which he must prove faithful.—1Co 1:8; 4:2-5; Heb 4:13.

TRIBUTE. Generally, money or other valuable consideration, such as livestock, paid by a state or a ruler to a foreign power in acknowledgment of submission, to maintain peace, or to gain protection. (For a consideration of the original-language words, see TAXATION.) Nations exacting tribute from other peoples frequently received gold and silver or products that were in short supply in their own land. In this way they strengthened their economic position while keeping the subjugated nations weak by drawing heavily on their resources.

Judean Kings David (2Sa 8:2, 6), Solomon (Ps 72:10; compare 1Ki 4:21; 10:23-25), Jehoshaphat (2Ch 17:10, 11), and Uzziah (2Ch 26:8), as well as Israelite King Ahab (2Ki 3:4, 5), received tribute from other peoples. However, on account of unfaithfulness, the Israelites were often in an inferior or position and were forced to pay tribute to others. As early as the time of the Judges, while under the domination of Moabite King Eglon, they paid tribute. (Jg 3:12-17) In later years, both the kingdom of Judah and the northern kingdom of Israel paid tribute upon coming under the control of foreign powers. (2Ki 17:3; 23:35) At various times they paid what amounted to a form of tribute when buying off enemy nations or bribing others for military assistance.—2Ki 12:18; 15:19, 20; 18:13-16.

TRIUMPHAL PROCESSION. A formal procession in celebration of victory over an enemy. The Greek word *thri·am·beu'o*, meaning "lead in a triumphal procession," occurs only twice in the Scriptures, each time in a somewhat different illustrative setting.—2Co 2:14; Col 2:15.

Triumphal Processions Among the Nations. Egypt, Assyria, and other nations commemorated their military victories with triumphal processions. In the days of the Roman republic, one of the highest honors the Senate could bestow on a conquering general was to allow him to celebrate his victory with a formal and costly procession of triumph in which no detail of pomp and glory was overlooked.

The Roman procession moved slowly along *Via Triumphalis* and up the winding ascent to the temple of Jupiter atop the Capitoline Hill. Musicians playing and singing songs of victory were at the front, followed by young men leading the sacrificial cattle. Then came open carts loaded with booty, and tremendous floats illustrating battle scenes or the destruction of cities and temples, and perhaps topped with a figure of the vanquished commander. The captive kings, princes, and generals taken in the war, with their children and attendants, were led along in chains, often stripped naked, to their humiliation and shame.

Next came the general's chariot, decorated in ivory and gold, wreathed with laurel, and drawn by four white horses or, on occasion, by elephants, lions, tigers, or deer. The conqueror's children sat at his feet or rode in a separate chariot behind him. Roman consuls and magistrates followed on foot, then the lieutenants and military tribunes with the victorious army—all bedecked with garlands of laurel and gifts, and singing songs of praise to their leader. In the vanguard were the priests and their attendants bringing along the chief victim for sacrifice, a white ox.

As the procession passed through the city, the populace threw flowers before the victor's chariot, and burning incense on temple altars perfumed the way. This sweet odor signified honors, promotion, wealth, and a more secure life for the victorious soldiers, but it signified death to the unpardoned captives who would be executed at the end of the procession. This fact throws light on Paul's spiritual application of the illustration at 2 Corinthians 2:14-16.

Triumphal arches were built in honor of some generals. The Arch of Titus in Rome still commemorates the fall of Jerusalem in 70 C.E. (Picture, Vol. 2, p. 536) Accompanied by his father, Emperor Vespasian, Titus celebrated his victory over Jerusalem by a triumphal procession. Some arches served as city gates, but for the most part their function was only monumental. The design of the arches may have represented the yoke of submission under which captives were forced to march.

Christians Share in Triumphal Procession. It was from such examples and general knowledge of the times that Paul drew his metaphor when writing to the Corinthians: "Thanks be to God who always leads us in a triumphal procession in company with the Christ." (2Co 2:14-16) The picture presents Paul and fellow Christians as devoted subjects of God, "in company with the Christ," as sons, ranking officers, and victorious soldiers, all following in God's train and being led by him in a grand triumphal procession along a perfumed route.

At Colossians 2:15, the situation is quite different. Here the enemy governments and authorities under Satan are described as the captives and prisoners in the triumphal procession. These Jehovah the Conqueror strips naked and exhibits in open public as defeated ones, the ones conquered "by means of it," that is, by means of "the torture stake" mentioned in the previous verse. Christ's death on the torture stake not only provided the basis for removing "the handwritten document," the Law covenant, but also made it possible for Christians to be freed from bondage to the satanic powers of darkness.

Other Processions. The Bible also refers to other processions, occasions when throngs moved along together in celebration of outstanding events. David described Jehovah's victorious procession from Sinai to the holy temple site in Jerusalem—war chariots of God, captives, singers and musicians, and congregated throngs blessing the Holy One of Israel. (Ps 68:17, 18, 24-26) A procession was included in the inaugural celebration at the time of completion of the rebuilding of

Jerusalem's walls in the days of Nehemiah. (Ne 12:31) And a "festival procession" is referred to in Psalm 118:27, evidently in connection with the annual Festival of Booths.

TROAS (Troʹas). The principal seaport of NW Asia Minor from which Paul departed on his first visit to Macedonia, and to which he later returned on occasion. It was located about 30 km (19 mi) S of the Hellespont (Dardanelles) and about 25 km (15 mi) S of the traditional site of ancient Troy. The same Greek term rendered "Troas" also applied to the Troad, a region in Mysia that surrounded Troy.

The city of Troas was first built during the latter part of the fourth century B.C.E. by Antigonus, one of the generals of Alexander the Great. In 133 B.C.E. it came under Roman control, and thereafter the region of Mysia became part of the Roman province of Asia. Julius Caesar for a time considered transferring the seat of the Roman government to Troas. Emperor Augustus further favored the city by making it a *colonia*, independent of the provincial governor of Asia, and by exempting its citizens from both land and poll taxes.

On Paul's second journey, probably in the spring of 50 C.E., and after passing through Phrygia and Galatia, the apostle and his companions came to Troas, for "the spirit of Jesus did not permit them" to go into Bithynia. (Ac 16:6-8) Here in Troas, Paul had an unusual vision, one of a man calling to him: "Step over into Macedonia and help us." Immediately it was concluded, "God had summoned *us* to declare the good news to them." The occurrence of "us" in this text (and "we" in the following verses) must mean that, here in Troas, Luke first joined Paul's party and made the voyage with them across the Aegean to Neapolis.—Ac 16:9-12.

After leaving Ephesus on his third journey, Paul stopped in Troas and there preached the good news about the Christ, for as he says, "A door was opened to me in the Lord." But after an undisclosed period of time, the apostle became concerned that Titus had not arrived, and so he departed for Macedonia, hoping to find him there. —Ac 20:1; 2Co 2:12, 13.

Evidently Paul spent that winter in Greece before returning again to Troas in the spring of 56 C.E. (Ac 20:2-6) This time Paul stayed seven days ministering and spiritually building up the Christian brothers in Troas. The night before leaving, Paul assembled with them and "prolonged his speech until midnight." A young man in attendance named Eutychus, who was seated at the third-story window, fell asleep and tumbled to his death. The apostle miraculously brought the boy back to life and continued conversing with the group until daybreak.—Ac 20:6-12.

It is likely that Paul visited Troas again after being released from house arrest in Rome in 61 C.E. Paul wrote to Timothy during the apostle's second imprisonment in Rome, about the year 65 C.E., asking that Timothy bring a cloak and certain scrolls and parchments that Paul had left with Carpus in Troas. It seems very unlikely that such a request would have been made some nine years later, as the case would have been if Paul's last visit to Carpus' home had been on his third journey in about 56 C.E.—2Ti 4:13.

TROPHIMUS (Troph′i·mus) [Feeding; Nourishing]. A coworker of the apostle Paul; an Ephesian Gentile Christian. (Ac 21:29) Trophimus became a Christian perhaps during Paul's extended Ephesian ministry on his third missionary journey. Afterward Trophimus was one of Paul's traveling companions on the return leg of the trip through Macedonia into Asia Minor and on to Jerusalem. (Ac 20:3-5, 17, 22) There Trophimus was seen with Paul, and when Paul took several others along with him into the temple grounds, the Jews thought that Trophimus, a Gentile, went beyond the Court of the Gentiles, thereby defiling the temple. On this false assumption they mobbed Paul. (Ac 21:26-30; 24:6) Some years later, after Paul's first imprisonment, Trophimus traveled with him again. But when they got to Miletus, not far from Trophimus' hometown, Trophimus became sick and was unable to continue.—2Ti 4:20.

TRUMPET. A wind instrument consisting of a mouthpiece, a long metal tube, and a funnel-shaped end.

In the wilderness, before Israel had broken camp for the first time, Jehovah commanded Moses to make "two trumpets of silver . . . of hammered work." (Nu 10:2) Although no further description of these instruments is given, coins circulated at the time of the Maccabees and a relief on the Arch of Titus picture the trumpets as being from about 45 to 90 cm (1.5 to 3 ft) in length, straight, ending in a bell. Josephus states that what Moses made was a kind of clarion with "a narrow tube, slightly thicker than a flute, with a mouthpiece wide enough to admit the breath and a bell-shaped extremity such as trumpets have." (*Jewish Antiquities*, III, 291 [xii, 6]) At the

inauguration of Solomon's temple, 120 trumpets were played.—2Ch 5:12.

Three signals are described, employing two methods of playing: (1) Blowing both trumpets called all the representative men of the whole assembly of Israel to the tent of meeting; (2) blowing one trumpet would summon only the chieftains who were heads over thousands; and (3) blowing fluctuating blasts signaled the breaking up of camp.—Nu 10:3-7.

Jehovah further directed that in times of war the trumpets should sound "a war call." (Nu 10:9) This was done thereafter by the priest accompanying the army. (Nu 31:6) Abijah of Judah, when seeking to avert war with Jeroboam of Israel, pointed to these "trumpets for sounding the battle alarm" as a divine assurance of Judah's victory in warfare. When Jeroboam stubbornly persisted in his aggression, his forces were defeated by a Judean army that had been greatly encouraged by the priests' "loudly sounding the trumpets."—2Ch 13:12-15.

Trumpets were included among the musical instruments in the temple. (2Ch 5:11-13) The trumpeters were sons of Aaron, the priests. (Nu 10:8; 2Ch 29:26; Ezr 3:10; Ne 12:40, 41) Every account where the trumpet (Heb., *chatso·tserah′*) is mentioned without the priests being clearly identified as the players is an event of national importance when the presence of the priests would be expected. It is therefore reasonable to suppose that they were the ones playing the trumpets. (2Ch 15:14; 20:28; 23:13; compare 1Ch 15:24 with vs 28.) There is a possibility, though, that a variety of trumpets existed, and some of these may have been possessed by nonpriests.

Jesus told his hearers not to "blow a trumpet" (Gr., *sal·pi′zo*, related to *sal′pigx*, meaning "trumpet") to attract attention to one's acts of charity in imitation of hypocrites. (Mt 6:2) It is generally suggested that the trumpeting is here figurative, Jesus warning against ostentatiousness in making gifts of mercy.

TRUTH. The Hebrew term *'emeth′*, often rendered "truth," may designate that which is firm, trustworthy, stable, faithful, true, or established as fact. (Ex 18:21; 34:6; De 13:14; 17:4; 22:20; Jos 2:12; 2Ch 18:15; 31:20; Ne 7:2; 9:33; Es 9:30; Ps 15:2; Ec 12:10; Jer 9:5) The Greek word *a·le′thei·a* stands in contrast with falsehood or unrighteousness and denotes that which conforms to fact or to what is right and proper. (Mr 5:33; 12:32; Lu 4:25; Joh 3:21; Ro 2:8; 1Co 13:6; Php 1:18; 2Th 2:10, 12; 1Jo 1:6, 8; 2:4, 21) A number of other original-language expressions can, depending upon the context, also be translated "truth."

Jehovah, the God of Truth. Jehovah is "the God of truth." (Ps 31:5) He is faithful in all his dealings. His promises are sure, for he cannot lie. (Nu 23:19; 1Sa 15:29; Ps 89:35; Tit 1:2; Heb 6:17, 18) He judges according to truth, that is, *according to the way things really are,* and not on the basis of outward appearance. (Ro 2:2; compare Joh 7:24.) Everything that emanates from him is pure and without defect. His judicial decisions, law, commandments, and word are truth. (Ne 9:13; Ps 19:9; 119:142, 151, 160) They are always right and proper, and they stand in opposition to all unrighteousness and error.

Creation's testimony. The creative works testify to the fact that God exists. But, according to Paul, even certain of those people who "knew God" suppressed this truth. Rather than serving God in harmony with the truth concerning his eternal power and Godship, they made idols and worshiped these. Not being real gods, idols are an untruth, a lie or falsehood. (Jer 10:14) Hence, these persons, though having the truth of God, exchanged it "for the lie and venerated and rendered sacred service to the creation rather than the One who created." Their turning to the falsehood of idolatry led them into all kinds of degraded practices.—Ro 1:18-31.

In contrast to man's sinfulness. The degraded practices of non-Jews and the disobedience of the Jews to God's law in no way brought harm to the Creator personally. Instead, his truthfulness, holiness, and righteousness stood out in sharp contrast, and this to his glory. But the fact that man's wrongdoing makes God's righteousness stand out in even greater prominence provides no basis for claiming that God is unjust in executing an adverse judgment against wrongdoers. Being a creation of God, a person has no right to harm himself by sinning.

The above is the argument that Paul used in his letter to the Romans, saying: "If our unrighteousness brings God's righteousness to the fore, what shall we say? God is not unjust when he vents his wrath, is he? (I am speaking as a man does.) Never may that happen! How, otherwise, will God judge the world? Yet if by reason of my lie [compare Ps 62:9] the truth of God has been made more prominent to his glory, why am I also yet being judged as a sinner? And why not say, just as it is falsely charged to us and just as some men state that we say: 'Let us do the bad things that the good things may come'? The judgment against those men is in harmony with justice." (Ro 3:5-8) God has delivered his people, not for a course of sin, but for a life of righteousness, that they may glorify Him. The apostle says later in his letter: "Neither go on presenting your members to sin as weapons of unrighteousness, but present yourselves to God as those alive from the dead, also your members to God as weapons of righteousness."—Ro 6:12, 13.

What is the meaning of the statement that Jesus Christ is himself "the truth"?

Like his Father Jehovah, Jesus Christ is "full of undeserved kindness and truth." (Joh 1:14; Eph 4:21) While on earth, he always spoke the truth as he had received it from his Father. (Joh 8:40, 45, 46) "He committed no sin, nor was deception found in his mouth." (1Pe 2:22) Jesus represented things as they really were. Besides being 'full of truth,' Jesus was himself "the truth," and truth came through him. He declared: "I am the way and the truth and the life." (Joh 14:6) And the apostle John wrote: "The Law was given through Moses, the undeserved kindness and the truth came to be through Jesus Christ."—Joh 1:17.

John's words do not mean that the Law given through Moses was erroneous. It, too, was truth, conforming to God's standard of holiness, righteousness, and goodness. (Ps 119:151; Ro 7:10-12) However, the Law served as a tutor leading to Christ (Ga 3:23-25) and had a shadow, or prophetic picture, of greater realities. (Heb 8:4, 5; 10:1-5) Providing a shadow, the Law, though truthful, was not the full truth and, therefore, had to give way to the realities that it foreshadowed. This point is emphasized by the apostle Paul in his letter to the Colossians: "Let no man judge you in eating and drinking or in respect of a festival or of an observance of the new moon or of a sabbath; for those things are a shadow of the things to come, but the reality belongs to the Christ." (Col 2:16, 17) Accordingly, "the truth came to be through Jesus" in the sense that he put the things foreshadowed by the Law into the realm of actual truth. As he himself was no shadow but the reality, Jesus was "the truth." Jesus also became 'a minister in behalf of God's truthfulness' in that he fulfilled God's promises made to the forefathers of the Jews by ministering to the circumcised Jews and proselytes.—Ro 15:8; see JESUS CHRIST ('Bearing Witness to the Truth').

Similarly, the apostle Paul's reference to "the

truth in the Law" does not imply that there was any falsehood in it (Ro 2:20) but shows that the Law was not the full truth.

"The Spirit of the Truth." The spirit that proceeds from Jehovah God is pure and holy. It is "the spirit of the truth." (Joh 14:17; 15:26) Jesus Christ told his disciples: "I have many things yet to say to you, but you are not able to bear them at present. However, when that one arrives, the spirit of the truth, he will guide you into all the truth, for he will not speak of his own impulse, but what things he hears he will speak, and he will declare to you the things coming."—Joh 16: 12, 13.

God's spirit would teach them everything they needed to know to carry out their work, recalling and opening up to their understanding things they had previously heard from Jesus but had not understood. (Joh 14:26) God's spirit would also declare to them "the things coming." This could include bringing to light the significance of Jesus' death and resurrection, as these events were then yet future and were among the things that his disciples did not understand. (Mt 16:21-23; Lu 24:6-8, 19-27; Joh 2:19-22; 12:14-16; 20:9) Of course, God's spirit later also enabled Christ's followers to foretell future happenings. (Ac 11:28; 20:29, 30; 21:11; 1Ti 4:1-3) Being "the spirit of the truth," God's holy spirit could never be the source of error but would protect Christ's followers from doctrinal falsehoods. (Compare 1Jo 2:27; 4:1-6.) It would bear witness to the truth regarding Jesus Christ. From Pentecost 33 C.E. onward, God's spirit bore witness by helping Jesus' disciples to understand the prophecies that clearly proved that Jesus was the Son of God. On the basis of these prophecies, they bore witness to others. (Joh 15:26, 27; compare Ac 2:14-36; Ro 1:1-4.) Even before Pentecost, though, "the spirit of the truth" had been bearing witness to the fact that Jesus is the Son of God (1Jo 5:5-8), for it was by this spirit that Jesus was anointed and enabled to perform powerful works.—Joh 1:32-34; 10:37, 38; Ac 10:38; see SPIRIT.

God's Word Is Truth. God's Word presents things as they really are, revealing Jehovah's attributes, purposes, and commands, as well as the true state of affairs among mankind. God's Word of truth shows what is required for one to be sanctified or made holy, set apart for use by Jehovah in his service, and then to remain in a sanctified state. Hence, Jesus could pray respecting his followers: "Sanctify them by means of the truth; your word is truth." (Joh 17:17; compare Jas 1:18.) Their obedience to the revealed truth of God's Word led them into sanctification, the truth being the means by which they purified their souls. (1Pe 1:22) Thus they stood out as "no part of the world" that did not adhere to God's truth. —Joh 17:16.

'Walking in the Truth.' Those who desire to gain God's approval should walk in his truth and serve him in truth. (Jos 24:14; 1Sa 12:24; Ps 25:4, 5; 26:3-6; 43:3; 86:11; Isa 38:3) This would include abiding by God's requirements and serving him in faithfulness and sincerity. To a Samaritan woman Jesus Christ said: "The hour is coming, and it is now, when the true worshipers will worship the Father with spirit and truth, for, indeed, the Father is looking for suchlike ones to worship him. God is a Spirit, and those worshiping him must worship with spirit and truth." (Joh 4:23, 24) Such worship could not be based on imagination but would have to conform to what is in harmony with the actual state of things, consistent with what God has revealed in his Word about himself and his purposes.

Christianity is "the way of the truth" (2Pe 2:2), and those who assist others in furthering the interests of Christianity become "fellow workers in the truth." (3Jo 8) The entire body of Christian teachings, which later became part of the written Word of God, is "the truth" or "the truth of the good news." Adherence to this truth, 'walking' in it, is essential if an individual is to gain salvation. (Ro 2:8; 2Co 4:2; Eph 1:13; 1Ti 2:4; 2Ti 4:4; Tit 1:1, 14; Heb 10:26; 2Jo 1-4; 3Jo 3, 4) In the case of those who conduct themselves aright, the truth —the conformity of their ways to God's Word and the actual results of their course—testifies to the fact that they are examples worthy of imitation. (3Jo 11, 12) On the other hand, a person who departs from the basic teachings of Christianity, either by conducting himself improperly or by advocating false doctrine, is no longer "walking" in the truth. This was the situation of those who insisted that circumcision was necessary in order for one to gain salvation. Their teaching was contrary to Christian truth, and those who accepted it ceased to obey the truth or walk in it. (Ga 2:3-5; 5:2-7) Similarly, when the apostle Peter, by his actions, made an improper distinction between Jews and non-Jews, the apostle Paul corrected him for not "walking" in harmony with "the truth of the good news."—Ga 2:14.

"A Pillar and Support of the Truth." The Christian congregation serves as "a pillar and support of the truth," preserving the purity of the truth and defending and upholding it. (1Ti 3:15)

For this reason it is especially important that those entrusted with oversight in the congregation be able to handle "the word of the truth" aright. Proper use of God's Word enables them to combat false teaching in the congregation, instructing "those not favorably disposed; as perhaps God may give them repentance leading to an accurate knowledge of truth." (2Ti 2:15-18, 25; compare 2Ti 3:6-8; Jas 5:13-20.) Not all qualify to do this kind of instructing, or teaching, in the congregation. Men who have bitter jealousies and are contentious have no basis for bragging about their being qualified to teach. Their claim would be false. As the disciple James wrote: "Who is wise and understanding among you? Let him show out of his fine conduct his works with a mildness that belongs to wisdom. But if you have bitter jealousy and contentiousness in your hearts, do not be bragging and lying against the truth."—Jas 3:13, 14.

For the Christian congregation to be "a pillar and support of the truth," the members thereof must, through fine conduct, manifest the truth in their lives. (Eph 5:9) They have to be consistent and undeviating in right conduct, as if "girded about with truth." (Eph 6:14) Besides maintaining personal purity, Christians must be concerned about congregational purity. When emphasizing the need to keep the Christian congregation clean from the defilement of lawless persons, the apostle Paul wrote: "Clear away the old leaven, that you may be a new lump, according as you are free from ferment. For, indeed, Christ our passover has been sacrificed. Consequently let us keep the festival, not with old leaven, neither with leaven of badness and wickedness, but with unfermented cakes of sincerity and truth." (1Co 5:7, 8) Since Jesus Christ was sacrificed only once (compare Heb 9:25-28) as the reality of the Passover lamb, the entire life course of the Christian, comparable to the Festival of Unfermented Cakes, should be free from injuriousness and wickedness. There must be a willingness to remove what is sinful to maintain personal and congregational purity and thus to 'keep the festival with unfermented cakes of sincerity and truth.'

TRYPHAENA (Try·phae′na) [from a Gr. root meaning "live in luxury"]. A Christian woman in Rome whom Paul greets in his letter and commends for her hard labor. (Ro 16:12) Tryphaena and Tryphosa, with whom she is listed, may have been fleshly sisters, for it was not unusual for family members to have names derived from the same root word, as in this case. Both names were common among women of Caesar's household;

but the record is silent as to whether these two women belonged to that household.—Php 4:22.

TRYPHOSA (Try·pho′sa) [from a Gr. root meaning "live in luxury"]. A Christian woman of Rome greeted and commended by Paul.—Ro 16:12; see TRYPHAENA.

TSADHEH [**Ү**; final, **Ү**] (tsa·dheh′). The 18th letter of the Hebrew alphabet. It is one of the five Hebrew letters that have a different form when used as the final letter of a word. It has a strong hissing sound similar to the sound of "ts" in English. In the Hebrew, it appears as the initial letter in each of the eight verses in Psalm 119:137-144.

TSOHAR. See ARK No. 1.

TUBAL (Tu′bal).

1. One of the seven sons of Japheth.—Ge 10:2; 1Ch 1:5.

2. A people or a land usually mentioned along with Meshech, the name of another of Japheth's sons. Tubal, along with Javan and Meshech, engaged in trading with Tyre, dealing in slaves and copper articles. (Eze 27:13) In Ezekiel's dirge over Egypt, Tubal was included among the "uncircumcised" ones with whom the Egyptians would lie in Sheol, because of the terror they had wrought. (Eze 32:26, 27) The people of Tubal also are included among those uniting with "Gog of the land of Magog" who is called "the head chieftain of Meshech and Tubal" and who comes storming out of "the remotest parts of the north" in a fierce attack against Jehovah's people. (Eze 38:2, 3; 39:1, 2; see GOG No. 2.) In another prophecy, Jehovah foretells that he will send envoys to proclaim his glory to Tubal, Javan, and other lands.—Isa 66:19.

Tubal thus lay to the N of Israel but not so distant as to be out of commercial contact with Tyre in Phoenicia. Most scholars consider the name to refer to the same people as the *Tabalu* of Assyrian inscriptions, where *Tabalu* and *Mushku* (evidently Meshech) are mentioned together. (*Ancient Near Eastern Texts*, edited by J. Pritchard, 1974, p. 284) Some centuries later, Herodotus (III, 94) also listed them together as the Tibareni and the Moschi. On this basis the land of Tubal is considered to have been situated (at least in Assyrian times) to the NE of Cilicia in eastern Asia Minor. The existence of copper mines in this region coincides with the Bible account.

TUBAL-CAIN (Tu′bal-cain). Son of Lamech by his second wife Zillah; therefore, a descendant of Cain and half brother of Jabal and Jubal. He had a sister named Naamah. (Ge 4:17-22) Tubal-cain was "the forger of every sort of tool of copper and iron," which can be taken to mean that either he invented such tools or he founded or was prominent in the occupation.

TURBAN.   See HEADDRESS.

TURNING AROUND.   See REPENTANCE.

TURQUOISE (tur'quoise).   A semiprecious, opaque, porous gemstone, ranging in color from pale sky blue to dull green. It is composed of hydrous phosphate of aluminum with traces of copper (the blue color source) and iron (the green color source). When the blue stones are heated or exposed to the weather, they turn green, which sometimes happens when the stones lose their natural moisture with the passing of time. This may account for the seeming popularity of green turquoise stones in ancient times. The early Egyptians used turquoise for jewelry, and it is found on the Sinai Peninsula as nodules in a red sandstone.

Turquoise is easy to engrave because it is a comparatively soft stone. The high priest Aaron wore an engraved turquoise stone on his "breast-piece of judgment." Inscribed upon it was the name of one of Israel's 12 tribes, and it was positioned first in the second row of stones on the breastpiece. (Ex 28:2, 15, 18, 21; 39:11) The figu-rative "covering" worn by the king of Tyre is depicted as being adorned with turquoise along with every other sort of precious stone. (Eze 28: 12, 13) Edom was Tyre's "merchant" for turquoise, for which Tyre was willing to give some of its stores in exchange.—Eze 27:2, 16.

TURTLEDOVE   [Heb., *tor, tohr*; Gr., *try'gon'*]. A small wild pigeon, usually with strong migrato-ry habits. The Hebrew name evidently imitates the plaintive cry of "tur-r-r tur-r-r" made by the bird.

The varieties of turtledove most frequently found in Palestine are the common turtledove (*Streptopelia turtur*) and the collared turtledove (*Streptopelia decaocta*), the latter so named from a narrow black collar at the back of the neck. Another variety, the palm turtledove or laughing dove (*Streptopelia senegalensis*), has steadily ex-tended its range in Israel in recent decades.

The turtledove is mentioned in Jeremiah 8:7 among the birds that "observe well the time of each one's coming in," evidently indicating an-nual migration. Reference must be to the common turtledove, since the others found in Palestine do not migrate but stay there all year round. The

common turtledove was an unerring harbinger of spring in Palestine, arriving there from the S in early April and 'making its voice heard in the land.'—Ca 2:12.

A shy, gentle bird, the turtledove relies on speedy flight as a means of escaping its enemies. (Ps 74:19) During their season turtledoves are quite abundant throughout Palestine; and since they feed on grain, seeds, and clover, they are easily captured by ground snares. Abraham in-cluded a turtledove in his offering at the time Jehovah 'concluded a covenant' with him (Ge 15:9, 10, 17, 18), and thereafter the Mosaic Law either specified or allowed for the use of turtle-doves in certain sacrifices and purification rites. (Le 1:14; 5:7, 11; 12:6, 8; 14:22, 30; 15:14, 15, 29, 30; Nu 6:10, 11) Mary offered either two turtle-doves or two young pigeons at the temple follow-ing Jesus' birth.—Lu 2:22-24; see DOVE; PIGEON.

TUTOR.   The tutor of Bible times was general-ly, not the actual teacher, but the one who accom-panied the child to and from school and possibly in other activities as well. He would turn the child over to the instructor. This continued from child-hood to perhaps puberty or longer. He was to keep the child from physical or moral harm. (So, too, the old French *tuteur* and Latin *tutor* mean, literally, "a protector or guardian.") However, the duties of the tutor also involved the matter of discipline, and he might be charged with instruct-ing the child in matters of conduct. The tutors' discipline could be severe, whether they were slaves or were paid tutors.

Therefore, Galatians 3:24, 25 points out that "the Law has become our tutor [Gr., *pai·da·go·gos'*, literally "child leader"] leading to Christ, that we might be declared righteous due to faith. But now that the faith has arrived, we are no longer under a tutor." The Law was strict. It revealed the Jews to be transgressors and condemned them. (Ga 3:10, 11, 19) It, in effect, handed over the Jews who were properly disciplined to their In-structor, Jesus Christ. The apostle Paul says: "Be-fore the faith arrived, we were being guarded under law, being delivered up together into cus-tody, looking to the faith that was destined to be revealed."—Ga 3:23.

The apostle Paul told the Corinthians: "For though you may have ten thousand tutors in Christ, you certainly do not have many fathers; for in Christ Jesus I have become your father through the good news." (1Co 4:14, 15) Paul had initially brought the message of life to Corinth and hence was like a father to the congregation of

Christian believers there. Though others might subsequently care for their interests, like tutors to whom children are entrusted, this did not change Paul's relationship to the Corinthians. The "tutors," such as Apollos, might have genuine interest in the congregation, but Paul's interest had an added factor because he experienced the labor of spiritual parenthood with them.—Compare Ga 4:11, 19, 20; see EDUCATION; INSTRUCTION.

TWELVE, THE. See APOSTLE.

TYCHICUS (Tych′i·cus) [from a root meaning "fortune; success"]. One of Paul's aides, a "beloved brother and faithful minister and fellow slave in the Lord" from the District of Asia. (Col 4:7) Tychicus was a member of Paul's party returning from Greece through Macedonia into Asia Minor; but whether or not Tychicus went all the way to Jerusalem is not stated. (Ac 20:2-4) Tychicus is one of several persons suggested as "the brother" who, while in Greece, helped Titus to arrange the collection for the brothers in Judea. (2Co 8:18, 19; 12:18) From his prison in Rome, Paul sent Tychicus with letters to Ephesus and Colossae, promising that Tychicus would tell them more about his state of affairs and be of comfort to them; Onesimus is mentioned in the letter to the Colossians as accompanying him. (Eph 6:21, 22; Col 4:7-9) Following Paul's release from prison, he contemplated sending either Artemas or Tychicus to Crete. (Tit 3:12) When the apostle was back in a Roman prison for the second time, he dispatched Tychicus to Ephesus.—2Ti 4:12.

TYRANNUS (Ty·ran′nus) [Absolute Ruler; Sovereign]. A name connected with the Ephesian school auditorium in which Paul preached for two years after having encountered resistance in the Jewish synagogue.—Ac 19:9, 10.

TYRE [Rock]. The principal Phoenician seaport; identified with present-day es-Sur, situated about 50 km (30 mi) N of Mount Carmel and 35 km (22 mi) SSW of Sidon. (PICTURE, Vol. 2, p. 531) Tyre was an ancient city (Isa 23:1, 7), but just when it was founded as a colony by the Sidonians is not known. It is first mentioned after the conquest of the Promised Land in about 1467 B.C.E., and at that time it was a fortified city. This mention of Tyre was in connection with the boundaries of Asher's tribal territory. From the start, and all through its history, Tyre apparently remained outside Israel's borders as an independent neighbor.—Jos 19:24, 29; 2Sa 24:7.

Friendly relations existed at times between Tyre and Israel, notably during the reigns of

Ancient coin bearing the name Tyre

David and Solomon. Skilled Tyrian workmen engaged in building David's royal palace with cedar timber sent by Hiram the king of Tyre. (2Sa 5:11; 1Ch 14:1) The Tyrians also supplied David with cedar later used in the temple's construction. —1Ch 22:1-4.

After David's death King Hiram of Tyre furnished Solomon with materials and assistance for the construction of the temple and other government buildings. (1Ki 5:1-10; 7:1-8; 2Ch 2:3-14) A half-Israelite son of a Tyrian worker in copper, who himself was a skilled craftsman, was employed in the construction of the temple. (1Ki 7:13, 14; 2Ch 2:13, 14) For their assistance the Tyrians were paid with wheat, barley, oil, and wine. (1Ki 5:11, 12; 2Ch 2:15) In addition, Solomon gave the king of Tyre 20 cities, though the Tyrian monarch was not overly pleased with the gift.—1Ki 9:10-13.

Tyre in time became one of the great sea powers of the ancient world, and her mariners and commercial fleet of "Tarshish" ships were famous for their voyages to faraway places. Solomon and the king of Tyre cooperated in a joint shipping venture for the importing of precious things including gold from Ophir.—1Ki 9:26-28; 10:11, 22; 2Ch 9:21.

In all the dealings the Tyrians had with Israel, there is no indication that, as a people, they were interested in the worship of Jehovah; their association was particularly a commercial one. Racially they were Canaanites, and religiously they practiced a form of Baal worship, their chief deities being Melkart and Astarte (Ashtoreth). When Ethbaal was king of the Sidonians (including Tyre), his daughter Jezebel married Ahab, the king of the northern kingdom of Israel. Jezebel was infamous in her determination to blot out the worship of Jehovah.—1Ki 16:29, 31; 18:4, 13, 19.

Condemned by God. It was not, however, for the personal wickedness of Jezebel and her daughter Athaliah that Tyre came under heavy divine condemnation. Tyre grew to be very great at the expense of other peoples, including Israel. She was a manufacturer of metal objects, glassware, and purple dyes and was a trading center for the overland caravans as well as a great import-export depot. Along with this industrial and commercial growth came riches, conceit, and pride. Her merchants and tradesmen boasted of being princes and honorable ones of the earth. (Isa 23:8) Tyre in time also developed an attitude of opposition to Jehovah and conspired with neighboring nations against God's people. (Ps 83:2-8) So it was her bold defiance of Jehovah that eventually brought upon the city adverse judgment, downfall, and destruction.

In the latter part of the ninth century B.C.E., Jehovah took note of this city's arrogant attitude. He therefore warned her that she would be paid back in kind for robbing his people of the gold, silver, and many other desirable things that she had used to beautify her temples. There was also to be an accounting for Tyre's having sold God's people into slavery.—Joe 3:4-8; Am 1:9, 10.

Later the prophet Isaiah recorded a further pronouncement against Tyre, which indicated that she would be forgotten for "seventy years." (Isa 23:1-18) Years thereafter the prophet Jeremiah included Tyre among those nations that were singled out to drink the wine of Jehovah's rage. (Jer 25:8-17, 22, 27; 27:2-7; 47:2-4) Since the nations mentioned in the prophecy of Jeremiah were to "serve the king of Babylon seventy years" (Jer 25:8-11), this suggests that both the prophecy of Isaiah and that of Jeremiah related to Nebuchadnezzar's campaign against Tyre.

Also through Ezekiel, a contemporary of Jeremiah, Jehovah pointed to calamity for Tyre at the hands of Nebuchadnezzar. (Eze 26:1–28:19) Though Tyre had been compared to a pretty ship with multicolored sails and deck coverings and a prow inlaid with ivory, she would sink in the open sea. (Eze 27:3-36) Tyre's 'king' (apparently the line of Tyrian rulers) haughtily boasted: "I am a god. In the seat of god I have seated myself." But he was to be removed as profane and destroyed by fire.—Eze 28:2-19.

Destruction of City. In the course of Nebuchadnezzar's long siege against Tyre, the heads of his soldiers were "made bald" from the chafing of their helmets, and their shoulders were "rubbed bare" from carrying materials used in the construction of siegeworks. Since Nebuchadnezzar received no "wages" for serving as His instrument in executing judgment upon Tyre, Jehovah promised to compensate him with the wealth of Egypt. (Eze 29:17-20) According to the Jewish historian

Josephus, the siege lasted 13 years (*Against Apion,* I, 156 [21]), and it cost the Babylonians a great deal. Secular history does not record exactly how thorough or effective Nebuchadnezzar's efforts were. But the loss in lives and property to the Tyrians must have been great.—Eze 26:7-12.

When the Israelites returned from Babylonian exile, however, the Tyrians were able to assist in supplying cedar timbers from Lebanon for a second temple, and they resumed their trade with the rebuilt city of Jerusalem.—Ezr 3:7; Ne 13:16.

Tyre's conflict with Nebuchadnezzar, though great, was not to be the complete end for Tyre. A later prophetic pronouncement indicated that, though Tyre would build a rampart and pile up silver and gold, Jehovah himself would destroy her completely.—Zec 9:3, 4.

Nearly 200 years after Zechariah's prophecy was given, it was fulfilled. In 332 B.C.E. Alexander the Great marched his army across Asia Minor and, in his sweep southward, paused long enough to give his attention to Tyre. When the city refused to open its gates, Alexander in his rage had his army scrape up the ruins of the mainland city and throw it into the sea, thus building a causeway out to the island city, all of this in fulfillment of prophecy. (Eze 26:4; DIAGRAM, Vol 2, p. 531) With his naval forces holding the Tyrian ships bottled up in their harbor, Alexander set about constructing the highest siege towers ever used in ancient wars. Finally, after seven months the 46-m-high (150 ft) walls were breached. In addition to the 8,000 military men killed in battle, 2,000 prominent leaders were killed as a reprisal, and 30,000 inhabitants were sold into slavery.

Mentioned in the Greek Scriptures. Despite the city's total destruction by Alexander, it was rebuilt during the Seleucid period, and in the first century C.E. it was a prominent port of call on the Mediterranean. During Jesus' great Galilean ministry, a number of people from around Tyre and Sidon came to hear his message and to be cured of their diseases. (Mr 3:8-10; Lu 6:17-19) Some months later Jesus personally visited the region around Tyre, on which occasion he cured the demon-possessed child of a Syrophoenician woman. (Mt 15:21-29; Mr 7:24-31) Jesus observed that, had he performed in Tyre and Sidon the powerful works that he did in Chorazin and Bethsaida, the pagans of Tyre and Sidon would have been more responsive than those Jews.—Mt 11:20-22; Lu 10:13, 14.

TYRIAN. See TYRE.

U

UCAL (U'cal). One to whom Agur spoke the words found in Proverbs chapter 30. Ucal may have been a son or disciple of Agur, but nothing definite is known about him.—Pr 30:1.

UEL (U'el). One of the sons of Bani who sent away their foreign wives and sons in response to Ezra's counsel.—Ezr 10:10, 11, 34, 44.

ULAI (U'lai). A "watercourse" flowing through or near Shushan (Susa) in Elam. Along the Ulai, Daniel received the vision of the ram and the he-goat. It cannot be determined whether the prophet actually went there from Babylon or was transported to that location in a visionary way. (Da 8:1-3, 6, 16) Conjectures about the Ulai vary considerably, and identification is difficult because rivers in the vicinity seem to have changed course somewhat through the centuries. One view is that the Ulai is the Karkheh River. According to another, it was an artificial canal to the N or NE of Shushan connecting the Karkheh with another river.

ULAM (U'lam).

1. Father of Bedan; of the tribe of Manasseh. —1Ch 7:14, 16, 17.

2. A distant descendant of Saul, of the tribe of Benjamin, whose sons were outstanding archers. Ulam's descendants, "sons and grandsons," numbered some 150 in the time of the chronicler. —1Ch 8:33, 39, 40.

ULCER. An open bodily sore other than a direct wound, though the inflammatory type usually results from a minor injury, such as a skin abrasion. Ulcers are either external or internal, developing on the skin or on mucous surfaces. They often discharge pus and cause progressive disintegration and death of tissue in the affected area. Inflammatory ulcers, with their hot, aching sensation, often develop on the lower part of a person's leg.

In the Hebrew Scriptures, the word sometimes translated "ulcer" is *ma·zohr'*, which can apply to an ulcer, a sore, or a boil. Certain scholars believe that it refers to a wound of the kind that might require the pressing out of matter within it. The Greek word *hel'kos*, denoting an ulcer, is used in the Christian Greek Scriptures; it appears in the Greek *Septuagint* at Exodus 9:9 and Job 2:7 for the Hebrew word *shechin'*, which signifies a boil. —See BOIL.

Figurative Use. Prophetically, Ephraim (Israel) was depicted as being sick and Judah as having an "ulcer," conditions resulting from their wrongdoing and consequent loss of God's favor. But, instead of trusting in Jehovah for protection from their foes, they futilely sought aid from the king of Assyria, who was unable to heal them of their 'ulcerous' condition. (Ho 5:13) Later, Zion, her people having been taken into Babylonian exile, was represented as being afflicted with an ulcer.—Jer 30:12-15, 17; compare Lu 16:20, 21; Re 16:2, 10, 11.

ULLA (Ul'la). An Asherite whose three sons were tribal family heads and valiant warriors. —1Ch 7:39, 40.

UMMAH (Um'mah). A city of undetermined location on the boundary of Asher's territory. (Jos 19:29-31) Some scholars think that "Ummah" resulted from a textual alteration of "Acco" (the latter name appearing here in some manuscripts of the Greek *Septuagint* and in the list at Jg 1:31), but this is not certain.

UNCLE. The Hebrew term *dohdh,* at times rendered "uncle" or "father's brother" (Le 10:4; 20:20; 25:49; Nu 36:11; 1Sa 10:14-16; 14:50; Es 2:7, 15; Jer 32:7-9, 12; Am 6:10), is much broader in its application than the English word "uncle." It not only applies to a kinsman, usually the father's brother, but can also denote (in the singular or plural) "love" (Pr 7:18), expressions of endearment or of love (Ca 1:2, 4; Eze 16:8; 23:17), and a dear one or loved one (Ca 1:14, 16; Isa 5:1). The context or other related scriptures, however, often establish the family relationship designated by the Hebrew word *dohdh*. For example, *dohdh* is used to describe the relationship of King Jehoiachin to King Zedekiah. Since Zedekiah was the brother of Jehoiachin's father Jehoiakim, the word *dohdh* in this case obviously designates an uncle, or a father's brother. (2Ki 24:6, 15, 17; 1Ch 3:15) A different family relationship is described at 1 Chronicles 27:32, where the counselor Jonathan is said to be David's *dohdh*. Second Samuel 21:21 and 1 Chronicles 20:7 indicate that Jonathan was the son of David's brother Shimei. Accordingly, the reference to David's *dohdh* must be to David's nephew and not to his uncle.

The feminine form of *dohdh* is used for one's aunt. (Ex 6:20; Le 18:14; 20:20) An uncle on the mother's side of the family is designated in Hebrew by the expression "mother's brother."—Ge 29:10.

"The son of Paul's sister" revealed to Paul and then to the Roman commander of Jerusalem the plot that had been hatched against his uncle's life. —Ac 23:16-22.

UNCLEAN ANIMALS. See ANIMALS.

UNCLEANNESS. See CLEAN, CLEANNESS.

UNDERSTANDING. The original-language words rendered "understanding" can refer to comprehension of a rather simple kind or can describe a full and profound realization of the inner nature, underlying reasons, and significance of complex matters. Insight, discernment, and perception are all closely connected to understanding.

The Hebrew verb *bin* and the noun *bi·nah'* are most frequently related to understanding. At times *bin* and *bi·nah'* may more particularly emphasize the specific aspects of discerning (1Sa 3:8; 2Sa 12:19; Ps 19:12; Da 9:2), giving thoughtful consideration (De 32:7; Pr 14:15; 23:1; Jer 2:10; Da 11:37) or attention (Job 31:1; 32:12; 37:14; Ps 37:10) to a matter, and may be so rendered. Professor R. C. Dentan, writing in *The Interpreter's Dictionary of the Bible* (edited by G. Buttrick, 1962, Vol. 4, p. 733), says: "The root בין [*bin*] means primarily 'to discern with the senses,' 'to perceive distinctions,' then 'to give close attention to,' and finally—particularly in the derived stems —'to gain comprehension' or 'give' it to others." Hebrew scholar Gesenius gives the basic sense as "*to separate, to distinguish; . . .* hence *to discern, to mark, to understand,* all [of] which depend on the power of separating, distinguishing, discriminating." (*A Hebrew and English Lexicon of the Old Testament,* translated by E. Robinson, 1836, p. 140) Another noun, *tevu·nah',* comes from the same root as *bi·nah'* and may be appropriately rendered "discernment" (Pr 10:23; 11:12) or "understanding" (Ex 31:3; De 32:28), according to the context.

The basic meaning of these terms reveals the understanding person to be one able to see into a matter and discern its composition by separating the individual factors or features that compose or act together to form the whole, then to perceive the relationship between them and thus comprehend, or grasp, the significance or meaning of the matter. This may be illustrated with a language. If a person is to understand what is spoken in a certain tongue, he must be able to distinguish the individual words composing the sentences, know their meaning, and see how they relate to one another. (De 28:49) However, even though a person may basically comprehend what is said to him, understanding can also go beyond such simple comprehension; it means that he gets the real significance and sense of the message, then is able to evaluate it, benefit by it, and know what action it calls for. When Ezra the priest read the Law before the people in Jerusalem, "all intelligent [from Heb., *bin*] enough to listen" were gathered. Even though these had mature minds able to understand all the words, the Levites "were explaining the law to the people [instructing the people in the law, or giving understanding (form of *bin*)], . . . reading aloud from the book, from the law of the true God, it being expounded, and there being a putting of meaning into it; and they continued giving understanding in the reading." —Ne 8:2, 3, 7, 8.

In the Greek Scriptures, "understanding," as signifying perception, getting the sense of a matter, is represented especially by the verb *sy·ni'e·mi* (literally, put together) and the related noun *sy'ne·sis.* Other terms are *e·pi'sta·mai,* meaning, basically, "know well," and *gi·no'sko,* meaning "know."

Source of Understanding. Jehovah God is both the Source of understanding and the Supreme Example of its use. The splendid coordination and functioning of the universe, in which each creation serves a particular and harmonious purpose, with no clashes or problems resulting from a lack of discernment on their Creator's part, manifest God's understanding. (Job 38:36; Ps 136:5-9; Pr 3:19, 20; Jer 10:12, 13) God has given the animals instinctive understanding, each according to its kind. Men may spend years gaining understanding of aerodynamics, but the falcon instinctively knows just how to "read" and utilize the different types of air currents. (Job 39:26) Animals, however, do not have certain other aspects of understanding that are peculiar to man. —Compare Ps 32:9.

Despite intensive research over centuries, many features and cycles operating according to divine laws still elude man's full comprehension. (Job 36:29; 38:19, 20) What men can grasp from their study of the material creation only approaches 'the fringes of God's ways,' and is but "a whisper" as compared to "mighty thunder." This is even more true of God's works of judgment and salvation, his thoughts being too deep for ungodly persons to grasp. (Job 26:7-14; Ps 92:5, 6) Consideration of the divine wisdom and understanding manifest in the material creation, however, enabled Job to discern his proper relationship to the

Creator and humbly recognize his own lack of understanding.—Job 42:1-6.

As regards man, Jehovah can exercise insight into the thoughts and doings of all mankind (1Ch 28:9; Ps 139:1-6), and as he chooses, he 'gives thoughtful consideration' (Heb., *bin*) or attention to individuals and classes. (Pr 21:12; Ps 5:1, 2) He knows his own invincible purpose and what he will do in the future. His righteous standards are fixed, unchangeable. Hence, "there is no wisdom, nor any discernment, nor any counsel in opposition to Jehovah." (Pr 21:30; compare Isa 29:13, 14; Jer 23:20; 30:24.) He needs to consult no one to understand a matter, such as how to help his servants effectively or how to relieve them from distress and oppression.—Isa 40:10-15, 27-31.

Knowledge of Jehovah God and discernment of his will combined with faith and trust therefore form the foundation of all true understanding on the part of his intelligent creatures. "Knowledge of the Most Holy One is what understanding is," and this includes understanding "righteousness and judgment and uprightness, *the entire course of what is good.*" (Pr 9:10; 2:6-9; 16:20) No matter of real importance can be fully understood unless all the factors are viewed from Jehovah's standpoint and seen in relation to his standards, qualities, and eternal purpose.

Those turning from the Source. The person who turns to transgression begins to discount God as a factor to be considered when making decisions and plans. (Job 34:27) Such a person allows his heart to blind him to the wrongness of his ways and he loses insight. (Ps 36:1-4) Even if claiming to worship God, he puts men's precepts above God's; he prefers them. (Isa 29:13, 14) He rationalizes and excuses his loose conduct as mere "sport" (Pr 10:23) and becomes perverted, brutish, stupid in his reasoning, to the extreme of assuming that the invisible God does not see or discern his wrongdoing, as though God's powers of perception had failed. (Ps 94:4-10; Isa 29:15, 16; Jer 10:21) By his course and actions he says, in effect, "There is no Jehovah" (Ps 14:1-3) and leaves him 'out of the picture.' Not being guided by divine principles, he cannot judge matters correctly, see the issues clearly, evaluate the factors involved, and arrive at right decisions.—Pr 28:5.

Fields of Human Understanding. Understanding may relate to knowledge and skill in mechanical activities, such as construction and designing of buildings or the making of articles of wood, metal, stone, or cloth. The Tyrian worker Hiram was "a skillful man, experienced in understanding" as a craftsman working with a wide range of materials. (2Ch 2:13, 14; 1Ki 7:13, 14) Such understanding contributes to effective work, resulting in products of enduring quality.

Others may be "expert [form of *bin*]" in matters of transportation or music due to their understanding. (1Ch 15:22; 25:7, 8; 2Ch 34:12) Some may show understanding in linguistics, writing, or other scholarly subjects. (Da 1:4, 17, 20) Such understanding can be gained through natural abilities and effort. Of course, God's spirit can augment, or enhance, such understanding in persons and qualify them to teach others their craft or profession.—Ex 31:2-5; 35:30-35; 36:1; 1Ch 28:19.

Some may have keen discernment of human nature, being observant and able to 'put two and two together.' David, noting the way his servants were whispering, 'discerned' that his child by Bath-sheba had died. (2Sa 12:19) Rehoboam was guided by his understanding of fallen human nature and its tendency toward envy and jealousy when assigning his sons' inheritances.—2Ch 11:21-23.

Similarly, men or communities of men may show considerable discernment in business operations, a factor in their successfully enriching themselves, as did "the leader" of Tyre. (Eze 28: 2, 4) Rulers may have understanding of military warfare and strategy (Isa 10:12, 13) or be expert in political diplomacy. (Da 8:23) Yet their understanding may be narrow and of short-range benefit, as in the foregoing cases.

It can be seen, then, that the Scriptures refer to understanding obtainable by natural means. Yet any such "comprehension" (*sy'ne·sis*) of worldly 'intellectual men' (*sy·ne·toi'*) becomes foolishness, in vain, when God's purposes are not considered. (1Co 1:19, 20, *Int*) The Scriptures, therefore, primarily urge a superior understanding, one that is *spiritual,* having God as its foundation. No matter how much men may exploit the earth's resources, exploring its depths and the depths of the seas or studying the skies, they can never by their own efforts find "the place of understanding" and wisdom that leads to successful life in righteousness and happiness. (Job 28:1-21, 28) Such understanding is 'better than silver' and can bring the desired future that fleeting worldly riches and honor fail to bring.—Pr 16:16, 22; 23:4, 5; Ps 49:6-8, 14, 20.

Relationship to Knowledge and Wisdom. Understanding must be based on knowledge, and it works with knowledge, though it is itself more than mere knowledge. The extent and worth of one's understanding is measurably affected by the quantity and quality of one's knowledge. Knowledge is acquaintance with facts, and the greatest and most fundamental facts relate to God, his existence, his invincible purpose, his ways. Understanding enables the person to relate the knowledge he acquires to God's purpose and standards, and thereby he can assess or evaluate such knowledge. The "understanding heart is one that searches for knowledge"; it is not satisfied with a mere superficial view but seeks to get the full picture. (Pr 15:14) Knowledge must become 'pleasant to one's very soul' if discernment is to safeguard one from perversion and deception. —Pr 2:10, 11; 18:15; see KNOWLEDGE.

Proverbs 1:1-6 shows that the "man of understanding is the one who acquires skillful direction, to understand a proverb and a puzzling saying, the words of wise persons and their riddles." These must not be things said merely to pass the time away in idle conversation, for wise persons would not customarily waste time in such manner, but must refer to instruction, questions, and problems that discipline and train the mind and heart in right principles, thereby equipping the learner for wise action in the future. (Compare Ps 49:3, 4.) Knowledge and understanding together bring wisdom, which is "the prime thing," the ability to bring a fund of knowledge and keen understanding to bear on problems with successful results. (Pr 4:7) The person who is rightly motivated seeks understanding, not out of mere curiosity or to exalt himself, but for the very purpose of acting in wisdom; 'wisdom is before his face.' (Pr 17:24; see WISDOM.) He is not like those in the apostle Paul's day who assumed to be teachers of others but were "puffed up with pride, not understanding anything," unwisely letting themselves become "mentally diseased over questionings and debates about words," things that produce disunity and a host of bad results.—1Ti 6:3-5.

Gaining True Understanding. The person seeking true understanding prays to God: "Make me understand, that I may observe your law and that I may keep it with the whole heart . . . that I may keep living." (Ps 119:34, 144, also 27, 73, 125, 169) This is the right motive. The apostle prayed that the Colossian Christians might be "filled with the accurate knowledge of [God's] will in all wisdom and spiritual comprehension [sy·ne′sei], in order to walk worthily of Jehovah."—Col 1:9, 10.

Age and experience are natural factors that can help one to develop greater understanding. (Job 12:12) Age and experience alone are not the decisive factors, however. Job's comforters prided themselves on the understanding they and their aged associates had, but they were reproved by the younger man Elihu. (Job 15:7-10; 32:6-12) Jehovah, "the Ancient of Days" (Da 7:13), has understanding infinitely superior to that of all mankind, whose days cover only a few thousand years and who do not even understand just how the planet they live on came to be formed. (Job 38:4-13, 21) Hence, God's written Word is a principal means for gaining understanding.—Ps 119:30.

Children and young persons should thoughtfully consider the instruction of their older and more experienced parents, particularly so when these are devoted servants of God. (Pr 2:1-5; 3:1-3; 4:1; 5:1) Serious 'consideration' (Heb., bin) of the history of earlier generations can bring understanding, and older persons are often familiar with this. (De 32:7) Association should be sought, not with "inexperienced ones," but with the wise, feeding on their counsel and instruction so as to "keep living, and walk straight in the way of understanding." (Pr 9:5, 6) Listening and also observing, the person can cease to be naive and credulous, can "understand shrewdness," and can avoid many bitter experiences.—Pr 8:4, 5.

Diligence in studying and applying God's Word and commands can enable a person to have greater insight than those set as his teachers and more understanding than those who are older men. (Ps 119:99, 100, 130; compare Lu 2:46, 47.) This is because wisdom and understanding are, in effect, built into God's pure regulations and judicial decrees; hence Israel's faithful observance of these would cause surrounding nations to view them as "a wise and understanding people." (De 4:5-8; Ps 111:7, 8, 10; compare 1Ki 2:3.) The understanding person recognizes the inviolability of God's Word, wants to see his own course in relation thereto, and petitions God's aid in this. (Ps 119:169) He lets God's message sink down deep (Mt 13:19-23), writes it on the tablet of his heart (Pr 3:3-6; 7:1-4), and comes to develop a hatred for "every false path" (Ps 119:104). God's Son, when on earth, showed understanding in this way, even refusing to seek escape from death on the stake because the fulfillment of the Scriptures called for his dying in that manner.—Mt 26:51-54.

Time and meditation essential. The "overhasty" person usually fails to "consider [or give thoughtful attention to; form of Heb. bin] knowledge." (Isa 32:4; compare Pr 29:20.) The understanding person characteristically knows when to keep quiet (Pr 11:12), does not speak rashly, and keeps cool even though the discussion may become heated. (Pr 14:29; 17:27, 28; 19:11; Job 32: 11, 18; compare Jas 3:13-18.) He meditates on counsel so as to determine the significance of the words and message. (Job 23:5; Ps 49:3) He asks questions aimed at discerning the whys and wherefores so he can determine the cause of success or failure, divine blessing or cursing; he ponders the logical future consequences to which each course will lead. (Ps 73:2, 3, 16-18; Jer 2:10-19; compare Isa 44:14-20.) Israel failed to do this and did not give consideration in their hearts as to what would be "their end afterward."—De 32:28-30.

Accept discipline. Pride, stubbornness, self-will, and independence are enemies of understanding. (Jer 4:22; Ho 4:14, 16) The person with true understanding does not think he knows everything; hence Proverbs 19:25 says, "There should be a reproving of the understanding one, that he may discern knowledge." (Compare Job 6:24, 25; Ps 19:12, 13.) Because he *is* an understanding person, he is ready to listen, discerns the basis for the reproof, and benefits by it more than a stupid one would from a hundred strokes.—Pr 17:10; compare 29:19.

Understanding Prophecy. Inspired prophetic messages are understood only by those cleansed ones who humbly pray for understanding. (Da 9:22, 23; 10:12; 12:10) Though the general time period of their fulfillment may be comprehended, full discernment of the prophecy's application may have to await God's due time for its being carried out. (Da 8:17; 10:14; 12:8-10; compare Mr 9:31, 32; Lu 24:44-48.) Those placing their confidence in men and disdaining God's power and discounting his purpose as a factor worth considering cannot understand the prophecies, and they remain blind to their significance until the disastrous effects of their fulfillment begin to hit them.—Ps 50:21, 22; Isa 28:19; 46: 10-12.

UNDESERVED KINDNESS. See KINDNESS.

UNFERMENTED CAKES, FESTIVAL OF.
See FESTIVAL OF UNFERMENTED CAKES.

UNKNOWN GOD.
Part of an inscription on an altar seen by the apostle Paul while at Athens. The Athenians expressed their fear of deities by building many temples and altars. They even went so far as to deify the abstract, erecting altars to Fame, Modesty, Energy, Persuasion, and Pity. Perhaps fearing that they might possibly omit a god and thereby incur that one's disfavor, the men of Athens had erected an altar inscribed with the words, "To an Unknown God." At the outset in his

discourse to the Stoics, Epicureans, and others assembled at the Areopagus (Mars' Hill), Paul tactfully drew their attention to this altar, telling them that it was this God, heretofore unknown to them, about whom he was preaching.—Ac 17:18, 19, 22-34.

That altars of this nature existed in Greece is testified to by the Greek writers Philostratus (170?-245 C.E.) and Pausanias (second century C.E.). Pausanias mentions altars of "gods named Unknown." (*Description of Greece*, Attica I, 4) Philostratus, in his work *The Life of Apollonius of Tyana* (VI, III), writes: "It is a much greater proof of wisdom and sobriety to speak well of all the gods, especially at Athens, where altars are set up in honour even of unknown gods."

UNNI (Un'ni).

1. A Levite musician who played a stringed instrument in the procession that brought the ark of the covenant to Jerusalem.—1Ch 15:3, 16, 18, 20.

2. A postexilic Levite assigned to guard duty under High Priest Jeshua.—Ne 12:1, 9.

UNRIGHTEOUS RICHES. See RICHES.

UPHAZ (U'phaz).
A presently unidentified location where gold was found in ancient times. —Jer 10:9; Da 10:5.

UPPER ROOM. See HOUSE.

UR.

1. [Light]. 'Father' of Eliphal, one of the mighty men of David's military forces. (1Ch 11:26, 35) Ur appears to be the same person as Ahasbai.—2Sa 23:34.

2. "Ur of the Chaldeans," the city in Mesopotamia where Abram's (Abraham's) brother Haran (and likely Abraham himself) was born. (Ge 11:28; Ac 7:2, 4) Jehovah appeared to Abraham and directed him to leave Ur. The Bible, crediting Terah with the move because he was the family head, says that Terah took his son Abraham, his daughter-in-law Sarah, and his grandson Lot, moving from Ur to Haran.—Ge 11:31; 12:1; Ne 9:7.

Usually Ur is identified with Muqaiyir, which is W of the present bed of the Euphrates and some 240 km (150 mi) SE of Babylon. Ruins there cover an area that is about 910 by 730 m (3,000 by 2,400 ft). Once a center of worship of the moon-god Nanna (or Sin), the site's most prominent feature is still a temple tower, or ziggurat, some 61 m long, 46 m wide, and 21 m high (200 by 150 by 70 ft).—PICTURE, Vol. 2, p. 322.

Though at present the Euphrates River runs about 16 km (10 mi) E of the site of Ur, evidence indicates that in ancient times the Euphrates ran just W of the city. Historian and geographer Henri Gaubert, in his book *Abraham, Loved by God*, stated: "At the time of Abram the three great rivers (Karun, Tigris and Euphrates) flowed into the waters of the Persian Gulf by three separate estuaries. It is well to point out here the site of the city of Ur . . . on the left [east] bank of the Euphrates. The Hebrew tribe of Abram, originating in the city-state of Ur, could, in consequence, be perfectly correctly designated by the phrase 'the people from beyond the river.'"—1968, p. 8.

Also, a revised and updated edition of Sir Leonard Wooley's *Excavations at Ur* shows that the Euphrates was definitely W of Ur. Speaking of Ur's defenses, it states: "This massive fortification was further strengthened by the fact that the river Euphrates (as can be seen from the sunken line of its old bed) washed the foot of the western rampart while fifty yards from the foot of the eastern rampart there had been dug a broad canal which left the river immediately above the north end of the town, so that on three sides Ur was ringed with a moat." (*Ur 'of the Chaldees,'* by P. R. S. Moorey, 1982, p. 138) Thus it can be appropriately stated that Jehovah took Abraham "from the other side of the River," that is, the Euphrates.—Jos 24:3.

In royal tombs at Ur, excavators have found many objects of gold, silver, lapis lazuli, and other costly materials, as well as indications that early Sumerian kings and queens of the city were buried with their retinue of male and female servants.

Ruins of what appear to be private houses excavated at Ur (suggested by some as belonging to the period between the 20th and 16th centuries B.C.E.) show that they were constructed of brick, were plastered and whitewashed, and had 13 or 14 rooms surrounding a paved courtyard. Among clay tablets found at the site were some used to teach cuneiform writing. Other tablets indicate that students there had multiplication and division tables and worked at square and cube roots. Many of the tablets are business documents.

From excavations at Ur, it thus appears clear that Abraham made notable material sacrifices when leaving that city. But, in faith, the patriarch was "awaiting the city having real foundations, the builder and creator of which city is God." —Heb 11:8-10.

URBANUS (Ur·ba′nus) [from Lat., meaning "Refined; Elegant"]. A Roman Christian greeted in Paul's letter. (Ro 16:9) The name is found frequently in inscriptions of Caesar's household, but the record is silent as to whether this Urbanus was an imperial servant.

URI (U′ri) [from a root meaning "light"].

1. A descendant of Judah through Perez, Hezron, Caleb, and Hur. Uri's son Bezalel was a noted tabernacle craftsman.—Ex 31:2; 35:30; 38:22; 1Ch 2:4, 5, 9, 18-20; 2Ch 1:5.

2. Father of Geber, who was one of Solomon's food deputies.—1Ki 4:7, 19.

3. One of the three Levite gatekeepers who sent away their foreign wives and sons as a result of Ezra's counsel.—Ezr 10:10, 11, 24, 44.

URIAH (U·ri′ah) [My Light Is Jehovah].

1. The Hittite husband of Bath-sheba. Uriah was one of David's foreign warriors. (2Sa 23:39; 1Ch 11:41) His words, conduct, marriage to a Jewess, and residence in Jerusalem close to the king's palace all suggest that he adopted the worship of Jehovah God as a circumcised proselyte. —2Sa 11:3, 6-11.

While Uriah was engaged in the battle against Ammon at Rabbah, David committed adultery with his wife Bath-sheba, about which Uriah never learned. David then sent and had Uriah come to Jerusalem, whereupon the king asked him about the progress of the war and sent him out to go to his home so that his wife's child might appear to be Uriah's. However, Uriah refused to go there because the army was out in the field. (De 23:9-11; compare 1Sa 21:5.) Even when David made him drunk, he still refused to sleep at home. (2Sa 11:1-13) David's crime against Uriah then doubled, for David sent him back to the war with instructions to Joab that he should maneuver Uriah's death in battle.—2Sa 11:14-26.

2. A priest who witnessed Isaiah's writing the name of his son Maher-shalal-hash-baz on a tablet. (Isa 8:1, 2) Uriah's name is elsewhere spelled Urijah.—2Ki 16:10; see URIJAH No. 1.

3. Presumably a priest, one who stood at Ezra's right when he read from the Law to the returned exiles assembled at the Water Gate in Jerusalem. —Ne 8:1-4.

URIEL (U·ri′el) [God Is Light].

1. A Levite descendant of Kohath; son of Tahath.—1Ch 6:22, 24.

2. Chief of the Kohathites at the time David had the ark of the covenant brought to Jerusalem. —1Ch 15:5, 11, 12, 15.

3. Father of Micaiah (Maacah), who was the wife of King Rehoboam and mother of Abijah. (2Ch 13:1, 2; 11:21) Maacah was Absalom's grand-

daughter. Since Absalom's three sons apparently died young and childless (2Sa 14:27; 18:18), Micaiah must have been the child of Absalom's daughter Tamar and of Uriel, not the son of Absalom, but the son-in-law.

URIJAH (U·ri'jah) [My Light Is Jehovah].

1. A priest during the reign of King Ahaz of Judah (761-746 B.C.E.). When Ahaz went to Damascus to offer tribute to Tiglath-pileser III, he sent Urijah the design and pattern of the great altar he saw there and told him to build one like it, later instructing him to use it instead of Jehovah's altar. Urijah complied. (2Ki 16:8-16) Urijah (Uriah) also witnessed a writing of Isaiah. (Isa 8:1, 2) Though not so identified, he was presumably high priest, in view of his importance and the absence of any other person so titled at this time.

2. A prophet of Jehovah, son of Shemaiah from Kiriath-jearim. During the reign of Jehoiakim, Urijah prophesied against Judah and Jerusalem just as Jeremiah did. However, when Urijah learned that Jehoiakim sought his death, he fled to Egypt, but he was brought back and slain, his body being cast into a common graveyard.—Jer 26:20-23.

3. Son of Hakkoz; a priest whose son Meremoth was one of the priests in whose care Ezra entrusted the gold and silver and temple vessels brought to Jerusalem. Urijah's son Meremoth later helped to repair Jerusalem's wall.—Ezr 8:33; Ne 3:4, 21.

URIM AND THUMMIM. Objects used to ascertain the divine will when questions of national importance needed an answer from Jehovah.

As recorded at Leviticus 8:8, Moses, after placing the breastpiece upon Aaron, put the Urim and the Thummim in the breastpiece. While the Hebrew preposition here translated "in" can be rendered "upon," the same word is used at Exodus 25:16 in speaking of placing the two stone tablets *in* the ark of the covenant. (Ex 31:18) Some have proposed the suggestion that the Urim and the Thummim were the 12 stones affixed to the breastpiece. That this was not the case is shown by the fact that, in the priestly inauguration ceremony, the completed breastpiece with the 12 stones sewn on it, was put upon Aaron, and *then* the Urim and Thummim were put in it. Also, a comparison of Exodus 28:9, 12, 30 refutes the theory that they consisted of the two onyx stones on the shoulder pieces of the high priest's ephod. (Ex 28:9-14) They evidently were separate objects.

Their Use. It is notable that the Urim and the Thummim were to be over Aaron's heart when he went "in before Jehovah," doubtless referring to Aaron's standing in the Holy before the curtain to

the Most Holy compartment when inquiring of Jehovah. Their location, "over Aaron's heart," would appear to indicate that the Urim and the Thummim were placed in the fold, or pouch, formed by the doubled construction of the breastpiece. They were for "the judgments of the sons of Israel" and were used when a question of importance to the national leaders and consequently to the nation itself needed an answer from Jehovah. Jehovah, Israel's Lawgiver, would give an answer to the high priest as to the right course to pursue on any matter.—Ex 28:30.

David called upon Abiathar to employ the Urim and the Thummim when Abiathar, after escaping the slaughter of the priests of Nob in which his father died, came to David with the ephod. Apparently this was *the* ephod of the high priest.—1Sa 22:19, 20; 23:6-15.

May Have Been Lots. From the instances recorded in the Scriptures in which Jehovah was consulted by Urim and Thummim, it appears that the question was so framed that a "yes" or "no" answer, or at least a very brief and direct reply, could be given. In one instance (1Sa 28:6) the Urim is mentioned alone, evidently with the Thummim also understood to be included.

A number of Bible commentators believe that the Urim and the Thummim were lots. They are called "the sacred lots" in James Moffatt's translation of Exodus 28:30. Some suppose that they consisted of three pieces, one inscribed with the word "yes," one with "no," and the other blank. These would be drawn, giving the answer to the question propounded, unless the blank piece was drawn, in which case no answer was forthcoming. Others think that they may have been two flat stones, white on one side and black on the other. When thrown down, two white sides up would mean "yes," two black sides "no," and a black and a white would mean no answer. On one occasion, when Saul had inquired through the priest as to whether to resume an attack on the Philistines, he received no answer. Feeling that someone among his men had sinned, he petitioned: "O God of Israel, do give Thummim!" Saul and Jonathan were taken from among those present; after that, lots were cast to decide between the two. In this account the appeal, "Do give Thummim," seems to be separate from the lot casting, though it may give indication that there was some connection between the two.—1Sa 14:36-42.

Served to Link Kingdom With Priesthood. The Aaronic priesthood is referred to at Deuteronomy 33:8-10, which says: "Your Thummim and your Urim belong to the man loyal to you." The reference to these as belonging "to the man loyal to you [Jehovah]" perhaps alludes to the loyalty of the tribe of Levi (from which the Aaronic priesthood came) that was demonstrated in connection with the incident of the golden calf.—Ex 32:25-29.

Jehovah wisely provided the Urim and the Thummim and placed them in the hands of the high priest. This made the king dependent to a great extent on the priesthood, avoiding the concentration of too much power in the hands of the king. It brought about the necessity of cooperation between the kingship and the priesthood. (Nu 27:18-21) Jehovah made known his will to Israel by his written Word, also by prophets and by dreams. But it seems that prophets and dreams were used for special occasions, whereas the high priest with the Urim and the Thummim was always present with the people.

Use Ceased in 607 B.C.E. According to Jewish tradition, use of the Urim and the Thummim ceased when Jerusalem was desolated and her temple destroyed in 607 B.C.E. by the Babylonian armies under King Nebuchadnezzar. (Babylonian Talmud, *Sotah* 48*b*) This view is supported by what we read regarding these objects in the books of Ezra and Nehemiah. There, certain men who were claimants to priestly descent, but who could not find their names in the public register, were told that they could not eat from the most holy things provided for the priesthood until a priest stood up with Urim and Thummim. But there is no record of their use at that time, and thereafter the Bible makes no further reference to these sacred objects.—Ezr 2:61-63; Ne 7:63-65.

Greater High Priest Consults Jehovah. Jesus Christ is described in Paul's letter to the Hebrews as the great King-Priest according to the manner of Melchizedek. (Heb 6:19, 20; 7:1-3) In him kingship and priesthood are combined. His priestly work was foreshadowed by that of the high priest of ancient Israel. (Heb 8:3-5; 9:6-12) All judgment of mankind is committed into his hands as such a High Priest. (Joh 5:22) Nevertheless, when on earth Jesus declared: "The things I say to you men I do not speak of my own originality; but the Father who remains in union with me is doing his works" (Joh 14:10) and, "I do nothing of my own initiative; but just as the Father taught me I speak these things." (Joh 8:28) Also, he said: "If I do judge, my judgment is truthful, because I am not alone, but the Father who sent me is with me." (Joh 8:16) Certainly in his exalted heavenly position, perfected as High Priest forever, he continues in this course of subjection to his Father, looking to him for guidance in judgment.—Heb 7:28; compare 1Co 11:3; 15:27, 28.

UTENSILS. The Hebrew term *keli'* is very broad in its application and can refer to articles (Ge 24:53; Ex 3:22; Le 13:49, 52, 57-59; 15:4, 6), implements (Ge 27:3), goods (Ge 31:37), receptacles (Ge 42:25; 43:11), equipment (Ge 45:20), instruments (Ge 49:5; 1Ch 15:16), furnishings (Ex 25:9), utensils (Ex 25:39; 27:3, 19; 30:27, 28; 31:7-9), vessels (Le 6:28; 11:32-34), garb (De 22:5), weapons (Jg 9:54; 18:11, 16, 17), luggage (1Sa 10:22), baggage (1Sa 17:22), bags (1Sa 17:40, 49), organisms (1Sa 21:5), and tools (1Ki 6:7).

Often *keli'* designates the various utensils used in connection with the sanctuary. These utensils included such items as dishes, pitchers, shovels, bowls, forks, fire holders, extinguishers, snuffers, basins, and cups. (Ex 25:29, 30, 39; 27:3, 19; 37:16, 23; 38:3; 1Ki 7:40-50; 2Ch 4:11-22) Being used for a sacred purpose, these utensils were "holy." (1Ki 8:4) Accordingly, since the Jews who left Babylon in 537 B.C.E. were privileged to carry with them the sacred utensils that King Nebuchadnezzar had taken from Jerusalem, they had to keep themselves clean religiously and morally. The prophetic command applied to them: "Turn away, turn away, get out of [Babylon], touch nothing unclean; get out from the midst of her, keep yourselves clean, you who are carrying the utensils of Jehovah." (Isa 52:11) This required more than cleanness in an outward ceremonial way. It called for a cleanness of heart. The apostle Paul, when writing to the Corinthians, applied the words of Isaiah 52:11 in showing that Christians must likewise be free from defilement of flesh and spirit.—2Co 6:14-18; 7:1.

The founder of Christianity, Jesus Christ, set the example in this regard by remaining "loyal, guileless, undefiled, separated from the sinners." (Heb 7:26) While on earth he demonstrated zeal for maintaining the sanctity of Jehovah's temple, as when he twice cleansed it of commercialism. (Joh 2:13-25; Mt 21:12, 13; Mr 11:15-17; Lu 19:45, 46) In connection with the second temple cleansing, Mark reports that Jesus did not "let anyone carry a utensil through the temple." (Mr 11:16) Thus Jesus evidently did not allow anyone to detract from the sanctity of the temple courtyard by using it as a mere shortcut when carrying items to another part of Jerusalem.

UTHAI (U'thai).

1. A postexilic resident of Jerusalem; descendant of Judah through Perez.—1Ch 9:3, 4.

2. Head of a paternal house among the sons of Bigvai who came with Ezra to Jerusalem in 468 B.C.E.—Ezr 8:1, 14.

UZ.

1. A son of Aram and great-grandson of Noah through Shem.—Ge 10:22, 23; 1Ch 1:17.

2. Firstborn son of Nahor and Milcah; nephew of Abraham.—Ge 22:20, 21.

3. Son of Dishan and descendant of Seir the Horite.—Ge 36:20, 21, 28.

4. Homeland of Job (Job 1:1), settled by Uz, but it cannot be stated with certainty whether that Uz was Aram's son or Nahor's son. (Ge 10:22, 23; 22: 20, 21) Its exact location is unknown. Uz seemingly was near Edom, allowing for a later extension of Edomite domain into Uz, or for some later Edomites to be dwelling in the "land of Uz," as is indicated at Lamentations 4:21. Jeremiah was commissioned to pass the cup of God's wrath to "all the kings of the land of Uz," and the immediate context includes references to Philistia, Edom, Moab, and Ammon. (Jer 25:15, 17, 20, 21) Job's homeland was vulnerable to attack by Sabeans (from the S) and Chaldeans (from the E). (Job 1:15, 17) Taken together, these factors would indicate a location E of the Promised Land and near Edom, somewhere in N Arabia.

UZAI (U'zai) [shortened form of Azaniah]. A man whose son Palal helped Nehemiah to rebuild Jerusalem's wall.—Ne 3:25.

UZAL (U'zal).

1. The sixth named of Joktan's 13 sons, and also the tribe descended from him. (Ge 10:26-29; 1Ch 1:21) According to Arabian tradition, San'a (capital of Yemen Arab Republic) was anciently called 'Azal and was connected with Uzal.

2. A place referred to in connection with Tyre's traders, at Ezekiel 27:19. A suggested identification is the region Izalla, in NE Syria, near the upper Tigris River.

UZZA (Uz'za) [possibly a shortened form of Uzziah, meaning "My Strength Is Jehovah"].

1. A Benjamite.—1Ch 8:1, 7.

2. A name connected with a garden. Kings Manasseh and Amon of Judah were buried in the garden of Uzza instead of the usual royal burial places. (2Ki 21:18, 23, 26) Neither Uzza nor the garden are otherwise known. Since persons were buried there, the place could not have been in the temple grounds, and since the royal palace adjoined the temple, the "house" of Manasseh in the garden of Uzza may have been a summer residence.

3. Head of a family of Nethinim, some of whom returned to Jerusalem with Zerubbabel in 537 B.C.E.—Ezr 2:1, 2, 43, 49; Ne 7:51.

UZZAH (Uz'zah) [possibly a shortened form of Uzziah, meaning "My Strength Is Jehovah"].

1. A Merarite Levite.—1Ch 6:29.

2. A son of Abinadab, undoubtedly a Levite. Uzzah and his brother Ahio led the wagon carrying the ark of the covenant from their house when David wanted it brought to Jerusalem. When the bulls pulling the wagon nearly caused an upset, Uzzah reached out and grabbed hold to steady the Ark, for which Jehovah struck him dead on the spot. David named the place Perez-uzzah because there Jehovah had broken through in "a rupture against Uzzah."—2Sa 6:3-8; 1Ch 13:7-11.

Notwithstanding Uzzah's presumably good intentions to prevent the Ark from falling, it was judged as an "irreverent act." (2Sa 6:7) This was because deliberate disobedience was involved. Jehovah had instructed that under no circumstances was the Ark to be touched by unauthorized persons, a warning of public knowledge that carried with it the death penalty for violators. (Nu 4:15, 19, 20) Had authorized ones, Kohathite Levites, carried it with the poles on their shoulders as God had directed, God's anger would not have been incurred.—Ex 25:13, 14; Nu 7:9.

UZZEN-SHEERAH (Uz'zen-she'e·rah) [possibly, Ear of Sheerah]. A city that Sheerah, an Ephraimite woman, built. In what sense she 'built' is not stated; perhaps this was in the sense of her contributing in some major way to the progress and development of it as well as other places listed. (1Ch 7:22-24) Uzzen-sheerah's location is not definitely known. However, some geographers identify it with Beit Sira, about 4 km (2 mi) W of the suggested site of Lower Beth-horon and about 21 km (13 mi) NW of Jerusalem.

UZZI (Uz'zi) [shortened form of Uzziah].

1. A son or descendant of Tola in the tribe of Issachar. Uzzi and several of his descendants became heads of ancestral houses.—1Ch 7:1-3.

2. A descendant of Benjamin through Belah. Uzzi was a tribal family head.—1Ch 7:6, 7.

3. A descendant of Aaron through Eleazar in the high-priestly line; possibly great-grandson of Phinehas; forefather of the Bible writer Ezra. —1Ch 6:3-6, 51; Ezr 7:1-5.

4. A Benjamite whose son or descendant lived in postexilic Jerusalem.—1Ch 9:3, 7-9.

5. Overseer of the Levites in Jerusalem sometime after the exile; descendant of Asaph.—Ne 11:22.

6. Head of the priestly paternal house of Jedaiah during the time of High Priest Jeshua's successor Joiakim. (Ne 12:1, 12, 19) Possibly identical with No. 7.

7. A priest positioned with Nehemiah at the temple for the inauguration of Jerusalem's rebuilt wall. (Ne 12:27, 40-42) Perhaps the same person as No. 6.

UZZIA (Uz·zi′a) [shortened form of Uzziah]. A mighty man in David's forces. Uzzia was an Ashterathite, that is, probably from the town of Ashtaroth E of the Jordan.—1Ch 11:26, 44; Jos 9:10.

UZZIAH (Uz·zi′ah) [My Strength Is Jehovah].

1. A Kohathite Levite; "son" of Uriel.—1Ch 6:22-24.

2. One whose son Jonathan was an official of King David.—1Ch 27:25.

3. King of Judah, also called Azariah. The son of Amaziah by his wife Jecoliah, Uzziah is credited with a reign of 52 years (829-778 B.C.E.). During this period Jeroboam (II), Zechariah, Shallum, Menahem, Pekahiah, and Pekah ruled in succession over the northern kingdom. (2Ki 15:1, 2, 8, 10, 13, 14, 17, 23, 25, 27; 2Ch 26:3) The prophets Isaiah (1:1; 6:1), Hosea (1:1), Amos (1:1), and perhaps Joel were contemporaries of Uzziah. This king's reign witnessed an unusually great earthquake.—Zec 14:5.

After the death of his father, 16-year-old Uzziah was made king by the people of Judah. (2Ki 14:21; 2Ch 26:1) According to 2 Kings 15:1, however, Uzziah became king in the 27th year of Israelite King Jeroboam (II). As this would place the beginning of Uzziah's rule approximately 12 years after the death of his father, this must refer to his 'becoming king' in a special sense. It may be that in the 27th year of King Jeroboam, the two-tribe Judean kingdom was freed from subjection to the northern kingdom, a subjection that perhaps began when Israelite King Jehoash defeated Uzziah's father Amaziah. (2Ch 25:22-24) So it may be that Uzziah became king a second time in the sense of being free from the domination of Israelite King Jeroboam (II).

Uzziah did what "was upright in Jehovah's eyes." This was largely because he heeded the good instruction of a certain Zechariah (not the prophet by that name who lived in a later period). But his subjects continued improper sacrificing at high places.—2Ki 15:3, 4; 2Ch 26:4, 5.

Uzziah became famous for his military successes, attained with Jehovah's help. He restored Elath (Eloth) to the kingdom of Judah and rebuilt that city located at the head of the Gulf of 'Aqaba. He warred successfully against the Philistines, breaking through the walls of Gath, Jabneh, and Ashdod, after which he built cities in the territory of Ashdod. Uzziah gained victories over the Arabians and Meunim, and he made the Ammonites tributaries to Judah. His powerful, well-equipped fighting force came to consist of 307,500 men under the control of 2,600 heads of paternal houses. Uzziah strengthened the fortifications of Jerusalem and built engines of war there.—2Ki 14:22; 2Ch 26:2, 6-9, 11-15.

This king also had great interest in agriculture and raising livestock. Uzziah hewed out many cisterns to provide an ample water supply for the livestock and erected towers in the wilderness, likely to protect the grazing herds and flocks from marauders. Farming and vinedressing operations were carried on under his direction in the mountains and in Carmel.—2Ch 26:10.

It appears that Uzziah's brilliant successes resulted in his becoming haughty to the point of invading the Holy compartment of the temple to burn incense. High Priest Azariah, accompanied by 80 underpriests, immediately followed the king into the temple and censured him for this unlawful act, urging him to leave the sanctuary. With the censer for burning incense in his hand and raging against the priests, Uzziah was miraculously stricken with leprosy in his forehead, whereupon the priests excitedly ushered him out of the temple. As an unclean leper, Uzziah was cut off from all worship at the sanctuary and could not perform the kingly duties. Therefore, while Uzziah remained in a certain house until the day of his death, his son Jotham administered the affairs of state.—2Ch 26:16-21.

Concerning his death and burial, 2 Chronicles 26:23 reports: "Finally Uzziah lay down with his forefathers; and so they buried him with his forefathers, but in the burial field that belonged to the kings, for they said: 'He is a leper.'" This may mean that, because of his leprosy, Uzziah was buried in the ground of a field connected with the royal cemetery instead of being placed in a rock-hewn tomb.

A limestone plaque, found at Jerusalem and thought to date from the first century C.E., bears the following inscription: "Hither were brought the bones of Uzziah, king of Judah. Not to be opened."—PICTURE, Vol. 1, p. 960.

4. A Levite priest of "the sons of Harim" (1Ch 24:8; Ezr 2:36, 39) among those dismissing their foreign wives in compliance with Ezra's exhortation.—Ezr 10:10, 11, 21, 44.

5. A descendant of Judah through Perez whose "son" Athaiah is listed among the residents of Jerusalem in Nehemiah's time.—Ne 11:4.

UZZIEL (Uz'zi·el) [God Is Strength].

1. Last named of Kohath's four sons; grandson of Levi; uncle of Moses and Aaron. Uzziel's three sons, Mishael, El(i)zaphan, and Sithri, became heads of tribal families in Levi.—Ex 6:16, 18, 20, 22; Le 10:4; Nu 3:19, 30; 1Ch 6:2, 18; 23:12; see UZZIELITES.

2. Family head in the tribe of Benjamin; son or descendant of Bela.—1Ch 7:6, 7.

3. A Levite musician of the family of Heman, appointed to head David's 11th musical service division; also called Azarel.—1Ch 25:4, 18.

4. Levite descendant of Jeduthun who helped dispose of the unclean objects removed from the temple at the beginning of Hezekiah's reign.—2Ch 29:12, 14, 16.

5. One of four Simeonite sons of Ishi who led 500 men into Mount Seir to wipe out the remnant of Amalekites and take up living there; a contemporary of Hezekiah.—1Ch 4:41-43.

6. A goldsmith who helped repair Jerusalem's wall under Nehemiah's direction; son of Harhaiah.—Ne 3:8.

UZZIELITES (Uz·zi'el·ites) [Of (Belonging to) Uzziel]. Levite descendants of Kohath's fourth son Uzziel. (Nu 3:19, 27) They camped to the S of the tabernacle, and one of the Uzzielites, El(i)zaphan, was chieftain of all the Kohathites. (Nu 3:29, 30) One hundred and twelve Uzzielites under Amminadab accompanied the ark of the covenant when David had it brought to Jerusalem. (1Ch 15:3, 4, 10) Uzzielites were further involved in David's organization of temple service.—1Ch 23:6, 20; 24:24; 26:23, 24.

V

VAHEB (Va'heb). Apparently a now unknown place near the Arnon, "in Suphah."—Nu 21:14.

VAIZATHA (Vai·za'tha). One of Haman's ten sons.—Es 9:9, 10.

VALLEY. A depression between bluffs, hills, or mountains. Jehovah God is properly credited with the development of earth's topographical features, including its many valleys. (Ps 104:8) In Scripture, some were called merely valleys. (Jos 8:11; 1Sa 13:18) Others were "valley plains," low-lying level areas between mountains and hills. (De 11:11; see PLAIN.) There were also "torrent valleys," sometimes having perennial streams but often flowing with water only in the rainy season. (De 8:7; see TORRENT VALLEY.) Certain translations use "vale" or "valley(s)" where the references are to "low plain(s)" (Ge 14:3; 1Ch 12:15), and "vale" or "lowland(s)" for the "Shephelah," the hilly lowland between the Philistine coastal plain and the highlands of central Palestine.—De 1:7; 1Ki 10:27.

Among the notable valleys mentioned in the Scriptures are the Valley of Moab "in front of Beth-peor" (De 3:29; 34:6) and the Valley of Salt (2Sa 8:13), as well as those of Hinnom (Ne 11:30), Iphtah-el (Jos 19:14), Zeboim (1Sa 13:18), and Zephathah (2Ch 14:10). The 'valley plains' of Scriptural record include those of Shinar (Ge 11:2),

Jericho (De 34:3), Mizpeh (Jos 11:8), Lebanon (Jos 12:7), Ono (Ne 6:2), and Megiddo (2Ch 35:22; Zec 12:11).

Figurative and Prophetic Use. A dark valley, or ravine, with pitfalls and wild beasts would be perilous to a flock, especially at night, were it not for the care of a good shepherd. Though similarly faced with the threat of various calamities, David was secure in the knowledge that Jehovah was his Shepherd. Therefore, he could declare: "Even though I walk in the valley of deep shadow, I fear nothing bad."—Ps 23:1, 4.

"The pronouncement of the valley of the vision" evidently relates to ancient Jerusalem. Though of considerable elevation, the city is like a "valley" in being surrounded by higher mountains.—Isa 22:1, 5.

Evidently by clearing out all obstacles that stood in the way of the return of his people from Babylonian exile, Jehovah, in effect, 'raised up every valley,' 'leveled hills and mountains,' and made "rugged ground a valley plain" for them. (Isa 40:4) En route, the Jewish remnant did not suffer thirst. Jehovah's words through Isaiah were fulfilled: "Upon bare hills I shall open up rivers, and in the midst of the valley plains, springs."—Isa 41:18; compare Isa 35:6, 7, 10; 43:19-21; 48:20, 21.

VALLEY GATE. See Gate, Gateway.

VALLEY OF HINNOM. See Hinnom, Valley of.

VALLEY PLAIN. See Plain.

VANIAH (Va·ni′ah). Postexilic son of Bani. He and numerous other persons had married foreign wives but dismissed them at Ezra's admonition. —Ezr 10:10, 11, 34, 36, 44.

VAPOR. See Mist.

VASHTI (Vash′ti). The queen of Ahasuerus (Xerxes I) the king of Persia. In the third year of his reign, Ahasuerus called in all the nobles, princes, and servants from the jurisdictional districts. At the end of the conference, he held a seven-day banquet. Similarly, Vashti held a banquet for the women at the royal house. On the seventh day, Ahasuerus ordered his court officials to bring in Vashti in royal headdress, that all might see her loveliness. (It seems that the queen would ordinarily eat meals at the king's table, but history does not give proof of this as being the case at great banquets. Besides, at the time, Vashti was holding a banquet with the women.) For some unstated reason, Vashti persistently refused. Ahasuerus turned to his wise men who knew the law, and he was advised by Memucan, a prince, that it was not the king alone that Vashti had wronged but also all the princes and people in the jurisdictional districts. He said that when the princesses should hear what the queen had done (which news would quickly be spread in the castle), they would follow Vashti's action as a precedent for contemptuous action on their own part. (Es 1:1-22) Vashti was deposed, and about four years later, Esther the Jewess was selected to become the wife of Ahasuerus and to take the royal office of Vashti.—Es 2:1-17.

VAT. See Press.

VEDAN (Ve′dan). One of the places with which Tyre had commercial intercourse. (Eze 27:19) Its exact location is uncertain. However, it has been tentatively identified with Wadden near Medina, near the middle of the western side of the Arabian Peninsula.

VEGETATION. Plants in general. On the third creative "day," God caused the earth to bring forth "vegetation bearing seed according to its kind"; thus it was able to reproduce. (Ge 1:11-13) Genesis 2:5, 6 apparently describes conditions on that "day" just after God made dry land appear but before the production of grass, seed-bearing vegetation, and fruit-bearing trees. To supply needed moisture for coming plant life, Jehovah provided that mist should regularly rise from the earth to water the ground. It kept vegetation flourishing earth wide, even though there was then no rain. Although the luminaries in the heavens did not become clearly discernible in the expanse until the fourth creative "day" (Ge 1:14-16), an ample amount of diffused light was evidently available by the third "day" to foster the growth of vegetation.—See Ge 1:14, *Ro,* ftn.

God gave green vegetation to man and the animals as part of their original food supply, later expanding mankind's diet to include meat from which the blood had been drained. (Ge 1:29, 30; 9:3, 4) Sinful man was compelled to toil for the vegetation he ate (Ge 3:18, 19), but Jehovah remained the Provider of it for man and beast alike, for He is the Provider of the sunshine and rain essential to its growth.—Ps 104:14; 106:20; Mic 5:7; Zec 10:1; Heb 6:7; compare De 32:2.

Growth of vegetation can be controlled by God according to his purpose. He assured the Israelites that their obedience would be rewarded with rain and vegetation for their domestic animals. (De 11:13-15) However, if they abandoned their covenant with God, he would make their land devoid of vegetation. (De 29:22-25; compare Isa 42:15; Jer 12:4; 14:6.) One blow from Jehovah against ancient Egypt consisted of hail that struck all sorts of vegetation. In another God-sent blow, locusts devoured all the vegetation the hail had left.—Ex 9:22, 25; 10:12, 15; Ps 105:34, 35; compare Am 7:1-3.

Figurative Use. During the Palestinian dry season, vegetation, when subjected to the scorching heat of the sun or a parching east wind, quickly dries up. Accordingly, people about to be subjugated by military conquest are likened to "vegetation of the field and green tender grass, grass of the roofs, when there is a scorching before the east wind." (2Ki 19:25, 26; Isa 37:26, 27) Similarly, when severely afflicted, the psalmist exclaimed: "My heart has been struck just like vegetation and is dried up." "I myself am dried up like mere vegetation."—Ps 102:4, 11.

Under favorable conditions vegetation sprouts in great profusion, making it an appropriate figure to represent numerous descendants. (Job 5:25) During Solomon's reign, for example, "Judah and Israel were many" and flourished, "eating and drinking and rejoicing." (1Ki 4:20) This is evidently alluded to in a psalm regarding Solomon: "Those who are from the city will blossom like the vegetation of the earth." (Ps 72:16) On the other hand, though the wicked for a time may sprout like vegetation, they are not flourishing because of God's blessing but are in line to be "annihilated forever."—Ps 92:7.

In the Scriptures, trees at times represent those who are prominent and lofty (compare Eze 31:2-14), whereas the lowly vegetation, like the bramble, grass, or rushes, can represent people generally. (Compare Jg 9:8-15; 2Ki 14:8-10; Isa 19:15; 40:6, 7.) This aids in understanding the significance of Revelation 8:7, which speaks of the burning up of "a third of the trees" and "all the green vegetation."

VEIL. See DRESS.

VENGEANCE.

Infliction of punishment in return for an injury or offense; retributive action. The Greek word ek·di·ke′o, rendered "avenge," literally means "from justice," suggesting that the action represents justice achieved. As used in the Bible, "vengeance" usually applies to retribution paid by God in behalf of justice, but it may also refer to a person's executing that which he may view as just or as equalizing matters to his own satisfaction.

Belongs to Jehovah. Unless a person is qualified as executioner of vengeance by appointment of Jehovah, or by being designated as such by his Word, he does wrong if he attempts to avenge himself or others. "Vengeance is mine, and retribution," says Jehovah. (De 32:35) God is addressed by the psalmist: "O God of acts of vengeance, Jehovah." (Ps 94:1) Accordingly, the individual is condemned by God if he bears a grudge or seeks personal vengeance for real or fancied wrongs done to himself or to someone else.—Le 19:18; Ro 12:19; Heb 10:30.

The Scriptures point out that God's anger rests upon all sinners and transgressors, and that only through God's undeserved kindness in providing the ransom sacrifice of Jesus Christ is there a basis for mitigating or withholding the full retributive justice against the sinner. (Ro 5:19-21; 2Co 5:19; Heb 2:2, 3; see RANSOM.) God acts in full harmony with his righteousness when thus forgiving sin, and he is also righteous in bringing judgment upon sinners who reject his provision; such cannot escape divine vengeance.—Ro 3:3-6, 25, 26; compare Ps 99:8.

Jehovah's vengeance has a purpose. Jehovah's vengeance brings relief and benefit when he acts in behalf of those who trust in him; additionally, it procures praise to him as the just Judge. The psalmist says: "The righteous one will rejoice because he has beheld the vengeance. . . . And

mankind will say: 'Surely there is fruitage for the righteous one. Surely there exists a God that is judging in the earth.'" (Ps 58:10, 11) Therefore, the primary purpose for God's taking vengeance is to vindicate and glorify his own name and sovereignty. (Ex 14:18; Ps 83:13-18; Isa 25:1-5; Eze 25:14, 17; 38:23) His action also vindicates his servants as being truly his representatives and delivers them from undesirable circumstances. —Ex 14:31; 15:11-16; Eze 37:16, 21-23; Ps 135:14; 148:14; Pr 21:18.

A fixed time for God's vengeance. The Scriptures indicate that God has a due time for large-scale expressions of his vengeance upon his enemies. The prophet Isaiah was commissioned to proclaim "the day of vengeance on the part of our God." God's vengeance was expressed against ancient Babylon, the oppressor of his people, when the armies of Medo-Persia were used to break her power in 539 B.C.E. (Isa 61:1, 2; 13:1, 6, 9, 17) Jesus Christ, when on earth, quoted part of Isaiah's prophecy (61:1, 2) and applied it to himself. (Lu 4:16-21) Though the record does not say that he quoted the part concerning "the day of vengeance," in actuality he did proclaim that "day," which came upon Jerusalem in 70 C.E. Jesus foretold the encampment by armies (of the Romans) around the city, telling his followers to flee from Jerusalem when they saw this, "because these are days for meting out justice ["days of vengeance"], that all the things written may be fulfilled."—Lu 21:20-22, Int; compare AT, KJ, Ro, RS.

Jesus Christ further said, before his death and resurrection: "Concerning that day and hour [of executing judgment on the present-day system of things] nobody knows, neither the angels of the heavens nor the Son, but only the Father." (Mt 24:36) He thereby revealed that vengeance was sure to be executed at a time known and set by God. He illustrated the sureness of God's action in his due time in behalf of his name and his servants, speaking of a judge who, because of a widow's persistence in asking for justice, decided: "I will see that she gets justice ["I shall exact vengeance for her"]." Jesus applied the illustration to God, saying: "Certainly, then, shall not God cause justice to be done for ["do the vengeance of"] his chosen ones who cry out to him day and night, even though he is long-suffering toward them?" —Lu 18:2-8, Int.

Furthermore, in the apostle John's vision recorded in the book of Revelation, John saw the souls of those slaughtered because of the word of God and because of the witness work they used to have, crying out: "Until when, Sovereign Lord holy and true, are you refraining from judging and avenging our blood upon those who dwell on the earth?" The answer they received shows that there is a definite time for the vengeance to be carried out, namely, when "the number [would be] filled also of their fellow slaves and their brothers who were about to be killed as they also had been."—Re 6:9-11.

The Scriptures reveal that this execution of vengeance begins on Babylon the Great, then proceeds to come upon "the wild beast and the kings of the earth and their armies."—Re 19:1, 2, 19-21.

Appointed Executioners. The Lord Jesus Christ is God's Chief Executioner of vengeance. The apostle Paul comforts Christians with the words: "It is righteous on God's part to repay tribulation to those who make tribulation for you, but, to you who suffer tribulation, relief along with us at the revelation of the Lord Jesus from heaven with his powerful angels in a flaming fire, as he brings vengeance upon those who do not know God and those who do not obey the good news about our Lord Jesus. These very ones will undergo the judicial punishment of everlasting destruction from before the Lord and from the glory of his strength."—2Th 1:6-9.

In the Christian congregation. The apostles were appointed under Jesus Christ to care for the Christian congregation and to protect it from uncleanness and loss of Jehovah's favor. In harmony with his God-given authority, the apostle Paul wrote to the congregation at Corinth, which was experiencing divisions and troubles from "false apostles": "We are holding ourselves in readiness to inflict punishment for ["to avenge"] every disobedience."—2Co 10:6, *Int;* 11:13; 13:10.

Older men appointed to care for the congregation were authorized to carry out "vengeance" to the extent that they could take steps to bring about justice and to reestablish the congregation in righteousness before God, by correcting the wrong that had been done. This the governing members of the Corinthian congregation did, after Paul corrected them, and thus Paul wrote in his second letter to them: "What a great earnestness it produced in you, . . . yes, righting of the wrong ["vengeance"]!" These men showed godly repentance after Paul's first letter and cleared out the wicked man therein referred to, doing all they could to right matters before Jehovah. (2Co 7:8-12, *Int*) However, those men were not authorized to carry out on the wrongdoer the full penalty demanded by justice—full vengeance in putting him to death, as had been the prerogative of the judges under the Mosaic Law. (Le 20:10; Heb 10:28) They merely expelled such unrepentant bad persons from the congregation. (1Co 5:13) If such ones remained unrepentant, they would eventually receive full justice for their misdeeds in everlasting death. (Heb 10:29, 30) Indeed, the Christian who takes up unrighteousness, as, for example, fornication, is in danger, "because Jehovah is one who exacts punishment [literally, is the "avenger"] for all these things."—1Th 4:3-6, *Int.*

Rulers. Governmental rulers, whose duty it is to see that justice is carried out, may be the ones who execute vengeance upon evildoers, including any Christians who break the laws of the land that are in harmony with what is right and that are consistent with the authority allowed those rulers by God. In such case, these rulers are indirectly executing God's vengeance, as the apostle Paul writes: "For those ruling are an object of fear, not to the good deed, but to the bad . . . it is God's minister, an avenger to express wrath upon the one practicing what is bad."—Ro 13:3, 4; 1Pe 2:13, 14; compare Ge 9:6.

Imperfect Man's Tendency to Seek Vengeance. It is a tendency of fallen, imperfect men to seek vengeance upon those who do them injustice or upon persons whom they hate. The man who commits adultery with another man's wife is in danger of retributive vengeance from the husband, as the Proverbs say: "For the rage of an able-bodied man is jealousy, and he will not show compassion in the day of vengeance. He will have no consideration for any sort of ransom, neither will he show willingness, no matter how large you make the present." (Pr 6:32-35) Nonetheless, vengeance taken by a person on his own initiative is usually carried out in uncontrolled anger and is to no good purpose, but brings God's anger against the avenging individual.—Jas 1:19, 20.

Enemies of God and of his servants. Those who hate God have shown hostility toward God's servants, seeking to wreak vengeance upon them. This is not a true bringing about of justice, but it is a desire or action as a result of people's hostility toward what is right and righteous, and it is an attempt to get rid of those righteous ones whose words and course of action convict them of wickedness. (Ps 8:2; 44:15, 16) In some instances God's servants have been killed with the perverted idea that justice was being carried out. (Joh 16:2) In executing this claimed or supposed "vindictive justice," however, they have not pleased God but, rather, have stored up vengeance for themselves. At times, it is true, Jehovah used the nations, such as Babylon, to bring his own vengeance on his people Israel when they broke their covenant with him. (Le 26:25) But those nations, on their part, acted because of hatred and malice, expressing their own vengefulness, and for this Jehovah, in turn, took vengeance upon them.—La 3:60; Eze 25:12-17.

See also AVENGER OF BLOOD; CITIES OF REFUGE.

VENOM. Poisonous fluid secreted by certain snakes and some other creatures. (Nu 21:4-9; De 8:15; Ac 28:3-6) One Hebrew word for the venom of reptiles is *che·mah'* (De 32:24), which is also used to denote "rage," "fury," and the like. (De 29:28; Eze 19:12) It is from a root meaning "be hot" (De 19:6) and may allude to the inflammation or burning sensation associated with the bite of a venomous snake. Another Hebrew word (*ro'sh*, or *rohsh*) is applied to the "poison," or "venom," of cobras, "poisoned" water, and a "poisonous plant." —De 32:32, 33; Job 20:16; Jer 8:14; 9:15; 23: 15; La 3:19; see COBRA; POISONOUS PLANT; VIPER, HORNED.

Though some animal poisons may seem to be only for protection or killing, of interest is this statement by H. Munro Fox: "In some cases we know that poisons play a role in the functioning of the body of the animal which manufactures them. In many instances this may be the real *raison d'être* [reason for existence] of the venoms, quite apart from any protective value. The poisonous spittle of snakes, for example, has work to do in the digestion of the snake's food."—*Marvels & Mysteries of Our Animal World,* by The Reader's Digest Association, 1964, p. 259.

Figurative Use. The lying, slanderous statements of the wicked, so damaging to the victim's reputation, are likened to the deadly venom of the serpent. (Ps 58:3, 4) Of slanderers, it is said, "The venom of the horned viper is under their lips" (or, "behind their lips"), even as the viper's venom gland lies behind the lip and fangs of its upper jaw. (Ps 140:3; Ro 3:13) The human tongue, misused in slanderous, backbiting, false teaching, or similarly harmful speech, "is full of death-dealing poison."—Jas 3:8.

VERMILION. See COLORS.

VERSIONS. Translations of the Bible from Hebrew, Aramaic, and Greek into other tongues. Translation work has made the Word of God available to thousands of millions of persons unable to understand the original Biblical languages. The early versions of the Scriptures were handwritten and were therefore in the form of manuscripts. However, since the advent of the printing press, many additional versions, or translations, have appeared, and these have generally been pub-

lished in great quantities. Some versions have been prepared directly from Hebrew and Greek Bible texts, whereas others are based on earlier translations.—CHART, Vol. 1, p. 321.

The Scriptures have been published, the whole or in part, in more than 1,800 languages. From the standpoint of language coverage, this means that some 97 percent of the earth's population can have access to at least some part of the Bible. An account of versions, or translations, of the Scriptures will engender gratitude to Jehovah God for the wonderful way in which he has preserved his Word for the benefit of mankind's millions.

Ancient Versions of the Hebrew Scriptures. Extant today are possibly 6,000 ancient manuscripts of all or portions of the Hebrew Scriptures, written in Hebrew (with the exception of a few Aramaic sections). Known to be still in existence are also many manuscripts of old versions, or translations, of the Hebrew Scriptures in various languages. Some versions were in themselves translations of earlier translations from the Hebrew. For instance, the Hebrew Scripture portion of the Old Latin version was rendered from the *Septuagint,* a Greek translation of the Hebrew Scriptures. On the other hand, some ancient versions of the Hebrew Scriptures (the Greek *Septuagint,* Aramaic Targums, the Syriac *Peshitta,* and the Latin *Vulgate*) were made directly from the Hebrew and not through the medium of a version in Greek or some other language.

Samaritan "Pentateuch." After the deportation of most of the inhabitants of Samaria and the ten-tribe kingdom of Israel by Assyria in 740 B.C.E., pagans from other territories of the Assyrian Empire were settled there by Assyria. (2Ki 17:22-33) In time the descendants of those left in Samaria and those brought in by Assyria came to be called Samaritans. They accepted the first five books of the Hebrew Scriptures, and in about the fourth century B.C.E. they produced the Samaritan *Pentateuch,* not really a translation of the original Hebrew Pentateuch, but a transliteration of its text into Samaritan characters, mixed with Samaritan idioms. Few of the extant manuscripts of the Samaritan *Pentateuch* are older than the 13th century C.E. Of about 6,000 differences between the Samaritan and the Hebrew texts, by far the majority are unimportant. One variation of interest appears at Exodus 12:40, where the Samaritan *Pentateuch* corresponds to the *Septuagint.*

Targums. The "Targums" were free translations or paraphrases of the Hebrew Scriptures into Aramaic. They likely assumed their present final form no earlier than about the fifth century C.E. One of the principal Targums, the "Targum of Onkelos" on the Pentateuch, is rather literal. Another, the so-called Targum of Jonathan, or Jerusalem Targum, for the Prophets, is less literal. Extant today are Targums on the Pentateuch, the Prophets, and, of later date, the Hagiographa.

The Greek "Septuagint." The Greek *Septuagint* (often designated *LXX*) was used by Greek-speaking Jews and Christians in Egypt and elsewhere. Reportedly, work on it commenced in Egypt in the days of Ptolemy Philadelphus (285-246 B.C.E.), when, according to tradition, the Pentateuch thereof was translated into Greek by 72 Jewish scholars. Later, the number 70 somehow came to be used, and the version of the Pentateuch was referred to as the *Septuagint,* meaning "Seventy." The other books of the Hebrew Scriptures (by various translators whose style varied from quite literal to rather free rendition) were gradually added until translation of the entire Hebrew Scriptures had finally been completed during the second century B.C.E. and perhaps by 150 B.C.E. Thereafter the entire work came to be known as the *Septuagint.* This version is often quoted by writers of the Christian Greek Scriptures. Apocryphal writings were evidently inserted in the Greek *Septuagint* sometime after it was first completed.—See APOCRYPHA.

One of the oldest extant manuscripts of the Greek *Septuagint* is Papyrus 957, the Rylands Papyrus iii. 458, preserved in the John Rylands Library, Manchester, England. It is of the second century B.C.E. and consists of fragments of Deuteronomy (23:24–24:3; 25:1-3; 26:12, 17-19; 28:31-33). Another manuscript, of the first century B.C.E., is Papyrus Fouad 266 (possessed by the Société Egyptienne de Papyrologie, Cairo), containing parts of the second half of Deuteronomy according to the Greek *Septuagint.* In various places therein, the Tetragrammaton (YHWH in English) of the divine name is found in a form of Old Hebrew characters right within the Greek script.—See PICTURE, Vol. 1, p. 326; JEHOVAH.

The Greek *Septuagint* has thus been preserved in numerous manuscripts, many fragmentary, others fairly complete. Notably, the *Septuagint* texts are preserved in the three famous uncial manuscripts written on vellum—the Vatican Manuscript No. 1209 and the Sinaitic Manuscript, both of the fourth century C.E., and the Alexandrine Manuscript of the fifth century C.E. The *Septuagint* as found in the Vatican Manuscript No. 1209 is almost complete; part of the Hebrew Scriptures once included in the Sinaitic Manuscript has been lost; that in the Alexandrine Manuscript is rather complete, though lacking parts of Genesis, First Samuel, and Psalms.

Later Greek versions. In the second century, Aquila, a Jewish proselyte of Pontus, made a new and very literal Greek translation of the Hebrew Scriptures. Except for fragments and quotations thereof by early writers, it has perished. Another Greek translation of the same century was produced by Theodotion. His was apparently a revision of the *Septuagint* or some other Greek version of the Hebrew Scriptures, though he considered the Hebrew text itself. No complete copy of Theodotion's version is extant. Another Greek version of the Hebrew Scriptures of which no complete copy is extant was that of Symmachus. His rendition, probably translated about 200 C.E., endeavored to convey the right sense rather than to be literal.

About 245 C.E., Origen, the noted scholar of Alexandria, Egypt, completed a mammoth multiple version of the Hebrew Scriptures called the *Hexapla* (which means "sixfold"). Though fragments of it are extant, no complete manuscript copy has survived. Origen arranged the text in six parallel columns containing (1) the consonantal Hebrew text, (2) a Greek transliteration of the Hebrew text, (3) Aquila's Greek version, (4) Symmachus' Greek version, (5) the *Septuagint,* revised by Origen to correspond more exactly to the Hebrew text, and (6) Theodotion's Greek version. In the Psalms, Origen used anonymous versions he called Quinta, Sexta, and Septima. The Quinta and Sexta were also employed in other books.

Christian Greek Scriptures. Translations of the Christian Greek Scriptures into Syriac (an Aramaic dialect) were produced from the second century onward. A Syriac version of particular note is Tatian's *Diatessaron,* a Gospel harmony of the second century C.E. It may have been written originally at Rome in Greek and later translated into Syriac in Syria by Tatian himself, but that is uncertain. The *Diatessaron* is extant today in an Arabic translation, in addition to a small third-century vellum fragment in Greek and an Armenian translation of a fourth-century commentary on it that contains lengthy quotations from its text.

Only incomplete manuscripts of an Old Syriac version of the Gospels (a translation other than the *Diatessaron*) are extant, the Curetonian and the Sinaitic Syriac Gospels. Though these manuscripts were probably copied in the fifth century, they likely represent an older Syriac text. The original version may have been made from the Greek about 200 C.E. Quite likely, Old Syriac renditions of other books of the Christian Greek Scriptures once existed, but there are no extant manuscripts thereof. All books of the Christian Greek Scriptures except Second Peter, Second and Third John, Jude, and Revelation were included in the Syriac *Peshitta* of the fifth century. In about 508 C.E. Philoxenus, bishop of Hierapolis, had Polycarp make a revision of the *Peshitta* Christian Scriptures, and this was the first time Second Peter, Second and Third John, Jude, and Revelation were added to a Syriac version.

The Christian Greek Scriptures had already been translated into Latin by the end of the second century C.E. They were also available in Egyptian by about the middle of the third century.

Ancient Versions of the Entire Bible. The *Peshitta* of Syriac-speaking people professing Christianity was in general use from the fifth century C.E. onward. The word "Peshitta" means "simple." The Hebrew Scripture portion was basically a translation from the Hebrew, probably made during the second or third century C.E., though a later revision involved comparison with the *Septuagint.* Numerous *Peshitta* manuscripts are extant, the most valuable being a sixth- or seventh-century codex preserved at the Ambrosian Library in Milan, Italy. One *Peshitta* manuscript of the Pentateuch (lacking Leviticus) has a date corresponding to about 464 C.E., making it the oldest *dated* Bible manuscript in any tongue.

Old Latin versions. These probably appeared from the latter part of the second century C.E. onward. The whole Bible in Latin seems to have been used in Carthage, North Africa, at least by 250 C.E. The Hebrew Scriptures were translated into Old Latin from the Greek *Septuagint* (not yet revised by Origen), but the Christian Scriptures were rendered, not from a translation, but from the Greek. Various translations may have been made, or at least a number of translators worked on the Old Latin version. Scholars usually refer to two basic types of Old Latin text: the African and the European. No complete manuscripts are extant; only about 30 fragments.

Latin "Vulgate." The Latin *Vulgate* (*Vulgata Latina*) is a version of the entire Bible by the foremost Biblical scholar of that time, Eusebius Hieronymus, otherwise known as Jerome. He first undertook a revision of the Old Latin version of the Christian Scriptures in comparison with the Greek text; he began with the Gospels, which were published in 383 C.E. Between about 384 and 390 C.E., he made two revisions of the Old Latin Psalms, in comparison with the Greek *Septuagint;* the first was called the Roman Psalter and the second the Gallican Psalter, because of their adoption first in Rome and Gaul. Jerome also translated the Psalms directly from Hebrew, this work being called the Hebrew Psalter. Just when he completed his revision of the Old Latin Christian Scriptures is uncertain. He began to revise the Hebrew Scripture portion but apparently never completed such a revision, preferring to translate directly from Hebrew (though also referring to Greek versions). Jerome labored on his Latin translation from the Hebrew from about 390 to 405 C.E.

Jerome's version was originally received with general hostility, and only gradually did it gain wide approval. With its later general acceptance in western Europe, it came to be called the *Vulgate,* denoting a commonly received version (the Latin *vulgatus* meaning "common, that which is popular"). Jerome's original translation underwent revisions, the Roman Catholic Church making the one of 1592 its standard edition. Thousands of *Vulgate* manuscripts are extant today.

Other ancient translations. As Christianity spread, other versions were required. At least by the third century C.E., the first translation of the Christian Greek Scriptures had been made for the Coptic natives of Egypt. Various Coptic dialects were used in Egypt, and in time various Coptic versions were produced. The most important are the Thebaic, or Sahidic, Version of Upper Egypt (in the S) and the Bohairic Version of Lower Egypt (in the N). These versions, containing both the Hebrew and Christian Greek Scriptures, were probably produced in the third and fourth centuries C.E.

The Gothic version was produced for the Goths during the fourth century C.E. while they were settled in Moesia (Serbia and Bulgaria). Missing from it are the books of Samuel and Kings, reportedly deleted because Bishop Ulfilas, who made the translation, thought it would be dangerous to include for use by the Goths these books that consider warfare and that contain information against idolatry.

The Armenian version of the Bible dates from the fifth century C.E. and was probably prepared from both Greek and Syriac texts. The Georgian version, made for the Georgians in the Caucasus, was completed toward the end of the sixth century C.E. and, while revealing Greek influence, has an Armenian and Syriac basis. The Ethiopic version, used by the Abyssinians, was produced perhaps about the fourth or fifth century C.E. There are several old Arabic versions of the Scriptures.

Translations of parts of the Bible into Arabic may date from as early as the seventh century C.E., but the earliest record is that of a version made in Spain in 724 C.E. The Slavonic version was made in the ninth century C.E. and has been attributed to two brothers, Cyril and Methodius.

VESSELS.

Hollow receptacles, some having lids (Nu 19:15), used to hold liquids or dry materials. (1Ki 17:10; Es 1:7; Jer 40:10) Many were made of clay, wood, metal, or stone. (Le 6:28; 15:12; Nu 7:85; 1Ki 10:21; Mt 26:7) Common containers included jars and vessels "of the bowl sort" (Isa 22:24), bags or sacks (Ge 42:25; Hag 1:6), baskets (Mr 8:19, 20; 2Co 11:33), skin bottles (Jg 4:19; Lu 5:37, 38), and buckets.—Nu 24:7; Joh 4:11; see UTENSILS.

Jars, Jugs, and Flasks. The jar, generally a deep cylindrical vessel having one, two, or even four handles, was usually earthenware (Isa 30:14; La 4:2) and, sometimes, made of stone. (Joh 2:6) A common large jar in the days of the kingdoms of Judah and of Israel may have been approximately 65 cm (25 in.) high with a diameter of about 40 cm (16 in.). Some jars were equipped with spouts. (2Ki 4:2) Jars might be kept on a stand (Le 11:35) and were used to hold such liquids as water or oil (1Ki 18:33; 2Ki 4:2), large ones often being employed for wine. (1Sa 10:3; 25:18; 2Sa 16:1; Jer 13:12) Also dry materials, such as flour, were stored in jars. (1Ki 17:12) Sometimes documents, including deeds of purchase, were placed in earthenware jars, or vessels, for safekeeping. (Jer 32:13-15) A number of ancient manuscripts were thus preserved in jars in the Qumran area near the Dead Sea, among the manuscripts being the well-known Dead Sea Scroll of Isaiah.

Water jugs (1Sa 26:11, 12, 16; 1Ki 19:6) and flasks (1Sa 10:1; 1Ki 14:3; 2Ki 9:3; Jer 19:1, 10) were commonly earthenware.

Bowls, Dishes, and Platters. Bowls were used to hold such liquids as wine (Am 6:6), milk (Jg 5:25), and water (Jg 6:38). They were made of clay, stone, and metal. Some banquet bowls were ceramic. As indicated by finds of archaeologists, in the days of the kingdoms of Judah and of Israel ceramic bowls averaged about 20 cm (8 in.) in height, had a diameter inside the rim of approximately 40 cm (16 in.), and sometimes had four handles. In comparison with bowls, dishes and platters likely were shallow.—Ex 25:29; 37:16; Nu 4:7; 7:84, 85; Mt 14:8, 11; Mr 6:25, 28.

Cups. The cup, a comparatively small vessel for drinking liquids, was usually made of clay, though sometimes of metal. (Pr 23:31; Jer 35:5;

Mr 9:41) Some cups were molded to fit the hand. Usually they were handleless shallow bowls. Those equipped with handles could also serve as dippers.

Figurative Use. The congregator indicated that at death "the jar at the spring is broken." Apparently this jar is the heart, which in death ceases to receive and transmit the flow of blood throughout the body. It becomes as useless as a broken jar that can hold no water. Also the brain, alluded to in connection with the figure of a "golden bowl" (evidently the cranium with its brain content), ceases to function and undergoes dissolution, "gets crushed."—Ec 12:6, 7.

Vessels. The Scriptures often refer to people as vessels. (Ac 9:15) Christians are frail earthen vessels entrusted with a glorious treasure, the ministry. (2Co 4:7) Women are designated as the "weaker vessel." Therefore, Christian husbands, by taking into consideration their wives' physical and biological limitations, as did Jehovah in the Law given to Israel (Le 18:19; 20:18), act "according to knowledge, assigning them honor as to a weaker vessel, the feminine one."—1Pe 3:7.

An individual should keep separate from vessels "lacking honor" (persons who do not conduct themselves aright) and should pursue a course in harmony with Jehovah's will. Thus he can be "a vessel for an honorable purpose, sanctified, useful to his owner, prepared for every good work." (2Ti 2:20, 21) Jehovah's refraining from bringing immediate destruction upon "vessels of wrath," wicked persons, serves to spare righteously disposed ones because it gives them time to be molded as "vessels of mercy."—Ro 9:17-26.

Cup. The cup is often symbolic of divine retribution or of God's anger. From such a cup wicked individuals, cities, or even peoples and nations might drink. (Ps 11:6; 75:8; Isa 51:17, 22; Jer 25:12-29; 51:41; La 4:21; Re 14:9, 10; 16:19; 18:5-8) Ancient Babylon, for example, was a symbolic "golden cup in the hand of Jehovah," from which many nations had to drink the bitter potion of defeat.—Jer 51:7.

When destruction was in store for Jerusalem, the inhabitants were told that people would not "give them the cup of consolation to drink on account of one's father and on account of one's mother." This was possibly an allusion to a cup of wine given to a person mourning over his deceased parents.—Jer 16:5-7; compare Pr 31:6.

The symbolic "cup" that Jehovah poured for Jesus Christ was His will for Jesus. Doubtless because of Christ's great concern over the reproach his death as one charged with blasphemy and sedition would bring to God, Jesus prayed that this "cup" pass away from him, if possible. Nevertheless, he was willing to submit to Jehovah's will and drink it. (Mt 26:39, 42; Joh 18:10, 11) Jehovah's assigned portion, or "cup," for Jesus meant not only suffering but also Jesus' baptism into death climaxed by his being resurrected to immortal life in heaven. (Lu 12:50; Ro 6:4, 5; Heb 5:7) It was, therefore, also "the cup of grand salvation" for Christ. (Ps 116:13) According to the divine will, the "cup" that Jesus Christ was given to drink he also shares with the "little flock" of his joint heirs of the Kingdom.—Lu 12:32; Mr 10:35-40.

VILLAGE. See CITY.

VINE.
A plant with long, slender twining stems that creep along the ground or climb by means of tendrils, the most common variety being the grapevine (*Vitis vinifera*). The Hebrew word *ge'phen* generally refers to "the wine vine" (Nu 6:4; Jg 13:14), an exception being the "wild vine" that produced wild gourds.—2Ki 4:39.

The history of viticulture begins with the statement: "Noah . . . proceeded to plant a vineyard." (Ge 9:20) Melchizedek, king of Salem, brought out "bread and wine" to set before Abraham, proving that grapes were grown in the land of Canaan before 1933 B.C.E. (Ge 14:18) Egyptian inscriptions depict grape picking and the treading of winepresses in the second millennium B.C.E.; the Pharaohs of the time had official cupbearers. (Ge 40:9-13, 20-23) The Egyptian wine-making industry, however, suffered a severe blow when Jehovah "went killing their vine" with a plague of hail.—Ps 78:47; 105:33.

The spies who entered the Promised Land, "a land of . . . vines and figs and pomegranates," brought back from the torrent valley of Eshcol a cluster of grapes so large that it had to be carried on a bar between two men. (De 8:8; Nu 13:20, 23, 26) Grape clusters from this region are commonly said to weigh 4.5 to 5.5 kg (10 to 12 lb). One cluster was recorded as weighing 12 kg (26 lb); another, more than 20 kg (44 lb).

Besides the torrent valley of Eshcol, other grape-growing regions mentioned in the Bible are En-gedi by the Dead Sea (Ca 1:14), Shechem (Jg 9:26, 27), Shiloh (Jg 21:20, 21), and across the Jordan, Sibmah, Heshbon, and Elealeh.—Isa 16: 7-10; Jer 48:32.

Planting and Care. Vineyards were often planted on hillsides. It was customary to fence or wall in vineyards (Nu 22:24; Pr 24:30, 31) and also to build booths or watchtowers (Isa 1:8; 5:2) to protect the vineyards against thieves or animal

intruders such as foxes and wild boars. (Ps 80:8, 13; Ca 2:15) The Mosaic Law allowed a passerby to eat his fill but not to carry any off in a receptacle, for this would be thievery.—De 23:24.

For convenience a winepress and a vat were dug near the vineyard, since usually the bulk of the crop was crushed to make wine. (Isa 5:2; Mr 12:1; see WINE AND STRONG DRINK.) Of course, fresh grapes were eaten in considerable quantity, and some sun-dried raisins were produced.—1Sa 25: 18; 30:12; 2Sa 16:1; 1Ch 12:40.

Ancient vineyards were laid out in several different ways. Sometimes the vines were systematically planted in rows 2.5 m (8 ft) or more apart in well-prepared soil. No other seeds were to be planted in a vineyard, according to the Mosaic Law, though trees, such as the fig, might be planted there. (De 22:9; Lu 13:6, 7) Sometimes the vines were allowed to grow along the ground down a hillside, with only the clusters being raised by forked sticks, but more often the vines were trained over wooden arbors or piles of stones.

Pruning is necessary for production of good grapes. Jesus said that "every branch . . . not bearing fruit he takes away, and every one bearing fruit he cleans [by pruning], that it may bear more fruit." (Joh 15:2) The pruning of productive branches and the cutting off of fruitless ones allow the plant to use its full strength in producing fruit of higher quality. Pruning in Bible lands began in the spring, about March, and was repeated in April and again in May if necessary.—2Ch 26:10; Isa 18:5; Lu 13:7.

A fruitful vine with proper care and good pruning may reach unusual age and size. For example, it is reported that one such vine in Jericho was over 300 years old and had a trunk diameter of nearly 46 cm (18 in.). Sometimes these old vines reached a height of more than 9 m (30 ft) and were veritable 'vine trees.' But in spite of such stature among the trees of the forest, such vine wood is not serviceable either as "a pole with which to do some work" or "a peg on which to hand any kind of utensil," for it is too soft; and it is not straight enough for lumber. Indeed, vine wood served as a fitting illustration of the unfaithful inhabitants of Jerusalem, good only as fuel for the fire, the eventual destiny, Jesus said, of unfruitful vines.—Eze 15:2-7; Joh 15:6.

A successful vintage season was one of song and gladness that was shared in by the grape gatherers and the treaders of the winepresses. (Jg 9:27; Isa 16:10; Jer 25:30; see PRESS.) It was also a joyful time for the poor and alien residents of the land, who were permitted to glean the vineyards after the general harvest. (Le 19:10; De 24:21) The opposite was also true—when the vines had withered, or when they produced no grapes, or when the vineyards became desolate wastes of thorns, these were calamitous times of great sorrow.—Isa 24:7; 32:10, 12, 13; Jer 8:13.

Sabbatical laws required owners to leave their vineyards uncultivated, unpruned, and unharvested every seventh year and during the Jubilee. (Le 25:3-5, 11) But during those years any persons (owners, slaves, aliens, the poor), as well as the animals, were welcome to eat freely of what grew by itself.—Ex 23:10, 11; Le 25:1-12.

Illustrative and Figurative Use. The familiarity of the grapevine—the general knowledge people had of its cultivation and productivity as well as the vintage and the gleaning activities connected therewith—made it an object of frequent reference by Bible writers. Vineyards producing an abundance of fruitage reflected Jehovah's blessing. (Le 26:5; Hag 2:19; Zec 8:12; Mal 3:11; Ps 128:3) The expression 'sitting everyone under his own vine and under his own fig tree' became proverbial of peace and security.—1Ki 4:25; 2Ki 18:31; Isa 36:16; Mic 4:4; Zec 3:10.

Unproductive vines would be a manifestation of God's disfavor. (De 28:39) Israel was like grapes in the wilderness, but it became like a degenerate vine (Ho 9:10; 10:1), like a foreign vine producing wild grapes. (Isa 5:4; Jer 2:21) A common proverbial saying in the time of Jeremiah and Ezekiel referred to the fact that unripe grapes set the teeth on edge, because of their sourness.—Jer 31:29, 30; Eze 18:2.

Attempts have been made to link the "vine of Sodom" with various plants found native to the Dead Sea area, but the setting of this expression in its only occurrence (De 32:32) clearly indicates a figurative use. Sodom is repeatedly used in the Bible to represent moral corruption and wickedness.—Isa 1:10; 3:9; Jer 23:14.

Jesus spoke on a number of occasions about vineyards and their grapes. (Mt 20:1-16) Just three days before his death, he gave the illustration of the wicked cultivators.—Mr 12:1-9; Lu 20:9-16; see ILLUSTRATIONS.

When instituting the Lord's Evening Meal, Jesus used wine, the "product of the vine," as a symbol of his "blood of the covenant." On that final night of his earthly life, he also spoke of himself as "the true vine" and of his Father as "the cultivator." His disciples he likened to "the branches" who would be either pruned so as to bear more fruit or lopped off completely.—Mt 26:27-29; Mr 14:24, 25; Lu 22:18; Joh 15:1-10.

Prophetic Use. When Jacob blessed Judah, there was prophetic meaning in his words: "Tying his full-grown ass to a vine [*lag·ge'phen*] and the descendant of his own she-ass to a choice vine [*welas·so·re·qah'*], he will certainly wash his clothing in wine and his garment in the blood of grapes. Dark red are his eyes from wine." (Ge 49:8-12) The Hebrew word *so·re·qah'* denotes a red vine yielding the richest or choicest fruit. (Compare Isa 5:2; Jer 2:21, where the related term *so·req'* occurs.) A few days before the sign reading "The King of the Jews" was posted above him on the torture stake (Mr 15:26), Jesus Christ, who was of the tribe of Judah, rode into Jerusalem on a colt, the foal of an ass, thereby being presented to Jerusalem as her king. (Mt 21:1-9; Zec 9:9) While Jesus did not tie the colt of the she-ass to a literal vine, he did bind his kingly claims to a symbolic vine, a spiritual one, namely, God's Kingdom.—Compare Mt 21:41-43; Joh 15:1-5.

In addition to this greater significance, Jacob's prophecy had a literal application in the inheritance given to the tribe of Judah in the Promised Land. This included the mountainous region, with its productive valleys and elevated 'fruitful hillsides' that were terraced in vineyards.—Isa 5:1.

In the book of Revelation, after the mention of "the harvest of the earth," an angel is heard giving the command: "Gather the clusters of the vine of the earth, because its grapes have become ripe." Thereupon "the vine of the earth" was gathered and hurled "into the great winepress of the anger of God." This vine is different from "the true vine," which produces fruit to God's glory. "The vine of the earth" evidently produces hurtful fruitage, for it is destroyed at God's command.—Re 14:15, 18, 19.

VINEGAR. A sour liquid produced in ancient times by the fermenting of wine or other alcoholic drinks. Nazirites were forbidden to drink "the vinegar of wine or the vinegar of intoxicating liquor," which indicates that vinegar (probably diluted) was sometimes consumed as a beverage. (Nu 6:2, 3) Harvesters dipped their bread into vinegar, perhaps finding it a refreshing condiment in the heat of the day.—Ru 2:14.

The acetic acid contained in vinegar produces a sour taste in the mouth and causes one's teeth to feel very sensitive. (Pr 10:26) This acid content is apparent from the vigorous foaming action that results when vinegar is mixed with the weak alkali sodium carbonate, a reaction apparently alluded to at Proverbs 25:20.

When Jesus Christ was on earth, the Roman soldiers drank a thin, tart, or sour, wine known in

Latin as *acetum* (vinegar), or as *posca,* when it was diluted with water. This was likely the drink offered to Jesus Christ while he was on the torture stake. Jesus refused the sour wine drugged with myrrh (or gall) that was presented to him to alleviate his suffering. (Mr 15:23; Mt 27:34; compare Ps 69:21.) However, just before he expired, he received plain sour wine from a sponge when it was put to his mouth.—Joh 19:28-30; Lu 23: 36, 37.

VINE OF SODOM. See VINE.

VINEYARD. See VINE.

VIPER
[Heb., *'eph·'eh'; tsiph·'o·ni';* Gr., *e'khi-dna*]. A poisonous snake equipped with highly specialized fangs that can be tilted back against the roof of the mouth when they are not being used. The venom of vipers varies according to types, several of which exist in Palestine. One of the most dangerous is the sand viper (*Vipera ammodytes*) of the Jordan Valley. Another kind is the Palestine viper (*Vipera palaestina*). The Hebrew *'eph·'eh'* is commonly connected with the Arabic *'af'an,* which refers to the carpet viper, a poisonous snake of the sandy Jericho plains.

The potency of the viper's poison is alluded to at Job 20:16, where Zophar speaks of "the tongue of a viper" as having the power to kill. Shipwrecked on the island of Malta, the apostle Paul was collecting a bundle of sticks and laying them upon a fire when a viper came out and fastened itself on Paul's hand. However, Paul "shook the venomous creature off into the fire and suffered no harm," though the people standing by expected Paul to swell up with inflammation or suddenly die.—Ac 28:3-6.

Illustrative Use.   The dangerous bite of the viper is used in an illustrative way at Proverbs 23:32, where the wise man describes the effects of the excessive use of wine, saying: "It bites just like a serpent, and it secretes poison just like a viper [Heb., *u·khetsiph·'o·ni'*]." Describing the wickedness that God's people Israel had come to practice, the prophet Isaiah wrote: "The eggs of a poisonous snake are what they have hatched . . . Anyone eating some of their eggs would die, and the egg that was smashed would be hatched into a viper." (Isa 59:5) Most snakes lay eggs, and while the majority of the vipers are not oviparous (egg laying), certain types are.

John the Baptizer called the Pharisees and Sadducees "offspring of vipers." (Mt 3:7; Lu 3:7) And Jesus Christ called the scribes and Pharisees "offspring of vipers" because of their wickedness and the deadly spiritual harm they could inflict upon unsuspecting persons.—Mt 12:34; 23:33.

VIPER, HORNED
[Heb., *'akh·shuv'; shephi-phon'*]. One of the viperous poisonous snakes that inhabit Palestine, distinguished by a small pointed horn above each eye. Raymond Ditmars reports that the horned viper (*Cerastes cornutus*) is found in N Africa from Algeria to Egypt and also in Arabia and S Palestine.

Because the venom of the horned viper is potent (though not usually fatal to humans), David fittingly speaks of violent men as having sharpened their tongue "like that of a serpent; the venom of the horned viper is under their lips."—Ps 140:3; see ASP.

Reaching a maximum length of about 0.8 m (2.5 ft), the horned viper is of a pale, sandy hue and thus conceals itself in sand, waiting for prey. The untrained eye finds it most difficult to spot a lurking horned viper. In his book *Reptiles of the World* (1953, pp. 234, 235), Raymond Ditmars describes some horned vipers he saw in captivity: "Like all desert vipers, they were continually seeking to throw sand over their backs, thus hiding their bodies. If the cage were to be provided with several inches of fine sand, nothing would be seen of the snakes during the day but the tops of their heads. In shoveling sand the reptile flattens the body to such an extent, the lower edge acts as a scoop, then by a remarkable series of wave-like motions traveling the length of the body, on either side, the snake sinks into the sand or works this over its back."

Figurative Use.   The horned viper, which is alert and strikes with great swiftness, has been known to attack horses; thus the comparison given at Genesis 49:17 of the tribe of Dan with the "horned snake" is most fitting. There Jacob likened Dan to a serpent, a horned snake, "that bites the heels of the horse so that its rider falls backward." This was not to downgrade Dan, as if he were a vile snake in the grass fit only to be crushed under the heel. Rather, in the capacity of a snake, Dan would serve a great national purpose. By lying in wait like the horned viper, he could, in effect, bite the heels of the horse carrying an enemy warrior and cause it to rear up and dump its rider off backward. So, though small, Dan would be as dangerous as a horned viper to Israel's disturbers.

VIRGIN.
The Hebrew word *bethu·lah'* signifies a woman who has never been united to a man in marriage and has never had sexual intercourse. (Ge 24:16; De 32:25; Jg 21:12; 1Ki 1:2; Es 2:2, 3,

17; La 1:18; 2:21) The Greek term *par·the′nos,* however, can apply to both single men and single women.—Mt 25:1-12; Lu 1:27; Ac 21:9; 1Co 7:25, 36-38.

According to the Law, a man who seduced an unengaged virgin had to give her father 50 silver shekels ($110), was to marry her (if her father permitted), and was not allowed to divorce her "all his days." (Ex 22:16, 17; De 22:28, 29) But an engaged virgin, being viewed as already belonging to a husband, was to be stoned to death if she did not scream when sexually attacked. Her failure to scream would have denoted consent and thus would have constituted her an adulteress. (De 22:23, 24; compare Mt 1:18, 19.) The fact that an engaged virgin was regarded as being 'owned' by a husband also explains why Joel 1:8 could refer to "a virgin" as wailing over "the owner of her youth."

As greater freedom in the Lord's service is enjoyed by those retaining their virginity, the apostle Paul recommended singleness as the better course for Christians having self-control. (1Co 7:25-35) However, regarding those lacking self-control, he observed: "If anyone thinks he is behaving improperly toward his virginity, if that is past the bloom of youth, and this is the way it should take place, let him do what he wants; he does not sin. Let them marry."—1Co 7:36.

The Greek word rendered "virginity" at 1 Corinthians 7:36-38 literally means "virgin." For this reason the thought has been advanced that Paul was talking about a father's or guardian's duty toward a marriageable daughter. Thus *The Jerusalem Bible* reads: "If there is anyone who feels that it would not be fair to his daughter to let her grow too old for marriage, and that he should do something about it, he is free to do as he likes: he is not sinning if there is a marriage." Another view is that this text pertains to a man's deciding to marry the girl to whom he is engaged. The *American Translation* states: "If a man thinks he is not acting properly toward the girl to whom he is engaged, if his passions are too strong, and that is what ought to be done, let him do as he pleases; it is no sin; let them be married."

The context, however, suggests that the reference is not to a virgin girl but to a person's own virginity. One commentator observed: "I think the apostle is here continuing his former discourse, and advising unmarried persons, who are at their own disposal, what to do; the man's virgin being meant of his virginity." (*Matthew Henry's Commentary on the Whole Bible,* 1976, Vol. III, p. 1036) Since the Greek word *par·the′nos* can include sin-

gle men, the rendering "virginity," as found in the translations by J. B. Rotherham and J. N. Darby as well as in the *New World Translation,* is appropriate and seems to fit the context best.

Spiritual Virginity. Even as the high priest in Israel could take only a virgin as his wife (Le 21:10, 13, 14; compare Eze 44:22), so the great High Priest, Jesus Christ, must have only a "virgin" as his spiritual "bride" in heaven. (Re 21:9; Heb 7:26; compare Eph 5:25-30.) Hence, the apostle Paul was deeply concerned about the purity of the Corinthian congregation, desiring to present it "as a chaste virgin to the Christ." (2Co 11:2-6) The bride of Christ is composed of 144,000 spirit-anointed persons who individually maintain their 'virginity' by remaining separate from the world and by keeping themselves morally and doctrinally pure.—Re 14:1, 4; compare 1Co 5:9-13; 6: 15-20; Jas 4:4; 2Jo 8-11.

Messianic Prophecy. Although the Hebrew word *bethu·lah′* means "virgin," another term (*′al·mah′*) appears at Isaiah 7:14: "Look! The maiden [*ha·′al·mah′*] herself will actually become pregnant, and she is giving birth to a son, and she will certainly call his name Immanuel." The word *′al·mah′* means "maiden" and can apply to a nonvirgin or a virgin. It is applied to "the maiden" Rebekah before marriage when she was also called "a virgin" (*bethu·lah′*). (Ge 24:16, 43) Under divine inspiration, Matthew employed the Greek word *par·the′nos* (virgin) when showing that Isaiah 7:14 found final fulfillment in connection with the virgin birth of Jesus, the Messiah. Both Matthew and Luke state clearly that Jesus' mother Mary was then a virgin who became pregnant through the operation of God's holy spirit.—Mt 1:18-25; Lu 1:26-35.

Cities, Places, and Peoples. Often the term "virgin" is used in connection with cities, places, or peoples. Reference is made to the "virgin" or "virgin daughter" of "my people" (Jer 14:17), as well as of Israel (Jer 31:4, 21; Am 5:2), Judah (La 1:15), Zion (2Ki 19:21; La 2:13), Egypt (Jer 46:11), Babylon (Isa 47:1), and Sidon (Isa 23:12). The sense of this figurative use appears to be that the various peoples or locations thus referred to either had not been seized and ravished by foreign conquerors or at one time enjoyed an unsubdued state like a virgin.

VISION

VISION. A sight or scene presented to a person's mind by day or by night, usually through other than ordinary means, and sometimes while the recipient was in a trance or was dreaming. (Ac 10:3; Ge 46:2) It is often difficult to establish a clear demarcation between visions and dreams described in the Bible, and at times they are combined.

When a person received a vision from God during waking hours, it appears that the impression was made upon the conscious mind. The vision could later be recalled and described or recorded by the recipient, in his own words. Some persons, such as Daniel and Nebuchadnezzar, also had nocturnal visions, or 'visions of the night.' These seem to have been impressed upon the subconscious mind while the recipient slept.

Trance. Apparently God's spirit at times superimposed on the mind a picture of God's purpose or a vision while a person was in a trance, a state of deep concentration or a sleeplike condition. The Greek word rendered "trance" in the Christian Scriptures is *ek'sta·sis.* Defined literally as a putting away or displacement, it carries the figurative idea of a throwing of the mind out of its normal state. An individual in a trance would be oblivious of his literal surroundings and would be receptive to a vision.—Ac 22:17, 18.

Assurances of Divine Favor. Certain visions from God revealed to Jehovah's servants how he was dealing with them and gave them assurance of divine favor. The word of Jehovah came to Abram (Abraham) in a vision, and the patriarch was assured: "Do not fear, Abram. I am a shield for you. Your reward will be very great." (Ge 15:1) Thereafter, Jehovah made a covenant with Abraham. (Ge 15:2-21) Some years later, God talked to Jacob in visions of the night, telling him not to be afraid to go down to Egypt, for God would constitute him a great nation there and would eventually bring him up from that land.—Ge 46:1-4; compare 2Sa 7:1-17; 1Ch 17:1-15.

Direction in Serving the Divine Purpose. Some visions from God gave the recipients direction in the doing of Jehovah's will. After the glorified Jesus Christ appeared to Saul of Tarsus, Saul, though temporarily blinded, had a vision in which he saw a man named Ananias lay his hands upon him so that he might recover sight. Also by means of a vision, Ananias was directed to the very house where Saul was in Damascus.—Ac 9:1-19.

In Caesarea in 36 C.E., the devout Gentile Cornelius received a vision in which an angel told him to send to Joppa for Simon Peter. (Ac 10:1-8) At Joppa, Peter fell into a trance and had a vision in which he saw descending from heaven a vessel containing various unclean creatures. By this means the apostle was taught that he should not consider defiled the things God had cleansed. This prepared Peter to initiate the work of preaching the good news to uncircumcised Gentiles.—Ac 10:9-23; 11:5-12.

Divine direction in the preaching work was also given to Paul by means of visions. At Troas, during Paul's second missionary tour, at night the apostle had a vision of a Macedonian man who entreated: "Step over into Macedonia and help us." (Ac 16:8-12) Later, as a result of a reassuring vision by night in which the Lord spoke to him, the apostle remained in Corinth for a year and six months, teaching the Word of God.—Ac 18:8-11.

Prophecy. Some visions from God were prophetic or were given to enable the recipient to interpret prophecies communicated in visions and dreams. The prophet Daniel "had understanding in all sorts of visions and dreams." (Da 1:17) It was in "a night vision" that God revealed to Daniel the content and meaning of King Nebuchadnezzar's dream about an immense image pictorial of world powers.—Da 2:19, 28; compare Da 4:5, 10, 13, 20-22.

In a prophetic dream and "visions during the night," Daniel beheld four huge beasts coming out of the sea, indicating that four "kings" would stand up from the earth. (Da 7:1-3, 17) The prophet was also privileged to behold in vision "someone like a son of man" obtaining rulership, dignity, and kingdom from the Ancient of Days.—Da 7:13, 14.

Visions from God were also received by such Bible writers as Isaiah (1:1; 6:1-13), Amos (7:1-9, 12; 8:1, 2), and Ezekiel (1:1). Obadiah's inspired prophetic declaration against Edom opens with the words: "The vision of Obadiah." (Ob 1) "The vision of Nahum" contains a pronouncement against Nineveh.—Na 1:1.

The book of Revelation contains a series of visions seen by the aged apostle John. The book's Greek name, *A·po·ka'ly·psis,* meaning "Uncovering" or "Disclosure," is apropos, for Revelation does uncover matters, disclosing many events of the distant future, far beyond the time of its composition.—Re 1:1, ftn.

False Visions. Prior to Jerusalem's destruction in 607 B.C.E., that city's false prophets spoke "the vision of their own heart," their messages not originating with Jehovah. (Jer 23:16) Having no vision from Jehovah, what they visioned was worthless. (La 2:9, 14) Because they spoke untruth and "visioned a lie," Jehovah was against them. —Eze 13.

Some Foretold to See Visions. In contrast with false visions and in addition to the God-given visions already discussed, Joel was divinely inspired to foretell that, under the influence of God's spirit, young men would "see visions." (Joe 2:28) Peter showed that there was a fulfillment of this prophecy on the day of Pentecost in 33 C.E., when the holy spirit was bestowed upon followers of Jesus Christ and they miraculously declared in many languages "the magnificent things of God." —Ac 2:1-4, 11, 15-17.

VISIONARY. A man who had or claimed to have visions from God regarding concealed or future matters. The Hebrew word for "visionary" is cho·zeh', from cha·zah', meaning "behold; vision." Cha·zah' and its derivatives are employed with reference to seeing visions.—Nu 24:4; Isa 1:1; 21:2; 22:1; Eze 13:7; Da 8:1; see SEER.

Some visionaries were false and were opposed by God. (Isa 29:10; Mic 3:7) Others were sent by Jehovah and spoke in his name. (2Ki 17:13; 2Ch 33:18) The term "visionary" is applied to several men, namely, Heman, Iddo, Hanani, Gad, Asaph, Jeduthun, and Amos. (1Ch 25:5; 2Ch 12:15; 19:2; 29:25, 30; 35:15; Am 7:12) Some, such as Gad and Iddo, recorded their visions or wrote other accounts. (1Ch 29:29; 2Ch 9:29; 33:19) Not all of Jehovah's prophets were visionaries. However, Gad was called both a "prophet" and "David's visionary," apparently because at least some of the messages he received from God came by means of visions containing divine instruction or counsel for King David.—2Sa 24:11; 1Ch 21:9.

VOICE. The sounds uttered by persons in speaking, singing, and the like, as well as those made by animals, are denoted in Scripture by the Hebrew word qohl, its Aramaic equivalent qal, and the Greek word pho·ne'. (Ge 3:8, 10; 21:17; Job 4:10; Da 4:31; Mt 27:46) Besides "voice," qohl can also denote "thunder," "sound," "noise," "news," and so forth. (Ge 45:16; Ex 9:28; 20:18; 32:17) Similarly, pho·ne' can have such meanings as "sound," "cry," "speech sound," and "blast," as well as "voice."—Joh 3:8; Ac 19:34; 1Co 14:10, 11; Heb 12:26; Re 8:13.

Spirit Persons. The apostle Paul speaks of "the tongues of men and of angels," indicating that spirit persons have language and speech. (1Co 13:1) Angels, and Jehovah God himself, have been heard to speak in voice sounds and languages audible to men and understandable by them. But it is not to be supposed that such would be the voice with which they communicate with one another in the heavens, for an atmosphere such as exists around the earth is necessary for propagating the sound waves of voice that is audible and understandable to the human ear.

The instances in which God or angels spoke in a voice in the hearing of men would therefore be a manifestation of their speech as transformed into sound waves, just as appearances of angels to the vision of man required either a materialization or a transmitting to the human mind of a pictorial image. Today even human scientists can convert the sound-wave pattern of an individual's voice into electric impulses that can be transmitted to a receiver, which can change those impulses back to sounds closely resembling the individual's voice.

Have any humans actually heard the voice of God himself?

In three instances in the Bible record, Jehovah is reported as speaking audibly to humans. These are: (1) At the time of Jesus' baptism (29 C.E.), when Jehovah said: "This is my Son, the beloved, whom I have approved." Both Jesus and John the Baptizer undoubtedly heard this voice. (Mt 3:17; Mr 1:11; Lu 3:22) (2) At Jesus' transfiguration (32 C.E.), with the apostles Peter, James, and John present, when virtually the same words were uttered. (Mt 17:5; Mr 9:7; Lu 9:36) (3) In 33 C.E., shortly before Jesus' last Passover, when, responding to Jesus' request that God glorify his name, a voice from heaven said: "I both glorified it and will glorify it again." The crowd thought that it had thundered or that an angel had spoken to Jesus.—Joh 12:28, 29.

On those occasions it was Jehovah God who made himself manifest by means of audible sounds of speech understandable to his servants. Evidently in the last-named instance the crowd did not hear the voice distinctly, since some compared it to thunder. Jehovah undoubtedly was the speaker on those occasions, because Jesus, in connection with whom the statements were made, was God's own Son, closer to the Father than any other creature was.—Mt 11:27.

Speaking to a group of unbelieving Jews, about the time of the Passover of 31 C.E., Jesus told them: "Also, the Father who sent me has himself borne witness about me. You have neither heard his voice at any time nor seen his figure; and you do not have his word remaining in you, because the very one whom he dispatched you do not believe." (Joh 5:37, 38) This unbelieving crowd had never heard God's voice, and they were not obeying his word or even the obvious witness they received through God's support of Jesus' works. For that matter, apparently only Jesus and John the Baptizer had heard the audible voice of Jehovah, for the last two instances of Jehovah's speaking had not yet occurred at this point.

Biblical mention of Jehovah's "voice" sometimes refers to the authoritativeness of his command as "the voice of God Almighty."—Eze 10:5, RS.

Angelic voices. On other occasions when God 'spoke,' angels were used as his representatives to provide the vocal manifestation. Angels represented God in speaking to Moses in Mount Horeb and to Israel, assembled near the foot of the mountain. (Ex 34:4-7; 20:1-17; Ga 3:19) These angels sometimes did not present any visible appearance of a form, as when the voice came from the quaking, smoking mountain. (Ex 20:18, 19; De 4:11, 12; Heb 12:18, 19) At times they made visionary appearances (Da 8:1, 15, 16; Re 14:15-18) and on several occasions materialized in human form to bring spoken messages to men.—Ge 18: 1-3, 20; 19:1; Jos 5:13-15.

Hearing the Voice of God. To 'hear the voice of God' does not necessarily mean the hearing of a literal, audible voice. It more often means recognizing and hearing with obedience what God has caused to be written in his Word and transmitted through his earthly servants who represent him. (1Jo 2:3, 4) Thus, "voice" is used as applying to "every utterance coming forth through Jehovah's mouth," his commands whether presented to the individual verbally by God himself or by angels or men, or in inspired writing.—Ps 103:20; Mt 4:4; see OBEDIENCE.

Hearing Jesus' Voice. Jesus Christ spoke of himself as "the fine shepherd" whose sheep "listen to his voice, . . . and the sheep follow him, because they know his voice. . . . they do not know the voice of strangers." (Joh 10:2-5, 11) Those who are Christ's "sheep" "know" his voice in that they recognize and acknowledge as true what Christ says as recorded in the Bible. They refuse to acknowledge the teaching of 'strangers,' false shepherds. They "listen" to his voice in that they obey his commands as set forth in the Scriptures. (Joh 15:10, 15) Since Christ Jesus is God's Chief Representative, who always listens to Jehovah's voice and speaks what Jehovah directs, the one following Christ will be in union with Jehovah. —Joh 5:19; 1Jo 2:6.

The voice of the resurrected Jesus Christ. After Christ's resurrection and ascension, he appeared to Saul of Tarsus (later the apostle Paul), speaking to him in a voice that Saul understood, but that the men accompanying him did not understand. (Ac 9:1-9; 22:6-11; 26:12-18) At Acts 9:7, the account states that the men with Saul heard "a voice ["sound," *Da, Ro,* ftns]." Here the Greek word *pho·nes'*, the genitive case of *pho·ne'*, is used, with the sense of 'hearing *of* the voice.' This allows for the meaning that the men heard only the *sound of the voice,* but did not understand. When Paul later related the experience, he said that the men "did not hear the voice of the one speaking." (Ac 22:9) In this account the accusative (objective) case *pho·nen'* is used. This can give the sense that, although the *sound* registered on their ears, they did not hear the voice as being *distinct words that they understood* as did Saul, to whom Christ was speaking.

The apostle Paul said, when writing to the Thessalonian congregation about the gathering of God's anointed holy ones: "The Lord [Jesus Christ] himself will descend from heaven with a commanding call, with an archangel's voice and with God's trumpet." (1Th 4:16) The term "archangel" means "chief angel" or "principal angel." Paul's expression "archangel's voice" evidently focuses attention on the authoritativeness of Jesus' voice of command. Jesus, when on earth, revealed the authority that God invested in him, when he said: "For just as the Father has life in himself, so he has granted also to the Son to have life in himself. And he has given him authority to do judging, because Son of man he is. . . . The hour is coming in which all those in the memorial tombs will hear his voice and come out."—Joh 5:26-29.

Use of Human Voice. Voice, along with language, is a gift of God. Therefore, the voice should be lifted in praise to God. This can be done by speaking "the magnificent things of God," upbuilding others with information from God's Word of truth, or in songs of praise and thanksgiving.—Ac 2:11; Ps 42:4; 47:1; 98:5; Eph 5:19; Col 3:16.

God hears his servants' voice. Those who serve God with spirit and truth can call upon God with the assurance that he hears their voice, regardless of the language in which they call upon him. Moreover, even though the literal voice is not used, the petition to God being a silent one, God, who knows the hearts of men, "hears" or gives attention nevertheless. (Ps 66:19; 86:6; 116:1; 1Sa 1:13; Ne 2:4) God hears afflicted ones who cry to him for help, and he also hears the voice and knows the intentions of men who oppose him and plot evil against his servants.—Ge 21:17; Ps 55:18, 19; 69:33; 94:9-11; Jer 23:25.

Inanimate Things. Among the numerous things of God's creation, many do not make a voice sound. But the Hebrew word *qohl* ("voice," "sound") is used with regard to the witness these voiceless things give to the majesty of their Creator. (Ps 19:1-4) In a personified sense wisdom is said to keep "giving forth its voice" in the public squares, because it is available to all who seek it, and God has had wisdom proclaimed before all, so that there is no excuse for the one not listening. —Pr 1:20-30.

Figurative Use. The anguish of Jerusalem's inhabitants in the face of Babylonian attack is compared with the distressed voice of a sick woman, "the voice of the daughter of Zion" being likened to that of a woman giving birth to her first child. (Jer 4:31) The enemy would reduce Jerusalem to such a low state that any utterances made with her voice would come up from her position of debasement as in the dust and would be like the low voice of a spirit medium. (Isa 29:4) Through the prophet Jeremiah, God also prophesied that Egypt would be vanquished by the Babylonians, who would come in force as woodcutters, to chop her down. She would lie on the ground, deeply humbled, weeping softly and moaning, her "voice" being low like that of a hissing serpent in retreat. —Jer 46:22.

VOPHSI (Voph'si). A Naphtalite whose son Nahbi was one of the 12 Israelites sent to spy out Canaan.—Nu 13:2, 14.

VOW. A solemn promise made to God to perform some act, make some offering or gift, enter some service or condition, or abstain from certain things not unlawful in themselves. A vow was a voluntary expression made of one's own free will. Being a solemn promise, a vow carried the force of an oath or a swearing, and at times the two expressions accompany each other in the Bible. (Nu 30:2; Mt 5:33) "Vow" is more the declaration of intent, while "oath" denotes the appeal made to a higher authority attesting to the truthfulness or binding nature of the declaration. Oaths often accompanied attestation to a covenant.—Ge 26:28; 31:44, 53.

The earliest record of a vow is found at Genesis 28:20-22, where Jacob promised to give Jehovah one tenth of all his possessions if Jehovah would continue with him and bring him back in peace, thereby proving to be Jacob's God. Jacob was not bargaining with God, but he wanted to be sure that he had God's approval. As this example points out, vows were made by the patriarchs (see also Job 22:27), and as with so many other patriarchal customs, the Mosaic Law, rather than introduce these already-existing features of worship, defined and regulated them.

Many vows were made as appeals to God for his favor and success in an undertaking, as in Jacob's case. Another example of such is the vow by Israel to devote the cities of the Canaanite king of Arad to destruction if Jehovah gave Israel the victory. (Nu 21:1-3) Vows were also made as expressions of devotion to Jehovah and his pure worship (Ps 132:1-5) or to indicate that a person was setting himself or his possessions apart for special service. (Nu 6:2-7) Parents could make vows in connection with their children, as Hannah did regarding Samuel. (1Sa 1:11; compare Jg 11:30, 31, 39.) In these instances the children cooperated in carrying out the vow.

Voluntary, but Binding When Once Made. Vows were wholly voluntary. However, once a man made a vow, fulfillment was compulsory by divine law. Thus a vow was spoken of as being 'bound upon his soul,' implying that his very life became surety for the performance of his word. (Nu 30:2; see also Ro 1:31, 32.) Since life is at stake, it is understandable why the Scriptures urge one to use extreme caution before making a vow, carefully considering the obligations to be assumed. The Law stated: "In case you vow a vow to Jehovah . . . God will without fail require it of you, and it would indeed become a sin on your part. But in case you omit making a vow, it will not become a sin on your part."—De 23:21, 22.

As later expressed by the Congregator: "What you vow, pay. Better is it that you vow not than that you vow and do not pay. Do not allow your mouth to cause your flesh to sin, neither say before the angel that it was a mistake." (Ec 5:4-6) A vow rashly made on the impulse of momentary enthusiasm or mere emotion might very well prove to be a snare. (Pr 20:25) Under the Law one making such a thoughtless vow was guilty before God and had to present a guilt offering for his sin. (Le 5:4-6) In the final analysis, a vow has no merit in the eyes of God unless it is in harmony with his righteous laws and issues from the right kind of heart and spirit.—Ps 51:16, 17.

Vows of women, under the Law. The laws regulating vows made by women are outlined at Numbers 30:3-15: The vow of a daughter was binding once her father heard it and raised no objection; or, instead, he could annul it. The vow of a wife (or an engaged girl) likewise depended on her husband (or fiancé) for validation. If the man annulled the vow after first letting it stand, he bore her error. (Nu 30:14, 15) In the case of a widow or a divorced woman, "everything that she has bound upon her soul will stand against her." —Nu 30:9.

Disposition of Things Vowed. In fulfillment of a vow, any person or possession, including land, could be offered to Jehovah, except what had already been set apart for Him by the Law—the firstborn, firstfruits, tithes, and the like. (Le 27:26, 30, 32) That which was vowed as "sanctified" (Heb., qo'dhesh, something set aside as holy, for sacred use) could be redeemed by a certain payment to the sanctuary (except clean animals). (Le 27:9-27) However, anything "devoted" (Heb., che'-rem) could not be redeemed, but it was to be completely and permanently the property of the sanctuary or, if devoted to destruction, was to be destroyed without fail.—Le 27:28, 29.

Wrong or Unclean Vows. The vows of heathen religions many times involved unclean, immoral practices. Throughout Phoenicia, Syria, and Babylon, the proceeds of temple prostitution were dedicated to the idol or temple. Such degenerate vows were outlawed in Israel: "You must not bring the hire of a harlot or the price of a dog [likely, a pederast (sodomite)] into the house of Jehovah your God for any vow."—De 23:18, ftn.

After Jerusalem's destruction, Jeremiah reminded the Jews in Egypt that one reason for the calamity that befell them was their making vows to the "queen of the heavens" and offering sacrifices to her. The women who were taking a prominent part in this idol worship were quick to point out that their vows and worship to the "queen of the heavens" had been approved by their husbands and that they were determined to carry out their vows to this goddess. They thus made the excuse that they were acting in harmony with the Law regarding vows for women (Nu 30:10-15), but Jeremiah denounced their actions as being really law defying, since they were idolatrous. —Jer 44:19, 23-25; 2Co 6:16-18.

Hypocritical vows. The Jews did not slip back into outright idol worship after the exile. However, they "made the word of God invalid because of [their] tradition." Their specious reasoning in interpreting the Law affected the matter of vows as well as other features of worship, their religious leaders hypocritically teaching "commands of men as doctrines." (Mt 15:6-9) For example, Jewish tradition stated that if a man said to his father or mother, "Whatever I have by which you might get benefit from me is a gift dedicated to God" (a pronouncement of dedication or sanctification), he thereby vowed to sanctify all he had spoken of to God and was not to use these things to help his parents; this was on the theory that now the temple had the prior claim to these possessions, although he was actually allowed full liberty to keep them for himself.—Mt 15:5, 6.

Sacrifices Connected With Vows. Under the Law, a burnt offering at times accompanied other sacrifices, to denote complete dedication and an appeal to Jehovah to accept the sacrifice with favor. (Le 8:14, 18; 16:3) Such was true in connection with vows. (Nu 6:14) Burnt offerings were sacrificed to perform special vows. (Nu 15:3; Ps 66:13) And concerning a "communion sacrifice to Jehovah in order to pay a vow," the requirement was that an unblemished animal be offered, part of which was burned on the altar.—Le 22:21, 22; 3:1-5.

As regards Jephthah's vow before fighting the Ammonites (Jg 11:29-31), see JEPHTHAH.

Paul's Observance of Law as to Vows. The apostle Paul made a vow, whether a Nazirite vow or not is uncertain; also, whether he had made the vow before becoming a Christian is not stated. He may have concluded the period of his vow at Cenchreae, near Corinth, when he had his hair clipped (Ac 18:18) or, as some believe, when he went to the temple in Jerusalem with four other men who were completing their vows. However, this latter action was taken by Paul on the advice of the Christian governing body to demonstrate that Paul was walking orderly and not teaching disobedience to the Law, as rumored in the ears of some of the Jewish Christians. It was common practice for a person to pay for others the expenses involved in the ceremonial cleansing at the expiration of the period of a vow, as Paul here did. —Ac 21:20-24.

As to why the apostle Paul and his associates in the Christian governing body approved the carrying out of certain features of the Law, even though the Law had been moved out of the way by the sacrifice of Jesus Christ, the following things may be considered: The Law was given by Jehovah God to his people Israel. Accordingly, the apostle Paul said, "The Law is spiritual," and of its regulations he said, "The Law is holy, and the commandment is holy and righteous and good." (Ro 7:12, 14) Consequently, the temple and the services carried on there were not despised by Christians, or looked down upon as wrong. They were not idolatrous. Furthermore, many of the practices had become ingrained as custom among those who were Jews. Moreover, since the Law was not merely religious but was also the law of the land, some things, such as the restrictions on work on the Sabbaths, had to be followed by all those living in the land.

But in considering this matter, the main point is that the *Christians did not look to these things for salvation.* The apostle explained that certain things, such as the eating of meat or vegetables, the observing of certain days as above others, even the eating of meat that had been offered to idols before being put up for regular sale in the marketplaces, were matters of conscience. He wrote: "One man judges one day as above another; another man judges one day as all others; let each man be fully convinced in his own mind. He who observes the day observes it to Jehovah. Also, he who eats, eats to Jehovah, for he gives thanks to God; and he who does not eat does not eat to Jehovah, and yet gives thanks to God." Then he summed up his argument by stating the principle: "For the kingdom of God does not mean eating and drinking, but means righteousness and peace and joy with holy spirit," and he concluded: "Happy is the man that does not put himself on judgment by what he approves. But if he has doubts, he is already condemned if he eats, because he does not eat out of faith. Indeed, everything that is not out of faith is sin."—Ro 14:5, 6, 17, 22, 23; 1Co 10:25-30.

An enlightening comment is made on this point by Bible scholar Albert Barnes, in his *Notes, Explanatory and Practical, on the Acts of the Apostles* (1858). Making reference to Acts 21:20 —which reads: "After hearing this [an account of God's blessing on Paul's ministry to the nations] they began to glorify God, and they said to him: 'You behold, brother, how many thousands of believers there are among the Jews; and they are all zealous for the Law'"—Barnes remarks: "The reference here is, to the law respecting circumcision, sacrifices, distinctions of meats and days, festivals, &c. It may seem remarkable that they should still continue to observe those rites, since it was the manifest design of Christianity to abolish them. But we are to remember, (1.) That those rites had been appointed by God, and that they were trained to their observance. (2.) That the apostles conformed to them while they remained in Jerusalem, and did not deem it best to set themselves violently against them. [Ac 3:1; Lu 24:53] (3.) That the question about their observance had never been agitated at Jerusalem. It was only among the Gentile converts that the question had risen, and there it *must* arise, for if they were to be observed, they must have been *imposed* upon them by authority. (4.) The decision of the council (ch. xv.) related only to the *Gentile* converts. [Ac 15:23] . . . (5.) It was to be presumed, that as the Christian religion became better understood —that as its large, free, and [universal] nature became more and more developed, the peculiar institutions of Moses would be laid aside of course, without agitation, and without tumult. Had the question been agitated [publicly] at Jerusalem, it would have excited tenfold opposition to Christianity, and would have rent the Christian church into factions, and greatly retarded the advance of the Christian doctrine. We are to remember also, (6.) That, in the arrangement of Divine Providence, the time was drawing near which was to destroy the temple, the city, and the nation;

which was to put an end to sacrifices, and *effectually* to close for ever the observance of the Mosaic rites. As this destruction was so near, and as it would be so effectual an *argument* against the observance of the Mosaic rites, the Great Head of the church did not suffer the question of their obligation to be needlessly agitated among the disciples at Jerusalem."

VULTURE [Hebrew, *ra·cham'*; *ra·cha'mah*], **BLACK VULTURE** [Hebrew, *'oz·ni·yah'*]. A large carrion-eating bird that renders a very valuable service in lands of warm climate, consuming the dead carcasses and putrefying flesh that might otherwise cause disease. This bird is listed among those declared 'unclean' in the Mosaic Law.—Le 11:13, 18; De 14:12, 17.

In Arabic, a language that is cognate with Hebrew, a word similar to *ra·cham'* designates the Egyptian vulture (*Neophron percnopterus*), often called Pharaoh's chicken. This bird is white except for its black wings and yellow bill and legs. It is the smallest of the vultures found in Bible lands, being about 65 cm (26 in.) in length. With its bare wrinkled face, large eyes, hooked beak, and curved talons, it is quite repulsive in appearance. Because of its willingness to eat refuse disdained even by other vultures, it is considered the foulest scavenger of the Middle East and, by the same token, the most useful because of the service it performs.

The griffon vulture (*Gyps fulvus*) is a yellowish-brown bird measuring about 1.2 m (4 ft) in length, with a wingspan of some 2.7 m (9 ft). The griffon vulture was the symbol of the Egyptian goddess Nekhebet and also appeared on the battle standards of the Egyptians, Assyrians, and Persians.

The lammergeier, or bearded vulture (*Gypaetus barbatus*), is a large bird of prey, standing about 1.2 m (4 ft) high. With its long pointed wings that span almost 3 m (10 ft), the lammergeier flies with unusual grace, and wheels effortlessly as it searches the land below for food. Unlike other vultures, the lammergeier has feathers on its head and a beard resembling that of a goat. It has a preference for marrow bones, carrying these to great heights and then dropping them on rocks so that they split open, allowing the bird to reach the marrow within.

The Hebrew word *'oz·ni·yah'* evidently refers to the black vulture (*Aegypius monachus*), the largest bird of prey occurring in Israel. More brown than black, it has the vulture's characteristic naked head; the neck is blue, the tail wedge-shaped.

W

WAGES. See HIRE, WAGES.

WAGON. The wagon or cart of ancient times was a simple vehicle, usually wooden, having spoked or solid wheels. (1Sa 6:14) Some were little more than two-wheeled open platforms fitted with a horizontal tongue or pole in front. Others had sides, and some were covered, such as the six covered wagons (drawn by two bulls each) used to transport tabernacle articles. (Nu 7:2-9) The "coaches" of Revelation 18:13 may denote four-wheeled wagons or carriages.

In Israel, especially in earlier times, the wagon was usually drawn by cattle rather than horses, the latter being used especially for chariots and in warfare. (2Sa 6:3, 6; 15:1; 1Ch 13:7, 9; Pr 21:31) Wagons were employed to transport persons (Ge 45:19, 21, 27; 46:5), grain, and other loads. (1Sa 6:7-14; Am 2:13) Those used in warfare (as mentioned at Ps 46:9) may have been military baggage wagons. In the time of Isaiah, when the Israelites had many horses (Isa 2:7), wagons pulled by horses were used in threshing.—Isa 28:27, 28.

The prophet Isaiah pronounced woe upon persons 'drawing sin as with wagon cords,' possibly indicating that such individuals were attached to sin just as animals were tied with cords to wagons they pulled.—Isa 5:18.

WALLS. Masonry structures that serve as barriers, mark boundaries, or form enclosures. As long as man has been constructing houses and cities, he has been building walls out of many materials, in a variety of designs, to serve a number of purposes. The size and strength of structures largely depend on the construction of the walls and the materials used in making them.

The walls of David's palace were of cut stone. (2Sa 5:11) Similarly, the outside walls of Solomon's temple, it appears, were of quarried stone, with some of their interior surfaces covered over with cedar boards. (1Ki 6:2, 7, 15) These interior wooden panels, in turn, were elaborately decorated with carvings and overlays of gold. (1Ki 6:29; 1Ch 29:4; 2Ch 3:4, 7) The interior wall surfaces of Belshazzar's palace were plastered. (Da 5:5) The walls of the homes of the people in general were usually of simple construction—sun-dried bricks, uncut stones, or plastered material over a wooden framework. Sometimes the surface was whitewashed.—Ac 23:3.

City Walls. In ancient times fear caused people to erect protective walls around large cities to prevent enemy invasion. (1Ki 4:13; Isa 25:12) The inhabitants of the small "dependent towns" round about (Nu 21:25) likewise took refuge within the walled city if attacked. The Mosaic Law made a legal distinction between walled and unwalled towns, as to the rights of house owners. (Le 25:29-31) The walls not only provided a physical barrier between city residences and an enemy but also afforded an elevated position atop which the defenders could protect the walls from being undermined, tunneled through, or breached by battering rams. (2Sa 11:20-24; 20:15; Ps 55:10; Ca 5:7; Isa 62:6; Eze 4:1, 2; 26:9) As a countermeasure, attacking forces sometimes threw up siege walls as shields behind which to assault the city walls.—2Ki 25:1; Jer 52:4; Eze 4:2, 3; 21:22; see FORTIFICATIONS.

Other Walls. Stone walls were often built to hedge in vineyards or fields, and to form corrals or sheep pens. (Nu 22:23-25; Pr 24:30, 31; Isa 5:5; Mic 2:12; Hab 3:17) And there were also walls that served for embankment purposes along terraced hillsides. (Job 24:11) These walls were of a fairly permanent nature, built of undressed fieldstones and sometimes set in clay or mortar.

Symbolic Walls. In the Scriptures, walls are sometimes mentioned in a figurative way as pictorial of protection and safety (1Sa 25:16; Pr 18:11; 25:28) or as a symbol of separation. (Ge 49:22; Eze 13:10) In this latter sense Paul wrote the Ephesians: "For he [Christ] is our peace, he who made the two parties one and destroyed the wall in between that fenced them off." (Eph 2:14) Paul was well acquainted with the middle wall in Jerusalem's temple courtyard, which carried a warning sign to the effect that no non-Jew was to go beyond that wall under penalty of death. However, when Paul wrote to the Ephesians in 60 or 61 C.E., though he may have alluded to it in an illustrative way, he actually did not mean that the literal wall had been abolished, for it was still standing. Rather, the apostle had in mind the Law covenant, which had acted as a dividing wall between Jews and Gentiles for centuries. On the basis of Christ's death nearly 30 years previously, that symbolic "wall" had been abolished.

Jeremiah was told he would be like fortified walls of copper against those that opposed him. (Jer 1:18, 19; 15:20) In another illustration, God's people, though dwelling as in a city without literal walls, therefore seemingly defenseless, enjoy peace and security because of God's invisible help. (Eze 38:11) Or from another point of view, a strong city would be one having Jehovah as "a wall of fire" (Zec 2:4, 5), or having walls of salvation set up by Jehovah, rather than ones of mere stone and brick. (Isa 26:1) "The holy city, New Jerusalem," which comes down out of heaven, is said to have "a great and lofty wall" of jasper, the height of which is 144 cubits (64 m; 210 ft), and it is said to have 12 foundation stones consisting of precious jewels engraved with the names of the 12 apostles.—Re 21:2, 12, 14, 17-19.

WAR. A state of hostility accompanied by actions designed to subjugate or to destroy those viewed as the enemy. A number of Hebrew words involve waging war; one of these, from the verb root *qa·rav'*, means basically "come near," that is, to fight. The Greek noun *po'le·mos* means "war"; and the verb *stra·teu'o* is from a root that refers to an encamped army.

The Bible says that Nimrod "went forth into Assyria," which was evidently an act of aggression, into the territory of Asshur the son of Shem. There Nimrod built cities. (Ge 10:11) In Abraham's day Chedorlaomer, king of Elam, subjected a number of cities (all apparently around the southern end of the Dead Sea) for a period of 12 years, forcing them to serve him. After they rebelled, Chedorlaomer and his allies warred against them, vanquishing the forces of Sodom and Gomorrah, taking their possessions, and capturing Abraham's nephew Lot and his household. At that Abraham mustered 318 trained servants and, together with his three confederates, pursued Chedorlaomer and recovered the captives and the plunder. However, Abraham did not take any of the booty for himself. This is the first record of a war waged by a servant of God. Abraham's warring to recover his fellow servant of Jehovah had Jehovah's approval, for, on Abraham's return, he was blessed by Melchizedek, priest of the Most High God.—Ge 14:1-24.

God-Ordained Warfare. Jehovah is "a manly person of war," "the God of armies," and "mighty in battle." (Ex 15:3; 2Sa 5:10; Ps 24:8, 10; Isa 42:13) Not only has he the right as Creator and Supreme Sovereign of the universe but he is also obligated by justice to execute or authorize execution of the lawless, to war against all obstinate ones who refuse to obey his righteous laws. Jehovah was therefore just in wiping out the wicked at the time of the Flood, in destroying Sodom and Gomorrah, and in bringing destruction upon Pha-

raoh's forces.—Ge 6:5-7, 13, 17; 19:24; Ex 15:4, 5; compare 2Pe 2:5-10; Jude 7.

Israel used as God's executioner. Jehovah assigned the Israelites the sacred duty of serving as his executioners in the Promised Land to which he brought them. Prior to Israel's deliverance from Egypt, the nation had not known warfare. (Ex 13:17) By victoriously directing Israel against "seven nations more populous and mighty" than they were, God magnified his name as "Jehovah of armies, the God of the battle lines of Israel." This proved that "neither with sword nor with spear does Jehovah save, because to Jehovah belongs the battle." (De 7:1; 1Sa 17:45, 47; compare 2Ch 13:12.) It also gave the Israelites the opportunity to demonstrate obedience to God's commandments to the point of endangering their lives in God-ordained warfare.—De 20:1-4.

No aggression beyond the God-given limits. However, God strictly commanded Israel that they were not to engage in wars of aggression or conquest beyond the territory that he granted to them and that they were not to fight any nations except the ones he ordered them to fight. They were not to engage in strife with the nations of Edom, Moab, or Ammon. (De 2:4, 5, 9, 19) But they were attacked by these nations in later times and were forced to defend themselves against them in warfare. In this they had God's help.—Jg 3:12-30; 11:32, 33; 1Sa 14:47.

When, during the period of the Judges, the king of Ammon tried to justify his aggressions against Israel by falsely charging Israel with taking Ammonite land, Jephthah refuted him by recalling the historical facts. Jephthah then proceeded to fight against these aggressors, on the principle that 'every one whom Jehovah dispossesses before us we will dispossess.' Jephthah would not relinquish an inch of Israel's God-given land to any intruder.—Jg 11:12-27; see JEPHTHAH.

Sanctified warfare. Anciently, the fighting forces, before they entered battle, were customarily sanctified. (Jos 3:5; Jer 6:4; 51:27, 28) During warfare Israel's forces, including non-Jews (for example, Uriah the Hittite, who was probably a circumcised proselyte), had to remain ceremonially clean. They could not have sexual relations, even with their own wives, during a military campaign. Accordingly, there were no prostitutes who followed Israel's army. Moreover, the camp itself had to be kept clean from defilement.—Le 15:16, 18; De 23:9-14; 2Sa 11:11, 13.

When it was necessary to punish unfaithful Israel, those foreign armies bringing the destruction were viewed as 'sanctified,' in the sense that they were 'set apart' by Jehovah for the execution of his righteous judgments. (Jer 22:6-9; Hab 1:6) Similarly, those military forces (principally the Medes and Persians) who brought destruction on Babylon were spoken of by Jehovah as "my sanctified ones."—Isa 13:1-3.

The false prophets in Israel, in their greediness, were said to "sanctify war" against anyone who did not put something into their mouths. Undoubtedly they sanctimoniously claimed divine sanction for their acts of oppression, which included sharing in the responsibility for the persecution and even the death of true prophets and servants of God.—Mic 3:5; Jer 2:8; La 4:13.

Conscription. At Jehovah's command Israel's able-bodied males 20 years old and upward were conscripted for military service. According to Josephus, they served up to the age of 50 years. (*Jewish Antiquities*, III, 288 [xii, 4]) The fearful and fainthearted were rejected because Israel's wars were wars of Jehovah, and those displaying weakness of faith in fearfulness would tend to weaken the army's morale. Exemptions were given to men who had just completed a new house, as well as to those who had planted a vineyard and had not used its fruitage. These exemptions were based on the right of a man to enjoy the fruitage of his work. The newly married man was exempt for one year. During this time the man might be able to have and to see an heir. Here Jehovah revealed his concern and consideration for the family. (Nu 1:1-3, 44-46; De 20:5-8; 24:5) The Levites, who took care of the service at the sanctuary, were exempt, showing that Jehovah considered the spiritual welfare of the people more important than military defense.—Nu 1:47-49; 2:32, 33.

Laws concerning assault and siege of cities. Jehovah instructed Israel as to military procedure in the conquest of Canaan. The seven nations of Canaan, named at Deuteronomy 7:1, 2, were to be exterminated, including women and children. Their cities were to be devoted to destruction. (De 20:15-17) According to Deuteronomy 20:10-15, other cities were first warned and terms of peace extended. If the city surrendered, the inhabitants were spared and put to forced labor. This opportunity to surrender, together with the assurance that their lives would be spared and their women would not be raped or molested, was an inducement to such cities to capitulate to Israel's army, thus avoiding much bloodshed. If the city did not surrender, all males were killed. Killing the men removed danger of later revolt by the city. "The women and the little children" were spared. That

"women" here no doubt means *virgins* is indicated by Deuteronomy 21:10-14, where prospective war brides are described as mourning for parents, not for husbands. Also, earlier, when Israel defeated Midian, it is specifically stated that only *virgins* were spared. Such sparing of only virgins would serve to protect Israel from false worship and no doubt from sexually transmitted diseases. (Nu 31:7, 17, 18) (As to the justice of God's decree against the Canaanite nations, see CANAAN, CANAANITE [Conquest of Canaan by Israel].)

Food-producing trees were not to be cut down for siegeworks. (De 20:19, 20) Horses of the enemy were hamstrung during the heat of battle to incapacitate them; after the battle they undoubtedly were killed.—Jos 11:6.

Not All of Israel's Wars Were Proper. Israel's lapsing into a course of unfaithfulness was accompanied by conflicts that were little more than power struggles. This was the case with Abimelech's warring against Shechem and Thebez in the time of the Judges (Jg 9:1-57), as well as Omri's warfare against Zimri and Tibni, which led to his being firmly established in the kingship over the ten-tribe kingdom. (1Ki 16:16-22) Also, instead of relying on Jehovah for protection from their enemies, the Israelites began to trust in military might, horses and chariots. Thus, in the time of Isaiah, the land of Judah was "filled with horses" and there was "no limit to their chariots." —Isa 2:1, 7.

Ancient War Strategy and Tactics. Spies were sometimes sent out ahead of the attack to ascertain conditions existing in the land. Such spies were not sent to initiate unrest, revolt, or subversive underground movements. (Nu 13:1, 2, 17-19; Jos 2:1; Jg 18:2; 1Sa 26:4) Special trumpet calls were employed for mustering forces, for war calls, and for signaling unified action. (Nu 10:9; 2Ch 13:12; compare Jg 3:27; 6:34; 7:19, 20.) On occasion forces were divided and deployed in flanking attacks, or in ambush and decoy operations. (Ge 14:15; Jos 8:2-8; Jg 7:16; 2Sa 5:23, 24; 2Ch 13:13) In at least one instance, at Jehovah's direction, singers of praise to God were put in the vanguard, ahead of the armed forces. God fought that day for Israel, throwing the camp of the enemy into confusion so that the enemy soldiers killed one another.—2Ch 20:20-23.

Fighting was to a great extent hand to hand, man against man. A variety of weapons were used—swords, spears, javelins, arrows, slingstones, and so forth. During the conquest of the Promised Land, Israel did not rely on horses and chariots; their trust was in the saving power of Jehovah. (De 17:16; Ps 20:7; 33:17; Pr 21:31) Not until later times did the armies of Israel employ horses and chariots, as did the Egyptians and others. (1Ki 4:26; 20:23-25; Ex 14:6, 7; De 11:4) Foreign armies were sometimes equipped with war chariots having iron scythes extending from their axles.—Jos 17:16; Jg 4:3, 13.

War tactics changed during the course of the centuries. Generally, Israel did not concentrate on developing instruments of offensive warfare, though considerable attention was given to fortification. King Uzziah of Judah is noted for building "engines of war, the invention of engineers," but these were primarily for the defense of Jerusalem. (2Ch 26:14, 15) In order to be able to attack the higher and weaker part of a city's wall, the Assyrian and Babylonian armies, particularly, were known for their siege walls and their siege ramparts. These ramparts served as inclined planes up which towers with battering rams were brought; from these towers, the archers and slingers fought. Along with these were other forms of siege engines, including giant rock throwers. (2Ki 19:32; Jer 32:24; Eze 4:2; Lu 19: 43) At the same time the defenders of the city attempted to hold off the attack by means of archers, slingers, as well as by soldiers who would throw firebrands from their walls and towers and from missile-throwing engines inside the city. (2Sa 11:21, 24; 2Ch 26:15; 32:5) In assaulting walled fortifications, one of the first things attempted was the cutting off of the city's water supply, while the city about to be besieged often stopped up water sources around the city to deprive the attackers of their use.—2Ch 32:2-4, 30.

On defeating an enemy, the victors sometimes stopped up wells and springs in the area and spread stones over the ground, occasionally sowing the ground with salt.—Jg 9:45; 2Ki 3:24, 25; see ARMS, ARMOR; FORTIFICATIONS.

Jesus Foretells War. Jesus, the man of peace, observed that "those who take the sword will perish by the sword." (Mt 26:52) He declared to Pilate that, had his Kingdom been of this world, his attendants would have fought to prevent his being delivered up to the Jews. (Joh 18:36) Yet he foretold that Jerusalem, because of rejecting him as the Messiah, would in time suffer siege and desolation, during which her "children" (inhabitants) would be dashed to the ground.—Lu 19: 41-44; 21:24.

Shortly before his death, Jesus gave prophecies that applied to that generation and also to the time when his presence in Kingdom power would

begin: "You are going to hear of wars and reports of wars; see that you are not terrified. For these things must take place, but the end is not yet. For nation will rise against nation and kingdom against kingdom."—Mt 24:6, 7; Mr 13:7, 8; Lu 21:9, 10.

Christ Wages War as "King of Kings." The Bible reveals that the resurrected Lord Jesus Christ, with 'all authority in heaven and on earth' granted to him by his Father, will engage in a warfare that will destroy all of God's enemies and establish everlasting peace, as his title "Prince of Peace" implies.—Mt 28:18; 2Th 1:7-10; Isa 9:6.

The apostle John had a vision of things to take place after Christ's enthronement in heaven. The words of Psalms 2:7, 8 and 110:1, 2 had foretold that God's Son would be invited to 'ask of Jehovah the nations as his inheritance,' and that Jehovah would respond by sending him forth to 'go subduing in the midst of his enemies.' (Heb 10:12, 13) John's vision depicted a war in heaven in which Michael, that is, Jesus Christ (see MICHAEL No. 1), led the armies of heaven in a war against the Dragon, Satan the Devil. The outcome of that war was the hurling of the Devil and his angels to the earth. This war immediately followed the 'birth of the male child' who was to rule the nations with a rod of iron. (Re 12:7-9) A loud voice in heaven then announced: "Now have come to pass the salvation and the power and the kingdom of our God and the authority of his Christ." This brought relief and joy to the angels; but it presaged troubles, including wars, for the earth, as the declaration continued: "Woe for the earth and for the sea, because the Devil has come down to you, having great anger, knowing he has a short period of time."—Re 12:10, 12.

After Satan was hurled to the earth, he made God's servants on earth, the remaining ones of the 'seed of the woman,' "who observe the commandments of God and have the work of bearing witness to Jesus," his chief target. Satan initiated warfare against them that included both a spiritual conflict and actual persecution, even resulting in death for some. (Re 12:13, 17) Succeeding chapters of Revelation (13, 17-19) describe the agents and instruments Satan uses against them, as well as the victorious outcome for God's holy ones under their Leader Jesus Christ.

'War of the great day of God Almighty.' The 19th chapter of Revelation gives a view of the greatest war of all human history, surpassing anything that men have ever witnessed. Earlier in the vision it is called "the war of the great day of God the Almighty." Aligned against Jehovah and the Lord Jesus Christ as the Commander of God's armies, the hosts of heaven, are the symbolic "wild beast and the kings of the earth and their armies" assembled to the site of this war by "expressions inspired by demons." (Re 16:14; 19:19) None of God's earthly servants are pictured as having part in this battle. The earthly kings "will battle with the Lamb, but, because he is Lord of lords and King of kings, the Lamb will conquer them." (Re 17:14; 19:19-21; see HAR–MAGEDON.) Following this fight, Satan the Devil himself is to be bound for a thousand years, "that he might not mislead the nations anymore until the thousand years were ended."—Re 20:1-3.

With the conclusion of this war, the earth will enjoy peace for a thousand years. The psalm that declares "[Jehovah] is making wars to cease to the extremity of the earth. The bow he breaks apart and does cut the spear in pieces; the wagons he burns in the fire," had initial fulfillment in God's bringing peace to Israel's land by wrecking the enemy's war instruments. After Christ defeats the promoters of war at Har–Magedon, the extremity of this earthly globe will enjoy full and satisfying peace. (Ps 46:8-10) Persons favored with eternal life will be those who have beaten "their swords into plowshares and their spears into pruning shears" and who do not "learn war anymore." "For the very mouth of Jehovah of armies has spoken it."—Isa 2:4; Mic 4:3, 4.

War threat forever ended. Revelation's vision goes on to show that at the end of the thousand years Satan the Devil will be brought back from his binding in the abyss and will again induce many to come up to wage war against those remaining loyal to God. But no damage will be done, for 'fire will come down out of heaven' and devour these enemies, thereby removing all threat of war forever.—Re 20:7-10.

Christian Warfare. While the Christian does not engage in a physical war against blood and flesh (Eph 6:12), he is engaged in warfare nonetheless, a spiritual fight. The apostle Paul describes the war waged within the Christian between "sin's law" and "God's law," or 'the law of the mind' (the Christian mind in harmony with God).—Ro 7:15-25.

This warfare of the Christian is an agonizing one, requiring the exertion of every effort for a person to come off winner. But he can be confident of victory through the undeserved kindness of God through Christ and the help of God's spirit. (Ro 8:35-39) Jesus said of this fight: "Exert yourselves vigorously to get in through the narrow door" (Lu 13:24), and the apostle Peter counseled:

"Keep abstaining from fleshly desires, which are the very ones that carry on a conflict [or, "are doing military service" (*stra·teu'on·tai*)] against the soul."—1Pe 2:11, *Int;* compare Jas 4:1, 2.

Against wicked spirits. In addition to this warfare against sin's law, the Christian has a fight against the demons, who take advantage of the tendencies of the flesh by tempting the Christian to sin. (Eph 6:12) In this warfare the demons also induce those under their influence to tempt or to oppose and persecute Christians in an effort to get them to break their integrity to God.—1Co 7:5; 2Co 2:11; 12:7; compare Lu 4:1-13.

Against false teachings. The apostle Paul also spoke of a warfare that he and his associates were waging, in carrying out their commission as those appointed to care for the Christian congregation. (2Co 10:3) The congregation at Corinth had been wrongly influenced by presumptuous men called by Paul "false apostles" who, by giving undue attention to personalities, had caused divisions, sects, in the congregation. (2Co 11:13-15) They became, in effect, followers of men such as Apollos, Paul, and Cephas. (1Co 1:11, 12) The members of the congregation lost the spiritual viewpoint, that these men were merely representatives of Christ, unitedly serving the same purpose. They became *fleshly.* (1Co 3:1-9) They viewed men in the congregation 'according to what they were in the flesh,' their appearance, natural abilities, personalities, and so forth, instead of regarding them as spiritual men. They failed to recognize that God's spirit was operating in the congregation, and that men such as Paul, Peter, and Apollos were accomplishing what they did by God's spirit, for His glory.

Therefore, Paul was impelled to write them: "Indeed I beg that, when present, I may not use boldness with that confidence with which I am counting on taking bold measures against some who appraise us as if we walked according to what we are in the flesh. For though we walk in the flesh, we do not wage warfare according to what we are in the flesh. For the weapons of our warfare are not fleshly, but powerful by God for overturning strongly entrenched things. For we are overturning reasonings and every lofty thing raised up against the knowledge of God; and we are bringing every thought into captivity to make it obedient to the Christ."—2Co 10:2-5.

Paul wrote to Timothy, whom he had left in Ephesus to care for the congregation there: "This mandate I commit to you, child, Timothy, in accord with the predictions that led directly on to you, that by these you may go on waging the fine warfare; holding faith and a good conscience." (1Ti 1:18, 19) Not only did Timothy have before him conflicts because of sinful flesh and because of the opposition of the enemies of the truth but he also had to wage warfare against the infiltration of false doctrine and of those who would corrupt the congregation. (1Ti 1:3-7; 4:6, 11-16) His actions would fortify the congregation against the apostasy that Paul knew would occur after the apostles passed off the scene. (2Ti 4:3-5) So it was a real fight that Timothy had to wage.

Paul was able to say to Timothy: "I have fought the fine fight, I have run the course to the finish, I have observed the faith." (2Ti 4:7) Paul had maintained his faithfulness to Jehovah and Jesus Christ by right conduct and service in the face of opposition, suffering, and persecution. (2Co 11: 23-28) He had additionally discharged the responsibility of his office as an apostle of the Lord Jesus Christ, fighting the war to keep the Christian congregation clean and spotless, as a chaste virgin, and as "a pillar and support of the truth." —1Ti 3:15; 1Co 4:1, 2; 2Co 11:2, 29; compare 2Ti 2:3, 4.

God's material support of the Christian. In the warfare of the Christian, God views the Christian as His soldier and, therefore, provides him with the necessary material things. The apostle argues, with regard to the authority of one serving as a minister to others: "Who is it that ever serves as a soldier at his own expense?"—1Co 9:7.

Christians and Wars of the Nations. Christians have always maintained strict neutrality as to fleshly warfare between nations, groups, or factions of any kind. (Joh 18:36; 1Co 5:1, 13; Eph 6:12) For examples of the attitude of the early Christians in this respect, see ARMY (Those Known As Early Christians).

Other Uses. In the song of Barak and Deborah, after the victory over the army of Jabin, king of Canaan, a circumstance is recalled that sets forth a principle: "They [Israel] proceeded to choose new gods. It was then there was war in the gates." (Jg 5:8) As soon as they forsook Jehovah for false worship, trouble came, with the enemy pressing at the very gates of their cities. This is in harmony with the psalmist's declaration: "Unless Jehovah himself guards the city, it is to no avail that the guard has kept awake."—Ps 127:1.

At Ecclesiastes 8:8, Solomon wrote: "There is no man having power over the spirit to restrain the spirit; . . . nor is there any discharge in the war." In the day of death the dying person cannot restrain the spirit, or force of life, and keep it from returning to God the Giver and Source, so as to live longer. Dying humans cannot control the day of death and prevent it from ever reaching them. They cannot, by any human efforts, be discharged from the war that the enemy Death wages against all mankind without exception. Sinful man cannot get some other sinful man to substitute for him in death and thus enjoy a furlough from death. (Ps 49:6-9) Only through Jehovah's undeserved kindness by means of Jesus Christ is relief possible. "Just as sin ruled as king with death, likewise also undeserved kindness might rule as king through righteousness with everlasting life in view through Jesus Christ our Lord."—Ro 5:21.

WAR CLUB. See ARMS, ARMOR.

WARP. In weaving, the group of threads running the length of the fabric. The set of threads woven alternately over and under these at right angles across the cloth constitutes the woof. When Israel's priests tested woven materials for leprosy, they inspected both the warp and the woof.—Le 13:47-59; see LEPROSY (In garments and houses); WEAVING.

Upon completing the cloth, the weaver cuts across the warp threads, removing the material and leaving the "thrums," or ends of the warp threads, fastened to the loom. King Hezekiah alluded to this in recalling his severe illness when he thought that God was about to cut short his life, cutting Hezekiah off "from the very threads of the warp" in untimely death.—Isa 38:9-12.

WARS OF JEHOVAH, BOOK OF THE. See BOOK.

WASHING OF FEET. A welcome and hospitable act that often preceded the eating of a meal in the generally warm climate of the ancient Middle East, where persons customarily wore open sandals, walked on dry soil, and traveled on foot along dusty roads. In the average home of the common people, the host provided needed vessels and water, and visitors washed their own feet. (Jg 19:21) A wealthier host usually had his slave do the foot washing, and this was considered a menial task. Abigail indicated her willingness to comply with David's wish that she become his wife by saying: "Here is your slave girl as a maidservant to wash the feet of the servants of my lord." (1Sa 25:40-42) Especially was it a display of humility and affectionate regard for guests if the host or hostess personally washed the visitors' feet.

Not only were feet washed as a host's gesture of hospitality toward his guest but they were also customarily washed before a person retired to bed. (Ca 5:3) Especially noteworthy was the requirement that Levite priests wash their feet and hands before going into the tabernacle or before officiating at the altar.—Ex 30:17-21; 40:30-32.

When Jesus Christ was on earth, a host might offer his guest water for washing the feet, give him a kiss, and grease his head with oil. Simon the Pharisee neglected these three expressions of hospitality while entertaining Jesus. Thus, when a weeping sinful woman wet Jesus' feet with her tears, wiped them with her hair, kissed his feet, and then greased them with perfumed oil, Christ pointed out Simon's failure and then told the woman: "Your sins are forgiven."—Lu 7:36-50.

Jesus Christ washed his apostles' feet on the last night of his earthly life, Nisan 14, 33 C.E., doing so to teach them a lesson and "set the pattern," rather than to establish a ceremony. (Joh 13:1-16) That evening there had been a discussion among the apostles as to who was the greatest (Lu 22:24-27), and the spirit then prevailing apparently led to Jesus' washing of his disciples' feet as a lesson in humility and willingness to serve one another in the humblest way. On that night Jesus and the apostles were merely using a room and were not someone's guests. So, there were no servants on hand to wash their feet, which would undoubtedly have been the case had they been guests. None of the apostles took the initiative to perform this menial service for the others. However, at an appropriate time during the meal, Jesus rose, laid aside his outer garments, girded himself with a towel, put water in a basin, and washed their feet. He thus showed that in humility each one should be the servant of the others and should show love in practical ways, doing things for the comfort of others. Christian hostesses did so, as is evident from the apostle Paul's reference to the hospitable act of foot washing among other fine works performed by Christian widows. (1Ti 5:9, 10) The Christian Greek Scriptures do not list formal washing of feet as a required Christian ceremony. Nonetheless, the example Jesus Christ set by this act stands as a reminder to Christians to serve their brothers lovingly, even in small ways and by performing humble tasks in their behalf.—Joh 13:34, 35; see BATHING.

WASHING OF HANDS.

Rather than being plunged into a container filled with water, in ancient times the hands were often washed with water poured upon them. The dirty water then ran into a container or basin over which the hands were held.—Compare 2Ki 3:11.

The Law prescribed that the priests wash their hands and their feet at the copper basin located between the sanctuary and the altar before ministering at the altar or entering the tent of meeting. (Ex 30:18-21) The Law also stated that in case someone slain was found and it was impossible to ascertain who the murderer was, the older men of the city nearest the slain person were to take a young cow, one that had never been worked with or had never pulled a yoke, to a torrent valley of running water and there break its neck. After this, the older men were to wash their hands over the young cow, denoting their innocence in regard to the murder. (De 21:1-8) Also, according to the Law, a person was rendered unclean if touched by someone with a running discharge who had not rinsed his hands. —Le 15:11.

David desired morally clean hands so as to be able to worship before Jehovah's altar. (Ps 26:6) On the other hand, Pilate vainly tried to clear himself of bloodguilt in connection with the death of Jesus by washing his hands before the people. But in this way he really could not escape responsibility for Jesus' death, since he, not the howling mob, had the authority to determine the judgment.—Mt 27:24.

The scribes and Pharisees in the first century C.E. attached great importance to the washing of hands and took issue with Jesus Christ concerning his disciples' overstepping the traditions of men of former times by not washing their hands when about to eat a meal. This involved no ordinary hand washing for hygienic purposes but was a ceremonious ritual. "The Pharisees and all the Jews do not eat unless they wash their hands up to the elbow." (Mr 7:2-5; Mt 15:2) The Babylonian Talmud (*Sotah* 4b) puts the one eating with unwashed hands on the same plane as one having relations with a harlot, and it states that the one lightly esteeming hand washing will be "uprooted from the world."—See BATHING.

WATCH. See NIGHT.

WATCHMAN.

One who guards against possible harm to persons or property, often during the night, and who may sound an alarm in the face of threatened danger. In military service a watchman is usually called a guard or sentry. —Jer 51:12, ftn; Ac 12:6; 28:16; see GUARD.

As a protection against thieves and vandals, persons often were stationed to watch over ripening vineyards or flocks of animals, positioning themselves perhaps in booths or elevated watchtowers built for that purpose. (2Ki 17:9; 2Ch 20:24; Job 27:18; Isa 1:8) Siege forces attacking fortified places had watchmen or sentries to give their commanders military intelligence. (Jer 51:12) When King Saul was in the field camp with his army he also had personal watchmen whose responsibility was to look out for their king's welfare.—1Sa 14:16; 26:15, 16.

Watchmen were often stationed on the city walls and towers to observe those approaching before they got close. (2Sa 18:24-27; 2Ki 9:17-20) At times watchmen made their inspection rounds through the city streets as well. (Ca 3:3; 5:7) Fearful persons, awake during the dangerous hours of the night, might repeatedly inquire of the watchmen if all was well (Isa 21:11, 12), and it was only natural for watchmen themselves to long for the daylight to come. (Ps 130:6) Happy the city that, in addition to the watchmen, had Jehovah watching over it.—Ps 127:1.

Figurative Use. Jehovah raised up prophets who served as figurative watchmen to the nation of Israel (Jer 6:17), and they, in turn, sometimes spoke of watchmen in a symbolic way. (Isa 21:6, 8; 52:8; 62:6; Ho 9:8) These prophet-watchmen had the responsibility to warn the wicked of impending destruction, and if they failed to do so, they were held accountable. Of course, if the people were unresponsive and failed to heed the warning, their blood was upon themselves. (Eze 3:17-21; 33:1-9) An unfaithful prophet was about as worthless as a blind watchman or a voiceless dog.—Isa 56:10.

WATCHTOWER. A place of lookout or post of observation, often built on a city wall. (See TOWER.) Other watchtowers were constructed in wilderness areas or on frontiers. They were principally designed for military purposes and served to protect a city or a boundary; they were also constructed as places of refuge for shepherds and farmers in isolated areas and enabled a watchman to warn of marauders so that flocks and ripening crops in the area might be protected. —2Ch 20:24; Isa 21:8; 32:14.

A number of cities were named Mizpeh (Heb., *mits·peh'*, "Watchtower"), probably because of being on high elevations or because of notable towers erected there. Sometimes the Bible distinguished these cities by naming their location, as "Mizpeh of Gilead" (Jg 11:29) and "Mizpeh in Moab."—1Sa 22:3.

A pile of stones was set up by Jacob and called "Galeed" (meaning "Witness Heap") and "The Watchtower." Laban then said: "Let Jehovah keep watch between me and you when we are situated unseen the one from the other." (Ge 31:45-49) This pile of stones would testify to the fact that Jehovah was watching to see that Jacob and Laban carried out their covenant of peace.

WATER. The liquid that is a major constituent of all living matter. Jehovah is the Source of this liquid (Re 14:7) so essential to the life of man, animals, and vegetation on earth. (Ex 17:2, 3; Job 8:11; 14:7-9; Ps 105:29; Isa 1:30) He provides it and can control it. (Ex 14:21-29; Job 5:10; 26:8; 28:25; 37:10; Ps 107:35) God furnished the Israelites with water, miraculously when necessary (Ex 17:1-7; Ne 9:15, 20; Ps 78:16, 20; Isa 35:6, 7; 43:20; 48:21); gave them a land having plenty of water (De 8:7); and promised to bless their water supply as long as they obeyed him (Ex 23:25).

Jehovah was responsible for the original watering of the ground by means of a mist arising from the earth, and he established the laws governing evaporation of water and its precipitation as rain. (Ge 2:5, 6; Job 36:27; Am 5:8; see CLOUD; MIST; RAIN.) On the second creative day, God produced an expanse by having some water remain on earth while raising a great quantity high above the globe; the waters above the expanse undoubtedly supplied the water whereby the wicked were later destroyed in the Flood of Noah's day.—Ge 1:6-8; 7:11, 17-24; Isa 54:9.

The Law given at Mount Sinai prohibited making images of things "in the waters under the earth," apparently meaning aquatic creatures in earth's waters, which are below the level of the land. This would include rivers, lakes, seas, and subterranean waters.—Ex 20:4; De 4:15-18; 5:8.

Illustrative and Figurative Uses. There are numerous illustrative and figurative references to water in the Scriptures. People, especially the restless masses alienated from God, are symbolized by waters. Babylon the Great, in her earthwide domination, is said to sit "on many waters." These waters are explained in John's vision of the great harlot to "mean peoples and crowds and nations and tongues."—Re 17:1, 15; compare Isa 57:20.

Because of the power of water as a destructive agent (causing drowning, washing away, or similar effects), it is often employed as a symbol of some destructive force. (Ps 69:1, 2, 14, 15; 144:7, 8) It is used of a military force at Jeremiah 47:2.

Water was used at the tabernacle both for physical cleanness and in a symbolic way. At the installation of the priesthood, the priests were washed with water, and symbolically, "sin-cleansing water" was spattered on the Levites. (Ex 29:4; Nu 8:6, 7) Priests washed before ministering at Jehovah's sanctuary and before approaching the altar of burnt offering. (Ex 40: 30-32) Water was employed to wash sacrifices (Le 1:9) and in ceremonial purifications. (Le 14:5-9, 50-52; 15:4-27; 17:15; Nu 19:1-22; see CLEAN, CLEANNESS.) The "holy water" used in the case of jealousy, where a wife was suspected of adultery, evidently was pure, fresh water, into which dust from the tabernacle was put before she drank it. —Nu 5:17-24.

Life-giving water. Jehovah is "the source of living water." Only from him and through his Son, Jesus Christ, the Chief Agent of life, can men receive everlasting life. (Jer 2:13; Joh 17:1, 3) Jesus told a Samaritan woman at a well near Sychar that the water he would give would become in its receiver "a fountain of water bubbling up to impart everlasting life."—Joh 4:7-15.

The apostle John records his vision of "a new heaven and a new earth" in which he saw flowing out from the throne of God "a river of water of life." On each side of this river there were trees producing fruit, the leaves of the trees being used for the curing of the nations. (Re 21:1; 22:1, 2) After this feature of the vision was completed, Jesus spoke to John about his purpose in sending his angel with the vision. Then John heard the proclamation: "And the spirit and the bride keep on saying: 'Come!' And let anyone hearing say: 'Come!' And let anyone thirsting come; let anyone that wishes take life's water free." Evidently this invitation would be extended by God's servants for thirsty ones to *begin* drinking of God's provisions for gaining eternal life through the Lamb of God. (Joh 1:29) They could get what is now available of this water of life. The invitation is to be extended to everyone who can be reached, not for the purpose of commercial gain by selling the water, but free to all desiring it.—Re 22:17.

Before Jesus' death and resurrection, he spoke of his followers who would receive holy spirit, beginning at Pentecost 33 C.E., saying that out from their inmost parts "streams of living water will flow." (Joh 7:37-39) The record in the Christian Greek Scriptures provides abundant evidence that, impelled by the activating force of God's spirit, the apostles and disciples accomplished marvels in bringing life-giving waters to other people, starting from Jerusalem and expanding throughout the then known world.

Nourishing the implanted word. Using a different figure in writing to the congregation at Corinth, the apostle Paul likened the work of the Christian minister to that of a farmer, who first plants the seed, waters and cultivates it, then waits for God to make the plant grow to maturity. Paul brought the good news of the Kingdom to the Corinthians, planting seed in the Corinthian "field." Apollos came afterward and by his further teaching nourished and cultivated the seed sown, but God, by his spirit, brought growth. Paul used this illustration to emphasize the fact that no individual human is important in himself, but all are ministers, working together as God's workmen. God is the important One, and he blesses such unselfish, unified work.—1Co 3:5-9.

God's word of truth. God's word of truth is likened to water that cleanses. The Christian congregation is clean in the sight of God, like a chaste bride for Christ, who cleansed it "with the bath of water by means of the word." (Eph 5:25-27) In a similar usage, Paul speaks to his fellow Christians who have the hope of being underpriests of Christ in the heavens. Referring back to the tabernacle and the requirement that the priests wash in water before entering the sanctuary to serve, he says: "Since we have a great priest [Jesus Christ] over the house of God, let us approach with true hearts in the full assurance of faith, having had . . . our bodies bathed with clean water." (Heb 10:21, 22) This cleansing involves not only the knowledge of God's word but also its application in their daily lives.

The water of baptism. Jesus explained to Nicodemus: "Unless anyone is born from water and spirit, he cannot enter into the kingdom of God." (Joh 3:5) Jesus was apparently speaking of the water of baptism, when a person repents of his sins and turns away from his former course of life, presenting himself to God through baptism in the name of Jesus Christ.—Compare Eph 4:4, 5, which speaks of the "one baptism."

The apostle John later wrote: "This is he that came by means of water and blood, Jesus Christ . . . For there are three witness bearers, the spirit and the water and the blood, and the three are in agreement." (1Jo 5:5-8) When Jesus came "into the world," that is, when he began his ministerial and sacrificial course as God's Messiah, he came to John the Baptizer to be immersed in water (not in repentance for sins, but in presentation of himself to God, to carry out God's will for him). (Heb 10:5-7) After this, God's spirit came down upon him, a testimony that he was God's Son and the Messiah. (Lu 3:21, 22) It is the water of his baptism that is in harmony with the blood of his sacrifice and with God's spirit in unanimously testifying to this great Messianic truth.

Other figurative uses. David said concerning the wicked: "May they dissolve as into waters that go their way." (Ps 58:7) David may have had in mind the torrent valleys common in Palestine, many of which are filled with a swelling, threatening torrent during a flash flood. But the water quickly runs off and disappears, leaving the valley dry.

When attacking the city of Ai, the Israelites sent out a small force that was defeated. This had a demoralizing effect on the Israelites, for the account says that the hearts of the people of Israel "began to melt and became as water," meaning that they sensed they had somehow incurred Jehovah's displeasure and were without his help. Joshua was very upset, evidently because Israel, the army of Jehovah, had fled in fear before their enemies, thus bringing reproach upon Jehovah's name.—Jos 7:5-9.

WATER GATE. See GATE, GATEWAY.

WATERMELON [Heb., *'avat·ti'ach*]. A large oblong or roundish fruit with a hard rind, many seeds, and a sweet pulp having high water content. It was one of the items of diet for which the mixed crowd and the Israelites expressed a longing while in the wilderness after leaving Egypt. (Nu 11:4, 5) Watermelons (*Citrullus vulgaris*) have long been cultivated in Egypt and other parts of the Middle East.

WAVE OFFERING. See OFFERINGS.

WAW [ו]. The sixth letter of the Hebrew alphabet. In pronunciation this letter corresponds generally to the English "w," as in "wine"; at times, however, in modern Hebrew it is given the sound of English "v." In this work it is transliterated as "w" (ו), "u" (ו), and "oh" (ו). It is rarely used as an initial letter, usually being substituted for by the letter *yohdh* (י). In the Hebrew, it appears at the beginning of each of the eight verses of Psalm 119:41-48.

WAX. Biblical references to wax are apparently to beeswax, a dark-yellow substance that bees use in forming walls of honeycomb cells where they deposit honey or larvae. Wax is produced by worker bees, which, after consuming large amounts of honey, manufacture wax in special glands in their abdomens. The wax is excreted through tiny pores and forms as small white flakes on the exterior of the abdomen. The flakes of wax are then transferred to the bee's mouth, where they are chewed prior to construction use. The bee has control over the production of wax and makes it only when a supply is needed.—See BEE.

The wax is easily separated from the honey by melting it in warm water. This causes the wax to rise to the surface, where it can be skimmed off. The melting of wax is used in poetic Scriptural illustrations to express a distressed condition of the heart (Ps 22:14), the dissolution of mountains and of plains (Ps 97:5; Mic 1:4), and the destruction of God's enemies; the psalmist exclaimed: "As wax melts because of the fire, let the wicked ones perish from before God."—Ps 68:1, 2.

WAY, THE. This expression can be applied to a road, street, track, or path; a mode of action or conduct; or a normal course, manner, or method. In the Scriptures it is often used with reference to a course of conduct and action that is either approved or disapproved by Jehovah God. (Jg 2:22; 2Ki 21:22; Ps 27:11; 32:8; 86:11; Isa 30:21; Jer 7:23; 10:23; 21:8) With the coming of Jesus Christ, an individual's enjoying a proper relationship with God and approaching him acceptably in prayer depended on acceptance of Jesus Christ. As the Son of God stated: "I am the way and the truth and the life. No one comes to the Father except through me." (Joh 14:6; Heb 10:19-22) Those who became followers of Jesus Christ were spoken of as belonging to "The Way," that is, they adhered to a way or manner of life that centered around faith in Jesus Christ, following his example.—Ac 9:2; 19:9, 23; 22:4; 24:22.

WEANING. The process of training a nursing child to take food in another way. In ancient times, a mother usually breast-fed her child for some time, unless such circumstances as inability to produce sufficient milk or her untimely death required that a nursing woman be acquired for that purpose. (Ex 2:5-10) The time when breast-feeding was discontinued marked a significant point in the young one's life. (Isa 11:8; 28:9) This happy event could call for a feast such as the one Abraham arranged at the weaning of Isaac.—Ge 21:8.

In those days, women nursed their children much longer than they do now in most parts of the earth. Upon being weaned, Samuel was old enough to be placed in the care of High Priest Eli and to serve at the tabernacle. (1Sa 1:24-28) He must have been at least three years old then, for the registration of Levite males began at that age. (2Ch 31:16) In his book *Family, Love and the Bible* (London, 1960, p. 175), Raphael Patai says of Arab children: "Cases are known where a child was suckled until his tenth year." The evidence indicates that Isaac was about five years old when weaned.—See ISAAC.

A weaned child, though no longer yearning for nourishment from its mother, still finds security and satisfaction in her arms. Comparably, David had soothed and quieted his soul "like a weanling upon his mother," and his soul was 'like a weanling upon him.' Apparently it was soothed, quieted, and satisfied because he did not desire prominence, had manifested humility, avoided haughtiness, and refrained from walking in things too great for him. He urged Israel to act similarly, humbly 'waiting for Jehovah to time indefinite.'—Ps 131:1-3.

WEAPONS. See ARMS, ARMOR.

WEAVING.

The process of interlacing sets of threads lengthwise and crosswise to make cloth. The group of threads running the length of the fabric is the warp, and the set running across it is the woof, or weft. Woof thread is woven alternately over and under the warp threads. (Le 13:59) Weaving was often done by women but was also apparently an occupation of men. (2Ki 23:7; 1Ch 4:21) The loom that the Hebrews, Egyptians, and others used for weaving was basically a frame.—Jg 16:13, 14; Isa 19:1, 9, 10.

Ancient looms were either vertical or horizontal. One type of vertical loom consisted of two upright stakes with a crossbeam at the top. The warp threads hung from it and had weights attached to keep them straight. In some looms a lower beam took the place of weights, and in others this beam could be rotated to serve as a roller for the woven cloth. A common horizontal loom consisted of two parallel beams kept in place some distance apart by four pegs driven into the ground at their extremities. Warp threads were stretched between these beams. The wooden shaft of Goliath's spear was possibly being compared to such a heavy beam when it was likened to "the beam of loom workers."—1Sa 17:4, 7.

On the loom the warp threads were usually separated into two sets, so that the woof thread would pass over one set when drawn across the warp in one direction and under that set when moved across it in the opposite way. For this, two "sheds," or passages, were needed. In a simple horizontal loom a flat "shed stick" was placed across the warp under alternate warp threads, and by turning it on edge, one "shed" was made, through which the woof thread was passed in one direction. Alternate warp threads attached by loops of thread to a "lease rod" lying on top of the warp were next raised by lifting the "lease rod" vertically from the warp, making another "shed" through which the weft was drawn in the oppo-

site direction across the warp. After each movement across the warp, the woof thread was pressed against the growing cloth with a peg. The weaver drew the weft across the warp with a shuttle, basically a rod carrying the thread. Since the skillful weaver moved the shuttle rapidly, Job could say: "My days themselves have become swifter than a weaver's shuttle."—Job 7:6.

After the cloth had been woven to the desired length and rolled up, the loom worker cut it from the warp threads. (Isa 38:9, 12) Materials commonly used by weavers included animal hair (Ex 36:14; Mt 3:4), wool, and linen.—Compare Pr 31:13.

Fabrics of varying patterns could be made by using threads of different colors in the warp or the woof or in both. Or woof thread of a particular color might be run only partway in the warp. (Ge 37:23; 2Sa 13:18; Pr 7:16) The loom worker might weave in an irregular manner—running a set of woof threads over one warp thread and then under two across the warp, and then running the next set over two warp threads, under two, then over one for the width of the warp, as in weaving gabardine today. By variations in weaving methods, a pattern is developed in the fabric even when warp and woof threads are the same color. Aaron, for instance, was provided with a white robe of fine linen woven "in checkerwork."—Ex 28:39.

WEEDS.

Generally, troublesome plants that serve no apparent useful purpose where they grow. While some scholars have endeavored to link with specific plants the various original-language words rendered "weeds" in the Bible, no certain identification is possible.

The Hebrew word bo'shah' is considered to be derived from a root meaning "stink" and therefore probably embraces a variety of foul-smelling plants, "stinking weeds." Faithful Job, in effect, stated that if his life course had not been one of integrity, then, instead of barley, let stinking weeds grow.—Job 31:40.

Another Hebrew term, choh'ach, is understood to designate thorny plants generally, thorny weeds that grow on cultivated ground and quickly take possession of desolated land. (Job 31:40; Isa 34:13; Ho 9:6) The same word appears at Job 41:2, where the allusion seems to be to a thorn put into the gills of a fish for carrying purposes. Choh'ach is also employed in an illustrative sense. (Ca 2:2) A thorny weed in the hand of a drunkard can bring injury to him and to others; so it is with stupid people who use a proverb wrongly because of not understanding it. (Pr 26:9) King Jehoash of

Israel compared the action of proud King Amaziah of Judah in wanting to fight him to a thorny weed's asking for a marriage alliance with a cedar of Lebanon.—2Ki 14:8, 9; 2Ch 25:18.

The Hebrew designation *sha'yith* appears to denote a variety of weeds that grow on neglected or desolated land. (Isa 5:6; 7:23-25; 27:4) This term, rendered "weeds," is used figuratively to represent people who by their unfaithfulness have become worthless and fit only for destruction.—Isa 9:18, 19; 10:17-19; compare Da 4:20-22.

At Proverbs 24:31, the plural form of the Hebrew term *qim·mohs'*, which is commonly rendered "nettle," appears to denote weeds of all kinds.—See NETTLE.

The weeds (Gr., *zi·za'ni·a*) of Jesus' illustration at Matthew 13:24-30, 36-43 are generally considered to be bearded darnel (*Lolium temulentum*), which very much resembles wheat until maturity, when it can be readily distinguished from wheat by its smaller black seeds. This, together with the fact that the roots of these weeds become entwined with the wheat, would make it most inadvisable to pull up the weeds at an early stage. If darnel seeds become mixed with wheat kernels after the harvest, this can have a serious effect upon the eater. Dizziness and even fatal poisoning have been attributed to eating bread containing too much darnel flour. The poisonous properties of darnel seeds are generally believed to stem from a fungus growing within them.

WEEK.

The Hebrew word for "week" (*sha·vu'a'*) literally refers to a sevenfold unit or period. The Greek word *sab'ba·ton*, in turn, is derived from the Hebrew word for Sabbath (*shab·bath'*).

The counting of days in cycles of seven goes far back into man's history. The precedent for such time division was set by Jehovah God in dividing his creative work period into six days, or units of time, crowned by a seventh day of rest. (Ge 2: 2, 3) Following this, the next reference we find to a seven-day cycle is in the case of Noah at the time of the Flood, but no seventh-day rest is mentioned. (Ge 7:4, 10; 8:10, 12) Seven-day periods were observed with regard to marriages in Paddan-aram and in Philistia. (Ge 29:27, 28; Jg 14:12, 17) A seven-day period was also observed at the funeral of Jacob. (Ge 50:10) However, the Bible record does not show that these early seven-day periods conformed to a weekly arrangement, having a regular starting day and being followed by other comparable seven-day periods. Among some ancient peoples the seven-day cycles were governed by the four phases of

the moon and started again with each new moon. Since a lunar month runs either 29 or 30 days, this would not allow for completely consecutive seven-day cycles.

One early reference to a ten-day period is found at Genesis 24:55. In ancient Egypt the time was divided into ten-day cycles (three such to each month), and the Israelites obviously became familiar with this during their long sojourn in Egypt.

Under the Law. It is first in conjunction with the instructions regarding the Passover that we find a divine ordinance requiring the observance of a specific seven-day period. This period became the annual Festival of Unfermented Cakes that was thereafter celebrated by the Israelites after the Passover. Both the first day and the seventh, or last, day were to be days of rest.—Ex 12:14-20; 13:6-10.

Sabbath day instituted. However, following the inauguration of this special week there ensued a period of about one month during which the Israelites were traveling on their Exodus from Egypt, and in this period no mention is made of a weekly observance by them terminating with a seventh day of rest. Following the 15th day of the second month of their coming out of the land of Egypt, Jehovah began to give them manna, and it was at this time that they were first instructed as to a regular Sabbath observance every seventh day. (Ex 16:1, 4, 5, 22-30) Such Sabbath observance necessarily resulted in a *consecutive* weekly division of days not bound by the lunar monthly periods. It was thereafter made a legal statute by God in the Law covenant given through Moses to the nation of Israel.—Ex 20:8-11; De 5:12-15.

Festival periods. There were, of course, certain festival periods of seven days' duration that were set out in the Law and that did not necessarily begin or end in conformity with the regular week governed by the Sabbath. They began on a particular day of the lunar month; therefore, the starting day fell on different days of the week from year to year. This was true of the Festival of Unfermented Cakes, which followed the Passover and came on Nisan 15-21, and of the Festival of Booths on Ethanim 15-21. Also, the Festival of Weeks, or Pentecost, was based on a count of seven weeks plus one day, but the seven weeks began counting from Nisan 16 and so did not always run concurrently with the regular weeks ending with the regular Sabbath days.—Ex 12:2, 6, 14-20; Le 23:5-7, 15, 16; De 16:9, 10, 13.

The days of the week were not given names but were simply designated by number, the exception being the seventh day called "the sabbath."

(Ex 20:8) This was also true in the days of Jesus and his apostles, although the day before the Sabbath came to be called "Preparation."—Mt 28:1; Ac 20:7; Mr 15:42; Joh 19:31.

Seven-day and seven-year periods. Because of the importance that the Law covenant attached to the Sabbath, or the seventh day, the word "sabbath" was commonly used to represent the entire week of seven days. (Le 23:15, 16) It was likewise used to refer to the seventh year, which was a Sabbath year of rest for the land. And it also stood for the entire seven-year period, or week of years, ending in a Sabbath year. (Le 25:2-8) The Jewish Mishnah repeatedly uses the expression "week of years."—Shevi'it 4:7-9; Sanhedrin 5:1; see SEVENTY WEEKS (A Messianic Prophecy).

WEEKS, FESTIVAL OF. See PENTECOST.

WEEPING.

An expression of strong emotion (such as grief) by shedding tears. Both men and women of the past, including mighty warriors like David, wept, not considering it a sign of weakness. (Ge 42:24; 43:30; 45:2, 3, 14, 15; 46:29; Ru 1:9, 14; 2Sa 13:36; Job 30:25; Ps 6:6-8) The death of a loved one or a friend was one of the chief causes for weeping. (2Sa 18:33–19:4; Lu 7:11-15; 8:49-56; Joh 20: 11-15) And the death of respected and beloved individuals might give rise to national weeping (2Sa 3:31-34), long periods sometimes being devoted to such expression of grief. (Ge 50:1-3, 10, 11; Nu 20:29; De 34:8) Other circumstances that occasioned weeping were defeat in warfare (De 1:44, 45; Jer 31:15; La 1:16), captivity (Ps 137:1), oppression (Ec 4:1), great calamity (Es 3:13, 14; 4:1-4), and remorse over sin (Ezr 10:1-4; Jer 3:21, 22; 31:9; Joe 2:12; Lu 22:54-62; Jas 4:8, 9; see MOURNING). Weeping in religious ceremony was associated with worship of the Babylonian god Tammuz.—Eze 8:14.

Aside from feelings of personal loss or affliction, deep concern and intense feeling for others often prompted weeping. Thus the apostle Paul spoke of admonishing and correcting fellow believers with tears. (Ac 20:31; 2Co 2:4) With weeping, he mentioned those who were "walking as the enemies of the torture stake of the Christ." (Php 3:18, 19) And because of the close bond of love existing between Paul and the overseers of the Ephesus congregation, all wept upon learning of the possibility that they might not see the apostle's face again.—Ac 20:36-38.

There were times when worshipers of Jehovah wept during prayer, as did Hannah, Hezekiah, and Nehemiah. (1Sa 1:9-11; 2Ki 20:1-5; Ne 1:2-4; Ps 39:12) Even Jesus Christ, while on earth, supplicated and petitioned his Father "with strong outcries and tears."—Heb 5:7.

WEIGHTS AND MEASURES.

Archaeological evidence, the Bible itself, and other ancient writings provide the basis for assigning approximate values to the various weights and measures used by the Hebrews.

Linear Measures. The linear measures employed by the Hebrews were evidently derived from the human body. Since the ratio in length or width of one part of the body to another can be determined, it is possible to ascertain the relationship of one linear measurement to another; and based on archaeological evidence pointing to a cubit of about 44.5 cm (17.5 in.), approximate modern values can be given to the linear measurements mentioned in the Bible. (See CUBIT.) The chart that follows presents the relationship of the Hebrew linear measures to one another as well as their approximate modern equivalents.

Linear Measures		
		Modern Equivalent
1 fingerbreadth	= ¼ handbreadth	1.85 cm (0.72 in.)
1 handbreadth	= 4 fingerbreadths	7.4 cm (2.9 in.)
1 span	= 3 handbreadths	22.2 cm (8.75 in.)
1 cubit	= 2 spans	44.5 cm (17.5 in.)
1 long cubit*	= 7 handbreadths	51.8 cm (20.4 in.)
1 short cubit		38 cm (15 in.)
1 reed	= 6 cubits	2.67 m (8.75 ft)
1 long reed	= 6 long cubits	3.11 m (10.2 ft)
*Possibly the same as the "former" cubit of 2Ch 3:3.		

There is some uncertainty about the measure designated by the Hebrew term go'medh, appearing solely at Judges 3:16 with reference to the length of Ehud's sword. In numerous translations this word is rendered "cubit." (KJ, Le, JB, NW, Ro, RS) Some scholars believe that go'medh denotes a short cubit roughly corresponding to the distance from the elbow to the knuckles of the clenched hand. This would be about 38 cm (15 in.).—NE.

Other linear measurements mentioned in the Scriptures are the fathom (1.8 m; 6 ft); the sta'dion, or furlong (185 m; 606.75 ft); and the mile, probably the Roman mile (1,479.5 m; 4,854 ft). The word "journey" is often used in connection with a general distance covered. (Ge 31:23; Ex 3:18; Nu 10:33; 33:8) A day's journey was perhaps 32 km (20 mi) or more, while a Sabbath day's journey appears to have been about

1 km (0.6 mi).—Mt 24:20; Ac 1:12; see FATHOM; FURLONG; JOURNEY; MILE.

Measures of Capacity. Based on jar fragments bearing the designation "bath" in ancient Hebrew characters, the capacity of the bath measure is reckoned at approximately 22 L (5.81 gal). In the charts that follow, dry and liquid measures are figured in relation to the bath measure. The relationship of one measure to another, when not stated in the Bible, is drawn from other ancient writings.—See BATH; CAB; COR; HIN; HOMER; LOG; OMER; SEAH.

Dry Measures

			Modern Equivalent
1 cab	=	4 logs	1.22 L (2.2 dry pt)
1 omer	=	1⅘ cabs	2.2 L (2 dry qt)
1 seah	=	3⅓ omers	7.33 L (6.66 dry qt)
1 ephah	=	3 seahs	22 L (20 dry qt)
1 homer	=	10 ephahs	220 L (200 dry qt)

Liquid Measures

			Modern Equivalent
1 log	=	¼ cab	0.31 L (0.66 pt)
1 cab	=	4 logs	1.22 L (2.58 pt)
1 hin	=	3 cabs	3.67 L (7.75 pt)
1 bath	=	6 hins	22 L (5.81 gal)
1 cor	=	10 baths	220 L (58.1 gal)

Other dry and liquid measures. The Hebrew word *'is·sa·rohn'*, meaning "tenth," often denotes a tenth of an ephah. (Ex 29:40; Le 14:10; 23:13, 17; Nu 15:4) According to Targum Jonathan, the "six measures of barley" (literally, six of barley) mentioned at Ruth 3:15 are six seah measures. On the authority of the Mishnah and the *Vulgate*, the Hebrew term *le'thekh* is understood to designate a half homer. (Ho 3:2; *AS, KJ, Da, JP, Le, NW; Bava Mezia* 6:5 ftn and appendix II, D, translated by H. Danby) The Greek terms *me·tre·tes'* (appearing in the plural at John 2:6 and rendered "liquid measures") and *ba'tos* (found in the plural at Lu 16:6) are equated by some with the Hebrew bath measure. The Greek *khoi'nix* (quart) is commonly thought to be slightly more than a liter or a little less than a U.S. dry quart.—Re 6:5, 6.

Weights. Archaeological evidence suggests that a shekel weighed approximately 11.4 g (0.403 oz avdp; 0.367 oz t). Using this as a basis, the chart that follows sets forth the relationship of the Hebrew weights and their approximate modern equivalent.

The Greek word *li'tra* is generally equated with the Roman pound (327 g; 11.5 oz avdp). The mina

Weights

		Modern Equivalent
1 gerah	= 1/20 shekel	0.57 g (0.01835 oz t)
1 bekah (half shekel)	= 10 gerahs	5.7 g (0.1835 oz t)
1 shekel	= 2 bekahs	11.4 g (0.367 oz t)
1 mina (maneh)	= 50 shekels	570 g (18.35 oz t)
1 talent	= 60 minas	34.2 kg (75.5 lb avdp; 91.75 lb t; 1101 oz t)

of the Christian Greek Scriptures is reckoned at 100 drachmas. (See DRACHMA.) This would mean that the Greek mina weighed 340 g (10.9 oz t) and the Greek talent, 20.4 kg (44.8 lb avdp; 54.5 lb t; 654 oz t).—See MINA; MONEY; SHEKEL; TALENT.

A set of inscribed Hebrew weights

Area. The Hebrews designated the size of a plot of land either by the amount of seed needed to sow it (Le 27:16; 1Ki 18:32) or by what a span of bulls could plow in a day.—1Sa 14:14, ftn.

WELL. The Hebrew word *be'er'*, translated "well," usually designates a pit or hole sunk into the ground to tap a natural supply of water. The term *be'er'* appears in such place-names as Beer-lahai-roi (Ge 16:14), Beer-sheba (Ge 21:14), Beer (Nu 21:16-18), and Beer-elim (Isa 15:8). This word may also mean "pit" (Ge 14:10) and, at Psalms 55:23 ("pit") and 69:15 ("well"), seems to denote the grave. It is used metaphorically to refer to a wife or a beloved woman. (Pr 5:15; Ca 4:15) And Proverbs 23:27, where the foreign woman is likened to a narrow well, may allude to the fact that obtaining water from such a well often involves difficulties, as earthenware jars break readily on its sides.—See FOUNTAIN, SPRING.

In lands having a long dry season, particularly wilderness regions, from earliest times wells have been of great importance. Anciently, the unauthorized use of wells appears to have been viewed as an invasion of property rights. (Nu 20:17, 19; 21:22) The scarcity of water and the labor entailed in digging wells made them valuable property. Not infrequently did the possession of wells give rise to violent disputes and strife. For this reason the patriarch Abraham, on one occasion, formally established his ownership of a well at Beer-sheba. (Ge 21:25-31; 26:20, 21) After his death, however, the Philistines disregarded the rights of his son and heir Isaac and stopped up the very wells that Abraham's servants had dug. —Ge 26:15, 18.

Wells were frequently surrounded by low walls and were kept covered with a large stone, doubtless to keep out dirt and to prevent animals and persons from falling into them. (Ge 29:2, 3; Ex 2:15, 16) Near some wells, there were drinking troughs or gutters for watering domestic animals. (Ge 24:20; Ex 2:16-19) Throughout the hills of Palestine, wells were dug in the limestone, and steps, leading down to the water, were often cut in the rock. In some wells, after descending, the one drawing water simply dipped a vessel directly into it. However, from very deep sources, water was commonly drawn up by means of a leather bucket (Nu 24:7) or an earthenware jar (Ge 24:16) suspended from a rope.—See JACOB'S FOUNTAIN.

WEST. The Hebrews indicated direction from the viewpoint of a person facing east. Thus the west was behind them and might be implied by the Hebrew word *'a·chohr'*, meaning "behind." —Isa 9:12.

Most often, "west" ("westward," or "western") is denoted by the Hebrew word *yam* (meaning "sea," as at Jos 1:4), evidently because the Mediterranean, or Great Sea, lay in that direction from the Promised Land. (Ge 28:14; Ex 10:19; 38:12; Nu 34:6; Zec 14:4) The context must be considered to determine whether *yam* means "sea" or denotes the west.—Jos 15:8-12; 2Ch 4:2-4, 15.

Another Hebrew word (*ma·'arav'*) is used to denote either the sunset (Isa 43:5; 59:19) or the west. (1Ch 26:30; 2Ch 32:30) It is used to help convey the thought of great distance in the comforting assurance of Jehovah's mercy toward imperfect humans: "As far off as the sunrise is from the sunset, so far off from us he has put our transgressions."—Ps 103:12.

When Jesus said that many would come "from eastern parts and western parts" to recline at the table in the Kingdom with Abraham, Isaac, and Jacob, the Greek text at Matthew 8:11 says literally "from risings and settings." Here the Greek word *dy·sme'* relates to the direction of the sun-

set, that is, the west. (*Int*) *Dy·sme'* is also used elsewhere to denote the west.—Mt 24:27; Lu 12: 54; 13:29; Re 21:13.

WHEAT. An important cereal crop that has long supplied man with a valuable item of diet and has at times, in recent years as anciently, been sold at a price double or triple that of barley. (Compare 2Ki 7:1, 16, 18; Re 6:6.) Wheat (Heb., *chit·tah'*; Gr., *si'tos*), either by itself or mixed with other grains, was commonly made into bread. (Ex 29:2; Eze 4:9) This cereal could also be eaten raw (Mt 12:1) and was made into grits by crushing its kernels. Especially the green ears of wheat were prepared by roasting. (Le 2:14; 2Sa 17:28) Wheat was exacted as tribute from defeated tribes or nations (2Ch 27:5), and it figured in offerings made to Jehovah.—1Ch 23:29; Ezr 6:9, 10.

The plant itself, when young, resembles grass and is bright green. Mature wheat, however, may measure from 0.6 to 1.5 m (2 to 5 ft) in height and is golden brown. Its leaves are long and slender, and the central stem terminates in a head of kernels. One variety of wheat (*Triticum compositum*) cultivated in Egypt of old, and still encountered there, has several ears per stalk. (Compare Ge 41:22, 23.) The varieties of wheat that have been commonly cultivated in Palestine in more recent years, and likely also in Bible times, are bearded, that is, they have coarse, prickly hairs on the husks of the kernels.

True to God's promise, the Israelites found Palestine to be a land of wheat and barley. (De 8:8; 32:14; Ps 81:16; 147:14) Not only did they have enough for themselves but they also were able to export grain. (2Ch 2:8-10, 15) In Ezekiel's time, commodities from Judah and Israel, including "wheat of Minnith," were being traded in Tyre. —Eze 27:17.

Wheat was sown in Palestine about the same time as the barley, in the month of Bul (October-November), after the early fall rains had sufficiently softened the soil for plowing. (Isa 28:24, 25) The wheat harvest followed the barley harvest (Ru 2:23; compare Ex 9:31, 32) and was closely associated with the Festival of Weeks, or Pentecost, in the month of Sivan (May-June), at which time two leavened loaves made of wheat flour were presented as a wave offering to Jehovah. (Ex 34:22; Le 23:17) After the wheat was threshed, winnowed, and sifted, it was often stored in underground pits, a practice perhaps alluded to at Jeremiah 41:8.

The Bible also makes illustrative reference to wheat. It is used to represent persons acceptable to Jehovah, "the sons of the kingdom." (Mt 3:12;

13:24-30, 37, 38; Lu 3:17) Both Jesus and the apostle Paul mentioned wheat in illustrating the resurrection. (Joh 12:24; 1Co 15:35-38) And Jesus likened the test to come upon his disciples, as a result of the trials he was about to undergo, to the sifting of wheat.—Lu 22:31.

WHEEL. A circular frame of hard material that may be solid or spoked and that is capable of turning on an axle. Anciently, wooden planks were pegged together, rounded, and furnished with a rim (felly, or felloe) to form the early wheel. The spoked type was used on chariots, wagons, and other vehicles. (Ex 14:25; Isa 5:28; 28:27) The ten copper carriages that Solomon made for use at Jehovah's temple each had a copper axle and four chariotlike copper wheels 1.5 cubits (67 cm; 26 in.) high, with hubs, spokes, and rims.—1Ki 7:27-33.

The potter fashioned earthenware vessels on a revolving horizontal disk called a potter's wheel. (Jer 18:3, 4) Also, a bucket might be lowered and raised in a cistern by means of rope attached to some type of wheel or windlass.—Ec 12:6.

Illustrative and Figurative Use. According to the Hebrew Masoretic text, Proverbs 20:26 reads: "A wise king is scattering wicked people, and he turns around upon them a wheel." This seems to allude to an action of a king comparable to the use of the wheel in threshing grain. (Compare Isa 28:27, 28.) The metaphor appears to indicate that the wise king acts promptly in separating wicked persons from righteous ones and in punishing the wicked. Thereby evil is suppressed in his domain. (Compare Pr 20:8.) However, by a slight alteration, this verse says that a wise king turns around upon the wicked "their own hurtfulness."

The uncontrolled tongue is a "fire" that "sets the wheel of natural life aflame." The entire round or course of natural life into which a person came by birth can be set aflame by the tongue, making life become a vicious circle, possibly even resulting in its own destruction as if by fire.—Jas 3:6.

By the river Chebar in the land of the Chaldeans during the fifth year of King Jehoiachin's exile, Ezekiel envisioned Jehovah riding upon a swift-moving chariotlike celestial vehicle. Its four wheels had rims filled with eyes, and within each wheel was another wheel apparently at right angles, making it possible to go forward or to either side without changing the angle of the wheels. Beside each wheel was a cherub, the cherubic living creatures and wheels moving in unison as they were directed by the spirit. (Eze 1:1-3, 15-21; 3:13) The following year, Ezekiel had a similar vision, this time being transported, evidently by the spirit of inspiration, to a place before the temple that Solomon had built in Jerusalem. The vision that he saw indicated that soon that city and the temple would be destroyed in execution of Jehovah's judicial decision. (Eze 8:1-3; 10:1-19; 11:22) Some 60 years thereafter, Daniel envisioned the Ancient of Days, Jehovah, seated upon a heavenly, wheeled throne. Both throne and wheels were aflame, suggesting the approach of fiery divine judgment upon world powers.—Da 7:1, 9, 10; Ps 97:1-3.

WHIP. Usually a flexible cord or leather lash with a handle. This instrument has been used since ancient times to beat humans (2Ch 10:11, 14) as well as to drive and direct animals.—Pr 26:3; Na 3:2.

King Rehoboam boasted that, whereas his father Solomon had chastised the Israelites with "whips," he would do so with "scourges." Rehoboam's expression was figurative, but the scourges alluded to may have been lashes equipped with sharp points, since the Hebrew word ('aq·rab·bim') for "scourges" literally means "scorpions." —1Ki 12:11, 14, ftn; 2Ch 10:11, 14.

Eliphaz the Temanite spoke of "the whip of a tongue." (Job 4:1; 5:21) Apparently the allusion was to the use of the tongue to inflict injury, as in slandering and speaking abusively.—Compare Pr 12:18; Jas 3:5-10.

At Passover time of 30 C.E., "after making a whip of ropes, [Jesus] drove all those with the sheep and cattle out of the temple." Indicating that Jesus used the whip only on the animals, not on the men with the sheep and cattle, is the fact that he evicted the sellers of doves verbally, not with the whip. Also, by driving out the cattle with the whip, he upset their business activity, and the men would naturally follow after their cattle, to round them up.—Joh 2:13-17.

WHITE. See COLORS.

WICKEDNESS. That which does not conform to God's standard of moral excellence is wicked, bad, evil, or worthless. Like the Greek word po·ne·ri'a (Mt 22:18; Mr 7:22; Lu 11:39; Ac 3:26; Ro 1:29; 1Co 5:8; Eph 6:12), the Hebrew verb ra·sha'' and related forms designate that which is wicked. (Ge 18:23; 2Sa 22:22; 2Ch 20:35; Job 34:8; Ps 37:10; Isa 26:10) Po·ne·ros' (related to po·ne·ri'a) often signifies that which is evil or wicked in a moral sense (Lu 6:45) and can apply to something that is bad or worthless in a physical sense, as when Jesus Christ spoke of "worthless fruit." (Mt

7:17, 18) This word can also describe something that is hurtful and, at Revelation 16:2, has been rendered "painful" (*AT, TEV*) and "malignant." —*NE, NW.*

Why has God permitted wickedness?

Satan the Devil, who caused the first man and woman, Adam and Eve, to rebel against God, stands in opposition to God's righteous standard and is appropriately termed "the wicked one." (Mt 6:13; 13:19, 38; 1Jo 2:13, 14; 5:19) The rebellion initiated by Satan called into question the rightfulness and righteousness of God's sovereignty, that is, whether God's rulership over his creatures is exercised righteously and in their best interests. The fact that Adam and Eve rebelled also raised another issue: Would all other intelligent creatures prove unfaithful and disloyal to God when obedience appeared to bring no material benefits? Satan's claim respecting faithful Job implied that they would do so. Satan said: "Skin in behalf of skin, and everything that a man has he will give in behalf of his soul. For a change, thrust out your hand, please, and touch as far as his bone and his flesh and see whether he will not curse you to your very face."—Job 2:4, 5; see SOVEREIGNTY.

Time was required to settle the issues that had been raised. Hence, Jehovah God, by permitting wicked persons to continue living, made it possible for others to share in proving Satan's claim false by serving God faithfully under unfavorable and trialsome circumstances. God's permission of wickedness has also provided an opportunity for individuals to abandon a wrong course and to subject themselves willingly to God's righteous laws. (Isa 55:7; Eze 33:11) So God's holding back for a time from destroying the wicked serves to spare the righteously disposed ones by allowing time for them to prove their love and devotion to Jehovah.—Ro 9:17-26.

Additionally, Jehovah God makes use of circumstances in such a way that the wicked themselves unwittingly serve his purpose. Though they oppose God, he can restrain them to the extent necessary for the preserving of his servants in their integrity, and can cause the actions even of such persons to bring his righteousness to the fore. (Ro 3:3-5, 23-26; 8:35-39; Ps 76:10) This thought is expressed at Proverbs 16:4: "Everything Jehovah has made for his purpose, yes, even the wicked one for the evil day."

A case in point is the Pharaoh on whom Jehovah, through Moses and Aaron, served notice for the release of the enslaved Israelites. God did not make this Egyptian ruler wicked, but he did allow him to continue living and also brought about circumstances that caused Pharaoh to manifest himself as being wicked and deserving of death. Jehovah's purpose in doing this is revealed at Exodus 9:16: "For this cause I have kept you in existence, for the sake of showing you my power and in order to have my name declared in all the earth."

The Ten Plagues visited upon Egypt, climaxed by the destruction of Pharaoh and his military forces in the Red Sea, were an impressive demonstration of Jehovah's power. (Ex 7:14–12:30; Ps 78:43-51; 136:15) For years afterward the nations round about were still talking about it, and God's name was thus being declared throughout the earth. (Jos 2:10, 11; 1Sa 4:8) Had Jehovah killed Pharaoh immediately, this grand display of God's power to His glory and for the deliverance of His people would not have been possible.

The Scriptures give assurance that the time will come when wickedness will no longer exist, as all those who stand in opposition to the Creator will be destroyed when his permission of wickedness will have served its purpose.—2Pe 3:9-13; Re 18:20-24; 19:11–20:3, 7-10.

WIDOW. A woman who has lost her husband in death and has not remarried. Death of the husband severs the marriage bond, leaving the widow free to remarry if she chooses to do so. (Ru 1:8-13; Ro 7:2, 3; 1Co 7:8, 9) Under the patriarchal arrangement, and later under the Mosaic Law, the brother of a man who had died childless was to take his brother's widow as his wife and have a child by her, to carry on the line of her deceased husband.—Ge 38:8; De 25:5-10; Ru 4:3-10; see BROTHER-IN-LAW MARRIAGE.

Upon the death of their mate, widows could return to the house of their father. (Ge 38:11) In the Law, specific provision to this effect was made for the daughter of a priest who became widowed or was divorced. Since the priest received tithes for his household's sustenance, the daughter could share in this provision. This assured that she would not face poverty, and thus averted reproach that might otherwise have come upon the priesthood. (Le 22:13) For those widows who had no such support or protection, provisions were made in God's law for them to enjoy gleaner's rights in the fields, olive groves, and vineyards (De 24:19-21); to participate in the bounteous celebration each year at festivals (De 16:10-14); and, every third year, to share in the tithes that were contributed by the nation (De 14:28, 29; 26:12, 13).

Concern of Jehovah and Christ for Widows.

Jehovah spoke of himself as the One "executing judgment for the fatherless boy and the widow." (De 10:18) Strong injunctions are given in the Law as to the administration of full and equal justice to widows. (Ex 22:22-24; De 24:17) A curse was pronounced upon those perverting the judgment of widows (De 27:19), and proper treatment of widows was urged in the writings of the prophets.—Isa 1:17, 23; 10:1, 2; Jer 22:3; Eze 22:7; Zec 7:9, 10; Mal 3:5.

Jesus displayed his concern for the welfare of the widows in Israel when he condemned the scribes as "the ones devouring the houses of the widows."—Mr 12:38-40; Lu 20:46, 47.

Christian Assistance to Widows.

During the emergency that arose in the Christian congregation shortly after the day of Pentecost 33 C.E., the Greek-speaking widows were being overlooked in the daily distribution. When this was brought to the attention of the apostles, they considered the matter so important that they appointed "seven certified men . . . full of spirit and wisdom" to supervise the distribution of food with equity.—Ac 6:1-6.

The apostle Paul, at 1 Timothy 5:3-16, gave complete instructions for the loving care of widows in the Christian congregation. The congregation was to care for destitute widows. But if the widow had children or grandchildren, they should assume the responsibility of providing for her needs, or, as Paul instructed, "if any believing woman has widows [that is, widows related to her], let her relieve them, and let the congregation not be under the burden. Then it can relieve those who are actually widows [that is, actually bereaved, without help]." A widow put on the list for material help by the congregation was one "who has become not less than sixty years old," having a good record of morality, of faithful and loving devotion to Jehovah, and of hospitality and love toward others. On the other hand, the apostle recommends that young widows remarry, bear children, and manage a household, thereby avoiding a snare because of sexual impulses and the danger of being "unoccupied, . . . gossipers and meddlers in other people's affairs."

Jesus' half brother James highlighted the importance of looking after orphans and widows in their tribulation when, as a requisite for worship that is clean and undefiled from God's standpoint, he set it parallel with keeping oneself without spot from the world.—Jas 1:27.

Among the widows of notable faith are Tamar (Ge 38:6, 7), Naomi and Ruth (Ru 1:3-5), Abigail (1Sa 25:37, 38, 42), the widow of Zarephath (1Ki 17:8-24), and Anna the prophetess (Lu 2:36, 37; compare Luke's description of Anna with the qualifications of a worthy widow as outlined by Paul at 1Ti 5:3-16). Also, an unnamed widow was highly commended by Jesus because she contributed all of what she had to the temple.—Mr 12:41-44.

Figurative Use.

Cities, when cast off and desolated, are symbolically likened to widows. (La 1:1; compare Jer 51:5.) Babylon the Great, "the great city that has a kingdom over the kings of the earth," boasts, like her type, ancient Babylon, that she will never become a widow. Nevertheless, just as ancient Babylon did indeed become a "widow," so will modern Babylon the Great.—Isa 47:8, 9; Re 17:18; 18:7, 8.

WIFE. A married woman. In Hebrew, 'ish·shah' means "woman" (literally, a female man) or "wife"; the wife was referred to as one "owned by a husband." (Isa 62:4, ftn) In Greek, gy·ne' can mean "wife," or it can mean "woman," whether married or not. Jehovah God provided the first man Adam with a wife by taking a rib from him and building it into the woman. She thereby became bone of his bones and flesh of his flesh. She was the counterpart of Adam and was created as a helper for him. (Ge 2:18, 20-23) God dealt directly with Adam, and in turn, Adam passed on God's commandments to his wife. By reason of his prior creation and his being created in God's image, he had the priority as head and was the spokesman for God to her. His headship was to be exercised in love, and the woman as a helper was to cooperate in the procreative mandate issued to the pair.—Ge 1:28; see WOMAN.

After the sin, first of Eve, who instead of being a helper to her husband proved to be a temptress, and then of her husband Adam, who followed her in transgression, God pronounced judgment on the woman, saying: "I shall greatly increase the pain of your pregnancy; in birth pangs you will bring forth children, and your craving will be for your husband, and he will dominate you." (Ge 3:16) Since that time, among many peoples of the earth the woman has indeed been dominated, often in a very harsh way, by her husband, and instead of being a companion and helper, she has in many cases been treated more like a servant.

Among the Ancient Hebrews.

Among the ancient Hebrews the man was the head of the house and was his wife's owner (Hebrew, ba''al), and the woman was the one owned (be·u·lah'). Among servants of God the wife occupied a dignified and honorable place. Godly women of spirit and ability, while subject to their husbandly head, had much latitude and freedom of action and were happy in their place; they were blessed in being used by Jehovah God to perform special services for him. Examples among the many faithful wives of the Bible are Sarah, Rebekah, Deborah, Ruth, Esther, and Mary the mother of Jesus.

Wife protected under the Law. While the husband occupied the superior position in the marriage arrangement, God's requirements were that he was to provide for and care for the family in a material and spiritual way. Also, any wrongdoings of the family reflected on him; consequently he had a heavy responsibility. And while he had greater privileges than the wife, God's law protected the wife and gave her certain unique privileges, so that she was able to live a happy, productive life.

A few examples of the Law's provisions involving the wife were: Either husband or wife could be put to death for adultery. If the husband was suspicious of secret infidelity on the part of his wife, he could bring her to the priest, for Jehovah God to judge the matter, and if the woman was guilty, her reproductive organs would atrophy; on the other hand, if she was not guilty, the husband was required to make her pregnant, thereby publicly acknowledging her innocence. (Nu 5:12-31) A husband could divorce his wife if he found something indecent on her part. This would likely include such things as showing him gross disrespect or bringing reproach upon the household or that of his father. But the wife was protected by the requirement that he must write out for her a certificate of divorce. She was then free to marry another man. (De 24:1, 2) If the wife made a vow that her husband thought unwise or detrimental to the family's welfare, he could nullify it. (Nu 30:10-15) This, however, was a safeguard for the wife, keeping her from any hasty action that might bring her into difficulty.

Polygamy was allowed under the Mosaic Law but was regulated so that the wife was protected. The husband could not transfer the right of the firstborn from the son of a less-loved wife to the son of his favorite wife. (De 21:15-17) If an Israelite daughter was sold by her father as a servant and the master took her as a concubine, her owner could allow her to be redeemed if she did not please him, but he could not sell her to a foreign people. (Ex 21:7, 8) If either he or his son had taken her as a concubine and then married another wife, she was to be provided with food, clothing, and shelter, as well as the marriage due. —Ex 21:9-11.

If a husband maliciously charged his wife with having falsely claimed to be a virgin at the time of marriage and his charge was proved false, he was punished and had to pay her father twice the marriage rate for virgins and could never divorce her all his days. (De 22:13-19) If a man seduced an unengaged virgin, he was required to pay the marriage price to her father and, if the father permitted, to marry her, after which he could never divorce her all his days.—De 22:28, 29; Ex 22:16, 17.

While the position of the wife in Hebrew society was somewhat different from a wife's status in Western society today, the faithful Hebrew wife enjoyed her position and her work. She helped her husband, raised the family, managed the household, and found many things of satisfaction and delight, being able to express her womanly nature and talents to the full.

Description of a Good Wife. The happy state and activities of the faithful wife are described at Proverbs 31. She is said to be of more value to her husband than corals. He is able to put trust in her. She is industrious—weaving, making clothing for her family, attending to the buying of household needs, working in the vineyard, managing a household with the servants, aiding others who need help, clothing her family attractively, even bringing in some income by her handiwork, equipping her family against future emergencies, expressing herself in wisdom and loving-kindness, and, through fear of Jehovah and good works, receiving praise from her husband and from her sons, thereby honoring her husband and her family in the land. Truly he who has found a good wife has found a good thing and gets goodwill from Jehovah.—Pr 18:22.

In the Christian Congregation. The standard in the Christian congregation is that a husband should have only one living wife. (1Co 7:2; 1Ti 3:2) Wives are commanded to be in subjection to their husbands, whether these husbands are Christian believers or not. (Eph 5:22-24) Wives are not to withhold the marital due, for as with the husband, so with the wife, she does not "exercise authority over her own body." (1Co 7:3, 4) Wives are instructed to let their primary adornment be that of the secret person of the heart, producing the fruitage of the spirit, that perhaps through their conduct alone the unbelieving husband may be won over to Christianity.—1Pe 3:1-6.

Figurative Use. In a figurative sense Jehovah spoke of Israel as his wife by reason of his covenant with the nation. (Isa 54:6) The apostle

Paul speaks of Jehovah as the Father of spirit-begotten Christians, and he speaks of "the Jerusalem above" as their mother, as though Jehovah were married to her for the purpose of bringing forth spirit-begotten Christians. (Ga 4:6, 7, 26) The Christian congregation is spoken of as the bride, or wife, of Jesus Christ.—Eph 5:23, 25; Re 19:7; 21:2, 9.

WILD ASS.   See Ass.

WILD BULL.   See Bull.

WILDERNESS.   The Hebrew term for wilderness (*midh·bar'*) in general refers to a sparsely settled, uncultivated land. (Jer 2:2) It might include pasture grounds (Ps 65:12; Jer 23:10; Ex 3:1), cisterns (2Ch 26:10), houses, and even some cities (1Ki 2:34; Jos 15:61, 62; Isa 42:11). While often designating simply steppelands with brush and grass, *midh·bar'* may also apply to waterless regions that could be termed true deserts. Other Hebrew terms used to designate such areas more specifically are often found in poetic parallel with *midh·bar'*.—Ps 78:40; Jer 50:12.

The word *yeshi·mohn'* denotes a natural waste place or desert. (Ps 68:7; Isa 43:19, 20) It is apparently a stronger term than *midh·bar'*, indicating greater barrenness, as in the expression the "empty, howling desert [*yeshi·mon'*]." (De 32: 10) Used with the definite article, it refers to specific wilderness areas.—Nu 21:20; 1Sa 23:19, 24; see JESHIMON.

'*Ara·vah'* describes arid and sterile tracts, like those across the Jordan from Jericho. (Nu 22:1) Such desert plains could be the result of forest destruction and lack of proper conservation and cultivation, or they could be the result of prolonged drought, these conditions converting productive terrain into unfruitful wastelands. (Isa 33:9; Jer 51:43) With the definite article, the word also denotes a specific part of the Promised Land. (See ARABAH; ARABAH, TORRENT VALLEY OF.) Another term, *tsi·yah'*, describes any "waterless region" and is used in parallel with the previously mentioned words.—Ps 107:35; Isa 35:1.

Even those regions meriting the description "desert" in the Bible were rarely of the sandy type, as certain portions of the Sahara Desert are with their rolling sand dunes. Usually they were relatively treeless, arid or semiarid flatlands, rocky plateaus, or desolate waterless valleys hemmed in by high mountains and barren peaks. —Job 30:3-7; Jer 17:6; Eze 19:13.

The nation of Israel, making their Exodus from Egypt, were guided by God into the wilderness along the Red Sea, causing Pharaoh to assume that they had lost their bearings. (Ex 13:18-20; 14:1-3) On the other side of the Red Sea, and for the remainder of 40 years, Israel passed from one wilderness section to another, including the wilderness regions of Shur, Sin, Sinai, Paran, and Zin (Ex 15:22; 16:1; 19:1; Nu 10:12; 20:1), at times encamping at oases, such as at Elim, with its 12 springs and 70 palm trees (Ex 15:27), and at Kadesh.—Nu 13:26; De 2:14; MAP, Vol. 1, p. 541.

The Promised Land itself, forming part of the so-called Fertile Crescent, lay like a finger of well-cultivated land bounded on one side by the Mediterranean Sea and on two sides by vast wilderness regions—the Syro-Arabian Desert on the E and the Sinai Peninsula on the S. (Ex 23:31) Within the land's boundaries were smaller wilderness sections, for example, that by Dothan, just S of the Valley of Jezreel, where Joseph was cast into the waterpit by his brothers (Ge 37:17, 22); the Wilderness of Judah, with certain sections around the cities of Ziph, Maon, and En-gedi, wildernesses in which David sought refuge from Saul (Jg 1:16; 1Sa 23:14, 24; 24:1); and wilderness regions on the E side of the Jordan, merging with the Syro-Arabian Desert (Nu 21:13; De 1:1; 4:43). Much of the rift valley through which the Jordan River runs (today called The Ghor) is basically desert land.

While many of the wilderness regions mentioned in the Bible are today completely barren wastelands, there is evidence that some were not always so. Denis Baly, in *The Geography of the Bible* (1957, p. 91), says that "the nature of the vegetation pattern must have undergone very great changes since Biblical times." The original well-balanced conditions on which soil, climate, and vegetation formed a stable environment, with little soil erosion, were thrown out of balance by destruction of forests that were never replanted. With shade gone, and roots no longer holding the soil, the burning summer heat and slashing winter rains destroyed it. The earth was baked by the sun, swept by the wind, flaked by extreme temperature variations, and washed away by the rains. Archaeological investigation shows that many areas now completely barren once "included pasture lands, plains, and oases where springs and occasional rains plus careful water conservation made possible the building of villages and the maintaining of important caravan routes." (*The Interpreter's Dictionary of the Bible*, edited by G. Buttrick, 1962, Vol. 1, p. 828) Even today many of such wilderness areas are covered with a heavy green turf in the spring, though by the end of summer they have been burned bare by heat and drought.

Conditions in Wilderness of Wandering.

Although the conditions in some of the wilderness regions were quite possibly more favorable in the ancient past than at the present time, Moses could speak of Israel's trek through Sinai as "through the great and fear-inspiring wilderness, with poisonous serpents and scorpions and with thirsty ground that has no water." (De 1:19; 8:15; PICTURES, Vol. 1, p. 542) It was a "land of fevers" (Ho 13:5), a land of pit and deep shadow. (Jer 2:6) The more barren wilderness regions either were uninhabited (Job 38:26) or were places where tent dwellers resided and nomads roamed. (1Ch 5:9, 10; Jer 3:2) Here were brambles and thornbushes (Ge 21:14, 15; Ex 3:1, 2; Jg 8:7), thorny lotus trees, and thickets of prickly acacia trees. —Ex 25:10; Job 40:21, 22.

Weary travelers traversing the beaten paths (Jer 12:12) might seek shade under the thin, rodlike branches of a broom tree (1Ki 19:4, 5), or under a gloomy-looking dwarf juniper (Jer 48:6), or by the gnarled trunk of a tamarisk with its featherlike foliage of tiny evergreen leaves (Ge 21:33). High above, eagles and other birds of prey wheeled around in cloudless skies (De 32:10, 11), while horned vipers and arrow snakes slithered over rocks and under bushes, sand lizards scurried about, and big monitor lizards lumbered along on short, powerful legs. (Le 11:30; Ps 140:3; Isa 34:15) Mountain goats appeared on rocky crags (1Sa 24:2); wild asses, zebras, camels, and ostriches foraged on the sparse vegetation; and even pelicans and porcupines might be seen. (Job 24:5; 39:5, 6; Jer 2:24; La 4:3; Zep 2:13, 14) At night, the howling of jackals and wolves was joined by the hooting of owls or the whirring cry of the nightjar, adding to the feeling of wildness and isolation. (Isa 34:11-15; Jer 5:6) Those who slept in a wilderness region generally did so with little sense of security.—Compare Eze 34:25.

With the exception of scattered oases, the Sinai Peninsula is largely a region of sand, hard gravel, and rock. Meager vegetation grows in the wadis. Anciently there may have been a greater amount of rainfall and also more vegetation. However, without God's care, the Israelites, possibly numbering three million, could never have survived in this barren region. As Moses told them on the Plains of Moab: "Watch out for yourself that you may not forget Jehovah your God . . . who brought you out of the land of Egypt, out of the house of slaves; who caused you to walk through the great and fear-inspiring wilderness, with poisonous serpents and scorpions and with thirsty ground that has no water; who brought forth water for you out of the flinty rock; who fed you with manna in the wilderness, which your fathers had not known, in order to humble you and in order to put you to the test so as to do you good in your afterdays."—De 8:11-16.

Wilderness in the Greek Scriptures.

Here the Greek term e're·mos corresponds generally to the Hebrew midh·bar'. (Lu 15:4) It describes the wilderness setting of John the Baptizer's preaching (Mt 3:1) and the lonely places into which a certain demonized man was driven. (Lu 8:27-29) Jesus, after being baptized, fasted and was tempted by Satan in a wilderness region. (Mt 4:1; compare Le 16:20-22.) During his ministry, at times Jesus retired to the wilderness to pray. (Lu 5:16) He assured his disciples, however, that his presence with kingly power would not be limited to some lonely wilderness but would be made manifest everywhere. (Mt 24:26) The wilderness still had its own special dangers when the apostle Paul made his missionary journeys.—2Co 11:26; compare Ac 21:38.

Figurative Uses.

The wilderness regions to the E and SE of Palestine were also the source of fierce hot winds now called siroccos, from the Arabic word (sharquiyyeh) for "east wind." These winds blowing in from the desert have a tremendous parching effect, absorbing all the moisture in the air and often carrying with them fine, yellowish dust. (Jer 4:11) The siroccos occur principally in the spring and fall, and those in the spring can be very destructive to vegetation and crops. (Eze 17:10) Speaking of Ephraim, as the tribe representing the apostate northern kingdom of Israel, Jehovah foretold that though Ephraim "should show fruitfulness, an east wind . . . will come. From a wilderness it is coming up, and it will dry up his well and drain his spring. That one will pillage the treasure of all desirable articles." This devastating east wind out of the wilderness symbolized the attack on Israel by Assyria out of the E, plundering and carrying the Israelites captive.—Ho 13:12-16.

Wilderness regions themselves, characteristically thinly inhabited and manifesting a lack of human attention and cultivation, were often used to depict the destructive results of enemy invasion. Because of Judah's unfaithfulness, the armies of Babylon would make her 'holy cities a wilderness, Zion a sheer wilderness, Jerusalem a desolate waste' (Isa 64:10), her orchards and cultivated fields all taking on a wilderness appearance. (Jer 4:26; 9:10-12) Her princely rulers, who had been like majestic cedars of a forest, would be felled. (Jer 22:6, 7; compare Eze 17:1-4, 12, 13.) On the other hand, in retribution for their hatred and opposition to God's kingdom arrangement, the enemy nations, such as Babylon, Egypt, Edom, and others, were to undergo a similar experience. Particularly Babylon was singled out as due to become a "waterless wilderness and a desert plain," uninhabited, forgotten in her desolation.—Jer 50:12-16; Joe 3:19; Zep 2:9, 10.

By contrast, the restoration of Judah, after the 70-year exile, would be like converting a wilderness region into an Edenic garden, with fruitful orchards and productive fields watered by streams and rivers, and with reedy plants, leafy trees, and blossoming flowers, all making the land appear to rejoice.—Isa 35:1, 2; 51:3.

Individuals. Similar references to individuals show that such prophecies apply primarily in a spiritual, rather than a literal, way. Thus, the one trusting in men rather than in Jehovah is likened to a solitary tree in a desert plain, with no hope of seeing good. But the one trusting in Jehovah is like "a tree planted by the waters," fruitful, luxuriant, secure. (Jer 17:5-8) These contrasts also provide the basis for a mental picture of what constituted a wilderness region.

"Wilderness of the sea." The "wilderness [*midh·bar'*] of the sea" at Isaiah 21:1 has been understood by some commentators to be an expression referring to the southern part of ancient Babylonia. When the Euphrates and Tigris rivers annually overflowed their banks, this region became as a 'wilderness sea.'

In Revelation. In the book of Revelation, the wilderness is used in a dual sense: to represent solitude and refuge from attackers in the case of the symbolic woman who gives birth to the royal male child (Re 12:6, 14), and to represent the home of wild beasts in the case of the symbolic woman "Babylon the Great," who rides the sevenheaded wild beast.—Re 17:3-6, 12-14.

WILDERNESS OF JUDAH. See JUDAH, WILDERNESS OF.

WILD GOAT. See GOAT.

WILLOW [Heb., *tsaph·tsa·phah'*]. The name of this tree in Hebrew corresponds to the Arabic *safsaf*, which is applied to the willow tree. There are two types of willow growing in Israel; one is designated by the botanical term *Salix alba*, but the most common is the *Salix acmophylla*.

The Hebrew word occurs only once, at Ezekiel 17:5, where the symbolic "seed of the land," evidently referring to Zedekiah, is figuratively planted by the king of Babylon as "a willow by vast waters." The willow trees are found along the banks of rivers and shallow streams and in other moist places, where they sprout quickly from cuttings or slips and grow rapidly. They never attain the height of poplar trees but grow as shrubs or small trees and often form thickets along the watercourses. Their beauty is in their slender long leaves, hanging gracefully from the slender twigs and branches.

WIND. The Hebrew word *ru'ach*, often rendered "spirit," can also denote air in motion, wind. (Ec 1:6) Other Hebrew terms and expressions may be translated "storm wind" (Ho 8:7), "tempest," "whirling tempest" (Jer 25:32; 23:19), "tempestuous wind," and "windstorm" (Ps 148:8; 2Ki 2:11). Although at John 3:8 *pneu'ma* (generally translated "spirit") means "wind," the Greek term *a'ne·mos* is the more frequently used designation for wind. (Mt 7:25, 27; 11:7; Joh 6:18) "The breezy part [Heb., *ru'ach*] of the day" apparently referred to the evening hours just before sunset, when refreshing cool breezes commonly arise in the region where the garden of Eden is thought to have been.—Ge 3:8; see SPIRIT.

Jehovah God is the Creator of the wind. (Am 4:13) Though not literally in it (1Ki 19:11; compare Job 38:1; 40:6; Ps 104:3), God can control the wind and use it to serve his purposes, as when he employed it as an agent to cause the waters of the Flood to subside. (Ge 8:1; Ex 14:21; Nu 11:31; Ps 78:26; 107:25, 29; 135:7; 147:18; Jer 10:13; Jon 1:4) His Son, when on earth, likewise displayed power to control the winds, causing them to abate. (Mt 8:23, 27; 14:24-32; Mr 4:36-41; 6:48, 51; Lu 8:22-25) It was apparently only by Jehovah's allowance that Satan was able to produce or control "a great wind" that brought death to Job's children.—Job 1:11, 12, 18, 19.

Usually winds were named for the direction from which they came, the "east wind" blowing westward from the E. (Ex 10:13, 19; Ps 78:26; Ca 4:16) All four directions, N, S, E, and W, are embraced by references to "the four winds" of heaven or earth. (Jer 49:36; Eze 37:9; Da 8:8; Mt 24:31) At Revelation 7:1, "four angels" are depicted as "standing upon the four corners of the earth, holding tight the four winds of the earth." By standing at the "corners," the "angels" would let loose the winds obliquely from diagonal directions, sparing no quarter of the earth from the disastrous blowing of the winds.

North winds were cool and brought heavy rains. (Job 37:9; Pr 25:23) The S wind blew over hot desert areas into Palestine and, therefore, could produce a heat wave (Lu 12:55); storm winds might also originate in the S. (Isa 21:1; Zec

9:14) In the dry season, the E wind, in moving toward Egypt and Palestine, crossed vast desert areas and so was hot and dry, scorching or drying up vegetation. (Ge 41:6, 23, 27; Eze 17:7-10; compare Ho 13:15; Jon 4:8.) During the rainy season, W winds carried moisture into Palestine from the Mediterranean Sea and brought rain to the land. (1Ki 18:42-45) When observers there saw a cloud rising in the W, they could expect a storm. (Lu 12:54) In the dry summer, daily breezes from the Mediterranean made the weather more tolerable.—See CLOUD; EUROAQUILO.

Figurative Use. Winds can spring up quickly and just as quickly die down, thus appropriately representing the transitoriness of man's life. (Job 7:7) Having no solid substance, wind can denote vain knowledge and labor, empty words and hopes (Job 15:1, 2; 16:3; Ec 5:16; Ho 12:1), as well as nothingness. (Isa 26:18; 41:29; Jer 5:13) As vain works end up in futility, pursuing them is like "striving after wind." (Ec 1:14; 2:11) And the man who brings ostracism upon his house takes "possession of wind." He gains nothing that is worth while or has real substance.—Pr 11:29.

Winds scatter and toss objects about, and so being 'scattered to every wind' or 'divided toward the four winds' signifies complete dispersion or division. (Jer 49:36; Eze 5:10; 12:14; 17:21; Da 11:4) Like a vessel that is tossed about by the winds, with no set course, persons lacking Christian maturity are subject to being "carried hither and thither by every wind of teaching by means of the trickery of men, by means of cunning in contriving error."—Eph 4:13, 14.

WINDOW. See HOUSE.

WINE AND STRONG DRINK.
There are a number of original-language terms that usually designate some kind of wine (Heb., ti·rohsh' [Ge 27:28, 37; Ho 2:8, 9, 22]; Heb., che'mer [De 32:14; Isa 27:2] and its corresponding Aramaic term chamar' [Da 5:1, 2, 4, 23]; as well as Gr., gleu'kos [Ac 2:13]). But the Hebrew word ya'yin is found most frequently in the Scriptures. It first appears in Genesis 9:20-24, where the reference is to Noah's planting a vineyard after the Flood and then becoming intoxicated on the wine therefrom. The Greek word oi'nos (basically corresponding to the Hebrew term ya'yin) first occurs in Jesus' comments on the inadvisability of using old wineskins for new, partially fermented wine, as the pressure developed through fermentation would burst the old wineskins.—Mt 9:17; Mr 2:22; Lu 5:37, 38.

Various strong alcoholic liquors, apparently derived from pomegranates, dates, figs, and the like, were usually designated by the Hebrew term she·khar'. (Nu 28:7; De 14:26; Ps 69:12) The Hebrew word 'a·sis', at The Song of Solomon 8:2, refers to "the fresh juice" of pomegranates, but in other passages the context points to wine. (Isa 49:26; Joe 1:5) Beer may have been designated by the Hebrew word so've'.—Isa 1:22; Na 1:10.

Wine Making. In Palestine the grapes were gathered during August and September, depending on the type of grapes and the climate of the region. The vintage season was practically over by the time "the festival of booths" was celebrated in the early part of autumn. (De 16:13) After being picked, the grapes were placed in limestone vats, or troughs, where men usually crushed them barefoot, singing songs as they trod the winepress. (Isa 16:10; Jer 25:30; 48:33) With such comparatively gentle crushing methods, the stems and seeds were not broken down, so that little of the tannic acid in the skins was expressed; this, in turn, made for a high-quality wine, one that was smooth and soft on the palate. (Ca 7:9) Sometimes heavy stones were used instead of feet.—See PRESS.

The first "must," or fresh juice, that flows from the broken skins of the grapes, if kept separate from the greater volume of juice extracted under pressure, makes the richest and best wines. Fermentation begins within six hours after the crushing, while the juice is still in the vats, and slowly progresses for a period of several months. The alcohol content of the natural wines varies from 8 to 16 percent by volume, but this can be increased by adding alcoholic spirits later on. If grapes are low in sugar content, and fermentation continues too long, or if the wine is not properly protected from oxidizing, it turns to acetic acid, or vinegar.—Ru 2:14.

During the aging period the wine was kept in jars or skin bottles. (Jer 13:12) These containers were probably vented in such a way as to allow the carbon dioxide gas (a by-product in the conversion of the sugars to alcohol through fermentation) to escape without admitting oxygen from the air to contact and react with the wine. (Job 32:19) As the wines were left undisturbed they gradually clarified, the dregs falling to the bottom, with an improvement in the bouquet and flavor. (Lu 5:39) Thereafter wines were usually transferred to other vessels.—Isa 25:6; Jer 48:11; see DREGS.

Uses. From time immemorial wine has been used as a beverage at mealtimes. (Ge 27:25; Ec 9:7) Wine, bread, and other foods are often associated together. (1Sa 16:20; Ca 5:1; Isa 22:13;

55:1) Melchizedek set "bread and wine" before Abraham. (Ge 14:18-20) Jesus drank wine with his meals when it was available. (Mt 11:19; Lu 7:34) Wine was very much a part of banquets (Es 1:7; 5:6; 7:2, 7, 8), wedding feasts (Joh 2:2, 3, 9, 10; 4:46), and other festive occasions (1Ch 12:39, 40; Job 1:13, 18). The royal commissaries were stocked with wines (1Ch 27:27; 2Ch 11:11); it was the customary beverage of kings and governors. (Ne 2:1; 5:15, 18; Da 1:5, 8, 16) Travelers often included it in their provisions for a journey.—Jos 9:4, 13; Jg 19:19.

Its wide usage made wine a commodity of trade (Ne 13:15), "the wine of Helbon" (preferred by the kings of Persia) and "the wine of Lebanon" being particularly famous. (Eze 27:18; Ho 14:7) Wine was a medium of payment for workers employed in providing wood used in building the temple. (2Ch 2:8-10, 15) It was considered an excellent gift for one's superiors (1Sa 25:18; 2Sa 16:1, 2) and was included in the tithing contribution given for the support of the priests and Levites. (De 18:3, 4; 2Ch 31:4, 5; Ne 10:37, 39; 13:5, 12) And wine was among the choice things offered up to Jehovah in connection with sacrificial worship of him.—Ex 29:38, 40; Le 23:13; Nu 15:5, 7, 10; 28:14; 1Sa 1:24; 10:3; Ho 9:4.

Wine was not at first a part of the Passover meal but was added later, perhaps after the return from Babylonian exile. It was therefore on the table when Jesus celebrated the Passover the last time with his apostles and was conveniently used by him in instituting the Memorial of his death. The red "blood of grapes" was a fitting representation of Jesus' own sacrificial blood. On that occasion Jesus spoke of such wine as "this product of the vine," and since it was perhaps seven months after the grape harvest, there can be no question but that it was fermented juice of the vine.—Ge 49:11; Mt 26:18, 27-29.

As indicated by Jesus and reported by the physician Luke, wine had certain medicinal value as an antiseptic and mild disinfectant. (Lu 10:34) The Bible also recommends it as a curative remedy in cases of certain intestinal disturbances. Paul counseled Timothy: "Do not drink water any longer, but use a little wine for the sake of your stomach and your frequent cases of sickness." (1Ti 5:23) This was sound medical advice. As Dr. Salvatore P. Lucia, professor of medicine, University of California School of Medicine, writes: "Wine is the most ancient dietary beverage and the most important medicinal agent in continuous use throughout the history of mankind. . . . Actually, few other substances available to man have

been as widely recommended for their curative powers as have wines."—*Wine as Food and Medicine,* 1954, p. 5; see DISEASES AND TREATMENT.

Contrary to the erroneous opinions of some, alcoholic liquors are not mental stimulants but are in reality sedatives and depressants of the central nervous system. "Give intoxicating liquor, you people, to the one about to perish and wine to those who are bitter of soul," not as a mental stimulant to make such ones more conscious of their misery, but, rather, as the proverb says, that they may 'forget their troubles.' (Pr 31:6, 7) There was an ancient custom among the Romans of giving criminals drugged wine to blunt the pain of execution. Perhaps this is why Roman soldiers offered Jesus drugged wine when impaling him.—Mr 15:23.

It is apparent that wine is one of the gifts included among Jehovah's blessings to mankind. Wine "makes the heart of mortal man rejoice"; it puts the heart in "a merry mood." (Ps 104:15; Es 1:10; 2Sa 13:28; Ec 2:3; 10:19; Zec 10:7) Hence, Daniel when in mourning drank no wine. (Da 10:2, 3) An abundant supply of wine, symbolized by the "vine" in the oft-repeated expression 'sitting under one's own vine and fig tree,' denotes prosperity and security under Jehovah's righteous rule. (1Ki 4:25; 2Ki 18:31; Isa 36:16; Mic 4:4; Zec 3:10) Wine is also included in the restoration blessings promised by Jehovah.—Joe 3:18; Am 9:13, 14; Zec 9:17.

Temperate Use. Moderation in all things is a Bible principle. Even honey is no exception—in moderation it is good; used to excess, it is injurious. (Pr 25:27) So also with Jehovah's gifts of wine and strong drink, they must be used as he directs. Overindulgence and disregard for Bible principles in the use of these provisions brings Jehovah's disapproval and leads to debauchery and death. The Bible is very emphatic on this matter, both in its precepts and its examples.—Pr 23:29-31; see DRUNKENNESS.

There may be cases where drinking alcohol, even in small quantities, would be ill-advised and detrimental to one's health. On other occasions one may refrain from drinking intoxicating liquor to avoid stumbling others and out of love and consideration for others.—Ro 14:21.

Jehovah forbade the priests and Levites, when on duty at the tabernacle or temple, to drink alcohol in any form, under penalty of death. (Le 10:8, 9; Eze 44:21) Off duty they were free to drink in moderation. (1Ch 9:29) So too it was a divine regulation that a Nazirite was not to drink any alcoholic beverage while under this special vow. (Nu 6:2-4, 13-20; Am 2:12) Because Samson was to be a Nazirite from birth, his mother was not allowed to touch wine or liquor during her pregnancy. (Jg 13:4, 5, 7, 14) When officiating, "it is not for kings to drink wine or for high officials to say: 'Where is intoxicating liquor?'" lest they "forget what is decreed and pervert the cause of any of the sons of affliction." (Pr 31:4, 5) Overseers in the Christian congregation should not be 'drunken brawlers,' and ministerial servants "should likewise be serious, . . . not giving themselves to a lot of wine."—1Ti 3:3, 8.

Pictorial. Ancient Babylon, when acting as Jehovah's executioner, made all the nations 'drunk on wine,' symbolic of Jehovah's wrath against the nations. (Jer 51:7) Also, in other texts, opponents of Jehovah are depicted as being forced to drink of God's righteous indignation, likened to "wine [that] is foaming," "the wine of rage," "the wine of the anger of God." (Ps 75:8; Jer 25:15; Re 14:10; 16:19) A bitter potion that has no relationship to divine anger is "the wine of her [spiritual] fornication" that "Babylon the Great" makes all the nations drink.—Re 14:8; 17:2; 18:3, 13.

WINEPRESS. See PRESS.

WINESKINS.

The Greek word *a·skos'* designates a bag or bottle made of a whole animal skin. Jesus Christ said: "Neither do people put new wine into old wineskins [skin bags, *Int*]; but if they do, then the wineskins burst and the wine spills out and the wineskins are ruined. But people put new wine into new wineskins, and both things are preserved." (Mt 9:17; Mr 2:22; Lu 5:37, 38) As new wine ferments, it generates carbon dioxide gas that exerts pressure on the skin bottles. New skins expand; old, inflexible ones burst under the pressure.

This illustration was part of Jesus' answer as to why his disciples did not conform to all the old customs and practices of the Pharisees. Jesus evidently implied that the truth of Christianity was too powerful and energetic to be retained by the old system of Judaism, which lacked vitality and elasticity and which was fast passing away. (Mt 9:14-16) For a general discussion of skin bottles and their uses, see BOTTLE.

WINNOWING.

The final step in separating cereal grains such as barley and wheat from their chaff and straw. After threshing has broken the grain kernels loose from the chaff, and the straw has been cut into small pieces, the whole mixture is winnowed by tossing it into the air against the wind with a winnowing shovel or fork. (Isa 30:24) The breeze, especially strong in the evening, blows the chaff away, carries the straw off to the side, and lets the heavy kernels fall back onto the threshing floor. (Ru 3:2; PICTURE, Vol. 2, p. 953) After the grain is passed through a sieve to remove pebbles and the like, it is ready for grinding or storage.—Am 9:9; Lu 22:31.

Figurative Use. Often 'winnowing' is used in a figurative sense. For example, Jehovah purposed to send "winnowers" against Babylon and her inhabitants so that these might winnow her. (Jer 51:1, 2) The "winnowers" proved to be the Medes and the Persians under Cyrus. In effect, they tossed Babylon and her inhabitants into the air, that the wind might catch them and blow them away like chaff to be burned. (Mt 3:12; Lu 3:17) Similarly, as foretold, Jehovah had earlier used Babylon to winnow his people, scattering them in defeat. (Jer 15:7) And, through the prophet Isaiah, Jehovah gave the assurance to his people that the time would come when they would reduce their enemies to chaff and winnow them. (Isa 41:14-16) At Jeremiah 4:11 "a searing wind" to come against Jerusalem is said to be "not for winnowing, nor for cleansing." A tempestuous, searing wind would not be suitable for winnowing, so this points to its destructive nature.

WISDOM.

The Biblical sense of wisdom lays emphasis on sound judgment, based on knowledge and understanding; the ability to use knowledge and understanding successfully to solve problems, avoid or avert dangers, attain certain goals, or counsel others in doing so. It is the opposite of foolishness, stupidity, and madness, with which it is often contrasted.—De 32:6; Pr 11:29; Ec 6:8.

The basic terms signifying wisdom are the Hebrew *chokh·mah'* (verb, *cha·kham'*) and the Greek *so·phi'a*, with their related forms. Also, there are the Hebrew *tu·shi·yah'*, which may be rendered "effectual working" or "practical wisdom," and the Greek *phro'ni·mos* and *phro·ne·sis* (from *phren*, the "mind"), relating to "sensibleness," "discretion," or "practical wisdom."

Wisdom implies a *breadth* of knowledge and a *depth* of understanding, these giving the soundness and clarity of judgment characteristic of wisdom. The wise man 'treasures up knowledge,' has a fund of it to draw upon. (Pr 10:14) While "wisdom is the prime thing," the counsel is that "with all that you acquire, acquire understanding." (Pr 4:5-7) Understanding (a broad term that frequently embraces discernment) adds strength to wisdom, contributing greatly to discretion and foresight, also notable characteristics of wisdom.

Discretion implies prudence and may be expressed in caution, self-control, moderation, or restraint. The "discreet [form of *phro'ni·mos*] man" builds his house on a rock-mass, foreseeing the possibility of storm; the foolish man builds his on sand and suffers disaster.—Mt 7:24-27.

Understanding fortifies wisdom in other ways. For example, a person may obey a certain command of God because he recognizes the rightness of such obedience, and this is wisdom on his part. But if he gets real understanding of the *reason* for that command, the good purpose it serves, and the benefits accruing from it, his heart determination to continue in that wise course is greatly strengthened. (Pr 14:33) Proverbs 21:11 says that "by one's giving insight to a wise person he gets knowledge." The wise person is happy to get any information that will grant him a clearer view into the underlying circumstances, conditions, and causes of problems. Thereby he "gets knowledge" as to what to do regarding the matter and knows what conclusions to draw, what is needed to solve the existing problem.—Compare Pr 9:9; Ec 7:25; 8:1; Eze 28:3; see INSIGHT.

Divine Wisdom. Wisdom in the absolute sense is found in Jehovah God, who is "wise alone" in this sense. (Ro 16:27; Re 7:12) Knowledge is acquaintance with fact, and since Jehovah is the Creator, who is "from time indefinite to time indefinite" (Ps 90:1, 2), he knows all there is to know about the universe, its composition and contents, its history till now. The physical laws, cycles, and standards upon which men rely in their research and invention, and without which they would be helpless and have nothing stable upon which to build, are all of His making. (Job 38:34-38; Ps 104:24; Pr 3:19; Jer 10:12, 13) Logically, his moral standards are even more vital for stability, sound judgment, and successful human living. (De 32:4-6; see JEHOVAH [A God of moral standards].) There is nothing beyond his understanding. (Isa 40:13, 14) Though he may allow things that are contrary to his righteous standards to develop and even temporarily prosper, the future ultimately rests with him and will conform precisely to his will, and the things spoken by him "will have certain success."—Isa 55:8-11; 46:9-11.

For all these reasons it is evident that "the fear of Jehovah is the start of wisdom." (Pr 9:10) "Who should not fear you, O King of the nations, for to you it is fitting; because among all the wise ones of the nations and among all their kingships there is in no way anyone like you." (Jer 10:7) "He is wise in heart and strong in power. Who can show

stubbornness to him and come off uninjured?" (Job 9:4; Pr 14:16) In his mightiness he can intervene at will in human affairs, maneuvering rulers or eliminating them, making his prophetic revelations prove infallible. (Da 2:20-23) Biblical history recounts the futile efforts of powerful kings with their astute counselors to pit their wisdom against God, and it highlights the way he has triumphantly vindicated his servants who loyally proclaimed his message.—Isa 31:2; 44:25-28; compare Job 12:12, 13.

"God's wisdom in a sacred secret." The rebellion that broke out in Eden presented a challenge to God's wisdom. His wise means for ending that rebellion—wiping out its effects and restoring peace, harmony, and right order in his universal family—formed "a sacred secret, the hidden wisdom, which God foreordained before the systems of things," that is, those systems that have developed during man's history outside Eden. (1Co 2:7) Its outlines were contained in God's dealings with, and promises to, his faithful servants during many centuries; it was foreshadowed and symbolized in the Law covenant with Israel, including its priesthood and sacrifices, and was pointed to in innumerable prophecies and visions.

Finally, after more than 4,000 years, the wisdom of that sacred secret was revealed in Jesus Christ (Col 1:26-28), through whom God purposed "an administration at the full limit of the appointed times, namely, to gather all things together again in the Christ, the things in the heavens and the things on the earth." (Eph 1:8-11) God's provision of the ransom for the salvation of obedient mankind and his purpose for a Kingdom government, headed by his Son and able to end all wickedness, were revealed. Since God's grand purpose is founded on and centered in his Son, Christ Jesus "has become to us [Christians] wisdom from God." (1Co 1:30) "Carefully concealed in him are all the treasures of wisdom and of knowledge." (Col 2:3) Only through him and by faith in him, God's "Chief Agent of life," can salvation and life be attained. (Ac 3:15; Joh 14:6; 2Ti 3:15) There is, therefore, no true wisdom that fails to consider Jesus Christ, that does not base its judgment and decisions solidly on God's purpose as revealed in him.—See JESUS CHRIST (His Vital Place in God's Purpose).

Human Wisdom. Wisdom is personalized in the book of Proverbs, depicted there as a woman inviting persons to receive what she has to offer. These accounts and related texts show that wisdom is indeed a blend of many things: knowledge, understanding (which includes discernment), thinking ability, experience, diligence, shrewdness (the opposite of being gullible or naive [Pr 14:15, 18]), and right judgment. But since true wisdom begins with the fear of Jehovah God (Ps 111:10; Pr 9:10), this superior wisdom goes beyond ordinary wisdom and includes holding to high standards, manifesting righteousness and uprightness, as well as adhering to truth. (Pr 1:2, 3, 20-22; 2:2-11; 6:6; 8:1, 5-12) Not all wisdom measures up to that superior wisdom.

Human wisdom is never absolute but is relative. Wisdom on a limited scale is attainable by man through his own efforts, though he must in any case use the intelligence with which God (who even gave the animals certain instinctive wisdom [Job 35:11; Pr 30:24-28]) initially endowed man. Man learns from observation of, and working with, the materials of God's creation. Such wisdom may vary in type and extent. The Greek word so·phi′a is often applied to skill in a certain trade or craft, to skill and sound administrative judgment in governmental and business fields, or to extensive knowledge in some particular field of human science or research. Similarly, the Hebrew chokh·mah′ and cha·kham′ are used to describe the 'skillfulness' of sailors and ship caulkers (Eze 27:8, 9; compare Ps 107:23, 27) and of workers in stone and wood (1Ch 22:15), as well as the wisdom and skill of other craftsmen, some having great talent in a wide variety of crafts. (1Ki 7:14; 2Ch 2:7, 13, 14) Even the skilled image carver or idol maker is described by such terms. (Isa 40:20; Jer 10:3-9) The shrewd practice of the business world is a form of wisdom.—Eze 28:4, 5.

All such wisdom may be had even though the possessors lack the spiritual wisdom the Scriptures particularly advocate. Nevertheless, God's spirit may enhance some of these types of wisdom where they are useful in accomplishing his purpose. His spirit activated those constructing the tabernacle and its equipment as well as those weaving the priestly garments, men and women, filling them with both 'wisdom and understanding.' Thereby they not only understood what was desired and the means for accomplishing the work but also displayed the talent, artistry, vision, and judgment necessary to design and produce superb work.—Ex 28:3; 31:3-6; 35:10, 25, 26, 31, 35; 36:1, 2, 4, 8.

Ancient wise men. Men noted for their wisdom and counsel were anciently prized by kings and others, even as in modern times. Egypt, Persia, Chaldea, Edom, and other nations had their bodies of "wise men." (Ex 7:11; Es 1:13; Jer 10:7;

50:35; Ob 8) Such bodies evidently included the priests and government officials but were not restricted to such; they probably included all those 'elders' of the nations who were particularly known for their wisdom and who resided near the capital so as to be available for counseling. (Compare Ge 41:8; Ps 105:17-22; Isa 19:11, 12; Jer 51:57.) The monarchs of Persia had a privy council of seven wise men for quick consultation (Es 1:13-15), and lesser Persian officials might have their own staff of wise men.—Es 6:13.

Joseph, by the help of God's spirit, displayed such discretion and wisdom that Egypt's ruling Pharaoh made him his prime minister. (Ge 41:38-41; Ac 7:9, 10) "Moses was instructed in all the wisdom of the Egyptians" and was "powerful in his words and deeds" even prior to God's making him his spokesman. But this human wisdom and ability did not qualify Moses for God's purpose. After his first attempt (at the age of about 40) to bring relief to his Israelite brothers, Moses had to wait another 40 years before God sent him forth, a spiritually wise man, to lead Israel out of Egypt.—Ac 7:22-36; compare De 34:9.

Solomon was already wise before entering into full kingship (1Ki 2:1, 6, 9), yet he humbly acknowledged himself "but a little boy" in prayer to Jehovah and sought his aid in judging God's people. He was rewarded with "a wise and understanding heart" unequaled among Judah's kings. (1Ki 3:7-12) His wisdom surpassed the famed wisdom of the Orientals and of Egypt, making Jerusalem a place to which monarchs or their representatives traveled to learn from the Judean king. (1Ki 4:29-34; 10:1-9, 23-25) Certain women of ancient times were also noted for their wisdom. —2Sa 14:1-20; 20:16-22; compare Jg 5:28, 29.

Not always used for good. Human wisdom can be used for good or for bad. In the latter case it definitely betrays itself as wisdom that is only fleshly, not spiritual, not from God. Jehonadab was "a very wise man," but his counsel to David's son Amnon was based on shrewd strategy and manipulation of people by deceit, bringing dubious success and disastrous consequences. (2Sa 13:1-31) Absalom cunningly campaigned to unseat his royal father David (2Sa 14:28-33; 15:1-6) and, upon occupying Jerusalem, solicited the advice of two of his father's counselors, Ahithophel and Hushai, concerning what further steps he might shrewdly take. Ahithophel's wise advice was consistently of such accuracy that it appeared as if it came from God. Nevertheless, he had become a traitor to God's anointed, and Jehovah caused his wise battle plan to be rejected in favor of faithful Hushai's plan, which skillfully played on Absalom's vanity and human weaknesses to bring about his downfall. (2Sa 16:15-23; 17:1-14) As Paul wrote of God: "'He catches the wise in their own cunning.' And again: 'Jehovah knows that the reasonings of the wise men are futile.'"—1Co 3:19, 20; compare Ex 1:9, 10, 20, 21; Lu 20:19-26.

Apostate priests, prophets, and wise men of the Israelite nation in time led the people to oppose God's counsel and commands as spoken by his loyal servants. (Jer 18:18) As a result, Jehovah caused 'the wisdom of their wise men to perish and the understanding of their discreet men to conceal itself' (Isa 29:13, 14; Jer 8:8, 9), bringing the 500-year-old kingdom to ruin (as he later did to Jerusalem's proud destroyer, Babylon, and to the boastful dynasty of Tyre). (Isa 47:10-15; Eze 28:2-17) They rejected spiritual wisdom in favor of fleshly wisdom.

The vanity of much of human wisdom. Investigating "the calamitous occupation" that sin and imperfection have brought mankind, King Solomon weighed the value of the wisdom that men in general develop and attain and found it to be "a striving after wind." The disorder, perversion, and deficiencies in imperfect human society were so far beyond man's ability to straighten out or compensate for, that those 'getting an abundance of wisdom' experienced increased frustration and irritation, evidently because they became acutely conscious of how little they could personally do to improve matters.—Ec 1:13-18; 7:29; compare Ro 8:19-22, where the apostle shows God's provision for ending mankind's enslavement to corruption and subjection to futility.

Solomon also found that while such human wisdom produced varied pleasures and proficiency that brought material wealth, it could not bring true happiness or lasting satisfaction. The wise man dies along with the stupid, not knowing what will become of his possessions, and his human wisdom ceases in the grave. (Ec 2:3-11, 16, 18-21; 4:4; 9:10; compare Ps 49:10.) Even in life, "time and unforeseen occurrence" might bring sudden calamity, leaving the wise without even such basic needs as food. (Ec 9:11, 12) By his own wisdom man could never find out "the work of the true God," never gain solid knowledge of how to solve man's highest problems.—Ec 8:16, 17; compare Job chap 28.

Solomon does not say human wisdom is utterly without value. Compared with mere foolishness, which he also investigated, the advantage of wisdom over folly is like that of 'light over darkness.' For the wise man's eyes "are in his head," serving his intellectual powers, whereas the stupid man's eyes do not see with thoughtful discernment. (Ec 2:12-14; compare Pr 17:24; Mt 6:22, 23.) Wisdom is a protection of greater value than money. (Ec 7:11, 12) But Solomon showed that its worth is all relative, entirely dependent on its conformity to God's wisdom and purpose. (Ec 2:24; 3:11-15, 17; 8:12, 13; 9:1) A person can be excessive in striving to manifest wisdom, pushing himself beyond the limits of his imperfect ability in a self-destructive course. (Ec 7:16; compare 12:12.) But by obediently serving his Creator and being content with food, drink, and the good that his hard work brings him, God will give him the needed "wisdom and knowledge and rejoicing."—Ec 2:24-26; 12:13.

Contrasted with God's sacred secret. The world of mankind has developed a fund of wisdom over the centuries—much of it is taught through its schools and by other means of instruction, while some is acquired by individuals through personal association with others or by experience. For the Christian there is need to know the right attitude to adopt toward such wisdom. In an illustration of an unrighteous steward who manipulated his master's accounts with certain creditors so as to gain a secure future, Jesus described the steward as 'acting with practical wisdom [phro·ni'mos, "discreetly"].' This shrewd foresight, however, was the practical wisdom of "the sons of this system of things," not that of "the sons of the light." (Lu 16:1-8, Int) Earlier, Jesus praised his heavenly Father for hiding certain truths from the "wise and intellectual ones" while revealing them to his disciples, who were by comparison like "babes." (Lu 10:21-24) The scribes and Pharisees, educated at rabbinic schools, were among such wise and intellectual ones.—Compare Mt 13:54-57; Joh 7:15.

In that first century, the Greeks were especially renowned for their culture and accumulated knowledge, their schools and philosophic groups. Probably for that reason Paul paralleled 'Greeks and Barbarians' with 'wise and senseless ones.' (Ro 1:14) Paul strongly emphasized to the Christians at Corinth, Greece, that Christianity is not reliant on nor characterized by "the wisdom [so·phi'an] of the world," that is, the world of mankind alienated from God. (1Co 1:20; see WORLD [The world alienated from God].) Not that among the multiple facets of the world's wisdom there was nothing useful or beneficial, for Paul sometimes made use of skill learned in the tentmaking trade and also quoted on occasion from literary works of worldly authors to illustrate certain points of truth. (Ac 18:2, 3; 17:28, 29; Tit 1:12) But the overall outlook, methods, standards, and goals of the world—its philosophy—were not in harmony with the truth, were contrary to 'God's wisdom in the sacred secret.'

So the world in its wisdom rejected God's provision through Christ as foolishness; its rulers, though they may have been able and judicious administrators, even "impaled the glorious Lord." (1Co 1:18; 2:7, 8) But God, in turn, was now proving the wisdom of the worldly wise to be foolishness, putting their wise men to shame by using what they considered "a foolish thing of God," as well as persons they deemed 'foolish, weak, and ignoble,' to accomplish His invincible purpose. (1Co 1:19-28) Paul reminded the Corinthian Christians that "the wisdom of this system of things [and] that of the rulers of this system of things" would come to nothing; hence such wisdom was not part of the apostle's spiritual message. (1Co 2:6, 13) He warned Christians in Colossae against being ensnared by "the philosophy [phi·lo·so·phi'as, literally, love of wisdom] and empty deception according to the tradition of men."—Col 2:8; compare vss 20-23.

Despite its temporary benefits and successes, the world's wisdom was doomed to produce failure. But the Christian congregation of God's anointed had spiritual wisdom that led to "the unfathomable riches of the Christ." Since that congregation formed part of God's sacred secret, by his dealings with it and his purposes fulfilled in it, he made known or revealed "the greatly diversified wisdom of God" through the congregation, even to "the governments and the authorities in the heavenly places." (Eph 3:8-11; 1:17, 18; compare 1Pe 1:12.) Its members, having "the mind of Christ" (compare Php 2:5-8), had knowledge and understanding vastly superior to that of the world, hence they could speak, "not with words taught by human wisdom, but with those taught by the spirit," with "a mouth and wisdom" opposers could not refute, though such Christians might be looked down upon as "unlettered and ordinary" by worldly standards.—1Co 2:11-16; Lu 21:15; Ac 4:13; 6:9, 10.

Waging spiritual warfare. The apostle Paul relied on godly wisdom in waging spiritual warfare against any who threatened to pervert Christian congregations, such as the one in Corinth. (1Co 5:6, 7, 13; 2Co 10:3-6; compare 2Co 6:7.) He knew that "wisdom is better than implements for fighting, and merely one sinner can destroy much good." (Ec 9:18; 7:19) His reference to "overturning strongly entrenched things" (2Co 10:4) corre-

sponds in idea to the Greek *Septuagint* rendering of part of Proverbs 21:22. Paul knew the human tendency to give prime attention to those having impressive manner, obvious talent, or powerful personality and speech; he knew that the 'quiet speech of a wise man of little material wealth' is often ignored in favor of those giving greater appearance of mightiness. (Compare Ec 9:13-17.) Even Jesus, who did not have the earthly wealth and position Solomon possessed but who had vastly superior wisdom, was shown little respect and attention by the rulers and people.—Compare Mt 12:42; 13:54-58; Isa 52:13-15; 53:1-3.

To some who boasted in fleshly abilities (contrast Jer 9:23, 24) rather than in the heart, Paul's personal appearance was viewed as "weak and his speech contemptible." (2Co 5:12; 10:10) Yet he avoided any extravagance of speech or display of human wisdom and its power to persuade, so that his hearers' faith would be built up through God's spirit and power and be founded on Christ rather than on "men's wisdom." (1Co 1:17; 2:1-5; 2Co 5:12) With spiritual foresight, Paul was "a wise director of works," not of material construction but of spiritual construction, working with God to produce disciples that manifested truly Christian qualities.—1Co 3:9-16.

Hence, no matter how much of the world's wisdom one might have by virtue of skill in trades, shrewdness in commerce, administrative ability, or scientific or philosophic learning, the rule was: "If anyone among you thinks he is wise in this system of things, let him become a fool, that he may become wise." (1Co 3:18) He should be proud only of 'having insight and knowledge of Jehovah, the One exercising loving-kindness, justice, and righteousness in the earth,' for in this Jehovah takes delight.—Jer 9:23, 24; 1Co 1:31; 3:19-23.

Wise administration. As wisdom personified states: "I have counsel and practical wisdom. I—understanding; I have mightiness. By me kings themselves keep reigning, and high officials themselves keep decreeing righteousness. By me princes themselves keep ruling as princes, and nobles are all judging in righteousness. Those loving me I myself love, and those looking for me are the ones that find me." (Pr 8:12, 14-17) The Messianic King displays such superior wisdom from God. (Isa 11:1-5; compare Re 5:12.) This surpasses the ability men may have or develop naturally, making one wise in the principles of God's law and, with the aid of his spirit, making it possible to render judicial decisions that are right and free from partiality. (Ezr 7:25; 1Ki 3:28; Pr

24:23; compare De 16:18, 19; Jas 2:1-9.) Such wisdom is not apathetic toward wickedness but wars against it.—Pr 20:26.

Men selected for responsibility within the Christian congregation qualified, not on the basis of worldly success, fleshly wisdom, or natural abilities, but because of being "full of spirit and [godly] wisdom." (Ac 6:1-5; compare 1Ti 3:1-13; Tit 1:5-9.) Such ones were among the "prophets and wise men and public instructors" Jesus had promised to send out, and they could also serve as judges and counselors within the congregation, even as fleshly Israel had had its wise men who served in similar ways. (Mt 23:34; 1Co 6:5) They recognized the value of consulting together.—Pr 13:10; 24:5, 6; compare Ac 15:1-22.

Acquiring True Wisdom. The proverb counsels: "Buy truth itself and do not sell it—wisdom and discipline and understanding." (Pr 23:23) Jehovah, the Source of true wisdom, grants it generously to those who sincerely seek it and ask for it in faith, showing a wholesome, reverential fear of him. (Pr 2:1-7; Jas 1:5-8) But the seeker must spend time in study of God's Word; learn His commands, laws, reminders, and counsel; consider the history of God's acts and doings; then apply these in his life. (De 4:5, 6; Ps 19:7; 107:43; 119:98-101; Pr 10:8; compare 2Ti 3:15-17.) He wisely buys out the opportune time, not acting unreasonably in a wicked time, but "perceiving what the will of Jehovah is." (Eph 5:15-20; Col 4:5, 6) He must develop firm faith and unshakable conviction that God's power is invincible, that His will is certain of success, and that His ability and promise to reward faithfulness are sure.—Heb 11:1, 6; 1Co 15:13, 14, 19.

Only in this way can the person make right decisions as to his life course and not be swayed by fear, greed, immoral desire, and other damaging emotions. (Pr 2:6-16; 3:21-26; Isa 33:2, 6) As wisdom personified says: "Happy is the man that is listening to me by keeping awake at my doors day by day, by watching at the posts of my entrances. For the one finding me will certainly find life, and gets goodwill from Jehovah. But the one missing me is doing violence to his soul; all those intensely hating me are the ones that do love death."—Pr 8:34-36; 13:14; 24:13, 14.

Wisdom and the heart. Intelligence is obviously a major factor in wisdom, yet the heart, which relates not just to thinking but to motivation and affection as well, is clearly a more important factor in gaining true wisdom. (Ps 49:3, 4; Pr 14:33; see HEART.) God's servant wants to get "sheer wisdom" in his "secret self," have wise

motivation in planning his life course. (Compare Ps 51:6, 10; 90:12.) "The heart of the wise is at his right hand [that is, ready to help and protect him at critical moments (compare Ps 16:8; 109:31)], but the heart of the stupid [is] at his left hand [failing to direct him in the course of wisdom]." (Ec 10:2, 3; compare Pr 17:16; Ro 1:21, 22.) The truly wise person has trained and disciplined his heart in the way of wisdom (Pr 23:15, 16, 19; 28:26); it is as though he had written righteous commandments and law 'upon the tablet of his heart.'—Pr 7:1-3; 2:2, 10.

Experience and right association. Experience contributes measurably to wisdom. Even Jesus grew in wisdom as he passed through childhood. (Lu 2:52) Moses assigned as chieftains men who were "wise and discreet and *experienced.*" (De 1:13-15) While one learns a measure of wisdom from suffering punishment or by observing others receive it (Pr 21:11), a superior and time-saving way to wisdom is profiting by and learning from the experience of those already wise, preferring their company to that of "inexperienced ones." (Pr 9:1-6; 13:20; 22:17, 18; compare 2Ch 9:7.) Older persons are more likely to have such wisdom, particularly those who give evidence of having God's spirit. (Job 32:7-9) This was illustrated notably at the time of Rehoboam's kingship. (1Ki 12:5-16) However, "better is a needy but wise child [relatively speaking] than an old but stupid king, who has not come to know enough to be warned any longer."—Ec 4:13-15.

The city gates (often having adjacent public squares) were places where older men gave wise counsel and judicial decisions. (Compare Pr 1:20, 21; 8:1-3.) The voice of foolish persons usually was not heard in such an atmosphere (either in soliciting wisdom or offering it), their chatter being elsewhere. (Pr 24:7) Though association with wise ones brings discipline and occasional rebuke, this is far better than the song and laughter of the stupid. (Ec 7:5, 6) The person who isolates himself, pursuing his own narrow, restricted view of life and his own selfish desires, eventually goes off on a tangent contrary to all practical wisdom.—Pr 18:1.

Revealed in personal conduct and speech. Proverbs 11:2 states that "wisdom is with the modest ones"; James speaks of the "mildness that belongs to wisdom." (Jas 3:13) If jealousy, contention, bragging, or stubbornness is present in a person, it indicates that he is lacking true wisdom and is being guided, rather, by wisdom that is "earthly, animal, demonic." True wisdom is "peaceable, reasonable, ready to obey." (Jas 3:

13-18) "The rod of haughtiness is in the mouth of the foolish one, but the very lips of the wise ones will guard them." They wisely hold back from presumptuous, harsh, or rash speech. (Pr 14:3; 17:27, 28; Ec 10:12-14) From the tongue and lips of the wise comes well-thought-out, healing, pleasant, beneficial speech (Pr 12:18; 16:21; Ec 12:9-11; Col 3:15, 16), and instead of stirring up trouble, they seek to bring calm and to 'win souls' by wise persuasion.—Pr 11:30; 15:1-7; 16:21-23; 29:8.

Those who become 'wise in their own eyes,' elevating themselves above others (even above God), are worse off than the person who is stupid but does not pretend to be otherwise. (Pr 26:5, 12; 12:15) Such self-assuming persons are too proud to accept correction. (Pr 3:7; 15:12; Isa 5:20, 21) Paradoxically, both the lazy man and the man who gains riches tend toward this attitude. (Pr 26:16; 28:11; compare 1Ti 6:17.) But "an earring of gold, and an ornament of special gold, is a wise reprover upon the hearing ear" (Pr 25:12); yes, "give a reproof to a wise person and he will love you."—Pr 9:8; 15:31-33.

Wisdom in the family. Wisdom builds up a household, not just a building, but the family and its successful life as a unit. (Pr 24:3, 4; compare Pr 3:19, 20; Ps 104:5-24.) Wise parents do not hold back the rod and reproof, but by discipline and counsel they protect their children against delinquency. (Pr 29:15) The wise wife contributes greatly to the success and happiness of the family. (Pr 14:1; 31:26) Children who wisely submit to parental discipline bring joy and honor to the family, upholding its reputation against slander or accusation, and give proof to others of their fathers' wisdom and training.—Pr 10:1; 13:1; 15:20; 23:24, 25; 27:11.

WITNESS. See Legal Case.

WOLF [Heb., *ze'ev'*; Gr., *ly'kos*]. A carnivorous animal resembling a dog, a large German shepherd, but having longer legs, larger feet, a broader head, and stronger jaws. It is reported that in Palestine and Syria wolves usually hunt singly or in twos or threes, not in packs. They seek their prey under the cover of darkness, remaining in hiding during the day. (Hab 1:8; Zep 3:3) Wolves are fierce, voracious, bold, and greedy, often killing more sheep than they can eat or drag away. The shepherd of ancient times therefore had to be courageous and resourceful to protect the flock from wolves.—Joh 10:12, 13.

Most of the Scriptural references to the wolf are illustrative. In his deathbed prophecy, Jacob lik-ened his son Benjamin to a wolf, this undoubtedly with reference to the tribe's fighting abilities. (Ge 49:27; see Benjamin No. 2.) The unscrupulous princes of Judah (Eze 22:27), false prophets (Mt 7:15), vicious opposers of the Christian ministry (Mt 10:16; Lu 10:3), as well as false teachers that would endanger the Christian congregation from within (Ac 20:29, 30), are compared to wolves. In contrast with the well-known despoilings by wolves (Jer 5:6), the wolf and the lamb are depicted as being at peace during Messiah's rule, feeding together as one; in addition to its application to changes in the lives of people, this prophetic picture doubtless indicates that such peace will prevail among animals.—Isa 11:6; 65:25.

WOMAN. An adult human female, one beyond the age of puberty. The Hebrew expression for woman is *'ish·shah'* (literally, a female man), which is also rendered "wife." Similarly, the Greek term *gy·ne'* is translated both "woman" and "wife."

Creation. Before the man Adam ever asked for a human companion, God his Creator made provision. After placing Adam in the garden of Eden and giving him the law respecting the tree of the knowledge of good and bad, Jehovah said: "It is not good for the man to continue by himself. I am going to make a helper for him, as a complement of him." (Ge 2:18) He did not oblige the man to go seeking a companion among the animals, but he brought the animals to Adam for naming. Adam was not inclined toward bestiality and was able to determine that there was no suitable companion for him among these. (Ge 2:19, 20) "Hence Jehovah God had a deep sleep fall upon the man and, while he was sleeping, he took one of his ribs and then closed up the flesh over its place. And Jehovah God proceeded to build the rib that he had taken from the man into a woman and to bring her to the man. Then the man said: 'This is at last bone of my bones and flesh of my flesh. This one will be called Woman, because from man this one was taken.'"—Ge 2:21-23.

Position and Responsibilities. The woman, being created out of the man, was dependent upon the man for being brought into existence. Being part of the man, "one flesh" with him, and a complement and helper to him, she was subject to him as her head. She was also under the law that God had given Adam about the tree of the knowledge of good and bad. She was responsible to work for the good of the man. Together they were to have children and to exercise dominion over the animals.—Ge 1:28; 2:24.

Since the normal course for women in Bible

times was to marry, the scriptures that treat of the woman's responsibilities usually have reference to her position as a wife. The primary duty of all women in Israel was to serve Jehovah God in true worship. Abigail, who became the wife of David after her good-for-nothing husband Nabal died, was an example of this. Even though Nabal took a bad course, refusing to use his material goods to help David, the anointed of Jehovah, Abigail realized that she, as Nabal's wife, was not obligated to follow her husband in such action contrary to Jehovah's will. Jehovah blessed her when her assisting his anointed one showed her persistence in right worship.—1Sa 25:23-31, 39-42.

Secondarily, the woman was to obey her husband. She was responsible to work hard for the good of the household and to bring honor to her husbandly head. This would bring the greatest glory to her. Proverbs 14:1 says: "The truly wise woman has built up her house, but the foolish one tears it down with her own hands." She should always speak well of her husband and increase the respect of others for him, and he should be able to take pride in her. "A capable wife is a crown to her owner, but as rottenness in his bones is she that acts shamefully." (Pr 12:4) The honorable position and the privileges she has as a wife, together with the blessings to her because of faithfulness, industriousness, and wisdom, are described in Proverbs chapter 31.—See WIFE.

A Hebrew woman who was a mother had much to do with the training of her children in righteousness, respectfulness, and industriousness and often did much in counseling and influencing older sons for good. (Ge 27:5-10; Ex 2:7-10; Pr 1:8; 31:1; 2Ti 1:5; 3:14, 15) Girls, especially, were trained to be good wives by learning from their mothers the arts of cooking, weaving, and general household management, while the father taught the son a trade. Wives also were free to express themselves to their husbands (Ge 16:5, 6) and at times aided their husbands in arriving at right decisions.—Ge 21:9-13; 27:46–28:4.

The bride was usually selected for a man by the parents. But, doubtless under the Law, as it was earlier in Rebekah's case, the girl had an opportunity to voice her feelings and will in the matter. (Ge 24:57, 58) Although polygamy was practiced, God not yet acting to restore the original state of monogamy until the Christian congregation was established (Ge 2:23, 24; Mt 19:4-6; 1Ti 3:2), polygamous relationships were regulated.

Even the military laws favored both wife and husband in exempting a newly married man for one year. This gave the couple the opportunity to exercise their right to have a child, which would be a great comfort to the mother when the husband was away, and even more so if he should die in battle.—De 20:7; 24:5.

Laws applied with equal force to both men and women who were guilty of adultery, incest, bestiality, and other crimes. (Le 18:6, 23; 20:10-12; De 22:22) Women were not to wear the clothing of a man or a man the clothing of a woman, a practice that might open the way for immorality, including homosexuality. (De 22:5) Women could participate in the benefits of the Sabbaths, the laws governing Nazirites, the festivals, and, in general, all the provisions of the Law. (Ex 20:10; Nu 6:2; De 12:18; 16:11, 14) The mother, as well as the father, was to be honored and obeyed.—Le 19:3; 20:9; De 5:16; 27:16.

Privileges in the Christian Congregation. For those called by God to the heavenly calling (Heb 3:1) to be joint heirs with Jesus Christ, there is no distinction between men and women in a spiritual sense. The apostle writes: "You are all, in fact, sons of God through your faith in Christ . . . there is neither male nor female; for you are all one person in union with Christ Jesus." (Ga 3:26-28) These all must receive a change of nature at their resurrection, being made partakers together of "divine nature," in which state none will be women, for there is no female sex among spirit creatures, sex being God's means for reproduction of earthly creatures.—2Pe 1:4.

Proclaimers of the good news. Women, spoken of as "daughters" and "women slaves" in Joel's prophecy, were among those receiving the gifts of holy spirit on the day of Pentecost 33 C.E. From that day forward the Christian women who were favored with these gifts talked in foreign tongues that they had not understood before, and they 'prophesied,' not necessarily making predictions of important future events, but speaking forth Bible truths.—Joe 2:28, 29; Ac 1:13-15; 2:1-4, 13-18; see PROPHETESS.

Their speaking about Bible truths to others was not to be limited to fellow believers. Before his ascension to heaven, Jesus had told his followers: "You will receive power when the holy spirit arrives upon you, and you will be witnesses of me both in Jerusalem and in all Judea and Samaria and to the most distant part of the earth." (Ac 1:8) Thereafter, on the day of Pentecost 33 C.E., when holy spirit was poured out upon them, the entire group of some 120 disciples (including some women) were empowered as his witnesses (Ac 1: 14, 15; 2:3, 4); and the prophecy of Joel (2:28, 29) quoted by Peter on that occasion included reference to such women. So they were numbered among those who bore the responsibility to be witnesses of Jesus "in Jerusalem and in all Judea and Samaria and to the most distant part of the earth." Consistent with that, the apostle Paul later reported that Euodia and Syntyche, in Philippi, had "striven side by side with [him] in the good news"; and Luke mentioned Priscilla as sharing with her husband Aquila in 'expounding the way of God' in Ephesus.—Php 4:2, 3; Ac 18:26.

Congregational meetings. There were meetings when these women could pray or prophesy, provided they wore a head covering. (1Co 11:3-16; see HEAD COVERING.) However, at what were evidently *public* meetings, when "the whole congregation" as well as "unbelievers" assembled in one place (1Co 14:23-25), women were to "keep silent." If 'they wanted to learn something, they could question their own husbands at home, for it was disgraceful for a woman to speak in a congregation.'—1Co 14:31-35.

While not permitted to teach in congregational assembly, a woman could teach persons outside the congregation who desired to learn the truth of the Bible and the good news about Jesus Christ (compare Ps 68:11), as well as be a 'teacher of what is good' to younger women (and children) within the congregation. (Tit 2:3-5) But she was not to exercise authority over a man or dispute with men, as, for example, in the meetings of the congregation. She was to remember what happened to Eve and how God expressed the matter of woman's position after Adam and Eve had sinned.—1Ti 2:11-14; Ge 3:16.

Men serve as overseers, ministerial servants. In the discussion of "gifts in men" given by Christ to the congregation, there is no mention of women. The words "apostles," "prophets," "evangelizers," "shepherds," and "teachers" are all in the masculine gender. (Eph 4:8, 11) Ephesians 4:11 is rendered by the *American Translation:* "And he has given us some *men* as apostles, some as prophets, some as missionaries, some as pastors and teachers."—Compare *Mo, NW;* also Ps 68:18.

In full accord with this, when the apostle Paul wrote to Timothy about the qualifications for the service positions of "overseers" (*e·pi'sko·poi*), who were also "older men" (*pre·sby'te·roi*), and of "ministerial servants" (*di·a'ko·noi*) in the congregation, he specifically states that they must be men and, if married, 'the husband of one wife.' No discussion by any of the apostles discusses any office of "deaconess" (*di·a·ko·nis'sa*).—1Ti 3:1-13; Tit 1:5-9; compare Ac 20:17, 28; Php 1:1.

Although Phoebe is mentioned (Ro 16:1) as a "minister" (*di·a'ko·nos*, without the Greek definite article), it is evident that she was not an appointed female ministerial servant in the congregation, because the Scriptures make no provision for such. The apostle did not tell the congregation to receive instructions from her but, rather, to receive her well and to 'assist her in any matter where she might need them.' (Ro 16:2) Paul's reference to her as a minister evidently has something to do with her activity in the spreading of the good news, and he was speaking of Phoebe as a female minister who was associated with the congregation in Cenchreae.—Compare Ac 2:17, 18.

In the home. The woman is described in the Scriptures as "a weaker vessel, the feminine one." She is to be treated accordingly by her husband. (1Pe 3:7) She has many privileges, such as sharing in teaching the children and generally managing the internal affairs of the household, under her husband's approval and direction. (1Ti 5:14; 1Pe 3:1, 2; Pr 1:8; 6:20; chap 31) She has the duty of submission to her husband. (Eph 5:22-24) She owes him the marital due.—1Co 7:3-5.

Adornment. The Bible throughout does not condemn adornment in clothing or the wearing of jewelry, but it commands that modesty and propriety be the governing factors. The apostle instructs that feminine dress be well arranged and that women adorn themselves "with modesty and soundness of mind." Emphasis should not be put on hairstyles, ornaments, and expensive clothing but, rather, on the things contributing to spiritual beauty, namely, "good works" and "the secret person of the heart in the incorruptible apparel of the quiet and mild spirit."—1Ti 2:9, 10; 1Pe 3:3, 4; compare Pr 11:16, 22; 31:30.

The apostle Peter tells such submissive women who display chaste, respectful, godly conduct that "you have become [Sarah's] children, provided you keep on doing good and not fearing any cause for terror." So these wives have a grand opportunity, not by being descended from faithful Sarah in a fleshly way but by imitating her. Sarah was privileged to bear Isaac and become an ancestress of Jesus Christ, who is primarily the 'seed of Abraham.' (Ga 3:16) Thus Christian wives, proving themselves to be figurative daughters of Sarah even toward unbelieving husbands, are sure to receive a rich reward at God's hands.—1Pe 3:6; Ge 18:11, 12; 1Co 7:12-16.

Women Ministered to Jesus. Women enjoyed privileges in connection with Jesus' earthly ministry, but not the privileges given to the

12 apostles and the 70 evangelizers. (Mt 10:1-8; Lu 10:1-7) A number of women ministered to Jesus from their belongings. (Lu 8:1-3) One anointed him a few days before his death, and for her act Jesus promised: "Wherever this good news is preached in all the world, what this woman did shall also be told as a remembrance of her." (Mt 26:6-13; Joh 12:1-8) Women were among those to whom Jesus especially appeared on the day of his resurrection, and women were among those to whom he appeared later.—Mt 28:1-10; Joh 20:1-18.

Figurative Use. In several instances women are used symbolically to represent congregations or organizations of people. They also are employed to symbolize cities. Christ's glorified congregation is spoken of as his "bride," also called "the holy city, New Jerusalem."—Joh 3:29; Re 21:2, 9; 19:7; compare Eph 5:23-27; Mt 9:15; Mr 2:20; Lu 5:34, 35.

Jehovah spoke to the congregation or nation of Israel as his "woman," he being as "a husbandly owner" to her by reason of the Law covenant relationship between them. In restoration prophecies he speaks to Israel in this way, sometimes directing his words to Jerusalem, the governing city of the nation. The "sons" and "daughters" (Isa 43:5-7) of this woman were the members of the nation of Israel.—Isa 51:17-23; 52:1, 2; 54:1, 5, 6, 11-13; 66:10-12; Jer 3:14; 31:31, 32.

In many instances other nations or cities are referred to as feminine or as women. A few are: Moab (Jer 48:41), Egypt (Jer 46:11), Rabbah of Ammon (Jer 49:2), Babylon (Jer 51:13), and symbolic Babylon the Great.—Re 17:1-6; see BABYLON THE GREAT; DAUGHTER.

The "woman" of Genesis 3:15. At the time that he sentenced humankind's parents, Adam and Eve, God gave the promise of a seed that would be brought forth by the "woman," and who would crush the serpent's head. (Ge 3:15) Here was a "sacred secret" that God purposed to reveal in his due time. (Col 1:26) Some factors in the circumstances existing at the time of the prophetic promise provide clues as to the 'woman's' identity. Since her seed was to crush the serpent's head, he would have to be more than a human seed, for the Scriptures show that it was not to a literal snake on the ground that God's words were aimed. The "serpent" is shown at Revelation 12:9 to be Satan the Devil, a spirit person. Consequently, the "woman" of the prophecy could not be a human woman, such as Mary the mother of Jesus. The apostle sheds light on the matter at Galatians 4:21-31.—See SEED.

In this passage the apostle speaks of Abraham's free wife and of his concubine Hagar and says that Hagar corresponds to the literal city of Jerusalem under the Law covenant, her "children" being the citizens of the Jewish nation. Abraham's wife Sarah, Paul says, corresponds to "the Jerusalem above," who is the spiritual mother of Paul and his spirit-begotten associates. This heavenly "mother" would be also the "mother" of Christ, who is the oldest among his spiritual brothers, all of whom spring from God as their Father.—Heb 2:11, 12; see FREE WOMAN.

It would follow logically and in harmony with the Scriptures that the "woman" of Genesis 3:15 would be a spiritual "woman." And corresponding to the fact that the "bride," or "wife," of Christ is not an individual woman, but a composite one, made of many spiritual members (Re 21:9), the "woman" who brings forth God's spiritual sons, God's 'wife' (prophetically foretold in the words of Isaiah and Jeremiah as cited in the foregoing), would be made up of many spiritual persons. It would be a composite body of persons, an organization, a heavenly one.

This "woman" is described in John's vision, in Revelation chapter 12. She is shown as bringing forth a son, a ruler who is to "shepherd all the nations with an iron rod." (Compare Ps 2:6-9; 110:1, 2.) This vision was given to John long after Jesus' human birth and also after his anointing as God's Messiah. Since it obviously has to do with the same person, it must have reference, not to Jesus' human birth, but to some other event, namely, his being installed in Kingdom power. So the birth of God's Messianic Kingdom was here pictured.

Satan is shown later as persecuting the "woman" and making war with "the remaining ones of her seed." (Re 12:13, 17) The "woman" being heavenly, and Satan by this time being hurled down to the earth (Re 12:7-9), he could not reach those heavenly persons of whom the "woman" was made up, but he could reach the remaining ones of her "seed," her children, the brothers of Jesus Christ still on earth. In that way he persecuted the "woman."

Other uses. In foretelling famine conditions to come upon Israel if they disobeyed and broke his covenant, God said: "Ten women will then actually bake your bread in but one oven and give back your bread by weight." The famine would be so great that ten women would need only one oven, whereas they would each use one in normal times.—Le 26:26.

After warning Israel of the calamities that would come upon her for unfaithfulness, Jehovah said, through Isaiah the prophet: "And seven women will actually grab hold of one man in that day, saying: 'We shall eat our own bread and wear our own mantles; only may we be called by your name to take away our reproach.'" (Isa 4:1) In the preceding two verses (Isa 3:25, 26), God had pointed out that Israel's men would fall by war. So he was telling Israel of the inroads such conditions would make on the manpower of the nation, creating such a shortage that several women would attach themselves to one man. They would be glad to take his name and have some male attentions, even if they had to share him with other women. They would accept polygamy or concubinage to have some little part in a man's life. Thereby some of the reproach of widowhood or of the unmarried state, and childlessness, would be removed.

In a prophecy comforting Israel, Jehovah said: "How long will you turn this way and that, O unfaithful daughter? For Jehovah has created a new thing in the earth: A mere female will press around an able-bodied man." ("The woman woos the man!" *AT*) (Jer 31:22) Up until then Israel, with whom God was in the relationship of marriage by reason of the Law covenant, was turning "this way and that" in unfaithfulness. Now Jehovah invites the "virgin of Israel" to set up road marks and signposts to guide her back and to fix her heart upon the highway that leads back. (Jer 31:21) Jehovah will put his spirit in her so that she will be most eager to come back. Thus, as a wife would press around her husband in order to get back into good relations with him, so Israel would press around Jehovah God in order to get back into good relations with him as her husband.

"The desire of women." Of "the king of the north," Daniel's prophecy says: "To the god of his fathers he will give no consideration; and to the desire of women and to every other god he will give no consideration, but over everyone he will magnify himself. But to the god of fortresses, in his position he will give glory." (Da 11:37, 38) "Women" here may represent the weaker nations who become 'handmaids' of "the king of the north," as weaker vessels. They have their gods that they desire and worship, but the "king of the north" disregards them and pays homage to a god of militarism.

The symbolic "locusts." In the vision of the symbolic "locusts" at Revelation 9:1-11, these locusts are depicted as having "hair as women's hair." In harmony with the Scriptural principle that the woman's long hair is a sign of her subjection to her husbandly head, the hair of these symbolic "locusts" must represent the subjection of those whom they symbolize to the one who is shown in the prophecy to be head and king over them.—See ABADDON.

144,000 'not defiled with women.' In Revelation 14:1-4, the 144,000 described as standing with the Lamb on Mount Zion are said to have been "bought from the earth." These are the ones that did not defile themselves with women; in fact, they are virgins." These are shown as having a more intimate relationship with the Lamb than any others do, being the only ones to master the "new song." (Re 14:1-4) This would indicate that they make up the "bride" of the Lamb. (Re 21:9) They are spiritual persons, as revealed by the fact that they stand on the heavenly Mount Zion with the Lamb. Therefore their 'not defiling themselves with women' and their being "virgins" would not mean that none of these 144,000 persons had ever been married, for the Scriptures do not forbid persons on earth who are to be joint heirs with Christ to marry. (1Ti 3:2; 4:1, 3) Neither would it imply that all the 144,000 were men, for "there is neither male nor female" as far as the spiritual relationship of Christ's joint heirs is concerned. (Ga 3:28) The "women" therefore must be symbolic women, doubtless religious organizations such as Babylon the Great and her 'daughters,' false religious organizations, the joining of and participation in which would prevent one from being spotless. (Re 17:5) This symbolic description harmonizes with the requirement in the Law that the high priest of Israel take only a virgin for his wife, for Jesus Christ is Jehovah's great High Priest.—Le 21:10, 14; 2Co 11:2; Heb 7:26.

With reference to Jesus' addressing Mary as "woman," see MARY No. 1 (Respected, Loved by Jesus).

WOMB. An organ of the female in which the young are nourished and grow prior to birth. Jehovah is the Creator of the womb (Ge 2:22), and he is the One able to make it fruitful (Ge 29:31; 30:22; 49:25) or unproductive. (Ge 20:18) Sarah's womb was 'dead,' or beyond power of childbearing, when Jehovah restored that power to her. (Ro 4:19; Ge 18:11, 12; 21:1-3) The Bible points out that Jehovah is responsible for the process of formation of an embryo in the womb, showing that the design of the human in the womb is according to God's pattern and not by chance or evolution. (Job 31:15; compare Job 10:8; Ps 139:13-16; Isa 45:9.) The womb being created specifically for the propagation of the race, the "restrained womb" is listed as one of four things that have not said: "Enough!"—Pr 30:15, 16.

Since the womb is located in the general area of the body known as the belly, the Hebrew word for "belly" is often used with primary reference to the womb, as at Genesis 25:23; Deuteronomy 7:13; Psalm 127:3.—See BELLY.

God, as the womb's Designer, can also see exactly what is being formed in it. He can read the hereditary traits being built into the unborn child and determine what use He wants to make of the individual, if He so desires.—Jer 1:5; Lu 1:15; compare Ro 9:10-13.

Jehovah commanded Israel: "Sanctify to me every male firstborn that opens each womb among the sons of Israel, among men and beasts. It is mine." (Ex 13:2) In human births, this had reference to the *father's* first male child.—See FIRSTBORN, FIRSTLING.

Jesus pointed out that his mother Mary was not to be honored above others who serve God. On an occasion when he was teaching, a woman cried out: "Happy is the womb that carried you and the breasts that you sucked!" Jesus replied: "No, rather, Happy are those hearing the word of God and keeping it!" (Lu 11:27, 28) Later, as Jesus was led away to the torture stake, he gave a prophecy concerning Jerusalem's coming destruction, telling the women weeping for him that days were coming in which people would say: "Happy are the barren women, and the wombs that did not give birth." (Lu 23:27-29) This was fulfilled in 70 C.E. when more than a million Jews, including young children, perished, and thousands were taken into captivity, to be sold into slavery.

The Jewish ruler and Pharisee Nicodemus, on hearing Jesus' statement, "Unless anyone is born again, he cannot see the kingdom of God," asked: "How . . . ? He cannot enter into the womb of his mother a second time and be born, can he?" Jesus then explained that this new birth is, not from a human womb, but "from water and spirit."—Joh 3:1-8.

Figurative Use. "Womb" is employed at times with reference to the source of something. In speaking about creative works involving the earth, Jehovah speaks of the sea as bursting forth "from the womb." (Job 38:8) Jehovah says to David's Lord that in the day of his military force this one will have willing volunteers "like dewdrops" from "the womb of the dawn" (from where comes the morning dew).—Ps 110:1-3.

WOOF. See WARP.

WOOL. The soft curly hair that forms the fleece of certain animals, particularly sheep. It was shorn and used extensively by the Hebrews and others of ancient times to make clothing and for doing embroidery. (Ex 35:4-6, 25; 36:8, 35, 37; 38:18; 39:1-8, 22-29; Le 13:47; Pr 31:13, 22; Eze 34:3) Woolen clothing provides insulation from heat and cold and is comfortable, imparting warmth without great weight and absorbing moisture though not feeling damp to the wearer.

Under the Law, the Israelites were required to give "the first of the shorn wool" of their flocks to the priests. (De 18:3-5) The people who were not priests were forbidden to "wear mixed stuff of wool and linen together."—De 22:11; Le 19:19; see CLOTH (Other Uses).

The importance of wool in ancient times is indicated by the fact that Moabite King Mesha paid "a hundred thousand lambs and a hundred thousand *unshorn* male sheep" to the king of Israel as tribute. (2Ki 3:4) Wool was also a valuable item of trade.—Eze 27:1, 2, 7, 16, 18.

Since wool is often white in its natural state, it is sometimes associated with whiteness and purity. For example, through the prophet Isaiah, Jehovah likened forgiven sins to white wool, saying: "Though the sins of you people should prove to be as scarlet, they will be made white just like snow; though they should be red like crimson cloth, they will become even like wool."—Isa 1:18-20.

Jehovah gives "snow like wool," blanketing the land as with a warm covering of white wool.—Ps 147:16.

"The Ancient of Days," Jehovah God, is depicted symbolically in vision as having hair like clean wool. (Da 7:9) This suggests great age and wisdom, which are associated with gray-headedness. (Compare Job 15:9, 10.) Similarly, the apostle John saw "someone like a son of man" and observed that "his head and his hair were white as white wool, as snow." (Re 1:12-14) His hair being described in this manner may indicate that it had become white in the way of righteousness.—Pr 16:31.

WORD, THE. The term "word" in the Scriptures most frequently translates the Hebrew and Greek words *da·var'* and *lo'gos.* These words in the majority of cases refer to an entire thought, saying, or statement rather than simply to an individual term or unit of speech. (In Greek a 'single word' is expressed by *rhe'ma* [Mt 27:14], though it, too, can mean a saying or spoken matter.) Any message from the Creator, such as one uttered through a prophet, is "the word of God." In a few places *Lo'gos* (meaning "Word") is a title given to Jesus Christ.

The Word of God. "The word of Jehovah" is an expression that, with slight variations, occurs hundreds of times in the Scriptures. By "the word of Jehovah" the heavens were created. God said the word and it was accomplished. "God proceeded to say: 'Let light come to be.' Then there came to be light." (Ps 33:6; Ge 1:3) It should not be understood from this that Jehovah himself does no work. (Joh 5:17) But he does have myriads of angels that respond to his word and carry out his will.—Ps 103:20.

Creation, animate and inanimate, is subject to God's word, and can be used by him to accomplish his purposes. (Ps 103:20; 148:8) His word is dependable; what God promises he also remembers to do. (De 9:5; Ps 105:42-45) As he himself has said, his word "will last to time indefinite"; it will never return without accomplishing its purpose.—Isa 40:8; 55:10, 11; 1Pe 1:25.

Jehovah is a communicative God, in that he reveals to his creatures in a variety of ways what his will and purposes are. God's words were spoken, doubtless through an angel, to such men as Adam, Noah, and Abraham. (Ge 3:9-19; 6:13; 12:1) At times he used holy men like Moses and Aaron to make known his purposes. (Ex 5:1) "Every word" that Moses commanded Israel was in effect the word of God to them. (De 12:32) God also spoke through the mouth of prophets such as Elisha and Jeremiah, and prophetesses such as Deborah.—2Ki 7:1; Jer 2:1, 2; Jg 4:4-7.

Many of the divine commandments were committed to writing from the time of Moses forward. The Decalogue, commonly called the Ten Commandments and known in the Hebrew Scriptures as "the Ten Words," was first delivered orally and later 'written by the finger of God' on stone tablets. (Ex 31:18; 34:28; De 4:13) These commandments were called the "Words" at Deuteronomy 5:22.—See TEN WORDS.

Joshua wrote additional *words in the book of God's law*" under divine inspiration, and this was true with other faithful Bible writers. (Jos 24:26; Jer 36:32) Eventually all such writings were collected together and made up what is called the Sacred Scriptures or Holy Bible. "All Scripture . . . inspired of God" would include, today, all the canonical Biblical books. (2Ti 3:16; 2Pe 1:20, 21) In the Christian Greek Scriptures, God's inspired word is often spoken of as simply "the word."—Jas 1:22; 1Pe 2:2.

There are many synonyms for God's word. For example, in Psalm 119, where references to Jehovah's "word(s)" occur more than 20 times, synonyms are found in poetic parallelisms—such terms as law, reminders, orders, regulations, commandments, judicial decisions, statutes, and sayings of Jehovah. This also shows that the expression "word" means a complete thought or message.

The word of God is also described in a number of other ways that give it breadth and meaning. It is "the 'word' [or "saying" (*rhe'ma*)] of faith" (Ro 10:8, *Int*), "the word [or message (form of *lo'gos*)] of righteousness" (Heb 5:13), and "the word of the reconciliation" (2Co 5:19). God's word or message is like "seed," which, if planted in good soil, brings forth much fruitage (Lu 8:11-15); his sayings are also said to 'run with speed.'—Ps 147:15.

Preachers and Teachers of the Word. The greatest exponent and supporter of Jehovah's inspired word of truth was the Lord Jesus Christ. He astounded people by his methods of teaching (Mt 7:28, 29; Joh 7:46), yet he took no credit to himself, saying, "the word that you are hearing is not mine, but belongs to the Father who sent me." (Joh 14:24; 17:14; Lu 5:1) Faithful disciples of Christ were those who remained in his word, and this, in turn, set them free from ignorance, superstition, and fear, also from slavery to sin and death. (Joh 8:31, 32) Often it was necessary for Jesus to take issue with the Pharisees, whose traditions and teachings made void "the word [or declaration] of God."—Mt 15:6; Mr 7:13.

It is not just a matter of hearing the word of God preached. Rather, acting upon and showing obedience to that message is also essential. (Lu 8:21; 11:28; Jas 1:22, 23) After being well trained for the ministry, the apostles and disciples, in turn, obeyed the word and took up the preaching and teaching themselves. (Ac 4:31; 8:4, 14; 13:7, 44; 15:36; 18:11; 19:10) As a result, "the word of God went on growing, and the number of the disciples kept multiplying."—Ac 6:7; 11:1; 12:24; 13:5, 49; 19:20.

The apostles and their associates were no peddlers of the Scriptures, as the false shepherds were. What they preached was the straight, unadulterated message of God. (2Co 2:17; 4:2) The apostle Paul told Timothy: "Do your utmost to present yourself approved to God, a workman with nothing to be ashamed of, handling the word of the truth aright." Furthermore, Timothy was commanded: "Preach the word, be at it urgently in favorable season, in troublesome season." (2Ti 2:15; 4:2) Paul also counseled Christian wives to watch their conduct, "so that the word of God may not be spoken of abusively."—Tit 2:5.

Ever since the Devil contradicted what God had said in the garden of Eden, there have been many satanic opponents of God's word. Many persons who have upheld God's word have lost their lives for doing so, as both Bible prophecy and history testify. (Re 6:9) It is also a fact of history that persecution has failed to stop the proclamation of God's word.—Php 1:12-14, 18; 2Ti 2:9.

The Power of God's Word and Spirit. God's word exerts tremendous power upon its hearers. It means life. God demonstrated to Israel in the wilderness that "not by bread alone does man live but by every expression of Jehovah's mouth does man live." (De 8:3; Mt 4:4) It is "the word of life." (Php 2:16) Jesus spoke the words of God, and he said: "The sayings [*rhe'ma·ta*] that I have spoken to you are spirit and are life."—Joh 6:63.

The apostle Paul wrote: "The word [or message (*lo'gos*)] of God is alive and exerts power and is sharper than any two-edged sword and pierces even to the dividing of soul and spirit, and of joints and their marrow, and is able to discern thoughts and intentions of the heart." (Heb 4:12) It reaches the heart and reveals whether one is actually living according to right principles.—1Co 14:23-25.

The word of God is the truth and can sanctify one for God's use. (Joh 17:17) It can make a person wise and happy; it can accomplish whatever work God purposes for it. (Ps 19:7-9; Isa 55:10, 11) It can equip a person *completely* for every good work and can enable him to conquer the wicked one.—2Ti 3:16, 17; compare 1Jo 2:14.

Of Jesus' preaching it is said: "God anointed him with holy spirit and *power,* and he went through the land doing good and healing all those oppressed by the Devil; because God was with him." (Ac 10:38) The apostle Paul accomplished conversions of persons, even pagans, "not with persuasive words of [men's] wisdom but with a demonstration of spirit and *power.*" (1Co 2:4) The words that he spoke by God's holy spirit, based on the Scriptures, the Word of God, worked powerfully to make the conversions. He told the congregation at Thessalonica: "The good news we preach did not turn up among you with speech alone but also with *power* and with holy spirit and strong conviction."—1Th 1:5.

John the Baptizer came "with Elijah's spirit and power." He had Elijah's "spirit," his drive and force. Jehovah's spirit also directed John, so that he spoke the words of God, words that exerted strong power; he was able very successfully to "turn back the hearts of fathers to children and the disobedient ones to the practical wisdom of righteous ones, to get ready for Jehovah a prepared people."—Lu 1:17.

The message of the good news from God's Word the Bible should therefore not be underrated. These words are more powerful than any words men can devise or speak. The ancient Beroeans were commended for "carefully examining the Scriptures" to see whether what an apostle taught was correct. (Ac 17:11) God's ministers, speaking God's powerful Word, are energized and backed up by "power of holy spirit."—Ro 15:13, 19.

"The Word" as a Title. In the Christian Greek Scriptures "the Word" (Gr., *ho Lo'gos*) also appears as a title. (Joh 1:1, 14; Re 19:13) The apostle John identified the one to whom this title belongs, namely, Jesus, he being so designated not only during his ministry on earth as a perfect man but also during his prehuman spirit existence as well as after his exaltation to heaven.

"The Word was a god." Regarding the Son's prehuman existence, John says: "In the beginning *the Word* was, and *the Word* was with God, and *the Word* was a god." (Joh 1:1, *NW*) The *King James Version* and the *Douay Version* read: "In the beginning was the Word, and the Word was with God, and the Word was God." This would make it appear that the Word was identical with Almighty God, while the former reading, in the *New World Translation,* indicates that the Word is not *the* God, Almighty God, but is a mighty one, a god. (Even the judges of ancient Israel, who wielded great power in the nation, were called "gods." [Ps 82:6; Joh 10:34, 35]) Actually, in the Greek text, the definite article *ho,* "the," appears before the first "God," but there is no article before the second.

Other translations aid in getting the proper view. The interlinear word-for-word reading of the Greek translation in the *Emphatic Diaglott* reads: "In a beginning was the Word, and the Word was with the God, and a god was the Word." The accompanying text of the *Diaglott* uses capital and small capital letters for *the* God, and initial capital and lowercase letters for the second appearance of "God" in the sentence: "In the Beginning was the Logos, and the Logos was with God, and the Logos was God."

These renderings would support the fact that Jesus, being the Son of God and the one used by God in creating all other things (Col 1:15-20), is indeed a "god," a mighty one, and has the quality of mightiness, but is not the Almighty God. Other translations reflect this view. *The New English Bible* says: "And what God was, the Word was." The Greek word translated "Word" is *Lo'gos;* and so Moffatt's translation reads: "The Logos was divine." The *American Translation* reads: "The Word was divine." Other readings, by German translators, follow. By Böhmer: "It was tightly bound up with God, yes, itself of divine being." By Stage: "The Word was itself of divine being." By Menge: "And God (= of divine being) the Word was." And by Thimme: "And God of a sort the Word was." All these renderings highlight the *quality* of the Word, not his identity with his Father, the Almighty God. Being the Son of Jehovah God, he would have the divine quality, for divine means "godlike."—Col 2:9; compare 2Pe 1:4, where "divine nature" is promised to Christ's joint heirs.

The Four Gospels—A New Translation, by Professor Charles Cutler Torrey, says: "In the beginning was the Word, and the Word was with God, and the Word was god. When he was in the beginning with God all things were created through him; without him came no created thing into being." (Joh 1:1-3) Note that what the Word is said to be is spelled without a capital initial letter, namely, "god."

This Word, or *Lo'gos,* was God's only direct creation, the only-begotten son of God, and evidently the close associate of God to whom God was speaking when he said: "Let *us* make man in *our* image, according to *our* likeness." (Ge 1:26) Hence John continued, saying: "This one was in the beginning with God. All things came into existence through him, and apart from him not even one thing came into existence."—Joh 1:2, 3.

Other scriptures plainly show that the Word was God's agent through whom all other things came into existence. There is "one God the Father, out of whom all things are, . . . and there is one Lord, Jesus Christ, through whom all things are." (1Co 8:6) The Word, God's Son, was "the beginning of the creation by God," otherwise described as "the firstborn of all creation; because by means of him all other things were created in the heavens and upon the earth."—Re 3:14; Col 1:15, 16.

Earthly ministry and heavenly glorification. In due time a change came about. John explains: "So *the Word* became flesh and resided among us [as the Lord Jesus Christ], and we had a view of his glory, a glory such as belongs to an only-begotten son from a father." (Joh 1:14) By becoming flesh, the Word became visible, hearable, feelable to eyewitnesses on earth. In this way men of flesh could have direct contact and association with *"the word* of life," which, John says, "was from the beginning, which we have heard, which we have seen with our eyes, which we have viewed attentively and our hands felt."—1Jo 1:1-3.

The glorified Lord Jesus Christ continues to carry the title "the Word," as noted in Revelation 19:11-16. There in a vision of heaven John says he saw a white horse whose rider was called "Faithful and True," "The Word of God"; and "upon his outer garment, even upon his thigh, he has a name written, King of kings and Lord of lords."

Why God's Son is called "the Word." A title often describes the function served or the duty performed by the bearer. So it was with the title *Kal-Hatzé,* meaning "the voice or word of the king," that was given an Abyssinian officer. Based on his travels from 1768 to 1773, James Bruce describes the duties of the *Kal-Hatzé* as follows. He stood by a window covered with a curtain through which, unseen inside, the king spoke to this officer. He then conveyed the message to the persons or party concerned. Thus the *Kal-Hatzé* acted as the word or voice of the Abyssinian king. —*Travels to Discover the Source of the Nile,* London, 1790, Vol. III, p. 265; Vol. IV, p. 76.

Recall, too, that God made Aaron the word or "mouth" of Moses, saying: "He must speak for you to the people; and it must occur that he will serve as a mouth to you, and you will serve as God to him."—Ex 4:16.

In a similar way God's firstborn Son doubtless served as the Mouth, or Spokesman, for his Father, the great King of Eternity. He was God's Word of communication for conveying information and instructions to the Creator's other spirit and human sons. It is reasonable to think that prior to Jesus' coming to earth, on many of the occasions when God communicated with humans he used the Word as his angelic mouthpiece. (Ge 16:7-11; 22:11; 31:11; Ex 3:2-5; Jg 2:1-4; 6:11, 12; 13:3) Since the angel that guided the Israelites through the wilderness had 'Jehovah's name within him,' he may have been God's Son, the Word.—Ex 23:20-23; see JESUS CHRIST (Prehuman Existence).

Showing that Jesus continued to serve as his Father's Spokesman, or Word, during his earthly ministry, he told his listeners: "I have not spoken out of my own impulse, but the Father himself who sent me has given me a commandment as to what to tell and what to speak. . . . Therefore the things I speak, just as the Father has told me them, so I speak them."—Joh 12:49, 50; 14:10; 7:16, 17.

WORK. The exercise of physical or mental effort to accomplish a purpose or to produce something; work is commended in the Scriptures. (Ec 5:18) It is a gift of God for man to eat, drink, and "see good for all his hard work," and it is the divine will that man "rejoice in his works." (Ec 3:13, 22) Work was not first instituted in man's case after he sinned, for Jehovah gave the perfect, sinless man and woman a work assignment when he commanded them to subdue the earth. (Ge 1:28) However, vain work resulted from sin.—Ge 3:19; compare Ro 8:20, 21.

Under the Mosaic Law, periods of rest from labor were decreed. The Israelites were not to work on the weekly Sabbath day. (Ex 20:8-11) Also, "no sort of laborious work" was to be done at times of holy convention.—Le 23:6-8, 21, 24, 25, 34-36.

Jehovah and His Son Are Workers. Jehovah is a worker whose works include creation of such things as the heavens, the earth, animals, and man. (Ge 1:1; 2:1-3; Job 14:15; Ps 8:3-8; 19:1; 104:24; 139:14) It is fitting to acknowledge the greatness of Jehovah's works, extolling and thanking him for them. (Ps 92:5; 107:15; 145:4-10; 150:2) God's works are faithful and incomparable, are wrought in wisdom, and are "truth and judgment."—Ps 33:4; 86:8; 104:24; 111:7.

Jehovah did a "great work" in effecting the Israelites' deliverance from Egyptian bondage and enabling them to take possession of Canaan. (Jg 2:7) His works sometimes involve the execution of divine judgment. (Jer 50:25) Thus, through Isaiah, it was foretold: "For Jehovah will rise up . . . that he may work his work—his work is unusual." (Isa 28:21) Such an 'unusual work' took place in 607 B.C.E. and again in 70 C.E., when Jehovah worked, or brought about, the destruction of Jerusalem and her temple.—Hab 1:5-9; Ac 13:38-41; see POWER, POWERFUL WORKS.

Wisdom personified is represented as being beside Jehovah in creative work as his "master worker." (Pr 8:12, 22-31; compare Joh 1:1-3.) When on earth as a man, God's wise Son, Jesus Christ, showed that he was a worker and that, though material creative works relating to the earth had concluded, Jehovah continued to work, for Jesus said: "My Father has kept working until now, and I keep working." (Joh 5:17) To Jesus it was nourishing, satisfying, and refreshing as food to do the work he was assigned by Jehovah. (Joh 4:34; 5:36) Christ's works were done in his Father's name; they were from the Father and showed he was "in union with the Father." (Joh 10:25, 32, 37, 38; 14:10, 11; 15:24; Ac 2:22) Jesus successfully finished his God-assigned work on earth.—Joh 17:4.

Jesus said: "He that exercises faith in me, that one also will do the works that I do; and he will do works greater than these, because I am going my way to the Father." (Joh 14:12) Evidently, Christ did not mean that his followers would do works of a more miraculous kind than he did, for there is no Biblical record that any of them performed a miracle surpassing that of Jesus in raising Lazarus who had been dead for four days. (Joh 11:38-44) But, since Jesus was going to the Father, and his followers would receive the holy spirit to be witnesses of him "both in Jerusalem and in all Judea and Samaria and to the most distant part of the earth" (Ac 1:8), they would cover a greater area and work for a longer time than did Jesus, in this sense doing greater works than he did.

Necessity of Working. Jesus Christ said that "the worker is worthy of his wages," thereby indicating that those who labored in connection with spiritual matters would not lack necessities of life. (Lu 10:7) However, as the apostle Paul pointed out to the Thessalonians, the lazy person who refuses to work does not deserve to eat at the expense of others but should learn to work with his hands to care for his needs. (1Th 4:11; 2Th 3:10, 12) Likewise, the stealer should "steal no more" but "do hard work."—Eph 4:28.

Quality of the Work of God's Servants. When doing any work, the servant of Jehovah should remember his relationship with God, doing everything "whole-souled as to Jehovah, and not to men." (Col 3:23) This calls for industriousness (Pr 10:4; 13:4; 18:9), honesty, and fidelity. Manifesting such traits brings glory to God, as is evident from the admonition given to Christian slaves: "Let slaves be in subjection to their owners in all things, and please them well, not talking back, not committing theft, but exhibiting good fidelity to the full, so that they may adorn the teaching of our Savior, God, in all things."—Tit 2:9, 10; Eph 6:5-8; Heb 13:18.

Proper Evaluation of Acquisitions. Christians should appreciatively look to God for his blessing on their work and not be unduly anxious about their material needs. Jesus advised his followers to seek first the Kingdom. (Mt 6:11, 25-33) He also urged: "Work, not for the food that perishes, but for the food that remains for life everlasting." (Joh 6:27) Hence, God's servants wisely view the money and material things obtained as a result of their work as subordinate to the much more important spiritual riches. They also use material resources acquired by labor to advance spiritual interests, and they thus "make friends" with God and Christ.—Ec 7:12; Lu 12:15-21; 16:9.

Improper Works to Be Avoided. Jehovah determines which works are proper and which works are improper. He "will bring every sort of work into the judgment in relation to every hidden thing, as to whether it is good or bad." (Ec 12:13, 14) God will also deal with each person according to that one's work. (Ps 62:12) This and especially love for Jehovah God are good reasons for shunning improper works and doing works that are pleasing in his sight.—1Jo 5:3; Ps 34:14; 97:10; Am 5:14, 15.

To experience divine favor, Christians must avoid the "works of the flesh," which include such things as fornication, loose conduct, idolatry, practice of spiritism, hatreds, fits of anger, and drunken bouts. Such practices would bar one from inheriting God's Kingdom and are evidently included among the "unfruitful works that belong to the darkness," works that result in no benefit. —Ga 5:19-21; Eph 5:3-14; 1Pe 4:3; compare Joh 3:20, 21.

Proper Works. Dependence upon Jehovah God is essential if one's works are to succeed. (Ps 127:1; Pr 16:3) It is God who backs up and strengthens those who work at doing his will. (2Co 4:7; Php 4:13) Whereas the lives of humans abound with vain works (Ec 2:10, 11), works relating to true worship are not in vain. Hebrew Christians were given the assurance: "God is not unrighteous so as to forget your work and the love you showed for his name, in that you have ministered to the holy ones and continue ministering." (Heb 6:10) Such work evidently included rendering material assistance or other kindnesses to those in need or to those experiencing suffering and persecution. (Compare Eph 4:28; Php 4:14-19; 1Ti 6:17, 18; Jas 1:27.) Other fine works include sharing in making disciples (Mt 28:19, 20; 1Co 3:9-15) and, in the case of men, serving as an overseer in a Christian congregation and teaching fellow believers.—1Th 5:12, 13; 1Ti 3:1; 5:17.

Faith and Works. Works of the Mosaic Law, which included such things as sacrificial offerings, purifications, and circumcision, did not make a person righteous. (Ro 3:20; 4:1-10; Ga 3:2) Yet, the disciple James—who is not discussing works of Mosaic Law—says "a man is to be declared righteous by works, and not by faith alone" (Jas 2:24), for there must be practical works that demonstrate one's faith, giving proof of it. (Compare Mt 7:21-27; Eph 2:8-10; Jas 1:27; 2:14-17; 4:4.) For example, Abraham had works that proved his faith, such as his willingness to offer up Isaac. Rahab also proved her faith by her works of hiding the Israelite spies.—Heb 11:17-19; Jas 2:21-25.

WORLD. This is the usual English term for translating the Greek *ko′smos* in all of its occurrences in the Christian Greek Scriptures except 1 Peter 3:3, where it is rendered "adornment." "World" can mean (1) humankind as a whole, apart from their moral condition or course of life, (2) the framework of human circumstances into which a person is born and in which he lives (and in this sense it is at times quite similar to the Greek *ai·on′*, "system of things"), or (3) the mass of mankind apart from Jehovah's approved servants.

The *King James Version* used "world" to render not only *ko′smos* but also three other Greek words in some of its renderings of them (*ge; ai·on′; oi·kou·me′ne*) and five different Hebrew words (*'e′rets; che′dhel; che′ledh; 'oh·lam′; te·vel′*). This produced a blurring or confused blending of meanings that made it difficult to obtain correct understanding of the scriptures involved. Later translations have served to clear up considerably this confusion.

The Hebrew *'e′rets* and the Greek *ge* (from which come the English words "geography" and "geology") mean "earth; ground; soil; land" (Ge 6:4; Nu 1:1; Mt 2:6; 5:5; 10:29; 13:5), although in some cases they may stand in a figurative sense for the people of the earth, as at Psalm 66:4 and Revelation 13:3. Both *'oh·lam′* (Heb.) and *ai·on′* (Gr.) relate basically to a period of time of indefinite length. (Ge 6:3; 17:13; Lu 1:70) *Ai·on′* may also signify the "system of things" characterizing a certain period, age, or epoch. (Ga 1:4) *Che′ledh* (Heb.) has a somewhat similar meaning and may be rendered by such terms as "life's duration" and "system of things." (Job 11:17; Ps 17:14) *Oi·kou·me′ne* (Gr.) means the "inhabited earth" (Lu 21: 26), and *te·vel′* (Heb.) may be rendered "productive land." (2Sa 22:16) *Che′dhel* (Heb.) occurs only at Isaiah 38:11, and in the *King James Version* it is rendered "world" in the expression "inhabitants of the world." *The Interpreter's Dictionary of the Bible* (edited by G. Buttrick, 1962, Vol. 4, p. 874) suggests the rendering "inhabitants of (the world of) cessation," while pointing out that most scholars favor the reading of some Hebrew manuscripts that have *che′ledh* in place of *che′dhel*. The *New World Translation* reads "inhabitants of [the land of] cessation."—See AGE; EARTH; SYSTEMS OF THINGS.

"Kosmos" and Its Various Senses. The basic meaning of the Greek *ko′smos* is "order" or "arrangement." And to the extent that the concept of beauty is bound up with order and symmetry, *ko′smos* also conveys that thought and therefore was often used by the Greeks to mean "adornment," especially as regards women. It is used in that way at 1 Peter 3:3. Hence also the English word "cosmetic." The related verb *ko·sme'o* has the sense of 'putting in order' at Matthew 25:7 and that of 'adorning' elsewhere. (Mt 12:44; 23:29; Lu 11:25; 21:5; 1Ti 2:9; Tit 2:10; 1Pe 3:5; Re 21:2, 19) The adjective *ko'smi·os,* at 1 Timothy 2:9 and 3:2, describes that which is "well-arranged" or "orderly."

Evidently because the universe manifests order, Greek philosophers at times applied *ko'smos* to the entire visible creation. However, there was no real unanimity of thought among them, some restricting it to the celestial bodies only, others using it for the whole universe. The use of *ko'smos* to describe the material creation as a whole appears in some Apocryphal writings (compare Wisdom 9:9; 11:17), these being written during the period when Greek philosophy was making inroads in many Jewish areas. But in the inspired writings of the Christian Greek Scriptures this sense is virtually, perhaps entirely, absent. Some texts may appear to use the term in that sense, such as the account of the apostle's address to the Athenians at the Areopagus. Paul there said: "The God that made the world [form of *ko'smos*] and all the things in it, being, as this One is, Lord of heaven and earth, does not dwell in handmade temples." (Ac 17:22-24) Since the use of *ko'smos* as meaning the universe was current among the Greeks, Paul might have employed the term in that sense. Even here, however, it is entirely possible that he used it in one of the ways discussed in the rest of this article.

Linked With Mankind. Richard C. Trench's *Synonyms of the New Testament* (London, 1961, pp. 201, 202), after presenting the philosophic use of *ko'smos* for the universe, says: "From this signification of κόσμος [*ko'smos*] as the material universe, . . . followed that of κόσμος as that external framework of things in which man lives and moves, which exists for him and of which he constitutes the moral centre (John xvi. 21; I Cor. xiv. 10; I John iii. 17); . . . and then the men themselves, the sum total of persons living in the world (John i. 29; iv. 42; II Cor. v. 19); and then upon this, and ethically, all not of the ἐκκλησία [*ek·kle·si'a;* the church or congregation], alienated from the life of God and by wicked works enemies to Him (I Cor. i. 20, 21; II Cor. vii. 10; Jam. iv. 4)."

Similarly, the book *Studies in the Vocabulary of the Greek New Testament,* by K. S. Wuest (1946, p. 57), quotes Greek scholar Cremer as saying: "As *kosmos* is regarded as that order of things whose center is man, attention is directed chiefly to him, and *kosmos* denotes mankind within that order of things, humanity as it manifests itself in and through such an order (Mt. 18:7)."

All humankind. *Ko'smos,* or the "world," is therefore closely linked and bound up with *mankind.* This is true in secular Greek literature and is particularly so in Scripture. When Jesus said that the man walking in daylight "sees the light of this world [form of *ko'smos*]" (Joh 11:9), it might appear that by "world" is meant simply the planet Earth, which has the sun as its source of daylight. However, his next words speak of the man walking at night who bumps into something "because the light is not *in him.*" (Joh 11:10) It is primarily for mankind that God gave the sun and other heavenly bodies. (Compare Ge 1:14; Ps 8:3-8; Mt 5:45.) Similarly, using light in a spiritual sense, Jesus told his followers they would be "the light of the world" (Mt 5:14), certainly not meaning they would illuminate the planet, for he goes on to show their illuminating would be for mankind, "before men." (Mt 5:16; compare Joh 3:19; 8:12; 9:5; 12:46; Php 2:15.) The preaching of the good news "in all the world" (Mt 26:13) also means preaching it to mankind as a whole, even as in some languages "all the world" is the common way of saying "everybody" (compare French *tout le monde;* Spanish *todo el mundo*).—Compare Joh 8:26; 18:20; Ro 1:8; Col 1:5, 6.

In one basic sense, then, *ko'smos* refers to all humankind. The Scriptures therefore describe the *ko'smos,* or world, as being guilty of sin (Joh 1:29; Ro 3:19; 5:12, 13) and needing a savior to give it life (Joh 4:42; 6:33, 51; 12:47; 1Jo 4:14), things applicable only to mankind, not to the inanimate creation nor to the animals. This is the world that God loved so much that "he gave his only-begotten Son, in order that everyone exercising faith in him might not be destroyed but have everlasting life." (Joh 3:16, 17; compare 2Co 5:19; 1Ti 1:15; 1Jo 2:2.) That world of mankind forms the field in which Jesus Christ sowed the fine seed, "the sons of the kingdom."—Mt 13:24, 37, 38.

When Paul says that God's "invisible qualities are clearly seen from the world's creation onward, because they are perceived by the things made," he must mean from the creation of mankind forward, for only when mankind appeared were there minds on earth capable of 'perceiving' such invisible qualities by means of the visible creation. —Ro 1:20.

Similarly, John 1:10 says of Jesus that "the world [*ko'smos*] came into existence through him." While it is true that Jesus shared in the production of all things, including the heavens and the planet

Earth and all things in it, *ko'smos* here applies primarily to humankind in whose production Jesus likewise shared. (Compare Joh 1:3; Col 1: 15-17; Ge 1:26.) Hence, the rest of the verse says: "But the world [that is, the world of mankind] did not know him."

"The founding of the world." This clear connection of *ko'smos* with the world of mankind also aids one in understanding what is meant by "the founding of the world," as referred to in a number of texts. These texts speak of certain things as taking place 'from the founding of the world.' These include the 'shedding of the blood of the prophets' from the time of Abel onward, a 'kingdom prepared,' and 'names being written on the scroll of life.' (Lu 11:50, 51; Mt 25:34; Re 13:8; 17:8; compare Mt 13:35; Heb 9:26.) Such things relate to human life and activity, and hence "the founding of the world" must relate to the beginning of mankind, not of the inanimate creation or the animal creation. Hebrews 4:3 shows that God's creative works were, not *started*, but "finished" from the founding of the world." Since Eve was evidently the last of Jehovah's earthly creative works, the world's founding could not precede her.

As shown under ABEL (No. 1) and FOREKNOWLEDGE, FOREORDINATION (Foreordination of the Messiah), the Greek term (*ka·ta·bo·le'*) for "founding" can refer to the conceiving of seed in human conception. *Ka·ta·bo·le'* literally means "a throwing down [of seed]" and at Hebrews 11:11 may be rendered "conceive" (*RS, NW*). Its use there evidently refers to Abraham's 'throwing down' human seed for the begetting of a son and Sarah's receiving that seed so as to be fertilized.

Therefore "the founding of the world" need not be taken to mean the beginning of the creation of the material universe, nor does the expression "before the founding of the world" (Joh 17:5, 24; Eph 1:4; 1Pe 1:20) refer to a point of time prior to the creation of the material universe. Rather, these expressions evidently relate to the time when the human race was 'founded' through the first human pair, Adam and Eve, who, outside of Eden, began to conceive seed that could benefit from God's provisions for deliverance from inherited sin.—Ge 3:20-24; 4:1, 2.

'Spectacle to world, both to angels and men.' Some have understood the use of the word *ko'smos* in 1 Corinthians 4:9 to include both invisible spirit creatures and visible human creatures, by the rendering: "We are made a spectacle unto the world, both to angels and men." (*AS*) However, the footnote offers an alternative reading saying: "Or, *and to angels, and to men.*" This latter rendering is also the way in which other versions render the Greek text here. (*KJ; La; Mo; Vg; CC; Murdock*) Young's translation reads: "A spectacle we became to the world, and messengers, and men." Just preceding this, in 1 Corinthians 1:20, 21, 27, 28; 2:12; 3:19, 22 the writer uses the word *ko'smos* to mean the world of humankind, so that evidently he does not depart from that sense immediately afterward in 1 Corinthians 4:9, 13. Hence, if the rendering "both to angels and men" is admitted, the expression is merely an intensification, not to enlarge the meaning of the word *ko'smos,* but to enlarge on the spectatorship as going beyond the world of mankind, so as to include "angels" as well as "men."—Compare *Ro.*

The human sphere of life and its framework. This does not mean that *ko'smos* loses all of its original sense of "order" or "arrangement" and becomes merely a synonym for mankind. Mankind itself reflects a certain order, being composed of families, tribes, and having developed into nations and language groups (1Co 14:10; Re 7:9; 14:6), with their wealthy and poor classes and other groupings. (Jas 2:5, 6) A framework of things that surround and affect mankind has been built up on earth as mankind has grown in number and in years of existence. When Jesus spoke of a man as 'gaining the whole world but forfeiting his soul in the process,' he evidently meant gaining all that the human sphere of life and human society as a whole could offer. (Mt 16:26; compare 6:25-32.) Of similar significance are Paul's words about those "making use of the world" and the married persons' 'anxiety for the things of the world' (1Co 7:31-34), as also is John's reference to "this world's means for supporting life."—1Jo 3:17; compare 1Co 3:22.

In the sense of signifying the framework, order, or sphere of human life, *ko'smos* has a meaning similar to that of the Greek *ai·on'.* In some cases the two words can almost be interchanged. For example, Demas is reported to have forsaken the apostle Paul because he "loved the present system of things [*ai·o'na*]"; while the apostle John warned against 'loving the world [*ko'smon*]' with its way of life that appeals to the sinful flesh. (2Ti 4:10; 1Jo 2:15-17) And the one who is described at John 12:31 as "the ruler of this world [*ko'smou*]" is identified at 2 Corinthians 4:4 as "the god of this system of things [*ai·o'nos*]."

At the close of his Gospel, the apostle John says that if all the things Jesus did were set down in full detail, he supposed "the world [form of *ko'smos*] itself could not contain the scrolls written."

(Joh 21:25) He did not use *ge* (the earth) or *oi·kou·me'ne* (the inhabited earth) and thereby say that the *planet* could not contain the scrolls, but he used *ko'smos,* evidently meaning that human society (with its then existing library space) was not in position to receive the voluminous records (in the book style then used) that this would have entailed. Compare also such texts as John 7:4; 12:19 for similar uses of *ko'smos.*

Coming "into the world." When one is 'born into this world,' then, he is not merely born among mankind but also comes into the framework of human circumstances in which men live. (Joh 16:21; 1Ti 6:7) However, while references to one's going or coming into the world may refer to one's birth into the human sphere of life, this is not always the case. Jesus, for example, in prayer to God said: "Just as you sent me forth into the world, I also sent them [his disciples] forth into the world." (Joh 17:18) He sent them into the world as grown men, not as newborn babes. John speaks of false prophets and deceivers as having "gone forth into the world."—1Jo 4:1; 2Jo 7.

The many references to Jesus' 'coming or being sent forth into the world' evidently do not refer primarily, if at all, to his human birth but more reasonably apply to his going out among mankind, publicly carrying out his assigned ministry from and after his baptism and anointing, acting as a light bearer to the world of mankind. (Compare Joh 1:9; 3:17, 19; 6:14; 9:39; 10:36; 11:27; 12:46; 1Jo 4:9.) His human birth was solely a necessary means to that end. (Joh 18:37) In corroboration of this, the writer of Hebrews represents Jesus as speaking words from Psalm 40:6-8 "when he comes into the world," and Jesus logically did not do this as a newborn babe.—Heb 10:5-10.

When his public ministry among mankind came to its close, Jesus knew "that his hour had come for him to move out of this world to the Father." He would die as a man and would be resurrected to life in the spirit realm from which he had come. —Joh 13:1; 16:28; 17:11; compare Joh 8:23.

"The elementary things of the world." At Galatians 4:1-3, after showing that a child is like a slave in the sense of being under the stewardship of others until he is of age, Paul states: "Likewise we also, when we were babes, continued enslaved by the elementary things [*stoi·khei'a*] belonging to the world." He then proceeds to show that God's Son came at the "full limit of the time" and released those becoming his disciples from being under the Law that they might receive the adoption of sons. (Ga 4:4-7) Similarly at Colossians 2:8,

9, 20 he warns the Christians at Colossae against being carried off "through the philosophy and empty deception according to the tradition of men, according to the elementary things [*stoi·khei'a*] of the world and not according to Christ; because it is in him that all the fullness of the divine quality dwells bodily," stressing that they "died together with Christ toward the elementary things of the world."

Of the Greek word *stoi·khei'a* (plural of *stoi·khei'on*) used by Paul, *The Pulpit Commentary* (Galatians, p. 181) says: "From the primary sense of 'stakes placed in a row,' . . . the term [*stoi·khei'a*] was applied to the letters of the alphabet as placed in rows, and thence to the primary constituents of speech; then to the primary constituents of all objects in nature, as, for example, the four 'elements' (see 2 Pet. iii. 10, 12); and to the 'rudiments' or first 'elements' of any branch of knowledge. It is in this last sense that it occurs in Heb. v. 12." (Edited by C. Spence, London, 1885) The related verb *stoi·khe'o* means "walk orderly."—Ga 6:16.

In his letters to the Galatians and Colossians, Paul was evidently not referring to the basic or component parts of the material creation but, rather, as German scholar Heinrich A. W. Meyer's *Critical and Exegetical Hand-Book* (1884, Galatians, p. 168) observes, to "the elements of non-Christian humanity," that is, to its fundamental, or primary, principles. Paul's writings show this would include the philosophies and deceptive teachings based purely on human standards, concepts, reasoning, and mythology, such as the Greeks and other pagan peoples reveled in. (Col 2:8) However, it is clear that he also used the term as embracing things of a Jewish nature, not only non-Biblical Jewish teachings calling for asceticism or "worship of the angels" but also the teaching that Christians should put themselves under obligation to keep the Mosaic Law.—Col 2:16-18; Ga 4:4, 5, 21.

True, the Mosaic Law was of divine origin. However, it had now been fulfilled in Christ Jesus, "the reality" to which its shadows pointed, and it was therefore obsolete. (Col 2:13-17) Additionally, the tabernacle (and later temple) was "worldly" or of human construction, hence, "mundane" (Gr., *ko·smi·kon';* Heb 9:1, *Mo*), that is, of the human sphere, not heavenly or spiritual, and the requirements related thereto were "legal requirements pertaining to the flesh and were imposed until the appointed time to set things straight." Christ Jesus had now entered into the "greater and more perfect tent not made with hands, that is, not of this creation," into heaven itself. (Heb 9:8-14, 23, 24) He himself had told a Samaritan woman that the time was coming when the temple at Jerusalem would no longer be used as an essential part of true worship but that the true worshipers would "worship the Father with spirit and truth." (Joh 4:21-24) So the need to employ such things that were only "typical representations" (Heb 9:23) within the human sphere picturing the greater things of a heavenly nature had ceased with Christ Jesus' death, resurrection, and ascension into heaven.

Hence the Galatian and Colossian Christians could now worship according to the superior way based on Christ Jesus. He, and not humans and their principles or teachings, or even the "legal requirements pertaining to the flesh" as found in the Law covenant, should be recognized as the appointed standard and the full means of measuring the truth of any teaching or way of life. (Col 2:9) Christians should not be like children by voluntarily placing themselves under that which was likened to a pedagogue or tutor, namely, the Mosaic Law (Ga 3:23-26), but they were to be in a relationship with God like that of a grown son with his father. The law was elementary, "the A B C of religion," as compared with the Christian teaching. (H. Meyer's *Critical and Exegetical Hand-Book,* 1885, Colossians, p. 292) Anointed Christians, because of their being begotten to heavenly life, had, in effect, died and been impaled to the *ko'smos* of the human sphere of life, in which regulations such as fleshly circumcision had been in force; they had become "a new creation." (2Co 5:17; Col 2:11, 12, 20-23; compare Ga 6:12-15; Joh 8:23.) They knew that Jesus' Kingdom was not from a human source. (Joh 18:36) They certainly should not turn back to "the weak and beggarly elementary things" of the human sphere (Ga 4:9) and thereby be deluded into giving up the "riches of the full assurance of their understanding" and "accurate knowledge of the sacred secret of God, namely, Christ," in whom are concealed "all the treasures of wisdom and of knowledge."—Col 2:1-4.

The world alienated from God. A use of *ko'smos* unique to the Scriptures is in making it stand for the world of mankind apart from God's servants. Peter writes that God brought the Deluge "upon a world of ungodly people," while preserving Noah and his family; in this way "the world of that time suffered destruction when it was deluged with water." (2Pe 2:5; 3:6) It may again be noted that the reference here is not to the destruction of the planet or of the celestial bodies of the universe, but it is restricted to the human sphere,

in this case the unrighteous human society. It was that "world" that Noah condemned by his faithful course.—Heb 11:7.

The pre-Flood unrighteous world, or human society, ended, but mankind itself did not end, being preserved in Noah and his family. After the Flood the majority of mankind again deviated from righteousness, producing another wicked human society. Still there were those who took a separate course, adhering to righteousness. In course of time God designated Israel as his chosen people, bringing them into covenant relationship with himself. Because the Israelites were thus made distinct from the world in general, Paul could use *ko'smos*, "world," as equivalent to the non-Israelite "people of the nations," or "Gentiles," at Romans 11:12-15. (*NW; KJ*) He there pointed out that Israel's apostasy led to God's revoking his covenant relationship with them and that it opened up the way for the Gentiles to enter into such relationship and its riches, by being reconciled to God. (Compare Eph 2:11-13.) The "world," or *ko'smos*, then, during this post-Flood and pre-Christian period again designated all humanity outside of God's approved servants, and specifically those outside Israel during the period of its covenant relationship with Jehovah.—Compare Heb 11:38.

In a similar manner and with great frequency, *ko'smos* is used to signify all non-Christian human society, regardless of race. This is the world that hated Jesus and his followers because they bore witness concerning its unrighteousness and because they maintained separateness from it; such world thereby showed hatred for Jehovah God himself and did not come to know him. (Joh 7:7; 15:17-25; 16:19, 20; 17:14, 25; 1Jo 3:1, 13) Over this world of unrighteous human society and its kingdoms, God's Adversary, Satan the Devil, exercises rulership; in fact, he has made himself "the god" of such world. (Mt 4:8, 9; Joh 12:31; 14:30; 16:11; compare 2Co 4:4.) God did not produce such unrighteous world; it owes its development to his chief Opposer, in whose power "the whole world is lying." (1Jo 4:4, 5; 5:18, 19) Satan and his "wicked spirit forces in the heavenly places" act as the invisible "world rulers [or, cosmocrats; Gr., *ko·smo·kra'to·ras*]" over the world alienated from God.—Eph 6:11, 12.

Not simply humanity, of which Jesus' disciples were a part, but the whole organized human society that exists outside the true Christian congregation is meant in such texts. Otherwise Christians could not cease to be a "part of the world" without dying and ceasing to live in the flesh. (Joh 17:6; 15:19) Though unavoidably living in the midst of that society of worldly persons, including those engaging in fornication, idolatry, extortion, and similar practices (1Co 5:9-13), such Christians must keep themselves clean and unspotted by that world's corruption and defilement, not entering into friendly relations with it, lest they be condemned with it. (1Co 11:32; Jas 1:27; 4:4; 2Pe 1:4; 2:20; compare 1Pe 4:3-6.) They cannot be guided by worldly wisdom, which is foolishness in God's sight, nor can they 'breathe in' the "spirit of the world," that is, its selfish and sinful activating force. (1Co 1:21; 2:12; 3:19; 2Co 1:12; Tit 2:12; compare Joh 14:16, 17; Eph 2:1, 2; 1Jo 2:15-17; see SPIRIT [Impelling Mental Inclination].) Thus, through their faith they 'conquer the world' of unrighteous human society, even as did God's Son. (Joh 16:33; 1Jo 4:4; 5:4, 5) That unrighteous human society is due to pass away by divine destruction (1Jo 2:17), even as the ungodly pre-Flood world perished.—2Pe 3:6.

Ungodly world ends; humankind preserved. Thus, the *ko'smos* for which Jesus died must mean the world of mankind viewed simply as the human family, *all human flesh.* (Joh 3:16, 17) As to the world in the sense of *human society alienated from God* and in actual enmity toward God, Jesus did not pray on behalf of such world but only for those who came out of that world and put faith in him. (Joh 17:8, 9) Even as human flesh survived the destruction of the ungodly human society, or world, in the Deluge, so Jesus showed that human flesh is to survive the great tribulation that he likened to that Flood. (Mt 24:21, 22, 36-39; compare Re 7:9-17.) "The kingdom of the world" (evidently meaning of humankind) is, in fact, promised to become "the kingdom of our Lord and of his Christ," and those reigning with Christ in his heavenly Kingdom are due to "rule as kings over the earth," hence over humankind apart from the deceased ungodly human society dominated by Satan.—Re 11:15; 5:9, 10.

WORM [Heb., *toh·le·'ah'* or *toh·la''ath*]. Any of a great variety of slender crawling or creeping animals, usually having soft bodies and being legless or virtually so. In Scripture, "worm" often appears to denote the larval stage of insects, particularly maggots. (Ex 16:20, 24; Isa 14:11; 66:24) At other times the reference is not to maggots but to worms that feed on vegetation.—De 28:39; Jon 4:7.

The term "worm" also appears in an illustrative setting. Bildad disparagingly spoke of man as a worm (Job 25:6), and it was foretold that the Messiah would be viewed as a reproach and despicable, as a worm. (Ps 22:6) Jehovah God referred to Israel as a worm, a lowly and helpless creature, seemingly at the mercy of anyone passing by. But Jehovah assured the Israelites of his help and encouraged them not to be afraid.—Isa 41:14.

WORMWOOD [Heb., *la·'anah'*; Gr., *a'psinthos*]. This designates many, frequently somewhat woody, plants having an intensely bitter taste and a strong aromatic odor. Several varieties of wormwood are found in Palestine, particularly in desert areas. The most common is the *Artemisia herba-alba,* a small shrub growing 40 cm (16 in.) tall. In Scripture, wormwood is compared to the aftereffects of immorality (Pr 5:4) and the bitter experience that was to come and did come upon Judah and Jerusalem at the hands of the Babylonians. (Jer 9:15; 23:15; La 3:15, 19) It also represents injustice and unrighteousness (Am 5:7; 6:12) and is used with reference to apostates. (De 29:18) At Revelation 8:11, wormwood denotes a bitter and poisonous substance, also called absinthe.

WORSHIP. The rendering of reverent honor or homage. True worship of the Creator embraces every aspect of an individual's life. The apostle Paul wrote to the Corinthians: "Whether you are eating or drinking or doing anything else, do all things for God's glory."—1Co 10:31.

When Jehovah God created Adam, He did not prescribe a particular ceremony or a means by which perfect man might approach Him in worship. Nevertheless, Adam was able to serve or worship his Creator by faithfully doing the will of his heavenly Father. Later, to the nation of Israel, Jehovah did outline a certain way of approach in worship, including sacrifice, a priesthood, and a material sanctuary. (See APPROACH TO GOD.) This, however, had only "a shadow of the good things to come, but not the very substance of the things." (Heb 10:1) The primary emphasis has always been on exercising faith—doing the will of Jehovah God—and not on ceremony or ritual.—Mt 7:21; Jas 2:17-26.

As the prophet Micah put it: "With what shall I confront Jehovah? With what shall I bow myself to God on high? Shall I confront him with whole burnt offerings, with calves a year old? Will Jehovah be pleased with thousands of rams, with tens of thousands of torrents of oil? Shall I give my firstborn son for my revolt, the fruitage of my belly for the sin of my soul? He has told you, O earthling man, what is good. And what is Jehovah asking back from you but to exercise justice and to love kindness and to be modest in walking with your God?"—Mic 6:6-8; compare Ps 50:8-15, 23.

Hebrew and Greek Terms. Most Hebrew and Greek words that can denote worship can also be applied to acts other than worship. However, the context determines in what way the respective words are to be understood.

One of the Hebrew words conveying the idea of worship ('a·vadh') basically means "serve." (Ge 14:4; 15:13; 29:15) Serving or worshiping Jehovah required obedience to all of his commands, doing his will as a person exclusively devoted to him. (Ex 19:5; De 30:15-20; Jos 24:14, 15) Therefore, for an individual to engage in any ritual or act of devotion toward any other gods signified his abandoning true worship.—De 11:13-17; Jg 3:6, 7.

Another Hebrew term that can denote worship is hish·ta·chawah', which primarily means "bow down" (Pr 12:25), or do obeisance. (See OBEISANCE.) Whereas such bowing could at times simply be an act of respect or of courteous regard toward another person (Ge 19:1, 2; 33:1-6; 37:9, 10), it could also be an expression of worship, indicating one's reverence and gratitude to God and submission to his will. When used with reference to the true God or false deities, the word hish·ta·chawah' is at times associated with sacrifice and prayer. (Ge 22:5-7; 24:26, 27; Isa 44:17) This would indicate that it was common to bow down when praying or offering sacrifice.—See PRAYER.

The Hebrew root sa·ghadh' (Isa 44:15, 17, 19; 46:6) basically signifies "prostrate oneself." The Aramaic equivalent is usually associated with worship (Da 3:5-7, 10-15, 18, 28), but it is used at Daniel 2:46 to refer to King Nebuchadnezzar's paying homage to Daniel, prostrating himself before the prophet.

The Greek verb la·treu'o (Lu 1:74; 2:37; 4:8; Ac 7:7) and the noun la·trei'a (Joh 16:2; Ro 9:4) convey the idea of rendering not merely an ordinary, mundane service but sacred service.

The Greek word pro·sky·ne'o corresponds closely to the Hebrew term hish·ta·chawah' in expressing the thought of obeisance and, at times, worship. The term pro·sky·ne'o is used in connection with a slave's doing obeisance to a king (Mt 18:26) as well as the act Satan stipulated when he offered Jesus all the kingdoms of the world and their glory. (Mt 4:8, 9) Had he done obeisance to the Devil, Jesus would thereby have signified submission to Satan and made himself the Devil's servant. But Jesus refused, saying: "Go away, Satan! For it is written, 'It is Jehovah your God you must worship [form of Gr. pro·sky·ne'o or, in the Deuteronomy account that Jesus was quoting, Heb. hish·ta·chawah'], and it is to him alone you must render sacred service [form of Gr. la·treu'o or Heb. 'a·vadh'].'" (Mt 4:10;

De 5:9; 6:13) Similarly, worship, obeisance, or bowing down to "the wild beast" and its "image" is linked with service, for the worshipers are identified as supporters of "the wild beast" and its "image" by having a mark either on the hand (with which one serves) or on the forehead (for all to see). Since the Devil gives the wild beast its authority, worshiping the wild beast means, in reality, worshiping or serving the Devil.—Re 13:4, 15-17; 14:9-11.

Other Greek words associated with worship are drawn from eu·se·be'o, thre·skeu'o, and se'bo·mai. The word eu·se·be'o means "give godly devotion to" or "venerate, revere." (See GODLY DEVOTION.) At Acts 17:23 this term is used with reference to the godly devotion or veneration that the men of Athens were giving to an "Unknown God." From thre·skeu'o comes the noun thre·skei'a, understood to designate a "form of worship," whether true or false. (Ac 26:5; Col 2:18) The true worship practiced by Christians was marked by genuine concern for the poor and complete separateness from the ungodly world. (Jas 1:26, 27) The word se'bo·mai (Mt 15:9; Mr 7:7; Ac 18:7; 19:27) and the related term se·ba'zo·mai (Ro 1:25) mean "revere; venerate; worship." Objects of worship or of devotion are designated by the noun se'ba·sma. (Ac 17:23; 2Th 2:4) Two other terms are from the same verb stem, with the prefix The·os', God. These are the·o·se·bes', meaning "God-revering" (Joh 9:31), and the·o·se'bei·a, denoting "reverence of God." (1Ti 2:10) These two terms correspond somewhat to the German word for "public worship," namely, Gottesdienst (a combination of "God" and "service").

Worship That Is Acceptable to God. Jehovah God accepts only the worship of those who comport themselves in harmony with his will. (Mt 15:9; Mr 7:7) To a Samaritan woman Christ Jesus said: "The hour is coming when neither in this mountain [Gerizim] nor in Jerusalem will you people worship the Father. You worship what you do not know; we worship what we know . . . Nevertheless, the hour is coming, and it is now, when the true worshipers will worship the Father with spirit and truth, for, indeed, the Father is looking for suchlike ones to worship him. God is a Spirit, and those worshiping him must worship with spirit and truth."—Joh 4:21-24.

The words of Jesus clearly showed that true worship would not depend upon the presence or use of visible things and geographic locations. Instead of relying on sight or touch, the true worshiper exercises faith and, regardless of the place or things about him, maintains a worshipful attitude. Thus he worships, not with the aid of something that he can see or touch, but with spirit. Since he has the truth as revealed by God, his worship is in agreement with the truth. Having become acquainted with God through the Bible and evidence of the operation of God's spirit in his life, the person who worships with spirit and truth definitely 'knows what he is worshiping.'

WRATH. See ANGER.

WRITING.

The act of inscribing on a surface letters or characters that convey words or ideas. The first man, Adam, was endowed with the ability to speak a language. Initially, however, there would have been little, if any, need for him to write. Adam was then able to handle all communication by word of mouth and, as a perfect man, did not have to depend on a written record to offset an imperfect memory. Nevertheless, Adam must have had the ability to devise some means of making a written record. But the Bible provides no direct proof that he wrote either before or after his transgression.

The thought has been advanced that the words, "this is the book of Adam's history," may indicate that Adam was the writer of this "book." (Ge 5:1) Commenting on the phrase "this is the history" ("these are the origins"), occurring frequently throughout Genesis, P. J. Wiseman notes: "It is the concluding sentence of each section, and therefore points backward to a narrative already recorded. . . . It normally refers to the writer of the history, or the owner of the tablet containing it."—*New Discoveries in Babylonia About Genesis,* 1949, p. 53.

Examination of the contents of these histories casts considerable doubt on the correctness of the view advanced by Wiseman. For example, according to this view, the section beginning with Genesis chapter 36, verse 10, would conclude with the words of Genesis 37:2, "This is the history of Jacob." However, nearly the entire record pertains to Esau's offspring and makes only incidental reference to Jacob. On the other hand, the information that follows presents extensive information about Jacob and his family. Moreover, if the theory were correct, this would mean that Ishmael and Esau were the writers or possessors of the most extensive documents about God's dealings with Abraham, Isaac, and Jacob. This does not appear to be reasonable, for it would make those who had no share in the Abrahamic covenant the ones who had the greatest interest in that covenant. It would be hard to conceive that Ishmael had such concern about events associated with Abraham's

household that he put forth efforts to get a detailed record of them, a record that spanned many years after his being dismissed along with his mother Hagar.—Ge 11:27b–25:12.

Similarly, there would have been no reason for Esau, who had no appreciation for sacred things (Heb 12:16), to have written or to have been the possessor of an account dealing extensively with events in Jacob's life, events to which Esau was not an eyewitness. (Ge 25:19–36:1) Also, it does not seem logical to conclude that Isaac and Jacob would have largely ignored God's dealings with them, being content to have only brief records about someone else's genealogies.—Ge 25:13-19a; 36:10–37:2a.

Writing Before the Flood. There is no way to establish definitely that some of the histories mentioned in the book of Genesis were committed to writing before the Flood, and the Bible contains no references to pre-Flood writing. However, it should be noted that the building of cities, the development of musical instruments, and the forging of iron and copper tools had their start long before the Flood. (Ge 4:17, 21, 22) Reasonably, therefore, men would have had little difficulty in also developing a method of writing. Since there was only one language originally (which later became known as Hebrew; see HEBREW, II) and since those who continued to speak that language, the Israelites, are known to have used an alphabet, this suggests that alphabetic writing could have existed before the Flood.

Assyrian King Ashurbanipal spoke of reading "inscriptions on stone from the time before the flood." (*Light From the Ancient Past,* by J. Finegan, 1959, pp. 216, 217) But these inscriptions may have simply preceded a local flood of considerable proportions or could have been accounts that purported to relate events prior to the Flood. For example, what is termed "The Sumerian King List," after mentioning that eight kings ruled for 241,000 years, states: "(Then) the Flood swept over (the earth)." (*Ancient Near Eastern Texts,* edited by J. Pritchard, 1974, p. 265) Such record, clearly, is not authentic.

According to Bible chronology, the global Flood of Noah's day occurred in 2370 B.C.E. Archaeologists have assigned dates earlier than this to numerous clay tablets they have excavated. But these clay tablets are not dated documents. Hence the dates that have been assigned to them are merely conjectural and provide no solid basis for establishing a relationship in time to the Biblical Flood. None of the artifacts that have been excavated are definitely known to date from pre-Flood times. Archaeologists who have assigned items to the pre-Flood period have done so on the basis of findings that, at best, can only be interpreted to give evidence of a great local flood.

Writing After the Flood. After the confusion of man's original language at Babel, various systems of writing came into existence. The Babylonians, Assyrians, and other peoples used cuneiform (wedge-shaped) script, which is thought to have been developed by the Sumerians from their pictographic writing. There is evidence that more than one writing system was used at the same time. For example, an ancient Assyrian wall painting depicts two scribes, one making cuneiform impressions on a tablet with a stylus (likely in Akkadian) and the other writing with a brush on a piece of skin or papyrus (possibly in Aramaic). Egyptian hieroglyphic writing consisted of distinct pictorial representations and geometric forms. Though hieroglyphic writing continued to be employed for inscriptions on monuments and wall paintings, two other forms of writing (first hieratic and then demotic) came into use. (See EGYPT, EGYPTIAN.) In nonalphabetic systems, a pictorial representation (or its later, often irrecognizable, linear or cursive form) could stand for the object depicted, an idea conveyed by the object, or another word or syllable having the same pronunciation. By way of illustration, a simple drawing of an eye could be used in English to designate an "eye," the personal pronoun "I," the verb "see," the noun "sea," or the initial syllable of "season."

The alphabetic system employed by the Israelites was phonetic, with each written consonant symbol representing a particular consonant sound. The vowel sounds, however, had to be supplied by the reader, the context determining the word intended in the case of terms having the same spelling but a different combination of vowel sounds. This posed no real problem; even modern Hebrew magazines, newspapers, and books omit vowel points almost entirely.

Literacy Among the Israelites. Priests of Israel (Nu 5:23) and prominent persons, like Moses (Ex 24:4), Joshua (Jos 24:26), Samuel (1Sa 10:25), David (2Sa 11:14, 15), and Jehu (2Ki 10:1, 6), knew how to read and write, and the people in general, with some exceptions, were literate also. (Compare Jg 8:14; Isa 10:19; 29:12.) Though apparently figurative, the command for the Israelites to write upon the doorposts of their houses implied that they were literate. (De 6:8, 9) And the Law required that the king, upon taking his throne, write out for himself a copy of the Law and read in it daily.—De 17:18, 19; see BOOK.

Although Hebrew written material was evidently quite common, few Israelite inscriptions have been found. Likely this is because the Israelites did not erect many monuments to extol their achievements. Most of the writing, including the books of the Bible, was doubtless done with ink on papyrus or parchment and, therefore, would not have lasted long in the damp soil of Palestine. The message of the Scriptures, however, was preserved throughout the centuries by painstaking copying and recopying. (See COPYIST; MANUSCRIPTS OF THE BIBLE; SCRIBE.) The Bible's history alone reaches to man's very beginning and even beyond. (Ge chaps 1, 2) The records engraved on stone and inscribed on clay tablets, prisms, and cylinders may, in some cases, be much older than the most ancient extant Bible manuscript, yet those records have no real effect on the lives of people today—many of them (like The Sumerian King List) contain outright falsehoods. Hence, among ancient writings, the Bible stands out as unique in presenting a meaningful message that deserves much more than passing interest.

Y

YAH. See JAH.

YAHWEH. See JEHOVAH.

YEAR. The principal Hebrew word for "year," *sha·nah'*, comes from a root meaning "repeat; do again" and, like its Greek counterpart *e·ni·au·tos'*, carries the idea of a cycle of time. On earth it is the recurrence of the seasons that visibly marks the completion of the annual periods; the seasons, in turn, are governed by the earth's revolutions around the sun. The Creator, therefore, provided the means for measuring time in terms of years by placing the earth in its assigned orbit, with the earth's axis positioned at an inclined angle in relation to its plane of travel around the sun. A convenient means for subdividing the year into shorter periods is also provided by the regular phases of the moon. These facts are indicated early in the Bible record.—Ge 1:14-16; 8:22.

From the beginning, man made use of these

divinely provided time indicators, measuring time in terms of years subdivided into months. (Ge 5: 1-32) Most ancient peoples used a year of 12 lunar months. The common lunar year has 354 days, with the months having 29 or 30 days, depending on the appearance of each new moon. It is, therefore, about 11¼ days short of the true solar year of 365¼ days (365 days 5 hours 48 minutes and 46 seconds).

In Noah's Time. In Noah's time we have the first record of the ancient reckoning of the length of the year. He evidently divided the year into 12 months of 30 days each. At Genesis 7:11, 24 and 8:3-5 the "log" that Noah kept shows 150 days to be equal to five months. In this account the second, seventh, and tenth months of the year of the Flood are directly mentioned. Then, following the tenth month and its first day, a period of 40 days occurs, as well as two periods of 7 days each, or a total of 54 days. (Ge 8:5-12) There is also an indeterminate time between the sending forth of the raven and the first sending forth of the dove. (Ge 8:6-8) Likewise another indeterminate period is indicated following the third and final sending forth of the dove at Genesis 8:12. In the following verse, we find the first day of the first month of the following year mentioned. (Ge 8:13) What method Noah or those prior to him used to reconcile a year made up of 30-day months with the solar year is not revealed.

Egypt and Babylon. In ancient Egypt the year was made up of 12 months of 30 days each, and five additional days were added annually to bring the year into harmony with the solar year. The Babylonians, on the other hand, held to a lunar year but added a 13th month, called Veadar, during certain years to maintain the seasons in line with the months to which they normally corresponded. Such a year is called a lunisolar or bound year and obviously is sometimes shorter and sometimes longer than the true solar year, depending on whether the lunar year has 12 or 13 months.

The Metonic Cycle. At some point the system of adding an intercalary, or 13th, month seven times every 19 years was developed, giving almost exactly the same result as 19 true solar years. This cycle came to be called the Metonic cycle after the Greek mathematician Meton of the fifth century B.C.E.

The Hebrews. The Bible does not say whether this was the system the Hebrews originally employed to reconcile their lunar year with the solar year. The fact that the recorded names of their lunar months are seasonal names shows

they did make some such reconciliation. Twice each year the sun's center crosses the equator, and at those times day and night are everywhere of equal length (approximately 12 hours of daylight and 12 hours of darkness). These two times are called the vernal, or spring, equinox and the autumnal, or fall, equinox. They occur about March 21 and September 23 of each of our present calendar years. These equinoctial occurrences could logically provide the means for noting when the lunar months were running too far ahead of the related seasons and thus serve as a guide for making the needed adjustment by the addition of an intercalary month.

The years were anciently reckoned as running from autumn to autumn, the first month starting around the middle of our present month of September. This coincides with the Jewish tradition that the creation of man took place in the autumn. Since the Bible provides a record of Adam's age in terms of years (Ge 5:3-5), it is reasonable that the count began with the time of his creation, and if this indeed occurred in the autumn, it would explain to some extent the ancient practice of beginning the new year at that time. Additionally, however, such a year would be particularly suited to the agricultural life of the people, especially in that part of the earth where both the pre-Flood and early post-Flood peoples were concentrated. The year closed with the final harvest period and began with the plowing and sowing toward the first part of our month of October.

A sacred and a secular year. God changed the year's beginning for the nation of Israel at the time of their Exodus from Egypt, decreeing that it should begin with the month of Abib, or Nisan, in the spring. (Ex 12:1-14; 23:15) The autumn, or fall, of the year, however, continued to mark the beginning of their secular or agricultural year. Thus, at Exodus 23:16, the Festival of Ingathering, which took place in the autumn in the month of Ethanim, the seventh month of the sacred calendar, is spoken of as being at "the outgoing of the year" and at Exodus 34:22 as "at the turn of the year." Likewise, the regulations concerning the Jubilee years show that they began in the autumn month of Ethanim.—Le 25:8-18.

The Jewish historian Josephus (of the first century C.E.) says that the sacred year (beginning in the spring) was used with regard to religious observances but that the original secular year (beginning in the fall) continued to be used with regard to selling, buying, and other ordinary affairs. (*Jewish Antiquities,* I, 81 [iii, 3]) This double system of a sacred and a secular year is especially prominent in the postexilic period following the release of the Jews from Babylon. The first day of Nisan, or Abib, marked the start of the sacred year, and the first day of Tishri, or Ethanim, marked the beginning of the secular year. In each case, what was the first month of one calendar became the seventh of the other.—See CALENDAR.

Calendar correlated with festivals. The major points of each year were the three great festival seasons decreed by Jehovah God: The Passover (followed by the Festival of Unfermented Cakes) on Nisan 14; the Festival of Weeks, or Pentecost, on Sivan 6; and the Festival of Ingathering (preceded by the Atonement Day) on Ethanim 15-21. The Festival of Unfermented Cakes coincided with the barley harvest, Pentecost with the wheat harvest, and the Festival of Ingathering with the general harvest at the close of the agricultural year.

The Sabbath and Jubilee years. Under the Law covenant every seventh year was a year of complete rest for the land, a Sabbath year. The period or week of seven years was called a 'sabbath of years.' (Le 25:2-8) Each 50th year was a Jubilee year of rest, in which all Hebrew slaves were set free and all hereditary possessions of land were returned to their original owners.—Le 25:10-41; see SABBATH YEAR.

Method of counting rule of kings. In historical records it was the usual practice in Babylon to count the reigning, or regnal, years of a king as full years, beginning on Nisan 1. The months during which the king might have actually started to rule prior to Nisan 1 were regarded as forming his *accession* year, but they were historically credited to, or counted as belonging to, the full regnal years of the king who had preceded him. If, as Jewish tradition indicates, this system was followed in Judah, then, when the Bible speaks of Kings David and Solomon as each reigning for "forty years," the reigns cover full 40-year periods.—1Ki 1:39; 2:1, 10, 11; 11:42.

In Prophecy. In prophecy the word "year" is often used in a special sense as the equivalent of 360 days (12 months of 30 days each). (Re 11:2, 3) It is also called a "time" and is occasionally represented symbolically by a "day."—Re 12:6, 14; Eze 4:5, 6.

YEAST. See LEAVEN.

YIRON

(Yi′ron). One of the fortified cities in the territory of Naphtali. (Jos 19:32, 35, 38) Its location is uncertain, but it has tentatively been identified with present-day Yaroun, about 30 km (19 mi) SW of Dan, in Galilee.

YOHDH

[י]. The tenth letter of the Hebrew alphabet. It is the smallest of the Hebrew letters. The name of the smallest letter of the Greek alphabet, *i·o′ta,* evidently is akin to the Hebrew *yohdh.* Since the Law of Moses was originally written and subsequently preserved in Hebrew, it is likely that Jesus was referring back to the Hebrew *yohdh* when he said that the "smallest letter [Gr., *i·o′ta*]" would not pass away without its due fulfillment. (Mt 5:18) This letter occurs as the initial letter in the Tetragrammaton, or sacred name Jehovah (reading from right to left: יהוה), and as such was carried over into the earliest copies of the Greek *Septuagint.* A papyrus fragment of the third century C.E. (P. Oxyrhynchus vii. 1007) containing a portion of the *Septuagint* translation of Genesis represented the divine name Jehovah by a doubled *yohdh.*—Ge 2:8, ftn.

Because of the similarity between the letters *yohdh* (י) and *waw* (ו), they were sometimes confused by copyists. In the Hebrew, at Psalm 119:73-80 each verse begins with the letter *yohdh.*

YOKE.

A bar borne upon a person's shoulders, from each side of which loads were suspended (compare Isa 9:4), or a wooden bar or frame placed over the necks of two draft animals (usually cattle) when drawing a farm implement or a wagon. (Nu 19:2; De 21:3; 1Sa 6:7) The latter crossbeam was generally held in position by two bands, each encircling the neck of one animal. Some yokes, instead of having bands, had straight bars that projected down along each side of the animals' necks and were secured by thongs tied across their throats. Yokes were also fastened to the animals' foreheads at the base of their horns. Yokes borne across the shoulders of humans in ancient Egypt to carry water and other burdens were about 1 m (3 ft) long and were equipped with straps at the ends for attaching loads.

Original-Language Terms. The Greek terms (*zy·gos′, zeu′gos*) that convey the idea of a yoke are drawn from the word *zeu′gny·mi,* which means "yoke; couple; join; bind; unite together." Usually two animals were yoked together, so the Greek word *zeu′gos* can denote a "pair" or "yoke" of animals, such as a "pair of turtledoves." (Lu 2:24; 14:19) The Hebrew term *tse′medh* somewhat corresponds to the Greek word *zeu′gos* and can designate a "couple" (Jg 19:3, 10), a "pair" (1Sa 11:7), a "span" (1Ki 19:19, 21), or an "acre," the measure of land that a span of bulls can plow in a day (1Sa 14:14; Isa 5:10). An entirely different Hebrew word (*'ol* or *'ohl*), however, refers to the instrument used for yoking or uniting things together.

(Nu 19:2) Another Hebrew term (*moh·tah'*, yoke bar) is associated with yokes (Le 26:13; Isa 58: 6, 9; Jer 27:2; 28:10, 12, 13; Eze 30:18; 34:27) and at 1 Chronicles 15:15 refers to the poles by means of which the Ark was carried. The Greek word *zy·gos'*, besides designating a yoke, can apply to various objects that unite two or more things. For example, the beam of a pair of scales 'yokes' two pans together; thus, *zy·gos'* is rendered "pair of scales" at Revelation 6:5. Like the Hebrew *'ol* (Ge 27:40; Isa 9:4), *zy·gos'* could also describe the yoke bar used by an individual for carrying loads, equally distributed on either side of the bar.

Figurative Use. Slaves often had to carry burdens (compare Jos 9:23; 1Ti 6:1), and for this reason the yoke appropriately represented enslavement or subjection to another person, such as Esau's subjection to Jacob (Ge 27:40), or subjection to a ruler or nation (1Ki 12:4-14; 2Ch 10:4-14; Eze 34:27), as well as oppression and suffering. (Isa 58:6-9) An iron yoke denoted severer bondage than a wooden yoke. (De 28:48; Jer 28:10-14) And removing or breaking the yoke signified liberation from bondage, oppression, and exploitation.—Le 26:13; Isa 10:27; 14:25; Jer 2:20; 28:2, 4; 30:8; Eze 30:18.

When the city of Jerusalem fell to King Nebuchadnezzar, the inhabitants came under the heavy yoke of submission to Babylon. This yoke was especially hard on the old men, who had not endured such a thing earlier in life. (Compare Isa 47:6.) Evidently alluding to this in his lamentation over the destruction of Jerusalem, Jeremiah said: "Good it is for an able-bodied man that he should carry the yoke during his youth." By learning to bear a yoke of suffering while young, an individual will find it much easier to bear a yoke in later life, and that without losing hope.—La 3:25-30.

Whereas individuals and nations have dealt oppressively with others, Jehovah God has never placed an oppressive, hurtful yoke upon his faithful servants. Through the prophet Hosea, Jehovah reminded Israel of his merciful treatment: "With the ropes of earthling man I kept drawing them, with the cords of love, so that I became to them as those lifting off a yoke on their jaws, and gently I brought food to each one." (Ho 11:4) So in Jehovah's treatment of the Israelites, he acted as one who lifted off or pushed back a yoke far enough to enable an animal to eat comfortably. It was only when they broke their yoke of submission to God (Jer 5:5) that they came under the oppressive yoke of enemy nations.—Compare De 28:48; Jer 5:6-19; 28:14.

The Law given to the nation of Israel was a yoke, for it placed them under obligations and responsibilities to Jehovah God. Being holy, righteous, and good, what the Law prescribed did not work injury to the Israelites. (Ro 7:12) Because of their sinfulness and imperfection, however, they were unable to keep it perfectly, and therefore it proved to be a yoke that 'neither they nor their forefathers were able to bear' (for it resulted in condemnation to them for breaking the Law). This point was made by Peter, when showing that it was not necessary to impose upon non-Jewish Christians the obligation to observe "the law of Moses." (Ac 15:4-11) The Law itself did not bring slavery, but sin did. (Ro 7:12, 14) So for an individual to try to gain life by keeping the Mosaic Law perfectly not only would be impossible but would also mean letting himself "be confined again in a yoke of slavery," because, being a sinner and a slave to sin, he would be condemned by the Law, which provided no truly effective sacrifice for sins, as did Christ's ransom.—Ga 5:1-6.

In the time of Jesus' earthly ministry, the Jews found themselves under the yoke of the Mosaic Law and, additionally, burdened down with many traditions of men. Concerning the scribes and Pharisees, Jesus Christ said: "They bind up heavy loads and put them upon the shoulders of men, but they themselves are not willing to budge them with their finger." (Mt 23:4) Hence, from a spiritual viewpoint, the common people especially were "loaded down." So Jesus could say: "Come to me, all you who are toiling and loaded down, and I will refresh you. Take my yoke upon you and learn from me, for I am mild-tempered and lowly in heart, and you will find refreshment for your souls. For my yoke is kindly and my load is light." (Mt 11:28-30) If the "yoke" Jesus had in mind was one that had been placed upon him by his heavenly Father, then this would signify that others could get under the yoke *with him* and he would assist them. On the other hand, if the yoke is one that Jesus himself puts on others, then the reference is to submitting oneself to Christ's *authority* and *direction* as his disciple. At Philippians 4:3 the apostle Paul was likely referring to a particular brother in the Philippian congregation as a "genuine yokefellow," that is, one under Christ's yoke.

Since marriage binds husband and wife together, it is like a yoke. (Mt 19:6) Hence, for a Christian to marry an unbeliever would result in an 'unequal yoking' (2Co 6:14), making unity in thought and action very difficult.

Z

ZAANAN (Za'a·nan). A town mentioned by the prophet Micah as among places due to experience the foretold invasion of Judah. (Mic 1:11) Many scholars consider it to be the same as Zenan at Joshua 15:37. It is tentatively identified with 'Araq el-Kharba, in the Shephelah region of Judah, about 6 km (3.5 mi) NW of Lachish.

ZAANANNIM (Za·a·nan'nim). "The big tree in Zaanannim" was a point apparently at the S boundary of Naphtali's tribal territory. (Jos 19:32, 33) Sisera met death in the tent of Jael, the wife of Heber the Kenite, "near the big tree in Zaanannim, which is at ["by" (*JP*) or "near" (*AT, RS*)] Kedesh," perhaps the Kedesh SE of Megiddo in Issachar. (Jg 4:11, 17, 21; 5:19) However, Zaanannim's actual site remains unidentified.

ZAAVAN (Za'a·van). Second-named son of Horite Sheik Ezer and grandson or descendant of Seir the Horite.—Ge 36:20, 21, 27; 1Ch 1:42.

ZABAD (Za'bad) [[God] Has Endowed].

1. An Ephraimite in the family of Shuthelah.—1Ch 7:20, 21.

2. A descendant of Judah through Jerahmeel; his great-grandfather was an Egyptian; son of Nathan.—1Ch 2:3, 25, 34-37.

3. One of David's mighty men; son of Ahlai.—1Ch 11:26, 41.

4. One of the assassins of King Jehoash of Judah; son of Shimeath the Ammonitess. (2Ch 24:26) He is also called Jozacar.—2Ki 12:21; see JOZACAR.

5, 6, 7. Three of the Israelites whom Ezra encouraged to dismiss their foreign wives and sons; sons of Zattu, Hashum, and Nebo, respectively.—Ezr 10:10, 11, 27, 33, 43, 44.

ZABBAI (Zab'bai) [possibly a shortened form of Zebadiah, meaning "May Jehovah Endow"]. A postexilic son of Bebai, among those who terminated their foreign marriage alliances, on Ezra's counsel. (Ezr 10:28, 44) He was probably the father of the Baruch who did work on Jerusalem's walls.—Ne 3:20.

ZABBUD (Zab'bud) [Endowed]. One of the two leaders of the sons of Bigvai, a paternal house whose members went to Jerusalem with Ezra in 468 B.C.E.—Ezr 8:1, 14.

ZABDI (Zab'di) [shortened form of Zabdiel].

1. A descendant of Judah in the family of Zerahites; grandfather of Achan.—Jos 7:1, 17, 18.

2. Head of a Benjamite family dwelling in Jerusalem; son or descendant of Shimei.—1Ch 8:1, 19-21, 28.

3. Officer of King David's wine supplies in the vineyards; a Shiphmite. Another officer, Shimei, had oversight of the vineyards themselves.—1Ch 27:27.

4. A Levite of the sons of Asaph and forefather of Mattaniah, a postexilic music leader. (Ne 11:17) Zabdi appears to be elsewhere called Zichri (1Ch 9:15) and possibly Zaccur.—1Ch 25:2, 10; Ne 12:35.

ZABDIEL (Zab'di·el) [God Has Endowed].

1. Father of the Jashobeam who was over the first monthly division ministering to King David.—1Ch 27:2.

2. A prominent priest appointed as an overseer in Jerusalem after the Babylonian exile.—Ne 11:10, 14.

ZABUD (Za'bud) [Endowed]. A priestly adviser of King Solomon; son of Nathan. (1Ki 4:5) It is not certain, but Zabud's father Nathan may have been the prophet who was a close adviser of King David.—2Sa 7:3; 12:1.

ZACCAI (Zac'cai) [possibly a shortened form of Zechariah, meaning "Jehovah Has Remembered"]. Founder of a family in Israel. Seven hundred and sixty of his male descendants returned from the Babylonian exile in 537 B.C.E.—Ezr 2:1, 2, 9; Ne 7:14.

ZACCHAEUS (Zac·chae'us) [from Heb., possibly from a root meaning "clean; pure"]. A chief tax collector at Jericho who became one of Christ's disciples. As such an official, Zacchaeus was likely over the other tax collectors in and around Jericho. The district around Jericho was fertile and productive, yielding considerable tax returns as a result of commerce, and Zacchaeus, in the manner of most tax collectors, had probably employed questionable practices in connection with his position to procure part of his notable wealth, for, indeed, "he was rich."—Lu 19:1, 2, 8; see TAX COLLECTOR.

When Jesus came to Jericho in the spring of 33 C.E., just before going to Jerusalem and to his

ZACCUR

death, Zacchaeus wanted to get a glimpse of him, but being small in stature, he could not see over the crowd. So, running ahead to an advance position, he resourcefully gained a vantage point by climbing a tree. This interest, of course, impressed Jesus, who told Zacchaeus that he would stay with him while in Jericho. The townspeople objected, however, saying that Jesus was making himself a friend of sinners. Showing a changed attitude, Zacchaeus declared that he would restore fourfold whatever he had got unjustly and that he would give half his belongings to the poor. Jesus then acknowledged that his household was now in line for salvation. (Lu 19:3-10) Also, while visiting Zacchaeus, Jesus spoke the illustration of the minas.—Lu 19:11-28.

ZACCUR (Zac'cur) [from a root meaning "remember"].

1. A Reubenite whose son Shammua was one of the 12 spies that Moses sent into the Promised Land.—Nu 13:3, 4.

2. A Simeonite whose descendants through Shimei became numerous.—1Ch 4:24-27.

3. A Merarite Levite; son of Jaaziah.—1Ch 24: 26, 27.

4. Head of the third group of Levite musicians; a son of Asaph, a Gershonite. (1Ch 25:2, 10; 6:39, 43; Ne 12:35) Zaccur may possibly be called Zabdi (Ne 11:17) and Zichri.—1Ch 9:15.

5. One who worked building Jerusalem's wall under Nehemiah's direction; son of Imri.—Ne 3:2.

6. A Levite represented in the signatures to the covenant of faithfulness proposed during Nehemiah's governorship. Zaccur may have been there himself, or perhaps one of his descendants signed, in his name. (Ne 9:38; 10:1, 9, 12) Possibly the same as No. 7.

7. A Levite whose son Hanan was entrusted with proper distribution of the tithes during Nehemiah's governorship. (Ne 13:10-13) Perhaps the same as No. 6.

ZADOK (Za'dok) [from a root meaning "be righteous"].

1. A priest prominently associated with King David. Zadok was a descendant of Aaron through the high-priestly line of Eleazar. (1Ch 6:3-8, 50-53) He is also called a seer. (2Sa 15:27) Zadok, as a young man mighty in valor, was one of the tribal chiefs who threw in his support for David's kingship. (1Ch 12:27, 28) From that time on he was loyal to David.—2Sa 8:15, 17; 20:25; 1Ch 18:16.

Zadok and Abiathar (whenever the two are mentioned, Zadok is named first, perhaps because he was also a prophet) accompanied the ark of the covenant when David had it brought up to Jerusalem, after which Zadok continued to serve for a time at Gibeon, where the tabernacle was located. (1Ch 15:11, 14; 16:39) When Absalom rebelled, Zadok and the Levites started to bring the Ark along as they accompanied David in his flight from Jerusalem, but David sent them back to the city, designating Zadok and others to act as intelligence intermediaries. (2Sa 15:23-29, 35, 36; 17: 15, 16; 18:19-27) After the rebellion was over, Zadok and Abiathar were instrumental in securing David's favorable reception in Jerusalem. (2Sa 19:11-14) When, late in his reign, David organized the Levitical services for the temple, both Zadok and Ahimelech the son of Abiathar assisted him. —1Ch 24:3, 6, 30, 31.

In contrast with Abiathar, Zadok did not support the attempted usurpation of the throne by Adonijah; for this, David appointed Zadok as the one to anoint Solomon as king. (1Ki 1:7, 8, 26, 32-46) During the reigns of Saul and David, Zadok served only as an associate priest, but for his loyalty as contrasted with the wavering allegiance of High Priest Abiathar, Solomon expelled Abiathar from Jerusalem and made Zadok high priest. This fulfilled Jehovah's prophecy spoken against Eli's house. (1Ki 2:26, 27, 35) The later listing of "Zadok and Abiathar" at 1 Kings 4:4 is probably in a historical sense. Josephus claims that Zadok was the first high priest at Solomon's temple. (*Jewish Antiquities*, X, 152 [viii, 6]) At 1 Chronicles 27:16, 17, Zadok is listed as leader over the house of Aaron. The Bible provides a basis for tracing the line of Zadok as holding the office of high priest down to the time of Darius the Persian (likely Darius II). (1Ki 4:2; 1Ch 6:8-15; 2Ch 31:10; Ne 12:22) The priests seen in Ezekiel's visionary temple were "sons of Zadok." —Eze 40:46; 43:19; 44:15; 48:11.

2. Maternal grandfather of King Jotham of Judah.—2Ki 15:32, 33; 2Ch 27:1.

3. A descendant of Aaron through No. 1 in the high-priestly line, and an ancestor of the "skilled copyist" Ezra.—1Ch 6:3, 8, 12, 13; 9:11; Ezr 7:1-6; Ne 11:11.

4. One of Jerusalem's postexilic wall rebuilders; son of Baana. (Ne 3:4) Either he or a representative of a family of the same name signed the national covenant proposed shortly thereafter.—Ne 9:38; 10:1, 14, 21.

5. Another who helped rebuild Jerusalem's wall; son or descendant of Immer, who possibly belonged to the priestly family.—Ne 3:29.

6. A copyist whom Nehemiah made jointly responsible with Shelemiah and Pedaiah for the Levitical stores. (Ne 13:13) Perhaps the same as No. 5.

7. A postexilic ancestor of Jesus' adoptive father Joseph.—Mt 1:14.

ZAHAM (Za'ham) [Loathsome One]. A son of King Rehoboam (presumably by his wife Maha-lath).—2Ch 11:18, 19, 23.

ZAIR (Za'ir). A site in or near Edom. In the vicinity of Zair, Judah's King Jehoram, by night, struck down a surrounding military force of Edomites. (2Ki 8:20-22) Zair's actual location is not known.

ZALAPH (Za'laph). Father of at least six sons, one of whom helped Nehemiah to repair Jerusalem's wall.—Ne 3:30.

ZALMON (Zal'mon).

1. An Ahohite warrior of David. (2Sa 23:8, 28) Apparently called Ilai at 1 Chronicles 11:29.

2. A mountain near Shechem. From Mount Zalmon, Abimelech and his forces cut wood with which to burn down the vault belonging to the city of Shechem. (Jg 9:48, 49) As the only mountains near Shechem are Ebal and Gerizim, Zalmon was either a peak or slope of one of these, or else it was some other less important hill nearby.

3. A lofty peak evidently in Bashan, E of the Jordan. (Ps 68:14, 15) It was perhaps the highest peak of Mount Hauran (Jebel ed Druz).

ZALMONAH (Zal·mo'nah). A wilderness site where the Israelites encamped after leaving Mount Hor and before moving on to Punon. (Nu 33:41, 42) Zalmonah is tentatively identified by Y. Aharoni with es-Salmaneh, about 20 km (12 mi) NNW of the suggested site of Punon.

ZALMUNNA (Zal·mun'na). One of the kings of Midian whose forces and allies oppressed Israel for seven years prior to Gideon's judgeship. (Jg 6:1) Gideon's small band routed the invaders and, in pursuit of the fleeing forces, captured and put to death Kings Zebah and Zalmunna.—Jg 6:33; 8:4-21; Ps 83:11, 12; see ZEBAH.

ZAMZUMMIM (Zam·zum'mim) [possibly from a root meaning "have in mind; scheme"]. The Ammonite name for the Rephaim; a people dispossessed by the Ammonites. (De 2:19, 20) There is no definite connection between them and the Zuzim.—Ge 14:5; see REPHAIM.

ZANOAH (Za·no'ah) [possibly from a root meaning "stink"].

1. A Judean city in the Shephelah. (Jos 15:20, 33, 34, 36) It was among the cities reinhabited after the Babylonian exile. (Ne 11:25, 30) The residents of this Zanoah may have been the ones who did repair work on Jerusalem's southern wall and its Valley Gate. (Ne 3:13) It is identified with Khirbet Zanu' (Horvat Zanoah), about 5 km (3 mi) SE of Beth-shemesh.

2. A city in the mountainous region of Judah. (Jos 15:20, 48, 56, 57) This is apparently the Zanoah referred to at 1 Chronicles 4:18 as being 'fathered' by Jekuthiel. (See JEKUTHIEL.) It is tentatively identified with Khirbet Beit Amra, about 10 km (6 mi) SSW of Hebron.

ZAPHENATH-PANEAH (Zaph'e·nath-pa-ne'ah). The name that Pharaoh gave to Joseph when elevating him in authority to a position next to himself. (Ge 41:45) To those who spoke Hebrew, the pronunciation of the name evidently meant "Revealer of Hidden Things," but to the Egyptians it perhaps meant "The God Said: He Will Live!"

ZAPHON (Za'phon) [from a root meaning "keep watch"]. A city assigned to Gad. (Jos 13: 24, 27) Some favor identifying it with Tell es-Sa'idiyeh, about 10 km (6 mi) NNW of Succoth. The name also appears in some translations at Judges 12:1 instead of "northward."—JB, NE, RS.

ZAREPHATH (Zar'e·phath) [possibly from a root meaning "refine"]. A Phoenician town 'belonging to' or apparently dependent upon Sidon in Elijah's day. At Zarephath the prophet was shown hospitality by a poor widow, whose flour and oil were miraculously sustained during a great famine and whose son Elijah, in God's power, subsequently raised from death. (1Ki 17:8-24; Lu 4:25, 26) It later marked an extremity of former Canaanite territory foretold to become the possession of Israelite exiles. (Ob 20) The name is preserved in that of Sarafand, about 13 km (8 mi) SSW of Sidon, though the ancient site may have been a short distance away on the Mediterranean shore.

ZARETHAN (Zar'e·than). The first reference to it is at Joshua 3:16, where the account is given of the miraculous damming up of the waters of the Jordan "at Adam, the city at the side of Zarethan." Later the record states that at the time of the casting of copper items for the temple, such casting was done in the District of the Jordan, "in the clay mold, between Succoth and Zarethan." (1Ki 7:46) The clay available in the Jordan Valley contributed toward the feasibility of such copper-casting operations in this area.

Since the site of Adam is generally placed at Tell ed-Damiyeh (on the E side of the Jordan opposite the entrance to the Wadi Far'ah) and since Succoth is considered to be located about 13 km (8 mi) NNE of Adam, these texts would indicate that Zarethan lay on the W side of the Jordan not far from Adam and Succoth. The 82-m-high (270 ft) summit known as Qarn Sartabeh, which is called "the great landmark of the Jordan valley," is suggested by some as the probable location of Zarethan. (*Encyclopædia Biblica*, edited by T. Cheyne, London, 1903, Vol. IV, col. 5382) It lies across the Jordan from Adam, at the entrance to the Wadi Far'ah.

This identification, however, is somewhat difficult to harmonize with the description of Solomon's fifth administrative district as given at 1 Kings 4:12, which refers to "Taanach and Megiddo and all Beth-shean, which is beside Zarethan below Jezreel, from Beth-shean to Abelmeholah to the region of Jokmeam." Qarn Sartabeh lies much farther S than the other places there listed and not "beside" Beth-shean in the sense of neighboring it. *The Jerusalem Bible* endeavors to adjust the geographic order of the places listed at 1 Kings 4:12, referring to "all Beth-shean below Jezreel, from Beth-shean as far as Abel Meholah, which is beside Zarethan," thus relating Zarethan to Abel-meholah rather than to Beth-shean. However, since the reference is to "all Beth-shean," it doubtless indicates a region rather than the city itself. If Zarethan was indeed connected with the prominent summit of Qarn Sartabeh, it may be that the region of Beth-shean embraced the valley plain around it and extending southward to a point from which Zarethan became visible, thus serving to indicate a separate, but neighboring, region.

Other sites suggested for Zarethan lie E of the Jordan and therefore do not seem to fit the context. Excavations at one of them, Tell es-Sa'idiyeh, produced unusual quantities of articles made of bronze (an alloy formed chiefly of copper and tin), which may confirm the location of Solomon's copper-casting activity in this general area.

In the account at 2 Chronicles 4:17, which parallels that of 1 Kings 7:46, "Zeredah" appears in place of Zarethan, perhaps representing a variant spelling of the name.

ZATTU (Zat'tu). Forefather of a large family that returned to Jerusalem with Zerubbabel in 537 B.C.E. (Ezr 2:1, 2, 8; Ne 7:13) When Ezra came to Jerusalem some of their descendants

dismissed the foreign wives they had taken. (Ezr 10:10, 11, 27, 44) Shortly thereafter, a representative of this family, or someone else named Zattu, sealed the "trustworthy arrangement."—Ne 9:38; 10:1, 14.

ZAYIN [ז] (za'yin). The seventh letter in the Hebrew alphabet. It corresponds generally to the English letter "z" and, in the Hebrew, is found at the beginning of each verse of Psalm 119:49-56.

ZAZA (Za'za). A son of Jonathan among the descendants of Jerahmeel in the tribe of Judah. —1Ch 2:3-5, 25, 33.

ZEAL. See JEALOUS, JEALOUSY.

ZEALOUS ONE, THE. A designation distinguishing the apostle Simon from the apostle Simon Peter and evidently corresponding to the term "Cananaean" used by Matthew and Mark. (Mt 10:4; Mr 3:18; Lu 6:15; Ac 1:13) Simon's being called "the zealous one" does not necessarily mean that he was at one time associated with the political group called Zealots. The designation may simply have been an appellative appropriate to his personality.

ZEBADIAH (Zeb·a·di'ah) [May Jehovah Endow].

1. A Benjamite, son or descendant of Beriah. —1Ch 8:1, 15, 16.

2. A Benjamite, son or descendant of Elpaal. —1Ch 8:1, 17, 18.

3. A Benjamite warrior who joined David's forces at Ziklag; son of Jeroham from Gedor. —1Ch 12:1, 2, 7.

4. Joab's nephew and chief of the fourth monthly rotational army division. His being 'after his father Asahel' may indicate that he succeeded to the post after Asahel was put to death. (2Sa 2:23) Or if these monthly courses were organized after Asahel's death, then it could mean that Zebadiah was put over a division named after Asahel.—1Ch 27:1, 7; see ASAHEL No. 1.

5. A gatekeeper involved in David's organization of the Levitical services; son of Meshelemiah, a Korahite.—1Ch 26:1, 2.

6. One of the Levites whom Jehoshaphat in his third year, 934 B.C.E., dispatched to teach Jehovah's law in the cities of Judah.—2Ch 17:7-9.

7. A leader of the house of Judah, son of Ishmael, among those whom King Jehoshaphat appointed over legal cases.—2Ch 19:8-11.

8. Head of the paternal house of Shephatiah.

Zebadiah, son of Michael, led 80 males of his paternal house back to Jerusalem with Ezra in 468 B.C.E.—Ezr 8:1, 8.

9. One of the priests of the house of Immer who was among those encouraged by Ezra to dissolve their foreign marriage alliances.—Ezr 10: 19, 20.

ZEBAH (Ze′bah) [Sacrifice]. A king of Midian who shared in oppressing Israel. Zebah and Zalmunna were rulers presumably for the seven years that Midian made raids against Israel, ruining fields and bringing about poverty. (Jg 6:1-6) At some unspecified time they also killed members of Gideon's household.—Jg 8:18, 19.

When Gideon defeated their army of 135,000, Zebah, Zalmunna, and 15,000 managed to escape under hot pursuit and made their way to Karkor, quite some distance, but there they were again defeated and finally captured. As Gideon was bringing Zebah and Zalmunna back as humiliated captives at least as far as Succoth, they must have been reminded of their boastful words (or at least the expression of their attitude) preserved in the psalm: "Let us take possession of the abiding places of God for ourselves." (Ps 83:11, 12) After they admitted to having killed his brothers, Gideon personally put to death the two Midianite kings.—Jg 8:4-21.

ZEBEDEE (Zeb′e·dee) [possibly from a Heb. root meaning "endow"]. Father of Jesus' apostles James and John. (Mt 4:21, 22; 10:2; 26:37; Mr 3:17; 10:35; Lu 5:10; Joh 21:2) Zebedee's wife Salome is generally believed to have been the sister of Jesus' mother Mary. This would mean that Zebedee was Jesus' uncle by marriage, and James and John, Jesus' cousins.—Mt 27:56; Mr 15:40; Joh 19:25; see SALOME No. 1.

Zebedee was in the fishing business on the Sea of Galilee and apparently did quite well with it, for there were hired men working with him. (Mr 1:16, 19, 20) His wife Salome was able to render material services to Jesus. (Mr 15:40, 41) So while there is no indication that Zebedee himself followed Christ, his family freely did so.—Mt 20:20.

ZEBIDAH (Ze·bi′dah) [from a root meaning "endow"]. A wife or concubine of King Josiah and mother of King Jehoiakim. Zebidah was the daughter of Pedaiah from Rumah.—2Ki 23: 34, 36.

ZEBINA (Ze·bi′na) [Gained [that is, bought]]. A postexilic son of Nebo. Zebina and six of his brothers had married foreign wives but sent them away, as counseled by Ezra.—Ezr 10:43, 44.

ZEBOIIM (Ze·boi′im). A site named in connection with the boundary of Canaanite territory. (Ge 10:19) Zeboiim was one of the five city-states of the District that rebelled after 12 years of domination by Chedorlaomer. Its King Shemeber joined forces with the rulers of Sodom, Gomorrah, Admah, and Bela (Zoar) and apparently was vanquished with them in the Low Plain of Siddim by Chedorlaomer and his three confederates. This defeat resulted in the capture of Lot and in Abraham's subsequent victory over the invaders. (Ge 14:1-16) Later, Zeboiim was one of the wicked cities of the District destroyed by Jehovah along with Sodom and Gomorrah. (Ge 19:24, 25; De 29:22, 23; Ho 11:8) Its exact site is unknown. Many scholars believe that the original site now lies beneath the waters of the Dead Sea, though some others have recently claimed that the ruins of the city may be identified with a site along one of the wadis to the SE of the Dead Sea.

ZEBOIM (Ze·bo′im) [Hyenas].

1. A valley in the territory of Benjamin, near Michmash. In King Saul's day, a band of Philistine pillagers would sally forth from Michmash and "turn to the road to the boundary that looks toward the valley of Zeboim, toward the wilderness." (1Sa 13:16-18) Though there is uncertainty about its location, the valley of Zeboim may be the Wadi Abu Daba′ (meaning, "Valley of the Father of Hyenas") about 10 km (6 mi) ESE of Michmash and about 13 km (8 mi) ENE of Jerusalem.

2. A town inhabited by Benjamites after their return from Babylonian exile. It is mentioned between Hadid and Neballat and with Lod (Lydda). (Ne 11:31, 34, 35) The exact site is now unknown.

ZEBRA [Heb., pe′re′]. An animal of the horse family resembling the wild ass in appearance and habits, though easily distinguished from the latter by its dark or black stripes. The stripes distort the shape and unity of the zebra's outline to such an extent that even sharp-eyed natives are often unaware of its presence just 40 or 50 m (130 or 160 ft) away. Aside from its camouflage, the zebra's keen senses of sight and smell, as well as its ability to run swiftly, serve as a protection from carnivores. The animal has been reported to travel at 64 km/hr (40 mph) after its initial burst of speed. Also, its hooves and teeth are effective weapons of defense.

The zebra is a wild animal that is hard to tame. (Job 24:5; 39:5; Isa 32:14) Zebras feed chiefly on grasses. (Job 6:5; Jer 14:6) They regularly quench their thirst (Ps 104:11) and are seldom found more than 8 km (5 mi) away from water.

The obstinacy of the zebra and the strong impulse that drives the female when in sexual heat were used to illustrate the independent and adulterous course of wayward Israel. (Jer 2:24; Ho 8:9) Jehovah's angel foretold that Abraham's son Ishmael would be "a zebra of a man." Likely this had reference to a fiercely independent disposition, as suggested by the words: "His hand will be against everyone."—Ge 16:12.

"Onager" and "wild ass" are appropriate alternate renderings of the Hebrew *pe're'*.—Job 6:5, ftn.

ZEBUL (Ze'bul) [Toleration; or, possibly, Lofty Abode (Habitation)]. A commissioner of the city of Shechem, subservient to Gideon's son Abimelech. When a certain Gaal and his brothers came to Shechem and attempted to arouse the city against Abimelech, Zebul informed Abimelech and later challenged the rebel leader Gaal to prove his boasts by fighting. The Shechemite rebels were defeated and Zebul drove Gaal and his brothers from the city.—Jg 9:26-41.

ZEBULUN (Zeb'u·lun) [Toleration; or, possibly, Lofty Abode (Habitation)].

1. The sixth son of Jacob's wife Leah. Being the less-loved wife, Leah was especially pleased about the birth of the boy. The name she gave him reflected the hope that her standing with Jacob would be enhanced. Leah exclaimed: "At last my husband will tolerate me, because I have borne him six sons." (Ge 30:20; 35:23; Ex 1:1-3; 1Ch 2:1) Zebulun eventually became the father of three sons—Sered, Elon, and Jahleel. (Ge 46:14) A distant descendant of Zebulun bearing the same name as one of these three sons, Elon, served as a judge in Israel.—Jg 12:11, 12.

2. The name Zebulun also designates the tribe descended from him through his three sons. About a year after the Israelites were liberated from enslavement in Egypt, this tribe's able-bodied men from 20 years old upward numbered 57,400. (Nu 1:1-3, 30, 31) A second census taken at the close of Israel's 40 years' wandering in the wilderness revealed an increase of 3,100 registered males.—Nu 26:26, 27.

In the wilderness, the tribe of Zebulun, alongside the tribes of Judah and Issachar, camped on the E side of the tabernacle. This three-tribe division was first in the order of march. Eliab the son of Helon served as the chieftain of the Zebulunite army.—Nu 1:9; 2:3-7; 7:24; 10:14-16.

Tribal Inheritance. Regarding the inheritance of the tribe of Zebulun, the dying patriarch Jacob stated: "Zebulun will reside by the seashore, and he will be by the shore where the ships lie anchored; and his remote side will be toward Sidon." (Ge 49:13) Since Sidon was to the N of Israel and since Zebulun's territory was to be toward Sidon, the location of Zebulun's territory was to be a northern one. While not bordering directly on the sea, the area assigned to Zebulun was situated between the Sea of Galilee on the E and the Mediterranean on the W and thus gave the Zebulunites easy access to both bodies of water. Hence, they could easily engage in commercial trade, which may be alluded to by Moses' words of blessing: "Rejoice, O Zebulun, in your going out."—De 33:18.

At the time the distribution of the Promised Land continued from Shiloh, the third lot was drawn for Zebulun. (Jos 18:8; 19:10-16) To assist in the division of the land, Elizaphan the son of Parnach was the divinely appointed representative of the tribe of Zebulun. (Nu 34:17, 25) When the territorial boundaries were established, Zebulun was surrounded by Asher (Jos 19:24, 27), Naphtali (Jos 19:32-34), and Issachar.

Several Levite cities were situated in the territory of Zebulun. (Jos 21:7, 34, 35; 1Ch 6:63, 77) From one of these, Nahalol (Nahalal), the Zebulunites failed to drive out the Canaanites, as was also true of the city of Kitron.—Jg 1:30.

Outstanding Warriors. The tribe of Zebulun produced courageous warriors. Ten thousand men from Naphtali and Zebulun responded to Barak's call to fight against the forces under the command of Sisera. (Jg 4:6, 10) Following the victory, Barak and Deborah sang: "Zebulun was a people that scorned their souls to the point of death." (Jg 5:18) Among those supporting Barak were Zebulunites "handling the equipment of a scribe," evidently men in charge of numbering and enrolling the warriors. (Jg 5:14; compare 2Ki 25:19; 2Ch 26:11.) Zebulunites also came to Judge Gideon in response to his call for warriors. (Jg 6:34, 35) Among David's supporters were 50,000 Zebulunites, loyal men not having "a double heart." (1Ch 12:33, 38-40) During David's reign Zebulunites evidently had a notable share in subduing the enemies of Israel.—Ps 68:27.

Attitude Toward True Worship. In the latter half of the eighth century B.C.E., individuals from the tribe of Zebulun humbled themselves and responded to Judean King Hezekiah's invitation to attend the Passover celebration at Jerusalem. (2Ch 30:1, 10, 11, 18, 19) Centuries later, in fulfillment of Isaiah's prophecy (Isa 9:1, 2), Christ Jesus preached in the territory of ancient Zebulun and apparently found hearing ears there.—Mt 4:13-16.

Referred to in Visions. In Ezekiel's vision, Zebulun's land assignment was situated between Issachar and Gad (Eze 48:26, 27), and one of the gates of the city "Jehovah Himself Is There" bears the name Zebulun. (Eze 48:33, 35) The apostle John, in vision, heard that 12,000 had been sealed out of the (spiritual) tribe of Zebulun.—Re 7:4, 8.

ZEBULUNITE (Ze·bu′lu·nite) [Of (Belonging to) Zebulun]. A member of the tribe of Zebulun. (Nu 26:26, 27) Judge Elon was a Zebulunite.—Jg 12:11, 12.

ZECHARIAH (Zech·a·ri′ah) [Jehovah Has Remembered].

1. One of the ten sons of Jeiel in the tribe of Benjamin. (1Ch 9:35-37) His name is abbreviated as Zecher in the parallel list at 1 Chronicles 8:31.

2. A Reubenite who possibly warred against the Hagrites in the days of Saul.—1Ch 5:6, 7, 10.

3. A Levite gatekeeper also commended as "a counselor with discretion." He had been a gatekeeper at the entrance of the tent of meeting, and when David reorganized the Levitical services for the future temple, Zechariah's lot fell to the north. He was the firstborn son of Meshelemiah, a Korahite, in the Kohathite family of Levites.—1Ch 9:21, 22; 26:1, 2, 14.

4. A Levite assigned to play a stringed instrument with other Levites in the procession that brought the ark of the covenant to Jerusalem. Zechariah thereafter played in front of the tent that housed the Ark.—1Ch 15:18, 20; 16:1, 4, 5.

5. A priestly trumpeter in the procession accompanying the ark of the covenant to Jerusalem. —1Ch 15:24.

6. A Levite of the family of Uzziel who was involved in the reorganization of service for the house of Jehovah.—1Ch 24:24, 25.

7. A Merarite Levite, son of Hosah, appointed to the corps of gatekeepers during David's reign. —1Ch 26:1, 10, 11.

8. A Manassite whose son Iddo was tribal chieftain in Gilead during David's reign.—1Ch 27:16, 21.

9. A Levite whose son Jahaziel assured Jehoshaphat and the people of Judah that Jehovah would fight their war for them.—2Ch 20:13-17.

10. One of the princes of the people whom Jehoshaphat, in 934 B.C.E., charged to teach Jehovah's law throughout the cities of Judah.—2Ch 17:7, 9.

11. Son of King Jehoshaphat. Zechariah and his brothers had all received generous gifts from Jehoshaphat, but the kingship passed to the first-born Jehoram. In order to make his position strong, Jehoram, after his enthronement, killed Zechariah and the rest of his brothers as well as some of the princes.—2Ch 21:1-4.

12. Son of High Priest Jehoiada. After Jehoiada's death, King Jehoash turned away from true worship, listening to wrong counsel rather than to Jehovah's prophets. Zechariah, Jehoash's cousin (2Ch 22:11), sternly warned the people about this, but instead of repenting, they stoned him in the temple courtyard. Zechariah's dying words were: "Let Jehovah see to it and ask it back." This prophetic request was granted, for not only did Syria do great damage to Judah but also Jehoash was killed by two of his servants "because of the blood of the sons of Jehoiada the priest." The Greek *Septuagint* and the Latin *Vulgate* say that Jehoash was killed to avenge the blood of the "son" of Jehoiada. The Masoretic text and the Syriac *Peshitta*, however, read "sons," possibly using the plural number to denote the excellence and worth of Jehoiada's son Zechariah the prophet-priest.—2Ch 24:17-22, 25.

Zechariah the son of Jehoiada is most likely the one whom Jesus had in mind when prophesying that "the blood of all the prophets spilled from the founding of the world" will be required "from this generation [the Jews of the time of Jesus' earthly ministry], from the blood of Abel down to the blood of Zechariah, who was slain between the altar and the house." (Lu 11:50, 51) The places mentioned as the site of the slaying correspond. In the first century C.E., Chronicles was the last book in the canon of the Hebrew Scriptures. So Jesus' phrase, "from Abel . . . to Zechariah," was similar to our expression, "from Genesis to Revelation." In the parallel account at Matthew 23:35, Zechariah is called the son of Barachiah, possibly another name for Jehoiada, unless, by chance, it indicates a generation between Jehoiada and Zechariah or is the name of an earlier ancestor. —See BARACHIAH.

13. An adviser of King Uzziah, who reigned from 829 to 778 B.C.E. Zechariah is described as an "instructor in the fear of the true God."—2Ch 26:5.

14. King of Israel. Zechariah was a son of Jeroboam II and the last of Jehu's dynasty to rule. His recorded reign of six months was terminated when he was murdered by Shallum. (2Ki 15:8-12) Zechariah's father died in about 803 B.C.E., in the 27th year of Uzziah's reign (2Ki 14:29), but some

11 years passed before Zechariah's stated rule of six months' duration occurred starting in Uzziah's 38th year (c. 792 B.C.E.). (2Ki 15:8, 13) This may have been because he was very young when his father died, or it may have been due to considerable opposition (typical of the northern kingdom of Israel) that had to be overcome before he was firmly established in the kingdom.

15. A witness to Isaiah's writing the name of his son on a tablet; son of Jeberechiah.—Isa 8:1, 2.

16. Maternal grandfather of King Hezekiah. —2Ki 18:1, 2; 2Ch 29:1.

17. One of the Levites of the sons of Asaph who helped to dispose of the unclean objects removed from the temple at the beginning of Hezekiah's reign.—2Ch 29:13, 15-17.

18. A Kohathite Levite appointed to help oversee the temple repairs sponsored by King Josiah. —2Ch 34:8, 12.

19. One of three leading priests who made generous contributions of animal victims for the great Passover celebration arranged by Josiah. —2Ch 35:1, 8.

20. A postexilic prophet and writer of the book bearing his name. Zechariah calls himself "the son of Berechiah the son of Iddo" (Zec 1:1, 7), but in other references made to him, this middle linkage is omitted. (Ezr 5:1; 6:14; Ne 12:4, 16) Zechariah was probably born somewhere in Babylon, for his prophetic activity began only 17 years after the return from exile and reasonably he was at that time older than 17, though still called a "young man."—Zec 2:4.

Zechariah and Haggai were used by Jehovah to stimulate Zerubbabel, High Priest Jeshua, and the returned exiles to finish rebuilding Jehovah's temple even though a Persian government ban was still in effect. (Ezr 5:1, 2; 6:14, 15) Zechariah's prophecy contains messages that he delivered to that end over a period of two years and a month. (Zec 1:1, 7; 7:1, 8) Any other prophetic activity he performed is not recorded.—See ZECHARIAH, BOOK OF.

Though this Zechariah's father's name was Berechiah, Jesus' reference to "Zechariah son of Barachiah" (Mt 23:35; note the difference in spelling) more likely refers to a high priest who lived at an earlier time.—See No. 12.

21. One of the "head ones" whom Ezra sent to gather some ministers for the house of God at the time of the journey to Jerusalem in 468 B.C.E. (Ezr 8:15-17) He is possibly the same as No. 22 or No. 23.

22. Head of the paternal house of Parosh. Zechariah and 150 males of that paternal house came to Jerusalem with Ezra. (Ezr 8:1, 3) Possibly the same as No. 21.

23. Head of the paternal house of Bebai who led 28 males of his family on the return with Ezra. (Ezr 8:1, 11) Possibly the same as No. 21.

24. One of those sons of Elam who dissolved their foreign marriage alliances, upon the advice of Ezra.—Ezr 10:10, 11, 26, 44.

25. An associate of Ezra when he read and expounded the Law to the people. Zechariah, probably a priest, stood on Ezra's left.—Ne 8:1, 2, 4.

26, 27. Two men of Judah, the son of Amariah and of the Shelanite respectively, whose descendants lived in Jerusalem after the Babylonian exile.—Ne 11:4, 5.

28. A priest, the son of one named Pashhur, whose descendants lived in postexilic Jerusalem. —Ne 11:10, 12.

29. A priestly trumpeter in the procession at the inauguration of Jerusalem's rebuilt wall; son of Jonathan.—Ne 12:27, 31, 35.

30. Another trumpeter, also a priest, at the same inauguration attended by No. 29.—Ne 12: 40, 41.

31. Priestly father of John the Baptizer. (Lu 3:2) He and his wife Elizabeth, a relative of Jesus' mother Mary, lived in the Judean hills. They both feared God and obeyed his commandments. Though advanced in years, they had no children. —Lu 1:5-7, 36.

When it was Zechariah's turn to offer incense during "the division of Abijah," probably around late spring or early summer of 3 B.C.E., he entered the sanctuary as usual. On this occasion Jehovah's angel Gabriel appeared to him, informing him that his supplication had been favorably heard, that his wife Elizabeth would bear a son to him, and that the boy was to be called John. Gabriel instructed Zechariah about how the boy should be raised and what this son was to accomplish. (Lu 1:5-17) Zechariah asked the angel for a sign as a further assurance. Because of his weakness as to believing the angel, he was informed that he would be struck with dumbness until after John's birth. (Lu 1:18-23) On the eighth day after the baby was born, Elizabeth rejected suggestions from neighbors and relatives and insisted that her son be named John. Upon their appealing to the father, Zechariah took a tablet and wrote on it: "John is its name." Instantly his speech was restored and he uttered a prophecy concerning the work of his son and that of the Messiah.—Lu 1:13, 57-79.

ZECHARIAH, BOOK OF.

This book of the Hebrew Scriptures identifies its writer as "Zechariah the son of Berechiah the son of Iddo the prophet." (Zec 1:1) It also provides a basis for establishing the time period covered and an approximate date for the composition. The last time indicator found in the book of Zechariah is the fourth day of Chislev in the fourth year of Darius' reign (about December 1, 518 B.C.E.). (7:1) Accordingly, this book could not have been committed to writing before the close of 518 B.C.E. Since it was in the "eighth month in the second year of Darius" (October/November 520 B.C.E.) that "the word of Jehovah occurred to Zechariah" (1:1), the book covers a period of at least two years.

From chapter 9 onward the subject matter found in the book of Zechariah appears to differ considerably from the earlier section. No further reference is made to angels and visions or to Governor Zerubbabel and High Priest Joshua. There is no mention of the temple-rebuilding work, and not even the name of Zechariah appears. In view of this and the nature of the prophecies contained in the latter chapters of the book, a number of critics maintain that this section could not have been written by Zechariah. However, it should be noted that Zechariah, like other prophets, wrote according to divine inspiration and did not receive all revelations at the same time or in the same manner. (2Pe 1:20, 21) Also, prophecies did not have to fit within a particular framework of existing circumstances and incorporate the name of the prophet or of some of his contemporaries for an entire book to be the work of the prophet. That the book of Zechariah forms one harmonious whole, instead of consisting of separate and unrelated parts

HIGHLIGHTS OF ZECHARIAH

Prophetic messages encouraging the Jews to resume temple rebuilding, also providing foregleams of the Messiah's coming and his rule as King-Priest

Written by Zechariah during the reign of Persian King Darius I, about 19 years after the first Jews arrived home from Babylon in 537 B.C.E.

A call to repentance, followed by eight visions and a prophecy about "Sprout" (1:1–6:15)

First vision: A rider on a red horse standing with three other horsemen among the myrtle trees; the vision concludes with an assurance that Jerusalem will be shown mercy and the temple rebuilt

Second vision: The four horns that dispersed Judah are cast down by four craftsmen

Third vision: A young man with a measuring rope prepares to measure Jerusalem, but an angel foretells more growth as well as Jehovah's protection for the city

Fourth vision: High Priest Joshua's befouled garments are removed and replaced with robes of state

Fifth vision: Zechariah sees a gold lampstand with seven lamps supplied with oil from two olive trees; Zerubbabel will complete the temple rebuilding with the help of God's spirit

Sixth vision: A flying scroll represents the curse going forth because of all those stealing and those swearing falsely in Jehovah's name

Seventh vision: A woman named Wickedness is transported in an ephah measure to Shinar

Eighth vision: Four chariots proceed from between two copper mountains to move about in the earth

The man named Sprout will build Jehovah's temple and serve as king-priest

Question about the observance of fasts commemorating the calamities that befell Jerusalem (7:1–8:23)

Calamities came as punishment for disobedience; fasting in commemoration of these was not really done to Jehovah

Jerusalem will enjoy divine favor; the former days of fasting will be transformed into "an exultation and a rejoicing and good festal seasons"; many from the nations will come to her to seek Jehovah's favor

Judgment upon nations, Messianic prophecies, and the restoration of God's people (9:1–14:21)

Many cities and nations will experience Jehovah's adverse judgment

Zion's righteous, humble King will come into the city on an ass

Jehovah expresses anger against the false shepherds

The scattered people of God will be brought out of Egypt and Assyria

Zechariah is called to be a shepherd; the people are given an opportunity to pay for his work, and they value it at 30 silver pieces

Jerusalem will become a burdensome stone that severely scratches anyone tampering with it

A well will be opened for cleansing from sin; the shepherd will be struck, and the sheep will be scattered

Jerusalem will come under attack, but Jehovah will war against the aggressors

Those remaining out of the attacking nations will celebrate the Festival of Booths each year, bowing down before Jehovah as King

recorded by different writers, is evident from the thoughts expressed therein. Throughout, the book highlights that Jerusalem would be restored and that Jehovah would come to the defense of the city.—Zec 1:13-21; 2:4, 5; 8:14-23; 9:11-17; 12:2-6; 14:3-21.

Historical Background. About February 9, 519 B.C.E., the prophet Zechariah heard the words: "The whole earth is sitting still and having no disturbance." (Zec 1:7, 11) At that time Jerusalem was not a disturbing factor to the nations, but it appeared to observers that Jehovah had forsaken the city. Although the temple's foundation had been laid in 536 B.C.E., the rebuilding work made slow progress on account of enemy opposition and finally, in 522 B.C.E., came under an official ban. (Ezr 4:4, 5, 24) Additionally, plagued by droughts and crop failures because of having neglected the temple rebuilding work, the repatriated Jews found themselves in very difficult circumstances. (Hag 1:6, 10, 11) They needed encouragement to continue the construction work despite mountainous obstacles.

Jehovah's words, through Zechariah, must therefore have been a real source of comfort and inspiration to them. The visions seen by Zechariah clearly showed that it was the divine will for Jerusalem and its temple to be rebuilt. (Zec 1:16; chap 2) The power of the nations that had dispersed Judah would be shattered. (1:18-21) High Priest Joshua would gain an acceptable appearance before Jehovah (3:3-7), and Governor Zerubbabel would, with the help of God's spirit, finish rebuilding the temple.—4:6-9.

Agreement With Other Bible Books. The book of Zechariah is in complete harmony with the rest of the Scriptures in identifying Jehovah as the Protector of his people. (Zec 2:5; compare De 33:27; Ps 46:11; 125:2.) He rewards or punishes individuals or nations according to their dealings and returns to those who repentantly return to him. (Zec 1:2-6; 7:11-14; compare Isa 55:6, 7; Jer 25:4-11; Eze 33:11; Mal 3:7; 2Pe 3:9.) Jehovah requires that those who desire his favor must speak truth and manifest obedience, justice, loving-kindness, and mercy. (Zec 7:7-10; 8:16, 17; compare De 24:17; Ps 15:1, 2; 82:3, 4; Pr 12:19; Jer 7:5, 6; Eph 4:25.) He does not respond to calls for aid from those who do not obey him. —Zec 7:13; compare Isa 1:15; La 3:42-44.

Also, noteworthy similarities are readily apparent by comparing passages in Zechariah with other scriptures.—Compare Zec 3:2 with Jude 9; Zec 4:3, 11-14 with Re 11:4; Zec 4:10 with Re 5:6;

Zec 8:8 with Re 21:3; Zec 14:5 with Jude 14; Zec 14:7 with Re 21:25; Zec 14:8 with Re 22:1, 17.

Fulfillment of Prophecy. The fulfillment of prophecies recorded in the book of Zechariah testifies to its authenticity. What is known about Alexander the Great's campaign in Syria, Phoenicia, and Philistia, including the conquest of Tyre and Gaza, fits the words of Zechariah 9:1-8 and, therefore, can be understood as a fulfillment of this prophecy. Numerous other prophecies contained in the book of Zechariah find their fulfillment in Christ Jesus—his entry into Jerusalem as king, "humble, and riding upon an ass" (Zec 9:9; Mt 21:5; Joh 12:15), his betrayal for "thirty silver pieces" (Zec 11:12, 13; Mt 26:15; 27:9), the subsequent scattering of his disciples (Zec 13:7; Mt 26:31; Mr 14:27), Jesus' being pierced with a spear while on the stake (Zec 12:10; Joh 19:34, 37), and his role as King-Priest (Zec 6:12, 13; Heb 6:20; 8:1; 10:21).

ZECHER (Ze'cher) [shortened form of Zechariah]. A descendant of Jeiel, the "father" of Gibeon. (1Ch 8:29-31) Zecher is an abbreviation for Zechariah, the name appearing in the parallel account at 1 Chronicles 9:37.

ZEDAD (Ze'dad). A point at Israel's northern boundary. (Nu 34:8; Eze 47:15) It is tentatively identified with Sadad, some 105 km (65 mi) NE of Damascus.

ZEDEKIAH (Zed·e·ki'ah) [Jehovah Is Righteousness].

1. "Son of Chenaanah"; a false prophet who assured King Ahab that he would succeed in his effort to wrest Ramoth-gilead from the Syrians. Zedekiah "made for himself horns of iron" to illustrate that Ahab would push the Syrians to their extermination. Thereafter, when Jehovah's true prophet Micaiah foretold calamity for Ahab, Zedekiah struck Micaiah upon the cheek.—1Ki 22:11, 23, 24; 2Ch 18:10, 22, 23.

2. A prince in the time of King Jehoiakim.—Jer 36:12.

3. "Son of Maaseiah"; an adulterous, lying prophet among the exiles in Babylon. Jehovah's prophet Jeremiah foretold that King Nebuchadnezzar would roast Zedekiah and his associate Ahab in the fire.—Jer 29:21-23.

4. Son of Josiah by his wife Hamutal; last of the Judean kings to reign at Jerusalem. Upon his being constituted vassal king, his name was changed by Babylonian King Nebuchadnezzar from Mattaniah to Zedekiah. During the 11 years of his reign, Zedekiah "continued to do what was

bad in Jehovah's eyes."—2Ki 24:17-19; 2Ch 36:10-12; Jer 37:1; 52:1, 2.

At 1 Chronicles 3:15, Zedekiah is listed as the "third" son of Josiah. Whereas he was actually the fourth son in the order of birth (compare 2Ki 23:30, 31; 24:18; Jer 22:11), he may here be placed before his full brother Shallum (Jehoahaz) because of having ruled much longer.

When his father, King Josiah, was mortally wounded in the attempt to turn back the Egyptian forces under Pharaoh Nechoh at Megiddo (c. 629 B.C.E.), Zedekiah was about nine years old, or about three years older than his nephew Jehoiachin. At that time the people made Zedekiah's full brother, 23-year-old Jehoahaz, king. Jehoahaz' rule lasted a mere three months, because Pharaoh Nechoh removed him as king, replacing him with Eliakim (renamed Jehoiakim), the 25-year-old half brother of Jehoahaz and Zedekiah. Following the death of his father Jehoiakim, Jehoiachin began ruling as king. It appears that at this time the Babylonian armies under King Nebuchadnezzar were besieging Jerusalem. After having reigned three months and ten days, Jehoiachin surrendered to the king of Babylon (617 B.C.E.).—2Ki 23:29–24:12; 2Ch 35:20–36:10.

Early Years of Reign. Subsequently, Nebuchadnezzar placed Zedekiah on the throne at Jerusalem and had him take an oath in Jehovah's name. This oath obligated Zedekiah to be a loyal vassal king.—2Ch 36:10, 11; Eze 17:12-14; compare 2Ch 36:13.

Evidently, early in Zedekiah's reign messengers arrived from Edom, Moab, Ammon, Tyre, and Sidon, perhaps with the intention of getting Zedekiah to join them in a coalition against King Nebuchadnezzar. (Jer 27:1-3; the reference to Jehoiakim in verse 1 may be a transcriber's error for Zedekiah; see NW ftn.) The Scriptures do not reveal just what the messengers accomplished. Possibly their mission did not succeed, as Jeremiah urged Zedekiah and his subjects to remain submissive to the king of Babylon and also presented yoke bars to the messengers to symbolize the fact that the nations from which they had come should likewise submit to Nebuchadnezzar. —Jer 27:2-22.

It was also early in his reign that Zedekiah (for some reason not stated in the Bible) sent Elasah and Gemariah to Babylon. If the incident is presented in chronological order, this would have been in the fourth year of Zedekiah's kingship. —Jer 28:1, 16, 17; 29:1-3.

Zedekiah personally went to Babylon in the fourth year of his reign. Likely this was to present tribute and thereby to reassure Nebuchadnezzar of his continued loyalty as a vassal king. On that occasion Zedekiah was accompanied by his quartermaster Seraiah, whom the prophet Jeremiah had entrusted with a scroll setting forth Jehovah's judgment against Babylon.—Jer 51:59-64.

About a year later, Ezekiel began serving as a prophet among the Jewish exiles in Babylonia. (Eze 1:1-3; compare 2Ki 24:12, 17.) In the sixth month of Zedekiah's sixth year as king (612 B.C.E.), Ezekiel saw a vision that revealed the idolatrous practices, including the worship of the god Tammuz and of the sun, being carried on at Jerusalem.—Eze 8:1-17.

Rebels Against Nebuchadnezzar. Approximately three years later (c. 609 B.C.E.), contrary to Jehovah's word through Jeremiah and the oath that the king himself had taken in Jehovah's name, Zedekiah rebelled against Nebuchadnezzar and sent to Egypt for military assistance. (2Ki 24:20; 2Ch 36:13; Jer 52:3; Eze 17:15) This brought the Babylonian armies under Nebuchadnezzar against Jerusalem. The siege of the city began "in the ninth year, in the tenth month, on the tenth day of the month."—Eze 24:1-6.

It may have been at the commencement of this siege that Zedekiah sent "Pashhur the son of Malchiah and Zephaniah the son of Maaseiah, the priest," to Jeremiah in order to inquire of Jehovah whether Nebuchadnezzar would withdraw from Jerusalem. Jehovah's word through Jeremiah was that the city and its inhabitants would experience calamity at the hands of the Babylonians. (Jer 21:1-10) It appears that after this, Jeremiah, in compliance with divine direction, personally went to Zedekiah to advise him that Jerusalem would be destroyed and that the king would be taken to Babylon, there to die in peace.—Jer 34:1-7.

In besieged Jerusalem, Zedekiah and his princes deemed it advisable to do something to comply with Jehovah's law and gain His favor. Although it was not the Jubilee year, they concluded a covenant to release their Hebrew slaves from servitude. Later they broke this covenant by enslaving those whom they had set free. (Jer 34:8-22) This appears to have taken place at the time a military force from Egypt came to the defense of Jerusalem, causing the Babylonians to lift the siege temporarily to meet the Egyptian threat. (Jer 37:5) Apparently believing that the Babylonians would be defeated and unable to resume the siege, those who had released enslaved Hebrews felt that the danger was over and, therefore, again brought freed Hebrew slaves into servitude.

During this general period Zedekiah dispatched "Jehucal the son of Shelemiah and Zephaniah the son of Maaseiah the priest to Jeremiah" with the request that the prophet pray to Jehovah in behalf of the people, evidently so that the foretold destruction of Jerusalem would not come. But Jehovah's answer, as conveyed by Jeremiah, showed that the divine judgment remained unchanged. The Chaldeans would return and destroy Jerusalem.—Jer 37:3-10.

Later, when Jeremiah decided to leave Jerusalem to go to Benjamin, he was seized at the Gate of Benjamin and falsely accused of falling away to the Chaldeans. Though Jeremiah denied the charge, Irijah, the officer having the oversight, did not listen to him but brought the prophet to the princes. This led to Jeremiah's being imprisoned in the house of Jehonathan. After a considerable period had passed and Jerusalem was evidently again being besieged by the Babylonians, Zedekiah sent for Jeremiah. In reply to the king's inquiry, Jeremiah told Zedekiah that he would be given into the hand of the king of Babylon. When Jeremiah pleaded that he not be returned to the house of Jehonathan, Zedekiah granted his request and had him put in custody in the Courtyard of the Guard.—Jer 37:11-21; 32:1-5.

Indicating that Zedekiah was a very weak ruler is the fact that, when the princes later requested that Jeremiah be put to death for allegedly weakening the morale of the besieged people, Zedekiah said: "Look! He is in your hands. For there is nothing at all in which the king himself can prevail against you." However, afterward Zedekiah granted Ebed-melech's request to rescue Jeremiah and directed that Ebed-melech take along 30 men to assist in this. Later Zedekiah again had a private audience with Jeremiah. He assured the prophet that he would neither kill him nor deliver him into the hands of those seeking his death. But Zedekiah feared reprisals from the Jews who had fallen away to the Chaldeans and, therefore, did not heed Jeremiah's inspired advice to surrender to the princes of Babylon. In further display of his fear, the king requested that Jeremiah not reveal the subject of their private discussion to the suspicious princes.—Jer 38:1-28.

Fall of Jerusalem. Finally (607 B.C.E.), "in the eleventh year of Zedekiah, in the fourth month, on the ninth day of the month," Jerusalem was broken through. By night Zedekiah and the men of war took to flight. Overtaken in the desert plains of Jericho, Zedekiah was taken to Nebu-

chadnezzar at Riblah. Zedekiah's sons were slaughtered before his eyes. As Zedekiah was only about 32 years of age at the time, the boys could not have been very old. After witnessing the death of his sons, Zedekiah was blinded, bound with copper fetters, and taken to Babylon, where he died in the house of custody.—2Ki 25:2-7; Jer 39:2-7; 44:30; 52:6-11; compare Jer 24:8-10; Eze 12:11-16; 21:25-27.

5. Son of Jeconiah (Jehoiachin) but apparently not one of the seven borne to him as a prisoner in Babylon.—1Ch 3:16-18.

6. A priest or the forefather of one among those attesting by seal the "trustworthy arrangement" that was drawn up during Nehemiah's governorship.—Ne 9:38; 10:1, 8.

ZEEB (Ze′eb) [Wolf]. A prince of Midian in the forces that Gideon and the Israelites defeated. After their initial loss, Zeeb and his fellow prince Oreb fled, only to be captured and slain by the Ephraimites. The wine vat where Zeeb was killed came to be called by his name.—Jg 6:33; 7:23-25; 8:1-3; Ps 83:11.

ZELA(H) (Ze′la[h]) [possibly from a root meaning "rib; side"]. A city in Benjamin. (Jos 18:21, 28) The bones of Saul and Jonathan were buried at Zela. Earlier, Saul's father Kish had been interred there. (2Sa 21:14) Its exact location is unknown. Some scholars think that in Joshua "Zelah" should be combined with the name that follows, "Ha-eleph"; however, see HA-ELEPH.

ZELEK (Ze′lek). An Ammonite warrior who joined David's "mighty men of the military forces."—1Ch 11:26, 39; 2Sa 23:37.

ZELOPHEHAD (Ze·lo′phe·had) [meaning, possibly, "Shadow (Shelter) From Dread"]. A descendant of Manasseh through Machir, Gilead, and Hepher. (Nu 26:29-33) Zelophehad died during the 40-year wilderness wandering, not with "those who ranged themselves against Jehovah in the assembly of Korah, but for his own sin." (Nu 27:3) He had no sons but was survived by five daughters: Mahlah, Noah, Hoglah, Milcah, and Tirzah, all of whom survived to enter the Promised Land.—Nu 27:1; 1Ch 7:15.

This special situation raised problems concerning the inheritance. When Zelophehad's daughters requested their father's share of the land in Manasseh, Moses brought their case before Jehovah. God's judicial decision was that brotherless daughters should receive the family inheritance. (Nu 27:1-9; Jos 17:3, 4) Later, it was stipulated that these daughters had to marry men of their father's tribe so that the inheritance would remain within the tribe.—Nu 36:1-12.

ZELZAH (Zel'zah). A location in Benjamin. As one sign confirming Saul's leadership over Israel, he was to meet and receive a message about his father's lost she-asses from two men "close by the tomb of Rachel in the territory of Benjamin at Zelzah." (1Sa 10:1, 2, 7) The Greek *Septuagint* has been translated to read "leaping mightily" instead of "Zelzah," though the latter term appears in the Hebrew Masoretic text. Rachel was buried at an unknown point 'on the way from Bethel to Bethlehem' (Ge 35:16-20), and the site of Zelzah remains undetermined.

ZEMARAIM (Zem·a·ra'im).

1. An unidentified Benjamite city mentioned with Bethel. (Jos 18:21, 22) It has been suggested that it was a site NE of Bethel.

2. An eminence in the mountainous region of Ephraim. From this mountain, King Abijah of Judah spoke, pointing out that Jeroboam and the ten tribes of Israel had rejected Jehovah's kingdom covenant with David. Apparently, Bethel was in the same neighborhood. (2Ch 13:4, 19) Possibly Mount Zemaraim was named for the Benjamite city of Zemaraim, but the mountain's precise location remains undetermined.

ZEMARITE (Zem'a·rite). A family or tribe that descended from Ham's son Canaan. (Ge 10: 15, 18; 1Ch 1:13, 16) Mention of this Canaanite people between "Arvadite" (linked with Arvad off the Phoenician coast) and "Hamathite" (likely associated with Hamath in Syria) indicates that the Zemarites settled along the N Phoenician coast. According to an emendation, Ezekiel 27:8 mentions "skilled [wise] men of Zemer" (*RS; BE*), suggested by some as the city of the Zemarites and tentatively identified with Tell Kazel, about 35 km (22 mi) NE of Tripoli. However, here the Hebrew text reads: "Your skilled ones [men], O Tyre." (*AT; RS*, ftn) Pointing to another location, others would link the Zemarites with Sumra, a seacoast town between Tripoli and Arvad.

ZEMIRAH (Ze·mi'rah) [possibly from a root meaning "melody"]. A family head in the tribe of Benjamin; son or descendant of Becher.—1Ch 7:6, 8, 9.

ZENAN (Ze'nan). A town in the Shephelah region of Judah. (Jos 15:33, 37) Many scholars consider it likely to be the same as Zaanan of Micah 1:11 and tentatively identify it with 'Araq el-Kharba, about 6 km (3.5 mi) NW of Lachish.

ZENAS (Ze'nas). An acquaintance of Paul, concerning whom Titus was told: "Carefully supply Zenas . . . and Apollos for their trip." (Tit 3:13) At the time Zenas was evidently on the island of Crete, but where he and Apollos were going, whether to Nicopolis, where Paul hoped to meet Titus (Tit 3:12), or to some other place, is not stated. Paul says that Zenas was "versed in the [Mosaic] Law," which may mean that he was either a Jew or a Jewish proselyte who had been converted to Christianity. His Greek name might favor the latter conclusion, but this is by no means decisive, since in the first century C.E., it was not uncommon for Jews to have Greek names. Other such examples include Justus, Dorcas, and Mark.—Ac 1:23; 9:36; 12:25.

ZEPHANIAH (Zeph·a·ni'ah) [Jehovah Has Concealed (Treasured Up)].

1. A Levite in the genealogical line from Kohath to Samuel and Heman.—1Ch 6:33-38.

2. A prophet of Jehovah in Judah during the early part of Josiah's reign; writer of the book bearing his name. Zephaniah was possibly a great-great-grandson of King Hezekiah.—Zep 1:1; see ZEPHANIAH, BOOK OF.

3. A leading priest during the last decade of the kingdom of Judah; son of Maaseiah. Zephaniah was twice sent by Zedekiah to Jeremiah, first to inquire of Jehovah about Judah's future and later to request him to pray on their behalf. (Jer 21:1-3; 37:3) From a false prophet in Babylon, Zephaniah received a letter urging him to rebuke Jeremiah, but instead of complying, Zephaniah read the letter to Jeremiah, who then wrote Jehovah's reply. (Jer 29:24-32) Following the fall of Jerusalem, Zephaniah, then second priest under Seraiah, was taken to Nebuchadnezzar at Riblah and killed.—Jer 52:24, 26, 27; 2Ki 25:18, 20, 21.

4. Father of Josiah, or Hen, a postexilic contributor of precious metals to make a crown for High Priest Joshua.—Zec 6:10, 11, 14.

ZEPHANIAH, BOOK OF. This book of the Hebrew Scriptures contains the word of Jehovah by means of his prophet Zephaniah. It was in the days of Judean King Josiah (659-629 B.C.E.) that Zephaniah carried on his prophetic work. (Zep 1:1) In the 12th year of Josiah's reign, he being about 20 years of age, the king began an extensive campaign against idolatry, and from the 18th year of his rule until its conclusion, his subjects "did not turn aside from following Jehovah." (2Ch 34:3-8, 33) Therefore, since the book of Zephaniah mentions the presence of foreign-god priests and the worship of Baal and heavenly bodies in

Judah, the time for its composition may reasonably be placed before the start of Josiah's reforms about 648 B.C.E.—Zep 1:4, 5.

Idolatry, violence, and deception abounded in Judah when Zephaniah began prophesying. Many were saying in their heart: "Jehovah will not do good, and he will not do bad." (Zep 1:12) But Zephaniah's prophesying made it clear that Jehovah would execute vengeance upon unrepentant wrongdoers. (1:3–2:3; 3:1-5) His adverse judgments would be visited not only upon Judah and Jerusalem but also upon other peoples—the Philistines, Ammonites, Moabites, Ethiopians, and Assyrians.—2:4-15.

The prophecy of Zephaniah would have been especially comforting to those who were endeavoring to serve Jehovah and who must have been greatly distressed about the detestable practices of Jerusalem's inhabitants, including her corrupt princes, judges, and priests. (Zep 3:1-7) As rightly disposed persons would have looked forward to the execution of divine judgment upon the wicked, they are evidently addressed with the words: "'Keep yourselves in expectation of me,' is the utterance of Jehovah, 'till the day of my rising up to the booty, for my judicial decision is to gather nations, for me to collect together kingdoms, in order to pour out upon them my denunciation, all my burning anger.'" (3:8) Eventually, Jehovah would turn favorable attention to the remnant of his people Israel, restoring them from captivity and making them a name and a praise among all other peoples.—3:10-20.

Authenticity. The authenticity of the book of Zephaniah is well established. Often the thoughts expressed in this book find a parallel in other parts of the Bible. (Compare Zep 1:3 with Ho 4:3; Zep 1:7 with Hab 2:20 and Zec 2:13; Zep 1:13 with De 28:30, 39 and Am 5:11; Zep 1:14 with Joe 1:15; and Zep 3:19 with Mic 4:6, 7.) It harmonizes completely with the rest of the Scriptures in emphasizing vital truths. For example: Jehovah is a God of righteousness. (Zep 3:5; De 32:4) Although providing opportunity for repentance, he does not indefinitely allow transgression to go unpunished. (Zep 2:1-3; Jer 18:7-11; 2Pe 3:9, 10) Neither silver nor gold can deliver wicked persons in the day of Jehovah's fury. (Zep 1:18; Pr 11:4; Eze 7:19) To be favored with divine protection, a person must conduct himself in harmony with God's righteous judgments.—Zep 2:3; Am 5:15.

Another outstanding evidence of the book's canonicity is the fulfillment of prophecy. The

---

HIGHLIGHTS OF ZEPHANIAH

Messages of divine judgment against Judah and Jerusalem, as well as against other nations; also an announcement of restoration for Jerusalem

Written by Zephaniah early in Josiah's reign, before the reforms that he began in about 648 B.C.E.

Jehovah's day of judgment is near (1:1–2:3)

Jehovah will finish everything off the surface of the ground

All in Judah and Jerusalem who practice idolatry, who swear to Jehovah as well as by a false god, who draw back from serving Jehovah, or who have not sought him will be cut off

Princes, violent ones, deceivers, will be among those sought out for attention; all who feel that Jehovah will not act for good or for bad will see their wealth and property come to nothing

Jehovah's day is coming, a day of fury; neither silver nor gold to provide escape

Meek ones of the earth should seek Jehovah as well as meekness and righteousness; then, probably, they will be concealed in the day of his anger

Punishment for Judah's neighbors and more distant Ethiopia and Assyria (2:4-15)

The Philistines will be destroyed; Moab will become desolate like Sodom, and Ammon will be like Gomorrah for reproaching Jehovah's people

Ethiopians will fall by the sword; Assyria will be destroyed; Nineveh will be devastated, with wild animals taking possession of its ruins

Jerusalem's rebellion and corruption (3:1-7)

The oppressive city, Jerusalem, is also marked for judgment; she did not trust Jehovah and draw near to him; her princes, judges, prophets, and priests all acted corruptly instead of using their influence for good

The people did not fear Jehovah and change their ways even after witnessing his judgment on other nations

The outpouring of Jehovah's anger and the restoration of a remnant (3:8-20)

Jehovah's anger will be poured out on nations and kingdoms

Peoples will be given a pure language so as to call on Jehovah's name and serve him shoulder to shoulder

Only the humble and lowly will remain among God's people Israel and enjoy security under His protection

All those responsible for afflicting Israel will be punished; the regathered remnant will be made "a praise among all the peoples of the earth"

foretold destruction came upon the Assyrian capital Nineveh in 632 B.C.E. (Zep 2:13-15) and upon Judah and Jerusalem in 607 B.C.E. (Zep 1:4-18; compare 2Ki 25:1-10.) As allies of the Egyptians, the Ethiopians evidently experienced calamity at the time Nebuchadnezzar conquered Egypt. (Zep 2:12; compare Eze 30:4, 5.) And the Ammonites, Moabites, and Philistines eventually ceased to exist as a people.—Zep 2:4-11.

ZEPHATH (Ze′phath) [possibly from a root meaning "keep watch"]. A royal Canaanite city in the southern part of Judah's territory, apparently S of Arad, captured by the combined forces of Judah and Simeon. (Jg 1:16, 17; compare Jos 15:30; 19:4.) The city was renamed "Hormah," meaning "A Devoting to Destruction." This city, like the other cities of the Canaanites, had been placed 'under ban' by Jehovah and was to be devoted to destruction. (De 7:1-4) The tribes of Judah and Simeon were now applying the terms of that ban to Zephath. Zephath may have been the principal Canaanite city of that district or area.—See HORMAH.

ZEPHATHAH (Zeph′a·thah). A valley near Mareshah where Jehovah enabled the forces of Judah's King Asa to defeat those of Zerah the Ethiopian (967 B.C.E.). (2Ch 14:9-12) Zephathah is apparently one of the valleys N of Mareshah. The Greek *Septuagint* has been translated to read "in the valley north of Maresa" (Bagster), but "Zephathah" appears in the Hebrew Masoretic text.

ZEPHO (Ze′pho). Third-named son of Eliphaz; grandson of Esau and sheik of an Edomite tribe. —Ge 36:10, 11, 15; 1Ch 1:36.

ZEPHON (Ze′phon). The first-named son of Gad and founder of the family of Zephonites; also called Ziphion.—Ge 46:16; Nu 26:15.

ZEPHONITES (Ze′phon·ites) [Of (Belonging to) Zephon]. A family descended from Gad through Zephon.—Nu 26:15.

ZER. A fortified city in Naphtali's territory. (Jos 19:32, 35) Its site is unknown.

ZERAH (Ze′rah) [possibly a shortened form of Zerahiah].

1. An Edomite sheik. Zerah was the son of Reuel and grandson of Esau and Basemath, Ishmael's daughter. (Ge 36:3, 4, 13, 17; 1Ch 1:37) Possibly the same as No. 2.

2. Father of the second Edomite king, Jobab; he was from Bozrah. (Ge 36:33; 1Ch 1:44) Possibly the same as No. 1.

3. A son of Judah and Tamar; twin brother of Perez. (Ge 38:27-30; Mt 1:3) Zerah was one of those "who came to Jacob into Egypt." (Ge 46:12, 26) His five sons (1Ch 2:4, 6) grew into a Judean tribal family (Nu 26:20) and eventually included persons such as Achan (Jos 7:1, 17, 18, 24; 22:20), two of David's army leaders (1Ch 27:11, 13), and some postexilic residents of Jerusalem (1Ch 9:3, 6; Ne 11:22, 24).

4. A son of Simeon and founder of a family in that tribe. (1Ch 4:24; Nu 26:12, 13) He is called Zohar at Genesis 46:10 and Exodus 6:15.

5. A descendant of Gershon the son of Levi. (1Ch 6:16, 20, 21; compare Ge 46:11.) In 1 Chronicles 6:41 reference may be made to the same person.

6. An Ethiopian, or Cushite, who led a huge army of a million men and 300 chariots into Judah during Asa's reign, in 967 B.C.E. Zerah met defeat, and his fleeing forces were pursued and slaughtered "as far as Gerar." (2Ch 14:1, 9-15) Identification of Zerah with any secularly known Egyptian or Ethiopian ruler remains uncertain.

ZERAHIAH (Zer·a·hi′ah) [Jah Has Flashed Forth; Jah Has Shone Forth].

1. A descendant of Aaron through Eleazar and Phinehas in the high-priestly line.—1Ch 6:3, 4, 6, 50, 51; Ezr 7:4.

2. Father of Elieho-enai who headed the paternal house of Pahath-moab, 200 males of whom returned to Jerusalem with Ezra in 468 B.C.E. —Ezr 8:1, 4.

ZERAHITES (Ze′rah·ites) [Of (Belonging to) Zerah].

1. Descendants of Simeon's son Zerah.—Nu 26:12, 13; see ZERAH No. 4.

2. The tribal family that sprang from Judah's son Zerah.—Nu 26:20; Jos 7:17; 1Ch 27:11, 13; see ZERAH No. 3.

ZERED, TORRENT VALLEY OF (Ze′red). A torrent valley at which the Israelites camped on their way around the frontier of Moab, at the end of the 38 additional years of wandering from the time of the rebellion at Kadesh-barnea. (Nu 21:12; De 2:13, 14) It is generally identified with the Wadi el-Hasa′, the southernmost tributary of the Dead Sea. This valley formed the boundary between Moab and Edom, and over a 56-km (35 mi) stretch, it descends some 1,190 m (3,900 ft), entering the Dead Sea at the SE end. The valley is some 5 to 6 km (3 to 4 mi) across at the top. There is evidence there of a series of Edomite fortresses that served to guard the natural approaches to the S of the Wadi el-Hasa′.

ZEREDAH

ZEREDAH (Zer′e·dah).

1. The hometown of Jeroboam, first king of the northern kingdom of Israel. (1Ki 11:26) The only indication of its location is the statement: "And there was Jeroboam the son of Nebat an Ephraimite from Zeredah." It is generally identified with Deir Ghassana (in the region of Ephraim) where the nearby spring called ʽAin Seridah preserves the name. This site is about 25 km (16 mi) SW of Shechem.

2. Reference is made to Zeredah in "the District of the Jordan" in connection with the casting of copper utensils for the temple constructed by Solomon. (2Ch 4:17) The parallel text at 1 Kings 7:46 indicates this to be the same place as Zarethan, Zeredah perhaps being a variant spelling of the name.—See ZARETHAN.

ZERERAH (Zer′e·rah). The flight of the defeated Midianites, as they were pursued by Gideon's forces, is described as continuing "as far as Beth-shittah, on to Zererah, as far as the outskirts of Abel-meholah by Tabbath."—Jg 7:22.

Twenty Hebrew manuscripts here read "Zeredah" rather than Zererah. Since Zeredah and Zarethan are used in a parallel sense at 2 Chronicles 4:17 and 1 Kings 7:46, some suggest the location of Zererah to be the same as that of Zarethan.—See ZARETHAN.

Such location, however, would seem to be possible only if the expression "on to Zererah" were to be taken in the sense of 'in the direction of Zererah,' inasmuch as the location of Zarethan seems to have been considerably S of Abel-meholah. Otherwise, Zererah would necessarily be viewed as lying between Beth-shittah and Abel-meholah; in such case its precise location is unknown.

ZERESH (Ze′resh). The wife of Haman. Zeresh and Haman's friends proposed that he erect a stake to a height of 50 cubits (22 m; 73 ft) on which to hang Mordecai. (Es 5:10, 14) But when reversals set in, Zeresh, along with Haman's wise men, said: "If it is from the seed of the Jews that Mordecai is before whom you have started to fall, you will not prevail against him, but you will without fail fall before him."—Es 6:13.

ZERETH (Ze′reth). First-named son that Helah bore to Asshur; of the tribe of Judah.—1Ch 4:1, 5, 7.

ZERETH-SHAHAR (Ze′reth-sha′har). A site in Reuben situated "in the mountain of the low plain." (Jos 13:15, 19) It is tentatively identified with ez-Zarat, situated at the hot springs of Callirrhoe on the E shore of the Dead Sea.

ZERI (Ze′ri). One of Jeduthun's six sons, all of whom were temple musicians. (1Ch 25:1, 3) With the Hebrew letter *yohdh* prefixed, his name is spelled "Izri" in 1 Chronicles 25:11, where he is identified as head of the fourth of David's 24 divisions of temple musical service.

ZEROR (Ze′ror) [from a root meaning "flint"]. An ancestor of King Saul; listed as son of Becorath and father of Abiel; of the tribe of Benjamin. —1Sa 9:1.

ZERUAH (Ze·ru′ah) [from a root meaning "be leprous"]. Mother of King Jeroboam (I); a widow at the time that Jeroboam began to lift up his hand against King Solomon.—1Ki 11:26.

ZERUBBABEL (Ze·rub′ba·bel) [from Akkadian, meaning "Seed (Offspring) of Babel"]. First governor of the repatriated Jews (Hag 2:21); a descendant of King David and an ancestor of Jesus Christ; likely reckoned as the son of Pedaiah but legally reckoned as the son of Shealtiel. (1Ch 3:19; Mt 1:12, 13; Lu 3:27; see GENEALOGY OF JESUS CHRIST [Problems in Matthew's Genealogy of Jesus].) The genealogical listing of 1 Chronicles (3:19, 20) names seven sons of Zerubbabel (Meshullam, Hananiah, Hashubah, Ohel, Berechiah, Hasadiah, Jushab-hesed) and one daughter (Shelomith). Zerubbabel's official or Babylonian name appears to have been Sheshbazzar.—Ezr 1:8, 11; 5:14, 16; compare Ezr 3:8.

After the liberation from Babylonian exile, Zerubbabel, in 537 B.C.E., led a Jewish remnant back to Jerusalem and Judah. (Ezr 2:1, 2; Ne 7:6, 7; 12:1; MAP, Vol. 2, p. 332) As the governor appointed by King Cyrus, Zerubbabel had been entrusted with sacred gold and silver vessels that had years earlier been taken from the temple by Nebuchadnezzar. (Ezr 5:14, 15) At Jerusalem, the temple altar was erected in the seventh month (Ethanim, or Tishri, September-October), under the direction of Zerubbabel and High Priest Jeshua (Ezr 3:1, 2), and in the second year in the second month (Ziv, or Iyyar, April-May, of 536 B.C.E.), the actual construction of the temple began. (Ezr 3:8) Recognizing the bad motive of the non-Jews who asked to have a share in the rebuilding work, Zerubbabel, Jeshua, and the heads of the paternal houses stated: "You have nothing to do with us in building a house to our God, for we ourselves shall together build to Jehovah the God of Israel, just as King Cyrus the king of Persia has commanded us."—Ezr 4:1-3.

These non-Jews, however, continued to dishearten the temple rebuilders and finally (in 522 B.C.E.) succeeded in having an official ban placed on the work. Two years later, stirred up by the prophets Haggai and Zechariah, Zerubbabel and Jeshua (Joshua) courageously resumed the construction of the temple despite the ban. (Ezr 4:23, 24; 5:1, 2; Hag 1:1, 12, 14; Zec 1:1) Thereafter an investigation of the Persian archives vindicated the legality of their work. (Ezr 6:1-12) Throughout, the prophets Haggai and Zechariah continued to encourage Zerubbabel, strengthening him for the work and assuring him of divine favor. (Hag 2:2-4, 21-23; Zec 4:6-10) Finally (in 515 B.C.E.) the temple was completed. (Ezr 6:13-15) Also during Zerubbabel's governorship the needs of the Levites were cared for, the singers and gatekeepers receiving their portion "according to the daily need."—Ne 12:47.

ZERUIAH (Ze·ru'iah) [possibly from a root meaning "balsam"]. King David's sister or half sister and the mother of Joab, Abishai, and Asahel. Zeruiah's sister Abigail is said to be "the daughter of Nahash," though that is not directly stated of Zeruiah. (2Sa 17:25) Zeruiah and Abigail are also said to be "sisters" of the sons of Jesse. (1Ch 2:16) It is possible, therefore, that they were daughters of Jesse's wife by a previous marriage to Nahash, therefore only half sisters of David. (See ABIGAIL No. 2; NAHASH No. 2.) Apparently Zeruiah was considerably older than David, for her sons seem to have been about the same age as David. Zeruiah's name is usually associated with her three sons, who were all valiant fighters for David. (2Sa 2:13, 18; 16:9) The only reference made to the boys' father is that he was buried at Bethlehem.—2Sa 2:32.

ZETHAM (Ze'tham) [possibly from a root meaning "olive; olive tree"]. A Gershonite Levite descended from Ladan. He headed a paternal house and was assigned to care for the temple treasures.—1Ch 23:7-9; 26:22.

ZETHAN (Ze'than) [from a root meaning "olive; olive tree"]. A descendant of Benjamin through Jediael and Bilhan.—1Ch 7:6, 10.

ZETHAR (Ze'thar). One of the seven court officials whom Ahasuerus sent to bring Vashti before him.—Es 1:10, 11.

ZEUS. The supreme god of the polytheistic Greeks, corresponding to Jupiter of the Romans. Zeus was a god of the sky and was viewed as having control of the winds, clouds, rain, and thunder, exercising his power over these natural forces for both a destructive and a beneficial purpose. The ancient poet Homer (The Iliad, VIII, 1-25) represents Zeus as having greater strength than all the other gods combined. Zeus, however, was not regarded as being supreme in an absolute sense but is at times depicted as becoming a victim of deception and having to yield to the will of the Fates and Destiny.

Aside from relating the events of his birth, childhood, and acquisition of the throne, the legends are chiefly concerned with the many love affairs of Zeus. The mythological accounts tell of his seducing goddesses and earthly women and of his fathering a host of illegitimate children. Paradoxically, it is related that Zeus killed Iasion (a mortal) for having committed immorality with the goddess Demeter. Besides being marred by Zeus' many acts of unfaithfulness, the marriage of Zeus and Hera was beset by other troubles. Zeus, it is said, was so much plagued by incessant scolding from his wife Hera that he on occasion complained bitterly concerning this before the assembled deities.

At times the pure worship of Jehovah came into direct conflict with the worship of the false god Zeus. King Antiochus IV (Epiphanes), in his attempt to stamp out the Jewish religion, directed that the temple at Jerusalem be profaned and rededicated to Zeus of Olympus. See the Apocryphal book of 2 Maccabees 6:1, 2.

In the first century C.E., the townspeople of Lystra, upon seeing Paul heal a lame man, considered Paul and Barnabas to be gods, identifying Paul with Hermes and Barnabas with Zeus. The priest of Zeus even brought out bulls and garlands in order to offer sacrifices with the crowd. (Ac 14:8-13) Two ancient inscriptions discovered in 1909 in the vicinity of Lystra testify to the worship of these two gods in that city. One of the inscriptions refers to the "priests of Zeus," and the other mentions "Hermes Most Great" and "Zeus the sun-god."—The International Standard Bible Encyclopaedia, edited by J. Orr, 1960, Vol. III, p. 1944.

The ship on which Paul as a prisoner set sail from the island of Malta bore the figurehead "Sons of Zeus," that is, the twin brothers Castor and Pollux.—Ac 28:11.

ZEUS, SONS OF. According to Greek and Roman mythology, Castor and Pollux were the twin sons of Leda and the offspring of the god Zeus (Jupiter), thus being called Dioscuri, or "Sons of Zeus." Among other things, they were regarded as protectors of mariners, able to save sailors imperiled at sea. It was believed that these deities manifested themselves during storms in the form of St. Elmo's fire. The Alexandrian boat on which the prisoner Paul sailed from Malta to Puteoli when en route to Rome bore the figure-head "Sons of Zeus." Perhaps the image or symbol and the name of Castor were on one side of the bow and the corresponding representation and name of Pollux on the other.—Ac 28:11.

ZIA (Zi'a) [possibly from a root meaning "tremble; quake; violently shake"]. A Gadite who lived in Bashan.—1Ch 5:11, 13.

ZIBA (Zi'ba). The servant of Saul's household from whom David, on inquiry, learned of Jonathan's lame son Mephibosheth. David brought Mephibosheth to Jerusalem and assigned Ziba, his 15 sons, and his 20 servants to care for Mephibosheth's inheritance. (2Sa 9:2-12 [The reference to "my table" in verse 11 is generally thought to be a scribal error for "David's table"; another possibility is that Ziba may have been *repeating* David's exact words.]) When David fled from Jerusalem on account of Absalom's rebellion, Ziba brought him much needed supplies of food and animals. However, he left Mephibosheth behind, even though he wanted to come, and told David that Mephibosheth deliberately stayed in Jerusalem, expecting to recover the kingdom for Saul's house. In response, without further investigation of the matter David transferred Mephibosheth's property to Ziba.—2Sa 16:1-4.

When David returned after the rebellion was crushed, Ziba was among the early ones to greet the king. Then Mephibosheth met David, welcomed him back, and informed him of Ziba's trickery and slander. In the light of these new developments, David now decided that the property should be divided between Mephibosheth and Ziba. Mephibosheth, however, declared: "Let him [Ziba] even take the whole, now that my lord the king has come in peace to his house."—2Sa 19:17, 24-30.

ZIBEON (Zib'e·on) [Hyena; possibly, Small Hyena]. A sheik in the land of Seir. (Ge 36:20, 29, 30; 1Ch 1:38, 40b) His granddaughter Oholibamah married Esau. (Ge 36:2, 14, 24, 25) For the suggested explanations as to why Zibeon is described as both a Hivite and a Horite, see HORITE.

ZIBIA (Zib'i·a) [Gazelle]. Family head in the tribe of Benjamin. Son of Shaharaim by his wife Hodesh.—1Ch 8:1, 8-10.

ZIBIAH (Zib'i·ah) [Female Gazelle]. Mother of King Jehoash of Judah, presumably the wife of King Ahaziah and therefore daughter-in-law of Athaliah. (2Ki 11:1, 2; 12:1; 2Ch 24:1) Zibiah was from Beer-sheba. Nothing is said of how she fared in Athaliah's purge of Judah's royal house.

ZICHRI (Zich'ri) [shortened form of Zechariah, meaning "Jehovah Has Remembered"].

1. Third-named son of Izhar; grandson of Kohath, a Levite.—Ex 6:18, 21.

2, 3, 4. Three family heads in the tribe of Benjamin, residents of Jerusalem. They were sons or descendants of Shimei, Shashak, and Jeroham respectively.—1Ch 8:1, 19, 21, 23, 25, 27, 28.

5. A son of Asaph, and forefather of the post-exilic musician Mattaniah. (1Ch 9:15) Elsewhere he may be called Zabdi (Ne 11:17) and Zaccur.—1Ch 25:2, 10; Ne 12:35.

6. A Levite descendant of Moses through Eliezer; father or ancestor of the Shelomoth appointed, during David's reign, over the treasures of the things captured in war.—1Ch 26:25-27; 23:15, 17.

7. A Reubenite whose son Eliezer was tribal chieftain during David's reign.—1Ch 27:16.

8. A man of Judah whose son Amasiah was a military chief for King Jehoshaphat.—2Ch 17:12, 14, 16.

9. Father of the Elishaphat who helped Jehoiada to overthrow Athaliah.—2Ch 23:1.

10. A mighty warrior from Ephraim in the army of the northern kingdom that invaded Judah around 760 B.C.E. Zichri killed three prominent members of King Ahaz' household, including a royal prince.—2Ch 28:6, 7.

11. A Benjamite whose son Joel was an overseer of the Benjamites living in Jerusalem after the exile.—Ne 11:3, 4, 7, 9.

12. Head of the priestly paternal house of Abijah during the time of High Priest Jeshua's successor Joiakim.—Ne 12:12, 17.

ZIDDIM (Zid'dim). A fortified city in the territory of Naphtali. (Jos 19:32, 35) Its exact location is not definitely known.

ZIHA (Zi'ha).

1. First-listed family of Nethinim who accompanied the exiled Israelites back to Judah in 537 B.C.E.—Ezr 2:1, 2, 43; Ne 7:46.

2. One of two overseers of the Nethinim who returned from Babylonian exile.—Ne 11:21.

ZIKLAG (Zik′lag). As originally assigned, this was a Simeonite enclave city in S Judah. (Jos 15:21, 31; 19:1, 2, 5; 1Ch 4:24-30) Later, Ziklag was under Philistine control. Achish, king of Gath, gave it to the fugitive David as a place of residence (and it thereafter became the possession of Judah's kings). (1Sa 27:6) The Amalekites raided and burned the city, taking captives, including David's wives Ahinoam and Abigail. After defeating the marauders and recovering the captives and things taken, David, from Ziklag, sent some of the spoil of battle to his friends, older men of Judah in various cities. (1Sa 30) Many armed mighty men joined David at Ziklag, and there he received news of King Saul's death. (2Sa 1:1, 2; 4:10; 1Ch 12:1, 2, 20-22) After the Babylonian exile, some of the sons of Judah settled in this city. (Ne 11:25, 28) Various sites have been suggested for the identification of Ziklag, but Y. Aharoni and others favor identifying it with Tell esh-Shari′ah (Tel Sera‵), about 7 km (4 mi) E of Gerar and 22 km (14 mi) NW of Beer-sheba.

ZILLAH (Zil′lah) [Shadow; Shelter]. One of the two wives of Lamech, the first polygamist of Bible record. She was the mother of Tubal-cain and of his sister Naamah. Lamech composed a poem for his wives Adah and Zillah.—Ge 4:19-24.

ZILLETHAI (Zil′le·thai) [from a root meaning "shadow; shelter"].

1. Head of a family of Benjamites that lived in Jerusalem; son of Shimei.—1Ch 8:1, 20, 21, 28.

2. A valiant Manassite chieftain who joined David's forces at Ziklag.—1Ch 12:19-21.

ZILPAH (Zil′pah). Leah's maidservant and one of Jacob's secondary wives. Zilpah had been a servant of Leah's father Laban until Leah and Jacob were married in 1774 B.C.E., when she was given to Leah. (Ge 29:24) After Leah had had four sons and thought she was through childbearing, she gave Zilpah to Jacob as a secondary wife. Zilpah then bore Gad and Asher, who, in turn, had many sons. (Ge 30:9-13; 35:26; 37:2; 46:16-18) Zilpah remained with Jacob's household through their many travels.—Ge 32:22; 33:1, 2.

ZIMMAH (Zim′mah). A Gershonite Levite. (1Ch 6:20) He is possibly the same Zimmah who is mentioned in 1 Chronicles 6:42. If this genealogy skips many names (as these lists commonly do), he may also be the one referred to at 2 Chronicles 29:12, whose descendant Joah helped to cleanse the temple in Hezekiah's day.

ZIMRAN (Zim′ran). First named of the six sons Keturah bore to Abraham. Zimran and his five full brothers were given gifts and sent into "the land of the East." (Ge 25:1, 2, 6; 1Ch 1:32) The conjecture of some is that Zimran's descendants were associated either with Zabram, a town situated W of Mecca on the Arabian shore of the Red Sea, or with Zimri, mentioned in Jeremiah 25:25.

ZIMRI (Zim′ri).

1. A son of Zerah and grandson of Judah. —1Ch 2:4, 6.

2. The Simeonite chieftain, son of Salu, who brought Cozbi the Midianitess into the camp of Israel, committing fornication with her in his own tent. For this, Zimri and Cozbi were slain by Phinehas, with Jehovah's approval. This quick action put an end to the scourge that had already caused the death of thousands of guilty Israelites. —Nu 25:6-8, 14-18.

3. Fifth king of the ten-tribe kingdom of Israel. Zimri ruled in Tirzah for seven days in about 951 B.C.E. He had previously been chief of half the chariots under King Elah, but when the army was away at Gibbethon, and King Elah had remained behind, Zimri killed him and all the rest of Baasha's house and made himself king. His rule was very short because the army made Omri king and immediately returned to besiege Tirzah, whereupon Zimri burned the king's house down over himself. Zimri is noted for doing what was bad in Jehovah's eyes. (1Ki 16:3, 4, 9-20) Jezebel's last words recalled the consequences that befell Zimri. As Jehu triumphantly rode into Jezreel, she taunted from the window: "Did it go all right with Zimri the killer of his lord?"—2Ki 9:30, 31.

4. A descendant of Saul and Jonathan. (1Ch 8:33-36; 9:42) It has been suggested that he may be the same as No. 3; the reason is that there is a possibility that this Zimri (No. 3) was trying to recover the kingship as a member of Saul's household.

5. An apparent geographic location that is unknown; sometimes, but without good authority, connected with Abraham's son Zimran.—Jer 25:25; Ge 25:1, 2.

ZIN.

1. A wilderness through which the Israelites traveled en route to Canaan; not synonymous with the Wilderness of Sin. (Nu 33:11, 36) In the second year after Israel's leaving Egypt, 12 Israelites spied out the Promised Land, starting out

from the Wilderness of Zin. At that time the Israelites were encamped at Kadesh. (Nu 13:21, 26) Later, after having wandered in the wilderness for years, the Israelites arrived at Kadesh in the Wilderness of Zin the second time. This area of the Wilderness of Zin was desolate, unsown, lacking figs, vines, pomegranates, and water. (Nu 20:1-5; compare Nu 20:28; 33:38; De 1:3.) It was in connection with the waters of Meribah at Kadesh in the Wilderness of Zin that Moses and Aaron failed to sanctify Jehovah before the people and lost the privilege of entering the Promised Land.—Nu 27:12-14; De 32:50, 51.

The Wilderness of Zin was "alongside Edom" (being immediately W of Edom) and at the SE extremity of Judah's assigned territory. (Nu 34:3; Jos 15:1) Since Kadesh was located in the wilderness areas of Zin and of Paran (Nu 13:26; 20:1), possibly these were adjoining wilderness regions, or that of Zin may have been part of the more extensive Wilderness of Paran.

2. Twice "Zin" appears without the term "wilderness." In these cases, it may designate a presently unidentified town in S Judah between the ascent of Akrabbim and Kadesh-barnea and from which the surrounding wilderness drew its name. Or it may mean the Wilderness of Zin itself.—Nu 34:4; Jos 15:3.

ZINA (Zi'na). A descendant of Gershon through Shimei. (1Ch 23:6, 7, 10) He is called Zizah in 1 Chronicles 23:11.—See ZIZAH.

ZION (Zi'on). Originally the Jebusite stronghold that came to be called "the City of David." (1Ki 8:1; 1Ch 11:5) After capturing Mount Zion, David established his royal residence there. (2Sa 5:6, 7, 9; see DAVID, CITY OF.) Alluding to David's ruling from Zion as God's anointed one are Jehovah's words: "I, even I, have installed my king upon Zion, my holy mountain." (Ps 2:6) Zion became a mountain especially holy to Jehovah when David had the sacred Ark transferred there. (2Sa 6:17) Later, the designation "Zion" embraced the temple area on Mount Moriah (where the Ark was moved during Solomon's reign) and the term was, in fact, applied to the entire city of Jerusalem. (Compare Isa 1:8; 8:18; see MOUNTAIN OF MEETING.) Since the Ark was associated with Jehovah's presence (Ex 25:22; Le 16:2) and because Zion was a symbol of heavenly realities, Zion was referred to as the place of God's dwelling (Ps 9:11; 74:2; 76:2; 78:68; 132:13, 14; 135:21) and the place from which help, blessing, and salvation would come.—Ps 14:7; 20:2; 50:2; 53:6; 134:3.

For unfaithfulness to him, Jehovah allowed the Babylonians to desolate Zion, or Jerusalem. (La 2:1, 4, 6, 8, 10, 13) Later, in fulfillment of prophecy, Jehovah restored a remnant of his repentant people to Zion, or Jerusalem. (Isa 35:10; 51:3; 52:1-8; Jer 50:4, 5, 28; 51:10, 24, 35) This made it possible for Jesus Christ to ride into Jerusalem on the colt of an ass and present himself to Zion as king, thus fulfilling the prophecy of Zechariah. (Zec 9:9; Mt 21:5; Joh 12:15) Only a remnant responded favorably, whereas the religious leaders rejected Jesus as king and sought his death. This pointed to calamity for earthly Jerusalem, or Zion, and its casting off by God.—Mt 21:33-46.

As Jesus had been rejected in earthly Jerusalem, it could not have been there that Jehovah laid his Son as "a tried stone, the precious corner of a sure foundation." (Isa 28:16; Ro 9:32, 33; 1Pe 2:6) Rather, it must have been in the Zion concerning which Hebrew Christians were told: "But you have approached a Mount Zion and a city of the living God, heavenly Jerusalem, and myriads of angels, in general assembly, and the congregation of the firstborn who have been enrolled in the heavens, and God the Judge of all, and the spiritual lives of righteous ones who have been made perfect, and Jesus the mediator of a new covenant." (Heb 12:22-24) It is evidently on this heavenly Mount Zion that the Lamb, Christ Jesus, stands with the 144,000 who have been purchased from the earth.—Re 14:1-3; see JERUSALEM; NEW JERUSALEM.

ZIOR (Zi'or) [from a root meaning "be insignificant"]. A city in the mountainous region of Judah. (Jos 15:20, 48, 54) It is identified with Si'ir, about 7 km (4 mi) NNE of Hebron.

ZIPH.

1. A descendant of Judah through Jehallelel. —1Ch 4:15, 16.

2. An unidentified city in the southern part of Judah.—Jos 15:21, 24.

3. A city in the mountainous region of Judah. (Jos 15:20, 48, 55, 57) It is apparently the Ziph 'fathered' by Mesha. (1Ch 2:42) Geographers generally connect it with Tell Zif, some 6 km (3.5 mi) SE of Hebron. David sought refuge from King Saul in the wilderness surrounding Ziph, and the men of the city twice revealed his whereabouts to the king. (1Sa 23:14, 15, 19, 24, 29; 26:1, 2; compare Ps 54:Sup.) This Ziph apparently was the one later fortified by Rehoboam.—2Ch 11:5-8.

ZIPHAH (Zi'phah). A 'son' of Jehallelel in the tribe of Judah.—1Ch 4:1, 16.

ZIPHION. See ZEPHON.

ZIPHITES (Ziph′ites) [Of (Belonging to) Ziph]. The inhabitants of Ziph in the mountainous region of Judah.—Psalm 54:Sup; see ZIPH No. 3.

ZIPHRON (Ziph′ron). A site at the northern border of the Promised Land. (Nu 34:9) Its exact location is not definitely known, although Y. Aharoni identifies it with Hawwarin, about 100 km (60 mi) SSE of Hamath.

ZIPPOR (Zip′por) [Bird]. Father of Moab's King Balak.—Nu 22:2, 4, 10, 16; 23:18; Jos 24:9; Jg 11:25.

ZIPPORAH (Zip·po′rah) [Bird; or, possibly, Small Bird]. The wife of Moses. Zipporah met Moses at a well, when she and her six sisters were watering their father's flocks. When certain shepherds came on the scene and, as was their custom, attempted to drive the girls away, Moses helped the girls out, even watering the flocks himself. For this kindness he was invited to the home of Zipporah, and eventually her priestly father Jethro gave her in marriage to Moses. (Ex 2:16-21) Zipporah bore two sons to Moses—Gershom and Eliezer.—Ex 2:22; 18:3, 4.

When Jehovah sent Moses back to Egypt, Zipporah and their two sons started out to accompany him. Along the way a very serious incident occurred, the rather obscure account of which says: "Now it came about on the road at the lodging place that Jehovah ["Jehovah's angel," LXX] got to meet him and kept looking for a way to put him to death. Finally Zipporah took a flint and cut off her son's foreskin and caused it to touch his feet and said: 'It is because you are a bridegroom of blood to me.' Consequently he let go of him. At that time she said: 'A bridegroom of blood,' because of the circumcision."—Ex 4:24-26.

Scholars have offered many interpretations of this passage, some of these being incorporated into modern Bible translations. (See CC, JB, Kx, La, NE, RS, as well as the German Zürcher Bibel, the Spanish Bover-Cantera and the French Crampon, Lienart, and Segond versions.) Such interpretations attempt to settle questions as to whether it was Moses' or the child's life that was threatened, whether Zipporah touched the feet of Moses or the feet of the child or the feet of the angel with the foreskin. They also venture opinions as to why Zipporah said (and to whom she said), "You are a bridegroom of blood to me."

It seems that it was the child's life that was in danger in view of what the law of circumcision

states at Genesis 17:14; that Zipporah circumcised the child because she realized what was needed to set matters right; that she cast the foreskin at the feet of the angel who was threatening the child's life to demonstrate her compliance with Jehovah's law; that Zipporah addressed Jehovah through his representative angel when she exclaimed, "You are a bridegroom of blood to me," doing so to show her acceptance of a wifely position in the circumcision covenant with Jehovah as the husband.—See Jer 31:32.

But there is no way of Scripturally settling such questions with certainty. The literal reading of the ancient Hebrew in this passage is veiled in the idioms used nearly 3,500 years ago. This is why literal translations (NW, Ro, Yg) and others (AS, KJ, Da, Dy, JP, Mo, Le), including the ancient Greek Septuagint, are not clear on these matters.

Apparently Zipporah returned to visit her parents, for, following the Exodus, Zipporah and her two sons accompanied Jethro back to Moses at the wilderness camp. (Ex 18:1-6) Zipporah's newly felt presence there apparently provoked Moses' sister Miriam to jealousy, and she (along with Aaron) seized upon Zipporah's Cushite background as an excuse for complaint against Moses. (Nu 12:1) This does not indicate that Zipporah had died and Moses had remarried an Ethiopian woman, as is commonly contended, for although "Cushite" usually refers to Ethiopians, it can also embrace those from Arabia.—See CUSH No. 2; CUSHITE.

ZITHER. The Bible gives no description of the musical instrument designated by the Aramaic word qath·rohs′, but it was probably a type of stringed instrument. If this term is related to the Greek ki·tha′ra (a stringed instrument), from which a number of English words, including "zither," are drawn, then "zither" is an approximate transliteration. The qath·rohs′ was one of the instruments of Nebuchadnezzar's orchestra.—Da 3:5, 7, 10, 15.

ZIV. The name of the second lunar month of the sacred calendar; the eighth of the secular calendar of the Israelites. (1Ki 6:1, 37) It corresponds to part of April and part of May. The comment on 1 Kings 6:1 in the Soncino Books of the Bible says concerning the month of Ziv: "Now known as Iyyar, the second month after Nisan. It was called Ziv (brightness) because it falls at the time of the year when the earth is 'brightened' with blossoms and flowers." (Edited by A. Cohen, London, 1950) The name Iyyar is found in the Jewish Talmud and other postexilic works.

By this month the barley harvest has reached up into the hill country and the wheat harvest is under way in the lowlands. The hills of Galilee are ablaze with flowers. The dry season begins during this month, and the early morning clouds soon disappear in the heat of the day. During this time the plants depend upon the nightly dews that form, and they await the end of the dry season in October.—Ho 6:4; Isa 18:4.

The 14th day of Ziv provided a second opportunity for the Israelites to celebrate the Passover in the event they, because of absence or ceremonial uncleanness, had been prevented from doing so on Nisan 14.—Nu 9:9-13; 2Ch 30:2, 3.

It was in the month of Ziv that Solomon began the construction of the temple, and nearly 500 years later in the same month, Zerubbabel initiated the work of rebuilding the temple.—1Ki 6:1; Ezr 3:8.

ZIZ. A pass by which the armies of Moab, Ammon, and the Ammonim came against Judah during the reign of King Jehoshaphat (936–c. 911 B.C.E.). It is usually identified with Wadi Hasasa (Nahal Hazezon), about 15 km (9.5 mi) SE of the suggested site of Tekoa and some 10 km (6 mi) NW of En-gedi.—2Ch 20:1, 2, 16, 20.

ZIZA (Zi′za).

1. A son of King Rehoboam by Absalom's granddaughter Maacah. When the royal succession was directed to Ziza's brother Abijah, Ziza received gifts of cities, food, and wives from Rehoboam.—2Ch 11:20, 22, 23.

2. One of the Simeonite chieftains who expanded their grazing land by annexing Hamite territory and destroying its inhabitants during the reign of Hezekiah; son of Shiphi.—1Ch 4:24, 37-41.

ZIZAH (Zi′zah). Second-listed son of Shimei, head of a paternal house of Gershonite Levites assigned to certain duties during David's reign. (1Ch 23:6, 7, 10, 11) In verse 10 the name is spelled Zina in the Masoretic text, Zizah in the Greek *Septuagint* and the Latin *Vulgate*.

ZOAN (Zo′an). An ancient Egyptian city, built seven years after Hebron, hence already in existence around the time of Abraham's entry into Canaan (1943 B.C.E.). (Nu 13:22; Ge 12:5; 13:18) The Bible name Zoan corresponds to the Egyptian name (*d′n·t*) of a town located in the northeastern part of the Delta region, about 56 km (35 mi) SW of Port Said. Better known by its Greek name,

Tanis (near present-day San el-Hagar), it was situated on the branch of the Nile called the Tanitic branch.

At Psalm 78:12, 43, "the field of Zoan" is used parallel to "the land of Egypt" in recounting Jehovah's miraculous acts on behalf of Israel leading up to the Exodus. This has caused some scholars to hold that Moses' meetings with Pharaoh took place at Zoan. Similarly, it has led to the effort to link Zoan (Tanis) with the city of Rameses, as well as with the city of Avaris, referred to by Manetho in his account about the so-called Hyksos kings. Thus, many modern reference works say that Zoan's name changed to Avaris under the "Hyksos," then changed to Rameses under the Rameses side dynasty, and finally reverted to Zoan (in the Greek form Tanis). It may be noted, however, that the Bible uses the name Zoan consistently as applying before the Exodus (back to Abraham's time), at the time of the Exodus, and as late as the eighth, seventh, and sixth centuries B.C.E. (in the time of the prophets Isaiah and Ezekiel).

If Zoan were the site of Moses' interviews with Pharaoh, this would certainly give some indication as to the starting point of the Exodus route. However, several factors place this view in doubt. For Zoan to refer to such a site, the expression "the field of Zoan" would have to be viewed, not as simply *paralleling* "the land of Egypt," but as a much more *specific* expression, designating the precise location where the miracles occurred. Such a limiting or restrictive sense would not actually fit the case, for the Ten Plagues did not occur in just one part of Egypt (such as a portion of the Delta) but throughout the entire land. This would seem to support the view that "the field of Zoan" is used as a parallel of "the land of Egypt."

Those modern scholars who endeavor to present Zoan (or, according to their attempted connection, Avaris or Rameses) as Pharaoh's residence at the time of the Exodus also face a lack of Biblical support and agreement in several respects. The Bible shows that Moses' first encounter took place at the edge of the Nile River. (Ex 7:14, 15) Zoan (Tanis) is not on the actual river but at the terminus of one of the ancient branches forking off from the main stream. In attempting to locate the city of Rameses at the same place as Zoan, or Tanis, they also pass over the fact that Zoan was already a city in Abraham's time, whereas the Biblical Raamses ("Rameses," *NE*) began to be built by the Israelites in Egypt about 400 years later (unless by "building" the Bible means "building up," or strengthening).—Ex 1:11.

These scholars would make Zoan (Avaris-Rameses, as they identify it) the Egyptian capital at the time of the Exodus, whereas the Bible identifies Rameses as merely a 'storage place.' And, in holding that Ramses II was the Pharaoh of the Exodus because of his claim that he was the builder of the city of Rameses (or, more accurately, a place called Per-Rameses), they ignore the fact that the building of the Biblical Rameses began 80 years or more before the Exodus (before the birth of Moses [Ex 1:11–2:10]), whereas historians credit Ramses II with a rule of only about 66 years.—See RAAMSES, RAMESES.

The question remains, then, why "the field of Zoan" is apparently used to parallel "the land of Egypt" with regard to Jehovah's performance of miraculous acts. While a possible connection with Pharaoh's court cannot be completely discounted, it is also entirely possible that the great age of the city caused the psalmist to use Zoan in such a way, it apparently being one of the earliest cities founded in Egypt. Its use, if this was the case, might be similar to the use of "Plymouth Rock" as representing the early colonizing of the United States. Or it may be due to its prominence and its location at the entrance to Egypt for those coming from Palestine, perhaps being the first major city Jacob's family encountered when coming into Egypt. (Compare Isa 30:2-4; see HANES.) Lying as it does near the northern extremity of Egypt, its "field" might even figuratively refer to all the Nile Valley stretching to the S thereof, as far as the southern boundary of Egypt.

There is no doubt as to the importance of the city of Zoan (Tanis), particularly with respect to commercial trade and religious structures. There is evidence of much royal building there from the time of the early "dynasties" of Egyptian kings onward. A great temple was constructed, measuring about 305 m (1,000 ft) long. Pharaoh Ramses II set up an immense monolithic statue of himself at Tanis measuring some 28 m (92 ft) in height and weighing over 800 metric tons. Assyrian Kings Esar-haddon and Ashurbanipal refer to Zoan (called *Sa'nu* or *Si'nu* in the cuneiform inscriptions) as a royal city under a prince. Before them, the prophet Isaiah, in the divine pronouncement against Egypt, had referred to "the princes of Zoan" and classed them with those of Noph (Memphis), thereby pointing up also the political importance of Zoan. (Isa 19:1, 11-13) Tirhakah, the Ethiopian ruler over Egypt and a contemporary of Isaiah, is said to have used Zoan (Tanis) as an administrative base for northern Egypt.

The Assyrian conquest of Egypt by Esarhaddon and Ashurbanipal proved the 'foolishness' of the counselors from Zoan. (Isa 19:13) Then, in about 591 B.C.E., the prophet Ezekiel warned of another conquest by Babylonian King Nebuchadnezzar, with a 'fire being set in Zoan.' (Eze 29:17; 30:1, 10, 14) Zoan (Tanis) evidently recovered, however, and continued to be the major Delta city of Egypt until the time of Alexander the Great. Thereafter the new city of Alexandria robbed Zoan (Tanis) of its commercial importance, and it steadily declined.

ZOAR (Zo'ar) [Smallness]. A city of the "District," evidently once at the edge of a fertile plain. (Ge 13:10-12; see DISTRICT OF THE JORDAN.) Apparently Bela was Zoar's earlier name. In Abraham's day, it was ruled by a king who rebelled with the four others of the District after 12 years of domination by Chedorlaomer, only to be defeated by the Elamite monarch and his three allies. (Ge 14:1-11) When Jehovah was about to destroy Sodom, Lot requested and received permission to flee from there to Zoar, and this city was spared. (Ge 19:18-25) Fear later caused him and his two daughters to leave Zoar and become cave dwellers in the nearby mountainous region.—Ge 19:30.

It was foretold that when catastrophe befell Moab, its runaways would flee to Zoar and that the cry over the nation's devastation would be heard "from Zoar clear to Horonaim, to Eglath-shelishiyah," perhaps indicating that Zoar was then a Moabite city. (Isa 15:5; Jer 48:34) The Greek *Septuagint* and certain modern translations (*AT, JB, NE, RS*) mention Zoar (Zogora) at Jeremiah 48:4 (31:4, *LXX*, Bagster), but the Hebrew Masoretic text there refers instead to "her little ones." (*NW, JP, Le, Ro*) Zoar marked the extreme S point that Moses saw when viewing the land from Mount Nebo. (De 34:1-3) Apparently the city was in or near Moab, close to the Moabite mountainous region and somewhere SE of the Dead Sea. (Compare Ge 19:17-22, 30, 37.) Some scholars would place Zoar N of the Dead Sea, others on the el-Lisan Peninsula, or just W or S of the S end of the sea. Yohanan Aharoni identifies it with es-Safi, situated on the delta of the torrent valley of Zered (Wadi el-Hasa'). In the Middle Ages the name was linked with an important site between Jerusalem and Elath. However, some scholars believe that the original Zoar and the other "cities of the District" lie beneath the waters of the S portion of the Dead Sea.—Ge 13:12.

ZOBAH (Zo'bah). A Syrian (Aramaean) kingdom otherwise known as Aram-Zobah. (Ps 60: Sup) One of its kings was Hadadezer. (1Ki 11:23) The compound form "Hamath-zobah" may designate adjoining kingdoms named Hamath and Zobah. (2Ch 8:3) Zobah seems to have been located N of Damascus with a domain extending to the region of Hamath on the N and to the river Euphrates on the E.—2Sa 8:3.

King Saul warred against the kings of Zobah. (1Sa 14:47) The Ammonites later hired Syrians of Zobah and other troops to fight against David, but all were defeated by his army. (2Sa 10:6-19; 1Ch 19:6-19) It was likely in this war that David vanquished and took spoil from Zobah's King Hadadezer, including much copper (eventually used in temple construction) from his cities Betah (apparently also named Tibhath) and Berothai (Cun?). (2Sa 8:3-12; 1Ch 18:3-9) One of the mighty men of David's military forces was Igal the son of Nathan of Zobah.—2Sa 23:8, 36; see ARAM No. 5; HADADEZER.

ZOBEBAH (Zo·be'bah). A descendant of Koz in the tribe of Judah.—1Ch 4:1, 8.

ZODIAC. The band of stars seen from the earth as appearing within nine degrees on either side of the plane of Earth's orbit around the sun. Concerning King Josiah of Judah, 2 Kings 23:5 says: "And he put out of business the foreign-god priests, whom the kings of Judah had put in that they might make sacrificial smoke on the high places in the cities of Judah and the surroundings of Jerusalem, and also those making sacrificial smoke to Baal, to the sun and to the moon and to the constellations of the zodiac and to all the army of the heavens." The expression here rendered "constellations of the zodiac" comes from the Hebrew word *maz·za·lohth'*, which occurs but once in the Bible, although the word *Maz·za·rohth'* found at Job 38:32 may be related. It is the context that helps make clear its meaning.

The discovery of what may be called the zodiacal zone is generally credited to the early Babylonians. They doubtless observed the apparent yearly path of the sun among the stars, which path is now known as the ecliptic. The astronomers could note that within a zone about 18 degrees wide, extending 9 degrees on each side of the ecliptic, lie the apparent paths of the sun, moon, and major planets, as viewed from the earth. It was not until the second century B.C.E., however, that a Greek astronomer divided the zodiac into 12 equal parts of 30 degrees each; these parts came to be called the signs of the

zodiac and were named after the related constellations. The word "zodiac" is from the Greek and means "circle of animals," since most of the zodiac's 12 constellations originally were designated by the names of animal or marine life.

These signs today no longer coincide with the constellations after which they were originally named. This is due to what is known as the precession of the equinoxes, which results in a gradual eastward shift of the constellations by about one degree every 70 years in a cycle that takes some 26,000 years to complete. Thus the sign of Aries, in the past 2,000 years, moved approximately 30 degrees, into the constellation Pisces.

Connection With Astrology. The zodiacal constellations were made objects of false worship from early Mesopotamian times onward. Certain qualities were attributed to each of the different constellations, and these were then used in astrological predictions based on the particular position or relationship of the celestial bodies to the signs of the zodiac at any given time. As shown by the text at 2 Kings 23:5, such use of astrology was introduced into Judah by foreign-god priests whom certain kings had brought into the country. Jehovah God long before had prohibited such star worship on penalty of death.—De 17:2-7.

Astrology was a predominant facet of Babylonian worship. The predictions based on the zodiac by her astrologers, however, did not save Babylon from destruction, even as the prophet Isaiah had accurately forewarned.—Isa 47:12-15; see ASTROLOGERS.

In modern times the zodiacal signs continue to play an important part in the worship of many people. Interestingly, the signs of the zodiac found their way into some of the religious cathedrals of Christendom and can today be seen in such places as the Cathedral of Notre Dame in Paris, as well as on the cathedrals of Amiens and Chartres, France.

ZOHAR (Zo'har).

1. A Hittite whose son Ephron sold the cave of Machpelah to Abraham.—Ge 23:7-9; 25:9.

2. Fifth-named son of Simeon and father of a tribal family; one of those numbered among the 70 of Jacob's household who "came into Egypt." (Ge 46:8, 10, 27; Ex 6:15) He is elsewhere called Zerah.—Nu 26:13; 1Ch 4:24.

ZOHELETH (Zo'he·leth) [from a root meaning "reptile"]. A stone beside En-rogel; its location is otherwise unknown. Near "the stone of Zoheleth," Adonijah did sacrificing and was proclaimed king by many of Israel's prominent men. However, his presumptuous attempt to succeed David to the throne was foiled.—1Ki 1:9, 10, 25, 49, 50.

ZOHETH (Zo'heth). A descendant of Ishi in the tribe of Judah.—1Ch 4:1, 20.

ZOPHAH (Zo'phah). A leading member of the tribe of Asher. Eleven "sons" of his are listed. —1Ch 7:35-37, 40.

ZOPHAI (Zo'phai) [possibly from a root meaning "honeycomb"]. A son of a certain Elkanah and ancestor of Samuel. The alternate form of the name is Zuph.—1Ch 6:26, 28, 33-35; see ZUPH.

ZOPHAR (Zo'phar). One of Job's three "companions"; a Naamathite. (Job 2:11) Zophar was the third in turn to speak in the debate with Job. His general line of reasoning followed that of Eliphaz and Bildad; he accused Job of wickedness, telling him to put away his sinful practices. (Job chaps 11, 20) But after two rounds Zophar desisted; he had spoken his words of denunciation and had nothing to add in the third round. In the end Jehovah commanded that he and his companions offer a great sacrifice and that Job pray in their behalf.—Job 42:7-9.

ZOPHIM (Zo'phim). A field on the top of Pisgah where Balaam built seven altars, where sacrifices were offered, and where the prophet took up one of his proverbial utterances regarding Israel. (Nu 23:14-24) The name Zophim seems to be preserved at Tela'at es-Safa near the suggested location of Pisgah, E of the N end of the Dead Sea. Some scholars, however, translate the word *tsohphim'* instead of considering it a proper name, using such expressions as "the field of the watchmen."—*Le;* compare *JB, NE.*

ZORAH (Zo'rah). A city in the Shephelah allotted to the tribe of Judah. (Jos 15:20, 33) Situated on the boundary between Dan and Judah, it was inhabited by people of Dan. (Jos 19:41, 48; Jg 18:2, 8, 11) The Danite Samson was born at Zorah and was buried nearby. (Jg 13:2, 24, 25; 16:31) The city was fortified by King Rehoboam, perhaps because of its strategic location about 25 km (16 mi) W of Jerusalem. (2Ch 11:5, 10) Zorah was repopulated by some sons of Judah who returned from Babylonian exile. (Ne 11:25, 29) It is identified with present-day Sar'ah (Tel Zor'a), on the N

side of what is suggested to be the Valley of Sorek.

ZORATHITES (Zo'rath·ites) [Of (Belonging to) Zorah]. Descendants of Shobal, of the tribe of Judah.—1Ch 2:3, 52, 53; 4:2.

ZORITES (Zor'ites) [Of (Belonging to) Zorah]. Descendants of Salma of the tribe of Judah.—1Ch 2:3, 54.

ZUAR (Zu'ar) [from a root meaning "be insignificant"]. A man of Issachar whose "son" Nethanel was a tribal chieftain in the wilderness.—Nu 1:8, 16; 2:5; 7:18, 23; 10:15.

ZUPH [possibly, Honeycomb].

1. A Kohathite Levite and ancestor of Samuel. (1Sa 1:1; 1Ch 6:33-38) He is also called Zophai, an alternate form of the same name.—1Ch 6:26.

2. A "land" outside the territory of Benjamin through which Saul went searching for his father's she-asses. In a city within the land of Zuph, Saul had his first meeting with Samuel. (1Sa 9:3-6, 15-18) The exact location of Zuph is not known.

ZUR [Rock].

1. One of the five kings of Midian at the time Israel approached the Promised Land. Zur is also called a chieftain and "a head one of the clans of a paternal house," as well as a 'duke of Sihon.' His daughter Cozbi was the Midianitess whom Zimri took for immoral relations and whom Phinehas slew. Zur himself was killed when the Israelites punished Midian for luring some men of Israel into immoral intercourse and false worship.—Nu 25:14-18; 31:1, 2, 7, 8; Jos 13:21.

2. A Benjamite, son of Jeiel and evidently a brother of Ner, Saul's grandfather.—1Ch 8:29, 30; 9:35, 36, 39.

ZURIEL (Zu'ri·el) [My Rock Is God]. Wilderness chieftain of the Merarite Levites; son of Abihail. —Nu 3:35.

ZURISHADDAI (Zu·ri·shad'dai) [My Rock Is the Almighty]. A Simeonite whose "son" Shelumiel was tribal chieftain during the wilderness journey.—Nu 1:6, 16; 2:12; 7:36, 41; 10:19.

ZUZIM (Zu'zim). A people E of the Jordan River whom Chedorlaomer's forces defeated in Ham.—Ge 14:5.

Subject Index

In the references below, bold numbers identify the volume; lightface numbers, the pages. References on heading lines lead to major discussions, and these often include aspects specified in subheads.

Aaron 1:9-11
golden calf: **1:**393
high priest: **1:**1207-8
Moses' mouthpiece: **2:**435-7

Abel 1:15
blood of Jesus and: **1:**345
faith: **1:**804
"founding of the world": **1:**858;
2:1207
offering: **1:**386, 832; **2:**525

Abihu 1:22
illegitimate fire: **1:**1174

Abishag 1:26
Adonijah's request for: **1:**49-50,
988

Abraham 1:28-32
Bethel encampment: **1:**295
burial place for family: **1:**377;
2:290, 715
Canaanites' relationship with:
1:400-1
circumcision covenant: **1:**469,
523
concubines: **2:**147
covenant: **1:**460-1, 522-3
kept in force "one week"
(Da 9:27): **2:**901
passed on: **1:**1217-18, 1242-3
covenants with others: **1:**75,
106
declared righteous: **1:**604-5
Egypt: **1:**694; **2:**863
faith: **1:**804-5
promise of seed: **1:**1138-9
resurrection: **2:**785
father of nations: **2:**473
Hebrew: **1:**1065-7
Isaac "sacrificed" by: **1:**1217;
2:432-3
Jehovah's relationship with:
2:161-2, 661-2
laughter about Isaac: **2:**208
Lot rescued by: **2:**1166
Sarah represented as sister:
2:863
seed of: **1:**522, 524; **2:**362-3,
887-90
400-year affliction: **1:**460-1,
776, 1216-17
Satan fights: **2:**867-8
travels: **1:**330-1
wealth: **2:**804

Absalom 1:32-5
usurpation attempt: **1:**1163-4;
2:103, 1191-2

Abusive Speech 1:35
backbiting: **1:**241
blasphemy: **1:**337-9
gossip, slander: **1:**989-91
reviling: **2:**801-2

Abyss 1:35-6
angel of (Re 9:11): **1:**12, 126
key of (Re 9:1): **2:**149

Accident 1:38
compensation: **1:**493-5

Accusation 1:39-40
self-justification: **2:**83-4
slander: **1:**990-1
suspicion of adultery: **1:**1261;
2:234-5, 1094

Acts of Apostles 1:42-4
authenticity: **1:**153-4, 476

Adam 1:44-6
bearded: **1:**266-7
creation: **2:**303-4, 1005-6,
1024-5
in God's image: **1:**1184;
2:247-8, 304, 962-3
Eve's relationship with: **2:**1182
complement: **2:**1195
Jehovah's name known by: **2:**13
Jehovah's relationship with:
2:160
long-suffering: **2:**263
personality revealed to:
2:14-16
son of God: **2:**997
Jesus a corresponding ransom:
2:735-6
knowledge of "good and bad":
2:181, 1011
language: **1:**1068, 1075
not ransomed: **2:**18, 736
perfection and free moral
agency: **2:**604
rib: **1:**352; **2:**803
sin: **2:**16, 304, 963-4, 1010
effect on Adam: **1:**479-80;
2:247, 964
effect on offspring: **2:**979-80
not foreknown: **1:**853-4
test of obedience: **1:**676-7;
2:67, 963
writing: **2:**1212

Administration 1:48-9
(See also GOVERNMENT; RULER)
Christian congregation:
1:128-9; **2:**549-51, 564-5
Israel: **1:**1228-9; **2:**549, 564
wisdom in: **2:**1193-4

Adonijah 1:49-50
conspiracy for throne: **2:**987-8

Adoption 1:50-1
anointed Christians: **1:**605;
2:998-9

Adornment 1:51-2
ornaments: **2:**559-61
women: **1:**515; **2:**1197

Adultery 1:53-4
suspicion of wife's: **1:**1261;
2:234-5, 1094

Affection 1:55
relationship to love: **2:**273-4

Agabus 1:55-6
famine foretold: **1:**476

Age 1:56-7
aion: **2:**1054, 1103
gray-headedness: **1:**995
life span: **2:**252
universe: **2:**1032

Agriculture 1:57-9
(See also PLANTS; TREES; VINE;
crops by name)
farming implements: **1:**810-11
field: **1:**829-30
grafting: **1:**993
harvest: **1:**1040-1; **2:**755-6
millstones: **2:**953
plowing: **2:**648-9
sowing: **1:**1178; **2:**1012-15
threshing: **1:**556; **2:**953,
1096-7
winnowing: **2:**953, 1189
year's beginning: **1:**765

Ahab 1:59-60
events during reign: **2:**845
palace: **1:**948
Shalmaneser's inscription:
1:454-5; **2:**907-8

**Ahasuerus (Husband of Queen
Esther) 1:61**
amnesty granted by: **1:**95-6
banquet for officials: **1:**763
chronology: **2:**613-16
identified: **1:**762-3
picture: **2:**331

Ahaz 1:61-2
alliance with Assyria: **2:**1101
unfaithfulness: **1:**1102-3, 1171

Alcoholic Beverages
(See WINE AND STRONG DRINK)

Alexander the Great 1:70-1
conquests: **1:**269, 1003
Persia: **2:**616
Tyre: **2:**531, 1136
empire: **2:**333-4

Alien Resident 1:72-5
proselyte: **2:**699-700
unbled meat: **1:**345

Altar 1:81-6
(See also TEMPLE)
blood at base and on horns:
1:344-5, 1207
fire: **1:**833
horns: **1:**1143-4
incense: **1:**1195-6; **2:**686
to "Unknown God": **2:**1141
water and wine at base: **1:**823

Ambassador 1:88-90
Christian: **2:**761-2

Ammonites 1:92-5
religion: **1:**430; **2:**27, 424-5

**Amon (Amon-Ra) 1:96-7, 976;
2:506, 554-5**

Amos 1:99-100, 296

Amusements 1:101-2
Christian view: **1:**888
dancing: **1:**574-5
games: **1:**887-9; **2:**335
theater: **1:**1089

**Ananias (Husband of Sapphira)
1:104; 2:200, 862**

Ancient of Days 1:105, 135

Angel 1:106-8
(See also DEMON)
cherubs: **1:**431-2
Jacob wrestles with: **1:**1245;
2:190
Jehovah represented by: **2:**1161
Jehovah's armies: **1:**176;
2:21-2
Jehovah's ministers: **2:**407
language: **2:**201
law: **2:**211
obeisance by: **2:**524
of abyss (Re 9:11): **1:**12, 126
seraphs: **2:**896-7
sons of God: **2:**996-7
spirit creatures: **2:**1018-19
voice of: **2:**1160

Anger 1:108-10
avoiding: **2:**706-7
gestures: **1:**218, 660
leads to presumptuousness:
2:680
nose symbolic of: **2:**510
rage: **2:**292
slowness to: **2:**262-4

Animals 1:110-12
(See also BEASTS, SYMBOLIC;
BIRDS; FISH; HUNTING AND
FISHING; INSECTS; OFFERINGS;
REPTILES)
Arabia: **1:**139
compensation for loss or injury:
1:494-5, 561
creeping thing: **1:**547
cud chewing: **1:**555; **2:**816
fear of humans: **1:**819
firstborn of: **1:**836
kinds: **2:**152-3
ark: **1:**164-5
life-force: **2:**1025-6
list:
antelope: **1:**115
ape: **1:**119
ass: **1:**195-6; **2:**954-5
bat: **1:**262
bear: **1:**265-6
Behemoth: **1:**280-1
boar: **1:**347
bull: **1:**374-5
calf: **1:**393-4
camel: **1:**140, 395-6; **2:**955
chamois: **1:**426
cow: **1:**480, 525, 1084-5
dog: **1:**644-5
fox: **1:**869
frog: **1:**874
gazelle: **1:**901-2; **2:**955
goat: **1:**965-6; **2:**955
greyhound: **1:**1010
hare: **1:**555-6, 1035
hind: **1:**1119
horse: **1:**1144-6
jackal: **1:**1241-2
jerboa: **2:**29-30, 642
leech: **1:**232
leopard: **2:**236-7

Scripture Index

In the references below, bold numbers identify the volume; lightface numbers, the pages.

Picture Credits

Pictures are listed below by page number and, where necessary, numbered in parentheses in order of appearance on page (clockwise from top left)

Volume One

Aleppo Codex, The; edited by Moshe H. Goshen-Gottstein (Jerusalem; Magnes Press, 1976). Copyright © by Hebrew University Bible Project and reprinted with their permission: 322 (2), 324 (3).
Archaeological Museum of Istanbul: 960 (2, 4).
British Library, The; by permission of: 324 (1).
British Museum, London; courtesy of: 47, 201, 203, 205, 265, 283, 323 (3), 325 (3), 534 (4), 661, 689, 690, 952 (1), 955 (2), 956 (1-3), 958 (1-4), 967, 1001, back left endsheet (1).
British Museum, London; courtesy of the Trustees of: 533 (2), 614 (2), 887, 952 (2), 955 (1), 957, back left endsheet (2, 4).
Crane, Ralph. Bardo Museum: 739 (2).
Curtis, Dr. J. E.: 958 (5).
Darom, Dr. David: 543 (3), 544 (3, 4, 6, 7).
Egyptian Museum, Cairo: 150, 532 (2).
Israel Department of Antiquities and Museums; photograph courtesy of the Shrine of the Book, Israel Museum, Jerusalem: 322 (3), 1221.
Israel Department of Antiquities and Museums; photograph from Israel Museum, Jerusalem: 325 (4), 403, 948 (1, 3, 4), 960 (1).
John Rylands University Library, The; Manchester; courtesy of: 323 (1).
Kreisssparkasse, Cologne: 614 (1).
Louvre Museum, Paris: 230 (1, 2), 532 (3), 946 (1, 5), 948 (6, 7), 955 (3).

Manley Studios: 692.
Musées Nationaux, France: 325 (1), 360.
Museo della Civiltà Romana, courtesy of: 171.
Museo Egizio, Turin; courtesy of Superintendence of: 351, 532 (4), 533 (4), 960 (3).
Museum of Delphi, Delphi, Greece: 886.
National Aeronautics and Space Administration, Washington, D.C.: 333, 541.
Pictorial Archive (Near Eastern History) Est.: front left endsheet, front right endsheet (3), 38, 58, 142, 177, 182, 303, 323 (2), 331 (4), 332 (1), 334 (1, 2), 335 (2), 336 (1), 384, 530 (3), 534 (2, 3), 535, 542 (2, 3), 543 (1), 574, 580, 741 (3, 4), 747 (1, 2), 946 (2, 3), 950 (1-3), 953 (2, 3), 959, 1090, 1093, 1098.
Pictorial Archive (Near Eastern History) Est. and Survey of Israel, based on a map copyrighted by: 953 (1).
Schrempp, Heinz: 740 (1).
Smithsonian Institution, Washington, D.C.; photo number 83-2259: 328.
Société Royale de Papyrologie du Caire: 324 (2), 326 (all).
Staatlichen Museen zu Berlin, DDR; used with the kind permission of: 758.
United States Department of Agriculture, Washington, D.C.: 741 (2).
Walters Art Gallery, Baltimore: 71.

Volume Two

American Bible Society Library, New York; courtesy of: 11 (2).
American Bible Society Library, New York; courtesy of. Excerpt from *A Literal Translation of the New Testament. . .From the Text of the Vatican Manuscript,* by Herman Heinfetter, London, 1863: 11 (4).
Ashmolean Museum, Oxford; by courtesy of Visitors of: 324 (2).
British Library, The; by permission of: 336 (3).
British Museum, London; courtesy of: 317, 324 (1, 4), 328 (2), 529 (1, 3), 530 (1-3, 6), 534 (3), 865, 908.
British Museum, London; courtesy of the Trustees of: front right endsheet, 323 (1), 325, 326 (1), 328 (4), 332, 459, 529 (5), 544, 751 (1), back left endsheet (4).
FAO photo: 261.
Holyland Hotel, Jerusalem; Reproduction of the City of Jerusalem at the time of the Second Temple—located on the grounds of: 535 (3), 538 (1, 4), 745 (1), 948 (4).
Israel Department of Antiquities and Museums; photograph courtesy of the Shrine of the Book, Israel Museum, Jerusalem: 7.
Israel Department of Antiquities and Museums; photograph from Israel Museum, Jerusalem: 5, 639, 741.
Kreisssparkasse, Cologne: 534 (2).
Levy, Epher: 178.
Louvre Museum, Paris: 335 (2), 529 (4).
"Man and His Work" Pavilion, Eretz Israel Museum, Tel Aviv: 952 (2), 953 (3).

Manley Studios: 329 (2), 748 (2), 948 (1), back left endsheet (3).
Musée de Normandie, Caen, France: 534 (5, 6).
Musée du Luxembourg, Paris, "La Voie Royale": 532 (2), 1135.
Musei Capitolini: 534 (4, 7).
Museo della Civiltà Romana, courtesy of: 536 (3), 666.
Museo Egizio, Turin; courtesy of Superintendence of: 529 (2).
National Aeronautics and Space Administration, Washington, D.C.: 738 (1).
National Archaeological Museum, Athens, Greece: 335 (1), 530 (5).
New York Public Library, The; Rare Books and Manuscripts Division; Astor, Lenox, and Tilden Foundations: 11 (1).
Pictorial Archive (Near Eastern History) Est.: 48 (1), 104, 107, 108 (1, 2), 194, 197 (1, 2), 335 (3), 433, 484, 500, 530 (4), 532 (4), 538 (2, 3), 724, 737, 739 (1, 3, 4), 740, 745 (3), 751 (2, 3), 844, 947, 948 (3), 950 (1), 952 (4-6), 953 (1, 2), 954 (1), 1061, 1064, 1080, 1178.
ROLOC Color Slides, photo by: 322 (1), 748 (1).
Smithsonian Institution, Washington, D. C.; courtesy of: 532 (3), 883.
Smithsonian Institution, Washington, D.C.; photo number 78-8738: 119.
Staatlichen Museen zu Berlin, DDR; used with the kind permission of: 323 (2), 380, 945 (2).
Uitgeversmaatschappij Elsevier; courtesy of: 531.
Vatican Museums photograph: 336 (2), 534 (1).

BIBLE EDITIONS
AND
STUDY HELPS

NEW WORLD TRANSLATION OF THE HOLY SCRIPTURES: This modern translation endeavors to convey faithfully what is in the original Bible languages. It is available in the following editions:

Regular Edition: Complete Bible. Printed in clear, legible type, two columns to the page. With hardbound vinyl cover, marginal references, an appendix, a concordance, and maps. $17 \times 12.4 \times 3.5$ cm ($6^3/_4 \times 4^7/_8 \times 1^3/_8$ in.).

Reference Edition: Genesis through Revelation. This larger edition, designed for the serious Bible student, has over 125,000 marginal references, more than 11,000 footnotes, an extensive concordance, and 43 appendix articles, plus maps; hardbound cover. $23.5 \times 18.7 \times 4.4$ cm ($9^1/_4 \times 7^3/_8 \times 1^3/_4$ in.). (Sample at right from Genesis 1:16-18)

Pocket Edition: Complete Bible. This edition is only 14×9.5 cm ($5^1/_2 \times 3^3/_4$ in.) and about 2 cm ($^3/_4$ in.) thick. It is bound in a pigskin cover, with gilt-embossed title.

THE KINGDOM INTERLINEAR TRANSLATION OF THE GREEK SCRIPTURES: With this word-for-word translation under the Greek Bible text compiled by Westcott and Hort you can get the literal sense of the words used in the original language. A modern-English rendering is provided in the right-hand column. With footnotes, appendix, maps, hard cover, and gilt-embossed title. $17 \times 12 \times 2.4$ cm ($6^3/_4 \times 4^7/_8 \times {}^{15}/_{16}$ in.).

COMPREHENSIVE CONCORDANCE OF THE NEW WORLD TRANSLATION OF THE HOLY SCRIPTURES: 1,280 pages, more than 333,000 Scripture entries, and over 14,700 word headings.

Sample from Reference Edition of the "New World Translation" (Actual size)

Ps 95:5
c Job 38:8
  Pr 8:29
d De 32:4
  1Ti 4:4
e Ge 1:29
  Ps 72:16
  Mt 13:32
f Lu 6:44
g Hag 2:19
  Jas 3:12
h Le 19:19
  Ps 104:14
i Ga 6:7
j De 4:19
  Ps 148:3
k Ge 8:22
  1Ch 23:31
  Ps 104:19
l Jer 33:25
  Eze 32:8
m Ps 8:3
  Ps 136:8
  Jer 31:35
n Isa 13:10
	And it came to be so. **16** And God proceeded to make* the two great luminaries, the greater luminary for dominating the day and the lesser luminary for dominating the night, and also the stars.ᵐ **17** Thus God put them in the expanse of the heavens to shine upon the earth,ⁿ **18** and to dominate by day
	
	Ge 1:11* Lit., "according to its **kind (genus).**" Heb., *lemi·noh'*; Gr., *ge'nos;* Lat., *ge'nus.* The term "kind" here means a created or family kind, its older meaning or definition and not as present-day evolutionists use it. **16*** "And . . . **proceeded to make.**" Heb., *wai·ya''as* (from *'a·sah'*). Different from "create" (*ba·ra'*) found in vss 1, 21, 27; 2:3. Progressive action indicated by the imperfect state. See App 3c.

All the above publications are available at modest prices. To order, write to WATCH TOWER, using the appropriate address on the final page.

CHIEF OFFICE AND OFFICIAL ADDRESS OF

Watch Tower Bible and Tract Society of Pennsylvania
Watchtower Bible and Tract Society of New York, Inc.
International Bible Students Association

25 Columbia Heights, Brooklyn, New York 11201, U.S.A.

ADDRESSES IN OTHER COUNTRIES:

ALASKA 99507: 2552 East 48th Ave., Anchorage.
ARGENTINA: Caldas 1551, 1427 Buenos Aires.
AUSTRALIA: Box 280, Ingleburn, N.S.W. 2565; Zouch Road, Denham Court, N.S.W. 2565.
AUSTRIA: Gallgasse 42-44, Postfach 67, A-1134 Vienna.
BAHAMAS: Box N-1247, Nassau, N.P.
BARBADOS: Fontabelle Rd., Bridgetown.
BELGIUM: rue d'Argile 60, B-1950 Kraainem.
BELIZE: Box 257, Belize City.
BOLIVIA: Casilla No. 1440, La Paz.
BRAZIL: Rodovia SP-141, Km 43, 18280 Cesario Lange, SP; Caixa Postal 92, 18270 Tatuí, SP.
BURMA: P.O. Box 62, Rangoon.
CANADA L7G 4Y4: Box 4100, Halton Hills (Georgetown), Ontario.
CHILE: Av. Concha y Toro 3456, Puente Alto; Casilla 267, Puente Alto.
COLOMBIA: Apartado Aereo 85058, Bogotá 8, D.E.
COSTA RICA: Apartado 10043, San José.
COTE D'IVOIRE (IVORY COAST): 06 B.P. 393, Abidjan 06.
CYPRUS: P. O. Box 4091, Limassol.
DENMARK: P.B. 340; Stenhusvej 28, DK-4300 Holbæk.
DOMINICAN REPUBLIC: Avenida Francia 33 (Apartado 1742), Santo Domingo.
ECUADOR: Casilla 4512, Guayaquil.
EL SALVADOR: Apartado 401, San Salvador.
ENGLAND NW7 1RN: The Ridgeway, London.
FIJI: Box 23, Suva.
FINLAND: Postbox 68, SF-01301 Vantaa 30.
FRANCE: 81 rue du Point-du-Jour, F-92100 Boulogne-Billancourt.
GERMANY, FEDERAL REPUBLIC OF: Postfach 20, D-6251 Selters/Taunus 1.
GHANA: Box 760, Accra.
GREECE: 77 Leoforos Kifisias, GR-151 24 Marousi.
GUADELOUPE: B.P. 239, 97156 Pointe-à-Pitre Cedex.
GUAM 96913: 143 Jehovah St., Barrigada.
GUATEMALA: 11 Avenida 5-67, Guatemala 1.
GUYANA: 50 Brickdam, Georgetown 16.
HAITI: Post Box 185, Port-au-Prince.
HAWAII 96819: 2055 Kam IV Rd., Honolulu.
HONDURAS: Apartado 147, Tegucigalpa.
HONG KONG: 4 Kent Road, Kowloon Tong.
ICELAND: P. O. Box 8496, IS-128 Reykjavík.
INDIA: Post Bag 10, Lonavla, Pune Dis., Mah. 410 401.
IRELAND: 29A Jamestown Road, Finglas, Dublin 11.
ISRAEL: P. O. Box 961, 61-009 Tel Aviv.
ITALY: Via della Bufalotta 1281, I-00138 Rome RM.
JAMAICA: Box 180, Kingston 10.
JAPAN: 1271 Nakashinden, Ebina City, Kanagawa Pref., 243-04.
KENYA: Box 47788, Nairobi.
KOREA, REPUBLIC OF: Box 33 Pyungtaek P. O., Kyunggido, 450-600.

LEEWARD ISLANDS: Box 119, St. Johns, Antigua.
LIBERIA: P.O. Box 171, Monrovia.
LUXEMBOURG: 41, rue du Père Raphaël, L-2413 Luxembourg, G. D.
MADAGASCAR: B.P. 511, Antananarivo 101.
MALAYSIA: 28 Jalan Kampar, Off Jalan Landasan; 41300 Klang, Sel.
MARTINIQUE: Cours Campeche, Morne Tartenson, 97200 Fort de France.
MAURITIUS: 5 Osman Ave., Vacoas.
MEXICO: Apartado Postal 42-048, 06471 México, D.F.
NETHERLANDS: Noordbargerstraat 77, 7812 AA Emmen.
NETHERLANDS ANTILLES: Oosterbeekstraat 11, Willemstad, Curaçao.
NEW CALEDONIA: B.P. 787, Nouméa.
NEW ZEALAND: P.O. Box 142; 198 Mahia Rd., Manurewa.
NIGERIA: PMB 001, Shomolu, Lagos State.
NORWAY: Gaupeveien 24, N-1914 Ytre Enebakk.
PAKISTAN: 197-A Ahmad Block, New Garden Town, Lahore 16.
PANAMA: Apartado 1835, Panama 9A.
PAPUA NEW GUINEA: Box 636, Boroko, N.C.D.
PERU: Av. El Cortijo 329, Monterrico Chico, Lima 33; Casilla 18-1055, Miraflores, Lima 18.
PHILIPPINES, REPUBLIC OF: P.O. Box 2044, Manila 2800; 186 Roosevelt Ave., San Francisco del Monte, Quezon City 3010.
PORTUGAL: Rua Conde Barão, 511, Alcabideche, P-2765 Estoril; Apartado 91, P-2766 Estoril Codex.
PUERTO RICO 00927: Calle Onix 23, Urb. Bucaré, Río Piedras.
SENEGAL: B.P. 3107, Dakar.
SIERRA LEONE: P. O. Box 136, Freetown.
SOLOMON ISLANDS: P.O. Box 166, Honiara.
SOUTH AFRICA: Private Bag 2067, Krugersdorp, 1740.
SPAIN: Apartado postal 132, E-28850 Torrejón de Ardoz (Madrid).
SRI LANKA, REP. OF: 62 Layard's Road, Colombo 5.
SURINAME: Wicherstraat 8-10; Box 49, Paramaribo.
SWEDEN: Box 5, S-732 00 Arboga.
SWITZERLAND: Ulmenweg 45; P.O. Box 225, CH-3602 Thun.
TAHITI: B.P. 518, Papeete.
TAIWAN: 109 Yun Ho Street, Taipei 10613.
THAILAND: 69/1 Soi 2, Sukhumwit Rd., Bangkok 10 110.
TRINIDAD AND TOBAGO, REP. OF: Lower Rapsey Street & Laxmi Lane, Curepe.
UNITED STATES OF AMERICA: 25 Columbia Heights, Brooklyn, N.Y. 11201.
URUGUAY: Francisco Bauzá 3372, Montevideo.
VENEZUELA: Apartado 20.364, Caracas, DF 1020A.
WESTERN SAMOA: P. O. Box 673, Apia.
ZAMBIA, REP. OF: Box 21598, Kitwe.
ZIMBABWE: 35 Fife Avenue, Harare.